NEW!

for Psychology

Engaging Every Student. Supporting Every Instructor. Setting the New Standard for Teaching and Learning.

Achieve for Psychology sets a whole new standard for integrating **assessments, activities,** and **analytics** into your teaching. It brings together all of the features that instructors and students loved about our previous platform, LaunchPad—interactive e-book, LearningCurve adaptive quizzing and other assessments, interactive learning activities, extensive instructor resources—in a powerful new platform that offers:

- A cleaner, more intuitive, mobile-friendly interface.
- Powerful analytics.
- Self-regulated learning and goal-setting surveys.
- A fully integrated iClicker classroom response system, with questions available for each unit or the option to integrate your own.
- A **NEW Video Collection for Introductory Psychology!**

Our resources were **co-designed with instructors and students**, on a foundation of *years* of **learning research**, and rigorous testing over multiple semesters. The result is superior content, organization, and functionality. Achieve's pre-built assignments engage students both *inside* and *outside of class*. And Achieve is effective for students of *all levels* of motivation and preparedness, whether they are high achievers or need extra support.

Macmillan Learning offers **deep platform integration** of Achieve with all LMS providers, including Blackboard, Brightspace, Canvas, and Moodle. With integration, students can access course content and their grades through one sign-in. And you can pair Achieve with course tools from your LMS, such as discussion boards and chat and Gradebook functionality. LMS integration is also available with Inclusive Access. For more information, visit MacmillanLearning.com/College/US/Solutions/LMS-Integration or talk to your local sales representative.

"I'd love to thank our Macmillan team.... They are truly fantastic and have been a lifesaver."

—Nicole Evangelista Brandt, *Columbus State Community College*

Achieve was built with accessibility in mind. Macmillan Learning strives to create products that are usable by all learners and meet universally applied accessibility standards. In addition to addressing product compatibility with assistive technologies such as screen reader software, alternative keyboard devices, and voice recognition products, we are working to ensure that the content and platforms we provide are fully accessible. For more information visit https://www.macmillanlearning.com/college/us/our-story/accessibility

Mobile: Based on user data, we know that lots of students use parts of Achieve on a mobile device. As such, activities such as e-book readings, videos, and LearningCurve adaptive quizzes are easily used across devices with different screen sizes.

Achieve for Psychology: Assessments

LearningCurve Adaptive Quizzing

Based on extensive learning and memory research and proven effective for hundreds of thousands of students, LearningCurve focuses on the core concepts in every chapter, providing individualized question sets and feedback for correct and incorrect responses. The system adapts to each student's level of understanding, with follow-up quizzes targeting areas where the student needs improvement. Each question is tied to a learning objective and linked to the appropriate section of the e-book to encourage students to discover the right answer for themselves. LearningCurve has consistently been rated the #1 resource by instructors and students alike. This fantastic learning tool was updated by Scott Cohn of Western Colorado University for the third edition.

- LearningCurve's game-like quizzing promotes retrieval practice through its unique delivery of questions and its point system.
- Students with a firm grasp on the material get plenty of practice but proceed through the activity relatively quickly.
- Unprepared students are given more questions, therefore requiring that they do what they should be doing anyway if they're unprepared—practice some more.
- Instructors can monitor results for each student and the class as a whole, to identify areas that may need more coverage in lectures and assignments.

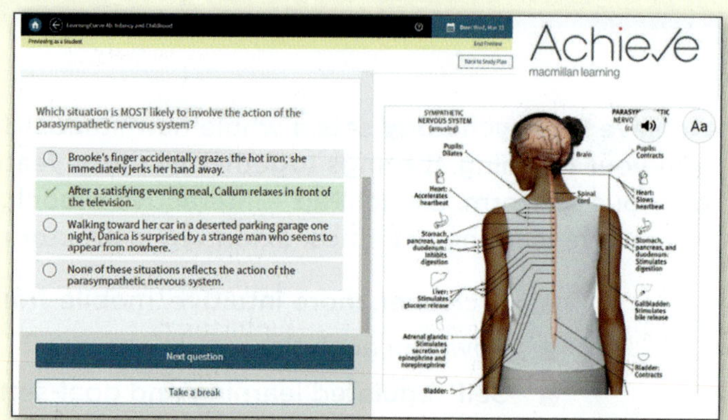

E-book

Macmillan Learning's e-book is an interactive version of the textbook that offers highlighting, bookmarking, and note-taking. Built-in, low-stakes self-assessments allow students to test their level of understanding along the way, and learn even more in the process thanks to the *testing effect*. Students can download the e-book to read offline, or to have it read aloud to them. Achieve allows instructors to assign chapter sections as homework.

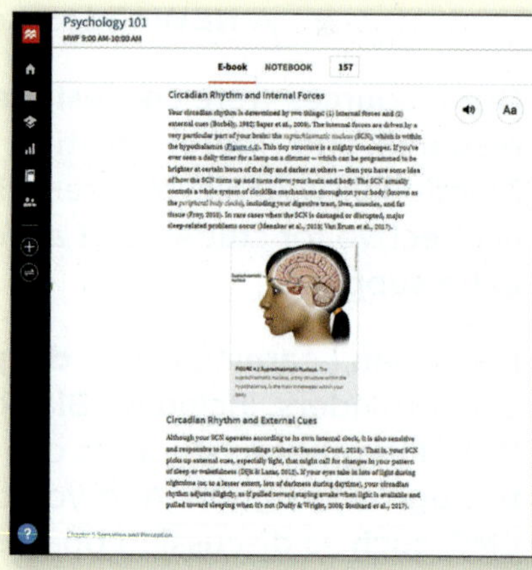

Test Bank

For the third edition of *My Psychology*, Clare Mathes of Baldwin Wallace University worked in consultation with textbook author Andrew Pomerantz to update an assessment package as carefully constructed as the book and media. Test banks for Macmillan Learning's psychology textbooks offer thousands of questions, all meticulously reviewed. Instructors can assign out-of-the-box exams or create their own by:

- Choosing from thousands of questions in our database.
- Filtering questions by type, topic, difficulty, and Bloom's level.
- Customizing multiple-choice questions.
- Integrating their own questions into the exam.

Exam/Quiz results report to a gradebook that lets instructors monitor student progress individually and classwide.

"[T]he test bank questions are great in that they're mostly application questions. I also like the ease of contacting technical support. It's a great resource. I have recommended it to most of my colleagues."

—Adebimpe Diji, *Century College*

Practice Quizzes

Jenn Knapp of Louisiana State University updated the Practice Quizzes, which mirror the experience of a quiz or test—with questions that are similar but distinct from those in the test bank. Instructors can use the quizzes as is or create their own, selecting questions by question type, topic, difficulty, and Bloom's level.

Achieve for Psychology: Activities

Achieve is designed to support and encourage active learning by connecting familiar activities and practices out of class with some of the most effective and approachable in-class activities, curated from a variety of active learning sources.

New! Video Collection for Introductory Psychology

This collection offers classic as well as current, in-demand clips from high-quality sources, with original content to support *My Psychology*, Third Edition. In fact, the Show Me More section of each chapter includes new, curated videos selected by the author, Andrew Pomerantz.

Accompanying assessment makes these videos assignable, with results reporting to the Achieve Gradebook. Our faculty and student consultants were instrumental in helping us create this diverse and engaging set of clips. All videos are closed-captioned and found only in **Achieve**.

Immersive Learning Activities

Focusing on student engagement, these immersive learning activities invite students to apply what they are learning to their own lives, or to play the role of researcher—exploring experimental methods, analyzing data, and developing scientific literacy and critical thinking skills.

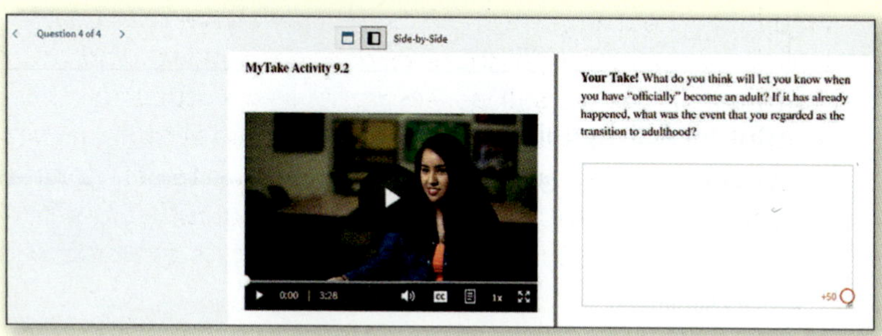

My Take Videos are professionally produced interviews in which real introductory psychology students provide their own takes on, or personal connections with, important concepts from each chapter. These student-centered videos come with assessment questions in Achieve, as well as a brand-new activity in which students can create a My Take Video of their own.

The new edition of *My Psychology* also includes the text-specific My Psychology Podcast activities, in which author Andrew Pomerantz speaks with other introductory psychology instructors about the most important and interesting concepts in each chapter. These podcasts are broken up into discrete, listenable chunks that are accompanied by assessment questions in Achieve for each segment of the podcast.

Concept Practice Tutorials

Achieve includes dozens of these dynamic, interactive mini-tutorials that teach and reinforce the course's foundational ideas. Each of these brief activities (only 5 minutes to complete) addresses one or two key concepts, in a consistent format—review, practice, quiz, and conclusion.

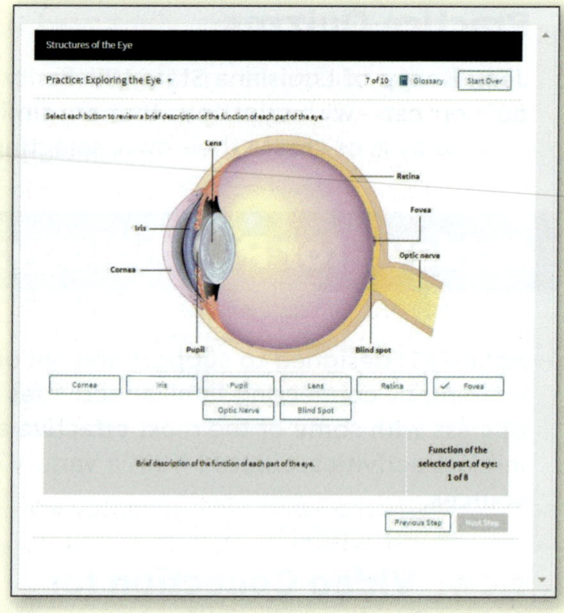

PsychSim6

The new release of *PsychSim* for Achieve redefines what's possible with interactive psychology simulations. With a new look, new format, and updates for accessibility, the *PsychSim* tutorials immerse students in the world of psychological research, placing them in the role of scientist or subject in activities that highlight important concepts, processes, and experimental approaches.

Instructor Activity Guides

Instructor Activity Guides provide instructors with a structured plan for using Achieve's active learning opportunities in both face-to-face and remote learning courses. Each guide offers step-by-step instructions—from pre-class reflection to in-class engagement to post-class follow-up. The guides include suggestions for discussion questions, group work, presentations, and simulations, with estimated class time, implementation effort, and Bloom's taxonomy level for each activity.

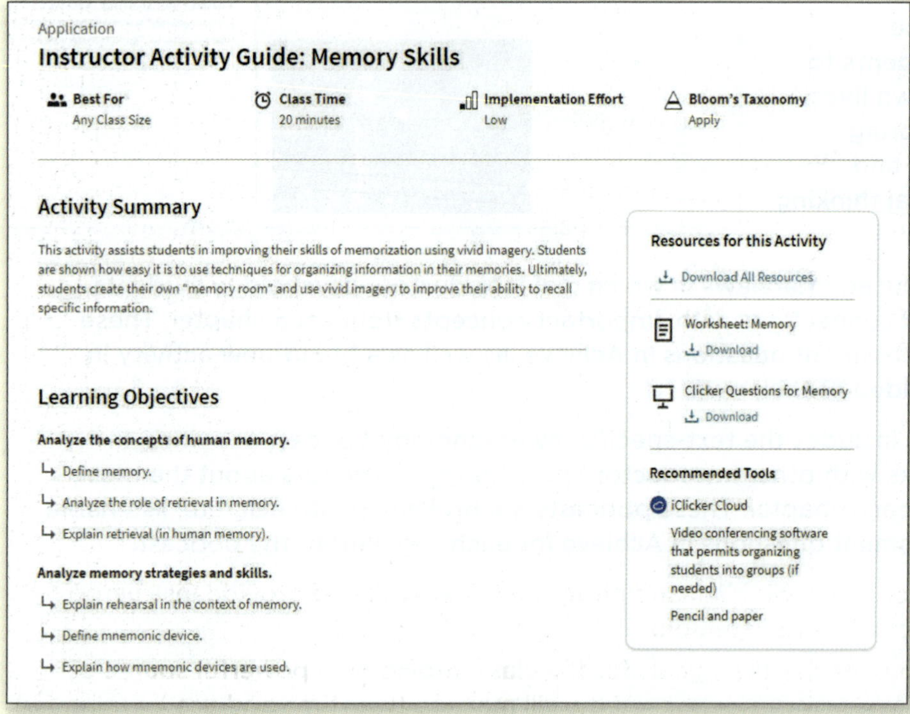

iClicker Classroom Response System

Achieve seamlessly integrates iClicker, Macmillan Learning's highly acclaimed classroom response system. iClicker can help make any classroom—in-person or virtual—more lively, engaging, and productive:

- ***New*** Author Andrew Pomerantz updated the set of iClicker questions for each chapter of the third edition—now with in-class discussion questions, diversity questions, and exit polls to help gauge student understanding.
- iClicker's attendance feature helps you make sure students are actually attending in-person classes.
- Instructors can choose from flexible polling and quizzing options to engage students, check their understanding, and get their feedback in real time.
- iClicker allows students to participate using laptops, mobile devices, or in-class remotes.
- iClicker easily integrates your instructors' existing slides and polling questions—there is no need to re-enter them.
- Instructors can take advantage of the questions in our In-Class Activity Guides, and our book-specific questions within Achieve to improve the opportunities for all students to be active in class.

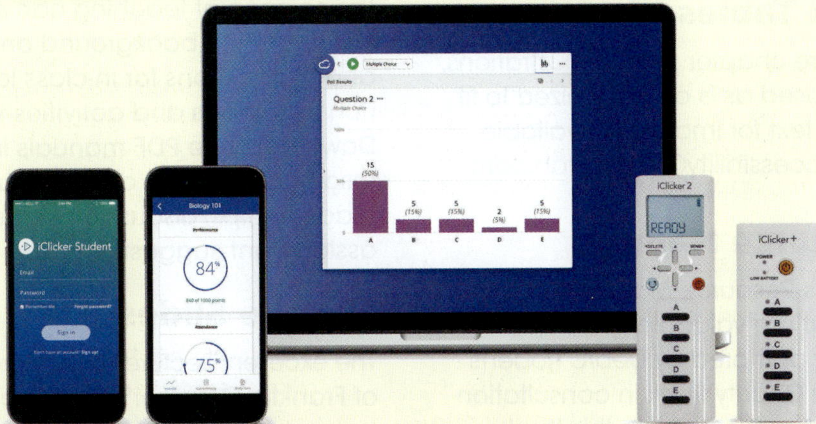

Achieve for Psychology: Analytics

Learning Objectives, Reports, and Insights

Content in Achieve is tagged to specific Learning Objectives, aligning the coursework with the textbook and with the APA Learning Goals and Outcomes. Reporting within Achieve helps students see how they are performing against objectives, and it helps instructors determine if any student, group of students, or the class as a whole needs extra help in specific areas. This enables more efficient and effective instructor interventions.

Achieve provides reports on student activities, assignments, and assessments at the course level, unit level, subunit level, and individual student level, so instructors can identify trouble spots and adjust their efforts accordingly. Within Reports, the Insights section offers snapshots with high-level data on student performance and behavior, to answer such questions as:

- What are the top Learning Objectives to review in this unit?
- What are the top assignments to review?
- What's the range of performance on a particular assignment?
- How many students aren't logging in?

Goal-Setting and Reflection surveys help students plan and direct their learning, and provide instructors with an unprecedented view into students' metacognition:

- The **Intro Survey** asks students to consider their goals for the class, providing a powerful source of intrinsic motivation. Students must then consider how they will manage their time and use learning strategies to achieve their plan.

- **Checkpoint surveys** ask students to monitor and assess their progress, and prompt them to make changes as necessary.
- **Each completed survey generates a report** for the instructor that reveals how the class is progressing—going well beyond the course grades.

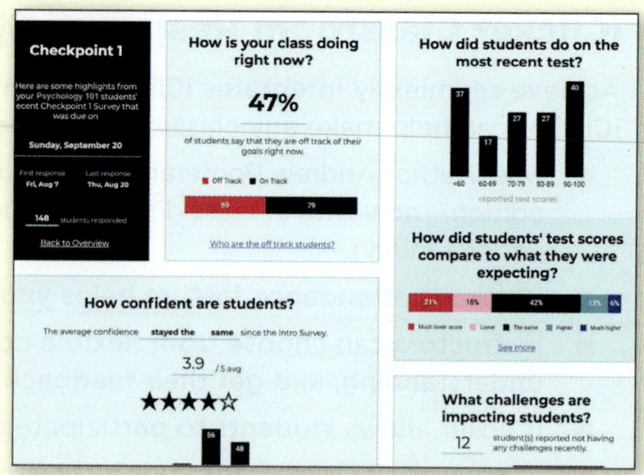

These tools help students develop control over their learning and foster a growth mindset to build long-lasting academic success.

Additional Instructor Resources in Achieve: All Within One Place

Image Slides and Tables

Presentation slides feature chapter photos, illustrations, and tables and can be used as is or customized to fit an instructor's needs. Alt text for images is available upon request via WebAccessibility@Macmillan.com

Instructor's Resource Manuals

The abundant *Instructor's Resource Manual* features a variety of materials that are valuable to new and veteran teachers. Initially authored by Debra Roberts of Howard University and Charity Peak in consultation with textbook author Andrew Pomerantz, this third edition was updated by Nere Ayu of Howard University. The manual serves as a concise introduction to how the science of teaching can enrich the classroom. In addition to background on the chapter reading and suggestions for in-class lectures, the manual is rich with ideas and activities to engage students. Downloadable PDF manuals include a range of resources, such as chapter outlines or summaries, teaching tips, discussion starters, sample syllabi, assignment suggestions, and classroom activities.

Lecture Slides

The excellent Lecture Slides were created by Kristin Flora of Franklin College. These accessible, downloadable presentation slides provide support for key concepts and themes from the text and can be used as is or customized to fit an instructor's needs.

Achieve Read & Practice

Achieve Read & Practice marries Macmillan Learning's mobile-accessible e-book with the acclaimed LearningCurve adaptive quizzing. It is an easy-to-use yet exceptionally powerful teaching and learning option that streamlines the process of increasing student engagement and understanding, and reduces cost. If students struggle with a particular topic, they are encouraged to re-read the material and answer a few short additional questions. The gradebook provides analytics for student performance individually and for the whole class, by chapter, section, and topic, helping instructors prepare for class and one-on-one discussions. Instructors can assign reading simply, and students can complete assignments on any device. See MacmillanLearning.com/ReadandPractice.

Customer Support

Our Achieve Client Success Team—dedicated platform experts—provides collaboration, software expertise, and consulting to tailor each course to fit your instructional goals and student needs. Start with a demo at a time that works for you to learn more about how to set up your customized course. Talk to your sales representative or visit https://www.macmillanlearning.com/college/us/contact-us/training-and-demos for more information.

Pricing and bundling options are available at the Macmillan student store: store.macmillanlearning.com/

THIRD EDITION

ANDREW M. POMERANTZ

Southern Illinois University Edwardsville

New York

Executive Vice President & General Manager: Charles Linsmeier
Vice President, Social Sciences & High School: Shani Fisher
Senior Executive Program Manager: Carlise Stembridge
Development Editor: Michael Kimball
Assistant Editor: Talia Green
Executive Marketing Manager: Katherine Nurre
Marketing Assistant: Claudia Cruz
Executive Director, Digital Workflow Strategy: Noel Hohnstine
Senior Media Editor, Social Sciences: Lauren Samuelson
Senior Director, Content Management Enhancement: Tracey Kuehn
Senior Managing Editor: Lisa Kinne
Lead Content Project Manager: Won McIntosh
Senior Media Project Manager: Eve Conte
Executive Permissions Editor: Robin Fadool
Photo Researcher and Lumina Project Manager: Krystyna Borgen
Assistant Director, Process Workflow: Susan Wein
Senior Workflow Project Manager: Paul Rohloff
Director of Design, Content Management: Diana Blume
Senior Design Services Manager: Natasha Wolfe
Interior Design: Patrice Sheridan
Senior Design Manager, Cover Design: John Callahan
Art Manager: Matthew McAdams
Composition: Lumina Datamatics, Inc.
Printing and Binding: Lakeside Book Company

Library of Congress Control Number: 2022934152

ISBN-13: 978-1-319-33944-9 (Paperback)
ISBN-10: 1-319-33944-1 (Paperback)
ISBN-13: 978-1-319-44958-2 (Loose-leaf Edition)
ISBN-10: 1-319-44958-1 (Loose-leaf Edition)

1 2 3 4 5 6   27 26 25 24 23 22

Worth Publishers
120 Broadway
New York, NY 10271
www.macmillanlearning.com

In My Psychology, *numerous examples describe clients with whom the author has personally worked in his clinical practice. In those cases, any identifying information has been changed, disguised, or omitted to maintain client confidentiality.*

To my kids, Benjamin and Daniel.

I love you and I'm proud of you every day!

About the Author

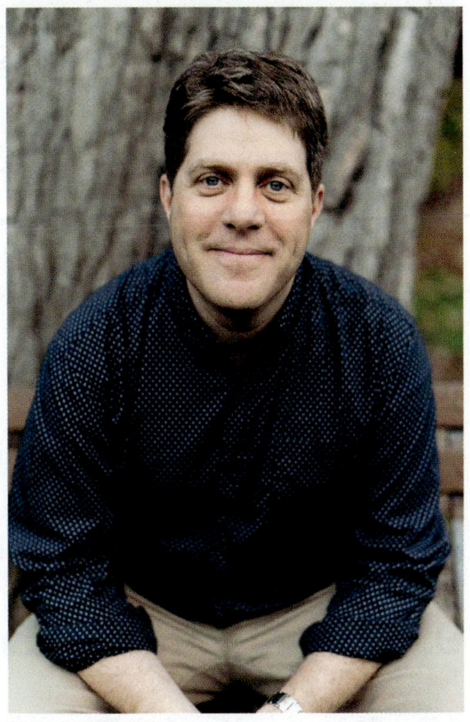

Photo by Felise Waxman

Andrew M. Pomerantz is Professor of Psychology and Director of the Clinical Psychology Graduate Program at Southern Illinois University Edwardsville (SIUE). For over twenty-five years, he has taught Introduction to Psychology as well as undergraduate and graduate courses related to clinical psychology. His research on teaching in psychology has been published in *Teaching of Psychology, Scholarship of Teaching and Learning in Psychology*, and *Training and Education in Professional Psychology*, and been presented at conferences of the American Psychological Association and the National Institute on the Teaching of Psychology. At SIUE, Pomerantz has received the Paul Simon Outstanding Teacher-Scholar Award and was an invited member of the Peer Consultant Team of the Excellence in Learning and Teaching Initiative. He is also the author of two textbooks that have won the Textbook Excellence Award ("Texty") from the Textbook & Academic Authors Association: *Clinical Psychology: Science, Practice, and Diversity* (2017) and this very text, *My Psychology* (2020).

His research focuses on various topics within clinical psychology, especially those related to ethical and professional issues in psychotherapy. He has served on the editorial boards of *Journal of Clinical Psychology, Ethics & Behavior*, and *Journal of Contemporary Psychotherapy*. He maintains a part-time private practice of psychotherapy in St. Louis, Missouri, where he sees adults and children with a wide range of issues and disorders. He also served two terms as president of Psychotherapy Saint Louis, a multidisciplinary therapist organization.

He earned his B.A. degree in psychology from Washington University in St. Louis and his M.A. and Ph.D. in clinical psychology from Saint Louis University. He completed his predoctoral internship at the Indiana University School of Medicine Psychology Training Consortium.

When Andy isn't doing psychology things, he likes hanging out with his two wonderful kids and his amazing wife. He enjoys discovering new music, either online or in record stores (while they still exist). He likes watching, coaching, and playing basketball, but he'll settle for walking, running, or riding his bike too. He also watches some high-quality TV shows and perhaps even more low-quality TV shows.

Brief Contents

Contents

Instructor's Preface

Why *My Psychology*?

Psychology is unique among academic disciplines — uniquely *personal*. Its concepts, theories, and research overlap with so much of our daily lives: how we perceive, remember, and learn about the world around us; how we experience and express thoughts and feelings; how our personalities and development shape our experience; how we relate to others; and how we experience hardship and healing, among others. College students may identify with elements of introductory courses in many disciplines, but more than any other course, Intro Psych is Intro *Me*. For that reason, *My Psychology* distinguishes itself from competing texts by inviting students to make a personal connection to the science of psychology.

Every time I teach Intro Psych, my students are eager to make that personal connection. Research illustrates that many other students share that eagerness. One study found that almost every major topic in the field — memory, learning, personality, social psychology, disorders, development, stress and health, and more — was rated by current Intro Psych students as "important" or "quite important" to their lives (McCann et al., 2016). Another study asked Intro Psych students the extent to which they agreed with statements about what they expect to learn from the course. The statements were all adapted from the first version of the American Psychological Association's *Guidelines for the Undergraduate Psychology Major* (American Psychological Association, 2007). Students agreed most enthusiastically with the statements that connected psychology to their personal lives: "I will be more insightful about my own behavior, and use some of the concepts studied during the course in my own life." "I will have improved my critical thinking skills when examining my own behavior and the behavior of others." "I will understand people better, especially regarding cultural differences and diverse viewpoints" (Landrum & Gurung, 2013).

"I use Pomerantz, and my students and I love it! The students genuinely enjoy reading the text, and I get comments about it every semester. I love the integration of diversity throughout the text, and the real-life examples that engage students better than any text I've ever used before."

—Eva Szeli, *Arizona State University*

My Psychology connects the science of psychology with the personal experience of students by engaging with them on their level. Indeed, student engagement is a primary theme of the text. From the students' point of view, one key to engagement is accessibility — a sense that the book is written in a way they can grasp, not at a level that outstrips their reading level and causes them to lose interest. *My Psychology* deliberately strikes this level of accessibility, using language that students at all levels find approachable and intelligible, not intimidating or bewildering. Another key to engagement in any educational endeavor is a sense of immediacy. Teachers create immediacy through "behaviors that promote students feeling heard, included, valued, and known" (Rogers, 2015, p. 20; see also McCroskey & Richmond, 1992). When teachers have high levels of immediacy, students tend to like them, and feel motivated to engage more fully and willingly in the material being taught (Allen et al., 2006; Mazer, 2015; Witt et al., 2004). Immediacy is a quality typically measured in teachers, but textbooks can deliver it, too. For your students and mine, I strove to maximize the level of engagement in *My Psychology* in four pioneering ways: technology (including smartphones), applications, diversity coverage, and pedagogy.

"[T]his book is outstanding in many respects. Most notably, it accomplishes the following: (1) It meets students where they are at—i.e., it is written in a way that is extremely easy for students to relate to (and to apply to their personal lives); and (2) it includes incredibly extensive coverage of diversity issues... It's an outstanding book (with excellent supplemental resources)."

—Craig J. Vickio, *Wright State University*

My Psychology includes a variet friendly tools, including Chapt Take videos, Show Me More li e-book. Alejandro Rivera/E+/Ge

Improvements for the Third Edition

A trove of carefully chosen improvements appears throughout the third edition of *My Psychology*. These improvements focus on ensuring comprehensive, current coverage of the evolving field of psychology, with specific emphasis on two important forces in the lives of contemporary students: (1) diversity, equity, and inclusion (DEI) and (2) the COVID pandemic.

Improvements in Diversity, Equity, and Inclusion

Diversity has been a hallmark of *My Psychology* since the first edition. Building on that already wide range of representation, we have made global improvements concerning diversity, equity, and inclusion throughout the third edition of the text. These improvements permeate every chapter, appearing in examples, research, photos, names, gender pronouns, and more. The text includes plenty of new coverage (marked by more Diversity Matters flags) that highlights differences and similarities between diverse groups on important psychological variables (based on ethnicity, age, sexual orientation, gender identity, and more). Highlights of that diversity coverage include new sections for the third edition with these headings: Cultural Humility; Antiracism; Coming Out and Mental Health; Diversity, Multiculturalism, and Personality; The ADDRESSING Model; Sexual Orientation and Sleep; Diversity and Dreams; and Socioeconomic Status and Memory.

"This is beyond a doubt the best intro psych book I've seen for its treatment of diversity and multiculturalism."
—Edwin Shriver, *Emmanuel College*

Along with these new sections for diversity coverage, there are new and revised examples and photos that expand representation to a wider range of people. The language has been revised throughout, including gender pronouns, to increase inclusiveness and sensitivity. Many specific diversity changes are noted below, in the curated, chapter-by-chapter list of changes.

Coverage of the COVID Pandemic

The COVID pandemic has shaped our students' world — including how they feel, think, and behave. And psychology is particularly well-suited to explain many of the pandemic's consequences. Throughout the third edition, well-curated inclusions of relevant research and examples address the psychological impact of COVID. New, judiciously selected COVID-related research appears in almost every chapter, touching on such topics as teletherapy, stigma, cognitive dissonance, locus of control, hardiness, stress, sleep problems, dreams, olfaction, memory problems, creativity, emotional intelligence, attachment, transitioning to adulthood, loneliness, self-actualization, self-efficacy, and the Big Five model of personality.

The third edition of *My Psychology* also includes hundreds of new references, most of them from 2020–2022. This infusion of new research spans all 15 chapters and incorporates new and enhanced coverage of a wide range of topics, ensuring that the text remains fresh, contemporary, and relevant. Here's a curated, chapter-by-chapter list of the most essential specific improvements (comprehensive list available on request):

… of Psychology

…ersity coverage: Inez Beverly
…nan to earn a PhD in psychology;
…l studies" by Kenneth Clark
…iffer Howes, a pioneering
…of psychology
…, which discusses
…ood, maximiz-
…o underserved
…next pandemic
…Will Your State Need

Chapter 2: Brain and Behavior

- New diversity coverage: Diversity Matters flags for content about brain plasticity and blindness, brain changes that correlate with individualism and collectivism, and the ways language usage can shape the brain
- New research: on fMRIs as potential tools to reveal biomarkers for psychological disorders and on the way the experience of violence or neglect in children can result in brain changes
- New feature: Show Me More 2.1: How Neurons Work

Chapter 3: Sensation and Perception

- New diversity coverage: new Diversity Matters flags for the names of colors across cultures; for cultural experiences and differences in olfaction abilities; for collectivism, individualism, and vision; and for gendered pain
- New COVID coverage: new section, Olfaction and COVID
- New chapter opener using microwave popcorn as an illustration of sensation and perception
- New features: Chapter App 3.3: GeoPain; Show Me More 3.1: Sensory Interaction: Combining Video and Audio; Show Me More: 3.4: The Science of Smell

Chapter 4: Consciousness

- New diversity coverage: new sections on Sexual Orientation and Sleep, and Diversity and Dreams; new Diversity Matters flags for sections on Gender and Sleep, Ethnicity and Sleep, Age and Sleep, and Solitary Sleep and Co-Sleeping; and new research on ethnicity and sleep
- New COVID coverage: new sections on COVID and Sleep Problems and on COVID and Dreams
- New features: My Take Video 4.3: Screens and Sleep; Show Me More 4.2: The Benefit of Naps

Chapter 5: Memory

- New diversity coverage: new section, Socioeconomic Status and Memory; new Diversity Matters flags for sections on Diversity and Flashbulb Memory, Culture and Memory, and Language and Memory
- New COVID coverage: new section, Memory Problems and COVID
- New chapter opener using "receipts" to illustrate memory and memory mistakes
- New section: Misinformation Effect and Fake News
- New features: Chapter App 5.1: 50 U.S. States; Show Me More 5.3: An App that Mimics the Hippocampus to Help Memory Functions

Chapter 6: Learning

- New diversity coverage: new section, Classical Conditioning and Diversity; new research on Charles Henry Turner, one of the first Black behavioral researchers
- New COVID coverage: new research on sniffer dogs being trained to detect COVID in humans
- New chapter opener using a trip to the dentist's office to illustrate learning concepts
- New research: on the new topic, informational learned helplessness
- New feature: Chapter App 6.2: OurHome

Chapter 7: Cognition

- New diversity coverage: new Diversity Matters flags for research about how culture can influence concept formation, for the one-word stage across cultures, and for the coverage of stereotype threat
- New COVID coverage: new section, Creativity and COVID; new research on the COVID pandemic and affective forecasting, and on emotional intelligence and COVID
- New chapter opener that uses a story about a friend needing help to illustrate key cognition concepts
- New section: Misinformation (and ways to address it)
- New features: Chapter App 7.1, HelloTalk; Show Me More 7.2: Why More Choices Don't Make You Happy; New Show Me More 7.4: Neuroscience and Language

Chapter 8: Motivation and Emotion

- New diversity coverage: new Diversity Matters flags for coverage of gender and eating, emotion and age, emotion and ethnicity, and emotion and gender
- New section: Social Situations, about the social influences of eating
- New COVID coverage: new section, Weight and COVID; new research on COVID, mask-wearing, and emotion recognition
- New research on weight stigma
- New features: Chapter App 8.2: Daylio, an app that tracks emotions; Show Me More 8.2, Obesity Guidelines Move Away from Focus on Weight Loss

Chapter 9: Development Across the Lifespan

- New diversity research: new Diversity Matters flags for coverage of gender and friends, gender and moral reasoning, gender and psychological disorders, and adolescent dating
- New COVID coverage: new research on COVID and disrupted attachment, and on COVID and young people entering adulthood
- New chapter opener that uses flashbacks and flashforwards in TV episodes to introduce key concepts in development over the lifespan
- New research on the psychological effects of acne
- New feature: Chapter App 9.1: Pregnancy Tracker

Chapter 10: Diversity in Psychology

- New section: Intersectionality
- New section: The ADDRESSING Model, an acronym for diversity variables
- New section: Cultural Humility
- New section: Antiracism (including a discussion of colorism)

- New section: Coming Out and Mental Health
- New section: Differences in Digital Communication
- Updated statistics throughout Diversity by the Numbers
- New key term: BIPOC
- New features: My Take Video 10.3: Gender and Gender Development; Show Me More 10.1: Healthy Ways to Discuss Issues of Race; Show Me More 10.3: Gender and Gender Roles

Chapter 11: Stress and Health

- New diversity coverage: on *familismo*, a type of social support in Latinx communities
- New COVID coverage: new section, Stress and COVID; new research about loneliness in the pandemic and on hardiness and the impact of COVID
- New features: Chapter App 11.2, The Mighty, about social support for health-related stressors; Show Me More 11.3: Toxic Stress in Young Children; Show Me More 11.4: Conquering Loneliness in a Lonely World

Chapter 12: Personality

- New diversity coverage: new section, Diversity, Multiculturalism, and Personality
- New COVID coverage: new research on COVID and self-actualization, self-efficacy, locus of control, and the Big Five

Chapter 13: Social Psychology

- New diversity coverage: new research on following instructions from authority figures during COVID; revised explanation in the "Discrimination" section
- New COVID coverage: new From Research to Real Life box: Can Cognitive Dissonance Increase Mask Wearing and Social Distancing During COVID; new research on political polarization and the pandemic
- New research on clothes and first impressions, on cyberbullying, on liking people who are similar to us, and on altruistic behaviors and the benefits for people who perform them

Chapter 14: Psychological Disorders

- New diversity coverage: new Diversity Matters flags for age ranges of people with anxiety disorders; for schizophrenia and geography; for schizophrenia and ethnicity; and for who gets disorders of childhood and autism spectrum disorder
- New COVID coverage: new section, The Influence of COVID
- New description and explanation of the DSM-5-TR (text revision) released in March 2022, including its one new disorder, prolonged grief disorder; DSM-5-TR updates throughout the chapter
- New sections: The Influences of Stigma (including a new key term, stigma)
- New features: Show Me More 14.1: Misconceptions about Obsessive-Compulsive Disorder; Show Me More 14.2: Smartphones as a Tool to Combat Depression; Show Me More 14.3: Mental Health Issues among Black Americans; New Show Me More 14.4: Men, Mental Health, and the "Man Up" Mentality

Chapter 15: Therapy

- New COVID coverage: new research on teletherapy and COVID
- DSM-5-TR updates throughout the chapter
- New key terms: behavioral activation and cultural competence
- New section: Stimulant Drugs
- New features: My Take Video 15.4: Teletherapy; Chapter App 15.1 FearTools; Chapter App 15.2: BetterHelp; Show Me More 15.3: Stand-up Comedy as Therapeutic? Show Me More 15.4: An African Perspective on the Importance of Psychological Treatment

Technology That Brings Psychology to Students' Lives

Our Intro Psych students live on their smartphones and computers. *My Psychology* meets them there.

My Psychology addresses the need for a contemporary textbook that recognizes not only what students experience in their daily lives, but also the mode of those experiences. Students can access this entire suite of technological features on their smartphones and computers. These features can also be assigned and assessed via Achieve, Macmillan's online learning environment.

"Students loved this book and I really enjoyed using this book. I found this semester easier to teach between the actual textbook and the accompanying [online learning platform]."

—Nicole Evangelista Brandt, *Columbus State Community College*

Chapter Apps are real apps that students can download onto smartphones, or use on computers. Each app demonstrates a real-life *app*lication of an important psychology concept to students' daily lives. Students read a brief description of the app and then consider applied and critical thinking questions. For example, a Chapter App in the Social Psychology chapter is *Waze*, a popular app that many drivers prefer to Google Maps and other navigation apps because it lets drivers share information about the roads (e.g., accidents, traffic jams, cheap gas stations) with each other as a "community" of drivers.

Whether they use the app or simply read the brief description in the textbook, students then consider questions about which theory of prosocial behavior (or altruism) best explains the behavior of contributing road information for the benefit of other *Waze* users. In the Learning chapter, one Chapter App (*stickK*) illustrates the use of punishment for failing to uphold commitments to change undesired behavior. In an extensive class test campaign with more than 500 students, more than 95% reported enjoying the Chapter App activities. Your use of Chapter Apps can span a wide range of engagement: for some, you may want your students to download and use the app and provide written answers to the questions that accompany it; for others, merely using the app as an example in class to help with understanding or to facilitate discussion may be ideal.

The third edition of *My Psychology* includes new Chapter Apps such as Chapter App 3.3: GeoPain (for the section on touch and pain), Chapter App 6.2: OurHome (about parenting, operant conditioning, and reinforcement), Chapter App 8.2: Daylio (an app that tracks emotions), Chapter App 11.1: The Mighty (about social support for health-related stressors), and Chapter App 15.2: BetterHelp (a therapy platform).

My Take Videos are brief, professionally produced interviews in which real Intro Psych students provide their own takes on, or personal connections with, important concepts from the chapter. For example, the Social Psychology chapter features "My Take on the Fundamental Attribution Error," in which several students recount personal stories about this concept in their own lives. One student tells the tale of attributing a fellow driver's decision to steal her parking space to unflattering personality traits until she later discovered that the driver was in an emergency situation. As with Chapter Apps, students can use smartphones to access these videos in multiple ways. The videos are a reminder of the diverse experiences students bring to the study of psychology and emphasize the power of connecting experience to the course concepts.

We added three new My Take Videos to the video program for the third edition: My Take Video 4.3: Screens and Sleep; My Take Video 10.3: Gender and Gender Development; and My Take Video 15.4: Teletherapy. And we've retained all the My Take Videos that have been favorites through the first two editions of the text, including My Take Video 3.2: Sensory Adaptation, My Take Video 7.1: Affective Forecasting, My Take Video 9.2: Parenting Styles, and My Take Video 13.3: Social Comparison.

Show Me More provides students with bonus material illustrating key concepts in the chapter. This feature takes students to brief videos (e.g., news clips, documentary YouTube videos) or interactive Web sites where they can delve more deeply into important, often personally relevant material. For example, in the Cognition chapter, one Show Me More link takes students to a brief video interview of Daniel Kahneman (author of *Thinking, Fast and Slow*) describing how dual process theory can affect their decision making.

In the Diversity chapter, Show Me More 10.1 is from Macmillan's new video collection and discusses healthy ways to discuss issues of race. In fact, each chapter of *My Psychology* 3e includes videos from the video collection for introductory psychology. Finally, each chapter's Show Me More includes the text-specific My Psychology

CHAPTER APP 8.2

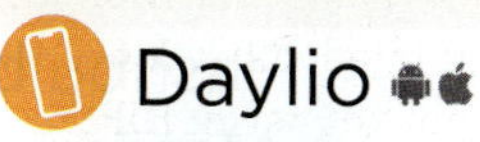

The Daylio app allows you to track your emotions. You enter your mood (rad, good, meh, bad, or awful), along with your recent activities (working, watching movies, cleaning, exercising, etc.). The app then provides you with stats and graphs showing how your mood changed as time passed and your activities changed.

How does it APPly to your daily life?
How could an app like Daylio help you understand the patterns of your emotions? How could it help you determine which activities evoke positive and negative emotions? How could the information it provides influence your decisions on activities to choose in the future?

How does it APPly to your understanding of psychology?
How could this app help you appreciate the range of your own emotions? How could it help you recognize or regulate your own emotions?

To learn more about this app or to download it to your phone, you can search for "Daylio" on Google, in the iPhone App store, or in the Google Play store.

Chapter Apps are apps that students can download onto smartphones or use on computers. They appear in every chapter, and they demonstrate applications of key psychological concepts in students' daily lives.

"Love the extra videos."
—Alan J. Whitehead, *Southern Virginia University*

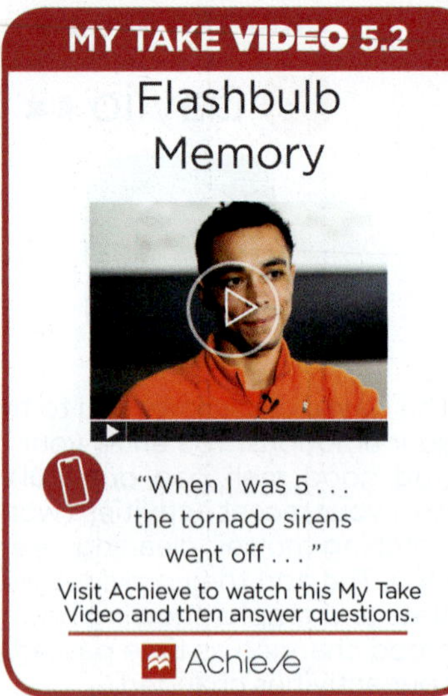

My Take videos are brief interviews with real Intro Psych students about their personal connection with important psychological concepts. My Take videos were custom-made for every chapter of *My Psychology*.

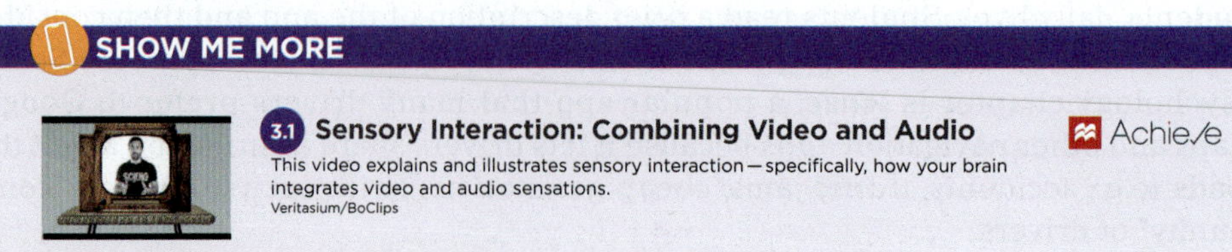

SHOW ME MORE
3.1 Sensory Interaction: Combining Video and Audio
This video explains and illustrates sensory interaction—specifically, how your brain integrates video and audio sensations.
Veritasium/BoClips
"When I was 5 . . . the tornado sirens went off . . ."
Achieve

The Show Me More links at the end of each chapter provide students with interesting bonus material for important psychological concepts.

Podcast activities, in which author Andrew Pomerantz speaks with other introductory psychology instructors about the most important and interesting concepts in each chapter. These podcasts are broken up into discrete, listenable chunks that are accompanied by assessment questions in Achieve for each segment of the podcast.

Applications That Make Psychology Personally Meaningful

Our Intro Psych students learn best when they see how psychology relates to their lives. *My Psychology* helps them understand how core concepts are personally meaningful.

These features recur in every chapter, highlighting the applicability of psychology concepts to students' own lives. They point out the parallels between students' own experiences and the science of psychology. They complement the coverage within each chapter by providing students with distinct, novel ways of understanding and personalizing important psychology concepts.

From Research to Real Life features directly connect psychological research to an aspect of the students' daily activities. In the Science of Psychology chapter, the From Research to Real Life application focuses on college student success, including studies that examine sleep patterns, extracurricular engagement, academic self-efficacy, study schedules, and class attendance. In the Motivation and Emotion chapter, the feature focuses on the relationship between financial success and happiness. And the Social Psychology chapter includes a new From Research to Real Life for our times: Can Cognitive Dissonance Increase Mask Wearing and Social Distancing During COVID?

LIFE HACK 8.3

If you want to feel happier, do something kind for someone else, or think about acts of kindness you've already done.

(Lyubomirsky & Layous, 2013; Otake et al., 2006; Pressman et al., 2015)

Life Hacks offer suggestions to students for how to improve their lives according to psychological research. They appear in every chapter of the text.

Life Hack mini-features offer direct suggestions to students for how to improve their lives according to the findings of psychological research. These quick tips, each of which is supported by research citations, steer students toward higher levels of well-being, productivity, and other desirable outcomes. For example, in The Science of Psychology chapter, a Life Hack describes how to avoid the correlation-causation fallacy. In the Consciousness chapter, students come across a Life Hack that instructs them to get a good night's sleep before a big test, because sleep enhances memory. And a Life Hack in the Personality chapter notes how difficult it can be to change another person's personality.

It's Like... features use the power of analogy to help students understand concepts that may be unfamiliar but share important similarities with concepts they already know well. For example, in the Development chapter, the concepts of assimilation and accommodation are likened to the process of sorting a basket of clean laundry into folded piles. In the Sensation and Perception chapter, top-down processing is likened to the autocomplete feature in texting apps and Google searches. And in the Stress and Health chapter, the fight-or-flight response is likened to working the gas and brake pedals in a vehicle.

Watching Psychology features use popular TV shows and movies to illustrate key concepts. For example, in the Social Psychology chapter, the feature focuses on *The Voice* (in which judges often hear singers without seeing them) and the impact of physical attractiveness on impression formation. In the Cognition chapter, Watching Psychology focuses on *Family Feud* and its demand for both convergent thinking (to get the top answers on the board) and divergent thinking (to get the lower or last remaining answers).

Current Controversy features encourage critical thinking and an appreciation of the scientific process by introducing students to ongoing debates and disagreements within personally relevant areas of psychology. For example, in the Consciousness chapter, Current Controversy focuses on whether high schools should start later in the morning to accommodate teens' circadian rhythms. In the Psychological Disorders chapter, Current Controversy focuses on whether premenstrual dysphoric disorder (PMDD) should qualify as a disorder. And the Social Psychology chapter discusses the contemporary issue of cyberbullying.

"I really like the approach of focusing on application. This is a course that is directly applicable to the lives of students and it is essential that a textbook makes that clear."

—Amy J. Ort, *Nebraska Wesleyan University*

New Ways of Emphasizing Diversity

Our Intro Psych students are increasingly diverse, as is the world in which they live. *My Psychology* emphasizes and embraces diversity in many forms.

Diversity is an essential element of psychology. It is also an essential element of students' lives, so, fittingly, diversity-related coverage is included in every chapter of the book, including a full chapter devoted to culture, sex, and gender.

Diversity Matters flags call attention to the role that diversity and culture play in many important psychology concepts. These Diversity Matters flags show that diversity is woven throughout the entire text rather than compartmentalized. Diversity is appreciated in broad terms — not just ethnicity or race, but other areas of individual difference as well, including age, gender, sexual orientation, socioeconomic status, religion, and more. As an example, a Diversity Matters flag in the Social Psychology chapter highlights coverage of the impact of individualism and collectivism on conformity.

***My Psychology* dedicates a full chapter to diversity.** The title of Chapter 10 — Diversity in Psychology: Multiculturalism, Gender, and Sexuality — indicates that its focus (relative to comparable chapters in other textbooks) is uniquely inclusive and focused on social awareness. Expert advice and feedback from a diverse panel of reviewers — such as Albert K. Toh of the University of Arkansas at Pine Bluff, Aaliyah Churchill of California State University Northridge, and Eva Szeli of Arizona State University — as well as recognized scholars of diversity in psychology — Rachel Farr of the University of Kentucky, Stephen Forssell of The George Washington University, and Debra Roberts of Howard University — ensure the quality of this important material. The chapter begins by recognizing many forms of diversity in the way students live, including race, ethnicity, language, religion, age, sexual orientation, education, income, ability/disability status, and big city versus small town. It then educates students about a variety of other broad-based concepts, including how cultures can be defined, diversity *within* groups (dynamic sizing), acculturation, cultural intelligence, and microaggressions. Of course, the chapter also delivers complete coverage of the topics of gender and sexuality, including discussion of the concepts of cisgender, transgender, and transition.

"I'm currently using Pomerantz's *My Psychology*, and I love how relatable this book is for students! It's very well-written and the examples are all very current and interesting. I also absolutely love that there's an entire chapter devoted to multiculturalism and diversity!"

—Jessamy Comer, *Rochester Institute of Technology*

Diversity is an essential part of psychology. *My Psychology* features unique coverage of diversity throughout the text as well as a full chapter (Chapter 10) dedicated to diversity.
(Top to bottom) Peathegee Inc/Blend Images/Getty Images; commerceandculturestock/Getty Images; mbbirdy/Getty Images

"My favorite aspect of the book is that it has an entire chapter dedicated to multiculturalism. This is particularly important to me as a faculty member of color, and I think it is critical to promote discussions of diversity within the field. I also enjoy that the book comes with an abundance of resources to allow students to engage with the material outside of simply reading the book."

—Aaliyah Churchill, *California State University Northridge*

TABLE 1: Diversity Coverage

CHAPTER 1: THE SCIENCE OF PSYCHOLOGY
Influential African Americans in the history of psychology, p. 10–11
Influential women in the history of psychology, p. 12
Differences across cultures in acceptance of Freud's ideas, p. 14
Differences across cultures in acceptance of behaviorism around the world, p. 15
How multiculturalism challenged assumptions held by some older schools of psychology, p. 16
How psychologists can fight racism, p. 19

CHAPTER 2: BRAIN AND BEHAVIOR
How poverty can influence brain development, p. 51
How the experience can influence brain development, pp. 51–52
How different languages may influence the brain differently, p. 52

CHAPTER 3: SENSATION AND PERCEPTION
How gender, age, ethnicity, and experience can influence an individual's absolute threshold, p. 67
How culture can influence vision, p. 82
How culture can influence audition, p. 86
How gender and ethnicity can influence olfactory abilities, p. 89
Why people from different cultures enjoy different foods, p. 91
Differences in gendered pain, p. 94

CHAPTER 4: CONSCIOUSNESS
How culture can influence circadian rhythms, p. 106
How gender, ethnicity, and age can influence sleep, pp. 109–110

CHAPTER 5: MEMORY
How culture impacts flashbulb memories, p. 156
How ethnicity can influence what we remember, p. 159
How language can influence what we remember, pp. 159–160
Differences in memory and socioeconomic status, p. 160

CHAPTER 6: LEARNING
Coverage of Charles Henry Turner, one of the first Black behavioral researchers, pp. 173–174
How classical conditioning can happen differently within diverse groups, p. 181
How ethnicity can influence perceptions of reinforcements, p. 187

CHAPTER 7: COGNITION: THINKING, LANGUAGE, AND INTELLIGENCE
How culture interacts with expertise, p. 213
How culture can influence concept formation, p. 213
How multiple cultural backgrounds and languages can influence creativity, p. 222
How figurative language isn't necessarily universal, pp. 229–230
How ethnicity and socioeconomic status can create test bias in measures of intelligence, p. 242
How culture-fair intelligence tests aim to minimize bias, p. 243
Coverage of stereotype threat, p. 243–244

CHAPTER 8: MOTIVATION AND EMOTION
How diversity influences experiences of intrinsic and extrinsic motivation, p. 251
How ethnicity can influence Maslow's hierarchy of needs, p. 258
How ethnicity can influence motivation, pp. 258–259
How gender can influence motivation, p. 259
How age can influence motivation, pp. 259–260
How sex, stress, and economic factors can influence eating behaviors, pp. 265–268
How age, ethnicity, and gender can interact with emotion, pp. 277–280

CHAPTER 9: DEVELOPMENT ACROSS THE LIFE SPAN
How culture can influence the development of mathematical abilities, p. 293
How culture can influence the likelihood of co-sleeping, p. 293
How television watching can foster stereotypes regarding ethnicity and gender, p. 307
How culture can influence the evaluation of various parenting styles, p. 310
How culture can interact with goodness-of-fit between kids and parenting styles, p. 311
How ethnicity can influence the development of childhood friendships, p. 312
How ethnicity can influence the moral sense of what is right, p. 317
Differences in gender and psychological disorders, p. 321
How ethnicity can influence dating patterns in teens, pp. 322–323
How ethnicity can influence perceptions of emerging adulthood, p. 324
How ethnicity can influence the experience of empty nest syndrome, p. 329

(Continued)

TABLE 1: Diversity Coverage (CONTINUED)

CHAPTER 10: DIVERSITY IN PSYCHOLOGY: MULTICULTURALISM, GENDER, AND SEXUALITY
This whole chapter focuses on diversity!
How race, ethnicity, language, religion, age, and other culture variables vary within the United States, pp. 337–339
Explanation and discussion of intersectionality, p. 339
What dynamic sizing is, and how it relates to understanding people from diverse cultures, p. 341
How the definition of culture has changed over the years, p. 341
How multiculturalism has come to play an important role in psychology, pp. 342–345
What acculturation is, and how acculturation strategies differ, pp. 344–345
What acculturative stress is, p. 345
Which specific variables differ between cultural groups, pp. 346–348
How cultural differences can translate into differences in daily life, pp. 348–351
Applying diversity with the ADDRESSING model, p. 351
What cultural intelligence is, pp. 351–352
What cultural humility is, pp. 352–353
What microaggressions are, pp. 353–355
What being an antiracist is, p. 355
What colorism is, p. 355
How gender, sex, gender identity, and nonbinary are defined, p. 356
What influences gender development, pp. 356–358
What cisgender, transgender, and transition mean, p. 358
How sexual orientation is defined, pp. 359–360
Coming out and mental health, p. 360
How cultural variables can influence attitudes toward sexual minorities, pp. 361–362
How gender differences translate into differences in daily life, pp. 362–365

CHAPTER 11: STRESS AND HEALTH
How culture can influence the appraisal of stressors, p. 373
How gender, culture, and age can influence the experience of stress, pp. 384–387
How ethnicity and gender can influence coping strategies, pp. 388–391

CHAPTER 12: PERSONALITY
How culture can influence the evaluation of humanistic theory, p. 418
Differences in external locus of control and mental health, p. 422
How research has confirmed the Big Five personality traits in countries around the world, p. 428
How multicultural experiences influence personality traits, p. 428
How cultural competence plays an important role in personality assessment, pp. 430–431

CHAPTER 13: SOCIAL PSYCHOLOGY
How ethnicity can influence the likelihood of the fundamental attribution error, pp. 441–442
How culture can influence the likelihood of conformity, pp. 449–450
Differences in obeying instructions from authority figures, p. 452
How ethnicity and gender can influence bodily attractiveness, p. 456
How ethnicity and gender can influence aggressive behavior, p. 465
Gender differences in perception of physical attractiveness, p. 466

CHAPTER 14: PSYCHOLOGICAL DISORDERS
How culture can influence perceptions of normality and abnormality, p. 478
Differences in psychological consequences during the pandemic, p. 483
How ethnicity can influence the experience of anxiety disorders, p. 496
How ethnicity can influence the experience of major depressive disorder, p. 503
How ethnicity can influence the experience of eating disorders, p. 507
How an urban or rural lifestyle can influence the experience of schizophrenia, p. 513

CHAPTER 15: THERAPY
How the lack of diversity in efficacy studies limits their generalizability, p. 550
How ethnicity, age, socioeconomic status, relations, sexual orientation, and other cultural variables are relevant to evidence-based psychotherapy, p. 551
How essential cultural competence is to therapists, pp. 553–555
How essential cultural self-awareness is to therapists, p. 554
Narrow versus broad definitions of what constitutes a culture, pp. 554–555

"[For] me, as an African American female, teaching in a school with quite a bit of diversity, but placed in a strong southern-based geographical region, I believed a textbook that spoke to multiculturalism explicitly was important for initiating much needed conversations."

—Bibia Redd, *University of North Georgia-Gainesville*

Pedagogy That Enriches the Learning Experience

Our Intro Psych students benefit from effective learning tools integrated into their reading experience. *My Psychology* provides a full, multifaceted program of these tools.

My Psychology is packed with pedagogical tools that maximize students' engagement with and understanding of the science of psychology. These tools aim to include students from all educational backgrounds, and many leverage personal connections to the material to boost memory and comprehension.

"Examples, examples, examples. If there is one thing that stands out to me about this text it is that it really does a nice job of providing various means for the student to connect concepts to real life."
—Elizabeth Arnott-Hill, *College of DuPage*

An example-rich approach. An Intro Psych textbook is only as good as its examples, and *My Psychology* stands out in both the quantity and quality of examples it offers. Every major concept is explained with at least one example, and minor concepts frequently receive the same treatment. These examples resonate with students by providing a real-world (*students'* real world) context to help them appreciate the material. For example, in the Motivation and Emotion chapter, when describing the theories of emotion, textbooks typically use the example of a dog or a wolf attacking a person as an event that evokes strong emotion. *My Psychology* instead uses the example of dropping a smartphone on a hard surface – something far more common and immediate to today's Intro Psych student. Collectively, the examples in *My Psychology* strike an ideal balance between accessibility and rigor. (Numerous examples describe clients with whom the author has personally worked in his clinical practice. In those cases, any identifying information has been changed, disguised, or omitted to maintain client confidentiality.)

In the Brain and Behavior chapter, an example of sensory and motor neurons concerns searching for your smartphone in a dark room by reaching through a crowded backpack. In the Memory chapter, chunking is illustrated with a condensed list of TV networks – NBCHBOTBSBETTNTCBS. In the Social Psychology chapter, the example for the fundamental attribution errors considers watching another vehicle speed versus speeding oneself.

"I like the three-step synced pedagogical system. It is a sound practice."
—Diana L. Ciesko, *Valencia College*

Three-step synced pedagogical system. Each major section of each chapter starts with learning objectives ("You Will Learn") and ends with a question about each one ("Check Your Learning"). The Chapter Summary then provides the answers to each of those questions. A simple, synchronized numbering system makes it easy for students to follow any particular concept through these three stages. This preview–question–answer process provides students with the core knowledge delivered in each chapter.

Each major section of each chapter starts with learning objectives ("You Will Learn") and ends with a corresponding question about each learning objective ("Check Your Learning"). The Chapter Summary then answers each question at the end of the chapter. The synchronized numbering system for the preview-question-answer process helps students to learn the core knowledge in every chapter.

YOU WILL LEARN:

5.1 how psychologists define memory.

5.2 about the role that memory can play in personal identity.

CHECK YOUR LEARNING:

5.1 How do psychologists define memory?

5.2 What role does memory play in personal identity?

CHAPTER SUMMARY

Defining Memory

5.1 Memory is the process of taking in information, saving it over time, and retrieving it later.

5.2 Memories define each individual as a unique person.

What's Your Take? Critical thinking questions invite the students to connect their own experiences to important psychological concepts. For example, in the Learning chapter, a What's Your Take? question prompts students to think about how their own pets have been classically conditioned. In the Development chapter, another question prompts students to think about how the college environment might represent a "strange situation" (often used in infant attachment research) for themselves or other students.

Addressing the student directly. As appropriate, *My Psychology* speaks straight to the student. The text does not shy away from using words like *you, your,* and *yours* to explain concepts to students. Such use of second-person language furthers the students' sense of engagement and interaction with the material. The second-person approach is used judiciously, woven tactfully in and out of more standard didactic language — enough to hook the student into persisting through the assigned reading, but not so much that more typical presentation of material is compromised.

Student dialogue questions. In my own experience teaching Intro Psych, I have noticed common questions that arise from my students when we cover particular topics. In *My Psychology*, those questions (and others) are embedded as student dialogue questions. Distinguished by a colorful font and an icon of a student with a raised hand, many student dialogue questions anticipate students' confusion or difficulties and provide clear-cut answers. Some student dialogue questions overlap with the concepts that instructors and students identify as especially challenging and likely to cause "bottlenecks" to learning (Gurung & Hackathorn, 2018; Gurung & Landrum, 2013). For example, in the Learning chapter, the distinction between negative reinforcement and punishment is notorious for tripping up students. A student dialogue question inserted at that very point in the text — "Wait, what's the difference between negative reinforcement and punishment?" — gives voice to the student's puzzlement and sets the stage for the clarifying answer that immediately follows.

"I really like the ease of reading and understanding that is presented in this text.... There are also the added pedagogical features that draw the student in and create a very relatable feel between the text and everyday life. These are definite pluses to using this text.... I would give it a 10."

—Vivian C. Hsu-Yang, *Penn State University - Abington*

"Student Dialogue Questions stand out as a valuable pedagogical feature."

—Celeste Favela, *El Paso Community College*

Wait, I'm confused. What's the difference between punishment and negative reinforcement?

These student dialogue questions are common questions that students have asked in Intro Psych courses. They give voice to the student's potential puzzlement and set the stage for clarifying answers.

Correspondence with APA's Introductory Psychology Initiative (IPI) and APA's Guidelines for the Undergraduate Psychology Major

For many years, the American Psychological Association has offered guidelines relevant to the teaching of introductory psychology. Initially, those guidelines took the form of the APA Guidelines for the Undergraduate Psychology Major, which centered on student learning goals in five areas (APA, 2013; Hettich, 2014):

- Knowledge base in psychology
- Scientific inquiry and critical thinking
- Ethical and social responsibility in a diverse world
- Communication
- Professional development

Of course, many students who take introductory psychology will major in another field and some may never take another psychology course. In response, the APA developed its Introductory Psychology Initiative (IPI) with recommendations aimed more directly at this specific course (Gurung & Neufeld, 2022). Those recommendations emphasize student learning outcomes based on seven Key Integrative Themes of psychology (Altman, 2021; APA, 2021). *My Psychology* thoroughly addresses each theme:

- *Psychological science relies on empirical evidence and adapts as new data develop.* Every chapter of *My Psychology* is rich with empirical research. Chapter 1 describes the importance of empirical research and the process by which it is conducted, using a uniquely effective combination of relatable examples, My Take videos featuring actual introductory psychology students, text boxes, and visuals.

- *Psychology explains general principles that govern behavior while recognizing individual differences.* The strong emphasis on diversity throughout *My Psychology* thoroughly addresses this theme. The text features a full chapter on diversity and related issues (Chapter 10), and diversity coverage is infused throughout every chapter (highlighted by Diversity Matters flags).
- *Psychological, biological, social, and cultural factors influence behavior and mental processes.* Coverage of these four factors is woven throughout the book. Of course, most chapters emphasize psychological factors, but *My Psychology* includes full chapters emphasizing biological (Chapter 2), social (Chapter 13), and cultural (Chapter 10) factors.
- *Psychology values diversity, promotes equity, and fosters inclusion in pursuit of a more just society.* Again, the strong emphasis on diversity, including a full chapter on the topic and meaningful material woven throughout every chapter, reflects these values. Diversity coverage spans many characteristics, including ethnicity, race, gender, age, sexual orientation, ability/disability status, religion, socioeconomic status, and more. Moreover, an especially diverse photo and figure program, as well as inclusive language, enhance all students' experiences of connecting with the material.
- *Our perceptions and biases filter our experiences of the world through an imperfect personal lens.* Often, coverage in *My Psychology* contrasts empirical findings of psychology researchers with the perceptions and biases that students may carry. Numerous sections specifically address the kinds of imperfect perceptions that our personal lens can produce, including belief perseverance and the correlation/causation fallacy (Chapter 1), sensory illusions (Chapter 3), the impact of sleep deprivation on ethnic/racial bias (Chapter 4), memory mistakes and hindsight bias (Chapter 5), heuristics, confirmation bias, and affective forecasting (Chapter 7), the influence of diversity variables on perception and experience (Chapter 10), prejudice, first impressions, and ingroup bias (Chapter 13), the influence of various psychological disorders on experience (Chapter 14), and cognitive distortions that can contribute to psychological disorders (Chapter 15).
- *Applying psychological principles can change our lives, organizations, and communities in positive ways.* Life Hacks, a feature unique to *My Psychology*, offer direct, evidence-based suggestions to students in every chapter for how their own lives can be improved by applying the psychological principles they are studying. Moreover, positive outcomes offered by the application of psychology appear repeatedly throughout *My Psychology*. For example, Chapter 15 explains the benefits of various forms of psychotherapy and biomedical treatments in detail; Chapter 13 features coverage of strategies for overcoming prejudice; Chapter 11 includes a wide range of strategies for coping with stress; Chapter 10 includes suggestions for increasing cultural intelligence, handling microaggressions, and being an antiracist; Chapter 8 includes suggestions for eating healthy and exercise; Chapter 5 includes tips for improving memory; Chapter 4 includes sleep hygiene suggestions; and Chapter 1 includes evidence-based tips for academic success in college.
- *Ethical principles guide psychology research and practice.* Ethical principles—specifically, the American Psychological Association Code of Ethics—take center stage several times in *My Psychology*. For example, Chapter 1 features a section on ethical issues in psychology research, and Chapter 15 includes extensive coverage of ethical issues in psychotherapy such as multiple relationships, confidentiality, and informed consent.

My Psychology delivers content that corresponds strongly with both sets of APA guidelines. Table 2 offers details of that correspondence for the Guidelines for the Undergraduate Psychology Major, and Table 3 offers details of that correspondence for the IPI Key Integrative Themes.

TABLE 2: How *My Psychology* Covers the APA's Guidelines for the Undergraduate Psychology Major

Goal 1: Knowledge Base in Psychology

1.1 Describe key concepts, principles, and overarching themes in psychology

1.2 Develop a working knowledge of psychology's content domains

1.3 Describe applications of psychology

TEXT CONTENT

Chapter 1: 1.1–1.15
Chapter 2: 2.1–2.34
Chapter 3: 3.1–3.31
Chapter 4: 4.1–4.25
Chapter 5: 5.1–5.27
Chapter 6: 6.1–6.31
Chapter 7: 7.1–7.34
Chapter 8: 8.1–8.17
Chapter 9: 9.1–9.26
Chapter 10: 10.1–10.24
Chapter 11: 11.1–11.24
Chapter 12: 12.1–12.29
Chapter 13: 13.1–13.20
Chapter 14: 14.1–14.49
Chapter 15: 15.1–15.30
Appendix A: A.1–A.4 Appendix B
1.4—1.7; Psychology's Many Subfields, pp. 5–8
11.10; The Future of Psychology, pp. 18–19
4.8; Treating and Preventing Sleep Problems, pp. 116–118
4.24–4.25; Meditation and Mindfulness, pp. 130–133
5.21; Socioeconomic Status and Memory, p. 160
5.22; Efforts to Improve Memory, pp. 157–159
Applying Classical Conditioning to Your Life, pp. 182–183
Applying Operant Conditioning to Your Life, pp. 194–195
8.11; Promoting Healthy Eating, pp. 269–270
8.15; Emotion Regulation, pp. 280–281
8.16; Why Emotion Regulation Matters, pp. 281–283
10.9–10.10: Acculturation: Managing Multiple Cultures, pp. 344–345
11.16–11.21; Coping with Stress: Psychological Strategies and Social Strategies, pp. 388–396
11.22–11.24; Coping with Stress: Physical and Medical Strategies, pp. 396–399
13.4; Attitude Persuasion Strategies, pp. 443–445
13.15; Toward Fairness and Cooperation: Fighting Prejudice, pp. 458–460
14.4–14.7; Why Do Psychological Disorders Develop?, pp. 480–486

FEATURE CONTENT

The knowledge base and major topics of psychology are further reinforced by all Chapter Apps, My Take videos, From Research to Real Life text features, Watching Psychology text features, Current Controversy text features, It's Like... text features, Diversity Matters flags, Life Hack text features, Show Me More links, student dialogue questions, the study guide, Achieve resources, the LearningCurve quizzing system, and the Instructor's Resource Manual.

Goal 2: Scientific Inquiry and Critical Thinking

2.1 Use scientific reasoning to interpret psychological phenomena

2.2 Demonstrate psychology information literacy

2.3 Engage in innovative and integrative thinking and problem solving

2.4 Interpret, design, and conduct basic psychological research

2.5 Incorporate sociocultural factors in scientific inquiry

TEXT CONTENT

1.10; Multiculturalism, p. 16
1.10; Biopsychosocial Theory, p. 18
1.10; The Future of Psychology, pp. 18–19
1.11–1.15; The Science of Psychology, pp. 20–29
2.30–2.34; How We Know All of This: Viewing the Brain, pp. 56–59
3.15; How Diversity Influences Vision, pp. 81–82
3.21; How Diversity Influences Hearing, pp. 86–87
4.5–4.6; Diversity in Normal Sleep, pp. 109–113
5.21; Diversity and Memory, pp. 159–160
6.14; Reinforcement and Diversity, p. 187
Expertise, Culture, and Concepts, pp. 212–213
7.5–7.8; Problem Solving and Decision Making, pp. 213–217
7.14; Creativity and Culture, p. 222
7.14; Creativity and COVID, p. 222
7.32; Test Bias, pp. 242–243
7.33; Stereotype Threat, pp. 243–244
7.34; Group Differences, p. 244
8.6; Motivation and Diversity, pp. 258–260
8.10; Environmental and Sociocultural Factors in Hunger and Eating, pp. 265–269
8.17; Emotion and Diversity, pp. 284–286
9.12–9.14; Psychosocial Development in Infancy and Childhood, pp. 307–312
9.19–9.23; Psychosocial Development in Adolescence, pp. 317–324
9.26; Psychosocial Development in Adulthood, pp. 327–332
10.1–10.24: Chapter 10, Diversity in Psychology: Multiculturalism, Gender, and Sexuality, pp. 336–365
11.12; Stress and COVID, p. 383
11.13–11.15; Stress and Diversity, pp. 384–387
11.17; Diversity and Coping, pp. 388–389
12.24; Diversity, Multiculturalism, and Personality, pp. 428–429
13.13–13.14; Prejudice: Us Versus Them, pp. 456–458
13.15; Toward Fairness and Cooperation: Fighting Prejudice, pp. 458–460
14.6; The Sociocultural Theory of Psychological Disorders, pp. 481–482
14.7; The Biopsychosocial Theory of Psychological Disorders, p. 482
The Influence of COVID, p. 483
The Influence of Stigma, pp. 484–486
15.16–15.17; The Importance of Culture and Diversity in Psychotherapy, pp. 553–555
A.1–A.5; Appendix A: An Introduction to Statistics in Psychological Research

(Continued)

TABLE 2: How *My Psychology* Covers the APA's Guidelines for the Undergraduate Psychology Major (CONTINUED)

FEATURE CONTENT

Chapter 1: Current Controversy: Should Psychologists Prescribe Medication?; From Research to Real Life: Psychologists' Research on College Success; Chapter App 1.1: MyHomework; My Take Video 1.1: Belief Perseverance; My Take Video 1.2: Correlation-Causation Fallacy; Life Hack 1.1; Watching Psychology: Survey Says? *Family Feud* and Random Sampling; Show Me More 1.1: Nature Versus Nurture; Show Me More 1.2: Will Your State Need Psychologists in the Future? Show Me More 1.3: The Placebo Effect; Show Me More 1.4: My Psychology Podcast

Chapter 2: Life Hack 2.1; My Take Video 2.1: Parts of the Brain; Watching Psychology: What Happens in Your Brain When You Watch Movies and TV; Chapter App 2.1: 3D Brain; It's Like...: Plasticity Is Like An Athlete Switching Positions; Chapter App 2.2: GlassesOff Life Hack 2.2; From Research to Real Life: The Murderer's Mind; Current Controversy: Neuroeverything?; Show Me More 2.1: How Neurons Work; Show Me More 2.2: A Split-Brain Patient; Show Me More 2.3 My Psychology Podcast

Chapter 3: My Take Video 3.1: Difference Threshold; My Take Video 3.2: Sensory Adaptation; From Research to Real Life: Variety, the Key to Happiness?; It's Like...: Top-Down Processing Is Like Autocomplete; Life Hack 3.1; Chapter App 3.1: BioDigital Human; Chapter App 3.2: Be My Eyes; Life Hack 3.2; Chapter App 3.3: GeoPain; Life Hack 3.3; Watching Psychology: More Touch, More Wins?; Show Me More 3.1: Sensory Interaction: Combining Video and Audio Show Me More 3.2: The McGurk Effect: Does Lipreading Override Hearing?; Show Me More 3.3: Mudsplashes, Gorillas, and Change Blindness; Show Me More 3.4: The Margaret Thatcher Effect on More Faces; Show Me More 3.5: The Science of Smell; Show Me More 3.6: My Psychology Podcast

Chapter 4: It's Like...: Consciousness Is Like a Light Controlled by a Dimmer; Life Hack 4.1; My Take Video 4.1: Sleep Deprivation; From Research to Real Life: Do You Realize What Sleep Deprivation Does to You?; My Take Video 4.2: Circadian Rhythm; Watching Psychology: What (Body Clock) Time Is Kickoff?; Chapter App 4.1: Sleep Cycle Current Controversy: Should High School Start Later in the Day?; Life Hack 4.2; My Take Video 4.3: Screens and Sleep; Chapter App 4.2: Insight Timer; Show Me More 4.1: Natural Light and Circadian Rhythms; Show Me More 4.2: The Benefits of Naps; Show Me More 4.3: My Psychology Podcast

Chapter 5: From Research to Real Life: Is Forgetting Good?; It's Like...: Your Smartphone Is Like a Flash Drive for Your Brain; Chapter App 5.1: 50 US States; My Take Video 5.1: Recall Versus Recognition; Life Hack 5.1; Watching Psychology: The Serial Position Effect on *American Idol*; My Take Video 5.2: Flashbulb Memory; Life Hack 5.2; From Research to Real Life: Improving Your Memory; Life Hack 5.3; Chapter App 5.2: Elevate; Current Controversy: Can Head Injuries in Sports Cause Memory Loss?; My Take Video 5.3: Memory Mistakes; Show Me More 5.1: Moonwalking with Einstein; Show Me More 5.2: Sports Head Injuries and Memory Loss; Show Me More 5.3: An App that Mimics the Hippocampus to Help Memory Functions; Show Me More 5.3: My Psychology Podcast

Chapter 6: My Take Video 6.1: Classical Conditioning; From Research to Real Life: Classical Conditioning in Advertising; It's Like...: The Classic Study of Dogs Discriminating Between Similar Shapes Is Like You Discriminating Between Similar Logos; Chapter App 6.1: Aqualert Water Intake Tracker and Reminder; Chapter App 6.2: OurHome; My Take Video 6.2: Reinforcement Schedules; Watching Psychology: Home Runs and Schedules of Reinforcement; Chapter App 6.3: stickK; Life Hack 6.1; Current Controversy: Does Violence in the Media Cause Violence in Real Life?; Life Hack 6.2; Show Me More 6.1: Classical Conditioning; Show Me More 6.2: My Psychology Podcast

Chapter 7: Chapter App 7.1: Hello Talk; My Take Video 7.1: Affective Forecasting; Life Hack 7.1; Watching Psychology: Convergent and Divergent Thinking on *Family Feud;* Life Hack 7.2; Current Controversy: What Is Texting Doing to Language?; My Take Video 7.2: Emotional Intelligence; From Research to Real Life: Intelligence Correlates with...; Show Me More 7.1: Daniel Kahneman Discusses Dual-Process Theory; Show Me More 7.2: Why More Choices Don't Make You Happy; Show Me More 7.3: Is Texting Killing Language?; Show Me More 7.4: Neuroscience and Language; Show Me More 7.5: My Psychology Podcast

Chapter 8: My Take Video 8.1: Intrinsic and Extrinsic Motivation; Chapter App 8.1: Space; Chapter App 8.2: Daylio; It's Like...: The Thrifty Gene Hypothesis Is Like Buying Gas for a Nickel a Gallon; My Take Video 8.2: Emotion Regulation; Life Hack 8.2; From Research to Real Life: Does Money Buy Happiness?; Life Hack 8.3; Watching Psychology: This Show Is Scary; Show Me More 8.1: Derek Redmond and His Father Cross the Finish Line; Show Me More 8.2: Obesity Guidelines Move Away from Focus on Weight Loss; Show Me More 8.3: Serving Size Versus What You Really Eat; Show Me More 8.4: My Psychology Podcast

Chapter 9: Chapter App 9.1: Pregnancy Tracker—BabyCenter; From Research to Real Life: A Well-Running Brain; Life Hack 9.1; It's Like...: Assimilation and Accommodation Are Like Sorting Laundry; Watching Psychology: Screen Time and Kids' Development; My Take Video 9.1: Parenting Styles; Chapter App 9.2: Twitter; Current Controversy: Social Media; My Take Video 9.2: Emerging Adulthood; Life Hack 9.2; Show Me More 9.1: Newborns Can Make Sense of Hearing and Sight Together; Show Me More 9.2: Piaget's Conservation Task; Show Me More 9.3: Moral Decision Making and a Legendary Producer's Records; Show Me More 9.4: My Psychology Podcast

Chapter 10: My Take Video 10.1: Culture; Life Hack 10.1; Chapter App 10.1: Culture Guide; Chapter App 10.2: Vent; My Take Video 10.2: Microaggressions; It's Like...: Dynamic Sizing Is Like Appreciating Breanna Stewart's Height; Life Hack 10.2; My Take Video 10.3: Gender and Gender Development; Watching Psychology: TV, Sexual Attitudes, and Sexual Behaviors; Chapter App 10.3: Refuge Restrooms; Current Controversy: How Does Social Media Affect Body Image?; Show Me More 10.1: Healthy Ways to Discuss Issues of Race; Show Me More 10.2: Microaggressions; Show Me More 10.3: Gender and Gender Roles; Show Me More 10.4: My Psychology Podcast

Chapter 11: It's Like...: Stopping Your Fight-or-Flight Response Is Like Stepping on the Gas and Brake at the Same Time; My Take Video 11.1: Appraisal; Chapter App 11.1: Serenita; Current Controversy: What Counts as a Trauma?; Life Hack 11.1; My Take Video 11.2: Coping; Life Hack 11.2; From Research to Real Life: Don't Stress Out about Stress; Chapter App 11.2: The Mighty; Life Hack 11.3; Chapter App 11.3: Runkeeper; Show Me More 11.1: Human Versus Animal Experience of Stress; Show Me More 11.2: Type A Personality Explained; Show Me More 11.3: Toxic Stress in Young Children; Show Me More 11.4: Conquering Loneliness in a Lonely World; Show Me More 11.5: My Psychology Podcast

Chapter 12: Life Hack 12.1; My Take Video 12.1: Locus of Control; Chapter App 12.1: Freedom; From Research to Real Life: What's Happening to Our Locus of Control?; Current Controversy: Is There an Upside to Neuroticism?; My Take Video 12.2: Five-Factor Model of Personality; Watching Psychology: Personality and Preferences in Movies and TV; Life Hack 12.2; Show Me More 12.1: Locus of Control and Academic Potential; Show Me More 12.2: The Big Five and College Majors; Show Me More 12.3: My Psychology Podcast

TABLE 2: How *My Psychology* Covers the APA's Guidelines for the Undergraduate Psychology Major (CONTINUED)

Chapter 13: My Take Video 13.1: The Fundamental Attribution Error; From Research to Real Life: Can Cognitive Dissonance Increase Mask Wearing and Social Distancing During COVID?; Life Hack 13.1; My Take Video 13.2: Conformity; Chapter App 13.1: HabitShare; Life Hack 13.2; My Take Video 13.3: Social Comparison; It's Like...: Fighting Prejudice Is Like Treating Phobias; Life Hack 13.3; Chapter App 13.2: ReThink; Current Controversy: Cyberbullying and Social Psychology; Watching Psychology: *The Voice, American Idol,* and Attractiveness; Chapter App 13.3: Waze; Show Me More 13.1: An App to Stop Bullying at Its Source; Show Me More 13.2: The Give and Take of the Reciprocity Norm; Show Me More 13.3: My Psychology Podcast

Chapter 14: My Take Video 14.1: Categorical Versus Dimensional Models of Psychopathology; Current Controversy: Premenstrual Dysphoric Disorder? it's Like...: The Categorical Model Is Like an HIV Test, and the Dimensional Model Is Like a Blood Pressure Test; Life Hack 14.1; Chapter App 14.1: MindShift CBT; Chapter App 14.2: Moodtrack Diary; Life Hack 14.2; From Research to Real Life: How Powerful Is Social Media in the Development of Eating Disorders?; Show Me More 14.1: Misconceptions about Obsessive Compulsive Disorder; Show Me More 14.2: Smartphones as a Tool to Combat Depression; Show Me More 14.3: Mental Health Issues among Black Americans; Show Me More 14.4: Men, Mental Health, and the "Man Up" Mentality; Show Me More 14.5: My Psychology Podcast

Chapter 15: My Take Video 15.1: Exposure Therapy; Chapter App 15.1: FearTools; My Take Video 15.2: Cognitive Distortions; It's Like...: Eclectic Therapy Is Like Fruit Salad, and Integrative Therapy Is Like a Smoothie; My Take Video 15.3: Understanding Psychotherapy; From Research to Real Life: Psychotherapy Changes the Brain; Current Controversy: Therapies That Work... for Whom?; It's Like...: Common Factors in Therapy Are Like the Common Active Ingredient in Toothpaste; Life Hack 15.1; My Take Video 15.4: Telepsychology; Chapter App 15.2: BetterHelp; Show Me More 15.1: Judith Beck and Cognitive Therapy; Show Me More 15.2: Virtual Reality Exposure Therapy for Phobias; Show Me More 15.3: Stand-up Comedy as Therapeutic?; Show Me More 15.4: An African Perspective on the Importance of Psychological Treatment; Show Me More 15.5: My Psychology Podcast

Scientific inquiry and critical thinking in psychology are reinforced with the three-step synched pedagogical system (You Will Learn, Check Your Learning, and Chapter Summary), the Self-Assessment quiz, What's Your Take? critical thinking questions, the study guide, Achieve, LearningCurve, and the Instructor's Resource Manual.

Goal 3: Ethical and Social Responsibility in a Diverse World

3.1 Apply ethical standards to evaluate psychological science and practice

3.2 Build and enhance interpersonal relationships

3.3 Adopt values that build community at local, national, and global levels

TEXT CONTENT

11.10; The Future of Psychology, pp. 18–19
1.15; Ethics in Psychological Studies, p. 29
4.5–4.6; Diversity in Normal Sleep, pp. 109–113
4.11; Diversity and Dreams, p. 121
5.21; Socioeconomic Status and Memory, p. 160
6.10; Classical Conditioning and Diversity, pp. 181–182
6.14; Reinforcement and Diversity, p. 187
7.15–7.21; Language, pp. 223–234
8.5; One Motivation after Another: Maslow's Hierarchy, pp. 256–257
9.12–9.13; Psychosocial Development, pp. 307–312
9.14; Friend Relationships, pp. 311–312
9.22; Relationships with Parents, pp. 320–321
9.22; Relationships with Peers, pp. 321–323
10.1–10.24; Chapter 10, Diversity in Psychology: Multiculturalism, Gender, and Sexuality, pp. 336–365
10.13; The ADDRESSING Model, p. 351
10.15; Cultural Humility, pp. 352–353
10.17; Microaggressions, pp. 353–355
10.16; Antiracism, p. 355
10.22; Coming Out and Mental Health, p. 360
10.24; Differences in Digital Communication, p. 364
11.12; Stress and COVID, p. 383
11.20; Decreasing Stress by Improving Relationships, pp. 392–393
11.21; Decreasing Stress by Behaving Differently, pp. 394–396
12.24; Diversity, Multiculturalism, and Personality, pp. 428–429
13.1–13.5; Social Cognition: How We Think about Each Other, pp. 440–447
13.6–13.11; Social Influence: How We Influence Each Other, pp. 447–455
13.12–13.17; Social Relations: How We Relate to Each Other, pp. 455–469
13.18–13.20; Prosocial Behavior: Helping Each Other, pp. 469–472
14.4–14.7; Why Do Psychological Disorders Develop?, pp. 480–486
14.7; The Influence of COVID, p. 483
14.7; The Influence of Stigma, pp. 484–486
15.15; What Makes Therapy Work?, pp. 552–553
15.16–15.17; The Importance of Culture and Diversity in Psychotherapy, pp. 553–555
15.18–15.20; Ethics in Psychotherapy, pp. 555–556

FEATURE CONTENT

Chapter 2: Show Me More 2.2: A Split-Brain Patient?

Chapter 3: Watching Psychology: More Touch, More Wins?

Chapter 7: Show Me More 7.3: Is Texting Killing Language?; Show Me More 7.4: Neuroscience and Language

Chapter 8: My Take Video 8.2: Intrinsic and Extrinsic Motivation

Chapter 9: Show Me More 9.3: Moral Decision Making and a Legendary Producer's Records

Chapter 10: My Take Video 10.1: Culture; Life Hack 10.1; Chapter App 10.1: Culture Guide; Chapter App 10.2: Vent; My Take Video 10.2: Microaggressions; It's Like...: Dynamic Sizing Is Like Appreciating Breanna Stewart's Height; Life Hack 10.2; Watching Psychology: TV, Sexual Attitudes, and Sexual Behaviors; Chapter App 10.3: Refuge Restrooms Show Me More 10.1: Show Me More 10.2: Healthy Ways to Discuss Issues of Race Microaggressions; Show Me More 10.3: Gender and Gender Roles

Chapter 11: Chapter App 11.2: The Mighty; Life Hack 11.3

Chapter 12: Life Hack 12.1

Chapter 13: My Take Video 13.1: The Fundamental Attribution Error; From Research to Real Life: Can Cognitive Dissonance Increase Mask Wearing and Social Distancing During COVID?; Life Hack 13.1; My Take Video 13.2: Conformity; Chapter App 13.1: HabitShare; Life Hack 13.2; My Take Video 13.3: Social Comparison; Chapter App 13.2: ReThink; Current Controversy: Cyberbullying and Social Psychology; It's Like...: Fighting Prejudice Is Like Treating Phobias; Life Hack 13.3; Chapter App 13.3: Waze; Show Me More 13.1: An App to Stop Bullying at Its Source; Show Me More 13.2: The Give and Take of the Reciprocity Norm

Chapter 14: From Research to Real Life: How Powerful Is Social Media in the Development of Eating Disorders?; Show Me More 14.2: Smartphones as a Tool to Combat Depression; Show Me More 14.3: Mental Health Issues among Black Americans; Show Me More 14.4: Men, Mental Health, and the "Man Up" Mentality

Chapter 15: My Take Video 15.4: Telepsychology; Show Me More 15.3: Stand-up Comedy as Therapeutic?; Show Me More 15.4: An African Perspective on the Importance of Psychological Treatment

Ethical responsibility and social responsibility in a diverse world are reinforced by dozens of Diversity Matters flags throughout the entire text.

(Continued)

TABLE 2: How *My Psychology* Covers the APA's Guidelines for the Undergraduate Psychology Major (CONTINUED)

Goal 4: Communication

4.1 Demonstrate effective writing for different purposes

4.2 Exhibit effective presentation skills for different purposes

4.3 Interact effectively with others

TEXT CONTENT

1.14; How Psychologists Share Their Results, pp. 28–29
5.25; The Misinformation Effect and Fake News, pp. 164–165
7.15–7.21; Language, pp. 223–234
8.14; Communicating Emotions, pp. 275–280
9.14; Friend Relationships, pp. 311–312
9.22; Relationships with Parents, pp. 320–321
9.22; Relationships with Peers, pp. 321–323
10.1–10.24; Chapter 10, Diversity in Psychology: Multiculturalism, Gender, and Sexuality, pp. 336–365
13.12–13.17; Social Relations: How We Relate to Each Other, pp. 455–469
13.18–13.20; Prosocial Behavior: Helping Each Other, pp. 469–472
15.16–15.17; The Importance of Culture and Diversity in Psychotherapy, pp. 553–555

FEATURE CONTENT

Chapter 3: Watching Psychology: More Touch, More Wins?; Show Me More 3.3: Mudsplashes, Gorillas, and Change Blindness

Chapter 7: Current Controversy: What Is Texting Doing to Language?; Show Me More 7.3: Is Texting Killing Language?; Show Me More 7.4: Neuroscience and Language

Chapter 10: My Take Video 10.1: Culture; Life Hack 10.1; Chapter App 10.1: Culture Guide; Chapter App 10.2: Vent; My Take Video 10.2: Microaggressions; It's Like...: Dynamic Sizing Is Like Appreciating Breanna Stewart's Height; Life Hack 10.2; My Take Video 10.3: Gender and Gender Development; Watching Psychology: TV, Sexual Attitudes, and Sexual Behaviors; Chapter App 10.3: Refuge Restrooms; Current Controversy: How Does Social Media Affect Body Image?; Show Me More 10.1: Healthy Ways to Discuss Issues of Race; Show Me More 10.2: Microaggressions; Show Me More 10.3: Gender and Gender Roles

Chapter 11: Chapter App 11.2: The Mighty

Chapter 13: My Take Video 13.1: The Fundamental Attribution Error; From Research to Real Life: Can Cognitive Dissonance Increase Mask Wearing and Social Distancing During COVID?; Life Hack 13.1; My Take Video 13.2: Conformity; Chapter App 13.1: HabitShare; Life Hack 13.2; My Take Video 13.3: Social Comparison; It's Like...: Fighting Prejudice Is Like Treating Phobias; Life Hack 13.3; Chapter App 13.2: ReThink; Current Controversy: Cyberbullying and Social Psychology; Chapter App 13.3: Waze; Show Me More 13.1: An App to Stop Bullying at Its Source; Show Me More 13.2: The Give and Take of the Reciprocity Norm

Chapter 15: My Take Video 15.4: Telepsychology; Show Me More 15.3: Stand-up Comedy as Therapeutic?; Show Me More 15.4: An African Perspective on the Importance of Psychological Treatment

Communication skills are reinforced through What's Your Take? critical thinking questions and essay questions in the Test Bank, as well as Achieve, LearningCurve, and the Instructor's Resource Manual.

Goal 5: Professional Development

5.1 Apply psychological content and skills to career goals

5.2 Exhibit self-efficacy and self-regulation

5.3 Refine project management skills

5.4 Enhance teamwork capacity

5.5 Develop meaningful professional direction for life after graduation

TEXT CONTENT

1.10; The Future of Psychology, pp. 18–19
1.2; What Psychology Is *Not*, pp. 2–4
1.4–1.7; Psychology's Many Subfields, pp. 5–8
5.7; Effortful Processing, pp. 141–142
7.5–7.8; Problem Solving and Decision Making, pp. 213–217
8.1–8.6; Motivation, pp. 250–260
8.15; Emotion Regulation, pp. 280–281
8.16; Why Emotion Regulation Matters, pp. 281–283
11.8; How Stress and Your Body Affect Each Other, pp. 374–377
11.9–11.11; How Stress and Your Mind Affect Each Other, pp. 377–383
11.12; Stress and COVID, pp. 383–384
11.20; Decreasing Stress by Improving Relationships, pp. 392–393
11.21; Decreasing Stress by Behaving Differently, pp. 394–396
12.10–12.14; Humanistic Theory of Personality, pp. 416–419
12.18; Albert Bandura, Reciprocal Determinism, and Self-Efficacy, pp. 420–421
13.1–13.5; Social Cognition: How We Think about Each Other, pp. 440–447
13.13–13.15; Prejudice: Us Versus Them, pp. 456–458
13.20; Why *Don't* People Help?, pp. 471–472
15.12–15.15; How Well Does Psychotherapy Work?, pp. 549–553
15.24–15.30; Biomedical Therapies, pp. 558–563

FEATURE CONTENT

Chapter 1: Current Controversy: Should Psychologists Prescribe Medication?; My Take Video 1.1: Belief Perseverance; My Take Video 1.2: Correlation-Causation Fallacy; Show Me More 1.2: Will Your State Need Psychologists in the Future?; how Me More 1.3: The Placebo Effect

Chapter 2: It's Like...: Plasticity Is Like an Athlete Switching Positions; Chapter App 2.2: GlassesOff; Life Hack 2.2

Chapter 3: From Research to Real Life: Variety, the Key to Happiness?; Life Hack 3.1; Chapter App 3.1: BioDigital Human; Life Hack 3.2; Chapter App 3.3: GeoPain; Life Hack 3.3; Watching Psychology: More Touch, More Wins?

Chapter 4: Life Hack 4.1; My Take Video 4.1: Sleep Deprivation; From Research to Real Life: Do You Realize What Sleep Deprivation Does to You?; My Take Video 4.2: Circadian Rhythm; Chapter App 4.1: Sleep Cycle; Life Hack 4.2

Chapter 5: From Research to Real Life: Is Forgetting Good?; Life Hack 5.1; Life Hack 5.2; From Research to Real Life: Improving Your Memory; Life Hack 5.3; Chapter App 5.2: Elevate Current Controversy: Can Head Injuries in Sports Cause Memory Loss?; My Take Video 5.3: Memory Mistakes; Show Me More 5.1: Moonwalking with Einstein; Show Me More 5.2: Sports Head Injuries and Memory Loss

Chapter 6: Life Hack 6.1; Life Hack 6.2

Chapter 7: My Take Video 7.1: Affective Forecasting; Life Hack 7.1; Watching Psychology: Convergent and Divergent Thinking on *Family Feud;* Life Hack 7.2; Current Controversy: What Is Texting Doing to Language?; My Take Video 7.2: Emotional Intelligence; From Research to Real Life: Intelligence Correlates with...; Chapter App 7.1: HelloTalk

Chapter 8: My Take Video 8.1: Intrinsic and Extrinsic Motivation; My Take Video 8.2: Emotion Regulation; Chapter App 8.1: Motivation; Chapter App 8.2: Daylio; Life Hack 8.1; Life Hack 8.2; From Research to Real Life: Does Money Buy Happiness?; Life Hack 8.3

Chapter 9: From Research to Real Life: A Well-Running Brain; Life Hack 9.1; Watching Psychology: Screen Time and Kids' Development; My Take Video 9.1: Parenting Styles; Current Controversy: Social Media: Good or Bad for Adolescent Development?; My Take Video 9.2: Emerging Adulthood; Life Hack 9.2

TABLE 2: How *My Psychology* Covers the APA's Guidelines for the Undergraduate Psychology Major (CONTINUED)

Chapter 10: Life Hack 10.1; Chapter App 10.1: Culture Guide; Chapter App 10.2: Vent; My Take Video 10.2: Microaggressions; It's Like...: Dynamic Sizing Is Like Appreciating Breanna Stewart's Height; Life Hack 10.2; Chapter App 10.3: Refuge Restrooms; Show Me More 10.1: Healthy Ways to Discuss Issues of Race; Show Me More 10.2: Microaggressions; Show Me More 10.3: Gender and Gender Roles

Chapter 11: My Take Video 11.1: Appraisal; Chapter App 11.1: Serenita; Current Controversy: What Counts as a Trauma?; Life Hack 11.1; My Take Video 11.2: Coping; Life Hack 11.2; From Research to Real Life: Don't Stress Out about Stress; Chapter App 11.2: The Mighty; Life Hack 11.3; Chapter App 11.3: Runkeeper

Chapter 12: My Take Video 12.1: Locus of Control; Chapter App 12.1: Freedom; From Research to Real Life: What's Happening to Our Locus of Control?; Current Controversy: Is There an Upside to Neuroticism?; Life Hack 12.1; My Take Video 12.2: Five-Factor Model of Personality; Show Me More 12.1: Locus of Control and Academic Potential; Show Me More 12.2: The Big Five and College Majors

Chapter 13: My Take Video 13.1: The Fundamental Attribution Error; From Research to Real Life: Can Cognitive Dissonance Increase Mask Wearing and Social Distancing During COVID?; Life Hack 13.1; My Take Video 13.2: Conformity; Chapter App 13.1: HabitShare; Life Hack 13.2; My Take Video 13.3: Social Comparison; It's Like...: Fighting Prejudice Is Like Treating Phobias; Life Hack 13.3; Chapter App 13.2: ReThink; Current Controversy: Cyberbullying and Social Psychology; Chapter App 13.3: Waze; Show Me More 13.1: An App to Stop Bullying at Its Source; Show Me More 13.2: The Give and Take of the Reciprocity Norm

Chapter 14: Life Hack 14.1; Life Hack 14.2

Chapter 15: My Take Video 15.2: Cognitive Distortions; From Research to Real Life: Psychotherapy Changes the Brain; Current Controversy: Therapies That Work... for Whom?; Life Hack 15.1; My Take Video 15.4: Telepsychology; Show Me More 15.3: Stand-up Comedy as Therapeutic?; Show Me More 15.4: An African Perspective on the Importance of Psychological Treatment

Professional development is further reinforced by Achieve, LearningCurve, and the Instructor's Resource Manual.

TABLE 3: How *My Psychology* Covers the Key Integrative Themes of the APA's Introductory Psychology Initiative (IPI)

IPI'S SEVEN "INTEGRATIVE THEMES"	IPI'S "SAMPLE CONCEPTS OR IDEAS"	*MY PSYCHOLOGY*, THIRD EDITION COVERAGE
A. Psychological science relies on empirical evidence, and adapts as new data develop.	• Experimental methods • Statistics • Memory models • Cognition • Development across the life span • Therapy interventions	• The importance of **empirical research** and the scientific process by which it is conducted are introduced in Chapter 1, and are carried throughout every chapter, with regular discussions of research studies and supporting pedagogical features. • A combination of rich, relatable examples; My Take videos featuring real students; From Research to Real Life boxes; Current Controversy boxes; and Watching Psychology boxes effectively demonstrate how central is empirical evidence in psychological science. • *My Psychology* includes a full Appendix (A), covering statistics in psychological research. Additionally, the Third Edition features well-curated research and examples relating to the psychological impact of the COVID-19 pandemic, responding to psychology in today's world and new data as it continues to evolve.
B. Psychology explains general principles that govern behavior while recognizing individual differences.	• Intelligence • Resilience • Personality testing • Supertasters • Diversity • Culture	• **Diversity** and how it relates to the key concepts and ideas in psychology is strongly emphasized throughout *My Psychology*, featured in sections designated to explore the impact of diversity on core topics (for example, "Diversity and Dreams" in Chapter 4, "Diversity and Memory" in Chapter 5, "Diversity and Coping" in Chapter 11). • The text features an entire chapter covering diversity and related issues (Chapter 10). • **Diversity Matters flags** highlight important diversity topics in diversity in each chapter. • The Third Edition includes new coverage that highlights differences and similarities between diverse groups (based on ethnicity, age, sexual orientation, gender identity and more) on important psychological variables.

(*Continued*)

TABLE 3: How *My Psychology* Covers the Key Integrative Themes of the APA's Introductory Psychology Initiative (IPI) (CONTINUED)

IPI'S SEVEN "INTEGRATIVE THEMES"	IPI'S "SAMPLE CONCEPTS OR IDEAS"	*MY PSYCHOLOGY,* THIRD EDITION COVERAGE
C. Psychological, biological, social, and cultural factors influence behavior and mental processes.	• Psychological disorders • Development across the life span • Aging • Health and wellness • Attachment • Personality theories	• The **biopsychosocial theory** is first introduced in Chapter 1, and is woven throughout the book. The text highlights the biological, psychological, social, and cultural factors that influence understanding of behavior and mental processes, and also includes full chapters dedicated to emphasizing each separately: biological (Chapter 2), social (Chapter 13), and cultural (Chapter 10). • The text's narrative examples, as well as the My Take Videos featuring real-life students discussing core ideas in psychology (including **two new My Take Videos in this Third Edition**), the variety of visuals, and the text boxes in each chapter, expand thoroughly on the biopsychosocial influences on behavior and mental processes, including drug use (Chapter 4), motivation (Chapter 8), development (Chapter 9), and more. • This edition features new coverage on psychology during COVID-19, presenting, for example, COVID-19 and Sleep Problems (Chapter 4), Memory Problems and COVID-19 (Chapter 5), and new research on the influence of COVID-19 on the development of psychological disorders (Chapter 14).
D. Psychology values diversity, promotes equity, and fosters inclusion in pursuit of a more just society.	• Racial and cultural identity • Stereotypes • Racism • Biases • Prejudice, implicit and explicit • Emotional regulation	• *My Psychology* emphasizes **diversity as a core responsibility** in each chapter, featuring meaningful material, unassuming language, new research from and featuring minoritized groups, and expanded representation in narrative examples to ensure *everyone* is included: regardless of ethnicity, race, gender, age, sexual orientation, ability/disability status, religion, socioeconomic status, and other diverse characteristics. • Along with featuring a full chapter on diversity and related topics (Chapter 10), *My Psychology* makes no gender assumptions in pronoun use, and is curated with especially diverse photos, figures, and cartoons to enhance all students' experience in connecting with the materials.
E. Our perceptions and biases filter our experiences of the world through an imperfect personal lens.	• Perceptual illusions • Schemas • Cognitive errors • Self-serving bias • Ingroup bias	• Using relatable examples and features that spotlight students themselves, *My Psychology* presents scientific research and examines how it contrasts with **perceptions and biases** that students may carry. • Numerous sections directly address theme, including belief perseverance and the correlation/causation fallacy (Chapter 1), sensory illusions (Chapter 3), the impact of sleep deprivation on ethnic/racial bias (Chapter 4), and more. • The Third Edition includes a new section on The Misinformation Effect and Fake News (Chapter 5), and is expanded with new and revised examples and diversity coverage to represent a wider range of people, emphasizing in each chapter how our own personal experiences influence our perception of the world. • Schemas and cognitive errors are covered in Chapter 7. Ingroup bias is covered in Chapter 13.
F. Applying psychological principles can change our lives, organizations, and communities in positive ways.	• Psychotherapy • Study skills • Coping • Conflict resolution • Behavioral change	• **Life Hacks** appear throughout each chapter to offer students direct evidence-based suggestions to apply what they are learning and improve their lives—helping make the content meaningful and memorable. • Integrated throughout *My Psychology* are frequent reminders and examples of how **applying psychology to everyday life** improves one's self and one's community. Students can turn to Chapter 15 to examine the benefits of forms of psychotherapy and biomedical treatments; they can find strategies for overcoming prejudice in Chapter 13; and importantly, in the first few pages of Chapter 1, they can learn useful tips that can contribute to their academic success.

TABLE 3: How *My Psychology* Covers the Key Integrative Themes of the APA's Introductory Psychology Initiative (IPI) (CONTINUED)

IPI'S SEVEN "INTEGRATIVE THEMES"	IPI'S "SAMPLE CONCEPTS OR IDEAS"	*MY PSYCHOLOGY,* THIRD EDITION COVERAGE
G. Ethical principles guide psychology research and practice.	• Beneficence (do good) and nonmaleficence (do no harm) • Fidelity and responsibility • Integrity • Justice • Respect for people's rights and dignity	• The **ethical principles** in psychology are discussed throughout the book. Along with Chapter 1's expansive section introducing the ethical obligations that psychology researchers have, Chapter 10 features a discussion on the profession's Code of Ethics in regard to multiculturalism, necessitating cultural sensitivity in therapy, assessment, and research. • Chapter 15 includes a thorough section on Ethics in Psychotherapy and, in Chapter 15's section covering The Importance of Culture and Diversity in Psychotherapy, discusses the ethical responsibility of psychotherapists to work with diverse clients in a way that respects their cultural background, values, and practices.

Correspondence with the MCAT Categories for Psychology

In recent years, the Medical College Admissions Test (MCAT) started including psychology topics on its exam. Coverage within *My Psychology* matches with many MCAT categories, as outlined in Table 4. A full correspondence document is available upon request.

TABLE 4: Sample Correspondence to MCAT Categories

MCAT 2015: CATEGORIES IN SENSATION AND PERCEPTION	*MY PSYCHOLOGY,* THIRD EDITION
CONTENT CATEGORY 6A: SENSING THE ENVIRONMENT	**SECTION TITLE AND PAGE NUMBERS**
SENSORY PROCESSING	**SENSATION AND PERCEPTION, PP. 64–98**
Sensation	The Difference Between Sensation and Perception, pp. 65–66
Thresholds	Thresholds: What Your Senses Can and Cannot Do, pp. 66–68 Absolute Threshold, pp. 66–67 Difference Threshold, pp. 67–68
Weber's Law	Difference Threshold, pp. 67–68
Sensory adaptation	Sensory Adaptation, pp. 68, 70 (From Research to Real Life feature)
Sensory receptors	Rods and cones (vision receptor cells), pp. 75–76 Olfactory receptor cells, pp. 87–88 Taste buds, pp. 90–91 Somatosensory receptor cells (touch, temperature), pp. 92–94
Types of sensory receptors	Rods and cones (vision receptor cells), pp. 75–76 Olfactory receptor cells, pp. 87–88 Taste buds, pp. 90–91 Somatosensory receptor cells (touch, temperature), pp. 92–94
Vision	Vision, pp. 74–82
Structure and function of the eye	Your Eye: Its Parts and Their Functions, pp. 74–76
Visual Processing	How You See: Eye Movements, Depth Perception, Color Perception, and More, pp. 76–81
Hearing	Hearing, pp. 83–87
Auditory Processing	Your Ear: Its Parts and Their Functions, pp. 83–84
Other Senses	Smell and Taste, pp. 87–91 Other Senses, pp. 91–95
Somatosensation	Skin Deep: Your Somatosenses, pp. 92–94
Pain perception	Pain, pp. 93–94
Taste	Detectable as Delectable: Your Sense of Taste, pp. 90–91

(Continued)

TABLE 4: Sample Correspondence to MCAT Categories (CONTINUED)

Taste buds, chemoreceptors that detect specific chemicals	Taste Buds: The Gustation Receptor Cells, pp. 90–91
Smell	The Nose Knows: Your Sense of Smell, pp. 87–90
Olfactory cells, chemoreceptors that detect specific chemicals	How Olfaction Receptor Cells Work, pp. 87–88
Pheromones	Olfaction and Sex, p. 88
Olfactory pathways in the brain	How Olfaction Receptor Cells Work, pp. 87–88
Kinesthetic sense	On the Move and in Balance: Your Kinesthetic Sense and Vestibular Sense, p. 95
Vestibular sense	On the Move and in Balance: Your Kinesthetic Sense and Vestibular Sense, p. 95
Perception	The Fundamentals of Sensation and Perception, pp. 65–73 Vision, pp. 74–82 Hearing, pp. 83–87 Smell and Taste, pp. 87–91 Other Senses, pp. 91–95
Perception	The Difference Between Sensation and Perception, pp. 65–66
Bottom-up/top-down processing	Bottom-Up and Top-Down Processing, pp. 71–73
Perceptual organization (e.g., depth, form, motion, constancy)	Perceptual Constancy, p. 68 Perceptual Set, p. 72 Depth Perception, p. 77 Separating and Grouping Objects, p. 80
Gestalt principles	Separating and Grouping Objects, p. 80

Acknowledgments

In the coverage of psychotherapy in Chapter 15, you'll find the *therapeutic alliance*. Defined as a trusting and collaborative relationship in which therapist and client work toward shared goals, the alliance is the cornerstone of success for therapy of all kinds. In the psychotherapy field, the alliance has earned its place as a key active ingredient in the realization of goals that require tremendous, sustained, and concerted effort.

What's true about alliances between clients and their therapists is also true for alliances between authors and their publishing teams. I have been exceedingly fortunate to feel a tremendous alliance with so many people who have supported, championed, and contributed to this book. At the top of the list is Michael Kimball, development editor. For all aspects of this project, from the biggest picture to the smallest detail, Michael has delivered exactly what I needed (even though I often didn't realize I needed it until after I received it). Somehow, Michael brings to our shared work the ideal combination of reliability, expertise, wisdom, constructive criticism, support, respect, advice, and camaraderie. His dedication to the success of this project improved both my writing and my thinking, and his touch is evident in all of the best parts of this book.

Dan DeBonis, executive program manager for the first two editions of *My Psychology*, was a vitally important and valued ally throughout the publishing process. Every textbook author should be fortunate enough to work with someone like Dan, who blends the professional talents of broad editorial expertise and astuteness with the personal assets of cooperativeness, openness, and thoughtfulness. I have been continually impressed by Dan's ability to keep the ship steered toward what's best for the book. Carlise Stembridge, executive program manager for the current edition, is fantastic as well. I am thankful for her skillful, expert, personable, and collaborative oversight of the project. Even the many challenges created by the COVID pandemic could not hinder Carlise's remarkable commitment to doing what's best for the book. I am also deeply appreciative of Talia Green, assistant editor, for all of her thoughtful support with diversity-related issues throughout the text, for her guidance through the review process, and for her immense help with preparing the chapters for production.

Chuck Linsmeier was actually my senior acquisitions editor for a short time at the beginning of this project, before he was promoted to his current position of executive vice president & general manager. Chuck's willingness to take a chance on me in the first place, to have faith in my ability as an author for a project of this scope, is something I will always deeply appreciate. I similarly appreciate the perspective he now offers through his continued involvement and dedication to the project.

I am also indebted to video producer Kate Super and her team, whose video-making talents and cooperative spirit were the key ingredients in the My Take videos throughout the book.

For the look of the book, I owe tremendous gratitude to many people for their talents: Eli Ensor for the consistently outstanding illustrations; Matthew McAdams for the diligent management of the art program; John Callahan for the amazing cover; Natasha Wolfe and Diana Blume for the excellent design work; and Krystyna Borgen and Robin Fadool for their conscientious help with photo selection. Thanks for working so collaboratively with me.

Many thanks also go to those who, in various ways, expertly converted the words on my computer screen into the fully produced pages of this textbook. First on the list is lead content project manager Won McIntosh, who guided this text through production with a patient mastery (as she always does). Senior managing editor Lisa Kinne, senior workflow project manager Paul Rohloff, copyeditor Daniel Nighting, and proofreader Lakshmi Suresh were also key contributors at different stages of production.

Additional thanks to those who helped with media and print supplements, including executive director for digital workflow strategy, Noel Hohnstine and senior media editor, social sciences, Lauren Samuelson, who brought a fresh perspective to the media program.

To those whose efforts involved publicizing and promoting the book, I am tremendously grateful: senior marketing manager Kate Nurre and director of advertising Todd Elder.

Of course, there are many people outside of the Worth family toward whom I also feel great appreciation. That list begins with my own family. To my wife, Melissa Lynn Pomerantz: Your love, support, confidence, understanding, belief, and patience made this book (and most of what I do) possible. To my kids, Benjamin and Daniel Pomerantz: I love you and I'm proud of you every day! To my parents, Carol and Bill Pomerantz: Thank you for a lifetime of love and support.

The SIUE Department of Psychology has been a wonderful place to work. Thanks for the opportunity and collegiality you have always provided. My undergrad professors at Washington University in St. Louis sparked my interests in both psychology and academic writing. My graduate professors at Saint Louis University fostered and nurtured those interests. Thanks to all of you.

Long before I reached college, many teachers spent many hours cultivating my writing skills. At Parkway Central High School, Parkway Central Middle School, Green Trails Elementary, and even at Lucky Lane Preschool, you encouraged and shaped my ability to express myself through the written word. Your time, effort, and care played a significant role in the skill and confidence I needed to create this book. I sincerely thank you.

Another important boost in my ability to write textbooks came from Mary Ellen Lepionka, whose book about writing and developing college textbooks I found invaluable. Thanks for sharing your expertise with me.

To my own students, especially those in my Intro Psych courses, thanks for everything you have taught me. I extend the same thanks to all of the clients with whom I have had the privilege to work.

Thanks to the staff at my various library hangouts, who provided a variety of resources: SIUE, St. Louis County Library, and University City Public Library, among others.

Thanks to the musicians who inhabit my music libraries, many of whom were my frequent companions throughout my work on this project.

Special thanks to all of the professors, instructors, and experts who offered their feedback on various drafts and components of this textbook. Your time, effort, and expertise provided tremendously valuable guidance in reviews, focus groups, surveys, and class testing.

Jennifer Ackil, *Gustavus Adolphus College*
Jonathan Adams, *The University of Alabama at Birmingham*
Maria Anderson, *Farmingdale State College*
Gene Ano, *Mt. San Antonio College*
Elizabeth Arnott-Hill, *College of DuPage*
Melanie Arpaio, *Sussex County Community College*
Sherry Ash, *San Jacinto College*
Diane Ashe, *Valencia College*
Sheryl Attig, *Tri-County Technical College*
Kevin Autry, *California State Polytechnic University*
Wendy Jo Bartkus, *Albright College*
Dave Baskind, *Delta College*
Laura Beavin, *Rio Hondo College*
Karen Beck, *Rio Hondo College*
Dan Bellack, *Trident Technical College*
Lisamarie Bensman, *Windward Community College*
Or'Shaundra Benson, *College of DuPage*
David Beseda, *Southern Maine Community College*
Andrew Blair, *Palm Beach State College*
Kristen Bonwell, *San Diego Miramar College*
Pamela C. Bradley, *Sandhills Community College*
Nicole Evangelista Brandt, *Columbus State Community College*
Jennifer Breneiser, *Valdosta State University*
Deborah Briihl, *Valdosta State University*
Salena Brody, *The University of Texas at Dallas*
Jamie Bromley, *Franklin College of Indiana*
Myra Beth Bundy, *Eastern Kentucky University*
Anthony Carboni, *St. Johns River State College*
Leighann Chaffee, *University of Washington Tacoma*
Rachelle Chaykin, *Pennsylvania Institute of Technology*

Aaliyah Churchill, *California State University–Northridge*
Diana Ciesko, *Valencia College*
Jonathan Cleveland, *University of Cincinnati Blue Ash College*
Doreen Collins-McHugh, *Seminole State College*
Jessamy E. Comer, *Rochester Institute of Technology*
Kyle Conlon, *Stephen F. Austin State University*
Robin Cooper-Wilbanks, *Nashville State Community College*
Roger Copeland, *El Centro College*
Laurie Corey, *Westchester Community College*
Carmen Culotta, *Wright State University*
Martha Deen, *Kilgore College*
Stacie DeFreitas, *University of Houston–Downtown*
Victoria DeSensi, *Wilmington College*
Maysa De Sousa, *Springfield College*
David C. Devonis, *Graceland University*
Adebimpe Diji, *Century College*
Angela B. Dortch, *Ivy Tech Community College*
Natalie Dove, *Eastern Michigan University*
Davido Dupree, *Community College of Philadelphia*
C. Jeff Dykhuizen, *Delta College*
Rebecca M. Eaker, *Georgia Gwinnett College*
John E. Edlund, *Rochester Institute of Technology*
Amanda ElBassiouny, *California Lutheran University*
Kecia L. Ellick, *Clayton State University*
Nolen Embry-Bailey, *Bluegrass Community and Technical College*
Brandi Emerick, *Indiana University*
Andrea Ericksen, *San Juan College*
Sarah Etezadi, *Marianopolis College*
Rebecca Jane Ewing, *Western New Mexico University*
Celeste Favela, *El Paso Community College*
Keith Feigenson, *Albright College*
Rebecca D. Foushee, *Lindenwood University*
Lisa Fozio-Thielk, *Waubonsee Community College*
Alyssa Francis, *University of Rhode Island*
Stacey Frank, *Tri-County Technical College*
Perry Fuchs, *University of Texas at Arlington*
Jill Fultz, *Lansing Community College*
Amanda Gabriele, *Forsyth Technical Community College*
Janice Gallagher, *Ivy Tech Community College*
Tina Garrett, *Holmes Community College*
Marc Gentzler, *Valencia College*
Jeffrey K. Gray, *Charleston Southern University*
Alexis Green, *Charleston Southern University*
Sharon Griffin, *San Jacinto College*
Elin Grissom, *Loyola University New Orleans*
Thomas Hancock, *University of Central Oklahoma*
Greg Harris, *Polk State College*
Anna Harvey, *St. Johns River State College*
Brett Heintz, *Delgado Community College*
Debora Herold, *Indiana University–Purdue University Indianapolis*
Brooke Hindman, *Greenville Technical College*
Ryan J. Hjelle, *University of Minnesota Duluth*
Ei Hlaing, *University of Lynchburg*
Jericho Hockett, *Washburn University*
Vivian Hsu-Yang, *Penn State Abington*
Regina M. Hughes, *Collin College*
Alishia Huntoon, *Oregon Institute of Technology*
Elgrie J. Hurd III, *Brookhaven College*
Lisa Jackson, *Schoolcraft College*
Benjamin Jee, *Worcester State University*
Stephanie Jesseau, *University of Nebraska Omaha*
Erin Johnson, *Coastline Community College*
Chizara Jones, *Clayton State University*
Todd Joseph, *Hillsborough Community College*
Hilary Kalagher, *Drew University*
Andrew Kelly, *Georgia Gwinnett College*
Serita R. Kelsey, *University of the District of Columbia Community College*
Linda Kieffer, *Delgado Community College*
Franz Klutschkowski, *North Central Texas College*
Brenda E. Koneczny, *Minnesota State University Moorhead*
Dana Kuehn, *Florida State College at Jacksonville*
Julia Lazzara, *Paradise Valley Community College*
Marvin W. Lee, *Tennessee State University*
Kristen Leverentz-Brady, *Coastal Carolina Community College*
Mary Lewis, *Columbus State Community College*
Qin Li, *Mt. San Antonio College*
Peter D. Lifton, *Northeastern University*
Lindsey Lilienthal, *Penn State Altoona*
Tammy Lochridge, *Itawamba Community College*
Mark Ludorf, *Stephen F. Austin State University*
Lynda Mae, *Arizona State University*
George Martinez, *Somerset Community College*
Michele Mathis, *Cape Fear Community College*
Danielle McAneney, *Southwestern College*
Donna McCarty, *Clayton State University*
Jason McCoy, *Cape Fear Community College*
Stacy A. McDonald, *Holy Family University*
Aradhana Mehta, *Rhode Island College*
Peter G. Mezo, *University of Toledo*
Elizabeth Moseley, *Cleveland State Community College*
Kristen Mudge, *Jackson College*
Tonya Nascimento, *University of West Florida*
Hayley Kleitz Nelson, *Delaware County Community College*
Dennis Norman, *Owens Community College*
Toni Norris, *Calhoun Community College*
Gina O'Neal-Moffitt, *Florida State University*
Amy Ort, *Nebraska Wesleyan University*
Nicha Otero, *University of Arkansas–Fort Smith*
Eirini Papafratzeskakou, *Mercer County Community College*
Cari Paterno, *Oakton Community College*
Christina Pedram, *Arizona State University*
Jeffrey Pedroza, *Santa Ana College*
Joseph Pelletier, *Houston Baptist University*
Sandra Prince-Madison, *Delgado Community College*
Ruth E. Propper, *Montclair State University*
Caroline Pyevich, *Pima Community College*
Vaidehi Rajagopalan, *St. Charles Community College*
Allexcia Rankin, *Carl Albert State College*
Stacey Ray, *Bluegrass Community and Technical College*
Bibia Redd, *University of North Georgia–Gainesville*
Jill Rinzel, *University of Wisconsin–Milwaukee at Waukesha*
Marylou Robins, *San Jacinto College South*
David L. Roby, *Texas Southmost College*
Joshua S. Rodefer, *Valdosta State University*
James Rollins, *Nashville State Community College*

Jeffrey Rudski, *Muhlenberg College*
Vasiliy Safin, *Stony Brook University*
Cherry H. Sawyerr, *Lone Star College*
Kathleen Schmidt, *Southern Illinois University Carbondale*
Gwendolyn Scott-Jones, *Delaware State University*
Laurence Segall, *Housatonic Community College*
Elisa Setmire, *Moorpark College*
Melonie Sexton, *Valencia College*
Edwin R. Shriver, *Emmanuel College*
Aisha Patrice Siddiqui-Adams, *Columbus State University*
Nancy Simpson, *Trident Technical College*
Stacey Souther, *Cuyahoga Community College*
Jonathan Sparks, *Vance-Granville Community College*
Kathleen Stellmach, *Pasco-Hernandez State College*
Jamie Stone, *Lansing Community College*
Mary Hughes Stone, *San Francisco State University*
Terry Stone, *University of Nebraska at Omaha*
Melissa St. Pierre, *Community College of Philadelphia*
Nathan Swink, *Butler Community College*
Éva Szeli, *Arizona State University*
Shai Tabib, *Kean University*
Cheryl L. Todd, *Wor-Wic Community College*
Albert K. Toh, *University of Arkansas at Pine Bluff*
Jeremy Tost, *Valdosta State University*
Dunja Trunk, *Bloomfield College*
Lora Vasiliauskas, *Virginia Western Community College*
Wendy Valentine, *Ellsworth Community College*
Enrique Velasquez, *San Antonio College*
Craig J. Vickio, *Wright State University*
Susan Villalobos, *North Lake College*
Jeffrey B. Wagman, *Illinois State University*
Stephanie Weigel, *University of North Dakota*
Mark Whatley, *Valdosta State University*
Jason Whetten, *Northern Arizona University*
Alan J. Whitehead, *Southern Virginia University*
Chrissy Whiting-Madison, *Rogers State University*
Ralph Worthing, *Delta College*
James Thomas Wright, *Forsyth Technical Community College*
Andrew Wrobel, *University of Rhode Island*
Tomas Yufik, *St. Edward's University*
Anna Zaborowski, *San Jacinto College*
Carla A. Zimmerman, *Colorado State University Pueblo*

Student Preface

Welcome to psychology! More accurately, welcome to *My Psychology*!

To help you succeed in this course, you'll find lots of tools and strategies throughout the pages of *My Psychology*. Here are a few specific suggestions for success in this course (and perhaps other courses as well) to keep in mind from the beginning. All of these are based on research that is explained and referenced in Chapter 1 or 5:

- Show up to class. Students who attend class, even when attendance is not mandatory, get better grades.
- When studying for a test, it is better to start early and space your study sessions with some time between them than it is to study by cramming.
- Get plenty of sleep and exercise, and eat healthy. These healthy habits set the stage for academic success.
- Believe in your ability to succeed in this class. Self-efficacy of this kind, specifically applied to this class, makes it more likely that you will actually achieve that success.
- Set a specific goal for yourself from the outset. Aiming for a specific letter grade or percentage often produces better results than a less-focused effort toward success.
- Minimize multitasking. Even among people who think they are good at it, doing multiple things at once usually results in lower levels of performance on each thing.
- Make the material as personally meaningful as you can. If it's relevant to your life, it's easier to remember.

That last point — making the material as personally meaningful as you can — is something that *My Psychology* prioritizes. Since I taught my first Intro Psych class over 20 years ago, I have always tried to make connections between the textbook's presentation of psychology and my students' experience of psychology in their own personal lives. After all, psychology is already woven into your life. Its concepts are the ideas and behaviors that explain what you do and why you do it (probably more than any other class you'll take in college). That's why I wrote a textbook that maximizes your personal connection to the science of psychology: *My Psychology*.

As you'll see, this book includes lots of features to maximize that connection, to engage you with the material in a way that recognizes the experiences you've had and the way you live your life. Here's a preview of those features — categorized as technology (including smartphones), applications, diversity coverage, and learning tools — that can serve as a guide for how to get the most out of the book:

"[T]he perfect text for first-year students."

— Chrissy Whiting-Madison, *Rogers State University*

Technology

My Psychology meets you where you live — on your smartphones and computers. As a textbook for the contemporary college student, *My Psychology* recognizes not only what you experience in your daily lives, but also how you experience those things. You can access all of these technological features on your smartphone or computer.

Chapter Apps Most of you have smartphones, and if you do, you probably use apps all the time. I do, and along the way I have noticed that quite a few apps do a great job illustrating important psychology concepts. So, in each chapter, I provide two or three Chapter Apps, each placed near the concept it illustrates. You can download each app on your smartphone. For those you don't download, you can still learn a lot about them and their connection to psychology by reading the brief description in the Chapter App feature.

CHAPTER APP 8.2

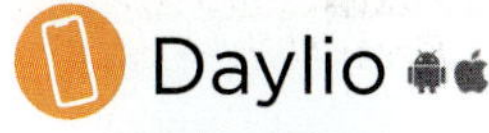

The Daylio app allows you to track your emotions. You enter your mood (rad, good, meh, bad, or awful), along with your recent activities (working, watching movies, cleaning, exercising, etc.). The app then provides you with stats and graphs showing how your mood changed as time passed and your activities changed.

How does it APPly to your daily life?
How could an app like Daylio help you understand the patterns of your emotions? How could it help you determine which activities evoke positive and negative emotions? How could the information it provides influence your decisions on activities to choose in the future?

How does it APPly to your understanding of psychology?
How could this app help you appreciate the range of your own emotions? How could it help you recognize or regulate your own emotions?

To learn more about this app or to download it to your phone, you can search for "Daylio" on Google, in the iPhone App store, or in the Google Play store.

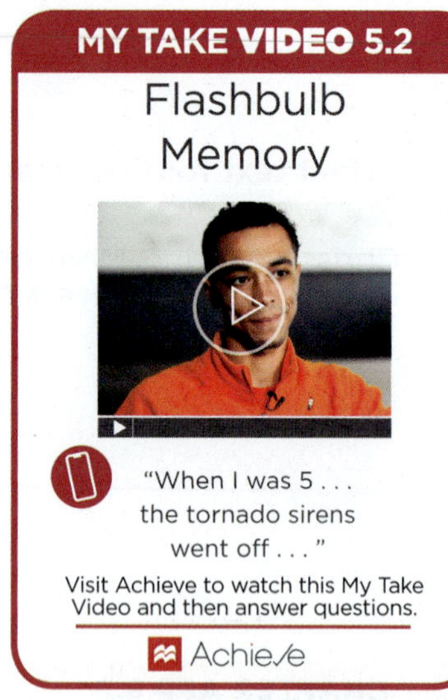

My Take Videos In my own classes, students' own personal stories are among the most memorable moments, especially when those stories are on-target examples of a key concept. My Take Videos, which you'll see two or three times per chapter, provide exactly that experience — real Intro Psych students sharing their own stories, or takes, regarding a psychology concept. These are brief, professionally made videos, created exclusively for this textbook, in which students like you reveal their own connections to psychology and prompt you to think of your own.

Show Me More links The Internet is full of wonderful videos, articles, and Web sites that give you the chance to delve deeper and learn even more about many important psychology concepts. Show Me More links appear at the end of each chapter to guide you toward them. This bonus material includes news clips and articles, TED Talks, documentary footage, Web sites that invite interaction, and over 100 new psychology videos. Like My Take Videos, Show Me More links are accessible with your smartphone or on your computer through Achieve.

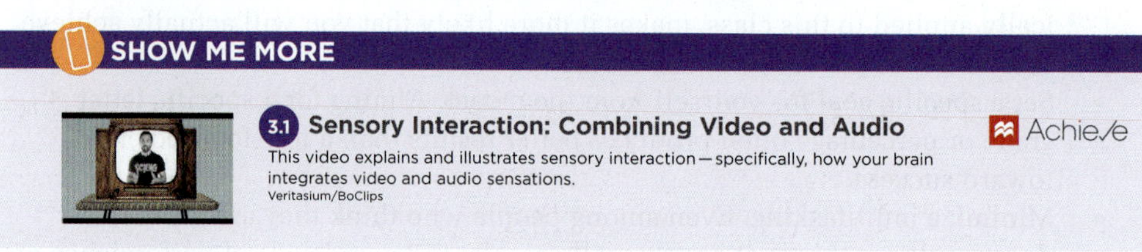

SHOW ME MORE
3.1 Sensory Interaction: Combining Video and Audio
This video explains and illustrates sensory interaction — specifically, how your brain integrates video and audio sensations.
Veritasium/BoClips
"When I was 5 . . . the tornado sirens went off . . ."
Achieve

Applications

The applications in every chapter highlight the parallels between your experiences and the science of psychology. These applied features complement the coverage within each chapter by providing you with distinct, fresh ways of understanding psychological concepts and making them personally relevant.

From Research to Real Life We zoom in on a particular area within psychology and explain how research on that topic directly applies to your real life.

FROM RESEARCH TO REAL LIFE

Psychologists' Research on College Success

Among the many, many questions that psychologists study, one might be of particular interest to you: what predicts academic success in college students? As you read through the findings listed below, keep in mind that most of them come from correlational studies. That means causal relationships are not definite, and none of the correlations are perfectly positive or negative, so they do not necessarily apply to every student.

- Students who stay up later and wake up later get lower GPAs. In one study, GPAs dropped 0.13 points (on a standard 0–4.0 scale) for each hour the sleep cycle was pushed back (Trockel et al., 2000).
- Students who are more engaged in college life — involved in more curricular and extracurricular activities for longer periods — get higher GPAs (Kuh et al., 2008; Wolf-Wendel et al., 2009).
- Students who believe that they can succeed with effort earn higher GPAs (Robbins et al., 2004).
- Students who use performance goals — specifically setting out to achieve a high standard in a course — earn higher GPAs than those who don't (Harackiewicz et al., 2002).
- Students who spend more time on social media get lower GPAs than students who don't (Liu et al., 2017).
- Students who cram for tests get lower GPAs than those whose study sessions are spaced out and consistent (Landauer, 2011; Roediger & Karpicke, 2011).
- Students whose life goals are more superficial tend to fall below their own GPA expectations more often than students whose life goals are more focused on helping others and driven by a meaningful purpose (Beattie et al., 2018).
- Just showing up makes a big difference. Students who attend class regularly earn higher GPAs than those who don't. In fact, one study concluded that attendance was a better predictor of college students' grade in a course than their SAT or ACT score, high school GPA, study habits, or study skills (Credé et al., 2010).
- Participation matters too. Students who participate in class tend to earn higher grades than students who don't (Kim et al., 2020). •

Life Hacks Life hacks are quick hits — just a sentence or two to offer a recommendation for how to live your life according to psychology research, which is included as a citation. They appear as brightly colored little boxes on the page, and they draw a direct line between the conclusions of psychological studies and your own attempts to live happier, more productive lives.

LIFE HACK 8.3

If you want to feel happier, do something kind for someone else, or think about acts of kindness you've already done.

(Lyubomirsky & Layous, 2013; Otake et al., 2006; Pressman et al., 2015)

It's Like... You already have a wealth of knowledge and understanding of the world around you. Sometimes, a psychology concept runs parallel to something you already know. It's Like..., which appears once per chapter, points out those parallels.

IT'S LIKE...

Plasticity Is Like an Athlete Switching Positions

Imagine asking a talented 7-year-old softball player who has only played first base to switch positions. That probably won't be much of a problem. As a beginner, that girl probably can take her general athletic skills to shortstop, centerfield, or any other position on the diamond because she hasn't specialized too much yet. By contrast, imagine asking a 30-year-old Major League veteran first baseman to become a shortstop, a centerfielder, or play any other position. He would find it challenging, maybe even impossible. For years, he has spent every game and practice, day after day, exclusively at first base. His skills have become so highly specialized to the first base position that he might not be able to play another position well. Of course, there is a chance that it *could* work, at least to a limited extent. But all of that time spent playing just one position makes a change much tougher than it would be for a player with less experience.

Brain plasticity works the same way. In very young brains, many parts of the brain haven't specialized much yet. So if there is a need to cover for a damaged brain region (an injured teammate, so to speak), those parts of the brain have the flexibility necessary to make the switch. In older brains, however, the brain parts have specialized more, which means that their ability to adapt and change is more limited. Thankfully, even in adults, there is often some plasticity among brain parts, just like some athletes can take on a new position when pressured to do so later in their careers.

Watching Psychology Lots of TV shows and movies directly relate to psychology concepts. Watching Psychology explores these on-screen experiences.

WATCHING PSYCHOLOGY

Survey Says? *Family Feud* and Random Sampling

The *Family Feud* host says it each time there is a new question: "100 people surveyed, top answers on the board." But which 100 people? Are those 100 people a random sample of the U.S. population? Or are certain people more likely to be sampled and others less likely to be sampled, based on how *Family Feud* recruits them? If they call random phone numbers, the 100 people could be reasonably close to a random sample, although it would be tilted toward those who are willing to pick up the phone from an unknown number and spend time answering a stranger's questions. But if *Family Feud* surveys its own studio audience, the 100 people would all be those who live near or visit the city where it happens to be filmed, who may not represent the country at large in terms of likes, dislikes, experiences, and other factors that could influence their answers.

Think about how different the top answers to these *Family Feud* questions could be depending on which groups the 100 people surveyed came from:

- *Name a movie you enjoy watching over and over again.* Think you'd get different top answers from 20-somethings and 60-somethings?
- *Name a food you have on special occasions.* Think you'd get different top answers in Hawaii and Maine?
- *Name a feature of a car that would make you want to buy it.* Think you'd get different top answers from men and women?

When psychologists conduct research, they sample as randomly as possible to make sure that the data they collect is representative of the population they are studying. And when random sampling isn't entirely possible, they explain this fact, being careful not to overestimate the range of people for whom their results might be true.

Current Controversy In many areas of psychology, the experts (and their research results) don't agree. In Current Controversy, we examine these areas, with special emphasis on how the controversy might affect your life or the lives of people you know.

CURRENT CONTROVERSY

Should Psychologists Prescribe Medication?

Traditionally, a primary distinction between psychiatrists and psychologists was that psychiatrists prescribed medication but psychologists did not (Balon et al., 2004). However, a movement within psychology has blurred that distinction a bit.

The movement started in the 1980s, when a handful of practicing psychologists argued that with extra training they should be allowed to prescribe medications to their clients. Their movement has gained momentum over the past few decades, and many states considered legislation that specifies exactly what a psychologist would have to do to earn the right to prescribe. So far, only a small number of states, including New Mexico, Louisiana, Illinois, Iowa, and Idaho, have approved such legislation, and in those states, only a small number of psychologists have become prescribers. Some states have rejected similar legislation, and the debate continues in others (Levin, 2017; Sammons, 2011).

Those who argue that psychologists *should* be allowed to prescribe medication focus on a few key points:

- In many states, particularly in rural areas, there's a shortage of psychiatrists (Long, 2005).
- Most psychiatric medications (e.g., Prozac, Xanax, and Zoloft) are prescribed not by psychiatrists but by primary care doctors and pediatricians (Cummings, 2007). Those physicians don't receive much specialized training in mental health issues. Psychologists could gain more training than those physicians and provide more effective prescriptions.
- There are other professions whose members are not physicians but who can prescribe medication, including dentists, podiatrists, optometrists, and advance practice nurses.
- Seeing a psychologist for both therapy and medication is more convenient for clients than seeing a psychologist for therapy and a medical doctor for medication.

Those who say that psychologists *should not* be allowed to prescribe medication focus their arguments on a few key points:

- It isn't clear how much extra training psychologists would need to be qualified to prescribe. Some argue that it's necessary to go all the way through medical school—in addition to getting a doctoral degree in psychology (Griffiths, 2001; Robiner et al., 2002). Others say that less training is enough (Resnick & Norcross, 2002).
- It isn't clear that all psychologists would become prescribers. If it's optional, then the general public might get confused about what psychologists do.
- There is a concern that prescriptions could phase out talk therapy if more psychologists could prescribe. Psychologists would see more clients per hour for med checks than for talk therapy, thereby making more money. If so, that might be a disservice to some clients (McGrath, 2004).

The controversy about prescription privileges for psychologists continues today (Linda & McGrath, 2017; Nasrallah, 2017; Robiner et al., 2020). •

Diversity Coverage

Diversity is an important part of psychology and all of its subfields. Diversity is also an important part of your life and all its aspects.

Diversity Matters Dozens of times throughout the book, diversity takes center stage. When it does, a Diversity Matters flag calls your attention to it. Often, diversity is characterized by ethnicity or race, but it takes many other forms too, including age, gender, sexual orientation, socioeconomic status, ability/disability status, religion, and more. As an example, a Diversity Matters flag in the Social Psychology chapter highlights the ways that individualism and collectivism can influence conformity to social norms. Diversity Matters flags in the Motivation and Emotion chapter highlight coverage of the influence that gender and age can have on motivation.

A full chapter dedicated to diversity Diversity takes center stage most prominently in the Diversity in Psychology chapter, which is dedicated entirely to the topic. The title of Chapter 10—Diversity in Psychology: Multiculturalism, Gender, and Sexuality—indicates its inclusive focus. The chapter was developed in consultation with experts in the diversity field and begins by recognizing many forms of diversity with which you live, including race, ethnicity, language, religion, age, sexual orientation, education, income, ability/disability status, and big cities versus small towns. It then covers a variety of concepts to help you appreciate diversity in a broad sense, including how cultures can be defined, diversity within groups (dynamic sizing), acculturation, cultural intelligence, and microaggressions. The chapter also offers detailed coverage of the topics of gender and sexuality, including discussion of the concepts of cisgender, transgender, and transition.

Learning Tools

My Psychology is packed with learning tools that will maximize your engagement with and understanding of the science of psychology. These learning tools make use of personal connections to the material to boost memory and comprehension.

"I was impressed based on the content of the material, the various extra features embedded within the chapters and the ease of readability. I am still delighted with the textbook and having changed with the results in terms of improved grades my students are consistently earning."

—Bibia Redd, *University of North Georgia-Gainesville*

An example-rich approach Simply put, the book has *lots* of examples designed to relate to your day-to-day life. The goal is for these examples to resonate with you by connecting to your real world.

Three-step synced pedagogical system As a learning strategy designed to boost your understanding of the material, the sections of each chapter feature a three-step method for previewing, questioning, and confirming what you learn. Each section starts with a "You Will Learn" list—essentially a preview of major points the section will cover. At the end of that section, you'll see a corresponding list of questions, one for each item on the list ("Check Your Learning"). At the end of the chapter, in the Chapter Summary, all of those questions are answered. In all three places, a synchronized numbering system keeps you organized, so you know which preview points go with which question and which answers. Of course, this system doesn't cover every detail—there's no shortcut for a thorough reading of the full chapter—but it does highlight the core knowledge.

YOU WILL LEARN:

5.1 how psychologists define memory.

5.2 about the role that memory can play in personal identity.

CHECK YOUR LEARNING:

5.1 How do psychologists define memory?

5.2 What role does memory play in personal identity?

CHAPTER SUMMARY

Defining Memory

5.1 Memory is the process of taking in information, saving it over time, and retrieving it later.

5.2 Memories define each individual as a unique person.

What's Your Take? At the end of each chapter, you'll encounter questions that invite you to offer your perspective or your experience with a particular concept. For example, you'll be asked if your pets have ever demonstrated the kinds of conditioning that you'll read about when we cover learning. You'll be asked if your experience as a new college student parallels the experience that some psychologists have used with babies to test their attachment to their parents and their reaction to new situations.

WHAT'S YOUR TAKE?

1. When you think about your own culture, your first thought may be your ethnicity or your race. But there may be many other cultural variables that are just as important. As a clinical psychologist, I have learned from some of my own clients that certain or diversity characteristics besides ethnicity or race were at the core of their identities. For one woman, it was her religion (she was a Modern Orthodox Jew); for one man, it was his sexual orientation (he was gay); for another woman, it was her geographical upbringing (she grew up and still lived in a tiny rural town). One teenage boy even proudly told me that he was from "skater culture"—not just that he skateboarded, but he had adopted the entire lifestyle that encompasses skateboarding—and that if I didn't get skater culture, I couldn't get him.

   If you saw a psychologist, which of your cultural or diversity characteristic(s) would the psychologist have to get in order to get you? Are you a typical member of that culture or diverse group, or do you differ from most others in some way?

2. I have noticed a strong positive correlation in my own life: when I do more laundry, I'm in a better mood. I first noticed this correlation in college, when I tended to feel a bit more upbeat during weeks when I found myself in the laundry room more than once and a bit more down on weeks when I didn't. What's up with that? Could it be that washing, drying, and folding *caused* my good mood? Or that my good mood *caused* me to do more laundry? Neither of those made much sense. Eventually, I settled on a more likely interpretation: there was a third factor—exercising—that caused both. In weeks when I ran, worked out, or played basketball more often, the exercise improved my mood, *and* it increased the amount of sweaty clothes in the hamper, which meant I needed to do laundry more often.

   How about you? Have you ever noticed two things correlating in your own life—increasing together, decreasing together, or one increasing when the other decreased in a predictable way—but without a causal relationship between them? If so, what were they, and how do you explain their correlation?

Student dialogue questions I teach Intro Psych, so I know what kinds of questions students often ask. I embedded many of them into the book itself. You'll see them—they feature an icon of a student with a raised hand, speaking in a different, colored font—and some of them may accurately anticipate questions that occurred to you as you were reading. Each of these questions is followed by a direct answer, enabling you to understand confusing or challenging concepts more clearly by means of a greater level of interaction with the material.

I know some very shy people, and this social anxiety disorder diagnosis sounds like it would fit them pretty well. What's the difference between social anxiety disorder and extreme shyness?

With the help of these many features focusing on technology, application, diversity, and learning tools, *My Psychology* helps you learn the science of psychology by helping you connect the material to your own life. It invites you into our rich field and makes you feel welcome by demonstrating how personally relatable, applicable, and comprehensible psychology can be.

1 The Science of Psychology

LaylaBird/E+/Getty Images

CHAPTER OUTLINE

This may be your first psychology course, but you've been a student of psychology—what people do and why they do it—since the day you were born.

As a baby, you focused your psychological research on the effects of crying. Specifically, you wondered, if I cry when I'm hungry, will someone feed me? Every day, you ran experiments on this question, keeping track of the results in your head, until eventually you had enough data to draw a conclusion about the connection between crying and food. You then moved on to more sophisticated experiments in which you explored what happened when you cried around certain people, at certain times, and in certain places.

As a young child, your research interests shifted toward toys. Specifically, you questioned, what happens when one kid yanks a toy out of another kid's hands? The scene played out before your eyes at your fourth birthday party, and the outcome was clear: the victim shrieks, and the toy bandit gets a scolding. You took note of this result, but wondered if that would be the outcome every time. Might the result change under different circumstances—another toy, another kid, another place, another parent?

In middle school and high school, your research focus expanded to academic performance. You questioned the relationship between the time you spend on social media the night before a test and the grade you receive. You manipulated social media time—some nights you stayed away from it completely, while some nights you used Twitter, Snapchat, or Instagram for hours. You noticed a strong pattern: more social media time usually meant lower grades. But you wondered whether the time spent on social media actually *caused* the lower grades—or were there other factors? For example, could it be that social media time takes away from sleeping time, and lack of sleep is what really caused the lower test scores?

As a college student, your psychology research continues. With this course, you take an important step toward becoming an expert in the field. Beginning with this chapter, you will learn the vocabulary of psychology. You will learn what psychologists specialize in, how they conduct research, and how they apply their knowledge to help real people.

You will learn how the field of psychology got its start, how it evolved, and where it is now. Together with the later chapters, this information will equip you to continue your work as a psychologist, whether amateur or professional, through the course of your life.

What Is Psychology?

YOU WILL LEARN:

1.1 what psychology is.

1.2 what psychology is *not*.

1.3 what big questions underlie much of the field of psychology.

As we embark on this journey into the vast world of psychology, we will explore its big questions and clear up some common misunderstandings about the field. Let's start with a clear definition of the word.

Defining Psychology

Psychology is the scientific study of behavior and mental processes. The *and* in that definition is important: it means that psychology focuses on *both* our outer actions and our inner experiences. Our behavior – what we do outwardly – tends to be observable and easy to measure. Our mental processes – the thoughts, feelings, and other experiences that occur inside our mind – tend not to be so observable or easy to measure. For psychologists, both topics deserve attention.

As an example, consider Jessica, a young woman who struggled with but is now overcoming *bulimia nervosa*, an eating disorder we'll cover more in the chapter on disorders. Whether psychologists are treating Jessica or studying her disorder, they are interested in both her behavior and her mental processes. Psychologists want to know about Jessica's observable behaviors as she improves: for example, the increased frequency of healthy meals and snacks and the decreased frequency of binges and purges. Psychologists also want to know what mental processes might trigger those behaviors: positive feelings Jessica has about her body, reasonable thoughts about the influence of her weight on her self-worth, and so on. Considering only her behavior or only her mental processes would produce an incomplete understanding of Jessica.

AP Images/zz/SL/AAD/STAR MAX/IPx

AP Images/zz/KGC-247/STAR MAX/IPx

Psychology, as the scientific study of behavior *and* mental processes, focuses on both what we do and why we do it. Consider bulimia, an eating disorder with which many people, including singers Lady Gaga and Elton John, have struggled. In the treatment of bulimia, psychologists are interested in improvements in eating behavior *and* improvements in the thoughts that underlie those behaviors.

Another important word in the definition of psychology is *scientific*. Psychologists don't just speculate about behavior and mental processes, accepting guesses and gut feelings as the truth. Instead, we measure the merit of those ideas by applying the *scientific method*. Psychologists put their ideas to the test, share the results, and – together with all the other psychologists doing similar work – accumulate knowledge about behavior and mental processes. There is much more on the scientific method in psychology coming up later in this chapter.

What Psychology Is *Not*

To accurately understand what psychology *is*, it's essential to understand what psychology is *not*. The portrayal of psychology in the media – in movies, on TV shows, in the news – can be quite misleading. So let's correct some misconceptions that you may have about psychology.

Psychology is *not* just therapy. Check the table of contents of this psychology textbook: it has 15 chapters, but just one on therapy. Of course, many psychologists do therapy, but many do not. In fact, about one-third of psychologists have specializations that have nothing to do with therapy or any other kind of helping services. Of the two-thirds who become experts in therapy, some teach, supervise, or study it rather than practice it (Norcross et al., 2005; Norcross & Karpiak, 2012). We'll look at specializations in psychology later in this chapter, but for now, the point is that psychology covers much more than just therapy.

On a related note, psychology is *not* exclusively about people with mental disorders. Most of the research that psychologists do focuses on normal processes that occur in all of us: how we think, learn, develop, remember, speak, interact, and do other everyday activities. So despite the fact that psychologists frequently appear on television shows or movies – often helping the police track down a crazed killer or doing therapy with severely disturbed people – that portrayal of psychologists is more Hollywood than reality (Gabbard, 2001; Gharaibeh, 2005; Young, 2012).

psychology
The scientific study of behavior and mental processes.

Psychology is also *not* all about Sigmund Freud. Freud may be the first name that pops up for many people when they think about psychology, but that's way out of date. Yes, there was a time when Freud's ideas dominated the field, but that time — the early 1900s, basically — is long gone (Wegenek et al., 2010). Today, only a small minority of psychologists — fewer than 10% — practice what Freud preached (Stanovich, 2013). Of course, it would be an overstatement to call Freud irrelevant. He was, after all, *the* central figure of psychology for decades, but psychology today is much more varied, and Freud's voice is now just one of many.

psychiatry
The medical specialization that focuses on the brain and its disorders.

Psychology is also *not* **psychiatry**, the medical specialization focusing on the brain and its disorders. Many people mistakenly lump the two professions together, but there are important distinctions (Balon et al., 2004; Jorm et al., 1997). Psych*iatrists* are medical doctors. They go to medical school and earn MD degrees to become physicians. In fact, they do much of their medical training alongside med students on their way to becoming other kinds of physicians — such as pediatricians, obstetrician-gynecologists, dermatologists, and cardiologists — before they specialize in psychiatry. Like the rest of these physicians, psychiatrists prescribe medication.

Bettmann/Getty Images

Sigmund Freud's ideas dominated the field of psychology many years ago. Some people mistakenly believe that psychology is still all about Freud, but that way of thinking is out of date. Today, psychology is much more varied, and Freud's voice is just one among many.

Psych*ologists* are different kinds of doctors. They are not medical doctors. Their graduate training is focused on behavior and mental processes, not on the physical and biological systems emphasized in medical school. Psychologists earn PhD or PsyD degrees, not MDs. Psychologists generally don't prescribe medication (see the Current Controversy box). Instead, psychologists use talk therapies and other forms of behavioral intervention to help clients (Burns et al., 2008; DeLeon et al., 2011; Harris, 2011). The training of psychologists includes more emphasis on research methods than does the training of psychiatrists, which results in more psychologists pursuing careers in research than psychiatrists (Abrams et al., 2003).

CURRENT CONTROVERSY

Should Psychologists Prescribe Medication?

Traditionally, a primary distinction between psychiatrists and psychologists was that psychiatrists prescribed medication but psychologists did not (Balon et al., 2004). However, a movement within psychology has blurred that distinction a bit.

The movement started in the 1980s, when a handful of practicing psychologists argued that with extra training they should be allowed to prescribe medications to their clients. Their movement has gained momentum over the past few decades, and many states considered legislation that specifies exactly what a psychologist would have to do to earn the right to prescribe. So far, only a small number of states, including New Mexico, Louisiana, Illinois, Iowa, and Idaho, have approved such legislation, and in those states, only a small number of psychologists have become prescribers. Some states have rejected similar legislation, and the debate continues in others (Levin, 2017; Sammons, 2011).

Those who argue that psychologists *should* be allowed to prescribe medication focus on a few key points:

- In many states, particularly in rural areas, there's a shortage of psychiatrists (Long, 2005).
- Most psychiatric medications (e.g., Prozac, Xanax, and Zoloft) are prescribed not by psychiatrists but by primary care doctors and pediatricians (Cummings, 2007). Those physicians don't receive much specialized training in mental health issues. Psychologists could gain more training than those physicians and provide more effective prescriptions.
- There are other professions whose members are not physicians but who can prescribe medication, including dentists, podiatrists, optometrists, and advance practice nurses.
- Seeing a psychologist for both therapy and medication is more convenient for clients than seeing a psychologist for therapy and a medical doctor for medication.

Those who say that psychologists *should not* be allowed to prescribe medication focus their arguments on a few key points:

- It isn't clear how much extra training psychologists would need to be qualified to prescribe. Some argue that it's necessary to go all the way through medical school — in addition to getting a doctoral degree in psychology (Griffiths, 2001; Robiner et al., 2002). Others say that less training is enough (Resnick & Norcross, 2002).
- It isn't clear that all psychologists would become prescribers. If it's optional, then the general public might get confused about what psychologists do.
- There is a concern that prescriptions could phase out talk therapy if more psychologists could prescribe. Psychologists would see more clients per hour for med checks than for talk therapy, thereby making more money. If so, that might be a disservice to some clients (McGrath, 2004).

The controversy about prescription privileges for psychologists continues today (Linda & McGrath, 2017; Nasrallah, 2017; Robiner et al., 2020). •

Perhaps most important, psychology is *not* just a bunch of ideas with nothing to back them up. Too often, psychology is wrongly associated with unsupported guesswork and unproven opinions – from psychics who claim to know people's innermost thoughts and feelings via extrasensory perception (ESP) to the Dr. Phils of the world, who claim to understand people based on a 3-minute TV interview in front of a live studio audience. Instead, the enduring ideas in psychology are backed up by science. In fact, the scientific method is the cornerstone of psychology, and it transforms ideas from speculation to scholarship.

Psychology's Big Questions

Psychology is a huge field of study, with researchers taking it in many directions. There is no single overarching question that captures psychology, but a few big questions underlie the topics psychologists explore most.

Nature or Nurture? Were you born that way, or were there factors in your upbringing that made you the person you are? Is your behavior genetic, stemming from the DNA you inherited from your biological parents, or is it environmental, stemming from the experiences you've had over the years? These questions drive research in many areas of psychology.

For example, psychologists who study language have long asked whether our ability to speak is inborn or learned through observation and reinforcement (Oliver & Plomin, 2007; Perszyk & Waxman, 2018; Plomin & Dale, 2000; Saxton, 2010). Similarly, psychologists who study psychological disorders have conducted thousands of studies to determine the extent to which genes or environment contribute to schizophrenia, depression, borderline personality disorder, and almost every other kind of mental illness (Keller & Miller, 2006; McClellan & King, 2010; Mehta-Raghavan et al., 2017; Sullivan et al., 2012). These studies often involve adopted children or twins separated at birth, whose unique childhood circumstances allow us to untangle nature from nurture. Of course, the answer always involves an interaction of both nature and nurture – a phenomenon we will explore throughout the text (Rutter, 2006; Sasaki & Kim, 2017; Wermter et al., 2010).

Change or Stability? To what extent do you change over time? To what extent do you remain the same? When you change, how does it happen – slowly and surely, or in abrupt spurts? Many specializations in psychology focus on questions like these. For example, developmental psychologists explore how we change from birth through old age in many ways: how we reason, how we interact, and how our morals influence our decisions at every age (Erikson, 1950, 1959; Kesselring, 2009; Kohlberg, 1984; Moshman, 2009; Piaget, 1954, 1983). Personality psychologists, who study the traits that define us, also focus on change versus stability – examining the extent to which our personality changes over time or stays the same (Borghuis et al., 2017; Caspi et al., 2003; Nave et al., 2010; Schwaba & Bliedorn, 2018).

Universal or Unique? When psychological researchers come to a conclusion, for whom is it true? Do some psychological truths apply universally? Or are such truths unique to certain people in certain places at certain times? Consider emotions. When psychologists study them, one of their primary questions has been whether there are basic emotions – and basic facial expressions to go along with them – that are similar around the globe, as opposed to specific emotions that occur only in certain cultures (Ekman, 2003; Ekman & Cordaro, 2011; Gendron et al., 2018; Kayyal & Russell, 2013; Russell, 1994). Similarly, questions of culture occur when researchers evaluate how beneficial a particular form of psychotherapy is. Most often, the people included in such studies are Americans who are not members of underrepresented groups. So the question is, if it works for some people, will it also work for underrepresented groups in the United States or people in other countries (Bernal et al., 2009; Castro et al., 2010; Griner & Smith, 2006; Soto et al., 2018)?

DIVERSITY MATTERS

CHECK YOUR LEARNING:

1.1 What is psychology?

1.2 What are the primary differences between psychology and psychiatry?

1.3 What are the three big questions that underlie the field of psychology?

To check your understanding of these questions, click show the answers or refer to the answers in the Chapter Summary.

Psychology's Many Subfields

YOU WILL LEARN:

1.4 about the size and breadth of the field of psychology.

1.5 how applied and basic research specializations differ.

1.6 about specific applied specializations within psychology, such as clinical psychology, counseling psychology, and industrial/organizational psychology.

1.7 about specific basic research specializations within psychology, such as personality psychology, developmental psychology, and social psychology.

As a profession, psychology is immense and diverse (Norcross, Kohout, & Wicherski, 2005). In 2019, 70% of psychologists were women and 30% were men. Five percent had disabilities. The average age was 48.4, but there were sizable numbers of psychologists at every age between their mid-20s and their mid-70s (APA, 2020). In terms of ethnicity, there is a strong recent trend toward increased diversity. Specifically, 84% of the current psychology workforce is White, but among the people who earned psychology doctoral degrees in 2018, only 69% are White. Importantly, this means the numbers of psychologists who are Latinx, Black, Asian American, and from other underrepresented groups are very likely to rise, suggesting that the population of psychologists will come closer to matching the population of the United States (Lin et al., 2020).

Over a hundred thousand people, including both professionals and students, belong to the American Psychological Association (APA), the country's largest organization of psychologists (Winerman, 2017). APA includes 54 divisions, each of which focuses on a particular topic within psychology. That large number of divisions shows you the tremendous breadth of topics contained within psychology — from child and adolescent psychology to media psychology, from the psychology of women to the psychology of religion and spirituality, from exercise and sport psychology to military psychology, and so many more.

The major specializations in psychology can be divided into two big categories: *applied* specializations and *basic research* specializations. Let's consider both, along with specific examples of each.

Applied Specializations

Applied psychology specializations are areas in which psychologists apply their expertise to real-world problems. These are the psychologists who *practice.* In other words, they use their knowledge of mind and behavior to enhance some important aspect of their clients' lives. They work in hospitals, clinics, schools, companies, agencies, private practices, and other organizations.

Before we consider specific types of applied psychologists, it is important to note that not *all* of them practice, at least not full-time. A few teach or conduct research *about* practicing, often as professors in university psychology departments (Prinstein et al., 2013). After all, someone has to train the next generation of applied psychologists and do research on the techniques they will use. Take me, for example: I'm a psychologist with an applied specialization (clinical). Although I see a small number of clients in private practice, I also work full-time as a professor teaching and doing research related to clinical psychology.

applied psychology specializations Areas in which psychologists apply their expertise to real-world problems, using their knowledge of mind and behavior to enhance some important aspect of their clients' lives.

clinical psychology An applied specialization in which psychologists focus on psychological disorders.

Clinical Psychology. **Clinical psychology** is an applied specialization in which psychologists focus on psychological disorders. Clinical psychologists do many professional activities, but psychotherapy is at the top of the list. About three-quarters of

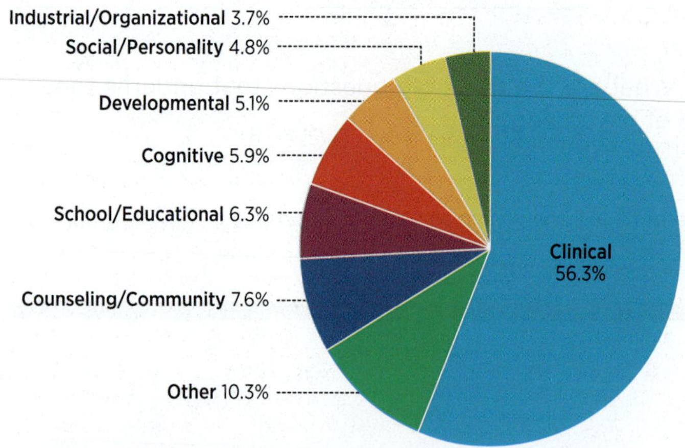

FIGURE 1.1 Doctoral Degrees in Psychology. Psychology contains many specializations. Basic research specializations focus on conducting investigations, while applied specializations like clinical psychology (the largest specialization) apply their expertise to real-world problems. (Source: APA, 2017b).

this therapy is done with individual clients, and the rest with groups, families, or couples. Clinical psychologists also do psychological assessment, including intelligence tests and personality tests, often to diagnose people with psychological disorders. Clinical psychologists work in lots of settings, including hospitals, clinics, and mental health agencies, but private practice is the most common (Norcross, Karpiak, & Santoro, 2005). As illustrated in **Figure 1.1**, clinical psychology is by far the most popular specialization in psychology.

Counseling Psychology. **Counseling psychology** is an applied specialization in which psychologists focus on improving the functioning of people who are struggling through difficult times in their lives.

Counseling psychology sounds a lot like clinical psychology. What's the difference?

You're right about the overlap: counseling psychologists are similar to clinical psychologists. They both do psychotherapy, often in private practice settings, with individuals, groups, families, and couples (Norcross, 2000; Sayette & Norcross, 2018). Decades ago, there was a noticeable difference between counseling psychologists and clinical psychologists. Clinical psychologists saw people with more serious, diagnosable problems, while counseling psychologists saw people who generally functioned quite well but were going through a rough time in their lives. To help you remember this historical distinction: *clinical* comes from the same root as *recline*, as in a patient so impaired that they need bedside care; *counseling* comes from the same root as *consult*, as in a person who just needs guidance or advice (Roger & Stone, 2014).

Today, that distinction is still true to some extent, but the two specializations have drifted toward each other and now share professional territory (Morgan & Cohen, 2008; Neimeyer et al., 2011). In many agencies — university counseling centers and mental health clinics, for example — counseling psychologists and clinical psychologists work side by side, serving the same clients. Counseling psychologists are still less likely to seek jobs in places like inpatient psychiatric units, where the clients are likely to have relatively debilitating problems. Another distinction is that counseling psychologists tend to do more career counseling and vocational (job) counseling than clinical psychologists (Sayette & Norcross, 2018).

Industrial/Organizational Psychology. **Industrial/organizational (I/O) psychology** is an applied specialization focused on the workplace. Some I/O psychologists concentrate on issues of personnel — helping companies hire the right people, place them in jobs that fit their abilities, and train them to maximize their performance. Other I/O psychologists focus on the organization as a whole — its management structure, leadership style, work environment (including minimization of stress, harassment, and discrimination), and development over time. I/O psychologists typically work as consultants, sharing their expertise with businesses, school districts, governmental agencies, or other organizations who seek their services (Blanton, 2007; Pass, 2007). For example, they might help a Fortune 500 corporation develop a training program for new employees hired straight out of college, or they might meet with the managers in a small business to advise them about how they can interact with their employees in a way that increases morale and production.

Community Psychology. **Community psychology** is an applied specialization in which psychologists focus on the wellness of entire communities. Rather than helping individuals with a problem one by one as they experience it, community psychologists try to address community-wide problems that make its members vulnerable to that problem in the first place. As a result, community psychologists often participate

counseling psychology
An applied specialization in which psychologists focus on improving the functioning of people who are struggling through difficult times in their lives.

industrial/organizational (I/O) psychology
An applied specialization in which psychologists focus on the workplace.

community psychology
An applied specialization in which psychologists focus on the wellness of entire communities.

in large-scale efforts to empower people and enhance their lives through prevention (American Psychological Association, 2007a; Society for Community Research and Action, 2016). For example, the community psychologists' approach to the problem of teen suicide emphasizes educating large groups of people within the community (high school students, teacher groups, parent groups) about risk factors, warning signs, and resources, as opposed to waiting until a teen becomes suicidal and then (hopefully) intervening to save that one person.

forensic psychology
An applied specialization in which psychologists focus on legal and criminal justice issues.

educational psychology
An applied specialization in which psychologists focus on learning and teaching.

basic research psychology specializations
Areas in which psychologists conduct research for the sake of enhancing the understanding of behavior and mental processes.

physiological psychology
A basic research specialization in which psychologists focus on the neural basis of behavior.

Forensic Psychology. **Forensic psychology** is an applied specialization in which psychologists focus on legal and criminal justice issues. Forensic psychologists — whose degrees are often actually in clinical psychology, with a concentration in forensic issues — often do psychological assessments (DeMatteo et al., 2009; Otto & Heilbrun, 2002; Otto et al., 2003). For example, they may give psychological tests to children and parents in a custody dispute, to a defendant whose competence to stand trial is in question, or to a prisoner who is eligible for parole. Forensic psychologists do psychotherapy too, for victims, offenders, and law enforcement officers. They also serve as expert witnesses in trials, as well as consultants to lawyers and to companies or individuals in court cases (Sullivan & Pomerantz, 2017).

Educational Psychology. **Educational psychology** is an applied specialization in which psychologists focus on learning and teaching. Together with the members of the closely related (and more applied) specialization *school psychology*, they improve students' performance by examining how students organize their materials, study, motivate themselves, and deal with challenges. There is significant overlap between educational psychologists and school psychologists, but there is one major difference. Educational psychologists tend to do more research and focus on the big picture of how people generally learn. School psychologists tend to work more directly with kids, parents, and teachers, and they focus on how particular kids learn. Many educational psychologists and school psychologists work in schools, often providing services like testing for learning styles or learning problems. They also coordinate efforts between parents, teachers, and administrators to meet a student's special needs, such as coping with specific learning disorders (Barringer & Saenz, 2007; Helms & Rogers, 2015).

Basic Research Specializations

Basic research psychology specializations are areas in which psychologists conduct research for the sake of enhancing the understanding of behavior and mental processes. These are the psychologists who *run studies*. They don't do therapy, conduct assessments, or consult with organizations. Psychology is not something they practice; it's something they investigate. They conduct research that collectively builds psychology's knowledge base. Interestingly, basic research specializations existed long before applied specializations — that is, in the earliest days of the field, psychology was a topic of study, not a human service industry (Jakobsen, 2012; Matthews & Matthews, 2012; Smith & Davis, 2003).

Most basic research psychologists have academic jobs in universities, typically in psychology departments but occasionally in medical schools, business schools, or other parts of the university (Calfee, 2007; Grigorenko, 2007; Roediger, 2007; Vroom, 2007). Let's examine the specific academic subjects in which they work.

Physiological Psychology. **Physiological psychology** is a basic research specialization in which psychologists focus on the neural basis of behavior. It goes by many names: biological psychology, behavioral neuroscience, and neuropsychology, among others. Physiological psychologists conduct studies to determine the roles of various parts or processes within the brain in various behaviors, from hearing and sight to memory and sleep. They also explore how the various parts of the brain communicate with each other and how the brain communicates with the rest of the body. Additionally, they study the biological underpinnings of psychological disorders like schizophrenia, depression, and bipolar disorder (Garrett, 2009).

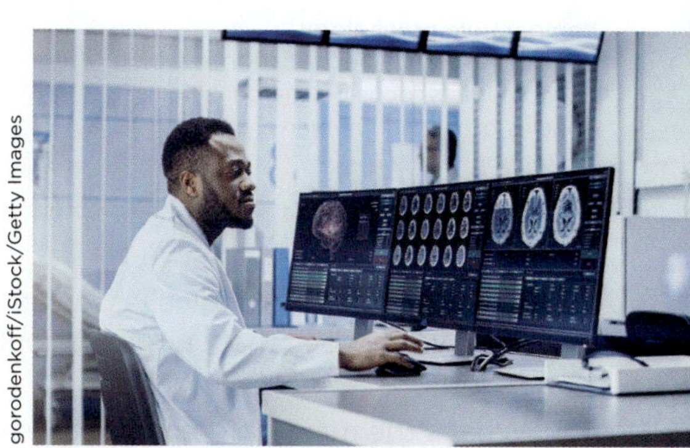
gorodenkoff/iStock/Getty Images

Physiological psychologists study the parts of the brain and their connections to mental processes and behavior.

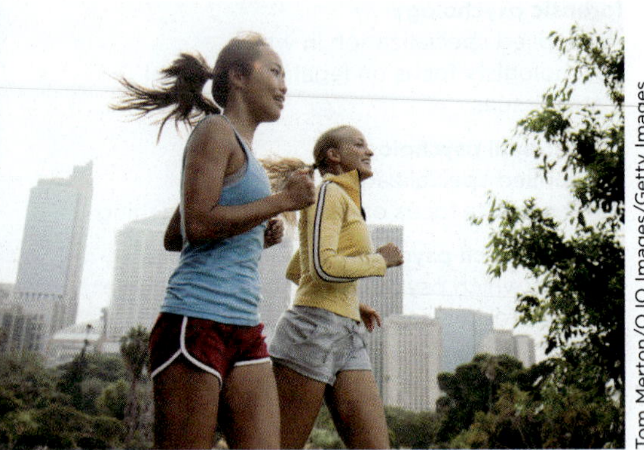
Tom Merton/OJO Images/Getty Images

Health psychologists study the relationship between physical and mental wellness, including the connection between exercise and mood.

Developmental Psychology. **Developmental psychology** is a basic research specialization in which psychologists focus on how people change throughout the life span. In the early days, developmental psychologists focused exclusively on childhood and adolescence, but in recent decades, they have also focused on development during the adult years. Developmental psychologists conduct research on how our reasoning, thinking, relationships, emotions, and other aspects of our lives evolve as we age. They are interested in discovering how these processes normally take place, how they may differ across cultures, and how they can be influenced by such factors as parenting, peers, media, and technology (Kuther & Morgan, 2013).

Personality Psychology. **Personality psychology** is a basic research specialization in which psychologists focus on people's traits. Personality psychologists try to determine what personality is made of — its basic ingredients, essentially. They also explore factors that influence personality, including genes and family environment, in an attempt to understand how those traits develop. Additionally, they study the ways that personality may interact with culture (does it have the same basic ingredients around the world?) and with age (does personality change in predictable ways as we get older?) (Barenbaum & Winter, 2008).

Social Psychology. **Social psychology** is a basic research specialization in which psychologists focus on how people think about, influence, and relate to each other. Social psychologists explore our attitudes toward others, including prejudices and stereotypes, and how they relate to our interpersonal actions. They compare the way we explain the behavior of others to the way we explain the behavior of ourselves. They examine how other people — their mere presence, the actions they take, or the orders they give — can affect our behavior. They also try to understand what attracts us to each other as friends and romantic partners (American Psychological Association, 2007a; Aronson et al., 2013).

Health Psychology. **Health psychology** is a basic research specialization in which psychologists focus on the relationship between mind and body. Most health psychologists are researchers, but some work in other specialization areas (like clinical and counseling) directly with clients on health-related issues. They study eating, exercise, and other topics related to weight; smoking, drinking, and other topics related to harmful substances; and sexual behavior and sexually transmitted diseases. They also examine the relationship between mental health and physical health, especially the immune system and stress-related conditions like heart disease (Brownell & Salovey, 2007; Gurung, 2014; Wegenek et al., 2010).

Comparative Psychology. **Comparative psychology** is a basic research specialization in which psychologists focus on the behavior of species other than humans. They conduct experiments on a wide variety of species, from bees to birds to baboons. And the range of topics they study mirrors the topics studied in humans: social interactions, development through the life span, personality characteristics, cognitive processing, and even psychological disorders (Ferdowsian et al., 2013; Leighty et al., 2013; Manson & Perry, 2013; Pepperberg et al., 2013; Tu & Hampton, 2013). Comparative psychology research carries the dual purpose of understanding the behavior of the animals being studied and applying that understanding, as appropriate, to people as well.

developmental psychology
A basic research specialization in which psychologists focus on how people change throughout the life span.

personality psychology
A basic research specialization in which psychologists focus on people's personality traits.

social psychology
A basic research specialization in which psychologists focus on how people think about, influence, and relate to each other.

health psychology
A basic research specialization in which psychologists focus on the relationship between mind and body.

comparative psychology
A basic research specialization in which psychologists focus on the behavior of species other than humans.

CHECK YOUR LEARNING:

1.4 The largest psychological association has 54 divisions. What does that suggest about the field of psychology?

1.5 What's the main difference between applied psychology specializations and basic research psychology specializations?

1.6 What is the main focus of each of these applied psychology specializations: clinical psychology, forensic psychology, and industrial/organizational psychology?

1.7 What is the main focus of each of these basic research psychology specializations: developmental psychology, physiological psychology, and social psychology?

To check your understanding of these questions, click show the answers or refer to the answers in the Chapter Summary.

Psychology Then and Now

Psychology is relatively new, but its roots go way, way back.

YOU WILL LEARN:

1.8 how the older fields of philosophy and physiology influenced the creation of psychology.

1.9 what the early schools of psychology — structuralism, functionalism, psychoanalysis, behaviorism, and humanism — emphasized.

1.10 what the more contemporary schools of psychology — multiculturalism, evolutionary psychology, cognitive psychology, neuroscience, and biopsychosocial theory — emphasize.

Relatively new? Weren't there psychologists all the way back in the late 1800s?

Yes, there were. However, the late 1800s is not so long ago in the broad scope of history. For an academic field, being only a century and a half old is like being a toddler (Benjafield, 2012).

The *really* old academic fields, the ones that originated in ancient times, include the two from which psychology emerged: *philosophy* and *physiology* (Fuchs, 2002; Goodwin, 2003; Green & Groff, 2003; Robinson, 1997; Wertheimer, 2012). Philosophy, of course, is the seeking of wisdom about the world in which we live, the attempt to discover the truths that govern our lives. It has been around about as long as people have, with notable contributions from Greek, Roman, Chinese, Judaic, Hindu, and other cultures (Stagner, 1988).

Among the questions that the philosophers pondered, many touch on the inner workings of the mind and the reasons for our behavior. For example, in France in the 1600s, René Descartes famously pondered how our reflexes might work — what exactly happens within your brain and body when you touch a burning hot object and involuntarily yank your hand away. Their answers to those questions traditionally came from opinion and insight, not from scientific experiment. In fact, the questions themselves — for example, is human nature good or bad, how much free will do people really have — don't really lend themselves to scientific testing. So philosophers' wisdom, as perceptive as it may have been, had no science to back it up. That's the niche that psychology filled: the study of the human mind and behavior grounded in science rather than speculation (Malone, 2009; Watson & Evans, 1991).

Any study of the human mind would be incomplete without study of the human brain as well. After all, mental activity is a bodily function like any other. Physiology — another field with a history stretching back more than two millennia — focuses on these brain-body functions. (Today, we would probably use the term *biology* to describe much of what was traditionally called *physiology*.) As early as the Middle Ages, physiologists were making important discoveries about the human body, like how blood circulates, how the bones of the skeleton are arranged, and how diseases damage organs. But even by the late 1800s, physiology couldn't say much about the inner workings of the human brain. Imaging technologies, like magnetic resonance imaging (MRI), computed tomography (CT) scans, and even X-rays, were a long way away. Yet the desire to understand how the brain works, along with the scientific methods used by physiologists, inspired many of the earliest experiments in psychology.

Old-School Psychology

There are a few notes to keep in mind as we explore the history of psychology. First, the way that history is organized in this chapter — old-school versus new-school — may be a bit oversimplified. There is no clear-cut boundary or landmark event to separate the two. But as time has passed, some of the original *schools of thought* in psychology have faded and newer ones have taken their places. That's not to say that the older schools of thought aren't still influential — most of them are, in updated forms — but they don't dominate the field as they once did.

Second, although the history of psychology tends to highlight events and people from Europe and the United States, it's important to remember that psychology is a global science with a global history (Blowers, 2006; Brock, 2006; Danziger, 2006). The

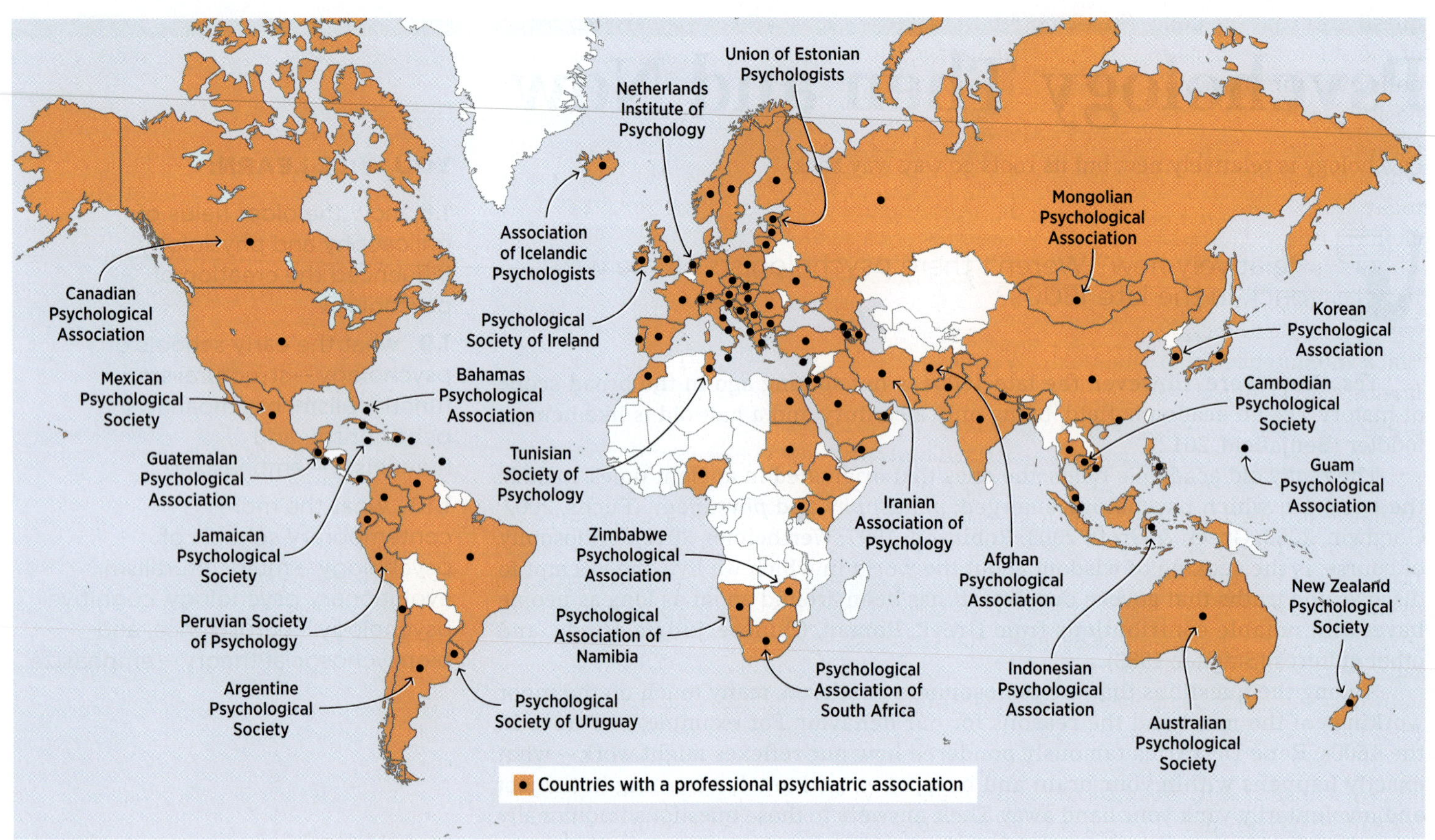

FIGURE 1.2 Psychology Worldwide. With national psychological associations around the globe, some of which have been around for nearly a century, it is clear that psychology is a global science with a global history.

American Psychological Association may be the largest and the oldest (founded in 1892), but about 100 other countries, including many outside of the Western world, have national psychological associations of their own. Some have been thriving for almost a century, like the Indian Psychological Association (founded in 1925), the Japanese Psychological Association (1927), and the Argentine Psychological Society (1930). Even the Association of Icelandic Psychologists has been around since the 1950s. **Figure 1.2** illustrates the many other national associations, which cover every continent except Antarctica and show just how worldwide psychology and its history are (Baker & Benjamin, 2012; Benjamin & Baker, 2012; Dodgen et al., 2013).

DIVERSITY MATTERS

Third, the history of psychology in the United States includes important contributions from diverse populations (Leong, 2009). For example, Black psychologists have made many notable historical achievements. In 1920, Francis C. Sumner became the first Black man to earn a PhD in psychology in the United States. He went on to become a professor and served as the chairperson of the Howard University psychology department for decades.

In 1933, Inez Beverly Prosser became the first Black woman to earn a PhD in psychology. Unfortunately, she died in a car accident a year later, but her research on the educational development of Black children was inspirational and influential. Prosser was soon followed by Alberta Banner Turner, who earned her PhD in psychology in 1935. Turner held a variety of academic positions despite race- and gender-based obstacles and fought valiantly for equal rights throughout her career.

In the 1950s, psychologists Kenneth Clark and Mamie Phipps Clark, a married couple, provided expert testimony about their own research on racial issues during the historic U.S. Supreme Court case *Brown v. Board of Education*, which led to public school desegregation. In that research, known as their famous "doll studies," the Clarks gave Black dolls and White dolls to Black children aged 3 to 7, then asked them questions about the dolls. The Black children's responses revealed the harmful impact of racism and segregation on their self-image: they frequently preferred the White dolls over the Black dolls; they also were more likely to label the White dolls with positive words (like "nice") and label the Black dolls with negative words (like "bad") (Clark & Clark, 1939, 1947). The Clarks also opened a child guidance clinic in Harlem, which Mamie Phipps Clark directed for over 30 years and which is still in operation today. In 1971, Kenneth Clark became the first Black president of the American Psychological Association (Benjamin & Crouse, 2002; Holliday, 2009).

In the late 1960s, Robert L. Williams helped to found the Association of Black Psychologists. In the 1970s, he coined the term and pioneered the study of *ebonics*, legitimizing the Black vernacular of the English language. Williams also developed the Black Intelligence Test of Cultural Homogeneity (BITCH), designed to illustrate how linguistic and cultural bias in intelligence tests placed Black and other underrepresented groups at a disadvantage (Belgrave & Allison, 2014; Williams, 1972).

The history of psychology in the United States has been significantly influenced by the work of members of other diverse groups as well (Sue, 2009). Carolyn Lewis Attneave founded the Society of Indian Psychologists in the 1970s and devoted her career to studying mental health needs and treatment among Native Americans (Trimble & Clearing-Sky, 2009). Also in the 1970s, Derald Sue was among the founders of the Asian American Psychological Association and served several years as its first president (Leong & Okazaki, 2009). George I. Sanchez was the first Latinx psychologist, earning his doctoral degree in 1934. He went on to conduct pioneering research on cultural issues regarding intelligence tests and other psychological assessment tools (Padilla & Olmedo, 2009).

Office of Public Affairs at Columbia University, publication permission granted by Columbia University Archives, Columbia Library

Psychologists Kenneth Clark and Mamie Phipps Clark were a husband-and-wife team who made significant contributions to the history of psychology. Their research and expert testimony played a key role in the historic United States Supreme Court case *Brown v. Board of Education*, which made it unconstitutional for states to establish separate public schools for Black students and White students.

Structuralism and Functionalism. Wilhelm Wundt lived in Germany from 1832 to 1920. He is considered by many to be the father of psychology, but before he focused on the mind at all, he focused on the body. He earned a medical degree in 1856 and worked as a research assistant for a famous medical researcher, Hermann Helmholtz, for years after. He even wrote a textbook on physiology during that time. But his interests steadily drifted into areas that physiology and medicine had not yet explored: the inner workings of the mind. Of course, philosophers had long been speculating about the inner workings of the mind, but with his background in physiology and medicine, Wundt approached it differently than the philosophers did: *as a science*. Wundt insisted that his new science — to which he gave the name *psychology* — should be conducted like any other science, emphasizing highly controlled methods of data collection. Wundt taught the first course in the new science of psychology in 1862 at the University of Heidelberg, wrote its first textbook (*Principles of Physiological Psychology*) in 1874, and established the first psychology research laboratory at the University of Leipzig in 1879 (Blumenthal, 1997; Capaldi & Proctor, 2003; Hunt, 2007; Stewart, 2008).

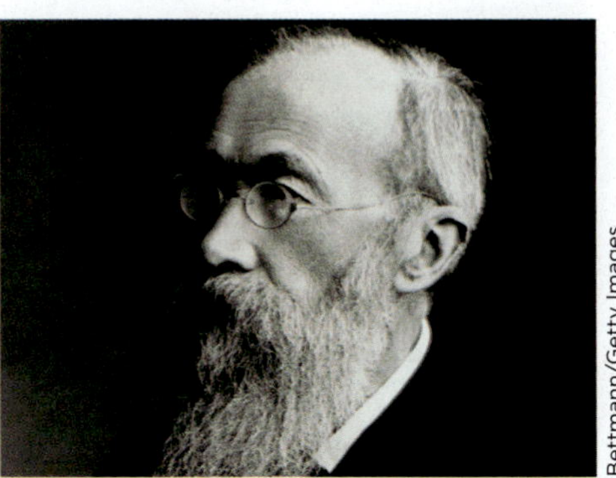

Bettmann/Getty Images

Wilhelm Wundt is widely considered to be the father of psychology. In Germany in the late 1800s, he was the first to approach the inner workings of the mind as a science. He taught the first psychology course, wrote the first psychology textbook, and established the first psychology research lab.

In that research laboratory, Wundt's experiments resembled experiments in physiology and medicine. They typically focused on such mental processes as reaction time, attention, and the way we perceive things around us through sight, hearing, touch, and other senses (Bringmann et al., 1997; Danziger & Ballyntyne, 1997; Popplestone & McPherson, 1998). Wundt used an approach similar to the way physiologists studied the human body: trying to determine its structure, what it was made of, what organs and bones it contained, and how everything connected to each other. But while physiologists could open the body to take a peek at the structure of the body (in surgeries or autopsies), Wundt lacked such a direct way to investigate the structure of mental processes like reaction time, perception, and attention. Instead, he relied on his research participants to *introspect*, or look inside themselves, and describe what was going on inside their own mind (Goodwin, 2003). Wundt asked participants to narrate exactly what mental activities took place when they felt a particular sensation or reacted to a particular stimulus.

Wait a minute — Wundt asked his participants to describe in detail the processes going on inside their own head? Were they any good at it?

structuralism
A perspective from the early history of psychology that focused on breaking down mental processes into their structure or basic parts.

No. In fact, Wundt's participants were terrible at it, as almost anyone would be. (How accurately, specifically, and completely could you use words to explain the lightning-fast and often complicated processes that take place in your brain when you think, feel, see, hear, or react?) For this reason, introspection has long been discredited and abandoned as a scientific method in psychology. In spite of the shortcomings of his introspective methods, Wundt's accomplishments are still recognized as groundbreaking for psychology as a scientific field, and he is still considered its original pioneer (Blumenthal, 2002; Pickren & Rutherford, 2010).

Structuralism. As an undergraduate student in the 1880s in England, Edward B. Titchener read Wilhelm Wundt's writings and became fascinated with Wundt's research. After graduating, he moved to Germany to become a graduate student in Wundt's lab. Titchener's own research continued to be guided by what he learned under Wundt. He tried to break down the structures of mental processes "in much the same way as a chemist breaks down chemicals into their component parts – water into hydrogen and oxygen, for example" (Stewart, 2008, p. 273). This approach evolved into **structuralism**: a perspective from the early history of psychology that focused on breaking down mental processes into their structure or basic parts.

After Titchener earned his doctoral degree, he moved to the United States in 1892 and became a professor at Cornell University in Ithaca, New York. So, more than any other single person, it was Titchener who brought Wundt's new science of psychology from Europe to the United States (Stagner, 1988; Tweney, 1997; Watson & Evans, 1991).

One more note about Titchener – his attitude toward women illustrates how the sexist attitudes common in his time made it difficult for talented women to fully participate in the early development of psychology (Stewart, 2008). In the early 1900s,

DIVERSITY MATTERS

Titchener established and led psychological organizations that deliberately kept women out. One woman, Christine Ladd-Franklin, fought back. Ladd-Franklin had fulfilled all requirements for a PhD at Johns Hopkins University but was denied the degree until 44 years later. The university, like many others at the time, allowed women to attend classes but would not formally enroll women in the psychology program.

Ladd-Franklin went on to conduct research and publish papers on such topics as the psychological processes of color vision. In 1912, Titchener excluded Ladd-Franklin from a conference for psychological researchers, and she responded, "I am shocked to know that you are still – at this year – excluding women from your meeting of experimental psychologists. It is such a very old-fashioned standpoint!" Two years later, Titchener again excluded Ladd-Franklin from a psychological conference, a move she called "so immoral – worse than that, so unscientific!" Titchener grumbled to colleague (another man), "I have been pestered . . . by Mrs. Ladd-Franklin for not having women at the meetings. . . . Possibly she will succeed in breaking us up, and forcing us to meet – like rabbits – in some dark place underground" (all quotations from Benjamin, 2006, pp. 131–133).

Titchener was certainly not the only man at the time with chauvinist attitudes (he actually became more open-minded later in his career), nor was Ladd-Franklin the only woman whose career was stifled by them. In spite of these attitudes, many women made significant early contributions to the field of psychology. In 1898, Ethel Puffer Howes completed all of the requirements for a psychology PhD at Harvard, but the university would not grant her the degree because of a policy (at the time) against PhD degrees for women. Howes then became a member of Harvard's faculty for many years despite the fact that the university refused to list her name among the men who were her colleagues (Johnston & Johnson, 2017). In 1905, Mary Whiton Calkins became the first woman to be president of the American Psychological Association. The same year, Margaret Floy Washburn became the first U.S. woman to officially earn a PhD in psychology, and she was named president of the American Psychological Association in 1921. The trailblazing by these women and others – done at a time when societal norms strongly pushed women away from careers and higher education and toward marriage and child-rearing – is a primary reason that the majority of today's doctoral degrees in psychology are earned by women (Carpenter, 1997; Furumoto & Scarborough, 2002; Kohout & Pate, 2013; Rutherford & Milar, 2017; Scarborough & Furumoto, 1987; Stewart, 2008).

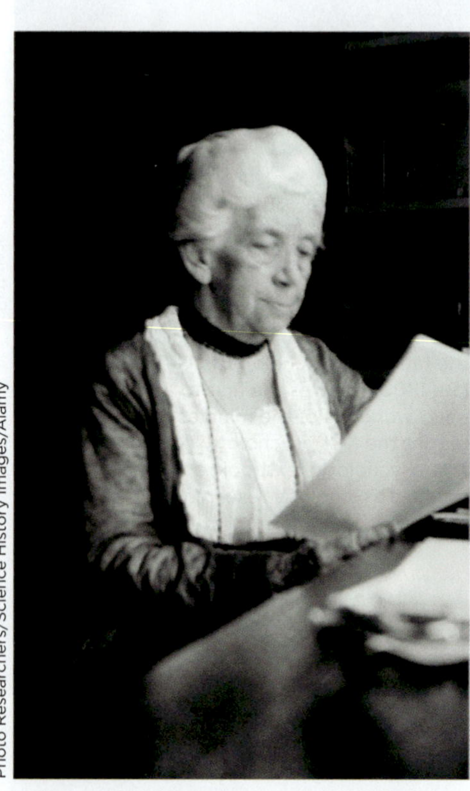

Christine Ladd-Franklin was among the first women to complete psychology PhD coursework and to conduct psychological research. Like Mary Whiton Calkins, Margaret Floy Washburn, and Ethel Puffer Howes, she overcame biases against women in the field to become a pioneer of psychology.

Functionalism. Structuralism faded rather quickly as psychology expanded in the United States. The approach that took its place was **functionalism**: a perspective from the early history of psychology that focused on the function of our mental processes and behaviors. Unlike structuralism, which tried to determine what the mental processes *are*, functionalism tried to determine what the mental processes are *for* — their purpose, or their value to the person performing them (Angell, 1907; Goodwin, 2012). Of course, functionalism was strongly influenced by Charles Darwin's theory of evolution, which was rapidly gaining acceptance at the time and which focused heavily on the function of various behaviors and physical attributes for survival and reproduction (Darwin, 1877; Fitzpatrick & Bringmann, 1997).

Functionalism was also promoted by William James, whom many consider to be the father of U.S. psychology. James was born in New York City in 1842, the son of a wealthy and prominent family. He earned a degree in medicine at Harvard University and landed a job there as a professor, a position he kept for 25 years. Beginning in 1874, he taught courses in psychology and ran a psychology lab, widely acknowledged as the first in the United States. Because psychology was such a new discipline, James had never taken a course in it himself. As he put it, "The first lecture in psychology that I ever heard was the first I ever gave" (quoted in Hunt, 2007, p. 150). But soon, psychology was being taught and studied around the country. There were about 20 psychology labs in the United States by 1892 and about 40 by 1900 — due in large part to James's popularization of the new field (Benjamin, 2007; Sokal, 2002).

Pictorial Press Ltd./Alamy

William James is widely considered to be the father of psychology in the United States. His psychology research lab at Harvard University was the first in the United States.

James promoted psychology through teaching and publishing research studies, many of which expanded the range of psychological research to new topics like children, animals, intelligence, and learning. But James's most significant single contribution was the landmark *Principles of Psychology*, a textbook he published in 1890 that gave this up-and-coming field its first authoritative source. The text remained popular and influential for many decades (Bruder, 1997; Hunt, 2007; James, 1890; Leary, 2002, 2003; Nordby & Hall, 1974; Simon, 1998).

Psychoanalysis. By the early 1900s, Wundt, Titchener, and James had put psychology on the map. But it was another pioneer — Sigmund Freud — who made psychology a household term. His ideas are collectively known as **psychoanalysis:** a perspective in psychology created by Sigmund Freud that emphasizes unconscious mental activity and the long-lasting influence of childhood experiences.

Freud was born in Austria, in an area now part of the Czech Republic, in 1856. By his early 20s, he had earned an MD in neurology. Early in his career, he began to specialize in what he called nervous disorders — basically, aches and pains for which doctors could find no biological basis. With the help of another physician, Joseph Breuer, Freud started to recognize that when people with nervous disorders discussed their symptoms, especially when they revealed thoughts and feelings that had previously been hidden (often stemming from painful childhood experiences), those symptoms improved. The discovery of this "talking cure" (as it was called by Anna O., a patient whose treatment was famously described by Breuer) led Freud to two historic ideas.

The first historic idea was the existence of the *unconscious*, thoughts and feelings of which the person is unaware that yet have the power to strongly affect the person's life. The second historic idea was *psychoanalytic psychotherapy*, a form of psychotherapy designed to make the unconscious conscious. (Both of these ideas are discussed in more detail in Chapter 12.) The term *psychoanalysis* was eventually used to capture all of Freud's ideas, whether they related to psychotherapy techniques or simply his theories of the inner workings of the mind (Fancher & Rutherford, 2012; Federn, 1997; Keen, 2001).

Psychoanalysis drew tremendous attention, not only from professors who studied it and physicians who used it but from the general public as well. This attention elevated Freud to a level of fame that was way beyond that of any psychology figure before (and perhaps since). In the process, it elevated psychology to a level of acceptance too. Freud came to the United States in 1909 to deliver a series of lectures, which were influential in spreading psychoanalysis beyond Europe (as were his many

functionalism
A perspective from the early history of psychology that focused on the function of our mental processes and behaviors.

psychoanalysis
A psychological perspective created by Sigmund Freud that emphasizes unconscious mental activity and the long-lasting influence of childhood experiences.

books). In the 1910s, articles on psychoanalysis increasingly appeared in journals, and by the 1920s, psychoanalytic training institutes and psychoanalytic professional associations were multiplying (Goodwin, 2012). Freud's popularity and influence, based largely on the notion of the unconscious and how it could be uncovered, continued to grow even after his death in 1939 (Hothersall, 2004; Stewart, 2008). Current interest in psychoanalysis is far below its peak levels – in fact, it is heavily criticized by some – but it retains some influence in certain pockets of the field (Axelrod et al., 2018; Gabbard, 2009).

It is worth noting that while the United States embraced Freud's ideas, other

countries resisted them. For example, Freud's ideas did not take hold in Argentina, Turkey, or China at anywhere near the level they did in the United States and other places (Gulerce, 2006; Hsueh & Guo, 2012; Taiana, 2006).

All that Freud stuff – like the unconscious and psychoanalysis – seems really unscientific. Did anybody point that out?

Behaviorism. Yes – the *behaviorists* pointed out that problem, and quite a few other problems, regarding psychoanalysis. **Behaviorism** is a perspective in psychology that emphasizes observable behavior over internal mental processes. The rationale behind behaviorism is simple: behavior can be seen and measured, but mental processes like feelings and thoughts cannot. Behaviorists believed psychology could be a science if it focused on behavior rather than mental processes – a point that Wundt, Titchener, James, and other pioneers of psychology had already highlighted.

Freud's theories, of course, delved much more deeply into mental processes than observable behavior. So you can understand how some people – behaviorists, specifically – would cringe when they saw Freud's theories stealing the spotlight. Freud's primary method was to look inside the mind and try to explain its inner workings. Some may have believed he had a talent for it, and his ideas may have been attention-grabbing, but it was just another form of introspection to the behaviorists – a method that had already been rejected as unscientific.

John Watson led the behaviorists' charge. Watson was born in 1878 in South Carolina. He grew up on a farm, which may explain why he became interested in research on animal behavior as a graduate student and continued that work during his career as a professor at the University of Chicago and Johns Hopkins (Stewart, 2008; Wozniak, 1997). He wrote an influential behaviorist "manifesto" in which he declared that for psychology, the "goal is the prediction and control of behavior [not mental processes]. Introspection forms no essential part of its methods" (Watson, 1913, p. 158).

By the 1920s and 1930s, behaviorism was picking up steam through Watson's continued promotion. Also, the research in Russia by Ivan Pavlov on conditioning in dogs was published in English for the first time. Pavlov's research focused on animals' behavior with strong implications for humans, a mode of study that U.S. behaviorists eagerly adopted (Goodwin, 2012). Behaviorism continued to flourish through the mid-1900s thanks to the work of B. F. Skinner, who became the new face of the movement. Skinner was both a researcher – he focused primarily on the relationship of reinforcement and behavior in rats, pigeons, and other animals – and a widely known behaviorism spokesperson. In fact, in the 1960s and 1970s, Skinner became a bestselling author, TV talk show regular, and overall academic celebrity (Coleman, 1997; Mills, 1998; Rutherford, 2009; Smith, 1996).

The heyday of behaviorism has passed, but it remains a force in psychology. This is true particularly for those interested in behavior change in animals (as in the training of service dogs), or in people with limited ability to identify and communicate their own thoughts (as in treatment of children at the severe end of the autism spectrum).

behaviorism
A psychological perspective that emphasizes observable behavior over internal mental processes.

Like psychoanalysis, behaviorism gained much more popularity in the United States than in some other countries. In fact, in much of Europe, behaviorism never had more than a minor influence. In India, it never overtook or even blended with the spiritual and mystical emphasis so prominent in that country's approach to psychology (Brock, 2006; Paranjpe, 2006).

DIVERSITY MATTERS

Carl Rogers was a pioneer of humanism, which emphasizes the notion that human nature is generally good and people are naturally motivated to grow toward their own potential.

Humanism. By the mid-1900s, psychology had two prominent schools of thought: psychoanalysis and behaviorism. Neither of them painted a favorable picture of human nature. The *unconscious* was the centerpiece of the psychoanalytic point of view, and it focused on the idea of destructive animalistic impulses in each of us. Behaviorists' portrayal was not quite so negative, but it certainly wasn't positive either. The behaviorists believed human nature, if it existed at all, was neutral, since we are no more than products of the environment around us. Psychology was ripe for a third approach that shined a light on what is good in all of us, and *humanism* became that approach (Cain, 2010). **Humanism** is a perspective in psychology that emphasizes the notion that human nature is generally good and people are naturally motivated to grow toward their own potential.

Carl Rogers led the humanistic movement. When Rogers went to graduate school in psychology, he was actually trained to do Freud's psychoanalysis, like most other graduate students of his time. Early in his therapy career, however, he found that his experiences with clients didn't match his Freudian training. To Rogers, people who experienced psychological problems weren't struggling with unconscious drives toward unrestrained aggression or desires. Rogers thought people were just stifled in their quest to grow. In other words, people just want to blossom and bloom into their true selves — to *self-actualize*, as Rogers put it — but sometimes obstacles got in the way of that natural process (Bohart & Tallman, 1999; Rogers, 1959, 1961).

What got in the way, according to Rogers, were *conditions of worth* imposed by others, which forced people to choose between being their true selves and being someone whom their loved ones would accept. For example, consider Dashon, a 10-year-old boy. Dashon loves ballet, but his parents feel that he should pursue more traditional hobbies for men, like football. In fact, they make it clear to Dashon that their acceptance of him as a son depends on which of these activities he pursues. Understandably, Dashon goes with football, but he doesn't enjoy it, and he feels a nagging unhappiness about his inability to pursue the dance that he feels is an essential part of his identity. From the humanistic point of view, ongoing experiences like this — having to sacrifice aspects of his true self to gain acceptance from important people in his life — can make Dashon vulnerable to depression, anxiety, and other psychological problems. The point here is that Dashon's original motivation was nothing evil or nasty — just the need to be true to himself. According to Rogers and the humanists who followed him, that's the fundamental need for all of us.

Another leading figure in the humanistic movement, Abraham Maslow, pointed out that the need to be true to yourself can emerge only after more basic needs are met. Maslow created a *hierarchy of needs* in which he listed these prerequisites, like hunger, thirst, safety, and feeling connected to other people (Maslow, 1968).

Humanism rose to prominence in the 1960s and 1970s. In fact, during that time it was often called *third force psychology* (Murray, 1988; Stagner, 1988), a nickname that showed how it had come to rival the psychoanalytic (first force) and behavioral (second force) approaches. The influence of humanism has faded since that time, particularly after Rogers's death in 1987. However, the basic ideas of humanism remain vital, especially among many psychologists who practice psychotherapy and who hold fundamentally positive views about human nature.

New-School Psychology

The past few decades have seen the rise of entirely new schools of thought in psychology. That doesn't mean that the older schools are long gone. In fact, all of them remain in one form or another, and among some groups of psychologists, the old schools of

humanism
A psychological perspective that emphasizes the notion that human nature is generally good and people are naturally motivated to grow toward their own potential.

Peathegee Inc/Blend Images/Getty Images

commerceandculturestock/Moment Select/Getty Images

zhang bo/iStock/Getty Images

Multicultural psychology is an approach that emphasizes the impact of culture on our thoughts, feelings, and actions. Culture can be defined by many variables, including race, ethnicity, gender, age, religion, spirituality, socioeconomic status, sexual orientation, geography, region, and ability or disability status.

thought remain quite influential. But the new schools — most notably, *multiculturalism*, *evolutionary psychology*, *cognitive psychology*, *neuroscience*, and *biopsychosocial theory* — more accurately capture the movements that characterize psychology's present and immediate future.

Multiculturalism. **Multiculturalism** is a perspective in psychology that emphasizes the influence of culture on behavior and mental processes. Multiculturalism — a term that overlaps a great deal with *diversity* — challenges an assumption held by the older schools of psychology (almost all of which were founded by White men from the United States and Europe) that an explanation of human behavior was equally true for *all* humans. That's simply not true. Increasingly, psychologists are recognizing that cultural variables have a powerful impact on what we think, feel, and do (Kirmayer et al., 2018; Matsumoto, 2003; Van de Vijver & Matsumoto, 2011).

DIVERSITY MATTERS

What, exactly, do psychologists mean when they say "culture"?

Psychologists think of a *culture* as a shared lifestyle with its own unique norms, expectations, and values. There are actually lots of characteristics on which a culture can center. For many of us, race or ethnicity may be the first examples that come to mind (Mio et al., 2009). But many other characteristics can be culturally important, including such forms of diversity as gender, religion/spirituality, age, socioeconomic status, sexual orientation, geographic region, and disability or ability status (Artman & Daniels, 2010; Lyons et al., 2010; McGoldrick et al., 2005; McKitrick & Li, 2008; Robinson-Wood, 2009; Sewell, 2009). This broader understanding of culture means that each of us has quite a few cultural characteristics. In fact, when you consider all of your cultural variables together, your combination may be rather unique. A research psychologist who develops theories to explain your behavior, or a practicing psychologist who conducts therapy with you when you are struggling, should consider your unique intersection of cultural variables rather than applying a one-size-fits-all approach (Johnson et al., 2011; Leong & Kalibatseva, 2013).

Evidence of the rise of multiculturalism is all over the field of psychology. Dozens of professional psychological journals that focus on multicultural issues (such as *Cultural Diversity & Ethnic Minority Psychology*, *Culture & Psychology*, and *Psychology of Sexual Orientation and Gender Diversity*) have sprung up in recent decades, rapidly earning respect and popularity among professionals. Divisions of the American Psychological Association, such as Division 44: Society for the Psychological Study of Lesbian, Gay, and Bisexual Issues, and Division 45: Society for the Psychological Study of Culture, Ethnicity, and Race, have been established. Our profession's ethical code has added new standards that require psychologists to consider a wide range of cultural variables when they conduct therapy, assessment, or research (American Psychological Association, 2002). The requirements for graduate programs in psychology to be accredited (that is, approved) by APA also include more emphasis on cultural diversity than they did previously (American Psychological Association, 2005).

For psychologists in the United States, the importance of multiculturalism is highlighted by the increasing diversity within the population. According to the U.S. Census Bureau, groups such as Latinx Americans and Asian Americans are likely to increase significantly in upcoming decades, while White European Americans are likely to decrease (Leong & Kalibetseva, 2013). With these population trends ahead, the importance of multiculturalism within psychology is likely to increase even more.

multiculturalism
A psychological perspective that emphasizes the influences of culture on behavior and mental processes.

evolutionary psychology
A psychological perspective that emphasizes Charles Darwin's theory of evolution as an influence on behavior.

Evolutionary Psychology. **Evolutionary psychology** is a perspective in psychology that emphasizes Charles Darwin's theory of evolution as an influence on behavior. Evolutionary theory is well over 100 years old, and its influence on psychology can be traced back as far as William James's functionalism, but its impact on psychology continues to grow. Contemporary psychologists increasingly turn to evolutionary theory to explain and predict all kinds of human behavior.

For example, psychologists use evolution to explain *altruism*, feeling concern for other people and helping them in an unselfish way. Why would you help when it brings you no benefit? According to evolutionary theory, it may be that among our ancestors, people who helped were more likely to receive help — perhaps even life-saving help — later. So, helpers had a better chance at survival because of the goodwill they had accumulated among friends and family (de Waal, 2008; Neuberg et al., 2010). Or, if Darwin's assumption that getting our genes into the next generation is what drives us, then altruism toward those who share at least some of our genes makes a lot more sense. According to this evolutionary theory, helping a relative is like helping part of yourself (Neyer & Lang, 2003; Van Vugt & Van Lange, 2006).

cognitive psychology
A psychological perspective that emphasizes cognitive processes such as thinking, language, attention, memory, and intelligence.

neuroscience
A psychological perspective that emphasizes the link between behavior and the biological functioning of the brain.

Cognitive Psychology. **Cognitive psychology** is a perspective in psychology that emphasizes processes such as thinking, language, attention, memory, and intelligence. These are the processes of acquiring and using information. Some cognitive psychologists do research to determine how these functions take place normally; others focus on how they can go wrong or how they can be improved (Sternberg & Sternberg, 2010).

The cognitive perspective arose largely as a reaction against the behavioral perspective, which came before it. In particular, psychologists associated with the cognitive perspective argue against the behavioral emphasis on issues *outside* of the mind, like observable behavior and external conditions. Instead, cognitive psychologists highlight the fact that what happens *inside* the mind is essential to understanding humans. Cognitive psychologists study a wide range of inside-the-mind questions, like how we solve problems and make decisions, how we learn languages, what stimulates creative thinking, and what influences intelligence.

Neuroscience. **Neuroscience** is a perspective in psychology that emphasizes the link between behavior and the biological functioning of the brain. This link has always been an important part of psychology, but technological advances in recent decades that allow researchers access to the inner workings of the brain — including functional magnetic resonance imaging (fMRI), CT, and positron emission tomography (PET) — have enabled this perspective to explode in popularity and influence (Gerber & Gonzalez, 2013). (By the way, neuroscience often goes by other names, such as *neuropsychology* and *biopsychology*.)

Neuroscience provides explanations for all kinds of behavior. For example, particular parts of the brain respond to addictive drugs (like morphine or meth), as well as addictive behaviors (like gambling and compulsive eating) (Everitt & Robbins, 2005; Kelley & Berridge, 2002; Potenza, 2006; Reuter et al., 2005). The hallucinations common to people with schizophrenia activate the same visual and auditory areas of the brain that are activated by normal sights and sounds (Allen et al., 2008; McGuire et al., 1993; Shergill et al., 2000; Silbersweig et al., 1995). People with out-of-control aggression, including some murderers, have unusually high activity of certain brain regions (Miczek et al., 2007; Raine et al., 1998). Certain kinds of intelligence seem to stem from certain brain areas. For example, your ability to do math depends on the activity of certain brain regions, while your ability to use language depends more on other brain regions (Dehaene, 2011; Dehaene et al., 1999).

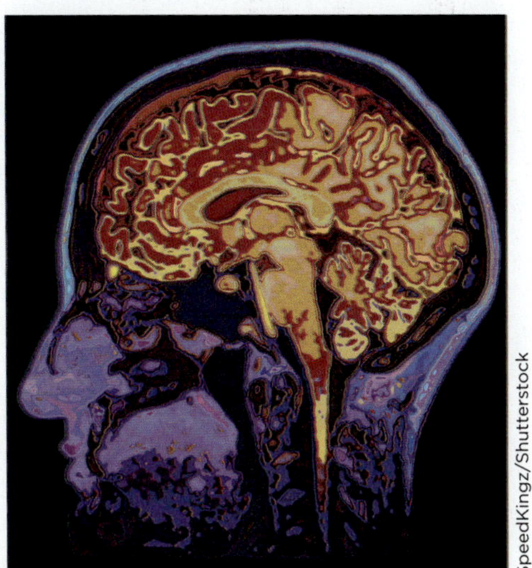
SpeedKingz/Shutterstock

Neuroscience (also known as neuropsychology or biopsychology) emphasizes the link between behavior and the biological functioning of the brain. Great advances in brain imaging technology have enabled great advances in neuroscience, which helps explain many different behaviors.

Neuroscience has become so hot in recent years that there is now a bit of backlash. Some critics of neuroscience point out that PET scans and fMRIs give us previously unimaginable images of the inner workings of the brain, but those images can make the link between brain and behavior seem simple when it is actually remarkably complex. The same critics also point out that just because a certain brain activity goes along with a certain behavior, that doesn't mean

positive psychology
A perspective in psychology that emphasizes people's strengths and successes.

biopsychosocial theory
A uniquely comprehensive psychological perspective that emphasizes biological, psychological, and social factors as influences on behavior.

that the brain activity *causes* the behavior (Burton, 2013; Halpern, 2017; Satel & Lilienfeld, 2013; Shulman, 2013).

Positive Psychology. **Positive psychology** is a perspective in psychology that emphasizes people's strengths and successes. When positive psychology rose to popularity in the 1990s and 2000s, it contrasted with the dominant focus within much of psychology: people's *problems*, in the forms of disorders, weaknesses, and failings. Much of mainstream psychology still maintains that focus, but those associated with the positive psychology movement promote a very different message. They conduct research and offer services designed to help people maximize their psychological assets and virtues. Positive psychologists see psychology as more than a tool for helping people overcome misery and impairment. They see it as an opportunity to help people flourish and be happy (Gable & Haidt, 2005; Seligman, 2018; Seligman et al., 2005; Seligman & Czikszentmihalyi, 2000; Snyder et al., 2011).

For example, positive psychologists have extensively studied positive emotions like happiness. They have explored such questions as how to bring more authentic happiness into your life, the health-related benefits of happiness, and the connection between happiness and parts of everyday life like job performance, relationship quality, and self-esteem (Frederickson, 2001; Lyubomirsky et al., 2005; Schiffer & Roberts, 2018; Seligman, 2004).

Biopsychosocial Theory. **Biopsychosocial theory** is a uniquely comprehensive popular perspective in psychology that emphasizes biological, psychological, and social factors as influences on behavior. Biopsychosocial theory is as inclusive as it gets among the schools of psychology. Unlike other old and new approaches, biopsychosocial theory does not claim that one factor alone explains your behavior. Instead, it recognizes that your brain and genetic inheritance (biological factors) *and* your thoughts and feelings (psychological factors) *and* your family and culture (social factors) all interact (Campbell & Rohrbaugh, 2006; Gask, 2018; Melchert, 2011).

Consider Leo, a young man in college who has panic attacks. What causes them? Biopsychosocial theory allows us to consider a wide range of factors. Regarding his biology, Leo may have inherited a tendency toward panic from his parents, who are quite panicky themselves. This inheritance may take the form of unique brain activity, such as overactivity in an area called the *amygdala* (Debiec & LeDoux, 2009; Faravelli et al., 2009; Forsyth et al., 2009; Liverant et al., 2007). Regarding his psychology, Leo may have a tendency to *catastrophize*, or make a mountain out of a molehill, especially when he notices minor changes in his own body. He may notice his heart rate going up a bit after climbing a few flights of stairs, mistakenly believe that he's about to have a heart attack, and bring a panic attack on himself (Clark & Beck, 2010). Regarding his social environment, the fact that Leo has watched not only his parents but also his older brother, older sister, and grandfather have panic attacks means that panic was modeled for him throughout his childhood (Ehlers, 1993; Mineka & Cook, 1993). Biopsychosocial theory does not require that all three of these factors be given equal weight. After all, in a specific case (like Leo's), one factor may outweigh the others. But biopsychosocial theory does enable psychologists to consider multiple factors rather than just one, which can produce a more accurate and complete explanation of what's really going on.

The Future of Psychology: Technology, Antiracism, Social Justice Advocacy, and More

It's impossible to know exactly what the future holds for psychology, but today's psychologists are well aware of the issues that shape our lives and have already started to tackle them in their work. Those issues include social justice, antiracism, technology, social media, and more (Marshall-Lee et al., 2020; Gray et al., 2020; Abrams 2020a, 2020b). In the midst of the COVID-19 pandemic and the social unrest that coincided with it, the APA offered a list of trending issues on which psychologists were likely to work in the years that followed (Spiner, 2021). Here are highlights of the issues they expect to emerge and what psychologists might do to address them:

DIVERSITY MATTERS

Fighting racism. Psychologists can conduct research on the ways that racist beliefs take hold, develop and test the effectiveness of antiracism efforts, and provide affirmative and healing mental health services for those who have experienced racism. Their research can also focus on the rates and reasons for racially biased or overly aggressive policing, and develop tests and interview techniques that can help police departments hire officers less likely to approach policing with that kind of bias or aggression. They can also address race-related problems within the psychology profession itself by exposing racial inequality in research practices, grad school admissions, and the way faculty members are hired and retained (Roberts et al., 2020).

Using social media for good. Psychologists can take advantage of the wide reach of Instagram, Twitter, and other social media by sharing easy-to-understand summaries of research results, evidence-based mental health tips, and more.

Maximizing mental health apps and online therapy. There are thousands of apps that claim mental health benefits, and their use has grown since the start of the pandemic. So has the use of online therapy. Psychologists can help by developing or improving existing apps themselves (rather than allowing the app stores to fill with options developed by less qualified people), and by conducting research on apps to determine which ones are most likely to provide direct benefit or supplement traditional therapy. Psychologists can also help by conducting research to see how well online therapy works, by lobbying legislators to ensure that sufficient devices and Internet access are widely available, and by pressuring insurance companies to pay for online therapy the same way they pay for in-person therapy.

DIVERSITY MATTERS

Reaching out to underserved communities. The COVID-19 pandemic emphasized that some segments of our society are more vulnerable than others to mental health problems that are often worsened by poverty, substance use, physical health problems, and other widespread inequities. Psychologists can help by promoting telehealth for communities where in-person access to psychologists is difficult, and can also pressure legislators to dedicate funds to mental health services.

Preparing for the next pandemic. If another pandemic hits, psychologists can help us be ready for it by conducting research on social and behavioral issues like social distancing, mask-wearing, and vaccination decisions. They can also conduct research on what works best for online/virtual activities (as opposed to in-person ones), including work and school.

CHECK YOUR LEARNING:

1.8 Which two older fields influenced the development of psychology?

1.9 What was the emphasis of each of the original schools of psychology — structuralism, functionalism, psychoanalysis, behaviorism, and humanism?

1.10 What is the emphasis of each of the more contemporary schools of psychology — multiculturalism, evolutionary psychology, cognitive psychology, neuroscience, positive psychology, and biopsychosocial theory?

To check your understanding of these questions, click show the answers or refer to the answers in the Chapter Summary.

The Science of Psychology

YOU WILL LEARN:

1.11 why psychology requires a scientific approach.

1.12 about the three primary types of research that psychologists do: descriptive, correlational, and experimental research.

1.13 the steps of the scientific method.

1.14 how psychologists share results.

1.15 what ethical obligations psychology researchers have.

Remember how we defined psychology at the beginning of this chapter: the scientific study of behavior and mental processes. The *scientific* part of that definition is crucial. It means that psychologists don't settle for answers that are just speculation, guesswork, or common sense. Instead, psychologists *test* any possible answer to determine how legitimate that answer actually is. So when clinical psychologists wonder whether genes cause bipolar disorder, they don't base their answer on a hunch or on their personal experience with a family that has both a parent and a kid with bipolar disorder. They measure the rate of bipolar disorder in identical twins raised apart, or in adopted kids whose biological parents are bipolar but whose adoptive parents are not, or conduct another type of scientific investigation. In other words, these clinical psychologists produce an answer based on data that they have carefully and purposefully collected (Craddock & Jones, 1999; Lichtenstein et al., 2009; McDonald, 2018).

When developmental psychologists wonder whether kids who play violent video games behave more violently in real life than kids who don't, they don't base their answer on a gut feeling or their observations of the kid next door who plays *Call of Duty* and throws rocks at the dog. They meticulously measure video game playing and violent behavior in hundreds of kids and calculate how strongly the two go together (Bushman & Huesmann, 2010; Carnagey et al., 2007; Polman et al., 2008; Verheijen et al., 2018).

As a psychology researcher myself, I have seen firsthand how a question can evolve from speculation into science. Once, during my undergrad clinical psychology class, my students and I were discussing how well psychotherapy works. The emphasis was on the beneficial effects of psychotherapy for the client, but soon the class discussion veered in a new and interesting direction: how therapy might affect the client's *partner*. Specifically, we started to speculate about the ways that psychotherapy could — unintentionally, of course — cause distress in the person who was dating or married to the client. I asked my students, what would make *you* feel uncomfortable about your own partner's therapy? Luke spoke up first: "If my girlfriend kept me in the dark about it — if she wouldn't even tell me why she was going to therapy or what she was talking about there — I would hate that!" Taylor responded, "I wouldn't even need to know exactly why my boyfriend's in therapy, but I definitely don't want him seeing some hot therapist!" Then Nathan chimed in, "If my partner was in therapy for just a few sessions, no problem. But if he's going for months and months, I'd get nervous."

When class ended, everyone left — except Elizabeth. She asked me some questions that advanced the conversation past speculation and into science: "Has anyone actually *investigated* that question? I mean, have any psychologists ever actually *conducted a study* to see what makes people feel uncomfortable about their partners' therapy? And if not, can *we* do that study?" Elizabeth was not satisfied with the hunches that her classmates had offered. She wanted to *scientifically* test possible answers. So we did exactly that.

Over the next few months, Elizabeth and I read other research related to the topic, designed our own original study, and ran it. We found some interesting results, too: our participants were especially uncomfortable with the idea of their partner keeping the reasons for therapy secret, refusing to talk about therapy sessions with them, being in therapy for more than 6 months, and seeing an attractive therapist. Other factors, like how much the client talked about the partner in therapy and the therapist's age and marital status, didn't make such a big difference. When our study was complete, Elizabeth and I wrote it up, submitted it to a journal, and got it published (Pomerantz & Seely, 2000).

Gorodenkoff/Shutterstock

Psychologists take a scientific approach to important questions. For example, psychologists conduct research on the possible connection between violent video games and violent behavior in kids.

The Need for Science in Psychology

When psychology got its start in the late 1800s, it was swimming in a sea of nonscientific thought (Cattell, 1895). That's why pioneers like Wundt, Titchener, and James had to work so hard to distinguish their new field *as a science*. These early psychologists worked to separate their new scientific field from nonscientific fields like philosophy, which around that time emphasized the theories of John Locke, David Hume, and John Stuart Mill. These philosophers covered important topics — how people learn, what knowledge and abilities we are born with, and how we are shaped by experience — but they covered it through ideas and debates, rather than testing (Benjamin, 2007).

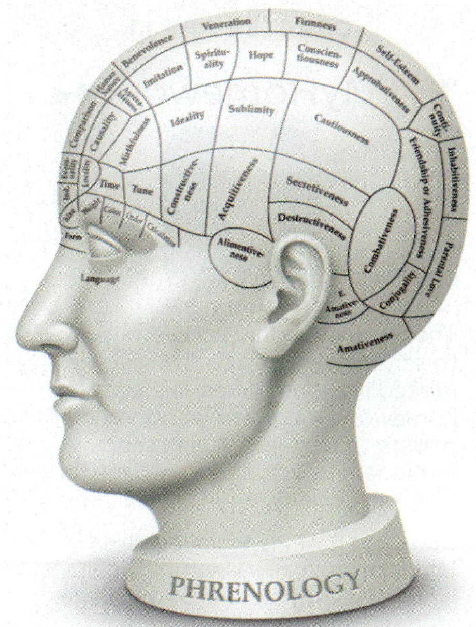

FIGURE 1.3 Pseudopsychology and Phrenology. In the late 1800s, many members of the public believed in phrenology, or the idea that bumps in the skull revealed personality characteristics and mental abilities. Disproving this kind of unsupported pseudopsychology is a major reason why it is important for psychology to be a science.

Pseudopsychology. An even bigger foe to the science of psychology was the popular psychology of the day. These were ideas the general public believed in, but that had no basis in science — like we have astrology, horoscopes, and the vaccines-cause-autism theory today. In the late 1800s, popular psychology included *phrenology*, *physiognomy*, and *mesmerism* (Benjamin, 2007).

Phrenology. According to phrenology, bumps in the skull revealed personality characteristics and mental abilities (**Figure 1.3**). Phrenologists would travel from town to town, run their hands over the heads of the townspeople, and inform them that a bump over their right ear meant they were selfish, a bump on the top of their head meant they were kind, and a bump on the back of their head meant they were friendly and loving.

Physiognomy. Physiognomy was like phrenology but focused on the face rather than the skull. Supposedly your eyelids indicated how sympathetic you were, and the area around your lips told how patriotic you were.

Mesmerism. Mesmerism (named after its inventor, Franz Anton Mesmer) was a practice in which a healer moved magnets or in some cases just empty hands over your body to adjust your balance of fluids or to induce a hypnotic trance.

These unsupported techniques were popular for some time, but they were bogus and have since been discredited. Perhaps more important, they were unscientific. In response, early psychologists fought hard to make sure that psychology was scientific, which made its claims more valid and respectable than those of all the nonscientific techniques.

FROM RESEARCH TO REAL LIFE

Psychologists' Research on College Success

Among the many, many questions that psychologists study, one might be of particular interest to you: what predicts academic success in college students? As you read through the findings listed below, keep in mind that most of them come from correlational studies. That means causal relationships are not definite, and none of the correlations are perfectly positive or negative, so they do not necessarily apply to every student.

- Students who stay up later and wake up later get lower GPAs. In one study, GPAs dropped 0.13 points (on a standard 0–4.0 scale) for each hour the sleep cycle was pushed back (Trockel et al., 2000).
- Students who are more engaged in college life — involved in more curricular and extracurricular activities for longer periods — get higher GPAs (Kuh et al., 2008; Wolf-Wendel et al., 2009).
- Students who believe that they can succeed with effort earn higher GPAs (Robbins et al., 2004).
- Students who use performance goals — specifically setting out to achieve a high standard in a course — earn higher GPAs than those who don't (Harackiewicz et al., 2002).
- Students who spend more time on social media get lower GPAs than students who don't (Liu et al., 2017).
- Students who cram for tests get lower GPAs than those whose study sessions are spaced out and consistent (Landauer, 2011; Roediger & Karpicke, 2011).
- Students whose life goals are more superficial tend to fall below their own GPA expectations more often than students whose life goals are more focused on helping others and driven by a meaningful purpose (Beattie et al., 2018).
- Just showing up makes a big difference. Students who attend class regularly earn higher GPAs than those who don't. In fact, one study concluded that attendance was a better predictor of college students' grade in a course than their SAT or ACT score, high school GPA, study habits, or study skills (Credé et al., 2010).
- Participation matters too. Students who participate in class tend to earn higher grades than students who don't (Kim et al., 2020).

CHAPTER APP 1.1

The MyHomework app allows you to schedule and track any school-related responsibilities, like classes, homework, long-term assignments, papers, and exams. It also sends reminders for classes, study sessions, and meetings.

How does it APPly to your daily life?
How could an app like this one help you be successful as a college student? In particular, how could it help you schedule consistently spaced study sessions rather than cramming?

How does it APPly to your understanding of psychology?
How does following consistently spaced study schedules and other advice supported by psychologists' research help you appreciate the need for science in psychology?

To learn more about this app or to download it to your phone, you can search for "MyHomework" on Google, in the iPhone App store, or in the Google Play store.

Today, we call unsupported theories and practices in popular psychology **pseudopsychology**: psychological information that is not supported by science but may appear to be. (*Pseudo-* is Greek for false.) Unfortunately, pseudopsychology is still around and still persuades lots of people. Some believe that psychics can predict their future. Some have faith in horoscopes or numerology. Some are sure that their dreams can be accurately analyzed or the TV ads they see contain subliminal messages that force them to buy products. Fortunately, real psychology — that is, scientific psychology — is now well established, producing thousands of empirical studies every year and disproving the myths of pseudopsychology loudly and often (e.g., Lawson, 2007; Lilienfeld, 2010, 2018; Lilienfeld et al., 2015).

Critical Thinking. Perhaps the greatest enemy to pseudopsychology and the greatest friend to real psychology is **critical thinking**: an inquisitive, challenging approach to ideas and assumptions. Critical thinking is essential to advancement in any kind of science. After all, somebody had to say, "Wait, maybe the earth isn't flat," or "Hey, maybe there's a way we can connect all our computers together in some kind of web." In psychology, critical thinking is vital. Without it, psychologists would never generate new ideas about how your personality was formed, how your memory works, what the various regions of your brain do, how your mood and your health affect each other, and what helps people with psychological disorders.

With critical thinking, we become less dependent upon "common sense" (or "folk wisdom," or the proverbs that everybody "knows" to be true), which is especially helpful when common sense contradicts itself. That actually happens quite a bit. Which is true: "There's no place like home," or "The grass is always greener on the other side"? "Better safe than sorry," or "Nothing ventured, nothing gained"? "Birds of a feather flock together," or "Opposites attract"? Common sense certainly has its place, but science, fueled by critical thinking, can help us confirm or disconfirm the commonsense explanations that occur to us.

Confirmation Bias. Critical thinking also helps us avoid some of the common errors in thinking that can lead us to conclusions that feel true but are actually false. One such error is the **confirmation bias**: a tendency to prefer information that confirms what you thought in the first place. You've experienced the confirmation bias in real life many times. For example, let's say Alex tries a new restaurant and hates it. Later, they come across that restaurant on Yelp and notice that it has 100 reviews. They scroll quickly past the many glowing five-star reviews but spend plenty of time on the few one-star reviews, agreeing enthusiastically with all of them. By the time Alex clicks away from that page, they're more convinced than ever that it is indeed a terrible restaurant despite the reality that the restaurant's average rating was 4.5 stars out of 5. In other words, thanks to the confirmation bias, they looked for and found information that confirmed what they originally thought.

As scientists, psychologists dedicate themselves to overcoming confirmation bias. That is, we have to be open to ideas different from our own, even if that means we have to admit those ideas weren't perfect. For example, for a while in the late 1960s and 1970s, many clinical psychologists believed it was a good idea to use *flooding* as a form of therapy for people with phobias and other anxiety disorders (Boulougouris et al., 1971; Emmelkamp & Wessels, 1975; Levis & Carrera, 1967; Willis & Edwards, 1969). Flooding involves exposing people to what they're afraid of — not little by little, but all at once, to "flood" them with anxiety. A client who is afraid of dogs gets put quickly into a room full of dogs, a client afraid of flying gets put directly onto a plane, and so on.

As the 1970s went by, the number of studies supporting flooding declined, but they didn't disappear altogether. Occasionally, into the 1980s and even in more recent years, studies would pop up with some kind of claim that flooding worked for particular clients (Keane et al., 1989; Levis, 2008; Marshall, 1985; Rychtarik et al., 1984; Zoellner et al., 2008). The point is this: a clinical psychologist who was pro-flooding from the beginning could fall victim to confirmation bias and with tunnel vision seek out those few studies that continued to support flooding as a treatment. In doing so, that clinical

pseudopsychology
Psychological information that is not supported by science but may appear to be.

critical thinking
An inquisitive, challenging approach to ideas and assumptions.

confirmation bias
A tendency to prefer information that confirms what a person thought in the first place.

psychologist would ignore the many studies that found flooding to be ineffective or harmful. That clinical psychologist would also have to ignore the many studies finding that other therapies worked much better – especially systematic desensitization, in which the exposure is more gradual and humane (Barlow et al., 2007; Gamble et al., 2010; Head & Gross, 2009; Morganstern, 1973; Pitman et al., 1991).

Belief Perseverance. Another error that critical thinking helps us overcome is **belief perseverance**: a tendency to maintain a belief even when evidence suggests it is incorrect. Belief perseverance happens when you can't avoid beliefs that prove yours wrong but you cling to yours anyway. Going back to that restaurant example, if several of Taylor's friends tell them that restaurant was their all-time favorite, they might think, "What do they know about good food? It was awful." If it wins awards from local restaurant critics, they might dig their heels in even more: "Restaurant critics are such idiots."

Psychologists don't like to admit they are wrong, either, but it's their responsibility to overcome any belief perseverance and let critical thinking and scientific evidence reign. Besides confirmation bias and belief perseverance, there are plenty of errors in thinking that psychologists, as scientists, use critical thinking to overcome. Table 1.1 explains some of them.

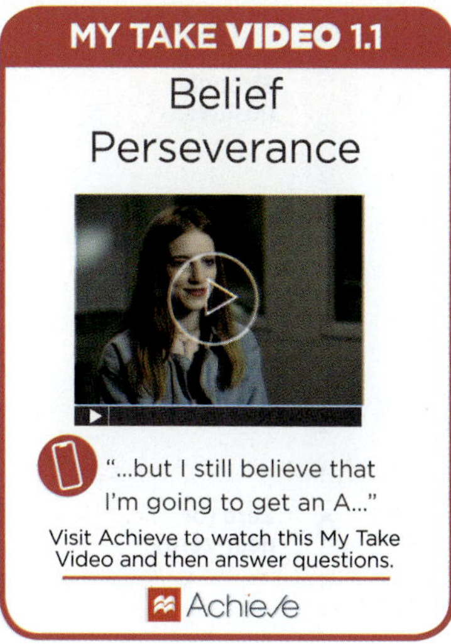

MY TAKE VIDEO 1.1
Belief Perseverance
"...but I still believe that I'm going to get an A..."
Visit Achieve to watch this My Take Video and then answer questions.
Achieve

A quick note about these My Take videos: you'll find them in every chapter, and they're usually just 2 to 4 minutes long. Each video features several students in introductory psychology classes like yours explaining how an important psychological concept connects to their own personal lives. In other words, they share their "take" on the concept in a way that helps you understand it and relate it to your own personal life. Check them out!

The Goals of Psychological Studies

When psychologists conduct scientific studies, they have one of three aims: (1) to *describe* people in terms of a particular variable, (2) to see how two variables *correlate* with each other, or (3) to *experiment* by manipulating one variable and measuring how another variable responds. Let's consider each of these goals separately.

Descriptive Research. **Descriptive research** is research in which the goal is simply to describe a characteristic of the population. The psychologist specifies a group of people and then measures some quality, behavior, or other feature within that group. Imagine yourself as a psychologist with a strong interest in social media usage among U.S. college students. Descriptive research on that topic might simply measure how many hours per day college students spend on social media – nothing more, nothing less.

belief perseverance
A tendency to maintain a belief even when evidence suggests it is incorrect.

descriptive research
A type of research in which the goal is simply to describe a characteristic of the population.

TABLE 1.1: Thinking Errors

THINKING ERROR	DEFINITION	EXAMPLE
Confirmation bias	You prefer information that confirms what you already believe.	You believe that the rash on your arm is nothing serious, so you seek out medical Web sites that say it's nothing serious and click away from those that say it could be serious.
Belief perseverance	You maintain a belief even when evidence suggests it is incorrect.	It has been raining hard all day, but you believe that your softball game in a couple of hours will not get rained out.
Bandwagon fallacy	You believe something because lots of other people believe it.	Many yards on nearby streets have signs endorsing the same candidate, so you think they must be worthy of your vote.
Emotional reasoning	You believe something because of how it makes you feel rather than how logical it is.	You believe your friend is a peaceful and well-behaved person, even though they have been in several unprovoked fistfights this semester.
Authority fallacy	You believe something because an authority figure believes it.	You change your beliefs about raising the minimum wage after hearing the opinion of an expert on the subject.
Antiquity fallacy	You believe something because people have believed it for a long time.	You believe that babies and young children in cars are just as safe unbuckled as they are in properly installed car seats because that is what people in your parents' or grandparents' generation thought.
Black-or-white fallacy	You take an absolute or extreme belief when a more moderate belief would be more accurate.	You believe that your weight gain was entirely caused by a side effect of your medication, when in fact it was due to many factors.

Information from Lepper et al. (1986), Wason and Johnson-Laird (1972), and Tindale (2007).

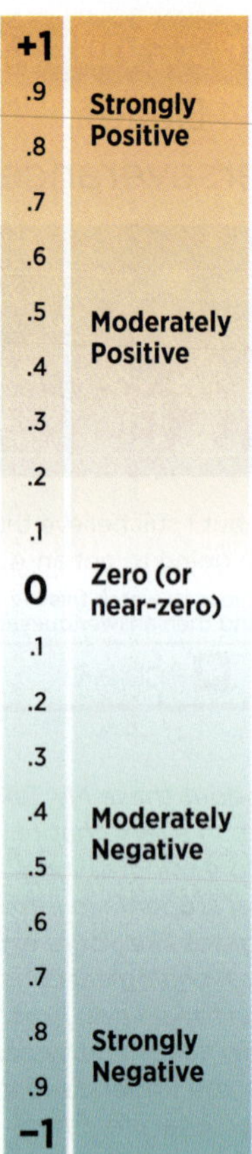

FIGURE 1.4 Correlation Coefficients. Correlation coefficients, which show how two variables relate to each other, range from +1.0 to −1.0. The closer they are to those extremes, the stronger they are. The closer they are to the middle (zero), the weaker they are.

You'd report your findings of this descriptive study in the form of a *measure of central tendency*, like the *mean*, *median*, or *mode*. You'd also report the scatter, or *variance*, around those measures of central tendency, such as the *standard deviation*. You can find more information about these concepts in Appendix A.

Correlational Research. **Correlational research** is research in which the goal is to determine the relationship between two variables. Descriptive research focuses on variables in isolation, but correlational research focuses on variables in tandem: how changes in one variable are linked to changes in the other variable, or how *predictive* one variable is for another. In other words, if you know how someone scores on one variable, how confidently can you predict how they score on the other variable?

As an example, let's say you have finished your descriptive research on social media usage by college students. Now you are interested in doing a new correlational study on college students' social media usage *and* their self-esteem (basically, how positively they think and feel about themselves). In other words, you want to find an answer to this question: if you know either the number of hours per day someone spends on social media *or* how much self-esteem that person has (as measured by a numeric questionnaire), how accurately can you predict the other variable?

To measure correlations, psychologists use the **correlation coefficient**: a statistic that shows the relationship between two variables, ranging from highly positive (+1) to highly negative (−1) (**Figure 1.4**). A *positive correlation coefficient* means that as one variable goes up, the other variable goes up with it. In your study, a positive correlation would mean that the more time a student spent on social media, the higher their self-esteem. The stronger the positive correlation is — the closer it falls to +1 — the more confidence you can have in the prediction. So if you had a correlation coefficient around +.9 (quite rare in psychology), you could conclude that the two variables move together very closely, but if you had a correlation coefficient around +.4 (more common in psychology), you could conclude that the two variables were connected but more loosely.

A *negative correlation coefficient* means that as one variable goes up, the other variable goes down, and vice versa. In your study, a negative correlation coefficient would mean that the more time a student spends on social media, the lower their self-esteem. The stronger the negative correlation is — the closer it falls to −1 — the more confidence you can have in the prediction. So if you have a correlation coefficient around −.9 (quite rare in psychology), you could conclude that the two variables were very much opposites. However, if you have a correlation coefficient around −.4 (more common in psychology), you could conclude that the two variables had a looser inverse relationship.

Between the positive and the negative, there's the *zero correlation coefficient*, also known as no correlation, or the absence of a correlation. In your study, a zero correlation coefficient would mean that the time a student spent on social media told you absolutely nothing about their self-esteem, and vice versa. The two variables would have nothing — or zero — to do with each other. Correlation coefficients that fall very close to zero, like +.1 or −.1, are often interpreted by psychologists as being essentially the same as a zero correlation coefficient. Even though such coefficients may lean in either a positive or negative direction, they lean so slightly that they have no real predictive value.

When a correlation is strong (in either a positive or negative direction), there is a temptation to think that one variable *made* the other variable change (Dickter, 2006; Thompson, 2013). But that would be an error that psychologists call the **correlation–causation fallacy**: the mistaken belief that when two variables correlate strongly with each other, one must cause the other (see My Take Video 1.2). Simply put, *correlation does not necessarily mean causation*. Let's say you find a strong negative correlation coefficient in your study: as social media hours increase, self-esteem decreases. Does that mean that spending more time on social media *causes* self-esteem to drop? Not necessarily. What about causation the other way around: does high self-esteem *cause* people to spend less time on social media? Again, not

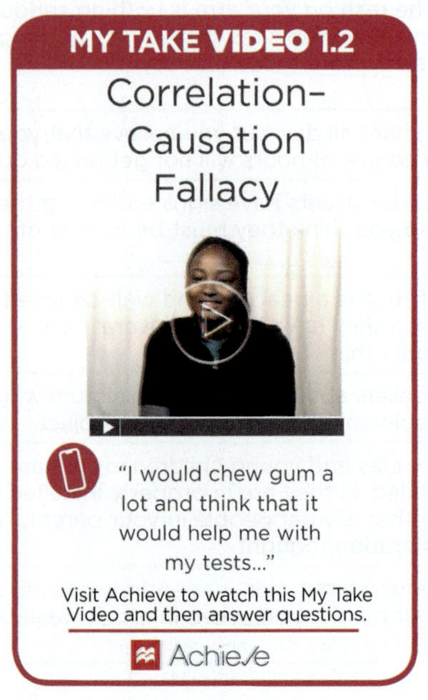

necessarily. You can't tell from a correlation coefficient. The correlation coefficient tells what *varies with* what, but not what *causes* what. In the case of this strong negative correlation, there could be four options: (1) the first variable could cause the second variable, (2) the second variable could cause the first variable, (3) both variables could cause each other, or (4) neither variable could cause the other (perhaps a third variable, outside of the focus of the study, causes both). To determine the causal relationship between variables, you'd have to upgrade from a correlational study to *experimental research*, which we turn to now.

LIFE HACK 1.1

When you notice a correlation between two things in your own life, don't automatically assume that one causes the other. You might have the cause and effect reversed, or they could both be caused by something else, or the connection could be coincidental rather than causal.

(Dickter, 2006; Thompson, 2013)

Experimental Research. **Experimental research** is research in which the goal is to determine the cause-and-effect relationship between two variables by manipulating one and observing changes in the other. In your work on social media and self-esteem, you'd be running experimental research if you controlled one of the two variables — that is, if you determined how much or how little of it your participants have — rather than simply measuring what was already there. In this case, neither variable is easy to manipulate, but your best bet would be to manipulate social media time. Changing a person's self-esteem is too much of a challenge, both practically and ethically. (Could you effectively lower your participants' self-esteem? Would it be ethical if you did?) Also, you may have reason to believe that social media time influences self-esteem more than self-esteem influences social media time, based on experts' theories or the results of previous studies on this topic. The difficulty of completely manipulating one of these variables highlights a common problem for psychologists: it's difficult to experiment on people. Unlike chemists experimenting on chemicals or physicists experimenting on objects, psychologists have to consider both what's realistically doable and what's morally permissible for those whom they study (Hock, 2013; Wampold, 2006).

With a research design based on the idea that changes in social media time cause changes in self-esteem, social media time would be your **independent variable (IV)**: in experimental research, a variable that is manipulated by the researcher. By contrast, self-esteem would be your **dependent variable (DV)**: in experimental research, a variable that is expected to depend upon the independent variable. In your study, you might initially measure both social media time and self-esteem in your participants and then double their social media time for a week, with the expectation that such an increase would cause changes in self-esteem.

Actually, you would only double social media time for half of your participants, and leave social media time unchanged for the other half. The group whose social media time you doubled would be your **experimental group**: in experimental research, the group of participants who receive the treatment that is the focus of the study. The group whose social media time remained the same would be your **control group**: in experimental research, the group of participants who do not receive the treatment that is the focus of the study.

Of course, you'd want to put participants into those two groups via **random assignment**: a procedure in experimental research by which the assignment of participants into either the experimental or control group happens entirely by chance. Assuming you did assign participants randomly, at the end of the study you'd measure whether your experimental group showed changes that your control group didn't. In other words, did those whose social media time got doubled demonstrate changes in their self-esteem, while those whose social media time remained the same stayed at the same level of self-esteem?

When possible, psychologists like to run their experiments using a **double-blind procedure**: a way of conducting experimental research in which neither the participants nor the researchers are aware of which participants are in each group. The purpose of keeping both the participants and the researchers "blind" is to minimize the **placebo effect**: the effect of expectations rather than the experimental manipulations. The double-blind procedure might not be possible for your study of social media and self-esteem, since your participants will notice any changes to their social media time. But in other studies, particularly those in which the placebo effect is a real

correlational research
A type of research in which the goal is to determine the relationship between two variables.

correlation coefficient
A statistic that shows the relationship between two variables, ranging from highly positive (+1) to highly negative (−1).

correlation–causation fallacy
A mistaken belief that when two variables correlate strongly with each other, one must cause the other.

experimental research
A type of research in which the goal is to determine the cause-and-effect relationship between two variables by manipulating one and observing changes in the other.

independent variable (IV)
A variable in experimental research that is manipulated by the researcher.

dependent variable (DV)
A variable in experimental research that is expected to depend upon the independent variable.

experimental group
The group of participants in experimental research who receive the treatment that is the focus of the study.

control group
The group of participants in experimental research who do not receive the treatment that is the focus of the study.

random assignment
A procedure in experimental research by which the assignment of participants into either the experimental or control group happens entirely by chance.

double-blind procedure
A way of conducting experimental research in which neither the participants nor the researchers are aware of which participants are in the experimental group and which are in the control group.

placebo effect
The effect of expectations in experimental research rather than the effect of experimental manipulations.

scientific method
A way of asking and answering questions that follows a predetermined series of steps: posing a question, conducting a literature review, developing a hypothesis, testing the hypothesis by collecting data, and analyzing the data and drawing conclusions.

literature review
A step in scientific research during which a researcher learns what previous research on the topic already exists.

theory
A proposed explanation for observed events.

hypothesis
A prediction, typically based on a theory, that can be tested.

risk, the double-blind procedure is both possible and desirable. For example, consider a team of clinical psychologists running an experiment on a new type of therapy for depression. They might give half of their participants (the experimental group) the new therapy, and the other half (the control group) a therapy already shown to work by previous studies. However, they would not tell any of the participants which group they were in. They might also ask other clinicians to conduct the interviews to assess clients' depression levels at the end of the study and keep those clinicians in the dark about which clients received which kind of therapy.

The Scientific Method

The **scientific method** is a way of asking and answering questions that follows a predetermined series of steps: posing a question, conducting a literature review, developing a hypothesis, testing the hypothesis by collecting data, and analyzing the data and drawing conclusions (**Figure 1.5**). Psychologists, like scientists in other disciplines, follow the scientific method as a primary way of learning more about the topic they study (Hershey et al., 1996, 2006). Let's consider each step of the scientific method as it might apply to your study on social media time and self-esteem.

Posing a Question. The question on which the study focuses depends on the kind of research you conduct (Leong et al., 2012). If the research is descriptive, the question might simply be "How many hours per day do students spend on social media?" If the research involves self-esteem and is correlational, the question could be "To what extent are social media time and self-esteem linked?" If it involves self-esteem and is experimental, the question could be "To what extent does time on social media cause changes in self-esteem?"

Conducting a Literature Review. Of course, the question a researcher poses should be informed by what other researchers have found before. So you will need to do a **literature review**: a step in scientific research during which a researcher learns what previous research on the topic already exists. You may not be the first researcher to study social media time and self-esteem. In fact, there may already be lots of other studies on the topic, and if so, your best contribution might be to add to what's already there rather than unnecessarily repeating what many others have done (Baumeister, 2013; Marczyk et al., 2005; Rothstein, 2012). (For the emerging body of literature on social media and self-esteem–related topics, see Andreassen et al., 2017; Chou & Edge, 2012; Cingel & Olsen, 2018; Gonzalez & Hancock, 2011; Junco, 2013a, 2013b, 2012; Kalpidou et al., 2011; Rozgonjuk et al., 2018; Saiphoo et al., 2020 among others.)

Developing a Hypothesis. Psychological research is typically based on a **theory**: a proposed explanation for observed events. For example, your experimental research on social media time and self-esteem might be based on the theory that as social media time goes up, self-esteem goes down. Ideally, this theory is influenced by previous research on the topic (Gelso, 2006). To see how strong your theory is, that theory must be translated into a **hypothesis**: a prediction, typically based on a theory, that can be tested.

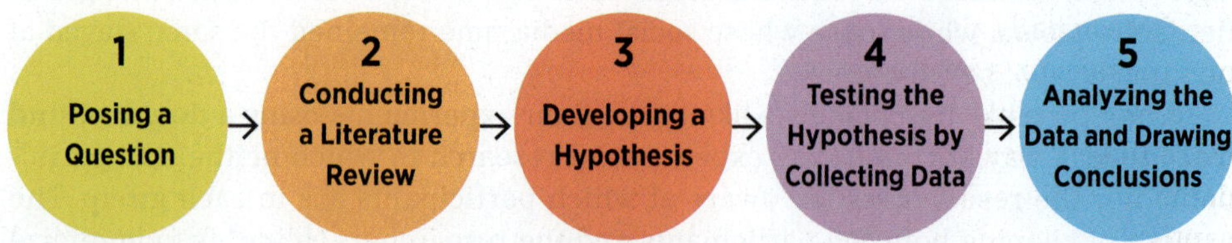

FIGURE 1.5 The Steps of the Scientific Method. When psychologists conduct scientific research, they move through certain steps in a certain order: posing a question, conducting a literature review, developing a hypothesis, testing the hypothesis by collecting data, and analyzing the data and drawing conclusions.

An important part of translating a theory into a hypothesis is to make the concepts in the theory more specific and easier to measure, often in numbers. In other words, for each concept you need an **operational definition**: a specific, measurable definition of a variable for the purpose of a scientific study. *Social media time* might be operationally defined as participants' response to the question "How many hours per day do you use social media?" Or, if your participants allow you to track their social media use directly by monitoring their devices, it might be the number of hours revealed by that method. *Self-esteem* might be operationally defined as participants' total score on a 10-item self-esteem questionnaire.

operational definition
A specific, measurable definition of a variable for the purpose of a scientific study.

population
The whole range of people on whom a study's research is focused.

sample
The subset of the population who actually participates in the research.

Testing the Hypothesis by Collecting Data. When you collect data for your study of social media and self-esteem, you'll have to decide whose social media time and self-esteem you want to research. In other words, you have to identify the study's **population**: the whole range of people on whom the research is focused. In this case, your population is U.S. college students. But you certainly won't be able to include all of them in your study; there are way too many, and you couldn't access them all.

That means you'll have to settle for a **sample**: the subset of the population who actually participates in the research. It's important for the sample to match the population (**Figure 1.6**). If the sample differs in a significant way from the population, your results may be true only for your sample, not more generally across your whole population. For example, if you recruited your sample only from a college that had a high proportion of students of a particular religion, race, gender, or major, then the data those students provide might not be generalizable to all college students. Your best bet in terms of matching your sample to the population is to obtain a *random sample*, which provides each member in the population an equal chance of being selected in the research, – a strategy that isn't always possible but that psychologists strive for nonetheless.

This social media study would be conducted as a *survey*, or a set of questions addressed to a group of people about their behavior or attitudes. Surveys are usually done in a *self-report* format, which means that the people completing the survey answers questions about themselves. Occasionally, psychologists conduct surveys in which the participant describes someone else's behavior or attitudes, as when a parent completes a survey about a young child.

Other methods for descriptive research include *laboratory observations* and *naturalistic observations*. With laboratory observations, the psychologist collects data from participants by watching their behavior in the psychologist's lab. With naturalistic observations, the psychologist collects data from participants by visiting them in the real-world location where their behavior happens naturally. For example, imagine a group of psychologists conducting a study to determine gender differences in physically aggressive behavior in kids. They could do a laboratory observation study in which the psychologists invite small groups of kids to their lab and monitor them while they interact. Or they could do a naturalistic observation study in which the psychologists visit elementary schools and monitor the kids at recess, at lunch, and in the classroom. A particular advantage of naturalistic observation is that it sidesteps any differences between how people might behave in the unique environment of a psychology lab and how they actually behave in their own environment.

FIGURE 1.6 The Importance of Random Sampling. If you want to taste the full range of Skittles, you could eat the entire large bag of them in the middle (the entire population of Skittles). A more feasible and efficient idea, though, might be to just eat the small bag on the left because it's a *random sample* of the large bag in the middle. (Eating the bag on the right, which is not a random sample, would just give you an idea of how green Skittles taste, but not the whole range of flavors.) Random sampling is the goal for psychologists conducting research — it allows them to learn the general "flavor" for some aspect of that population without the need to include all members of that population in the research.

Occasionally, psychologists conduct research in which the sample consists of just one person (or a very small group) studied in great depth. This type of research is called a *case study* (Davison & Lazarus, 2007; Kazdin, 2011). Often, case studies read more like stories than scientific research, with words rather than numbers used to detail what happened. Sigmund Freud, for example, was known for writing lengthy, captivating case studies about his clients (Gay, 1995). Other times, case studies are empirical. For instance, a clinical psychologist might count a particular behavior of a client — say, a disruptive child's verbal outbursts during class — both before and after a particular form of therapy has been implemented (Freeman & Eagle, 2011; Gallo et al., 2013; Photos et al., 2008).

WATCHING PSYCHOLOGY

Survey Says? *Family Feud* and Random Sampling

The *Family Feud* host says it each time there is a new question: "100 people surveyed, top answers on the board." But which 100 people? Are those 100 people a random sample of the U.S. population? Or are certain people more likely to be sampled and others less likely to be sampled, based on how *Family Feud* recruits them? If they call random phone numbers, the 100 people could be reasonably close to a random sample, although it would be tilted toward those who are willing to pick up the phone from an unknown number and spend time answering a stranger's questions. But if *Family Feud* surveys its own studio audience, the 100 people would all be those who live near or visit the city where it happens to be filmed, who may not represent the country at large in terms of likes, dislikes, experiences, and other factors that could influence their answers.

Think about how different the top answers to these *Family Feud* questions could be depending on which groups the 100 people surveyed came from:

- *Name a movie you enjoy watching over and over again.* Think you'd get different top answers from 20-somethings and 60-somethings?
- *Name a food you have on special occasions.* Think you'd get different top answers in Hawaii and Maine?
- *Name a feature of a car that would make you want to buy it.* Think you'd get different top answers from men and women?

When psychologists conduct research, they sample as randomly as possible to make sure that the data they collect is representative of the population they are studying. And when random sampling isn't entirely possible, they explain this fact, being careful not to overestimate the range of people for whom their results might be true. •

Analyzing the Data and Drawing Conclusions. Once the data is collected, it's time to make sense of it. Most often, that process begins by entering numbers into a data file in a statistics computer program and conducting a *data analysis* with the appropriate statistical tests. The best statistical tests are the ones that directly address the hypothesis. For example, if you ran a correlational study on social media time and self-esteem, a correlation coefficient would tell you exactly what you want to know. With the statistics in hand, the next step is to interpret them, or explain in a way that is understandable to others what it all means and why it matters.

Often, this final step in analyzing the data includes suggestions for **replication**: conducting a study again, for the purpose of confirming or disconfirming the results. A single study means something, but a bunch of studies conducted in a similar way that reach the same conclusions means much more. If your experimental study led to the conclusion that more time on social media caused self-esteem to drop, that's a conclusion with some impact. But if you or other researchers replicate your study — perhaps with different or larger samples — and got the same results again and again, the impact of your conclusion grows, as does the confidence you can have that it is true across time and place.

How Psychologists Share Their Results

So do psychologists just post their research results on their own Web site or a blog as soon as they're done?

No! Psychologists who have conducted research are certainly eager to share their results, but they do so in a way that ensures higher quality than simply putting those results out there without any oversight or scrutiny. Psychologists make their research known to others via the **peer review process**: the appraisal of research by people who are as expert on the subject as the researcher (or more so). The peers involved in the peer review process take an evaluative role: they receive submissions from researchers and decide whether they are worthy to be shared with the professional community (Kazdin, 2013).

There are two main outlets for psychologists (and their students) to share their research — presentations at professional conferences and articles in professional journals. The peer review process is a big part of both outlets. If you wanted to give a

replication
Conducting a study again to confirm or disconfirm the results.

peer review process
The appraisal of research by people who are at least as expert on the subject as the researcher.

talk or present a poster about your study on social media and self-esteem at a professional conference, you can't just show up and claim a time slot — it doesn't work that way. Instead, you would anonymously submit a proposal to the conferences' *reviewers*, other psychologists who know a lot about this particular subject and have probably done similar research themselves (Beins & Beins, 2008; Cohen et al., 2013). If you wanted to publish an article about your study, you couldn't just post it on a journal's site as easily as you would post on a blog. You'd have to submit your manuscript to the editor of a particular journal, who passes it along to reviewers to be read and evaluated (Drotar et al., 2013; Tesser & Martin, 2005). The reviewers at the conference or the journal would then provide you with feedback: a rejection, an acceptance, or often (for journals) something in between that researchers call a *revise-and-resubmit* (Nagata & Trierweiler, 2006; Osipow, 2006; Peterson, 2006).

The main point about the peer review process is this: for psychologists to share their research results with others in the field, that research has to be reviewed by professional peers with expertise in the same area. Those peers have to judge it as soundly designed, skillfully conducted, and providing results that are important to the field. This peer review system motivates researchers to produce high-quality studies and allows those who read or attend a presentation about the research to trust that the research is first-rate.

Ethics in Psychological Studies

When psychologists conduct research, they are required to do so ethically (Fisher & Vacanti-Shova, 2012; Fried, 2012; Koocher, 2013). This requirement comes from multiple sources, including an *Institutional Review Board* (IRB) and APA. The IRB is a group at each university or research center that makes sure that psychologists' studies don't put any participants at risk (Dell et al., 2006; Miller, 2003). (Early in the history of psychology, before IRBs were common, some studies with questionable ethics were conducted.)

Also, APA publishes a code of ethics that offers guidelines about conducting ethical psychological research (American Psychological Association, 2017a). In the APA Code of Ethics, the standards on research are essentially a list of important dos and don'ts. Namely, psychologists conducting research ethically *do*:

- Get approval from their own IRB, which requires proof that participants won't be harmed, before beginning any study.
- Tell any possible participants enough about the study beforehand to enable them to make an educated decision about whether to participate (Fischman, 2000). Researchers call this obtaining **informed consent to research**: an ethical requirement for psychologists by which they must inform people about the research and obtain their consent before participation can occur.
- Allow participants to withdraw without penalty if they feel uncomfortable.
- Keep confidential the information they collect from participants.
- When the study is over, offer the participant an explanation, or *debriefing*, of the study's purpose and the opportunity to learn about its results and conclusions (Eyde, 2000).
- If animals are used as subjects, treat them humanely.
- Include as authors those who made significant research contributions, with the order of authors reflecting the size of the contribution; the one who made the biggest contribution is the first author.

And psychologists conducting research ethically *don't*:

- Force people to participate against their will.
- Deceive possible participants about the research unless doing so won't cause them pain or distress, is essential to the study, is disclosed after participation, and is the only option (no undeceptive alternative is available).
- Fabricate, or make up, data.
- Plagiarize, or claim as their own, ideas or words that belong to someone else.

informed consent to research
An ethical requirement for psychologists by which they must inform people about the research and obtain their consent before participation can occur.

CHECK YOUR LEARNING:

1.11 Why does psychology require a scientific approach?

1.12 How do the three main types of psychology research — descriptive, correlational, and experimental — differ?

1.13 What are the five steps of the scientific method?

1.14 In what ways do psychologists share their research results?

1.15 What ethical obligations do psychology researchers have?

To check your understanding of these questions, click show the answers or refer to the answers in the Chapter Summary.

CHAPTER SUMMARY

What Is Psychology?

1.1 Psychology is the scientific study of behavior and mental processes, which means that psychology focuses on *both* our outer actions *and* our inner experiences.

1.2 Psychology is not just therapy, not exclusively about people with mental disorders, not all about Sigmund Freud, not psychiatry, and not just a bunch of ideas with no research to back them up.

1.3 Three big questions underlie the field of psychology: Nature or nurture? Change or stability? Universal or unique?

Psychology's Many Subfields

1.4 The field of psychology is large and diverse. Tens of thousands of people belong to the American Psychological Association, which has 54 divisions focusing on a wide variety of topic areas.

1.5 Applied psychology specializations are areas in which psychologists apply their expertise to real-world problems. Basic research psychology specializations are areas in which psychologists conduct research to further the understanding of behavior and mental processes.

1.6 Areas of applied psychology include clinical psychology, counseling psychology, community psychology, forensic psychology, educational psychology, and industrial/organizational psychology.

1.7 Areas of basic research in psychology include developmental psychology, personality psychology, physiological psychology, comparative psychology, social psychology, and health psychology.

Psychology Then and Now

1.8 Psychology evolved from two much older fields of study: philosophy, which focuses on questions about the inner workings of the mind, and physiology, which focuses on the biological functioning of brain and body.

1.9 Structuralism was a perspective in psychology that focused on breaking down mental processes in terms of their structure or basic parts. Functionalism was a perspective in psychology that emphasized the function of mental processes and behaviors. Psychoanalysis is a perspective in psychology that focuses on unconscious mental activity and the long-lasting influence of childhood experiences. Behaviorism is a perspective in psychology that insists on studying observable behavior instead of internal mental processes. Humanism is a perspective in psychology that concentrates on the notion that human nature is generally good and people are naturally motivated to grow toward their own potential.

1.10 Multiculturalism is a perspective in psychology that highlights the influence of culture on behavior and mental processes. Evolutionary psychology is a perspective in psychology that emphasizes Charles Darwin's theory of evolution as an influence on behavior. Cognitive psychology is a perspective in psychology that emphasizes cognitive processes such as thinking, language, attention, memory, and intelligence. Neuroscience is a perspective in psychology that studies the link between behavior and the biological functioning of the brain. Positive psychology is a perspective in psychology that emphasizes people's strengths and successes. Biopsychosocial theory is a popular and comprehensive perspective in psychology that acknowledges biological factors, psychological factors, and social factors as influences on behavior. The future of psychology is likely to include emphasis on technology, antiracism, and social justice advocacy.

The Science of Psychology

1.11 Psychology requires a scientific approach to make its claims more valid and respectable than all the nonscientific techniques of pseudopsychology.

1.12 In descriptive research, the goal is simply to describe a characteristic of the population. In correlational research, the goal is to determine the relationship between two variables. In experimental research, the goal is to determine the cause-and-effect relationship between two variables by manipulating one and observing changes in the other.

1.13 The five steps of the scientific method are (1) posing a question, (2) conducting a literature review, (3) developing a hypothesis, (4) testing the hypothesis by collecting data, and (5) analyzing the data and drawing conclusions.

1.14 Psychologists share results through a peer review process, the two main outlets of which are presentations at professional conferences and articles in professional journals.

1.15 Psychology researchers are ethically obligated to not harm participants, to obtain informed consent from them, to allow participants to withdraw, to keep their information confidential, and to debrief participants.

KEY TERMS

psychology, p. 2
psychiatry, p. 3
applied psychology specializations, p. 5
clinical psychology, p. 5
counseling psychology, p. 6
industrial/organizational (I/O) psychology, p. 6
community psychology, p. 6
forensic psychology, p. 7
educational psychology, p. 7
basic research psychology specializations, p. 7
physiological psychology, p. 7
developmental psychology, p. 8
personality psychology, p. 8
social psychology, p. 8
health psychology, p. 8
comparative psychology, p. 8
structuralism, p. 12
functionalism, p. 13
psychoanalysis, p. 13
behaviorism, p. 14
humanism, p. 15
multiculturalism, p. 16
evolutionary psychology, p. 16
cognitive psychology, p. 17
neuroscience, p. 17
positive psychology, p. 18
biopsychosocial theory, p. 18
pseudopsychology, p. 22
critical thinking, p. 22
confirmation bias, p. 22
belief perseverance, p. 23
descriptive research, p. 23
correlational research, p. 24
correlation coefficient, p. 24
correlation–causation fallacy, p. 24
experimental research, p. 25
independent variable (IV), p. 25
dependent variable (DV), p. 25
experimental group, p. 25
control group, p. 25
random assignment, p. 25
double-blind procedure, p. 25
placebo effect, p. 25
scientific method, p. 26
literature review, p. 26
theory, p. 26
hypothesis, p. 26
operational definition, p. 27
population, p. 27
sample, p. 27
replication, p. 28
peer review process, p. 28
informed consent to research, p. 29

SELF-ASSESSMENT

1. Psychology is defined as the scientific study of _____ and _____ _____.

2. Dr. Hernandez is a psychologist conducting research on shyness. Specifically, they compare the shyness of adopted children to the shyness of their adoptive parents and biological parents. Which of the big questions of psychology is most closely connected to Dr. Hernandez's study?

a. Nature or nurture
b. Change or stability
c. Universal or unique
d. All of the answers are correct.

3. Dr. Jenkins is a psychologist who works with corporations and organizations to help them with hiring decisions and provide advice about the best ways for managers to supervise employees. Dr. Jenkins is most likely a(n) _____ psychologist.

a. forensic
b. counseling
c. clinical
d. industrial/organizational

4. The two academic fields from which psychology emerged are _____ and _____.

5. The contemporary, or "new," schools of psychology include _____, _____, and _____.

a. psychoanalysis, multiculturalism, neuroscience
b. multiculturalism, neuroscience, evolutionary psychology
c. humanism, multiculturalism, evolutionary psychology
d. behaviorism, multiculturalism, neuroscience

6. According to the biopsychosocial theory, the three types of factors that influence behavior are _____ factors, _____ factors, and _____ factors.

7. Psychology is a _____, which means that psychologists test every theory that attempts to explain behavior and mental processes.

8. A group of psychologists conduct a research study to determine the connection between the number of hours of sleep teenagers get per night and their grade point average. This study is best described as _____ research.

a. correlational
b. experimental
c. descriptive
d. psychiatric

9. Dr. Matsumi is a psychologist who conducts research on how people make group decisions. Specifically, they are interested in learning more about how important it is to members of groups to avoid conflict with others even when they disagree. Which of the following psychology specializations does Dr. Matsumi's research best represent?

a. Comparative psychology
b. Clinical psychology
c. Physiological psychology
d. Social psychology

10. The goal of _____ research is to determine the cause-and-effect relationship between two variables by manipulating one variable and observing changes in the second variable.

To check your understanding of these questions, click show the answers in the e-book or refer to the answers in Appendix B.

Research shows quizzing is a highly effective learning tool. Continue quizzing yourself using LearningCurve, the system that adapts to *your* learning.

WHAT'S YOUR TAKE?

1. When you think about your own culture, your first thought may be your ethnicity or your race. But there may be many other cultural variables that are just as important. As a clinical psychologist, I have learned from some of my own clients that certain or diversity characteristics besides ethnicity or race were at the core of their identities. For one woman, it was her religion (she was a Modern Orthodox Jew); for one man, it was his sexual orientation (he was gay); for another woman, it was her geographical upbringing (she grew up and still lived in a tiny rural town). One teenage boy even proudly told me that he was from "skater culture"—not just that he skateboarded, but he had adopted the entire lifestyle that encompasses skateboarding—and that if I didn't get skater culture, I couldn't get him.

   If you saw a psychologist, which of your cultural or diversity characteristic(s) would the psychologist have to get in order to get you? Are you a typical member of that culture or diverse group, or do you differ from most others in some way?

2. I have noticed a strong positive correlation in my own life: when I do more laundry, I'm in a better mood. I first noticed this correlation in college, when I tended to feel a bit more upbeat during weeks when I found myself in the laundry room more than once and a bit more down on weeks when I didn't. What's up with that? Could it be that washing, drying, and folding *caused* my good mood? Or that my good mood *caused* me to do more laundry? Neither of those made much sense. Eventually, I settled on a more likely interpretation: there was a third factor—exercising—that caused both. In weeks when I ran, worked out, or played basketball more often, the exercise improved my mood, *and* it increased the amount of sweaty clothes in the hamper, which meant I needed to do laundry more often.

   How about you? Have you ever noticed two things correlating in your own life—increasing together, decreasing together, or one increasing when the other decreased in a predictable way—but without a causal relationship between them? If so, what were they, and how do you explain their correlation?

SHOW ME MORE

1.1 Nature Versus Nurture

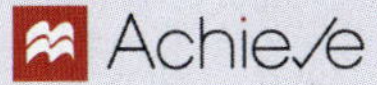

This video offers interesting ideas regarding the interacting roles of nature and nurture as influences on behavior.

HealthCentral Network

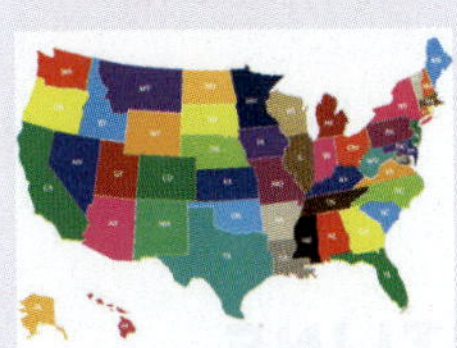

1.2 Will Your State Need Psychologists in the Future?

https://www.apa.org/workforce/data-tools/interactive-state-level

This interactive Web site predicts the supply and demand of psychologists for all 50 U.S. states through 2030. Enter a year, and the site tells you which states will need psychologists and which will have more than enough.

hamikus/Deposit Photos

This video is hosted by a third-party Web site (source). For accessible content requests, please reach out to the publisher of that site.

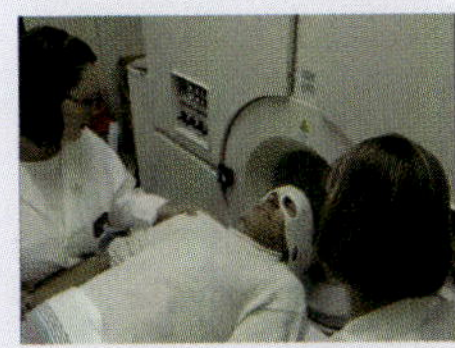

1.3 The Placebo Effect

This video presents a study of the placebo effect on levels of dopamine in the brain and other treatment outcomes.

© Worth Publishers

1.4 My Psychology Podcast

This podcast features the author of this textbook, psychologist Andy Pomerantz, speaking with other instructors of introductory psychology courses about the most important and interesting concepts in this chapter.

Macmillan Learning

2 Brain and Behavior

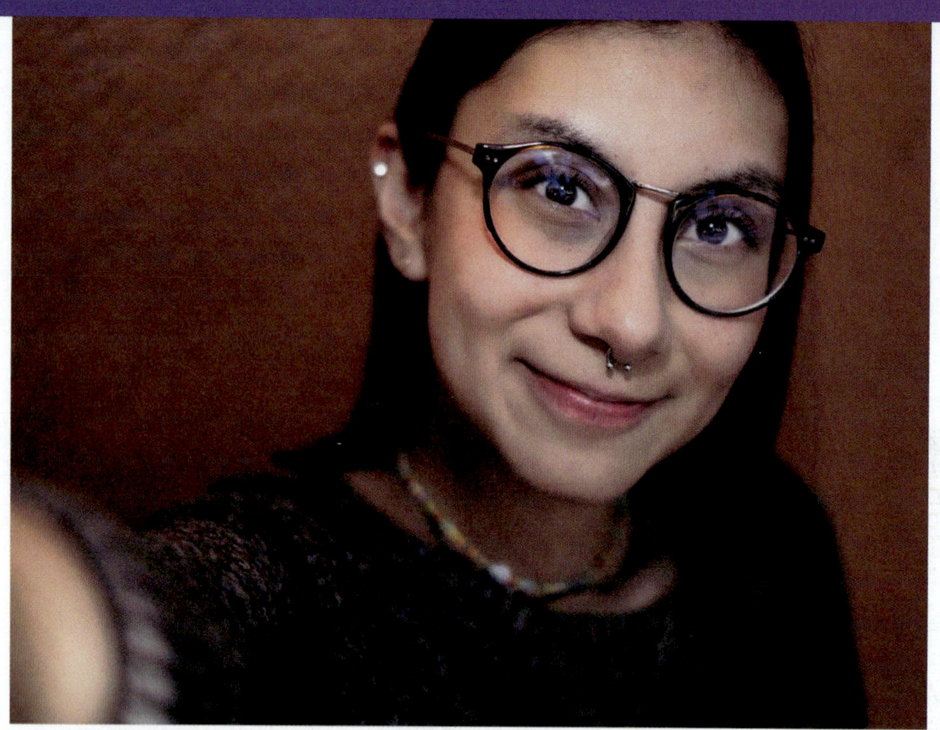

Sergio Mendoza Hochmann/Moment/Getty Images

CHAPTER OUTLINE

We live in an exciting time for studying the brain. Rapid advances in technology allow psychologists and other researchers to view the brain and its inner workings more vividly than ever before. These researchers make eye-popping discoveries that pinpoint specific brain structures or brain activities associated with specific behaviors or experiences. Their research is often accompanied by astonishingly brilliant images of the brain at work. Yet the finding that I find most striking is not one of these brain discoveries or brain images. It is a simple story that a team of brain researchers shared about a stray sick kitten that wandered into their lives.

The researchers named the 4-week-old male kitten Diesel. Diesel unfortunately lost both eyes to feline herpes, but he doesn't behave like a blind cat. In fact, Diesel rapidly developed a mental map of the lab that allows him to run and jump with remarkable speed. This is due, in part, to the "rapid processing of information from his whiskers, which are always a step in front of him when he is in motion" (Yeshurun et al., 2009, p. 321). Even more amazing is Diesel's ability to catch flies. This sightless cat can hear a fly buzzing through the lab, and then he tracks it even though he can't actually see it. Then, at exactly the right instant, Diesel springs up into "the air, catching the fly between his clapped paws" (Yeshurun et al., 2009, p. 321).

How does Diesel do all of that? More specifically, how does Diesel's *brain* help him to do all of that? Without sight, how does his brain capitalize so keenly on his remaining senses, like hearing and touch? Without sight, how does his brain create a mental map of the room? Without sight, how does his brain maneuver his legs to steer him around objects straight to the fly, and then coordinate his two front paws to rise and smack together at exactly the right moment in exactly the right spot to catch the fly? Come to think of it, even *with* sight, the ability of Diesel's brain to do any of those things would be pretty remarkable. And that's just a cat catching a fly. When you take the time to appreciate the additional things that the human brain empowers you to do—talking, planning, reasoning, creating, and computing, among many others—the abilities of your brain are absolutely mind- (or brain-) boggling.

In this chapter, we will examine what psychologists have learned about the brain. We'll learn how the brain interacts with the rest of the body, what various parts of the brain are responsible for, and how microscopic activities within the brain translate into thoughts and actions. We'll also learn about the tools and technologies that researchers use to uncover all of this knowledge about the brain.

Brain and Behavior Connections: An Introduction

Today, we take for granted the fact that the brain and behavior are closely connected. A couple of centuries ago, however, that connection wasn't so obvious. Let's examine some historic events that advanced the understanding of how the brain connects to behavior.

YOU WILL LEARN:

2.1 how a head injury and an autopsy discovery in the 1800s led to better understanding of brain and behavior connections.

2.2 how our approach to understanding the brain will start with microscopic activity within the brain, then expand to the parts of the brain, and then expand more to how the brain interacts with the whole body.

Phineas Gage's Accident and Paul Broca's Discovery

It's September 13, 1848, and a railroad crew lays new tracks across a small town in Vermont. Tools of the trade surround the railroad, including blasting powder (to blast through hills and mountains) and iron rods used to tightly pack that blasting powder into compact spaces. Suddenly, there's an unexpected explosion, followed by the anguished screams of the 25-year-old crew leader, Phineas Gage. His crew members rush toward Phineas and discover that an accidental explosion of blasting powder had shot one of those iron rods — over an inch thick and over three feet long — up through the roof of Phineas's mouth, *through his brain*, and out the top of his skull. Somehow, after just a momentary loss of consciousness, Phineas comes to his senses. He even talks, stands up, and walks with the support of his crew members.

When this accident took place — and yes, it really happened like that — people were fascinated that Phineas Gage survived at all (Macmillan, 2000a, b). But as the months and years went by, a different fascination emerged, one that focused on the way Phineas's brain injury impacted him as a person. In some ways, he remained the same. He retained his basic abilities (moving, walking, talking, etc.), and his intelligence and memory seemed intact, too. But in other ways, he was quite different. Specifically, his personality had changed. Before the accident, Phineas was a reliable, calm, kind man, but now he was irresponsible, hot-headed, and mean. He notably lacked the self-control he once had, which meant that he had a hard time keeping a job and living independently (Wilgus & Wilgus, 2009).

No autopsy was performed when Phineas Gage died, but many years later researchers exhumed and reexamined his skull with more modern technology. They concluded that the damaged regions of his brain were largely limited to those that heavily impact decision making and managing emotions. This was no surprise, considering what changed and what stayed the same about Phineas Gage in the aftermath of his accident (Damasio et al., 1994). There is still some debate about the exact parts of the brain that were injured in Phineas Gage's accident, the exact effects of the accident on his behavior, and exactly how long those effects lasted (Griggs, 2015; Kean, 2014; Macmillan & Lena, 2010). However, there is no debate about the basic lesson that his accident and its aftermath confirmed: certain parts of the brain are related to certain functions or abilities. After all, it is rare that a real-world event produces a situation in which a healthy person loses a specific part of their brain, and that loss corresponds to a specific change in behavior. Of course, the phrenologists (discussed in Chapter 1) made claims about such links, but their claims were unfounded speculations about how certain bumps on the skull might match certain characteristics and tendencies. Phineas Gage's accident focused the exploration not on the skull but on the brain inside of it.

Another important early step in understanding the connections between brain and behavior happened in 1861, when a French doctor named Paul Broca did an autopsy on a man who lost the ability to speak after he had a stroke. Broca found damage to only one small part near the front of the left side of the man's brain (LaPointe, 2013).

Warren Anatomical Museum in the Francis A. Countway Library of Medicine. Gift of Jack and Beverly Wilgus

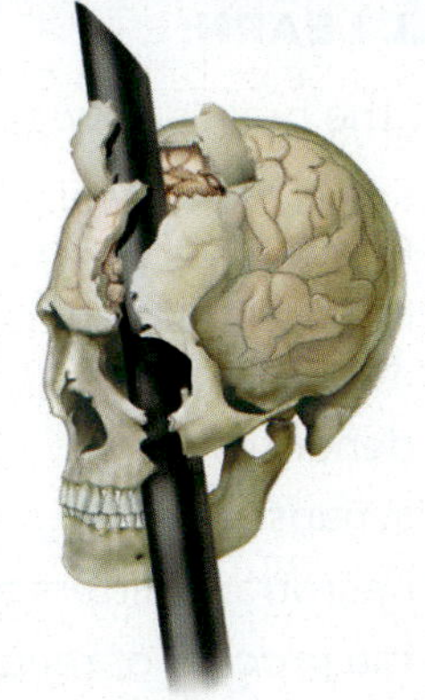

In 1848, a railroad worker named Phineas Gage experienced a horrible injury: an accidental explosion sent an iron rod up through the roof of his mouth, through his brain, and out the top of his skull. He survived the accident, and he retained many abilities, like walking, talking, and remembering. However, his personality changed drastically. The case of Phineas Gage provided early evidence that certain parts of the brain influence certain traits or abilities.

The identification of that part — still called *Broca's area* today — was another early step in determining connections between particular brain regions and particular behaviors.

Fast-forward to today, and we have traveled far down the path of understanding brain and behavior connections (Kandel & Hudspeth, 2013). In fact, the people who marveled at Phineas Gage's survival and subsequent transformation in the mid-1800s couldn't have imagined the modern technologies that now allow us to see the inner workings of the brain. Nor could they have predicted the surge of brain research happening today.

Learning the Brain: A Three-Step Strategy

There is a lot to learn about brain and behavior connections. In this chapter, we'll follow an easy, three-step organizational structure for understanding the brain:

1. We'll start with the microscopic activity *within* the brain that allows for communication throughout the brain and to other parts of the body.
2. We'll zoom out to the whole brain and its parts, examining their connections to various behaviors.
3. We'll zoom out even more to see the big picture: whole-body systems including the *nervous system* and the *endocrine system*, which both interact directly and continually with the brain.

CHECK YOUR LEARNING:

2.1 What is the story of Phineas Gage, and why is his story important to the relationship between brain and behavior?

2.2 In this chapter, our approach to understanding the brain is to start small and zoom out. What are the three levels of understanding?

To check your understanding of these questions, click show the answers or refer to the answers in the Chapter Summary.

Activity Within the Brain

YOU WILL LEARN:

2.3 about the brain's network of neurons.

2.4 what neurons do.

2.5 why the myelin sheath is important for axons.

2.6 what dendrites do.

2.7 what synapses are.

2.8 what neurotransmitters are.

2.9 what the process of reuptake is.

2.10 about action potentials.

On a microscopic level, your brain is bustling with activity. Let's take a close look. Specifically, let's examine how information travels deep within your brain.

Neurons

The building blocks of brain activity are **neurons**: the cells that facilitate communication within the nervous system. The neurons in your brain connect with parts of your body outside your brain — receiving sensory input from your hands, sending motor output to your feet, and so on. But your neurons actually do a tremendous amount of communicating *among each other* (Schwartz et al., 2013). In fact, most of the neurons in your brain are **interneurons**: neurons that serve only to connect to other nearby neurons rather than reaching farther out into the body. Interneurons are also known as *connector neurons* or *relay neurons*, names that reveal their function, like kids in the middle of a classroom passing along a note that was sent from a kid in the front to a kid in the back (Kandel et al., 2013).

neurons
The cells that facilitate communication within the nervous system.

interneurons
The neurons that serve only to connect to other nearby neurons rather than reaching farther out into the body.

The sheer number of neurons in your brain — nearly 100 *billion* — is staggering (Azevedo et al., 2009; Nolte, 2008; Pakkenberg & Gundersen, 1997; Post & Weiss, 1997). It is even more staggering to realize that these billions of neurons are interconnected, forming an astoundingly efficient and intricate web through which information travels. Picture a map of the United States that features its 100 biggest cities and all of the highway connections between each of them. That number of criss-crossing roads would certainly look complex, but now imagine how complex that network gets if the map included 1000 or 10,000 cities — still tiny numbers compared to the billions of neurons your brain contains. Even if a map connected every *house* in the United States to each other, it would connect only 100 million houses — still a thousand times fewer than the number of neurons interconnected in your 3-pound, 6.5-inch-long brain.

Sensory Neurons and Motor Neurons. Many of the neurons that extend beyond your brain fall into two categories: neurons that deliver messages *to* your brain and neurons that deliver messages *from* your brain (Kandel et al., 2013; Schwartz et al., 2013). Specifically, **sensory neurons** carry information to your brain from your senses (sight, hearing, smell, taste, and touch). And **motor neurons** carry messages from your brain to your muscles. (Sensory neurons are sometimes called *afferent neurons*, and motor neurons are sometimes called *efferent neurons*.) For example, if you accidentally touch a hot stove, you'll witness how quickly both sensory neurons and motor neurons can convey their messages. Your sensory neurons carry the message "This is hot!" to your brain and your motor neurons carry the message "Move away!" to the muscles controlling your hand — all within a fraction of a second (Pearson & Gordon, 2013). That kind of instant, no-thinking-required response is a **reflex**: an automatic motor response to sensory input.

Of course, most of the exchanges between your sensory neurons and your motor neurons are not so reflexive. Instead, the interaction involves a bit more control on your part. For example, imagine that you're trying to find your phone, which is in your backpack, while you're in a dark room. Because you can't see, you put your hand in and start feeling around. As your hand feels various things — a pen, a pair of sunglasses, a pack of gum — it's sending messages through sensory neurons to your brain about the shape, size, texture, and other tactile features of those items. Each time your hand does that, your brain sends back a message through your motor neurons to your hand that says, "Keep feeling around." Then, when your hand runs across the smooth glass rectangular surface of your phone screen, that sensation (communicated through your sensory neurons) causes your brain to respond (through your motor neurons), "Grab it!"

The Parts of a Neuron. As Figure 2.1 illustrates, the center of each neuron is the **cell body** (or **soma**): the large central region of a neuron that performs the basic activities, including the production of energy, to keep the neuron functional. The passageway extending from each neuron is the **axon**: the part of the neuron that carries information toward other neurons. At the end of the axon, the axon splits into **axon terminals**: small branches at the end of an axon that form connections with the next neuron. (The word *terminal* lets you know that it is the end of the first neuron.) On the receiving end of that next neuron, smaller passageways take in what the axon terminals deliver. Those smaller passageways are **dendrites**: branches at the end of

sensory neurons
The cells that carry information to the brain from the senses (sight, hearing, smell, taste, and touch).

motor neurons
The cells that carry messages from the brain to the muscles.

reflex
An automatic motor response to sensory input.

cell body (soma)
The large central region of a neuron that performs the basic activities, including the production of energy, to keep the neuron functional.

axon
The part of the neuron that carries information toward other neurons.

axon terminals
The small branches at the end of an axon that form connections with the next neuron.

dendrites
The branches at the end of neurons that receive signals from other neurons.

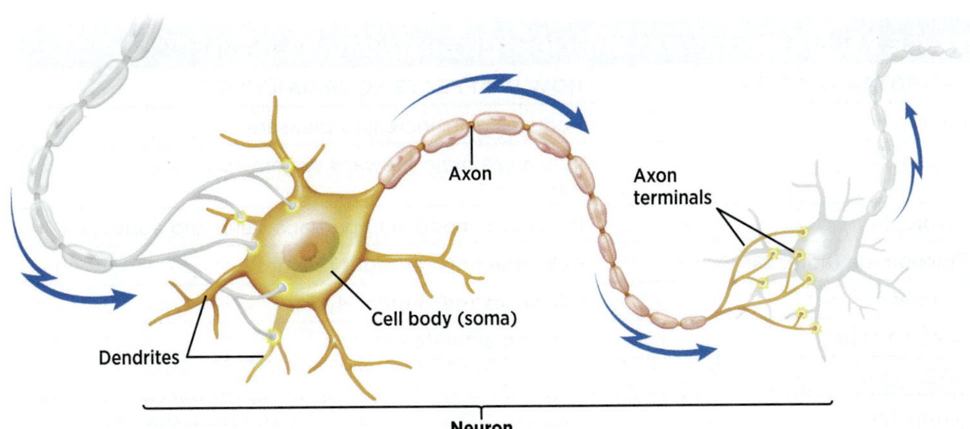

FIGURE 2.1 Neurons and Their Connections. The cell body (or soma) is the centerpiece of each neuron and keeps it functioning. Farther from the center, axons carry information away from the neuron and toward the next neuron in the chain. (In this illustration, as the arrow indicates, the movement is from left to right.) Near the end of each axon, it splits into axon terminals, the small branches that form connections with the next neuron. In that next neuron, the dendrites are the receiving branches that accept what the axon terminals deliver.

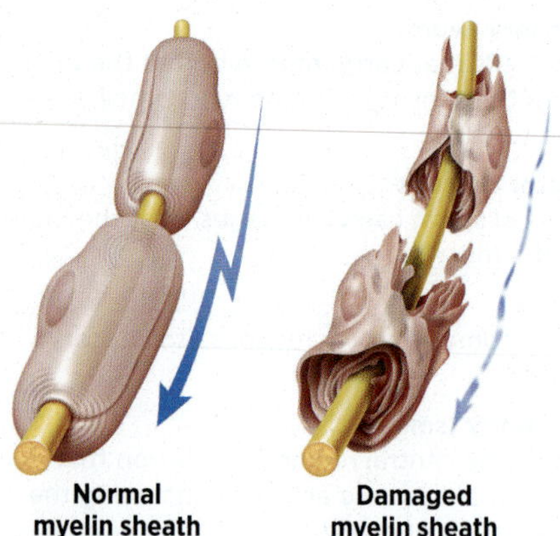

FIGURE 2.2 Myelin Sheath. The myelin sheath is a protective sleeve of fatty material that surrounds the axon. The myelin sheath makes sure that communication between neurons happens at maximum speed and with minimal loss. Deterioration of the myelin sheath is one feature of multiple sclerosis, a disease in which motion is impaired because of slowed signals from the body to the brain.

neurons that receive signals from other neurons. So, the signal shoots through the axon, into an axon terminal, and travels to a dendrite on the next neuron.

In many neurons, the axon is covered with a layer of insulation called the **myelin sheath**: a protective sleeve of fatty material that surrounds the axon (**Figure 2.2**). Myelin is just one of many substances manufactured by **glial cells**: cells that support and protect neurons throughout the brain (Jessell & Sanes, 2013). The myelin sheath has an important role in neuronal communication: it makes sure that messages travel through axons, which can be quite long in some cases, at maximum speed and with minimal loss (Bauman & Pham-Dinh, 2001; Filley, 2013). One problem that arises from deterioration of the myelin sheath is *multiple sclerosis* (MS), a disease that can affect both movement and sensation. Specifically, in people suffering from MS, the signals sent via motor neurons don't arrive as intended at the body part that is supposed to move, or the information sent via sensory neurons doesn't arrive as intended in the brain (Hurley et al., 1999; Kuhlmann et al., 2017; Laflamme et al., 2018).

Communication Between Neurons

When a signal from a neuron makes it successfully through the axon, the message travels from an axon terminal of one neuron to a dendrite of the next neuron. That trip is a vital part of neuronal communication (Siegelbaum & Kandel, 2013a; Siegelbaum et al., 2013b). Between the axon terminal and the dendrite — the space that needs to be crossed — is the **synapse**: a gap between two connecting neurons (**Figure 2.3**).

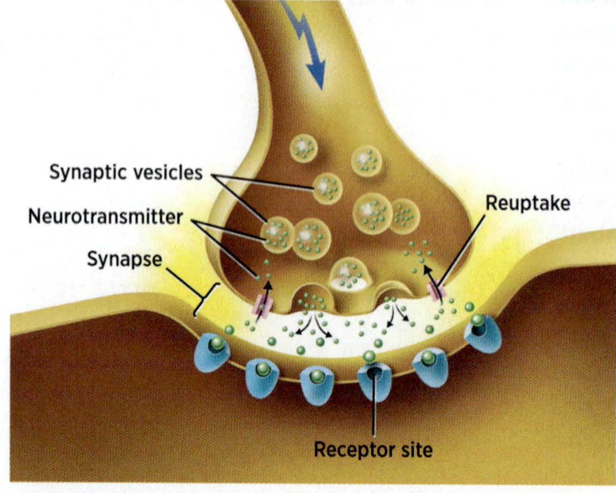

FIGURE 2.3 The Synapse. The synapse is the gap between two connecting neurons. Neurotransmitters cross the synapse and land in receptor sites, or openings in dendrites that match specific neurotransmitters as a lock fits a specific key. Neurotransmitters that don't find a receptor site may return to the sending neuron in a process called reuptake.

Neurotransmitters. The substances that actually travel across the synapse are **neurotransmitters**: chemical messengers that travel across synapses from one neuron to the next. You are probably familiar with quite a few specific neurotransmitters. For example, **endorphins** are neurotransmitters involved in reducing pain and increasing pleasure. They occur naturally in our brains in response to feel-good stuff like food, fun, sex, and exercise. (Our natural endorphins are mimicked closely by such pain-killing drugs as morphine and codeine.) Other neurotransmitters include *dopamine* (involved in the reward system and in movement), *serotonin* (involved in mood, and possibly sleep and appetite), *epinephrine* (involved in the fight-or-flight response), and *histamine* (involved in the immune system) (Schwartz & Javitch, 2013). See **Table 2.1** for a list of these and other important neurotransmitters.

Some drugs enhance the impact of a neurotransmitter. Those drugs are called *agonists*, and they include the morphine example mentioned previously. Other drugs interfere with the impact of a neurotransmitter. Those drugs are called *antagonists* (a word you may remember from a literature class to describe a character that puts up opposition or stands in the way). Examples of antagonists include common antihistamines like Benadryl, Claritin, and Zyrtec.

myelin sheath
A protective sleeve of fatty material that surrounds the axon.

glial cells
The cells that support and protect neurons throughout the brain.

synapse
The gap between two connecting neurons.

neurotransmitters
The chemical messengers that travel across synapses from one neuron to the next.

endorphins
The neurotransmitters involved in reducing pain and increasing pleasure.

TABLE 2.1: Some Important Neurotransmitters

NEUROTRANSMITTER	HOW IT AFFECTS YOUR DAILY LIFE
Endorphins	Reduces pain, increases pleasure
Dopamine	Influences brain's reward system and body's movement
Serotonin	Influences mood, and perhaps sleep and appetite
Epinephrine (adrenaline)	Helps the fight-or-flight response
Histamine	Influences the immune system
Acetylcholine	Helps to activate muscles
GABA (gamma-aminobutyric acid)	Helps to control anxiety
Glutamate	Helps with memory, learning, and brain development

Until they reach the synapse, neurotransmitters travel in **synaptic vesicles**: tiny, saclike containers for neurotransmitters (Kaeser & Regehr, 2017; Siegelbaum et al., 2013a). To complete their journey across the synapse, the neurotransmitters emerge from the synaptic vesicles and find their way to **receptor sites**: openings in dendrites that match specific neurotransmitters like a lock fits a specific key. That lock-and-key relationship means that not every neurotransmitter will find a home as it passes from the axon terminal of one neuron to the dendrite of the next neuron. Actually, even if the neurotransmitter could fit a lock, sometimes there are not enough receptor sites to accept them all.

LIFE HACK 2.1

When you are feeling sad or anxious, physical exercise can provide an endorphin boost and an improved state of mind.

(Daley, 2008; Salmon, 2001; Stathopoulou et al., 2006)

So what happens to neurotransmitters that don't cross the synapse and find a receptor site in the next neuron?

To handle some of these excess neurotransmitters, the first neuron carries out **reuptake**: the process when a neurotransmitter is taken back up by the sending neuron after failing to land in a receptor site in the receiving neuron. This tiny chemical interaction, in which some neurotransmitters successfully reach the receiving neuron while others get taken back up into the sending neuron, can have a significant impact on your day-to-day life experience. For example, consider the neurotransmitter serotonin. In some cases, low serotonin levels correlate with feelings of depression. One class of drugs commonly prescribed for depression is SSRIs, or selective serotonin reuptake inhibitors. (This class of drugs includes familiar brands like Paxil, Celexa, Zoloft, Prozac, and Lexapro.) As their name indicates, SSRIs inhibit the reuptake of serotonin that didn't make it across the synapse. By doing so, they can affect the amount of serotonin flowing through the brain, which can improve mood and decrease feelings of depression.

Action Potentials. Another important part of communication between neurons is how a neuron initiates the transmission of a signal. This start is called an **action potential**: the release, or *firing*, of an electrical impulse that travels through the axon. Action potentials either happen completely or don't happen at all, a phenomenon known as the *all-or-none response*. Most of the time, a neuron is not firing (Kandel et al., 2013). In those moments, the neuron is in a state of **resting potential**: the low-level electrical charge in a neuron that is not firing (Koester & Siegelbaum, 2013a). The neuron shifts from rest into action when the electrical charge reaches a certain **threshold**: the level of electrical charge required to trigger an action potential (Koester & Siegelbaum, 2013b). Each action potential is followed by a **refractory period**: a waiting time before another action potential can begin, during which the neuron is reset.

A final point about the way neurons connect: in humans, those connections depend heavily on experience, especially early in life. In nonhuman species, the brain is largely "hard-wired" at birth, meaning that certain axon terminals are connected to certain dendrites across synapses from day one. That enables those animals to "hit the ground running" more than humans can. For example, a newborn horse can walk within hours. The human brain is more "soft-wired" at birth, but this soft-wiring means it can be shaped to adapt to unique circumstances. That adaptability allows each of our brains to customize the synaptic connections we need as we determine that we need them, and our brains make that determination while we grow up (Sanes & Jessell, 2013a, b, c). It's like the difference between a computer with lots of preloaded software that fills almost its entire hard drive, and a computer with plenty of gigs available for the software it needs for whatever particular purposes may arise.

synaptic vesicles
The tiny, saclike containers for neurotransmitters.

receptor sites
The openings in dendrites that match specific neurotransmitters like a lock fits a specific key.

reuptake
The process when a neurotransmitter is taken back up by the sending neuron after failing to land in a receptor site in the receiving neuron.

action potential
The release, or *firing*, of an electrical impulse that travels through the axon.

resting potential
The low-level electrical charge in a neuron that is not firing.

threshold
The level of electrical charge required to trigger an action potential.

refractory period
A waiting time, during which the neuron is reset before another action potential can begin.

CHECK YOUR LEARNING:

2.3 What are neurons, and approximately how many of them does your brain contain?

2.4 How do sensory neurons and motor neurons differ?

2.5 What is the myelin sheath, and what function does it serve?

2.6 What is the function of dendrites?

2.7 What is the synapse, and how is it involved in communication between neurons?

2.8 What are neurotransmitters, and what do they do?

2.9 How does the process of reuptake work?

2.10 What is the role of an action potential in communication between neurons?

To check your understanding of these questions, click show the answers or refer to the answers in the Chapter Summary.

The Brain and Its Parts

YOU WILL LEARN:

2.11 what localization is.

2.12 how the human brain compares to the brains of other animals.

2.13 where the brainstem is located and what it does.

2.14 where the cerebellum is located and what its function is.

2.15 about the main function of the thalamus.

2.16 what the limbic system is and what its primary function is.

2.17 about the parts of the brain involved in the limbic system.

2.18 why the cerebrum and cerebral cortex are important parts of the human brain.

2.19 what the corpus callosum is.

2.20 why the corpus callosum is cut in split-brain surgery.

2.21 about the cerebrum's four lobes.

2.22 what association areas are and what they do.

2.23 what plasticity is and when it takes place.

Now we broaden our focus from the microscopic activity of neurons deep within the brain to the whole brain and its parts. As we do, let's keep two major ideas in mind. The first involves **localization**: the idea that specific parts of the brain do specific things. In this section, we will discuss examples of localization, but let's not oversimplify. When identifying what the various parts of the brain do, it is important to remember that no part of the brain does anything entirely by itself.

In fact, the brain is perhaps the most awesome display of cooperation and coordination that human beings have ever encountered. The brain's components interact in such a way that certain parts may play a significant role in a certain behavior, but that behavior still depends on other parts for its successful execution. Don't be fooled by media reports that dumb down this complexity of the brain, with headlines like "Scientists discover the part of the brain that controls" some behavior. The brain's parts are far too interconnected to be reduced to such isolated, one-to-one connections (Krakauer et al., 2017; Rose & Abi-Rached, 2013; Satel & Lilienfeld, 2013).

As an example, consider the simple act of drinking a can of soda. To make that happen, different parts of your brain have to do many things: experience thirst, recall where the refrigerator is, command your legs to walk there, command your hand to open the refrigerator, see and choose a can of soda, move your hand toward the can, grip the can, pull the tab on top of the can, lift the can to your mouth at the proper angle, enjoy the taste, and experience the quenching of thirst. That's a *lot* of microbehaviors, each of which relies on different combinations of brain parts, required to do a common and easy action (Amaral & Strick, 2013; Rizzolatti & Kalaska, 2013). (And we're not even counting the behind-the-scenes stuff your brain takes care of automatically while you're busy getting the soda, like making sure your heart keeps beating and your lungs keep inhaling and exhaling.) Even if the behavior is mental rather than physical (like *remembering* the soda you drank), multiple parts of the brain are almost always involved (Schacter & Wagner, 2013; Siegelbaum & Kandel, 2013b).

The second major idea to keep in mind as we consider the brain and its parts involves a comparison between our brains — *human* brains — and the brains of other animal species. Look at the shape of our heads and the shapes of their heads. What you'll notice is that our heads, and our brains, are proportionally bigger toward the top and front. (As **Figure 2.4** shows, that difference is evident with our close primate relatives, and even more obvious in reptiles and birds.) That means that our *brains* are bigger on top and up front. That difference provides a big hint about specific regions within the brain where certain functions are controlled, some of which are common to many species and others of which are more unique to humans (Preuss, 2009).

localization
The idea that specific parts of the brain do specific things.

brainstem
The part of the brain that connects to the spine and controls the functions most essential to staying alive.

reticular activating system
The collection of neurons in the brainstem involved in arousal.

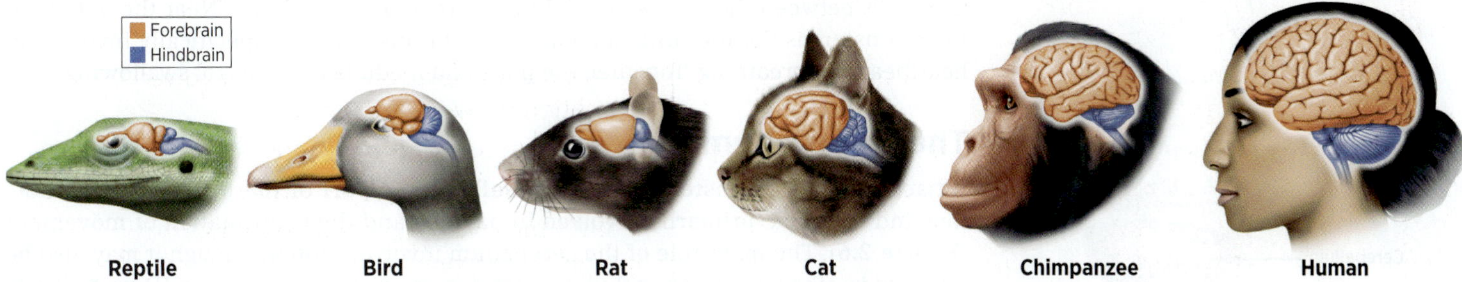

FIGURE 2.4 Comparing Heads and Brains Across Species. Compared to the heads of other species, the heads of humans are proportionally bigger on top and up front. That reflects the fact that our *brains* are proportionally bigger on top and up front. Generally, the parts on top and up front are involved in our uniquely human abilities, like planning, decision making, and complex cognitive tasks. By contrast, the parts near the back and the bottom of the brain—which all species have—are involved in the abilities common to both humans and other types of animals, like breathing, balancing, hunger, sleeping, and heartbeat.

As a rule of thumb, the parts of our brains that are closest to the back and the bottom (near the connection to the spine) control the basic functions that humans share with other species, especially stuff like heartbeat, hunger, arousal, breathing, and balancing. After all, other animals have those brain parts, just like we do (Saper et al., 2013). The farther we move up and out from the base of the brain (especially toward the front), the more we encounter parts of the brain that control functions more unique to humans, like decision making, planning, speech, and complex tasks involving emotions and learning. After all, those parts are much larger in us than in other animals. That difference is largely due to evolution, specifically the fact that our species emerged more recently than other species (Schneider, 2014; Sousa et al., 2017).

Following this rule of thumb can often help you figure out which parts of the brain are largely responsible for which kinds of behaviors. For example, if the question is what part of the brain is in charge of making you feel sleepy and waking you up, the fact that all animals do those things tells you that it's a part near the back and bottom of the brain, which all animals have. If the question is what part of the brain allows you to develop a strategy for a complex, long-term behavior (like creating an exercise plan for the upcoming months), the fact that nonhuman animals don't do that tells you that it's a part near the front or top of your brain, which only humans have. Combine this rule of thumb with the fact that many brain parts have names that indicate their location, like brain*stem* (at the bottom and back, near the spine) or *frontal* lobe (at the front of your brain, right behind your forehead), and you've got some helpful clues for learning which brain parts go with which functions.

As we now consider specific parts of the brain, let's start at the bottom and the back, and work our way up and toward the front.

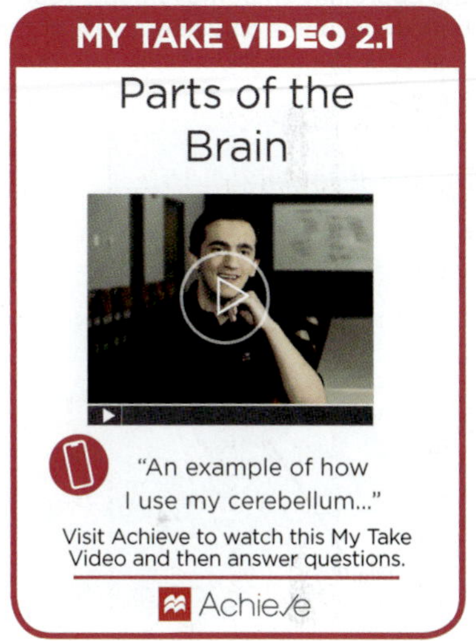

MY TAKE VIDEO 2.1
Parts of the Brain
"An example of how I use my cerebellum..."
Visit Achieve to watch this My Take Video and then answer questions.
Achieve

The Brainstem

The **brainstem** is the part of the brain that connects to the spine and controls the functions most essential to staying alive (**Figure 2.5**). These functions include not only 24/7 behaviors like breathing and heartbeat, but also other basic bodily functions that take place only at certain times, like sexual reproduction, swallowing, sneezing, and even vomiting (Anderson et al., 2013; Hurley et al., 2010). The *-stem* in the word *brainstem* accurately depicts how it fits into the larger structure of the brain—like a stem, with the rest of the brain blossoming up and around it like a flower.

The brainstem contains a few important brain structures within it. One of these is the **reticular activating system**: a collection of neurons in the brainstem involved in arousal. (*Reticular* means netlike, which is the shape this collection of neurons takes.) The *activating system* part of this key term refers to the activation of waking and sleeping, but the reticular activating system is also involved in related functions like alertness and attention (Saper et al., 2013). The brainstem also contains the **pons**: a part of the brainstem involved in transmitting information, sleep, breathing, and equilibrium. Because of its position near the top of the brainstem, the pons conveys

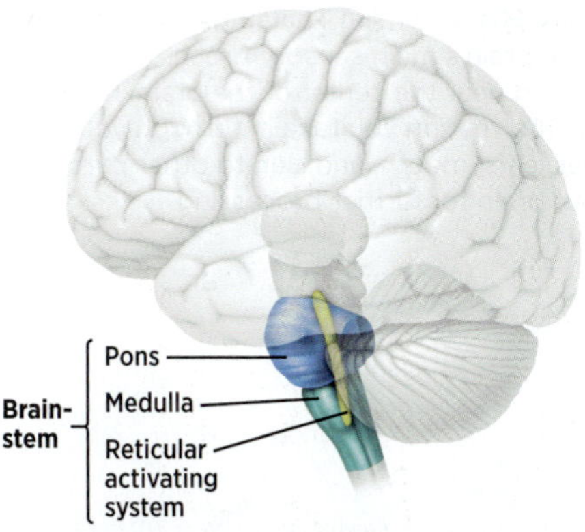

FIGURE 2.5 The Brainstem. The brainstem is the part of the brain that connects to the spine and controls the functions most essential to staying alive, like breathing, heartbeat, sexual reproduction, and swallowing. The brainstem includes the reticular activating system, pons, and medulla.

pons
The part of the brainstem involved in transmitting information, sleep, breathing, swallowing, and equilibrium.

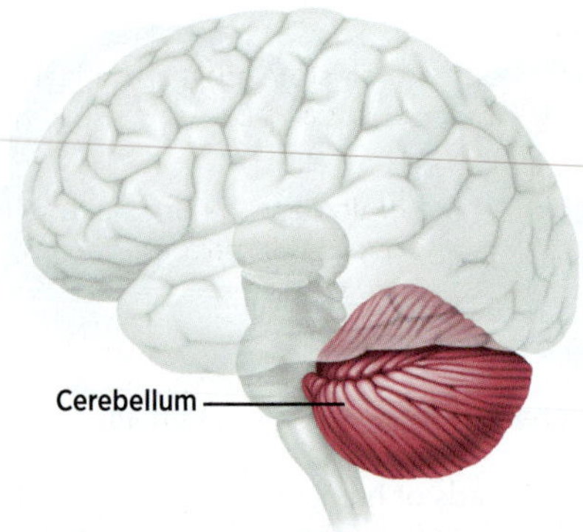

FIGURE 2.6 The Cerebellum. The cerebellum is near the bottom and back part of the brain. It is primarily involved in balance and the coordination of movement. Your cerebellum occupies only about 10% of the space in your brain but contains over half of its neurons.

messages between the brainstem and higher regions of the brain. Near the bottom of the brainstem is the **medulla**: the part of the brainstem most specifically involved in heartbeat and breathing. Together, the pons and medulla also control swallowing.

The Cerebellum

Adjacent to the brainstem is the **cerebellum**: the part of the brain near the bottom and the back, primarily involved in balance and the coordination of movement (Figure 2.6). The main role of the cerebellum involves motion, though it may also be involved in other functions, including attention, memory, and language (Dum & Strick, 2009; Graybiel & Mink, 2009; Sokolov et al., 2017). Your cerebellum does not initiate movement, but it regulates it. For example, imagine that Sam needs to slow down their car to about half its current speed, and Sam's brain sends the message "Step softly on the brake" to Sam's foot. Sam's cerebellum doesn't *create* that message (another part of the brain does that), but the cerebellum does make sure that Sam steps on the brake with just the right amount of force. Without Sam's cerebellum, a simple act like stepping on the brake could go wrong in many ways: they could tap it so weakly that the car doesn't slow down; they could slam on it so hard that the car comes to a jolting stop; or they could step on it in an inconsistent, herky-jerky way that makes the car lurch back and forth.

The cerebellum, which is about the size of a small fist, is only about 10% of your brain but contains over 50% of its neurons. Damage to the cerebellum creates serious problems across a wide range of everyday movement-related tasks, from tremors and spastic movements to severely impaired walking and talking (Manto, 2010; Shakkottai et al., 2017).

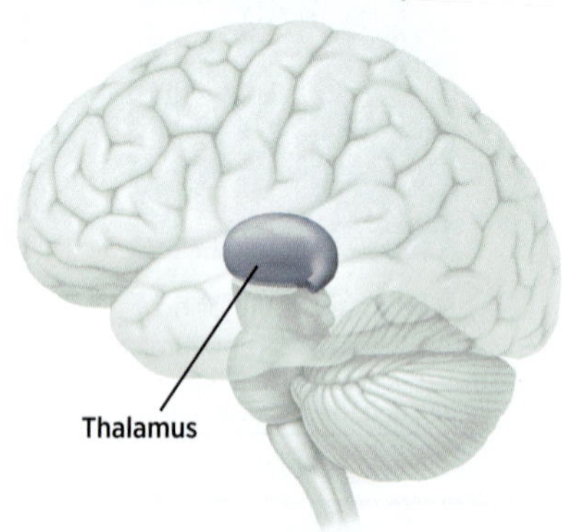

FIGURE 2.7 The Thalamus. The thalamus is the brain's main sensory processing center, located near the center of the brain. It directs the information you take in through your eyes, ears, mouth, and skin to other parts of your brain for further processing.

The Thalamus and the Limbic System

At this point we move up a level, from the "ground floor" of the brain (containing the brainstem and cerebellum) to its "middle floor." A centerpiece of this middle level is the **thalamus**: the brain's main sensory processing center, located near the center of the brain (Figure 2.7). The thalamus, which is shaped like a small egg, receives the information you take in through your eyes, ears, mouth, and skin, then directs this information to the parts of your brain that need to process it. Passing along sensory information is the main role of the thalamus, but it is also involved in arousal and movement in a limited way (Amaral, 2013; Gardner & Johnson, 2013; Taber et al., 2004). Its involvement in movement is a cooperative effort with a nearby brain structure, the *basal ganglia*.

Near the center of the brain and surrounding the thalamus is the **limbic system**: a cluster of brain areas involved primarily in emotion. (The word *limbic* means border, and as Figure 2.8 shows, the components of the limbic system do appear to form a border around the thalamus.) There is an old (but true) joke among people who study the brain that the limbic system is all about the "four f's": fleeing, fighting, feeding, and, um, sexual intercourse (Pinel, 2011; Pribram, 1960). Those four f's are all considered primary motivations of human beings. When you recognize that the words *emotion* and *motivation* come from the same root – *mot-*, which is Latin for move – it is easy to see that the limbic system is the part of the brain most responsible for initiating the impulses and feelings intended to move you. As Figure 2.8 illustrates, the limbic system includes several distinct parts: the *hypothalamus*, the *hippocampus*, and the *amygdala*.

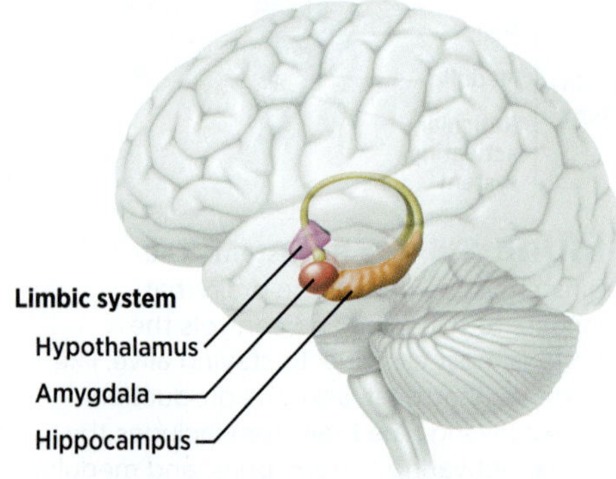

FIGURE 2.8 The Limbic System. The limbic system, located near the center of the brain, is a cluster of brain areas involved primarily in emotion. The limbic system includes the hypothalamus, the hippocampus, and the amygdala.

The Hypothalamus. The **hypothalamus** is the part of the limbic system involved in maintaining steadiness in bodily functions. One way the hypothalamus achieves this steadiness is by exerting control over the *pituitary gland*, which (as described in more detail later in this chapter) is the master gland of the endocrine system and therefore has tremendous influence on the release of hormones. The hypothalamus also has significant influence over the *autonomic nervous system*, which means that it affects your heartbeat, breathing, and other involuntary functions (Horn & Swanson, 2013). The hypothalamus also influences the triggers you feel to eat or drink. In this way, your hypothalamus helps you maintain *homeostasis*, or a relatively constant internal environment (Richerson et al., 2013; Shizgal & Hyman, 2013). For example, homeostasis ensures that your heartbeat increases while you run, and makes sure your heartbeat returns to normal soon after you stop. Homeostasis also means that your body temperature stays about the same, even when Mother Nature (or air conditioning or heating) causes great fluctuations in the temperature around you.

The Hippocampus. The **hippocampus** is the part of the limbic system involved in memory, especially spatial memory and long-term memory. Spatial memory is your memory for physical spaces, such as the layout of the home you grew up in, or the hallways of your high school. Those mental maps, including the emotional connections to those spaces, become long-term memories thanks to your hippocampus (Siegelbaum & Kandel, 2013b). Long-term memory takes place when things that you focus on temporarily (that is, things that are in short-term memory) become stored in such a way that they endure indefinitely. Your hippocampus is the part of your brain most responsible for that conversion (Aly & Ranganath, 2018; Kandel & Siegelbaum, 2013; Sekeres et al., 2018; Shrager & Squire, 2009; Squire, 1992; Suzuki, 2009).

Damage to the hippocampus impairs the ability to convert short-term memories to long-term memories — that is, to stop memories from simply fading away. In severe cases, it causes *anterograde amnesia*, a complete inability to form new long-term memories after a certain point in time (Winocur et al., 2001). We'll cover anterograde amnesia and other memory problems in more detail in Chapter 5. For now, just know that anterograde amnesia is fascinating to observe but devastating to live through. People who experience it can recall their long-term memories from before the onset of anterograde amnesia, but they can't create any new long-term memories after that point. So, if a 55-year-old woman who got married decades ago experiences this kind of damage to her hippocampus today, she'll have no problem continuing to recognize the person she married or recalling the wedding they had years ago, but she won't be able to form a new memory of her grandchild being born next week.

Henry Molaison is one of the people most responsible for our knowledge about the connection between the hippocampus and anterograde amnesia. Henry wasn't a researcher, but a man who suffered from severe epilepsy. In 1953, Henry was 27 years old and desperate for improvement in his symptoms. He underwent an experimental brain surgery in which the hippocampus was removed. That surgery improved his epilepsy, but it had another unexpected effect: for the 55 remaining years of his life, Henry could not form new memories. After the surgery, he couldn't learn people's names or remember new information he heard. He repeatedly completed the same puzzles without getting bored, because they were new to him every time he did them. Henry (and his family) allowed researchers to conduct hundreds of studies on him while he was alive, and donated his brain to science after his death. His contributions have greatly increased our understanding of the function of the hippocampus (Corkin, 2013; Ogden, 2012; Scoville & Milner, 1957).

One way the hippocampus can become damaged is through stress. In particular, high levels of stress that last for a long time can damage the hippocampus and, in turn, the ability to form new spatial and long-term memories (McEwen, 1999; Shields et al., 2017). One study of older adults found strong positive correlations between three things: levels of cortisol (the "stress hormone," as we will discuss later in this chapter), damage to the hippocampus, and impairment in simple memory tasks (Lupien et al., 1998). Other studies have found that people who have lived through traumatic experiences like childhood abuse or active combat during war show physical damage to the hippocampus and deficits in the ability to form new memories (Bremner, 1999; Calem et al., 2017; Nelson & Tumpap, 2017).

medulla
The part of the brainstem most specifically involved in heartbeat and breathing.

cerebellum
The part of the brain near the bottom and the back, primarily involved in balance and the coordination of movement.

thalamus
The brain's main sensory processing center, located near the center of the brain.

limbic system
The cluster of brain areas involved primarily in emotion, located near the center of the brain and surrounding the thalamus.

hypothalamus
The part of the limbic system involved in maintaining a steadiness in bodily functions.

hippocampus
The part of the limbic system involved in memory, especially spatial memory and long-term memory.

WATCHING PSYCHOLOGY

What Happens in Your Brain When You Watch Movies and TV?

Psychologists have conducted hundreds of studies on the impact of TV and movies, especially on cognitive development and likelihood of violent behavior. Recently, a fascinating collection of studies has emerged that focus on a more biologically based question: what happens *inside your brain* when you watch TV and movies? This growing body of research has the potential to identify connections between what (or how much) you watch and how you respond. Highlights from studies of this type include these findings:

- The amount of time that kids spend watching TV correlates with the size of certain parts of their developing brains (Fields, 2016). Specifically, studies found that a part of the frontal lobe (the frontopolar cortex, specifically) is thicker in kids who watch more TV. Thickness in that part of the brain correlates with lower levels of intellectual development, especially verbal abilities (Takeuchi & Kawashima, 2016; Takeuchi et al., 2015).
- When watching a movie, the parts of your brain involved in vision respond in a distinct way during suspenseful moments. In one study, participants watched 3-minute clips from 10 suspenseful movies (including *Alien*, a James Bond movie, and several by Alfred Hitchcock). The movies were played on a screen surrounded by a border that contained a black-and-white visual pattern. According to data from brain scans, when suspense was at its highest, there was reduced activity in the visual processing regions that control peripheral vision and increased activity in the visual processing regions that control vision in the center of the visual field. These changes suggest that the components of your brain work together when you watch something suspenseful, helping you to focus on the main action and disregard any distractions happening off to the side (Bezdek et al., 2015).
- When watching a movie, certain types of electrical activity within the brain correlate with that movie's success at the box office. Specifically, researchers measured the brain activity of college students while they watched a variety of movie trailers. Researchers also asked the participants to evaluate the movies by rating them on a 0–10 scale. Results showed that the box office performance correlated more strongly with the patterns of brain activity than with the 0–10 ratings of the films. This finding suggests that how your brain immediately reacts better predicts the widespread success of a film than how you rate it after having a chance to think about it (Boksem & Smidts, 2015; Christoforou et al., 2017).

The Amygdala. The **amygdala** is the part of the limbic system involved most directly in emotion, especially fear. There are certainly other parts of the brain involved in emotion, but the amygdala is perhaps the most important part of all (LeDoux & Damasio, 2013; Phelps, 2006; Phelps & LeDoux, 2005). For example, other parts of the brain may influence how the fight-or-flight response plays out (whether you fight, or fly, or do something else), but it's the amygdala that sounds the fight-or-flight alarm in the first place (LeDoux et al., 2009; Schafe & LeDoux, 2004).

Damage to the amygdala causes all kinds of problems with emotional processes, especially the experience of fear (Wang et al., 2017). For example, one case study found that a woman with a damaged amygdala could recognize the faces of people she knew, but failed to identify whether those faces showed fear (Adolphs et al., 1994). Another study of nine people with amygdala damage found that they struggled to recognize fear in the facial expressions of others but had no problems recognizing happiness in those faces (Adolphs et al., 1999). In another study, researchers used sudden, randomly timed, loud blasts of noise to startle a man with a damaged amygdala (and eight control participants as well). The researchers found that his startle reflex — his involuntary, immediate fear response — was weaker than the startle reflexes of the control participants (Angrilli et al., 1996).

Other researchers reached a different kind of finding about the amygdala by studying altruists, people who commit acts of kindness for others that provide no payoff for themselves. Specifically, these researchers examined the brains of 19 people whom they called "extraordinary altruists" because they had donated kidneys to strangers. Compared to the average member of a control group, the average extraordinary altruist had an amygdala that was not only larger but also more responsive to fearful facial expressions in other people. These results suggest that an extraordinary altruist is motivated to act by an amygdala that enhances the ability to recognize the fear of others (like medical patients needing kidney transplants) and to respond with compassion (Marsh et al., 2014).

amygdala
The part of the limbic system involved most directly in emotion, especially fear.

cerebrum (forebrain)
The front and upper part of the brain, consisting of two hemispheres and involved in sophisticated, often uniquely human, abilities.

cerebral cortex
The outer layer of the cerebrum, where sensory information is processed.

association areas
Brain material that is devoted to synthesizing and interpreting information rather than merely taking information in.

cerebral hemispheres
The left and right halves of the cerebrum.

corpus callosum
The bundle of neurons that connects and allows communication between the two cerebral hemispheres.

The Cerebrum and Cerebral Cortex

If the brainstem and cerebellum represent the brain's ground floor, and the thalamus and limbic system represent its middle floor, it is now time to move up to the top floor. The **cerebrum** (also known as the **forebrain**) is the upper front part of the brain, which consists of two hemispheres and is involved in sophisticated, often uniquely human, abilities. The cerebrum fits over the parts of the brain that we have already discussed (brainstem, cerebellum, thalamus, limbic system) like a thick helmet. So, when you see photos of the brain, looking wrinkled and resembling a walnut, what you're actually seeing is the cerebrum – the same way you see a football player's helmet covering their head (**Figure 2.9**). More specifically, you're seeing the **cerebral cortex**: the outer layer of the cerebrum, where sensory information is processed. *Cortex* comes from a Latin word that means bark of a tree, which describes its position on the outer layer of the brain. (Brain experts often use the terms *cerebrum* and *cerebral cortex* interchangeably.)

More than any other part of the brain, the cerebrum (especially its cerebral cortex) is what makes humans human. Compared to other animals, we simply have much more cerebrum than they do: ten times more than a macaque monkey, and a thousand times more than a rat (Rakic et al., 2004). Since our bodies are bigger than theirs, what's even more meaningful is a proportional comparison: the cerebrum occupies most of our brains but only a small fraction of the brains of many animals. That big cerebrum is what makes humans so, well, cerebral. The cerebrum gives us many distinctly human abilities, including thinking, reasoning, planning, creating, communicating, computing, multitasking, and so much more (Premack, 2010; Rakic et al., 2009).

The cerebrum contains lots of **association areas**: brain material that is devoted to synthesizing and interpreting information rather than merely taking in information. To understand what happens in association areas, imagine that an ambulance approaches your car from behind. There are specialized parts of your brain that take in the sight of the flashing lights in your rearview mirror and the sound of the blaring siren that grows louder as it gets closer. But somewhere in your brain, that information has to be integrated to make sense. That is what the association areas do. They associate, or combine, these various bits of information so they have meaning: there's an ambulance behind me, which means there's an emergency nearby, so I need to pull over to let the ambulance get to the person who needs help. Without the synthesis that the association areas provide, you would be limited simply to processing and reacting to isolated bits of sight, sound, and other information rather than understanding what they mean together.

The Cerebral Hemispheres and the Corpus Callosum

Just as the globe can be divided into Western and Eastern hemispheres, the cerebrum can be divided into two halves, or **cerebral hemispheres**: the left and right halves of the cerebrum. The link between the two hemispheres is the **corpus callosum**: the bundle of neurons that connects and allows communication between the two cerebral hemispheres.

The corpus callosum enables an interesting relationship to occur between the two halves of your brain and the two halves of your body: each is matched with its opposite. That is, your left cerebral hemisphere is paired with the right half of your body, and your right cerebral hemisphere is paired with the left half of your body. So, if you stub a toe on your left foot, it is your right hemisphere that receives the pain message. Or, if you want to give someone a high-five with your right hand, it's your left hemisphere that sends the message to raise that hand. This cross-relationship between brain and body also explains why an illness or injury to one side of the brain, such as a stroke, affects only the opposite side of the body. Tedy Bruschi, former Pro Bowl linebacker for the New England Patriots, suffered a mild stroke at the unusually young age of 31. The stroke was caused by a blood clot in his brain's right hemisphere, which caused damage to his body's entire left side. The day of the stroke, "there was total numbness in my left arm and leg. . . . My 5-year-old son came in from my left, and

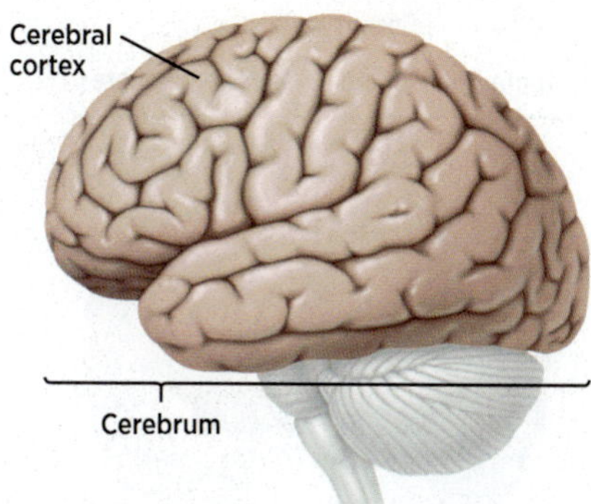

FIGURE 2.9 The Cerebrum and Cerebral Cortex. The cerebrum (also known as the forebrain) is the upper front part of the brain. It consists of two hemispheres and is involved in sophisticated, often uniquely human, abilities. The cerebrum contains lots of association areas, which are brain regions devoted to synthesizing and interpreting information rather than merely taking in information. The cerebral cortex is the outer layer of the cerebrum, where sensory information is processed.

CHAPTER APP 2.1

3D Brain

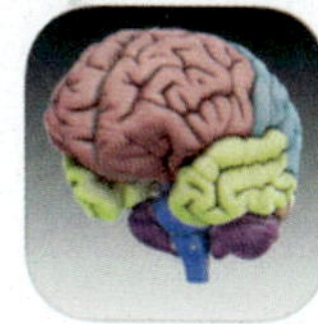

The 3D Brain app shows great 3D images of the brain—better than what is possible on textbook pages because they rotate on-screen and make outer parts of the brain transparent so you can see inner parts directly.

How does it APPly to your daily life?
How does such a high-tech, vivid, rotatable, 3D view of the brain affect your appreciation of your own brain? Will it increase the odds that you will do things to take care of it, like wearing a seat belt in the car, wearing a helmet on your bike, or eating or drinking healthy?

How does it APPly to your understanding of psychology?
How do these images improve your understanding of the brain, its parts, and their functions?

To learn more about this app or to download it to your phone, you can search for "3D Brain" on Google, in the iPhone App store, or in the Google Play store.

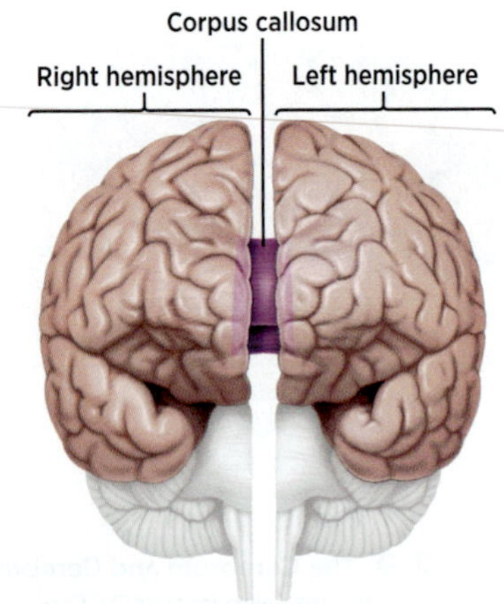

FIGURE 2.10 Split-Brain Surgery. The cerebrum consists of two halves, or hemispheres. The left and right hemispheres communicate through a bundle of neurons known as the corpus callosum. Each hemisphere controls the movement in the opposite half of the body. On rare occasions (typically as a last-resort effort to reduce severe epileptic seizures), split-brain surgery is performed by cutting the corpus callosum.

I couldn't see him." After a trip to the ER, Bruschi had surgery to fix the cause of the blood clot, "and the rest of my recovery was learning how to . . . use the left side of my body again" (Bruschi, 2014). Bruschi soon created "Tedy's Team," a charitable organization dedicated to increasing awareness of stroke symptoms and raising funds for stroke research and recovery.

On rare occasions, serious problems can emerge from faulty communication between the hemispheres. In such cases, one treatment option is a serious and infrequent operation called **split-brain surgery**: a surgical procedure in which the corpus callosum is cut, typically to reduce epileptic seizures (**Figure 2.10**). Epileptic seizures typically start in one hemisphere and then gain power as they bounce back and forth, across the corpus callosum, between both hemispheres. If the corpus callosum is cut, the seizures are restricted to one hemisphere, making them much less severe (Roland et al., 2017). (The vast majority of people with epilepsy improve with antiseizure medications. Split-brain surgery is a last resort.)

As you might imagine, some of the side effects of split-brain surgery are fascinating. People who have the operation typically retain most of their personality characteristics and intelligence. However, they demonstrate some peculiar abilities and inabilities based on the fact that the two sides of their brain have lost communication with each other. In some cases, for example, each side of the body does its own thing, with little or no awareness of what the other side is doing. Because the two hemispheres can't coordinate with each other, the right hemisphere tells the left side what to do, while the left hemisphere tells the right side what to do. In one particular case, a woman who had undergone a split-brain surgery found her hands competing with each other in the supermarket aisles — her right hand would reach for a box of cereal, but her left hand would stop her from putting it in her cart (Wolman, 2012).

The effects of split-brain surgery are evident not only in the hands, but in many other parts of the body as well. In some experiments, researchers asked split-brain patients to look at a dot on a screen and then flashed words to either the right or left of that dot, so the word was in the field of vision of only one eye. Let's imagine that the word was *banana* (**Figure 2.11**). When asked what word they saw, the patients were good at saying "banana" when the word was on the right (and processed by the left

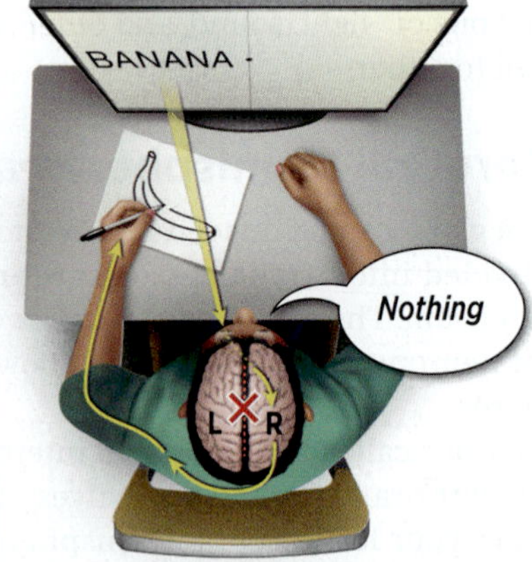

FIGURE 2.11 The Aftermath of Split-Brain Surgery. In patients who have undergone split-brain surgery, communication between the two hemispheres of the brain is impaired, resulting in some unusual effects. Numerous research studies support findings like the one illustrated here. If the word *banana* appears in the right side of their field of vision (and is processed by their left hemisphere), patients could correctly say the word "banana." If the word banana appears in the left side of their field of vision (and is processed by their right hemisphere), patients could not say "banana," but could draw a banana with their left hand. These results indicate not only the importance of communication between the hemispheres of the brain, but also that certain tasks are dominated by particular hemispheres. For example, the left hemisphere is dominant for language tasks, like word reading, while the right hemisphere is dominant for the recognition of objects (Gazzaniga, 1998, 2005; Gazzaniga et al., 1962).

split-brain surgery
A surgical procedure in which the corpus callosum is cut, typically to reduce epileptic seizures.

hemisphere). However, if the same word was on the left (and processed by the right hemisphere), the patients could not *say* "banana," but could *draw* a banana with their left hand. This curious finding helped researchers understand that each hemisphere may dominate certain tasks. As this example shows, the left hemisphere is dominant for language tasks, such as word reading. The right hemisphere, by contrast, is dominant for the recognition of objects and faces (Gazzaniga, 1998, 2005; Gazzaniga et al., 1962).

The Lobes

Figure 2.12 illustrates how the cerebrum consists of four distinct regions, or *lobes*, each of which has a right half and a left half. (As with your ear*lobe*, here the word *lobe* simply means rounded or curved part.)

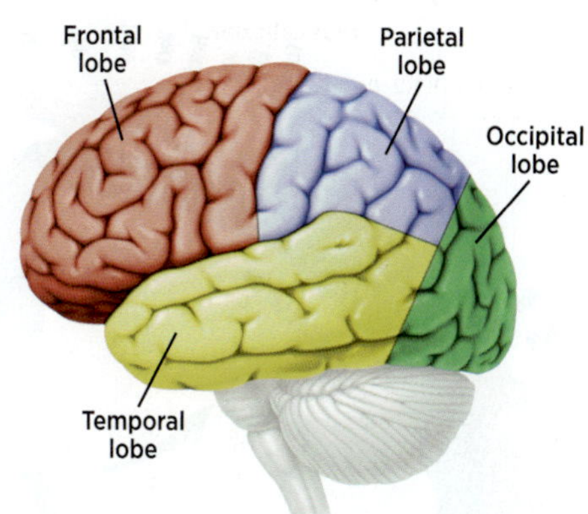

FIGURE 2.12 The Lobes. The cerebrum consists of four lobes. The occipital lobe is involved in vision. The temporal lobe is involved in hearing and speech production. The parietal lobe is involved in touch and perception. The frontal lobe is involved in complex thinking tasks, planning, and other advanced functions, most of which are unique to humans.

Occipital Lobe. If we begin at the back of the brain and move forward, we start with the **occipital lobe**: the lower back part of the brain involved in vision. Your occipital lobe connects (through the thalamus) with your eyes, taking in the raw images you see and beginning to process (or extract meaning from) them. Damage to the occipital lobe can cause a range of sight-related problems, including difficulty seeing certain parts of the visual field, difficulty seeing certain movements or colors, visual hallucinations (seeing things that aren't really there), or complete blindness (Anderson & Rizzo, 1994; Beniczky et al., 2002; Ferber & Karnath, 1999; Werth, 2006).

Temporal Lobe. As we move toward the front of the brain (but remain in the bottom half), we reach the **temporal lobe**: the lower middle part of the brain, involved in hearing and speech production. The location of the temporal lobe is near your ears, which makes sense considering how vital it is to the perception of sound. The temporal lobe is the first place sound goes after it moves through your ear, and also where the brain starts to make sense of those sounds.

The temporal lobe contains **Wernicke's area**: part of the temporal lobe specifically involved in understanding speech. Researchers know that Wernicke's area exists because they have seen people with damage to that specific area demonstrate **Wernicke's aphasia**: dysfunction in understanding or creating coherent speech, caused by damage to Wernicke's area. People with Wernicke's aphasia fail to understand even simple statements by others. They can produce words, but those words are often made up, and they can produce sentences, but the sentences are often gibberish or irrelevant to the conversation. In addition to its auditory emphasis, the temporal lobe appears to play some role in visual processing, including the identification of objects, as well as long-term memory for verbal material (Albright, 2013; Kandel & Siegelbaum, 2013; Schacter & Wagner, 2013; Wagner et al., 1998).

Parietal Lobe. Above the occipital and temporal lobes, we find the **parietal lobe**: the part of the brain near the top and back of the head involved in touch and perception. A particularly important part of the parietal lobe is the **somatosensory cortex**: a strip of brain matter near the front of the parietal lobe involved in receiving information from the senses. The somatosensory cortex takes in visual information that has been relayed from the occipital lobe, as well as auditory information that has been relayed from the temporal lobe. But one of the main functions of the somatosensory cortex is to directly monitor the sensation of touch (including contact, pressure, pain, temperature, and itch) everywhere on your body (Amaral, 2013). In fact, specific spots on the somatosensory cortex correspond to specific parts of your body.

Does the size of the body part match the amount of space it takes up on the somatosensory cortex?

occipital lobe
The lower back part of the brain, involved in vision.

temporal lobe
The lower middle part of the brain, involved in hearing and speech production.

Wernicke's area
The part of the temporal lobe specifically involved in understanding speech.

Wernicke's aphasia
The dysfunction in understanding or creating coherent speech caused by damage to Wernicke's area.

parietal lobe
The part of the brain near the top and back of the head, involved in touch and perception.

somatosensory cortex
The strip of brain matter near the front of the parietal lobe, involved in receiving information from the senses.

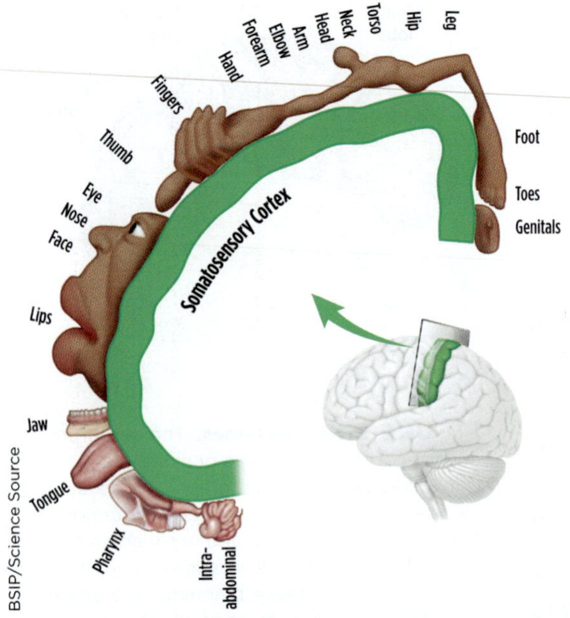

BSIP/Science Source

FIGURE 2.13 The Somatosensory Cortex. Within the parietal lobe is a strip of brain matter called the somatosensory cortex, which is involved in receiving information from the senses. The amount of space in the somatosensory cortex devoted to a particular body part is determined not by the size of that body part, but by its sensitivity. For example, your lips get more space than your torso, despite the fact that the lips are much smaller, because your lips are much more sensitive to touch.

Interestingly, no. The size of each spot does not correspond to the size of the corresponding part of your body. Instead, the size of each spot corresponds to the *sensitivity* of that part of your body (Gardner & Johnson, 2013; Nakamura et al., 1998).

Take a look at **Figure 2.13**, which illustrates how much space on the somatosensory cortex is devoted to various body parts. The first thing you'll notice is how out of proportion those body parts seem. For example, why would the somatosensory space for your lips, a tiny part of your body, be bigger than the space for a huge part like your whole torso? The answer is that the lips are far more sensitive — for good reason, Darwin would tell us, since what touches (and passes) the lips could affect human survival much more than what touches the abdomen or the back. Think about it this way — if a fly lands on your back, you might notice it, but you might not. But if the same fly lands on your lips, you'll instantly sense it. In other species, the somatosensory cortex reveals the evolutionary importance of their body parts too. For example, in rats, the somatosensory cortex devotes a huge amount of space to the whiskers, with each individual whisker having its own oversized corresponding spot (Pinto et al., 2000).

Frontal Lobe. The lobe located in the front of the brain is appropriately named the **frontal lobe**: the part of the cerebral cortex right behind the forehead, which is involved in complex thinking tasks, planning, purposeful actions, and other advanced functions. Remember one of the major points from earlier in this chapter — the abilities that are most uniquely human tend to be located in the part of the brain that we have much more of than other species. That part, more than any other, is the frontal lobe.

The frontal lobe does lots of things, some of which are still being discovered, but it is clear that most of those things are distinctively human, such as integrating multiple pieces of information, deciding what to do in response to that information, figuring out how to do it, and carrying out the task. For example, imagine that you were considering buying a new smartphone. There would be lots of steps involved: gathering information about different makes and models (such as price, features, size, etc.), weighing the pros and cons of each smartphone until you settle on one, determining exactly how you're going to buy it (at a store, through a Web site, etc.), and then taking the necessary actions to actually make the purchase (going to the store, ordering on the Web site, etc.). Every one of those steps relies on your uniquely human frontal lobe.

There is one part of the frontal lobe — the *prefrontal* region, located all the way up front — that is especially devoted to these kinds of uniquely human behaviors. The prefrontal region accounts for 29% of the human cerebral cortex, which makes it twice as big as it is in our closest primate relatives (Rilling, 2006; Schoenemann, 2006; Schoenemann et al., 2005; Semendeferi et al., 2001). The prefrontal region is often described as being important in executive control (Olson & Colby, 2013). To understand what *executive control* means, think about what an executive at a company does. The executive does *not* do routine, automatic tasks — that's what the lower-level employees do. Instead, the executive oversees those routine, automatic tasks, and handles any unusual issues that come up during the process. The executive's job might involve identifying and defining problems, considering multiple solutions, making tough decisions, forming strategies, and instructing others on how to implement those strategies.

The prefrontal region of the frontal lobe performs tasks similar to those of an executive (Arciniegas, 2013; Banich, 2009). It oversees the routine and automatic tasks that the other parts of the brain are doing, evaluates and integrates unusual situations on a case-by-case basis, and decides what to do about them. For example, if you hit a traffic jam on your way to an important doctor's appointment, many parts of your brain do their routine, automatic tasks: your occipital lobe sees the cars lined up bumper to bumper, your temporal lobe hears the traffic report on the radio, and your amygdala feels the fear of missing the exam and even sends out the initial fight-or-flight response.

frontal lobe
The part of the cerebral cortex right behind the forehead, involved in complex thinking tasks, planning, purposeful actions, and other advanced functions.

motor cortex
The strip of brain matter near the back of the frontal lobe, involved in voluntary movement.

Broca's area
The part of the left side of the frontal lobe heavily involved in speaking.

Broca's aphasia
The speech dysfunction caused by damage to Broca's area.

But it's your frontal lobe, particularly your prefrontal region, that integrates all of those sources of information, ponders them, generates options (Find another way to get there? Call to reschedule?), chooses one, and acts on that decision.

Another important part of the frontal lobe is the **motor cortex**: the strip of brain matter near the back of the frontal lobe involved in voluntary movement. The motor cortex lies just in front of the somatosensory cortex. Like the somatosensory cortex, it connects to parts throughout the body, but rather than taking information *from* them (in the form of sensations), the motor cortex sends information *to* specific parts of the body (in the form of motor instructions) (Chang et al., 2018; Rizzolatti & Strick, 2013; Wolpert et al., 2013). It is your motor cortex, with the help of your somatic nervous system, that tells your thumbs to move when you text and your feet to move when you dance.

Like the somatosensory cortex, the motor cortex allocates its space according to need rather than size, as shown in **Figure 2.14**. The parts of your body that need more motor control get more representation on the motor cortex, regardless of their size. That's why body parts like your fingers, thumb, and tongue — each of which is small but has tremendous range of motion — occupy lots of space on the motor cortex. That is also why your hips and thighs — which have a much more limited range of motion, but are much bigger — occupy very little space on the motor cortex. In nonhuman animals, the motor cortex reflects the movements typical for that species (Brown et al., 2013; Peters et al., 2017). In monkeys, for example, the space on the motor cortex for feet is much larger than the corresponding space for human feet, which makes sense when you consider that monkeys use their feet to grasp objects and swing from branches, while we don't use ours for much more than walking and wiggling our toes (Kalaska & Rizzolatti, 2013).

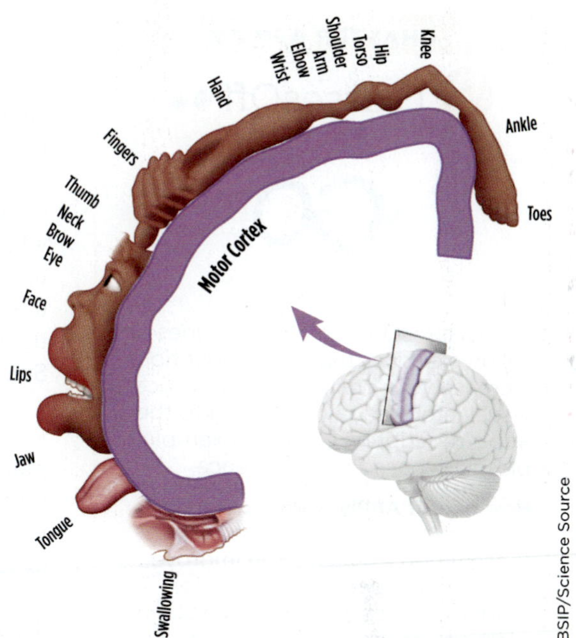

BSIP/Science Source

FIGURE 2.14 The Motor Cortex. Like space in your somatosensory cortex, space in your motor cortex depends not on the size of the body part but on its need for motor control. For example, your fingers, thumbs, and tongue are all small body parts but all require great motor control, so they have disproportionately large amounts of space in your motor cortex.

The frontal lobe also contains **Broca's area**: a part of the left side of the frontal lobe heavily involved in speaking. As described earlier, this area of the brain was discovered by French surgeon Paul Broca in the mid-1800s, when he conducted an autopsy on a person who had severely limited speech after a stroke. Broca found that this particular part of the frontal lobe, located near but not within the motor cortex, was the only part of the brain that had experienced any damage. **Broca's aphasia** is the speech dysfunction caused by damage to Broca's area. People with Broca's aphasia have no problem comprehending speech (assuming Wernicke's area remains intact), but have a difficult time producing speech (Kuhl & Damasio, 2013). There are very long pauses between their words, and when they put together a sentence, it often includes just the most essential words: "Need . . . bread. . . ." rather than "We need to go to the store to buy more bread." Broca's aphasia is often called an expressive aphasia, since the problems primarily involve getting language out. By contrast, Wernicke's aphasia is often called a receptive aphasia, since the problems primarily involve taking language in.

Aubrey Plaza, the actress from *Parks and Recreation*, *Legion*, and many other TV shows and movies, suffered a temporary expressive aphasia after a stroke when she was a 20-year-old student at New York University. She could understand everything happening around her but couldn't communicate any of her own thoughts: "You could say something and I would know what you meant but I couldn't express it or even write it. That was the weirdest part. When they gave me a piece of paper and a pen I just kept writing lines instead of words" (Patterson, 2016).

Hahn Lionel/ABACA/Newscom

When actress Aubrey Plaza had a stroke at the unusually young age of 20, she developed a temporary expressive aphasia in which she could not express herself through speech or writing. Her youth was a key to her quick recovery — her brain had a greater degree of plasticity than is typical in older stroke victims.

Brain Plasticity

Both Aubrey Plaza and Tedy Bruschi (the football player we discussed earlier in this chapter) experienced their strokes at unusually young ages. Their youth undoubtedly worked to their advantage when it came to recovery. Aubrey Plaza began regaining her ability to communicate within days. Tedy Bruschi relearned how to

CHAPTER APP 2.2

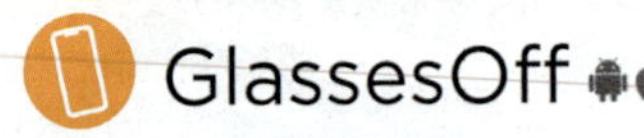

The GlassesOff app offers a series of vision exercises that, with repetition, increase your brain's ability to process visual information (according to the app's description), a great example of plasticity based on experience.

How does it APPly to your daily life? The makers of this app claim that these vision exercises can improve vision and decrease the need for reading glasses, which suggests plasticity of the brain based on experience. To what extent do you believe such innovations can replace reading glasses, Lasik, or other eye surgeries?

How does it APPly to your understanding of psychology? How do vision exercises like the ones in this app illustrate *plasticity*? At what age would these exercises be most effective?

To learn more about this app or to download it to your phone, you can search for "GlassesOff" on Google, in the iPhone App store, or in the Google Play store.

use the left side of his body within months. Their recoveries involved changes in the actual structure and function of their brains. In fact, before-and-after brain images of people who experience brain injury or illness (followed by successful treatment) show that certain parts of the brain modify their size, shape, or capabilities to help them regain lost brain function. In other words, both Aubrey Plaza's and Tedy Bruschi's brains demonstrated **plasticity**: the ability of the brain to adapt its structure or function in response to damage or experience. The word *plasticity* makes sense when you think of how versatile and adaptable plastic can be. We mold plastic into many different forms for many different purposes, from soda bottles to trash bags to smartphone cases to prosthetic limbs. Amazingly, the human brain shows some of the same versatility and adaptability (Bavelier et al., 2009; McEwen, 2004; Neville & Sur, 2009).

The younger you are, the more plasticity your brain has (Kolb & Gibb, 2011; Kolb & Whishaw, 1998; Van Horn, 2004). Young children's brains are especially plastic. That doesn't mean all kids will fully recover from a brain injury, but they typically recover better than adults with similar brain injuries. Kids' brains are more plastic because they are less fully developed. Specifically, the various parts of the brain haven't finished specializing yet, which means that sometimes they can switch to a different function that a damaged part of the brain can no longer do, at least to some extent.

Neurogenesis. Another advantage that young brains have over old brains is the capacity for **neurogenesis**: the creation of new neurons. Neurogenesis is an especially beneficial strategy for dealing with damage to a part of the brain. Rather than taking existing neurons and overhauling the way they work, neurogenesis involves the manufacture of neurons that didn't exist before. For many years, experts believed that children were the only ones capable of neurogenesis, but now it is clear that adults are too, although in a much more limited way and only in certain parts of the brain (such as the hippocampus) (Eriksson et al., 1998; Ming & Song, 2011; van Praag et al., 2002, 2004). This discovery is encouraging to researchers who seek answers to common brain malfunctions in adults (especially older adults), including certain memory impairments and psychological disorders (Deng et al., 2010).

Within the brain, perhaps the most plastic elements of all are **stem cells**: cells that have not yet specialized, and therefore can become a variety of different cells as the need arises. As the word *stem* implies, stem cells have begun to grow but have not finished. They are sensitive to demands within the brain to serve a certain purpose, perhaps based on specific parts of the brain that need help (Woodbury &

IT'S LIKE...

Plasticity Is Like an Athlete Switching Positions

Imagine asking a talented 7-year-old softball player who has only played first base to switch positions. That probably won't be much of a problem. As a beginner, that girl probably can take her general athletic skills to shortstop, centerfield, or any other position on the diamond because she hasn't specialized too much yet. By contrast, imagine asking a 30-year-old Major League veteran first baseman to become a shortstop, a centerfielder, or play any other position. He would find it challenging, maybe even impossible. For years, he has spent every game and practice, day after day, exclusively at first base. His skills have become so highly specialized to the first base position that he might not be able to play another position well. Of course, there is a chance that it *could* work, at least to a limited extent. But all of that time spent playing just one position makes a change much tougher than it would be for a player with less experience.

Brain plasticity works the same way. In very young brains, many parts of the brain haven't specialized much yet. So if there is a need to cover for a damaged brain region (an injured teammate, so to speak), those parts of the brain have the flexibility necessary to make the switch. In older brains, however, the brain parts have specialized more, which means that their ability to adapt and change is more limited. Thankfully, even in adults, there is often some plasticity among brain parts, just like some athletes can take on a new position when pressured to do so later in their careers.

Black, 2004). In this way, stem cells can repair damage and help brain regions recover functions they might otherwise lose (do Nascimento & Ulrich, 2015; Gage, 2000; Zhao, 2015).

plasticity
The ability of the brain to adapt its structure or function in response to damage or experience.

neurogenesis
The creation of new neurons.

stem cells
Cells that have not yet specialized, and therefore can become a variety of different cells as the need arises.

Plasticity after Brain Damage. Sometimes, as in the case of a stroke, the brain shows its plasticity in response to damage (Sanes & Jessell, 2013d). In one study, researchers simulated the amputation of fingers by using anesthetic (the same stuff your dentist injects to make your mouth numb) on two fingers of their research participants — specifically, their ring fingers and index fingers. They discovered that in the participants' somatosensory cortex, the amount of space dedicated to those two fingers decreased, and the amount of space dedicated to the pinky finger, middle finger, and thumb increased. The brain physically adapted to help functional parts to take over for nonfunctional parts (Rossini et al., 1994).

In a study with rats, researchers cut the facial neurons that carry movement commands to the whiskers. They soon observed some interesting reactions in the motor cortex of each rat: a decrease in the space dedicated to the whiskers, and a corresponding increase in the space dedicated to the front legs (Donoghue et al., 1990; Sanes & Donoghue, 2000; Sanes et al., 1990, 1992). It's as if the brain adopted the strategy that if it could no longer move the whiskers around, it would try the next best thing — increasing the dexterity of the front legs instead. That is a vital adaptation for rats, who constantly move their whiskers around to feel what is around them (the way people sometimes use their arms and hands in a dark room). In this situation, the plasticity in a rat's motor cortex might make the difference between living (by finding food and avoiding danger) and dying.

Plasticity after Life Experience. In addition to showing its plasticity in response to damage, the brain shows its plasticity in response to life experience (Sanes & Jessell, 2013c). One study examined the brains of people who read Braille, the writing system in which letters are represented by patterns of small dots or bumps, across which the visually impaired person moves their finger (Pascual-Leone & Torres, 1993). They discovered that in the somatosensory cortex of these individuals, the space dedicated to the "reading finger" (the right index finger) had become significantly larger than the space dedicated to the left index finger. That space was also larger than the space for either index finger in the somatosensory cortex of someone who doesn't read Braille at all.

DIVERSITY MATTERS

Poverty is another experience that, over time, may change the brain. Specifically, in the brains of people who spend long stretches of their lives in poverty, the average size of the hippocampus, occipital lobe, prefrontal cortex, and other brain regions is smaller than in people who live in wealthier conditions. In addition to those size differences, there are functional differences — those parts of the brain don't work as fast or as well for people in poor conditions (Hanson & Hackman, 2012). These findings are consistent across several different measurements of poverty, including socioeconomic status, family income, and education level. Violence and neglect — which often go hand-in-hand with poverty — also correlate with physical changes in the brain. Specifically, brain scans of kids exposed to high levels of violence or neglect show that certain brain regions (including the prefrontal cortex) are thinner than those of kids who did not live through these kinds of experiences (Colich et al., 2020).

DIVERSITY MATTERS

The experience of living in a specific cultural group may change the brain too (Dominguez et al., 2009; Freeman et al., 2009b; Rule et al., 2013). Several studies have found specific brain differences between members of Western cultures, who tend to be more individualistic (such as in the United States and many European countries), and members of Eastern cultures, who tend to be more collectivistic (such as in many Asian countries) (Tang & Liu, 2009). For example, one group of researchers found that

DIVERSITY MATTERS

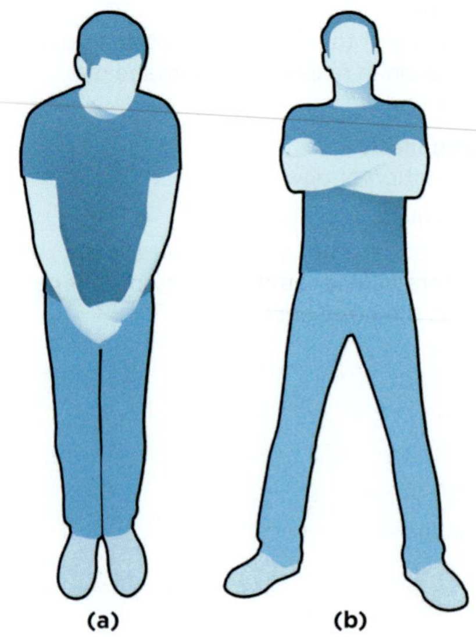

FIGURE 2.15 Culturally Distinct Brain Responses to Dominant and Submissive Body Language. Cultural experiences can influence brain activity. In one study, participants saw drawings of human figures displaying either submission (generally viewed more favorably in collectivistic cultures) or dominance (generally viewed more favorably in individualistic cultures). The parts of the brain linked to the feeling of reward (including parts in the prefrontal cortex) were more active in Japanese participants when they saw the submissive figure, but more active in American participants when they saw the dominant figure (Freeman et al., 2009a).

LIFE HACK 2.2

When you practice a behavior extensively, you change your brain in ways that enhance your ability to do that behavior well.

(Pascual-Leone & Torres, 1993; Sanes & Jessell, 2013c)

parts of the brain linked to the feeling of reward, including a part of the prefrontal cortex (the medial prefrontal cortex, to be specific), respond in different ways to contrasting body language. Specifically, researchers showed two kinds of drawings to both Japanese and American participants – some drawings of a person showing submission (more favored in collectivistic cultures), and some drawings of a person showing dominance (more favored in individualistic cultures). The reward systems in the brains of the Japanese participants were more active when they saw the submissive figure, but the reward systems in the brains of the American participants were more active when they saw the dominant figure (Freeman et al., 2009a) (**Figure 2.15**).

Even languages may affect the brain differently (Bolger et al., 2005; Chen et al., 2009; Gandour, 2005). For example, one study found that different parts

DIVERSITY MATTERS

of the occipital lobe are activated by English words (formed by a string of letters) versus Chinese characters (formed by holistic visual stimuli) (Tan et al., 2000). Other studies found that in English, verbs and nouns are each processed in specific parts of the brain, but in Chinese, a language that does not make distinctions between verbs and nouns like English does, a single word can be processed in many different parts of the brain depending on the context in which it is used (Li et al., 2004).

Plasticity after Psychotherapy. Another experience that changes the brain is psychotherapy. It probably comes as no surprise that the treatment of psychological problems with medication changes the brain. After all, that is what drugs like Xanax, Zoloft, and Concerta are designed to do. But studies show that psychotherapy – talk therapy, with no medication involved – changes the brain too, often in ways that mimic medication (Cozolino, 2010; Linden, 2012). For example, clients with phobias (an anxiety disorder covered in more detail in Chapter 14) showed similar changes in the activity of the limbic system and other parts of the brain whether they were treated with medication or cognitive-behavioral psychotherapy (Johanson et al., 2006; Linden, 2006; Paquette et al., 2003; Straube et al., 2006). Similar findings – that therapy and medication change the same parts of the brain in the same ways – have also been found in clients with obsessive-compulsive disorder, panic disorder, depression, borderline personality disorder, social anxiety disorder, and other disorders (Baxter et al., 1992; Brody et al., 2001; DeRubeis et al., 2008; Furmark et al., 2002; Goldapple et al., 2004; Mancke et al., 2018; Nakatani et al., 2003; Nascimento et al., 2018; Penades et al., 2002; Sakai et al., 2006; Steiger et al., 2017; Wykes et al., 2002).

CHECK YOUR LEARNING:

2.11 To what extent can specific brain functions be localized exclusively to specific parts of the brain?

2.12 In general, how do the parts near the base of the human brain differ from the parts near the outer regions of the human brain?

2.13 Where is the brainstem located, and what does it do?

2.14 Where is the cerebellum located, and what is its primary function?

2.15 What is the main function of the thalamus?

2.16 What is the limbic system, and what is its primary function?

2.17 What parts of the brain are contained in the limbic system, and what is the main function of each part?

2.18 What are the primary functions of the cerebrum and cerebral cortex?

2.19 What is the corpus callosum, and what is its primary function?

2.20 Why is the corpus callosum cut in split-brain surgery?

2.21 What are the four lobes of the cerebrum, and what is the focus of each lobe?

2.22 What are the association areas, and what do they do?

2.23 What is plasticity, and when is it most likely to occur?

To check your understanding of these questions, click show the answers or refer to the answers in the Chapter Summary.

The Nervous System and the Endocrine System

Your body features two fine-tuned communication systems, each designed to send and receive different kinds of information: the *nervous system* and the *endocrine system*.

YOU WILL LEARN:

2.24 how the nervous system connects the brain to the rest of the body.

2.25 the difference between the central nervous system and the peripheral nervous system.

2.26 the two parts of the peripheral nervous system.

2.27 the two divisions that make up the autonomic nervous system.

2.28 what the endocrine system is.

2.29 which gland is the "master gland."

The Nervous System

The **nervous system** is the full set of nerves that connect your brain with all the other parts of your body. The nervous system is what enables your brain to act as a command center, sending and receiving messages from all over your body. As described earlier in the chapter, the building blocks of your nervous system are *neurons*, the cells that facilitate communication within the nervous system.

The Central Nervous System and the Peripheral Nervous System. The core of the nervous system is known as the **central nervous system**: the brain and the spinal cord. All communication with the brain must move through the central nervous system, but often – as the example of searching for a smartphone in the dark from earlier in the chapter illustrates – the communication moves beyond the brain and spinal cord to other body parts, like your hands or feet (Brodal, 2010). That kind of communication requires not only your central nervous system, but also your **peripheral nervous system**: the neurons that connect the central nervous system to other parts of the body. You've heard the word *peripheral* before in the term *peripheral vision* – not what's in the center, but what's off to the side. Peripheral means the same thing here – the neuronal connections that extend from your center (your brain and spine) to all other parts of your body.

The Somatic Nervous System and the Autonomic Nervous System. The peripheral nervous system has two parts: the *somatic nervous system* and the *autonomic nervous system*. Your **somatic nervous system** is the part of the peripheral nervous system that connects the central nervous system to the parts of the body you control voluntarily. The example in which you move your hand around inside your backpack to find your phone illustrates the somatic nervous system. In fact, any sensation or action that you are aware of moves through your somatic nervous system.

By contrast, your **autonomic nervous system** is the part of the peripheral nervous system that connects the central nervous system to the parts of your body you control involuntarily. Your autonomic nervous system regulates the bodily functions that you never have to think about, like the beating of your heart and the digestion of your food. Unlike your somatic nervous system, which spreads throughout your entire body, your autonomic nervous system covers only your core, where most of your organs are (Amaral & Strick, 2013; Horn & Swanson, 2013).

As **Figure 2.16** illustrates, your autonomic nervous system has two parts of its own: one that helps you "turn up," and another that helps you "turn down" (Garrett, 2015). Specifically, the **sympathetic division** is the part of your autonomic nervous system that revs your body up in response to stressors. By contrast, the **parasympathetic division** is the part of your autonomic nervous system that calms your body down when stressors decrease. In Chapter 11, when we discuss stress in more detail, we'll delve into the fight-or-flight response, which is an autonomic emotional and physical reaction to a perceived threat that prepares us to either attack it or run away from it. For now, it is important to know that the sympathetic division cranks up your fight-or-flight response, and your parasympathetic division winds it down.

nervous system
The full set of nerves that connect the brain with all other parts of the body.

central nervous system
The brain and the spinal cord.

peripheral nervous system
The neurons that connect the central nervous system to other parts of the body.

somatic nervous system
The part of the peripheral nervous system that connects the central nervous system to the parts of the body controlled voluntarily.

autonomic nervous system
The part of the peripheral nervous system that connects the central nervous system to the parts of the body controlled involuntarily.

sympathetic division
The part of the autonomic nervous system that revs the body up in response to stressors.

parasympathetic division
The part of the autonomic nervous system that calms the body down when stressors decrease.

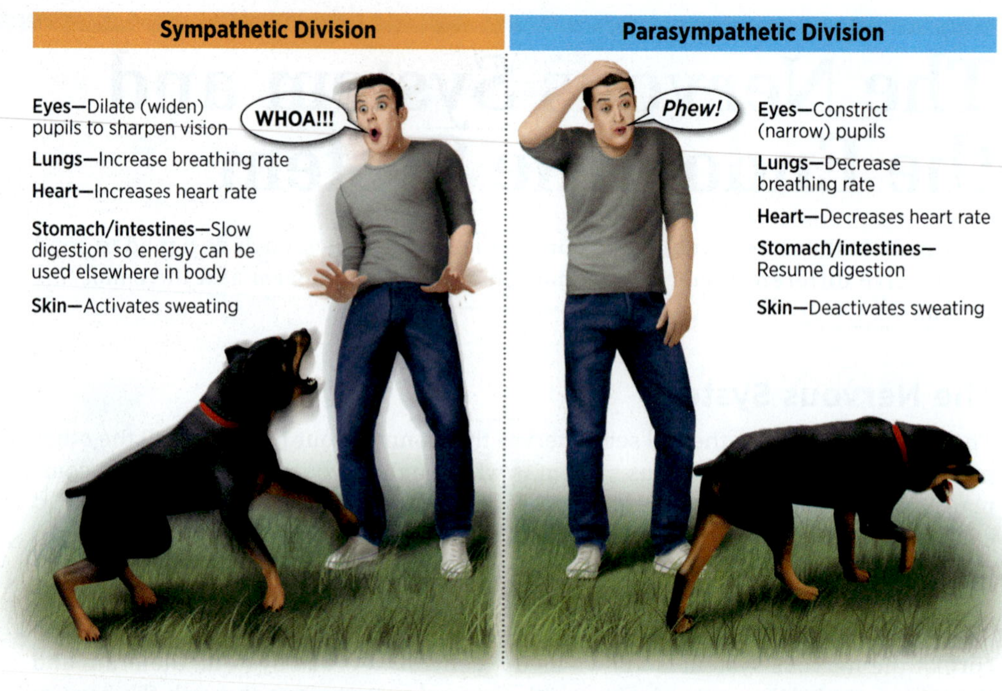

FIGURE 2.16 The Sympathetic and Parasympathetic Divisions. Within your autonomic nervous system, the sympathetic division helps your body "turn up" in response to stressors by widening your pupils, increasing your heart rate, and increasing your breathing rate. The parasympathetic division helps your body "turn down" when the stressors decrease by returning all of your body parts to their resting state.

You've probably noticed that your body's immediate response to stressors, especially sudden stressors, is largely outside of your control (or autonomic). For example, if you're walking alone through a neighborhood and without warning you see a huge, growling, unleashed dog sprinting toward you, your sympathetic division triggers a set of bodily changes: your heart races and beats more strongly, you breathe more heavily and quickly, and you start to sweat. (Actually, the changes include others that are less noticeable too: your pupils dilate [enlarge], your stomach slows digestion, and your liver and kidney produce more of certain substances as well.) All of these changes are designed to help you do what the term *fight or flight* suggests: either fight the threat or fly away from it as fast as possible. As the dog gets close, however, you notice the dog's owner calling it. The dog suddenly turns around and runs back. Within a few seconds, you're past that house, past that dog, past that threat.

That is when your parasympathetic division activates, undoing all of the bodily changes that the sympathetic division revved up. It brings your heart, lungs, stomach, and everything else back to normal. But it doesn't happen instantly. Even though your mind knows the threat is no longer there, it may take your body many minutes to return to normal. In fact, you may notice that the sweating, heart-pounding, and heavy breathing are still with you even when you've had enough time to get several blocks away from that dog. As Figure 2.17 shows, that is the nature of the autonomic nervous system and its sympathetic and parasympathetic divisions: they automatically control your reactions to stressors (and their absence) to maximize your chances of survival, but you don't have much voluntary control over the process.

The Endocrine System

endocrine system
The set of glands that sends hormones throughout the body via the bloodstream.

hormones
The chemicals made by the glands of the endocrine system that affect certain tissues throughout the body.

Unlike the nervous system, which sends messages between the brain and the rest of the body via neurons, the **endocrine system** is the set of glands that sends hormones throughout the body via the bloodstream. **Hormones**, chemicals made by the glands of the endocrine system, affect certain tissues throughout the body. Hormones influence virtually every important function within your body,

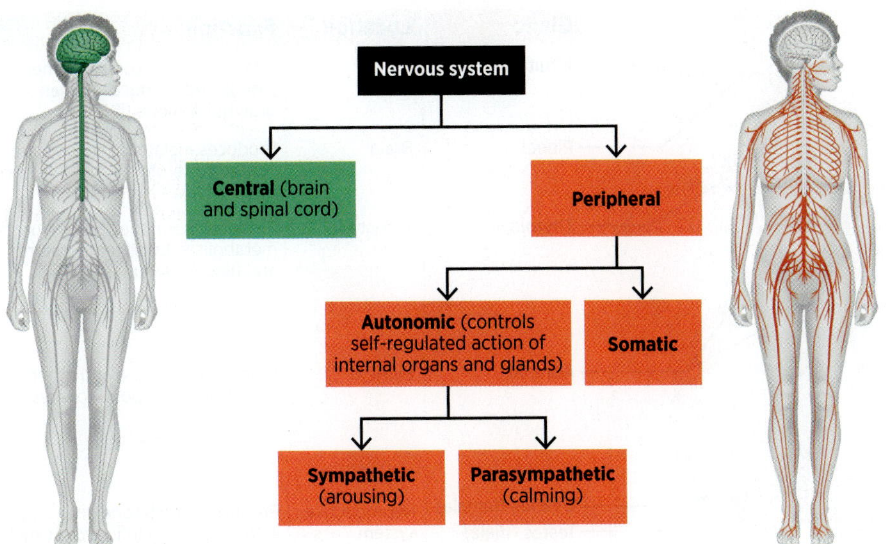

FIGURE 2.17 The Organization of the Nervous System. The most basic division of the human nervous system is between the central and peripheral nervous systems. The peripheral nervous system is further divided between the somatic and autonomic nervous systems. The autonomic nervous system is even further divided into the sympathetic and parasympathetic divisions.

including your appetite, mood, energy level, sleep schedule, sex drive, metabolism, digestion, and more.

Does the endocrine system operate at the same speed as the nervous system?

No. The endocrine system operates much more slowly than the nervous system. Messages dart through neurons, but hormones ooze through the bloodstream, often taking a long time to get started, build up, and ultimately stop. Consider the familiar hormones most closely tied to sexual development (puberty): *testosterone* and *estrogen*. If you recall your middle school years, you'll remember that those hormones kicked in over months, not seconds. Little by little, those hormones had the expected effect on the appropriate body parts, and eventually (in some cases, quite a few years after they started), the messages slowed and stopped.

The endocrine system features many glands, but the most important is the **pituitary gland**: the "master gland" in the brain, which produces human growth hormone and also controls all of the other glands in the body. Although it is no bigger than the eraser on the end of a pencil, your pituitary gland is in charge, either directly or via control of other glands, of some remarkably important stuff: how tall you grow, your metabolism rate, the ratio of muscle to fat in your body, when puberty kicks in, your blood pressure, your body temperature, the production of breast milk after childbirth, and much more.

Figure 2.18 includes the pituitary gland among a list of important glands in the endocrine system. Also on that list are the **adrenal glands**: glands located on top of the kidneys that produce hormones to arouse the body in response to stress. One of those hormones, named after the gland itself, you know well: adrenaline. When you notice that your "adrenaline is pumping" – when you're gearing up for a big game, or walking through a haunted house, or biking down a steep hill – that is actually your adrenal glands working overtime.

Another hormone produced by the adrenal gland is cortisol, which is nicknamed the stress hormone (Cozolino, 2008). Psychologists who study stress often use cortisol levels as an objective way of measuring stress – not only because cortisol levels are good stress indicators, but also because cortisol is easy to measure. It doesn't require a blood test (although that works too): all it takes is an analysis of someone's hair or saliva. For example, one study found that the hair of women in the third trimester of pregnancy – a time notorious for high stress levels – has double the cortisol content

pituitary gland
The "master gland" in the brain that produces human growth hormone and controls all of the other glands in the body.

adrenal glands
The glands located on top of the kidneys that produce hormones to arouse the body in response to stress.

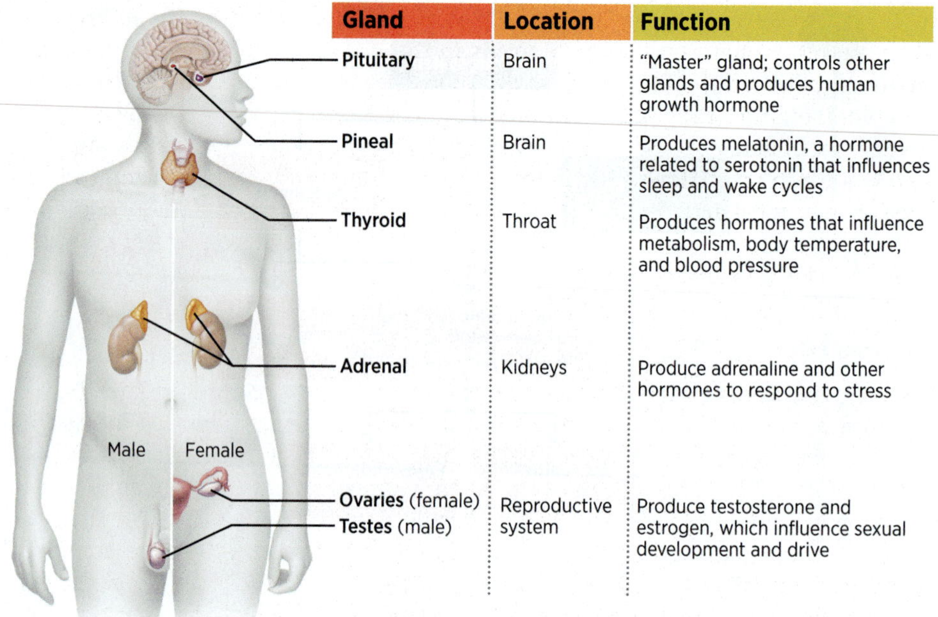

Gland	Location	Function
Pituitary	Brain	"Master" gland; controls other glands and produces human growth hormone
Pineal	Brain	Produces melatonin, a hormone related to serotonin that influences sleep and wake cycles
Thyroid	Throat	Produces hormones that influence metabolism, body temperature, and blood pressure
Adrenal	Kidneys	Produce adrenaline and other hormones to respond to stress
Ovaries (female) Testes (male)	Reproductive system	Produce testosterone and estrogen, which influence sexual development and drive

FIGURE 2.18 Selected Glands of the Endocrine System. The endocrine system includes a variety of glands. Some are located in the brain, and others are located in other parts of the body. The pituitary gland, or "master gland," controls all of the other glands.

of women who were not pregnant (Kirschbaum et al., 2009). Studies of infants have found that their saliva contains more cortisol in the immediate aftermath of experiences that they find stressful, including separation from a parent and unexpected physical pain (Kirschbaum & Hellhammer, 1994; Larson et al., 1991; Lewis & Thomas, 1990).

CHECK YOUR LEARNING:

2.24 How does the nervous system connect the brain with all other parts of your body?

2.25 What is the difference between the central nervous system and the peripheral nervous system?

2.26 What are the two parts of the peripheral nervous system, and what does each part do?

2.27 What are the two divisions of the autonomic nervous system, and what does each division do?

2.28 What is the endocrine system?

2.29 Which gland is called the master gland, and why does it deserve that label?

To check your understanding of these questions, click show the answers or refer to the answers in the Chapter Summary.

How We Know All of This: Viewing the Brain

YOU WILL LEARN:

2.30 how electroencephalography (EEG) works.

2.31 how computed tomography (CT) works.

2.32 how magnetic resonance imaging (MRI) works.

2.33 how positron emission tomography (PET) works.

2.34 how functional magnetic resonance imaging (fMRI) works.

How did we gain all of this knowledge about the brain, including the parts and activity within it? How has psychology evolved from phrenology (guessing the connections between brain regions and abilities based on the shape of the skull) to vivid, detailed, stunning images of the brain's inner workings in just over a century? The answer is closely linked to the advancement of technology (Van Horn, 2004). Let's consider various ways of viewing the brain and its activity, beginning with the oldest form of brain-viewing technology still being used today and making our way to the newest.

Electroencephalography (EEG)

Electroencephalography (EEG) is a technique in which electrodes are placed on the scalp to record electrical activity in the brain. EEGs, which were first used in the 1920s, don't produce pictures of the brain, but graphs that illustrate the activity between any two points in the brain (Millett, 2001). Specifically, EEGs measure the difference in electrical voltage between any two points in the brain, which indicates the activity of neurons between them (Coburn et al., 2006; Frey & Spitz, 2013; Olejniczak, 2006). Psychologists and other professionals who use EEGs know what normal graphs between particular points look like, and they use that knowledge as a comparison when examining a patient's EEGs for abnormalities. If that comparison indicates excessive electrical activity in certain neuronal connections, that activity could indicate a likelihood of seizures. For that reason, EEGs are well suited for the assessment of seizure-based disorders like epilepsy (Westbrook, 2013).

electroencephalography (EEG)
A technique in which electrodes are placed on the scalp to record electrical activity in the brain.

computed tomography (CT)
A technique in which multiple X-rays are combined to make a 3D image of the brain.

lesion
The damage or destruction of brain tissue.

magnetic resonance imaging (MRI)
A technique in which magnetic fields and radio waves are used to make images of brain structure.

positron emission tomography (PET)
A technique in which activity in various brain structures is illustrated by a radioactive sugar injected into the body.

Computed Tomography (CT)

Psychologists' abilities to see brain activity, especially to locate it in specific parts of the brain, took a big step forward from EEGs with the introduction in the 1970s of **computed tomography (CT)**: a technique in which multiple X-rays are combined to make a 3D image of the brain. Each X-ray provides a 2D image of a "slice" of the brain; when computers combine these 2D images, they can make the image 3D. (That process actually resembles to the way 3D printers work — combining 2D slices of an object to make a 3D whole.) CT scans produce images of the brain in shades of gray. These images allow psychologists to distinguish brain matter (which is dense and appears nearly white) from ventricles or space in the brain (which appears black). This distinction is important when assessing whether a patient has a disease that features enlarged ventricles, like Alzheimer's disease or schizophrenia (Hurley et al., 2013). Subtle differences in the shades of gray also allowed psychologists to detect the specific location of a **lesion**: damage or destruction of brain tissue.

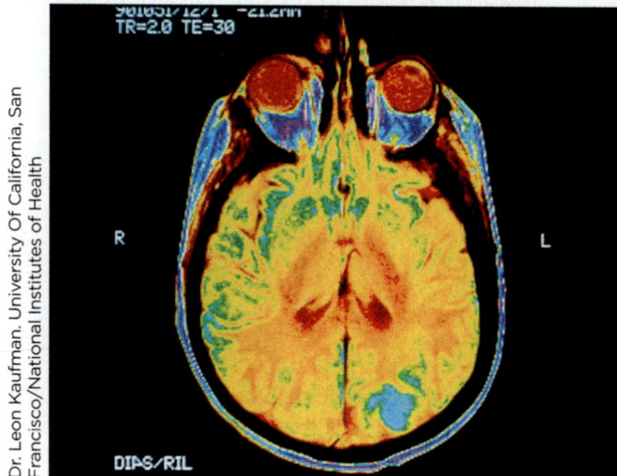

Dr. Leon Kaufman, University Of California, San Francisco/National Institutes of Health

Magnetic resonance imaging (MRI) is a technique in which magnetic fields and radio waves are used to make images of brain structure. MRIs offer much more detail than computed tomography (CT) scans.

Magnetic Resonance Imaging (MRI)

The next step forward in brain imaging, which came along in the 1980s, was **magnetic resonance imaging (MRI)**: a technique in which magnetic fields and radio waves are used to make images of brain structure. MRIs offer much more detail than CT scans. The *magnetic* in its name indicates that MRIs work by putting a strong magnetic field around the brain to measure the radio waves that naturally come from hydrogen atoms (remember, like the rest of the body, the brain is mostly H_2O). This magnetic field is contained in a large tube in which the patient lies down (or, in some machines, stands or sits up) — a procedure that can cause problems for people who are too big for the tube or too fidgety to stay still. Like CT scans, MRIs are good for finding lesions as well as tumors and other abnormalities in brain structures. Although MRIs can take longer (30–60 minutes, typically) and cost more than CT scans, the higher resolution provides psychologists with a better view of the brain (Erhart et al., 2005; Gupta et al., 2004; Symms et al., 2004).

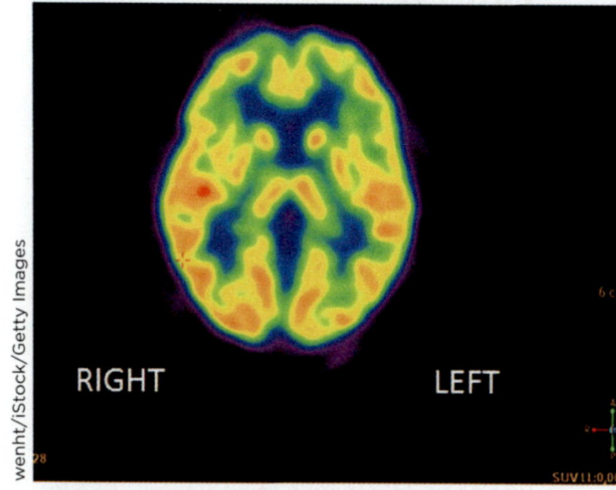

wenht/iStock/Getty Images

Positron emission tomography (PET) is a technique in which activity in various brain structures is illustrated by a radioactive sugar injected into the body. Unlike MRIs and CT scans, PET scans show brain function, not just brain structure.

Positron Emission Tomography (PET)

MRIs provide images of *brain structure*, meaning that they (along with CT scans) show the brain's parts, but not the activity within those parts — like seeing the architectural blueprint of a building but not the movement patterns of the people within it. Two more recent innovations in brain imaging make the jump from brain structure to brain *function*, which means they are able to illustrate activity within the brain. One recent innovation is **positron emission tomography (PET)**: a technique in which activity in various brain structures is illustrated by a radioactive sugar injected into the body. That radioactive sugar is typically injected into a vein near the elbow, but can also be inhaled as a gas if necessary. Once in your bloodstream, the radioactive sugar travels throughout your body, including your brain. In your brain, blood rushes to each part according to how heavily that part is being used — when a part of the brain is being used a lot, it pulls a lot of blood.

When the blood is carrying a radioactive sugar, PET scanners can detect it. So, PET scans are good for making connections between particular activities and particular parts of the brain (Little et al., 2013; Miletich, 2009). For example, certain parts of the brain will light up on a PET scan when you are watching an exciting

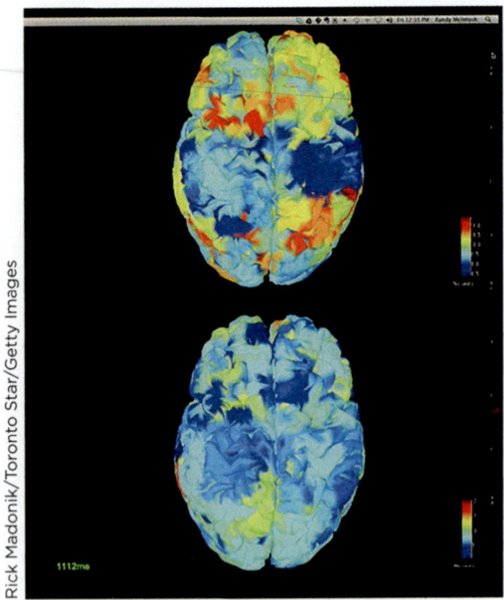

Rick Madonik/Toronto Star/Getty Images

Functional magnetic resonance imaging (fMRI) is a technique in which magnetic fields are used to make images of brain activity. Like PET scans, fMRIs show brain function, not just brain structure.

basketball game on TV, others when you are feeling hungry, and others when you are recalling a childhood memory. One study found that PET scans of the brains of people listening to their favorite music featured very high levels of activity in parts of the brain involved in reward and emotion, including the prefrontal cortex and amygdala (Blood & Zatorre, 2001). In another study, PET scans of the brains of 10 long-distance runners after running a half-marathon showed that the euphoric feeling of the runner's high is based in heightened activity in certain parts of the brain, including the prefrontal cortex and the limbic system (Boecker et al., 2008).

Functional Magnetic Resonance Imaging (fMRI)

Similar to PET in its ability to illustrate brain function rather than just brain structure is **functional magnetic resonance imaging (fMRI)**: a technique in which magnetic fields are used to make images of brain activity.

fMRIs use the same kind of magnet-based technology as regular MRIs, but they can detect metabolism (energy use) in particular parts of the brain at particular times (Dickerson, 2007; Small & Heeger, 2013). That metabolism is indicated by oxygen in the blood, which has unique magnetic properties that respond to the magnetic field used in fMRI. As such, fMRIs can identify which parts of the brain are most active when we talk, think, or perform other activities (Bandettini, 2012). In one fMRI study, participants were excluded from playing a game with others, and researchers found that the pain of social rejection activates the same parts of the brain (including parts of the cerebral cortex and prefrontal cortex) as physical pain (Eisenberger et al., 2003).

With fMRIs, can psychologists "see" psychological disorders in the brain?

Not yet, at least not reliably enough to use for diagnosis. Many people are eager for the day that fMRIs or other types of brain scans will show *biomarkers* — definitive biological indicators — of particular disorders like schizophrenia, bipolar disorder, or obsessive-compulsive disorder. Researchers using fMRIs are finding more and

functional magnetic resonance imaging (fMRI) A technique in which magnetic fields are used to make images of brain activity.

FROM RESEARCH TO REAL LIFE

The Murderer's Mind

The new generation of brain imaging, including PET scans, illuminates not just the parts of the brain, but what is going on inside of them. So what is going on inside the brain of a killer?

Psychologist Adrian Raine has dedicated his career to that question. He describes the method that he and his team used to study convicted killers in one study:

. . . complete with shackles and chains, and flanked by guards, our forty-one murderers trooped into the brain-scanning facility. . . . The technique we used to scan their brains was positron-emission tomography — PET for short. . . . We used the continuous performance task to activate or "challenge" the prefrontal cortex. The subject had to press a response button every time they saw the figure "o" flashed on a computer screen. This went on for thirty-two minutes.

— Raine (2013, p. 66)

What they found was that the PET scans of these murderers looked just like PET scans of nonmurderers in some ways, such as activation of the occipital lobe. But the PET scans showed a couple of important differences: an overactive limbic system and an underactive prefrontal cortex (Amen et al., 2007; Raine et al., 1997). Think about that combination. The limbic system is all about emotion and impulse — it is the part of the brain that says, "Let's do this!" (Barrash et al., 2000). The prefrontal cortex is all about executive control and decision making — it is the part of the brain that says, "Wait a minute — is this a good idea?" (Bechara et al., 1997; Bechara & Demasio, 2005; Blair, 2007). When the balance between those two is off, the result could be behavior that satisfies a momentary urge but lacks judgment and forethought. In the terrible cases of these murderers, that behavior is homicide.

Studies have found that this balance of the limbic system versus prefrontal cortex is often an important factor not just in murderous behavior, but in other kinds of aggressive behavior such as assault, domestic abuse, and even social insensitivity (Damasio, 1994; Haycock, 2014; Raine, 2013). Current research points to an underactive prefrontal cortex as the single strongest correlate of antisocial and violent behavior (Yang & Raine, 2009). Assuming this finding is confirmed by further research, it suggests that among murderers, the brain's inability to keep impulses in check is as dangerous as the brain's ability to produce those impulses in the first place. •

CURRENT CONTROVERSY

Neuroeverything?

One by-product of the newest brain imaging technology, including PET scans and fMRIs, is that those images appear all over the popular media. New psychological findings—whether presented in a TV news story, news or magazine article, or blog post—are often accompanied by a high-tech picture of a human brain with certain parts glowing bright red, orange, yellow, or blue. Often, the words that accompany these pictures include *neuropsychology* (or *neuropsychiatry*, *neuroscience*, or another *neuro-* term) along with an explanation of how these pictures explain all kinds of human experiences. As stated by Sally Satel and Scott O. Lilienfeld in their book *Brainwashed: The Seductive Appeal of Mindless Neuroscience*:

> *You've seen the headlines: This is your brain on love. Or God. Or envy. Or happiness. And they're reliably accompanied by articles boasting pictures of color-drenched brains—scans capturing Buddhist monks meditating, addicts craving cocaine, and college sophomores choosing Coke over Pepsi. The media—and even some neuroscientists, it seems—love to invoke the neural foundations of human behavior to explain everything from the Bernie Madoff financial fiasco to slavish devotion to our iPhones, the sexual indiscretions of politicians, conservatives' dismissal of global warming, and even an obsession with self-tanning.*
>
> —*Satel and Lilienfeld (2013, p. ix)*

The problem is that those brain pictures can be quite misleading (Illes et al., 2009; Rose & Abi-Rached, 2013). To be more accurate, the people explaining the brain imaging can overreach and oversimplify. Too often, they make the leap from what the pictures actually show—for example, certain brain regions working harder than others—to very specific conclusions about exactly what thoughts or feelings are taking place (Racine et al., 2010). (It is one thing to see that it is raining in Michigan, but another thing to claim that your cousin in Kalamazoo is getting wet.) Too often, they also reduce a feeling or behavior down to activity in a solitary part of the brain, glossing over the fact that almost everything we do involves a complex web of brain regions, even if one plays the biggest role (Racine et al., 2005).

One study found that participants considered brain-related scientific findings more credible if they saw a version of the story with fMRI images than participants who saw the same story with either bar graphs or no visuals (McCabe & Castel, 2008). Another study found that just adding neuropsychology explanations, even without the images, powerfully influenced many readers to believe the results (Weisberg et al., 2008). In other words, the words and images of neuropsychology are remarkably persuasive. However, before fully believing the neuro-news you encounter in the popular media, think critically about the limitations of this technology and how findings should be responsibly interpreted.

more biological features of some disorders, but current research still shows too much inconsistency between fMRIs of people with the same disorder to reach any conclusions with certainty (Elliott et al., 2020). For now, the main point is that fMRIs provide amazing views of the inner workings of the brain, but researchers can't yet "see" specific disorders in the brain distinctively enough to use them as a diagnostic tool.

Although fMRIs provide perhaps the most breathtaking images yet of the inner workings of the brain, the technology is relatively new and has limitations. For example, fMRIs may not be entirely reliable across time (Caceres et al., 2009). One study conducted fMRIs on participants viewing fearful faces at three different points in time (the initial session, 2 weeks later, and 8 weeks later) and got significantly different results at each point (Johnstone et al., 2005). Also, some researchers have conducted exploratory fMRI studies. *Exploratory* here means that the researchers have participants perform a particular behavior and simply see what lights up (instead of forming a hypothesis ahead of time about specific parts of the brain that should light up). This kind of research can produce connections that appear strong in a single study but are not replicated because they were due to chance rather than actual relationships between variables (Yarkoni, 2009).

CHECK YOUR LEARNING:

2.30 How does an electroencephalography (EEG) work?

2.31 How does computed tomography (CT) work?

2.32 How does magnetic resonance imaging (MRI) work?

2.33 How does positron emission tomography (PET) work?

2.34 How does functional magnetic resonance imaging (fMRI) work?

To check your understanding of these questions, click show the answers or refer to the answers in the Chapter Summary.

CHAPTER SUMMARY

Brain and Behavior Connections: An Introduction

2.1 Phineas Gage's tragic brain injury changed his personality and behavior, and Paul Broca's autopsy of a stroke victim found damage to just one part of the man's brain. These two findings helped researchers understand that certain parts of the brain are related to certain functions or abilities.

2.2 A good way to understand the brain is to start small and then zoom out. In this chapter, we begin with microscopic activity within the brain. Then, we focus on the brain itself, its parts, and how different parts are connected to different behaviors. Finally, we cover the whole body and how it interacts with the brain.

Activity Within the Brain

2.3 Your brain contains a network of about 100 billion neurons, the building blocks of brain activity.

2.4 Sensory neurons carry information from the senses to the brain, while motor neurons carry information from the brain to the muscles. Neurons send messages through their axons, which end with axon terminals.

2.5 Axons are often covered with a myelin sheath, a sleeve of fatty material that protects the message from getting lost as it travels.

2.6 Dendrites receive messages from the axon terminals of the previous neuron.

2.7 Between the axon terminal of one axon and the dendrites of the next axon, there is a small space called a synapse that must be crossed.

2.8 The substances that cross the synapse are neurotransmitters, which travel from synaptic vesicles to specific receptor sites within the dendrites.

2.9 When neurotransmitters don't successfully cross the synapse, they return to the sending neuron through a process called reuptake.

2.10 The process of sending a message between neurons starts with an action potential, which happens when the electrical charge within the neuron exceeds a certain threshold.

The Brain and Its Parts

2.11 Certain brain functions can be localized to certain parts of the brain, but no part of the brain does anything entirely by itself.

2.12 As a rule of thumb, the parts of the human brain that control functions most other animals can do are located near the base of the brain. The parts of the human brain that control uniquely human functions are closer to the outer regions, especially the front, of the brain.

2.13 The brainstem connects to the spine and controls the functions most essential to staying alive.

2.14 The cerebellum is located near the base of the brain and primarily controls balance and coordination of movement.

2.15 The thalamus is the brain's main sensory processing center.

2.16 The limbic system is a cluster of brain areas surrounding the thalamus and involved primarily in emotion.

2.17 The limbic system contains the hypothalamus, which maintains a steadiness in bodily functions; the hippocampus, which is involved in memory; and the amygdala, which controls fear and other emotions.

2.18 The cerebrum and cerebral cortex are involved in sophisticated, often uniquely human, abilities.

2.19 The corpus callosum is the bundle of neurons that connects and allows communication between the right and left halves, or hemispheres, of the cerebrum.

2.20 On rare occasions, the corpus callosum is cut in a surgery called split-brain surgery, which can alleviate seizures but often results in decreased communication between the two hemispheres.

2.21 The cerebrum consists of four lobes: (1) the occipital lobe, which focuses on vision; (2) the temporal lobe, which focuses on hearing and speech production; (3) the parietal lobe, which focuses on touch and perception; and (4) the frontal lobe, which focuses on complex thinking tasks and other advanced functions.

2.22 The cerebrum and its lobes contain high concentrations of association areas, which synthesize and interpret information taken in by other parts of the brain.

2.23 Plasticity refers to the ability of the brain to adapt its structure or function. It can take place after injury or life experience, including psychotherapy or cultural experiences. Plasticity is greater in younger brains than older brains, due in part to younger brains' greater ability for neurogenesis, or creation of new neurons.

The Nervous System and the Endocrine System

2.24 The nervous system connects your brain with all other parts of your body through neurons.

2.25 The central nervous system consists of the brain and spinal cord, and the peripheral nervous system consists of the neurons that connect the central nervous system to other parts of the body.

2.26 The peripheral nervous system has two parts: (1) the somatic nervous system, which oversees voluntary movement; and (2) the autonomic nervous system, which oversees involuntary movement.

2.27 The autonomic nervous system consists of two divisions: (1) the sympathetic division, which revs your body up; and (2) the parasympathetic division, which calms your body down.

2.28 The endocrine system is the set of glands that uses hormones to communicate through the bloodstream to various tissues throughout the body.

2.29 Among the glands, the pituitary gland is the "master gland," which controls many systems in your body.

How We Know All of This: Viewing the Brain

2.30 Electroencephalography (EEG) is a technique that involves electrodes placed on the scalp to record electrical activity within the brain.

2.31 Computed tomography (CT) is a technique in which multiple X-rays are combined to make a 3D image of the brain.

2.32 Magnetic resonance imaging (MRI) is a technique in which magnetic fields and radio waves are used to make images of brain structures.

2.33 Positron emission tomography (PET) is a technique in which activity within various brain structures is visible after a radioactive sugar is injected into the body.

2.34 Functional magnetic resonance imaging (fMRI) is a technique in which magnetic fields are used to make images of brain activity.

KEY TERMS

neurons, p. 36
interneurons, p. 36
sensory neurons, p. 37
motor neurons, p. 37
reflex, p. 37
cell body (or soma), p. 37
axon, p. 37
axon terminals, p. 37
dendrites, p. 37
myelin sheath, p. 38
glial cells, p. 38
synapse, p. 38
neurotransmitters, p. 38
endorphins, p. 38
synaptic vesicles, p. 39
receptor sites, p. 39
reuptake, p. 39
action potential, p. 39
resting potential, p. 39
threshold, p. 39
refractory period, p. 39
localization, p. 40
brainstem, p. 41
reticular activating system, p. 41
pons, p. 41
medulla, p. 42
cerebellum, p. 42
thalamus, p. 42
limbic system, p. 42
hypothalamus, p. 42
hippocampus, p. 43
amygdala, p. 44
cerebrum (forebrain), p. 45
cerebral cortex, p. 45
association areas, p. 45
cerebral hemispheres, p. 45
corpus callosum, p. 45
split-brain surgery, p. 46
occipital lobe, p. 47
temporal lobe, p. 47
Wernicke's area, p. 47
Wernicke's aphasia, p. 47
parietal lobe, p. 47
somatosensory cortex, p. 47
frontal lobe, p. 48
motor cortex, p. 49
Broca's area, p. 49
Broca's aphasia, p. 49
plasticity, p. 50
neurogenesis, p. 50
stem cells, p. 50
nervous system, p. 53
central nervous system, p. 53
peripheral nervous system, p. 53
somatic nervous system, p. 53
autonomic nervous system, p. 53
sympathetic division, p. 53
parasympathetic division, p. 53
endocrine system, p. 54
hormones, p. 54
pituitary gland, p. 55
adrenal glands, p. 55
electroencephalography (EEG), p. 56
computed tomography (CT), p. 57
lesion, p. 57
magnetic resonance imaging (MRI), p. 57
positron emission tomography (PET), p. 57
functional magnetic resonance imaging (fMRI), p. 58

SELF-ASSESSMENT

1. The cells that facilitate communication within your nervous system are called _____.

2. What's the main function of the parasympathetic division of your autonomic nervous system?

a. to rev up your body in response to stressors
b. to calm down your body when stressors decrease
c. to control your sense of vision
d. to help you comprehend human speech

3. The _____ is the part of your limbic system most directly involved in emotion, especially fear.

a. cerebellum
b. corpus callosum
c. amygdala
d. pons

4. Compared to the brains of other species, human brains have a high proportion of _____, which are devoted to synthesizing and interpreting information rather than just taking information in.

a. association areas
b. dendrites
c. myelin sheaths
d. synaptic vesicles

5. In split-brain surgery, what gets cut?

a. the parietal lobe
b. Wernicke's area
c. the medulla
d. the corpus callosum

6. Ashley experienced a brain injury in a car accident. Since the injury, her ability to see is impaired. Damage to which lobe of Ashley's brain is most likely to be responsible for the sight impairment?

a. occipital
b. temporal
c. parietal
d. adrenal

7. Which of the following is true about your frontal lobe?

a. It is located at the back and base of your brain, near the spinal cord.
b. It is involved in complex thinking tasks, planning, and other advanced functions that many nonhuman animal species cannot perform.
c. It controls breathing and heartbeat.
d. It controls patterns of waking and sleeping.

8. Jayla experienced a brain injury as a young child. Fortunately, her brain demonstrated an ability to adapt its structure or function in response to the injury. That ability is called ______.

9. When information passes from one neuron to the next, it specifically moves through the ______ of the first neuron into the ______ of the second neuron.

a. interneurons; myelin sheath
b. receptor sites; stem cells
c. axon terminals; dendrites
d. dendrites; glial cells

10. What's the main difference between magnetic resonance imaging (MRI) and functional magnetic resonance imaging (fMRI)?

a. An MRI shows the brain's structure, but an fMRI shows the brain's activity.
b. An MRI can be conducted on the brain of any species, but an fMRI can be conducted only on human brains.
c. An MRI can only provide images of microscopic parts of the brain, but an fMRI can only provide images of the whole brain.
d. An MRI involves electrodes being placed on the head, but an fMRI does not.

To check your understanding of these questions, click show the answers in the e-book or refer to the answers in Appendix B.

Research shows quizzing is a highly effective learning tool. Continue quizzing yourself using LearningCurve, the system that adapts to *your* learning.

WHAT'S YOUR TAKE?

1. If you saw a psychotherapist, you'd probably measure your improvement by describing changes in your behaviors, thoughts, or feelings. However, those ways of assessing improvement can be difficult to quantify and vulnerable to subjectivity. Would measuring changes in your brain be better? There are plenty of research studies that show how psychotherapy changes the brain, but in the "real world" of outpatient psychotherapy—counseling centers, clinics, private practice offices—measuring progress with brain imaging technology is still rare (Barsaglini et al., 2014; Etkin et al., 2005; Weingarten & Strauman, 2015). As the years go by, however, it may become more common, especially if scanning equipment becomes more convenient and less expensive. If you were the client, how would you want your therapy progress to be measured—by changes that a scanner detects in your brain, or by changes that you notice in your day-to-day behaviors, thoughts, or feelings? What are the pros and cons of each?

2. Increasingly, lawyers use brain images to defend their clients in court (Bonnie & Scott, 2013; Farah, 2010; Meixner, 2015; Teitcher, 2011). In three recent court cases, juries deciding whether a convicted killer should receive the death penalty were provided (by the defendant's attorneys) PET scans, MRIs, and fMRIs of the killer's brain. In each case, experts explained that those images illustrated a variety of abnormalities involving parts of the brain such as the frontal lobe, amygdala, cerebellum, and corpus callosum, among others. In two cases, the jury decided against the death penalty. In one, the jury decided for the death penalty (Miller, 2013). If you were on the jury, how much impact would brain scan evidence have on you? Would it matter if the crime was murder or something less serious? Would it matter if you were determining guilt or sentencing someone who had already been found guilty?

SHOW ME MORE

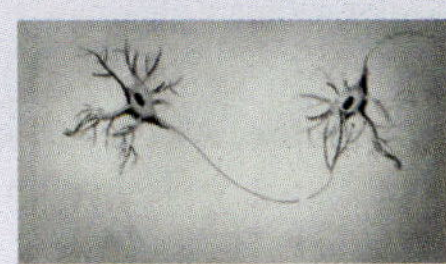

2.1 How Neurons Work

In this video, experts provide a detailed explanation of how neurons work, including explanations of action potential and how some psychiatric drugs work.
Macmillan Learning

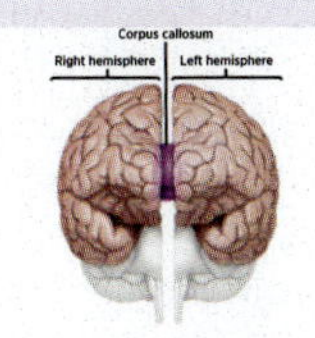

2.2 A Split-Brain Patient

http://tiny.cc/showmemore2e

In this video, a patient who underwent split-brain surgery explains and illustrates the effect of the surgery on their functioning.
Macmillan Learning

This video is hosted by a third-party Web site (source). For accessible content requests, please reach out to the publisher of that site.

2.3 My Psychology Podcast

This podcast episode features the author of this textbook, psychologist Andy Pomerantz, speaking with other instructors of introductory psychology courses about the most important and interesting concepts in this chapter.
Macmillan Learning

3 Sensation and Perception

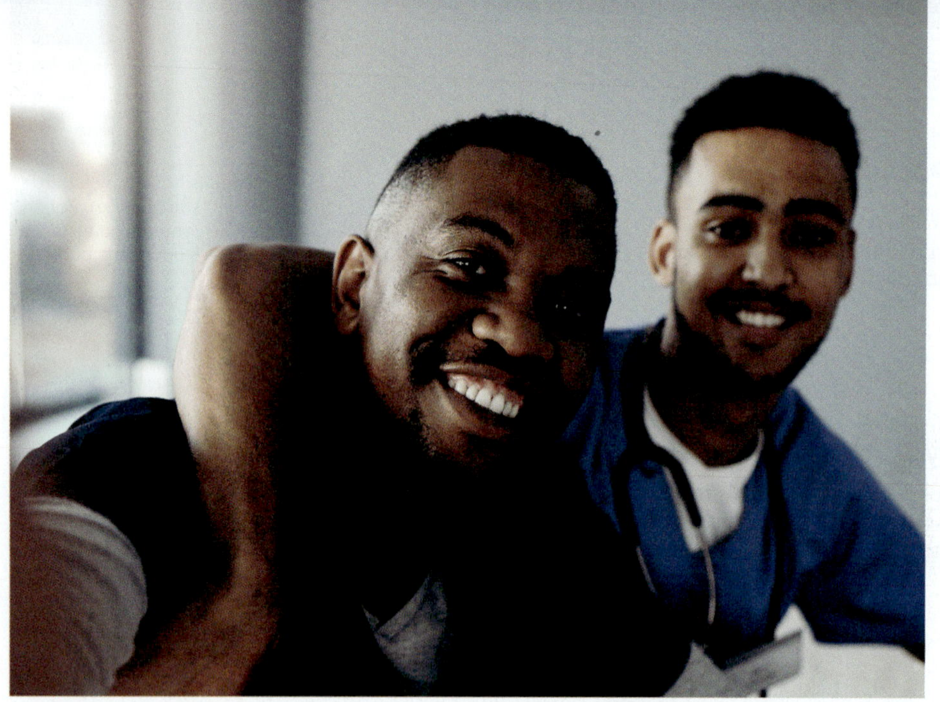

PeopleImages/E+/Getty Images

CHAPTER OUTLINE

Let's talk about microwave popcorn.

Specifically, let's talk about how you *sense* and *perceive* microwave popcorn. There's plenty for your sensory organs to take in: your eyes see the bag gradually expanding through the front window of the microwave; your ears hear the sounds of one kernel, then a few more, then lots of kernels popping; your nose smells that familiar, mouthwatering popcorn aroma; your fingers feel the scorching hot bag as you pull it open; and your tongue tastes the salty, buttery, yummy flavor of each piece. As all that *sensation* takes place, there's *perception* happening too, which is your brain's remarkable ability to attach meaning to all those raw sensations. Your brain doesn't just detect all of that sensory information; it also interprets what it detects. That way, you can use that information to understand what's going on around you (popcorn's ready!) and help you decide how to respond (get a big bowl!).

In this chapter, we will examine how your sensory organs (eyes, ears, nose, tongue, and skin) cooperate with your brain to sense and perceive the world around you — not just microwave popcorn, but everything. We will explore your ability to notice new sensations and stop noticing old ones. We will explore the way your senses interact with each other, as well as the impact your expectations and previous experiences can have on what you perceive. And we'll take an in-depth look at the specific senses of vision, hearing, smell, taste, and touch.

The Fundamentals of Sensation and Perception

Sensation and perception determine how we take in and make sense of the world around us. Let's begin our discussion by defining and distinguishing between these two concepts.

YOU WILL LEARN:

3.1 the difference between sensation and perception.

3.2 how evolution has influenced sensation and perception.

3.3 about the thresholds that mark the limits of sensory abilities.

3.4 how your senses adapt to unchanging stimuli.

3.5 how your perception deals with changing stimuli.

3.6 how simultaneous input from multiple senses can result in competition or integration.

3.7 how expectations and experiences can affect what you sense and perceive.

The Difference Between Sensation and Perception

Sensation is the ability of your sensory organs to pick up energy in the environment around you and transmit it to your brain. It's the way you absorb the information your surroundings have to offer. Because sensation happens so quickly and so automatically, you might take it for granted. To better appreciate how your body and brain do it, think about the ways your smartphone constantly "senses" its surroundings. It senses whether an Internet signal is present, and if so, how strong it is. It senses whether a cellular signal (for phone calls and texts) is present, and if so, how strong it is. It senses whether a Bluetooth device is in range to connect. Your body's senses work in very much the same way. Your eyes, ears, nose, tongue, and skin are constantly monitoring the environment, sending messages to your brain about what they detect around you.

An essential step in sensation is **transduction**: the conversion of energy outside your body, like light or sound, into neural energy, like brain activity. Transduction explains how that yellow banana on the table becomes a yellow banana *image* in your brain. Transduction explains how the blaring horn of an oncoming truck becomes a blaring horn *sound* in your brain. This process is much like when your phone's camera uses transduction to make a photo of an object, or when voicemail uses transduction to make a recording of a human voice. In a similar way, your senses and brain use transduction to make mental representations of what happens around you (Eatock, 2010; Gegenfurtner, 2010; Levine, 2001).

Be Good/Shutterstock

The sensations that your eyes and ears take in, including the colors of a lady bug, become perceptions when you begin to make sense of what they are.

Sensation, for both your phone and your body, involves only the detection of available information. What happens to that information next is **perception**: the ability of your brain to interpret the raw sensations it has taken in. Perception is your brain's ability to translate the sights, sounds, and smells into something meaningful or understandable. For example, if you're outside, your eyes may detect small, flying, bright objects — one that's red with black dots, another with yellow and black stripes, and yet another that glows off and on. Those sights are initially taken in through your eyes as simple sensations — colors and patterns.

Those sensations become perceptions when you start comprehending what they are. Rather than isolated or unfamiliar sights (or sounds, smells, etc.), perceptions are things you recognize and put into context. You might see that little red-and-black flying object and say, "Ooh, that's a ladybug!" You might see that one with the yellow and black stripes and say, "Look out, there's a bee!" And when the sun goes down and you see the one that glows, you might say, "Cool, a firefly!" Each of those statements requires that you perceive what those visual stimuli are, and what they mean. That's the difference between sensation and perception. Sensation is more passive, simply detecting information from the environment and making it available to your brain. Perception is more active, transforming that sensory information into something meaningful you can use.

The Evolution of Sensation and Perception. Sensation and perception *evolved*. Throughout human history, survival of the fittest often meant survival of those whose abilities to sense and perceive the world were most advanced. As a result, your brain devotes a lot of space and energy to sensation and perception. (Recall from Chapter 2 how many parts of the brain are involved in seeing, hearing, smell, taste, and touch.) So, it's clear that sensation and perception must serve an important purpose

sensation
The ability of the sensory organs to pick up energy in the environment around the body and transmit it to the brain.

transduction
The conversion of energy outside the body, like light or sound, into neural energy, like brain activity.

perception
The ability of the brain to interpret the raw sensations it has taken in.

extrasensory perception (ESP) The controversial notion of perception without sensation.

parapsychology The study of topics that fall outside the range of mainstream psychology.

absolute threshold The minimum level of a stimulus necessary for a person to detect its presence at least half of the time.

(Huber & Wilkinson, 2010). Many psychologists have argued that the important purpose is to help us respond to the world in ways that keep us alive. By accurately sensing and perceiving the world around us, our ancestors could take actions that increased their chances of survival (Zanker, 2010). Remember that example about the banana? Once you sense it and perceive it, you can reach for it, peel it, and eat it. Remember that example about the blaring horn of an oncoming truck? Once you sense it and perceive it, you can jump out of its path. Both of those actions help you survive.

Interestingly, the sensation and perception abilities of various species in the animal kingdom match perfectly with the kinds of sights, sounds, and other sensory stimuli that increase their survival chances (Snodderly, 2018). For example, elephants' ears are perfectly suited for picking up low-frequency sounds, like the rumble of a rival pack of elephants a long distance away. Insects' ears, by contrast, are perfectly suited for picking up higher-frequency sounds, such as the rapidly flapping wings of another insect just a centimeter away (McBurney, 2010a). Frogs have specialized cells within their eyes that serve as bug detectors — their only function is to spot small, quick-moving objects within range of the frog's jutting tongue and send a message straight to the part of the frog's brain that controls prey catching (Ewert, 1987; Goodale & Humphrey, 2001). Our own human ancestors may have developed color vision capabilities to enable them to better detect which fruits were ripe, as well as slight changes in other people's skin color (e.g., getting red in the face) that could indicate anger (Changizi et al., 2006; Dominy & Lucas, 2001; Greenlee et al., 2018; Jacobs, 2009; Nakajima et al., 2017; Regan et al., 2001).

Extrasensory Perception (ESP) and Parapsychology. As you read the words *sensation* and *perception*, you may be reminded of the term **extrasensory perception (ESP)**: the controversial notion of perception without sensation. Believers in ESP claim that it can supposedly take a number of forms: "mental telepathy," in which a person supposedly knows another person's thoughts through mind reading; "clairvoyance," in which a person can supposedly know what will happen in the future by merely imagining it; and a special ability to supposedly perceive ghosts that can't be seen, heard, or otherwise sensed by other people. As scientists, psychologists largely reject the notion of ESP. The controversy about ESP therefore pits psychologists against people who deal in **parapsychology**: the study of topics that fall outside the range of mainstream psychology. Parapsychology overlaps a lot with *pseudopsychology* (as discussed in Chapter 1), psychological information that is not supported by science but may appear to be.

Believers may call ESP a sixth sense, but scientists, including psychologists, who have studied it almost uniformly conclude that ESP is not a legitimate sense (McBurney, 2010b).

Thresholds: What Your Senses Can and Cannot Do

Even though your sensation and perception abilities are highly evolved, they do have limits.

Absolute Threshold. For one of your senses to notice something, there has to be enough of that something to detect. In other words, the amount has to exceed the **absolute threshold**: the minimum level of a stimulus necessary for you to detect its presence at least half of the time (**Figure 3.1**). In a silent room you would hear a dog barking, but could you hear it breathing? On a pitch-black night, you would see the brake lights of a car 100 feet ahead of yours, but could you see them a mile ahead? If you were drinking water, you would certainly notice if someone had dropped a spoonful of salt into it, but could you notice a single granule of salt? All of these are questions of absolute threshold.

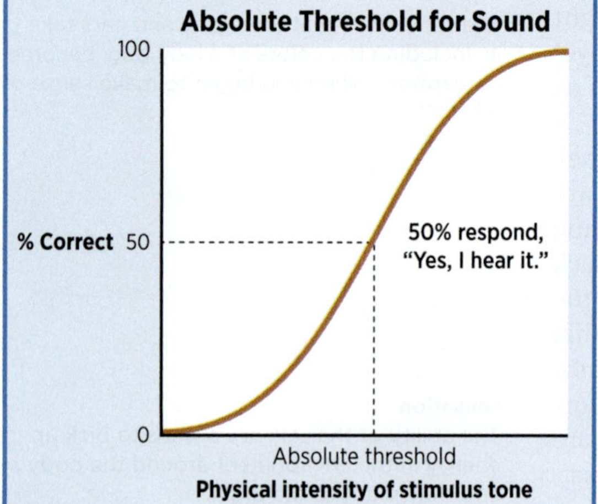

FIGURE 3.1 Absolute Threshold. Absolute threshold is the point at which the intensity of the stimulus (for example, the brightness of the light or the loudness of the sound) is strong enough to be detected at least 50% of the time.

So what *is* the absolute threshold for each human sense?

You might expect psychologists to have determined the specific measures of absolute threshold for each of our senses. However, these numbers vary so broadly from person to person, and even from situation to situation for the same person, that pinpointing any particular amount would be an oversimplification. For example, a common estimate of the absolute threshold of frequency for hearing is around 20 hertz (Krumbholz et al., 2000; Moller & Pedersen, 2004; Pressnitzer et al., 2001). But it can depend on quite a few factors. For example: (1) Women generally hear better than men (although men may hear better at the lowest frequencies). (2) Young adults generally hear better than older adults. (3) Hearing loss happens at a higher rate in White Americans than Black Americans. (4) Hearing tends to be worse in people who use firearms, smoke heavily, work for long periods near loud machinery or construction equipment, or have diabetes (Agrawal et al., 2008, 2009; Dement et al., 2018; Feder et al., 2017; Helzner et al., 2005; Morrell et al., 1996; Pearson et al., 1995).

DIVERSITY MATTERS

Absolute threshold for smell can also depend on numerous factors. For example: (1) Younger adults have more sensitive noses than older adults. (2) Women have more sensitive noses than men (even as newborns). (3) Women's sense of smell is most sensitive during ovulation. (4) People who are depressed, or even temporarily sad, often show decreased sensitivity to smell (Doty et al., 1985; Doty & Kamath, 2014; Flohr et al., 2017; Pause et al., 1996). Further, absolute threshold for all senses depends on a person's motivations and expectations in the moment: you're more likely to notice a sound, sight, or smell when you are instructed to seek it out ("What's that noise?" "Can you smell that?"), but more likely to miss it if no one calls your attention to it (Pagliano, 2012).

DIVERSITY MATTERS

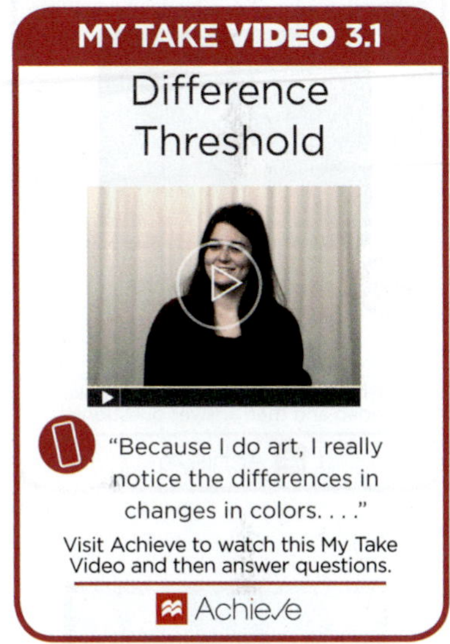

MY TAKE VIDEO 3.1
Difference Threshold
"Because I do art, I really notice the differences in changes in colors. . . ."
Visit Achieve to watch this My Take Video and then answer questions.
Achieve

Difference Threshold. Absolute threshold revolves around a common question regarding sensation: *is it there?* Another common question occurs when you know it's there, but you wonder, *has it changed?* That question involves the **difference threshold** (or **just noticeable difference**): the smallest change in a stimulus necessary for you to detect it at least half of the time. When the difference is well above this threshold — like the obvious difference between your phone screen at its minimum and maximum brightness settings — it's easy to notice. And when the difference is well below this threshold — like the tiny difference in yellowness between two yellow sticky notes from the same pack — it's impossible to notice.

The most interesting difference threshold questions are the ones for which the answer is not so obvious. For example, imagine that your flashlight is gradually getting dimmer over the course of several hours as its batteries run down. How much brightness will the flashlight have to lose before your eyes notice? Or maybe your old freezer has started to wear out. How many degrees will the temperature have to rise before you notice a difference in the coldness of ice cream on your tongue?

Like absolute threshold, difference threshold for various senses depends on a number of factors, often including age and gender (Kidd, 2010). Another important variable is experience. Specifically, we are much better at detecting differences in things with which we have plenty of experience (Green & Bavelier, 2007; Li et al., 2006). For example, if you drink a lot of cola, you may have a strong preference for a certain brand (Coke vs. Pepsi), type (diet vs. caffeine-free vs. regular), or even container (aluminum can vs. plastic bottle vs. glass bottle vs. fountain drink). A prerequisite for that preference is a low difference threshold, which can come from a lifetime of cola drinking. If you rarely drink cola, your difference threshold is likely to be much higher — essentially, they all taste the same to you.

The difference threshold for a particular stimulus is somewhat predictable according to the *Weber–Fechner law*, which is named after Ernst Heinrich Weber and Gustav Theodor Fechner, two early psychology researchers who studied the topic in the 1800s (Hoagland, 1930; Sobkowicz et al., 2013). The Weber–Fechner law states that the difference threshold is proportional to the amount of the stimulus present in the first place. The bigger the original amount, the bigger the difference will have to be for you to notice. For example, imagine that you frequently order small french fries from

difference threshold (just noticeable difference)
The smallest change in a stimulus necessary for a person to detect it at least half of the time.

sensory adaptation
The tendency of a person's sensation of a stimulus to decrease when the stimulus remains constant.

perceptual constancy
The brain's ability to maintain the same perception of an object even when conditions around it cause it to produce different sensations.

selective attention
When the brain pays more attention to one sensory channel than others.

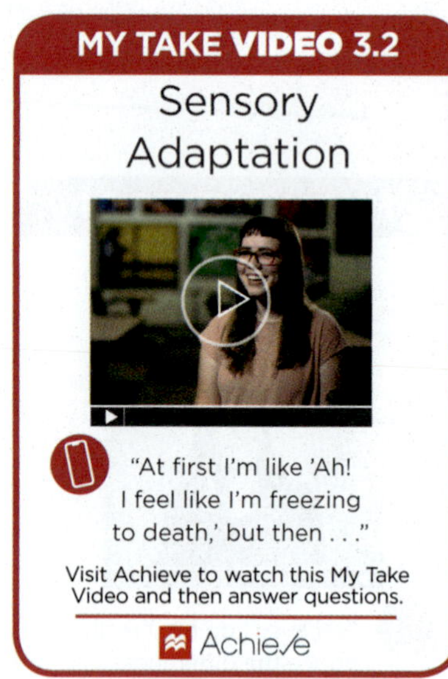
MY TAKE VIDEO 3.2
Sensory Adaptation
"At first I'm like 'Ah! I feel like I'm freezing to death,' but then . . ."
Visit Achieve to watch this My Take Video and then answer questions.
Achieve

the same restaurant drive-through. If they give you a large order by mistake, you'll probably notice the difference in weight as soon as you grab the bag, even though that difference may be just few ounces. But if you frequently bench-press 100 pounds, it will take much more than an ounce of extra weight — at least a couple of pounds, probably — for you to notice the extra weight.

Sensory Adaptation. In our discussion of difference thresholds, our focus was on sensory stimuli changing, but what about when stimuli stay the same? In those situations, you experience **sensory adaptation**: the tendency of your sensation of a stimulus to decrease when the stimulus remains constant. When you see, hear, or feel the same unchanging thing for a long time, you get used to it and eventually stop noticing it (He, 2010; Webster, 2010). (Sensory adaptation often goes hand in hand with *habituation* — when you decrease or stop *responding* to a stimulus that repeats or stays constant.) As an example of sensory adaptation, think about what you hear as the car you're in starts to drive on a highway. When the car accelerates on the entrance ramp, you hear the engine rev louder until you reach, say, 60 miles per hour. But if the car stays at 60 mph for a long time (like it would on cruise control), you'll stop noticing the sound of the engine. Of course, the engine is still making the same amount of noise as when the car first reached 60 mph, but you have become accustomed to the constant hum. Another example: You walk into a bakery and immediately smell the strong, wonderful fragrance of fresh-baked bread. But if you work in that bakery, by the time your 8-hour shift is over, you don't smell bread at all, even though every new customer does. See the From Research to Real Life box on page 70 for more about sensory adaptation and variety as a key to happiness.

Perceptual Constancy. Sometimes, the raw input that your senses detect may appear to change even when the object you're sensing actually stays the same. You have a remarkable ability to recognize that the object remains unchanged even though it may look, sound, or otherwise seem different (Goldstein, 2010a). This is **perceptual constancy**: your brain's ability to maintain the same perception of an object even when conditions around it cause it to produce different sensations (**Figure 3.2**). For example, imagine you're playing kickball and you're deep in the outfield. A powerful kicker sends a high pop-up your way. When it first leaves the kicker's foot, that red rubber ball looks tiny from your spot in the field. As it soars toward you, however, the ball seems to get bigger and bigger until your whole field of vision is nearly filled with the red ball when it reaches you. According to the sensation your eyes detect and send to your brain, that ball got bigger during its flight in your direction, but your brain converts that changing *sensation* into a constant *perception*. Your brain knows that red rubber ball is the same size whether it's leaving the kicker's foot or landing in your arms.

FIGURE 3.2 Perceptual Constancy. As this tablet tilts downward, the image it casts on your eye changes. It becomes increasingly narrow until it is eventually just a horizontal line. Thanks to perceptual constancy, however, you know that the tablet retains the same rectangular shape no matter how upright it is (Goldstein, 2010a).

Sensory Overload: When Senses Compete for Your Attention

Your senses don't take turns. They work concurrently, which means they send simultaneous messages to your brain. Somehow, your brain has to decide how to prioritize or blend all of this sensory input. Let's explore how that happens.

Selective Attention. With so much sensory information steadily arriving from your eyes, ears, nose, tongue, and skin, your brain constantly makes decisions about which sense to focus on (Dosher & Lu, 2010; Knudsen, 2018). Your brain often meets this challenge through **selective attention**: paying more attention to one sensory channel than others. Selective attention is necessary in most situations, especially those that engage all of your senses simultaneously. Consider a carnival, county fair, or state fair. Your eyes take in the sights of rides, games, animals, clowns, and crowds. Your nose takes in the smells of cotton candy and kettle corn. Your tongue takes in the tastes of funnel cake and fresh-squeezed lemonade. Your skin takes in the heat of the warm sun. But your friend is trying to ask you something, so just for the moment, your brain uses selective attention to "turn down" the inputs from your eyes, nose, tongue, and skin and "turn up" the input from your ears. All of those sensations are still coming through, of course, but some aren't registering as strongly as before. After you hear your friend say, "Ferris wheel next?" and you agree, your conversation ends. As you start walking together in that direction, your brain stops selectively attending to your hearing and returns to attending to all of your senses. (By the way, sometimes you boost your brain's selective attention ability by deliberately blocking off one of your senses, as when you choose to close your eyes to concentrate on a phone call or music.)

Sometimes, the competition for your brain's attention comes from two things being detected by the same sense. Like at the carnival – your friend's voice would not be the only sound you'd hear when they speak. At the same moment, your ears take in the shouts of kids on nearby rides, the music drifting out of the carousel, the chirps of birds flying above, and many other noises. The power to hear your friend in spite of all of this auditory competition is called the **cocktail party effect**: the ability to attend to certain stimuli within one sense (such as hearing) over other stimuli within the same sense.

cocktail party effect
The ability to attend to certain stimuli within one sense (such as hearing) over other stimuli within the same sense.

sensory interaction
The idea that the senses can influence each other.

The cocktail party effect got its name from the common experience of being in a crowded party, surrounded by loud conversations in all directions but focusing your attention only on the person in front of you (Cherry, 1953). An interesting thing often happens in such situations – you catch something meaningful, often personal, in a conversation you thought you were tuning out (Loebach et al., 2010; Wood & Cowan, 1995; Yost, 2001). For example, imagine you're at a party talking to a small group of friends and you hear someone in a nearby group mention your name (or your friend's name, your hometown, or anything else personally relevant to you). In fact, your name seems to jump out of that conversation, even though none of the words before it even seemed to register. But it's obvious that the sounds register at least at some shallow level, because you must be processing them enough to determine if they are personally meaningful to you.

One study found that the underlying principle of the cocktail party effect – that we pay more attention to what is personally meaningful – may be true even when we are not fully conscious. Researchers used two different methods to wake up surgery patients as their anesthesia began to wear off after surgery. In one method, the patients heard a repeating message through headphones every 10 seconds: "Patient, open your eyes." In the other method, the patients heard the same message at the same rate, but with the patient's own name replacing the word "patient" (for example, "Casey, open your eyes"). When the researchers used names, patients opened their eyes and regained consciousness significantly faster than when the researchers used "patient" (Jung et al., 2017). If you ever woke up someone by adding their name when you said "Wake up," perhaps you benefited from this strategy!

Humans are the only species who go to cocktail parties, but we're not the only ones who demonstrate the cocktail party effect. Researchers have identified many animals, including insects, birds, and more, who display a remarkable ability to pay attention to one sound while ignoring others (Bee & Micheyl, 2008; Brumm & Slabbekoorn, 2005). In a swamp full of dozens of different frog species, female frogs have an uncanny ability to pick out the mating calls from males of their own species (Gerhardt & Bee, 2006; Hulse, 2002). Bats, who rely on the echo of their own voice to determine exactly where to fly, somehow distinguish their own voice from the racket created by hundreds of nearby bat voices in the same cave (Moss & Surlykke, 2001). And in a crowded colony with hundreds of penguins, baby penguins have a remarkable ability to zoom in on the call of a parent above the constant call of all the other penguins, even when the parent is far away and relatively quiet (Aubin & Jouventin, 1998, 2002).

AWL Images/Masterfile

The cocktail party effect is your ability to attend to certain stimuli within one sense (such as hearing) over other stimuli within the same sense. Other species have this ability, too, including baby penguins, who can pick out the voices of their parents in a loud crowd (Aubin & Jouventin, 1998, 2002).

Sensory Interaction. Sometimes it's not about choosing one sensation over others – as illustrated by selective attention and the cocktail party effect – but about blending sensations. When that blending happens, sensations can affect each other in interesting ways. **Sensory interaction** is the idea that your senses can influence

FROM RESEARCH TO REAL LIFE

Variety, the Key to Happiness?

When you can't escape the rattle of a noisy air conditioner or the stench of a nearby trashcan, you're rooting for sensory adaptation to kick in. After a (hopefully short) time, you get used to it and don't notice how bad it is. But you're rooting *against* sensory adaptation when you do things we enjoy. You don't want the tenth bite of cake or the tenth sniff of freshly brewed coffee to be any less pleasurable than the first.

A team of psychologists offers a theory of happiness—the hedonic adaptation prevention model—that addresses this issue of sensory adaptation for things we enjoy (Fritz et al., 2017; Galak & Redden, 2018; Sheldon et al., 2012; Sylvester et al., 2018). According to this model, variety keeps most people happy. Repeatedly experiencing *different* enjoyable things prevents sensory adaptation from kicking in. (Check the name of the theory closely—it's all about "adaptation prevention.") Too often, researchers say, most people strive for happiness by seeking out the things that provided it in the past. The downside to "more of the same" is that sensory adaptation may have diminished our sensitivity to it; at the same time, expectations for happiness from it have gone up. The solution might be variety.

These researchers asked undergraduate participants to list acts of kindness they could perform (Sheldon et al., 2012). They came up with a varied list, including doing chores for roommates, lending books to classmates, cooking dinner for friends, and allowing cars to merge in front of them on the highway. The researchers then told them to do these kind acts for the next 10 weeks, but with a catch: half were told they had to stick with the same single kind act each week, while the other half were told to vary their kind acts each week so the acts wouldn't be repeated. At the end of 10 weeks, the high-variety group reported much higher levels of happiness than the low-variety group. In fact, the low-variety group was less happy than when the study began (a finding that could also partially reflect other factors, like the stress of an ongoing semester). The take-home message is this: in your own day-to-day life, it may be the *variety* of enjoyable activities, rather than repeatedly doing the same few over and over, that underlies your happiness. •

Melpomene/Shutterstock.com

According to the hedonic adaptation prevention model, variety increases happiness by limiting sensory adaptation to the things you like (Sheldon et al., 2012).

each other. One obvious example of sensory interaction is ventriloquism—when a performer (usually a comedian) gives voice to a dummy. You hear words that coordinate with the timing of the dummy's mouth moving (rather than the ventriloquist's mouth), and perceive that the dummy is talking, at least until you remind yourself that dummies can't talk. What you see influences what (you think) you hear. A similar thing happens when you watch a movie in a theater with speakers positioned on the sides of the room—you perceive the dialogue as coming from the mouths of the actors on the screen directly in front of you, when in reality it is coming from your left and right (Shams, 2010).

When sensory inputs don't match—as when overdubs in a movie don't match the mouth movements of the actors—we often experience the *McGurk effect*, in which the words we perceive others saying are influenced by our vision as well as our hearing (MacDonald, 2018; Moore, 2012; Soto-Faraco & Alsius, 2009; Summerfield, 1992). In the classic study that identified the McGurk effect, researchers created a brief video in which participants *heard* a person saying "ma ma" but simultaneously *saw* that person's lips form the sound "ta ta." In this particular case, many participants reported hearing "na na"—a curious and distinct blend of what they saw and what they heard (McGurk & MacDonald, 1976). In other cases, what goes in your eyes actually overrides what goes in your ears, and you report "hearing" what you see (perhaps with some influence of what you hear), even though the sound clearly differs from the sight.

The power that vision has over our other senses is illustrated not only by the McGurk effect but by many other situations as well (Zellner, 2013). For example, researchers have found that vision can influence and even transcend taste. In a study about candy, participants who ate lemon drops that had been colored purple frequently made the mistake of reporting that the candy had a grape taste

(Doty, 2010; Zellner et al., 1991). In a study of beverages, participants who drank a cherry-flavored drink that was colored orange often mistakenly labeled the flavor of the drink as orange (Zellner, 2010).

Some researchers have theorized that sensory interaction can, under certain circumstances, lead to feelings of queasiness and nausea. This idea is **sensory conflict theory**: a theory that states that motion sickness is a byproduct of sensory interaction. Sensory conflict theory is certainly not the only explanation of motion sickness, and there is research both supporting and disputing it (Oman, 1990; Stoffregen & Riccio, 1991; Warwick-Evans et al., 1998; Yardley, 1992). Basically, sensory conflict theory suggests that you feel sick when you are moving and what you see doesn't match what you otherwise sense, especially within your body in terms of balance, position, and touch (Bos et al., 2008; D'Amour et al., 2017). That's why you're at greater risk for motion sickness when you read, watch a screen, or close your eyes as a passenger in a moving car. Your eyes tell your brain you're sitting still, but your bodily senses tell your brain you're zooming ahead, slowing down, turning left, or turning right as your body leans due to the car's movements.

Chuck Wagner/Shutterstock.com

When multiple senses interact, vision has an especially strong impact. The color of a food or drink can strongly influence the way you perceive its taste.

Bottom-Up and Top-Down Processing

When you were a newborn baby, every sight, sound, smell, taste, and touch was new. You experienced the world purely through **bottom-up processing**: a way of processing information in which what you sense becomes a perception with no influence of expectations or previous experiences. With each passing day, however, you gained life experience, which you stored away as memories. Soon your mind was no longer a blank slate but full of expectations for what you might sense in any given situation. Those expectations then began to *shape* what you perceived, in much the same way that you can guess the ends of your best friend's sentences because your previous conversations have taught you what they tend to say. This is **top-down processing**: a way of processing information in which your expectations or previous experiences influence what you perceive.

Your current day-to-day experience involves a combination of bottom-up and top-down processing (Chun & Wolfe, 2001; Lewkowicz, 2010). In less familiar situations — like when you eat somewhere that features tastes, smells, sights, and sounds from a part of the world you've never seen — it's more bottom-up processing. In more familiar situations — like when you eat somewhere very familiar where you've learned exactly what to expect — it's more top-down processing.

Sometimes, both types of processing are easy to identify. Imagine that your friend Jaylin leaves your house to drive home, a 15-minute trip. The weather is terrible, so as you say goodbye, you tell Jaylin, "Text me when you get there." About 15 minutes later, a text comes through. Instantly, some bottom-up processing happens — you feel your phone vibrate against your skin or your ear picks up the sound of the text alert. These are sensations you would experience even if you had no expectation of an incoming text around that time. But you do have expectations, so almost as instantly, some top-down processing happens too. Even before you can raise the phone up to read the text, speculations flash into your mind: "It's probably Jaylin letting me know they made it home." The point is that your top-down processing uses expectations and experience to predict what you might see even before you actually see it, and sometimes those predictions can influence what you see (or think you see).

Top-down processing comes into play when you listen to digital music too. The sounds entering your ears are actually tiny, microsecond bits of sound alternating with tiny, microsecond bits of silence. Your top-down processing allows you to fill in the blanks, since the surrounding sounds tell you what to expect (Moore, 2010). The same thing happens in a more obvious way when you're on a phone call in which the other person's voice cuts in and out. You use top-down processing to guess, often with impressive accuracy, what words filled the seconds you couldn't catch (Loebach et al., 2010).

sensory conflict theory
The theory that explains motion sickness as a byproduct of sensory interaction.

bottom-up processing
A way of processing information in which what a person senses becomes a perception with no influence of expectations or previous experiences.

top-down processing
A way of processing information in which expectations or previous experiences influence what a person perceives.

IT'S LIKE...

Top-Down Processing Is Like Autocomplete

When you type the first few letters of a text into your phone, the phone's autocomplete (or autofill) feature offers to complete the word for you. The same thing happens when you google something—your computer guesses the rest of the word or phrase you might be typing. It's as if it knows what to expect, based on what you have typed in the past. Your brain uses top-down processing much like your devices use this autocomplete feature. Your brain knows what you might be sensing, based on what you have sensed in the past.

Of course, neither autocomplete nor top-down processing can function alone. Your phone or computer combines its top-down expectations with the bottom-up processing of the first few letters you actually type in, just as your brain combines its top-down expectations with the first few milliseconds of a sound sent to your ear (Carlson, 2010). The main point here is that it is not bottom-up processing alone that creates your sensation, but a combination of that bottom-up processing with the top-down processing that it triggers.

There is one important distinction between the way your devices and your brain do top-down processing: your phone gives you the *option* to autocomplete your words and phrases, but your brain doesn't always make it optional. In fact, sometimes, your brain acts like an autocomplete feature with too much power, jumping to a conclusion about what you're sensing before you've had a chance to fully sense it. For example, if you're expecting an important delivery to arrive in the mail, your brain might use "autocomplete" to convert a quick glance out the front window at a small white truck with red and blue trim to the conclusion that your delivery is here. But that might be a random white truck with red and blue trim, not the USPS mail truck, driving by. That's the double-edged sword of top-down processing—it offers shortcuts that can be helpful when accurate, but problematic when premature. •

FIGURE 3.3 Top-Down Processing and Perceptual Set. Is the number in the middle eleven or two? If you read across, so that the numerals are Hindu-Arabic, it looks like eleven. But if you read down, so that the numerals are Roman, it looks like two. This illustrates how the context around a stimulus influences your top-down processing and your perceptual set.

Perceptual Set. Top-down processing is a major contributor to your **perceptual set**: your tendency to perceive things in a certain way because of your previous experiences or your attention strategy (**Figure 3.3**). Your perceptual set helps you know what to expect, to quickly assess a situation, especially the parts of it that are most important to you, rather than slowly and methodically examining every detail as if it were unlike anything you'd ever encountered before. For example, consider how the perceptual set influenced the reaction of Hillary Anderson, a witness to the 2013 Boston Marathon bombing, when she heard the first of the terrorists' bombs explode near the finish line: "I remember looking up, looking for planes. I remember exactly where I was during 9/11, and my first instinct was to look up and see what was coming" (*New York Times*, 2013).

Change Blindness and Inattentional Blindness. Often, your perceptual set offers shortcuts that are beneficial, allowing you to extract the information you need more quickly and accurately than you could if you didn't have any particular expectations or goals in that moment. But sometimes, your perceptual set can be quite misleading. For example, consider **change blindness**: a failure to notice changes in your visual field simply because you expect otherwise. Some of the first instances of change blindness happened in Hollywood movies made back in the 1930s, when scenes were spliced together by literally cutting and pasting clips of film reels. Sometimes, two pasted-together clips would include blatant mistakes, like an actor delivering the first few words of a line with one shirt button open and the last few words of the same line with two shirt buttons open, because the two takes were recorded on different days. The interesting thing is not that these editing mistakes happened, but that almost none of the filmmakers or audience members noticed them (Rensink, 2010). The same kinds of continuity errors still happen today, and most of us are blind to these changes (until viral video clips point them out to us).

Closely related to change blindness is **inattentional blindness**: a failure to notice something in your visual field simply because your attention was focused elsewhere. With change blindness, you fail to see an item change, but with inattentional blindness, you fail to see the item *at all* (Mack, 2003; Rensink, 2000, 2013). For example, a distracted driver whose full attention is devoted to reading a text from a friend might completely fail to see a stop sign, even though that stop sign falls within the driver's field of vision. Similarly dangerous things are true for pedestrians too: numerous studies have found that people using smartphones to text (or for other purposes) make risky, often life-threatening street-crossing decisions and fail to notice "Don't Walk" signs at

perceptual set
The tendency to perceive things in a certain way because of a person's previous experiences or attention strategy.

change blindness
The failure to notice changes in the visual field simply because a person expects otherwise.

inattentional blindness
The failure to notice something in your visual field simply because your attention was focused elsewhere.

significantly higher rates than pedestrians who are not using a smartphone at all (Lin et al., 2017; Schwebel et al., 2012).

Change blindness and inattentional blindness have been the focus of much psychological research (Simons & Levin, 1997; Simons & Rensink, 2005). They also have serious implications for some real-world issues. For example, change blindness or inattentional blindness can undermine the validity of eyewitness testimony in a courtroom trial (Davies & Hine, 2007; Hyman et al., 2018; Jaeger et al., 2017). They can influence what police officers or security guards see and don't see when they monitor situations (Davis et al., 2018; Durlach, 2004; Graham et al., 2018). They can also affect what players and officials see during sporting events (Pazzona et al., 2018; Werner & Thies, 2000).

Some of the research on change blindness and inattentional blindness focuses on the role of distraction. Specifically, when your eye is drawn toward one part of a scene, how likely are you to miss something — even something big — in another part of the scene? One influential study used a "mudsplash" technique to illustrate how surprisingly strong change blindness and inattentional blindness can be. They showed participants a photo for three seconds and then "splashed" the photo for a fraction of a second with several small splotches at random places on the screen (to simulate a mudsplash on a car windshield). At the same time as the mudsplash, the experimenters also changed something else in the photo, and that new photo remained on the screen for 3 more seconds. When the change from photo 1 to photo 2 was blatantly obvious, most participants noticed it in spite of the mudsplashes. But when the change was moderate (completely noticeable without mudsplashes), most participants had to watch the sequence two or more times before they saw it. In about a quarter of these moderate cases, the changes were not seen at all, even after many repetitions (O'Regan et al., 1999). These findings have implications for numerous real-world activities, including drivers who miss something important on the road in front of them when something hits their windshield or their attention is otherwise drawn to just one part of their field of vision (Simons & Ambinder, 2005).

In another study of change blindness and inattentional blindness, researchers showed a video of two groups of people, some in white shirts and some in black shirts, passing basketballs back and forth within their groups. As the two groups weaved in and out of each other's paths, participants were told to count the number of passes made by the group in white shirts. A few seconds in, a person in a gorilla suit wandered into the scene, stopped in the middle of the players, did some chest-thumping, and then walked off. At the end of the 20-second scene, most participants accurately reported the number of passes made by the group in white shirts, but about half (!) completely failed to notice the person in the gorilla suit. Their concentration on the passes made them oblivious to other things happening in the scene that they weren't looking for (Simon & Chabris, 1999). The take-home message from these change blindness and inattentional blindness studies is this: when you allocate your attention to certain sensations (like using your phone while driving), you are surprisingly vulnerable to missing other sensations completely, no matter how obvious they might be.

LIFE HACK 3.1

When you're driving, minimize any potential distractions (like glancing at a phone) that might cause change blindness or inattentional blindness like mudsplashes do. In a very short time, you could fail to see something important and potentially dangerous.

(O'Regan et al., 1999; Simons & Ambinder, 2005)

CHECK YOUR LEARNING:

3.1 What is the difference between sensation and perception?

3.2 What role have sensation and perception played in evolution?

3.3 What is the difference between absolute threshold and difference threshold?

3.4 What is sensory adaptation?

3.5 How does perceptual constancy help you to perceive stimuli that produce changing sensations?

3.6 What is the difference between selective attention and sensory interaction?

3.7 What is the difference between bottom-up processing and top-down processing?

To check your understanding of these questions, click show the answers or refer to the answers in the Chapter Summary.

Vision

YOU WILL LEARN:

3.8 how vision dominates the senses.

3.9 the functions of various parts of the eye, including the cornea, iris, lens, retina, rods, cones, fovea, and blind spot.

3.10 how eye movements facilitate vision.

3.11 how depth perception works.

3.12 how color perception works.

3.13 how to determine whether objects that are seen together belong to a group.

3.14 how certain objects, including faces and bodies, are visually processed in a special way.

3.15 how diversity influences vision.

Vision – your sense of sight – dominates the human senses (Goodale & Milner, 2013). All of the senses are important, of course, but we are influenced by what we see more often and more powerfully than by what we hear, smell, taste, or touch. This dominance shows in many ways. For instance, vision occupies more brain space than any other sense (Medina, 2014). In an online poll asking, "If you had to give up a sense, which would it be?", vision ranked last among the 4000+ respondents (only 4% chose it) (quibblo.com). Even the use of visual terms in our language reflects how our visual sense permeates the way we think. For example, when we understand something, we "see what you mean." When we ignore something, we "turn a blind eye." When we expect something to happen, we "see the writing on the wall." And when we concentrate exclusively on one goal, we have "tunnel vision."

Earlier in the chapter, we mentioned that sensation and perception evolved, which implies that they provide some advantage for survival. In terms of vision, some researchers have argued that there are two main evolutionary advantages of vision: identification and action (Goodale & Westwood, 2004; Milner & Goodale, 2008). Identification of an object allows you to recognize it, categorize it, and think about it. Action, of course, means doing something in response to that object – for example, moving toward it, running away from it, holding it, hitting it, or talking to it.

Interestingly, neurological research has found that human and primate brains have two distinct pathways, or streams, of visual information within the brain that reflect these two distinct functions (Goodale, 2011; Goodale & Milner, 1992, 2013). One stream, the *ventral* stream, controls identification of an object – determining *what* it is. A second stream, the *dorsal* stream, controls action toward the object – specifically, determining *where* it is. If the ventral stream is damaged, the person cannot recognize an object but can pick it up; if the dorsal stream is damaged, the person can recognize an object but cannot pick it up (Goodale & Humphrey, 2001). So, when you see a dozen glazed circles in a cardboard box, it's your ventral stream that allows you to identify those objects as donuts and your dorsal stream that allows you to grab one.

CHAPTER APP 3.1

BioDigital Human

The BioDigital Human app enables you to see the human eye even better than the photos in this text. Its amazing images are 3D and can be rotated to view all parts of the eye from various angles.

How does it APPly to your daily life?
How do these rotatable 3D images of the human eye help you appreciate what your eyes do for you all the time? How could you take better care of your eyes to protect your vision for the long term?

How does it APPly to your understanding of psychology?
How do these images enhance your understanding of *depth perception* and *retinal disparity*?

To learn more about this app or to download it to your phone, you can search for "BioDigital Human" on Google, in the iPhone App store, or in the Google Play store.

Your Eye: Its Parts and Their Functions

The hardware of your eye is an engineering marvel. Let's go through your eye in the same order that a ray of light does – starting on the outer surface and moving toward the back, where the pathway to the brain begins.

Cornea. First, the light hits your **cornea**: a thin transparent cover for the whole eye (**Figure 3.4**). The cornea refracts (or bends) images to improve vision, but it cannot change its own shape to do so. (The purpose of refractive surgery, which helps with nearsightedness and farsightedness, is to alter the shape of the cornea.) The cornea also serves as a protective cover and tends to recover quickly from minor scratches that might do serious damage to inner parts of the eye if they were unprotected. However, a serious scratch can leave a scar on the cornea that obstructs vision. In many ways, the cornea functions as a built-in contact lens; in fact, the original contact lenses developed in the mid-1900s were called "corneal lenses" (Barr, 2005).

Iris. Just behind the cornea is the **iris**: a colored circular muscle situated in the center of the eye. The iris gives your eyes their unique shade; when someone says that Regina King has hazel eyes or Jake Gyllenhaal has blue eyes, they are really referring to the color of their irises. The iris acts as a diaphragm that opens and closes, and the **pupil** is the opening in the middle. The size of the pupil determines how much light the eye allows through. In the dark, the pupil expands to about 8 mm to let in as much scarce light as possible. In bright light, the pupil contracts to about 2 mm to keep the

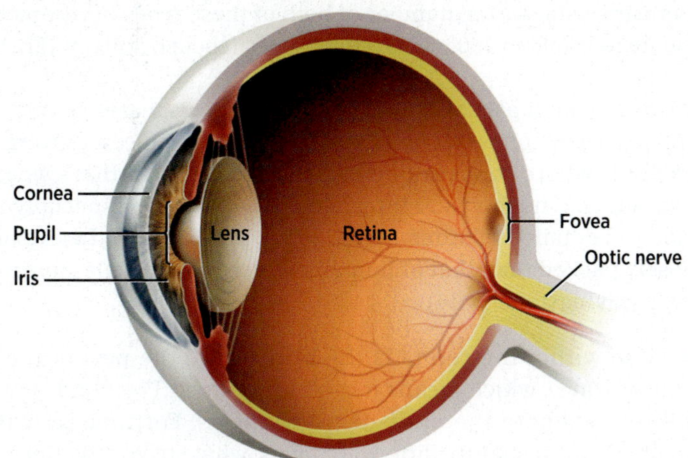

FIGURE 3.4 The Parts of the Human Eye. The human eye includes the cornea, a thin transparent cover; the iris, the circular muscle that gives the eye its unique color; the pupil, the opening inside the iris; the lens, which varies its shape to maintain focus; the retina, the rear part that receives visual stimulation; the fovea, an area in the center of the retina containing many cones but no rods; and the optic nerve, which delivers visual information from the retina to the brain.

vision
The sense of sight.

cornea
The thin transparent cover for the whole eye.

iris
The colored, circular muscle situated in the center of the eye.

pupil
The opening in the middle of the iris.

lens
The clear layer beneath the surface of the eye that maintains focus on an object by varying its own shape.

visual accommodation
The process by which the lens changes shape to focus on objects at varying distances from the eyes.

retina
The rear part of the eyeball, which receives visual stimulation and sends it to the brain via the optic nerve.

rods
Receptor cells in the retina that detect shades of gray and allow a person to see in low light.

cones
Receptor cells in the retina that detect color when light is plentiful.

amount of light manageable. The pupil also expands in moments of arousal, either sexual or intellectual (Fong, 2012).

Lens. After the light travels through the pupil, it moves on to the **lens**: a clear layer beneath the surface of your eye that maintains focus on an object by varying its own shape. Specifically, the lens changes its own curvature (the degree and shape of curve) to maximize focus. This is quite similar to the lenses you might choose for your glasses or your camera: you want the curve to be just right to produce the clearest, most focused image. Unlike the immobile lenses in your glasses or camera, your eye's lens can adjust its shape as necessary, shifting focus between near and far. This is called **visual accommodation**: the process by which the lens changes shape to focus on objects at varying distances from your eyes. As you age, the lens loses some of its elasticity, which is one reason why contacts, glasses, or surgery are likely to become more of a necessity. Also with age come *cataracts*: cloudy spots on the lens that can hamper vision, like cloudy spots on your car's windshield (Artal et al., 2006).

Retina. Once past the lens, light reaches the **retina**: the rear part of the eyeball that receives visual stimulation and sends it to the brain via the optic nerve. The retina is basically a screen at the back of your eye. The collective goal of all these parts of your eye is to cast a focused, clear image on that screen. That image includes miniature versions of all of the items in your field of vision. For example, a single letter in a newspaper headline held at arm's length makes an image about 1.5 mm high on your retina (Mather, 2011).

The retina is where visual *transduction* starts to happen, which means that outside stimuli (light) get converted into internal brain signals (neural activity) (Gegenfurtner, 2010). The passageway from the retina to your brain is the *optic nerve*. Visual information carried by your optic nerve makes its first stop at your thalamus and then moves farther back, to the occipital lobe (Goldstein, 2010b; Lee, 2010).

Rods and Cones. The retina contains receptor cells called *rods* and *cones* that are specially designed to detect certain kinds of visual stimuli under certain conditions (Gordon & Abramov, 2001). **Rods** are receptor cells in the retina that detect shades of gray and allow us to see in low light. **Cones** are receptor cells in the retina that detect color when light is plentiful. (Try to remember the *C* connection: *c*ones = *c*olor.) In the

For Regina King and the rest of us, eye color is actually the color of the iris: the circular muscle situated in the center of the eye.

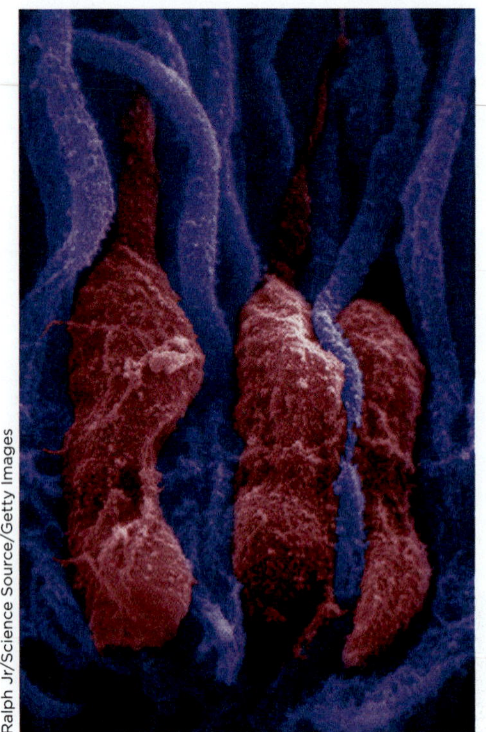

Ralph Jr/Science Source/Getty Images

Rods (red in this photo) are receptor cells in the retina that detect shades of gray and allow us to see in low light. Cones (purple in this photo) are receptor cells in the retina that detect color when light is plentiful.

human eye, there are a staggering number of both of these types of receptor cells in the retina, but far more rods (about 100 million) than cones (about 6 million) (Frishman, 2001).

Fovea. Occupying a small part of the retina is the **fovea**: an area in the center of the retina that contains many cones but no rods. The fovea (which comes from a Latin root meaning *small pit*) is where cones are most densely packed, so that's where the other parts of the eye send as much visual information as possible, especially information containing color and detailed features (Artal, 2010). The fovea in the eye of an eagle is even more densely packed than that of humans, which allows eagles to spot prey more than a mile away (Livingstone, 2014).

Blind Spot. Also within the retina is the **blind spot**: the part of the retina that contains no rods or cones, which means it can't sense light. The blind spot is basically the part of the retina where the optic nerve connects. Fortunately, with two eyes focusing on an object from slightly different angles, what strikes the blind spot in one of your eyes will probably be seen normally by your other eye. Check **Figure 3.5** for a demonstration of the blind spot in each of your eyes.

FIGURE 3.5 Blind Spot Demonstration. Cover one of your eyes and then focus your open eye on one of the letters. If your right eye is open, focus on the "R." If your left eye is open, focus on the "L." If you move your face toward or away from the image, you'll find a spot where the other letter disappears. That's the blind spot in that eye.

How You See: Eye Movements, Depth Perception, Color Perception, and More

We've covered the parts of the eye. Now, let's focus on how those parts work together to enable you to see.

Eye Movements. In order to see something, first it has to catch your eye — or, more precisely, first your eyes have to catch it. Thankfully, your eyes feature a sophisticated, coordinated system of movement that enables you to focus and refocus your gaze as necessary. You never notice it because it happens so automatically, but the movement within your eye is continual and impressive.

Vision researchers have identified many kinds of eye movements, but they place most of them in three categories: (1) *saccadic*, (2) *compensatory*, and (3) *vergence* (Kowler & Collewijn, 2010). Saccadic eye movements are "jumps" that take your gaze from one particular point to another. Between these jumps (actually called *saccades*) are pauses, known as *fixations*. Picture yourself sitting in a movie theater, waiting for the movie to start. Within just a few seconds, your eyes may jump through many sights — from the kid eating popcorn to the couple holding hands to the ads on the big screen to the smartphone in your hand. Between each of those saccades is a fixation, whether a fraction of a second or many seconds long.

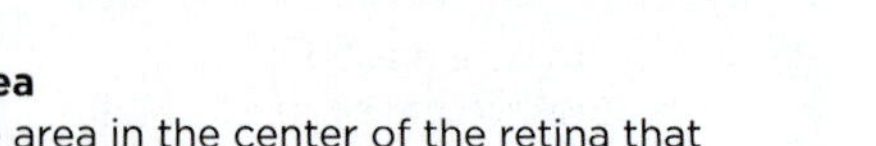

fovea
The area in the center of the retina that contains many cones but no rods.

blind spot
The part of the retina that contains no rods or cones and is therefore unable to sense light.

But some visual movements, like reading words across the page, are smooth rather than jumpy, right?

Not exactly. Even though reading seems like a smooth visual glide from one side of the page to the other, it actually involves lots of little saccades (about 20–30 milliseconds long) and fixations (about 200–300 milliseconds long). Fixations are a bit longer for unfamiliar or difficult words and a bit shorter for expected words. Your eyes actually suppress vision during the saccades and then restart it during the fixations. This eliminates the blur that you would see during those jumps (picture the moments in an amateur video in which the camera operator yanks the camera from one object to the next).

DIVERSITY MATTERS

In English, each fixation includes the target word plus about three or four letters to the left and 14 or 15 letters to the right (about three to four words total). The left–right pattern is reversed in Hebrew, Arabic, Farsi, and Urdu, all of which are languages that read right-to-left. In Chinese, in which each written character is denser than a typical English letter, the fixation is narrower, including the target word plus just one character to the left and two or three to the right (Rayner, 1998; Rayner & Pollatsek, 2010; Snell et al., 2018; Snowling & Hulme, 2008).

The second type of eye movements is *compensatory* eye movements, or movements that compensate for the movement of your head. Right now, as you focus on these words, shake your head no. Now shake it yes. Notice how effortless it is to maintain your focus on a particular word, even a particular letter, while your head moves up and down or side to side. (If you were wearing a GoPro camera mounted on your head, especially if that camera didn't feature image stabilization, just think about how jumpy the video would be from that simple head shake.) That's what compensatory eye movements do: they keep your eyes focused on a chosen image, even though your head containing your eyes moves around continuously.

The third type of eye movements is *vergence* eye movements, which move your two eyes in unison to focus on a single chosen image. Vergence comes from the same root as *converge*, which means *come together*. Imagine holding a flashlight in each hand and then adjusting them to converge upon various objects in front of you, one after the other: one near, one far, one up, one down, one slightly to the left, one slightly to the right. Those adjustments you would make to your wrists and hands to converge the lights on any particular object are the equivalent of vergence eye movements around your field of vision.

Depth Perception. **Depth perception** is your ability to judge the distance and depth of objects. Depth perception tells you whether you can reach the remote at the other end of the couch without getting up. It allows you to know whether the extra-large pizza box that just arrived will fit on the narrow countertop in your kitchen. It helps a driver to determine exactly how far they can back up into a parallel parking spot and then pull forward without bumping the cars in front and behind.

Monocular and Binocular Depth Cues. Depth perception depends on many features of visual information (Peterson, 2001). Some of these features are **monocular depth cues**: qualities of visual stimuli that indicate depth when you use only one eye. Monocular depth cues are the kinds of things you notice in a two-dimensional painting or photograph. For example, relative size, which is how big two things are in comparison to each other, can suggest depth.

Consider a photo taken at a baseball game at which the photographer is in the front row behind home plate, and the camera faces directly forward. The batter looks much bigger than the pitcher, who looks much bigger than the center fielder. Of course, those players are all probably of somewhat similar heights and weights, which means the different-sized images they cast on your retina are indicators of their distance from you, not actual size. Other monocular cues include linear perspective (as when you look at a road leading off into the distance), surface texture (the way a close-up of a face shows wrinkles and pores, but a more distant photo doesn't), and shading (how the sides of a cardboard box appear slightly different shades of brown because light from one direction hits them at different angles) (Timney, 2010).

Monocular depth cues are good for depth perception, but even better are **binocular depth cues**: qualities of visual stimuli that indicate depth when you use both eyes. Binocular depth cues help us when we look at things in three dimensions – consider the difference between watching a regular movie and a movie with 3D glasses. Binocular depth cues depend on **retinal disparity** (or **stereopsis**): your brain's

depth perception
The ability to judge the distance and depth of objects.

monocular depth cues
The qualities of visual stimuli that indicate depth when using only one eye.

binocular depth cues
The qualities of visual stimuli that indicate depth when using both eyes.

retinal disparity (stereopsis)
The brain's measurement of the difference between the images of a single object sent by each of the two eyes.

The Banks of the Seine or, Spring Through the Trees, 1878 (oil on canvas), Monet, Claude (1840–1926)/Musee Marmottan Monet, Paris, France/Bridgeman Images

Claude Monet was a master of using monocular cues to convey depth. In this painting, *Spring Through the Trees*, notice how he uses differences in relative size (among other features) to show that the branches are in front and the buildings are behind.

CHAPTER APP 3.2

Be My Eyes

The Be My Eyes app allows sighted people to help blind people—to "be their eyes"—for small tasks that require vision. If you are a sighted person who downloads the app and registers, you'll receive occasional requests for a video call from a blind person who could use your help. You might be asked to find the expiration date on food packaging, locate a power outlet in a hotel room, read instructions that came with a new product, identify items in a grocery store, put together an outfit that matches well, or provide help with any number of other tasks.

How does it APPly to your daily life? For sighted people, how does this app affect your appreciation of your ability to see? For people who are blind or who know someone who is, how might this app affect your day-to-day life?

How does it APPly to your understanding of psychology? How does this app enhance your understanding of the way vision dominates the senses? How does it enhance your understanding of the evolutionary advantages of vision?

To learn more about this app or to download it to your phone, you can search for "Be My Eyes" on Google, in the iPhone App store, or in the Google Play store.

measurement of the difference between the images of a single object sent by each of your two eyes. Retinal disparity is greater for objects that are close up than for objects that are far away. Your brain assesses that retinal disparity and then follows the logical rule that the more retinal disparity there is, the closer the object must be.

You can see retinal disparity by taking pairs of photos with your phone. First, take two photos of your doorknob just a few inches in front of your face – one with the phone in front of your right eye and the other with the phone in front of your left eye. Then repeat this two-photo process from across the room. You'll see that the difference between the left-eye and right-eye perspectives – the disparity – is much more noticeable when the doorknob is close than when it is far away. Researchers have found that the human ability to perceive depth using retinal disparity is quite impressive. For example, most people can tell that one coffee cup is closer than another (assuming they are both at about arm's length), even if the disparity is equivalent to the thickness of a fingernail (Wilcox & Allison, 2010).

Depth perception comes in handy for nonhuman species too – birds trying to land on a window ledge, giraffes extending their necks toward leaves on a tree branch, and dogs jumping down from the back of a pickup truck onto the ground, to name a few. Only some animals, however, can use binocular depth cues – the animals with overlap in the fields of vision in each eye (Fox et al., 1977; Timney, 2010). Cats, dogs, and primates – whose eyes are both on the front of their heads – have it. Horses have much less of it, because their eyes face different but not completely opposite directions (Timney & Keil, 1999). Many fish have no binocular depth vision, because their eyes face completely opposite directions, which means they have entirely distinct inputs coming from each eye (Sedgwick, 2001).

Color Vision. Your ability to tell a red light from a green light or pick your favorite flavor of Skittles from the pack is basically your ability to detect **hue**: the color of light, as determined by its wavelength.

The wavelengths that your eyes can detect represent just a small fraction of the full range of wavelengths. As **Figure 3.6** shows, your eyes can sense wavelengths ranging from 400 to 750 nanometers in length. The waves just outside our visible range have names that connect them to their neighboring colors: ultraviolet rays at the low end of the spectrum (just below the waves you perceive as violet) and infrared rays at the high end (just above the waves you perceive as red).

It may seem that hue is completely objective – purple is purple, yellow is yellow, and so on – but hue actually depends on context. For example, the colors surrounding an object can affect the way you perceive that object's color (Webster, 2010). Check **Figure 3.7** to see how a square of the same color looks different depending on the color of the circle surrounding it. You've probably noticed subtle real-life versions of this surround effect too, especially if you've ever tried the same picture or photo in different-colored frames or even tried on different-colored shirts or makeup to see which ones bring out the color of your eyes.

Another type of context that can influence your perception of color is the amount of time you spend looking at it. Remember *sensory adaptation* from earlier in this

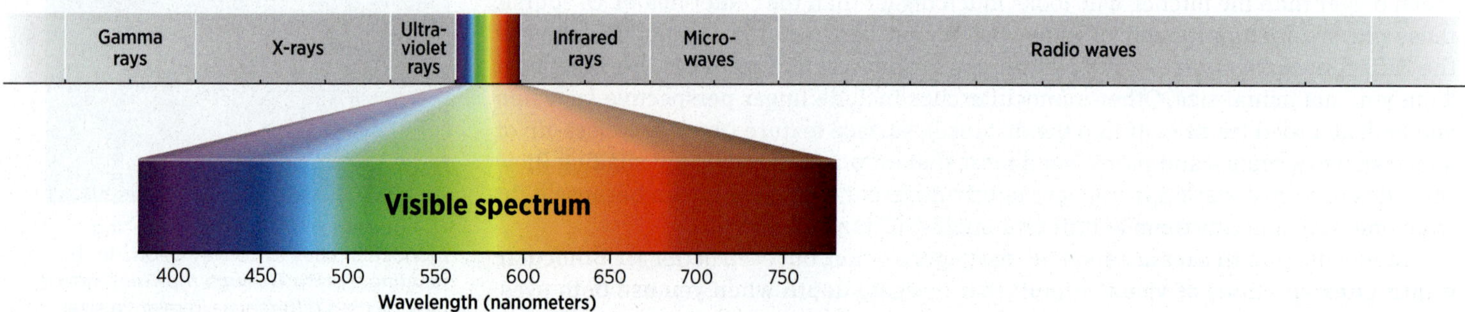

FIGURE 3.6 Visual Light and the Wavelength Spectrum. The rainbow of colors that your eyes can sense comes from just a small fraction of all wavelengths in the environment.

chapter? Just as your ears get used to the sound of an air conditioner and your nose gets used to the smell of coffee when you're around either for a long time, your eyes get used to certain colors if you stare at them long enough. For example, stare at the green circle in the red square in **Figure 3.8** for 30–60 seconds, then move your eyes to the white square. When you do this, the white will look like a red circle in a green square, because red is the opposite of green and your sensors for each get worn out by continuous use (Gordon & Abramov, 2001; Livingstone, 2014).

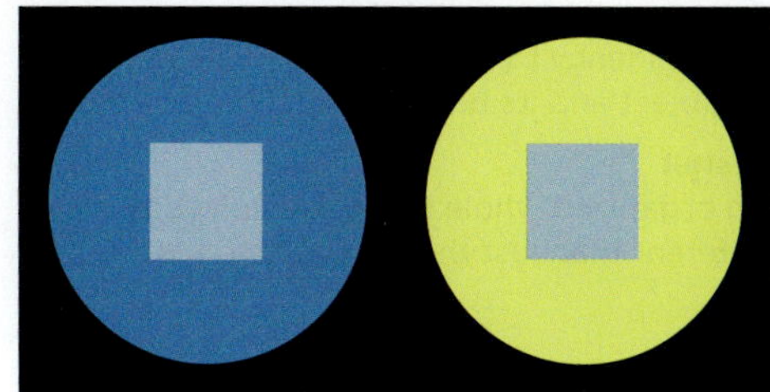

FIGURE 3.7 The Effect of the Surround. The squares inside the circles are exactly the same color, but the circles around them make them seem slightly different. That's the effect of the surround.

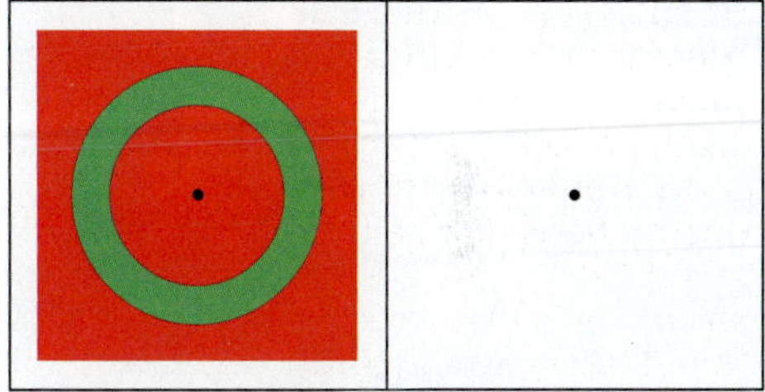

FIGURE 3.8 Sensory Adaptation in Vision. Stare continuously at the red and green figure for 30–60 seconds, then shift to the white square. The aftereffect you see, in which white appears either red or green (the opposite of what it had been before), happens because the cones that sense particular colors get temporarily exhausted, allowing the opposite color to emerge.
Information from Zanker (2010).

Trichromatic Theory of Color Vision. There have been many explanations of color vision throughout the history of psychology, including an influential color theory by Christine Ladd-Franklin, one of the pioneering women of early psychology we discussed in Chapter 1 (Furumoto, 1995; Shamey & Kuehni, 2020). Today, the dominant explanations focus on rods and cones. Earlier, we discussed the fact that cones are the specialized receptor cells in your retina that detect color. There are actually three types of cones, each capable of sensing only a certain range of colors: (1) *short-wavelength-sensitive* (*S*) cones, which pick up bluish colors; (2) *middle-wavelength-sensitive* (*M*) cones, which pick up greenish colors; and (3) *long-wavelength-sensitive* (*L*) cones, which pick up reddish colors (Gegenfurtner, 2010; Lee, 2010). (Recall the well-known *Roy G. Biv* mnemonic for the colors of the rainbow you may have learned in a science class years ago, and keep in mind that the sequence of colors in that acronym represents decreasing wavelengths.) The presence of these three distinct types of cones is the basis of the **trichromatic theory of color vision**: an explanation of color vision based on the idea that your cones are specialized to sense either red, green, or blue. In fact, many TV screens and computer monitors work the same way — portraying a full range of colors by mixing just a few (Stockman, 2010).

Deficiencies can occur in any one of the three kinds of cones, resulting in distinct kinds of colorblindness (including some that involve more than one deficiency). The most common form of colorblindness is red–green colorblindness, which happens when either the M cones or L cones (but not both) are deficient. This is relatively common (7–10%) in men of Western European descent. If the S cones are deficient, that's blue–green (or tritan) colorblindness, which occurs much more rarely (in just 1 of 10,000 people). Complete colorblindness (achromatopsia), in which none of the cones work properly and the person sees the world in shades of gray, is even rarer (1 in 30,000 people) (Mollon et al., 2003; Tait & Carroll, 2010).

Opponent-Process Theory of Color Vision. Trichromatic theory is not the only theory to explain color vision. Another is the **opponent-process theory of color vision**: an explanation of color vision based on the idea that your visual system is specialized to sense specific opposite pairs of colors (like red–green or blue–yellow). Among researchers of color vision, these two theories of color vision have a long history of rivalry dating back to the 1800s (Goldstein, 2001a; Helmholtz, 1852; Hering, 1878, 1964; Young, 1802). Supporters of the opponent-process theory emphasize that while certain pairs of colors can complement each other, other pairs can't. There's such a thing as bluish purple or reddish orange, but no such thing as reddish green or bluish yellow. (It's similar to the way we can combine certain directions on a map, like northeast or southwest, but not others, like northsouth or eastwest.) So according to opponent-process theory, the pairs that don't blend may be *opponents*. That means the process by which we see colors may depend heavily on specific *processes* within our eyes in response to the red–green or blue–yellow components of what we see.

Experts in color vision recognize that trichromatic theory and opponent-process theory both play roles in color vision. So the question is not which theory is correct, but how the two work together. Research indicates that they operate at different levels of the vision process. Trichromatic theory applies near the beginning of the color vision process, when the visual stimulus reaches the cones, while opponent-process theory kicks in later in the color vision process, after the stimulus passes cones and heads through the optic nerve toward the brain (Buchsbaum & Gottschalk, 1983; Gegenfurtner & Kiper, 2003).

hue
The color of light, as determined by its wavelength.

trichromatic theory of color vision
An explanation of color vision based on the idea that the cones are specialized to sense either red, green, or blue.

opponent-process theory of color vision
An explanation of color vision based on the idea that the cones are specialized to sense specific opposite pairs of colors (like red–green and blue–yellow).

figure–ground organization
The tendency to visually distinguish between an object and its background.

gestalt
An organized whole that is perceived as different than just the sum of its parts.

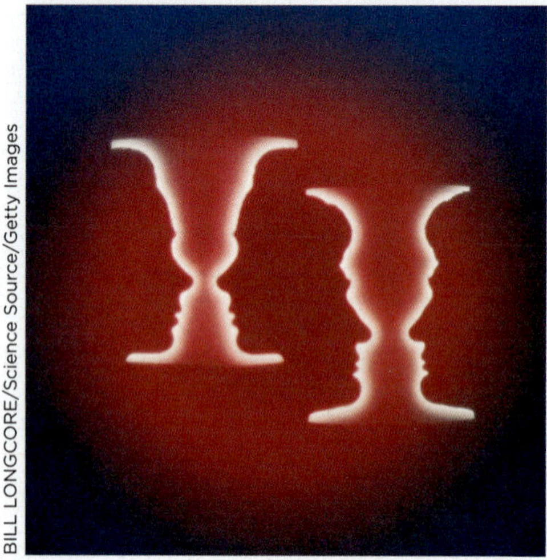

BILL LONGCORE/Science Source/Getty Images

FIGURE 3.9 Distinguishing Figure from Ground. Sometimes it's not easy to tell the figure (the focal item) from the background. Do you see faces or vases?

Separating and Grouping Objects. When your eyes take in a scene, how do you know which items have nothing to do with each other and which are part of a group? One key is your capability for **figure–ground organization**: your tendency to visually distinguish between an object and its background. Usually, distinguishing the *figure* (the item in front) and the *ground* (what's behind it) is easy—you see your pillow on top of your bed or your sandwich on top of your plate. But sometimes it can be tough, as in **Figure 3.9**. Researchers have found that when it's not obvious, we tend to rely on several rules of thumb. More often than not, the figure is smaller than the ground, the figure is more symmetrical than the ground, the figure appears closer than the ground, the figure is more likely to be convex (with outward curves or bulges) than the ground, and if there's anything moving, it's more likely to be the figure than the ground (Goldstein, 2001b; Lass et al., 2017; Pomerantz & Portillo, 2010; Vecera & Lee, 2010).

The figure–ground challenge involves separating items, but what about grouping them together? Again, it's often easy to know whether individual items belong together as a group. For example, one winter afternoon I was walking toward my college's athletic building and saw about a dozen young men walking off a bus and toward the door. All were wearing warm-up suits that were blue with white trim and carrying matching blue-and-white duffel bags over their shoulders. All appeared to be about 20 years old, give or take a couple of years. All were tall and athletically built. All were walking near each other in the same direction at the same time. I certainly did *not* think to myself, "What a coincidence! All of these tall athletes decided on their own to dress in blue-and-white warm-up suits, and now they all happen to be at the same place at the same time heading in the same direction!" Instead, I thought to myself, "I bet that's a visiting college basketball team that my college's team is playing tonight." When I got close enough to read the logo on their jackets and bags, I saw that I was right. When I group people or things together like that, you form a **gestalt**: an organized whole that you perceive as different from just the sum of its parts.

What features cause us to make a gestalt out of a collection of things we see?

Researchers who study visual organization have identified several characteristics of groups of objects that increase the odds that we will see them as a gestalt, or a whole rather than a collection of parts (Goldstein, 2010b; Pomerantz & Portillo, 2010; Schirillo, 2010):

- **Proximity.** The closer objects are to each other, the more likely they belong together. Lots of space between objects, especially if other things occupy that space, decrease the odds that you'll form a gestalt. Think about a tightly packed herd of sheep as opposed to the same sheep spread out across miles of land with lots of other animals in between them.
- **Similarity.** If objects share the same color, size, orientation (facing the same direction), or distance from you, they're probably a group rather than a collection of individuals. Think about uniformed soldiers marching in formation.
- **Common fate.** If objects change together rather than each changing on its own, they are likely to go together. Think about a group of birds flying: if their takeoffs, turns, and landings are all synchronized, you're likely to see them as a flock.
- **Connectedness.** If objects are touching, they probably go together. Two people sitting next to each other at a concert could be strangers, but if they're holding hands, they're probably a couple.
- **Closure.** If one part is missing in an otherwise complete shape, you're likely to overlook what's missing and assume the parts make a whole. Check out **Figure 3.10** in the margin: it's just a bunch of black pentagons, but your eyes fill in what's missing to make it a soccer ball.

FIGURE 3.10 Gestalt and Closure. A gestalt is an organized whole that you perceive as different from just the sum of its parts. For example, when your eyes see these patterns of black on a white background, you form a gestalt of a soccer ball.

Special Modes of Vision? In recent years, psychologists have increasingly discovered we perceive certain visual objects — namely, faces, bodies, and maybe words and numbers — in specialized ways (Gauthier, 2010, 2018; Goldstein, 2010b; Grill-Spector et al., 2017; Spunt & Adolphs, 2017; Stevens et al., 2017; Yeo et al., 2017). You have mechanisms in your brain specially designed to process faces, much like your smartphone (equipped with the right apps) has mechanisms specially designed to process bar codes, QR codes, and other special kinds of visual stimuli. One source of evidence for this specialized kind of perception — known as *modular* perception, or perception in a particular mode — is the fact that some people have visual inabilities that reflect these very specific tasks. For example, among people who have otherwise intact perception, a few can't perceive or recognize faces (prosopagnosia), and a few others can't perceive or recognize words (alexia) (Humphreys & Riddoch, 2001).

Some of the strongest evidence of modular vision involves faces (Kanwisher, 2017; Kanwisher et al., 1997; Morton & Johnson, 1991). Some researchers even argue that your brain has a *face processor*, a small spot in your temporal lobe called the *fusiform face area* that receives images of the faces you see (Nakayama, 2001; Sinha et al., 2010). **Figure 3.11** with the Margaret Thatcher photo illustrates the difference in perception your face processor makes. It's the same pair of photos — one right side up and the other upside down. The upside-down pair seems only slightly different from each other. But the right-side-up pair seems extremely different from each other, with one appearing grotesque because the eyes, nose, and mouth are inverted. Because of modular vision for faces, you notice that violation of expectation (those inverted features) much more strongly when your face processor is activated (when the photos are right side up) than when it isn't. Because the first photos demonstrating this effect featured a photo of the former British prime minister Margaret Thatcher, it's called the *Margaret Thatcher effect* (Thompson, 1980). (Check out Show Me More 3.4 at the end of the chapter to try the Margaret Thatcher effect.)

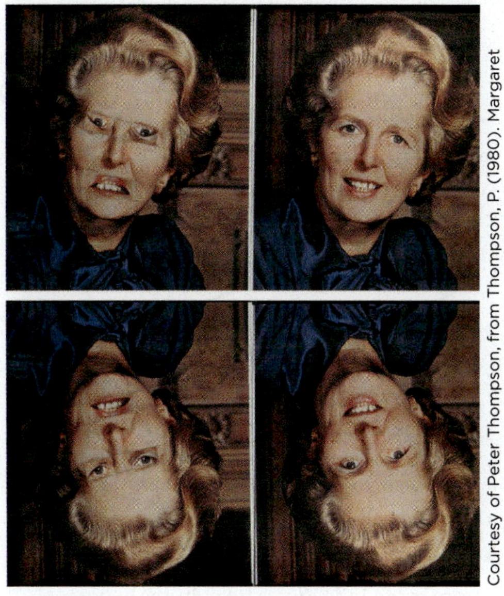

Courtesy of Peter Thompson, from Thompson, P. (1980). Margaret Thatcher: A New Illusion. *Perception, 9*, 383–384.

FIGURE 3.11 The Margaret Thatcher Effect. The irregularities in Margaret Thatcher's face are much more obvious when looking at her face right side up as opposed to upside down. That difference suggests specialized modular processing of faces in the brain.

Similarly, other studies have used upside-down photos to illustrate that human bodies and specific body parts (arms, legs, etc.) are also perceived in a modular way. Specifically, these studies found that the time it takes to compare two bodies (or two arms or two legs) is significantly shorter when those bodies are shown right side up rather than upside down. The same difference does not appear for other stimuli, such as houses (or parts of houses). This implies that our brains have a special way of fast-tracking the perception of human bodies as well as faces (Reed, 2010; Reed et al., 2003, 2006; Taylor et al., 2017).

How Diversity Influences Vision

Increasingly, psychologists are recognizing that your cultural background influences how, and even what, you perceive (Nisbett & Miyamoto, 2005). This is especially evident in cross-cultural studies of vision (Masuda, 2010).

Color Naming Across Cultures. In some ways, cultures around the world tend to name colors similarly. The same set of 11 colors appears in almost all languages:

DIVERSITY MATTERS

black, white, red, yellow, green, blue, gray, orange, brown, pink, and purple (Berlin & Kay, 1969; Kay & Regier, 2007; Lindsey & Brown, 2006; Regier et al., 2005).

In other ways, there are some differences in color naming from one culture to the next (Caskey-Sirmons & Hickerson, 1977; Roberson et al., 2000). For example, one group of researchers found that a small culture in Papua New Guinea used only five names to cover the whole spectrum of colors. Similarly, a tribal group in southern Africa had a list of color categories that didn't match with more widely used categories at all (Roberson et al., 2004, 2005a, b). Another study noticed that some languages fail to make a distinction between blue and green (using a combined term the researchers call *grue*). Those languages are typically spoken in very sunny parts of the world — in particular, regions where people are exposed to high levels of short-wavelength ultraviolet (UV) rays, which tend to wear out the cones involved in the perception of colors in the part of the spectrum around blue and green (Lindsey & Brown, 2002).

FIGURE 3.12 The Rod and Frame Test. In the rod and frame test, the task is to make the rod completely vertical, regardless of the orientation of the frame. People from more collectivistic cultures, where appreciation of context and relationships is emphasized, struggle with this task more than people from more individualistic cultures, where independence is emphasized (Ji et al., 2000; Kitayama et al., 2003).

The point here is not just that diverse cultures have unique ways of naming colors, but also that their ways of naming colors may influence how they see their world (Kay & Regier, 2006; Roberson, 2005; Roberson & Hanley, 2010). For instance, if you spoke a language that used the same word — *grue* — for what you now call blue *and* what you now call green, you might be more likely to see a blue shirt and a green shirt as being the same color.

Collectivism, Individualism, and Vision. Other diversity-based differences in vision relate to differences in individualism versus collectivism, or the extent to which the culture tends to emphasize the well-being of the individual person versus the well-being of the family or larger group. In collectivistic cultures, connections or relationships between people or objects — generally called *context* — are prioritized over the independence of each person or object. Some researchers have found that that visual perception of the members of individualistic and collectivistic cultures often reflects these priorities (Chiao & Harada, 2008).

DIVERSITY MATTERS

For example, consider the studies that use the rod and frame test, as illustrated in **Figure 3.12**. Participants in these studies receive a simple instruction: make the rod vertical. Sometimes the frame is at a right angle with the rod, but other times the frame is slightly tilted. Asian participants are more likely to make more mistakes than U.S. participants on this task. The mistakes tend to be in the direction of making the rod line up with the frame — parallel to the sides of the frame and perpendicular to the frame's top and bottom — even when the frame leans to one side. Researchers in these studies offer the interpretation that Asian participants, who come from more collectivistic cultures, have more difficulty separating the rod from its context (the frame) than U.S. participants, who come from a more individualistic culture (Ji et al., 2000; Kitayama et al., 2003).

Takahiko Masuda and Richard E. Nisbett

FIGURE 3.13 Cultural Differences in Vision: Focal Items Versus Background. When viewing images like this one, people from collectivistic cultures tend to pay more attention to items in the background, while people from individualistic cultures tend to pay more attention to the big fish up front.

Additional studies also demonstrate how people from collectivistic cultures (compared to people from individualistic cultures) tend to see the context more and the featured item within the context less (Nisbett & Masuda, 2003). For example, in one study, participants in Japan and the United States watched short video clips of underwater scenes or wildlife scenes before being quizzed about them. U.S. participants did better on questions regarding the items up front, like the big fish in **Figure 3.13**, and Japanese participants did better on questions regarding items in the background (Masuda & Nisbett, 2001). Similarly, East Asian participants did better at noticing changes in the background of rapidly flashing pictures, and participants from Western countries did better at noticing changes in the main objects in the front (Masuda & Nisbett, 2006). Studies of eye tracking show that when Westerners and East Asians look at the same photo, Westerners' eyes spend more time focused on the main objects in front, while East Asians' eyes spend more time focused on objects in the background (Chua et al., 2005; Rayner et al., 2007). Together, these studies suggest that people from collectivistic cultures tend to focus their vision more on contextual features or relationship-based features of the visual field than people from individualistic cultures.

CHECK YOUR LEARNING:

3.8 For most people, which of the five senses dominates?

3.9 What are the functions of the various parts of the eye, including the cornea, iris, lens, retina, and fovea?

3.10 What is the difference between these three kinds of eye movement: saccadic, compensatory, and vergence?

3.11 What is depth perception, and on what features in the stimulus does it depend?

3.12 What is hue, and what are the two competing theories of color vision?

3.13 What factors help people to determine if objects that are seen together belong to the same group?

3.14 What kinds of objects are processed in special ways?

3.15 How does diversity influence vision?

To check your understanding of these questions, click show the answers or refer to the answers in the Chapter Summary.

Hearing

YOU WILL LEARN:

3.16 what audition is.

3.17 about parts of the ear, including the pinna, tympanic membrane, ossicles, oval window membrane, and cochlea.

3.18 how you hear pitch.

3.19 how you determine the location from which a sound is coming.

3.20 how the perception of speech may be different from the perception of other sounds.

3.21 how diversity influences hearing.

Audition is your sense of hearing. When you think about the benefits of audition, you may think first about the pleasure that it brings. After all, your ears bring in the sounds of babies' laughter, ocean waves, a cheering crowd, and your favorite music booming through the speakers. But the sense of hearing is important for the necessities of life too. In fact, over the course of human history, hearing has been vital to survival, just like vision. It's interesting that you can easily turn off vision (close your eyes), but unless you stick your fingers in your ears, you can't turn off hearing. Similarly, you can see only what's in front of you, but you can hear what's coming from every direction. In these ways, the sense of hearing has always alerted humans, as well as other species, to predators and other dangers that may be nearby. Those auditory alerts enable us to turn toward what we hear so we can see it too, further increasing the chances of our survival (Moore, 2001a, 2010). If the screech of car tires, the beep of a smoke alarm, or the hiss of a snake has ever helped you avoid serious danger, you know the survival value of an intact sense of hearing.

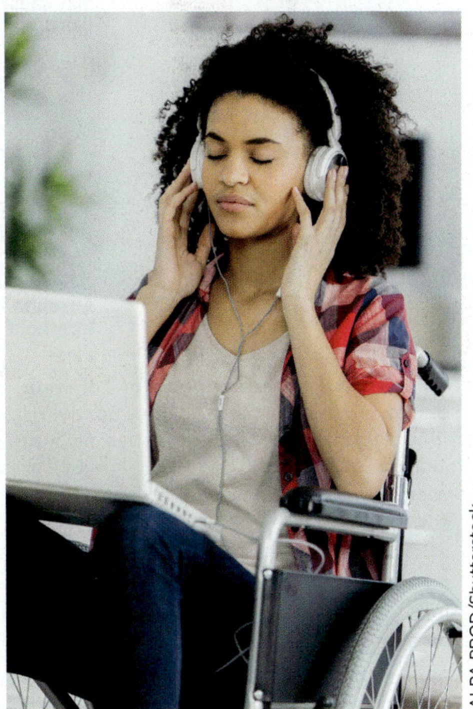

Audition is your sense of hearing. Your ears have some distinct advantages over your eyes. For example, your ears don't close, and they pick up sensation from every direction, rather than just in front of you. These advantages of our ears increased the chances of survival for our ancestors.

Your Ear: Its Parts and Their Functions

Now let's go through the parts of your ear in the same order that a sound does (**Figure 3.14**). We'll start on the outer surface and move toward the inner regions, where the ear ultimately connects to the brain. But first, let's consider exactly what sound is. Essentially, sound is vibration. Sometimes, you can actually see the vibration that sends the sound your way, like a single guitar string quivering after it's plucked. This vibration — or sound wave, as it is often called — travels through the air and reaches the edge of the ear. Your outer ear steers it toward the inner part, where the vibrations that started outside your ear start a chain reaction of vibration of tiny parts inside your ear (the details of which we will describe shortly). The vibration of those tiny parts gets translated, through *transduction*, into neural activity that your brain can process (Eatock, 2010). So, in short, you hear because your ears convert a vibration made around you into a vibration happening within you.

Some of those vibrations sound a lot louder than others. Loudness is measured in units called *decibels* (abbreviated *dB*). Exposing your ears to too many decibels, especially for too long a period of time, can damage your hearing. That's true whether the noise is something you can't control, like a thunderstorm, or something you can control, like the volume on your headphones. By the way, hearing loss due to wearing loud headphones for a long time is a real risk. It happens to a sizable number of people even at young ages, especially those who listen to music, games, or movies for many

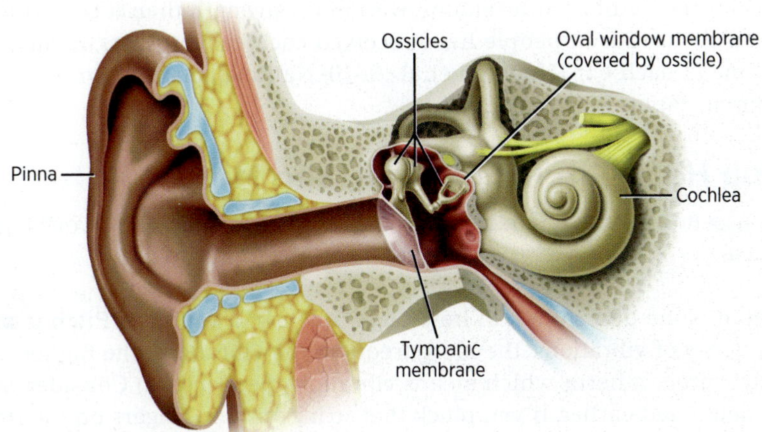

FIGURE 3.14 **The Parts of the Human Ear.** The parts of the human ear include the pinna, tympanic membrane, ossicles, oval window membrane, and cochlea.

audition
The sense of hearing.

LIFE HACK 3.2

Be smart about the volume of your headphones, especially if you wear them for long periods. If it's too loud for too long, it can damage your hearing.

(Breinbauer et al., 2012; Sulaiman et al., 2013, 2014)

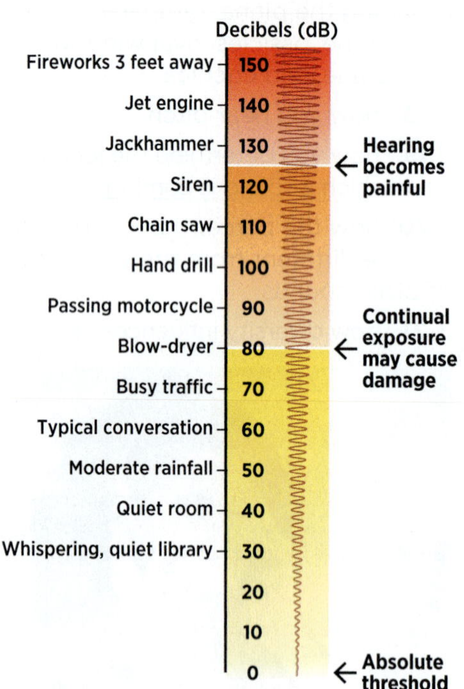

FIGURE 3.15 The Loudness of Common Sounds. As the decibel level goes up, the risk for hearing damage does too, especially if the loudness is chronic.

Source: American Speech-Language-Hearing Association (ASHA), http://www.asha.org/public/hearing/Noise/.

hours each day, year after year (Breinbauer et al., 2012; Sulaiman et al., 2013, 2014; Srihari et al., 2021). Check **Figure 3.15** for examples of sounds across the range of decibels.

Outer Ear. When sound moves toward your ears, it first reaches your **pinna**, or outer ear. Your pinna basically consists of the parts of your ear that you can easily touch with your fingers. Your pinna functions as a funnel that guides sound toward the inner ear, where the real work of hearing is done. When you cup your hand around your ear to strengthen a sound, you're enhancing the job your pinna always does automatically. In some animals, the pinna is huge relative to their body size. For example, consider bats and foxes. Both are nocturnal animals that move around in the dark and therefore rely disproportionately on hearing rather than sight, and with both animals, the pinna is disproportionately large, at least by human standards. Also, while your pinna is stationary, other animals like horses and cats have pinna that can pivot and move toward sound to better take it in (Wallace, 2010).

Middle Ear. The pinna leads to the **tympanic membrane**: a surface stretched taut across the ear canal to form the boundary between the outer ear and the middle ear. Your tympanic membrane is commonly called your eardrum (which is easy to remember if your high school band featured a *timpani*, a type of large drum). On the inner side of the tympanic membrane is a chain of very small bones called **ossicles** connected in ball-and-socket fashion. On the other side of the ossicles, there's a second membrane between the middle ear and the inner ear called the **oval window membrane**. In between those two membranes, your ossicles amplify sound to about 17 times its entry level (Hackney, 2010).

Inner Ear. Once the sound makes its way through your middle ear, it enters your inner ear. Your inner ear consists primarily of your **cochlea**, a spiral fluid-filled structure in the inner ear that sends sound waves to the brain via the auditory nerve. Vibrations of cochlear fluid are the final step of hearing within the ear. Everything else happens in the brain, beginning with the arrival of auditory information at the main auditory nucleus in the midbrain.

Disorders of the cochlea, which can be inborn or acquired via exposure to excessive noise, are a common source of hearing loss or deafness (Gomersall & Baguley, 2010). Such disorders can be treated with a *cochlear implant*, a small prosthetic device that includes parts both inside and outside of the ear. Specifically, cochlear implants consist of a microphone behind the ear that looks like a common hearing aid. The microphone picks up auditory information and sends it to a processor that is either attached to it or carried separately, often in a pocket. That processor sends the information to a receiver surgically implanted under the skin on the skull near the ear. That receiver is connected by electrodes to the cochlea and auditory nerve, which ultimately receive the auditory information with more strength than it could on its own. Hundreds of thousands of people have received cochlear implants, including many who have one in each ear (Houston et al., 2010; National Institute on Deafness and Other Communication Disorders, 2017).

How You Hear: Pitch, Location, and More

We've discussed the parts of your ear. Now, let's consider how they work together to help you hear.

Pitch. Pitch is the description of how "high" or "low" a sound is. Pitch is produced by the frequency of vibrations: the more frequent the vibrations, the higher the pitch. (Pitch is measured in hertz, which means vibrations per second.) Consider the guitar string we mentioned earlier. If you pluck that string with no fingers on the fret, it will produce a certain pitch. But if you pluck it again with a finger pressing down onto the fret — essentially shortening the vibrating part of the string — the pitch goes up

pinna
The outer ear.

tympanic membrane
A surface stretched taut across the ear canal to form the boundary between the outer ear and the middle ear.

ossicles
A chain of very small bones connected in ball-and-socket fashion on the inner side of the tympanic membrane.

oval window membrane
A membrane between the ossicles of the middle ear and the inner ear.

cochlea
The spiral fluid-filled structure in the inner ear that sends sound waves to the brain via the auditory nerve.

pitch
The description of how "high" or "low" a sound is.

because it doesn't take as much time for the shorter string to complete each full vibration. The same principle explains why violins and ukuleles are higher-pitch instruments than cellos and upright basses — it's all about how long it takes for the strings to vibrate.

If you couldn't perceive pitch, all music would sound like beats on the same drum and all speech would sound like a monotone drone. You'd still notice the loudness and length of each sound, but no variability in terms of highs or lows (Moore, 2012; Yost, 2010). Your ability to detect pitch differs from that of other species. You've noticed this if you've ever seen a dog respond to dog whistles, which produce a pitch they can hear but we can't. Your ability to detect pitch might also differ from that of people older than you, since high-pitch hearing is the first type of hearing to decline with age. (Want to check out a pitch-based auditory illusion? Search online for "Shepard tone" and you'll hear a sound that seems to continually get higher in pitch but never actually does.)

There are two prominent theories about exactly how you perceive pitch: *place theory* and *frequency theory* (Moore, 2001b). **Place theory** is an explanation of pitch perception based on the idea that you hear different pitches because tiny hairs in different places within the cochlea are stimulated. **Frequency theory** is an explanation of pitch perception based on the idea that you hear different pitches because nerve impulses travel with different frequencies through the auditory nerve. The names of these theories are good indicators of the difference between them: place theory emphasizes the specific *place* where the sound stimulates the cochlea, and frequency theory emphasizes the speed or *frequency* at which the sound makes a nerve impulse travel from the cochlea through the auditory nerve.

A big difference between the two theories about pitch is the location at which the sound is processed. According to place theory, the sound is processed in the inner ear and then sent to the brain. According to frequency theory, however, the sound moves unprocessed through the inner ear and the auditory nerve, and then is processed in the brain. There is evidence that both place theory and frequency theory explain pitch perception, but in different ways: at low frequencies, frequency theory is most supported; at high frequencies, place theory is more supported; and in the middle, they both play important roles (Horowitz, 2012; Moore, 2012; Pickles, 2013; Schnupp et al., 2012).

Zsolt Biczo/Shutterstock

A disorder of the cochlea can cause hearing loss but can be treated with a cochlear implant, a small prosthetic device featuring parts both inside and outside of the ear.

Sound Localization. **Sound localization** is your ability to perceive the location from which a sound originates. As an analogy for the way your ears and brain localize sound, imagine talking on the phone with a friend about a half-mile away as a thunderstorm develops. Lightning strikes, and you immediately hear a loud boom of thunder outside your window. You start to say, "Whoa, did you hear that?" but as soon as you get to "Whoa," your friend hears the same thunder outside their own window and interrupts you with their own, "Whoa, did you hear that?" That brief delay between the thunder reaching your ears and the thunder reaching their ears tells you a lot about the location of that lightning strike: it hit closer to you than to your friend, since it got to you sooner.

Your brain uses the same method to determine sound location, but your left ear and right ear take the place of you and your friend at different locations. In other words, your brain measures the discrepancy between the sound's arrival times at each of your ears. Your ears are only inches apart, so thankfully your brain can detect microseconds (millionths of a second) of difference between your two ears receiving the same sound. Of course, if the sound comes from directly in front or in back of you, the discrepancy will be zero. However, if the sound is even slightly to your right or left, your brain will register the difference and use that to determine where to look for the sound (Brand et al., 2002; Yost, 2001).

A sound coming from your left side would not only hit your left ear sooner than your right ear, but it would be louder in your left ear as well. Your brain also uses this discrepancy in volume to aid in sound localization. Your brain is highly sensitive to this difference in loudness, needing only a fraction of a decibel of extra volume to determine that the sound is louder in, and therefore closer to, one ear than the other (McAlpine, 2010).

place theory
The explanation of pitch perception based on the idea that a person hears different pitches because tiny hairs in different places within the cochlea are stimulated.

frequency theory
The explanation of pitch perception based on the idea that a person hears different pitches because nerve impulses travel with different frequencies through the auditory nerve.

sound localization
The ability to perceive the location from which a sound originates.

Speech Perception. In recent decades, an increasing amount of research has focused on whether human speech is perceived in a different way than all other sounds. Some evidence suggests that the way people hear speech may be a specialized process (somewhat similar to the modular kinds of visual perception we discussed earlier with regard to how you see faces, bodies, and perhaps words). However, the extent of this specialization is still unclear, and some experts have expressed doubt about it (Bowers & Davis, 2004; Fitch, 2018; Fowler & Magnuson, 2012; Hickock & Poeppel, 2007).

One interesting line of evidence in support of specialized perception of speech comes from studies in which participants wear earphones that present a different audio stream into each ear. When those streams contain music, participants tend to listen to what they hear in their left ear, but when those streams contain speech, participants tend to listen to what they hear in their right ear. This suggests that, at least in comparison to music, different regions in different hemispheres of the brain may be dedicated to speech perception (Broadbent & Gregory, 1964; Kimura, 1967; Moore, 2012). There is even some fMRI (functional magnetic resonance imaging) evidence that 3-month-old babies, who have not yet begun to speak, use certain parts of their brains more than other parts when they hear speech, which suggests that some specialized speech perception mechanisms may be present from birth (Dehaene-Lambertz et al., 2002).

How Diversity Influences Hearing

DIVERSITY MATTERS

Earlier, we examined how diversity variables influenced the way people see. The same question has been examined for hearing as well. The number of hearing studies is not as great, but the evidence is similar: at least in some ways, culture shapes how and what you hear.

Exposure to certain sounds within a culture, especially at an early age, seems to shape hearing. Numerous studies have used music to demonstrate this finding (Dowling, 2001; Hannon & Trainor, 2007; Lynch et al., 1990, 1991; Morrison & Demorest, 2009). Across cultures, there are certain similarities in how musical sounds are organized. For instance, the most pleasing combinations of tones are typically separated by exactly one octave, which means they are multiples of each other's frequency (Levitin & Tirovolas, 2010).

Within that octave, however, different cultures divide the pitch range into a different number of distinct tones, usually between 5 and 15 (Levitin & Tirovolas, 2010). Those distinct tones are collectively known as the *scale*, and — here's the impact of culture — listening to music in your culture's scale makes you more sensitive to that scale but less sensitive to other scales. One study found that both adults and 10- to 13-year-old kids from Western cultures were much better at noticing out-of-tune notes in familiar Western scales than in unfamiliar Indonesian scales (Lynch & Eilers, 1991). A follow-up study found the same results for children as young as a year old, but dissimilar results for 6-month-old babies, suggesting that it takes at least half a year of exposure to a certain musical scale for a child's pitch sensitivity to shift in that direction (Lynch &Eilers, 1992).

The findings are similar for rhythms too: kids from Western cultures, as long as they are at least a year old, are better at noticing rhythmic mistakes (an "off-beat" moment in a song) in familiar Western music than in unfamiliar Balkan music (Hannon & Trehub, 2005a). When people from Western cultures listened to the Balkan music over and over again, 1-year-olds gained an equal sensitivity to those newly familiar rhythms, but adults did not (Hannon & Trehub, 2005b).

Gender is another factor that seems to influence hearing. Around the world, men are more likely than women to experience hearing impairment, but that finding can largely be attributed to men more often working at high-decibel jobs (construction, for example) likely to damage hearing (Mathers et al., 2000; Nelson et al., 2005). However, there's evidence that even among newborn babies, girls hear better than boys — a finding that can't be explained by experience in the workplace or anywhere else (Popple, 2010).

CHECK YOUR LEARNING:

3.16 What is audition?

3.17 What are the functions of the various parts of the ear, including the pinna, middle ear, and inner ear?

3.18 What is pitch, and what are the two competing theories that explain it?

3.19 How do you determine the location from which a sound is coming?

3.20 How does the perception of speech differ from the perception of other sounds?

3.21 How does diversity influence hearing?

To check your understanding of these questions, click show the answers or refer to the answers in the Chapter Summary.

Smell and Taste

YOU WILL LEARN:

3.22 what olfaction is.

3.23 how olfaction receptor cells work.

3.24 how olfaction relates to sex.

3.25 how olfaction abilities vary across people.

3.26 what gustation is.

3.27 how gustation receptor cells, or taste buds, work.

3.28 how experience can influence taste.

Vision and hearing are crucial, but they are not the most universal senses among all the species. Smell and taste are. Even organisms as tiny and simple as the single-celled amoeba have them. They may not have recognizable noses or mouths, but they definitely have a way of sensing the chemicals around them (smell) and the substances they might consume (taste) (Sell, 2014). Let's examine your sense of smell and then your sense of taste.

The Nose Knows: Your Sense of Smell

Olfaction is your sense of smell. It's well known that other species (dogs, for example) have better olfaction than humans, but don't underestimate the sophistication of your sense of smell. Remember our discussion of receptor cells in your eyes? There were four kinds: rods and three types of cones. There are at least *350–450* kinds of receptor cells in your nose, and a total of about 6 million to 10 million receptor cells, the most for any sense other than vision (Doty, 2010; Munger, 2010). Equipped with so many receptor cells of so many different types, your nose can detect about a *trillion* different scents (Bushdid et al., 2014).

How Olfaction Receptor Cells Work. The presence of so many different kinds of receptor cells means that even a seemingly simple smell is actually a complex combination. It's like the three types of cones in your retina blending red, green, and blue to make other colors. With olfaction, however, hundreds of different kinds of receptor cells do the blending. So even a smell as basic as cinnamon or chocolate is the product of many different kinds of receptor cells combining their inputs.

Researchers have found that people use *internostril comparison* to determine the location of a source of a smell. Remember how your brain localizes sound by noticing the discrepancy in the arrival time and the volume in each ear? Your brain does the same thing with the scents coming through each nostril, even though they are right next to each other. Your brain can tell which nostril is picking up a scent sooner and more strongly, then use that information to deduce what direction that scent is coming from (Arzi & Sobel, 2010; Porter et al., 2005). Humans are not the only ones to use internostril comparison — there's evidence some sharks do it, too, in their search for prey. That evidence led some researchers to speculate that the hammerhead shark, with its nostrils far apart on opposite sides of its unusually wide head, might represent an extreme evolutionary adaptation based on this ability (Gardiner & Atema, 2010).

-101PHOTO-/iStock/Getty Images

Olfaction is your sense of smell. With 350–450 kinds of receptor cells, your nose can detect about a trillion different scents.

olfaction
The sense of smell.

cilia
Tiny scent-seeking threads that extend from olfactory receptor cells through the mucus of your nose.

The millions of olfactory receptor cells deep in your nose each extend about 20 **cilia**: tiny scent-seeking threads through the mucus of the nose. Those cilia sweep the nose for scent-carrying chemicals, then carry them through the receptor cells and

wildestanimal/Moment/Getty Images

People use internostril comparison, or the discrepancy in the times that a scent reaches each nostril, to determine the location of a smell. Other species do, too. Some researchers argue that the hammerhead shark, with its nostrils set very far apart, might be especially advanced in this ability (Gardiner & Atema, 2010).

onto the two **olfactory bulbs**: brain structures located on the underside of your brain (behind the bridge of your nose) that receive scent information from cilia. The olfactory bulbs then send the olfactory information to the **olfactory cortex**: a collection of brain regions involved in smell, which includes the amygdala and parts of the cerebral cortex (Cowart & Rawson, 2001; Doty, 2010; Shah et al., 2010). Remember how we learned that the amygdala plays a prominent role in emotion, especially fear (Chapter 2)? When it receives olfactory information, the amygdala determines the emotional meaning of smells. It responds strongly when a smell is associated with a feeling, especially a feeling of fear or anxiety, but it responds weakly when a smell has no emotional importance (Winston et al., 2005; Zald, 2003).

Olfaction and Sex. Sometimes the emotion associated with a smell is sexual excitement. For many species, olfaction plays a significant role in sexual attraction. (Ever seen dogs sniffing each other?) There is even evidence that in some species, like lizards, voles, spiders, and bees, the male can use olfaction to determine whether the female is a virgin, and if not, how many times she has mated. And in other species, such as moths, females who have just mated stop producing the scent that attracts males and start producing a scent that repels them (Thomas, 2011).

Humans rely on olfaction during the mating, or dating, process too. Two types of olfactory information can play a role. The first is *odors*, which are smells of which you are aware. If it's an odor, you realize you're smelling it, and you also probably realize the effect it has on you. The second type of olfactory information is *pheromones*, chemical signals detected by your nose without your awareness. You don't *smell* pheromones, exactly, at least not in the same way you smell odors. You are not conscious of them, but they can influence your behavior, especially in terms of attraction to others.

Of course, for humans, pheromones are just one of many attraction factors (many of which are visual and verbal), but for some other species, pheromones are the dominant attraction factor. For example, a male silk moth needs to smell just eight molecules of a particular pheromone from the female to set into motion a full sequence of mating behavior (Brennan, 2010). Research continues on particular human pheromones and their effects, but at the moment one of the most widely recognized is androstadienone, which is found in men's sweat and which increases positive mood and sexual arousal in people attracted to men (Lundström et al., 2003; Wyart et al., 2007; Zhou et al., 2014).

Olfaction and COVID. When the COVID pandemic emerged in early 2020, many of the symptoms that sufferers reported didn't really distinguish the potentially deadly virus from less threatening illnesses: fever, cough, achiness, fatigue, and shortness of breath. Soon, however, a distinctive symptom emerged: loss of smell. Many people diagnosed with COVID noticed a complete inability to smell (*anosmia*) or an impaired ability to smell (*micronosmia*) (Lima et al., 2020). Numerous studies verify that loss of smell is indeed a hallmark indicator of COVID (but perhaps not for the Delta variant). For example, one study collected the symptoms of over 7000 people who tested positive for COVID and found that 65% of them had experienced loss of smell (Menni et al., 2020). In a smaller-scale study, researchers gave a scratch-and-sniff smell test (the UPSIT) to 60 people who were hospitalized for COVID. Almost all — 59 out of 60 — had an impaired sense of smell. Of those 59, over half had either completely lost their sense of smell or had severe smell impairment — and their impaired sense of smell was not limited to certain odors. In fact, most of the participants were partially or completely unable to detect all 40 of the smells included in the test, including mint, cinnamon, onion, gasoline, rose, and dill pickle (Moein et al., 2020).

Fortunately, the majority of people who lost their sense of smell due to COVID have recovered it. Unfortunately, that recovered sense of smell is not always as good as before. For some, especially those who struggled with the virus for many months ("long-haulers"), the sense of smell returns either weakened (needing a much stronger odor for them to detect it) or distorted (such that things smell different than expected,

olfactory bulbs
Brain structures located on the underside of your brain (behind the bridge of your nose) that receive scent information from cilia.

olfactory cortex
A collection of brain regions involved in smell, including the amygdala and parts of the cerebral cortex.

usually in a negative way). In one study, researchers followed up with people who experienced loss of smell due to COVID to assess their smell abilities 6 months later. Only a few had not regained any sense of smell at all, but over 40% reported at least some distortion in their sense of smell (*parosmia*) (Hopkins et al., 2021).

How Diversity Influences Olfaction. About 1–2% of the U.S. population experiences either hyposmia (limited ability to smell) or anosmia (no ability to smell), which is usually temporary and often caused by the flu or a sinus infection (Gilbert, 2008). Rates of hyposmia and anosmia increase with age, as does the danger: among older adults, a declining sense of smell can be an early sign of more serious or even life-threatening diseases, like Alzheimer's or Parkinson's (Amrutkar et al., 2015; Doty, 2010, 2012; Picillo et al., 2015; Velayudhan et al., 2013). To illustrate, one study tested the olfactory abilities of over 1600 adults over age 60. Five years later, 21.8% of those with olfactory impairment had died, compared to fewer than 10% of those with an intact sense of smell (Gopinath et al., 2012). The good news is that regular exercise maintains, and in some cases improves, olfactory abilities (among many other abilities) in older adults (Schubert et al., 2013).

DIVERSITY MATTERS

Age is not the only predictor of a relatively weak sense of smell. Another predictor is gender: men are generally worse than women at noticing and identifying scents (Ferdenzi et al., 2013; Sorokowski et al., 2019). One study in the early 1980s asked men and women to predict which smells each gender would be better at identifying. The participants guessed that men would be better at identifying at-the-time stereotypical "man stuff" like motor oil, beer, and cigars, while women would be better at identifying at-the-time stereotypical "woman stuff" like nail polish remover, baby powder, and Ivory soap. The results? Women were better at identifying all the smells (Cain, 1982).

Another study gave smell identification tests to hundreds of men and women from four cultural groups: Black Americans, White Americans, Korean Americans, and people native to Japan. Across all four groups, women outperformed men to almost exactly the same extent (Doty et al., 1985). Additional research on smell and gender has indicated that women, especially at childbearing age, rate the importance of olfaction higher than men do (Murr et al., 2018).

DIVERSITY MATTERS

Cultural experiences can also influence olfactory abilities, as illustrated by studies that compare the senses of smell of people from diverse ethnic groups (Sorokawska et al., 2015). In one study of this type, researchers gave smell tests to equal numbers of adults from Japan and Germany. They asked all participants to identify odors in three categories: odors that were more common in Japanese culture (such as dried fermented soybeans and Japanese tea), odors that were more common in German culture (such as marzipan and blue cheese), and odors that were common in both cultures (such as coffee and peanuts). Perhaps not surprisingly, results showed that participants were much better at identifying odors common in their own homeland than from the other, but equally good at identifying the odors common in both. The main conclusion here is that your cultural experience provides you with an advantage in recognizing some smells but a disadvantage in recognizing others (Ayabe-Kanamura et al., 1998).

The impact of cultural experience on the ability to detect odors is further supported by the fact that one of the most widely used smell tests has been modified for use in different countries. That smell test is the University of Pennsylvania Smell Identification Test (UPSIT), and it has been used in many studies examining people's sense of smell. It's a scratch-and-sniff test that asks the smeller to identify 40 different odors, including coconut, lemon, root beer, ginger bread, lilac, leather, and pine. As usage of the test spread outside the United States, international researchers made changes to better match the olfactory experiences of people in their countries, including China, France, Italy, Korea, and others. For example, in the Iranian version, hami melon replaces root beer and jasmine replaces lilac (Taherkhani et al., 2015).

One more diversity variable that can influence smelling abilities is socioeconomic status (SES). Generally, people from lower SES groups tend to perform worse on smell tests than people in higher SES groups. In one study, researchers gave the UPSIT to over 1500 people in Brazil, a country with a wide range of SES levels. People in the lower SES groups consistently scored lower than people in the higher SES groups, both overall and on many specific odors. For example, when the odor was pizza, 74% of the highest SES group got it right, but only 59% of the lowest SES group did. The discrepancies were similar for other odors, like apple (74% vs. 48%) and rose (78% vs. 59%). The researchers explained that there could be several reasons for these olfactory differences, including differences in pollution, health, and familiarity with the odors on the test (Fornazieri et al., 2019).

Detectable as Delectable: Your Sense of Taste

Gustation is your sense of taste. *Gust*ation comes from the same root as dis*gust*ing and the Spanish verb *gust*ar (as in "*Me gustan las enchiladas*"), all of which generally refer to how pleasing something is (or tastes) to you. How good it tastes is important not just for enjoyment but for health too. Gustation allows you to sense, and spit out, toxins and other substances that would cause you disease or discomfort if you ate them. For example, if you have ever taken a swig of spoiled milk, you understand this reaction. Gustation also encourages you to take in what you need to maintain homeostasis, or a good balance of essential elements in your body. That's why sports drinks like Powerade and Gatorade taste so good after you work out – your body loses a lot of salt when you sweat, and those high-sodium sports drinks replace it (Di Lorenzo & Rosen, 2010).

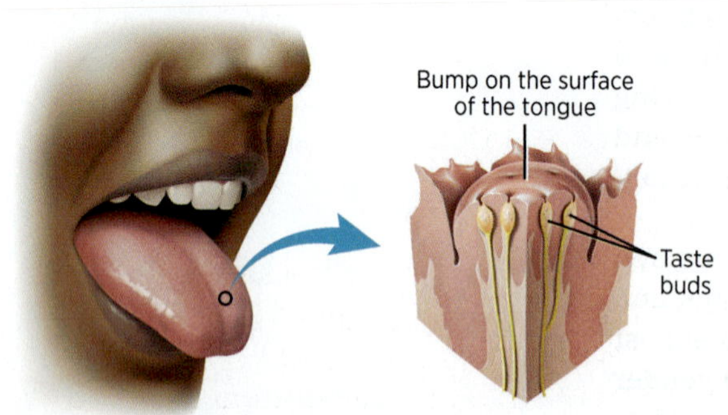

FIGURE 3.16 Taste Buds. Taste buds are the receptor cells of gustation. They are located on the edges of each papilla, or little bump, on the surface of your tongue.

Taste Buds: The Gustation Receptor Cells. The taste buds on your tongue, which regenerate about every 10 days, are your receptor cells for taste. As **Figure 3.16** and **Table 3.1** show, our taste buds can detect at least four basic qualities, and most likely a fifth, that combine to create the characteristic tastes of the foods and drinks you consume. The four definite taste qualities are sweet, sour, salty, and bitter. The fifth is *umami*, a Japanese word for *delicious taste* or *yummy* (Mather, 2011). In the gustatory world, for many years there was a controversy about umami and whether it is a basic taste quality of its own or a combination of others, but in recent years umami has become widely accepted as a full-fledged taste quality (Fleischman & Nguyen, 2018; Lawless, 2001; Yamaguchi & Ninomiya, 1999). Umami is a savory protein-rich flavor. You taste it when you eat foods like beef, chicken, tomatoes, mushrooms, soy, some cheeses, and some potatoes. You also taste it when you eat foods with MSG (monosodium glutamate), which has been used as a flavor enhancer in many foods (Di Lorenzo & Rosen, 2010).

We may all share the same kinds of taste buds, but our taste buds don't share the same levels of sensitivity. Indeed, there are a few supertasters among us. Supertasters

TABLE 3.1: Taste Receptor Cells and the Foods That Activate Them

TASTE RECEPTOR CELLS	TASTES DETECTED	FOOD EXAMPLES
Sweetness	Sugars	Sugary cereals, cookies, cakes, sweetened yogurts
Saltiness	Salts	Chips, crackers, popcorn, pretzels, macaroni & cheese
Sourness	Acids	Lemons, limes, sour candies
Bitterness	Plant alkaloids	Coffee, dark chocolate, arugula
Umami	Savory proteins	Beef, chicken, mushrooms, soy

gustation
The sense of taste.

are people with unusually sensitive palates. Supertasters were first identified by researchers examining high sensitivity to bitterness, but it soon became clear that the same people are often highly sensitive to other taste sensations too (Duffy & Bartoshuk, 2000). Supertasters are more likely to be women than men, a fact that's not surprising when you consider that women generally have more taste buds than men do (Bartoshuk et al., 1994). In experiments, supertasters can detect smaller changes in a food's ingredients ("This batch of cookies has a little more brown sugar than that one"), and are also better at determining whether a particular ingredient is present or absent within a mixture ("There's a dash of cayenne pepper in this chili") (Dinehart et al., 2006; LaTour et al., 2018).

There are both advantages and disadvantages to being a supertaster. On the upside, the bitterness of beer or "burn" of whiskey and other hard drinks is more intense, which decreases the likelihood of alcohol consumption and its negative consequences. Also, scrumptious foods taste extra-scrumptious. Actually, that could be a downside too: if chocolate chip cookies taste not just good, but amazing, there's a chance that supertasters will eat more than they should. Another downside has to do with green leafy vegetables like spinach and kale — their characteristic bitter tastes come across to supertasters as extra-bitter, which means supertasters are less likely to eat them and experience their health benefits (Prescott, 2010).

The Influence of Experience on Taste. Just as experience can shape how you see, hear, and smell, experience can shape how you taste as well (Prescott et al., 1997; Wardle et al., 2003). The main reason people from different cultures develop preferences for certain foods is exposure: that is, what they've had experience eating, especially as kids. Exposure, or lack thereof, may explain why certain tastes that typically come along later in life, like coffee, alcohol, and fancy chocolates and cheeses, often take a while to become acquired tastes.

DIVERSITY MATTERS

If your diet is less than perfect, the good news is that changing what you eat, and maintaining those changes over time, can actually change your preferences. If you lay off the Lay's potato chips for a while, you'll eventually find them less appetizing — too salty or too heavy for your new taste (Mattes, 1997; Tuorila, 2010). In one study, 4- and 5-year-old kids were given only one kind of tofu — sweetened, salty, or plain — 15 times over several weeks. By the end of the study, kids had developed a greater preference for the kind they were exposed to, but not the others — an important lesson for how we feed our kids and ourselves (Sullivan & Birch, 1990).

LIFE HACK 3.3

If you eat healthier foods consistently for a long time, your taste preferences will eventually change too. You'll like the healthier foods more and like the unhealthy foods less.

(Mattes, 1997; Sullivan & Birch, 1990; Tuorila, 2010)

CHECK YOUR LEARNING:

3.22 What is olfaction?

3.23 How do olfaction receptor cells work?

3.24 How does olfaction relate to sex?

3.25 How do olfaction abilities vary across diverse groups of people?

3.26 What is gustation?

3.27 What are the four basic qualities that taste buds can detect, and what is the fifth possible quality?

3.28 How can experience influence taste?

To check your understanding of these questions, click show the answers or refer to the answers in the Chapter Summary.

Other Senses

It's not just the holes in your head that draw in important sensory information. Your entire body does. Let's start our exploration of these bodily senses with a focus on what your skin takes in.

YOU WILL LEARN:

3.29 what your somatosenses are.

3.30 what your kinesthetic sense is.

3.31 what your vestibular sense is.

somatosenses
The senses experienced through the skin, primarily touch, temperature, and pain.

Skin Deep: Your Somatosenses

Your **somatosenses** are the senses you experience through your skin, primarily touch, temperature, and pain. Other senses, like itch, tickle, and tingle, are somatosenses too, but because they are so sparsely researched by psychologists, we won't cover them in detail (Carstens, 2010).

Touch. Your skin consists of two primary layers: the epidermis, visible on the outside, and the dermis below it (Linden, 2015; Weisenberger, 2001). Your skin has separate receptor cells for touch (mechanoreceptors), temperature (thermoreceptors), and pain (nociceptors) (Klatzky & Lederman, 2010). So if something makes you feel all three sensations – like a snowball in the face – it's because all three kinds of receptor cells were activated. You use those receptor cells to very quickly detect a lot of information about the objects you touch, including their size, shape, weight, texture, and more. Because of that, you're good at recognizing objects by touch when you can't see them. In fact, research shows that common household objects are typically recognized within 3 seconds with an accuracy rate of about 95% (Hsiao, 2010). For those who rely more on touch than other senses – like a person who is blind feeling the contours of the face of a loved one – recognition by touch is even more impressive.

Your touch (or tactile) receptors detect not only whether you are being touched, but how much pressure is being applied and whether the touch is accompanied by movement (Cholewiak & Cholewiak, 2010). People who study touch consider lots of variables about the way things feel against your skin, including how rough or smooth it is (consider sandpaper vs. satin sheets), how hard or soft it is (countertops vs. sofa cushions), and how sticky or slippery it is (chewed gum vs. a stick of butter). They also consider how the surface goes up and down in ridges, bumps, and other patterns (Hollins, 2010).

One measure of the strength of your sense of touch is called the *grating orientation discrimination test*. If you took this test, you'd be blindfolded and then touch objects that feature a pattern of ridges and grooves. The challenge is to say what direction the ridges and groove run. To get an idea of how this works, imagine closing your eyes and then running your fingers across potato chips with ridges of different sizes – the big, wide ridges in Lay's wavy chips versus the little, narrow ridges in Ruffles. The smaller the ridges and grooves are, the more difficult this task becomes. Generally, the limit is around the point when the grooves are narrower than 1 mm (Bensmaia, 2010).

Another measure of tactile sensory ability is the *two-point threshold test*. This is a simple test in which a device with two points – a lot like the compass you may have used in a geometry class – is placed on your skin. The question is how far apart the points need to be in order for you to perceive them as two points rather than one. Different parts of your body produce different results. Parts that are extremely sensitive to touch, like the fingers, lips, and cheeks, require a distance of just a few millimeters. Parts that are less sensitive, like the back, calf, and upper arm, require multiple centimeters (Bensmaia, 2010; Mather, 2011). Check **Figure 3.17** for more. And see the Watching Psychology box on sports and the benefits of touching.

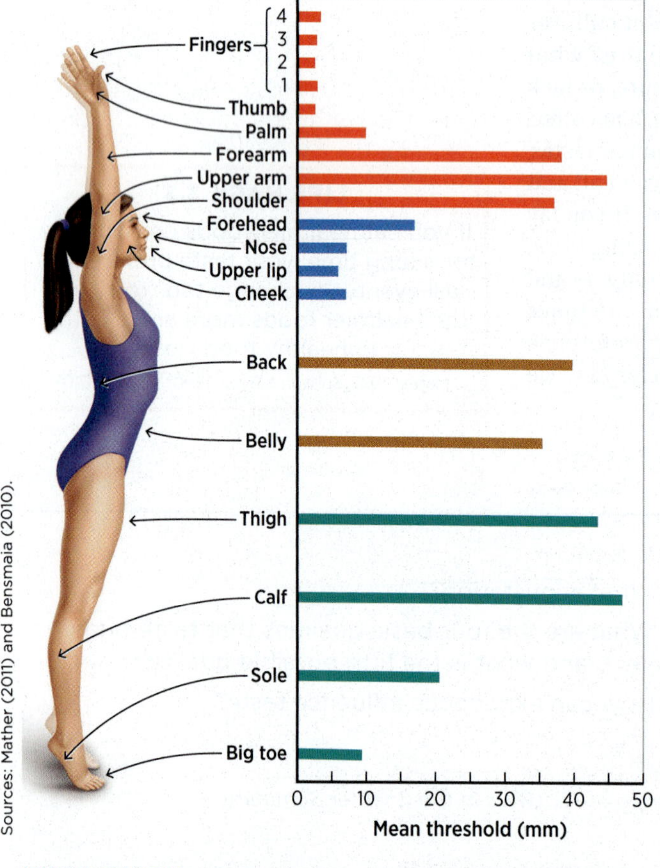

FIGURE 3.17 Touch Sensitivity of Different Skin Regions. How far apart do two simultaneous touches have to be for you to detect that they are two rather than one? On more sensitive areas of your skin, like your fingers and face, just a few millimeters. On less sensitive areas of your skin, like your legs and back, a lot more.

WATCHING PSYCHOLOGY

More Touch, More Wins?

When you watch basketball on TV, you see lots of touching—not just players committing fouls, setting screens, or boxing out for rebounds, which are all part of the game—but extra, intentional touching. To congratulate, console, or celebrate, teammates touch in all kinds of ways: high fives, chest bumps, flying shoulder bumps, head slaps, and bear hugs. A team of psychological researchers wondered, do teams that touch more win more (Kraus et al., 2010)?

To answer this question, these researchers watched TV broadcasts of a game featuring each of the 30 NBA teams early in the season. Every time two teammates touched, they counted it. Then they compared touchy-feely teams to non-touchy-feely teams in a couple of ways. First, they looked at just the five games immediately following the one they watched. They found that teams with winning records in that five-game span had touched about 50% more than teams with losing records. Next they waited until the season ended and correlated the amount of touch with the total number of wins. That correlation was strongly positive (.42), indicating that the extent to which teammates touched each other during that early-season game predicted the number of wins that team would earn throughout the season.

Of course, it's important to keep in mind that a strong correlation does not necessarily indicate cause. To assume that touch *causes* success on the basketball court, based only on the results of this study, would be flawed logic. It could be instead that success on the basketball court causes more touching, or that both variables are influenced by a third variable outside the scope of this study. However, the finding that NBA teammates who touch each other more also succeed more does raise some interesting questions. For example, to what extent might the same correlation be true for other teams as well, including not only sports teams, but teams or groups who work together in non-sports activities?

Ashley Landis-Pool/Getty Images

Touch is important even among professional sports teams. Research indicates that successful NBA teams tend to high-five, hug, and otherwise touch each other more than less successful teams (Kraus et al., 2010).

Temperature. Your skin senses temperature through two types of thermoreceptors, each of which is specially designed to detect either hot or cold (but not both). A cluster of these on a particular area of your skin is known as a cold spot or a hot spot. Overall, your skin has more cold spots than hot spots, and certain areas on your body, including some on your forearm, likely have regions about the size of a key on your computer keyboard where hot spots are completely absent (Green, 2004). Your cold thermoreceptors get their input to your brain about 10 times faster than your hot thermoreceptors do. Your face, especially your lips and cheeks, is among the most sensitive to temperature changes in either direction; your extremities, especially your feet, are least sensitive (Jones, 2010).

Pain. Unlike touch and temperature, pain is difficult to measure, which poses a significant challenge to researchers who try to study it (Cervero, 2013; Turk & Melzack, 2011). There is no such thing as an objective, accurate "pain meter," no equivalent to pounds of pressure for touch or degrees for temperature. Instead, the experience of pain is highly subjective, which means that each person uniquely determines their own experience of pain.

Sometimes, the same injury causes one person excruciating pain and another person none, such as two same-age children who receive the same shot from their pediatrician. Sometimes, an injury causes pain well after it occurs, when the person can shift attention away from the task at hand, such as when a soldier gets injured on the battlefield but only feels pain after reaching safety. Sometimes, the experience of pain

Jamie Kingham/Cultura RM/Alamy

A snowball in the face will activate all three types of receptor cells in your skin: touch (mechanoreceptors), temperature (thermoreceptors), and pain (nociceptors).

can depend upon expectation, such as the difference between the expected soreness that comes the day after a grueling workout and the similarly intense but unexpected soreness that arises for no apparent reason. It's clear that pain serves an adaptive purpose in the evolutionary sense, steering us away from things and situations that could harm or kill us, but it's unclear why we experience it in such idiosyncratic ways (Eccleston & Crombez, 1999).

DIVERSITY MATTERS The experience of pain varies widely across all groups, of course, but a growing number of studies have found that gender can influence the experience of pain. In general, women tend to experience greater sensitivity to pain and have a higher risk for chronic pain than men. Researchers believe there may be multiple factors behind this gender-based gap. One factor is biological differences in the way the brain processes pain (Bartley & Fillingim, 2013; Mogil, 2020). Another factor is the difference in socialization of gender roles, which encourage men to deny or distract themselves from pain and encourage women to acknowledge their pain and seek help or support (Wise et al., 2002).

Psychologists and other researchers have offered many theories to explain pain. None is perfect, but one that has powerfully influenced our understanding of pain for decades is the *gate control theory of pain* (Melzack & Wall, 1967; Moayedi & Davis, 2013; Nathan, 1976). The basic idea of the gate control theory of pain is that pain has three dimensions or "systems" (Melzack & Casey, 1968; Melzack & Wall, 2008; Rollman, 2010):

1. The sensory–discriminative system identifies where pain is and how bad it is (how the pain directly feels).
2. The motivational–affective system produces the emotions you have about pain (how having the pain makes you feel).
3. The cognitive–evaluative system determines your interpretation and response to pain (how you think about and what you do about the pain).

The presence of these three dimensions of pain can at least partially explain why pain can be so subjective. It's not just about what happened to your body, such as the severity of the ankle sprain, the number of stitches, or the size of the bruise. It's also about the thoughts and feelings you have about the pain ("Oh no – this is a catastrophe!" vs. "This will be a minor hassle for a couple of days"). Additionally, it's about your response ("I'm helpless – there's nothing I can do about it" vs. "I'll get medical attention, educate myself about it, and do what I can to minimize it"). Although gate control theory has needed some updates since its introduction in the 1960s, and improvements in technology have allowed for more details about the neurological basis of pain, it remains a strong guide to our understanding of pain (Mendell, 2014).

One particularly vexing question about pain that gate control theory (or any other theory) cannot fully explain is ***phantom limb pain***. Phantom limb pain is felt in a part of the body that no longer exists, such as someone with an amputation feeling pain in the arm or leg that was amputated. People with amputations feel other sensations in their phantom limbs as well, but pain, unfortunately, is relatively common and at times excruciating. Similar experiences are often described in people whose limbs are still there but do not function because of paralysis from a brain or spinal cord injury (Brugger, 2010; Chien & Bolash, 2017; Lackner, 2010a).

What little research has been done on phantom limb pain suggests that perhaps the pain has something to do with brain plasticity (as described in Chapter 2), or the brain's attempt to reorganize after the loss of the limb (Flor et al., 2006; Makin & Flor, 2020; Ramachandran & Hirstein, 1998). It also seems to relate to pain in that limb before it was lost – the more pain was present when the limb was there, the more phantom pain is likely after it's lost (Flor, 2002). Functional prostheses, or replacement body parts that keep the corresponding part of the brain active, can be helpful in some cases (Brugger, 2010; Foell & Flor, 2013; Lotze et al., 1999).

CHAPTER APP 3.3

The GeoPain app enables users suffering from physical pain to pinpoint their daily pain experiences on a 3D body map. They can track the intensity and frequency of their pain over time, choose terms to describe the pain specifically (burning, aching, shooting, etc.), identify triggers for their pain, receive suggestions from others who have experienced similar pain, and even export their pain data to share with their doctors on social media.

How does it APPly to your daily life?
If you were experiencing pain, especially recurring or chronic pain, how might an app like GeoPain be most helpful to you? With whom would you choose to share your pain data, and why?

How does it APPly to your understanding of psychology?
How would an app like GeoPain help you understand the ways pain can be described and measured? How would it help you understand the variability in the ways people describe pain?

To learn more about this app or to download it to your phone, you can search for "GeoPain" on Google, in the iPhone App store, or in the Google Play store.

On the Move and in Balance: Your Kinesthetic Sense and Vestibular Sense

kinesthetic sense
The sense of the position and movement of the body parts.

vestibular sense
The sense of balance.

Your **kinesthetic sense** is your sense of the position and movement of your body parts. Your kinesthetic sense comes from sensors in the muscles, tendons, and joints throughout your body (Lackner, 2010b; Reed, 2010). Closely related is your **vestibular sense**: your sense of balance. Your vestibular system is largely located in your inner ear (Lackner, 2010c). Together, your kinesthetic sense and vestibular sense provide you with constant feedback about the position of your body and each of its parts, including the direction each is moving and the speed with which that movement is happening.

You typically take kinesthetic sense and vestibular sense for granted, but you notice them from time to time. For example, if you are sitting in an adjustable office chair and you adjust the height, you notice yourself rising or sinking even if your eyes are closed. If your alarm beeps but you don't want to get up, you can reach your hand toward it to hit the snooze without even opening your eyes because you know where your hand is in space. If an earthquake rattles your room, even without any of the sights or sounds you'd notice at the time, your body would tell you that you're being shaken.

Even when you're taking in visual information, your kinesthetic and vestibular senses provide additional information about where you are, especially related to landmarks you come across (Chance et al., 1998). In one study, researchers led participants along an unfamiliar pathway on a college campus, passing landmarks like a water fountain, a courtyard, a fence, a restroom, and a set of stairs. These participants wore a video-recording device over both eyes that included a screen, so they saw only what was on the screen rather than seeing the environment directly. Later, a different group of participants sat in the lab and watched the videos that the first group made. Both groups were later tested on their knowledge of the route. The first group – those who actually walked the route – did much better. They made fewer mistakes when asked to point from one landmark to another, and also when they drew a map of the route. Both groups *saw* the route in the same way, but only the first group *felt* it with their bodily senses – kinesthetic and vestibular (Waller et al., 2004).

Researchers have found that certain experiences can affect your kinesthetic or vestibular senses in a negative or positive way. On the downside, multiple injuries can inhibit your kinesthetic sense. One study focused on participants who had sprained one ankle, but not the other, multiple times. These participants sat in a chair in which their vision of their lower bodies was blocked. The experimenter made slight turns of each ankle and found that it took much more of a turn for participants to notice a change in the position of their often-injured ankle than in their never-injured ankle. Their injuries had reduced their kinesthetic sensitivity in their bad ankles (Garn & Newton, 1988). On the upside, certain training experiences can boost your kinesthetic or vestibular senses. For example, practicing the martial art of tai chi can improve your kinesthetic sense and balance (Jacobson et al., 1997; Wu, 2002).

Tightrope walkers depend heavily on their kinesthetic sense to know precisely the location and movement of each body part and on their vestibular sense to maintain balance.

CHECK YOUR LEARNING:

3.29 What are your somatosenses?

3.30 What is your kinesthetic sense?

3.31 What is your vestibular sense, and where is it located?

To check your understanding of these questions, click show the answers or refer to the answers in the Chapter Summary.

CHAPTER SUMMARY

The Fundamentals of Sensation and Perception

3.1 Sensation is the ability of your sensory organs to pick up energy in the environment around you and transmit it to your brain. Perception is the ability of your brain to interpret the raw sensations it has taken in.

3.2 Human sensation and perception evolved in ways that have been critical for survival.

3.3 Absolute threshold is the minimum level of a stimulus necessary for you to detect its presence at least half of the time. Difference threshold (or just noticeable difference) is the smallest change in a stimulus necessary for you to detect that change at least half of the time.

3.4 Sensory adaptation is the tendency of your sensation of a stimulus to decrease when the stimulus remains constant.

3.5 Perceptual constancy is your brain's ability to maintain the same perception of an object even when conditions around it cause it to produce different sensations.

3.6 Selective attention is paying more attention to one sensory channel than others. Sensory interaction is the idea that your senses can affect each other in often interesting ways.

3.7 In bottom-up processing, what you sense becomes a perception with no influence from expectations or previous experiences. In top-down processing, your expectations or previous experiences influence what you perceive.

Vision

3.8 Each sense is important, but people are influenced by what they see more than by what they hear, smell, taste, or touch.

3.9 The cornea is a thin, transparent cover for the eye that bends images to improve vision. Just behind the cornea is the iris, a colored circular muscle in the center of the eye. The iris opens and closes the pupil in the middle of the eye. The lens is a clear layer beneath the surface of the eye that helps to maintain focus by varying its shape. The retina is the rear part of the eyeball, which receives visual stimuli and sends them to the brain via the optic nerve. The retina contains receptor cells called rods and cones, which help to see visual stimuli under varying conditions. The fovea is a part of the retina that contains many cones but no rods, and the blind spot is a part of the retina that contains no rods or cones.

3.10 Saccadic eye movements are "jumps" that take your gaze from one particular point to another. Compensatory eye movements make adjustments for the movement of your head. Vergence eye movements move your two eyes in unison to focus on a single chosen image.

3.11 Depth perception is the ability to judge the distance and depth of objects. It depends on monocular and binocular depth cues, as well as retinal disparity.

3.12 Hue is the color of light, as determined by its wavelength. The two competing theories of color vision are trichromatic theory, which is based on the idea that cones are specialized to sense either red, green, or blue, and opponent-process theory, which is based on the idea that cones are specialized to sense specific opposite pairs of colors (like red-green and blue-yellow).

3.13 Factors such as proximity, similarity, common fate, connectedness, and closure help people to determine whether objects are separate or part of a group.

3.14 People view certain objects in specialized ways, particularly faces, bodies, and maybe words.

3.15 Diversity influences how and what people perceive, including color vision and focus on isolated objects versus objects in relation to each other.

Hearing

3.16 Audition is your sense of hearing.

3.17 The outer ear, called the pinna, consists of the parts of the ear that you can easily touch. The middle ear is made up of the tympanic membrane, the ossicles, and the oval window membrane. The inner ear primarily consists of the cochlea, which sends sound waves to the brain by way of the auditory nerve.

3.18 Pitch is the description of how "high" or "low" a sound is. There are two competing theories that explain how we perceive pitch: place theory and frequency theory.

3.19 To determine sound location, or where a sound originates, your brain measures the discrepancy between the sound's arrival times at your left ear and right ear.

3.20 Research suggests that speech perception is a specialized human ability.

3.21 Many diversity variables influence hearing, including gender and exposure to specific cultural sounds.

Smell and Taste

3.22 Olfaction is your sense of smell.

3.23 Hundreds of types of olfaction receptor cells blend input to create each smell sensation.

3.24 Olfaction plays a significant role in sexual attraction and mating in many species, including humans.

3.25 Age and gender are variables that influence sense of smell.

3.26 Gustation is your sense of taste.

3.27 Your tongue's taste buds can detect at least four basic qualities (sweet, sour, salty, and bitter) and possibly a fifth (umami).

3.28 Experience shapes how people taste. People from different cultures enjoy different foods, which is largely due to exposure.

Other Senses

3.29 Somatosenses are the senses you experience through your skin, primarily touch, temperature, and pain.

3.30 Kinesthetic sense is your sense of the position and movement of body parts, which comes from sensors in the muscles, tendons, and joints.

3.31 Vestibular sense is your sense of balance. The vestibular system is largely located in the inner ear.

KEY TERMS

sensation, p. 65
transduction, p. 65
perception, p. 65
extrasensory perception (ESP), p. 66
parapsychology, p. 66
absolute threshold, p. 66
difference threshold (just noticeable difference), p. 67
sensory adaptation, p. 68
perceptual constancy, p. 68
selective attention, p. 68
cocktail party effect, p. 69
sensory interaction, p. 69
sensory conflict theory, p. 71
bottom-up processing, p. 71
top-down processing, p. 71
perceptual set, p. 72
change blindness, p. 72
inattentional blindness, p. 72
vision, p. 74
cornea, p. 74
iris, p. 74
pupil, p. 74
lens, p. 75
visual accommodation, p. 75
retina, p. 75
rods, p. 75
cones, p. 75
fovea, p. 76
blind spot, p. 76
depth perception, p. 77
monocular depth cues, p. 77
binocular depth cues, p. 77
retinal disparity (stereopsis), p. 77
hue, p. 78
trichromatic theory of color vision, p. 79
opponent-process theory of color vision, p. 79
figure–ground organization, p. 80
gestalt, p. 80
audition, p. 83
pinna, p. 84
tympanic membrane, p. 84
ossicles, p. 84
oval window membrane, p. 84
cochlea, p. 84
pitch, p. 84
place theory, p. 85
frequency theory, p. 85
sound localization, p. 85
olfaction, p. 87
cilia, p. 87
olfactory bulbs, p. 88
olfactory cortex, p. 88
gustation, p. 90
somatosenses, p. 92
kinesthetic sense, p. 95
vestibular sense, p. 95

SELF-ASSESSMENT

1. _____ is the ability of your sensory organs to pick up energy in the environment around the body and transmit it to your brain.

2. Your ability to determine whether the amount of salt varies between two potato chips indicates your _____. Your ability to determine whether salt is present at all on a potato chip indicates your _____.

a. difference threshold; absolute threshold
b. absolute threshold; difference threshold
c. perceptual constancy; extrasensory perception (ESP)
d. cocktail party effect; top-down processing

3. When you are in a noisy crowd of people, you have the ability to tune out other conversations to concentrate on yours, yet you may also notice your name if it is mentioned in another conversation. This experience describes

a. sensory conflict theory.
b. perceptual constancy.
c. the cocktail party effect.
d. change blindness.

4. When you tell someone your eye color, you're really telling them the color of your _____, the circular muscle in the center of your eye.

a. retina
b. lens
c. cornea
d. iris

5. Cones are receptor cells

a. in your nose.
b. in your ear.
c. in your eye that detect shades of gray.
d. in your eye that detect color.

6. _____ is an organized whole that is perceived as different from just the sum of its parts.

7. What's the function of your pinna?

a. to enhance the ability of your taste buds
b. to guide sound in the environment toward your inner ear
c. to enlarge or shrink the opening in your iris to adjust the amount of light your eye takes in
d. to form tiny scent-seeking threads that extend from olfactory receptors through the mucus of your nose

8. The _____ is the spiral fluid-filled structure in your inner ear that sends sound waves to the brain via the auditory nerve.

9. _____ is your sense of smell.

10. A person experiencing problems with the vestibular sense is most likely to have

a. a very high difference threshold when tasting food.
b. a tendency to fall down because of an inability to stay balanced.
c. extreme sensitivity to temperature.
d. an inability to detect scents.

To check your understanding of these questions, click show the answers or refer to the answers in Appendix B.

Research shows quizzing is a highly effective learning tool. Continue quizzing yourself using LearningCurve, the system that adapts to *your* learning.

WHAT'S YOUR TAKE?

1. Experience shapes your difference thresholds. What do you have a lot of experience with? Do you have a difference threshold to match? Do you have areas of expertise in which you can notice subtle differences where other people wouldn't? Perhaps you drink lots of bottled water and can detect differences between brands that your friends can't. Maybe you've used many different types of headphones, and you have developed a sensitivity to each pair's ability to deliver bass and treble, while your friends think they're all the same. Maybe you're a car expert who can recognize the difference between the hums of the engines of very similar models. Maybe you're a barbecue expert who tastes the difference between sauces, even if their labels say they are the same flavor.
2. Babies all respond similarly to various kinds of music, but they soon become accustomed to music from their own culture. Do you know how this worked in your life? Did your earliest months and years make you more familiar with certain scales, rhythms, or styles of music? If you were surrounded by rap, pop, country, classical, jazz, or any other kind of music, how does that shape the way you respond to those kinds of music now?

SHOW ME MORE

3.1 Sensory Interaction: Combining Video and Audio

Achieve

This video explains and illustrates sensory interaction—specifically, how your brain integrates video and audio sensations.
Veritasium/BoClips

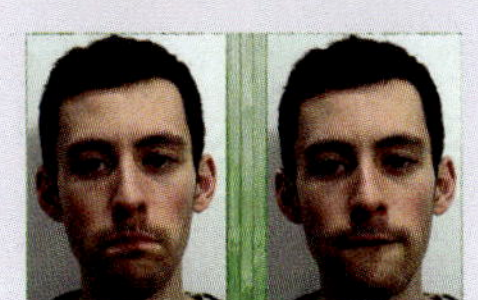

3.2 The McGurk Effect: Does Lipreading Override Hearing?

Achieve

This brief video illustrates the McGurk effect.
Timothy Revell

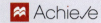

3.3 Mudsplashes, Gorillas, and Change Blindness

Achieve

This video gives you a chance to experience change blindness for yourself.
Visual Generation/Shutterstock.com

3.4 The Margaret Thatcher Effect on More Faces

http://tiny.cc/htd15y

This Web site allows you to connect to flip photos of Barack Obama, Justin Beiber, and Kate Middleton to see more examples of the Margaret Thatcher effect.
Courtesy of Peter Thompson, from Thompson, P. (1980). Margaret Thatcher: A New Illusion. *Perception, 9,* 383–384

This video is hosted by a third party Web site (source). For accessible content requests, please reach out to the publisher of that site.

3.5 The Science of Smell

https://www.npr.org/2020/11/11/933847587/a-nose-dive-into-the-science-of-smell

This podcast features an interview with Harold McGee, an expert on smell, explaining how smell and taste interact, how we perceive complex odors, and how the process of cooking releases scents.
-101PHOTO-/iStock/Getty Images

This video is hosted by a third party Web site (source). For accessible content requests, please reach out to the publisher of that site.

3.6 My Psychology Podcast

Achieve

This podcast episode features the author of this textbook, psychologist Andy Pomerantz, speaking with other instructors of introductory psychology courses about the most important and interesting concepts in this chapter.
Macmillan Learning

4 Consciousness

viviana loza/Shutterstock

CHAPTER OUTLINE

You can find Mammoth Cave National Park in southern Kentucky, about halfway between Louisville and Nashville. The cave attracts thousands of visitors every year to explore its 400-mile maze of pitch-black pathways. For over a hundred years, out-of-town visitors to the cave have stayed at the Mammoth Cave Hotel, where the rooms feature a mini-fridge, a coffee maker, and satellite TV.

In June 1938, Nathaniel Kleitman and Bruce Richardson visited Mammoth Cave, but they didn't stay at the Mammoth Cave Hotel. They stayed in the cave itself. In the dark. For over a month.

Kleitman was a professor at the University of Chicago and a pioneer of sleep research, and Richardson was his student. In an early attempt to understand why we sleep when we do, they lived in Mammoth Cave. They wondered: if we stay in a chamber deep inside a cave for weeks, with no sunlight or stars to indicate day or night, will we still sleep and awaken on the same 24-hour schedule? Could we shift to a different schedule—for example, one that repeats every 22 or 26 hours—and, if so, what would be the consequences of such a shift? The study produced mixed results, as the younger Richardson had more flexibility in his sleep–wake pattern, while the older Kleitman was more closely tied to the standard 24-hour schedule. More important, though, the study was a major early step into the largely unexplored science of sleep. In his later experiments, Kleitman took more adventurous steps in the study of sleep: keeping himself awake for a week straight, spending 2 weeks in a submarine, and taking his family to a town in Norway above the Arctic Circle to live for 2 months in constant sunlight (Gottesmann, 2013; Kleitman, 1963; Kleitman & Kleitman, 1953; Wolf-Meyer, 2013).

Research on sleep has progressed significantly since the Mammoth Cave experiment. Of course, research on sleep is just one type of research on *consciousness*, the focus of this chapter. Consciousness is basically awareness of what's happening around you and inside of you. And sleep is just one state of consciousness. In this chapter, we'll cover many varieties of consciousness. We'll examine what contemporary researchers have learned about sleep and the biological rhythms that affect it. We'll explore insomnia and other sleep-related problems, including why they happen and how they can be treated. We'll consider drugs, both legal and illegal, that influence consciousness. And we'll consider other topics related to consciousness too, including hypnosis, meditation, and mindfulness.

Consciousness is your awareness of yourself and your surroundings. That definition may make the concept seem simple, but different experts offer different definitions of consciousness (Gazzaniga, 2018; Revonsuo, 2018; Velmans, 2009; Vimal, 2009). Some experts say that the main ingredients of consciousness are the ability to monitor and control what's going on both inside and outside your mind (Kihlstrom, 2007). Other experts say the ability to think about thinking (yours and others') is at the heart of consciousness (Corballis, 2007). Still others say that what makes you conscious is your ability to pick up on intention: what you intend to do and what others intend to do (Bering & Bjorklund, 2007). Some experts have even wondered if animals or machines could possess a form of consciousness (Dehaene et al., 2017; Godfrey-Smith, 2017; Grinde, 2018). The common thread across the many definitions of consciousness is awareness, or an ability to recognize and be responsive to what's happening in and around you.

consciousness
A person's awareness of their self and surroundings.

Let's take a more detailed look at the state of consciousness that has been most extensively studied by psychologists and other researchers: sleep.

Sleep

Everybody sleeps. Not just people — other mammals, birds, and reptiles sleep too. There is some evidence that amphibians and fish also sleep (or at least do something very similar) (Lesku et al., 2006; Rattenborg, 2007; Rattenborg et al., 2009). In fact, sleep "appears to provide restoration for all living organisms. Even plants have a time-keeping . . . mechanism allowing them to 'anticipate' daily changes in light and temperature" (Espie & Morin, 2012, p. 1).

Some animals, including certain species of birds, whales, dolphins, and porpoises, can actually sleep with one eye open (Lyamin et al., 2008; Peigneux et al., 2012; Siegel, 2005). For example, consider mallard ducks. When they gather together to sleep, the mallards on the left edge of the pack sleep with their left eye open and the mallards on the right side sleep with their right eye open, all for the purpose of looking out for predators approaching from their side. Sleeping with one eye open is called *unihemispheric sleep*, a practice that allows the half of the brain opposite the closed eye to rest while the half opposite the open eye remains alert. By the way, the mallards in the middle sleep with both eyes shut (*bihemispheric sleep*), confident that their partners on the edges are protecting them (Lima et al., 2005; Rattenborg et al., 1999).

In humans, there have been some significant changes in sleep throughout our long history. For Neanderthals (70,000–40,000 B.C.), sleep was probably similar to the way nonhuman primates still sleep now — lots of brief sleeps instead of

YOU WILL LEARN:

4.1 why you sleep.

4.2 how sleep deprivation affects you.

4.3 what your circadian rhythm is and what influences it.

4.4 what the stages of normal sleep are.

4.5 how sleep differs across diverse groups of people.

4.6 what co-sleeping is and how common it is.

4.7 what various sleep abnormalities are.

4.8 how to prevent and treat sleep problems.

IT'S LIKE...

Consciousness Is Like a Light Controlled by a Dimmer

It is easy to think of consciousness like a light switch, something that is on when you're awake and off when you are asleep. But it would be more accurate to think of consciousness as a dimmer, something that can be adjusted to any level. Of course, sleep and wakefulness are common levels of consciousness, but they are not the only ones. There are lower levels of consciousness than sleep. Remember, even when you sleep, you are conscious enough to respond if the fire alarm blares in your ear or your phone's vibrations shake the bed or the bright sunlight streams through a crack in the blinds onto your closed eyes. That is not true for a person in a coma or under anesthesia for a medical operation.

There are also levels of consciousness between sleep and wakefulness — that gray area of brief experiences like daydreaming, half-sleeping before you actually drift off, and half-awakening as sleep comes to an end (Gillespie, 1997; Gurstelle & De Oliveira, 2004; LaBerge, 2007). And in some cultures, there are higher levels of consciousness than merely being awake. For example, Buddhists describe higher states of consciousness that stem from transcending the material world that can break the chains that bind us to suffering (Patel, 2012).

Anastasiia Markus/Shutterstock

All humans sleep. So do mammals, birds, reptiles, and many other forms of life.

just a long one, including many during daytime hours. (Ever go to the zoo and find the chimpanzees or baboons dozing through a sunny afternoon?) By the Neolithic period (around 10,000 B.C.), humans were increasingly getting all of their z's in one big nighttime session and staying awake through most, if not all, of the day (Espie & Morin, 2012). That was true until a recent development on the human timeline: the invention of the electric light bulb. Artificial light meant that the setting of the sun did not require the end of a day's activity. So, more than humans could before, we stayed up well into the night and slept well into the morning (Thorpy, 2010).

Why Do We Sleep?

We spend one-third of our lives sleeping, but researchers don't have a clear-cut explanation for why (Frank, 2006a). There are plenty of sleep theories, but so far, none of these theories can fully explain the function of sleep. An obvious answer is that we sleep to rest, to give the body and brain some time off from the heavy use they get during our busy days. But sleep is much more than rest. (If you're doubtful, spend a night just resting — awake — rather than sleeping, then see how refreshed you feel and how well you function the next day.)

Sleep Theories and Evolution. Many sleep theories emphasize evolution (Blumberg & Rattenborg, 2017; Keene & Duboue, 2018; Miyazaki et al., 2017). After all, this universal behavior must have provided some adaptive advantage to our species. But what, exactly, could that advantage be?

Staying Still. *Inactivity theory* suggests that the main advantage of sleep is simply staying still during the dark hours of night, which kept our ancestors out of danger. In the dark of night, early humans couldn't do much good in terms of hunting or gathering, but they could do a lot of harm in terms of getting injured, getting lost, or falling prey to animals that see well at night (Siegel, 2009). However, inactivity theory doesn't explain why sleep, which makes us mostly unaware of our surroundings, is better than merely resting while awake.

Saving Energy. *Energy conservation theory* highlights the fact that we spend far fewer calories when asleep than when awake. This was a crucial difference for our ancestors, for whom food was much more difficult to find and store (Penev, 2007; Schmidt, 2014). With this kind of food insecurity, a nightly mini-hibernation to save calories might have been a beneficial strategy.

Recharging the Body. *Restorative theory* suggests that sleep allows the body to recharge and strengthen itself, an idea supported by the fact that good sleep boosts the immune system, speeds recovery from injury and illness, and activates human growth hormone (Bryant et al., 2004; Siegel, 2005). Without good sleep, the body has less opportunity to restore itself, which helps to explain why people with abnormal sleep patterns are at greater risk for many diseases, some of which could be deadly (Abbott et al., 2018; Åkerstedt et al., 2017; Kwok et al., 2018; Lin et al., 2018; Liu et al., 2017).

Developing the Brain. *Brain plasticity theory* emphasizes the fact that sleep allows the brain to change, grow, and reorganize itself, which makes sense when you notice how much babies sleep during those early months when their brains are growing so quickly (Frank, 2006b; Page et al., 2018).

Enhancing Memory. *Evolutionary theory* points out that sleep is essential for consolidating memories and for resting our vision system (Diekelmann & Born, 2010; Kavanau, 2004, 2005, 2006, 2008; Paller et al., 2021; Walker, 2012). It is noteworthy that vision is the only sense that shuts off entirely when you sleep: hearing, smell, taste, and touch stay on, at least to a limited extent. By shutting off vision when you sleep, your brain gets time to process all of the visual images you've taken in during the day. It's like taking videos on your phone nonstop from the minute you wake up, and then giving your phone a break from recording at night while those many hours of continuous video get transferred into a storage system. Interestingly, researchers who studied a particular species of fish found that those who live near the surface of the water, where light allows them to see, sleep far more than those who live in caves, where darkness prevents sight (Duboué et al., 2011). Other researchers have refuted this idea, pointing out that some animals rely heavily on the visual system yet don't sleep as much as might be expected (Capellini et al., 2008; Harrison, 2012).

Sleep Deprivation. All of the sleep theories in the previous section make sense, and each is supported by some scientific evidence. However, no one sleep theory eclipses the others, so the puzzle of sleep remains incompletely solved. Most likely, the full answer involves a combination of these advantages, as well as others still to be identified by researchers (Frank, 2010; Walker, 2017). But there's one thing we know for sure: when you don't get enough sleep, you feel the consequences. **Sleep deprivation** is the failure to get enough sleep, regardless of the reason.

MY TAKE VIDEO 4.1

Sleep Deprivation

"I don't get enough sleep because. . ."

Visit Achieve to watch this My Take Video and then answer questions.

Achieve

Sleep deprivation is remarkably common in the United States, where about 35% of adults get too little sleep (defined as less than 7 hours per day) on a regular basis (Centers for Disease Control and Prevention, 2017). Unfortunately, the consequences of sleep deprivation are far-reaching in terms of how you feel and how you perform. For example, sleep deprivation causes irritability and moodiness (Hall et al., 2012). In one study of 750 teenagers, the day after a bad night's sleep featured significantly higher levels of anxiety than the day after a good night's sleep (Fuligni & Hardway, 2006). Similar results were found in studies of college students and medical residents (Galambos et al., 2009; Zohar et al., 2005).

Sleep deprivation harms not just your feelings but your performance, too. Your brain is simply not as sharp and not as quick when it operates on too little sleep. There are four reasons why (Monk, 2012):

1. **Cognitive slowing.** Your neurons and the connections between them just don't function as fast when you are sleep deprived. You may notice this if you play any video game that involves repetitive fast responding. Poor sleep the night before rarely results in good gaming.
2. **Cognitive rigidity.** Lack of sleep kills your creativity. You are less likely to create an original masterpiece or even offer witty comments when talking with your friends if you haven't slept well.
3. **Decreased motivation.** It is not just that you can't perform well when you're sleepy; it is also that you don't *care* that much about your poor performance when you're sleepy. As a result, your decreased effort compounds your poor performance.
4. **Likelihood of unintended sleep the next day.** The day after a sleepless night, there's a greater chance that you'll doze off — or at least daydream or space out a lot — which interferes with performance.

Aside from the occasional all-nighter, complete sleep deprivation is, thankfully, a relatively uncommon occurrence for most of us. What is far more common is partial sleep deprivation, caused by a night when you hit the sack too late, get up too early, or sleep fitfully throughout the night. String together a series of nights with partial sleep deprivation, and the negative effects accumulate (Krause et al., 2017; Lim & Dinges, 2010). One study tracked people who were limited to 5 hours of sleep per night for a week straight and found that their alertness, memory, attention, and reasoning all worsened throughout the week (Dinges et al., 1997). Another study extended the partial sleep deprivation to 2 weeks, and the effects were even worse. Those who slept 6 hours per night during the second week performed as poorly as someone who had just pulled an all-nighter, and those who slept only 4 hours per night during the second week performed as poorly as someone who had just pulled two consecutive all-nighters (Van Dongen et al., 2003). More recent research extended the partial sleep deprivation to 3 weeks and found significantly higher levels of ethnic bias and negative interpersonal evaluation. Specifically, sleep-deprived participants (about 90% of whom were either White or Black) displayed more negative views toward people with Arab or Muslim names and also judged people with certain facial features as more dangerous compared to when they slept enough (Alkozei et al., 2017, 2018).

LIFE HACK 4.1

Avoid sleep deprivation, which causes real impairment in memory, attention, reasoning, and mood. It happens not only if you pull one all-nighter, but also if you string together consecutive nights of insufficient sleep.

(Hall et al., 2012; Krause et al., 2017; Lim & Dinges, 2010; Monk, 2012; Von Dongen et al., 2003)

As the From Research to Real Life box shows, what is especially scary about these sleep deprivation studies is that sleep-deprived people often don't recognize how seriously sleep deprivation affects them (Pilcher & Walters, 1997; Van Dongen et al., 2003). When a sleep-deprived person drives a car, that lack of recognition gets dangerous (Horne & Reyner, 1999; Howard et al., 2004). One study of more than 5000 drivers found that the most sleep-deprived were the most likely to crash, whether the driver was professional (truck or bus operator) or nonprofessional (Carter et al., 2003). One study estimates that in the United States, 328,000 car crashes per year, including 6400 fatal car crashes, involve a drowsy driver (Tefft, 2014).

sleep deprivation
The failure to get enough sleep, regardless of the reason.

FROM RESEARCH TO REAL LIFE

Do You Realize What Sleep Deprivation Does to You?

Research shows that sleep deprivation leads to crabby moods, slowed thinking, and decreased motivation. People who are sleep-deprived don't always recognize that they are sleep-deprived and that their sleep deprivation might impair them significantly (Van Dongen et al., 2003). What about college students in particular? How well do they recognize their own sleep deprivation?

One study used an overnight method to answer this question (Pilcher & Walters, 1997). The study, which involved psychology students as participants, lasted from 10 P.M. on a Friday to 11 A.M. on Saturday. On Friday night, after everyone arrived at the sleep lab, the researchers randomly sent half of the students home with the instruction to sleep a full 8 hours and then come back the next day. The other half of the students stayed at the sleep lab—and stayed awake—all night. They hung out, talked with each other, played video games, watched movies, or did homework, but they were not allowed to sleep.

On Saturday morning, the students who slept at home came back, and both groups of students took the same tests. These tests measured their cognitive abilities (reasoning, reading comprehension, evaluating written arguments, and logic). The students also estimated their own level of performance on the tests. The results of the tests were no surprise: the students who stayed up all night in the sleep lab performed worse. The big surprise was in the students' estimates of their own performance: those who stayed up all night provided estimates that were *higher* than the participants who got a good night's sleep. In other words, the sleep-deprived students performed worse than their peers who got 8 hours of sleep but believed they performed better. These findings suggest sleep deprivation impairs both your cognitive abilities *and* your ability to recognize that impairment. •

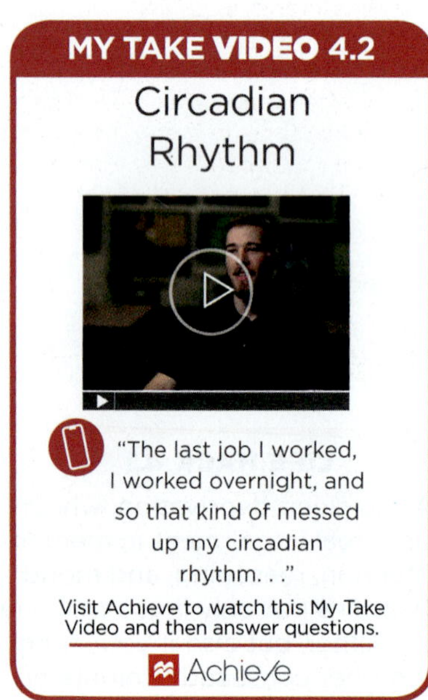

MY TAKE VIDEO 4.2
Circadian Rhythm
"The last job I worked, I worked overnight, and so that kind of messed up my circadian rhythm. . ."
Visit Achieve to watch this My Take Video and then answer questions.
Achieve

Circadian Rhythm: Your Biological Clock

A good understanding of sleep requires a broader understanding of the daily pattern in which sleep is included. That pattern is controlled by your **circadian rhythm**: the 24-hour cycle on which your brain and body function. (If you speak Spanish, it might help your memory for this term: *circadian* breaks down to *circa-*, which means around, and *-dia*, which means day, so *circadian* means *around a day*.) Your circadian rhythm is what makes you predictably sleepy at certain times of the day and predictably alert at others. Most of us have circadian rhythms that fall into step with each other, and with the rhythm of the sun as well, but there is some variability. For instance, you probably know a few night owls and a few morning people.

As **Figure 4.1** shows, our alertness tends to start at around midlevel when we wake up, then rise throughout the morning, peak sometime around noon, decline through the afternoon, and drop to its lowest levels through the evening until we're back in bed.

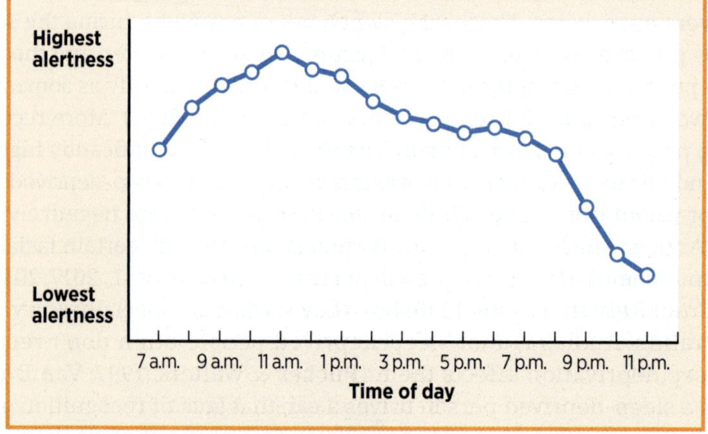

FIGURE 4.1 Alertness Through the Day and Night. During the waking hours of 7 A.M. to 11 P.M., alertness climbs through the morning, peaks around 11 A.M. or noon, fades slightly through the afternoon, and drops to its lowest levels before bedtime. Data from Monk (2012) and Monk et al. (1994).

circadian rhythm
The 24-hour cycle on which the brain and body function.

WATCHING PSYCHOLOGY

What (Body Clock) Time Is Kickoff?

Imagine that you had to play an intramural flag football game at 3 A.M. And imagine that the other team had already recalibrated their body clocks to be wide awake at that time of day. Would that seem fair?

To a lesser extent, the same kind of thing happens when NFL teams from across the country play each other: because of time zone differences, one of the teams is playing later on their own internal body clocks than the other team. That difference can be substantial, especially considering how our circadian rhythm begins to drop in the afternoon and then drops rapidly at night. One study examined 25 seasons' worth of *Monday Night Football* games, with special attention to games in which teams from the Pacific time zone (San Francisco 49ers, Seattle Seahawks, Los Angeles Chargers, etc.) played against teams from the Eastern time zone (New York Giants, Philadelphia Eagles, New England Patriots, etc.) (Smith et al., 1997). After taking into account other influences (the point spread, home field advantage, etc.), the researchers found that West Coast teams won more often and by more points than expected. In fact, they beat the spread about 68% of the time.

The researchers emphasized circadian rhythms in their explanations of their findings. Specifically, by kickoff at 9 P.M. Eastern time, the East Coast players' circadian rhythms have dropped much lower than those of their West Coast opponents. So if the San Francisco 49ers host a 6 P.M. game with the New England Patriots, the 49ers are playing at 6 P.M. on their body clocks, while the Patriots are playing at 9 P.M. on their body clocks. This 3-hour difference could translate into a lapse by the Patriots — a missed field goal or a missed tackle, for example — that makes the difference in the game.

A study of Major League Baseball found that circadian rhythms can influence who wins and who loses in that sport too (Winter et al., 2009). Over 10 years and 24,000 games, teams that had a *circadian advantage* — playing a game in which their circadian rhythm had been less disrupted in the past 24 hours than their opponent's — won significantly more often than expected. This effect is slightly stronger than home field advantage. In fact, home teams tend to *lose* games when they have just returned home from another time zone if they play a visiting team that has already adjusted to that time zone. For example, if the Chicago Cubs return home to Wrigley Field (in the Central time zone) from a West Coast trip to play the St. Louis Cardinals the next day, the Cubs are actually at a slight *disadvantage* if the Cardinals have played their most recent games in St. Louis, Milwaukee, or any other Central time zone location. So, the next time you watch sports, don't forget about the body clock factor as you predict a winner.

Research on professional football and baseball games shows that circadian rhythm can play a role in the outcome of sporting events in which one team travels across time zones to play another (Smith et al., 1997; Winter et al., 2009).

Sleep Studies. Since the early days of sleep research, scientists have tried to learn about circadian rhythm by conducting *free-running* sleep studies (Duffy & Dijk, 2002; Lack & Wright, 2012). In these sleep studies, people spend days or weeks in an environment devoid of time cues — no windows to reveal sunlight or darkness, no changes in internal lighting, no clocks or watches, no smartphones, and so on. With only their internal clock to guide them, how would these participants schedule their time? Early attempts at free-running sleep studies, which were done in caves, bunkers, and basements, showed varied results. In some, people stuck closely to a 24-hour clock. In others, people fell into a 25-hour rhythm, essentially waking up about an hour later every day, with a few people extending the day even more than that (Aschoff, 1965; Czeisler & Dijk, 2001; Kleitman, 1963; Webb & Agnew, 1974; Wever, 1984).

More recent studies, done in professional sleep labs under tightly controlled conditions, suggest that people in free-running studies tend to extend the day, but not by much. Instead, these participants sleep and wake on a cycle that averages about 24.2 hours, which means that they wake up about 12 minutes later every day (Czeisler et al., 1999; Dijk et al., 1999; Duffy et al., 2001). Explaining why the schedule strays from 24 hours at all — a result not found when free-running studies are conducted on mice and rats — remains a challenge for sleep researchers (Dijk & Lazar, 2012).

Circadian Rhythm and Internal Forces. Your circadian rhythm is determined by two things: (1) internal forces and (2) external cues (Borbély, 1982; Saper et al., 2005).

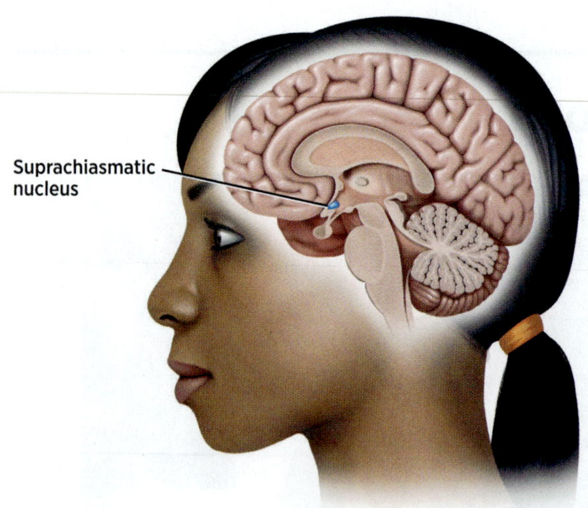

FIGURE 4.2 Suprachiasmatic Nucleus. The suprachiasmatic nucleus, a tiny structure within the hypothalamus, is the main timekeeper within your body.

The internal forces are driven by a very particular part of your brain: the *suprachiasmatic nucleus* (SCN), which is within the hypothalamus (**Figure 4.2**). This tiny structure is a mighty timekeeper. If you've ever seen a daily timer for a lamp on a dimmer — which can be programmed to be brighter at certain hours of the day and darker at others — then you have some idea of how the SCN turns up and turns down your brain and body. The SCN actually controls a whole system of clocklike mechanisms throughout your body (known as the *peripheral body clocks*), including your digestive tract, liver, muscles, and fat tissue (Froy, 2010). In rare cases when the SCN is damaged or disrupted, major sleep-related problems occur (Menaker et al., 2013; Van Erum et al., 2017).

Circadian Rhythm and External Cues. Although your SCN operates according to its own internal clock, it is also sensitive and responsive to its surroundings (Asher & Sassone-Corsi, 2015). That is, your SCN picks up external cues, especially light, that might call for changes in your pattern of sleep or wakefulness (Dijk & Lazar, 2012). If your eyes take in lots of light during nighttime (or, to a lesser extent, lots of darkness during daytime), your circadian rhythm adjusts slightly, as if pulled toward staying awake when light is available and pulled toward sleeping when it's not (Duffy & Wright, 2005; Stothard et al., 2017).

This adaptation to light and dark is probably a leftover from the evolution-based human tendency to stay awake when the sun shines and stay asleep when it doesn't. Interestingly, people who live in rural areas have circadian rhythms that match with natural sunrise–sunset patterns more than people who live in big cities, where artificial light is more inescapable (Roenneberg et al., 2007). One group of researchers took participants camping for a week, where their eyes saw no light other than the sun (and a nighttime campfire). The campers' circadian rhythms shifted noticeably during that week to synchronize with the rise and fall of the sun, which meant that they became early birds, going to sleep closer to nightfall and getting up closer to the crack of dawn than they typically did at home (Wright et al., 2013).

For you, the most important consequence of this circadian responsiveness to light might be the brightness with which you surround yourself in your day-to-day life. This light includes not just overhead lights and lamps, but the TVs, computers, and smartphones that you might stare at before bed. To your SCN, that bright light signals daytime, so it tries to keep your brain and body awake. Interestingly, treatment of circadian rhythm disorders often includes bright light therapy, in which people are exposed to bright lights — at the right times of day — to reset their body clocks (Figueiro et al., 2018; Lack & Wright, 2012).

Another external cue that can affect your circadian rhythm is food (Asher & Sassone-Corsi, 2015; Vetter & Scheer, 2017). The time at which you eat can determine how sleepy or alert you feel throughout the day. This effect may not be evident after just one oddly timed meal — like eating a sandwich at an all-night diner at 3 A.M. However, making a consistent shift to different eating times can disrupt your circadian rhythm (Wehrens et al., 2017). In a study of rats, researchers shifted mealtime for 1 week and found that the rats' circadian rhythm was disrupted, affecting not only activity levels but also blood sugar levels and metabolism (Yoon et al., 2012).

Of course, it is harder to manipulate mealtimes in humans than in rats, but one team of researchers used an innovative method to get around that inconvenience. They studied people observing Ramadan, the month on the Islamic calendar in which many people who practice Islam don't eat or drink between sunrise and sunset. Researchers found that several signs of circadian rhythm, including the timing and amount of certain hormones, were different during Ramadan than at other times of the year (Bogdan et al., 2001). However, more recent research on the topic suggests that other temporary lifestyle changes that take place during Ramadan, such as changes in the amount and timing of exercise, work, and other activities, may account for circadian rhythm changes as much as the intermittent fasting (Qasrawi et al., 2017).

Some researchers have suggested that persistently poor *chrononutrition*, in which the eating schedule mismatches the natural highs and lows in energy levels, can lead to health problems. Unfortunately, poor chrononutrition is common to many Western lifestyles and can contribute to obesity, diabetes, sleep disturbances, and cardiovascular disease (Crispim & Mota, 2018; Froy, 2010; Hart et al., 2020; Huang et al., 2011; Maury et al., 2010; Portaluppi et al., 2012; Pot, 2018).

One activity that can throw off your circadian rhythms significantly is *shift work*, particularly working the overnight shift (James et al., 2017; Richardson, 2006). Shift work often determines when you can eat, sleep, and do almost everything else. The number of shift workers who suffer from significant problems related to sleep and wakefulness is noteworthy: 14–32% of people who consistently work overnight and 8–26% of people whose shift rotates between overnight and other times (Drake et al., 2004). The obvious reason is that the human body can only adjust so much to a schedule that strays from the sleep-when-it's-dark strategy that evolution selected for us. However, there are other reasons for this disruption too. For example, shift work often causes strain on important relationships (Newey & Hood, 2004; Vallières & Bastille-Denis, 2012).

Trying to get all of your sleep during the day comes with practical problems too: neighbors making noise, kids demanding attention, and sunlight seeping through the windows. A variety of serious health problems, including obesity, heart problems, strokes, ulcers, and possibly cancer, happen at a high rate among shift workers (Haus & Smolensky, 2013; Manenschijn et al., 2011; Newey & Hood, 2004; Reid & Zee, 2004; Vyas et al., 2012). For women, even more health-related problems have been associated with shift work: increased menstrual pain and bleeding, irregular timing of the menstrual cycle, premature birth, and spontaneous abortion (Chung et al., 2005; Cone et al., 1998; Knutsson, 2003; Labyak et al., 2002; Mahoney, 2010; Nurminen, 1998). When shift work throws off circadian rhythms, the consequences can be much worse than just a little daytime sleepiness.

REM
Rapid eye movement, or the flitting of the eyeballs behind the eyelids during sleep.

REM sleep
The stage of sleep in which intense brain activity and vivid dreams are most likely to occur.

non-REM sleep
Any sleep other than REM sleep, when rapid eye movement, intense brain activity, and dreams are unlikely to occur.

Normal Sleep

We've already mentioned sleep problems, and soon we will be covering them in even more detail. Let's focus here on what happens during normal sleep.

Stages of Sleep. At its most basic, your sleep can be divided into two types, *REM sleep* and *non-REM sleep*. **REM** is rapid eye movement, or the flitting of the eyeballs behind the eyelids during sleep. **REM sleep** is the stage of sleep in which intense brain activity and vivid dreams are most likely to occur. By contrast, **non-REM sleep** is any sleep other than REM sleep, when rapid eye movement, intense brain activity, and dreams are unlikely to occur.

As **Figure 4.3** shows, non-REM sleep can be further divided into stages (Moore, 2006; Rama et al., 2006; Silber et al., 2007). *Stage 1 sleep* is the lightest sleep, which happens right when you fall asleep and for a short time afterward (Carskadon & Dement, 1996; Ohayon et al., 2004). When you're in stage 1 sleep, you've just drifted off. You stop responding when people call your name, but if you do wake up, you may say you hadn't even been sleeping yet. *Stage 2 sleep* is a bit deeper. Your body temperature drops, your heart rate slows, and it takes more to wake you up.

Stage 3 and *stage 4* are the deepest stages of sleep and together are often called *slow-wave sleep*. In slow-wave sleep, an EEG shows that brain activity produces big, slow waves that are markedly different from any other stage of sleep or wakefulness. In slow-wave sleep, you are difficult to wake up. If you do arise from slow-wave sleep, you are likely to be confused and disoriented for a short time, a condition sleep researchers sometimes call *sleep inertia*, or being "sleep drunk" (Jewett et al., 1999; Silva & Duffy, 2008; Wertz et al., 2006).

Following stages 3 and 4 sleep is REM sleep. Following REM sleep, the whole cycle repeats again. In a typical night of high-quality sleep, the cycle lasts about 90 minutes and repeats about five times. The cycle differs slightly throughout the night, such that

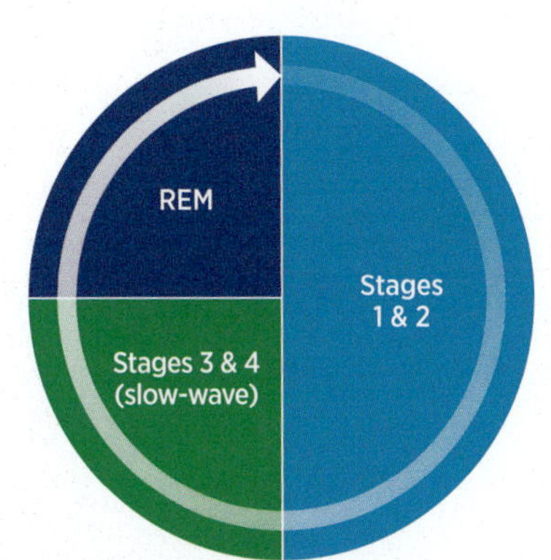

FIGURE 4.3 Type of Sleep Each Night. A typical 8-hour night of sleep consists of about five sleep cycles, each of which lasts about 90 minutes. As illustrated here, about half of each cycle consists of stage 1 and stage 2 sleep. About a quarter is stage 3 and stage 4 sleep, and about a quarter is REM sleep.

early cycles are heavier on stages 3 and 4 sleep, but later cycles are heavier on REM sleep (Feinberg & Floyd, 1979; Peigneux et al., 2012).

The discovery of REM sleep in the mid-1900s was a landmark of early sleep research, revealing a universal state of consciousness into which we all fall (Aserinsky & Kleitman, 1953). REM sleep features a fascinating combination of characteristics: the brain is very active (producing EEG waves that resemble those during waking hours), but the body is completely inactive (**Figure 4.4**). That is due to **REM paralysis**: temporary immobility during REM sleep. This discrepancy between the high level of activity of your brain and the complete inactivity of your body is the reason early sleep researchers also called REM sleep *paradoxical sleep*. There is a paradox, or contradiction, between the amount of action in brain and body (Jouvet et al., 1959).

That action in your brain during REM sleep is most likely a dream (Kramer, 2006). If sleep researchers wake up somebody during REM sleep, there is about an 80% chance of the sleeper recalling a dream, a much higher chance than if the sleeper woke up during non-REM sleep (Nielsen, 1995, 2000, 2004; Vogel, 1991). You probably have experienced this. Certain mornings, the alarm wakes you up from an intensely vivid dream. Other mornings, the alarm catches you at a non-REM point in your sleep cycle, and you wake up empty-minded, as if you haven't dreamed all night. Early sleep researchers argued that dreams happened exclusively during REM sleep, but more recent research suggests that at least some kind of dreamlike activity also happens during other stages (De Koninck, 2012; Dement, 1960).

REM Rebound. When you don't get enough dream time one night, the next night you experience **REM rebound**: an increase in REM sleep after a period of REM sleep deprivation. REM rebound is part of the more general experience of *sleep rebound* – catching up on sleep after a night (or more) in which sleep was scarce. When your body responds to a sleep debt in this way, it adds hours to your sleep total and fills those hours with a higher percentage of REM sleep than usual (Endo et al., 1998; Ocampo-Garcés et al., 2000). When sleep rebound happens, your body rushes past the non-REM sleep stages more quickly than usual to get to REM sleep sooner.

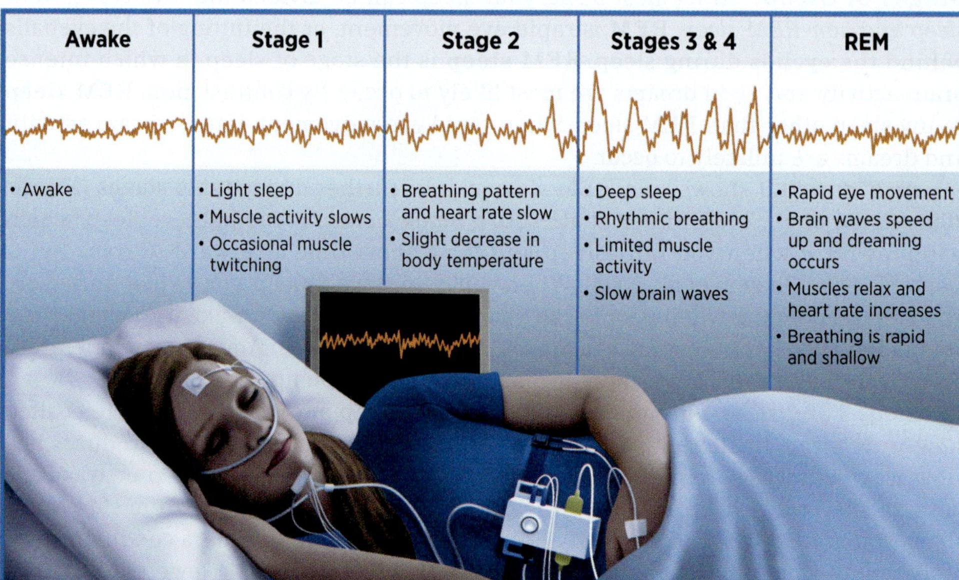

FIGURE 4.4 Sleep Waves. Stage 3 and stage 4 sleep earned the nickname *slow-wave sleep* because of the slower, bigger patterns they produce on EEG readings. Notice also the similarities between the waves of wakefulness and REM sleep.

REM paralysis
Temporary immobility during REM sleep.

REM rebound
An increase in REM sleep after a period of REM sleep deprivation.

In terms of more general sleep rebound, you never fully recover the lost hours of sleep. If you typically sleep 8 hours per night but pull an all-nighter on Sunday night, you won't sleep 16 hours on Monday, or somehow squeeze in all 8 of those missing hours during the rest of the week. One study found that people who were kept awake one night and were then given 24 hours straight in bed recouped only about 5–6 hours of extra sleep — far short of the full 8 hours that they lost (Rosenthal et al., 1991).

Diversity in Normal Sleep

We all progress through the stages of non-REM and REM sleep in the same way. However, many aspects of our sleep vary across different groups of people.

DIVERSITY MATTERS

Gender and Sleep. Consider gender differences in sleep. Women's sleep typically contains more slow-wave sleep than men's (Dijk & Lazar, 2012). Women generally sleep for slightly longer periods than men do, but they also experience more insomnia than men (Groeger et al., 2004; Morgan, 2012; Ursin et al., 2005; Yager, 2010). Men, on the other hand, experience more sleep apnea than women (Theorell-Haglöw et al., 2017). Women also experience more disruptive patterns of sleep when they are pregnant, nursing, experiencing PMS, or going through menopause, including difficulty falling asleep and staying asleep (Baker & Driver, 2004, 2007; Driver, 2012; Manber & Bootzin, 1997; Moline et al., 2003).

DIVERSITY MATTERS

Ethnicity and Sleep. Let's consider how sleep differs among people of various ethnicities. In certain groups of people around the world, sleep is almost exclusively limited to a single long nighttime slumber. That is called *monophasic* sleep, and it's most common in the United States and other Western countries. In other regions, sleep is more typically *biphasic*, meaning that it happens two times per day — overnight plus a nap in the afternoon. Spain and many Spanish-speaking countries, including Mexico, are good examples of this "siesta" culture. Lots of other places around the world are neither monophasic nor biphasic but *polyphasic*, which means that they sleep not only at night and at siesta time but at various other times, often for brief catnaps. Cultures in which polyphasic sleep is common include Japan, China, and a variety of other places around the world (Arber et al., 2012; Brunt, 2008; Richter, 2003; Steger, 2003; Steger & Brunt, 2003).

Sounds like naps are common in lots of cultures. Are naps beneficial?

Most of the research says yes, naps have benefits (Milner & Cote, 2009). Napping enables you to catch up on (at least some) of last night's lost sleep and maintain alertness through the afternoon and evening. Another less obvious benefit of naps may be avoidance of activity in the late afternoon. Early in human history, people lived exclusively in warm climates, and peak temperatures often reached dangerous levels, so less activity during that time could have kept people safe and alive (Takahashi & Kaida, 2006). That time of day — late afternoon, or siesta time — is the most popular time for naps, and it is a time that when many people around the world start to drag (Dinges & Broughton, 1989). In the United States, many of us are likely to grab a cup of coffee, gulp down an energy drink, or just power through it. But in other parts of the world, a nap is the answer, and sleep researchers are learning why.

To examine the impact of napping, a team of researchers examined the abilities of college students on a visual discrimination task throughout the course of the day and night. The task was relatively simple: basically, participants had to determine whether certain bars on a complex grid were vertical or horizontal. Students who took no nap

CHAPTER APP 4.1

Sleep Cycle

Sleep Cycle is one of numerous available apps that monitor your stages of sleep. Specifically, it tracks your sleep stages and provides you with feedback regarding how much time you spent in each stage. It can also wake you up in an ideal (lighter, rather than deeper) stage of sleep.

How does it APPly to your daily life?
How could this kind of app improve your sleep and, more broadly, your life?

How does it APPly to your understanding of psychology?
How does this kind of app enhance your understanding of the various stages of sleep, including REM?

To learn more about this app or to download it to your phone, you can search for "Sleep Cycle" on Google, in the iPhone App store, or in the Google Play store.

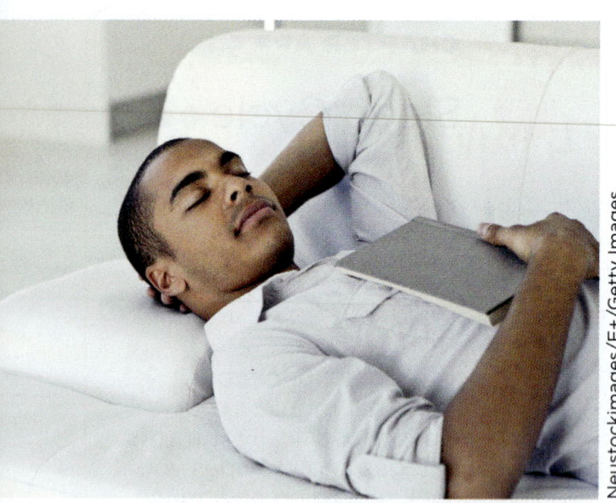
Neustockimages/E+/Getty Images

In many parts of the world, daytime naps are common.

got worse as the day went on. Students who took a half-hour nap at 2 P.M. didn't get any worse after they woke up. Students who took an hour-long nap at 2 P.M. actually got better after they woke up. And students who took a 90-minute nap — which contained both slow-wave and REM sleep — performed best of all (Mednick et al., 2002, 2003). Another study found that even a quick 10-minute nap had significant positive effects on both cognitive performance and feelings of fatigue (Tietzel & Lack, 2002). Other researchers have found similar results (Debarnot et al., 2011; Hayashi et al., 1999; Ji et al., 2018; Karni et al., 1994; Scullin et al., 2017). In fact, some researchers have suggested that strategic napping should become part of the daily regimen for such professionals as pilots, emergency room doctors, and train conductors (Cheng et al., 2014; Hartzler, 2014; Hursh & Drummond, 2017). Some college libraries have even installed "nap stations" or "nap pods" to help college students overcome or avoid sleep deprivation (Wise et al., 2018).

DIVERSITY MATTERS

In addition to the frequency of naps by adults, there are many other ways that sleep habits differ between ethnic groups. One review of studies compared the sleep habits of people from different countries. The review found that kids in Europe, North America, and Australia were likely to go to sleep earlier, wake up earlier, and sleep longer compared to kids in Asia and the Middle East. Also, infants in Asia took more frequent and longer naps than infants in other countries. Further, in some Asian countries (for example, Korea), the habit of daily naps for children extended years beyond the age at which those naps usually drop out of the daily schedules of kids from the United States and some European countries. There may be many reasons for these differences, including diet, parenting attitudes and practices, lifestyles, sleeping arrangements, and the presence of siblings or other family members in the room or home (Jeon et al., 2021).

DIVERSITY MATTERS

Within the United States, one review of sleep studies found a striking racial difference between the sleep behavior of kids from 2 to 5 years old. On average, White kids went to bed earlier, had more consistent bedtimes, slept longer at night, and napped less during the day than Black and Latinx kids. These differences, especially the lesser amount of nighttime sleep for Black and Latinx kids, were significant enough for the authors of the review to suggest that the children's development may be negatively affected (Smith et al., 2019). A separate study found similar patterns based not on race or ethnicity, but on socioeconomic status — with lower-income kids showing sleep patterns that resembled those of the Black and Latinx kids in the first study — highlighting the intersection of variables that can combine to influence sleep behavior (Ordway et al., 2020).

DIVERSITY MATTERS

Age and Sleep. In addition to gender and culture, age is another factor that can determine what normal sleep patterns look like. Of course, kids sleep more, especially when they're very young. In the first few weeks after birth, babies sleep about 16 hours per day. Those 16 hours, to the chagrin of new parents, are evenly distributed through the 24-hour day, which means babies awaken frequently during the night. By about 4 months, however, most of babies' sleep happens at night, and by about 6 months, most babies are giving their parents a solid 6-hour block of overnight sleep (Lee & Rosen, 2012; Rivkees, 2003). In the United States and culturally similar countries, two naps a day are the norm for most kids into the second year of life, with the first nap usually around 10 A.M. and the second usually around 3 P.M. Two-year-olds typically drop the morning nap, and between ages 3 and 5, most kids no longer need daytime naps to function well (Sadeh et al., 2009).

When kids hit puberty, an important shift happens. They don't seem to need more sleep, but they do seem to shift their sleep time to a later hour of the day (Carskadon & Tarokh, 2013; Feinberg & Campbell, 2010; Wolfson & O'Malley, 2012). As the preteen years begin, kids strongly prefer a later bedtime and a later wake-up call. This preference clashes with most high school schedules, which demand early wake-up times. This clash has led to significant debate regarding policies about high school start times (Au et al., 2013). Check the Current Controversy box for more.

CURRENT CONTROVERSY

Should High School Start Later in the Day?

Everybody knows that teenagers like to stay up later and wake up later than they did when they were younger. You may remember that shift happening yourself, perhaps in middle school but almost certainly by high school. It's not just a trend or a U.S. thing. Teens show this pattern around the world (Andrade & Menna-Baretto, 2002; Dorofaeff & Denny, 2006; Gibson et al., 2006; Reid et al., 2002; Saarenpaa-Heikkila et al., 1995; Thorleifsdottir et al., 2002; Yang et al., 2005). Neuropsychological research using EEGs found that the brain activity in teens indicated lower attentiveness in early morning classes than in classes later in the day (Dikker et al., 2020). There is even some evidence that other mammals, including monkeys, rats, and mice, exhibit the same circadian shift around the same point in their life span (Hagenauer et al., 2009). The reasons for this shift are not entirely clear, but puberty has a lot to do with it (Wolfson & O'Malley, 2012). Research on sixth-grade girls found that those who started puberty earlier had a stronger preference for later bedtimes and wake-up times (Carskadon et al., 1993, 2004).

Whatever the cause of this push toward later bedtimes in teens, it's a terrible match for early-morning start times in high school (Carskadon & Tarokh, 2013). According to researchers, many high schoolers are simply "expected to function at school at a time when their bodies were meant to sleep" (Wolfson & Richards, 2011, p. 269). School performance isn't the only undesirable outcome from this situation. So are car crashes. One study compared accident rates in two similar neighboring high schools in Virginia—one in Virginia Beach and the other in Chesapeake. Over a 2-year stretch, the accident rate for teen drivers in Virginia Beach, where school starts 75–80 minutes earlier, was about 35% higher than in Chesapeake (Vorona et al., 2011). Another study found that teen accident rates dropped 16% in the year after a school district pushed back its high school start times an hour (Danner & Phillips, 2008).

Delayed start times have produced other positive results for students, including better attendance, grades, and graduation rates; increased sleep time on weekends and less need for catch-up sleep on weekends; less tardiness and daytime sleepiness; lower self-reported levels of depressive feelings; and even healthier average body weights (Berry et al., 2021; Gariépy et al., 2018; McKeever & Clark, 2017; Wahlstrom, 2002a; Wahlstrom et al., 2017; Widome et al., 2020; Wolfson et al., 2007). But districts typically run into strong opposition when they suggest a shift to a later high school day. Arguments against the later start include complications with the scheduling of buses, interference with after-school sports, lack of child care for younger kids if they arrive home before their high school–age siblings, and the mistaken parental belief that teens would go to sleep an hour later if they had a later start time (Dunietz et al., 2017; Kirby et al., 2011; Nahmod et al., 2017; Owens et al., 2010; Wahlstrom, 2002b; Wolfson et al., 2007; Wolfson & Carskadon, 2005).

Whether caused by early start times or any other reason, insufficient sleep in teens correlates with all kinds of questionable, even dangerous decision making (Hershner, 2013). A study of over 12,000 high school students throughout the United States found that kids who sleep less than 8 hours a night are much more likely to smoke, drink, use drugs, and consider suicide (McKnight-Eily et al., 2011). Check **Table 4.1** for more details. Of course, this data is correlational, which means that we can't be sure that the lack of sleep *causes* the poor decision making. The explanation could instead be that these risky behaviors cause insufficient sleep (too busy partying to sleep), or that a third factor (stress, depression, etc.) causes both the risky behaviors and the insufficient sleep.

For healthy older adults, the amount of sleep is typically the same as when they were younger. The key word there is *healthy*, though. The increased frequency of injury and illness in older adults often produces less sleep and lower sleep quality, including more frequent awakenings at night and sleepiness during the day (Dijk et al., 2010;

TABLE 4.1: Teens, Sleep, and Risky Decisions

RISKY ACTIVITY	PERCENT WITH LESS THAN 8 HOURS OF SLEEP ON AN AVERAGE SCHOOL NIGHT	PERCENT WITH MORE THAN 8 HOURS OF SLEEP ON AN AVERAGE SCHOOL NIGHT
Smoked cigarettes in past month	24.0	15.0
Drank alcohol in the past month	50.3	36.7
Used marijuana in the past month	23.3	15.6
Had sexual intercourse in the past 3 months	39.1	27.8
Felt sad or hopeless almost every day for 2 weeks	31.1	21.6
Seriously considered suicide in the past 12 months	16.8	9.8

Data from McKnight-Eily et al. (2011).

This large-scale survey illustrates the connection between insufficient sleep and risky decisions about drugs, sex, and self-harm. Whether that connection is causal—that is, whether sleepiness causes teens to make different decisions—remains unclear.

solitary sleeping
Sleep in which only one person is in the bed or in the room.

co-sleeping
Sleeping in the same room or same bed with another person (usually a caregiver).

Foley et al., 2004; Schwarz et al., 2017). One study explored the importance of *subjective* age (as opposed to chronological age) on sleep in middle-aged and older adults in the United States. Results showed that subjective age correlated strongly with sleep problems, suggesting that as adults age, how old you *feel* may be just as important as how old you are in terms of getting a good night's sleep (Stephan et al., 2017).

DIVERSITY MATTERS

Sexual Orientation and Sleep. Recent studies, some of which included tens of thousands of participants, have found significant differences in sleep between adults who are straight and adults who are lesbian, gay, or bisexual. Consistently, the studies find that in people who are straight, sleep is longer and of higher quality, as measured by total amount of sleep, falling asleep, staying asleep, need for sleep medication, or sleep disorders confirmed by a health care professional. Some studies find that people who are bisexual have more sleep problems than people who are gay and lesbian, and that people who are gay and lesbian have more sleep problems than people who are straight. Other studies find that people who are bisexual, gay, or lesbian are all about equal in terms of sleep problems, but they all have more sleep problems than adults who are straight. The reasons for these sleep differences are not entirely clear, but researchers often point out the higher rates of stress, mental illness, and health problems among people who are lesbian, gay, and bisexual in comparison to people who are straight (Chen & Shiu, 2017; Dai & Hao, 2019; Galinsky et al., 2018; Patterson & Potter, 2019, 2020).

Solitary Sleeping and Co-Sleeping

We've discussed a lot about the differences in *how much* and *when* people sleep, but what about *with whom* they sleep? For many who grew up in mainstream U.S. culture, the childhood norm is **solitary sleeping**: sleep in which you are the only person in your bed or in your room. By contrast, in many cultures the childhood norm is **co-sleeping**: sleeping in the same room or same bed with another person (usually a caregiver).

Co-sleeping can take many forms (Ball et al., 1999; Worthman, 2011). The most common, especially with very young children, is the *family bed*, in which the child and parent(s) sleep together. Other arrangements include separate beds within reaching distance or separate beds on opposite sides of the same room. Worldwide, co-sleeping is actually more common than solitary sleeping (Burnham & Gaylor, 2011; Shweder et al., 1995). In fact, sleep researchers believe that the emphasis on solitary sleep prevalent in the United States and other Western cultures is a relatively recent development in the course of human history, and that human children typically haven't slept by themselves in their own rooms (Super & Harkness, 2013).

DIVERSITY MATTERS

As **Table 4.2** shows, co-sleeping rates vary around the world, but it tends to be especially common in Asian cultures (Sourander, 2001). One study found that among kids between 6 months and 6 years old, 59% of Japanese kids regularly co-slept with parents (and most of those fell asleep while physically touching a parent), but only 15% of American kids did (Latz et al., 1999). Some researchers believe that sleeping collectively rather than individually is an effect (and perhaps also a cause) of the collectivistic mindset common in Asian cultures. However, plenty of other factors, including the money to afford a home with separate bedrooms for each family member, influence the likelihood of family members sleeping together in any culture (Brenner et al., 2003; Giannotti et al., 2008; Weimer et al., 2002; Willinger et al., 2003). Perhaps because of this variety of factors, co-sleeping rates within the United States vary by ethnic group. For example, the rate for Black young children is at least double the rate for their White peers (Landrine & Klonoff, 1996; Wolf et al., 1996).

Some U.S. parents believe that co-sleeping will foster too much dependence, and possibly lead to problematic behaviors, in their children. When it is bedtime, these parents want kids to get to sleep on their own rather than relying on a caregiver for comfort. This belief supports the parental decision to gradually require babies to self-soothe, or "cry it out," at bedtime — an approach that 61% of Western parenting books endorse (Jenni & O'Connor, 2005; Ramos & Youngclarke, 2006). But sleep research

TABLE 4.2: Co-Sleeping Around the World

COUNTRY	PERCENT OF 3-MONTH-OLD BABIES SLEEPING IN THE SAME BED AS THEIR PARENT(S)
China	88
Sweden	65
Chile	64
United States	34
Germany	23
Canada	23
Argentina	15
Turkey	2

Data from Hauck et al. (2008) and Nelson et al. (2001).

doesn't support that belief (Burnham, 2013). For example, one study found that preschoolers who were co-sleepers from birth were actually better at making friends by themselves and getting dressed by themselves than their solitary-sleeping peers (Keller & Goldberg, 2004). Another longitudinal study that followed kids from birth through high school found that kids who co-slept when they were young had no more emotional, behavioral, relationship, criminal, drug-related, or sexual problems than their peers who slept in their own rooms (Okami et al., 2002).

Other U.S. parents believe that co-sleeping could increase the risk of injury or even sudden death (for example, by suffocation) to the baby. Research suggests this too is an assumption without strong support (McKenna & McDade, 2005; Nelson et al., 2001).

Sleep Abnormalities

You know from firsthand experience what it means to have a bad night's sleep. Perhaps you have occasionally had a scary dream after a slasher movie marathon or difficulty dozing off because the coffee you thought was decaf was not. But some people have persistent sleep problems that interfere with their daily functioning. Let's explore what they are and why they happen.

insomnia
A sleep disorder featuring consistent difficulty falling asleep, staying asleep, or achieving high-quality sleep.

Insomnia. **Insomnia** is a sleep disorder featuring consistent difficulty falling asleep, staying asleep, or achieving high-quality sleep. People with insomnia just can't sleep. No matter how much advice they get from friends and family, how many self-help books they read, or which pills they take, they can't string together a few consecutive nights – or, in some cases, even a few consecutive hours – of decent sleep. The consequences are awful, not just during the night spent staring at the ceiling, but also during the subsequent day.

Consider Gayle Greene, an English professor at Scripps College, who wrote a book about the anguish that severe bouts of insomnia caused her (Greene, 2008):

> I look at the clock and it's 6:05 A.M. The last time I looked it was 4:30, which, considering that I went to bed at 3:00, is not good. Must have been that cup of tea I had before class – no, one cup of tea doesn't do this. Maybe it was the wine I had with dinner – no, that was hours ago. It could be anything I did, it could be nothing I did, I have no idea – classes went fine, dinner with a friend, nothing on my mind . . . I give up and get up, and it is bad, bad as the worst hangover. . . . Head aches, eyes sting . . . back aches . . . I stare out the window at the blank, dead day . . . I tell myself, it will look better in the morning – tomorrow morning, that is, this day's a dead loss. . . . They call this a "sleep disorder," but it's actually an all-day disorder. Insomnia is not just something that happens to the night; it happens to the day. (pp. 26–28)

Insomnia is, unfortunately, common. About one-third of us experience at least some symptoms of insomnia, and 10% have full-blown cases (Ohayon et al., 2002). Many factors contribute to insomnia (Gehrman et al., 2012; Perlis et al., 1997; Taylor et al., 2014). As **Figure 4.5** illustrates, disorders of mind and body are common sources of sleeplessness, as you know if you've ever spent the night with a sore back, a queasy stomach, or relentless worry. Work can be a source of that worry. Studies have demonstrated that worrying about your job – or losing your job altogether – increases your odds for insomnia (Åkerstedt & Kecklund, 2012). One study of over 24,000 people in 31 countries found that as job insecurity increased, so did insomnia (Mai et al., 2018).

DIVERSITY MATTERS

Similarly, money (or a lack of it) can also be a source of that worry. People of low socioeconomic status have higher rates of insomnia than the rich – not just because they worry about how to pay the rent but also because they live in more crowded, noisy homes and often lack education about things that can disrupt sleep (like caffeine and cigarettes) (Anderson et al., 2017; Arber et al., 2009; Friedman et al., 2007; Paine et al., 2004).

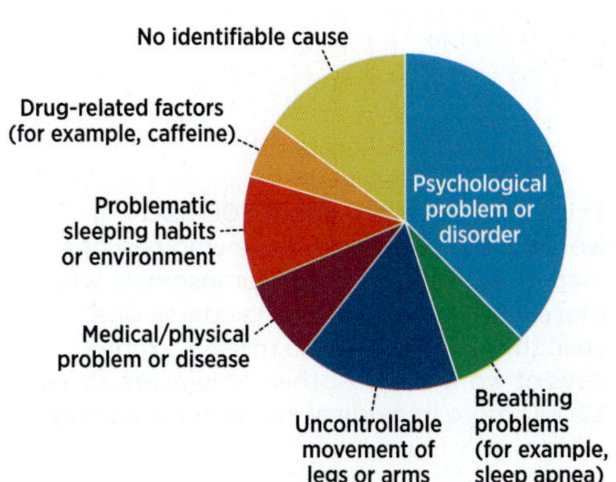

FIGURE 4.5 Sources of Insomnia. There are many sources of insomnia, with psychological disorders being the most common.
Information from Ohayon and Guilleminault (2006).

sleepwalking
Walking while asleep, or *somnambulism.*

The cost of insomnia is tremendous, not just in personal aftereffects of a sleepless night, but also in dollars and cents (Leger, 2012; Reynolds & Ebben, 2017). Sleep problems become workplace problems, such as absenteeism, on-the-job accidents, decreased productivity, and higher health care costs (**Table 4.3**) (Kleinman et al., 2009; Leger, 1994; Stoller, 1994). In total, insomnia-related work problems cost the United States over $100 billion per year (Wickwire et al., 2016).

Sleepwalking. **Sleepwalking (somnambulism)** is walking while asleep. Sleepwalkers usually can't be woken up easily. When sleepwalkers do wake up, they are often confused about what just happened (how they got to the living room, the basement, or the backyard, for example). Occasional sleepwalking happens to only about 3% of us, and sleepwalking at least once a week is even rarer (less than 0.5%) (Hublin et al., 1997). But when sleepwalking does happen, it can be a bizarre experience for the sleepwalker and anyone watching. Stand-up comedian Mike Birbiglia made a movie and wrote a book about his own struggles with sleepwalking (called *Sleepwalk with Me*) that led to him sleeping in a zipped-up sleeping bag with mittens on his hands to prevent him from unzipping it (Birbiglia, 2011). He even sleepwalked through a closed second-story hotel window (as he dreamed that a missile was heading for his room), waking up on the lawn below, and then walking through the front entrance covered with blood to explain to the front desk clerk what he had just done.

The cause of sleepwalking is still being researched, but it's clear that heredity is a factor (Cartwright, 2006; Petit et al., 2015). A study that examined almost 3000 pairs of twins found much higher correspondence rates of sleepwalking between identical twins than nonidentical twins, which means the odds of sleepwalking are higher when all of the a person's genes, rather than just half of them, are shared with a sleepwalker (Hublin et al., 1997; Hublin & Kaprio, 2003). More generally, about 80% of sleepwalkers have at least one biological relative who also sleepwalks (Zadra & Pilon, 2012). Stress and psychological problems also seem to correlate with sleepwalking, as suggested by the overlap between sleepwalking and anxiety, depression, and other mental disorders (Gau & Soong, 1999; Laganière, 2018; Lam et al., 2008; Ohayon et al., 1999; Zadra et al., 2018).

More recently, a couple of rare variations of disordered activities while sleeping have been more widely recognized. In *sleep-related eating behaviors*, the sleeper eats while staying asleep. This typically takes place during the first few hours of the night and is most common in young women (Auger & Morgenthaler, 2006; Chiaro et al., 2015; Howell et al., 2009; Schenck & Mahowald, 1994). People who sleep-eat have relatively high rates of other sleeping, eating, and psychological disorders (Auger, 2006; Inoue, 2015; Schenck et al., 1993; Winkelman, 1998).

In *sleep-related sexual behaviors* (also known as *sexsomnia*), the sleeper gropes another person, tries to have intercourse, masturbates, or performs other sexual behaviors while staying asleep. Typically, these behaviors are more unrestrained and inconsiderate than the sexual behaviors the person carries out while awake (Andersen et al., 2007; Dubessy et al., 2016; Organ & Fedoroff, 2015; Schenck et al.,

TABLE 4.3: Lost Sleep, Lost Money

TYPE OF EXPENSE	EMPLOYER'S AVERAGE ANNUAL INCREASED COST TO COVER AN EMPLOYEE WITH INSOMNIA
Medical care	$751
Prescription drugs	$735
Sick leave	$208
Short- and long-term disability	$189
Worker's compensation	$170
Total	$2053

Data from Kleinman et al. (2009).

This study examined about 300,000 U.S. workers and compared those who had been diagnosed with or treated for insomnia with those who had not. Over the course of a year, those with insomnia missed 3 more days of work and cost their employers about $2000 more in medical and other expenses.

2007; Shapiro et al., 2003). When they realize what they have done, sleepers with sleep-related sexual behaviors often feel ashamed and embarrassed, and their intimate relationships often suffer (Guilleminault et al., 2002; Mangan, 2004).

narcolepsy
A disorder of "sleep attacks" characterized by immediate and unexpected shifts from wakefulness to REM sleep.

sleep terrors
Brief, sudden awakenings in which the person feels frightened and confused.

sleep apnea
A sleep disorder caused by interruptions of breathing that cause repeated waking.

Narcolepsy. **Narcolepsy** is a disorder of "sleep attacks" characterized by immediate and unexpected shifts from wakefulness to REM sleep. (The *-lepsy* part of the word is the same as in *epilepsy* — it suggests a "seizure" of sleep.) Narcolepsy is rare, occurring in fewer than one-fourth of 1% of the population (Dauvilliers et al., 2007; Ohayon et al., 2002). When it happens, it typically begins in the teenage or early adult years and tends to continue through the life span (Dauvilliers et al., 2001).

Narcolepsy is an obvious disorder to recognize: the person goes from completely alert to completely asleep almost immediately, much like a boxer or MMA fighter getting knocked out. Muscle tone typically goes limp in these sleep attacks, which causes the person to sag in their seat or flop down on the ground. Sometimes, the sleep attacks are triggered by certain kinds of strong emotional reactions, such as laughter or surprise. The sleep attacks are usually brief — just 15–20 minutes — followed by a normal state of wakefulness (Pelayo & Lopes, 2006). The cause of narcolepsy is not known, and no cures are yet available. Some medications seem to bring minor reductions in the frequency of sleep attacks, however, as do good sleep habits and the avoidance of situations that trigger narcoleptic attacks (Dauvilliers & Bayard, 2012).

Sleep Terrors. **Sleep terrors** are brief sudden awakenings in which the person feels frightened and confused. Sleep terrors are often called *night terrors*, but many experts prefer the term *sleep terrors* because the experience can happen during daytime sleep as well (Zadra & Pilon, 2012). Sleep terrors are distinct from *nightmares* — the scary dreams that wake us up. Nightmares are quite common in the general population (Germain, 2012; Robert & Zadra, 2008). About 80% of college students in one survey experienced at least one nightmare in the previous year, and about 15% experience about one per month (Belicki, 1992a, 1992b; Belicki & Belicki, 1982). By contrast, sleep terrors have happened to only about 2% of adults (Zadra & Pilon, 2012). About three-quarters of children have nightmares, but only 1–6% have sleep terrors (Ivanenko & Larson, 2013; Mindell & Owens, 2015). Another distinction: nightmares happen during REM sleep, but sleep terrors happen during non-REM sleep.

A person experiencing a sleep terror is essentially having a panic attack while sleeping. It features intense fear, screaming, sweating, rapid breathing, and a pounding heart. It typically happens within the first 90 minutes of sleep and lasts just a few minutes. When it is over, the sleeper usually returns to normal sleep rather than waking up, and often can't remember the sleep terror when they do wake up. The cause of sleep terrors is not entirely known, but genetics appears to play a substantial role (Abe et al., 1993; Nguyen et al., 2008). Children with parents who have sleep terrors are twice as likely to have sleep terrors as their peers whose parents don't have sleep terrors (Abe et al., 1984). Sleep terrors also tend to overlap with psychological problems like anxiety and depression. Sleep terrors tend to begin in childhood and go away without treatment by adolescence or early adulthood (LaBerge, 2000; Ophoff et al., 2018; Petit et al., 2015; Thiedke, 2001).

Stokkete/Shutterstock

Sleep terrors are brief sudden awakenings during non-REM sleep in which the person feels frightened and confused.

Sleep Apnea. **Sleep apnea** is a sleep disorder caused by interruptions of breathing that cause repeated waking. Some degree of sleep apnea happens to about 20% of adults, but only about 5% experience serious levels of breathing problems and daytime sleepiness (Franklin & Lindberg, 2015). Sleep apnea is obvious (and often disturbing) to anyone who can see or hear the sleeper, with symptoms like loud snoring, snorting, gasping, choking, and breathless pauses (Sanders & Givelber, 2006). But sleep apnea is not always obvious to the sleepers themselves, because they are usually not awake enough to be fully aware of their surroundings. People suffering from sleep apnea feel sleepy the next day, but the sleepiness starts to seem normal because sleep apnea

sleep hygiene
Routine behaviors that promote healthy sleep.

DIVERSITY MATTERS

happens every night. Men experience sleep apnea more often than women, older adults more often than younger adults, and people of low-socioeconomic status more often than people of high socioeconomic status, but the biggest risk factor is obesity. That's because the excessive mass around the upper airway narrows or blocks the flow of breath in and out of the lungs (Eckert et al., 2009; Peppard & Hagen, 2018; Weaver & Ye, 2012; Young et al., 2004; Young & Peppard, 2005).

The most common treatment for sleep apnea is a *continuous positive air pressure*, or *CPAP*, machine (Ferguson et al., 2006; Gay et al., 2006; Hirshkowitz & Lee-Chiong, 2006). The CPAP typically sits on the sleeper's bedside table and pumps out a continuous flow of air, which is delivered through a tube connected to a mask that the sleeper wears all night. The mask completely covers the nose and mouth, delivering a steady stream of air that prevents the airway from closing. CPAP treatment can be life-changing for someone whose nights and days are ravaged by sleep apnea. One man who was probably "sleep deprived for 15 years" started using a CPAP machine. He describes waking up in the lab as "amazing": "I felt like a 10-year-old who had polished off a pot of coffee. I couldn't believe how completely refreshed I felt!" (American Sleep Apnea Association, 2015).

Another common treatment for sleep apnea is the mandibular advancement device, a mouth-guard-like device that keeps the airway open. Other treatments include surgery and weight loss programs (Bailey, 2006; Chan & Cistulli, 2009; Kapen, 2006; Schwartz et al., 2018; Sher, 2006).

COVID-19 and Sleep Problems. When the pandemic began, sleep problems began – or worsened – for many people around the world (Casagrande et al., 2020; Jahrami et al., 2021; Robillard et al., 2021). The sharpest rise was in the rate of insomnia, but other sleep problems rose too, including sleeping too much and sleeping at undesired times. One sign of the severity of COVID-related sleep problems is the fact that sales for melatonin (an over-the-counter sleep aid discussed in more detail in the next section) rose by over 42% in 2020 (Akhtar, 2021). There are many reasons why COVID-19 might cause sleep problems, including anxiety about the virus and its consequences, physical symptoms of the virus itself (for those infected), disrupted daily routines and mealtimes, relationship tension caused by extra time at home with family members, increased alcohol use, and blurred lines between professional and personal life due to many people working from home (Abrams, 2021).

Not all of the sleep-related consequences of COVID-19 have been negative, however. For many high school students, whose classes shifted from in-person to online, the pandemic offered a chance to get more sleep. Multiple studies found that high school students reported longer and higher-quality sleep after the shift to online classes, along with a circadian shift toward "eveningness" (a tendency to be more awake and alert in the evening rather than earlier in the day) primarily because they could sleep later in the morning than they had been when school was in-person (Genta et al., 2021; Gruber et al., 2020).

Treating and Preventing Sleep Problems. The best way to deal with sleep problems is to practice good **sleep hygiene**: routine behaviors that promote healthy sleep. For good sleep hygiene, experts generally include both behaviors you should do and those you shouldn't do (Gradisar & Short, 2013; Lichstein et al., 2012).

DO:

- Wake up and go to sleep at the same time every day.
- Exercise during daytime hours.
- Allow yourself no more than a light bedtime snack.
- Create a sleep environment that is comfortable, quiet, dark, and a comfortable temperature.

DON'T:

- Drink caffeine after noon.
- Take a nap in the late afternoon or evening.
- Smoke cigarettes, drink alcohol, eat a heavy meal, or exercise close to bedtime.
- Use any device with a bright screen (TV, computer, smartphone, etc.) close to bedtime.

The last of these tips — avoiding screens before bed — is increasingly problematic for many of us, especially teens and children. Decades ago, the brightest things anyone saw in their bedroom at night were a nightlight or the moon. Then came the TVs. Only 6% of sixth-graders had a TV in their bedroom in 1970, but that number jumped to 77% in 1999 and remained at 76% in 2010 (Rideout et al., 2010; Roberts et al., 1999). By 2009, even 17% of *toddlers* had a TV in their bedroom, and by 2019, 36% of kids age 3–6 did too (Mindell et al., 2009; Helm & Spencer, 2019). Studies have found that the presence of a TV in the bedroom correlates with more total screen time, fewer hours of sleep, and higher levels of daytime sleepiness, along with higher rates of other sleep-related problems (Gentile et al., 2017; Shochat et al., 2010; Van den Bulck, 2004).

Milan Ilic Photographer/Shutterstock

Looking at a bright screen around bedtime can disrupt sleep.

Today, many of us share our bedroom not only with our TV but also with our smartphone. A 2011 study found that 72% of teenagers used a phone as they tried to fall asleep — a number that has probably increased in the years since (National Sleep Foundation, 2011). The same study found that 28% of those teens leave their phone's ringer (or vibrate function) on all night, and 18% woke up at least a few nights a week to respond to a call, text, or other alert. A 2017 survey found that about 80% of us check our phone in the hour before bedtime, and about 50% of us check our phone in the middle of the night (Deloitte, 2017).

There are many ways that smartphones at bedtime can interfere with your sleep: (1) Time you spend doing smartphone activities (texts, social media, videos, etc.) can push back the time you actually fall asleep. (2) The content of what you see on your smartphone (exciting or upsetting news on a social media site, a funny YouTube video, a friend's reply to your earlier text, etc.) can make it difficult to wind down and drift off. (3) The bright light in your eyes can disrupt your circadian rhythm. (4) Waking up in the middle of the night to respond to an alert on your phone can reduce your overall sleep time (Gradisar & Short, 2013). Certainly, the increasing presence of tablets (iPads, etc.) and other screened devices multiplies the problems caused by TVs and smartphones.

LIFE HACK 4.2

Limit the amount of time you spend looking at screens, like TVs and smartphones, right before bed. Too much exposure to bright lights at bedtime can interfere with sleep.

(Gradisar & Short, 2013)

If prevention of sleep problems hasn't worked, there are plenty of popular treatments for sleep problems (Burman et al., 2015; Lee-Chiong & Sateia, 2006). Many treatments are pharmaceutical, including prescription drugs like Ambien and Lunesta, as well as over-the-counter drugs like Unisom and ZzzQuil. These drugs can be helpful short-term for certain people, but they don't work for everyone, and they are generally not considered long-term solutions to long-term sleep problems. Plus, the side effects can be awful, including grogginess the next day, a need for ever-increasing dosages, and potential for misusing or getting hooked on the drug (Riemann & Nissen, 2012).

Another popular drugstore option is melatonin tablets, which deliver extra amounts of the natural bodily hormone related to sleep and arousal. However, the data for melatonin is mixed. One meta-analysis covering hundreds of sleepers found that on average, melatonin enabled people to fall asleep just 4 minutes sooner and sleep a total of just 13 minutes longer (Brzezinski et al., 2005). Other studies show similar outcomes for the use of melatonin, yet still other studies show more positive effects (Li et al., 2019; Sadeghniiat-Haghighi et al., 2016). It is worth mentioning that the side effects of melatonin are generally less risky than for many medications (Ferracioli-Oda et al., 2014).

Many people have turned to herbal substances to help them sleep, such as chamomile, kava, and valerian, but again scientific data on their helpfulness is lacking. A meta-analysis covering over 1600 sleepers found no differences between those who used herbal sleep aids and those who didn't (Leach & Page, 2015).

As a result of the frequently less-than-ideal outcomes with the many substances used as sleep aids, many sleepy people have searched for nonmedical solutions. One such solution is to improve upon any shortcomings in sleep hygiene, as listed previously. Beyond that, more deliberate techniques for improving sleep can include counseling or psychotherapy focused on reducing worry, especially worry that happens at bedtime or worry about sleep itself (Bélanger et al., 2007; Hertenstein et al., 2018; Jacobs et al., 2004; Sivertsen et al., 2006).

Sleep-improving techniques can also include *stimulus control* and *sleep restriction* (Kaplan & Harvey, 2013; Lacks et al., 1983; Means & Edinger, 2006; Spielman et al., 1987). With stimulus control, the bed is used exclusively for sleeping (not for watching TV or using the phone or doing homework or lying awake through the night). With sleep restriction, the sleeper condenses sleep into a small number of hours (as if the bed is only "open" for a small, strictly controlled, and consistent period each night) and then gradually expands the open hours as needed. Research indicates that in general, nonpharmacological treatments for sleeping problems are as effective as pharmacological treatments (and may be significantly more effective and longer-lasting) and lack any of the unwanted side effects (Jacobs et al., 2004; Murtagh & Greenwood, 1995; Smith et al., 2002).

CHECK YOUR LEARNING:

4.1 Why do we sleep?

4.2 How does sleep deprivation affect people?

4.3 What is your circadian rhythm, and what influences it?

4.4 What are the stages of normal sleep?

4.5 Different sleep patterns have been found between which diverse groups of people?

4.6 What is co-sleeping, and how common is it?

4.7 How are the sleep abnormalities of insomnia, sleepwalking, narcolepsy, sleep terrors, and sleep apnea different from one another?

4.8 What strategies can you use to prevent and treat sleep problems?

To check your understanding of these questions, click show the answers or refer to the answers in the Chapter Summary.

Dreams

YOU WILL LEARN:

4.9 what theories of dreams have been proposed.

4.10 how dreams can affect daily functioning through such techniques as imagery rehearsal therapy and lucid dreaming.

4.11 how the COVID-19 pandemic influenced dreaming and how diverse groups dream differently.

Dreams have been a focus of psychologists since early in the history of the field—even before 1900, when Sigmund Freud's famous book *The Interpretation of Dreams* was published. Besides sleeping, breathing, eating, and drinking, dreaming is one of the few experiences you share with every other human being from every culture at all points in history. And dreaming is frequent too: you do it every single night. You'd think, then, that psychologists would know a lot about dreaming. The truth is, they don't.

Theories of Dreams

Dreaming has been studied extensively by sleep researchers, but much of that study has been theoretical. Many sleep experts have offered opinions about why we dream and what dreams mean, but the scientific study of dreams is relatively recent (Givrad, 2016).

Historically, many different tribes and cultures around the world have offered their own theories of dreaming. Many of these are "folk theories," supported by belief and tradition more than scientific evidence, but they are still powerful influences on the lives of those who accept them. Among these folk dream theories (Lohmann, 2007) are:

- **Nonsense theory.** Dreams are just imaginary nonsense, random images and stories to be enjoyed for what they're worth and then forgotten.
- **Message theory.** Dreams contain important messages, perhaps from others (family members, ancestors, etc.) or from parts of yourself that need to be heard.
- **Generative theory.** Dreams not only predict the future but generate or determine it.

- **Soul travel theory.** Dreams are the experience of your soul wandering outside of your body.
- **Visitation theory.** Dreams are visits by supernatural spirits to the dreamer.

Freud's theory of dreaming arrived in the early 1900s and had a tremendous impact on society that continues to a lesser extent today. Freud argued that dreams revealed the unconscious mind, particularly deep-down wishes of which you are largely unaware while awake. According to Freud, the wishes don't show themselves directly but get converted into stories that utilize lots of symbolism. In Freud's terms, the *latent content* of the dream (the unconscious wish) gets translated into the *manifest content* of the dream, which is the actual story you see acted out in your mind. He called that translation process *dream work*, and in therapy, Freud and his clients would try to undo that dream work to figure out what the dream meant (Cabaniss et al., 2011; Freud, 1900). Unfortunately, in terms of science, Freud's theory of dreaming lacks testability and therefore lacks empirical support. Although some people still expect the analysis of dreams to be a major part of psychotherapy, the truth is that as Freud's theories have declined, so has dream analysis, to the point where it is now a relatively uncommon therapy tool (Hill & Knox, 2010; Leonard & Dawson, 2018; Pesant & Zadra, 2004).

The Scientific Study of Dreaming

The scientific study of dreaming began in the post-Freud era with the observation in the late 1950s that dreaming usually happens during REM sleep. This connection was established by researchers watching sleepers' eyes and then waking them when their eyes moved rapidly beneath their eyelids. Those awakened during that rapid eye movement were far more likely to report that they had been dreaming than those in other sleep stages (Dement, 1960; Dement & Kleitman, 1957; Nielsen, 1995, 2000, 2004; Vogel, 1991).

This link between eye movement and dreaming led some researchers to take a more neuropsychological approach to dreaming, attempting to determine how the various parts of the brain function during REM sleep. This neuropsychological research led to the influential *activation–synthesis hypothesis* in the 1970s, which states that dreams are initiated by the pons, a structure in the brainstem (Hobson & McCarley, 1977). The occipital lobe then becomes involved, adding random visual elements to give the dream some structure. Those random visual elements are meaningless until the sleeper wakes up and assigns some meaning to them.

In more recent years, with great advances in technology, neuropsychological theories of dreaming have expanded from the activation–synthesis hypothesis. In fact, one researcher suggested that dreams during REM sleep represent a different level of consciousness from other types of sleep. His theory is that dreaming provides a virtual reality model of the world so the dreamer has an expanded library of images, concepts, and emotions with which to respond to daily life (Hobson, 2009). Another neurological finding regarding dreams is the fact that the amygdala and hypothalamus are quite active during dreams, suggesting that emotions (especially negative emotions such as fear) are especially relevant to dreaming (Maquet et al., 1996). Other neuropsychological researchers have pointed out that those parts of the brain are involved in memory formation, which suggests dreaming may function to create and solidify memories, especially memories that involve emotions (Nishida et al., 2009; Wagner et al., 2001).

The Effect of Dreams on Daily Functioning

Other dream research has focused on how dreams help a person function after waking up. Several studies suggest that your nighttime dreams help you function better in the morning, especially in terms of mood regulation. (The old saying that everything will look better in the morning may actually have some science behind it.) In a study of people with depression, the themes of their dreams were more negative in the first half of the night and more positive in the second half. When participants rated their moods, they were much more positive in the morning than the night before. This finding suggests that dreams perform a fresh-start function (Cartwright, 2005; Cartwright et al., 1998a).

Some research suggests that dreams can improve mental health (Cartwright et al., 1998b). Some people suffering from posttraumatic stress disorder (PTSD), including many military veterans who have recurring nightmares, have benefited from *imagery rehearsal therapy*. Imagery rehearsal therapy is a simple technique in which the nightmare sufferer retells the nightmare to a therapist or counselor — but with a better ending. The veteran goes through a process during waking hours in which they take control of the dream. It may start the same way as the nightmare usually starts, but the veteran gives it a happy finish. The veteran then reviews, or *rehearses*, the new and improved version of the dream several times a day, including right before bedtime. For example, one patient used imagery rehearsal therapy to change a nightmare about being chased by a dangerous enemy to a cheery, playful story about being chased by his brothers as a child. Results of imagery rehearsal therapy (either alone or in combination with other, more established forms of therapy) are encouraging, with many veterans eliminating or drastically reducing the occurrence of PTSD nightmares (Belleville et al., 2018; Krakow et al., 2001; Krakow & Zadra, 2006; Moore & Krakow, 2007).

It's interesting that you can influence your dreams by controlling aspects of your waking hours. But can you control your dreams *while* you're dreaming?

Lucid Dreaming

Some sleep experts believe that some people can control their dreams while they are dreaming, though it requires training and practice (Baird et al., 2019; LaBerge, 1985). They call this **lucid dreaming**: a dreaming experience in which you have some control over the dream while you remain asleep. Lucid dreaming happens most often during REM sleep but occasionally in stage 1 or stage 2 sleep as well (LaBerge, 1988). It is most likely when the person returns to sleep after being awakened during the first hour of sleep. Even then, lucid dreaming still often requires lots of training and practice and might remain impossible for many people (Gott et al., 2020; LaBerge, 1985).

The key element of lucid dreaming is the awareness that you are dreaming. The decision to control it is optional (LaBerge, 2007). It is a bit like watching a TV show with the remote in your hand. You know you're watching the show, so you can decide to pause, fast-forward, or rewind. But with lucid dreaming, you can also control the content, as if you are the director of the show. You can decide what happens as well as what the characters in the dream do or say. In a survey of people who experience lucid dreams, most reported using the opportunity to fulfill wishes, such as flying, dancing, having fun, or having sex. Most also reported that the lucid dream had a positive influence on their waking mood (Stumbrys & Erlacher, 2016). Like imagery rehearsal therapy, lucid dreaming has been used as a therapeutic tool to help people overcome recurring nightmares. Lucid dreaming has also been used by athletes such as tennis players, high divers, and long-distance runners to "practice" their sports (Erlacher, 2012; Spoormaker & Lancee, 2012). However, both of these applications of lucid dreaming are still relatively new and have little evidence of success at this point. Some experts have suggested that intentional lucid dreaming can sometimes disrupt sleep patterns (Vallat & Ruby, 2019).

Dreams and COVID-19

When the COVID-19 pandemic began, some researchers were very interested to see how the pandemic may have affected the way we dream. A small but growing number of their studies shows that the pandemic did in fact influence our dreams quite a bit, especially during the spring of 2020, when so many people started to feel its impact. For example, one study of over 3000 adults in the United States found a significantly increased frequency of dreams specifically related to COVID-19, especially in people whose lives were most drastically changed in terms of health, income, or relationships. Many of these dreams featured masks, social distancing, and the virus itself (Schredl & Bulkeley, 2020).

A similar study in Finland found a 26% increase in the frequency of nightmares compared to pre-pandemic times. Many of these nightmares featured pandemic-specific

lucid dreaming
A dreaming experience in which a person has some control over the dream while remaining asleep.

themes like becoming infected with the virus, failure to maintain social distance, and struggling to find personal protective equipment (Pesonen et al., 2020). An even larger-scale study in Italy also found an increase in nightmare frequency and dream recall, especially among those with high levels of depression or anxiety (Scarpelli et al., 2021). Researchers have previously noticed this general phenomenon, in which the collective dreams of a group of people reflect a recent or current shared major stressor, after numerous natural disasters and the terrorist attacks of September 11, 2001 (Bulkeley & Kahan, 2008; David & Mellman, 1997).

Diversity and Dreams

DIVERSITY MATTERS

Dream researchers have identified some differences in the dreams of people from diverse groups, particularly in terms of gender and age. Regarding gender, several studies have found consistent differences between the dream content of men and women. For example, studies of U.S. adults have found that women's dreams are much more likely to feature clothing, architecture, and acts of friendliness, while men's dreams are much more likely to feature weapons, tools, streets, and acts of physical aggression (Krippner & Weinhold, 2002; Mathes & Schredl, 2013; Schredl et al., 2004).

Regarding age, a survey of over 1500 people (ranging from 8 to 70 years old) found that the content of dreams tends to reflect the issues and challenges common to each stage of life. For example, children dream more often about magic; teens dream more often about school, teachers, and studying; young adults dream more often about sexual experiences; middle-age and older adults dream more often about trying again and again to successfully achieve something; and older adults dream more often about people who are now dead as if they are alive (Maggiolini et al., 2020).

CHECK YOUR LEARNING:

4.9 How have various theories attempted to explain dreams?

4.10 How do the themes of dreams tend to differ between bedtime and wake-up time, and how can dreams affect mental health?

4.11 How did the start of the COVID pandemic affect dreaming, and how do dreams differ between diverse groups of people?

To check your understanding of these questions, click show the answers or refer to the answers in the Chapter Summary.

Hypnosis

Hypnosis is an altered state of consciousness in which one person, the participant, becomes very suggestible to another person, the hypnotist. Many people new to psychology assume that hypnosis is a big part of what psychologists do, perhaps because Freud is widely known to have used it with his clients (Tinterow, 1970). Actually, it's not. Only a few researchers study it, and only a few practitioners use it with their clients. But hypnosis has been a part of psychology's history since the field began. For those who do study and apply it, hypnosis is a powerful technique.

The roots of hypnosis go back hundreds of years, all the way to the idea of animal magnetism (put forth by Franz Mesmer, of *mesmerism* fame in the late 1700s and early 1800s) and even the exorcism procedures of Johann Gassner decades earlier (Pattie, 1994; Peter, 2005). But hypnotism today bears little resemblance to either of those outdated practices or to the myths that most people believe about it. Hypnosis does not involve a suspicious or sinister character passing his hands across a helpless victim or instantly "putting under" anyone. Hypnosis does not require the hypnotist to have a special gift or personality. Hypnotized people are not weak, gullible, or faking it, either (Barnier & Nash, 2008; Kihlstrom, 2008a). Instead, hypnotism is simply a technique in

YOU WILL LEARN:

4.12 what hypnosis is and how it works.

4.13 what purposes hypnotism has been used for.

4.14 who can be hypnotized.

4.15 whether hypnotism is actually nothing more than people simply complying with the social and situational role they feel pressured to fill at that moment.

hypnosis
An altered state of consciousness in which one person, the participant, becomes very suggestible to another person, the hypnotist.

Savage Chickens

which one person alters the consciousness of another. Then the hypnotist suggests new behaviors (usually for the purpose of helping the client) that can be tried under hypnosis or after the client comes out of hypnosis (Kihlstrom, 2005; Kirsch & Braffman, 2001).

The Procedure of Hypnotism

The procedure of hypnotism begins with an *induction*, an attempt to change the consciousness of the person receiving the technique. The hypnotist typically conducts induction by reading or reciting a script that instructs the person to unwind and calm themselves to a point that approaches sleep (but does not drift into sleep). During induction, the client either focuses their eyes on a target or feels their muscles relax. Here's an example of an induction focusing on the eyes:

> Now I would like you to find a spot or an object on the wall. . . . Eyes comfortable and heavy. . . . Just concentrate on the target and listen to my words, allowing yourself to relax more and more . . . you find that your eyelids are beginning to get heavier and heavier. . . . Soon your eyes will close themselves and when they do, you can really allow yourself to relax completely . . . your eyes are closed now and they will remain closed for the duration of our work together. . . . In a moment I'm going to touch the very top of your head with my hand and, when I do, I would like you to notice these warm waves of relaxation that begin to emanate from the very top of your head and pass through your entire body . . . the muscles of your forehead, your eyes, your face become limp and relaxed . . . your breathing is becoming more and more slow and regular . . . it is so comfortable, so pleasurable to be so deeply hypnotized and relaxed. . . . (Nash, 2008, pp. 490–491)

Once the induction is complete, the next step in the hypnosis procedure is a *suggestion*, in which the hypnotist tells the person to perform a certain behavior. For example, the hypnotist may tell the person to extend his arm forward and imagine it being lifted by helium-filled balloons. The hypnotist can tell that the person is hypnotized not just because his arm goes up, but because his arm goes up in a way that seems involuntary. The person believes that rather than choosing to move their arm up, the arm simply moved up on its own (Barnier & Nash, 2008; Kihlstrom, 2008a). Once the suggestions are complete, the hypnotist terminates the hypnosis. This often happens by simply telling the person that at the count of 1 (after counting backward from 10), they will come out of hypnosis and be fully conscious (Nash, 2008).

Often, the first suggestion (like the arm levitation) is just a test to make sure that the induction has worked and the person is in a suggestible state. Once that test is passed, the hypnotist can offer all kinds of suggestions to try to improve all kinds of problems. For example, hypnosis can be used to help people with phobias (although there are other treatments used more frequently and with more empirical support, as we will see in Chapter 15) (Bryant, 2008; Valentine et al., 2019). Consider a person with a phobia of airplanes. The hypnotist can suggest that they picture, while they're hypnotized, going through the motions of getting on an airplane, beginning with walking through the airport, arriving at the gate, walking onto the plane, sitting in their seat, taking off, and so on. The hypnotist can also suggest that after they come out of hypnosis, they will complete these actions in an upcoming real flight. (That's a *posthypnotic* suggestion.)

If this use of hypnosis to treat phobias sounds a bit like an exercise in imagination, it is — but with the extra power that comes from a change in consciousness. Other problems to which hypnosis has been applied include depression, chronic pain, smoking, drinking, and obesity (Elkins & Perfect, 2008; Jensen & Patterson, 2008; Milling et al., 2018a, 2018b; Yapko, 2008).

Who Can Be Hypnotized?

There are wide differences in whether a person can become hypnotized (Elkins, 2021; Friedlander & Sarbin, 1938; Laurence et al., 2008; Piccione et al., 1989). A person who is not willing to be hypnotized or who strongly doubts that hypnosis will work generally can't be hypnotized. People who are more likely to be hypnotized have a more general open-mindedness and are high in absorption, or have the tendency to get wrapped up in immediate sensory experiences (Glisky et al., 1991; Roche & McConkey, 1990). Men and women are equally likely to be hypnotized (Kihlstrom et al., 1980).

One last note about hypnotism: it is not just role playing by the person being hypnotized (Barabasz & Barabasz, 2008; Oakley, 2008). That explanation was put forth by the **social-cognitive theory of hypnosis**: a theory of hypnosis that emphasizes pressure to play the role assigned to a person being hypnotized. The social-cognitive theory suggests that a "hypnotized" person is really just a person conforming to the social pressure (from the hypnotist or others watching) to act hypnotized, but brain studies say otherwise. Neuropsychological evidence shows that hypnosis does in fact affect many parts of the brain, including the regions that control arousal and attention (Rainville & Price, 2003; Speigel, 2003). In one study, half of the participants underwent hypnosis in which they received the suggestion that their left leg was paralyzed. The other half underwent the same hypnosis, but were told ahead of time to fake being hypnotized and fake the leg paralysis. PET scans revealed that completely different parts of the brain were activated by the two groups, which suggests that those who were truly hypnotized were engaged in something quite different from merely playing along with the social role of a person under hypnosis (Ward et al., 2003).

social-cognitive theory of hypnosis
A theory of hypnosis that emphasizes pressure to play the role assigned to a person being hypnotized.

psychoactive drugs
Substances that alter mental functioning.

CHECK YOUR LEARNING:

4.12 What is hypnosis, and how does it work?

4.13 What types of issues has hypnosis been used to treat?

4.14 What characteristics are associated with greater hypnotizability?

4.15 What is the social-cognitive theory of hypnosis, and how strongly is it supported by neuropsychological studies?

To check your understanding of these questions, click show the answers or refer to the answers in the Chapter Summary.

Psychoactive Drugs and Consciousness

Psychoactive drugs are substances that alter mental functioning. When you take psychoactive drugs, they alter not only your consciousness but other brain activities like thinking, mood, memory, and perception. Some psychoactive drugs are illegal, while others are legal. Some of the legal drugs require a prescription, while others are sold over the counter. Some are remarkably common, while others are obscure. Before we consider specific categories of psychoactive drugs, let's consider how those drugs work within your body.

YOU WILL LEARN:

4.16 what psychoactive drugs are.

4.17 how psychoactive drugs work.

4.18 what tolerance and withdrawal are.

4.19 what addiction is.

4.20 what depressants do.

4.21 what stimulants do.

4.22 what opioids do.

4.23 what hallucinogens do.

How Psychoactive Drugs Work

If we zoom in to the level of the neuron, we see that psychoactive drugs do their work on neurotransmitters. Recall from Chapter 2 that neurotransmitters are the chemical messengers (like endorphins, serotonin, and dopamine) that travel across the synapses between neurons. A psychoactive drug can affect neurotransmitters in one of four ways (Brick & Erickson, 2013):

1. Increase the release of a neurotransmitter from the sending neuron.
2. Block or activate the receptors of neurotransmitters in the receiving neuron.
3. Inhibit the reuptake of neurotransmitters that didn't complete the trip across the synapse back into the sending neuron.
4. Inhibit enzymes in or near the neuron that would break down the neurotransmitter.

tolerance
Decreased effectiveness of a particular amount of a drug.

withdrawal
Stressful and uncomfortable symptoms caused by discontinuing a drug that had become habitual.

physical dependence
A bodily need for a particular drug in order to function normally.

psychological dependence
A mental need for a particular drug in order to function normally.

addiction
Problematic drug use that persists in spite of serious negative consequences.

There is one thing shared by all four of these particular effects on neurotransmitters: a change in the amount of neurotransmitter that successfully makes the trip from one neuron to the next. Regardless of whether that change is an increase or a decrease, it alters brain functioning.

Tolerance and Withdrawal. Many psychoactive drugs, when taken repeatedly over time, cause the user to build up a **tolerance**: decreased effectiveness of a particular amount of a drug. A tolerance requires a user to seek out more and more of the drug to match the same effect that a smaller amount had earlier. This can become dangerous when the amount grows to levels that the body can't handle in a healthy way.

Another possible outcome of repeated use of certain drugs over time is **withdrawal**: stressful and uncomfortable symptoms caused by discontinuing a drug that had become habitual. Withdrawal symptoms vary from one drug to another, but they often include jumpiness, trembling, headaches, nausea, insomnia, anxiety, irritability, and fatigue. Depending on the drug, withdrawal symptoms can last hours, days, weeks, or longer.

Withdrawal is often a by-product of *dependence* on a drug, which can take two forms, physical and psychological. **Physical dependence** is a bodily need for a particular drug in order to function normally. **Psychological dependence** is a mental need for a particular drug in order to function normally. For people who have never experienced dependence before, it can be difficult to imagine or even understand. It may be easy for them to think, "What do you mean you absolutely *need* a drink? Just use some willpower and quit!" To understand dependence, try to imagine life without something that's an absolutely essential part of your day-to-day functioning, something that would make you panic if you lost it. Your smartphone? The Internet? Your TV? Playing video games? Like most psychoactive drugs, these things and activities are not necessities. People are not born with an inherent need for them. In fact, many people around the world live full and happy lives without ever using them. But for some of us, these activities become so deeply ingrained in our lives that they seem like requirements. That's what physical or psychological dependence feels like for people who continuously use certain psychoactive drugs. The drugs become a need, and the people using them establish a new, chemically enhanced normal for their brains and bodies.

Addiction. Physical and psychological dependence are major contributors to **addiction**: problematic drug use that persists in spite of serious negative consequences. A person becomes an addict by prioritizing the continued use of a psychoactive drug above just about everything else — work, relationships, family, money, health, even their own life. Their actions may make no sense to the people around them, who often intervene or plead with them to stop. Unfortunately, addiction gives people a sort of tunnel vision that limits their focus to the next hit, the next high, the next buzz.

Consider singer and actor Demi Lovato. At a very young age, they had an enormously successful career, with many hit songs and starring roles on popular TV shows. But they were also addicted to alcohol and cocaine, resulting in the first of numerous rehab stints and treatment attempts. In 2018, after 6 years sober, they relapsed with those (and other) substances and experienced an opioid overdose that was nearly fatal. The overdose caused a heart attack, strokes, and organ failure. It left them with serious health issues, including heart problems and vision problems that left them nearly blind for 2 months (and with continuing visual impairment). They have pledged to try to live a more balanced and well-adjusted life, but the cost of their addiction is already quite high (Ganz, 2021).

Ryan Pfluger/The New York Times/Redux Pictures

Demi Lovato has enjoyed tremendous success as a singer and actor, but they have struggled with serious addiction issues along the way.

Types of Psychoactive Drugs

Lots of substances affect the brain. Let's consider the four best-understood categories: *depressants*, *stimulants*, *opioids*, and *hallucinogens*.

Depressants. **Depressants** are drugs that slow bodily functions. One subset of depressants, *benzodiazepines*, reduce nervousness and are often prescribed for problems relating to anxiety or insomnia. Another subset of depressants, *barbiturates*, are depressant drugs that have a calming effect. Barbiturates were used for many years as prescription medications for sleep and anxiety (and often sold on the street as downers), but their popularity has decreased in recent decades because the more recent generation of sleep and anxiety medications are more effective and have fewer side effects.

depressants
Drugs that slow bodily functions.

By far, the most commonly used depressant, both in the United States and around the world, is alcohol.

Wait—alcohol is a depressant? When I see people drinking alcohol, they don't look depressed to me.

The effects of alcohol can seem to bring a relaxed, pleasant feeling (or buzz), but that is usually at low doses. At higher doses, the depressant effects of alcohol are much more obvious: speech, movement, coordination, reasoning, and reaction time all slow down. Alcohol also delays the drinker's inhibitions to the point where they can't keep up with the drinker's impulses. This often leads to behaviors that the drinker would have decided against if sober. Sometimes, these behaviors are aggressive or sexual acts that later bring regret, legal trouble, or even more traumatic consequences.

As an example, consider the connection between alcohol and sexual assault. Alcohol is a factor in half of all sexual assaults (Abbey et al., 1996, 2004). Multiple studies have found that college men who drink more alcohol are more likely to commit sexual assaults (Abbey et al., 1998, 2001, 2014; Abbey & McAuslan, 2004).

The dangers of alcohol extend far beyond sexual assault. Continued use of alcohol is toxic to many essential body parts, including the liver, pancreas, heart, stomach, and brain. It is well established as a contributor to birth defects in the babies of women who drink while pregnant. (See the section on *fetal alcohol syndrome* in Chapter 9.) Alcohol interacts dangerously with dozens of commonly taken medications, including aspirin, antihistamines, antidepressants, antianxiety medications, and more. An overdose of alcohol (also known as alcohol poisoning) kills hundreds of people in the United States every year (Brick & Erickson, 2013; Room et al., 2005). And as **Figure 4.6** illustrates, drunk driving kills thousands.

Because alcohol comes in so many different forms, it is important to understand how those forms compare to each other in terms of alcohol content. Generally speaking, the amount of alcohol is approximately the same in a 12-ounce beer, a 5-ounce glass of

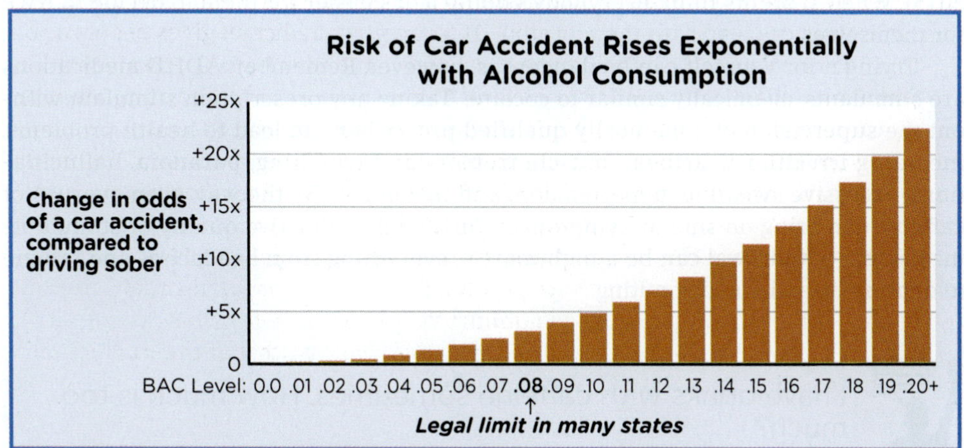

FIGURE 4.6 Crash Likelihood and Blood Alcohol Concentration. Just a few drinks raise the odds of a car crash. Many more multiply the odds.
Data from Ingraham (2015) and Compton and Berning (2015).

wine, and a 1.5-ounce shot of hard liquor. However, the impact of these drinks can differ because of the different rates at which they can be consumed. It typically takes longer to drink a whole bottle of beer or sip a whole glass of wine than it does to down a shot in a single gulp. That difference, multiplied by several (or many) drinks, leads to a different rate of absorption of alcohol by the body. The faster the alcohol gets into the body, the higher the peak level of blood alcohol concentration (BAC).

BAC also depends on the size of the person. Smaller people feel the effects of alcohol more quickly than bigger people. Remember when you were young and took children's medication in liquid form? The bottle had a dosage chart based on weight (or age, which correlates with weight in kids) because the appropriate dosage depends on how big the kid is. The same is true with alcohol — bigger people need more of it to feel the same effects as smaller people. That's one reason why alcohol affects an average-sized man and an average-sized woman differently.

Stimulants. **Stimulants** are drugs that speed up bodily functions. One of the best-known, and perhaps the most addictive, is cocaine, which is typically taken in powder or solid forms ("crack"). The stimulant category also includes amphetamines, which are most commonly found in prescription drugs for ADHD (like Adderall, Ritalin, Concerta, and Vyvanse), as well as in methamphetamine (or "meth"). Caffeine — found in coffee, tea, energy drinks, many sodas, and even chocolate — is also a low-grade stimulant. In low to moderate doses, stimulants make people feel more energetic. They quicken heart rate and breathing rate, as well as help to fight fatigue.

These effects explain why caffeine is so ever-present in our society (and many others around the world). They also explain why the abuse of prescription ADHD drugs, especially on college campuses, has become so rampant in recent years. A meta-analysis of over 30 studies on the subject, covering thousands of students across a wide range of colleges, found that 17% of college students misused or abused stimulant medications (Benson et al., 2015). The same team of researchers more recently found that a disproportionately high number of those students misusing or abusing ADHD medication actually have substantial symptoms of ADHD. However, they are taking the medication either without a prescription or in ways that vary from their prescription (Benson et al., 2017, 2018).

Studies that delve into those reasons for the misuse or abuse of stimulants find that academic performance is among the leading reasons. These drugs can help students stay awake and alert when studying, writing papers, and taking tests (Bennett & Holloway, 2017; DeSantis et al., 2008; Prosek et al., 2018; White et al., 2006). College students asked to estimate the percentage of their classmates who misuse or abuse ADHD stimulant medications generally overestimate the actual rate, and the amount by which they overestimate it correlates with their own odds of doing it (Kilmer et al., 2015). When students think everybody's doing it, it's easier for them to decide to try it for themselves.

Trying it for yourself can be dangerous, however. Remember: ADHD medications are stimulants, chemically similar to cocaine. Taking any prescription stimulant without the supervision of a medically qualified prescriber can lead to health problems, including irregular heartbeat, muscle tremors and twitching, paranoia, hallucinations, excessive sweating, hypertension, and insomnia. (By the way, even overuse of caffeine can bring on similar symptoms.) Further, the addictive quality of stimulants means that withdrawal can be a nightmare — everything from headaches and fatigue to depression, pain, and vomiting.

I have drinks with caffeine sometimes. How much is too much?

stimulants
Drugs that speed up bodily functions.

Researchers are still working on this question, but there is growing evidence that keeping caffeine intake below 400 mg per day seems to be best for your health. Studies indicate that the adverse effects of caffeine don't kick in until intake gets higher than that (de Mejia & Ramirez-Mares, 2014; Mayo Clinic Staff, 2017; Nawrot et al., 2003). Of course, that amount is based on an average-sized adult. For smaller adults, children, and pregnant women, the healthy amount of caffeine has a lower limit. If you're trying to convert that 400 mg total into a particular number of caffeinated drinks, the key is to know how much caffeine *your* drinks contain. Check **Table 4.4** – it lists common caffeine sources like sodas, energy drinks, coffee, tea, and more. When you do, pay attention not only to the amount of caffeine, but the serving size as well. If you drink big bottles of soda, venti cups of coffee, or tall cans of Red Bull, you might have to do some multiplying.

One last note about stimulants – nicotine, the key ingredient in tobacco, is also considered a stimulant. Surely, you've already been bombarded with knowledge of the health dangers of smoking and chewing tobacco. For example, nicotine is highly addictive, and many people who quit smoking end up starting again. It is the leading preventable cause of death in the United States: it kills hundreds of thousands of people every year in the United States and millions around the world. (For about half of the people who smoke continuously throughout their lives, the habit will kill them.) A pregnant woman who smokes does serious damage to her fetus, and secondhand smoke damages the people who inhale it.

Do you know about *thirdhand smoke*? Thirdhand smoke is not smoke itself, but the cancer-causing residue that smoke leaves behind. That residue embeds itself in almost everything the smoke touches – clothes, carpets, drapes, sofas, pillows, car seats, even human hair. And that residue remains there long after the smoke itself has cleared (Dreyfuss, 2010; Matt et al., 2017, 2018; Sleiman et al., 2010). So, if you smell cigarettes – on someone's jacket, in their car, in their apartment, anywhere at all – you're exposed to thirdhand smoke, even if there is no longer any smoke to be seen.

Unfortunately, far fewer people recognize the dangers of thirdhand smoke than secondhand smoke (Díez-Izquierdo et al., 2018a; Winickoff et al., 2009). Perhaps that

TABLE 4.4: How Much Caffeine?

PRODUCT		SERVING SIZE	AMOUNT OF CAFFEINE (MG)
Coke, Pepsi, Diet Coke, Diet Pepsi	Constantin Iosif/ Shutterstock	12 ounces	23–47
Mountain Dew, Diet Mountain Dew	Keith Homan/ Alamy	12 ounces	42–55
Red Bull, Rockstar, Amp	Steve Stock/ Alamy	8 ounces	70–80
Coffee	Stockforlife/ Shutterstock .com	8 ounces	100–200
5-Hour Energy Shot	Helen Sessions/ Alamy	2 ounces	200

How much caffeine do you consume per day? Remember, many experts suggest that the closer you get to 400 mg per day, the closer you get to health risks. Also, remember to compare these serving sizes to your actual drink sizes.

opiates
Pain-relieving drugs naturally derived from the poppy plant.

opioids
Drugs that include both naturally derived opiates and synthetically made substances that bind to the same receptors in the brain and have similar effects.

is because the evidence, and the public awareness, regarding the dangers of thirdhand smoke are just starting to grow (Tuma, 2010). But what researchers have already learned about those dangers is disturbing (Díez-Izquierdo et al., 2018b). For example, in one study, nonsmokers who moved into apartments that had previously been occupied by smokers showed significant jumps in their own nicotine levels, even if the apartment had been cleaned between residents and had stayed vacant for as long as 2 months (Matt et al., 2010). Another study measured thirdhand smoke in people who had stayed in two different kinds of "nonsmoking" hotel rooms: rooms in completely nonsmoking hotels and nonsmoking rooms in hotels that also contain some smoking rooms. People who stayed in the nonsmoking rooms in hotels that also contain some smoking rooms had higher levels of nicotine, presumably from breathing in thirdhand smoke from the other rooms and hallways of the hotel, than people who stayed in the completely nonsmoking hotel (Matt et al., 2014).

Opioids. *Opiates* and *opioids* are similar terms with similar meanings, but there is a distinction in terms of how they are created. **Opiates** are pain-relieving drugs naturally derived from the poppy plant. **Opioids** are a category of drugs that include both naturally derived opiates and synthetically made substances that bind to the same receptors in the brain and have similar effects. Opiates have been used by societies around the world for thousands of years, but synthetic opioids have been around for less than a century. (From this point on, for simplicity, we'll use the term *opioids* to describe all of these drugs.) Opioids include some street drugs, like heroin and opium, and also some prescription painkillers like morphine, codeine, fentanyl, hydrocodone (Vicodin), and oxycodone (OxyContin, Percocet, Percodan). Opioids activate the same receptors in our brains as *endorphins*. As we learned in Chapter 2, endorphins are neurotransmitters in the brain that occur naturally when we increase pleasure or reduce pain. So, using an opioid is like getting a powerful shot of the pleasure that comes naturally from good sex, good food, good exercise, or a good laugh.

That's the primary reason why opioids are so addictive. People who take opioids experience such an intense rush of pleasure (or relief from pain) that the previous state of mind seems undesirable, perhaps unbearable. They often focus exclusively on finding another dose of opioids (another hit, as some would say) to return them to the euphoric, often semiconscious state they were in when they had taken the opioid.

Decades ago, opioid addiction typically took the form of people hooked on illegal drugs like heroin or morphine. In recent decades, however, prescription opioid addiction has become much more common, to the point where its annual costs in the United States are approximately $50 billion and it has been labeled both a crisis and an epidemic (Fischer et al., 2014; Katz, 2017; Oderda et al., 2015; Popova et al., 2009). According to one estimate, in 2016–2017 (U.S. Department of Health and Human Services, 2018):

- On average, 130 people die of opioid-related drug overdoses every day.
- Over 11 million people misused prescription opioids.
- 2 million people misused prescription opioids for the first time.

Scott Dudelson/Getty Images

The death of Juice WRLD is one of many linked to overdoses involving opioids.

Celebrities whose deaths have been linked to addiction or overdose of opioids (often called "painkillers" in news reports) include Juice WRLD, Mac Miller, Prince, Tom Petty, Heath Ledger, Philip Seymour Hoffman, and Michael K. Williams. Other celebrities who have publicly described their problems with the drugs include rappers Eminem and Macklemore, actor Matthew Perry, and football players Brett Favre and Walter Payton.

In some cases of opioid addiction, the person becomes addicted after taking the drugs for a prescribed reason, such as severe back pain or postsurgical pain (Volkow et al., 2018). One study found that about a quarter of the people who received a prescription for opioids for back pain took the medication in a way that didn't match instructions (Martell et al., 2007). In other cases, the person becomes addicted with no history of legitimate opioid use. They obtain the pills from a friend, family member, unethical medical professional, or on the street. In fact, among physicians who treat patients with chronic pain, a significant challenge is distinguishing true pain sufferers from opioid addicts scamming for meds (Fields, 2011; Haller & Acosta, 2010). Increasing numbers who become addicted to prescription opioids later turn to heroin or other street forms of the drug (Jones, 2013).

There is no surefire treatment for addiction to opioids. A common treatment is methadone, a substance that is itself an opioid. It is safer than the drugs it typically treats, but it is not entirely safe, and its misuse can cause further problems or even death. Nonetheless, many people have recovered from addiction to opioids with the help of methadone, other substances, or nonmedical therapies.

Naloxone, a drug used in emergency situations to save the life of a person who has overdosed on opioids, is available in both injection and nasal-spray forms. The severity of the opioid crisis is reflected by the fact that the number of naloxone prescriptions doubled in just 1 year (2017 to 2018) (U.S. Department of Health and Human Services, 2021).

Hallucinogens. **Hallucinogens** are drugs that produce unrealistic sensations such as hallucinations. Hallucinogens were known as "psychedelic" drugs in past generations, when the most common examples were LSD (lysergic acid diethylamide, or "acid"), PCP, and certain psychoactive varieties of mushrooms. In recent years, "psychedelics" such as psilocybin have received renewed attention as potentially legitimate ways (if legal, taken responsibly, and supervised appropriately) to achieve a variety of psychological and medical benefits (e.g., Andersen et al., 2021; Carroll, 2017; Holson, 2018; Nutt & Carhart-Harris, 2021; Pollan, 2018). Currently, a common illicit hallucinogen is MDMA ("ecstasy"), which also has some stimulant qualities. Some other drugs that may or may not chemically qualify as hallucinogens but sometimes have hallucinogenic effects include "bath salts," cannabis (marijuana, "weed," or "pot"), and synthetic cannabis ("K2" or "spice").

Hallucinogens cause people to see, hear, and feel things that are not really there. During "trips" on these drugs, some people claim to experience unusual cross-sensory distortions, like seeing smells or hearing colors. Hallucinogens also cause a strong detachment from reality (often described as a dreamlike state) and impair people's judgment and reasoning, which causes them to do blatantly dangerous things that they would never otherwise do. For example, people tripping on hallucinogens might try to fly from a high story of a building or try to drive a car through a wall. Sometimes, people experience these hallucinations as "bad trips" in which the hallucinations feel scary and the person fears that they may be losing their mind.

Marijuana is included in this category, but it is different from the more "hard-core" hallucinogens in many ways. First, it is not always hallucinogenic. Many people do not report any drastically different sensations when on marijuana than when off it. Instead, the primary effect is often described as a pleasantly relaxed feeling, with any sensory changes secondary if present at all. Second, marijuana is much less toxic. A single overdose of MDMA, LSD, or another hallucinogen can cause serious damage or death, but there is little evidence of such risks for marijuana. In fact, some experts describe marijuana use as safer than such legal drugs as alcohol and nicotine (Brick & Erickson, 2013). Third, marijuana is prescribed by doctors for a number of conditions, including glaucoma (a disease involving excessive pressure in the eye) and nausea from chemotherapy. Fourth, marijuana is legal for recreational use in an increasing number of states. Marijuana is not without risk, however. It can become addictive. In higher doses or after long-term use, it often causes memory loss, impairs driving ability, and decreases overall motivation. Long-term smoking of marijuana can also lead to lung cancer.

One final note about psychoactive drugs: the drugs used to treat psychological disorders are psychoactive drugs too. They include *antipsychotic* drugs to help with hallucinations and other bizarre experiences; *antianxiety* drugs to help with fear and nervousness; *antidepressant* drugs to help with sadness and hopelessness (and anxiety as well); and *mood-stabilizing* drugs to help reduce the intensity of extreme emotional highs and lows. All of these drugs are described in Chapter 15 as treatments for psychological disorders. **Table 4.5** summarizes the effects of the various types of psychoactive drugs.

hallucinogens
Drugs that produce unrealistic sensations such as hallucinations.

TABLE 4.5: Types of Psychoactive Drugs

TYPE	EXAMPLES	COMMON EFFECTS
Depressants	Alcohol, benzodiazepines, barbiturates	Slow bodily functions; enhance relaxation
Stimulants	Cocaine, amphetamines (including many ADHD medications), methamphetamines, caffeine, nicotine	Speed up bodily functions; enhance energy and overcome fatigue
Opioids	Heroin, opium, morphine, codeine, hydrocodone, oxycodone, fentanyl	Relieve pain; enhance pleasure
Hallucinogens	LSD ("acid"), PCP, selected mushrooms, MDMA ("ecstasy"), "bath salts," cannabis, synthetic cannabis, peyote (mescaline), psilocybin	Produce hallucinations or dreamlike "trips"

CHECK YOUR LEARNING:

4.16 What are psychoactive drugs?

4.17 How do psychoactive drugs work?

4.18 What is the difference between tolerance and withdrawal?

4.19 What is addiction?

4.20 What do depressants do, and what are some common examples?

4.21 What do stimulants do, and what are some common examples?

4.22 What do opioids do, and what are some common examples?

4.23 What do hallucinogens do, and what are some common examples?

To check your understanding of these questions, click show the answers or refer to the answers in the Chapter Summary.

Other Altered States of Consciousness

YOU WILL LEARN:

4.24 what meditation is.

4.25 what mindfulness is.

Beyond sleep and wakefulness, even beyond hypnosis and psychoactive drugs, are other states of consciousness. For some people, certain occurrences temporarily put the mind in a different mode — including trances, out-of-body experiences, seizures, fasting- or fever-induced stupors, mystical revelations, and spiritual or religious visions (Barušs, 2003). Let's consider the examples of *meditation* and *mindfulness*.

Meditation and Mindfulness

Meditation is an activity designed to increase focused attention with the ultimate purpose of improving your mental state. Historically, that improvement of mental state emphasized a more direct connection with a higher being or spirit, such as Buddha or God. More recently, especially as practiced in the United States and other Western cultures, that emphasis on spiritual connection is accompanied by an emphasis on personal or psychological gain, such as lowered stress levels or improvement in symptoms of anxiety or depression, often with an eye toward improvement in physical health too (Das, 2014; Eberth & Sedlmeier, 2012; McMahan & Braun, 2017; Reangsing et al., 2021; Shapiro & Walsh, 2003).

meditation
An activity designed to increase focused attention with the ultimate purpose of improving a person's mental state.

Meditation has been around for thousands of years in cultures all around the world, often tied to religious or spiritual practices (Harrington, 2008; West, 1987). During that long history, meditation has taken many different forms, but most have one of two primary goals. In the first type of meditation, the goal is to empty the mind of all thoughts. The person meditating tries to achieve an entirely clear mind, a mind not occupied by thoughts or feelings. This clear mind then allows the person to experience the sensations of life as they arrive. The person meditating loses sense of time or space, and the world around the person begins to feel like a single, connected entity.

In the second type of meditation, the goal is to focus the mind wholly on one specifically chosen stimulus. This stimulus can be a word, phrase, or sound that the person says over and over again (a mantra, like "Om, om, om . . . "), a visual object that the person sees or imagines, or a concept that the person holds in mind. The idea is that the person reaches a transcendent, transformative state by becoming completely absorbed with this stimulus. By continuously focusing on this stimulus, all other thoughts and impulses fall away, leaving the mind to focus on inner experience (Gunaratana, 2014; Newberg, 2010; Simpkins & Simpkins, 2009; van Vugt, 2015).

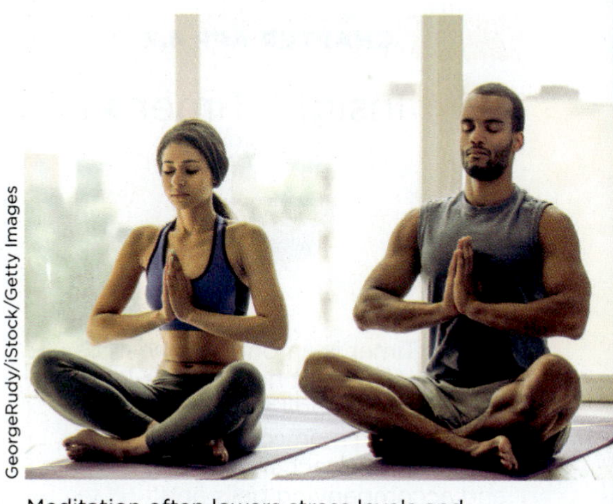
GeorgeRudy/iStock/Getty Images

Meditation often lowers stress levels and improves mental and physical health.

Meditation has grown in popularity in recent decades, and there are plenty of how-to books available, each providing its own methods for practicing meditation (e.g., Hanh, 1975; Kabat-Zinn, 2018; Siegel, 2018). One of those books is written by the Dalai Lama, the spiritual leader of all Tibetan Buddhism, a religion closely associated with meditation practices both currently and historically. Here are some of the Dalai Lama's insights and suggestions for beginning meditation (His Holiness the Dalai Lama, 2011):

- Meditation can be challenging when it is new, and it requires extensive practice.
- At first, aim for 10–15 minutes of meditation per day. Even a few minutes of successful meditation is a big accomplishment in the early stages.
- Meditate in the early morning hours, if possible, when the mind tends to be clearest and most unaffected by the events of the day.
- Meditation can be practiced anywhere, but it is better at first to find a quiet place free of visual and auditory distractions.
- Any comfortable position is fine, but sitting cross-legged is preferred because it is both comfortable and upright, decreasing the odds of drifting off to sleep.
- Start meditation by noticing your breath, deliberately concentrating on how it passes in and then out through your nostrils.

The goal of meditation is to achieve a neutral or blank state of mind, one that directly experiences the immediate inner sensations to such an extent that it can't get caught up in distracting thoughts about day-to-day life. Of course, those thoughts will at least occasionally occur, even if you don't want them to, but you can let go of them and gently remind yourself to refocus exclusively on your breathing. The Dalai Lama describes that process of letting mental events run their course rather than fighting them, as well as the benefits of doing so (His Holiness the Dalai Lama, 2011):

> When you initially engage in this meditation, inevitably you will find that your mind wanders off, thoughts and images float through your conscious awareness, or a memory pops up for no apparent reason. When this happens, do not get caught up in the energy of these thoughts and images by trying to suppress or reinforce them. Simply observe them and let them go, as if they are clouds appearing in the sky and fading from view . . . every now and then you will come to experience short intervals of what feels like an absence or a vacuum, when your mind has no particular content. Your first successes in this will only be fleeting. But with persistence . . . you can start to understand that the mind is like a mirror, or clear water, in which images appear and disappear. . . . Like a detached onlooker watching a spectacle, you will learn how to see your thoughts for what they are, namely constructs of your mind. So many of our problems arise because, in our naïve untrained state, we confuse our thoughts with actual reality. . . . In so doing, we tie ourselves ever tighter into a world that is essentially our own creation and become trapped in it, like a length of rope entangled in its own knots. (pp. 169–170)

CHAPTER APP 4.2

 Insight Timer

Insight Timer is among the most popular apps that help people learn and practice meditation. It lets users choose from many different guided meditations, teachers, durations, and accompanying bells and ambient sounds. It also allows users to create a meditation schedule, to track meditation history, and to connect with others using the same meditation practices on the app.

How does it APPly to your daily life?
If you have meditated before, how could an app like this influence the frequency with which you meditate and the benefits you receive from meditation? If you have never meditated before, how could an app like this influence the likelihood that you might try it?

How does it APPly to your understanding of psychology?
How do these apps enhance your understanding of the effects of meditation and mindfulness?

To learn more about this app or to download it to your phone, you can search for "Insight Timer" on Google, in the iPhone App store, or in the Google Play store.

Several parts of this description by the Dalai Lama illustrate that meditation leans heavily on the concept of **mindfulness**: awareness of your moment-to-moment experiences fully, deliberately, and without distraction. There is some discrepancy between the original Eastern definition of mindfulness and the way the term is used more recently in Western countries, but the essence remains largely the same (Carmody, 2015; Davis & Thompson, 2015; Gethin, 2015; Grossman, 2011; Grossman & Van Dam, 2011; Quaglia et al., 2015). That essence of mindfulness is all about experiencing what is happening in the present moment. This also means a mindful person does not focus on what happened in the past (even a minute or a day ago), and does not worry about what the future may bring. Experience of the present moment is without judgment or wishful thinking either. There is no approval or disapproval, no desire that what is happening will change or remain, just accepting it no matter how it makes you feel (Bishop et al., 2004; Brown & Ryan, 2004; Germer, 2005; Hick, 2008; Kabat-Zinn, 1994; Roemer & Orsillo, 2009).

As an example of an opportunity for mindfulness, consider brushing your teeth. Without mindfulness, you'd do it mindlessly: like a robot, zoned out, going through the motions, not noticing anything about the process at all. With mindfulness, there is a lot to notice: the colors on the toothpaste tube, the firmness of the toothbrush bristles against your teeth, the minty sting of the toothpaste on your tongue, the way the water swirls around the sink before it goes down the drain. Without mindfulness, you might distract yourself by listening to a podcast or peeking at your smartphone as you brush your teeth. With mindfulness, brushing your teeth gets your full attention. Without mindfulness, your mind might wander to the past or the future ("Did my friend understand that text I sent last night?" "Am I ready for that exam later today?"). With mindfulness, your mind stays zoomed in on today, on this moment, on the sensations of brushing your teeth.

The underlying idea of mindfulness has risen dramatically in terms of popularity in the United States since the 1990s (Brown et al., 2015; Crane, 2017). Psychologists and other kinds of therapists have used mindfulness as the basis of treatments for various problems, and have woven it into other forms of treatment too (Hayes-Skelton & Wadsworth, 2015; Irving et al., 2015; Segal et al., 2012; Shapiro, 2009). And those treatments have shown impressive results. In terms of biology, mindfulness changes the brain (Zeidan, 2015). In one particular study, participants were shown photos designed to evoke negative emotions, including funerals, people crying, burn victims, and dead animals. The fMRI images of participants showed that those higher in mindfulness had greater activation of the prefrontal cortex and lower activation of the amygdala as they viewed the pictures (Modinos et al., 2010). These results (and similar results from other studies) suggest that mindfulness helps the parts of the brain that interpret events to calm the part of the brain that produces anxiety (Brown et al., 2012; Creswell et al., 2007; Vago & Silbersweig, 2012; Zeidan et al., 2011). Brain differences like these can be obtained after a minimal amount of mindfulness training: just 20 minutes a day for 4 days (Zeidan et al., 2013).

The evidence of the power of mindfulness is not limited to brain scans. Many studies show that incorporating mindfulness into your life can make you significantly happier and healthier (Arch & Landy, 2015; Carsley et al., 2018; Chiesa & Serretti, 2011; Dawson et al., 2020; Gu et al., 2015; Khoury et al., 2013; Schumer et al., 2018). Specifically, there is evidence that mindfulness-based psychotherapies provide great benefits to people with anxiety, depression, eating disorders, personality disorders, addiction, and many other psychological diagnoses (Baer, 2006; Bowen et al., 2015; Goldberg et al., 2018; Hedman-Lagerlöf et al., 2018; Hofmann et al., 2010; Piet & Hougaard, 2011; Sala et al., 2020; Sedlmeier et al., 2012; Vøllestad et al., 2012). An increasing number of mindfulness apps (often incorporating meditation practices) are available via smartphone, some of which have shown at least short-term benefits (Flett et al., 2019; Gál et al., 2020).

mindfulness
Awareness of one's moment-to-moment experiences fully, deliberately, and without distraction.

Mindfulness brings psychological benefits to people without psychological disorders as well (Brown, 2015; Shapiro & Jazaieri, 2015). Higher levels of mindfulness in couples correlate with lower levels of hostility (even right after an argument) and higher levels of relationship satisfaction (Barnes et al., 2007; Carson et al., 2004). College students who underwent an 8-week mindfulness training program had significantly lower rates of daily hassles, stress, and medical symptoms 3 months after it ended (Williams et al., 2001). Middle-aged adults without psychological disorders who underwent a similar 8-week mindfulness training program reported significant gains in positive emotions and overall quality of life (Nyklíček & Kuijpers, 2008). Prisoners who practiced mindfulness meditation saw significant improvements in their overall well-being (Auty et al., 2017). A mindfulness-based program also helped physicians significantly lower their own levels of stress and emotional exhaustion (Schroeder et al., 2018). It is also noteworthy that mindfulness aids in the treatment of many physical and medical problems, including cancer, chronic pain, diabetes, hypertension, heart disease, and HIV/AIDS (Anheyer et al., 2017; Carlson, 2015; Grossman et al., 2004; Haller et al., 2017; Keng et al., 2011).

ESB Professional/Shutterstock.com

Mindfulness is awareness of your moment-to-moment experiences, fully, deliberately, and without distraction.

CHECK YOUR LEARNING:

4.24 What is meditation, and what purpose does it serve?

4.25 What is mindfulness, and what effects can it have?

To check your understanding of these questions, click show the answers or refer to the answers in the Chapter Summary.

CHAPTER SUMMARY

Sleep

4.1 The function of sleep is not entirely clear, but many theories emphasize evolutionary benefits like staying still to avoid harm, saving energy, recharging the body, developing the brain, and enhancing memory.

4.2 Partial sleep deprivation is quite common, and it has strong (but often unrecognized) negative consequences in terms of emotion and performance.

4.3 Your circadian rhythm is your internal body clock, which affects alertness and sleepiness throughout each day. It is primarily controlled by your suprachiasmatic nucleus, but it can be influenced by external cues like schedules of light exposure, eating, work shifts, and jet lag.

4.4 Normal sleep can be divided into rapid eye movement (REM) sleep and non-REM sleep. REM sleep involves intense brain activity and dreaming. Non-REM sleep involves stage 1, stage 2, and stages 3 and 4 (slow-wave sleep), which occur in increasing depth.

4.5 People from diverse groups exhibit different kinds of sleep patterns.

4.6 Co-sleeping involves family members sleeping in the same room or same bed (usually a child with an adult). For young children, co-sleeping is much more common in Asia and some other parts of the world than it is in most of the United States.

4.7 Sleep abnormalities include insomnia (difficulty sleeping), sleepwalking, narcolepsy (sleep attacks), sleep terrors (brief awakenings marked by fright and confusion), and sleep apnea (sleep interruptions caused by breathing difficulties). Physical illness often goes hand in hand with these sleep abnormalities.

4.8 To treat or prevent sleep problems, maintain a consistent sleep-wake schedule, exercise daily, don't eat much at night, and sleep in a comfortable, dark, quiet room. Also, close to bedtime avoid caffeine, naps, cigarettes, alcohol, exercise, and bright light.

Dreams

4.9 There are many theories of dreaming, including folk theories, Sigmund Freud's theory that dreams reveal unconscious wishes, and theories that focus on neuropsychological functioning.

4.10 Themes of dreams tend to be more positive closer to wake-up time than bedtime. In some cases, dreams can improve mental health through imagery rehearsal therapy and lucid dreaming.

4.11 The start of the COVID pandemic produced more COVID-related dreaming. The content of dreams tends to differ across gender and age.

Hypnosis

4.12 Hypnosis is an altered state of consciousness in which one person, the participant, becomes very suggestible to another person, the hypnotist. The procedure of hypnotism includes induction, suggestions (some of which can be posthypnotic), and termination.

4.13 Hypnosis has been used to treat various behavioral problems and mental disorders and to improve performance in other areas, including sports, but the evidence for its effectiveness is limited.

4.14 Some people are much more hypnotizable than others, especially those who are more open-minded and have a tendency to get engrossed in sensory experiences.

4.15 The social-cognitive theory of hypnosis, which states that a hypnotized person is really just conforming to social pressure to act hypnotized, is disconfirmed by neuropsychological studies showing that parts of the brain are actually affected by hypnosis.

Psychoactive Drugs and Consciousness

4.16 Psychoactive drugs are substances that alter mental functioning.

4.17 Psychoactive drugs work by changing the amount of neurotransmitter that travels between neurons.

4.18 Tolerance is the decreased effectiveness of a particular amount of a drug caused by repeated use of that drug. Withdrawal involves stressful and uncomfortable symptoms caused by discontinuing a drug that has become habitual, often after a person has become physically or psychologically dependent on that drug.

4.19 Addiction is problematic drug use that persists in spite of serious negative consequences.

4.20 Depressants are drugs that slow bodily functions, and include alcohol, benzodiazepines, and barbiturates. Alcohol has been linked to a variety of negative outcomes, including drunk driving, sexual assault, overdose, dangerous interaction with common medications, birth defects, and damage to vital organs.

4.21 Stimulants are drugs that speed up bodily functions. Stimulants include cocaine, amphetamines (such as those found in ADHD prescription medications), methamphetamine ("meth"), nicotine, and caffeine.

4.22 Opioids (a term that encompasses *opiates*) are drugs made from opium, or synthetic versions of those drugs, that relieve pain by activating the endorphin receptors in the brain. They are highly addictive and include heroin, morphine, codeine, hydrocodone, oxycodone, and fentanyl.

4.23 Hallucinogens, formerly known as psychedelics, are drugs that produce unrealistic sensations, or "trips," such as hallucinations. They include LSD ("acid"), PCP, certain varieties of mushrooms, MDMA ("ecstasy"), and psilocybin. Other drugs that sometimes have hallucinogenic effects include "bath salts" and cannabis.

Other Altered States of Consciousness

4.24 Meditation is an activity designed to increase focused attention with the ultimate purpose of improving your mental state, often for spiritual or psychological gain.

4.25 Mindfulness is an awareness of your moment-to-moment experiences, fully, deliberately, and without distraction. Mindfulness has been used to improve the mental health of people with and without mental disorders; neuropsychological studies show that it produces changes in the brain.

KEY TERMS

consciousness, p. 101
sleep deprivation, p. 103
circadian rhythm, p. 104
REM, p. 107
REM sleep, p. 107
non-REM sleep, p. 107
REM paralysis, p. 108
REM rebound, p. 108
solitary sleeping, p. 112
co-sleeping, p. 112
insomnia, p. 113
sleepwalking (somnambulism), p. 114
narcolepsy, p. 115
sleep terrors, p. 115
sleep apnea, p. 115
sleep hygiene, p. 116
lucid dreaming, p. 120
hypnosis, p. 121
social-cognitive theory of hypnosis, p. 123
psychoactive drugs, p. 123
tolerance, p. 124
withdrawal, p. 124
physical dependence, p. 124
psychological dependence, p. 124
addiction, p. 124
depressants, p. 125
stimulants, p. 126
opiates, p. 128
opioids, p. 128
hallucinogens, p. 129
meditation, p. 130
mindfulness, p. 132

SELF-ASSESSMENT

1. ______ is your awareness of yourself and your surroundings.

a. REM sleep
b. Consciousness
c. Insomnia
d. Circadian rhythm

2. Lanesha is dreaming. Lanesha is most likely to be in which stage of sleep?

a. REM sleep
b. stage 1 sleep
c. stage 2 sleep
d. stage 3 sleep

3. Anthony experiences ______, which involves sleep "attacks" happening at any time of day.

a. sleep terrors
b. sleep apnea
c. insomnia
d. narcolepsy

4. Research on the dreams of people with depression shows that

a. people with depression don't dream.
b. people with depression dream about five times as much as people without depression.
c. dreams that occur in the first half of the night tend to be more negative than dreams that occur in the second half, and dreamers report more positive moods when they wake up than when they went to bed.
d. depression is caused by nightmares.

5. _____ is an altered state of consciousness in which one person becomes very suggestible to another person.
   a. Hypnosis
   b. Sleep apnea
   c. Sleepwalking
   d. Déjà vu

6. Which of the following is true about psychoactive drugs?
   a. All psychoactive drugs are illegal.
   b. No psychoactive drugs cause tolerance or withdrawal.
   c. Psychoactive drugs are substances that alter mental functioning.
   d. All of the statements are correct.

7. Sean starts using a drug on a regular basis. Eventually, he needs higher doses of the drug to achieve the same effect that a lower dose had earlier. Sean is exhibiting a(n) _____ to this drug.

8. _____ is problematic drug use that persists in spite of serious negative consequences.

9. Barbiturates, benzodiazepines, and alcohol are all examples of _____.
   a. stimulants
   b. hallucinogens
   c. opioids
   d. depressants

10. _____ is awareness of your moment-to-moment experiences, fully, deliberately, and without distraction.

To check your understanding of these questions, click show the answers in the e-book or refer to the answers in Appendix B.

Research shows quizzing is a highly effective learning tool. Continue quizzing yourself using LearningCurve, the system that adapts to *your* learning.

WHAT'S YOUR TAKE?

1. Many undergraduate students have worked the night shift, either part-time or full-time. Some of you may be doing so currently. Others may have a friend or family member who has worked night shifts. What effect did it have on you (or your friend or family member)? Did it disrupt sleep? Did it negatively influence health or happiness? If so, how long did it take to notice these effects?

2. Consider the number of brightly lit screens to which you expose your eyes and your suprachiasmatic nucleus every night: TVs, computers, tablets, smartphones, and perhaps even more. How much time do you spend on these screens? How close to bedtime? Do you look at any screens while you're *in* bed? How have you noticed your sleep being influenced by screen time near bedtime? Will you (or do you) allow your kids to use screens when their bedtime approaches?

SHOW ME MORE

4.1 Natural Light and Circadian Rhythms

http://tiny.cc/sq5njy

Here's a video summary of a study on the effect of natural light (as experienced in a week-long camping trip in the Rocky Mountains) versus electrical light on circadian rhythms.

Jordan Siemens/Iconica/Getty Images

This video is hosted by a third-party Web site (source). For accessible content requests, please reach out to the publisher of that site.

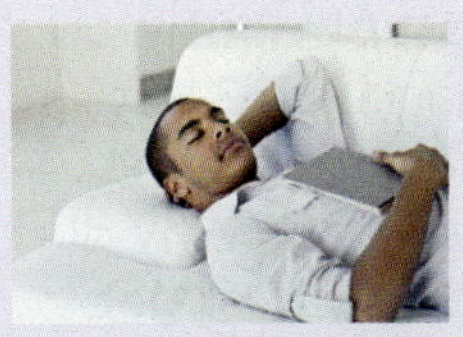

4.2 The Benefits of Naps

This video explains the benefits of naps and shows examples of "nap friendly spaces" available to students and employees during the day.

Neustockimages/E+/Getty Images

4.3 My Psychology Podcast

This podcast episode features the author of this textbook, psychologist Andy Pomerantz, speaking with other instructors of introductory psychology courses about the most important and interesting concepts in this chapter.

Macmillan Learning

5 Memory

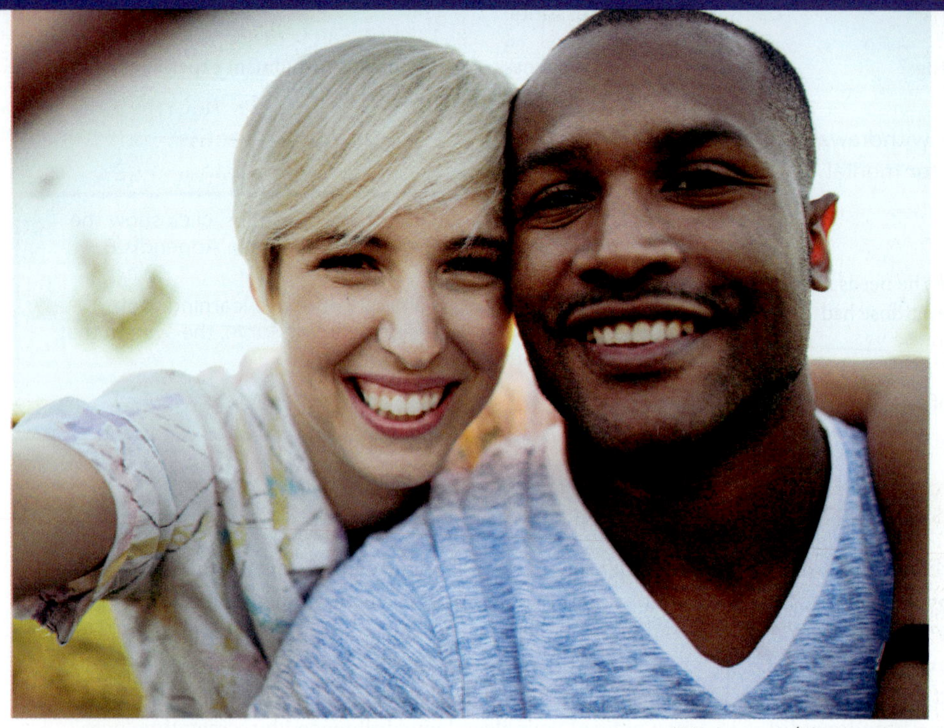

AYA images/Shutterstock

CHAPTER OUTLINE

Receipts is an interesting word. For many years, receipts just referred to proof of purchase, like the slip of paper a grocery store cashier hands you after you pay. More recently, the meaning of receipts has expanded to include proof that something happened, usually in a form you can show on your smartphone. When someone says "show me the receipts," you might pull up a screenshot, text, photo, video, voicemail, social media post, or some other piece of evidence to support your claim.

Receipts can show proof or catch someone lying. But sometimes, receipts can catch people remembering something inaccurately. Maybe it has happened to you: you remember something vividly and confidently, but when you see the receipts, it turns out your memory was somehow wrong. It has certainly happened to me. Once, I saw a commercial for a nearby pizza place and mentioned to my wife, "We should try that place—I heard it's really good." A bit puzzled, she responded, "We went there last year on my birthday—don't you remember?" "No, that was a different place," I said, certain that she was confused and my recollection was right. We went back and forth for a few minutes, and every time she offered a detail—what we ate, where we sat—none of it matched what I remembered. Then she pulled out her phone and showed me the receipts: photos of the two of us in that very restaurant, taken on the date of her birthday, eating what she said we ate, and sitting where she said we sat. She even started to search for the group text she sent that night to our friends to recommend the place, but I told her that wasn't necessary—there were already enough receipts to prove my memory was mistaken.

"Receipts" moments like that raise important questions about how memory works. Most obviously, how can some of our memories be so inaccurate? But more fundamentally, how do we form memories in the first place? How do we store and retrieve them? Why do some memories endure, while others fade away or get distorted? What enhances memory, and what distorts or impairs it? How do cultural and diversity factors impact memory? In this chapter, we explore all of these questions and more.

Defining Memory

YOU WILL LEARN:

5.1 how psychologists define memory.

5.2 about the role that memory can play in personal identity.

5.3 about the extremes in memory achievement.

Memory is the process of taking in information, saving it over time, and calling it to mind later. Memory is so essential that it would be difficult to imagine human life without it. Let's envision how the first 2 minutes of your day might go without a well-functioning memory. You wake up in your bed, but you have no recollection of where you are. The room seems completely unfamiliar. Disoriented, you wander to the next room, stand in front of the sink, and see a face in the mirror – but you don't recognize it. Looking down, you see a small plastic stick with bristles on the end of it next to a tube that says Crest, but you can't remember what those items are or how to use them. You hear something vibrate and ring on your bedside table. Bewildered, you track down the sound. It is some kind of glass-screened small rectangle connected by a cord to the power outlet on the wall, and it's lighting up. You wonder, "What is this rectangle, and what should I do with it?" Back in the bathroom, you catch another glimpse of yourself in the mirror, but again, that face is completely unfamiliar, as if you hadn't just stared at it a minute ago.

Memory and Identity

Memory is indispensable, not just to our functioning but to our identities. Your memories define you as a unique person. No one else has accumulated exactly the same knowledge, experienced exactly the same events, or achieved exactly the same abilities and skills as you. As a result, there's an overlap between your memory and your personality. What you remember shapes who you are today, including the way you think, feel, and behave.

To illustrate this connection between what you remember and who you are, consider the words of Nelson Dellis. He has one of the most impressive memories ever documented, having won numerous national memory contests and memorized many long lists of names and numbers along the way. However, even Dellis knows that memory is about much more than filing away facts:

> What's scary to me . . . about potentially losing memories is not forgetting all the stuff I learned . . . it's more those small moments with people we love and care about that make us who we are, and if you lose those memories . . . then who are you, and how can you enjoy life? (Dellis, 2012)

This link between memory and identity became clear to me as my family watched Alzheimer's disease increasingly overtake my grandma in the last years of her life. Toward the end, she even struggled to recognize her own children and recall her own name. It was painful and saddening to watch. As we discussed her condition and tried to comfort each other, some of my relatives lamented, "Her memory is really slipping now." Others used slightly different wording: "Grandma is really slipping now." We all meant the same thing, of course, but it's interesting that we were saying *her memory* and *Grandma* interchangeably. Without realizing it, we highlighted the fact that her lifetime of memories – who her family and friends were, what ingredients went into her chicken soup, the words to her favorite songs – is what made Grandma who she was.

The Extremes of Memory Achievement

When psychologists study memory, sometimes they focus on memory impairment like my grandma's. Such impairments can come not only from Alzheimer's but from other brain diseases, disorders, or injuries. Sometimes, researchers focus on the other extreme – memory excellence – including those rare people who have the ability to remember nearly everything (Hooper, 2018; Lockhart, 2000). In rare cases, they are born with this ability. For example, Kim Peek (the real person on whom Dustin Hoffman's character in *Rain Man*, which won the Oscar for Best Picture in 1989, was

memory
The process of taking in information, saving it over time, and calling it to mind later.

Dan Eckstein/ZUMA Press/Newscom

When journalist Joshua Foer wrote a book about the USA Memory Championship, he learned the memory enhancement techniques that the competitors use. The next year, Foer entered the contest himself—and won. (Check the Show Me More 5.1 feature at the end of the chapter for a video in which Foer describes his experiences.)

based) had a memory for facts that was nearly perfect and boundless. He could answer the most obscure trivia questions regarding history, music, sports, movies, religion, and many other subjects. He memorized, word for word, over 9000 books—more than some Kindles can hold! He knew the exact location of every zip code and every area code in the United States, and he knew the local TV stations in every one of them. He memorized calendars going back decades: if you told him your date of birth, he could instantly tell you the day of the week on which it fell. He memorized the exact wording of many of Shakespeare's plays (and would often stand up and correct the actors when they missed a word!) (Treffert & Christensen, 2009; Weber, 2009).

If you're not born with a mind like Kim Peek's, you can train your mind to excel in memory. The book *Moonwalking with Einstein* (Foer, 2011) describes the USA Memory Championship, an annual event in New York City where mental athletes from around the world gather to see who can most quickly and successfully memorize all kinds of information. They memorize astonishingly long lists of random numbers or words, 50-line poems they have never seen or heard before, and extensive sequences of photos of strangers' faces and names. Particularly impressive is Ben Pridmore, a competitor who can memorize a list of over 1500 random numbers in order, recite the first 50,000 digits of pi, and learn the order of a newly shuffled deck of cards in just over half a minute. Pridmore was not born with these abilities but learned them through training in memory enhancement techniques that any of us could use. The journalist who wrote *Moonwalking with Einstein*, Joshua Foer, had no special memory abilities himself when he began writing the book. However, while writing it, he became so intrigued and inspired by these mental athletes that he learned their techniques, entered the competition the next year—and won.

Much of the research that psychologists conduct on memory falls between the two extremes of memory impairment and memory excellence, where most of us spend our day-to-day lives (Bower, 2000; Kahana, 2000). Memory researchers strive to understand how memories form, how we access memories, how different kinds of memory work, and ways to help or hurt our ability to remember. Much of what we now know centers on the fundamental fact that memory generally involves a three-step process of getting information into our minds (*encoding*), holding onto it (*storage*), and taking it back out later (*retrieval*)—a process that we will now examine in detail.

CHECK YOUR LEARNING:

5.1 How do psychologists define memory?

5.2 What role does memory play in personal identity?

5.3 Is an extremely strong memory something you can train yourself to have, or does it depend entirely on inborn ability?

To check your understanding of these questions, click show the answers or refer to the answers in the Chapter Summary.

The Three Steps of Memory

YOU WILL LEARN:

5.4 what the three steps of memory are according to the information processing model.

5.5 what encoding is and how it involves sensory memory.

5.6 what echoic memory and iconic memory are.

Much of what we now understand about memory centers on the **information processing model**: a model of memory that involves the three steps of *encoding*, *storage*, and *retrieval* (**Figure 5.1**). We will examine these three steps in detail, but essentially, they involve getting information into our minds (*encoding*), holding onto that information (*storage*), and taking that information back out later (*retrieval*) (Baddeley, 2002; Brown & Craik, 2000; Cowan, 1988). This way of understanding human memory is similar to the way we understand computer memory. First, information enters your computer—for example, a document you open as an e-mail attachment. Then the computer saves that information within its gigs of available memory. And of course, that information then remains available for you to pull up later when you need it.

FIGURE 5.1 The Three Steps of Memory. The three big steps in the memory process are encoding (taking information in), storage (holding information), and retrieval (pulling information out).

YOU WILL LEARN: *(Continued)*

5.7 how encoding depends on level of processing and how level of processing can be enhanced.

5.8 how encoding involves the physiological changes of long-term potentiation.

5.9 what storage is and where it occurs.

5.10 what retrieval is and how it happens through recall or recognition.

5.11 how retrieval can be affected by retrieval cues.

5.12 how encoding specificity and priming can enhance retrieval.

It can be tempting to take this metaphor between human memory and computer memory too far, but that would be a mistake because they are not *exactly* the same (Draaisma, 2000; Randall, 2007). The three steps (encoding, storage, and retrieval) are definitely involved in our memory process, but the human mind is far more complex than any computer. So it is best to understand this computer metaphor as an oversimplified version of what goes on in your own memory — a good place to start but not a comprehensive explanation. That's why psychologists call it the information processing *model*, rather than the information processing *fact*. It's an approximation of how our memory works, but not a perfect description.

Encoding

Encoding is entering information into memory. Without encoding, the next steps of memory can't happen — that is, there's nothing to store and nothing to retrieve later (Brown & Craik, 2000; Shields et al., 2017). What you encode, of course, depends on what your senses detect. For that reason, encoding is closely related to **sensory memory**: the earliest part of the memory process, in which the senses take in and very briefly hold information. To explain, let's return to the computer metaphor for a moment. The exterior of your computer has numerous ports through which the computer can "sense," or take in, information from other devices. They allow your computer to "see" an image from a scanner plugged into a USB port or "hear" a voice through a microphone plugged into the minijack port.

Your head also has ports that take in information from around you — your eyes, ears, nose, and mouth. These sense organs are constantly monitoring all of the sights, sounds, smells, and tastes that surround you. The vast majority of this incoming data gets discarded. For example, in a crowded movie theater, your ears pick up lots of little sounds — the air conditioner blowing, chairs creaking, popcorn bags crinkling, people coughing — but because you're focused on the sounds of the movie, those sounds get filtered out before you encode them into memory. More specifically, these sounds last only as long as sensory memory can hold them — about 3 or 4 seconds for sounds, about half a second for sights — and then disappear (Turkington & Harris, 2001). The sounds of the movie, however, progress past sensory memory and get fully encoded, entering and sticking in your mind in such a way that you can remember them throughout the movie and perhaps for days, months, or years after the movie ends.

Echoic Memory. That brief sensory memory for the ambient sounds of the movie theater is an example of **echoic memory**: auditory sensory memory, or all the information your ears took in during the past few seconds. Echoic memory is what allows you to cover for yourself when you momentarily space out, or get distracted, while listening to someone speak. I've taken advantage of it many times, including a few when I was practicing therapy.

For example, one client of mine was tearfully telling me about the moment she caught her boyfriend cheating on her with his ex-girlfriend. "So I walk into the restaurant, and he's actually holding hands with her across the table! I couldn't believe it! I didn't know what to do at first, but then I decided to . . ." Suddenly I heard a dog bark. A dog? In my therapy office? What was going on? It took me a few seconds, but finally I figured out that the sound of the barking dog was coming from my client's purse, where she kept her phone. (Later, she explained to me that she loved dogs so much

information processing model
A model of memory that involves the three steps of *encoding*, *storage*, and *retrieval*.

encoding
The entering of information into memory.

sensory memory
The earliest part of the memory process, in which the senses take in and very briefly hold information.

echoic memory
The auditory sensory memory, or all the information the ears took in during the previous few seconds.

that she made barking her ringtone.) During those few seconds, she was still telling her story, but I was certainly not paying attention. Somehow, within an instant, the last few seconds of her story echoed in my mind. Without missing a beat, I said, "So you decided to march right over there and throw water in his face. How did he react?" Thank you, echoic memory.

Iconic Memory. Your eyes' version of this very temporary holding area for incoming information is **iconic memory**: visual sensory memory, or all the information your eyes took in during the last fraction of a second (Coltheart, 1980; Hollingworth, 2009; Jiang et al., 2009; Long, 1980).

In a classic study, George Sperling (1960; see also Irwin & Thomas, 2008) demonstrated that the amount of information we hold in iconic memory is much greater than researchers had previously believed (**Figure 5.2**). He flashed a 3-by-4 matrix (a tic-tac-toe board with an extra column, basically) with a different letter in each of the 12 boxes in front of participants for a very brief period – just one-twentieth of a second. He then asked them to list all the letters they remembered. In this free-recall situation, participants typically remembered only about half of the letters. However, Sperling had a hunch that many more than half of the letters were present in iconic memory. He guessed that the memory of certain letters faded away during those seconds in which participants were listing the ones that they first recalled. Sperling tested this hunch by sounding a tone immediately after the flash, which indicated a specific row that participants should recall (different tones for top, middle, and bottom). Their recall went up to 76% of the target row, supporting Sperling's hypothesis. A follow-up study (Averbach & Sperling, 1961) with larger grids found similar results with the use of a visual cue (a bar next to a particular row) rather than a tone.

Level of Processing. The likelihood that information progresses past sensory memory and becomes encoded, stored long-term, and retrieved depends upon its **level of processing**: how deeply information is processed. Also known as *depth of processing*, the idea here is that we tend to forget information quickly when we think about it in shallow ways, but we tend to remember information well when we think about it in deep ways (Baddeley & Hitch, 2017; Craik, 2002, 2007; Craik & Lockhart, 1972; Craik & Tulving, 1975). In this context, *shallow* means superficial, and *deep* means meaningful. So the more meaning we attach to information – the more we relate it to other information or connect it to emotion, for example – the more it becomes embedded in our memory.

For example, imagine shopping for wedding invitations. As you look through the dozens of samples, you pay attention to many features of the words – the font, the size, the color of the ink – but you don't pay attention to their meaning. In other words, even if every one of these invitation samples contains the same information – the same names, the same wedding date, the same wedding location – odds are you'll

L	G	Q	W
D	T	N	R
P	M	Z	K

FIGURE 5.2 Sperling's Iconic Memory Task. When asked to recall all of these letters after seeing them for a fraction of a second, most participants could recall no more than half. But when participants were asked to remember a particular row, their recall rates improved significantly, illustrating the capacity of iconic memory. Research from Sperling (1960).

iconic memory
The visual sensory memory, or all the information the eyes took in during the previous fraction of a second.

level of processing
How deeply information is processed.

quickly forget it because you were focusing on shallow characteristics of the words rather than deep ones.

By contrast, imagine your memory for an actual wedding invitation you receive from a friend, which causes you to think about what that wedding means to you. It may mean that you will travel a long distance, buy a wedding gift, or see old friends at the wedding. All of these meaningful thoughts enhance your memory for the information on the invitation. **Table 5.1** further explains the differences between shallow and deep processing.

Research using brain scanning technology has found that different levels of processing take place in different areas of the brain (Rose et al., 2015). Researchers presented words to participants, half of whom were asked whether the word contained the letter *A* (shallow processing), and half of whom were asked whether the word was a living or nonliving thing (deep processing). As expected, the deep processors remembered more of the words, but this study also discovered something new: the deep processors utilized their left prefrontal cortex much more extensively than the shallow processors (Kapur et al., 1994). The finding that shallow processing and deep processing rely on different parts of the brain suggests that they are distinct functions.

chunking
Grouping pieces of information together in a meaningful way to enhance memory.

rehearsal
Deliberately repeating information to enhance memory.

Effortful Processing. To some extent, we can deliberately control the level of processing that we apply to incoming information, which is known as *effortful processing* (Hasher & Zacks, 1979, 1984). One effective type of effortful processing is **chunking**: grouping pieces of information together in a meaningful way to enhance memory (Thalmann et al., 2018). For example, you might find it impossible to remember a string of letters this long: NBCHBOTBSBETTNTCBS. However, if you chunk it into three-letter codes — which are meaningful because they are TV networks — the task becomes much easier: NBC, HBO, TBS, BET, TNT, CBS. See **Table 5.2** for an example about chunking and grocery shopping.

We often chunk deliberately to boost our memories, but chunking happens automatically and outside of our awareness too (Gobet et al., 2001). This happens often in our memory for faces, in which we chunk numerous facial features into a package rather than viewing eyes, nose, mouth, hair, skin color, and so on as isolated features to be remembered separately (Thornton & Conway, 2013). Chunking may also happen automatically when experts in particular activities view and remember complex patterns. For example, chess champions chunk. They see the board not as a collection of isolated pieces (the way an inexperienced player might), but as a meaningful pattern — a whole rather than a collection of parts (Chase & Simon, 1973; Gobet & Simon, 1998; Sala & Gobet, 2017). Chunking also happens when experienced football, basketball, soccer, and field hockey players perceive and remember plays in their respective sports (Allard & Burnett, 1985; Garland & Barry, 1990, 1991; Weber & Brewer, 2003; Williams et al., 1993).

Another type of effortful processing is **rehearsal**: deliberately repeating information to enhance memory. Rehearsal commonly takes the form of saying verbal material over and over, either aloud or silently, to yourself. For example, imagine that while you are grocery shopping you are talking on the phone with your roommate and they ask you to pick up peanut butter, bananas, and bread. After you hang up, you might recite that short list to yourself again and again — "Peanut butter, bananas, and bread. Peanut butter, bananas, and bread. Peanut butter, bananas, and bread" — until you have those items in your cart. But rehearsal can involve nonverbal sounds as well as words, as when a guitarist mentally replays a riff again and again. Rehearsal can be

Belinda Pretorius/Shutterstock.com

Chunking involves grouping pieces of information together in a meaningful way. Chunking strengthens memory, and it also enables experts in chess (and other fields) to grasp complex patterns among a variety of parts.

TABLE 5.1: Shallow Processing Versus Deep Processing of Written Text

Shallow processing happens when you consider questions about superficial characteristics of the material, like these:	*Deep processing* happens when you consider questions about the significance of the material, like these:
• What type and size is the font?	• What does it mean?
• What color are the letters?	• What are its most important points?
• Are the letters in upper case or lower case?	• How does it relate to information I already know?
• How many words does it contain?	• How does it affect my life?

TABLE 5.2: Chunking at the Supermarket

WHAT YOU NEED TO REMEMBER IF YOU DON'T CHUNK	WHAT YOU NEED TO REMEMBER IF YOU CHUNK
Lettuce	Salad ingredients
Dressing	
Croutons	
Carrots	
Tomatoes	
Pizza crust	Pizza ingredients
Tomato sauce	
Shredded cheese	
Oregano	
Pepperoni	
Mushrooms	
Detergent	Laundry items
Fabric softener	
Dryer sheets	
Bleach	

visual too, such as when a wide receiver repeatedly envisions a pass route or a cheerleader repeatedly envisions a routine in an attempt to memorize it (Awh et al., 1998, 1999; Godijn & Theeuwes, 2012).

Psychologists who study memory make a distinction between two kinds of rehearsal, *maintenance rehearsal* and *elaborative rehearsal* (Craik & Watkins 1973). In **maintenance rehearsal**, information is repeated in exactly the same form it was originally encoded. By contrast, **elaborative rehearsal** involves adding meaning or associations to information, which enhances memory. Maintenance rehearsal (as exemplified by the grocery store example) can help a little, but elaborative rehearsal can help a lot more (Gardiner et al., 1994; Greene, 1987; Naveh-Benjamin & Jonides, 1984). The reason centers on *level of processing*: maintenance rehearsal is shallow, but elaborative rehearsal is deep (Craik & Tulving, 1975).

As an example of elaborative rehearsal, consider two high school students, Molly and Ellie, learning about the 2008 presidential election in their history class. Molly approaches it as nothing more than a list of unrelated bits of information to be committed to memory: Barack Obama was the Democratic nominee and John McCain was the Republican nominee. Obama's running mate was Joe Biden. McCain's running mate was Sarah Palin. The election took place on November 4. And so on. Ellie, on the other hand, uses a different strategy. She seeks out the context for these facts and the meaning they held for voters at the time: attitudes toward the outgoing president, George W. Bush; controversies over health care, the Iraq war, and the economic recession; the historical significance of a Black candidate; and so on. Even if Molly spends an equivalent amount of time doing rote memorization, her maintenance rehearsal will never be as deep or as effective as Ellie's elaborative rehearsal.

Long-Term Potentiation. When encoding takes place, the memory-based physiological changes of the brain have begun. One physiological change is **long-term potentiation**: the increased connectivity between simultaneously stimulated neurons that forms the biological basis of memory. Long-term potentiation is what memory looks like up close, at the neuron level, in the brain (Bliss & Collingridge, 1993; Malenka & Nicoll, 1999; Nicoll, 2017). Think of long-term potentiation like a path through the woods becoming more well-worn because of repeated use, making it easier and quicker to travel. That's similar to what long-term potentiation does to the axons that connect neurons to each other.

maintenance rehearsal
Information repeated in exactly the same form as it was originally encoded.

elaborative rehearsal
Adding meaning or associations to information to enhance memory.

long-term potentiation
The increased connectivity between simultaneously stimulated neurons that forms the biological basis of memory.

Interestingly, physical exercise helps long-term potentiation (Miller et al., 2018; Tsai et al., 2018). In one study, some rats were given the chance to run on exercise wheels, while others were not. Not only did the running rats memorize a maze more quickly than the others, but their brains also showed much more evidence of long-term potentiation — in particular the hippocampus, where much of memory is centered (van Praag et al., 1999). A later study found the same effect to be especially strong for rats whose mothers were given alcohol during pregnancy, a finding with hopeful implications for children whose mothers drank during their pregnancies and who now suffer with fetal alcohol syndrome (covered in Chapter 9). These children often struggle with cognitive impairments such as limited memory capacity (Christie et al., 2005).

More recently, researchers have discovered the process of *long-term depression*. (Although the word *depression* suggests a sadness that may last many months, that's not what it means in this discussion of the biological basis of memory.) Long-term depression is the opposite of long-term potentiation, which means it is a *decrease* in the connectivity between neurons in the brain that correlates with memory fading (Bear & Abraham, 1996; Linden, 1994; Linden & Connor, 1995; Malenka & Bear, 2004; Pinar et al., 2017). Long-term depression may be an important part of the process of forgetting (see the From Research to Real Life box), which is actually quite functional when applied to unimportant information (Malleret et al., 2010; Nicholls et al., 2008).

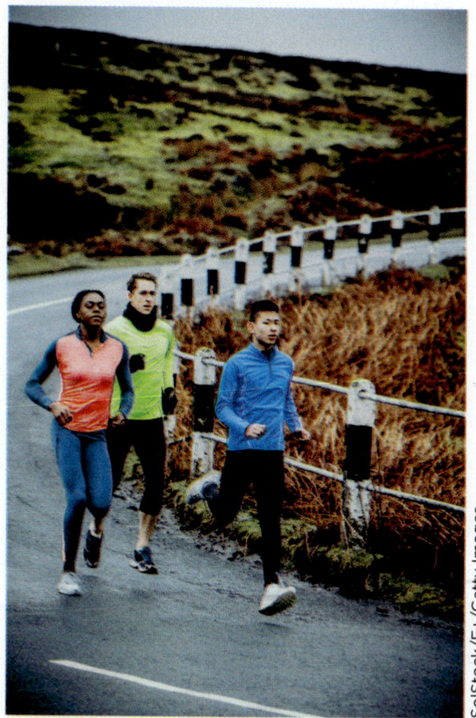
SolStock/E+/Getty Images

Exercise enhances long-term potentiation, the improvement in the connectivity of neurons in the brain that forms the biological basis of memory.

Wait — forgetting is functional? Isn't it bad to forget stuff?

Actually, forgetting stuff that is no longer important is beneficial. It makes more room for the important stuff, which enhances memory overall (Bjork, 2011, 2014; Bluck et al., 2010; Hupbach et al., 2018; Smith, 2011).

FROM RESEARCH TO REAL LIFE

Is Forgetting Good?

We hate to forget. As one author describes it, "To most people, forgetting is a terrible thing. To students taking exams, forgetting can mean poor grades. . . . To the elderly, forgetting can mean imminent cognitive decline. The downside of forgetting is quite clear to everyone" (Smith, 2011, p. 153).

But if forgetting has a downside, does that mean it has an upside too? One memory scholar, Bjork, strongly argues that it does (Bjork, 1972, 1978, 1989, 2014; Bjork et al., 1998). His argument is supported by this fact about human memory: our storage capacity (especially in long-term memory) is essentially limitless, but our retrieval capacity is severely limited. Our ability to retain information outpaces our ability to recall it. This may be a good thing, though: "We do not *want* everything in our memories to be accessible. . . . We need to remember our current phone number, not our prior phone number; we need to remember where we parked the car today, not yesterday or a week ago" (Bjork, 2011, p. 2).

He goes on to argue that forgetting actually helps remembering. Specifically, when you forget old stuff that is no longer important in your day-to-day life, it lets you remember new stuff that is important (Bjork, 2011). He emphasizes that with the help of retrieval cues, what is forgotten one day can be remembered the next. For example, if you forget how to shift gears on your old bike because you haven't ridden it in years, you will probably remember when you find yourself sitting on the bike with your hands on the handlebars. Bjork is certainly not the only memory expert to make the case that forgetting can be beneficial (Small, 2021). Other memory researchers go so far as to use the term *active forgetting* (as opposed to the more passive way many people may assume forgetting happens). They explain that what's "active" about active forgetting is the role played by the prefrontal cortex, which seemingly decides to strategically override and inhibit the hippocampus at times. In other words, the part of the brain that is most directly involved in planning and purposeful actions (the prefrontal cortex) sometimes takes over the part of the brain most directly involved in memory (the hippocampus). The prefrontal cortex can even cast little "amnesic shadows" to help us forget certain memories in ways that help us quickly access the most essential memories (Anderson & Hulbert, 2021).

It's certainly helpful that when I enter the first letter of a search term into Google, the autofill function on my computer "remembers" a few of my most recent search terms and fills them in. But it would be distinctly *un*helpful if autofill remembered *all* of the search terms I'd *ever* used. They would instantly fill the screen with so many options that I'd be overwhelmed. In other words, I'm glad autofill "forgets" some of the search terms that I used infrequently and long ago. This keeps things simple and keeps the focus on the most likely terms. When our brain forgets, it serves the same function. Suppressing information we don't need makes room to take in or highlight new information we do need. •

storage
Retaining information in memory.

short-term memory
A limited amount of new information being held briefly until it is either discarded or encoded into long-term memory.

long-term memory
A seemingly limitless amount of information being held for extensive periods of time.

Storage

Storage is retaining information in memory. It's the second of the three fundamental memory steps, or what happens to information between its intake (*encoding*) and its output (*retrieval*). It's a lot like saving files on a hard drive, a flash drive, or a cloud storage service like Google Drive, iCloud, or Dropbox – a process by which you hold onto information you've taken in until you need to open it later.

Traditionally, psychologists have divided the storage of memory into two basic types based on how long it lasts. The first type of storage is **short-term memory**: a limited amount of new information being held briefly until it is either discarded or kept long-term. The second type of storage is **long-term memory**: a seemingly limitless amount of information being held for extensive periods of time.

Short-Term Memory. Information in short-term memory is like a customer who has just entered a crowded restaurant. Imagine that customer is you. You've entered the restaurant, but you're not necessarily staying. What happens next could go either of two ways. After a short wait, you might sit, eat, and stay for a long time. Or after that short wait, you might turn around and leave. Either way, your "short-term" wait won't last long.

Information in short-term memory doesn't last long either (Baddeley, 2000). In a matter of seconds, short-term memory goes one of two ways (much like that customer in the crowded restaurant): it either fades or, if it is processed sufficiently, it enters long-term memory (Atkinson & Shiffrin, 1968; Baddeley et al., 2009; Brown, 1958; Peterson, 1966). A classic study established this finding by giving participants a random three-letter code to remember (for example, PQC) and then immediately requiring them to perform an unrelated distracter task. In this case, the distracter task was counting backward by either threes or fours from a three-digit number (e.g., 309) spoken by the experimenter, until the participants were told to recall the three-letter code. If the experimenters kept the participants counting for 15 seconds, almost none of them remembered the code (**Figure 5.3**). Even if the delay was only 3 seconds, recall was only about 50% (Peterson & Peterson, 1959).

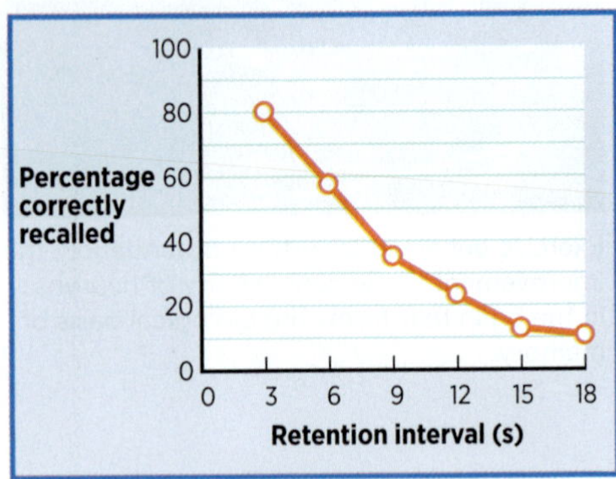

FIGURE 5.3 The Short Life of Short-Term Memory. This graph shows how quickly short-term memory fades. Participants trying to remember a three-letter code while counting backward from a random number started to falter significantly after just 3 seconds and had almost no success after just 15 seconds (Peterson & Peterson, 1959).

Even without a distracter task, information fades from memory quickly. A classic study by Ebbinghaus (1885) found that people who learned three-letter codes forgot over half of the items within an hour and about three-quarters of the items within a day. For the next month, the rate of recall continued to drop. See **Figure 5.4** for more on this "forgetting curve."

In addition to this limited duration, short-term memory features a limited capacity. In a review of some early memory studies, Miller (1956) consistently found that the maximum for short-term memory is seven items, plus or minus two. In other words, Miller concluded that most of us can hold about seven items at a time in short-term memory, with a range of five to nine. Miller referred to this finding of seven plus or minus two as the "magic number" of memory capacity. Some more recent researchers question just how magical this number is, however. Specifically, many more recent studies have found that our limit is actually lower than Miller estimated (Adam et al., 2017; Baddeley, 1994, 2000; Gobet & Clarkson, 2004; Green, 2017; Schweickert & Boruff, 1986; Shiffrin & Nosofsky, 1994). So, if there's a magic number of short-term memory capacity, research evidence now points to three or four much more strongly than seven (Cowan, 2001, 2005, 2010; see also Adams et al., 2018).

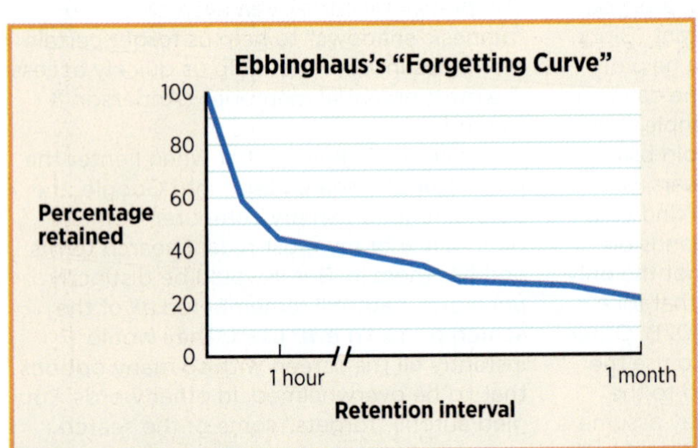

FIGURE 5.4 How Quickly We Forget. A classic memory study found that people who memorized a set of three-letter codes forgot half within an hour, three-quarters within a day, and more over the next month (Ebbinghaus, 1885).

An important determination in this debate over the magic number of items in memory capacity is how we define *item* – and relatedly, how the information to be remembered is *chunked* (Mathy & Feldman, 2012). As we discussed earlier, chunking allows us to take multiple bits of information and group them into a single item. By chunking, you can multiply the amount of information you remember. Phone numbers are a great example – if you consider each digit to be an item, as in 3-1-4-5-5-5-9-7-4-2, that's 10 items to remember. If you chunk them together as 314-555-9742, that's only three items. And if you can consider the whole series of digits to be a single meaningful

TABLE 5.3: Why Companies Chunk Phone Numbers

What's easier for you to remember?		
1-800 FLOWERS	or	1-800-356-9377
1-800 CONTACTS	or	1-800-266-8228
1-800 WALGREENS	or	1-800-925-4733
1-800 RITE AID	or	1-800-748-3243
1-800 GO UHAUL	or	1-800-468-4285
1-800 GOTJUNK	or	1-800-468-5865
1-800 PETMEDS	or	1-800-738-6337

piece of information, then that's just one item. That's why companies who want you to remember their phone number get a phone number that translates nicely to words (ideally, to a single word). Consider 1-800-FLOWERS. It's a lot easier to remember than 1-800-356-9377, because the word *flowers* is a single meaningful chunk, while that random series of seven numbers is, well, a random series of seven numbers (**Table 5.3**).

But I don't have to memorize phone numbers. My phone does that for me.

Yes, it does, and that's a big change in the way many of us use our memories. We have phones – not to mention computers, tablets, external drives, and other ways to store information digitally – doing memory tasks that the human brain used to do. This experience may have become totally familiar, but it's unprecedented in the larger time frame of human history. Check the It's Like . . . box for a discussion of the impact of this change.

IT'S LIKE...

Your Smartphone Is Like a Flash Drive for Your Brain

Years ago, if you had asked me for my best friend's phone number, I'd point to my head and say "I've got it up here."

Now, I point to my phone and say, "I've got it in here."

That's true for lots of people who grew up without smartphones, and for lots of information besides phone numbers too. Our smartphones (not to mention our computers, tablets, and other devices) are like flash drives for our brains – external storage devices that now hold information that we once carried within ourselves.

Numerous authors have debated the pros and cons of this "outsourcing" of human memory (e.g., Carr, 2008). One author laments the fact that "a third of people under 30 can't remember their own phone number. Their smartphones are smart, so they don't need to be. Today's young people are forgoing memory before they even have a chance to lose it" (Brooks, 2007).

Another writer admits the shortcomings of his own memory for big events in the lives of his close friends. Here he explains why he never deletes the text messages he receives from friends announcing the birth of their children:

> I know why I've kept them [on my phone]: *without referring to them, I have no idea of the names or the birthdays of most of my close friends' firstborn children.* I've replied to these texts, sometimes sent a card or gift as well, and then put the entire event out of mind. (Chatfield, 2012; italics added)

Flash drives and other external memory devices, including cloud-based storage, can improve the memory capacity of our computers tremendously. They allow us to store more information than our computers' built-in hard drives ever could. But when we use those devices, we run the risk of them malfunctioning or information getting lost. And they can actually become inconvenient if we rely on them for frequently needed information. Perhaps the same can be said for our smartphones: they greatly increase our brains' memory capacity, but overreliance on them can be an inconvenience if it becomes necessary too often. It also puts us in jeopardy of major problems if they get lost or damaged (or the battery dies).

Prostock-studio/Shutterstock

Increasingly, our smartphones hold information that we once carried within our brains.

working memory
A type of memory in which processing, or work, is done on briefly held information.

Working Memory. More recent research into short-term memory has offered a different way of understanding it. Specifically, new research suggests that in many cases short-term memory is not merely a holding cell where information passively waits to be either processed or forgotten. Instead, short-term memory often bustles with activity. That is, the information short-term memory contains is often manipulated, operated upon, and otherwise used during its short stay (Alloway & Alloway, 2013; Baddeley, 2000, 2003, 2007; Baddeley & Hitch, 1974; Christophel et al., 2017; Cowan, 2008; Gathercole, 2007; Oberauer et al., 2018). This now widely accepted idea is known as **working memory**: a type of memory in which processing, or work, is done on briefly held information.

Your working memory is operating almost all of your waking hours. For example, consider watching a TV show. As you take in all the images and words, they don't just sit there — you *do* something with them. You figure out what they mean; connect that meaning to other events that have already happened in the show; speculate about upcoming plot twists they might predict; evaluate the quality of the acting and writing; and much more. In other words, even if the words of a particular scene will occupy your memory for only a very short time, you work on them while they're there.

Working memory is crucial to learning and academic performance (Alloway & Gathercole, 2005; Alloway et al., 2005; Dehn, 2008; Gathercole et al., 2004; Morgan et al., 2018; Peng et al., 2018; Simone et al., 2018; Swanson & Berninger, 1996). First, consider the ability to follow a teacher's directions. One researcher found that most kids' working memories enable them to follow verbal instructions with about five specific pieces of information, but some kids with learning differences can only handle three pieces of information (Henry, 2001). Next, consider some of the many activities that those instructions might contain: hearing a spelling word aloud, thinking about its correct spelling, and writing those letters in order; or, hearing a phrase in one language, thinking about its proper translation, and saying it in another language; or, reading a long paragraph, comprehending it, and answering a question about it. All of these tasks and many more during a school day require the student not just to take new information into short-term memory but to do something with it while it is there (Gathercole & Alloway, 2008; Levin et al., 2010).

Researchers have linked working memory to a variety of complex tasks, including verbal comprehension, reasoning, decision making, and problem solving (Engle, 2002; Hambrick et al., 2005). As a specific example, researchers have found that working memory capacity predicts sight-reading ability among both novice and expert pianists (Hambrick & Meinz, 2011; Meinz & Hambrick, 2010). The task of playing written music is complex. The pianist must read the notes on the page; translate them into specific movements of fingers, hands, arms, and feet; and then execute those movements in the right order, time, and volume. So it makes sense that people who have greater ability to cognitively work on the musical notes they read would sight-read more successfully.

As the research on piano playing suggests, working memory is also closely related to multitasking. Consider watching that TV show again: Could you follow it while also texting? Or while talking on the phone? Or while studying? Researchers have found that multitasking ability, as measured by speed and accuracy of responses, depends heavily on working memory capacity (Bühner et al., 2006; Covre et al., 2018; Hambrick et al., 2010; Pollard & Courage, 2017; Redick et al., 2016). One study focused on multitasking among applicants for air traffic controller training courses and found that working memory, even more than overall intelligence, predicts how successfully they could multitask (Colom et al., 2010). Another study of emergency room doctors found that multitasking generally increased prescribing errors, but the extent of the errors depended on the working memory capacity of the doctor (Westbrook et al., 2018).

Skynesher/E+/Getty Images

The ability to read music and play it on the piano depends on working memory, which is the processing, or work, done on information you take in.

Long-Term Memory. Beyond short-term memory and working memory lies *long-term memory* (Bahrick, 2000). There isn't much research on the capacity of long-term memory, largely because most experts assume that it is limitless.

It may well be. This is one aspect of the memory-as-computer metaphor that does not fit. Every type of computer memory storage device, from old floppy disks to new high-capacity external hard drives or cloud storage services, has a finite limit that cannot be exceeded. Human long-term memory simply does not appear to have such a limit (Dudai, 1997; Voss, 2009).

The typical path to long-term memory involves a passage through short-term memory assisted by processing of some kind. If information doesn't get focused on, thought about, or used in some way, then it usually fails to enter long-term memory. But sometimes information takes a shortcut to long-term memory (Delorme et al., 2018; Hasher & Zacks, 1979, 1984). Psychologists call this shortcut **automatic processing** (or **automatic encoding):** the entrance of some information into long-term memory without any conscious processing. Comparing automatic processing to the effortful processing that we discussed earlier is like comparing a feeding tube to eating. The contents of a feeding tube bypass the processing that typically takes place in the mouth (chewing and swallowing). Likewise, automatically processed information bypasses the processing that typically takes place in short-term memory. For example, researchers have found that we automatically process the frequency with which events occur (Zacks et al., 1982; Zacks & Hasher, 2002). In other words, you don't deliberately count how often you do particular things — eat pumpkin pie, ride a roller coaster, hold a newborn baby, replace your phone, or any other activity — but unconsciously, you're keeping track, at least well enough to provide an approximation.

automatic processing (automatic encoding)
The entrance of some information into long-term memory without any conscious processing.

retrieval
Pulling information out of memory.

recall
A type of retrieval in which stored information is accessed without any comparison to external information.

recognition
A type of retrieval in which stored information is compared to external information to determine if it matches.

Retrieval

Retrieval is pulling information out of memory. It is the third and final step among the three basic steps of memory (Brown & Craik, 2000; Gardiner, 2007; Spear, 2007). When you consider the vastness of your long-term memory, your ability to retrieve memories quickly and accurately is truly astonishing. Imagine you come across an old photo of yourself from your 6th birthday party. So much related information, tucked away for so many years, suddenly comes back: the excitement you felt as the first friends and family arrived, the joy you felt as you ripped wrapping paper off your presents, the taste of the chocolate-with-chocolate-icing birthday cake, the bright balloons that covered the ceiling, and so much more. These details pour forth in a split second, and without much effort.

Psychologists make an important distinction between two kinds of retrieval, *recall* and *recognition* (Foster, 2009; Lockhart, 2000; Mandler, 1980; Tulving, 1976). **Recall** is a type of retrieval in which you access stored information without any comparison to external information. **Recognition** is a type of retrieval in which you determine whether stored information matches external information.

When I answer different kinds of exam questions, do I use those different kinds of retrieval?

Yes! In fact, the best way to understand the difference between recall and recognition is to think about your experiences with short-answer essay exams versus multiple-choice exams. Let's consider a specific exam question from a U.S. history test: who was president during the Civil War? If this was a short-answer question — if it was followed by just a blank, with no options to choose from — you would have to rely on recall. You'd be entirely on your own, scanning your memory for the answer, without the luxury of a list of possibilities to remind you of the right answer. That list of possibilities is exactly what a multiple-choice version of that question would provide. So with a multiple-choice question, you could rely on recognition rather than recall. In other words, if the same question was followed by choices — (a) George Washington, (b) Thomas Jefferson, (c) Abraham Lincoln, and (d) Theodore Roosevelt — you wouldn't have to generate the right answer entirely on your own but could merely spot the choice that matches what's stored in your memory (which, of course, is Lincoln).

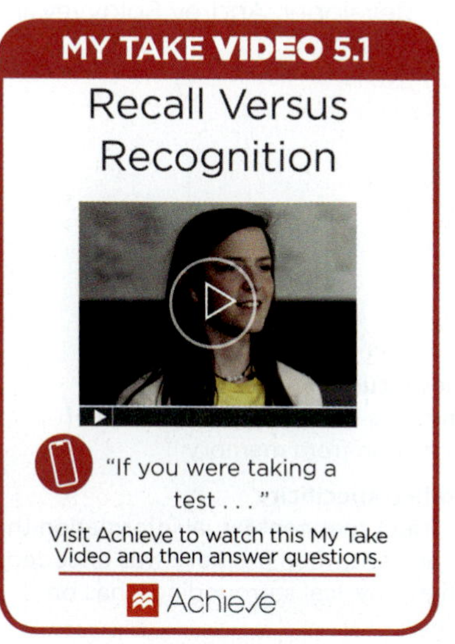
MY TAKE VIDEO 5.1
Recall Versus Recognition
"If you were taking a test . . ."
Visit Achieve to watch this My Take Video and then answer questions.
Achieve

CHAPTER APP 5.1

 50 US States

50 US States is a simple app in which users name an American state after seeing it highlighted on an unlabeled map. What makes it interesting in terms of memory is that it has two modes of game play. In "Quiz" mode, the user has to come up with the name of the state, so it depends on recall. In "4 States" mode, the user has to choose the correct state from four options, so it depends on recognition.

How does it APPly to your daily life? Which mode of game play—the one based on recall or the one based on recognition—would you find more difficult? Are there other examples in your life when the type of retrieval (recall versus recognition) influences how difficult a task is?

How does it APPly to your understanding of psychology? How could this app help you appreciate the difference between the two types of retrieval: recall and recognition? How might that appreciation influence the way you study or otherwise learn new material?

To learn more about this app or to download it to your phone, you can search for "50 US States" on Google, in the iPhone App store, or in the Google Play store; there are several apps with similar names, so it might be helpful to include the name of the app developer, Andrey Solovyev, in your search.

Exam questions are certainly not the only real-life situations that illustrate the difference between recall and recognition. Once I attended a wedding and saw a familiar face among the wedding party standing alongside the couple. "I know that guy," I said to myself, but I just could not come up with his name. Then it occurred to me that the entire wedding party was listed in the program I was handed when I walked in. I scanned the list, and there were the names of all six people in the wedding party: no, no, no, no, no, yes! Tommy Green! Even though I couldn't recall it, when his name was right there in front of my eyes, I recognized Tommy's name instantly.

Another time, a friend of mine called with this question: "You know that restaurant you found when you stopped in Effingham, Illinois, on your way to Chicago? The one that you said was so fantastic? We're on the road right now, and we're just a few minutes away from Effingham – what's the name of that place?" To my surprise, I drew a blank. "Um, uh, let me call you right back," I said. I immediately Yelped "Effingham restaurants" and scrolled through the links that popped up: not Ruby Tuesday, not El Rancherito, not TGI Fridays – yes, Firefly Grill! My recall may have failed me, but my recognition came through just in time to call my friend back before he passed the exit.

Retrieval Cues. Whether it takes the form of recall or recognition, retrieval depends upon a number of factors. One such factor is **retrieval cues**: reminders that facilitate retrieval of information from memory. Retrieval cues are things – often sights, sounds, or smells – that prompt you to remember. They make stored information pop into your mind when it otherwise might not (Bower, 2000; Thomson & Tulving, 1970; Tulving & Osler, 1968; Wiemers et al., 2014).

Let's consider that example about Firefly Grill, my favorite restaurant in Effingham, Illinois. Many months passed before I had another chance to drive through Effingham and stop there again. By that time, I remembered liking the restaurant a lot, but I couldn't remember exactly what I had ordered there. As I entered the parking lot, things started looking familiar. Retrieval cues were all over, and they were jogging my memory: the restaurant's logo on the front door, the big open kitchen, the high ceiling, the distinctive tables and chairs, the oversized photos on the walls, the unique uniforms of the servers. Suddenly, effortlessly, my first meal appeared in my mind with as much detail as if I had pulled up a digital photo: a grilled chicken sandwich on a pretzel bun, and thin-cut French fries with homemade ketchup. When the restaurant was many miles away, I couldn't retrieve what I had ordered the first time I went there – out of sight, out of mind. However, when I saw all the sights I had associated with it, they served as powerful retrieval cues.

Sometimes, as I did in Firefly Grill, you encounter retrieval cues by chance. But you can bring up retrieval cues on purpose as well. For example, picture yourself at a party where you see a woman across the room. You know you've met her before, but you can't remember her name or how you crossed paths with her. Asking yourself general questions like "Who is she?" or "Where do I know her from?" may not be enough to spark your memory. But more specific questions might. In other words, thinking of specific places or situations may provide the retrieval cues you need. "Was she in my chemistry class? Does she live near me? Did I meet her at that concert in the park? Did I play sports with her? Yes, that's it – she was on the team that beat us in softball last week. She made that great catch when I smashed a long fly ball into left-center field, and then I caught her line drive when I was playing third base the next inning. After the game, we briefly joked about how we robbed each other. Her name is Tamisha." If you hadn't brought softball to mind as a retrieval cue, Tamisha and everything you know about her might have remained buried in the storage of your mind.

retrieval cues
Reminders that facilitate retrieval of information from memory.

encoding specificity
The effect that contextual information that was present when memory was encoded, such as physical surroundings, has on retrieval.

Encoding Specificity. Related to retrieval cues is the idea of **encoding specificity**: the effect of contextual information present when memory was encoded, such as physical surroundings, on retrieval. Encoding specificity (also known as *context-dependent memory*) means that where you are when you are trying to remember something can make a difference. Specifically, if you're in the same location or situation where you learned the information, you have a better chance of recalling it (Brown & Craik, 2000; Fisher & Craik, 1977; Koriat, 2000; Smith et al., 2018; Tulving & Thomson, 1973). For example, picture a new employee, Kirsten, who shows up for her first day at work and meets her coworker, Drew, at the elevator to their office. Kirsten is more likely to remember Drew's name the next day if she bumps into him at the elevator again rather than in the conference room, in the parking lot, or in a grocery store.

Studies have found that encoding specificity works in all kinds of situations. In one early study, half of the participants memorized a list of words underwater, while the other half learned the same list on dry land. When they were quizzed, each group remembered more when they were in the same place where they learned it (Godden & Baddeley, 1975). Other studies have found similar results based on the odor in the room (flowers, peppermint, or fresh pine), the type of music being played (jazz or classical), whether the participant was riding an exercise bike, whether the participant was smoking, and even whether the participant was chewing a particular kind of gum (Baker et al., 2004; Balch & Lewis, 1996; Balch et al., 1992; Herz, 1997; Larsson et al., 2017; Mead & Ball, 2007; Miles & Hardman, 1998; Peters & McGee, 1982). For your own benefit as a college student who will take many tests, the take-home message is clear: study in an environment as similar as possible to the environment where you will take the test (Smith & Vela, 2001).

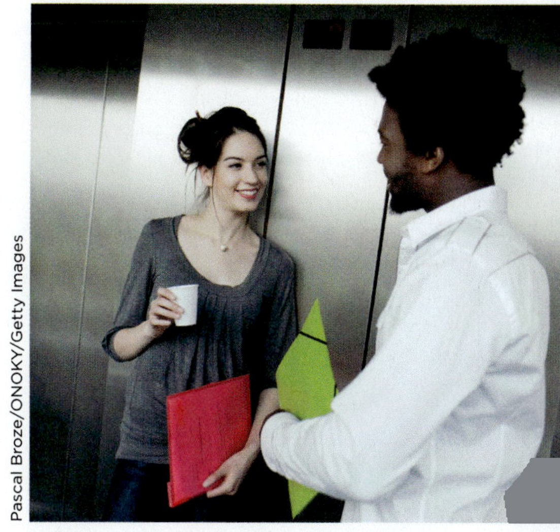
Pascal Broze/ONOKY/Getty Images

Encoding specificity (or context-dependent memory) means that you are more likely to remember something if you're in the same context as when you learned it. For example, if you meet someone at the elevator, you're more likely to remember that person's name at the same elevator than in a different location.

Just as being in the same location can help retrieval, so can being in the same state of mind, which psychologists call *state-dependent learning*. Studies have found that when you put yourself in the same mood or psychological state you were in when you learned new information, you are more likely to remember it (Bower, 1981; Eich, 1995a, b, 2007; Ucros, 1989). For example, one study put participants in either a good mood or bad mood by having them make statements about themselves that were either flattering or insulting. While in those moods, they memorized lists of words. Two days later, they were asked to recall their lists. Their recall performance depended on their mood when they were tested. Those in the same mood at both points in time, regardless of whether that mood was good or bad, remembered significantly more than those in one mood when they learned and in a different mood when they recalled (Beck & McBee, 1995).

Priming. A final type of influence on retrieval is **priming**: when recent experiences cause an increased likelihood of recalling certain memories. For example, spending time on any beach is likely to increase your recollection of all of your memories related to beaches. Priming can even influence the way that individual words enter our mind (Lukatela & Turvey, 1994a, b). For example, if you ask people to spell the word *flour/flower*, you're more likely to get the first spelling from a baker, and you're more likely to get the second spelling from a florist. Their different day-to-day experiences — most important, the words and concepts that occupy their minds on a regular basis — predispose them toward different recollections of the spelling of that homonym.

LIFE HACK 5.1

Take advantage of context-dependent memory and state-dependent learning. If you're struggling to remember something, try to put yourself back in the same situation or the same mood you were in when you first learned it.

(Eich, 2007; Fisher & Craik, 1977; Koriat, 2000; Tulving & Thomson, 1973)

When researchers study priming, they often show participants a list of words and then distract them for a few minutes. After the distraction, the researchers provide word stems — that is, the first few letters of a word — and then ask the participants to complete the word. So if the word stem is *tel-*, participants might come up with the word *tell*, *television*, or *telephone*, among others. However, if the original list included the word *telescope*, participants are especially likely to choose that word. What is especially interesting about priming is that they would also be likely to come up with *telescope* if the original word list contained words semantically related to telescopes (but not the word *telescope* itself), like *star*, *moon*, *planet*, and *constellation* (Turkington & Harris, 2001).

In a twist on this methodology, one group of researchers showed participants photos of celebrities whose names happened to sound exactly like ordinary words. For example, they used a photo of Brad Pitt, whose last name is a homophone for *pit* (**Figure 5.5**). The likelihood that participants correctly identified the celebrity depended upon whether they had been primed with a fill-in-the-blank task in which

priming
When recent experiences cause an increased likelihood of recalling certain memories.

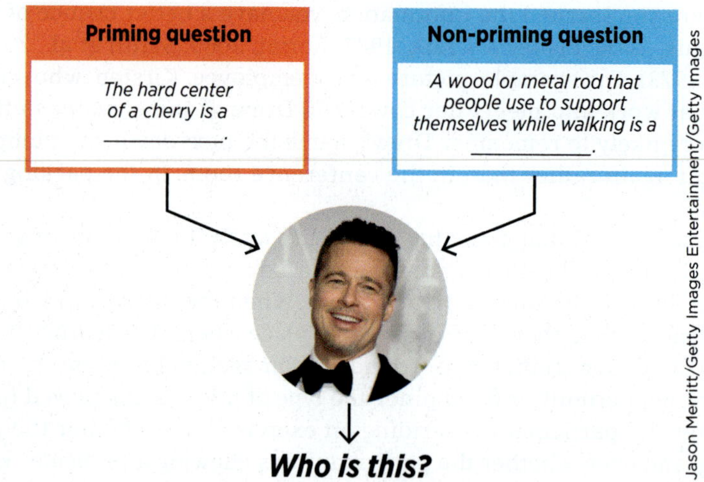
Priming question
The hard center of a cherry is a ________.
Non-priming question
A wood or metal rod that people use to support themselves while walking is a ________.
Who is this?
Jason Merritt/Getty Images Entertainment/Getty Images

FIGURE 5.5 **Brad Pitt and Cherry Pits.** Researchers found that the likelihood of correctly recognizing Brad Pitt increased if participants had been asked a question about pits (as in cherries) as opposed to a question about something unrelated to his name (like a cane). The sound of the word *pit* primed participants to remember similar-sounding words (Burke et al., 2004).

the homophone was the right answer. In other words, participants were more likely to correctly say "That's Brad Pitt" if they had previously been asked what the name of the hard inner part of a cherry or plum is rather than a different unrelated question (Burke et al., 2004).

Here's a personal example of priming. I once spent several hours shoveling foot-high snow from my driveway in single-digit temperatures. The whole time, all I could think about was how far below freezing it was and my increasing chances of frostbite. As I finally finished shoveling, I felt my phone vibrate. By the time I managed to pull off a snow-caked glove and reach my frozen fingers into my pocket, I had missed the call and had a very short new voicemail. It was from my next-door neighbor, and when I listened she said just one word: "Chilly?" Was she joking? Or mocking me from her toasty living room? She knew it was way past chilly – it was absolutely frigid. I disgustedly shoved the phone back in my pocket and trudged toward my door when I heard her knock on her kitchen window. I looked up and saw her holding a steaming bowl with a spoon in it, and she mouthed the word to me again: "Chili?" Oh, *chili*, not *chilly*. She wasn't mocking me – she was offering me lunch. I had been so focused on the cold that I was primed to bring to mind *chilly* when I heard that word. On any other day, without such priming, I would have been more likely to consider what she actually meant.

CHECK YOUR LEARNING:

5.4 What are the three steps of memory according to the information processing model?

5.5 What is encoding, and how does it involve sensory memory?

5.6 What is the difference between echoic memory and iconic memory?

5.7 How does encoding depend on the level of processing?

5.8 What is long-term potentiation, and how does it relate to encoding?

5.9 What is storage, and where in the brain does it occur?

5.10 What is retrieval, and what are the two ways it happens?

5.11 What are retrieval cues, and how do they affect retrieval?

5.12 What are encoding specificity and priming, and how does each enhance retrieval?

To check your understanding of these questions, click show the answers or refer to the answers in the Chapter Summary.

Types of Memory

Psychologists have identified many types of memory. One legendary memory researcher made a note of every type of memory he ever saw defined in any article or book. His final list included 256 types of memory, including such peculiar labels as particular *political memory*, *chemical memory*, and even the oxymoronic *forgotten memory* (Tulving, 2007). Since there's no way we can explore all of the types of memory, let's zoom in on the types that are most widely studied by memory experts.

One way of categorizing memory focuses on conscious awareness of memories. In other words, there are memories that we *know* we know (and can describe well), and there are other memories that we *don't know* we know (and can't describe well). In this section, we consider the two labels that capture these different kinds of memory — *explicit memory* and *implicit memory* — as well as some related concepts.

YOU WILL LEARN:

5.13 what explicit memory is.

5.14 about two types of explicit memory: semantic memory and episodic memory.

5.15 what implicit memory is.

5.16 about a type of implicit memory known as procedural memory.

Explicit Memory

Explicit memory is memory of which you are consciously aware. It is also called *declarative memory*, which refers to the fact that it is memory that you can declare (or, more simply, tell) to another person (Baddeley et al., 2009; Lockhart, 2000; Squire & Zola, 1996). (By the way, when you hear the word *explicit*, you may initially think that it means graphic in an adults-only way, as in some movies, music, and video games with "explicit content." That's not the meaning of the word here.) Explicit memory is memory that you *know* you know. It consists of all the factual knowledge you have accumulated, as well as all of the personal experiences you have tucked away.

Semantic Memory. There are two subtypes of explicit memory: *semantic memory* and *episodic memory* (Ryan et al., 2008; Tulving, 1983). **Semantic memory** is a type of explicit memory consisting of facts, figures, word meanings, and other general information. Semantic memory is what helps *Jeopardy!* contestants answer all those questions on all those subjects. It's the depository of available information and trivia that you have in mental storage: stuff you learned in school, like the seven continents; stuff you learned from friends and family, like what kind of car your cousin bought last year; stuff you learned through media, like who won the NBA or WNBA games last night; and much, much more.

Everett Collection

Semantic memory is a kind of explicit memory that consists of facts, figures, and other general information — the kind of knowledge that makes *Jeopardy!* contestants successful.

Episodic Memory. By contrast, **episodic memory** is a type of explicit memory consisting of personal firsthand experiences. Episodic memory is your internal autobiography, a record of the episodes of your life (Gershman & Daw, 2017; Mace, 2010; Neisser & Libby, 2000; Tulving, 1972, 1983, 1998; Wheeler, 2000). It's your recollection of what happened to you rather than what facts you happened to pick up along the way. Your episodic memory contains your replay of minor events in your life, like last night's dinner and last week's visit to the dentist. It also contains major events in your life, like your high school graduation and your last conversation with a dying relative. The small stuff often fades rather quickly from episodic memory, being replaced by more recent events, but the big stuff tends to endure (Conway, 2008).

Research suggests that different regions of the brain may be responsible for semantic memory and episodic memory (Brown et al., 2018; Moscovitch et al., 2016; Takashima et al., 2017). One study describes three children who experienced brain injuries with hippocampus damage. All three had severely limited episodic memory. They couldn't remember what took place in their own lives, but they still succeeded in mainstream schools and reached an average or slightly below-average level of achievement in areas like language competence, literacy, and factual knowledge. Their experiences indicate that the hippocampus is much more involved in episodic memory than semantic memory (Vargha-Khadem et al., 1997). Other studies have suggested that semantic memory relies more heavily on the prefrontal cortex, which makes

explicit memory
Memory of which one is consciously aware.

semantic memory
A type of explicit memory consisting of facts, figures, word meanings, and other general information.

episodic memory
A type of explicit memory consisting of personal firsthand experiences.

implicit memory
Memory of which one is not consciously aware.

procedural memory
A type of implicit memory consisting of how to perform tasks that are done automatically.

sense, since that part of the brain is also heavily involved with the kind of deliberate thought often used to form semantic memories (but not as often used to form episodic memories) (Gabrieli et al., 1998; Martin & Chao, 2001).

Implicit Memory

Implicit memory is memory of which you are not consciously aware. It is also called *non-declarative memory*, because you cannot easily declare (or tell) it to another person. Implicit memory is memory that you *don't know* you know. You can't explicitly state it, but you can *imply* its presence by your actions, which is why it is called *implicit* (Baddeley et al., 2009; Lockhart, 2000; Squire & Zola, 1996). For example, if you are an experienced driver, you might not be able to describe the exact steps involved in starting a car (e.g., turning the key in the ignition, stepping on the brake, putting it in gear, stepping on the gas, steering). However, the fact that the engine cranks and your car moves down the road within seconds of you sitting in the driver's seat implies that you clearly remember how to start a car.

Procedural Memory. Much of implicit memory is **procedural memory**: a type of implicit memory consisting of how to perform tasks that you do automatically. The key word in that definition is *how*. Procedural memory is your recollection of how to do things (Schacter et al., 2000). For example, you rely on your procedural memory to know how to ride a bike, how to brush your teeth, how to buckle a belt, how to use utensils, how to turn up the volume on your phone, and lots of other behaviors that you can do on autopilot. Procedural memory is remembering an action rather than an object.

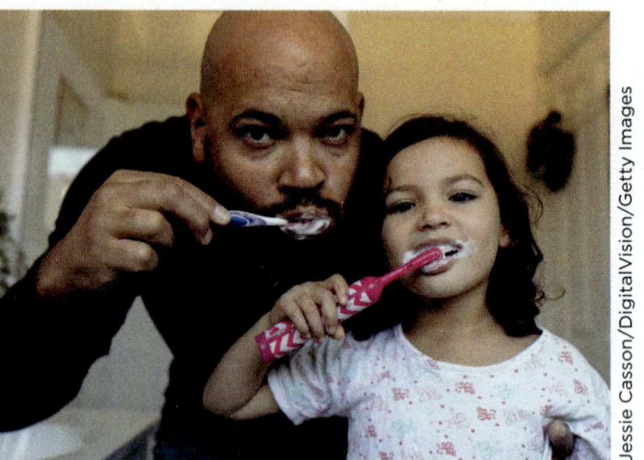

Jessie Casson/DigitalVision/Getty Images

Procedural memory is implicit memory for tasks you do automatically. Those tasks, like brushing your teeth, often enter your procedural memory through repetition.

It is important to remember that actions don't enter procedural memory the first time we do them. It takes many, many repetitions for them to become so ingrained that we no longer need to make a deliberate effort to complete them (Gupta & Cohen, 2002; Ofen-Noy et al., 2003). For example, new ballroom dancers trying to learn the cha-cha will definitely have to hear (from instructors, partners, or themselves) the "one, two, cha cha cha" count and work purposefully to make their feet take the correct steps on every beat. But after a little experience, the need to hear the count fades. After a lot of experience, they do the cha-cha without thinking, as if what was once entirely foreign has become entirely intuitive.

Sometimes we don't realize that our procedural memories are so deeply ingrained until we need to teach another person how to do the same procedure. (If a 4-year-old asked you how to tie shoes, could you explain every little step?) I was once filling my car with gas when a mother and her 15-year-old son, with a brand-new driver's permit, pulled up to the opposite side of the pump. Mom handed her son a credit card and said, "Go ahead — fill it up." The son looked completely bewildered, and in response the mom looked equally bewildered about the fact that her son was so bewildered. The son said, "How?" The mom said, "What do you mean, 'how'? You just fill it up. It's so easy." Eventually, the mom realized that she had filled the tank so many times that she could do it without thinking. It was embedded in her procedural memory. But she was going to have to take her inexperienced son step by step through this process: open the little fuel door on the side of the car, unscrew the gas cap, press the necessary buttons on the display, select a particular grade of gas, lift the nozzle, insert it in the tank, squeeze the handle to start the flow, and so on. By the time she was finished, the mom realized that you don't just "fill it up." You learn a series of steps that is initially complex but eventually becomes a procedure committed to memory.

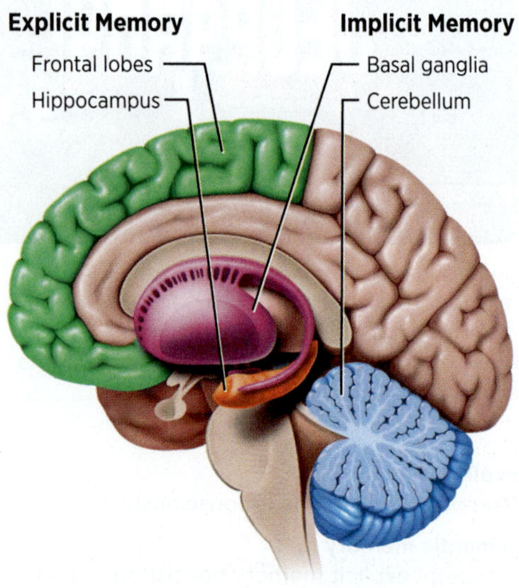

FIGURE 5.6 Localizing Implicit Memory and Explicit Memory. Implicit memory relies on the cerebellum and basal ganglia, but explicit memory relies on the frontal lobes and hippocampus.

Research indicates that implicit memory and explicit memory are very distinct processes in the brain (Loonis et al., 2017). In fact, they utilize different brain regions (**Figure 5.6**). Explicit memory relies primarily on the frontal lobes and hippocampus. Specifically, verbal information (like passwords for your social media accounts) is stored in the left side of the frontal lobes and hippocampus, but visual information (like what your backpack looks like) is stored on the right side of these brain structures. Implicit memory, on the other hand, relies primarily on the cerebellum and (at least for implicit memories involving motion) basal ganglia (Eichenbaum, 2010; Squire, 2004).

CHECK YOUR LEARNING:

5.13 What is explicit memory?

5.14 What are the two basic types of explicit memory, and how do they differ?

5.15 What is implicit memory?

5.16 What is procedural memory?

To check your understanding of these questions, click show the answers or refer to the answers in the Chapter Summary.

What Affects Memory?

YOU WILL LEARN:

5.17 how memory can be affected by decay over time.

5.18 how memory can be affected by context, or "other" information around it.

5.19 what retroactive interference and proactive interference are.

5.20 what the primacy effect and recency effect are.

5.21 how feelings can influence memory, such as the flashbulb memory of an especially emotional event.

5.22 how to improve memory, including mnemonics, study frequency, and sleep habits.

Sometimes your memory is amazing, pulling up a fact or trivial experience you buried deep many years ago and haven't thought about since. ("Wow, I can't believe I remember my kindergarten teacher's name.") Other times, your memory lets you down, leaving you fumbling for important facts ("What's the passcode for my phone?") or information you've used recently and regularly ("What's my neighbor's name again?"). Psychologists can't entirely explain why memory can be so fickle, but they have identified certain factors that often affect it.

Time and Memory

Time is generally the enemy of memory. Psychologists call the process by which time erodes memory **decay**: the dwindling or loss of information from memory due to the passing of time. Decay happens most often when information is not used. For instance, if it is not used, information that enters sensory memory will decay before it enters short-term memory. Similarly, unused information that enters short-term memory will decay before it enters long-term memory.

Once information is in long-term memory, its recall still depends on use. If you call it up once in a while (rather than leaving it untouched for long periods), the information is more likely to be there when you need it later (Barrouillet et al., 2009; Brown et al., 2007; Carrier & Pashler, 1992). For example, consider a family reunion at which you bump into a cousin whom you haven't seen in 5 years. If you haven't heard or thought their name in all that time, there's a decent chance their name has decayed from your long-term memory and you'll need to peek at their nametag. However, if you occasionally talk about them with other family members or you've seen their Instagram posts once in a while, those experiences have refreshed your memory enough to lessen the chances of decay.

Context and Memory: "Other" Information

Your ability to remember a particular piece of information depends on its context—that is, what other information surrounds it (Dewar et al., 2010; Roediger et al., 2010; Wixted, 2010). In general, other information interferes with the memory of the target information, much as a pocketful of coins makes it difficult to find the one dime you need.

One particular form of this interference is **retroactive interference**: problems remembering older information caused by newer information. Retroactive interference is what happens when you watch two movies in a row and have difficulty recalling the details of the first one. The second movie sort of bumps the first one (or at least parts of it) out of your mind. The opposite form of interference is **proactive interference**: problems remembering newer information caused by older information. Proactive interference is what happens when you watch two movies in a row and have difficulty recalling the *second* one. In this case, it's as if the first movie refuses to make room for the second one, so parts of the second one don't get processed into memory (Bäuml, 1996; Fatania & Mercer, 2017; Keppel & Underwood, 1962; Underwood, 1957).

Retroactive interference is usually considered problematic, but recent research suggests that it could be helpful when people are tormented by painful or upsetting memories. One group of researchers was studying the negative memories of children

decay
The dwindling or loss of information from memory due to the passing of time.

retroactive interference
Problems remembering older information caused by newer information.

proactive interference
Problems remembering newer information caused by older information.

serial position effect
The tendency to remember the first and last items in a series better than the items in the middle.

primacy effect
The tendency to remember the first items in a series particularly well.

recency effect
The tendency to remember the last items in a series particularly well.

who had lived through Hurricane Katrina in 2005, but Hurricane Gustav hit the same area in 2008 as they conducted the study. The researchers found that the experience of Hurricane Gustav reduced children's memories of Hurricane Katrina, even if their experience with Hurricane Gustav was not as severe (Weems et al., 2014).

Different researchers tried to replicate the 2008 study in a more controlled way. Researchers exposed participants to highly negative pictures (to mimic the hurricane), then exposed them to a second set of negative pictures, and, finally, asked participants to recall the first set of images. Memories of the first image set were reduced by seeing the second image set, even when the second image set was less negative than the first. The researchers speculated that people who *want* to forget a highly negative event might go through a new, less severe, negative event to create retroactive interference that at least partially displaces the unwelcome memories of the original event (Hensley et al., 2018). Of course, additional research will be necessary to determine how effective such a technique might be.

Position Effects. Related to both proactive and retroactive interference is the **serial position effect**: the tendency to remember the first and last items in a series better than the items in the middle. There are terms for the specific effects at either end of the series. The **primacy effect** is the tendency to remember the first items in a series particularly well. The **recency effect** is the tendency to remember the last items in a series particularly well. For the first items in the list, there's no chance of proactive interference, because nothing came before. For the last items, there's no chance of retroactive interference, because nothing came after — unless there's a delay before recall, when retroactive interference can take place so the recency effect is not so strong (Postman & Phillips, 1965). However, the items in the middle are susceptible to both proactive and retroactive interference, so they tend to be forgotten more often (Feigenbaum & Simon, 1962; Greene, 1986; Murdock, 1962; Raffel, 1936; Tzeng, 1973).

The serial position effect, primacy effect, and recency effect were described early in the history of psychology by Hermann Ebbinghaus (1885). For over a century, his findings about these effects have been replicated again and again (Bower, 2000; Craik & Watkins, 1973; Crowder & Greene, 2000). In a free recall situation immediately after hearing a list of about a dozen items ("Name all the words you can remember . . ."), participants typically begin with the last items, correctly naming the last three items about 80–90% of the time. Next, participants name the first couple of items on the list, correctly naming them about 60–70% of the time. Then, if they can, participants name items from the middle of the list, but only about 30–40% of them (**Figure 5.7**).

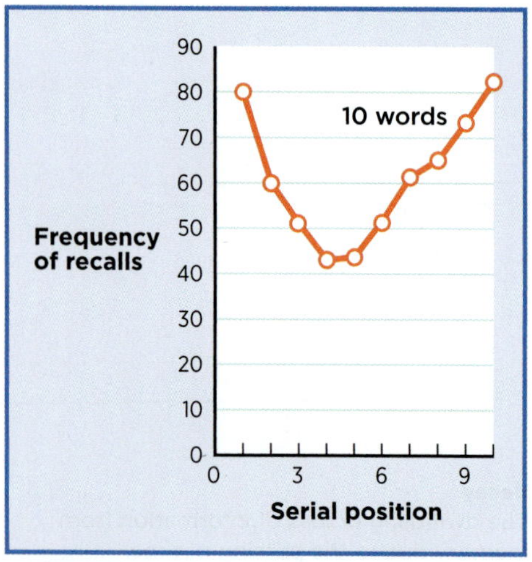

FIGURE 5.7 Serial Position Effect. When you recall a series right after it ends, you are much more likely to remember the first and last items than the items in the middle (Postman & Phillips, 1965).

Researchers often study the serial position effect by presenting a list of spoken or written words and then asking participants to recall all they can (Crowder & Greene, 2000). But serial position makes a difference in all kinds of situations in which there is a series of stimuli. For example, if you meet 10 people at a party, you are more likely to remember the names of the first few people and the last few people than the people in the middle. If you go to a concert and hear 20 songs, you are most likely to remember what the band opened with or what it played as an encore than what it played halfway through.

More recent research has explored these kinds of real-world applications of the serial position effect, primacy effect, and recency effect. As an example of the primacy effect, one study found that wine tasters who tried five wines tended to prefer the first wine they tasted, no matter which one that was — perhaps because their memory for the first one was stronger than for the others (Mantonakis et al., 2009). A meta-analysis of 11 studies on food preferences found the same result. The first food tasted is disproportionately chosen as the favorite, even when the order was randomly determined (Dean, 1980). By contrast, the recency effect was demonstrated in a study of figure skating results. Skaters who went last received the best ratings from the judges, even when their order was randomized according to their previous scores (Bruine de Bruin, 2005, 2006).

WATCHING PSYCHOLOGY

The Serial Position Effect on American Idol?

In many competitions, contestants take turns showcasing their talents: beauty contests, gymnastics, political debates, speed dating, and job interviews, among many others. Does it matter whether you go first, last, or somewhere in the middle?

A team of researchers explored this question in the results of the *Idol* singing series (Page & Page, 2010). They examined not just *American Idol* but also *Australian Idol*, *Canadian Idol*, *Indian Idol*, *X-Factor* (England), and similar shows from Brazil, the Netherlands, and Germany. Their dataset included over 1500 singing performances from 165 episodes.

Their basic finding? The later, the better. That is, *Idol* contestants who performed later in the show were most likely to survive to the next week. *Idol* contestants who performed earlier (with the exception of the very first contestant) were most likely to be voted off (as illustrated in **Figure 5.8**). Specifically, the researchers calculated that a contestant is 5 percentage points more likely to advance into the following week's competition for each position they are closer to the end of the show. The authors found that there is a small primacy effect, based on the fact that singers who go first are evaluated more positively than those who go second or third, but there is a huge recency effect.

Of course, if you think critically about these results, you can see numerous reasons other than serial position effects to explain them. The authors themselves point out many of them: The show's producers may save the best for last rather than presenting the singers in random order. Also, more viewers may watch the latter part of the show than the earlier part of the show. Further, later singers have the advantage of hearing earlier singers, as well as the judge's feedback, so they can make adjustments accordingly.

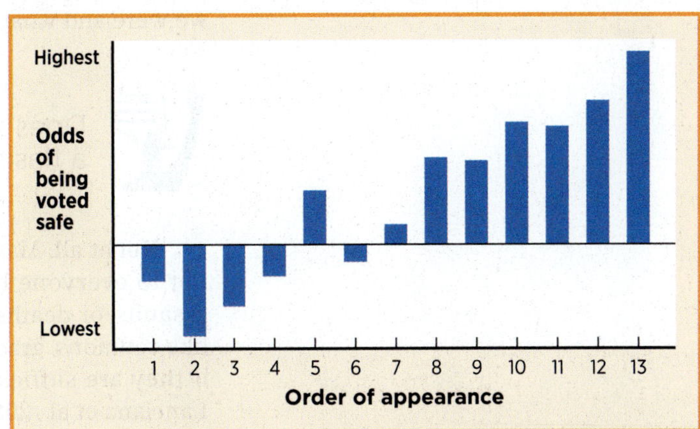

FIGURE 5.8 American Idol and the Serial Position Effect. On *American Idol*, singers who perform later in the show have better odds of receiving enough votes to survive to the next week. This finding may reflect the recency effect (among other factors). Data from Page and Page (2010).

Even with these alternative explanations, these researchers argue that the order of appearance may make a difference for each contestant. Other studies have offered similar results and conclusions (Li & Epley, 2009). •

Relearning. Sometimes your memory depends not so much on the presence of "other" information, but on the fact that you have already remembered and forgotten that particular information. Psychologists call this process *relearning*: the process of committing information to memory for a second time after it has been forgotten. A few paragraphs ago, we imagined a family reunion in which you forgot your cousin's name. If he reintroduces himself ("Johnny, of course! How have you been?"), a week later you are more likely to remember Johnny's name than you are to remember the name of Johnny's new baby whom you met for the first time at the reunion. At the reunion, you are learning Johnny's baby's name but *re*learning Johnny's name, so Johnny's is more likely to stick (MacLeod, 1988; Nelson, 1985).

Flashbulb Memory. Other times, your memory depends upon the emotional context of the information you learn. Specifically, information and events that arouse powerful feelings are especially likely to be recalled, often as if they happened yesterday (Fivush et al., 2009; Schmidt, 2007; Schooler & Eich, 2000). A memory of this type is a **flashbulb memory**: a distinctively clear and vivid memory of an emotionally charged and novel event (Brown & Kulik, 1977; Curci & Luminet, 2009; Luminet & Curci, 2009).

Flashbulb memories are often shared by those who experienced or witnessed them. For U.S. residents in recent years, that list might include the terrorist attacks of 9/11; the school shootings at Sandy Hook Elementary in Connecticut or Marjory

flashbulb memory
A distinctively clear and vivid memory of an emotionally charged and novel event.

mnemonic
A specific technique or strategy deliberately used to enhance memory.

Stoneman Douglas High School in Florida; Hurricane Katrina in New Orleans; the mass shooting at an outdoor concert in Las Vegas; the killing of George Floyd; the insurrection at the U.S. Capitol on January 6, 2021; even a championship victory by a favorite sports team. These major events contain so much emotional power that many of us not only remember them with detail and feeling but also can recall exactly where we were and what we were doing when they took place.

Does something have to be a society-wide event to be a flashbulb memory?

Not at all. Many of your flashbulb memories are personal: things that happened not to everyone but just to you. Bad things, like car accidents, robberies, sexual assaults, or deaths of loved ones, can produce flashbulb memories. But good things, like reunions, graduations, or surprise parties, can also produce flashbulb memories if they are sufficiently vivid, important, and emotionally intense (Davidson, 2008; Lanciano et al., 2018; May et al., 2020; Stone & Jay, 2018). For example, one study found that for women pledging the Greek system at a large state college, the moment they received a bid from a sorority was as capable of creating a flashbulb memory as any negative event they might have experienced (Kraha & Boals, 2014).

Flashbulb memories are more vivid than regular memories, but they are not any more accurate (Talarico & Rubin, 2009). One important factor about the reliability of flashbulb memories is how direct the experience is. If you experience the event firsthand, you are less likely to forget or distort the memory than if you see or hear it on the news (Er, 2003; Pillemer, 2009). In one study, researchers asked people to recall the earthquake that rocked the San Francisco area in October 1989, which killed over 60 and injured over 3000. Coincidentally, the World Series was taking place in the area at the time, featuring both Bay Area teams, the San Francisco Giants and the Oakland A's. For this reason, the earthquake was witnessed live by millions on TV and radio. People from California, who were more likely to have felt the earth move under their own feet, recalled their own experiences of the earthquake and the news reports about it with a high degree of accuracy. People from a distant city such as Atlanta, who could only learn about the earthquake secondhand, showed much lower rates of recall about the event (Neisser et al., 1996).

DIVERSITY MATTERS

Diversity and Flashbulb Memory. Culture can also have a strong impact on flashbulb memories (Wang & Aydin, 2018). Understandably, the importance of an event to members of a particular culture makes a difference in whether flashbulb memories form or not. For example, more Americans formed flashbulb memories of the 9/11 terrorist attacks than did residents of other countries, and Americans' memories remained more specific and accurate years later (Curci & Luminet, 2006; Luminet et al., 2004). Also, in 2013, Catholic churchgoers in Italy were more likely to form flashbulb memories when Pope Benedict XVI resigned than Catholic Italians who didn't attend church or Italians who were not Catholic (Curci et al., 2015).

Some researchers have even argued that forming a flashbulb memory for a particular event strengthens the ties between people within a particular social group. By claiming "I can remember exactly what I was doing when . . ." an event occurred, a person identifies as a member of the group especially affected by that event (Bernsten, 2018; Demiray & Freund, 2015; Hirst & Meksin, 2018). For example, by forming and sharing a flashbulb memory of Prince's sudden death in 2016, a fan of the singer can feel a closer bond to his larger community of fans around the world.

Whether flashbulb memories form or not can depend on how individualistic or collectivistic the cultural group tends to be – that is, how the event matters to *me*, as opposed to how the event matters to *us*. One study found that for participants from a more individualistic country (such as the United States) and a

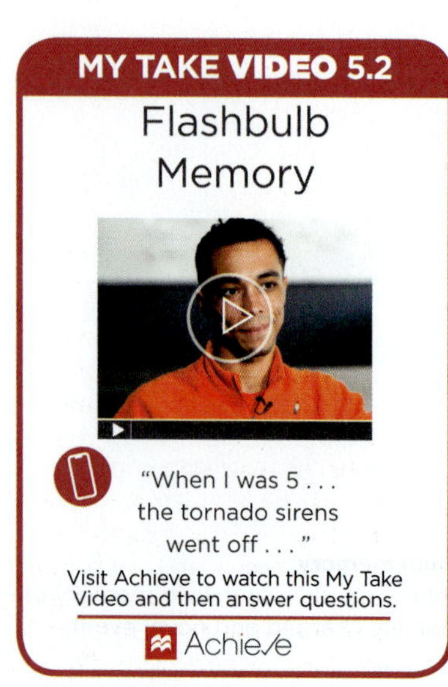
MY TAKE VIDEO 5.2
Flashbulb Memory
"When I was 5 . . . the tornado sirens went off . . ."
Visit Achieve to watch this My Take Video and then answer questions.
Achieve

more collectivistic country (such as China), the *national* importance of an event had a roughly equal impact on the likelihood of forming a flashbulb memory. However, the *personal* importance of the event had a different impact on the different groups: it mattered significantly less to participants from China than to participants from the United States and the United Kingdom (Kulkofsky et al., 2011).

Efforts to Improve Memory

So far, our discussion of what affects memory has focused on factors over which you often have no control, like the passage of time and the context that surrounds the information you hope to remember. But memory also depends on some factors you can control to a great extent, including deliberate efforts to enhance our memory of certain facts or events.

Mnemonics. A **mnemonic** is a specific technique or strategy deliberately used to enhance memory. Mnemonics are the mental devices, or tricks, commonly used by memory champions, such as the USA Memory Championship competitors described earlier in this chapter (Worthen & Hunt, 2011). You've probably used them too. For example, in a science class, you may have memorized the colors of the rainbow in order as *ROY G. BIV* (rather than directly remembering the sequence *r*ed, *o*range, *y*ellow, *g*reen, *b*lue, *i*ndigo, *v*iolet). If so, you were using an *acronym* as a mnemonic (Stalder, 2005). In a math class, you may have used a different acronym to learn the order of operations by memorizing the sentence *Please excuse my dear Aunt Sally*, the first letters of which correspond to *p*arentheses, *e*xponents, *m*ultiplication, *d*ivision, *a*ddition, and *s*ubtraction.

In addition to mnemonics that rely on letters and words, many mnemonics rely on rhythm and rhyme, such as making a song out of the 50 states and their capitals. Others rely on visual imagery — in particular, associating new information with distinct visual stimuli. Ben Pridmore, who won the USA Memory Championship, describes a mnemonic based on this kind of visualization called the *method of loci* (Moe & DeBeni, 2004, 2005). (*Loci* simply means locations or places.) He uses it to memorize the order of cards in a deck in a matter of seconds. In his mind, he converts each card "into a mental image of an object or person, and [I] visualize them at different points [or loci] along a journey — in this case, around the rooms of my grandma's old house" (Pridmore, 2007). Of course, his grandma's old house is something that Ben already knows by heart, so he's memorizing a series of new things by picturing each new thing with an already-memorized thing. For example, if Ben's first card is the king of hearts, he might picture a king with a visibly pounding heart opening his grandma's front door. If his next card is the three of diamonds, he might imagine a stack of three oversized glistening diamonds on the table in the living room of his grandma's house visible after walking in the front door. If the next card is the seven of clubs, he might picture seven actual clubs on the living room couch, and so on.

Similar to the method of loci is the *peg word method*, in which you pair images of the items you need to remember with a series of words (not locations) you already have committed to memory. For example, you might begin by memorizing the simple five-word sequence *run, blue, bee, door, drive*, which rhymes with 1, 2, 3, 4, 5 (Elliott & Gentile, 1986; Massen & Vaterrodt-Plunnecke, 2006; Wang & Thomas, 2000). Then, whenever you need to remember a series of five or fewer things, you can pair those things with this five-word sequence you already know. So, imagine that while jogging, you think of five people to whom you need to send party invitations. To remember them until you get home, just picture each of them interacting with the items on the previously memorized list: Tina running, Greg painted blue, Devonte being stung by a bee, Darren slamming a door, and Deya driving. Later, when you are back home, you are likely to recall those images of your five friends as you recite your memorized list.

CHAPTER APP 5.2

 Elevate

The Elevate app offers memory activities designed to keep your mind sharp and either maintain or enhance your memory if played on a regular basis. It includes a variety of personalized activities designed to enhance memory and other cognitive functions.

How does it APPly to your daily life?
Apps like Elevate often claim to improve users' memory capabilities. In your opinion, could it improve your memory? If so, which activities would be most effective, and how much time would you have to spend using them? As you consider apps like Elevate, how important is it to you to know that well-done scientific studies support their claims about memory?

How does it APPly to your understanding of psychology?
Of all of the various types of memory described in this chapter, which do you think would be most and least improvable by apps like Elevate?

To learn more about this app or to download it to your phone, you can search for "Elevate app" on Google, in the iPhone App store, or in the Google Play store.

Joseph Calev/iStock/Getty Images

One mnemonic that can boost memory for a list of items is the method of loci, in which you picture the items in particular locations you already have memorized. If you had the specific locations within this kitchen memorized, you could remember the countertop to your left first, then the sink, stove, and fridge. Then, if you needed to call four friends in a particular order, you could visualize each friend at a specific spot in the kitchen: Jasmine at the countertop, Ella washing her hands in the sink, Caleb turning on the stove, and Diego opening the fridge.

FROM RESEARCH TO REAL LIFE

Improving Your Memory

Much of the research on memory applies directly to your life during college and beyond. To maximize your ability to remember everything from the information that will be on tomorrow's exam to the names of the people you met at last night's party, follow these evidence-based memory tips:

- **Make it meaningful.** Think about what the information *means* to you—how you feel about it, what opinion you have about it. For example, if you're trying to remember the names of your friend's three dogs, think about your previous interactions with each of them (Princess startled you with a loud bark; Bailey grossed you out with bad breath; Bandit amazed you with Frisbee-catching abilities). Such deep processing helps memories sink in better than shallow, superficial processing.
- **Use mnemonics.** Mnemonics—like acronyms, or the method of loci—are great, as long as your goal is mere memorization, not comprehension. For example, HOMES is a great way to remember the names of the Great Lakes (Huron, Ontario, Michigan, Erie, and Superior), but it doesn't help with any meaningful information about them, like the size of each one or where they are in relation to each other.
- **Organize ideas.** Organize ideas into some kind of structure or groups, rather than just a random assortment. For example, to remember everyone on your softball team, categorize them by position: infielders, outfielders, pitchers, and catchers.
- **Visualize information.** Visualize information rather than just thinking about the word or repeating it verbally. This can even include drawing objects if you have the chance. For example, visualizing the things you still need to put in your bag for an overnight trip—a change of clothes, running shoes, toothbrush, phone charger, and jacket—will give you a better chance of remembering them than simply saying the list over and over to yourself.
- **Use context cues.** Go back to the same place you learned something to help you remember it now. Going back to the same mood (or at least imagining it) can help too.
- **Imagine teaching the information.** Imagine yourself teaching the information to someone else. By doing that, you'll think about (or process) the information especially deeply. You can even anticipate questions you might get from your students and answer those too.
- **Don't multitask.** Memory suffers significantly when you do more than one thing at once. You may see your friends "studying" with their eyes darting between their textbook and their phone (and maybe a TV too), but don't follow their lead—turn off all unnecessary screens.
- **Keep your mind healthy.** Keep your mind—and your memory capacity—healthy by getting enough sleep, eating right, and exercising. Some particularly memory-enhancing foods include fish (especially wild salmon), pomegranates and blueberries, green tea and coffee (in moderation), tree nuts (especially walnuts and almonds), and dark chocolate (with at least 70% cacao content). Exercise helps memory most when it is aerobic and happens outside in fresh air.
- **Exercise your mind.** Whether old-school, like crossword puzzles, or new-school, like memory-enhancing apps, brain activities keep your brain in shape and ready to form, store, and recall memories.

Sources: Alloway and Alloway (2013), Alloway (2011), and Baddeley (2004).

Spacing Effect. Studying is another memory enhancement effort. In your many years of school, you have undoubtedly tried a variety of study strategies. Researchers have found that some strategies work better than others. Specifically, they have identified the **spacing effect**: the tendency to have better long-term memory for information when your attempts to study it are spaced apart rather than crammed together. The spacing effect (also known as the advantage of *distributed practice* over *massed practice*) basically boils down to one important point for you as a test taker: cramming does not work as well as consistent, repeated studying. Cramming can certainly be effective to a limited extent. However, information learned through repeated exposures on multiple days becomes more deeply embedded in long-term memory, making it more likely to be recalled on test day and more likely to be retained long after the test (Bahrick, 2000; Geller et al., 2018; Landauer, 2011; Landauer & Bjork, 1978; Roediger & Karpicke, 2011).

The inferiority of cramming to spaced studying is a particularly important finding when you consider that it isn't obvious to everyone. When given a choice, many people choose cramming, even when they have the time for more spaced study and even though cramming produces lesser results (Son, 2004, 2005; Son & Kornell, 2008). In one study, the participants' task was to memorize random patterns on the number pad of a computer keyboard. They learned these patterns in one of two ways: cramming (many repetitions at once), or spaced practice (repetitions spread out over time). Participants who learned via cramming *predicted* higher levels of performance but *delivered* lower levels of performance than those who learned via spaced practice (Simon & Bjork, 2001).

spacing effect
The tendency to have better long-term memory for information when attempts to study it are spaced apart rather than crammed together.

One more note about spaced studying: college students underestimate how often their peers use this study strategy. Specifically, one study found that college students believed that about 57% of students intentionally space out their study sessions, but about 71% actually did. The researchers suggested that if students more accurately perceived how common spaced studying is, they might be more likely to do it themselves (Anthenian et al., 2018).

LIFE HACK 5.2

Use the spacing effect to your advantage. Rather than cramming for tests, study the material in multiple, spaced-apart sessions.

(Landauer, 2011; Roediger & Karpicke, 2011)

Diversity and Memory

DIVERSITY MATTERS

Culture and Memory. *What* you remember depends quite a bit on your specific cultural background (Cappeliez & Webster, 2017; Göz et al., 2017; Nakayama et al., 2017). A growing body of recent research has found interesting differences between the memories of people of European descent (often Americans), who tend to approach life with a more individualistic, self-focused orientation, and people of Asian descent, who tend to approach life with a more collectivistic, group-focused orientation (Ross & Wang, 2010; Wang, 2013; Wang & Aydin, 2009).

One group of researchers asked participants from China and the United States to freely recall any 20 specific memories from their own lives. The memories provided by the U.S. participants included twice as many memories in which they were the only person mentioned, while the memories provided by the Chinese participants included twice as many mentions of social interactions or group activities (Conway et al., 2005; Wang & Conway, 2004). In another study, Asian Americans were instructed to describe themselves as either Asian or American. Then, they were instructed to remember events from their own past. Those who had described themselves as American were much more likely to remember events that were self-focused and much less likely to remember events that involved social interaction (Wang, 2008). Similar cultural differences have been found in very young children. When asked to share their memories for things that had happened to them, European American preschoolers include far more of their own personal feelings, preferences, and opinions, while Asian preschoolers include far more discussion of other people (especially authority figures) and social correctness (Wang, 2004; Wang et al., 2000).

Another study with preschoolers produced a similar result. The preschoolers, half of whom were American and half of whom were Korean, played a "pizza game" together in which they made pretend pizzas using toy food ingredients. A few days later, when they were asked to remember the pizza game, the American kids told more stories that featured only themselves, and the Korean kids told more stories that featured other kids in the group (Chae et al., 2006).

In addition to affecting which events you remember, culture can affect *how* you remember events (Wang, 2021; Wang et al., 2017, 2018). Specifically, researchers have found that when people of European descent recall an event, they tend to tell the story from their own point of view. By contrast, people of Asian descent are more likely to tell the story from the point of view of other people (Cohen & Gunz, 2002; Leung & Cohen, 2007). For example, if they were remembering the day their city's team won a basketball championship, the person of European background would be more likely to describe what it was like for them as an individual: "I saw that shot go in at the last second, and I was ecstatic! I jumped and screamed and felt such a rush of happiness." The person of Asian background might incorporate a more collective point of view for a memory of the same event: "When we saw that shot go in at the last second, everyone in the gym cheered! The fans in the stands celebrated while the players and coaches ran to hug each other on the court."

DIVERSITY MATTERS

Language and Memory. Even the language you speak can influence what you remember. In a pair of studies, people who spoke both Russian and English were interviewed in one language or the other and then asked to share some of their personal memories. It was no surprise that those who were interviewed in Russian remembered more events from the time in their lives when they primarily spoke Russian, while those who were interviewed in English remembered more events from the time in their lives when they primarily spoke English. More noteworthy, however, was the difference in content of their memories: those interviewed in English provided memories that were much more about themselves, while those interviewed in Russian provided memories that were much more about other people and relationships (Marian & Kaushanskaya, 2004; Marian & Neisser, 2000).

DIVERSITY MATTERS

Socioeconomic Status and Memory. Researchers who study racial and ethnic differences in memory abilities among older Americans have often found that people of color (most often studied are Black and Latinx Americans) tend to perform slightly worse on some memory tasks and experience slightly higher rates of memory problems than White Americans (Dixon et al., 2021). One likely reason for that discrepancy is socioeconomic status (SES), which tends to differ along racial lines as well. Generally, people with higher SES throughout their lives tend to have higher-functioning memories as older adults than people with lower SES (Marden et al., 2017). Another likely reason for the discrepancy is discrimination: Black older adults who experience more daily discrimination tend to experience more memory problems (Johnson et al., 2020; Zahodne et al., 2019). Other likely reasons include race-related discrepancies in physical health and mental health (Zahodne et al., 2017).

Sleep and Memory

Sleep is an important but often overlooked factor that affects memory. One interesting aspect of the relationship between sleep and memory is that memories are typically stronger if the time interval between encoding and retrieval includes sleep than if it doesn't (Brown & Lewandowsky, 2010). In other words, "sleeping on it" helps memory. Researchers believe that sleep serves two important functions related to memory: (1) sleep allows for *consolidation* of memories, strengthening memory formation (Feld & Born, 2017; LeDoux, 2007); and (2) sleep prevents any kind of interference from taking place (Born et al., 2006; Ellenbogen et al., 2006; MacLeod & Hulbert, 2011). This effect is strongest if the sleep takes place closer to the time of encoding than the point of retrieval. Sleeping right after you study helps your mind form strong memories of the material (de Bruin et al., 2017; Ekstrand, 1972).

The flip side of sleep helping memory is that a *lack* of sleep hurts memory (Gais et al., 2006; Marshall & Born, 2007; Mu et al., 2005; Ratcliff & Van Dongen, 2018; Whitney & Rosen, 2013). You probably know this firsthand. The day after pulling an all-nighter studying for a test, your memory sputters. Your absent-mindedness extends even to things you typically remember with ease — where you put your keys, why you went into the kitchen, what time your friend said they'd pick you up. On these drowsy days, these kinds of memories are lost in a fog. However, on days when you are well rested, this stuff is easy to remember. Interestingly, research has found that information learned right before a sleepless night is frequently forgotten even if you sleep well the following two nights (Peigneux et al., 2010). So, if you don't sleep well on Monday night, you're likely to forget information you took in during the day on Monday — and sleeping well on Tuesday and Wednesday won't bring it back.

LIFE HACK 5.3

Get a good night's sleep before a big test, because sleep enhances memory and sleeplessness impairs it.

(Brown & Lewandowsky, 2010; Gais et al., 2006; LeDoux, 2007; Whitney & Rosen, 2013)

In kids, the link between sleep and memory has prompted some researchers to recommend taking a second look at kids with learning problems before diagnosing them with learning-related disorders. Their idea is that a sleep-related problem might underlie their struggles at school (Curcio, 2006; Maski et al., 2017; Steenari et al., 2003; Taras & Potts-Datema, 2005). This link has also fueled the debate about school start times (as discussed in Chapter 4), with some arguing that pushing back the opening bell to later in the morning would facilitate numerous benefits, including increased memory for what students learn during the school day (Wahlstrom, 2002; Wolfson & Carskadon, 2003).

CHECK YOUR LEARNING:

5.17 What is decay?

5.18 How is memory affected by context?

5.19 What's the difference between retroactive interference and proactive interference?

5.20 What's the difference between the primacy effect and the recency effect?

5.21 How can emotion influence memory, especially in relation to flashbulb memory?

5.22 How can mnemonics, the spacing effect, and sleep each improve memory?

To check your understanding of these questions, click show the answers or refer to the answers in the Chapter Summary.

Memory Problems

YOU WILL LEARN:

5.23 how psychologists define amnesia.

5.24 what the difference between retrograde amnesia and anterograde amnesia is.

5.25 about the misinformation effect and the types of memory mistakes it can produce.

5.26 how certain psychological disorders have a negative impact on memory.

5.27 how COVID-19 can contribute to memory problems.

In this section, we consider some of the ways that memory can go wrong. Each of us knows all too well about such memory problems. They take many forms, from distorted memories to intrusive memories to memory failure. Thankfully, these problems typically limit themselves to certain times and places, even among older adults showing the normal age-related reduction in memory capacity (Anderson & Craik, 2000). In severe cases, however, these memory problems can be disruptive to people's lives for extended periods of time (Hodges, 2000; Mayes, 2000).

Amnesia

Amnesia is the inability to remember some or all information, either temporarily or permanently. Most cases of amnesia have a definitive cause in the form of a brain injury or disease, but amnesia occasionally takes place without a physical cause (O'Connor & Verfaellie, 2002). In cases without physical cause, known as *dissociative amnesia*, the incidents often occur in the aftermath of psychological trauma, severe abuse, or overwhelming stress (Brand & Markowitsch, 2010; Brand et al., 2009; Staniloiu et al., 2018). Sometimes, amnesia is global, meaning that the person's entire memory is wiped out. Other times, amnesia is situation-specific, meaning that the lost memories are limited to a certain part of the person's life. For example, people suffering from psychogenic amnesia may not recall anything related to the trauma or abuse that preceded it, but their memories for unrelated material remain intact (Kopelman, 2002a).

People with amnesia often retain their implicit memory despite an obvious loss of explicit memory. In an illustration of this point from the early days of psychology, a Swiss psychiatrist named Edouard Claparède shook hands with an amnesia patient while holding a thumbtack that pricked the patient's hand. Claparède had shaken her hand on previous days too (with no thumbtack), but day after day the patient had no recollection of who Claparède was. However, the day after he used the thumbtack, the patient refused to shake Claparède's hand. She still did not explicitly recognize him and had no conscious recollection of the thumbtack, but her implicit memory of the pain held her back (Claparède, 1911).

Retrograde Amnesia. Psychologists have identified specific types of amnesia. **Retrograde amnesia** is the inability to retrieve information that took place before a certain point in time. When you hear a survivor of a car accident say, "I can't remember anything from before the accident," they are describing retrograde amnesia. For example, Scott Bolzan hit his head after slipping in the bathroom and lost all memory for what came before — his wife, his kids, and his career as an NFL player, pilot, and business owner.

Bolzan wrote a book (titled *My Life, Deleted*, coauthored by his wife and another writer), in which he explains the experience: "I'd lost my life as I'd known it — my knowledge, my experiences, and even my identity — when my skull hit that tile floor . . . on the way to the hospital, I could almost feel the information draining away, leaving me in a foggy, disoriented haze. From that point on, my life was forever changed"

amnesia
The inability to remember some or all information, either temporarily or permanently.

retrograde amnesia
The inability to retrieve information that took place before a certain point in time.

anterograde amnesia
The inability to form new memories after a certain point in time.

(Bolzan et al., 2011, p. 4). Speaking of his wife, he added, "She was the woman I'd fallen in love with, married, and fathered three children with, and yet I had forgotten everything there was to know about her and our life together. But one question was nagging me even more: Who the hell was *I*?" (p. 9).

Although Bolzan's retrograde amnesia appears long-lasting, other cases can last just minutes, hours, or days (Papagno, 1998). This is commonly seen in athletes who "get their bell rung," incurring mild head injuries and temporarily struggling to remember simple facts about themselves. Usually, these athletes soon return to full memory function (Kapur et al., 1998; Kopelman, 2002). See the Current Controversy box about sports head injuries and memory loss.

Anterograde Amnesia. In contrast to retrograde amnesia, **anterograde amnesia** is the inability to form new memories after a certain point in time. In this case, the memory for what took place before the life-changing event remains intact. People with retrograde amnesia can remember their childhood, family, job, and so on, but they can't create new memories. They don't remember what has happened since the onset of the amnesia, which means they don't remember what they just said or did or what others just said or did to them. This results in lots of repeating from people with anterograde amnesia — the same questions, the same stories, the same actions — because there's no recollection that they've already been done (Mayes, 2002). In one well-known case of anterograde amnesia, Clive Wearing, a music producer and conductor from England, suffered brain damage from a virus. In 1985, Wearing found himself feeling like he was waking up over and over, unable to remember that he had already woken up that day. His condition required hospitalization and ruined his career, although he has shown some memory improvement over the years (Wearing, 2005).

CURRENT CONTROVERSY

Can Head Injuries in Sports Cause Memory Loss?

Sydney Urzendowski was a ninth-grader in Nebraska playing on her high school soccer team. After one header, she had intense headaches and nausea that lasted for months. She also had significant memory loss: she not only can't remember the play on which the head injury occurred, but she can't remember *that entire soccer season*. (See the Show Me More link at the end of the chapter for a video featuring Sydney.)

Was Sydney's experience a fluke, or do head injuries from sports cause memory loss? This question is at the center of a major debate involving amateur and professional athletes and those who treat and care about them. In recent years, Major League Baseball has required first-base and third-base coaches to wear helmets at all times while on the field. The National Football League has introduced new rules to outlaw blows to the head and neck, as well as leading with one's own helmet while tackling or carrying the ball. The National Hockey League has similarly made new rules to penalize hits to the head. The rationale for all of these moves was to reduce the aftereffects of head injuries, one of which is memory loss.

Numerous studies support this rationale. For example, multiple studies have found a negative correlation between the number of headers by professional soccer players and memory ability: the more headers, the worse the memory ability (Allen & Karceski, 2017; Levitch et al., 2018; Lipton et al., 2013; Matser et al., 2001). Another soccer study found that frequent headers (including practices and games) better predicted memory problems than unintentional head-to-head or head-to-goalpost collisions (Stewart et al., 2018). A study on high school and college athletes across many sports (soccer, American football, basketball, baseball, and lacrosse) found that the aftereffects of a concussion depend strongly on how many concussions the athlete had before it: those with multiple prior concussions were over seven times more likely to show a significant drop in memory ability than those with no prior concussions (Iverson et al., 2004). A meta-analysis of over 500 retired athletes found that those with more concussions struggled more with multiple types of memory problems even a decade after their playing days were over (Zhang et al., 2019).

Other studies reach different conclusions, however. In one, researchers found no cumulative effects on memory after two concussions (Iverson et al., 2006). Another study of over 1000 college athletes found that those who had previous concussions demonstrated no impairment in memory as long as no concussion had taken place in the last 6 months (Bruce & Echemendia, 2009). A meta-analysis showed mixed results: no general memory loss due to multiple mild head injuries, but some possible effects on particular kinds of memory (Belanger et al., 2010). Another meta-analysis showed no direct correlation between concussions and memory problems in retired NFL players (Fields et al., 2020).

The bottom line is that despite extensive study, it is difficult to draw specific conclusions about the way sports head injuries affect memory, whether those injuries involve concussions or not (Martini & Broglio, 2018). Given the inconclusive research, and the fact that the connection certainly exists in at least *some* cases, perhaps the most important part of Sydney's story is her (eventual) honesty about her symptoms and the involvement of professional health care providers in her assessment and treatment. •

John Patriquin/Portland Press Herald/Getty Images

According to many studies, memory loss can come not only from concussions but also from repeated contact to the head (including headers in soccer) that doesn't cause concussions.

Source Amnesia. Sometimes people have no problem remembering information, but they can't recall how or where they learned it (Chen et al., 2018; Mitchell & Johnson, 2000). This is **source amnesia**: the inability to remember the source of, or how you obtained, a particular memory (but not the memory itself). Full-fledged cases of source amnesia involve a complete inability to remember the sources of any memories, but you may have experienced fleeting moments of source amnesia yourself. There might have been times when you were completely confident about a memory, but you couldn't identify how you came to know the information — where you heard it, saw it, read it, or otherwise took it in. For example, picture yourself in a car with friends trying to find a party to which you are all invited. No one else quite remembers the address, but you do: 7476 Gannon Avenue. "How do you know that?" they ask. "I don't know how I know — I just do," you reply. When you arrive, the party is happening so it's clear that your memory was correct, but you still can't remember how you knew. Did the host text you about the party? Call you? E-mail you? Tell you in person? Post it on social media? Or did you hear another friend mention it? Your inability to determine the source of the information you remembered is a brief moment of source amnesia.

The existence of source amnesia indicates that when our memory is working correctly, we engage in *source monitoring*. We pay attention not only to information but to where it comes from (Johnson et al., 1993; Ranganath et al., 2012).

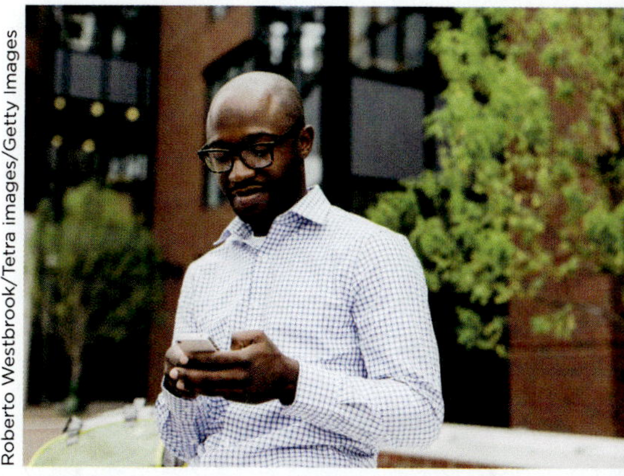
Roberto Westbrook/Tetra images/Getty Images

Source amnesia is the inability to remember the source of a particular memory. Unless source amnesia occurs, as a person forms a memory of the words or images they see on a smartphone screen, they will also form a memory of where they learned that information.

The Misinformation Effect

The **misinformation effect** is the tendency of false or misleading information presented after the fact to become mistakenly incorporated into memory. In other words, memories often become distorted when new information enters our minds, as if the new information somehow seeps into our original version of the memory (Calvillo & Mills, 2020; Pickrell et al., 2004; Volz et al., 2017). This is not an error of omission, in which memories are lost, but an error of commission, in which memories are twisted, revised, or supplemented with information that is not true (Roediger & McDermott, 2000).

To illustrate, one summer day, I took my 4-year-old son to Target. He had just received a gift card and was eager to spend it. But in the checkout line, with dinosaur Legos in his little hands, he looked up at me and burst into tears: "I lost my gift card!" The cashier tried to help by saying, "This happened to a little girl yesterday too, but she remembered where she was when she took her gift card out of her pocket, and then she went back to that part of the store and found it. What part of the store were you in when you took your gift card out of your pocket?" He sniffed, thought for a few seconds, and said, "The toy part, by the Legos." Back to the toy section we went, retracing his steps, looking on every shelf, but no gift card. After a long search, we headed back to the car to see if the gift card might be there. And as he climbed in, my son's misery turned to delight — "Daddy, here's my gift card! On the back seat!" As he excitedly pulled me back into the store with the gift card clutched tightly in his little hand, I noticed that his shorts and t-shirt actually had no pockets at all. He couldn't have taken the gift card out of his pocket anywhere in the store. The truth was that he held the card in his hand as he got in the car at home and dropped it before we got to the store. Yet the cashier's question ("What part of the store were you in when you took your gift card out of your pocket?") *suggested* that he took it out of his pocket somewhere in the store, and that suggestion was powerful enough to create a misinformed, false memory in my son's mind.

To some, it may seem surprising or disturbing to acknowledge the misinformation effect, the very idea that our memories are so imperfect. But they are. A leading memory researcher, Daniel Schacter, describes it this way:

> [W]e now know that we do not record our experiences the way a camera records them. Our memories work differently. We extract key elements from our experiences and store them. We then recreate or reconstruct our experiences rather than retrieve copies of them. Sometimes, in the process of reconstructing we add on feelings, beliefs, or even knowledge we obtained after the experience. In other words, we bias our memories of the past by attributing to them emotions or knowledge we acquired after the event. (Schacter, 2001, p. 9)

source amnesia
The inability to remember the source of a particular memory (but not the memory itself) or how it was obtained.

misinformation effect
The tendency of false or misleading information presented after the fact to be mistakenly incorporated into memory.

The misinformation effect can be especially important if the memory was a crucial element of a courtroom trial. Specifically, the misinformation effect is particularly relevant — and threatening — to the validity of eyewitness testimony. Elizabeth Loftus, a leading researcher on this topic, and a colleague describe the limitations of eyewitness testimony:

> [An] honest and sincere witness cannot be presumed to be entirely accurate. Human information processors are simply overwhelmed by the magnitude of incoming information and efforts to process and remember it accurately, leaving us vulnerable to error. Some information is necessarily lost, and other information may be confused or distorted. (Davis & Loftus, 2007, pp. 223–224)

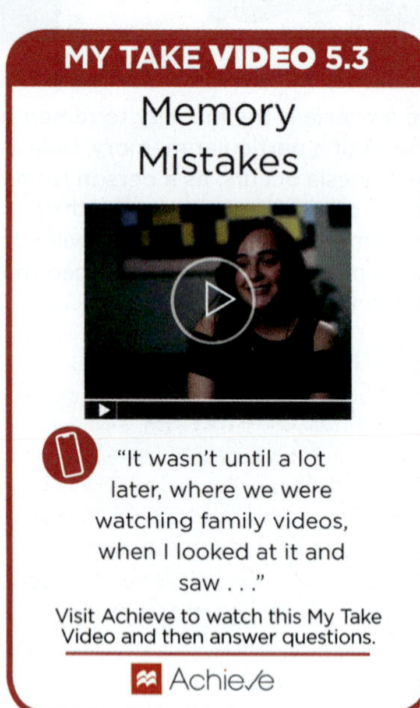

MY TAKE VIDEO 5.3
Memory Mistakes
"It wasn't until a lot later, where we were watching family videos, when I looked at it and saw . . ."
Visit Achieve to watch this My Take Video and then answer questions.
Achieve

The story of the wrongful conviction and imprisonment of Clarence Elkins illustrates how unreliable eyewitness testimony can be (Neuschatz et al., 2007). Elkins was convicted of killing his mother-in-law and raping and beating his 6-year-old niece in 1998. There was no physical evidence to connect Elkins to the crime. His conviction was based on the testimony of the niece, who supposedly witnessed Elkins murdering his mother-in-law and of course experienced her own traumatic events firsthand. After his sentencing, Elkins continued to claim his innocence. As a jail inmate, Elkins got a hold of a cigarette butt discarded by a fellow inmate, Earl Mann. At the time of the attack, Mann had been living next door to Elkins, and Mann was a convicted sex offender. DNA evidence from the cigarette butt matched evidence from the crime scene. Mann, not Elkins, was the murderer. Elkins was exonerated, but not before he spent 7 years in prison, largely because of eyewitness testimony tainted with misinformation. Elkins's case resembles many others overturned by the Innocence Project, an organization that since 1992 has used DNA evidence to free hundreds of people who have been wrongly convicted of serious crimes. In many of these cases, misinformed eyewitness testimony contributed to the original, mistaken conviction (Medwed, 2007).

Research suggests that young children (like my son, from the example a few paragraphs ago) are particularly suggestible to new information as they recall their memories of events (Melnyk et al., 2007). At the other end of the age spectrum, elderly adults are particularly prone to making memory errors when they serve as eyewitnesses (LaVoie et al., 2007), which can cause concern when they offer their version of events during a courtroom trial. People with psychological disorders such as schizophrenia, posttraumatic stress disorder, and alcohol abuse are also especially prone to memory inaccuracies (Soraci et al., 2007). Also, emotional arousal matters: people in a highly emotional state tend to get the central feature of the memory right but often forget or distort the peripheral details (Reisberg & Heuer, 2004, 2007). For example, a witness to an assault may accurately describe the type of weapon used (gun, knife, etc.), but inaccurately describe the clothing or eye color of the attacker.

The Misinformation Effect and Fake News. More recently, the increasing presence of "fake news" has prompted some researchers to explore how much that type of misinformation can contribute to memory mistakes. Some researchers have focused on "push polls" as a specific technique for fake news. Push polls are a deceptive way of spreading information in the form of a poll or survey. When the push poll is spreading misinformation, the person answering the questions may assume the poll is a genuine attempt to gather their opinion, but the real purpose of the poll is to suggest (or "push") the falsehoods within the questions themselves.

For example, supporters of Candidate A in an upcoming election might conduct a push poll in which they ask "If Candidate B was arrested for child abuse, how would that affect your likelihood to vote for them?" despite the fact that there's no reason for this speculation about Candidate B. In one study, researchers conducted push polls on participants who were later (in some cases, many days later) asked if they remembered a fake news story (which the researchers had since fabricated) that corresponded with the falsehood. Results showed that indeed, those who had participated in the push poll were much more likely to mistakenly "remember" a fake news story than those who had not (Murphy et al., 2021).

A similar study was conducted in the United Kingdom, at a time when the population was bitterly divided on the Brexit issue (whether the UK should leave or remain in the European Union). Over 40% of the more than 1000 participants mistakenly "remembered" a fake news story about Brexit. Perhaps more importantly, the odds of such a false memory were especially high when the fake news story matched with the participants' beliefs (Greene et al., 2021).

Types of Memory Mistakes. Psychologists have identified a number of specific kinds of memory mistakes based on the misinformation effect. For example, the *Moses illusion* is named after this famous question: how many animals of each kind did Moses take on the ark? Most people recall that Moses took two of each animal, but that's wrong – not the number, but the person. In the famous biblical story it was Noah, not Moses, who took animals on the ark, but the incorrect information embedded in the question might convince you otherwise (Park & Reder, 2004).

The *orientation illusion* occurs when you remember the orientation or other physical attributes of an item incorrectly (**Figure 5.9**). For example, when asked to remember what common coins look like, people often remember the heads facing the wrong direction or other features on the wrong part of the coin (Jones & Martin, 2004).

FIGURE 5.9 Orientation Illusion. One common memory mistake is the orientation illusion, in which people mistakenly remember which direction something faces. Consider coins, for example: although George Washington faces left on the quarter, people sometimes mistakenly remember him facing right (Rubin & Kontis, 1983).

The *association illusion* works this way: you remember things associated with what you saw or heard, even though you did not actually see or hear those particular things. In studies of the association illusion, researchers typically present a list of words that all relate to a target word, but the target word itself is intentionally left out. For example, the list of words may include *cola, drink, pop, bubbles, bottle, can, cup, machine, beverage* – all words that relate to *soda*, but *soda* is not on the list. When the participants did a free recall of the list – just remembering any words they could, in any order – they recalled the target word 55% of the time. When they did a recognition task – saw words one by one, and replied yes or no about whether they were on the list – they said yes to the target word 57% of the time (Roediger & Gallo, 2004). These are remarkably high recall rates when you consider that the word being remembered was not actually on the list. The lesson of the association illusion is this: your memory may have a hard time distinguishing between what you actually witnessed and closely associated things that you didn't witness. These and other common memory mistakes are summarized in **Table 5.4**.

Such memory distortion can be small and simple, like falsely remembering a word that was not actually presented among a list of related words, but it can also be much bigger and more elaborate – a memory mistake called *rich false memory*

TABLE 5.4: Common Memory Mistakes

MEMORY MISTAKE	DESCRIPTION	EXAMPLE
Moses illusion	Allowing mistaken information in the question or prompt to influence the memory	When asked, "In which part of New York did Drake grow up?" you "remember" that Drake grew up in Brooklyn, but he actually grew up in Toronto.
Orientation illusion	Remembering aspects of spatial orientation, such as what direction something faces	When asked what side the face on a penny or nickel looks toward, you mistakenly say left for penny and right for nickel.
Associative illusion	Remembering things that you never actually saw or heard because you saw or heard similar things	After hearing a word list containing *sandals, sneakers, high heels, clogs, cleats, pumps,* and *boots*, you mistakenly "remember" hearing the word *shoe*.
Labeling effects	Remembering things differently because of the labels others use for them	After watching a video of a car accident, you are likely to report higher speeds if asked, "How fast were they going when they *smashed into* each other?" rather than "How fast were they going when they *made contact with* each other?"
Hindsight bias	Remembering your predictions incorrectly after the outcome is determined	After the basketball season ends, you mistakenly remember correctly predicting the team that won the championship, when you really predicted another team to win it.

Information from Park and Reder (2004), Jones and Martin (2004), Roediger and Gallo (2004), Pohl (2004a, b), and Loftus and Palmer (1974).

(Loftus, 2005). In the 1990s, research by Elizabeth Loftus and others focused on news stories featuring court cases in which people claimed to have been abused or otherwise victimized by family members or friends. In some cases, their stories were lengthy and detailed but either highly unlikely or impossible based on the available evidence (Loftus & Cahill, 2007).

For example, some people claimed to have been abused for long periods of time by large numbers of people who were Satanic cult members and murdered hundreds of young children. However, no evidence of these Satanic cults was found, nor was there evidence of any murdered children to corroborate their stories. Many of these accusers later retracted their stories. In many cases, they were found to have "recovered" these formerly "repressed memories" when in therapy with clinicians who convinced the clients that they were true by strongly suggesting that the events took place. In other words, these false memories were aided by input from others who were attempting to shape the client's thinking (Bottoms et al., 1996; Goodman et al., 2007). Stories like these, which expose many "repressed memories" to be exaggerated, fabricated, or the results of persuasion by other people, may contribute to the fact that memory experts hold skeptical views about the validity of these "repressed memories" (Patihis et al., 2021).

In one study related to this false memory phenomenon, Loftus gave participants descriptions of events that actually happened to them as children (as collected from participants' family members), but she mixed in one false story too. The false story went something like this: "One time, when you were 5 or 6 years old, you got lost in a shopping mall. You got very upset, but an elderly woman stopped to help you, and she brought you back to us." A quarter of the participants mistakenly "remembered" (completely or partially) this story happening to them, even though their family members had previously confirmed to Loftus that it never did (Loftus & Pickrell, 1995)! Similar studies followed, with similar percentages of people mistakenly "remembering" being attacked by animals or being pulled out of the water by a lifeguard despite the fact that these events never took place (Heaps & Nash, 2001; Porter et al., 1999).

Other researchers have used edited photos for the same effect. After confirming with participants' family members that they had never been on a hot air balloon as a child, the researchers essentially Photoshopped a childhood image of the participant onto a hot air balloon background. They then interviewed the participants, on three occasions, about the experience. Most participants couldn't remember the hot air balloon ride at first, but about half mistakenly "remembered" it either fully or partially by the third interview. A few participants even included details in their false recollections: "basically for $10 or something you could go up in a hot air balloon and go up about 20 odd meters" (Wade et al., 2002, p. 600). It is noteworthy that the researchers in these studies were actively encouraging the participants to remember all they could about the event, which illustrates that false memories can be the product of people's suggestible memory suggestibility and the "nudges" they receive from other people to recall certain things in a certain way.

One study illustrated how false memories can be created by showing participants a Photoshopped image of the participant as a child on a hot air balloon ride. (The participants did not know that their family members had told the researchers no such event ever happened.) About half of the participants "remembered" this hot air balloon ride—that never happened—after being interviewed about it several times. Some even recalled specific details (Wade et al., 2002). Data from Using false photographs to create false childhood memories. Wade, Garry, Read, and Undsay. Psychonomlc Bulletin & Review 2002, Springer.

Research on false and recovered or repressed memory, like the kind Elizabeth Loftus conducted, has slowed in recent years. However, there continues to be at least some interest in the related topic of *motivated forgetting*, or the notion that some experiences may be so unpleasant or traumatic that people choose, perhaps unconsciously, to forget them. One study found that people who cheated at a game had "forgotten" the rules they broke—a convenient slip, considering that if they remembered the rules, they'd feel more guilty (Shu et al., 2011). Some researchers have speculated that motivated forgetting makes evolutionary sense, particularly if the forgotten event is a major betrayal by a loved one, like a child who has been abused by a parent. In such a situation, an accurate memory of the abuse could prompt the child to confront or run away from the parent, either of which could threaten the child's well-being or survival. Wiping the abuse from memory, although it leaves the child with an unrealistic view of the parent, might actually serve the child's best interests (DePrince et al., 2012).

Memory and Psychological Disorders

Some psychological disorders are largely defined by memory problems. *Dissociative amnesia* is essentially the clinical name for the amnesia that we have already discussed, with an emphasis on the loss of autobiographical information. *Major neurocognitive disorder* and *mild neurocognitive disorder*, which can stem from Alzheimer's disease, brain injury, excessive substance use, and various medical illnesses, are also characterized by serious memory problems (American Psychological Association, 2013a; Becker & Overman, 2002). These memory-based disorders can worsen other psychological problems as well. Imagine how your life might be affected if your memory became significantly impaired. You might experience bouts of sadness about your memory difficulties or nervousness about your ability to function at school, at work, and in relationships. Your self-image might worsen as you begin to see yourself as incompetent. Indeed, the frequency of depression and anxiety disorders increases when people experience significant memory disorders (Tate, 2002).

Anxiety, Depression, and Memory. Memory can also play an important role in more common psychological problems in which memory problems are not the defining symptoms (Burt et al., 1995). For example, many studies have linked anxiety to memory problems. Specifically, these studies find that working memory capacity is often quite low in people high in anxiety. This is true especially when the material to be remembered is verbal (as opposed to visual) and they feel pressure to respond quickly (Crowe et al., 2007; Hayes et al., 2008; Ikeda et al., 1996; Leigh & Hirsch, 2011; Visu-Petra et al., 2011). The attention that the anxiety demands is attention that the person can't devote to working memory, so distraction takes place (Rapee, 1993; Visu-Petra et al., 2013). This finding is particularly important for anxious kids, because working memory is crucial to learning and school performance (Alloway & Gathercole, 2005; Alloway et al., 2005; Dehn, 2008; Gathercole et al., 2004; Swanson & Berninger, 1996).

Interestingly, people with anxiety disorders (generalized anxiety disorder and phobias, among others) tend to remember the events of their lives rather accurately. Their memories do not center on anxiety, even though their current feelings might (MacLeod & Mathews, 2004). The story is different for people with depression, however. Numerous studies indicate that people in depressed moods remember depressing things (Dalgleish & Cox, 2002; Hertel, 2004; Urban et al., 2018). For example, when presented with a long list of words that includes some that suggest positive feelings (*happy, smile, delighted,* etc.) and some that suggest negative feelings (*miserable, cry, gloomy,* etc.), people in depressed moods recalled significantly more negative than positive words, including some negative words that weren't even on the list (Bower, 1981; Howe & Malone, 2011; Watkins et al., 1996). People suffering from depression tend to recall their unfortunate experiences and emotions frequently but fail to recall the good stuff (Hertel, 2004; Watkins et al., 1992; Wenzlaff et al., 2002). Psychologists call this tendency *rumination*, and it can be a difficult habit to break, keeping some people locked into a melancholy mindset for extended periods (Connolly & Alloy, 2018; Nolen-Hoeksema, 2000).

A meta-analysis of this relationship between memory and depression confirms that clinically depressed people remember depressing things disproportionately (Matt et al., 1992). Some researchers have even suggested that therapy for depression should include deliberate attempts to recall more positive memories (Josephson, 1996; Rusting & DeHart, 2000; Werner-Seidler et al., 2017).

tommaso79/Shutterstock

Memory can play an important role in psychological disorders. For instance, people who are depressed tend to ruminate about their most unfortunate past moments.

PTSD and Memory. Posttraumatic stress disorder (PTSD) is another psychological disorder in which memory plays a prominent role. Of course, in some cases, traumatic events can disrupt memory (Levin & Hanten, 2002). But more typically, people with PTSD remember too much, too often. In other words, they are tormented by **involuntary memory**: spontaneous retrieval of information in the absence of any intention to retrieve it. For example, a person who witnessed a murder might rehear the bang of the gun, or a survivor of a serious traffic accident might re-see the oncoming car months afterward, even though neither person has any desire to recall these events. Sometimes these involuntary memories are triggered by external cues like sights or sounds, or internal cues like thoughts or feelings, but other times they just seem to pop into the sufferer's head (Bernsten, 1996, 2001; Helstrup et al., 2007; Kvavilashvili & Mandler, 2004; Mace, 2004; Williams & Moulds, 2010). In PTSD, these memories are often experienced as flashbacks, as they take the person, at least in their mind, right back to the traumatic event even though they would strongly prefer to avoid it. It's one thing to experience an assault, robbery, accident, or other trauma in the first place, but to relive it again and again through such vivid memory can turn a one-time event into an extended nightmare. Sadly, some people suffering from PTSD have little control over when the memory interrupts their daily life (Grey & Holmes, 2008; Holmes et al., 2005; Iyadurai et al., 2019; Krans et al., 2010).

Schizophrenia and Memory. Research has also found significant memory impairment in people with schizophrenia, a debilitating disorder featuring hallucinations, delusions, and other symptoms that indicate a detachment from reality (Aleman et al., 1999; Danion et al., 2004). Specifically, people with schizophrenia show remarkably low levels of episodic memory and long-term memory and somewhat low levels of short-term memory. However, procedural memory and implicit memory typically remain at normal levels (Aleman et al., 1999; Bazin & Perruchet, 1996; Brebion et al., 1997; McKenna et al., 2000). So people with schizophrenia are more likely to remember *how* to do things (like button up a jacket), but less likely to remember *what* they did (like where they left their jacket). These kinds of memory deficits can cause significant day-to-day problems for these individuals. In one study, caregivers of schizophrenics completed a questionnaire that asked about forgetfulness and daily functioning, with questions like "Did they forget where things are normally kept or look for things in the wrong places?" These caregivers reported rates much higher than those found for people without schizophrenia, and similar to those found in people with brain damage due to strokes (McKenna et al., 2002).

Memory Problems and COVID-19

Researchers have begun to explore memory problems related to the COVID-19 pandemic. Some of those studies focus on memory and social distancing. In one study, researchers found a positive correlation between working memory capacity and the likelihood of social distancing — that is, people with higher working memory capacity were more likely to socially distance (Xie et al., 2020). In another study, researchers found that people who did socially distance — especially those who experienced high levels of loneliness as a result — were more likely than others to experience memory-related problems after about a month (Zhang et al., 2020).

Memory problems can also increase after being infected with COVID-19. Specifically, one study found that 8 months after testing positive, 11% of people reported that they had experienced memory problems, compared to just 4% of people who had never tested positive (Søraas et al., 2021).

A final issue connecting COVID-19 and memory involves contact tracing, which is the process of figuring out how a person became infected by asking them to remember any recent interactions with specific people (contacts). The key word there is *remember*. Problems with remembering such as inaccuracy, incompleteness, distortion, and suggestibility can all limit the extent to which contact tracing is successful (Garry et al., 2021).

involuntary memory
The spontaneous retrieval of information in the absence of any intention to retrieve it.

CHECK YOUR LEARNING:

5.23 What is amnesia?

5.24 What is the difference between retrograde amnesia and anterograde amnesia?

5.25 What is the misinformation effect, and what kinds of memory mistakes can it produce?

5.26 How do anxiety, depression, PTSD, and schizophrenia each involve memory?

5.27 How can COVID-19 contribute to memory problems?

To check your understanding of these questions, click show the answers or refer to the answers in the Chapter Summary.

CHAPTER SUMMARY

Defining Memory

5.1 Memory is the process of taking in information, saving it over time, and retrieving it later.

5.2 Memories define each individual as a unique person.

5.3 Research on memory excellence shows that some people are born with the ability to remember nearly everything and that other people can train their mind to do amazing memory tasks as well.

The Three Steps of Memory

5.4 The information processing model of memory involves three steps: encoding, storage, and retrieval.

5.5 Encoding is entering information into memory. It depends on sensory memory, in which the senses take in and very briefly hold information.

5.6 Echoic memory is auditory sensory memory, and iconic memory is visual sensory memory.

5.7 The likelihood that information gets encoded depends upon how deep the level of processing is. That depth can be enhanced by effortful processing such as chunking and rehearsal.

5.8 When encoding takes place, long-term potentiation occurs, which is an increase in connectivity between neurons that form the biological basis of memory.

5.9 Storage is retaining information in memory. It occurs in short-term (or working) memory and long-term memory.

5.10 Retrieval is pulling information out of memory. It happens in two ways: recognition, in which there is comparison to external information, and recall, in which there is not.

5.11 Retrieval cues are reminders that facilitate retrieval of information from memory.

5.12 Due to encoding specificity, memories are easier to retrieve when there is similar contextual information present. Because of priming, recent experiences create an increased likelihood of recalling particular memories.

Types of Memory

5.13 Explicit memory is memory of which one is consciously aware.

5.14 There are two basic types of explicit memory: semantic memory and episodic memory. Semantic memory consists of facts, figures, word meanings, and other general information, while episodic memory consists of personal firsthand experiences.

5.15 Implicit memory is memory of which one is not consciously aware.

5.16 Procedural memory is a type of implicit memory consisting of how to perform tasks that one does automatically.

What Affects Memory?

5.17 Decay is the dwindling or loss of information from memory due to the passing of time.

5.18 The ability to remember a particular piece of information depends on its context. Surrounding information can interfere with remembering the target information.

5.19 Retroactive interference is the difficulty remembering older information that is caused by newer information. Proactive interference is the difficulty remembering newer information that is caused by older information.

5.20 The primacy effect is the tendency to remember the first items in a series particularly well, while the recency effect is the tendency to remember the last items in a series particularly well.

5.21 A memory that arouses powerful feelings is especially likely to be recalled and is known as a flashbulb memory.

5.22 Three ways to improve one's memory are mnemonics, spacing apart study sessions, and getting enough sleep.

Memory Problems

5.23 Psychologists define amnesia as the inability to remember some or all information, either temporarily or permanently.

5.24 Retrograde amnesia is the inability to recall information acquired before a certain point in time, while anterograde amnesia is the inability to form new memories after a certain point in time.

5.25 The misinformation effect is the tendency of false or misleading information presented after the fact to become mistakenly incorporated into memory. The different types of memory mistakes based on the misinformation effect include the orientation illusion, the association illusion, and rich false memory.

5.26 Anxiety, depression, PTSD, and schizophrenia each impair memory in ways that are particular to the specific psychological disorder.

5.27 COVID-19 can contribute to memory problems in several ways. Infections can increase the likelihood of memory problems; social distancing can be less likely in people with limited working memory capacity; and imperfect memory for social interactions can hinder contact tracing.

KEY TERMS

memory, p. 137
information processing model, p. 138
encoding, p. 139
sensory memory, p. 139
echoic memory, p. 139
iconic memory, p. 140
level of processing, p. 140
chunking, p. 141
rehearsal, p. 141
maintenance rehearsal, p. 142
elaborative rehearsal, p. 142
long-term potentiation, p. 142
storage, p. 144
short-term memory, p. 144
long-term memory, p. 144
working memory, p. 146
automatic processing, p. 147
retrieval, p. 147
recall, p. 147
recognition, p. 147
retrieval cues, p. 148
encoding specificity, p. 148
priming, p. 149
explicit memory, p. 151
semantic memory, p. 151
episodic memory, p. 151
implicit memory, p. 152
procedural memory, p. 152
decay, p. 153
retroactive interference, p. 153
proactive interference, p. 153
serial position effect, p. 154
primacy effect, p. 154
recency effect, p. 154
flashbulb memory, p. 155
mnemonic, p. 157
spacing effect, p. 158
amnesia, p. 161
retrograde amnesia, p. 161
anterograde amnesia, p. 162
source amnesia, p. 163
misinformation effect, p. 163
involuntary memory, p. 168

SELF-ASSESSMENT

1. According to the information processing model, the three steps of memory are _____.
   a. encoding, processing, and storage
   b. encoding, storage, and retrieval
   c. processing, retrieval, and forgetting
   d. chunking, short-term memory, and recall

2. _____ _____ is an early part of the memory process in which the senses take in and very briefly hold information.

3. Level of processing refers to _____.
   a. how severe a case of amnesia is
   b. how strongly certain contextual stimuli may prime recall of a memory
   c. how many numbers a person can recall in a particular order
   d. how deeply and meaningfully information is thought about

4. _____ _____ is the increased connectivity between simultaneously stimulated neurons that form the biological basis of memory.

5. _____ is grouping pieces of information together in a meaningful way to enhance memory.
   a. Priming
   b. Recognition
   c. Recall
   d. Chunking

6. A group of students take an exam in the same room where they studied for it. The match between where they learned the information and where they remember it is called _____ _____.
   a. semantic memory
   b. episodic memory
   c. encoding specificity
   d. implicit memory

7. Jamia, a server at a restaurant, has a problem remembering older information that is caused by receiving newer information. Specifically, when a customer asks her for something, it causes her to forget what the previous customer asked for. Jamia is experiencing _____ _____.
   a. proactive interference
   b. retroactive interference
   c. the spacing effect
   d. the misinformation effect

8. A _____ _____ is a distinctively clear and vivid memory of an emotionally charged and novel event.

9. After Tony injured his head in a car accident, he could remember events from before the accident but couldn't create memories of events after the accident. Tony suffered from _____ _____, the inability to form new memories after a certain point in time.
   a. retrograde amnesia
   b. anterograde amnesia
   c. source amnesia
   d. encoding specificity

10. _____ _____ is the spontaneous retrieval of information without any intention to retrieve it.
   a. Involuntary memory
   b. Semantic memory
   c. Proactive interference
   d. Long-term memory

To check your understanding of these questions, click show the answers in the e-book or refer to the answers in Appendix B.

Research shows quizzing is a highly effective learning tool. Continue quizzing yourself using LearningCurve, the system that adapts to *your* learning.

WHAT'S YOUR TAKE?

I was cleaning out the basement when I came across an old photo: my basketball team from kindergarten. I hadn't seen that photo, or thought about that team, in decades. But that photo served as a retrieval cue, and memories came flooding back. I remembered how itchy the uniforms were. I remembered how impossibly high the basket seemed, and how big and heavy the ball felt in my little 6-year-old hands. I remembered the sound of parents erupting with cheers on the rare occasion one of us made a basket during a game. I even remembered the taste of the basketball-shaped cake we got at our end-of-the-season party.

How about you? Has a particular retrieval cue — a particular sight, sound, smell, or taste from your past — ever opened a door to a world of memories you had otherwise tucked away?

SHOW ME MORE

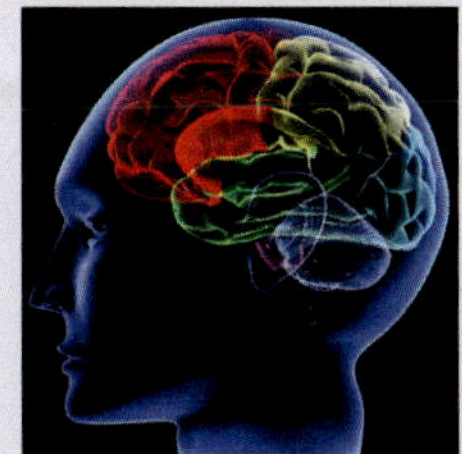

5.1 Moonwalking with Einstein

http://tiny.cc/showmemore2e

In this video, author Joshua Foer explains how he wrote a book about memory championship competitions and ultimately learned their techniques to become a memory champion himself.

Yakobchuk Vasyl/Shutterstock

This video is hosted by a third-party Web site (source). For accessible content requests, please reach out to the publisher of that site.

5.2 Sports Head Injuries and Memory Loss

This video illustrates the potential dangers of sports head injuries by telling the story of high school soccer player Sydney Urzendowski.

John Patriquin/Portland Press Herald/Getty Images

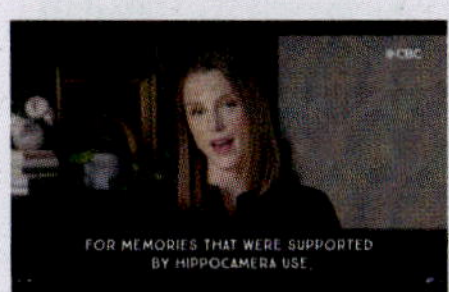

5.3 An App that Mimics the Hippocampus to Help Memory Functions

This video explains the role of the hippocampus in memory and describes the development of a new app, HippoCamera, intended to mimic what the hippocampus struggles to do in people with memory problems.

Courtesy Second Peninsula

5.4 My Psychology Podcast

This podcast episode features the author of this textbook, psychologist Andy Pomerantz, speaking with other instructors of introductory psychology courses about the most important and interesting concepts in this chapter.

Macmillan Learning

6 Learning

Dubova/Shutterstock

CHAPTER OUTLINE

As you walk into the dentist's office, that unique dentist-office smell hits you. You immediately react with a twinge of anxiety and a quickened heartbeat. You can hear the sound of the dentist's drill as you check in at the front desk, which immediately raises your anxiety level and your heart rate.

Soon, they call your name, and you settle into the dentist's chair. You do a few things to make yourself more calm and comfortable before the dentist starts working on your teeth. You ask for a quick description of everything the dentist will do and how long it will take, which the dentist happily provides. You ask if you can wear earbuds, and when the dentist says yes, you put them in and press play on your favorite playlist. You close your eyes and take intentional, deep breaths as the dentist begins their work, which turns out to be much less scary than you had imagined.

Your behaviors during this visit to the dentist display your remarkable ability to learn from experience. Think about it: Why did your heart rate immediately jump and your anxiety immediately kick in as soon as you sensed the smell and sound of the dentist's office? How did you know that asking the dentist those questions, distracting yourself with earbuds, and breathing deeply would be so helpful?

The answer to all of these questions is *learning.* When psychologists use this term, they don't typically mean the kind of deliberate learning that happens in schools through reading textbooks or attending lectures. Instead, we use *learning* to refer to the process by which the events of everyday life influence future behavior. This kind of learning can happen when we notice that certain things occur in tandem, so we associate them with each other — like the smell or sound of the dentist's office and the fear or pain those sensations can often predict. Or it can happen when we notice that certain actions bring about certain consequences — like asking questions, using earbuds, and breathing deeply brought about a reduction in your anxiety. These are behaviors you learned through life experience.

The same general rules that explain the way animals learn explain the way humans learn, too. This similarity enables psychologists to conduct research on animals, as well as humans, to better understand the learning process. That learning research forms the foundation of this chapter, which emphasizes classical conditioning, operant conditioning, and observational learning, as well as biological and cognitive influences on learning.

What Is Learning?

YOU WILL LEARN:

6.1 how psychologists define learning.

6.2 how learning fits into the nature–nurture debate.

6.3 that learning occurs universally across species.

Learning is the process by which life experience causes change in the behavior or thinking of an organism. You adjust your behavior accordingly as consequences happen to you, especially those that result from your own actions. Consider Jenny, a 9-year-old girl with two uncles. Uncle Joe always takes Jenny out for ice cream in his red pickup truck. Now, whenever Jenny sees a red pickup truck coming down her street, she gets excited. Her Uncle Carl doesn't take Jenny out for ice cream when he comes over, but Jenny has noticed something else – whenever she asks to play basketball with Uncle Carl, he quickly and happily says yes. Now she asks him to shoot hoops as soon as he arrives.

In both of these situations, Jenny has *learned* what goes with what. Through her own experience, she has learned to associate two things that occur together, or a behavior that is followed by a consequence. And Jenny remembers what she has learned about each uncle. What you've learned tends to endure unless new experiences come along to change it.

Learning is the essence of the nurture side of the nature–nurture debate that surrounds all of human behavior. On the nature side of the argument is *maturation*, which causes some behaviors to take place because the person's or animal's biological clock says it's time for them. For example, potty training works with most kids at age 2 or 3 – but not earlier – because younger children simply don't have the mental or physical capabilities to learn this behavior, no matter the efforts of their parents. Dating follows a similar pattern: the main reason it emerges in the teenage years – and not, say, around kindergarten – is puberty. Of course, maturation and learning (that is, nature and nurture) often interact. For example, when the toddler starts potty training or when the teenager starts to date, positive experiences will accelerate the process and negative experiences will delay it.

So far, all of the examples have featured people, but don't let that mislead you: learning isn't unique to humans. All species learn. Consider the California sea slug (also known as California sea hare), which lives in the ocean off the west coast of the United States and Mexico. Researchers study the way this little animal learns because it learns through life experience, just as larger, more complex animals (including humans) do. For example, researchers poked one part of a sea slug's body and then immediately delivered electric shock to another part. When they tried it again later, the sea slug withdrew its second body part as soon as it felt the poke in its first body part, showing that it had learned from the earlier experience (Carew et al., 1983, 1981). In a separate study, researchers delivered electric shock when the sea slug allowed its gill to fall below a certain height. In these cases, the sea slug began keeping its gill raised high much longer than normal, which it apparently learned to do in order to avoid the shock (Hawkins et al., 2006).

Darren J. Bradley/Shutterstock.com

All species learn. Even the California sea slug, a biologically small, simple animal found in the Pacific Ocean, shows the ability to learn to avoid electric shock by behaving in particular ways in response to particular conditions.

As implied by the studies of the California sea slug, researchers who study learning don't make many distinctions between species. That's because the processes by which one species learns are basically the same for any other species (although there are some biological factors that make a difference – we'll discuss them later). For this reason, a lot of learning studies use animals as participants – often pigeons, rats, dogs, or cats with the assumption that the findings can be applied to humans too (Ator, 1991; Barad, 2005; Delgado et al., 2006).

DIVERSITY MATTERS

One pioneering researcher even studied the learning processes of insects, including bees, ants, and cockroaches. His name was Charles Henry Turner, and he was one of the first Black behavioral researchers in the United States. He published numerous studies on the ways insects learned in the late 1800s and early 1900s. And he accomplished this work despite the fact he spent the bulk of his career working as a high school

learning
The process by which life experience causes change in the behavior or thinking of an organism.

science teacher rather than a professor, perhaps because of the racial bias in colleges and universities at the time (Abramson, 2003, 2009; Turner, 1913).

Some of the earliest and most important learning research was stumbled upon by Ivan Pavlov in his work with dogs. Let's consider Pavlov's pioneering work next.

CHECK YOUR LEARNING:

6.1 How do psychologists define learning?

6.2 How does learning fit into the nature–nurture debate?

6.3 Is learning unique to humans?

To check your understanding of these questions, click show the answers or refer to the answers in the Chapter Summary.

Classical Conditioning

YOU WILL LEARN:

6.4 who Ivan Pavlov was and why his research with dogs was important.

6.5 what classical conditioning is and how it occurs in your life.

6.6 the components of classical conditioning.

6.7 how we generalize or discriminate what we learn.

6.8 how learned associations can be acquired and extinguished.

6.9 how multiple learned associations can be linked to produce higher-order conditioning.

6.10 how we learn vicariously through others' life experiences.

Ivan Pavlov, one of the most prominent figures in the history of psychology, was actually not a psychologist at all. He was a Russian medical researcher who in the late 1800s devoted his professional life to the study of the digestive system (Babkin, 1949; Todes, 2014; Windholz, 1997). Pavlov examined secretions made by various parts of the digestive tract, including saliva, which is produced in the mouth to start the digestive process. Pavlov was measuring the amount of saliva that dogs produced when food entered their mouths when he made an accidental discovery.

Pavlov's Accidental Discovery

Initially, everything in Pavlov's digestive research was going well. Pavlov had the dogs in their harnesses to keep them from running around. His assistants would bring the food to the dogs, and they would measure how much the dogs' mouths watered with the help of specialized equipment.

But a problem arose. After a few attempts, the dogs started salivating too soon. They weren't salivating *when* the food arrived, but *before* the food arrived. The dogs had picked up on cues that the food was on the way – perhaps the sight of the assistant who brought the food or the sound of the door opening as the assistant entered the room – and were salivating in *anticipation* of the food (Mook, 2004). At first, this problem of too-early mouth-watering frustrated and perplexed Pavlov. But soon, he realized this "problem" was actually a fascinating phenomenon that happened in various forms to dogs, to humans, and to other species as well. By the early 1900s, Pavlov decided to shift the direction of his research entirely to the study of what he called *conditioned reflexes* – a bold move for a researcher who had won the Nobel Prize for his studies of digestion (Fancher & Rutherford, 2012). His learning studies had a tremendous and lasting impact on the field of psychology and our understanding of behavior.

Sovfoto/UIG/Getty Images

Ivan Pavlov and his colleagues were conducting research on the digestive system in the late 1800s in Russia when they shifted their focus to learning and, more specifically, classical conditioning.

In his research, Pavlov focused on **classical conditioning**: a form of learning in which animals or people make a connection between two stimuli that have occurred together such that one predicts the other. Essentially, Pavlov designed studies that *intentionally* created the kind of anticipatory salivation in dogs that originally happened by accident (Pavlov, 1927, 1928). His first step was to identify a **neutral stimulus**: a stimulus that causes no response at all. He used sounds such as a bell for the neutral stimulus because its sound produced no salivation (or any other reaction) in the dog (**Figure 6.1**). Next, he identified food as the **unconditioned stimulus**: a stimulus that causes a response automatically, without any need for learning. Food certainly fits that description, since a dog instinctively salivates to food as a natural

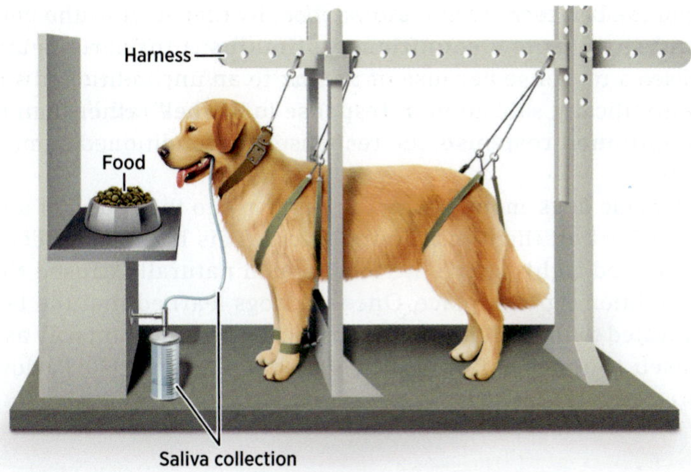
Harness
Food
Saliva collection

FIGURE 6.1 Pavlov's Classical Conditioning. For his research on classical conditioning, Pavlov placed dogs in an apparatus that allowed him to measure their salivation. At first, dogs salivated only when food was placed in front of them, but after Pavlov repeatedly paired the food with the sound of a bell, dogs eventually salivated to the sound of the bell by itself.
Sovfoto/UIG via Getty Images

biological reflex. That salivation in response to the food is the dog's **unconditioned response**: the automatic response to a stimulus that occurs naturally, without any need for learning.

Next, the conditioning happened. In other words, Pavlov paired the neutral stimulus and the unconditioned stimulus by ringing the bell and then immediately putting food by the dog's mouth (**Figure 6.2**). The dog eventually noticed the repetition of this sequence: *bell–food, bell–food, bell–food*. Soon enough, the dog salivated

Before Conditioning
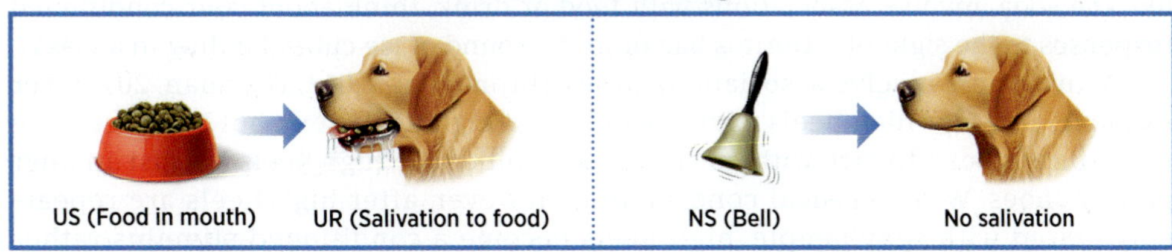
US (Food in mouth)
UR (Salivation to food)
NS (Bell)
No salivation
An unconditioned stimulus (US) produces an unconditioned response (UR).
A neutral stimulus (NS) produces no salivation response.
During Conditioning
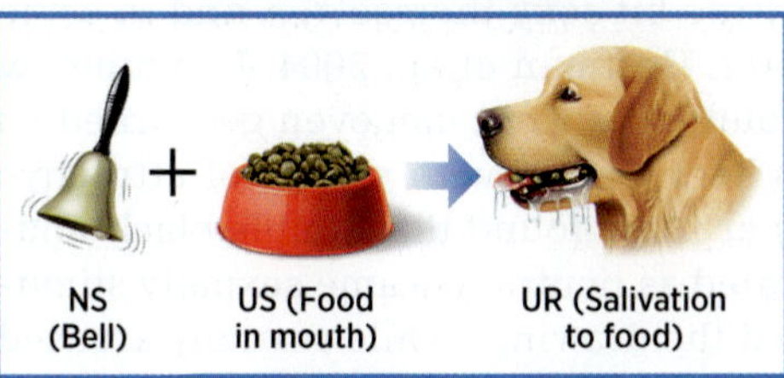
NS (Bell)
US (Food in mouth)
UR (Salivation to food)
The US is repeatedly presented just after the NS. The US continues to produce a UR.
After Conditioning
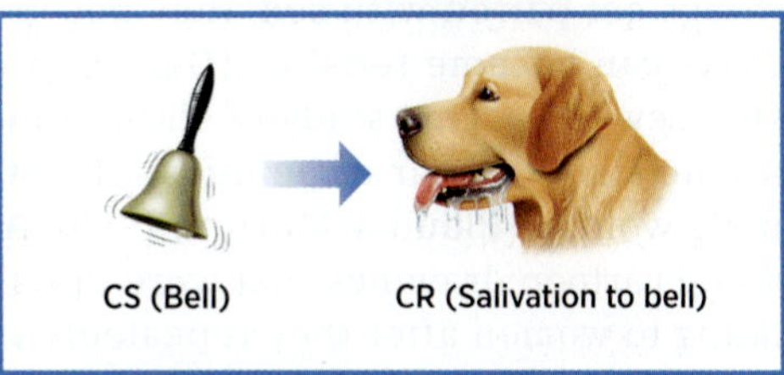
CS (Bell)
CR (Salivation to bell)
The previously neutral stimulus alone now produces a conditioned response (CR), thereby becoming a conditioned stimulus (CS).

FIGURE 6.2 Pavlov's Classical Conditioning Experiment. *Before* a dog undergoes any conditioning, it salivates to food. In other words, food is an unconditioned stimulus, and salivating to food is an unconditioned response. Before conditioning, the sound of a bell causes no response in the dog at all. *During* conditioning, the food and bell are presented at the same time over and over again (*bell–food, bell–food, bell–food . . .*). *After* conditioning, because of what the dog has learned by the repeated pairing of the bell and the food, the dog salivates to the bell alone (without food). The bell, which used to be a neutral stimulus, is now a conditioned stimulus. And salivating to the bell is now a conditioned response.

classical conditioning
A form of learning in which animals or people make a connection between two stimuli that have occurred together, such that one predicts the other.

neutral stimulus
A stimulus that causes no response at all.

unconditioned stimulus
A stimulus that causes a response automatically, without any need for learning.

unconditioned response
The automatic response to a stimulus that occurs naturally, without any need for learning.

to the sound of the bell *even if there was no food*. By this process, the bell transforms from a neutral stimulus to a **conditioned stimulus**: a formerly neutral stimulus that now causes a response because of its link to an unconditioned stimulus. This salivation — specifically, salivation in response to the bell rather than the food — is called the **conditioned response**: the response to a conditioned stimulus acquired through learning.

So Pavlov made dogs' mouths water in response to the sound of a bell that had absolutely no effect on them just hours before. This happened because the bell repeatedly sounded right before the food, which naturally caused the salivation before any conditioning took place. Once the dogs learned that the bell predicted food, they salivated to the bell just as automatically and involuntarily as they always had to food itself (Gottlieb & Begej, 2014; Kehoe & Macrae, 1998; Pavlov, 1927, 1928; Weiss, 2014).

That may happen to dogs in a lab study, but does it happen to people in the real world too?

Yes! Ever notice your mouth water when you hear the *pffst* of a soda can opening? It's the same phenomenon. Soda automatically makes your mouth water. It is an unlearned biological response to good-tasting liquids entering your mouth. In this case, soda is the unconditioned stimulus, and your salivation to soda is the unconditioned response. Over time, you have learned that the *pffst* sound is consistently followed by the cold, sweet sensation of the soda on your tongue. Just as Pavlov's dogs experienced *bell–food, bell–food, bell–food*, you have experienced *pffst–soda, pffst–soda, pffst–soda*. As a result, the *pffst* sound has transformed from a neutral stimulus (*pffst*) to a conditioned stimulus, and your salivation in response to the *pffst* sound is the conditioned response.

Other examples of classical conditioning are all around us. Many examples, like the soda, involve associations with food or drink; think about your conditioned responses to the sight of a Doritos bag or to the sound of ice cubes landing in a glass.

Many others involve associations to sex (Brom et al., 2014; Hoffman, 2017). For example, consider high heels. Many people find high heels sexy, but high heels are not naturally sexy. In fact, without classical conditioning, high heels are just another pair of shoes. With classical conditioning, however, after high heels are repeatedly paired with sexy people, high heels become a conditioned stimulus rather than a neutral stimulus. The same sexy-by-association description can be true for any number of sights (certain clothes), sounds (certain music), or smells (certain colognes or perfumes) (Brom et al., 2015; Hoffman et al., 2012, 2014). If these things get paired with sex, they become a little bit sexy themselves, and in some cases can become fetishes (Darcangelo, 2012; Hoffman et al., 2004; Lalumiere & Quinsey, 1998). One study of straight men found that some can even get turned on by the sight of a jar of pennies after it has been paired with photos of attractive nude women (Plaud & Martini, 1999). Another study found that simple black-and-white cartoon drawings that were initially rated as neutral became sexually stimulating to women after they repeatedly viewed the drawings while sexually aroused (Both et al., 2011).

Processes Related to Classical Conditioning

Once Pavlov established the basics of classical conditioning, he examined a variety of processes related to it so he could better understand exactly how it works (Babkin, 1949; Fancher & Rutherford, 2012; Windholz, 1997).

Generalization and Discrimination. For example, Pavlov noticed that a dog conditioned to salivate to a particular bell might also salivate to another bell as long as

conditioned stimulus
A formerly neutral stimulus that now causes a response because of its link to an unconditioned stimulus.

conditioned response
The response to a conditioned stimulus acquired through learning.

generalization
The learning process by which stimuli that are similar to the conditioned stimulus cause the same conditioned response.

discrimination
The learning process by which stimuli that are different from the conditioned stimulus fail to cause the same conditioned response.

FROM RESEARCH TO REAL LIFE

Classical Conditioning in Advertising

If Pavlov's dogs had money, they might have spent it on bells. That's quite odd, given that dogs are usually indifferent to bells. But Pavlov did such a good job pairing bells with food, which the dogs inherently liked, that he transformed bells from neutral to exciting. It's as if some of the thrill dogs naturally feel toward food rubbed off on the bell.

Advertisers do the same thing to us every day. They don't call it classical conditioning, though. They call it branding. Just as Pavlov did, they pair their product (which is originally pretty neutral to us) with something we inherently like or find exciting. With repetition, the product begins to take on the qualities of the well-liked, exciting person or thing with which it has been paired (Bergkvist & Zhou, 2016; De Houwer et al., 2001; Knoll & Matthes, 2017; Schachtman et al., 2011; Till & Priluck, 2000).

Dylan Buell/Getty Images

Icon Sports Wire/Corbis/Getty Images

Why does Nike pay millions of dollars to athletes like Giannis Antetokounmpo and Serena Williams? It's simple: classical conditioning. Nike knows that if it pairs its swoosh with exciting, successful athletes frequently enough, you'll learn to respond to the swoosh as exciting and successful too. This happens in much the same way that Pavlov's dogs learned to salivate to a sound that was originally neutral to them.

Let's consider Nike, with its iconic swoosh logo, as an example. This may be difficult to imagine, but there was a time early in your life when that swoosh meant absolutely nothing to you. It was just a random, meaningless shape, much as the bell was a random, meaningless sound to a dog entering Pavlov's lab for the first time. Over time, though, you saw the swoosh again and again. And Nike was very selective about who you saw it paired with: athletes like Michael Jordan, Pete Sampras, Michelle Wie, LeBron James, Roger Federer, Serena Williams, Carli Lloyd, Rory McIlroy, Maria Sharapova, Cristiano Ronaldo, Russell Westbrook, Giannis Antetokounmpo, Alex Morgan, Brooks Koepka, Nyjah Huston, and Rayssa Leal. In short, you saw the Nike swoosh paired over and over again with exciting and successful athletes. In time, some of that excitement and success rubbed off onto the swoosh, so that the swoosh itself carried those qualities.

If Pavlov had worked for Nike, he would have explained it this way: the athlete is the unconditioned stimulus, and your positive reaction to the athlete is the unconditioned response. Nike knows that you already have that reaction built in. Nike's strategy is to pair its swoosh with the athlete, so the swoosh (to which you are neutral at first) eventually becomes the conditioned stimulus. Your positive response to the swoosh is the conditioned response—the advertising equivalent of a dog salivating to a bell.

But I don't salivate when I see a Nike swoosh. I don't have any reaction at all.

Your response may not be as obvious as the dogs' response to the bell, but if you find yourself responding more positively to Nike shoes and clothes than you would to the same items without the swoosh—if you like them more, or would pay more money for them—you've been conditioned. Of course, the Nike swoosh is just one example. You may also have immediate reactions to shirts with the Polo Ralph Lauren or Hollister logo, purses with the Chanel logo, headphones with the Beats logo, or many other branded products.

the sound of the second bell was similar enough to the sound of the first one. In other words, the dog might exhibit **generalization**: the process by which stimuli that are similar to the conditioned stimulus cause the same conditioned response. On the other hand, if the dog detected that the second bell's sound was quite different from the first bell's sound, the dog would not salivate to the second bell at all. This non-response illustrates **discrimination**: the process by which stimuli that are different from the conditioned stimulus fail to cause the same conditioned response.

MY TAKE VIDEO 6.1
Classical Conditioning
"Classical conditioning was involved when I was working in the Marine Corps as a dog handler . . . "
Visit Achieve to watch this My Take Video and then answer questions.
Achieve

Generalization and discrimination are complementary processes. When generalization stops, discrimination begins (Brown, 1965; Wyrwicka, 2000). A classic study illustrates the extent to which animals can learn to discriminate between stimuli even when they are remarkably similar (**Figure 6.3**) (Shenger-Krestovnikova, 1921, as described in Gray, 1979, 1987). First, dogs were repeatedly shown a circle immediately before receiving food. As a result, the dogs began salivating to the sight of the circle. They were then shown an oval (taller than it was wide) immediately before receiving food, and as expected, salivated to that too. The dogs generalized what they learned about the circle to another figure that resembled a circle. The researchers then presented the circle and the oval many more times, but with an important difference: the circle was always followed by food, but the oval was never followed by food. The dogs soon learned to discriminate: they continued to salivate to the circle but stopped

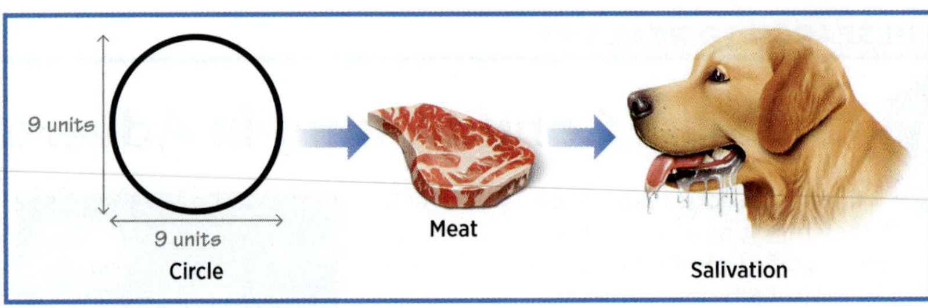

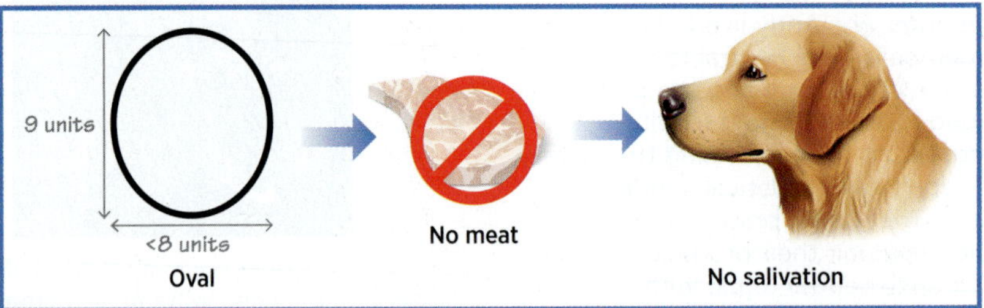

FIGURE 6.3 Generalization and Discrimination. In a classic study of generalization and discrimination, dogs learned to respond differently to very similar shapes (a circle and a nearly circular oval). Those two shapes served as meaningful predictors to the dogs: the circle meant that food was coming, but the oval did not (Shenger-Krestovnikova, 1921, as described in Gray, 1979, 1987).

salivating to the oval. Finally, the experimenters showed the dogs new ovals that were closer and closer to the shape of a circle. The dogs only began to salivate to the oval when the oval's height became very close to its width — specifically, when the height-to-width ratio was 9 to 8 — but not any sooner.

One of the most famous — and controversial — studies in the history of psychology attempted to explore the generalization and discrimination processes in classical conditioning. It was conducted by John B. Watson, a U.S. psychologist who promoted the results of Pavlov's studies in the United States in the early 1900s in the form of *behaviorism*, and his collaborator Rosalie Rayner (Benjafield, 2015; Buckley, 1989; Smirle, 2013; Watson, 1913, 1914). In his 1920 Little Albert study, Watson and Rayner worked with an 11-month-old baby boy. Sitting on the floor with him, they presented Albert with a variety of things to see and touch. Among them was a white rat, to which Albert showed no fear at all. In fact, he seemed rather curious about it, reaching his hand out to touch it. However, the next time they presented the white rat to Albert, Watson made a sudden, loud noise right behind Albert's head by whacking a steel bar with a hammer. Of course, Albert's natural reaction to the unexpected loud noise was fear, illustrated by his immediate startle response and crying. Watson then repeated the pairing — *rat–loud noise, rat–loud noise, rat–loud noise* — until he eventually presented the rat by itself, without the loud noise. As you might expect, Albert began to cry and show fear of the rat — the same one he had earlier not feared at all — thanks to the association it now had with the loud noise.

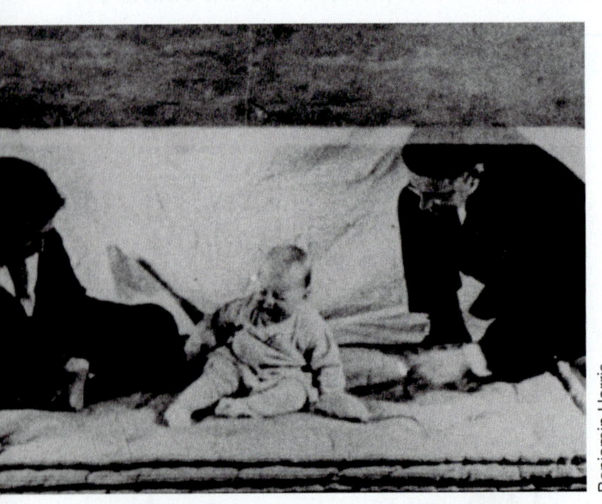

Benjamin Harris

In the Little Albert study (which would not be allowed by today's ethical standards), a baby boy was classically conditioned to fear one white fuzzy thing (a rat), and then he generalized his fear to other white fuzzy things. He discriminated, or did not feel fear of, things that were not white and fuzzy.

The Little Albert study was a vivid early example of classical conditioning, but the part most specifically relevant to the ideas of generalization and discrimination was that Albert began to fear objects similar to the white rat. Almost anything that Watson or Rayner presented that was white and furry like the rat made Albert cry, including a rabbit, a dog, a fur coat, and even (to some extent) Watson's own hair. However, items that did not resemble the white rat, such as toy blocks, caused no negative reaction in Albert at all. He reacted positively to them, just as he had before any conditioning took place. In other words, Albert showed generalization by fearing things that were furry and white (like the rat), and he showed discrimination by *not* fearing things that were *not* furry and white.

It is important to emphasize that the methods Watson and Rayner used would never be approved by the ethics committees that oversee psychological research

IT'S LIKE...

The Classic Study of Dogs Discriminating Between Shapes Is Like You Discriminating Between Logos

In the classic study of generalization and discrimination described earlier, dogs viewing circles and nearly circular ovals learned to discriminate between those two shapes only when the difference between the two stimuli became *meaningful* to them (Shenger-Krestovnikova, 1921, as described in Gray, 1979, 1987). At first, the dogs generalized. They salivated to both circles and ovals, presuming that since circles predicted food, ovals would too. Only when their experience taught them that circles predicted food, but ovals did not, did discrimination become important.

Our own discrimination behaviors are a lot like those of the dogs in that study. We discriminate more when the difference between items means a lot to us. Think for a minute about the number of times in a typical day that you make important distinctions between things that appear alike but have different meanings to you. Your backpack may look just like many other people's backpacks, but a quick check of its details (zippers, handles, pockets) makes it obvious which is yours. Your phone, your jacket, your shoes—they probably look a lot like many others', but you zoom in on the particulars of your items because they mean so much to you. When the difference between the items doesn't mean that much—two nearly identical empty carts at the grocery store, for example—you might not discriminate between them at all.

Erich Haefele/ullstein bild/Getty Images

KAREN BLEIER/AFP/Getty Images

Ekaterina Minaeva/Alamy

We often generalize what we've learned, but when slight differences between stimuli suggest big differences in terms of their meaning, we often discriminate instead. McDonald's, Monster, and M&M'S all share M logos, but those M's mean very different things—french fries versus energy drink versus candy—so discriminating between them happens easily.

The same rules of discrimination apply to your responses to the many logos you see every day. You associate each of them with a distinct product or place (at least you should, if the advertisers have done their jobs well). Some are similar to each other, but you will discriminate between them and react in different ways if they represent things that hold some meaning in your life. Consider the three logos of McDonald's, Monster, and M&M'S: all consist of nothing but the letter M, but you probably find yourself reacting differently to each. One M means fries, one M means energy drink, and one M means candy. At one point early in your life, none of them meant anything to you. Only when each logo was paired with the product it represents did you begin to learn what it meant and discriminate it from the other M's you encountered. •

today. Their treatment of Little Albert caused far too much harm to the participant to justify its use. In fact, this methodology has been the subject of significant controversy, not only for the way Watson and Rayner conditioned this infant but also for the fact that they did nothing afterward to try to reduce the fears they had created in him (Fridlund et al., 2012). Indeed, studies of this type sparked the movement toward putting *institutional review boards* in place to examine and possibly prohibit potentially risky or unethical studies before they can be conducted (Ceci et al., 1985; Rosnow et al., 1993).

Acquisition. In addition to generalization and discrimination, Pavlov identified other components of the classical conditioning process. For example, he recognized that there is a particular moment when the animal initially makes the link between the two stimuli (Gleeson, 1991). We call this **acquisition**: the point in the learning process at which the neutral stimulus becomes a conditioned stimulus because it causes the conditioned response. An important point regarding acquisition is that it is based on the ability of one stimulus to *predict* the other. Specifically, the conditioned stimulus (formerly the neutral stimulus) predicts the unconditioned stimulus. For Pavlov's dogs, the bell predicts the food. For Jenny (in the example earlier in this chapter), a red pickup truck predicts ice cream. As with any prediction, it makes sense only if the

acquisition
The point in the learning process at which the neutral stimulus becomes a conditioned stimulus because of its link to the conditioned response.

order of events is correct. If the sequence were reversed – if the dogs heard the bell *after* they received food or if Jenny saw her uncle's red pickup truck *after* she ate ice cream – then the neutral stimulus would not serve as a predictor, and conditioning would be far less likely to occur (Rescorla, 1988a, b).

For acquisition to take place, it is also important that the two stimuli happen within a very brief time of each other. If a long delay separates the neutral stimulus from the unconditioned stimulus, the two may never become associated with each other, so learning may never take place. Remember the study in which straight men became sexually turned on by a jar of pennies after it was paired with photos of attractive naked women? The researchers got those results by presenting the photos *immediately* after the pennies (Plaud & Martini, 1999). If they had allowed significant time to pass between the pennies and the photos, the men might not have made the link between the two, and the pennies would not have caused arousal. Similarly, imagine that you give your dog a new kind of food before the dog gets a painful shot at the vet's office. The dog is much more likely to associate the taste of the food with the pain of the shot if only 5 seconds, rather than 5 minutes or 5 hours, separate the two events.

Extinction. At the other end of the classical conditioning timeline from acquisition is **extinction**: the point in the learning process at which the conditioned stimulus no longer causes the conditioned response because it is no longer linked to the unconditioned stimulus. To study extinction, Pavlov took dogs that had been conditioned to salivate to the bell and then repeatedly presented the bell without food. Eventually, the bell no longer predicted food. In fact, the bell predicted the absence of food. As a result, the dogs eventually stopped salivating to the bell, so the conditioned response was extinguished.

Extinct sounds so permanent. Once extinction happens, is that learning gone forever?

Spontaneous Recovery. When extinction happens, that learning is not necessarily gone forever. The learned association between the two stimuli seems to be hidden rather than deleted entirely. We know this because of Pavlov's discovery of **spontaneous recovery**: after a temporary period of inactivity, the return of a conditioned response that had become extinct. After he extinguished the dog's conditioned response of salivating to the bell, Pavlov waited a while (several hours at least) and then presented the bell again. The dog salivated – not as much as it had when the bell–food connection was at its strongest, but certainly more than it had before the bell was ever paired with food. This response suggests that the dog, after the pause, is unsure whether the bell predicts food, as it did a while ago, or the absence of food, as it did more recently. As a result, the dog quickly reacquires the connection between bell and food, but less powerfully than the original connection (Falls, 1998; Pavlov, 1927, 1928; Rescorla, 1997; Vurbic & Bouton, 2014).

Spontaneous recovery happens to people too. Consider Ron, a 55-year-old man who just helped his elderly mother move into Autumn View, an assisted living facility. Ron programs his smartphone with customized rings, and he chose the old-fashioned *brrrringgg* of analog phones for Debbie, the director of Autumn View. The first few times Debbie called Ron, the news was alarming: his mother had fallen and broken her arm; his mother was having trouble breathing; his mother was experiencing chest pain. Soon, via classical conditioning, Ron was responding to Debbie's *brrrringgg* with panic before he even answered the phone. However, the next several calls from Debbie were not alarming at all. In fact, they were quite mundane: a call to let Ron know he had left his sunglasses there when he last visited, a reminder about an upcoming Mother's Day party at the facility, a minor question about the bill. Soon, the *brrrringgg* that had predicted panic was predicting, well, not much at all. At that point, Ron's

extinction
The point in the learning process at which the conditioned stimulus no longer causes the conditioned response because it is no longer linked to the unconditioned stimulus.

spontaneous recovery
After a temporary period of inactivity, the return of a conditioned response that had become extinct.

panic response to the *brrrringgg* became extinct. He reacted to that ring no differently than to any other ring. He then received no calls from Debbie for quite a while, until one morning he heard the *brrrringgg* for the first time in weeks. Ron reacted with mild anxiety – not the full-fledged panic he had felt after the first few calls from Debbie, but certainly more anxiety than he would have felt if he had never associated her ring with alarming news.

Higher-Order Conditioning. Pavlov also found that sometimes during classical conditioning, the number of associated stimuli is not limited to two. The stimuli can be linked in a chain of three or more. This is called **higher-order conditioning**: classical conditioning that involves three or more stimuli. (Higher-order conditioning is also known as *second-order conditioning* [Holland & Rescorla, 1975; Nairne & Rescorla, 1981; Rescorla, 1976, 1980].) Specifically, in higher-order conditioning, a conditioned stimulus from a previous learning process serves as an unconditioned stimulus for a new learning process, producing a new conditioned stimulus that causes the same conditioned response as the previous learning process.

To illustrate, let's think again about the way the *pffst* of opening a can of soda causes you to salivate. As a reminder, this response is caused by the fact that you have repeatedly heard the sound right before you taste the soda. That's a two-step process (*pffst–soda*), but could it be extended to three steps? In other words, is there another stimulus that might repeatedly happen right before (and predicts) the *pffst* sound? If you typically get your soda from a vending machine, the thud sound that the can makes as it falls to the machine's opening could be that third stimulus. In this three-step sequence – *thud–pffst–soda* – the thud predicts the *pffst*, and the *pffst* predicts the soda. With enough repetition, the thud produces a salivation response directly, even without hearing the *pffst*. The sequence could even be extended to four steps if we consider the sound of the dollar bill sliding into the slot at the beginning of the process, such that the sound of the bill sliding in causes salivation through a four-step *bill–thud–pffst–soda* connection.

Vicarious Conditioning. Classical conditioning can happen not only because of what happens directly to you, but also because of what you see happening to the people around you. We call this second type of classical conditioning **vicarious conditioning**: conditioning that takes place via observation of others' life experiences rather than one's own. Jenny – whose Uncle Joe takes her out for ice cream in his red pickup truck – has a close friend named Seiko. Jenny has told Seiko stories about how Uncle Joe takes her for ice cream in his red pickup truck, and in fact, once Seiko was at the ice cream shop herself when she saw Jenny and Uncle Joe pull up. On several occasions, Seiko has been playing with Jenny in her front yard when a red pickup truck drives by, and she has noticed Jenny's excitement when she sees it. Now, if Seiko happens to see a red pickup truck before Jenny does, she feels a twinge of excitement too – even though she's never actually been taken to an ice cream shop in a red pickup truck herself.

Classical Conditioning and Diversity. As we've discussed, classical conditioning is a remarkably universal phenomenon: it happens to all people (and all animals too). There is some evidence, though, that it happens differently within diverse groups.

DIVERSITY MATTERS

For example, one study that took place in both New York and Israel showed that people from different cultures showed different learning capabilities. As a bit of background info, in the Hebrew language (spoken by all Israeli participants), letters and words read from right to left, the opposite direction of English (spoken by all New York participants).

In this study, researchers sat the participants in front of a computer screen and asked them to learn seven simple pairings. Each pairing involved one letter spoken aloud at the same moment that a random shape appeared on screen for a couple of seconds. For example, in the English version, participants might hear a D and see a triangle, then hear a G and see an oval, then hear an R and see a square, and so on. The

higher-order conditioning
Classical conditioning that involves three or more stimuli.

vicarious conditioning
Conditioning that takes place via observation of others' life experiences rather than one's own.

Hebrew version was similar: participants might hear a ז and see a triangle, then hear a נ and see an oval, then hear a ר and see a square. Half of the English-speaking participants saw the shapes appear in a familiar, left-to-right way: the first shape appeared on the left edge of the screen for a couple of seconds, then the second shape appeared slightly to the right, then the third shape appeared slightly further to the right, and so on. But for the other half of the English-speaking participants, the shapes appeared in the unfamiliar, right-to-left way. The process was similar for the Hebrew-speaking participants: half saw the shapes appear in the familiar, right-to-left way, and the other half saw the shapes appear in the unfamiliar, left-to-right way.

Results showed that each group of participants learned the pairs better when they appeared in the way familiar to them. In other words, they were better at this classical conditioning task when it was consistent with their cultural experience (the direction they read and write). So, when classical conditioning happens to us, the degree to which it matches our previous experiences – cultural, linguistic, or otherwise – may impact the way or the extent to which the conditioning happens (McCrink & Shaki, 2016).

CHAPTER APP 6.1

Aqualert Water Intake Tracker and Reminder

The Aqualert app is designed to help you drink sufficient amounts of water throughout the day. You input your personal information (weight, sex, activity level) and the app helps you develop a schedule for how much water you should drink. At scheduled times, you hear alerts sent by the app that remind you to drink water. It also gives you feedback on your water consumption, allowing you to track your progress.

How does it APPly to your daily life? Think about the way Pavlov's dogs learned through *classical conditioning* to salivate to the sound of a bell when it was followed by food. What do you think will happen if you use this app in which the sound of the alert is followed by water? Does some version of this classical conditioning already happen in your day-to-day life? In other words, have certain sounds (or sights or other stimuli) become predictors of certain foods or drinks?

How does it APPly to your understanding of psychology? There are four essential parts of classical conditioning for the Pavlov bell-food studies: the *unconditioned stimulus*, the *unconditioned response*, the *conditioned stimulus*, and the *conditioned response*. Can you identify those four parts of classical conditioning from the experience you would have with this app?

To learn more about this app or to download it to your phone, you can search for "Aqualert" on Google, in the iPhone App store, or in the Google Play store.

Applying Classical Conditioning to Your Life

Classical conditioning is often an important part of efforts to improve people's lives. For example, psychologists use principles of classical conditioning to help clients overcome *phobias*. Phobias are strong, irrational fears of a particular thing or situation. Most psychologists believe that a phobia is produced by a learned pairing of a specific thing with an extremely unpleasant feeling, so the best way to overcome a phobia is to break that pairing (Duits et al., 2015; Fanselow & Sterlace, 2014; Hazlett-Stevens & Craske, 2008; Spiegler & Guevremont, 2010). For example, consider Teresa, a young woman with a phobia of buses, which developed after she was robbed on a bus. She learned to avoid buses through her experience of the bus–robbery pairing, which is problematic because she needs to take a bus to her job. Her psychologist, Dr. Sumule, helps Teresa overcome her phobia by encouraging her to gradually expose herself to buses – getting near them, then getting on them briefly, then staying on for longer periods. As she completes these steps, she repeatedly finds that the learned pairing of the bus with the robbery doesn't occur. In other words, Teresa experiences the bus without the fear of robbery. As she spends more time on buses *without* being robbed, the pairing of buses with robberies extinguishes and Teresa's phobia diminishes. (We will discuss phobias and their treatment in much more detail in Chapters 14 and 15.)

Classical conditioning can be used in the treatment of physical disorders too. The basic idea is that if a drug improves a disorder, what's paired with that drug can bring about similar improvement. It's just like Pavlov's dogs, which learned to salivate to a bell because the bell had been paired with food, but for human beings, the reaction can take many other physical forms besides salivation (Ader & Cohen, 1982; Cohen et al., 1994; Exton et al., 2000; Longo et al., 1999; Tekampe et al., 2017).

For example, in studies of patients with serious airborne allergies (like pollen, for example), patients took an effective allergy drug and simultaneously drank a very unusual drink – let's imagine it's pineapple soda. After this pairing of effective drug with pineapple soda was repeated a number of times, the researchers gave the patients the pineapple soda by itself. The patients' reactions to the pineapple soda by itself were similar to their reactions to the effective allergy drug with which it had been paired. Not only did the patients describe similar improvements in their allergy symptoms, but their bodies had similar physiological reactions in terms of producing antibodies, as well. The formerly neutral stimulus of pineapple soda had come to have a medical effect in these patients because of its learned association with a drug that had a medical effect (Gauci et al., 1994; Goebel et al., 2008).

This research raises the question of the power of *placebos*, medically inactive substances that somehow have a positive effect on patients (Peiris et al., 2018; Vits et al., 2011; Wager & Atlas, 2015). In one study examining the placebo effect, researchers treated patients with psoriasis, a common skin disease in which the elbows, knees, or other areas become very red and itchy. At first, all patients were treated repeatedly with an ointment that had a unique smell and color. The ointment contained a steroid as its active ingredient. Then the patients were divided into two groups. (The patients did not know which group they were in.) Group 1 continued to get the exact same ointment they had been using, including the steroid. Group 2 got a slightly different ointment, one that smelled the same but only contained the active ingredient 25% to 50% of the time. As you would expect, Group 1 got better. Specifically, 78% of them were cured of their psoriasis. Group 2 – whose ointment *lacked the medicine* most of the time – got better at almost the same rate (73%). Through classical conditioning, the patients in Group 2 had learned the pairing of the steroid with the unique smell and color of the ointment. The pairing was so strong that the smell and color of the ointment caused the patients' skin to react as if it were actually receiving the medicine (Ader et al., 2010).

In a more recent study on the placebo effect, children 5–12 years old who were having difficulty falling asleep were given melatonin, which helped. Every time they took the melatonin before bed, they drank a distinctive drink (lemonade with peppermint) and saw a distinctive sight (a dim red light). In the week after the melatonin treatment ended, researchers divided the kids into two groups. Group 1 continued to drink the lemonade with peppermint and see the dim red light at bedtime, but Group 2 did not. Many more kids in Group 1 than Group 2 experienced continued benefits during that week. Even though the active ingredient (melatonin) was no longer present, the things that had been paired with the melatonin (the lemonade with peppermint and the red light) served as placeboes for the kids in Group 1 (van Maanen et al., 2017).

CHECK YOUR LEARNING:

6.4 Who was Ivan Pavlov, and why is his research with dogs important?

6.5 What is classical conditioning, and how commonly does it occur in your life?

6.6 What are the five main components of classical conditioning?

6.7 With regard to classical conditioning, what do generalization and discrimination mean?

6.8 With regard to classical conditioning, what do acquisition and extinction mean?

6.9 What is higher-order conditioning?

6.10 How does learning take place through vicarious conditioning?

To check your understanding of these questions, click show the answers or refer to the answers in the Chapter Summary.

Operant Conditioning

YOU WILL LEARN:

6.11 what operant conditioning is.

6.12 how operant conditioning relates to the law of effect.

6.13 who B. F. Skinner was and why his research on operant conditioning was important.

6.14 how psychologists define reinforcement.

You may have noticed that learning via classical conditioning is quite passive. In Pavlov's classic studies, the dogs weren't really *doing* anything voluntarily. Things were being done *to* them. Food was placed near their mouths and bells were rung in their ears, but the dogs' role was simply to stand there and allow any natural involuntary reflexes (like salivation) to occur.

Often, learning is a more active process. In these moments, you learn by connecting what you do with what happens to you as a result. Psychologists call this **operant conditioning**: a form of learning in which the consequences of a voluntary behavior affect the likelihood that the behavior will recur. The word *operant* shares its root with the word *operate*, so *operant conditioning* refers to what you learn when you operate on the environment around you (Flora, 2004; Murphy & Lupfer, 2014). As you

YOU WILL LEARN: (*Continued*)

6.15 the differences between various types of reinforcement.

6.16 the differences between various schedules of reinforcement.

6.17 how psychologists define punishment.

6.18 how discriminative stimuli affect operant conditioning.

6.19 how shaping takes place.

6.20 the relevance of some classical conditioning concepts to operant conditioning.

FIGURE 6.4 Thorndike's Puzzle Box. When Edward Thorndike placed hungry cats inside puzzle boxes, they learned which behaviors caused the door to open and allowed them to eat the food outside. Thorndike explained that the cats' learning process illustrated the law of effect, or the idea that a behavior is likely to be repeated if its outcome is desirable but unlikely to be repeated if its outcome is undesirable (Thorndike, 1911, 1927).

operate on your environment, you develop your own personal if–then statements that explain past behavior and govern future behavior. These if–then statements are called *contingencies*. Here are a few examples of possible contingencies: (1) If I run outside without shoes, then I get a cut on my foot. (2) If I answer the phone when my friend Jayden calls, then I laugh at his jokes. (3) If I blow off my math homework, then I bomb the test.

If one of Pavlov's dogs had whimpered and then received a treat (and then learned to whimper more and more), perhaps Pavlov would have focused on operant conditioning rather than classical conditioning. As it happens, though, operant conditioning has a different pioneer: Edward L. Thorndike. Thorndike was a U.S. psychologist who conducted many studies on animal behavior in the late 1800s and early 1900s (Thorndike, 1898, 1900). In the best known of these studies, he placed cats inside a small box he called a puzzle box. As **Figure 6.4** illustrates, the cat could open the door to the puzzle box by performing a particular behavior, such as stepping on a button on the box's floor. Thorndike gave the cats food when they escaped, and he timed how long it took them to do so. He found that the first escape took quite a while as the cats moved randomly around the box, but each escape after the first one took a shorter and shorter time. Through trial and error, the cats seemed to be learning an important contingency: if I step on this button, then the door opens and I get to exit and eat.

Thorndike explained that the cats were demonstrating the **law of effect**: the observation that a behavior is more likely to be repeated if its effects are desirable but less likely to be repeated if its effects are undesirable (Thorndike, 1911, 1927). It's a simple but powerful rule by which all of us (animals and people) live: we pay attention to the outcome of each of our actions. If we like the outcome, we are more likely to repeat that action; if we don't like the outcome, we are less likely to repeat the behavior.

operant conditioning
A form of learning in which the consequences of a voluntary behavior affect the likelihood that the behavior will recur.

law of effect
The observation that a behavior is more likely to be repeated if its effects are desirable but less likely to be repeated if its effects are undesirable.

B. F. Skinner: Operant Conditioning for Everyone

B. F. Skinner was a psychology professor at the University of Minnesota, Indiana University, and Harvard. Inspired by Thorndike, Skinner spent his career conducting extensive studies on animal behavior, trying to expand what we know about the law of effect and operant conditioning (Mills, 1998; Richelle, 1993). While Thorndike's

FIGURE 6.5 **Skinner Box.** B. F. Skinner's Skinner boxes (or operant chambers) were new and improved versions of Edward Thorndike's puzzle boxes. They allowed animals to bring food or water into the box by pressing a lever or button. Also, because the boxes were wired for electricity, they could automatically record the frequency of animals' behavior and control lights that indicated whether a reward was available at a particular time.

work remained relatively unknown to most people outside of academia, Skinner's work made him a household name. By the 1960s and 1970s, Skinner was as much of a rock star as a psychology professor could be: he frequently appeared on TV talk shows, wrote two books that sold millions of copies and made the *New York Times* bestseller list, was on *Esquire* magazine's 1970 list of the 100 most important people, and was the subject of a cover story in *Time* magazine in September 1971 (Mills, 1998; Rutherford, 2009; Smith, 1996). Most of Skinner's fame stemmed from his ability to apply his findings about animal behavior to human behavior. Perhaps the most controversial of these was his claim that *all* behavior is determined by its consequences (that is, by operant conditioning), which means we have no free will to act as we want. This claim that free will doesn't really exist — which may be easier to accept as applied to other animals than to humans — remains controversial today (Altus & Morris, 2009; Baer et al., 2008; McKenna & Pereboom, 2016; Vervoort & Blusiewicz, 2020).

Skinner's first step as a researcher was to improve upon Thorndike's puzzle box. The **Skinner box** (originally called an *operant chamber*) is a container into which animals such as pigeons or rats could be placed for the purpose of observing and recording their behavior in response to consequences (**Figure 6.5**). Many of the advantages of the Skinner box had to do with automation and the use of electricity, which were a big deal at the time it was first used (1930s). For example, the Skinner box automatically dispensed food or water when the animal pressed the right lever or button. It recorded the animal's lever-pressing behavior automatically (through an electrical device), which meant there was no need for a person to observe continuously. And it could use a light to indicate that a reward was available if a behavior was performed. It also kept the animal in the box, so the experimenter didn't have to catch the escaped animal and wrestle it back into the box for another trial (as was required for Thorndike's cats) (Ator, 1991; Toates, 2009).

Reinforcement. With his new boxes, Skinner ran a multitude of studies on how consequences shape actions. The type of consequence upon which he focused most was **reinforcement**: any consequence of a behavior that makes that behavior more likely to recur. In general, reinforcement can be described as anything that helps the animal experience pleasure or avoid pain (Donahoe, 1998; Flora, 2004). Usually, what's reinforcing to one member of a species is reinforcing to all members of that species. But sometimes, what we expect to be reinforcing to a person or animal is not. In other

Skinner box
(Originally called an *operant chamber*) A container into which animals such as pigeons or rats could be placed for the purpose of observing and recording their behavior in response to consequences.

reinforcement
Any consequence of a behavior that makes that behavior more likely to recur.

s5iztok/E+/Getty Images

Reinforcement is an essential part of animal training. Dogs learn to fetch, shake hands, roll over, or jump over a bar by associating those behaviors with the reinforcements, such as treats, that come after them.

words, reinforcement, like beauty, is in the eye of the beholder. For example, Joanne, who lives alone in an apartment building offers two 13-year-old neighbors — Suveer and Bianca — peanut butter cookies for helping her carry some heavy items up the steps. Suveer finds cookies reinforcing and quickly volunteers to help. Bianca, on the other hand, is allergic to peanuts, so she does not find the cookies reinforcing at all and the offer does not motivate her to help.

Positive and Negative Reinforcement. Reinforcement can be categorized in many ways. For example, it can be labeled as either *positive* or *negative*. **Positive reinforcement** involves getting something desirable. **Negative reinforcement** involves removing something undesirable. Positive reinforcement comes in many forms — for example, a restaurant server receiving a tip for providing good service, a 5-year-old child getting a hug for successfully tying their shoes, or a college sports team earning a trophy for winning a championship. Negative reinforcement also takes many forms — for example, a homeowner getting rid of bugs by calling an exterminator, a harassment victim stopping unwelcome calls and texts by obtaining a restraining order, or a child overcoming strep throat by taking an antibiotic. Remember that in this context, *positive* doesn't mean good and *negative* doesn't mean bad. In terms of reinforcement, positive means plus (plus something desirable, to be specific) and negative means minus (minus something undesirable, to be specific). Keep in mind that both positive reinforcement and negative reinforcement are in fact reinforcing, which means that they both increase the likelihood of the behavior happening again in the future.

Primary and Secondary Reinforcers. Reinforcement can also be categorized as either *primary* or *secondary*. A **primary reinforcer** is an innate reinforcer that requires no learning to have a reinforcing effect because it satisfies a biological need. A few basic things serve as primary reinforcers, not only to humans, but to most species, because they have value to keep us alive and healthy: food, water, physical touch, sex, reduction in pain or discomfort.

Through your life experience (and classical conditioning), you come to associate those core primary reinforcers with other stimuli. We call a stimulus that has been paired with a primary reinforcer a **secondary reinforcer**: a reinforcer that requires a learned link to a primary reinforcer to have a reinforcing effect. For many of us, money is the ultimate secondary reinforcer (Bell & McDevitt, 2014; Delgado et al., 2006). Any value that a rectangular green piece of paper or a small silver circle may have to you is something that you had to learn, because none of us is born with an appreciation for dollar bills or coins. The same is true for money in any other form. For example, picture two children, a 1-year-old and a 12-year-old, receiving identical Amazon gift cards. The 12-year-old reacts with excitement. She has learned, through her experience, that the gift card can be exchanged for books, music, toys, and lots of other cool stuff online. The 1-year-old tries to eat the gift card for a minute and then discards it with complete indifference. To the baby, a gift card is not yet paired with the fun things it can bring, so it hasn't become a secondary reinforcer. Plenty of other powerful reinforcers in your day-to-day life are secondary rather than primary reinforcers — from applause to grades to plaques.

Another example of secondary reinforcement is the use of clickers by dog trainers. Specifically, a dog trainer teaches a dog to perform a behavior (heel, sit, and so on) by following the behavior with not only a treat (primary reinforcer) but also a click (secondary reinforcer). Soon enough, the dog forms such a strong association between the treat and the click that the click alone becomes a powerful reinforcer (Pryor, 2009).

Immediate and Delayed Reinforcement. It is also possible to describe reinforcement as *immediate* or *delayed*. This is an important distinction, as a single behavior can have very different short-term effects and long-term effects. For example, eating a whole lot of pizza can feel like a wonderful indulgence at the time

positive reinforcement
A type of reinforcement that involves getting something desirable.

negative reinforcement
A type of reinforcement that involves removing something undesirable.

primary reinforcer
An innate reinforcer that requires no learning to have a reinforcing effect because it satisfies a biological need.

secondary reinforcer
A reinforcer that requires a learned link to a primary reinforcer to have a reinforcing effect.

but can cause a stomachache later on. The later consequence (stomachache) should probably outrank the earlier consequence (good taste). However, the immediacy of the first consequence paired with the delay of the second consequence can cause you to behave in ways that you later regret. Just imagine if the order of the immediate and delayed reinforcers were somehow reversed: your behavior would likely change if the stomachache came immediately but the good taste of the pizza came hours later.

Reinforcement and Diversity. What is reinforcing to people from one culture might not be reinforcing to people from a different culture (Gelfand et al., 2007; Pantalone et al., 2010; Spiegler, 2016). For example, consider money. Money is a powerful reinforcer, but different types of money mean different things to different people. Currency used in one country may be valuable to people within that country but worthless to people outside of it.

DIVERSITY MATTERS

Individualism and collectivism can also play a role in the way reinforcements are perceived in various cultures. Specifically, reinforcements for individual achievements are often more well-received in cultures that emphasize individualism — such as the United States, Australia, and some European countries — than in cultures that emphasize collectivism — such as many Asian, Latinx, and Native American groups (Baruth & Manning, 1992; Kallam et al., 1994; Nelson, 1995). In fact, among more collectivistic cultures, a person who is singled out for an individual award might be teased or belittled by their peers for standing out from the crowd. For teachers, coaches, employers, or anyone else who might use reinforcements to influence the behavior of people from diverse backgrounds, this is an important point to keep in mind (Moran et al., 2014; Pierangelo & Giuliani, 2008).

Speaking of employers and reinforcements, one study asked undergraduate business students in three countries (United States, Australia, and Mexico) what they would find most reinforcing about a job offer. There were some common preferences, including good pay and recognition for high levels of performance. But there were some differences between the groups too. In particular, Mexican students expressed stronger preferences for the opportunity to get jobs for their relatives and the opportunity to contribute to society and the well-being of others. These preferences may reflect the fact that Mexico is generally more collectivistic and less individualistic than either the United States or Australia (McGaughey et al., 1997). A similar study of undergraduate students regarding the job characteristics they would find most reinforcing found interesting gender-based differences. Specifically, women from both countries placed more reinforcement value on good working conditions and convenient working hours than men (Corney & Richards, 2005).

A study of high school students' perceptions of reinforcements covered an especially broad range of ethnicities (Homan et al., 2012). The researchers asked 750 teenagers from seven countries (United States, Australia, Tanzania, Denmark, Honduras, Korea, and Spain) to rate dozens of potentially reinforcing activities, including sports, social activities, Internet use, games, and sleep, on a scale of 1 to 5. Higher scores meant that they found the activity more rewarding. There were some consistencies across cultures, but the results showed plenty of cultural differences too. For example, in Tanzania, shopping received the highest rating of all, but shopping didn't rate higher than eighth in any other country. In Honduras, visiting relatives was the second-highest rated activity, but its rating was nowhere near as high in any other country. In Denmark, downhill skiing was the highest-rated sport, but it didn't crack the top five sports of any other country. In the United States, the top five sports included two (American football and fishing) that didn't appear in the top five of any other country. Soccer, on the other hand, did not make the American top five, but it made the top five in most other countries. The lesson here is that the reinforcement value of any particular item or activity can depend on the cultural background of the person who receives it.

CHAPTER APP 6.2

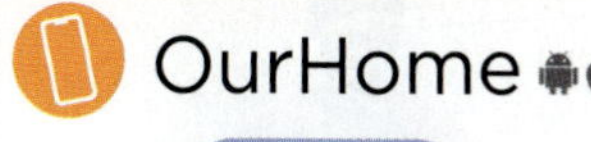

There are lots of apps designed to help parents use operant conditioning — and reinforcement in particular — to make changes in their children's behavior. For example, OurHome allows parents to reinforce their kids' behavior with points that the kids can later exchange for things they like. The parent chooses the particular behavior for the child to perform, like cleaning their room, walking the dog, doing their homework, washing the dishes, or practicing a musical instrument. The parent also determines how many points the behavior is worth and how many points are needed to earn specific reinforcers, like 10 points for a half-hour of screen time, 20 points for extra dessert, or 30 points for an extra $5 in their allowance.

How does it APPly to your daily life?
What are the most important decisions for the parent using this kind of app: the specific behaviors the child needs to perform, the specific reinforcements available to the child, the exchange rate between points and reinforcements, or something else? If you were the kid, which of these factors would have the most powerful influence on your behavior?

How does it APPly to your understanding of psychology?
Consider what you have learned about various types of reinforcement. If your parents had used an app like OurHome when you were a young child, which type of reinforcement would have influenced your behavior more powerfully: Positive or negative? Primary or secondary? Immediate or delayed? If you are a parent of a young child now, would your kids respond the same way as you?

To learn more about this app or to download it to your phone, you can search for "OurHome" on Google, in the iPhone App store, or in the Google Play store.

MY TAKE VIDEO 6.2

Reinforcement Schedules

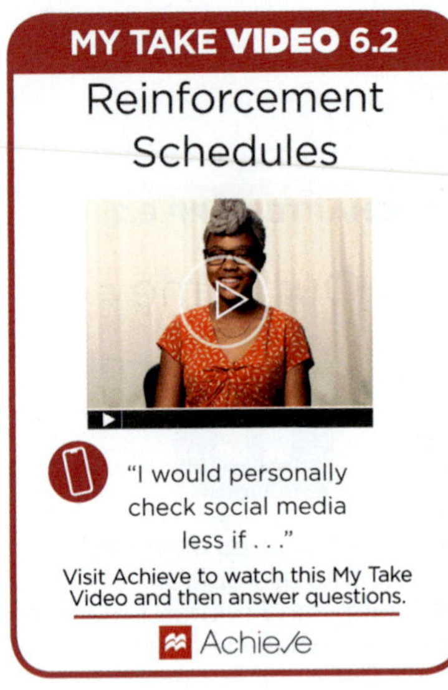

"I would personally check social media less if . . ."

Visit Achieve to watch this My Take Video and then answer questions.

Achieve

Reinforcement Schedules

When it comes to reinforcement, timing is everything. In fact, Skinner identified a variety of specific **reinforcement schedules**: a pattern by which reinforcements occur in response to a particular behavior. The most basic distinction is between *continuous* and *partial* reinforcement. **Continuous reinforcement** is a pattern by which a behavior is reinforced every time it occurs. By contrast, **partial reinforcement** (also known as *intermittent* reinforcement) is a pattern by which a behavior is reinforced only some of the time. For example, let's say a father (Ramon) wants his young daughter (Isabella) to clean her room. If Ramon takes Isabella to the park every day Isabella cleans her room, that's continuous reinforcement. If Ramon takes Isabella to the park only on some of the days Isabella cleans her room, that's partial reinforcement.

The distinction between continuous and partial reinforcement is important in terms of *acquisition* and *extinction*, which we discussed earlier. (Those terms appeared in the section on classical conditioning, but they apply to operant conditioning as well.) Acquisition happens more quickly with continuous reinforcement – after just a couple of times cleaning her room, Isabella will have learned that "If I clean my room, I get to go to the park" is a hard-and-fast rule. But continuous reinforcement results in faster extinction too – if Ramon forgets to reinforce Isabella just once or twice, Isabella will realize quickly that the reinforcement doesn't always happen, and she will be less likely to perform the behavior.

With partial reinforcement, acquisition happens more slowly if at all, because it can be difficult to detect a connection between the behavior and the outcome. But once that connection has been acquired, the behavior is quite resistant to extinction. If Isabella has learned that cleaning her room leads to going to the park only some of the time, she won't necessarily quit if she doesn't get rewarded the next time she cleans her room. She might not even quit after two or perhaps even 10 room cleanings don't bring about the reward. This reluctance to quit the behavior happens because she has learned that the next room cleaning might still bring the reward. The bottom line is that continuous reinforcement is best for making acquisition happen initially, but partial reinforcement is best for maintaining that behavior over time.

Within the broad category of partial reinforcement, Skinner (1961) identified four more specific reinforcement schedules: *fixed-ratio*, *variable-ratio*, *fixed-interval*, and *variable-interval* (**Table 6.1**). They differ from each other in two important ways – whether the reinforcement is predictable (*fixed*) or unpredictable (*variable*), and whether it is based on the number of repetitions of the behavior (*ratio*) or the passage of time (*interval*). These differences can powerfully influence behavior.

Ratio Schedules: Fixed Versus Variable. A **fixed-ratio schedule** is a reinforcement schedule in which a behavior is reinforced after a consistent, predictable number of occurrences. By contrast, a **variable-ratio schedule** is a reinforcement schedule in which a behavior is reinforced after an inconsistent, unpredictable number of occurrences. Consider soda machines versus slot machines. With a soda machine, you know with great confidence that if you put the money in once and press the button once, you'll get your reinforcement. There's no mystery, no uncertainty – this is an example of a fixed-ratio schedule. With a slot machine, you *don't* know what will happen after you put your money in and press the button. There *is* mystery and uncertainty – you could get nothing, or a little something, or a lot. And you don't know how many times you'll need to play before you get any kind of reinforcer, so there's always the thought that it could be the next one.

The difference between *fixed ratio* and *variable ratio* is important, particularly in terms of extinction, which is essentially giving up on the possibility that your behavior will bring about the reward. With the soda machine, if you put in your money, press the button, and get nothing, you are extremely unlikely to insert money even once more. But with the slot machine, if you put in your money, press the button, and get nothing,

reinforcement schedule
A pattern by which reinforcements occur in response to a particular behavior.

continuous reinforcement
A pattern by which a behavior is reinforced every time it occurs.

partial reinforcement
(Also called *intermittent* reinforcement) A pattern by which a behavior is reinforced only some of the times it occurs.

fixed-ratio schedule
A reinforcement schedule in which a behavior is reinforced after a consistent, predictable number of occurrences.

variable-ratio schedule
A reinforcement schedule in which a behavior is reinforced after an inconsistent, unpredictable number of occurrences.

TABLE 6.1: Summary of Reinforcement Schedules

	FIXED	VARIABLE
RATIO	Reinforcement comes when you perform the behavior a predictable number of times. *Example: soda machine*  Graham Oliver/Alamy	Reinforcement comes when you perform the behavior an unpredictable number of times. *Example: slot machine*  Folio Images/Alamy
INTERVAL	Reinforcement comes when you perform the behavior after a predictable amount of time has passed. *Example: mail* 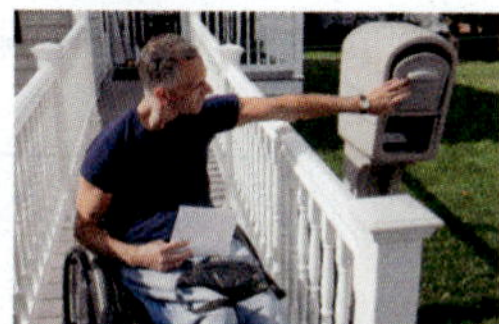 Huntstock/DisabilityImages/Getty Images	Reinforcement comes when you perform the behavior after an unpredictable amount of time has passed. *Example: e-mail*  m-imagephotography/iStock/Getty Images

you might insert money again and again, because you have learned from previous experience (your own or someone else's) that you might hit the jackpot on the next try (Horsley et al., 2012).

Interval Schedules: Fixed Versus Variable. A **fixed-interval schedule** is a reinforcement schedule in which a behavior can be reinforced after a time interval that is consistent and predictable. By contrast, a **variable-interval schedule** is a reinforcement schedule in which a behavior can be reinforced after a time interval that is inconsistent and unpredictable. Consider mail versus e-mail. (For the sake of this discussion, let's assume that you find your mail and your e-mail to be equally reinforcing in terms of the amount of pleasure each gives you.) With mail, you know to check your mailbox at a certain time – say, around 2:00 P.M. every day but Sunday. In other words, your mail arrives on a fixed-interval schedule. If you receive your mail at 2:00 P.M. on Monday, will you check the mailbox again at 2:30 P.M. that day? At 7:00 P.M.? At 9:00 A.M. on Tuesday? Of course not – you know that you can't possibly receive the next batch of mail until Tuesday around 2:00 P.M., so you'll wait until then to check again.

E-mail, on the other hand, doesn't arrive at predictable times. Instead, it is on a variable-interval schedule. If you receive e-mail at 2:00 P.M. on Monday, will you check it again at 2:30 P.M.? You very well might, and you might check it several times that night and Tuesday morning too. After all, there's no need to wait until 2:00 P.M. Tuesday (or any other predetermined time) to check, because for e-mail the time of arrival varies unpredictably. Since you never know when the next one might arrive, you are likely to check your e-mail far more frequently than you check your snail mail. (The same variable-interval reinforcement schedule holds true for Instagram, Twitter, Snapchat, Facebook, texts, voicemail, and anything else that could arrive at any time of day. Can you imagine how your phone usage might change if you only felt the need to check your phone at certain, predictable times of day?)

fixed-interval schedule
A reinforcement schedule in which a behavior can be reinforced after a time interval that is consistent and predictable.

variable-interval schedule
A reinforcement schedule in which a behavior can be reinforced after a time interval that is inconsistent and unpredictable.

WATCHING PSYCHOLOGY

Home Runs and Schedules of Reinforcement

One of the joys of tuning in to a baseball game on TV is the thrill of the home run. Some sluggers deliver the long ball at an amazing rate—a feat measured by the statistic *at-bats per home run*. This number reflects the average number of at-bats you'd have to wait to see a particular batter send one over the fence.

Babe Ruth, Mark McGwire, Josh Gibson, and Barry Bonds are among the best in baseball history for at-bats per home run. Among more current players, one of the best is Fernando Tatis Jr. In his best season so far, Tatis has earned a ratio of about 11:1. So, as a fan, you have a one in 11 chance of seeing a homer when Tatis takes an at-bat.

Now think about how important the schedule of reinforcement is to baseball-viewing habits. You can't predict when Fernando Tatis Jr. will hit his next homer. That means his home runs provide reinforcement on a *variable-ratio* schedule. You have a general idea that he hits one about once every 11 at-bats (roughly one every two or three games), but you can't know which at-bats specifically will produce a home run. Let's imagine that you are a huge fan of Fernando Tatis Jr. and his home runs. In fact, they're the main reason you watch the game. If he hits a homer in the first inning, will you continue to watch the game? Of course! He might hit another in a later inning. If he hasn't hit one in a week, will you watch? Of course! He could smash a home run (or even two or three of them) tonight. Because the schedule of reinforcement is variable, you keep watching.

Now imagine if Tatis' home runs were delivered on a *fixed-ratio* schedule instead of a variable-ratio schedule. He still hits them at the same rate—one home run every 11 at-bats—but now they're predictable. Tonight, if he hits one in the first inning, will you continue to watch the game? Of course not! He's going to go homerless in his next 10 at-bats, so he definitely won't hit another one out of the park tonight. You'll only regain interest 11 at-bats from now, which might be days away. Imagine the massive changes in game attendance, TV ratings, and advertisement revenue if home runs in baseball somehow switched from a variable-ratio schedule to a fixed-ratio schedule—not because the total number of home runs would decrease, but because their predictability would increase.

Of course, such a hypothetical switch is entirely unrealistic. The excitement of sports (and many other activities) lies not just in the thrill of the next big moment but in the fact that you never know when that thrill might come. •

Punishment

So far, our discussion of operant conditioning has focused on behaviors followed by reinforcements, but of course, many behaviors are followed instead by **punishment**: any consequence of a behavior that makes that behavior less likely to recur.

Wait, I'm confused. What's the difference between punishment and negative reinforcement?

Many students find the terminology confusing. But there's a simple rule to clarify it: if the term includes the word *reinforcement*, it makes the behavior happen *more* often, whether it's positive or negative; if the term includes the word *punishment*, it makes the behavior happen *less* often, whether it is positive or negative (**Table 6.2**). Like reinforcement, punishment can be positive (adding something undesirable) or negative (subtracting something desirable). For example, a parent who spanks a child for cursing is using positive punishment. But a parent who takes away a child's video game console for cursing is using negative punishment. Of course, both punishments are intended to reduce the cursing behavior.

Some consequences that are meant to be punishments can actually be experienced as insignificant (having no effect on the frequency of the behavior) or even reinforcing (increasing its frequency). A parent who "punishes" a teenager for lying by sending them to their room may not see a reduction in lying behavior if the child's room includes a TV and computer. A kindergarten teacher who "punishes" a child for hitting a classmate by scolding them in the hallway is also giving the child plenty of

TABLE 6.2: Responses to a Behavior That Influence Its Frequency

	REINFORCEMENT	PUNISHMENT
POSITIVE	*Increase* frequency of behavior by getting something good	*Decrease* frequency of behavior by getting something bad
NEGATIVE	*Increase* frequency of behavior by removing something bad	*Decrease* frequency of behavior by removing something good

punishment
Any consequence of a behavior that makes that behavior less likely to recur.

one-on-one attention. The child may actually find this attention to be a reinforcement rather than punishment.

Drawbacks of Punishment. Skinner and other researchers who have studied operant conditioning warn that the use of punishment to change behavior has quite a few drawbacks that the use of reinforcement does not (Gershoff et al., 2018; Grogan-Kaylor et al., 2018). For example, punishment teaches people (and animals) what behavior to avoid, but not what behavior to choose instead (Lerman & Toole, 2011). Punishment also provides a model of aggressiveness, and in some cases violence, that the recipients (especially children) might follow when it is their turn to influence others' behavior. In fact, children who were physically disciplined are particularly likely to become physically aggressive (Elgar et al., 2018; Gershoff, 2002, 2008, 2010; Gershoff & Bitensky, 2007; King et al., 2018). And punishment can encourage lying and other kinds of deceptiveness — hiding the punished behavior rather than eliminating it ("I didn't do it!") (Rotenberg et al., 2012).

Punishment can also create high levels of anxiety and fear, which can interfere with the desired behavior change. For example, a child punished harshly for failing to take out the trash might anxiously withdraw altogether rather than step up to complete the chore. In families where harsh physical punishment is common, children are at greater risk for developing anxiety disorders and other kinds of mental disorders as adults, as illustrated in **Figure 6.6** (Afifi et al., 2012; Österman et al., 2014). ("The harsh physical punishment" we're discussing here goes way beyond spanking; it includes pushing, shoving, grabbing, and slapping. Spanking is generally not associated with such negative effects on children, especially when parents use it in moderation and only after other punishments, like time-outs, have failed [Ferguson, 2013; Larzelere & Kuhn, 2005; Oas, 2010].)

The message accompanying the punishment must be very clear to avoid confusion about which behavior brought it on (Johnston, 1972; Wacker et al., 2009). For example, consider a teenage boy who spends an evening on his computer checking social media, watching YouTube videos, listening to music, and shopping for clothes. He then gets grounded by his parent "for what you did on the computer last night." Would he know exactly how to change his behavior? Perhaps it was one particular online activity, or just a couple of them, or the total amount of time he spent doing all of them. His parent's vague explanation does not offer enough information for him to determine specifically what he did wrong.

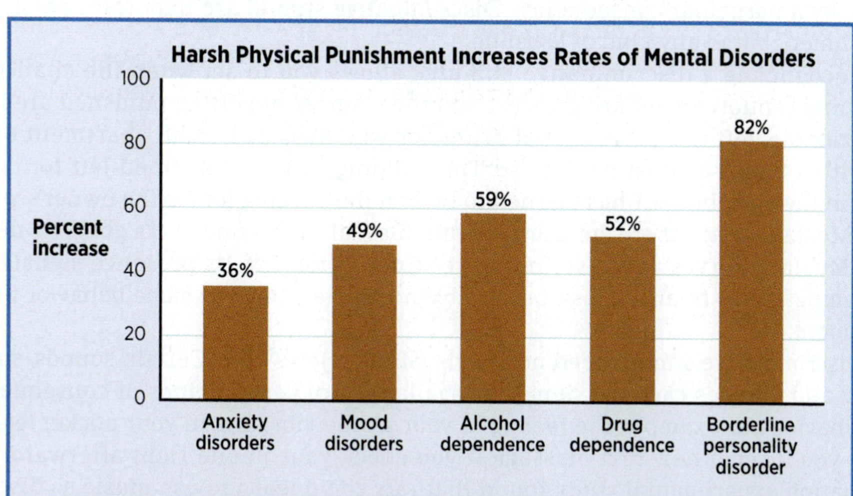

FIGURE 6.6 Harsh Physical Punishment Increases Rates of Mental Disorders. Adults who experienced harsh physical punishment as children are at significantly greater risk for many mental disorders than adults who did not. They have an approximately 36% greater chance of anxiety disorders, 49% greater chance of mood disorders, and 82% greater chance of borderline personality disorder. Data from Afifi et al. (2012)

CHAPTER APP 6.3

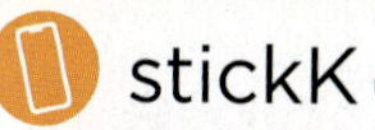

The stickK app helps individuals change their own behavior, and it relies on punishment rather than reinforcement. Specifically, stickK allows you to set a behavioral goal—exercising four times a week, losing 10 pounds, studying 2 hours a day, or whatever you choose—and then "bet" your own money that you will succeed. You can specify where the money goes if you fail, including an "anti-charity" (a cause that you personally oppose) of your choosing. This arrangement increases your commitment to complete your chosen behavior so you can avoid the punishment of contributing to a political party, a social movement, or some other organization that you dislike.

How does it APPly to your daily life?
Consider what you've learned about *punishment*. If you used an app like stickK, would the threat of punishment motivate you to change your behavior? How would the specifics of the punishment (the amount of money, who receives it, etc.) influence the power of the punishment? stickK also has a searchable list of users, including their behavioral goals and their track record of success and failure. For you, how would the punishment of people knowing you failed compare to the punishment of losing money?

How does it APPly to your understanding of psychology?
Unlike many apps that utilize reinforcement to change behavior, stickK utilizes *punishment*. Which strategy would you expect to be more effective? Why? What do your answers tell you about the difference between the concepts of reinforcement and punishment? What do your answers tell you more generally about wise use of *operant conditioning*?

To learn more about this app or to download it to your phone, you can search for "stickK" on Google, in the iPhone App store, or in the Google Play store.

For all of these reasons, experts in operant conditioning tend to recommend the use of reinforcement of wanted behaviors over punishment of unwanted behaviors. Among many other examples, reinforcement has been successfully applied to increase desired behaviors in children with autism (Kern & Kokina, 2008; Thompson, 2014), as well as corporate workers' compliance with computer security procedures (Villamarin-Salomon & Brustoloni, 2010).

LIFE HACK 6.1

When you use punishment to change someone else's behavior, provide a specific suggestion for a better behavior they can do instead.

(Hanley et al., 2005; Mayhew & Harris, 1979; Murphey et al., 1979; Petscher et al., 2009)

Effective Use of Punishment. Punishment can certainly be effective if used wisely. For example, when punishing a behavior, recommend a better behavior, and then strongly reinforce the better behavior when it occurs (Hanley et al., 2005; Mayhew & Harris, 1979; Murphey et al., 1979; Petscher et al., 2009). Make sure the punishment happens immediately after the bad behavior, and explain specifically what the punishment is for (Tanimoto et al., 2004; Walters & Demkow, 1963). This increases the odds that the individual will make the right connection between the behavior and the consequence. If you threatened a punishment, make sure you deliver it as promised, or the individual learns that the threats are meaningless. Finally, punish the same bad behavior consistently each time it happens.

As an example, consider the parent who takes away a child's video game console as a punishment for cursing. That punishment is most likely to be effective if the parent takes the console away within seconds of the offensive word, explains that it's because of the cursing, suggests better words to use, and handles future incidents similarly. If the parent waits hours or days to take away the video game console, offers no explanation why it is happening, provides no suggestions for better behavior, and later ignores similar cursing, the punishment is likely to be ineffective.

When used the right way, punishment can even have a vicarious effect. In other words, effective punishment often decreases the unwanted behavior not only in the person receiving the punishment but in other people who observe the punishment too (Malouff et al., 2009). Consider the child from the previous paragraph who had their video game console taken away because they used bad language. If their sibling sees how they got punished, the sibling is less likely to use bad language too.

Allen Creative/Steve Allen/Alamy

This Krispy Kreme *Hot Doughnuts Now* sign is a discriminative stimulus, letting doughnut lovers know that they can receive the reinforcement of a new batch fresh out of the oven.

Discriminative Stimuli

One of the problems associated with punishment is that individuals may learn to change their behavior only in the specific situations when they know they'll get caught. The ability to identify these specific situations hinges on the presence of a **discriminative stimulus**: a signal that indicates that a particular behavior will be followed by a particular consequence. Discriminative stimuli are important not only to punishment but to any kind of learning.

Recognizing a discriminative stimulus allows you to act when the chances of obtaining reinforcement are greatest and the chances of getting punished are least. For example, Jeff is a professional drummer who lives in a small apartment building with a policy against loud noise. The building's owner has fined Jeff for drumming in the past, but Jeff has learned to look in the parking lot for the owner's yellow Ford Mustang. If it's there, he doesn't drum for fear of the fine. If it's gone, he drums. That Mustang serves as a discriminative stimulus for Jeff. Its presence signals that drumming brings financial loss, but its absence signals that the same behavior brings enjoyment.

Discriminative stimuli need not be visual, as in Jeff's case. Certain sounds, smells, tastes, and touches can also signal the availability of certain kinds of consequences for behavior. For example, the feeling of your phone vibrating in your pocket lets you know you'll see a new text message if you check your phone right afterward. One fascinating experimental study found that rats could learn to use music as discriminative stimuli. First, researchers placed rats in a Skinner box in which they could earn food by pressing a lever. Then, they added a new rule for the rats. Lever pressing brought about food when the Beatles' "Yesterday" was playing but not when Mozart's *The Magic Flute* was playing. Sure enough, with enough experience, the rats became

discriminative stimulus
A signal indicating that a particular behavior will be followed by a particular consequence.

careful listeners and pressed the lever when they heard the Beatles but not Mozart (Okaichi & Okaichi, 2001).

kvkirillov/iStock/Getty Images

To get an animal (or a person) to learn a complex behavior, it is most effective to use shaping, or reinforcing each of the small steps of the behavior.

Shaping

Sometimes, the behavior to be learned isn't as simple as pressing a lever or pecking at a button. For these multi-step behaviors, the behavior isn't learned all at once, but *shaped*, little by little (Krueger & Dayan, 2009; Pryor & Ramirez, 2014; Skinner, 1938, 1974). **Shaping** is the process of gradually learning a complex behavior through the reinforcement of each of its small steps. Animal trainers are experts in shaping, especially those who work in a circus or zoo where the animals perform. For example, if the trick calls for a dolphin to circle the pool and then jump out of the water through a hoop, the trainer begins by reinforcing the first step in that behavior — say, swimming halfway around the pool. Then the trainer ups the ante, offering reinforcement only when the dolphin circles three-quarters of the pool, then the whole pool. Next, to earn the reinforcement the dolphin must peek its beak out of the water after circling the pool, then its fins, then its whole body, then touch the hoop, then go through the hoop. By reinforcing each "baby step," the dolphin learns to do the full trick.

Does shaping happen with people as well as animals?

Yes, human behavior is often shaped as well. Consider DeAndre, a youth basketball coach trying to teach his first-grade player, Derrick, to shoot a layup. A layup may look easy, but it's actually a complex behavior, particularly for a young child. Consider the parts: jump off the proper foot, shoot with the correct hand, and bounce the ball off the backboard. If DeAndre's plan is to wait for Derrick to spontaneously shoot a perfect layup and then reinforce him for it, he may be waiting forever. Derrick may never do the whole thing correctly on his own. Instead, DeAndre teaches the first part in isolation — jumping off the proper foot as he approaches the basket. Every time Derrick gets it right, he gets a heartfelt "Good job!" from his coach. After some repetition and success with the feet, DeAndre adds the next step, shooting with the correct hand, praising Derrick only when he does both steps well. Once Derrick masters these first two steps, DeAndre shows Derrick the spot to hit on the backboard and praises him only when he puts all three steps together — good foot, good hand, and good backboard.

Operant Conditioning Versions of Some Classical Conditioning Concepts

Many of the terms we introduced earlier in this chapter when we discussed classical conditioning apply to operant conditioning too. For example, *generalization* and *discrimination* happen in operant conditioning. Let's consider Derrick, the first-grade basketball player, one more time. When he receives praise for successfully performing the layup and all of its parts, he's receiving it from a particular coach in a particular gym. Let's imagine that Derrick's next opportunity for a layup takes place in a different gym and with a different coach. Would Derrick expect to receive similar praise in this new setting? To the extent he does, he's generalizing what he learned from DeAndre. To the extent he doesn't, he's discriminating between the original situation and the new one.

Acquisition and *extinction* are also important concepts in operant conditioning. In this context, acquisition refers to the point when the learner makes the connection between a particular behavior and its consequence. Extinction refers to the point when the learner realizes that that connection no longer applies. Remember our discussion of the operant conditioning involved with soda machines? Acquisition occurs when we learn that "If I insert money and press a button, then I get a soda." Extinction occurs when we later learn — from a broken soda machine — that "If I insert money and press a button, then I *don't* get a soda."

shaping
The process of gradually learning a complex behavior through the reinforcement of each small step that is a part of the complex behavior.

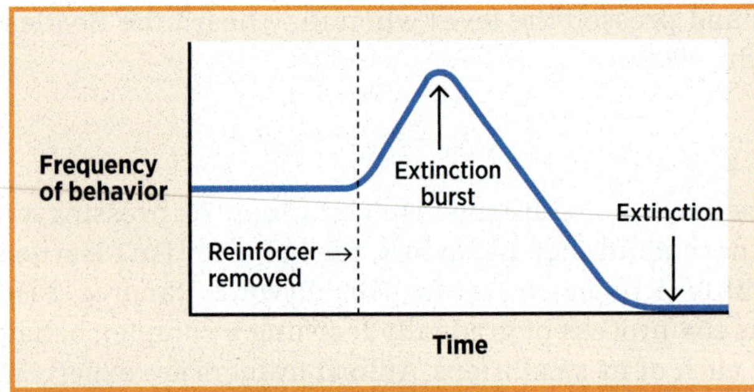

FIGURE 6.7 **Extinction.** Here's how extinction works: When you've learned that a behavior that used to bring you reinforcement no longer brings any reinforcement, you'll eventually decrease that behavior. However, before that decrease starts, your first reaction will be an *increase* in the frequency or intensity of the behavior to try harder to get what you've learned to expect. That increase is called the extinction burst. As long as that extinction burst doesn't result in the return of the reinforcement, extinction will follow.

When extinction occurs in operant conditioning, it follows a predictable pattern – the behavior actually *increases* first and dies out later, as shown in Figure 6.7. Psychologists call the first part of this pattern, when the behavior gets more intense or frequent, an *extinction burst*. Picture yourself at that broken soda machine. When you insert the money, press the button, and get nothing, you press the button again and again, try the other buttons, and maybe even kick or shake the machine – all efforts to get the reinforcement you learned to expect. Only after all of these extra behaviors fail do your efforts to get a soda extinguish.

Imagine for a minute that intensifying your behavior made the soda come out. You would learn that when you don't get the reinforcer you expect, you should just try harder and you'll eventually get it. This is a powerful lesson to keep in mind when you *are* the soda machine – that is, when you are the source of reinforcement for someone else. For example, let's say you have a regular babysitting gig for a 6-year-old boy. He has learned from experience that if he says, "I'm not tired," after you tuck him in, you let him get out of bed and watch TV. If his parents instruct you to be stricter, what should you expect the boy to do the first time you don't let him watch TV? He certainly won't go down without a fight. He'll ask repeatedly, scream, cry, throw a fit – anything he can think of to get his reinforcer (watching TV). If you stand firm, he'll eventually give up, having learned that there's a new rule in place. If you give in, however, he'll simply learn that he has to ramp up his efforts to get what he wants, and that's what he'll do in the future.

Applying Operant Conditioning to Your Life

Anywhere you find a person receiving a consequence for an action, operant conditioning is at work. Many psychologists who do therapy use operant conditioning to help clients reduce unwanted behaviors. (This approach, known as *contingency management*, is discussed in more detail in Chapter 15.) The logic goes like this: the client is behaving a certain way because of the consequences that follow the behavior, so if the consequences change, then the behavior will change too (Davis et al., 2016; Drossel et al., 2008; Kearney & Vecchio, 2002; Sayegh et al., 2017; Villamar et al., 2008).

For example, consider Braden, a 7-year-old boy who lives with his mother and father. Braden has been behaving in a problematic way: he refuses to go to school. When his parents try to get him out of bed in the morning, he cries, "I don't want to go!" and pulls the covers over his head. His mother responds to Braden's behavior by cuddling with him in his bed for 30 minutes, while his father brings him breakfast in bed. Whether they realize it or not, Braden's parents' behaviors are positive reinforcement for Braden's school refusal behavior. The family seeks help from a psychologist, Dr. Abrams, who suggests that they stop providing such reinforcers and possibly replace them with reasonable punishments (like losing TV time) when Braden refuses to go to school. Dr. Abrams also suggests that Braden's parents shape Braden's behavior by reinforcing small steps in the right direction, like getting out of bed, getting dressed, getting his backpack on, and so on. After a short adjustment period, Braden learns the new consequences for his behavior and his behavior then changes — he refuses school far less often and attends school far more often.

Operant conditioning may also play a role in the experience of major depressive disorder (which we will cover in more detail in Chapter 14). Specifically, researchers have found that some people with major depressive disorder tend to be less sensitive to reinforcement and more sensitive to punishment (Eshel & Roiser, 2010). In other words, their feelings of pleasure tend to be muted when their behavior produces a good outcome, but their feelings of pain tend to be amplified when their behavior produces a bad outcome. More recent research suggests that less sensitivity to reinforcement is more likely to be an active ingredient in their depression than the greater sensitivity to punishment (Mukherjee et al., 2020). This kind of research has the potential to help therapists work effectively with clients who have major depressive disorder by encouraging them to reevaluate the feedback they receive for their actions.

Sometimes, operant conditioning can affect human lives even though it's not humans who are being conditioned. For example, dogs can be trained through operant conditioning to help people with a variety of physical disabilities, such as impairments of sight, hearing, or mobility. The dog's training consists of reinforcements and punishments for particular behaviors that correspond with the needs of the person with a disability. For example, trainers reward these dogs for heeling (staying alongside the leg or wheelchair of their owner) through the use of reinforcements. Similar training underlies bomb-sniffing and drug-sniffing dogs, which are reinforced for barking or otherwise notifying their owners when they smell a particular scent.

Researchers have even trained giant African rats to find landmines. The rats' excellent sense of smell helps them to pick up the scent of TNT, the explosive used in most landmines. The researchers reinforce the rats by offering food when the rats hold their noses over a landmine for a 5-second period. The rats are then motivated to scurry across a field and pause over any landmines they find, allowing their owners to deactivate or remove them. This is a vital application of operant conditioning, especially considering that landmines are found in dozens of countries and cause a great deal of injury and death (Poling et al., 2010, 2011).

Taylor Weidman/Getty Images

Operant conditioning has been applied in many creative ways. For example, animal trainers have used operant conditioning to teach giant African rats to respond in a particular way to the scent of TNT, an explosive found in landmines. By doing so, they help people locate them so they can be deactivated or removed.

Along the same lines, researchers trained sniffer dogs to detect COVID in humans. Sniffer dogs have been trained to detect other diseases in humans with at least a moderate degree of reliability, including several types of cancer and low blood sugar (hypoglycemia) in people with diabetes. When COVID arose in 2020, one group of researchers in Iran hoped they might train dogs to do the same with this new virus. They had dogs sniff the clothing, masks, and mucus samples of hundreds of people, some of whom had tested positive for COVID. And the researchers used classical conditioning techniques to allow the dogs to react differently when they did or did not detect the virus. Within weeks, the dogs could identify positive and negative COVID cases with impressive accuracy. Of course, this research was just a start (a single study using just six dogs), but it could represent an important early step toward developing a new tool to battle the pandemic (Eskandari et al., 2021).

CHECK YOUR LEARNING:

6.11 What is operant conditioning?

6.12 How does operant conditioning relate to the law of effect?

6.13 Who is B. F. Skinner, and why was his research on operant conditioning important?

6.14 How do psychologists define reinforcement?

6.15 What are the differences between positive and negative reinforcement?

6.16 What are the differences between these pairs of schedules of reinforcement: continuous versus partial; fixed-ratio versus variable-ratio; and fixed-interval versus variable-interval?

6.17 How do psychologists define punishment?

6.18 What role do discriminative stimuli play in operant conditioning?

6.19 With regard to operant conditioning, what is shaping?

6.20 Which classical conditioning concepts also occur in operant conditioning?

To check your understanding of these questions, click show the answers or refer to the answers in the Chapter Summary.

Observational Learning

YOU WILL LEARN:

6.21 what observational learning is.

6.22 how Albert Bandura studied observational learning.

6.23 the relationship between observational learning and brain cells called mirror neurons.

So far, our discussion of learning in this chapter has focused primarily on the individual's direct experiences — in other words, how you learn from what happens to *you*. But the truth is that you also learn a lot from what you see happening to other people. We call this **observational learning**: learning that occurs as a result of observing others' behavior and consequences rather than your own. For example, if your close friend has a frustrating experience with their new smartphone — short battery life, overheating, dropped calls, random crashes, and so on — you'll avoid that model if you get one for yourself. If your older cousin has a great experience working for a particular organization — good pay, fair treatment, opportunity for advancement, and so on — you may be likely to apply there as well if you're looking for a job. Other people's experience counts for you as well.

The Bobo Doll Studies

A classic series of studies by Albert Bandura and his colleagues, known as the Bobo doll studies, illustrates the power of observational learning (Bandura et al., 1961, 1963). Here's the scene: children between 3 and 6 years old playing with toys watch an adult (the *model*) interact with a Bobo doll, a large standup inflatable punching bag figure with a clown painted on it. Half of the children saw the model ignore the Bobo doll; the other half saw the model act physically aggressive toward it. The aggressive models kicked the doll, yelled at it, punched it, and hit it with a hammer. All of the children then had their own toys unexpectedly taken away in an attempt to frustrate them and were placed alone in the room with the Bobo doll. How did the children deal with their frustration? It depended on what they had observed in the model. The children who saw the model act aggressively toward the Bobo doll were more likely to act aggressively themselves than the children who saw the model ignore the Bobo doll. They kicked it, yelled at it, punched it, and hit it with a hammer — just as they had seen the model do moments earlier.

Did the models in those studies get anything — a reinforcement or a punishment — after they acted aggressively toward the Bobo doll?

In these early Bobo doll studies, the model's aggressive behavior did not bring about any consequences. But what if it did? What if the children saw the model receive either reinforcement or punishment after beating up the Bobo doll? Would *vicarious learning* take place? Bandura examined this question in later studies and found that the observed consequences do make a difference: children who saw the model get rewarded for aggressive behavior acted more aggressively themselves than did children who saw the model get punished. However, Bandura then offered sticker booklets and juice to the children who saw the model get punished — but only if they repeated the aggressive behavior that they saw the model get punished for. Most of them had no problem doing so. This suggests that these children had added the model's aggressive behavior to their own behavioral repertoire even if they had chosen not to display it at first (Bandura, 1965).

The Bobo doll studies demonstrate the often-overlooked power of *modeling*, or imitation of observed behavior. The behavior we watch can strongly influence the behavior we exhibit. And we watch a lot, not only in person but on screens of various kinds: TV, movies, YouTube, video games, and so on. For instance, exposure of children to movies that include smoking has been shown to significantly predict established smoking patterns when the children reach their late teens (Dalton et al., 2009;

observational learning
A type of learning that occurs as a result of observing others' behavior and consequences rather than our own.

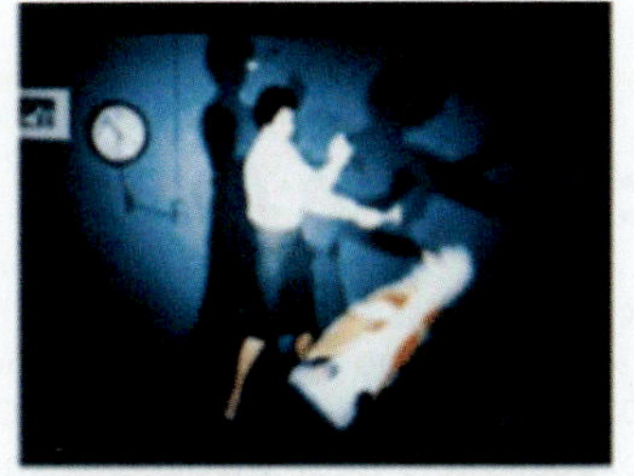

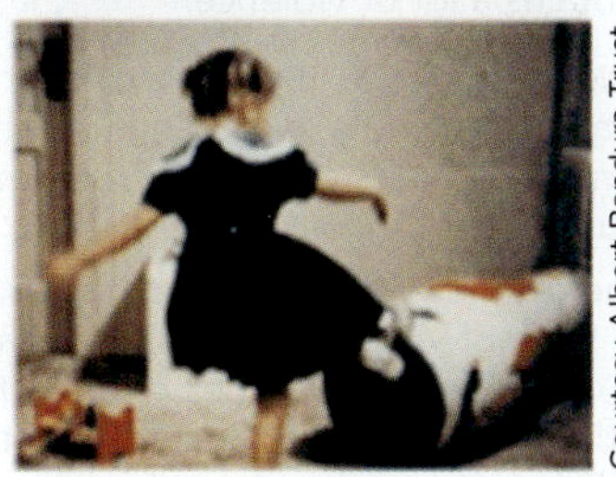

Courtesy Albert Bandura Trust

The classic Bobo doll studies by Albert Bandura illustrated that the way kids interact with a doll was strongly influenced by what they learned when they observed adults interacting with the same doll. In each of these pairs of photos, the upper photo shows an adult doing something to the Bobo doll and the lower photo shows a child doing the same thing.

Heatherton & Sargent, 2009). In another study, children age 8–12 watched a 20-minute clip of a PG-rated movie that either did or did not contain guns. They then played in a room with one cabinet full of toys (Legos, Nerf items, checkers and other board games) and another cabinet containing a disabled .38-caliber handgun. The kids who had watched the clip featuring guns found the gun much more often, held it for much longer periods of time, and squeezed the trigger many more times (Dillon & Bushman, 2017). Does the observation of violence in the media contribute to violent behavior in real life? The Current Controversy box examines this issue in detail.

It is important to consider observational learning not only from the perspective of the learner, but from the perspective of the model as well. What behaviors do you model, and who's watching you? If you are a parent (or an aunt, uncle, older sibling, older cousin, etc.), this is a particularly relevant question. You may not identify yourself as a model for the children around you, and you may not have invited them to follow your lead, but they may do so anyway. For example, parents who overeat are more likely to have children who overeat; parents who smoke are more likely to have children who will smoke; and parents who use verbal or physical aggression are more likely to have children who do the same (Francis et al., 2007; Gilman et al., 2009; Hiemstra et al., 2017; Lydecker & Grilo, 2017; Pagani et al., 2004, 2009).

On the other hand, parents who read are more likely to have children who read; parents who do charity work are more likely to have children who do charity work; and parents who exercise and eat healthy are more likely to have children who exercise and eat healthy (Anzman et al., 2010; Bekkers, 2007; Bus et al., 1995; Martire & Helgeson, 2017; Skibbe et al., 2008; van Bergen et al., 2017). Simply put, observational learning can lead to behavior that is good or bad, productive or wasteful, prosocial or antisocial. Remember that it's not the parents' *instruction* that we're talking about but the parents' *behavior*. (It's not parents who *tell* their kids to read but parents who *actually* read who are most likely to have kids who read.) Of course, parents' instructions can be powerful messages too, but often not as powerful as the behavioral example they set.

LIFE HACK 6.2

Remember the Bobo doll studies when kids are around. Kids are learning and making decisions about their own behavior by observing your behavior and the consequences it brings.

(Bandura et al., 1961, 1963; Francis et al., 2007; Gilman et al., 2009; Pagani et al., 2004, 2009)

Mirror Neurons

In recent years, researchers who focus on the biology of the brain have discovered particular cells that relate directly to observational learning. These brain cells, known as **mirror neurons**, are thought to underlie empathy and imitation and

mirror neurons
Neurons that are thought to underlie empathy and imitation and that activate when a person performs or observes a particular behavior.

CURRENT CONTROVERSY

Does Violence in the Media Cause Violence in Real Life?

Few topics in psychology have created as much public controversy as the impact of violence in the media (Ball-Rokeach, 2016; Ferguson & Kilburn, 2010; Huesmann, 2010; Kirsh, 2012; Plante et al., 2020). We are certainly exposed to a lot of media, and it contains a lot of violence:

- American teens (13–18 years old) spend an average of 9 hours per day using media, excluding use at school or for homework. Tweens (8–12 years old) average 6 hours per day (Common Sense Census, 2015).
- By one estimate, 85% of video games on the market include some form of violence (American Psychological Association, 2020). Among video games rated T (for Teen), 98% involve intentional violence, 90% reinforce the player for causing injury, and 69% reinforce the player for killing (Haninger & Thompson, 2004). Among video games rated E (for Everyone), 64% involve intentional violence, and 60% reinforce the player for causing injury (Thompson & Haninger, 2001).
- On American TV, 70% of shows contain acts of violence. TV ratings such as TVY7, TVPG, TV14, and TVMA are poor indicators of how much violence a show contains, especially non-gory violence (like punching or pointing a gun). This means that such violence is widespread across all ratings (Gabrielli et al., 2016).

Hundreds of studies have been conducted to explore what behavior accompanies and follows viewing media violence. Overall, the results of these studies are mixed. Some of these studies find strong connections between watching media violence and violent or aggressive behavior (Anderson et al., 2010, 2017; Anderson & Bushman, 2001, 2018; Bender et al., 2018; Bushman & Anderson, 2001; Calvert et al., 2017; Ferguson & Kilburn, 2009). But some studies find little or no connection between media violence and aggressive behavior (Ferguson, 2018; Ferguson & Colwell, 2018; Ferguson et al., 2020; Przybylski & Weinstein, 2019). Some researchers who have found no connection have suggested that the researchers who do find a connection are influenced by organizations and political forces that want to condemn violent video games as a result of public pressure (Copenhaver & Ferguson, 2018; Ferguson & Beresin, 2017). Another aspect of the controversy involves all video games being lumped together with the most violent as "bad," when there is indeed strong evidence that some video games produce beneficial or even prosocial effects for those who play them, including improved problem-solving skills and intergroup relations (Adachi & Willoughby, 2017; Granic et al., 2014; Lobel et al., 2017).

One of the significant challenges in determining the impact of media violence is figuring out how to study it (Ferguson & Savage, 2012). Many studies use correlational methods, simply determining the extent to which media violence and aggressive behavior occur together. (Remember from Chapter 1—correlation does not necessarily mean that one variable caused the other. In fact, at least one study has found that whether a video game features direct competition against another player is a better predictor of real-world aggression than the violence the game contains [Hawk & Ridge, 2021].) Other researchers have used more experimental methods, in which they manipulate people's exposure to media violence and then observe their reactions (Bushman & Anderson, 2015). In one experimental study, for example, participants played either a violent or nonviolent video game and then watched a video of real-life violence. For the participants who played a nonviolent video game, heart rates went up when they watched the video. However, for the participants who played a violent video game, heart rates did not go up, suggesting that the video game violence had desensitized them (Carnagey et al., 2007).

In another experimental study, researchers had children age 8 to 12 play either a violent E-rated Xbox game (*Spiderman*) or nonviolent one (*Finding Nemo*). Next, researchers assessed the kids in two ways. The first way was biological: they measured the amount of cortisol, a hormonal sign of the fight-or-flight response, in their saliva. These results showed that kids who had played the more violent video game had significantly higher levels of cortisol. The second way involved the use of a word-completion task: kids saw the first letters of a word and were asked to add letters to complete the word. Kids who played the more violent video game were significantly more likely to create aggressive words. For example, when the partial word was K I __ __, kids who played the more violent video game were significantly more likely to spell KILL than KISS or KITE. The researchers concluded that violent video games were more likely to both elicit a biological fight-or-flight response and increase access to aggressive words and thoughts compared to less violent video games (Gentile et al., 2017).

Other researchers have taken a more longitudinal approach to studying the impact of media violence. They follow participants over a period of years, rather than testing them in just one sitting, to see how video game violence affected them. One group of researchers studied teens over a 3-year period and found that those who played violent video games more often were no more likely to behave aggressively than those who played them less often. Other variables, such as violence in their home and the extent to which they were depressed, were much better predictors of aggressive behavior (Ferguson et al., 2012). •

activate when a person performs *or* observes a particular behavior (**Figure 6.8**). The key phrase in that definition is *performs or observes*. In other words, the same neuron in your brain fires whether you perform the behavior yourself or watch someone else do it. If a bowling ball drops on your toe, you cringe. If you see a bowling ball fall on the toe of a stranger a few lanes away, you cringe too. Of course, you don't feel that person's pain to the same extent that they do, but you feel it a little bit, thanks to your mirror neurons (Ferrari & Coudé, 2018; Heyes, 2010; Iacoboni, 2009; Rizzolatti & Craighero, 2004).

Mirror neurons were actually discovered in monkeys, and our understanding of them in monkey brains is far more advanced than our understanding of them in

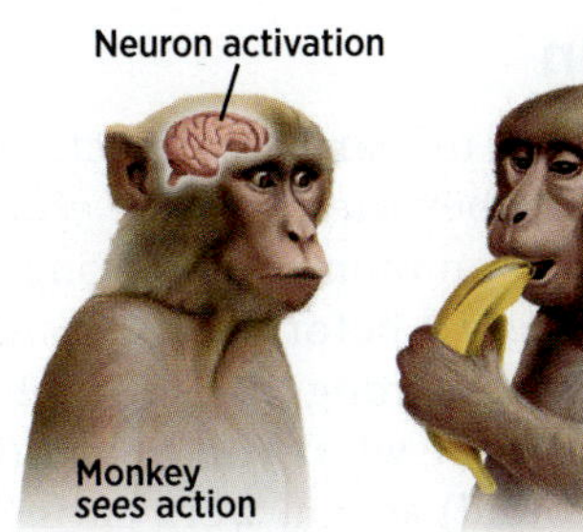

FIGURE 6.8 Mirror Neurons in the Brain. The discovery of mirror neurons revealed that behavior causes very similar activation of neurons whether you perform the behavior yourself or watch the behavior performed by someone else. Mirror neurons are a relatively recent discovery, but researchers believe that they may play a significant role in observational learning, empathy, and imitation.

human brains (Fabbri-Destro & Rizzolatti, 2008; Keysers & Gazzola, 2018). In these studies, wires are connected directly to the motor cortex in the frontal lobe of monkeys. This allows researchers to identify particular mirror neurons that fire in monkey A when it sees monkey B perform particular behaviors, such as breaking a peanut shell open or grasping a ball. Researchers have identified mirror neurons and located them within the brain, but they still have a lot left to learn. However, researchers are closer to understanding the biological mechanism by which what we observe becomes what we do. Perhaps the old saying, "Monkey see, monkey do," skipped a step. "Monkey see, monkey mirror neurons fire, monkey do" is less catchy but probably more accurate.

CHECK YOUR LEARNING:

6.21 What is observational learning?

6.22 Who conducted the Bobo doll studies, and what concept did those studies most clearly demonstrate?

6.23 What role do mirror neurons play in observational learning?

To check your understanding of these questions, click show the answers or refer to the answers in the Chapter Summary.

Biological Influences on Learning

YOU WILL LEARN:

6.24 what biological preparedness is and how it affects learning.

6.25 how John Garcia and others have studied biological preparedness.

6.26 how learning can be limited by instinctive drift.

The impressive findings of Pavlov, Skinner, and others during the early days of learning research led some experts to believe that any animal could be conditioned to learn any behavior (Kimble, 1981). At the time, researchers assumed that animals (and people too) enter the world as blank slates, available to be conditioned (classical or operant conditioning) by any life experience that they might encounter. It turns out to not be entirely true. We actually enter the world with an inborn head start toward certain learning experiences — especially those that increase the chances that we will stay healthy and safe (Krause & Domjan, 2017; Logue, 1979; Seligman, 1970; Seligman & Hager, 1972). The phrase that psychologists use to describe this head start is **biological preparedness**: an animal's evolutionary predisposition to learn what is most relevant to the survival of that species. It's as if we have been primed by our ancestors to have *almost* learned certain connections before we have any experience at all. Then, just a little learning is enough to complete the connection.

biological preparedness
An animal's evolutionary predisposition to learn that which is most relevant to the survival of that species.

Taste Aversion

Consider how easy it is to learn a connection between what you eat and how your stomach feels. Remember the last time you had food poisoning? There's a good chance you developed an immediate strong dislike, or *taste aversion*, to what you ate (say, blueberry yogurt) before you got sick. But there's a poor chance that you developed an immediate strong dislike to what you saw (the tables and chairs, the people you were with) or what you heard (the topic of conversation, the music or TV in the background) as you were eating. You were much more likely to learn that the blueberry yogurt, rather than the sights and sounds in the room, made you sick. The reason is that evolution primed — or biologically prepared — you to do so. Your ancestors had a predisposition toward making this taste–sickness connection. Just as they passed down other survival-of-the-fittest characteristics, they passed down that predisposition to future generations, including you (Parker, 2014).

John Garcia and his colleagues conducted classic studies with rats that parallel this taste aversion experience. Their research illustrated that certain learning connections are more likely than others because of biological preparedness (e.g., Garcia et al., 1966, 1989). They began by giving rats either "sweet water" (water with a sugary substance mixed in) or "bright noisy water" (water that tasted plain but was accompanied by a bright light and a loud sound). Soon after drinking, the rats received one of two consequences: nausea (caused by radiation), or mildly painful electric shock. Rats who drank the sweet water and then experienced nausea avoided the sweet water when it was offered again. However, rats who drank the sweet water and then received an electric shock didn't hesitate to drink the sweet water when it was offered again. It seems they were predisposed to link the water's sweet taste to nausea but not to physical pain.

On the other hand, rats who drank the bright noisy water and then experienced nausea were eager to drink bright noisy water again, but rats who drank the bright noisy water and then experienced electric shock avoided bright noisy water from that point on. They were more likely to connect sights and sounds to physical pain than to nausea (Garcia & Koelling, 1966). Both of these findings are consistent with the evolution of rats (and most other animals). In other words, Garcia's rats seem to have been born, thanks to their genetic inheritance, with a head start toward connecting food with nausea and sights or sounds with physical pain, connections that would enhance their ability to survive in the wild.

Garcia and other researchers have put their research on taste aversion to practical use (Garcia & Gustavson, 1997; Gustavson et al., 1974, 1976). The real-world problem was that sheep farmers were losing large parts of their flocks to nearby packs of wolves. To stop the wolves from attacking the sheep, the researchers offered the wolves a sheep carcass tainted with a tasteless substance that made them very ill. Of course, the wolves devoured the carcass, but they developed a taste aversion to sheep in the process. They very quickly stopped preying on the sheep at all, to the farmers' delight. Similar taste aversion strategies have also been applied to keep raccoons from preying on chickens and to keep blackbirds from devouring sunflower crops (Gustavson et al., 1982; Nicolaus et al., 1982).

When doctors know that chemotherapy will cause nausea, they will often give patients a very unusual food — perhaps cucumber popsicles — as a scapegoat food. The intention is to allow patients to develop a taste aversion to something they may never eat again rather than a food they commonly eat.

For another real-world illustration of the biological preparedness that underlies the learning of food aversions, consider cancer patients going through chemotherapy. Chemotherapy causes nausea, among other side effects. Many patients develop an aversion to food they ate immediately before chemotherapy treatments. They may realize intellectually that the chemo caused the nausea, but the biological predisposition to link food rather than other stimuli with stomach problems is so strong that it's hard *not* to connect the nausea to food they recently ate (Bernstein, 1978; Bernstein & Webster, 1985; Hong et al., 2009; Wang et al., 2017). Fortunately, physicians have developed a technique to make sure that chemotherapy patients don't develop aversions to their favorite foods: they give patients a "scapegoat food" — often an unusual kind of ice cream, candy, or fruit juice that the patients have never had before — with the intention that the patient will develop an aversion to that new food instead of an old favorite (Bernstein, 1999; Broberg & Bernstein, 1987; Kwok et al., 2017; Scalera & Bavieri, 2008).

instinctive drift
The tendency of animals' behavior to return to innate, genetically programmed patterns.

Are food aversions the only way biology influences learning?

Food aversions are not the only evidence of biological preparedness. Consider phobias (see Chapter 14), especially the things people are most commonly afraid of: spiders, snakes, heights, enclosed spaces, the dark, dogs, and other animals. Even today, we remain quick to learn to fear these objects because evolution has biologically predisposed us to do so. For thousands of years they were life-threatening, and we inherited the same readiness to steer clear of them that kept our ancestors alive and well. The fact that these things and situations aren't usually life-threatening anymore, or that other things and situations have taken their place in the most recent generations, hasn't had time to register in our collective DNA, so we remain very likely to develop these highly unnecessary phobias. Even though objects like guns, knives, and speeding cars are much greater threats in our modern lives, phobias to these contemporary dangers are rare (Cook et al., 1986; Flannelly, 2017; Gamble et al., 2010; Gerdes et al., 2009; Hoehl et al., 2017; McNally, 1987; Rakison, in press; Scher et al., 2006; Seligman, 1971).

Cathy Keifer/Shutterstock.com

The most common phobias involve objects that no longer pose threats to our daily lives, like spiders, snakes, and heights. The fact that humans are still predisposed to develop these specific phobias, rather than phobias toward things that actually pose greater contemporary danger, illustrates the biological (and evolutionary) influence on learning.

Instinctive Drift

As a final example of the influence of biology on learning, consider **instinctive drift**: the tendency of animals' behavior to return to innate, genetically programmed patterns. If you offer an animal reinforcement in a way that is inconsistent with its instinct, the reinforcement may work temporarily, but the animal will inevitably gravitate back toward the behaviors that come naturally. In a classic paper, two former students of Skinner who had gone on to become animal trainers in a zoo describe how they were occasionally unable to train animals to perform the desired behavior (Breland & Breland, 1961). The problems always involved the animals doing what instinct rather than reinforcement told them to do. For example, when the trainers tried to teach a raccoon to pick up coins and drop them into a piggy bank, the raccoon couldn't stop rubbing the coins together and dipping them in and out of the piggy bank rather than simply dropping them in — just as the raccoons would instinctively dip the food in and out of water before eating. Similarly, when they tried to train pigs to do the same drop-the-coin-in-the-bank trick, the pigs too often rooted the coins — that is, dropped them and pushed them around on the ground with their snout — as they would do naturally when searching for food.

tbkmedia.de/Alamy

Instinctive drift is the tendency of an animal's behavior to return to innate, genetically programmed patterns. Researchers who tried to train raccoons to drop coins into a slot ran into difficulties because the raccoons couldn't stop rubbing the coins together and dipping them in and out of the slot, as they naturally do with food in water.

CHECK YOUR LEARNING:

6.24 What is biological preparedness, and how is it relevant to learning?

6.25 How have John Garcia and others studied biological preparedness?

6.26 What is instinctive drift, and how is it relevant to learning?

To check your understanding of these questions, click show the answers or refer to the answers in the Chapter Summary.

Cognitive Influences on Learning

YOU WILL LEARN:

6.27 that cognition, or thought, influences learning.

6.28 how cognitive maps help us learn.

6.29 that what we learn can remain latent until given the chance to emerge.

6.30 that we sometimes use insight to enhance trial-and-error learning.

6.31 that experiences in which we perceive no control over unpleasant events can lead to learned helplessness.

The pioneers of learning research overlooked not only the importance of biology but also the importance of cognition — or *thinking* — on learning. Early researchers seemed to believe that we learned mechanically, automatically, without thought — whether associating stimuli in classical conditioning or associating a behavior with its outcome in operant conditioning. If we reconsider a few of the examples from earlier in this chapter, it's easy to see how some kind of cognition actually plays an important role in learning. Remember Jenny, whose Uncle Joe drives a red pickup truck and takes her out for ice cream? It's not a stretch to imagine that — between Jenny's sight of a red pickup truck and her feeling of excitement — there's a quick thought about what a red pickup truck means to her. Remember Isabella, whose father, Ramon, reinforced her by taking her to the park when she cleaned her room? The contingency Isabella learns ("If I clean my room, then I get to go to the park") is actually a thought, an interpretation that explains the connection between his actions and their consequences. Even when we discuss the way animals learn, we use verbs like *associate* and *expect* and *predict* — all of which suggest that there's some kind of cognitive activity going on in the mind that affects the process.

Cognitive Maps

Edward Tolman conducted some important early studies that provide evidence of cognition during learning (Tolman, 1932, 1948; Tolman & Honzik, 1930). Tolman put one rat (rat A) in a maze and offered it no reinforcement. Rat A explored the various alleys and corners of the maze. Tolman later replaced rat A with a second rat (rat B) and placed food at the exit. With time, rat B eventually learned to make its way through the maze to reach the food. Finally, Tolman removed rat B, put rat A back in the maze, and placed the food at the exit. That's when Tolman observed the key result of this study: rat A reached the food for the first time *much more quickly* than rat B did. It was as if rat A had been taking mental notes about the maze as it wandered around earlier. Rat A seemed to have developed a **cognitive map** — a mental diagram of the physical environment — while it initially explored when no reinforcement was available (Epstein et al., 2017; Schiller et al., 2015). Rat A then used that map to take a very quick route through the maze to the food it smelled.

Rat A's cognitive map clearly improved its ability to navigate the maze to reach the food. Comparing the abilities of rat A and rat B to reach the food for the first time is like comparing two people trying to find a newly opened coffee shop in a downtown area of a city: an out-of-towner wandering the city for the first time (rat B), and a hometowner whose experience on those streets has created a mental map they can use to help them navigate (rat A). Tolman's main conclusion was that rat A — and all other rats, animals, and humans — have the ability to use cognitive maps and other types of cognition to speed up the learning process.

Rat A seemed to be mentally stockpiling what it had learned as it explored the maze: where the dead ends were, what sequence of rights and lefts led to a particular spot, and so on. Only after the food was offered did rat A have the opportunity to demonstrate what it knew. Rat A's quick solving of the maze once food was offered showed evidence that it was engaged in *latent learning* during its initial time in the maze. **Latent learning** is learning that has taken place but cannot be directly observed.

Here's an example that shows both the cognitive map and latent learning: Destiny, a teenage girl driving a car for the first time. Destiny has never been behind the wheel before, but for more than 15 years she has been a passenger and learned

cognitive map
A mental diagram of the physical environment as it is initially explored when no reinforcement is available.

latent learning
A type of learning that has taken place but cannot be directly observed.

quite a bit — the layout of the local streets, the functions of various controls around the steering wheel, and what the pedals do. When her father starts the lesson by saying, "Let's just take a short trip to school," Destiny has at least a rough idea what to do: turn on the ignition, put the car in drive, move her right foot from the brake to the gas, make a left and then two rights to arrive at school. Her father is there to talk her through the details, but thanks to all of the latent learning she has done over the years, Destiny learns to drive in a much shorter period of time than she would if she had never been in a car before. And the cognitive map is there too: she knows to take a left and two rights to get to school not because she's getting directions from Waze or Google Maps, but because she has her own internal mental GPS from her years driving the neighborhood streets with others (or walking or riding her bike along those streets).

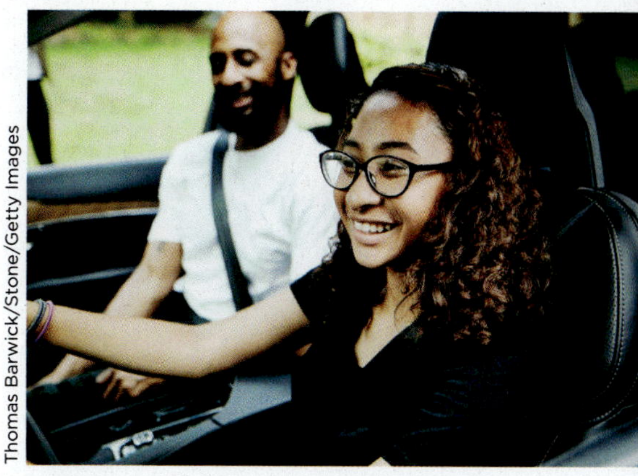
Thomas Barwick/Stone/Getty Images

Latent learning is learning that has taken place but has not yet been demonstrated. For example, a teenager who takes the wheel for the first time may show that she has picked up some knowledge of driving but hasn't had a chance to show it yet.

Insight

Another type of cognitive activity that can influence learning is **insight**: the perception of a solution to a problem that results from cognitive understanding rather than from trial and error. Simply put, sometimes you figure out problems because you use your analytic abilities or creativity to come up with a solution (Weisberg, 2015, 2018a, 2018b). Picture yourself in a grocery store receiving an important phone call from your doctor. As your doctor is telling you your medical test results, your phone battery runs out. Your charger is lost, and the doctor's office closes in 10 minutes. What will you do?

If cognition played no role in learning, you would have no choice but to operate on your environment in a random, hit-and-miss way until one of your actions charges your phone by chance. You might push your grocery cart back and forth, or high-five another customer, or pick up a box of Cheerios, hoping that one of those behaviors somehow recharges your phone. Of course, you don't behave so randomly, and that's because you have cognition on your side. You *think* about a solution. After a minute, you remember that a friend of yours has a part-time job at that grocery store. You ask the manager if your friend is working, and fortunately, the answer is yes. You quickly find your friend, explain the situation, and ask for a favor: "Do you have a charger I can borrow? Or can I just use your phone for a minute?" Your friend lets you borrow a charger and points you toward an outlet as well. You plug in, call back your doctor, and finish your call just in time. That experience of suddenly coming up with a solution is called an *aha moment* (as in "Aha! I figured it out!").

A survey of over 1000 adults found that about 80% of people report experiencing aha moments, and that they most commonly take place at night, at work, or in the shower (Ovington et al., 2018). Neuropsychological studies using fMRI (functional magnetic resonance imaging) show that aha moments rely heavily on activity in certain parts of the brain, including parts of the frontal lobe like the prefrontal cortex and the anterior cingulate, as well as the thalamus, hippocampus, and midbrain (Aziz-Zadeh et al., 2009; Kounios & Beeman, 2009; Tik et al., 2018; Topolinski & Reber, 2010).

In the 1920s in Berlin, Wolfgang Kohler conducted classic studies on chimps who seemed to use their own cognitions to solve problems in a similar way. When Kohler placed a banana outside the chimp's cage, just farther away than its arm could reach, the chimp used a stick inside the cage to pull the banana closer. When Kohler placed another banana a bit farther out, beyond the reach of the first stick, the chimp fastened two sticks together to form a double-length stick, which enabled it to retrieve the banana. When Kohler hung a banana from the ceiling, the chimp stacked crates to form a tower that it could climb to grab the banana. In each of these cases, the chimp's action was preceded by a period of frustration that simpler efforts did not bring about the reward, as well as a period of inactivity in which the chimp appeared to be thinking about the situation. There were also failed attempts at each of the strategies that eventually proved successful (Gould & Gould, 1994; Kohler, 1924). The point is that Kohler's chimps didn't perform random acts and wait for the bananas to land in their laps. The chimps used cognition, or thought, to supplement what they learned from the consequences of their actions.

insight
The perception of a solution to a problem that results from cognitive understanding rather than from trial and error.

Learned Helplessness

A lot of animal research illustrates the influence of cognition on learning, but the studies by Martin Seligman and his colleagues are especially relevant to human suffering and wellness (Overmier & LoLordo, 1998; Overmier & Seligman, 1967; Seligman, 1975; Seligman & Maier, 1967). Seligman used dogs in his studies, and he placed them in an apparatus known as a shuttle box, as shown in **Figure 6.9**. The shuttle boxes were divided into two halves by a short wall (no taller than the dogs' legs) that the dogs could easily jump over. One side of the shuttle box (the shock side) contained an electrified floor through which Seligman could shock the dogs' feet; the other side (the safe side) did not.

In one of their best-known studies (Maier et al., 1969), Seligman and his colleagues divided the dogs into three groups, and each group went through two phases of the study. In the first phase, Group 1 received controllable shock: they were placed on the shock side but were free to jump to the safe side, which they quickly learned to do upon the first sign of the shock. Group 2 received uncontrollable shock: they were restrained on the shock side in harnesses that prevented them from crossing to the safe side when shock was delivered. Group 3 received no shock at all.

In the second phase, every dog received controllable shock. As you might expect, Group 1 quickly learned to jump to the safe side during the second phase, just as they had in the first. Group 3 also learned to jump to the safe side. But Group 2 – the dogs who were powerless to do anything to avoid the shock in the first phase – never learned to avoid the shock in the second phase at all. They just stayed there and took it. Sometimes they whimpered and cried, but they never made any effort to alleviate their pain, despite the fact that all they needed to do was make a quick jump over a short nearby wall.

Seligman (1975) later explained that even after he tried to lure the dogs in Group 2 to the safe side – by removing the short wall altogether, by calling to the dogs from the safe side, even by luring them to the safe side with food – the dogs did nothing to help themselves. Seligman called the dogs' reaction to this situation **learned helplessness**: the absence of any attempt to help oneself that results from previously learning that such attempts are useless. Seligman explained that the dogs in Group 2 (who were the main focus of this study) had apparently learned, through their experience in the first phase, that their pain was entirely outside of their control. This lesson was so strong that even when the situation changed and they could, in fact, exert some control, they didn't realize or accept this fact. In other words, they continued to *believe*

FIGURE 6.9 Learned Helplessness. In a series of classic studies, dogs that were free to avoid shock when they saw a warning light learned to do so. But dogs that were prevented from avoiding shock stopped trying, even when they were no longer being prevented. That failure to try to avoid the shock was labeled *learned helplessness*. Some psychologists believe that learned helplessness explains depression in people who have learned that they can't control the negative experiences in their lives (Maier et al., 1969; Seligman, 1975).

learned helplessness
The absence of any attempt to help oneself that results from previously learning that such attempts are useless.

they were helpless even when they weren't, and that cognition had a powerful influence on their behavior.

What do these learned helplessness studies with dogs have to do with people?

Seligman and others believed that the findings of their learned helplessness studies offered an explanation for human depression. They suggested that people who are depressed resemble the dogs from Group 2: at some point in their lives, they experience pain (often emotional rather than physical) that they perceived as uncontrollable. Through that process, they learn they are helpless. As a result, they stop trying to help themselves — despite new life circumstances and encouragement from friends and family that they really can help themselves — and resign themselves to endless days of sadness and apathy. As we will discuss in Chapter 14, many factors can contribute to depression, but learned helplessness may be one of those factors for many people (Smallheer et al., 2018).

More recently, some experts have wondered if learned helplessness might also explain some people's inaction regarding the environment. Their thinking goes like this: even for somebody who cares a great deal about the environment, they will be less likely to participate in behaviors that might improve the environment if their own life experience has led to a strong sense of learned helplessness. That means these people will participate in fewer activities that are good for the environment such as recycling, buying items that include recycled materials, promoting awareness of climate change, or donating money to pro-environment causes. A study of over 400 participants found support for this idea: high levels of learned helplessness served as a barrier between participants' concern about the environment and taking action to improve it (Landry et al., 2018).

Another study examined the correlation between environmental concern and environmental action among 32 countries around the world. Researchers found that the correlation depended on the residents' sense of external control. Specifically, in countries where residents have a high sense of external control, they were less likely to take environmental action even if they had high levels of environmental concern (Tam & Chan, 2017). External control, of course, resembles learned helplessness: both suggest that the person lacks internal control over their own situation.

Some researchers have stretched the concept of learned helplessness in new ways to capture the way misinformation and fake news can overwhelm many people. They have coined the term *informational learned helplessness* and explain it this way: people are so bombarded with bad information about current events like politics and social issues that they eventually feel helpless to separate the good from the bad and just passively take it all in (much like the dogs in Group 2 just accepted the electric shock and didn't attempt to avoid it). Their attempts to find the truth among the torrent of social media posts, online news stories, and TV reports feel futile, so they simply accept whatever information comes their way — including a huge amount of misinformation. One study that focused on informational learned helplessness and belief in COVID misinformation found a positive correlation between these two variables: people who scored high in informational learned helplessness were more likely to agree with false beliefs about COVID (Nisbet & Kamenchuk, 2019, 2021).

A final note about learned helplessness: later in his career, Seligman shifted his focus to the flip side of learned helplessness, *learned optimism*, in which people can, via their own cognitions, emphasize positive interpretations of life experiences to enhance their own sense of power and ward off depression (Kobau et al., 2011; Seligman, 1991, 2011). As an example, consider the ways an employee can interpret a job layoff. They can blame themselves and consider it a permanent setback, which could lead to depression based on the belief that there is nothing they can do to help themselves. Or they can blame external circumstances (the decision-makers in the organization, the economy, etc.) rather than themselves and consider the layoff a temporary problem. The second explanation suggests that there's reason to be hopeful that things may work out, and that the employee can play an active role in making that happen. Seligman (1991) argues that even if the "helpless" interpretation is the first one that occurs to this employee, they can train themselves to reject that interpretation and replace it with the more optimistic and self-empowering way of thinking. This increases the odds that not only will they work to solve their own problem but they're happy while doing so.

CHECK YOUR LEARNING:

6.27 How much does cognition influence learning?

6.28 What are cognitive maps, and how are they relevant to learning?

6.29 What is latent learning?

6.30 What is insight, and how is it relevant to both cognition and trial-and-error learning?

6.31 What is learned helplessness, and what experiences are likely to produce it?

To check your understanding of these questions, click show the answers or refer to the answers in the Chapter Summary.

CHAPTER SUMMARY

What Is Learning?

6.1 Psychologists define learning as the process by which life experience causes change in the behavior or thinking of an organism.

6.2 Learning is the essence of the nurture side of the nature-nurture debate that surrounds all of human behavior. (Maturation is the nature side of the debate.)

6.3 Learning isn't unique to humans. It occurs across all species.

Classical Conditioning

6.4 Ivan Pavlov was a Russian medical researcher studying the digestive system of dogs. Pavlov's accidental discovery of the learning process led to studies that shaped the field of psychology.

6.5 Classical conditioning is a form of learning in which animals or people make a connection between two stimuli that have occurred together, such that one predicts the other. Classical conditioning occurs in everyday life. People have all sorts of conditioned responses to things they see and hear.

6.6 The components of classical conditioning include a neutral stimulus, unconditioned stimulus, unconditioned response, conditioned stimulus, and conditioned response.

6.7 Generalization is the process by which stimuli that are similar to the conditioned stimulus cause the same conditioned response. Discrimination is the process by which stimuli that are different from the conditioned stimulus fail to cause the same conditioned response.

6.8 Acquisition happens when the neutral stimulus becomes a conditioned stimulus by its link to the conditioned response. Extinction happens when the conditioned stimulus no longer causes the conditioned response because it is no longer linked to the unconditioned stimulus.

6.9 Higher-order conditioning is a learning process in which a conditioned stimulus from a previous learning process serves as an unconditioned stimulus, producing a new conditioned stimulus that causes the same conditioned response.

6.10 Vicarious conditioning is conditioning that takes place by way of observation of others' life experiences rather than one's own.

Operant Conditioning

6.11 Operant conditioning is a form of learning in which the consequences of a voluntary behavior affect the likelihood that the behavior will recur.

6.12 The law of effect suggests that the likelihood of repeating a behavior depends on the effects of that behavior.

6.13 B. F. Skinner was a U.S. psychologist who conducted extensive operant conditioning studies on animal behavior. Skinner's research on operant conditioning made him a household name, in part because he applied his findings about animal behavior to human behavior.

6.14 Reinforcement is any consequence of a behavior that makes that behavior more likely to recur.

6.15 Positive reinforcement involves getting something desirable, while negative reinforcement involves removing something undesirable.

6.16 A reinforcement schedule is a pattern by which reinforcement occurs in response to a particular behavior. Continuous reinforcement is a pattern by which a behavior is reinforced every time it occurs, while partial reinforcement is a pattern by which a behavior is reinforced only some of the times it occurs. A fixed-ratio schedule is a reinforcement schedule in which a behavior is reinforced after a consistent, predictable number of occurrences. By contrast, a variable-ratio schedule is a reinforcement schedule in which a behavior is reinforced after an inconsistent, unpredictable number of occurrences. A fixed-interval schedule is a reinforcement schedule in which a behavior can be reinforced after a time interval that is consistent and predictable. By contrast, a variable-interval schedule is a reinforcement schedule in which a behavior can be reinforced after a time interval that is inconsistent and unpredictable.

6.17 Punishment is any consequence of a behavior that makes that behavior less likely to recur.

6.18 Recognizing a discriminative stimulus allows a person to act when the chances of obtaining reinforcement are greatest and the chances of getting punished are least.

6.19 Shaping is the process of gradually learning a complex behavior through the reinforcement of each of its small steps.

6.20 Generalization, discrimination, acquisition, and extinction are all concepts that occur in both classical conditioning and operant conditioning.

Observational Learning

6.21 Observational learning is learning that occurs as a result of observing others' behavior and consequences rather than our own.

6.22 Albert Bandura's Bobo doll studies demonstrated the power of modeling, imitation of observed behavior.

6.23 Mirror neurons are thought to underlie empathy and imitation and to activate when a person performs or observes a particular behavior.

Biological Influences on Learning

6.24 Biological preparedness is an animal's evolutionary predisposition to learn what is most relevant to the survival of that species.

6.25 John Garcia's research on taste aversion provided solid evidence for biological preparedness.

6.26 Instinctive drift is the tendency of animals' behavior to return to genetically programmed patterns, making it difficult to teach animals behavior that is inconsistent with instinct.

Cognitive Influences on Learning

6.27 Cognition, or thought, influences learning more than the original learning researchers believed it did.

6.28 A cognitive map is a mental diagram of a physical environment that can speed up the learning process.

6.29 Latent learning is learning that has taken place but cannot be directly observed until it is given a chance to be performed.

6.30 Insight is the perception of a solution to a problem that results from cognitive understanding and that allows one to skip some of the steps of trial-and-error learning.

6.31 Learned helplessness is the absence of any attempt to help oneself, resulting from previously learning that the situation is outside of one's control.

KEY TERMS

learning, p. 173
classical conditioning, p. 174
neutral stimulus, p. 174
unconditioned stimulus, p. 174
unconditioned response, p. 175
conditioned stimulus, p. 176
conditioned response, p. 176
generalization, p. 177
discrimination, p. 177
acquisition, p. 179
extinction, p. 180
spontaneous recovery, p. 180
higher-order conditioning, p. 181
vicarious conditioning, p. 181
operant conditioning, p. 183
law of effect, p. 184
Skinner box, p. 185
reinforcement, p. 185
positive reinforcement, p. 186
negative reinforcement, p. 186
primary reinforcer, p. 186
secondary reinforcer, p. 186
reinforcement schedule, p. 188
continuous reinforcement, p. 188
partial reinforcement, p. 188
fixed-ratio schedule, p. 188
variable-ratio schedule, p. 188
fixed-interval schedule, p. 189
variable-interval schedule, p. 189
punishment, p. 190
discriminative stimulus, p. 192
shaping, p. 193
observational learning, p. 196
mirror neurons, p. 197
biological preparedness, p. 199
instinctive drift, p. 201
cognitive map, p. 202
latent learning, p. 202
insight, p. 203
learned helplessness, p. 204

SELF-ASSESSMENT

1. When a person salivates to the sight of a familiar logo on a pizza box, that salivation is a(n) ______ ______.
   a. unconditioned response
   b. conditioned response
   c. unconditioned stimulus
   d. conditioned stimulus

2. A child has learned through experience that a certain bell sound means that the ice cream truck is nearby, and she responds to that bell with excitement. When that child reacts with similar excitement to a similar-sounding bell, she's exemplifying ______.
   a. extinction
   b. generalization
   c. biological preparedness
   d. shaping

3. Conditioning that takes place through observation of others' life experiences rather than one's own is known as ______ ______.

a. vicarious conditioning
b. higher-order conditioning
c. operant conditioning
d. classical conditioning

4. ______ is any consequence of a behavior that makes that behavior more likely to recur.

a. Reinforcement
b. Acquisition
c. Generalization
d. Punishment

5. A ______ ______ schedule is a reinforcement schedule in which a behavior is reinforced after an unpredictable number of occurrences — like winning money by buying lottery tickets.

a. fixed-ratio
b. variable-ratio
c. fixed-interval
d. variable-interval

6. A ______ ______ is a signal indicating that a particular behavior will be followed by a particular consequence.

7. When an animal trainer teaches a dolphin to jump out of the water and through a hoop by reinforcing each of the smaller behaviors required to do that action, the learning process is known as ______.

8. ______ ______ is an animal's evolutionary predisposition to learn what is most relevant to the survival of that species.

9. If a teenager — who has never driven a car before but has watched others driving many times — can drive well on their first attempt, then they are probably exhibiting ______ ______.

a. biological preparedness
b. classical conditioning
c. latent learning
d. spontaneous recovery

10. ______ ______ is the absence of any attempt to help oneself after learning through experience that the situation is outside of one's control.

To check your understanding of these questions, click show the answers in the e-book or refer to the answers in Appendix B.

Research shows quizzing is a highly effective learning tool. Continue quizzing yourself using LearningCurve, the system that adapts to *your* learning.

WHAT'S YOUR TAKE?

1. Before Pavlov intentionally conditioned his dogs to salivate to previously neutral stimuli (like the bell), they were classically conditioned by accident. The dogs picked up on sights and sounds that regularly occurred before they were given food in the lab, and soon those sights and sounds triggered anticipatory mouth-watering. Our own pets get classically conditioned by accident too. My childhood dog came running and jumped with excitement whenever she heard the crinkle of her bag of treats. We never intended for her to make this association, but over time, she learned that the crinkling sound of that particular bag meant that a treat would soon follow.

   How have your own pets demonstrated this kind of accidental classical conditioning? What kinds of previously neutral stimuli—the sight of the leash, the sound of the electric can opener, or others—have they identified as precursors to food? What kinds of conditioned reactions do your pets show to those stimuli now? Are there other unconditioned stimuli besides food that your pet has been conditioned to anticipate? If so, what are they, and what conditioned responses have they developed?

SHOW ME MORE

6.1 Classical Conditioning

This video offers some good examples and explanations of classical conditioning.
© Worth Publishers

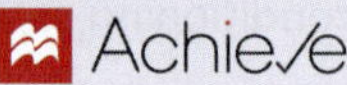

6.2 My Psychology Podcast

This podcast episode features the author of this textbook, psychologist Andy Pomerantz, speaking with other instructors of introductory psychology courses about the most important and interesting concepts in this chapter.
Macmillan Learning

7 Cognition: Thinking, Language, and Intelligence

Igor Kardasov/Shutterstock

CHAPTER OUTLINE

Imagine your best friend calls you in a panic: "I have job interview in an hour, and my suit is a wrinkled mess!" You ask for more info, and they explain that the suit is crumpled, creased, and crinkled so badly that there's no way they can wear it. They just tried to use their iron, but it's not working. Frantically, they ask "What can I do?"

Thankfully, you have the *cognitive* abilities—*thinking*, *intelligence*, and *language*—to help your friend with this problem. To start, you need to generate possible solutions. Is there another outfit available? Is there another way besides ironing to make that suit look presentable? You have to be creative enough to think of many possible solutions, and smart enough to narrow the list to the best ones. All the while, you need to appreciate your friend's emotional state and stop yourself from getting caught up in it.

Throughout your problem-solving and decision-making process, you need to communicate clearly with your friend. You need to understand the language they use to describe the problem, and then use language effectively enough for them to understand any solution you propose.

You think about your friend's problem and settle on a strategy: they can hang the suit in the bathroom while they run the hot shower, and the steam will get the wrinkles out. As clearly as you can, you explain this strategy to your friend. Your friend understands, and with a little bit of hope in their voice, they tell you they'll try it. Ten minutes later, your friend lets you know the solution worked and tells you how thankful they are.

Successfully solving your friend's problem illustrates the value of *cognition*—your ability to use information productively. Exactly how we use information, especially our capacities to think and use language in intelligent ways, is a focus of many psychology researchers. It will be our focus in this chapter as well.

cognition
What the brain does with information, including understanding it, organizing it, analyzing it, and communicating it.

Cognition is what your brain does with information, including understanding it, organizing it, analyzing it, and communicating it. Simply put, cognition is all about *knowledge* and what you do with it. In fact, the root of the word (*cogn-*) means *to know* in Latin. You're already familiar with other words that come from the same root, like re*cogn*ize (to re-know something), *cogn*izant (being knowledgeable of something), and in*cogn*ito (unknowable because of a disguise).

Cognition is something you do so continuously and so automatically that it's easy to take it for granted. Perhaps the best way to appreciate cognition is to notice what happens when people experience problems with it. Sometimes, these cognitive problems are fleeting. For example, you may have noticed that a friend or family member wasn't "thinking straight" in the hours after surgery, before the anesthesia had worn off. Other times, cognitive problems can last longer, as when someone develops Alzheimer's disease or another form of dementia. During interactions with people experiencing cognitive problems, the striking thing is their limited ability to use knowledge. They just don't seem as capable as you might expect to understand it, communicate it, or reason intelligently about it.

Psychologists who study cognition focus on three main areas: thinking, language, and intelligence. (Psychologists who study cognition focus on memory too, but that topic had its own chapter earlier in this book.) We'll consider all three topics in this chapter, beginning with thinking.

Thinking

YOU WILL LEARN:

7.1 how psychologists define and research cognition.

7.2 how psychologists define the term *concept*.

7.3 about the three main types of concepts.

7.4 the three levels psychologists use to organize concepts.

7.5 the difference between problem solving and decision making.

7.6 the difference between an algorithm and a heuristic.

7.7 the different ways people stray from reason when solving problems.

7.8 about the different types of heuristics.

7.9 about the two types of thinking involved in dual-process theory.

7.10 whether people are good at affective forecasting.

7.11 how psychologists define creativity.

7.12 the difference between divergent thinking and convergent thinking.

7.13 about functional fixedness.

7.14 about other factors that are linked to creativity.

Any discussion of thinking has to start with an explanation of the term **concept**: a mental representation of a category of similar things, actions, or people. Concepts are the most basic building blocks of thinking, the pieces that you use to string together thoughts. For example, to have even a simple thought such as "My cousin borrowed my hoodie," first you'd need to understand the concept of *cousin*, the concept of *borrow*, and the concept of *hoodie*. You've known these concepts so long that you probably can't remember not knowing them, but there are probably other concepts that you can remember picking up more recently. Did you always understand the concept of cancel culture? Side hustle? Gig worker? ASMR?

Concepts facilitate thinking in two important ways. First, they allow us to apply what we already know to something new (Markman & Rein, 2013). Let's go back to the concept of "hoodie." Once you have that concept, you have a pretty good idea about what it means for an item to belong to it: the item is clothing, it covers the top half of your body, it has a hood, and so on. So when you get a new hoodie as a gift, you don't find yourself bewildered or perplexed. You recognize it as a hoodie, and you know exactly what it's for and what to do with it. (Imagine how differently you might react if you opened the gift and found a completely unfamiliar item, for which you had no concept.) Second, concepts facilitate communication (Rips et al., 2012). Imagine a phone call in which you tell your friend about the gift you received. Without the concept of "hoodie," you'd struggle through a lengthy description that might or might not be effective: "It's a piece of clothing that covers my chest and arms, and it's got this part that covers my head. . . ." With both of you grasping the concept of "hoodie," that single word precisely conveys to your friend the gift you received.

Concepts: What Holds Them Together?

Each concept must have some kind of "gl0ue" that holds it together, some similarity among the items that concept contains. What exactly is that glue? Psychologists have studied this question extensively. The answer that has received the most attention has been *features*, characteristics that the items have in common. However, other answers include the *goals* shared by the items and the *relationships* between the items

(Markman & Rein, 2013). Let's consider all three of these ways that concepts can be held together (**Table 7.1**).

concept
A mental representation of a category of similar things, actions, or people.

prototype
The most typical or best example within a concept.

Feature-Based Concepts. Originally, psychologists believed that all concepts were defined by a list of characteristic features. This was an all-or-nothing way of understanding concept membership: if an item had all the features, it was in, but if it was missing any of those features, it was out (Smith & Medin, 1981). Logically, this understanding of concepts made a lot of sense, but it didn't work well practically. As an example, let's consider the concept of a *ball*. If you were going to make a list of the features required for something to belong to this concept, it might include these: it's round, it bounces, and it's used in sports. That would certainly capture most balls: soccer balls, basketballs, baseballs, volleyballs, tennis balls, kickballs. But it doesn't capture all of them. Footballs aren't round. Neither are rugby balls. Bowling balls don't bounce. And plenty of balls, such as wrecking balls, cotton balls, meatballs, and matzah balls, aren't used in sports.

So psychologists started looking for other ways to understand how people form concepts. In the 1970s, researcher Eleanor Rosch proposed that the object only needs the *most representative* features rather than *all* of the features to become a member of a concept (Hampton, 1995; Kinsella et al., 2015; Rosch, 1975; Rosch & Mervis, 1975; Rosch et al., 1976). Rosch argued that our minds form a **prototype**: the most typical or best example within a concept. The prototypes we form are averages, or abstract blends, of the best members of the category. This means that a prototype is something we imagine, rather than some specific thing we have actually encountered (Posner & Keele, 1970; Reed, 1972). So we don't choose any specific ball to serve as the prototype of a *ball*. Instead, we morph together these good examples of balls into a new mental creation that falls right in the middle of all of them. Then we compare any new ball-like items to that prototype to see if they belong in the concept of a *ball*.

Other researchers disagreed with Rosch's prototype theory, especially the "imagined" or "morphed together" quality of prototypes (Brooks, 1978; Hampton, 2016; Kruschke, 2005; Medin & Schaffer, 1978; Murphy, 2002, 2016b; Murphy & Hoffman, 2012; Nosofsky et al., 1989; Nosofsky & Johansen, 2000; Smith & Minda, 1998, 2000). These other researchers argued that you choose a real "textbook example" of the definition of the concept — the best example you have actually seen, heard, or touched — rather than morphing several of them together into an imaginary prototype. They call this "best example" an *exemplar* to distinguish it from a prototype. This exemplar theory states that one type of real ball you have encountered — let's say a soccer ball — serves as the exemplar in your mind for the concept of *ball*. Whether you include a new ball-like object in that concept — let's say a golf ball or a racquetball — depends on how closely that new object resembles a soccer ball.

Feature-based concept formation has proven to be a complex and challenging area of research for psychologists. As a result, the debate about how we form concepts is far from over. A couple of conclusions are certain, however. One conclusion is that

TABLE 7.1: Types of Concepts

TYPE OF CONCEPT	WHAT HOLDS THE CONCEPT TOGETHER	FOR EXAMPLE...
Feature-based	Similar features or characteristics	Beagles, bulldogs, Great Danes, Chihuahuas, and huskies are all *dogs*.
Goal-based	The same goal or purpose	Cash, credit cards, debit cards, gift cards, checks, money orders, Paypal, Venmo, and Apple Pay are all *methods of payment*.
Relationship-based	The same relationship or connection between people or things	Uber, Lyft, taxis, buses, and limos are all *ride services*.

Information from Markman and Rein (2013).

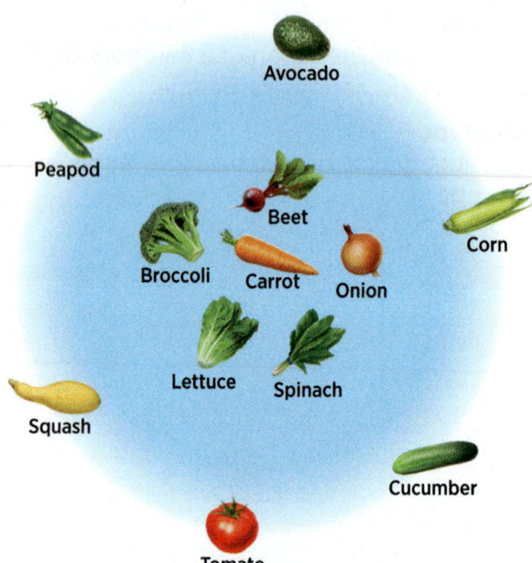

FIGURE 7.1 Fuzzy Boundaries: Is It a Vegetable? Some foods are just more vegetable-ish than others. In other words, the vegetable concept has fuzzy boundaries, with some items definitely in and others possibly in and possibly out. The foods on the fuzzy boundary of this figure are sometimes considered vegetables, but sometimes not.

concepts often have fuzzy boundaries, with some items definitely in, some items definitely out, and some items in between (**Figure 7.1**). This means that some items are simply better or more typical members of concepts than others (Hampton, 1995). For example, consider the concept of *soup*. Tomato soup definitely fits within that concept. Hamburgers definitely don't. But what about chili? Maybe it belongs to the concept of *soup*, but if it does, it's not the most typical member.

Goal-Based Concepts. It's possible that the most distinctive thing shared by items within a concept is not a feature but the goal that those items accomplish. That is, objects may be tied together by what purpose they collectively serve (Barsalou, 1983, 1985, 2003, 2012; Chrysikou, 2006). As an example, consider the concept of exercise equipment (as discussed in Markman & Rein, 2013). The items within this category span a wide range of examples, and can even possess contrasting characteristics. Some pieces of exercise equipment, like treadmills and elliptical machines, are big things that you stand on and pay a lot of money for. Other exercise equipment, like dumbbells and jump ropes, are small things that you hold in your hand and pay less money for. Stationary bikes and rowing machines are things you sit on; activity trackers (FitBit, Apple Watch, Garmin, etc.) and running shoes are things you wear. But all of these items belong to the concept of exercise equipment because they all share a goal: promoting exercise and physical fitness.

Relationship-Based Concepts. Sometimes, a concept hangs together because the items in it all describe similar kinds of relationships or interactions between things or people (Gentner & Kurtz, 2005; Goldwater et al., 2011; Kurtz et al., 2013; Markman, 1999). For example, the concept of "teaching" evokes a certain type of relationship: one person who is more knowledgeable in a particular subject area sharing that knowledge with another person who is less knowledgeable. The concept includes a wide assortment of examples — a kindergarten teacher, a middle school basketball coach, an ACT tutor, a law school professor — but in every case, the example belongs to the concept because it is based on the same kind of relationship.

Expertise, Culture, and Concepts

Psychologists often organize concepts into three levels: *superordinate*, *basic*, and *subordinate* (Johnson, 2013; Neisser, 1987). The kind we tend to use most in our thinking are the *basic* concepts. As **Figure 7.2** shows, those *basic* concepts fall within much broader, *superordinate* concepts, and they also contain many more specific, *subordinate* concepts (Bauer & Just, 2017; Murphy, 2016a). As an example, consider the basic concept of a bicycle. Bicycle falls within the superordinate concept of vehicle, along with cars, trucks, motorcycles, boats, and spaceships. Bicycle also contains many subordinate concepts, such as mountain bikes, road bikes, racing bikes, BMX bikes, and cruiser bikes.

Superordinate Concept (Vehicle)
Basic Concept (Bicycle)
Subordinate Concept (Mountain Bike)

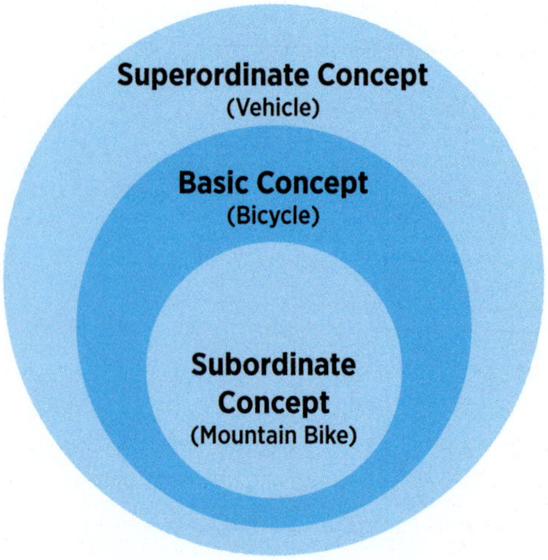

FIGURE 7.2 Superordinate, Basic, and Subordinate Concepts. We tend to focus our thinking on basic concepts (bicycle) rather than zooming out to superordinate concepts (vehicle) or zooming in to subordinate concepts (mountain bike). But for a person with specific expertise in mountain bikes, mountain bike could become the basic concept, with specific kinds of mountain bikes occupying the subordinate level.

But what you consider basic — in other words, the conceptual level at which you typically think — depends on your level of expertise and your cultural background. If you're an expert on a topic, you tend to zoom in on concepts in such a way that what's subordinate to most people is basic to you (Hajibayova & Jacob, 2017; Johnson & Mervis, 1997; Medin et al., 2002; Tanaka & Taylor, 1991). Let's consider bicycles again, but from the perspective of Jada, who owns a bike shop specializing in mountain bikes. For Jada, who spends hours every day reading about, discussing, repairing, and riding mountain bikes, *mountain bike* isn't a subordinate concept; it is a basic concept. Jada is so immersed in mountain bikes, rather than bikes in general, that mountain bikes represent her typical level of thinking. (She may not have even ridden another type of bike for years.) Jada's subordinate concepts would be specific subtypes of mountain bikes, like cross-country, downhill, trail, or dirt-jumping styles.

DIVERSITY MATTERS

Culture works much the same way as expertise, providing knowledge that focuses your thinking to an extent that people outside of the culture simply can't match (Park et al., 2018). For example, consider someone who has no Indian heritage and who only rarely eats Indian food. For this person, *Indian food* may be a subordinate concept, under the basic concept *Asian food* (along with *Chinese food* and *Japanese food*). But for someone of Indian heritage, who eats or cooks Indian food every day, *Indian food* could be basic, or even superordinate. It could contain the more specific concepts *North Indian cuisine* and *South Indian cuisine* (the latter of which is typically more spicy), and either of those concepts could include concepts based on more specific regions or states within India, such as *Hyderabadi cuisine*, *Bihari cuisine*, *Maharashtrian cuisine*, and *Goa cuisine*. The point here is that culture, because of the expertise it brings, can powerfully influence whether a particular concept is superordinate, basic, or subordinate for you.

DIVERSITY MATTERS

Culture can influence concept formation in other ways as well. Researchers have found that people of Asian descent and people of European descent often show differences in how they organize items into concepts. Generally, when organizing objects into concepts, people of Asian descent tend to take a more relationship-based approach, while people of European descent tend to take a more feature-based approach (Chiu, 1972; Nisbett, 2003). Some have speculated that this distinction stems from the greater emphasis on collectivism in Asian cultures than European cultures (Miyamoto & Wilken, 2013).

In a study illustrating these tendencies, Chinese and U.S. college students were given lists of three items and asked to group a pair of the items together conceptually (Ji et al., 2004). The lists were constructed such that some pairs of items related to each other in some relationship-based way, but other pairs of items were similar in terms of features. Chinese students tended to put items together because they related to or interacted with each other. U.S. students tended to put items together because they had similar features. For example, one list contained the words *monkey*, *panda*, and *banana* (**Figure 7.3**). Chinese students were more likely to group together *monkey* and *banana* (based on the monkeys-eat-bananas relationship). U.S. students were more likely to group together *monkey* and *panda* (based on the shared feature that both monkeys and pandas are animals).

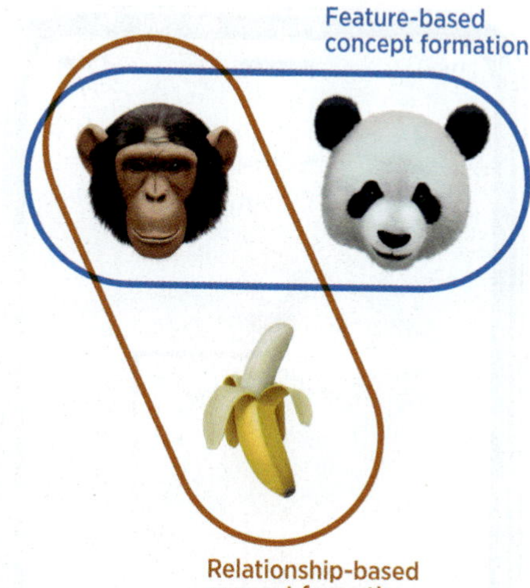

FIGURE 7.3 Cultural Influence on Concept Formation. In one study, Chinese students were more likely to group monkeys and bananas together conceptually, while U.S. students were more likely to group monkeys and pandas together conceptually. That difference in concept formation may indicate a tendency toward relationship-based concepts (monkeys eat bananas) versus feature-based concepts (monkeys and pandas are both animals). Research from Ji et al. (2004).

Problem Solving and Decision Making

Problem solving is using cognition to find a way to achieve a goal. Problem solving is closely related to **decision making**, which is using cognition to choose between available options. To help distinguish between problem solving and decision making, keep this in mind: when you solve problems, you often have to create the answers from scratch, but when you make decisions, the possible answers are usually already presented to you.

Another distinction between problem solving and decision making is how badly the right answer is *needed*. For problem solving, the need is pressing, but for decision making, the need may be less urgent or even absent (Bassok & Novick, 2012; Mayer, 2013).

Algorithms. A key question in the study of both problem solving and decision making is the extent to which they are based on reason. For a long time, psychologists assumed that when it comes to problem solving, we are all about reason (Evans, 2012). In fact, they believed that we solve problems like machines, using an **algorithm**, or a formula-like method of problem solving. Algorithms are what Google Maps and other GPS/navigation apps use to give you directions from point A to point B — an entirely logic-based set of rules based on essential data (distance, roads, traffic) that produces the most rational, sensible, practical route. But psychologists soon recognized that people are not entirely algorithmic as problem solvers (Arkes, 1991; Evans, 2013; McKenzie, 2005; Speekenbrink & Shanks, 2013).

problem solving
Using cognition to find a way to achieve a goal.

decision making
Using cognition to choose between available options.

algorithm
A formula-like method of problem solving.

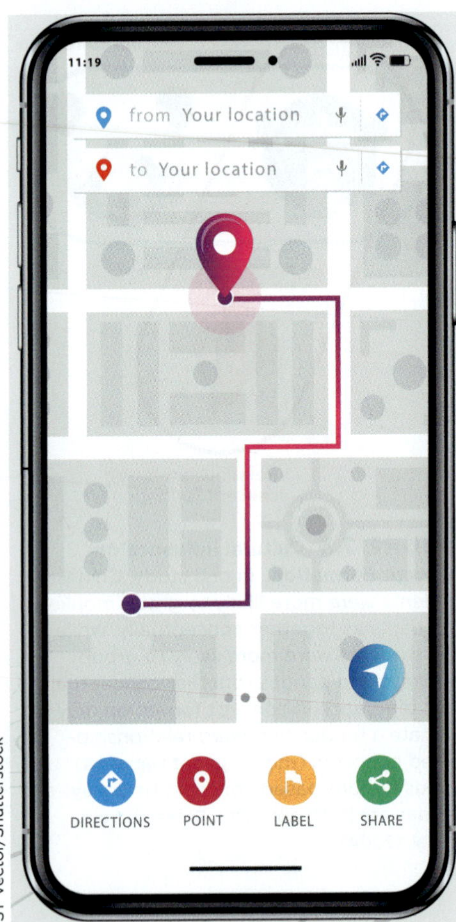

PST Vector/Shutterstock

To give you directions from point A to point B, Google Maps (and other GPS/navigation apps) uses an algorithm, a method of problem solving based entirely on logic and rationality. Humans, however, often combine algorithms with other factors, like preferences and values, to solve problems. That is why you may choose to take the scenic route rather than the most efficient one.

Whether you are choosing a candy bar or a college, your values and preferences mix with your reasoning to determine your response (Chater et al., 2005; Oaksford et al., 2012). Sometimes, we stray pretty far from solid reasoning, as the problems described below illustrate.

Problems with Problem Solving. A number of different factors can cause us to stray from reason when solving problems. One such factor is your **mental set**, or the limits you place on your approach to problem solving based on what has worked in the past. For example, consider Tommy and his TV remote. When his TV remote at home doesn't work, Tommy has discovered that tapping it a few times on the coffee table usually fixes the problem. Tommy tried the same technique at his new job at a restaurant with TVs, but it didn't work. Unable to think of another solution, Tommy just kept tapping. Finally, his coworker Natalia helped him solve the problem by replacing the batteries. If Tommy wasn't so limited by his mental set, he also might have considered other solutions like checking to see if any buttons on the remote are jammed, cleaning off the part of the remote that the signal comes out of, or cleaning off the part of the TV that receives the signal.

Another factor that overrides reason in many problem-solving situations is **confirmation bias**: a tendency to prefer information that confirms what you thought in the first place. For example, if you're looking to replace your broken phone, your first thought might be to get the kind that your best friend has, since they rave about it constantly. You do a little research online, and you find that there are plenty of positive reviews of your best friend's phone, but plenty of negative ones too. You also notice other phones that have plenty of positive reviews with fewer negative reviews. But you find yourself playing down the good reviews of competing phones (and the bad reviews of your best friend's phone), and playing up the good reviews of your best friend's phone (and the bad reviews of competing phones). In the end, you convince yourself of what you half-believed when you started, even if reason suggests otherwise — your best friend's phone is the one to get.

Social media is another place where confirmation bias often occurs, especially when we stay within our "bubble" of ideas, beliefs, and preferences (Westerwick et al., 2017; Workman, 2018). In fact, confirmation bias may play a role in the acceptance of the "fake news" that fills our Twitter and Facebook feeds (and perhaps the accounts we choose to follow) when it validates what we already believed in the first place (Lazer et al., 2018; Sunstein, 2018).

In one study related to the online experience of confirmation bias, U.S. college students were asked to browse an online news magazine that displayed headlines on topics that often divide people whose political beliefs are conservative from people whose political beliefs are liberal (abortion, universal health care, defense spending, gay marriage, etc.). Each headline was worded to clearly favor either a conservative or liberal point of view. Results showed a strong confirmation bias: participants clicked on a significantly greater number of headlines that agreed with their own political opinions (Knobloch-Westerwick et al., 2020).

Your reasoning can also be swayed by **framing**: the particular way a question or problem is presented, which can influence how you respond to it. You can see the importance of framing in the way people on either side of an argument try to define the argument itself. For example, in the debate over fracking, those in favor of fracking frame it as an exploration of new homegrown oil resources that can create jobs and stimulate the economy now, while those opposed to fracking frame it as a threat to natural resources that can damage water quality and human health in the future (Lakoff, 2016; Mercado et al., 2014; Nyberg et al., 2020; Thompson, 2013; Wehling, 2018).

Numerous studies have found that the way a problem is framed can indeed have a powerful influence on the way people solve it (Brugman et al., 2017; LeBoeuf & Shafir, 2012; Slovic, 1975; Thibodeau et al., 2017a, 2017b; Tversky & Kahneman, 1981, 1986). One study found that more people are willing to undergo a medical procedure when they hear about how successful it is (for example, "This operation has an 85% success

mental set
The limits a person places on an approach to problem solving based on what has worked in the past.

confirmation bias
A tendency to prefer information that confirms what a person thought in the first place.

framing
The particular way a question or problem is presented, which can influence how a person responds to it.

rate") rather than its chance of failure ("This operation fails 15% of the time") (Levin et al., 1988). Another study found that a package of ground beef is viewed more positively when it is labeled as "75% lean" instead of "25% fat" (Levin, 1987).

More recently, researchers have found that participants respond with different action plans when asked how they might "fight against developing cancer" versus "reduce your risk of developing cancer." Specifically, framing cancer as an enemy that people must "fight against" actually reduces the likelihood of important prevention behaviors (which many people might not associate with a "fight"), such as drinking less alcohol and eating a healthier diet (Hauser & Schwartz, 2015, p. 69). Even our understanding and strategy against the COVID pandemic is affected by the way the issue is framed (Semino, 2021; Wicke & Bolognesi, 2020). In one study, researchers framed the vaccine decision in two different ways: emphasizing loss or emphasizing gain. To emphasize loss, they told participants that choosing not to get vaccinated could mean sacrificing their health, the health of their family and friends, and their opportunities to travel and socialize. To emphasize gain, they told participants that a decision to get vaccinated could bring them health, help to end lockdown-related restrictions, and provide the opportunity to go to clubs and theaters. Results showed that the frame made a difference among young adult participants (age 18–30). Those who received the loss frame had significantly more positive vaccination attitudes than those who received the gain frame (Reinhardt & Rossman, 2021).

In another COVID-related study of over 1400 U.S. residents, researchers framed the origin of the pandemic in two ways, one that mentioned China and its food markets, and another that described it as a mutation of previous viruses with no mention of China. Results showed that participants who heard the China frame expressed stronger beliefs that Asian Americans were a threat and higher levels of general xenophobia (dislike of people from outside the country) than those who heard the frame that did not mention China (Dhanani & Franz, 2021).

Heuristics. As we've seen, our reasoning can be affected by such contextual factors as what we've done before (mental set), what we thought in the first place (confirmation bias), and how the problem is presented (framing). Even when reasoning isn't affected by these contextual factors, we still tend to use shortcuts when we solve problems. Although we're generally unaware of it, our minds commonly jump to quick thought processes that could be logically flawed rather than grinding out more time-consuming answers that might be more accurate. That is, instead of relying on an algorithm when we solve problems, we more often rely on a **heuristic**: an educated guess or rule-of-thumb method of problem solving. Pioneering researchers Daniel Kahneman and Amos Tversky in the early 1970s were the first to identify the role of heuristics. Since that time, their many studies offer compelling and often disconcerting evidence of just how illogical we can be, usually without even realizing it (Ceschi et al., 2018; Griffin et al., 2012; Kahneman & Tversky, 1972, 1973, 1979, 1996, 2000; Rakow & Skylark, 2018; Tversky & Kahneman, 1971, 1974, 1986). Let's examine the four heuristics that have received the most attention from Kahneman, Tversky, and other researchers: the *representativeness heuristic*, the *availability heuristic*, the *affect heuristic*, and the *anchoring heuristic*.

The **representativeness heuristic** is an educated guess based on similarity to a prototype. According to the representativeness heuristic, we tend to draw conclusions about people or things based on how closely they resemble a "textbook case" of a certain category, even if those conclusions might be illogical (Gilovich & Savitsky, 2002; Gualtieri & Denison, 2018; Tversky & Kahneman, 1982). It is basically a more scholarly version of the old saying known as the "duck test": "If it looks like a duck, swims like a duck, and quacks like a duck, then it's probably a duck." The key word in that expression is *probably* — it's often an appropriate leap to make, but not always. For example, if you meet a woman who is a college student and 6 feet tall, you might assume that she's on her school's basketball team, since many women of similar height play basketball. However, when you chat with her you discover that she doesn't play basketball at all.

heuristic
An educated guess or rule-of-thumb method of problem solving.

representativeness heuristic
An educated guess based on similarity to a prototype.

availability heuristic
An educated guess based on the information that most quickly and easily comes to mind.

anchoring heuristic
An educated guess in which the starting point has a strong influence on the conclusion that is ultimately reached.

Jim Cumming/Moment/Getty Images

If you thought this animal was a duck, you were misled by the representativeness heuristic, the tendency to take an educated guess based on similarity to a prototype. It may look like a duck, but it's actually a loon.

The leap your mind made – that she must play basketball, based on how representative her height was of the basketball-player category in your mind – proved inaccurate.

The **availability heuristic** is an educated guess based on the information that most quickly and easily comes to mind. Just because an answer pops into your head first doesn't necessarily make it more accurate than another answer that would require a little more digging. In one study of the availability heuristic, Kahneman and Tversky (1973) asked participants if there were more words that started with the letter R or words that have R as their third letter. Most participants quickly responded that there were more words that start with R, but the truth is that there are three times as many words that have R as the third letter. The explanation is that the words that start with R were more *available*, or easy to bring to mind.

As another illustration of the availability heuristic, Tversky and Kahneman (1973) read aloud a list of names that included more women's names than men's names, but they were deliberate about which specific names they chose. If the study were done today, the list might look like this: Sofi Abdul, Tonya Brown, Lakisha Smith, Gabriela Rodriguez, Muhammad Ali, Teresa McKee, Catherine Meyer, Darius Templeton, Michelle Goldman, Matt Damon. They then asked the participants if the list included more men's names or women's names. Participants were likely to answer incorrectly when the gender with fewer names included more famous names. (The seven women's names in this list don't include any famous women, but the three men's names include one sports champion and one movie star.) This mistake happens because the famous names are more available, or easier to recall, than the unfamiliar names.

The **anchoring heuristic** is an educated guess in which the starting point has a strong influence on the conclusion you ultimately reach. When you're not sure what to think, but someone else provides a suggestion (an *anchor*), it is unlikely that your response will stray too far from their suggestion. Tversky and Kahneman (1974) illustrated the anchoring heuristic by asking U.S. participants what percentage of African nations were in the United Nations – a fact that most of them did not know. Before letting the participants answer, they spun a roulette-style wheel to give the participants a random percentage to consider as a possible answer. This random percentage was the anchor, and the anchor had a big influence on the participants' guesses. When the anchor was 10%, the median guess by participants was 25%. When the anchor was 65%, the median guess by participants was 45%. Clearly, the participants' guesses were strongly influenced by the anchor they were provided, even though they knew that anchor was randomly determined. In another study, half of the participants were asked if Mahatma Gandhi died before or after the age of 140, and the other half were asked if he died before or after the age of 9. Both anchors were extremely inaccurate, of course (Gandhi died at 78), but they nonetheless pulled participants' later guesses about Gandhi's actual age at death in their respective directions: those who heard the anchor of 140 had an average guess of 67, while those who heard the anchor of 9 had an average guess of 50 (Strack & Mussweiler, 1997).

The anchoring heuristic even has a powerful effect on how much you might be willing to pay for an item at the store. One study asked students to use the last two digits in their Social Security numbers – essentially, a completely random number between 00 and 99 – as the anchor. They were then shown a variety of retail products, from a wireless computer keyboard to a fancy box of chocolates (**Table 7.2**). First, they

Imagine that you were asked if you would spend a dollar amount equivalent to the last two digits of your Social Security number on a product. Then, with that two-digit number still fresh in your mind, you were asked the maximum you would pay for that product. In one study, that maximum was anchored remarkably closely to a random two-digit number. In fact, people using the highest last two digits of their Social Security numbers would pay two or three times the amount of money as people with the lowest two-digit numbers for the same item.

TABLE 7.2: Anchored

LAST TWO DIGITS OF SOCIAL SECURITY NUMBER	WHAT THEY'D PAY FOR A CORDLESS KEYBOARD	WHAT THEY'D PAY FOR A BOX OF FANCY CHOCOLATES
00–19	$16.09	$9.55
20–39	26.82	10.64
40–59	29.27	12.45
60–79	34.55	13.27
80–99	55.64	20.64

Data from Ariely et al. (2003).

were asked if they would pay their anchor (in dollars) for the objects. Then, they were asked the maximum they would pay for them. Their responses to the second question were most fascinating: people with high anchors were willing to pay significantly more — sometimes even double or triple the price — than people with low anchors. For example, participants with anchors below 20 were willing to pay only $16.09 for the wireless keyboard and $9.55 for the chocolates, while participants with anchors above 80 were willing to pay $55.64 for the wireless keyboard and $20.64 for the chocolates (Ariely et al., 2003).

The **affect heuristic** is an educated guess in which the worth of something is strongly influenced by how you feel toward it. (Here "affect" means feelings.) So if you like something a lot, you tend to conclude that it is worthwhile and good, but if you dislike it a lot, you tend to conclude that it is worthless and bad (Kahneman & Fredrick, 2002).

In one study, whether participants preferred tap water or bottled water depended more on their positive or negative emotions toward either type of water than on environmental impact, taste, concern about chemicals or other contaminants, health benefits, and social norms for water preferences (Etale et al., 2018). The affect heuristic undoubtedly plays a role in your judgment of things of which you are a fan. Your passion for any particular thing makes you more likely to judge it in a positive way. For example, if you love the Chicago Cubs, you expect the Cubs to win even when a purely objective, logical analysis (for example, the Cubs are having a terrible season so far and several of their best players are injured) would lead to a more negative, and more accurate, conclusion.

affect heuristic
An educated guess in which the worth of something is strongly influenced by how a person feels toward it.

dual-process theory
The notion that every person possesses two separate types of thinking, one automatic and one deliberate.

Cognition and Emotion

The affect heuristic is just one attempt to explain the impact that emotions can have on thinking. The contemporary theory that best captures this combination of emotion with reason is **dual-process theory**: the notion that each of us possesses two separate types of thinking, one automatic and one deliberate. As indicated by the title of Daniel Kahneman's influential book *Thinking, Fast and Slow* (2011), dual-process theory states that when you face a problem or a decision, you can respond in two distinct ways: one based on fast thinking and the other based on slow thinking (Evans & Over, 1996; Helm et al., 2018; Sloman, 1996; Stanovich, 2011).

Type 1 and Type 2 Thinking. Type 1 thinking is thinking fast. It happens instantly, effortlessly, and often without your full awareness. It is your impulse, your gut response, your intuition. It produces quick responses that can be fueled primarily by emotion (**Table 7.3**). In fact, it often activates the heuristics that we just discussed. By contrast, Type 2 thinking is thinking slowly. It happens more deliberately and purposefully. It is your ability to analyze, evaluate, and think things through. Type 2 thinking takes longer and requires more effort than Type 1 thinking, but it does a much better job of emphasizing reason over emotion (Evans, 2018; Evans & Stanovich, 2013; Laird-Johnson, 2012; Toplak, 2018).

When you're trying to solve problems or make decisions, both types of thinking can be beneficial. Type 1 thinking happens first, and it can be persuasive. Type 2 thinking

TABLE 7.3: Dual-Process Theory: Type 1 Versus Type 2 Thinking

TYPE 1 THINKING IS...	TYPE 2 THINKING IS...
Fast	Slow
Automatic	Effortful
Outside your awareness	Under your control
More emotional	More logical
Your immediate impulse	Your careful analysis

Information from Evans (2013) and Evans and Stanovich (2013).

FIGURE 7.4 I'll Get a Green One; I Can *Feel* It. In one study where the goal was to pick out a green jellybean without looking, participants could choose their odds: one in 10 in the small jar, or nine in 100 in the big jar. According to logic, this should be a no-brainer: go for the small jar, where your chances are 10%, rather than the big jar, where your chances are only 9%. But 61% of participants went for the big jar, presumably because they felt like it gave them more chances to win. Even when the experimenters dropped the number of green jellybeans in the big jar to five, many participants still chose the big jar rather than the small jar. Research from Epstein (1991) and Denes-Raj and Epstein (1994).

sometimes comes up with a better solution, but you may have started to follow the instructions of your Type 1 thinking by the time it does (Kahneman & Fredrick, 2005). As an example, imagine that a friend invites you to take an overnight road trip to see a concert. Your immediate reaction to that idea is your Type 1 thinking. Perhaps your Type 1 thinking leans in a positive direction: going on the road trip would be a good idea. Your Type 1 thinking probably produces this response because of emotion (more than reason): the excitement of the concert, the fun you'd have with your friend, and so on. If your Type 1 thinking is more negative, that too would be based on emotion more than reason: boredom on the long drive, disappointment if the band puts on a bad show, and so on.

If you give yourself a little time, however, Type 2 thinking will have a chance to kick in. Like Type 1 thinking, Type 2 thinking may come down either in favor of or against the road trip. Whatever your Type 2 thinking decides, that decision will be based primarily on reason rather than emotion. Type 2 thinking may prompt you to consider questions like these: Can I afford money for food, gas, a hotel, and a ticket to the concert? How much work would I have to miss, and how much would I fall behind on school assignments? Is there another way for my friend and me to see this band that might be less costly in terms of time and money? With such a thorough analysis, based on data rather than feelings, Type 2 thinking is likely to arrive at a more rational decision — if you can wait for it.

Type 1 thinking can be quite valuable in terms of producing rapid responses to situations in which overthinking can be detrimental, such as reacting to loud noises to avoid danger or responding to a greeting from another person in a quick and appropriate way. However, lots of studies indicate how Type 1 thinking, with its emotional influence, can take over the reasoning process, even when Type 2 thinking could generate a more logical answer. For example, in one study participants see two jars of jellybeans of various colors (Denes-Raj & Epstein, 1994; Epstein, 1991). The smaller jar contains 10 jellybeans, one of which is green (**Figure 7.4**). The larger jar contains 100 jellybeans, nine of which are green. The researchers explain these numbers to the participants and then allow them to reach their hand into one jar, with their eyes closed, to try to select a green jellybean. Type 2 thinking says go for the smaller jar, since the odds are greater than for the larger jar (10% vs. 9%). But 61% of participants chose the larger jar, presumably because they couldn't resist the temptation of nine chances of winning (versus just one chance). The researchers then reduced the number of green jellybeans in the larger jar to five out of 100. Even in this situation, in which odds of pulling a green jellybean from the smaller jar were double the odds of pulling one from the larger jar (10% vs. 5%), about a quarter of the participants still chose the larger jar. A few of them even said out loud that they knew their decision didn't make logical (or mathematical) sense, but the exciting feeling of having more chances to win was too strong to override.

Additional research has examined whether training people to use their Type 2 thinking — to think through their actions rather than responding impulsively — can have a positive real-life influence. For example, in one study thousands of economically disadvantaged teenage boys from high-crime areas of Chicago learned about thinking fast and thinking slow through a weekly, in-school program called "Becoming a Man." The primary message taught through this program was that slowing down and reflecting on a situation (and the possible responses), rather than thinking and acting automatically, might be beneficial in lots of real-world scenarios. Results were impressive: arrest rates decreased by about 30%, violent crime arrests decreased by about 50%, and graduation rates increased by about 15% (Heller et al., 2017).

Affective Forecasting. Another important note regarding the role of emotion in cognition: When trying to solve a problem or make a decision, you're not just hoping that the situation will turn out well. You're also hoping that *your feelings* about the situation will turn out well. The question isn't just "What will happen if I ...?" but also "How will I feel if I . . . ?" (Schwartz & Sommers, 2013). Psychologists call this emphasis on the subjective results of decisions, rather than the objective results, **affective forecasting**: predicting how you will feel about the outcomes of your decisions.

affective forecasting
Predicting how a person will feel about the outcomes of their decisions.

Research on affective forecasting suggests that we are not very good at it, and that the a common mistake is an overestimation of how intense our feelings will be (Gautam et al., 2017; Kahneman, 1999, 2000; Kahneman et al., 1993; Redelmeier et al., 2003; van Dijk et al., 2017). One study illustrated this tendency to mistakenly predict our own emotions by focusing on college students who experienced a breakup. The participants were first-year college students who were in a romantic relationship. Researchers asked the participants to predict how distressed they would feel if they broke up with their partners. Within the next 6 months, many of them did break up with their partners, and researchers then asked those participants how distressed they actually were. Results showed they were significantly less distressed than they predicted, not just immediately after the breakup, but a couple of weeks and a couple of months afterward too (Eastwick et al., 2008).

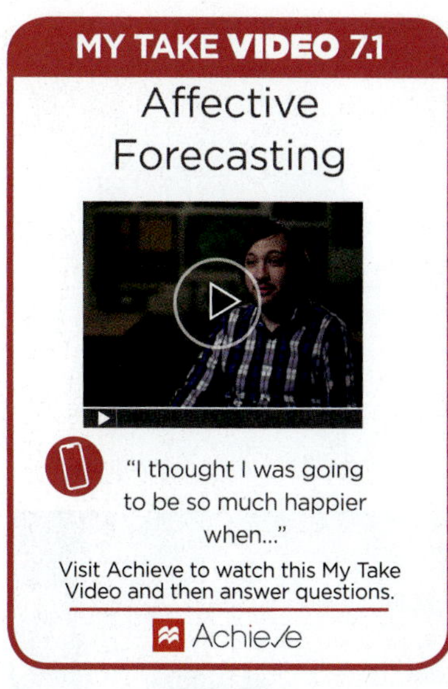

MY TAKE VIDEO 7.1
Affective Forecasting
"I thought I was going to be so much happier when..."
Visit Achieve to watch this My Take Video and then answer questions.
Achieve

The COVID pandemic has also provided opportunities to show how our affective forecasting can be mistaken. As the reality of the pandemic sank in, many of us expected our experience of the lockdown to be all bad. But research suggests that along with the bad, there was plenty of unexpected good that many of us experienced — a silver lining of sorts that didn't initially occur to us. In one study of over 9000 Americans, 89% reported that the pandemic had a negative impact on some aspect of their lives. But 73% also reported that the pandemic had a *positive* impact on some aspect of their lives. Similar patterns were found when the researchers asked more specific questions about relationships, jobs, free time, and even health. Many people reported negative consequences of the pandemic, and a sizable (although smaller) number of people also reported *positive* consequences. Those positive consequences spanned a wide range, including unforeseen benefits of working from home (like less time in highway traffic or airports), spending more time with partners and kids, saving money and eating healthier because restaurants were closed, and more (DeAngelis, 2021; van Kessel et al., 2021). The point here is not to deny the negative effects of the lockdown — as expected, those effects undeniably happened, and participants acknowledged them in this study. The point is that lots of pleasant surprises happened too, in ways that had meaningful positive impacts on lots of people. That fact illustrates how off-base or incomplete our affective forecasts can be.

Affective forecasting can be influenced by a person's particular psychological characteristics (Hansenne & Christophe, 2019). For example, one study asked participants to predict the emotions they would have when they experienced a wide range of events, including football games, an election, Valentine's Day, birthdays, and movies. Those who tend to worry and feel distress more often predicted more unpleasant feelings, while those who worry less predicted more pleasant feelings (Hoerger et al., 2016). Similarly, the affective forecasts of people with major depressive disorder included high levels of bad feelings and low levels of good feelings — both forecasts that match the nature of the disorder (Thompson et al., 2017).

Affective forecasting is also influenced by the **durability bias**: the overestimation of the expected length of the feeling produced by the outcome of a decision. When looking ahead to a big decision, you expect that the outcome will influence your emotions for a long time, but it often doesn't. Instead, you get used to whatever happens, and the feeling passes (Gilbert, 2006; Gilbert & Wilson, 2000, 2007; Gilbert et al., 1998). Think of how great you thought your life would be after you got that new hairstyle, that new device, that new job, or that new romantic partner. You may have imagined "happily ever after," but "happily" probably didn't last that long. What was new became routine, and eventually didn't bring as much excitement as you expected it to.

LIFE HACK 7.1

Keep the durability bias in mind the next time you consider spending lots of money on something to make yourself happy. There is a good chance that the happiness it brings will not last as long as you expect.

(Gilbert, 2006; Gilbert & Wilson, 2000, 2007; Gilbert et al., 1998)

In one study of the durability bias, researchers asked students from the University of Virginia and Virginia Tech how the outcome of a big Saturday football game between the two rival schools would make them feel, and how long they would feel that way (Wilson et al., 2000). Most expected the outcome to have a major impact on their happiness well into the next week. It didn't. Win or lose, by Monday, most students' happiness was no longer impacted.

durability bias
The overestimation of the expected length of the feeling produced by the outcome of a decision.

In another study of the durability bias, first-year college students took a survey about the impact of a housing lottery that would determine the buildings in which they would live for their remaining years on campus (Dunn et al., 2003). The lottery did not determine roommates, just location. Before the lottery, students predicted that its outcome would have a huge impact on their happiness for years to come. They were wrong. Follow-up questionnaires 1 year and 2 years after the housing lottery found that the students' level of happiness at that time had nothing to do with where the housing lottery had placed them.

Cognition and Creativity

Creativity is the capacity to come up with original ideas or approaches to a problem. Creative acts can be something as small and personal as the invention of the Internet-famous "popcorn hoodie" — a hoodie worn backward with the hood full of popcorn — or as big and globally transformative as the development of Facebook (Kaufman & Beghetto, 2009). Either way, creativity goes beyond selecting among preexisting solutions to a problem — it is the invention of a completely new solution.

Anjali Prasertong

Creativity is the capacity to come up with original ideas or approaches to a problem. In some cases, creative solutions change the world. In other cases, creative solutions just give you a convenient place to hold your popcorn.

As an example of a creative solution, consider this real-world problem: when first responders (police officers, firefighters, search-and-rescue workers) arrive at a building, how can they get a good look at what's inside? The obvious solution is to enter, but sometimes that's too risky. (Is there a shooter inside? A fire? A bomb?) Other times, entering is simply impractical, such as when a building has been damaged so badly that debris blocks access to survivors. Another solution might involve sending in a trained dog or a robot, but dogs' ability to communicate is limited, and robots can be expensive and clunky. A team of inventors has created a device — the Bounce Imaging Explorer — as a solution for this problem. The Bounce Imaging Explorer is a small ball — no bigger than a softball — equipped with six digital cameras, a thermometer, an oxygen sensor, and flashing LED lights. First responders can toss it into any space — a burning building, a hostage situation, the rubble caused by a natural disaster — and it automatically transmits panoramic photos and information about the environment to any linked device, such as a smartphone or tablet in the hands of a first responder. The creation was inspired by rescue efforts after the massive earthquake in Haiti in 2010, when rescuers had difficulty determining from the outside whether partially collapsed buildings contained survivors or were structurally sound enough to enter. The inventors demonstrated some genuine outside-the-box creativity when they conceived of this relatively inexpensive and potentially life-saving device.

Divergent Thinking and Convergent Thinking. When the creators of the Bounce Imaging Explorer saw a need for a better way to see inside hazardous situations, they probably generated a variety of ideas before settling on that particular solution. They engaged in **divergent thinking**: a problem-solving strategy in which you come up with lots of different possible solutions. Divergent thinking is essentially brainstorming, even if you do it alone. It's most evident in that early part of the creative process when the goal is to think open-mindedly and generate many ideas, even if you know that many will be discarded in the process of choosing the best one (Sternberg, 2006; Sternberg & Lubart, 1991). The opposite of divergent thinking is **convergent thinking**: a problem-solving strategy in which you use logic to deduce the single best solution.

As you might expect, creative people tend to be divergent thinkers rather than convergent thinkers (An et al., 2016; Runco, 2018; Smith & Ward, 2012). To assess creativity, psychologists sometimes use the "brick test," in which people think of as many uses for a brick as they can (Carson et al., 2005; Gallagher & Grimm, 2018; Lichtenfeld et al., 2018; Silvia et al., 2009). (The same kind of test can focus on other common objects too — a chair, a paper clip, etc.) Convergent thinkers tend to think that bricks are for building houses. That is appropriate, certainly, but not creative. Divergent thinkers would imagine many other additional uses for a brick: some innovative (a doorstop, a bookend, a paperweight), some imaginative (a hammer, a garden stepping stone, a weight for arm exercises), and some way out there (a weapon, a canvas on which to paint, an alternative to chalk for writing on the sidewalk).

creativity
The capacity to come up with original ideas or approaches to a problem.

divergent thinking
A problem-solving strategy in which a person comes up with lots of different possible solutions.

convergent thinking
A problem-solving strategy in which a person uses logic to deduce the single best solution.

functional fixedness
Thinking about something in only the way it is most typically used rather than other possible uses.

Functional Fixedness. To engage in divergent thinking (about bricks or anything else), it is important to overcome the tendency toward **functional fixedness**:

WATCHING PSYCHOLOGY

Convergent and Divergent Thinking on *Family Feud*

The beginning of each round of *Family Feud*, when a member of each family walks up front and puts a hand on the buzzer, is all about convergent thinking. The goal, after all, is to guess the most common answer provided in a survey of 100 people.

After one contestant wins that face-off, the host moves down the line of that family, posing the same question to each one. Eventually, most of the answers on the board have been uncovered, but it's often difficult to get those last few. That's when the contestants need to get creative and use divergent thinking. They need to think past the first several answers that come to mind, and come up with that less obvious answer (often hiding near the bottom of the board). That's what the other family is doing as they huddle up, hoping for a chance to steal — brainstorming possible answers beyond the ones already on the board.

For example, consider this *Family Feud* question: Name a food that goes well with peanut butter. Convergent thinking leads you right away to the obvious #1 answer: jelly. Then it starts getting tougher, especially if the list of top answers on the board is long. You may have to think a bit more divergently to come up with bread or crackers, then even more divergently to come up with honey or chocolate, and then very divergently to come up with celery or apples. That divergent thinking — moving past the first and most obvious answer to other answers that may work — is what creativity is all about. •

thinking about something in only the way it is most typically used, rather than other possible uses. Thinking of an object's most typical use (like bricks for houses) doesn't thwart creativity, but *stopping* there does (Glucksberg & Weisberg, 1966; Maier, 1931; Munoz-Rubke et al., 2018; Simonton & Damian, 2013). If you've ever seen magazines or Web sites with those lists of creative uses (or "hacks") for household items and thought "Wow, that really is a good idea," then you appreciate the creativity that can flow when people get past functional fixedness. Examples of getting past functional fixedness include using a drinking straw as a protective covering for a necklace to keep it from tangling or kinking, using uncooked rice (or kitty litter) to dry out a wet smartphone, using a piece of uncooked spaghetti as a long match for tough-to-reach candle wicks, and using a comb to hold a nail in place so you don't smash your fingers. All of these ideas originally popped into the head of someone who thought past the most obvious use of an object and was not restrained by functional fixedness.

Getting past functional fixedness can lead to exciting artistic developments too. Consider the turntable. For decades, it was used solely for its intended function: playing music. But in the late 1970s, a few pioneering DJs — Kool Herc and Grandmaster Flash, most notably — forged a new function for turntables: *making* music (Hill, 2013; Piskor, 2013). Grandmaster Flash had noticed that at his parties, dancers' favorite parts of the songs he played were the brief stretches when the vocals and often some of the instruments dropped out, leaving just the groove from the rhythm section. He wished that those stretches — the breaks, as he called them — lasted more than just a few seconds. He wondered if he could somehow use two turntables to fuse these breaks into a long-lasting beat. As he describes it:

> I knew I wanted a continuous groove.... I need to stop the record on the left and start the record on the right at a precise moment in time so that you, the listener, can't tell where one stops and the next one starts.... Finally, I found a way to start the first record with my hand physically on the vinyl itself. The platter would turn but the music wouldn't play because the needle wouldn't be traveling through the groove. However, when I took my hand off the record ... BAM! The music started right where I wanted it.... What if I could do this with two turntables at once? It wasn't easy, but I kept winding the second record back and forward until I got it just right and ... BAM!... The break played twice without missing a beat.... I'd gone from breaking a song apart in my head to breaking it apart on the turntable. The possibilities were endless. (Flash & Ritz, 2008, pp. 74–79)

Rick Diamond/WireImage/Getty Images

A key to creativity is overcoming functional fixedness, or thinking about something in only the way it is most typically used. In the 1970s, Grandmaster Flash (shown here) and a few other DJs overcame functional fixedness with regard to turntables and treated them as devices for making music rather than only devices for playing music.

Those possibilities include looping, in which the same break is juggled between two turntables for as long as the DJ wants (and often used by rappers to rhyme over), and blending, in which different breaks are strung together into an overlapping syncopated mix. These innovations with turntables as musical instruments paved the way for the sample-based method of music making (now used by music makers in every genre), in which computer programs are used to combine segments from different songs (McLeod & DiCola, 2011; Schloss, 2004).

DIVERSITY MATTERS

Creativity and Culture. Another factor linked to creativity is culture (Gocłowska et al., 2018; Lubart, 1999). People who experience multiple cultures or speak multiple languages are relatively high in creativity, presumably because their diverse experiences help them think in multiple ways (Fürst & Grin, 2018; Leung et al., 2008; Ricciardelli, 1992; Simonton, 2008). A number of studies suggest that people from Western cultures tend to think more divergently than people from Eastern cultures, which leads to a higher level of creativity (Kharkhurin & Motalleebi, 2008; Niu & Sternberg, 2001). In fact, the number of patents per capita — an interesting way to measure how many new ideas a culture creates — is higher in cultures with high individualism, which is generally more prominent in Western than Eastern cultures (Shane, 1992, 1993). However, there is also research suggesting that the difference in creativity between Western and Eastern cultures is smaller than previously thought, and might depend on how people from each culture define creativity in the first place (Adair & Xiong, 2018; Güss et al., 2018; McCarthy et al., 2018; Palmiero et al., 2017).

Johnny Green/PA Images/Getty Images

The magnificent glass sculptures of artist Dale Chihuly are a product of creativity that depends on both individualism and collectivism. Individualism tends to promote the kind of divergent thinking that leads to creative ideas. Collectivism tends to promote the kind of teamwork necessary to carry out those ideas. Chihuly's sculptures require a large team of people to blow, hold, turn, and assemble the many separate pieces of glass.

Also, while individualism may facilitate many creative ideas, it doesn't necessarily facilitate implementation of those ideas (Hofstede, 2001). So if genius is 1% inspiration and 99% perspiration (as the old saying goes), pure individualism may be good for the start but not necessarily the follow-through. Often, what produces the best results is a partnership of "idea people," who come up with creative plans, and hard workers who translate those plans into reality. Consider the work of Dale Chihuly, who is recognized as one of the premier glass sculptors in U.S. history. He is the designer of many enormous and intricate works, many of which contain hundreds of specially made pieces of glass arranged in a particular way. As an artist, Chihuly is the main creative force behind his glass sculptures, but the execution of his art — the conversion of the idea in Chihuly's mind into actual sculpted glass — requires a team of coworkers (Chihuly, 2007). The shaping of even a single piece of glass often involves the coordinated efforts of dozens of people to blow, hold, and turn the glass in its liquefied state. The assembly of his finished works in museums, which involves painstakingly arranging hundreds of smaller glass pieces to form the large work of art, is another major group effort. Without all of these teammates, Chihuly's creations would remain uncreated.

Creativity and COVID. The COVID pandemic created unprecedented challenges for people around the world, whether due to experiences with the virus itself or the quarantine that the virus required. Some researchers have already begun studying how people responded in terms of creativity. One study of over 1000 people in France in April and May 2020 found that everyday creativity-creativity regarding common household and family tasks and activities, rather than creativity focused on specific professional tasks — significantly increased during the pandemic. Interestingly, the largest increase happened among people who were low in everyday creativity before the pandemic, suggesting that the pandemic either forced or allowed this group to behave more creatively than they had in the past (Mercier et al., 2021). Another study of over 1000 employees in China, Germany, and the United States found that those who gave the highest rating to the impact of COVID responded with the most creativity at work, which correlated with feelings of professional growth and positive well-being (Tang et al., 2021). Similar positive effects of creativity were also found in a study that focused on home-schooling during the pandemic. Parents who were more creative in their attempts to manage the challenge of home-schooling experienced lower stress levels and fewer disciplinary problems than parents who were less creative (Aznar et al., 2021).

CHECK YOUR LEARNING:

7.1 How do psychologists define cognition, and what are the three main areas of research?

7.2 How do psychologists define the term *concept*?

7.3 What are the three main types of concepts?

7.4 What three levels do psychologists use to organize concepts?

7.5 What is the difference between problem solving and decision making?

7.6 What is the difference between an algorithm and a heuristic?

7.7 What are three ways in which people stray from reason when solving problems?

7.8 What are the four main types of heuristic?

7.9 According to dual process theory, what are the two types of thinking, and how do they differ?

7.10 What is affective forecasting, and, in general, how good are people at it?

7.11 How do psychologists define creativity?

7.12 What is the difference between divergent thinking and convergent thinking?

7.13 What is functional fixedness?

7.14 What types of factors contribute to creativity?

To check your understanding of these questions, click show the answers or refer to the answers in the Chapter Summary.

Language

Language is your ability to communicate with others using words or other symbols combined and arranged according to rules. Language, if you stop and think about it, is absolutely amazing. Just think about the word-related things you could *not* do at all when you were born — say them, write them, read them, or understand them. Somehow, just a few years later, you were doing all of those things fluently. And now, your brain uses language as easily and automatically as your lungs use air. One expert illustrates the often-overlooked marvels of linguistic ability by detailing, in slow motion, what happens in just a brief snippet of conversation:

> Without any real effort, we identify over a dozen speech sounds ... per second, recognize the words they constitute, almost immediately understand the message generated by the sentences they form, and often elaborate appropriate verbal and nonverbal responses before the utterance ends. (Mattys, 2013, p. 391)

Let's examine many aspects of language, such as how it evolved in our species, how it develops during childhood, how it is structured by grammatical rules, and how it interacts with thinking.

YOU WILL LEARN:

7.15 how psychologists define language.

7.16 how researchers speculate that language evolved.

7.17 about different theories of language development.

7.18 about the various stages of a child's language development.

7.19 about the four levels of grammar.

7.20 how extralinguistic information can influence communication.

7.21 whether language influences thinking.

The Evolution of Language

How did humans get so good at language? Other animals communicate, of course, but how did our use of language become so sophisticated? The truth is that we don't know for sure. In fact, we may never know for sure, since the evolution of language took place so many thousands of years ago (Aitchison, 1996; Bickerton & Szathmáry, 2009; Carstairs-McCarthy, 2001; Christiansen & Kirby, 2003; Gibson & Tallerman, 2012). But that hasn't stopped speculation.

Some experts believe that early in human history, there was a kind of "protolanguage" — a primitive way of communicating that was just a step or two beyond grunting (Bickerton, 1992, 2009; Zywiczynski et al., 2017). This protolanguage may have been made up of isolated sounds, each of which carried a complete message that was fundamentally important to survival at that time. For example, one sound

language
The ability to communicate with others using words or other symbols combined and arranged according to rules.

may have declared "LookOutAPredatorIsBehindYou!" while another sound may have communicated "Don'tEatThatItWillMakeYouSick!" (Bickerton, 2013). These sounds might have functioned like the language of car horns now – isolated blasts of communication that lack detail but quickly convey crucial information that makes sense in context. Over long periods of time, humans may have broken down these single sounds into smaller parts – rudimentary words – that could be combined in new ways (Pleyer et al., 2017; Wray, 1998, 2000). But again, this protolanguage theory is an educated guess rather than a proven fact, and not all experts agree with it (Arbib, 2008; Bichakjian et al., 2017).

But how did language grow to include so many words?

That is a good observation: the languages we use today are far more expansive than the isolated single sounds of our ancestors. The average U.S. adult has a vocabulary of between 60,000 and 100,000 English words (Pinker, 1994), and that's just a fraction of the complete English language. The English language adds new words all the time – see **Table 7.4** for some of the newest dictionary entries. That gives us many options for saying what our ancestors said with their single sounds.

Why would our language produce so many ways to convey the same basic message? Some experts have speculated that language is a social indicator, and the use of certain kinds of language can impress or attract certain kinds of people (Kinzler, 2021). According to this viewpoint, if you use a rich vocabulary when you speak, including words often used by highly educated people, then listeners will not only understand your message but also be impressed by the manner in which you communicated it (Lange et al., 2013; Rosenberg & Tunney, 2008). Think of it this way: you're exchanging messages with someone on a dating app, and they offer an opinion about a new movie: "Yeah, I seen that movie. I hated it. I don't know what them people was thinking when they was talking about how good it was." Would you get a different impression if they wrote this instead? "Yes, I have seen that film. To be honest, I didn't care for it. I'm aware of the glowing praise it has received from critics, yet I fail to see how they could have come to such a conclusion." Both messages carry the same content, but the *way* that content is carried differs greatly. That difference, in turn, tells you something about the speaker. In this way, complex language can function for humans like decorative feathers function for a peacock or elaborate songs for a songbird – a way of displaying attractiveness and status to others (Locke, 2012).

TABLE 7.4: What's the Word? Terms Added to the Dictionary in Recent Years

1. Pickleball	a. A person who experiences long-term effects following initial improvement from a serious illness
2. Long hauler	b. A hybrid of a zebra and a donkey
3. Flex	c. A firm refusal or rejection
4. Hard pass	d. To delay or prevent progress by acting in a deliberately unhurried way
5. Deepfake	e. Sport played with short-handled paddles and a plastic ball
6. Slow-walk	f. Revealing a strong desire for attention, approval, or publicity
7. Thirsty	g. An image or recording that has been convincingly altered and manipulated
8. Zonkey	h. Bragging or showing off to impress other people

Can you match these recent additions to the dictionary with their meanings?
Answers: 1-e; 2-a; 3-h; 4-c; 5-g; 6-d; 7-f; 8-b.

Information from https://www.merriam-webster.com/words-at-play/new-words-in-the-dictionary-september-2019; https://www.merriam-webster.com/words-at-play/new-words-in-the-dictionary-april-2020; and https://www.merriam-webster.com/words-at-play/new-words-in-the-dictionary.

DIVERSITY MATTERS

Of course, sophisticated language is in the eye of the beholder: what one person views as sophisticated and impressive may seem snobbish or unlikeable to someone else. This is especially true when considering language as it is spoken within a particular culture or subculture, where a certain way of speaking, whether sophisticated or not, can signal membership within the group (Keblusek et al., 2017). For example, in the subculture of Latina gangs in California, young women learn to use specific words carefully, pronouncing them in specific ways, to communicate their gang affiliations (Mendoza-Denton, 2008). Also, one study showed 5-year-old American children pictures of other 5-year-olds and played them a recording of the pictured child saying a sentence in English. The children strongly preferred the child who spoke with an American accent, rather than a French one, whether or not the pictured child was of a different race than the participant (Kinzler et al., 2009). American kids of the same age also showed more trust in adults who spoke English with an American accent, rather than a Spanish one, even when the words they spoke were nonsense words (Kinzler et al., 2011).

Language benefits groups who live together, and that may be another reason why the complexity of language has grown over the course of human history. Some theories state that language may have evolved beyond single sounds so information could be shared with family members about food, tools, and other basic elements of survival (Gibson, 2012). A single sound couldn't explain how best to use a small hand axe or how best to connect an arrowhead to a shaft when those primitive tools were first used. A single sound can't communicate "There is no fresh water past those hills" or "There are plenty of animals to hunt and berries to pick on the other side of that lake" — crucial information for finding food and water early in human history. So, in the same way we take full advantage of our vast vocabulary on the Yelp app to share our news about the quality of food and drink at various places where we forage now, early humans may have expanded their linguistic skills to yelp similar information to their kin to help them survive.

The Development of Language

We've discussed the way language might have evolved over the course of human history. Now let's discuss the way language develops over the course of *each* human's history, starting at birth. When you enter the world, your language skills are practically nonexistent. Within months, however, you understand many words and sentences. By your first birthday, you're chiming in with a few words of your own. In just the next couple of years, you become fluent as both a listener and a speaker, with an extensive vocabulary and the ability to form all kinds of sentences. How is that possible? How can such a young child master the incredibly complex task of language acquisition so quickly?

Felise Waxman

Babies understand language within their first few months, and use words themselves by the time they reach their first birthday. Within the next couple of years, their linguistic abilities expand greatly.

Nativist Theory of Language Development. Maybe you're simply born with the ability to acquire language. Maybe there is something built into human beings, similar to the abilities to see and to breathe, that enables you to acquire language. That's the basic idea behind **nativist theory**: a theory of language development that says the ability to use language is inborn. Nativist theory, which overlaps with the more recent theories of *universal grammar* or *linguistic universalism*, has been at the center of a long-lasting debate in psychology. Renowned linguist Noam Chomsky (1959, 1995) has been among the most vocal champions of nativist theory for many decades. On the other side of the debate, some experts say that learning language is about nurture just as much as it is about nature. From their point of view, language is not an inborn ability but learnable, just like anything else (Bybee & McClelland, 2005; Elman et al., 1996). This debate illustrates how language, like many other topics within psychology, is a hot spot for the nature–nurture issue.

Those who support nativist theory typically believe that every person is born with a **language acquisition device**: a specific capacity within the brain that provides the ability to use language. Like software that comes preloaded on a new computer, the language acquisition device would empower you to learn language quickly from day

nativist theory
A theory of language development that says the ability to use language is inborn.

language acquisition device
A specific capacity within a person's brain that provides the ability to use language.

social-pragmatic theory
Suggests that a child's use of language develops from a desire to interact socially.

one. The word *device* makes it sound like the language acquisition device is literally a small piece of equipment implanted in your brain, but, as we learned back in Chapter 2, such a device would actually be a circuit of numerous brain regions that interact to produce language.

Nativist theory (or at least the general idea that there is an inborn component to language acquisition) gets some support from observations of children who are deaf. One observation involves the way children who are deaf often interact with their parents. When these parents do not use standard sign language, the families often develop an idiosyncratic "home sign" language of their own. Typically, these languages feature many of the same properties as any human language (signed or spoken), such as the ways words are combined and the structures of sentences. Moreover, they are quite complex and enable expression of a wide range of thoughts and feelings — way beyond anything found in any nonhuman species. It is also notable that the child is typically better at this home sign language than their parents, suggesting that it was the kid who primarily created it (Goldin-Meadow, 2005). All of this suggests that language emerges naturally, even in an environment in which it is not spoken aloud.

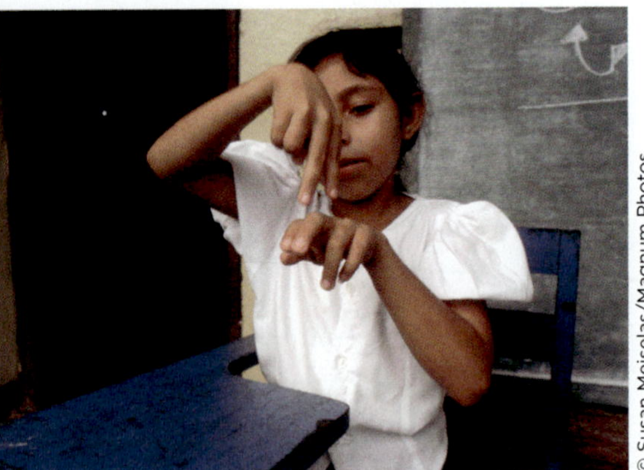

© Susan Meiselas/Magnum Photos

In the 1980s, Nicaragua introduced its first schools for deaf children. These children had never used standard sign language. When they were brought together, they quickly developed their own sign language. That occurrence supports nativist theory, the idea that the ability to use language is inborn rather than learned.

Another observation involves children who were deaf and living in Nicaragua in the 1980s, when schools for the deaf were first created in that country. None of the children who entered the school had ever been exposed to standard sign language. Quickly and spontaneously, these kids formed their own sign language. At first, teachers dismissed it as simplistic and limited. However, further research indicated that the kids' indigenous sign language featured a wide vocabulary and a complex structure that resembled many other languages (Kegl et al., 1999; Pyers et al., 2014; Senghas et al., 2004). Today, that indigenous sign language is recognized as Nicaraguan Sign Language and is widely considered a legitimate version of sign language. Again, it seems that in the absence of a shared language, a new one emerged naturally. Such stories suggest that, at least to some extent, we humans have an innate disposition to develop and use our linguistic abilities (Jackendoff, 2012).

Nonnativist Theories of Language Development. Just because our linguistic abilities are strongly influenced by nature doesn't mean that nurture is uninvolved (Baldwin & Meyer, 2007; Fitch, 2012). Numerous studies show that rewarding kids for language-related behaviors leads to an increase in those behaviors. In one such study, 2- to 4-year-old kids with serious language delays heard a parent make a particular sound. The kids then immediately received something from that parent that made them happy — such as tickling, clapping, or the parent saying "Yay!" With repetition of this sequence, each of the children began to make that particular sound themselves (Sundberg et al., 1996). Studies like this support the *formalist theory* of language development, which suggests that kids learn language through the process of hearing others speak it (Bruner, 1975, 1981).

More recently, another nonnativist theory of language development has received more attention from researchers. **Social-pragmatic theory** suggests that a child's use of language develops from a desire to interact socially. Beginning with their earliest nonverbal communications, kids want to be part of the conversation that their parents, grandparents, and older siblings are having. Improving their language abilities by emulating the language they hear helps them accomplish that (Brooks & Meltzoff, 2005; Gopnik & Meltzoff, 1997; Ramirez-Esparza et al., 2014; Tomasello, 2004).

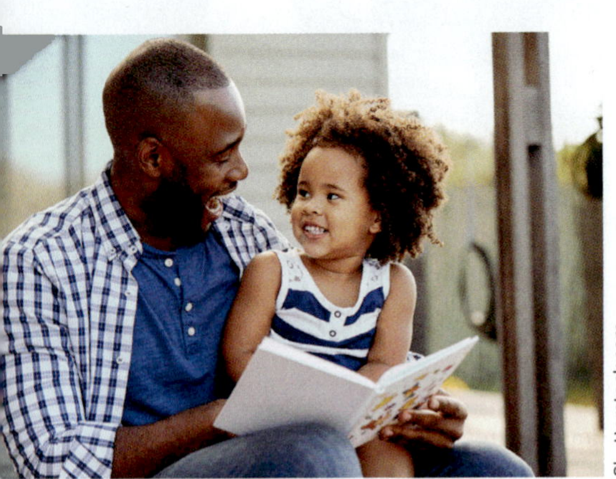

Shutterstock.com

Social-pragmatic theory suggests that a child's use of language develops from a desire to interact socially. Reading books with young children, especially in a way that encourages lots of questions and commentary about the book (rather than just sticking to the script), has been found to improve language use in children (Whitehurst et al., 1988).

In a study that illustrates this process, one group of parents read picture books to their young kids for a month at home in their typical way. The second group of parents was instructed to read picture books to their young kids in a way that was specifically designed to get kids talking: ask lots of open-ended questions about the book, frequently stop to discuss with the child what happened on a particular page (rather than strictly sticking to the text), and encourage the child to answer their own questions. Afterward, kids from the second group outperformed kids from the first group on a number of linguistic tasks. They used language more expressively, spoke in longer utterances, and more frequently used phrases than single words to get their points across (Whitehurst et al., 1988).

Parentese. Regardless of whether nature or nurture is actually more prominent, it's clear that language development starts in the earliest days of life. Around that time, parents speak to babies in that special way: sing-songy, high-pitched, with elongated vowel sounds and lots of repetition. Many people call this baby talk, but psychologists prefer the terms *infant-directed speech*, *motherese*, or the more gender-neutral *parentese* (Fernald, 1994; Mithen, 2012). As the first form of verbal communication, parentese strengthens bonds between infants and their caretakers. It is often accompanied by physical touch, such as hugging, caressing, and kissing.

Research suggests that parentese helps babies to develop language more rapidly and fully. In one study, some parents of 6- to 10-month-old babies received expert coaching on parentese while others did not. (The parents and babies were otherwise matched on other important variables, like socioeconomic status and gender.) Babies of the parents who received the coaching vocalized significantly more in the months that followed, and they spoke a significantly larger number of full words at age 14 months (Ramírez et al., 2018). Additional research suggests that these advances in language development are still significant when the children reach 24 and 33 months old (Ramírez-Esparza et al., 2017).

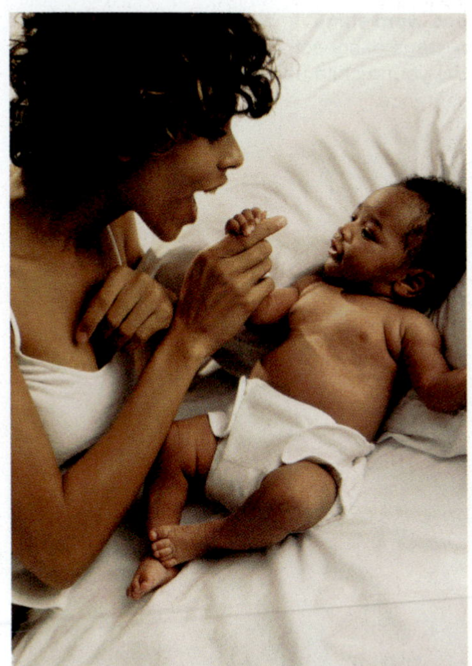
Purestock/Getty Images

Parentese (commonly known as *baby talk*) is a sing-songy, high-pitched, repetitive way of speaking that strengthens bonds between babies and caretakers.

Babbling. The baby's role in responding to parentese is **babbling**: an early stage of speech development during which the baby vocalizes a wide variety of nonword sounds. Babbling begins just a few months after birth, with single-syllable sounds like *ba*. A few months later, babies' babbling becomes *reduplicated*, which is a fancy way of saying a single-syllable sound gets repeated over and over: *ba* becomes *ba-ba-ba-ba*. A few months after that, babies string together a variety of different single-syllable sounds (*variegated babbling*) to make longer babbles like *ba-ga-mi-nu* or *pa-go-ki-ba* (Benders & Altvater-Mackensen, 2017; Fenson et al., 1994; Levey, 2013; Oller, 2000). Each babble itself may be meaningless, but the process of babbling is important to the baby's development of spoken language. Babbling elicits verbal responses from caregivers, which babies then hear and mimic. This is how babies learn how to shape their babbles into the words, phrases, and sentences that they will ultimately use (Albert et al., 2018; Goldstein & West, 1999; Goldstein et al., 2003; Gros-Louis et al., 2006; Morgan & Wren, 2018).

The best language learning happens when caregivers reply immediately and responsively to the babies' babbles. Language develops much better when babies genuinely *interact* with adults (as in a face-to-face exchange) than when they merely hear random adult voices (as in overhearing conversations or the chatter on TV or radio) (Goldstein & Schwade, 2008). When babies do have those direct, back-and-forth interactions with adults, they are doing some pretty intense listening.

Wait, how can you tell how intensely a baby is listening? Obviously, they can't just tell you.

LIFE HACK 7.2

When you care for a baby, talk with them. The baby will learn more from conversing with you, even if the conversation contains lots of baby talk, than from hearing voices on TV or hearing nothing at all.

(Goldstein & Schwade, 2008; Goldstein & West, 1999; Gros-Louis et al., 2006)

We can tell how intensely babies listen to language from some creative studies in which babies hear a certain kind of babble many times in a row — enough to get used to it — and then hear either a similar type of babble or a different type. At that moment, they spend much more time looking in the direction of the different type of babble — their nonverbal way of saying "Huh?" when they hear something unfamiliar (Gerken, 2007; Gómez & Gerken, 2000; Saffran & Thiessen, 2003). It is a similar reaction to the one you would have if you were with a group of friends speaking one language and then someone started speaking a completely foreign language. You'd turn your head toward that person, taking some time to try to understand what's going on.

In one study of this type, some babies heard a 2-minute recording containing only babbles that followed an A-B-A syllable pattern, like *ga-ti-ga* or *li-na-li*. Other babies heard a 2-minute recording containing only babbles that followed an A-B-B syllable pattern, like *ga-ti-ti* or *li-na-na*. Next, each group of babies heard new babbles that

babbling
An early stage of speech development during which the baby vocalizes a wide variety of nonword sounds.

one-word stage
A stage of speech development during which the young child uses a single word as a full sentence.

were either consistent or inconsistent with the patterns of the babbles they had just heard for 2 minutes. The babies whose new babbles were inconsistent stared much longer at the speaker that those babbles came from — as if intrigued or puzzled by the different sound — than the babies whose new babbles were consistent (Marcus et al., 1999). Studies like this one indicate that babies pick up speech patterns more quickly than we might realize, which helps them learn what kinds of sounds are common in their native languages (Koenig & Cole, 2013).

One-Word Stage. After the babbling stage, usually around the first birthday, comes the **one-word stage**: a stage of speech development during which the young child uses a single word as a full sentence. If you've ever spent time around a 1-year-old, you know that you have to rely on context to understand these one-word exclamations. Babies' imperfect pronunciation can make it even tougher (MacWhinney, 2001). For example, consider 1-year-old Megan saying, "Ca!" She could be referring to *cat*, and if she is, she could mean, "I want to pet the cat" or "I'm afraid of the cat." Or, she could be referring to her big sister, Catherine, and if she is, she could mean, "Yay, Catherine just walked into the room!" or "That's Catherine's toy." Or, she could be doing her best to say *clap*, which could be her recognition of someone clapping or her request to play a patty-cake clapping game. Your knowledge of what might be going on inside little Megan's mind — what's going on around her at the moment, what she's been learning about recently, what she's looking or pointing at — can be essential in deciphering what her one-word utterances mean.

DIVERSITY MATTERS

There is remarkable similarity in the first words spoken by babies around the world. One study asked caregivers of hundreds of babies around a year old from three cultures that speak three different languages (Hong Kong, Beijing, and the United States) to report the first 10 words the babies said (Tardif et al., 2008). As **Table 7.5** illustrates, six words (listed here in their English forms) appeared in the top 20 for all three cultures: *mommy, daddy,*

TABLE 7.5: First Words Around the World

UNITED STATES	HONG KONG	BEIJING
Daddy	**Daddy**	**Mommy**
Mommy	Aah	**Daddy**
Baa baa	**Mommy**	Grandma — paternal
Bye	Yum yum	Grandpa — paternal
Hi	Sister — older	**Hello**
Uh oh	**Uh oh**	Hit
Grr	Hit	Uncle — paternal
Bottle	**Hello**	Grab
Yum yum	Milk	Auntie — maternal
Dog	Naughty	**Bye**
No	Brother — older	**Uh oh**
Woof woof	Grandma — maternal	Wow
Vroom	Grandma — paternal	Sister — older
Kitty	**Bye**	**Woof woof**
Ball	Bread	Brother — older
Baby	Auntie — maternal	Hug/hold
Duck	Ball	Light
Cat	Grandpa — paternal	Grandma — maternal
Ouch	Car	Egg
Banana	**Woof woof**	Vroom

Information from Tardif et al. (2008).

Babies in various cultures, speaking various languages, share some of the same first words. Here's a rank-ordered list of the words (translated into English from the Cantonese of Hong Kong and the Putonghua of Beijing) that appear most commonly among babies' first 10 words in three of those cultures. The words in bold print appear in all three lists.

hi/hello, *bye*, *uh oh*, and *woof woof*. *Mommy* and *daddy* were actually in the top three in all three cultures. Also, babies in all three cultures produced far more nouns (words for things, people, etc.) among their first words than verbs, adjectives, or other kinds of words. The differences between the lists show interesting cultural trends: babies in the more collectivistic cultures of Beijing and Hong Kong produce more family-related words, like sister, brother, grandma, grandpa, auntie, and uncle, than babies in the more individualistic United States. Babies in the United States are also the only ones for whom the word *no* ranks in the top 20.

Expanding Language Use. Within months, those one-word utterances become two- and three-word utterances until kids form full sentences by age 3. Of course, kids' mastery of language is far from complete at that early age. Their vocabulary expands greatly during childhood, with a base of about 10,000 words by kindergarten (Anglin, 1993). Their ability to use language effectively – forming complex sentences accurately, mastering irregular verbs (*went* rather than "*goed*"), even pronouncing tough words correctly (*spaghetti* rather than "*psgetti*") – continues to develop throughout childhood.

Parent–child interaction remains important to language development as the child's language development expands, but cell phones represent one possible disruption to this process. One team of researchers decided to conduct a study to explore this possibility. They had 38 parents teach their 2-year-old kids two new words at two different times. For each parent, one of the two teaching sessions was interrupted by a cell phone call, which the parent answered. Not surprisingly, kids learned the new words significantly more often in the uninterrupted condition. The main reason for this result was not that the call took time away from the parent–child interaction, but that the call broke the flow of the interaction between the parent and child. The researchers conclude that we can't expect toddlers to pause and then return to their conversations with adults without sacrificing some language development in that moment (Reed et al., 2017).

Figurative Language. From around age 9 through the teenage years, kids master the challenges of *figurative language* – the metaphors, idioms, and proverbs that mean something different from what they literally say (Cacciari & Padovani, 2012; Levorato & Cacciari, 2002; Levorato et al., 2004; Nippold & Duthie, 2003). Our language is full of these figures of speech – about six of them per minute of conversation, according to one estimate – so wrapping your head around them (hey, "wrapping your head around" – there's one right there) is essential to fully understanding language (Gibbs et al., 2012; Glucksberg, 1989).

For example, if you say, "Break a leg!" to a 6-year-old before the kindergarten songfest, they might burst into tears, thinking that you hope they get injured. But 10 years later, that same kid will know exactly what you mean when you use the same figurative language before the high school musical. Similarly, older kids are much better than younger kids at recognizing that having "butterflies in your stomach" does not mean that insects have actually flown into your open mouth, and that "We're all in the same boat" does not mean that anyone needs to put on a lifejacket. By the end of high school, kids have not only picked up hundreds of examples of figurative language, but have also expanded their vocabulary to about 50,000 words and growing (Gabig, 2014).

"Butterflies in your stomach" is an example of figurative language, in which metaphors, idioms, and proverbs are used to mean something different from what they literally say.

DIVERSITY MATTERS

It is important to remember that any particular example of figurative language is not necessarily universal. Two people from different cultures may not understand certain figures of speech the same way even if they speak the same language (Yagiz & Izadpanah, 2013). For example, one study asked English speakers from the United States and India how closely they associate emotion words (like *happy* and *sad*) with specific colors, temperatures, and other descriptors. The researchers found plenty of overlap between the two cultures: over 95% from both groups associated happiness with up and sadness with down, so figurative language like "I'm flying high" or "I feel so low" probably makes sense across cultures. But there was plenty of difference too: 73% of Americans associated happiness with warmth, but only 30% of Indians did. So, a phrase like "That movie warmed my heart" might cause confusion when spoken across cultures. Similarly, 66% of Americans associated sadness with blue, but only 15% of Indians did. So, saying "I have the blues today" could mean different things to different people (Barchard et al., 2017).

The Rules of Language: Grammar

Grammar is the set of rules within a language. If you're fluent in any language, you know its grammar by heart. Though grammar rulebooks may have helped, it's likely that you learned grammar primarily through immersion, or lots of experience listening to and speaking your language. Grammar is so woven into language that it's easy to take it for granted. In fact, the best reminders that grammar governs language take place when we hear someone break grammatical rules. For example, when native Spanish or English speakers begin to learn the other language, their speech often contains some minor differences from the speech of native speakers. English words that start with the letters "st-" may be pronounced by native Spanish speakers as if they start with "est-," so "study" sounds like "estudy." The wording of questions can also seem out of order to native speakers, like "You are hungry?" versus "Are you hungry?" These distinctions, of course, stem from differences between Spanish and English grammar. The fact that they sound unusual to native speakers of the other language highlights the fact that there are some powerful underlying rules to the way each language operates (Wasow, 2001).

Phonemes. A **phoneme** is the smallest distinct unit of speech. You might automatically equate phonemes with the letters of the alphabet, but phonemes are the *sounds* the letters make, not the letters themselves. In English, the same phoneme can be produced by multiple letters, such as the *k* sound in these words: *c*ar, *k*angaroo, *ch*orus, plu*ck*, Ira*q*. Or the same letter can produce different phonemes, such as the way *j* is used in these words: *j*ump, *j*alapeño, hallelu*j*ah. Or multiple letters can combine to form a single phoneme, as in *sh* (*sh*op), *ph* (*ph*one), and *ch* (*ch*ill). That is why *Wheel of Fortune* can be so tough when only a few letters are showing — you can't always be sure what phonemes those letters represent.

When words are short and simple, combining phonemes is easy. For example, the three phonemes represented by the letters *c*, *u*, and *p* combine to form the word *cup*. Longer and more complex words are more challenging, but the rules of phonemes help you sound them out (Cohn, 2001). Words borrowed from other languages containing phonemes that English doesn't feature can also be difficult. For example, the first sound in the French-derived word *genre* (softer than the *g* in *giant*) or the last sound in the Vietnamese soup *pho* (shorter than the *o* in *go*) can be tough for some English speakers to say.

Morphemes. A **morpheme** is the smallest meaningful unit of a language. Morphemes can be full words (like *play*), but they can also be parts of words, like the prefix *re-* to signify something happening again (*re*play) or the suffix *-ed* to signify that something happened in the past (play*ed*). More morphemes can be linked together to form more complex words.

People new to a language often have a difficult time learning when *not* to use certain morphemes (Levey, 2013). For example, in English we usually add the morpheme *-s* at the end of a word to make it plural, but there are some cases when we change a letter before the *-s* as well (*knife* becomes *knives*, not *knifes*), and other cases in which we abandon that grammatical rule altogether (*child* becomes *children*, not *childs*).

Syntax. The next level of grammar is **syntax**: the rules by which words are put together to make phrases and sentences. Syntax helps you put together your statements in ways that others will understand, especially regarding the order of the nouns, verbs, adjectives, and other types of speech (Baker, 2001; Garnham, 2005).

grammar
The set of rules within a language.

phoneme
The smallest distinct unit of speech.

morpheme
The smallest meaningful unit of a language.

syntax
The rules by which words are put together to make phrases and sentences.

For example, if you said, "Your shoe is untied," your syntax would be perfectly understandable. Slight bendings of syntax rules are typically easy enough to understand. For example, Yoda from *Star Wars* might say, "Untied your shoe is." However, if you said, "Shoe your untied is," you'd be breaking the rules of syntax so badly that it could confuse others.

semantics
The rules by which a person extracts meaning from words and sentences.

extralinguistic information
Components of language other than the literal meaning of the words.

Semantics. A final level of grammar involves the comprehension of language rather than the production of it. **Semantics** is the rules by which you extract meaning from words and sentences. Semantics is at work when you automatically translate the words and sentences that you've heard other people say into the meaning they are trying to convey (Lappin, 2001). For example, if your friend Kara utters the words, "I might dye my hair," you instantly know five things: (1) "I" is Kara. (2) "Might" indicates the following action is a possibility rather than a sure thing. (3) "Dye" means color (as opposed to "die," meaning the ending of life). (4) "My" refers to something belonging to Kara. And (5) "hair" refers to what's growing out of Kara's head. You also can synthesize those five individual meanings into the single idea that she is trying to convey: she's considering a change to her look, and she's apparently interested in your thoughts about it. If you think of Kara's statement as a package she delivered to you, semantics is what allows you to unpack it. She had that idea in her mind, translated it into language, and sent that language aloud to you. Then, you used semantics to decode the language so that you could comprehend her idea and hold it in your mind. That's pretty impressive, especially considering that the whole semantic process happens in just a fraction of a second.

Extralinguistic Information. Even more impressive, when listening to Kara, you appreciate not only *what* she said but also *how* she said it. That is because in addition to paying attention to her language, you're paying attention to her **extralinguistic information**: components of language other than the literal meaning of the words. Extralinguistic information can include the volume, pitch, or speed of spoken words. Often, it communicates a speaker's emotions or intentions just as powerfully as the words themselves. (Of course, if you can see the speaker, extralinguistic information can also include facial expressions, gestures, and other visual cues.)

Extralinguistic information is the difference between reading a screenplay and watching the play acted out. The way the speakers say the lines can bring meaning to them that the written page simply can't provide. That is why you feel the need to add facial-expression emojis to your texts sometimes (**Figure 7.5**) — without those hints about how you mean the words you're texting, the recipient might understand the message incompletely or incorrectly. That is also why, in some cases, you feel the need to call or videochat rather than text — when it's important that the other person appreciate *how* your words come out. In Kara's case, if she exclaims, "I might dye my hair!" with excitement and quickness in her voice, she's letting you know that she's leaning toward doing it and she's hoping you will support her. If she mutters, "I *miiiight* dye my hair...," emphasizing "might" and trailing off at the end, she's letting you know that she's thinking about the idea, but she's definitely not sold on it.

FIGURE 7.5 How It Feels to Go Home. Extralinguistic information like tone of voice and nonverbal cues is crucial to human speech. When we text, we often include emojis to communicate exactly how we mean what we say. These texts provide very different information about how this person feels about going home, even though the words remain exactly the same.

Research has found that extralinguistic information can have a powerful influence on communication. One study played brief audio clips of politicians speaking on C-SPAN. These clips were specifically edited to omit any meaningful political comments, but to include just enough words to give the participant a chance to rate the attractiveness of the politician's voice. Politicians with more attractive voices were rated as more competent and trustworthy than politicians with less attractive voices, even when both voices were paired with identical photos (Surawski & Ossoff, 2006). Another study found that participants listening to 2-second clips of phone calls between two other people — just the question "How are you?" — could reliably guess whether the speaker was addressing a friend or a romantic partner based on vocal qualities like tone and pitch (Farley et al., 2013).

CURRENT CONTROVERSY

What Is Texting Doing to Language?

"Texting is bleak, bald, sad shorthand, which masks dyslexia, poor spelling and mental laziness." This statement comes from a prominent professor in England (Crystal, 2008), but you may have heard your parents, high school teachers, or college professors similarly say that texting is the demise of language, reducing young people's literacy.

Texting is so new that research on its effects has only begun, but most of the available evidence suggests that the negative claims are false. Some studies have found that reading textisms (words spelled or abbreviated the way they are in texts, like "LOL," "l8r," "NVM," and "RU") have no negative effects on the ability to spell properly or on other literacy skills (Plester et al., 2008; Powell & Dixon, 2011; Zebroff, 2018). In one study, 9- and 10-year-old kids who hadn't yet gotten their first phone were given one for a 10-week period. Their spelling actually improved, and they continued to develop their reading and writing skills as their classmates without phones did (Wood et al., 2011). Other studies found that among college students, larger numbers of texts correlated with better reading accuracy and fluency (Drouin, 2011; Kemp, 2010). Some experts have argued that any decrease in literacy among young people is more likely due to a decrease in traditional reading (of books and other longer pieces) than an increase in texting (Zebroff & Kaufman, 2017).

Language expert John McWhorter makes the argument that texting is not the destruction of standard language, but is the development of an entirely new language with a grammar all its own (McWhorter, 2013a). In a widely viewed TED Talk (see Show Me More 7.3), McWhorter calls texting "fingered speech," and claims that it actually comes closer to oral speech—the original form of language, and the only one that humans had throughout most of their history—than any other kind of writing does. He also claims that people who text are becoming bilingual, and their fluency in texting language will enhance their overall cognitive abilities. He even describes texting as a "linguistic miracle happening right under our noses" (McWhorter, 2013b). •

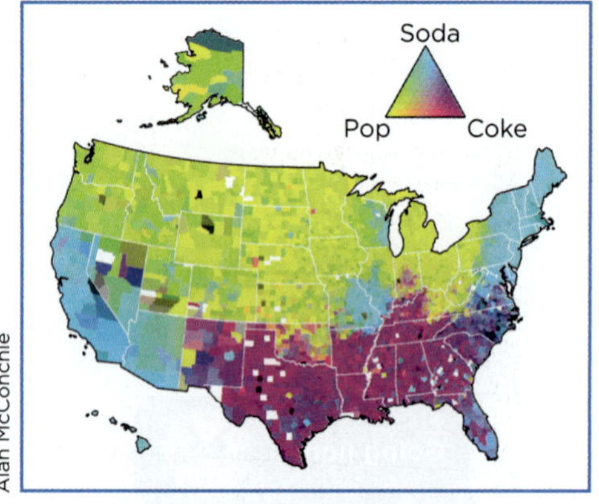

Alan McConchie

FIGURE 7.6 Soda, Pop, or Coke? What word do you use for soft drinks? Throughout the United States, it depends on dialect. It's *soda* in Maine, *pop* in Montana, and *Coke* in Mississippi. Information from popvssoda.com.

Dialect. Another illustration of the importance of *how* language is spoken comes from **dialect**: a group's particular version of a language with its own unique characteristics. Dialect includes accent, but it is much more than that. Dialect can influence the way we shape our sentences, the way we conjugate verbs, the expressions we use, and the words we choose as well. U.S. English features a wide variety of dialects. Many are based on region, but dialects can also center around ethnicity, age, social class, or other variables (Akmajian et al., 2010; Labov et al., 2006).

Imagine that you're standing on a street corner and you notice that across both streets, there is a boy wearing sleeping clothes. If you were raised in the northern United States, you're likely to say. "Look *kitty-corner, you guys*! He's wearing pa-*jah*-mas!" But if you were raised in the South, you're likely to say, "Look *catty-corner, y'all*! He's wearing pa-*ja*-mas!" (Katz, 2016; Vaux, 2003). Dialects of English are often even more distinct when we compare the United States to other countries that speak the language, such as Australia, Canada, and England (where gasoline is petrol, an apartment is a flat, and an elevator is a lift). **Figure 7.6** illustrates one of the linguistic questions that divides the U.S. dialects most clearly: what do you call carbonated soft drinks?

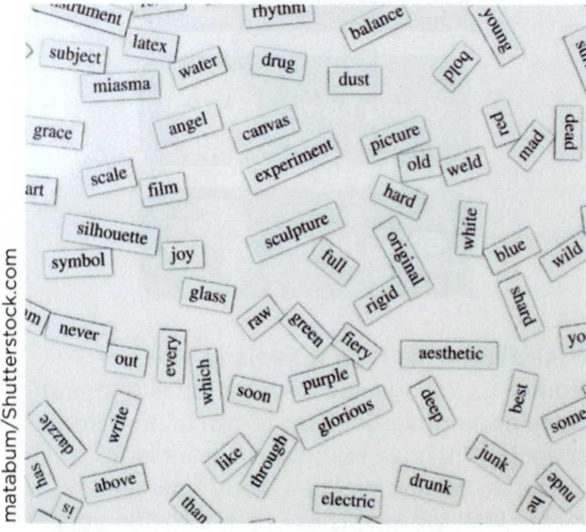

matabum/Shutterstock.com

The theory of linguistic relativity states that language influences thought. To the extent this theory is correct, the size of your vocabulary affects the breadth of your thinking.

Does Language Influence Thinking?

Think of your vocabulary as a box of those magnet words that you may have seen scattered on a refrigerator door. The number and type of words contained in the box would certainly affect the sentences you could create. But would they also affect the thoughts you could think? Would a huge box of words enable you to think more broadly? Would lots of words in a particular category—for example, dozens of words for colors, rather than just a few—make you more likely to be an expert on that topic? These are the questions surrounding **linguistic relativity**: the theory that language influences thought.

A well-known early study of linguistic relativity strongly claimed that language did in fact influence, and often limit, thinking (Whorf, 1956). But current experts continue to debate the issue (Athanasopoulos et al., 2016; Gleitman & Papafragou, 2013; Pederson et al., 1998; Reiger et al., 2010). Those who oppose linguistic relativity point out that your language could never keep up with your thoughts, no matter what kind of vocabulary you possess. Even if you are an eloquent speaker, your words are just a rough sketch of the full range of thoughts rapidly running through your mind (Bloom, 2002; Clark, 1992; Gleitman & Papafragou, 2013; Papafragou, 2007).

For example, if you send a text that says, "Home at 7," that language is really an abbreviation of the full-length thought you had: "I'm leaving my current location now, and I estimate travel between my current location and home to require 25 minutes. It's 6:35 now, so according to the laws of mathematics, I should arrive home at 7 P.M."

To illustrate the controversy over linguistic relativity, consider the people who speak North Saami. They live near the Arctic Circle in Sweden, Finland, and Norway, where they herd reindeer across wide swaths of land. Ice and snow are major parts of their daily lives. To get by, they need to know whether ice on a lake is thick enough to walk on without cracking, or thin enough for their reindeer to break through to graze on the grass underneath. They need to know whether snow has fallen evenly or in random drifts, and whether snow has a path from previous travelers or remains untouched. It should come as no surprise, then, that North Saami features dozens of words for what English speakers simply call "ice," and dozens more for what English speakers simply call "snow." For example, *rovda* is ice too thin to support the weight of a reindeer; *čođđi* is ice over stones or trees; *oppas* is snow that has not yet been walked across; and *čahki* is snow in hard lumps (Magga, 2006). But regarding linguistic relativity, the key question is this: does that linguistic difference mean that North Saami speakers think differently about ice and snow than English speakers do?

Those who support the theory of linguistic relativity would say yes to that question, and they offer some fascinating examples of the relationship between language and thought (Boroditsky, 2011). For example, in a language (Kuuk Thaayorre) spoken by an Australian aboriginal tribe, there are no words for left or right. Instead, speakers of this language rely much more on the directions you'd see on a compass – north, south, east, and west – to orient themselves. One researcher asked a group of Kuuk Thaayorre–speaking 5-year-olds to point southeast, and they did it instantly and correctly. Later at a professional conference, the same researcher asked a room full of English-speaking adults to point southeast, and they hesitated, struggled, and mostly got it wrong. (By the way, she didn't ask Kuuk Thaayorre–speaking adults to point southeast because she didn't want to insult their intelligence: it would be like testing your ability to point to the left [Boroditsky, 2012]!)

In another study by the same researcher with the same Kuuk Thaayorre–speaking tribe, participants saw a sequence of cards that depicted an action (like frames of a cartoon) and were asked to put them in order from start to finish. For example, a set of five cards may have shown a person picking up a banana, peeling it, holding the banana with one bite missing, holding the banana with several bites missing, and then holding the empty peel (**Figure 7.7**). When English speakers put the cards in order, they automatically arranged them left to right. When Kuuk Thaayorre speakers put the cards in order, they automatically arranged them east to west – corresponding to the way the sun moves as time progresses – no matter what direction they happened to be facing at that moment (Boroditsky & Gaby, 2006).

CHAPTER APP 7.1

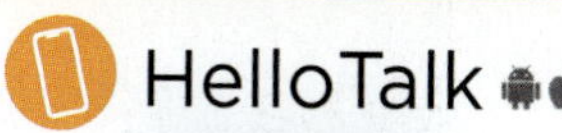

The HelloTalk app allows users to chat with someone who speaks a language other than their own. Each partner then teaches the other how to speak their native language. Through text, voice calls, or video calls, you can learn a new language from someone who has been speaking it their entire lives.

How does it APPly to your daily life?
In your daily life, how helpful would it be to become more fluent in another language? What advantages and disadvantages would learning by chatting with a native speaker have over more traditional ways of learning a language, like classes you may have taken in high school?

How does it APPly to your understanding of psychology?
How could this app help you appreciate the nature-nurture debate about the way language develops (nativist vs. non-nativist)? How could it help you better understand the importance of grammatical features of language, like phonemes, morphemes, semantics, and dialect?

To learn more about this app or to download it to your phone, you can search for "HelloTalk" on Google, in the iPhone App store, or in the Google Play store.

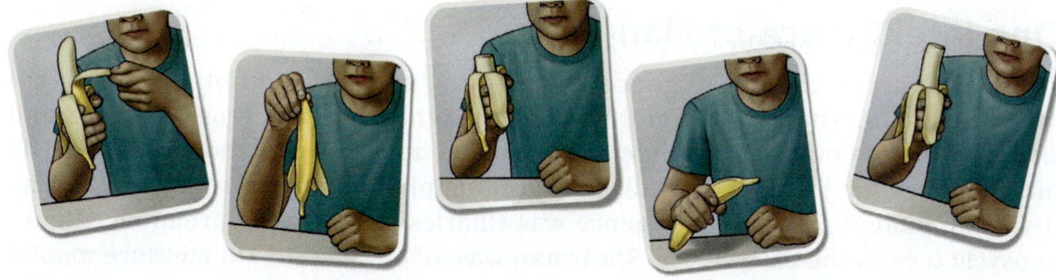

FIGURE 7.7 Left to Right or East to West? When given sets of cards like these, English speakers had no problem arranging them in sequential order. Neither did Kuuk Thaayhorre speakers. But while English speakers automatically arranged the sequence from left to right, Kuuk Thaayorre speakers arranged the sequence from east to west, no matter what direction they were facing when they did it. Kuuk Thaayorre has no words for left or right, so they rely on the movement of the sun (east to west) to orient themselves, suggesting some degree of linguistic relativity. Information from Boroditsky and Gaby (2006).

dialect
A group's particular version of a language with its own unique characteristics.

linguistic relativity
The theory that language influences thought.

Another study of linguistic relativity focused on German and Spanish, two languages that are *gendered*, which means some nouns are feminine and some are masculine (Boroditsky et al., 2003). The researchers found a few nouns that are masculine in one language and feminine in the other, and then asked native speakers of each language to describe those objects. The word for *key* is masculine in German, and German speakers described keys with words like hard, heavy, jagged, and useful — a traditionally masculine-sounding set of adjectives. The word for *key* is feminine in Spanish, and Spanish speakers described keys with traditionally feminine-sounding adjectives like lovely, little, golden, shiny, and intricate. Then the researchers tried *bridge*, which is feminine in German and masculine in Spanish. German speakers described bridges as beautiful, elegant, pretty, and fragile. Spanish speakers described bridges as big, strong, sturdy, and dangerous. Not all studies of gendered language come to such strong conclusions about the idea that language shapes thought (Samuel et al., 2019). But those that do suggest that language may at times influence thought in meaningful ways, though it would certainly be an overstatement to say that "language is a straitjacket for thought" (Boroditsky, 2012, p. 628).

CHECK YOUR LEARNING:

7.15 How do psychologists define language?

7.16 How do researchers think language may have evolved?

7.17 What is the difference between the nativist theory and nonnativist theories of language development?

7.18 What are the stages of a child's language development?

7.19 What is grammar, and what are its four levels?

7.20 What forms of extralinguistic information can influence communication?

7.21 What is linguistic relativity, and how widely is it accepted among experts in the field?

To check your understanding of these questions, click show the answers or refer to the answers in the Chapter Summary.

Intelligence

YOU WILL LEARN:

7.22 how psychologists define intelligence.

7.23 about the difference between general intelligence and specific intelligences and how they fit into a hierarchical model of intelligence.

7.24 about multiple intelligences.

7.25 what emotional intelligence is.

7.26 how the nature-nurture debate applies to intelligence.

7.27 how psychologists measure intelligence.

7.28 about different types of intelligence tests.

7.29 how psychologists evaluate measures of intelligence.

Intelligence is the ability to gain knowledge and learn from experience. Actually, the word *ability* in that definition has been controversial since the early days of psychology. Specifically, the controversy centers around whether the singular word *ability* in that definition should be replaced with the plural word *abilities* (Burkart et al., 2017; Sternberg, 2000; Wasserman & Tulsky, 2005). In other words, is intelligence one thing or many separate things?

One Intelligence or Many?

Those who argue that intelligence is one thing support the notion of **general intelligence** (or simply ***g***): overall intelligence that applies across all tasks and situations. Those on the other side of the argument support the notion of **specific intelligences** (or simply ***s***): intelligences that apply to only a particular area. The first champion of general intelligence was Charles Spearman, a prominent figure in psychology in the early 1900s. Spearman was among the first to measure mental abilities (like reading, writing, math ability, and sensory abilities) scientifically. He observed that there were strong positive correlations among those various abilities for most of his participants. If the person was good at one of the mental abilities, that person was probably good at all of them. Spearman reasoned that a single factor must underlie the connectedness of these abilities, and he called that factor *g* (Spearman, 1904, 1923). If you think about your high school classmates, you may remember that many of the kids who excelled in one subject excelled in others too. If so, you might come to a conclusion similar to Spearman's: how smart you are, in the most fundamental sense, influences your performance across the board.

But you may also remember from high school that some students excelled in certain classes while they struggled in others. Those kids' patterns of abilities support the viewpoint of Louis Thurstone, Spearman's primary opponent in the intelligence debates. Thurstone relied on a statistical process called *factor analysis*, which determines which variables in a long list tend to cluster together. If intelligence is in fact a single thing, a factor analysis of different cognitive tasks would reveal one big cluster. But if intelligence is made up of different things, a factor analysis would reveal several different clusters (like verbal ability, math ability, and memory), and that's what Thurstone found. Thurstone's findings led him to claim that there isn't a single underlying intelligence that determines how well you perform across the board. Instead, he argued that there are different specific intelligences, some of which may be stronger than others, that cause your abilities to potentially differ (Brody, 2000; Mackintosh, 2011; Thurstone, 1938).

Both Spearman and Thurstone eventually acknowledged that the other one had a point. There is no denying the existence of general intelligence or specific intelligences, they reasoned, so a *hierarchical model of intelligence* seems ideal: one that contains numerous specific intelligences, each of which is considered a part of a single general intelligence (**Figure 7.8**).

In the years since the intelligence debates between Spearman and Thurstone, other experts have offered specific versions of the hierarchical model (Davidson & Kemp, 2011; Willis et al., 2011). In the 1960s and 1970s, James Cattell argued that general intelligence is made up of two primary specific intelligences: *fluid intelligence*, or the ability to solve new problems, and *crystallized intelligence*, or stored knowledge (Cattell, 1971; Horn & Cattell, 1966; Kent, 2017).

In the 1990s, John Carroll developed a *three-stratum theory* of intelligence, in which a singular general intelligence contains a handful of broad specific intelligences, and then each of those broad specific intelligences contains several much more specific intelligences (Carroll, 1993). (*Stratum* means layer, and Carroll's theory says that intelligence contains three layers: *g*, big *s*, and little *s*.) For example, you may have a certain overall intelligence (*g*), a certain memory ability (big *s*) within that, and a more particular short-term memory ability (little *s*) within that.

More recently, Carroll's work has been integrated with that of others into the *Cattell–Horn–Carroll (CHC) theory of intelligence*, which proposes a single general intelligence, 10 broad abilities, and over 70 more narrow abilities (Benson et al., 2018; Flanagan et al., 2000, 2013; Horn & Noll, 1997; Kaufman et al., 2013; Schneider & McGrew, 2018). The main point here is that these various hierarchical models of intelligence all include a general or overall intelligence, as well as one or two levels of more specific intelligences contained within it.

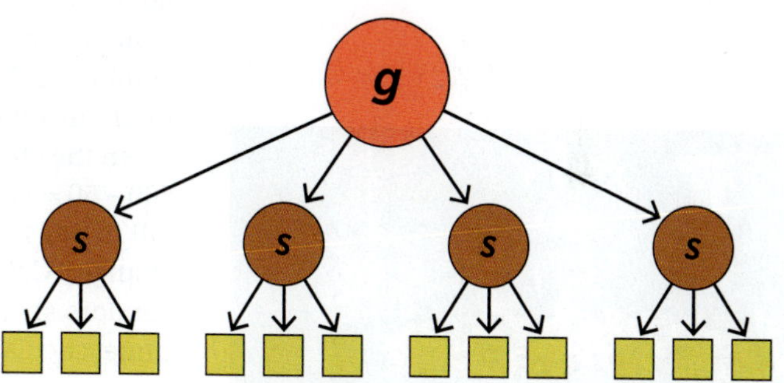

FIGURE 7.8 Hierarchical Model of Intelligence. According to the hierarchical model of intelligence, you have a general intelligence (g) that is made up of several specific intelligences (s), each of which can be further broken down into more particular abilities.

Multiple Intelligences

According to the hierarchical theories of intelligence described previously, your overall intelligence is essentially a combination of your separate intelligences. Some experts disagree with the notion that those separate intelligences should be combined (Davis et al., 2011). These experts believe that our separate intelligences are as distinct as apples and oranges. This belief is known as the *multiple intelligences* approach, and its most widely respected proponent is Howard Gardner (Chen & Gardner, 2018; Gardner, 1985, 1995, 1999). In the 1980s, Gardner identified and defined eight distinct intelligences (he added a ninth more recently) that each of us possess to one degree or another. Gardner required an ability to have certain characteristics to count as an intelligence. For example, it must correspond to specific locations in the brain (as

7.30 about the difference between intelligence tests and achievement tests.

7.31 about the extremes of intelligence.

7.32 what test bias is and why intelligence tests should avoid it.

7.33 how stereotype threat can negatively influence test-taking.

7.34 about group differences on intelligence tests and the controversy that surrounds them.

intelligence
The ability to gain knowledge and learn from experience.

general intelligence (*g*)
Overall intelligence that applies across all tasks and situations.

specific intelligences (*s*)
Intelligences that apply to only a particular area.

TABLE 7.6: Gardner's Theory of Multiple Intelligences

INTELLIGENCE	PEOPLE WITH HIGH LEVELS EXCEL AT...
Linguistic	Writing, speaking, and understanding language.
Logico-mathematical	Math, science, logic, and problem solving.
Spatial	Reasoning about physical objects in three-dimensional space.
Musical	Playing instruments, singing, and creating and appreciating music.
Bodily-kinesthetic	Dancing, sports, and movement-related tasks.
Interpersonal	Interacting with others, as well as understanding others' thoughts and feelings.
Intrapersonal	Self-awareness.
Naturalistic	Understanding and appreciating plants, animals, weather, and other aspects of the environment.
Existential	Contemplating the meaning of life and other deep philosophical topics.

indicated by the connections between certain kinds of brain damage and certain kinds of impairment), and it must be something in which at least a few people (savants) have naturally exceptional capabilities.

Gardner's multiple intelligences are described in **Table 7.6**. They include the kinds of intelligences that relate to success in school or standardized tests — such as *linguistic* intelligence and *logico-mathematical* intelligence — but also nonacademic intelligences such as *bodily–kinesthetic* intelligence (at which athletes and dancers would excel) and *naturalistic* intelligence (at which farmers, hikers, and other outdoorsy types would excel) (Gardner, 2006).

Some intelligence experts have argued that even Gardner's broad view of multiple intelligences is too limited. They assert that other abilities — some of which matter little at school, but a lot in other settings — deserve to be recognized as parts of the intelligence puzzle (Austin & Saklofske, 2005; Niu, 2020). For example, some have pointed out that *relationship* intelligence, or the ability to maintain harmonious relationships with friends and family, is a core element of intelligence as defined in many parts of the non-Western world (Niu & Brass, 2011). Other researchers have proposed *cultural* intelligence (how well you respond to situations of cultural diversity) and even *mating* intelligence (how good you are at dating and forming romantic relationships) (Ang et al., 2011; Ang & Van Dyne, 2008; Earley & Ang, 2003; Geher & Kaufman, 2011).

Still other intelligence experts argue for the acknowledgment of more real-world kinds of intelligence, often called *practical* intelligence or *successful* intelligence — the kind of street smarts that help you get by in your day-to-day lives just as much as book smarts do (Sternberg, 1999, 2018; Wagner, 2011; Wagner & Sternberg, 1985). One study illustrated the distinctiveness of real-world intelligence by asking child street vendors in Brazil to make change — something they do many times every day when their customers pay for goods with large bills (Carraher et al., 1985). When they were given the change-making task as a pencil-and-paper arithmetic problem (for example, 500 – 50 = ?), only 37% got it right. But when they were actually handed a 500-cruzeiros bill to pay for a 50-cruzeiros item, 98% of them correctly handed back 450 cruzeiros in change. (Cruzeiros were the currency in Brazil at the time of the study.) These street vendors struggled to do an abstract written problem but had little problem doing the same calculation as a practical real-world task.

Alex Treadway/National Geographic/Getty Images

Practical intelligence is the street smarts needed to successfully complete the tasks necessary in daily life. For street vendors, practical intelligence involves making change correctly, whether or not they can do a corresponding math problem with pencil and paper.

Emotional Intelligence

Of all of the nontraditional types of intelligence proposed by researchers, the most prominent is **emotional intelligence**: the ability to sense and manage emotions in yourself and others. Emotional intelligence is a relatively recent development in psychology — the first articles and books on the topic came out in the 1990s — but it has received lots of attention since that time (Fiori & Vesely-Maillefer, 2018; Goleman, 1998, 2006; Mayer & Salovey, 1997; Salovey, 2005; Salovey & Mayer, 1989). Emotional intelligence has four branches (Mayer et al., 2008):

- **Accurately perceiving emotions in yourself and others.** How well can you read your friend's facial expressions or tone of voice? How sensitive are you to your own stress level?
- **Using emotions to facilitate thinking.** If you sense that your friend is sad, will you rethink your plan to ask them for a big favor, and instead invite them to talk about her own problems? If you sense that you are stressed out, will you make it a priority to figure out how to reduce your stress?
- **Understanding emotions.** If your friend is indeed sad, what might this mean— problems with their job, their friends or family, their health, or something else?

emotional intelligence
A person's ability to sense and manage their own emotions as well as the emotions of others.

If you are indeed stressed out, what could this signify about the lifestyle you've been living?

- **Managing emotions.** What actions can you intentionally take to help lift your friend's sadness? What behaviors can you deliberately do to reduce your own stress levels?

ONOKY - Eric Audras/Brand X Pictures/Getty Images

Emotional intelligence is the ability to sense and manage emotions in yourself and others. Your emotional intelligence can influence the success of many of your interactions, including job interviews.

Advocates of emotional intelligence claim that it is a vital and often underrated factor across most areas of your life, from school to work to health to relationships (Neubauer & Freudenthaler, 2005; Schulze et al., 2005; Villanueva et al., 2017). As an example, consider the importance of emotional intelligence in one important situation: a job interview. Robert's education, experience, and résumé all suggest to the interviewer that he is smart enough to handle the job – that's how he landed the interview in the first place. During the interview, however, he shows some signs of low *emotional* intelligence. At one point, Robert misreads the interviewer's facial expressions, mistakenly thinking she disapproves of his answer when she's just giving it serious thought. He becomes overly concerned about this perceived disapproval, so he decides to tell a joke, which backfires and confuses the interviewer. The interview still might be salvageable at this point, but Robert gets so angry at himself that he pounds the desk and shouts, "I'm so stupid!" At that point, he begins to cry while begging the interviewer for another chance. No matter how impressive his credentials might be, these mistakes in terms of reading emotions, using emotions as cues for behavior, and controlling his own emotions made it clear that Robert might not be the best person for the job.

Research suggests that emotional intelligence correlates with job performance (Abraham, 2005; O'Boyle et al., 2011; Van Rooy & Viswesvaran, 2004). Employees who are high in emotional intelligence are more likely to emerge as leaders among their coworkers, and leaders high in emotional intelligence are more effective in managing their workers than leaders low in emotional intelligence (Côté et al., 2010; George, 2000; Mandell & Pherwani, 2003; Miao et al., 2017a, 2017b, 2018; Rosete & Ciarrochi, 2005). Emotional intelligence correlates with other desirable outcomes too, including physical health, mental health, high-quality relationships with friends and family, academic achievement, and avoidance of alcohol and tobacco by teens (Mayer et al., 2008; Petrides et al., 2016; Schutte et al., 2007; Trinidad & Johnson, 2002).

Research has even begun to emerge on the ways that emotional intelligence buffered people from the stress of the COVID pandemic. In one study that collected data during the first week of lockdown in Poland (mid-March 2020), results showed that people with higher levels of emotional intelligence experienced significantly less anger, disgust, anxiety, and sadness than those with lower levels (Moron & Biolik-Moron, 2021). A similar study around the same time in Israel found a negative correlation between emotional intelligence and worry – that is, the higher the level of emotional intelligence, the lower the level of worry (Zysberg & Zisberg, 2020). Another study that focused on nurses working through the pandemic found that those with higher levels of emotional intelligence were less likely to experience burnout regarding their jobs, physical problems that can be worsened by stress (like stomach aches), and sleep difficulties (Soto-Rubio et al., 2020).

The value of emotional intelligence has become so widely recognized that many schools now deliberately teach emotional intelligence to their students (Goetz et al., 2005). For example, medical students doing their residency at the University of Kansas Medical Center underwent emotional intelligence training, which produced not only increased levels of emotional intelligence but also higher satisfaction rates from their patients (Dugan et al., 2014). (Who wouldn't want their doctor to have high emotional intelligence?) Some researchers have quibbled that emotional intelligence is perhaps more of a personality trait than an intelligence, but, regardless of how it is labeled, there is little doubt of its significance or its impact on day-to-day functioning (Austin & Saklofske, 2005; Perez et al., 2005; van der Linden et al., 2017).

MY TAKE VIDEO 7.2

Emotional Intelligence

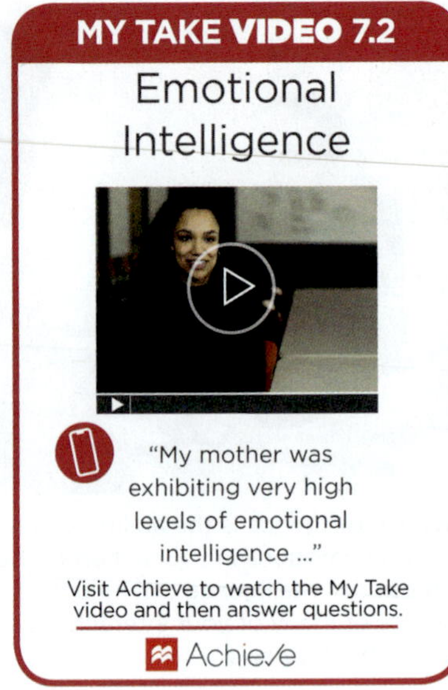

"My mother was exhibiting very high levels of emotional intelligence ..."

Visit Achieve to watch the My Take video and then answer questions.

Achieve

Nature, Nurture, and Intelligence

The nature–nurture debate that runs through psychology applies to intelligence as much as any other variable. What determines your intelligence – your genes or your environment? The short answer is both. There is simply no way to dismiss either the genes with which you are born or the surroundings in which you live as influences on your intelligence (**Table 7.7**).

A better question, then, is how much influence does each factor have? This question has been answered primarily through twin studies and adoption studies. In twin studies, researchers can compare identical (monozygotic) twins to non identical (dizygotic) twins. Identical twins share all of their genes, but non identical twins share only half. If identical twins' intelligence levels match more often than non identical twins' intelligence levels match, that would suggest that genes play a powerful role. In adoption studies, researchers can compare the intelligence levels of adopted kids with their adoptive parents and biological parents. To the extent that kids' intelligence levels are similar to their adoptive parents', environment matters; to the extent that kids' intelligence levels are similar to their biological parents', genes matter. These studies have produced a number of key findings (Bartels et al., 2002; Bouchard, 2013; Bouchard et al., 1990; Bouchard & McGue, 1981, 2003; Deary et al., 2006; Mandelman & Grigorenko, 2011; Neisser et al., 1996; Nisbett et al., 2012; Plomin & von Stumm, 2018; Rizzi & Posthuma, 2013; Sauce & Matzel, 2018):

- **Overall, genes have a substantial influence on intelligence.** Estimates of the heritability of intelligence vary across studies but tend to hover in the 50–75% range. This suggests that to a significant extent, when it comes to intelligence, you're born with it. However, it also leaves plenty of room for impact by the environment.
- **Heritability rates depend on when intelligence is measured.** Compared to a young child's intelligence, an adult's intelligence is much more likely to follow predictions based on genetic inheritance. It is not uncommon to find a 3-year-old whose intelligence doesn't match their biological parents' intelligence, but it is quite uncommon to find a 30-year-old who shows such a mismatch with their parents.
- **There are many important environmental variables.** The way you were raised, the schools you attend, the jobs you get, the food you eat, the socioeconomic level at which you live, and the people with whom you interact all have the power to affect your intelligence.
- **Genes and environment interact in complex ways.** Consider Mateo, a boy who, because of his genetic inheritance of intelligence, is one of the smartest kids in his elementary school. His parent notices his intelligence and fosters it with after-school activities and brain-training computer games. His teachers also notice his intelligence and challenge him with customized class work and advanced educational opportunities. These new environmental influences further boost Mateo's intelligence. As a young man, Mateo enrolls in an academically rigorous college and surrounds himself with classmates and professors who keep his mind sharp. Mateo genes not only affect his intelligence directly, they also influence the kinds of environments in which he lives, and those environments further influence his intelligence.

As the amount of shared genes increases, the correlation between siblings' IQ increases. That correlation gets very high for identical twins, but it doesn't reach 1.00, suggesting that the environment has some influence. The fact that pairs raised together have higher correlations than the same type of pairs raised apart also points to the importance of the environment.

TABLE 7.7: Gene-ius

TYPE OF SIBLINGS	CORRELATION BETWEEN SIBLINGS' INTELLIGENCE LEVELS
Monozygotic (identical) twins raised together	0.86
Monozygotic (identical) twins raised apart	0.72
Dizygotic (non identical) twins raised together	0.60
Nontwin siblings raised together	0.47
Nontwin siblings raised apart	0.24

Data from Bouchard and McGue (1981) and Deary et al. (2006).

As we've seen in the previous sections, there are plenty of psychologists who study intelligence, but there are even more who measure it in their clients. In fact, among clinical psychologists (like me), measuring intelligence is among the most common professional activities besides conducting interviews and therapy (Archer & Newsom, 2000; Camara et al., 2000; Cashel, 2002; Curry & Hanson, 2010; Watkins et al., 1995; Wright et al., 2017). We do this by administering an **intelligence test**: an assessment technique used by psychologists to numerically measure intelligence.

intelligence test
An assessment technique used by psychologists to numerically measure intelligence.

intelligence quotient (IQ)
A single number used to represent a person's overall intelligence.

When you picture a psychologist giving a client an intelligence test, don't picture the psychologist handing the client a question booklet, an answer sheet, and a #2 pencil (as if it was just like the standardized tests you took in school as a child, or like the college entrance exams you might have taken). Also, do not picture the client taking a quick, poorly crafted, online quiz. Many of the so-called "intelligence tests" floating around on the Internet make psychologists cringe. Some of them are more about making money from Web site ads than giving you a legitimate measure of your intelligence (Burnett, 2013).

Legitimate intelligence tests – the ones psychologists give to their clients – are face-to-face interactions. To learn to give them, the psychologist takes one course (or more) in graduate school in which the focus is learning to administer, score, and interpret these tests (Mihura et al., 2017; Raiford et al., 2010). Typically, the psychologist and the client sit on opposite sides of a table or desk. The psychologist's setup generally includes a test manual to guide them through all parts, or *subtests*, of the test in a standardized way; a blank form on which to write down the client's responses; and often a small collection of items such as pictures, objects, and brief written activities that the psychologist will share with the client at various points in the test. Most subtests involve the psychologist asking questions out loud, the client responding out loud, and the psychologist writing down what the client says. The whole intelligence test typically lasts between 30 minutes and 3 hours. When it is over, the psychologist assigns points to the client's responses, calculates the appropriate scores, and writes up the results in the form of a report.

Intelligence Quotient (IQ). The primary result of the intelligence test is the **intelligence quotient (IQ)**: a single number used to represent a person's overall intelligence. IQ has a median of 100. As scores move up from 100, they indicate above-average intelligence. As scores move down from 100, they indicate below-average intelligence. Those scores have to move up or down a sizable amount to

FROM RESEARCH TO REAL LIFE

Intelligence Correlates With...

Experts may debate the definition of intelligence, but there is little debate about how powerfully it correlates with a number of real-world outcomes. It is probably no surprise that intelligence is linked to how well students do in school and how many adults do in their careers (Amdurer et al., 2014; Deary et al., 2007; Kaufman et al., 2012; Naglieri & Bornstein, 2003; Rohde & Thompson, 2007; Schmidt & Hunter, 2004; Schnieder et al., 2018). But intelligence also correlates with many other things. (Keep in mind that correlation does not necessarily mean causation.) Specifically, higher intelligence correlates with:

- Higher socioeconomic status (SES) (Damian et al., 2015; Neisser et al., 1996; Strenze, 2007)
- Higher income (several hundred dollars annually per IQ point increase) (Zagorsky, 2007)
- Higher levels of academic achievement (Lynn et al., 2018)
- Higher levels of extraversion and lower levels of neuroticism and psychoticism (Ackerman & Heggestad, 1997; Furnham & Chang, 2017)
- Longer life span (Arden et al., 2015; Batty et al., 2007)
- Better physical health (Gottfredson & Deary, 2004; Lynn et al., 2018)
- Higher likelihood of having an opinion about politics and higher likelihood of that opinion being near the center of the political spectrum rather than at an extreme (Rindermann et al., 2012)
- Younger "biological age" around midlife, including younger-looking faces, healthier cardiovascular systems, and better cholesterol levels (Schaefer et al., 2015)
- Lower levels of fertility and crime (Lynn et al., 2018)

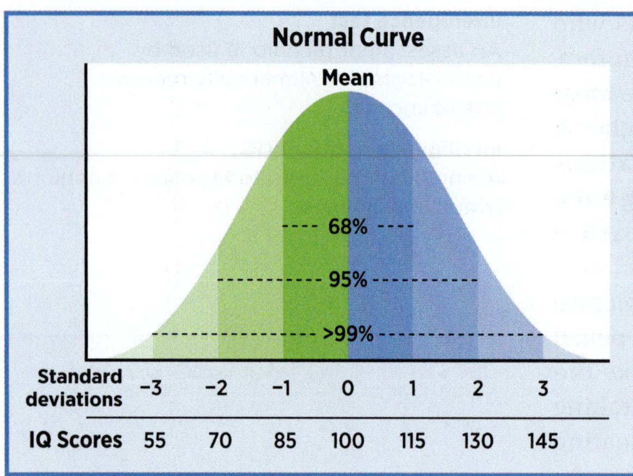

FIGURE 7.9 The Normal Curve. When they are graphed, intelligence scores of the population create a normal curve, in which scores near the mean are most common. The farther from the mean in either direction, the more uncommon the score is. Data from Urbina (2011).

make a meaningful difference. A person whose IQ is just a couple of points above or below 100 is still in the average range. As **Figure 7.9** indicates, over two-thirds of people have IQs that fall within 15 points of 100. (The *standard deviation*, which we covered back in Chapter 1, of IQ tests is 15.) About 95% fall within 30 points of the mean, and about 99% within 45 points of the mean. The illustration of this finding, as featured in Figure 7.9, is known as the **normal curve**: a graph showing that the frequency of scores on a test is greatest in the middle and decreases toward the extremes. The normal curve has also been called a *bell curve*, since it is shaped like a bell. The main idea communicated by the normal curve of intelligence is that we, as a population, tend to cluster around the middle of the IQ range. IQ is a lot like height in that way: most of us are within a couple of inches of average height, just as most of us are within a small number of points of average IQ.

Intelligence Tests Used by Psychologists. Among the specific intelligence tests that psychologists use, most prominent are the **Wechsler Intelligence Tests**: a widely used and highly respected set of intelligence tests originally developed by David Wechsler (Drozdick et al., 2018; Goldstein, 2008; Lichtenberger & Kaufman, 2009; Raiford, 2018; Wahlstrom et al., 2018). When Wechsler created his first IQ test in the early 1900s, it was designed for adults only, but now there are three separate versions to cover nearly the entire life span:

- The *Wechsler Adult Intelligence Scale* (*WAIS*), appropriate for people age 16–90
- The *Wechsler Intelligence Scale for Children* (*WISC*), appropriate for people age 6–16
- The *Wechsler Preschool and Primary Scale of Intelligence* (*WPPSI*), appropriate for people age 2.5–7

The Wechsler intelligence tests each include about a dozen subtests, many of which are shared by all three tests. These subtests are grouped into four or five categories. In the adult version of the test, those categories are

- **Verbal comprehension.** Subtests that assess how well you understand and use words and sentences
- **Perceptual reasoning.** Subtests that assess your ability to solve visual problems, often including designs and puzzles
- **Working memory.** Subtests that assess your ability to hold, manipulate, and retrieve information from short-term memory
- **Processing speed.** Subtests that assess how quickly and accurately you can scan and make decisions about simple visual information

An alternative to the Wechsler tests is the **Stanford–Binet Intelligence Test**: a widely used and highly respected intelligence test originally developed by Alfred Binet and then revised by Lewis Terman and appropriate across the life span. In terms of structure, the Stanford–Binet is similar to the Wechsler tests, with many subtests grouped into a smaller number of categories, which are then pulled together to form the full-scale IQ score. One big difference is that the Stanford–Binet is a single test for clients age 2 to 85 rather than three tests for various age groups, as with the Wechsler. Another difference is that the hardest items are harder and the easiest items are easier on the Stanford–Binet (compared to the Wechsler tests). That's an advantage for a psychologist testing a client at the very high end or the very low end of the range of intelligence (Kamphaus & Kroncke, 2004).

When psychologists measure intelligence (or anything else, for that matter), they use only tests that meet their high professional standards. Specifically, they seek tests that are high in *reliability* and *validity*.

An intelligence test should be high in **reliability**: the extent to which an assessment technique provides consistent, repeatable results. A reliable intelligence test

normal curve
A graph showing that the frequency of scores on a test is greatest in the middle and decreases toward the extremes.

Wechsler Intelligence Tests
A widely used and highly respected set of intelligence tests originally developed by David Wechsler.

Stanford–Binet Intelligence Test
A widely used and highly respected intelligence test originally developed by Alfred Binet and Lewis Terman and appropriate across the life span.

reliability
The extent to which an assessment technique provides consistent, repeatable results.

doesn't depend on who administers it, where it was administered, or when it was administered. You might remember that when psychologists give IQ tests, they keep a manual in front of them. That manual tells them exactly what to do at every step, which increases reliability, since differences in the way the test is given could lead to differences in scores.

An intelligence test should also be high in **validity**: the extent to which an assessment technique measures what it claims to measure. A valid intelligence test provides results that are similar to what other well-established intelligence tests measure, and results that are different from what tests of other abilities measure.

validity
The extent to which an assessment technique measures what it claims to measure.

achievement test
An assessment technique used by psychologists to numerically measure the level of learning a person has attained.

giftedness
Significantly above-average intelligence.

specific learning disorder
A mental disorder in which achievement in reading, writing, or math is significantly below age expectations.

Achievement Tests. Often, when a client takes an intelligence test, the client also takes an **achievement test**: an assessment technique used by psychologists to numerically measure the level of learning a person has attained.

Achievement tests sound pretty similar to intelligence tests. What's the difference?

The main difference is that intelligence tests measure what a person *can* accomplish, but achievement tests measure what a person *has* accomplished, particularly in school-related areas like reading, writing, and math (Mayer, 2011). Generally, these two scores match pretty closely: smart people are usually high achievers, and not-so-smart people are usually low achievers. Occasionally, a person's achievement falls significantly below their intelligence level, which typically comes to light when that person struggles in school ("Alyssa's so bright — I wonder why she's having such a hard time learning long division").

Extremes of Intelligence. There is a wide range of reasons why psychologists give intelligence tests. One is to test for **giftedness**: significantly above-average intelligence. The term *giftedness* was coined in the early 1900s by Leta Hollinger, a pioneering woman in the history of psychology (Held, 2010). The official definition of giftedness differs between states or school districts, but a common definition is two standard deviations above the mean on an intelligence test. On a Wechsler test, that would mean a score of at least 130, which is obtained by only the top 2–3% of students. (Often, there are other factors besides a single IQ score that affect whether a student receives the giftedness designation.) Kids who are labeled as gifted often participate in school activities and classes that are designed to provide them with cognitive challenges that they might not otherwise experience (Little, 2018; Reis & Renzulli, 2011). Many gifted students attain high levels of achievement at school and eventually as professionals, but some do not, especially when they find school unchallenging, when they have trouble applying their intelligence to the kinds of tasks demanded of them, or when poverty or obstacles in their home or school environment interfere (Olszewski-Kubilius & Corwith, 2018; Reis & McCoach, 2000; Renzulli & Park, 2002).

Another reason why psychologists use intelligence tests is to determine whether a client has a **specific learning disorder**: a mental disorder in which achievement in reading, writing, or math is significantly below age expectations. The term *dyslexia* is often used to refer to a specific learning disorder that focuses on reading. As with giftedness, the official cutoff for "significantly below age expectations" varies across states and districts. The diagnosis of a specific learning disorder often gives a kid access to educational resources that might not have been available otherwise — specially designed teaching or tutoring sessions, an individualized educational plan for teachers to follow, and other accommodations intended to help maximize the student's achievement. Children with specific learning disorders have an increased likelihood of other diagnoses, including attention-deficit/hyperactivity disorder (ADHD), anxiety, and depression (McDonough et al., 2017; Tannock, 2013; Willcutt & Pennington, 2000). However, a diagnosis of a specific learning disorder does not necessarily predict

Karwai Tang/WireImage/Getty Images

Gabriel Olsen/FilmMagic/Getty Images

Both Keira Knightley and Magic Johnson have overcome specific learning disorders to achieve remarkably successful careers.

long-term hardship: many people, including actor Keira Knightley and former basketball star Magic Johnson, have overcome learning disorders to reach high levels of success.

A third reason why psychologists give intelligence tests is to test for **intellectual disability**: a mental disorder based on significantly below-average intelligence and impaired day-to-day functioning. Prior to 2013, intellectual disability was called *mental retardation*, a term that is now considered by many to be inappropriate or disrespectful. The diagnosis is based not just on an IQ score approximately two standard deviations below the mean (around 70), but also on significant problems doing basic tasks independently — like getting dressed, communicating, exhibiting appropriate social skills, and other adaptive behaviors. Intellectual disability can only be diagnosed when it arises in childhood (American Psychiatric Association, 2013). Down syndrome, which occurs once per every 800–1000 births, is the most common genetic problem leading to intellectual disability (Hodapp et al., 1999, 2011).

DIVERSITY MATTERS

Test Bias. In addition to having high levels of reliability and validity, the best intelligence tests have *low* levels of **test bias**: the tendency of a test to produce scores in a consistently inaccurate way for members of particular groups. Unfortunately, the history of intelligence testing has featured controversies about test bias. In particular, critics of intelligence tests have accused the test makers of including items that give certain groups an advantage (typically middle- to upper-class Whites, which also describes most of the test *makers*, historically), while giving a disadvantage to other groups (typically ethnic and racial minorities and people of relatively low socioeconomic status).

This type of bias happens when intelligence tests tap into aspects of life that some groups have more access to and familiarity with than others (Helms, 2006). For example, imagine that a 15-year-old boy is asked to define *quinoa* as a vocabulary question on an intelligence test. If that boy is from certain socioeconomic or cultural groups in which quinoa (a grain-like seed with high nutritional value) is popular, he's more likely to have eaten, or at least heard of, quinoa than if he's from other groups. Imagine that later in the test, the same boy faces this question: "What are some advantages and disadvantages to taking a gap year?" Again, if the boy is from a cultural or economic background in which college is a common path, he has a decent chance of knowing that *gap year* refers to a year between high school and college when young people often seek additional experiences or education. But if his background is different, a *gap year*, or any other term related to college, is less likely to be familiar to him. A higher proportion of ethnic and racial minorities fall into a lower socioeconomic category, so intelligence tests can be unfair to entire cultural groups when they are loaded with items that reflect higher socioeconomic categories (Bornstein & Bradley, 2003; Suzuki et al., 2011).

In the 1970s, one researcher decided to make a statement about how test bias disadvantages some cultural groups. A pioneer in the field of Black psychology named Robert Williams turned the tables by creating an intelligence test based entirely on knowledge familiar to people who grew up in the Black community. He called it the Black Intelligence Test of Cultural Homogeneity, or the BITCH. Not surprisingly, Whites found the test much more difficult than Blacks did and scored much lower on it. One question asked what *Jet* is (a news and entertainment magazine focused on the Black community); another asked what Juneteenth commemorates (the freeing of the slaves); another asked what deuce-and-a-quarter means (a Buick Electra 225). The BITCH has not been widely used, but its impact was certainly felt. Specifically, the test enabled one minority group to show the majority group what it feels like to be evaluated by a test that values others' social and cultural experiences over their own (Thaler et al., 2015; Williams, 1972; Wingate, 2011).

intellectual disability
A mental disorder based on significantly below-average intelligence and impaired day-to-day functioning.

test bias
The tendency of a test to produce scores in a consistently inaccurate way for members of particular groups.

Thankfully, today's widely used intelligence tests are far less biased than the intelligence tests from decades ago. Their authors have repeatedly revised them, making special efforts to reduce test bias. These authors strive to create **culture-fair intelligence tests**: intelligence tests that aim to reduce or remove any cultural factors leading to bias. A few more recently created tests adopt the strategy of minimizing the use of words at all, since words are the primary source of test bias. For example, the Universal Nonverbal Intelligence Test (UNIT) is an intelligence test originally published in 1996 that is completely language-free (Bracken & McCallum, 2009; McCallum & Bracken, 2005). All of the instructions are given with hand gestures, and clients respond by pointing to answers or arranging items in a particular way. None of the items involve words at all. Its subtests involve mazes, puzzles, visual memory games, and similar tasks. As with other tests of this type, the UNIT is not (yet) widely used, it is only appropriate for clients in a limited age range (school-aged children), and data on its reliability and validity are limited (McCallum & Bracken, 2018; Ortiz & Dynda, 2005). But the existence of the UNIT and other tests like it indicates that psychologists are increasing their efforts to minimize test bias and maximize cultural fairness.

Marijus Auruskevicius/Shutterstock.com

Culture-fair intelligence tests use tasks that do not depend heavily on language, such as mazes, puzzles, and visual memory games, to assess intelligence without the influence of cultural factors.

Stereotype Threat. In addition to test bias, minority groups often face the obstacle of **stereotype threat**: the expectation that others may judge you according to stereotypes about a group to which you belong. When you sense that others are stereotyping you in a negative way — they think people like you are stupid, for example — your awareness of their stereotype can interfere with your abilities (Spencer et al., 2016; Steele, 1997; Steele & Aronson, 2004). You could become so preoccupied with the stereotype, and so worried that anything you say or do might be misinterpreted to confirm it, that your intelligence can't shine through (Lewis & Sekaquaptewa, 2016; Schmader & Johns, 2003; Schmader et al., 2008). It is a self-fulfilling prophecy of sorts. They prejudge you as unintelligent, and your awareness of that prejudice distracts you and makes you seem less intelligent than you really are. One study of racial and ethnic minority medical students included an explanation of the stereotype threat from a Black student, who felt like he was at a disadvantage compared to "a White student who doesn't have to constantly survey. And they can probably think about what they're supposed to be thinking about" (Bullock et al., 2020, p. S62).

Since stereotype threat was originally identified in the 1990s, a growing body of research has demonstrated how real it is. Separate studies have found that when people feel judged by others who hold stereotypical expectations, test-takers who are women, Black, Latinx, poor, or older adults all earn significantly lower scores on intelligence-related tests than they otherwise would (Armstrong et al., 2017; Cadinu et al., 2005; Croizet & Claire, 1998; Gonzales et al., 2002; Hess et al., 2003; Spencer et al., 1999; Taylor & Walton, 2011).

Stereotype threat can influence performance in all kinds of situations, not just intelligence tests (Gentile et al., 2018; Liu et al., 2021; Lamont et al., 2015). For example, one study focused on the gender-based stereotype that women are less knowledgeable than men about cars. Researchers showed women a video in which a criminal takes a hostage and demands that the hostage tell the criminal exactly where to find a particular car. The criminal then drives their own car to the car and finds money in its trunk. After watching the video, the women who watched it were asked to recall all of the details about the two cars (a black Volkswagen Golf and a gray Peugeot convertible). Half of the women were simply asked to describe the cars, but the other half were given an instruction intended to activate the stereotype that women are relatively bad at car knowledge: "... the aim of this study is actually to evaluate your knowledge about cars and your ability to describe them . . . remember that your knowledge about cars will determine how well you do." The women who received the second instruction produced significantly less accurate information and significantly more mistakes in

culture-fair intelligence tests
Intelligence tests that aim to reduce or remove any cultural factors that could lead to bias.

stereotype threat
The expectation that others may judge you according to stereotypes about a group to which you belong.

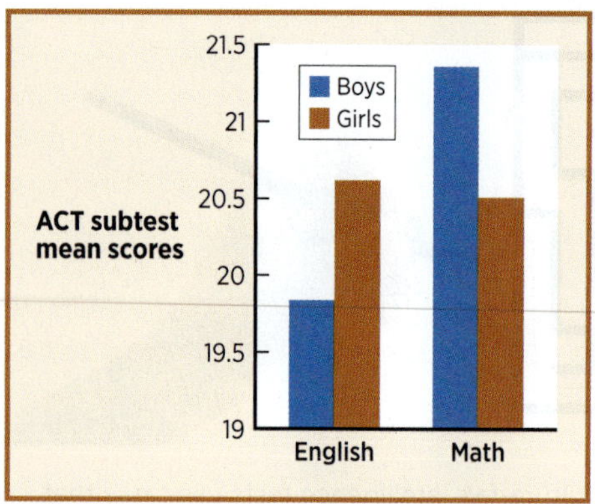

FIGURE 7.10 English, Math, and Gender: Average Scores on the ACT Subtests. Although overall intelligence does not differ between genders, men and boys as a group tend to perform slightly better on mathematical tasks, and women and girls as a group tend to perform slightly better on verbal tasks (Halpern, 2012; Halpern et al., 2011). That group difference is reflected in these ACT subtest means for English and Math, which are for 2013 but are typical of other years as well. Research from Buddin (2014).

their descriptions of the cars. The researchers point out that stereotype threats of this kind could have real-world consequences, such as when witnesses to crimes are questioned by police, judges, or attorneys (Brelet et al., 2018).

Group Differences. With such factors as test bias and stereotype threat in the mix, many findings about intelligence differences between groups — especially racial groups — have been the subject of great controversy. In particular, the finding in the 1990s that Black people tend to score lower than White people on intelligence tests — and the claim that these lower scores were due in part to genetics rather than environment — was met with swift and effective criticism (Daley & Onwuegbuzie, 2011; Fraser, 1995; Gardner, 1995; Herrnstein & Murray, 1994; Lind, 1995; Nisbett, 1995).

Nonetheless, researchers have explored questions of intelligence differences between groups of various kinds. One particularly well-studied question focuses on the differences in intelligence between men and women. In terms of general or overall intelligence, there is no difference. Men's and women's averages are remarkably similar in many particular areas of intelligence too. However, there are a few particular areas of intelligence in which slight but consistent differences have been identified across many countries and cultures (**Figure 7.10**). Specifically, women tend to have a slight advantage in most verbal abilities, including reading and writing, while men tend to have a slight advantage in math and most tasks that involve visual or spatial orientation (Halpern, 2012; Halpern et al., 2011; Hedges & Nowell, 1995; Hegarty & Waller, 2005; Schultheis & Carlson, 2013; Torres et al., 2006).

It is important to keep in mind that just because a group of people tend to score a certain way on intelligence tests, a particular person from that group won't necessarily follow that trend. In other words, the differences *within* a group can be as large and as important as the differences *between* groups. Think of it this way: men tend to be taller than women, but it is entirely possible that the next man you meet will be shorter than most women (like comedian Kevin Hart, who stands 5′2″) or that the next woman you meet will be taller than most men (like Taylor Swift, who stands 5′11″). In much the same way, any particular woman could excel at math or visual–spatial abilities, and any particular man could excel at verbal abilities.

Misinformation. **Misinformation** is information that is false, deceptive, or misleading. Misinformation — or "fake news," as it's sometimes called — has always been present in our society, often created and spread intentionally. Of course, the importance of misinformation has risen in recent years, especially in the areas of politics and the COVID pandemic. In fact, the term *infodemic* has been used to describe the crisis of misinformation that parallels the COVID pandemic itself. Their relevance to our discussion of intelligence in this chapter becomes clear when you remember that we defined intelligence as "the ability to gain knowledge and learn from experience." The first part of that definition — the ability to gain knowledge — is directly endangered when that knowledge is untrue.

Psychologists who study misinformation have found that there are certain factors that affect how likely we are to believe it. Some of those factors are characteristics of the information itself: we're more likely to believe misinformation when it matches other information we already accept, when we think the source is reliable, when we think lots of other people believe it, when it doesn't contradict itself, and when there's some evidence put forth to support it (Schwarz, 2015). Other factors are characteristics of the person receiving the information: people who are more likely to believe misinformation are those who tend to accept weak claims without evaluating them critically, those who rely more on intuition than analytical reasoning, those who hold extreme political beliefs, and those with relatively low levels of education and general cognitive functioning (Bago et al., 2020; Baptista & Gradim, 2020; Batty et al., 2021; Pennycook & Rand, 2019; Scherer et al., 2021).

Misinformation
Information that is false, deceptive, or misleading.

Influenced by the urgency of recent issues such as the pandemic and increasing political divisions, psychologists have explored strategies for reducing the impact of misinformation. Debunking misinformation after people have heard it can work, but some researchers have argued that getting out ahead of misinformation and warning people that what they may hear later is wrong — a tactic informally known as *prebunking*, or inoculating — can be even more effective (Maertens et al., 2021; van der Linden, 2017; Jolley & Douglass, 2017). Other promising strategies include deliberately encouraging people to think about the truthfulness of the information they encounter — that is, sometimes just a little nudge to question whether information is false can be enough to prevent people from mistakenly believing it (Pennycook et al., 2020).

CHECK YOUR LEARNING:

7.22 How do psychologists define intelligence?

7.23 What is the difference between general intelligence (g) and specific intelligences (s), and how do they fit into the hierarchical model of intelligence?

7.24 What is the theory of multiple intelligences?

7.25 What is emotional intelligence?

7.26 How does the nature–nurture debate apply to intelligence?

7.27 How do psychologists measure intelligence?

7.28 What are the two main intelligence tests that psychologists use?

7.29 What is the role of reliability and validity in measures of intelligence?

7.30 What is the difference between intelligence tests and achievement tests?

7.31 What are the two extremes of intelligence?

7.32 What is test bias, and why is it detrimental to intelligence tests?

7.33 How can stereotype threat negatively influence test-taking?

7.34 Are there group differences between men and women in terms of intelligence?

To check your understanding of these questions, click show the answers or refer to the answers in the Chapter Summary.

CHAPTER SUMMARY

Thinking

7.1 Psychologists define cognition as what your brain does with information, including understanding it, organizing it, analyzing it, and communicating it. Psychologists study cognition by focusing on three main areas: thinking, language, and intelligence.

7.2 Psychologists define the term *concept* as a mental representation of a category of similar things, actions, or people.

7.3 The three main types of concepts are feature-based concepts, goal-based concepts, and relationship-based concepts.

7.4 Psychologists often organize concepts into three levels: superordinate, basic, and subordinate.

7.5 Problem solving is using cognition to find a way to achieve a goal (when the options are unknown), while decision making is using cognition to choose between available options.

7.6 An algorithm is a formula-like method of problem solving, while a heuristic is an educated guess, or rule-of-thumb, method of problem solving.

7.7 People stray from reason in a variety of ways when solving problems, including mental set, confirmation bias, and framing.

7.8 Four main types of heuristic are the representative heuristic, the availability heuristic, the affect heuristic, and the anchoring heuristic.

7.9 Dual-process theory is the idea that people possess two separate types of thinking, one automatic (Type 1 thinking) and one deliberate (Type 2 thinking).

7.10 People are not good at affective forecasting, which is predicting how we will feel about the outcomes of our decisions.

7.11 Psychologists define creativity as the capacity to come up with original ideas or approaches to a problem.

7.12 Divergent thinking is a problem-solving strategy in which you come up with lots of different possible solutions, while convergent thinking is a problem-solving strategy in which you use logic to deduce the single best solution.

7.13 Functional fixedness is thinking about something in the one way it is most typically used, rather than other possible uses.

7.14 A number of factors contribute to creativity, including culture.

Language

7.15 Psychologists define language as the ability to communicate with others using words or other symbols combined and arranged according to rules.

7.16 Some experts believe a "protolanguage" of isolated sounds evolved into rudimentary words that could then be combined in new ways.

7.17 The nativist theory of language development argues that the ability to use language is inborn, while nonnativist theories suggest that nurture has a strong influence on language development.

7.18 The stages of a child's language development include babbling, one-word stage, expanding language use, and use of figurative language.

7.19 Grammar is the set of rules within a language, and it has four levels: phonemes, morphemes, syntax, and semantics.

7.20 Extralinguistic information such as facial expressions, gestures, and how the language is spoken can influence communication.

7.21 Current experts continue to debate linguistic relativity, which is the theory that language influences thought.

Intelligence

7.22 Psychologists define intelligence as the ability to gain knowledge from experience.

7.23 General intelligence (g) is overall intelligence that applies across all tasks and situations, while specific intelligences (s) are intelligences that apply to only a particular area. The hierarchical model of intelligence suggests that people contain numerous specific intelligences, each of which is considered a part of a single general intelligence.

7.24 The theory of multiple intelligences, put forth primarily by Gardner, states that every person has many distinct intelligences, including some that contribute to traditional success in school and others that focus on nonacademic parts of life.

7.25 Emotional intelligence is the ability to sense and manage emotions in yourself and others.

7.26 Overall, genes have a substantial influence on intelligence, but there are many important environmental variables. Genes and environment interact in complex ways to influence intelligence.

7.27 An intelligence test is an assessment technique used by psychologists to numerically measure intelligence.

7.28 Psychologists mostly use the Wechsler Intelligence Tests to measure intelligence, while a respected alternative is the Stanford–Binet Intelligence Test.

7.29 For psychologists, measures of intelligence must be high in reliability and validity.

7.30 Intelligence tests measure what a person can accomplish, while achievement tests measure what a person has accomplished.

7.31 One extreme of intelligence is giftedness, significantly above-average intelligence, while the other extreme is intellectual disability, a mental disorder based on significantly below-average intelligence and impaired day-to-day functioning.

7.32 Test bias is the tendency of a test to produce scores in a consistently inaccurate way for members of particular groups. Unfortunately, the history of intelligence testing has featured controversies about test bias.

7.33 When people sense others are stereotyping them in a negative way, it can detract from their ability to perform well on tests.

7.34 In terms of general intelligence, there is no difference between men and women. However, there are a few particular areas of intelligence in which one sex slightly, but consistently, outperforms the other.

KEY TERMS

cognition, p. 210
concept, p. 210
prototype, p. 211
problem solving, p. 213
decision making, p. 213
algorithm, p. 213
mental set, p. 214
confirmation bias, p. 214
framing, p. 214
heuristic, p. 215
representativeness heuristic, p. 215
availability heuristic, p. 216
anchoring heuristic, p. 216
affect heuristic, p. 217
dual-process theory, p. 217
affective forecasting, p. 218
durability bias, p. 219
creativity, p. 220
divergent thinking, p. 220
convergent thinking, p. 220
functional fixedness, p. 220
language, p. 223
nativist theory, p. 225
language acquisition device, p. 225
social-pragmatic theory, p. 226
babbling, p. 227
one-word stage, p. 228
grammar, p. 230
phoneme, p. 230
morpheme, p. 230
syntax, p. 230
semantics, p. 231
extralinguistic information, p. 231
dialect, p. 232
linguistic relativity, p. 232
intelligence, p. 234
general intelligence (*g*), p. 234
specific intelligences (*s*), p. 234
emotional intelligence, p. 236
intelligence test, p. 239
intelligence quotient (IQ), p. 239
normal curve, p. 240
Wechsler Intelligence Tests, p. 240
Stanford–Binet Intelligence Test, p. 240
reliability, p. 240
validity, p. 241
achievement test, p. 241
giftedness, p. 241
specific learning disorder, p. 241
intellectual disability, p. 242
test bias, p. 242
culture-fair intelligence tests, p. 243
stereotype threat, p. 243
misinformation, p. 244

SELF-ASSESSMENT

1. Psychologists define the term _____ as a mental representation of a category of similar things, actions, or people.

2. _____ _____ is using cognition to find a way to achieve a goal.
   a. Decision making
   b. Concept creation
   c. Problem solving
   d. Affective forecasting

3. A(n) _____ is a formula-like method of problem solving.
   a. algorithm
   b. heuristic
   c. frame
   d. semantic

4. The _____ heuristic is an educated guess based on the information that most quickly and easily comes to mind.
   a. availability
   b. representative
   c. anchoring
   d. affect

5. Rachel was searching for a new apartment. She found one she liked, and expected that after she moved in, she would be happy for a long time. However, the happiness didn't last long. Within a week, the new apartment was just a place to live. Rachel's misjudgment of how she'd feel after an event in her life is an example of which of the following?
   a. affective forecasting
   b. durability bias
   c. functional fixedness
   d. confirmation bias

6. _____ is the capacity to come up with original ideas or approaches to a problem.

7. _____ is the set of rules within a language.
   a. Grammar
   b. Syntax
   c. Semantics
   d. Phonemes

8. A _____ is the smallest distinct unit of speech.

9. _____ is the tendency of a test to produce scores in a consistently inaccurate way for members of particular groups.
   a. Test bias
   b. Validity
   c. Divergent thinking
   d. Syntax

10. _____ _____ is the expectation that others may judge you according to stereotypes about a group to which you belong.

To check your understanding of these questions, click show the answers in the e-book or refer to the answers in Appendix B.

Research shows quizzing is a highly effective learning tool. Continue quizzing yourself using LearningCurve, the system that adapts to *your* learning.

WHAT'S YOUR TAKE?

1. Are we getting smarter? James Flynn and other researchers found that average IQ scores in the United States continue to get higher (Flynn, 1984, 1987). The average score on Wechsler tests in 1947 was 100, but without adjustments, the average would have increased to 107.5 in 1972, 111.7 in 1989, and 115.1 in 2001 (Flynn, 2011). We're smarter than the generations that came before us, at least as measured by standard IQ tests. Some interesting theories have emerged as to why this increase, known as the Flynn effect, has taken place, including better diet, better medical care, better technology, more education, more familiarity with IQ tests, and other lifestyle changes that have taken place over the decades (Rinderman et al., 2017; Urbina, 2011). Why do you think your generation performs better on IQ tests than your parents' or your grandparents' generation?

SHOW ME MORE

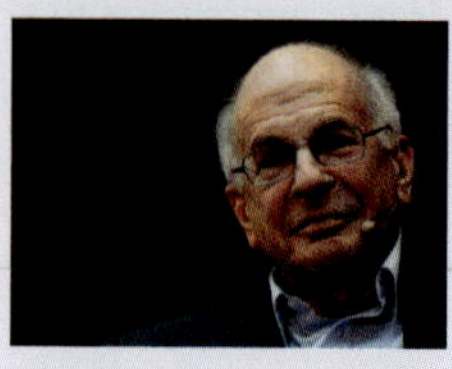

7.1 Daniel Kahneman Discusses Dual-Process Theory

http://tiny.cc/722ojy

In this video, Daniel Kahneman explains dual-process theory and how the difference between thinking fast and thinking slow can influence decision making.

Sean Gallup/Getty Images

This video is hosted by a third-party Web site (source). For accessible content requests, please reach out to the publisher of that site.

7.2 Why More Choices Don't Make You Happy

This video explains research on decision making—specifically, how the number of options you have can influence your happiness about the choice you make.

SciShow Psych/BoClips

7.3 Is Texting Killing Language?

http://tiny.cc/69d15y

This TED Talk features language expert John McWhorter discussing the relationship between texting and language.

B Christopher/Alamy

This video is hosted by a third-party Web site (source). For accessible content requests, please reach out to the publisher of that site.

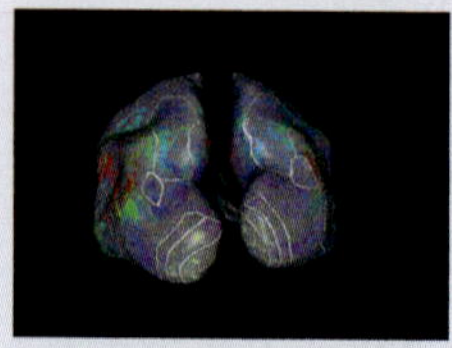

7.4 Neuroscience and Language

This video offers a glimpse into neuropsychological research that helps us understand where language is processed within the brain.

National Science Foundation

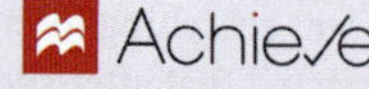

7.5 My Psychology Podcast

This podcast episode features the author of this textbook, psychologist Andy Pomerantz, speaking with other instructors of introductory psychology courses about the most important and interesting concepts in this chapter.

Macmillan Learning

8 Motivation and Emotion

Alessandro Biascioli/iStock/Getty Images

CHAPTER OUTLINE

Imagine that you are Derek Redmond.

You are a track champion and a record-holding sprinter in your own country. Now, you are going for the gold at the Olympics.

When the real Derek Redmond bolted out of the starting blocks for the 400-meter semifinals representing Britain in the 1992 Olympics, he felt great. But in the middle of the race, it happened: a torn hamstring. Redmond grabbed the back of his leg and limped along, but after a few steps he dropped to the ground. Olympic officials ran over to help as Redmond knelt on the track, his head hanging. But within seconds, he stood up and continued the race. He was essentially hopping on his left leg, since his right leg was so injured he couldn't place much weight on it. Redmond was determined to cross the finish line, even though his dreams of an Olympic medal were shattered. As he hobbled forward, another runner approached him from behind—not a competitor, but Derek's father, who had witnessed his son's injury from the stands. Jim Redmond caught up to his son, put his arm around him, and joined him as he continued around the track. As Derek wept, father and son finished the race (Redmond, 2012; Weinberg, 2004). (See Show Me More 8.1 at the end of the chapter for a video of this iconic Olympic moment.)

Derek Redmond's story is considered one of the most memorable and inspirational moments in Olympic history, largely because it is so rich with *motivation* and *emotion*, the two primary topics of this chapter. Consider the motivations that fueled the sprinter: to train for years to become a world-class athlete and fight through severe injury to finish the race. Consider the motivations of his father: to comfort his son and help him reach his goal in spite of devastating circumstances. Consider the emotions of the sprinter: excitement and nervousness before the race, then

PASCAL PAVANI/AFP/Getty Images

Derek Redmond displayed intense motivation and emotion when he experienced an injury as an Olympic athlete.

heartbreak and anguish at the worst possible moment. Consider the emotions of his father: alarmed at seeing his son motionless on the track, pride when his son rises up to continue the race, and compassion when his son cries in his arms.

You may not be an Olympic sprinter, but you have undoubtedly experienced your own extraordinary moments of motivation and emotion. In this chapter, we will cover classic and contemporary explanations for what motivates us to behave the way we do. We will also consider how different motivations interact with one another, and explore the universal motivation of hunger and eating. We will also discuss many aspects of emotions: how they arise, how we communicate them, how we regulate them, and how they interact with ethnicity, gender, and age.

Motivation

YOU WILL LEARN:

8.1 what motivation is.

8.2 the difference between intrinsic motivation and extrinsic motivation.

8.3 about classic theories of motivation.

8.4 about contemporary theories of motivation.

8.5 about Abraham Maslow's hierarchy of needs.

8.6 how motivation is experienced by people of diverse backgrounds.

Motivation is a desire that stimulates and steers behavior. Your motivation is what stirs you to take action. In some cases, the goal behind a motivation is something specific and short-term. For example, your energy level is dragging, so you are motivated to find something caffeinated. That motivation may translate into the behavior of getting in line at a nearby coffee shop or grabbing a soda out of the fridge. In other cases, the goal behind a motivation is more abstract and long-term. For example, you experience an ongoing sense of loneliness, so you are motivated to find a romantic partner. That motivation may translate into the behavior of downloading a dating app to find a match. Of course, motivation does more than simply prompt you to act: it prompts you to act *with purpose* toward a goal (Fiske, 2008; Ryan, 2012).

Sometimes, a behavior is its own motivation. You do it because you enjoy it. That's **intrinsic motivation**: the desire to perform a behavior because the behavior itself is rewarding. Other times, a behavior is a means to an end. You do it not because you enjoy the behavior itself, but because you enjoy what that behavior delivers. That's **extrinsic motivation**: the desire to perform a behavior to obtain an external reward (Kruglanski 2018; Ryan et al., 1990; Ryan & Deci, 2000a, b). That external reward is an **incentive**: an object or situation outside yourself that you are motivated to acquire.

Let's consider some examples, beginning with intrinsic motivation. Danielle, a tenth-grader, is intrinsically motivated to play on the JV basketball team because of her love for the game. Javier, a college senior majoring in education, is intrinsically motivated to do his student teaching at a local elementary school because of the thrill he gets from educating young kids. In both cases, the behavior begins because the behavior itself brings pleasure. As time goes by, there is a chance that intrinsic motivation will continue to fuel their behavior. However, there is also a chance that the same behavior could become extrinsically motivated. For example, maybe Danielle continues to play basketball because of the social status it gives her among her peers or for the chance to earn a college scholarship. Maybe Javier continues teaching because the job provides him with a salary and health insurance.

A real-world example of the difference between intrinsic motivation and extrinsic motivation comes from RZA (Robert Diggs), the leader of hip-hop supergroup Wu-Tang Clan since the 1990s and producer of hundreds of songs. In a 2020 interview in which he looked back on his long career, RZA explained that in the early days, before he signed a record contract, he made beats "with no economic goal," just to "entertain myself" and "have fun." But after he signed a deal and was making beats to

motivation
A desire that stimulates and steers behavior.

intrinsic motivation
A desire to perform a behavior because the behavior itself is rewarding.

extrinsic motivation
A desire to perform a behavior to obtain an external reward.

incentive
An object or situation outside the person that the person is motivated to acquire.

earn paychecks, "I'm not even making music unless you call me with that money … the money became the dictator of my creativity." That shift from the early days when he made music because he loved it to the mid-career days when he made music because it provided income illustrates the difference between intrinsic and extrinsic motivation (Rubin, 2020).

Johnny Nunez/Getty Images

RZA, long-time producer and leader of the Wu-Tang Clan, explained in an interview that his motivation to make beats shifted from intrinsic to extrinsic when he started getting paid for his work.

Does it really matter whether the motivation for a behavior is intrinsic or extrinsic?

Yes, it really does. Research shows that extrinsic motivation can undermine intrinsic motivation. That is, your behavior on an intrinsically motivated task may decrease if that behavior becomes extrinsically motivated. That decrease can take the form of less frequent behavior, lower quality performance, or diminished interest in the behavior (Deci et al., 1999). For example, one large-scale study examined thousands of employees from a variety of fields, including banking, insurance, medical technology, and retail. Across the board, higher levels of intrinsic motivation correlated with better work performance and stronger commitment to their organizations. Higher levels of intrinsic motivation also correlated with lower levels of burnout, work–family conflict, and intention to quit (Kuvaas et al., 2017).

The lesson from studies like this one is this: Don't lose sight of why you chose a behavior in the first place — what you enjoyed about your partner, your major, your job, your hobby, or your pet. That's intrinsic motivation, and that — more than any extrinsic motivation that may come along — has the best chance of maintaining that behavior long-term. In addition, behaving according to intrinsic motivation, as opposed to extrinsic motivation, is linked to higher self-esteem and well-being, less depression, and less anxiety over time (Kasser & Ryan, 1993, 1996; Niemiec et al., 2009; Twenge et al., 2010; Williams et al., 2000).

Of course, extrinsic motivation can play an important role too. It fuels behaviors that might be boring or unpleasant (like a kid earning an allowance for taking out the trash, washing dishes, and vacuuming). And recent research suggests that under certain circumstances, the incentives you earn through extrinsic motivation — whether payment, praise, or prizes — can complement rather than undermine your own intrinsic motivation (Cerasoli et al., 2014; Gerhart & Fang, 2015; Henderlong & Lepper, 2002). For example, one study compared two weight-loss strategies for obese people. The strategies were identical except that one method included small financial rewards if participants met their goals ($1–10 per week, plus a raffle for $50–100 at the end of the study). Researchers found that the participants who were extrinsically motivated by financial rewards actually lost more weight than the group whose motivation was only intrinsic. Further, these researchers found that participants who received financial rewards had higher levels of both extrinsic and intrinsic motivation (Leahey et al., 2017).

DIVERSITY MATTERS Some research suggests that there may be diversity-based differences in the extent to which people experience intrinsic and extrinsic motivation. For example, one study found that extrinsic motivation decreased with age, especially between the mid-30s and the mid-60s. The researchers speculated that this finding may reflect a declining interest in superficial signs of success like wealth, popularity, and social status as people move from young adulthood toward older adulthood. The same study also found that for adults in their 20s and 30s, extrinsic motivation was higher in men than women. The researchers speculated that social pressures on young men to achieve power, professional status, and high income may partially explain this gender difference (LeFebvre & Huta, 2021).

MY TAKE VIDEO 8.1

Intrinsic and Extrinsic Motivation

"Something that motivated me intrinsically is…"

Visit Achieve to watch the My Take video and then answer questions.

Achieve

Classic Theories of Motivation

Early psychologists who studied motivation offered a number of theories that have stood the test of time and remain relevant today. A more recent generation has also

JHVEPhoto/iStock/Getty Images

An instinct is a motivation that is biologically innate, such as a bird's motivation to build a nest. Humans are motivated by instincts too, but ours are typically more flexible than those of other species.

produced intriguing theories of motivation. Let's consider the old-school theories first, and then move on to the new-school theories in the next section.

Instinct Theory. An **instinct** is a motivation that is biologically innate. Some instincts, like eating and reproducing, are common across species. Others are more particular to a type of animal, like a newborn kangaroo climbing into its mother's pouch the moment it's born, or birds building nests for their eggs (Keeping, 2006). As these examples illustrate, instincts are not limited to simple, short behaviors. Sometimes, they take the form of elaborate routines or patterns that play out over hours or days.

Instincts are at the core of **instinct theory**: a theory of motivation stating that humans, like all other animals, are motivated primarily by instinct. Instinct theory was one of the first motivation theories, and it was held in high regard through the early and mid-1900s (Gillespie, 1971; Moltz, 1965; Tolman, 1923; Wells, 1923). Today, however, instinct theory is widely acknowledged as incomplete. That does not mean it's wrong. After all, humans are an animal species, and all animals have instincts. But we've come to understand that instinct can't explain everything about a person's behavior. For example, we have an instinct to make homes for ourselves, much like birds have an instinct to nest. However, the ways we behave to achieve that outcome are far more adaptable than the rigid behavior of many bird species, whose nest building seems to happen largely on autopilot. People aren't limited to gathering building materials and assembling them in a safe location, as birds do when they build nests. People can drive down streets looking for "for rent" signs on apartment buildings, search the Internet for listings of houses or condos, remodel or repaint rooms, and shop in stores and garage sales for sofas, tables, and chairs. Instinct is certainly in the mix, but there are other motivations influencing human behavior too.

Drive Reduction Theory. **Drive reduction theory** is a theory of motivation stating that unmet biological drives cause unpleasant sensations that motivate you to meet those needs. You have a short list of basic biological drives, including hunger, thirst, sex, and physical comfort. According to drive reduction theory, satisfying these drives is what motivates your behavior. The bad feelings your body experiences when those needs get neglected, like hunger, thirst, and pain, are increasingly loud alerts to satisfy these drives. After you satisfy them, you have regained **homeostasis**: steadiness or balance in your bodily state.

Like instinct theory, drive reduction theory was most prominent in the early and mid-1900s (Hull, 1943, 1952). Also like instinct theory, drive reduction theory has been criticized for being incomplete, and specifically for reducing human motivation to something too simplistic and too biologically based to account for all human behavior (Ryan, 2012). For example, drive reduction theory can't account for *curiosity*. Curiosity fuels all kinds of behavior, from stalking an old friend's social media pages to wandering around an unfamiliar park to trying new foods you come across at the grocery store. Curiosity isn't a drive and doesn't stem from a biological need. But curiosity (and the related concept of *interest*) does motivate people to gather information and learn about otherwise new situations and things (Loewenstein, 1994; Renninger & Hidi, 2011; Renninger & Su, 2012; Sakaki et al., 2018; Silvia, 2008, 2012).

Arousal Theory. **Arousal theory** is a theory of motivation stating that you are motivated to obtain and maintain an optimal level of arousal. You may have heard the term *arousal* used in a sexual context, but here it refers to a more general excitement or attentiveness. Actually, arousal is how some people explain the curiosity motivations we just discussed. Specifically, they say that curiosity allows you to stay at least mildly aroused in situations in which you might otherwise become completely bored.

The ideal level of arousal differs across people and across situations, but it's clear that the ideal falls somewhere in the middle rather than at either extreme. That is, your best performance happens when you are mildly or moderately aroused, not when you are minimally or maximally aroused (Berlyne, 1960; Fiske & Maddi, 1961; Hunt, 1965). This finding is described by the **Yerkes–Dodson law**: the finding that

instinct
A motivation that is biologically innate.

instinct theory
A theory of motivation stating that humans, like all other animals, are motivated primarily by instinct.

drive reduction theory
A theory of motivation stating that unmet biological drives cause unpleasant sensations that motivate the person to meet those needs.

homeostasis
Steadiness or balance in the person's bodily state.

arousal theory
A theory of motivation stating that the person is motivated to obtain and maintain an optimal level of arousal.

Yerkes–Dodson law
The finding that moderate levels of arousal are linked to higher levels of performance than high or low levels of arousal.

moderate levels of arousal are linked to higher levels of performance than high or low levels of arousal. Yerkes and Dodson actually performed their research in 1908, long before arousal theory appeared, but they did find that a moderate level of electric shock was more beneficial than high or low levels of shock when teaching rats to behave in particular ways, so arousal theorists adopted it (Teigen, 1994; Winton, 1987; Yerkes & Dodson, 1908).

As an example of the Yerkes–Dodson law, consider Josh, a teenager taking his driver's license test. He has already passed the written exam, and now he is behind the wheel about to start the driving portion with the examiner. Josh doesn't want to be overly aroused – so nervous that he loses his focus or freezes up. He also doesn't want to be under-aroused – so uninterested that he hardly tries. He wants to be optimally aroused – enough to keep him alert and help him make a genuine effort, but not so much that he panics. Many of the things you do on a regular basis – studying, taking exams, meeting new people, playing video games, competing in sports, completing your work at your job – similarly benefit from just the right level of arousal.

Contemporary Theories of Motivation

Now, let's consider some of the more contemporary theories of motivation that have had the greatest impact.

Self-Determination Theory. **Self-determination theory** is a theory of motivation stating that the strongest and healthiest motivations are those that come from within yourself. According to self-determination theory, it is best to be *autonomous* – to do what you do because you find it naturally rewarding, rather than behaving in ways that bring external rewards. If that sounds a lot like an endorsement of intrinsic motivation, it should: self-determined and autonomous motivations are almost equivalent to intrinsic motivation. There is one important difference, though: sometimes, extrinsic motivations can become autonomous too. The key is how *controlling* those extrinsic motivations feel to you. If they feel very controlling, they will never become integrated into yourself, never become part of what fundamentally fuels you. But if they don't feel controlling, they can become integrated into yourself, and you can find yourself motivated autonomously by them (Deci & Ryan, 2012; Ryan & Deci, 2003, 2017; Ryan et al., 1990).

As an example, consider Antonio, an eleventh-grader who becomes a member of his school's chapter of the National Honor Society (NHS). To maintain his NHS membership, he needs to participate in community service. Specifically, he needs to spend every Wednesday afternoon tutoring second-graders who struggle with basic math skills. At first, he sees the tutoring as a meaningless chore. He drags himself to the first tutoring session at the elementary school, and rolls his eyes when he finds out that he has been assigned to a small group of students who need help with simple addition and subtraction. Soon enough, however, Antonio starts to enjoy the tutoring. The progress the kids make, and the interpersonal connections Antonio makes with them, generate an unexpected sense of satisfaction. Now when he tutors every Wednesday, it's not because he *has* to, but because he *wants* to. An extrinsic motivation that initially made Antonio feel like he was being controlled has now become integrated into Antonio's own autonomous, self-determined motivation.

Research on self-determination theory shows that *autonomous motivation*, compared to *controlled motivation*, produces superior behavior in terms of both quality and quantity. For example, compared to students who study just to get good grades, students who are autonomously motivated actually learn the material in a deeper and longer-lasting way (Benware & Deci, 1984; Ryan et al., 1990; Wang, 2008). Similar results have been found for healthy eating, increasing exercise, and quitting cigarettes too. People who make these changes because they want to for themselves, rather than making them to impress friends or follow doctor's orders, make more significant

self-determination theory
A theory of motivation stating that the strongest and healthiest motivations are those that come from within the person.

improvements that last longer (Dwyer et al., 2017; Williams et al., 1996, 1998, 2006a, b). In fact, in the broadest sense, people who allow autonomous motivation to guide their lives have higher levels of psychological wellness than people who feel controlled by outside forces (Ryan et al., 2017; Sheldon et al., 2004).

Autonomous motivation has become so well-established as an influence on behavior that some researchers now have tried it as a technique for intentional behavior change. For example, in one study, dental hygienists attempted to persuade young adult patients to have higher levels of autonomous motivation regarding their own dental health. The goal was for participants to see checkups as something they value and want to do for themselves, rather than something they must do to follow "doctors' orders" and avoid getting in trouble. Results showed that those patients were significantly more likely to attend dental visits in the future compared to similar patients who did not receive this intervention (Halvari et al., 2017).

Regulatory Focus Theory. **Regulatory focus theory** is a theory of motivation stating that there are two primary motivation systems — promotion and prevention — that affect different people in different ways. *Promotion motivation* is all about getting more good stuff: advancing, accomplishing, acquiring, and maximizing. By contrast, *prevention motivation* is all about holding on to what you have: staying vigilant, avoiding risk, and preventing loss (Crowe & Higgins, 1997; Higgins, 1997, 2000, 2002, 2011; Scholer & Higgins, 2012). According to regulatory focus theory, the key is living a life that matches your balance of promotion and prevention motivations, or achieving *regulatory fit* (Higgins, 2008).

carballo/Shutterstock

Promotion motivation focuses on getting something good. Prevention motivation focuses on not losing what you already have. We all have some of both, but not necessarily in equal amounts. The dominating type of motivation can influence the way you experience many things, such as a camping trip: it can be an opportunity for new adventures or a challenge to avoid pain.

To better understand the difference between promotion motivation and prevention motivation, imagine two friends, Owen and Evan, planning a camping trip. Owen is motivated more by promotion, and Evan is motivated more by prevention. As they drive out to the campsite, Owen is eager: "I can't wait to get out there! Maybe we'll see some wild animals up close! And food always tastes better when cooked over an open fire." By contrast, Evan is cautious: "I just hope neither one of us gets hurt — camping can be dangerous. Let's make sure we extinguish the campfire completely. The last thing we want is a forest fire. And if we do see any animals, I hope it's from a safe distance." For Owen, camping (and everything else) is an exciting opportunity, an experience full of delight and exhilaration if they have any luck. For Evan, camping (and everything else) is a risky responsibility, an experience full of disappointment and pain if they're not careful.

Most of us have a nice balance between promotion and prevention motivations, but some of us lean one way or the other pretty strongly. As you might expect, Evan and other prevention-oriented people are vulnerable to worry and anxiety disorders (Klenk et al., 2011; Scott & O'Hara, 1993; Strauman, 1989). On the other hand, Owen and other promotion-oriented people are vulnerable to depression when their hopes fall flat or their efforts fail (Cornette et al., 2009; Strauman, 2002). These two types of people also respond differently to common situations. In one study, researchers interviewed 52 employees of businesses that were switching to entirely new computer systems. Promotion-oriented employees were much more accepting of the big switch than their more prevention-oriented coworkers (Stam & Stanton, 2010).

In another study, researchers presented two kinds of antismoking ads: one ad emphasized obtaining positive outcomes, like better breath, whiter teeth, and improved physical endurance; a second ad emphasized avoiding negative results, like lung cancer, bad breath, and yellow teeth. (Notice that some of those outcomes are the same things phrased in alternative ways.) Each type of ad had its most powerful effect when there was good fit between the ad's approach and the participant's promotion orientation or prevention orientation (Kim, 2006). Similar studies have found that a good fit between the person and the message they receive — either promoting positive outcomes or preventing negative ones — can increase the likelihood of all kinds of behaviors, such as taking prescribed medication, believing a Yelp review, or purchasing what they put in their online cart at stores like Amazon (Ashraf & Thongpapanl, 2015; O'Connor et al., 2018; Pentina et al., 2018).

regulatory focus theory
A theory of motivation stating that there are two primary motivation systems — promotion and prevention — that affect different people in different ways.

Achievement Goal Theory. **Achievement goal theory** is a theory of motivation stating that when you are motivated to achieve a goal, certain goals (*mastery goals*) produce better outcomes than other goals (*performance goals*). Achievement goal theory is actually the most recent version of an achievement-based motivation theory that has been around since the mid-1900s (Atkinson, 1964; McClelland, 1961). In those early days, the basic idea was simply that the achievement of goals was a primary human motivation. Today, that idea is accepted as a given, and the focus of the theory has shifted to two different kinds of goals (mastery vs. performance) and the different results they yield (Ames, 1992; Dweck & Leggett, 1988). Mastery goals involve doing something well, or *mastering* it. By contrast, performance goals involve *demonstrating* that you can do something well, or *performing* for others (Ames & Archer, 1987, 1988; Murayama et al., 2012).

That distinction between mastery and performance has proven to be important in terms of its influence on behavior. There is a big difference in what you'll do when you're motivated to *actually* achieve something versus *showing* that you have achieved it (Senko et al., 2008). For example, consider Pamela and Malika, two seventh-graders in the same introductory Spanish class. Pamela is motivated to do what she needs to do to get a good grade in the class — attend class, memorize vocabulary words, cram before the exams, and so on. Those are performance goals. Malika, on the other hand, is motivated to actually learn Spanish — speak it meaningfully with others and appreciate the language and the culture surrounding it (whether or not an exam is coming up). Those are mastery goals.

Studies show that students motivated by mastery goals like Malika are much more likely to sustain motivation for a longer time, remain persistently interested in the material, and understand the material more deeply than students like Pamela (Elliott & Dweck, 1988; Elliot et al., 1999; Fong et al., 2018; Harackiewicz et al., 2002b; Heyman & Dweck, 1992; Kaplan & Midgley, 1997; Maehr & Midgley, 1991; Matos et al., 2017; Pintrich & De Groot, 1990; Wolters, 2004). However, students motivated by performance goals like Pamela are more likely to learn the material only superficially through rote memorization, and to cheat to get good grades (Anderman et al., 1998; Harackiewicz et al., 2000; Meece & Holt, 1993). Even so, performance goals like Pamela's often produce exam scores that are as good as, or even better than, mastery goals like Malika's (Harackiewicz et al., 2002a; Koestner et al., 1987; Miller & Hom, 1990; Senko et al., 2008). This sets up a dilemma for educators. They want students to be motivated by mastery goals, but exams and other evaluations of students often encourage more of a performance goal motivation.

The consequences of mastery versus performance goals extend beyond just achievement in the classroom. They influence self-esteem too. People motivated by mastery goals tend to view their abilities (for example, intelligence) and personality characteristics (for example, shyness) as changeable. They believe they can actually improve themselves. As a result, over time, their self-esteem tends to rise (Dweck & Grant, 2008). People motivated by performance goals tend to view their abilities as unchangeable. They believe they can't learn more to improve themselves, and that their only hope is to better demonstrate their ability on tests. As a result, over time, self-esteem tends to drop for people motivated by performance goals (Robins & Pals, 2002).

In some studies, researchers have actually trained students to have more of a mastery mindset — also known as a growth mindset — than a performance mindset. The researchers teach participants to see their own abilities as changeable (or *incremental*) as opposed to seeing their abilities as fixed (or an *entity*). They often use the terms *growth mindset* and *fixed mindset* to capture the difference between these terms. The results of these studies are remarkably positive (Cury et al., 2008; DaFonseca et al., 2008; DeBacker et al., 2018; Howell et al., 2016; Miu & Yeager, 2015; Yeager et al., 2019). For example, in one study, researchers taught a group of middle school students about the incremental improvements their own brains can make — including how their brains form new connections every time they learn, how challenging themselves with new material could improve their brain power, and so on. Compared to another group of students who received no such training, this mastery mindset–trained group showed improved scores on math tests, and their teachers noticed that they had become more motivated to actually learn the material (Blackwell et al., 2007).

achievement goal theory
A theory of motivation stating that when the person is motivated to achieve a goal, certain goals (mastery goals) produce better outcomes than other goals (performance goals).

hierarchy of needs
An explanation of motivation created by Abraham Maslow based on the idea that certain needs must be satisfied before others.

One Motivation after Another: Maslow's Hierarchy

With so many possible motivations fueling our behaviors, it wouldn't be surprising if someone offered a meta-theory of motivation, one that focuses on not just a single motivation but on many motivations working in a particular order. In fact, there is such a meta-theory, and it has remained influential since its introduction in the mid-1900s. The **hierarchy of needs** is an explanation of motivation created by Abraham Maslow based on the idea that certain needs must be satisfied before others (**Figure 8.1**). Maslow argued that some basic needs demand more of your focus and attention than others at first. Only when those needs are met will you move on to others (Fiske, 2008; Maslow, 1943, 1954, 1967, 1968). You don't need to deliberately think about this sequence, according to Maslow. Instead, you experience it automatically. In a way, this sequence resembles a sequence of college courses in which one is a prerequisite for the next. You have to pass the 100-level class before you can register for the 200-level class. Then you have to pass the 200-level class before you can register for the 300-level class, and so on. Maslow's theory originally included five needs, but he later added a sixth. Let's consider them in order, starting with the most basic.

Physiological Needs. *Physiological needs* include food, water, sleep, and sex. They focus on keeping your body alive and healthy. So, it makes sense that these are the most primary needs, the ones that must be met before any others. Without a well-functioning body, nothing else matters. People who are unfortunate enough to live on the brink of starvation are driven entirely by physiological needs — for example, figuring out where their next meal is coming from. If you've ever been temporarily desperate for food or water, you know the feeling too. As the need becomes more pressing, it is difficult to even think about anything else but getting that physiological need met right now.

Safety Needs. *Safety needs* include security and stability in your daily life. People who are unfortunate enough to live in war zones or in neighborhoods with a constant threat of gun violence feel the press of safety needs — securing a life in which they can feel protected and free of danger. If you've ever found yourself in a threatening

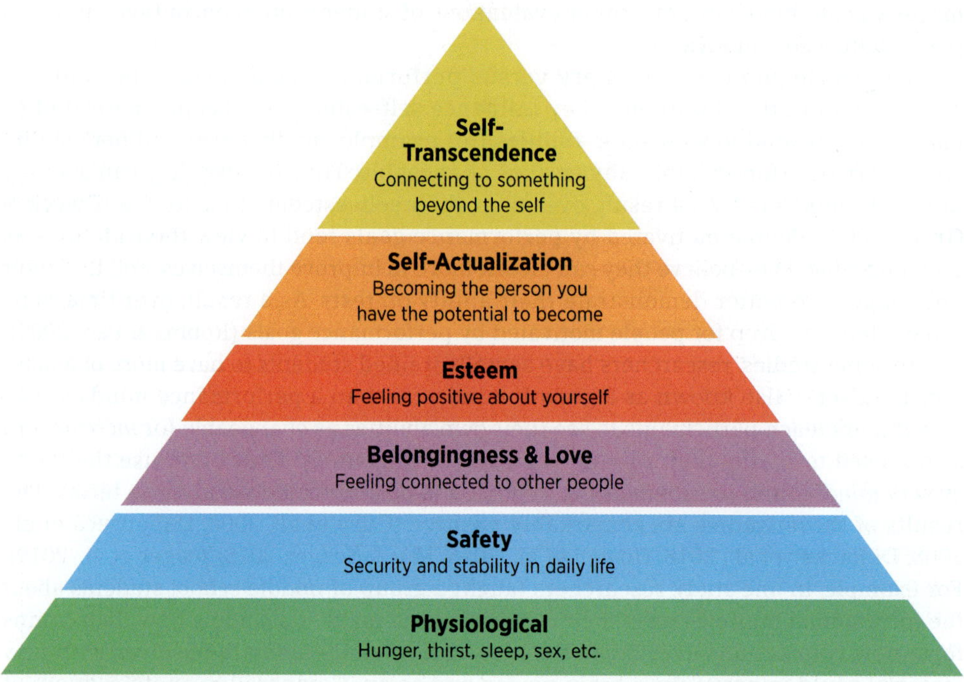

FIGURE 8.1 Maslow's Hierarchy of Needs. According to Abraham Maslow's hierarchy of needs, you must satisfy your basic needs (toward the bottom of the hierarchy) before moving on to others.

situation, like an assault or a car skidding out of control, you know the feeling too. You might also know the feeling if you've suddenly heard fire alarms or tornado sirens. You drop everything else and refocus entirely on getting yourself to a safe place.

MOHAMAD ABAZEED/AFP/Getty Images

Safety needs include security and stability in daily life. Unfortunately, meeting safety needs remains a struggle for many people.

Belongingness and Love Needs. *Belongingness and love needs* involve connections with other people, making connections and keeping them. These needs push people toward togetherness, as opposed to living in isolation and solitude. The need to connect with other people is remarkably strong and universal. In every culture around the world, people tend to congregate and share their lives with small groups of friends and family. Throughout the course of evolution, belonging to a cooperative group made any individual more fit to survive (Barash, 1982).

Once those social bonds form, we work hard to keep them and feel pain and sadness if they break. And if broken social bonds ever reconnect, the reunion is usually considered cause for celebration (Baumeister & Leary, 1995; Leary et al., 2001; Richman & Leary, 2009). If you've ever experienced periods of genuine loneliness, had a falling-out with a close friend, or broken up with a romantic partner, you know how strong the drive to belong can be. Prolonged periods in which the need for belonging and love go unmet often produce stress, depression, and physical illness (Leary & Cox, 2008; van Winkel et al., 2017). That is something that many prisoners, who often fear solitary confinement even more than living among a community of criminals, understand.

Esteem Needs. *Esteem needs* involve feeling positive about yourself — having a good sense of self-worth and the confidence that you can live your life competently and effectively. This is the need that drives you to do things that make you feel proud. For young children, that might mean behaving well enough to get approval or praise from parents. For teens, that might mean getting good grades or excelling on a sports team, a school club, or a part-time job. For adults, that might mean making a living or a meaningful contribution to society. Any activity that enhances your sense of self satisfies your esteem needs: this enhancement can come from others in the form of popularity and acceptance, or it can come from within yourself in the form of self-respect and honor.

Self-Actualization Needs. *Self-actualization needs* involve living a life that matches who you truly are. These needs are based, of course, on **self-actualization**: fully becoming the person you have the potential to become. As the term suggests, self-actualization means making actual, or real, your unique capabilities. You don't meet your self-actualization needs by becoming what other people want you to become. You meet your self-actualization needs by becoming what *you*, deep down, want to become. If you've ever had a job or been in a relationship in which you spent too much time meeting other people's demands, you know how it feels to have your self-actualization needs go unmet. But if you've ever had a job, a relationship, or any experience in which you felt yourself truly being yourself, you know how it feels to have your self-actualization needs met.

Sometimes, you're lucky enough to have a **peak experience**: a moment of self-actualization that produces strong, often mystical, feelings of personal fulfillment. In these blissful moments, you typically lose track of time and space, as well as any problems or concerns that were troubling you (Maslow, 1970). Peak experiences often take place during periods of **flow**: performing a behavior with complete immersion and enjoyment, or feeling like you're "in the zone." Flow involves total absorption in an activity, usually one in which you are quite skilled and also optimally challenged, as opposed to overwhelmed or bored (Csikszentmihalyi, 1975; Jackson, 2012; Seligman & Csikszentmihalyi, 2000; Yaden et al., 2017). Any activity can produce flow or a peak experience as long as it is intrinsically motivated, but some activities that do so frequently include playing sports, creating art (music, visual art, writing, etc.), interacting with others, learning something new, and even certain uses of the Internet (Chen, 2006; Chen et al., 1999, 2000; Csikszentmihalyi, 1990; Jackson, 1995; Jackson & Csikszentmihalyi, 1999; Mouton & Montijo, 2017). Not surprisingly, people who are

self-actualization
Fully becoming the person one has the potential to become.

peak experience
A moment of self-actualization that produces strong, often mystical, feelings of personal fulfillment.

flow
Performing a behavior with complete immersion and enjoyment, or feeling like one is "in the zone."

CHAPTER APP 8.1

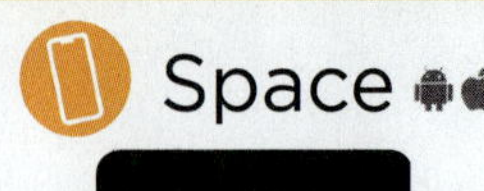

The Space app is designed to help improve your "phone/life balance" by tracking and managing your smartphone usage. The app's home screen shows two of its main features: the number of times you have unlocked your phone that day, and how much time you have spent on your phone that day. The app can also provide summaries of those two statistics over weeks or months.

How does it APPly to your daily life? How many times per day do you unlock your phone, and how much time per day do you spend on it? How does that number compare to the number of times you'd like to unlock your phone, and how much time you'd like to spend on it? If there's a mismatch between how much you use your phone and how much you'd like to use it, what can you do to change your behavior?

How does it APPly to your understanding of psychology? Which theory of motivation discussed in this chapter (the classic theories of motivation, the contemporary theories of motivation, or the motivations included in Maslow's hierarchy of needs) best explains your phone usage behavior?

To learn more about this app or to download it to your phone, you can search for "Space app" on Google, in the iPhone App store, or in the Google Play store.

extraverted tend to experience flow more often when interacting with other people in activities like group projects at work and team sports. And people who are introverted tend to experience flow more often when they are alone, in activities like reading, art, working solo, or solitary sports (Liu & Csiskzentmihalyi, 2020; Magyaródi & Oláh, 2015).

Self-Transcendence Needs. *Self-transcendence needs* were added to Maslow's hierarchy of needs long after it was originally proposed (Maslow, 1969, 1971). They involve needs beyond the self, often involving religious or mystical transformation or a connection to something larger than the self. Positioned at the highest end of the hierarchy, self-transcendence needs arise only when all of the other needs are met. They focus on a feeling of unity with all other people, but not in the same way as the need for belonging. Instead of a connection between you and one other person, or even a group of people, self-transcendence involves connection with the universe and all beings (not just people) in it (Koltko-Rivera, 1998). People can meet self-transcendence needs in a variety of ways. For example, they might dedicate their lives to spiritual activity in which they feel a connection to a higher power, to a social or political cause in which they deeply believe, or to selflessly serving others in need (Koltko-Rivera, 2006). Sometimes, people experience self-transcendence through especially meaningful experiences with movies, books, or other media (Dale et al., 2017; Oliver et al., 2018).

Motivation and Diversity

Many theories of motivation are limited because they assume that the same motivations drive everyone. That is simply not true. Different groups of people, as defined by ethnicity, gender, age, and other factors, are motivated by different forces. Thankfully, that fact is increasingly recognized and researched by psychologists.

DIVERSITY MATTERS

Motivation and Ethnicity. A cornerstone of Maslow's hierarchy of needs is the need for esteem. In the United States and other individualistic societies, the quest for self-esteem is hardly questioned. We often assume everyone wants it and suffers if they don't have it. However, there is growing evidence that the need for self-esteem does not apply equally around the world. Specifically, in East Asian countries and other collectivist cultures, the need for an accurate view of the self, even if it is unflattering or critical, often outweighs the need for a positive view of the self (Crocker & Park, 2004; Heine et al., 1999; Smith et al., 2016).

In studies in which Western and Eastern participants are asked to predict the future events of their lives, Western participants are much more likely to look ahead with unrealistic optimism (for example, to expect an exceptionally high salary), while Eastern participants are much more likely to predict an ordinary future filled with events that are more likely and common (Heine & Lehman, 1995; Ohashi & Yamaguchi, 2004). When researchers ask participants about their views of their *relationships* (with close friends, family members, and romantic partners) rather than their views of themselves, Eastern participants' views are as positive as Western participants' views (Endo et al., 2000). This finding is consistent with the collectivistic value of connectedness with others rather than the individualistic value of independence and self-promotion.

These differences in the need for individual self-esteem also show up in the way people from different cultures respond to challenges. Generally, people from individualistic cultures tend to work harder on tasks they know they can do well, but people from collectivistic cultures tend to work harder on tasks they know they *can't* do well (Morling & Kitayama, 2008). In one study, participants worked on a series of word games (for example, coming up with one word that connects to three others, such as *sleep*, *fantasy*, and *day* all connecting to *dream*). The key question was what participants did when they got feedback that they failed. Participants from the United States and Canada didn't persist much. Instead, they gave up rather quickly. By contrast, participants from Japan persisted much longer, and they also assigned more importance to the task than the U.S. and Canadian participants did. The researchers interpreted these results as consistent with a self-enhancing strategy by the Western participants (consistent with the need to maintain self-esteem), but a self-improving strategy by the Eastern participants, which is easier to do when the need for self-esteem is not so strong (Heine et al., 2001).

DIVERSITY MATTERS

Motivation and Gender. The idea that some groups are more motivated by goals focusing on relationships than by goals focusing on the self may apply to gender as well. Specifically, women appear to be more motivated by goals that emphasize working together and helping others, than men. However, men appear to be more motivated by goals that emphasize personal power over other people and things, than women (Diekman & Eagly, 2008). These differences probably stem from gender-based roles that society has historically promoted, in which women are encouraged to become caretakers and men are encouraged to become authority figures (Eagly, 1987; Eagly et al., 2000; Eagly & Crowley, 1986). In recent decades, as women have increasingly taken on jobs formerly dominated by men (especially leadership positions), women's personal power goals have increased somewhat, but the change in the opposite direction for men working together and helping others has not been as strong (Eagly & Diekman, 2003).

This discrepancy between these goals (helping vs. power) may play a significant role in the decisions of girls and women regarding STEM (science, technology, engineering, and mathematics) careers. In one study, researchers asked hundreds of college students how well they believed they would meet both types of goals if they chose a STEM career. The helping goals included things like helping others, serving humanity, serving community, caring for others, and connection with others. The personal power goals included things like recognition, achievement, status, focus on the self, and financial rewards. The difference was drastic: participants believed that with a STEM career, they would be significantly more likely to fulfill personal power goals than helping goals. The researchers concluded that even though interest in STEM careers has risen among women, the perception that such careers may impede helping goals may prevent some women from sticking with that interest long-term (Diekman et al., 2010).

Besides STEM, politics is another career field in which gender differences in motivation can influence interest. In one study of college students, researchers described political careers in two different ways: the first emphasized power and independence, while the second emphasized helping the community. When they were described the first way, men rated the careers as more attractive than women. But when they were described the second way, women's opinions increased so much that the gender gap closed (Schneider et al., 2016).

DIVERSITY MATTERS

Motivation and Age. Adults at different stages of their lives are likely to experience different motivations (Heckhausen & Heckhausen, 2018). Younger adults tend to be more motivated to gain, while older adults tend to be more motivated to avoid loss (Ebner et al., 2006; Freund et al., 2012; Freund & Ebner, 2005; Heckhausen, 2006). Consider Adriana, a 20-year-old woman, and her 70-year-old grandmother, Mary. Adriana is looking to build a life, so her primary motivations are to get new things, like job skills, a romantic relationship, financial independence, and material possessions. If Mary already has at least some of those things, her primary motivations are to hold on to them (along with her health), especially as she notices her same-age peers losing some of theirs.

Even when younger and older adults engage in the same behavior, they might be driven by different motivations. Younger adults tend to value the outcome more, while older adults tend to value the process more. In one study, among adults who were starting a new exercise program, younger adults reported that they were exercising because of the results that the exercise provided (like sexual attractiveness, muscle tone, and weight loss), but older adults reported that they were exercising because of the process of exercise itself (like the fun of the workouts and the interaction with other people at the gym) (Freund et al., 2010). Further, with social interactions, younger adults tend to be more motivated to establish new relationships, while older adults tend to be more motivated to minimize or eliminate current relationships that cause tension (Nikitin et al., 2014; Nikitin & Freund, 2018).

CHECK YOUR LEARNING:

8.1 What is motivation?

8.2 What is the difference between intrinsic motivation and extrinsic motivation?

8.3 What are the basic ideas of the classic theories of motivation: instinct theory, drive reduction theory, and arousal theory?

8.4 What are the basic ideas of the contemporary theories of motivation: self-determination theory, regulatory focus theory, and achievement goal theory?

8.5 What is the sequence of levels in Abraham Maslow's hierarchy of needs?

8.6 What are some forms of diversity that can influence motivation?

To check your understanding of these questions, click show the answers or refer to the answers in the Chapter Summary.

A Primary Motivation: Hunger and Eating

YOU WILL LEARN:

8.7 what body mass index (BMI) is, and how it is used to define being overweight or obese.

8.8 consequences of being overweight or obese.

8.9 biological factors that can contribute to being overweight or obese.

8.10 environmental and sociocultural factors that can contribute to being overweight or obese.

8.11 tips for eating healthy.

There are many competing theories of motivation, and many diversity-related factors that might influence how any of those theories apply to any particular person. But there is one fundamental motivation that we all share: to eat. Let's explore the many reasons why we eat, with special emphasis on why we might sometimes eat too much.

Obesity and Overweight

Words like *obese* and *overweight* are thrown around a lot, so let's begin by defining them clearly. Both definitions will be based on **body mass index (BMI)**: a number calculated from a person's height and weight that indicates body fat and overall fitness level. Your BMI is calculated by dividing your body weight (in kilograms) by the square of your height (in meters) (Centers for Disease Control and Prevention, 2015). Of course, your BMI depends on your ratio of food intake (especially fats and added sugars) to physical activity – in other words, the number of calories you consume versus the number of calories you burn (Must et al., 2006). If you're interested to learn your own BMI, there are plenty of simple BMI tables and calculators available online, including this one from the National Institutes of Health: http://www.nhlbi.nih.gov/health/educational/lose_wt/BMI/bmi_tbl.htm.

BMIs are placed into four categories (Must & Evans, 2011). *Normal/healthy weight* is defined as a BMI between 18.5 and 24.9. A BMI below 18.5 is considered *underweight*. **Overweight** is a BMI between 25 and 29.9. **Obesity** is a BMI of 30 or higher. As an example, consider Dylan, who stands 5′8″. If he weighs 145 pounds, his BMI is 22, which puts him in the normal/healthy category. If he weighs 180 pounds, his BMI is 27.4, which puts him in the overweight category.

It is important to note that some experts consider BMI an imperfect, or even significantly flawed, measurement tool. Specifically, they argue that BMI does not reliably predict health (Banack et al., 2018; Maffetone et al., 2017a). One study measured blood pressure, cholesterol, and several other indicators of overall health in over 40,000 people and found that 47% in the BMI overweight category and 26% in the BMI obese category were in good health. Additionally, 31% of people in the BMI

body mass index (BMI)
A number calculated from a person's height and weight that indicates body fat and overall fitness level.

overweight
A BMI between 25 and 29.9.

obesity
A BMI of 30 or higher.

normal category were in poor health. One reason may be that when BMI considers weight, it does not distinguish between muscle and fat, so it categorizes two people of the same height and weight the same way even if one has much more muscle and less fat than the other. These researchers recommend that BMI should not, by itself, be considered an indicator of overall health, but instead should be considered in combination with other measurement tools like blood tests, amount of regular physical activity, or body fat percentage (Tomiyama et al., 2016).

Related to the idea that BMI does not perfectly summarize a person's health status is the *Health at Every Size* movement. The roots of this movement reach back decades, but it has risen in popularity in recent years to fight fat shaming and promote positive self-images, especially for women. Well-known supporters, such as body activist and supermodel Ashley Graham, help to bring attention to the movement. The viewpoint at the core of the Health at Every Size movement is that weight does not define health. Instead, health is defined by healthy behaviors like nutritious eating habits and regular exercise, even if they don't result in thinness.

Within the movement, the pressure to achieve a certain size (or BMI), along with the dieting that often accompanies it, is considered detrimental to both physical and mental health. The Health at Every Size movement is controversial, with both enthusiastic supporters and outspoken critics (Bacon, 2010; Bacon & Aphramor, 2014; Bombak et al., 2018; Cara, 2016; Katz, 2012; Mundasad, 2017). Research on the effects of the Health at Every Size movement has produced mostly positive results on a wide range of outcomes, including anti-fat attitudes, body esteem, intuitive eating habits, body image, and self-esteem (Bacon & Aphramor, 2011; Bégin et al., 2018; Humphrey et al., 2015; Penney et al., 2015; Ulian et al., 2018a, b).

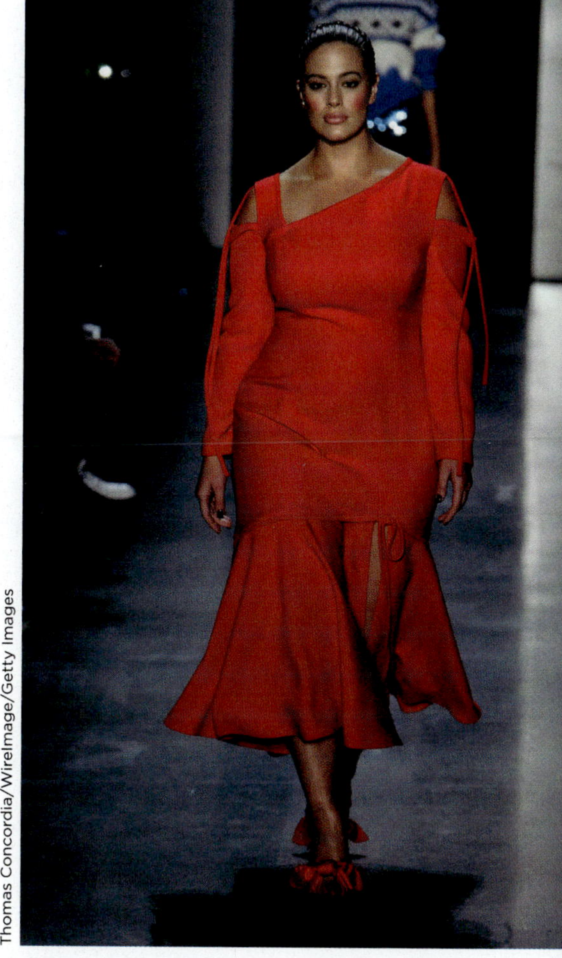

Thomas Concordia/WireImage/Getty Images

Body activist and supermodel Ashley Graham supports the Health at Every Size movement, which is based on the idea that health is not defined by weight or BMI.

Consequences of Overweight and Obesity. As we consider the consequences that often happen to people who are overweight or obese, remember that the causal relationship is not always a one-way street. That is, the research discussed in this section presents a convincing case that these are indeed *consequences* of overweight and obesity, but some of these consequences could be causes too.

Perhaps the most firmly established and widely known consequence of being overweight or obese is physical disease. People who carry excess weight — especially in the form of fat — are at heightened risk for a long list of medical problems, including diabetes, cardiovascular disease, cancer, hypertension, arthritis, stroke, gallbladder disease, and high cholesterol (Adams et al., 2006; Anderson et al., 2007; Bray, 2004; Calle et al., 2003; Lavie et al., 2009; Maffetone et al., 2017b; Maffetone & Khopkar, 2018; Must et al., 1999). Diabetes has an especially close link to being overweight and obese, and given the rise in overweight and obesity rates in recent decades, the rate of diabetes is correspondingly expected to double between 2000 and 2030 (Hartz et al., 1983; Schwartz & Porte, 2005; Wild et al., 2004).

In addition to the physical costs of these diseases, there are also financial costs: People who are overweight or obese have far more doctor's office visits, overnight stays in hospitals, and prescription medications than people of healthy weight, which add up to significantly higher medical expenses (Finkelstein & Yang, 2011; Quesenberry et al., 1998; Sturm, 2002; Thompson et al., 2001; Tremmel et al., 2017). In total, obesity-related illnesses account for more than 20% of medical spending in the United States, with an annual cost near $190 billion (Hruby & Hu, 2015).

Besides physical health problems, people who are overweight or obese suffer with mental health problems at high rates too (Naslund et al., 2017; Simon et al., 2006). Several longitudinal studies show that obesity is often followed by depression, especially in women (Bjerkeset et al., 2008; Quek et al., 2017; Roberts et al., 2003). In one review of longitudinal studies of obesity and depression, researchers found far more evidence for an obesity-then-depression sequence than a depression-then-obesity sequence (Faith et al., 2011). Even when excess weight does not result in diagnosable depression, it often lowers self-esteem, which reduces happiness (Murray et al., 2017; Wardle & Cook, 2005). Anxiety is also relatively common in overweight and obese adults, especially among women and the very obese (Baker et al., 2017; Scott et al., 2008).

Obesity has even been linked to dementia later in life. One longitudinal study explored the medical records of over 10,000 people over a 30-year span — in particular, their weight when they were in their 40s, and whether they had been diagnosed with dementia by their 70s. They found that those who were overweight or obese in middle age had significantly higher rates of dementia as older adults. Specifically, compared to people who were of normal weight in their 40s, overweight people had a 35% greater risk of developing dementia, and obese people had a 74% greater chance (Whitmer et al., 2005).

Weight-Related Stigma. The increased risk of depression, anxiety, and other mental disorders among people who are overweight or obese is probably connected to the stigma and discrimination that they face on a regular basis (Moskovich et al., 2011; O'Brien et al., 2013). By any name — "anti-fat bias," "fat shaming," "weight stigma," or "sizeism," for example — disapproving or hateful attitudes toward overweight and obese people cause significant damage (Chrisler & Barney, 2017; McHugh & Kasardo, 2012). Unfortunately, these attitudes are often present among many groups of people. For example:

- These attitudes are present among children: One study of 5- to 10-year-old kids found that they were much less likely to want to be friends with another kid who was overweight, or even a normal-weight girl standing next to other girls who were overweight (Penny & Haddock, 2007).
- These attitudes are present among doctors: Over one-third of physicians view obese patients as lazy, sloppy, weak-willed, and unattractive (Foster et al., 2003; Wear et al., 2006). As a result, many obese patients (especially women) hold negative or fearful attitudes toward the health care system and avoid visiting doctors even when they have real medical needs (Mensinger et al., 2018).
- These attitudes are present in employers and supervisors: In one study, overweight or obese workers were much more likely to be viewed as potentially weak workers, and to receive negative performance evaluations from their supervisors (Polinko & Popovich, 2001; Rudolph et al., 2009). And in another, participants who read about an employee making a mistake were more likely to punish that employee by withholding a raise or promotion if the employee was obese than if the employee was of average weight (Lindeman et al., 2018).

Researchers have identified many unfortunate correlations with weight stigma. For example, people who experience more moments of weight stigma throughout a particular day feel less motivation to eat healthy, exercise, or lose weight at the end of the day (Vartanian et al., 2018). People who experience high levels of weight stigma also tend to turn to unhealthy eating as a coping strategy (Puhl et al., 2020a). Weight stigma can also discourage people from exercising. Multiple studies have found that people who experience weight stigma (at the gym or elsewhere), especially those who are socially anxious, tend to avoid the gym and other places where exercise could be observed by others. Instead, they may choose to exercise alone or not at all (Horenstein et al., 2021; Thedinga et al., 2021; Schvey et al., 2017). Weight stigma even influenced the way some people handled the COVID quarantine: in one study, young adults who had experienced high levels of weight stigma before the pandemic were more likely to binge eat during the pandemic (Puhl et al., 2020b).

Biological Factors in Hunger and Eating

Within your body, there are numerous factors that cause you to feel hungry, eat, and, under certain circumstances, overeat. Let's consider the primary factors.

Hormones. Your body contains hunger-related hormones that respond to your need for food at any particular time. One pair of these hormones, *leptin* and *ghrelin*, is especially important. **Leptin** is a hormone that signals feelings of fullness.

leptin
A hormone that signals feelings of fullness.

Ghrelin is a hormone that signals feelings of hunger. These two hormones essentially monitor the amount of food in your stomach and send messages to your brain about what action to take next. Leptin's message, which happens after you eat a big meal, is "Stop eating — your stomach is full." Ghrelin's message, which happens when many hours have passed since that big meal, is "Start eating — your stomach is empty" (Berk, 2008a; Wren et al., 2001).

Set Point, Settling Point, and Thrifty Genes. Another biological factor that influences your eating behavior is your **set point**: a particular weight to which your body tends to return after increases or decreases. Your set point is like the temperature to which a thermostat is set. If the room gets a little too hot, cold air blows, and if the room gets a little too cold, hot air blows. The goal is to return to the predetermined temperature without ever straying far from it. In much the same way, your body (especially through its use of leptin and ghrelin) returns your body to its set point of weight by increasing or decreasing appetite as necessary.

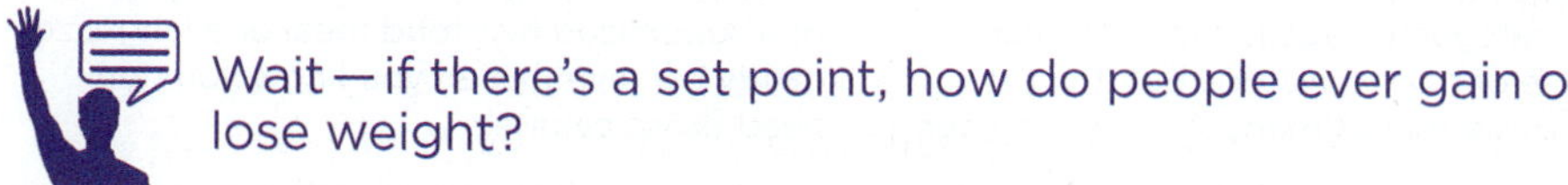
Wait — if there's a set point, how do people ever gain or lose weight?

Actually, set point is one reason why losing a significant amount of weight — and, more importantly, *keeping* it off — is so difficult. One study found that the average contestant on TV's *The Biggest Loser* lost plenty of weight during the show, but had gained most of it back six years later (Fothergill et al., 2016). But there are some people who manage to lose weight and keep it off. There are also people who gain significant weight and keep it on. To explain these drastic and long-lasting weight changes, some experts argue that the set point may better be described as a *settling point*, a term intended to sound more flexible and more responsive to external factors than *set point*. Set point, as it was originally conceived, focused exclusively on what happens inside your body, but ignored external factors. So, according to set point, your body is "hard-wired" to retain roughly the same weight whether you live where food is sparse or plentiful. But that's not how it actually works. People tend to gain weight when the environment enables them to do so. *Settling point* suggests that those environmental influences do matter, especially in terms of weight gain (Egger & Swinburn, 1997; Pinel et al., 2000; Speakman et al., 2011).

If you live in a developed country like the United States, your environmental influences are probably quite different from the way they were thousands of years ago. For most of human history, food was scarce. It was especially difficult to find foods rich in calories, fats, and salts. (Vegetables and fruits were easier to come by.) So, our ancestors stuffed themselves when they found rich foods, intentionally trying to build up fat that might enable them to survive the next period of food deprivation. They would feast now to survive famine later.

You are a descendant of those opportunistic overeaters, which means that your body and brain inherited the same strategy: when you find rich foods, eat as much as possible and accumulate fat, since food may not be available later. But in a daily American lifestyle, there's a good chance that food *is* available later. In fact, you may spend most of your life with quick and easy access to fast food restaurants, 24-hour convenience stores, or pizza delivery. So instead of occasional opportunities for overeating, as your ancestors had, you may have continual opportunities for overeating. You may never encounter the famine that would burn off the fat resulting from such eating habits, so that fat stays with you, potentially creating numerous health risks. This phenomenon is known as the *thrifty gene hypothesis*: you inherited genes that promote an eating strategy to build up fat whenever possible. This strategy may have kept your ancestors alive, but it can backfire and contribute to your illness or death if left unchecked (Berk, 2008b; Chakravarthy & Booth, 2004; Myles et al., 2011; Neel, 1962, 1999).

ghrelin
A hormone that signals feelings of hunger.

set point
A particular weight to which the person's body tends to return after increases or decreases.

IT'S LIKE...

The Thrifty Gene Hypothesis Is Like Buying Gas for a Nickel a Gallon

After a lifetime of high gas prices, imagine how you'd feel if you saw a gas station selling gas for a nickel a gallon. You'd grab that deal, assuming that you won't soon find it again. You'd fill your tank, and you might also fill up so many gas cans that they'd fill the trunk, the back seat, the roof rack, and maybe even a trailer. If you could, you'd make your car fat with gas.

But what if you went around the corner and saw another gas station also selling gas for a nickel a gallon? And what if that price remained consistent for the rest of your life, available at gas stations everywhere you go? If you maintained the same mentality—stock up as much as you can every chance you get—your car would soon become seriously obese with gas. No matter how much you drove, there's no way your car could burn gas at the same rate you acquire it.

Thankfully, your logic would take over and prevent this stockpiling of gas. But when it comes to food intake, your logic is up against thousands of years of evolution. As the thrifty gene hypothesis states, your genes motivate you to stock up on high-calorie, high-fat foods because they have been scarce and valuable safeguards against famine over the course of human history. But if your lifestyle is like that of many Americans, your world is not like the world humans inhabited many millennia ago. All kinds of high-calorie, high-fat foods are inexpensive and readily available at many restaurants, supermarkets, convenience stores, and vending machines. Thanks to your evolutionary inheritance, you may feel the urge to stock up on calories even if you don't need them. According to the thrifty gene hypothesis, that's a big reason why obesity has become such a problem in countries like the United States. It's an inherited challenge to resist the temptation of a supersized fast food meal or a king-size candy bar, even when you know you don't need those calories. •

The problems related to the thrifty gene hypothesis are made worse by the fact that your daily lifestyle may require far less exercise than your ancestors' lifestyles. You may choose to exercise, but exercise was built into your ancestors' lifestyle. They had unavoidable workouts every day while foraging for and running after food. In some less developed societies today, people still live a lifestyle similar to that of our shared human ancestors, spending much of their day in pursuit of food and eating a relatively low-fat, low-salt, low-calorie diet. Obesity, and the many health problems that come with it, are extremely rare in those societies.

The thrifty gene hypothesis is not the only explanation for our tendency toward obesity, nor is it without criticism. One such criticism is that there are many people in our contemporary society who remain thin, despite having the same access to fattening foods and an exercise-free lifestyle as people who become overweight or obese (Qasim et al., 2018; Speakman, 2013).

Genetics. The thrifty gene hypothesis applies broadly to all humans, but the specific genes you inherit from your parents also play a significant role in your eating behavior and your weight (Bell et al., 2005; Locke et al., 2015). The heritability of being overweight is 40–70%, meaning that roughly half (or more) of the variability in your BMI is due to your genes rather than your environment (Flier, 2004; Samaras, 2008). Adoption studies find that when adopted kids grow up, their BMIs correlate positively with the weights of their biological parents, but don't correlate at all with the weights of their adoptive parents (Stunkard et al., 1986b; Vogler et al., 1995). Twin studies reach similar results: identical (monozygotic) twins have a much higher BMI correlation than fraternal (dizygotic) twins (Bouchard et al., 1994; Stunkard et al., 1986a). In fact, the more genes you share with someone, the higher the correlation between their weight and yours (Maes et al., 1997). Check **Figure 8.2** for details.

By the way, in spite of oversimplified reports you may hear in news stories about a single "fat gene" or "obesity gene," the genetic influence on weight comes from a collection of many genes (Alfredo Martínez et al., 2007; Loos & Janssens, 2017; Marti et al., 2004). Those genes influence many things related to your eating and weight, including how you experience hunger, how you experience fullness, and how your body stores nutrients (Stein, 2008).

metabolic rate (or metabolism)
The rate at which one's body burns energy.

Metabolic Rate. Additionally, those genes influence your **metabolic rate (or metabolism)**: the rate at which your body burns energy. Of course, your metabolic rate

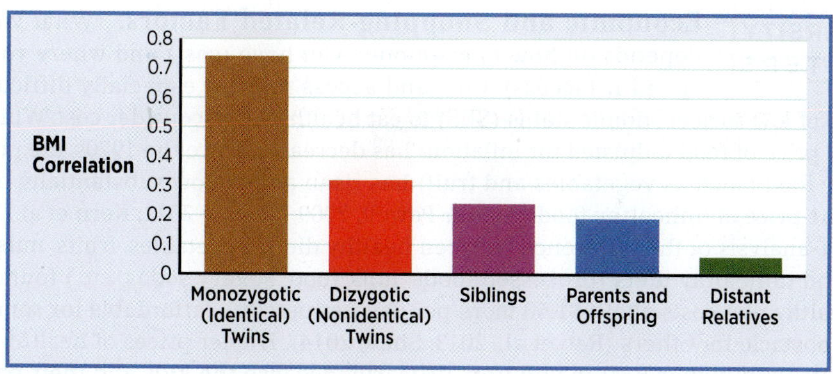

FIGURE 8.2 Genes and BMI. Genes play a significant role in BMI. The correlation between BMIs of people who share a larger percentage of their genes is substantially higher than the correlation between BMIs of people who share a smaller percentage of their genes.
Information from Maes et al. (1997).

varies. It is lower when you rest, higher when you exercise, and tends to vary across the life span. But it also differs between you and other people. Your metabolic rate is simply faster or slower than the metabolism of some other people. You may have a friend who overeats and doesn't exercise yet never gains a pound, and another friend who exercises and eats reasonably yet never loses a pound. Difference in metabolic rate is a likely explanation.

Psychological Factors in Hunger and Eating

Eating may be driven by biology, but it is affected by many psychological factors as well, including stress (Moskovich et al., 2011). There is little doubt that stress affects eating (Greeno & Wing, 1994; Hill et al., 2018; Masih et al., 2017). You may assume that stress *increases* eating, especially if you've seen scenes in TV shows or movies where emotionally distraught people scarf down a whole tub of ice cream or a big bag of chips. However, that increase in eating isn't automatic (Steere & Cooper, 1993). In fact, some research has found that among people experiencing stress, a *decrease* in eating is actually more common than an increase in eating. But the same research finds that gender and the amount of stress make big differences too.

If the stress levels are only moderate, both men and women tend to eat less, but if the stress levels are high, women tend to eat more while men still tend to eat less (Stone & Brownell, 1994).

In addition to influencing *how much* you eat, stress can influence *what* you eat. Generally, stress causes less healthy food choices (Oliver & Wardle, 1999; Wallis & Hetherington, 2009). One study that asked teachers and nurses to keep a personal food and stress journal for 8 weeks found that they ate at fast food restaurants more often when they were highly stressed (Steptoe et al., 1998). A survey of over 4000 adolescents found that when they were highly stressed, they ate more fatty foods, fewer fruits and vegetables, and skipped breakfast more often (Cartwright et al., 2003). Another study found that negative mood (which frequently accompanies stress) significantly increases the focus on short-term goals like feeling immediate comfort rather than long-term goals like staying healthy. That increased focus on short-term goals translates into choosing candy bars, cookies, and chips over carrots, apples, and rice cakes (Gardner et al., 2014).

Environmental and Sociocultural Factors

Besides the biological and psychological factors *within* you, factors *outside* of you influence your eating and your weight. Let's consider some of the most important.

DIVERSITY MATTERS

Economic and Shopping-Related Factors. What you eat depends on how much money you have (cost) and where you can spend it (access). Cost and access make it especially difficult for people of low socioeconomic status (SES) to eat healthy. First, consider cost. While the overall price of food (adjusted for inflation) has decreased since the 1970s, the price of *healthy* food (such as vegetables and fruit) has risen and is now substantially higher than the price of unhealthy food (Auld & Powell, 2009; Cawley, 2011; Kern et al., 2017). A meta-analysis of the difference between healthy diets (vegetables, fruits, nuts, fish, etc.) and unhealthy diets (processed foods, junk food, sugary sodas, etc.) found that the healthy diet costs about $1.50 more per day per person — affordable for some, but a real obstacle for others (Rao et al., 2013; Shaw, 2014). Higher prices of healthy foods correlate with higher BMI in children, primarily because the kids and their parents buy cheaper, more fattening foods instead (Powell & Bao, 2009; Sturm & Datar, 2005).

Those cheaper, more fattening foods often come from fast food restaurants. Where fast food restaurants are prevalent, BMIs tend to increase (Niemeier et al., 2006; Polsky et al., 2016). Specifically, in the United States, there is a strong correlation between a state's obesity rate and its concentration of fast food restaurants (**Figure 8.3**). In states where it is easier to find a McDonalds, Wendy's, Burger King, or Taco Bell, it is also easier to find obese people (Burgoine et al., 2016; Maddock, 2004). On the other hand, if the prices of fast food and healthy food are closer together, healthy eating slightly increases: specifically, when fast food prices go up 10% (approaching the prices of healthier foods), the likelihood of teenagers frequently eating fruits and vegetables increases 3% and the likelihood of teenagers being overweight drops 6% (Powell et al., 2007).

Even if you can afford healthy food, you need access to stores that sell it. That is not easy in a *food desert*, an area with few if any stores and restaurants offering healthy options. If you're affluent, the chances are higher that you live near supermarkets and restaurants where healthy, nutritious food is sold. You also probably have a car, or can afford an Uber or bus fare, to get to those kinds of places. But if you're struggling financially, your best (or only) nearby options may be convenience stores, dollar stores, and fast food restaurants, and you may not have access to transportation

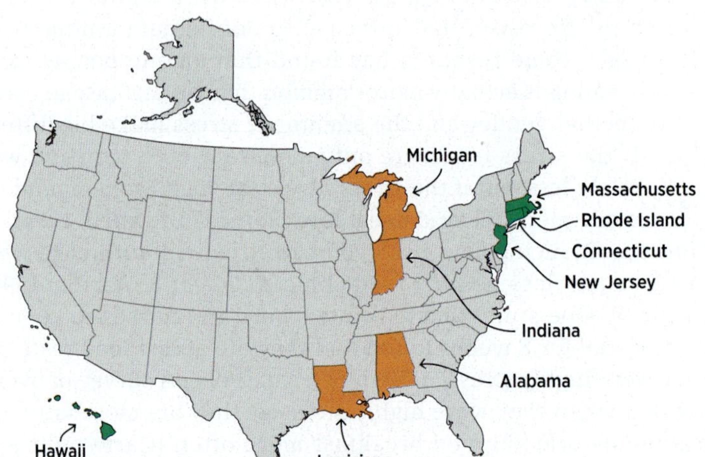

FIGURE 8.3 Obesity Rates and Fast Food, State by State. Among U.S. states, there's a strong correlation between the obesity rate and the concentration of fast food restaurants (as measured by the number of residents per fast food restaurant). Five states are among the 10 lowest in obesity rates *and* among the 10 lowest in concentration of fast food restaurants: Hawaii, Connecticut, Massachusetts, Rhode Island, and New Jersey. Four other states are among the 10 highest in obesity rates *and* among the 10 highest in concentration of fast food restaurants: Alabama, Louisiana, Michigan, and Indiana. In some cases, the concentration in one state is double that in another state. For example, Louisiana has one fast food restaurant for every 8000 people, but Hawaii has one for every 16,000 people.
Information from Maddock (2004).

to get you to another part of town (Burgener & Thomsen, 2018; Smith & Cummins, 2011). As a result, people who live in food deserts tend to have higher obesity rates (Fiechtner et al., 2013; Morland et al., 2006).

Interestingly, obesity rates also tend to be relatively high in *food swamps*, or small areas where there are some healthy food options (unlike in food deserts). In food swamps, those options are greatly outnumbered by unhealthy food options like convenience stores, fast food restaurants, and junk food outlets. (If you've ever seen a busy street where there's a grocery store with healthy food, but it's practically eclipsed by signs for Burger King, Dunkin' Donuts, 7-11, KFC, and Dairy Queen, you've seen a food swamp.) One study found that the food swamps actually predict obesity better than food deserts do (Cooksey-Stowers et al., 2017). Another study examined the eating habits of hundreds of middle-school kids in different Baltimore neighborhoods and found that those living in food swamps ate significantly more snacks and desserts than those who did not (Hager et al., 2016).

Lifestyle Factors. Many aspects of day-to-day life can affect how an individual or a family eats. Researchers have paid special attention to the amount of time spent watching TV. As the amount of time watching TV (or computers, or any other screens) expands, so do waistlines (Vandewater & Wartella, 2011). Not only is TV watching sedentary (you're often a couch potato while you do it), but it is often accompanied by snacking on unhealthy foods (Crespo et al., 2001; Matheson et al., 2004). To make matters worse, the ads during those shows often promote unhealthy foods too. Shows marketed to children and Black viewers have especially high rates of ads for fast food, candy, soda, and similarly unhealthy foods (Henderson & Kelly, 2005; Tirodkar & Jain, 2003; Vandewater & Wartella, 2011).

The constant barrage of ads for unhealthy foods on kids' shows contributes to obesity in kids (World Health Organization, 2003). In fact, the relationship is so strong, and has received so much attention, that some children's advocacy groups have called for limitations (or a complete ban) on advertising for unhealthy food on kids' shows, like the ban that exists for cigarettes during adult programming (Institute of Medicine, 2006). In one study, researchers surveyed parents of children age 3 to 5 about two things: which TV shows the kids watched and which cereals they ate. Results showed a strong positive correlation: the more time kids spent watching shows that advertised high-sugar cereals (like Cocoa Puffs, Froot Loops, and Cinnamon Toast Crunch), the more often they ate those cereals (Emond et al., 2018). And of course, the more often kids eat unhealthy foods like these, the greater the odds of obesity (and other health problems).

More recent research on the relationship between watching TV and eating accounts for the fact that today, TV watching happens in many different ways than simply watching shows on the couch at home as they are broadcast live. Unlike in your parents' or grandparents' generation, your generation can binge-watch on Netflix, Hulu, Amazon Prime, Disney+, or with shows recorded on a DVR — and TV watching doesn't necessarily happen on a TV at home, but anywhere on computer screens, smartphones, tablets, and other devices. These studies produce very similar results: regardless of how or where it is watched, excessive TV time and high rates of overweight and obesity go together (e.g., Falbe et al., 2017).

Hero Images/Getty Images

In social situations, the way we eat can make an impression on others. Research suggests that both women and men change their eating habits depending on who they're eating with.

Social Situations. The way you eat can depend on who you're eating with (Higgs & Ruddock, 2020). Research suggests that people often model their own food intake on the intake of others — that is, we adjust the amount and type of food we eat to match what we see others eating (Vartanian et al., 2015). Research also suggests that eating behaviors depend on whether we are eating alone or with others. Specifically, being with other people tends to increase the amount we eat compared to what we would eat alone, especially if we're with family and friends and the meal lasts a long time (de Castro, 1994; Pliner et al., 2006).

DIVERSITY MATTERS

The social influences on eating can depend on a number of factors, including gender. For example, women tend to be more concerned than men about looking gluttonous while they're eating

(Vartanian et al., 2007). Both men and women change their eating habits depending upon characteristics of the people they're eating with, but the most significant changes are the decreases in food intake by women when they eat with an eligible, attractive, unfamiliar man – perhaps to create an impression of traditional femininity (Mori et al., 1987; Pliner & Chaiken, 1990; Salvy et al., 2007).

Opportunities for Exercise. The flip side to consuming calories is burning them off through exercise. Unfortunately, some people simply don't have as much opportunity for exercise as others. Of course, some of the obstacles involve time and money. Some people just don't have enough of either to join a gym or dedicate themselves to a regular exercise program. But another factor is the *built environment*, or the exercise opportunities built into the physical surroundings and day-to-day life in a particular neighborhood. Ideally, the built environment facilitates exercise by containing a number of features: a good quality and quantity of parks, streets that are walkable (well-lit, low traffic, with well-maintained sidewalks and traffic lights designed for pedestrians as well as cars), shops and restaurants within walking distance, and low levels of crime. These features promote walking, jogging, bike riding, and other nonmotorized ways of getting around that burn calories and combat obesity. Sadly, lower-SES neighborhoods (the same ones less likely to have supermarkets and healthy restaurants) tend not to have such picturesque built environments (Burke et al., 2009; Morland et al., 2002a, b). As a result, weight problems are even more difficult to overcome in these areas (Garfinkel-Castro, 2017; Sallis et al., 2011).

Portion Size. The amount of food in front of you influences how much you eat: We eat more when we are offered more. Researchers have confirmed this tendency in so many studies that it even has a name: the *portion size effect* (Hetherington, 2019; Hetherington & Blundell-Birtill, 2018; Zuraikat et al., 2019). The portion size effect shows up in all kinds of ways for both children and adults: at home and in restaurants, with foods that come in distinct pieces (like chicken nuggets or graham crackers), and with foods that are unstructured (like mac and cheese or pudding; Reale et al; 2019, Steenhuis & Poelman, 2017). The portion size effect becomes an obesity risk when we receive much more food than we need in terms of calories. A meta-analysis that combined the results of 14 studies found that larger portions led to greater weight gain, suggesting that if portion sizes were reduced, then weight gain could slow or stop (Robinson et al., 2022).

We often receive much more than what we need from fast food restaurants, especially in recent years. Consider a McDonald's customer, for example, ordering a burger, fries, and soda in the late 1950s. Now picture yourself doing the same, all supersized to the largest on the menu. Your burger is *5 times* as big, your fries *2.5 times* as big, and your soda *4.5 times* as big (Young & Nestle, 2002, 2007)! It's no wonder newer generations have more of an obesity problem than earlier generations. In fact, in recent years the amount of money that Americans spend eating out has risen to double its level in the 1950s, matching the amount we spend eating at home (U.S. Department of Agriculture, 2014).

You might expect that eating a larger portion would lead to more enjoyment, but research suggests otherwise (de Ridder & Gillebaart, 2022). In one study, researchers offered a couple of different snacks (applesauce some days, brownies other days) to kids age 8 to 11 in an after-school program. At the beginning of the study, researchers asked the kids to predict how much they would enjoy different portion sizes of the snacks: the recommended serving size, 50% larger, and 125% larger. Then, over a couple of months, the researchers offered the snacks of various sizes to the kids. On the days when the kids ate the snacks, the researcher asked the kids how much they enjoyed them. Results showed that the kids did not enjoy the larger portions of applesauce or brownies more than the smaller portions, even though they predicted that they would. Results also showed that the kids enjoyed smaller portions of both foods more than they predicted. The researchers concluded that it's a good strategy to remind kids (and older people) that eating a smaller portion can provide just as much enjoyment as eating a larger portion, which can counteract the portion size effect and reduce obesity-related problems (Schwartz et al., 2020).

Another effective strategy for counteracting the portion size effect focuses on the tools we use to eat: plates, bowls, spoons, cups, etc. A meta-analysis that combined the results of 28 studies showed that changing the size of the tools we use to eat usually changes the number of calories we take in, especially using smaller bowls and cups (Vargas-Alvarez et al., 2021). Think about how much cereal you'd pour into (and eat out of) a big bowl versus a small bowl, or how much soda you'd drink if you chose the Super Big Gulp versus a smaller cup.

LIFE HACK 8.1

To limit how much you eat, limit your portion size, both at home and when you eat out. Bigger portions lead to greater caloric intake and potential weight gain. Research shows that your enjoyment of eating doesn't necessarily depend on the amount you eat.

(Hetherington, 2019; Robinson et al., 2022; Schwartz et al., 2020)

Weight and COVID. The COVID quarantine, with its disruption of normal routines and exercise opportunities, had a measurable effect on our weight (Zachary et al., 2020). One longitudinal study of over 700 U.S. adults found that both body weight and BMI increased significantly, on average, between April 2020 and October 2020 (Bhutani et al., 2021). Another study of about 700 young adults compared exercise habits during 2018 (long before the pandemic began) and during 2020 (soon after the pandemic began). Results showed that exercise at all levels of intensity (mild, moderate, and vigorous) dropped significantly during the pandemic, and that the primary reasons were closed gyms, inconsistently available outdoor exercise opportunities (because of weather, etc.), and limited at-home exercise options (Folk et al., 2021). One survey of over 1800 young adults found that about 30% reported that they had overeaten to cope with the pandemic, and about 35% had eaten more unhealthy foods than usual during the pandemic (Mason et al., 2021).

Promoting Healthy Eating

With so many factors influencing how and what you eat — and so many of those influences leading to people being overweight and obese — what is the best strategy for healthy eating? Experts and researchers offer lots of suggestions, ranging from how you can manage your own eating to how organizations, including the government, can make large-scale social changes (Roberto et al., 2015).

Individual Strategies. There are quite a few individual strategies for promoting healthy eating — including shopping smart, lifestyle changes, and professional help.

Shop smart. The grocery store is just as important as the kitchen table in terms of healthy food choices. Filling your fridge and cupboard with healthy food will prevent you from potentially making unwise choices when you get that late-night craving for double fudge brownies. And take advantage of your knowledge about portion size: if you must eat too much once in a while, eat too much of something healthy. One study found that when kids were served double portions of vegetables with their meals, they ate much more of them (Mathias et al., 2012).

Think lifestyle change, not quick fix. Crash diets and short-term exercise programs don't work, at least not long-term. A better approach involves bigger changes in how you live your life. These changes can include not only what you eat, but also the social support you get from friends and family regarding weight loss and how much you prioritize exercise and integrate it into your regular schedule (Jeffrey et al., 2003; Perri & Corsica, 2002; Wadden, 1995; Wadden et al., 2007).

Consider professional help. If you continue to have serious struggles with weight, numerous options are available. For example, there are therapies based on behavioral change, like keeping a record of your eating and exercise behavior and rewarding yourself for meeting specific goals (Jones-Corneille et al., 2011). There are also therapies based on changing irrational thoughts about weight, like

XiXinXing/Thinkstock/Getty Images

Healthy school lunches are one of many social strategies to promote healthy eating.

"I'll never get in shape" or "I'm such a loser for letting myself get to this point" (Brownell, 2004; Castelnuovo et al., 2017). Of course, there are also pills and surgeries to consider as weight loss strategies. Unfortunately, those pills often have unwanted side effects and questionable effectiveness (especially long-term), and the surgeries are often expensive and produce other medical complications (Encinosa et al., 2009, 2011).

Social Strategies. There are also many social strategies for promoting healthy eating – including better food labeling, limiting advertising of unhealthy foods, taxing unhealthy foods, and increasing community interventions.

Require more prominent and realistic food labeling. Packaged food already includes food labels, but often the serving sizes are unrealistically small. (One serving of Tostitos is just *seven* chips? [FritoLay, 2016] One serving of Haagen-Dazs vanilla ice cream is just *2/3 of a cup*? [Haagen-Dazs, 2021]) Also, the nutrition information on restaurant menus could be more easily available and complete (Kersh & Morone, 2011).

Limit advertising of unhealthy foods. Numerous experts and advocacy groups have called for limitations on the advertising of unhealthy foods, especially on kids' shows (Ippolito, 2011). Similar efforts were part of the plan that worked well in changing behaviors regarding tobacco, seat belt use, and recycling, which has prompted some experts to suggest using them against unhealthy foods as well (Chaloupka, 2011; Economos et al., 2001).

Tax unhealthy food. In some states, there are already taxes on some unhealthy foods, like soda, potato chips, and candy, but these policies could be expanded and improved (Powell & Chaloupka, 2009). Speaking of taxes, the government could provide tax incentives to supermarket chains (and any other seller of healthy foods) for opening stores in food deserts, and for existing stores in those neighborhoods to get the equipment and inventory necessary to supply healthier food to their customers (Roberto & Brownell, 2011).

Increase community-wide interventions. These efforts could include more offerings from the parks & recreation department (such as exercise and recreation classes), community classes on healthy food and cooking, and health education campaigns (Economos & Sliwa, 2011).

Promote healthy eating at schools and workplaces. Schools could place more emphasis on food and nutrition education, offer more opportunity for physical education and after-school sports, and offer healthier options in the cafeteria and vending machines (Brown, 2011). Employers could offer educational programs; create workplaces that promote physical activity (make gyms available, encourage stairs over elevators, and limit sedentary activity); financially reward employees who participate in fitness programs; offer inexpensive healthy snacks at meetings, at meals, and in vending machines; install bike racks; and create walking trails nearby (Goetzel et al., 2011).

CHECK YOUR LEARNING:

8.7 What is body mass index (BMI), and how does it define being overweight or obese?

8.8 What are the negative consequences of being overweight or obese?

8.9 What biological factors contribute to being overweight or obese?

8.10 What environmental and sociocultural factors contribute to being overweight or obese?

8.11 Do healthy eating strategies occur at the individual level, the social level, or both?

To check your understanding of these questions, click show the answers or refer to the answers in the Chapter Summary.

Emotion

Emotion is all aspects of feeling, including changes to the body, behavior, and consciousness. Notice that the letters *mot* in the word e*mot*ion also appear in the word *mot*ivation. Both words come from the same root, which means *to move*. The purpose of emotion is to move you, to stir you into action (Frijda, 2008; Solomon, 2008). That action may be obvious, like when joy inspires a child to run and hug a parent returning from a long time away. Or it may be subtle, like when anger sets off a low-key glare at your friend or family member. Throughout human history (and still today), those actions often produced survival advantages. For example, people who ran away from something that made them feel scared, or who avoided food that made them feel disgust, were more likely to live (Montag & Pankseep, 2017; Plutchik, 2001, 2003). You are a descendant of those people whose emotions moved them to survive, and you have inherited many of the genes that predisposed them to behave according to their emotions.

YOU WILL LEARN:

8.12 what emotion is.

8.13 about a variety of theories that explain the connection between the physical and mental aspects of emotion.

8.14 how people communicate emotions, and whether certain emotions are communicated by all people.

8.15 what emotion regulation is, and how different strategies of emotion regulation compare to each other.

8.16 why emotion regulation is important, especially in relation to positive emotions.

8.17 how emotion interacts with age, ethnicity, and gender.

Theories of Emotion

Emotions are both mental and physical experiences. Consider sadness, for example. One of my psychotherapy clients, Cody, had an appointment with me the day after the death of his dog, who had provided 12 years of loving companionship. Cody tried to describe what was going through his mind: he was enduring pure despair, thinking about how much he would miss her, and remembering great times they shared. But he also communicated his sadness through tears, stomach aches, and physical exhaustion that made him look like he was dragging himself around. His sadness saturated not just his mind, but his body as well.

As psychologists have studied emotions over the years, some of their main questions have focused on this combination of mind and body experiences that emotions produce. Specifically, the question of *which comes first* — the sequence in which emotions affect the mind and the body — has prompted a variety of theories, each backed by its own research. Let's explore the main theories by examining how each of them would explain what happens to you in a very specific situation: you drop your phone down a flight of concrete steps (see **Figure 8.4**).

James–Lange Theory. **James–Lange theory** is a theory of emotion stating that you experience emotion by noticing bodily changes first and then interpreting them as particular feelings. The *James* in James–Lange theory is William James, whom you may remember from Chapter 1 as the father of U.S. psychology. Back in 1884, James wrote one of the earliest psychology papers about emotion, which argued that the physical sensation comes first and that the sensation is followed by the feeling (James, 1884).

How does James–Lange theory explain the fear you feel when your phone falls down the steps? It says that first, your heart starts pounding, your breathing quickens, and your muscles tense up. *After* that bodily reaction, you become consciously aware of the emotion, and your mind feels fear. The key here is that your physical reaction, and your awareness of it, trigger the mental reaction.

There is research supporting the notion that certain emotions are characterized by certain patterns of biological reactions. For example, most participants in a study who saw unpleasant pictures involuntarily flexed their "frown" muscle (in their eyebrows) and also revealed subtle differences in the amount of electric energy contained within the skin. However, not all participants reacted this way. In fact, a sizable number did not (Lang, 1994; Lang et al., 1993). Also working against the James–Lange theory is the fact that, often, the physical reaction simply can't happen as quickly as the mental reaction because the human body doesn't respond that quickly. (Think about it — if you saw your phone fall down the steps, would your heart, breathing, and muscles

emotion
All aspects of feeling, including changes to the body, behavior, and consciousness.

James–Lange theory
A theory of emotion stating that the person experiences emotion by noticing bodily changes first and then interpreting them as particular feelings.

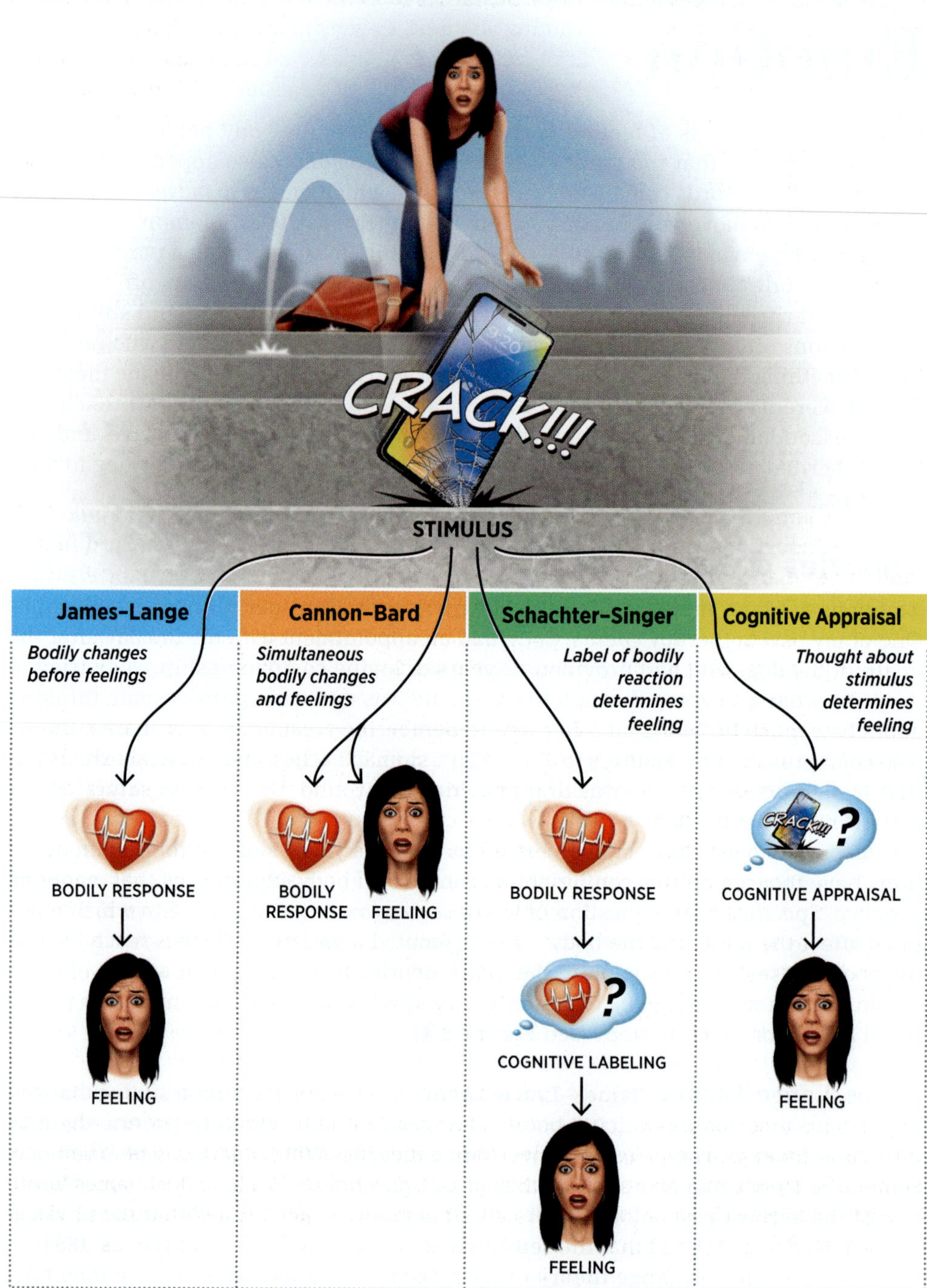

FIGURE 8.4 Theories of Emotion. If your phone fell down a set of concrete steps, you'd probably feel fear. But how exactly would that emotion arise? Four major theories of emotion offer different explanations, especially in terms of the role of bodily arousal and the sequence of events.

even have a chance to react in that first instant before your mind registered fear?) So, the James–Lange theory has garnered significant support in the many years since its introduction, but it also received significant criticism — much of which led to the theories of emotion we consider next.

Cannon–Bard theory
A theory of emotion stating that the person experiences emotion by simultaneously becoming aware of bodily changes and feelings.

Cannon–Bard Theory. The first prominent alternative to James–Lange theory was developed by Walter Cannon and Philip Bard in the early 1900s. **Cannon–Bard theory** is a theory of emotion stating that you experience emotion by simultaneously becoming aware of bodily changes and feelings. So, rather than the physical part of emotion hitting you first and the mental part hitting you next, they hit at the same time.

In our example, dropping your phone down the steps would simultaneously produce the conscious experience of fear in your mind and produce the heart rate, breathing, and muscle changes in your body. Cannon and Bard, who were physiologists and tested their theory by experimenting on the brains of cats, explained that their theory reflected the important role of the thalamus within the brain (Bard, 1934). Specifically, the thalamus is where the processing of the image of the stimulus – in this case, dropping your phone down the steps – divides into two separate and simultaneous streams, one that heads toward the cerebral cortex to produce the conscious experience of fear and another that heads toward the hypothalamus to produce the bodily changes (LeDoux, 1996).

Like the James–Lange theory before it, the Cannon–Bard theory received some support from research (Bard, 1928; Cannon, 1931; Dror, 2014). For example, in their own studies, Cannon and Bard found that a cat with its sensory cortex and motor cortex removed could still have emotional reactions. This experience should not be possible, according to the James–Lange theory, since it depends on the perception of bodily change (Bard & Rioch, 1937; Cannon, 1927; Dalgleish, 2004).

The Cannon–Bard theory also received criticism, including the fact that it doesn't allow for thought to influence the emotion process. According to Cannon–Bard theory (and James–Lange theory too, for that matter), emotions happened automatically. That may be true for most animals, but not for humans: we have the ability to think about how events affect us. That is why the theories of emotion that came next historically focus on how thinking might influence the experience of emotion.

Schachter–Singer Theory. **Schachter–Singer theory** is a theory of emotion stating that the label you assign to your bodily reaction determines your mental reaction. (Schachter–Singer theory is also known as *two-factor theory*, with the two factors being your bodily reaction and your label for it.) When Stanley Schachter and Jerome Singer created their theory in the mid-1900s, they pointed out that the physical component of many emotions is quite similar. For example, consider the physical reactions we've been discussing in our example about dropping your phone down the steps: increased heart rate, rapid breathing, and tensed muscles. So far, we've tied those physical reactions specifically to fear, but they actually could signal any number of emotions: excitement, anger, surprise, and more.

As an alternative example, consider Ronnie, a high school basketball player taking the court for a big game immediately after finding out that a scout from a local college team is in the crowd to check him out for a potential scholarship. Ronnie notices that his heart is pounding, and (perhaps unconsciously and instantly) wonders why. The options are many: shock (from just learning about the scout), nervousness (about the stakes of his performance in this particular game), exhilaration (about the opportunity to earn a college scholarship), or irritation (that he didn't get any advance notice about the scout). It is not the physical reaction itself, but the label that Ronnie places on it after he notices it, that determines how he experiences it mentally.

Schachter–Singer theory has been quite influential, but it has been criticized as well (Reisenzein, 1983; Sinclair et al., 1994). Some researchers who tried to replicate the classic Schachter–Singer study got different results (Marshall & Zimbardo, 1979; Maslach, 1979). Also, emotions don't necessarily require labels to be felt: when you were a baby and lacked the vocabulary necessary for labeling, you still experienced emotions all the time, and it still might happen once in a while today when you have a feeling that you can't quite describe in words.

Cognitive Appraisal Theory. **Cognitive appraisal theory** is a theory of emotion stating that what you think about a stimulus causes the emotion. The key difference between this theory (developed largely by Richard Lazarus) and other theories of emotion is that it deemphasizes physical reactions. Unlike the other three theories we have considered, the definition of cognitive appraisal theory doesn't mention bodily or physical reactions. According to cognitive appraisal theory, you experience an emotion

Schachter–Singer theory
A theory of emotion stating that the label one assigns to one's bodily reaction determines your mental reaction.

cognitive appraisal theory
A theory of emotion stating that what the person thinks about a stimulus causes the emotion.

facial feedback theory
A theory of emotion stating that one's brain can influence one's emotions by monitoring one's facial expressions.

because of your interpretation of the event that brought it on (Folkman et al., 1986; Lazarus, 1964, 1982, 1984; Lazarus & Alfert, 1964). In our example of dropping your phone down the steps, cognitive appraisal theory explains that your reaction of fear happens simply because you interpret what you see — a drop that could break your phone — but *not* because you interpret any bodily reaction.

Cognitive appraisal theory leaves lots of room for interpretation of events, which could differ between one person and another, or even differ for one person under different circumstances. For example, imagine that you dropped your phone while you happened to be at the store buying a new one. Would your emotional reaction differ if you dropped the one you were finished with or the one you just bought? Or, imagine that you dropped your phone, but you had purchased a free-replacement protection plan when you bought the phone. Would your emotional reaction differ from the same drop of your phone without that protection plan?

A criticism of the cognitive appraisal approach centers on the notion that thought must take place before emotion. Instead, in some cases, emotion may actually come first (Zajonc, 1980, 1984). The reason for this may be that in some situations, the mind generates emotions more automatically and easily than it generates thoughts. For example, you may occasionally hear a sound (perhaps the voice of an old friend) or smell a scent (perhaps a food you ate often as a young child) and for a brief moment have an emotional reaction to it *before* you can identify it ("I like that! What is it?").

Facial Feedback Theory. **Facial feedback theory** is a theory of emotion stating that your brain can influence your emotions by monitoring your facial expressions. Facial feedback theory is the most recent theory of emotion we'll discuss, having been developed in the 1970s and 1980s and researched heavily in the 1990s and 2000s (Buck, 1980; Davis et al., 2009; Söderkvist et al., 2018). The logic goes like this: your face sensitively responds to situations around you in all kinds of ways — smiles, frowns, winces, squints, raised eyebrows, flared nostrils, and more. Those expressions don't *result* from emotion, however. Instead, they *cause* emotion.

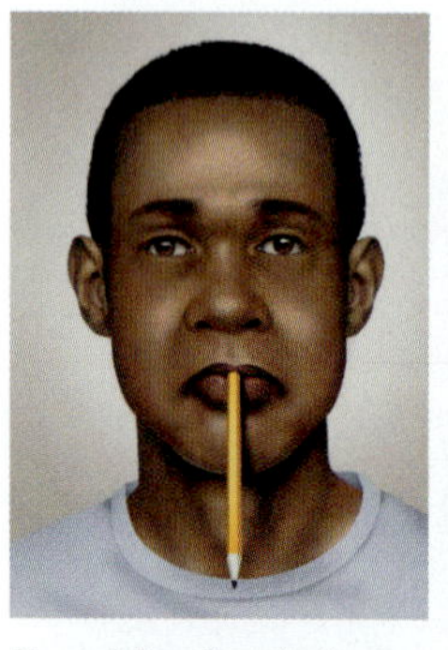
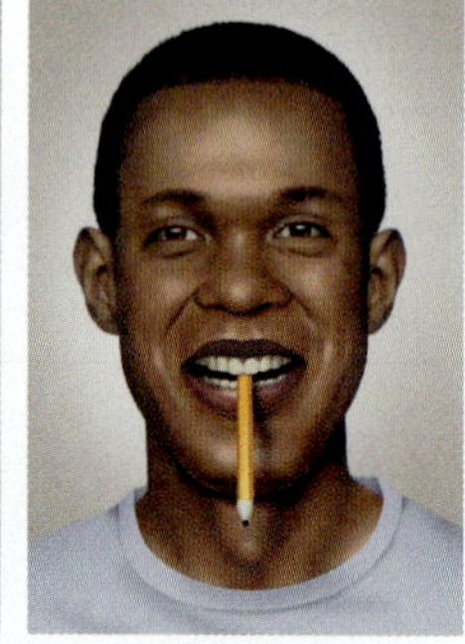

Facial feedback theory states that your brain can influence your emotions by monitoring your facial expressions. Researchers have tested this theory by having participants hold a pencil in their mouths in such a way that it forces either a pout or a smile, and then asking them to rate the funniness of cartoons. Smilers rated the same cartoons as funnier than pouters, presumably because their facial expressions influenced their mood (Soussignan, 2002). More recent research suggests that the facial feedback effect may not be as strong as indicated by earlier research, and that it may depend on the method by which researchers study it — specifically, whether the participant knows they are being watched or being recorded on video (Coles et al., 2019; Noah et al., 2018).

Wait, my face makes an expression *before* I feel the emotion?

According to the facial feedback hypothesis, yes. Consider again our example of dropping your phone down the steps. The facial feedback hypothesis states that *first*, your face shows fear: your eyes widen, your eyebrows slant upward, and your mouth opens. Soon *after*, your brain notices that your face has made these adjustments, and comes to the conclusion that you must be feeling fear. (It's a bit like catching a glimpse of the bags under your eyes in the mirror and realizing "Wow, I must be tired," but instead of a mirror, your brain monitors your facial expressions.) In a way, the facial feedback theory resembles the James–Lange theory, but emphasizes the face, rather than the entire body, as what determines emotion (McIntosh, 1996).

When researchers study facial feedback theory, they come across an unusual challenge: how do they get participants to make particular facial expressions and then measure how those expressions influence the participants' emotions? In some studies, researchers simply tell participants to smile, frown, or hold their faces in a particular position. For example, in one study researchers told participants to lower their eyebrows, and participants reported a worsening of mood as a result (Lewis, 2012).

Many emotion researchers have used a remarkably simple method to get participants to make facial expressions: putting a pen in their mouths (Soussignan, 2002). The trick is in *how* the pen is held by the mouth. Holding the pen with your teeth only (no lips) forces your face into a smiling position, but holding it with your lips only (no teeth) prevents your face from smiling (by forcing it into a pouting position). In one study, participants rated the funniness of cartoons while holding the pen in one of those ways. Those whose mouths were forced into a smile rated the cartoons as significantly funnier than those whose mouths were prevented from smiling, presumably because smiling put them in a happier mood. Similar results have been found in studies in which participants' facial expressions were controlled by having them repeat the same vowel sound over and over again. Participants who repeated the *ee* sound (which produces a smile, like when a photographer tells you to say *cheese*) reported more pleasant emotional experiences than those who repeated other vowel sounds that don't produce smiles (McIntosh et al., 1997; Zajonc et al., 1989).

Other studies have explored whether the effects of "putting on a happy face" might extend to other parts of the body as well. In one study, participants read a brief story about a man named Donald whose behavior was vaguely aggressive (he demanded his money back from a cashier after buying something, and he got into a conflict with his landlord, among other things). Some participants read the story with their index finger extended; others read it with their middle finger extended (yes, "flipping the bird"). Those with their middle finger extended not only rated Donald as more hostile, they also rated themselves as feeling less happy — again, presumably because that hand gesture indicating anger and displeasure prompted them toward negative emotions (Chandler & Schwarz, 2009; Srull & Wyer, 1979).

In a facial feedback study relevant to the COVID pandemic, researchers examined whether smiling through a needle injection very similar to receiving a COVID vaccine made a difference in terms of stress and pain. They found that it did. Specifically, participants who smiled through the shot reported feeling less pain and also showed less of an increase in heart rate than participants who did not (Pressman et al, 2020).

More recent research on facial feedback theory suggests that the effect is not as powerful as earlier research may have implied (Coles et al., 2019). Also, numerous studies that attempted to replicate the earlier facial feedback studies found that it matters quite a bit whether the participant knows they are being observed or recorded on video. In the later (but not earlier) studies, participants were aware of the video recording and the facial feedback effect was largely absent. This difference in results between studies of the same topic shows the importance of the method by which researchers run their studies: even a slight change in the method can produce very different results (Noah et al., 2018).

Communicating Emotions

It is almost impossible to experience emotions without communicating them. When your friend whispers something funny to you during class, it is hard to hold in that laugh. When you accidentally bite the inside of your mouth at dinner, it is hard to mask that pain from the others at the table. Communicating emotion is so automatic that even when you talk on the phone, you might gesture just as much as you would if you were talking in person. Poker players know how automatic the communication of emotions can be — that's why they often wear sunglasses or hoods in an attempt to hide any slight automatic facial reactions (or "tells") about the hand they've been dealt.

Many psychologists believe that sharing emotions has an evolutionary social function (Shiota, 2014). In particular, the communication of emotions strengthens the bonds that you have with the people around you (Fischer & Manstead, 2008; Gervais & Fessler, 2017). Let's go back to that example about dropping your phone down the steps. The fearful look on your face serves as a warning to the others around you. In general, that fearful look says, "Something dangerous is happening, so watch out!" In this particular case, it says, "Hold on tight to your own phone, because it could drop and get damaged!" If you discovered that your phone was indeed broken, your fear might turn to sadness. Expressing that sadness may draw helpful responses from those around you, such as compassion for your loss, offers to use their phones, or suggestions for repairing or replacing it (Batson & Shaw, 1991; Bonanno et al., 2008; Eisenberg et al., 1989; Keltner & Kring, 1998).

David Becker/ZUMA Press, Inc./Alamy

Nonverbal communication of emotions is so powerful that card players have to make great effort to maintain a "poker face" that reveals no emotion about the hand they hold.

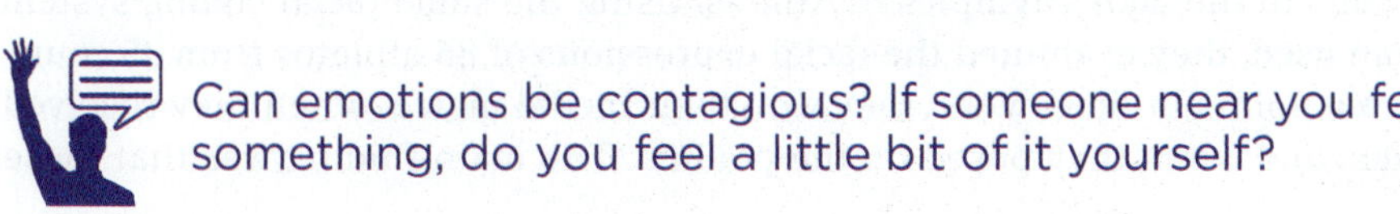
Can emotions be contagious? If someone near you feels something, do you feel a little bit of it yourself?

That happens, and psychologists call it *empathy* — the tendency to identify with and to some extent experience the emotions of others. Empathy varies from one person to the next. Bullies, child abusers, and violent criminals typically experience little empathy for the feelings of others (Jolliffe & Farrington, 2006; Miller & Eisenberg, 1988; Perez-Albeniz & de Paul, 2003; Schaffer et al., 2009; Walters & Espelage, 2018). Those at the other end of the empathy scale can be so empathic that they can't help but mirror the facial expressions of those around them. One study found that high-empathy people smiled slightly when they saw photos of happy faces and frowned slightly when they saw photos of angry faces, while low-empathy people kept a straight face no matter which photo they saw. The high-empathy people also rated the faces they saw as more emotional than the low-empathy people did. The happy faces struck them as very happy and the angry faces struck them as very angry, as if the emotions were coming through at a higher intensity (Dimberg et al., 2011). Other studies have found that this facial mimicry by high-empathy people happens automatically, unconsciously, and accurately within just a fraction of a second (Dimberg & Thunberg, 2012; Rymarczyk et al., 2016; Sonnby-Borgström, 2002).

Let's take a closer look at the two specific components of communicating emotions: expressing them and recognizing them.

Expressing Emotions. From day one, human beings express emotions. If you've ever held a baby for even a few minutes, you've seen their faces show a wide range of feelings, from miserable to happy, and from alert to sleepy. By the age of 2 or 3, young children typically show the full range of adult emotions, differentiated to a greater extent than in their first months (Lewis, 2008). What may come across as a more general "sad" in a baby is a bit more distinguishable as a particular kind of sad in a toddler: heartbroken because someone they love just left the house, gloomy because a rainy day is keeping them from going to the park, or dejected because they can't find the last piece to their puzzle.

Not only do babies express emotion, they express the *same* basic emotions around the world (Hess & Thibault, 2009). Many studies find this to be true even in blind babies, who obviously can't be imitating faces they've seen, which leads many experts to conclude that all humans are born with the capacity to experience and express certain feelings (Camras et al., 1991; Eibl-Eibesfelt, 1973; Valente et al., 2017). The research on babies' emotional expression is just a small part of the research on how people of all ages express emotion. In general, the conclusion is the same: human beings around the world express the same basic set of emotions (Matsumoto et al., 2008a).

A leading researcher on emotional expression, Paul Ekman, conducted classic studies in the early 1970s that examined whether people from a wide range of countries and cultures showed the same facial expressions. In one, he showed American and Japanese participants the same films and (without their knowledge, initially) recorded their facial reactions. He found that participants from both cultures showed basically the same facial reactions at the same moments in each film. Ekman also categorized the emotional expressions of the participants into six basic categories, each thought to be a basic human emotion: anger, disgust, fear, happiness, sadness, and surprise (Ekman, 1972).

Many more recent studies support Ekman's early findings that there are a small number of basic emotions that people express around the world (Celeghin et al., 2017; Ekman, 1974, 1993, 2003; Harris & Alvarado, 2005; Mauss et al., 2005; Ruch, 1995). In one such study, researchers took advantage of a situation in which people from around the world come together and are likely to experience similar emotions: the Olympics. Researchers analyzed the facial expressions of athletes immediately after winning a medal in judo in the 2004 Olympics in Athens. Using the same facial coding system that Ekman used, they examined the facial expressions of 85 athletes from 35 countries at three points in time: when they won their medal match, when they received their medal, and when they posed on the podium. The main finding was that these

BONNINSTUDIO/iStock/Getty Images

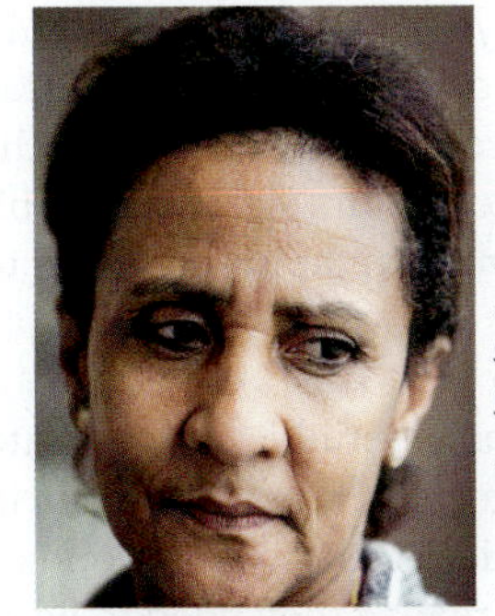

Juanmonino/E+/Getty Images

Gogosvm/iStock/Getty Images

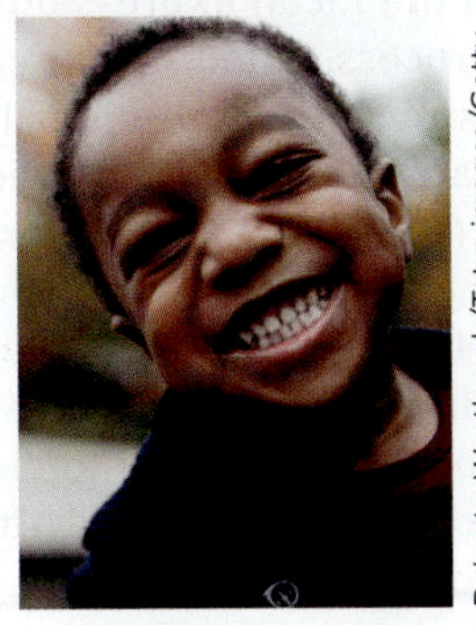

Roberto Westbrook/Tetra images/Getty Images

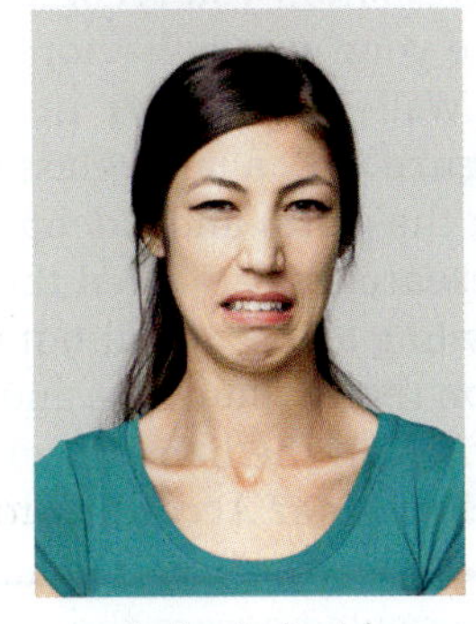

ozgurdonmaz/iStock/Getty Images

Paul Burns/Blend Images/Getty Images

People around the world show the same six basic facial expressions: anger, sadness, fear, happiness, disgust, and surprise.

athletes' facial expressions were so similar to each other that they must represent basic universal human emotions (Matsumoto & Willingham, 2006).

Is it possible that people have such similar expressions of emotion because they see other people displaying them?

That possibility — that people's facial expressions are shaped by the facial expressions they see in the people around them — also occurred to those researchers who studied the Olympic athletes. So, they also visited the 2004 Paralympic Games in Athens and did the same study with blind athletes. In this case, there were 59 blind judo competitors from around the world, about half of whom had been blind their entire lives. The results were essentially the same: the spontaneous emotions expressed on the faces of these blind athletes when they won their matches, received their medals, and stood on the podium were the same as each other, and the same as the sighted athletes from the Olympic study (Matsumoto & Willingham, 2009). These findings provide even stronger support for the idea that basic human emotions are universal and innate.

DIVERSITY MATTERS

Not all researchers agree with the idea that all humans express the same basic emotions. At the very least, they argue, important differences exist in the particular, customary ways that basic emotions are expressed. To describe these differences, researchers often use the term *dialect* (Elfenbein, 2013, 2017; Elfenbein et al., 2007; Hess & Thibault, 2009). You have probably heard the word *dialect* used to describe spoken language, but here it refers to unspoken language, such as facial expressions and other nonverbal communications of emotion. Consider happiness as an example: people from diverse groups may all express happiness, but the specific way that happiness shows itself varies according to expectations and norms within that group (Hareli & Hess, 2017). These varied expressions can include the type of smile (big and beaming vs. small and closed-lipped), the small movements around the eyes, how long the facial expression lasts, and whether the smile is accompanied by bodily movements like clapping excitedly or jumping up and down. Picture the differences between the ways that people of different genders, ages, ethnicities, or social statuses might feel comfortable expressing happiness if they received wonderful news, and you can appreciate the wide differences in these types of dialogues.

Recognizing Emotions. To successfully communicate emotions, you must be able to not only express them, but also recognize them. Earlier, in the example of dropping your phone down the steps, we mentioned that your friends around the table might benefit from your facial expression and realize they need to be careful with their phones too.

Research indicates that the emotion you recognize in the facial expressions of others can powerfully influence your own behavior — a process called *social referencing* (Clément & Dukes, 2017; Walle et al., 2017). In one study, 12-month-old babies were placed on a *visual cliff* (**Figure 8.5**), a large glass surface that has a shallow end (where wallpaper is right under the glass) and a deep end (where wallpaper is many inches below the glass). The researchers adjusted the deep end to be deep enough to make the babies hesitate crawling across it, but not necessarily refuse. To start the experiment, the baby is placed on the shallow side, and their mom stands by the edge of the deep side. The question is, Will the baby crawl across the deep end to mom, or will the baby stay on the shallow side? According to the results of this study, it all depends on mom's facial expression. When mom made a happy or interested facial expression, most of the babies crawled across the deep end, but when mom made an angry or sad facial expression, few of the babies crawled across. And when mom looked fearful, *none* of the babies crawled across (Sorce et al., 1985). The main point of these findings is that babies — and perhaps the rest of us, to some extent — refer to other people's facial expressions to help decide what actions to take, especially when the right answer is unclear.

In real life, you may have seen this influence of others' facial expressions play out when a child sees an adult express emotion about the child's injury. For example, picture Amit, a 7-year-old boy at soccer practice falling and scraping his knee. In that brief moment immediately after the fall, Amit is silent, but scans eagerly for his coach.

FIGURE 8.5 The Power of Facial Expression. The emotions expressed in the faces of those around you can have a powerful influence on your behavior. In one study, most babies crawled across the deep end of a glass-topped visual cliff (which made them at least somewhat unsure about their safety) if mom's face looked happy or interested. Few of them crossed if mom's face looked angry or sad, and none crossed if mom looked fearful. Information from Sorce et al. (1985).

If he sees a look of panic come over the coach's face, Amit may panic too, complete with screaming and crying. But if the coach's face stays calm and cool, communicating that the injury is no big deal, odds are that Amit will gather himself after a minute and resume playing, without any screaming or crying. It is as if Amit is unsure how badly he is hurt, so he waits for the cue of the coach's facial expression to nudge his own emotional reaction in one direction or the other.

Just as researchers have explored whether the expression of emotion is universal, they have also explored whether recognition of those emotions is universal. Again, the predominant answer seems to be yes. In another classic study by Paul Ekman and his colleagues, over 500 participants from 10 countries in Europe, Asia, and North America were shown 18 photos of the faces of White people expressing a basic emotion (anger, disgust, fear, happiness, sadness, or surprise). When asked what emotion was being expressed, they made few mistakes. The percentage of participants from a particular country who correctly identified the target emotion never fell below 60%, and about a third of the time it was above 90%. As **Table 8.1** indicates, participants were especially good at identifying happiness. In most countries, over 90% of participants got it right. The participants also agreed with each other quite strongly about how intense the emotion was in each photo. Overall, the results of this study suggest that people around the world recognize facial expressions in largely the same way (Ekman et al., 1987).

Other studies have also supported the recognition of emotions as universal (Ekman & Friesen, 1971; Matsumoto et al., 2002). Remember that 2004 Olympic study we discussed earlier? Those authors also showed those photos to participants from around the world to see how accurately they could recognize the emotion in the athletes' faces. Overall, they were quite good at it, with the majority of participants making the correct choice the majority of the time (Matsumoto & Willingham, 2009). Kids make the correct choices too: they have roughly the same accuracy rates as adults for sad and angry expressions, and lag only slightly behind in the other emotions (Lawrence et al., 2015). Another study used mimes to silently express 25 different emotions to 1200 participants who spoke three different languages (English, Hindi, and Malayalam). No matter what language they spoke, participants accurately identified at least 23 of those mimed feelings (Ershadi et al., 2018). A meta-analysis of many studies confirms that recognition of emotion through facial expressions is universal, but also points out that people from the same country or ethnic group were slightly better at recognizing the emotions of people within their group than people outside that group (Elfenbein & Ambady, 2002).

DIVERSITY MATTERS

Not all researchers agree with the idea that the recognition of human emotions is universal. Examining similar questions as the classic studies by Ekman with different methods, some researchers have found that people in diverse groups often interpret facial expressions differently than other groups do (Fernández-Dols & Russell, 2017; Gendron, 2017; Gendron et al., 2018; Russell et al., 2017a, b; Yuki et al., 2007). In one such study, members of a small-scale indigenous society in Papua New Guinea saw photos of faces from an unfamiliar culture expressing various emotions. Those photos were actually from Ekman's book *The Face of Man* (1980) and are intended to illustrate the emotions that he argued were universally recognized (happiness, sadness, etc.). In this study, the participants were allowed to describe the emotions with whatever word they wanted (rather than a multiple-choice format, as in the original studies), and the experimenter spoke the native language (which made translation into English less problematic). The results differed significantly from the universal emotion recognition that Ekman would have predicted: well under half of the participants' descriptions matched the emotion supposedly portrayed in the photo (Crivelli et al., 2017).

DIVERSITY MATTERS

In addition to language, race can also play a role in emotion recognition. In one study, researchers asked 178 future teachers to identify the emotions expressed on the faces of Black and White kids aged 9–13. The participants, who were predominantly White, were generally good at recognizing the kids' emotions, but their most frequent mistake was misperceiving

TABLE 8.1: A Smile Is a Smile Around the World

COUNTRY	PERCENTAGE OF PARTICIPANTS WHO CORRECTLY IDENTIFIED HAPPINESS IN THE SAME TARGET PHOTO
Estonia	90
Germany	93
Greece	93
Hong Kong	92
Italy	97
Japan	90
Scotland	98
Sumatra	69
Turkey	87
United States	95

Data from Ekman et al. (1987).

When participants from countries around the world were shown a photo of the same face expressing happiness, the vast majority from every country identified the emotion correctly. They identified other basic emotions, such as surprise, sadness, fear, disgust, and anger, with only slightly less accuracy.

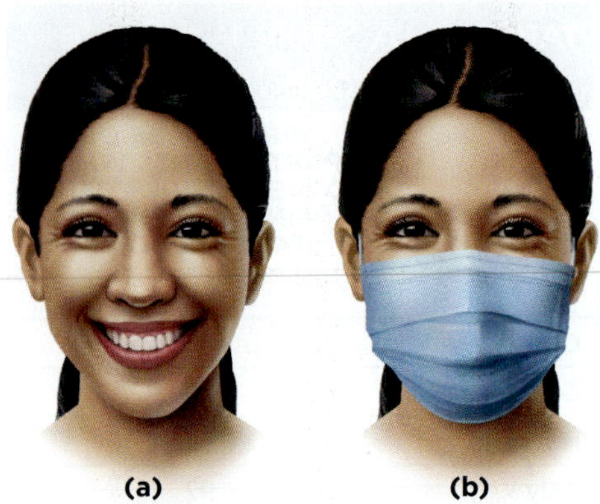

FIGURE 8.6 Research Suggests that Mask-Wearing can Interfere with Emotion Recognition. Wearing masks is important for slowing the spread of COVID. However, masks can make it difficult to identify which emotion a person is feeling and how intense that emotion is. They can also make observers less confident about how the person wearing the mask is feeling. To compensate, some experts suggest relying on verbal communication and body language, and also openly acknowledging the difficulties that masks can cause.

Black kids (both boys and girls) as angry when they were not (Halberstadt et al., 2020).

Since the start of the COVID pandemic, researchers have studied the impact of mask-wearing on emotion recognition. Essentially, these researchers are trying to answer the question illustrated in **Figure 8.6**: does wearing a mask that covers the mouth and nose interfere with other people's ability to recognize the mask-wearer's emotions? Generally, the answer appears to be yes, at least to some extent (Bani et al., 2021; Grundmann et al., 2021). One study found that observers could still recognize happy and sad faces behind masks, but struggled to recognize exactly *how* happy or sad the person was (Kastendieck et al., 2021). Another study found that observers recognized the emotion in masked faces less accurately and had less confidence in their guesses. The most common mistakes were *missing* emotions – believing a face showed no emotion when it was actually happy, sad, angry, and so on – rather than misperceiving one emotion when the face was actually expressing a different emotion (Carbon, 2020).

To compensate for this impaired ability to read facial expressions through face masks, some experts recommend that we pay more attention to small facial changes visible above the mask (for example, changes in the area around the eyes or eyebrows during a smile or frown), rely more on verbal communication and body language, and openly acknowledge the difficulties of emotion recognition to each other during masked conversations (Carbon, 2020; Mheidly et al., 2020).

Emotion Regulation

Emotion regulation is your ability to manage the type, intensity, length, and expression of your own emotions. Of course, you're never in complete control of your emotions. For example, you can't force yourself to be happy when you hear about the death of a relative, or force yourself to be calm when a fire alarm shrieks. But you can have some control over your emotions. For example, you might try to limit your sadness about a relative's death when other family members need you for support, or you might try to avoid panicking when you hear the fire alarm so you can calmly find safety. That ability to not let your emotions get the best of you is emotion regulation (Gross, 1998a, b; Yih et al., 2018).

Methods of Regulating Emotions. James Gross, a leading researcher on emotion regulation, describes five strategies for emotion regulation (Gross, 2008, 2014). The strategies occur at different points in time, beginning before the emotion has a chance to occur and ending when you're already starting to feel it. Let's walk through them with one particular example in mind: your cousin Bryan, whom you find annoying but to whom you owe a favor, has left you a voicemail asking you to have lunch with him next Saturday.

MY TAKE VIDEO 8.2

Emotion Regulation

"A time when I used an emotion regulation strategy was..."

Visit Achieve to watch the My Take video and then answer questions.

Achieve

- *Situation selection.* If you use situation selection to regulate emotion, you will say no to Bryan. Or you might not even return his call. Situation selection means that you deliberately put yourself in situations where you are likely to experience positive emotions and avoid negative emotions (like the annoyance you feel around Bryan). This is a strategy that involves lots of planning and anticipating. It can, if taken to the extreme, cause you to make significant adjustments to your daily schedule.
- *Situation modification.* If you use situation modification to regulate emotion, you will see Bryan on Saturday, but you will structure your time together in such a way that it minimizes your feelings of annoyance. For example, you might tell Bryan that you'd rather see a movie than get lunch, because at the movie you won't have to interact with him as much. Situation modification is not quite as proactive as situation selection, but it can still involve some planning.
- *Attentional deployment.* If you use attentional deployment to regulate emotion, you will have lunch with Bryan, but you will distract yourself. You will draw your attention to other things besides Bryan's annoying personality. Perhaps

emotion regulation
The ability to manage the type, intensity, length, and expression of one's own emotions.

you will concentrate hard on the food you order and the Yelp review you plan to post about it, or perhaps you will daydream about how you will be spending the next day doing more enjoyable things, or perhaps you will sneak peeks at your phone during lunch. Any of these behaviors would draw your attention away from the annoyance you would otherwise feel.

- *Cognitive change.* If you use cognitive change to regulate emotion, you will have lunch with Bryan. If you start to feel annoyed, then you will rethink the situation or your capacity to deal with it. For example, instead of thinking about how annoying he is, you might think it is nice to keep the family ties close. And if you start to think you can't stand it, you might remind yourself that it's only for a couple of hours. If you can't escape or reshape your situation, rethinking it in this way can take the edge off of negative emotions, and perhaps even flip them into positive emotions.
- *Response modulation.* If you use response modulation, you will go to lunch with Bryan, and feel annoyed, but you will try to suppress it (or "hold it in"). You might take deep breaths, put a fake smile on your face, or just suffer through it. Response modulation is a strategy for dealing with the emotion after it happens. You're just trying to control how intensely you feel it.

LIFE HACK 8.2

To minimize negative emotions in your life, it is better to prevent them by rethinking, changing, or avoiding the situations that cause them than to suppress the negative emotions after you start to feel them.

(Demaree et al., 2006; Gross & Levenson, 1993, 1997; Webb et al., 2012)

Research indicates that some of these five emotion regulation strategies work better than others — a key point to keep in mind for managing your own emotions in your daily life. One clear finding is that response modulation doesn't work well, especially the kind that involves suppression of negative feelings. Suppression isn't particularly effective in reducing negative emotions, and in some cases it actually compounds (or worsens) them (Compas et al., 2017; Demaree et al., 2006; Gross & Levenson, 1993, 1997). Suppression also interferes with memory, as if your brain's effort to suppress the feeling subtracts from its ability to form memories of what actually happened (Richards & Gross, 2000, 2006). Suppression has bad social consequences too — the people around you often notice you doing it, and when they do they are likely to feel stressed, like you less, and distance themselves from you (Butler et al., 2003; English et al., 2013; Srivastava et al., 2009).

On the other hand, the emotion regulation strategies that take place earlier than suppression — that is, before you begin to feel the feeling — tend to work better. In particular, situation selection has been found to be helpful, especially for people who would struggle to regulate their emotions if they found themselves in an undesirable situation (Webb et al., 2018). Cognitive change also tends to produce desirable results, especially when it involves rethinking the situation and your capacity to deal with it (Gross, 1998a; Hayes et al., 2010; Koole, 2009). In fact, a meta-analysis of almost 200 studies that compared the results of the five different strategies for regulating emotion found that cognitive change or rethinking proved much more effective overall than the other available strategies (Webb et al., 2012).

CHAPTER APP 8.2

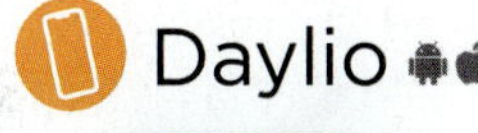

The Daylio app allows you to track your emotions. You enter your mood (rad, good, meh, bad, or awful), along with your recent activities (working, watching movies, cleaning, exercising, etc.). The app then provides you with stats and graphs showing how your mood changed as time passed and your activities changed.

How does it APPly to your daily life?
How could an app like Daylio help you understand the patterns of your emotions? How could it help you determine which activities evoke positive and negative emotions? How could the information it provides influence your decisions on activities to choose in the future?

How does it APPly to your understanding of psychology?
How could this app help you appreciate the range of your own emotions? How could it help you recognize or regulate your own emotions?

To learn more about this app or to download it to your phone, you can search for "Daylio" on Google, in the iPhone App store, or in the Google Play store.

Why Emotion Regulation Matters

It is easy to see why emotion regulation matters in your everyday life — it maximizes your positive feelings, such as happiness, contentment, enthusiasm, pride, amusement, and awe. Beyond those fleeting emotional moments, however, there are more enduring reasons why emotion regulation matters too: positive emotions improve the long-term quality of your life.

For example, consider your physical health. As the Twitter-based study illustrated in **Figure 8.7** shows, experiencing happiness and other positive feelings improves your physical wellness and decreases your susceptibility to both serious diseases and the common cold (Cohen & Pressman, 2006; Cohen et al., 2003; Fredrickson & Cohn, 2008; Frederickson & Joiner, 2018; Moskowitz & Saslow, 2014; Ong & Allaire, 2005). The more positive emotions a person has, the lower the odds of stroke or heart disease (Davidson et al., 2010; Ostir et al., 2001). Among people with chronic diseases, those who experience more positive emotions experience lower levels of pain and disability

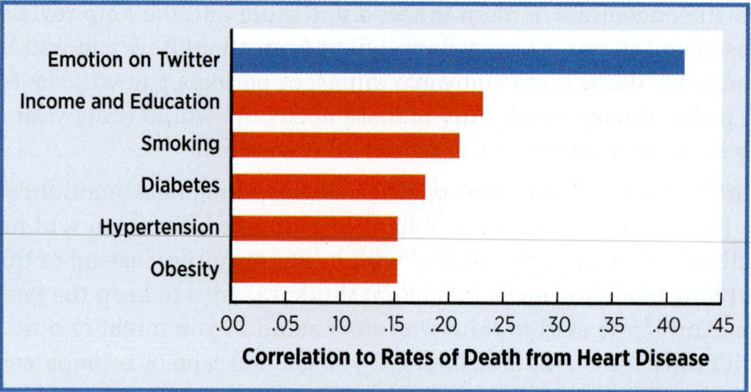

FIGURE 8.7 Twitter, Happiness, and Heart Disease. Researchers explored the connection between the emotional language used in 148 million tweets (collected over a 10-month period) to the rates of death from heart disease. Those death rates were highest in U.S. counties where the tweets contained lots of words expressing negative emotions like hostility and tension (*hate*, *grrr*, *despise*, *jealousy*, *stupid*, and plenty of curse words). Those rates were lowest in counties where the tweets contained lots of words expressing positive emotions like optimism and happiness (*wonderful*, *great*, *hope*, *fantastic*, *enjoyed*, etc.). The emotional tone of the tweets correlated with a county's rate of death by heart disease better than smoking, diabetes, obesity, and other variables. Bottom line: negative emotions seem to go hand in hand with disease, while positive emotions seem to go hand in hand with wellness. Data from Eichstaedt et al. (2015).

(Gil et al., 2004). And among older adults living on their own, more positive emotions correlate with higher levels of functioning regarding daily activities (Cabrita et al., 2017).

In a unique study concerning the connection between positive emotions and health, researchers found that baseball players who were smiling in their 1952 baseball cards were half as likely to die in any specific year within the next five decades as those who were not smiling (Abel & Kruger, 2010). More generally, reviews of studies on positive emotions and mortality consistently find a strong positive correlation between positive emotions and age of death: simply put, happier people live longer (Chida & Steptoe, 2008; Diener & Chan, 2011).

In addition to improving your long-term physical health, positive emotions promote an open-minded approach to life that makes people better at solving problems and interacting with other people. Recent research supports the *broaden-and-build theory of positive emotions*, which states that from an evolutionary standpoint, positive emotions mean safety, and safety allows you to expand your thinking beyond mere survival or avoidance of harm. So, when you're happy, you explore new ways of thinking and new ways of interacting with others. This leads to more creative solutions to problems and more helpful connections to the people around you (Fredrickson & Branigan, 2005; Isen, 2008; Johnson & Fredrickson, 2005; Tugade et al., 2014).

Focus On Sport/Getty Images Sport/Getty Images

Focus On Sport/Getty Images

Positive emotions correlate with longer lives. A study of baseball cards from the mid-1900s supports this finding, showing that smiling players tended to live longer than nonsmiling players (Abel & Kruger, 2010). For example, Roger Maris (top) died at 51, while Stan Musial (bottom) lived to 92.

Wow, the benefits of positive emotions are impressive. How can I maximize positive emotions in my own life?

You know yourself better than anyone, so you probably know plenty of ways to boost your own happiness. But psychologists have conducted research on a number of specific ways to increase positive emotions, and they have found a few techniques that work for most people (Myers & Diener, 2018; Nelson & Lyubomirsky, 2014; Seligman et al., 2006):

- *Perform acts of kindness.* People who do nice things for others feel happier themselves (Lyubormirsky et al., 2005; Lyubomirsky & Layous, 2013; Weinstein & Ryan, 2010). Ever hear of "paying it forward"? It happens when people do random acts of kindness for strangers, like paying for the coffee of the stranger behind you in line or sending an uplifting text to a friend or relative you haven't seen in a while. Researchers studied the effects of paying it forward by sending dozens of college students out to do kind things for strangers. They did all kinds of things—gave away small gift cards and candies, helped people carry heavy items, gave compliments, put money in parking meters, and more. The results showed that the people who paid it forward experienced significant increases in positive emotions (Pressman et al., 2015). Another study found that people can feel happier just by deliberately counting the acts of kindness they have already performed for others. When you can't give to others, it helps to remind yourself of what you've already given (Otake et al., 2006).

- *Write letters of gratitude.* If you've been the *recipient* of acts of kindness, writing letters in which you express your appreciation can heighten your positive emotions (Rash et al., 2011; Seligman et al., 2005; Toepfer et al., 2012; Wood et al., 2010). One 8-month longitudinal study found that people who spent 15 minutes a week writing letters to people in their lives who had done things that made them feel grateful (but not sending the letters) experienced more positive emotions than a control group who did not (Lyubomirsky et al., 2011). Another study of kids from third to twelfth grade found that those who generally experienced few positive emotions experienced a significant increase in positive emotions when they wrote and sent gratitude letters (Froh et al., 2009).
- *Count your blessings.* People who make an effort to count their blessings, or appreciate what they have, as opposed to focusing on what they don't have, generally experience more positive emotions (Emmons & McCullogh, 2003; Froh et al., 2008; Lyubomirsky et al., 2005). One study of college students found that those who counted their blessings were significantly more likely to remember positive events from their lives, which are likely to boost happiness (Watkins et al., 2004). Another study found that the more people count their blessings, the fewer symptoms of depression they experience (Lambert et al., 2012).
- *Visualize a bright future.* People who picture the future as a happy time tend to experience happiness in the present (Boehm et al., 2011; Sin & Lyubomirsky, 2009). One study found that college students who wrote essays once a week about the best version of themselves they could imagine in the future felt happier than those who did not (Layous et al., 2013). Another found that students who wrote similar essays every day for just 4 days experienced a similar increase in happiness even 3 weeks later (King, 2001).

LIFE HACK 8.3

If you want to feel happier, do something kind for someone else, or think about acts of kindness you've already done.

(Lyubomirsky & Layous, 2013; Otake et al., 2006; Pressman et al., 2015)

FROM RESEARCH TO REAL LIFE

Does Money Buy Happiness?

Does money necessarily equal happiness? This question produces mixed results (Boyce et al., 2017; Diener & Biswas-Diener, 2002; Lucas & Diener, 2008).

Some studies have found that the connection between money and happiness is strongest for people on the border of meeting their basic needs (Biswas-Diener & Diener, 2001; Diener et al., 1993). If more money means the difference between food and hunger, or between home and homelessness, or between medical care and sickness, having it produces much more happiness. But if your basic needs like food, shelter, safety, and medical care are met, getting more money probably won't produce the same increase in happiness. However, other studies have found that the connection between income and happiness remains consistently strong at all SES levels (Twenge & Cooper, 2020). And other research has found that the connection between SES and happiness depends on how SES is measured. If SES is measured by how wealthy you perceive yourself to be (especially compared to others around you), it correlates much more strongly with happiness than if it is measured by actual dollar amounts (Tan et al., 2020).

Some research has found that when money does buy happiness, it happens not by buying material things, but by buying experiences (like a trip, or a night at the movies), services that give you extra free time (like maid service or prepared meals), or gifts to friends or charities (Aknin et al., 2018; Gilovich et al., 2015; Helliwell et al., 2017a, b; Whillans et al., 2016).

It is also important to point out that even when money does affect happiness, it is just one of many factors. Good relationships with family and friends, a good marriage, and a healthy spiritual life are among many other factors that play a role (Diener & Diener, 2009; Diener et al., 1993; Ellison, 1991; Lucas et al., 2003; Suh et al., 1998).

One more note about the connection between finances and happiness—certain kinds of debt cause more unhappiness than others. Specifically, one study of thousands of U.S. adults found that student loan debt was negatively correlated with happiness, but credit card debt and mortgages were not (Greenberg & Mogilner, 2021).

display rules
Norms within a group about the acceptable verbal and nonverbal expression of emotion.

Emotion and Diversity

We all experience emotion, but we all experience it differently. Let's explore differences in emotion according to age, ethnicity, and gender. As we get into each of those differences, it is important to keep in mind the idea of **display rules**: norms within a group about the acceptable verbal and nonverbal expression of emotion. Many different kinds of groups have their own sets of display rules, including ethnic groups, age groups, gender-based groups, and even work organizations (Brody, 2000; Dahling, 2017; Matsumoto, 1990; Nixon et al., 2017; Safdar et al., 2009). We begin to pick up on display rules during infancy and continue to incorporate these rules throughout our lives (Malatesta & Haviland, 1982; Misailidi, 2006). You've noticed the effects of these different display rules if you've ever seen a diverse group of people experience the same event at the same time. For example, imagine an audience in a crowded movie theater. If a sad scene happens, some people openly weep, some quietly shed a single tear, some show a slightly sorrowful facial expression, and others may reveal no emotion at all. How you respond depends not only on the amount of sadness you actually feel, but also on display rules, the unwritten social guidelines that tell you how, or whether, you are allowed to display it.

One large-scale study of over 5000 people from 32 countries asked participants what they should do if they feel certain emotions in front of other people. Results indicated that participants from more individualistic cultures (such as the United States, Canada, and Australia) were much more likely to approve of expressing happiness and surprise, but not sadness, than people from more collectivistic cultures (such as Indonesia and Hong Kong) (Matsumoto et al., 2008b). A review of literature on gender-based display rules found that throughout childhood, girls are likely to show more happiness, sadness, anxiety, and sympathy than boys, while boys are likely to show more anger than girls (Chaplin & Aldao, 2013). Another study illustrated that display rules can depend on who is watching: elementary school–aged kids reported a much lower likelihood of expressing anger, sadness, or pain in front of peers than when they were alone or with a parent (Zeman & Garber, 1996).

WATCHING PSYCHOLOGY

This Show Is Scary: The Effect on Children of Frightening TV and Movies

Between R-rated movies, 24-hour news stations, and even network programming (like any of the *CSI* shows), there is plenty on TV that could produce fear in children. What's the effect of watching scary stuff on TV?

Some research suggests that the long-term effects could be quite strong in terms of anxiety and fear (Cantor, 2011; Hoekstra et al., 1999). In one study of college students, about 25% of them reported that they still felt significant emotional impact of a scary show or movie they watched when they were much younger (Harrison & Cantor, 1999). Another study found that among college students who had seen either *Jaws* or *Poltergeist* before age 12, 37% said the fright or other emotions caused by that movie were still negatively affecting some aspect of their waking life (Cantor, 2004). A survey of elementary school–aged kids found that over 75% had been scared by something they had seen on TV or other media. Of these, 38% of them had such significant fear that immediately afterward they couldn't perform a behavior they had previously performed (like being alone in a bedroom), and almost 25% said the effects were still at least somewhat with them at the time of the study even though months or years had gone by (Cantor et al., 2010).

There is other research that reports different findings — that any effects of scary media on kids are fleeting and largely inconsequential, especially in kids over 10 years old (Pearce & Field, 2016). Still other research has emphasized that the emotional vulnerability of the particular child may play a key role. One study of kids from New Orleans found that those who experienced Hurricane Katrina in 2005 had a more fearful reaction to the media coverage of Hurricane Gustav in 2008 than those kids who had not experienced Katrina (Weems et al., 2012). Of course, the way parents handle scary images on TV makes a difference too. Kids who discuss scary shows with their parents generally respond better than kids whose parents take a more passive approach (Browne & Hamilton-Giachritsis, 2005; Buijzen et al., 2007). •

DIVERSITY MATTERS

Emotion and Age. Many people assume that older adults feel less positive emotion than younger adults. In fact, several studies have found that some facial features common in older adults, like wrinkles and sagging skin, often give younger adults the impression that the older adults are unhappy (Ebner, 2008; Hess et al., 2012; Hummert, 2014). However, the opposite appears to be true: other than those who are very near death, older adults tend to experience more positive emotions than younger adults (Carstensen & DeLiema, 2018; Carstensen et al., 2000, 2011; Gerstorf et al., 2010; Magai, 2001, 2008; Riedeger et al., 2009). Older adults also tend to experience less emotional variability than younger adults, staying more "even-keeled" and less reactive to life events (Brose et al., 2013; Riediger & Rauers, 2014; Röcke et al., 2009; Steptoe et al., 2011).

diego_cervo/iStock/Getty Images

Other than those who are very near death, older adults tend to experience more positive emotions than younger adults (Carstensen et al., 2000, 2011; Gerstof et al., 2010; Magai, 2001, 2008; Riedeger et al., 2009).

There are several possible explanations for these emotional tendencies in older adults. Compared to younger adults, they may have learned through life experience to "choose their battles," which enables them to stay happy when daily hassles happen rather than blowing them out of proportion (Mikels et al., 2014). Especially if they are retired and have grown, independent children, they may experience fewer obligations than younger adults who are being pulled in multiple directions by work and family (Charles et al., 2010; Riedeger & Freund, 2008). The explanation most supported by research relates to the five strategies of emotion regulation we discussed earlier: older adults have learned to improve their emotion regulation, particularly by dealing with emotions before they occur rather than after (Gross & John, 2003; John & Gross, 2004; Riffin et al., 2014). Remember that example about your annoying cousin Bryan asking you to have lunch with him next Saturday? Because of their extensive life experience, older adults are more likely to use the emotion regulation techniques that fall earlier in the sequence, like situation selection or situation modification, rather than one that falls later in the sequence, like response modulation (Morgan & Scheibe, 2014). Older adults have been there and done that with Bryan (and others), and they know right away how annoying he can be, so they're wise enough to avoid him.

Emotion and Ethnicity. What makes people in one culture happy does not necessarily make people in another culture happy (Mitamura et al., 2014).

In individualistic cultures like the United States, people typically attribute their happiness to personal achievements, like doing well on an exam or getting a raise at work. By contrast, in collectivistic cultures, people typically attribute their happiness to interpersonal harmony, like getting along well with family members or improving the quality of a friendship (Diener & Suh, 2003; Uchida et al., 2004). In the United States, maximizing happiness is often seen as the goal, but in Asian countries, such a one-sided emphasis on positive emotions is often discouraged, especially since it can lead to jealousy and interpersonal conflict (Uchida & Kitayama, 2009). The correlation between positive emotions and physical wellness is stronger in the United States than Japan, but the correlation between balanced positive/negative emotions and physical wellness is stronger in Japan than the United States (Miyamoto & Ryff, 2011).

Regarding emotion regulation, research shows that suppression (which is common to the fifth strategy of emotion regulation, response modulation) is viewed quite differently in collectivistic cultures (primarily Asian countries) versus individualistic cultures (primarily the United States). Specifically, suppression has fewer negative consequences in collectivistic cultures (Butler et al., 2003; Matsumoto et al., 2008b, c; Pilch et al., 2018). In one study, researchers had pairs of participants—both Asian American women, or both European American women—watch and discuss a disturbing, graphic documentary about bombings during World War II. When European American women expressed emotion about what they saw, their blood pressure went down, but when Asian American women expressed emotion about what they saw, their blood pressure went up (Butler et al., 2003). Overall, suppression seems more acceptable, and perhaps even beneficial, in collectivistic cultures than in individualistic cultures (Huwaë & Schaafsma, 2018).

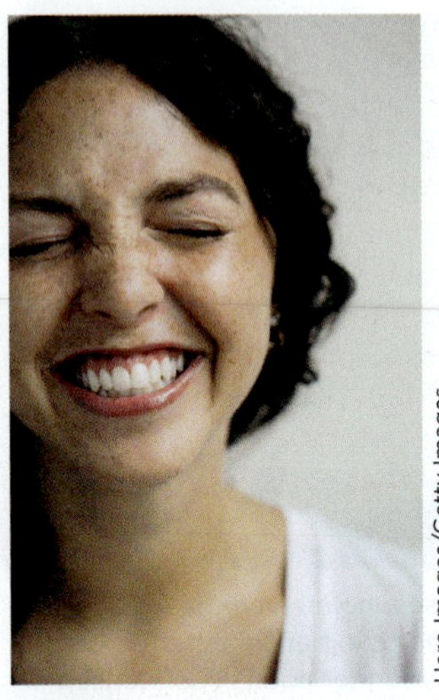
Hero Images/Getty Images

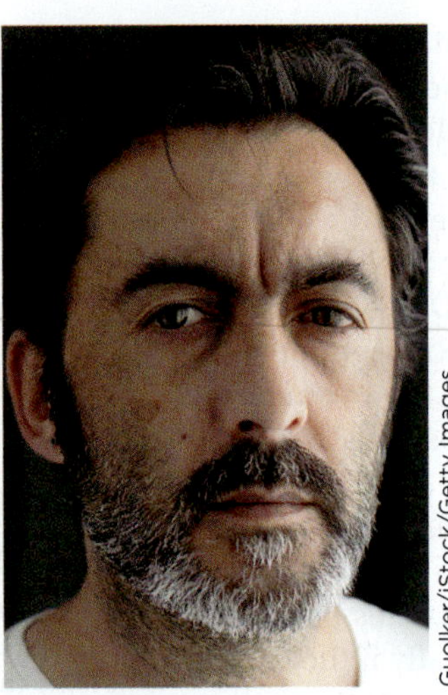
Guolker/iStock/Getty Images

Around the world, women tend to express emotion more openly than men (Fischer & Manstead, 2000).

Emotion and Gender In general, emotion plays different roles in the lives of men and women. Women describe their emotional experiences as more intense, express their emotions more freely, and pick up on others' emotions more accurately (Briton & Hall, 1995; Brody & Hall, 2008; Robinson & Johnson, 1997; Timmers et al., 2003). Gender differences such as these appear early in childhood and increase through adolescence into adulthood (Chaplin & Aldao, 2013). Although they tend to differ somewhat according to ethnicity, some basic gender-based differences in emotion tend to be rather universal (Gong et al., 2018). In one study involving participants from 37 countries, women had more intense, longer-lasting, more openly expressed feelings than men in every country (Fischer & Manstead, 2000).

DIVERSITY MATTERS

Women also have a wider range of people with whom they will discuss their emotions (Rimé et al., 1991). For example, let's say James and Cassandra are both laid off from their jobs at the same time and feel sad about it. James is more likely to limit his discussion of his sadness to his romantic partner or his closest friends (or to keep it entirely to himself), while Cassandra is more likely to share her sadness with a larger number of friends and family. To some extent, decisions about sharing feelings with particular people depends on the gender of the recipient too: both men and women report greater comfort sharing their emotions with women than with men (Timmers et al., 1998). Women also report a greater likelihood of "emotional contagion," or experiencing the same emotions as the people around them (Dimberg & Lundquist, 1990; Doherty, 1997).

CHECK YOUR LEARNING:

8.12 What is emotion?

8.13 Compare and contrast the five theories that explain the connection between the physical and mental aspects of emotion (James-Lange theory, Cannon-Bard theory, Schachter-Singer theory, cognitive appraisal theory, and facial feedback theory).

8.14 What is a probable evolutionary benefit of communicating emotions? To what extent are the communication and recognition of facial expressions universal?

8.15 What is emotion regulation, and what are the best strategies of emotion regulation?

8.16 Why is emotion regulation important, especially in relation to positive emotion?

8.17 How does emotion interact with age, ethnicity, and gender?

To check your understanding of these questions, click show the answers or refer to the answers in the Chapter Summary.

CHAPTER SUMMARY

Motivation

8.1 Motivation is a desire that stimulates and steers your behavior.

8.2 Intrinsic motivation is the desire to perform a behavior because the behavior itself is rewarding. Extrinsic motivation is the desire to perform a behavior to obtain an external reward.

8.3 Classic theories of motivation include instinct theory (behaving according to innate instincts), drive reduction theory (reducing unpleasant biological sensations), and arousal theory (maintaining an optimum level of arousal).

8.4 Contemporary theories of motivation include self-determination theory (behaving autonomously), regulatory focus theory (achieving regulatory fit between promotion and prevention motivations), and achievement goal theory (pursuit of mastery goals vs. performance goals).

8.5 Abraham Maslow's hierarchy of needs states that certain needs must be met before others. Specifically, needs must be met in this sequence: physiological needs, safety, belongingness and love, esteem, self-actualization, and self-transcendence.

8.6 People of diverse ethnicities, genders, and ages experience different motivations.

A Primary Motivation: Hunger and Eating

8.7 Body mass index (BMI) is a number calculated from a person's height and weight that indicates overall fitness level. Overweight people have BMIs between 25 and 29.9. Obese people have BMIs at or above 30.

8.8 Being overweight or obese increases the odds of many medical problems, mental health problems, and stigma.

8.9 Biological factors contributing to being overweight or obese include hormones, set point or settling point, genetics, and metabolic rate.

8.10 Environmental and sociocultural factors contributing to being overweight or obese include economic and shopping-related factors, lifestyle factors, opportunities for exercise, portion size, and food presentation.

8.11 Healthy eating can incorporate strategies at the individual level and the social level.

Emotion

8.12 Emotion is all aspects of feeling, including changes to the body, behavior, and consciousness.

8.13 James–Lange theory states that you experience emotion by noticing bodily changes first and then interpreting them as particular feelings. Cannon–Bard theory states that you notice the bodily changes and feelings simultaneously. Schachter–Singer theory states that the label you assign to your bodily reaction determines your mental reaction. Cognitive appraisal theory states that what you think about a stimulus causes the emotion. Facial feedback theory states that your brain determines your emotions by monitoring your facial expressions.

8.14 Communicating emotions happens automatically and probably had the evolutionary benefit of social bonding. People around the world use facial expressions to show the same basic emotions from the day they are born. People around the world also recognize the same basic emotions in the faces of others.

8.15 Emotion regulation is your ability to manage the type, intensity, and expression of your own emotions. The best emotion regulation strategies are those that enable you to avoid, change, or rethink situations that cause negative emotions before you actually feel them, rather than suppressing them after the feeling has begun.

8.16 Emotion regulation is important because it maximizes positive emotion, which improves physical health, problem solving, and social interactions.

8.17 Older adults generally tend to experience more positive emotions than younger adults. People from different ethnicities often experience different patterns of emotion, even in response to the same situations. Women tend to express emotions more freely and recognize emotions more accurately than men.

KEY TERMS

motivation, p. 250
intrinsic motivation, p. 250
extrinsic motivation, p. 250
incentive, p. 250
instinct, p. 252
instinct theory, p. 252
drive reduction theory, p. 252
homeostasis, p. 252
arousal theory, p. 252
Yerkes–Dodson law, p. 252
self-determination theory, p. 253
regulatory focus theory, p. 254
achievement goal theory, p. 255
hierarchy of needs, p. 256
self-actualization, p. 257
peak experience, p. 257
flow, p. 257
body mass index (BMI), p. 260
overweight, p. 260
obesity, p. 260
leptin, p. 262
ghrelin, p. 263
set point, p. 263
metabolic rate (metabolism), p. 264
emotion, p. 271
James–Lange theory, p. 271
Cannon–Bard theory, p. 272
Schachter–Singer theory, p. 273
cognitive appraisal theory, p. 273
facial feedback theory, p. 274
emotion regulation, p. 280
display rules, p. 284

SELF-ASSESSMENT

1. A 7-year-old basketball player plays for the love of the game. A veteran professional basketball player plays for the money it brings. The 7-year-old is motivated by _____. The pro is motivated by _____.
   a. intrinsic motivation; intrinsic motivation
   b. extrinsic motivation; extrinsic motivation
   c. intrinsic motivation; extrinsic motivation
   d. extrinsic motivation; intrinsic motivation

2. _____ is a theory of motivation stating that the strongest and healthiest motivations are those that are autonomous, or come from within yourself.
   a. Self-determination theory
   b. Achievement goal theory
   c. Arousal theory
   d. Drive reduction theory

3. Kianna's primary motivation in life is to find a close group of friends and a dating partner to whom she feels truly connected. According to Maslow's hierarchy of needs, Kianna is focused on _____ needs.

a. physiological
b. self-actualization
c. self-transcendence
d. belongingness and love

4. Body mass index indicates overall fitness level and amount of body fat. To determine body mass index, which of the following pieces of information is necessary?

a. Weight only
b. Height and weight
c. Height, weight, and ethnicity
d. Height, weight, ethnicity, and age

5. Jonathan is a middle-aged adult who is obese. As Jonathan gets older, if he remains obese he will be at high risk for

a. physical problems, including diabetes.
b. psychological problems, including anxiety and dementia.
c. both a and b.
d. neither a nor b.

6. Which of the following is true about the hormones leptin and ghrelin?

a. They signal feelings related to fullness and hunger.
b. They signal feelings related to fear and relaxation.
c. They control sleep and wakefulness.
d. Leptin triggers self-actualization; ghrelin triggers self-transcendence.

7. Hannah has a difficult time losing weight no matter how little she eats. Tianna has a difficult time gaining weight no matter how much she eats. In terms of biology, it is likely that Hannah and Tianna have different _____.

8. Which of these choices best describes the concept of display rules?

a. Display rules influence the amount of food people eat when they are with other people.
b. Display rules influence the way people dress when they exercise in front of other people.
c. Display rules influence the extent to which fast food restaurants show people photos of the food they sell.
d. Display rules influence the way people from diverse groups express emotion.

9. _____ theory is a theory of emotion stating that you experience emotion by simultaneously becoming aware of bodily changes and feelings.

10. Which of the following are emotion regulation strategies?

a. Cognitive change and response modulation
b. Situation selection and situation modification
c. Both a and b
d. Neither a nor b

To check your understanding of these questions, click show the answers in the e-book or refer to the answers in Appendix B.

Research shows quizzing is a highly effective learning tool. Continue quizzing yourself using LearningCurve, the system that adapts to *your* learning.

WHAT'S YOUR TAKE?

1. When have you had peak experiences? When have you experienced flow? What kinds of activities facilitate these experiences for you? Are they planned or spontaneous? Do they involve other people, or just you? How can you experience more peak experiences and flow in the future?

SHOW ME MORE

8.1 Derek Redmond and His Father Cross the Finish Line

http://tiny.cc/showmemore2e

This video shows the emotion and motivation that the opening page of this chapter describes: sprinter Derek Redmond's famous moment from the 1992 Olympics, including his father's efforts to help his injured son reach the finish line.

PASCAL PAVANI/AFP/Getty Images

This video is hosted by a third-party Web site (source). For accessible content requests, please reach out to the publisher of that site.

8.2 Obesity Guidelines Move Away from Focus on Weight Loss

This video explains how some health professionals are changing the ways they understand and help people address obesity-related problems.

MoMo Productions/DigitalVision/Getty Images

8.3 Serving Size Versus What You Really Eat

http://tiny.cc/showmemore2e

In this video, see the difference between the serving size listed on the packages of popular foods and the amount that many people actually eat.

Pamela D. Maxwell/Shutterstock.com

This video is hosted by a third-party Web site (source). For accessible content requests, please reach out to the publisher of that site.

8.4 My Psychology Podcast

This podcast episode features the author of this textbook, psychologist Andy Pomerantz, speaking with other instructors of introductory psychology courses about the most important and interesting concepts in this chapter.

Macmillan Learning

9 Development Across the Life Span

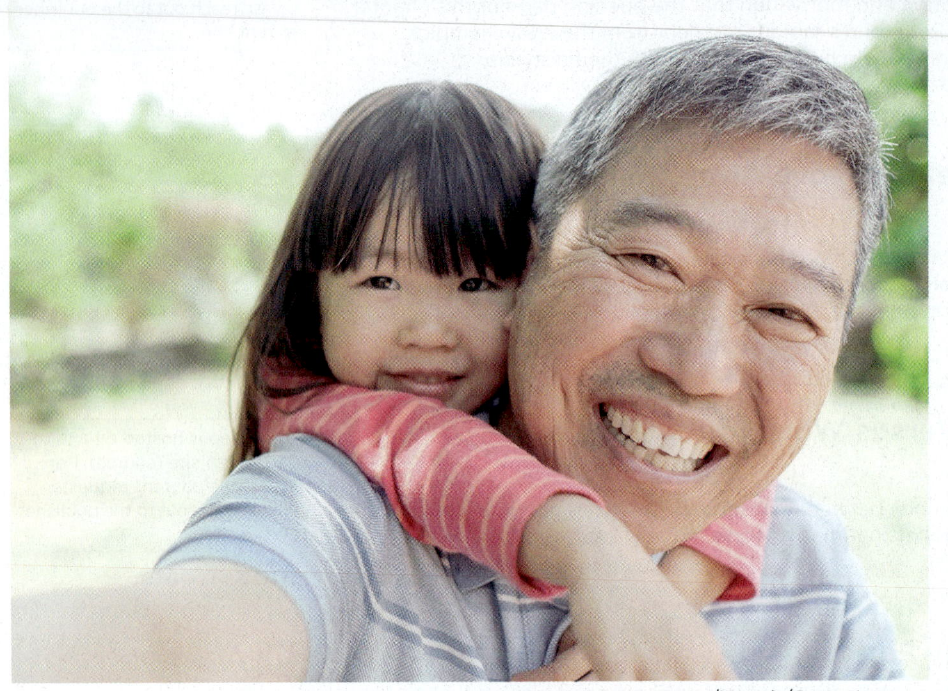

PonyWang/iStock/Getty Images

CHAPTER OUTLINE

Some of my favorite TV episodes are the ones that feature flashbacks and flashforwards—those moments when we see the characters we know so well at different times in their lives. In *black-ish*, we glimpse scenes of Bow's and Dre's childhoods—long before they found each other, got married, and started a family. In *Orange Is the New Black*, we see the characters in scenes as children or teens, years before the criminal activity that would land them in prison. *Friends* shows us high school versions of Ross, Rachel, and the rest of the group. *The Simpsons* is full of scenes imagining Homer, Marge, Bart, Lisa, and Maggie at some point in the distant past or distant future. *This Is Us* frequently shifts the timeframe in which we see Randall, Kevin, Kate, and other members of the Pearson family navigate through their lives. *Breaking Bad, Westworld, Jane the Virgin,* and *The Walking Dead* are among the other TV shows that tell their characters' stories by offering a peek into their lives at various ages.

Flashbacks and flashforwards have a distinct power: to show how people *develop* the course of their lives. Development over a lifetime is exactly what developmental psychologists study and what we will examine in this chapter. We will explore the theories and research that developmental psychologists use to explain how our bodies, brains, and relationships transform as we move through life. First, we'll consider some of the big issues relevant to development at any age, like the impact of nature and nurture on development, whether development happens gradually or in spurts, and whether anything about us stays the same amid all of these developmental changes. Then, we'll move chronologically through the life span and examine what happens along the way, from the prenatal months through infancy, childhood, and adolescence. We'll look at the phases of adulthood too, from its emergence to the end of the life cycle.

Big Questions about Developmental Psychology

YOU WILL LEARN:

9.1 what developmental psychology is.

9.2 the difference between cross-sectional and longitudinal research designs.

9.3 what developmental psychology's three big questions are.

Developmental psychology is the study of the changes to body, mind, and interpersonal interaction that people experience across the life span. The phrase "across the life span" means that development happens at every age. Early in the history of the field, developmental psychologists focused almost exclusively on children, with the assumption that when people reached adulthood, development was done. In fact, in 1890, psychology pioneer William James said that "for most of us, by age 30, the character has set like plaster and will never soften again" (James, 1890, p. 124). In recent decades, the focus of developmental psychology has changed drastically (Bennett, 1999; Cairns & Cairns, 2006). Kids still receive lots of attention from developmental psychologists, but adults now do as well (Bennett, 1999; Cairns & Cairns, 2006; Lerner, 2006; Orth & Robins, 2019; Overton, 2006, 2010).

Developmental psychologists focus on how people change over time. To examine these changes, they design their studies in two distinct ways, each with its own benefits: *cross-sectional designs* and *longitudinal designs*. A **cross-sectional design** is a research design in which people of different ages are compared to each other at the same point in time. By contrast, a **longitudinal design** is a research design in which the same group of people is compared to itself at different points in time (**Table 9.1**). As an example, consider Dr. Khan, a developmental psychologist who is interested in how digital literacy — basically, how tech-savvy a person is — changes as people get older. The quickest way to answer that question would be for Dr. Khan to design a cross-sectional study in which she measures the digital literacy of people who are, say, 10, 30, 50, 70, and 90 years old *right now*. The quickness of the study is the main upside of the cross-sectional design. It provides an immediate answer to the research question without having to wait until people actually get older.

Of course, the longitudinal design has an upside too: higher validity, or a better chance of measuring what the study actually intends to measure (Little et al., 2009). If Dr. Khan designed a longitudinal study, she would measure the digital literacy of people who are 10 years old right now, and then measure digital literacy of *the same people* again at 30, 50, 70, and 90 years old. By doing so, researchers can notice *cohort effects*, or unique influences on certain groups of people because of their common age (Cavanaugh & Whitbourne, 2003). Your childhood may have been full of computers, tablets, and smartphones, but the childhood of someone 25 or 50 years older than you probably wasn't. Each generation moves through history at a distinctive point in time, and its members form a *cohort* whose experiences are unlike those of any other generation. A cross-sectional study that simultaneously compares your generation to the generations that are 25 and 50 years older than you might make it look like digital literacy drops drastically across the life span, but that drop may be a *cohort effect* rather than true development. A longitudinal study, even though it takes many years, could account for cohort effects.

developmental psychology
The study of the changes to body, mind, and interpersonal interaction that people experience across the life span.

cross-sectional design
A research design in which people of different ages are compared to each other at the same point in time.

longitudinal design
A research design in which the same group of people is compared to itself at different points in time.

TABLE 9.1: Cross-Sectional Versus Longitudinal Design

	CROSS-SECTIONAL DESIGNS	LONGITUDINAL DESIGNS
Advantages	• Can be done quickly • Since data is collected only once from each participant, no concerns about dropout	• Not vulnerable to cohort effects negatively affecting validity
Disadvantages	• Vulnerable to cohort effects negatively affecting validity	• Takes a long time • Some original participants drop out • Often expensive

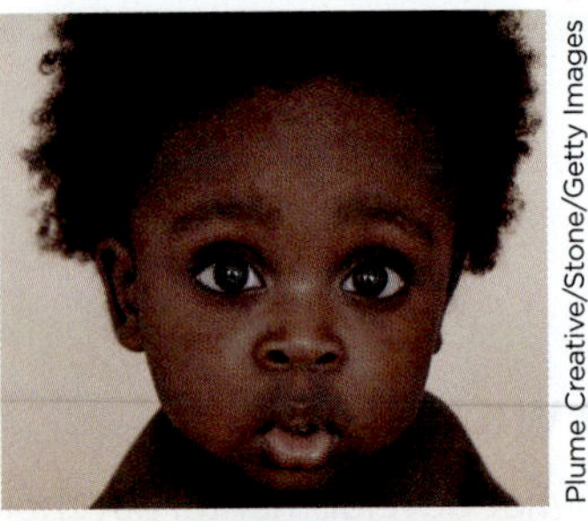
Plume Creative/Stone/Getty Images

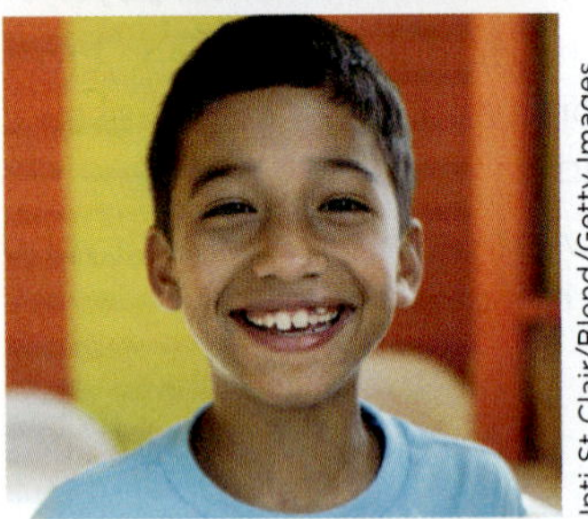
Inti St Clair/Blend/Getty Images

massimo colombo/Moment/Getty Images

diego cervo/iStock/Getty Images

Developmental psychology is the study of the changes to body, mind, and interpersonal interaction that people experience across the life span.

Of course, not all longitudinal studies are decades long — some last just a few months or years — but the benefits of tracking the same group of people through time are similar regardless of length.

Developmental psychologists conduct lots of cross-sectional studies *and* lots of longitudinal studies (Card & Little, 2007). However, they also use other research methods, from observing babies and making educated guesses about their thoughts and feelings to using MRIs to see how the brain changes over time (Bornstein, 1999; Paus, 2009; Perrin et al., 2008). Regardless of how research is conducted, developmental psychologists often focus on a few big questions: *stability versus change*, *stage development versus continuous development*, and *nature versus nurture* (Lerner et al., 2005).

Stability Versus Change

As we get older, how much do we change, and how much do we stay the same? We do plenty of both, of course (Bleidorn & Hopwood, 2019; Magnusson & Stattin, 2006; Orth & Luciano, 2018; Roberts et al., 2003). Think of relatives or friends you see only once in a while. You probably notice new developments as they get older — not just how they look, but also how they think, react, and interact with others — and you probably notice qualities that stay the same year after year. For example, a 4-year-old boy who sings and dances in his own homemade talent shows at every family get-together might become a 14-year-old adolescent who acts in school plays and sings in the choir. At both ages, the core characteristic of attention-seeking through performance drives his behavior. But he may show changes in his behavior as well. For example, perhaps the attention-seeking increases or decreases in intensity, or his ways of showing it shift.

Stage Development Versus Continuous Development

When we change, do we change suddenly or gradually? The way a caterpillar changes into a butterfly provides a good example of sudden — or *stage* — development (**Figure 9.1**). The caterpillar stays a caterpillar for quite a while, then abruptly transforms into a butterfly, staying in that form for the rest of its life. Developmental psychologists point to certain changes — the bodily changes of puberty, for example — as being stage developments. Children have child bodies for the first 11–13 years or so, then enter the brief cocoon of adolescence in which the body rapidly transforms into its adult version. However, many of the changes that people go through are more gradual than puberty. For example, our decline in intelligence (as discussed in Chapter 7) doesn't happen overnight, but little by little during the latter half of adulthood. This decline in intelligence is an example of *continuous* development.

Nature Versus Nurture

The nature versus nurture question, which is central to the entire field of psychology, holds a prominent place in developmental psychology (Beauchaine et al., 2008).

FIGURE 9.1 Stage Development Versus Continuous Development. One of the major questions for developmental psychologists is whether people develop in stages or continuously. Stage development is like running your hand up a staircase — it stays level for a while, then suddenly jumps up to a new level, then stays at that level for a while. Continuous development is like running your hand up a ramp — steady, slow movement upward.

What determines how we change over time: an inborn genetic blueprint that unfolds inevitably (nature), or the influences of the people and the world around us (nurture)? Of course, an interaction of nature and nurture underlies most of the changes we experience (Ehrlich & Feldman, 2003; Kandler & Zapko-Willmes, 2017; Marcus, 2004). We are born with certain personality characteristics (nature), but those characteristics are affected by powerful experiences (nurture) (Wrzus & Roberts, 2017). For example, people whose long-term jobs and relationships bring satisfaction show increases in emotional stability, while the opposite is true of people whose long-term jobs and relationships bring them aggravation (Roberts, 1997; Roberts et al., 2003; Robins et al., 2002).

DIVERSITY MATTERS

The influence of nurture on our development often depends greatly on the cultural circumstances in which we live (Cole, 2005; Fung, 2011; Quintana, 2011; Schlegel, 2009). For example, the ability to do math problems develops, to some extent, according to the type of math that our culture demands of us. Children in Brazil who work as street vendors are experts in the type of math that job requires – on-the-fly, in-your-head addition, subtraction, and multiplication. They often have trouble, however, doing written math problems that tap into the same types of calculations (Carraher et al., 1985; Sternberg, 2011).

DIVERSITY MATTERS

As another example of cultural influence on development, consider this question: at what age do children begin to sleep in their own bed rather than the same bed as their parent(s)? For many in the United States, the answer may seem obvious: immediately. Babies have their own cribs in their own rooms when they come home from the hospital. In fact, babies even sleep in a separate crib for those first days *in* the hospital. In many other parts of the world (and for some in the United States), however, the "family bed" is the norm (Alexeyeff, 2013; Shweder et al., 1995, 2006). Specifically, young kids and parents co-sleeping is common in many parts of Asia, Africa, and Central America. Members of these families often prefer this even when there are other beds available in other rooms. Some longitudinal studies find that young children who co-sleep are just as well-adjusted and well-behaved later in childhood or adolescence as their peers who sleep separately from their parents (Beijers, 2018; Okami et al., 2002). Other studies, especially those citing risk of injury or death (via suffocation) of infants in bed with adults, offer more negative recommendations (Chen et al., 2018; Goldberg & Keller, 2007).

**Note about terminology: throughout this chapter, you'll see the word "parent" many times in different forms (parents, parenting, etc.), just as you would if you read many of the research studies cited in the chapter. When you come across these words, please keep in mind that the people who fill "parent" roles for some children often include a wide range of caregivers, not only mothers and fathers.*

CHECK YOUR LEARNING:

9.1 What is developmental psychology?

9.2 What is the difference between cross-sectional and longitudinal research designs?

9.3 What are the three big questions for developmental psychologists?

To check your understanding of these questions, click show the answers or refer to the answers in the Chapter Summary.

Development Before Birth

As we start our exploration of development across the life span, we start well before the baby's grand entrance. Lots of important developmental events take place during pregnancy.

YOU WILL LEARN:

9.4 about the sequence of prenatal development.

9.5 what teratogens are.

9.6 what fetal alcohol syndrome is.

Conception

You probably don't need your psychology textbook to tell you how conception typically happens, but here's a quick refresher: About midway through a woman's menstrual cycle, her body ovulates, or releases an ovum (egg) capable of being fertilized. If she

Zygote	Embryo	Fetus
First two weeks after fertilization	Two weeks to two months after fertilization	Two months after fertilization to birth

FIGURE 9.2 Stages of Prenatal Development. The stages of prenatal development progress from zygote to embryo to fetus.

has sexual intercourse with a man during that time, the sperm contained in his ejaculation — hundreds of millions of them — race toward the egg. As the leading sperm (it only takes one) reaches the egg, it passes through the egg's outer layer, and within hours, the nucleus of the sperm joins with the nucleus of the egg to form a new single cell. At this point, conception has occurred, and this new cell will double millions of times over the next 9 months to develop a human baby.

From the moment the sperm and egg merge into a new single cell, that cell typically contains 46 chromosomes, 23 from the egg and 23 from the sperm. As the cells multiply, every cell contains the same set of chromosomes. Each chromosome contains deoxyribonucleic acid, or *DNA*. The DNA contains the *genes*, which drive every aspect of development through the life span.

Prenatal Development

Different terms describe the organism at various points during prenatal development (**Figure 9.2**). The first term is **zygote**: the prenatal human organism from the moment the egg is fertilized by sperm to about 2 weeks. At that point, we begin to use the term **embryo**: the prenatal human organism from about 2 weeks to about 2 months after conception. For the remainder of the pregnancy, we use the term **fetus**: the prenatal human organism from about 2 months after conception to birth.

zygote
The prenatal human organism from the moment the egg is fertilized by sperm to about 2 weeks.

embryo
The prenatal human organism from about 2 weeks to about 2 months after conception.

fetus
The prenatal human organism from about 2 months after conception to birth.

Zygotes don't always reach the embryo stage. (In many of these cases, women at this early stage of pregnancy will not know they have conceived.) Among the zygotes that do survive, a few divide into two (for reasons that are not entirely clear). Each of these new zygotes develops into a separate embryo, fetus, and eventually baby. You know these pairs as identical twins, but the more scientific name is *monozygotic twins*, with *mono-* referring to the fact that they started as one zygote. In contrast, fraternal (or nonidentical) twins are *dizygotic twins*, with *di-* referring to the fact that they started as two separate zygotes — that is, two eggs fertilized by two sperm.

During the embryonic period, the cells specialize more than they had during the zygotic period. Each cell is devoted to a specific body part, beginning with the most essential, such as the spinal cord, heart, and brain. Facial features and arms and legs start to develop too. Assuming that no complications arise, the formation of a fully functioning human body is well under way.

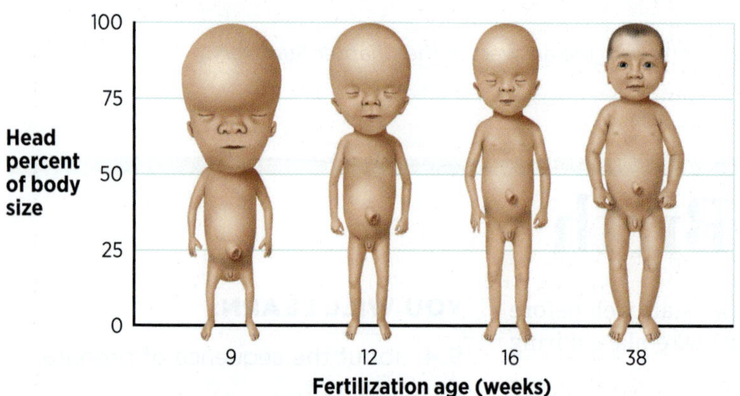

FIGURE 9.3 The Fetus Takes Shape. At the beginning of the fetal period of prenatal development, the head comprises about 50% of the fetus' length. As the weeks go by, that percentage decreases to about 25%.

During the fetal period — the last 7 months or so of pregnancy — the sheer increase in size is extraordinary. Around the end of the embryonic period (about 2 months into pregnancy), the embryo has a length of just 1 inch and a weight of just 1 ounce. The size of a newborn baby carried to a full 9-month term is typically 20 inches long and 7–8 pounds! Along with this tremendous growth in size, the fetus' internal organs begin to function more independently. The fetus starts moving around too, with the mother feeling an increasing number of friendly kicks (Hepper, 2003). The ratios of the various body parts also change (as **Figure 9.3** illustrates): the legs and torso stretch out quite a bit, making the head seem less oversized in comparison to the rest of the body (Adolph & Berger, 2005).

Another fascinating finding about fetuses: they pay attention and respond to what happens around them. We know this because researchers have studied fetuses' *habituation*, the tendency to ignore stimuli that repeat or stay constant (as discussed in Chapter 3). How did researchers study this? They played specific sounds through small speakers placed on the pregnant mom's belly near the fetus' head. Using the same ultrasound technology that allows parents-to-be to know which sex to expect, they observed the fetuses' reactions. At first, the fetuses responded noticeably, by blinking or moving their arms or legs. But eventually, after hearing the sounds repeatedly, they no longer responded – the same way you might learn to disregard a false car alarm (Bellieni et al., 2005; Hepper et al., 2012; Joy et al., 2012; Leader, 2016). Fetuses even showed a memory for the sound to which they had habituated by not responding as strongly when they were reintroduced to it after a delay of several weeks (Dirix et al., 2009).

Teratogens: Dangers in the Womb

A **teratogen** is any substance that harms the embryo or fetus. Teratogens can enter the pregnant woman's body in many forms (Fryer et al., 2008; Georgieff et al., 2018; Holbrook & Rayburn, 2014):

- Drugs that can be abused, like alcohol, nicotine, tobacco, amphetamines, opioids, or cocaine
- Prescription drugs, like the acne drug Accutane and many others
- Environmental pollution, like pesticides, mercury, and lead
- Diseases, like chickenpox, rubella, Zika, and other viruses

Teratogens can cause a wide range of physical and psychological problems, including cognitive difficulties, physical disabilities, congenital disabilities, sensory difficulties, memory difficulties, and disruptive behavior. Because some women are unaware of their pregnancy until well into the embryonic stage, they may expose themselves to teratogens without realizing they are pregnant at the time. This is true particularly in unplanned pregnancies, which constitute more than half of the pregnancies in the United States (Finer & Zolna, 2011).

By far, the most studied teratogen is alcohol (Jones & Streissguth, 2010; Popova et al., 2017). The most hazardous consequence of alcohol during pregnancy is **fetal alcohol syndrome**: a pattern of physical and behavioral difficulties common in people whose mothers drank alcohol excessively during pregnancy. Fetal alcohol syndrome affects about 1 per 1000 children, but *fetal alcohol effects* – basically a less extreme version of fetal alcohol syndrome – affect another 9 per 1000. (Some researchers combine all consequences arising from alcohol consumption during pregnancy into the broader term *fetal alcohol spectrum disorder* [Lange et al., 2018].) Fetal alcohol syndrome involves a number of physical characteristics that include small size, both before and well after birth. There is also a distinct set of facial features, including small eyes, a thin upper lip, and a near absence of the groove between the bottom of the nose and the upper lip.

The psychological and behavioral features of fetal alcohol syndrome are actually often far more problematic than the physical features (Popova et al, 2016; Riley & McGee, 2005). One study found that 87% of children with fetal alcohol syndrome were diagnosable with a mental disorder (O'Connor et al., 2002). The most common disorders are attention-deficit/hyperactivity disorder (ADHD), oppositional-defiant disorder, conduct disorder, anxiety, and depression (Fryer et al., 2007; Weyrauch et al., 2017). Many of these disorders are associated with disruptive or illegal behavior, so it may come as no surprise that among people with juvenile delinquency issues, 23% have fetal alcohol syndrome or fetal alcohol effects. For comparison, among the general population, only 1% have either fetal alcohol syndrome or fetal alcohol effects (Fast et al., 1999; Fast & Conry, 2004). In addition to psychological disorders, kids with fetal alcohol syndrome also show many school-related difficulties, including difficulties with attention, memory, mathematical abilities, and language development (Fast & Conry, 2009; Mattson & Riley, 1998; Meintjes et al., 2010).

What happens to kids with fetal alcohol syndrome? Do they grow out of it?

CHAPTER APP 9.1

Pregnancy Tracker – BabyCenter

The "Pregnancy Tracker – BabyCenter" app is one of many apps for expectant parents that provides developmental information about pregnancy. It explains (often with photos or videos) what's typical at each week and month, such as the size of the fetus. It even offers developmental information for the first year of the baby's life. It offers advice for a healthy pregnancy, including what to seek out and what to avoid. Users can also connect with each other to provide information and support.

How does it APPly to your daily life?
If you (or someone close to you) were expecting or were parenting a baby, would this app help you? If so, what specific benefits would it provide?

How does it APPly to your understanding of psychology?
How could the information provided by this app help you appreciate development before birth (including teratogens and fetal alcohol syndrome) and during infancy?

To learn more about this app or to download it to your phone, you can search for "Pregnancy Tracker BabyCenter" on Google, in the iPhone App store, or in the Google Play store.

teratogen
Any substance that harms the embryo or fetus.

fetal alcohol syndrome
A pattern of physical and behavioral difficulties common in people whose mothers drank alcohol excessively during pregnancy.

Kids with fetal alcohol syndrome often don't outgrow their psychological or behavioral difficulties. Research has found that 92% of adults with fetal alcohol syndrome were diagnosable with a mental illness, most often drug problems, alcohol problems, or depression (Barr et al., 2006; Famy et al., 1998). The difficulties that made schoolwork especially challenging in childhood also tend to persist and cause problems in adulthood.

More recently, researchers have turned their attention to another teratogen on the rise: methamphetamines, or "meth." Results of their studies indicate that meth may do as much damage as alcohol, and possibly more. Children of women who used meth during pregnancy have at least double the risk for behavior difficulties by the time they are just 5 years old, including ADHD, disruptive or rule-breaking behavior, and social withdrawal (LaGasse et al., 2012; Twomey et al., 2013). These kids also show significant shortcomings in controlling their emotions and actions, paying attention, solving problems, and using short-term memory (Abar et al., 2013).

A final note about teratogens: Education is the key. Teaching everyone, especially women who are pregnant (or could become pregnant), about the substances that could cause serious, lifelong problems for their children is essential to reducing the teratogen risk (Conover & Polifka, 2011; Shahin & Einarson, 2011). Along the same lines, doing healthy things to combat the effects of teratogens helps women who are pregnant (or could become pregnant). For example, folic acid (which is contained in many green vegetables, like spinach and broccoli, and can also be taken as a supplement) has been shown to reduce the risk of disabilities and difficulties evident from birth (Hernández-Díaz et al., 2000).

CHECK YOUR LEARNING:

9.4 What is the sequence of prenatal development?

9.5 What are teratogens?

9.6 What is fetal alcohol syndrome?

To check your understanding of these questions, click show the answers or refer to the answers in the Chapter Summary.

Infancy and Childhood

YOU WILL LEARN:

9.7 what abilities newborns have.

9.8 how physical development proceeds through predictable stages.

9.9 how, according to Piaget, children develop schemas (or mental categories) and either assimilate new information into them or accommodate the schemas to account for the new information.

9.10 how, according to Piaget, children develop through cognitive stages.

For developmental psychologists, a new bundle of joy is a new bundle of research opportunities. To learn about what infants think and feel, developmental psychologists often rely on *inferences*, educated guesses based on what babies *can* communicate (Bornstein, 1999; Cohen & Cashon, 2006). Developmental psychologists infer that a particular behavior by a baby — for example, how long they stare at something, their facial expressions and actions, or whether they cry — tells us something about the workings of their mind. As we consider studies that rely on inference, keep in mind that this approach requires researchers to take some logical leaps, so it's far from perfect. With babies, however, it is the best we can do. (We certainly can't expect them to fill out surveys about their beliefs or explain their behaviors in an interview with a researcher!)

The Abilities of Newborns

Brand-new babies can do a lot. For starters, all five senses work remarkably well from day one (Bornstein et al., 2005). A baby's ability to smell is particularly impressive. When researchers placed foods that people generally like (such as butter or bananas) near the noses of newborns, the babies gave them a smile. However, when the researchers presented rotten eggs, the babies gave them a "yucky" face (Steiner, 1977).

In another study, researchers had the mothers of 2-week-old babies, as well as other women, sleep with gauze pads under their arms. The next day, they gave each baby a "smell test" by placing the mother's gauze pad and the other woman's gauze pad near the baby's head. Then, researchers measured how long the baby turned its head toward each gauze pad. Consistently, the babies turned toward the mother's gauze pad, which contained the mother's odor, for much longer than the non-mother's gauze pad. Researchers interpreted this finding as an ability to distinguish odors and show a preference for one smell over the other (Cernoch & Porter, 1985). In a more recent study of premature newborns ("preemies"), those whose noses were stimulated with the smell of cinnamon switched from their feeding tube to breastfeeding more quickly and went home sooner than their peers who had no such stimulation (Van et al., 2018).

Newborn babies' vision isn't as sharp as their sense of smell, but it is good enough for the important (to them) stuff. Babies can't focus at every distance, but they can focus quite well at objects about 8–12 inches away — the very distance between baby's face and the face of the person holding and feeding them (Slater & Johnson, 1998). Within a few days of birth, babies prefer their mother's face to the faces of other women — a finding that researchers inferred from the fact that they stare longer at mom's face (Bushnell, 2001; Bushnell et al., 1989; Pascalis et al., 1995; Sugden & Marquis, 2017; Sugden & Moulson, 2018). Babies have other preferences regarding faces too: open eyes over closed eyes, attractive over unattractive, and direct eye contact over no eye contact (Reynolds & Roth, 2018). Actually, newborn babies prefer looking at faces of any kind over looking at other types of images, even within the first few hours of their lives (Legerstee, 1992; Opfer & Gelman, 2011). Specifically, their eyes follow a moving face-like image for a longer period of time than they follow a moving image resembling a scrambled or blank face (**Figure 9.4**). This finding was discovered in babies as young as 9 *minutes* old (Fantz et al., 1975; Goren et al., 1975; Johnson et al., 1991; Mondloch et al., 1999; Nelson et al., 2006; Rakison & Poulin-Dubois, 2001; Valenza et al., 1996).

In terms of hearing, newborns are born with limited but essential abilities. They can tell the difference between their mother's voice and the voices of other women. Researchers came to this conclusion by measuring the rate at which babies suck on a pacifier-like device when hearing different voices. They suck faster when hearing the voice of their mom than for a stranger's voice (DeCasper & Fifer, 1980; DeCasper & Spence, 1986). Newborns can also make sense of combined hearing and visual sensory experiences. In one study, researchers showed a brief video to babies who were less than a week old. On the left side of the screen, a ball moved toward the baby; at the same time, on the right side, an identical ball moved away from the baby. The video's sound either increased or decreased in volume as the ball moved. As you

9.11 about the ways researchers have challenged some of Piaget's conclusions.

9.12 about the three distinct types of attachment and why secure attachment to others is so important.

9.13 about different types of parenting styles.

9.14 what temperament is and how it can affect parent-child relationships.

SelectStock/Vetta/Getty Images

Newborn babies have strong sensory abilities. For example, at just 2 weeks of age, a baby can distinguish the smell of their own mother from the smell of other women (Cernoch & Porter, 1985).

FIGURE 9.4 What Newborn Babies See. Just minutes after birth, babies stare longer at the figure on the left than the figure on the right, which suggests that they can tell the difference between face-like images and other images.

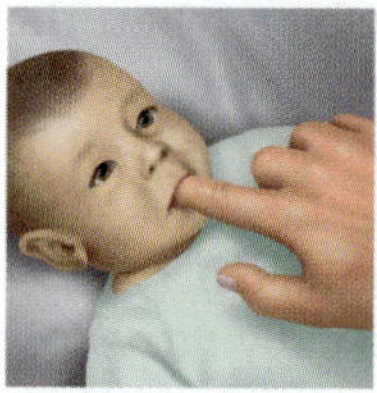

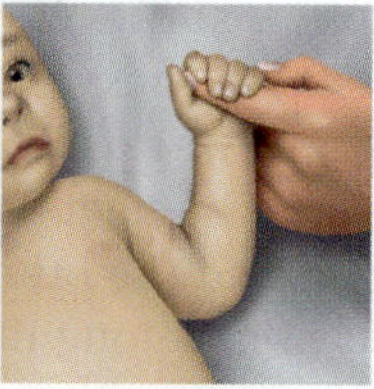

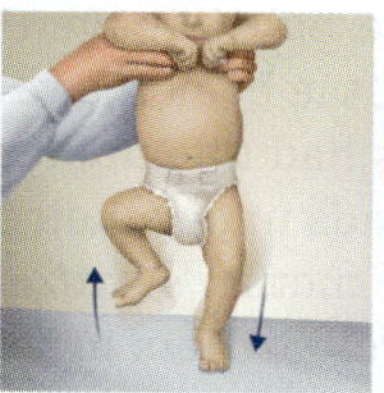

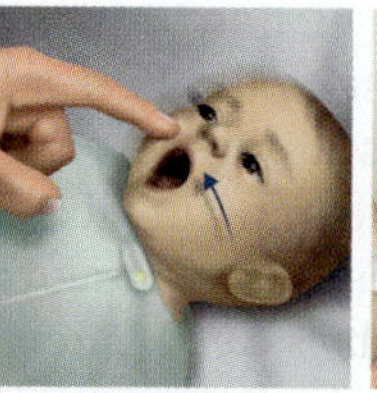

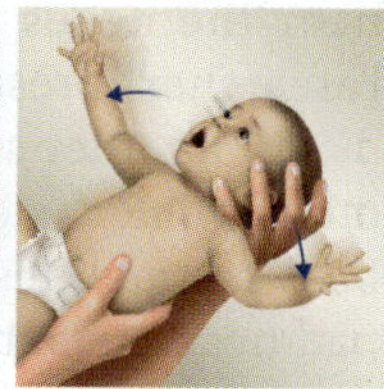

FIGURE 9.5 The Reflexes of Newborns. Newborn babies exhibit many reflexes, including sucking, grasping, stepping, rooting (turning their heads and opening their mouths when an object touches the cheek), and the Moro reflex (flinging arms outward when startled).

might expect, babies looked longer at the ball moving toward them when the volume went up, but longer at the ball moving away from them when the volume went down. That is, the babies looked longer at the ball that matched the change in volume (Orioli et al., 2018). (To try this task yourself, see Show Me More 9.1 at the end of the chapter.)

Beyond their sensory abilities, babies can do lots of other things. They exhibit a variety of reflexes, as shown in **Figure 9.5**. Babies *suck* when a nipple (or fingertip, or almost anything) is placed inside their mouths. They *grasp* when a finger is placed in their palms and *step* with their legs when they are held upright with their feet touching the ground. Babies *root* (turn their heads and open their mouths) when an object brushes one of their cheeks. They also fling their arms out in response to a sudden surprise, a reaction called the *Moro reflex* (Adolph & Berger, 2005; Kisilevsky et al., 1991; von Hofsten, 2003). And of course, we're all very familiar with babies' ability to cry to make their needs known. Clearly, babies' brains and bodies function at an impressive level as soon as they arrive.

Physical Development

At some point in your life, someone has probably said to you, "Wow, I can't believe how much you've grown!" The physical development that takes place during infancy and childhood is remarkable. Let's consider three facets of that physical development: brain development, sensory development, and motor development.

Brain Development. In the first 3 years of life, a child's brain triples in weight. It continues growing at a slower pace until about age 10. Between a child's first and second birthdays, the number of synapses (connections between neurons) increases by 40,000 *per second*, for a total of about 1 quadrillion through early childhood (Zelazo & Lee, 2010).

This exuberant formation and connection of neurons occurs in a predictable order. The first surge takes place in the visual cortex, followed by the areas of the brain that help with hearing and language. Eventually, the prefrontal cortex develops, which enables thought, planning, and problem solving (Huttenlocher & Dabholkar, 1997). The neurons in the frontal lobe that shape the memory system take a while longer to fully develop, which explains *infantile amnesia*, our inability to remember what happened to us before ages 2–4 (Bauer et al., 2011; Madsen & Kim, 2016; Schneider, 2011).

Nature may drive the development of the young brain, but nurture steers it. The experiences a child has during these early years affect the way a child's brain grows (Cole, 2006; Le Grand et al., 2001; Maurer et al., 2005). For example, researchers examined the visual abilities of people who, as very young children, were successfully treated for serious vision problems such as severe cataracts (Le Grand et al., 2004).

Their ability to see human faces accurately later in life still fell far below normal. The reason is that *prior* to their treatment, their lack of visual stimulation caused the vision-related areas of the brain to be underdeveloped, and those brain areas never entirely caught up.

Similarly, a baby's babbling contains the basic sounds of every human language, but within the first years of life, babies typically hear only one language (or perhaps two or three, which would still be a very small portion of the thousands that exist). As a result, the wiring in their brain for that one language gets strengthened while the unused parts fall away. The neurons and synapses go through a natural *pruning* process, in much the same way that a gardener might prune certain branches of a bush but allow others to grow larger and more complex (Kuhl, 2004; Nelson et al., 2006). That is also why young children are so much better at picking up new languages than adults — their pruning process isn't complete yet, so they still have the "branches" to enable the new connections in their brains.

A series of classic experiments highlight the impact of environment on brain development (e.g., Diamond et al., 1966, 1975; Globus et al., 1973; Krech et al., 1966; Renner & Rosenzweig, 1987; Rosenzweig et al., 1962). In the 1960s and 1970s, a group of researchers placed young rats in either an *enriched environment* or an *impoverished environment*. The enriched environment featured a wide array of things to see, hear, and do, along with some other rats with whom to interact. The impoverished environment featured nothing besides food and water — no sights, no sounds, no activities, and no rat buddies. The researchers examined the brains of all these rats and found that rats from the enriched environments showed enriched brain wiring — including more neurons, bigger neurons, and more synaptic connections between neurons. The greatest effect happens at the youngest ages, but more recent studies have demonstrated that even older rats' brains can be affected by the amount of stimulation in the environment (Kempermann et al., 1997; Song et al., 2005; van Praag et al., 2000). Perhaps it should be no surprise that the brains of children who grow up in poverty, where the environment is often more impoverished, develop significantly less fully than the brains of their more financially fortunate peers (Hair et al., 2015; Johnson et al., 2016; Kim et al., 2019).

FROM RESEARCH TO REAL LIFE

A Well-Running Brain

Research on enriched environments versus impoverished environments provides clear evidence that activity — especially exercise — physically enhances the brains of rats. What about the brains of people? Do our brains respond the same way when we keep ourselves active?

A growing body of research suggests that physical exercise increases the physical condition of the human brain (Voss et al., 2011). One study randomly assigned 120 older adults to one of two groups: 60 walked at a moderate pace 3 days a week for up to 40 minutes, and the other 60 simply stretched instead. Researchers found that the hippocampus, which is closely linked to memory and which shrinks with age, actually increased in size by 2% in the walkers but not in the stretchers (Erickson et al., 2011). Other studies have found that the volume of the whole brain increases in older adults who participate in moderate aerobic exercise walking — again, a finding that runs counter to the typical course of brain development (Colcombe et al., 2006; Erickson & Kramer, 2009). In addition to a sheer increase in brain size, older adults also show increased connections between different regions of their brains after a year of walking exercise (Voss et al., 2010).

These physical improvements in the brain translate into improvements in day-to-day brain function as well (Bray et al., 2021; Chen et al., 2020; Zhang et al., 2021). For example, 6 months of a regular exercise regimen (4 days a week, 45–60 minutes a day on a treadmill, bike, or elliptical machine) boosted the memory, attention, and processing speed of older adults. A control group who participated in stretching classes for the same amount of time showed no such gains (Baker et al., 2010). This result is typical. A meta-analysis that combined the results of 29 studies and over 2000 participants, age 18 and over, found that memory, attention, and processing speed all improve with aerobic exercise (Smith et al., 2010).

Researchers suggest that the positive effects could be maximized by linking physical exercise to cognitive activity (Fabel & Kempermann, 2008; Gheysen et al., 2018). Rather than mindless time on a treadmill (like a mouse on a running wheel), exercise accompanied by social interaction (like walking while talking with friends) or a cognitive challenge (like reading a thought-provoking article while riding a stationary bike) is likely to be most beneficial to the brain.

LIFE HACK 9.1

To maximize the functioning of your brain, exercise your body.

(Smith et al., 2010 ; Voss et al., 2011)

Sensory Development. The rapidly increasing brainpower in babies allows them to improve their sensory skills. In the first months of life, babies increase their ability to perceive facial expressions in the people around them. In fact, some research has found that babies of depressed moms show a preference for different intensities of smiles and frowns — presumably to match the downcast faces they often see in their moms — than did babies of non-depressed moms (Kellman & Arterberry, 2006). Newborns' visual preference for faces over non-faces becomes even more obvious as the months go by. At 2 months, newborns smile and coo more at people than at toy monkeys (Legerstee et al., 1987). At 3 months, they gaze longer at (and have more rapid heartbeats when viewing) a real person than at a mannequin or a doll (Brazelton et al., 1974; Field, 1979; Klein & Jennings, 1979). In terms of hearing, babies also develop a strong preference for speech over non-speech sounds in their first few months of life (Vouloumanos et al., 2001, 2010; Vouloumanos & Werker, 2004, 2007).

Motor Development. Many parents can attest to the fact that the immobile infant becomes a scampering toddler seemingly overnight. Many parents can also describe the sequence of motor skills the child develops in the process. Specifically, babies use these movements to get around (in this order): rolling, sitting up, crawling, standing, cruising (getting around on two feet while holding onto still objects like chairs or low tables), and finally walking (Adolph & Berger, 2005, 2006). Children around the world follow the same sequence, at around the same points in time, with only minimal influences by family or culture. This suggests that motor development is determined more by biology than environment, more by nature than by nurture.

Cognitive Development

Our understanding of children's cognitive development — the changes in the way children think about and understand the world around them — has long been dominated by the ideas of legendary researcher Jean Piaget (Beins, 2012; Messerly, 2009; Smith, 2009). Piaget, who lived in Switzerland from 1896 to 1980, shared his comprehensive theory of childhood development in more than 100 books and more than 600 published papers (e.g., Piaget, 1924, 1926, 1929, 1936/1952, 1983). His theories have inspired empirical research by generations of developmental psychologists. Whether this research supports his ideas (as much of it has) or refutes them (as some has, especially more recently), Piaget founded the study of how kids' minds work. Let's consider some of Piaget's most important ideas, including *schemas* and *stages of cognitive development*. Then, let's consider an alternative to Piaget's theories, as well as more recent research that tests Piaget's theories.

Schemas. One of Piaget's most fundamental observations was that a primary task for each of us is to sort the vast range of things we encounter into categories, or mental

David A Land/Blend Images/Getty Images

khoa vu/Moment/Getty Images

Miodrag Gajic/E+/Getty Images

The motor development of babies follows the same sequence around the world. Three of the major milestones are (in order) sitting up, crawling, and walking.

"boxes" (Birney et al., 2005; Halford & Andrews, 2006; P. H. Miller, 2011). According to Piaget, each category or box is a **schema**: a concept or mental representation that guides the way you make sense of new information. Once the schema is in place, it can be reused endlessly to classify the new things you encounter. That classification process is **assimilation**: making sense of new information by sorting it into already existing schemas. Of course, sometimes an item doesn't fit into an existing schema, or a schema needs to be subdivided or redefined to better sort items (Gelman & Kalish, 2006). We deal with these situations by using **accommodation**: making sense of new information by revising or creating new schemas.

To illustrate schemas, assimilation, and accommodation, let's consider Eli, a young boy just learning what a sandwich is. At an early age, Eli first sees an object with two pieces of bread and something between them, which he hears described as a sandwich. At that point, Eli's mind creates a new "sandwich" schema. Later that day, when he sees his sister's PB&J, he shouts, "Sandwich!" The next day, when he sees his mom's turkey on wheat, he shouts, "Sandwich!" Thanks to the schema, Eli can assimilate every sandwich he sees into this new mental box, even though sandwiches had no name or category in his mind just a few days earlier (Golinkoff et al., 1995; Quinn, 2011; Waxman & Leddon, 2011).

The next day, Eli sees a taco and says, "Sandwich!" Of course, he's misusing his "sandwich" schema, and his mom kindly corrects him: "No, Eli, that's a taco." So Eli accommodates his system of schemas by creating a new one: the "taco" schema. In upcoming months and years, Eli further accommodates new knowledge by creating separate schemas for "burger," "calzone," "samosa," "empanada," and "knish." And Eli breaks down his original "sandwich" schema into more specific minischemas, such as "BLT," "sub," and "Philly cheesesteak."

As Eli grows up, his collection of schemas develops from simple to complex — not just with sandwiches, but with everything he comes across. Chairs (rocking chairs vs. recliners vs. high chairs), precipitation (rain vs. snow vs. hail), technology (smartphone vs. TV remote vs. video game controller), and feelings (anger vs. jealousy vs. disgust) — these are just a few of the different kinds of things that Eli will use schemas to categorize.

Piaget's Stages of Cognitive Development. Piaget believed that children's thinking progressed through distinct stages (rather than more gradual, continuous development). According to his observations, kids stick with the same way of thinking for years, then shift to a new way of thinking in a very short time. He argued that these different stages were biologically determined and only minimally influenced by environment or experience. The idea is that kids around the world move through the

schema
A concept or mental representation that guides the way a person makes sense of new information.

assimilation
A classification process that makes sense of new information by sorting into already existing schemas.

accommodation
A classification process that makes sense of new information by revising or creating new schemas.

IT'S LIKE...

Assimilation and Accommodation Are Like Sorting Laundry

When you take a load of laundry out of the dryer and dump it into a basket, it's a jumbled mess. As you fold it, you categorize it. The first item you pull out of the muddle is a shirt, so you start a shirt pile. The second item is a pair of pants, so you start a pants pile. The third item is a sock, so you start a sock pile. As you make your way through the basket, many of the items fit easily into one of the three piles you've started. For different items, you start a new pile. For example, when you come across your first pair of underwear, it doesn't fit into any of the existing piles, so you start an underwear pile. Eventually, you have separate piles for towels and sheets, and you've divided the pants pile into two piles: long pants and shorts. When you're done folding the laundry, the jumbled mess is now organized and functional.

Each separate pile of clothes — that is, each category — corresponds to what Piaget called a *schema*. When you put an item in a pile you've already started, that's *assimilation*. When you start a new pile for an item that doesn't fit into an existing pile, that's *accommodation*. Without schemas, assimilation, and accommodation, a young child might experience the world like a jumbled mess of laundry. However, by using assimilation and accommodation, the world becomes much more orderly and understandable.

Digital Vision/Getty Images

During the sensorimotor stage, which lasts through the first 2 years of life, children understand the world through sensory experience. For example, the way they experience Cheerios involves taste, smell, touch, and sight.

same stages in the same order at around the same ages (Keil, 2006; Messerly, 2009; P. H. Miller, 2011). **Table 9.2** offers a summary of Piaget's stages: the *sensorimotor stage*, the *preoperational stage*, the *concrete operational stage*, and the *formal operational stage*. Let's examine each in detail.

Sensorimotor Stage. The **sensorimotor stage** is the first stage in Piaget's theory of development, from birth to about age 2, when babies understand the world through sensory experience. Babies know something is real by seeing, hearing, smelling, touching, or tasting it. That direct experience is crucial because babies can't yet imagine or remember much. For example, consider how a baby might learn about Cheerios – their taste, texture, color, size, and shape. They don't yet have the brainpower to imagine Cheerios when the Cheerios are not around, or to understand someone's verbal description of Cheerios well enough to picture them. Babies need to interact with Cheerios in direct sensory ways: see them with their eyes, feel them on their fingers, and taste them with their tongues.

Does that explain why babies love peek-a-boo so much?

Yes! Peek-a-boo, a favorite of kids during the sensorimotor stage, makes a lot of sense in terms of that need for direct sensory experience (Parrott & Gleitman, 1989; Singer & Revenson, 1996). Think of it this way: If someone plays peek-a-boo with you today, you obviously understand that they continue to exist even when they hide their face. But when you were a baby, when they hid their face they weren't just momentarily out of sight – they were *gone*. That's what made their reappearance so miraculous and exciting!

Peek-a-boo doesn't work on you anymore because you developed **object permanence**: the ability to realize that an object continues to exist even when you can't see, hear, or otherwise sense it. Object permanence is a milestone within the sensorimotor stage. Piaget argued that object permanence emerges around a child's first birthday (Piaget, 1936/1952, 1954). As evidence of young infants' lack of object permanence, Piaget pointed to his experiments in which he hid toys from children in simple ways (under a cloth, for example). The younger children who had not yet achieved object permanence didn't even look for the toy (remember, it is *gone* to them), but the older children did. The object permanence that the older children had developed enabled them to know that the toy continued to exist even if they temporarily couldn't see it.

Preoperational Stage. After the sensorimotor stage comes the **preoperational stage**, from about age 2 to about age 7, when children can use language and other

sensorimotor stage
The first stage in Piaget's theory of development, from birth to about age 2, when babies understand the world through sensory experience.

object permanence
The ability to realize that an object continues to exist even when a person can't see, hear, or otherwise sense it.

preoperational stage
The second stage in Piaget's theory of development, from about age 2 to about age 7, when children can use language and other symbols for real objects but still can't complete many mental operations.

TABLE 9.2: Piaget's Stages of Cognitive Development

STAGE	AGE (APPROX.)	DESCRIPTION	KEY CHALLENGES
Sensorimotor	0–2	Use sensory experience (touch, taste, sight, etc.) to understand the world.	Object permanence
Preoperational	2–7	Use language and other symbols but have limited mental operations.	Pretend play Conservation Theory of mind Egocentrism
Concrete operational	7–11	Think logically about concrete, but not abstract, things.	Reversibility Transitive reasoning
Formal operational	11–adulthood	Think logically about abstract things.	

symbols for real objects but still can't complete many mental operations. This is the period when kids develop the ability to represent things in their mind, because they no longer need actual direct sensory experience. One sure sign of the preoperational stage is *pretend play*, which takes place when kids assign fictional roles to people (telling a friend, "You be the mommy and I'll be the little girl ... ") or give fictional powers to objects (singing into a hairbrush as if it is a microphone) (Lillard, 2017; Müller, 2009; Müller & Racine, 2010). In each of these cases, the child demonstrates the ability to break free of the literal meaning of an object and instead imagine that the object is something or someone else.

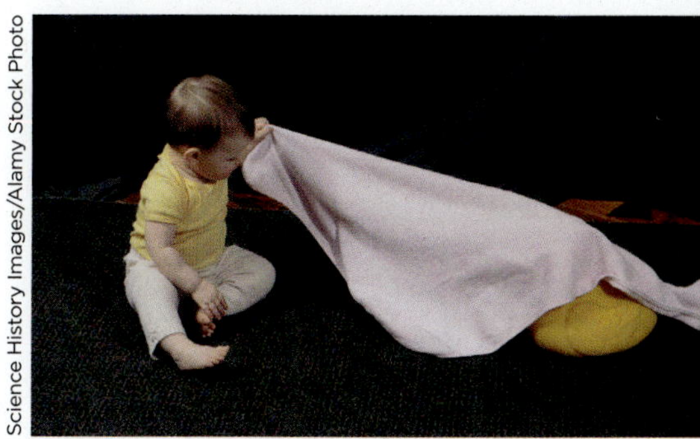
Science History Images/Alamy Stock Photo

Object permanence, which emerges around the age of 1 year, is the ability to realize that an object continues to exist even when you can't see or otherwise sense it. Without a sense of object permanence, a young child (unlike this one, who is removing a cloth to find a hidden toy) would not look for a missing object, because the child would assume that the object was gone.

During the preoperational stage, children's mathematical abilities bloom. However, through much of this stage, children continue to struggle with **conservation**, a mental operation in which an amount or quantity remains the same regardless of the shape it takes. One of Piaget's best-known observations involved a young child looking at two glasses filled with exactly the same amount of liquid. When the liquid in one of those glasses was poured into a taller, thinner glass, a child who had not yet attained the ability to conserve would immediately — and mistakenly — say the new glass had "more" because the liquid rose higher in the comparison glass. Likewise, to a child who has not yet mastered conservation, a ball of dough becomes "more" when it is rolled out into a bigger-looking pizza crust (Martí, 2003).

Another hallmark of the preoperational stage is the child's development of **theory of mind**: the understanding of the thoughts, feelings, intentions, and other mental activities of oneself and others. Simply put, kids in the preoperational stage gain an ability to "get inside the head" of other people (and themselves) that they did not have when they were younger (Carpenter, 2011; Lewis & Carpendale, 2011; Meltzoff, 2011; Perner, 1999; Schaafsma et al., 2015; Wellman et al., 2003). Their language certainly reflects this newfound ability, as they use words to refer to mental events — like *want, think*, and *feel* — increasingly during this period (Bartsch & Wellman, 1997; Wellman, 2011).

In one study that illustrates the emergence of theory of mind, a 6- or 18-month-old child sat next to a woman with a toy that the child could see. The woman did not give the child the toy, either because she accidentally dropped it or because she played with it herself. The older children showed much more impatience and frustration when the woman played with the toy herself than when she dropped it, even though the time the child was kept waiting was the same in both cases. Apparently, the older children were able to read the woman's intentions, so they were more upset by her selfishness than by her accidental mishandling of the toy. The younger children showed no such difference. They were equally mad regardless of the reason for the wait, presumably because they hadn't yet developed theory of mind, so they couldn't yet appreciate the woman's intentions (Behne et al., 2005; see also Carpenter et al., 1998; Tomasello et al., 2005).

Some researchers have explored whether an underdeveloped theory of mind relates to autism spectrum disorders, a core characteristic of which is a difficulty seeing the world through others' eyes (Baron-Cohen, 1995, 2000; Bowler, 1992; Leppanen et al., 2018; Perner et al., 1987; Wimmer & Perner, 1983). Several studies of this

© Maya Barnes Johansen/TopFoto

© Maya Barnes Johansen/TopFoto

The preoperational stage is when children achieve a sense of conservation, or the understanding that an amount or quantity remains the same regardless of the shape it takes. Before developing a sense of conservation, children (like this girl) commonly make the mistake of assuming that a substance becomes "more" or "less" according to its size or shape.

conservation
A mental operation in which an amount or quantity remains the same regardless of the shape it takes.

theory of mind
The understanding of the thoughts, feelings, intentions, and other mental activities of oneself and others.

This is Sally.
This is Anne.
Sally puts her ball in the green box.
Sally goes away.
Anne moves the ball to the blue box.
Where will Sally look for her ball?

FIGURE 9.6 The False-Belief Task. The false-belief task is a research method often used to test for theory of mind. In the false-belief task, the child hears a story about Sally, who puts an object in one container and then leaves the room. When she's gone, another girl moves the object to another container. When Sally returns, where will she look for the object? Kids with an intact theory of mind typically understand that Sally will look in the first container, but kids without an intact theory of mind (including many kids on the autism spectrum) will mistakenly think that Sally will look in the second container. This mistake indicates a failure to appreciate how their own view of a situation differs from another person's view.

connection use a research method based on the *false-belief task*, as shown in **Figure 9.6**. The method involves telling children a story about a girl, Sally, who puts an object (usually a toy or a piece of chocolate) in a basket and then leaves the room. While she's out, another girl moves the object from the basket to a box. When Sally comes back, where will she look for the object? Among kids without developmental problems, 85% get it right and say that Sally will look in the basket, where she left it. But among kids with autism spectrum disorder, 80% get it wrong and say that Sally will look in the box, where it is now. (It's important to point out that the kids in this study were well beyond the age of the preoperational stage, so the expectation for some degree of theory of mind was reasonable.)

The researchers interpreted this finding to suggest that kids with autism spectrum disorder (whose IQs were equal to or higher than those of the kids without the disorder) lack the theory of mind that would enable them to see the situation as *Sally* would. The suggestion is that kids with autism spectrum disorder assume that the way *they* see the situation is the way everyone (including Sally) must see it (Baron-Cohen et al., 1985, 1997). Other researchers have argued against this interpretation, saying that autism spectrum disorder is more complex than the mere lack of theory of mind. Specifically, they argue that kids with autism spectrum disorder may lack the motivation, along with or instead of the ability, to appreciate the mental activity of others (Carpendale & Lewis, 2010; Chevallier, 2012; Chevallier et al., 2011; Schultz, 2005).

Until kids develop theory of mind, their thinking is dominated by **egocentrism**: the inability to understand a situation from a point of view other than their own. Kids influenced by both egocentrism and theory of mind often show a blend of the two perspectives — they kind of see the world as others see it, but kind of see it their own way too. For example, imagine that 3-year-old Kenny's elderly grandfather slips and falls during a visit, breaking his hip. The adults try to make Kenny's grandfather comfortable until the ambulance arrives. Kenny tries to help too, by giving his grandfather Kenny's own teddy bear and a Band-Aid and saying, "Here Grandpa, this will make it all better!" Kenny's theory of mind allows him to recognize the pain that his grandpa must be suffering, but Kenny's egocentrism limits him to considering what helps *Kenny* (and not what might help other people) to overcome pain.

Concrete Operational Stage. Piaget's third stage is the **concrete operational stage**, from about age 7 to about age 11, in which children acquire the ability to think logically about concrete things. They master conservation completely. Also, their ability to perform mental manipulations on things, even when those things are just representations in their heads rather than real items in their hands, increases dramatically (Bibok et al., 2009). One such mental manipulation is *reversibility*, which involves an understanding of how certain pairs of mathematical calculations (addition–subtraction or multiplication–division) are opposite. Picture an 11-year-old girl who knows she had $2.50 cash in her room but who only counts $1.50 right now. She does a subtraction problem in her head to calculate that $1.00 is missing. Later, she finds the missing $1.00 in the pocket of the jeans she wore yesterday. To know how much she has after this discovery, she doesn't need to recalculate that 1.50 + 1.00 = 2.50. Instead, she can jump immediately to the correct conclusion that she has $2.50 again, since she understands that addition reverses subtraction.

Another achievement of the concrete operational stage is *transitive reasoning* (Halford & Andrews, 2006). You might remember from a math class that the transitive property goes like this: if A equals B, and B equals C, then A must equal C. In the concrete operational stage, kids come to understand not only this mathematical version, but other versions of transitive reasoning as well. For example, if Ms. Alexander is as tough a science teacher as Mr. Bakir, and Mr. Bakir is as tough as Ms. Cruz, then Ms. Alexander must be as tough as Ms. Cruz.

Formal Operational Stage. Piaget's fourth and final stage is the **formal operational stage**, beginning around age 11 and lasting through adulthood, in which the person becomes able to think logically about abstract things. The key difference between this stage and the concrete operational stage is that mental operations are

egocentrism
The inability to understand a situation from a point of view other than your own.

concrete operational stage
The third stage in Piaget's theory of development, from about age 7 to about age 11, in which children acquire the ability to think logically about concrete things.

formal operational stage
The final stage in Piaget's theory of development, beginning around age 11 and lasting through adulthood, in which the person becomes able to think logically about abstract things.

not limited to concrete things. Mental operations can be theoretical, figurative, or conceptual. For example, during the formal operational stage kids develop the ability to appreciate political approaches (such as liberal or conservative), religious beliefs (not just visible objects and symbols of religion), and philosophical points of view. Recall your own experiences with political, religious, and philosophical ideas. You probably didn't start seriously considering such issues, either in school or with family or friends, until you were nearing the end of elementary school, or perhaps later.

Piaget argued that not everyone reaches the formal operational stage. Several empirical studies indicate that he was correct (Neimark, 1975; Renner et al., 1976; Sutherland, 1992), and one study estimates that only about one-third of U.S. high school students fully complete the formal operational stage (Kuhn et al., 1977). More recent research has found that people who can perform this abstract thinking have significant advantages in certain professions, especially those related to math and computer science (Frorer et al., 1997; Kramer, 2007).

scaffolding
A process by which a person learns new words, ideas, and ways of thinking by interacting with a more advanced person who provides decreasing levels of help.

Vygotsky's Alternative to Piaget's Theories. Long before contemporary researchers relied on empirical methods to challenge Piaget, Lev Vygotsky challenged Piaget with a theory of his own. Vygotsky, who was born in Russia the same year that Piaget was born in Switzerland, argued that social interaction was the primary force behind cognitive development (Daniels, 2011; Rogoff, 2003; van der Veer & Valsiner, 1994; Vygotsky, 1978, 1986; Yasnitsky, 2012). Piaget never denied that children's social interactions could have some influence on the development of their thinking, but he always considered that influence secondary (Piaget & Inhelder, 1969). Piaget believed biology was the primary force. Vygotsky's theory switched the emphasis, stating that kids' interactions with older kids and adults were the main force for changes in thinking. That is, Vygotsky believed that kids' thinking changes mostly because the adults around those kids foster that change.

Vygotsky explained that often, a child's way of thinking was pushed along by **scaffolding**: a process by which a person learns new words, ideas, and ways of thinking by interacting with a more advanced person who provides decreasing levels of help. Consider two children of the same age who live in neighboring apartments, each working on a difficult jigsaw puzzle. The child in apartment A works entirely alone, but the child in apartment B interacts with a parent or older sibling who is more expert in puzzles. The child in apartment B hears these comments in the process: "That can't be an edge piece. It doesn't have any straight sides." "That has to be a corner piece because it has two straight sides." Notice that the parent or older sibling doesn't do the puzzle for the child, but makes comments that nudge the child to use logic slightly beyond the child's current level of thinking. Just as scaffolding on a construction site provides a temporary way for people to climb to new heights, Vygotsky's scaffolding allows kids to climb to higher levels of cognition with the help of people whose thinking is more advanced (Langford, 2005; R. Miller, 2011).

Of course, scaffolding won't help if the next step is too high for the child to reach, so Vygotsky also emphasized the *zone of proximal development*, which is essentially the range of learning just above what a kid can do alone (Daniels, 1996; Emerson, 1983, Hedegaard, 1992; Wersch & Tulviste, 1992). This is a particularly important idea for those who work directly with children, like teachers or tutors. They should know the kid's starting point and then offer challenges a bit beyond it, along with the support to help them meet those challenges (Fischer & Bidell, 2006; Rose & Fischer, 2009). For example, a child who recently mastered addition for one-digit numbers should probably be prodded to try addition problems in which one of the numbers has two digits, not addition problems in which each number has five digits.

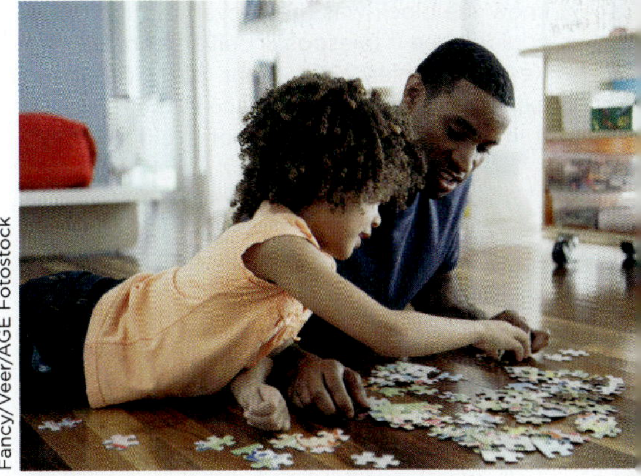
Fancy/Veer/AGE Fotostock

Scaffolding is a process by which a person (like this child) learns new words, ideas, and ways of thinking by interacting with a more advanced person (like this young adult) who provides decreasing levels of help. Scaffolding was an idea of Lev Vygotsky, who believed that children's cognitive development was primarily influenced by nurture, or interactions with others. By contrast, Jean Piaget believed that children's cognitive development was primarily influenced by nature, or biologically determined stages.

Piaget Now: Empirical Findings. In some ways, Piaget's original theories have held up quite well, especially considering that about a century has passed since he began to offer them. However, more contemporary researchers have tested Piaget's ideas extensively, and some of their results contradict his predictions.

Often, results that don't support Piaget come from studies using methods Piaget didn't use. That is, modern researchers have tested Piaget's theories in different ways than he did, and some of their tests yielded different results (Kesselring, 2009). As an example, consider Piaget's concept of object permanence. In his own studies, he relied

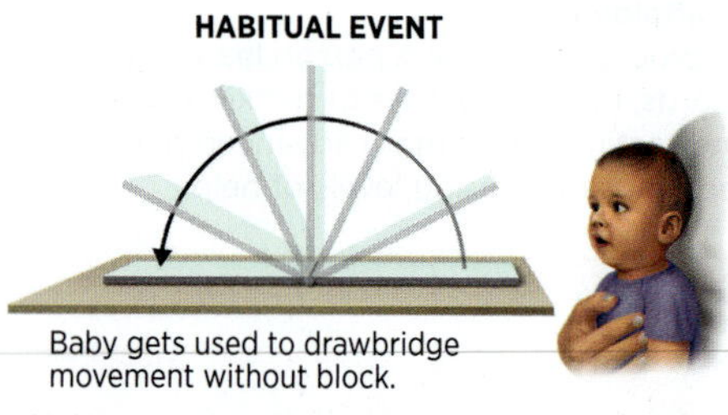

HABITUAL EVENT
Baby gets used to drawbridge movement without block.

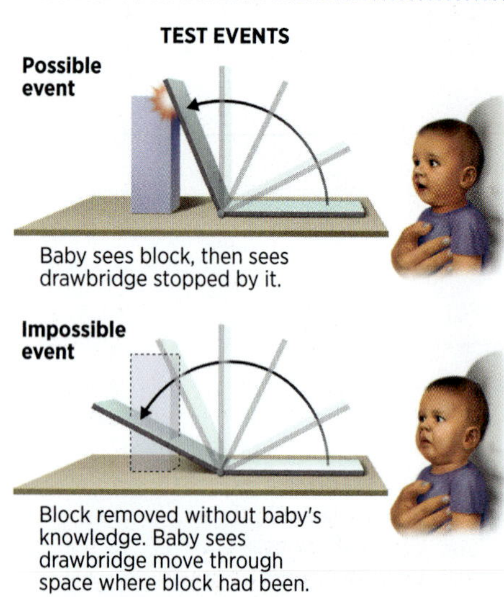

TEST EVENTS
Possible event
Baby sees block, then sees drawbridge stopped by it.
Impossible event
Block removed without baby's knowledge. Baby sees drawbridge move through space where block had been.

FIGURE 9.7 Testing Object Permanence with the Drawbridge Method. The drawbridge method was developed as a new way to test Piaget's theory of object permanence. The "drawbridge" goes up and down, much as a pizza box opens and closes. Babies as young as 3.5 months old stared for an extra-long time at the drawbridge when it passed through a space where it should bump into a block—an indication that they knew the block was there, even though they couldn't see it (Hespos & Baillargeon, 2008; Keen & Berthier, 2004; Klahr, 2012). (The expression on the baby's face in the third frame is another indication of this finding.)

on the method of hiding a toy under a cloth and observing whether the child moved the cloth in an attempt to find it. His results indicated that kids couldn't develop object permanence until after their first birthday (Piaget, 1952, 1954, 1983). But what if younger babies really do have a sense of object permanence, and they just couldn't show it in the way Piaget required? Perhaps younger babies didn't yet have the necessary hand–eye coordination to lift the cloth, or the toy wasn't interesting enough for them to seek it (Cohen & Cashon, 2006; P. H. Miller, 2011; Müller, 2009).

Is there a different way that very young babies could show their sense of object permanence?

A group of researchers thought there might be a different way, so they tested Piaget's object permanence idea using an innovative *violation-of-expectation* method. It was based on the simple idea that babies will stare longer at events that surprise them (or violate their expectations) than events that they expect (Baillargeon, 1987, 2004; Baillargeon et al., 1985, 1990; Baillargeon & Graber, 1987, 1988; Mareschal & Kaufman, 2012). Specifically, these researchers showed babies a "drawbridge" video in which they repeatedly saw the moving part of the drawbridge drop toward them until it hit the ground, then lift away from them until its opposite side hit the ground. To understand the drawbridge movement, imagine seeing a pizza box opening and closing all the way across its full 180-degree range. Better yet, see **Figure 9.7** for a side view.

After the babies became used to the opening and closing motion, the researchers inserted the image of a block behind the drawbridge. From that point on, the drawbridge either stopped when it would hit the block (as if your pizza box bumped into a block hidden behind it as you pushed it wide open), or it moved right through that space, as if the block had disappeared. Here's the key finding: babies as young as 3.5 months old stared longer at the drawbridge passing through the block space (a violation of their expectations) than the drawbridge stopping at the point when it would bump into the block (what they expected). This finding suggests that these babies have a sense of object permanence about the block, even though it becomes invisible to them behind the drawbridge, at a much younger age than Piaget claimed (Hespos & Baillargeon, 2008; Keen & Berthier, 2004; Klahr, 2012).

In a different kind of violation-of-expectation study, babies see a doll on a table. Next, they see the researcher cover the doll with a blanket, put a second doll under the blanket, and then remove the blanket. When the blanket is lifted, babies as young as 2.5 months old stare longer if there is only one doll behind the blanket (that is, if the first doll has been secretly removed) than if both dolls are there. This long stare suggests that they expect the second doll to be there even though it was temporarily out of sight — again, at an age far younger than Piaget's methods would have allowed them to display (Baillargeon et al., 2011; Wynn, 1992).

The idea that Piaget's methods underestimated how quickly kids develop object permanence (and other cognitive abilities) is just one of the criticisms that his theories receive from modern researchers. Two other criticisms are common. One is that Piaget's theory emphasized stages too much. Kids in the real world don't develop their cognitive abilities in the caterpillar-to-butterfly stage-based way that Piaget and other stage theorists described. There may be spurts of cognitive growth at certain times, but kids tend to show gradual, continuous change to a greater extent than Piaget described (Bibok et al., 2009).

The second criticism is related to the first: Piaget emphasized that his stages occurred because of biology (nature), or a sequence of changes that was inborn and relatively unaffected by environment (nurture). However, as Vygotsky argued, modern research indicates that the environment, especially the interactions kids have with older people, can influence the rate at which their thinking develops (Birney et al., 2005; Kingsley & Hall, 1967; Legerstee, 1994; Müller, 2009). Screen time on TV, computers, smartphones, and other media is another environmental influence: check the *Watching Psychology* box for how it affects kids' development.

WATCHING PSYCHOLOGY

Screen Time and Kids' Development

U.S. children spend a tremendous amount of time using screens, including phones, tablets, computers, video games, and TVs. How does all of this screen time affect kids' development? Researchers have concluded that it can have both positive and negative effects — effects that may only grow with the increasing integration of media into daily lives (Huntemann & Morgan, 2012; Subrahmanyam & Greenfield, 2012). Certainly, there can be a developmental upside to certain screen activities. For example, some computer games can enhance kids' ability to pay attention for long periods of time and pay attention to multiple stimuli at the same time. Some argue that when used wisely, such screen time can allow parents to cope with busy schedules and be more emotionally available when the screens are off (Rideout & Hamel, 2006). Also, kids who watch media with prosocial content — for example, TV shows or movies that include acts of kindness or help — have higher levels of helping and empathy, and lower levels of aggressive behavior (Coyne et al., 2018; Padilla-Walker et al., 2015). Additionally, some studies have found little or no connection between screen time and mental health issues in teens (Ferguson et al., 2021).

Morrowind/Shutterstock

Research suggests that some screen time for children can have positive effects, but when screen time is excessive, the effects tend to be negative.

On the other hand, excessive screen time can have quite a developmental downside. At the very least, screen time displaces time that could be spent exercising, sleeping, and socializing in person with friends and family — all essential to health and happiness in childhood (García-Hermoso et al., 2020; Hale & Guan, 2015; Herman et al., 2015; Kremer et al., 2014; Oswald et al., 2020; Wartella & Robb, 2007; Whiting et al., 2021). Also, some studies suggest that kids who text a lot — particularly with textisms like *lol* and *brb* — often struggle with the formal writing necessary to succeed in high school, college, and some workplaces (Rosen et al., 2010). However, other studies actually suggest that texting correlates with strong literacy skills (Kemp & Bushnell, 2011; McWhorter, 2013a, b; Plester et al., 2009). More generally, some studies have found a negative correlation between screen time and cognitive abilities, especially for very young children (2 and younger) (Madigan et al., 2019; Walsh et al., 2018).

Smartphones receive criticism for outcomes other than literacy, however. A series of large-scale surveys of eighth-, tenth-, and twelfth-graders in the United States took place every year from 1991 to 2016 (and included over a million total participants). It found that overall psychological well-being — including things like self-esteem, happiness, and overall life satisfaction — decreased suddenly around 2012. That's right around the time that smartphones sharply increased in popularity, especially among teens. The same study found that the happiest teens were the ones who spent the least time on screens, and that teens' happiest years were the ones that had the most nonscreen activities like in-person socializing, sports and exercise, and in-person religious activities (Twenge et al., 2018).

Another downside to excessive screen time involves TV in particular. TV can expose kids to a much more diverse range of people than they would encounter in real life, but it often promotes stereotypes while doing so (Asamen & Berry, 2012). For example, across all ages of childhood, kids who watch more TV hold more stereotypical views about gender roles (regarding work, child care, etc.) than kids who watch less TV (Signorielli, 2012). TV stereotypes of ethnic groups have a particular power to shape kids' thinking when kids don't have real-world opportunities to see members of that ethnic group. If the only Indian man a child ever sees on TV or in real life is Raj Koothrappali from *The Big Bang Theory*, that child may mistakenly come to believe that all Indian men are like him — highly intelligent but socially clueless and petrified of women. •

Psychosocial Development

Just as children's bodies and brains develop, so do their relationships with other people. The first and most fundamental of these relationships are those within the immediate family, so let's begin with concepts related to family: *attachment, parenting styles, and temperament*. Then, we'll move on to relationships with friends.

Attachment. **Attachment** is a close emotional bond between two people, particularly a young child and a caregiver. Two researchers — Mary Ainsworth and John Bowlby — devoted their careers to the study of attachment between children and parents. Their work forms the foundation of our understanding of the subject (Ainsworth, 1989; Ainsworth & Bowlby, 1965; Bowlby, 1969, 1973). Their research was based on the idea of the **critical period**: a period of time during which a particular developmental task is especially likely to be influenced by outside events. Of course, there are all kinds of critical periods. The focus for these researchers, however, was the critical period of a baby's first months of life for attachment to caregivers.

attachment
A close emotional bond between two people, particularly a young child and a caregiver.

critical period
A period of time during which a particular developmental task is especially likely to be influenced by outside events.

Attachment is a close emotional bond between a young child and a caregiver. The first months of life are often crucial to the development of attachment.

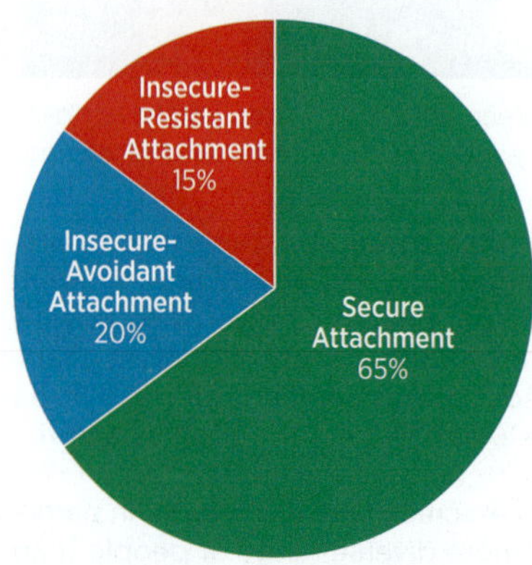

FIGURE 9.8 Attachment Styles of American Babies. Most American babies show a secure attachment to their caregivers. Data from Teti and Teti (1996) and Thompson (1998).

stranger anxiety
The fear of unfamiliar people that emerges in children at about 8 months of age.

The primary way researchers examined parent–child attachment was the *strange situation* method. Basically, they observed babies' reactions when they spend a few minutes in four different situations: with the caregiver (typically mom), with a stranger who enters the room, with both the caregiver and the stranger, or alone. They observed several aspects of the babies' behavior: how much they explored the room (played with toys, etc.), how they reacted when mom left, how they reacted when the stranger approached in mom's absence, and how they reacted when mom came back (Bosma & Gerlsma, 2003; Thompson, 2006). Based on these observations, Ainsworth and her colleagues identified three distinct types of attachment: *secure attachment, insecure-avoidant attachment*, and *insecure-resistant attachment* (Ainsworth et al., 1978; Lamb & Lewis, 2005):

- **Secure attachment.** These babies appeared the most stable and well-adjusted. When mom was present, they were comfortable enough to explore the new toys and interact with the stranger. In general, these babies seemed to use mom as a secure home base. For the most part, they felt comfortable straying from that secure home base as long as they knew they could return to it. Of course, they did cry at times when mom left or when the stranger spoke to them. All babies, even those with secure attachment, exhibit **stranger anxiety**: the fear of unfamiliar people that emerges in children at about 8 months of age. But when securely attached babies got upset, the crying was relatively brief and ended quickly when mom returned. Thankfully, most American babies develop secure attachment (Teti & Teti, 1996; Thompson, 1998) (**Figure 9.8**).
- **Insecure-avoidant attachment.** These babies didn't seem to care much when mom left, and they avoided her when she returned.
- **Insecure-resistant attachment.** These babies got quite upset when mom left, and they didn't entirely welcome her return. They had a mixed reaction involving both seeking out mom and angrily resisting the comfort she offered.

Some researchers have also proposed a fourth type of attachment, *disorganized attachment*, in which babies seem confused about how to respond when mom leaves and returns. At different times, these babies may resemble babies in each of the three other types (Duschinsky, 2015; Main & Solomon, 1986, 1990).

In very young children, attachment styles can vary from one time to another and from one caregiver to another. Around the age of 4 or 5, kids generally settle on one attachment style. That attachment style makes a big difference — not just during childhood with their parents, but for many years to come in many kinds of relationships (Baryshnikov et al., 2017; Belsky & Fearon, 2002; O'Connor et al., 2018; Widom et al., 2018). In fact, Bowlby once wrote that attachment style "is a characteristic of human nature throughout our lives — from the cradle to the grave" (1988, p. 82).

A secure attachment style yields the most benefits as kids grow up: more self-reliance, a better self-concept, healthier relationships with peers, better at handling unpleasant feelings, more resilient when facing stress, more likely to help and comfort others, and a happier overall mood (Brumariu & Kerns, 2011; Gross et al., 2017; Reich & Vandell, 2011; Schore, 2001; Seibert & Kerns, 2015; Sroufe, 2005; Sroufe et al., 2005). One longitudinal study of 1000 kids found that 3-year-olds with secure attachments had the most social success, including the highest-quality friendships, when they reached first- and third-grades (McElwain et al., 2008). A meta-analysis covering over 3500 kids found a strong link between secure mother–child attachment in preschool and the number of close friendships in older childhood (Schneider et al., 2001). Researchers have even found that secure attachment predicts high levels of self-worth and low levels of depression well into adulthood (Kenny & Sirin, 2006).

Research suggests that the COVID pandemic disrupted attachment between infants and mothers in several ways, especially before vaccines were available (Mayopoulos et al., 2021). The experience of pregnancy and childbirth were especially stressful during the pandemic, which led to an increase in the rate of postpartum depression and anxiety among new moms, which in turn interfered with those mothers' attachment behaviors with their infants (Oskovi-Kaplan et al., 2021; Yan et al., 2020). Some hospitals followed policies that kept mothers and infants separate to a greater extent than usual, which prevented or reduced opportunities for breastfeeding and skin-to-skin contact, both of which can provide important opportunities for attachment (Gribble et al., 2020).

Attachment is not uniquely human. It happens in many species, including monkeys, which were the focus of a classic study on the topic. Harry Harlow and colleagues placed infant monkeys in a room containing two fake "mothers" — one made of cold, hard wire mesh, and the other made of soft, warm terry cloth fabric (Blum, 2002; Harlow, 1958; Harlow & Harlow, 1962; Harlow & Zimmerman, 1958, 1959). The wire mesh mother provided a bottle of milk; the terry cloth mother provided no food or drink at all. The researchers' main question was this: with which mother would the young monkeys form an attachment?

The answer was clear: unless the young monkeys needed nourishment, they attached to the terry cloth mother. They spent much more time with the terry cloth mother, and they explored a new room more eagerly when the terry cloth mother was in the room with them. They even stretched to reach the bottle attached to the wire mesh mother's body while clinging to the terry cloth mother. Their preference for the terry cloth mother was particularly strong when the young monkeys were frightened. They would run and hold tight to the terry cloth mother, even though it had never provided food. This study was inspired by Harlow's knowledge of orphans raised in institutions where they got little physical attention and became adolescents and adults with significant emotional and behavioral problems. Harlow's research highlights how fundamentally important attachment is in humans and other animals as well (Kobak, 2012).

Nina Leen/The LIFE Picture Collection/Getty Images

In classic studies by Harry Harlow and colleagues, infant monkeys formed attachments to soft terry cloth-covered "mothers" even though they did not provide food. The attachment was especially evident when the monkeys were frightened.

Parenting Styles. Your own experience with parents — your own and others you know — has probably shown you that parenting styles can differ greatly. In fact, based on your experience with various parents, you could probably create numerous categories of *parenting styles* into which most of them could be placed. Developmental psychologists have done the same thing. While researchers acknowledge that each parent has their own unique approach, they argue that there are three big categories that describe most of them — *authoritarian, permissive,* and *authoritative* (Baumrind, 1966, 1967, 1971, 1978, 1996; Laursen & Collins, 2009):

- An **authoritarian parenting style** is an approach to parenting in which parents require children to obey unquestionable strict rules. These "because-I-said-so" parents demand compliance without explanation and with the threat of harsh punishment. When an authoritarian parent tells their 16-year-old newly driver's-licensed child that they must be home by 9 P.M. on a Saturday, there is no negotiation, no discussion, no debate. There is just a respectful "Yes, I understand" from the child, because the price of any kind of resistance would be high.
- A **permissive parenting style** is an approach to parenting in which parents place minimal demands on children and allow them to run their own lives. These "whatever" parents either lack the time or energy to involve themselves in their children's lives, or choose to indulge them by agreeing to what they want. When the new 16-year-old driver goes out on a Saturday night, a permissive parent either tells them to stay out as late as they want, or says nothing at all.
- An **authoritative parenting style** is an approach to parenting in which parents set rules, but also explain and negotiate those rules with their children. These "here's why" parents are much more engaged in their kids' lives than permissive parents, but not as inflexibly controlling as authoritarian parents. They provide firm boundaries and limits for their kids and exert power at appropriate times. However, these authoritative parents also explain their rationale and consider their kids' input when making their decisions. In short, they raise their kids through a balance of clout and cooperation. When the 16-year-old child heads out on a Saturday night, an authoritative parent might tell them to be home by 10:30. When the teen explains that the movie won't end until 10:45, the parent extends the deadline to 11, but reminds the teen that they'll be grounded if they are late.

authoritarian parenting style
An approach to parenting in which parents require children to obey unquestionable, strict rules.

permissive parenting style
An approach to parenting in which parents place minimal demands and allow children to run their own lives.

authoritative parenting style
An approach to parenting in which parents set rules, but also explain and negotiate those rules with their children.

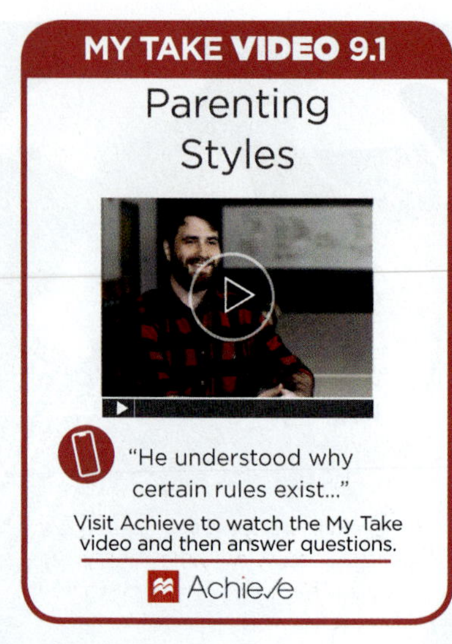

Many studies on parenting styles shows that often, authoritative parents produce well-adjusted kids. Compared to kids raised by authoritarian or permissive parents, kids raised by authoritative parents tend to be more independent, autonomous, socially competent, appropriately assertive, and academically successful, and less likely to be anxious, depressed, delinquent, obese, or secretive (Baumrind, 1967, 2013; Hartman et al., 2015; Lamb & Lewis, 2005; Pinquart, 2016, 2017; Sokol et al., 2017; Steinberg et al., 1989, 1991, 1992). Teens raised by authoritative parents are also more likely than their peers to maintain healthy eating habits and weight, and to have candid and open discussions of sexual issues (Askelson et al., 2012; Berge et al., 2010).

Some research suggests that the positive outcomes associated with authoritative parents are true across many cultural groups within the United States, including Black, Asian American, and Mexican American families, and with U.K. families as well (Carlo, 2018; Chan & Koo, 2011; Cheah et al., 2009; Pinquart & Kauser, 2018; Querido et al., 2002). However, other research suggests that the authoritative style may not yield the same advantages in certain cultures. For example, one study of over 1000 teens in Spain found that children raised by permissive parents (specifically, parents who indulge their children) rate as highly on many desirable characteristics as those raised by authoritative parents (Garcia & Gracia, 2009; Garcia et al., 2021). Other studies have found that the authoritarian style of parenting may benefit some Black youth as much as the authoritative style (Baumrind, 1972; Deater-Deckard et al., 1996; LeCuyer et al., 2011; Valentino et al., 2012).

Temperament

Could a parenting style depend on the type of kid they have?

Absolutely. Parenting is a relationship between two people, so it is not just the parent's behavior that determines its style. The child's behavior matters too (Groh et al., 2017). A major factor in the child's behavior is the child's **temperament**: the basic emotional responsiveness that characterizes a person throughout their life span. Ask any parent with several kids and they'll tell you that kids are different from each other from the very beginning. In their first days, way before the world around them has had time to exert any real influence, some kids are content and some kids are cranky. Some are easy to soothe, some endlessly fussy, some high-energy, and some relaxed. These qualities are biologically based, noticeable from an early age, and likely to form the foundation of the personalities that will carry through childhood and adulthood (Caspi & Shiner, 2006; Kagan & Fox, 2006; Rothbart, 2007; Sanson et al., 2011; Thomas et al., 1970).

Each kid has their own temperament, but classic research by Alexander Thomas and Stella Chess identifies three categories into which most (but certainly not all) kids fall: *easy temperament*, *difficult temperament*, and *slow-to-warm-up temperament* (Chess & Thomas, 1986; Thomas & Chess, 1977):

- Kids with an *easy temperament* are, well, easy-going. They are generally optimistic and positive. They acclimate quickly to new situations and can be calmed in a predictable and manageable way.
- Kids with a *difficult temperament* give their parents a much harder time. They are quick to react negatively (crying, screaming, etc.) to unfamiliar people and things. They don't fall into predictable sleeping or eating patterns. They are also harder to please or comfort when they get upset.
- Kids with a *slow-to-warm-up temperament* take a long time to get used to new people or new situations, and their typical first reaction is to shy away. They are generally quiet and have low levels of activity.

temperament
The basic emotional responsiveness that characterizes a person throughout their life span.

More recent research suggests that there are a couple of factors, or basic ingredients, of temperament that underlie these three categories: reactivity and self-regulation. *Reactivity* is a tendency to react with negative emotions such as irritability and anxiety, and *self-regulation* is control over one's own moods and behavior (Rothbart, 2007; Rothbart & Bates, 2006). These basic elements of temperament reflect the way each of us is "wired," and they are relatively stable across the life span. For example, numerous studies have found that babies with high levels of reactivity grow up to become grade schoolers, high schoolers, and adults with higher-than-average chances of experiencing anxiety disorders (Clark et al., 1994; Fox & Pine, 2012; Kagan & Snidman, 1999; Rapee et al., 2005).

Inti St Clair/Blend Images/Getty Images

A child with an easy temperament is easy to get along with, especially in comparison to a child with a difficult or slow-to-warm-up temperament.

But you are not entirely stuck with a particular temperament from birth to death. Your life experiences can alter your temperament a little, or at least loosen it up enough that you can choose to react differently from your first impulse (Fox et al., 2008; Kagan & Snidman, 2004; Kagan et al., 1994). For example, imagine that Diego is a highly reactive baby boy. If Diego's parent makes a deliberate and appropriate effort to challenge his natural anxiety around unfamiliar people, then Diego is likely to become more comfortable around people than if his parent always allows him to avoid new people altogether. Carefully introducing Diego to new people as the months and years go by gives him the opportunity to disprove his first reaction that new people are scary without overwhelming him.

As this example illustrates, it is the interaction between parenting styles and temperament that matters, not just the parenting style or the child's temperament. Researchers call this interaction between the natural ways of kids and parents *goodness-of-fit* (Chess & Thomas, 1991; Mangelsdorf et al., 1990; Newland & Crnic, 2017). If you've ever played team sports, you've experienced goodness-of-fit with your coach. Coaches who adapt their styles to match the abilities of their players, rather than imposing their preferred style regardless of who is on the roster, have an advantage in fostering the successful development of the team. In the same way, parents who adapt their parenting style to the temperament of their kids have an advantage in fostering the successful development of their kids. Research shows this is true in the classroom too: children in preschool and elementary school show fewer behavior problems when there is goodness-of-fit between their temperament and the teacher's style (Hipson & Séguin, 2016; Roubinov et al., 2017).

Culture can play a significant role in goodness-of-fit between kids and parents. One study of 2-year-olds in China and Canada found that mothers from each country reacted differently when the kids acted shy around a stranger (probably demonstrating a difficult or slow-to-warm-up temperament). Canadian moms were more likely to disapprove of the shyness and encourage their kids to overcome it, while Chinese moms were more likely to approve of the shyness and not push their kids to interact with the stranger (Chen et al., 1998). When kids in these countries reach elementary school, they reflect the same preferences toward each other that their moms did toward them as toddlers: Canadian kids tend to dislike shyness in their peers, but Chinese kids tend to like it (Chen et al., 1992).

Friend Relationships. A child's psychosocial development depends not only on family, but on friends too. Developmental psychologists haven't studied friend relationships as much as family relationships. However, the studies conducted confirm the experience you may have had yourself: during childhood, friendships matter a lot (Erdley & Day, 2017; Hymel et al., 2011). Compared to kids without close friendships, kids with close friendships have higher self-esteem and fewer behavioral and emotional problems (Buhrmester, 1990; Ladd et al., 1997; Raboteg-Saric & Sakic, 2014). Kids with close friendships experience less loneliness, depression, and victimization by peers (Bukowski et al., 1993; Hodges et al., 1999; Parker & Asher, 1993; van Harmelen et al., 2016). They have higher levels of school involvement and earn better grades (Kingery & Erdley, 2007; Kingery et al., 2011). They have decreased chances of dropping out of school and committing crime, and they are more likely to function well as young adults (Parker & Asher, 1987; van Harmelen et al.,

2017). Among psychologists who treat kids with ADHD, it is widely recognized that improving the child's social skills often leads to better friendships, which in turn often leads to improvements in ADHD symptoms and other areas of the child's life (Hoza et al., 2003; Mikami, 2010; Normand et al., 2017).

DIVERSITY MATTERS

Gender matters in childhood friendship, regarding both who you are likely to befriend and how you are likely to interact. Starting at around age 3 or 4 and lasting until puberty, boys generally play with boys and girls generally play with girls. With few exceptions, this is how it happens in cultures around the world (Pellegrini et al., 2007; Whiting & Edwards, 1988). From the same age, boys usually prefer toy trucks and guns, and girls usually prefer dolls. Researchers have found these toy preferences in infants as young as 3–8 *months* by tracking eye movements to see which toys they look at longer, and have found that those preferences remain stable for years (Alexander et al., 2009; Jadva et al., 2010; Lauer et al., 2018). Boys' play is typically more rough-and-tumble, with plenty of physical aggression, and often outside in large groups. Girls' play is typically more cooperative, inside, and in small groups (Pasterski et al., 2011). Girls' play often involves aggression too, but unlike the boys' punches and tackles, girls often hurt each other with gossip or backstabbing — acts of relationship betrayal (Schneider et al., 2011).

DIVERSITY MATTERS

Ethnicity matters in childhood friendships too. Kids in Asia tend to be more cooperative with each other, while kids in Europe and the United States tend to be more competitive (Chen et al., 2011; Farver et al., 1995; Orlick et al., 1990). Another Eastern–Western culture distinction is the function of friendship. In the West, kids typically value their friendships because friendships increase their own self-worth. In the East (as well as some Black and Latinx groups in the United States), the main benefit of friendship is the opportunity to serve your friends, not yourself. So, Western kids tend to seek friendships for what their friends can do for them, but Eastern kids tend to seek friendships for what they can do for their friends (Chen et al., 2004; French et al., 2005; Rubin et al., 2006; Way, 2006).

As an example, let's say a friendship emerges between two sixth-grade girls in the same science class, one struggling with a D– and the other excelling with an A+. In Western countries, it is more likely that the girl with a D– initiated the friendship, with the hope that the girl with an A+ might help her to raise her grade. In an Eastern country, it is more likely that the A+ student initiated the friendship, with the intention of lending a hand to her classmate.

A final note on childhood friendships: often, the most important friendship is the one with your siblings. Your brothers and sisters are family, but those sibling relationships often double as close friendships, especially if they are close to your age. Sibling relationships are "a natural laboratory for learning about the social world" — a safe place to develop skills in cooperation, assertiveness, conflict resolution, empathy, and many other relationship skills, which could be valuable in important relationships through the life span (Howe et al., 2011, p. 368; see also Dirks et al., 2015). In fact, one study found that the odds of a married person getting a divorce slightly decrease as the number of siblings that person has increases (Bobbitt-Zeher et al., 2016).

CHECK YOUR LEARNING:

9.7 Newborn babies' abilities include which senses and reflexes?

9.8 How do nature and nurture influence physical development?

9.9 According to Piaget, how do children use assimilation and accommodation to develop schemas?

9.10 According to Piaget, what is the series of cognitive stages through which children develop?

9.11 In what ways have researchers challenged some of Piaget's conclusions?

9.12 What are three distinct types of attachment, and why is secure attachment to others so important?

9.13 What are the three parenting styles into which most parents can be categorized?

9.14 What is temperament, and how early in life does it appear?

To check your understanding of these questions, click show the answers or refer to the answers in the Chapter Summary.

Adolescent Development

YOU WILL LEARN:

9.15 how psychologists define adolescence.

9.16 about the changes that occur in girls and boys during puberty.

9.17 how the brain continues to grow during adolescence.

9.18 about characteristics of adolescent thinking.

9.19 about Kohlberg's stages of moral thinking.

9.20 how psychologists define identity.

9.21 about Erik Erikson's eight-stage psychosocial theory of development.

9.22 why relationships with both parents and peers are key elements of adolescence.

9.23 about the emerging adulthood stage.

Adolescence is the developmental period that encompasses the transition from childhood to adulthood. Some people define adolescence as the teenage years or the years spent in middle school and high school. This is generally accurate, but adolescence has no official start or end time. Some of your peers probably showed the physical, cognitive, or psychosocial signs of adolescence while still in elementary school. At the other end of the timeline, there are those whose adolescence extends well past their teenage years. Developmental psychologists have learned a great deal about the physical, cognitive, and psychosocial changes that take place during adolescence (Jessor, 2018; Kuhn & Franklin, 2006; Lerner & Steinberg, 2009).

Physical Development

Every time you walked among kids your age during middle school and high school, you saw the tremendous range of physical development that takes place during adolescence. Let's consider the changes that take place in both the body and the brain.

Bodily Changes. The most observable sign that childhood is ending and adulthood is on the horizon is the beginning of **puberty**, the time period featuring physical changes that mark the onset of adolescence and enable sexual reproduction. You know from your own experience (and your biology or sex ed classes) the outward hallmarks of puberty. Most of them involve **secondary sex characteristics**: the parts of the body that characterize sexual maturation but are not directly involved in reproduction. In girls, hips widen, breasts develop, and body fat increases in certain areas. In boys, shoulders broaden, facial hair grows, muscles develop, and the voice deepens. In everyone, height surges, underarm and pubic hair appears, and acne does too, at least for some.

Other changes that are not as apparent to the outside observer involve the **primary sex characteristics**: the parts of the body directly involved in sexual reproduction, such as genitals, ovaries, and testes. For example, a boy's penis and testes enlarge, and he experiences his first ejaculation. A girl experiences enlargement of her uterus, clitoris, and labia, and she also experiences **menarche**: her first menstrual period. All of these changes to both primary and secondary sex characteristics are driven by the hormones that the pituitary gland produces.

Girls typically begin puberty about 2 years before boys — around age 10–11 for girls, around age 12–13 for boys. The length of puberty varies a bit, but generally it is complete within 4 or 5 years. The age at which puberty starts actually varies a bit across cultures and across time periods. Girls in many parts of the world now hit puberty sooner than they did about a hundred years ago (Euling et al., 2008). The reasons for this shift are unclear, but some researchers point to correlations with obesity, stress, abuse, poverty, the absence of a father in the home, and exposure to chemicals that disrupt endocrine regulation (Kaplowitz, 2008; Kelly et al., 2017; Noll et al., 2017; Sun et al., 2017; Toppari & Juul, 2010; Walvoord, 2010; Webster et al., 2014).

With puberty comes the child's own emotional reaction to it. Researchers have found that kids who reach puberty before their peers experience a higher rate of unwelcome psychological and behavioral problems. Boys who hit puberty before their male friends are more likely to smoke, use alcohol and drugs, and feel high levels of hostility and stress. Girls who are among the first of their friends to reach puberty have similarly high rates of substance abuse, and also have higher rates of psychological disorders (especially depression), abuse victimization by dating partners, and risky behavior (Chen et al., 2017; Dimler et al., 2015; Platt et al., 2017; Susman & Dorn, 2009; Wang et al., 2016). Possible causes for these problems

adolescence
The developmental period that encompasses the transition from childhood to adulthood.

puberty
The time period featuring physical changes that mark the onset of adolescence and enable sexual reproduction.

secondary sex characteristics
The parts of the body that characterize sexual maturation but are not directly involved in reproduction.

primary sex characteristics
The parts of the body directly involved in sexual reproduction, such as genitals, ovaries, and testes.

menarche
A girl's first menstrual period.

include (1) body image dissatisfaction, primarily for girls who believe their bodies are developing "too soon"; (2) increased odds of hanging out with older kids, whose bodies may be similar, but whose personal activities may be far ahead of the younger child; and (3) increased rates of conflict with parents, who may disagree with the child that a grown-up body merits grown-up levels of freedom (Collins & Steinberg, 2006; Winer et al., 2016). Acne is another feature of puberty for which the psychological effects can be real, despite the fact that they are often overlooked. Research suggests that acne can contribute to serious psychological problems in teens, with strong correlations to depression and anxiety (Samuels et al., 2020). The psychological effects of acne appear especially strong for girls and for teens with darker skin (Natsuaki & Yates, 2021).

Brain Changes. Adolescence means big changes in the brain as well as in the body. Within the brain, white matter in particular continues to grow during adolescence (Paus, 2009). In addition to the sheer increase in size, the adolescent brain features a marked increase in *myelination* (insulation, basically) of axons, which enhances the connections between neurons, which in turn improves cognitive ability (see Chapter 2; Zelazo & Lee, 2010).

This increase in myelination is actually part of a larger process taking place. The adolescent brain selects and improves the most often used neuronal pathways, and eliminates the ones that are rarely or never used. This use-it-or-lose-it strategy is another step in the *pruning* process that began in infancy and childhood. Pruning results in the adolescent brain having fewer connections between neurons than the younger brain, but the connections that remain are more effective (Kuhn, 2009). The primary lesson here is that experience shapes the brain. Adolescents choose their own experiences, which means they determine which neural pathways will flourish and which will waste away (Kuhn & Franklin, 2006; Nelson et al., 2006; Thomas & Johnson, 2008).

For example, consider two classmates, Garrett and Ben, who are 14 years old and finishing eighth grade. Until this time, Garrett's and Ben's parents made the big decisions for them, including what they would do during their summer breaks. But this year, the boys decided for themselves how they would spend their summers. Garrett spends his summer on one thing: video games. No camps, no organized activities, no jobs, little socializing — just hour after hour in a dark basement playing *Fortnite*, *Madden*, *Overwatch*, *Minecraft*, or other video games. Ben spends his summer on lots of things: a couple of weeks at an outdoor sleepaway camp, a week of robotics activities, lots of time at the local pool with friends, practices and games with his baseball team, some lawn-cutting to earn some money, and a little video game playing of his own. At the end of the summer, an MRI would show connections between neurons in Garrett's brain to have grown extensively in areas that relate to video game playing, but that connections between neurons in other parts of his brain have weakened or wasted away. On the other hand, Ben's brain probably shows many brain areas with significant growth between neurons and far fewer dwindling, but no single type of neuron would be as well developed as Garrett's video game neurons. If Garrett and Ben continue to make similar choices through their teens, their brains will reflect even more drastic differences than what this single summer produces.

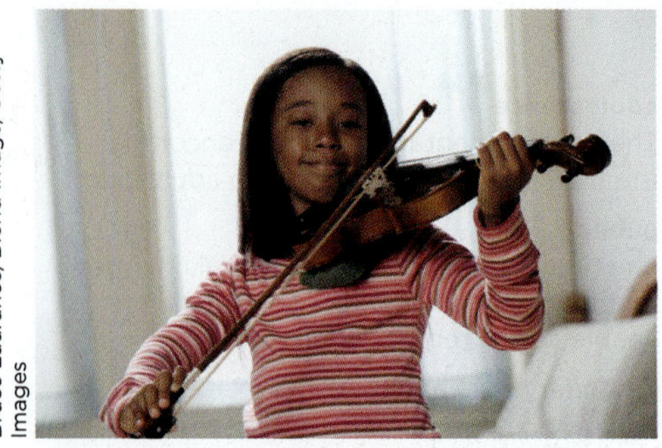

Bruce Laurance/Blend Image/Getty Images

Experience shapes the brain, especially early in development. In one study, the parts of the brains of violin players that correspond to the four fingers (but not the thumb) of the left hand were larger and more complex than the same brain parts in people who don't play the violin (Elbert et al., 1995).

One study offering empirical support for this idea involves the impact of playing an instrument on the brains of teens. Researchers conducted MRIs on the brains of expert violin players and found that the parts of their cortexes that correspond specifically to the four fingers (but not the thumb) of the left hand (the body parts to which violinists must devote so much attention to play the correct notes) were much larger and involved much richer webs of neurons than those of non–violin players (Elbert et al., 1995). This finding was especially strong for violinists who began playing before the age of 12 — that is, those whose violin training likely took place over the course of adolescence.

Cognitive Development

According to Piaget's timetable, adolescents should have entered the last cognitive stage, the formal operational stage. That stage enables adolescents to think logically about all kinds of things, both tangible and abstract. Of course, anyone who has spent time around adolescents knows their thinking is often far from fully developed. Many adolescents think in ways that are quite similar to the *egocentrism* they exhibited when they were much younger children (Elkind, 1967, 1985; Frankenberger, 2000; Lin, 2016; Smetana & Villalobos, 2009; Somerville, 2013).

This teen version of egocentrism, which we defined earlier in this chapter as the inability to understand a situation from a point of view other than their own, shows itself in several different ways. For example, many adolescents' thinking features an **imaginary audience**, in which they believe that their lives are continuously being watched and evaluated by other people. If thoughts like "What will people think?" or "I'm so embarrassed!" were prominent during your middle school and high school years, then you know all about the concept of imaginary audience. Often, these concerns are about trivial things — which shoes you wear with a particular outfit, who you sit with at lunch on a given day, whether your friends see you with your parents at the movie theater. But to adolescents, these events seem hugely important and often spark significant drama, as if a reality show crew is following them with cameras, broadcasting their lives to millions. Today, the not-so-imaginary audiences represented by followers and friends on Twitter, TikTok, YouTube, Snapchat, Instagram, and Facebook probably reinforce adolescents' sense that their every move is being anticipated and scrutinized (Ranzini & Hoek, 2017). Studies have found that teens with a greater sense of imaginary audience tend to disclose more about themselves on Facebook and other social media platforms, including a greater number of selfies (Cingel et al., 2015; Krcmar et al., 2015). That tendency is especially strong among teen girls with a strong sense of self-objectification, which means that they favor physical appearance over other personal characteristics and competencies (Zheng et al., 2019).

Another example of egocentrism in adolescence is the **personal fable**: a common way of thinking among adolescents in which they believe themselves to be special or invulnerable. It is as if the adolescent is the hero in a fairy tale that can only have a happy ending, despite the fact that this is real life, in which tragic endings happen too. In fact, kids whose thinking includes the personal fable engage in more high-risk behaviors than other kids and believe that they are at unrealistically low risk for harmful outcomes (Alberts et al., 2007; Greene et al., 2000; Kim et al., 2018). For example, the personal fable can convince adolescents that *my* car won't crash if I text while driving, *I* won't get suspended if I skip school repeatedly, or nothing bad will happen to *me* if I experiment with addictive substances. In addition to underestimating the chances of bad endings, the personal fable can sway adolescents toward overestimating the chances of good endings. For example, consider the high school sophomore who's a second-string offensive lineman on the JV football team but is certain that he is a lock for the NFL, or the eighth-grade girl who couldn't sing or dance well enough to qualify for her middle school talent show but has no doubt she is the next Beyoncé. One study found that teens with a strong sense of personal fable are especially likely to disclose information about themselves on Facebook, especially by checking in at various locations and updating their personal profile. These teens are apparently unaffected by the fact that these behaviors could harm them by threatening their privacy (Cingel et al., 2015).

Kohlberg and Moral Development. When Piaget examined the development of kids' thinking, he emphasized *logical* thinking. But logic is certainly not the only aspect of thinking that develops. Particularly around the adolescent years, *moral* thinking develops too (Helwig & Turiel, 2011; Moshman, 2009; Turiel, 2006, 2010). Lawrence Kohlberg, a psychologist from New York who was born in 1927 and died in 1987,

CHAPTER APP 9.2

You know Twitter. You may be one of the millions who use it every day to share your thoughts with followers.

How does it APPly to your daily life?
When the concept of *imaginary audience* was first proposed, Twitter didn't exist. Now that it does, the imaginary audience of adolescence has been replaced by a real audience of followers. (The same is true for Facebook or Snapchat friends, Instagram followers, etc.) When you were an adolescent, how did your use of Twitter or other social media affect your sense of imaginary audience — that your life is continuously being watched and evaluated by other people?

How does it APPly to your understanding of psychology?
How do Twitter and other social media help you appreciate the concept of imaginary audience? How might the concept of imaginary audience need to be adapted for today's adolescents?

To learn more about this app or to download it to your phone, you can search for "Twitter" on Google, in the iPhone App store, or in the Google Play store.

imaginary audience
A common way of thinking among adolescents in which they believe their lives are continuously being watched and evaluated by other people.

personal fable
A common way of thinking among adolescents in which they believe themselves to be special or invulnerable.

Michael Krinke/iStock/Getty Images

Adolescents commonly believe in a personal fable, or a way of thinking in which they believe themselves to be special or invulnerable. Personal fables can be dangerous because they make dangerous behaviors, like texting while driving, seem safe.

Fotosenmeer/Shutterstock

Moral development refers to changes in the way you determine right and wrong. For example, your stage of moral development can influence your decisions about whether or not to steal from a store.

extended Piaget's work by proposing a theory of moral development that has inspired many developmental researchers (Carpendale, 2009).

Kohlberg's basic idea is that the way we think about moral issues – especially how we determine right and wrong – evolves as we move through childhood and into adulthood. Specifically, Kohlberg argues that we move through three stages of moral reasoning – *preconventional morality, conventional morality*, and *postconventional morality* (Kohlberg, 1973a, b, 1974, 1984; Kohlberg & Candee, 1984):

- **Preconventional morality** is a moral decision-making strategy driven by the potential rewards and punishments of the decision. In this stage, what's right is what maximizes benefit and minimizes hardship for *you*. You make decisions to serve your own needs.
- **Conventional morality** is a moral decision-making strategy driven by the desire to follow society's norms and laws. In this stage, what's right is what puts you in line with your culture's expectations of you. You make decisions to ensure that others will approve of you, and when you consider doing something bad you realize that the system would fall apart "if everyone did it."
- **Postconventional morality** is a moral decision-making strategy driven by fundamental rights and ethical principles. The personal consequences of the decision, as well as how well the decision fits with society's preferences, take a backseat at this point. In this stage, what's right is what's *right* in the larger sense. You make decisions because ethical principles that steer all people toward such collective values as justice, dignity, and equality instruct you to do so.

Kohlberg (1984, pp. 177–178) offers the example of Joe, a participant in one of his longitudinal studies. Joe answered the same moral question at ages 10, 17, and 24: why shouldn't you steal from a store? His answers show a progression through Kohlberg's three stages. At 10, Joe explains that "someone could see you and call the police." So, you don't steal because if you do, bad things can happen to *you*. This kind of preconventional moral reasoning is common to children. By 17, adolescent Joe has entered the conventional morality stage. This is shown by his consideration of society's expectations and what it would mean if he and others didn't meet them: "It's one of our rules.... If we didn't have these laws, people would steal, they wouldn't have to work for a living, and our whole society would get out of kilter." At 24, adult Joe has progressed even further, with reasoning that refers to what is fundamentally and universally right, rather than what the rules or the law say: "It's violating another person's rights, in this case, to property."

For another real-life example of moral decision making, consider the story of a Detroit record shop owner named Jeff Bubeck (Saunders, 2012). Jeff stumbled upon a huge, valuable record and tape collection left behind in a storage unit by J Dilla, a legendary hip-hop producer who had died several years earlier. Jeff knew there was a market to sell what he had discovered, but he also knew that J Dilla's mother, Maureen Yancey, was in deep debt from the medical bills related to her son's lengthy terminal illness. So, he had a moral decision to make: sell his newfound bounty for a profit, or give it to J Dilla's mother. Jeff decided to give the records to J Dilla's mother, and his reasoning reflects Kohlberg's postconventional stage of moral decision making: "I was just trying to do the right thing ... it was her son's stuff, you know?... I told her take it with you. It's yours.... I was like, 'Yeah, back in the right hands'" (National Public Radio, 2014). See Show Me More 9.3 to hear a podcast that tells this story, including Jeff explaning his moral reasoning and J Dilla's mother's reaction to his decision.

There are a few other important features of Kohlberg's theory. First, the important thing is not necessarily the decision you make, but the reasoning you use to arrive at that decision. Second, age does not always predict moral thinking. Third, not everyone progresses all the way to the third stage. In fact, Kohlberg labeled the second stage

preconventional morality
A moral decision-making strategy driven by the potential rewards and punishments of the decision.

conventional morality
A moral decision-making strategy driven by the desire to follow society's norms and laws.

postconventional morality
A moral decision-making strategy driven by fundamental rights and ethical principles.

"conventional" because he concluded that moral thinking stops at that level for most people (Kohlberg, 1963, 1984).

Kohlberg believed that moral reasoning should be a focus of the educational system. In addition to the traditional academic subjects, Kohlberg thought schools should offer classes in "character education" to advance the ability to think about issues of right and wrong (Snarey, 2012).

Kohlberg's ideas have been used in educational settings, and have had a powerful impact on the developmental psychology field, but they also have received some sharp criticism. One criticism of Kohlberg's theory is the same that Piaget's theory received: it is too stage-based, and it doesn't reflect the reality that our moral reasoning inches forward gradually rather than suddenly leaping forward and then stalling for years (Nucci & Gingo, 2011).

A second criticism points out that moral reasoning and moral behavior — what you think is right and what you actually do in that situation — don't always match. In fact, one study found that the correlation between moral reasoning and moral action is just .3. That's positive, but far from perfect (Krebs & Denton, 2005).

DIVERSITY MATTERS

A third criticism focuses on culture: What seems universally "right" (and therefore determines the highest level of moral reasoning) may not be universal at all, but dependent upon ethnicity and other variables (Cowell et al., 2017; Menon, 2003; Turiel, 2002, 2006, 2008, 2015). What's "right" in your culture may not be "right" in another. One study posed this moral question to 10- and 11-year-old students: Should you mention your score to your classmates if you did much better on an exam than they did? The answer depended heavily on culture: 86% of U.S. kids believed it was right not to mention your own score, because by doing so you were showing off, but 68% of Chinese kids believed it was right to mention your own score, because by doing so you were offering to help your classmates (Heyman et al., 2008).

DIVERSITY MATTERS

A fourth criticism focuses not on ethnicity but on gender: Males and females may go about moral reasoning differently. Specifically, males tend to emphasize fair treatment, while females tend to emphasize caring for others in need (Eisenberg et al., 2009; Gilligan, 1982, 1987; Gilligan & Wiggins, 1987; Walker, 2006). Also, compared to males' moral decisions, females' moral decisions tend to be more influenced by the emotional responses related to harm that may come to someone in the situation (Friesdorf et al., 2015). These findings are especially important in light of the fact that the participants in Kohlberg's research were more often male than female, so the stages of moral reasoning that he proposed may describe moral development more accurately for males than females (Heyman & Lee, 2012; Jaffee & Hyde, 2000).

Photo by B+

J Dilla (James Yancey), a legendary hip-hop producer and DJ, passed away in 2006 after years of serious illness. Months later, a record store owner named Jeff Bubeck bought a record collection out of an abandoned storage unit. He soon discovered that he had bought J Dilla's record collection, as well as some of J Dilla's own unreleased beats. Those items were highly collectible and sought after by hip-hop fans. Bubeck faced a moral decision: sell them for a profit, or give them to J Dilla's mom (Maureen Yancey), who was in deep debt because of her son's medical bills. He decided to give them to Ms. Yancey, and his rationale demonstrated moral reasoning that exemplifies Kohlberg's postconventional stage (National Public Radio, 2014; Saunders, 2012).

Psychosocial Development

A primary challenge of adolescence is figuring out who we are as individuals. Erik Erikson, a German psychologist whose developmental theories became prominent in the 1950s and 1960s (and remain influential today), focused extensively on this process of forming an **identity**: a person's stable sense of who they are. Actually, identity is just a small part of Erikson's psychosocial theory of development, which features eight stages that cover the entire life span (Coles, 2000; Erikson, 1950, 1959; Erikson & Erikson, 1998). In the following paragraphs, we'll focus on the stages most relevant to adolescence, but **Table 9.3** offers a description of all eight stages, from birth through late adulthood.

As the table indicates, each stage is characterized by a *crisis*. If the crisis is successfully met, it produces a *virtue* that can benefit the person from that point forward. For example, in the infancy stage (0–18 months), Erikson identifies the crisis as *trust versus mistrust*. Babies can't take care of themselves, so they have to rely on other people to meet all their needs: to feed them, keep them warm, change their diapers, respond to their cries, and so on. Their experience during these early months teaches

identity
A part of Erikson's psychosocial theory of development; a person's stable sense of who they are.

TABLE 9.3: Erikson's Psychosocial Stages

STAGE	AGE	CRISIS	CENTRAL QUESTION	VIRTUE
Infancy	0–18 months	Trust vs. mistrust	"Will the people around me take care of me?"	Hope
Early childhood	2–3 years	Autonomy vs. shame and doubt	"Can I control myself?"	Will
Preschool	3–5 years	Initiative vs. guilt	"Can I do things on my own?"	Purpose
Elementary school	6–11	Industry vs. inferiority	"Can I keep up with my peers?"	Competence
Adolescence	12–18	Identity vs. role confusion	"Can I determine who I am?"	Fidelity
Young adulthood	19–40	Intimacy vs. isolation	"Can I form a lasting connection with another person?"	Love
Middle adulthood	40–65	Generativity vs. stagnation	"Can I contribute something valuable?"	Care
Older adulthood	65+	Ego integrity vs. despair	"Was my life well lived?"	Wisdom

According to Erik Erikson, at every age from birth through older adulthood, we experience a psychological crisis centering on a question that is particularly relevant at that time in our lives. Ideally, we answer that question in a positive way and develop the corresponding virtue.

them whether they can depend upon, or *trust*, other people. If it is a positive experience, they emerge with the virtue of *hope*, or a sense that things will work out and other people will come through for them.

For adolescence, Erikson identified the challenge as *identity versus role confusion* (Côté, 2009; Erikson, 1959, 1968; Marcia, 1966, 1980). The aim during those years is to develop an answer to a fundamental question: who am I? (see Table 9.3). That answer, of course, stems from answers to many more specific questions, each crucial to a person's individuality: Who am I in terms of religion? Ethnicity? Politics? Sexual orientation? Career? Style of dress? Social group? Music, sports, and other interests? At first, the options can seem overwhelming, especially as we begin to look beyond our immediate family and see the vast range of choices available not just among our peers but among people across the country or around the world. We may "try on" a variety of these options during adolescence, only to replace each one quickly with another. Society seems to allow for these temporary phases of identity during adolescence, at least to a greater extent than if they took place later. For example, a teenager who goes through a new look, a new set of friends, and a new passion every few months probably just gets an eye roll and a head shake from friends and family, but an equally fickle 35-year-old gets more serious disapproval. Erikson called this tolerance of rapidly shifting identities a *moratorium*, suggesting that we suspend judgment of adolescents as they work their way through this process of identity formation.

You probably remember lots of kids from your high school class, perhaps including yourself, who exemplified Erikson's description of an adolescent experiencing role confusion while forming an identity. The best example I've encountered is Steven, a psychotherapy client of mine who was a highly anxious kid. I saw Steven off and on throughout high school — a few sessions when he's struggling, followed by stretches of no therapy when he's doing fine. This gave me the unique opportunity to get close looks at his life in different stages during his teen years. When I first met Steven, he was intensely academic: lots of advanced classes, lots of concern about standardized test scores, little interest in fashion, friends, or much else that didn't involve classroom success. In fact, the original reason for Steven's therapy was intense anxiety about getting into an elite university — anxiety that was happening pretty early, considering he was just starting ninth grade. "I'm a serious student," he told me. "I'm pretty much all about my grades."

Just 6 months later, Steven was all about something else: skateboarding. He looked different, with a new haircut and new clothes; he spoke differently, with lots of skate lingo. He had plenty of skater friends and spent a lot of time at local skate parks or skate shops. His parents were now worried about his grades, but Steven was now worried about ankle injuries he might get while trying to impress his friends. Skateboard Steven lasted until the summer before tenth grade, at which point his interests shifted to politics. Political Steven wrote about political issues in his high school's newspaper, read lots of articles on political Web sites, and planned for a career in office. He hung out with kids on student council and sat at a lunch table where the main topic of conversation (and Steven's main anxiety) was how to help his preferred candidates win their upcoming elections. The skateboard gear was now in the back of the closet, replaced by a neater, more traditional wardrobe and haircut.

Steven's "lifelong" dedication to politics lasted through most of tenth grade. At that point, a growth spurt got him noticed by the coach of his school's basketball team, who encouraged Steven to attend a summer basketball camp. He did, and then made the varsity team in eleventh grade. Now we had Basketball Steven: hanging with his teammates exclusively, following NCAA and NBA teams enthusiastically, decked out in Nike hoops gear from head to toe, and focusing his worries on how many points, rebounds, and assists he was accumulating. All was well until a knee injury prevented Steven from playing basketball during his senior year, but a new passion found him: DJing. Steven bought a starter set of DJ equipment and started making mixes and beats on his laptop. New clothes, friends, and values followed (as did new anxieties, about his ability to get enough paying DJ gigs to pay for upgraded equipment).

Ideally, by the time his adolescence ends, Steven will have developed a coherent sense of who he is to carry him through the rest of his life. If so, he will earn the virtue of *fidelity*, the ability to stay true to who he is even when his life circumstances change. If not, he will remain in a state of role confusion, in which he continues to search for himself and test out different ways of living.

The importance of the outcome of this identity versus role confusion stage is especially clear when you consider Erikson's next stage: *intimacy versus isolation*. **Intimacy** is long-term emotional closeness with a romantic partner. According to Erikson, the intimacy versus isolation stage is when young adults seek monogamous, loving relationships that will last a lifetime. Erikson believed that success at the young adult stage depends heavily on success at the adolescent stage: Those who have formed a strong identity are most likely to create successful couples, while those still in a state of role confusion are most likely to struggle. (Would you want to be in a long-term relationship with someone still unable to commit to a single identity?)

Research on Erikson's ideas confirms the importance of identity formation during adolescence. One study found that teens who struggle to form an identity are much more likely than their peers to experience high levels of anxiety (Crocetti et al., 2009). Another study found that teens with low levels of identity development are especially likely to experience high levels of distress (Wiley & Berman, 2013). Another longitudinal study followed participants from age 15 to age 25 to see if the teens' levels of identity formation predicted their ability to form intimate romantic relationships 10 years later. These researchers found a significant positive correlation of .33 between these two variables. Correlation doesn't necessarily mean cause (there may be outside factors influencing both identity formation and romantic intimacy), but this correlation supports Erikson's basic idea that success at the adolescent and young adult stages go together (Beyers & Seiffge-Krenke, 2010).

dekazigzag/Shutterstock

Image Source Trading Ltd/Shutterstock

Achieving intimacy, or long-term emotional closeness with a romantic partner, is a major challenge of young adulthood.

intimacy
A part of Erikson's psychosocial theory of development; long-term emotional closeness with a romantic partner.

CURRENT CONTROVERSY

Social Media: Good or Bad for Adolescent Development?

Social media has become ever-present in adolescence, with the vast majority of U.S. teens using Instagram, Snapchat, Facebook, TikTok, Twitter, or other platforms (Statista, 2018). With the rise of social media (and smartphones), psychologists have studied their impact on the lives of teens. Most reviews of this research conclude that social media can have both positive and negative effects (Allen et al., 2014; Best et al., 2014; Uhls et al., 2017; Underwood et al., 2018; Wood et al., 2016). Among the findings are these:

Positive Effects of Social Media:

- **Social media can help teens develop friendships.** Teens often use social media to make new friends and enhance the friendships they already have (Borca et al., 2015; Lenhart, 2015).
- **Social media can help teens build social support.** When teens go through difficult times, social media can provide encouragement, assistance, and a sense of community (Frison & Eggermont, 2016; Maier et al., 2015).
- **Social media can allow for beneficial identity exploration.** Deciding what to disclose and how to present themselves (through photos, status updates, etc.) can help teens develop a stronger and more coherent sense of who they are (Craig & McInroy, 2014; James, 2009; Subrahmanyam & Smahel, 2012).
- Social media can help teens find others going through similar struggles. For teens with specific issues, including those related to sexual identity, academic challenges, physical problems, and psychological disorders, the sheer volume and variety of people who can relate may be much greater on social media than in face-to-face interactions (Fuchs, 2017; Naslund et al., 2016; Perales et al., 2016).

Negative Effects of Social Media:

- **Social media provides a platform for cyberbullying.** The perception of being anonymous, or at least somewhat removed from the target, can lead some teens to cyberbully. At the least, it can perpetuate "digital drama" in which harassment, cruelty, insults, rumors, or humiliation are used to harm others (Barlett et al., 2018; Chen et al., 2017; Hamm et al., 2015; Whittaker & Kowalski, 2015).
- **Social media can cause depression or anxiety through social comparison.** Teens who believe their own social lives, attractiveness, wealth, or other parts of their lives are inferior to the ones they see in their social media feeds are more likely to develop psychological problems including depression and anxiety (Davila et al., 2012; Fardouly et al., 2017; Nesi & Prinstein, 2015; Verduyn et al., 2015).
- **Social media can expose teens to inappropriate content.** Especially for younger teens, the sex, violence, substance use, and other high-risk content they may see and hear on social media, especially if it comes across as normal and expected behavior, can be more than they are ready to handle (Daniels & Zurbriggen, 2016; Winpenny et al., 2013).
- **Social media can interfere with healthy behaviors like sleeping, exercising, and in-person socializing.** When social media is used excessively, it can take time away from other essential activities (Hale & Guan, 2015; Herman et al., 2015; Kremer et al., 2014; Wartella & Robb, 2007).

Research suggests that using social media can have both positive and negative effects on adolescents.

Relationships with Parents. The teenage years are notorious for parent–child conflicts. Certainly, it is a time of tension for everyone involved. After over a decade of dependence, in which young children rely on their parents to do everything from wipe their noses to tie their shoes, adolescents begin to do many big things (driving, dating) and make many big decisions (career, college, sex) for themselves. But they still can't do everything on their own, so inevitably, there is a push and pull between teens' need for autonomy ("Stop bugging me about my homework!") and their need for help ("Can you help me with my homework?") (McElhaney et al., 2009).

This push and pull does not mean that adolescence is doomed to become an all-out conflict between parents and kids. In fact, research suggests that in about 85–95% of families, the level of turmoil is not extreme (Lamb & Lewis, 2005). There is typically a modest increase in conflict around the beginning of adolescence, but these conflicts usually don't threaten the relationships that hold the family together (Branje et al., 2009; Steinberg, 1981, 1990). Families generally find a way to adjust to these adolescent changes and to renegotiate the roles and responsibilities of each member. (This is true especially for families with authoritative parents, who set rules but are willing to alter them in response to the increasing independence of their kids.) Conflict between parents and adolescents is generally less extensive for second-born kids than for first-born kids, suggesting that parents learn from their experiences with the oldest child, then adjust their parenting to minimize conflict with younger siblings (Whiteman et al., 2003). The few families that are most likely to be torn apart by adolescence are those that were starting to tear well before their kids reached that age (Laursen & Collins, 2009; Stattin & Klackenberg, 1992).

DIVERSITY MATTERS

In some cases, difficulties with parents can relate to another phenomenon of adolescence: gender differences in psychological disorders. Starting in adolescence, girls (compared to boys) show an increase in *internalizing* disorders. These are disorders in which they direct their distress toward themselves, either bodily (cutting, for example) or more often emotionally (depression or anxiety, for example). Adolescent girls also develop much higher levels of body dissatisfaction (often seeing themselves as too fat), accompanied by potentially harmful weight control efforts from dieting to bulimia and anorexia (Barker & Galambos, 2003; Karazsia et al., 2017; May et al., 2006; Morken et al., 2018; Phelps et al., 1993).

Adolescent boys, on the other hand, demonstrate more *externalizing* disorders — disorders in which they direct their distress toward other people, like conduct disorder, oppositional defiant disorder, and, to some extent, attention-deficit/hyperactivity disorder (ADHD). This gender gap in disorders emerges at about age 13, grows until about age 18, and then remains throughout adulthood (Galambos et al., 2009). Keep in mind that any of these psychological disorders can be either the cause or the effect of difficulties in the parent–adolescent relationship. Of course, in some cases, psychological disorders can arise for reasons completely unrelated to parenting.

Researchers who examine adolescents' relationships with their parents often find that teens who have more than one parent develop a distinct relationship with each parent. In particular, teens tend to relate differently to their moms than their dads. Of course, it varies from one family to the next, but among teens with a mom and a dad, they generally spend more time with mom and seek more support from her (Doyle et al., 2009; Markiewicz et al., 2006). Teens also tend to feel closer to mom and share more of their thoughts and feelings with her (Doyle et al., 2009). On the other hand, teens tend to disagree with mom more, showing her less respect and obedience than they do with dad (Maccoby, 1998; McHale et al., 2003; Steinberg & Silk, 2002).

Relationships with Peers. Just as crucial as teens' relationships with their parents are teens' relationships with each other. Adolescents spend twice as much time with peers as with their parents. Compared to early childhood, more of this time is unsupervised, in larger groups, directed by the kids themselves (as opposed to parents determining what kids do), and involves all genders (Rubin et al., 2006).

Researchers have found that these peer relationships have important consequences for functioning and well-being (Hartup, 1999; Lamblin et al., 2017; Rubin et al., 2005). For example, adolescents who struggle socially tend to struggle in lots of other ways: bad grades, poor self-image, depression, delinquency, and substance abuse (Gazelle & Ladd, 2003; Ollendick et al., 1992; Sandstrom et al., 2003; Wentzel, 2003; Wentzel et al., 2004). Of course, there are exceptions to this rule. Some isolated kids do very well in many areas of life, and some popular kids do quite poorly. And it is often hard to tell which came first: social isolation or the problems (like bad grades, depression, etc.) that often come with it. In many cases, these circumstances feed off of each other. A "loner" kid becomes depressed, which further isolates them from their peers, which worsens their depression, and the cycle continues.

kali9/E+/Getty Images

Relationships with peers become extremely important during the adolescent years.

In some cases, the particular group of friends you hang out with — your crowd — can influence the odds of experiencing certain kinds of psychological problems as you move through adolescence. Researchers studied about 250 diverse high school students who labeled themselves as Populars, Jocks, Brains, Burnouts, Nonconformists, or Average kids (Prinstein & La Greca, 2003). They found that Burnouts experience significantly higher rates of depression than Populars and Jocks; Brains experience much higher rates of social anxiety than Populars and Jocks; and Brains, Burnouts, and Average kids

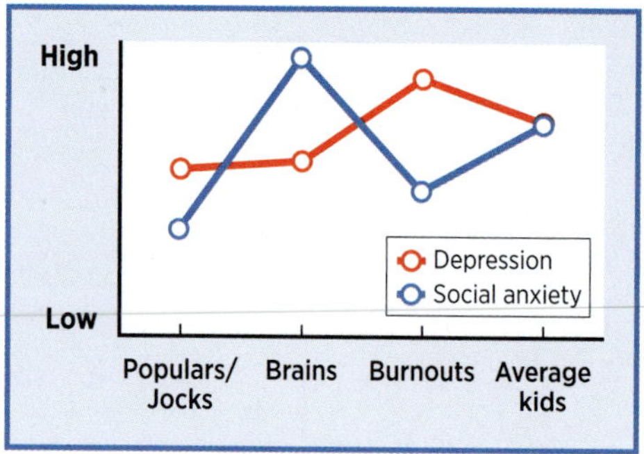

FIGURE 9.9 Your Friend Group and Your Mental Health. During adolescence, different friend groups experience different psychological problems, like depression and social anxiety, at different rates. Burnouts experience the highest levels of depression, but Brains experience the highest levels of social anxiety. Does this match what you and your peers experienced in adolescence? Data from Prinstein and La Greca (2003).

experience more loneliness than Populars and Jocks. **Figure 9.9** illustrates some of these findings. Also, if many of your friends experience a particular problem, then the odds that you will experience that same problem increase. For example, teens who hang out with depressed friends are more likely to become depressed themselves, and kids whose friends have eating disorders are more likely to develop eating disorders themselves (Ellis & Dumas, 2019; O'Connor et al., 2016; Schacter & Juvonen, 2017).

One problem with adolescent crowds and the friendships within them is that they are unstable. Kids tend to move through a number of "BFFs" and peer groups during their middle school and high school years (Jiang & Cillesen, 2005). One study asked adolescents to list the names of their friends once per month. The boys' answers were a bit more stable than girls', but all of them demonstrated a high level of instability. Overall, about one-third of the friends on a typical adolescent's list one month didn't make that adolescent's list the very next month (Chan & Poulin, 2007). Over the course of a 9-month school year, that's a high level of turnover, possibly resulting in completely different groups of friends at the beginning of the year and at the end. Additionally, teens' self-perceptions of peer relationships are not reliable. This means that teens are likely to overestimate or underestimate how close they are with their friends, which in turn could lead to further social problems (Brown & Larson, 2009).

Friendships take on added importance in adolescence, but another kind of peer relationship – dating – is important as well. As your own experience may reflect, the way kids date changes significantly within just the brief span of high school. Here is a summary of a common progression (Connolly & McIsaac, 2009):

- At 14, dating relationships typically last just a few weeks and rarely last more than a few months. Dating often takes place in large groups rather than couples, and social status is often a major motivator. You can become more popular because you're going out with someone popular. There are lots of crushes and infatuations too, the reason for which is often to have something to talk about with your friends as much as it is "true love" with your partner.
- At 16, dating is a bit more serious, with less of it happening in large groups and more of it happening in couples. The average dating relationship lasts 6 months. Couples often get together because their friends help to arrange the relationships by asking "Do you like...?" for each other.
- At 18, dating is again more serious, with the average relationship lasting a full year. Dating activities are almost all couple-based, with only a few big group outings. The relationships are more exclusive, so emotional bonds between couples are more lasting and adult-like. At times, people at this age can find themselves engulfed in romantic relationships, sometimes so much that they eclipse friends, family, or individual goals. For example, both members of a high school senior couple applying to college may limit their applications to only the specific schools where the partner is also applying.

DIVERSITY MATTERS It is important to keep in mind that the way dating changes throughout adolescence depends on a number of cultural variables, including ethnicity. For example, Asian American teens tend to start dating later than White, Black, and Latinx teens, perhaps due to differences in cultural norms based on individualism and collectivism (Connolly & McIsaac, 2011; Connolly et al., 2004).

DIVERSITY MATTERS Most of the data on adolescent dating focuses on heterosexual relationships, but in recent years, research has emerged on homosexual and bisexual relationships among adolescents as well. About 5% of adolescents report same-sex attraction, and they appear to have as many dating experiences as those who are attracted to the opposite sex (Carver et al., 2003; Williams et al., 2003). However, a sizable number of the dating experiences of adolescents who identify as gay or lesbian are actually with opposite-sex partners, possibly reflecting a fluctuating sexual orientation during the teen years or pressure from peers to participate in straight dating behaviors (Diamond, 2008; Russell & Consolacion, 2003). Among younger adolescents – middle schoolers in grades 6–8, to be specific – approximately

3.8% identify as gay, lesbian, or bisexual, and another 12.1% as "not sure" (Shields et al., 2013).

Unfortunately, adolescent dating relationships are not immune to relationship violence (Vagi et al., 2013). Alarmingly, every year about 1 in 10 high school girls experiences violence from a dating partner (Howard et al., 2013). One large-scale longitudinal study of over 600 adolescents identified several factors that predict dating violence: adverse living conditions (such as poverty), violence-tolerant attitudes, and, perhaps most notably, watching violent media (Connolly et al., 2010). Another study points out the importance of the peer group norms: teens whose friends are violent toward their romantic partners tend to be violent toward their own (Ellis & Dumas, 2019; Foshee et al., 2013). Child abuse is also a factor. Kids who are abused are at increased likelihood to become perpetrators of dating violence as adolescents (and adults as well) (Gómez, 2011).

On a more uplifting note, some recent research on adolescence has focused on *positive youth development*, efforts to build on teens' strengths by involving them in organized, constructive peer-based activities (Grusec et al., 2011; Lerner & Steinberg, 2009). In positive youth development programs, kids are offered group activities that allow them to participate in the simultaneous improvement of society and themselves (Damon, 2004; Larson, 2000; Lerner et al., 2009; Snyder et al., 2011). For example, a high school may create a club for kids to boost a community's voter registration or beautify its parks, a town may start a Girls on the Run council, or a religious institution's youth group may organize a charity drive or a Habitat for Humanity effort.

By design, positive youth development programs try to enhance the "5 C's": competence, confidence, connection, character, and caring/compassion. Some research indicates that these programs work. One meta-analysis found that positive youth development programs produce meaningful improvements in competence, confidence, and life skills (Bruner et al., 2021). Other research found that high-risk kids experience fewer psychological problems when they participate in these group activities (Holland & Andre, 1987; Masten, 2004, 2006). Other research finds additional positive effects on school performance, but finds no impact on other important variables, like risky sexual behavior, problem behaviors, or positive social behaviors (Ciocanel et al., 2017).

DIVERSITY MATTERS

Of course, beneficial outcomes of any program for teens can only take place if the teens have the chance to participate. Unfortunately, the availability of extracurricular programs of any kind (both at school and elsewhere) depends on socioeconomic status (Fredricks & Eccles, 2006; Theokas & Bloch, 2006). For example, kids from poor families participate in organized sports at a rate far below that for kids from more affluent families, not only because the sports themselves cost money (registration, equipment, etc.), but because they require rides and free time from parents who simply may not have enough of it (Mahoney et al., 2009).

Emerging Adulthood. When does adolescence end and adulthood begin? Traditionally, adolescence has been roughly defined as the middle school and high school years. According to that definition, adulthood would begin by the time a person reaches the age of 18 (or perhaps a bit later). But some contemporary developmental psychologists, led by J. J. Arnett, have put forward the idea of **emerging adulthood**: a recently proposed developmental stage during which the person gradually moves from adolescence to adulthood, typically during the late teens and twenties in modern Western cultures (Arnett, 2000, 2007, 2014; Schwartz, 2016). As an example of emerging adulthood, consider Joshua, who went away to college for a couple of years after high school but returned to his parents' house at the age of 20. He continues to take classes at the local college on a part-time basis, and holds a part-time job as well, but still relies on his parents for money, food, and emotional support. Through his twenties, he occasionally moves into an apartment with friends, but only with his parents' backing. He typically moves back home after a short stint. He's now approaching 30, still striving toward self-sufficiency.

Doug Savage

emerging adulthood
A recently proposed developmental stage during which the person gradually moves from adolescence to adulthood.

MY TAKE **VIDEO 9.2**

Emerging Adulthood

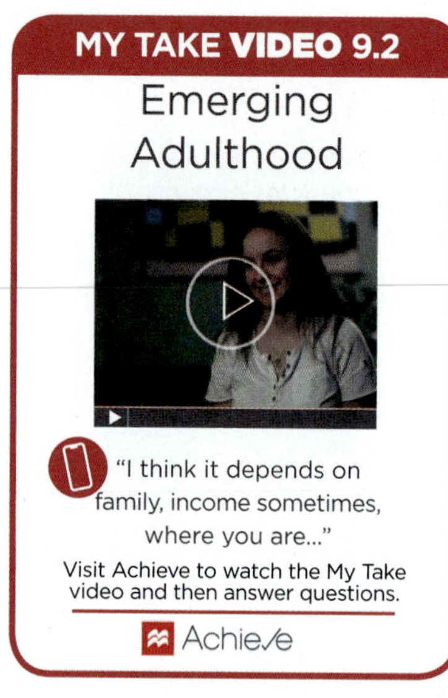

"I think it depends on family, income sometimes, where you are..."

Visit Achieve to watch the My Take video and then answer questions.

Achieve

The notion that adulthood *emerges* suggests that we become adults slowly, little by little. This differs from the conventional idea that we become adults more abruptly, perhaps around the time we reach a particular birthday that signifies changes to our legal status (18? 21?) or when we achieve a particular milestone, such as graduation, marriage, or a first job (Kerckhoff, 2003). If adulthood emerges slowly, that means adolescence fades slowly. If a 20-something (or perhaps 30-something or even older) has not yet fully become an adult, then they must remain partially an adolescent, which means that they may still be searching for their own identity, as Erikson described. As a result, emerging adults may delay such tasks as finding a mate and starting a family, and they may stay somewhat dependent on their parents or others for support.

DIVERSITY MATTERS

Some researchers dispute the notion of emerging adulthood as a developmental stage through which everyone passes (Côté, 2014; Kloep & Hendry, 2011). These researchers argue that emerging adulthood (if it exists at all) exists only in cultures where 20-somethings can financially afford it and the people around them endorse it, such as higher-SES segments of the United States and other Western countries (du Bois-Reymond, 2016; Galambos & Martinez, 2007; Hendry & Kloep, 2007; Hill & Redding, 2021; Syed, 2015). They suggest we shouldn't necessarily accept emerging adulthood as the norm, even if we accept it as a possibility, since that would imply that making a quicker jump from adolescence to full adulthood is somehow abnormal (Côté & Bynner, 2008).

Shifts in living arrangements during the COVID pandemic support the idea that the financial climate has to be right for young people to enter adulthood. In just the 5-month period from February to July in 2020, the percentage of U.S. residents aged 18–29 living with one or both parents jumped from 47% to 52%. The jump was even greater for the younger half of that age bracket (18–24 years old), 63% to 71%. It is probably not coincidental that around the same time (February–May 2020), 25% of people aged 16 to 24 lost their jobs, resulting in twice as many young people who were neither working nor enrolled in school (DeAngelis, 2021). Critics of the idea that emerging adulthood is a normal developmental stage might point to these numbers and argue that a young person whose psychological development is complete might still wait to launch their adult lives if the economy is bad, as it became during the pandemic.

CHECK YOUR LEARNING:

9.15 How do psychologists define adolescence?

9.16 During puberty, what physical changes occur in girls and boys?

9.17 How does the brain develop during adolescence?

9.18 How are egocentric thinking, imaginary audience, and personal fable relevant to adolescent thinking?

9.19 What is the sequence of Kohlberg's stages of moral thinking?

9.20 How do psychologists define identity?

9.21 What is Erikson's eight-stage psychosocial theory of development, how does it apply to adolescence?

9.22 What role do relationships with parents and peers play during adolescence?

9.23 What is the proposed stage called emerging adulthood, and how is it relevant to adolescence?

To check your understanding of these questions, click show the answers or refer to the answers in the Chapter Summary.

Adulthood

YOU WILL LEARN:

9.24 how the functioning of our bodies and brains changes throughout the stages of adulthood.

Our final phase of development, adulthood, covers a long stretch of time: from the late teens or early twenties all the way through the eighties, nineties, and beyond. The earliest developmental psychologists focused exclusively on kids, but the assumption that development stalls in adulthood has been shattered. Current developmental psychologists acknowledge that development continues all the way through the life span (Baltes et al., 2006; Elder & Shanahan, 2006; Moshman, 2003).

Physical Development

Let's consider the physical changes that predictably happen to us as we move through young adulthood, middle adulthood, and older adulthood.

9.25 how cognitive performance changes throughout the stages of adulthood.

9.26 about the highlights of psychosocial development throughout adulthood.

Young Adulthood. In early adulthood, the body and the brain peak. In most sports, elite athletes reach their prime in their twenties, with a quick decline often looming in their thirties. Your own athletic prowess might follow a similar path. If you haven't yet experienced it, you will soon learn why rec centers have separate "30 and over" or "40 and over" leagues in many sports!

The health-related habits of young adulthood are especially important, not just while you're a young adult, but for the rest of your life. The routines that you establish for yourself in your twenties – what you eat, how often you exercise, how much you sleep, how much you smoke, drink, or use drugs – may be hard to break when you're in your thirties, forties, and beyond (Daniels et al., 2005). You might get by with unhealthy habits while you're younger, but the consequences will probably catch up with you later – often in the form of obesity, high blood pressure, heart disease, or other serious health risks (Mozaffarian et al., 2011). For example, according to one study of over 15,000 young adults, those who were overweight or obese in their teens or early twenties were significantly more likely to gain more weight and develop diabetes in their late twenties and early thirties (Nagata et al., 2018).

Gary Burchell/DigitalVision/Getty Images

Exercise and other health-related habits of young adulthood are important because they often extend into middle adulthood and older adulthood.

Middle Adulthood. Starting in the thirties and accelerating with every decade, the functioning of our brains and bodies gradually declines. Age spots, wrinkles, thinning hair, creaky joints, and loss of muscle tone creep in. Bone loss causes breaks to happen more easily and heal more slowly. It also causes us to lose height – about 1–2 inches between our thirties and our seventies (Sorkin et al., 1999). We also get fatter, or more specifically, fat comprises much more of our body weight in middle adulthood than it did in adolescence (Kyle et al., 2001). Our need for glasses and contacts increases dramatically in our forties and fifties due to our eyes' decreased ability to focus. For some, hearing begins to slip too. Of course, healthy habits related to eating, exercise, and sleeping can reduce the rate at which any of these changes take place, at least to some degree. A 40-year-old who eats healthily, runs 5Ks, avoids alcohol, and gets a solid 8–10 hours of sleep each night is much more likely to avoid serious physical problems than a 40-year-old who eats unhealthily, rarely exercises, drinks heavily, and pulls all-nighters.

LIFE HACK 9.2

Make healthy choices about diet, exercise, sleep, and substance use when you're a young adult. Those choices often become habits that continue for decades.

(Daniels et al., 2005; Mozaffarian et al., 2011)

For women, a hallmark of middle adulthood is **menopause**: the time in a woman's life when she stops having menstrual periods. The average age for menopause is 51, but it can take place as early as the late thirties or as late as the late fifties (Gold et al., 2001; Morabia & Costanza, 1998). Menopause is associated with a drop in estrogen levels and other physical changes that vary from woman to woman, including hot flashes, fatigue, and stomach and heart irregularities. Typically, these changes do not cause severe or lasting disruption to the woman's life. Some researchers have also found that depression rates increase after menopause, but others have found no such evidence (Hunter, 1990; Llaneza et al., 2012; Matthews et al., 1990). Among the factors that increase the likelihood that a woman will experience depression after menopause are previous episodes of depression, stressful life events (like health problems or children leaving home) that happen around the same time, menopause occurring relatively early in the woman's life, and negative attitudes toward menopause and aging (Georgakis et al., 2016; Vivian-Taylor & Hickey, 2014). Another factor that can have an impact on a woman's experience of menopause is her partner's attitude toward it. Those women whose partners are more knowledgeable and supportive about menopause symptoms tend to experience higher quality of life during menopause (Zhang et al., 2020).

Men don't experience anything quite as definitive as menopause, but they do experience *andropause* starting in their late thirties and continuing through their fifties. The gradual hormonal changes of andropause happen primarily because of lower levels of testosterone. Andropause does not eliminate a man's ability to

menopause
The time in a woman's middle adulthood when she stops having menstrual periods.

Ryan McGinnis/Alamy

Studies of the brains of taxi drivers, who accumulate vast knowledge of a city's streets as they shuttle passengers, show that experience continues to shape the brain even during middle adulthood.

reproduce, but it does decrease it — a fact that is receiving increased attention among couples and their doctors considering the biological clocks of couples trying to conceive (Lewis et al., 2006).

The interaction of nature and nurture — specifically, the notion that experience shapes the biology of the brain — remains true well into middle adulthood. In an innovative study, researchers used MRIs to examine the brains of London taxi drivers in middle adulthood and found that the volume of their hippocampus was significantly greater than that of control participants (Maguire et al., 2000). This is important because the hippocampus controls spatial representation, which is where we keep maps of streets and other spaces. So, these London taxi drivers' brains actually expanded in such a way that reflects the knowledge they accumulated as they navigated the streets of London during their middle adulthood years. In a 2006 follow-up study, these researchers compared the brains of London taxi drivers to the brains of London bus drivers. Both drive full-time, but the bus drivers follow the same predictable route day after day while the taxi drivers traverse the city on unpredictable routes. The bus drivers' brains did not show the same increased volume in the hippocampus as the taxi drivers' brains. This finding confirmed that spatial knowledge (which taxi drivers need far more than bus drivers), as opposed to any other aspect of driving, affects brain development, even when the brain belongs to a middle-aged adult.

Older Adulthood. Older adulthood — generally, your sixties and beyond — is a life stage that extends further today than it ever has in the past. With a current life expectancy in the United States of 78.6 years (about 81 for women, about 76 for men), and with the number of people reaching 100 more than tripling in the last few decades, there is a good chance that your older adulthood will last as long as your young or middle adulthood (Xu et al., 2018).

Jupiterimages/Stockbyte/Getty Images

Healthy habits like regular exercise can reduce the chances of serious medical problems during older adulthood.

Generally, the decline in physical abilities that began in middle adulthood continues as we move through our sixties and beyond. Just as the body shrinks during older adulthood, the brain does as well, losing about 10–15% of its peak volume by the age of 90 (Shan et al., 2005; Zelazo & Lee, 2010). The parts of the brain that are most likely to shrink include the frontal lobes, a fact that correlates with the decline of memory and other cognitive abilities (Pardo et al., 2007). The sensory abilities weaken, with such vision problems as glaucoma and cataracts increasingly common and deterioration of the cochlea in the inner ear causing an increased need for hearing aids. There's also an increase in medical conditions such as arthritis (joint inflammation) and osteoporosis (excessive bone loss). Because of weakening bones and immune systems, simple falls can lead to serious injuries that require extensive recovery time or surgery. More serious and potentially fatal diseases like cancer and cardiovascular disease also become more common. Just as in earlier stages of adult life, healthy habits can reduce the chances of many of these unfortunate events (Mattson, 2012).

Cognitive Development

Like physical functioning, cognitive functioning generally peaks during young adulthood. Memory, speed of information processing, creativity, and other measures that developmental psychologists use to assess the sharpness of our minds all land at their highest levels around our twenties (Park et al., 2002; Salthouse & Babcock, 1991; Verhaeghen & Salthouse, 1997).

Things begin to change during middle adulthood. We process information a bit more slowly, meaning that we need just a bit more time to respond to stimuli that we see and hear. Also, our working memory becomes a bit more restricted, so we take more time to solve problems, formulate responses to other people, and make decisions.

What happens to intelligence during middle adulthood is more complicated, largely because intelligence consists of so many distinct abilities. Also, age-based comparisons can be made via either cross-sectional or longitudinal research methods, which sometimes produce different results (O'Connor & Kaplan, 2003; Salthouse, 2009). In the large-scale Seattle Longitudinal Study, researchers measured various intelligence-related abilities of thousands of participants over many decades (Schaie, 2012). The study concludes that some components of intelligence – particularly processing speed and fluency with words and numbers – seem to peak in early adulthood and decline in middle adulthood, especially toward its tail end (in our fifties). But many other components of intelligence – verbal meaning, reasoning, spatial abilities – seem to remain as high during middle adulthood as they were in young adulthood. Overall, the findings suggest that noticeable declines in intelligence typically don't occur in healthy adults until our sixties or seventies, and that many of us will retain intelligence comparable to many young adults well into our 80s or beyond.

Of course, diseases of the brain can significantly disrupt the cognitive process. The risk for such diseases – most often, *dementia* – greatly increases during older adulthood. Dementia is a term used to cover any brain disorder in which the main symptom is a steep decline in overall mental functioning. *Alzheimer's disease* is a particular kind of dementia in which basic cognitive functions like memory, language, and reason worsen irreversibly. Alzheimer's disease is devastating and, unfortunately, increasingly common: In the United States, over 11% of people over 65, and 35% of people over 85, have Alzheimer's disease, for a total of over 5 million (Alzheimer's Association, 2021). Researchers are actively searching for ways to cure Alzheimer's, or even slow its progress, but with little success. The result is a tremendous burden on families' time, finances, and emotions as they struggle to provide their older loved ones with the care they deserve.

The causes of Alzheimer's disease also remain under investigation. Some of the suspected risk factors are outside of our control (genes), but many other risk factors are at least partially within our control, particularly by exercising, eating, and sleeping right: obesity, smoking, diet, cholesterol levels, heart health, and sleep quality (Ahlskog et al., 2011; Daviglus et al., 2011; Li et al., 2011; Lutsey et al., 2018; Shi et al., 2018). One study estimates that half of Alzheimer's disease cases are attributable to these controllable risk factors, and that even moderate improvement in them could prevent millions of cases in the future (Barnes & Yaffe, 2011).

Psychosocial Development

As we move from young adulthood through older age, we also move through a sequence of psychological and social experiences. Let's consider them chronologically, from young adulthood through middle adulthood and older adulthood.

Young Adulthood. As Erik Erikson emphasized, one of the primary tasks of young adulthood is to form loving, lasting couples that will provide intimacy and stave off isolation. Traditionally, this meant marriage, but in recent decades, marriage has been happening less often and later in life (Teachman et al., 2013). At a wedding in 1960 between a woman and man (in which the marriage was the first for both the bride and groom), the median age of the woman was 20.3 and the median age of the man was 22.8. By 1980, those numbers had climbed to 22.0 (woman) and 24.7 (man), and by 2018, they had further climbed to 27.8 (woman) and 29.8 (man) (U.S. Census Bureau, 2018).

One reason for the differences in marriage patterns is the rise of *cohabitation*, or romantically involved couples living together while unmarried. Since 1970, the number of cohabiting couples has multiplied by 10, and the stigma that once followed cohabiting is largely gone. In recent years, at least 75% of young adults live together with a partner before they get married (Popenoe, 2009). Cohabiting households are now as likely to include children as married households, and the percentage of babies born to cohabiting couples has more than tripled since 1980 (Kroeger & Smock, 2014; Sassler & Miller, 2017).

In spite of the trends toward extended singlehood and cohabitation, over 90% of U.S. adults marry, and the vast majority of these marriages take place during young adulthood (Popenoe, 2009). But a sizable number of these marriages end in divorce, most often in years 5–10 of the marriage (Amato, 2010). The divorce rate almost tripled between 1980 and 2006, but it has stopped growing in more recent years (Hoelter, 2009; National Vital Statistics, 2010). **Table 9.4** lists some of the most powerful predictors of divorce in couples.

TABLE 9.4: Factors That Increase the Likelihood of Divorce

YOUR SITUATION	YOUR (OR YOUR PARTNER'S) CHARACTERISTICS
Marrying young Low education level Low socioeconomic status No religious affiliation Baby before marriage Divorced parents	Psychological problems Alcohol or substance use Violent toward partner Cheating, infidelity Unfair division of household labor

Information from Hoelter (2009).

Whether married, cohabiting, or single, parenthood is another defining challenge of young adulthood (Azar, 2003; Stern et al., 2018). In most cases, young adults rise to the challenge posed by their bundle of joy, but the process can also produce significant distress, especially when the new-baby excitement wears off, helpful relatives leave, work hours increase, or the parent has little confidence in their parenting abilities (Gross & Marcussen, 2017; Wallace & Gotlib, 1990). Other studies have found new parents, particularly new moms, are most likely to struggle with depression and other psychological problems when their pre-baby expectations – how much they would enjoy parenthood, how difficult it would be, how much their partner would help – did not match their post-baby experiences (Hackel & Ruble, 1992; Harwood et al., 2007; Kalmuss et al., 1992; Riggs et al., 2018).

One of my own therapy clients, Marci, illustrated this unhappy reaction to unfulfilled expectations. Early in her first pregnancy, she came to see me for help overcoming some mild OCD (obsessive-compulsive disorder) issues. She had a fear of germs that sent her to the sink to wash her hands about 10–20 times a day. She'd be facing lots of germs when the baby (and dirty diapers) arrived, so she proactively sought my help, and the treatment was successful. A few months before her due date, Marci no longer washed her hands excessively, and she was optimistic that motherhood would be joyful. I didn't hear from her until about 6 months after she had given birth, and when I did, she did not sound joyful at all. In fact, she sounded disillusioned and depressed. Caring for this baby was much more difficult than she anticipated. This wasn't like when she held her friend's babies and made goo-goo eyes at them until she saw a big toothless smile, she told me. She couldn't hand her own baby back to anyone when they started crying or spitting up. The middle-of-the-night feedings, the fussiness, the never-ending laundry, and the limited help she received – none of it was what she expected when she was expecting. We restarted therapy and saw each other for a few more sessions. With some compassion, some adjustments in her expectations, and some suggestions for communicating with others about help and support they could provide, she was well on her way to feeling content and, at times, joyful.

iStock/Getty Images

Middle adulthood is marked by the stress of multiple obligations, often including work and caring for young children and other family members.

Middle Adulthood. By middle adulthood, many of us have moved past finding partners and entered parenthood. We have entered Erikson's *generativity versus stagnation* stage, which means that our work becomes a primary focus (Wapner & Demick, 2003). Work, in this sense, should be understood broadly: not only traditional careers or jobs, but also stay-at-home parenting or other essential roles, whether directly paid or not. In any of these capacities, a goal of work during middle adulthood is to produce something that the individual deems lasting and worthy – perhaps healthy and happy children, or positive change in the world, or a profit.

There is a unique set of circumstances surrounding this pursuit of meaningful work during middle adulthood. In some ways, dedication to work becomes easier in middle adulthood than it was during early adulthood, largely because of family circumstances. Specifically, teenagers require a lot less direct care than babies, preschoolers, or elementary schoolers, which frees up time and energy for parents to devote to work (Moen & Roehling, 2005; Sterns & Huyck, 2001). On the other hand, middle adulthood comes with its own family stressors that can interfere with work productivity. For example, a 50-year-old adult might have a 25-year-old child who moves back home, regularly borrows money to pay back student loans, or needs a grandparent to watch the grandkids on a regular basis. Or, they might have an ailing parent or partner of their own to take care of (Climo & Stewart, 2003). Whether they are an entry-level employee or an executive in the peak earning years of their life, a combination of these factors can detract from their efficiency and add to their stress level (Aazami et al., 2018; Michel et al., 2011; Simon-Rusinowitz et al., 1996; Steiner & Fletcher, 2017).

A large-scale study of workers at various stages of adulthood illustrates the realities of working during middle adulthood. Researchers surveyed over 41,000 male and female employees of a huge corporation (IBM) from 79 countries in North America, Latin America, Europe, and Asia (Erickson et al., 2010). Their main finding was that workers at either end of the parenting spectrum – workers who never had kids, or workers whose kids were grown and out of the house – had the lowest levels of work–family stress. Workers in the middle of the spectrum had the highest levels of work–family stress. These workers are the parents in their thirties and early forties with young kids – kids who need not only the income that a parent brings home, but also rides to soccer practice, attendance at dance recitals, and quality time reading bedtime books. As the years pass, these kids get more independence and eventually move out. Under most circumstances, this increase in their kids' independence reduces the workers' level of work–family stress.

For example, consider the Tolliver family, which includes Phoebe (mom, age 35), Samantha (age 8), and Owen (age 6). Mom works full-time, and both kids are quite active: school, piano lessons, soccer teams, and plenty of birthday parties. At this age, Samantha and Owen need Phoebe for almost everything – they simply can't function on their own yet. But as they get older, they gain skills that free up their mom little by little. They start to clean up after themselves, and eventually do the dishes and the laundry. They can stay at home alone, first for just an hour or so, then for longer stretches. They can get themselves snacks and eventually cook meals. They can soon get to places on their own, either by driving or by arranging rides for themselves. A decade down the road, Phoebe will have largely made it through the period of middle adulthood when the work–parenting combination is at its most demanding.

Speaking of children leaving home, you may be familiar with the *empty nest syndrome*, in which parents in middle adulthood may become depressed or otherwise struggle emotionally to adjust to a home without kids. The media and popular literature may portray the empty nest syndrome as universal, but in fact, it is not (Raup & Myers, 1989). In one study of over 300 parents in Vancouver whose kids had recently moved out, only about a quarter (32% of moms and 23% of dads) experienced the negative symptoms associated with the empty nest syndrome (Mitchell & Lovegreen, 2009). In fact, most parents described positive effects of the empty nest, including increased personal growth and leisure time, improved quality of their romantic life, and pride in raising and launching their children – a finding that echoes the findings of similar studies (Dennerstein et al., 2002; Schmidt et al., 2004).

DIVERSITY MATTERS

Culture mattered a lot in the Vancouver study, with some parents of Asian descent reporting much higher rates of empty nest syndrome than those of European descent. Other studies have similarly found that the reaction by middle adulthood to the possibility of an empty nest depends on ethnic background (Mitchell & Wister, 2015). Some researchers have speculated that the impact of culture relates to individualism and collectivism. Parents from individualistic cultures may celebrate a child's departure as a graduation to independent life. However, parents from more collectivistic cultures may mourn a child's departure as a weakening or betrayal of their family bonds, particularly if it happened sooner than the parents had expected or under adverse circumstances. For example, parents may react this way if their children marry or move in with a partner the parents don't like, or leave home primarily to "run away" from family conflicts (Goldscheider & Goldscheider, 1999).

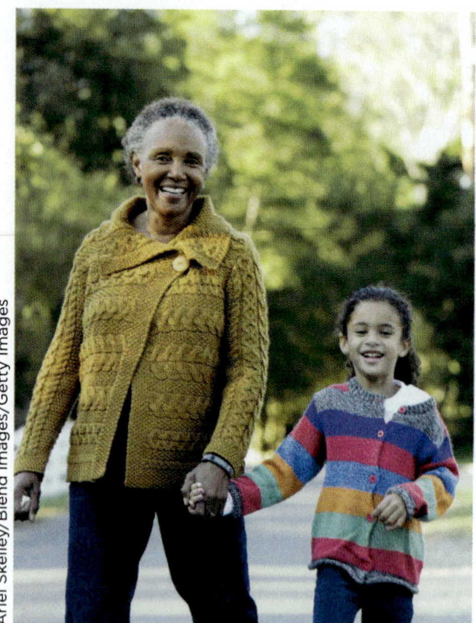
Ariel Skelley/Blend Images/Getty Images

Becoming a grandparent is a significant event that often occurs toward the end of the middle-adulthood phase of life.

For some middle-aged adults, the nest doesn't become empty as soon as they may have expected. Increasingly, adult children live at home well into their twenties or beyond. Research suggests that middle-aged adults whose nests remain full often experience a mix of closeness and tension with these adult children (Dor, 2013; Kloep & Hendry, 2010). Many kids return home when economic times are tough, a phenomenon known as "boomerang kids" or "accordion families" (Newman, 2012). These experiences are also likely to bring a blend of renewed attachment and heightened strain to the parent–child relationship (Mitchell & Gee, 1996).

Adding to the caregiving burdens of middle adulthood is *eldercare*, providing help to aging parents or other family members. As life expectancies increase, larger numbers of middle-aged adults give significant time, energy, or money to caring for their own parents. It is especially stressful when the middle generation supports both the generation above (their aging parents) and the generation below (their grown children), an experience that has earned this middle generation the nickname of the *sandwich generation*. One study (Fingerman et al., 2011) surveyed over 600 men and women in Philadelphia who ranged in age from 40 to 60 and who had both grown kids and living parents. Results indicated that these middle-aged adults provided frequent support both "upstream" and "downstream," but most provided significantly more support to their kids than their parents. Most participants viewed their kids as more important than their parents and said that their kids were in greater need. Those who supported their parents more than their kids frequently had parents with illness or disability.

An important landmark for middle-aged adults happens the first time their kids have kids of their own: grandparenthood (Brown & Roodin, 2003; Taubman-Ben-Ari et al., 2018). Becoming a grandparent brings great joy, but it is not without its challenges (Shlomo et al., 2010). One study followed about 100 first-time grandparents from the time their child (or child's partner) was expecting to 1–2 years after the child was born (Somary & Strieker, 1998). Compared to grandfathers, grandmothers had more of their expectations for grandparenthood fulfilled and found more personal meaning in their relationships with their grandchildren. Grandfathers, however, felt more comfortable offering parenting advice. It also mattered whose parent the grandparent was: parents of the baby's mother experienced more satisfaction as grandparents than they expected, but parents of the baby's father did not. Another study found that the amount of time that grandparents spent babysitting their grandchildren correlated positively with improved mental health in the grandparents (Condon et al., 2018).

Older Adulthood. At some point, typically in our sixties, we move past middle adulthood and into older adulthood. According to Erikson, the crisis we face at this stage is *ego integrity versus despair*, which means that we spend much of our time looking back and deciding if our life was well-lived. Perhaps the best way for a college student to appreciate this reflective experience is to imagine yourself at your graduation ceremony. There may be a moment, between waving to family in the crowd and listening to speeches by university administrators, when you quietly reminisce about the years you just spent in college. Did I make smart decisions? Choose the right school? Choose the right major? Work hard enough? Make good friends? Grow as a person? If your answers are negative, you'll feel regret and anguish about wasting your college years. If your answers are positive, you'll feel gratification and pride because you believe you spent your time intelligently. Now, imagine the intensity of these feelings if you were looking back on not just your college years, but *all* of your years, from the age of 70, 80, or more.

This looking-back process is so powerful for older adults that clinical psychologists have developed a psychotherapy based on it. Called *life review* (or *reminiscence*), this technique involves asking older adults to recall the major events of their lives, and to reevaluate whether their decisions benefited themselves or others or led to an important life lesson. Meta-analyses of these therapies indicate that they are often successful in improving well-being and reducing depression levels in older adults, including those with dementia symptoms (Bohlmeijer et al., 2003, 2007; O'Philbin et al., 2018; Westerhof & Bohlmeijer, 2014).

According to Erikson, adults who move successfully through their older years develop *wisdom*, a sense of expertise and good judgment about life decisions that comes from the lessons of their own experiences (Kramer, 2003). As a result, wisdom is one cognitive ability in which older adults actually exceed younger adults. In one study, adults of various ages read stories about interpersonal conflicts and were asked to predict how those conflicts would unfold (Grossman et al., 2010). Some of the conflicts involved political or social issues, such as U.S. immigration policies. Other conflicts were more personal, like a woman who bought an expensive headstone for her deceased parents' graves and expected her siblings to share the cost even though they had not agreed to buying it. The oldest participants considered the largest number of perspectives on the conflicts (as opposed to being one-sided), which facilitates compromise. The older adults' superiority on this task was so strong that the authors recommended that older adults should be assigned to key roles in high-stakes conflict resolution, such as in negotiations between rival groups or contentious legal cases.

Shutterstock

During older adulthood, many older adults enter retirement, a task that can bring both great satisfaction as well as some new stressors.

Another task that many older adults face is retirement. You might think that *task* is the wrong word to describe retirement, especially if you view it as an ongoing vacation. However, research suggests that retirement can be fraught with its own stressors, even as it brings great satisfaction and new opportunities to many older adults (Kim & Moen, 2001; Schwaba & Bleidorn, 2018). One study found that for men, being recently retired correlates with higher levels of morale, but being retired for longer periods correlates with more serious depressive symptoms (Kim & Moen, 2002). Of course, it is difficult to know how to interpret this shift as retirement is prolonged. The increase in depressive symptoms could be caused by dissatisfaction with retirement itself, but it could also be caused by deteriorating health, loss of a partner, financial difficulties, or other factors. Other studies have found that those who struggle in retirement are also likely to have long job histories, strong emotional connections to work, anxiety about retirement, and a lack of control over the retirement process. For example, a worker who developed a strong attachment to a company over a career spanning many decades and who is forced to retire without a plan for his upcoming years may struggle in retirement (Van Solinge & Henkens, 2005, 2007).

Death. For all of us who reach the older adulthood stage, we realize that the stage must end in death. Interestingly, death anxiety does not peak in older adulthood. Research indicates that anxiety about death is actually higher in younger adulthood (perhaps when thoughts of death occur for the first time, or when dependent children enter the picture) and may also be higher in middle adulthood (when heart attacks and other serious health risks increase) (Gesser et al., 1987; Russac et al., 2007). For those older adults who do experience death anxiety, it is less severe when the adult is physically and psychologically healthy, feels a strong sense of gratitude toward life, and has a strong belief in God and the afterlife (Fortner & Neimeyer, 1999; Harding et al., 2005; Lau & Cheng, 2011; Missler et al., 2011; Neimeyer et al., 2011). At any age, death anxiety can be a contributing factor to a variety of mental health problems, including panic disorder and other anxiety-based disorders and depression (Iverach et al., 2014).

Numerous theorists have offered explanations of how we experience the awareness of our own dying. The best-known of these is Elisabeth Kübler-Ross, a psychiatrist who has cared for many dying patients. She identified a common five-stage sequence that begins when we learn that we have a terminal illness (Kübler-Ross, 1969). Here are the five stages she proposed, along with an example of what a person diagnosed with terminal cancer might say:

1. Denial: "No way — the test results must be wrong!"
2. Anger: "It's so unfair! Why should *I* have to die?"
3. Bargaining (often in prayer with a higher power): "If I never drink or smoke again, and I eat healthy and exercise, and I do the chemo, can I stay alive?"
4. Depression: "It's no use. I can't beat it. I'm as good as dead."
5. Acceptance: "I understand that death is inevitable. I'm ready."

The appeal of Kübler-Ross's stages has helped them gain a strong following among health professionals and the general public, but research indicates that they are not universal, especially when multiple ethnicities are involved (Boerner et al., 2015; Irish et al., 1993; Klass & Hutch, 1985; Metzger, 1979; Stroebe et al., 2017). Instead, there is a wide variety of reactions to impending death, some of which may incorporate some of Kübler-Ross's stages, and some of which may not.

CHECK YOUR LEARNING:

9.24 How does the level of functioning of our bodies and brains change throughout the stages of adulthood?

9.25 How does the level of cognitive performance change throughout the stages of adulthood?

9.26 What are the highlights of the psychosocial development throughout the stages of adulthood?

To check your understanding of these questions, click show the answers or refer to the answers in the Chapter Summary.

CHAPTER SUMMARY

Big Questions about Developmental Psychology

9.1 Developmental psychology is the study of changes to body, mind, and interpersonal interaction across the life span.

9.2 In a cross-sectional research design, people of different ages are compared to each other at the same point in time. In a longitudinal research design, the same group of people is compared to itself at different points in time.

9.3 Developmental psychologists often focus on three big questions: stability versus change, stage development versus continuous development, and nature versus nurture.

Development Before Birth

9.4 The sequence of prenatal development proceeds from conception to zygote to embryo to fetus.

9.5 Teratogens are substances in a pregnant woman's body—such as drugs, pollutants, and diseases—that can harm the embryo or fetus.

9.6 Fetal alcohol syndrome is a pattern of bodily and behavioral problems common in people whose mothers drank heavily during pregnancy.

Infancy and Childhood

9.7 Newborns' abilities include the use of all five senses, as well as a variety of reflexes such as sucking, grasping, rooting, crying, and the Moro reflex.

9.8 Physical development proceeds through predictable stages, but it can be influenced by the amount of stimulation in the environment.

9.9 According to Piaget, children develop schemas (or mental categories) and either assimilate new information into them or accommodate the schemas to account for the new information.

9.10 According to Piaget, children develop through a series of cognitive stages—sensorimotor stage, preoperational stage, concrete operational stage, and formal operational stage—in which their ways of thinking change in predictable ways.

9.11 Researchers have challenged some of Piaget's conclusions, suggesting that cognitive stages may be less rigid and less biologically based than Piaget argued.

9.12 The three distinct types of attachment are secure attachment, insecure-avoidant attachment, and insecure-resistant attachment. Secure attachment to others is essential to healthy psychosocial development.

9.13 The three categories that capture most parenting styles are authoritarian, permissive, and authoritative, each of which can produce distinct outcomes in children.

9.14 Temperament is a person's basic emotional responsiveness, which is typically evident from a very early age and can have a big effect on parent-child relationships.

Adolescent Development

9.15 Psychologists define adolescence as the developmental period that encompasses the transition from childhood to adulthood.

9.16 During puberty, which girls typically reach before boys, both primary and secondary sex characteristics emerge.

9.17 The brain continues to grow during adolescence, including a marked increase in myelination and improved connections between frequently used neurons.

9.18 Adolescent thinking can involve the egocentric thinking of younger children, often featuring an imaginary audience or personal fable.

9.19 Kohlberg's stages of moral thinking progress through preconventional morality to conventional morality and then postconventional morality.

9.20 Psychologists define identity, which often solidifies during adolescence, as a person's stable sense of who they are.

9.21 Erik Erikson's eight-stage psychosocial theory of development explains crises faced at every age from infancy through late adulthood. The way an adolescent handles the challenge of identity versus role confusion is important for the next stage, intimacy versus isolation.

9.22 Relationships with both parents and peers are key and often challenging elements of adolescence.

9.23 Some developmental psychologists have recently proposed a new stage, emerging adulthood, as the transition between adolescence and adulthood. The validity of this stage is still being debated.

Adulthood

9.24 The functioning of our bodies and brains typically peaks during young adulthood, starts to decline during middle adulthood, and declines further in older adulthood.

9.25 Cognitive performance typically follows a similar pattern to physical performance: highest during young adulthood and declining through middle adulthood and older adulthood.

9.26 The highlights of psychosocial development through adulthood include forming couples, becoming parents, working, launching children, caring for older relatives, grandparenting, retirement, and facing death.

KEY TERMS

developmental psychology, p. 291
cross-sectional design, p. 291
longitudinal design, p. 291
zygote, p. 294
embryo, p. 294
fetus, p. 294
teratogen, p. 295
fetal alcohol syndrome, p. 295
schema, p. 301
assimilation, p. 301
accommodation, p. 301
sensorimotor stage, p. 302
object permanence, p. 302
preoperational stage, p. 302
conservation, p. 303
theory of mind, p. 303
egocentrism, p. 304
concrete operational stage, p. 304
formal operational stage, p. 304
scaffolding, p. 305
attachment, p. 307
critical period, p. 307
stranger anxiety, p. 308
authoritarian parenting style, p. 309
permissive parenting style, p. 309
authoritative parenting style, p. 309
temperament, p. 310
adolescence, p. 313
puberty, p. 313
secondary sex characteristics, p. 313
primary sex characteristics, p. 313
menarche, p. 313
imaginary audience, p. 315
personal fable, p. 315
preconventional morality, p. 316
conventional morality, p. 316
postconventional morality, p. 316
identity, p. 317
intimacy, p. 319
emerging adulthood, p. 323
menopause, p. 325

SELF-ASSESSMENT

1. In a _____ research design, the same group of people is compared to itself at different points in time.

2. _____ are substances in the pregnant woman's body that harm the embryo or fetus, including alcohol, pesticides, and some prescription drugs.

3. Ha-joon is a newborn baby. When he is surprised, he displays a reflex in which he flings his arms to the side. This reflex is known as
   a. rooting.
   b. grasping.
   c. the Moro reflex.
   d. blinking.

4. _____ is making sense of new information by sorting into already existing schemas, while _____ is making sense of new information by revising or creating new schemas.

5. _____ is a mental operation in which an amount or quantity remains the same regardless of the shape it takes.
   a. Object permanence
   b. Egocentrism
   c. Accommodation
   d. Conservation

6. _____ is a process by which a person learns new words, ideas, and ways of thinking by interacting with a more advanced person who provides decreasing levels of help.

a. Assimilation
b. Scaffolding
c. Accommodation
d. Attachment

7. Bobby is a parent of two children. He typically sets rules for his kids but also explains the rules and negotiates them with his kids. Bobby's parenting style is best described as

a. authoritative.
b. authoritarian.
c. permissive.
d. negligent.

8. Sierra is a teenager who makes lots of risky and dangerous decisions, including texting while driving and trying certain drugs, because she believes herself to be special or invulnerable. The term that best describes this decision-making tendency in Sierra and other adolescents is

a. theory of mind.
b. assimilation.
c. object permanence.
d. personal fable.

9. ____________ ____________ eight-stage psychosocial theory of development explains crises faced at every age from infancy through late adulthood.

a. Jean Piaget's
b. Lev Vygotsky's
c. Erik Erikson's
d. Lawrence Kohlberg's

10. The functioning of the body and the brain typically peak in

a. childhood.
b. young adulthood.
c. middle adulthood.
d. older adulthood.

To check your understanding of these questions, click show the answers in the e-book or refer to the answers in Appendix B.

Research shows quizzing is a highly effective learning tool. Continue quizzing yourself using LearningCurve, the system that adapts to *your* learning.

WHAT'S YOUR TAKE?

1. When Mary Ainsworth created the *strange situation* research design, her intent was to see how babies responded when they found themselves separated from their caretakers, then either left alone or approached by new people. For many first-year college students, the college experience might be an adult version of a strange situation, with plenty unfamiliar situations and challenges. Some researchers noticed this parallel and pointed out the upside: that college can be a time for young adults whose parental attachment gave them a sense of security to explore and master the new environment (Kenny & Barton, 2003). Of course, the downside is that new college students whose parental attachment is not so secure might shy away from exploration (for example, choose not to meet new classmates or join new clubs) or experience high levels of distress (anxiety, depression, eating disorders, etc.). These researchers have conducted numerous studies that support this connection between parental attachment and well-being in first-year college students (Kenny, 1987; Kenny & Donaldson, 1991; Kenny & Perez, 1996). Do you think your own experience as a first-year college student was influenced by the type of attachment you had to your parents as a young child? What about your siblings, high school friends, or roommates? Did they handle the "strange situation" of college as you would have predicted based on their attachments to their parents?

SHOW ME MORE

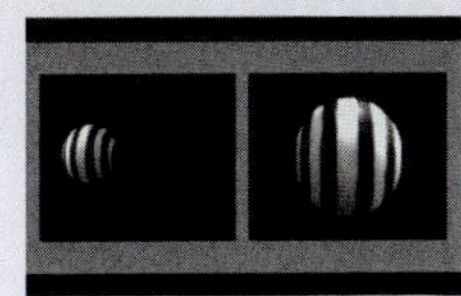

9.1 Newborns Can Make Sense of Hearing and Sight Together

http://tiny.cc/dee15y

Here's the brief video shown to newborns in the study described in "The Abilities of Newborns" section of this chapter. On the left, you will see a ball move toward you, and on the right, you will see a ball move away from you. The sound will match one of those movements. Your ability to determine which sight matches the sound was present even when you were a newborn baby.

Giulia Orioli, Andrew J. Bremner, TeresaFarroni.

This video is hosted by a third-party Web site (source). For accessible content requests, please reach out to the publisher of that site.

9.2 Piaget's Conservation Task

Here's a pair of videos illustrating Piaget's concept of conservation: an older kid grasps the concept, and a younger kid who is not quite there yet.

© Worth Publishers

9.3 Moral Decision Making and a Legendary Producer's Records

http://tiny.cc/lj7njy

This segment from the radio show *Snap Judgment* tells the tale of the moral challenge faced by a record store owner who stumbled across the valuable record collection and original recordings of J Dilla, a legendary DJ and producer.

Chalffy/iStock/Getty Images

This video is hosted by a third-party Web site (source). For accessible content requests, please reach out to the publisher of that site.

9.4 My Psychology Podcast

This podcast episode features the author of this textbook, psychologist Andy Pomerantz, speaking with other instructors of introductory psychology courses about the most important and interesting concepts in this chapter.

Macmillan Learning

10 Diversity in Psychology: Multiculturalism, Gender, and Sexuality

Gustavo Frazao/Shutterstock

CHAPTER OUTLINE

If you went to see a psychologist who was different from you, would you be concerned about the psychologist's ability to understand you and your issues? A conversation I had with my 20-year-old Latina neighbor, Gabriela, highlights the importance of this question. Knowing that I was a psychologist (and that I shouldn't work with her myself, since we already knew each other well), Gabriela asked me if I could refer her to another psychologist to help her with some personal issues. I was happy to help and gave her a list of a few names of colleagues I highly recommended. She thanked me, looked down at the list, and asked, "Um, do you know how old they are? And are any of them the same ethnicity as me? And this one whose first name is Jordan — what's their gender?" Gabriela explained, "I just want to find someone like me. I'm afraid that someone who is too different — someone who is not Latina, someone who is much older than me, someone who is not a woman — won't really appreciate what I'm going through or where I'm coming from. I just won't be as comfortable talking to them. They might not 'get' me."

Is there truth to what Gabriela was thinking? In your experience, are people of different ethnicities, ages, or genders so different that they can't fully "get" each other? If so, is it also true about differences in religion, socioeconomic status, sexual orientation, disability status, and other variables? If it's true between a client and a therapist, is it true in other kinds of relationships too? Perhaps the underlying question is this: how different, and how similar, are we?

These are the kinds of questions that underlie the main topic of this chapter, *diversity*. We'll consider lots of issues regarding the diverse range of people that surround you in your neighborhood, your city, your country, and your planet. For example, we'll explore what a culture is and the various characteristics of a culture. We'll examine some of the differences that exist between, and within, cultural groups. We'll learn how people adapt when they find themselves immersed in a different culture. We'll investigate ways that you can maximize your capability to live successfully in a multicultural world. Finally, we'll take a detailed look at particular sources of diversity — gender and sexuality — that are especially impactful in all of our lives.

Diversity Surrounds You

YOU WILL LEARN:

10.1 how diverse the United States is in terms of race, ethnicity, language, religion, age, and other variables.

10.2 what intersectionality is.

10.3 what a culture is.

10.4 what dynamic sizing is.

10.5 how the definition of *culture* has changed within psychology over the years.

You live in an increasingly diverse world. Whether you define that world narrowly, like your neighborhood or town, or more broadly, like your state or country, the world's population is mixing and mingling like never before. To understand why the field of psychology has devoted so much attention to the issue of diversity, let's consider some of the numbers that show what a varied assortment we have become. (Please note: In most chapters, Diversity Matters tags appear when the material highlights diversity issues. This entire chapter highlights diversity in many forms, so the tags are not used.)

Diversity by the Numbers

According to the U.S. Census Bureau, the following is how U.S. residents collectively answered questions about themselves in terms of race and ethnicity, language, religion, age, education, income, and other topics relating to diversity (United States Census Bureau [USCB], 2011, 2017a, 2019 with specific tables noted where applicable; plus other sources as marked):

Race and Ethnicity. About 60% of the U.S. population describes itself as White (non-Hispanic), 19% as Hispanic or Latinx, 13% as Black, 6% as Asian, 1% as Native American or Alaska Native, 0.2% as Native Hawaiian or other Pacific Islander, and 3% as multiracial. These numbers are changing, however, with percentages of Latinx, multiracial, Asian, and Native Hawaiian/Pacific Islander people rising most rapidly (Henry J. Kaiser Family Foundation, 2014; USCB, 2017a).

In recent years, especially after the 2020 protests over the death of George Floyd, a new term has been increasingly used to refer collectively to people of racial or ethnic minorities. That term is **BIPOC**: Black, Indigenous, and People of Color. While BIPOC refers broadly to people of color, the fact that Black and Indigenous people are specifically mentioned (BIPOC rather than simply POC) reflects the especially oppressive and racist treatment those groups of people have received at times during U.S. and Canadian history (Garcia, 2020).

Language. With so many racial and ethnic groups, many of which include large numbers of new immigrants, it should come as no surprise that a sizable number of U.S. residents — 21.6%, to be specific — speak a language other than English at home (USCB, 2019). The number is higher in large U.S. cities, where new immigrants tend to congregate. In fact, in each of the largest U.S. cities, there are well over 100 different languages spoken at home, and in some of those cities the percentage of residents who speak a language other than English at home exceeds 50% (USCB, 2015). See Table 10.1 for details.

Religion. The most prevalent religion in the United States is Christianity (about 65%). About 1–2% of the population subscribes to each of these religions: Judaism, Islam, Buddhism, and Hinduism. A number of other religious groups and belief systems are represented in smaller numbers as well. About 26% of people in the United States describe themselves as religiously unaffiliated (for example, atheist, agnostic, or "nothing"). In recent years, the trends in the country's religious diversity have included a decrease in the number of people subscribing to Christianity and an increase in the number of people subscribing to other religions or to no religion (Pew Research Center, 2019).

Age. In the United States, about 5–7% of the population falls into each 5-year age range starting with the youngest children (0–4 years old) and continuing through

BIPOC
Black, Indigenous, and People of Color.

TABLE 10.1: Linguistic Diversity in the United States

CITY	PERCENT OF THE POPULATION WHO SPEAK A LANGUAGE OTHER THAN ENGLISH AT HOME	TOTAL NUMBER OF LANGUAGES SPOKEN IN DIFFERENT HOMES
Los Angeles	54	185
Miami	51	128
Riverside, CA	40	145
San Francisco	40	163
New York	38	192
Houston	37	145
Dallas	30	156
Chicago	29	153
Phoenix	26	163
Washington, DC	26	168

The linguistic diversity of the United States is especially great in its biggest cities. These 10 cities rank highest in terms of the percentage of residents who speak a language other than English at home — over 25% in each city. The total number of languages spoken by the residents of each of these cities is well over 100 (USCB, 2015).

middle adulthood (54–59 years old). About 18% of the population is over 60, including about 6% over 75. That older demographic has grown in recent decades and is projected to continue to grow in the future. Since 1980, the average age of Americans has risen from 30 to almost 37 (USCB, 2011, Table 7).

Sexual Orientation. Sexual orientation rates depend on who is surveyed and how the surveys are conducted (as described in detail later in this chapter), but experts on the subject typically agree that about 2–4% of the U.S. population identify as gay, lesbian, or bisexual (Gates & Newport, 2013). Rates differ widely across various parts of the country, with higher gay, lesbian, and bisexual rates in certain cities (for example, San Francisco, California; Portland, Maine; and Austin, Texas) than in other cities or rural areas (Laumann et al., 2004; Newport & Gates, 2015). By the way, the categories mentioned here — gay, lesbian, and bisexual, along with straight — are the options typically used in large-scale surveys of sexuality. The options in those surveys may change as an increasingly wide range of sexual orientations are more widely recognized.

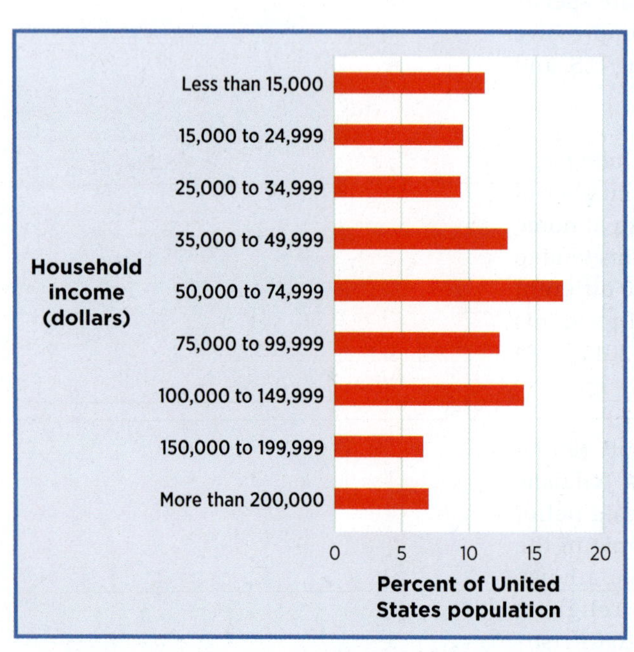

FIGURE 10.1 Economic Diversity in the United States. The economic diversity among U.S. families is great, ranging from extreme poverty to extreme wealth. Data from the United States Census Bureau (2017b, Table A1, https://www.census.gov/content/dam/Census/library/publications/2017/demo/P60-259.pdf).

Education. About 88% of U.S. adults have a high school diploma or GED. About 59% have completed some college, and about 33% have a bachelor's degree. About 12% have more advanced degree, such as a master's or doctorate (USCB, 2016).

Socioeconomic Status (SES). The median household income in the United States is about $58,000, but the range is tremendous, as illustrated in **Figure 10.1**. When you consider the sizable number of people near the lower end of the range, along with the fact that the highest income category (over $200,000 per year) doesn't have an upper limit — it includes some families making many *millions* per year — you get a sense of the tremendous economic diversity within the U.S. population (USCB, 2017b).

Big City or Small Town. About 31% of the U.S. population lives in urban areas, about 55% in suburban areas, and about 14% in rural areas

(Pew Research Center, 2018). Another illustration of the diversity of cities, suburbs, and small towns throughout the United States is reflected by a state-by-state comparison of population density. The roomiest states — such as Wyoming, Montana, and Alaska — have fewer than 7 people per square mile. The most crowded states — like Massachusetts, New Jersey, and Rhode Island — have over 900 people per square mile (USCB, 2021).

Disability Status. About 27% of the U.S. population has a disability, with about two-thirds of them describing their disability as "severe" and one-third as "nonsevere." Common disabilities span a wide range, including challenges with seeing or hearing; challenges with mobility such as walking or climbing stairs; challenges with personal care such as bathing, eating, or preparing meals; and psychological challenges such as dementia or severe depression or anxiety (USCB, 2018).

Intersectionality. We have been discussing each of these diversity variables separately, but they exist in different combinations in different people. Each of us has a race/ethnicity *and* religious/spiritual beliefs *and* an economic level *and* a sexual orientation, and so on. Sometimes, a particular combination of these variables creates a distinctively unfortunate set of circumstances. To discuss that combination, psychologists often use the term **intersectionality**: the way any one person's unique combination of social and cultural categories intersect or overlap, especially as related to discrimination, unequal treatment, or social disadvantage.

When psychologists (and researchers in other fields) study intersectionality, they often focus on the struggles of people whose combination of diversity factors is the least privileged or most oppressed within a society. For example, researchers might study people who face discrimination because of both race *and* gender, or both ethnicity *and* sexual orientation, or both disability *and* poverty, or some other combination of two or more factors. When the study of intersectionality began in the late 1980s and early 1990s, it focused primarily on the experience of being both Black and a woman (Cole, 2009; Crenshaw, 1989). In recent years, the study of intersectionality has broadened. Today, psychologists increasingly explore ways to work toward social justice and equity — an effort to minimize the negative psychological consequences experienced by many people living at societal intersections where they experience oppression or marginalization (Carbado et al., 2013; Cho et al., 2013; Cole, 2009; Crenshaw, 1991; Lewis et al., 2015; Mays & Ghavami, 2018; Moradi & Grzanka, 2017; Rosenthal, 2016; Warner et al., 2018).

In one study of intersectionality, researchers focused on people who are both lesbian/gay/bisexual and a member of a racial/ethnic minority group. The researchers measured which factor was the more accurate predictor of health issues for people with those intersecting identities: their experiences with heterosexism and racism considered *separately*, or those experiences considered *in combination*. The clear answer was those two factors *in combination*. That finding suggests that if you want to begin to understand how different types of inequalities might impact someone, it's important to acknowledge how those inequalities work together rather than how each might work on its own (Fattoracci et al., 2021).

The COVID pandemic further illustrated how intersecting factors can contribute to suffering. Of course, the pandemic caused difficult losses of many kinds including jobs, relationships, routines, and physical and mental health. But those losses didn't occur in equal proportion across the population. Instead, those losses happened disproportionately among people who live at the intersections of poverty, preexisting conditions, and limited access to health care. This intersection of factors tends to be more common within BIPOC communities than the White population in the United States (Blustein et al., 2021; Bowleg, 2020; Hankivsky & Kapilashrami, 2020).

intersectionality
The way any one person's unique combination of social and cultural categories intersect or overlap, especially as related to discrimination, unequal treatment, or social disadvantage.

culture
A group of similar people who share beliefs, values, and patterns of behavior.

worldview
A comprehensive, culturally influenced way of approaching and understanding the world around you.

dynamic sizing
The ability to simultaneously know the norm for a group and recognize that the norm might not apply to every member of that group.

The main point of all the information we reviewed in this section is to demonstrate just how much diversity surrounds you. Each of the diversity variables we considered – race and ethnicity, language, religion, age, sexual orientation, education, money, population density, and disability status – span wide ranges. Collectively, these variables (and many others) produce an incredibly diverse national profile. All of these variables can contribute to *culture* as well, a topic to which we turn now.

What Constitutes a Culture?

A **culture** is a set of shared beliefs, values, and patterns of behavior within a group of people. The qualities that tie a cultural group together can be any number of things. For example, culture can form around any type of diversity – including sex, gender, race, ethnicity, religion, age, education, and so on. Any of those qualities, and many others too, can have an important impact on how you live your life. Specifically, those qualities can shape your **worldview**: a comprehensive, culturally influenced way of approaching and understanding the world around you.

MY TAKE VIDEO 10.1

Culture

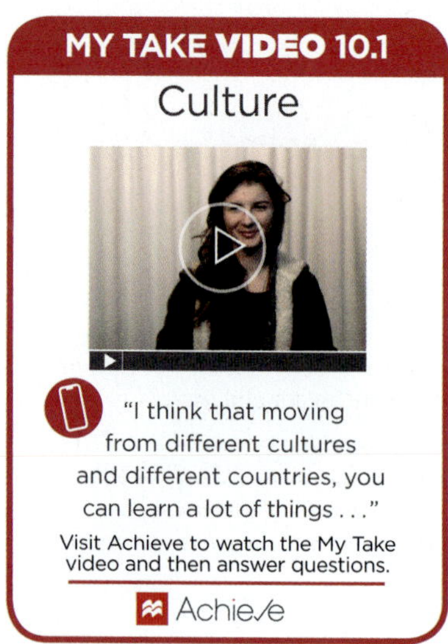

"I think that moving from different cultures and different countries, you can learn a lot of things . . ."

Visit Achieve to watch the My Take video and then answer questions.

Achieve

To illustrate some real differences between people in terms of their culture and worldview, let's consider two people of different backgrounds. To keep it simple, let's focus on just three characteristics: age, race/ethnicity, and religion. Jasmin is 25 years old, Black, and Christian. Asmita is 75 years old, Indian, and Hindu. Based on these three qualities alone, what differences might you expect between Jasmin's and Asmita's beliefs and behaviors? The religious difference could affect what either woman believes about higher powers and what happens after we die. The race/ethnicity difference could affect the holidays the women celebrate and the roles they fill within their families. The age difference could affect their approaches to education, technology, and family. Even if we limit ourselves to considering just these three qualities, it is clear that Jasmin and Asmita may have very different cultural experiences. Just imagine if there were even more differences – if one were high-income and the other low-income, if one lived in a huge city and the other lived in a rural area, if one had little education and the other had a lot, or if one had a severe disability and the other did not. Their cultural worlds might be incredibly different.

Wait, if we assume that people are different just because of their cultural qualities, aren't we prejudging them?

LIFE HACK 10.1

Use dynamic sizing when you meet someone from a different cultural background. Think of what is common in that person's culture, but remember that this particular person might be uncommon in any number of ways.

(Sue, 1998, 2006)

Great point. We certainly don't want our efforts to appreciate culture to accidentally morph into prejudice (or stereotyping or discrimination, for that matter). That is why it is so important to use **dynamic sizing**: the ability to simultaneously know the norm for a group *and* recognize that the norm might not apply to every member of that group. When you consider another person's culture, you want to know what is typical for that culture, but you don't want to assume that every person is typical (Roysircar, 2013; Sue, 1998, 2006).

The important point here is that there are differences not only between but also *within* cultural groups. Let's consider Jasmin and Asmita again. Without dynamic sizing, someone might look at their ages and assume that they live in different worlds when it comes to technology: Jasmin practically lives online, while Asmita has far less interest in anything computer-related. But with dynamic sizing, you would consider the possibility that Jasmin or Asmita doesn't fit the norm for her respective generation. Perhaps Asmita uses social media and talks to her family on Skype or Facetime, while Jasmin doesn't even have a smartphone. You can't be sure until you get to know each of them. Dynamic sizing doesn't mean ignorance of cultural norms, just flexibility in applying them to specific people.

IT'S LIKE...

Dynamic Sizing Is Like Appreciating Breanna Stewart's Height

Women, as a group, are shorter than men. Your experience tells you that, and so do the facts: average height for grown women in the United States is 5 feet, 3.8 inches, compared to 5 feet, 9.3 inches for men (Centers for Disease Control and Prevention, 2012). But that doesn't mean that every woman falls near the women's average, and every man falls near the men's average. Consider Breanna Stewart. She's the 6-foot, 4-inch basketball star who earned three Naismith College Player of the Year awards and won four NCAA championships at University of Connecticut, then became an all-star, MVP, and WNBA champion with the Seattle Storm. At her height, Breanna Stewart towers over almost every person she meets.

So, two things are true: (1) *as a group*, women tend to be about 5 feet, 4 inches tall; and (2) *as an individual member of that group*, Breanna Stewart is much taller than that. Appreciating both of those facts at the same time is just like dynamic sizing.

When psychologists consider culture, they simultaneously consider what is common within that culture and the possibility that a particular member of that culture might not be so common. For example, someone from an individualistic culture might be very collectivistic. Or, someone who is older might act very young. Or, someone from a big city might have small-town values. On any variable, there is variation *within* a cultural group, just like there is height variation within a gender. Dynamic sizing reminds us that not everyone within a group has characteristics typical of that group, which helps us to avoid stereotyping and prejudice. •

AP Photo/Nick Wass

On average, women tend to be shorter than men. But at 6 feet, 4 inches, WNBA star Breanna Stewart is taller than almost everyone, regardless of gender. Her exceptional height serves as a reminder of the importance of dynamic sizing: the ability to simultaneously know the norm for a group *and* recognize that the norm might not apply to every member of that group. Dynamic sizing can be especially helpful in appreciating differences within a cultural group.

Defining Culture. What, exactly, constitutes a culture? Over the history of psychology, there has been some debate and some change in the answer to that question. When psychology began to give cultural issues serious attention (around the 1960s and 1970s), culture was almost entirely defined as race/ethnicity. But as time has gone by, psychologists have expanded the definition of culture (Arredondo et al., 1996; Fukuyama et al., 2014; Pedersen, 1999; Sue et al., 1996; Sue & Sue, 2016; Triandis, 2007).

Today, there are lots of variables besides race/ethnicity that psychologists consider culturally relevant. We discussed many of them earlier in this chapter as we considered the diversity of the population: age, religion, education level, socioeconomic status, sexual orientation, urban or rural setting, and disability status. But the list certainly expands beyond that. Gender, of course, is an important cultural variable (and one to which we will devote significant time later in this chapter). Some have also argued for the importance of other cultural variables too, like politics (for example, liberal versus conservative culture) or region of the country (for example, the culture of the Pacific Northwest versus the Deep South, the Midwest, or the East Coast).

One way to determine whether a characteristic is culturally important is to ask yourself whether you would experience *culture shock* if your situation changed tomorrow. Culture shock is feeling disoriented or bewildered with an unfamiliar situation. For example, consider a 78-year-old man who lives in a retirement home. If he moved to a college residence hall, would he experience culture shock? How about a woman who has lived her entire life on the south side of Chicago: would she experience culture shock if she found herself living in a small mining town in West Virginia? Or a prisoner who has been incarcerated for years: would culture shock accompany a shift to life on the outside? There's a good chance that these situations would cause culture shock, at least to some degree, since they would both involve significant change in some fundamental aspects of daily life.

Subcultures. Regarding the question of what constitutes a culture, the list could include what some people would consider *subcultures*: for example, military culture,

multiculturalism
An approach in psychology that highlights the importance and value of multiple cultural groups within a society.

prison culture, even cultures based on specific activities or interests. In my own therapy practice, I have learned to appreciate not only my clients' cultures, but their subcultures as well. With Dylan, a 19-year-old college sophomore, I learned not to even offer 8 A.M. Friday appointments. The college student culture in which they lived – in the college residence hall where students often stayed up late studying, talking, or partying on Thursday nights – made it practically impossible for them. As they once reminded me: "You know 8 A.M. on Friday is like the middle of the night for me, right?" With Amy, a stay-at-home mom of twin 6-month-olds, I came to respect the "baby culture" in which she and so many of her friends were immersed. In this baby culture, parents' work, sleep, and sex lives revolved around nap times, bath times, and diaper changes. With Brianna, a high-ranking executive at a Fortune 500 firm, I realized that the overriding expectation in her corporate culture was that the job always comes first. Brianna often missed out on important family events and even took phone calls from her coworkers during our therapy sessions. Dylan, Amy, and Brianna each live in a world affected by not only widely recognized cultural variables, but also specific subcultures.

Studies have shown that clients like and benefit from a therapist's cultural sensitivity and competence, because they feel like the therapist respects them, cares about them, and "gets" them (Atkinson et al., 1992; Constantine, 2002; Davis et al., 2018; Fuertes et al., 2006; Gim et al., 1991; Mosher et al., 2017). This cultural appreciation is not just for the benefit of therapists and their clients, however. It is also for anyone who hopes to better understand the factors that influence the lives of the people around them.

CHECK YOUR LEARNING:

10.1 In what ways is the United States a diverse nation?

10.2 What is intersectionality?

10.3 What is culture, and how does it influence a person's worldview?

10.4 What is dynamic sizing, and why is it important to appreciating differences within a group?

10.5 How has the definition of *culture* changed within psychology over the years?

To check your understanding of these questions, click show the answers or refer to the answers in the Chapter Summary.

Multiculturalism

YOU WILL LEARN:

10.6 what multiculturalism is and how important it has become in psychology.

10.7 how the understanding of cultural differences has changed over the years.

10.8 how multiculturalism is reflected in psychology today.

10.9 what acculturation is.

10.10 about different acculturation strategies.

10.11 what acculturative stress is.

10.12 about specific ways in which cultures differ from each other.

Multiculturalism is a psychological approach that highlights the importance and value of multiple cultural groups within a society. Let's explore the topic of multiculturalism, beginning with a consideration of the role multiculturalism has played over the years.

The Importance of Multiculturalism in Psychology

In the earliest years of psychology, cultural issues received almost no attention. With rare exceptions, psychology was a science by and for White men (Guthrie, 2004; Hilgard et al., 1991; Scarborough & Furumoto, 1987). In the 1960s and 1970s, issues of culture, especially race/ethnicity and gender, started to appear in the field. This happened, in part, because more ethnic minorities and women were contributing to psychological research, and their contributions were increasingly focused on topics related to their own cultural characteristics. The prominence of cultural issues grew through the 1980s and then exploded in the 1990s and 2000s, as the U.S. population and the members of the psychology profession continued to become more diverse (Betancourt & López, 1993; Hall, 1997; Oh et al., 2017; Pickren & Burchett, 2014).

Today, multiculturalism is undoubtedly a dominant movement in psychology. In fact, some have called it *the* dominant movement in psychology, going so far as to label it the "fourth force" in psychology's history (David et al., 2014; Pedersen, 1990, 1999, 2008). The three major forces that came before – Sigmund Freud's psychoanalysis, B. F. Skinner's behaviorism, and Carl Rogers's humanism (all of which are covered in Chapter 12) – can all be enhanced by multiculturalism (Bugental, 1964; Hall, 2014). That is, multiculturalism blends with other approaches to psychology, enabling them to be adapted and customized for members of diverse cultural groups.

10.13 about differences that diversity makes in everyday life.

10.14 what cultural intelligence is.

10.15 what cultural humility is.

10.16 what antiracism is.

10.17 what microaggressions are.

Understanding Cultural Differences. The way that psychologists understand cultural differences has changed as multiculturalism has become more integrated in the field. This change has taken place in four stages (Leong, 2014; Leong et al., 2012a, b). At first, psychologists used a *deficit model* to understand cultural differences. This model suggested that a difference – specifically, a difference from the predominant White male perspective – is a deficit. So, if psychologists recognized that members of gender minorities and racial/ethnic minorities did anything differently, that difference was seen as an inherent, built-in shortcoming in comparison to the "right" way – the way that White men did it. The obvious problem with this approach is that no one group does things in an objectively "right" way, which means that other ways shouldn't be viewed as deficits.

The deficit model was replaced by the *culturally disadvantaged model*, which said that the shortcomings were socially created, rather than inherent or built-in. The idea of the deficit was still there, but now nurture (rather than nature) produced the deficits – including poverty, malnutrition, poor parenting, second-rate schooling, and so on. The same problem still existed, though: no single group's behavior should be seen as "right," with other groups being inferior by comparison, whether that inferiority supposedly came from nature or nurture.

A big shift came with the *cultural pluralism model*, the basic idea of which is that a cultural difference is *not* a deficiency. According to cultural pluralism, neither the White male way of doing things, nor any other particular way of doing things, is better than any other. Each cultural group brings its own unique approach, and each cultural group represents naturally occurring variation within the human species.

The most recent model is the *positive psychology model*, which not only rejects the idea that cultural difference is deficiency, but goes a step further and argues that the unique qualities of each culture are strengths worthy of acknowledgment or even celebration. As an example, consider speech patterns. Specifically, consider how the typical speech patterns of White men might differ from those of women or racial/ethnic minority groups – everything from sentence structure to vocabulary to the underlying purpose of conversations. Decades ago, that different style of speaking would have been viewed as an inborn deficit, or a bit later, as a deficit caused by an inferior environment. More recently, those different styles of speaking would be recognized as equally legitimate to any other, or applauded as uniquely impressive and worthy.

kali9/Getty Images

PeopleImages/Getty Images

FatCamera/E+/Getty Images

Multiculturalism is a psychological approach that highlights the importance and value of multiple cultural groups within a society. The approach has become increasingly common, and multiculturalism has become an important topic of study in the field of psychology.

Multiculturalism in Contemporary Psychology. Today, the importance of multiculturalism in psychology is evident in many ways. The American Psychological Association now includes quite a few divisions devoted to multicultural or diversity-related topics, including Division 35 (Society for the Psychology of Women), Division 36 (Society for the Psychology of Religion and Spirituality), Division 44 (Society for the Psychology of Sexual Orientation and Gender Diversity), Division 45 (Society for the Psychological Study of Culture, Ethnicity, and Race), and Division 51 (Society for the Psychological Study of Men and Masculinities). There are dozens of professional psychology journals that regularly publish articles on multicultural topics, and the number of psychology books on multicultural topics is huge and continues to grow.

Recent revisions of the profession's Code of Ethics have added numerous standards requiring psychologists to do therapy, assessment, and research with sensitivity

acculturation
Managing a life that involves the coexistence of more than one culture.

assimilation
An acculturation strategy in which the person adopts the new culture and rejects the old culture.

separation
An acculturation strategy in which the person retains the old culture and rejects the new culture.

to cultural issues (American Psychological Association, 2010). For example, if Dr. Diggs (who is Christian) has a therapy session with Aaron (who is Jewish), Dr. Diggs has an ethical obligation to appreciate and respect Aaron's viewpoint and his experience of religiously relevant events. Likewise, if Dr. Diggs (a U.S. psychologist) is going to give an intelligence test to Reka, who recently moved to the United States from Hungary, Dr. Diggs has an ethical obligation to think about several factors regarding the choice, administration, and interpretation of the results of the test: Reka's linguistic abilities, Reka's understanding of the purpose of the test, and how Reka's cultural background might influence some of her answers.

Speaking of tests, the makers of psychology's most widely respected intelligence tests, personality tests, and other assessment tools have gone to great lengths to make their tests more culture-fair than those tests were in the early and mid-1900s. Rather than asking questions that only people with certain cultural backgrounds might answer correctly, or using images much more familiar to one cultural group than to others, test-makers have deliberately created questions and images that are more accessible and recognizable to a wider range of people (Gregory, 2004).

The *Diagnostic and Statistical Manual of Mental Disorders–5-TR* (DSM–5-TR), the book that lists and defines all of the disorders that psychologists use to diagnose their clients, covers more culture than it ever has, too (American Psychiatric Association, 2022). Compared to earlier editions, DSM–5-TR now includes lots of information about how various disorders might be experienced differently by members of different cultures. For example, in some Asian countries, social anxiety centers on making *others* uncomfortable in social situations rather than feeling uncomfortable oneself. DSM–5-TR also gives psychologists a heads-up about certain psychological issues that are unique to certain cultures ("Cultural Concepts of Distress"). For example, *susto* (an experience in which psychological and physical symptoms follow a frightening event that causes the soul to leave the body) is uniquely prevalent in some Latinx groups. For another example, *maladi dyab* (an experience in which a malicious or envious person can "send" depression or other psychological issues to another) is uniquely prevalent in some Haitian communities. Together, all of these developments across psychology show that multiculturalism has earned a prominent place in the field.

Acculturation: Managing Multiple Cultures

Consider the Zhang family, who immigrated from China to the United States. Their move raises the issue of **acculturation**: managing a life that involves the coexistence of more than one culture. Acculturation is basically deciding how much to hold on to your old culture and how much to accept the new one. It is an important issue for increasing numbers of people in countries around the globe. Some may seek a new culture by choice, but many others are forced from their homelands due to conditions made unlivable like natural disasters, war, poverty, or famine (Berry, 2017; Sam & Berry, 2006a; Ward & Geeraert, 2016).

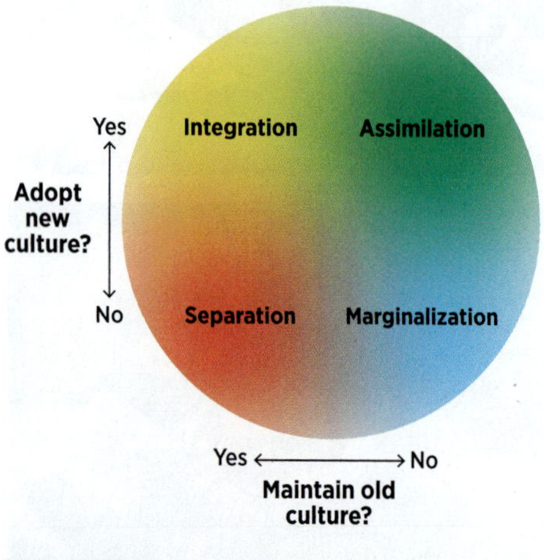

FIGURE 10.2 Acculturation Strategies. There are four acculturation strategies, involving a combination of attitudes toward the old and new cultures. Notice that the boundaries between them are fuzzy, to represent how people often choose a middle ground, or drift from one strategy to another. Information from Berry (2003).

Acculturation Strategies. Acculturation strategies are determined by how the person answers two questions: (1) To what extent will I retain my previous culture? (2) To what extent will I embrace my new culture? As **Figure 10.2** shows, there are four distinct strategies for approaching acculturation: *assimilation*, *separation*, *marginalization*, and *integration* (Berry, 1980, 2003; Rivera, 2010):

- **Assimilation** is an acculturation strategy in which the person adopts the new culture and rejects the old culture. For members of the Zhang family, assimilation might mean dropping any connection to language, religion, customs, clothing, food, or other elements of their life in China and entering the U.S. mainstream as much as possible.
- **Separation** is an acculturation strategy in which the person retains the old culture and rejects the new culture. For the Zhang family, separation might

involve choosing to live among Chinese neighbors, to speak Mandarin rather than English, and to eat exactly what they ate in China, all without adopting any part of a more mainstream U.S. lifestyle.

- **Marginalization** is an acculturation strategy in which the person rejects both the new culture and the old culture. For the Zhang family, marginalization might mean not celebrating any U.S. or Chinese holidays and not forming close connections with the Chinese or mainstream American communities.
- **Integration** is an acculturation strategy in which the person adopts both the new culture and the old culture. For the Zhang family, integration might mean embracing the holidays, sports, food, and other elements of both mainstream U.S. and Chinese lifestyles.

marginalization
An acculturation strategy in which the person rejects both the new culture and the old culture.

integration
An acculturation strategy in which the person adopts both the new culture and the old culture.

acculturative stress
Stress associated with the process of managing old and new cultures.

Think of these four approaches to acculturation along two dimensions, one that measures attachment to new culture, and another that measures attachment to old culture. Over time, people might adjust their acculturation strategies, moving up or down one of the dimensions, as they spend more time in the new culture (Rudmin, 2003; Rudmin & Ahmadzadeh, 2001; Ryder et al., 2000).

Acculturative Stress. Living between two cultures often causes **acculturative stress**: stress associated with the process of managing old and new cultures. Acculturative stress can include lots of things that immigrants and other newcomers to cultural groups often experience: language difficulties; pressure to dress, speak, or behave in a certain way; harassment and discrimination; and lack of necessary skills or knowledge (Berry, 1970, 2006c; Birman & Simon, 2014; Romero & Piña-Watson, 2017).

Many acculturation stressors come from members of the new, larger culture (in the Zhangs' case, mainstream U.S. culture). But there can also be pressure from within the person's smaller group (in the Zhangs' case, other Chinese or Asian immigrants) to stay true to their roots (Contrada et al., 2001; French & Chavez, 2010). One study found that among Latinx college students, pressure to conform to their own group was a significant factor in their overall life satisfaction (Ojeda et al., 2012). These pressures to conform could include dating and hanging out with other people who are Latinx, listening to the music that other people who are Latinx listen to, or dressing like other people who are Latinx dress. Another study found similar results for U.S. college students of Asian descent: the pressure to conform to their own group predicted anxiety better than any other variable the researchers examined, including perceived discrimination and concern about fulfilling stereotypes (French et al., 2013). Similar observations have been made about Black and other students of color teasing each other for "acting White" when they get good grades (Bergin & Cooks, 2002; Contrada et al., 2000; Davis et al., 2018; Fordham & Ogbu, 1986). Studies of Black and Latinx young adults have found that those who more often heard accusations of assimilation from their friends and family were more likely to experience psychological symptoms of depression, anxiety, or stress (Durkee & Williams, 2015; Thornhill et al., 2021).

Among the four acculturation strategies, integration has consistently been linked with the best adaptation to stress and the fewest psychological difficulties. Marginalization, on the other hand, typically produces the worst results in terms of stress management and overall mental health. The two strategies that involve choosing one culture over the other – assimilation and separation – typically fall somewhere in between (Berry, 2015; Berry 2006b; Berry & Sam, 1997; Nguyen, 2006). Other factors that predict good adjustment to acculturation stress include an agreeable, extraverted, stable personality; young age (younger kids often adjust better than older kids and adults); plenty of education and money; and high levels of social support from both the new and the old cultures (Berry, 2006c; Berry et al., 1987; Kealey, 1989; Kosic, 2006; Ra & Trusty, 2017; Ward et al., 2004; Wong et al., 2017).

mbirdy/Getty Images

Acculturative stress takes many forms. Sometimes, it comes from the person's new culture. Other times, it comes from members of the person's culture, such as pressure to stay true to one's roots.

individualism
A worldview that emphasizes the well-being of the individual over the well-being of the group.

collectivism
A worldview that emphasizes the well-being of the group over the well-being of the individual.

How Do Cultures Differ?

It is pretty clear that there are differences between cultures. But how, specifically, do they differ?

Of course, there are differences in the outward signs of culture, like the clothes people wear, the food they eat, the religious texts they read, and the customs they maintain. But what about the differences underlying cultural values that shape those outward signs of culture and the beliefs that maintain them?

One researcher, Geert Hofstede, conducted a massive, long-term study of IBM employees beginning in the late 1960s that answers this question. (IBM is a huge, global company, with over a quarter-million workers in dozens of countries, so it provides a very multicultural sample for research on multicultural issues.) In the study, Hofstede asked IBM workers from 50 different countries to describe the characteristics they noticed in their colleagues from other countries. From thousands of their responses, he started to piece together the underlying values of people from many different cultures. He then boiled these values down to just four fundamental values that diverse cultures hold (Hofstede, 1980). In recent years, Hofstede and other researchers have continued this line of research with other populations in even more countries, and (with a few exceptions) this more recent research has confirmed the existence of his four original cultural values and also suggested two more (Hofstede et al., 2010; Hofstede, 2001; Minkov, 2013, 2018; Minkov & Hofstede, 2010, 2011). Let's discuss each of those six values.

Individualism Versus Collectivism. **Individualism** is a worldview that emphasizes the well-being of the individual over the well-being of the group. Its opposite, **collectivism**, is a worldview that emphasizes the well-being of the group over the well-being of the individual. As **Figure 10.3** shows, generally, U.S. culture leans strongly toward individualism. By contrast, some other countries, especially many from Asia, South America, and Africa, lean toward collectivism (Oyserman et al., 2002; Triandis et al., 1988). (Of course, there's plenty of variation *within* the cultural groups too – some people within each culture lean the opposite way.)

The contrast between strongly individualistic cultures and strongly collectivistic cultures is striking. People from individualistic cultures tend to be driven more by the question, "What's best for *me*?" People from collectivistic cultures tend to be driven instead by the question, "What's best for *us*?" For people in collectivistic cultures, *us* can be defined in a variety of ways, including family, friends, partners, or groups of coworkers (Brewer & Chen, 2007; Hui & Triandis, 1986).

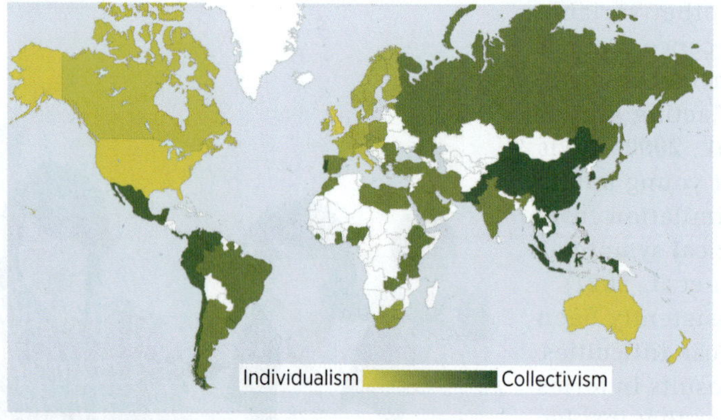

FIGURE 10.3 Individualism and Collectivism Around the World. Collectivism is much higher in Asia, South America, the Middle East, and Africa. Individualism is much higher in Western countries such as the United States, Canada, Australia, and some parts of Europe. (Measurements from many countries are missing, as indicated in white on this map.) Information from Hofstede (2001).

To illustrate the difference between individualism and collectivism, consider two clients in my psychotherapy practice, each of whom was a college senior. Both were applying to law school, and both were equally strong applicants. David, who had more individualistic values, told me about how he decided where to apply: "Here's what I'm looking for: a law school with a great reputation, that specializes in the areas of law I want to practice, and is located in a big city." He applied to about 10 such schools, all around the country, and was thrilled when he got into his top choice, which was a thousand miles away. Mia, who had more collectivistic values, approached her application decisions differently: "I'm only applying to law schools here in town. My parents are nearby, and I might need to help take care of them. They're getting older, you know. Plus, there's that family I nanny for part-time. I don't want to make them go through the hassle of finding someone else. And my partner, she didn't exactly come out and say it, but she made it pretty clear that she doesn't want to do a long-distance relationship." She was thrilled to get into a local law school, where she attended classes while maintaining all of those previous relationships.

Large Versus Small Power Distance. A culture with a large power distance has a power structure, or hierarchy, in which the people on the top have way more power than the people on the bottom. This cultural power structure is similar to the culture within many large corporations: the boss can make big changes that have major effects on lower-level workers, and there is little or nothing the lower-level workers can do about it.

By contrast, in a culture with a small power distance, the distance between people with varying levels of power is much smaller. In fact, in some of these cultures, there is little difference in power: everyone has nearly the same amount of power, and leadership is often shared or rotating. As an example of the difference between large and small power structures, consider how a family might decide the age at which a child should be allowed to begin dating. In a family with a large power difference, the decision belongs to the parent absolutely. In a family with a small power difference, the decision may ultimately be the parent's to make, but the child may have much more input on the decision.

Assertiveness Versus Caring. Some cultures are much more assertive and cutthroat than others. In these cultures, many interactions are competitions, with clear winners and losers. Strangers are rarely to be helped, or even trusted. Instead, the best strategy is typically to remain vigilant and protect yourself. In these cultures, assertiveness is the undercurrent of daily life.

In other cultures, that undercurrent is caring. Strangers are typically befriended, and even those who might otherwise be seen as inferior because of their low social or economic status are typically respected. Vigilance is not a pressing need, because other people are generally viewed as trustworthy.

Avoidance Versus Acceptance of Uncertainty. Cultures differ in how they handle uncertainty. In some cultures, tradition is everything and pressures people to think, feel, and behave in certain ways in certain situations. This way, there is no uncertainty to cause anxiety. Other cultures embrace that uncertainty. They welcome new ideas and novel situations, even if they cause confusion or discomfort sometimes. They have fewer laws and social guidelines (both official and unspoken) to restrict people's behavior. They allow plenty of debate between various viewpoints, rather than insisting that one particular viewpoint is the only truth.

Long- Versus Short-Term Orientation. People in cultures with a long-term orientation keep an eye on distant goals, and they work hard to reach them, often by saving their money and adapting when the going gets tough. By contrast, in cultures with shorter-term orientations, quick results are more important, and goals that bring immediate results are a high priority. In other words, rather than savers, they are spenders.

Indulgence Versus Restraint. In some cultures, it's all about the current moment and it's generally OK to indulge in what feels good now. In other cultures, the mentality is much more controlled and reserved. People in these cultures tend to put off immediate pleasure and instead prefer a stoic, muted way of life.

No short list of cultural characteristics can capture all of the complex and subtle differences between cultures, but these six characteristics describe a good portion of those differences. **Figure 10.4** shows a profile for the United States on all six of these cultural characteristics. (You can compare the United States to any other country with Chapter App 10.1.) You'll see that the United States is remarkably high in individualism, has a short-term orientation, and is a bit more indulgent than

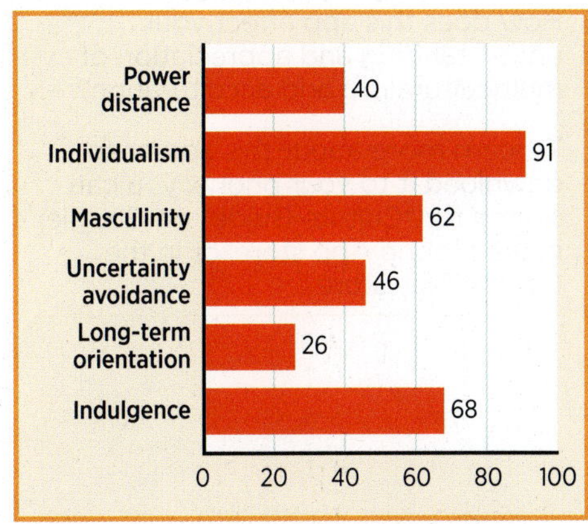

FIGURE 10.4 The Cultural Characteristics of the United States. The United States, according to this profile, has a culture high in individualism and indulgence, and low on long-term orientation. Data from The Hofstede Center (https://exhibition.geerthofstede.com/hofstedes-globe/).

CHAPTER APP 10.1

Culture Guide

For many years, the U.S. Air Force's Culture and Language Center has been writing culture guides to keep members of the military informed about the wide variety of cultures they may encounter around the world. The Culture Guide app makes all of these guides available digitally to the general public. This app allows you to scroll through dozens of countries and learn a wealth of information about each one. For each country, tapping "Information" reveals such aspects of culture as family structure, gender roles, religion and spirituality, language and communication style, social relationships, food and drink, clothing, arts, sports, and more.

How does it APPly to your daily life?
How could this app help you become more knowledgeable about cultures around the world? Whether or not you travel to these countries, how could this app help you become more appreciative of diverse cultures? For psychologists and other mental health professionals who work with diverse clients, how could this app be helpful?

How does it APPly to your understanding of psychology?
How does this app affect your understanding and appreciation of multiculturalism and acculturation?

To learn more about this app or to download it to your phone, you can search for "Culture Guide" on Google, in the iPhone App store, or in the Google Play store.

restrained. If you compare the United States to another country, you may notice drastic differences in some of these variables. The point here is that countries around the world differ widely on some important, measurable cultural characteristics.

What Difference Does Diversity Make?

It is clear that cultural groups differ from each other in many meaningful ways, but what does all that difference mean in your day-to-day life? Which specific behaviors, thoughts, and feelings might relate to your membership in a particular ethnicity, religion, gender, or other cultural group? Some answers are actually sprinkled throughout this book. Every chapter offers information (usually highlighted by a *Diversity Matters* tag) about how culture influences different experiences. Now let's take a look at a sampling of the many ways that diversity makes a difference.

Differences in Defining Identity. When people from more individualistic cultures are asked to describe themselves, they tend to do so, well, individualistically. On the other hand, when people from more collectivistic cultures are asked to describe themselves, they describe themselves in connection to others (Rhee et al., 1995; Smith, 2011). In one study, researchers gave both Mexican American and White American middle-schoolers the same simple, open-ended prompt: describe yourself. The Mexican American kids were more likely to use adjectives that implied a relationship to another person, like helpful or cooperative. The White kids were more likely to use adjectives that described personal, independent qualities, like smart and energetic (Dabul et al., 1995).

In another study, people from Malaysia (collectivistic) were compared to people from Australia and Britain (individualistic) in terms of how they chose to finish this sentence: "I am _____." Participants from Malaysia were much more likely to give responses that showed membership in a family or group, like "I am a daughter" or "I am a Muslim person." Participants from Australia and Britain were more likely to describe their personal traits or characteristics, with no reference to other people: "I am honest," "I am intelligent," and so on (Bochner, 1994). In a similar study, college students from India were more likely to mention a social role when describing themselves ("I am a student," "I am an Indian person"), but college students from the United States were more likely to evaluate themselves ("I am trustworthy," "I am clever," "I am good-looking") (Dhawan et al., 1995).

Differences in Raising Children. Parents with either low levels of education or low socioeconomic status are more likely to use physical punishment such as spanking than parents with higher levels (Dietz, 2000; Ryan & Deci, 2017). Physical punishment is also most common in the Southern region of the United States and least common in the Northeast; more common among certain ethnicities (Black and Latinx, in most studies) than others; and more common among members of certain conservative religious groups (Gershoff, 2002; Straus & Stewart, 1999).

On a separate note, kids in less industrialized countries (like Guatemala and Republic of the Congo) often have very different day-to-day experiences than kids in more industrialized countries such as the United States (Medin et al., 2007). Among other things, their parents often give them more household duties, including babysitting their younger siblings, at a much younger age, even 5–7 years old (Morelli et al., 2003).

Differences in Feelings. An annual large-scale survey asks residents of 149 countries to rate their overall level of happiness on a scale of 1 to 10. Most of the countries' average scores fall within a point of the middle of the scale, but some are much higher and others are much lower. As **Table 10.2** illustrates, the ten countries with the highest averages all fell above 7 (and are mostly located in Europe), and the ten countries with the lowest averages all fell below 4 (including several in Africa and the Middle East) (Helliwell et al., 2021).

Interestingly, this annual happiness survey demonstrated little change when the COVID pandemic arrived. Separate ratings of negative feelings like sadness and worry did reveal a slight change in 2020 (compared to 2017–2019), but only in about one-third of the countries surveyed. Overall, the survey showed a remarkable resilience and stability of emotion, considering the scope and seriousness of the pandemic (Helliwell et al., 2021). (Table 10.2 has some specific examples.)

There are other cultural differences in happiness too, especially in terms of what makes people happy and just how happy they tend to get (Mesquita & Leu, 2007; Tov & Diener, 2007). For example, in one study, U.S. and East Asian students read another student's diary entry that included some positive events, like getting the highest score in the class on a test. When asked what that student is feeling when the positive event happens, the U.S. students reported only good feelings. However, the East Asian students reported a mix of good and bad feelings — with the bad feelings often related to interpersonal consequences like jealousy or envy (Leu et al., 2010).

In another study, U.S. and Japanese students filled out questionnaires about their emotions four times a day (3 P.M., 6 P.M., 9 P.M., and midnight) for eight consecutive days. They were asked to write down and rate the last feeling they had right before completing the questionnaire. Overall, the Japanese students reported feelings near a neutral level (neither pleasant nor unpleasant), but the U.S. students reported feelings significantly above neutral and well into the "pleasant" range (Mesquita & Karasawa, 2002).

Even particular feelings can take on different connotations in different cultures. For example, people in more individualistic cultures like the United States and Australia typically experience pride as a good feeling and guilt as a bad feeling. However, in more collectivistic cultures like China and Taiwan, pride is not always so good, and guilt is not always so bad (Eid & Diener, 2001).

TABLE 10.2: How Happy Are You with Your Life?

COUNTRY	MEAN RATING (0 = UNSATISFIED; 10 = SATISFIED)
Top Ten Countries	
Finland	7.8
Denmark	7.6
Switzerland	7.6
Iceland	7.6
Netherlands	7.5
Norway	7.4
Sweden	7.4
Luxembourg	7.3
New Zealand	7.3
Austria	7.3
...	...
Bottom Ten Countries	
Burundi	3.8
Yemen	3.7
Tanzania	3.6
Haiti	3.6
Malawi	3.6
Lesotho	3.5
Botswana	3.5
Rwanda	3.4
Zimbabwe	3.1
Afghanistan	2.5

On a scale of 0–10, residents of most countries around the world produced a mean above the midpoint of 5 when asked how happy they were with their current lives. The range was wide, however, with some countries producing means well above or below the midpoint. Of the 149 countries surveyed in 2018 through 2020, the top 10 and bottom 10 are listed in the table. By the way, the United States ranked 19th, with a mean of 7.0. Data from Helliwell et al. (2021).

Differences in Memory. Culture often creates differences in what people remember and how they remember it, especially regarding childhood experiences (Nelson, 2018; Wang, 2014, 2018). When asked to share as many early childhood memories as they could in 5 minutes, people from the United States and Britain came up with about twice as many memories as people from China (Wang et al., 2004). The content of the memories differs as well. People from collectivistic cultures tend to remember group actions and interpersonal relationships, such as a family trip, or a special connection with a teacher. However, people from individualistic cultures tend to remember individual successes and failures, such as winning an award, or performing poorly on a test (Mullen, 1994; Wang, 2006; Wang & Conway, 2004; Wang & Ross, 2005). Also, when asked to remember past emotional experiences, people from individualistic cultures tend to focus on the positive feelings like their team winning a championship, or graduating from high school. People from collectivistic cultures, however, tend to focus more equally on positive and negative feelings (Oishi, 2002; Ross et al., 2002; Wang & Ross, 2005).

Differences in Seeing. People from diverse cultures actually see the world in different ways. For example, consider the *Müller–Lyer illusion*, which demonstrates that the figures attached to the ends of a line can influence how long you estimate the line to be. In **Figure 10.5** the two lines are actually the same length, but one may look longer than the other depending on whether the ends fold in (making a two-headed arrow) or fold out. Actually, the extent to which one looks longer than the other depends on the culture in which you have lived. People who spend their lives in "carpentered" environments — where the buildings feature lots of rectangular walls, doors, and windows, and the rooms feature lots of picture frames, bookshelves, and TVs, all of which have manufactured right angles — are much more susceptible to this illusion than people from "noncarpentered" environments, where the huts, tepees, and household items are more handmade and feature far fewer right angles (Keith, 2012; Norenzayan et al., 2007; Pedersen & Wheeler, 1983; Segall et al., 1966).

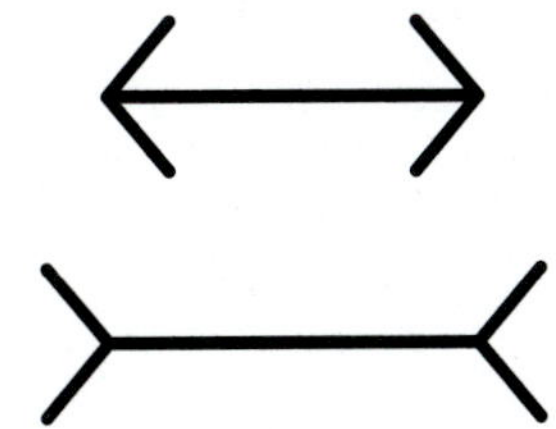

FIGURE 10.5 The Müller–Lyer Illusion. The extent to which these identical lines appear to be of different lengths actually depends on cultural background. People from cultures that are more "carpentered" — that is, people who have spent their lives around buildings and objects that are cut to exact specifications and feature plenty of perfect fits and clean angles — are more susceptible to this illusion than people from less "carpentered" cultures (Keith, 2012; Pedersen & Wheeler, 1983; Segall et al., 1966).

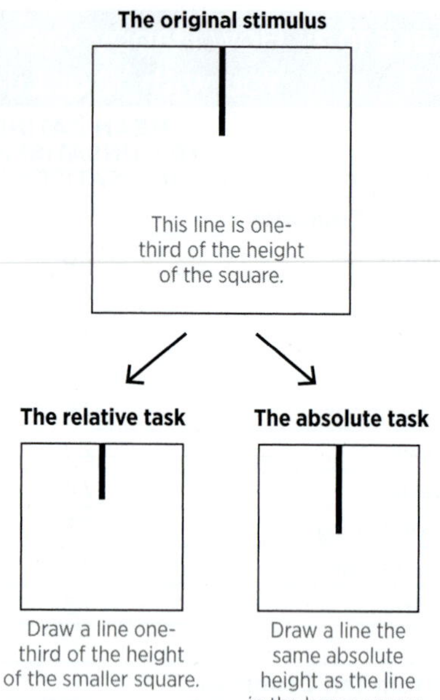
The original stimulus
This line is one-third of the height of the square.
The relative task
The absolute task
Draw a line one-third of the height of the smaller square.
Draw a line the same absolute height as the line in the larger square.

FIGURE 10.6 Seeing Parts in Isolation or in Context. People from collectivistic cultures are better at drawing the hanging line at the same proportion it was in the original square (as shown on the bottom left). However, people from individualistic cultures are better at drawing the hanging line at the same absolute height it appeared in the original square, regardless of the size of the second square (as shown on the bottom right). Information from Kitayama et al. (2003).

Another cultural difference in vision appears when people of Asian or U.S. backgrounds see a square with a small line hanging from the top (see **Figure 10.6**). When given a blank square of a different size and asked to add the hanging line to it, Americans are better at matching the exact length of the first hanging line (regardless of the size of the new square). However, Asians are better at matching the proportion of the hanging line to the new square (one-third the length of a new side). This difference suggests that people from collectivistic cultures tend to see items in context, while people from individualistic cultures tend to see items in isolation (Kitayama et al., 2003).

Differences in Seeking Help. In the United States, when people struggle with mental health, the odds that they seek professional help and stick with it depend on ethnicity and race (Meyer & Takeuchi, 2014). In general, people from ethnic and racial minority groups seek help at much lower rates than White people. Specifically, people who are Black or Asian American are least likely to seek professional help for mental health issues, with people who are Latinx only slightly higher (Dobalian & Rivers, 2008; Garland et al., 2014; Meyer et al., 2009; Padgett et al., 1994; Virnig et al., 2004). People from ethnic and racial minority groups are also more likely than White people to end treatment early (Wang, 2007).

Researchers are trying to uncover the reasons for these differences, but the possibilities are many. The reasons include turning to family, friends, or religious leaders rather than mental health professionals; lack of trust in the mental health system; inability to find therapists culturally or linguistically similar to themselves; cultural values regarding shame and stigma of mental issues; and lack of the necessary money, insurance, transportation, or time (Snowden, 2007, 2012; Snowden et al., 2007, 2011; Snowden & Yamada, 2005).

Differences in Sex Life. Compared to college students in the United States, college students in China are often less knowledgeable and less experienced with sex. Specifically, Chinese college students tend to lose their virginity later, have less premarital sex, have less oral sex, and participate in a narrower range of sexual activities than their U.S. counterparts (Tang et al., 1997). A study of ethnically diverse medical students found that those from the United States, Canada, Western Europe, and South Africa were generally much more sexually liberal, while those from the Middle East and Asia were generally much more sexually conservative (Leiblum et al., 2003).

Culture even impacts why people have sex (Hatfield et al., 2010). In one study, U.S. and Chinese college students both reported a high motivation to please their partners and strengthen the relationship, but the U.S. college students reported much higher rates of self-centered motives for sex, such as pleasure, stimulation, or stress reduction (Tang et al., 2012).

For "hooking up" on college campuses, ethnicity and race don't seem to influence the likelihood much, but religion does. Specifically, students with higher levels of religious activity are much less likely to engage in hookups than the rest of their college classmates (Brimeyer & Smith, 2012; Fielder et al., 2013; Penhollow et al., 2007). Similarly, teens who attend religious services or youth activities, or whose families emphasize religion around the house, tend to become sexually active later and have fewer sexual partners (Haglund & Fehring, 2010; Hernandez et al., 2014; Manlove et al., 2008; Miller & Gur, 2002; Rostosky et al., 2003).

Differences in Social Media Usage. People from different cultural and demographic groups handle social media in different ways (Alpizar et al., 2012; Li et al., 2018; Nadkarni & Hofmann, 2012; Park et al., 2012). For example, a study examining Facebook pages of 120 college students found that Black students revealed more about themselves in the "About Me" section, listed more group affiliations, and offered more extensive self-descriptions than White and Asian American students (DeAndrea et al., 2010).

Another study found that students who are White tend to post fewer selfies than students who are Black or Latinx Black people (Williams & Marquez, 2015). The specifics of selfies differ by culture too. Also, compared to Facebook users in Asia, Facebook users in the United States tend to post photos in which their face takes up a larger proportion of the frame, features of the background are blocked or cropped out, and their face is more emotionally expressive (Huang & Park, 2013). Facebook users in the United States tend to post far more positive self-presentations – photos and messages that emphasize how happy their life is and avoid any mention of negative events or feelings – than Facebook users in South Korea (Lee-Won et al., 2014).

There are Facebook differences based on gender and age too. Women tend to disclose more to their Facebook friends than men do (just as they tend to do with in-person relationships) (Sheldon, 2013). Older Facebook users tend to spend more time looking at family pictures and less time looking at posts from their same-age friends than younger Facebook users (McAndrew & Jeong, 2012).

One study examined what motivates college students from an individualistic culture (United States) and a collectivistic culture (Croatia) to use Instagram. Results showed that the Americans' main motivation was self-promotion, while the Croatians' main motivation was social interaction. The researchers suggest that these results reflect that Americans' use of Instagram is more "me-focused," with followers considered fans, while Croatians' use is more "we-focused," with followers considered friends (Sheldon et al., 2017, p. 648).

Applying Diversity Knowledge in Your Daily Life

It's great to *have* all of this knowledge about diversity, but it's even better to *use* it. Let's consider some ways you can apply this knowledge to your day-to-day life.

The ADDRESSING Model. An important early step to applying your diversity knowledge is to recognize diversity when you encounter it. To do so, it helps to have diversity variables "on your radar" so you can appreciate them in the people around you. The *ADDDRESSING model* is a list of diversity variables designed to heighten awareness and acknowledgement of other people's identities. No such list is comprehensive, but the ADDRESSING model covers a wide range of characteristics, each of which could be important to how other people understand themselves and the sense of power or powerlessness they experience in their daily lives. The model was originally designed to help therapists better appreciate their clients, but it can help any of us appreciate other people in much the same way (Hays, 1996, 2013, 2022). ADDRESSING is an acronym in which each letter stands for a characteristic of diversity:

- **A**ge/generation
- **D**isabilities present since birth
- **D**isabilities acquired later in life
- **R**eligion/spiritual orientation
- **E**thnicity/race
- **S**ocioeconomic status (SES)
- **S**exual orientation
- **I**ndigenous heritage
- **N**ational origin
- **G**ender

Taking these characteristics into account and discussing them to learn more (in appropriate and respectful ways) can help you appreciate the diverse range of people and identities you encounter in your life.

Cultural Intelligence. **Cultural intelligence** is your ability to live and interact effectively in a multicultural society. Similar to *cultural competence* (a term used by mental health professionals about their ability to work with diverse clients), cultural

cultural intelligence
A person's ability to live and interact effectively in a multicultural society.

intelligence is what enables you to get along happily and productively with people of different ethnicities, races, religions, geographic locations, genders, sexual orientations, and more.

For example, consider Hannah, a White Christian woman who grew up in rural Minnesota. When she was a child, the people in her life were, with few exceptions, homogeneous – same ethnicity, same religion, same lifestyle. That remained true through high school, but when she went to a college with much more diversity than her hometown, Hannah met and developed friendships with students with different characteristics and backgrounds.

After college, Hannah got a job in the marketing department at Ford Motor Company. That job not only took her to a big city (Detroit), but also introduced her to an even more diverse array of people, both at her site and on her travels around the United States and to many other parts of the world. At every step of her personal journey, Hannah relied on her cultural intelligence to appreciate the backgrounds of the people with whom she interacted, to form healthy and respectful relationships with them, and to work fruitfully together. In recent years, the realization that workers are more successful and satisfied when they have high levels of cultural intelligence has increasingly found its way into many industries, from business, military, and engineering to education, law enforcement, and health care (Anand & Lahiri, 2009; Cushner & Mahon, 2009; Dresser, 2005; Earley & Mosakowski, 2004; Grandin & Hedderich, 2009; Livermore, 2015; Moran et al., 2009; Ott & Michailova, 2018).

To be culturally intelligent, you need to know information about a cultural group *and* apply that information correctly (Ang & van Dyne, 2008). Imagine Hannah in her first months on the job at Ford. She meets Mohammed, a Muslim man, on a business trip. Should she shake his hand? (Many people who are Muslim shun body contact between men and women who are not related.) Her behavior might differ greatly when she meets Javier, from Spain, where not only a handshake but a brief hug and a kiss on the cheek are customary. Later, Hannah hosts a business dinner, and her guests will include Namit, who is Hindu. What should she consider as she chooses a restaurant? (Many people who are Hindu don't eat beef, so a steakhouse may not be a good idea.) Another time, she interviews Haru, a Japanese applicant for an entry-level position. Haru makes very little eye contact with Hannah throughout the interview. Should Hannah consider Haru's lack of eye contact rude? (It's not uncommon for people from Japan to make less eye contact than people from the United States do, especially toward someone in a position of authority, as a sign of respect.) A lack of cultural intelligence in these kinds of situations could lead Hannah to behave in ways that offend or confuse the people with whom she is interacting, and could damage her relationships with them (Axtell, 2007; Dresser, 2005; Hofstede et al., 2002).

Studies have found that cultural intelligence correlates with many positive outcomes, including better adjustment in a new culture, more trust in relationships between members of different cultures, better negotiation skills when doing business with a member of another culture, better job performance for international employees, and simply more interactions with members of other cultures (Ang et al., 2007, 2015; Chen et al., 2012; Imai & Gelfland, 2010; Ng et al., 2012; Rockstuhl & Ng, 2008; Shu et al., 2017; Templer et al., 2006). You can increase your cultural intelligence by reading books, watching videos, or going through training specifically designed to do so. However, just having multicultural encounters – interacting with people different from yourself and learning from those interactions – can raise your cultural intelligence as well (Crowne, 2008; Raver & Van Dyne, 2018; Shannon & Begley, 2008; Tarique & Takeuchi, 2008; Young et al., 2018).

LIFE HACK 10.2

You can boost your own cultural intelligence by reading about different cultures, undergoing multicultural training, or directly interacting with people from cultural groups different from your own.

(Crowne, 2008; Shannon & Begley, 2008; Tarique & Takeuchi, 2008)

Cultural Humility. Cultural intelligence is great, but no one should presume they know everything about the cultural factors that might play a role in another person's life. For that reason, it's also important to have **cultural humility**: an attitude based on self-reflection, recognizing the limits of your own knowledge about diversity, and educating yourself about the identities and experiences of other people (Hook et al., 2017; Mosher et al., 2017; Tervalon & Murray-Garcia, 1998).

cultural humility
An attitude based on self-reflection, recognizing the limits of your own knowledge about diversity, and educating yourself about the identities and experiences of other people.

To understand the importance of showing cultural humility to other people, imagine how it would feel if someone treated you *without* cultural humility, assuming they completely "get" you in terms of diversity. They might act like they know the particulars of your gender, age, ethnicity, sexual orientation, religion, and socioeconomic status (among other characteristics). And they might jump to conclusions about how all of those characteristics impact your day-to-day experience — and in the process, they might even come across as arrogant or insensitive.

Now imagine if this person treated you *with* cultural humility. Their attitude would be drastically different. Instead of making assumptions about everything they *do* know about you, they would recognize how much they *don't* know. They would seek to learn more about you, rather than presuming they already know everything they need to know. They would be respectful, patient, and open-minded as they attempt to understand the different facets of your identity and how they impact your life. And they would explore the diverse facets of their own identity too, since that kind of self-awareness can help them appreciate the diversity of other people.

CHAPTER APP 10.2

The Vent app allows you to express your emotions to a community of others. First, you choose a broad category (fear, sadness, happiness, etc.). Then you choose a specific feeling within that category (within happiness, you can choose excited, proud, relieved, etc.) and write a brief post to explain. Other Vent users respond to your emotions by tapping "hug," "same," "omg," "yay," "ugh," or other buttons to express support. In some ways, it's like posting your feelings on social media like Twitter, Instagram, or Facebook, but in a forum specifically dedicated to emotional expression.

How does it APPly to your daily life? How valuable would you find this app? Which emotions would you be most likely and least likely to express? How likely would you be to express support for the emotions of others?

How does it APPly to your understanding of psychology? How might members of different groups (like different genders, different ethnicities, or different levels of individualism and collectivism) use this app differently? How does an appreciation of those differences help you understand the ways that people from diverse cultures experience and express feelings? How does that appreciation affect your cultural intelligence?

To learn more about this app or to download it to your phone, you can search for "Vent app" on Google, in the iPhone App store, or in the Google Play store.

Microaggressions. One sign of an increase in cultural intelligence is a decrease in **microaggressions**: everyday actions or comments that, often unintentionally, contain hostile or off-putting messages for members of certain cultures. The *micro* in microaggressions refers to the fact that these are typically not big, attention-grabbing actions — no direct slurs, no physical attacks, no vandalism or destruction of property. Instead, microaggressions are little things that people do or say that have a negative impact on others, often because they reveal an "ism" (racism, ageism, sexism, heterosexism, weightism, lookism, etc.) that makes the recipient feel insulted, demeaned, or marginalized (Harrell, 2000; Sue, 2010a, b; Sue et al., 2007).

Often, microaggressions are subtle, and may even be unconscious to the person delivering it, who believes that they are saying something neutral or kind. For example, consider Sophia, a fourth-grader who just completed her science fair project. A judge evaluating the kids' projects says "Nice work!" to the boy whose project is next to Sophia's. Then, to Sophia, the judge says, "Nice work! How did *you* get so good at science?" The way the judge emphasizes *you* communicates to Sophia that there is something about her, presumably her gender, that the judge finds incompatible with scientific ability — a message that could damage her self-confidence and discourage her from pursuing science in the future.

As another example, consider Sam, a 19-year-old young man and college student. Sam has struggled with depression off and on, and finally decided to see a counselor in his university's counseling center. In the first session, Sam's counselor asks him a series of typical background questions — family, friends, medical history, and so on. The counselor then asks about Sam's dating life: "Do you have a girlfriend?" By specifying "girlfriend" in the question (rather than asking a more general and inclusive question, like "Are you dating anyone?"), the counselor subtly communicates to Sam that heterosexuality is the expectation, the norm, the standard. Sam, who is gay, isn't exactly sure how to respond, but he is sure that he feels uncomfortable with this counselor.

Here's is one more example: Joe, a 45-year-old accountant, is having a conversation with coworkers at the office holiday party in mid-December. One coworker shares a fond recollection of a childhood Christmas morning with his parents. The coworker then turns to Joe: "So Joe — what did your mom and dad do for Christmas when you were a kid?" Joe feels slighted for two reasons: first, when Joe was a kid, he didn't have both a mom and a dad, and second, Joe is Jewish and doesn't celebrate Christmas. His coworker's assumptions that everyone has two parents and that everyone celebrates Christmas were part of a well-meaning question, but they communicate an assumption about how things are that might make Joe feel marginalized and "less-than."

Like many microaggressions, these examples are not so blatantly offensive that they would automatically cause the recipient to storm out of the room, burst into tears, or hurl insults (or fists) in retaliation. But being on the receiving end of *many* microaggressions — which is the experience of many members of minority groups — can be hurtful, or as one group of authors put it, "death by a thousand cuts"

microaggressions
Everyday actions or comments that, often unintentionally, contain hostile or off-putting messages for members of certain cultures.

MY TAKE VIDEO 10.2

Microaggressions

"It's really important because . . ."

Visit Achieve to watch the My Take video and then answer questions.

Achieve

(Nadal et al., 2011a, p. 234). Numerous studies have examined the accumulated effect of microaggressions on minority groups, including people who are Black, Latinx, Asian American, multiracial, women, sexual minorities, gender minorities, and others. The findings are consistent: higher rates of stress, depression, anxiety, anger, alcohol use, physical illness, and other negative consequences are the result of consistent microaggressions (Blume et al., 2012; Donovan et al., 2013; Huynh, 2012; McCabe, 2009; Nadal et al., 2011b, c, 2016; Ong et al., 2013; Owen et al., 2019; Torres et al., 2010; Wang et al., 2011; Wong et al., 2014; Wong-Padoongpatt et al., 2017).

So what's the best way to avoid committing microaggressions?

Some people believe that the best strategy is to "bite your tongue." They argue that catching a biased or prejudiced thought before it escapes through your mouth is the way to prevent microaggressions. That strategy may help, but it doesn't get to the root of the problem (and it also discourages you from talking to people who are different from you, which would only lessen your opportunities for increased cultural intelligence). Instead, a better strategy is to explore your underlying beliefs, including any "isms" that might linger in your mind, and change them to be more inclusive of diversity. That is easier said than done, but an admirable and worthwhile goal nonetheless. To achieve it, open discussions with others about these issues (including humble admissions of your own less-than-ideal beliefs) and ongoing interactions with a diverse range of people can be quite helpful (Hook et al., 2013; Nadal, 2013; Owen et al., 2011, 2014; Sue & Sue, 2012). Additionally, schools and workplaces are increasingly providing education about the issue of microaggressions, and teachers are increasingly being trained to respond effectively when they take place in the classroom (Holder, 2019; Kohli et al., 2019; Pearce, 2019; Young & Anderson, 2019).

Another important question about microaggressions is how to respond to them when you see them happen to someone around you. How does one shift from passive bystander to active ally? Numerous experts have offered suggestions (Nadal, 2014; Sue et al., 2021; Abrams, 2021):

- Focus on the person's behavior, not the person themselves. Questioning a specific statement or action is less likely to make another person react defensively than questioning their character (by accusing them of being a racist or a sexist, for example).
- Decide whether it's best to respond now or to wait until later. Responding immediately can work well sometimes, but other times it might heighten tensions and lead to defensiveness or even physical danger. Keep in mind that the person who committed the microaggression might be more receptive if you wait to discuss the issue privately, rather than in front of others.
- Consider stating your disapproval, perhaps with a phrase like "I actually disagree," or "That's not OK, in my opinion," or "I know you didn't mean to hurt anyone, but what you said could have been hurtful."
- A question might be more appropriate than a statement in some situations, perhaps along the lines of "How is their [diversity variable] relevant to this situation?"
- Try to state only your own reaction, rather than presuming that others (including the person who you think may have been hurt by the microaggression) feel the way you would expect.
- If you are the person who committed the microaggression (and none of us are immune from doing so), acknowledge it, apologize, and try to learn from it.

The concept of microaggressions has risen quickly in popularity and acceptance in recent years. Some researchers believe that rise has been *too* quick and that scholars have been too eager to endorse the idea of microaggressions. These researchers wonder if the definition of the term *microaggression* is clear enough and shared by all who study it; if microaggressions always reflect prejudice or aggression in the person committing them; and if microaggressions are always experienced negatively by people on the receiving end (Haidt, 2017; Lilienfeld, 2017a, b, 2020). Other researchers have responded to these criticisms by arguing that microaggressions reflect life as it is actually lived, especially by members of oppressed minorities, and that evidence for microaggressions as a valid concept is growing quickly (Ong & Burrow, 2017; Sue, 2017; Williams, 2020).

antiracist
A person whose beliefs and actions oppose racism and promote racial equality.

colorism
Prejudice or discrimination based on the darkness of a person's skin, often within a single racial or ethnic group.

Antiracism. Another way to apply diversity knowledge in your day-to-day life is to live as an **antiracist**: a person whose beliefs and actions oppose racism and promote racial equality. *Racism* is the belief that race strongly determines a person's value and that some racial groups are inherently inferior to others, which often leads to prejudice and discrimination. The opposite of racism is not the absence of racism, but *anti*racism – a more active confrontation of racist actions, biases, policies, systems, and institutions (Kendi, 2019; Roberts & Rizzo, 2021).

Antiracism has the potential to reduce the negative psychological effects that racism can have, which have been well documented by researchers (Williams et al., 2019; Schmitt et al., 2014). One meta-analysis combined the results of over 60 studies that examined the connection between perceived racism among Black American adults and mental health. Results showed that those with higher levels of perceived racism had higher levels of psychological distress, especially in the form of anxiety, depression, and other psychological disorders (Pieterse et al., 2012). Another meta-analysis – this one combining the results of over 200 studies – focused on perceived racism and discrimination in adolescents. Its findings were similar: those with higher levels of perceived racism had higher levels of psychological distress, depression, and substance use (Benner et al., 2018). A study of racism in college students found similar results too: Asian American and Latinx college students with higher perceived racism had higher levels of anxiety, depression, and suicidal thoughts (Hwang & Goto, 2008).

Any discussion of racism should include **colorism**: prejudice or discrimination based on the darkness of a person's skin, often within a single racial or ethnic group. Colorism exists within numerous groups, including the Black, Asian American, and Latinx communities (Figuereo & Calvo, 2021; Harvey et al., 2017; Monk, 2021). Research indicates that colorism can have harmful psychological effects. For example, one review of 28 articles found that Black Americans with darker skin were more likely to experience depression and anxiety (and a wide range of physical health issues) than Black Americans with lighter skin (Keyes et al., 2020). In another study, Black and White participants were asked to rate the traits of either darker-skinned or lighter-skinned Black people whose photos they saw. Both Black and White participants demonstrated colorism: they rated the darker-skinned Black people as more criminal, less intelligent, less attractive, more aggressive, and of lower income than lighter-skinned Black people (Maddox & Gray, 2002). Colorism has also been identified as a factor in school punishments: among Black girls in middle school and high school, those with darker skin were significantly more likely than those with lighter skin to receive out-of-school suspension as a consequence for misbehavior (Blake et al., 2017).

CHECK YOUR LEARNING:

10.6 What is multiculturalism, and how has its importance within psychology changed?

10.7 How has the understanding of cultural differences changed throughout the history of psychology?

10.8 How is the importance of multiculturalism reflected in the profession of psychology today?

10.9 What is acculturation?

10.10 What are the key variables in the various acculturation strategies?

10.11 What is acculturative stress?

10.12 In what specific ways do cultures differ from each other?

10.13 In which areas of daily life can cultural diversity produce differences?

10.14 What is cultural intelligence?

10.15 What is cultural humility?

10.16 What is antiracism?

10.17 What are microaggressions?

To check your understanding of these questions, click show the answers or refer to the answers in the Chapter Summary.

Gender and Sexuality: Essential Forms of Diversity

YOU WILL LEARN:

10.18 how gender and sex are defined.

10.19 what influences gender development.

10.20 what cisgender, transgender, and transition mean.

10.21 what sexual orientation is, and how some sexual orientations are defined.

10.22 what coming out is.

10.23 about some influences on attitudes toward sexual minorities.

10.24 about some differences that gender makes in daily life.

Any cultural variable could have a meaningful impact in the life of any one person. Some, however, seem especially prominent. Let's take a closer look at two variables — *gender* and *sexuality* — that play central roles in many of our lives.

Defining Gender and Sex

We've already listed many of the qualities around which culture can center, but one of the most fundamental is **gender**: your culture's social, psychological, and behavioral expectations related to the sex you were assigned at birth. Gender is not equivalent to **sex**: your biological assignment at birth (often male or female) based on a combination of genitals, chromosomes, and hormones. Some individuals are born with a combination of male and female sex traits and are called *intersex*. Gender is also not equivalent to **gender identity**: your internal sense of yourself as man, woman, both, or neither. Some people describe their gender identity as **nonbinary**: a gender identity that does not fall within the categories of woman or man, and may fall between those categories or be entirely distinct from them. (American Psychological Association 2012, 2015a, b; GLAAD, 2018).

In casual conversation, you've probably heard people use gender and sex interchangeably, assuming that the two always match. Maybe you've even filled out forms that ask for either your gender or your sex but not both, assuming that your answer for one would be the same as your answer for the other. These assumptions are not always correct. A person's gender does not always match the body parts with which that person was born (Eagly, 2013; Pryzgoda & Chrisler, 2000; Smith et al., 2013).

Gender Development

Of course, gender doesn't appear all at once at birth, or puberty, or any other particular point in a person's life. Instead, gender evolves over time through a process called *gender development*, and that process depends on lots of factors beyond simple biology (Bussey, 2013; Martin & Ruble, 2010; Martin et al., 2017; Ruble & Martin, 1998; Steensma et al., 2013; Zosuls et al., 2011).

gender
Your culture's social, psychological, and behavioral expectations related to the sex you were assigned at birth.

sex
A person's biological assignment at birth (often male or female) based on a combination of genitals, chromosomes, and hormones.

gender identity
Your internal sense of yourself as man, woman, both, or neither.

nonbinary
A gender identity that does not fall within the categories of woman or man, and may fall between those categories or be entirely distinct from them.

Parents and Gender Development. Parents play a major role in gender development. Some parents would never allow their sons to set foot in the "pink" toy aisle, or might discourage their daughters if they were interested in playing or even watching football. Other parents wouldn't mind, and still others would actively encourage it. These parental responses to interests that don't conform to popular gender norms powerfully shape a child's understanding and sense of masculinity or femininity (Bussey & Bandura, 1999). This shaping happens not just with toys and games, but also with occupational interests (engineering vs. nursing, for example) and household responsibilities (cooking vs. lawn mowing, for example).

Peers and Gender Development. Peers influence gender development too, especially as kids enter the preteen years, when fitting in and maintaining popularity become more important (Kornienko et al., 2016; Ruble et al., 2006). One review of studies on peers and gender development concluded that, generally, peer groups push kids strongly toward traditional gender roles and often provide negative feedback when a child's behavior varies from those roles (Witt, 2000).

How would you respond if you were a fifth-grade boy getting taunted by other fifth-grade boys for your interest in fashion design? Or if you were a seventh-grade girl being teased by other seventh-grade girls for your interest in joining a wrestling team? One study of hundreds of U.S. elementary school students found that getting picked on by peers for doing things that didn't conform to gender stereotypes produced different results for different picked-on kids. Specifically, for boys and girls with many friends who are boys, getting picked on led to more behaviors consistent with gender stereotypes. For boys with many friends who are girls, however, getting picked on led to more behaviors *in*consistent with gender stereotypes (Lee & Troop-Gordon, 2011).

The Media and Gender Development. In addition to parents' and peers' influence on gender development, there is the influence of the media. The way people of different genders are depicted on TV, in video games, in magazines, on billboards, and elsewhere has a strong influence on kids' gender development. Let's consider TV as a prime example (see the Watching Psychology box as well). It might be an obvious point, but there is a real difference in the way men and women are typically portrayed on TV shows. Men are more often portrayed as authoritative, powerful, expert, dominant, and physically muscular, while women are more often portrayed as lower in status, helpless, caring for others, provocative, and concerned about sexual attractiveness (Coltrane & Messineo, 2000; Ellemers, 2018; Rivadeneyra, 2011; Sink & Mastro, 2017; Turow, 2012).

Commercials reinforce gender stereotypes too. One study found that in commercials, women are significantly more likely than men to be suggestively dressed, at home, or advertising cosmetics and retail stores, while men are significantly more likely than women to be fully dressed, at work, or advertising financial services and technology products (Prieler, 2016).

WATCHING PSYCHOLOGY

TV, Sexual Attitudes, and Sexual Behaviors

There are plenty of good reasons for parents to be concerned about how TV might affect their kids. For example, too much TV could interfere with homework, physical fitness, or socializing with friends. Recent research highlights another risk associated with excessive TV watching: influences on sexual attitudes and behaviors. Generally speaking, there is a correlation between how many hours teens spend watching TV and how likely they are to engage in sexual behaviors (Ward et al., 2014). More specifically, longitudinal studies that track people through the teen and young adult years find that those who watch lots of TV, especially TV with lots of sexual content, are more likely to have sex at all, have sex without a condom, and have sex with multiple partners (Collins et al., 2004; Fisher et al., 2009; Gottfried et al., 2013; O'Hara et al., 2012).

The type of sexual content matters too. When teens watch TV that promotes common sexual stereotypes (women as sex objects, men as driven primarily by sex, casual sex as safe and without negative consequences), they are more likely to believe those stereotypes are true, and also more likely to engage in sexual behaviors (Ward & Friedman, 2006; Ward et al., 2016). It is not just TV either. In one study, straight college men who had more exposure to a wide variety of entertainment media (TV, movies, music videos, and men's magazines) had more casual sex partners, less consistent use of condoms, and stronger beliefs that promiscuity and hookups are acceptable (Ward et al., 2011).

It is particularly concerning that some of the common themes in the sex-laden shows targeted toward teens and adults are also common themes in shows targeted toward children and preteens (Rousseau & Eggermont, 2018). One study examined multiple episodes of seven popular Nickelodeon and Disney shows from 2004–2012: *Drake and Josh*, *Suite Life of Zack and Cody*, *Wizards of Waverly Place*, *Hannah Montana*, *iCarly*, *Sonny with a Chance*, and *Jonas*. The study's results indicated a high frequency of portraying stereotypical heterosexual interactions — in some cases, as often as in shows aimed at an older audience. For example, it was common to find boys objectifying girls and valuing them for their appearance ("she is so hot..."); girls concerned about their own looks ("wait — let me fix my hair..."); girls offering flirtatious compliments to boys ("my friend didn't tell me how cute you are..."); and boys using material items (gifts) or status (as popular rock stars or TV stars) to impress girls. The shows that relied most heavily on these themes were the ones with lead characters who were boys and men (Kim et al., 2007; Kirsch & Murnen, 2015). So, even younger TV viewers are being introduced to scripts of sexual interactions that, according to a growing body of research, predict early and risky sexual behavior. •

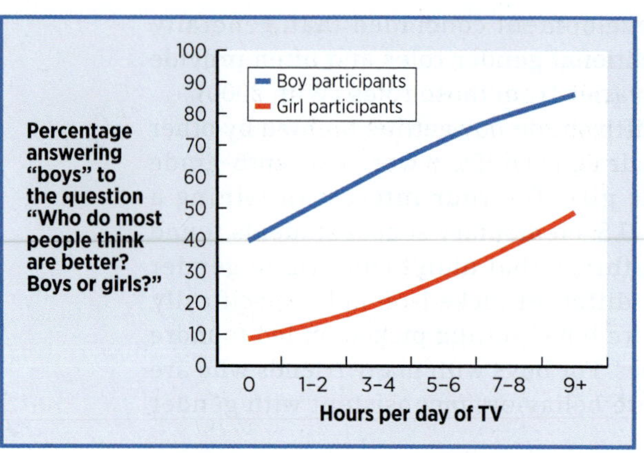

FIGURE 10.7 TV Watching and Gender Development in 4-Year-Olds. When 4-year-old children were asked "Who do most people think are better? Boys or girls?" their answers depended on how much TV they watched per day. For both boys and girls, the more TV they watched, the more likely they were to answer "boys." "Boys" was the answer for less than 10% of the girls who watch no TV, but almost half of the girls who watch 9+ hours of TV per day.
Data from Halim et al. (2013).

Those TV portrayals make a real difference in how kids see and experience gender. In fact, the more time kids spend watching TV, the more strongly they buy into the gender stereotypes they see on the screen (Durkin & Nugent, 1998; McGhee & Frueh, 1980; Ward & Friedman, 2006). The effects are evident even at very early ages. In one study, researchers asked 4-year-old kids this question: "Who do most people think are better? Boys or girls?" The kids' responses depended on how much TV they watched. As **Figure 10.7** shows, the more TV that participants watched, the more likely they were to answer "boys." In fact, a kid who watched 3–4 hours of TV per day was twice as likely to answer "boys" as a kid who watched no TV at all (Halim et al., 2013, p. 130). In another study, researchers found that 4-year-old children who spent more time watching Disney princess movies and shows were more likely to behave in stereotypically female ways, and that likelihood had grown even stronger a year later (Coyne et al., 2016).

Cisgender and Transgender. When someone's sense of gender corresponds to their assigned sex at birth, that person is **cisgender**: a person whose gender matches the sex they were assigned at birth. When someone does not experience that correspondence, that person may be **transgender**: a person whose gender differs from the sex they were assigned at birth. (In Latin, *cis-* means on the same side, and *trans-* means on opposite sides.) Knowing that someone is cisgender or transgender doesn't tell you anything about their sexual orientation — they could be attracted to anyone.

People who are transgender often experience significant distress or unhappiness from the pressure to conform to a different gender than their own. In some cases, a person who is transgender will **transition**: choose to take steps to live as the gender that matches their identity rather than their biologically assigned sex. Transitioning can include name changes, pronoun changes (he, she, they, or others), clothing changes, long-term hormone treatments (androgens and estrogens) to cause changes to the body, or surgeries to change the genitals, chest, face, vocal cords, and other body parts that differ between men and women (National Center for Transgender Equality, 2014; Sánchez & Vilain, 2013).

Jennifer Finney Boylan is an English professor who was born James Boylan. She transitioned male-to-female in her early forties, years after marrying and having two children with a woman. In her autobiography *She's Not There*, Boylan explains how her identification with the female gender (and the stress that accompanied it) started decades before her hormones and surgeries, when she was a 3-year-old boy (Boylan, 2003, pp. 19–22):

> Since then, the awareness that I was in the wrong body, living the wrong life, was never out of my conscious mind.... And at every moment as I lived my life, I countered this awareness with an exasperated companion thought, namely, Don't be an *idiot*. You're *not* a girl. Get over it. But I never got over it.... After I grew up and became female, people would often ask me, How did you *know*, when you were a child?... It seemed obvious to me that this was something you understood intuitively, not on the basis of what was between your legs, but because of what you felt in your heart. Remember when you woke up this morning — I'd say to my female friends — and you knew you were female? *That's* how I felt. *That's* how I knew. Of course, knowing with such absolute certainty something that appeared to be both absurd and untrue [was] ... a crushing burden, which was, simultaneously, invisible.

The burden that Jennifer Finney Boylan describes — combined with high rates of discrimination, oppression, and poverty — often translates into serious psychological issues for people who are transgender (James et al., 2016). One study of over 500 people

cisgender
A person whose gender matches the sex they were assigned at birth.

transgender
A person whose gender differs from the sex they were assigned at birth.

transition
Taking steps to live as the gender that matches one's identity rather than one's biologically assigned gender.

sexual orientation
A person's pattern of romantic attraction to a particular group or groups of other people.

heterosexual or straight
The sexual orientation of a person who is attracted to people with a sex or gender different than their own.

gay/lesbian
The sexual orientation of a person who is attracted to people with a sex or gender different than their own.

bisexual or bi
The sexual orientation of a person who is attracted to people of more than one sex or gender.

LGBTQ+
A community of members of sexual minorities, including lesbian (L), gay (G), bisexual (B), transgender (T), queer/questioning (Q), and other people.

who are transgender found that over half were clinically depressed, and about a third had attempted suicide at some point in their lives — both rates way above those found in the general population (Clements-Nolle et al., 2001). Other studies have found similar results, especially among people who are transgender and were socially outcast, harassed, bullied, or rejected by their families (Bockting et al., 2013; Grant et al., 2010; Witcomb et al., 2018).

Sexual Orientation

Sexual orientation is a person's pattern of romantic attraction to a particular group (or groups) of other people. Your sexual orientation is who you'd like to be intimate with. A person with a **heterosexual** (or **straight**) orientation is attracted to people with a sex or gender different than their own. A person with a **gay/lesbian** orientation is attracted to people with a sex or gender the same as their own. A person with a **bisexual** (or **bi**) orientation is attracted to people of more than one sex or gender.

You're probably already familiar with those terms, but it would be a mistake to think that they capture everyone. Sexual orientations also include *pansexual* (attracted to anyone, regardless of the other person's gender), *sex fluid* (attracted to different people at different times), *questioning* (still in the process of examining or reexamining who they find attractive), and *asexual* (sexually attracted to no one) (Zea & Nakamura, 2014). Collectively, people whose sexual orientations or gender identities differ from that of the majority of the population identify as **LGBTQ+**: a community of members of sexual minorities, including lesbian (L), gay (G), bisexual (B), transgender (T), queer/questioning (Q), and other people.

How many people have each sexual orientation?

It depends on both who and how you ask (**Table 10.3**). In terms of *who*, more open-minded cultures in which varieties of sexual orientations are widely accepted are more likely to produce higher estimates of gay, lesbian, and bi. In terms of *how*, questions that ask how a person labels themselves ("What's your sexual orientation?") produce lower estimates of gay, lesbian, and bi identity than questions that ask what behaviors a person has done ("Have you ever had sexual interactions with _____?") or who they find attractive ("Have you ever been attracted to _____?"). Also, surveys conducted via the Internet tend to produce higher estimates of gay, lesbian, and bi identity than those conducted by other means, perhaps because of a higher sense of anonymity (Chandra et al., 2011; Harris Interactive & Witeck-Combs, 2010). Collectively, most researchers tend to settle on a range of 2–4% of the general U.S. population (give or take a percentage point or two) as a reasonable estimate of how many of us identify as gay, lesbian, or bi (Gates, 2013).

Within that range, there are gender-based differences. Specifically, men tend to identify as gay more often than bisexual, but women tend to identify as bisexual more often than lesbian (Dworkin, 2013; Herek et al., 2010). In other words, women tend to have a nonexclusive sexuality more often than men. (Here, *nonexclusive* means that just because

CHAPTER APP 10.3

Refuge Restrooms

The Refuge Restrooms app helps users locate public restrooms that are safe and comfortable for people who are transgender, intersex, and nonbinary. Users can add new locations as they find them.

How does it APPly to your daily life?
How valuable would this app be to a transgender, intersex, or gender-nonconforming person? How valuable could it be to someone who is cisgender or otherwise does not fall into any of those categories, in terms of appreciating difficulties that people who are transgender experience?

How does it APPly to your understanding of psychology?
How does this app help you understand the concepts of transgender, cisgender, and intersex?

To learn more about this app or to download it to your phone, you can search for "Refuge Restrooms" on Google, in the iPhone App store, or in the Google Play store.

TABLE 10.3: Sexual Orientation Rates: It Depends How You Ask

	ALL PARTICIPANTS (%)	MEN (%)	WOMEN (%)
Do you *identify* as lesbian, gay, or bisexual?	3.7	2.8	4.6
Do you have any *sexual experience* with a person of same sex?	8.8	5.2	12.5
Do you have any *attraction* to a person of same sex?	11.0	6.5	16.7

Data from Chandra et al. (2011) and Gates and Newport (2013).

Researchers trying to determine how many people are lesbian, gay, or bisexual get different answers when they ask the question in different ways. In this large-scale U.S. study, the rates were lowest when the question asked about *identifying* as lesbian, gay, or bisexual; higher when the question asked about same-sex *behaviors*; and higher still when the question asked about same-sex *attraction*.

Wavebreak Media ltd/Alamy

Sexual orientations span a wide range. They include heterosexual (straight), gay/lesbian, and bisexual (bi), as well as pansexual, fluid, questioning, asexual, and others.

a person is attracted to one gender, that doesn't mean that the person isn't also attracted to another gender [Bailey et al., 2000; Dickson et al., 2003; Laumann et al., 2004; Thompson & Morgan, 2008; Vrangalova & Savin-Williams, 2012].) In one large-scale survey of over 14,000 young adults, the researchers gave the participants several middle-ground options to define their sexuality — not just straight or gay/lesbian, but in-between options like "mostly straight," "bisexual", and "mostly gay." As **Table 10.4** shows, far more men placed themselves at one end of the scale or the other (definitively straight or gay), and far more women placed themselves in one of the middle categories (Udry & Chantala, 2006).

Another gender-based difference in sexual orientation has to do with *fluid* sexuality, or the likelihood for sexual attraction to change over time. Women are much more likely to experience a fluid sexuality than men over the course of their lives (Diamond, 2000; Kanazawa, 2017; Peplau & Garnets, 2000). This is especially evident in longitudinal studies, which track people across many years. More often than men, women find their patterns of attraction changing, sometimes dividing their adult lives into two long, distinct periods, and other times dividing them into many briefer periods that involve returning to previous attractions (Diamond, 2005, 2007, 2009; Kinnish et al., 2005). An increasing recognition of the fluidity of sexual orientation has caused many experts in this field to wonder if it may be a mistake to assume that sexual orientation is a trait for everyone — something that develops early in life and remains constant — and instead consider that at least for some people, it is a characteristic that can vary throughout the life span (Diamond, 2013).

Coming Out and Mental Health. A critical decision in the lives of LGBTQ+ people is to the degree to which they *come out* (reveal their identity to themselves and eventually others), as opposed to concealing it. Of course, that decision is not necessarily all-or-nothing, since an LGBTQ+ person can decide to come out to certain people but not others or can decide at various points in time to reveal certain aspects of their identity and keep other aspects concealed.

It's not easy to predict how coming out might influence mental health outcomes. There can be pros and cons to both high and low levels of outness. A high level of outness can enable a person to be authentic and find partners and friends who can provide social support, but it can also expose them to prejudice and discrimination. A low level of outness can protect a person from that prejudice and discrimination, but it can also prevent the opportunity to experience that authenticity and find those partners and friends who could provide social support (Camacho et al., 2020).

A meta-analysis combined the results of almost 200 studies that measured the experiences of over 92,000 people who identify as lesbian, gay, or bisexual. The results suggested a wide range of outcomes for people who had largely come out or had not. Those who had not come out had a slightly higher risk of depression and anxiety (especially among lesbian and gay people rather than bisexual people), but a slightly lower risk of substance use issues (Pachankis et al., 2020). Another study across 28 countries found that the amount of structural stigma — laws, policies, and attitudes toward people who are lesbian, gay, or bisexual — can make a big difference in decisions related to coming out and the consequences of those decisions. Specifically, in countries with high levels of structural stigma, people who are lesbian, gay, or bisexual are much less likely to choose to come out, a decision that results in lower life satisfaction despite protecting them from overt discrimination and oppression (Pachankis & Bränström, 2018).

Often, questions about sexual orientation are worded in all-or-none ways. By contrast, in one large-scale study (about 14,000 participants), there were five options: completely heterosexual, mostly heterosexual, bisexual, mostly gay/lesbian, and completely gay/lesbian. The percentages were higher for men at the two extremes but higher for women in the three middle-ground categories.

TABLE 10.4: Sexual Orientations of Men and Women

SEXUAL ORIENTATION	MEN (%)	WOMEN (%)
Completely heterosexual	94.03	85.10
Mostly heterosexual	3.18	10.65
Bisexual	0.57	2.55
Mostly gay/lesbian	0.63	0.70
Completely gay/lesbian	1.18	0.47

Data from Udry and Chantala (2006).

Drazen_/Getty Images

Attitudes toward same-sex relationships have generally become more positive and affirming in recent decades, but those attitudes still vary widely and relate to numerous factors such as ethnicity, age, religious and political beliefs, and other factors.

Attitudes Toward Sexual Minorities. Attitudes toward sexual minorities have changed drastically in recent decades — just ask the older people in your life. Not long ago, any kind of same-sex romantic relationship was viewed with disdain by many (but certainly not all) within mainstream U.S. culture. Gay marriage was illegal across the country, and being gay or lesbian was even considered a psychological disorder (American Psychiatric Association, 1952, 1968).

Today, positive and affirming views toward diverse sexual orientations are more common. However, they are not universal (Kite & Bryant-Lees, 2016). Research indicates that views toward diverse sexual orientations depend on a number of factors. For example, within the United States, ethnicity seems to make a difference. In general, people who are White hold more favorable attitudes toward non-straight orientations than people who are Black or Latinx. Age and gender seem to make a difference as well, with more positive attitudes generally held by younger adults and women (Costa et al., 2015; Dodge et al., 2016; Horn, 2013; Twenge et al., 2016). Other predictors of negative views toward sexual minorities include conservative religious and political beliefs; high levels of commitment to religion; traditional beliefs about gender roles (how men and women "should" behave); the belief that sexuality is a choice (and therefore changeable); and lack of direct contact with lesbian women or gay men (Cárdenas et al., 2018; Eliason, 2001; Harbaugh & Lindsey, 2015; Haslam & Levy, 2006; Hegarty & Pratto, 2001; Israel & Mohr, 2004; Mohr & Rochlen, 1999). Negative views of same-sex relationships seem to depend on the gender of the people in those relationships too: gay men draw more disapproval than lesbian women, especially from straight men (Cárdenas & Barrientos, 2008; Copp & Koehler, 2017; Herek, 2000).

The fact that many people still respond to gay, lesbian, and bisexual orientations with scorn and ridicule contributes to the high rate of psychological disorders among sexual minorities (Cochran & Mays, 2013). Depression, anxiety, alcohol and drug issues, and other psychological struggles occur in sexual minorities at two to three times the rate in the general population (Bostwick et al., 2014; Cochran et al., 2003; Fergusson et al., 1999, 2005; Meyer, 2003; Mustanski et al., 2016; Russell & Fish, 2016). Unsurprisingly, the rates of unpleasant and unfortunate experiences that often contribute to mental disorders — assault, bullying, discrimination, stress, hopelessness, and lack of social support, among others — are also in greater abundance in the lives of sexual minorities (Berlan et al., 2010; Burton et al., 2013; Hatzenbuehler et al., 2010).

Research has identified several factors that improve attitudes toward sexual minorities. For example, friendships can make a big difference. Specifically, high-quality relationships in which a straight person really gets to know a sexual minority as a real person go along with more agreeable attitudes toward sexual minorities overall (Heinze & Horn, 2009; Lemm, 2006; Vonofakou et al., 2007). One study found that straight college students with LGBTQ+ friends were more likely than their straight peers without LGBTQ+ friends to intervene when they witness discrimination or harassment against LGBTQ+ students on campus. That finding was true whether or not the straight student with LGBTQ+ friends personally knew anyone involved in the situation (Dessel et al., 2017).

Learning about the achievements and fame of sexual minorities can improve relationships toward them too. In one study, researchers showed participants pictures of gay/lesbian celebrities and offered a description of each. For half of the participants, the description included the fact that the celebrity was gay or lesbian; for the other half, the description omitted that fact. The celebrities — who included filmmaker Pedro Almodóvar, author Michael Cunningham, singer Melissa Etheridge, U.S. Congress member Barney Frank, actor Rupert Everett, civil rights leader Bayard Rustin, and tennis star Martina Navratilova — got more favorable ratings from the participants who learned about their sexual orientations (Dasgupta & Rivera, 2008).

Another promising factor for attitudes toward sexual minorities is the presence of *gay–straight alliances* (GSAs) in U.S. high schools. GSAs are extracurricular organizations that offer a safe, supportive environment for teens to come together to share experiences, socialize, and engage in advocacy and activism. They welcome students who are (or who think they may be) LGBTQ+, as well as students who are straight. GSAs began to appear in a few high schools on the East and West coasts around 1990. Today, there are thousands of GSAs in high schools throughout the United States and in many other countries (Fetner & Kush, 2008).

A growing body of research finds that GSAs have lots of positive effects (Russell et al., 2009). One study found that belonging to a GSA made members more comfortable with diverse sexual orientations, as well as boosted academic performance, family relationships, and a sense of belonging to the school community (Lee, 2002). Another study found that schools with GSAs had lower rates of hopelessness and suicide attempts among sexual minority students (Davis et al., 2014). Other studies have also found a wide range of positive effects — not just for members of GSAs, but also for students who didn't belong to a GSA but simply went to schools that had them (Poteat et al., 2018; Toomey et al., 2011; Walls et al., 2010; Worthen, 2014).

Finally, simply talking with peers about issues related to sexual orientation tends to go along with positive or affirming attitudes toward people of diverse sexual orientations (Duhigg et al., 2010; Sorensen et al., 2009). This is especially true when those conversations have a positive, respectful tone and are accompanied by critical thinking and self-reflection (Poteat, 2015).

What Difference Does Gender Make?

There are plenty of ways in which people of all genders are remarkably similar — overall intelligence, self-esteem, moral reasoning, leadership capabilities, mathematical ability, and other variables (Bussey, 2013; Hyde, 2005, 2014; Hyde et al., 2008; Priess & Hyde, 2010). But there are also plenty of examples of big differences between the genders. As we consider a few of them, remember that just because these differences exist, that doesn't necessarily mean that gender *caused* them. There could be other explanations. And of course, these differences don't apply to *all* members of a gender. These are broad overall trends, but you shouldn't assume they apply to any one person in particular.

Differences in Communication. Often, women and men use speech for different reasons. Specifically, women tend to speak to maintain relationships and build new connections, with an emphasis on listening and compassion. Men, on the other hand, tend to speak to assert dominance or to hold someone else's attention, with an emphasis on taking control or solving problems (Carli, 2013; McHugh & Hambaugh, 2010).

When researchers examine specific communication behaviors in men and women, they typically find differences that make sense in terms of how men and women use speech. For example, compared to women, men tend to interrupt more often (especially to redirect the conversation) and speak both louder and longer (Anderson & Leaper, 1998; Mast & Sczesny, 2010; West & Zimmerman, 1983). Women, compared to men, tend to apologize more often, offer more compliments, use more verbal reinforcers of others' speech ("mm hm," "right," "yeah," etc.), and sprinkle in more terms to soften their language such as "kinda," "sorta," "like," "I mean," and "y'know?" (Carli, 1990; Farley et al., 2010; Hannah & Murachver, 2007; Laserna et al., 2014; Leaper & Robnett, 2011; Stubbe & Holmes, 1995). Women's communication typically focuses on emotion more often than men's, including the use of emojis in texts at a significantly higher rate (Chaplin, 2015; Ogletree et al., 2014; Rosen et al., 2010; Tossell et al., 2012).

Even nonverbal communication reflects clear gender differences. Women tend to smile, nod, and lean forward more often, while men tend to fidget, stretch out, and demonstrate visual dominance (more eye contact when speaking than when listening) more often (Dovidio et al., 1988a, b; Hall, 2006; Hall et al., 2000; Mast & Sczesny, 2010). **Table 10.5** shows a summary.

Custom Life Science Images/Alamy

Research indicates that gay-straight alliances, which are increasingly common in U.S. high schools, can have positive effects on attitudes toward sexual minorities.

Differences in Expressing Emotion. Around the world, women tend to cry more often than men, not only when sad things happen to them, but also when happy things happen, or when they empathize while seeing sad or happy things happen to others (De Fruyt, 1997; Peter et al., 2001; Vingerhoets & Bylsma, 2016; Vingerhoets et al., 2000; Vingerhoets & Scheirs, 2000). Women also tend to smile more often than men, for reasons that may be complex. In some situations, a woman's smile may convey her happiness, but in others, it may communicate agreement in an attempt to build relationships (Fischer & Evers, 2013). This gender difference in smiling is even evident on social media: a study of Facebook profile photos found that women were significantly more likely to choose photos of themselves smiling than men were (Tifferet & Vilnai-Yavetz, 2014).

TABLE 10.5: He Says, She Says: Gender Differences in Speaking Behaviors

MEN MORE OFTEN...	WOMEN MORE OFTEN...
Interrupt (especially to change the topic)	Apologize
Speak loudly	Offer compliments
Hold the floor for long periods of time	Use verbal reinforcers like "mm hm" and "right"
Stretch out	Soften language with words like "kinda" and "y'know?"
Fidget	Smile, nod, and lean forward
Maintain visual dominance (more eye contact when speaking than listening)	Include emojis and emoticons in texts

Information from Mast and Sczesny (2010), Carli (1990, 2013), McHugh and Hambaugh (2010), West and Zimmerman (1983), Anderson and Leaper (1998), Farley et al. (2010), Hannah and Murachver (2007), Stubbe and Holmes (1995), Leaper and Robnett (2011), Laserna et al. (2014), Dovidio et al. (1988a, b), Hall (2006), Hall et al. (2000), Ogletree et al. (2014), Rosen et al. (2010), and Tossell et al. (2012).

Women and men often have different motivations for speaking: women to connect, and men to compete. Research on specific speech behaviors (both verbal and nonverbal) reflects this gender difference.

It is not just crying and smiling, either. Women generally demonstrate more emotion through facial expression than men (Kring & Gordon, 1998). That's especially true with certain emotions, like happiness, sadness, fear, and embarrassment, but less true with other emotions, like anger and pride. The explanation for that distinction may be that cultural norms pressure women and men to show or hide different feelings (Brody & Hall, 2008, 2010).

People tend to interpret facial expressions of men and women differently too, especially when the feeling being expressed is negative. In one study, researchers showed pictures of the faces of men and women feeling anger, sadness, fear, or disgust. They also offered explanations for why the person might feel that way: got yelled at by boss, heard footsteps in the dark, got some bad news, saw an animal get run over by a car, and so on. Participants were then asked whether the people in the pictures were "emotional" or simply "having a bad day." In other words, participants were asked whether the emotions of the people in the pictures were attributable to their personalities, or to their situation. Results showed that women in the pictures were more often labeled as "emotional," and men in the pictures were more often labeled as "having a bad day" (Barrett & Bliss-Moreau, 2009).

Differences in Personality. As we will cover in Chapter 12, the most widely accepted model of personality features five distinct traits (Costa & McCrae, 1992; McCrae & Costa, 2003, 2013). In some of these traits, men and women have equal amounts. For example, in *conscientiousness* (being organized, responsible, and deliberate), there are no gender differences. But in other traits, there are small but consistent gender differences. Women tend to be slightly higher in *agreeableness* (cooperating and complying with others) and *neuroticism* (experiencing anxiety, sadness, and similar emotions) (Lynn & Martin, 1997; Rubinstein & Strul, 2007). Men and women have roughly equal levels of *openness to experience* (receptiveness to new things). However, when you break that trait down into its component parts, women have greater openness to feeling new emotions, but men have greater openness to hearing new ideas. In terms of the components of *extraversion* (outgoingness), women are higher in friendliness and warmth toward others, but men are higher in excitement seeking and assertiveness toward others (Costa et al., 2001; Feingold, 1994; Lodhi et al., 2002; Stake & Eisele, 2010).

Differences in Education. In both school and work, girls and women are underrepresented in the *STEM* areas – science, technology, engineering, and math (Sadler et al., 2012). This is especially true in certain areas of STEM (computer science, engineering, and physics) and less so in others (biology, chemistry, and math) (Cheryan et al., 2017). But that's not because of any inherent gender difference in abilities. The difference occurs because our society has traditionally steered girls away from these stereotypically male fields. This has often lowered both girls' interest and belief in their capabilities. And it can lead to girls fearing that if they struggle in a STEM course, they will confirm stereotypes about their gender (Betz et al., 2013; Bussey, 2013; Spencer et al., 1999; Steele, 1997, 2010; Wang & Degol, 2017).

Jupiterimages, Brand X Pictures/Getty Images

Recruitment of girls and women into STEM fields has increased in recent years.

Thankfully, efforts to recruit girls into STEM fields and women into STEM careers have increased, but results of these efforts have been mixed (Glass & Minnotte, 2010; Milgram, 2011; Watt, 2010). At the college level, women tend to be underrepresented in STEM majors, but overrepresented in education, nursing, humanities, and social sciences (including psychology) (Basow, 2010). More generally, gender differences in education show that girls tend to earn slightly better grades throughout school, but boys tend to slightly outperform them on standardized tests (Downey & Vogt Yuan, 2005; Duckworth & Seligman, 2006; Legewie & DiPrete, 2012).

Differences in Navigating. Researchers haven't shed much light on the old stereotype about men refusing to stop for directions. However, they have found many gender differences in the strategies we use to navigate from place to place (Lawton, 1994; Saucier & Ehresman, 2010). Men tend to rely more on directions that remain constant, especially distances and compass directions. For example: go north for 3 miles, then turn east and go 2 miles. Women, on the other hand, tend to rely more on directions that depend on the person's perspective at the time, including landmarks and relative directions. For example: go straight until you see the McDonalds, then turn right and keep going until you see the park on your left (Choi & Silverman, 2003; Lawton, 1994; Lawton & Kallai, 2002; Nowak et al., 2015; Saucier et al., 2002).

This gender difference in giving and using directions shows up as early as middle school (Choi & Silverman, 2003). In one study, about 100 kids age 10–17 completed a walk-through maze set up in a huge room with big, portable wall pieces. The maze included over 30 opportunities to go right or left and over 20 landmarks. After walking through the maze five times, each kid was asked to draw a bird's-eye-view map of the maze or make a written list of step-by-step instructions for navigating it. The girls' drawings and written instructions included far more mentions of landmarks, and far fewer mentions of directions, than the boys' (Schmitz, 1997).

Differences in Digital Communication. A study about college women and men taking selfies found an interesting difference: women took far more selfies with others (about 14 per week) than alone (about 8), but the men took more selfies alone (about 9 per week) than with others (about 6). The researchers suggested that the gender difference likely reflects socialization patterns that steer women toward collaboration and men toward independence (Koterba et al., 2021).

Another study examined differences in college women and men in how they use and respond to emojis. Results showed that the women were more familiar with emojis and used them more often in their texts, social media, and emails. Results also showed that there was no difference in how women and men rated the strength of positive emojis like these 😀 😊. But when they saw negative emojis like these 😞 😨, the women rated them as more negative than the men did. The researchers interpreted that difference as consistent with the tendency of many women to interpret faces (real faces, not emojis) and other stimuli as more negative than many men do (Jones et al., 2020).

Differences in Sex Life. Men generally report more interest in sex than women – more frequency, more variety, and more partners (Graham et al., 2017; Peplau, 2003; Petersen & Hyde, 2010a). Men also report higher rates of almost every specific sexual activity than women, with masturbation and pornography at the top of the list of things that men do more often than women (Hald et al., 2014; Oliver & Hyde, 1993; Petersen & Hyde, 2010b). Higher frequency of sex in men is true for gay as well as straight relationships, with gay men reporting higher rates of sex than lesbian women (Peplau & Fingerhut, 2007). Men also report a higher frequency of orgasm than women during both sex and masturbation (Laumann et al., 1994).

The reasons for sexual activity differ between the genders too: women more often seek emotional and interpersonal connection, while men more often seek physical gratification (Baumeister, 2013; Leigh, 1989; Meston & Buss, 2007; Patrick et al., 2007). Gender differences also apply to *hookups* (one-time sexual encounters between people who don't know each other well). In college, where most research on hookups is done, men tend to be more comfortable with hookups than women (Lambert et al., 2003). Women tend to experience more worry and distress after hookups, and also show more interest in converting their hookups to long-term relationships than men do (Fielder & Carey, 2010; Owen & Fincham, 2011; Townsend & Wasserman, 2011). Hookups also involve a greater risk to women's reputations than to men's. Studies find that the responses of college students to hookup stories depend on who the story is about. If it's about a woman, there is a greater chance that the reader will lose respect for her. However, if the story is about a man, the odds are lower that such a negative evaluation will take place (Allison & Risman, 2013; Bogle, 2008).

There are also differences between men and women regarding sexual consent. Among straight college students, men more often express consent nonverbally (using body language to show they want to have sex), but women more often express consent verbally (saying they want to have sex). However, when considering whether a woman is consenting, men tend to rely more often on their own perception of her nonverbal signs of consent, which could lead to miscommunication and even sexual assault or acquaintance rape (Jozkowski et al., 2014). To address these gender differences in consent, some experts recommend consent education efforts that promote equality and power for every person involved in a sexual encounter, regardless of gender. Experts also emphasize the importance of active consent communication (rather than making assumptions about the other person's consent decisions based on the absence of resistance) (Willis & Smith, 2021).

CURRENT CONTROVERSY

How Does Social Media Affect Body Image?

For many of us, checking social media often means checking out how other people look. Recent research suggests that for many social media users, especially women and girls, those experiences are often followed by harsh evaluations of their own bodies (Eckler et al., 2017; Fardouly et al., 2018).

In one study of over 1000 eighth- and ninth-grade girls, those who used Facebook were more concerned about how thin, pretty, and physically attractive they were than those who did not (Tiggemann & Slater, 2013). Similarly, among college women, Facebook time correlates positively with worries about body image, especially among those with strong tendencies to compare their own appearance to the appearance of their friends (Fardouly & Vartanian, 2015).

One study asked women age 17–25 to spend 10 minutes either browsing their own Facebook page or browsing a "neutral" control Web site (a site about handmade crafts and other Etsy-ish ideas). Those who browsed Facebook reported a lower mood and reported more flaws with their own hair, skin, and face (Fardouly et al., 2015). Other studies have found that among young adults (especially women), those who use social media more tend to compare and evaluate themselves against others and have higher levels of body dissatisfaction, as also more frequently make unhealthy eating choices including behaviors characteristic in bulimia like binging and purging. (Rounsefell et al., 2020; Smith et al., 2013).

These findings connecting Facebook usage to negative body experiences aren't limited to women. One study found that for college men and women, high Facebook usage correlates with self-consciousness and shame about their bodies (Manago et al., 2014). A large-scale study of over 11,000 adults (from their 20s to their 60s) in New Zealand found that both men and women who use a Facebook account have lower levels of body satisfaction than those who don't (Stronge et al., 2015).

In one creatively designed study, researchers handed college women an iPad and told them to do one of two things: (1) take a single selfie and upload it without editing it to Facebook or Instagram; or (2) take several selfies, choose one, edit it, and then upload it to Facebook or Instagram. Results showed that both conditions caused the women to experience increased anxiety, decreased confidence, and decreased feelings of physical attractiveness. Those effects were stronger in the first condition (single unedited selfie), but they were still strong in the second condition (selected and edited selfie), suggesting that simply *posting* a selfie, separate from viewing the selfies of others, can have undesirable effects (Mills et al., 2018).

urbazon/E+/Getty Images

Multiple studies point to a relationship between Facebook usage, including viewing selfies (like this one), and issues with body image. This connection is especially evident among girls and young women.

Speaking of Instagram, one study that randomly asked young women to use either Facebook or Instagram on an iPad for 7 minutes found that the participants who used Instagram made significantly more comparisons based on appearance than those who use Facebook. The experience also caused more body dissatisfaction and more negative emotion for people who use Instagram than those who use Facebook. The researchers explained this finding by pointing out that Instagram may cause more harm than Facebook because it relies more on photos and less on text (Engeln et al., 2020).

In another Instagram-focused study, young women age 18 to 26 were shown Instagram images of women, half of which featured body-positive captions (like "You can be whatever size and be beautiful inside and out #body positivity" or "My life is so much more than my jean size #bodypositivity"). Results showed that those captions actually had no effect: the women who saw the photos with captions experienced just as much body dissatisfaction as the women who saw the same photos without the captions (Tiggemann et al., 2020). •

CHECK YOUR LEARNING:

10.18 What is the difference between gender and sex?

10.19 What influences gender development?

10.20 What do cisgender, transgender, and transition mean?

10.21 What is sexual orientation?

10.22 What is coming out?

10.23 What influences attitudes toward sexual minorities?

10.24 What aspects of daily life can be influenced by gender?

To check your understanding of these questions, click show the answers or refer to the answers in the Chapter Summary.

CHAPTER SUMMARY

Diversity Surrounds You

10.1 The United States is a diverse nation in terms of race, ethnicity, language, religion, age, sexual orientation, education, income, and rural or urban location.

10.2 Intersectionality is the way any one person's unique combination of social and cultural categories intersect or overlap, especially as related to discrimination, unequal treatment, or social disadvantage.

10.3 A culture is a group of similar people who share beliefs and patterns of behavior. Culture can powerfully influence worldview, your comprehensive way of understanding the world around you.

10.4 Dynamic sizing is the ability to simultaneously know the norm for a group *and* recognize that the norm might not apply to every member of that group.

10.5 In the early days of psychology, culture was essentially equated to race or ethnicity. Today, psychologists consider many other variables as culturally important, such as gender, age, religion, sexual orientation, and socioeconomic status.

Multiculturalism

10.6 Multiculturalism is a psychological approach that highlights the importance and value of multiple cultural groups within a society. Multiculturalism has become increasingly important in psychology in recent decades. Some call it the dominant movement in contemporary psychology.

10.7 In earlier years, cultural differences were often defined as deficits or disadvantages of one culture compared to another. More recently, the unique qualities of each culture have been viewed as strengths and virtues.

10.8 Today, many areas of psychology reflect an emphasis on multiculturalism, including professional organizations, journals, books, ethical guidelines, assessment tools, and the DSM-5-TR.

10.9 Acculturation is managing a life that involves the coexistence of more than one culture.

10.10 There are a variety of different acculturation strategies based on how much a person retains their previous culture and how much they embrace their new culture.

10.11 Acculturative stress is the physical or psychological stress that comes from acculturation.

10.12 Specific ways in which cultures differ from each other include individualism and collectivism, power distance, long-term orientation and short-term orientation, and more.

10.13 Cultural diversity can produce differences in many areas of daily life, including how you define your identity, raise children, experience feelings, remember events, and more.

10.14 Cultural intelligence is your ability to live and interact effectively in a multicultural society.

10.15 Cultural humility is an attitude based on self-reflection, recognizing the limits of your own knowledge about diversity, and educating yourself about the identities and experiences of other people.

10.16 The opposite of racism is not the absence of racism, but antiracism—a more active confrontation of racist actions, biases, policies, systems, and institutions.

10.17 Microaggressions are everyday actions or comments that, often unintentionally, contain hostile or off-putting messages for members of certain cultures.

Gender and Sexuality: Essential Forms of Diversity

10.18 Gender is your psychological and behavioral experience of the sex you were assigned at birth. Sex is your biological assignment at birth (often male or female) based on a combination of genitals, chromosomes, and hormones.

10.19 Gender development can be influenced by parents, peers, and the media.

10.20 Cisgender refers to a person whose gender matches the sex they were assigned at birth. Transgender refers to a person whose gender differs from the sex they were assigned at birth. Transition refers to a person taking steps to live as the gender that matches their identity rather than their biologically assigned sex, often through name changes, pronoun (he/she/they) changes, clothing changes, or significant biological changes like surgeries or hormone treatments.

10.21 Sexual orientation is a person's pattern of romantic attraction to a particular group (or groups) of other people. Some common sexual orientations include heterosexual/straight (toward members of the other sex), gay/lesbian (toward members of the same sex), and bisexual/bi (toward members of both the other and the same sex).

10.22 Coming out is when a person who is LBGQT+ reveals their identity to themselves and eventually to others, as opposed to concealing it.

10.23 Attitudes toward sexual minorities vary widely. They can be influenced by familiarity or friendships with sexual minority members, as well as by involvement in organizations like gay-straight alliances.

10.24 Gender can influence many aspects of daily life, including communication styles, expression of emotion, personality, education, direction following, and sex life.

KEY TERMS

BIPOC, p. 337
intersectionality, p. 339
culture, p. 340
worldview, p. 340
dynamic sizing, p. 340
multiculturalism, p. 342
acculturation, p. 344
assimilation, p. 344
separation, p. 344
marginalization, p. 345
integration, p. 345
acculturative stress, p. 345
individualism, p. 346
collectivism, p. 346
cultural intelligence, p. 351
cultural humility, p. 352
microaggressions, p. 353
antiracist, p. 355
colorism, p. 355
gender, p. 356
sex, p. 356
gender identity, p. 356
nonbinary, p. 356
cisgender, p. 358
transgender, p. 358
transition, p. 358
sexual orientation, p. 359
heterosexual (straight), p. 359
gay/lesbian, p. 359
bisexual (bi), p. 359
LGBTQ+, p. 359

SELF-ASSESSMENT

1. Language is one way to measure diversity in the United States. Approximately _____% of U.S. residents speak a language other than English at home.

a. 1
b. 10
c. 20
d. 50

2. _____ is a group of similar people who share beliefs and patterns of behavior.

3. _____ is the ability to simultaneously know the norm for a group *and* recognize that the norm might not apply to every member of that group.

a. Dynamic sizing
b. Microaggression
c. Culture shock
d. Acculturation

4. Andrzej moves from Poland to the United States. He retains his Polish culture and also adopts U.S. culture. The acculturation strategy that best describes this behavior is

a. assimilation.
b. separation.
c. marginalization.
d. integration.

5. Amber comes from a culture that emphasizes what's best for the individual. Kyong comes from a culture that emphasizes what's best for the group. Which of the following descriptions most accurately characterizes this difference?

a. Amber's culture is individualistic; Kyong's culture is collectivistic.
b. Amber's culture has a large power distance; Kyong's culture has a small power distance.
c. Amber's culture is more caring; Kyong's culture is more assertive.
d. Amber's culture has a shorter-term orientation; Kyong's culture has a longer-term orientation.

6. _____ is your ability to live and interact effectively in a multicultural society.

a. Integration
b. Assimilation
c. Cultural intelligence
d. Worldview

7. Travis puts a bumper sticker on his car that makes a joke about a minority group. He intends it to be funny, but his next-door neighbor, who belongs to that group, finds it slightly hostile and offensive. Although he may not realize it, Travis' behavior could be labeled as

a. acculturative stress.
b. a microaggression.
c. collectivism.
d. dynamic sizing.

8. _____ is your biological assignment at birth (often male or female) based on a combination of genitals, chromosomes, and hormones.

9. Heather is a person whose gender and sex match. Which of these words best describes Heather?

a. transgender
b. transition
c. heterosexual
d. cisgender

10. Which of the following is true regarding surveys of sexual orientation?

a. Most researchers tend to settle on a range of about 2–4% of the general U.S. population identifying as gay, lesbian, or bisexual.
b. Rates of sexual orientation are completely consistent regardless of the way the researchers ask participants about their sexual orientation.
c. Compared to women, men tend to have much more fluid sexual orientations, meaning that their sexual orientations change over time.
d. Within the United States, the rates of gay, lesbian, and bisexual people are consistent across all 50 states.

To check your understanding of these questions, click show the answers in the e-book or refer to the answers in Appendix B.

Research shows quizzing is a highly effective learning tool. Continue quizzing yourself using LearningCurve, the system that adapts to *your* learning.

WHAT'S YOUR TAKE?

1. In this chapter, you've read what the experts have to say about cultural differences between different groups. How do your own experiences match with their descriptions? Have you met people very culturally different from yourself? Did those differences fit into one of the cultural characteristics described in this chapter (for example, individualism vs. collectivism)? Did you notice other important differences besides the ones described in this chapter?
2. How has cultural intelligence affected you? Have there been times in your life when you were glad your cultural intelligence was as strong as it was, or when you wished it was stronger? How have you been influenced by the cultural intelligence of people around you?

SHOW ME MORE

10.1 Healthy Ways to Discuss Issues of Race

https://macmillan.app.box.com/s/wn2zf8bbfxgilz25h2wad8lbf4181m6z/folder/143194010039

This video features a discussion between people of different races and genders about healthy ways to approach difficult conversations about race.

CNN

10.2 Microaggressions

http://tiny.cc/showmemore2e

In this brief video, Derald Wing Sue, a leading scholar on the topic of microaggressions, offers explanations and illustrations of the concept.

Rawpixel.com/Shutterstock

This video is hosted by a third-party Web site (source). For accessible content requests, please reach out to the publisher of that site.

10.3 Gender and Gender Roles

https://macmillan.app.box.com/s/wn2zf8bbfxgilz25h2wad8lbf4181m6z?page=1

This video features men in prison reexamining issues related to gender and gender roles.

Courtesy CNN

10.4 My Psychology Podcast

This podcast episode features the author of this textbook, psychologist Andy Pomerantz, speaking with other instructors of introductory psychology courses about the most important and interesting concepts in this chapter.

Macmillan Learning

11 Stress and Health

FG Trade/E+/Getty Images

CHAPTER OUTLINE

My dentist finishes the tooth cleaning and hands me a mirror. As I check out my bright white grin, she says, "You may notice a little bleeding. Don't worry about it. It's just that sharp-pointed tool I have to use. Happens to everybody."

"No problem," I reply. I leave the dentist's office with glistening teeth but a tiny cut or two around my gums. I don't give it a second thought.

An hour later, I'm writing this chapter, searching for articles about the connection between stress and health. As I run my tongue across one of those tiny cuts in my mouth, I come across a study in which—believe it or not—the researchers gave people those cuts on purpose (Marucha et al., 1998).

I read the study eagerly. The researchers made a 3.5-millimeter cut on the roof of the mouth of each college-student participant. This happened twice: once during summer break, and once a couple of months later, just a few days before a major exam during the fall semester. The researchers took close-up photos of each cut every day until it healed. Their findings? For every student, the cut healed much more quickly during vacation time than it did during exam time. It took about a week to disappear during summer, but almost 11 days around exams. The difference was obvious early in the process: after just one or two days, the cut made during summer break was already noticeably smaller than the cut made before the exam. It was the same students, the same mouths, and the same kinds of cuts, but different healing rates. What was the researchers' explanation? *Stress*. The high stress brought on by exams made the students' cuts heal much more slowly than identical cuts did during low-stress summer vacation time.

I was amazed at how the healing of such little cuts, just like the ones in my own mouth, could depend so much on stressors like exams. But then I wondered, what if the stakes were higher? What if it wasn't a tiny cut that the body was trying to heal, but a big wound or surgery incision? What if the body was trying to fight off a serious disease, like the flu or HIV? And what if the stressor was bigger or more unpredictable than an exam, like the death of a loved one or the loss of a job? Especially when the stakes are so high, what can we do to enhance our ability to handle stress well?

This chapter addresses the broad issue that underlies all of those questions: how stress affects health. We'll begin by defining stress and identifying some of its common causes. Then we'll explore how stress affects the body and the mind, including the role that culture can play. Finally, we'll discuss the ways we cope with the stress we experience.

Stress: What Is It and What Causes It?

YOU WILL LEARN:

11.1 how psychologists define stress.

11.2 about the difference between stress and a stressor.

11.3 what the fight-or-flight response is.

11.4 how appraisal is involved in stress.

11.5 how everyday hassles cause significant stress when they accumulate.

Before we explore the connection between stress and health, let's define stress and consider some of the factors that make us feel it.

What Is Stress?

Stress is an unpleasant physical or psychological reaction to circumstances you perceive as challenging. You may know the reaction well, perhaps too well. Your muscles may tense, your stomach may churn, your pulse may quicken, or your teeth may grind. You may feel anger, irritability, sadness, or nervousness (Folkman, 2011; Smyth et al., 2018; Theil & Dretsch, 2011).

It's important to clarify that when psychologists talk about stress, they are talking about that unpleasant reaction, *not* the event or situation that caused it. Sometimes, in everyday speech, we use the word *stress* for both the reaction and the situation that caused it, which can get confusing (Monat et al., 2007). For example, you might say, "I'm feeling so much stress about that PowerPoint presentation I have to give" and "That PowerPoint presentation is such a stress." Psychologists make a distinction: the reaction you have about the PowerPoint presentation is indeed stress, but the presentation itself is a *stressor*. We'll examine stressors in more detail a bit later, but for now, the important point is that psychologists use different terms for the feeling of stress and the thing that causes that feeling.

Since the mid-1900s, psychologists have studied stress, along with its effects on health and ways to cope with it. A big reason why the study of stress arose around that time was that soldiers returning from World War II were demonstrating the physical and psychological toll of the stress they experienced in battle (Cooper & Dewe, 2004; Lazarus, 1999). Some soldiers were even traumatized by their stress, which eventually led psychologists to create the diagnosis of *posttraumatic stress disorder* (PTSD), a topic we'll discuss later. Of course, psychologists quickly recognized that war wasn't the only thing that caused stress, so their study of stress expanded to include experiences common to all of us.

The Fight-or-Flight Response. An important part of the experience of stress is the **fight-or-flight response**: an automatic emotional and physical reaction to a perceived threat that prepares you to either attack it or run away from it. Your fight-or-flight response has long been recognized as a product of evolution (Cannon, 1932). It was essential to the survival of early human beings, and it is still beneficial today. Basically, it's your body quickly gearing up to respond to a perceived danger by taking it on (fight) or taking off (flight). To be specific, it's your sympathetic nervous system that gears up, as we learned in Chapter 2. Your heart rate speeds up, your breathing quickens, you start to sweat, and your muscles tense. When this fight-or-flight response is followed by actual fight or flight — when you actually take on the threat or take off running — your body spends this energy effectively and then calms down naturally. But when the fight-or-flight response is restrained, the result is stress (McEwen & Lasley, 2002; Taylor, 2011b).

Consider this example: David hears someone trying to break into his home at night. At the first sound of this danger, his fight-or-flight response kicks in: He instantly sits up in bed, amped by adrenaline. His body is ready to either confront the intruder or run. But if he does neither, his body will have gotten revved up for nothing. That unnecessary revving won't do much damage if it happens just once. But if it happens over and over, or it never really goes away (as it would if David felt like intruders were constantly after him), it will cause excessive wear and tear on the body. That is the key to how stress, over time, damages health. Repeated or continuous wear and tear from the frustration of the fight-or-flight response damages the heart, weakens the immune system, and generally breaks down health.

stress
An unpleasant physical or psychological reaction to circumstances perceived as challenging.

stressor
Any event or change in one's life that causes stress.

fight-or-flight response
An automatic emotional and physical reaction to a perceived threat that prepares you to either attack it or run away from it.

IT'S LIKE...

Stopping Your Fight-or-Flight Response Is Like Stepping on the Gas and Brake at the Same Time

There's a good reason driving instructors teach new drivers to drive with one foot rather than two. Using two feet would allow you to press the gas and the brake at the same time, which is no good for the car. Especially if both pedals were pushed to the floor, you could expect the simultaneous stop-and-go commands to damage important parts inside your car, like your transmission or your brakes (Magliozzi & Magliozzi, 2011).

The same is true for important parts inside your body when it comes to stress. Your body's natural response to stressors is to *go*, in the form of battling the stressor (fight) or running away (flight). When you prevent yourself from doing either, you are essentially sending a *stop* message at the same time. The problem gets worse as the stressor gets more chronic — which is like keeping a foot on the gas and the brake for days on end.

Realistically, society prevents people from responding as naturally to stressors as other animals do. You *have* to tap the brakes on your fight-or-flight response, at least some of the time, in order to get along with others. But it's also important to give yourself an outlet (like regular exercise) for that fight-or-flight response, or to rethink the stressor so the fight-or-flight response doesn't affect you as negatively or last as long as it otherwise might.

Digital Stress. Recently, psychologists and other researchers have coined a term for a new type of stress: *digital stress*, or the stress that results from online interactions and other uses of Internet-based technology. In one study of digital stress, researchers examined thousands of anonymous posts to *A Thin Line*, a Web site on which teens and young adults share their stressful digital experiences with peers. From these posts, the researchers identified six distinct types of digital stressors. Three types focus on hostility and cruelty — (1) mean and harassing personal attacks, (2) public shaming and humiliation, and (3) impersonation. Three more types of digital stress focus on managing the closeness of relationships — (1) feeling smothered, (2) pressure to comply with requests, and (3) breaking into digital accounts and devices (a partner reading your texts without permission, etc.) (Weinstein & Selman, 2016).

The same researchers also explored what kinds of advice teens give each other for handling these digital stressors. For digital stressors focused on hostility and cruelty, the most common advice was to seek help from others (parents, school administrators, police, etc.). For digital stressors focused on managing the closeness of relationships, the most common advice was to cut ties (break up, end the friendship, "ghost" the person, etc.) (Weinstein et al., 2017).

Another group of researchers identified other sources of digital stress, including communication load (too many texts, social media messages, and e-mails); Internet multitasking (communicating online while doing other things); perceived social pressure to be available 24/7; and fear of missing out (FOMO). They found that higher levels of these digital stressors were associated with higher levels of burnout, anxiety, and depression (Reinecke et al., 2017). Other studies have found that *problematic social media use* — being overly concerned about social media, spending excessive time on social media, and allowing social media to interfere with other aspects of life such as jobs, school, and relationships — is positively correlated to depressive symptoms (Shensa et al., 2017).

Doug Savage

What Causes Stress?

A **stressor** is any event or change in your life that causes you stress. Anything *can* be a stressor, depending upon what *you* perceive to be challenging. Of course, there are certain events and changes that almost all of us would experience as stressors. Most are major unfortunate life events like the death of a loved one, a divorce or breakup, a serious injury or illness, or a job loss. (Major life events that are generally seen as positive can be common stressors too, like retiring, getting a new job, finishing school, experiencing pregnancy, and starting a romantic relationship.) Back in the 1960s and 1970s, the leading stress researchers made a questionnaire out of these major life events in which they assigned each event a specific point value (Holmes & Masuda, 1974; Holmes & Rahe, 1967). Participants checked the

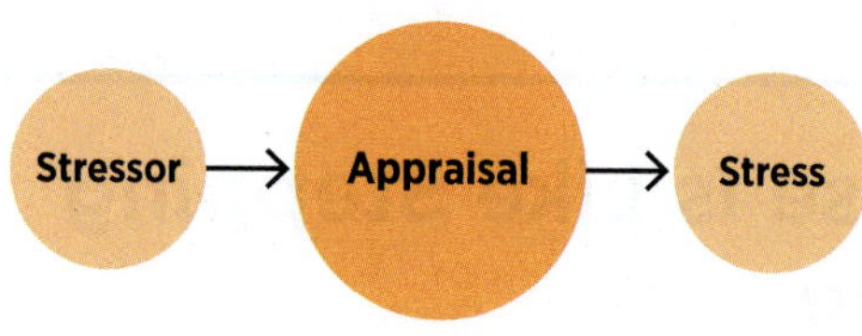

FIGURE 11.1 The Importance of Appraisal. Stressors don't cause stress directly. Between the stressor and the stress, your appraisal—your evaluation of how bad the stressor is and how capable you are of handling it—plays an important role.

events that had happened to them in the previous year, added up their points, and that total predicted their risk for serious health problems.

Appraisal. That questionnaire, titled the Social Readjustment Rating Scale, did a decent job of predicting stress-related health problems, but it was far from perfect. There were plenty of people who racked up high point totals but didn't experience much stress or health problems. There were also plenty of people with low point totals who were stressed out and sick all the time. By the 1980s, researchers had identified at least two reasons why an objective count of stressor points might not always match actual stress experiences. As **Figure 11.1** shows, the first reason involves **appraisal**, or the way you evaluate the things that happen to you (Benyamini, 2011; Kemeny, 2011; Lazarus et al., 1985, 1999; Tomaka & Blascovich, 1994). (You may have heard the word *appraisal* when someone is selling a house, or assessing the value of an antique. It means the same thing here—basically, how much it is worth—but how much stress rather than how much money.)

Psychologists break down the stress appraisal process into two parts, *primary appraisal* and *secondary appraisal*. **Primary appraisal** is determining how stressful an event is to you. **Secondary appraisal** is determining how capable you are of coping with the event. Think of it this way: primary appraisal is how hard you think the big bad wolf can huff and puff; secondary appraisal is knowing whether your house is built of straw, wood, or brick.

As an example, let's consider Tyler and Navya, two single 20-somethings who have worked as sales reps in Peoria, Illinois, for the same big company for several years. They get the same news at the same time: they're being transferred to Chicago. Their reactions are very different. Let's consider their primary appraisals first—what they think about the transfer. Tyler sees the transfer as extremely stressful: "Ugh! I'll have to pack up everything, say goodbye to all my friends, and find a new place to live in Chicago, which is expensive and crowded. Plus, my new job responsibilities might be too much." Navya's primary appraisal of the transfer is much more positive: "Cool! I get to live in the big city, make new friends, and have the chance for even more success than I've had here."

In terms of secondary appraisal, or what they think about their own abilities to handle the transfer, Tyler and Navya differ again. Tyler worries to himself: "I can't handle this. New situations make me nervous, and I'm not the kind of person who will thrive with a new supervisor in a city I don't know." Navya is more confident: "I can do this. I'm good at my job. It may take a little adjusting, but I'm sure I'll find a way to be happy and successful in Chicago. It's a great opportunity." As you can tell, Tyler is in much worse shape than Navya in terms of this move. Not only is he likely to experience more stress (due to a big gap between his perceptions of the stressor and his ability to handle it), but he is also more likely to experience physical health problems as a consequence.

Research supports the notion that appraisal of stressors influences health (Gianaros & Wager, 2015; Kruse & Sweeny, 2018; Petrie & Weinman, 2006). For example, one study followed 65 people who had just experienced their first heart attack. All got standard hospital treatment, but half got something extra: three sessions with a psychologist whose goal was to make sure the patients left the hospital with rational and accurate appraisals about their heart condition and their ability to recover from it. Those patients left the hospital thinking something like this: "That heart attack was serious, but I'm recovering, and I can live a long and healthy life." However, patients who didn't get those sessions might think something like this: "That heart attack means I'm going to die soon, and there's nothing I can do about it." The patients whose treatment included their heads as well as their hearts viewed their heart condition as more controllable and less stressful. They also had fewer ongoing heart-related symptoms and returned to work faster (Petrie et al., 2002). Other studies have found similar

CHAPTER APP 11.1

Serenita

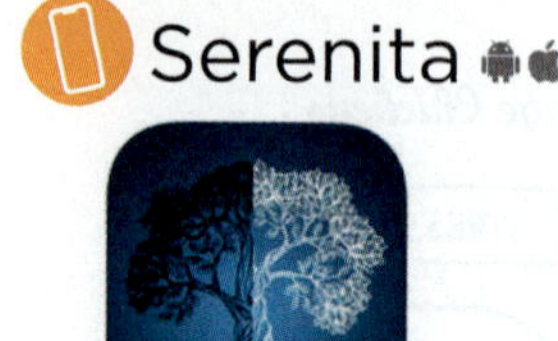

The Serenita app measures your heart rate pattern, breathing, and blood flow through the tip of your finger, which you place on the camera lens of your smartphone. Serenita then translates those biological measurements into a stress level. It also offers tips for breathing-based techniques to reduce stress, but our focus here is on how it measures stress.

How does it APPly to your daily life?
How valid are biological measures like breathing, heart rate, and blood flow as indicators of stress? Can your experience of stress be accurately assessed by such objective measures, or is it more subjective? Could two people with similar heart rates, breathing, and blood flow be experiencing different amounts of stress?

How does it APPly to your understanding of psychology?
How does this app influence your appreciation of *appraisal* of stress, including *primary appraisal* and *secondary appraisal*?

To learn more about this app or to download it to your phone, you can search for "Serenita" on Google, in the iPhone App store, or in the Google Play store.

results when the patient's partner is included in the discussions of beliefs about the illness. In fact, in these cases stress levels are lower in both members of the couple (Broadbent et al., 2009a, b).

appraisal
The way you evaluate the things that happen to you.

primary appraisal
The way you determine how stressful an event is to you.

secondary appraisal
The way you determine how capable you are of coping with an event.

hassles
The common, minor annoyances or aggravations of day-to-day life.

DIVERSITY MATTERS

Appraisal and Diversity. Diversity variables like ethnicity, gender, and age can influence the way we appraise stressors. For example, while a college entrance exam like the ACT or SAT is probably stressful for many high school students, it might be especially stressful for students from certain cultural groups, including many Asian cultures, who sometimes place unusually high emphasis on academic achievement (Lee, 1997; Lee & Mock, 2005; Sue & Consolacion, 2003). Similarly, a healthy 16-year-old boy who catches the flu may experience less stress about the disease than his 80-year-old grandfather with serious health issues who also catches the flu; the boy doesn't worry as much about recovering as his grandfather does.

Hassles. Another reason why a simple list or point total of your major stressors doesn't always reflect your actual stress level is that the list leaves out **hassles**, the common, minor annoyances or aggravations of day-to-day life. Hassles add up, and cumulatively, they can add significantly to your stress level (DeLongis et al., 1988; Kanner et al., 1981; Keles et al., 2017; Mize & Kliewer, 2017; Serido et al., 2004). One study of couples found that one person's daily hassles can even increase the stress level of that person's romantic partner, as well as the tension in the relationship (Falconier et al., 2015). Hassles vary from person to person, but some common ones include transportation problems (traffic, car trouble, late buses or subways); losing your keys, phone, or wallet; conflict (or "drama") with friends or family members; crowded or uncomfortable living conditions; excessive or bothersome school or work responsibilities; a too-long to-do list; and running low on essentials like money, food, or sleep.

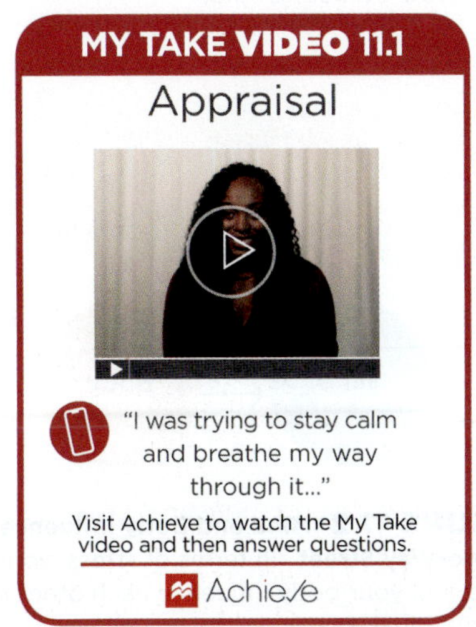

MY TAKE VIDEO 11.1
Appraisal
"I was trying to stay calm and breathe my way through it..."
Visit Achieve to watch the My Take video and then answer questions.
Achieve

CHECK YOUR LEARNING:

11.1 How do psychologists define stress?

11.2 What is the relationship between stress and stressors?

11.3 What is the fight-or-flight response?

11.4 What is appraisal, and what is the difference between primary appraisal and secondary appraisal?

11.5 What are hassles, and how do they relate to stress?

To check your understanding of these questions, click show the answers or refer to the answers in the Chapter Summary.

Stress and the Mind–Body Connection

Both mind and body suffer the consequences of stress. As we learned in Chapter 1, psychology has an entire specialization devoted to this connection: *health psychology*, the psychological specialization that focuses on the relationship between mind and body. Many health psychologists are researchers, conducting studies like the ones described in this chapter. Their findings often apply to the practice of psychology and medicine, so health psychology has become increasingly influential in how people are treated for stress-related problems. (As a side note, the term *behavioral medicine* is also used to mean roughly the same thing as *health psychology*.)

YOU WILL LEARN:

11.6 about the different ways stress damages a person's health.

11.7 what the general adaptation syndrome is.

11.8 how stress affects the immune system and contributes to illness.

YOU WILL LEARN: (*Continued*)

11.9 how different personality types experience different levels of stress-related consequences.

11.10 how certain personality traits correlate with high or low stress levels.

11.11 how stress is the basis of different psychological disorders.

11.12 how the COVID pandemic affected stress levels.

Most often, we think of the mind affecting the body, but actually the relationship between mind and body is bidirectional, or a two-way street, as **Figure 11.2** illustrates (Kemeny, 2011). For example, think of the stress Mateo would feel in the weeks after breaking his thumb — aggravation with the cast, difficulty using his phone and the keyboard on his computer, and issues with using silverware. Or consider Jessica's migraine headaches: they come and go without warning, causing not only physical pain but also feelings of frustration and helplessness. So, not only do these bodily problems cause bodily pain, they also cause mental anguish with their unpredictability or their power to impair basic daily activities. Sometimes, the mental stress caused by physical problems actually makes the physical problems even worse, creating a cycle of stress.

To keep things simple, we'll separate the body and the mind in the upcoming sections. One section will discuss how stress and the body affect each other, and another section will discuss how stress and the mind affect each other.

How Stress and Your Body Affect Each Other

In recent years, psychological research has identified many ways in which stress can make you sick. These ways fall into three general categories (Holroyd & Lazarus, 1982; Monat et al., 2007):

1. **Stress damages your health directly.** As we discussed earlier in this chapter, repeatedly revving up your fight-or-flight response, without addressing the stress that causes that response, causes excessive wear and tear on your heart, cardiovascular system, and other important parts of your body.
2. **Reactions to stress can damage your health directly.** This type of harm is not about the stress itself, but how you deal with it. Responding to stress by relying too much on alcohol or other harmful drugs, working too much, sleeping too little, or eating too much unhealthy food can put you at increased risk for injury or illness.
3. **Reactions to stress can damage your health indirectly.** Responding to signs of stress by ignoring them, denying them, or insisting you never need help can heighten the chances that your stress and its negative influence on your body will continue unchecked.

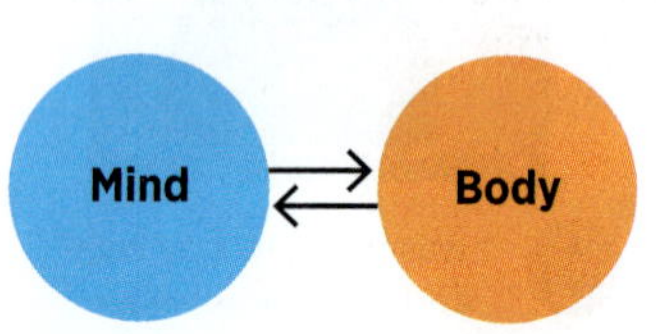

FIGURE 11.2 Mind and Body Influence: A Two-Way Street. In terms of stress, your mind and your body influence each other in a bidirectional way.

When stressors persist over time, the response follows a predictable pattern. That pattern, first identified by Hungarian medical researcher Hans Selye in the early and mid-1900s (Selye, 1936, 1952, 1956), is known as the **general adaptation syndrome**: a widely accepted understanding of the way bodies respond to ongoing stress, consisting of the three-step sequence of *alarm*, *resistance*, and *exhaustion*. Those first two stages — alarm and resistance — help us to handle short-term stressors (**Figure 11.3**). Again, think of the adrenaline rush that comes with your fight-or-flight response. When you face a short-term stressor (also known as an *acute* stressor) like a job interview, a big exam, or a speech to a large crowd, your body's built-in strategy of sounding an alarm and resisting the stress is probably enough to get you geared up for the event (without causing any negative effects). The problems come when the stressor is unrelenting, or *chronic*, rather than short-term. With chronic stressors, the body's alarm keeps sounding, but eventually the resistance wears off, like an army simply overwhelmed by never-ending waves of enemy attacks. The result is exhaustion, which leaves you vulnerable to disease.

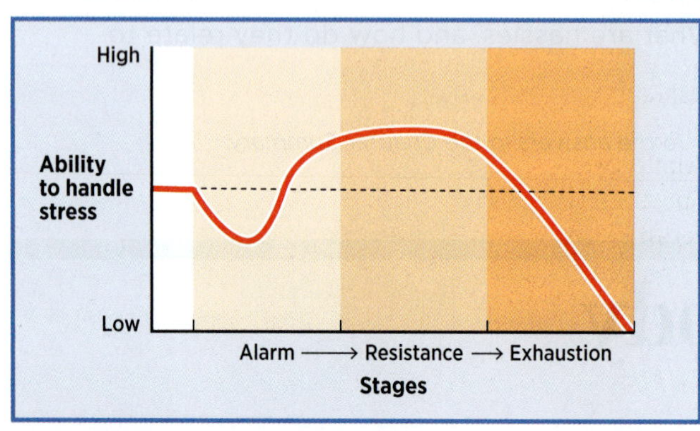

FIGURE 11.3 General Adaptation Syndrome. According to Selye's concept of the general adaptation syndrome, our ability to ward off the effects of stress stays strong for a while (during the resistance stage), but eventually plummets (during the exhaustion phase).

general adaptation syndrome
A widely accepted understanding of the way the body responds to ongoing stress, consisting of the sequence of alarm, resistance, and exhaustion.

Chronic Stress: Examples and Evidence. Examples of chronic stressors include living in an unstable environment, like a war zone or an extremely violent neighborhood; living in ongoing poverty, where the next meal is uncertain; living with an abusive partner or parent who could hurt you at any time; and working as a first responder, such as a police officer or paramedic, and witnessing terrible things nearly every day (Davies et al., 2013; Straker, 2013; Straker et al., 1988). Consider these examples of evidence linking chronic stress to physical health problems:

- A study of over 9500 adults found that experiencing more chronic stressors during childhood increases the rate of serious medical diseases during adulthood, including heart disease, chronic lung disease, diabetes, and cancer. For adults who grew up experiencing at least four kinds of chronic stressors (like psychological, physical, or sexual abuse; or living in a home with criminal activity, substance abuse, or violence), the risk of serious medical diseases during adulthood was often two to four times the normal rate (Felitti et al., 1998; Shonkoff et al., 2009). (See **Table 11.1** for more details.)
- In Operation Iraqi Freedom (2003–2010), over 83% of the medical evacuations of soldiers were not for battle injuries, but for diseases, including pneumonia and tuberculosis, that increased in likelihood as the soldiers experienced stress-related exhaustion (Fischer, 2013; Wool, 2013).
- Among people who test positive for COVID, those who have experienced chronic stress tend to have more severe cases and higher chances of fatality than those who have not (Lamontagne et al., 2021).
- Men with chronic stress have a lower sperm count and quality than similar men without chronic stress (Nargund, 2015). In pregnant women, chronic stress correlates with higher levels of high blood pressure (preeclampsia), preterm birth, and low birthweight (Barrett et al., 2018).
- In a study of over 850 elementary-school-age kids with asthma from big U.S. cities, the more the kids were exposed to violence, the greater the amount of stress-related asthma symptoms the kids exhibited. Higher stress meant more days of significant wheezing and disrupted play activities for the kids, as well as more lost nights of sleep for the parents. This study controlled for other variables like socioeconomic status and nonviolent negative life events (Wright et al., 2004).
- Kids in the most violent Chicago neighborhoods were twice as likely to *develop* asthma in the first place as kids in the least violent Chicago neighborhoods (Sternthal et al., 2010).

TABLE 11.1: Multiple Stressors in Childhood Lead to Health Problems in Adulthood

ADULT HEALTH PROBLEM	INCREASED LIKELIHOOD
Severe obesity	1.6 times
Diabetes	1.6 times
Cancer	1.9 times
Heart disease	2.2 times
Stroke	2.4 times
Chronic lung disease	3.9 times
Depression	4.6 times
Alcoholism	7.4 times

Researchers found that when people experienced at least four serious chronic stressors during childhood, their risk for serious health problems during adulthood multiplied (Felitti et al., 1998).

The Immune System. Your **immune system** is your body's innate method of defending against bacteria, viruses, infections, injuries, and anything else that could cause illness or death. When ongoing stress outlasts your resistance and exhaustion sets in, your *immune system* gets compromised. Researchers who focus on this phenomenon call their field **psychoneuroimmunology (PNI)**: the study of the relationship between psychological factors, including stress, and the immune system. Specifically, these researchers examine how certain hormones, like cortisol, epinephrine, and norepinephrine, increase with stress and interfere with the production of *antibodies*, which are the cells that fight off disease in your body (Kaye & Lightman, 2005; Rabin, 2005). In one study, parents of kids with disabilities (whose parenting stress was presumed to be unusually high) and parents of kids without such disabilities were given a vaccination for pneumonia. The parents of kids with disabilities produced fewer pneumonia antibodies, which means that even with the boost of the vaccination, their stress levels suppressed the production of the cells that fight off the disease (Gallagher et al., 2009).

Stress and Illness. The physical problems that psychoneuroimmunologists focus on are **psychophysiological illnesses**: any illness that stress can cause, worsen, or maintain. When research on stress and health was in its early stages, in the mid-1900s, it was considered newsworthy when an illness was discovered to be psychophysiological. Now, it is difficult to find an illness that *isn't* psychophysiological. Research has established psychological or stress-related connections to almost every physical malady that you can imagine (Contrada & Baum, 2011; O'Connor et al., 2021; Segerstrom & Miller, 2004). Perhaps the best-established connection is with **coronary heart disease** — a common and often fatal disease in which the arteries that lead to

immune system
The body's innate method of defending against bacteria, viruses, infections, injuries, and anything else that could cause illness or death.

psychoneuroimmunology (PNI)
The study of the relationship between psychological factors, including stress, and the immune system.

psychophysiological illnesses
Any illness that stress can cause, worsen, or maintain.

coronary heart disease
A common and often fatal disease in which the arteries that lead to the heart are clogged or blocked.

the heart are clogged or blocked — and other cardiovascular conditions (Cohen et al., 2015; Sparrenberger et al., 2009; Wirtz & von Känel, 2017). Of course, as **Figure 11.4** illustrates, a long list of other diseases have been connected to stress, from the common cold to cancer, from the flu to HIV, from arthritis to pneumonia, from migraines to irritable bowel syndrome, from diabetes to asthma, and many, many more (Cohen et al., 1991, 1993; Cohen & Williamson, 1991; Irwin, 2008; Marsland et al., 2017; Nagaraja et al., 2016; Segerstrom & Miller, 2004; Snast et al., 2018; Vedhara & Irwin, 2005).

Even wounds are affected by stress. Wounds are actually a favorite of researchers in this field, since they can be created and measured so much more conveniently than many other diseases or conditions. There are quite a few studies in which researchers give people wounds of a very specific size and location, measure the decrease in size of the wound over time, and see if stress levels predict how quickly that decrease will happen. (By the way, the word *wound* may make it sound worse than it is — it is typically a small cut or blister that causes the participant very little pain.) Over and over, these studies have found that stress slows wound healing (Bosch et al., 2007; Ebrecht et al., 2004; Gouin & Kiecolt-Glaser, 2011; Walburn et al., 2009, 2018). One study found that blisters on the forearm healed less quickly in high-stress people than in low-stress people, and that the high-stress people's bodies also produced fewer of the cell proteins (cytokines) that promote wound healing (Glaser et al., 1999). In another study, researchers gave identical small wounds (near the elbow) to 13 people who took care of a relative with Alzheimer's and to 13 people who didn't. The two groups were matched in terms of gender, age, and socioeconomic status. The caregivers' wounds took 9 days longer to heal completely, but the noncaregivers' wounds healed faster and were noticeably smaller within the first few days, presumably due to the difference in stress levels between the groups (Kiecolt-Glaser et al., 1995).

Sometimes, these researchers don't need to wound their participants themselves. Instead, they focus on wounds that the participants obtained some other way.

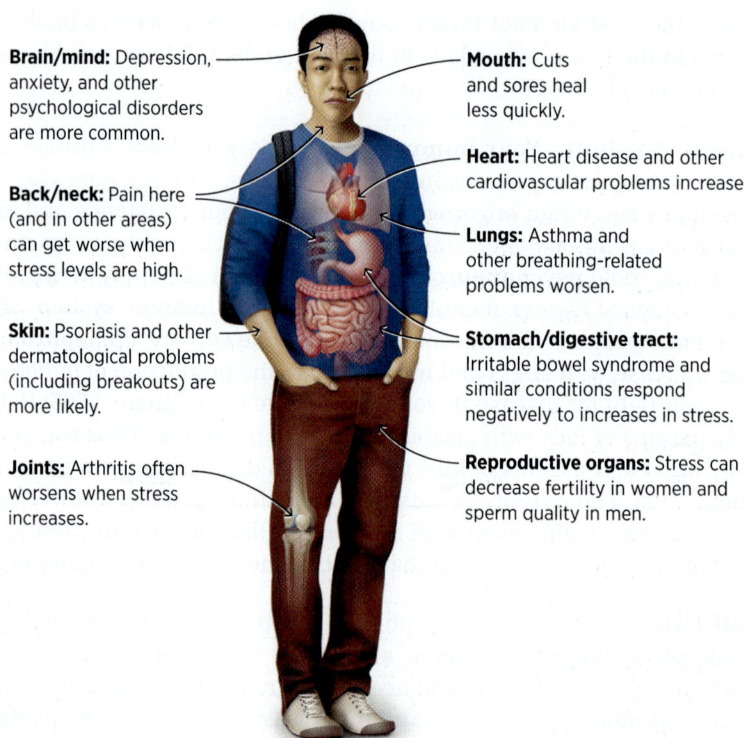
Brain/mind: Depression, anxiety, and other psychological disorders are more common.
Mouth: Cuts and sores heal less quickly.
Heart: Heart disease and other cardiovascular problems increase.
Back/neck: Pain here (and in other areas) can get worse when stress levels are high.
Lungs: Asthma and other breathing-related problems worsen.
Skin: Psoriasis and other dermatological problems (including breakouts) are more likely.
Stomach/digestive tract: Irritable bowel syndrome and similar conditions respond negatively to increases in stress.
Joints: Arthritis often worsens when stress increases.
Reproductive organs: Stress can decrease fertility in women and sperm quality in men.

FIGURE 11.4 Stress from Head to Toe. Chronic, severe stress can take its toll on many parts of the body. The conditions listed here, and many more that can affect the whole body (like cancers and viruses), can be worsened by stress. Information from O'Malley et al. (2011), Linton (2000), Gollenberg et al. (2010), Sanders and Bruce (1997), Contrada and Baum (2011), Vedhara and Irwin (2005), Irwin (2008), Segerstrom and Miller (2004), and Danoff-Burg and Revenson (2005).

For example, one group of researchers tracked people undergoing hernia surgery, which requires an incision. They found that the incisions of patients who were highly stressed about their surgery healed much more slowly than the incisions of patients who were less stressed about the same surgery (Broadbent et al., 2003). Building on that finding, the same researchers later developed a technique to lower stress before and after surgery. Patients took part in a 45-minute presurgery meeting with a psychologist who taught them relaxation and deep breathing skills, helped them imagine a successful recovery, and provided them with relaxation recordings that the patients listened to in the days before and after the surgery. They tested this technique on 30 patients having surgery to remove their gallbladders. Compared to 30 patients who underwent the same surgery but did not receive the stress reduction technique, these patients' surgery wounds healed much more quickly (Broadbent et al., 2012).

How Stress and Your Mind Affect Each Other

Stress disrupts not only your body, but your mind as well. Think of the most stressful times in your life. Most likely, your stress eclipsed any chance you had of feeling happiness. For example, if you've ever been unlucky in love, you know firsthand how the stress of relationship conflict can bring down your mental state. It is no surprise that researchers have found that experiencing these kinds of relationship conflicts — and even recalling such conflicts long after they've ended — increases levels of stress hormones like epinephrine and norepinephrine (Kiecolt-Glaser et al., 1997; Malarkey et al., 1994). What may be more surprising is that the levels of those stress hormones in newlywed couples predict how happy the members of those couples will be with their marriages *10 years later*. In fact, they even predict whether the couple will be married or divorced by that time (Kiecolt-Glaser et al., 2003).

Let's consider other ways that your mind and your stress level interact, with a focus on the role of your personality and the psychological disorders most closely related to stress.

Personality, Stress, and Health. Back in the late 1800s, a Canadian physician named William Osler was treating people with heart problems. He noticed that many of these heart patients seemed to have similar personalities, most typically an "ambitious [person] . . . whose engines are set at full speed ahead" (cited in Chesney & Rosenman, 1980, p. 188). This was one of the first written observations by a medical professional that linked a particular personality style with a particular physical illness. As the decades went by, others added to Osler's observation about the connection between heart problems and personality traits. For example, in the 1930s, Karl and William Menninger (famous U.S. psychiatrists whose Menninger Clinic is now a well-known mental health care institution in Houston) pointed out that many patients with heart problems were also very aggressive.

Stress and Personality Types. In the late 1950s, a cardiologist named Meyer Friedman noticed that in his waiting room, the chairs were showing signs of wear in unusual places — on the front edges of the seats and armrests. He eventually figured out that his patients — who, by definition, had heart trouble — were literally sitting on the edges of their seats and grasping the armrests tensely as they barely tolerated the wait to see the doctor. These impatient patients inspired Friedman and his colleagues to give a formal name to this personality style that predisposed people to heart disease: **Type A personality**, or a personality featuring high levels of competitiveness, drive, impatience, and hostility (Friedman & Rosenman, 1959). People with Type A personality find themselves in a "constant struggle to do more and more things in less and less time, and [are] often quite hostile or aggressive in their efforts to achieve them" (Friedman, 2011, p. 218). They are hurried and cutthroat in their attempts to attain their goals — not just when such qualities might be beneficial or necessary, but all the time.

I once agreed to go holiday shopping in December with some relatives. My aunt's new boyfriend, Cole, was driving. I didn't know him at all, but it only took a few minutes

Type A personality
A personality featuring high levels of competitiveness, drive, impatience, and hostility.

for me to guess that he might have a Type A personality. As we pulled into the parking lot of the crowded shopping center, he leaned forward with his hands clenched the steering wheel. A look of intensity came over his face. The race for a parking spot was on, and Cole wasn't about to lose. There were a few open spaces near the back, but he would never settle for those. He sped toward the front, scanning intensely. He patrolled the rows, up and down, up and down. "Come on, *come on*!" he muttered angrily. My aunt pleaded for him to just take one of the spaces open near the back of the lot, but Cole, with determination in his voice and a possessed look in his eye, cut her off: "Don't distract me. I'll get us a good spot. I can promise you that." She tried to explain to him that we were in no hurry, but her words fell on deaf ears. Eventually, he saw a shopper walking toward her car. He crept behind her until she got to her car in a row near the front. He immediately put his blinker on and exclaimed "Yes!" as if he had just won the parking championship. It took this shopper a few minutes to vacate her spot – she had a baby and stroller to load into the car, not to mention lots of shopping bags – so Cole gave her an annoyed honk and barked, "Let's go already!"

Through the late 1900s, Type A personalities (like Cole's) received a lot of attention from researchers, and for good reason: heart disease had become the greatest cause of premature death in the Western world. And according to much of the research around that time, the connection was confirmed: Type A personality was correlated with heart trouble. For example, researchers conducted an 8-year longitudinal study on 3500 men, which found that those with Type A personalities had significantly higher incidence of heart disease (Rosenman et al., 1964, 1975). More recent research has produced results that are not so definitive, however (Houston & Snyder, 1988; Miller et al., 1991). These recent studies still generally support the link between Type A personality and heart disease, but they try to determine a more particular connection: what, specifically, are the toxic ingredients within Type A personality? Type A personality is a broad cluster of characteristics; perhaps particular characteristics contribute more than others to heart disease (Friedman & Booth-Kewley, 1987). So far, the prime suspects seem to be hostility and competitiveness (Booth-Kewley & Friedman, 1987; Cooper & Bright, 2001; Friedman, 2011; Ganster et al., 1991; Lohse et al., 2017). Being driven and even impatient are not so bad for your health. In fact, they can be quite productive in certain circumstances. However, an ever-present hostile attitude and competing constantly with others are more likely to be bad for your health.

When researchers identified Type A personality, they also identified **Type B personality**: a personality very much unlike Type A personality, in which the person is noncompetitive, easygoing, relaxed, and rarely angry (Cooper & Dewe, 2004). People with Type B personalities are more "chill" than their Type A counterparts. For example, unlike Cole, someone with a Type B personality might choose to park in the distant corner of a crowded parking lot to avoid the competition in the front rows – or might even skip the shopping center on a crowded day altogether.

Other personality types have been identified more recently (Friedman, 2011). **Type C personality** is a personality featuring a low level of emotional expression, a high level of agreeableness with other people, and a tendency to feel helpless. For example, consider Phoebe: whenever she gets together with her family, she holds her feelings in and goes along with whatever they want to do, but she is bothered by a sense that she doesn't have as much control over her life as she would like. **Type D personality** (sometimes called *distressed personality*) is a personality featuring high levels of negative emotions, like depression and anxiety, and a reluctance to share those emotions with others. For example, consider Ronnie: he worries a lot, and tends to feel blue pretty often, but he keeps these feelings to himself rather than talking about them with his friends or family.

Researchers have hypothesized that Type B personality should correlate with low risk of heart disease, and that Type C personality should correlate with high risk of cancer. However, research testing those hypotheses has not been extensive, and the research that has been done offers little support (Temoshok, 1986; Temoshok et al., 1985). However, there is increasing research support for the hypothesis that Type D personality correlates with high levels of heart disease (Denollet, 2000; Du et al., 2016; Kupper & Denollet, 2018; Lin et al., 2018; Mols & Denollet, 2010; Pedersen & Denollet, 2003, 2006).

Type B personality
A personality in which the person is noncompetitive, easygoing, relaxed, and rarely angry.

Type C personality
A personality featuring a low level of emotional expression, a high level of agreeableness with other people, and a tendency to feel helpless.

Type D personality
A personality featuring high levels of negative emotions, like depression and anxiety, and a reluctance to share those emotions with others.

Stress and Personality Factors. Most recently, research exploring the link between personality and stress (and health) has focused on *the five-factor model of personality*, also known as the *Big Five*. We will explore the Big Five in depth in Chapter 12, but for now it is important to know that it is a prominent way that psychologists currently understand personality. The Big Five is based on the idea that each person's personality consists of five fundamental traits, or that there are five basic "ingredients" in human personality. What differentiates us from each other is the amount of each ingredient that each person has (Digman, 1990; Hunt, 1993; McCrae & Costa, 1996). Those five ingredients are:

- *Neuroticism*, the tendency to experience negative emotions such as anxiety and depression
- *Extraversion*, the tendency to be socially outgoing
- *Openness to experience*, the tendency to be receptive to new or unconventional ideas
- *Conscientiousness*, the tendency to be organized, responsible, and deliberate
- *Agreeableness*, the tendency to cooperate and comply with other people

Lots of studies have found connections between these five personality traits and health-related issues. High levels of conscientiousness and extraversion generally correlate with positive health outcomes. For example, people who are high in conscientiousness as children tend to live longer, healthier lives than people low in conscientiousness (Friedman et al., 2003; Kern & Friedman, 2008).

In another study, researchers tracked 883 older adults for 5 years, during which 182 died. Those with low conscientiousness were twice as likely to die as those with high conscientiousness (Wilson et al., 2004). High extraversion is also commonly found in people with good health, but can occasionally be harmful to health when it leads to hazardous social behaviors like excessive drinking, risky sex, or long-term smoking (Booth-Kewley & Vickers, 1994; Friedman, 2011). High levels of openness to experience can be good too: studies have found that people with higher levels of it tend to have lower levels of heart and cardiovascular diseases (Lee et al., 2014; Ó Súilleabháin et al., 2018).

On the other hand, neuroticism has repeatedly been linked to illness and disease. In the previously mentioned study of 883 older adults, those with high neuroticism were twice as likely to die during the 5-year period as those with low neuroticism (Wilson et al., 2004). Additional research has found that neuroticism correlates negatively with healthy behaviors like exercise and eating fruits and vegetables, but positively with unhealthy behaviors and outcomes like smoking, obesity, diabetes, high cholesterol, and heart disease (Jokela et al., 2014; Pesta et al., 2012). (See **Table 11.2** for more on this link between neuroticism and health.)

There is much more to learn about the connection between personality and health, but perhaps the clearest finding so far is that people who are generally unhappy and irritated, as indicated by high levels of neuroticism, tend to have more health problems (especially heart problems) than people who are generally happy and calm (Cacioppo & Berntson, 2011; Friedman & Martin, 2011; Jokela, 2018; Smith & MacKenzie, 2006). As described by Meyer Friedman, the cardiologist who first identified Type A behavior back in the 1950s and who has spent over half a century studying it, the full body of research on personality and health has taught us:

> . . . that a person who is chronically irritated, depressed, hostile, impulsive, bored, frustrated, unstable, lonely, or powerless is indeed more likely to develop illnesses and to die prematurely than is someone who is generally emotionally balanced and effective, . . . has stable and supportive social relationships, and is well integrated into the community. (Friedman, 2011, p. 215)

TABLE 11.2: Neuroticism, Stress, and Illness

THE CORRELATION BETWEEN NEUROTICISM AND...	IS...
High blood pressure	.62
Heart disease	.61
Diabetes	.57
High cholesterol	.53
Stroke	.40
Obesity	.28
Activity and exercise	–.50

Neuroticism, a personality trait defined by a tendency to think and feel negatively, can play a significant role in your experience of stress. It correlates in a strong positive way with stress-related illnesses and in a strong negative way with health-promoting behaviors like exercise.
Data from Pesta et al. (2012).

Stress-Related Psychological Disorders. Stress can contribute to almost any psychological disorder. Depression, anxiety, eating disorders, attention-deficit/hyperactivity disorder (ADHD), schizophrenia — all of them can be worsened in times of high stress. But a few psychological disorders are actually built around the concept of stress. In the diagnostic manual that psychologists use, the *Diagnostic and Statistical Manual of Mental Disorders*

posttraumatic stress disorder (PTSD) A psychological disorder lasting at least a month characterized by feeling continuously on edge, avoiding reminders of the traumatic event, having difficulty sleeping and concentrating, and frequently recalling or reliving the event.

(DSM-5-TR, which we discuss in detail in Chapter 14), those disorders appear in the section "Trauma- and Stressor-Related Disorders" (American Psychiatric Association, 2022).

Posttraumatic Stress Disorder. One of the disorders in the "Trauma- and Stressor-Related Disorders" section of *DSM* describes the lingering stress and other aftereffects caused by traumatic events. That disorder is **posttraumatic stress disorder (PTSD)**: a psychological disorder lasting at least a month characterized by feeling continuously on edge, avoiding reminders of the traumatic event, having difficulty sleeping and concentrating, and frequently recalling or reliving the event. People with PTSD experience a variety of symptoms. Sometimes, they re-experience the trauma through frightening dreams and flashbacks. They may experience hyperarousal, which means they stay keyed up all the time, making it difficult to sleep. They may be highly sensitive to sights or sounds that remind them of the trauma. In some cases, people with PTSD become emotionally numb and seem to "blank out" for periods of time (Keane et al., 2009; Weathers, 2018).

I've been through some very distressing events myself, but I'm not sure if they were traumas. What exactly qualifies as a trauma?

DSM-5-TR explains that a trauma involves exposure to actual or threatened death, serious injury, or sexual violence (American Psychiatric Association, 2022). The PTSD diagnosis was originally created to capture the "shell shock" experience of

CURRENT CONTROVERSY

What Counts as a Trauma?

The first requirement for a diagnosis of PTSD is the *T*, or the trauma. But what, exactly, counts as a trauma? PTSD first appeared as a disorder in DSM in 1980, after lobbying efforts by people seeking official recognition of what had informally been called *shell shock* or *combat fatigue* in soldiers (Friedman et al., 2007; Resick et al., 2008; Watters, 2010). Undoubtedly, wartime experiences can be traumas. So can other life-changing tragedies, like natural disasters, assaults, bombings, and serious car accidents.

Scott Olson/Getty Images

Some events, like the tornado that caused this damage, are undoubtedly traumatic. But where should the line be drawn?

But where's the line between a trauma and an event that is merely unfortunate or unpleasant? This question has been at the heart of a controversy among psychologists that continues today (Chou et al., 2017; Friedman, 2009; Larson & Pacella, 2016). It is important for many reasons, primarily because important things can depend on whether a person is diagnosed with PTSD: health insurance benefits (to pay for treatment), disability benefits, the outcomes of lawsuits for personal injury and worker's compensation, and much more (Sparr & Pitman, 2007).

According to the DSM-5-TR definition of PTSD, a trauma consists of "exposure to actual or threatened death, serious injury, or sexual violence" in at least one of these ways (American Psychiatric Association, 2022, p. 301):

- "Directly experiencing the traumatic event"
- "Witnessing, in person, the event as it occurred to others"
- "Learning that the traumatic event occurred to a close family member or close friend"
- "Experiencing repeated or extreme exposure to aversive details of the traumatic event" (like what first responders often see on the job)

This definition is certainly helpful, but a lot of questions remain. How is the phrase "threatened death, serious injury, or sexual violence" defined? (Does it count if you narrowly avoid an oncoming car that could have killed or hurt you?) And who defines the threat? What is threatening to one person might be uneventful or even enjoyable to the next. (Consider skydiving or storm chasing.) Similarly, can words rather than actions constitute such threats? One researcher argues that an individual can experience trauma "simply from a word being spoken," offering the example of certain racial slurs to some members of minority racial and ethnic groups in the United States (Brown, 2008, p. 97). On another note, how close does the family member or friend have to be for their trauma to become your trauma when you find out about it? Also, what does the "in person" phrase in the definition mean about witnessing something tragic (like a terrorist attack or a tornado) on television or through social media?

Because of questions like these, psychologists and others continue to debate what constitutes the traumas upon which the PTSD (and acute stress disorder) diagnoses are based. •

soldiers returning from live combat, but people who are diagnosed with PTSD today have experienced a wide range of harrowing events, including acts of violence (shooting incidents, sexual assaults), natural disasters (tornadoes, earthquakes, tsunamis), or accidents (car wrecks, plane crashes) (Friedman et al., 2007; Kessler, 2018; Krupnick, 2017; Resick et al., 2008; Shalev & Marmar, 2018).

Of course, just because a person experiences a trauma does not mean they will develop PTSD (or any other mental disorder, for that matter) (Briere et al., 2016; Fink et al., 2017; Galatzer-Levy et al., 2018). Human beings are often quite resilient in the aftermath of traumatic events. In fact, some researchers have estimated that as many as 90% of us will experience some kind of traumatic event in our lifetimes, but only 6.8% of us will develop PTSD in our lifetimes (Breslau, 2009; Kessler et al., 2005a, b; McFarlane, 2010).

Many studies have tracked people after specific potential traumas and found that only a small fraction developed or continued to suffer from PTSD. For example, one longitudinal study tracked over 1000 people who spent at least 24 hours in the hospital for traumatic injuries, including car accidents and assaults. About three-quarters of them showed no signs of PTSD at any follow-up point (3 months, 1 year, 2 years, or 6 years) after the accident. Of those that did, only 4% had serious PTSD symptoms that persisted across that full time period (Bryant et al., 2015). Another longitudinal study tracked Northern Illinois University students for 31 months after a 2008 mass shooting in a classroom there that left six dead and 21 injured. It found that even after such a horrific event, the vast majority of students showed minimal or no PTSD symptoms, and only about 2% showed continuous serious symptoms (Orcutt et al., 2014). And a study of over 2000 New Yorkers found that more than one-third of the people who lost a loved one in the September 11, 2001, terrorist attacks reported either no symptoms or just one symptom of PTSD — a remarkable finding when you consider that the diagnosis had at least a dozen possible symptoms at the time, and to qualify for the diagnosis, at least six symptoms were required (Bonanno et al., 2007).

Acute Stress Disorder and Adjustment Disorder. Two additional DSM disorders are based primarily on stress reactions. One is **acute stress disorder**: a psychological disorder that takes place in the days and weeks immediately after a trauma in which the person feels dazed and anxious and experiences flashbacks. Essentially, acute stress disorder is like PTSD but occurs more *immediately* after the traumatic stressor. (By definition, acute stress disorder can only be diagnosed 3 days to 1 month after the trauma, and PTSD can only be diagnosed after at least 1 month has passed.) The other related disorder is **adjustment disorder**: a psychological disorder defined by an excessively disruptive stress reaction to an identifiable stressor. Adjustment disorder differs from PTSD and acute stress disorder because it does not require a trauma. Essentially, it is the appropriate diagnosis for a person whose reaction to a nontraumatic or common stressor is way out of proportion, someone who is debilitated by something that most people would overcome more quickly and easily (American Psychiatric Association, 2022).

Three of my own therapy clients, each of whom experienced disruptive levels of stress, illustrate the difference between PTSD, acute stress disorder, and adjustment disorder:

- **Posttraumatic stress disorder.** Holly, a flight attendant, started working with me 5 months after she was assaulted and robbed in the airport parking lot after working a late-night flight. She told me that since the event, she had a difficult time relaxing at all. She was always nervous, and found it hard to sleep or concentrate on anything. She also had flashbacks almost every day—unwelcome daydreams in which she relived the event—and was scared to park in the same lot or walk alone anywhere inside or outside of the airport. She was going through the motions at work, barely able to get herself to her flights on time and serve the passengers adequately, in a near-panic state the whole time. Because of the severity and duration of her symptoms, PTSD was the appropriate diagnosis for Holly.

acute stress disorder
A psychological disorder that takes place in the days and weeks immediately after a trauma in which the person feels dazed and anxious and experiences flashbacks.

adjustment disorder
A psychological disorder defined by an excessively disruptive stress reaction to an identifiable stressor.

- **Acute stress disorder.** Esteban, an elementary school teacher, called me 5 days after a terrifying incident in his home. During a thunderstorm, lightning struck a huge, 20-foot tree in his yard, sending it crashing through Esteban's house, within feet of crushing Esteban, his partner, and their baby, who were in the kitchen at the time. The tree destroyed the kitchen table: "If we had been sitting there, we'd be gone," Esteban told me. Esteban had been experiencing similar symptoms to Holly's—lots of anxiety and fear, difficulty relaxing and sleeping, flashbacks in which he saw the tree falling over and over again. Every time another thunderstorm happened, his symptoms got even more intense. Esteban was significantly affected by the stress he was experiencing, and he certainly lived through a trauma, but it was so recent—just 5 days ago—that PTSD wasn't an appropriate diagnosis. Instead, acute stress disorder was. (If his symptoms had lasted longer than a month, Esteban's diagnosis could have been changed to PTSD. Thankfully, they didn't.)
- **Adjustment disorder.** Shantelle was a 16-year-old high school sophomore whose Spanish teacher, Ms. Rosales, moved away in the middle of the school year. Now, 6 weeks later, Shantelle was still absolutely devastated. That is why her parents brought her to me—they couldn't understand why the loss of Ms. Rosales was so upsetting to their daughter, especially because the new Spanish teacher seemed quite competent and kind. Of course, they understood why Shantelle would be affected a *little*—Ms. Rosales had been an excellent teacher for the first half of the year, and Shantelle had enjoyed learning from her. But Shantelle wasn't affected a little; she was affected a *lot*. She cried often, worried about her grades and her future. Sometimes, she was so distressed that she passed on opportunities to hang out with friends and missed shifts at her part-time job at Subway. Shantelle hadn't experienced a trauma, but she was having significant trouble adjusting to a stressor, so the appropriate diagnosis for her was adjustment disorder.

Prolonged Grief Disorder. When DSM-5-TR was published in 2022, it included a new disorder: **prolonged grief disorder**, a psychological disorder in which the person experiences the death of someone close to them followed by grief that is excessively intense or long-lasting. Prolonged grief disorder is an appropriate diagnosis when a person's loss took place at least 12 months ago (or for children, at least 6 months ago), yet they continue to feel intense yearning for the loss or spend an unusually large amount of time thinking about the person who has died. Other features of prolonged grief disorder can include avoidance of reminders that the person is dead; intense bitterness, sorrow, or loneliness; and difficulty getting back to normal activities and relationships, even after this long period of time. Of course, cultural norms and customs are important context for determining whether a person's grief should be labeled as prolonged grief disorder (American Psychiatric Association, 2022; Prigerson et al., 2021).

Is there any chance that major stressors could actually improve your state of mind?

Thankfully, yes. In fact, psychologists have recently been paying a lot more attention to the possible upside of the aftermath of traumatic stress. They have found that some trauma survivors actually experience **posttraumatic growth**: when people experience trauma, but find a way to benefit, improve, or enrich themselves from that point forward (Davis & Nolen-Hoeksema, 2009; Tedeschi et al., 2017; Zautra & Reich, 2011).

prolonged grief disorder
A psychological disorder in which the person experiences the death of someone close to them followed by grief that is excessively intense or long-lasting.

posttraumatic growth
When people experience trauma and then find a way to benefit, improve, or enrich themselves from that point onward.

How, exactly, do these people show such resilience? Some psychologists point to *benefit finding*, or deliberately looking for the advantages of the experience of the trauma. For example, although a soldier may lose a leg to a roadside bomb, they may also gain a more appreciative outlook on life, closer relationships with their support network, and greater self-respect for having been tough enough to survive and recover (Elderton et al., 2017; Lechner et al., 2009; Pakenham, 2011). Benefit finding has actually been linked to increased rates of improvement across a range of health-related stressors (Affleck & Tennen, 1996; Danoff-Burg & Revenson, 2005; Tennen et al., 2006).

Other people who experience a traumatic stressor focus on *meaning making*, trying to create some sense out of what may have made no sense at first (Casellas-Grau et al., 2017; Park, 2011; Zeligman et al., 2018). Sometimes, religion plays an important role in meaning making, as when people accept a stressor as a test that God or another higher power has given them for a good if unknown reason (Pargament, 2011; Tsai et al., 2015). Researchers also point to positive emotions — love, joy, gratitude, humor, and so on — and say that the more a person feels them, the more they can grow from stressors (Biggs et al., 2017; Bonanno, 2004, 2009; Folkman, 1997, 2011; Folkman & Moskowitz, 2000; Kong et al., 2018; Rabkin et al., 2009; Rzeszutek, 2017; Tugade, 2011; Yu et al., 2014).

Scott Olson/Getty Images

Only a small fraction of people who live through a trauma, such as this soldier's loss of a limb, experience posttraumatic stress disorder. Fortunately, some experience posttraumatic growth by finding a way to benefit, improve, or enrich themselves after the trauma.

The idea that a person could find benefit or make meaning from a traumatic event illustrates the more general notion of *eustress*, the interpretation of stress as an opportunity rather than a threat (Lazarus, 1993; Simmons & Nelson, 2007). (The *eu-* in eustress means good, as in *eu*phoria. It is the opposite of *dis*tress, or the interpretation of stress as bad or threatening.) Whether the stressor is minor or major, viewing it as a chance to improve yourself, learn something new, or meet a challenge is better for you than viewing it as a looming danger. One study of hundreds of social workers found that those who view their on-the-job responsibilities as eustress report lower levels of exhaustion and cynicism and greater levels of dedication and enthusiasm for their jobs than their colleagues who view those same activities less positively (Kozusznik et al., 2015; Rodriguez et al., 2013).

LIFE HACK 11.1

Whenever possible, view stress as eustress — an opportunity rather than a threat. That mind-set will increase the chances that you will benefit rather than suffer from the experience.

(Kozusznik et al., 2015; Lazarus, 1993; Simmons & Nelson, 2007)

Stress and COVID

The COVID pandemic caused a notable increase in stress for many of us — not just those who tested positive, but those whose lives were upended by the quarantine and changes to daily life (Alzueta et al., 2021). Research conducted during the pandemic on Americans and their stress levels have produced some striking findings. For example, one survey found that the percentage of people who considered themselves in "serious distress" (the highest category in the study) jumped from just 3.4% in 2018 to 27.7% in April 2020 (Twenge & Joiner, 2020). Another study found 80% identified the pandemic as a significant source of stress in their lives (American Psychological Association, 2021a). The consequences of that stress were extensive too: over 60% reported unwanted changes in weight and sleeping patterns, and 48% said their overall level of stress had increased since prepandemic times (American Psychological Association, 2021b).

On the other hand, there was some evidence that Americans showed an impressive resilience (or ability to cope) with the stress of the pandemic as it persisted. One study measured stress levels at three points in time: April 2020, 5 weeks later, and 10 weeks later. Results showed that stress levels decreased across those points in time, returning to a level that's comparable with nonpandemic times. This pattern of decreasing stress was true for overall stress, as well as for specific categories of stress — such as stress about money, stress about daily activities, and stress about COVID itself. Participants who were older, more mindful, and had more social support were especially likely to show this pattern of resilience or decreasing stress over time (Park et al., 2021).

CHECK YOUR LEARNING:

11.6 What are the different ways that stress damages a person's health?

11.7 What is general adaptation syndrome?

11.8 How does stress affect the immune system and contribute to illness?

11.9 What are the main characteristics of Type A and Type B personality, and how do they relate to the experience of stress?

11.10 How do the personality traits of conscientiousness, extraversion, and neuroticism correlate with stress levels?

11.11 How does stress relate to psychological disorders?

11.12 How did the COVID pandemic affect stress levels?

To check your understanding of these questions, click show the answers or refer to the answers in the Chapter Summary.

Stress and Diversity

YOU WILL LEARN:

11.13 about the different ways people of different genders experience stress.

11.14 how people of different ethnic backgrounds experience stress.

11.15 about the ways in which people experience stress at different ages.

As twins, Scarlett Johansson and her brother, Hunter, have undoubtedly experienced many of the same stressors. As members of different genders, however, they have undoubtedly experienced some different stressors too.

Different people experience different stressors. Even when people experience the same stressors, they can experience them differently. The same event can bring about different meanings or challenges for people from diverse groups. Let's consider how some of our diverse characteristics – gender, ethnicity, and age – shape the stress we experience.

Stress and Gender

DIVERSITY MATTERS

One way to consider the differences in stressors that men and women face is to find a pair of twins in which each is a different gender from the other and speculate about the stress in each of their lives. For example, did you know that actress Scarlett Johansson has a twin brother named Hunter? Growing up in the same family at the same time, they must have encountered many of the same stressors. But would you expect that what stressed out Scarlett stressed out Hunter too, and vice versa? More generally, are there some stressors that are more likely to impact people because of their gender?

Psychologists have actually collected lots of data on men's and women's experiences of stress. In terms of trauma, men experience more traumatic stressors than women, but women experience PTSD more often than men (Olff et al., 2007; Silove et al., 2017; Tang & Freyd, 2012). Specifically, men are 3.5 times more likely to experience war-related trauma and 1.5 times more likely to experience a physical assault. Women, however, are six times more likely to experience sexual assault during adulthood, and 2.5 times more likely to have experienced sexual assault during childhood (Basile, 2005; Dallam, 2005; Tolin & Foa, 2006). Whether the stress is traumatic or more common, women tend to appraise stressors as more severe than men do (Davis et al., 1999). As a result, the overall self-reported stress level for women tends to be higher than that for men (Matud, 2004).

Men and women also tend to get stressed about different things. In some cases, biology may play a role. For example, women are more vulnerable to stressors related to pregnancy and childbirth, while men are more vulnerable to stressors related to impotence (Kendall-Tackett, 2005c). In other cases, as **Table 11.3** shows, social norms and expectations may play a significant role: women tend to experience much more caregiving-related stress (for their children or elderly or sick relatives) and housework-related stress, while men tend to experience more stress related to money and work (Kendall-Tackett, 2005b; Matud, 2004). In one study, college students experienced two kinds of stressors: achievement stressors (math problems and verbal memorization) and social stressors (being excluded by two other people in the room who

TABLE 11.3: Stressors Endorsed More Often by Women or Men

THIS STRESSOR...	...WAS LISTED BY THIS PERCENTAGE OF WOMEN...	...AND THIS PERCENTAGE OF MEN.
Separation, divorce	**4.4**	2.3
Change in religious attendance or beliefs	**10.0**	7.5
Death in the immediate family	**30.7**	27.0
Birth in family	**27.7**	20.1
Serious illness of a close friend or relative	**18.1**	14.0
Engagement	14.8	**21.6**
Starting a serious relationship (not marriage)	17.8	**25.0**
Ending a serious relationship (not marriage)	11.2	**23.8**
Making new friends	52.7	**57.3**
Major change in financial status	30.6	**37.0**
Change in commitment to work	27.5	**35.3**
Dealings with staff or supervisor	15.1	**19.2**
Change in work pressure	22.6	**29.4**
Increase or decrease in workload	25.2	**30.7**

Data from Matud (2004).

When over 2800 women and men were given a checklist of 31 stressors that could have happened to any of them over the past 2 years, many of those stressors were equally endorsed by both groups. But the rest of the stressors — the ones listed in this table — were endorsed by one group significantly more often than the other, illustrating the fact that stress experiences often depend on gender.

were actually actors told to speak to each other while ignoring the participant). Men had higher levels of cortisol, a hormone that indicates stress, after the achievement stressors, and women had higher levels of cortisol after the social stressors (Stroud et al., 2002).

In another study of kids age 8–17, girls found performance-based experiences (such as giving a speech, answering math problems correctly, etc.) more stressful than rejection-based experiences (such as being left out of a social interaction by other girls) before puberty. However, the opposite pattern was true for girls after puberty. For boys, puberty didn't matter: the two kinds of experiences produced about the same levels of stress at all ages (Stroud et al., 2017).

When men and women experience the same stressor, they often react differently. For example, when married couples argue, women feel more stress, not only by their own description, but also by biological measurements like blood pressure (Kendall-Tackett, 2005a). In one interesting pair of studies, researchers actually put men and women through the same stressor — keeping their hand immersed in ice water for 2 minutes — but attached a different description to that stressor for different participants. Researchers told some participants that success indicated a high level of qualities that women stereotypically value, like nurturing and forming intimate relationships. They told other participants that success indicated a high level of qualities that men stereotypically value, like willpower and physical strength. Researchers found that women experienced more stress (as shown by blood pressure increases) when the task was described the first way, but men experienced more stress when the task was described the second way (Lash et al., 1991, 1995). So, across genders, it is not just the task that causes us stress, but how we perceive the task.

Stress and Ethnicity

Just as people of different genders experience stress differently, so do people of different ethnic backgrounds (Slavin et al., 1991). First of all, minority or immigrant groups in the United States are simply more likely to face certain real-world stressors than people in the majority. For example, Latinx families have higher odds of encountering poverty, language barriers, limited education, and unemployment (Padilla & Borrero, 2006). Black families contend with many of the same experiences at similarly high rates, plus the legacy of personal and institutional racism that remains from the slavery era (McCreary, 2006). Studies have found that this increased stress due to ethnic or racial factors takes its toll in terms of both physical and mental health (Perry et al., 2013).

For example, one study found that among almost 800 Black people in the United States, the higher the rate of perceived racial discrimination, the higher the rate of psychological distress (Brown et al., 2000). Another study with over 5000 participants found similar connections between perceived racial discrimination and both depression and cardiovascular disease (Chae et al., 2012). Other studies have found that the higher rates of pregnancy- and birth-related complications among Black women — nearly twice that of White women — is due in large part to race-based stress (Rosenthal & Lobel, 2011). Race-related stress may even cause Black people in the United States to age more quickly. One biologically focused study examined *telomeres* — tiny parts of our chromosomes that indicate age like rings on a tree trunk. Researchers found that middle-aged Black women are, on average, 7.5 years "older" than White women according to their telomeres, and that the difference was due at least in part to stressors that Black women are more likely to experience, many of which are based in racism and poverty (Geronimus et al., 2010). In another study of over 6000 adults above the age of 52, participants who are Latinx and participants who are Black reported much higher levels of chronic stress than White participants, but lower likelihood of being upset by those stressors (Brown et al., 2018).

Collectivism, Individualism, and Stress. One significant characteristic of culture is whether it leans toward the well-being of the group over the individual, or *us* over *me*. Individualistic cultures, which often come from the United States, Canada, Western Europe, and Australia, emphasize the well-being of the individual over the group, or *me* over *us* (Hofstede, 2001; Hofstede et al., 1997; Kim et al., 1994; Oyserman, 2017; Triandis, 1995, 2001).

Research shows that people from collectivistic and individualistic cultures often have different experiences of stress (Yeh et al., 2006). For example, people from individualistic cultures are more likely to feel stress about personal achievements, like school or job challenges, while people from collectivistic cultures are more likely to feel stress about family harmony, like how much support they are providing or how strong their relationships are (Chun et al., 2006; Heine & Lehman, 1995; Tafarodi & Smith, 2001).

Another stress-related difference between individualistic and collectivistic cultures involves the issue of "standing out" versus "standing in" (Weisz et al., 1984). Generally, in individualistic cultures, it is considered good to stand out from the crowd, to distinguish yourself by your accomplishments. In collectivistic cultures, however, standing out is more likely to be experienced as highly stressful. Instead, collectivistic cultures tend to favor behavior that is more conventional, or in agreement with others. You know the saying, popular in the United States, that "the squeaky wheel gets the grease"? In Japan, there is a different saying: "The nail that sticks out gets pounded down" (Tweed & Conway, 2006). As an example, imagine that you get a job in which you quickly learn that your supervisor expects you to work a few extra hours without extra pay. You also realize that all of your coworkers are already used to this expectation. If you're from an individualistic culture, your impulse may be to stand up for the extra pay that is rightfully yours, asserting yourself even if you single yourself out as disruptor in the process. In fact, simply accepting the arrangement you see as unfair might cause you stress. However, if you're from a collectivistic culture, it may be *less* stressful to accept the arrangement than to fight it, because, by fighting it, you may threaten harmony in your relationships with your coworkers and your supervisor. If you're from a collectivistic culture, you may be willing to sacrifice some personal gains if it meant keeping the peace with those around you.

Hill Street Studios/Blend Images/Getty Images

People from collectivistic cultures (including many from Asia, Africa, and South America) often have different experiences of stress than people from individualistic cultures. In collectivistic cultures, stress is more likely to come from threats to relationship harmony than shortcomings in personal achievement. Also, standing out from the crowd is more likely to cause stress for people in collectivistic cultures than people in individualistic cultures.

A final note on people from individualistic and collectivistic cultures: Stress often affects their bodies and minds differently. Specifically, when people from individualistic cultures get stressed out, they tend to feel it mentally. They tend to report unpleasant thoughts and emotions (sadness, despair, anxiety, anger, etc.). On the other hand, when people from collectivistic cultures get stressed out, they tend to feel it physically. They tend to report headaches, stomach discomfort, fatigue, and bodily pain. This cultural difference, at least to some degree, appears across a wide range of individualistic and collectivistic cultures (Chun et al., 1996; Takeuchi et al., 2002).

Stress and Age

DIVERSITY MATTERS

What stressed you out when you were 5? 10? 15? What stresses you out now? Perhaps some of your stressors have remained consistent, but undoubtedly, some have changed. At least in mainstream U.S. culture, there are certain sources of stress that are more likely to have an impact on us at various ages (Aldwin, 2011; American Psychological Association, 2014a):

- **Ages 2–5**—the behavioral demands of preschool or day care; power struggles with parents ("I want to do it myself!")
- **Elementary school**—academic achievement, making friends
- **Middle school**—academic achievement, starting to date, popularity
- **High school**—academic achievement, dating, arguing with parents, popularity, family financial issues
- **Young adulthood**—finishing school, committed relationship or marriage, work, money, raising young kids
- **Middle to older adulthood**—health problems, health problems of loved ones, work, financial issues, divorce, caregiver burdens, death of parents or others

When intensive, chronic stress takes place early in the life span, it can have long-lasting effects. A review of studies on the biological effects of stress on people and animals found that there appear to be certain critical periods of development when the long-term potential of stress is especially likely, including the prenatal period (when the fetus feels mom's stress), the first year of life (when stress often comes from poor parental care), and adolescence (Lupien et al., 2009). Numerous studies have found that when major stressors – especially family conflict, abuse, and the absence of a father – are persistent throughout a girl's childhood, she is more likely to experience her first period (menarche) earlier than her peers (Belsky et al., 1991; Boynton-Jarrett et al., 2013; Moffitt et al., 1992; Romans et al., 2003; Wierson et al., 1993). Evolutionary theory argues that this would happen because earlier menarche enables earlier childbirth, which might be necessary because girls under perpetually high stress could be expected to have shorter life spans. One study supports this theory quite strongly: not only did women with high-stress childhoods have their first period sooner, they also had their first baby sooner and expected their own life spans to be shorter than peers with lower-stress childhoods (Chisholm et al., 2005).

Stress levels tend to be lower in older adults than in younger adults or middle-aged adults (Birditt et al., 2005; Neupert et al., 2007). This may reflect the wisdom of experience, a "been there, done that" attitude that prevents older adults from getting overly upset about day-to-day occurrences. However, when older adults do find themselves facing chronic and unavoidable stressors, the effects can be especially damaging (Esterling et al., 1994). In one study, researchers gave the influenza virus vaccine (flu shots) to older adults, some of whom were taking care of their spouses with dementia. They found that the caregivers' bodies responded more poorly to the vaccine, producing far fewer antibodies and leaving the older adults more susceptible to a disease that could be serious or fatal, especially at that age (Kiecolt-Glaser et al., 1996). Another study of about 400 such spousal caregivers, age 66–96, found that over a 4-year period, they were 63% more likely to die than same-age peers who did not have that ongoing, serious stressor in their lives (Schulz & Beach, 1999). And in a study of older adults caring for their husbands or wives with cancer, these caregivers were significantly more likely to experience heart disease or stroke than peers who were not in similar caregiving situations (Ji et al., 2012).

Anita_Bonita/iStock/Getty Images

Older adults tend to have lower overall stress levels than younger or middle-aged adults, but when their stress does increase, the health-related consequences can be significant.

CHECK YOUR LEARNING:

11.13 How do people of different genders experience stress in different ways?

11.14 How do people of different ethnic backgrounds, including individualistic and collectivistic cultures, experience stress differently?

11.15 How can age influence the experience of stress?

To check your understanding of these questions, click show the answers or refer to the answers in the Chapter Summary.

Coping with Stress: Psychological Strategies and Social Strategies

YOU WILL LEARN:

11.16 how psychologists define *coping*.

11.17 how coping styles differ by ethnicity and gender.

11.18 about ways to decrease stress by evaluating it differently.

11.19 how mindfulness can influence stress levels.

11.20 about the importance of social support to emotional and physical health.

11.21 about ways to decrease stress by behaving differently.

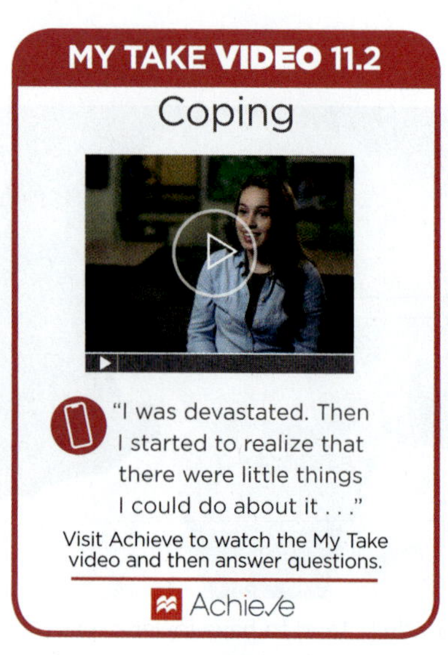
MY TAKE VIDEO 11.2
Coping
"I was devastated. Then I started to realize that there were little things I could do about it . . ."
Visit Achieve to watch the My Take video and then answer questions.
Achieve

coping
Efforts to reduce or manage an experience of stress.

So far, this chapter has focused heavily on what stresses you out and what effects that stress can have — in other words, what stress does to you. It's time to turn the tables and focus on what you can do about stress. So, we turn to the topic of **coping**: efforts to reduce or manage your experience of stress.

Diversity and Coping

DIVERSITY MATTERS

There is no single formula for how best to cope with stress. What works for your friends or family might not work for you (and vice versa) (Klienke, 2002). In fact, coping strategies often vary according to factors like ethnicity and gender. People from collectivistic cultures tend to cope by changing things within themselves, like their own thoughts and feelings (which often allows them to avoid conflict with others). People from individualistic cultures tend to cope by changing things outside of themselves, like the stressor itself (Chun et al., 2006; Tweed et al., 2004; Yeh & Inose, 2002). Even when friends and family are available, people from collectivistic cultures may choose not to burden them (because they fear that the burden could threaten harmony in the relationship), and they may benefit simply from knowing help is available without actually using it. People from individualistic cultures, on the other hand, are more likely to directly ask friends and family for help, and to take whatever they can get (Kim et al., 2008; Taylor et al., 2004).

Regarding gender, women tend to cope by talking about their feelings, often repeatedly, with other women. By contrast, men tend to cope by problem solving and avoid discussing their emotions with anyone (Brougham et al., 2009; Frydenberg & Lewis, 1993; Helgeson, 2011; Marceau et al., 2015; Rose, 2002; Rose et al., 2007). With this difference in mind, some researchers have argued that the classic notion of fight-or-flight as a response to stress actually doesn't fit women's coping strategies as well as it fits men's. Fight-or-flight is good if you're fighting a stressor solo, but not if you're fighting it with your family in tow, as women have more often found themselves throughout human history. These researchers argue that for women, *tend-and-befriend* may be a more accurate description of the fundamental coping response (Nickels et al., 2017; Tamres et al., 2002; Taylor, 2002, 2011b; Taylor et al., 2000b). According to the tend-and-befriend theory, evolution would have favored a coping response in women that favors cooperation rather than competition. It would incorporate their families, especially their kids, since women have typically been the primary caregivers. So, *tending* (or nurturing) relationships with children, and *befriending* (or enhancing

TABLE 11.4: Knowing Yourself: Stress Tips

Understand how you stress. What stress signs do you notice in yourself?
Identify your sources of stress. Who or what stresses you out?
Learn your own stress signals. Are they physical symptoms (like headache or muscle tension), mental symptoms (like anger or fatigue), or both?
Recognize how you deal with stress. Do you engage in unhealthy behaviors like overeating or smoking?
Find healthy ways to manage stress. Do you need to exercise, meditate, or talk it out?
Take care of yourself. Get enough sleep, good food, and water. Take breaks or vacations when possible. Make time for things you enjoy.
Reach out for support. Let friends, family, or a mental health professional help you through especially stressful times.

Information from the American Psychological Association (2007).

fizkes/Shutterstock

Coping strategies often differ across groups based on ethnicity, gender, or other variables. For example, women tend to cope with stress by talking about their feelings, but men tend to cope with stress by problem solving and avoiding discussion of emotion.

and using social connections, especially with other women) creates a safety net big enough to protect women and their children in times of high stress.

In my private practice, I have worked with numerous therapy clients who got laid off from their jobs. Sometimes, their responses have illustrated the gender differences in coping with stress. For Yolanda, I was probably the tenth person she had turned to for support, after her mom, her sisters, her cousins, and her friends. Support is what she wanted most from therapy — someone to listen, understand, and empathize. For Greg, I was the only person he had talked with about the layoff. He hadn't even told his closest family and friends. What he wanted most from his therapist was not emotional support but strategic advice on what actions to take to overcome his feelings of sadness and to secure a new job.

As illustrated previously, there is a wide range of coping strategies, especially among diverse populations. But psychologists have been studying coping strategies for decades, and collectively, their research offers some guidance for ideas that are likely to help you handle your own stress more effectively. **Table 11.4** offers a summary of tips from the American Psychological Association.

Decreasing Stress by Thinking Differently

Remember earlier in this chapter when we discussed *appraisal*? We defined it as the way you evaluate the things that happen to you. If you made a deliberate effort to change that evaluation, you might feel less stress. There is a form of psychotherapy, *cognitive therapy*, that is based on the notion of thinking about the things that happen to you in more realistic and logical ways (see Chapter 15 for more details) (Leahy, 2017). Actually, according to the two different types of appraisal, you have two opportunities to change the way you think about your stressors — how bad the stressor is (*primary appraisal*), and how capable you are to deal with it (*secondary appraisal*). Recall the example from earlier in the chapter — the two sales reps who get transferred to Chicago. One of them, Tyler, considered the stressors huge, focusing on lost friends, financial strain, and added job responsibilities. He also considered his ability to cope as weak, expecting that he'd crumble under the pressure. But what if Tyler's thoughts are more negative than they need to be? What if he instead believed that the stressors are tolerable, and that his coping ability is adequate? If he says to himself, "I might actually be OK in Chicago. I may lose some friends, but I'll meet a lot of new people too. Things might be tough financially for a while, but the new job gives me more earning potential. My supervisors wouldn't transfer me to this new position if they didn't think I could succeed." These thoughts might be more accurate than the thoughts that first popped into Tyler's head, and if he believes them, he may experience less unnecessary stress.

Mindfulness. A final way in which thinking differently can reduce your stress involves *mindfulness*. Mindfulness comes from the Buddhist tradition, but psychologists now often use it with no connection to religion at all. As we discussed in Chapter 4,

FROM RESEARCH TO REAL LIFE

Don't Stress Out about Stress

Stress may contribute to health problems, but *believing* that stress causes health problems can make those health problems much worse (Crum et al., 2013; Fischer et al., 2016; Jamieson et al., 2013). A huge study of over 28,000 people examined these two variables — how much stress a person has, and how strongly that person believed that stress affects health — and found that people who were high on both were in the worst shape. People with that combination had significantly higher rates of psychological problems, physical health problems, and even death, than those who had high stress but didn't believe that stress harmed their health. Specifically, those who thought stress affected their health "some" were about twice as likely to be in poor physical health, and those who thought stress affected their health "a lot" were about four times as likely to be in poor physical health compared to people who thought that their stress affected their health either hardly or not at all (Keller et al., 2012).

These results point to the tremendous value of thinking positively about stress. Viewing stress as a challenging opportunity or a chance to rise to the occasion, rather than unbeatable pressure that will inevitably harm you, is key. One study examined an intervention designed to change people's thinking in this positive direction. The researchers put people in a series of stressful situations, including delivering a speech in front of an audience of experts. Some of them were taught ahead of time by psychologists to interpret their stress response as "not harmful . . . and that increased arousal actually aids performance" (Jamieson et al., 2012, p. 418). Others were given no such instructions, or were told to distract themselves by thinking about something else when they felt stressed. Those who got the stress-is-helpful instructions responded to the stressors in a significantly healthier way. So, improving the way you think about stressors — including, perhaps most importantly, the stressor of stress itself — has the power to positively impact your well-being. •

mindfulness is awareness of your moment-to-moment experiences fully, deliberately, and without distraction. Mindfulness involves an increased acceptance of what's going on inside of you — your physical and psychological experiences — with an emphasis on just feeling it rather than analyzing it or avoiding it. People with high levels of mindfulness don't live on autopilot, numbly going through the motions of life. Instead, they actively pay attention to what's happening to them, with full engagement and acceptance of that experience. Whether they face joy or pain, they purposefully stay in touch with their emotions rather than repressing them or evading them (Hayes et al., 2011; Hick, 2008; Roemer & Orsillo, 2009; Shapiro, 2009a, b; Shapiro & Carlson, 2017).

Numerous studies have found that stress decreases as mindfulness increases. Many reviews and meta-analyses of these studies conclude that mindfulness-based therapies significantly reduce not only stress levels, but all kinds of mental and physical problems associated with stress, like depression, anxiety, chronic pain, and fibromyalgia (Alsubaie et al., 2017; Baer, 2003; Grossman et al., 2004; Koncz et al., 2021; Parsons et al., 2017; Zhou et al., 2020; see also Bohlmeijer et al., 2010, de Abreu Costa et al., 2018; Hoffman et al., 2010; Kiken et al., 2017; and Pascoe et al., 2017). Furthermore, these positive effects of mindfulness often last. One longitudinal study found that organ transplant recipients who received mindfulness training around the time of the transplant were lower in depression, anxiety, and insomnia 6 months later (Kreitzer et al., 2005). Another longitudinal study found that diabetic patients who received mindfulness training were significantly better both medically and psychologically a full year later compared to similar patients who didn't receive the training (Hartmann et al., 2012). So, evidence suggests that making a mindfulness-based change in your thinking can decrease stress and many of its consequences.

problem-focused coping
A style of coping with stress that emphasizes changing the stressor itself.

emotion-focused coping
A style of coping with stress that emphasizes changing your emotional reaction to the stressor.

Problem-Focused Coping and Emotion-Focused Coping. Changing the way we think also decreases stress if we make smart choices about focusing on the stressor itself or our inner reaction to it. Psychologists have names for these two approaches to coping: *problem-focused coping* and *emotion-focused coping*. **Problem-focused coping** is a style of coping with stress that emphasizes changing the stressor itself. This kind of coping involves tackling the problem head-on in an attempt to solve or minimize it (Carroll, 2013). By contrast, **emotion-focused coping** is a style of coping with stress that emphasizes changing your emotional reaction to the stressor (rather than changing the stressor itself). With emotion-focused coping, you basically accept the stressor as unchangeable, so you instead focus on changing the way you feel while facing it (Carver & Connor-Smith, 2010; Carver & Vargas, 2011; Folkman & Moskowitz, 2004). The key point here is that relying too much on only problem-focused coping or only emotion-focused coping can unnecessarily increase stress. By contrast, allowing yourself the flexibility to switch from one style of coping to the other can decrease stress (Carver, 2013; Gilbertson-White et al., 2017).

LIFE HACK 11.2

Both problem-focused coping (changing the stressor itself) and emotion-focused coping (changing how you feel about the stressor) can be beneficial. Try to use both types of coping, rather than relying too much on only one.

(Carver, 2013)

Switching between coping strategies works best when you consider how *controllable* the stressor is (Aldridge & Roesch, 2007; Austenfeld & Stanton, 2004; Clarke, 2006; Penley et al., 2002). Problem-focused coping tends to work best when the stressor is controllable. For example, let's say you're applying to college and the SAT or ACT is coming up. If you're stressed about the SAT or ACT, there are lots of things you can do about it. You can buy study guides, take a prep course, make a study schedule, search the Web for tips, take practice tests, or join a study group, among other things. Any of these problem-focused actions has the potential to change your impression of the SAT or ACT, from an overwhelming threat to a challenging opportunity. In problem-focused coping, the point is that you can take action to deal with the situation in a constructive way.

On the other hand, emotion-focused coping tends to work best when the stressor is not so controllable. For example, consider a situation that you will hopefully never have to encounter: a friend from high school dies in a car accident. In this situation, sadly, nothing can change the stressor. The worst has already happened. Your best strategy in terms of managing your stress would be to focus on your own feelings about the event. Some ways of managing those feelings could make this terrible situation more tolerable for you. Perhaps you'd benefit from talking about it with friends, family, or a therapist; or from journaling or blogging about your experience; or from offering kind words about your friend at the funeral; or from engaging in physical exercise to clear your mind. (Other attempts to manage your emotions might be less beneficial, such as drinking excessively, ruminating endlessly, or refusing to acknowledge that it happened at all.) The point here is that once the opportunity for controlling the stressor itself has passed, trying to control it would be futile and maybe even harmful. A better option is to accept it, but manage your feelings as well as possible.

Research indicates that this sequence — consider problem-focused coping first, then resort to emotion-focused coping if necessary — is in fact what people often do (Rothbaum et al., 1982). For example, one study took a close look at the kinds of coping strategies used by people struggling with rheumatoid arthritis. Researchers found that emotion-focused coping was over four times more likely to happen on days when the participants had also tried problem-focused coping. They also found that emotion-focused coping was much more common on days when the previous day featured problem-focused coping. Together, these findings suggest that emotion-focused coping is relatively uncommon as a first-line strategy, but much more common as a follow-up to problem-focused coping that didn't do much good (Tennen et al., 2000).

One more note on the controllability of stressors: when stress is *uncontrollable*, it is especially likely to be toxic, both physically and psychologically. In one study, participants received 30 brief, mild electric shocks to their forearms. Half of them decided for themselves when the shocks would happen (controllable stressor); for the other half, the researchers decided when (uncontrollable stressor). Even though the voltage was identical for both groups, the second group reported feeling significantly more intense pain (Müller, 2013). In another study, rats' tails were shocked in a way that they could learn to escape (controllable stressor) or that was inescapable (uncontrollable stressor). Although these shocks took place when the rats were adolescents, serious consequences lasted through adulthood. Specifically, adult rats who had experienced the controllable stressor demonstrated healthier patterns of brain growth throughout their lives. Also, those rats that had experienced the controllable stressor as adolescents were more resilient in the face of uncontrollable stressors when they eventually experienced them as adults (Kubala et al., 2012).

social support
The relationships one has with friends, family, and others that can be beneficial when experiencing stress.

Decreasing Stress by Improving Relationships

Generally speaking, if the quality of the important relationships in your life is poor — if you're in conflict with your family and friends, or if they've rejected you altogether — your stress level will be high. In fact, researchers have found that prolonged social isolation, or *loneliness*, is one of the most toxic stressors of all, often producing serious physical and psychological health problems (Brown et al., 2018; Cacioppo et al., 2003; Cohen, 2004; Courtin & Knapp, 2017; Holt-Lunstad et al., 2015; Segrin et al., 2018). One study found that widows who were socially isolated were significantly more likely to develop heart disease than widows who were well-connected with others (Sorkin et al., 2002). Another study found that a flu shot given to lonely first-year college students produced far fewer antibodies (and was therefore much less effective) than the same shot in first-year college students with more friends (Pressman et al., 2005). A study of about 2000 Americans conducted May 2020, when the social distancing efforts of the COVID-19 pandemic were in full effect, found that those efforts may have contributed to higher levels of loneliness. Specifically, levels of loneliness at that time were significantly higher than they had been in the same participants pre-pandemic in 2018 (Philpot et al., 2021).

CHAPTER APP 11.2

The Mighty

The Mighty app is designed to help people give and receive social support for health-related stressors they share. Users choose an issue for which they want support, which can be a psychological disorder (depression, anxiety, etc.), a physical disease (cancer, COVID, rare diseases, etc.), or a challenging experience (sleep problems, relationship problems, parenting problems, etc.). The Mighty then suggests groups for the user to join where they can share thoughts, feelings, and support with others who have been through the same thing.

How does it APPly to your daily life?
If you or a loved one were struggling with a health-related stressor, in which ways could an app like The Mighty be beneficial? What kinds of social support would you expect to find most and least valuable?

How does it APPly to your understanding of psychology?
How can The Mighty app help you understand the concept of social support, and its three specific types: informational social support, instrumental social support, and emotional social support?

To learn more about this app or to download it to your phone, you can search for "The Mighty" on Google, in the iPhone App store, or in the Google Play store.

DIVERSITY MATTERS A number of diversity variables may influence the chances that a person experiences loneliness. One large-scale study measured loneliness in over 46,000 participants living in 237 countries. Its results showed that loneliness happened more frequently in men than in women, in younger adults than in older adults, and in people from individualistic cultures than in people from collectivistic cultures. In combination, those results suggest that young men in individualistic cultures may be especially vulnerable to loneliness (Barreto et al., 2021).

Simply put, staying connected to other people is vitally important to your emotional and physical health. Psychologists call these connections with others **social support**: the relationships you have with friends, family, and others that can benefit you when you experience stress. Social support can take many forms, but it is often categorized in three ways (Taylor, 2011b):

- *Informational social support* occurs when you gain knowledge or understanding from your family and friends. For example, consider Molly, a young adult stressed out about doing her own taxes for the first time. She calls her uncle, her big sister, and her older friend Angelina for help. Collectively, they tell her all kinds of things: what forms need to be filled out, what counts as a deduction for her, how much help TurboTax or H&R Block might be able to provide, and more. After those conversations, doing her taxes is no longer the major stressor that Molly first thought it was. It is a chore, but one she can manage without too much worry because of the new information she picked up.
- *Instrumental social support* occurs when you gain something more tangible from your family and friends. For example, let's imagine that Molly loses her job. Informational social support might be helpful (where to find another job, advice on writing a résumé, etc.), but she has more pressing needs right now: a place to live, food to eat, and money to spend on necessities. If her friend Angelina loans Molly some cash and lets her crash at her place for a few weeks, just until Molly can get back on her feet, Angelina will have provided vital instrumental social support.
- *Emotional social support* occurs when you receive warmth, reassurance, or other expressions of feeling from friends and family. If Angelina offered Molly money and a place to stay, but was completely unfriendly and indifferent about doing so, her social support would be incomplete. If, however, she did what good friends do—provide help not only in the form of stuff, but also in the form of compassion, kindness, and encouragement—she would be supplying Molly with valuable emotional social support.

Many studies illustrate the tremendous benefits of social support. Regarding physical health, a high level of social support has been linked to lower risk of heart attack, susceptibility to viruses, diabetes complications, pregnancy problems, and many other conditions (Heinze et al., 2015; Schwarzer & Leppin, 1991; Taylor, 2011b; Uchino, 2006). A high level of social support also has been shown to slow the progression of diseases after they have been diagnosed, such as HIV and breast cancer (Friedman et al., 2017; Leserman et al., 1999; Leung et al., 2014). One study focused on a particular way of providing social support: hugs. Researchers asked 400 adults to track the number of hugs they received over a 2-week period. Then, the researchers exposed those adults to a virus that causes the common cold. Participants who received more hugs were less likely to catch a cold, and for participants who did, those who had received more hugs had less severe symptoms (Cohen et al., 2015).

Motortion Films/Shutterstock

Social support—your relationships with friends, family, and others—provides an important buffer from stress and its harmful effects.

Perhaps the most striking studies on social support and physical health are the longitudinal studies that follow patients for years or decades, which typically find that social support extends the life span. People with continuously high levels of social support are significantly less likely to die early, while continuously low levels of social support predict early death as strongly as chronic health problems like smoking, obesity, or high blood pressure (Herbst-Damm & Kulik, 2005; House et al., 1988; Olaya et al., 2017; Rutledge et al., 2004; Seeman, 1996). Regarding mental health, social support has been found to be a powerful buffer from depression, anxiety, eating disorders, and many other psychological problems (Ginter et al., 1994; Hakulinen et al., 2016; Rueger et al., 2010, 2016; Stice, 2002; Stice et al., 2004; Tiller et al., 1997).

LIFE HACK 11.3

Take advantage of available social support when you are stressed out. Research strongly suggests that your relationships with friends and family can protect your emotional and physical well-being when stress levels are high.

(Rueger et al., 2010; Stice, 2002; Stice et al., 2004; Taylor, 2011b; Uchino, 2006)

Women tend to be more involved in social support (especially emotional social support) than men, both as givers and takers in times of stress (Tamres et al., 2002; Taylor, 2011a; Taylor et al., 2000b). One interesting study followed college students who stayed in their mostly empty residence halls through the entire winter break—an experience likely to create feelings of loneliness. The researchers found that many students did in fact get lonely, but those who experienced the least loneliness were the ones who had the most contact with women. The gender of the participants didn't matter, and it didn't matter how much contact they had with men. Only contact with women was related to a reduction in loneliness, suggesting that many women may have a way of generating social support that is uniquely effective in helping others get through stressful situations (Wheeler et al., 1983). Also, social support may have more of an effect on women's health than men's health (Elliot et al., 2018; Milner et al., 2016). One meta-analysis found that the correlation between social support and health is positive for all of us, but it is stronger for women (.20) than for men (.08) (Schwarzer & Leppin, 1991).

DIVERSITY MATTERS In many cultural groups, social support is built into the values that form the foundation of the culture. For example, *familismo* is a value often identified as a cornerstone of Latinx culture. Familismo involves an emphasis on loyalty and closeness among family members, such that family takes priority over individual interests and its members provide mutually supportive relationships. Variations of familismo exist in other cultures, too. For example, in many Asian cultures, the value of *filial piety* promotes interconnectedness and support among family members, especially from children to parents.

Research on familismo suggests that the high levels of social support it provides are indeed beneficial (Campos et al., 2014).One meta-analysis that combined the results of 39 studies found that high levels of familismo corresponded to lower levels of depression, suicidal thinking, and anxiety (Valdivieso-Mora et al., 2016). A more recent study of ninth-grade adolescents who are Latinx found that those with higher levels of familismo experienced fewer depressive symptoms, and that their familismo helped to buffer the stressful effects of financial hardship (Montoro & Ceballo, 2021).

The takeaway message of this section is that stress is not something you need to endure alone. The better your relationships with other people, in terms of both quantity and quality, the better your chances of withstanding stressful situations.

Decreasing Stress by Behaving Differently

There is no substitute for action in the struggle to minimize stress. *Early* action is especially important – the kind of action you take when you anticipate problems before they happen and take measures to prevent them or minimize their impact.

Proactive Coping. When we cope with stressors in a forward-looking way, psychologists call it **proactive coping**: a coping style that focuses on future goals and the stressors that could get in the way of them. The major advantage to proactive coping is that it targets stressors that haven't happened yet. That gives you the chance to either avoid them or prepare for them, either of which can be a more effective strategy than waiting for the stressor to happen (Aspinwall, 1997, 2003, 2005, 2011). Proactive coping means that addressing future problems now takes much less time and effort than waiting for them to arrive (Aspinwall & Taylor, 1997). One study of college students found that those who use more proactive coping tend to experience less stress and self-blame (Straud & McNaughton-Cassill, 2018).

To illustrate proactive coping, consider Isabella, a young woman who just found out that she is expecting her first baby. Isabella is a planner. Within hours of the positive pregnancy test, Isabella started thinking about the stressors she would soon face, and what she could do about them in advance. In fact, the first thing Isabella did was read a couple of pregnancy books that helped her know what to expect. Those books, plus some advice from friends, relatives, and Web sites, provided Isabella with enough information to make a list of pregnancy-related stressors and baby-related stressors. The list included getting maternity clothes, getting baby furniture, finding a pediatrician, and arranging her maternity leave with her employer. At first, the list seemed overwhelming, but Isabella tackled these tasks one by one, *ahead of time*. She borrowed some maternity clothes from her sister and bought some more online; she picked up a gently used crib and changing table from some neighbors whose kids had outgrown them; she selected a pediatrician based on friends' recommendations; and she made specific plans with her boss about taking time off from work.

By contrast, consider Isabella's cousin, Julia, who got pregnant around the same time as Isabella. Julia knows that pregnancies and babies come with plenty of stressors, but she figures she'll deal with them as they come up. She has always responded well "on the fly" to other challenging situations, and she is confident that she can do the same as she moves through her pregnancy. She might be right, but think of the stress that Julia will face as she makes last-minute, high-pressure decisions. A proactive coping style could make Julia's experience less stressful.

Proactive coping can certainly have disadvantages, especially if you take it too far. For example, if you worry too much about things that probably won't happen and probably won't be a big deal even if they do, then you can cause yourself more work than necessary (Newby-Clark, 2004). Also, if you're too public about your proactive coping efforts, you run the risk of annoying other people (Ashford et al., 2003; Grant & Ashford, 2008). But overall, a healthy amount of proactive coping has more upside than downside. That is, a little stress now can save a lot of stress later.

Hardiness and Optimism. Sometimes, there are stressors you can't anticipate, so there's no way for proactive coping to help. In such situations, it can be beneficial to respond with **hardiness**: behaviors that reflect resilience under stressful circumstances. Hardy people welcome stress. They see it as an opportunity for improvement and success rather than failure and pain. Hardiness is closely related to the concepts of *posttraumatic growth* and *eustress* that we discussed earlier in the chapter. Hardiness has three key ingredients, known by psychologists as the "three C's" – commitment, controlling, and challenge (Maddi, 2002; Maddi & Harvey, 2006; Maddi & Kobasa, 1984; Ouellette & DiPlacido, 2001):

- A *commitment* to staying involved in a tough situation even when it gets stressful, as opposed to looking for an easy escape (or "bailing out").

proactive coping
A style of coping that focuses on future goals and the stressors that could get in the way of them.

hardiness
Behaviors that reflect resilience under stressful circumstances.

- *Controlling* the situation as much as possible and exerting whatever influence you can, rather than being passive.
- Seeing a stressor as a *challenge* to face courageously rather than a threat to be avoided fearfully.

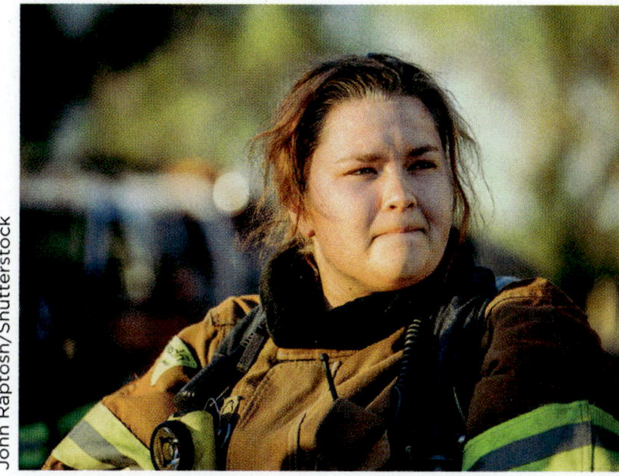
John Raptosh/Shutterstock

Hardiness is a set of behaviors that reflect resilience under stressful circumstances. Hardy people tend to see stress as an opportunity for success rather than a threat of failure.

Studies have found that high levels of hardiness correlate with low levels of stress in people experiencing many serious stressors, including parents whose children have cancer, military veterans going through or returning from active duty, West Point cadets undergoing military training, and former prisoners of war readjusting to freedom (Bartone et al., 2017; Maddi et al., 2017; Stoppelbien et al., 2017; Thomassen et al., 2018; Zerach et al., 2017). Fortunately, hardiness is not something you are simply born with or without – it can be cultivated. When you face stressors, you can make deliberate efforts to respond with hardy behaviors. In fact, psychologists have successfully used hardiness training to improve this ability in clients (Bartone et al., 2016; Khoshaba & Maddi, 2001; Maddi, 1987, 2017; Maddi et al., 2002; Stein & Bartone, 2020).

As an example of hardiness, consider this situation: due to a mix-up in the campus housing office, Kelvin, a college sophomore living on campus, is placed in a suite with three other students even though he requested a single room. At first, Kelvin might react with frustration, look for ways out of the situation, or experience overwhelming anxiety about getting along with three new roommates. But if Kelvin can respond with more hardiness, he might realize that he has the opportunity to turn this mix-up into a blessing in disguise. He can give his suitemates a chance and do his best to build friendships with them rather than just seeing what happens. He can remind himself that he's resilient and flexible enough to handle this situation. All the while, he can keep in mind the best possible outcome of this surprise situation: new friends and an enjoyable year living together, when he otherwise would have been living alone. Such a hardy attitude will not guarantee Kelvin a great outcome, but it certainly increases the likelihood that his stress levels will stay low.

Many of us showed an impressive level of hardiness during the COVID pandemic. One study found that while 89% of Americans reported that the pandemic had a negative impact on their lives, 73% of those Americans reported that the pandemic also had a *positive* impact on their lives. Specifically, 33% reported that their relationships improved; 26% reported that how they spend their free time improved; 14% reported that their health improved; and 13% reported that their jobs improved (van Kessel et al., 2020). It's important to note that many of those positive changes didn't just happen to us – instead, we *made* them happen, thanks to hardiness. Many of us deliberately worked on staying close to the people in our lives (perhaps with lots of Zoom calls), intentionally started or stuck to an exercise plan, or creatively made job-related changes for the better.

Related to hardiness is **optimism**: an attitude toward the future characterized by hope or expectation of a positive outcome. Like hardiness, optimism buffers us from stress (Archana & Kumar, 2016; Kim et al., 2017; Scheier & Carver, 2018; Seligman, 1991). One study of college students found a strongly negative correlation between participants' optimism levels and the extent to which they experienced about 40 physical symptoms of various kinds. The more optimistic they were, the less they were bothered by all kinds of headaches, stomachaches, fatigue, aches, and pains (Scheier & Carver, 1985). Another study of residents of Mississippi and Alabama who lived through the 2011 tornado outbreak (one of the costliest and deadliest natural disaster events in U.S. history) found that those with higher levels of optimism experienced significantly fewer symptoms of PTSD and other mental health problems (Carbone & Echols, 2017). Additional studies have come to similar conclusions about the power of optimism to minimize stress and its negative effects for a wide range of potentially stressful situations – including starting college, caring for a relative with Alzheimer's disease, having a newborn baby, and battling diseases like cancer, arthritis, asthma, and AIDS (Carver & Scheier, 2017; Segerstrom et al., 1998; Segerstrom & Miller, 2004). Optimism is a key part of the recent movement toward *positive psychology*, a perspective in psychology that emphasizes people's strengths and successes. Such an emphasis

optimism
An attitude toward the future characterized by hope or expectation of a positive outcome.

michaeljung/iStock/Getty Images

Optimistic people look toward the future with hope and an expectation of a positive outcome. Research has repeatedly found that optimism reduces stress.

(including optimism as well as other aspects of a positive outlook) has been linked to high levels of overall physical health (Boehm & Kubzansky, 2012; Gable & Haidt, 2005; Kok et al., 2013; Taylor et al., 2000a; Wright, 2017).

Many people assume that anyone who has high levels of optimism automatically has low levels of pessimism (an attitude toward the future characterized by hopelessness or expectation of a negative outcome). But the authors of one interesting study challenged that assumption. They combined the results of over 60 studies that measured both optimism and pessimism in their participants, along with the participants' physical health. As expected, they found that the presence of optimism was strongly correlated with good physical health. But they also found that the absence of pessimism was *more* strongly correlated with good physical health (Scheier et al., 2021). So, if you want to adjust your attitude in a way that improves your physical health, you may have better results by decreasing your pessimistic thoughts than by increasing your optimistic thoughts.

As good as optimism is for fending off stress, hardiness may be even better. Both optimistic people and hardy people share a positive outlook even when the future seems bleak, but hardy people tend to work more actively to make that outlook a reality (Maddi & Hightower, 1999). For example, consider Inez and Thomas, two restaurant servers who lose their jobs when their restaurant goes out of business. Inez is an optimist, so she truly believes that "things will work out – I'm sure another job will come along." Thomas is hardy, so he *works* to make sure that things work out and the other job comes along – he checks the online job ads and sends out his résumé more often than Inez does. Of course, there is no reason why optimism and hardiness can't go hand in hand. Expecting a positive outcome *and* working to make it happen may be the best strategy for keeping your stress at bay.

CHECK YOUR LEARNING:

11.16 How do psychologists define coping?

11.17 How do coping styles differ by ethnicity and gender?

11.18 What is the difference between problem-focused coping and emotion-focused coping?

11.19 How can mindfulness influence stress levels?

11.20 How can different types of social support be categorized, and what role does social support play in emotional and physical health?

11.21 What kinds of changes in thinking and behavior can decrease stress?

To check your understanding of these questions, click show the answers or refer to the answers in the Chapter Summary.

Coping with Stress: Physical Strategies and Medical Strategies

YOU WILL LEARN:

11.22 about the stages of change model.

11.23 how to decrease stress with exercise.

11.24 how to decrease stress with medicine and healing techniques.

Taking care of your body is essential for reducing stress and maintaining physical and mental health. Most of us know that getting enough sleep, eating healthy, and exercising are important for reducing stress, but only *half* of us actually do these self-care behaviors at a "very good" or "excellent" level (American Psychological Association, 2014a). (For more details, see **Figure 11.5**.)

Why don't people take better physical care of themselves even though they know it would decrease their stress?

There are plenty of real-world reasons: we don't have enough time to exercise, healthy food is too expensive or inconvenient, or busy schedules rob us of sleep. But another reason may be that our minds are just not ready to commit to those kinds of lifestyle changes. The *stages of change model* is a way that psychologists think about that readiness to make big changes. It is widely accepted by psychologists who focus on health-related issues, and it includes five specific stages that identify how ready someone might be to make major life improvements (DiClemente & Prochaska, 1982; Mauriello et al., 2017; Prochaska et al., 1992; Prochaska & Velicer, 1997; Schwarzer, 2011). **Table 11.5** lists those five stages of change, which basically range from "not even on my radar" to "I've made the change and I want to keep it that way." Research shows that when trying to help someone make major lifestyle changes in diet, exercise, or other health-related behaviors, tailoring efforts to a person's current stage of change is often helpful (Krebs et al., 2018; Noar et al., 2007). For example, an extremely overweight friend not thinking about exercise is at Stage 1 (not even on their radar). The most beneficial action may be to move them to Stage 2 (starting to think about exercise) rather than trying to push them immediately to Stage 4 (taking action, or committing to an exercise schedule).

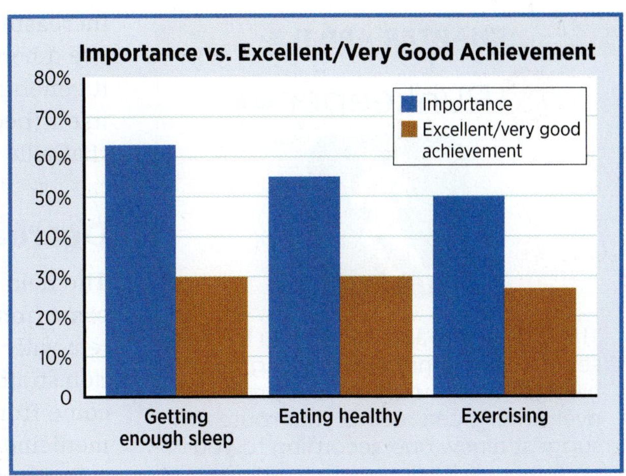

FIGURE 11.5 What We Know Versus What We Do about Managing Stress. Regarding the stress-reducing behaviors of sufficient sleep, healthy eating, and exercising, more of us understand their importance than actually do the behaviors consistently. Data from the American Psychological Association (2014a).

Decreasing Stress with Exercise

Exercising reduces stress and the health risks associated with it (Crews & Landers, 1987; Edenfield & Blumenthal, 2011; Puterman et al., 2018; Wang et al., 2014). Particularly beneficial is **aerobic exercise**: physical exercise that maintains an increased heart rate for a prolonged time. Aerobic exercise brings oxygen to the muscles (*aero-* means air or oxygen). Examples include running, walking, hiking, swimming, cycling, rowing, jumping rope, and using an elliptical training machine.

aerobic exercise
Physical exercise that maintains an increased heart rate for a prolonged time.

If you think back to the fight-or-flight roots of the stress response, the benefits of aerobic exercise make a lot of sense. The "flight" impulse in particular matches your behavior when you run, bike, swim, or otherwise put your body in continuous motion. (Boxing or MMA forms of exercise probably match the "fight" impulse as well.) This may explain why studies have found that exercise has both immediate and long-term benefits. So, if you look at the big timeline, running several times a week will help you maintain a low stress level over time. But if you zoom in on a more specific point in time, running when you wake up tomorrow will help you feel less stressed through the morning (Forcier et al., 2006; Hamer et al., 2006).

Of course, there is such a thing as too much aerobic exercise (Ishikawa-Takata et al., 2003; La Gerche & Prior, 2007). There is no formula for how much is right for everyone in terms of health benefits and stress reduction. Your exercise habits should be customized to your current fitness and health levels. In the United States, with its

According to the stages of change model, people move through a series of stages in terms of their readiness to make health-related changes in their lives. Matching efforts to help with the person's current stage makes a big difference.

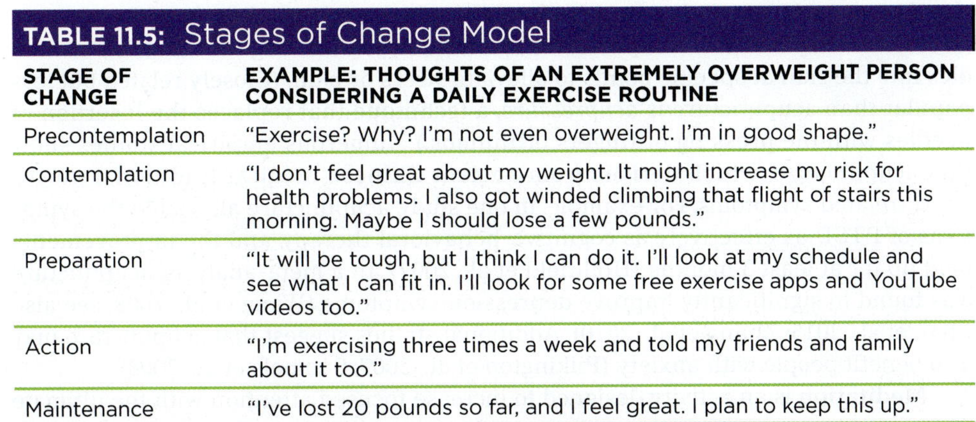
TABLE 11.5: Stages of Change Model

STAGE OF CHANGE	EXAMPLE: THOUGHTS OF AN EXTREMELY OVERWEIGHT PERSON CONSIDERING A DAILY EXERCISE ROUTINE
Precontemplation	"Exercise? Why? I'm not even overweight. I'm in good shape."
Contemplation	"I don't feel great about my weight. It might increase my risk for health problems. I also got winded climbing that flight of stairs this morning. Maybe I should lose a few pounds."
Preparation	"It will be tough, but I think I can do it. I'll look at my schedule and see what I can fit in. I'll look for some free exercise apps and YouTube videos too."
Action	"I'm exercising three times a week and told my friends and family about it too."
Maintenance	"I've lost 20 pounds so far, and I feel great. I plan to keep this up."

Information from Prochaska and Velicer (1997), DiClemente and Prochaska (1982), Prochaska et al. (1992), Schwarzer (2011), and Krebs et al. (2018).

CHAPTER APP 11.3

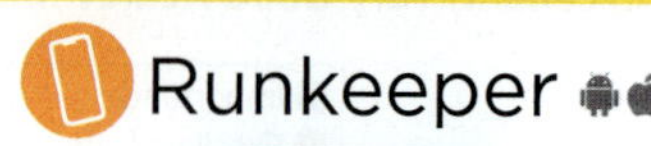

The Runkeeper app allows you to set specific running (or walking, or hiking) goals and track your progress over time. It can record your route or suggest a new one according to your preferences. It allows you to share your running achievements on social media, and even tracks your running speed according to the song playing on your phone at the time (in case you want to see which song made you pick up the pace).

How does it APPly to your daily life?
Exercise is a powerful way to decrease stress and maintain health. How can apps like this one influence the amount of exercise you get? How would you improve upon the features of this app?

How does it APPly to your understanding of psychology?
How does this app help you understand *aerobic exercise* and its benefits? Also, since there can be too much exercise, what's the best way to use this app to decrease rather increase stress?

To learn more about this app or to download it to your phone, you can search for "Runkeeper" on Google, in the iPhone App store, or in the Google Play store.

increasingly sedentary lifestyle (in other words, we sit too much), many of us could use a boost in our exercise levels. In terms of stress, exercise becomes too much if it generates more stress than it relieves. If your exercise routine becomes a stressor itself (because of pressure or competition), it may be time to take it down a notch (LaCaille & Taylor, 2013).

Decreasing Stress with Medical and Healing Techniques

The field of medicine offers countless suggestions for stress reduction. Many of them come from *conventional medicine* — basically, the mainstream Western health care system with its doctors, nurses, and hospitals. But an increasing number of stress reduction strategies have their origins outside of that system. In some cases, these strategies come from **complementary medicine**: health care that complements conventional medicine. In other cases, these strategies come from **alternative medicine**: health care that is used instead of conventional medicine. Together, complementary medicine and alternative medicine are often called *CAM* (*c*omplementary and *a*lternative *m*edicine). When the best of CAM is combined with the best of conventional medicine, the term *integrative medicine* is often used.

In recent years, mainstream U.S. culture has embraced CAM to a greater extent than ever before. Most U.S. medical schools offer CAM courses as electives, and about a quarter require CAM courses (Jacobs & Gundling, 2009). Rates of CAM usage among cancer patients range between 40% and 85% (Bardia et al., 2009; Ebel et al., 2015). About 60% of HIV patients use CAM, as do about 51% of patients with diabetes, 36% of patients with cardiovascular disease, and 41% of patients with lower back pain (Alzahrani et al., 2021; Bloedon & Szapary, 2009; Ghildayal et al., 2016; Tokumoto, 2009). Large-scale surveys of tens of thousands of U.S. adults found that 36–38% had used some form of CAM in the past year (excluding prayer, which is sometimes included in such studies as a CAM), mostly for common problems like colds, neck pain, joint pain, sinus problems, asthma, and hypertension. Those who were most likely to use CAM were women, highly educated, middle-aged, open-minded, and living in cities; the most likely users were confident that CAM would be safe and helpful, and dissatisfied with conventional medicine (Barnes et al., 2004, 2007; Galbraith et al., 2018; Harris et al., 2012; Tangkiatkumjai et al., 2021). Studies of college students have found their usage of CAM in the previous year to be much higher than that of the general public (Nguyen et al., 2016; Nowack & Hale, 2012; Nowack et al., 2015).

Generally, CAM is more prevention-based than conventional medicine. It also tends to emphasize the idea that what underlies most illness (and stress) is an imbalance among certain energies or bodily regions, as opposed to the conventional view emphasizing malfunction at the cellular, biochemical, or molecular level (Chiappelli, 2012; Ernst et al., 2006; Micozzi, 2011).

Some of the most common specific CAM practices — *acupuncture, meditation, homeopathic medicine*, and *biofeedback* — are each used for a wide range of stress-related problems. **Acupuncture** is a technique involving the insertion of needles into the skin at specific points to alleviate stress or pain. (Closely related but less popular than acupuncture is *acupressure*, a technique that replaces the insertion of needles with the pressing of fingers or thumbs.) Numerous empirical studies show that acupuncture, which derives from ancient Chinese medical tradition, reduces stress-related symptoms. For example, in one study, acupuncture alleviated the symptoms of PTSD as effectively as cognitive-behavioral therapy, and the improvements held up for at least 3 months (Hollifield et al., 2007). In a meta-analysis, acupuncture was found to significantly improve depression symptoms (Wang et al., 2008; see also Chan et al., 2015; Zhang et al., 2010). Additional studies suggest that acupuncture may also benefit people with anxiety (Pilkington et al., 2007; Samuels et al., 2008).

Meditation is an activity designed to increase focused attention with the ultimate purpose of improving your mental state. Like acupuncture, meditation originates in Eastern spiritual practice but is now often practiced in the West without a specific

complementary medicine
Health care that complements, or is used along with, conventional medicine.

alternative medicine
Health care that is used instead of conventional medicine.

acupuncture
A technique involving the insertion of needles into the skin at specific points to alleviate stress or pain.

meditation
An activity designed to increase focused attention with the ultimate purpose of improving your mental state.

religious emphasis. Meditation takes many forms, but two of the most common are *concentrative meditation* and *mindfulness meditation*. Concentrative meditation involves a focus on a single stimulus, often coming from within the person (breathing patterns, a repeated sound, etc.). *Mindfulness meditation* involves increased attention to all stimuli in the internal and external environment (Shapiro, 2009a). (Mindfulness meditation obviously shares an emphasis with the mindfulness-based thinking described a earlier in this chapter.) When practiced on a regular basis, meditation lowers stress and the risk of stress-related problems, including anxiety and depression (Beauchamp-Turner & Levinson, 1992; Blanck et al., 2018; Goyal et al., 2014; MacLean et al., 1997; Oman et al., 2008; Walsh & Shapiro, 2006). Studies have found that meditating on a regular basis increases the immune system's ability to battle diseases ranging from the flu to cancer, and promotes healthy aging (Carlson et al., 2003; Conklin et al., 2018; Davidson et al., 2003). One study focused specifically on 91 full-time teachers in elementary, middle, or high schools – a population for whom high stress levels are notoriously common. Its primary finding was that teachers' stress levels dropped significantly when they started practicing meditation, even just twice a week for 20 minutes per session (Anderson et al., 1999).

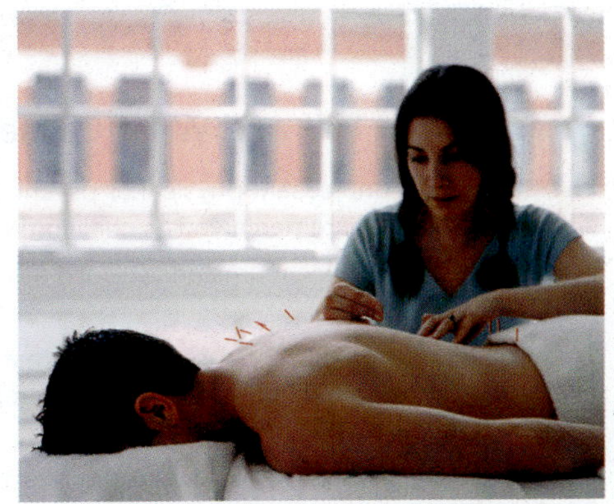

Creatas/Getty Images

An increasing number of people consider complementary medicine or alternative medicine to reduce stress. A common example of these approaches is acupuncture, a technique involving the insertion of needles into the skin at specific points to alleviate stress or pain.

Homeopathic medicine is health care based on the idea that the human body has the ability to heal itself and characterized by low-dose medications made from natural sources. Homeopathic medicine has been practiced in European countries for hundreds of years but is still considered outside of the mainstream by many in the United States. Homeopathic medicine presumes that your body doesn't need medication made of synthesized ingredients or in large doses, as is common in conventional medicine. (In fact, such medication could worsen your health, according to the homeopathic approach.) Instead, homeopathic medicine believes that your body has an impressive and often underestimated ability to fix itself, but it may need just a little "nudge" from a small dose of a medicine (often made from a plant or mineral) to kick-start the healing process. Advocates of homeopathic medicine believe in it strongly, but there is little empirical evidence that homeopathic medicine improves stress levels and related conditions (Davidson et al., 2011; Pilkington et al., 2006). Also, there is some criticism stating that its benefits are due primarily to the *placebo effect*, or mere expectations of benefit rather than any actual healing properties of the homeopathic medicine (Shang et al., 2005; Smith, 2012).

Biofeedback is using a monitor to see information about your physiological functions (like heartbeat or muscle tension), with the intention of influencing those functions in a healthy direction. If you've ever checked your own heart rate while exercising (with a smartphone app, or with the metal sensors on the handles of the treadmill, or even with your finger on your pulse), you have an understanding of biofeedback. For people with stress-related conditions like cardiovascular disease, biofeedback can be an important tool, primarily because knowing your heart rate in real time is the first step to controlling it. Biofeedback allows people to see or hear what their heart is doing (through a graph on a screen, or beeps from the machine), which can prompt them to do something to change it. That "something" might be slowing their breathing, using visual imagery, or taking another deliberate action to bring down a dangerously high heart rate (Khazan, 2013; Schwartz & Andrasik, 2005). Research on the stress-related benefits of biofeedback has been sparse, especially in recent decades, but there are at least a few small-scale supportive studies (Leahy et al., 1997; Reiner, 2008; Teufel et al., 2013).

homeopathic medicine
Health care based on the idea that the human body has the ability to heal itself and characterized by very low-dose medications made from natural sources.

biofeedback
Use of a monitor that provides information about physiological functions (like heartbeat or muscle tension), with the intention of influencing those functions in a healthy direction.

CHECK YOUR LEARNING:

11.22 What are the stages in the stages of change model, and how does this model relate to stress reduction efforts?

11.23 What effect does exercise have on stress?

11.24 What are some techniques of complementary medicine and alternative medicine that can decrease stress?

To check your understanding of these questions, click show the answers or refer to the answers in the Chapter Summary.

CHAPTER SUMMARY

Stress: What Is It and What Causes It?

11.1 Stress is an unpleasant physical or psychological reaction to circumstances that are perceived as challenging.

11.2 Stressors are the circumstances, such as events or changes in your life, that cause stress.

11.3 The fight-or-flight response is an automatic emotional and physical reaction to a perceived threat that prepares you to either attack or run away.

11.4 Appraisal is how you evaluate the things that happen to you. Primary appraisal determines how stressful the event is, and secondary appraisal determines how capable you are to handle it.

11.5 Hassles are the minor annoyances or aggravations of day-to-day life that add up to cause significant stress.

Stress and the Mind–Body Connection

11.6 Both the body and the mind suffer the consequences of stress. The relationship between the body and the mind is bidirectional.

11.7 The general adaptation syndrome is a widely accepted understanding of the way bodies respond to ongoing stress, consisting of the sequence of alarm, resistance, and exhaustion.

11.8 Stress can wear down a person's immune system, which defends the body against bacteria, viruses, infections, injuries, and anything else that could cause illness or death.

11.9 People with Type A personality, who are competitive, driven, and hostile, experience more stress-related health consequences than people with Type B personality, who are noncompetitive, easygoing, and relaxed.

11.10 People with high levels of the personality traits conscientiousness and extraversion tend to experience less stress, while people with high levels of the personality trait neuroticism tend to experience more stress.

11.11 Stress can contribute to almost any psychological disorder. And stress is the basis of several psychological disorders, including posttraumatic stress disorder, acute stress disorder, adjustment disorder, and prolonged grief disorder.

11.12 Stress levels rose for many people during the COVID pandemic, but many people also showed an impressive level of resilience.

Stress and Diversity

11.13 People of different genders often experience different types of stressors and get stressed out about different things. Men and women tend to react differently to the same stressor, with women often appraising stressors as more severe than men do.

11.14 Minority or immigrant groups in the United States are more likely to face certain real-world stressors than people in the majority. People from collectivistic and individualistic cultures often have different experiences of stress.

11.15 In mainstream U.S. culture, different sources of stress are more likely to impact people at various life stages.

Coping with Stress: Psychological Strategies and Social Strategies

11.16 Coping is any effort to reduce or manage the experience of stress.

11.17 People from collectivistic ethnicities tend to cope by changing things within themselves (like their own thoughts and feelings), while people from individualistic ethnicities tend to cope by changing things outside of themselves (like the stressor itself). Women tend to cope by talking with others about their feelings, while men tend to cope by problem solving and by not discussing their emotions.

11.18 Problem-focused coping emphasizes changing the stressor itself, while emotion-focused coping emphasizes changing one's emotional reaction to the stressor.

11.19 Practicing mindfulness can reduce stress through an increased awareness of moment-to-moment physical and psychological experiences.

11.20 Social support is often categorized in three ways—informational, instrumental, and emotional—and it is important to both emotional and physical health.

11.21 People can decrease stress through positive ways of thinking and behaving such as proactive coping, hardiness, and optimism.

Coping with Stress: Physical Strategies and Medical Strategies

11.22 The stages of change model—which includes precontemplation, contemplation, preparation, action, and maintenance—can explain why people don't always do things that would likely reduce stress.

11.23 Exercise, particularly aerobic exercise, reduces stress and the health risks associated with it.

11.24 Complementary medicine and alternative medicine offer a variety of techniques to decrease stress, including acupuncture, meditation, homeopathic medicine, and biofeedback.

KEY TERMS

stress, p. 370
fight-or-flight response, p. 370
stressor, p. 371
appraisal, p. 372
primary appraisal, p. 372
secondary appraisal, p. 372
hassles, p. 373
general adaptation syndrome, p. 374
immune system, p. 375
psychoneuroimmunology (PNI), p. 375
psychophysiological illnesses, p. 375
coronary heart disease, p. 375

Type A personality, p. 377
Type B personality, p. 378
Type C personality, p. 378
Type D personality, p. 378
posttraumatic stress disorder (PTSD), p. 380
acute stress disorder, p. 381
adjustment disorder, p. 381
prolonged grief disorder, p. 382
posttraumatic growth, p. 382
coping, p. 388
problem-focused coping, p. 390
emotion-focused coping, p. 390
social support, p. 392
proactive coping, p. 394
hardiness, p. 394
optimism, p. 395
aerobic exercise, p. 397
complementary medicine, p. 398
alternative medicine, p. 398
acupuncture, p. 398
meditation, p. 398
homeopathic medicine, p. 399
biofeedback, p. 399

SELF-ASSESSMENT

1. Vanessa is about to give a speech to a large group of people. The unpleasant feeling Vanessa has about giving the speech is ____, while the speech itself is ____.

a. stress; appraisal
b. a stressor; stress
c. stress; a stressor
d. coping; stress

2. ____ is determining how stressful an event is. ____ is determining how capable you are to cope with the stressful event.

3. Isaiah is noncompetitive, easygoing, relaxed, and rarely angry. Which of these personality types best describes him?

a. Type A personality
b. Type B personality
c. Type C personality
d. Type D personality

4. People whose personalities feature high levels of ____ tend to experience less stress.

a. anxiety
b. extraversion
c. neuroticism
d. isolation

5. ____ occurs when people experience trauma but find a way to benefit, improve, or enrich themselves from that point forward.

6. Keeping the old culture while embracing the new culture is the acculturation strategy of ____.

a. assimilation
b. separation
c. marginalization
d. integration

7. ____ is an effort to reduce or manage the experience of stress.

a. Coping
b. Projection
c. Posttraumatic stress disorder
d. Psychoneuroimmunology

8. ____ coping is a style of coping with stress that emphasizes changing the stressor itself, while ____ coping is a style of coping with stress that emphasizes changing your reaction to the stressor.

9. ____ refers to an increased awareness of what's going on inside of a person — the moment-to-moment physical and psychological experiences — with an emphasis on just feeling it rather than analyzing it or avoiding it.

10. ____ is health care based on the idea that the human body can heal itself with low-dose medications made from natural sources.

To check your understanding of these questions, click show the answers in the e-book or refer to the answers in Appendix B.

Research shows quizzing is a highly effective learning tool. Continue quizzing yourself using LearningCurve, the system that adapts to *your* learning.

WHAT'S YOUR TAKE?

1. The "Stress and Gender" section of this chapter describes how stress can be experienced differently by people of different genders. How well does that description match the stress experiences of you and people you know well?
2. As mentioned in the chapter, we have all heard many messages about how important it is to take care of our bodies (to manage stress, and for other reasons too). However, many of us don't do what we should to stay in good physical shape. In your opinion, why don't we? Which factors affect which groups within our population the most? How can you motivate yourself to improve your own physical self-care?

SHOW ME MORE

11.1 Human Versus Animal Experience of Stress

This video offers an explanation of important differences between how animals and humans experience stress.
laurien/Getty Images

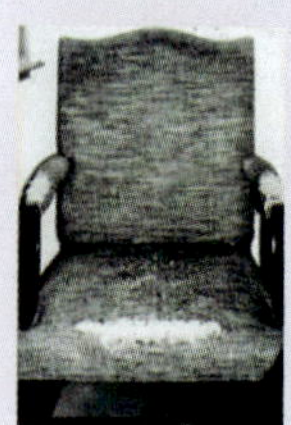

11.2 Type A Personality Explained

This video offers an entertaining version of the origins of Type A personality.
Greater Good Science Center

11.3 Toxic Stress in Young Children

This video illustrates how stress can become toxic for young children, and strategies for helping them cope.
Associated Press

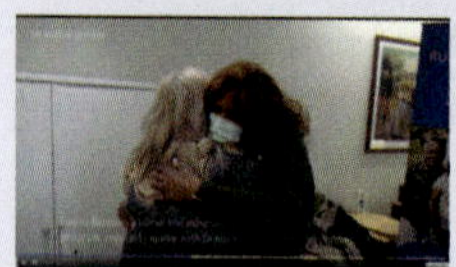

11.4 Conquering Loneliness in a Lonely World

This video explains how loneliness, during the pandemic or any time, can have harmful effects, and how social support can be a beneficial way of addressing it.
Associated Press

11.5 My Psychology Podcast

This podcast episode features the author of this textbook, psychologist Andy Pomerantz, speaking with other instructors of introductory psychology courses about the most important and interesting concepts in this chapter.
Macmillan Learning

12 Personality

GaudiLab/Shutterstock

CHAPTER OUTLINE

I was enjoying in my seventh-grade Spanish class. Learning vocabulary words, conjugating verbs, even rolling my r's — everything was going well. Then we got to the translation for the word *is*, and I found myself quite confused. The textbook had two translations: *está* and *es*. How could a single verb in English translate into two different verbs in Spanish?

My teacher, Señora Fernandez, explained that Spanish speakers make an important distinction between two kinds of *is*. There's the kind of *is* that's momentary and fleeting (*está*), which describes someone's temporary state. There's also the kind of *is* that's more stable and unchanging (*es*), which describes someone's essential character. I started to get it: the two verbs distinguished how someone happens to be right now versus how someone is every day.

Señora Fernandez offered some examples to help us distinguish the two kinds of *is* in Spanish. She started with an English sentence: Miranda is quiet. Does that mean that Miranda is being quiet right now, or that Miranda is generally a quiet person? In Spanish, the choice of verb clarifies it. *Miranda está callada* means she's quiet right now; *Miranda es callada* means she's usually quiet, an introvert at heart. Here's another example: Alex is happy. Does that mean Alex is happy like he just received a nice text from a friend, or happy like he is always optimistic? Again, the Spanish verbs tell the tale: *Alex está feliz* means he's wearing a smile right now; *Alex es feliz* means he's a generally cheerful, glass-half-full kind of person.

I didn't realize it at the time, but when Señora Fernandez explained the difference between those two Spanish verbs, she also taught an important lesson about personality. Psychologists use the term *personality* to refer to each person's enduring character. It is what Spanish speakers refer to when they describe someone with the verb *es*: what a person *is* at their essence, across time and situations. Personality encompasses each person's unique and enduring patterns of thoughts, feelings, and actions. Personality is what makes you *you*.

In this chapter, we will explore numerous theories that psychologists use to explain how your personality developed and how it differs from the personalities of other people. We will also consider the tests and other techniques that psychologists use to measure personality.

What Is Personality?

YOU WILL LEARN:

12.1 what the definition of personality is.

12.2 how psychologists study personality.

12.3 how twin studies and adoption studies illustrate the biological contributions to personality.

In this section, we will consider three attempts to explain how personality is formed over time: *psychodynamic* theory, *humanistic* theory, and *behavioral and social-cognitive* theory. We will also consider *trait* theory, which emphasizes the ingredients that make personality rather than the way personality is formed over time. But first, let's define personality.

Defining Personality

Personality is a person's distinctive and stable way of thinking, feeling, and behaving. It is the psychological equivalent of your fingerprint: a unique set of characteristics that differentiates you from other people and stays with you long-term. For example, if you've ever gotten together with a friend or relative you haven't seen in years, you can appreciate what personality means. In spite of the time apart, the person probably hasn't changed enough to surprise you. There may be some superficial changes, but rarely are there changes in who the person *is*. Personality – a person's tendencies, predispositions, and singular way of interacting with the world – generally remains stable (Anusic & Schimmack, 2016).

A fascinating study illustrates just how stable personality tends to remain, even over long stretches of time (Nave et al., 2010). Personality researchers found teachers' ratings of students' personalities in an ethnically diverse Hawaii elementary school. The personality ratings were made between 1959 and 1967. *Four decades later*, the researchers located 144 of these students and recruited them for another personality assessment, which involved a video-recorded interview that was scored by trained observers using standardized rating scales. Results indicated that the participants' personalities hadn't changed much. Talkative kids talked a lot as adults; adaptable kids handled new situations well now; humble kids had remained modest; and impulsive kids still acted spontaneously in their 40s and 50s. Similar conclusions have come from other studies, including one of almost 1000 people assessed first at age 3 and again at age 26 (Caspi et al., 2003). The conclusion illustrates the way psychologists understand personality:

> [P]ersonality resides *within* people . . . . [T]he same individual . . . separated by many years . . . remains recognizably the same person. (Nave et al., 2010, p. 333; italics in original.)

LIFE HACK 12.1

In relationships, if you think you can easily change the other person's personality, think again. Research suggests that personality generally remains stable over time.

(Caspi et al., 2003; Nave et al., 2010)

Isn't it possible that people think, feel, and act the way they do because of the situation around them rather than the personality within them?

The situation can play a powerful role in how a person behaves. For example, if Vanessa stops her car at an intersection, she's probably not doing so because she has a timid personality, but because the light is red. Of course, if you spend some time in Vanessa's passenger seat, you'll notice that personality characteristics influence her driving style too. She might make sudden lane shifts and dart out into busy traffic, suggesting that she's a bold risk taker. She might yield a lot or let other drivers take parking spaces she's heading toward, suggesting a strong tendency to accommodate others and avoid conflict. She might explode with road rage at other drivers for minor infractions, suggesting a deep-seated impatience and self-importance. The main point is that the way you behave depends on an interaction of the situation and what your personality brings to it. What surrounds you can affect behavior, but psychologists recognize that what is *inside* of you – your personality – is also a strong influence on what you do and how you do it (Furr & Funder, 2021).

personality
A person's distinctive and stable way of thinking, feeling, and behaving.

Typically, psychologists explain personality with a *theory*. There are plenty of personality theories, offered by Freud, Rogers, Bandura, and others. Unfortunately, we can't crown one personality theory as "correct" and eliminate all the others (Barenbaum & Winter, 2008; Newman & Larsen, 2011). There is a reason why experts still use the term personality *theory* rather than personality *fact*: psychologists are still figuring out human personality, and will be doing so for many years to come.

James Woodson/DigitalVision/Getty Images

Jessica Holden Photography/Moment/Getty Images

Research on behavioral genetics reveals the strong impact of genes on personality. Identical twins (like the top pair), who share all of their genes, show more similarity in their personalities than nonidentical twins (like the bottom pair), who share only half of their genes.

Biological Contributions to Personality

Some people believe there is a simple answer to why you have a particular personality: you were born with it. There is certainly some truth to that notion (Bouchard, 2004; Floderus-Myrhed et al., 1980; Kendler et al., 2009; Krueger, 2008). The genetic influence is apparent in some aspects of personality from birth (DeYoung & Allen, 2019; Fish et al., 1991; Rothbart et al., 2000). If you've spent time around newborn babies, you know this firsthand. Some newborns are energetic, others sluggish. Some babies are fussy, others easygoing. Some babies are very responsive to other people, others much less so. All of these differences are apparent from day one, before the newborn babies have had any life experiences that might have influenced them.

Twin studies and adoption studies also indicate biological contributions to personality. Such research comes from the field of **behavioral genetics**: the study of the impact of genes (nature) and environment (nurture) on personality and behavior. Numerous studies of behavioral genetics have found that identical twins, who share all of the same genes, have a much higher likelihood of matching each other on many personality traits than fraternal twins, who share only some of the same genes (Loehlin & Nichols, 1976; Pedersen et al., 1988; Segal, 2011; Tellegen et al., 1988). This is true whether the twins are raised together or separated at birth and raised apart. Many adoption studies also show that genes influence personality. Researchers consistently find that adopted kids have personalities that are more similar to their biological parents' than their adoptive parents' (Daniels & Plomin, 1985; Pedersen et al., 1991; Rhee & Waldman, 2002). This is true even though adopted kids spend most days with their adoptive parents and may never have met their biological parents.

Figure 12.1 illustrates the impact of genes on personality characteristics (Jang et al., 1996). Notice how the bars for identical (monozygotic) twins extend farther than the bars for nonidentical (dizygotic) twins. This indicates that twins who share all the same genes are more likely to match on personality characteristics than twins who share only half the same genes.

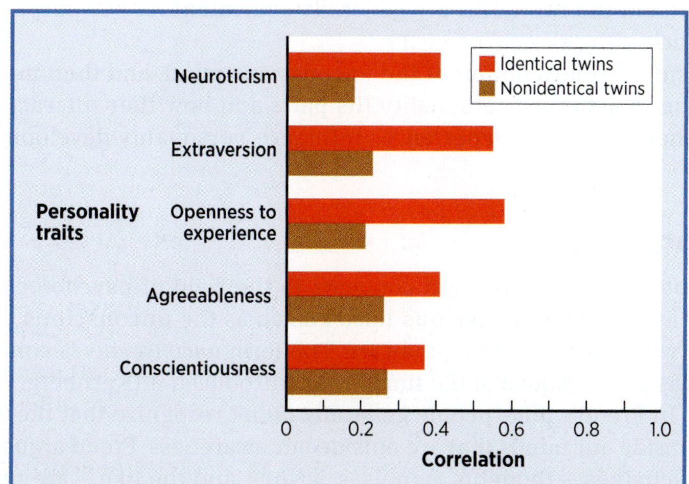

FIGURE 12.1 Correlations of Personality Characteristics Within Twin Pairs. Genes clearly influence personality, as indicated by the longer bars for identical twins than for nonidentical twins. But that space between the ends of the longest bars and the 1.0 line indicates that many nongenetic factors influence personality too. Data from Jang et al. (1996).

behavioral genetics
The study of the impact of genes (nature) and environment (nurture) on personality and behavior.

An important fact about the correlations presented in Figure 12.1 is that none of them is even close to the maximum correlation of 1.0. Even the correlations describing identical twins, who are genetic clones, fall far short. If genes completely determined personality — if it was all about biology — the identical twin correlations would be 1.0. The correlations for nonidentical twins would be much higher as well. This is why numerous researchers have estimated that about 50% of personality is determined by genes (Nettle, 2007; Tellegen et al., 1988). That is a sizable amount, but it also means there must be a lot more to personality than just biology (Rutter, 2000, 2006, 2011; Tremblay, 2011). That nonbiological contribution is what the theories in this chapter attempt to explain, beginning with the psychodynamic theory of Sigmund Freud.

CHECK YOUR LEARNING:

12.1 What is the definition of personality?

12.2 What is the role of theory in the study of personality?

12.3 What do behavioral genetics studies (twin studies and adoption studies) suggest about the roles of biology and environment in the development of personality?

To check your understanding of these questions, click show the answers or refer to the answers in the Chapter Summary.

Psychodynamic Theory of Personality

YOU WILL LEARN:

12.4 what the psychodynamic theory of personality is.

12.5 what the unconscious is, and why it is important.

12.6 what the id, ego, and superego are.

12.7 about the psychosexual stages of development.

12.8 how Sigmund Freud's followers offered revised new psychodynamic theories.

12.9 about current thoughts on psychodynamic theory.

The **psychodynamic theory of personality** is an explanation of personality, based on the ideas of Sigmund Freud, that emphasizes unconscious forces and early childhood experiences. The study of personality was founded on Freud's psychodynamic theory. Developed in the late 1800s and early 1900s in Vienna, Austria, it was among the first personality theories historically and has been hugely influential in both academic and popular culture (Routh, 1996, 2011). In fact, many other personality theories were developed by psychologists who learned psychodynamic theory as students but were dissatisfied with it (Engel, 2008; Hollon & DiGiuseppe, 2011). (A brief note on terminology — the word *psychoanalytic* is often used to refer to Freud's theories. Among serious Freudian scholars, there are distinctions between psychodynamic and psychoanalytic, but the two terms are generally equivalent for our purposes. For simplicity, we'll stick with *psychodynamic*.)

Let's consider Freud's notion of the unconscious mind, and then move on to his ideas about the structure of personality (its parts and how they interact). After that, we'll discuss how childhood experiences influence personality development at various stages.

The Unconscious

Freud contributed many important concepts to the field of psychology, but one of the most essential is the **unconscious** (also known as the **unconscious mind**): mental activity of which the person is unaware. The term *unconscious* is commonly used today, but it was a radical idea at the time Freud introduced it (Kernberg, 2004; Lane & Harris, 2008). In Freud's time, people generally didn't recognize that there are activities going on inside our minds that are outside our awareness. Freud argued that these unconscious activities — thoughts, impulses, wishes, and the like — are not meaningless or negligible. They powerfully drive us, influence our thoughts and actions, and affect our lives (Karon & Widener, 1995; Kris, 2012).

psychodynamic theory of personality
An explanation of personality, based on the ideas of Sigmund Freud, that emphasizes unconscious forces and early childhood experiences.

unconscious (unconscious mind)
Mental activity of which the person is unaware.

According to Freud, the impact of the unconscious is so great that it can explain our actions that are otherwise unexplainable. In other words, "random" things we do aren't random at all. Instead, they are caused by unconscious thoughts, wishes, or urges. Freud called this idea **psychic determinism**: the belief that all thoughts and behaviors, even those that seem accidental, arbitrary, or mistaken, are determined by psychological forces. For example, consider Terrell, a sales rep who has a big presentation today. His coworker arrives to carpool to work with him, and as Terrell is about to step into the car, he notices his shoe is untied. Terrell takes his computer bag off his shoulder, sets it down, and ties his shoe. He then gets into the passenger seat and drives off, leaving the computer bag on the ground. Even if Terrell can't come up with a conscious reason why he would do that (after all, he needs that laptop for his presentation), that doesn't mean there is no reason for it. According to Freud, the reason lies in Terrell's unconscious (Cabaniss et al., 2011; Rycroft, 1968). Perhaps deep down, Terrell is terrified about this presentation and desperately wants to avoid it. Or maybe he has some unrecognized hatred for his job, so a ruined presentation might get him fired and force him to find another one, an outcome that may be exactly what he wants on some level.

Sigmund Freud Copyrights/ullstein bild/Getty Images

Sigmund Freud created the psychodynamic theory of personality, which emphasizes unconscious forces and early childhood experiences.

As incidents like Terrell's suggest, your unconscious doesn't always do a perfect job of locking in the material that you hope to keep hidden. Sometimes, that unconscious material makes itself evident through errors in your words or actions. Psychologists call such leaks **Freudian slips**: verbal or behavioral mistakes that reveal unconscious thoughts or wishes. If you're a fan of the old TV show *Friends*, you know that Jennifer Aniston's character, Rachel, and Ross (played by David Schwimmer) have had strong romantic feelings for each other since the sitcom began. In the episode in which Ross marries another woman (Emily), he absentmindedly says Rachel's name instead of Emily's during the wedding vows ("I, Ross, take thee, Rachel . . ."). As you can imagine, Emily doesn't laugh it off as if it were a meaningless mistake that Ross just happened to make at the altar. Emily knew exactly where the Freudian slip came from, as did everyone else watching the wedding: Ross's unconscious, where he deeply wished that he was marrying Rachel instead of Emily.

Psychologists sometimes commit Freudian slips themselves. In my own private practice, I once arrived at my office for a 9 A.M. appointment with a particularly ornery client — Curtis, a physically intimidating man who not only accused me of being incompetent on many occasions, but also threatened to sue me during our appointment the week before. I arrived about 20 minutes early and went through my usual routine upon arrival: enter my office through the side door, turn on all the lights, unlock the waiting room door, and wait for my client to arrive. By 9 A.M., he hadn't arrived. I started playing a game on my phone to pass the time. By 9:05, 9:10, 9:15, still no Curtis. At 9:20, my phone rang, and I answered. A furious Curtis shouted: "Where are you! I've been outside your office for 20 minutes but the damn door is locked!" Apparently, I had "forgotten" to unlock the waiting room door. In the thousands of times I have arrived at my office to see clients and gone through my usual office-opening routine, this was the only time I ever made such a mistake, and also the only time Curtis was my first client of the day. Coincidence? Accident? Freud certainly would believe otherwise: my failure to open the waiting room door exposed an unconscious wish — to keep Curtis away from me. (Of course, *proving* that my mistake with Curtis, or Ross's mistake at his wedding, was *definitely* a Freudian slip is impossible. It may seem true, but there's no scientifically valid way to test it, and no way to collect data to support or refute it. That inability to test ideas in a scientific way is a major shortcoming of Freud's theories in general, and something we will consider in more detail later in this section.)

The Structure of Personality

Freud believed that personality was a by-product of the interaction of three components of the mind: the *id*, the *ego*, and the *superego* (**Figure 12.2**). Keep in mind that these three components lie in the unconscious mind, at least partially if not totally hidden. Freud believed that these three components of the mind are engaged in a continuous battle we can't control or even directly observe. He was also confident this battle determines to a significant extent how we think, feel, and behave — in fact, our very personalities (Freud, 1923, 1932; Kernberg, 2004; Moore & Fine, 1990; Skelton, 2006).

psychic determinism
The belief that all thoughts and behaviors, even those that seem accidental, arbitrary, or mistaken, are determined by psychological forces.

Freudian slips
Verbal or behavioral mistakes that reveal unconscious thoughts or wishes.

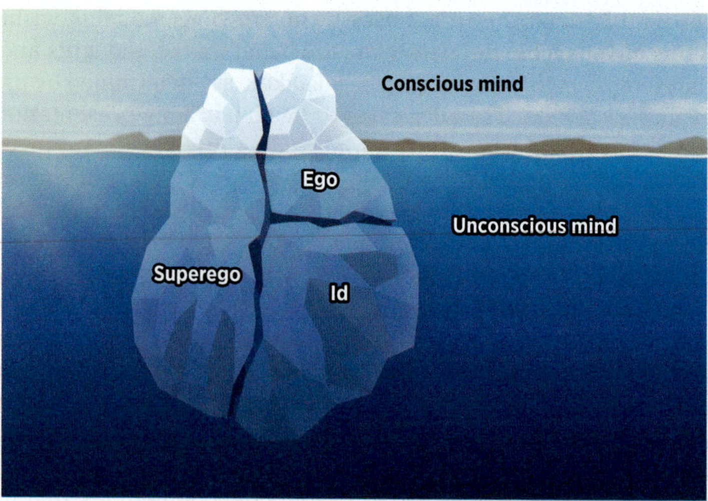

FIGURE 12.2 The Unconscious Nature of the Id, Ego, and Superego. All three of Freud's components of the mind lie at least partially "beneath the surface," in the unconscious mind.

Id. The first component is the **id**: the animalistic part of the mind that generates our most primal, biologically based impulses such as sex and aggression. To understand the id, imagine a wild animal walking down the hallway outside a psychology classroom, a ferocious bear guided entirely by primal instinct. And the bear is hungry. How will the bear behave in response to being hungry? Will the bear kindly ask a few students if they have any snacks in their backpacks? Will the bear patiently slip a dollar into the vending machine? Absolutely not. The bear will devour any food the students happen to have, and perhaps devour a student too. The bear will smash the glass of the vending machine, slash open the packages, and gorge on all of the chips, candy bars, and mini-donuts inside. And the bear certainly won't feel any need to apologize afterward.

Freud believed that each of us is driven by an id that generates impulses just like those of this wild animal. In fact, he argued that the id is the only component of the mind present at birth. You may never have thought about a cute, cuddly newborn in quite this way before, but it is hard to deny: Babies do seem to be driven solely by their immediate desires. When a newborn wants something – food, a new diaper, to be held – the baby screams and wails in a selfish attempt to get what would feel good at the moment. The *pleasure principle* – the force that guides the id toward immediate gratification – fuels babies' behavior entirely (Moore & Fine, 1990).

But as babies grow up, they stop acting so selfishly and start being more considerate and socially appropriate. How does that happen?

Superego. As children get older, the people who care for them – parents, grandparents, or other relatives – gradually start to expect them to keep their id impulses in check. The caretakers teach children what is right and wrong, what is acceptable and unacceptable. Those guidelines eventually become a built-in part of the child's mind. So, with the help of others, the child develops a **superego**: the part of the mind that opposes the id by enforcing rules, restrictions, and morality. A toddler who yanks a toy out of another child's hand may be told disapprovingly by their caregiver at the time: "No, Mateo. It's not OK to take toys away from your friends. Ask if you can have a turn with it next." As Mateo hears comments like this repeatedly, they become part of his own standards of conduct – his own set of "shoulds" – which he carries with him

id
According to Freud, the animalistic part of the mind that generates our most basic, biologically based impulses, such as sex and aggression.

superego
According to Freud, the part of the mind that opposes the id by enforcing rules, restrictions, and morality.

regardless of who (if anyone) may be supervising him in a particular situation. Mateo will behave properly not just to gain the approval of those around him, but to gain the approval of himself as well. In this way, Freud's concept of the superego matches the more common notion of the *conscience*, the internal monitor that tells us how acceptable our actions are.

Maskot/Getty Images

According to psychodynamic theory, the superego is the part of the mind that opposes the id by enforcing the rules, restrictions, and morality learned from caretakers. For example, this child is learning rules about how to treat others on the playground.

Ego. The job of the superego – to counteract the ongoing stream of powerful id impulses – is certainly a difficult one. This rivalry between the id's drive for gratification and the superego's restraint makes for never-ending conflict within the mind. Freud believed this conflict was managed by the third component of the mind, the **ego**: the part of the mind that serves as a realistic mediator between the id and superego. The ego makes compromises. Its task is to find ways to satisfy both the id and the superego, while also meeting the demands of the real world (Gabbard, 2005). The ego works according to the *reality principle*: the force that guides a person toward rational, reality-based behavior (Fodor & Gaynor, 1950).

Defense Mechanisms. Sometimes, the compromises formed by the ego are quite simple: if the id wants to eat a big piece of cake, but the superego says no way, the ego says eat a smaller piece. Other times, the ego resorts to more creative methods to deal with id-versus-superego conflict. Freud and his followers (including his daughter, psychoanalyst Anna Freud) identified a number of these methods and called them **defense mechanisms**: techniques used by the ego to manage conflict between the id and superego. When a person leans heavily on a particular defense mechanism, it can influence or even dominate their personality (Dewald, 1964; Freud, 1905, 1936; Sandler & Freud, 1985).

For example, consider Rick, who repeatedly accuses his partner, Jing of wanting to cheat on him. There is absolutely no evidence for it, and Jing completely denies it, but Rick remains sure that Jing is sick of him and actively wants to see other people. Freud would argue that Rick's belief about Jing wanting to cheat actually began as an id impulse deep within Rick's own unconscious: *Rick* wants to cheat. His superego, of course, rejected that impulse ("Cheating is wrong!"), which left his ego to deal with the resulting id-versus-superego conflict. Rick's ego uses a defense mechanism called *projection*, in which the ego "projects" the id's impulse to cheat onto other people instead of keeping it within Rick. (Think of it like an old-school movie projector – even though the film is projected onto the screen, the true location of the film is within the projector.) It's as if Rick's ego, in an attempt to deal with this id-versus-superego conflict, converted "*I* want to cheat" into "*My partner* wants to cheat."

As this example suggests, a person who uses projection as a defense mechanism all the time could develop a distrustful, paranoid personality. Other defense mechanisms handle the id-versus-superego conflict in different ways. For example, when an ego uses *reaction formation*, it does the opposite of the original id impulse – as when an employee who is furious at his boss praises her intelligence instead of shouting insults at her. In *displacement*, the ego steers an id impulse to a different, safer target. (This is sometimes known by the nickname "kicking the dog.") For example, an athlete with an impulse to physically assault her coach reroutes her aggression and starts a fight with a teammate who may not deserve it. Psychodynamic theorists consider *sublimation* one of the most successful defense mechanisms: it's just like displacement, but the redirection of the id impulse actually helps other people (Gabbard, 2005; Karon & Widener, 1995). Consider a woman who channels her impulses to hurt others into the profession of dentistry – she inflicts pain on others, but in a way that benefits them. **Table 12.1** offers further explanation and examples of many of the defense mechanisms put forth by Freud and his followers.

A final note about Freud's three components of the mind may make them easier to understand and remember: Freud wrote in German, and his writings were translated into many languages. When his ideas were translated into English, the translators (for some reason) chose the Latin words *id*, *superego*, and *ego* as the labels for Freud's

ego
According to Freud, the part of the mind that serves as a realistic mediator between the id and superego.

defense mechanisms
According to Freud, techniques used by the ego to manage conflict between the id and superego.

TABLE 12.1: Selected Defense Mechanisms

DEFENSE MECHANISM	WHAT THE EGO DOES	EXAMPLE
Repression	Hides your id impulse in the unconscious to keep you unaware of it	You have an id impulse to insult your parent/caregiver, but it never reaches consciousness.
Denial	Blocks external events from consciousness because they are too threatening	You learn that your good friend has a fatal disease but act as if everything is OK.
Regression	Retreats to an earlier time in your life when the current stressor was absent	Soon after you take a stressful new job, you find yourself craving the comfort foods and TV shows you enjoyed as a kid.
Projection	"Projects" your id impulse onto others, so it appears they have it rather than you	You have an id impulse to cheat on your partner, but you accuse your partner of wanting to cheat on you.
Rationalization	Comes up with seemingly acceptable explanations for behaviors actually based on id impulses	You give in to your impulse to order (and eat) many boxes of Girl Scout cookies, but tell yourself that you only did so to support a worthy cause.
Reaction formation	Overreacts against the id impulse by doing the exact opposite, as if overcompensating	You have an id impulse to damage your friends' new house, but instead you buy them a housewarming gift.
Displacement	Redirects the id impulse toward a safer target in order to minimize the consequences to you	You have an id impulse to scream at your supervisor, but instead you scream at your dog.
Sublimation	Redirects the id impulse in a way that actually benefits others	You have an id impulse to hurt other people, so you become a soldier who can do so for the sake of national security.

three components of the mind. As **Table 12.2** shows, if the translators had stuck with ordinary English words instead, the id would be known as the *it*, or the thing inside each of us. (Not *he*, *she* or *they*, but *it* — as if referring to something nonhuman.) The superego would be the *above-me*, that is, the rules and restrictions that came from those in positions of power above each of us. And the ego would be the *me*, the person, negotiating between the two powerful forces on either side (Karon & Widener, 1995; Truscott, 2010). In other words, Freud intended to say your ego is *you*, which underscores the notion that the way your ego handles conflict largely defines your personality.

Stages of Development

According to Freud, the experiences we have as young children shape our personalities. He placed special emphasis on the way our parents/caregivers and other caregivers interact with us in the earliest years of life. He divided these early years into periods called **psychosexual stages**: the five biologically based developmental stages of childhood during which personality characteristics are formed. **Figure 12.3** presents all of these stages.

According to Freud, each psychosexual stage centers on a particular body part that is the focus of the child's life during that period (Freud, 1905). Kids typically move successfully through each psychosexual stage. However, sometimes a **fixation** can occur: a lingering psychological difficulty directly related to unsuccessful experience of a particular psychosexual stage. A fixation tends to stay with a person long after the psychosexual stage is over, stirring up psychological issues (and possibly shaping

TABLE 12.2: Alternate Translations of Freudian Terms

STANDARD TERM	ALTERNATE TRANSLATION	MEANING
Id	*It*	Not *he*, *she* or *they*, (person), but *it* (animal or thing) within you driven toward immediate pleasure
Superego	*Above-me*	The rules that come from those in power over you (parents/caregivers, etc.)
Ego	*Me*	Your personality, shaped by the way it handles conflict between the two other components of the mind

psychosexual stages
Freud's five biologically based developmental stages of childhood, during which personality characteristics are formed.

fixation
Freud's term for a lingering psychological difficulty directly related to unsuccessful experience of a particular psychosexual stage.

oral stage
The first of Freud's psychosexual stages, which takes place from birth to about 18 months and focuses on the psychological consequences of feeding behavior.

anal stage
Freud's second psychosexual stage, which lasts from about age 18 months to about age 3, and focuses on the psychological consequences of toilet training.

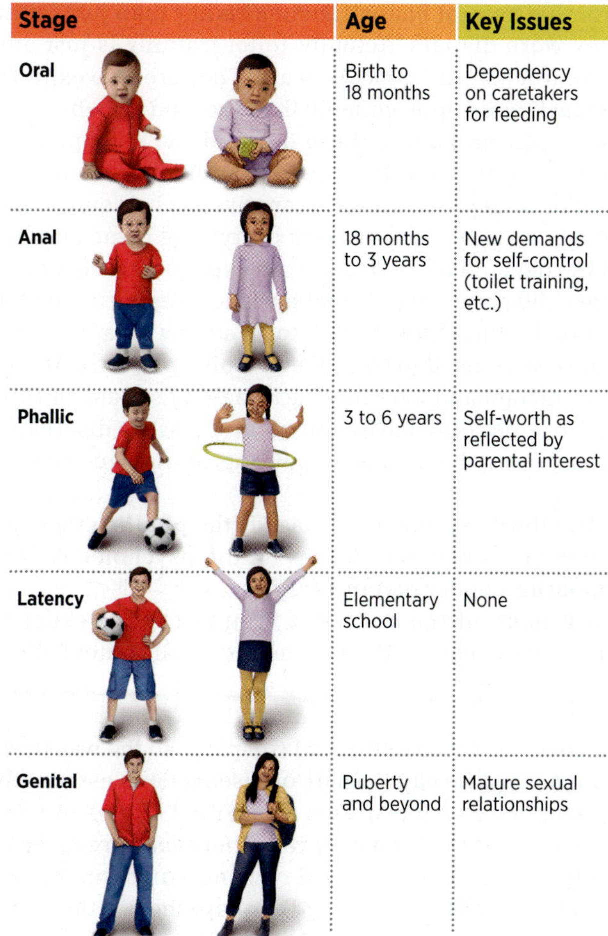

Stage	Age	Key Issues
Oral	Birth to 18 months	Dependency on caretakers for feeding
Anal	18 months to 3 years	New demands for self-control (toilet training, etc.)
Phallic	3 to 6 years	Self-worth as reflected by parental interest
Latency	Elementary school	None
Genital	Puberty and beyond	Mature sexual relationships

FIGURE 12.3 Freud's Psychosexual Stages. According to the theories of Sigmund Freud, people move through important stages during childhood that impact the formation of their adult personality.

personality) long into adulthood. It's like snagging your sweater as you walk past a doorway: you keep moving forward, but you're caught on something and you can't fully move on until you untether yourself (Westen et al., 2008).

Oral Stage. The first of Freud's psychosexual stages is the **oral stage**, which takes place from birth to about 18 months and focuses on the psychological consequences of feeding behavior. Babies experience much of the world through their mouths, and breastfeeding or bottle-feeding is a primary activity. Babies learn what to expect from others by the way their parents/caregivers respond to their need for food. Most of the time, parents/caregivers handle feeding just right, and babies learn they can expect to get food when they ask (cry) for it. However, if parents/caregivers provide too much food too often, babies may come to expect that others — friends, romantic partners, and others they form relationships with as they grow up — will do the same for them. This attitude — "Other people are great! They always come through and give me exactly what I need!" — can lead to a naïve and overly optimistic personality. On the other hand, if parents/caregivers provide too little food too infrequently, babies may come to expect that others will do the same as they grow up. This attitude — "Other people are terrible! They couldn't care less about me!" — can lead to a mistrusting and overly pessimistic personality.

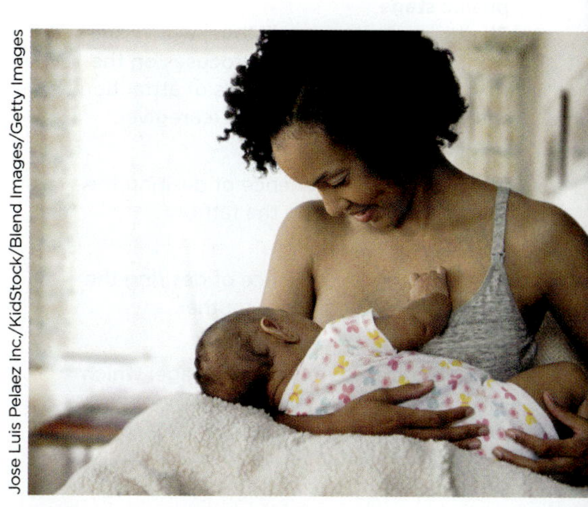

Jose Luis Pelaez Inc./KidStock/Blend Images/Getty Images

The oral stage is the first of Freud's psychosexual stages. It focuses on the long-term psychological consequences of the feeding behavior experienced during infancy.

Anal Stage. Freud's second psychosexual stage is the **anal stage**, which lasts from about age 18 months to about age 3, and focuses on the psychological consequences of toilet training. Toilet training is all about control. For the first time, children are expected to control this natural bodily function rather than just letting it happen as they did when they wore diapers. Actually, toilet training is just one of many new demands for self-control placed on kids this age. They are also expected to sit still, be quiet, and behave much more appropriately than they did as babies.

Most parents/caregivers handle these demands well, by placing just the right amount of demand for control on the child, but problems can arise when parents/caregivers overdo it or underdo it. Parents/caregivers who demand too much control cause kids to become overly concerned about everything being perfect. It may start in the bathroom, but the demand for perfection can expand — to cleaning up their clothes and toys, and as the child grows, to personal hygiene, keeping a schedule, and all other aspects of life. Eventually, this child grows into an adult with a "neat freak" personality dominated by the obsessive need to control everything perfectly. At the other extreme, parents/caregivers who demand too little teach their kids that control is unimportant. This attitude can cause not only messes in bathrooms, but disorganization in other areas of life, including messy bedrooms, sloppy appearance, and chaotic schedules.

Phallic Stage. The third psychosexual stage is the **phallic stage**, which runs from approximately 3 to 6 years old and focuses on the psychological consequences of attraction to the opposite-gender parent/caregiver.

Before we learn more of the details of Freud's psychosexual stages, let's put Freud's whole approach to personality in some historical context. When Freud developed his ideas (Europe in the late 1800s and early 1900s), it was assumed that most children would grow up with a mother and a father. Gender was generally seen as binary, and gender roles were also quite rigid compared to the way they are today. Also, the idea that a person could be gay, lesbian, or bisexual was essentially unacceptable. Of course, our contemporary society differs from Freud's in all of these ways. For that reason, Freud's phallic stage and some of his other ideas are often criticized today. Here, let's try to consider Freud's ideas and recognize any importance they may still hold, while understanding that we may need to adapt them if they are to apply to our own lives. Freud believed young children strive to have a special relationship with their opposite-gender parent/caregiver, but see their same-gender parent/caregiver as a rival. For boys, Freud called this experience the **Oedipus complex**: the childhood experience of desiring the mother and resenting the father. For girls, he called it the **Electra complex**: the childhood experience of desiring the father and resenting the mother. (Both terms are borrowed from Greek mythology.)

We can actually understand the possible consequences of this stage without emphasizing the gender of the child or parent/caregiver at all. Most parents/caregivers respond well to their child's wish to have a special relationship with them, but those who respond with too much or too little interest can cause the child psychological challenges related to self-worth. Specifically, a parent/caregiver who drops everything, to invest in the relationship with the child overinflates the child's self-worth. These children often grow into adults with exaggeratedly wonderful views of themselves — not healthy self-esteem, but conceit and arrogance. On the other hand, a parent/caregiver who ignores the child's wish for a special relationship deflates the child's self-worth. These children often grow into adults who undervalue themselves, lack confidence, and feel insecure.

Latency Stage. Freud's fourth psychosexual stage was the **latency stage**, which lasts through roughly age 6 to 11 or 12, when puberty has not yet kick-started the child's sexual drive, and the child's energies are focused primarily on school and other tasks that have little to do with the sexual or bodily issues that are so prominent in other stages. (As the name of the stage implies, the child's sexuality is *latent* during this time.) As a result, there is relatively little of psychological consequence that takes place during the latency stage, and Freud deemphasized it in his writings (Etchegoyen, 1993).

Genital Stage. The fifth and final psychosexual stage is the **genital stage**, which lasts from puberty through adulthood and focuses on mature, adult sexual relationships.

phallic stage
The third psychosexual stage, which runs from 3 to 6 years old and focuses on the psychological consequences of attraction to the opposite-gender parent/caregiver.

Oedipus complex
The childhood experience of desiring the mother and resenting the father.

Electra complex
The childhood experience of desiring the father and resenting the mother.

latency stage
Freud's fourth psychosexual stage, which lasts through the elementary school years, when the child's energies are focused primarily on school and other tasks that have little to do with sexual or bodily issues.

genital stage
The fifth and final psychosexual stage, which lasts from puberty through adulthood and focuses on mature, adult sexual relationships.

Freud believed that the personality is already set by the time a person enters the genital stage. Freud believed that people who had navigated successfully through the earlier stages (especially the first three) would have the greatest chance of success, which he defined as a long-term romantic relationship with an opposite-sex partner. Those who had become fixated would, by contrast, struggle.

neo-Freudian theories
Theories that revised, but did not entirely reject, the basics of Freud's original psychodynamic theory.

Freud's Followers

Sigmund Freud attracted many disciples, many of whom became well-respected personality theorists themselves. Some knew Freud personally; others came along after his death. Their **neo-Freudian theories** revised, but did not entirely reject, the basics of Freud's original psychodynamic theory. Freud's most prominent followers held on to his core ideas: the unconscious, the significance of early childhood experiences, and the notion that the mind contained id, ego, and superego. However, they let go of some of his ideas too. For example, they deemphasized the biology that was so prominent in Freud's theories, such as the id's bodily drives and the explicit sexuality of the phallic stage (Orlinsky & Howard, 1995; Skelton, 2006; Terman, 2012).

Alfred Adler. Alfred Adler, a psychiatrist colleague of Freud's, offered a different perspective on early child development. He pointed out that young children — particularly in comparison to the stronger, more capable adults they see in their lives — develop an *inferiority complex* that profoundly influences their development. In fact, according to Adler, our primary motivation — which carries past childhood and into adulthood — is to strive for *superiority* over our own perceived weaknesses (Adler, 1927; Mosak & Maniacci, 1999; Tan, 2019). For example, a person who sees themself as stupid is driven to complete a graduate degree to prove their intelligence, or someone who sees themself as unlikeable is driven to seek a huge number of friends and followers on social media. Adler's own serious childhood illnesses, including rickets and a nearly fatal case of pneumonia, probably prompted him to develop a theory with this emphasis on overcoming perceived weaknesses (Sweeney, 1998).

Golden Pixels LLC/Shutterstock

The theories of Alfred Adler regarding birth order influenced much research on the subject.

Adler also shined the light on how personality is influenced by *birth order*, or the place in the family into which a child is born (Adler, 1928). Adler's theories about being the oldest, the middle, the baby, or the only child have spawned hundreds of empirical studies. Collectively, these birth order studies suggest that firstborns tend to be more conservative and conventional, while laterborns (any sibling born into a family with an older brother or older sister) tend to be more liberal and unconventional. "Laterborns seek to discover unique family niches that have not already been taken by older siblings," which requires more out-of-the-box thinking and risk taking (Sulloway, 2011, p. 107). Not surprisingly, laterborns have more open-minded personalities and a greater likelihood to vote for liberal political candidates. Over the course of history, a disproportionately high number of revolutionary thinkers (such as Copernicus, who told us the Earth was not the center of the solar system, and Darwin, who told us that humans were just another species produced by evolution) have been laterborns. Laterborns are also twice as likely to support a radical political upheaval (Booth & Kee, 2009; Paulhus et al., 1999; Sulloway, 1996, 2001, 2009).

Laterborns are more likely to be risk takers in sports too. As **Figure 12.4** illustrates, laterborns are 1.48 times more likely to play a dangerous sport — football, rugby, ice hockey, lacrosse, gymnastics, boxing, downhill skiing, car racing, and so on — than firstborns. A more detailed analysis of baseball reveals that the difference is even greater when it comes to a particular risky play: stolen-base attempts. Specifically, researchers examined the statistics of 700 Major League Baseball players whose brothers also played in the league and found that younger brothers were 10.6 times more likely to attempt stolen bases than older brothers (Sulloway & Zweigenhaft, 2010). In addition, kid brothers were 4.7 times more likely to be hit by a pitch than big brothers, indicating their increased willingness to risk pain or injury.

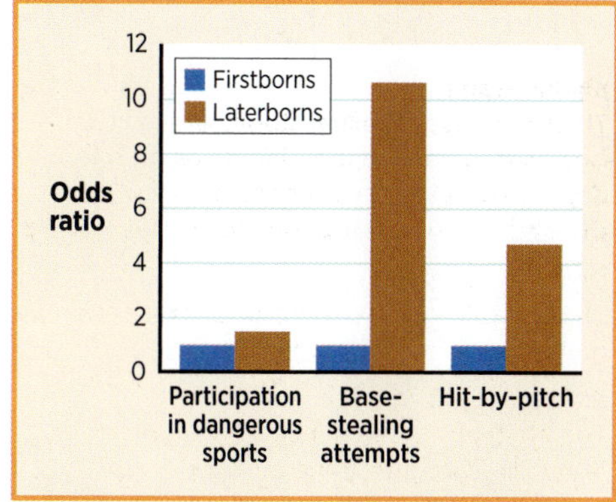

FIGURE 12.4 Birth Order and Risk Taking in Sports. Laterborns tend to take more dangerous risks than firstborns. As athletes, they more often choose dangerous sports, like boxing or gymnastics. As baseball players, they more often attempt to steal bases, which risks making an out, and allow pitches to hit them, which risks getting hurt.
Data from Sulloway and Zweigenhaft (2010).

It's worth mentioning that not all empirical research on birth order and personality supports Adler's theories (Rohrer et al., 2015). One large-scale study of 377,000 high school students measured correlations between birth order and several personality traits such as extraversion, impulsivity, and leadership characteristics. The average correlation was just .02, and none of the correlations extended higher than .05 or lower than –.05. In other words, each correlation between birth order and a particular personality trait fell very close to zero (remember, correlations can range all the way up to +1 and all the way down to –1), suggesting that your place among your siblings (if you have any) may not predict your personality much at all (Damian & Roberts, 2015).

Carl Jung. Carl Jung was once so in line with Freud's way of thinking that Freud personally chose Jung as his successor, but their views eventually diverged so much that Freud changed his mind (Bair, 2004; Shiraev, 2011). Among the big differences in their ways of thinking was the understanding of the unconscious. In contrast to Freud's notion that each of us created our own unique unconscious, Jung proposed the **collective unconscious**: common, inherited memories that are present in the minds of people of every culture. The idea is that the collective unconscious equips every person with basic, primal concepts (like a computer comes equipped with basic software) that have become central to human life throughout the ages (Jung, 1963).

Jung called these primal concepts **archetypes**: specific symbols or patterns within the collective unconscious that appear consistently across cultures and time periods. Examples of Jung's archetypes include the child, the hero, the great mother, the devil, the anima (femininity), and the animus (masculinity), among others. He pointed out that these archetypes emerge in some form in the art (paintings, stories, etc.) of cultures from every region and time period (Jung, 1964). For example, the hero archetype appears again and again in different forms from ancient Greece and China to contemporary Western society. Even as the specific appearance of the hero varies so widely, the universal essence of the hero — a courageous, noble person fighting for what they believe is right — remains unchanged.

Jung was also among the first to use the terms *introvert* and *extravert* to describe people with different personality types (Jung, 1971). Introverts are people who tend to focus inward and need little interaction with others. Extraverts are people who tend to focus outward and need lots of interaction with others.

Karen Horney. Karen Horney was one of very few women among the first generation of neo-Freudians. Among her pioneering ideas was the notion that women develop differently than men, and that it would be a mistake to assume that Freud's theories apply equally to both. For example, Horney disagreed with the emphasis on men in Freud's theories, such as the fact that he labeled the third psychosexual stage the "phallic" stage even though half of the people in the world don't have that body part.

Horney's theories served as a springboard for other feminist personality theorists. For example, Nancy Chodorow points out that the primary caretaker for children is typically the mother, which means that boys and girls face different challenges when they become old enough to form their own identity. Boys must form their identities by separating from mom and adopting a separate role model (usually dad or a male caregiver, if he's available), but girls must form their identities by remaining connected to mom yet developing their own individuality (Chodorow, 1978, 1989).

Similarly, Carol Gilligan highlights that women and men may develop different values and morals as they grow up — with women emphasizing the importance of interpersonal relationships more than men — but both are equally legitimate and normal (Gilligan, 1982, 1992). For example, when faced with the moral dilemma of turning in a friend who has done something wrong, women may focus more on maintaining the relationship, while men may focus more on justice.

Erik Erikson. Erik Erikson, whose theories we covered in Chapter 9 (Development Across the Life Span), was also a neo-Freudian. His greatest contribution, the eight-stage theory of psychosocial development, was closely related to Freud's

collective unconscious
Common, inherited memories that are present in the minds of people of every culture.

archetypes
Specific symbols or patterns within the collective unconscious that appear consistently across cultures and time periods.

five psychosexual stages. Erikson's first five stages correspond directly to Freud's, but the emphasis on biology and sex is replaced by an emphasis on social interaction with significant others. Erikson's next three stages extend all the way through adulthood, indicating his disagreement with the Freudian idea that personality is completely shaped by the time childhood ends (Erikson, 1946, 1950; Welchman, 2000).

Current Thoughts on Psychodynamic Theory

Psychodynamic theory remains a powerful force in psychology, but it's well past its heyday. It has been criticized broadly and sharply, and many different theories have arisen as alternative explanations of personality.

Perhaps the most damaging criticism aimed at psychodynamic theory is that it's not scientific enough (Michael, 2019; Tallis, 1996). Psychodynamic concepts are not easily defined, which makes it difficult to translate them into hypotheses that can be tested. For example, how can we be sure that the id, ego, and superego actually interact the way Freud said they did? Can we even be sure they exist? The three components certainly don't show up on CAT scans or MRIs of the brain. In Freud's day, when psychology was a younger field, speculations about the inner workings of the mind often went unchallenged. However, as psychology evolved, it has become a field of science rather than guesswork or speculation. Today, many psychologists dismiss Freud's theories, at least in part, because they can't be proven true or false. As such, they are often labeled as a faith rather than a science (Gabbard, 2009).

DIVERSITY MATTERS

Contemporary psychologists also criticize Freud for overgeneralizing his ideas (Grayling, 2002). He developed theories of personality that may have been a good fit for people like Freud himself: White men from Europe who lived during a historical period when sexuality was quite repressed, gender roles were quite rigid, almost every family included a mother and a father, and same-sex attraction was considered a disease. The problem is that when he proposed his theories, he claimed they held true for everyone, everywhere, at every time period. The work of Horney, Chodorow, and Gilligan (described previously) underscores the notion that for people of different genders, especially women in different times and places from Freud's own, Freud's theories may not apply.

Even some of Freud's core ideas seem to have softened over the years. Psychodynamic psychologists today are likely to agree with Freud's basic idea that early childhood experiences *influence* adult personality, but not that those experiences *completely determine* adult personality (Roberts et al., 2008). Neo-Freudians are likely to agree that the unconscious is an important force, but emphasize that it has numerous roles, including some that Freud didn't identify. For example, contemporary writings on the unconscious are likely to focus on information processing of which we are unaware (for instance, keeping track of how frequently events happen to us without trying to do so) in addition to id-versus-superego battles (Kaufman et al., 2010; Kihlstrom, 2008; Power & Brewin, 2011; Salti et al., 2019; Stadler & Frensch, 1998; Vlassova & Pearson, 2018). Contemporary psychodynamic psychologists are likely to agree that sexuality is a key element in human motivation, but insist that all sexual orientations can be equally healthy (Erwin, 2002; Lewes, 1995; Malark, 2017; Sand, 2017).

CHECK YOUR LEARNING:

12.4 What is the psychodynamic theory of personality?

12.5 What is the unconscious, and why is it important?

12.6 What are the id, superego, and ego?

12.7 What are the psychosexual stages of development?

12.8 How have Sigmund Freud's followers revised psychodynamic theories?

12.9 What is the contemporary view of psychodynamic theory?

To check your understanding of these questions, click show the answers or refer to the answers in the Chapter Summary.

Humanistic Theory of Personality

YOU WILL LEARN:

12.10 what the humanistic theory of personality is.

12.11 what self-actualization is.

12.12 how positive regard and conditions of worth can affect it.

12.13 how self-concept develops.

12.14 about current thoughts on humanistic theory.

The **humanistic theory of personality**, based on the ideas of Carl Rogers, emphasizes our inherent tendencies toward healthy, positive growth and self-fulfillment. Rogers became a psychologist at a time when the psychodynamic view was dominant, but he (like many others) soon grew weary of Freud's negative view of human nature. He simply didn't see people as fueled by biological, id-based desires like sex, aggression, and an insatiable drive for instant pleasure. Rogers had a much more positive, optimistic view of human nature and believed people were driven by the desire to reach their full potential (Cain, 2010).

Self-Actualization

Imagine a new plant just peeking out of the ground in the spring. We assume this plant has an inborn tendency to grow, to blossom and bloom. Likewise, Rogers assumed you have an inborn tendency toward **self-actualization**: fully becoming the person you have the potential to become. To grow, the plant needs water and sunlight. To self-actualize, you need what Rogers called **positive regard**: warmth, acceptance, and love from those around you. Rogers liked to use the word *prizing* as a less formal alternative to the term *positive regard*. Prizing captures the tender and full appreciation of another person (Rogers, 1959). For example, Rogers might say that Dinah prizes her granddaughter Melissa: that is, she cherishes Melissa without any kind of evaluation, simply because she is Melissa.

Bettmann/Getty Images

Carl Rogers developed the humanistic theory of personality, which emphasizes inherent tendencies toward healthy, positive growth and self-fulfillment.

Why does positive regard matter?

Problems arise when those around you don't provide *unconditional* positive regard, as Dinah provided Melissa, but instead make their positive regard *conditional* on certain behaviors or characteristics. In other words, they impose **conditions of worth**: requirements that you must meet to earn their positive regard. For example, some parents'/caregivers' love for their children depends on the grades they get, the sports they play, or the friends they choose. Because the parents'/caregivers' love and approval are so essential, the children will often meet those conditions of worth, even if it means straying from the interests or passions that come naturally to them. Like a plant that only gets sunlight from certain directions, certain "branches" of the child flourish while others wither. So, a child may sacrifice an important part of their true self in order to maintain their parents'/caregivers' approval. Or, as Rogers put it, the child's *real self* and *ideal self* would not match. The **real self** is the version of yourself that you actually experience in your day-to-day life. By contrast, the **ideal self** is the self-actualized version of yourself that you naturally strive to become (Cain, 2010).

Incongruence. Rogers believed that this **incongruence** – a mismatch between your real self and your ideal self – leads to unhappiness and mental illness. People experiencing incongruence feel like they can't be true to themselves but instead must change themselves to gain others' approval (or even pretend to be someone they are not). For example, the third-grade boy who plays hockey to win his parent's/caregiver's affections when he would much rather be practicing his violin; the teenager who does drugs to impress her friends, even though she doesn't really want to; the actor who auditions not because she enjoys theater but because her significant other pushed her to do so – all of these people will eventually sense a disconnect between who they really *are* and who they are *acting like* (Cain, 2010). (Think about that lopsided plant imagining, longingly, how it would feel to have all of its branches blooming.)

humanistic theory of personality
A theory based on the ideas of Carl Rogers that emphasizes people's inherent tendencies toward healthy, positive growth and self-fulfillment.

self-actualization
Fully becoming the person you have the potential to become.

positive regard
Warmth, acceptance, and love from those around you.

conditions of worth
Requirements that you must meet to earn a person's positive regard.

real self
The version of yourself that you actually experience in day-to-day life.

ideal self
The self-actualized version of yourself that you naturally strive to become.

incongruence
A mismatch between your real self and your ideal self.

Congruence. According to Rogers, the root of mental wellness is **congruence**: a match between your real self and your ideal self. People feel good when they are allowed to grow organically, according to their own natural tendencies. In our plant analogy, congruence happens when the sunlight comes from every direction. In human terms, congruence happens when you get unconditional positive regard from important people in your life, no matter how you behave. That doesn't mean that those important people approve of everything you do, but that they continue to value and appreciate you even when they may disapprove of a particular behavior of yours (Rogers, 1980; Tudor & Worrall, 2006).

The important point here is that your personality depends, in large part, on the way the people around you respond to your self-actualization tendency. If they nurture it, and allow all of your branches to flourish, you are likely to fully develop into the person you naturally are. If they stifle it, and allow only some of your branches to flourish, you are likely to develop into a person who only partially resembles your true self and otherwise portrays the kind of person others want you to be (Bohart & Tallman, 1999; Rogers, 1961, 1980). For example, consider Bhavna, a student in ninth grade who naturally tends to be cooperative with other people. If she has a parent/caregiver who makes their love (or positive regard) contingent on Bhavna defeating others (beating all her rivals at her chess tournament, earning first chair in violin in her school band, winning the election for class president), Bhavna may develop a competitive streak that betrays her naturally cooperative style.

paladin13/iStock/Getty Images

Carl Rogers believed that each person—just like a plant emerging from the ground—has an inborn tendency to grow, blossom, and bloom. He called that tendency self-actualization—fully becoming the person you have the potential to become.

Abraham Maslow. Abraham Maslow, whose hierarchy of needs we covered in Chapter 8, was another leading humanistic theorist. Like Rogers, Maslow emphasized that self-actualization is a primary motivation. However, Maslow reminded us that more basic needs (such as food, water, safety, and a feeling of belonging) must be secured before a person attempts to self-actualize (Maslow, 1968). According to Maslow, only when you feel fed, safe, and loved can you move on to fulfilling your full potential as a human being.

Speaking of Maslow's hierarchy of needs, one creative study found that self-actualization was not as important as the more fundamental physiological and safety needs when the COVID pandemic initially hit. These researchers examined billions of search engine entries in the United States during the first 4 weeks of the pandemic, then compared those online searches to online searches during pre-pandemic times. They found huge increases in Internet searches that reflected physiological needs, like grocery availability, restaurant delivery, health equipment, and toilet paper. Similarly, they found huge increases in Internet searches that reflected safety needs, like COVID protective equipment (masks, cleaning supplies, etc.), economic stimulus information, and unemployment benefits. On the other hand, they found sizable decreases in Internet searches that reflected self-actualization needs, like wedding-related purchases and topics related to life goals (Suh et al., 2021).

Maslow also believed that we experience a higher number of *peak experiences* as we move closer to self-actualization. These peak experiences are moments in which we are overcome with transcendent joy and fulfillment. People often use words like *mystical* or *ecstatic* to describe their peak experiences. They also describe a sense of exceptional harmony with the world around them, as well as a strong sense of purpose. The kinds of activities that bring about peak experiences vary widely, but for many people, music, art, religion, sports, or intimate interactions are the most likely sparks (Gabrielsson et al., 2016; Privette, 1983; Yaden et al., 2016). As Maslow (1968) explained it, a peak experience is "the most wonderful experience or experiences of your life; happiest moments, ecstatic moments, moments of rapture, perhaps from being in love, or from listening to music or suddenly 'being hit' by a book or painting, or from some great creative moment" (p. 83).

Self-Concept

Your **self-concept** is your view of who you are. The way important people in your life treat you, particularly how they respond to your self-actualization tendencies, has tremendous power in shaping that view of yourself. For example, the conditions of worth that others place on you become conditions of worth that you place on yourself (Hattie, 1992;

congruence
A match between your real self and your ideal self.

self-concept
Your view of who you are.

Rogers, 1959). Think again about the fifth-grader whose dad pushes him to excel at hockey despite the boy's lack of passion for the game. Over time, the condition he has learned from his dad (*You are* a worthy person only if *you* continue to pursue sports over the arts) is likely to become a rule he will apply to himself (*I am* a worthy person only if *I* continue to pursue sports over the arts). By the same token, someone who receives unconditional positive regard (*You* are a good person no matter what) is likely to internalize that message and have unconditional positive *self*-regard (*I* am a good person no matter what).

According to Rogers, other common terms that refer to our opinions of ourselves — for example, *self-esteem*, *self-image*, and *self-worth* — all follow the same pattern. The ways we think about ourselves are not inborn, but molded by the opinions of us that we receive from the most important people in our lives. These important people are often parents/caregivers or other family members when we are kids, but they can also be friends, romantic partners, or coworkers when we grow up. For example, someone whose partner repeatedly provides the feedback that "You are lazy" will be hard-pressed not to incorporate that message into their own self-image. By contrast, a person whose partner consistently tells them through words and actions that "You are wonderful" will build that message into their own self-esteem.

Current Thoughts on Humanistic Theory

Like psychodynamic theory, humanistic theory has been hugely influential in both academia and popular culture. Humanistic theory set the stage for the emphasis on self-concept and self-worth, which were largely neglected before its emergence in the 1960s. Now self-concept and self-worth receive attention from child-raising experts, educators, and couples counselors. Humanistic theory also gave rise to the positive psychology movement and continues to significantly influence the way that many psychotherapists practice (Angus et al., 2015; Cook et al., 2009; Rogers, 2018). More specifically, an increasing number of therapists are now utilizing *positive interventions* or *strength-based counseling*. These treatments differ from more traditional styles, which focus on clients' challenges and disorders, by emphasizing and building on clients' assets and abilities (Magyar-Moe et al., 2015; Nichols & Graves, 2018; Rashid, 2015; Seligman, 2011; Seligman et al., 2005; Snyder et al., 2011).

The current view of humanistic theory also includes many criticisms. Perhaps the most common critique is that humanistic theory is simply too optimistic and naïve. Remember, the bedrock of humanism is the idea that people are basically good. If this is true, and people simply want to live their own true, full lives, why do horrific crimes committed by one person against another fill newscasts on a daily basis? Can stifled self-actualization explain assault, murder, and war, or is there something more sinister in human nature than the mere desire to blossom and bloom? Perhaps that plant receiving sunlight from every direction will not blossom into a beautiful rose or even a harmless fern, but a vicious Venus flytrap.

Humanistic theory, like psychodynamic theory, has also been criticized for being unscientific. It's difficult to empirically define and confirm the mere existence of humanism's core concepts — the self-actualization tendency, the real and ideal selves, congruence and incongruence — let alone test the specific ways that Rogers proposed they work.

DIVERSITY MATTERS Humanistic theory is also criticized today for its strong endorsement of individualism. Some argue that Rogers's perception of the healthy individual as someone who follows only their own growth potential is a bit self-indulgent. We are individuals, of course, but we are also members of important groups (couples, families, communities, etc.), and we have obligations to balance what fosters our own personal growth with what fosters the well-being of the group. Along the same lines, collectivistic cultures that emphasize harmony in interpersonal relationships and obedience to parents/caregivers, such as many Asian cultures, may have a different take on what Rogers called incongruence. They may view the sacrifice of certain aspects of self-growth as commendable and selfless decisions that show respect for others rather than an inevitable source of personal unhappiness (Heine et al., 1999).

CHECK YOUR LEARNING:

12.10 What is the humanistic theory of personality?

12.11 What is self-actualization?

12.12 What is positive regard, and how does it relate to conditions of worth?

12.13 What is self-concept, and how does it develop?

12.14 What is the contemporary view of humanistic theory?

To check your understanding of these questions, click show the answers or refer to the answers in the Chapter Summary.

Behavioral and Social-Cognitive Theories of Personality

Behavioral and social-cognitive theories of personality offer a perspective much more grounded in science than either psychodynamic or humanistic theory. The **behavioral theory of personality** emphasizes the influence of the environment and the importance of observable, measurable behavior. The **social-cognitive theory of personality** emphasizes the interaction of environment, thought processes, and social factors.

YOU WILL LEARN:

12.15 what the behavioral theory of personality is.

12.16 what the social-cognitive theory of personality is.

12.17 about reciprocal determinism, or the interaction of behavior, environment, and cognitions.

12.18 about self-efficacy, or belief about one's abilities.

12.19 about locus of control, or the belief about internal and external influences on one's fate.

12.20 about current thoughts on behavioral and social-cognitive theories.

Behavioral Theory: The Importance of the Environment

You are already quite familiar with behavioral theory. In fact, behaviorism was the main focus of Chapter 6 (Learning), with its emphasis on classical conditioning and operant conditioning as explanations for what we do. Based on what you know about learning, it may come as no surprise that behaviorists think there is no such thing as personality.

Wait—how could they say there's no such thing as personality?

Let's revisit our definition of personality from the beginning of this chapter: "a person's distinctive and stable way of thinking, feeling, and behaving." Behaviorists have trouble with at least a few words in that definition. To begin, thinking and feeling are both activities that take place inside the mind and therefore can't be directly observed or measured. That means they are impossible to study empirically, so (according to behaviorists) they should not receive our attention. Only behavior *can* be observed and measured, so behavior should define personality by itself (Hunt, 1993; Kazdin, 1978; Watson, 1924). The other word in the definition that behaviorists have a problem with is *stable*, because *stable* implies there is something deep *within* the person — a trait, a characteristic, a quality — that causes them to consistently behave in a certain way. Ivan Pavlov's dogs didn't salivate because of some internal, stable characteristic; they salivated because of classical conditioning — specifically, the way sounds such as a bell were paired with food. B. F. Skinner's pigeons didn't peck at a button in the Skinner box because of some internal, stable characteristic; they pecked because of operant conditioning — specifically, the way the pecking was followed by a reinforcer. The animals' behavior was determined by factors outside

behavioral theory of personality
A theory that emphasizes the influence of the environment and the importance of observable, measurable behavior.

social-cognitive theory of personality
A theory that emphasizes the interaction of environment, thought processes, and social factors.

reciprocal determinism
The theory that three factors — behavior, environment, and cognitions — continually influence each other.

of them, not because of anything internal (Evans, 1968; Pavlov, 1927, 1928; Skinner, 1938).

According to behaviorists, people are no different from Pavlov's dogs or Skinner's pigeons. People behave a certain way because of the conditioning *outside* them rather than any stable force *inside* of them. As long as the conditioning remains the same, the behavior stays the same. If the conditioning changes, then the behavior changes. It's hard to believe that personality exists if behavior is so malleable by external conditions (Skinner, 1971).

For example, consider Josh, a 7-year-old child living with his father in a single-parent home. Josh whines a lot. A traditional view of personality might suggest that Josh has a deep-seated, unwavering characteristic — whininess — that causes him to whine as much as he does. But behaviorists would point out that Josh's dad reinforces the whining by giving Josh what he wants. Behaviorists would agree that Josh has a *habit* of whining a lot, but this habit developed because Josh received a reinforcing response for it, and it could be reversed if Josh received punishment for it, or even if it was simply ignored.

The idea that "personality" is really just habit controlled by external conditions indicates another core idea of the behavioral approach: the absence of free will. For behaviorists, external conditions determine all of your behavior. You do what you do because your conditioning experiences determine it, not because of any "choices" you make based on deep-rooted "personality" characteristics (Skinner, 1938, 1976). According to behaviorists, you have no more free will than a beach ball blown by the wind (Al-Hoorie, 2015).

Social-Cognitive Theory: Social Factors and Thoughts Are Important Too

Even the most die-hard behaviorists have to admit that behavior — *human* behavior — can't be entirely explained by external conditions. Compared to rats, pigeons, or dogs, there is a lot more thinking going on between our ears. We don't move through life without thinking, letting reinforcements and punishments shape us as if we were simple California sea slugs. We talk about the things that happen with other people and change our behavior based on what we observe. We form expectations, interpretations, beliefs, and plans rather than just responding automatically to what goes on around us. For social-cognitive theorists, personality blends the behavioral emphasis on external conditioning and these mental activities that involve our interactions with others ("social") and our thought processes ("cognitive"). These social and cognitive ingredients are not as observable and measurable as strict behaviorists would prefer, but social-cognitive theorists recognize that they are powerful influences on personality.

Albert Bandura, Reciprocal Determinism, and Self-Efficacy. Albert Bandura, the most prominent social-cognitive theorist, argues that your personality involves an ongoing *interaction* of multiple forces (Bandura, 1977a, 1986, 2001). He calls this idea **reciprocal determinism**: the theory that three factors — your behavior, your environment, and your cognitions — continually influence each other. **Figure 12.5** illustrates this interaction. Notice the double-sided arrows between all three boxes in the figure. These indicate that the relationships between behavior, environment, and cognitions are two-way streets — in other words, they all affect each other. As an example, consider Yolanda, who decides to adopt a more active lifestyle by taking a boot-camp exercise class at a nearby gym. By attending that class, Yolanda puts herself in an environment where she receives reinforcement (encouragement from fellow boot-campers) for her exercise behavior and also observes a group of dedicated exercisers who can serve as models. That environment is likely to affect both her cognitions ("This is actually enjoyable," and "I can do this") and her behavior (returning for more classes). She then puts herself in the boot-camp environment even more frequently (that is, her behavior changes), and the cycle continues.

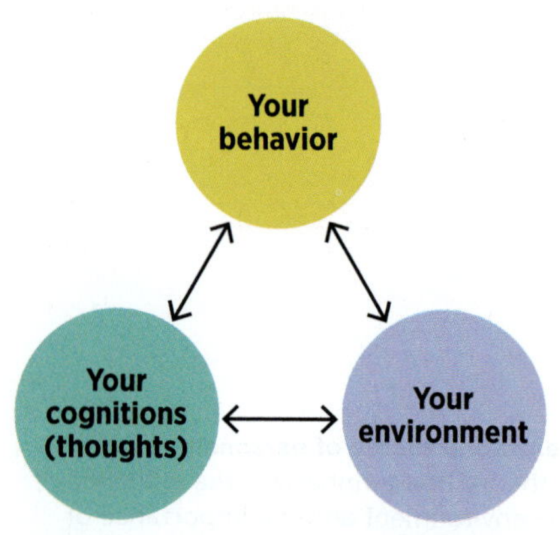

FIGURE 12.5 Reciprocal Determinism. According to Albert Bandura's concept of reciprocal determinism, your thoughts, your environment, and your behavior all influence each other.

The point here is that it's not just your environment that influences your behavior, as behaviorists would argue. Your behavior also shapes the environment in which you find yourself, and your cognitions enter the mix along the way as well.

Speaking of cognitions, Bandura emphasized one kind especially: **self-efficacy**, or your beliefs about your own capabilities (Bandura 1977b, 1982, 1997; Stajkovic et al., 2018). Yolanda's cognition — "I can do this" — reflects the importance of self-efficacy. If she left the first boot-camp classes overwhelmed and intimidated, thinking, "No way — this is too hard for me," she would be unlikely to return. But she did return, thanks to her belief that she could succeed. The key here is that Yolanda's self-efficacy (what she believes she can do) might be just as important as her actual physical ability or the difficulty level of the class. (I wonder if Albert Bandura read *The Little Engine That Could* when he was a kid: "*I think I can, I think I can . . .*")

The COVID pandemic took a toll on the self-efficacy of many people whose jobs suddenly became different or more challenging than they had been pre-pandemic. For example, one study of hundreds of teachers in the United States found that their self-efficacy regarding teaching was lower during the pandemic than before, especially among those teachers who were teaching virtually as opposed to in-person (Pressley & Ha, 2021). Another study of over one thousand nurses working in hospitals during the pandemic found that about half had low levels of self-efficacy regarding their jobs, and the rate of low self-efficacy was even higher among nurses with relatively little experience and less education (Simonetti et al., 2021).

self-efficacy
Your beliefs about your own capabilities.

locus of control
Your belief about how much control you have over what happens to you.

internal locus of control
The belief that your life is under the control of forces inside of yourself.

external locus of control
The belief that your life is under the control of forces outside of yourself.

Julian Rotter and Locus of Control. Julian Rotter, another important social-cognitive theorist, highlighted another kind of cognition that influences personality: **locus of control**, or your belief about how much control you have over what happens to you. The Latin word *locus* is the root of the word *location*, and according to Rotter, there are two locations for locus of control: within yourself and outside yourself. He gave each location a label: an **internal locus of control** is the belief that your life is under the control of forces inside of you, and an **external locus of control** is the belief that your life is under the control of forces outside of you (Galvin et al., 2018; Rotter, 1966, 1975, 1989).

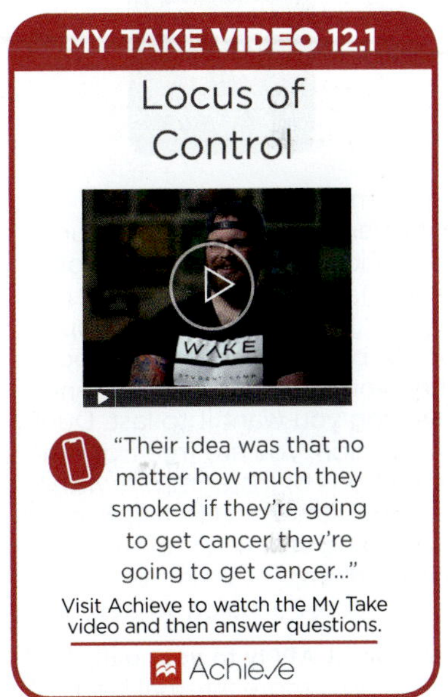

MY TAKE VIDEO 12.1
Locus of Control
WAKE
"Their idea was that no matter how much they smoked if they're going to get cancer they're going to get cancer..."
Visit Achieve to watch the My Take video and then answer questions.
Achieve

Locus of control can powerfully influence what we choose to do. Consider bike helmets. Isabella chooses to wear one, demonstrating her internal locus of control: "There are actions I can take to protect myself from injury on this bike ride." Eve chooses not to wear one, demonstrating her external locus of control: "If an accident happens, it happens. I can't really do anything about it." When you consider the vast array of everyday decisions that locus of control can affect — whether to eat healthy, whether to recycle, whether to apply for a job, whether to vote, whether to try anything at all — it's easy to see how it can shape the behaviors that form Isabella's and Eve's personalities. In Eve's case, if her external locus of control became extreme and she applied it to many areas of her life, it could resemble *learned helplessness*. (Remember Seligman's dogs from Chapter 6?) This in turn could lead to feelings of depression based on her belief that any action she might take to help herself will be futile.

Here are more examples of how your locus of control could influence the way you look at important issues in your daily life:

- *Will my relationship with my partner last?* If your locus of control is internal, you're likely to think it depends on how much time and effort you spend on the relationship, or on your judgement about who to begin to date in the first place. If your locus of control is external, you're likely to think it depends on your partner's personality, your friends' and family's acceptance of your partner, or just random chance.
- *Will I get good grades in college?* If your locus of control is internal, you're likely to think it depends on how you prioritize school among your other

activities, how much time you dedicate, and how effectively you study. If your locus of control is external, you're likely to think it depends on how difficult your instructors make your classes, how you are graded (exams vs. papers, multiple choice vs. essays, etc.), or how much other people in your life interfere with or support your college experience.

- *Will I be physically fit?* If your locus of control is internal, you're likely to think it depends on the eating and exercise habits that you create for yourself. If your locus of control is external, you're likely to think it depends on the genes you inherited, the side effects of medicines you need to take, or other factors you can't control.
- *Will I become wealthy?* If your locus of control is internal, you're likely to think it depends on how hard you work, how wisely you save, or how smartly you invest. If your locus of control is external, you're likely to think it depends on luck (like winning the lottery, or stumbling into a high-paying job), inheritances that you may not even know to expect, or the generosity of friends and family.

DIVERSITY MATTERS Research generally supports the idea that people with an external locus of control are more likely to experience symptoms of depression and other psychological disorders (Bjørkløf et al., 2013; Garlovsky et al., 2016; Harrow et al., 2009). However, that correlation depends to some extent on cultural factors. Specifically, the connection is weaker for people in more collectivistic cultures than for people in more individualistic cultures. This may reflect the relative importance that each type of culture places on the perception that each person controls their own personal lives (Cheng et al., 2013).

Locus of control can also shape personality by powerfully influencing how we explain what happens to us. For example, imagine that both Isabella and Eve were passed over for a promotion at work. Isabella is more likely to blame herself: "I didn't do enough to earn it." On the other hand, Eve is more likely to blame forces outside of herself: "My supervisor is unfair," or "My coworker who got the promotion is a cheater." More recent research on locus of control has indicated that people have not only a general locus of control, but specific ones too. For example, you may feel that you control your fate at work or school, but that your health, finances, and romantic life are not up to you (Hummer et al., 2011; Ng et al., 2006). The From Research to Real Life box explores an additional research finding about how locus of control has shifted over the years.

Researchers have explored a variety of ways that locus of control may influence a person's experience of the COVID pandemic. For example, in one study of over 400 U.S. residents, researchers measured locus of control regarding the pandemic by asking participants if they agreed with statements like "I am in control of whether I get COVID" and "If I take care of myself, I can avoid COVID." They also measured the extent to which participants adhered to COVID safety guidelines (social distancing, masks, hand washing, etc.). Results showed that people who agreed more with those kinds of statements – that is, people whose locus of control was more internal – were much more likely to stick to COVID safety guidelines (Devereux et al., 2021).

Other studies of locus of control have focused on the mental health effects of the pandemic and have generally found that an internal locus of control is beneficial. For example, one pandemic study of over 1700 adults in the United States and five European countries found that those with an internal locus of control had fewer symptoms of depression, anxiety, and stress than those with an external locus of control (Sigurvinsdottir et al., 2020). Another pandemic study found that among hundreds of people in the Middle East and North Africa who worked in the hospitality industry (in restaurants, hotels, etc.), those with an internal locus of control experienced much lower levels of depression, anxiety, and alienation than their coworkers with an external locus of control (Mahmoud et al., 2021).

CHAPTER APP 12.1

Freedom

Freedom is one of many apps that offer you control over your smartphone (or computer, or other devices). You schedule a "Freedom session" by deciding which apps and Web sites you want to block, when you want it to happen, and how long you want it to last. During that session, you are free from the distractions of Instagram, Twitter, YouTube, Amazon, Netflix, e-mail, or anything else you choose. As it says on the app's Web site: "Control distractions. Focus on what matters."

How does it APPly to your daily life?
If you had a more internal locus of control regarding your phone and how continuously it could distract you—the basic purpose of this app—would you interact differently with your phone? What differences would you expect to see in your productivity or your well-being?

How does it APPly to your understanding of psychology?
How does this app help you to understand the concept of *locus of control*? Do you think this app would appeal more to someone whose locus of control was internal or external?

To learn more about this app or to download it to your phone, you can search for "Freedom app" on Google, in the iPhone App store, or in the Google Play store.

FROM RESEARCH TO REAL LIFE

What's Happening to Our Locus of Control?

Has our locus of control shifted in recent generations? Compared to older generations, to what extent do you believe that your actions (rather than outside forces) can impact your life? According to research, your locus of control is probably more external than theirs.

Researchers conducted a massive review of studies conducted since 1930 in which participants' locus of control was measured (Twenge & Campbell, 2008). Combined, these studies included over *1.4 million* participants. The conclusion? Over time, the average score on measures of locus of control has drifted consistently and significantly toward the external extreme. This trend was equally strong across genders, and appears in children as well as adults. The trend toward a more external locus of control is especially strong in recent decades, such that it is clear in comparisons of studies from the 2000s to studies just two decades earlier (Twenge et al., 2004).

Where does this trend come from? Researchers see a connection between the trend toward external locus of control and societal changes in the United States toward greater individualism, alienation, and cynicism (Twenge et al., 2004). The current generation seems to have some doubt (perhaps a lot of doubt) about the idea that their lives depend on their own actions. Instead, they seem resigned to the notion that their fate is not in their own hands.

This resignation about external locus of control has bad implications for mental health. Researchers combined data from over 40 years of studies across 18 cultures and found positive correlations between locus of control and depression and between locus of control and anxiety (with some variation across cultural groups) (Cheng et al., 2013). Such a connection between locus of control and mental illness, especially depression, has been found by numerous other researchers as well (Harrow et al., 2009; Richardson et al., 2012; Twenge et al., 2010).

Have you noticed any indications of this trend toward external locus of control in your own life, or the corresponding increases in depression? Do your friends accept truths from previous generations such as "Life is what you make it" or "With hard work, anything's possible"? To what extent have those truths been replaced by feelings of apathy and powerlessness? What can we expect for future generations? •

Current Thoughts on Behavioral and Social-Cognitive Theories

Behavioral theories of personality are held in high regard by those who insist that all aspects of psychology should be empirically based. It is, after all, the most grounded in science of the personality theories we have covered. But many current psychologists find that pure behaviorism doesn't tell the whole story. By assuming that people behave just as animals do, it plays up the influence of the environment to the exclusion of uniquely human factors, especially the way we think and interact. And the behavioral notion that personality doesn't exist at all doesn't fly with most current psychologists. Even if conditioning and the environment are major factors in shaping our behavior, few agree that they are the only actors (Goldfried, 1995; O'Donohue, 2009).

Social-cognitive theories of personality consider factors beyond environment, especially the way we think and the social interactions we have. More than other personality theories, social-cognitive theory identifies many possible influences on personality. This "diversified" approach is both a strength and a weakness. On one hand, it makes social-cognitive theory particularly comprehensive; on the other hand, it makes social-cognitive theory seem less focused than some other theories. It is noteworthy that certain concepts within social-cognitive theory have been quite well supported by empirical literature. Self-efficacy, for example, has been shown to enhance achievement in a wide variety of areas, including memory abilities, work performance, exercise, breastfeeding, quitting smoking, reducing obesity, and overcoming cancer (Ashford et al., 2010; Beaudoin & Desrichard, 2011; Brockway et al., 2017; Gwaltney et al., 2009; Herts et al., 2017; Sadri & Robertson, 1993; Teixeira et al., 2015).

CHECK YOUR LEARNING:

12.15 What is the behavioral theory of personality?

12.16 What is the social-cognitive theory of personality?

12.17 According to the theory of reciprocal determinism, which three factors continually influence each other?

12.18 What is self-efficacy?

12.19 What is locus of control?

12.20 What is the contemporary view of the behavioral theory of personality and the social-cognitive theory of personality?

To check your understanding of these questions, click show the answers or refer to the answers in the Chapter Summary.

Trait Theory of Personality

YOU WILL LEARN:

12.21 what the trait theory of personality is.

12.22 how trait theorists strive to identify the basic ingredients of personality.

12.23 about the traits included in the five-factor, or Big Five, model of personality.

12.24 about current thoughts on trait theory.

The **trait theory of personality** emphasizes the discovery and description of the basic components of personality. All other personality theories attempt to explain *why* personality develops the way it does. By contrast, trait theory attempts to explain *what* personality is made of (John et al., 2008).

Many of the other personality theories, especially psychodynamic and humanistic, rely heavily on speculations about the inner workings of the mind that can't be empirically proven or disproven. Trait theory – especially the *five-factor model* (or *Big Five*), which we will examine in detail – has emerged in recent decades as a more scientific alternative. For that reason, while research on some other approaches to personality has dwindled in recent decades, research on trait theory has flourished.

A New Approach to Understanding Personality

When you eat an oatmeal cookie, you probably notice differences between that particular cookie and other oatmeal cookies you have eaten in the past. Why does one taste different from another? Most oatmeal cookies are made from the same short list of ingredients – oats, flour, sugar, eggs, butter – but each batch contains a different amount of each ingredient. More sugar in one batch or less butter in another batch will produce a noticeable difference in taste.

Trait theorists believe that our personalities, like oatmeal cookies, are all made from the same short list of ingredients. The aim of their research is to uncover those ingredients. They call these ingredients **traits**: stable elements of personality that influence thoughts, feelings, and behavior across most situations. Trait theorists assume that varying amounts of each trait account for differences in personality, just as varying amounts of each baking ingredient account for differences in taste. Trait theorists don't concern themselves much with how a particular trait develops over the course of a person's life. (That is a big difference from the psychodynamic, humanistic, behavioral, and social-cognitive theorists who we covered earlier.) Instead, trait theorists try to figure out exactly what those traits are, thereby understanding exactly what makes up human personality (Digman, 1996).

One of the main challenges in identifying the basic traits of human personality is narrowing down the massive number of possibilities. Just think of all the words in the English language that could describe the personalities of the people you know. Gordon Allport, an early trait theorist, actually read through the dictionary and found about 18,000 descriptive words (Allport, 1937; Allport & Odbert, 1936). Researchers who followed him took on the task of reducing this enormous number to a more manageable size. (Imagine that you signed up for an online dating service and got 18,000 different personality ratings of each potential date!)

This task – boiling down a huge list of personality traits to a shorter list of "supertraits" – would become a theme of trait theory as the years went by. For example, in the 1940s, Raymond Cattell reduced the personality descriptors to just 16 clusters (Cattell, 1943). From this list, he created a personality questionnaire called the *16PF* that was widely used for some time. As time went by, trait theorists used increasingly sophisticated statistical procedures (and increasingly powerful computers to run them). The most important of these is *factor analysis*, which takes a long list of variables and forms clusters that correlate with each other (Wright, 2017). Factor analysis shows that certain adjectives that describe

trait theory of personality
A theory that emphasizes the discovery and description of the basic components of personality.

traits
Stable elements of personality that influence thoughts, feelings, and behavior across most situations.

personality tend to hang together — for example, *shy, reserved, introverted, bashful,* and *withdrawn* — suggesting that those words all describe the same underlying trait.

The Five-Factor Model

Today, the leaders of trait theory are Paul Costa and Robert McCrae, who have continued the work of identifying the underlying "supertraits" of personality that was started by Allport and Cattell. Their work, along with related work by other researchers, has produced the **five-factor model of personality** (also known as the **Big Five**): an explanation of personality that emphasizes five fundamental traits present in all people to varying degrees. So, decades after Cattell reduced Allport's list of 18,000 personality ingredients to only 16 clusters, Costa and McCrae further reduced it to just five traits (Costa & McCrae, 1985, 1992a, 2008, 2017; McCrae & Costa, 2003, 2008; Widiger & Costa, 2012).

The Big Five have received so much attention and generated so much research in recent decades that they have become absolutely central to the study of personality (Digman, 1990; McCrae & Costa, 1996; Widiger, 2017). One researcher boldly stated that "most personality psychologists have come to agree that the Big Five *are* the basic dimensions of personality" (Hunt, 1993; italics added). Let's take a close look at those five traits here and in **Figure 12.6** (Jackson & Hill, 2019; Schwaba, 2019; Shiner, 2019; Smillie et al., 2019; Tackett et al., 2019):

- **Neuroticism**—the tendency to experience negative emotions such as anxiety, depression, and stress
- **Extraversion**—the tendency to be socially outgoing
- **Openness to experience**—the tendency to be receptive to new or unconventional ideas
- **Conscientiousness**—the tendency to be organized, responsible, and deliberate
- **Agreeableness**—the tendency to cooperate and comply with other people

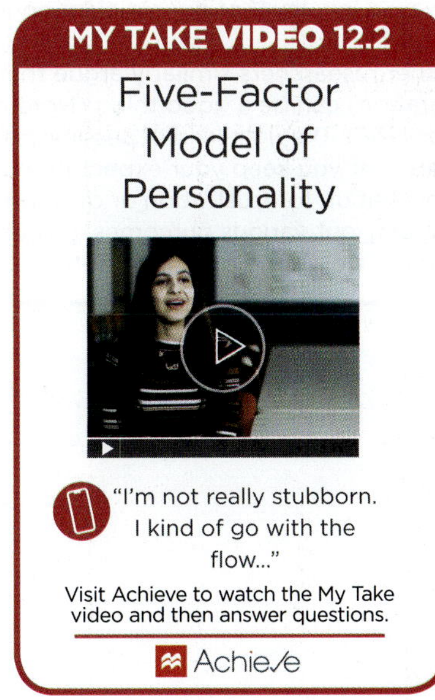

MY TAKE VIDEO 12.2
Five-Factor Model of Personality
"I'm not really stubborn. I kind of go with the flow..."
Visit Achieve to watch the My Take video and then answer questions.
Achieve

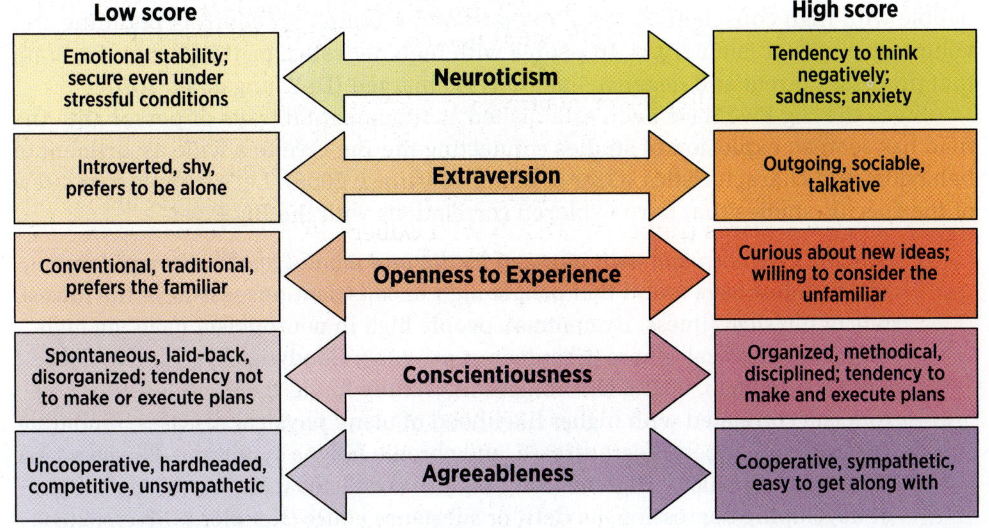

FIGURE 12.6 Descriptions of High and Low Levels of Big Five Personality Traits. Everyone lands somewhere on the dimension of each of the Big Five traits of personality—high, low, or somewhere between.

Five-Factor Model of personality (Big Five)
An explanation of personality that emphasizes five fundamental traits present in all people to varying degrees.

neuroticism
A personality trait emphasizing the tendency to experience negative emotions such as anxiety, depression, and stress.

extraversion
A personality trait emphasizing the tendency to be socially outgoing.

openness to experience
A personality trait emphasizing the tendency to be receptive to new or unconventional ideas.

conscientiousness
A personality trait emphasizing the tendency to be organized, responsible, and deliberate.

agreeableness
A personality trait emphasizing the tendency to cooperate and comply with other people.

CURRENT CONTROVERSY

Is There an Upside to Neuroticism?

At first glance, neuroticism seems all bad. The negative thinking, the self-doubt, the worry, the glass-half-empty mentality—who would want it?

Turns out, everybody might, at least a little bit. A number of psychologists have offered a defense of neuroticism, at least in small doses. For example, researchers argue that neuroticism can foster vigilance—a watchfulness or alertness that could provide an early warning of dangerous situations (Watson & Casillas, 2003). Who is more likely to try to avoid a dimly lit parking lot in a high-crime area or sidestep a doctor's waiting room full of contagious diseases—someone with high or low neuroticism? Viewed this way, a low level of neuroticism could actually leave you more vulnerable.

Other researchers similarly argue that pessimism (again, in moderation) can be a good thing (Norem, 2003, 2008; Norem & Cantor, 1986). The right kind of pessimism—"defensive pessimism"—ensures that you keep your expectations reasonable and don't set yourself up for frustration or disappointment. It also enables you to play out various outcomes in your head, which helps you determine whether a particular option is too risky to your physical or psychological well-being. Compared to an impulsive headfirst dive into a potentially harmful situation, a little defensive pessimism sounds pretty good.

The upside of neuroticism is just one part of the larger picture of pros and cons of the Big Five. High levels of any of these five traits carry advantages and disadvantages (Chang & Sanna, 2003). One researcher contends that these benefits and costs have evolutionary, survival-of-the-fittest connotations (Nettle, 2011). For example, high levels of extraversion probably gave our ancestors increased chances for sexual encounters that could lead to offspring, but also greater risks of infectious diseases or interpersonal conflicts that could lead to bodily harm or death. High levels of openness to experience probably gave our ancestors increased creativity in solving problems (upon which their lives may have depended), but also greater risks of bizarre or disorganized thinking that could lead to life-threatening mistakes. High levels of agreeableness probably gave our ancestors increased ability to form alliances with other individuals and groups (which could enhance survival), but also greater chances of being targeted when those other people turned out to be liars or thieves. •

With the Big Five traits (which the acronym OCEAN can help you remember), the question is not *whether* a person has them, but *to what extent* a person has each one. Each trait exists on a continuum, like a light bulb controlled by a dimmer rather than an on–off switch. Consider agreeableness as an example. The question is not whether a person has agreeableness or doesn't have it; instead, the question is how much agreeableness the person has. According to this approach, your unique combination of the five traits is what makes your personality different from everyone else's.

The Big Five emerge during childhood and remain rather consistent throughout the life span, suggesting that they may have genetic or biological roots (De Pauw, 2017; Jarnecke & South, 2017; McCrae & Costa, 2003; Soldz & Vaillant, 1999). Additional evidence of the biology behind the Big Five comes from MRI studies, which show that the size of a particular brain region corresponds to the level of each trait. For example, in people with high conscientiousness, the part of the brain that controls planning and voluntary behavior is enlarged. In people with high neuroticism, the part of the brain that processes threat and negative emotions is enlarged (DeYoung et al., 2010).

Since the Big Five have been established as fundamental traits of personality, the field has seen an explosion of studies connecting the Big Five to a wide assortment of behaviors and characteristics (Ozer & Benet-Martinez, 2006). Let's sample just a few of the specific studies that have explored correlations with the Big Five:

- *The Big Five correlate with physical health and mental health.* Several large-scale studies have found that people high in conscientiousness have the lowest rate of physical illness. By contrast, people high in neuroticism have the highest rate of physical illness (Chapman et al., 2013; Goodwin & Friedman, 2006; Kern & Friedman, 2017). One longitudinal study found that high levels of neuroticism correlated with higher likelihood of many physical diseases, including chronic pain, ulcers, heart disease, and chronic fatigue syndrome, 25 years later (Charles et al., 2008). High neuroticism also correlates with increased chances of developing depression, anxiety, or substance abuse (Kendler & Myers, 2010; Kotov et al., 2010). The Big Five even correlate with your *beliefs* about your health: people high in neuroticism (and, to a lesser extent, people low in agreeableness) believe more strongly than others that they will catch infectious diseases or pick up germs from others if they stand near them, shake their hands, or share a water bottle with them (Duncan et al., 2009).

WATCHING PSYCHOLOGY

Personality and Preferences in Movies and TV

Advertisers and marketers in the entertainment field often rely on demographics (age, gender, ethnicity, etc.) to predict who will like particular television shows or movies. Research suggests that psychological variables, especially the Big Five personality traits, may actually do a better job as predictors (Sandy et al., 2013). Among the specific connections made between personality and preferences are these:

- People with high levels of openness to experience tend to like movies and TV shows that present different worlds or provoke new thoughts, such as foreign films, indie movies, artsy pieces, and intellectually challenging documentaries (Chamorro-Premuzic et al., 2014; Kraaykamp & Van Eijck, 2005).
- People with high levels of agreeableness tend to dislike movies in which people have violent disagreements, so they typically avoid action movies and instead choose movies and TV shows where people get along nicely, like romances and comedies (Chamorro-Premuzic et al., 2014; Hall, 2005).
- People with high levels of neuroticism tend to prefer movies and shows that provide an escape from the real world, like sci-fi films and soap operas (Chamorro-Premuzic et al., 2014; Kraaykamp & Van Eijck, 2005).
- People high in extraversion tend to watch less TV (which is done at home, often alone) and tend to watch more movies (which is often done by going out, usually with others) than people low in extraversion (Krcmar & Kean, 2005; Weaver, 2003). When people high in extraversion do watch TV, they tend to prefer reality TV shows (Shim & Paul, 2007). •

- *The Big Five correlate with grades.* In studies ranging from young children to college students, conscientiousness, agreeableness, and openness positively correlate with GPA. Conscientiousness was by far the most important of these personality traits; in fact, high conscientiousness predicts high grades just as accurately as intelligence does (Caprara et al., 2011; Poropat, 2009; Rimfield et al., 2016). Conscientiousness also correlates with academic *motivation*—how badly you want to do well in school—which could certainly be an important part of its link to the grades you get (Komarraju et al., 2009).
- *The Big Five correlate with job performance.* Many studies have found that high conscientiousness correlates with high levels of job performance, but more recent studies have begun to find that too much conscientiousness can actually interfere, at least for some jobs (Carter et al., 2014; Judge & Zapata, 2015; Le et al., 2011). People with high levels of extraversion perform especially well at jobs that involve lots of social interaction, like managers, flight attendants, hair stylists, and salespeople. People who are easiest to train for a new job are high in openness and extraversion (Barrick & Mount, 1991; Hurtz & Donovan, 2000).
- *The Big Five correlate with romantic relationships.* According to a meta-analysis, the Big Five predictors of satisfaction in romantic relationships are low neuroticism, high agreeableness, high conscientiousness, and high extraversion (Malouff et al., 2010). Similarly, another study found that members of married couples who eventually divorced had relatively high levels of neuroticism and relatively low levels of agreeableness and conscientiousness (Solomon & Jackson, 2014).
- *The Big Five correlate with popularity and likeability.* Researchers asked 500 teen classmates to rate each other on likability and popularity. The teens also rated themselves on the Big Five. The teens rated most likeable and popular by their peers had low levels of neuroticism and high levels of extraversion and agreeableness (van der Linden et al., 2010).
- *The Big Five correlate with prejudice.* A meta-analysis of personality and prejudice found that people low in openness to experience and low in agreeableness are most likely to hold prejudices against other groups of people (Sibley & Duckitt, 2008).
- *The Big Five correlate with following "shelter-in-place" orders during the pandemic.* One study found that people with high levels of neuroticism were more likely to worry about COVID than people with low levels of neuroticism. The same study also found that people with higher levels of agreeableness and conscientiousness were more likely to follow COVID safety guidelines (masks,

social distancing, hand washing, etc.) than people with lower levels of those traits (Zettler et al., 2021).

- *The Big Five correlate with problematic use of social media.* A study of social media users found that people with high levels of extraversion, high levels of neuroticism, and low levels of conscientiousness were especially likely to use Facebook in problematic ways—for example, allowing it to interfere with other life activities or experiencing withdrawal symptoms when forced away from it for brief periods. High levels of extraversion were also correlated with problematic use of Instagram and WhatsApp (Sindermann et al., 2020).
- *The Big Five correlate with the way people use their smartphones.* One group of researchers tracked the specific ways that people used their smartphones and found many correlations to the personality traits of the people using them. For example, people high in openness tend to have longer text messages and take more photos. People high in conscientiousness tend to spend more time checking weather apps and health-monitoring apps. People high in extraversion tend to make and receive more calls, both at night and during the day (Stachl et al., 2020).

Diversity, Multiculturalism, and Personality

DIVERSITY MATTERS

Is the five-factor model of personality a good fit for people around the world? Somewhat, but not exactly. Researchers have explored this question in a wide variety of countries including Germany, China, the Czech Republic, Greece, Israel, the Philippines, and many more. Generally, the findings suggest that the five-factor model does a good job describing personality in many Western countries, especially where English (or German, or Dutch) is the most widely spoken language. But in many non-Western countries, the fit of the five-factor model is not as good.

Specifically, in many non-Western countries, there are often additional traits that need to be included. That is, it's the Big Five *plus* one or more additional traits. Or, one of the Big Five traits needs to be divided into two distinct traits to adequately capture personality differences. Or, one of the Big Five traits doesn't rank as "big" or prominent enough (Ashton et al., 2004; John, 2021; Saucier et al., 2000). The fit of the five-factor model also seems to depend on language. When the English version of the five-factor model is translated into another language, the model tends to fit the culture better. However, when the researchers develop a new model from scratch using a dominant, non-English language in the culture, that new model tends to include culture-specific personality traits beyond the Big Five (Oishi et al., 2021).

DIVERSITY MATTERS

Here's another question that researchers have explored: could multicultural experiences influence personality traits? That is, if you had the opportunity to spend time in a culture different than your own, might you develop different levels of Big Five traits from that experience? Numerous studies suggest that the answer is yes. In one study, researchers measured the Big Five traits in college students both before and after they spent 1-2 semesters abroad (in a study abroad program or an international exchange program). They found that when these students returned from their months-long stay in a new culture, they had higher levels of openness and agreeableness, and lower levels of neuroticism, than when they left home (Zimmermann & Neyer, 2013).

Another group of researchers found a similar result for a different, less intensive multicultural experience: a PowerPoint slideshow. These researchers showed students from the University of Arkansas one of two slideshows: one that featured the culture of Arkansas towns (with which most students were familiar), or one that featured the cultures of Zambia, Bolivia, and Oman (with which most students were unfamiliar). The slideshows were matched to make sure that each group of students saw similar activities and information: people eating, people having a conversation, maps of the area, brief historical facts, and so on. The students then completed personality questionnaires after the slideshow ended. Results show that those students who watched the Zambia/Bolivia/Oman slideshow had higher levels of openness than those who watched the Arkansas slideshow (Sparkman et al., 2016).

In another study, researchers measured the Big Five in three similar groups of young women in their late 20s and early 30s: people who had lived their entire lives in the United States, people who had lived their entire lives in Japan, and Japanese immigrants to the United States. For the Japanese immigrants, the longer they had lived in the United States, the more similar their Big Five personality scores were to the people who had lived in the United States their entire lives. In other words, their experience in a new culture seemed to have nudged them toward personality traits that resembled those of the people around them (Güngör et al., 2013).

Current Thoughts on Trait Theory

Trait theory dominates current research on personality. Among contemporary psychologists, it's generally viewed quite favorably as a scientifically well-grounded explanation of personality.

Trait theory also receives significant criticism (Block, 1995; Boyle, 2008; Epstein, 1994; McAdams, 1992; Pervin, 1994; Saucier & Srivastava, 2015). Let's return to our oatmeal cookie metaphor. It begins with the assumption that all oatmeal cookies are made of the same ingredients, so differences between them must be due to different amounts of one or more of those ingredients. But the truth is that oatmeal cookies often include ingredients beyond the "big five" of oats, flour, sugar, eggs, and butter. It may be the presence of one of those extra ingredients — cinnamon, raisins, chocolate chips, or walnuts, for example — that explains that oatmeal cookie's unique taste. In the same way, the Big Five may not capture all the flavors of personality (Norem, 2010; Shedler & Westen, 2004). Some examples of personality characteristics that may fall beyond the Big Five include how funny, honest, cheap, humble, narcissistic, or manipulative a person is (Ashton & Lee, 2008; De Vries et al., 2009; Paunonen & Jackson, 2000; Veselka et al., 2011). Earlier in the chapter, we joked about how learning 18,000 personality ratings about another person would be far too many. Some critics argue that five is too few.

The notion that traits endure across the life span has also come under fire. There is significant support for Costa and McCrae's argument that they do endure (McCrae & Costa, 1994), but there is also support for the argument that they don't (Roberts et al., 2006). For example, researchers conducted a huge cross-sectional study of over 132,000 adults aged 21–60 and found that conscientiousness and agreeableness both increased slightly with age (Srivastava et al., 2003). They also found that neuroticism in women decreased slightly with age. The researchers concluded that personality is not "set like plaster" (p. 1041) but changes, at least somewhat, as we enter new phases of life or go through powerful experiences.

A final criticism of trait theory focuses on the overemphasis of the traits themselves, as opposed to external circumstances. If traits were all-powerful, people would behave exactly the same way in all situations. Consider your behavior in a classroom: you walk in, sit down, stay quiet, take notes, and only speak up after raising your hand and being called on. If traits were the only determinants of behavior, you would behave this way not only in your class, but everywhere all the time. My guess is that your behavior at last Saturday night's party or tomorrow's soccer game would disprove this notion and would confirm the importance of the situation in addition to any of your own traits (Funder, 2008; Mischel, 1979; Mischel & Shoda, 1995).

CHECK YOUR LEARNING:

12.21 What is the trait theory of personality?

12.22 How do trait theorists strive to identify the basic ingredients of personality?

12.23 What is the Five-Factor Model of personality, and which five traits does it include?

12.24 What is the contemporary view of the trait theory of personality?

To check your understanding of these questions, click show the answers or refer to the answers in the Chapter Summary.

Assessing Personality

YOU WILL LEARN:

12.25 how and why psychologists assess personality.

12.26 what clinical interviews are, and how psychologists use them.

12.27 what objective personality tests are, and how some specific ones work.

12.28 what projective personality tests are, and how some specific ones work.

12.29 what behavioral assessment is, and how psychologists use it.

You assess personality every day. You communicate with people, observe what they do, and notice how they respond to various situations. Psychologists assess personality too. In some ways, their methods are similar: conversing with clients in interviews, observing their behavior, and measuring their responses to situations. But psychologists' methods are more extensive and formal, in part because their methods must be both *valid* and *reliable* (as discussed in reference to intelligence testing in Chapter 7). Any tool that assesses personality must measure what it claims to measure (validity), and it must do so in a way that produces consistent results (reliability) (Ayearst & Bagby, 2010; Wood et al., 2007). Validity and reliability are what separate the professional assessment tools that psychologists use from the amateur "personality tests" floating around social media and posted on random Internet sites by people with unknown qualifications (Buchanan, 2002; Buchanan & Smith, 1999).

Psychologists assess personality for a variety of purposes (Butcher, 2010). In many cases, the person being assessed is seeking treatment, and the personality assessment helps the psychologist determine the client's issues or diagnoses, which leads to the right treatment or referral. Such personality assessments take place anywhere psychologists practice, including psychiatric institutions, hospitals, clinics, community mental health centers, and private practices. In other cases, the assessment is part of a legal case. This type of psychology practice, in which legal issues are involved, is known as *forensic psychology* (Marczyk, Krauss, & Burl, 2012; Ogloff, 2002). For example, in court cases where the defendant pleads not guilty by reason of insanity, the psychologist may use personality assessment tools to explore the defendant's mental state. Likewise, some psychologists may use personality assessment tools as part of a custody evaluation when a couple with children is going through a divorce (Melton et al., 2018). Additionally, some psychologists assess personality as part of the employment process, usually to help employers make hiring or placement decisions. This use of personality tests appears to have grown in recent years. Nearly a third of U.S. companies use personality tests for this reason; that number jumps to 40% among Fortune 100 companies, and 100% among the top 100 companies in Great Britain (Rothstein & Goffin, 2006).

LIFE HACK 12.2

Be skeptical of so-called "personality tests" you find on random Web sites. They often lack the validity and reliability of personality tests used by psychologists.

(Buchanan, 2002; Buchanan & Smith, 1999)

Regardless of the purpose, a psychologist typically relies on several tools when assessing a client's personality. Psychologists prefer **multimethod assessment**: an approach to personality assessment that emphasizes the use of multiple methods rather than only one method. Multimethod assessment acknowledges that no single personality assessment tool is perfect. Using more than one assessment tool allows for the methods to offset each other's weaknesses, and in many cases, they converge upon similar conclusions. (In your personal life, as you get to know someone's personality, you are probably more confident if your impressions are based on more than one type of interaction with them.)

DIVERSITY MATTERS

Also, personality assessment depends heavily on the psychologist's **cultural competence**: the ability to work sensitively and expertly with members of a culturally diverse society. For example, let's say Murjanah takes a personality test and scores very low on a measure of extraversion. Murjanah's psychologist should know what is generally expected among people of Murjanah's ethnicity, gender, age, and other variables before making an interpretation of what that low score means, especially if a mental disorder might be diagnosed.

multimethod assessment
An approach to personality assessment that emphasizes the use of multiple methods rather than only one method.

cultural competence
The ability to work sensitively and expertly with members of a culturally diverse society.

clinical interview
A method of personality assessment in which the psychologist engages in conversation with the client.

Clinical Interviews

A **clinical interview** is a method of personality assessment in which the psychologist engages in conversation with the client. This conversation varies in terms of its *structure*, or the extent to which it is planned. Highly structured interviews typically follow a scripted list of questions that are asked in a particular order for a particular purpose (such as a mental disorder diagnosis). Unstructured interviews allow for much more improvisation by the psychologist and much more elaboration by the client (Maruish, 2008; O'Brien & Tabaczynski, 2007). A strength of structured interviews is that they are reliable and provide exactly the information the psychologist wants; a strength of unstructured interviews is that they let clients feel comfortable and expand upon what they think is most important (Sommers-Flanagan & Sommers-Flanagan, 2009; Villa & Reitman, 2007). To capture both of these strengths, many psychologists compromise and conduct *semistructured* interviews, which strike a balance between a predetermined plan and a spontaneous conversation (Morrison, 2008).

DIVERSITY MATTERS

Cultural competence is especially important during the clinical interview (Dana, 2005; Hays, 2008; Suzuki & Ponterotto, 2008). In a one-on-one, face-to-face interaction, it is essential for the psychologist to know and appreciate the cultural norms of communication for the client. For example, consider eye contact. The expected behavior could differ according to ethnicity, age, gender, and other variables (Sue & Sue, 2016). Some Asian American clients tend to avoid direct, prolonged eye contact, especially with people they perceive as authority figures (including, perhaps, the psychologist). If the psychologist is ignorant of this tendency, the lack of eye contact could mistakenly be interpreted as a sign of disinterest, disrespect, or dishonesty rather than simply a common behavior among members of their cultural community.

Objective Personality Tests

Psychologists use a wide variety of personality tests, but they are generally categorized as either *objective* or *projective* personality tests. In **objective personality tests**, the client responds to a standardized set of questions, usually in multiple-choice or true–false format. Typically, these are pencil-and-paper tests (although some can be taken on computers as well) in which clients read a list of brief statements about their thoughts, feelings, or behaviors. After each statement, the client marks the response that best describes them (Morey & Hopwood, 2008). The response options are often true–false, or a broader range of agreement, such as strongly agree, somewhat agree, neutral, somewhat disagree, and strongly disagree. The scoring of objective personality tests is straightforward and can often be done by computer.

Minnesota Multiphasic Personality Inventory-2. The **Minnesota Multiphasic Personality Inventory-2 (MMPI-2)** is a widely used and respected objective personality test that emphasizes mental disorders. It was originally created in 1943; the second edition came out in 1989. It is used with adult clients, but in 1992, a separate version for adolescents (MMPI-Adolescent, or MMPI-A) was published (Butcher & Williams, 2009; Williams & Butcher, 2011). In 2008, a shortened version of the adult form (MMPI-Restructured Form, or MMPI-RF) was also offered (Ben-Porath & Tellegen, 2008).

The MMPI-2 is a list of 567 self-descriptive statements to which the client answers true or false on a separate answer sheet. The statements cover a wide range of behavior, thoughts, and feelings. When the client is finished, the psychologist (perhaps with the help of a computer or answer sheet scanner) tallies up the patterns of true and false responses. These tallies translate into scores on a wide variety of scales. The most important of these are the 10 *clinical scales*, which include such categories as depression and paranoia, and indicate (either alone or in two- or three-scale combinations) the kinds of psychological challenges the client is likely to experience.

Couldn't the client just fake their way through a test like the MMPI-2?

objective personality tests
Personality tests in which the client responds to a standardized set of questions, usually in multiple-choice or true–false format.

Minnesota Multiphasic Personality Inventory-2 (MMPI-2)
A widely used and respected objective personality test that emphasizes mental disorders.

In some cases, clients may try to respond to MMPI-2 items in ways that would create a false impression (MacCann et al., 2012; Sackett, 2012; Ziegler et al., 2012). For example, a person on trial who has pleaded not guilty by reason of insanity may want to come across as having more serious mental illness symptoms than they really do. To address this, the MMPI-2 contains *validity scales*, which assess not the client's personality but their approach to taking this test. These validity scales indicate the likelihood that the client is "faking good," "faking bad," or filling in answers randomly. If any of the validity scales is too high, the psychologist will consider the clinical scales invalid and will not use them to make any interpretations (Butcher, 2011).

The MMPI-2 is the most frequently used personality test for hiring decisions. It has been used for this purpose with the U.S. military since the 1940s, and now it's especially common in the hiring process for jobs that involve public safety, like police officers, airline pilots, and nuclear power plant technicians (Butcher, 2012; Butcher & Williams, 2009; Sellbom et al., 2007; Zapata Sola et al., 2009). A large number of empirical studies support the reliability and validity of the MMPI-2. It has been translated into many languages and is among the most popular tests of any kind used by psychologists (Butcher et al., 2006; Butcher & Beutler, 2003; Garrido & Velasquez, 2006; Greene & Clopton, 2004; Wright et al., 2017).

NEO-Personality Inventory-3. Also widely used is the **NEO-Personality Inventory-3 (NEO-PI-3):** an objective personality test that measures the Big Five personality factors. Created by the theorists who developed the Five-Factor Model (Paul Costa and Robert McCrae), the NEO-PI-3 emphasizes normal personality traits rather than problematic characteristics like the MMPI-2. For that reason, psychologists do not use the NEO-PI-3 as often as the MMPI-2 when the task is to diagnose a client with a disorder. The NEO-PI-3 includes 240 items in a multiple-choice format, with choices ranging from strongly agree to strongly disagree. The NEO-PI-3 lacks the validity scales of the MMPI-2, but it's frequently used by psychologists seeking to assess how much of each of the Big Five traits a person has (Costa & McCrae, 1992b, 2008; Simms et al., 2017).

Current Thoughts on Objective Personality Tests. Objective personality tests are generally viewed by contemporary psychologists as reliable and valid assessment tools. These tests are standardized, which means the results won't depend on who administers the test, or where or when it is taken. The primary downside of objective personality tests is their *self-report* format, which means clients answer questions about themselves. As we discussed previously, some clients may knowingly give inaccurate answers in an attempt to deliberately fake a personality, which they may be able to do with some success in spite of validity scales and other attempts to catch them. In other cases, clients simply may not know themselves very accurately, and may unknowingly give answers that do not reflect their true personalities. Researchers have actually compared self-report and *other-report* versions (filled out by family or friends) of personality assessment tools, with the intention of discovering how closely the two ratings match and which is a better predictor of behavior (Yalch & Hopwood, 2017). Results indicate that the correlation between self-report and other-report measures of the Big Five is in the .40–.60 range – quite positive, but far from perfect (Vazire & Carlson, 2010). Of the two, other-report ratings are actually better predictors than self-report ratings of some behaviors, including job performance. In other words, at least in terms of work-related behavior, the way your friends or family members describe you is more accurate than the way you describe yourself (Connelly & Ones, 2010; Connolly et al., 2007).

Projective Personality Tests

In **projective personality tests**, clients respond to ambiguous stimuli in a free-form way. Projective personality tests are based on the assumption that the way you interpret what you see reveals something about your personality. You "project" your

NEO-Personality Inventory-3 (NEO-PI-3)
An objective personality test that measures the Big Five personality factors.

projective personality tests
Personality tests in which clients respond to ambiguous stimuli in a free-form way.

personality onto the world around you, especially when the world gives you the chance to make interpretations that may differ from those of others. Rather than forcing clients into a multiple-choice or true–false response, projective tests allow them to respond however they choose, with no restrictions (Smith & Archer, 2008; Tuber, 2012).

Picture yourself accompanying a group of sixth-graders on a school field trip to a modern art museum, where many of the paintings are abstract. As you stand in front of an abstract painting, you ask the kids what they see. Kevin says, "The red part is a pool of blood, like after someone has been stabbed." Deja says, "I see a face laughing at me." Julio points to a tiny black oval in the corner and says, "That little dot in the corner looks like a bug." Of course, you wouldn't make much of their responses to this single painting. But as you continue the tour, the same kids make similar responses to painting after painting. Kevin keeps seeing violence, Deja keeps seeing people persecuting her, and Julio keeps focusing on minuscule details in the painting rather than seeing the big picture. For psychologists who use projective tests, each person's pattern of responses reveals something important about that person's personality.

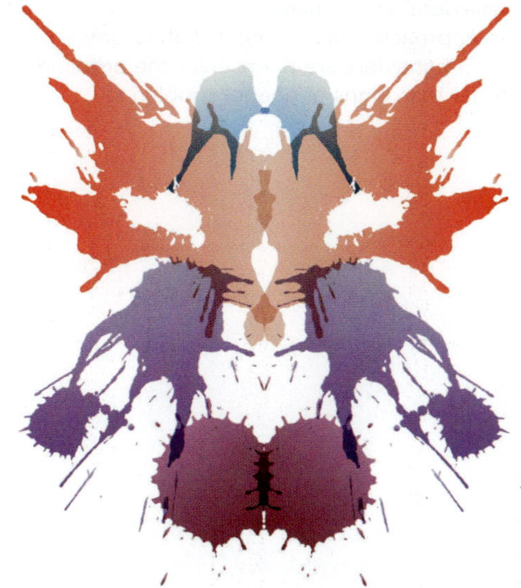

Blackspring/Shutterstock

Some psychologists believe that personality is revealed by the way a person responds to inkblots like this one, which resembles those in the Rorschach inkblot technique.

Rorschach Inkblot Technique. An assessment instrument that resembles this abstract art scenario is the **Rorschach inkblot technique**: a projective personality test in which the client responds to 10 inkblot images. Created in 1921 by Hermann Rorschach, a Swiss psychiatrist, it is administered in two phases. In the first phase, the psychologist shows the client each inkblot and asks what the client sees. In the second phase, the psychologist asks the client for an explanation of each response: what was it about the inkblot (its color, its shape, etc.) that made the client offer that response? Later, the psychologist codes the client's responses and calculates a variety of scores to describe the client's personality (Exner, 1986; Weiner, 2004).

Thematic Apperception Test. Inkblots are not the only things ambiguous enough to allow people's personalities to come through. Interpersonal scenes — basically, drawings of people without any caption — can serve the same purpose. That is the approach taken by the **Thematic Apperception Test (TAT)**: a projective personality test in which the client creates stories in response to cards that show people in undefined situations. The stories a client tells may include what's happening in the scene, what led up to it, what may happen next, and what the people in the scene are thinking or feeling (Ackerman et al., 2008; Morgan & Murray, 1935; Murray, 1943). The administration of the TAT is not standardized. Psychologists can choose different combinations of cards and present them in any order. Scoring processes also vary widely, and in many cases, the psychologist simply makes subjective interpretations of the client's stories rather than scoring them in any systematic way (Moretti & Rossini, 2004).

Kenney Mencher

When psychologists use the Thematic Apperception Test, they present a series of pictures like this one and ask clients to tell a story about each. Some psychologists believe that they can learn a lot about the client's personality by examining the themes of their stories.

Since the TAT's publication in 1943, a number of other story-telling projective tests have emerged. Most of these offer more standardized scoring procedures and more cultural diversity among the people depicted in the drawings than the TAT, which features primarily White people, often in rural settings (Malgady & Colon-Malgady, 2008; Teglasi, 2010). For example, the Tell-Me-a-Story (TEMAS) test features Latinx and Black characters in primarily urban settings (Malgady et al., 1984; Malone et al., 2020).

Current Thoughts on Projective Personality Tests. Projective personality tests are not as popular or respected as they once were, primarily because they lack the validity and reliability of many objective tests. This means that psychologists can't be completely confident that projective tests really measure the personality characteristics they claim to measure. It also means that psychologists can't be sure that the conclusions one psychologist would make about a client's projective test would match the conclusions another psychologist would make. (If a different person heard the sixth-graders' responses in the modern art museum, would that person come up

Rorschach inkblot technique
A projective personality test in which the client responds to 10 inkblot images.

Thematic Apperception Test (TAT)
A projective personality test in which the client creates stories in response to cards that show people in undefined situations.

behavioral assessment
An approach to assessment that assumes client behaviors are themselves the problems, rather than signs of deeper problems.

with exactly the same hypotheses as you about the kids' personalities?) This lack of standardization draws significant criticism and controversy for projective tests, and for many psychologists that lack is a deal breaker (Holt, 1999; Lilienfeld et al., 2010, 2000; Wood et al., 2003, 2010).

Supporters of projective tests point out that although objective tests may have more data to support their reliability and validity, projective tests do have some (Meyer, 2004; Mihura et al., 2013, 2015; Rose et al., 2001). Also, since projective tests do not rely on self-report, they are not as fakeable as objective tests, and this provides a unique way to tap into underlying personality characteristics.

Behavioral Assessment

Objective and projective personality tests both try to uncover something within the person that is presumed to be at the root of their behavior – personality characteristics, traits, disorders. So why not simply assess the behavior itself? That's the rationale behind **behavioral assessment**: an approach to assessment that assumes client behaviors are themselves the problems, rather than signs of deeper problems. As its name suggests, behavioral assessment is typically conducted by behaviorists – the same psychologists who question whether anything as internal or stable as "personality" even exists. It makes sense that they would devise and use an assessment method that focuses on observable behavior itself rather than any possible "cause" or "source" of it, which couldn't be empirically proven to exist.

To illustrate the behavioral assessment approach, let's say Thomas, an 8-year-old third-grader, refuses to go to school. For a behaviorist, the problem is *not* social anxiety, depression, conduct disorder, neuroticism, or anything else inside Thomas' mind. His behavior – his refusal to go to school – *is* the problem, and we shouldn't look any deeper than that. So, a behavioral assessment of Thomas would involve watching the behavior directly, a practice called *behavioral observation*. Ideally, the observation would happen not in the psychologist's office, but in the real-world environment where the problem behavior takes place (Thomas' house on a weekday morning, his bus stop, or the front door of his school). If such *naturalistic observation* is not possible, the psychologist can try to replicate the situation in the office, or use technology such as video cameras or smartphones to record Thomas' actions as they happen in their natural settings (Heiby & Haynes, 2004; Ollendick et al., 2004; Richard & Lauterbach, 2003).

Behavioral assessment typically involves a precise definition of the problem behavior and a systematic way of measuring how often it happens. It also involves noting the events that happen right before and right after the behavior – in order to understand any conditioning that may maintain the behavior (Cipani & Schock, 2007; O'Brien et al., 2016). (What does Thomas get when he refuses to go to school? Hugs and pancakes? A scolding and a time-out? What does he get when he *does* go to school?) Behavioral assessment may also involve interviewing and questionnaires, but if so, it is geared exclusively toward identifying the problem behavior and its function for the client (Haynes & Kaholokula, 2008).

CHECK YOUR LEARNING:

12.25 How and why do psychologists assess personality?

12.26 What are clinical interviews?

12.27 How do objective personality tests work?

12.28 How do projective personality tests work?

12.29 What is behavioral assessment, and how does it differ from other kinds of assessment?

To check your understanding of these questions, click show the answers or refer to the answers in the Chapter Summary.

CHAPTER SUMMARY

What Is Personality?

12.1 Personality is a person's distinctive and stable way of thinking, feeling, and behaving.

12.2 Personality is not fully understood by psychologists, so they attempt to explain it with different personality theories.

12.3 Behavioral genetics studies of twins and adoptive families suggest that both biology (nature) and environment (nurture) play important roles in the development of personality.

Psychodynamic Theory of Personality

12.4 The psychodynamic theory of personality is an explanation of personality, based on the ideas of Sigmund Freud, that emphasizes unconscious forces and early childhood experiences.

12.5 The unconscious is the mental activity of which a person is unaware. According to Freud, it can explain actions that are otherwise unexplainable.

12.6 The id is the animalistic part of the mind, which generates primal, biologically based impulses such as sex and aggression. The superego is the part of the mind that opposes the id by enforcing rules, restrictions, and morality. The ego is the part of the mind that serves as a realistic mediator between the id and superego.

12.7 Freud divided early childhood into five phases called psychosexual stages, each of which can have lasting effects on personality: (1) the oral stage, (2) the anal stage, (3) the phallic stage, (4) the latency stage, and (5) the genital stage.

12.8 Neo-Freudians held onto Freud's core ideas — the unconscious, the significance of early childhood experiences, and the notion that the mind contains the id, ego, and superego — but they deemphasized the biology that was so prominent in Freud's theories.

12.9 Psychodynamic theory is well past its heyday. Contemporary critics point out that it is not scientific enough and that Freud overgeneralized his ideas.

Humanistic Theory of Personality

12.10 The humanistic theory of personality is based on the ideas of Carl Rogers and emphasizes people's inherent tendencies toward healthy, positive growth and self-fulfillment.

12.11 Self-actualization is fully becoming the person one has the potential to become.

12.12 Positive regard is the warmth, acceptance, and love of people around us, while conditions of worth are the requirements that a person must meet to earn positive regard.

12.13 Self-concept is a person's view of who they are, and it develops in response to the ways that other people treat them.

12.14 Humanistic theory gave rise to the positive psychology movement and continues to significantly influence the way that many psychotherapists practice, though it has been criticized for being too optimistic and for being unscientific.

Behavioral and Social-Cognitive Theories of Personality

12.15 The behavioral theory of personality emphasizes the influence of the environment and the importance of observable, measurable behavior.

12.16 The social-cognitive theory of personality emphasizes the interaction of environment, thought processes, and social factors.

12.17 Albert Bandura's theory of reciprocal determinism suggests that three factors — behavior, environment, and cognitions — continually influence each other.

12.18 Bandura emphasized a type of cognition known as self-efficacy, a person's beliefs about their own abilities.

12.19 Julian Rotter highlighted a type of cognition known as locus of control, which is a person's belief about how much control they have over what happens in their life.

12.20 Behavioral theories of personality are held in high regard by those who insist that all aspects of psychology should be empirically based, but most current psychologists do not accept the behavioral notion that environment, rather than personality, determines all behavior. More than other personality theories, social-cognitive theory identifies many possible influences on personality, and self-efficacy has been shown to enhance achievement in a wide variety of areas.

Trait Theory of Personality

12.21 The trait theory of personality emphasizes the discovery and description of the basic components of personality.

12.22 Identifying the basic traits of human personality required narrowing down the massive number of possibilities to a much shorter list of "supertraits."

12.23 The Five-Factor Model of personality emphasizes five fundamental traits present in all people to varying degrees (the Big Five) — neuroticism, extraversion, openness to experience, conscientiousness, and agreeableness.

12.24 Trait theory dominates current research on personality, but some theorists feel the Big Five may not capture all the aspects of personality, that traits may not endure across the life span, and that trait theory underestimates the impact of external circumstances.

Assessing Personality

12.25 Psychologists assess personality through many valid and reliable methods, including interviews, observation of behavior, and personality tests. Psychologists assess personality for a variety of purposes, including diagnosis and treatment, employment, and forensic (legal or court-related) reasons.

12.26 A clinical interview — which can be structured, unstructured, or semistructured — is a method of personality assessment in which the psychologist engages in conversation with the client.

12.27 In an objective personality test such as the MMPI-2, the client responds to a standardized set of questions, usually in multiple-choice or true-false format.

12.28 In projective personality tests like the Rorschach inkblot technique, clients respond to ambiguous stimuli in a free-form way.

12.29 Behavioral assessment is an approach to assessment that assumes client behaviors are the problems (rather than signs of deeper problems).

KEY TERMS

personality, p. 404
behavioral genetics, p. 405
psychodynamic theory of personality, p. 406
unconscious, p. 406
psychic determinism, p. 407
Freudian slips, p. 407
id, p. 408
superego, p. 408
ego, p. 409
defense mechanisms, p. 409
psychosexual stages, p. 410
fixation, p. 410
oral stage, p. 411
anal stage, p. 411
phallic stage, p. 412
Oedipus complex, p. 412
Electra complex, p. 412
latency stage, p. 412
genital stage, p. 412
neo-Freudian theories, p. 413
collective unconscious, p. 414
archetypes, p. 414
humanistic theory of personality, p. 416
self-actualization, p. 416
positive regard, p. 416
conditions of worth, p. 416
real self, p. 416
ideal self, p. 416
incongruence, p. 416
congruence, p. 417
self-concept, p. 417
behavioral theory of personality, p. 419
social-cognitive theory of personality, p. 419
reciprocal determinism, p. 420
self-efficacy, p. 421
locus of control, p. 421
internal locus of control, p. 421
external locus of control, p. 421
trait theory of personality, p. 424
traits, p. 424
Five-Factor Model of personality (Big Five), p. 425
neuroticism, p. 425
extraversion, p. 425
openness to experience, p. 425
conscientiousness, p. 425
agreeableness, p. 425
multimethod assessment, p. 430
cultural competence, p. 430
clinical interview, p. 430
objective personality tests, p. 431
Minnesota Multiphasic Personality Inventory-2 (MMPI-2), p. 431
NEO-Personality Inventory-3 (NEO-PI-3), p. 432
projective personality tests, p. 432
Rorschach inkblot technique, p. 433
Thematic Apperception Test (TAT), p. 433
behavioral assessment, p. 434

SELF-ASSESSMENT

1. _____ is a person's distinctive and stable way of thinking, feeling, and behaving.

2. _____ is the study of the impact of genes (nature) and environment (nurture) on personality and behavior.

a. Self-actualization
b. Factor analysis
c. Behavioral genetics
d. Identification

3. Morgan is working as a cashier, and an extremely attractive customer makes a purchase. Morgan tries to say to the customer, "Your total is six dollars." However, Morgan mistakenly says, "Your total is sex dollars." If this mistake reveals an unconscious wish of Morgan's, the mistake is an example of a(n):

a. superego.
b. Freudian slip.
c. incongruence.
d. identification.

4. According to Sigmund Freud, the _____ is the animalistic part of the mind that generates our most basic, biologically based impulses such as sex and aggression.

a. id
b. ego
c. superego
d. ideal self

5. The correct sequence of Freud's five psychosexual stages is:

a. oral, anal, phallic, latency, genital.
b. latency, oral, phallic, genital, anal.
c. phallic, anal, oral, genital, latency.
d. oral, anal, genital, phallic, latency.

6. According to Carl Rogers, _____ leads to unhappiness and mental illness.

a. self-actualization
b. cultural incompetence
c. extraversion
d. incongruence

7. The _____ theory of personality emphasizes the interaction of environment, thought processes, and social factors.
   a. social-cognitive
   b. humanistic
   c. behavioral
   d. trait

8. Trina believes that her own actions determine what happens in her life. Terrence believes that outside forces, rather than his own actions, determine what happens in his life. Trina has a(n) _____ locus of control, while Troy has a(n) _____ locus of control.

9. The Five-Factor Model of personality emphasizes five fundamental traits present in all people to varying degrees. Which of these is NOT included among those five traits?
   a. Intelligence
   b. Neuroticism
   c. Conscientiousness
   d. Agreeableness

10. Dr. Velsor is a psychologist conducting a personality assessment. If she's using an objective personality test, which of the following might she be using?
   a. Rorschach inkblot technique
   b. Minnesota Multiphasic Personality Inventory-2
   c. Wechsler Adult Intelligence Scale
   d. Thematic Apperception Test

To check your understanding of these questions, click show the answers in the e-book or refer to the answers in Appendix B.

Research shows quizzing is a highly effective learning tool. Continue quizzing yourself using LearningCurve, the system that adapts to *your* learning.

WHAT'S YOUR TAKE?

1. When I was a young kid, I attended a sports camp in which we played different sports each week. After a few days of track and field week, my best long jump was 9 feet. The next day, the counselor marking our distances in the sand pit laid a stick in the sand and shouted out to me before I started my run up to the pit—"Here's the 9-foot mark!" I landed about a foot short of it. Frustrated, I went back to the starting line, built up more speed, timed my takeoff, and jumped a little farther, but still landed about 6 inches short of the stick. As I walked back for my third try, I told myself, "I *know* I can jump 9 feet. I did it yesterday!" Sure enough, on my third attempt, I cleared that stick. As I smiled and brushed off the sand, my counselor whispered, "Hey, I'll let you in on a little secret. The stick is actually at *10* feet." I had jumped past that stick not because of a new technique or a training regimen, but because I *believed* I could. Albert Bandura would have been proud of my counselor for knowing how to maximize the effects of self-efficacy in his campers. Can you recall any situations in which your own self-efficacy—your belief that you could achieve something—was a primary reason why you were able to actually achieve it?
2. When psychologists do personality assessments, they increasingly offer their services—including clinical interviews—via videoconference (usually via apps similar to Zoom or FaceTime). The COVID pandemic was a big reason for this trend, but it's likely to continue even after the pandemic ends. Some people view this trend positively, as a step forward with benefits for both client and therapist. Others are more wary about psychological assessment happening through screens rather than in-person. How about you? If you (or a friend or a family member) called a psychologist to schedule a clinical interview and were offered both videoconference and in-person options, which would you prefer? Why? What circumstances might influence your opinion?

SHOW ME MORE

12.1 Locus of Control and Academic Potential

This article describes how some colleges are now using tests of personality characteristics, including locus of control, to measure academic potential and influence admissions decisions.
http://tiny.cc/ip7njy
Peter Muller/Getty Images

This video is hosted by a third party Web site (source). For accessible content requests, please reach out to the publisher of that site.

12.2 The Big Five and College Majors

This article describes research on the correlation between college students' majors and their Big Five personality traits.
http://tiny.cc/0p7njy
Nerthuz/Shutterstock

This video is hosted by a third party Web site (source). For accessible content requests, please reach out to the publisher of that site.

12.3 My Psychology Podcast

This podcast episode features the author of this textbook, psychologist Andy Pomerantz, speaking with other instructors of introductory psychology courses about the most important and interesting concepts in this chapter.
Macmillan Learning

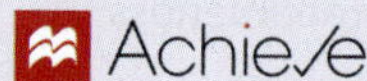

13 Social Psychology

Mix Tape/Shutterstock

CHAPTER OUTLINE

Your neighbor is a famous and respected professor. His list of academic achievements is extraordinary: He has written books, directed research institutes, and done expert appearances on TV shows viewed by millions. *Time* magazine even included him on its list of the "25 Most Influential Americans."

One afternoon, as you look out your window, the professor returns home with a friend. He finds his front door jammed, so he enters through the back door. Once inside, he and his friend work together on the front door to make sure it won't be jammed in the future. Soon, a police car pulls up. A jogger who saw your neighbor and his friend adjusting the front door called 911 to report what they thought was a burglary attempt. Your neighbor shows the officer his driver's license and university ID, but the officer remains suspicious. As the officer asks your neighbor more questions, the conversation becomes heated. Your neighbor is handcuffed on his porch and ultimately arrested for disorderly conduct.

This story actually happened to Henry Louis Gates, a Harvard professor, in July 2009 (Thompson, 2009). You may have seen Professor Gates as host of the PBS TV show *Finding Your Roots*. Professor Gates is Black. The police officer, Sgt. James Crowley, is White. Their interaction attracted so much media attention—often with "racial profiling" in the headline—that President Barack Obama and Vice President Joe Biden personally intervened. At the president's request, the four men sat down together to discuss the matter (Cooper, 2009). The charges were eventually dropped.

For months following these events, many questions arose on TV, radio, and social media (Phillips, 2009). Almost all of those questions involve key issues in *social psychology*. What prompted the jogger to call 911? Why did the police officer behave that way? Was prejudice, stereotyping, or discrimination involved? What opinions did we form about possible reasons the officer responded the way he did—his deep-seated personality characteristics, the demands of that particular situation, or instructions from his superiors? What are the best ways to reduce, or even prevent, such tensions?

Social psychologists study exactly these kinds of questions. Most psychologists explore how each of us behaves as an individual, but social psychologists explore how we behave *together*: how we think about each other, influence each other, and relate to each other. Your day-to-day life is inescapably social, so these are vitally relevant topics.

social psychology
The scientific study of how people think about, influence, and relate to each other.

social cognition
A person's thoughts about other people and the social world.

attribution
An explanation of the cause of behavior.

In the Personality chapter, we zoomed in to focus on the individual. In this chapter, we zoom out to focus on the individual *among other people*. Human behavior happens in the context of other humans. Your actions are affected by the people around you, just as their behavior is affected by you (Funder & Fast, 2010; Ross et al., 2010; Snyder & Deaux, 2012, 2019). To fully understand behavior, we need to consider **social psychology**: the scientific study of how people think about, influence, and relate to each other.

Sometimes, this scientific study takes place in the lab, where social psychologists design and manipulate situations. Participants are placed among other people and asked to perform a particular task while researchers observe and measure what happens (Crano & Lac, 2012). A social psychologist may place an individual in a group of people performing a particular behavior in a particular way — for example, responding to a puzzle with the same wrong answer — and see whether the individual follows along or resists. Or, they may present individuals with pictures or videos of other people and then assess the individuals' judgments about the other people's attractiveness, personality, or other qualities.

In addition to controlled lab studies, social psychologists conduct real-world (or *naturalistic*) studies, in which researchers observe how people behave in situations from their day-to-day lives (Reis & Gosling, 2010; Wilson et al., 2010). For example, researchers may observe who sits together in a high school cafeteria, or they may observe when and where people are most likely to help on a public street. Together, lab studies and real-world studies by social psychologists shed light on many areas of our lives: how other people affect the ways we work, play, help, hurt, love, hate, and otherwise behave (Kruglanski & Stroebe, 2012).

The social nature of our lives is not a new phenomenon. In fact, group existence has been a fact of life throughout the evolution of our species (Brewer, 2007; Foley, 1995; Gangestad, 2019). For the vast majority of human history, our ancestors lived their whole lives in bands of hunter-gatherers that probably included about 50–200 members (Barrett et al., 2002; Van Vugt & Van Lange, 2006). These bands, and the smaller groups that formed within them, were essential to human survival (Caporael, 2007; Kenrick, 2012). Living among other people has always provided important, even life-saving, advantages: other people can help you find food, water, and shelter; they can help care for your children (and yourself); and they can protect you against danger. But living among other people has always carried risks too: other people can hurt you, sicken you, or freeload off you (Neuberg & Cottrell, 2006). Today, as products of many thousands of years of evolution, we find ourselves unavoidably connected to the people around us, both for better and for worse. As we'll see, many of social psychology's core concepts remain connected to this evolutionary inheritance.

Social Cognition: How We Think about Each Other

YOU WILL LEARN:

13.1 what social cognition is.

13.2 what attributions are.

13.3 how people often make the fundamental attribution error.

13.4 what attitudes are, and how people try to change them.

13.5 what cognitive dissonance is, and how it can be resolved.

Our thoughts about other people strongly influence our feelings and behavior. Social psychologists use the term **social cognition** to refer to a person's thoughts about other people and the social world. In this section, we focus on forms of social cognition that social psychologists have studied extensively, including *attributions*, *attitudes*, and *cognitive dissonance*.

Attributions

Our thoughts about other people frequently focus on why they behave as they do. We develop an **attribution**: an explanation of the cause of behavior. A single behavior can generate a wide range of attributions. For example, imagine yourself in line at a coffee shop. As you wait to order, you see a person walk in, stroll past the line straight over to the "Pick Up Orders Here" counter, grab a coffee, and go. You ask the person in front of you, just to make sure: "Did that person really just steal a cup of coffee?" When they confirm that they saw the same thing, you wonder: "*Why*?"

LightField Studios/Shutterstock

Attribution is an explanation of the cause of behavior. If you saw a person walk into a coffee shop and take a cup of coffee without paying, multiple attributions could explain their behavior.

Attribution Theory: Is It the Person or the Situation? Answers to that question – whether it's the person or the situation that's responsible for the behavior – could span a wide range, but social psychologists believe that they fall into two distinct categories. These two categories are specified by **attribution theory**: a theory that behavior is caused either by traits within the individual or by the situation surrounding the individual. Sometimes people are driven to behave a certain way because of who they are – their personalities, essentially – but other times people are driven to behave a certain way by temporary, situational factors outside themselves (Heider, 1958; Kelley, 1973; Malle, 2006, 2011; Reis & Holmes, 2019). For example, if we attribute the behavior of the person who walked in and took the cup of coffee to enduring qualities within them – they're cheap, eccentric, or a thief – we're pointing at their personality traits. But maybe there's a better explanation based on their situation. Perhaps they're on a new prescription medicine that is causing confusion and erratic behavior. Perhaps they ordered at the counter before you came in, then ran out to say hi to a friend outside the shop, and then came back in for their coffee. Perhaps they ordered and paid on their phone before they came in. Any of these explanations point to their situation, not their disposition.

The Fundamental Attribution Error. Research on attribution theory has repeatedly found that the way we explain the behavior of other people tends to differ from the way we explain our own behavior (e.g., Gilbert & Malone, 1995; Ross, 1977). Specifically, we often commit the **fundamental attribution error**: overestimating the importance of traits and underestimating the importance of the situation when explaining the behavior of other people. According to the fundamental attribution error, when *I* do something, it's because of the situation around me, but when *you* do the same thing, it's because of who you are (Funder & Fast, 2010; Ross & Nisbett, 1991). Driving offers some common examples: *I'm* speeding because the traffic made me late, but *they're* speeding because they're reckless; *I* ran the red light because the light is malfunctioning, but *they* ran the red light because they're absentminded; *I* use my phone while driving because I'm pressed for time, but *you* use your phone while driving because you're irresponsible. For our own behavior, we can often identify many extenuating circumstances that caused us to behave as we did. That is, for ourselves, "it's complicated." For others, we assume it's simple: their personality traits explain it all. Of course, that assumption is often completely wrong – there's a reason it's called the fundamental attribution *error*.

LIFE HACK 13.1

It's called the fundamental attribution *error* for a reason. You might be making a mistake if you judge other people by considering only their personality traits and overlooking their circumstances.

(Funder & Fast, 2010; Jones & Harris, 1967; Ross & Nisbett, 1991)

A classic experiment from the 1960s illustrates the fundamental attribution error. Researchers had participants read "pro" or "con" essays about controversial topics of the time – for example, racial segregation (Jones & Harris, 1967). Then participants were asked for their opinions about why the authors wrote the essays. Participants overwhelmingly attributed the content of the essays to the authors' personalities, not any external circumstances – even when the experimenters told them that the authors had been *assigned* to take the viewpoint.

DIVERSITY MATTERS

Since the early days of research on fundamental attribution error, evidence has suggested that it occurs more in some cultural groups more than others. Specifically, the fundamental attribution error occurs more often in individualistic cultures (like the United States and most other Western countries) than in collectivistic cultures (like many Asian countries) (Bhawuk, 2018; Crittenden, 1991; Shweder & Bourne, 1982). In one study, researchers read sports articles and editorials in newspapers from the United States (including the *New York Times* and the *Boston Globe*) and Hong Kong (the *South China Morning Post*) (Lee et al., 1996). They then categorized each article in terms of how it attributed the action described: to the personalities of the people who did it, or to the circumstances

attribution theory
A theory that behavior is caused either by traits within the individual or by the situation surrounding the individual.

fundamental attribution error
Overestimating the importance of traits and underestimating the importance of the situation when explaining the behavior of other people.

attitude
A viewpoint, often influenced by both thoughts and emotions, that affects a person's responses to people, things, or situations.

surrounding those people. For example, did a tennis player win a match because that player had grit and willpower, or because of the opponent's mistakes or bad calls by the umpire? The results indicated that the Asian newspapers made far more attributions to the situation and far fewer attributions to personalities. This difference may stem from the fact that in collectivistic cultures, there is a general understanding that people often do things for the sake of others, and that actions done for this reason may not accurately reflect the personality of the person who does them.

MY TAKE VIDEO 13.1
Fundamental Attribution Error
Macmillan Learning
"Someone rudely cut in front of me and took my parking spot. I thought they were mean, but in reality. . ."
Visit Achieve to watch the My Take video and then answer questions.
Achieve

Attitudes

An **attitude** is a viewpoint, often influenced by both thoughts and emotions, that affects your responses to people, things, or situations. Attitudes land somewhere between what you know and how you feel (Banaji & Heiphetz, 2010; Petty et al., 1997, 2009a). Consider your attitude toward capital punishment (the death penalty). It probably consists of more than mere facts, such as how much capital punishment decreases crime rates, or the financial costs of capital punishment versus life in prison. It's also probably more than pure emotion, such as your gut reaction to the idea of a convicted criminal being put to death. Instead, your attitude is most likely a hybrid of thoughts and emotions, informed by facts and infused with sentiment.

As **Figure 13.1** shows, attitudes predict action, especially when those attitudes are strong (Fazio, 1990; Howe & Krosnick, 2017; Kraus, 1995; Kruglanski et al., 2015). Consider Marco, an overweight 40-year-old man with a very negative attitude toward exercising. The whole idea of working out seems unpleasant to Marco: It's a hassle, an unpleasant, sweaty, boring, time-consuming chore. Not surprisingly, he hasn't worked out in years. But if Marco's partner, friends, or coworkers can effectively persuade him that exercise is enjoyable and rejuvenating, then it's much more likely Marco will go to the gym or run outside. And it works the other way too: Actions predict attitudes. Let's imagine that Marco drags himself to the gym or the park for a run, forcing himself to exercise. If he sticks with it, his attitude toward exercise is likely to shift in a positive direction to match his new exercise routine.

Research supports the idea that the stronger an attitude, the more likely behavior will match it. In one study, researchers surveyed hundreds of Chicago residents about five social issues that were prominent at the time: affirmative action, immigration, school funding, gentrification, and the Iraq War. The researchers didn't just ask the participants what their attitudes were about each issue – they also asked how strong each attitude was, and whether they took action related to each issue (for example, attending rallies, signing petitions, or contacting a government official about that issue). Results showed a significant positive correlation: the stronger the attitude toward a particular issue, the more likely it was that the person took action regarding that issue (Holbrook et al., 2016).

Attitudes and actions typically correspond, but not always (Ajzen, 2000; Sheeran & Webb, 2016; Wallace et al., 2005). There are instances in which a person's stated attitudes disagree with the behaviors they perform. A meta-analysis of research on the attitude–action connection found that attitudes are least likely to predict behavior when the person lacks confidence in the attitude, the attitude is inconsistent, and contradictory attitudes are also present (Glasman & Albarracín, 2006). In a classic study of the disconnect between attitudes and actions, a Chinese couple traveled by car through the United States during the early 1930s (a time when prejudice in the United States toward Chinese people was high), seeking food and lodging at many stops along the way. Almost every restaurant and hotel welcomed them. Six months later, the same restaurants and hotels received a survey in the mail asking if they would serve Chinese customers, and most said they would *not* – an attitude opposite of the behavior they had just exhibited (LaPiere, 1934). The explanation for this discrepancy is not entirely clear, but it could involve social pressures against admitting to a hospitable attitude toward certain underrepresented groups at that time in U.S. history. The disconnect also might be explained by the difficulty of turning down any paying customer in tough economic times, regardless of attitudes toward them.

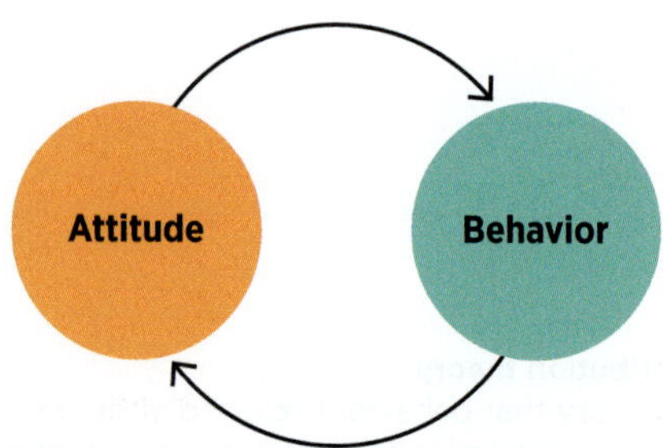

FIGURE 13.1 Reciprocal Influence of Attitude and Behavior. Attitudes and behavior influence each other. For example, consider exercising. Positive attitudes toward exercising can increase exercise frequency, and increased exercise frequency can improve attitudes toward exercising.

Explicit Attitudes and Implicit Attitudes. Social psychologists distinguish between *explicit* attitudes and *implicit* attitudes (Albarracín & Vargas, 2010). Explicit attitudes are the attitudes we *know* we have, the ones we can easily and accurately describe. Implicit attitudes are much more automatic and involuntary, lying below the surface of our awareness, a bit more difficult to acknowledge (Petty et al., 2009b). As an example of explicit and implicit attitudes, consider your attitude toward people of a race or ethnicity different from your own. It's possible that your explicit and implicit attitudes differ a bit. You may prefer to see yourself as open-minded, but perhaps you are actually a bit more closed-minded than you would like to admit. As **Figure 13.2** illustrates, the biology of explicit and implicit thoughts reflects this distinction: They take place in different parts of the brain. Neuroimaging studies show that explicit attitudes come from the frontal cortex (specifically, the orbitofrontal cortex region), which allows for deliberate cognitive processing, but implicit attitudes emerge straight from the amygdala, which processes emotion (Phan et al., 2002; Wright et al., 2008).

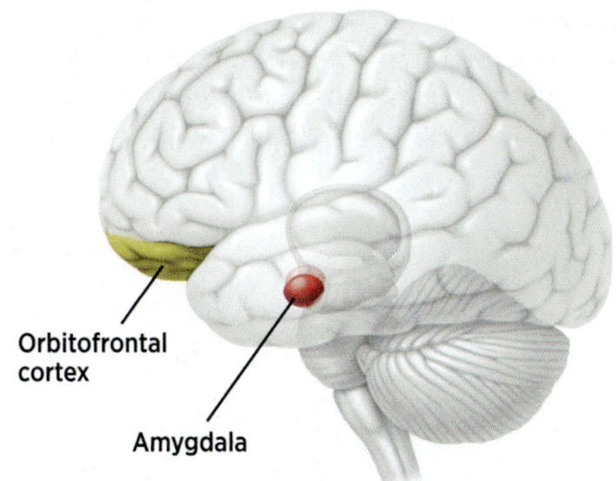

FIGURE 13.2 Explicit and Implicit Attitudes in the Brain. Explicit attitudes, which we have consciously thought through, activate the orbitofrontal cortex, where cognition takes place. Implicit attitudes, which we may not be so aware of, activate the amygdala, which processes emotion. Information from Wright et al. (2008) and Phan et al. (2002).

Which would you expect to be a better predictor of behavior — explicit attitudes or implicit attitudes? Social psychologists were somewhat surprised to find that, in general, the two are roughly equivalent in predicting behavior. They expected implicit attitudes to be better predictors, "truer" indicators, of how a person genuinely thinks and feels toward a topic than explicit attitudes (Ajzen, 2012; Greenwald et al., 2009; McCartan et al., 2018). An important exception to this equivalence was found in the area of racial attitudes and discrimination. In numerous studies, implicit racial attitudes were at least slightly better predictors than explicit racial attitudes of nonverbal behaviors — for example, making eye contact, smiling at, and sitting near people of diverse races (Fazio & Olson, 2003; Kurdi et al., 2018; Olson & Fazio, 2009).

Why are we covering attitudes in a chapter on *social* psychology? Aren't attitudes an individual thing?

Attitudes are important to social psychologists for a couple of reasons. First, we hold many attitudes toward other people (as individuals or groups), and they hold many attitudes toward us. Those attitudes can powerfully influence our behavior toward each other. Second, social psychologists study attitudes because we spend so much time and effort trying to *change* each other's attitudes. Just think of how often someone tries to alter your attitude on a daily basis. Your friend pleads with you to change your plans so the two of you can watch a movie together this weekend. Your neighbor's yard sign tries to sway your vote toward their preferred candidate. The voiceover on a commercial tries to convince you to switch to a newer, better smartphone.

Attitude Persuasion Strategies. Social psychologists have identified a variety of specific strategies that we use in attempts to change the attitudes of those around us. For example, **central route persuasion** is a persuasion strategy that emphasizes the message's content. By contrast, **peripheral route persuasion** is a persuasion strategy that emphasizes factors other than the message's content. Advertisers have undoubtedly made you familiar with both persuasion strategies. For example, when you see a TV commercial that directly explains the advantages of a particular car — good gas mileage, high safety rating, plenty of leg room — the advertisers are using central route persuasion. However, when you see a TV commercial for another car that simply pairs the car with a hot celebrity or trendy music, the advertisers are using peripheral route persuasion. The first ad, because of its direct approach, is more likely to be effective in the long run, especially if it gets the viewer to think about the advantages mentioned in its message.

central route persuasion
A persuasion strategy that emphasizes the message's content.

peripheral route persuasion
A persuasion strategy that emphasizes factors other than the message's content.

Social psychologists use the term *elaboration* to refer to this "thinking about it" process by the listener, and the more elaboration, the more effective the message (Petty & Briñol, 2012; Petty et al., 1995). When the strategy emphasizes stuff around the message (in its "periphery") rather than the message itself, elaboration tends to be minimal, so any attitude change tends to be superficial and short-term (Petty & Cacioppo, 1986; Wagner & Petty, 2011).

Other strategies for attitude change also resemble sales tactics. The **foot-in-the-door technique** is a persuasion strategy in which one person gets another person to agree to a small request before asking for a bigger one. Of course, the bigger request is the target, the change the first person wanted all along (Cialdini & Trost, 1998; Dillard et al., 1984; Dolinski, 2000; Gorassini & Olson, 1995; Hogg, 2010; Lee & Liang, 2019). For example, let's imagine that you want to borrow your friend Hector's car for an overnight trip to a city several hours away. Asking for such a big favor out of the blue may strike your friend as a bit much. But if you start by asking Hector to borrow his car for a 2-mile trip to the grocery store, he's more likely to say yes. Once he's agreed to that little request, he's more likely to say yes to a medium-sized request — say, a 20-mile trip to the doctor's office. Eventually, he might even agree to a large request like the overnight trip.

In one study of the foot-in-the-door technique, researchers sent e-mails to about 1000 participants asking them to click a link to a Web site designed to help children who had been injured by landmines in war zones (Guéguen & Jacob, 2001). For half, clicking the link in the e-mail immediately brought up a "donation" Web page. For the other half, clicking the link first brought up a petition against landmines that participants were asked to sign, which was then followed by the same "donation" Web page. Results indicated that getting participants to sign the petition — a foot-in-the-door — more than tripled the likelihood that the participant would click to donate.

Opposite to the foot-in-the-door technique is the **door-in-the-face technique**: a persuasion strategy in which one person gets another person to reject a large request before making a smaller one. In this case, the smaller request is the target that the first person has in mind from the beginning. The name of this term reflects the second person slamming the door in the face of the first person, only to reopen it when the more reasonable request follows (Pascual & Guéguen, 2005). For example, a teenage boy who wants a particular pair of expensive shoes for his birthday might begin by asking his parents/caregivers for a different pair that is *twice* as expensive. When they respond "Absolutely not!" his subsequent request for the pair he really wanted, which only cost half as much, may seem much more reasonable by comparison.

In a classic study of the door-in-the-face technique, researchers asked participants for a big, long-term commitment — to be a voluntary counselor at a juvenile detention center for 2 hours a week for 2 years — and almost none of them said yes. But when they followed that request with a smaller one — taking kids from the juvenile detention center on a single trip to the zoo — half agreed to do so. Other participants simply received the zoo request alone, and only 17% complied (Cialdini et al., 1975).

A final persuasion strategy used both on the sales floor and in day-to-day interactions is the **lowball technique**: a persuasion strategy in which one person quotes another person a low price to get an initial agreement and then raises the price (Burger & Caputo, 2015; Pascual et al., 2016). Some car dealers are notorious for lowballing customers — luring them into the dealership with a low advertised price and then adding hundreds or thousands for undercoating, delivery, and various mystery fees. It happens elsewhere too. A friend moving to a new apartment asks you to help move a couch and promises free pizza as a reward. You agree, but once you finish with the couch, your friend asks for help with the bed, the furniture, the TV, and dozens of boxes of clothes and other stuff. Hours later, sweaty and exhausted, you realize that you've worked much harder and longer than you expected to earn that "free" pizza.

foot-in-the-door technique
A persuasion strategy in which one person gets another person to agree to a small request before asking for a bigger one.

door-in-the-face technique
A persuasion strategy in which one person gets another person to reject a large request before making a smaller one.

lowball technique
A persuasion strategy in which one person quotes another person a low price to get an initial agreement and then raises the price.

social role
A title, position, or status that carries expectations for acceptable behavior.

Social Role. Our attitudes are also shaped by our sense of who we are and what we are supposed to do. Our attitudes and ultimately our actions are often influenced by our **social role**: a title, position, or status that carries expectations for acceptable behavior. The power of the social role is often most evident right after our role changes.

When a person becomes something new — a high school graduate, an employee, a parent, a boss, a retiree — they often feel a new pressure to behave as someone with that label should behave (Hogg et al., 1995; Stryker & Statham, 1986). For example, a recent college graduate starts to rethink the clothes they wear and the music they listen to, eventually switching to something a bit more "grown-up." After all, they think, they're leaving the student world and entering the professional world now.

A well-known and disturbing study from the 1970s illustrates the power that social roles can have on our attitudes and behavior. Social psychologist Phillip Zimbardo asked a couple of dozen college students (all men) to volunteer to spend time in a fake prison. (It was actually a basement of a building at Stanford University, where Zimbardo worked.) The researchers randomly assigned some of the men to be guards, while the others were randomly assigned to be inmates. The guards got uniforms, clubs, and mirrored sunglasses; the inmates got prison outfits, ID numbers, and cells.

FilippoBacci/E+/Getty Images

Social roles often carry expectations that encourage people to behave in certain ways. For example, the social role of first responder encourages people to perform often heroic acts to help others.

The experiment was scheduled to go on for weeks, but, within a few days, there were serious problems: The guards' behavior became degrading, humiliating, and abusive toward the prisoners. At times, they punished prisoners' behavior by denying them food and access to bathrooms, stripping their clothes off, spraying them with fire extinguishers, taking their beds away, and forcing them to clean toilets with their bare hands. When the complaints from the inmates about mistreatment by the guards intensified into rebellion — and it was clear that the physical and psychological health of the prisoners were at risk — the experimenters stopped the study after only 6 days (Banuazizi & Movahedi, 1975; Zimbardo, 1972; Zimbardo et al., 1973). The important point here is that the "prison guards" were just *playing the role* of prison guard. In real life, they were Stanford University students, but the role of prison guard altered their attitudes and behaviors to the point of intimidating and endangering their own classmates.

Let's remember that social roles can push people to perform wonderful behaviors too. We often see people performing heroic actions that may be influenced by the fact that their positions carry expectations of that kind of behavior. For example, first responders of all kinds, including firefighters and police officers, ran into the twin towers on 9/11 when everyone else was running out, sacrificing their lives in the name of their roles. Sully Sullenberger, the pilot who saved all 155 aboard by landing his powerless plane on the Hudson River in January 2009, walked up and down the passenger aisle to make sure all passengers and crew were out safely. He made this walk *twice* before exiting the plane himself, all in the name of doing his job. Scott Beigel, Aaron Fies, and Chris Hixon — all teachers and coaches at Stoneman Douglas High School in Parkland, Florida, who took their roles as caretakers for students seriously — lost their lives in a February 2018 mass shooting at the school as they tried to protect their students.

Cognitive Dissonance: Attitudes in Conflict

Cognitive dissonance is the discomfort caused by having an attitude or behavior that contradicts another attitude or behavior (**Figure 13.3**). You may be familiar with "dissonance" in music: a pair of sounds that are not in harmony with each other that can be unpleasant to experience. The same holds true for cognitive dissonance. We prefer for our attitudes and behaviors to be in harmony with each other. At times, however, we can sense that they are not, and that experience is indeed unpleasant. Like saying one thing when you believe another, it's an inner hypocrisy that demands to be resolved (Aronson, 1999; Cooper, 2012; Nail & Boniecki, 2011).

For example, consider Keith, a serious long-distance runner and new father. For years, Keith has trained 6 days a week year-round and has completed two marathons per year. This commitment reflects Keith's attitude toward his sport: "Running is my life. It's my top priority." A few months ago, Keith became a father to his first child, a daughter. Keith has long wanted to have children, and is thrilled about the baby. His attitude about fatherhood? "Fatherhood is my life. It's my top priority." Obviously, the

cognitive dissonance
The discomfort caused by having an attitude or behavior that contradicts another attitude or behavior.

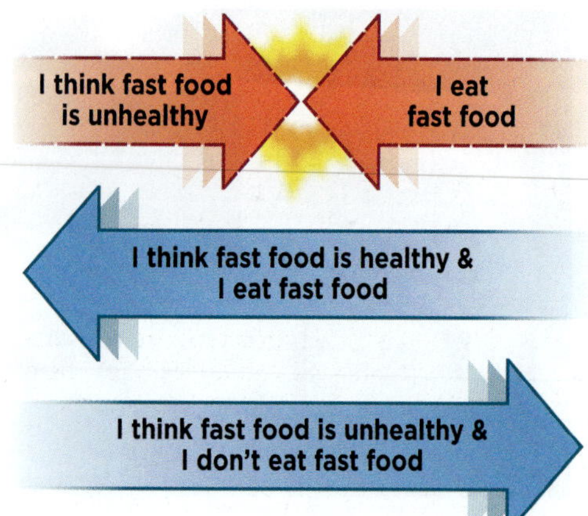

FIGURE 13.3 Cognitive Dissonance. The first row illustrates cognitive dissonance: an attitude and a behavior at odds with each other. The next two rows show two ways that cognitive dissonance could be resolved—either a change in the attitude or a change in the behavior.

baby's arrival has caused Keith some cognitive dissonance. He can't have two top priorities, and the coexistence of his commitments to his daughter and his sport has him stressed out. When he chooses running, he feels bad about neglecting his daughter; when he chooses his daughter, he feels bad about neglecting his running.

How can Keith resolve his cognitive dissonance? Social psychologists see three solutions: (1) change the first attitude, (2) change the second attitude, or (3) come up with a third attitude to resolve the tension between the first and second attitudes (Cooper, 1999; Harmon-Jones & Mills, 1999). In Keith's case, changing his first attitude would mean that he no longer considers running his top priority and becomes a fully devoted father. Changing his second attitude would mean that he no longer considers being a father his top priority and becomes a fully devoted runner. A new, third attitude could take a number of forms, each of which is effective only if it's believable: "I should keep running, at least a little bit, for my daughter's sake. It keeps me happy and healthy as a dad, and sets a great example for her." Or, "Not running 6 days a week doesn't mean I'm not dedicated to the sport. I'm just taking a break, for a very good reason." Or, "I'll try to find a good jogging stroller and take her along with me!"

The study of cognitive dissonance has a long history, stretching back to the classic 1950s work of Leon Festinger (1957, 1964). This field of study centers on the question that begins one of Festinger's most famous studies: "What happens to a person's private opinion if he is forced to do or say something contrary to that opinion?" (Festinger & Carlsmith, 1959, p. 203). In this study, participants were required to do monotonous, hour-long tasks that involved placing wooden pegs into slots over and over. The task was boring, but when it was over, the researchers asked each participant to tell the next set of participants waiting outside the room that the task was enjoyable. Half of the participants were paid $1 to offer this false opinion; the other half were paid $20. Guess which group had a more positive attitude about the task? You might expect the $20 group, since they were paid so much more, but the results indicated that the $1 group actually had a much more positive attitude about the task. Researchers suggested the $1 group had to convince themselves that they actually liked the task to resolve the cognitive dissonance between "I thought that task was boring" and "I'm not a liar." The $20 group didn't experience cognitive dissonance, because they could rationalize their behavior with the large sum of money.

In the decades since Festinger's studies, many other researchers have reconfirmed the power of cognitive dissonance to motivate changes in attitude and behavior (Cooper, 2007). In many cases, this cognitive dissonance has pushed individuals not toward lying, but toward more desirable or healthy behaviors (Freijy & Kothe, 2013; Stone & Fernandez, 2008). The basic idea is that confronting an incompatibility between your good attitude and your bad behavior can inspire you to change the behavior for the better. For example, researchers asked college women to perform actions inconsistent with eating disorders – such as speaking highly of their own bodies while in front of a mirror – and those women later had lower levels of attitudes consistent with eating disorders than college women who had not performed those actions (Becker et al., 2010). Also, people recycle more when they are made aware of the cognitive dissonance between their positive attitude toward recycling and their lack of recycling at times, such as throwing aluminum cans or plastic bottles in the trash rather than finding a recycling bin (Fried & Aronson, 1995). Similarly, people who see themselves as financially responsible but notice some out-of-control spending on their credit card statements can be motivated to spend more responsibly (Davies & Lea, 1995).

There is an alternative explanation for the attitude change found with cognitive dissonance: self-perception theory. Self-perception theory states that our attitudes form after our actions, rather than before them (Bem, 1967). According to this theory, people behave in a particular way, then work backward to figure out what attitude they must have held before performing that behavior. For example, if a driver finds themself driving way over the speed limit and weaving through traffic without wearing a seatbelt, they might conclude, "I guess I value excitement over safety."

FROM RESEARCH TO REAL LIFE

Can Cognitive Dissonance Increase Mask Wearing and Social Distancing During COVID?

Scientific evidence has shown that wearing masks and social distancing are two important behaviors for reducing the spread of COVID. There are many people who agree with this scientific finding but are not always consistent with their own mask wearing and social distancing. One team of researchers wondered if those people might be more consistent with these behaviors if they felt the contradiction between their beliefs and the way they actually behaved—that is, if they experienced cognitive dissonance (Pearce & Cooper, 2021).

These researchers ran a study in which the participants all agreed on the importance of these COVID safety behaviors beforehand. Next, the participants were randomly placed into four groups. The group in which the researchers were most interested—which they called the "dissonance group"—wrote a paragraph about why it's important to follow COVID safety guidelines *and* wrote a paragraph about a time when they failed to follow those guidelines. Among the other three groups, one just wrote the first paragraph, one just wrote the second paragraph, and one wrote neither. The researchers followed up with all participants a week later to ask how often they had worn masks and maintained social distance. Results showed that the dissonance group reported much more mask wearing and social distancing (about twice as much) than the other three groups. Additionally, the dissonance group reported a significantly higher number of vaccinations during the week before the follow-up than the other three groups.

The researchers pointed to cognitive dissonance as the primary explanation for their results. Essentially, they argued that participants in the dissonance group, more than participants in other groups, felt the difference between their COVID safety beliefs and their failure to behave consistently with those beliefs. Presumably, that difference—or cognitive dissonance—was unpleasant in the week that followed. To reduce that unpleasantness, those participants changed their behavior to match their COVID safety beliefs. The researchers even argued that these kinds of "dissonance-based behavior change" strategies could be used on the population more widely. •

CHECK YOUR LEARNING:

13.1 What is social cognition?

13.2 What are attributions?

13.3 What is the fundamental attribution error?

13.4 What are attitudes, and how do people try to change them?

13.5 What is cognitive dissonance, and how can people resolve it?

To check your understanding of these questions, click show the answers or refer to the answers in the Chapter Summary.

Social Influence: How We Influence Each Other

Intentionally or unintentionally, human beings influence each other's behavior. In some cases, a group sways you. In other cases, one person commands you. In still others, your mere awareness of other people modifies how you think and act. To illustrate, imagine yourself spending a full week completely *alone*. You are absolutely inaccessible, with no contact (in person, by phone, online) with anyone else. The difference between the way you would behave in such isolation and the way you behave in your usual, day-to-day life illustrates **social influence**: any way in which the presence of other people influences your thoughts, feelings, or behavior. Let's explore some ways that having others around you could cause you to conform or obey, or otherwise affect what you do.

YOU WILL LEARN:

13.6 what social influence is.

13.7 what conformity is, and when and why it happens.

13.8 what obedience is.

13.9 to what extent people obey authority.

13.10 how groups can help or hinder individual performance.

13.11 what processes affect group decision making.

Conformity: Going Along with the Group

You walk into the psychology experiment and take a seat. There are about a half-dozen other participants in the room with you. The experimenter explains that they will show you a straight line of a particular length (the "standard" line), and then show you three "comparison" lines of varying lengths. Your job is to identify which comparison line is closest in length to the standard line. No problem, you say to yourself.

social influence
Any way in which the presence of other people influences one's thoughts, feelings, or behavior.

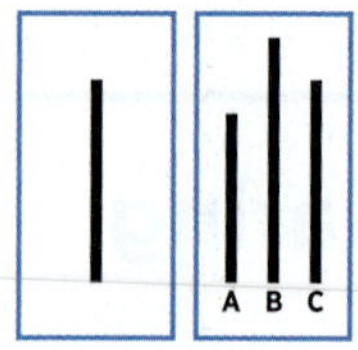

FIGURE 13.4 Asch's Classic Studies of Conformity. The person in the middle of the photo is the actual participant in Asch's classic study. The other two are actors (confederates) instructed to provide the same incorrect answer when asked to choose a line (A, B, or C) that matches the length of the target line (to the left). Reproduced with permission. Copyright © 2019 Scientific American, a division of Nature America, Inc. All rights reserved. Source: Asch (1951, 1955, 1956).

You take a look at the first set of lines, and the correct answer is obvious: Line A. The experimenter calls on four other participants first, and gets the same response four times in a row: "Line A, Line A, Line A, Line A." It's your turn now. You say Line A. It's a no-brainer.

The second set of lines has an equally obvious correct answer: Line B (**Figure 13.4**). The experimenter calls on participants in the same order as before. The first participant answers: Line C. You're surprised. You take a closer look, and, from what you see, the answer is still obviously Line B. The next participant agrees with the first participant: Line C. Now you're puzzled. The next two participants concur with the first two: Line C, Line C. Now it's your turn, and you're bewildered. Your eyes are telling you that absolutely, without question, Line B is correct. But the group has spoken: unanimously, they say Line C. How do you answer? Do you go with what you think you know, despite being the only one in the group to do so, or do you go along with the consensus?

This is precisely the methodology used by Solomon Asch in his classic 1950s studies (Asch, 1951, 1955, 1956). Asch was examining **conformity**: changes in an individual's behavior to correspond to the behavior of a group of other people. In these studies, Asch made it seem like there was a roomful of participants. In reality, there was only one participant: you. The other people in the room were actors whom Asch had instructed to provide particular answers to set you up for the decision about conforming. His findings were quite interesting. About 37% of the time, participants conformed. They went along with the group's opinion even when that opinion was obviously wrong. Only about 25% of participants never conformed to any of the 12 situations in which all the confederates answered incorrectly.

Asch's studies apply to many situations in our daily lives, most of which are much more consequential than choosing among straight lines. For example, Phoebe, a 16-year-old high school junior, knows very well the dangers of bulimia. She fully realizes that the pattern of bingeing on huge amounts of food and then purging to prevent weight gain is associated with great physical and psychological dangers. But many of the girls on her cheerleading squad binge and purge. Some make themselves vomit, some exercise excessively, and one even abuses laxatives. They all see it as a smart way to stay thin. What will Phoebe do? What would you do? Researchers have found that for young women who develop bulimia, conformity to peers' behavior is often a powerful reason why (Mason & Chaney, 1996; VanHuysse et al., 2016).

A more recent study creatively adapted Asch's method of studying conformity, using medical students as the participants (Beran et al., 2013). The medical students' task was to choose the right location to insert a needle. Specifically, the students were learning to insert a syringe into a specific spot near the kneecap to draw fluid, which is commonly done when testing for arthritis. Some students practiced on a fake knee that was brand new; others practiced on a fake knee that already had holes – in an incorrect location – supposedly from previous students working on the same task. The results? Students working on the "used" knee were more than 50% more likely than students working on the "new" knee to make an insertion in the wrong location (most often, near the holes that were already there). Those preexisting holes served the same function as the actors' answers in Asch's original experiment: they caused the participants to doubt their own judgment and feel pressure to go along with what others had done.

Why do people conform? Why don't they just do what they think is best and ignore the group?

conformity
Changes in an individual's behavior to correspond to the behavior of a group of other people.

Inclusion in social groups is such a primary, vital human need that it often outweighs other demands (Baumeister & Leary, 1995; Fiske, 2010). We touched on group inclusion under a different name – belongingness – in our discussion of Abraham

Maslow's hierarchy of needs back in Chapter 8 (Motivation and Emotion). This need may have evolved from our prehistoric ancestors, for whom exclusion from the social group could mean exclusion from food, shelter, and possibly even life itself. Our brains certainly reveal biological indicators of the importance of group inclusion: getting kicked out of a group activates the same pain-related brain areas as getting kicked in the shin, and forming friendships produces the same pain-killing substance (opioids) as morphine (Eisenberger et al., 2003; MacDonald & Leary, 2005; Panksepp et al., 1985; Wang et al., 2017). Similarly, the brains of people shown photos of social interaction after 10 hours of isolation react in similar ways as the brains of people shown photos of pizza after fasting for 10 hours (Tomova et al., 2020). No wonder the drive to stay connected to the group makes us question our own better judgment. Asch and many more recent researchers have identified certain factors that can increase or decrease the chances that a person will conform to a group, including the number of people in the group, whether any of those people are already dissenting, and the self-esteem of the person deciding whether to conform. See **Table 13.1** for a summary of those factors.

Another reason why people may conform is that they don't know how to behave on their own, so they mimic those around them. This type of conformity stems from a different kind of situation from the one in the Asch studies. If you were a participant in the Asch studies, you would know which line was correct, but you might choose to override that knowledge to fit in with the norm of the group. That kind of conformity is *normative conformity*. In other situations, you are clueless about what is correct. There is no knowledge to override. You seek information from those around you about how to behave, and by following their lead, you conform to their way of behaving. Your main goal isn't so much to be liked by everyone else as simply to do what you need to do to get through the situation. That kind of conformity is *informational conformity* (Cialdini & Goldstein, 2004; Deutch & Gerard, 1955; Madon et al., 2008; Sherif, 1936; Toelch & Dolan, 2015).

DIVERSITY MATTERS

A final note about conformity: it may be a universal human need, but it varies from one culture to the next (Horita & Takezawa, 2018). Researchers looked back on 133 conformity studies from 17 countries that used similar methodologies to Asch's line judgment task (Bond & Smith, 1996). They found that conformity levels were consistently higher in collectivist countries than in individualistic countries. This finding may come as no surprise, since collectivist cultures (such as China, Japan, and other Asian countries) emphasize group harmony and value compliance to a greater extent than individualistic cultures (like the United States, England, and other Western countries). Similarly, researchers have found that people from individualistic and collectivistic cultures tend to interpret conformity in different ways. Specifically, adults from collectivistic cultures may view highly conforming kids as intelligent and well-behaved, but adults from individualistic cultures may view the same kids as lacking creativity (Clegg et al., 2017). Studies have also found that conformity rates in the United States

MY TAKE VIDEO 13.2

Conformity

"I tend to witness a lot of conformity using social media. . ."

Visit Achieve to watch the My Take video and then answer questions.

Achieve

TABLE 13.1: A Person Is Most Likely to Conform to a Group When. . .

the group includes at least three to five members.
the group contains no other dissenting members.
the group is highly valued by the person.
the group is working toward a single, shared goal.
the person has low self-esteem.
the person has low status within the group.
the person's behaviors are visible to the group.
the person's alternatives outside the group are minimal.

As summarized in Levine and Kerr (2007) and Hogg (2010).

have dropped since the 1950s, when Asch's studies were conducted, presumably because the values of our society have moved toward greater individualism (Bond & Smith, 1996; Lalancette & Standing, 1990; Nicholson et al., 1985).

Obedience: Following Orders

Solomon Asch had a graduate student, Stanley Milgram, whose own research in social psychology became even more widely known than Asch's (Prislin & Crano, 2012). Milgram studied **obedience**: changes in an individual's behavior to comply with the demands of an authority figure. Obedience differs from conformity in important ways. We conform to groups of peers, whose status is equal to ours. We obey superiors, who hold positions of power over us (Hogg, 2010). Milgram's obedience studies focused on following orders.

As a Jewish person whose parents grew up during the Holocaust, Milgram felt compelled to understand how Nazi soldiers could have committed so many heartless, vicious murders of Jewish people. Some people presumed these Nazi soldiers were driven by pure evil, but Milgram wondered about the role of obedience to authority. Milgram's idea was reflected in the comments of Adolf Eichmann, a prominent Nazi who was responsible for the death of millions. Specifically, Eichmann explained that he was "just following orders" of those who ranked above him (Blass, 2004; Cesarani, 2004).

Milgram's method of studying obedience was both ingenious and controversial (Lunt, 2009; Milgram, 1963, 1965, 1974). (In fact, his studies, which took place in the 1960s, deceived and distressed participants. They would almost certainly not be allowed today.) Here's how the Milgram experiments worked, step by step, from the participants' point of view:

1. You respond to a newspaper ad for a study at Yale University involving "memory and learning." As a participant, you will be paid $4.00 plus 50¢ for travel expenses.
2. When you arrive, you meet two men. One, wearing a white coat, is clearly in charge of the study; we'll call him the Authority. The other is a man who appears to be another participant, just like you. The Authority explains that one of the participants will be the "Teacher" and the other the "Learner" in this study. You randomly choose slips of paper to determine who will play each role, and you get "Teacher."
3. What you don't realize at this point is that the slips of paper were rigged, and the "Learner" is actually an actor (confederate) who is in on Milgram's scheme. The study actually has nothing to do with memory or learning, but everything to do with obedience to authority.
4. The Authority explains that you will read pairs of words to the Learner. Then you will quiz him by saying the first word and expecting him to say the second (for example, "table/chair" or "solid/striped"). When the Learner gets a pair right, you will do nothing. When he gets a pair wrong, you will jolt him with electric shock as punishment.
5. You see the Authority take the Learner into the next room and attach his arm to a metal plate that delivers the shock. (In reality, no shock is delivered, but you don't know that yet.) The Learner mentions that he has a slight heart condition; the Authority replies that the shocks will be painful but not cause permanent damage. In your room, you sit before an electric shock generator that can deliver a range of shocks, labeled both in numbers (15–450 volts) and in words (from "Slight Shock" to "Danger: Severe Shock" to the highest level, "XXX," as shown in **Figure 13.5**). You can't see the Learner in the next room, but you can hear him.
6. The Authority instructs you to begin the word-pair learning exercise. You do so, and the Learner gets the first few correct. But then he starts making mistakes. The Authority tells you to deliver the lowest level of shock for the first mistake. With each additional mistake, he tells you to increase the voltage by 15 volts. If you resist, the Authority insists, stating, "It is absolutely essential that you continue," or "You have no other choice. You must go on."

obedience
Changes in an individual's behavior to comply with the demands of an authority figure.

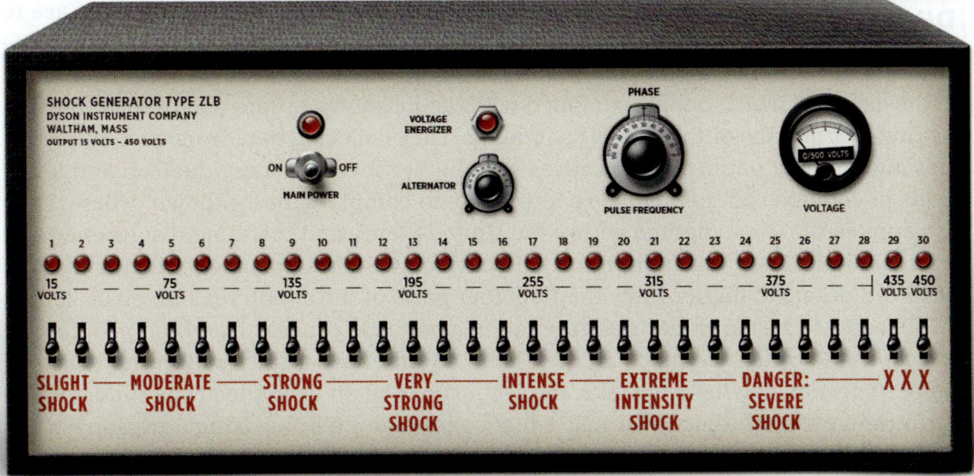

FIGURE 13.5 Milgram's "Shock Generator." Most participants in Milgram's famous study obeyed orders to shock another person all the way up to the XXX level on the far right of this machine.

7. As the voltage increases, so do the Learner's reactions to the shock you deliver (all of which, of course, are simulated and performed according to a script of which you are unaware). At 75 volts, he grunts in pain; at 150 volts, he says, "Experimenter! That's all. Get me out of here. . . . My heart's starting to bother me. I refuse to go on." At 300 volts, the Learner screams, "I absolutely refuse to answer any more. . . . You can't hold me here." At 330 volts, he shrieks, "Let me out of here. My heart's bothering me. . . . Let me out of here! Let me out!" From 330 volts all the way up to the maximum of 450 volts, he's completely silent, leaving you to perhaps wonder if he's still conscious or even alive.

The big question, of course, was how far the Teacher would go in delivering the electric shocks to the Learner. At what point would the Teacher refuse to obey? Prior to the study, Milgram posed this question to mental health professionals and college students, and they unanimously agreed that no participants would obey all the way to the maximum shock. Many predicted that they would disobey as soon as the Learner made his first request to stop (Funder & Fast, 2010; Milgram, 1974). Those predictions were shockingly wrong. The vast majority of the Teachers went well past the Learner's first request to stop. None of them stopped before 300 volts. Only 38% stopped at all — which means that 62% shocked the Learner all the way to the maximum, 450-volt, "XXX" level. Many participants tried to reason or argue with the Authority, and some showed signs of anxiety or anguish, but still did not stop obeying the Authority (Milgram, 1974).

Later studies by Milgram and others (often using methods that were more humane to participants) found similar results under similar conditions, confirming Milgram's original findings (Blass, 1999a, b, 2009; Burger, 2009; Milgram, 1965). Those later studies did, however, identify certain factors that influence the likelihood of obedience. Some factors involved characteristics of the person being ordered to act (the "Teacher"). For example, people who have progressed to high levels of Kohlberg's moral development scale (as covered in Chapter 9) were more likely to disobey the authority figure than those whose sense of morality was less developed (Feather, 1988; Kohlberg, 1981).

Other factors that influenced obedience involved characteristics of the authority figure. Obedience is greater when the authority figure is physically close and visible (as opposed to far away or invisible), viewed as an expert possessing legitimate power (as opposed to being a fraud), and associated with a respected institution, like Yale in Milgram's studies (Blass, 1999a; Blass & Schmidt, 2001). Still other factors that influence obedience involve characteristics of the situation. Disobedience grows when others disobey, when the victim can be seen and heard, or when the authority figure is challenged by another authority figure (Milgram, 1974).

social facilitation
An increase in individual performance caused by the presence of other people.

social loafing
A decrease in individual performance when tasks are done in groups.

DIVERSITY MATTERS Diversity factors may play a role in how likely people are to obey instructions from authority figures, especially if obeying the instructions might affect others. In one study, researchers focused on the extent to which people complied with the lockdown orders that occurred within the first few months of the COVID pandemic. They collected data from over 100 countries and found a pattern: in countries with higher levels of individualism and lower levels of collectivism, people were less likely to comply with lockdown orders. They also applied the same method within the United States, and the same results emerged: where individualism was higher and collectivism was lower, people tended to disobey lockdown orders at higher rates than in other parts of the country (Chen et al., 2021).

Obedience research has enlightened us about the process by which people may do despicable things. To place all the blame on inherent cruelty within the hearts of the perpetrators may be a mistake. In fact, it could be an example of the fundamental attribution error we discussed just a few pages ago — emphasizing a person's traits over the situation when explaining the behavior of others. At times, those people may be following the orders of authority figures rather than their own beliefs when they commit monstrous acts such as the Holocaust killings, which inspired Milgram's experiments.

CHAPTER APP 13.1

There are many apps designed to help you develop a good habit by tracking a behavior you want to do more often: work out, eat healthy, study a particular subject, practice a musical instrument, etc. With HabitShare, you can share the new habit you're trying to create with friends from your phone's contact list, so they know what behavior you're trying to change (and they may even choose to change the habit in their own lives). By sharing, friends can monitor each other's successes and failures, and send messages of encouragement through the app.

How does it APPly to your daily life?
If you were trying to change a particular behavior, how much of a difference would it make to know that other people were keeping an eye on your progress? Would you expect to do better or worse if you tried to build this new habit without sharing it with anyone?

How does it APPly to your understanding of psychology?
How does this app affect your appreciation of *social facilitation*? In your opinion, what *specifically* about the presence of other people monitoring you (or joining in with you) is most likely to facilitate your behavior?

To learn more about this app or to download it to your phone, you can search for "HabitShare" on Google, in the iPhone App store, or in the Google Play store.

Performing Tasks in Groups

Performing a behavior alone can be different from performing the same behavior in front of other people.

Social Facilitation. Sometimes, the company of others enhances a behavior. Social psychologists call this boost **social facilitation**: an increase in individual performance caused by the presence of other people. Social facilitation is most likely to occur when the task is easy and simple (Hackman & Katz, 2010; Levine & Moreland, 2012). For example, runners typically run faster times at meets, surrounded by spectators and other runners, than they do on solo training runs (Strube et al., 1981; Worringham & Messick, 1983). Call it adrenaline or simply being hyped up: the energy of the other people causes an arousal that translates into improved performance.

But don't people sometimes choke when they perform in front of crowds?

People do choke sometimes, but that's typically when the task is challenging, and something they haven't fully mastered yet. In those cases, the arousal caused by the presence of other people causes them to stumble rather than pick up the pace. For example, consider people chosen to sing the national anthem before sporting events. Some are experienced vocalists who have sung the anthem in similar circumstances many times; others are novices singing live in front of a big crowd for the first time. It's easy to guess who's more likely to fumble through it.

Social Loafing. Sometimes, the presence of others hinders a behavior. Social psychologists call this **social loafing**: a decrease in individual performance when tasks are done in groups. The difference between choking and social loafing is that choking takes place when we feel we are being watched and evaluated by an audience, but social loafing takes place when we simply find ourselves in a group of people that is collectively responsible for the task (Ingham et al., 1974; Karau & Williams, 1993; Latané et al., 1979; Simms & Nichols, 2014). Think about group projects you've worked on with classmates for which all members of the group will receive the same grade. Or if a parent with four kids asks them as a group to clean up the house, with no individual chores assigned. Those are the kinds of situations much more likely to produce the kind of slacking off that social psychologists call social loafing.

Researchers have found that social loafing is especially likely to take place when the individual feels their output is not distinguishable from the output of others (Harkins & Jackson, 1985). For example, when participants in one study were asked to shout as loudly as possible, the volume of each individual shouter depended significantly on the number of people in their group of shouters and whether the experimenters said they were being measured as a group or as individuals. Specifically, they shouted less loudly when they were in large groups and when they were told the volume was going to be measured only as a group rather than individually (Williams et al., 1981).

deindividuation
A loss of identity and accountability experienced by individuals in groups that can lead to atypical behavior.

groupthink
A phenomenon that occurs when group members value getting along with each other more than finding the best solution.

Deindividuation. Sometimes, we find ourselves in groups in which we don't stand out in any particular way — that is, we're just another face in the crowd. Such situations are likely to produce **deindividuation**: a loss of identity and accountability experienced by individuals in groups that can lead to atypical behavior. For example, imagine being at a stand-up comedy show in which the lights above the audience are down but the stage is brightly lit. A heckler's voice emerges, an unidentifiable voice shrouded by the darkness. The heckling continues unmercifully until suddenly the comedian breaks from their routine, points, and says "Turn all the lights up. Let's find this person." Not surprisingly, the heckling stops. The heckler's bravery was fueled by anonymity, but now that they can be identified, they are silent.

Deindividuation inspires other behaviors that are far more potentially harmful than bothering a comedian (Vilanova et al., 2017). Some experts have argued that soldiers can feel deindividuated in their uniforms and short haircuts, which make them difficult to distinguish from their fellow fighters and therefore more likely to behave aggressively. (Stanar, 2021; Watson, 1973). Along the same lines, **Figure 13.6** shows data from a study of violent crimes in Ireland, which found that attackers in disguises hurt more people more severely and made more threats for future harm than those without disguises (Silke, 2003). People who illegally buy and sell music, movies, and other materials online may be similarly fueled by the sense of anonymity that the Internet can provide (Hinduja, 2008; Zimmerman & Ybarra, 2016). The common thread to all of these examples is the lack of inhibition that we often place on our own behavior, which can occur when we perceive ourselves as an indistinguishable member of a crowd. When we know we can't be individually identified, and therefore are unlikely to get caught or punished, we sometimes act in ways we never would otherwise (Bushman & Huesmann, 2010). Deindividuation doesn't happen every time it could, however. Numerous studies have shown that in many potentially aggressive situations, people actually behave in basically the same way they would under normal circumstances (Postmes & Spears, 1998; Spears, 2017).

Group Decision Making

When groups work together, they often make different decisions than what any individual member might have made. For example, picture a city council meeting in which seven council members discuss how to spend the money in their budget: new playground equipment, a new police car, improvements to highway signs, better exercise equipment at the community center, or something else?

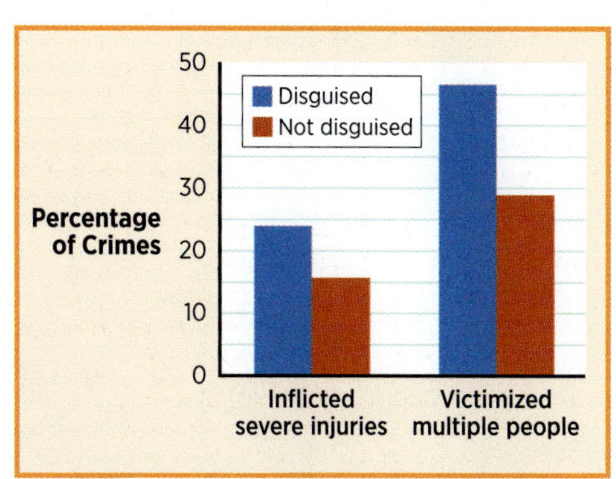

FIGURE 13.6 Deindividuation and Crime. Compared to violent criminals whose identities were visible, those in disguise — in other words, those more likely to experience deindividuation — are more likely to hurt multiple victims and to hurt them severely. Data from Silke (2003).

Groupthink. The obvious goal for the city council just described is to make a wise decision, but another goal (often unspoken) is for the group members to behave cooperatively toward each other. Usually, both goals can be accomplished, but if cooperation starts to outweigh wise decision making, the group may find themselves caught up in **groupthink**: a phenomenon that occurs when group members value getting along with each other more than finding the best solution. If this happened in the city council meeting, there is a good chance that the first suggestion — such as "Let's get the kids a new playground!" — will be met by one "yes" after another. Eventually, the group is unanimous and happy, and the meeting is adjourned. However, the police force may have needed that new car much more desperately than the kids needed a new playground. Pushing for the new police car would have caused an interpersonal clash among the council members at the meeting, and that's to be avoided at all costs when groupthink takes over.

When groupthink happens at higher levels of government, the consequences can be severe. The term *groupthink* was actually coined as a description of the massive Bay of Pigs debacle that President John F. Kennedy and his inner circle collectively decided upon in 1961. The idea was to enlist hundreds of Cuban immigrants to invade Cuba and overthrow Fidel Castro, but it failed miserably. Many of the invaders were captured or killed, and no political ground was gained by the United States. In retrospect, it seems obvious that someone involved in the planning should have spoken up about the plan's flaws, but no one did. They were too concerned with maintaining the unity and togetherness they felt as a group to raise a different point of view (Janis, 1982).

Groupthink happens in the workplace as well. In 1985, Coca-Cola decided to change its formula and replace its signature drink, one of the most successful products in history, with "New Coke." It was a disaster. Loyal Coke drinkers resented the company for changing their beloved drink, and many flocked to rival Pepsi. (Shortly afterward, "New Coke" was gone, and Coca-Cola classic was back.) Prior to the switch to New Coke, there were signs in the market research that a backlash might happen, but the executives at Coca-Cola remained in agreement — in part because groupthink discouraged those executives from disagreeing — and a bad group decision was made (Jones et al., 2016; Schindler, 1992).

To combat groupthink, it's wise to encourage disagreement within a group, and to reassure members that they will be valued, rather than shunned, for offering opposing opinions. It's helpful to run a group's decision past other experts on the subject — outsiders for whom getting along with those group members is unimportant — to see if they too would give it the go-ahead (Janis, 1982; Nemeth et al., 2001; Nemeth & Rogers, 2011). Additionally, it's beneficial to make sure the group includes members who feel strongly about the group's mission and are willing to speak out even when they know it will cause conflict with other members (Jetten & Hornsey, 2014; Packer, 2009; Packer et al., 2014, 2018).

LIFE HACK 13.2

When you are part of a group, remember the potential problems of groupthink. Allow everyone to voice their opinions, even if those opinions differ from the opinions of others.

(Janis, 1982; Nemeth et al., 2001; Nemeth & Rogers, 2011)

Group Polarization. Another common occurrence in group decision making is **group polarization**: the tendency for a group's attitudes to become more extreme as a result of group discussions. For example, at first, a group of neighbors *kind of* lean toward a particular candidate for mayor, but then after several discussions and group texts about the subject, they become that candidate's most hardworking campaigners. Or, at first, a group of people are *kind of* prejudiced against a particular type of people, but then after sharing their opinions with each other, they become even more prejudiced (Gabbay et al., 2018; Myers & Bishop, 1970; Myers & Lamm, 1976).

Group polarization can happen to two opposing groups at the same time, causing them to distance themselves from each other even more. (The term *polarization*, after all, refers to *poles*, or extreme opposites, like the North Pole and South Pole on a globe.) For example, politics today are much more polarized than they were a generation or two ago, largely because of the growth of media in which people can immerse themselves in exclusively one side of the debate. News channels, Web sites, radio shows, podcasts, social media posts, and other information sources filter in their own opinion and filter out any viewpoint that doesn't conform. As a result of these "echo chambers," conservatives get more conservative, liberals get more liberal, and the middle ground becomes more barren (Del Vicario et al., 2016; Druckman et al., 2018; Evans, 2009; Iyengar & Westwood, 2015).

One study examined this political polarization during the early months of the pandemic (March-August, 2020). Specifically, these researchers examined the many thousands of Twitter posts in the United States that included pro-mask hashtags (#WearAMask and #MaskUp) or anti-mask hashtags (#NoMasks and #MasksOff). They found that as the months went by, the number of both types of hashtags increased exponentially. They explained this increase in part by pointing to the fact that people on both sides increasingly heard the opinions of others within their group, which caused many people within each group to dig in their heels and become more passionate about their stance (Lang et al., 2021).

group polarization
The tendency for a group's attitudes to become more extreme as a result of group discussions.

CHECK YOUR LEARNING:

13.6 What is social influence?

13.7 What is conformity, and how does it differ between cultures?

13.8 What is obedience?

13.9 What did the classic obedience studies by Stanley Milgram reveal about the extent to which people obey authority?

13.10 How can the presence of other people help or hinder individual performance?

13.11 How can groupthink or group polarization influence group decision making?

To check your understanding of these questions, click show the answers or refer to the answers in the Chapter Summary.

Social Relations: How We Relate to Each Other

YOU WILL LEARN:

13.12 how first impressions are made.

13.13 what prejudice, stereotypes, and discrimination are.

13.14 how prejudice, stereotypes, and discrimination develop.

13.15 how to overcome prejudice.

13.16 why people behave aggressively.

13.17 what attracts people to one another.

Love, hate, and everything in between: We form all kinds of relationships with each other. Social psychologists study how these relationships develop, and uncover the reasons why we help or hurt each other. Specifically, they examine how we form *first impressions*, how we develop (and fight against) *prejudices*, why we behave *aggressively*, and why we feel *attraction* and *romantic love*.

First Impressions

All relationships begin with **impression formation**: the initial appraisal, or "first impression," that a person forms of another person. You know from firsthand experience how quickly you form impressions of other people, and how strong those impressions can be. Imagine meeting someone new at a party. Within seconds, you've gathered a massive amount of information (Eiser, 2012; Kelley, 1950; Uleman & Saribay, 2012). You realize that this information – their clothes, their hairstyle, their attractiveness, their age, their voice, the way they carry themself – is all superficial and preliminary. Although you don't really *know* this person, you can't help but to start forming an impression of them.

According to research by social psychologists, the factors that influence that first impression are quite predictable. Physical attractiveness, for example, is a powerful predictor of a positive first impression. Compared to less attractive people, highly attractive people have more money, more jobs, and more sex (Macrae & Quadflieg, 2010). These findings may relate to the fact that good looks enable a person to make a good first impression with people who might provide these benefits. Your attractiveness is defined in large part by your face, which people may size up in as little as one-tenth of a second (Locher et al., 1993; Olson & Marshuetz, 2005). One study found that when people judge the attractiveness of a person within a fraction of a second, they are also simultaneously judging that person's trustworthiness and status (Palomares & Young, 2018). (This high-speed face processing is undoubtedly another evolutionary gift from our ancestors – the quicker you can assess the face of another person, the quicker you can react if that face indicates danger [Kenrick, 2012; Neuberg et al., 2010].) In general, the attractiveness of a face depends upon its bilateral symmetry (how equivalent the left and right halves are) and the extent to which each facial feature falls close to the average or prototype for the person's age, gender, and ethnicity (Rhodes, 2006; Thornhill & Gangestad, 1999). Other key facial features include healthy skin and teeth, good grooming, and a friendly expression (Jones et al., 2004; Willis et al., 2008).

impression formation
The initial appraisal, or "first impression," that a person forms of another person.

Kevin Mazur/KCA/Getty Images

As Chris Rock has joked about impression management, "You can't get nobody being *you*. You got to *lie* to get somebody. You can't get nobody looking like you look, acting like you act, sounding like you sound. That's right — when you meet somebody for the first time, you're not meeting *them*: you're meeting their *representative*." (*Source:* Chris Rock, "Women Lie.")

DIVERSITY MATTERS

Of course, your body is important too. Culturally, there is quite a bit of variation in terms of bodily attractiveness. Across genders, ethnicities, countries, and time periods, different body types have been preferred (Anderson et al., 1992; Swami, 2015). However, in contemporary Western culture, people who are obese or overweight are often viewed in unflattering ways. Specifically, obese and overweight people receive higher ratings of laziness, incompetence, and boringness than physically fit people (Brochu & Morrison, 2007; Hebl & Turchin, 2005; Puhl & Brownell, 2012). In one study, participants saw bodies of various weights and were asked to rate the Big Five personality traits (as we discussed in Chapter 12) that they expected to go along with them. Compared to bodies of average weight, overweight and obese bodies were rated as lower in conscientiousness (more careless and disorganized, less self-disciplined) and lower in extraversion (more shy and reserved) (Hu et al., 2018). Body attractiveness depends not only on its size and shape, but also on how it moves. In particular, men with a masculine gait and women with a feminine gait are viewed more positively than those whose walking style doesn't match their gender (Johnson & Tassinary, 2007; Morrison et al., 2018).

Clothes can also be a powerful factor in first impressions. In one study, researchers showed hundreds of participants photos of the same men, dressed either in "richer" clothes or "poorer" clothes (as judged prior to the study by a different group of participants). The men in "richer" clothes were consistently rated as more competent than the men in "poorer" clothes. This finding was true even when the photos were only shown for a fraction of a second, when the participants were explicitly told to ignore the clothes, and when the participants were told specific information about the person's socioeconomic status that may have contrasted with their clothes (Oh et al., 2020).

We know the power of first impressions from both sides — as the person *forming* the first impression of someone else, and as the person *making* the first impression on someone else. As the maker of first impressions, we often engage in *impression management*, or attempts to improve the way we strike other people in an effort to enhance our first impression (Koslowsky & Pindek, 2011). In those crucial first seconds, we control whatever we can about what others will think of us: our hairstyle and color, our clothes, our posture, our greeting, our facial expression, and more.

Prejudice: Us Versus Them

Sometimes, our impression of a person is influenced by the groups to which they belong. In these cases, we have preconceived ideas about the group that prevent us from appreciating the person as an individual (Dovidio et al., 2012; Yzerbyt & Demoulin, 2010). These preconceived ideas are better known as **prejudice**: an often negative attitude toward a social group that is formed before getting to know group members. As an example, Justine is a 20-year-old with a prejudice against older adults that wrongly casts all older adults as forgetful.

Stereotypes. Once a prejudice is in place, it produces **stereotypes**: beliefs about a group's characteristics that are applied generally, and often inaccurately, to group members. Prejudice is a general bias toward the group as a whole; stereotyping is a specific application of that bias to a person within the group. For example, Justine's prejudice against older adults becomes a stereotype when she meets 65-year-old Jasmine and presumes that Jasmine is forgetful before giving Jasmine a chance to prove otherwise.

Stereotypes can focus on any number of characteristics, but the surface characteristics that can't be hidden — especially gender, race, and age — are the most common targets (Brewer, 1988; Fiske & Neuberg, 1990). We typically don't realize when we stereotype others. This may relate to the fact that stereotyping occurs largely in the amygdala, a part of the brain dedicated to emotional (rather than cognitive) processing. This suggests that we don't explicitly "think" stereotypes as much as we implicitly "feel" them (Amodio et al., 2004; Andersen et al., 2007; Izuma et al., 2019; Lieberman et al., 2005; Schultheiss & Pang, 2007).

prejudice
An often negative attitude toward a social group that is formed before getting to know group members.

stereotypes
Beliefs about a group's characteristics that are applied very generally, and often inaccurately, to group members.

Discrimination. Together, these kinds of biased thinking lead to **discrimination**: action based on prejudice or stereotypes toward a social group. Justine's prejudice and stereotyping toward Jasmine produce discrimination when Justine visits the restaurant where Jasmine works as a server and assumes that Jasmine will make mistakes with Justine's order. Prejudice and stereotypes occur inside the mind, and might remain unknown to others. Discrimination is a behavior that others can see (Allport, 1954; Dovidio & Gaertner, 2010). Prejudice is thinking "Black people are dangerous." Stereotyping is thinking "DeMarco is dangerous because he's Black." Discrimination is stepping off the elevator when DeMarco steps in.

discrimination
Action based on prejudice or stereotypes toward a social group.

ingroup
A social group to which a person believes they belong ("us").

outgroup
A social group to which a person believes they do not belong ("them").

ingroup bias
The tendency to hold a more positive attitude toward the ingroup than the outgroup.

outgroup homogeneity
The assumption that all members of an outgroup are essentially similar.

Contemporary American society may feature less obvious prejudice, stereotypes, and discrimination than it once did, but those problems still exist in various forms. Compared to the days when the U.S. government enslaved Black people, locked Japanese people in internment camps, or denied women the right to vote, today the bias is often (but not always) more subtle. (Coates, 2011; Fisher et al., 2017; Ozturk & Berber, 2020; Pager & Shepherd, 2008; Ross et al., 2010). For example, researchers sent résumés to companies in Chicago and Boston on which the job qualifications were equivalent, but the first names suggested Black or White race. "Brett" and "Allison" received 50% more callbacks than "Rasheed" and "Tamika" (Bertrand & Mullainathan, 2003). In another study (called "Shopping While Black"), shoppers in high-end retail stores asked a White salesperson to remove the security tag from a pair of sunglasses so they could try them on (**Figure 13.7**). The salesperson always removed the security tag, but Black shoppers were three times more likely to be stared at or followed to the mirror than White shoppers (Schreer et al., 2009). A review of 42 studies on bias held by health care professionals (doctors, nurses, etc.) found that the vast majority of them revealed bias — most often related to race or ethnicity, but sometimes related to gender, age, weight, or other variables. In every one of those studies that asked whether higher levels of bias correlated with lower quality of care, the answer was yes (FitzGerald & Hurst, 2017).

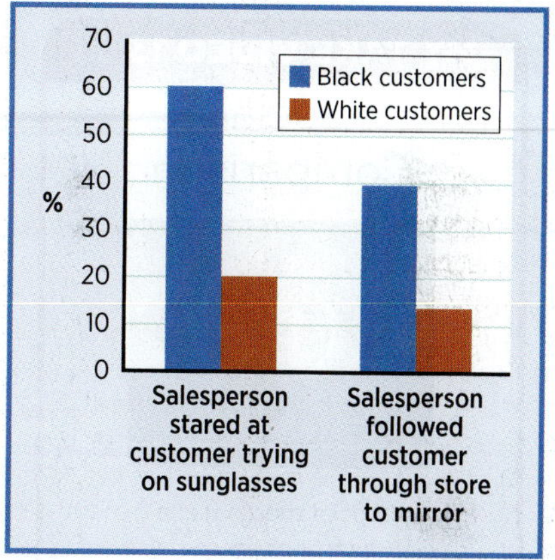

FIGURE 13.7 Shopping While Black. Salespeople at high-end stores stared at and followed a far greater percentage of Black customers than White customers, suggesting prejudice, stereotyping, and discrimination. Data from Schreer et al. (2009).

How do people become prejudiced?

In order for prejudice to have the opportunity to form in the first place, there has to be an "us" and a "them." Social psychologists use the terms *ingroup* and *outgroup* to refer to these classifications.

Ingroups and Outgroups. An **ingroup** is a social group to which you believe you belong ("us"). An **outgroup** is a social group to which you believe you do not belong ("them"). Each of us identifies with many ingroups; for example, Michelle Obama may consider herself part of the ingroups of Black Americans, women, wives, moms, Christians, Chicagoans, and former first ladies.

People have a strong tendency to favor the groups to which they belong (Brewer & Silver, 2006; Mullen et al., 1992). Social psychologists call this **ingroup bias**: the tendency to hold a more positive attitude toward the ingroup than the outgroup. At the same time, we tend to overlook the diversity within outgroups, mistakenly presuming that all of its members are alike (Mullen & Hu, 1989; Simon & Mummendey, 2012). This misperception is called **outgroup homogeneity**: the assumption that all members of an outgroup are essentially similar. Social psychologists have argued that of these two biases, ingroup bias comes first, and that outgroup homogeneity occurs only when that outgroup is perceived as a threat (Brewer, 2007; Stephan & Stephan, 2000). In other words, it's more about rooting for your own group to succeed than rooting for the other group to fail, unless the other group is directly challenging something your group holds dear, such as resources, values, or well-being. This idea may explain why most sports fans cheer for their own team to win much more often than they cheer for an opposing team to lose.

Leon Halip/Getty Images

One reason why sports fans may root for their team is the ingroup bias: the tendency to hold a more positive attitude toward the ingroup (often their hometown team) than the outgroup (other teams).

Once the ingroup–outgroup distinction breeds prejudice, additional factors allow it to thrive. One factor that enables prejudice is the natural human tendency to think *categorically* (Allport, 1954; Blashfield & Burgess, 2007; Satpute et al., 2016). Thinking categorically means making sense of the world by placing everything and everyone we encounter in separate "boxes." For example, we categorize just about everything: vehicles (car/truck/SUV), computers (laptop/desktop), dogs (beagles/greyhounds/poodles, etc.), music (pop/rap/country/R&B/metal/punk/jazz/classical,etc.), seasons (winter/spring/summer/fall), and so on. But people are all unique, and when we engage in social categorization, we tend to overlook that uniqueness (Crisp & Maitner, 2011; Dovidio & Gaertner, 2010; Fiske, 2012; Young, 2016).

A second factor that fosters prejudice when judging other people is the *smoke detector principle* — the idea that it's better to be oversensitive and produce many "false alarms" than to be undersensitive and allow even one catastrophe to take place. This oversensitivity is not a conscious decision, but a deep-seated tendency rooted in evolution (Nesse, 2005, 2019b; Neuberg & Schaller, 2016). Think about it from the point of view of your ancestor living thousands of years ago. Life in your hunter-gatherer band is good. The immediate and extended family helps to provide you with everything you need. When an unknown face appears — which was not as common as it is now — should you take a chance and get to know the person before making any judgments? There could be an upside — form a new alliance that might help to provide resources and share responsibilities. But the downside may be too great to take the chance. The new person could hurt you or the others in your hunter-gatherer band. It may be wiser, or at least safer, to err on the side of prejudice.

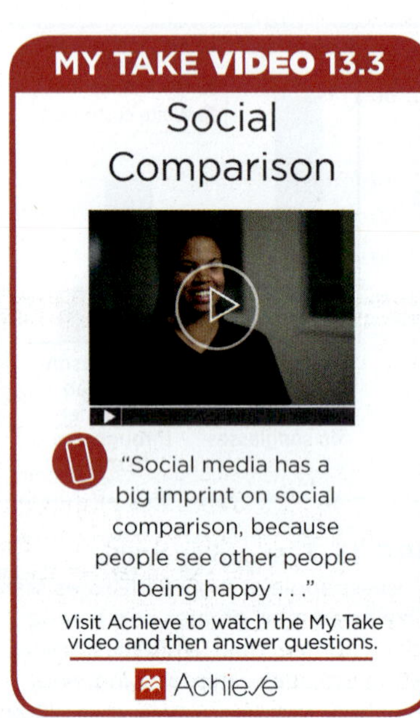

MY TAKE VIDEO 13.3
Social Comparison
"Social media has a big imprint on social comparison, because people see other people being happy . . ."
Visit Achieve to watch the My Take video and then answer questions.
Achieve

No wonder studies have found that humans still have a tendency to prejudge negatively other people who look unhealthy or dirty (and could sicken us), those who have angry facial expressions (and could injure us), and those who are unfamiliar (and could threaten the ingroup) (Neuberg & Cottrell, 2006). That last example — negatively prejudging people who are unfamiliar — goes a long way toward explaining the roots of racism, or any other prejudice based on obvious physical differences (Kurzban et al., 2001).

A third factor that promotes prejudice is **social comparison**: assessing yourself by determining how you measure up to other people. When you prejudge outgroups negatively, you seem better by contrast (Carrillo et al., 2011; Festinger, 1954; Suls & Wheeler, 2012). If you label other people as dishonest, you seem more truthful; if you dismiss other people as lazy, you seem more energetic. Research has shown that we compare ourselves to other people in many ways that could lead to prejudice, including weight, health, attractiveness, relationship satisfaction, and Instagram likes (Buunk et al., 1990; Corcoran et al., 2011; Gerber et al., 2018; Poran, 2002; Robinson et al., 2019; Tiggeman et al., 2018).

Rationalizing Prejudices. When individuals realize that they hold prejudices, they often try to rationalize them, or explain why they are justified to think that way. One such rationalization is the **just-world hypothesis**: the notion that the world is fair and that unfortunate events happen to those who deserve them (Dalbert, 2009; Hafer & Bègue, 2005; Lerner, 1965; Lerner & Miller, 1978). For example, consider Jalen, who hears that his neighbor Louisa lost her job. Jalen thinks, "I guess Louisa must have made a lot of mistakes at work." Jalen's assumption that Louisa caused the job loss, and his failure to consider that the job loss might have nothing to do with Louisa's behavior, illustrate the just-world hypothesis. Others who similarly "blame the victim" with "just-world" thinking often target members of particular ethnicities, genders, or age groups, as well as people who have experienced sexual assault, robbery, or other crimes (Felson & Palmore, 2018; Pinciotti & Orcutt, 2021).

Another rationalization for prejudice is the **scapegoat hypothesis**: the notion that prejudice can be fueled by the need to find someone to blame. By pawning off negative characteristics onto other groups, we try to convince ourselves that we couldn't have any such negative characteristics.

Toward Fairness and Cooperation: Fighting Prejudice

Thankfully, social psychologists' efforts to understand prejudice have generated strategies for overcoming it. Let's take a look at some of them.

social comparison
Assessing oneself by determining how one measures up to other people.

just-world hypothesis
The notion that the world is fair and that unfortunate events happen to those who deserve them.

scapegoat hypothesis
The notion that prejudice can be fueled by the need to find someone to blame.

Intergroup Contact. **Intergroup contact** is a strategy for fighting prejudice based on direct interpersonal interaction between members of multiple groups. People who hold strong prejudices against certain groups have, in many cases, never even met someone from that group. When they do, those prejudices often dissolve (Berger et al., 2018; Pettigrew & Tropp, 2006; Tropp & Barlow, 2018). In one study that illustrates the benefits of intergroup contact, researchers followed 2000 White, Asian, Latinx, and Black students through their college years. They found that first-year students with more outgroup friendships showed less anxiety about outgroups, as well as less ingroup bias, by the end of college (Levin et al., 2003). The same researchers also found that students who had a first-year roommate of a different ethnicity than their own were less prejudiced about their roommate's ethnicity, and usually about other ethnicities as well, by the end of college compared to students who shared the same ethnicity as their first-year roommate (Laar et al., 2005).

WESTEND61/Media Bakery

Intergroup contact is a strategy for fighting prejudice based on direct interpersonal interaction between members of multiple groups.

In recent years, some researchers have explored whether intergroup contact could still reduce prejudice if that contact is not in person. For example, in one study, participants read an online news story about either same-sex marriage or undocumented immigrants' rights and the comments section beneath it. In the comments section, participants came across one of two comments: (1) a comment by someone who identified themselves as a member of the group from the study (either a gay man or an undocumented immigrant) and shared their own story, or (2) a similar comment written in more general terms without the commenter identifying themselves. Results showed that the group who read the comment in which the writer identified themselves and told their own story had improved attitudes toward that group based on increased positive emotions and decreased negative emotions (Kim & Wojcieszak, 2018). The lesson of this study is that intergroup contact may not need to take place in person to have an effect: common online interactions may, under the right circumstances, produce similar outcomes.

Common Group Identity. **Common group identity** is a strategy for fighting prejudice based on the creation of a larger group that includes multiple smaller groups. Think of the U.S. Men's Olympic basketball team. Members of different professional teams – players who typically view each other as opponents – come together to play for a bigger common goal. They are no longer the Nets versus the Celtics or Kevin Durant versus Jayson Tatum. The antagonism disappears as competitors become teammates to form a single team representing their country.

Tim Clayton/Corbis/Getty Images

Common group identity is a strategy for fighting prejudice. It's based on the creation of a larger group that includes multiple smaller groups – for example, when WNBA stars who typically play on opposing teams, like Diana Taurasi and Sue Bird, join forces during the Olympics.

DIVERSITY MATTERS

When members of religious, ethnic, or cultural groups come together for a common cause, they too can overcome prejudice in the process. For example, after one of the most devastating tornadoes in U.S. history hit Joplin, Missouri, in May 2011, local religious organizations came together to help. They all had a common group identity now: survivors. The interfaith experience was so successful that a year later, they planned an interfaith remembrance service involving Christian, Jewish, and Muslim congregations. An organizer commented, "One of the things that struck me after the tornado was how different groups of people, who don't normally do things together, were cooperating and working together. . . . It was really inspiring" (Kennedy, 2012).

The odds of success for common group identity are highest when the common group is just as important and meaningful as the smaller groups, and when none of the smaller groups rank above the others in terms of power or prestige (Dovidio et al., 2009; Gaertner & Dovidio, 2012; Hornsey & Hogg, 2000). Numerous studies have shown how successful the common group identity approach can be. For example, executives from two competing banks who suddenly found themselves working together after a merger cooperated most effectively when they identified with the new, larger bank rather than the separate banks from which they came (Gaertner et al., 1996). Similarly, members of blended families get along better if they see themselves as one big family rather than two separate, cohabiting families (Banker & Gaertner, 1998).

intergroup contact
A strategy for fighting prejudice based on direct interpersonal interaction between members of multiple groups.

common group identity
A strategy for fighting prejudice based on the creation of a larger group that includes multiple smaller groups.

IT'S LIKE. . .

Fighting Prejudice Is Like Treating Phobias

The intergroup contact approach to overcoming prejudice is a lot like the way psychologists help a client overcome a phobia. We'll discuss phobia treatment in more detail in Chapter 15 (Therapy), but basically, the best way to treat a phobia is to gradually *expose* yourself to the source of your anxiety. In other words, take steps toward facing your fear. People can conquer a fear of dogs, for example, by choosing to face dogs instead of avoiding them. Little by little, the fear goes away through repeated exposure.

Intergroup contact works the same way: through *exposure*. People with strong prejudices toward a group of people typically avoid that group, just as a person with a dog phobia avoids dogs. In both cases, the avoidance denies the person the chance to disprove their irrational belief. Avoidance of dogs makes it impossible for the person to learn that they're wrong about dogs being dangerous. Similarly, avoidance of an ethnic, racial, or other diverse group makes it impossible for the person to learn that they're wrong about that group having the unfavorable quality they presumed.

Interacting with someone from an unfamiliar group serves the same purpose as that first step in phobia treatment: a shift from avoidance to *exposure*, which gives real-life experience a chance to prevail over any ignorance-based prejudices (Pettigrew & Tropp, 2006). This might mean that some prejudices (and the stereotyping and discrimination that they initiate) may be irrational fears at their core, just like any phobia. •

aggression
Behavior intended to cause harm or death.

Education. Straightforward information about an outgroup can be helpful in reducing prejudice. Sources like books, videos, and Web sites that present accurate, unbiased information enhance knowledge and challenge negative assumptions. This kind of education can also prepare people for the intergroup contact described previously.

Interestingly, prejudice can also fade when you educate yourself about *your own* group — particularly the opinions and experiences of your fellow ingroup members. In one study, researchers found that when a person learned that an ingroup friend was friends with an outgroup member, that person became less prejudiced toward that outgroup (Wright et al., 1997). For example, if Nathan and Steve are part of the same ingroup, and Nathan finds out that Steve hangs out with members of the outgroup on the weekends, Nathan is more likely to be less biased toward that outgroup. That is, Nathan is likely to think, "If Steve hangs out with them, maybe I should be open to hanging out with them too." Another researcher found that cross-group friendships actually decrease prejudice toward outgroups in general, not just the outgroup to which the friend belongs (Pettigrew, 1997). In other words, venturing out of your ingroup for even one meaningful relationship can have a ripple effect on your openness to people from many diverse groups.

LIFE HACK 13.3

To reduce your own prejudices, spend time and develop relationships with people different from yourself.

(Levin et al., 2003; Pettigrew, 1997; Pettigrew & Tropp, 2006)

Aggression

Two of the forces that most passionately draw human beings together are complete opposites of one another, *aggression* and *interpersonal attraction*. **Aggression** is behavior intended to cause harm or death. In *interpersonal attraction*, people who like or love each other feel a desire to enhance their relationship. Let's consider both in detail, beginning with aggression.

Biological Influences on Aggression. Whether or not we want to admit it, aggression is inherent to human behavior. Some of the earliest historical evidence of interaction between people includes irrefutable evidence of lethal brutality. Consider these artifacts: archeologists in Egypt uncovered a group of 59 human skeletons dating back 12,000–14,000 years. Almost half had stone projectiles embedded in their bones. Many had multiple broken bones, most of which were on the left side of the skull and rib cage, where right-handed attackers would have most likely landed their punches and weapon strikes (Buss, 2005). There is little doubt that these archeologists had stumbled into an ancient war zone. Similarly, some traditional, indigenous tribes living in Venezuela, Africa, and Australia — groups that have never experienced the violent video games, movies, or music available in the United States — actually have higher homicide rates than many U.S. cities (Buss & Duntley, 2006; Chagnon, 1988; Daly & Wilson, 1988).

More evidence that aggression is part of our nature comes from the fact that it appears as soon as we are physically capable of producing it. Before our first birthday, well before we fully soak up the influences around us, we behave aggressively. In fact, some psychologists have argued that the toddler years (ages 1–3) are the most aggressive of any during the life span, because about 25% of interactions between kids at this age are aggressive (Bushman & Huesmann, 2010; Tremblay & Nagin, 2005). Thankfully, young kids usually can't do much damage, but that doesn't mean we should discount their hitting, kicking, biting, scratching, hair pulling, and name calling. All of it supports the idea that aggression is innate in human beings.

Richard Drury/Getty Images

The role of biology in aggression is supported by the fact that toddlers, and even babies, often behave aggressively even though they have had little time to be influenced by other factors.

Highly aggressive kids tend to become highly aggressive adults (Hay, 2017; Huesmann & Moise, 1998). Researchers tracked 230 people from a small town in New York state for 40 years, measuring their aggressiveness at four ages: 8, 19, 30, and 48 (Huesmann et al., 2009). Their primary finding was that aggressiveness at age 8 was a strong predictor of aggressiveness at every later age, especially for men. By the time participants reached 48, highly aggressive 8-year-olds were much more likely to have committed a wide variety of aggressive acts, from spousal abuse to dangerous traffic violations. These results imply that aggression is more of a stable trait within each of us than a temporary state caused solely by factors around us.

There are also twin and adoption studies that find genes to be major contributing factors to aggression. A meta-analysis of 24 studies found that genes account for up to 50% of each person's level of aggressiveness (Miles & Carey, 1997). A more recent large-scale study found similar results, and specified that they apply to both impulsive ("heat-of-the-moment") aggression and premeditated ("cold and calculated") aggression (Baker et al., 2008).

Psychological Influences on Aggression. Genetics may form the foundation of aggression, but psychological factors play a role too. For example, certain personality traits have been linked to aggressive behavior. People low in *empathy* (the capacity to feel compassion for another person) tend to be highly aggressive (Castano, 2012; Miller & Eisenberg, 1988; Sergeant et al., 2006). People who lack empathy tend to dehumanize others, which opens the door to behaving hurtfully toward them.

Being impulsive is another personality variable that correlates with aggressiveness. Highly impulsive people lack the self-control, or "brakes," that less impulsive people use to stop themselves from committing acts of aggression. As a result, highly impulsive people find themselves lashing out with spur-of-the-moment aggressiveness at a high frequency (Duran-Bonavila et al., 2017; Hinshaw et al., 1992). Among the specific aggressive behaviors linked to both low empathy and high impulsivity is *bullying*, which is discussed in the Current Controversy box in more detail (Endresen & Olweus, 2001; Espelage et al., 2018; Jagers et al., 2007; Jolliffe & Farrington, 2011; Mayberry & Espelage, 2007).

Aggressive behavior is also influenced by observational learning (which we discussed in Chapter 6). Just as kids in Albert Bandura's studies imitated models' behavior toward a Bobo doll, they also imitate parents'/caregivers' behavior (Bandura, 1977, 1986). Whether the parents'/caregivers' aggressive behavior is aimed at the child, at each other, or at others, it becomes one of the child's behavioral options. Actually, the person modeling the aggression doesn't even need to be a parent/caregiver. Aggressive behavior by any family member or friend, especially if it appears to produce benefits and no cost, is likely to be imitated by children.

CURRENT CONTROVERSY

Cyberbullying and Social Psychology

Cyberbullying is a major social problem. It involves intentional harm of another person via computers, smartphones, or other devices, and is typically done to and by teenagers. Facebook, Twitter, Snapchat, YouTube, Instagram, texts, and e-mails are just some of the media used by cyberbullies. Specific acts of cyberbullying can include posting humiliating videos or photos, spreading rumors about the victim to a wide circle of peers, and sending cruel written messages directly to the victim.

AntonioGuillem/iStock/Getty Images

Cyberbullying, typically done by and to teenagers, has become a major social problem.

Cyberbullying is startlingly widespread and has grown rapidly in recent years. A 2010 survey asked 4400 kids ages 11–18 if they had ever experienced repeated cyberbullying, and about 20% said yes. About the same percentage admitted to doing the cyberbullying (Hinduja & Patchin, 2010). A survey of 5700 teens just 6 years later found that 25.7% had experienced repeated cyberbullying, and 33.8% had been cyberbullied at least once, with girls more likely to experience cyberbullying than boys (Patchin, 2016). A large-scale review of studies confirms that children and teens who experience cyberbullying have an increased likelihood of depression, anxiety, substance use, and suicidal thoughts or behaviors (Kwan et al., 2020). Other research shows that many people are both cybervictims and cyberbullies, with the first role often preceding the second (Lozano-Blasco et al., 2020).

Significant controversy exists over how our society should address cyberbullying. Indeed, it's difficult to know where to start: with the kids who might commit cyberbullying, the schools that allow for social environments that can lead to it, or parents/caregivers who could discourage it. Many key concepts in social psychology are relevant to choosing strategies to combat cyberbullying:

- First and foremost, cyberbullying is a form of *aggression*. It can be direct (when insults or threats are texted straight to the victim) or indirect (when one teen starts a rumor about another who initially knows nothing about it).
- Unlike older forms of bullying, in which the behavior took place face-to-face, cyberbullying often happens anonymously. The ability to hide behind a screen name or a hidden identity is a form of *deindividuation*, which heightens aggressiveness.
- *Social comparison* may play a role in cyberbullying behavior. Cyberbullies may attempt to pull someone else down to make themselves seem better by contrast.
- Teens have always been concerned with *ingroups* and *outgroups* among their peers, and cyberbullying may be seen as a way to get themselves included among a sought-after social group or get a rival ousted from theirs.
- The *scapegoat theory* suggests that people tend to look for someone to blame, and by doing so, they protect themselves from receiving such blame. Victimizing a peer via cyberbullying can serve exactly the scapegoat function.
- When an act of cyberbullying represents a group effort rather than one teen's idea, *groupthink* can be a factor. For example, one friend might say to a few others, "Hey, should I start a rumor about Tianna?" If the others respond with a chorus of "Yes," because they value their friendship with each other more than doing the right thing, then Tianna is likely to get bullied.
- Cyberbullying could be motivated by revenge, especially if a bully believes the *reciprocity norm* has been violated. For example, 13-year-old Zach invites his friend Jake to spend the night. Jake never reciprocates, and in fact, he ignores Zach entirely after the sleepover. Feeling wronged, Zach sends a threatening e-mail to Jake from a new account with a mysterious address that Zach created solely for that purpose.
- The *bystander effect* is also applicable here. How many of us know about cyberbullying, or even know someone who has perpetrated or been victimized by it, but have done nothing to reduce it? •

Situational Influences on Aggression. Biological factors and psychological factors are both internal, but external circumstances play a role in aggressiveness too. For example, unpleasant events often trigger angry action (Berkowitz, 1989, 1993; Berkowitz & Harmon-Jones, 2004). Some unpleasant events seem like minor nuisances, but these "little things" can add up to aggression when they are long-lasting, uncontrollable, and produce frustration (Donnerstein & Wilson, 1976; Fernandez & Turk, 1995; Geen & McCown, 1984). Second-hand smoke, bad smells, overcrowded spaces, nagging pain, and loud noises are all examples of negative situational factors that might trigger aggression.

Other unpleasant events that might produce aggression are not minor nuisances but "big things." For example, social rejection often results in angry outbursts. A friend who has been ostracized from the group, a player who has been kicked off the team, an employee who has been let go, or a romantic partner who has been dumped — any of these people is at increased likelihood for hostility, especially if they are sensitive to rejection (Ayduk et al., 2008; MacDonald & Leary, 2005; Warburton et al., 2006). Many of the shooters who have committed mass murders in schools and other public places, such as the shooters at Columbine High School in 1999, had reportedly experienced social rejection (Leary et al., 2003; Raitanen et al., 2017).

Even the weather can be a situational contributor to aggression. The most well-established weather-related predictor of aggression is temperature: When the weather gets hotter, so do people's tempers (Agnew, 2012; Anderson et al., 2000; Rinderu et al., 2018). This holds true not only in terms of crime statistics but even in sports. For example, consider Major League Baseball: pitchers hit more batters with pitches on hot days than cool days, particularly as retaliation after one of their own teammates has been hit (Larrick et al., 2011; Reifman et al., 1991). Or the National Football League: aggressive penalties like unnecessary roughness, unsportsmanlike conduct, and face mask (in which one player grabs and yanks the front of an opposing player's helmet) are more frequent in games with the hottest temperatures (Craig et al., 2016). Some social psychologists have pointed out that among the other risks of climate change, a warmer Earth is likely to be a more violent one (Miles-Novelo & Anderson, 2019). According to some predictions, by the mid-2100s, the United States could see nearly 100,000 more serious assaults per year if climate change continues (**Table 13.2**) (Anderson, 2001; Anderson et al., 1997).

The presence of weapons encourages aggressive behavior as well. In fact, in study after study, just the *sight* of weapons serves as a cue that translates into increased aggressive behavior (Anderson et al., 1998; Benjamin et al., 2017; Carlson et al., 1990). In one innovative real-world study from the 1970s, researchers had the driver of a pickup truck intentionally remain stopped when a red light turned green (Turner et al., 1975). The researchers then measured aggressive behavior in the driver behind the pickup, which they defined as honking the horn. In some cases, the pickup truck had a visible rifle in a gun rack and a bumper sticker that read "Vengeance." In others, it had neither. Drivers who saw the gun and sticker honked more often — a finding that defies logic (at least given today's possibility of road rage), but indicates the power that weapons have to prime feelings of anger.

In a more recent study on how exposure to weapons increases aggressiveness, researchers randomly assigned men to hold either a gun (a replica of a Desert Eagle automatic handgun) or a children's toy (the game Mouse Trap) for 15 minutes. They were then instructed to add as much hot sauce as they wanted to a glass of water that another person (unseen by the participant) would have to drink. The gun holders added three times as much hot sauce as the toy holders — a finding the experimenters interpreted as a sign of aggressiveness (Klinesmith et al., 2006).

No discussion of the situational causes of aggression would be complete without mention of alcohol. Many studies have found a link between alcohol consumption and aggressive behavior, including domestic violence, sexual assault, and violence outside of the home (Bushman & Cooper, 1990; Crane et al., 2016; Lipsey et al., 1997;

TABLE 13.2: Temperature and Violence: The Possible Effects of Global Warming

REGION OF THE WORLD	% HOMICIDE RATE CHANGE FOR ONE DEGREE (CELSIUS) INCREASE IN TEMPERATURE
All	+5.92
Africa	+17.94
Latin America	+4.39
North America/Australia/New Zealand	+2.84
Asia	+1.82
Europe	+1.82
Former USSR	−0.30

Data from Mares and Moffett (2016).

CHAPTER APP 13.2

ReThink is an app that stops cyberbullying at the source—the phone, tablet, or computer of the potential bully—before the damage is done. While the potential bully is typing a text, e-mail, or social media post, ReThink detects content in real time that might be hurtful or offensive. Then, the app instantly makes a "ReThink" alert pop up on the screen: "ReThink! Don't say things you might regret later!" Inserting this "brake," an opportunity to reconsider, may stop the potential bully from posting or sending the message, which in turn might protect the potential victim from cyberbullying. The teenage creator of the app, Trisha Prabhu, claims that it is very successful in doing so: it causes teens to change their mind (and not send or post the message) over 90% of the time; furthermore, the overall willingness of teens to send or post offensive messages drops from over 70% to below 5%. (Check out the Show Me More section at the end of the chapter for a link to her TED Talk video for the details.)

How does it APPly to your daily life?
Consider the people you know, or have known in the past, who might be likely to cyberbully someone else. Would they be willing to use ReThink? If they did, how effective would you expect it to be?

How does it APPly to your understanding of psychology?
How does this app help you understand *aggression*, *bullying*, and *cyberbullying*?

To learn more about this app or to download it to your phone, you can search for "ReThink app" on Google, in the iPhone App store, or in the Google Play store.

Miller & Pollock, 1996; Parrott & Eckhardt, 2018). In fact, over half of violent crimes are committed by people who were under the influence of alcohol (Innes, 1988; Pernanen, 1991). In another creative study using the "hot sauce" method described earlier, researchers illustrated that it's not only how much alcohol you consumed, but how much alcohol you *think* you consumed — how intoxicated you expect to be, that is — that can affect aggressiveness. Researchers gave participants either a nonalcoholic, weak, or strong drink. They also told participants that they just had a nonalcoholic, weak, or strong drink, but what they were told had nothing to do with what they actually drank. The result? Hot sauce levels depended directly upon what the participants were told they drank, but not at all upon how much alcohol they actually drank. The participants who *thought* they drank the most alcohol added the most hot sauce to the glass of water (Bègue et al., 2009).

Especially among teens and young adults, alcohol is often combined with energy drinks like Red Bull and Monster (Linden-Carmichael & Lau-Barraco, 2017; Martz et al., 2015; Spangler et al., 2018). In some cases, researchers studying the link between alcohol-plus-energy-drinks and aggression have found that link to be even stronger than the link between alcohol-only and aggression. One study interviewed people who had been in conflicts at a bar and found that alcohol-plus-energy-drink consumption was a better predictor of the number of verbal and physical acts of aggression — in other words, how intense or violent the conflict got — than alcohol-only consumption (Miller et al., 2016).

Violence in the media can also contribute to aggressive behavior. As mentioned in Chapter 6, there are some studies that cast doubt on the connection between violence in the media and aggressive behavior (Ferguson & Kilburn, 2009), but there are many more that establish that connection strongly (Anderson et al., 2010; Anderson & Bushman, 2001; Huesmann & Kirwil, 2007). Particularly when the people experiencing the violent TV, movies, and video games are kids, the link can be powerful and troubling. Some social psychologists have examined the short-term effects of media violence on behavior. For example, one researcher had 9-year-old boys watch either a violent or a nonviolent movie before they played floor hockey against each other. Those who watched the violent movie committed acts of aggression during the hockey game — hitting, tripping, elbowing, and so on — much more often than those who watched the nonviolent movie (Josephson, 1987).

Other researchers have taken a more long-term approach, and have typically found that exposure to violence in the media desensitizes people to real-world aggression and makes them more likely to behave aggressively (Carnagey et al., 2007). For example, researchers who studied a group of boys and men from age 8 through age 30 found that those who viewed the most violence on TV as youngsters were most likely to act aggressively and commit criminal acts, even after controlling for other factors that could predict aggressiveness (Eron et al., 1972; Huesmann, 1986; Huesmann & Miller, 1994).

Among the various forms of violent media, violent video games may be especially potent in terms of stimulating aggressive behavior. They involve active participation in violence rather than just passive observation, and they offer direct rewards for violent behavior, including points, progression to the next level of the game, and even verbal praise ("Great shot!") (Bushman & Huesmann, 2010). In one study, boys around 14 years old played either a violent or nonviolent video game for 20 minutes and then competed against a partner in a reaction-time task (pressing a button as quickly as possible after a signal). The winner of the reaction-time task was allowed to blast the loser with noise through headphones. Boys who had played the violent video game chose to blast their opponents with much louder noises than boys who had played the nonviolent video game, even though the researchers told the boys that such loud noises could cause permanent hearing damage (Konijn et al., 2007).

In an innovative study of the role of active participation in violent video games, one group of 10–13-year-old kids played violent video games, while another group watched (but did not play) the same games. When they were then sent out to recess, those who had played the games behaved much more violently than those who merely watched (Polman et al., 2008).

DIVERSITY MATTERS

Diversity-Related Influences on Aggression. Aggression varies across cultural and demographic groups in terms of how often it occurs and whether it is *direct* or *indirect* (Bond, 2004). Consider gender, for example. By the time children enter kindergarten, boys are more physically aggressive than girls (Hay, 2017; Loeber & Hay, 1997). Physical aggression such as punching or kicking is called *direct* aggression: the person you hurt is right there, and their reaction is immediately obvious. Around the same time that boys begin to engage in more direct aggression, girls begin to engage in more *indirect* or *relational* aggression, in which the victim is not present and their reaction may be delayed (Archer & Coyne, 2005; Björkqvist, 2018; Card et al., 2008). Many examples of indirect or relational aggression involve social "drama" such as telling rumors or gossiping, either in person or online. This gender-specific pattern — boys toward direct physical aggression, and girls toward indirect and relational aggression — increases throughout the school years and continues into adulthood (Côté et al., 2007; Crick & Grotpeter, 1995; Lagerspetz et al., 1988). However, the gender-specific pattern does not cover all kids at all times. Even though it may often be overlooked, there is still a sizable amount of relational aggression among boys and physical aggression among girls (Babinski & McQuade, 2018; Eriksen & Lyng, 2018; Hunt & Rhodes, 2018; Kraft et al., 2018).

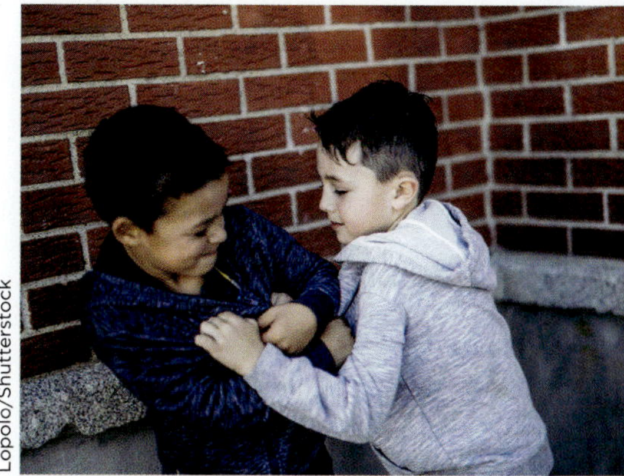
Lopolo/Shutterstock

KidStock/Blend Images/Getty Images

Beginning in the school years and continuing into adulthood, boys and men behave with more physical aggression, while girls and women behave with more relational aggression.

Attraction

After so much focus on people hurting each other, it's refreshing to remember that we often like or even love each other! Social psychologists place liking, loving, and any similarly warm and fuzzy interaction into the broad category of **interpersonal attraction**: the desire to enhance a relationship with another person. Lots of factors influence the attractiveness of one person to another, including nearness, sameness, beauty, and the odds of being liked back. Let's consider them one by one.

Proximity. Physical closeness often produces emotional closeness. If you are like most people, some of your best friendships and most serious romantic relationships began when you were neighbors of one kind or another. For example, maybe you lived in the same apartment building, sat near each other in classrooms or school buses, or played on the same sports teams. In one study, four equally attractive women were instructed to attend a college class (but not interact with students) at different rates: 15 times, 10 times, five times, or not at all. When the semester ended, students in the class were given photos of the four women and asked to rate the attractiveness of each. The more often they had been in class, the higher their attractiveness was rated (Moreland & Beach, 1992).

What is it about proximity that causes people to become attracted to each other? Seeing them (often) may actually be the key. Social psychologists call this the **mere exposure effect**: an increase in the attractiveness of a person (or object) resulting from nothing more than repeated contact. Many studies point to the fact that we feel positive toward what is familiar — not just people, but things too, including shapes, words, photographs, songs, and sounds (Albarracín & Vargas, 2010; Bornstein, 1989; Kunst-Wilson & Zajonc, 1980; Zajonc, 1968).

It's important to recognize that more recent research on the mere exposure effect suggests there is sometimes an opposite effect. In some cases, there may come a point at which increased exposure stops increasing attractiveness, and perhaps even begins to decrease attractiveness. The reasons are not entirely clear — perhaps we get bored, overly familiar, or just plain sick of it — but sometimes, overexposure does happen (Montoya et al., 2017).

Physical Attractiveness. We like beautiful people. We may like to tell ourselves that we are attracted to a person's inner beauty, but outward beauty (*looks*) has generated much more social psychology research.

interpersonal attraction
The desire to enhance a relationship with another person.

mere exposure effect
An increase in the attractiveness of a person (or object) resulting from nothing more than repeated contact.

DIVERSITY MATTERS

As the saying goes, beauty is in the eye of the beholder, but people of different genders tend to behold it quite differently. One researcher surveyed over 10,000 straight men and women from 33 countries on six continents — a massive, culturally diverse sample — to determine what each of these genders finds attractive in potential mates (Buss, 1989). Results indicate that there are some undeniable gender-specific themes that exist around the world. Across cultures, men place a higher premium on physical attractiveness in women as potential mates. Specifically, men who are attracted to women seek women who appear youthful and healthy, and have appealing figures (waist-to-hip ratio especially) — all features that suggest fertility, or the ability to conceive, give birth to, and nurture a child. On the other hand, women who are attracted to men place less emphasis on a potential mate's physical appearance and instead prefer potential mates who have wealth, status, and power — all features that suggest the ability to provide resources.

These results have been confirmed by other large-scale, cross-cultural studies (Shackelford et al., 2005). The primary explanation for the gender difference in preferences for potential mates focuses on evolution: among straight people, the man's strategy for passing along his genes is to mate with any woman who can successfully bear and raise his child. By contrast, the straight woman's strategy is to selectively choose a man with the means to feed, clothe, and protect the family once the children had arrived (Buss, 1994, 1995).

Some fascinating research results provide support for this evolutionary explanation. For example, straight men and women tend to experience jealousy for different reasons. Generally, a straight man is more likely to become jealous if a woman cheats on him sexually, because it could mean that she will focus on another man's child instead of their own. Generally, a straight woman is more likely to become jealous if a man cheats on her emotionally, because it could mean that he will develop a connection with another woman that would steer his resources toward the "other woman" rather than her and her children (Buss et al., 1992; Buunk et al., 1996; Sagarin et al., 2003). Along the same lines, when asked to describe their greatest regrets, men more often wished they had slept with more women, but women more often wished they had slept with fewer men (Roese et al., 2006).

Other studies have extended the conversation about the patterns of attractiveness among straight women and straight men. For example, researchers have found that the gender differences in mate preferences that we just discussed occur only if straight men or women need to prioritize. In other words, straight men and straight women actually value both physical attractiveness and resourcefulness, but if forced to choose, men tend to go with physical attractiveness and women tend to go with resourcefulness (Li et al., 2002). Additionally, some researchers have found that both men and women highly value some other qualities just as much as physical attractiveness and resourcefulness, including intelligence, kindness, honesty, and sense of humor (Fletcher et al., 2006; Lippa, 2007). Also, *social role theory* suggests that any difference in what men and women find attractive actually stems from the more basic desire to find a partner who can bring things to the relationship that we can't bring ourselves. So, among straight people, a traditional man may seek a traditional woman, and vice versa, but if either is untraditional — a man who sees himself as a homemaker, or a woman who sees herself as a breadwinner — they may adjust their preferences accordingly (Eagly & Wood, 1999; Wood & Eagly, 2010).

One last point on physical attractiveness: When it comes to faces, we tend to rate "average" way above average. That is, a person's facial attractiveness depends upon how unremarkable its features are within their age group, gender, and ethnicity (Langlois & Roggman, 1990). This may be counterintuitive, since we often think of "average"-looking people as plain or run-of-the-mill. But in this kind of research, social psychologists define "average" as the computerized combination of multiple faces, and in this way an "average" face could have a real upside. Specifically, this type of "average" face will have no odd or peculiar facial features that might be unappealing. It would also have no signs of possible illness or injury, such as scars,

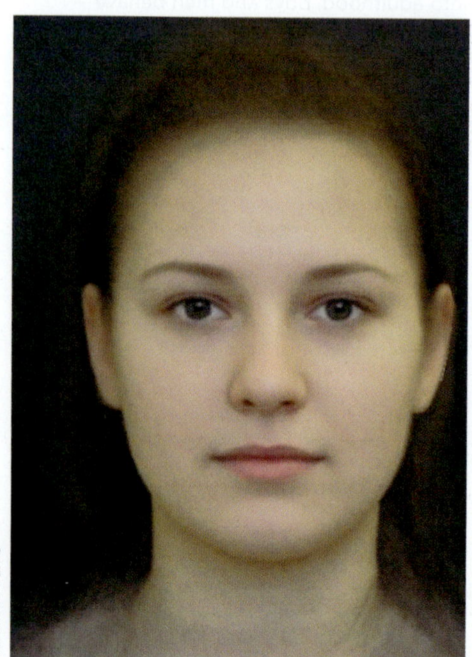

Indrikis Krams

This is a composite of photos of over 50 young Latvian women (Jakobsen, 2013; Rantala et al., 2013). Although researchers call it an "average" of those women's faces, it is typically rated as significantly above average in studies of facial attractiveness. The reasons for high attractiveness ratings of "average" faces may include the fact that they lack any idiosyncratic features — scars or blemishes, for example — that could signal illness or injury.

sores, or blemishes. Multiple studies have found that this type of "average" face has been rated as highly attractive in a wide range of cultures (Gangestad & Scheyd, 2005; Jones & Hill, 1993; Rhodes, 2006).

Similarity. "Opposites attract" is common wisdom for how we form friendships and romantic partnerships. But according to social psychology research, it is not often accurate (Montoya & Horton, 2013). A much more accurate description is that "birds of a feather flock together."

Many studies have found that we like other people if they are similar to us (Montoya & Horton, 2013). For example, one study of newlyweds found that people have a strong likelihood to choose a marriage partner who is equal to them in terms of both educational level and facial attractiveness (Stevens et al., 1990). In another study, ninth-graders and their teachers completed "get to know you" surveys in which they answered 28 questions about their own beliefs and preferences, including what sporting event they would most like to attend, what quality was most important in a friend, what languages they spoke, and what they would do with an unexpected day off from school. Students then learned how similar their teachers' answers were to their own. It turns out that the greater the similarity, the stronger the relationship between the student and teacher, and the higher the student's grades (Gehlbach et al., 2016).

A meta-analysis of many studies on similarity found that both *perceived* similarity and actual similarity predict attraction, meaning that you are likely to find yourself drawn to those who you *think* are similar to you just as much as those who are in fact similar to you (Montoya et al., 2008). One study found that this experience — liking people who you perceive as similar to yourself — may even apply to the music you like and the musicians who perform it. These researchers asked thousands of participants to rate how much they liked 50 popular musicians, including Beyoncé, Taylor Swift, Lil Wayne, and Justin Bieber. The participants then rated the personality traits they perceived in those musicians, as well as their own personality traits. Results showed that people tended to be fans of musicians who they perceived as having personalities similar to their own (Greenberg et al., 2021).

Reciprocal Liking. Remember your days in middle school, when you told your friends who you "liked" and then sent them across the lunchroom to find out if your crush "liked you back"? Social psychologists have examined the same question — whether the other person is attracted to *you* — and have found that it often makes quite a difference in your attraction toward the other person. If they like you, your attraction to them is likely to rise; if they don't, it's likely to drop (Curtis & Miller, 1986; Knobloch et al., 2008). One study found that in speed-dating situations, participants reported increased interest in the other person if they knew the other person was interested in them (Eastwick et al., 2007).

WATCHING PSYCHOLOGY

The Voice, *American Idol*, and Attractiveness

The Voice and *American Idol* each feature aspiring singers trying to impress celebrity judges. The shows are similar in many ways, but one of their most obvious differences is also one of the most intriguing to anyone with an interest in social psychology: the judges on *The Voice* sometimes can't see their contestants, but the judges on *American Idol* always can.

What influence might this difference have on the judges' decisions, such as who advances past the first round, who makes the finals, and even who wins the top prize? Facial attractiveness could make a big difference, especially in the first round of *American Idol*. Considering how quickly people tend to form first impressions based on facial attractiveness, the judges could be leaning toward or away from sending a contestant to Hollywood before they sing their first note. What about contestants' bodies? From time to time, *American Idol* judges during the first round have made side comments to each other about how "hot" a particular contestant was. (A Season 9 sensation, "Bikini Girl," seemed to sway some judges quite a bit with her nonvocal qualities.)

To social psychologists, the way new contestants are judged on *The Voice* — with the judges facing the opposite direction, able to hear but not see them — is a more valid way to select the best voices. Looks, in this case, might confuse judgment of the singer's voice.

Doug Savage

Romantic Love

Most of our discussion of attraction so far has covered all kinds of liking or loving. But one kind of love — *romantic love* — deserves special attention. Social psychologists have distinguished two distinct types of romantic love, one more typical of the early stages of a relationship, and the other more typical of long-term commitment. Let's explore both.

Passionate love is characterized by arousal and desire, and often experienced early in relationships. Couples feeling passionate love *burn* for each other. They are smitten by the thought of each other, by being together, and are distraught at the thought of being apart (Feybesse & Hatfield, 2019; Hatfield & Rapson, 1993).

Sometimes, couples who burn for each other burn out. But when they don't, their passionate love often evolves to a more mature love in which the raging fire becomes a steady warm flame (**Figure 13.8**). This is **companionate love**: love characterized by deep commitment and affection, and often experienced later in long-term relationships. These companion couples still describe themselves as being "in love," but the love they share is different than it was when they initially dated: less exhilarating, perhaps, but more stable and secure (Fehr, 2019; Hatfield & Sprecher, 1986; Sprecher & Regan, 2007).

Researchers have identified a key reason why companionate love develops: *equity*, or the belief by each partner that they are giving and getting a fair amount in the relationship (Polk, 2011). Actually, equity is important at every stage of a romantic relationship, but in the early stages, passion can hide many relationship flaws. As things get more serious, equity becomes even more important, and the perception by either partner that they are being treated unfairly can be a deal breaker (Hatfield & Rapson, 1993). *Self-disclosure*, or openness about yourself to your partner, is another important ingredient of lasting romantic relationships. It tends to be a mutual process: as one partner shares private thoughts and feelings, so does the other, but if one partner withholds, the other does as well (Kito, 2005; Sprecher, 1987).

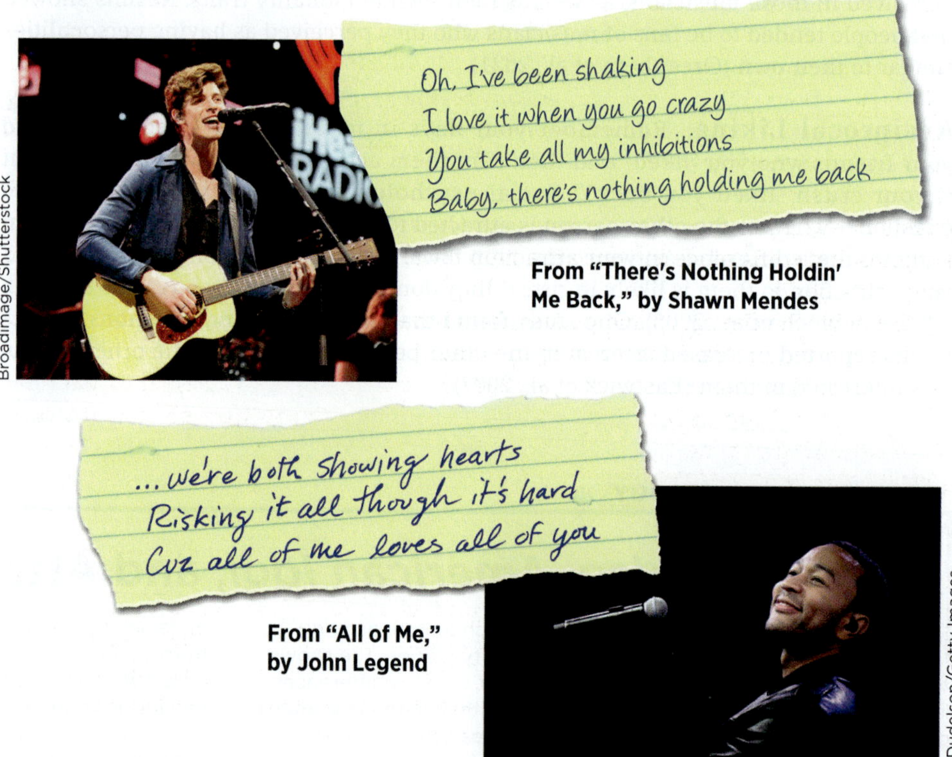

Oh, I've been shaking
I love it when you go crazy
You take all my inhibitions
Baby, there's nothing holding me back
From "There's Nothing Holdin' Me Back," by Shawn Mendes
Broadimage/Shutterstock
...we're both showing hearts
Risking it all though it's hard
Cuz all of me loves all of you
From "All of Me," by John Legend
Scott Dudelson/Getty Images

FIGURE 13.8 Passionate Love and Companionate Love in Popular Music. Shawn Mendes's lyrics capture the passionate love common in early stages of relationships, while John Legend's lyrics capture the companionate love common in more mature relationships.

passionate love
Love characterized by arousal and desire, and often experienced early in relationships.

companionate love
Love characterized by deep commitment and affection, and often experienced later in long-term relationships.

CHECK YOUR LEARNING:

13.12 When we create first impressions, how long does it take and what role does physical attractiveness play?

13.13 What is the difference between a prejudice, a stereotype, and discrimination?

13.14 How are each of these concepts relevant to prejudice: ingroup bias, outgroup homogeneity, categorical thinking, and social comparison?

13.15 How can people overcome prejudice?

13.16 What is aggression, and why do people behave aggressively?

13.17 What attracts people to one another?

To check your understanding of these questions, click show the answers or refer to the answers in the Chapter Summary.

Prosocial Behavior: Helping Each Other

YOU WILL LEARN:

13.18 what altruism is.

13.19 why people help others.

13.20 why people don't help others.

Prosocial behavior is behavior intended to help others. Social psychologists have explored many questions surrounding prosocial behavior, but two of these questions – *why* people help others and why people *don't* help others – have received the most attention. Let's discuss both.

Altruism

The purest motivation for prosocial behavior is **altruism**: completely unselfish concern for others. Earlier in this chapter, we recognized the extent to which aggression comes naturally to human beings. Thankfully, altruism seems to come naturally too. For example, after Hurricane Harvey hit the Houston area in August 2017, thousands of people offered their displaced neighbors a place to stay and food to eat. Victims received help not just from government agencies and organizations whose job it is to help, but from ordinary citizens as well. Those citizens used their own boats and jet skis to travel house to house saving people they had never met. They formed human chains to reach people who otherwise might have drowned. They donated money and supplies to dozens of charities so the help could continue after the waters receded (Reynolds, 2017).

But *why*? Psychologists and philosophers have long considered altruism a paradox. It's hard to understand why a person would behave altruistically, since altrustic behavior brings no benefit to the person who performs it. Or does it? Some have argued that any apparently altruistic act, if examined closely enough, actually does bring some kind of benefit to the person who performs it. (Feigin et al., 2018; Ghiselin, 1974; Maner et al., 2002). Let's consider Hurricane Harvey again. Imagine that you watch the events unfold on TV – people in Houston losing their homes, their cars, in some cases their loved ones – and you visit the Web site of a reputable charity to donate money. This is a completely selfless act, right? Maybe not. Maybe your donation relieves your guilt. Maybe it makes you feel proud of yourself. Maybe it makes you feel, vicariously, the same hopefulness that the recipients of that donation will feel (Schaller & Cialdini, 1988; Smith et al., 1989). In any of these cases, *you* benefit. Of course, your benefit doesn't lessen the positive impact of the donation, but it does cast some doubt on the utter selflessness of altruism.

Bass Fishing Club at WCU

Altruism, such as helping others after a natural disaster like Hurricane Harvey in Houston, is completely unselfish concern for others.

Researchers have examined the connection between altruistic behavior and benefits to the person who performs them. A meta-analysis of this research found that the connection between altruistic behavior and overall well-being was quite strong. Specifically, people who do more altruistic things tend to have higher levels of well-being, meaning that they are generally happier and healthier (Hui et al., 2020). Of course, it

prosocial behavior
Behavior intended to help others.

altruism
Completely unselfish concern for others.

can be difficult to determine causality here. Does behaving altruistically cause people to feel happier and healthier? Or does being happier and healthier in the first place cause people to behave altruistically? Maybe altruistic behavior and well-being both cause each other? There also could be a third factor that causes both.

Social Exchange Theory. Whether the altruistic motivation is purely selfless or not, people provide help to others all the time. Social psychologists have put forth a number of theories to explain *why*. One explanation is **social exchange theory**: the comparison of benefits and costs to the individual for helping. This explanation emphasizes what you get out of the helping behavior in comparison to what you give away. Imagine Hasan and Alex, a couple out on a dinner date. They leave the restaurant with their leftovers boxed up. Outside the restaurant, they pass a homeless person. Hasan gives the leftovers to the homeless person — a truly kind act, but not without some benefit to Hasan. As he recounted to his friend the next day, "That box was gonna spill all over my car. Plus, Alex smiled and told me I was sweet when I did it." By helping, he lost half an order of pasta but kept his car clean and got kind words from his partner — not a bad exchange for Hasan.

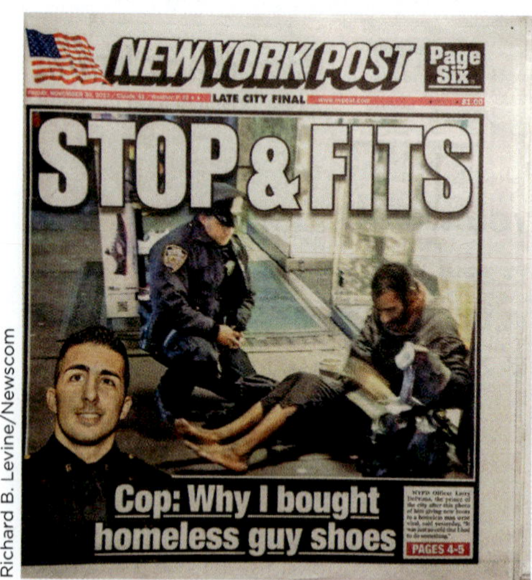
NEW YORK POST

Page Six

LATE CITY FINAL

STOP & FITS

Cop: Why I bought homeless guy shoes

PAGES 4-5

Richard B. Levine/Newscom

When New York City Police Officer Lawrence DePrimo bought a brand-new pair of boots for a barefoot homeless man on a frigid night, his act of kindness was front-page news. The officer's explanation captured the essence of the social responsibility norm: "It was freezing out. . . . I don't care what the price is. We just got to help him out" (Kim, 2012).

Reciprocity Norm. Another theory of helping is the **reciprocity norm**: the expectation that those who provide help will receive help in the future. Remember why Bill Withers offers his help in his classic song "Lean on Me": ". . . for it won't be long 'til I'm gonna need somebody to lean on." You may be the one providing help now, but you may also be the one seeking it in the future, so it can't hurt to bank some good will. The key difference between the reciprocity norm and social exchange theory is how certain the repayment is. In social exchange theory, the repayment happens right away — it's a sure thing. When you bank on reciprocity, however, you're taking a chance that if you help others, they'll return the favor in the future. Restaurant servers who bring candies or mints with the bill know all about the reciprocity norm. As **Figure 13.9** shows, providing a small gift of this type can increase tips by 20% (Strohmetz et al., 2006).

Is it possible that an act of kindness stimulates an act of kindness by the recipient, but not necessarily back to the original helper? In other words, when someone does a nice thing for you, might you "pay it forward" to a completely different person? In an innovative study, researchers had two actors walk through a supermarket, one a few steps behind the other (Guéguen & De Gail, 2003). The first actor smiled at half of the 800 strangers they passed, and did not smile at the other half. The second actor then dropped a pile of computer parts, scattering them all over the floor. The primary question was this: would those customers who just received a smile from one person be

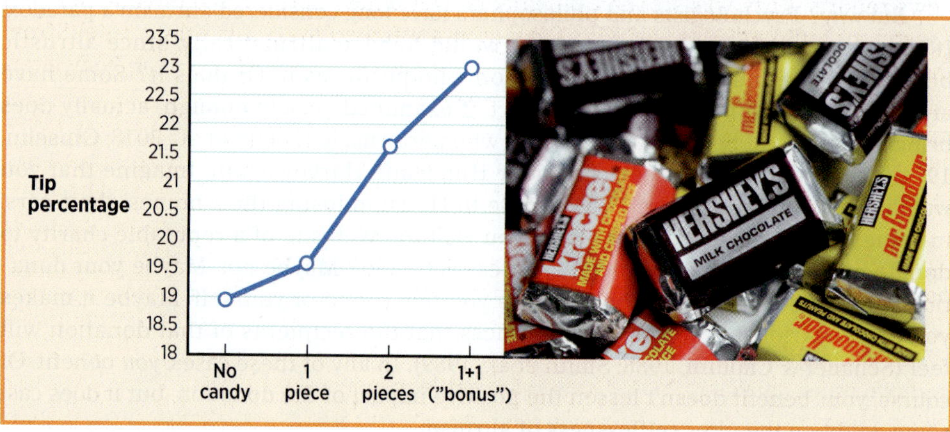

FIGURE 13.9 If You Give (Candy), You Shall Receive (Bigger Tips). Diners reciprocated with larger tips when servers offered mini Hershey bars with the bill. The highest tips came when the server offered one piece and then returned to offer a second "bonus" piece, which diners may have perceived as a particularly kind gesture. Data from Strohmetz et al. (2006); © Kristoffer Tripplaar/Alamy.

social exchange theory
An explanation of helping that emphasizes the comparison of benefits and costs to the individual for helping.

reciprocity norm
An explanation of helping that emphasizes the expectation that those who provide help will receive help in the future.

more likely to help clean up a another person's mess than those who did not receive a smile? The answer was yes. In fact, people who received a smile helped about 50% more often than people who did not.

Social Responsibility Norm. A third theory of helping is the **social responsibility norm**: the notion of duty to help those who need it, regardless of any potential payback to the helper. According to the social responsibility norm, you help because you are supposed to, period. It's your job as a citizen of your city, country, or the world to take care of other people, especially when they can't take care of themselves. New York City Police Officer Lawrence DePrimo illustrated the social responsibility norm when, on a particularly frigid night, he bought a brand-new pair of boots for a homeless, barefoot man. He explained: "It was freezing out and you could see the blisters on the man's feet. . . . I said, I don't care what the price is. We just got to help him out" (Kim, 2012).

Kinship Theory. A fourth theory of helping is more evolutionary in nature. **Kinship theory** emphasizes the importance of passing your genes on to future generations. To understand the way kinship theory explains helping behavior, consider this question: to whom would you be most likely to donate a kidney? For most of us, a relative would definitely outrank a stranger, and the closer the relative, the higher they rank. The tendency to help family first is evident throughout the animal kingdom. Bees, ants, and termites often give up their own lives for the sake of their colonies of relatives (Crawford, 1998; Hamilton, 1964). We similarly feel the impulse to help when doing so could benefit someone who carries at least some of our genes, such as our biological siblings, children, parents, or cousins. By helping them survive, we help part of ourselves survive (Neyer & Lang, 2003; Van Vugt & Van Lange, 2006). Even if it's not a life-or-death situation, some impulse to help kin remains, which can extend to those with whom we feel a closeness. As we develop relationships with people outside our biological families, close friends and adopted relatives can also qualify as family somewhere deep in our minds, despite the fact that we may not share genetic material (Korchmoros & Kenney, 2001, 2006).

Why *Don't* People Help?

We've seen a lot of explanations for helping, but often, people choose not to help when the opportunity arises. Why not?

In some cases, it may be because there are other people around. This is the **bystander effect**: the decrease in likelihood that you will help another person caused by the presence of others also available to help. Research on the bystander effect was triggered by the murder of Kitty Genovese in Queens, New York, in 1964. According to news reports, Kitty was stabbed repeatedly over a half-hour period outside her own apartment building. Many of Kitty's neighbors watched the 3 A.M. crime unfold from their own apartments, hearing her cries for help the whole time. However, nobody intervened, and only some even called police. Some facts of this particular case, including the number of bystanders and the lack of help offered, have since come into question (Cook, 2014; Manning et al., 2007). There have been numerous, more recent situations, however, in a which a person clearly needs help but no one from a group of onlookers offers it.

Especially because of the attention this case attracted at the time, social psychologists began exploring the possible reasons behind onlookers' decisions to help or not help in similar situations (Latané & Darley, 1970). In a classic study, participants were filling out questionnaires when smoke began to fill the room (Latané & Darley, 1968). When participants were alone, they reported the smoke 75% of the time. When they had two other participants with them, the percentage dropped to 38%. When they had two actors with them who clearly noticed the smoke but chose to do nothing, the percentage plummeted to 10%. This research resulted in a list of the five steps necessary for a bystander to intervene (**Table 13.3**) (Darley & Latané, 1968). Keep in mind that failure to take *any* single step would stop the bystander from helping.

Cases like Kitty Genovese's continue to occur. Some are smaller crimes against individuals (a backpack is snatched, a car is broken into), but others are large-scale

CHAPTER APP 13.3

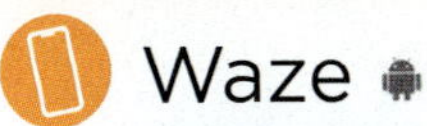

There are lots of apps to help you drive from Point A to Point B, but Waze is unique among them. As its Web site describes, Waze is "community—based," which means that drivers share info about the roads with each other. For example, Waze users can alert each other to the specific locations of police cars, accidents, traffic jams, cars on the shoulder, and even cheap gas stations they encounter. The Waze Web site explains that Waze users are "outsmarting traffic, together" by getting a "heads-up from a few million of your friends on the road."

How does it APPly to your daily life? Would you use an app like Waze? If so, would you share road information with other drivers, or only use the road information they shared with you?

How does it APPly to your understanding of psychology? Which explanation of *prosocial behavior* (or *altruism*) best explains the decision by a Waze user to voluntarily give a heads-up to other drivers without any external reward (money, etc.)?

To learn more about this app or to download it to your phone, you can search for "Waze app" on Google, in the iPhone App store, or in the Google Play store.

social responsibility norm
An explanation of helping that emphasizes the notion of duty to help those who need it, regardless of any potential payback to the helper.

kinship theory
An explanation of helping that emphasizes the importance of passing genes on to future generations.

bystander effect
The decrease in likelihood that one person will help another person caused by the presence of others also available to help.

TABLE 13.3: Five Steps Necessary for Bystander Intervention

STEP	EXAMPLE
Notice the event.	I hear my elderly next-door neighbor screaming in pain.
Interpret it as an emergency.	I think they have fallen and might be hurt.
Assume responsibility to intervene.	Whether other people hear this or not, I need to do something to help them.
Decide how to intervene.	I'm going to call 911 and go next door to help.
Take action.	Call 911, enter neighbor's apartment, and offer help.

Information from Latané and Darley (1968) and Darley and Latané (1968).

crimes against humanity (genocides, oppression, or exploitation of large segments of a population). Why do some people choose to stand by and do nothing? The reason may involve a **diffusion of responsibility**: a decreased sense of obligation to help when others are present. People presume that others will take care of it, so they dismiss any sense of obligation. The larger the group, the greater the diffusion of responsibility, and the lower the chances that people will help.

Another reason why people choose not to help relates closely to the concept of *attribution* that we covered earlier in this chapter. In this case, however, the crucial question is whether the bystander feels the need for help is deserved (Rudolph et al., 2004; Weiner, 1993). Consider someone who uses GoFundMe to raise money to help with huge medical bills resulting from a car accident. The car accident happened when they were driving on icy roads at a time when local news channels were advising people to stay off the roads. Some people may think, "That poor person! It's terrible that this tragedy happened to them." Other people may think, "It's their fault. They should not have been driving in those conditions." Of course, the first attribution is more likely to lead to GoFundMe donations than the second attribution.

In one study regarding attribution and helping, researchers gave participants fake news reports about the underlying causes of obesity. For some participants, the news report said obesity was genetic, which implied that obese people "can't help it." For other participants, the news report said obesity was behavioral, which implied that obese people choose to behave in ways that make them obese (overeating, not exercising, etc.). Participants who heard the genetic explanation were much more willing to help obese people (Jeong, 2007). Similarly, research has also shown that people are more willing to help a sick person than a drunk person, and a person with Alzheimer's disease more than a person with a drug addiction (Piliavin et al., 1969; Weiner et al., 1988).

diffusion of responsibility
A decreased sense of obligation to help when others are present.

CHECK YOUR LEARNING:

13.18 What is altruism?

13.19 Why do people help others?

13.20 Why don't people help others?

To check your understanding of these questions, click show the answers or refer to the answers in the Chapter Summary.

CHAPTER SUMMARY

Social Cognition: How We Think about Each Other

13.1 Social cognition refers to your thoughts about other people, including attributions, attitudes, and cognitive dissonance.

13.2 An attribution is an explanation for the cause of behavior, and social psychologists put attributions into two distinct categories: the person or the situation.

13.3 When explaining the behavior of other people, we often make the fundamental attribution error, in which we overestimate the importance of traits and underestimate the importance of the situation.

13.4 An attitude is a viewpoint, often influenced by both thoughts and emotions, that affects a person's responses toward people, things, or situations. Social psychologists have identified a variety of strategies people use to change other people's attitudes, including central route persuasion, peripheral route persuasion, the foot-in-the-door technique, the door-in-the-face technique, and the lowball technique.

13.5 Cognitive dissonance is the discomfort caused by having an attitude or behavior that contradicts another attitude or behavior. Social psychologists see three solutions to cognitive dissonance: (1) changing the first attitude, (2) changing the second attitude, or (3) creating a third attitude to resolve the tension between the first and second attitudes.

Social Influence: How We Influence Each Other

13.6 Social influence is any way in which the presence of other people influences a person's thoughts, feelings, or behavior.

13.7 Conformity occurs when a person changes their behavior to correspond to the behavior of a group of other people. Conformity may occur out of a universal human need for group inclusion, but it varies from one culture to the next. Conformity levels are generally higher in collectivist cultures than in individualistic cultures.

13.8 Obedience occurs when a person changes their behavior to comply with the demands of an authority figure.

13.9 Classic studies by Stanley Milgram revealed that many people will obey authority figures to a surprising extent, even when their obedience hurts other people.

13.10 Social facilitation is an increase in individual performance caused by the presence of other people, while social loafing is a decrease in individual performance when tasks are done in groups.

13.11 Groupthink is a phenomenon that occurs when group members value getting along with each other more than finding the best solution. Group polarization is the tendency for a group's attitudes to become more extreme as a result of group discussions.

Social Relations: How We Relate to Each Other

13.12 First impressions are made in the first seconds of meeting a person and are influenced by physical attractiveness.

13.13 A prejudice is an often negative attitude toward a social group that is formed before getting to know group members. Once a prejudice is in place, it produces stereotypes, which are beliefs about a group's characteristics that are applied to group members. Discrimination is any action based on prejudice or stereotypes toward a social group.

13.14 People's tendency to favor the groups to which they belong is known as ingroup bias, and people's tendency to overlook the diversity within outgroups is known as outgroup homogeneity. Prejudice is enabled by the natural tendency to think categorically, the predisposition to negatively prejudge people who are unfamiliar, and social comparison.

13.15 People can overcome prejudice through intergroup contact, common group identity, and education about outgroups.

13.16 Aggression is behavior intended to cause harm or death, and is influenced by genetics, personality traits, external circumstances, and cultural factors.

13.17 People are attracted to one another for a variety of reasons, including proximity, physical attractiveness, similarity, and reciprocal liking.

Prosocial Behavior: Helping Each Other

13.18 Altruism is completely unselfish concern for others.

13.19 Social psychologists have put forth a number of theories to explain why people help others, including social exchange theory, the reciprocity norm, the social responsibility norm, and kinship theory.

13.20 Social psychologists have suggested a number of explanations for why people don't help others, including the bystander effect and diffusion of responsibility.

KEY TERMS

social psychology, p. 440
social cognition, p. 440
attribution, p. 440
attribution theory, p. 441
fundamental attribution error, p. 441
attitude, p. 442
central route persuasion, p. 443
peripheral route persuasion, p. 443
foot-in-the-door technique, p. 444
door-in-the-face technique, p. 444
lowball technique, p. 444
social role, p. 444
cognitive dissonance, p. 445
social influence, p. 447
conformity, p. 448
obedience, p. 450
social facilitation, p. 452
social loafing, p. 452
deindividuation, p. 453
groupthink, p. 453
group polarization, p. 454
impression formation, p. 455
prejudice, p. 456
stereotypes, p. 456
discrimination, p. 457
ingroup, p. 457
outgroup, p. 457
ingroup bias, p. 457
outgroup homogeneity, p. 457
social comparison, p. 458
just-world hypothesis, p. 458
scapegoat hypothesis, p. 458
intergroup contact, p. 459
common group identity, p. 459
aggression, p. 460
interpersonal attraction, p. 465
mere exposure effect, p. 465
passionate love, p. 468
companionate love, p. 468
prosocial behavior, p. 469
altruism, p. 469
social exchange theory, p. 470
reciprocity norm, p. 470
social responsibility norm, p. 471
kinship theory, p. 471
bystander effect, p. 471
diffusion of responsibility, p. 472

SELF-ASSESSMENT

1. Yolanda is driving and sees another driver run a red light. According to the _____, Yolanda is likely to underestimate the importance of the situation and overestimate the importance of that driver's traits when explaining why that driver made that driving error.

2. A(n) _____ is a viewpoint, often influenced by both thoughts and emotions, that affects your responses to people, things, or situations.
   a. attribution
   b. attitude
   c. action
   d. none of the above

3. Which of the following is a persuasion technique?
   a. The foot-in-the-door technique
   b. The lowball technique
   c. The door-in-the-face technique
   d. All of the answers are correct.

4. _____ is the discomfort caused by having an attitude or behavior that contradicts another attitude or behavior.
   a. Implicit attitude
   b. Social role
   c. Cognitive dissonance
   d. Group polarization

5. When a person changes their behavior to comply with the demands of an authority figure, that person is _____.
   a. conforming
   b. obeying
   c. attributing
   d. discriminating

6. _____ is an increase in individual performance caused by the presence of other people.
   a. Social facilitation
   b. Social cognition
   c. Social loafing
   d. The smoke detector principle

7. _____ is the tendency for a group's attitudes to become more extreme as a result of group discussions.
   a. Social loafing
   b. Group polarization
   c. Groupthink
   d. Obedience

8. Inez believes that the world is fair and that unfortunate events happen to people who deserve them. Her belief illustrates:
   a. common group identity.
   b. reciprocal liking.
   c. diffusion of responsibility.
   d. the just-world hypothesis.

9. _____ love is characterized by arousal and passion, while _____ love is characterized by deep commitment and affection.

10. The idea that people help others because of a duty to do so, regardless of any potential payback to the helper, is known as the _____.
    a. reciprocity norm
    b. social exchange norm
    c. social responsibility norm
    d. none of the above

To check your understanding of these questions, click show the answers in the ebook or refer to the answers in Appendix B.

Research shows quizzing is a highly effective learning tool. Continue quizzing yourself using LearningCurve, the system that adapts to *your* learning.

WHAT'S YOUR TAKE?

1. We've all experienced salespeople who try many strategies to make a sale. A bicycle shop once tried to lowball me by advertising an unbelievably low price for a nice mountain bike and then, after they had my credit card in hand, mentioned that a few things were "extra"—including pedals and tires! Another time, I was shopping for a TV and the salesperson started with the biggest, most expensive TV in the store. After I said no, they showed me one at about half the price, which I bought. I thought I was getting quite a deal, but I actually spent more than I had planned because it seemed so cheap compared to the first one they showed me. Turns out they had used the door-in-the-face strategy on me: the model they sold me had a high profit margin, and it was the one they probably hoped to sell me all along. Have you had any experiences with salespeople who tried to use any of the strategies described in this section? Be sure to label the strategy (central route persuasion, peripheral route persuasion, foot-in-the-door, door-in-the-face, lowball technique), and describe how effective it was on you.
2. The research on attraction patterns comes to some pretty strong conclusions about what attracts us to each other as couples. Some of the biggest findings: men who seek women prioritize looks; women who seek men prioritize ability to provide resources; and everyone prioritizes intelligence, kindness, honesty, and sense of humor. How does your own personal experience match with these research results? Do these findings describe who you are attracted to? Do they describe who your friends find themselves attracted to? Do they describe the reasons why others are attracted to you?

SHOW ME MORE

13.1 An App to Stop Bullying at Its Source

http://tiny.cc/dxe15y

This TED Talk video features Trisha Prabhu describing her creation (and the effectiveness) of the ReThink app, which helps people to reconsider before posting or sending hurtful messages.

This video is hosted by a third-party Web site (source). For accessible content requests, please reach out to the publisher of that site.

13.2 The Give and Take of the Reciprocity Norm

http://tiny.cc/gq7njy

This radio clip (which is also presented in written form) offers detailed explanation, and additional examples, of the reciprocity norm theory.

Carolyn Franks/Shutterstock

This video is hosted by a third-party Web site (source). For accessible content requests, please reach out to the publisher of that site.

13.3 My Psychology Podcast

This podcast episode features the author of this textbook, psychologist Andy Pomerantz, speaking with other instructors of introductory psychology courses about the most important and interesting concepts in this chapter.

Macmillan Learning

14 Psychological Disorders

DavideAngelini/Shutterstock

CHAPTER OUTLINE

It can be difficult to decide which experiences should be labeled as psychological disorders. For example, consider the way psychologist Frank Tallis describes a client showing up for an appointment (Tallis, 2004, pp. ix–x):

> He collapsed on the couch and allowed his body to slide from a seated to an almost horizontal position. . . . The shadows beneath his eyes betrayed a week of sleepless nights—long hours, worrying in darkness.
>
> Only a few weeks earlier he had been a different person. He had burst through the door like a hurricane, shaking my hand vigorously and illuminating the room with a broad, fixed smile. . . . His enthusiasm was feverish. He was boiling over with plans, schemes, and ideas.
>
> Yet, some fourteen days later, the hurricane had blown itself out. He was inert, cheerless, and exhausted. His face had dropped like melted wax and his eyes were made of glass.
>
> What was wrong with him? Was he clinically depressed? Had his preoccupations turned into obsessions?

Dr. Tallis soon learned what was wrong with the client: his partner, with whom he was in love, was considering a breakup. Dr. Tallis uses this tale to start a book in which he proposes that being in love should be considered a mental disorder. He details the common "symptoms" of being in love: extreme mood swings, uncontrollable and obsessive thoughts, difficulty concentrating, impaired judgment, changes in sleeping and eating habits, and more. He compares these symptoms to the symptoms of established disorders, especially depression, and concludes that being in love often causes just as much impairment and disruption in the lives of those it afflicts.

Of course, Dr. Tallis's argument was unsuccessful. Being in love is *not* a mental illness. But the idea raises some interesting questions about psychological disorders that we explore in this chapter. First, what are psychological disorders? The question may seem simple, but determining which experiences should be labeled as disorders can be remarkably challenging—as illustrated by the experience of Dr. Tallis's lovesick client (and perhaps the experiences of you or someone close to you). Next, how do experts define psychological disorders? To address this question, we discuss the diagnostic manual that describes all psychological disorders and is used by psychologists and other mental health professionals. Finally, what are some specific psychological disorders?

What Are Psychological Disorders?

YOU WILL LEARN:

14.1 what the definition of a psychological disorder is.

14.2 about the criteria psychologists use to distinguish psychological disorders.

14.3 about the strengths and weaknesses of these criteria.

A **psychological disorder** is a pattern of behavior that interferes with a person's life by causing significant distress or dysfunction. There are lots of different psychological disorders, many of which we'll cover in this chapter. Some will strike you as familiar – perhaps you or someone close to you has been diagnosed with one. Some will strike you as less familiar – perhaps you've heard of them, but you're not sure exactly what they are.

For each disorder we cover in this chapter, you'll learn *what* it is (its characteristics, symptoms, etc.), *who* has it, and *why* it occurs. You will also come to understand important issues that surround psychological disorders in general – including how they are defined, how those definitions have changed over the years, and controversies that swirl around many of them.

Medical Student Syndrome: How This Chapter Might Affect You

Before we dive into psychological disorders, let's start with a quick note of caution about an effect this material may have on you. This effect is so well known among medical students that it has earned the nickname **medical student syndrome**: an experience common among medical students, and perhaps psychology students, in which they start to believe that they have the disorders or illnesses about which they are learning. Medical students may study ulcers and suddenly feel sharp stomach pains; they may study skin cancer and become convinced that their freckles are fatal. Fortunately, the medical students usually do not have the diseases they are studying, despite any fleeting or phantom symptoms they might experience (Boysen et al., 2016; Candel & Merckelbach, 2003).

You might have a similar experience as you learn about psychological disorders in this chapter. At some point, you may say to yourself, "I've felt that way at times," or even "That's me! I have that disorder!" At those moments, remember medical student syndrome. Even if a few of your symptoms are real, they may not be severe or long-lasting enough to qualify as a psychological disorder (Deo & Lymburner, 2011; Hardy & Calhoun, 1997).

Of course, it would be a mistake to dismiss serious symptoms of a psychological disorder. Some students may truly be struggling with a disorder they read about in this chapter, but there may also be plenty of false alarms. If you find yourself in need of reassurance or want to explore your own issues further, seek the opinion of a mental health professional, who you might find through your college's counseling center.

psychological disorder
A pattern of behavior that interferes with a person's life by causing significant distress or dysfunction.

medical student syndrome
An experience common among medical students, and perhaps psychology students, in which they start to believe that they have the disorders or illnesses about which they are learning.

Distinguishing Psychological Disorders

You may know people who you would label as psychologically disordered. For example, if your friend's grief over their aunt's death consisted of days or weeks of sadness, you would probably view that reaction as typical or expected. However, if your friend's sadness lasted years, included suicidal thoughts or behaviors, was accompanied by hallucinations and delusions, and interfered with working, studying, and socializing, then you might begin to view their reaction as psychologically disordered. Likewise, you can make a distinction between your slightly shy neighbor and your neighbor whose shyness is so severe that they spend years completely alone and immediately panic at the thought of interacting with another person.

Psychologists have long faced the challenge of identifying exactly what distinguishes people with and without psychological disorders (Kendler, 2018; Krueger et al., 2018; Maddux et al., 2005; Zachar & Kendler, 2010). In fact, over the years, psychologists have changed their minds about whether certain experiences are labeled as psychological disorders. For example, homosexuality was once considered a psychological disorder, but now it is not (Drescher, 2010; Strong, 2017). Until the 1980s, social anxiety disorder didn't exist as a psychological disorder: people with high levels of anxiety about social situations were thought to be extremely shy, but not mentally ill (Crocq, 2015; Wessely, 2008). The fact that psychologists have reversed their thinking on numerous disorders highlights how difficult it is to distinguish people who have psychological disorders from people who don't. Let's consider some of the standards that psychologists have used to make that distinction, all of which are helpful, but none of which are perfect: *infrequency, deviation from social norms, personal distress,* or *impairment in daily functioning*.

Infrequency. Perhaps the simplest way to determine if a behavior adds up to a psychological disorder is to consider how statistically infrequent it is. By this definition, infrequent essentially means disordered. This distinction makes sense for some psychological issues, such as the hallucinations of schizophrenia or the food refusal of anorexia, since these behaviors are quite infrequent. However, lots of behaviors that are not problematic (or are even desirable) would be classified as disordered if infrequency were the only factor. For instance, a person with an unusually good memory or a great capacity to handle stress would be considered disordered. Generally, psychologists do not categorize desirable rare qualities as disorders. So, infrequency is a useful, but imperfect, way to define psychological disorders. It works for many disorders, but not all.

Deviation from Social Norms. Psychological disorders can also be defined by the extent to which they deviate from social norms. For example, the social norm is to wash your hands several times a day. However, some people with obsessive-compulsive disorder (OCD) wash their hands dozens or even hundreds of times a day. In those cases, the handwashing behavior would be disordered. But there are also situations in which people can deviate from social norms and not be considered to have a disorder. For instance, an elite athlete who trains excessively for an upcoming big game or competition, neglecting work, school, family, or friends in the process, is usually described as dedicated or committed rather than disordered. Like infrequency, deviation from social norms can help to identify disorders in many cases, but by itself it is an imperfect standard.

DIVERSITY MATTERS

Here's another complication regarding deviation from social norms: Which social norms should be used? Our society is so diverse that the social norms within one group might differ greatly from the social norms in another group. For example, the social norms among younger people might differ from the social norms among older people; the social norms in the Bronx might differ from the social norms in rural South Dakota; and the social norms among Asian Americans might differ from the social norms of Latinx Americans. As a specific example, consider a behavior as simple as two men greeting each other: for many American men, a firm handshake is the social norm, but in more traditional Italian or Spanish cultures, kissing on the cheek may be expected, and in many Asian cultures, the greeting may include a bow or nod rather than any kind of verbal exchange or physical contact. The social norms get even more complicated when we consider more than one variable, like if we consider two people who differ in ethnicity *and* gender *and* age greeting each other. For this reason, it is crucial to consider the cultural context of behaviors before labeling a deviation from social norms as disordered (Gone & Kirmayer, 2010; McGoldrick et al., 2005).

lambada/E+/Getty Images

Jupiterimages/Stockbyte/Getty Images

For judging whether a behavior deviates from social norms, whose social norms should apply? In some social groups (but not others), the choice to have these piercings and tattoos could be viewed as signs of a psychological disorder.

Personal Distress. It is often assumed that personal distress accompanies most psychological disorders. It is true that many people genuinely *suffer* from some psychological disorders, like depressive disorders, anxiety disorders, and eating disorders — aching to escape or overcome them, seeking out treatment to alleviate their symptoms. This experience of suffering is not true of *everyone* with a psychological disorder, though. For example, a person with antisocial disorder might rob or even kill another person without the slightest trace of anxiety or anguish before or after.

Impairment in Daily Functioning. The definition of psychological disorder also includes the extent to which a thought, feeling, or behavior interferes with day-to-day life — that is, how much it impairs work, school, and relationships. The hopelessness and weariness of depressive disorders can certainly interfere with daily life, as can the restlessness and impulsiveness of ADHD. Many other disorders involve a similar level of impairment. However, there are some that do not. Some people with psychological disorders actually function at a high level. For example, prior to his suicide in 2014, actor Robin Williams reportedly struggled off and on for decades with substance abuse and various psychological disorders (Itzkoff, 2014). Yet during that time, he became a major movie and TV star, earning millions of dollars and winning an Academy Award for Best Supporting Actor in *Good Will Hunting*. So even impairment in daily functioning is, by itself, an imperfect standard.

Mark Sagliocco/Getty Images Entertainment/Getty Images

It's difficult to distinguish people with and without psychological disorders. Impairment with daily functioning is one way to make the distinction, but even that way is not always accurate. In the years before her suicide in 2018, Kate Spade had been suffering with anxiety and depression, yet she was also an extremely successful fashion designer and businessperson (Carras, 2018).

Seems like none of these criteria is a perfect rule for determining what's a psychological disorder. So how do the experts decide?

That's right: None of these four criteria is perfect. Each of them applies to many, but not all, psychological disorders. Experts consider each of the four factors when defining a psychological disorder, but the last two factors (personal distress and impairment in daily functioning) are generally given more weight than the first two factors (infrequency or deviation from social norms). This emphasis is reflected in the definition of mental disorder offered by the American Psychiatric Association in its manual of mental disorders, the ***Diagnostic and Statistical Manual of Mental Disorders*** **(DSM)**, which is the most commonly used manual of its kind among American mental health professionals. That definition states that mental disorders "are usually associated with significant distress or disability in social, occupational, or other important activities" (American Psychiatric Association, 2013, p. 20).

Diagnostic and Statistical Manual of Mental Disorders **(DSM)**
The book in which mental disorders are officially defined.

Whether or not they agree with the four criteria we have covered, some people believe that *dangerousness* is another way to determine psychological disorder. The belief that mental illness is linked with dangerousness is actually more myth than fact (Corrigan & Watson, 2005; Large et al., 2011; Varshney et al., 2016). Of course, movies, television, and news reports often promote this myth by portraying stories of mentally ill people committing an unrealistic number of violent or criminal acts, and their creators have often been criticized for doing so (Maiorano et al., 2017; Ross et al., 2018, 2019). The people who believe this myth tend to be those who are least familiar with people who have psychological disorders. In other words, the more direct contact someone has with people who have psychological disorders, the less likely that person is to believe the myth of dangerousness (Jorm & Reavley, 2014; Lee & Seo, 2018).

CHECK YOUR LEARNING:

14.1 What is a psychological disorder?

14.2 What are the criteria that psychologists use to distinguish people with and without psychological disorders?

14.3 What are the strengths and weaknesses of the criteria that psychologists use to define psychological disorders?

To check your understanding of these questions, click show the answers or refer to the answers in the Chapter Summary.

Why Do Psychological Disorders Develop?

YOU WILL LEARN:

14.4 about the biological theory of psychological disorders.

14.5 about the psychological theory of psychological disorders.

14.6 about the sociocultural theory of psychological disorders.

14.7 about the biopsychosocial theory of psychological disorders.

Why do people develop psychological disorders? Centuries ago, explanations centered on forces that we largely dismiss today: evil spirits inhabiting the body or soul, witches casting spells, or the consequences of sin leading to a person's suffering (George, 2007; Stone, 1997). In historical periods when more than one explanation existed, leaders in the field often argued about which explanation was most accurate (Fancher, 1995; Shorter, 1997). The same is true today. That is, a variety of explanations for psychological disorders compete with each other, and each one has researchers and other experts supporting it. Four theories dominate: (1) *biological*, (2) *psychological*, (3) *sociocultural*, and (4) *biopsychosocial*.

The Biological Theory of Psychological Disorders

The **biological theory of psychological disorders** asserts that biological factors within the human body, such as brain structures, neurochemicals, and genes, are the primary causes of psychological disorders. This theory fits well with a medical approach, in which psychological disorders are viewed as diseases of the brain (Clinton & Hyman, 1999; Howland, 2005; Kihlstrom, 2002). For that reason, psychiatrists and other medically trained experts tend to agree with this theory.

biological theory of psychological disorders
A theory asserting that biological factors within the human body, such as brain structures, neurochemicals, and genes, are the primary causes of psychological disorders.

Let's consider the example of Jamie, a person with major depressive disorder (defined later in this chapter). Psychologists who favor the biological theory would assume that Jamie's major depressive disorder is an illness in their brain. These psychologists would suggest that the disorder stems perhaps from too much or too little of a particular neurochemical, or a malfunction in a particular region of Jamie's brain, or a genetic tendency toward depression. These psychologists would also argue that biological treatment methods — such as medications — are necessary to treat Jamie's disorder.

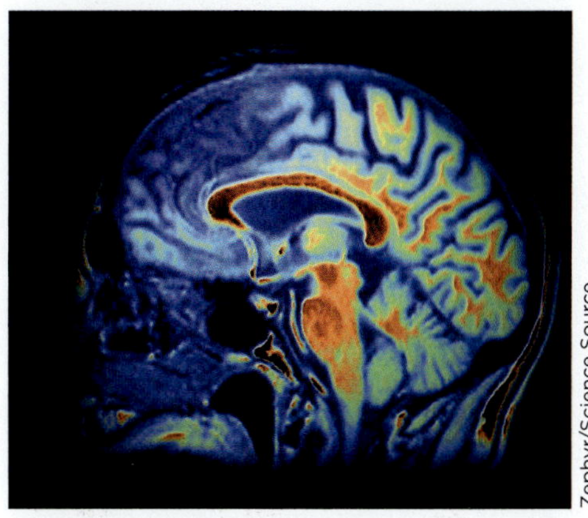

Zephyr/Science Source

There are many theories that offer explanations of how psychological disorders arise. The biological theory focuses on brain structures, neurochemicals, and genes.

The Psychological Theory of Psychological Disorders

The **psychological theory of psychological disorders** asserts that psychological factors — including emotions, thoughts, behaviors, and traits — are the primary causes of psychological disorders. When the inner workings of our minds are flawed in a significant way, they can produce psychological disorders. Within the psychological theory, there are a variety of more specific explanations, including *psychodynamic*, *behavioral*, *cognitive*, and *trait* explanations.

Psychodynamic explanations of psychological disorders (which we also covered in Chapter 12) emphasize the influence of unconscious feelings and thoughts, much of which stems from early childhood experiences and primal instincts like sex and aggression (Mitchell & Black, 1995). As Sigmund Freud suggested, unconscious feelings and thoughts can affect our lives even though they are out of our awareness. Sometimes, these feelings and thoughts affect our lives in such a way that we develop a psychological disorder (Freud, 1922). According to the psychodynamic approach, Jamie's major depressive disorder might represent feelings of anger that they have turned inward toward themself — rather than directing the feelings at the person toward whom they truly (but unconsciously) feels anger.

Behavioral explanations of psychological disorders emphasize learning and conditioning (which we discussed in Chapter 6). According to behavioral approaches, psychological disorders are behaviors that have been shaped by the reinforcements and punishments an individual has experienced as a result of their own behaviors (Skinner, 1974). From this point of view, Jamie's major depressive disorder consists of specific actions on their part that have brought about reinforcements they find valuable. For example, crying has elicited compassion and attention from friends and family, and absences from work have resulted in the opportunity to sleep in and watch TV.

Cognitive explanations of psychological disorders point to the way we think, particularly our illogical thoughts, as major contributors to psychological disorders. If we don't think logically about the events that happen to us, then we are susceptible to feelings that are more unpleasant than they need to be (Beck, 1976). In Jamie's case, depressive feelings may stem from the way they think about their recent failed job application. Let's say they think, "I'm completely unemployable. I'll never be able to get a job and I'll end up homeless." Of course, such negative thoughts are not justified by one failed attempt to get a job. These kinds of illogical thoughts may lead Jamie to feel much more dejected than necessary.

Trait explanations of psychological disorders highlight extremely high or low levels of a particular personality trait as the main reason behind a psychological disorder. The five-factor model of personality (which we covered in Chapter 12) offers a short list of broad and enduring personality traits — neuroticism, openness, extraversion, conscientiousness, and agreeableness — too much or too little of which could make a person vulnerable to certain psychological disorders (Claridge, 1995; Costa & Widiger, 2001). In this way, Jamie's major depressive disorder could be viewed as a by-product of very high levels of neuroticism, a personality trait that centers on a negative, pessimistic outlook on life.

psychological theory of psychological disorders
A theory asserting that psychological factors, including emotions, thoughts, behaviors, and traits, are the primary causes of psychological disorders.

The Sociocultural Theory of Psychological Disorders

The **sociocultural theory of psychological disorders** asserts that social and cultural factors surrounding the person, rather than factors within the person, are the primary causes of psychological disorders. The person may behave in a disordered way, but the underlying reasons can be found in the social or cultural context in which that person lives (Caplan, 1995; Eshun & Gurung, 2009). That context can be large, such as

sociocultural theory of psychological disorders
A theory asserting that social and cultural factors surrounding the person, rather than factors within the person, are the primary causes of psychological disorders.

the person's city or country, or it can be small, such as the person's immediate family or romantic partnership. Regardless of the scope, those who promote the sociocultural theory of psychological disorders believe that a faulty system will produce psychological problems in the individuals who live within it. Common social and cultural factors that are thought to contribute to psychological disorders include poverty, oppression, political unrest, prejudice, and abuse. From this viewpoint, Jamie's major depressive disorder doesn't originate within Jamie. Instead, the depression may be a consequence of economic hardship stemming from widespread unemployment in a weak economy, or dysfunction in relationships with their partner or family members.

The Biopsychosocial Theory of Psychological Disorders

The **biopsychosocial theory of psychological disorders** is a contemporary theory acknowledging that a combination of biological, psychological, and sociocultural factors contribute to psychological disorders. According to this comprehensive theory, neither the body (biological), nor mind (psychological), nor life circumstances (sociocultural) of a person should be ignored in attempts to explain psychological disorders. Instead, all three factors interact to cause psychological disorders (Campbell & Rohrbaugh, 2006; Wade & Halligan, 2017). As **Figure 14.1** shows, the biopsychosocial theory has become widely accepted in recent decades. Today, most psychologists recognize that each of these three perspectives offers important insights into psychological disorders.

Psychologists often use the *diathesis–stress model* as a specific explanation of how biological, psychological, and social factors interact to produce psychological disorders (Belsky & Pluess, 2009; Colodro-Conde et al., 2018; Monroe & Simmons, 1991; Zuckerman, 1999). In this model, *diathesis* refers to a vulnerability with which a person is born; *stress* is an event (or series of events) that turns that vulnerability into a full-blown psychological disorder.

According to the biopsychosocial theory, multiple factors underlie Jamie's major depressive disorder. They may have inherited a slight genetic predisposition to depression (biological), think a bit illogically about events in their life (psychological), and struggle economically due to a shortage of available jobs (sociocultural).

biopsychosocial theory of psychological disorders
A contemporary theory acknowledging that a combination of biological, psychological, and sociocultural factors contribute to psychological disorders.

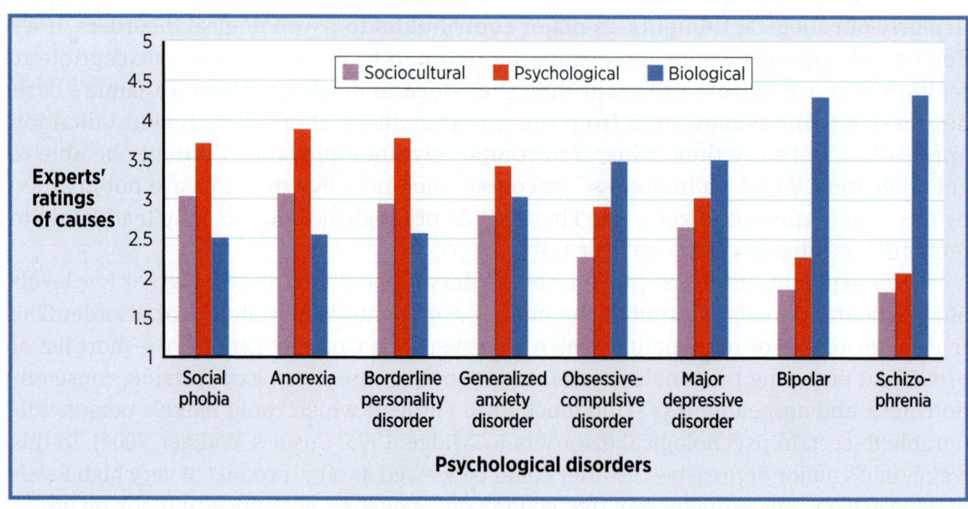

FIGURE 14.1 Experts' Beliefs about the Causes of Psychological Disorders. Researchers asked psychologists and other mental health professionals to rate, on a scale of 1 (lowest) to 5 (highest), whether various disorders were caused by biological, psychological, or sociocultural factors (Ahn et al., 2009). Different disorders received very different ratings. However, even for disorders that received a high rating in one of the three categories, the other two categories were still at least somewhat endorsed. For example, schizophrenia was rated as highly biological, but its ratings for psychological and sociocultural factors were well above the bottom of the scale. In general, this pattern endorses a biopsychosocial model, in which neither biology, psychology, nor sociocultural context is ruled out as a contributing factor to any disorder. Data from Ahn et al. (2009).

The Influence of COVID

The COVID pandemic produced a tremendous amount of psychological hardship, not just for those who tested positive for the virus but for many whose daily lives were disrupted by changes in school, work, finances, relationships, and so much more (Gruber et al., 2021). COVID may not have always been a direct *cause* of psychological disorders, but it interacted with the other factors listed in this section (biological factors, psychological factors, sociocultural factors) to increase the likelihood that people would experience serious symptoms or fully develop a diagnosable psychological disorder.

Several studies paint a picture of large increases in rates of serious psychological issues. One study found that in the early months of the pandemic, U.S. adults were eight times more likely to report serious mental distress than they were just 2 years earlier (Twenge & Joiner, 2020). Similar studies in the United Kingdom and China came to similar conclusions: the number of people with high levels of anxiety and depression in the early months of the pandemic was significantly higher than a few years earlier (Ahmed et al., 2020; Kwong et al., 2021; Rettie & Daniels, 2020). A more global study, which surveyed over 6000 people in 59 countries, also found unusually high rates of depression anxiety in the early months of the pandemic (Alzueta et al., 2021). A huge study that tracked hospital records of over 62,000 people diagnosed with COVID in the United States found that the chances of a diagnosis of a psychological disorder were remarkably high in the 3 months following the COVID diagnosis — not just higher than in healthy times, but higher than in the months following other serious medical problems (Taquet et al., 2021).

DIVERSITY MATTERS

The psychological consequences of the pandemic hit some groups harder than others. In the 59-country study mentioned above, the people most likely to experience high levels of anxiety or depression were those whose lives were most seriously affected by COVID, including those whose finances, job, or family relationships became more unstable (Alzueta et al., 2021). Often, instability of those kinds happened to people who were of lower socioeconomic status or those who identify as BIPOC (Black, Indigenous, and people of color) (Lund, 2020). Another study found that essential workers — those people who kept working during the pandemic while most of us stayed home, including health care workers, first responders, grocery store and restaurant employees, pharmacy employees, truck drivers, trash collectors, and more — reported higher levels of both stress and suicidal thoughts during summer 2020 than nonessential workers. And among the essential workers, the stress and suicidal thinking were higher among people who identified as BIPOC than people who identified as White (Bond et al., 2021).

For many people who were already diagnosed with a psychological disorder, the pandemic made it worse. In one study, researchers asked about 500 people with prepandemic psychological disorders the extent to which the pandemic had influenced their symptoms. Participants with all kinds of disorders reported a moderate impact, but the impact was strongest for those with generalized anxiety disorder and obsessive-compulsive disorder (Miller et al., 2021). Other studies have found that the worsening can work the other way too — that is, having a psychological disorder can make the experience of COVID infection more severe. One meta-analysis of these types of studies found that compared to COVID patients who were not diagnosed with a psychological disorder, COVID patients who were diagnosed with a psychological disorder were significantly more likely to require hospitalization and to die (Vai et al., 2021).

Notably, the impact of COVID on mental health was not bad for everyone. Many people showed remarkable resilience, and some even thrived, especially after they had time to adjust after the pandemic initially hit (Daly & Robinson, 2021; Park et al., 2021). In the study described previously that found that COVID tended to worsen prepandemic psychological disorders, many of the participants also described a significant upside of the pandemic (Miller et al., 2021). For example, one participant said, "my social anxiety has drastically decreased because I haven't been exposed to the outside world as much as I usually am" (p. 9). Another said that the pandemic "allowed me the space to really take care of myself . . . I'm finally on a regular sleeping schedule . . . I'm eating normally and exercising" (p. 14). And another described the impact of the pandemic as "positive in that my partner and I have reconnected and spent more time together" (p. 14).

stigma
A judgment of shame or disgrace directed toward a person because of a particular characteristic that person has.

The Influence of Stigma

Just as the pandemic can worsen the experience of mental illness, so can **stigma**: a judgment of shame or disgrace directed toward a person because of a particular characteristic that person has. Stigma toward people with mental illness has been an unfortunate part of many societies around the world throughout the course of human history, and it's an unfortunate part of American society today (Hinshaw, 2007). Wherever and whenever it appears, stigma toward people with mental illness shares four key features:

- Stigma degrades the person with mental illnesses by portraying them as flawed, threatening, tainted, "less than," or otherwise unacceptable. This portrayal goes hand-in-hand with an "us versus them" mentality, along with the unjustified stereotypes of people with mental illness as dangerous, incompetent, permanently mentally ill, unpredictable, and worthy of blame for their own mental illness (Goffman, 1963; Link & Stuart, 2017; Parcesepe & Cabassa, 2013; Pescosolido et al., 2019; Sheehan et al., 2017; Yeh et al., 2017).
- Stigma is based not on facts, but on social constructions, which are ideas that many members a society accept. That is, the stigma reflects what certain people—especially people with power—*believe* about people with mental illness, not what's actually true about people with mental illness (Major et al., 2018; Pescosolido et al., 2008).
- Stigma depicts people with mental illness as a homogenous group, as if everyone with mental illness is the same. As a result, it can be difficult for a person with mental illness to be recognized as the unique individual they are, and it can be easy for others to stereotype or prejudge them (Corrigan, 2007).
- Stigma worsens the mental illness for the stigmatized person. In addition to their mental illness, the stigma requires the person with mental illness to *also* cope with other people's disapproval. That extra layer of stress is the opposite of the social support that the person with mental illness would find helpful, and it can intensify the symptoms of any mental illness (Hinshaw, 2017).

To illustrate the way that stigma can worsen mental illness, consider Kevin Love. Kevin is a professional basketball player who has made the NBA all-star team five times as a member of the Minnesota Timberwolves and Cleveland Cavaliers, and who won the championship with LeBron James in 2016. Kevin has struggled with panic disorder, and had a panic attack that forced him to leave the court during a game against the Atlanta Hawks. For years, he told no one about his panic, primarily because of the stigma he thought other people, including his teammates, would hold toward him. But eventually he went public with his struggles, with the hope of freeing himself from the stigma – and inspiring others to do the same. In the quote below, notice how Kevin describes the stigma as more of a challenge than the panic attacks themselves:

> I distinctly remember being more relieved than anything that nobody had found out why I had left the game against Atlanta . . . *Why was I so concerned with people finding out?* . . . I'd thought the hardest part was over after I had the panic attack. It was the opposite. Now I was left wondering why it happened – and why I didn't want to talk about it. Call it a stigma or call it fear or insecurity . . . but what I was worried about wasn't just my own inner struggles but how difficult it was to *talk about* them. . . . (Love, 2018)

Layne Murdoch Jr./2021 NBAE/Getty Images

Kevin Love, an NBA All-Star and champion, has spoken out about his experience with mental illness and the stigma that often surrounds it.

People generally agree that people with mental illness deserve care and support, but research also shows that stigma against people with mental illness is quite widespread (Angermeyer & Deitrich, 2006; Parcesepe & Cabassa, 2013; Pescosolido, 2013). In one study, researchers asked over 6000 participants from 16 countries (including the United States) to read brief descriptions of a person with schizophrenia or a person with major depressive disorder. Across both of those disorders, over half of the participants agreed with each of these statements:

- The person is likely to be violent toward themselves.
- The person is unpredictable.
- The person should not teach children.
- I would be unwilling to allow this person to care for my children.
- I would be unwilling to be related to this person as an in-law.

Over 20% also agreed that neither the person with schizophrenia nor the person with major depression should be hired, befriended, or trusted (Pescosolido et al., 2013). Similar studies have produced similar results, with large percentages of participants reporting an unwillingness to become friends with, work with, or even spend a single evening socializing with a person who has a mental illness (Martin et al., 2000; Pescosolido, 2013).

Experts have identified four primary forms of stigma, each of which can be quite harmful: public stigma, self-stigma, structural stigma, and courtesy stigma. *Public stigma* is a shared, societal endorsement of stigma toward people with mental illness. It's probably what you think of first when you think of stigma — basically, the "common knowledge" about people with mental illness that "everyone" knows (but which is often untrue). Public stigma is spread not just through word of mouth but through TV, movies, and social media as well. *Self-stigma* is internalized endorsement, by a person with mental illness, of stigma toward people with mental illness. It's essentially public stigma accepted and turned inward by the person with mental illness. *Structural stigma* is stigma embedded in policies or practices that restrict opportunities for people with mental illness. It happens when stigma becomes part of the system or a feature of our institutions. Examples include health companies refusing to sell policies or charging unaffordable rates, employers refusing to hire or provide accommodations, landlords refusing to rent homes, and the legal system (the courts or law enforcement officers) providing unfair treatment. *Courtesy stigma* is stigma experienced by family members, friends, partners, or other people in close contact with the person with mental illness. Also known as "stigma by association," it's an indication of how strong stigma toward people with mental illness can be — strong enough to spread to people who do not have mental illnesses themselves but are simply connected to someone who does.

Research illustrates the negative effects that stigma often has on people who are already struggling with a mental illness. For example, numerous studies have found a negative correlation between self-stigma and willingness to seek treatment for a mental illness. That is, the more a person applies mental illness stigma to themselves, the less likely they are to seek help for that mental illness, and that lack of treatment can cause the mental illness to worsen (Clement et al., 2015; Nam et al., 2013).

Other studies have documented the *why try effect* — a sense of futility experienced by a person with mental illness whose self-stigma causes them to believe that they can't or don't deserve to reach their personal goals (Corrigan et al., 2009, 2019). When people with mental illness experience the why try effect, they basically give up, presuming that any efforts to help themselves overcome their mental illness (or perhaps to achieve anything at all) are hopeless. In one study of hundreds of people with mental illness, there was a strong positive correlation between self-stigma and the why try effect. In fact, that correlation was stronger than the correlation between depression and the why try effect, suggesting that stigma saps hope from people even more than the depression to which it might be connected (Corrigan et al., 2016). One unfortunate result of the why try effect is that people with mental illness may withdraw from society either partially or completely, which means they won't contribute to society in ways that might benefit others. For this reason, some experts have described mental illness stigma as a social justice issue that affects not just people with mental illness but all community members who might gain from their active engagement (Corrigan, 2004; Yanos, 2018).

The good news about stigma toward people with mental illness is that there are numerous strategies to overcome it, and evidence showing how well those strategies work. Most of the strategies focus on public stigma, and those strategies focus on either education, protest, or contact (Roe et al., 2014; Rüsch & Xu, 2017). *Education antistigma strategies* rely primarily on teaching people about mental illness to combat ignorance and misinformation. They can be social media campaigns, videos, Web sites, billboards, radio public service announcements, articles, books, or other forms of information. *Protest antistigma strategies* rely primarily on condemning and objecting to beliefs and behaviors that stigmatize people with mental illness. They are more directly oppositional than educational strategies, and they often involve calling out stigma when it occurs. For example, after the TV show *Modern Family* aired a Halloween episode that some people viewed as mocking and disrespectful toward people with mental illness, the National Alliance on Mental Illness (NAMI) posted an online letter opposing it, created a press release in which they scolded ABC-TV, posted about it on Twitter and Facebook, and encouraged their followers to take similar action (Greenstein, 2015). *Contact antistigma strategies* rely primarily on direct interactions between people with and without mental illness. This strategy is based on the idea that people who stigmatize people with mental illness probably don't know many people with mental illness. Providing them with opportunities to make direct contact, to get to know real people with names and faces, humanizes people with mental illness and makes it more difficult for ignorance to prevail.

Plenty of studies have put these antistigma strategies to the test, and many of the results are encouraging. In general, antistigma strategies tend to be effective, as shown in multiple meta-analyses (Corrigan et al., 2012; Griffiths et al., 2014; Morgan et al., 2018). When the three types of strategies are compared against each other, results sometimes differ, but most often the contact strategy is most successful, followed by the education strategy (Casados, 2017; Corrigan, 2014; Corrigan et al., 2001; Couture & Penn, 2003; Dovidio et al., 2013).

CHECK YOUR LEARNING:

14.4 According to the biological theory of psychological disorders, what factors are primary causes of psychological disorders?

14.5 According to the psychological theory of psychological disorders, what factors are primary causes of psychological disorders?

14.6 According to the sociocultural theory of psychological disorders, what factors are primary causes of psychological disorders?

14.7 How does the biopsychosocial theory of psychological disorders, combine the other three theories of psychological disorders?

To check your understanding of these questions, click show the answers or refer to the answers in the Chapter Summary.

The Diagnostic Manual: DSM

YOU WILL LEARN:

14.8 what DSM is.

14.9 who uses DSM and for what purposes.

14.10 how DSM is organized and how it has changed over the years.

14.11 about the difference between the categorical and dimensional models of psychopathology.

DSM (*Diagnostic and Statistical Manual of Mental Disorders*) is the book in which mental disorders are officially defined. DSM is used by psychiatrists, psychologists, social workers, counselors, even physicians and nurses – anyone in the United States who might diagnose or treat an individual with a mental disorder. (Outside the United States, mental health professionals often use other manuals, like the *International Classification of Diseases* or the *Chinese Classification of Mental Disorders*.) When health insurance companies pay for a person's psychological treatment, including therapy or medication, they typically do so after the person has been given a DSM diagnosis. With so many professionals using it and so many of our lives affected by it, DSM has become a powerful force in

U.S. society (Widiger, 2005; Zachar, 2018). Its contents determine the psychological diagnoses professionals can assign to us, which in turn influences not only the treatments we might receive, but our own views of ourselves as well (Eriksen & Kress, 2005; Langenbucher & Nathan, 2006).

The current edition of DSM is a hefty book – over 1000 pages describing hundreds of psychological disorders (American Psychiatric Association, 2022). It organizes these psychological disorders into about 20 categories based on similar characteristics and common themes. Within each category, specific disorders are named and defined (see **Table 14.1**). For example, within the eating disorders category, DSM lists the specific disorders anorexia nervosa, bulimia nervosa, and binge eating disorder. Within the anxiety disorders category, DSM lists panic disorder, specific phobia, social anxiety disorder, generalized anxiety disorder, and others.

For each disorder it names, DSM describes the nature of the disorder, how common it is, how it may appear differently across cultures, and how it may develop over time. At the end of this description, DSM lists the *diagnostic criteria* for the disorder, an itemized list of exactly what symptoms are necessary to qualify for the diagnosis. The diagnostic criteria are presented as a checklist, with rules regarding how many items on the list must be checked for the diagnosis to apply. For example, the diagnostic criteria for borderline personality disorder include nine possible symptoms, and the person must have at least five of them to qualify. As another example, the diagnostic criteria for generalized anxiety disorder include six possible symptoms, and the person must have at least three of them to qualify.

TABLE 14.1: Categories of Disorders in DSM-5-TR

CATEGORY	EXAMPLES OF DISORDERS
Neurodevelopmental disorders	Autism spectrum disorders, specific learning disorder, intellectual disability, attention-deficit/hyperactivity disorder
Schizophrenia spectrum and other psychotic disorders	Schizophrenia, brief psychotic disorder, schizoaffective disorder
Bipolar and related disorders	Bipolar disorder, cyclothymic disorder
Depressive disorders	Major depressive disorder, persistent depressive disorder (dysthymia), premenstrual dysphoric disorder
Anxiety disorders	Specific phobia, social anxiety disorder, panic disorder, generalized anxiety disorder
Obsessive-compulsive and related disorders	Obsessive-compulsive disorder, hoarding disorder, body dysmorphic disorder
Trauma- and stressor-related disorders	Posttraumatic stress disorder, acute stress disorder, adjustment disorder; prolonged grief disorder
Dissociative disorders	Dissociative identity disorder, dissociative amnesia
Somatic symptom and related disorders	Somatic symptom disorder, illness anxiety disorder, conversion disorder
Feeding and eating disorders	Anorexia nervosa, bulimia nervosa, binge eating disorder
Elimination disorders	Enuresis, encopresis
Sleep-wake disorders	Insomnia, narcolepsy
Sexual dysfunctions	Erectile disorder, female orgasmic disorder
Gender dysphoria	Gender dysphoria in children, gender dysphoria in adolescents and adults
Disruptive, impulse control, and conduct disorders	Oppositional defiant disorder, conduct disorder, intermittent explosive disorder
Substance-related and addictive disorders	Alcohol use disorder, cannabis use disorder
Neurocognitive disorders	Major neurocognitive disorder, mild neurocognitive disorder
Personality disorders	Antisocial personality disorder, borderline personality disorder, narcissistic personality disorder
Paraphilic disorders	Voyeuristic disorder, exhibitionistic disorder

Information from DSM-5-TR (American Psychiatric Association, 2022).

How has DSM changed over the years?

DSM wasn't always such a big book. When it was originally published in 1952, it included only 106 disorders — a small fraction of the number the current edition includes. As new editions of DSM came out, sometimes a single disorder was split into many, and sometimes entirely different problems were included as new disorders. Among the disorders that weren't included in the original DSM are many of today's most common or familiar disorders, including attention-deficit/hyperactivity disorder (ADHD), social anxiety disorder, bulimia nervosa, and posttraumatic stress disorder (PTSD) (Blashfield et al., 2010; Langenbucher & Nathan, 2006).

The Current Edition: DSM-5-TR

A major event for the mental health field took place in 2013 when the fifth edition of DSM was published. It was the first revision of the definitions of mental disorders in almost 20 years, the result of an extensive, multistep process that lasted more than a decade and involved hundreds of experts from at least a dozen countries (American Psychiatric Association, 2013; Kupfer et al., 2013; Paris, 2013a, b; Regier et al., 2013). In 2022, another new edition was published: DSM-5-TR. This edition did not include as many changes as some earlier editions did. In fact, it only introduced one entirely new disorder: *prolonged grief disorder*, which we covered in Chapter 11 and which involves intense grief after the death of someone close that continues to disrupt their lives for a long time after the death (at least a year for adults, or 6 months for children) (American Psychiatric Association, 2021, 2022; Appelbaum et al., 2021). Besides this new disorder, the text changes in DSM-5-TR mostly cover recent research on various disorders (the "TR" in the title stands for "text revision").

Although DSM-5-TR introduced only one new disorder in 2022, DSM-5 introduced quite a few new disorders in 2013. The disorders that appeared for the first time in DSM-5 include these:

- *Premenstrual dysphoric disorder* is a severe form of premenstrual syndrome (PMS). It requires a combination of at least five emotional symptoms and physical symptoms to occur during most menstrual cycles. Those symptoms must cause clinically significant distress or interfere with work, school, social life, or relationships with others (American Psychiatric Association, 2013; Freeman, 2017; Paris, 2013a; Regier et al., 2013; Wakefield, 2013).
- *Disruptive mood dysregulation disorder* occurs in children 6–18 years old who have an excessive number of temper tantrums per week over the course of a year. The tantrums must take place in at least two settings (like home and school), and the children are often irritable or angry between the tantrums (American Psychiatric Association, 2013; Copeland et al., 2013; Frances & Bastra, 2013; Pierre, 2013).
- *Binge eating disorder* involves at least one out-of-control food binge per week for 3 months. The binges often feature rapid eating, eating alone, and feelings of guilt (American Psychiatric Association, 2013; Ornstein et al., 2013; Stice et al., 2013).
- *Mild neurocognitive disorder* is a less intense version of more serious neurocognitive problems like amnesia or dementia. It features minor problems with cognitive functions like memory or attention — for example, forgetting what you wanted to buy at the grocery store, or losing track of the plot of a movie — but nothing serious enough that it prevents the person from living independently (American Psychiatric Association, 2013; Blazer, 2013; Frances, 2013).

CURRENT CONTROVERSY

Premenstrual Dysphoric Disorder?

For some women, the symptoms of premenstrual syndrome (PMS) can be quite severe. If these symptoms significantly disrupt daily life or cause substantial distress, is the person experiencing a psychological disorder? When DSM-5 came out in 2013, the authors added a new disorder: *premenstrual dysphoric disorder* (PMDD). (Versions of PMDD had been considered, but rejected, for earlier editions of DSM; Zachar & Kendler, 2014.) PMDD is not "ordinary" PMS, but a premenstrual experience that substantially interferes with aspects of life such as work, school, and relationships with others (American Psychiatric Association, 2013). PMDD is much less common and more severe than PMS. Its psychological symptoms include depression, anxiety, mood swings, and decreased interest in activities (Freeman, 2017). Some physical symptoms are also included.

Is it a good thing or a bad thing that PMDD is now included in DSM as a psychological disorder? On the good side, women with severe premenstrual symptoms may finally receive acknowledgment from the mental health field that their experience is legitimate. They may also receive more compassion and understanding from those around them, who otherwise might have thought they were complaining about "nothing" or "making up" their problem (Alevizou et al., 2018; Gallant & Hamilton, 1988). Also, these women will be more likely to receive treatment and less likely to be misdiagnosed with a different disorder.

Those who have argued that adding PMDD as a psychological disorder is a bad thing tend to focus on the idea that premenstrual symptoms, as unpleasant as they may be, are a part of life. They suggest that people who experience them are not psychologically disordered, but simply going through a difficult experience, and not all difficult experiences are psychological disorders. Receiving a diagnosis of PMDD might cause some to see themselves differently—specifically, to see themselves as a person with a psychological disorder when they had not seen themselves that way before. There could be some practical, real-world consequences to the disorder too. Consider a woman in a custody battle whose ex-husband's lawyer points out to the judge that the woman is mentally ill because she has received a PMDD diagnosis. This argument could not happen if PMDD were not a DSM diagnostic category in the first place (Browne, 2017; Caplan, 1992; Caplan & Cosgrove, 2004; Eriksen & Kress, 2005).

Again, the question here is not whether anyone experiences severe, life-disrupting premenstrual symptoms. Unfortunately, we know that to be true for some people. The question is whether those people should be diagnosed with a psychological disorder. Perhaps the broader question is where we should draw the line between common (but troubling) life experiences and psychological disorders. After all, PMDD is just one example. Other new disorders added to DSM-5 and DSM-5-TR include disorders based on excessive versions of some common experiences, like temper tantrums (disruptive mood dysregulation disorder), overeating (binge eating disorder), grief after the death of someone close (prolonged grief disorder), and concern about physical illnesses (somatic symptom disorder). •

Criticisms of DSM

Some people have criticized DSM authors for the manual's continued expansion with each new edition (Barry, 2022; Blashfield et al., 2014; Browne, 2017). Such criticism was especially common around the time DSM-5 was released in 2013, when there were letters of protest from numerous mental health organizations and plenty of media coverage regarding its controversial new disorders (Caccavale, 2013; Fabiano & Haslam, 2020; Greenberg, 2013; Wakefield, 2013; Whooley & Horwitz, 2013). One of the most outspoken critics of DSM-5 was Allen Frances, the psychiatrist in charge of the previous edition, DSM-IV (Frances, 2012). One of Frances's main complaints, shared by many other critics as well, is that the experiences that DSM-5 labeled as new disorders might actually fall within the range of daily, non-disordered life (Frances, 2013). Critics made similar complaints about previous revisions of DSM as well (Caplan, 1995; Kutchins & Kirk, 1997). The critics' point is that not every unpleasant or problematic human experience should qualify as a psychological disorder.

Other experiences are receiving plenty of research attention in recent years too, and could appear as disorders in future editions of DSM. One example is "cyberchondria," or excessive online searches for health-related information that cause distress or anxiety. A second example is "orthorexia," or sticking to a particular healthy diet so strictly that it disrupts daily life or causes health problems. And a third example is "internet gaming disorder," or excessive gaming that involves an inability to stop playing and continues in spite of disrupting other aspects of life. (Airoldi et al., 2021; Dunn & Bratman, 2016; Hay et al., 2021; Hayatbini & Oberle, 2019; McMullan et al., 2019; Petry & O'Brien, 2013; Starcevic & Aboujaoude, 2015; Strahler et al., 2018; te Poel et al., 2016; Zajac et al., 2017). These experiences happen to many people, but

categorical model of psychopathology
A model in which psychological disorders exist as either totally present or totally absent, as opposed to present to a certain extent.

dimensional model of psychopathology
A model of psychopathology in which psychological issues exist on a continuum, as opposed to being fully present or absent.

Categorical Versus Dimensional Models of Psychopathology

"The dimensional model of psychopathology is like a dimmer on a light switch . . ."

Visit Achieve to watch the My Take video and then answer questions.

are not currently included as disorders in DSM. So, at some point in the future, DSM authors will need to decide whether to add them as new disorders.

DSM has also received other criticisms (Khoury et al., 2014; Raskin, 2018; Raskin & Gayle, 2016). Some find fault with the all-or-nothing way it defines disorders, which is similar to the way physicians define many medical problems. That is, with many medical diseases, you either have it or you don't. For example, you either have cancer or you don't. Likewise, you either have COVID or you don't. It is a black-or-white question rather than a shades-of-gray question. (That's why the tests for these disorders come back "positive" or "negative.") Does the same logic apply to psychological disorders? According to DSM, it does. DSM says *whether or not* a person has a particular disorder. This approach illustrates a **categorical model of psychopathology**: a model in which psychological disorders exist as either totally present or totally absent, as opposed to present to a certain extent. Some psychologists think that this categorical model of psychopathology, with its distinct "yes" and "no" categories, doesn't fit psychological issues as well as it fits many medical problems.

Some psychologists have promoted an alternative to the categorical model of psychopathology: the **dimensional model of psychopathology**, in which psychological issues exist on a continuum as opposed to being fully present or absent. If the categorical model is a light switch — either totally on or totally off — then the dimensional model is a dimmer. The dimensional model of psychopathology suggests that rather than DSM helping psychologists determine *whether or not* a person has a disorder, it should help psychologists determine *the extent to which* a person has its symptoms (Kraemer, 2010; Simonsen, 2010; Widiger & Trull, 2007). The authors of DSM-5 considered a more dimensional diagnostic system, especially for the personality disorders, but ultimately stuck with the categorical model used in all previous editions of DSM (De Fruyt et al., 2013; Gore & Widiger, 2013; Phillips, 2013; Whooley & Horwitz, 2013). Check out the "It's Like . . ." box for further discussion.

IT'S LIKE...

The Categorical Model Is Like an HIV Test, and the Dimensional Model Is Like a Blood Pressure Test

Some medical tests give you definitive yes-or-no, black-or-white, all-or-none results. An HIV test is a great example: It comes back either positive or negative. These possible results match the underlying nature of what is being tested. HIV is a virus that is either in your body or not.

For other medical tests, the results might not be so either-or. The results might tell you where you fall within a range, or how high or low your scores are. A blood pressure test is a great example: It comes back as a pair of numbers that indicate how forcefully your heart is pumping blood through your veins. These results match the underlying nature of what is being tested. Blood pressure is something that is present in all of us, so the issue is not whether we have blood pressure or not, but how much blood pressure we have.

The contrast between yes-or-no tests (like HIV) and how-much tests (like blood pressure) is a lot like the contrast between the categorical model and the dimensional model of psychopathology. The categorical model resembles an HIV test: It places individuals in either the yes category or the no category regarding a particular disorder. DSM has always used a categorical model, and you can hear categorical thinking reflected in the common language we use to discuss psychological issues: "He *has* bipolar disorder," "She *doesn't have* obsessive-compulsive disorder," "I wonder if they *have* ADHD." On the other hand, the dimensional model resembles a blood pressure test: It asks how much, or to what extent, the problem is present in a person's life. Just like blood pressure scores are points on a continuum, people would receive ratings for psychological issues on, say, a 1–10 scale rather than being placed in a yes-or-no category.

Are psychological disorders something that we either have or don't have, like a virus? Or are psychological disorders something that we all have but in different amounts, like blood pressure? Is the answer different for different disorders? DSM has always used a categorical approach, but in recent years, many researchers have pushed for changes toward a dimensional model for at least some diagnoses (Bagby & Widiger, 2018; Blashfield et al., 2009; Hopwood et al., 2018; Morey & Hopwood, 2019; Widiger & Edmundson, 2011; Widiger & Trull, 2007).

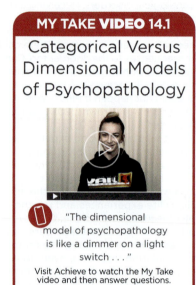

CHECK YOUR LEARNING:

14.8 What is DSM?

14.9 Who uses DSM, and why?

14.10 How is DSM organized, and how has it changed over the years?

14.11 What is the difference between the categorical and dimensional models of psychopathology?

To check your understanding of these questions, click show the answers or refer to the answers in the Chapter Summary.

Anxiety Disorders and Obsessive-Compulsive Disorder

YOU WILL LEARN:

14.12 what anxiety disorders are.

14.13 what generalized anxiety disorder is.

14.14 what specific phobia is.

14.15 what social anxiety disorder is.

14.16 what panic disorder is.

14.17 what obsessive-compulsive disorder is.

14.18 who gets anxiety disorders and obsessive-compulsive disorder.

14.19 why anxiety disorders and obsessive-compulsive disorder develop.

Anxiety disorders are the group of DSM disorders in which the experience of excessive, unjustified anxiety is the primary symptom. Although the focus of this section is anxiety *disorders*, it is important to keep in mind that often, anxiety can be a good thing. Anxiety is a built-in alarm system that alerts you to danger so you can react, perhaps by avoiding it or fighting against it (Blanchard et al., 2008; Hofer, 2010; McKay, 2016). You can probably recall many times when a little bit of anxiety served you well. At the time, you may have called the feeling nervousness, worry, apprehension, or just plain fear. Sometimes people get these feelings before a big test, a big date, or a big game. In situations like these, a little anxiety may improve your performance by keeping you focused and motivating you to perform well.

Anxiety becomes problematic when it occurs needlessly or excessively – that is, when there is more of it than the situation calls for (Craske et al., 2009; Stein & Nesse, 2015). DSM includes quite a few anxiety disorders, all of which share the same core of physical symptoms (heart racing, palms sweating) and psychological symptoms (worry, fear). Let's examine four of them: *generalized anxiety disorder, specific phobia, social anxiety disorder*, and *panic disorder*. We'll also examine *obsessive-compulsive disorder*, which used to fall within the anxiety disorders category in previous editions of DSM, but currently has its own separate category. (*Posttraumatic stress disorder*, which also features anxiety as a prominent symptom, was covered in Chapter 11.)

LIFE HACK 14.1

A little bit of anxiety is not necessarily a bad thing. As long as it is not excessive, anxiety can work to your benefit by alerting you to danger or improving your performance.

(Blanchard et al., 2008; Hofer, 2010)

Generalized Anxiety Disorder

Generalized anxiety disorder (GAD) involves anxiety symptoms that persist for a long time across a wide range of situations and activities (Brown & Lawrence, 2009; Dugas et al., 2018). People with generalized anxiety disorder worry about almost everything. Even when there isn't a good reason to do so, as **Figure 14.2** shows, a person with GAD worries about work, school, family, friends, health, money, appearance, life decisions, and world events. This never-ending worry leaves a person with GAD feeling continually nervous and stressed.

Wait, I worry about a lot of that stuff. Do I have GAD?

What separates most people from those with GAD is that people with GAD worry excessively – far more than they need to, to the point that it significantly interferes with their lives (Hazlett-Stevens et al., 2009; Papp, 2010). People with GAD often describe their worry as out of control. When they consider things that may happen in

anxiety disorders
The group of DSM disorders in which the experience of excessive, unjustified anxiety is the primary symptom.

generalized anxiety disorder
A disorder involving anxiety symptoms that persist for a long time across a wide range of situations and activities.

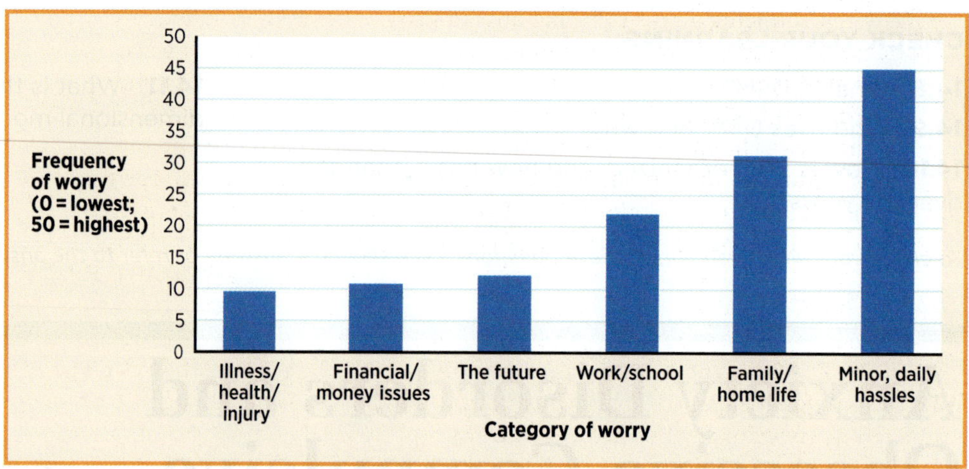

FIGURE 14.2 What Do People with Generalized Anxiety Disorder Worry About? Researchers interviewed almost 100 people with GAD and asked them what they worry about. Their answers spanned a remarkably wide range from the minor hassles of daily life to physical illness, from family and home life to travel, from finances to the future. Data from Roemer et al. (1997).

the future, they fear the worst despite knowing that the worst is extremely unlikely to happen (Holmes & Newman, 2006).

Consider your own experience as you approach a big exam. Your mind might generate a few worrisome thoughts: "Did I study enough? What if I bomb it?" You can probably calm those worrisome thoughts, though, by reminding yourself that you have attended class, read the assigned material, and spent time studying for the test. However, the student with GAD can't stop the barrage of what-ifs no matter how prepared for the test: "Did I study enough? What if I bomb it? What if that bad grade makes me fail this class? What if failing this class makes me drop out of college? What if I do OK on this test, but I bomb the next one? Wait, I think I'm getting a headache. What if it's actually a brain tumor?" With GAD, the worry continues and expands far more than it reasonably should.

Patricia Pearson, a news journalist, wrote a book about her struggle with GAD that reveals the psychological disorder's almost unlimited reach into a person's life:

> I would prefer not to be afraid of the following: phone bills, ovarian cancer, black bears, climate change, walking on golf courses at night, being blundered into by wild insects; unseemly heights, running out of gas, having the mole on my back that I can feel, but not see, secretly morph into a malignant melanoma. Plus, flying. This is a big problem. Also, on occasion, the prospect that the supervolcano underlying Yosemite National Park will erupt and kill us all. Certainly, in addition, unexpected liver failure. And cows. Also, but only occasionally, when I'm really over the edge with anxiety, the fear that the car I'm driving will simply explode. (Pearson, 2008, pp. 1–2)

Like all anxiety disorders, the signs of GAD are physical as well as psychological. Bodily symptoms like muscle tension, fatigue, restlessness, and difficulty sleeping accompany the worried thought processes. Even more serious medical problems like arthritis, back pain, migraines, ulcers, and heart disease are common among people with GAD (Csupak et al., 2018; Rygh & Sanderson, 2004).

Specific Phobia

Aretha Franklin, the legendary R&B performer who sang "Respect" and "I Say a Little Prayer," had a serious fear of airplanes. She traced the fear back to 1983, when she was on a small plane that experienced severe turbulence:

> We were bouncing all over the sky, and, to say the least, I had an anxiety attack. . . . I kiddingly told my road manager. . . . "You don't have to worry about getting me on another plane soon." However, I didn't feel it would be permanent. All I needed was a little time and I'd start flying again. But that never happened. . . . My fear of flying has had an impact on my tour scheduling. I haven't been back to California since I left in the early eighties. It's been even longer since I've been in Europe. I have had to turn down hundreds of offers to appear all over the world. Africa, Japan, Egypt, Australia, and China are just a few of the places I did not go. (Franklin & Ritz, 1999, pp. 200–201)

Aretha Franklin's fear of airplanes provides an excellent illustration of a **specific phobia**: a disorder characterized by excessive anxiety toward a specific object or situation. A specific phobia involves intense anxiety triggered by a single known stimulus (unlike GAD, in which anxiety can stem from almost any situation). People with specific phobias may live without much disruption as long as they avoid the feared object or situation. But that avoidance can itself become a major hassle — or, in Aretha Franklin's case, disruption to her career and her life — and when the avoidance fails, the anxiety can be overwhelming (Gamble et al., 2010; Hofmann et al., 2009a; Rowa et al., 2018).

You are probably quite familiar with some of the most common phobias, such as fear of heights (acrophobia), fear of snakes (ophidiophobia), fear of thunder and lightning (astraphobia), fear of dogs (cynophobia), fear of spiders (arachnophobia), fear of germs (mysophobia), or fear of enclosed spaces (claustrophobia). Thousands more specific phobias — some common, most very rare — have been identified.

Social Anxiety Disorder

People with **social anxiety disorder** (also called *social phobia*) have an intense and irrational fear of situations in which they may be judged or scrutinized. Some people with social anxiety disorder are anxious across most social situations — one-on-one conversations, small-group interactions, parties, and many others. For others, social anxiety disorder is more limited, occurring only when they must perform in front of others in such situations as public speaking, athletic contests, or other events. They worry excessively about doing something in front of other people that will cause them embarrassment or humiliation. The anxiety this disorder produces includes both psychological symptoms (like worry and dread) and physical symptoms (like sweating, quickened breathing, and a racing heart) (Beidel & Turner, 2007; Rowa et al., 2018; Taylor et al., 2009).

Emily Ford, a high school English teacher, wrote a memoir about her experience with social anxiety disorder. Here, she recalls a typical day from her own experience as a high school student, bombarded by the imagined criticisms of everyone around her:

> In first-period chemistry, I was up to my ears in dread. . . . The imagined thoughts of my classmates bombarded me from all sides: "Her hair is so ugly." "Yeah, but did you see those yellow teeth?" "Look at what she's wearing." "She's covered in cat hair." "She's covered in her own hair. Did you see her arms?" "She better not be my lab partner."
>
> Meanwhile, Mrs. H. set a pile of graded papers on the edge of her desk, ready to return them to the class. *What did she think of my answers?* I wondered. *Were they silly, messy, too long, too short, too precise, or just plain wrong? Did my work look like I was trying too hard or not hard enough?*
>
> I was the only one in my class not to fly to Disney World for the senior class trip. . . . I dreaded having to team up with roommates who would undoubtedly cringe at the thought of rooming with me. . . . It seemed simpler to stay home. (Ford, 2007, pp. 28–29, 35)

specific phobia
An anxiety disorder characterized by excessive anxiety toward a specific object or situation.

social anxiety disorder
An anxiety disorder characterized by an intense and irrational fear of situations in which one may be judged or scrutinized.

As this example illustrates, people with social anxiety disorder pay close attention to their behavior and are critical of themselves, often condemning themselves much more than others around them do (Hofmann et al., 2009b). As a result, people with social anxiety disorder often choose to avoid social interaction, which costs them friends and dating relationships (Ledley et al., 2008). Speaking of dating relationships, people with social anxiety disorder often perceive their partners as being more critical than they really are. In one study, researchers observed couples having a 10-minute discussion in which they try to solve a problem. Some of the couples included a person with social anxiety disorder. Results showed that people with social anxiety disorder perceived a much higher rate of criticism coming from their partners than people without social anxiety disorder did. Additionally, the researchers observing the discussions did not perceive the excessive criticism that the people with social anxiety disorder perceived in their partners (Porter et al., 2019).

I know some very shy people, and this social anxiety disorder diagnosis sounds like it would fit them pretty well. What's the difference between social anxiety disorder and extreme shyness?

Actually, that's a tough distinction, and one that has caused some controversy. Some experts have questioned whether social anxiety disorder should be considered a disorder at all, since it is essentially a very high level of a personality trait — shyness, or introversion — that is very common (Lane, 2007; Moynihan & Cassels, 2005; Poole et al., 2017). As with other disorders, DSM emphasizes that symptoms of social anxiety disorder must cause significant distress or disruption to qualify for the diagnosis.

Panic Disorder

People with phobias know when the anxiety is coming. However, there is often no identifiable cause for people with **panic disorder**: an anxiety disorder characterized by sudden, intense, unpredictable brief bursts of anxiety. In panic disorder, no object or situation sets off the fear reaction. And these episodes are called panic *attacks* for a reason: the reaction is unexpected and overwhelming, with powerful physical components (heart pounding, profuse sweating, gasping for air, dizziness) accompanying equally scary thoughts like "I'm having a heart attack!" or "I'm going to die!" (Craske & Barlow, 2008; Sewart & Craske, 2018).

If panic attacks happened to me, I'd become totally preoccupied about when the next attack might come.

That actually happens to many people with panic disorder. Sometimes, they become so concerned about the next panic attack they develop *agoraphobia*. A person with agoraphobia avoids situations from which escape might be difficult or impossible if they feel a panic attack coming on. This leaves people with agoraphobia essentially imprisoned at home, so scared of having a panic attack at the grocery store, the movie theater, a friend's house, or anywhere else that they don't venture out at all (Arch & Craske, 2008; Roest et al., 2019; Smits et al., 2006). Robert Rand, a dancer who wrote a book about his struggles with panic disorder, describes both the terrifying attacks (which landed him in the emergency room on at least one occasion) and the paralyzing agoraphobia that came along with it:

> The [panic attacks] . . . struck with increasingly terrible persistence. Day in and day out, for weeks at a time . . . the racing heart, the imploded mind, a feeling that surely I would faint or, even worse, would die — all this poked and jabbed at my mind. . . .

panic disorder
An anxiety disorder characterized by sudden, intense, unpredictable brief bursts of anxiety.

> My fear of panic attacks had become overwhelming. Anticipatory anxiety controlled every single aspect of my life. . . . Working, shopping, driving, socializing, even exercising – I gauged these activities by their potential to trigger uncontrollable, terrifying panic. There was much, very much, I didn't do for fear of bringing on attacks. (Rand, 2004, pp. 28–29, 33)

Many people with panic disorder also experience a hypersensitivity to small changes within their own bodies – slight increases in heart rate, light perspiration, a second or two of light-headedness, or a few heavy breaths. These sorts of bodily changes might happen to you if you climb a few flights of stairs or even stand up too quickly, but if you notice them at all, you can probably dismiss them easily. However, a person with panic disorder often misinterprets these sensations as early signs of an impending panic attack. Unfortunately, this misinterpretation often intensifies the anxiety, which in turn increases the physical sensations, which actually brings on a panic attack (Ohst & Tuschen-Caffier, 2018; Pollack et al., 2010).

Obsessive-Compulsive Disorder

Obsessive-compulsive disorder (OCD) is a disorder characterized by unwanted, repetitive thoughts and uncontrollable actions done in response to those thoughts. OCD can make the simple tasks of daily life remarkably difficult.

Such difficulties filled every day of high school for Jenny Traig, as she explained in her memoir:

> Head toward locker to retrieve calculus book. En route, accidentally brush against classmate. Pause. Is this classmate . . . unclean? What do you know about this classmate? . . . Head to girls' room to wash. . . . Wash hands for a count of one hundred and eighty Mississippi's. On the way out, accidentally touch the door handle. Go back inside and wash three minutes more. Proceed to locker. Realize you forgot paper towels you'll need to touch locker with. Return to girls' room. (Traig, 2004, pp. 221–222)

As Jenny's ordeal illustrates, OCD centers on the interaction of two things: obsessions and compulsions. Obsessions are thoughts – unwanted, intrusive, anxiety-provoking thoughts that seem to appear out of nowhere. Compulsions are actions – actions done with the intention of reducing the anxiety caused by the obsessions. It is a cycle: The obsession causes anxiety, and the compulsion reduces that anxiety. The problem is that the obsession occurs again, and again, and again, which makes the person feel the need to perform the compulsion again, and again, and again. A person with OCD can't stop the obsession from popping up, and then can't resist performing the compulsion that soothes the anxiety that the obsession caused (Abramowitz & Mahaffey, 2011; Blakey & Abramowitz, 2018; Eisen et al., 2010; Mathews, 2009).

Here's a more detailed description of the process of Jenny's OCD. She has a thought that involves a threat, such as "My hands have germs on them. I might get sick." That thought makes her feel anxious, and the only behavior that calms the anxiety is washing her hands at the sink. She washes her hands and feels better, but only temporarily. The next time that thought about germs on her hands occurs to her – which might be just a few minutes later – she will again feel the anxiety, and again feel the need to wash her hands to relieve the anxiety. If this pattern happens frequently, she may find her life – work, school, relationships, and everything else – continually interrupted.

Other common forms of OCD – checking to see if the door is locked, making sure the stove is turned off – follow similar patterns. An anxiety-provoking obsession ("I left the stove on and the house is going to burn down") is followed by a ritualized compulsion (checking the stove), with the pattern recurring many times. With less common versions of OCD, the link between obsession and compulsion can be a senseless but powerful superstition. In these cases, the compulsions can be strange. For example, some people with OCD believe that they can perform a ritual involving a certain pattern of tapping or

CHAPTER APP 14.1

The MindShift CBT app enables users to enter their anxiety symptoms and get help in the form of relaxation exercises, challenges to irrational thoughts, and actions that can provide immediate help. It helps users identify and overcome worry, phobias, panic disorder, social anxiety, and other anxiety-based experiences.

How does it APPly to your daily life?
In your opinion, to what extent can apps like this replace face-to-face help with anxiety that might otherwise come from family or friends? Or from a psychologist or another mental health professional?

How does it APPly to your understanding of psychology?
In your opinion, what distinguishes disordered anxiety – the kind that underlies *generalized anxiety disorder*, *specific phobia*, *social anxiety disorder*, *panic disorder*, and other anxiety disorders – from the kind of anxiety we all feel as part of day-to-day life?

To learn more about this app or to download it to your phone, you can search for "MindShift CBT" on Google, in the iPhone App store, or in the Google Play store.

obsessive-compulsive disorder (OCD) A disorder characterized by unwanted, repetitive thoughts and uncontrollable actions done in response to those thoughts.

touching to "undo" the anxiety caused by an obsessive thought. They might feel the need to tap a table, say, five times with each index finger. Or, the ritual might be entirely mental and undetectable by others, such as when a person with OCD silently counts to themselves in a particular way—perhaps, say, counting by fours to 100. When friends and family learn of these compulsive behaviors, the person with OCD can appear quite eccentric. Nonetheless, the person can't stop believing that those compulsions are the only option for undoing the anxiety caused by the recurring obsessions.

Who Gets Anxiety Disorders and Obsessive-Compulsive Disorder?

Lots of people develop anxiety disorders, especially in comparison to other types of psychological disorders (Remes et al., 2016). In fact, anxiety disorders are the single most common category of psychological disorders. In the U.S. population, 28.8% will experience some anxiety disorder at some point in their lifetime, and almost 18.1% will experience some anxiety disorder within any calendar year. Specific phobia and social anxiety disorder each occur at some point in the lives of more than 12% of people, which puts those disorders at the top of the list not only for anxiety disorders but for all psychological disorders (Kessler et al., 2005a, b, 2009).

Are certain people more likely than others to get anxiety disorders?

DIVERSITY MATTERS

Anxiety disorders happen to people of all ages, from young children to older adults (Ayers et al., 2009; Canuto et al., 2018; Essau et al., 2018; Moore et al., 2010; Rapee et al., 2009). Anxiety disorders occur two to three times more often in women and girls than in men and boys (Tolin et al., 2010). Interestingly, specific phobias follow that gender pattern only after the age of 10. Some experts have speculated that socialization may play a role in the development of specific phobias. They suggest that society allows boys and girls to experience fear equally when kids are young, but then encourages boys to behave more fearlessly than girls around the time kids reach age 10 (Emmelkamp & Wittchen, 2009; Woody & Nosen, 2009).

DIVERSITY MATTERS

Anxiety disorders happen across all ethnicities, both in the United States and around the world. In fact, the lifetime prevalence rates for anxiety disorders tend to hover around 25–30% in most countries, which is remarkably consistent with the rate for the U.S. population (Clark & Beck, 2010). In many cases, anxiety disorders look similar across cultures, but sometimes anxiety can take on unique forms. In many non-Western cultures, the experience of anxiety emphasizes physical discomfort rather than mental discomfort (Asmal & Stein, 2009). For example, GAD in Nigeria and some other African countries often involves the sensation that an insect is crawling inside the person's head or body (Stein & Williams, 2010). In Cambodia, panic attacks can feature neck pain and a sensation in the ears as if wind is shooting out (Good & Hinton, 2009; Hinton et al., 2009). Additionally, some specific phobias have emerged as common in certain parts of the world but remain rare or unheard of elsewhere. For example, in parts of Asia (including Thailand and China), many people have experienced *koro*, a sudden and intense fear that a part of the body (the penis in men, the vulva or nipples in women) will retract into the body and possibly cause death (Chiang, 2015; Dan et al., 2017; Greener, 2017).

Why Do Anxiety Disorders and Obsessive-Compulsive Disorder Develop?

Psychologists are still exploring the reasons behind anxiety disorders, but numerous factors have emerged. The most prominent are psychological factors and biological factors. Specific psychological factors that underlie anxiety disorders include illogical thoughts, learned reinforcements and punishments, the personality trait of neuroticism, and overprotective parenting/caregiving.

sanjagrujic/Getty Images

Illogical thoughts can contribute to anxiety disorders. For example, if a person illogically thinks that a harmless dog will viciously attack, that person is more likely to develop a specific phobia of dogs.

Illogical Thoughts. Illogical thoughts (also known as illogical or irrational cognitions) often take the form of if-then statements that are unlikely to be true and lead to unnecessary anxiety (Clark & Beck, 2010). For example, a person with a specific phobia might think: "If I go near a dog, the dog will definitely attack me." A person with a social anxiety disorder might think: "If I go to the party, there's a 100% chance that I'll humiliate myself." A person with OCD might think: "I know I just made sure the stove was off a minute ago, but if I don't check it again, then the house will burn down."

Learned Reinforcements and Punishments. In addition to illogical thoughts, learned reinforcements and punishments can also contribute to the development of anxiety disorders. Behavioral psychologists argue that people learn anxiety-related behaviors through experience, just like we learn any other behavior (Lissek et al., 2005; Lissek & Grillon, 2010). For example, consider Ali, who had a frightening experience on an elevator when they were young. Ali may choose to consistently avoid elevators in the future, and that avoidance feels reinforcing. As they repeat this behavior for months and years, they develop a specific phobia of elevators.

Neuroticism. Anxiety disorders can also be influenced by the personality trait of neuroticism (Merino et al., 2016; Pagura et al., 2009). Neuroticism, or the tendency to think and react negatively to the events that happen to us, is a personality trait that we all have to some degree. Individuals with high levels of neuroticism tend to remain so from childhood through the life span, and are more susceptible to developing anxiety disorders (Lawrence et al., 2009; Sauer-Zavala et al., 2017; Zinbarg et al., 2009). Consider, for example, a group of friends on their way to a softball game who hear on the radio a weather forecast calling for a slight chance of rain. Those with low or moderate levels of neuroticism might think, "It's probably not even going to happen," or "Maybe we'll get a little bit wet, or maybe we'll have to cut the game short — no big deal." But the friend high in neuroticism will react in a much more anxious way: "We could get hit by lightning! We could slip and fall and get seriously injured! The roads could flood, and we could end up stranded!"

Overprotective Parenting/Caregiving. Overprotective parenting/caregiving can also contribute to anxiety-related problems that arise in childhood and perhaps persist into adulthood (Howard et al., 2017; Hudson & Rapee, 2009; Lebowitz et al., 2016; Meyer et al., 2021). When parents/caregivers prevent or discourage their kids from experiencing any anxiety, they deny the kids the chance to realize how resilient they may be, and how much control they might have over a situation. Instead, the kids may get the message that even the smallest amount of anxiety can overwhelm them, which could lead to a lifetime of avoidance and fear. For example, 9-year-old Elbia expresses excitement about sleeping over at a friend's house for the first time tomorrow night. She also mentions that she might have a couple of moments of homesickness during the sleepover. If Elbia's parent/caregiver responds in an overprotective manner and denies Elbia the chance to go to the sleepover (especially if they do so repeatedly), they communicate to her that the homesickness might devastate her. In reality, being a little homesick may have been an experience that Elbia could have handled, which in turn might have helped her to grow. Considering the opposite of overprotection, one study found that parent/caregivers who challenge their kids to push their limits and do things that might initially cause a bit of anxiety have kids who develop fewer symptoms of anxiety (Majdandžić et al., 2018).

Genetic Factors. Biological factors that underlie anxiety disorders include genetics, brain differences, and evolution. The biological heritability of anxiety disorders

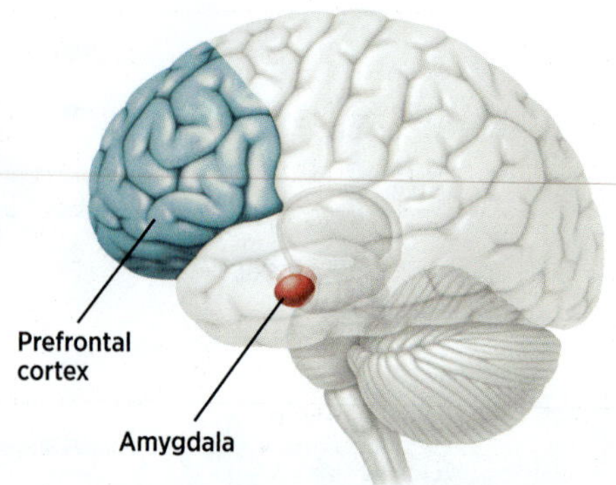

FIGURE 14.3 Anxiety Disorders and the Brain. In people with anxiety disorders, the amygdala is often overactive, and the prefrontal cortex is often underactive.

has been estimated at around 20–40%. This suggests that the likelihood of developing an anxiety disorder depends to a significant extent on the genes inherited from biological parents (Eley, 2009; Gelernter & Stein, 2009). It seems unlikely, however, that the genetic transmission is specific to a particular anxiety disorder. Instead, what gets passed on is a generally anxious disposition. This anxious disposition then reveals itself in any number of ways — maybe the same type of anxiety as a biological parent, but maybe a different type (Maron et al., 2008; Smoller et al., 2008). For example, a parent with panic disorder may pass along to their kids a broad tendency to be anxious rather than panic disorder specifically. If one of their kids develops an anxiety disorder, that disorder might be specific phobia or generalized anxiety disorder rather than panic disorder.

Brain Differences. Brain differences are also evident in many people with anxiety disorders. In fact, most of the anxiety disorders share the same physiological differences within the brain. Specifically, as **Figure 14.3** shows, researchers have found that in many people with anxiety disorders, the amygdala, a part of the brain that "sounds the alarm" when danger approaches, is overactive, and the prefrontal cortex, which often responds to the amygdala by signaling that all is well, is underactive (Britton & Rauch, 2009; Fischer & Tsai, 2009; Shackman & Fox, 2016). Additionally, certain neurochemicals tend to function in less than optimal ways in the brains of people with anxiety disorders. These neurochemicals include serotonin, dopamine, norepinephrine, and GABA. The particular problem with these neurochemicals is the subject of ongoing research (Bremmer & Charney, 2010; Malizia & Nutt, 2008).

Evolution. Evolution — in the natural selection, survival-of-the-fittest sense — is also widely recognized as a factor in the development of anxiety disorders (Bracha & Maser, 2008; Debiec & LeDoux, 2009; Nesse et al., 2019a). Our brains and bodies have evolved over the course of human history to predispose us to anxious responses. Think of it this way: If there ever were primitive tribes of humans who were *not* equipped with at least a little anxiety, they didn't survive. They weren't afraid of much, and as a result, they put themselves in more dangerous situations, which killed them off at a faster rate than people with at least a little anxiety. The anxious ones survived, and we are their descendants. The problem with anxiety arises when our evolved tendencies toward anxiety are exaggerated or applied at the wrong times. When that happens, we go into fight-or-flight mode unnecessarily.

For example, throughout human history it has been adaptive to experience intense anxiety when immediate danger emerges. In ancient times, the danger may have been a wild animal attacking or an enemy tribe approaching. Today, it might be a tornado siren wailing or car tires screeching. In any of these cases, people can actually benefit from the rush of adrenaline that intense anxiety brings: it gears them up to do battle or run away. However, when intense anxiety repeatedly occurs in the absence of any apparent threat, it can be disruptive rather than helpful.

Triple Vulnerability Theory. The best understanding of the cause of anxiety disorders would take both psychological and biological factors into account. A leading theory does exactly that. **Triple vulnerability theory** is an explanation for anxiety disorders that emphasizes the interaction of biological factors, general psychological factors, and specific psychological factors. According to David Barlow, the theory's primary author, the "recipe" for an anxiety disorder consists of three "ingredients": (1) a biological predisposition based on genes and brain differences; (2) a general perceived lack of control over life events that may be caused by parenting/caregiving styles or illogical thoughts; and (3) life experience that teaches the person which particular things or situations are specifically threatening. For example, if that third factor turns out to be dogs, a specific phobia to dogs may develop; or, if it turns out to be judgment by other people, social anxiety disorder may develop (Barlow, 2002; Barlow et al., 2007; Brown & Naragon-Gainey, 2013; Liverant et al., 2007; Sauer-Zavala & Barlow, 2021; Suarez et al., 2009).

triple vulnerability theory
An explanation for anxiety disorders that emphasizes the interaction of biological factors, general psychological factors, and specific psychological factors.

CHECK YOUR LEARNING:

14.12 What are anxiety disorders?

14.13 What is generalized anxiety disorder?

14.14 What is specific phobia?

14.15 What is social anxiety disorder?

14.16 What is panic disorder?

14.17 What is obsessive-compulsive disorder?

14.18 How common are anxiety disorders, and in which groups are they most frequently diagnosed?

14.19 Why do anxiety disorders and obsessive-compulsive disorder develop?

To check your understanding of these questions, click show the answers or refer to the answers in the Chapter Summary.

Depressive and Bipolar Disorders

YOU WILL LEARN:

14.20 what depressive and bipolar disorders are.

14.21 what major depressive disorder is.

14.22 what bipolar disorder is.

14.23 who gets depressive and bipolar disorders.

14.24 why depressive and bipolar disorders develop.

Depressive and bipolar disorders are the category of psychological disorders based on extreme moods or emotional states. Of course, some variation in mood is part of life for all of us. We experience good moods or bad moods every day, and we casually use terms like *sad*, *down*, or *blue* to describe our state of mind when things are not going well. There is a difference, however, between these common, passing struggles with mood and full-fledged depressive or bipolar disorders. For people with these disorders, the emotional experiences are so intense or long-lasting that they significantly disrupt daily life (Craighead et al., 2008; Klein et al., 2006). According to DSM, these disorders can occur in one of two specific ways: when a person becomes stuck at the low end of the mood range, where sadness prevails (as in *major depressive disorder* and *persistent depressive disorder* [*dysthymia*]), or when a person skips over the middle range of mood and alternates between the low end and the high end (as in *bipolar disorder* and *cyclothymic disorder*) (American Psychiatric Association, 2013).

Danny Evans was a young man with a wife, a baby, and a good job in advertising. He was living a happy, healthy life in Southern California – until he rather suddenly found himself experiencing a serious depressive episode. In his book (Evans, 2009, pp. 42–47), he captures depression's powerful impact:

> . . . the energy depletion that overcame me as I awoke that morning was far beyond anything I'd ever known. [The depression] must have tripped on an electrical cord that connected me to anything in life that gave me energy or optimism or pleasure. My mind felt physically heavy. I had an all-consuming sense of desolation, as though my soul was made of lead, but it also left me feeling empty. Vacant. It was as though I was dying from the inside out. . . .
>
> Only a few months earlier I was playing full-court basketball for forty minutes straight. I was fit. I was strong. . . . Yet there I was that morning, maybe a hundred days later, struggling just to get up. . . .
>
> . . . sadness duplicated itself so many times over that every fiber of my emotional fabric was occupied by this single sensation. My spirit was so heavy that the emotions one would normally summon to pull oneself out of depression – hope, enthusiasm, pride – had nowhere to go. They atrophied. They shriveled up and died. And that was sad, too.

depressive and bipolar disorders
The category of psychological disorders based on extreme moods or emotional states.

Stock Montage/Getty Images

Gary Gershoff/WireImage/Getty Images

Jim Spellman/Getty Images

Among well-known people who have struggled with depressive disorders or bipolar disorder are Abraham Lincoln (left), Kanye West (middle), and Kristen Bell (right).

Danny's experience vividly illustrates **major depressive disorder**: a psychological disorder in which a person experiences at least 2 weeks of depressed mood and a loss of interest in most activities. Major depressive disorder goes by many other names among mental health professionals and the general public: clinical depression, unipolar depression, or, simply, depression. Although major depressive disorder has many possible symptoms, its cornerstone is sadness — an unshakable, persistent, relentless sadness that pervades the person's life. In addition, activities that used to bring pleasure no longer do so. Weight changes are common, either because the person has little appetite or because they become unusually inactive while eating more than usual. Sleep is also frequently disrupted — sometimes more, sometimes less than usual. Energy levels, physical activity, and the ability to concentrate tend to dwindle, while feelings of worthlessness and thoughts of death often increase (American Psychiatric Association, 2013; Mondimore, 2006; Strunk & Sasso, 2017; Thase, 2006).

I feel sad sometimes. Pretty often, actually. And some of those other symptoms have happened to me too. Could I have major depressive disorder?

Perhaps, but keep in mind that the sadness that characterizes major depressive disorder is much more than common, everyday sadness. It is more forceful, resulting in genuine distress and real disruption in day-to-day life. Attending class, being productive at work, hanging out with friends, even getting out of bed can seem like insurmountable challenges to a person with major depressive disorder. Also, it is important to remember that for most of us, even intense feelings of sadness tend to last hours or days, far short of the 2-week duration that is required by the DSM definition of major depressive disorder. Having said that, if you do experience sadness or depression that is especially intense or long-lasting, seeking help from a mental health professional is a good idea.

Speaking of duration, DSM also includes a separate disorder that shares the same core of sadness as major depressive disorder, but it is much longer-lasting. **Persistent depressive disorder (dysthymia)** is a psychological disorder characterized by a chronic, relatively low-intensity depressed mood. The diagnosis of persistent depressive disorder requires the symptoms to be present for 2 *years* rather than 2 weeks. It is essentially a perpetual mild gloominess that can eclipse any memories of happier times (Klein & Black, 2017). Meri Nana-Ama Danquah, a poet, playwright,

major depressive disorder
A depressive disorder in which a person experiences at least 2 weeks of depressed mood and a loss of interest in most activities.

persistent depressive disorder (dysthymia)
A depressive disorder characterized by a chronic, relatively low-intensity depressed mood.

performance artist, and social activist, captures the essence of this disorder in her description of her own struggle:

> There are times when I feel like I've known depression longer than I've known myself. It has been with me since the beginning, I think. Long before I learned to spell my name. No, even longer than that. I'm sure that before I could even speak my own name or learn to love the color of my skin, this hollow heartache was following me, patiently awaiting the inevitable crossing of our paths, planning my future unhappiness . . . this terrible sickness . . . has cost me lovers and friendships, money and opportunities, time and more time. So much wasted time. (Danquah, 2002, pp. 174–175; see also Danquah, 1999)

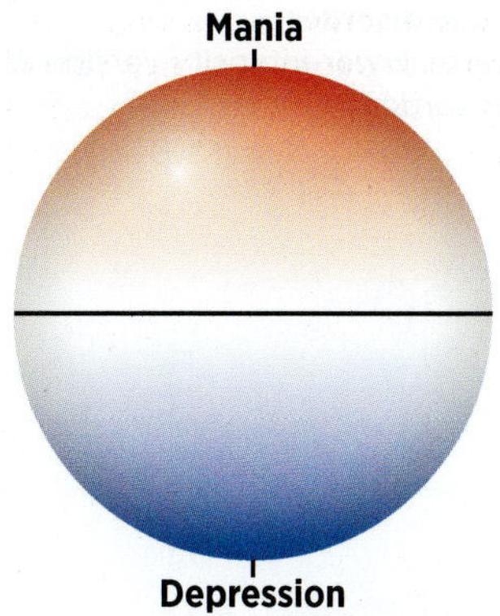

FIGURE 14.4 The Poles of Bipolar Disorder. People with bipolar disorder alternate between the poles of mood: the highs of mania and the lows of depression.

Bipolar Disorder

The term *bipolar* refers to the two poles of mood. Picture them as the North Pole of elation and the South Pole of sadness. We all experience mood swings, but most of us tend to stay pretty close to the equator in the middle most of the time. Some people, however, don't spend much time in the middle at all. These people may have **bipolar disorder** (formerly known as *manic depression*): a psychological disorder characterized by alternating between extremely high moods and extremely low moods. As **Figure 14.4** illustrates, their emotional state fluctuates back and forth from elation to sadness, and with little explanation or control over the shifts from one emotional extreme to the other (Otto & Applebaum, 2011; Strunk & Sasso, 2017).

You are already familiar with one of the poles of bipolar disorder — depression — from our discussion of major depressive disorder. (Remember that an alternate term for major depressive disorder is *unipolar* depression.) The other pole is **mania**, an emotional state of excessively elated mood and overabundant energy (Johnson et al., 2009; Miklowitz & Craighead, 2007; Miklowitz & Johnson, 2008). There are two variations of bipolar disorder, distinguished largely by the intensity and length of the mania experience. *Bipolar I disorder* features full-fledged manic episodes that last at least a week and cause significant impairment in daily functioning. In *bipolar II disorder*, the mania symptoms are typically briefer and less debilitating (and are called hypomanic episodes rather than manic episodes).

If mania is the opposite of depression, wouldn't mania be a good thing? I certainly like feeling elated and energetic.

Actually, people with bipolar disorder often find their manic episodes quite disturbing. In small doses and at appropriate times, periods of intense exhilaration can be great: imagine your reaction if you scratch off a winning lottery ticket, or land the job of your dreams, or score backstage passes to a concert by your favorite band. But mania can make a person feel out of control if the exhilaration doesn't have an identifiable reason behind it, or goes on far too long. During manic episodes, which can last for days on end, people can't seem to hit the brakes. They feel continuously full of energy, with little need for sleep. They are without inhibition, and may find themselves engaging in behaviors with harmful consequences, like indiscriminate talking, spending, working, substance use, or sex. If this uninhibited behavior goes on for a while, serious problems can arise. Consider the experience of Terri Cheney, a lawyer with bipolar disorder who wrote a book about her disorder in which she offers this first-hand description of a manic episode:

> The mania came at me in four-day spurts. Four days of not eating, not sleeping, barely sitting in place for more than a few minutes at a time. Four days of constant shopping . . . and four days of indiscriminate, nonstop talking: first to everyone I knew on the West Coast, then to anyone still awake on the East Coast, then to Santa Fe itself, whoever would listen. . . . Mostly, however, I talked to men. Canyon Road has a number of extremely lively, extremely friendly bars and clubs. . . . It wasn't hard for a redhead with a ready smile and a feverish glow in her eyes to strike up a conversation and then continue that conversation well into the early-morning hours, at his place or mine. (Cheney, 2009, pp. 6–7)

bipolar disorder
A psychological disorder characterized by alternating between extremely high moods and extremely low moods.

mania
An emotional state of excessively elated mood and overabundant energy.

cyclothymic disorder
A long-term, lower-intensity version of bipolar disorder.

Many people with bipolar symptoms experience extreme manic episodes like Terri, but some people describe milder episodes. In these milder cases, the ongoing up-and-down mood cycle can still interfere with daily life in significant ways, particularly when the ups and downs continue for a prolonged period. DSM has a different diagnostic label for this experience: **cyclothymic disorder**, a long-term, lower-intensity version of bipolar disorder. Essentially, cyclothymic disorder is to bipolar disorder what persistent depressive disorder is to major depressive disorder — the same core symptoms, but less intense and longer lasting. A person with cyclothymic disorder alternates between emotional ups that aren't quite manic and emotional downs that aren't quite depressive for 2 years or more (DeRubeis et al., 2016; Ketter & Wang, 2010; Newman, 2006; Stewart et al., 2006; Van Meter et al., 2018).

In serious cases, the despair brought on by bipolar disorder or depressive disorders can drive people to contemplate or commit acts of self-harm. The most serious concern, of course, is suicide. Compared to the general public, people with major depressive disorder are 20 times more likely to die by suicide. For people with bipolar disorder, the ratio is even higher (Michaels et al., 2017; Newman, 2006; Osby et al., 2001; Swartz, 2007). Thankfully, in spite of these statistics, the majority of people who struggle with depressive and bipolar disorders don't attempt to take their own lives. (If you or someone you know is in crisis, you can call the National Suicide Prevention Lifeline at 1-800-273-8255, or contact the Crisis Text Line by texting HELLO to 741741.)

CHAPTER APP 14.2

 Moodtrack Diary

The Moodtrack Diary app allows users to input information about their mood. They can enter this information as often as they want, in the form of both a numeric rating and a verbal description. The app provides charts and other kinds of feedback to show how mood changes over the course of days, weeks, or months.

How does it APPly to your daily life? How could this be helpful to people with or without psychological disorders? How could this be helpful to psychologists seeing clients with depressive disorders or bipolar disorder?

How does it APPly to your understanding of psychology? How does this app affect your appreciation of the difficulty in drawing the line between people with and without psychological disorders? For example, how low would a person's mood need to be, and for how long, before that person should be considered to have major depressive disorder (as opposed to just feeling blue or down)?

To learn more about this app or to download it to your phone, you can search for "Moodtrack Diary" on Google, in the iPhone App store, or in the Google Play store.

Who Gets Depressive and Bipolar Disorders?

Depressive and bipolar disorders are remarkably common. In fact, only anxiety disorders are more widespread. Among Americans, 20.8% have been diagnosed with a depressive or bipolar disorder at some point in their lives, and 9.5% have been diagnosed in the last year (Kessler et al., 2008). As **Figure 14.5** shows, these disorders take a tremendous toll: including treatment costs, lost productivity at work, and other expenses, the price tag for major depressive disorder and bipolar disorder in the United States alone is approximately $100 billion annually (Wang & Kessler, 2006). Dollars are not the only costs: people with depressive and bipolar disorders suffer through higher rates of marital conflict, divorce, and job loss than the general public (Constantino et al., 2006; Kessler & Wang, 2009; Murray & Lopez, 1996; Newman, 2006; Thase, 2006).

Within the depressive disorders and bipolar disorders categories, specific disorders occur at different rates. For example, major depressive disorder is far more common than bipolar disorder. Major depressive disorder has a lifetime prevalence rate of 17% and a 1-year prevalence rate of 6.6%. For bipolar disorder, those numbers are just 3.9% and 2.6%, respectively (Kessler et al., 2005a, b, 2008; Kessler & Wang, 2009). Major depressive disorder is about twice as common in women as in men, but bipolar disorder is diagnosed with about equal frequency across the sexes (Goodwin et al., 2006; Hatzenbuehler & McLaughlin, 2017; Kornstein & Sloan, 2006). As with phobias, the sex difference in rates of major depressive disorder occurs only after the age of about 12 or 13. Experts have offered many possible explanations for that finding, including biological differences that emerge at puberty, socialization that encourages women to express sadness but encourages men to hide it, and greater pressure on women to take on multiple responsibilities (Hankin et al., 2008; Hyde & Mezulis, 2020; Lara, 2008; Nolen-Hoeksema & Hilt, 2009).

Some experts argue that the high rate of major depressive disorder relates to the fact that the line between its DSM definition and ordinary, everyday sadness can be blurry. Specifically, they argue that depressive symptoms that appear in situations where such symptoms are expected, like after the death of a loved one or a similar major stressor, should be considered an expected (but unfortunate) experience rather than a psychological disorder. These experts also point out that people who experience this version of depression that comes after a recognizable cause — "uncomplicated" depression, as they call it — may be more likely to recover on their own without treatment than people whose depression doesn't have such a recognizable cause.

(Horwitz, 2015, 2017; Horwitz et al., 2017; Horwitz & Wakefield, 2007; Wakefield & Demazeux, 2016; Wakefield et al., 2017).

DIVERSITY MATTERS

Some version of major depressive disorder happens in every society around the world. However, the way people experience it can vary greatly (Ryder et al., 2017). Generally, non-Western cultures tend to experience depression as more physical than psychological, just as they do anxiety disorders. In some African countries, depression is sometimes expressed as a sensation of heat in the head; in Iran, as a heavy heart or tightness in the chest; and in India, as a sinking feeling (Kirmayer & Jarvis, 2006). Additionally, non-Western cultures may not view the experience of sadness as a sign of disorder; in fact, in Japan, sadness is often viewed as an important part of human experience that produces self-understanding and gives meaning to life (Watters, 2010). Depression is experienced and defined in different ways around the world, which might explain why it occurs at different rates in different places: relatively low in Japan, China, and Nigeria, but relatively high in the Netherlands, the United Kingdom, and Chile (Ustun & Sartorius, 1995).

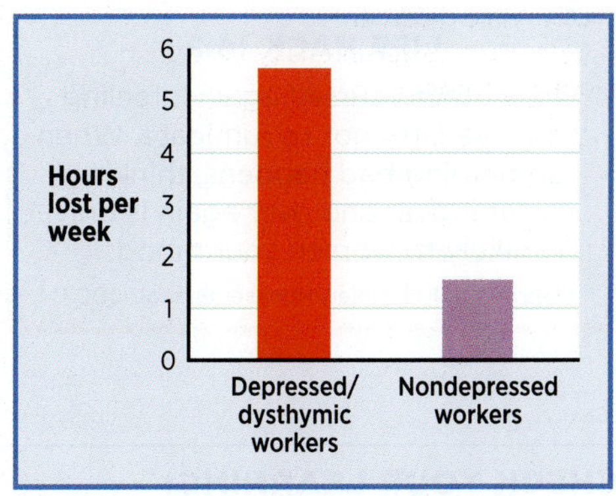

FIGURE 14.5 The Costs of Depression and Persistent Depressive Disorder (Dysthymia) at Work. Researchers found that U.S. workers with major depressive disorder or persistent depressive disorder (dysthymia) experience over three times as many hours of lost production (either absent, or present but not fully productive) as their peers (Stewart et al., 2003).

Why Do Depressive and Bipolar Disorders Develop?

Like anxiety disorders, depressive and bipolar disorders can develop for a variety of reasons. Research suggests that both biological factors and psychological factors play a role.

The biological factors that underlie these disorders include genetics, brain differences, and neurochemicals. In terms of genetics, bipolar disorder appears to be one of the most heritable psychological disorders, and major depressive disorder is not far behind (Berrettini & Lohoff, 2017; Miklowitz & Johnson, 2008). Brain differences are also present in both major depressive disorder and bipolar disorder, especially in the parts of the brain that process emotions, including the hippocampus, amygdala, and prefrontal cortex. So, when people with one of these disorders experience an unfortunate event, their brains may generate more intensely negative emotions than the brains of those without such disorders.

The focus on biological factors underlying depressive and bipolar disorders often takes the form of the *chemical imbalance* theory, which states that the levels of certain brain chemicals are awry in people with these disorders. The chemical imbalance theory has been promoted by pharmaceutical companies and is quite popular, but many experts who study and treat depression and bipolar disorders have reservations about how completely or accurately it explains these disorders (Read et al., 2020). So, levels of serotonin, norepinephrine, and dopamine may play some role in major depressive disorder and bipolar disorder; however, they are certainly not the sole cause, and their exact role remains under investigation (Delgado & Moreno, 2006; Hammen & Watkins, 2008; Johnson et al., 2009; Lacasse & Leo, 2015). Additionally, studies have found that people with depression and bipolar disorder who believe strongly in the chemical imbalance theory tend to have relatively low expectations for improvement and relatively high rates of ongoing symptoms after treatment has ended (Salem et al., 2019; Schroder et al., 2020).

An especially prominent psychological factor behind depressive and bipolar disorders is the presence of illogical thoughts, especially pessimistic and cynical thoughts. For people with depressive disorders, illogical thinking stems from a *depressive schema*, which is a mental framework that biases a person toward viewing the environment in a negative way (Alloy et al., 2017; Beck, 1976; Beck et al., 1979; Joorman, 2009). A depressive schema can darken the experience of life like sunglasses that never come off. They cause a person to believe that they are worthless, unlikable, or a failure, and that the world around them is exclusively gloomy, even if those beliefs are actually false (Beck, 1976; McBride et al., 2007). For people who struggle with depression, negative thoughts tend to stick around once they get in. People with major depressive disorder tend to *ruminate*, or think about their perceived shortcomings or the stressors they face over and over again, unable to let

LIFE HACK 14.2

To protect yourself against feeling depressed, try not to ruminate. When something bad happens, thinking about it over and over again is only likely to worsen your mood.

(Beevers, 2005; Nolen-Hoeksema et al., 2007)

them go, which further worsens their mood (Beevers, 2005; Nolen-Hoeksema et al., 2007). For example, one study of over one thousand college students conducted in the early months of the COVID pandemic found a strong positive correlation between rumination about the pandemic and depressive symptoms (Ye et al., 2020). Also, the personality trait of neuroticism can play a role in the development of depressive and bipolar disorders, just as it does in anxiety disorders (Barlow et al., 2021; Fournier & Tang, 2017).

CHECK YOUR LEARNING:

14.20 What are depressive and bipolar disorders?

14.21 What is major depressive disorder?

14.22 What is bipolar disorder?

14.23 How common are depressive and bipolar disorders, and in which groups are they most frequently diagnosed?

14.24 Why do depressive and bipolar disorders develop?

To check your understanding of these questions, click show the answers or refer to the answers in the Chapter Summary.

Eating Disorders

YOU WILL LEARN:

14.25 what eating disorders are.

14.26 what anorexia nervosa is.

14.27 what bulimia nervosa is.

14.28 what binge eating disorder is.

14.29 who gets eating disorders.

14.30 why eating disorders develop.

Food is central to human survival, and the drive to obtain it is one of our most primal instincts. But there is also psychological and social meaning attached to food that can derail even this most fundamental drive. Food means weight, and weight can have powerful consequences, especially in American culture. For some people, weight and body image translate into attractiveness and self-worth. These people are especially vulnerable to **eating disorders**: the category of psychological disorders that involve significant disturbances in behaviors related to eating or food.

Eating disorders, like other psychological disorders, range in severity. In some cases, they become so severe that the person with the eating disorder must stay for days, weeks, or months in a hospital. There, mental health professionals work with physicians and dieticians toward the primary goal of ensuring that the person takes in enough calories to stay alive and healthy. Let's examine the three most common eating disorders: anorexia nervosa, bulimia nervosa, and binge eating disorder.

Anorexia Nervosa

Anorexia nervosa (often called simply **anorexia**) is an eating disorder based on a refusal to eat enough food to maintain a minimally healthy body weight, based on the person's height and age. This refusal to eat usually starts with a distorted view of one's own body as fat. Additionally, people with anorexia typically base their entire self-image on their physical appearance, with thinness at the top of the list of desirable qualities. People with anorexia can be shockingly thin — sometimes to the point that they risk starving themselves to death — but refuse to eat adequately because they wrongly see themselves as overweight (Keel & McCormick, 2010; Steiger & Bruce, 2009; Stice et al., 2016; Sysko & Alavi, 2018).

Lisa Himmel wrote a book in which she tells the story of her fight against anorexia. In this excerpt, Lisa describes going out to lunch with her mom during her senior year of high school. Notice the inflexibility in her thinking about food and her strategy for tricking her mom into thinking she ate more than she did:

> They had plenty of suitable menu items: fresh soups, large salads, and fancy sandwiches. But I freaked out. Nothing appealed to me — or rather nothing fit in the strictures of my rigid diet plan.

eating disorders
The category of psychological disorders that involve significant disturbances in behaviors related to eating or food.

anorexia nervosa
An eating disorder based on a refusal to eat enough food to maintain a minimally healthy body weight, based on the person's height and age.

> I know she just wanted to have a pleasant lunch with her daughter. But I stared at the menu board overhead, while she carefully made suggestions, and I said, "No! That will make me fat, Mom!" She read out one option after the other, and I rejected everything. I wanted to give up, and let my hunger wallow in my tiny stomach, but I could tell I was acting like a child. I settled on a grilled vegetable sandwich on wheat bread, which I broke apart around the edges. The sandwich was fine, but I left most of it on the plate. . . .
>
> As I got older I began to stray from family dinners and my formerly adventurous appetite. My weight dropped and I seemed to become more noticeable to those who before had never or rarely acknowledged my presence. Words like "fit" and "thin" joined in their compliments of my body . . . receiving praise about my body was better than a fancy restaurant meal. Even when praise turned into worry as I lost more weight, I only heard "skinny" or "thin" . . . and I had to keep going. (Himmel & Himmel, 2009, pp. 116–117)

Peter Dazeley/Getty Images

People with anorexia have a distorted view of their own bodies as fatter than they really are, and often place a very high importance on their own body image. As a result, they refuse to eat enough to maintain a minimally healthy body weight.

Anorexia sounds like a psychological disorder that can have some serious physical consequences. Can it?

It definitely can. There are many dangerous consequences for the body when there is prolonged malnutrition from anorexia: irregular heart rate, chest pain, hypothermia, hair loss, dry skin, bone density loss, and constipation, among others (Cass et al., 2020). It is also common for women with anorexia to stop having menstrual periods (Katzman et al., 2010; Mitchell & Crow, 2010). Unfortunately, anorexia proves to be fatal in about 5% of cases — among the highest rates of mortality of any mental disorder — whether due directly to self-starvation or due indirectly to medical complications (Chesney et al., 2014; Chidiac, 2019; Keel, 2010).

Bulimia Nervosa and Binge Eating Disorder

Bulimia nervosa (often called simply **bulimia**) is an eating disorder in which an individual exhibits a pattern of overeating followed by drastic attempts to prevent weight gain. Decades ago, bulimia was considered a variation of anorexia, but now experts recognize it as a distinct disorder (Dell'Osso et al., 2016; Russell, 1979). People with bulimia are overly concerned about their weight, but find themselves trapped in a pattern of bingeing and purging (rather than flatly refusing food, as people with anorexia do). They overeat (binge) and then try to "undo" that overeating by quickly subtracting those calories from their bodies (purge). The overeating episode feels out of control and involves eating far more than others would eat in the same situation, at least once per week for 3 months. Often, the foods that people with bulimia choose to binge on are high-calorie sweets, like cakes, cookies, or ice cream. Also, people with bulimia often feel quite embarrassed by their binges and prefer to binge when they are alone or can hide the evidence (wrappers, packages, etc.). The most common form of purging is self-induced vomiting, but other forms include excessive exercise, misuse of laxatives or other medications, and temporary fasting (Stice et al., 2016; Sysko & Alavi, 2018; Sysko & Wilson, 2011).

People with bulimia are not necessarily underweight. As a result, people with bulimia may keep their symptoms undetected for longer periods of time than extremely thin people with anorexia. Frank Bruni, a journalist with *The New York Times*, wrote a book about his struggles with disordered eating and his desire to hide bulimic symptoms from friends and family. This passage is about a dinner at a restaurant with friends while he was a freshman at college:

> I'd eaten too much. . . . No way was I going to let all of that linger in my stomach. The bathroom at Sadlack's was for one person only, and it locked, so I had the privacy I needed. I ran the water from the sink to camouflage any sound I might make. I got to work immediately. I kept getting speedier and speedier at this.

bulimia nervosa
An eating disorder in which an individual exhibits a pattern of overeating followed by drastic attempts to prevent weight gain.

binge eating disorder
An eating disorder with the overeating pattern of bulimia but without the purging.

> Within forty-five seconds the sandwich was gone. I flushed the toilet, then went to the sink and scooped some cold water into my mouth to rinse it. I splashed some water on my face. I studied myself in the mirror. I needed to wait a bit longer before returning to the booth. I was still too red.
>
> After a minute, I made a fresh appraisal: pink now. Much better. Almost there.
>
> Thirty seconds later, I was good to go. My eyes were still watery, and faintly bloodshot. But how much of a giveaway, really, was that? Eyes could look the way mine did for any number of reasons. (Bruni, 2009, pp. 94, 98)

The physical toll of bulimia is severe. Not only can people with bulimia experience any of the medical problems associated with anorexia, but they may also experience problems tied to the specific way they purge. For example, a person with bulimia who forces themselves to vomit on a regular basis can do serious damage to their body, including dental problems, chronic sore throat, heartburn, fluid retention, and swelling of the glands involved in salivation and vomiting (Mehler et al., 2010). And abusing laxatives can cause a person with bulimia to develop diseases of the colon (Gibson et al., 2021).

Binge eating disorder is an eating disorder with the overeating pattern of bulimia but without the purging. Binge eating disorder is an appropriate diagnosis for people who binge on food at least once a week for 3 months but do not engage in calorie-subtracting behaviors like self-induced vomiting, overexercising, using laxatives, or fasting. Like people with bulimia, people with binge eating disorder feel a lack of control over their eating, and often choose to binge alone to avoid embarrassment. Binge eating disorder has been informally recognized by clinicians for many years, often as a variation of bulimia, but it became an official disorder of its own with the release of DSM-5 in 2013 (Fairburn et al., 2000; Hudson et al., 2012; Kessler et al., 2013; Stice et al., 2016; Sysko & Alavi, 2018).

Who Gets Eating Disorders?

Eating disorders typically develop around the middle school, high school, or young adult years. They are about 10 times more common in women and girls than in men and boys (Gordon, 2000; Keel, 2010). Eating disorders are relatively rare. In the United States, the combined rate for all three eating disorders is less than 2% of the population, with anorexia less common than bulimia and binge eating disorder (Agras, 2010; Crow & Brandenburg, 2010; Erskine & Whiteford, 2018; Kessler et al., 2013).

There is no doubt that Western cultural influences such as the glorification of thin women in the popular media push some people, especially girls and young women, toward eating disorders, but versions of eating disorders have been found elsewhere in the world (Keel, 2010). In some cases, the rise of eating disorders in a particular location happened right after people there gained access to Western media. There is actually quite a list of countries — Ukraine, Belize, South Korea, South Africa, and others — in which eating disorders quickly jumped from almost nonexistent to prevalent as soon as the country was exposed to U.S. pop culture (Levine & Smolak, 2010). Consider this example: The island nation of Fiji (in the South Pacific, east of Australia) — where full-figured women were traditionally viewed as symbols of beauty — had virtually no eating disorders until 1995. That year, U.S. and British television, with exceedingly thin women prominently featured, reached the island. Within a few years, 74% of teenage girls in Fiji reported that they viewed themselves as too fat, and 15% reported that they had intentionally vomited to lose weight (Becker et al., 2002).

testing/Shutterstock

In Fiji, eating disorders such as anorexia and bulimia were essentially nonexistent until its residents were able to watch American television. Soon after, some girls and women started evaluating their bodies in more negative ways, and there was a rise in eating disorders (Becker et al., 2002).

Why Do Eating Disorders Develop?

The development of eating disorders involves biological, psychological, and social factors. A small amount of research, including twin studies, points to biological factors, such as heritability (Bulik et al., 2006; Klump et al., 2001; Wade, 2010). There is also a small body of evidence from neuropsychological research suggesting that people with eating disorders may have disturbances in the regions of the brain responsible for taste and reward processing (Kaye & Oberndorfer, 2010).

Psychological factors that play a role in the development of eating disorders include a tendency toward perfectionism, especially among people with anorexia (Norris et al., 2019). This perfectionism often translates into an all-or-none attitude toward one's weight: either perfectly thin or unacceptably fat, with no in-between. In this way, the idea that "you can never be too thin," which is all too widely accepted in the United States, can become a dangerous obsession (Ghandour et al., 2018; Jacobi & Fittig, 2010; Vogele & Gibson, 2010). Among people with bulimia and binge eating disorder, impulsiveness is typically a more important risk factor than perfectionism. Acting on impulses can result in bingeing, and those binges, for some people, can lead to purging (Couturier & Lock, 2006; Oliva et al., 2019).

By far, social and cultural influences (such as those related to Western media) have received the most attention as possible causes of eating disorders. Our TV shows, films, and magazines can convince some people, especially girls and women, that thinness equals beauty. A never-ending parade of slender models and movie stars, combined with harsh criticism of those who gain a few pounds, encourages some people to pursue thinness at all costs (Brown & Tiggemann, 2021; Grabe et al., 2008; Levine & Murmen, 2009). In past decades, numerous studies found a strong correspondence between how often girls and young women read magazines that feature extremely thin women and their dissatisfaction with their own bodies, which can lead to an eating disorder (Field et al., 1999a, b; Groesz et al., 2002; van den Berg et al., 2007). More recently this type of research has extended to social media, with largely similar results: girls and women (along with a smaller number of boys and men) who spend a lot of time comparing themselves to photos of people whose bodies they find thin and attractive are at higher risk of developing eating disorders (Holland & Tiggemann, 2016; Saunders & Eaton, 2018; Sidani et al., 2016). Check out the From Research to Real Life box for a more detailed discussion of this topic.

All of the girls and women I know watch TV, see movies, and read magazines, but only a small number of them develop eating disorder symptoms. Why does the media affect some people differently than others?

The media message that thinness equals beauty is especially toxic when it is combined with another belief: beauty is everything. For people whose self-concept is built around the way their bodies look — not their intelligence, or abilities, or relationships, or anything else — the quest to lose weight can become life's primary goal.

DIVERSITY MATTERS

This belief that beauty is everything can come from a variety of sources. For example, researchers have found that girls whose parents/caregivers overemphasize their daughters' physical appearance and criticize their weight are much more likely to develop eating disorders than girls whose parents/caregivers do not (Davison et al., 2000; de León-Vázquez et al., 2018; Field et al., 2005; Rienecke, 2018). Also, girls whose mothers or friends serve as role models for eating disorders are at an increased risk (Eisenberg et al., 2005; Stice, 2002). Culture plays a powerful role too: American women from ethnicities in which body dissatisfaction rates are relatively low, such as Black women, tend to have low rates of eating disorders. By contrast, White women tend to have among the highest rates of both body image dissatisfaction and eating disorders (Field & Kitos, 2010; Roberts et al., 2006).

FROM RESEARCH TO REAL LIFE

How Powerful Is Social Media in the Development of Eating Disorders?

Researchers have published many studies about the impact that the media can have on the development of eating disorders. For many years, they focused on traditional media like magazines, TV, and movies (e.g., van den Berg et al., 2007). More recently, researchers have focused on social media, with largely similar results: social media tends to involve a lot of upward comparisons (comparing yourself with others you find more attractive, and often more thin or fit), which produces a higher rate of eating disorders (Cohen et al., 2017; Holland & Tiggemann, 2017; Marks et al., 2020).

For example, in one study of first-year college women, researchers sent participants a text at five random times per day over a 5-day period. Each text prompted them to click a link to a brief survey in which they reported the kinds of "appearance comparisons" they had been making and how they made them feel. Upward comparisons were much more common than lateral comparisons (to equally attractive people) or downward comparisons (to less attractive people). In addition, upward comparisons correlated with lower satisfaction about the participants' own appearance and increased thoughts about diet and exercise, both of which are strong predictors of eating disorders. Importantly, these results were more significant when the upward comparisons were made on social media than on traditional media or in person (Fardouly et al., 2017). In a similar study, researchers found that the number of upward comparisons on Snapchat, Instagram, and Facebook correlated positively with eating disorder symptoms, including bingeing, purging, excessive exercise, and body dissatisfaction (Saunders & Eaton, 2018).

Another study of over 1700 young adults divided them into four groups based on how much time they spend on social media. Results showed that compared to people who spent the least time on social media, people who spent the most time on social media had more than twice the rate of eating concerns. Those eating concerns include losing control over how much they eat; being told by a family member, friend, or professional that their eating patterns are concerning; feeling like food dominates their life; and their weight negatively affecting the way they feel about themselves (Sidani et al., 2016).

A review of 20 articles on this subject found strong overall evidence for an association between social media usage, especially involving photos, and disordered eating (Holland & Tiggemann, 2016). Collectively, this growing collection of studies strongly suggests that social media now has the impact on the likelihood of developing eating disorders that magazines, TV, and movies have long had, perhaps in an even more powerful way. •

CHECK YOUR LEARNING:

14.25 What are eating disorders?

14.26 What is anorexia nervosa?

14.27 What is bulimia nervosa?

14.28 What is binge eating disorder?

14.29 How common are eating disorders, and in which groups are they most frequently diagnosed?

14.30 Why do eating disorders develop?

To check your understanding of these questions, click show the answers or refer to the answers in the Chapter Summary.

Schizophrenia

YOU WILL LEARN:

14.31 what schizophrenia is.

14.32 about the differences between positive, negative, and cognitive symptoms of schizophrenia.

14.33 who gets schizophrenia.

14.34 why schizophrenia develops.

Schizophrenia is a severe psychological disorder in which the person exhibits bizarre disturbances in thinking, perception, feelings, and behavior.

Wait—isn't schizophrenia the disorder in which the person has multiple personalities?

No—that's a common belief, but it's wrong (Duckworth et al., 2003). (*Dissociative identity disorder*, which we'll discuss later in this chapter, comes closest to that description.) An accurate description of a person with schizophrenia centers on the fact that they have a take on reality that is blatantly, sometimes wildly, unrealistic. This obvious break from reality differs from the slight distortions of reality common in other disorders. It is more extreme than in the person with a phobia who overestimates the danger of a friendly dog or the person with major depressive disorder who

schizophrenia
A severe psychological disorder in which the person exhibits bizarre disturbances in thinking, perception, feelings, and behavior.

distorts a good job interview into a disaster. To describe this blatantly unrealistic way of perceiving the world, psychologists use the word **psychosis**: a significant impairment in the basic ability to tell the difference between the real world and imagination. As a result, people with schizophrenia often seem to have created their own personal world. They see things others don't see, hear things others don't hear, think things others don't think, and believe things others don't believe. In short, people with schizophrenia often don't live in the same reality as those around them (Lieberman et al., 2006; Mueser & Duva, 2011; Mueser & Roe, 2016).

Consider Elyn Saks, a law professor at the University of Southern California who has schizophrenia. She wrote a book in which she describes the experience of living with schizophrenia, including this striking passage in which she is a law school student at the library working on an assignment with her classmates. Notice how her grip on reality appears to slip, and how her speech and actions reveal an illogical and bizarre thought process:

> "I don't know if you're having the same experience of words jumping around the pages as I am," I say. "I think someone's infiltrated my copies of the cases. We've got to case the joint. I don't believe in joints. But they do hold your body together." I glance up from my papers to see my two colleagues staring at me. "I . . . I have to go," says one. "Me, too," says the other. . . .
>
> Later, Elyn finds herself in her professor's office, discussing the assignment:
>
> "The memo materials have been infiltrated," I tell him. "They're jumping around. I used to be good at the broad jump, because I'm tall. I fall. People put things in and then say it's my fault. I used to be God, but I got demoted." I begin to sing my little Florida juice jingle, twirling around his office, my arms thrust out like bird wings. (Saks, 2007, pp. 1–3)

Elyn's episodes illustrate just some of the more obvious symptoms of schizophrenia, including seeing things that aren't really there, believing in ideas that are bizarre and untrue, and thinking that jumps from one topic to another without obvious connections. The many symptoms of schizophrenia can be divided into three types: *positive symptoms, negative symptoms,* and *cognitive symptoms* (Lewis & Buchanan, 2007).

Positive Symptoms of Schizophrenia

Positive symptoms of schizophrenia are experiences that are present or excessive in people with schizophrenia but largely absent in people without it. (Think of "positive" as "plus" here – something added beyond the typical range of experiences that most people have.) Positive symptoms are the most visible signs of schizophrenia, especially *delusions* and *hallucinations*.

Delusions. **Delusions** are completely false beliefs that a person with schizophrenia believes to be reality. It doesn't matter that no one else among the person's family, friends, or cultural group holds those beliefs, or that they seem magical or peculiar to others, or that they defy logic. In spite of all of this, the person with schizophrenia accepts these beliefs as completely legitimate, often without questioning them at all. For example, one man with schizophrenia believed that the streetlights (and presumably the people who control them) were communicating directly with him, threatening him as he drove under them. When his family members tried to convince him otherwise, he not only refused to believe them, but suspected that they were in on the streetlights' plot (McLean, 2003).

Certain types of delusions can be especially prominent in certain cases of schizophrenia (Lindenmayer & Khan, 2006; Vahia & Cohen, 2008). For example, those with *delusions of persecution* believe that others are out to get them. ("My neighbors are all spying on me, conspiring to steal everything I own.") Those with *delusions of grandeur* believe that they have superhuman powers, or that they are a famous person

psychosis
A significant impairment in the basic ability to tell the difference between the real world and imagination.

positive symptoms
Experiences that are present or excessive in people with schizophrenia but largely absent in people without it.

delusions
Completely false beliefs that a person with schizophrenia believes to be reality.

such as a past president or a religious icon. ("I am George Washington, and I will start a new country.") And those with *delusions of reference* believe that random events have personal meaning specifically intended for them. ("A bluebird just flew by — that must be a warning for me not to leave the house.")

Hallucinations. **Hallucinations** are false sensations or perceptions. Hallucinations are sounds, images, scents, or other physical sensations that the person with schizophrenia experiences even though those sensations do not exist in reality (Castle & Buckley, 2008; Guillin et al., 2007).

The most common type of hallucination is auditory, often described as "voices." Hearing voices is quite different from the common experience of a train of thought or even a two-sided argument going back and forth within your mind. Instead, during an auditory hallucination, the person with schizophrenia hears the voice as entirely separate and distinct. The voice is like another person talking to them, but the person with schizophrenia can't recognize that the voice is in fact coming from within their own head. They have a hard time dismissing what these voices say, and often respond to them aloud, which can strike observers as odd or disturbing.

For example, I once worked in a psychiatric hospital with Janet, a patient with schizophrenia who repeatedly heard a voice telling her that her "insides" were dirty, so she should drink liquid soap to cleanse herself. Any attempt to convince Janet not to listen to the voice was hopeless. To Janet, that voice was as real, powerful, and believable as any. I vividly recall one quiet evening when the patients were in the lounge watching TV, only to be suddenly interrupted by Janet. "No! I just drank soap this morning! I don't need to drink more tonight!" she shouted out of the blue. She paused for a few seconds, apparently listening. "I said NO!" Another pause. Finally, she gave in. "Fine — I'll drink some, if it will shut you up." Defeated by the voice inside her head, she stomped in the direction of the soap dispensers in the restroom, only to be intercepted by staff members.

Visual hallucinations involve seeing something that isn't actually there. No one else sees it, yet the person with schizophrenia sees it, accepts it as real, and interacts with it accordingly. In the same psychiatric hospital where I worked with Janet, another patient, Miguel, had frequent visual hallucinations. For a while, he "saw" holes spontaneously open up in solid walls. On more than one occasion, he repeatedly tried to reach his hand through the hole he "saw," only to grow increasingly frustrated and confused as it proved impossible. When hospital staff asked him what he was doing, Miguel was quite surprised that the holes were not obvious to them too. Another patient, Tony, often "saw" cats come into the room, when in fact there were no cats in the hospital at all. It was quite clear when Tony had one of his cat hallucinations, because he also happened to be allergic to cats: he would suddenly jump back in fright or scurry from the room in response to something that no one else could see.

Beyond auditory and visual hallucinations, there are less common types of hallucination as well. These include olfactory hallucinations (involving false smells) and tactile hallucinations (involving false feelings of an object touching one's body). In one example of an olfactory illusion, a person with schizophrenia detected a foul body odor on himself — which no one else could smell — so often that he felt the need to take six showers a day (O'Neal, 1984). As an example of a tactile illusion, another patient with whom I worked in the psychiatric hospital often experienced the feeling of bugs crawling up and down his arm, when there were in fact never any bugs at all.

Negative Symptoms of Schizophrenia

Negative symptoms of schizophrenia are behaviors that are lacking in people with schizophrenia, but that are usually present in people without the disorder. (Think of "negative" as "minus" here — something missing from the experience of a person with schizophrenia that most people have.) In general, negative symptoms don't draw as

hallucinations
False sensations or perceptions.

negative symptoms
Behaviors that are lacking in people with schizophrenia, but that are usually present in people without the disorder.

flat affect
The absence of appropriate emotion.

cognitive symptoms
The disturbed, illogical ways that people with schizophrenia think.

much attention as positive symptoms, but their impact on day-to-day functioning can be quite strong. Usually, negative symptoms involve a withdrawal from life's activities, especially interpersonal interaction and emotional involvement. People with schizophrenia often find themselves disengaged, not only from others, but from their own emotions as well.

One specific negative symptom of schizophrenia is **flat affect**, the absence of appropriate emotion. For example, a person with schizophrenia may be the only one who doesn't laugh during a funny movie or cry at a funeral. Instead, this person may stare vacantly, expressing no emotion through words or facial expressions. When people with schizophrenia do express emotion, it can be way off-base. For example, they might be angry at a drinking fountain, surprised by a flower, or joyful about a tornado.

People with schizophrenia also exhibit some negative symptoms involving an absence of certain social behaviors. They may display *alogia*, an almost complete absence of speaking. They may also demonstrate *avolition*, a lack of initiative to take even the smallest action. Or, they may find themselves exhibiting *anhedonia*, an inability to experience happiness even when in the most joyful situations. Together, these negative symptoms can strongly hinder social interactions for people with schizophrenia (Andia et al., 1995; Nisenson et al., 2001). (Imagine the difficulties you might have when trying to have a friendship, or in some cases just a conversation, with a person who displays all of these symptoms.) These negative social impairments are often the first signs of schizophrenia, appearing long before the more obvious positive symptoms like hallucinations and delusions (Hollis, 2003).

In a fascinating study illustrating the early appearance of social impairment in schizophrenia, researchers obtained the childhood family home movies of people who went on to develop schizophrenia as adults. Of course, these family home movies included footage of not only the person who developed schizophrenia, but many other family members as well. Then, the researchers showed these movies to viewers who did not know which member of the family developed schizophrenia. The viewers guessed, with remarkable accuracy, which family member it was. When the researchers asked them how they knew, the viewers cited many negative symptoms, including lack of positive emotion, lack of social responsiveness, and other lacking interpersonal behaviors (Walker & Lewine, 1990).

When people with schizophrenia create art, their works often suggest the unusual perceptions and thought patterns that characterize the symptoms of the disorder. For example, consider this self-portrait by Bryan Charnley. He explains the inclusion of a second "mouth" covering his forehead by suggesting that his brain was sending messages to others in a way that he could not control: "My mind seemed to be thought broadcasting very severely and it was beyond my will to do anything about it. I summed this up by painting my brain as an enormous mouth, acting independently of me" (Charnley, 1991).

Cognitive Symptoms of Schizophrenia

Cognitive symptoms of schizophrenia involve the disturbed, illogical ways that people with schizophrenia think. The behavior and speech of people with schizophrenia often seem blatantly disorganized and disordered to others (Keefe & Eesley, 2006). For example, people with schizophrenia often display loose associations, thoughts that proceed with little apparent logical connection from one to the next. People with schizophrenia may jump nonsensically from a casual comment about last night's basketball game to a harsh criticism of their neighbors to a list of their favorite foods. If there is an identifiable reason for jumping from one sentence to the next, it may be the sounds of the words rather than their meaning. Some psychologists use *derailment* as a synonym for loose associations, a word that offers a visual image of a train (of thought) going off the tracks.

Sometimes, the speech or writing of someone with schizophrenia is so jumbled that even a single sentence is baffling, a phenomenon known as *word salad*. For example, a person exhibiting word salad might say something like this: "This pillow empowers the rejection of every word of those who fall behind. The difference? The streets order blue pencils for the animals." At other times, the speech of a person with schizophrenia may be sprinkled with *neologisms*, entirely new words of their own creation (Minzenberg et al., 2008; Noll, 2007). Loose associations, word salad, and neologisms are all on display in this excerpt from the writings of Pamela Spiro Wagner, an award-winning poet who developed schizophrenia:

> I am seeking truth and seeing it, which is Holy See-ing, a sacred pun, meaning I'd been given a nod of approval from the Vatican, the Vat-I-Can. I can see that I am at sea, that I will get Cs in all my classes, the gentlewoman's Cs, for good attendance and sitting for every test, though I am no Ladybird Johnson, I don't wear white gloves or send invitations for tea. I don't garden or beautify America's highways. But there is the matter of the piano's high C and canned orange juice drink, and high seas and . . . seven seas and . . . seize the day and. . . . Eat drink be merry for tomorrow we die, and . . . konk [*sic*] out. (Wagner & Spiro, 2005, pp. 104–105)

Schizophrenia sounds like it can be a pretty devastating disorder. How can a person with schizophrenia function in the real world with such serious symptoms?

Schizophrenia – which typically arises in late adolescence or early adulthood and can endure for years or even a lifetime – is an especially incapacitating psychological disorder in its severe form(Charlson et al., 2018; Hafner & an der Heiden, 2008; Kopelowicz et al., 2007; Mueser & Jeste, 2008). In many cases, people with schizophrenia don't function well in the real world. Some are so impaired that they must spend time – often long periods – in mental institutions. Some can live independently in the community, but they might struggle to hold jobs, maintain relationships, or take basic care of themselves (Hooley, 2009; Nordstroem et al., 2017).

There is some reason for optimism regarding the treatment of schizophrenia, however. Antipsychotic medication provides significant improvement for some (especially regarding positive symptoms). In some cases, people with schizophrenia can lead self-sufficient and productive lives. In fact, the movie *A Beautiful Mind* (which won the Academy Award for Best Picture in 2002) tells the true story of John Nash, a man with schizophrenia who earned a doctoral degree at Princeton, got married, and became a Nobel Prize–winning mathematician and economist.

Everett Collection, Inc./Alamy

The award-winning 2002 film *A Beautiful Mind* tells the story of John Nash, a mathematician with schizophrenia who won a Nobel Prize.

Who Gets Schizophrenia?

Schizophrenia is not a common psychological disorder. It occurs in around 1% of individuals, a finding that has been rather consistent across countries and cultures (Cornblatt et al., 2009; Mueser et al., 2006; Wu et al., 2018). Schizophrenia is about equally common across genders, but far more common and long-lasting in urban areas than nonurban areas (Conde et al., 2017; Eaton & Chen, 2006; Jongsma & Jones, 2018; Saha et al., 2005). In fact, the bigger the city, the greater the likelihood of schizophrenia (Colodro-Conde et al., 2018; Van Os et al., 2001, 2003). The reasons for this finding about population density are unclear, and researchers continue to explore a variety of possibilities, including higher rates of environmental toxins in big cities, social pressures and exclusion, infectious diseases (including those that pregnant women may experience that could affect the fetus), and migration of people with schizophrenia to big cities, among others (Pedersen, 2015; Plana-Ripoll et al., 2018; Selten et al., 2016; van Os et al., 2010).

One interesting theory focuses on the work role, and how it differs between urban and rural areas. Specifically, when people in a rural area or developing country suffer from schizophrenia, there is a good chance they can still work in some capacity, primarily because of employers' willingness to adjust responsibilities to match abilities. (That willingness may be associated with the likelihood that the person with schizophrenia has some social connection to the employer, or with the employer's difficulty in finding someone else to do the work, due to the small size of the community.) By contrast, in a big city, people suffering from schizophrenia may be more likely to simply get fired and replaced. The resulting unemployment, possible homelessness, and other stressors may increase the likelihood of ongoing schizophrenia in a way that doesn't happen in less urban areas (Warner, 2004).

DIVERSITY MATTERS There has been some debate about the schizophrenia rates of various ethnic groups in the United States. Specifically, Black people in America have a greater risk of a schizophrenia diagnosis — in some studies, four times greater — than White Americans (Barnes, 2004; Blow et al., 2004; Chen et al., 2021). However, some research suggests that the schizophrenia diagnoses of Black Americans have historically been mistaken, with mental health professionals overestimating the severity of symptoms or failing to follow diagnostic criteria (Lawson, 2008).

Why Does Schizophrenia Develop?

Thousands of studies have explored possible causes of schizophrenia. Collectively, they point to two main conclusions: (1) there are many causes of schizophrenia, and (2) the most prominent causes are biological (Mueser & Roe, 2016).

We know that schizophrenia has biological roots because of a couple of different types of research — research on genetics and research on the brain itself. Genetic studies typically examine psychiatric records of people who are related to each other in some way to calculate the odds that a particular person will develop schizophrenia. The primary findings of these studies? An adopted child who develops schizophrenia is far more likely to have biological parents with schizophrenia than to have adoptive parents with schizophrenia (Kendler & Diehl, 1993). This finding strongly suggests that genes contribute to schizophrenia.

Another way researchers have examined the genetics of schizophrenia is through twin studies. Basically, twin studies center on the fact that monozygotic (identical) twins are much more genetically similar than dizygotic (fraternal) twins. Twin studies consistently find that the odds of a person developing schizophrenia are much higher if their monozygotic twin has the disorder than if their dizygotic twin has the disorder. This finding actually extends to other relatives too, as illustrated in **Figure 14.6**. Basically, the more genes a person shares with someone with

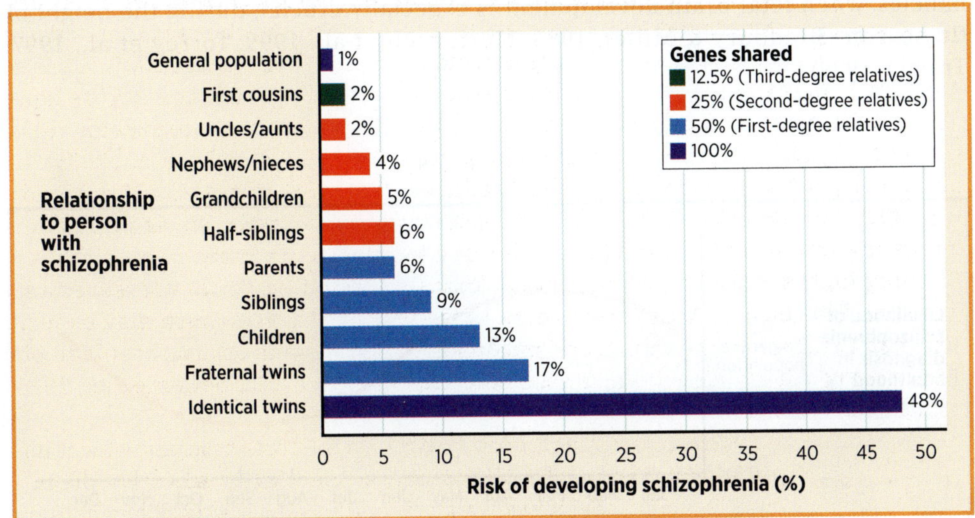

FIGURE 14.6 Shared Genes and Schizophrenia. The odds that a person will develop schizophrenia increase significantly with the percentage of genes that person shares with someone else who has schizophrenia. Data from Gottesman (2001).

schizophrenia, the greater the odds that they also will develop the disorder (Cardno & Gottesman, 2000; Gottesman, 1991).

A second type of research that highlights biological causes of schizophrenia focuses on the physical brain itself. Brain studies involving magnetic resonance imaging (MRI), functional MRI (fMRI), and other imaging technologies have consistently found some structural differences between the brains of people with schizophrenia and the brains of people without it. For example, the ventricles — basically, fluid-filled spaces within the brain — tend to be larger in the brains of people with schizophrenia than in people without it. A few other areas, including the hippocampus, amygdala, thalamus, and whole brain, are slightly smaller in people with schizophrenia than in people without it (Eyler, 2008; Schmajuk, 2001; Stewart & Davis, 2008).

Researchers have also found that there are unusual amounts of certain neurochemicals in the brains of people with schizophrenia. One neurochemical that has received a lot of attention in studies of this type is dopamine, but its exact role is still being determined. Through the 1970s and 1980s, research suggested that excess dopamine caused schizophrenia (Baumeister & Francis, 2002; Javitt & Laruelle, 2006). Later, that theory was revised to state that too much dopamine in certain (subcortical) regions of the brain caused positive symptoms of schizophrenia, while too little dopamine in other (prefrontal cortex) regions of the brain caused negative symptoms (Downar & Kapur, 2008; Guillin et al., 2007). Still, this revised dopamine theory cannot explain why some people with schizophrenia experience no change in symptoms when they take medication that changes their dopamine level (Noll, 2007).

Biological causes are not entirely responsible for schizophrenia (Mueser et al., 2013). Certain patterns of interaction in families also contribute to the disorder. This is true especially when family members are overinvolved in each other's lives and openly hostile toward each other. Researchers often call this pattern of interaction *expressed emotion*, and it seems to be a factor in the relapse of people with schizophrenia. When a person hospitalized with schizophrenia returns home, they are 2.5 times more likely to relapse if the family shows high levels of expressed emotion than if the family shows low levels of expressed emotion (Bebbington & Kuipers, 2008; Butzlaff & Hooley, 1998).

Other factors that play a role in the development of schizophrenia occur even before the person is born. Children of pregnant women who are malnourished or have a viral infection are at increased risk of eventually developing schizophrenia (Brown et al., 2004; Susser & Opler, 2006). Interestingly, as **Figure 14.7** shows, the birthdays of people with schizophrenia fall disproportionately in winter and early spring. This means their mothers went through months 4–6 of their pregnancies, when fetal brain development is especially crucial, during the height of flu season (Bradbury & Miller, 1985; Mortensen et al., 1999; Torrey et al., 1997; Tramer, 1929).

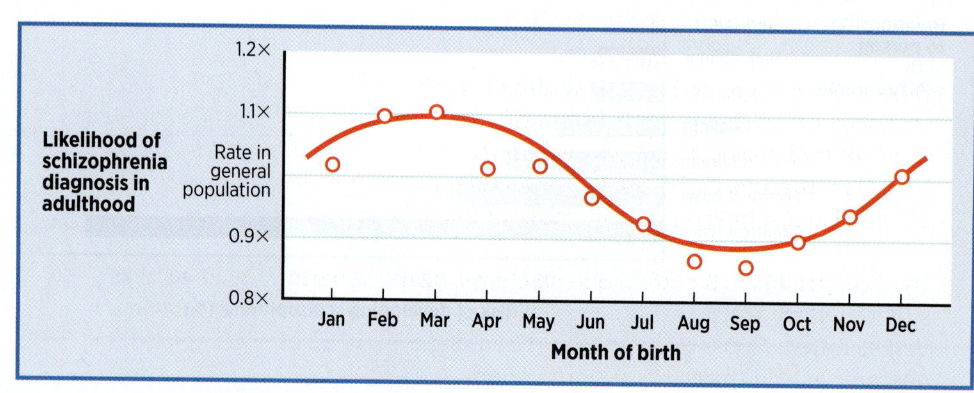

FIGURE 14.7 Birthdays of People with Schizophrenia. The month in which a person is born influences the risk of developing schizophrenia, with spring births at the highest risk. The underlying reason may be the increased risk of flu in expectant mothers during the middle months of pregnancy. Data from Mortensen et al. (1999).

CHECK YOUR LEARNING:

14.31 What is schizophrenia?

14.32 What is the difference between the positive, negative, and cognitive symptoms of schizophrenia?

14.33 How common is schizophrenia, and in which groups is it most frequently diagnosed?

14.34 Why does schizophrenia develop?

To check your understanding of these questions, click show the answers or refer to the answers in the Chapter Summary.

Disorders of Childhood

YOU WILL LEARN:

14.35 what disorders of childhood are.

14.36 what attention-deficit/hyperactivity disorder (ADHD) is.

14.37 what autism spectrum disorder is.

14.38 who gets disorders of childhood.

14.39 why disorders of childhood develop.

Many psychological disorders can occur in children, but there are some that emerge during childhood by definition. In the current DSM, these disorders fall in the category of *neurodevelopmental disorders*. These disorders include school-related problems such as specific learning disorders (formerly called learning disabilities) and developmental delays such as intellectual disability (formerly called mental retardation). Let's focus on two other well-known disorders in this category: *attention-deficit/hyperactivity disorder* (ADHD) and *autism spectrum disorder*.

Attention-Deficit/Hyperactivity Disorder

Attention-deficit/hyperactivity disorder (ADHD) is a disorder emerging in childhood that features significant problems with attention, hyperactivity/impulsivity, or both. Symptoms must be present before the age of 12 (even if the diagnosis comes later) and must occur in at least two settings, such as school and home. For some people with ADHD, the main problem is inattention: they are easily distracted or sidetracked, struggle to listen effectively, forget things easily, and make careless mistakes. For other people with ADHD, the main problem is hyperactivity or impulsivity: they have trouble staying seated or still, waiting their turn, and preventing themselves from interrupting others' words or actions (American Psychiatric Association, 2013; Roberts et al., 2015).

attention-deficit/hyperactivity disorder (ADHD)
A disorder emerging in childhood that features significant problems with attention, hyperactivity/impulsivity, or both.

For many kids with ADHD, the core symptoms of the disorder often lead to additional problems (Beauchaine & Hayden, 2016). For example, ADHD symptoms can cause problems in relationships with important people: teachers who want students to pay attention and follow rules, parents/caregivers who expect kids to display patience and self-control, and other kids who prefer to become friends with peers who wait their turn and use appropriate social skills. Turbulent relationships can in turn increase the likelihood of anxiety, depression, and rule-breaking behavior (Pliszka, 2015). Given the nature of the symptoms, academic struggles are understandably common in kids with ADHD, and rates of substance abuse are high as well (Kent et al., 2011; Pfiffner & Haack, 2015).

Katherine Ellison, a Pulitzer Prize–winning journalist, wrote a book about raising a son with ADHD. Here, she describes some of her son's struggles, beginning with core symptoms of inattentiveness but eventually expanding into interpersonal difficulties common in kids with ADHD (Ellison, 2010, pp. 7–8):

> Buzz was an eager, successful student right up until second grade. . . . It was then that he started forgetting to write down his assignments, or to do them, or to get them back to school. He lost permission slips, field trip forms, bulletins, thermoses, notebooks, sweaters, coats, and lunch boxes. Worst of all: he also lost every single member of his former pack of friends.
>
> By sixth grade . . . he refused to do chores or his homework, and wouldn't stop pinching and punching [his brother] Max. Our conflicts escalated. Bribes failed; "consequences" backfired. Sent to his room, Buzz roared obscenities and threw shoes at the door.

Samir Hussein/Getty Images

Actor Channing Tatum received an ADHD diagnosis as a child.

By contrast to Buzz's inattentive version of ADHD, consider this firsthand account of a more hyperactive/impulsive version. It was written by Blake Taylor as he neared the end of high school and looked back on his childhood with ADHD. (Taylor has since graduated from the University of California–Berkeley and medical school at Columbia University.) In this recollection of a day when he was 8 years old, notice his inability to put the brakes on his own behavior at dinnertime, even when his caregiver insists (Taylor, 2007, pp. 7–8):

> I am building a section of a robot on the family room floor. It is dinnertime, and Gloria, our babysitter, calls from the kitchen.
>
> "Blakey, come back and sit down and eat. . . . You are eight years old. It is time to behave. . . ."
>
> I return to the table for one bite. . . . I chew it, then get up and leave the dinner table again.
>
> "Blake! Come and eat [your] dinner!" Gloria commands this time.
>
> "I don't want to," I whine. I am thinking, "I don't want to sit down, and I have better things to do." I reluctantly return for another bite. . . .
>
> [My food] is getting cold on its plate — it has been on the dinner table for an hour — and I have been continually leaving the table to play with my K'nex and Legos on the family room floor.
>
> Finally . . . with the help of Gloria . . . I am actually able to sit still long enough to finish dinner.

What happens to kids with ADHD when they grow up?

For many years, the assumption was that kids commonly grow out of ADHD. Research strongly suggests that such an outcome is, unfortunately, not so common (Resnick, 2005). Many adults who struggled with ADHD as kids continue to struggle well into adulthood (Barbaresi et al., 2018; Kessler et al., 2006). When the disorder persists into adulthood, it correlates with many of the same problems that correlate with childhood ADHD, including anxiety, depression, and substance abuse (Molina et al., 2018; Uchida et al., 2015). It also correlates with some uniquely adult problems: adults with ADHD lose jobs, experience marital problems, engage in partner violence, struggle financially, and experience unplanned pregnancies at unusually high rates (Eakin et al., 2004; Kuriyan et al., 2013; Owens et al., 2017; Owens & Hinshaw, 2019; Pelham et al., 2020; Wymbs et al., 2012).

Autism Spectrum Disorder

Autism spectrum disorder is a disorder emerging in childhood that features significant social interaction deficits and rigid, repetitive patterns of behavior. Autism spectrum disorder was introduced in DSM-5 as a combination of several disorders that were listed separately in previous editions of DSM, including autistic disorder and Asperger's disorder. The inclusion of the word *spectrum* in the name of the disorder reflects the fact that its severity can vary greatly from one child to another. (It is also the root of the informal term *on the spectrum*, often used to describe people with this diagnosis.) Symptoms of autism spectrum disorder typically appear before the child turns 2 years old (American Psychiatric Association, 2013; Matson et al., 2013).

autism spectrum disorder
A disorder emerging in childhood that features significant social interaction deficits and rigid, repetitive patterns of behavior.

The social struggles of kids with autism spectrum disorder span a wide range. Sometimes, they show little or no interest in approaching others to begin an interaction, or don't respond receptively when others approach them. When interactions do happen, the conversation sometimes lacks a natural back-and-forth or any real sharing of interests or emotions. Nonverbal cues are often impaired too, with minimal eye contact, facial expression, or body language.

In terms of rigid, repetitive patterns of behavior, some kids with autism make the same physical movements over and over again – for example, spinning in a circle, flapping their hands, or opening and closing a door. In rare cases, the rigid, repetitive behavior can be dangerous – for example, a child slapping themself or hitting their head against a wall. This preference for rigid, repetitive behavior often extends to routines that involve the child and other people. For example, kids with autism spectrum disorder may react with extreme displeasure if they have to ride in an unfamiliar car or eat meals at an unusual time or place. When they reach adulthood, some people with autism spectrum disorder do live independent lives, while others continue to require help and support.

Who Gets Disorders of Childhood?

DIVERSITY MATTERS

When researchers conduct surveys to determine how many kids actually qualify for the ADHD diagnosis according to DSM criteria, the results consistently show a rate of about 5–7%. However, the actual rate of kids receiving the diagnosis in the community is much higher – around 11–15% overall (Polanczyk et al., 2007, 2014; Schwarz, 2016; Wilcutt, 2012). The rate is even higher in certain populations, including boys, those with lower socioeconomic status, kids who speak English as their first language, kids in single-parent/caregiver families, and kids in the South and Midwest regions of the United States (Bloom et al., 2013; Owens et al., 2015; Visser et al., 2014). The reason for this discrepancy between the smaller number of kids who *should* get the diagnosis and the larger number of kids who *do* get the diagnosis is not entirely clear. It may relate to the fact that parents/caregivers, teachers, and kids are familiar with the diagnosis, so when they seek help from a professional, "Is it ADHD?" may be the question that guides the conversation. Also, despite the need for a thorough evaluation, too often pediatricians or other health professionals diagnose ADHD after a brief visit including just a few questions about the child's behavior (Hinshaw & Ellison, 2016; Hinshaw & Scheffler, 2014).

DIVERSITY MATTERS

Autism spectrum disorder affects about 1–2% of kids, with about five times as many boys as girls receiving the diagnosis (Centers for Disease Control and Prevention, 2014). The rate is relatively consistent throughout most countries in the world (Baxter et al., 2015). Autism spectrum disorder rates are significantly higher now than they were decades ago, a finding that may be attributed to a number of factors, including increased awareness of the disorder, changes in the way it is defined, and changes in the way it is assessed (Dawson, 2013; Hansen et al., 2015).

Why Do Disorders of Childhood Develop?

The factors behind both ADHD and autism spectrum disorders remain the focus of extensive research. For ADHD, it's clear that there is no single cause. Genes are likely a powerful factor, as are brain differences (especially in parts of the brain involved in inhibition, like the frontal lobe), low birth weight, and prenatal exposure to toxins such as lead and nicotine (Beauchaine & Hayden, 2016; Cortese et al., 2012; Thapar et al., 2013). Environmental factors such as excessive video game use, excessive TV watching, and abusive parenting/caregiving styles can worsen ADHD in kids who already have it, but do not cause the disorder in otherwise healthy kids (Barkley, 2015). Factors such as these combine to create a brain that struggles to focus, plan, and give thought to impulses before acting on them (Barkley, 1997; Hinshaw & Ellison, 2016).

Genes seem to play a significant role in the development of autism spectrum disorder, especially genes related to the development of brain regions that influence social interaction (Dawson, 2008; Lichtenstein et al., 2010). Prenatal problems (including the mother's use of certain drugs) and childbirth complications also increase the risk. Certain members of the popular media have promoted theories that autism spectrum disorder can be caused by vaccines, but extensive research debunks this claim (Donovan & Zucker, 2016; Hupp & Jewell, 2015; Knopf, 2017, 2021; Madsen et al., 2002).

CHECK YOUR LEARNING:

14.35 What are disorders of childhood?

14.36 What is ADHD?

14.37 What is autism spectrum disorder?

14.38 How common are ADHD and autism spectrum disorder, and in which groups are they most frequently diagnosed?

14.39 Why do ADHD and autism spectrum disorder develop?

To check your understanding of these questions, click show the answers or refer to the answers in the Chapter Summary.

Dissociative Disorders

YOU WILL LEARN:

14.40 what dissociative disorders are.

14.41 what dissociative identity disorder is.

14.42 what dissociative amnesia and dissociative fugue are.

14.43 who gets dissociative disorders.

14.44 why dissociative disorders develop.

Dissociative disorders are the category of psychological disorders in which the person loses awareness of, or becomes disconnected from, essential parts of the self such as memories, emotions, or identity. When people dissociate in this way, they lose touch with some component of their own mental processes to such an extent that their day-to-day lives are significantly impacted. Their minds become fragmented rather than integrated, with certain facets seemingly split off from others (American Psychiatric Association, 2013; Pole et al., 2016; van der Hart & Nijenhuis, 2009).

Dissociative Identity Disorder

The most widely known and sensational dissociative disorder is **dissociative identity disorder** (or DID), in which a person exhibits two or more distinct personalities. (You may know of it by its former name, *multiple personality disorder*.) Instead of having a single coherent "self," a person with DID has two or more selves that are not integrated. These are entirely separate selves that seemingly share nothing other than the body in which they are located. These personalities typically alternate, with only one operating at a time. The shifts from one personality to the next are often sudden and unpredictable, and the contrast between personalities is often striking. When any particular personality is in control, the person can find it difficult or impossible to remember any details, or even the existence, of the other personalities. Most people with DID also experience a more general memory impairment for events that took place before the onset of DID (Lilienfeld & Lynn, 2003). For example, some have no recollection of long periods of their childhood.

A particularly well-publicized case of DID is that of "Sybil," a client whose real name was Shirley A. Mason. In the early 1970s, her case was the subject of a bestselling book and TV movie that brought this psychological condition to the awareness of the general public. Sybil had 16 personalities (or *alters*, as they are often called), including a whiny toddler, two devious young boys, two girls in elementary school, and a sad older woman. Her various personalities were so fractured that each was unaware of what the others did. For example, when Sybil looked in her closet, she often found clothes that she didn't remember buying and didn't even like because she had purchased them while a different personality was in control. She also struggled to do arithmetic at times, because the personality that was present when she learned to do arithmetic didn't share that ability with the others (Nathan, 2011; Schreiber, 1973).

dissociative disorders
The category of psychological disorders in which the person loses awareness of, or becomes disconnected from, essential parts of the self such as memories, emotions, or identity.

dissociative identity disorder
A psychological disorder in which a person exhibits two or more distinct personalities.

Dissociative Amnesia

Dissociative amnesia occurs when a person becomes unable to recall important information from their past. Essentially, they blank out regarding a particular period of their lives. In most cases, dissociative amnesia represents a gap in an otherwise intact memory, and almost always, the gap includes something horrific that happened to (or perhaps was done by) the person with the disorder. As an example, a person involved in a terrible car wreck may be unable to recall anything from the day of the wreck. Or, a person who violently attacks a loved one may have no recollection of the episode (American Psychiatric Association, 2013).

Now imagine a case of dissociative amnesia that is accompanied by unplanned and unexplained travel to a new location. That is a *dissociative fugue*. You may have heard occasional stories of dissociative fugues on the news, involving people who turn up in a random, unfamiliar location and can't explain to the locals who they are or offer any other personal details. A captivating 2009 case involved Hannah Emily Upp, a 23-year-old middle school teacher who went for a jog in one section of New York on August 28 and was found swimming in a harbor in a completely different part of the city on September 16 — with no memories at all of what happened between. Security cameras at Apple computer stores, Starbucks coffee shops, and several gyms showed that Hannah had visited those places, but she had no recollection of those visits. As she put it, "It was like 10 minutes had passed, but it was almost three weeks" (Marx & Didziulis, 2009). More recent articles about Hannah reveal that she may have experienced additional dissociative fugues since that time (Aviv, 2018; Barcella, 2021; Marx, 2017).

Nicole Bengiveno/The New York Times/Redux

Hannah Upp is a New York schoolteacher who experienced a dissociative fugue.

Who Gets Dissociative Disorders?

Dissociative disorders are extremely rare, with estimates of their frequency typically falling no higher than about 1% of the population (Johnson et al., 2006). There was a surge of reports of DID in the 1970s and 1980s, but current researchers believe that verifiable cases of the disorder are exceedingly scarce. In fact, some experts have argued that DID may not even be a valid disorder at all, or that it's a variation of borderline personality disorder (which we cover later in this chapter), or that it's posttraumatic stress disorder (PTSD, which we covered in Chapter 11) (Arrigo & Pezdek, 1998; Clary et al., 1984; Korzekwa et al., 2009; Lauer et al., 1993; Şar et al., 2017; Wilkinson & DeJong, 2021). Some of these experts also suggest that many patients who report multiple personalities are actually responding to a mental health professional's encouragement to do so. A mental health professional who is motivated to have a client with such a fascinating disorder might ask leading questions to persuade a client that they have multiple personalities, even if multiple personalities are not part of the client's original reason for seeking therapy (McHugh, 1995). (Of course, such behavior by a psychotherapist would be considered unethical and unprofessional.)

In fact, Sybil's therapist, Dr. Cornelia Wilbur, has been criticized for asking Sybil questions that might have led Sybil to believe in the idea that she had multiple personalities. Dr. Wilbur also recommended that Sybil read a book about multiple personality disorder — perhaps another nudge toward persuading her to believe that she might have the disorder herself (Nathan, 2011). In response to such criticisms of the DID diagnosis, other experts continue to argue that the diagnosis is legitimate and that the criticisms are largely based on myths (Brand et al., 2016; Reinders & Veltman, 2021). The controversy over the status of this phenomenon continues today.

Why Do Dissociative Disorders Develop?

When dissociative disorders occur, the people receiving the diagnosis almost always have personal histories featuring severe abuse or trauma. In the case of DID, the abuse or trauma often happened during childhood, in some cases decades before the emergence of the dissociative symptoms. With dissociative amnesia, the abuse or trauma is often a recent event, such as an assault, act of war, or natural disaster (American Psychiatric Association, 2013). In any of these cases, the person's coping skills seem to

dissociative amnesia
A psychological disorder in which a person becomes unable to recall important information from their past.

be overwhelmed by the horrific things they experienced. As a result, they disconnect from their own identities, either by forgetting themselves or reinventing themselves as a collection of other people because they can't function as the person they originally were (Gleaves et al., 2001; Ross, 1997).

CHECK YOUR LEARNING:

14.40 What are dissociative disorders?

14.41 What is dissociative identity disorder?

14.42 What are dissociative amnesia and dissociative fugue?

14.43 How common are dissociative disorders?

14.44 Why do dissociative disorders develop?

To check your understanding of these questions, click show the answers or refer to the answers in the Chapter Summary.

Personality Disorders

YOU WILL LEARN:

14.45 what personality disorders are.

14.46 what borderline personality disorder is.

14.47 what antisocial personality disorder is.

14.48 who gets personality disorders.

14.49 why personality disorders develop.

As we discussed in Chapter 12, your personality is your unique, longstanding way of behaving, thinking, and feeling. In some people, these longstanding characteristics are the very qualities that are disordered. According to DSM, these people have **personality disorders**: the category of psychological disorders based on an enduring pattern of inflexible and maladaptive behavior that appears across a wide range of situations and interferes with interpersonal interaction (Levy & Johnson, 2016; Millon, 2004; South et al., 2011; Sperry, 2016; Widiger & Lowe, 2010).

People with personality disorders can be frustrating or exasperating to friends, family members, and coworkers. They often have trouble getting along with others because their personality traits are so rigid. People with personality disorders lack the ability to vary their typical perception and reaction to the world, no matter how blatantly it doesn't work in a given situation. They usually have a hard time seeing their own role in interpersonal problems, even though people around them point it out repeatedly (Carlson & Oltmanns, 2018; Millon, 2009; Strijbos & Glas, 2018; Widiger & Mullins-Sweatt, 2008). Personality disorders are evident by late childhood or early adulthood and become woven into the person's enduring character (American Psychiatric Association, 2013).

From my own psychotherapy practice, one client with a personality disorder, Felicia, was especially memorable. Felicia's problematic personality was evident not only in the stories she told about her interactions with other people, but also in the way she interacted with me during the sessions. On the day I met this 28-year-old woman, she took over from the first minute of the initial interview. "Get rid of that list of questions," she barked as she scowled at my clipboard. "*I'll* decide what you need to know." What I needed to know, apparently, was that Felicia was furious with both her husband and an employee. She explained why: "So, for the last 6 months I've been cheating on my husband with this guy who worked for me. No big deal, right? But neither one of them can get over it! I ended it as soon as my husband found out 3 days ago, but he's *still* upset. I did what *he* wanted by ending it, and he doesn't even appreciate it! And my employee — he's upset too! I fired him when I ended the affair, and now he's saying that I treated him unfairly! I mean, I give this guy a paycheck for years, and this is the thanks I get. They both need to get over this *now*. They are making my life too difficult." Throughout her explanation, Felicia repeatedly interrupted my attempts to ask questions, and when I told her we were running out of time, she shot me a glare and corrected me: "*I'll* tell you when we're done."

personality disorders
The category of psychological disorders based on an enduring pattern of inflexible and maladaptive behavior that appears across a wide range of situations and interferes with interpersonal interaction.

Obviously, Felicia thought the world revolved around her. Feelings of privilege and self-importance dominated her personality. She believed that she had the right to cheat on her husband, mistreat her employee, decide how each of them should react to the situation, and even tell her psychologist how to conduct the interview. I eventually learned that Felicia had been like this since childhood, and that almost all of her meaningful relationships had suffered because her personality was so inflexible. In short, she had a personality disorder — narcissistic personality disorder, to be specific — that interfered significantly with her ability to get along with other people (Miller et al., 2017; Ronningstam, 2009).

Narcissistic personality disorder is just one of 10 separate personality disorders included in DSM, each distinct in its emphasis. Each personality disorder focuses on a different personality characteristic, but in each case that characteristic is inflexible and causes problems in relationships with others. **Table 14.2** includes a brief description of all 10 personality disorders. Let's focus on two personality disorders that are especially well known and well researched: borderline personality disorder and antisocial personality disorder.

Borderline Personality Disorder

Borderline personality disorder is a psychological disorder based on instability in many areas of the person's life, including interpersonal relationships, mood, and self-image. For many people with borderline personality disorder, everything is tumultuous — their view of themselves, their relationships with others, and their emotional reactions to the world around them. As a result of this instability, life can feel chaotic and uncertain, as if things could change drastically at any moment, not only for the person with borderline personality disorder but for others around that person as well (Hooley & St. Germain, 2008; Paris, 2007, 2018). A leading expert in the disorder, psychologist Marsha Linehan, explains it this way: People with borderline personality disorder are "the psychological equivalent of third-degree burn patients. They simply have, so to speak, no emotional skin. Even the slightest touch or movement can create immense suffering" (Linehan, 1993a, p. 69).

In romantic relationships, people with borderline personality disorder may love their partner at times, perhaps in an unrealistic, idealized way, and then hate their

TABLE 14.2: DSM Personality Disorders: A Brief Summary

PERSONALITY DISORDER	DOMINANT TRAITS, CHARACTERISTICS, AND BEHAVIORS
Antisocial personality disorder	Exploits others; self-serving; frequent illegal behaviors
Avoidant personality disorder	Socially fearful; self-conscious; easily embarrassed in front of others; sees self as incompetent and likely to be criticized or rejected by others
Borderline personality disorder	Unstable and unpredictable; rapidly and drastically changing view of self and others; impulsive and tumultuous
Dependent personality disorder	Submissive; needs others' reassurance and approval; follows others' lead rather than acting independently
Histrionic personality disorder	Excessive and dramatic display of emotions; seeks to be the center of attention; theatrical but emotionally shallow
Narcissistic personality disorder	Egotistical, entitled, and self-important; sees self as superior to others; needs others to admire him or her
Obsessive-compulsive personality disorder	Orderly, a perfectionist; overly controlling and detail-oriented; rigid and stubborn
Paranoid personality disorder	Distrustful and suspicious; feels justified in never letting guard down; views others as dangerous or deceptive
Schizoid personality disorder	Solitary; loner with little or no desire for relationships with others; detached and unemotional
Schizotypal personality disorder	Eccentric, quirky, peculiar, odd; blurred line between reality and fantasy; engages in magical thinking

Information from Millon (2004), Sperry (2016), and American Psychiatric Association (2013).

borderline personality disorder
A psychological disorder based on instability in many areas of the person's life, including interpersonal relationships, mood, and self-image.

partner soon after with no reason for the dramatic shift other than an unjustified sense that their partner abandoned them. This tendency toward *splitting*, or seeing others as all good or all bad, is also often applied to other people and events, making the emotional lives of people with borderline personality disorder volatile and unpredictable (Clarkin et al., 2006).

As a clinical psychologist, I once worked with Bianca, a woman with borderline personality disorder. Bianca was a bright 25-year-old unmarried woman whose family referred her to me after she made suicide threats. This was not the first time she had openly discussed suicide. In fact, on numerous occasions since her teens, Bianca had made similar threats and had overdosed on pills. Most of these attempts happened after she became upset with a family member, friend, or boyfriend and then plummeted into a state of extreme rage and sadness. The latest suicide threats fell into the same pattern. She had been dating David for about a month and was madly in love with him, but his slight hesitation when she began discussing marriage sent her quickly in the opposite direction. Within minutes, she went from adoring David to despising him, and from feeling wonderful about her future to feeling hopeless.

As Bianca shared these experiences with me, I noticed that she was relating to me in a way that paralleled the way she had related to David. Just a few sessions in, she told me I was the most caring and competent therapist she had ever had. She felt much happier, and was confident that with my help, her life would stay on course. Her happiness and optimism were encouraging to me, but they felt fragile. Sure enough, a few sessions later, a power outage in my office building caused me to reschedule all of my appointments for the day, including one with Bianca. She responded furiously, screaming through tears that I had deserted her and accusing me of being uncaring and incompetent. She spiraled downward for some time after that, bogged down in the false belief that she was worthless and no one cared about her.

As Bianca's case suggests, people with borderline personality disorder often require significant care from mental health professionals. In fact, this single disorder accounts for a full 20% of hospitalized psychiatric patients (Bradley et al., 2007). Bianca's case is also typical in that people with borderline personality disorder have a high likelihood of self-harm or suicidal behavior (Michaels et al., 2017). In fact, about 75% of people with this diagnosis have a history of at least one attempt to hurt or kill themselves (Clarkin et al., 1983; Paris, 2009).

Antisocial Personality Disorder

Antisocial personality disorder is a psychological disorder based on a disregard for, and violation of, the rights of other people (American Psychiatric Association, 2013; Olson-Ayala & Patrick, 2018; Patrick, 2007). In this diagnosis, *antisocial* does not mean that a person prefers not to be social, or would choose to stay home alone rather than go to a party. Instead, *antisocial* means something closer to *antisociety* — a threat to society and the people living in it. Essentially, having antisocial personality disorder is like having no conscience, particularly regarding the welfare of others. To someone with antisocial personality disorder, other people are tools to be used for one's own benefit, or obstacles to be pushed aside on the way to a selfish goal, with no concern or empathy for what happens to those people in the process.

People with antisocial personality disorder have long histories of deceiving, exploiting, and ripping off other people. If someone stands in the way of what the person with antisocial personality disorder wants, that someone might get manipulated, assaulted, or even killed. Extreme cases may have caught your attention on the news: stories of people, often labeled by media members as psychopaths, who commit terrible crimes against others yet seem to feel no remorse about it.

antisocial personality disorder
A psychological disorder based on a disregard for, and violation of, the rights of other people.

You mean they don't feel guilty about these acts afterward?

Correct: they don't feel guilty. That is the most striking characteristic of people with antisocial personality disorder: They show a heartless lack of guilt, as if they have committed their crimes against inanimate objects rather than human beings.

Who Gets Personality Disorders?

DIVERSITY MATTERS

Each of the 10 personality disorders occurs at its own rate, with specific rates for each hovering between 1% and 5% of the population. Collectively, about 10% of the population could be diagnosed with a personality disorder (Coker & Widiger, 2005; Lenzenweger et al., 2007). Borderline personality disorder occurs in about 1–2% of the population, and about 75% of those who receive the diagnosis are women (Coid et al., 2006; Gunderson, 2001; Lenzenweger et al., 2007). Antisocial personality disorder occurs in about 2% of the population, and about two-thirds of those who receive the diagnosis are men. There are also some small gender differences among the other personality disorders, but none as lopsided as borderline personality disorder and antisocial personality disorder (Paris, 2004).

Why Do Personality Disorders Develop?

The causes of personality disorders are still largely unknown, but research continues. Regarding borderline personality disorder, some evidence points to both a genetic predisposition and a serious disruption in the relationship between parent/caregiver and child – such as abuse, loss of a parent/caregiver, or poor attachment in early childhood (Hooley & St. Germain, 2008; Lenzenweger & Clarkin, 2005). Genetics also appears to play a role in antisocial personality disorder, but other factors do as well. For example, people with antisocial personality disorder are quite insensitive to punishments that would discourage a behavior (such as arrest or prison), but quite sensitive to rewards that would encourage a behavior (such as money or thrills). Additionally, people with antisocial personality disorder were often raised in families in which exploitation and manipulation of others were modeled by parents/caregivers, while empathy and remorse were met with disapproval (Coker & Widiger, 2005; Patrick, 2007; Patrick & Brislin, 2018).

CHECK YOUR LEARNING:

14.45 What are personality disorders?

14.46 What is borderline personality disorder?

14.47 What is antisocial personality disorder?

14.48 How common are borderline and antisocial personality disorders, and in which groups are they most frequently diagnosed?

14.49 Why do personality disorders develop?

To check your understanding of these questions, click show the answers or refer to the answers in the Chapter Summary.

CHAPTER SUMMARY

What Are Psychological Disorders?

14.1 A psychological disorder is a pattern of behavior that interferes with a person's life by causing significant distress or dysfunction.

14.2 The task of distinguishing psychological disorders is a significant challenge for psychologists. At times, psychologists have reversed their opinions about whether particular experiences are psychological disorders. Multiple criteria are used to define psychological disorders, including infrequency, deviation from social norms, personal distress, and impairment in daily functioning.

14.3 None of these criteria is perfect, but personal distress and impairment in daily functioning are most clearly emphasized by the authors of DSM. Culture should play an important role when considering whether a behavior is disordered.

Why Do Psychological Disorders Develop?

14.4 A variety of explanations offer answers to the question of what causes psychological disorders. The biological theory proposes that factors such as brain structures, neurochemicals, and genes are the primary causes of psychological disorders.

14.5 The psychological theory proposes that factors such as emotions, thoughts, behaviors, and traits are the primary causes of psychological disorders. Different psychological theories – including psychodynamic, behavioral, cognitive, and trait theories — emphasize particular psychological factors.

14.6 The sociocultural theory proposes that the social and cultural contexts in which a person lives, rather than factors within the person, are the primary causes of psychological disorders.

14.7 The biopsychosocial theory proposes that all of these factors — biological, psychological, and sociocultural — contribute to psychological disorders, often in an interactive way. This theory is particularly comprehensive and widely accepted by contemporary psychologists.

The Diagnostic Manual: DSM

14.8 DSM (*Diagnostic and Statistical Manual of Mental Disorders*) is the book in which mental disorders are officially defined.

14.9 In the United States, DSM is used by all major mental health professions and all other professionals who diagnose or treat mental disorders.

14.10 The most recent edition of DSM, DSM-5-TR, was published in 2022. A more substantive revision, DSM-5, was published in 2013. DSM-5-TR added only one new disorder, but DSM-5 added numerous new disorders and revised definitions of existing disorders. Since it was originally published in the 1950s, DSM has expanded greatly. The great increase in the number of psychological disorders has been criticized by some as labeling common but unfortunate experiences as disorders.

14.11 DSM uses a categorical model of psychological disorders, in which psychologists provide a yes-or-no answer to the question of whether a person has a particular disorder. The dimensional model is an alternative approach that poses questions about psychopathology such as "How much?" rather than "Yes or no?"

Anxiety Disorders and Obsessive-Compulsive Disorder

14.12 Anxiety disorders are the category of DSM disorders in which the primary symptom is anxiety, which is also known as worry, apprehension, nervousness, or fear.

14.13 Generalized anxiety disorder is characterized by anxiety, particularly in the form of worry, about a wide range of situations and activities.

14.14 Specific phobia is characterized by excessive anxiety toward a specific, identifiable object or situation.

14.15 Social anxiety disorder is characterized by an intense and irrational fear of the scrutiny of others and the embarrassment or humiliation that would follow.

14.16 Panic disorder is characterized by sudden, intense, unpredictable brief bursts (attacks) of anxiety that lack an identifiable trigger.

14.17 Obsessive-compulsive disorder is characterized by unwanted recurring anxiety-producing thoughts (obsessions) and uncontrollable actions (compulsions) done to reduce the anxiety produced by the obsessions.

14.18 Anxiety disorders are more common than any other category of psychological disorder. They are similarly common in the United States and other parts of the world. They occur two to three times more often in women than men.

14.19 Anxiety disorders and obsessive-compulsive disorder develop for a variety of reasons, often in combination. The reasons involve psychological factors — such as illogical thinking, learned reinforcements and punishments, neuroticism, and overly protective parenting/caregiving — and biological factors — such as genes, brain differences, and evolution.

Depressive and Bipolar Disorders

14.20 Depressive disorders and bipolar disorders are a category of psychological disorders characterized by extreme moods or emotional states that significantly disrupt daily functioning.

14.21 Major depressive disorder is characterized by depressed mood, loss of interest in most activities, and an assortment of other symptoms lasting at least 2 weeks. A much longer, less intensive version of these symptoms is known as persistent depressive disorder (dysthymia).

14.22 Bipolar disorder, formerly known as manic depressive disorder, is characterized by alternating between extremely high moods and low moods (the "poles" of emotion).

14.23 Collectively, depressive disorders and bipolar disorders are quite common, second only to anxiety disorders. Major depressive disorder is more common in women than men, and far more common than bipolar disorder.

14.24 Depressive disorders and bipolar disorders develop for a variety of reasons, including biological factors — such as genetics, brain differences, and neurochemicals — and psychological factors — such as illogical thinking stemming from a depressive schema.

Eating Disorders

14.25 Eating disorders are a category of psychological disorders that involve significant disturbances in behaviors related to eating or food.

14.26 Anorexia nervosa is characterized by a refusal to eat enough food to maintain a healthy body weight. It almost always stems from a distorted, inaccurate view of one's own body as fat.

14.27 Bulimia nervosa is characterized by a pattern of overeating (bingeing) followed by dangerous or drastic attempts to prevent weight gain (purging).

14.28 Binge eating disorder is essentially the bingeing pattern of bulimia without the purging. Eating disorders are relatively rare, but they occur about 10 times more often in girls and women than in boys and men. They typically develop in young women who live in the United States or countries similarly influenced by Western values.

14.29 Biological and psychological factors can also play a role in the development of eating disorders, but sociocultural factors have received much more attention from researchers.

14.30 Specifically, the emphasis in Western TV, movies, and magazines that thinness determines beauty, and to some extent worth, contributes to eating-related problems.

Schizophrenia

14.31 Schizophrenia is a severe psychological disorder characterized by bizarre disturbances in thinking, perception, feelings, and behavior. It involves a blatantly unrealistic take on reality that is held only by the person with the disorder.

14.32 Positive symptoms of schizophrenia are experiences that are present or excessive in people with the disorder but largely absent in people without the disorder. They include the most visible signs of schizophrenia, such as delusions (false beliefs) and hallucinations (false sensations or perceptions). Negative symptoms of schizophrenia are behaviors that are lacking in people with schizophrenia, but usually present in people without the disorder. A specific negative symptom is flat affect, the absence of feelings appropriate to a situation or being disengaged from social and emotional aspects of life. Cognitive symptoms of schizophrenia involve the disturbed, illogical ways that people with the disorder think, speak, and behave, all of which are often disorganized and disordered.

14.33 Schizophrenia is rare, but occurs around the world and at approximately equal rates across genders. It occurs more often in urban areas than rural areas.

14.34 Biological factors loom large as primary contributors to the development of schizophrenia. These factors include genes, structural differences in the brain, and possibly neurochemical differences. Other factors include hostile, overinvolved family interaction and prenatal complications during fetal development.

Disorders of Childhood

14.35 Many psychological disorders can occur during childhood, but disorders of childhood are those that begin during childhood by definition. They include specific learning disorders, intellectual disability, attention-deficit/hyperactivity disorder (ADHD), and autism spectrum disorder.

14.36 Attention-deficit/hyperactivity disorder (ADHD) is a disorder emerging in childhood that features significant problems with attention, hyperactivity/impulsivity, or both.

14.37 Autism spectrum disorder is a disorder emerging in childhood that features significant social interaction deficits and rigid, repetitive patterns of behavior.

14.38 Research suggests that 5–7% of children meet criteria for ADHD, but rates of actual diagnosis in the community are significantly higher. Rates of autism spectrum disorder are lower—around 1–2%. Both disorders are much more common in boys than girls.

14.39 The reasons why ADHD and autism spectrum disorder arise continue to be investigated. Genes appear heavily involved in both, but multiple causes are likely.

Dissociative Disorders

14.40 Dissociative disorders are a category of psychological disorders in which the person loses awareness of, or becomes disconnected from, essential parts of themselves such as memories, emotions, or identity.

14.41 Dissociative identity disorder, formerly known as multiple personality disorder, involves a person exhibiting two or more distinct personalities rather than a single, coherent self.

14.42 Dissociative amnesia is characterized by an inability to recall important information from one's past. The particular period about which the person blanks out almost always includes a horrific occurrence. A case of dissociative amnesia accompanied by unplanned and unexplained travel to a new location is a dissociative fugue.

14.43 Dissociative disorders are exceptionally rare; in fact, some experts doubt whether some of these disorders, particularly dissociative identity disorder, are valid diagnoses at all.

14.44 The primary reason for the development of most dissociative disorders appears to be severe abuse or trauma, either immediately before or long before the onset of the disorder.

Personality Disorders

14.45 Personality disorders are psychological disorders characterized by an enduring pattern of inflexible, maladaptive behavior occurring across a wide range of situations and interfering with interpersonal interaction. People with personality disorders have unbending, rigid personality traits in spite of the problems those traits cause in various situations.

14.46 Borderline personality disorder centers on instability in many areas of the person's life, including interpersonal relationships, mood, and self-image. It is characterized by a view of the self, relationships with others, and emotional reactions that are tumultuous and volatile.

14.47 Antisocial personality disorder centers on a disregard for, and violation of, the rights of other people. It often involves the exploitation or use of others for one's own benefit, with no concern or empathy for how those others are hurt or otherwise affected.

14.48 Each personality disorder occurs at its own rate. Borderline and antisocial personality disorders are both relatively uncommon. Borderline personality disorder occurs more often in women; antisocial personality disorder occurs more often in men.

14.49 The reasons why personality disorders develop are still largely undetermined. For borderline personality disorder, a serious disruption in the relationship between parent/caregiver and child appears to be a factor. For antisocial personality disorder, an insensitivity to punishment and a family background in which exploitation of others was modeled or encouraged appear to be factors. Genes may also play a role in the development of personality disorders.

KEY TERMS

psychological disorder, p. 477
medical student syndrome, p. 477
Diagnostic and Statistical Manual of Mental Disorders (DSM), p. 480
biological theory of psychological disorders, p. 480
psychological theory of psychological disorders, p. 481
sociocultural theory of psychological disorders, p. 481
biopsychosocial theory of psychological disorders, p. 482
stigma, p. 484
categorical model of psychopathology, p. 490
dimensional model of psychopathology, p. 490
anxiety disorders, p. 491
generalized anxiety disorder, p. 491
specific phobia, p. 493
social anxiety disorder, p. 493
panic disorder, p. 494
obsessive-compulsive disorder (OCD), p. 495
triple vulnerability theory, p. 498
depressive and bipolar disorders, p. 499
major depressive disorder, p. 500
persistent depressive disorder (dysthymia), p. 500
bipolar disorder, p. 501
mania, p. 501
cyclothymic disorder, p. 502

eating disorders, p. 504
anorexia nervosa, p. 504
bulimia nervosa, p. 505
binge eating disorder, p. 506
schizophrenia, p. 508
psychosis, p. 509
positive symptoms, p. 509
delusions, p. 509
hallucinations, p. 510
negative symptoms, p. 510
flat affect, p. 511
cognitive symptoms, p. 511
attention-deficit/hyperactivity disorder (ADHD), p. 515
autism spectrum disorder, p. 516
dissociative disorders, p. 518
dissociative identity disorder, p. 518
dissociative amnesia, p. 519
personality disorders, p. 520
borderline personality disorder, p. 521
antisocial personality disorder, p. 522

SELF-ASSESSMENT

1. The _____ theory of psychological disorders asserts that factors within the human body — such as brain structures, neurochemicals, and genes — are the primary causes of psychological disorders.
   a. sociocultural
   b. biological
   c. psychological
   d. categorical

2. The book used by U.S. mental health professionals to diagnose mental disorders is _____.

3. The number of psychological disorders has _____ since the mid-1900s.
   a. increased
   b. decreased
   c. remained the same
   d. alternated each decade between about a dozen and about 100

4. Qiang has an anxiety disorder. Which of these specific diagnoses could Qiang have?
   a. social anxiety disorder, panic disorder, or generalized anxiety disorder
   b. schizophrenia or dissociative identity disorder
   c. anorexia nervosa or bipolar disorder
   d. All of the answers are correct.

5. _____ is characterized by an intense and irrational fear of the scrutiny of others and the embarrassment or humiliation that would follow.

6. Hector has bipolar disorder. His mood goes back and forth between the two emotional "poles" of bipolar disorder, which are _____ and _____.

7. Which of the following is true?
   a. Eating disorders occur equally often across genders.
   b. Binge eating disorder involves a pattern of overeating followed by drastic attempts to avoid weight gain.
   c. Both a and b
   d. Neither a nor b

8. Hallucinations, delusions, flat affect, and loose associations are all symptoms of:
   a. anorexia nervosa.
   b. major depressive disorder.
   c. schizophrenia.
   d. obsessive-compulsive disorder.

9. _____ are psychological disorders in which the person loses awareness of, or becomes disconnected from, essential parts of themselves such as memories, emotions, or identity.
   a. Eating disorders
   b. Dissociative disorders
   c. Personality disorders
   d. Anxiety disorders

10. The core characteristic of antisocial personality disorder is _____.
    a. excessive shyness
    b. a very high level of anxiety
    c. a very high level of sadness
    d. a disregard for, and violation of, the rights of other people

To check your understanding of these questions, click show the answers in the e-book or refer to the answers in Appendix B.

Research shows quizzing is a highly effective learning tool. Continue quizzing yourself using LearningCurve, the system that adapts to *your* learning.

WHAT'S YOUR TAKE?

1. Psychologists and other experts in mental health use different strategies to create definitions of psychological disorders. They might use infrequency, deviation from social norms, personal distress, or impairment in daily functioning as a way to draw the line between people with and without psychological disorders. In your opinion, how should that line be drawn? What criteria should be used?
2. The rates of phobias and major depressive disorder are roughly equal across genders until kids reach a certain age (around 10 to 13), after which rates are higher for girls and women than for boys and men. In your opinion (informed by the theories presented in this chapter), what explains this pattern?

SHOW ME MORE

14.1 Misconceptions about Obsessive Compulsive Disorder

Achieve

This video explains common misconceptions about OCD, and clarifies the distinction between diagnosable OCD and less extreme "OCD-ish" habits or tendencies.

SciShow Psych/BoClips

14.2 Smartphones as a Tool to Combat Depression

Achieve

This video explains how smartphones, which at times can contribute to depressive symptoms, can actually be used to help identify depression or behaviors that might predict it.

Associated Press

14.3 Mental Health Issues among Black Americans

Achieve

This video discusses commonly held stigmas and attitudes toward psychological difficulties among Black people in the United States, and offers suggestions for overcoming them.

This video was produced and originally published by the Clay Center for Young Healthy Minds, a free, online educational resource to support the mental and emotional well-being of young people.

14.4 Men, Mental Health, and the "Man Up" Mentality

Achieve

This video depicts stigmatizing beliefs that men often hold regarding mental disorders, and ideas for moving past them.

Canadian Broadcasting Corporation/BoClips

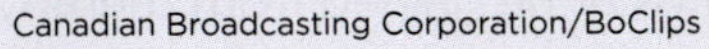

14.5 My Psychology Podcast

Achieve

This podcast episode features the author of this textbook, psychologist Andy Pomerantz, speaking with other instructors of introductory psychology courses about the most important and interesting concepts in this chapter.

Macmillan Learning

15 Therapy

Roman Samborskyi/Shutterstock

CHAPTER OUTLINE

Every year, therapy improves the lives of millions of people, including, perhaps, you or someone close to you. Some who benefit from therapy have diagnosed disorders like the ones we covered in Chapter 14, while others simply have stressors, struggles, or challenges in daily living. In one eye-opening study, 60 clients with a wide range of reasons for seeking therapy offered an insider's view of the kinds of positive effects that therapy can have (Kassan, 1999). Some clients emphasized how they benefited from the accepting and caring relationship with a therapist:

- "It's having someone accept you, whatever you're saying, without judgment, that allows you to accept yourself." (p. 407)
- "It was her warmth. She really gave off such humanity and sincere caring. It made it possible for me to be so trusting of her as to visit some very dark places. I felt very safe." (p. 370)

Some clients overcame specific symptoms or improved a particular behavior:

- "I got over my fear of flying. . . ." (p. 398)
- "I'm less anxious when presenting things in public. . . ." (p. 397)

Some clients achieved insight during therapy, realizing something new and important about themselves:

- "I got more of an understanding of why I do what I do. I've become more aware of how I am." (p. 396)
- "She made me aware of relationships in my childhood that very much affected my adult relationships. She helped me realize a lot of things that I was just oblivious to." (p. 360)

Jay-Z, the rapper, record executive, and entrepreneur, explained what he gained from therapy this way: "I grew so much from the experience. But I think the most important thing I got is that everything is connected. Every emotion is connected and it comes from somewhere. And just being aware of it. Being aware of it in everyday life puts you at such ... an advantage" (Baquet, 2017, p. 135).

Treatments for psychological challenges can enhance the lives of most who seek them. In this chapter, we will explore a variety of styles and formats of psychotherapy, including many you might be likely to encounter if you seek therapy yourself. We will also consider how well treatments work, how cultural variables can influence treatment, ethical issues that can arise during treatment, the impact of modern technology on treatment, and biomedical treatments including psychiatric medications.

History of Treatment of Psychological Disorders

YOU WILL LEARN:

15.1 how psychological disorders were treated centuries ago.

15.2 how and when the treatment of psychological disorders began to change toward the current approach.

15.3 about the definitions of psychotherapy and biomedical therapy.

Treatment for psychological issues has existed in one form or another since ancient times (Alexander & Selesnick, 1966; Benjamin, 2005, 2007). By today's standards, early treatments were often bizarre and brutal. People suffering from psychological disorders were sometimes thought to be possessed by the devil or evil spirits. Some were imprisoned in dungeon-like conditions or subjected to torturous interventions designed to rid their bodies of these spirits – including bloodletting and cutting holes in their skulls (Routh, 2011; Tallis, 1998). In many cases, the treatment was far worse than the disorder.

Thankfully, in the late 1700s and early 1800s, a new sentiment toward people with psychological issues began to grow – one that recognized them as human beings deserving real treatment and humane living conditions. In England, philanthropist William Tuke was so appalled by the miserable living conditions in homes for people with mental illness that he raised funds to open York Retreat. There, residents found more day-to-day freedoms, better food, more opportunities for physical exercise, and staff members who actually cared about them (Reisman, 1991; Rosner, 2018).

In France, as **Figure 15.1** illustrates, physician Philippe Pinel convinced those in power that people with mental illness deserved better treatment than they had been receiving (Ehrenwald, 1991). Among other things, Pinel successfully argued that staff members should create a case history for each patient, which included treatment notes and a label for the patient's psychological illness. These aspects of care are routine now, but were unheard of at the time. The changes that Pinel created reflected a changing attitude toward people with mental illness, one focused on improving their lives rather than simply locking them away (Cautin, 2011; Charland, 2018; Weiner, 1994). As Pinel himself wrote in 1801, "The mentally sick, far from being guilty people deserving punishment, are sick people whose miserable state

Bettmann/Getty Images

FIGURE 15.1 Philippe Pinel and Better Treatment. The title of this 1849 painting by Charles Müller – *Pinel Orders the Removal of Iron Shackles from the Insane Men at Bicêtre Hospice* – captures the role that Philippe Pinel and others played in promoting more humane treatment of people with mental illness in the late 1700s and early 1800s.

FLHC 90/Alamy Stock Photo

Dorothea Dix was one of numerous pioneers who worked to provide more resources for people with mental illness. Her efforts sparked the creation of dozens of public institutions throughout the 1800s.

psychotherapy
A treatment that involves a mental health professional using various techniques to help a person overcome a psychological disorder or improve some aspect of emotional, cognitive, or behavioral functioning.

biomedical therapy
A treatment for psychological disorders that involves medications or medical procedures to directly change the biology of the brain.

deserves all the consideration that is due to suffering humanity" (cited in Zilboorg & Henry, 1941).

In the United States, the Connecticut physician Eli Todd was inspired by the progress being made in Europe. Todd's own sister had died by suicide, and he believed that a better system of mental health treatment might have saved her life. Unfortunately, effective treatment was scarce in those days. In fact, before 1800 only three states had mental hospitals at all (Reisman, 1991). For decades, Todd campaigned for improved treatment of people with mental illness, and his efforts resulted in the first mental hospital in Connecticut opening in 1824 (Goodheart, 2003; Whitaker, 2015). For the first time, many families of people with mental health issues had a place where they could seek around-the-clock care for their loved ones.

Like Todd, Dorothea Dix recognized the need for mental hospitals. Dix was a Sunday school teacher in a Boston jail where she noticed that many of her students had been imprisoned because of mental illness rather than criminal activity. The authorities simply had nowhere else to take people with mental illnesses, so they often threw them in jail alongside convicts. Dix devoted the rest of her life to solving this problem. She traveled to city after city pleading with local community leaders to provide more adequate treatment to people with mental illness. She even had an ongoing exchange of letters with Millard Fillmore, the U.S. president from 1850 to 1853, about this issue (Colman, 2007; Snyder, 1975). Her efforts were remarkably successful: Dix was responsible for the creation of 30 public institutions for people with mental illness in various states throughout the 1800s.

Collectively, the efforts of reformers like Tuke, Pinel, Todd, and Dix changed society's attitude toward the treatment of people with mental illness — from scorn and punishment to compassion and respect (Cautin, 2011). This movement paved the way for the two primary forms of treatment used today — *psychotherapy* and *biomedical therapy* — that will be the focus of the rest of this chapter. **Psychotherapy** involves techniques used by a mental health professional to help a person overcome a psychological disorder or improve some aspect of emotional, cognitive, or behavioral functioning. **Biomedical therapy** involves medications or medical procedures that treat psychological disorders by directly changing the biology of the brain.

CHECK YOUR LEARNING:

15.1 How were psychological disorders treated centuries ago?

15.2 When and how did the treatment of psychological disorders begin to change toward the current approach?

15.3 What are the differences between psychotherapy and biomedical therapy?

To check your understanding of these questions, click show the answers or refer to the answers in the Chapter Summary.

Psychotherapies for Individual Clients

YOU WILL LEARN:

15.4 who seeks psychotherapy.

15.5 about the basics of psychodynamic therapy, including transference.

Psychotherapy often goes by the name *talk therapy* to distinguish it from treatments that involve medications. *Counseling,* at least in some of its forms, is another term that means something similar to psychotherapy. The most common type of psychotherapy is individual therapy — in which only the client and the therapist are involved (Norcross et al., 2005).

Who seeks psychotherapy?

Lots of people seek psychotherapy for lots of reasons. Over half of Americans will undergo some form of psychotherapy in their lifetimes — some to treat a psychological disorder, and others to help with day-to-day struggles with emotions, behaviors, or relationships (Engel, 2008). In recent years, the number of people entering therapy has increased. In 2019 alone, about 10% of U.S. adults saw a therapist, and that number increased further when the stress of the COVID pandemic hit in 2020 (Elflein, 2021; Terlizzi & Zablotsky, 2020). As shown in **Figure 15.2**, people enter therapy for lots of different reasons, including anxiety, depression, stress, family concerns, academic performance, and relationship issues (Pérez-Rojas et al., 2017).

There are many varieties of individual psychotherapy, but we will focus on four major ones — *psychodynamic therapy*, *person-centered therapy*, *behavior therapy*, and *cognitive therapy*. We'll start with psychodynamic therapy, which stems from Sigmund Freud's theories. Historically, Freud came first. In fact, until the mid-1900s, Freud's therapy dominated the field. The other therapies in this chapter came along later, often with the intention of offering something different than Freud did (Farreras et al., 2016; Gold & Stricker, 2017; Guadiano, 2008; Hollon & DiGiuseppe, 2011; Karpiak et al., 2016; Routh, 1996).

15.6 about the basics of person-centered therapy, including empathy, unconditional positive regard, and genuineness.

15.7 about the basics of behavior therapy, including exposure techniques and token economies.

15.8 about the basics of cognitive therapy, including the ABCDE model and cognitive distortions.

15.9 how therapies can be combined, including eclectic and integrative approaches.

Psychodynamic Therapy

Sigmund Freud, whose theory of personality we explored in Chapter 12, was a pioneer of psychotherapy in the late 1800s and early 1900s. He developed **psychoanalysis**: an approach to psychotherapy in which the main goal is to make the unconscious conscious — that is, helping the client become more aware of thoughts and feelings of which they were unaware at the start of therapy (Cabaniss et al., 2011; Karon & Widener, 1995). *Insight* is a single word often used to describe this process of looking inside oneself and seeing something that had previously gone unnoticed (Gibbons et al., 2007; Høglend & Hagtvet, 2019; Lacewing, 2014; McAleavey & Castonguay, 2014). For example, clients in psychoanalysis might realize for the first time that their low self-esteem today stems from an early childhood relationship with a parent/caregiver who ignored or belittled them.

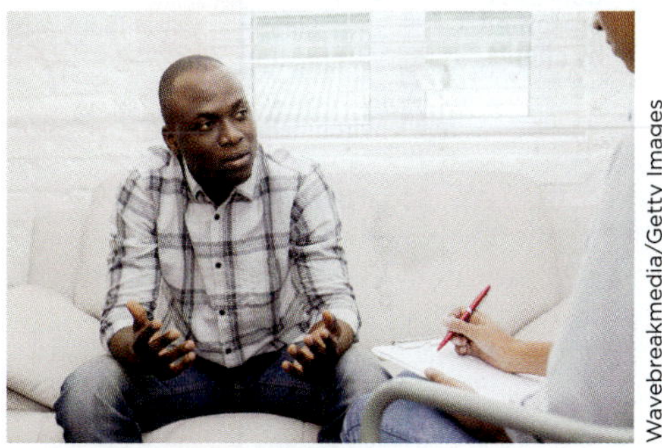

Wavebreakmedia/Getty Images

There are many kinds of individual therapy, including psychodynamic therapy, person-centered therapy, behavior therapy, and cognitive therapy.

In the 100-plus years since Freud created psychoanalysis, the treatment has been revised many times, usually to make the approach to therapy a quicker, more direct way of addressing psychological issues, which makes it a better match for contemporary society. Collectively, we now call all of these revisions of Freud's original approach **psychodynamic therapy**: therapy that has the goal of making the unconscious conscious, but more briefly and with more focus on the client's current life than psychoanalysis. Although classic psychoanalysis is rarely practiced today, many forms of psychodynamic therapy are very common (Barber & Solomonov, 2016; Gabbard, 2009a).

Psychodynamic therapists face two big challenges as they help their clients become more aware of unconscious thoughts and feelings. First, the therapist needs to access or "get at" the unconscious material, the innermost workings of the client's mind that are outside of even the client's awareness. Second, the therapist needs to help the client recognize this unconscious material and deal with it consciously.

To deal with the first of these challenges — gaining access to the client's unconscious — psychodynamic therapists use a variety of techniques, including *dream analysis*, working with a client's *resistance*, and working with a client's *transference*.

Dream Analysis. In **dream analysis**, the therapist and client attempt to find the underlying meaning of the client's dreams. Many psychodynamic therapists see dreams as symbolic expressions of unconscious wishes (Civitarese, 2014; Freud, 1900; Kernberg, 2004). So, consider a client who shares a dream in which a dog scratches and whines desperately to escape from a small locked cage. The therapist may

psychoanalysis
An approach to psychotherapy developed by Sigmund Freud in which the main goal is to make the unconscious conscious — that is, helping the client become more aware of thoughts and feelings of which they were unaware at the start of therapy.

psychodynamic therapy
Therapy that has the goal of making the unconscious conscious, but more briefly and with more focus on the client's current life than psychoanalysis.

dream analysis
A psychodynamic technique in which the therapist and client attempt to find the underlying meaning of the client's dreams.

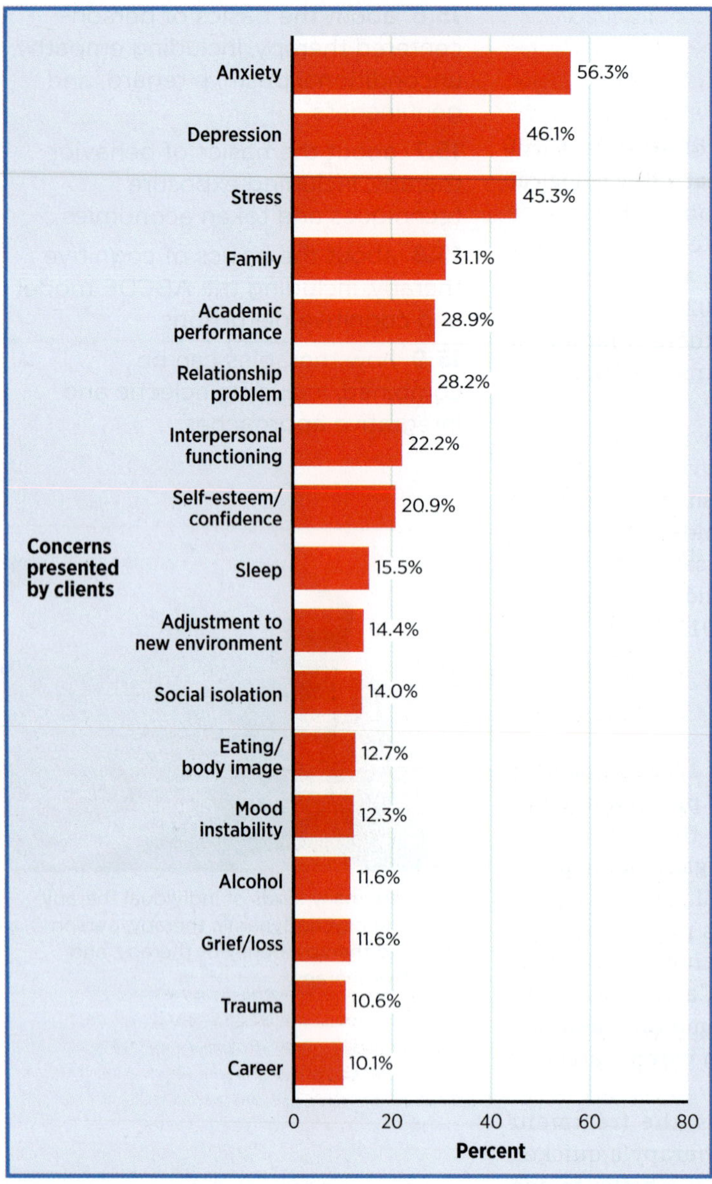

FIGURE 15.2 For What Kinds of Problems Do College Students Visit the Counseling Center? In a massive study of over 53,000 clients seeing 1300 college counselors at 84 schools, the range of concerns was very wide. The most common concerns were anxiety, depression, stress, family concerns, academic performance, and relationship issues (Pérez-Rojas et al., 2017). Data from Pérez-Rojas et al. (2017).

encourage the client to consider the dog as a symbol for themself and think about what part of their life — perhaps their job, their romantic relationship, or their family — represents the cage from which they want to be freed.

Resistance. Sometimes, the way the client relates to the therapist can reveal some of the client's unconscious issues. For example, when difficult or anxiety-provoking topics come up during therapy, clients often find a way to steer clear of discussing them. They may change the subject, or suddenly think of an entirely different problem that demands immediate attention. If the next session promises to include more discussion of the difficult or anxiety-provoking topic, clients may arrive late or not show up at all. Psychodynamic therapists call this behavior **resistance**: client behavior that blocks discussion or conscious awareness of anxiety-provoking topics. The client is typically unaware of the reason behind the resistance and, in some cases, unaware that they are using the resistant behavior at all. It's up to the psychodynamic therapist to point it out to the client, to help make it conscious (Dewald, 1964; Gabbard, 2009b; Karon & Widener, 1995; LaFarge, 2012; Lane & Harris, 2008).

One of my own psychotherapy clients, Ana, provided me with a real-life example of resistance. Ana was in her early 20s, and the main reason she sought therapy was to deal with feelings of sadness and low self-esteem that had lingered since she was a young child. She spent several early sessions expressing a bitter anger toward her older brother, who mistreated her as they grew up. This mistreatment was more serious and abusive than mere sibling rivalry: Ana's brother insulted her relentlessly, hit her until she was bruised, and sometimes fondled her. During our third session, I empathically listened to Ana continue to offer more details of what her brother had done and how it had affected her. At one point, I asked her if anyone else in her family knew about her brother's mistreatment of her. At that moment, Ana abruptly changed the subject to some new responsibilities her boss had given her at work that week, and proceeded to talk about work-related issues until we ran out of time. She missed our next appointment altogether, and was 15 minutes late to the appointment after that.

A psychodynamic explanation of Ana's behavior might go something like this: she was comfortable discussing her brother, despite his abusive behavior, but the idea of other people in her family being aware of it made Ana so uncomfortable that she resisted talking about it. Much later in therapy, Ana revealed that their mother knew about her brother's abusive behavior toward Ana, but did nothing to protect her. Ana was so scared to acknowledge her feelings of anger toward her mother during that third session that she prevented the conversation from going there without fully realizing why she was doing so.

Transference. Perhaps the most powerful tool that psychodynamic therapists have for accessing the client's unconscious is *transference* (Galatzer-Levy et al., 2000; Karon & Widener, 1995; Wolitzky, 2016). **Transference** happens when the client unconsciously and unrealistically expects the therapist to behave like an important person from the client's past. Without realizing it, the client *transfers* what they learned from previous relationships onto the relationship with the therapist. In a way, the client unconsciously assumes the therapist to be a certain kind of person — usually similar to mom, dad, or some other "big" figure from the client's own past — when in

resistance
Client behavior that blocks discussion or conscious awareness of anxiety-provoking topics.

transference
A client's unconscious and unrealistic expectations for the therapist to behave like an important person from the client's past.

reality, the client doesn't have enough evidence to know whether such an assumption is true at all (Diamond et al., 2022; Gabbard, 2005; S. H. Goldberg, 2012; A. Harris, 2012). For example, a client who grew up with a critical, fault-finding mom might presume — without realizing it — that their new therapist will have the same qualities (especially if the therapist is a woman). Or, a client whose dad always demanded that they keep their opinions to themself might enter a relationship with a therapist (especially a therapist who is a man) assuming — without being aware of it — that the therapist will make similar demands on them.

So, when clients experience transference, are they hallucinating? Do they actually think that their therapist is their mom or dad?

No, transference is not a hallucination at all. There is nothing bizarre about it. In fact, transference is a pretty common experience in all kinds of relationships, not just therapy. You have probably been on the receiving end of transference yourself. For example, maybe you dated someone who suspected you of cheating, despite the fact that you had given them no real reason to think so. Or maybe you worked for a supervisor who thought you were trying to steal their job, despite the fact that you had no such intentions at all. Why would these people have these false beliefs? According to psychodynamic therapists, the answer lies in their previous relationships. If their previous romantic partners cheated on them or their previous employees stole their jobs, then they may have a hard time expecting you not to do the same. They may have transferred what they learned from earlier relationships onto their relationship with you, without realizing that they were doing so.

One of my own clients comes to mind as an example of a client displaying transference toward their therapist. Juan was a 30-year-old man who came to see me for mild anxiety and occasional panic attacks. As we began our initial session together, Juan offered some background about his job and his family, then started to describe his symptoms. About 10 minutes in, he stopped himself and, to my surprise, he apologized to me: "I'm so sorry. I can tell you're bored, and that I am wasting your time. You are probably thinking, 'I wish this guy would shut up so I could go home.'" Then, he stood up and started to walk out of my office. I encouraged Juan to stay and assured him that I was very interested in him. After a moment of hesitation, he did. But then, 15 minutes later, he again interrupted himself, apologized for wasting my time, and started to leave. Altogether, Juan interrupted himself and started to leave four times during the first session.

RossHelen/iStock/Getty Images

Transference happens when the client unconsciously and unrealistically expects the therapist to behave like an important person from the client's past. Psychodynamic therapists try to help clients become aware of their transference tendencies, which may affect many of the client's other relationships outside of therapy.

It is important to note that I did nothing to give Juan a reason to believe that I was uninterested or annoyed with him. I didn't glance at my phone, stare at the clock, gaze out the window, or yawn as he spoke. So why did Juan presume that I was so uninterested and annoyed by him? The psychodynamic explanation might go like this: Without realizing that he was doing so, Juan presumed that I would be like some other important person in his life who did, in fact, find him uninteresting and annoying. He unconsciously jumped to the conclusion that I would too, despite the fact that there was no evidence that I felt that way. As therapy progressed, Juan shared many more details about his family, including his father who — you guessed it — found Juan to be an uninteresting and annoying nuisance throughout Juan's whole childhood.

Interpretation. Once psychodynamic therapists have gained access to clients' unconscious material, their next challenge is helping the client recognize it too. The primary technique for this is **interpretation**: the psychodynamic therapist's attempt to make a connection between the client's unconscious material and their current behavior, thoughts, or feelings (P. Goldberg, 2012; Johansson et al., 2010; Petraglia et al., 2017). Let's consider again the examples of my clients Ana and Juan. Ana won't benefit if I don't help her become aware of what I notice about the way she resists

interpretation
The psychodynamic therapist's attempt to make a connection between the client's unconscious material and their current behavior, thoughts, or feelings.

talking about her mother's role in the abuse. Likewise, Juan won't benefit if I don't help him become aware of the way he expects me to relate to him like his dad did. In both cases, good interpretations, statements in which I tactfully share with the client what I'm noticing, could provide the client with an "aha" moment, a powerful insight in which they come to know something about themselves that they didn't know before. Ana could recognize her hidden feelings toward her mother, and Juan could recognize his tendency to transfer expectations of his father onto other people in his life.

Working Through. Of course, this interpretation may not have an immediate impact. Even the most powerful insight takes some getting used to. So, after a psychodynamic therapist offers an insight, there is typically a need for **working through**: a lengthy phase of therapy in which interpretations are repeated, reconsidered, and given a chance to gradually sink in (Gabbard, 2009b). For both Ana and Juan, the first time I offered my interpretations they had a difficult time fully understanding or accepting them. But over time, with ongoing conversations, both Ana and Juan worked through my interpretations and incorporated them into their way of thinking and their views of themselves. Little by little, Ana accepted her feelings of anger and disappointment toward her mother, and she also recognized how avoiding those feelings had been interfering with her life. Bit by bit, Juan recognized that he transferred expectations of his father onto me and, more importantly, onto other people in his life, including his friends, coworkers, and supervisors. From that point on, he was able to catch himself when he started to transfer those expectations onto other people, and in those moments he reminded himself to relate to other people for who they truly were. In most cases, those people were actually far more accepting of Juan than his father was.

Psychodynamic Therapy Today. The number of therapists practicing traditional, "old school" psychoanalysis has dropped drastically since its heyday many decades ago, but the number practicing "new school" variations of psychodynamic therapy remains sizeable (Gabbard, 2009a; Jaimes et al., 2015; Norcross & Karpiak, 2012). One particular form of psychodynamic therapy, *interpersonal therapy*, is especially highly regarded. Studies have shown that it is especially beneficial for clients with depression, and perhaps some with other disorders as well (Cuijpers et al., 2021; Lipsitz & Markowitz, 2016; Markowitz & Weissman, 2012; Stuart, 2017; Swartz & Markowitz, 2009; Zhou et al., 2015). Interpersonal therapy is a short-term therapy (usually 14–18 sessions) built around the assumption that depression grows out of stressful interpersonal relationships. The therapist therefore attempts to improve the client's ability to form healthy relationships, particularly by making the client more aware of their own thoughts, feelings, and expectations regarding those relationships (Didie, 2015; Frank & Levenson, 2011; Klerman et al., 1984; Weissman, 1995).

Person-Centered Therapy

Person-centered therapy is a psychotherapy approach based on the theories of Carl Rogers that emphasizes the tendency toward healthy growth inherent in each person (a tendency we labeled *self-actualization* in Chapter 12). Person-centered therapy has also been called *humanistic therapy* and *client-centered therapy*. Person-centered therapists believe that most psychological disorders happen because the self-actualization tendency gets blocked. Therapy, then, is focused on helping clients return to their own self-actualization process, which will guide them back to happiness and psychological health (Cain, 2002, 2010; Erekson & Lambert, 2015; Maslow, 1968; Rogers, 1957; Watson & Bohart, 2015).

The notion that clients have the capacity within themselves to overcome their own psychological issues is a unique characteristic of person-centered therapy. Other forms of therapy typically assume that the client needs the therapist to apply a special technique to them. In person-centered therapy, the therapist's role is more of a facilitator, someone who helps clients help themselves by reconnecting with their

working through
A lengthy phase of psychodynamic therapy in which interpretations are repeated, reconsidered, and given a chance to gradually sink in.

person-centered therapy
A psychotherapy approach based on the theories of Carl Rogers that emphasizes the tendency toward healthy growth inherent in each person.

own tendencies toward healthy growth. As a result, person-centered therapy tends to be described as **nondirective therapy**: a style of therapy in which the client, rather than the therapist, determines the course of therapy. Person-centered therapists trust that if the therapist follows the client's lead, rather than vice versa, the client's own tendency toward self-actualization will guide them wisely.

How, exactly, do person-centered therapists accomplish this? According to Rogers, it's all about the relationship that the therapist forms with the client. Specifically, there are three essential characteristics, or "ingredients," that the therapist must bring to the therapeutic relationship in order to help the client self-actualize: *empathy, unconditional positive regard*, and *genuineness* (Cain, 2002, 2010; Rogers, 1959; Tudor & Worrall, 2006; Velasquez & Montiel, 2018; Watson & Pos, 2017). Let's consider all three in more detail.

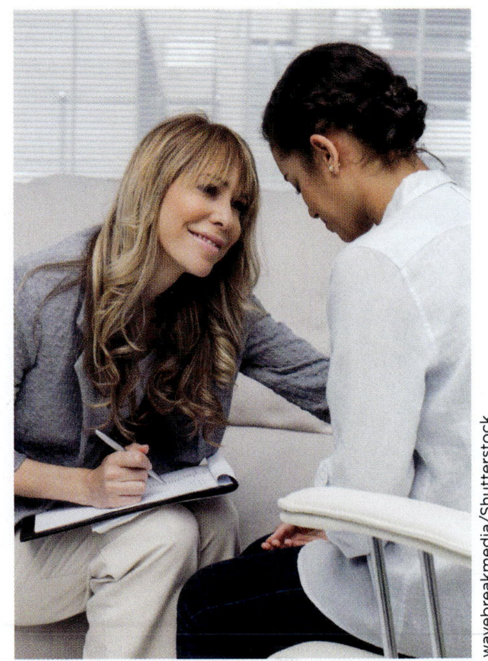

wavebreakmedia/Shutterstock

In person-centered therapy, one of the key elements is empathy, or the therapist's ability to sense the client's emotions and respond compassionately and nonjudgmentally.

Empathy. **Empathy** is the therapist's ability to sense the client's emotions just as the client would, and to then respond compassionately. Empathy is a deep, nonjudgmental understanding of "what it's like" to be the client (Bozarth, 1997; Elliott et al., 2018; Rogers, 1980). With empathy from the therapist, the client doesn't have to worry about the other person forming negative opinions or finding fault in them (which could happen in other relationships). Empathy makes clients feel supported and helps them clarify their own feelings (Gillon, 2007).

Unconditional Positive Regard. The second essential ingredient that the person-centered therapist provides is **unconditional positive regard**, or full acceptance of the client "no matter what," without any conditions or limitations. Rogers liked to say that the therapist should *prize* the client – that is, fully value and appreciate the client as a human being regardless of what the client does, thinks, or feels. (Rogers, 1959). Such full acceptance communicates to clients that they can be themselves completely, so there's no need to pick and choose which aspects of themselves they can show and which they must hide. Such a relationship is quite unique. (With how many friends or family members can you be completely yourself, with no need to monitor or edit what you say and do, and with no concern that you might be judged or rejected?) Over time, unconditional positive regard from the therapist can convince the client to have unconditional positive regard for themselves, which can lead to self-actualization and psychological well-being (Farber et al., 2018).

Genuineness. The third essential ingredient of the therapeutic relationship that the person-centered therapist offers is **genuineness**: the therapist's truthfulness, realness, and honesty, as opposed to falsely playing the therapist role. (Genuineness is also known as *congruence*.) Simply put, the other two ingredients we just discussed – empathy and unconditional positive regard – are worthless if they're fake. You've probably been the recipient of phony empathy before, and you've probably had others pretend to accept you no matter what. If so, you know how those experiences left you feeling – poorly understood and not valued for who you really are. Person-centered therapists aren't acting or otherwise faking it, and they're not just going through the motions of therapy because that's their job. Instead, they truly feel compassion for their clients and sincerely offer them complete acceptance. Such genuineness by the therapist encourages clients to be more engaged in the therapy process, which improves the outcome of therapy (Gillon, 2007; Kolden et al., 2018; Rogers, 1961).

Rogers was extremely confident about the combined power of empathy, unconditional positive regard, and genuineness. In fact, he boldly claimed that a therapist who provided those three ingredients, without any additional specific techniques, could help any client no matter what the problem might be – depression, anxiety, eating disorder, whatever (Rogers, 1957). Research generally supports the notion that these three ingredients are requirements for a good therapeutic relationship, which is a key factor in any kind of therapy (Elliott et al., 2011, 2018; Farber & Doolin, 2011; Farber et al.,

nondirective therapy
A style of therapy in which the client, rather than the therapist, determines the course of therapy.

empathy
The therapist's ability to sense the client's emotions just as the client would, and to then respond compassionately.

unconditional positive regard
The therapist's full acceptance of the client without any conditions or limitations.

genuineness
The therapist's truthfulness, realness, and honesty, as opposed to falsely playing the therapist role.

2018; Kolden et al., 2011, 2018; Zuroff et al., 2010). And for some clients, just those three ingredients may be sufficient. However, the three ingredients alone are not sufficient to help all types of clients.

So, what exactly do person-centered therapists *do* during a session? What techniques do they use?

Actually, person-centered therapy is more about attitudes than techniques. Person-centered therapists believe that *how they are* with clients — not *what they do* to them — is the main source of the benefit in psychotherapy. While most other approaches emphasize the use of particular techniques by the therapist, person-centered therapy emphasizes the power of a compassionate, accepting attitude (Bozarth et al., 2002).

Reflection. The only element of person-centered therapy that resembles a technique is *reflection*. In **reflection**, the therapist listens closely and actively, then restates the client's words in a way that highlights the client's feelings. *Reflection* is actually a shortened form of Rogers's preferred term, *reflection of feeling* (Rogers, 1986). When done appropriately, reflections have the ability to communicate the empathy, unconditional positive regard, and genuineness that are so central to the person-centered therapy approach. They help clients recognize their own feelings more deeply, and consider the possibility that any feelings they have are important and acceptable.

As an illustration of reflection and all of the components of person-centered therapy we have discussed, let's consider my client, Talia. Talia grew up as an only child, and her single mother was loving but domineering. From an early age, Talia's mother told Talia how her life should go: finish high school, go to college, major in nursing, get a job, get married, and have children. Whenever Talia voiced any doubt about this life path, her mom dismissed her thoughts as nonsense: "Oh Talia, that's not you." But Talia sensed that there was, in fact, more to her than the nurse, spouse, and mom roles her mother had laid out for her. Now 23, Talia had followed the first few of her mother's preapproved steps. She had graduated from college with a nursing degree and had landed a good job in a hospital. But she was frustrated and unfulfilled. She wanted to take her life in directions that her mother didn't even know about, she told me, and would certainly frown upon if she did.

Little by little, as our relationship strengthened, Talia revealed to me an astonishing array of yet-unexplored interests: She wanted to join a roller-derby team, create first-person shooter video games, and open a sushi restaurant. She yearned to travel through Australia, study architecture, and volunteer for a pet rescue organization. Hesitantly, she even shared that she might never want to get married or have children — decisions that would definitely stray from her mother's master plan for her.

It seemed clear to me that Talia's self-actualization was stifled. Following her mother's orders had provided Talia with an education and a job, but thwarted many of her other interests, leaving her quite unhappy. As I worked with Talia, I did a number of things that were characteristic of person-centered therapists. I expressed empathy for her situation, often through reflection: "It sounds like you're OK with your job, but you have all of these other passions that seem 'against the rules,' like you're not allowed to pursue them. It seems like that could leave you frustrated or depressed. Is that how you feel?" I practiced unconditional positive regard and was careful to accept Talia no matter what. I prized Talia as a human being — whether she was a mild-mannered nurse, a roller-derby bruiser, or an Australian adventurer. And I did all of this genuinely: I honestly felt empathy and unconditional positive regard toward her, rather than just acting like I did.

Over time, these therapeutic ingredients blended to create a therapy relationship in which Talia felt she could be herself completely. This was a new, liberating experience for Talia. In therapy, she didn't need to follow anyone's preapproved path or censor any of her thoughts or wishes — she could simply say what she really felt, and

reflection
A technique in which the therapist listens closely and actively, then restates the client's words in a way that highlights the client's feelings.

be who she really was. Eventually, Talia felt more free to be who she actually was — not only with her therapist, but with everyone else, including her mother and herself. As our therapy wrapped up, she had signed up for a roller-derby class and had booked a trip to Australia — with no concern about disapproval by anyone.

Zivica Kerkez/Shutterstock

In motivational interviewing, a contemporary version of person-centered therapy, therapists try to tap into the client's own motivation to change.

Motivational Interviewing. In recent years, *motivational interviewing*, a contemporary variation of person-centered therapy, has become quite prominent (Arkowitz et al., 2015; Miller & Moyers, 2017). (Don't let the word *interviewing* in the name mislead you: this is a form of psychotherapy that lasts multiple sessions, not just an initial interview.) Motivational interviewing was originally developed to help people with addiction problems (for example, substance abuse), but it is now used to help people with many other problems as well (Pace et al., 2017; Van Horn et al., 2021; Watson & Schneider, 2016).

A key element of motivational interviewing is tapping into the client's own motivation to change (Dennhardt et al., 2015; Hettema et al., 2005; Miller & Rose, 2009). Too often, the need to change has been imposed by the therapist on the client. For example, picture a rehab center where therapists tell clients that the clients need to stop drinking or using drugs. Clients often resist such orders from outsiders. They are more likely to make genuine, long-lasting change if the desire to do so comes from within themselves.

Therapists who use motivational interviewing try to generate that desire. They openly discuss the mixed feelings the clients may have about a big change in their behavior or lifestyle, such as giving up alcohol, drugs, overeating, gambling, smoking, or any other unhealthy behavior. In fact, therapists empathize with their client's ambivalence about changing, as any good person-centered therapist would. They also highlight discrepancies between the client's values and the way the client is actually living their life — to enhance the motivation to change. For example, the therapist might highlight how the client values their family and work but has put both at risk through substance use. After compassionately listening to the client's own struggle between the pros and cons of changing, the therapist essentially asks how the client would like to proceed. If the client decides to take the steps necessary to make the change, the motivation to change is the client's own, and success is more likely than if the therapist had strong-armed the client into it (Arkowitz et al., 2015; Frey & Hall, 2021; Magill et al., 2018; Miller & Rollnick, 2013; Miller & Rose, 2015).

Behavior Therapy

Behavior therapy is the application of operant and classical conditioning to change outward behavior, with little to no emphasis on the mental processes affecting that behavior. One of the primary reasons behavior therapy developed was to provide a more observable, measurable alternative to the therapies that came before it (Hunt, 1993; Newman et al., 2017; Shikatani et al., 2015; Watson, 1924). After all, many of the core concepts of psychodynamic therapy — the unconscious, resistance, transference, and so on — are impossible to observe or measure in an objective way. And progress in psychodynamic therapy — the extent to which the client's unconscious has been made conscious — is also impossible to directly see or calculate. Similarly, a person-centered therapist would have a difficult time measuring the effects of empathy, unconditional positive regard, or genuineness in a concrete way, because all of these concepts are inside the mind. Behavior therapy shifts the focus away from inner mental processes that can't be seen or measured and toward outward, visible behaviors that can. As a result, behavior therapy lends itself to scientific testing to a greater extent than other kinds of psychotherapy (Fishman, 2016; Grant et al., 2005; Kazdin, 1978; Silverman, 1996; Wenzel, 2017).

The first step of behavior therapy is to define the client's problem in behavioral terms — that is, in words that describe observable, measurable behaviors, rather than inside-the-mind experiences that can't be seen. This process differs drastically from how other kinds of therapists define problems (Spiegler & Guevremont, 2010; Truax,

behavior therapy
The application of operant and classical conditioning to change outward behavior, with little to no emphasis on the mental processes affecting that behavior.

2002). For example, consider Jamal, who seeks therapy from Dr. Lin, a behavior therapist. Jamal initially defines his problem as "social anxiety." When Dr. Lin asks Jamal to describe his social anxiety, Jamal says that he "feels really nervous around other people" and he "always thinks that other people are being critical of me." To Dr. Lin, those descriptions aren't very useful, because they are all inside of Jamal's head. Jamal's *feelings* of nervousness and his *thoughts* about the way other people judge him can't be directly observed or measured, so they aren't good targets for behavior therapy. So, Dr. Lin asks Jamal: "What *behaviors* do you want to change? What do you want to *do* differently?" After initially struggling with the question, Jamal provides some answers — he wants to call and text friends more often, go out to restaurants with friends and coworkers more often, and attend more parties on weekends. These are outward, observable, and measurable behaviors that Jamal and Dr. Lin can easily count. As such, they are much better goals for behavior therapy. After determining a *baseline* — the number of times that Jamal already performs each of those behaviors — Jamal and Dr. Lin can work toward increasing those numbers, and measure Jamal's progress at any point during therapy.

As Jamal's case illustrates, behavior therapists don't see unwanted behaviors (such as his avoidance of social situations) as symptoms of some deeper, underlying problem. Instead, they believe the unwanted behaviors *are* the problem to be fixed in therapy. Think of it this way: If your dog developed the bad habit of chewing up your shoes, would you need to explain that behavior by labeling it as a particular kind of disorder in the dog's mind? Or would you simply try to change your dog's shoe-chewing behavior regardless of where it may have come from? To a behavior therapist, it's as unproductive to look within the human mind as it is to look within the dog's mind.

Once they define problems behaviorally, behavior therapists use a variety of techniques to change the frequency or intensity of that behavior. All of these techniques are based on either classical conditioning or operant conditioning (which we covered in Chapter 12). The idea is that classical conditioning or operant conditioning shaped the problem behavior in the first place, so classical conditioning or operant conditioning can be used to modify it (Craske, 2010).

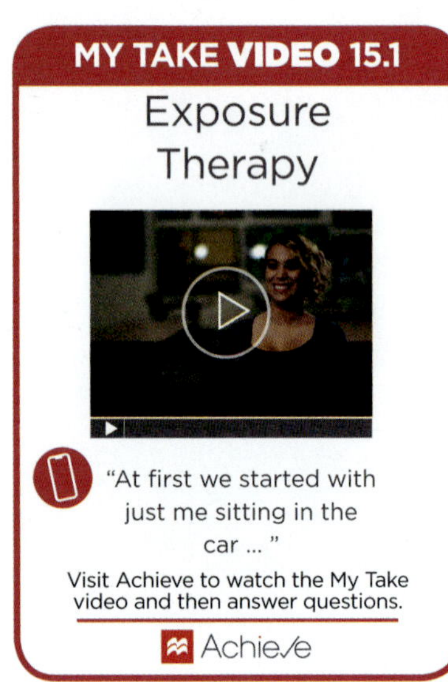

MY TAKE VIDEO 15.1
Exposure Therapy
"At first we started with just me sitting in the car ... "
Visit Achieve to watch the My Take video and then answer questions.
Achieve

Techniques Based on Classical Conditioning. **Exposure therapy** is a form of behavior therapy based on classical conditioning in which anxiety is treated by gradually exposing the client to the thing or situation that causes the anxiety. In short, exposure therapy makes clients gradually face their fears (Abramowitz et al., 2015; Foa & McLean, 2015; Garner et al., 2021; Hazlett-Stevens & Craske, 2008). Consider Zara a client who was badly bitten by a dog many years ago, in an incident that involved blood, stitches, and plenty of terror and pain. She has fearfully avoided dogs ever since. Now, Zara finds herself engaged to a partner who loves and owns dogs, so she is motivated to change. Her fear is the result of classical conditioning: Through real-life experience, dogs were paired with pain and terror. If Zara has new real-life experiences with dogs in which dogs are *not* paired with pain and terror, the original pairing will weaken, and dogs will not evoke such a strong fear reaction in her. Exposure therapy provides that new real-world experience.

It is important to note that the exposure to the anxiety-producing object or situation happens in small steps, each of which causes slightly more anxiety than the one before it. That is, clients face their fears little by little, rather than all at once (Gillihan & Foa, 2016). (*Flooding*, a behavioral treatment in which clients do face their worst fears all at once, was common decades ago but is rarely practiced today because it can be traumatic [Levis, 2008; Taylor, 2002; Zoellner et al., 2008].) Clients, together with their behavior therapists, define those small steps by creating an anxiety hierarchy. An *anxiety hierarchy* is a list of situations that involve the feared object or situation, ranked in order of least to most frightening. The first item on the list causes only mild anxiety, and is often seen by the client as quite achievable; the last item on the list would cause significant anxiety (at least at the time the list is made), and achieving it would indicate that the treatment has been successful. The items in between are like rungs on a ladder — evenly spaced and within reach from the previous step.

exposure therapy
A form of behavior therapy based on classical conditioning in which anxiety is treated by gradually exposing the client to the thing or situation that causes the anxiety.

TABLE 15.1: Example of an Anxiety Hierarchy Used in Treatment of Fear of Dogs

EXPOSURE	DISTRESS RATING (0 = NO FEAR; 100 = MAXIMUM FEAR)	TYPE OF EXPOSURE
1. Visualizing a dog on a leash far away	5	Imaginal
2. Visualizing a dog on a leash nearby	15	Imaginal
3. Visualizing an unleashed dog nearby	25	Imaginal
4. Hearing a dog bark in the next room	35	In vivo
5. Seeing a dog through a window	45	In vivo
6. Standing in the same room with a dog 20 feet away	55	In vivo
7. Standing in the same room with a dog 3 feet away	65	In vivo
8. Petting a dog for 1 second	75	In vivo
9. Petting a dog for 10 seconds	85	In vivo
10. Petting a dog for 1 minute	95	In vivo

Behavior therapists use anxiety hierarchies like this one to help clients take small steps toward facing and overcoming their fears. Notice that some of the exposures take place only in the client's mind (*imaginal*), and others take place in real life (*in vivo*).

As an illustration, **Table 15.1** shows the anxiety hierarchy used in the treatment of Zara's dog phobia. Notice that the first few items on the list don't involve real dogs at all. They involve Zara thinking about or imagining dog-related sights and sounds. These are *imaginal exposures*, and they are often good initial steps for clients to take when actual exposure of any kind would be overwhelming. As she moves through the hierarchy, Zara does start to interact with real dogs — first at a distance, then closer, then in physical contact. These are *in vivo exposures*, meaning that they happen in real life as opposed to Zara's imagination.

For Zara, successful exposure therapy would mean that dogs are paired with no emotional response instead of being paired with fear, which is a big improvement. Sometimes, instead of replacing fear with no emotional response, behavior therapists try to replace fear with a more pleasant feeling, such as relaxation. In Zara's case, the sights and sounds of dogs would gradually become linked to relaxation rather than fear, a difference that would make interaction with dogs much more possible in her day-to-day life. This process is known as **systematic desensitization**: a form of exposure therapy, primarily for phobias, in which the client experiences the new pairing of relaxation (rather than fear) with the thing or situation that previously caused the anxiety.

Systematic desensitization is a therapeutic application of the principle of **counterconditioning**: a classical conditioning technique in which the trigger for an unwanted response is paired with a new stimulus that prevents the unwanted response (Head & Gross, 2008; McGlynn, 2002; Wolpe, 1958, 1969). Systematic desensitization takes advantage of the fact that relaxation and anxiety are mutually exclusive, which means that you can't feel both at the same time. That is, in moments of deep relaxation, you are immune from anxiety. If an anxiety-provoking object were to appear in such a moment, you would have the experience of pairing that object with the relaxation you were feeling rather than the anxiety you used to feel. In Zara's case, seeing a dog while she's in a deeply relaxed state can create a new link between dogs and relaxation rather than the old link of dogs and anxiety.

The first step of systematic desensitization is *relaxation training*, which can take a variety of forms. Sometimes the therapist instructs the client to tense and then release various muscles in the body; sometimes the therapist helps the client envision a calming scene such as a beach or meadow; sometimes the therapist plays soothing music. Once clients can relax themselves during the session, the therapist gradually exposes them to the items on their anxiety hierarchy while they remain in that relaxed state.

systematic desensitization
A form of behavior therapy, primarily for phobias, in which the client experiences the new pairing of relaxation (rather than fear) with the thing or situation that previously caused the anxiety.

counterconditioning
A classical conditioning therapy technique in which the trigger for an unwanted response is paired with a new stimulus that prevents the unwanted response.

The result is that the client experiences things that were previously feared — snakes, heights, or germs, for example — in combination with relaxation, a new association that eclipses the old one in which those things were associated with fear.

Techniques Based on Operant Conditioning. Operant conditioning is all about the consequences that follow a behavior (as we discussed in Chapter 12) (Sturmey et al., 2007). If those consequences are good, we learn to do the behavior more often. If those consequences are bad, we learn to do the behavior less often. Behavior therapists often attempt to change those consequences, an approach known as *contingency management*. Contingencies are those personal "If ... , then ... " rules that we have each learned through our life experiences. Behaviors that turn out to be problematic are often learned in this way. For example, a child's experience may have taught them that if they insult classmates (the problem behavior), then they get laughs from classmates (the reinforcement). If behavior therapists can change these contingencies — particularly, the consequences (or the "then ... " part) that follow the behavior — the problem behaviors will change as well (Drossel et al., 2008; Kearney & Vecchio, 2002; Petry et al., 2013; Villamar et al., 2008).

One technique that behavior therapists use to change clients' contingencies is the **token economy**, in which clients earn tokens that are exchangeable for rewards when they perform target behaviors. (If you ever earned tickets or points by playing games at a place like Dave & Buster's or Chuck E. Cheese's, then traded those tickets or points for prizes, you temporarily experienced a token economy.) Token economies work best in settings where the client's behavior is under constant watch, like inpatient psychiatric hospitals, prisons, and residential schools. In these environments, supervisors pinpoint a target behavior for a particular person, and they provide a token (or chip, or ticket, or point) every time the behavior is performed (Ghezzi et al., 2008). As an example, consider Jeffrey, a man with severe depression living at an inpatient psychiatric hospital. Jeffrey often refuses to leave his room to participate in group activities, exercise, or socialize. However, the staff has noticed that he enjoys the cookies in the cafeteria, so they set up this token economy: Every time Jeffrey leaves his room, he gets a token. He can "buy" an extra cookie with three tokens. Soon, Jeffrey leaves his room more often, enticed by the reward of the cookies.

A challenge with token economies is *generalizability*, the idea that what the client learns in one setting will transfer to other settings (Stuve & Salinas, 2002). In Jeffrey's case, the goal isn't simply to get him to leave his room when he's in the hospital, but to continue to do so after he returns home. If Jeffrey becomes too dependent on a cookie contingency that doesn't exist in the real world, any improvement he shows in the facility may disappear when he returns home.

Token economies are based on reinforcement, but other forms of behavior therapy are based on punishment. For example, **aversive conditioning** is a form of behavior therapy that aims to reduce unwanted behavior by pairing it with an unpleasant experience. Aversive conditioning punishes undesired behaviors. Typically, the punishment used in aversive conditioning is a physically unpleasant sensation such as nausea or electric shock. It is delivered immediately after the client performs a clearly defined unwanted behavior, such as drinking alcohol, smoking, or self-injury (Emmelkamp & Kamphuis, 2002). It is important to note that in any therapy involving punishment, therapists must be extremely careful to use it ethically and with concern for the client's overall well-being. Aversive conditioning therapies tend to have less evidence supporting their effectiveness than reinforcement-based strategies. They are used rarely, and typically, they are only considered after reinforcement-based strategies have failed (Poling et al., 2002; Tahiri et al., 2012).

A form of operant-conditioning-based behavior therapy that has become more widely used in recent years is **behavioral activation**. A type of behavior therapy for people with depression in which they deliberately increase the frequency of reinforcing behaviors. Behavioral activation is based on the simple idea that when people are depressed, they don't do the enjoyable, reinforcing things they typically do. So, the goal of behavioral activation is to get clients to do those enjoyable things more often — to

token economy
A behavior therapy technique in which clients earn tokens that are exchangeable for rewards when they perform target behaviors.

aversive conditioning
A form of behavior therapy that aims to reduce unwanted behavior by pairing it with an unpleasant experience.

behavioral activation
A type of behavior therapy for people with depression in which they deliberately increase the frequency of reinforcing behaviors.

behave the way they do when they are not depressed, with the expectation that their mood will "come around" to match their behavior (Dimidjian et al., 2011; Hopko et al., 2016; Simmonds-Buckley et al., 2019).

Consider my client Shanice, for example, who typically enjoys riding her bike, texting with her sister, and reading graphic novels. When Shanice came to my office, her depression had lowered her mood and motivation so much that she wasn't doing those things much at all. Shanice and I worked together to create a plan for her to do more of those enjoyable activities: ride her bike twice a week, have at least one text exchange with her sister every day, and read graphic novels three times a week. Initially, Shanice said these activities would be difficult while she was feeling depressed – as she put it, "I'm just not feeling it." I assured her that by doing these things, even if they seemed a bit forced at first, she would be giving herself opportunities for happiness, and, as a result, her motivation would increase and her mood would lift. She agreed to try it, and it worked – within a couple of weeks, her depression was less intense, and after several more weeks, she was back to normal. (If you've ever dragged yourself to the gym when your energy level was low, and then noticed that your energy level picked up after your workout, then you have some idea of how behavioral activation can work.) Many studies show that behavioral activation works well for depression, and a few studies suggest that it may also benefit people with anxiety disorders or other problems (Boswell et al., 2017; Cuijpers et al., 2007; Dimaggio & Shahar, 2017; Mazzucchelli et al., 2009; Santos et al., 2021; Stein et al., 2021).

A final point about behavior therapy based on operant conditioning: sometimes, a client's behavior can improve significantly as a result of observing *other* people's behavior. Seeing another person receive reinforcements or punishments for a particular action can have powerful effects (Bandura, 1977; Freeman, 2002; Spiegler & Guevremont, 2010). Behavior therapists call the therapeutic use of this kind of observation **participant modeling**: a technique in which a client watches a model (in some cases, the therapist) perform the target behavior with the intent of the client imitating the model.

As an example of participant modeling, consider Julian, a client struggling with a fear of elevators. His elevator phobia became a significant problem when his company transferred him to a big city, where his office was located on the thirty-third floor of a high-rise office building. Julian's behavior therapist, who specializes in this issue, has a video recording of a model successfully riding an elevator. They watch it repeatedly, discussing the particular components of the behavior that the model displays. Julian's therapist also models the behavior himself, live in front of Julian. His therapist makes sure that Julian notices not only the behaviors involved in riding the elevator (button pressing, entering, waiting, exiting, etc.), but the absence of any negative consequences to any of the behaviors. Then, it is Julian's turn: With his therapist's encouragement and support, he initially rides the elevator in the therapist's building, with his therapist along for the ride, just one floor at a time. Soon, he applies his newly acquired behavior to the real world and finds himself independently riding up to and down from his thirty-third-floor office every day.

Cognitive Therapy

Cognitive therapy is a psychotherapy approach in which therapists help clients change the way they think about life events. What we think about the things that happen to us – our *cognitions* about them – has a huge impact on the way we feel. In fact, feelings like sadness and anxiety that underlie many psychological disorders are often caused by the way we think about the events that take place in our lives, rather than the events themselves (Beck, 2002, 1995, 1976; Beck & Haigh, 2014; Bermudes et al., 2009; Clark et al., 2009; DeRubeis et al., 2019; Dobson, 2012; Dozois & Brinker, 2015; A. Fernandez et al., 2021; Hofmann et al., 2013; Purdon, 2021; Wenzel, 2017). (See **Figure 15.3** for a cognitive model of emotions.)

We tend to overlook the importance of our cognitions about events, and mistakenly believe that the events directly caused our emotions. For example, I once had a client,

participant modeling
A technique in which a client watches a model (in some cases, the therapist) perform the target behavior with the intent of the client imitating the model.

cognitive therapy
A psychotherapy approach in which therapists help clients change the way they think about life events.

cognitive-behavioral therapy
A hybrid therapy approach that combines an emphasis on logical thinking with the use of conditioning principles to directly change behavior.

rational-emotive behavior therapy (REBT)
A form of cognitive therapy in which the therapist challenges the client's illogical beliefs and encourages the client to adopt more logical beliefs.

ABCDE model of cognitive therapy
A type of rational-emotive behavior therapy in which the therapist and client identify the sequence that leads from illogical thinking to logical thinking about particular life events.

FIGURE 15.3 Cognitive Model of Emotions. We often assume that the events in our lives lead directly to feelings, including depression and anxiety. However, according to cognitive therapists, there's an important step — our thoughts (or cognitions) about the events — that intervenes and actually causes us to feel certain emotions. For example, a breakup doesn't directly cause sadness — the *thoughts* about the breakup do.

Catrina, whose depression had lasted for weeks and had significantly interfered with her work and social life. She explained her reason for seeking therapy this way: "I'm miserable because my application for a promotion at work got rejected." According to cognitive therapists, a statement like that overlooks the middle step that occurs between the event and the feeling. A more complete explanation might go like this: "I'm miserable *because I see myself as a complete failure* because my application for a promotion got rejected." Here, it is easy to see that the cognition about the rejection is the link between the rejection and Catrina's misery about it.

Cognitive therapy tends to be rather short-term and structured, qualities it shares with behavior therapy (Olatunji & Feldman, 2008; Pretzer & Beck, 2004; Roth et al., 2002). Actually, cognitive therapy began as a variation of behavior therapy, after some behavior therapists realized that behavior therapy didn't always work as predicted. They recognized that mental processes, as difficult as they can be to define and measure, do in fact play a powerful role in determining people's behavior. Techniques based on classical conditioning and operant conditioning sometimes failed because they didn't take into account what the client was thinking. For that reason, cognitions were given much more attention (Goldfried, 1995; O'Donohue, 2009). The relationship between cognitive and behavioral forms of therapy is reflected in the fact that many therapists today describe themselves as practicing **cognitive-behavioral therapy**, a hybrid therapy approach that combines an emphasis on logical thinking with the use of conditioning principles to directly change behavior.

There are two pioneers of cognitive therapy, Albert Ellis and Aaron Beck (Dryden, 2015; Rosner, 2015). Their approaches differ a bit, but both emphasize improving psychological well-being by changing thought processes. Let's consider both of these approaches.

CHAPTER APP 15.1

 FearTools

The FearTools app uses cognitive therapy techniques, among others, to help users overcome anxiety that could lead to phobias, generalized anxiety disorder, and social anxiety disorder. Among its features is a Thought Diary, which allows users to enter thoughts (cognitions) that cause them anxiety and then pull up a list of cognitive distortions — like all-or-nothing thinking, generalizing, and catastrophizing — to challenge those thoughts. Next, the user can come up with alternative thoughts that would cause less anxiety, all in a process that closely parallels the ABCDE cognitive therapy model.

How does it APPly to your daily life?
If you were struggling with anxiety, could the cognitive therapy techniques in this app be helpful? Could it complement or replace a human therapist?

How does it APPly to your understanding of psychology?
Consider the anxiety disorders you learned about in Chapter 14. In your opinion, which of those disorders would be most and least improvable with the cognitive therapy approach used in this app?

To learn more about this app or to download it to your phone, you can search for "FearTools" on Google, in the iPhone App store, or in the Google Play store.

Rational-Emotive Behavior Therapy. Albert Ellis's approach to cognitive therapy is called **rational-emotive behavior therapy (REBT)**: a form of cognitive therapy in which the therapist challenges the client's illogical beliefs and encourages the client to adopt more logical beliefs (David et al., 2018; Ellis, 1962, 2008; Ellis & Ellis, 2011; O'Kelly & Collard, 2016). (Don't get confused — REBT has "behavior therapy" in its name, but it is a form of cognitive therapy.) Therapists who use REBT argue with clients — respectfully but forcefully — pointing out when clients' thoughts are unreasonable or irrational. Therapists also explain how those unreasonable or irrational thoughts may contribute to their depression, anxiety, or other psychological symptoms. They eventually encourage clients to challenge their own thoughts, with the ultimate goal of replacing those thoughts with more sensible ones (DiGiuseppe & Doyle, 2019; Dryden, 2009; Lorenzo-Luaces et al., 2015; Onken, 2015).

REBT utilizes the **ABCDE model of cognitive therapy**, in which the therapist and client identify the sequence that leads from illogical thinking to logical thinking about particular life events. In the ABCDE model, each letter stands for a step in the therapeutic sequence: *activating event, belief, consequence (emotional), dispute*, and *effective new belief* (David et al., 2019; Dryden, 1995, 2009; Ellis & Grieger, 1977; Ellis & Harper, 1975). Often, to teach clients to use this model, therapists ask clients to fill out a five-column form with each of these letters at the top of a column (**Figure 15.4**). Let's go back to Catrina's case as an example. The *activating event* for Catrina was

Activating event	Belief	Consequence (emotional)	Dispute	Effective new belief
My heart was pounding when I got to my seat at the concert.	"I'm probably having a heart attack."	Anxiety, panic	My seat was way up in the highest level of the arena, so it's normal for my heart to pound a little after all that stair climbing.	"I'm fine—it's just a slightly stronger heartbeat, and it'll go away in a few minutes."
The brakes on my bike squeaked when I stopped just now.	"My brakes will go out completely at any minute, and I'll crash and get seriously hurt."	Anxiety, panic	One little squeak does not mean the brakes are completely shot.	"The squeak is cause for a little concern, but not too much. I'll keep listening for it, and if the squeaking continues, I'll take it into the bike shop."

FIGURE 15.4 Sample ABCDE Form for Cognitive Therapy Clients. This form shows how a client in cognitive therapy might learn to identify and dispute the beliefs that lead to anxiety or other troublesome emotions and replace them with new beliefs that are more logical.

getting turned down for the job. Her *belief* about this event was "I see myself as a complete failure." This belief caused the *consequence* (*emotional*) of misery in Catrina's case. Steps A, B, and C illustrate how Catrina's problem developed: the job rejection led to her belief about being a complete failure, which led to the feeling of misery.

Steps D and E are where the therapeutic change happens. The *dispute* was the argument I made (with Catrina's help) against the illogical belief that she was a "complete failure." We disputed it with more logical, reasonable arguments like "Just because you didn't get this particular promotion doesn't mean you are a complete failure," and "Many aspects of your life are actually very successful, even without that promotion." Finally, we moved on to the *effective new belief*—a way of thinking about what happened that replaces the original belief (from step B). As Catrina put it, her effective new belief was this: "Losing that promotion is a letdown, but it doesn't mean I'm a failure at all. Actually, I'm a success in many ways, and I'll have many more chances to succeed too."

Cognitive Distortions. In Aaron Beck's approach to cognitive therapy, therapists teach their clients terminology to label their **cognitive distortions**: descriptive, memorable names for various kinds of irrational thinking (Beck, 1976, 2002; Beck et al., 1979; DiGiuseppe et al., 2016; Leahy, 2003; Newman, 2016). Let's highlight some of the cognitive distortions that apply to Catrina's case. **All-or-nothing thinking** is a cognitive distortion in which the client mistakenly evaluates events as either absolutely flawless or completely awful, with no middle ground in between. Catrina's belief that she was a complete failure for not receiving the promotion could be described as all-or-nothing thinking. Catrina's illogical belief of being a *complete* failure might also be an example of **overgeneralization**, in which the client comes to a very broad-based conclusion based on just a single unfortunate event. After all, Catrina's misery stemmed from just one lost promotion, not an endless series of them. Allowing that single event to define her as a complete failure simply isn't logical.

Another of Beck's cognitive distortions, **catastrophizing**, occurs when the client exaggerates the negative consequences of an event, or makes a "catastrophe" out of a minor mishap. For Catrina, maybe a lost promotion is a letdown, but it's certainly not catastrophic. **Mental filtering** describes the client's tendency to ignore, or "filter out," the positive while focusing excessively on the negative. Catrina had actually been promoted several times to obtain her current position, but ignored those promotions when she labeled herself a failure. When the client takes too much of the blame and responsibility for unfortunate events, that's called **personalization**. That promotion may have gone to someone else for

cognitive distortions
Descriptive names for various kinds of irrational thinking.

all-or-nothing thinking
A cognitive distortion in which the client mistakenly evaluates events as either absolutely flawless or completely awful, with no middle ground in between.

overgeneralization
A cognitive distortion in which the client comes to a very broad-based conclusion based on just a single unfortunate event.

catastrophizing
A cognitive distortion in which the client exaggerates the negative consequences of an event, or makes a "catastrophe" out of a minor mishap.

mental filtering
A cognitive distortion in which the client ignores, or "filters out," the positive while focusing excessively on the negative.

personalization
A cognitive distortion in which the client takes too much of the blame and responsibility for unfortunate events.

MY TAKE VIDEO 15.2

Cognitive Distortions

"I used to always believe that it was my fault ... "

Visit Achieve to watch the My Take video and then answer questions.

Achieve

any number of reasons that have nothing to do with Catrina, so it would be irrational to assume that Catrina is personally responsible for the way things worked out.

When clients understand cognitive distortions, they can reexamine the first thoughts that popped into their minds about the things that happen to them and, when appropriate, label them as illogical. By doing so, clients discredit that illogical thought, and give themselves the opportunity to replace it with a more logical one. That more logical thought, in turn, improves their emotional and psychological well-being.

Another trademark of cognitive therapy (particularly Aaron Beck's approach) is the idea that our beliefs are actually just hypotheses waiting to be tested (Dobson & Hamilton, 2008; Kuehlwein, 1993). Too often, we accept our beliefs as proven facts when, actually, we have not tested them at all. For that reason, cognitive therapists often encourage clients to put their beliefs to the test in real life. Just as scientists conduct experiments in a lab to test their hypotheses about chemistry or physics, clients should conduct experiments in their real lives to test their hypotheses about themselves.

For example, one of my clients, Elbia, was a 65-year-old grandmother who lived a sad, lonely life despite having two children and five grandchildren in town. "I'm a nuisance," she told me. "My kids and grandkids are busy with their own lives. They don't want to be bothered with this old lady." "How do you know that?" I kindly asked. At first, she was very confident that it was true, but as I repeated the question, she realized that she had no proof for her belief. Bravely, she decided to test it. In our next session, Elbia told me that she had asked her daughter if she and her kids might want to have dinner together, and her daughter happily accepted. Soon, she asked her son the same question, and he responded positively too. Within weeks, she was seeing her kids and grandkids frequently. Most importantly, Elbia felt much happier. Had she never tested her belief — the hypothesis that she was a nuisance to her family members — she would have never given herself the chance to prove it false.

Third-Wave and Mindfulness-Based Therapies. The most recent versions of cognitive therapy are collectively known as *third-wave therapies*, following behavior therapy as the first wave and traditional cognitive therapy as the second wave. One of the core elements of third-wave therapies is *mindfulness*, an increased awareness of internal experiences with an emphasis on just experiencing them rather than analyzing or avoiding them (as we discussed in Chapter 11). Therapists who promote mindfulness in their clients help them pay attention to and fully accept their thoughts and feelings, rather than relying on distractions or numbness to get them through their days (Dimidjian & Linehan, 2009; Fruzzetti et al., 2019; Morgan & Roemer, 2015).

The big difference between third-wave therapists and traditional cognitive therapists is their strategy toward irrational thoughts (Follette & Hazlett-Stevens, 2016; Olatunji & Feldman, 2008; Orsillo et al., 2016). For traditional cognitive therapists, the strategy is to confront and dispute irrational thoughts, with the intent of preventing the unpleasant emotions they may bring. For third-wave therapists, the strategy is not to confront or dispute those thoughts, but to simply let them run their course. Third-wave therapists believe that those irrational thoughts will pass, and any unpleasant feelings they bring will subside as well. With third-wave therapies, clients learn that they don't need to avoid these irrational thoughts or feelings: clients are resilient enough to endure them and emerge unscathed.

Consider Tyler, a client of mine with generalized anxiety disorder. Among the many things that Tyler worried about irrationally was his health: *what if I catch pneumonia or break my leg or develop heart disease?* These thoughts caused Tyler a lot of anxiety. He usually avoided them by distracting himself with video games, TV, and social media. A traditional cognitive approach would encourage Tyler to fight those irrational thoughts by labeling them as cognitive distortions and replacing them with more rational thoughts. By contrast, a mindfulness-based approach would encourage Tyler to experience the thoughts, but not get caught up in them or grant them too much authority. Those thoughts may occur, and they may produce anxiety, but they will be temporary and any anxiety they produce will fade away. That means Tyler doesn't need to dread the fleeting moments when he does experience those thoughts and feelings, or find some distraction to avoid them. Those moments may be slightly unpleasant, but Tyler is strong enough to withstand them until they pass.

There are many specific varieties of third-wave therapies. One popular third-wave therapy is *acceptance and commitment therapy* (ACT), which helps people with anxiety and other disorders to focus on accepting the emotions and thoughts they experience, as well as making strong commitments to behave according to one's own personal values (Forman et al., 2015; Forsyth & Eifert, 2016; Hayes, 2004; Hayes et al., 2011, 2012; Lee et al., 2021; Strosahl & Robinson, 2017; Swain et al., 2013). Another well-established third-wave therapy is *dialectical behavior therapy*, which helps people with borderline personality disorder and other disorders to regulate and tolerate intense emotional experiences (Cameron, 2015; Granato et al., 2021; Koerner, 2012; Linehan, 1993a, b; Lungu & Linehan, 2016; Rizvi & King, 2019).

Combining Therapies: Eclectic and Integrative Approaches

Psychodynamic therapy, person-centered therapy, behavior therapy, and cognitive therapy are four major approaches to psychotherapy. As you read about them in this chapter, you might have gotten the impression that a therapist has to choose one of these and abandon the others. That's actually not true at all. In fact, most therapists combine approaches (Cook et al., 2010; Norcross et al., 2005, 2019).

When therapists combine approaches, they typically follow an *eclectic* or *integrative* strategy. In the **eclectic approach to therapy**, the psychotherapist selects the best treatment for a particular client based on evidence from studies of similar clients (Gold, 1996; Norcross et al., 2016, 2017; Stricker, 2010). These eclectic therapists rely heavily on studies of "what works" for specific diagnoses to determine what kind of therapy they will conduct. The therapists' own personal preference is not the determining factor. Instead, eclectic therapists master a variety of different approaches, and shift gears between them as they work with clients with various problems. For example, an eclectic therapist might practice exposure therapy with her 9:00 A.M. client because that client has a specific phobia and the scientific studies suggest that exposure therapy works best for that disorder. If the therapist's 10:00 A.M. client has generalized anxiety disorder, the therapist may shift to cognitive therapy, because that's the therapy with the most evidence for that disorder. The eclectic approach has also been called the *prescriptive* approach because it resembles the way that physicians prescribe particular medications for particular illnesses (Antony & Barlow, 2010).

In contrast to the eclectic approach, some therapists adopt an **integrative approach to therapy**: a strategy in which the psychotherapist blends styles or techniques to create a new form of psychotherapy. Integrative therapists recognize that psychodynamic, person-centered, behavioral, and cognitive therapies need not be mutually exclusive. Their components can complement each other quite well and can be combined to create a unique blend. When they are expertly combined, the hybrid can be effective for a variety of clients (Beitman & Manring, 2009; Norcross, 2005; Wachtel, 1977).

For example, I once saw a client, Bobby, an extremely shy man who struggled with anxiety and depression. He was 30 years old and interested in dating, but was nervous about asking anyone out on a date and felt increasingly hopeless about his difficulty doing so. My therapy with Bobby included, at various times, elements of each of the major approaches to therapy. I expressed genuine empathy with his nervousness about asking someone out and the subsequent hopelessness, as a person-centered therapist would. I offered interpretations about how his early relationships with his parents may contribute to difficulty trying to start new relationships — ideas of which he had been unconscious — as a psychodynamic therapist would. I helped him create and progress through an anxiety hierarchy — including many behaviorally defined small steps along the way to asking someone out — as a behavior therapist would. And I challenged the logic of his thinking about asking someone out — he might not get rejected, after all, and if rejection did happen, it wouldn't destroy him — as a cognitive therapist would. (Check the "It's Like ... " box for further explanation about the difference between eclectic and integrative approaches.)

eclectic approach to therapy
A strategy in which the psychotherapist selects the best treatment for a particular client based on evidence from studies of similar clients.

integrative approach to therapy
A strategy in which the psychotherapist blends styles or techniques to create a new form of psychotherapy.

IT'S LIKE...

Eclectic Therapy Is Like Fruit Salad, and Integrative Therapy Is Like a Smoothie

When you eat a fruit salad, each bite delivers a distinct flavor: pineapple first, strawberry second, raspberry third. When you drink a smoothie, the same ingredients blend into a unique flavor that comes through in every sip.

An eclectic approach to psychotherapy is a lot like a fruit salad. Eclectic therapists bring a distinct approach to each client, based on the empirical evidence for what works best with that client's disorder. During the course of a workday, an eclectic therapist may be behavioral with their first client, psychodynamic with their second, and cognitive with their third.

On the other hand, an integrative approach to psychotherapy is a lot like a smoothie. Rather than offering them separately, the therapist blends these same ingredients—for example, behavioral, psychodynamic, and cognitive approaches—to form a unique combined type of therapy that comes through with every client. Like a well-mixed smoothie, the flavor of this type of therapy remains more constant from client to client, as opposed to the contrasting flavors of an eclectic therapist shifting therapy approaches for each client.

Shutterstock

Shutterstock

In an eclectic approach to therapy, the therapist provides each client with a single form of psychotherapy based on evidence that it works for a particular disorder—similar to a fruit salad in which each bite contains a single piece of fruit, and each has just one taste. In an integrative approach to therapy, the therapist blends styles or techniques to create a new form of psychotherapy—similar to a sip of a smoothie that contains tastes of several blended fruits.

CHECK YOUR LEARNING:

15.4 Who seeks psychotherapy?

15.5 What is the main goal of psychodynamic therapy, and what techniques do therapists use to help the client reach that goal?

15.6 What are the most important aspects of person-centered therapy, including its three essential characteristics?

15.7 How do behavior therapists use techniques based on classical conditioning (like exposure techniques) and techniques based on operant conditioning (like token economies) to help clients?

15.8 What is the main goal of cognitive therapy, and how are the ABCDE model and cognitive distortions relevant to that goal?

15.9 What are the similarities and differences between the eclectic and integrative approaches to psychotherapy?

To check your understanding of these questions, click show the answers or refer to the answers in the Chapter Summary.

Psychotherapies for Groups and Families

YOU WILL LEARN:

15.10 about the basics of group therapy.

15.11 about the basics of family therapy.

So far, we have focused on forms of psychotherapy in which there is only one client working with the therapist. Let's shift our focus to two kinds of therapy that involve multiple clients, *group therapy* and *family therapy*.

Group Therapy

group therapy
Psychotherapy conducted with a group of clients and with an emphasis on interpersonal interaction.

Group therapy is psychotherapy conducted with a group of clients and with an emphasis on interpersonal interaction. Group therapy can follow any of the approaches discussed as individual therapies, but it offers the additional unique opportunity to focus on interpersonal interaction, the way people get along with each other (Burlingame & Baldwin, 2011; Markin & Kasten, 2015; Yalom, 1983; Yalom & Lezcz, 2020). Many group therapists assume that a client's difficulties with interpersonal interaction are major reasons for their psychological struggles. People whose relationships with close friends and family members are full of conflict, tension, and mistreatment are especially vulnerable to developing psychological disorders. Group therapy gives these clients the chance to relate to new people (fellow group members), get feedback from them about the interaction, and then decide if they want to change the way they behave (Brabender, 2002; Corey & Corey, 2016; Goldberg & Hoyt, 2015; Ormont, 1992; Rutan & Shay, 2017).

For example, I once led a group that included Steven, an extremely insecure 30-year-old client with social anxiety, and Deja, a 48-year-old recently divorced woman with depression. Steven didn't speak up in the group for many sessions. He was timid and thought others would be angry at him for taking up valuable group time when they had problems of their own to discuss. On the other hand, Deja did not hesitate to dominate the conversation. In fact, she seemed to presume that the group revolved around her. More than any other client, she discussed her personal problems at great length and volume – including the four divorces she had experienced, and the many other friends who had moved on from her, leaving her lonely.

As one session started, Steven surprised us all by meekly saying that he would like to spend a minute discussing his issues, "if that's OK." Most of us encouraged Steven to speak, but Deja rolled her eyes and exhaled disapprovingly. Steven tearfully began describing how he had few friends and had never made efforts to meet new people because he was terrified to "put himself out there." He was sure that others would reject him, and he wouldn't be able to handle it. Most of us were on the edge of our seats as we listened to Steven, but Deja was checking her watch. After just a few minutes, she interrupted Steven mid-sentence: "Are you about done? Can someone else have a turn to talk? I have important stuff to bring up."

Steven apologized, returned to his silence, and let Deja take over. Before she did, though, I posed a question to the whole group: "What do you think of the way Deja and Steven communicate with each other?" One by one, the group members shared their opinions, which formed a consensus: Deja's behavior was too domineering, which made them dislike her; Steven's behavior was too unassertive, which made them lose respect for him. Neither Deja nor Steven had ever received such candid feedback. With further discussion, both Deja and Steven realized that the interpersonal tendencies they showed in the group were exactly the same ones that contributed to their problems in their real lives: Deja's failed marriages and friendships were largely due to her domineering behavior; Steven's loneliness was largely due to his lack of assertiveness. I then posed another question to Deja and Steven: "Do you want to change your interpersonal tendency? Or the ways you often act toward other people?" They both agreed that they did, and our group spent the remaining group sessions practicing different styles of interacting. The goal was for Deja and Steven (and the others) to develop healthier interaction skills with their fellow group members and, more importantly, to translate those skills to their real lives (which, I'm happy to say, they eventually did).

As this example illustrates, some groups include clients with a variety of diagnoses. Other groups include clients who share similar diagnoses (for example, bulimia groups, substance abuse groups, or bipolar disorder groups). Both types of groups have unique advantages (Yalom & Lezcz, 2020). Groups with a variety of diagnoses offer a wider variety of individuals with whom to interact; those with similar diagnoses offer a more immediate sense of *universality*, or the feeling that "we're all in the same boat." The number of clients in groups varies, but in most cases, it falls between 5 and 10 (Brabender, 2002). The number of therapists can vary as well – sometimes one, sometimes two. The presence of two therapists allows for two perspectives on clients' problems, as well as two sets of eyes and ears to capture clients' many verbal and nonverbal messages and an

Phynart Studio/E+/Getty Images

Group therapy is psychotherapy conducted with an emphasis on interpersonal interaction.

self-help group
A type of group therapy in which the group members run the session without a professional therapist leading them.

family therapy
Psychotherapy that aims to improve how the family system functions, which in turn will improve the mental health of its individual members.

opportunity to model healthy two-person interactions (Clark et al., 2016; Shapiro, 1999).

In other cases, the group is a **self-help group**, in which the group members run the session without a professional therapist leading them. Self-help groups typically center around a particular problem – substance use or depression, for example – and often consist of low-cost or free meetings organized by a veteran member of the group.

Family Therapy

Family therapy is psychotherapy that aims to improve how the family system functions, which in turn will improve the mental health of its individual members. In family therapy, the idea is that the entire family system is flawed – even if only one person shows symptoms (Bernal & Gomez-Arroyo, 2017; Davis et al., 2015; Goldenberg & Goldenberg, 2007; Kaslow, 2011; Lebow & Stroud, 2016; Rolland & Walsh, 2009). This is why family therapy focuses on improving the ways family members communicate and relate to each other.

Think of it this way: if something was wrong with a tire on your car, would you take the tire off the car and take the tire to a mechanic to repair it? The mechanic might tell you that was a bad idea. The same problem could occur again after you put the repaired tire back on the same car, because the problem may actually be in the car, not the tire. Perhaps the car's suspension or axles are bad, or perhaps the alignment is off. Repairing the car's system more broadly could address the problem better than a narrow-minded focus on just the tire alone. Family therapists think in much the same way. For example, treating any individual – a teenager with anorexia, a fourth-grader with panic disorder, a parent/caregiver with major depression – in isolation from the family system in which they live is like taking the tire off the car.

Family therapists utilize a wide range of styles, including family versions of the individual therapies we have already covered (psychodynamic, person-centered, behavioral, and cognitive). But they also try to take advantage of opportunities that are available only when the family participates in treatment. For example, family therapists often examine the family's *structure*, the rules by which it operates (Minuchin, 1974; Sexton & Stanton, 2016). Family rules are rarely explicit (they aren't posted as a list on the refrigerator door), but they are still powerful influences on how individuals behave within families. Think of the eye-opening experience you had as a kid when you first spent time, or perhaps slept over, at a friend's house. You may have gotten an insider's view on your friend's family's structure and realized just how different it was from your own family's structure. For example, some families encourage children to become independent thinkers who might disagree with parents/caregivers; others encourage children to behave obediently and agree with parents/caregivers at all times. The unspoken rule in Family A might be "Always think for yourself," while the unspoken rule in Family B might be "Do as you're told – because I said so." Regardless of the particular family rules, they may not be working well if they contribute to a member of the family developing a psychological disorder. With the whole family in therapy, a family therapist has the unique chance to help clarify and change the family rules.

CHECK YOUR LEARNING:

15.10 What is group therapy, and how does its emphasis differ from the emphasis of individual therapy?

15.11 What is the main goal of family therapy?

To check your understanding of these questions, click show the answers or refer to the answers in the Chapter Summary.

How Well Does Psychotherapy Work?

YOU WILL LEARN:

15.12 about the challenges involved in testing the results of psychotherapy.

15.13 how well psychotherapy works.

15.14 how the outcomes of different kinds of psychotherapy compare to each other.

15.15 what makes psychotherapy work.

In the early days of psychotherapy, there weren't many questions about how well it worked. Therapists and clients generally assumed that it was beneficial, and that was that (Weissmark & Giacomo, 1998). But in 1952, a prominent researcher named Hans Eysenck wrote a summary of the small amount of research on the outcome of psychotherapy available at that time. His conclusion was surprising and controversial: psychotherapy *didn't* work, he claimed, at least not any better than muddling through one's problems without psychotherapy (Eysenck, 1952). It turns out that Eysenck's methods were flawed, and his conclusion was wrong. Thousands of studies of psychotherapy since Eysenck's time undoubtedly support the conclusion that psychotherapy *does* work, but Eysenck's claim did inspire many researchers to study the question and provide data to answer it (Routh, 2011; Wampold, 2010a).

When researchers examine how well psychotherapy works, they face a number of important questions in terms of the research methods they use. For example, whom should they ask: the client, the therapist, or an outside observer (Holmqvist, 2016; Strupp, 1996; Strupp & Hadley, 1977)? When should they ask: during therapy, right when it ends, or long afterward (Lambert, 2011)? How should they ask: questionnaires, interviews, or even brain scans? (See the From Research to Real Life box for more on how therapy changes the brain.) Any of these methods can provide meaningful and important data. The point here is that determining how well psychotherapy works is a complex undertaking, full of methodological choices that can have a powerful influence on the results researchers obtain.

FROM RESEARCH TO REAL LIFE

Psychotherapy Changes the Brain

A fascinating way to measure the outcome of therapy—in addition to the more common methods of asking the client, asking the therapist, or observing the client's behavior—is to see how psychotherapy changes the brain itself. Studies using functional magnetic resonance imaging (fMRI) and positron emission tomography (PET) neuroimaging technologies to view clients' brains have shown that psychotherapy produces biological changes in the brain. In many cases, psychotherapy and medication appear to change the brain in similar ways. These studies typically compare clients with the same diagnosis, half of whom get therapy and half of whom get drugs. Among their findings:

- For clients with OCD, behavior therapy and Prozac both resulted in decreased metabolism in the right caudate nucleus, which corresponds with clients' reports of decreased anxiety (Baxter et al., 1992).
- For clients with social phobia, cognitive-behavior therapy and Celexa both resulted in decreased activation in the amygdala and hippocampus, which corresponds to lower anxiety levels (Furmark et al., 2002).
- For clients with major depressive disorder, interpersonal therapy and Paxil both resulted in decreased activation in the prefrontal cortex and increased activation in the inferior temporal lobe and insula, brain changes that suggest an improvement in mood (Brody et al., 2001).

For many, it comes as no surprise that medication changes the brain: after all, it is a biological intervention. But accumulating evidence suggests that psychotherapy changes the brain as well, often in much the same way as the corresponding medication (Arden & Linford, 2009; Barsaglini et al., 2014; Brooks & Stein, 2015; Cozolino, 2017; Fronzo et al., 2021; Mancke et al., 2018; Roffman et al., 2005; Stahl, 2012; Viamontes & Beitman, 2009). Some forward-thinking researchers have speculated that, if the technology becomes less expensive, therapists could routinely use fMRI or PET scans to examine the effects that the therapy has had on the client's brain (Cozolino, 2017). For now, most measurements of therapy outcome continue to rely on the tried-and-true (and inexpensive) methods of client feedback, surveys, or behavior observations, but it will be interesting to see how brain scans are involved in the future.

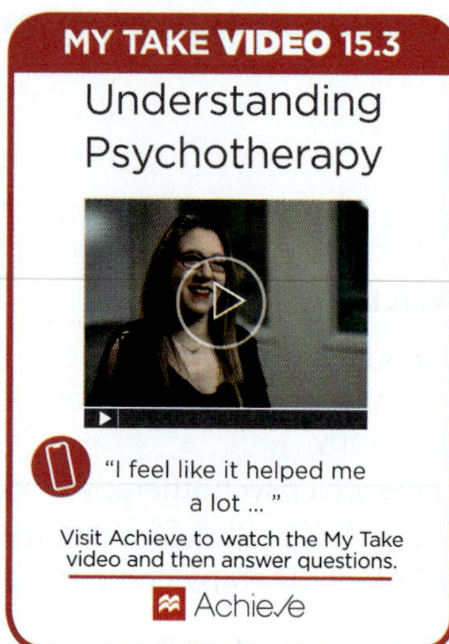
MY TAKE VIDEO 15.3
Understanding Psychotherapy
"I feel like it helped me a lot ... "
Visit Achieve to watch the My Take video and then answer questions.
Achieve

Fortunately, the thousands of studies on the benefits of psychotherapy collectively represent all of these methodological choices. Together, these studies point to one undeniable conclusion: psychotherapy works. Large-scale reviews of psychotherapy outcome studies have repeatedly confirmed this finding for decades (Lambert & Simon, 2008; Lipsey & Wilson, 1993; Luborsky et al., 2002; Shapiro & Shapiro, 1982; Smith & Glass, 1977; Wampold, 2010a; Wampold & Imel, 2015; Weiner, 2016). In general, the average person who receives psychotherapy for a particular issue is better off afterward than 80% of people who did not receive psychotherapy for a similar issue (Smith et al., 1980). Researchers have also repeatedly found that the benefits of psychotherapy tend to last for long periods of time, and that those benefits represent real-world improvement in the quality of the clients' lives (Bandelow et al., 2018; Lambert & Ogles, 2004). Of course, psychotherapy is not a cure-all. Some psychotherapy clients don't benefit, others drop out, and a small number actually get worse over the course of therapy (Cuijpers et al., 2018; Lebow, 2006; Rozental et al., 2016, 2018; Striano, 1988). However, these negative outcomes are the exception to the rule of successful outcome.

Studies that explore how well psychotherapy works generally fall into two categories: *efficacy* studies and *effectiveness* studies (Dalrymple et al., 2015; Spokas et al., 2008; Truax & Thomas, 2003). (See the Current Controversy box for more on efficacy studies.) Efficacy studies examine how well psychotherapy works in controlled studies — in other words, how well it works "in the lab" (Durand & Wang, 2011; Rosqvist et al., 2011). In an efficacy study, researchers test a specific type of therapy for a specific diagnosis, typically by selecting only clients who perfectly match the criteria for that diagnosis ("textbook cases" of the disorder) and treating them with a therapy manual that directs the therapist. For example, researchers might recruit people who meet the diagnostic criteria for obsessive-compulsive disorder (OCD) and treat them with a manual for a behavior therapy known as *exposure and response prevention* (*ERP*). ERP is a specific version of exposure therapy (which we discussed earlier in this chapter) in which the therapist also prevents clients from responding as they typically would — for example, making clients touch dirt and then preventing them from washing their hands. Numerous studies of ERP for OCD have demonstrated success, so psychologists now recognize ERP as a therapy that works for obsessive-compulsive disorder (Carr, 2008; Dougherty et al., 2015; Nathan & Gorman, 2007; Roth & Fonagy, 2005).

DIVERSITY MATTERS

The notion of using "therapy that works" for a particular problem is a cornerstone of **evidence-based practice**: an approach to psychotherapy in which the therapist makes decisions based on a combination of three factors: research evidence, therapist expertise, and client characteristics (APA Presidential Task Force on Evidence-Based Practice, 2006; Barlow et al., 2013; Buscemi & Spring, 2015). Increasingly, psychologists rely on evidence-based practice to help their clients. They consider "what works" according to efficacy studies, but also their own unique abilities as therapists and the unique characteristics of their clients as well — not just their diagnosis, but their ethnicity, age, gender, socioeconomic status, religion, sexual orientation, and other diversity variables (David et al., 2018; Norcross et al., 2011, 2017; Spring & Neville, 2011).

In contrast to efficacy studies, effectiveness studies examine how well psychotherapy works in the real world, in the clinics, counseling centers, hospitals, and private practices where clients are rarely textbook cases of any particular disorder (Chambless et al., 1998; Garske & Anderson, 2003; Lambert, 2013). Effectiveness studies are less tightly controlled than efficacy studies. They involve clients with varied diagnoses, and therapies that don't always strictly follow one manualized technique. However, they often do a better job of capturing the hodgepodge of clients that actual therapists see and the medley of treatment methods that they use in their day-to-day practices. One large-scale effectiveness study appeared in *Consumer Reports* magazine, in which readers described their experiences as psychotherapy clients ("Mental Health," 1995; Seligman, 1995). Of course, the respondents had a tremendous range of psychotherapy experiences — different types, lengths, therapist professions, and so on — but the results were very positive. The overwhelming majority reported that their psychotherapy experience was beneficial and that their lives were improved as a result. Effectiveness studies such as this one suggest that the benefits of psychotherapy are evident in real-world settings as well as lab studies.

evidence-based practice
An approach to psychotherapy in which the therapist makes decisions based on a combination of three factors: research evidence, therapist expertise, and client characteristics.

CURRENT CONTROVERSY

Therapies That Work . . . For Whom?

Efficacy studies are a great way to determine how well a particular form of psychotherapy works for a particular disorder. In efficacy studies, researchers carefully recruit only those clients who definitely meet the criteria for the disorder (and are often "textbook cases," with no co-occuring problems to complicate the diagnosis). Such research methods create a tightly controlled study in which there is a clear link between the therapy and the outcome.

But there are drawbacks to efficacy studies as well, especially for real-world psychotherapists — those who practice in clinics, counseling centers, hospitals, and private practices rather than in controlled studies — and their clients. Consider these issues:

- The clients in real-world settings often have messier diagnoses than those in the efficacy studies. In other words, textbook cases are not very common (Durand & Wang, 2011). For example, some clients may have some symptoms of major depressive disorder, but not quite enough to qualify for the diagnosis. Or, if clients do have enough symptoms, they may also have symptoms of anxiety disorders, eating disorders, or personality disorders, which complicate the diagnosis. Efficacy studies exclude these types of cases, even though large percentages of people who actually show up in clinics, counseling centers, private practices, and other real-world therapy settings are similar (Shedler, 2015; Westen et al., 2004).

DIVERSITY MATTERS

- The clients in real-world settings often come from a wider range of cultural backgrounds than the clients in the efficacy studies (Rosqvist et al., 2011). Few efficacy studies include significant numbers of clients from diverse backgrounds in terms of ethnicity, disability status, or sexual orientation; in fact, most clients in these studies are White and from middle or upper socioeconomic backgrounds (Brown, 2006; Munoz & Mendelson, 2005; Olkin & Taliaferro, 2006; Sue & Zane, 2006).

These drawbacks are among the reasons that certain therapies gain empirical support, but are not necessarily adopted by all therapists (Boswell et al., 2011; Safran et al., 2011; Stewart et al., 2012; Wolfe, 2012). As a result, there is a gap between the findings that psychotherapy researchers make and the way that many psychotherapists actually practice (Gyani et al., 2014). •

Which Therapy Works Best?

After researchers established that psychotherapy generally works, the battle over which type of psychotherapy works best began (Lambert, 2011; Smith et al., 1980). Psychodynamic therapists, person-centered therapists, behavioral therapists, cognitive therapists, and others — all of them claimed that their approach was uniquely beneficial. To settle the score, researchers designed studies in which clients were divided into two groups, one of which received Therapy A and the other of which received Therapy B. Over and over again, these studies yielded an unexpected result: a tie. The competing therapies both worked, with about equal rates of success (Lambert & Ogles, 2004; Luborsky et al., 2002; Norcross & Newman, 1992; Wampold, 2010b). Researchers called this finding the **dodo bird verdict** — a nickname (from *Alice in Wonderland*) for the research finding that different forms of psychotherapy are equally effective (Elliott et al., 2015; Luborsky et al., 1975). (As **Figure 15.5** illustrates, in *Alice in Wonderland*, the dodo bird character watches a race between many contestants and announces that "Everybody has won and all must have prizes.")

Universal History Archive/Getty Images

FIGURE 15.5 Dodo Bird Verdict. In *Alice in Wonderland*, the dodo bird character judges a race and declares, "Everybody has won and all must have prizes." In studies comparing the outcomes of various kinds of therapy, the finding has often been similar: different therapies generally produce positive results at about the same rate. That finding has been nicknamed the *dodo bird verdict*.

Psychotherapy researchers have confirmed the dodo bird verdict many times, but it is not without controversy (Asarnow & Ougrin, 2017; de Felice et al., 2019; Wampold, 2001). Some researchers point to the more recent generation of studies that are much more targeted — which *specific* kinds of therapy work for which *specific* problems — in which the findings are not equal across therapies (Antony & Barlow, 2010; Chambless, 2002; Chambless & Ollendick, 2001; Cuijpers et al., 2018; Siev & Chambless, 2007). Some of these specifically targeted studies have found that particular therapies (most often behavioral and cognitive techniques) have benefits with particular diagnoses that other therapies have not been able to match. As a result, while the major forms of therapy are all recognized as generally beneficial, certain therapies may be especially beneficial for certain problems (Mulder et al., 2017; Norcross, 2005; Paul, 2007).

Lists of which particular therapies work best for which particular disorders are available to therapists (and anyone else) in several different ways (Norcross et al., 2017). The American Psychological Association (APA) publishes *clinical practice guidelines* that describe the best treatments for various disorders. Two divisions of APA that focus on therapy — the clinical psychology division (Division 12) and the

dodo bird verdict
A nickname (from Alice in Wonderland) for the research finding that different forms of psychotherapy are equally effective.

child & adolescent psychology division (Division 53) — each maintain Web sites that allow users to search by disorder for evidence-based treatments. And books, with titles like *A Guide to Treatments That Work* and *Clinical Handbook of Psychological Disorders*, offer chapter-by-chapter explanations of the therapies that work best for particular problems written by experts on each disorder (Barlow, 2021; Nathan & Gorman, 2015).

What Makes Therapy Work?

The finding that many forms of psychotherapy may be beneficial highlights the presence of **common factors**: elements found in all forms of effective psychotherapy that play an important role in client improvement (Brown, 2015; Elkins, 2016; Messer & Wampold, 2002; Stricker, 2010; Wampold, 2010b, 2015). The idea that different therapies all work because of the same underlying mechanisms has actually been around since the 1930s, but only in the last few decades has the scientific study of psychotherapy been able to back it up with data (Frank, 1961; Rosenzweig, 1936; Torrey, 1986).

The best-supported common factor in psychotherapy is the **therapeutic alliance**: a trusting and collaborative relationship in which therapist and client work toward shared goals (Alavi & Sanderson, 2015; Budge & Wampold, 2015; Crits-Christoph et al., 2011; Flückiger et al., 2018; Halfon, 2021; Horvath et al., 2011; Kaiser et al., 2021; Karver et al., 2018; Norcross & Lambert, 2011; Norcross & Wampold, 2011). The therapeutic alliance is the single best predictor of success in psychotherapy. If you want to know whether therapy is going to work, it is more important to know about the strength of the therapeutic alliance than it is to know what type of therapy is being conducted, how much experience the therapist has, what type of training the therapist has, or anything else about the therapy (Beitman & Manring, 2009; Laska & Wampold, 2014; Wampold, 2010a). The therapeutic alliance is especially important from the client's point of view. It is crucial for the client to experience this sense of coalition and partnership as a foundation of therapy (Orlinsky, 2017; Rosenfeld, 2009; Wampold, 2001). The therapeutic alliance is vital not only in individual therapy, but in family therapy and group therapy too (Burlingame et al., 2018; Escudero & Friedlander, 2017; Friedlander et al., 2018). In group therapy, the therapeutic alliance is often called *cohesion*, which suggests an alliance between the client and all others in the group, including both therapists and fellow clients.

Other common factors of effective psychotherapy have been recognized as well. For example, *positive expectations* (or, more simply, *hope*) are provided by good therapists across all styles of therapy. The idea that things will change for the better, by whatever techniques the therapist uses, can be therapeutic in and of itself (Constantino et al., 2011, 2018). When a physician tells you what's wrong and hands you a prescription, you may start to feel better even before you pick up the medication. In this situation, improvement begins when hope replaces despair. The same is true in psychotherapy, regardless of the therapist's particular approach. When the therapist gives you reason for hope, the hope itself can have benefits.

A final common factor across therapies is *attention* — simply focusing on a problem rather than ignoring or neglecting it offers an opportunity for improvement. Any kind of therapy involves attention to the client's problem (Prochaska & Norcross, 2018). For example, consider Kelly, a teenager who developed bulimia nervosa. Kelly and their family may initially find their bingeing and purging so difficult to accept that they pretend it isn't so bad, convince themselves that it will simply go away on its own, or deny it altogether — anything to avoid dealing with it. On the other hand, taking her to any competent therapist would require, at the very least, that Kelly and their family acknowledge the problem — that is, to pay attention to it. That mere decision to address the bulimic behavior rather than disregard it would provide Kelly the opportunity for improvement.

common factors
Elements found in all forms of effective psychotherapy that play an important role in client improvement.

therapeutic alliance
A trusting and collaborative relationship in which therapist and client work toward shared goals.

IT'S LIKE...

Common Factors in Therapy Are Like the Common Active Ingredient in Toothpaste

All toothpastes work about equally well in preventing cavities, though their advertisements suggest otherwise. Those ads try to convince us that some special ingredient—baking soda, whiteners, sparkles, mouthwash, etc.—makes their brand uniquely effective. But the truth is that the various flavors of Crest, Colgate, Aim, and Aquafresh all prevent cavities quite well, and equivalently. That's because these toothpastes all share the same active ingredient: fluoride.

Toothpaste is like psychotherapy in this way. As the dodo bird verdict indicates, all major forms of psychotherapy generally work about equally well. The reason for this equality is the same as well: common factors are what make various kinds of therapy work. This is true in spite of the fact that the supporters of each kind of therapy usually point to its unique qualities or techniques—the ingredients that set it apart from the others. They may be important in terms of making the therapy palatable to certain clients, but they are not the active ingredients. So, what is the common active ingredient—the fluoride—of psychotherapy? Therapy seems to have a few active ingredients rather than just one, including the therapeutic alliance, positive expectations, and attention to problems.

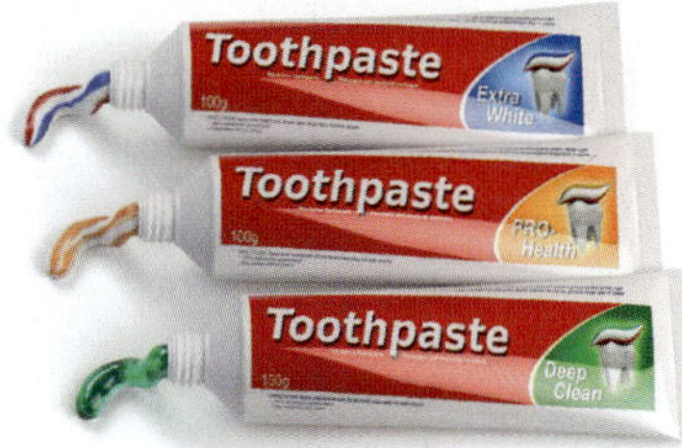

Maxx-Studio/Shutterstock

Across brands of toothpaste, fluoride is a common factor, an active ingredient that makes them all effective. Research suggests that there are common factors across types of psychotherapy too: a good therapeutic alliance, positive expectations, and attention to problems. •

CHECK YOUR LEARNING:

15.12 When they research how well psychotherapy works, how do researchers address the issues of who, when, and how to ask?

15.13 According to research, does psychotherapy work?

15.14 How do different types of psychotherapy generally compare to each other in terms of effectiveness?

15.15 What are the common factors that make various kinds of psychotherapy work?

To check your understanding of these questions, click show the answers or refer to the answers in the Chapter Summary.

The Importance of Culture and Diversity in Psychotherapy

YOU WILL LEARN:

15.16 what cultural competence is, and why it is important in the practice of psychotherapy.

15.17 what cultural self-awareness is, and why it is important for psychotherapists to have.

Good therapists recognize the importance of their clients' diverse backgrounds. They know that numerous cultural and diversity factors can influence the way clients interact with others, the meanings they attach to life events, and their expectations of psychotherapy as well. As a result, they use psychotherapy in a way that honors each client's unique combination of qualities.

DIVERSITY MATTERS

Psychotherapists in the United States and many other parts of the world practice in an increasingly diverse population. Psychotherapists have an ethical and moral responsibility to work with diverse clients in a way that respects their cultural background, values, and practices (Chu et al., 2016; Comas-Díaz, 2011, 2012; Melton, 2018; Pedersen, 2008; Vasquez, 2010). Essential to the success of therapy is **cultural competence**: the ability to work sensitively and expertly with members of a culturally diverse society.

Without cultural competence, a client might feel misunderstood and could miss out on the gains that therapy might bring (Comas-Díaz & Brown, 2016; Huey et al., 2014; McGoldrick et al., 2005; Owen et al., 2011; Sue & Sue, 2008). For

cultural competence
The ability to work sensitively and expertly with members of a culturally diverse society.

example, consider Saalim, a Muslim man who is in regularly scheduled therapy with Dr. Martels, a Christian psychologist. Saalim's upcoming appointment happens to fall at the end of Ramadan, a month in which Muslims traditionally fast during daylight hours. Specifically, the appointment conflicts with Eid al-Fitr, a three-day celebration marking the end of Ramadan during which the fast is broken with family and friends. Ideally, Dr. Martels would foresee the possibility of a scheduling conflict and gladly offer Saalim a different appointment. At the very least, he should be respectful and receptive if Saalim points out the scheduling conflict. He certainly should not become annoyed about the time conflict or belittle the religious observance — to do so would indicate an insensitivity that could jeopardize his relationship with Saalim, possibly resulting in a premature end to therapy (Brown & Pomerantz, 2011).

An important component of cultural competence is **cultural self-awareness**: the therapist's recognition that their own perspective is not necessarily that of others. Cultural self-awareness also requires the therapist to understand their own cultural background and the values and beliefs it has influenced (Fouad & Arredondo, 2007; Gelso, 2010; Graham & Roemer, 2015; Mirsalimi, 2010; Nezu, 2010). Closely related to cultural self-awareness is *cultural humility*: an attitude based on self-reflection, recognizing the limits of your own knowledge about diversity, and educating yourself about the identities and experiences of other people (discussed in Chapter 10; Hook et al., 2017; Mosher et al., 2017; Tervalon & Murray-Garcia, 1998). Therapists with cultural humility recognize that there's a lot to learn about the cultural background of their clients, and with respect and an open mind they try to learn more about that background and how it influences the client's day-to-day experience.

To illustrate the importance of cultural self-awareness and cultural humility in therapists, consider the experience I had with my client, Kumar, who moved to the United States from India as a child. When I worked with him, he was 32 years old and was married to an Indian woman with whom he had two young children. In large part, they held traditional Indian beliefs about many things, including the roles of husbands and wives within families. Kumar sought therapy for depressive symptoms. Rather quickly, he had gone from a happy, productive person to someone who felt sad most of the time, lost all interest in his pastimes, and had trouble eating and sleeping. At first, he was reluctant to offer any explanations for his sudden downturn, but as our relationship grew stronger, he told me about the event that devastated him: His wife had received a raise. In fact, his wife (who happened to work for the same large company as Kumar) had been promoted to a higher-ranking position than Kumar, with correspondingly higher pay. As he told me of his wife's promotion, Kumar felt intense shame and embarrassment. In traditional Indian culture (as in many others), the expectation in a family with a husband and a wife is for the husband to be the primary (or only) breadwinner. From Kumar's point of view, to be a husband out-earned by one's wife is to be emasculated and even humiliated.

My own cultural beliefs differed from Kumar's. As far as I'm concerned, my wife's promotion would be cause for celebration, regardless of whether her new position or pay exceeded my own. But thankfully, I had enough cultural self-awareness to recognize that my reaction to that situation was just my own, and not necessarily Kumar's (or anyone else's, for that matter). My responsibility was to recognize and respect Kumar's experience through his eyes, not mine.

The examples involving Saalim and Kumar happen to focus on religion and ethnicity, respectively, but there are many other types of diversity that culturally competent therapists recognize. For certain clients, issues related to gender, race, sexual orientation, language, socioeconomic status, age, disability status, urban/rural background, or other variables may be essential for the therapist to appreciate. There may be particular combinations of these variables that therapists should recognize because they can contribute to discrimination, unequal treatment, or social disadvantage — that is, examples of *intersectionality*, as we discussed in

cultural self-awareness
The therapist's recognition that their own perspective is not necessarily that of others.

Chapter 10. There may even be subcultures that are crucial to understanding certain clients, especially for therapists who work within those subcultures, such as therapists who work in the military or in the prison system (Atuel & Castro, 2018; Kupers, 2001).

When therapists show cultural competence, clients benefit. Multiple studies show that clients who believe their therapists appreciate their culture tend to have lower dropout rates and achieve better outcomes in therapy (Anderson et al., 2019; Owen et al., 2017; Rogers-Sirin et al., 2015; Soto et al., 2018).

LIFE HACK 15.1

If you seek therapy, make sure to choose a therapist who "gets" your cultural background. It's important to the success of therapy.

(McGoldrick et al., 2005; Owen et al., 2011; Sue & Sue, 2008)

CHECK YOUR LEARNING:

15.16 Why is cultural competence important in the practice of psychotherapy, and how is it valuable to clients?

15.17 Why is cultural self-awareness important for psychotherapists?

To check your understanding of these questions, click show the answers or refer to the answers in the Chapter Summary.

Ethics in Psychotherapy

YOU WILL LEARN:

15.18 why confidentiality is crucial to psychotherapy, and when psychotherapists might break it.

15.19 what informed consent is, and why it is important to psychotherapy.

15.20 what multiple relationships are, and how they can be harmful to clients.

Psychologists have many ethical standards to uphold when they conduct psychotherapy. That's true not just for psychologists, but for all mental health professionals who conduct therapy, including professional counselors and social workers, among others. Each mental health profession has its own *ethical code*, a document that sets the expectations for ethical behavior within that profession (Hummel et al., 2017; Koocher & Keith-Spiegel, 2016; Pope & Vasquez, 2016). The APA, for example, originally published an ethical code in the 1950s, and has updated it on a regular basis since that time (American Psychological Association, 2010; Behnke & Jones, 2012; Koocher & Campbell, 2016; Vasquez, 2015). The vast majority of psychotherapists maintain consistently high ethical standards. Those who violate their ethical obligations run the risk of harming clients as well as the reputation of the profession.

Confidentiality – maintaining the privacy of client information – is among the most essential ethical responsibilities of psychotherapists, without which the practice of psychotherapy might be impossible (Fisher, 2012). Clients expect psychotherapists to keep the content of their sessions secret; in fact, they often believe that confidentiality is absolute (Miller & Thelen, 1986). That is, clients often assume psychotherapy is a "vault" from which therapists never release any of their information. They are right for the most part, but on rare occasions, therapists are obligated to break confidentiality to protect the well-being of the client or someone else. For example, state laws require therapists to break confidentiality to report ongoing child abuse (Kenny et al., 2017; Knapp & VandeCreek, 2006; Koocher & Daniel, 2012; Tribbensee & Claiborn, 2003). Also, if the therapist learns that the client intends to harm someone – including themselves – the therapist is required to break confidentiality to warn those who may be at risk (Benjamin & Beck, 2018; DeMers & Siegel, 2016; Pope, 2011; Welfel et al., 2012). (Imagine, for example, that a client with a detailed plan to carry out a school shooting tells a therapist about their intentions.)

Another ethical requirement for psychotherapists is to obtain **informed consent**: permission given by the client, after the therapist educates the client about the therapy process, to move forward with the therapy. You may already be familiar with the idea of informed consent in research studies (especially if you are a participant in research studies as a component of this psychology course). If you do participate in a study, you will probably read informed consent forms before those studies begin. The forms give you a description of what the research entails and give you the option of going ahead or backing out. The informed consent process is similar with psychotherapy, but there

confidentiality
When a therapist maintains the privacy of client information.

informed consent
Permission given by the client, after the therapist educates the client about the therapy process, to move forward with the therapy.

multiple relationship
A situation in which a therapist has both a professional relationship and a nonprofessional relationship with the same person.

are often a few differences too. For example, informed consent for psychotherapy often involves both a written form and a verbal discussion. This discussion gives the client the chance to receive answers to any questions about the therapy process, and also gives the therapist the opportunity to begin to form a therapeutic alliance with the client by ensuring that the client genuinely understands what therapy will involve (Murphy & Pomerantz, 2016; Pomerantz, 2012, 2015, 2017; Pomerantz & Handelsman, 2004). Additionally, informed consent to therapy is often more of an ongoing process than a one-time event. Researchers usually know exactly what participation in an experiment will involve, but therapists can't always have such foresight. They don't always know at the outset how long therapy will last, or exactly what techniques might be included, or even what all the goals will be. So, psychotherapists often provide as much information as they can at the very beginning, and then more information as they get to know the client and their issues in greater detail (Pomerantz, 2005).

A particularly treacherous ethical issue that psychotherapists face is the **multiple relationship**: a situation in which a therapist has both a professional relationship and a nonprofessional relationship with the same person. The nonprofessional part of the multiple relationship might involve sexual interaction, nonsexual friendship, or a business partnership (Anderson & Kitchener, 1996; Cohen-Filipic, 2015; Sommers-Flanagan, 2012; Zur, 2007, 2017). Not every multiple relationship is unethical; in small communities where everyone knows everyone, for example, they can be unavoidable (Barnett, 2017; Johnson & Johnson, 2016; Juntunen et al., 2018; Schank et al., 2010; Werth et al., 2010). In many cases, however, multiple relationships are clearly unethical, especially when they have the potential to exploit the client or impair the therapist's ability to function competently and objectively (Gutheil & Brodsky, 2008; Schank et al., 2003; Zur, 2009). Sexual multiple relationships always fall in this unethical category, and it is the therapist's responsibility to avoid them entirely. Unfortunately, the media have often depicted therapists engaging in multiple relationships: sleeping with clients, becoming friends with them, or getting involved in their business activities. While movies and TV shows may portray such multiple relationships as normal or even helpful to clients, in the real world they pose significant risk to clients' well-being, and they are definitely not part of standard treatment by competent professionals (Pope, 1994; Sonne, 2012).

CHECK YOUR LEARNING:

15.18 Why is confidentiality crucial to psychotherapy, and under what circumstances might psychotherapists break it?

15.19 What is informed consent, and why is it important to psychotherapy?

15.20 How can multiple relationships be harmful to psychotherapy clients?

To check your understanding of these questions, click show the answers or refer to the answers in the Chapter Summary.

Telepsychology: Psychotherapy via Modern Technology

YOU WILL LEARN:

15.21 what telepsychology is.

15.22 what the pros and cons of telepsychology are.

15.23 how one example of telepsychology, virtual reality exposure therapy, works.

Traditional, face-to-face, in-person psychotherapy now has a rapidly growing counterpart: **telepsychology**, psychotherapy that takes place via technological devices over the Internet. Telepsychology can take a variety of forms, including videoconferencing and text-, e-mail, or app-based interactions. It can take place via computer, tablet, smartphone, or similar devices (Andersson, 2015, 2016; Barnett, 2018; Campbell et al., 2018; Campbell & Norcross, 2018; Dimeff et al., 2011; Eonta et al., 2011; Larson, 2018; Marks & Cavanagh, 2009; McCord et al., 2020; Riper & Cuijpers, 2016).

Telepsychology has a few undeniable advantages (Maheu et al., 2005). For example, it enables people who live a great distance from a psychotherapist to access the help they need. Regardless of distance, it offers convenience of therapy from home (or wherever the client may be with a mobile device), avoiding the hassles, time, and expense of a drive to the therapist's office. It can also make therapy available to people whose disorders prevent them from leaving home to go to a therapist's office, including those with agoraphobia, severe social phobia, or debilitating depression (Kraus, 2004; Luxton et al., 2016; Nelson & Bui, 2010).

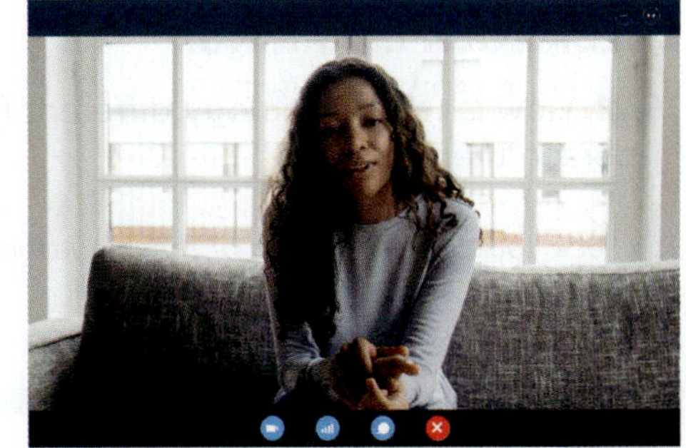

fizkes/Shutterstock

Videoconferencing with a therapist is one of many forms of telepsychology, or psychotherapy that takes place via technological devices over the Internet.

Telepsychology also has significant limitations, and it raises new legal and ethical concerns for therapists (Barnett & Kolmes, 2016; Fisher & Fried, 2003; Glueckauf et al., 2018; Hames et al., 2020; Koocher, 2009; Lustgarten & Elhai, 2018; Martin et al., 2020; Naglieri et al., 2004). For example, therapists must be expert enough in technology to deal with technology-related problems when they arise and use encryption or similar methods to ensure confidentiality (Barnwell et al., 2018; Poole & Crow, 2018). Even when the technology works as it should, telepsychology still cannot match in-person visits in terms of picking up on nonverbal communication (Rummell & Joyce, 2010). Especially when tele therapy happens in written form (e-mail or text), it can be easy for a therapist or a client to misunderstand each other's tone or emotional state. (That's why we so often resort to emoticons or emojis when e-mailing and texting, but sometimes those still fail to do the trick.)

Many studies have found that telepsychology works well – often just as well as traditional face-to-face therapies (Berryhill et al., 2018; Reger & Gahm, 2009; Spence et al., 2011; Varker et al., 2018). In fact, there has been so much recent research on the effectiveness on telepsychology that numerous reviews and meta-analyses – big, overarching studies that combine the results of lots of previous studies – have been published. This research indicates that telepsychology is generally about as beneficial as in-person therapy for both adults and children (E. Fernandez et al., 2021; McClellan et al., 2021; Poletti et al., 2020; Venturo-Conerly et al., 2021).

The fact that telepsychology works so well is especially great news in the context of the COVID pandemic. Since the pandemic hit in early 2020, a huge number of therapists around the world have transitioned to doing therapy either partially or completely online (mostly through videoconference), including many who had never tried it before (Owings-Fonner, 2020; Simpson et al., 2021; Waldroff, 2020). Many of these therapists who were forced into teletherapy by the pandemic found the experience to be much better than they expected, and most continue to see at least some of their clients online even as in-person therapy becomes safer and more feasible (Békés & Aafjes-van Doorn, 2020; Calkins, 2021; MacMullin et al., 2020). As technology and mobile devices continue to permeate our lives, it's likely that online therapy options will become even more prevalent. In fact, a 2021 survey asked leading experts in psychotherapy to predict changes in the next decade of psychotherapy, and one of the strongest predictions was the continued rise of teletherapy, especially through videoconferencing (Norcross et al., 2021).

One particular form of telepsychology that has earned positive reviews is **virtual reality exposure therapy**: a form of exposure therapy in which clients use electronic means to experience simulations of the situations that cause them anxiety. Perhaps the best way to describe virtual reality exposure therapy is to compare it to a video game that has been created with the specific goal of gradually helping clients face what they fear. For example, a client with a phobia of spiders can see virtual 3D spiders at increasingly close distances. A child afraid of thunderstorms can see and hear virtual storms at increasing levels of intensity. A military veteran with posttraumatic stress disorder (PTSD) can experience virtual flashbacks of the trauma, with increasing intensity, until the power of those flashbacks to cause anxiety wears off. A number of studies on virtual reality exposure therapy have demonstrated positive effects, especially on PTSD, phobias, and other anxiety disorders (Carl et al., 2019; Emmelkamp & Meyerbröker, 2021; Gerardi et al., 2008; Powers & Rothbaum, 2019; Reger et al., 2011). It will be interesting to see the role that virtual reality exposure therapy and other forms of therapy that depend on technology play in the future of psychotherapy.

telepsychology
Psychotherapy that takes place via technological devices over the Internet.

virtual reality exposure therapy
A form of exposure therapy in which clients use electronic means to experience simulations of the situations that cause them anxiety.

CHECK YOUR LEARNING:

15.21 How is telepsychology different from face-to-face, in-person therapy?

15.22 What are the pros and cons of telepsychology?

15.23 What is virtual reality exposure therapy?

To check your understanding of these questions, click show the answers or refer to the answers in the Chapter Summary.

Biomedical Therapies

YOU WILL LEARN:

15.24 who prescribes psychiatric drugs.

15.25 about antipsychotic drugs, including their benefits and drawbacks.

15.26 about antianxiety drugs, including their benefits and drawbacks.

15.27 about antidepressant drugs, including their benefits and drawbacks.

15.28 about mood-stabilizing drugs, including their benefits and drawbacks.

15.29 about stimulant drugs, including their benefits and drawbacks.

15.30 about brain stimulation techniques and psychosurgery, including their benefits and drawbacks.

In addition to psychotherapy, biomedical therapies are frequently used to treat psychological disorders by directly altering the biology of the brain. *Drug therapies* are by far the most common form of biomedical therapy, but other forms include *psychosurgery* and electric or magnetic forms of *brain stimulation*.

Can psychologists prescribe drugs?

In recent years, some psychologists have tried to obtain the privilege to prescribe drugs, but they have been successful only in a handful of states. Even in those states, prescribing psychologists are very rare (Brown et al., 2021; Burns et al., 2008; DeAngelis, 2017; DeLeon et al., 2011; Linda & McGrath, 2017; McGrath, 2010; Robiner et al., 2020; Tryon, 2008). So, generally speaking, the vast majority of psychologists do not prescribe drugs. *Psychiatrists* do. Psychiatrists are trained as medical doctors, and their approach to mental disorders emphasizes the biological abnormalities of the brain. Other medical doctors and nurse practitioners who people tend to see more often – primary care physicians, pediatricians, OB/GYNs, and so on – also prescribe drugs for psychological issues. Actually, these nonpsychiatrist prescribers and nurse practitioners write more prescriptions for psychiatric medications than psychiatrists do, as illustrated in **Figure 15.6** (Barkil-Oteo, 2013; Morris et al., 2021; Sultan et al., 2018). Psychologists often work collaboratively with these prescribers to provide comprehensive treatment for their clients (Ruddy et al., 2008).

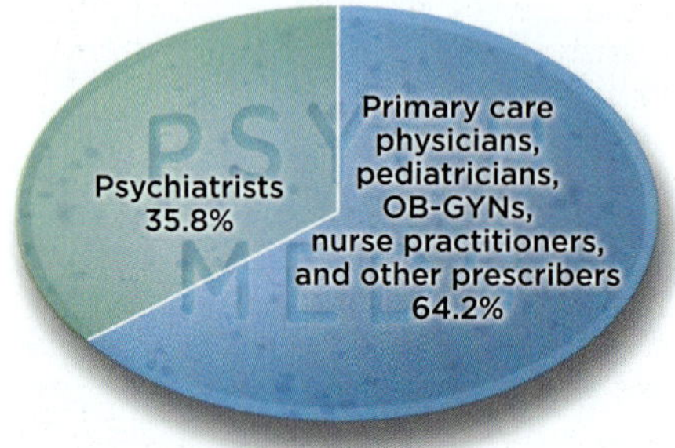

FIGURE 15.6 Who Prescribes Psychiatric Medications? The majority of prescriptions for psychiatric medications are written not by psychiatrists, but by the "first line" health care professionals that patients most often see: primary care physicians, OB/GYNs, pediatricians, nurse practitioners, and others with prescription privileges. Data from Morris et al. (2021).

Note: Data collected from over 300,000 college students in 2018–2019.

psychopharmacology
The treatment of psychological disorders with medications.

antipsychotic drugs
Medications used to reduce psychotic symptoms such as delusions, hallucinations, and bizarre behavior.

Drug Therapies

Psychopharmacology is the treatment of psychological disorders with medications. Often, clients who receive such medication also receive psychotherapy, and in many cases this combination can be better than either medication or therapy alone. Medication for psychological disorders is very common. According to one estimate, over 600 million prescriptions were written for such medications in the United States in 2018 (Grohol, 2019). Another estimate of Americans in 2019 found that 15.8% of Americans had taken medication for psychological issues in the past 12 months (Terlizzi & Zablotsky, 2020). And the number seems to be increasing too: one large-scale survey of college students found that the percent who take a psychiatric medication jumped from 13.5% in 2007 to 23.5% in 2019 (Morris et al., 2021).

Medication can be especially helpful in the reduction of psychological symptoms, often rather quickly. However, symptoms often come back after the medication is discontinued, especially if the client has not addressed underlying issues that contributed to the problem (Sammons, 2016). As **Figure 15.7** shows, there are five primary types of drugs used to treat psychological disorders: *antipsychotic, antianxiety, antidepressant, mood-stabilizing*, and *stimulant* drugs.

Antipsychotic Drugs. **Antipsychotic drugs** are medications used to reduce psychotic symptoms such as delusions, hallucinations, and bizarre behavior. Common brand names of antipsychotics include Risperdal, Zyprexa, Abilify, and Haldol. They

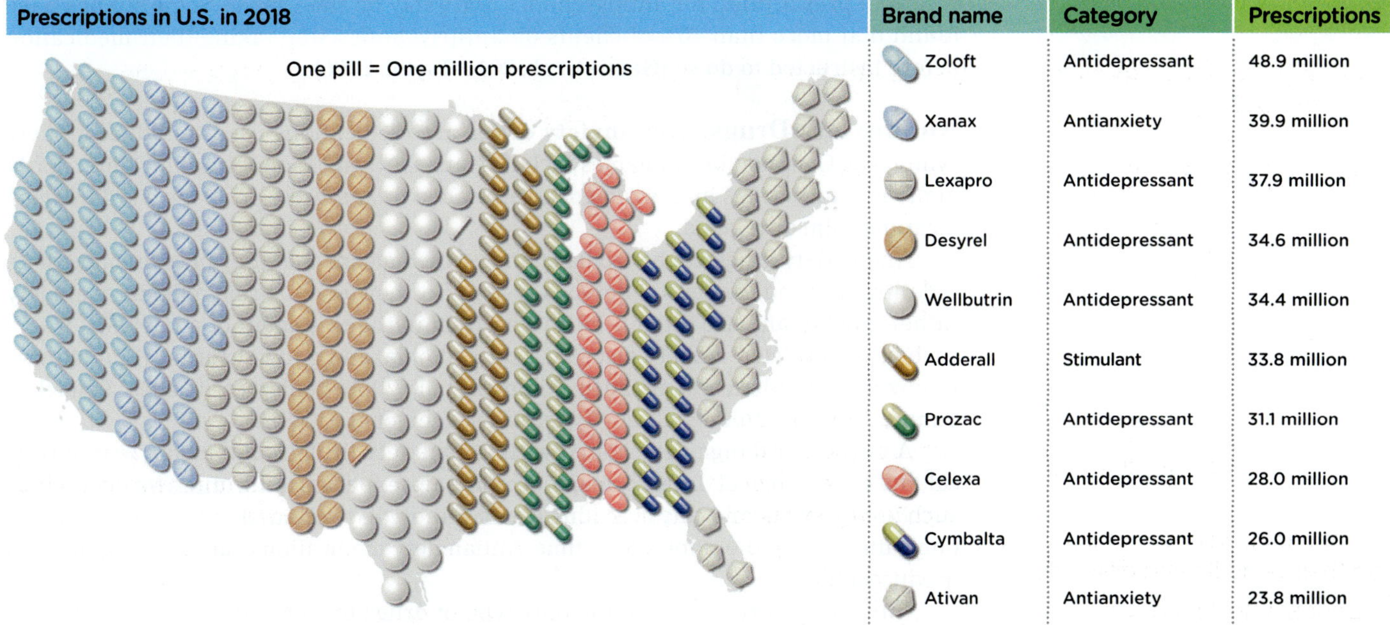

Brand name	Category	Prescriptions
Zoloft	Antidepressant	48.9 million
Xanax	Antianxiety	39.9 million
Lexapro	Antidepressant	37.9 million
Desyrel	Antidepressant	34.6 million
Wellbutrin	Antidepressant	34.4 million
Adderall	Stimulant	33.8 million
Prozac	Antidepressant	31.1 million
Celexa	Antidepressant	28.0 million
Cymbalta	Antidepressant	26.0 million
Ativan	Antianxiety	23.8 million

FIGURE 15.7 Commonly Prescribed Psychiatric Medications. Psychiatric medications are prescribed many millions of times per year in the United States. Information from Grohol (2019).

are prescribed primarily to clients with schizophrenia, but can also benefit clients with other disorders whose symptoms involve a loss of connection with reality. They work primarily by affecting the levels of dopamine in the brain. Most antipsychotics lower dopamine levels, but some recently introduced antipsychotics actually raise them (Kutscher, 2008). Some antipsychotics also affect serotonin levels (Sharif et al., 2007).

When the first antipsychotic drugs were discovered in the 1950s, they transformed the lives of many people who had been debilitated by schizophrenia their entire lives. There was a drastic drop in the population of U.S. mental hospitals after these drugs enabled people with schizophrenia to function well enough to manage their lives on their own. Consider this: from 1955 to 2006, when the U.S. population nearly doubled from 164 million to nearly 300 million, the number of people in public mental hospitals *dropped* drastically, from 558,000 to 40,000 (Torrey, 2008). Many of these "deinstitutionalized" people lived independently, held jobs, and formed meaningful relationships. Today, antipsychotics remain the treatment of choice for schizophrenia for all of these reasons (Abbas & Lieberman, 2015; Castle & Buckley, 2008; Lally & MacCabe, 2015; Sajatovic et al., 2008).

In spite of their upside, antipsychotics have a significant downside too. For example, they do not help everyone who takes them, with researchers routinely finding that sizable numbers of people who take antipsychotics either experience no benefit or experience more drawbacks than benefits (Hegarty et al., 1994; Hopper et al., 2007; Vanasse et al., 2016). For those who do benefit, the gains are often limited to the positive symptoms of schizophrenia, with the less obvious negative symptoms, such as social withdrawal, remaining unaffected. The side effects of antipsychotics are often quite severe (Kingdon & Turkington, 2005). For example, the earliest antipsychotics disrupt the way the central nervous system coordinates bodily movements. As a result, people taking these drugs often have involuntary restless movement in their legs and feet; tremors that resemble Parkinson's disease; and *tardive dyskinesia*, a condition that involves spastic, repetitive movements of the mouth, face, trunk, or extremities (Dolder, 2008; Stroup et al., 2006). A newer generation of antipsychotics has lessened these movement-related side effects to some extent, but they (like the first generation) often cause significant weight gain and the accompanying health risks diabetes and heart disease, as well as dangerous cholesterol levels (Lehman et al., 2004; Lieberman et al., 2005). With side effects like these, it is not surprising that many people who

CHAPTER APP 15.2

BetterHelp

This app is one of many telepsychology apps that have become popular in recent years. Basically, it enables the user to see a therapist on a computer, tablet, or smartphone. The forms of therapy include videoconference, live chat, messages, and phone calls. (This app is not free to use, but you don't need to actually use the app, or even download it, to understand it and answer the questions, below. Reading about it here, and perhaps exploring the way the app works at its Web site, will be enough.)

How does it APPly to your daily life? If you decided to see a therapist, would you prefer meeting via telepsychology or in person? Why? If you were to do telepsychology, which form would you prefer (videoconference, live chat, messages, phone call)?

How does it APPly to your understanding of psychology? In your opinion, how do the pros and cons of telepsychology (especially through videoconference) match up with the essential ingredients of successful therapy?

To learn more about this app or to download it to your phone, you can search for "BetterHelp" on Google, in the iPhone App store, or in the Google Play store.

receive a prescription for antipsychotics don't stay on their meds. Some studies have found that more than 40% of clients on antipsychotics stop taking their medication before instructed to do so (Garcia et al., 2016; Taylor, 2006).

Antianxiety Drugs. **Antianxiety drugs** are medications used to reduce anxiety symptoms. Common brand names include Xanax, Ativan, Klonopin, and Valium. Early in their history, drugs in this category were called *tranquilizers*, from the word *tranquil*, meaning calm or relaxed.

Antianxiety drugs are benzodiazepines, which means that they have an immediate sedating effect on the central nervous system. So, they tend to bring relief from anxiety rather quickly, and are often used successfully in the treatment of anxiety disorders such as generalized anxiety disorder, social phobia, and panic disorder (Bandelow & Baldwin, 2010; Blanco et al., 2010; Kimmel et al., 2015; Ledley et al., 2008; Pollack & Simon, 2009; Shinfuku et al., 2019; Van Ameringen et al., 2009).

A particular danger associated with antianxiety drugs is addiction, both physical and psychological. Indeed, many people have experienced withdrawal symptoms such as insomnia and physical illness when they discontinued antianxiety medications after taking them for a long time. Antianxiety medications can also be abused to produce a high.

Antianxiety drugs are not the only type of drugs prescribed to people with anxiety symptoms. Although the name may suggest otherwise, *antidepressant* drugs are actually even more common than antianxiety drugs in the treatment of anxiety. The success of antidepressants for people with anxiety symptoms highlights the overlap between depression and anxiety, and indicates that the two problems may be nearly indistinguishable biologically.

Antidepressant Drugs. **Antidepressant drugs** are medications used to reduce depression symptoms, and are also sometimes effective in reducing anxiety symptoms. Common brand names include Prozac, Paxil, Zoloft, Effexor, Lexapro, Celexa, Cymbalta, Wellbutrin, and Elavil. Antidepressants improve mood by increasing the activity of serotonin or norepinephrine, both of which are underactive in the brains of people diagnosed with depression.

The first widely used antidepressants were MAOIs (monoamine oxidase inhibitors), followed closely by TCAs (tricyclic antidepressants). Both treated the symptoms of depression with some success, but side effects were a significant problem: MAOIs have serious interactions with certain common foods, drinks, and other drugs; and TCAs can cause heart irregularities and can be quite toxic in overdoses (Denko & Thase, 2006; Potter et al., 2006). In the late 1980s and early 1990s, SSRIs (selective serotonin reuptake inhibitors) entered the U.S. market, reducing depressive symptoms with far fewer side effects than MAOIs and TCAs. With the help of massive direct-to-consumer ad campaigns, SSRIs have become massively popular (Barber, 2008; Nemeroff & Schatzberg, 2007).

In spite of their popularity, SSRIs remain a controversial topic (Murphy et al., 2021; Shelton & Lester, 2006). Some researchers have serious doubts about the actual ability of SSRIs to help reduce depression symptoms beyond the *placebo effect*, or the benefits generated by the expectation for improvement rather than any truly active ingredient in the drug (Hammen & Watkins, 2008; Sammons, 2016). Also, while SSRIs certainly cause fewer side effects than MAOIs or TCAs, they still cause some that can be quite significant, including increased suicidal thinking or self-harm in youth, weight gain, and sexual desire performance problems (Hieronymus et al., 2021; Kaslow et al., 2009). Given these iffy success rates and these potentially serious side effects, it is understandable that people stop taking their antidepressant meds before the prescription runs out — 40% within a month, and 75% within 3 months, according to some studies (Ho et al., 2016; Olfson et al., 2006).

Mood-Stabilizing Drugs. **Mood-stabilizing drugs** are medications used to lessen the extreme emotional highs and lows of bipolar disorder. *Lithium* is by far the most

antianxiety drugs
Medications used to reduce anxiety symptoms.

antidepressant drugs
Medications used to reduce depression symptoms (which are also sometimes effective in reducing anxiety symptoms).

mood-stabilizing drugs
Medications used to lessen the extreme emotional highs and lows of bipolar disorder.

common mood stabilizer, and has been for about half a century. Lithium is a salt-based substance that affects sodium neurons. Lithium helps people with bipolar disorder stay closer to the middle of the mood spectrum during all phases of the disorder: when depression or mania are in full swing, or as a preventive measure between episodes (Keck & McElroy, 2006; Ketter & Wang, 2010). People with bipolar disorder often take other drugs in addition to lithium, including antidepressants during depressive episodes and antipsychotics during manic episodes (Keck & McElroy, 2007; Sachs, 2004; Strakowski & Shelton, 2006).

The drawbacks of lithium include a number of side effects, including weight gain, sedation, hand tremors, and extreme thirst (Miklowitz, 2009; Miklowitz & Johnson, 2008). Sometimes, anticonvulsant medications – the kind more often used to treat seizure disorders like epilepsy, including Depakote and Lamictal – are also used to treat people with bipolar disorder (Muzina & Calabrese, 2006).

stimulant drugs
Medications used to treat children and adults with attention-deficit/hyperactivity disorder (ADHD).

electroconvulsive therapy (ECT)
A biomedical therapy for severe disorders in which an electric current passes through the brain of the client.

Stimulant Drugs. **Stimulant drugs** are medications used to treat children and adults with attention-deficit/hyperactivity disorder (ADHD). Common brand names include Adderall, Concerta, Vyvanse, and Ritalin. For people with ADHD, stimulant drugs can increase the ability to pay attention and focus, and also reduce hyperactive and impulsive behaviors. Generally, they work by increasing the production of norepinephrine in the brain. These drugs are effective for many, but not all, people with ADHD. As with many other categories of medications for psychological disorders, it may take multiple rounds of trial and error to find the right medication and dosage.

Drawbacks of stimulant drugs include decreased appetite, stomach pain, sleep difficulties, headaches, and feeling jittery. It should also be mentioned that stimulant drugs can be misused, either by people who receive a prescription taking more than necessary, or people who do not receive a prescription taking them recreationally. This misuse, which is especially common among college students, can be extremely dangerous and can cause serious health issues (Clemow & Walker, 2014; Faraone et al., 2020; McCabe et al., 2018; Schepis et al., 2021).

There are also a small but growing number of nonstimulant drugs for ADHD, including brand names like Strattera and Kapvay. They were introduced more recently than many stimulants and are less commonly prescribed, but they provide benefits to some people with ADHD.

Brain Stimulation and Psychosurgery

More drastic and controversial options are available when psychotherapy and medication have repeatedly failed as treatment efforts. One such option is **electroconvulsive therapy (ECT)**: a biomedical therapy for severe disorders in which an electric current passes through the brain of the client (**Figure 15.8**). The current is delivered via electrodes attached to the patient's head as the patient lies in a hospital bed, and it causes a seizure or a convulsion. ECT is used primarily for severe depression, but it has also been used for severe schizophrenia, severe bipolar disorder, and some other conditions (Carney et al., 2003; Elias et al., 2021; Fink, 2009; Gevirtz et al., 2016).

Contemporary ECT is nowhere near as brutal as its earliest versions (Shorter & Healy, 2007). When it began in the 1930s, patients received no anesthetic, no protection from injury induced by the seizure or convulsion (such as broken bones and bitten tongues), and sometimes excessive voltages of electric shock. In 1975, the film *One Flew Over the Cuckoo's Nest* (which won five Academy Awards, including Best Picture) popularized the harsh image of ECT when a rather uncaring mental hospital staff

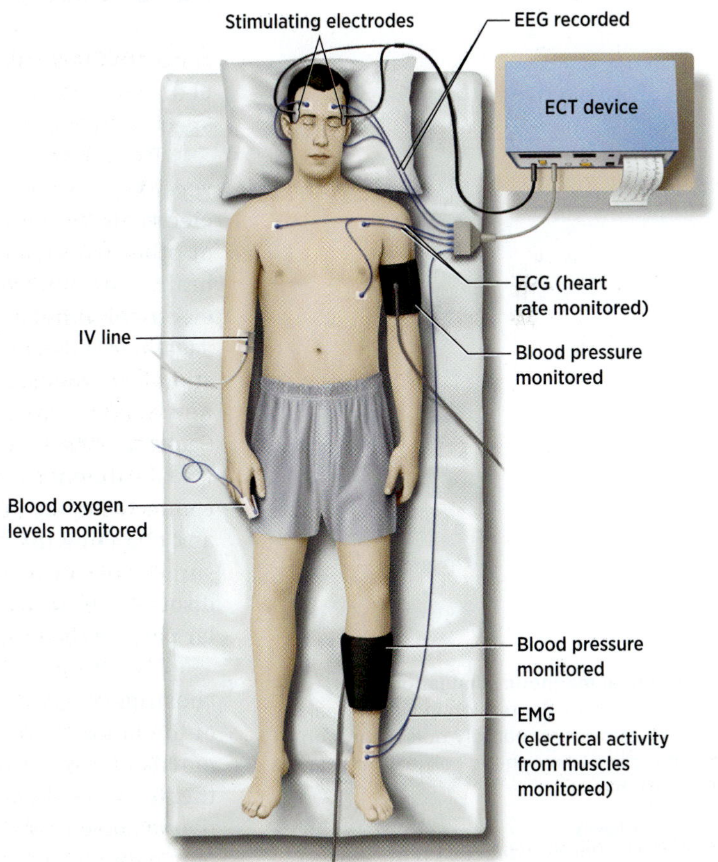

FIGURE 15.8 Electroconvulsive Therapy. Electroconvulsive therapy (ECT) is a biomedical therapy for severe disorders in which an electric current passes through the brain of the client.

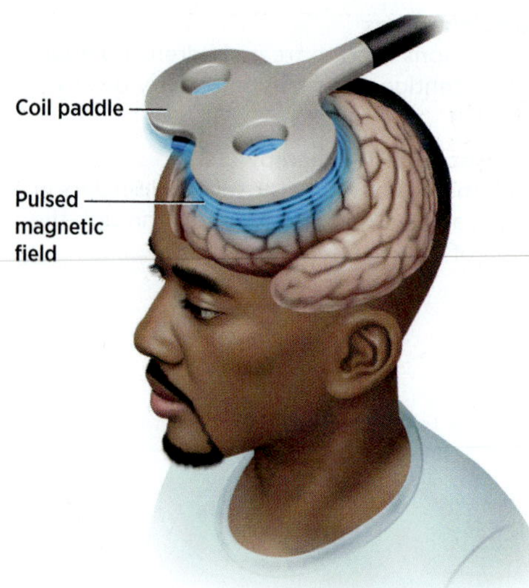

FIGURE 15.9 Transcranial Magnetic Stimulation. Transcranial magnetic stimulation (TMS) is a treatment for depression in which weak electric current repeatedly pulses through a paddle-shaped magnetic coil just outside the person's head.

administered ECT to Jack Nicholson's character (Abrams, 2002; Kneeland & Warren, 2002). Today, any patient receiving ECT is far more safeguarded before any volts of electricity cross their brains. ECT patients now get anesthesia, muscle relaxant (to lessen the extremity of the bodily seizure, which can cause injuries), and attention from a full team of medical personnel (Fink, 2001, 2009).

ECT seems to work rather well in terms of alleviating severe symptoms of severe schizophrenia, depression, and bipolar disorder (Bahji et al., 2019; Sanghani et al., 2018). This improvement can be life-changing for clients who have been completely debilitated or suicidal despite ongoing therapy and medication (Pinna et al., 2018). However, researchers are still working to figure out the exact mechanisms by which this improvement happens (UK ECT Review Group, 2003; Kellner, 2019; Nobler & Sackeim, 2006). Researchers know that the jolt of electricity causes a seizure or convulsion, but they can't make a definitive connection between the seizure or convulsion and the subsequent improvement in functioning (McClintock et al., 2008). Drawbacks to ECT, at least for some people, include short-lived gains (many patients who improve relapse weeks or months later) and memory loss for the period (in some cases, weeks or months) immediately before and after the treatment (Fink, 2009; Kneeland & Warren, 2002). It remains a highly controversial treatment (Andre, 2009; Breggin, 2008; Donohue & Keogh, 2021; Sadowsky, 2016).

More recently, alternatives to ECT have emerged. They offer different kinds of brain stimulation in forms that are less objectionable to some people, largely because they lack the seizures and convulsions inherent in ECT (Abrams, 2002; Shorter & Healy, 2007). These alternatives include **transcranial magnetic stimulation (TMS)**: a treatment for depression in which weak electric current repeatedly pulses through a paddle-shaped magnetic coil just outside the person's head (**Figure 15.9**). (The precise location of the coil depends on the client's symptoms.) TMS is noninvasive. It does not cause pain, memory loss, or any of the other side effects common in ECT, and some studies suggest it can alleviate symptoms of severe depression and PTSD (Cirillo et al., 2019; Fink, 2009; McClintock et al., 2018; Sehatzadeh et al., 2019). Like ECT, the specific mechanisms by which TMS works are still being explored by researchers.

Two additional brain stimulation treatments, *deep brain stimulation* (DBS) and *vagal nerve stimulation* (VNS), both involve surgically implanted devices that deliver electricity within the body with the intention of alleviating symptoms of depression or other psychological disorders. In DBS, a wire is surgically implanted deep in the brain and connected to a device surgically implanted near the collarbone that sends electrical impulses on a regular basis. In VNS, a surgically implanted device on the vagal nerve delivers electrical energy to the brain. Much like an implanted pacemaker stimulates the heart with electric charges, the VNS device does the same to the vagal nerve, which runs through the neck to the brainstem (George et al., 2006; Nobler & Sackeim, 2006).

Treatments such as DBS and VNS involve surgically implanting devices that are connected to the brain. These treatments do not involve the surgeon directly accessing and changing the brain itself. That kind of intervention is known as **psychosurgery**: surgery performed directly on the brain in an effort to improve severe psychological disorders. In many psychosurgeries, surgeons deliberately remove or disable particular parts of the brain.

One of the original forms of psychosurgery was the **lobotomy**: a historical psychosurgery in which the prefrontal lobes were disconnected from the inner regions of the brain that control emotions. Lobotomies began in the 1930s on patients whose moods or violent behavior were so disordered that they became serious threats to themselves or other people (Andre, 2009). Lobotomy results were considered positive in some cases, but they were undoubtedly negative in many others. Some lobotomy patients didn't survive the surgery at all. Among survivors, the changes included severe and permanent personality changes that left the person sluggish, unintelligent, dependent, and in some cases emotionless and unresponsive. By the 1960s, the use of lobotomies had stopped entirely, not only because of these horrific side effects, but also because drugs had been discovered that could control symptoms less dangerously (Braslow, 1997). Today, psychosurgeries of any kind are extremely rare and only used as a last-chance treatment when all else has failed.

transcranial magnetic stimulation (TMS)
A treatment for depression in which weak electric current repeatedly pulses through a paddle-shaped magnetic coil just outside the person's head.

psychosurgery
Surgery performed directly on the brain in an effort to improve severe psychological disorders.

lobotomy
A historical psychosurgery in which the prefrontal lobes are disconnected from the inner regions of the brain that control emotions.

CHECK YOUR LEARNING:

15.24 Who prescribes psychiatric drugs?

15.25 What are antipsychotic drugs, and what are their benefits and drawbacks?

15.26 What are antianxiety drugs, and what are their benefits and drawbacks?

15.27 What are antidepressant drugs, and what are their benefits and drawbacks?

15.28 What are mood-stabilizing drugs, and what are their benefits and drawbacks?

15.29 What are stimulant drugs, and what are their benefits and drawbacks?

15.30 What are electroconvulsive therapy (ECT), transcranial magnetic stimulation (TMS), and psychosurgery, and when might each be used?

To check your understanding of these questions, click show the answers or refer to the answers in the Chapter Summary.

CHAPTER SUMMARY

History of Treatment of Psychological Disorders

15.1 Centuries ago, people with psychological disorders were often thought to be possessed by evil spirits and were treated with barbaric interventions like bloodletting and cutting holes in the skulls of patients.

15.2 The treatment of psychological disorders started to become more humane in the late 1700s, changing the attitude toward people with mental illness from shunning and punishment to compassion and respect.

15.3 Psychotherapy involves techniques used by a mental health professional to help a person overcome a psychological disorder or improve some aspect of emotional, cognitive, or behavioral functioning. Biomedical therapy involves medications and medical procedures that treat psychological disorders by directly changing the biology of the brain.

Psychotherapies for Individual Clients

15.4 Psychotherapy clients come from all backgrounds, and about half of Americans will undergo some form of psychotherapy in their lifetimes.

15.5 In psychodynamic therapy, the main goal is to make the unconscious conscious through a process that results in insight. Psychodynamic therapists use a variety of techniques, including dream analysis, working with the client's resistance, and working with the client's transference.

15.6 In person-centered therapy, the therapist–client relationship is especially important. Person-centered therapists conduct nondirective therapy and emphasize the tendency toward healthy growth that exists in every person. The three essential characteristics of person-centered therapy are empathy, unconditional positive regard, and genuineness.

15.7 Behavior therapy is the application of operant conditioning and classical conditioning to change outward behavior. Behavior therapists use exposure therapy (a technique based on classical conditioning) and token economies (a technique based on operant conditioning).

15.8 Cognitive therapy is a psychotherapy approach in which a therapist helps clients change the way they think about life events. In the ABCDE model of cognitive therapy, the therapist helps the client identify illogical thinking and replace it with more logical thinking. Cognitive therapists teach their clients to recognize cognitive distortions such as all-or-nothing thinking, overgeneralization, catastrophizing, mental filtering, and personalization.

15.9 In the eclectic approach to therapy, the therapist selects the best treatment for a particular client based on evidence from studies of similar clients. In the integrative approach to therapy, the therapist blends different therapeutic techniques to create a new form of psychotherapy.

Psychotherapies for Groups and Families

15.10 Group therapy is psychotherapy conducted with a group of clients and an emphasis on interpersonal interaction.

15.11 Family therapy is psychotherapy that aims to improve how the family system functions, which in turn will improve the problems of its individual members.

How Well Does Psychotherapy Work?

15.12 To determine how well psychotherapy works, researchers have varied whom they ask (clients, therapists, or outside observers), when they ask (during, right after, or long after therapy), and how they ask (questionnaires, interviews, or other methods).

15.13 Thousands of studies on the benefits of psychotherapy point to one undeniable conclusion: psychotherapy works.

15.14 Generally, different types of therapy have about equal rates of success, a finding that researchers call the dodo bird verdict. However, particular therapies can be especially beneficial for particular diagnoses.

15.15 There are a few common factors in all forms of effective therapy, including the therapeutic alliance, positive expectations, and attention.

The Importance of Culture and Diversity in Psychotherapy

15.16 Cultural competence is the ability to work sensitively and expertly with members of a culturally diverse society. If the therapist lacks cultural competence, the client might feel misunderstood or miss out on the benefits of therapy.

15.17 With cultural self-awareness, a therapist recognizes that their perspective is not necessarily that of others. Having cultural self-awareness helps a therapist to recognize that a client's culture can influence their experience.

Ethics in Psychotherapy

15.18 Confidentiality is maintaining the privacy of client information. Therapy might be impossible without that trust between a client and a therapist. Therapists are obligated to break confidentiality to protect the well-being of the client or another person.

15.19 After the therapist explains the therapy process, the client gives informed consent, which is permission to move forward with the therapy. Providing informed consent is important to therapy because it allows the client to ask questions about the process and gives the therapist the opportunity to begin forming a therapeutic alliance.

15.20 A multiple relationship is a situation in which a therapist has both a professional relationship and a nonprofessional relationship with the same person. A multiple relationship can impair the therapist's ability to function competently and objectively, and can cause harm or exploitation to the client.

Telepsychology: Psychotherapy via Modern Technology

15.21 Telepsychology is psychotherapy that takes place via technological devices like computers or smartphones over the Internet, including videoconferencing (similar to Zoom or FaceTime) and e-mail.

15.22 Telepsychology has a couple of significant benefits, in particular allowing people who live a great distance from a psychotherapist to access help, as well as providing people with disorders that prevent them from leaving home an opportunity to see a therapist.

15.23 Limitations of telepsychology include the burden on the therapist to be technologically proficient and limitations in noticing nonverbal communication. A form of telepsychology, virtual reality exposure therapy, allows the client to experience the situation that causes them anxiety via electronic means.

Biomedical Therapies

15.24 Psychiatrists and other medical doctors prescribe drugs for psychological issues. Psychologists, with the exception of a very small number with extra training in a handful of U.S. states, do not prescribe medication.

15.25 Antipsychotic drugs are used to reduce psychotic symptoms such as delusions, hallucinations, and bizarre behavior. They have transformed the lives of some people with schizophrenia, but the side effects can be severe.

15.26 Antianxiety drugs are used to reduce anxiety symptoms and bring relief quickly, but they can be addictive.

15.27 Antidepressant drugs are used to reduce depression symptoms (as well as some anxiety symptoms), but their success rate is questionable, and they can have serious side effects, including increased suicidal thinking.

15.28 Mood-stabilizing drugs are used to lessen the extreme emotional highs and lows of bipolar disorder, but they can have significant side effects.

15.29 Stimulant drugs are used to treat attention-deficit/hyperactivity disorder (ADHD), but they sometimes cause a wide range of side effects and can be misused in harmful ways.

15.30 Electroconvulsive therapy (ECT) is a biomedical therapy for severe depression and some other disorders in which an electric current passes through the brain of the client. Unfortunately, the gains can be short-lived, and the side effects can include memory loss. In transcranial magnetic stimulation (TMS), a weak electric current repeatedly pulses though a coil outside the client's head. It is a noninvasive treatment for depression and other disorders and typically doesn't have the severe side effects of ECT. When other efforts prove ineffective, psychosurgery can be performed directly on the brain in an effort to improve severe psychological disorders. Decades ago, some lobotomy patients didn't survive the surgery, and survivors often had severe personality changes.

KEY TERMS

SELF-ASSESSMENT

1. Psychodynamic therapists use a variety of techniques, including:
   a. transference, dream analysis, and self-actualization.
   b. dream analysis, catastrophizing, and interpretation.
   c. reflection, token economy, and working with a client's resistance.
   d. transference, dream analysis, and interpretation.

2. Person-centered therapy emphasizes the tendency toward healthy growth inherent in each person, which is also known as _____.
   a. self-actualization
   b. cognition
   c. exposure
   d. participant modeling

3. _____ is a form of exposure therapy primarily used to treat phobias in which the client experiences relaxation and the anxiety-provoking thing or situation at the same time.

4. _____ is a psychotherapy in which therapists help clients change the way they think about life events.

5. There are various types of cognitive distortions, including:
   a. all-or-nothing thinking, mental filtering, and operant conditioning.
   b. personalization, overgeneralization, and unconditional positive regard.
   c. all-or-nothing thinking, overgeneralization, and catastrophizing.
   d. personalization, effectiveness, and catastrophizing.

6. There are two types of studies concerning how well psychotherapy works: _____ studies that focus on how well it works in a highly controlled study, and _____ studies that focus on how well it works with real clients and real therapists.

7. _____ are elements found in all forms of effective psychotherapy that play an important role in client improvement.

8. _____ is the ability to work sensitively and expertly with members of a culturally diverse society.
   a. Operant conditioning
   b. Token economy
   c. Cultural competence
   d. Counterconditioning

9. _____ is maintaining the privacy of client information and an essential ethical responsibility of a psychotherapist.

10. The five primary types of drugs used to treat psychological disorders are:
    a. antipsychotic, antianxiety, antidepressant, stimulant, and antidissociative.
    b. anticognitive, antianxiety, mood-stabilizing, stimulant, and antipersonality.
    c. antipsychotic, antianxiety, antidepressant, mood-stabilizing, and stimulant.
    d. anticognitive, antianxiety, antidepressant, antipersonality, and antidissociative.

To check your understanding of these questions, click show the answers in the e-book or refer to the answers in Appendix B.

Research shows quizzing is a highly effective learning tool. Continue quizzing yourself using LearningCurve, the system that adapts to *your* learning.

WHAT'S YOUR TAKE?

1. As technology improves and psychotherapists become more competent using it, the option of seeing a therapist via a videoconference app (similar to Zoom or FaceTime) is increasingly available. If you were the client, which would you prefer: in-person meetings or telepsychology? For you, what are the most important pros and cons of each? How important would the telepsychology option be when choosing a therapist?

SHOW ME MORE

15.1 Judith Beck and Cognitive Therapy

In this video, prominent cognitive therapist Judith Beck explains the cognitive approach to therapy.
Courtesy Freedom from Fear

Achieve

15.2 Virtual Reality Exposure Therapy for Phobias

This video provides a peek into virtual reality exposure therapy.
Courtesy CNN

Achieve

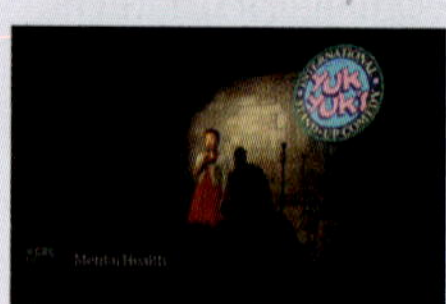

15.3 Stand-Up Comedy as Therapeutic?

This video presents an innovative program in which people perform stand-up comedy routines that focus on their own mental disorders, with the intent of providing a destigmatizing, therapeutic experience.
Canadian Broadcasting Corporation/BoClips

Achieve

15.4 An African Perspective on the Importance of Psychological Treatment

This TED Talk, performed in Nigeria, blends a personal account of the consequences of mental illness stigma with encouragement to adapt more accepting and affirming beliefs.
TED Talks/BoClips

Achieve

15.5 My Psychology Podcast

This podcast episode features the author of this textbook, psychologist Andy Pomerantz, speaking with other instructors of introductory psychology courses about the most important and interesting concepts in this chapter.
Macmillan Learning

Achieve

Appendix: An Introduction to Statistics in Psychological Research

Measures of Central Tendency

YOU WILL LEARN:

A.1 about measures of central tendency, including mean, median, and mode.

A.2 about variability, including range and standard deviation.

A.3 about types of distributions of data, including normal distribution, positively skewed distributions, and negatively skewed distributions.

A.4 about statistical significance and practical significance.

In Chapter 1, we discussed the three types of psychological research: *descriptive research, correlational research*, and *experimental research*. In descriptive research, it is important to describe the main characteristic of your population with one number. So, psychological researchers often include a **measure of central tendency**: a single number used to summarize or represent a group of numbers. Let's recall the descriptive study we considered in Chapter 1: how many hours per day college students spend on social media. If you collect data on daily social media hours from many students, you'll want a single number that shows how many hours per day, on average, that group of students spent on social media. The most commonly used measure of central tendency is the **mean**: the average of a group of numbers.

Another common measure of central tendency is the **median**: the number that falls at the midpoint in a group of numbers listed in order, such that half the numbers fall above it and half the numbers fall below it. The median of a list of numbers does the same thing as the median of a highway—divides it in half, with an equal amount of numbers (or lanes) on either side. The median is a good measure of central tendency when a handful of extremely high or low numbers might pull the mean in one direction, possibly making the mean deceptive. For example, if a few of your participants reported an extremely high number of hours per day on social media—15 or more hours, perhaps—those few participants could push the mean up to a number that gives a misleading impression of the overall group. The median—the line that splits the population in half—doesn't get pulled up or down by extreme numbers.

A final measure of central tendency often used in descriptive psychological research is the **mode**: in a group of numbers, the one that occurs most often. The mode is easy to find: it is just a matter of counting, with no calculations needed. In our study of daily social media usage among college students, if the most common response is 2 hours, then the mode is 2.

The median of a group of numbers performs the same function as the median of a highway: split the numbers (or lanes) such that the same amount falls on either side.
junyyeung/iStock/Getty Images

measure of central tendency
A single number used to summarize or represent a group of numbers.

mean
The average of a group of numbers.

median
The number that falls at the midpoint in a group of numbers listed in order, such that half fall above it and half fall below it.

mode
The number that occurs the most often in a group of numbers.

variability
The degree to which numbers in a group differ from the mean.

range
The difference between the highest score and the lowest score in a group of numbers.

standard deviation
A statistic that measures the variability around a mean.

normal distribution
A symmetrical distribution of numbers in which the mean, median, and mode all fall exactly in the middle.

Variability

The mean (and other measures of central tendency) is important, but so is the scatter around the mean. Psychologists call that scatter **variability**: the degree to which numbers in a group differ from the mean. The most basic measure of variability is **range**: the difference between the highest score and the lowest score in a list of numbers. A large range suggests a lot of scatter around the mean, and a small range suggests little scatter around the mean. However, range can be deceptive, since it takes just one high number or one low number to extend it in either direction.

A more sophisticated measure of variability is **standard deviation**: a statistic, commonly used in psychology research, that measures the variability around a mean. Standard deviation is basically the mean of the difference (or deviation) between each number in the list and the mean of that list. (Actually, if you consider the mathematical details, standard deviation is slightly more complicated. To calculate standard deviation, you have to square the difference between each number and the mean; otherwise, the positive differences and the negative differences would simply cancel each other out for a total of zero. When the differences are squared, however, they become positive. You then add together those positive numbers and divide that total by the number of items in the list. Finally, you take the square root of that number, and you have the standard deviation.)

For example, let's say that among the students who provided data, the mean was 3 hours per day spent on social media. That mean of 3 could come from a list of numbers that consistently fall close to 3, such as this: 3, 3, 2, 3, 3, 4, 2, 3, 4, 5, 3, 2, 1, 3, 4, 3, 3, and 3. That list has little variability, so it produces a small standard deviation (about 0.9). It also has a small range, 4 (the difference between the highest score, of 5, and the lowest score, of 1). By contrast, that same mean of 3 could come from a list of numbers with much more scatter, such as this: 10, 3, 0, 1, 1, 9, 0, 1, 2, 5, 11, 1, 1, 2, 0, 1, 1, and 5. That list has much more variability, so it produces a much larger standard deviation (about 3.4). It also has a much larger range, of 11 (the difference between the highest score, of 11, and the lowest score, of 0). (See **Figure A.1**.)

One of the benefits of knowing the variability and standard deviation around a mean involves making sense of *outliers*, or numbers in a list that fall far from the mean. If your mean of 3 came from the first list, and you meet Austin, a college student who spends 9 hours a day on social media, then you can be sure that Austin's behavior is rare. But if your mean of 3 came from the second list, Austin's social media time is not quite so out of the ordinary. It is quite high, but he is clearly not the only one in the second list spending that much time on social media.

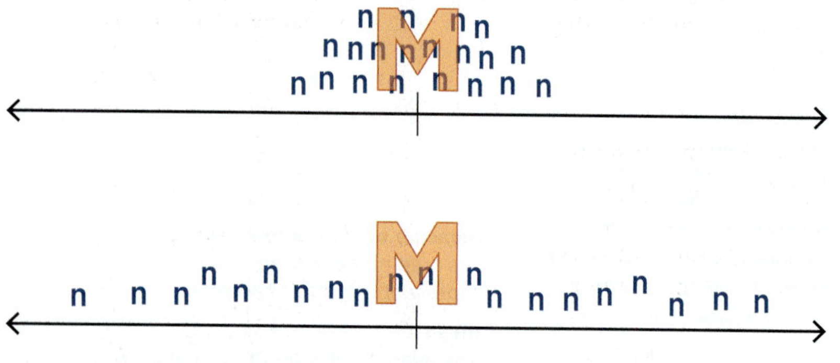

FIGURE A.1 Mean, Variability, and Standard Deviation. When a list of numbers clusters closely around their mean, as they do in the top scatterplot, the variability and standard deviation are small. When the list of numbers is spread widely around their mean, as they are in the bottom scatterplot, the variability and standard deviation are large. So, even if two lists of numbers produce the same mean, they can produce different variabilities and standard deviations, which indicate the amount of scatter.

Distribution of Data

The research data that psychologists collect can be distributed in various ways. Those distributions can be symmetrical around the mean, lean toward the high end, or lean toward the low end. The first of those distributions is the **normal distribution**: a symmetrical distribution of numbers in which the mean, median, and mode all fall exactly in the middle. The normal distribution is also called a *normal curve*, or *bell curve*, because in graph form it resembles a perfectly symmetrical bell (**Figure A.2**).

A common example of a normal distribution is height. The mean height for women in the United States is 5 feet, 4 inches. Lots of women are exactly that height, and many are within an inch of that height (5′3″ or 5′5″). As you move away from the mean toward shorter or taller heights, the number of women at each height declines. When you get to the extremes—many standard deviations above and below the mean—women at those

IT'S LIKE...

Standard Deviation Is Like the Variation in Daily High Temperature

Sometimes, the standard deviation tells us more than the mean does. In May, the mean high temperature in Los Angeles is about 75°F. In May, the mean high temperature in St. Louis is also about 75°F. But what about the standard deviation? In LA, the standard deviation is small. LA has such predictably consistent temperatures that if the high fell outside the 70s in May, it would be shocking. But St. Louis has a much larger standard deviation. In May, the temperature in St. Louis is all over the place. It could be a cool day with a high in the 50s, a scorcher that reaches the 90s, or anywhere between. That unpredictability is important to know if you're planning a May trip to one city or the other!

When psychologists conduct descriptive research, they routinely report the standard deviation along with the mean. Researchers know that the mean is generally a good use of a single number to summarize a group of numbers, but they know that the mean tells us a lot more when it is accompanied by a measure of how closely that group of numbers clusters around it. For example, imagine that a psychologist measured the overall anxiety levels of college students on two different campuses with a scale that ranged from 0 (no anxiety) to 100 (extreme anxiety). The two colleges produce the same mean of 20, not bad. But one has a tiny standard deviation, meaning that almost everybody lands right around 20. The other has a huge standard deviation, meaning that students land all over the place—some around 20, but some much lower and at least a few (gulp) much higher. If you were applying to colleges, could these standard deviations influence where you choose to apply? •

heights are quite rare. Among psychological variables, IQ (intelligence quotient) comes closest to a normal distribution, with most of us clustered at or around the mean level of IQ, and fewer and fewer of us landing at each score that is increasingly above or below the mean.

As illustrated in **Figure A.2**, in a normal distribution, we know the percentage of numbers that fall in each section as defined by standard deviations. Specifically, about 68% fall within one standard deviation of the mean, and roughly another 28% fall between one and two standard deviations from the mean. The sum of those two percentages is about 96%, meaning that only about 4% fall more than two standard deviations above or below the mean. The main point here is just how uncommon it is, within a normal distribution, for a number to fall two or more standard deviations from the mean. That's why it's so noteworthy when you see a woman who is nearly 6 feet tall, or meet someone with gifted-level IQ.

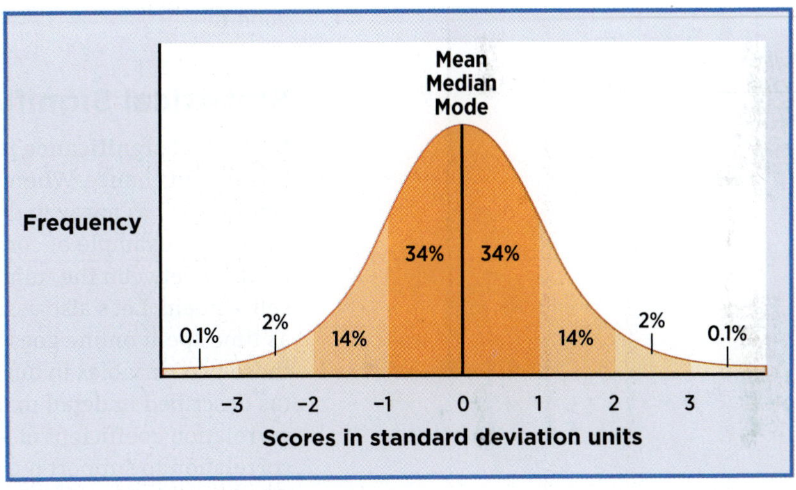

FIGURE A.2 The Normal Distribution. In a normal distribution, numbers are symmetrically distributed around a midpoint at which the mean, median, and mode all fall. Over two-thirds of the numbers fall within one standard deviation of the mean, and fewer than 5% fall more than two standard deviations away from the mean.

In psychological research, not all distributions are normal. Many distributions lean one way or the other. Psychologists call this a **skewed distribution**: a distribution of numbers that is not symmetrical around the mean. There are two types of skewed distributions, negative and positive. A **negatively skewed distribution** is a distribution of numbers that includes more numbers in the low end (toward the left on a graph) than in a normal distribution. A **positively skewed distribution** is a distribution of numbers that includes more numbers in the high end (toward the right on a graph) than in a normal distribution.

In a skewed distribution, the mean, median, and mode do not coincide. Instead, the skew (or the tail of the graph) pulls the mean, and to a lesser extent the median, in its direction. The mode remains at the peak of the graph (**Figure A.3**). The lesson to be learned here is that the mean can be a misleading statistic when the distribution is skewed. As an example, imagine that a used car dealership had 50 cars for sale. The vast majority of cars—45 out of 50—were priced between $10,000 and $12,000, with the most common price being $11,000. But the other five cars were high-end luxury cars, with price tags of $30,000, $40,000, $50,000, $60,000, and $70,000. That is a

skewed distribution
A distribution of numbers that is not symmetrical around the mean.

negatively skewed distribution
A distribution of numbers that includes more numbers in the low end (toward the left on a graph) than in a normal distribution.

positively skewed distribution
A distribution of numbers that includes more numbers in the high end (toward the right on a graph) than in a normal distribution.

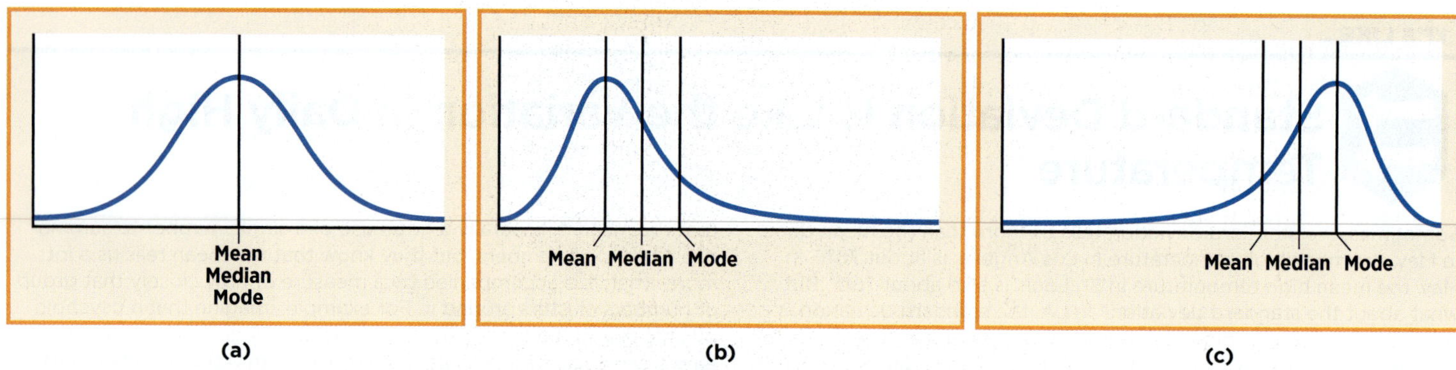

FIGURE A.3 Skewed Distributions. In a normal distribution, the mean, median, and mode are all the same. However, in a skewed distribution, extreme values at one end of the distribution pull the mean, and to a lesser extent the median, in their direction.

positively skewed distribution. Those five expensive cars would raise the mean price quite a bit. In fact, that mean price would fall several thousand dollars above the mode, $11,000. Used-car shoppers who see the mean price of cars at this dealership (but not the mode or median) and who have a budget of about $10,000–12,000 might assume that cars there are out of their price range, when most of them are actually a good fit.

Statistical Significance

Statistical significance is the probability that a statistic could have been obtained by random chance. When psychologists conduct research, they consider statistical significance as a way to determine whether their hypotheses were supported. Let's revisit the example of correlational research in Chapter 1, a study examining the correlation between the number of hours students spend on social media and a student's self-esteem. Let's also assume that we expect (or hypothesize) a negative correlation: as time spent online goes up, self-esteem goes down, and vice versa. After measuring those two variables in our participants, we calculate a *correlation coefficient*, a statistic (as described in detail in Chapter 1) that ranges from +1.0 to –1.0. Let's say we get a correlation coefficient of –0.3. That is a negative correlation, but is it a strong enough correlation to support our hypothesis? Someone skeptical of our study might claim that a correlation of –0.3 could have been obtained with random numbers. After all, –0.3 isn't far from 0, and 0 signifies no correlation at all.

That is where statistical significance comes in. Statistical significance is essentially a percentage of chance, or a *probability*, that the statistic happened by chance. The lower that probability, the higher the statistical significance. A low probability means that getting a statistic that strong rarely happens by chance, but a high probability means that getting a statistic that strong often happens by chance. Statistical significance is shades of gray rather than black and white, but psychologists have generally settled on 5% as a cutoff: if the statistical significance is less than 5% (often written as $p < 0.05$, with the p standing for probability), the result is considered statistically significant. In our example, if our correlation coefficient of –0.3 was accompanied by a statistical significance of 0.65, that would indicate a 65% probability of a correlation of that strength happening by chance. That is not impressive, and suggests no link between our two variables. However, if our correlation coefficient of –0.3 had a statistical significance of 0.02, that would indicate just a 2% probability of a correlation of that strength happening by chance. That is more impressive, and suggests a link between our two variables.

Statistical significance can be affected by many factors, but a major influence is *sample size*, the number of participants in the study (a number that psychologists abbreviate as n). Think of flipping coins. You always expect 50% heads and 50% tails, but sometimes your results differ. If you flip just 10 coins, getting 70% tails is not noteworthy.

statistical significance
The probability that a statistic could have been obtained by random chance.

In fact, it could be a fluke. But if you flip 1000 coins, getting 70% tails is noteworthy. It is different from what you would expect for such a large number of coin flips, and it suggests the influence of a factor other than just luck. In our study, a correlation of –0.3 would be more likely to have the statistical significance of 0.65 if we had a small number of participants, but the statistical significance of 0.02 if we had a much larger number of participants.

In addition to statistical significance, it is important for psychologists to consider *practical significance*. Practical significance is essentially real-world significance, or the impact of a statistic on the real lives of real people. Statistical significance and practical significance don't always match. As an example, imagine that a team of clinical psychologists creates a new therapy for panic disorder, and they test their new therapy on real clients who actually have panic disorder. Before the therapy starts, the mean number of panic attacks per week is 16. After the therapy ends, the mean number of panic attacks per week is 11. The psychologists run statistics (in this case, a comparison of pretherapy and posttherapy means known as a *t*-test) and find that this decrease of five panic attacks per week is a result with a less than 5% probability of happening by chance. That's impressive statistical significance, but what about practical significance? Clients who achieve this outcome would still be having about two-thirds of the panic attacks they had before they started, and would still average well over one panic attack per day. Many of them might argue that the therapy had only minimal practical significance in their day-to-day lives.

CHECK YOUR LEARNING:

A.1 What is the difference between the mean, median, and mode?

A.2 What do range and standard deviation measure, and how are they different from each other?

A.3 How does a normal distribution differ from positively and negatively skewed distributions?

A.4 What is statistical significance, and how does it differ from practical significance?

To check your understanding of these questions, click show the answers or refer to the answers in the Chapter Summary.

APPENDIX SUMMARY

A.1 For any group of numbers, the mean is the average, the median is the number that falls at the midpoint of the numbers listed in order, and the mode is the number that occurs most often.

A.2 Range and standard deviation are measures of variance. Range is the difference between the highest score and the lowest score in a group of numbers; standard deviation is a statistic that measures the variability around a mean.

A.3 In a normal distribution, the mean, median, and mode all fall exactly in the middle. In a negatively skewed distribution, there are more numbers in the low end, so the mean and median fall below the mode. In a positively skewed distribution, there are more numbers in the high end, so the mean and median fall above the mode.

A.4 Statistical significance is the probability that a statistic could have been obtained by random chance. By contrast, practical significance is the impact of a statistic on the real lives of real people.

KEY TERMS

measure of central tendency, p. A-1
mean, p. A-1
median, p. A-1
mode, p. A-1
variability, p. A-2
range, p. A-2
standard deviation, p. A-2
normal distribution, p. A-2
skewed distribution, p. A-3
negatively skewed distribution, p. A-3
positively skewed distribution, p. A-3
statistical significance, p. A-4

In fact, it would be a fluke. But if you flip 100 coins, getting 70% tails is noteworthy. It is different from what you would expect for such a large number of coin flips, and it suggests the influence of a factor other than just luck. In our study, a correlation of −0.3 would be more likely to have the statistical significance of 0.05 if we had a small number of participants, but the statistical significance of 0.02 if we had a much larger number of participants.

In addition to statistical significance, it is important for psychologists to consider *practical significance*. Practical significance is essentially real-world significance, or the impact of a statistic on the real lives of real people. Statistical significance and practical significance don't always match. As an example, imagine that a team of clinical psychologists creates a new therapy for panic disorder, and they test their new therapy on real clients who actually have panic disorder. Before the therapy starts, the mean number of panic attacks per week is 16. After the therapy ends, the mean number of panic attacks per week is 14. The psychologists run statistics (in this case, a comparison of pretherapy and posttherapy means known as a *t* test) and find that the decrease of two panic attacks per week is significant with a less than 5% probability of happening by chance. That's impressive statistical significance. But what about practical significance? Clients who achieve this outcome would still be having about two-thirds of the panic attacks as they had before they started, and would still average well over one panic attack per day. Many of them might argue that the therapy had only minimal practical significance in their day-to-day lives.

CHECK YOUR LEARNING:

A.1 What is the difference between the mean, median, and mode?

A.2 What do range and standard deviation measure, and how are they different from each other?

A.3 How does a normal distribution differ from positively and negatively skewed distributions?

A.4 What is statistical significance, and how does it differ from practical significance?

To check your understanding of these questions, click Show Me Answers or refer to the answers in the Chapter Summary.

APPENDIX SUMMARY

A.1 For any group of numbers, the mean is the average, the median is the number that falls at the midpoint of the numbers listed in order, and the mode is the number that occurs most often.

A.2 Range and standard deviation are measures of variation. Range is the difference between the highest score and the lowest score in a group of numbers; standard deviation is a statistic that measures the variability around a mean.

A.3 In a normal distribution, the mean, median, and mode all fall exactly in the middle. In a negatively skewed distribution, there are more numbers in the low end, so the mean and median fall below the mode. In a positively skewed distribution, there are more numbers in the high end, so the mean and median fall above the mode.

A.4 Statistical significance is the probability that a statistic could have been obtained by random chance. By contrast, practical significance is the impact of a statistic on the real lives of real people.

KEY TERMS

measure of central tendency, p. A-1

mean, p. A-1

median, p. A-1

mode, p. A-1

variability, p. A-2

range, p. A-2

standard deviation, p. A-2

normal distribution, p. A-2

skewed distribution, p. A-3

negatively skewed distribution, p. A-3

positively skewed distribution, p. A-3

statistical significance, p. A-4

B Appendix: Self-Assessment Answers

CHAPTER 1

1. behavior, mental processes; **2.** a; **3.** d; **4.** philosophy, physiology; **5.** b; **6.** biological, psychological, social; **7.** science; **8.** a; **9.** d; **10.** experimental

CHAPTER 2

1. neurons; **2.** b; **3.** c; **4.** a; **5.** d; **6.** a; **7.** b; **8.** plasticity; **9.** c; **10.** a

CHAPTER 3

1. Sensation; **2.** a; **3.** c; **4.** d; **5.** d; **6.** Gestalt; **7.** b; **8.** cochlea; **9.** Olfaction; **10.** b

CHAPTER 4

1. b; **2.** a; **3.** d; **4.** c; **5.** a; **6.** c; **7.** tolerance; **8.** Addiction; **9.** d; **10.** Mindfulness

CHAPTER 5

1. b; **2.** Sensory memory; **3.** d; **4.** Long-term potentiation; **5.** d; **6.** c; **7.** b; **8.** flashbulb memory; **9.** b; **10.** a

CHAPTER 6

1. b; **2.** b; **3.** a; **4.** a; **5.** b; **6.** discriminative stimulus; **7.** shaping; **8.** Biological preparedness; **9.** c; **10.** Learned helplessness

CHAPTER 7

1. concept; **2.** c; **3.** a; **4.** a; **5.** b; **6.** Creativity; **7.** a; **8.** phoneme; **9.** a; **10.** Stereotype threat

CHAPTER 8

1. c; **2.** a; **3.** d; **4.** b; **5.** c; **6.** a; **7.** metabolic rates; **8.** d; **9.** Cannon-Bard; **10.** c

CHAPTER 9

1. longitudinal; **2.** Teratogens; **3.** c; **4.** Assimilation, accommodation; **5.** d; **6.** b; **7.** a; **8.** d; **9.** c; **10.** b

CHAPTER 10

1. c; **2.** culture; **3.** a; **4.** d; **5.** a; **6.** c; **7.** b; **8.** Sex; **9.** d; **10.** a

CHAPTER 11

1. c; **2.** Primary appraisal, Secondary appraisal; **3.** b; **4.** b; **5.** Posttraumatic growth; **6.** d; **7.** a; **8.** Problem-focused, emotion-focused; **9.** Mindfulness; **10.** Homeopathic medicine

CHAPTER 12

1. Personality; **2.** c; **3.** b; **4.** a; **5.** a; **6.** d; **7.** a; **8.** internal, external; **9.** a; **10.** b

CHAPTER 13

1. fundamental attribution error; **2.** b; **3.** d; **4.** c; **5.** b; **6.** a; **7.** b; **8.** d; **9.** Passionate, companionate; **10.** c

CHAPTER 14

1. b; **2.** *Diagnostic and Statistical Manual of Mental Disorders* (DSM); **3.** a; **4.** a; **5.** Social anxiety disorder; **6.** depression, mania; **7.** d; **8.** c; **9.** b; **10.** d

CHAPTER 15

1. d; **2.** a; **3.** Systematic desensitization; **4.** Cognitive therapy; **5.** c; **6.** efficacy, effectiveness; **7.** Common factors; **8.** c; **9.** Confidentiality; **10.** c

Glossary

ABCDE model of cognitive therapy A type of rational-emotive behavior therapy in which the therapist and client identify the sequence that leads from illogical thinking to logical thinking about particular life events.

absolute threshold The minimum level of a stimulus necessary for a person to detect its presence at least half of the time.

accommodation A classification process that makes sense of new information by revising or creating new schemas.

acculturation Managing a life that involves the coexistence of more than one culture.

acculturative stress Stress associated with the process of managing old and new cultures.

achievement goal theory A theory of motivation stating that when the person is motivated to achieve a goal, certain goals (mastery goals) produce better outcomes than other goals (performance goals).

achievement test An assessment technique used by psychologists to numerically measure the level of learning a person has attained.

acquisition The point in the learning process at which the neutral stimulus becomes a conditioned stimulus because of its link to the conditioned response.

action potential The release, or *firing*, of an electrical impulse that travels through the axon.

acupuncture A technique involving the insertion of needles into the skin at specific points to alleviate stress or pain.

acute stress disorder A psychological disorder that takes place in the days and weeks immediately after a trauma in which the person feels dazed and anxious and experiences flashbacks.

addiction Problematic drug use that persists in spite of serious negative consequences.

adjustment disorder A psychological disorder defined by an excessively disruptive stress reaction to an identifiable stressor.

adolescence The developmental period that encompasses the transition from childhood to adulthood.

adrenal glands The glands located on top of the kidneys that produce hormones to arouse the body in response to stress.

aerobic exercise Physical exercise that maintains an increased heart rate for a prolonged time.

affect heuristic An educated guess in which the worth of something is strongly influenced by how a person feels toward it.

affective forecasting Predicting how a person will feel about the outcomes of their decisions.

aggression Behavior intended to cause harm or death.

agreeableness A personality trait emphasizing the tendency to cooperate and comply with other people.

algorithm A formula-like method of problem solving.

all-or-nothing thinking A cognitive distortion in which the client mistakenly evaluates events as either absolutely flawless or completely awful, with no middle ground in between.

alternative medicine Health care that is used instead of conventional medicine.

altruism Completely unselfish concern for others.

amnesia The inability to remember some or all information, either temporarily or permanently.

amygdala The part of the limbic system involved most directly in emotion, especially fear.

anal stage Freud's second psychosexual stage, which lasts from about age 18 months to about age 3, and focuses on the psychological consequences of toilet training.

anchoring heuristic An educated guess in which the starting point has a strong influence on the conclusion that is ultimately reached.

anorexia nervosa An eating disorder based on a refusal to eat enough food to maintain a minimally healthy body weight, based on the person's height and age.

anterograde amnesia The inability to form new memories after a certain point in time.

antianxiety drugs Medications used to reduce anxiety symptoms.

antidepressant drugs Medications used to reduce depression symptoms (which are also sometimes effective in reducing anxiety symptoms).

antipsychotic drugs Medications used to reduce psychotic symptoms such as delusions, hallucinations, and bizarre behavior.

antiracist A person whose beliefs and actions oppose racism and promote racial equality.

antisocial personality disorder A psychological disorder based on a disregard for, and violation of, the rights of other people.

anxiety disorders The group of DSM disorders in which the experience of excessive, unjustified anxiety is the primary symptom.

applied psychology specializations Areas in which psychologists apply their expertise to real-world problems, using their knowledge of mind and behavior to enhance some important aspect of their clients' lives.

appraisal The way you evaluate the things that happen to you.

archetypes Specific symbols or patterns within the collective unconscious that appear consistently across cultures and time periods.

arousal theory A theory of motivation stating that the person is motivated to obtain and maintain an optimal level of arousal.

assimilation A classification process that makes sense of new information by sorting into already existing schemas.

assimilation An acculturation strategy in which the person adopts the new culture and rejects the old culture.

association areas Brain material that is devoted to synthesizing and interpreting information rather than merely taking information in.

attachment A close emotional bond between two people, particularly a young child and a caregiver.

attention-deficit/hyperactivity disorder (ADHD) A disorder emerging in childhood that features significant problems with attention, hyperactivity/impulsivity, or both.

attitude A viewpoint, often influenced by both thoughts and emotions, that affects a person's responses to people, things, or situations.

attribution An explanation of the cause of behavior.

attribution theory A theory that behavior is caused either by traits within the individual or by the situation surrounding the individual.

audition The sense of hearing.

authoritarian parenting style An approach to parenting in which parents require children to obey unquestionable, strict rules.

authoritative parenting style An approach to parenting in which parents set rules, but also explain and negotiate those rules with their children.

autism spectrum disorder A disorder emerging in childhood that features significant social interaction deficits and rigid, repetitive patterns of behavior.

automatic processing (automatic encoding) The entrance of some information into long-term memory without any conscious processing.

autonomic nervous system The part of the peripheral nervous system that connects the central nervous system to the parts of the body controlled involuntarily.

availability heuristic An educated guess based on the information that most quickly and easily comes to mind.

aversive conditioning A form of behavior therapy that aims to reduce unwanted behavior by pairing it with an unpleasant experience.

axon The part of the neuron that carries information toward other neurons.

axon terminals The small branches at the end of an axon that form connections with the next neuron.

babbling An early stage of speech development during which the baby vocalizes a wide variety of nonword sounds.
basic research psychology specializations Areas in which psychologists conduct research for the sake of enhancing the understanding of behavior and mental processes.
behavior therapy The application of operant and classical conditioning to change outward behavior, with little to no emphasis on the mental processes affecting that behavior.
behavioral activation A type of behavior therapy for people with depression in which they deliberately increase the frequency of reinforcing behaviors.
behavioral assessment An approach to assessment that assumes client behaviors are themselves the problems, rather than signs of deeper problems.
behavioral genetics The study of the impact of genes (nature) and environment (nurture) on personality and behavior.
behavioral theory of personality A theory that emphasizes the influence of the environment and the importance of observable, measurable behavior.
behaviorism A psychological perspective that emphasizes observable behavior over internal mental processes.
belief perseverance A tendency to maintain a belief even when evidence suggests it is incorrect.
bisexual or bi The sexual orientation of a person who is attracted to people of more than one sex or gender.
binge eating disorder An eating disorder with the overeating pattern of bulimia but without the purging.
binocular depth cues The qualities of visual stimuli that indicate depth when using both eyes.
biofeedback Use of a monitor that provides information about physiological functions (like heartbeat or muscle tension), with the intention of influencing those functions in a healthy direction.
biological preparedness An animal's evolutionary predisposition to learn that which is most relevant to the survival of that species.
biological theory of psychological disorders A theory asserting that biological factors within the human body, such as brain structures, neurochemicals, and genes, are the primary causes of psychological disorders.
biomedical therapy A treatment for psychological disorders that involves medications or medical procedures to directly change the biology of the brain.
biopsychosocial theory A uniquely comprehensive psychological perspective that emphasizes biological, psychological, and social factors as influences on behavior.
biopsychosocial theory of psychological disorders A contemporary theory acknowledging that a combination of biological, psychological, and sociocultural factors contribute to psychological disorders.
BIPOC Black, Indigenous, and People of Color.
bipolar disorder A psychological disorder characterized by alternating between extremely high moods and extremely low moods.
blind spot The part of the retina that contains no rods or cones and is therefore unable to sense light.
body mass index (BMI) A number calculated from a person's height and weight that indicates body fat and overall fitness level.
borderline personality disorder A psychological disorder based on instability in many areas of the person's life, including interpersonal relationships, mood, and self-image.
bottom-up processing A way of processing information in which what a person senses becomes a perception with no influence of expectations or previous experiences.
brainstem The part of the brain that connects to the spine and controls the functions most essential to staying alive.
Broca's aphasia The speech dysfunction caused by damage to Broca's area.
Broca's area The part of the left side of the frontal lobe heavily involved in speaking.
bulimia nervosa An eating disorder in which an individual exhibits a pattern of overeating followed by drastic attempts to prevent weight gain.
bystander effect The decrease in likelihood that one person will help another person caused by the presence of others also available to help.
Cannon–Bard theory A theory of emotion stating that the person experiences emotion by simultaneously becoming aware of bodily changes and feelings.
catastrophizing A cognitive distortion in which the client exaggerates the negative consequences of an event, or makes a "catastrophe" out of a minor mishap.
categorical model of psychopathology A model in which psychological disorders exist as either totally present or totally absent, as opposed to present to a certain extent.
cell body (soma) The large central region of a neuron that performs the basic activities, including the production of energy, to keep the neuron functional.
central nervous system The brain and the spinal cord.
central route persuasion A persuasion strategy that emphasizes the message's content.
cerebellum The part of the brain near the bottom and the back, primarily involved in balance and the coordination of movement.
cerebral cortex The outer layer of the cerebrum, where sensory information is processed.
cerebral hemispheres The left and right halves of the cerebrum.
cerebrum (forebrain) The front and upper part of the brain, consisting of two hemispheres and involved in sophisticated, often uniquely human, abilities.
change blindness The failure to notice changes in the visual field simply because a person expects otherwise.
chunking Grouping pieces of information together in a meaningful way to enhance memory.
cilia Tiny scent-seeking threads that extend from olfactory receptor cells through the mucus of your nose.
circadian rhythm The 24-hour cycle on which the brain and body function.
cisgender A person whose gender matches the sex they were assigned at birth.
classical conditioning A form of learning in which animals or people make a connection between two stimuli that have occurred together, such that one predicts the other.
clinical interview A method of personality assessment in which the psychologist engages in conversation with the client.
clinical psychology An applied specialization in which psychologists focus on psychological disorders.
cochlea The spiral fluid-filled structure in the inner ear that sends sound waves to the brain via the auditory nerve.
cocktail party effect The ability to attend to certain stimuli within one sense (such as hearing) over other stimuli within the same sense.
cognition What the brain does with information, including understanding it, organizing it, analyzing it, and communicating it.
cognitive appraisal theory A theory of emotion stating that what the person thinks about a stimulus causes the emotion.
cognitive dissonance The discomfort caused by having an attitude or behavior that contradicts another attitude or behavior.
cognitive distortions Descriptive names for various kinds of irrational thinking.
cognitive map A mental diagram of the physical environment as it is initially explored when no reinforcement is available.
cognitive psychology A psychological perspective that emphasizes cognitive processes such as thinking, language, attention, memory, and intelligence.
cognitive symptoms The disturbed, illogical ways that people with schizophrenia think.
cognitive therapy A psychotherapy approach in which therapists help clients change the way they think about life events.
cognitive-behavioral therapy A hybrid therapy approach that combines an emphasis on logical thinking with the use of conditioning principles to directly change behavior.
collective unconscious Common, inherited memories that are present in the minds of people of every culture.
collectivism A worldview that emphasizes the well-being of the group over the well-being of the individual.

colorism Prejudice or discrimination based on the darkness of a person's skin, often within a single racial or ethnic group.
common factors Elements found in all forms of effective psychotherapy that play an important role in client improvement.
common group identity A strategy for fighting prejudice based on the creation of a larger group that includes multiple smaller groups.
community psychology An applied specialization in which psychologists focus on the wellness of entire communities.
companionate love Love characterized by deep commitment and affection, and often experienced later in long-term relationships.
comparative psychology A basic research specialization in which psychologists focus on the behavior of species other than humans.
complementary medicine Health care that complements, or is used along with, conventional medicine.
computed tomography (CT) A technique in which multiple X-rays are combined to make a 3D image of the brain.
concept A mental representation of a category of similar things, actions, or people.
concrete operational stage The third stage in Piaget's theory of development, from about age 7 to about age 11, in which children acquire the ability to think logically about concrete things.
conditioned response The response to a conditioned stimulus acquired through learning.
conditioned stimulus A formerly neutral stimulus that now causes a response because of its link to an unconditioned stimulus.
conditions of worth Requirements that you must meet to earn a person's positive regard.
cones Receptor cells in the retina that detect color when light is plentiful.
confidentiality When a therapist maintains the privacy of client information.
confirmation bias A tendency to prefer information that confirms what a person thought in the first place.
conformity Changes in an individual's behavior to correspond to the behavior of a group of other people.
congruence A match between your real self and your ideal self.
conscientiousness A personality trait emphasizing the tendency to be organized, responsible, and deliberate.
consciousness A person's awareness of their self and surroundings.
conservation A mental operation in which an amount or quantity remains the same regardless of the shape it takes.
continuous reinforcement A pattern by which a behavior is reinforced every time it occurs.
control group The group of participants in experimental research who do not receive the treatment that is the focus of the study.
conventional morality A moral decision-making strategy driven by the desire to follow society's norms and laws.
convergent thinking A problem-solving strategy in which a person uses logic to deduce the single best solution.
coping Efforts to reduce or manage an experience of stress.
cornea The thin transparent cover for the whole eye.
coronary heart disease A common and often fatal disease in which the arteries that lead to the heart are clogged or blocked.
corpus callosum The bundle of neurons that connects and allows communication between the two cerebral hemispheres.
correlation coefficient A statistic that shows the relationship between two variables, ranging from highly positive (+1) to highly negative (−1).
correlational research A type of research in which the goal is to determine the relationship between two variables.
correlation–causation fallacy A mistaken belief that when two variables correlate strongly with each other, one must cause the other.
co-sleeping Sleeping in the same room or same bed with another person (usually a caregiver).
counseling psychology An applied specialization in which psychologists focus on improving the functioning of people who are struggling through difficult times in their lives.
counterconditioning A classical conditioning therapy technique in which the trigger for an unwanted response is paired with a new stimulus that prevents the unwanted response.
creativity The capacity to come up with original ideas or approaches to a problem.
critical period A period of time during which a particular developmental task is especially likely to be influenced by outside events.
critical thinking An inquisitive, challenging approach to ideas and assumptions
cross-sectional design A research design in which people of different ages are compared to each other at the same point in time.
cultural competence The ability to work sensitively and expertly with members of a culturally diverse society.
cultural humility An attitude based on self-reflection, recognizing the limits of your own knowledge about diversity, and educating yourself about the identities and experiences of other people.
cultural intelligence A person's ability to live and interact effectively in a multicultural society.
cultural self-awareness The therapist's recognition that their own perspective is not necessarily that of others.
culture A group of similar people who share beliefs, values, and patterns of behavior.
culture-fair intelligence tests Intelligence tests that aim to reduce or remove any cultural factors that could lead to bias.
cyclothymic disorder A long-term, lower-intensity version of bipolar disorder.
decay The dwindling or loss of information from memory due to the passing of time.
decision making Using cognition to choose between available options.
defense mechanisms According to Freud, techniques used by the ego to manage conflict between the id and superego.
deindividuation A loss of identity and accountability experienced by individuals in groups that can lead to atypical behavior.
delusions Completely false beliefs that a person with schizophrenia believes to be reality.
dendrites The branches at the end of neurons that receive signals from other neurons.
dependent variable (DV) A variable in experimental research that is expected to depend upon the independent variable.
depressants Drugs that slow bodily functions.
depressive and bipolar disorders The category of psychological disorders based on extreme moods or emotional states.
depth perception The ability to judge the distance and depth of objects.
descriptive research A type of research in which the goal is simply to describe a characteristic of the population.
developmental psychology A basic research specialization in which psychologists focus on how people change throughout the life span.
developmental psychology The study of the changes to body, mind, and interpersonal interaction that people experience across the life span.
***Diagnostic and Statistical Manual of Mental Disorders* (DSM)** The book in which mental disorders are officially defined.
dialect A group's particular version of a language with its own unique characteristics.
difference threshold (just noticeable difference) The smallest change in a stimulus necessary for a person to detect it at least half of the time.
diffusion of responsibility A decreased sense of obligation to help when others are present.
dimensional model of psychopathology A model of psychopathology in which psychological issues exist on a continuum, as opposed to being fully present or absent.
discrimination Action based on prejudice or stereotypes toward a social group.
discrimination The learning process by which stimuli that are different from the conditioned stimulus fail to cause the same conditioned response.

discriminative stimulus A signal indicating that a particular behavior will be followed by a particular consequence.
display rules Norms within a group about the acceptable verbal and nonverbal expression of emotion.
dissociative amnesia A psychological disorder in which a person becomes unable to recall important information from their past.
dissociative disorders The category of psychological disorders in which the person loses awareness of, or becomes disconnected from, essential parts of the self such as memories, emotions, or identity.
dissociative identity disorder A psychological disorder in which a person exhibits two or more distinct personalities.
divergent thinking A problem-solving strategy in which a person comes up with lots of different possible solutions.
dodo bird verdict A nickname (from *Alice in Wonderland*) for the research finding that different forms of psychotherapy are equally effective.
door-in-the-face technique A persuasion strategy in which one person gets another person to reject a large request before making a smaller one.
double-blind procedure A way of conducting experimental research in which neither the participants nor the researchers are aware of which participants are in the experimental group and which are in the control group.
dream analysis A psychodynamic technique in which the therapist and client attempt to find the underlying meaning of the client's dreams.
drive reduction theory A theory of motivation stating that unmet biological drives cause unpleasant sensations that motivate the person to meet those needs.
dual-process theory The notion that every person possesses two separate types of thinking, one automatic and one deliberate.
durability bias The overestimation of the expected length of the feeling produced by the outcome of a decision.
dynamic sizing The ability to simultaneously know the norm for a group and recognize that the norm might not apply to every member of that group.
eating disorders The category of psychological disorders that involve significant disturbances in behaviors related to eating or food.
echoic memory The auditory sensory memory, or all the information the ears took in during the previous few seconds.
eclectic approach to therapy A strategy in which the psychotherapist selects the best treatment for a particular client based on evidence from studies of similar clients.
educational psychology An applied specialization in which psychologists focus on learning and teaching.
ego According to Freud, the part of the mind that serves as a realistic mediator between the id and superego.
egocentrism The inability to understand a situation from a point of view other than your own.
elaborative rehearsal Adding meaning or associations to information to enhance memory.
Electra complex The childhood experience of desiring the father and resenting the mother.
electroconvulsive therapy (ECT) A biomedical therapy for severe disorders in which an electric current passes through the brain of the client.
electroencephalography (EEG) A technique in which electrodes are placed on the scalp to record electrical activity in the brain.
embryo The prenatal human organism from about 2 weeks to about 2 months after conception.
emerging adulthood A recently proposed developmental stage during which the person gradually moves from adolescence to adulthood.
emotion All aspects of feeling, including changes to the body, behavior, and consciousness.
emotion regulation The ability to manage the type, intensity, length, and expression of one's own emotions.
emotional intelligence A person's ability to sense and manage their own emotions as well as the emotions of others.
emotion-focused coping A style of coping with stress that emphasizes changing your emotional reaction to the stressor.
empathy The therapist's ability to sense the client's emotions just as the client would, and to then respond compassionately.
encoding The entering of information into memory.
encoding specificity The effect that contextual information that was present when memory was encoded, such as physical surroundings, has on retrieval.
endocrine system The set of glands that sends hormones throughout the body via the bloodstream.
endorphins The neurotransmitters involved in reducing pain and increasing pleasure.
episodic memory A type of explicit memory consisting of personal firsthand experiences.
evidence-based practice An approach to psychotherapy in which the therapist makes decisions based on a combination of three factors: research evidence, therapist expertise, and client characteristics.
evolutionary psychology A psychological perspective that emphasizes Charles Darwin's theory of evolution as an influence on behavior.
experimental group The group of participants in experimental research who receive the treatment that is the focus of the study.
experimental research A type of research in which the goal is to determine the cause-and-effect relationship between two variables by manipulating one and observing changes in the other.
explicit memory Memory of which one is consciously aware.
exposure therapy A form of behavior therapy based on classical conditioning in which anxiety is treated by gradually exposing the client to the thing or situation that causes the anxiety.
external locus of control The belief that your life is under the control of forces outside of yourself.
extinction The point in the learning process at which the conditioned stimulus no longer causes the conditioned response because it is no longer linked to the unconditioned stimulus.
extralinguistic information Components of language other than the literal meaning of the words.
extrasensory perception (ESP) The controversial notion of perception without sensation.
extraversion A personality trait emphasizing the tendency to be socially outgoing.
extrinsic motivation A desire to perform a behavior to obtain an external reward.
facial feedback theory A theory of emotion stating that one's brain can influence one's emotions by monitoring one's facial expressions.
family therapy Psychotherapy that aims to improve how the family system functions, which in turn will improve the mental health of its individual members.
fetal alcohol syndrome A pattern of physical and behavioral difficulties common in people whose mothers drank alcohol excessively during pregnancy.
fetus The prenatal human organism from about 2 months after conception to birth.
fight-or-flight response An automatic emotional and physical reaction to a perceived threat that prepares you to either attack it or run away from it.
figure–ground organization The tendency to visually distinguish between an object and its background.
Five-Factor Model of personality (Big Five) An explanation of personality that emphasizes five fundamental traits present in all people to varying degrees.
fixation Freud's term for a lingering psychological difficulty directly related to unsuccessful experience of a particular psychosexual stage.
fixed-interval schedule A reinforcement schedule in which a behavior can be reinforced after a time interval that is consistent and predictable.
fixed-ratio schedule A reinforcement schedule in which a behavior is reinforced after a consistent, predictable number of occurrences.
flashbulb memory A distinctively clear and vivid memory of an emotionally charged and novel event.
flat affect The absence of appropriate emotion.
flow Performing a behavior with complete immersion and enjoyment, or feeling like one is "in the zone."
foot-in-the-door technique A persuasion strategy in which one person gets another person to agree to a small request before asking for a bigger one.

forensic psychology An applied specialization in which psychologists focus on legal and criminal justice issues.
formal operational stage The final stage in Piaget's theory of development, beginning around age 11 and lasting through adulthood, in which the person becomes able to think logically about abstract things.
fovea The area in the center of the retina that contains many cones but no rods.
framing The particular way a question or problem is presented, which can influence how a person responds to it.
frequency theory The explanation of pitch perception based on the idea that a person hears different pitches because nerve impulses travel with different frequencies through the auditory nerve.
Freudian slips Verbal or behavioral mistakes that reveal unconscious thoughts or wishes.
frontal lobe The part of the cerebral cortex right behind the forehead, involved in complex thinking tasks, planning, purposeful actions, and other advanced functions.
functional fixedness Thinking about something in only the way it is most typically used rather than other possible uses.
functional magnetic resonance imaging (fMRI) A technique in which magnetic fields are used to make images of brain activity.
functionalism A perspective from the early history of psychology that focused on the function of our mental processes and behaviors.
fundamental attribution error Overestimating the importance of traits and underestimating the importance of the situation when explaining the behavior of other people.
gay/lesbian The sexual orientation of a person who is attracted to people with a sex or gender different than their own.
gender Your culture's social, psychological, and behavioral expectations related to the sex you were assigned at birth.
gender identity Your internal sense of yourself as man, woman, both, or neither.
general adaptation syndrome A widely accepted understanding of the way the body responds to ongoing stress, consisting of the sequence of alarm, resistance, and exhaustion.
general intelligence (*g*) Overall intelligence that applies across all tasks and situations.
generalization The learning process by which stimuli that are similar to the conditioned stimulus cause the same conditioned response.
generalized anxiety disorder A disorder involving anxiety symptoms that persist for a long time across a wide range of situations and activities.
genital stage The fifth and final psychosexual stage, which lasts from puberty through adulthood and focuses on mature, adult sexual relationships.
genuineness The therapist's truthfulness, realness, and honesty, as opposed to falsely playing the therapist role.
gestalt An organized whole that is perceived as different than just the sum of its parts.
ghrelin A hormone that signals feelings of hunger.
giftedness Significantly above-average intelligence.
glial cells The cells that support and protect neurons throughout the brain.
grammar The set of rules within a language.
group polarization The tendency for a group's attitudes to become more extreme as a result of group discussions.
group therapy Psychotherapy conducted with a group of clients and with an emphasis on interpersonal interaction.
groupthink A phenomenon that occurs when group members value getting along with each other more than finding the best solution.
gustation The sense of taste.
hallucinations False sensations or perceptions.
hallucinogens Drugs that produce unrealistic sensations such as hallucinations.
hardiness Behaviors that reflect resilience under stressful circumstances.
hassles The common, minor annoyances or aggravations of day-to-day life.
health psychology A basic research specialization in which psychologists focus on the relationship between mind and body.
heterosexual or straight The sexual orientation of a person who is attracted to people with a sex or gender different than their own.
heuristic An educated guess or rule-of-thumb method of problem solving.
hierarchy of needs An explanation of motivation created by Abraham Maslow based on the idea that certain needs must be satisfied before others.
higher-order conditioning Classical conditioning that involves three or more stimuli.
hippocampus The part of the limbic system involved in memory, especially spatial memory and long-term memory.
homeopathic medicine Health care based on the idea that the human body has the ability to heal itself and characterized by very low-dose medications made from natural sources.
homeostasis Steadiness or balance in the person's bodily state.
hormones The chemicals made by the glands of the endocrine system that affect certain tissues throughout the body.
hue The color of light, as determined by its wavelength.
humanism A psychological perspective that emphasizes the notion that human nature is generally good and people are naturally motivated to grow toward their own potential.
humanistic theory of personality A theory based on the ideas of Carl Rogers that emphasizes people's inherent tendencies toward healthy, positive growth and self-fulfillment.
hypnosis An altered state of consciousness in which one person, the participant, becomes very suggestible to another person, the hypnotist.
hypothalamus The part of the limbic system involved in maintaining a steadiness in bodily functions.
hypothesis A prediction, typically based on a theory, that can be tested.
iconic memory The visual sensory memory, or all the information the eyes took in during the previous fraction of a second.
id According to Freud, the animalistic part of the mind that generates our most basic, biologically based impulses, such as sex and aggression.
ideal self The self-actualized version of yourself that you naturally strive to become.
identity A part of Erikson's psychosocial theory of development; a person's stable sense of who they are.
imaginary audience A common way of thinking among adolescents in which they believe their lives are continuously being watched and evaluated by other people.
immune system The body's innate method of defending against bacteria, viruses, infections, injuries, and anything else that could cause illness or death.
implicit memory Memory of which one is not consciously aware.
impression formation The initial appraisal, or "first impression," that a person forms of another person.
inattentional blindness The failure to notice something in your visual field simply because your attention was focused elsewhere.
incentive An object or situation outside the person that the person is motivated to acquire.
incongruence A mismatch between your real self and your ideal self.
independent variable (IV) A variable in experimental research that is manipulated by the researcher.
individualism A worldview that emphasizes the well-being of the individual over the well-being of the group.
industrial/organizational (I/O) psychology An applied specialization in which psychologists focus on the workplace.
information processing model A model of memory that involves the three steps of *encoding*, *storage*, and *retrieval*.
informed consent Permission given by the client, after the therapist educates the client about the therapy process, to move forward with the therapy.
informed consent to research An ethical requirement for psychologists by which they must inform people about the research and obtain their consent before participation can occur.
ingroup A social group to which a person believes they belong ("us").
ingroup bias The tendency to hold a more positive attitude toward the ingroup than the outgroup.

insight The perception of a solution to a problem that results from cognitive understanding rather than from trial and error.
insomnia A sleep disorder featuring consistent difficulty falling asleep, staying asleep, or achieving high-quality sleep.
instinct A motivation that is biologically innate.
instinct theory A theory of motivation stating that humans, like all other animals, are motivated primarily by instinct.
instinctive drift The tendency of animals' behavior to return to innate, genetically programmed patterns.
integration An acculturation strategy in which the person adopts both the new culture and the old culture.
integrative approach to therapy A strategy in which the psychotherapist blends styles or techniques to create a new form of psychotherapy.
intellectual disability A mental disorder based on significantly below-average intelligence and impaired day-to-day functioning.
intelligence The ability to gain knowledge and learn from experience.
intelligence quotient (IQ) A single number used to represent a person's overall intelligence.
intelligence test An assessment technique used by psychologists to numerically measure intelligence.
intergroup contact A strategy for fighting prejudice based on direct interpersonal interaction between members of multiple groups.
internal locus of control The belief that your life is under the control of forces inside of yourself.
interneurons The neurons that serve only to connect to other nearby neurons rather than reaching farther out into the body.
interpersonal attraction The desire to enhance a relationship with another person.
interpretation The psychodynamic therapist's attempt to make a connection between the client's unconscious material and their current behavior, thoughts, or feelings.
intersectionality The way any one person's unique combination of social and cultural categories intersect or overlap, especially as related to discrimination, unequal treatment, or social disadvantage.
intimacy A part of Erikson's psychosocial theory of development; long-term emotional closeness with a romantic partner.
intrinsic motivation A desire to perform a behavior because the behavior itself is rewarding.
involuntary memory The spontaneous retrieval of information in the absence of any intention to retrieve it.
iris The colored, circular muscle situated in the center of the eye.
James–Lange theory A theory of emotion stating that the person experiences emotion by noticing bodily changes first and then interpreting them as particular feelings.
just-world hypothesis The notion that the world is fair and that unfortunate events happen to those who deserve them.
kinesthetic sense The sense of the position and movement of the body parts.
kinship theory An explanation of helping that emphasizes the importance of passing genes on to future generations.
language The ability to communicate with others using words or other symbols combined and arranged according to rules.
language acquisition device A specific capacity within a person's brain that provides the ability to use language.
latency stage Freud's fourth psychosexual stage, which lasts through the elementary school years, when the child's energies are focused primarily on school and other tasks that have little to do with sexual or bodily issues.
latent learning A type of learning that has taken place but cannot be directly observed.
law of effect The observation that a behavior is more likely to be repeated if its effects are desirable but less likely to be repeated if its effects are undesirable.
learned helplessness The absence of any attempt to help oneself that results from previously learning that such attempts are useless.
learning The process by which life experience causes change in the behavior or thinking of an organism.
lens The clear layer beneath the surface of the eye that maintains focus on an object by varying its own shape.
leptin A hormone that signals feelings of fullness.
lesion The damage or destruction of brain tissue.
level of processing How deeply information is processed.
LGBTQ+ A community of members of sexual minorities, including lesbian (L), gay (G), bisexual (B), transgender (T), queer/questioning (Q), and other people.
limbic system The cluster of brain areas involved primarily in emotion, located near the center of the brain and surrounding the thalamus.
linguistic relativity The theory that language influences thought.
literature review A step in scientific research during which a researcher learns what previous research on the topic already exists.
lobotomy A historical psychosurgery in which the prefrontal lobes are disconnected from the inner regions of the brain that control emotions.
localization The idea that specific parts of the brain do specific things.
locus of control Your belief about how much control you have over what happens to you.
longitudinal design A research design in which the same group of people is compared to itself at different points in time.
long-term memory A seemingly limitless amount of information being held for extensive periods of time.
long-term potentiation The increased connectivity between simultaneously stimulated neurons that forms the biological basis of memory.
lowball technique A persuasion strategy in which one person quotes another person a low price to get an initial agreement and then raises the price.
lucid dreaming A dreaming experience in which a person has some control over the dream while remaining asleep.
magnetic resonance imaging (MRI) A technique in which magnetic fields and radio waves are used to make images of brain structure.
maintenance rehearsal Information repeated in exactly the same form as it was originally encoded.
major depressive disorder A depressive disorder in which a person experiences at least 2 weeks of depressed mood and a loss of interest in most activities.
mania An emotional state of excessively elated mood and overabundant energy.
marginalization An acculturation strategy in which the person rejects both the new culture and the old culture.
mean The average of a group of numbers.
measure of central tendency A single number used to summarize or represent a group of numbers.
median The number that falls at the midpoint in a group of numbers listed in order, such that half fall above it and half fall below it.
medical student syndrome An experience common among medical students, and perhaps psychology students, in which they start to believe that they have the disorders or illnesses about which they are learning.
meditation An activity designed to increase focused attention with the ultimate purpose of improving a person's mental state.
medulla The part of the brainstem most specifically involved in heartbeat and breathing.
memory The process of taking in information, saving it over time, and calling it to mind later.
menarche A girl's first menstrual period.
menopause The time in a woman's middle adulthood when she stops having menstrual periods.
mental filtering A cognitive distortion in which the client ignores, or "filters out," the positive while focusing excessively on the negative.
mental set The limits a person places on an approach to problem solving based on what has worked in the past.
mere exposure effect An increase in the attractiveness of a person (or object) resulting from nothing more than repeated contact.
metabolic rate (or metabolism) The rate at which one's body burns energy.
microaggressions Everyday actions or comments that, often unintentionally, contain hostile or off-putting messages for members of certain cultures.

mindfulness Awareness of one's moment-to-moment experiences fully, deliberately, and without distraction.
Minnesota Multiphasic Personality Inventory-2 (MMPI-2) A widely used and respected objective personality test that emphasizes mental disorders.
mirror neurons Neurons that are thought to underlie empathy and imitation and that activate when a person performs or observes a particular behavior.
misinformation Information that is false, deceptive, or misleading.
misinformation effect The tendency of false or misleading information presented after the fact to be mistakenly incorporated into memory.
mnemonic A specific technique or strategy deliberately used to enhance memory.
mode The number that occurs the most often in a group of numbers.
monocular depth cues The qualities of visual stimuli that indicate depth when using only one eye.
mood-stabilizing drugs Medications used to lessen the extreme emotional highs and lows of bipolar disorder.
morpheme The smallest meaningful unit of a language.
motivation A desire that stimulates and steers behavior.
motor cortex The strip of brain matter near the back of the frontal lobe, involved in voluntary movement.
motor neurons The cells that carry messages from the brain to the muscles.
multiculturalism A psychological perspective that emphasizes the influences of culture on behavior and mental processes.
multiculturalism An approach in psychology that highlights the importance and value of multiple cultural groups within a society.
multimethod assessment An approach to personality assessment that emphasizes the use of multiple methods rather than only one method.
multiple relationship A situation in which a therapist has both a professional relationship and a nonprofessional relationship with the same person.
myelin sheath A protective sleeve of fatty material that surrounds the axon.
narcolepsy A disorder of "sleep attacks" characterized by immediate and unexpected shifts from wakefulness to REM sleep.
nativist theory A theory of language development that says the ability to use language is inborn.
negative reinforcement A type of reinforcement that involves removing something undesirable.
negative symptoms Behaviors that are lacking in people with schizophrenia, but that are usually present in people without the disorder.
negatively skewed distribution A distribution of numbers that includes more numbers in the low end (toward the left on a graph) than in a normal distribution.
neo-Freudian theories Theories that revised, but did not entirely reject, the basics of Freud's original psychodynamic theory.
NEO-Personality Inventory-3 (NEO-PI-3) An objective personality test that measures the Big Five personality factors.
nervous system The full set of nerves that connect the brain with all other parts of the body.
neurogenesis The creation of new neurons.
neurons The cells that facilitate communication within the nervous system.
neuroscience A psychological perspective that emphasizes the link between behavior and the biological functioning of the brain.
neuroticism A personality trait emphasizing the tendency to experience negative emotions such as anxiety, depression, and stress.
neurotransmitters The chemical messengers that travel across synapses from one neuron to the next.
neutral stimulus A stimulus that causes no response at all.
nonbinary A gender identity that does not fall within the categories of woman or man, and may fall between those categories or be entirely distinct from them.
nondirective therapy A style of therapy in which the client, rather than the therapist, determines the course of therapy.
non-REM sleep Any sleep other than REM sleep, when rapid eye movement, intense brain activity, and dreams are unlikely to occur.
normal curve A graph showing that the frequency of scores on a test is greatest in the middle and decreases toward the extremes.
normal distribution A symmetrical distribution of numbers in which the mean, median, and mode all fall exactly in the middle.
obedience Changes in an individual's behavior to comply with the demands of an authority figure.
obesity A BMI of 30 or higher.
object permanence The ability to realize that an object continues to exist even when a person can't see, hear, or otherwise sense it.
objective personality tests Personality tests in which the client responds to a standardized set of questions, usually in multiple-choice or true–false format.
observational learning A type of learning that occurs as a result of observing others' behavior and consequences rather than our own.
obsessive-compulsive disorder (OCD) A disorder characterized by unwanted, repetitive thoughts and uncontrollable actions done in response to those thoughts.
occipital lobe The lower back part of the brain, involved in vision.
Oedipus complex The childhood experience of desiring the mother and resenting the father.
olfaction The sense of smell.
olfactory bulbs Brain structures located on the underside of your brain (behind the bridge of your nose) that receive scent information from cilia.
olfactory cortex A collection of brain regions involved in smell, including the amygdala and parts of the cerebral cortex.
one-word stage A stage of speech development during which the young child uses a single word as a full sentence.
openness to experience A personality trait emphasizing the tendency to be receptive to new or unconventional ideas.
operant conditioning A form of learning in which the consequences of a voluntary behavior affect the likelihood that the behavior will recur.
operational definition A specific, measurable definition of a variable for the purpose of a scientific study.
opiates Pain-relieving drugs naturally derived from the poppy plant.
opioids Drugs that include both naturally derived opiates and synthetically made substances that bind to the same receptors in the brain and have similar effects.
opponent-process theory of color vision An explanation of color vision based on the idea that the cones are specialized to sense specific opposite pairs of colors (like red–green and blue–yellow).
optimism An attitude toward the future characterized by hope or expectation of a positive outcome.
oral stage The first of Freud's psychosexual stages, which takes place from birth to about 18 months and focuses on the psychological consequences of feeding behavior.
ossicles A chain of very small bones connected in ball-and-socket fashion on the inner side of the tympanic membrane.
outgroup A social group to which a person believes they do not belong ("them").
outgroup homogeneity The assumption that all members of an outgroup are essentially similar.
oval window membrane A membrane between the ossicles of the middle ear and the inner ear.
overgeneralization A cognitive distortion in which the client comes to a very broad-based conclusion based on just a single unfortunate event.
overweight A BMI between 25 and 29.9.
panic disorder An anxiety disorder characterized by sudden, intense, unpredictable brief bursts of anxiety.
parapsychology The study of topics that fall outside the range of mainstream psychology.
parasympathetic division The part of the autonomic nervous system that calms the body down when stressors decrease.
parietal lobe The part of the brain near the top and back of the head, involved in touch and perception.
partial reinforcement (Also called *intermittent* reinforcement) A pattern by which a behavior is reinforced only some of the times it occurs.

participant modeling A technique in which a client watches a model (in some cases, the therapist) perform the target behavior with the intent of the client imitating the model.
passionate love Love characterized by arousal and desire, and often experienced early in relationships.
peak experience A moment of self-actualization that produces strong, often mystical, feelings of personal fulfillment.
peer review process The appraisal of research by people who are at least as expert on the subject as the researcher.
perception The ability of the brain to interpret the raw sensations it has taken in.
perceptual constancy The brain's ability to maintain the same perception of an object even when conditions around it cause it to produce different sensations.
perceptual set The tendency to perceive things in a certain way because of a person's previous experiences or attention strategy.
peripheral nervous system The neurons that connect the central nervous system to other parts of the body.
peripheral route persuasion A persuasion strategy that emphasizes factors other than the message's content.
permissive parenting style An approach to parenting in which parents place minimal demands and allow children to run their own lives.
persistent depressive disorder (dysthymia) A depressive disorder characterized by a chronic, relatively low-intensity depressed mood.
personal fable A common way of thinking among adolescents in which they believe themselves to be special or invulnerable.
personality A person's distinctive and stable way of thinking, feeling, and behaving.
personality disorders The category of psychological disorders based on an enduring pattern of inflexible and maladaptive behavior that appears across a wide range of situations and interferes with interpersonal interaction.
personality psychology A basic research specialization in which psychologists focus on people's personality traits.
personalization A cognitive distortion in which the client takes too much of the blame and responsibility for unfortunate events.
person-centered therapy A psychotherapy approach based on the theories of Carl Rogers that emphasizes the tendency toward healthy growth inherent in each person.
phallic stage The third psychosexual stage, which runs from 3 to 6 years old and focuses on the psychological consequences of attraction to the opposite-gender parent/caregiver.
phoneme The smallest distinct unit of speech.
physical dependence A bodily need for a particular drug in order to function normally.
physiological psychology A basic research specialization in which psychologists focus on the neural basis of behavior.
pinna The outer ear.
pitch The description of how "high" or "low" a sound is.
pituitary gland The "master gland" in the brain that produces human growth hormone and controls all of the other glands in the body.
place theory The explanation of pitch perception based on the idea that a person hears different pitches because tiny hairs in different places within the cochlea are stimulated.
placebo effect The effect of expectations in experimental research rather than the effect of experimental manipulations.
plasticity The ability of the brain to adapt its structure or function in response to damage or experience.
pons The part of the brainstem involved in transmitting information, sleep, breathing, swallowing, and equilibrium.
population The whole range of people on whom a study's research is focused.
positive psychology A perspective in psychology that emphasizes people's strengths and successes.
positive regard Warmth, acceptance, and love from those around you.
positive reinforcement A type of reinforcement that involves getting something desirable.
positive symptoms Experiences that are present or excessive in people with schizophrenia but largely absent in people without it.
positively skewed distribution A distribution of numbers that includes more numbers in the high end (toward the right on a graph) than in a normal distribution.
positron emission tomography (PET) A technique in which activity in various brain structures is illustrated by a radioactive sugar injected into the body.
postconventional morality A moral decision-making strategy driven by fundamental rights and ethical principles.
posttraumatic growth When people experience trauma and then find a way to benefit, improve, or enrich themselves from that point onward.
posttraumatic stress disorder (PTSD) A psychological disorder lasting at least a month characterized by feeling continuously on edge, avoiding reminders of the traumatic event, having difficulty sleeping and concentrating, and frequently recalling or reliving the event.
preconventional morality A moral decision-making strategy driven by the potential rewards and punishments of the decision.
prejudice An often negative attitude toward a social group that is formed before getting to know group members.
preoperational stage The second stage in Piaget's theory of development, from about age 2 to about age 7, when children can use language and other symbols for real objects but still can't complete many mental operations.
primacy effect The tendency to remember the first items in a series particularly well.
primary appraisal The way you determine how stressful an event is to you.
primary reinforcer An innate reinforcer that requires no learning to have a reinforcing effect because it satisfies a biological need.
primary sex characteristics The parts of the body directly involved in sexual reproduction, such as genitals, ovaries, and testes.
priming When recent experiences cause an increased likelihood of recalling certain memories.
proactive coping A style of coping that focuses on future goals and the stressors that could get in the way of them.
proactive interference Problems remembering newer information caused by older information.
problem solving Using cognition to find a way to achieve a goal.
problem-focused coping A style of coping with stress that emphasizes changing the stressor itself.
procedural memory A type of implicit memory consisting of how to perform tasks that are done automatically.
projective personality tests Personality tests in which clients respond to ambiguous stimuli in a free-form way.
prolonged grief disorder A psychological disorder in which the person experiences the death of someone close to them followed by grief that is excessively intense or long-lasting.
prosocial behavior Behavior intended to help others.
prototype The most typical or best example within a concept.
pseudopsychology Psychological information that is not supported by science but may appear to be.
psychiatry The medical specialization that focuses on the brain and its disorders.
psychic determinism The belief that all thoughts and behaviors, even those that seem accidental, arbitrary, or mistaken, are determined by psychological forces.
psychoactive drugs Substances that alter mental functioning.
psychoanalysis A psychological perspective created by Sigmund Freud that emphasizes unconscious mental activity and the long-lasting influence of childhood experiences.
psychoanalysis An approach to psychotherapy developed by Sigmund Freud in which the main goal is to make the unconscious conscious—that is, helping the client become more aware of thoughts and feelings of which they were unaware at the start of therapy.
psychodynamic theory of personality An explanation of personality, based on the ideas of Sigmund Freud, that emphasizes unconscious forces and early childhood experiences.
psychodynamic therapy Therapy that has the goal of making the unconscious conscious, but more briefly and with more focus on the client's current life than psychoanalysis.

psychological dependence A mental need for a particular drug in order to function normally.
psychological disorder A pattern of behavior that interferes with a person's life by causing significant distress or dysfunction.
psychological theory of psychological disorders A theory asserting that psychological factors, including emotions, thoughts, behaviors, and traits, are the primary causes of psychological disorders.
psychology The scientific study of behavior and mental processes.
psychoneuroimmunology (PNI) The study of the relationship between psychological factors, including stress, and the immune system.
psychopharmacology The treatment of psychological disorders with medications.
psychophysiological illnesses Any illness that stress can cause, worsen, or maintain.
psychosexual stages Freud's five biologically based developmental stages of childhood, during which personality characteristics are formed.
psychosis A significant impairment in the basic ability to tell the difference between the real world and imagination.
psychosurgery Surgery performed directly on the brain in an effort to improve severe psychological disorders.
psychotherapy A treatment that involves a mental health professional using various techniques to help a person overcome a psychological disorder or improve some aspect of emotional, cognitive, or behavioral functioning.
puberty The time period featuring physical changes that mark the onset of adolescence and enable sexual reproduction.
punishment Any consequence of a behavior that makes that behavior less likely to recur.
pupil The opening in the middle of the iris.
random assignment A procedure in experimental research by which the assignment of participants into either the experimental or control group happens entirely by chance.
range The difference between the highest score and the lowest score in a group of numbers.
rational-emotive behavior therapy (REBT) A form of cognitive therapy in which the therapist challenges the client's illogical beliefs and encourages the client to adopt more logical beliefs.
real self The version of yourself that you actually experience in day-to-day life.
recall A type of retrieval in which stored information is accessed without any comparison to external information.
recency effect The tendency to remember the last items in a series particularly well.
receptor sites The openings in dendrites that match specific neurotransmitters like a lock fits a specific key.
reciprocal determinism The theory that three factors—behavior, environment, and cognitions—continually influence each other.
reciprocity norm An explanation of helping that emphasizes the expectation that those who provide help will receive help in the future.
recognition A type of retrieval in which stored information is compared to external information to determine if it matches.
reflection A technique in which the therapist listens closely and actively, then restates the client's words in a way that highlights the client's feelings.
reflex An automatic motor response to sensory input.
refractory period A waiting time, during which the neuron is reset before another action potential can begin.
regulatory focus theory A theory of motivation stating that there are two primary motivation systems—promotion and prevention—that affect different people in different ways.
rehearsal Deliberately repeating information to enhance memory.
reinforcement Any consequence of a behavior that makes that behavior more likely to recur.
reinforcement schedule A pattern by which reinforcements occur in response to a particular behavior.
reliability The extent to which an assessment technique provides consistent, repeatable results.
REM Rapid eye movement, or the flitting of the eyeballs behind the eyelids during sleep.
REM paralysis Temporary immobility during REM sleep.
REM rebound An increase in REM sleep after a period of REM sleep deprivation.
REM sleep The stage of sleep in which intense brain activity and vivid dreams are most likely to occur.
replication Conducting a study again to confirm or disconfirm the results.
representativeness heuristic An educated guess based on similarity to a prototype.
resistance Client behavior that blocks discussion or conscious awareness of anxiety-provoking topics.
resting potential The low-level electrical charge in a neuron that is not firing.
reticular activating system The collection of neurons in the brainstem involved in arousal.
retina The rear part of the eyeball, which receives visual stimulation and sends it to the brain via the optic nerve.
retinal disparity (stereopsis) The brain's measurement of the difference between the images of a single object sent by each of the two eyes.
retrieval Pulling information out of memory.
retrieval cues Reminders that facilitate retrieval of information from memory.
retroactive interference Problems remembering older information caused by newer information.
retrograde amnesia The inability to retrieve information that took place before a certain point in time.
reuptake The process when a neurotransmitter is taken back up by the sending neuron after failing to land in a receptor site in the receiving neuron.
rods Receptor cells in the retina that detect shades of gray and allow a person to see in low light.
Rorschach inkblot technique A projective personality test in which the client responds to 10 inkblot images.
sample The subset of the population who actually participates in the research.
scaffolding A process by which a person learns new words, ideas, and ways of thinking by interacting with a more advanced person who provides decreasing levels of help.
scapegoat hypothesis The notion that prejudice can be fueled by the need to find someone to blame.
Schachter–Singer theory A theory of emotion stating that the label one assigns to one's bodily reaction determines your mental reaction.
schema A concept or mental representation that guides the way a person makes sense of new information.
schizophrenia A severe psychological disorder in which the person exhibits bizarre disturbances in thinking, perception, feelings, and behavior.
scientific method A way of asking and answering questions that follows a predetermined series of steps: posing a question, conducting a literature review, developing a hypothesis, testing the hypothesis by collecting data, and analyzing the data and drawing conclusions.
secondary appraisal The way you determine how capable you are of coping with an event.
secondary reinforcer A reinforcer that requires a learned link to a primary reinforcer to have a reinforcing effect.
secondary sex characteristics The parts of the body that characterize sexual maturation but are not directly involved in reproduction.
selective attention When the brain pays more attention to one sensory channel than others.
self-actualization Fully becoming the person you have the potential to become.
self-concept Your view of who you are.
self-determination theory A theory of motivation stating that the strongest and healthiest motivations are those that come from within the person.
self-efficacy Your beliefs about your own capabilities.

self-help group A type of group therapy in which the group members run the session without a professional therapist leading them.
semantic memory A type of explicit memory consisting of facts, figures, word meanings, and other general information.
semantics The rules by which a person extracts meaning from words and sentences.
sensation The ability of the sensory organs to pick up energy in the environment around the body and transmit it to the brain.
sensorimotor stage The first stage in Piaget's theory of development, from birth to about age 2, when babies understand the world through sensory experience.
sensory adaptation The tendency of a person's sensation of a stimulus to decrease when the stimulus remains constant.
sensory conflict theory The theory that explains motion sickness as a byproduct of sensory interaction.
sensory interaction The idea that the senses can influence each other.
sensory memory The earliest part of the memory process, in which the senses take in and very briefly hold information.
sensory neurons The cells that carry information to the brain from the senses (sight, hearing, smell, taste, and touch).
separation An acculturation strategy in which the person retains the old culture and rejects the new culture.
serial position effect The tendency to remember the first and last items in a series better than the items in the middle.
set point A particular weight to which the person's body tends to return after increases or decreases.
sex A person's biological assignment at birth (often male or female) based on a combination of genitals, chromosomes, and hormones.
sexual orientation A person's pattern of romantic attraction to a particular group or groups of other people.
shaping The process of gradually learning a complex behavior through the reinforcement of each small step that is a part of the complex behavior.
short-term memory A limited amount of new information being held briefly until it is either discarded or encoded into long-term memory.
skewed distribution A distribution of numbers that is not symmetrical around the mean.
Skinner box (Originally called an *operant chamber*) A container into which animals such as pigeons or rats could be placed for the purpose of observing and recording their behavior in response to consequences.
sleep apnea A sleep disorder caused by interruptions of breathing that cause repeated waking.
sleep deprivation The failure to get enough sleep, regardless of the reason.
sleep hygiene Routine behaviors that promote healthy sleep.
sleep terrors Brief, sudden awakenings in which the person feels frightened and confused.
sleepwalking Walking while asleep, or *somnambulism*.
social anxiety disorder An anxiety disorder characterized by an intense and irrational fear of situations in which one may be judged or scrutinized.
social cognition A person's thoughts about other people and the social world.
social comparison Assessing oneself by determining how one measures up to other people.
social exchange theory An explanation of helping that emphasizes the comparison of benefits and costs to the individual for helping.
social facilitation An increase in individual performance caused by the presence of other people.
social influence Any way in which the presence of other people influences one's thoughts, feelings, or behavior.
social loafing A decrease in individual performance when tasks are done in groups.
social psychology A basic research specialization in which psychologists focus on how people think about, influence, and relate to each other.
social psychology The scientific study of how people think about, influence, and relate to each other.
social responsibility norm An explanation of helping that emphasizes the notion of duty to help those who need it, regardless of any potential payback to the helper.
social role A title, position, or status that carries expectations for acceptable behavior.
social support The relationships one has with friends, family, and others that can be beneficial when experiencing stress.
social-cognitive theory of hypnosis A theory of hypnosis that emphasizes pressure to play the role assigned to a person being hypnotized.
social-cognitive theory of personality A theory that emphasizes the interaction of environment, thought processes, and social factors.
social-pragmatic theory Suggests that a child's use of language develops from a desire to interact socially.
sociocultural theory of psychological disorders A theory asserting that social and cultural factors surrounding the person, rather than factors within the person, are the primary causes of psychological disorders.
solitary sleeping Sleep in which only one person is in the bed or in the room.
somatic nervous system The part of the peripheral nervous system that connects the central nervous system to the parts of the body controlled voluntarily.
somatosenses The senses experienced through the skin, primarily touch, temperature, and pain.
somatosensory cortex The strip of brain matter near the front of the parietal lobe, involved in receiving information from the senses.
sound localization The ability to perceive the location from which a sound originates.
source amnesia The inability to remember the source of a particular memory (but not the memory itself) or how it was obtained.
spacing effect The tendency to have better long-term memory for information when attempts to study it are spaced apart rather than crammed together.
specific intelligences (*s*) Intelligences that apply to only a particular area.
specific learning disorder A mental disorder in which achievement in reading, writing, or math is significantly below age expectations.
specific phobia An anxiety disorder characterized by excessive anxiety toward a specific object or situation.
split-brain surgery A surgical procedure in which the corpus callosum is cut, typically to reduce epileptic seizures.
spontaneous recovery After a temporary period of inactivity, the return of a conditioned response that had become extinct.
standard deviation A statistic that measures the variability around a mean.
Stanford–Binet Intelligence Test A widely used and highly respected intelligence test originally developed by Alfred Binet and Lewis Terman and appropriate across the life span.
statistical significance The probability that a statistic could have been obtained by random chance.
stem cells Cells that have not yet specialized, and therefore can become a variety of different cells as the need arises.
stereotype threat The expectation that others may judge you according to stereotypes about a group to which you belong.
stereotypes Beliefs about a group's characteristics that are applied very generally, and often inaccurately, to group members.
stigma A judgment of shame or disgrace directed toward a person because of a particular characteristic that person has.
stimulant drugs Medications used to treat children and adults with attention-deficit/hyperactivity disorder (ADHD).
stimulants Drugs that speed up bodily functions.
storage Retaining information in memory.
stranger anxiety The fear of unfamiliar people that emerges in children at about 8 months of age.
stress An unpleasant physical or psychological reaction to circumstances perceived as challenging.
stressor Any event or change in one's life that causes stress.
structuralism A perspective from the early history of psychology that focused on breaking down mental processes into their structure or basic parts.

superego According to Freud, the part of the mind that opposes the id by enforcing rules, restrictions, and morality.
sympathetic division The part of the autonomic nervous system that revs the body up in response to stressors.
synapse The gap between two connecting neurons.
synaptic vesicles The tiny, saclike containers for neurotransmitters.
syntax The rules by which words are put together to make phrases and sentences.
systematic desensitization A form of behavior therapy, primarily for phobias, in which the client experiences the new pairing of relaxation (rather than fear) with the thing or situation that previously caused the anxiety.
telepsychology Psychotherapy that takes place via technological devices over the Internet.
temperament The basic emotional responsiveness that characterizes a person throughout their life span.
temporal lobe The lower middle part of the brain, involved in hearing and speech production.
teratogen Any substance that harms the embryo or fetus.
test bias The tendency of a test to produce scores in a consistently inaccurate way for members of particular groups.
thalamus The brain's main sensory processing center, located near the center of the brain.
Thematic Apperception Test (TAT) A projective personality test in which the client creates stories in response to cards that show people in undefined situations.
theory A proposed explanation for observed events.
theory of mind The understanding of the thoughts, feelings, intentions, and other mental activities of oneself and others.
therapeutic alliance A trusting and collaborative relationship in which therapist and client work toward shared goals.
threshold The level of electrical charge required to trigger an action potential.
token economy A behavior therapy technique in which clients earn tokens that are exchangeable for rewards when they perform target behaviors.
tolerance Decreased effectiveness of a particular amount of a drug.
top-down processing A way of processing information in which expectations or previous experiences influence what a person perceives.
trait theory of personality A theory that emphasizes the discovery and description of the basic components of personality.
traits Stable elements of personality that influence thoughts, feelings, and behavior across most situations.
transcranial magnetic stimulation (TMS) A treatment for depression in which weak electric current repeatedly pulses through a paddle-shaped magnetic coil just outside the person's head.
transduction The conversion of energy outside the body, like light or sound, into neural energy, like brain activity.
transference A client's unconscious and unrealistic expectations for the therapist to behave like an important person from the client's past.
transgender A person whose gender differs from the sex they were assigned at birth.
transition Taking steps to live as the gender that matches one's identity rather than one's biologically assigned gender.
trichromatic theory of color vision An explanation of color vision based on the idea that the cones are specialized to sense either red, green, or blue.
triple vulnerability theory An explanation for anxiety disorders that emphasizes the interaction of biological factors, general psychological factors, and specific psychological factors.
tympanic membrane A surface stretched taut across the ear canal to form the boundary between the outer ear and the middle ear.
Type A personality A personality featuring high levels of competitiveness, drive, impatience, and hostility.
Type B personality A personality in which the person is noncompetitive, easygoing, relaxed, and rarely angry.
Type C personality A personality featuring a low level of emotional expression, a high level of agreeableness with other people, and a tendency to feel helpless.
Type D personality A personality featuring high levels of negative emotions, like depression and anxiety, and a reluctance to share those emotions with others.
unconditional positive regard The therapist's full acceptance of the client without any conditions or limitations.
unconditioned response The automatic response to a stimulus that occurs naturally, without any need for learning.
unconditioned stimulus A stimulus that causes a response automatically, without any need for learning.
unconscious (unconscious mind) Mental activity of which the person is unaware.
validity The extent to which an assessment technique measures what it claims to measure.
variability The degree to which numbers in a group differ from the mean.
variable-interval schedule A reinforcement schedule in which a behavior can be reinforced after a time interval that is inconsistent and unpredictable.
variable-ratio schedule A reinforcement schedule in which a behavior is reinforced after an inconsistent, unpredictable number of occurrences.
vestibular sense The sense of balance.
vicarious conditioning Conditioning that takes place via observation of others' life experiences rather than one's own.
virtual reality exposure therapy A form of exposure therapy in which clients use electronic means to experience simulations of the situations that cause them anxiety.
vision The sense of sight.
visual accommodation The process by which the lens changes shape to focus on objects at varying distances from the eyes.
Wechsler Intelligence Tests A widely used and highly respected set of intelligence tests originally developed by David Wechsler.
Wernicke's aphasia The dysfunction in understanding or creating coherent speech caused by damage to Wernicke's area.
Wernicke's area The part of the temporal lobe specifically involved in understanding speech.
withdrawal Stressful and uncomfortable symptoms caused by discontinuing a drug that had become habitual.
working memory A type of memory in which processing, or work, is done on briefly held information.
working through A lengthy phase of psychodynamic therapy in which interpretations are repeated, reconsidered, and given a chance to gradually sink in.
worldview A comprehensive, culturally influenced way of approaching and understanding the world around you.
Yerkes–Dodson law The finding that moderate levels of arousal are linked to higher levels of performance than high or low levels of arousal.
zygote The prenatal human organism from the moment the egg is fertilized by sperm to about 2 weeks.

References

Aazami, S., Shamsuddin, K., & Akmal, S. (2018). Assessment of work-family conflict among women of the sandwich generation. *Journal of Adult Development, 25*(2), 135–140.

Abar, B., LaGasse, L. L., Derauf, C., Newman, E., Shah, R., Smith, L. M., Arria, A., Huestis, M., DellaGrotta, S., Dansereau, L. M, Neal, C., & Lester, B. M. (2013). Examining the relationships between prenatal methamphetamine exposure, early adversity, and child neurobehavioral disinhibition. *Psychology of Addictive Behaviors, 27*(3), 662–673.

Abbas, A. I., & Lieberman, J. A. (2015). Pharmacological treatments for schizophrenia. In P. E. Nathan & J. M. Gorman (Eds.), *A guide to treatments that work* (4th ed., pp. 175–216). Oxford University Press.

Abbey, A., & McAuslan, P. (2004). A longitudinal examination of male college students' perpetration of sexual assault. *Journal of Consulting and Clinical Psychology, 72*(5), 747–756.

Abbey, A., McAuslan, P., & Ross, L. T. (1998). Sexual assault perpetration by college men: The role of alcohol, misperception of sexual intent, and sexual beliefs and experiences. *Journal of Social and Clinical Psychology, 17*(2), 167–195.

Abbey, A., McAuslan, P., Zawacki, T., Clinton, A. M., & Buck, P. O. (2001). Attitudinal, experiential, and situational predictors of sexual assault perpetration. *Journal of Interpersonal Violence, 16*(8), 784–807.

Abbey, A., Ross, L. T., McDuffie, D., & McAuslan, P. (1996). Alcohol and dating risk factors for sexual assault among college women. *Psychology of Women Quarterly, 20*(1), 147–169.

Abbey, A., Wegner, R., Woerner, J., Pegram, S. E., & Pierce, J. (2014). Review of survey and experimental research that examines the relationship between alcohol consumption and men's sexual aggression perpetration. *Trauma, Violence, & Abuse, 15*(4), 265–282.

Abbott, S. M., Knutson, K. L., & Zee, P. C. (2018). Health implications of sleep and circadian rhythm research in 2017. *The Lancet Neurology, 17*(1), 17–18.

Abe, K., Amatomi, M., & Oda, N. (1984). Sleepwalking and recurrent sleeptalking in children of childhood sleepwalkers. *The American Journal of Psychiatry, 141*, 800–801.

Abe, K., Oda, N., Ikenaga, K., & Yamada, T. (1993). Twin study on night terrors, fears and some physiological and behavioural characteristics in childhood. *Psychiatric Genetics, 3*(1), 39–44.

Abel, E. L., & Kruger, M. L. (2010). Smile intensity in photographs predicts longevity. *Psychological Science, 21*(4), 542–544.

Abraham, R. (2005). Emotional intelligence in the workplace: A review and synthesis. In R. Schulze and R. D. Roberts (Eds)., *Emotional intelligence: An international handbook* (pp. 255–270). Hogrefe & Huber.

Abramowitz, J. S., Fabricant, L. E., & Jacoby, R. J. (2015). Exposure-based therapies. In R. L. Cautin & S. O. Lilienfeld (Eds.), *The encyclopedia of clinical psychology* (pp. 1183–1189). Wiley-Blackwell.

Abramowitz, J. S., & Mahaffey, B. L. (2011). The obsessive-compulsive disorder spectrum. In D. H. Barlow (Ed.), *The Oxford handbook of clinical psychology* (pp. 311–333). Oxford University Press.

Abrams, M. T., Patchcaran, K. M., Boat, T. F., & Institute of Medicine (U.S.). (2003). *Research training in psychiatry residency: Strategies for reform*. National Academies Press.

Abrams, R. (2002). *Electroconvulsive therapy* (4th ed.). Oxford University Press.

Abrams, Z. (2021a). Growing concerns about sleep. *APA Monitor on Psychology, 52*(4), 30. https://www.apa.org/monitor/2021/06/news-concerns-sleep

Abrams, Z. (2021b). How bystanders can shut down microaggressions. *APA Monitor on Psychology, 52*(6), 55. https://www.apa.org/monitor/2021/09/feature-bystanders-microaggressions

Abrams, Z. (2020b, April). Working together against racism. *Monitor on Psychology, 51*(3), 20. https://www.apa.org/monitor/2020/04/working-against-racism

Abrams, Z. (2020a, September). APA calls for true systemic change in US culture. *Monitor on Psychology, 51*(6), 20. https://www.apa.org/monitor/2020/09/systemic-change

Ackerman, P. L., & Heggestad, E. D. (1997). Intelligence, personality, and interests: Evidence for overlapping traits. *Psychological Bulletin, 121*(2), 219–245.

Ackerman, S. J., Fowler, J. C., & Clemence, A. J. (2008). TAT and other performance-based assessment techniques. In R. P. Archer & S. R. Smith (Eds.), *Personality assessment* (pp. 337–378). Routledge.

Adachi, P. J., & Willoughby, T. (2017). The link between playing video games and positive youth outcomes. *Child Development Perspectives, 11*(3), 202–206.

Adair, W. L., & Xiong, T. X. (2018). How Chinese and Caucasian Canadians conceptualize creativity: The mediating role of uncertainty avoidance. *Journal of Cross-Cultural Psychology, 49*(2), 223–238.

Adam, K. C. S., Vogel, E. K., & Awh, E. (2017). Clear evidence for item limits in visual working memory. *Cognitive Psychology, 97*, 79–97.

Adams, E. J., Nguyen, A. T., & Cowan, N. (2018). Theories of working memory: Differences in definition, degree of modularity, role of attention, and purpose. *Language, Speech, and Hearing Services in Schools, 49*(3), 340–355.

Adams, K. F., Schatzkin, A., Harris, T. B., Kipnis, V., Mouw, T., Ballard-Barbash, R., Hollenbeck, A., & Leitzmann, M. F. (2006). Overweight, obesity, and mortality in a large prospective cohort of persons 50 to 71 years old. *New England Journal of Medicine, 355*(8), 763–778.

Ader, R., & Cohen, N. (1982). Behaviorally conditioned immunosuppression and murine systemic lupus erythematosus. *Science, 215*(4539), 1534–1536.

Ader, R., Mercurio, M. G., Walton, J., James, D., Davis, M., Ojha, V., Kimball, A. B., & Fiorentino, D. (2010). Conditioned pharmacotherapeutic effects: A preliminary study. *Psychosomatic Medicine, 72*(2), 192–197.

Adler, A. (1927). *Understanding human nature*. Greenburg.

Adler, A. (1928). *The practice and theory of individual psychology*. Greenburg.

Adolph, K. E., & Berger, S. E. (2005). Physical and motor development. In M. H. Bornstein & M. E. Lamb (Eds.), *Developmental science: An advanced textbook* (5th ed., pp. 223–281). Lawrence Erlbaum.

Adolph, K. E., & Berger, S. E. (2006). Motor development. In D. Kuhn & R. Siegler (Vol. Eds.), *Handbook of child psychology* (6th ed., Vol. 2, pp. 161–213). Wiley.

Adolphs, R., Tranel, D., Damasio, H., & Damasio, A. (1994). Impaired recognition of emotion in facial expressions following bilateral damage to the human amygdala. *Nature, 372*(6507), 669–672.

Adolphs, R., Tranel, D., Hamann, S., Young, A. W., Calder, A. J., Phelps, E. A., & Damasio, A. R. (1999). Recognition of facial emotion in nine individuals with bilateral amygdala damage. *Neuropsychologia, 37*(10), 1111–1117.

Affleck, G., & Tennen, H. (1996). Construing benefits from adversity: Adaptational significance and dispositional underpinnings. *Journal of Personality, 64*(4), 899–922.

Afifi, T. O., Mota, N. P., Dasiewicz, P., MacMillan, H. L., & Sareen, J. (2012). Physical punishment and mental disorders: Results from a nationally representative U.S. sample. *Pediatrics, 130*(2), 184–192.

Agnew, R. (2012). Dire forecast: A theoretical model of the impact of climate change on crime. *Theoretical Criminology, 16*(1), 21–42.

Agras, W. S. (2010). Introduction and overview. In W. S. Agras (Ed.), *The Oxford handbook of eating disorders* (pp. 1–6). Oxford University Press.

Agrawal, Y., Platz, E. A., & Niparko, J. K. (2008). Prevalence of hearing loss and differences by demographic characteristics among U.S. adults: Data from the National Health and Nutrition Examination Survey, 1999–2004. *Archives of Internal Medicine, 168*(14), 1522–1530.

Agrawal, Y., Platz, E. A., & Niparko, J. K. (2009). Risk factors for hearing loss in U.S. adults: Data from the National Health and Nutrition Examination Survey, 1999 to 2002. *Otology & Neurotology, 30*(2), 139–145.

Ahlskog, J. E., Geda, Y. E., Graff-Radford, N. R., & Petersen, R. C. (2011, September). Physical exercise as a preventive or disease-modifying treatment of dementia and brain aging. *Mayo Clinic Proceedings, 86*(9), 876–884.

Ahmed, M. Z., Ahmed, O., Aibao, Z., Hanbin, S., Siyu, L., & Ahmad, A. (2020). Epidemic of COVID-19 in China and associated psychological problems. *Asian Journal of Psychiatry, 51*, 102092. https://doi.org/10.1016/j.ajp.2020.102092

Ahn, W., Proctor, C. C., & Flanagan, E. H. (2009). Mental health clinicians' beliefs about the biological, psychological, and environmental bases of mental disorders. *Cognitive Science, 33*(2), 147–182.

Ainsworth, M. D. S., Blehar, M. C., Waters, E., & Wall, S. (1978). *Patterns of attachment*. Lawrence Erlbaum.

Ainsworth, M. S. (1989). Attachments beyond infancy. *American Psychologist, 44*(4), 709–716.

Ainsworth, M., & Bowlby, J. (1965). *Child care and the growth of love*. Penguin Books.

Airoldi, S., Kolubinski, D. C., Nikčević, A. V., & Spada, M. M. (2021). The relative contribution of health cognitions and metacognitions about health anxiety to cyberchondria: A prospective study. *Journal of Clinical Psychology*. https://doi.org/10.1002/jclp.23252

Aitchison, J. (1996). *The seeds of speech: Language origin and evolution*. Cambridge University Press.

Ajzen, I. (2000). Nature and operation of attitudes. *Annual Review of Psychology, 52*, 27–58.

Ajzen, I. (2012). Attitudes and persuasion. In K. Deaux & M. Snyder (Eds.), *The Oxford handbook of personality and social psychology* (pp. 367–393). Oxford University Press.

Åkerstedt, T., & Kecklund, G. (2012). Sleep, work, and occupational stress. In C. M. Morin & C. A. Espie (Eds.), *The Oxford handbook of sleep and sleep disorders* (pp. 248–265). Oxford University Press.

Åkerstedt, T., Narusyte, J., Alexanderson, K., & Svedberg, P. (2017). Sleep duration, mortality, and heredity—a prospective twin study. *Sleep, 40*(10), zsx135.

Akhtar, A. (2021). Americans have turned to melatonin to soothe pandemic-induced stress. Experts worry high demand, little federal oversight, and insufficient data leave the industry ripe for scams. *Business Insider*. https://www.businessinsider.com/melatonin-sales-spiked-coronavirus-pandemic-2021-1

Akmajian, A., Demers, R. A., Farmer, A. K., & Harnish, R. M. (2010). *Linguistics: An introduction to language and communication* (6th ed.). MIT Press.

Aknin, L. B., Wiwad, D., & Hanniball, K. B. (2018). Buying well-being: Spending behavior and happiness. *Social and Personality Psychology Compass, 12*(5), e12386.

Alavi, S. B., & Sanderson, W. C. (2015). Mechanisms of action in psychotherapy. In R. L. Cautin & S. O. Lilienfeld (Eds.), *The encyclopedia of clinical psychology* (pp. 1745–1751). Wiley-Blackwell.

Albarracín, D., & Vargas, P. (2010). Attitudes and persuasion: From biology to social responses to persuasive intent. In S. T. Fiske, D. T. Gilbert, & G. Lindzey (Eds.), *Handbook of social psychology* (5th ed., Vol. 1, pp. 394–427). Wiley.

Albert, R. R., Schwade, J. A., & Goldstein, M. H. (2018). The social functions of babbling: Acoustic and contextual characteristics that facilitate maternal responsiveness. *Developmental Science, 21*(5), e12641.

Alberts, A., Elkind, D., & Ginsberg, S. (2007). The personal fable and risk-taking in early adolescence. *Journal of Youth and Adolescence, 36*(1), 71–76.

Albright, T. D. (2013). High-level visual processing: Cognitive influences. In E. R. Kandel, J. H. Schwartz, T. M. Jessell, S. A. Siegelbaum, & A. J. Hudspeth (Eds.), *Principles of neural science* (5th ed., pp. 621–637). McGraw-Hill.

Aldridge, A. A., & Roesch, S. C. (2007). Coping and adjustment in children with cancer: A meta-analytic study. *Journal of Behavioral Medicine, 30*(2), 115–129.

Aldwin, C. (2011). Stress and coping across the lifespan. In S. Folkman (Ed.), *Oxford handbook of stress, health, and coping* (pp. 15–34). Oxford University Press.

Aleman, A., Hijman, R., de Haan, E. H., & Kahn, R. S. (1999). Memory impairment in schizophrenia: A meta-analysis. *American Journal of Psychiatry, 156*(9), 1358–1366.

Alevizou, F., Vousoura, E., & Leonardou, A. (2018). Premenstrual dysphoric disorder: A critical review of its phenomenology, etiology, treatment and clinical status. *Current Women's Health Reviews, 14*(1), 59–66.

Alexander, F., & Selesnick, S. T. (1966). *The history of psychiatry: An evaluation of psychiatric thought and practice from prehistoric times to the present*. Harper & Row.

Alexander, G. M., Wilcox, T., & Woods, R. (2009). Sex differences in infants' visual interest in toys. *Archives of Sexual Behavior, 38*(3), 427–433.

Alexeyeff, K. (2013). Sleeping safe: Perceptions of risk and value in Western and Pacific infant co-sleeping. In K. Glaskin & R. Chenhall (Eds.), *Sleep around the world* (pp. 113–132). Palgrave MacMillan.

Alfredo Martínez, J., Enríquez, L., Moreno-Aliaga, M. J., & Marti, A. (2007). Genetics of obesity. *Public Health Nutrition, 10*(10A), 1138–1144.

Al-Hoorie, A. H. (2015). Human agency: Does the beach ball have free will? In Z. Dörnyei, P. D. MacIntyre, & A. Henry (eds.), *Motivational Dynamics in Language Learning*, pp. 55–72. Multilingual Matters.

Alkozei, A., Haack, M., Skalamera, J., Smith, R., Satterfield, B. C., Raikes, A. C., & Killgore, W. D. (2018). Chronic sleep restriction affects the association between implicit bias and explicit social decision making. *Sleep Health, 4*(5), 456–462.

Alkozei, A., Killgore, W. D., Smith, R., Dailey, N. S., Bajaj, S., & Haack, M. (2017). Chronic sleep restriction increases negative implicit attitudes toward Arab Muslims. *Scientific Reports, 7*(1), 4285.

Allard, F., & Burnett, N. (1985). Skill in sport. *Canadian Journal of Psychology, 39*(2), 294–312.

Allen, B., & Karceski, S. (2017). Soccer and head injuries: What is the risk? *Neurology, 88*(9), e74–e77.

Allen, K. A., Ryan, T., Gray, D. L., McInerney, D. M., & Waters, L. (2014). Social media use and social connectedness in adolescents: The positives and the potential pitfalls. *The Educational and Developmental Psychologist, 31*(1), 18–31.

Allen, P., Larøi, F., McGuire, P. K., & Aleman, A. (2008). The hallucinating brain: A review of structural and functional neuroimaging studies of hallucinations. *Neuroscience & Biobehavioral Reviews, 32*(1), 175–191.

Allison, R., & Risman, B. J. (2013). A double standard for "hooking up": How far have we come toward gender equality? *Social Science Research, 42*(5), 1191–1206.

Alloway, T. P. (2011). *Training your brain for dummies*. Wiley.

Alloway, T. P., & Alloway, R. (2013). *The working memory advantage: Train your brain to function stronger, smarter, faster*. Simon & Schuster.

Alloway, T. P., & Gathercole, S. (2005). Working memory and short-term sentence recall in young children. *European Journal of Cognitive Psychology, 17*(2), 207–220.

Alloway, T. P., Gathercole, S. E., Adams, A. M., Willis, C., Eaglen, R., & Lamont, E. (2005). Working memory and phonological awareness as predictors of progress towards early learning goals at school entry. *British Journal of Developmental Psychology, 23*(3), 417–426.

Alloy, L. B., Salk, R. H., Stange, J. P., & Abramson, L. Y. (2017). Cognitive vulnerability and unipolar depression. In R. J. DeRubeis & D. R. Strunk (Eds.), *The Oxford handbook of mood disorders* (pp. 142–153). Oxford University Press.

Allport, G. W. (1937). *Personality: A psychological interpretation.* Holt, Rinehart, & Winston.

Allport, G. W. (1954). *The nature of prejudice*. Addison-Wesley.

Allport, G. W., & Odbert, H. S. (1936). Trait-names: A psycho-lexical study. *Psychological Monographs, 47*(1), i–171.

Alpizar, K., Islas-Alvarado, R., Warren, C. R., & Fiebert, M. S. (2012). Gender, sexuality and impression management on Facebook. *International Review of Social Sciences and Humanities, 4*(1), 121–125.

Alsubaie, M., Abbott, R., Dunn, B., Dickens, C., Keil, T. F., Henley, W., & Kuyken, W. (2017). Mechanisms of action in mindfulness-based cognitive therapy (MBCT) and mindfulness-based stress reduction (MBSR) in people with physical and/or psychological conditions: A systematic review. *Clinical Psychology Review, 55*, 74–91.

Altman, W. S., Beers, M. J., Hammer, E. Y., Hardin, E. E., & Troisi, J. D. (2021). Reimagining how we teach introductory psychology: Support for instructors adopting the recommendations of the APA Introductory Psychology Initiative. *Scholarship of Teaching and Learning in Psychology, 7*(3), 181–191. https://doi.org/10.1037/stl0000289

Altus, D. E., & Morris, E. K. (2009). B. F. Skinner's utopian vision: Behind and beyond *Walden Two*. *Journal of Applied Behavioral Analysis, 32*(2), 319–335.

Aly, M., & Ranganath, C. (2018). New perspectives on the hippocampus and memory. *Neuroscience Letters, 680*, 1–3. https://doi.org/10.1016/j.neulet.2018.05.047

Alzahrani, A. S., Price, M. J., Greenfield, S. M., & Paudyal, V. (2021). Global prevalence and types of complementary and alternative medicines use amongst adults with diabetes: Systematic review and meta-analysis. *European Journal of Clinical Pharmacology, 77*(9), 1–16. https://doi.org/10.1007/s00228-021-03097-x

Alzheimer's Association. (2021). *Alzheimer's disease facts and figures.* https://www.alz.org/media/Documents/alzheimers-facts-and-figures.pdf

Alzueta, E., Perrin, P., Baker, F. C., Caffarra, S., Ramos-Usuga, D., Yuksel, D., & Arango-Lasprilla, J. C. (2021). How the COVID-19 pandemic has changed our lives: A study of psychological correlates across 59 countries. *Journal of Clinical Psychology, 77*(3), 556–570. https://doi.org/10.1002/jclp.23082

Amaral, D. G. (2013). The functional organization of perception and movement. In E. R. Kandel, J. H. Schwartz, T. M. Jessell, S. A. Siegelbaum, & A. J. Hudspeth (Eds.), *Principles of neural science* (5th ed., pp. 356–369). McGraw-Hill.

Amaral, D. G., & Strick, P. L. (2013). The organization of the central nervous system. In E. R. Kandel, J. H. Schwartz, T. M. Jessell, S. A. Siegelbaum, & A. J. Hudspeth (Eds.), *Principles of neural science* (5th ed., pp. 337–355). McGraw-Hill.

Amato, P. R. (2010). Research on divorce: Continuing trends and new developments. *Journal of Marriage and Family, 72*(3), 650–666.

Amdurer, E., Boyatzis, R. E., Saatcioglu, A., Smith, M. L., & Taylor, S. N. (2014). Long term impact of emotional, social and cognitive intelligence competencies and GMAT on career and life satisfaction and career success. *Frontiers in Psychology, 5*, 1447.

Amen, D., Hanks, C., Prunella, J., & Green, A. (2007). An analysis of regional cerebral blood flow in impulsive murderers using single photon emission computed tomography. *Journal of Neuropsychiatry and Clinical Neurosciences, 19*(3), 304–309.

American Psychiatric Association. (1952). *Diagnostic and statistical manual of mental disorders*. Author.

American Psychiatric Association. (1968). *Diagnostic and statistical manual of mental disorders: DSM-II*. Author.

American Psychiatric Association. (2013). *Diagnostic and statistical manual of mental disorders: DSM-5*. Author.

American Psychiatric Association. (2021, September 23). APA offers tips for understanding prolonged grief disorder. https://www.psychiatry.org/newsroom/news-releases/apa-offers-tips-for-understanding-prolonged-grief-disorder

American Psychiatric Association. (2022). DSM-5-TR collection. https://www.appi.org/getattachment/e7d9691a-7086-4307-9d36-64bf2bf4c895/APA-Publishing-DSM-5-TR-Core-Titles-Brochure.pdf

American Psychological Association. (2002). Ethical principles of psychologists and code of conduct. *American Psychologist, 57*(12), 1060–1073.

American Psychological Association. (2005). Guidelines and principles for accreditation of programs in professional psychology. http://www.apa.org/ed/G&P052.pdf

American Psychological Association. (2007a). *APA guidelines for the undergraduate psychology major*. Author.

American Psychological Association. (2007b). *Getting in: A step-by-step plan for gaining admission to graduate school in psychology* (2nd ed.). Author.

American Psychological Association. (2010). Ethical principles of psychologists and code of conduct, including 2010 amendments. http://apa.org/ethics/code/index.aspx

American Psychological Association. (2012). Guidelines for psychological practice with lesbian, gay, and bisexual clients. *American Psychologist, 67*(1), 10–42.

American Psychological Association. (2013). *APA guidelines for the undergraduate psychology major: Version 2.0*. Author. https://www.apa.org/ed/precollege/about/undergraduate-major

American Psychological Association. (2014a). Stress in America: Are teens adopting adults' stress habits? http://www.apa.org/news/press/releases/stress/2013/stress-report.pdf

American Psychological Association. (2015a). Guidelines for psychological practice with transgender and gender nonconforming people. *American Psychologist, 70*(9), 832–864. https://www.apa.org/practice/guidelines/transgender.pdf

American Psychological Association. (2015b). *APA dictionary of psychology* (2nd ed.). Washington, DC: Author.

American Psychological Association. (2017a). *Ethical principles of psychologists and code of conduct*. https://www.apa.org/ethics/code/

American Psychological Association. (2017b). *Graduate study in psychology*. American Psychological Association. https://www.apa.org/education/grad/survey-data/2017-admissions-applications

American Psychological Association. (2020a). *APA resolution on violent video games: February 2020 revision to the 2015 resolution*. https://www.apa.org/about/policy/resolution-violent-video-games.pdf

American Psychological Association. (2020b). *CWS data tool: Demographics of the U.S. psychology workforce*. https://www.apa.org/workforce/data-tools/demographics

American Psychological Association. (2021). *APA Introductory Initiative (IPI) student learning outcomes for introductory psychology*. https://www.apa.org/about/policy/introductory-psychology-initiative-student-outcomes.pdf

American Psychological Association. (2021b). APA: U.S. adults report highest stress level since early days of the COVID-19 pandemic. https://www.apa.org/news/press/releases/2021/02/adults-stress-pandemic

American Psychological Association. (2021c). One year later, a new wave of pandemic health concerns. https://www.apa.org/news/press/releases/stress/2021/one-year-pandemic-stress

American Sleep Apnea Association. (2015). Personal stories: Bill's story—it was a big deal after all. http://www.sleepapnea.org/learn/personal-stories/bills-story.html

Ames, C. (1992). Classrooms: Goals, structures, and student motivation. *Journal of Educational Psychology, 84*(3), 261–271.

Ames, C., & Archer, J. (1987). Mothers' beliefs about the role of ability and effort in school learning. *Journal of Educational Psychology, 79*(4), 409–414.

Ames, C., & Archer, J. (1988). Achievement goals in the classroom: Students' learning strategies and motivation processes. *Journal of Educational Psychology, 80*(3), 260–267.

Amodio, D. M., Harmon-Jones, E., Devine, P. G., Curtin, J. J., Hartley, S. L., & Covert, A. E. (2004). Neural signals for the detection of unintentional race bias. *Psychological Science, 15*(2), 88–93.

Amrutkar, C., Woodward, M., Shah, H., Benedict, R., Rajakrishnan, S., Doody, R., & Szigeti, K. (2015). Validation of olfactory deficit as a biomarker of Alzheimer's disease. Neurology, 84(14 Suppl.), P2-170.

An, D., Song, Y., & Carr, M. (2016). A comparison of two models of creativity: Divergent thinking and creative expert performance. *Personality and Individual Differences, 90*, 78–84.

Anand, R., & Lahiri, I. (2009). Intercultural competence in health care. In D. K. Deardorff (Ed.), *The Sage handbook of intercultural competence* (pp. 387–402). Sage.

Anderman, E. M., Griesinger, T., & Westerfield, G. (1998). Motivation and cheating during early adolescence. *Journal of Educational Psychology, 90*(1), 84–93.

Andersen, K. A., Carhart-Harris, R., Nutt, D. J., & Erritzoe, D. (2021). Therapeutic effects of classic serotonergic psychedelics: A systematic review of modern-era clinical studies. *Acta Psychiatrica Scandinavica, 143*(2), 101–118. https://doi.org/10.1111/acps.13249

Andersen, M. L., Poyares, D., Alves, R. S., Skomro, R., & Tufik, S. (2007). Sexsomnia: Abnormal sexual behavior during sleep. *Brain Research Reviews, 56*(2), 271–282.

Anderson, C. A., & Bushman, B. J. (2001). Effects of violent video games on aggressive behavior, aggressive cognition, aggressive affect, physiological arousal, and prosocial behavior: A meta-analytic review of the scientific literature. *Psychological Science, 12*(5), 353–359.

Anderson, C. A., & Bushman, B. J. (2018). Media violence and the general aggression model. *Journal of Social Issues, 74*(2), 386–413.

Anderson, C. A., Anderson, K. B., Dorr, N., DeNeve, K. M., & Flanagan, M. (2000). Temperature and aggression. *Advances in Experimental Social Psychology, 32*, 63–133.

Anderson, C. A., Arciniegas, D. B., Hall, D. A., & Filley, C. M. (2013). Behavioral neuroanatomy. In D. B. Arciniegas, C. A. Anderson, & C. M. Filley (Eds.), *Behavioral neurology & neuropsychiatry* (pp. 12–31). Cambridge University Press.

Anderson, C. A., Benjamin, A. J., Jr., & Bartholow, B. D. (1998). Does the gun pull the trigger? Automatic priming effects of weapon pictures and weapon names. *Psychological Science, 9*(4), 308–314.

Anderson, C. A., Bushman, B. J., Bartholow, B. D., Cantor, J., Christakis, D., Coyne, S. M., Donnerstein, E., Brockmyer, J. F., Gentile, D. A., Green, C. S., Huesmann, R., Hummer, T., Krahé, B., Strasburger, V. C., Warburton, W., Wilson, B. J., & Ybarra, M. (2017). Screen violence and youth behavior. *Pediatrics, 140*(Suppl. 2), S142–S147.

Anderson, C. A., Bushman, B. J., & Groom, R. W. (1997). Hot years and serious and deadly assault: Empirical tests of the heat hypothesis. *Journal of Personality and Social Psychology, 73*(6), 1213–1223.

Anderson, C. A., Shibuya, A., Ihori, N., Swing, E. L., Bushman, B. J., Sakamoto, A., Rothstein, H., & Saleem, M. (2010). Violent video game effects on aggression, empathy, and prosocial behavior in eastern and western countries: A meta-analytic review. *Psychological Bulletin, 136*(2), 151–173.

Anderson, J. L., Crawford, C. B., Nadeau, J., & Lindberg, T. (1992). Was the Duchess of Windsor right? A cross-cultural review of the socioecology of ideals of female body shape. *Ethology and Sociobiology, 13*(3), 197–227.

Anderson, K. J., & Leaper, C. (1998). Meta-analyses of gender effects on conversational interruption: Who, what, when, where, and how. *Sex Roles, 39*(3–4), 225–252.

Anderson, K. N., Bautista, C. L., & Hope, D. A. (2019). Therapeutic alliance, cultural competence, and minority status in premature termination of psychotherapy. *American Journal of Orthopsychiatry, 89*(1), 104–114.

Anderson, M. C., & Hulbert, J. C. (2021). Active forgetting: Adaptation of memory by prefrontal control. *Annual Review of Psychology, 72*, 1–36. https://doi.org/10.1146/annurev-psych-072720-094140

Anderson, N. D., & Craik, F. I. M. (2000). Memory in the aging brain. In E. Tulving & F. I. M. Craik (Eds.), *The Oxford handbook of memory* (pp. 411–425). Oxford University Press.

Anderson, S. E., Cohen, P., Naumova, E. N., Jacques, P. F., & Must, A. (2007). Adolescent obesity and risk for subsequent major depressive disorder and anxiety disorder: Prospective evidence. *Psychosomatic Medicine, 69*(8), 740–747.

Anderson, S. K., & Kitchener, K. S. (1996). Nonromantic, nonsexual posttherapy relationships between psychologists and former clients: An exploratory study of critical incidents. *Professional Psychology: Research and Practice, 27*(1), 59–66.

Anderson, S. W., & Rizzo, M. (1994). Hallucinations following occipital lobe damage: The pathological activation of visual representations. *Journal of Clinical and Experimental Neuropsychology, 16*(5), 651–663.

Anderson, V. L., Levinson, E. M., Barker, W., & Kiewra, K. R. (1999). The effects of meditation on teacher perceived occupational stress, state and trait anxiety, and burnout. *School Psychology Quarterly, 14*(1), 3–25.

Andersson, G. (2015). Computerized psychotherapy. In R. L. Cautin & S. O. Lilienfeld (Eds.), *The encyclopedia of clinical psychology* (pp. 712–716). Wiley-Blackwell.

Andersson, G. (2016). Internet-delivered psychological treatments. *Annual Review of Clinical Psychology, 12*, 157–179.

Andia, A. N., Zisook, S., Heaton, R. K., Hesselink, J., Jernigan, T., Kuck, J., Morganville, J., & Braff, L. (1995). Gender differences in schizophrenia. *Journal of Nervous and Mental Disease, 183*(8), 522–528.

Andrade, M., & Menna-Baretto, L. (2002). Sleep patterns of high school students living in Sao Paulo, Brazil. In M. A. Carskadon (Ed.), *Adolescent sleep patterns: Biological, social, and psychological factors* (pp. 118–131). Cambridge University Press.

Andre, L. (2009). *Doctors of deception: What they don't want you to know about shock treatment*. Rutgers University Press.

Andreassen, C. S., Pallesen, S., & Griffiths, M. D. (2017). The relationship between addictive use of social media, narcissism, and self-esteem: Findings from a large national survey. *Addictive Behaviors, 64*, 287–293.

Ang, S., & Van Dyne, L. (2008). Conceptualization of cultural intelligence: Definition, distinctiveness, and nomological networks. In S. Ang & L. Van Dyne (Eds.), *Handbook of cultural intelligence: Theory, measurement, and applications* (pp. 3–15). M. E. Sharpe.

Ang, S., Rockstuhl, T., & Tan, M. L. (2015). Cultural intelligence and competencies. In J. D. Wright (Ed.), *International encyclopedia of social and behavioral sciences* (2nd ed., Vol. 5, pp. 433–439). Elsevier.

Ang, S., Van Dyne, L., Koh, C., Ng, K.-Y., Templer, K. J., Tay, C., & Chandrasekar, N. A. (2007). Cultural intelligence: Its measurement and effects on cultural judgment and decision making, cultural adaptation and task performance. *Management and Organization Review, 3*(3), 335–371.

Ang, S., Van Dyne, L., & Ling Tan, M. (2011). Cultural intelligence. In R. J. Sternberg & S. B. Kaufman (Eds.), *The Cambridge handbook of intelligence* (pp. 582–602). Cambridge University Press.

Angell, J. R. (1907). The province of functional psychology. *Psychological Review, 14*(2), 61–91.

Angermeyer, M. C., & Dietrich, S. (2006). Public beliefs about and attitudes towards people with mental illness: A review of population studies. *Acta Psychiatrica Scandinavica, 113*(3), 163–179. https://doi.org/10.1111/j.1600-0447.2005.00699.x

Anglin, J. M. (1993). Vocabulary development: A morphological analysis. *Monographs of the Society for Research in Child Development, 58*(10), 1–165.

Angrilli, A., Mauri, A., Palomba, D., Flor, H., Birbaumer, N., Sartori, G., & di Paola, F. (1996). Startle reflex and emotion modulation impairment after a right amygdala lesion. *Brain, 119*(6), 1991–2004.

Angus, L., Watson, J. C., Elliott, R., Schneider, K., & Timulak, L. (2015). Humanistic psychotherapy research 1990–2015: From methodological innovation to evidence-supported treatment outcomes and beyond. *Psychotherapy Research, 25*(3), 330–347.

Anheyer, D., Haller, H., Barth, J., Lauche, R., Dobos, G., & Cramer, H. (2017). Mindfulness-based stress reduction for treating low back pain: A systematic review and meta-analysis. *Annals of Internal Medicine, 166*(11), 799–807.

Anthenien, A. M., DeLozier, S. J., Neighbors, C., & Rhodes, M. G. (2018). College student normative misperceptions of peer study habit use. *Social Psychology of Education, 21*(2), 303–322.

Antony, M. M., & Barlow, D. H. (Eds.). (2010). *Handbook of assessment and treatment planning for psychological disorders* (2nd ed.). Guilford Press.

Anusic, I., & Schimmack, U. (2016). Stability and change of personality traits, self-esteem, and well-being: Introducing the meta-analytic stability and change model of retest correlations. *Journal of Personality and Social Psychology, 110*(5), 766–781.

Anzman, S. L., Rollins, B. Y., & Birch, L. L. (2010). Parental influence on children's early eating environments and obesity risk: Implications for prevention. *International Journal of Obesity, 34*, 1116–1124.

APA Presidential Task Force on Evidence-Based Practice. (2006). Evidence-based practice in psychology. *American Psychologist, 61*(4), 271–285. https://doi.org/10.1037/0003-066X.61.4.271

Appelbaum, P. S., Leibenluft, E., & Kendler, K. S. (2021). Iterative revision of the DSM: An interim report from the DSM-5 steering committee. *Psychiatric Services, 72*, 1348–1349. https://doi.org/10.1176/appi.ps.202100013

Arber, S., Bote, M., & Meadows, R. (2009). Gender and socio-economic patterning of self-reported sleep problems in Britain. *Social Science & Medicine, 68*(2), 281–289.

Arber, S., Meadows, R., & Venn, S. (2012). Sleep and society. In C. M. Morin & C. A. Espie (Eds.), *The Oxford handbook of sleep and sleep disorders* (pp. 223–247). Oxford University Press.

Arbib, M. A. (2008). Holophrasis and the protolanguage spectrum. *Interaction Studies, 9*(1), 154–168.

Arch, J., & Craske, M. G. (2008). Panic disorder. In W. E. Craighead, D. J. Milkowitz, & L. W. Craighead (Eds.), *Psychopathology: History, diagnosis, and empirical foundations* (pp. 115–158). Wiley.

Arch, J. J., & Landy, L. N. (2015). Emotional benefits of mindfulness. In K. W. Brown, J. D. Creswell, & R. M. Ryan (Eds.), *Handbook of mindfulness: Theory, research, and practice* (pp. 208–224). Guilford Press.

Archana, V. P., & Kumar, U. (2016). Resilient personalities: An amalgamation of protective factors. In U. Kumar (Ed.), *The Routledge international handbook of psychosocial resilience* (pp. 91–103). Routledge.

Archer, J., & Coyne, S. M. (2005). An integrated review of indirect, relational, and social aggression. *Personality and Social Psychology Review, 9*(3), 212–230.

Archer, R. P., & Newsom, C. R. (2000). Psychological test usage with adolescent clients: Survey update. *Assessment, 7*(3), 227–235.

Arciniegas, D. B. (2013). Executive function. In D. B. Arciniegas, C. A. Anderson, & C. M. Filley (Eds.), *Behavioral neurology & neuropsychiatry* (pp. 225–249). Cambridge University Press.

Arden, J. B., & Linford, L. (2009). *Brain-based therapy with adults: Evidence-based treatment for everyday practice*. Wiley.

Arden, R., Luciano, M., Deary, I. J., Reynolds, C. A., Pedersen, N. L., Plassman, B. L., McGue, M., Christensen, K., & Visscher, P. M. (2015). The association between intelligence and lifespan is mostly genetic. *International Journal of Epidemiology, 45*(1), 178–185.

Ariely, D., Loewenstein, G., & Prelec, D. (2003). "Coherent arbitrariness": Stable demand curves without stable preferences. *Quarterly Journal of Economics, 118*(1), 73–105.

Arkes, H. R. (1991). Costs and benefits of judgment errors: Implications for debiasing. *Psychological Bulletin, 110*(3), 486–498.

Arkowitz, H., Miller, W. R., & Rollnick, S. (Eds.). (2015). *Motivational interviewing in the treatment of psychological problems* (2nd ed.). Guilford Publications.

Armstrong, B., Gallant, S. N., Li, L., Patel, K., & Wong, B. I. (2017). Stereotype threat effects on older adults' episodic and working memory: A meta-analysis. *The Gerontologist, 57*(Suppl. 2), S193–S205.

Arnett, J. J. (2000). Emerging adulthood: A theory of development from the late teens through the twenties. *American Psychologist, 55*(5), 469.

Arnett, J. J. (2007). Emerging adulthood: What is it, and what is it good for? *Child Development Perspectives, 1*(2), 68–73.

Arnett, J. J. (2014). Presidential address: The emergence of emerging adulthood: A personal history. *Emerging Adulthood, 2*(3), 155–162.

Aronson, E. (1999). Dissonance, hypocrisy, and the self-concept. In E. Harmon-Jones & J. Mills (Eds.), *Cognitive dissonance: Progress on a pivotal theory in social psychology* (pp. 103–126). American Psychological Association.

Aronson, E., Wilson, T. D., & Akert, R. M. (2013). *Social psychology* (8th ed.). Pearson.

Arredondo, P., Toporek, R., Brown, S. P., Jones, J., Locke, D. C., Sanchez, J., & Stadler, H. (1996). Operationalization of the multicultural counseling competencies. *Journal of Multicultural Counseling and Development, 24*(1), 42–78.

Arrigo, J. M., & Pezdek, K. (1998). Textbook models of multiple personality: Source, bias, and social consequences. In S. J. Lynn & K. M. McConkey (Eds.), *Truth in memory* (pp. 372–393). Guilford Press.

Artal, P. (2010). Eye: Structure and optics. In E. B. Goldstein (Ed.), *Encyclopedia of perception* (pp. 413–416). Sage.

Artal, P., Benito, A., & Tabernero, J. (2006). The human eye is an example of robust optical design. *Journal of Vision, 6*(1), 1–7.

Artman, L. K., & Daniels, J. A. (2010). Disability and psychotherapy practice: Cultural competence and practical tips. *Professional Psychology: Research and Practice, 41*(5), 442–448.

Arzi, A., & Sobel, N. (2010). Spatial perception: Time tells where a smell comes from. *Current Biology, 20*(13), R563–R564.

Asamen, J. K., & Berry, G. L. (2012). Television, children, and multicultural awareness: Comprehending the medium in a complex multimedia society. In D. G. Singer & J. L. Singer (Eds.), *Handbook of children and the media* (2nd ed., pp. 363–377). Sage.

Asarnow, J., & Ougrin, D. (2017). From efficacy to pragmatic trials: Does the dodo bird verdict apply? *The Lancet Psychiatry, 4*(2), 84–85.

Asch, S. E. (1951). Effects of group pressure upon the modification and distortion of judgments. In M. Henle (Ed.), *Documents of Gestalt psychology* (pp. 222–236). University of California Press.

Asch, S. E. (1955). Opinions and social pressure. *Scientific American, 193*(5), 31–35.

Asch, S. E. (1956). Studies of independence and conformity: I. A minority of one against a unanimous majority. *Psychological Monographs: General and Applied, 70*(9), 1–70.

Aschoff, J. (1965). Circadian rhythms in man: A self-sustained oscillator with an inherent frequency underlies human 24-hour periodicity. *Science, 148*, 1427–1432.

Aserinsky, E., & Kleitman, N. (1953). Regularly occurring periods of eye motility, and concomitant phenomena, during sleep. *Science, 118*(3062), 273–274.

Asher, G., & Sassone-Corsi, P. (2015). Time for food: The intimate interplay between nutrition, metabolism, and the circadian clock. *Cell, 161*(1), 84–92.

Ashford, S. J., Blatt, R., & VandeWalle, D. (2003). Reflections on the looking glass: A review of research on feedback-seeking behavior in organizations. *Journal of Management, 29*(6), 769–799.

Ashford, S., Edmunds, J., and French, D. P. (2010). What is the best way to change self-efficacy to promote lifestyle and recreational physical activity? A systematic review with meta-analysis. *British Journal of Health Psychology, 15*(Pt. 2), 265–288. https://doi.org/10.1348/135910709X461752

Ashraf, A. R., & Thongpapanl, N. T. (2015). Connecting with and converting shoppers into customers: Investigating the role of regulatory fit in the online customer's decision-making process. *Journal of Interactive Marketing, 32*, 13–25.

Ashton, M. C., & Lee, K. (2008). The HEXACO model of personality structure. In G. J. Boyle, G. Matthews, & D. H. Saklofske (Eds.), *The Sage handbook of personality theory and assessment* (Vol. 2, pp. 239–260). Sage.

Ashton, M. C., Lee, K., Perugini, M., Szarota, P., de Vries, R. E., Di Blas, L., Boies, K., & De Raad, B. (2004). A six-factor structure of personality-descriptive adjectives: Solutions from psycholexical studies in seven languages. *Journal of Personality and Social Psychology, 86*(2), 356–366. https://doi.org/10.1037/0022-3514.86.2.356

Askelson, N. M., Campo, S., & Smith, S. (2012). Mother–daughter communication about sex: The influence of authoritative parenting style. *Health Communication, 27*(5), 439–448.

Asmal, L., & Stein, D. J. (2009). Anxiety and culture. In M. M. Antony & M. B. Stein (Eds.), *Oxford handbook of anxiety and related disorders* (pp. 657–664). Oxford University Press.

Aspinwall, L. G. (1997). Where planning meets coping: Proactive coping and the detection and management of potential stressors. In S. L. Friedman & E. K. Scholnick (Eds.), *The developmental psychology of planning: Why, how, and when do we plan?* (pp. 285–320). Lawrence Erlbaum.

Aspinwall, L. G. (2003). Dealing with adversity: Self-regulation, coping, adaptation, and health. In A. Tesser & N. Schwarz (Eds.), *Blackwell handbook of social psychology: Intraindividual processes* (pp. 591–614). Wiley-Blackwell.

Aspinwall, L. G. (2005). The psychology of future-oriented thinking: From achievement to proactive coping, adaptation, and aging. *Motivation and Emotion, 29*(4), 203–235.

Aspinwall, L. G. (2011). Future-oriented thinking, proactive coping, and the management of potential threats to health and well-being. In S. Folkman (Ed.), *Oxford handbook of stress, health, and coping* (pp. 334–365). Oxford University Press.

Aspinwall, L. G., & Taylor, S. E. (1997). A stitch in time: Self-regulation and proactive coping. *Psychological Bulletin, 121*(3), 417–436.

Athanasopoulos, P., Bylund, E., & Casasanto, D. (2016). Introduction to the special issue: New and interdisciplinary approaches to linguistic relativity. *Language Learning, 66*(3), 482–486.

Atkinson, D. R., Casas, A., & Abreu, J. (1992). Mexican-American acculturation, counselor ethnicity and cultural sensitivity, and perceived counselor competence. *Journal of Counseling Psychology, 39*(4), 515–520.

Atkinson, J. W. (1964). *An introduction to motivation*. Van Nostrand.

Atkinson, R. C., & Shiffrin, R. M. (1968). Human memory: A proposed system and its control processes. *The Psychology of Learning and Motivation, 2*, 89–195.

Ator, N. A. (1991). Subjects and instrumentation. In I. H. Iverson & K. A. Lattal (Eds.), *Experimental analysis of behavior* (Pt. 1, pp. 1–62). Elsevier.

Atuel, H. R., & Castro, C. A. (2018). Military cultural competence. *Clinical Social Work Journal, 46*(2), 74–82. https://doi.org/10.1007/s10615-018-0651-z

Au, R., Appleman, E. R., & Stavitsky, K. (2013). Systematic strategies: Case of school start times. In A. R. Wolfson & H. Montgomery-Downs (Eds.), *The Oxford handbook of infant, child, and adolescent sleep and behavior* (pp. 559–571). Oxford University Press.

Aubin, T., & Jouventin, P. (1998). Cocktail-party effect in king penguin colonies. *Proceedings of the Royal Society of London. Series B: Biological Sciences, 265*(1406), 1665–1673.

Aubin, T., & Jouventin, P. (2002). How to vocally identify kin in a crowd: The penguin model. *Advances in the Study of Behavior, 31*, 243–277.

Auger, R. R. (2006). Sleep-related eating disorders. *Psychiatry (Edgmont), 3*(11), 64–70.

Auger, R. R., & Morgenthaler, T. I. (2006). Sleep-related eating disorders. In T. L. Lee-Chiong (Ed.), *Sleep: A comprehensive handbook* (pp. 457–462). Wiley-Liss.

Auld, M. C., & Powell, L. M. (2009). Economics of food energy density and adolescent body weight. *Economica, 76*(304), 719–740.

Austenfeld, J. L., & Stanton, A. L. (2004). Coping through emotional approach: A new look at emotion, coping, and health-related outcomes. *Journal of Personality, 72*(6), 1335–1364.

Austin, E. J., & Saklofske, D. H. (2005). Far too many intelligences? On the communalities and differences between social, practical, and emotional intelligences. In R. Schulze & R. D. Roberts (Eds.), *Emotional intelligence: An international handbook* (pp. 107–128). Cambridge, MA: Hogrefe & Huber.

Auty, K. M., Cope, A., & Liebling, A. (2017). A systematic review and meta-analysis of yoga and mindfulness meditation in prison: Effects on psychological well-being and behavioural functioning. *International Journal of Offender Therapy and Comparative Criminology, 61*(6), 689–710.

Averbach, E., & Sperling, G. (1961). Short-term storage of information in vision. In C. Cherry (Ed.), *Information theory* (pp. 196–211). Butterworth.

Aviv, R. (2018, April 2). How a young woman lost her identity. *The New Yorker.* https://www.nytimes.com/2017/09/29/nyregion/missing-teacher-virgin-islands.html

Awh, E., Jonides, J., & Reuter-Lorenz, P. A. (1998). Rehearsal in spatial working memory. *Journal of Experimental Psychology: Human Perception and Performance, 24*(3), 780–790.

Awh, E., Jonides, J., Smith, E. E., Buxton, R. B., Frank, L. R., Love, T., Wong, E. C., & Gmeindl, L. (1999). Rehearsal in spatial working memory: Evidence from neuroimaging. *Psychological Science, 10*(5), 433–437.

Axelrod, S. D., Naso, R. C., & Rosenberg, L. M. (2018). Introduction. In S. D. Axelrod, R. C. Naso, & L. M. Rosenberg (Eds.), *Progress in psychoanalysis* (pp. 1–14). Routledge.

Axtell, R. E. (2007). *Essential do's and taboos: The complete guide to international business and leisure travel*. Wiley.

Ayabe-Kanamura, S., Schicker, I., Laska, M., Hudson, R., Distel, H., Kobayakawa, T., & Saito, S. (1998). Differences in perception of everyday odors: A Japanese–German cross-cultural study. *Chemical Senses, 23*(1), 31–38. https://doi.org/10.1093/chemse/23.1.31

Ayduk, Ö., Gyurak, A., & Luerssen, A. (2008). Individual differences in the rejection–aggression link in the hot sauce paradigm: The case of rejection sensitivity. *Journal of Experimental Social Psychology, 44*(3), 775–782.

Ayearst, L. E., & Bagby, R. M. (2010). Evaluating the psychometric properties of psychological measures. In M. M. Antony & D. H. Barlow (Eds.), *Handbook of assessment and treatment planning for psychological disorders* (2nd ed., pp. 23–61). Guilford Press.

Ayers, C. R., Thorp, S. R., & Wetherell, J. L. (2009). Anxiety disorders and hoarding in older adults. In M. M. Antony & M. B. Stein (Eds.), *Oxford handbook of anxiety and related disorders* (pp. 625–635). Oxford University Press.

Azar, S. T. (2003). Adult development and parenthood: A social-cognitive perspective. In J. Demick & C. Andreoletti (Eds.), *Handbook of adult development* (pp. 417–431). Kluwer.

Azevedo, F. A., Carvalho, L. R., Grinberg, L. T., Farfel, J. M., Ferretti, R. E., Leite, R. E., & & Herculano-Houzel, S. (2009). Equal numbers of neuronal and nonneuronal cells make the human brain an isometrically scaled-up primate brain. *Journal of Comparative Neurology, 513*(5), 532–541.

Aziz-Zadeh, L., Kaplan, J. T., & Iacoboni, M. (2009). "Aha!": The neural correlates of verbal insight solutions. *Human Brain Mapping, 30*(3), 908–916.

Aznar, A., Sowden, P., Bayless, S., Ross, K., Warhurst, A., & Pachi, D. (2021). Home-schooling during COVID-19 lockdown: Effects of coping style, home space, and everyday creativity on stress and home-schooling outcomes. *Couple and Family Psychology: Research and Practice*. Advance online publication. https://doi.org/10.1037/cfp0000182

Babinski, D. E., & McQuade, J. D. (2018). Borderline personality features mediate the association between ADHD, ODD, and relational and physical aggression in girls. *Journal of Attention Disorders*, 23(8), 838–848. https://doi.org/1087054718797445.

Babkin, B. P. (1949). *Pavlov: A biography*. University of Chicago Press.

Bacon, L. (2010). *Health at every size: The surprising truth about your weight*. BenBella Books.

Bacon, L., & Aphramor, L. (2011). Weight science: Evaluating the evidence for a paradigm shift. *Nutrition Journal, 10*(1), 9.

Bacon, L., & Aphramor, L. (2014). *Body respect*. BenBella Books.

Baddeley, A. (1994). The magical number seven: Still magic after all these years? *Psychological Review, 101*(2), 353–356.

Baddeley, A. (2000). Short-term and working memory. In E. Tulving & F. I. M. Craik (Eds.), *The Oxford handbook of memory* (pp. 77–92). Oxford University Press.

Baddeley, A. (2003). Working memory: Looking back and looking forward. *Nature Reviews Neuroscience, 4*(10), 829–839.

Baddeley, A. (2007). Working memory: Multiple models, multiple mechanisms. In H. L. Roediger, Y. Dudai, & S. M. Fitzpatrick (Eds.), *Science of memory: Concepts* (pp. 151–153). Oxford University Press.

Baddeley, A. D. (2002). The psychology of memory. In A. D. Baddeley, M. D. Kopelman, & B. A. Wilson (Eds.), *The handbook of memory disorders* (2nd ed., pp. 3–15). Wiley.

Baddeley, A. D. (2004). *Your memory: A user's guide*. Carlton.

Baddeley, A. D., & Hitch, G. (1974). Working memory. *The Psychology of Learning and Motivation, 8*, 47–89.

Baddeley, A. D., Eysenck, M. W., & Anderson, M. C. (2009). *Memory*. Psychology Press.

Baddeley, A. D., Eysenck, M. W., & Anderson, M. C. (2009). *Memory*. Psychology Press.

Baddeley, A. D., Eysenck, M. W., & Anderson, M. C. (2009). *Memory*. Psychology Press.

Baer, J., Kaufman, J. C., & Baumeister, R. F. (Eds.). (2008). *Are we free? Psychology and free will*. Oxford University Press.

Baer, R. A. (2003). Mindfulness training as a clinical intervention: A conceptual and empirical review. *Clinical Psychology: Science and Practice, 10*(2), 125–143.

Baer, R. A. (Ed.). (2006). *Mindfulness-based treatment approaches: Clinician's guide to evidence base and applications*. Elsevier Academic Press.

Bagby, R. M., & Widiger, T. A. (2018). Five Factor Model personality disorder scales: An introduction to a special section on assessment of maladaptive variants of the Five Factor Model. *Psychological Assessment, 30*(1), 1–9.

Bago, B., Rand, D. G., & Pennycook, G. (2020). Fake news, fast and slow: Deliberation reduces belief in false (but not true) news headlines. *Journal of Experimental Psychology: General, 149*(8), 1608–1613. https://doi.org/10.1037/xge0000729

Bahji, A., Hawken, E. R., Sepehry, A. A., Cabrera, C. A., & Vazquez, G. (2019). ECT beyond unipolar major depression: Systematic review and meta-analysis of electroconvulsive therapy in bipolar depression. *Acta Psychiatrica Scandinavica, 139*(3), 214–226. https://doi.org/10.1097/YCO.0000000000000418

Bahrick, H. P. (2000). Long-term maintenance of knowledge. In E. Tulving & F. I. M. Craik (Eds.), *The Oxford handbook of memory* (pp. 347–362). Oxford University Press.

Bailey, D. R. (2006). Oral devices therapy for obstructive sleep apnea. In T. L. Lee-Chiong (Ed.), *Sleep: A comprehensive handbook* (pp. 373–379). Wiley-Liss.

Bailey, J. M., Dunne, M. P., & Martin, N. G. (2000). Genetic and environmental influences on sexual orientation and its correlates in an Australian twin sample. *Journal of Personality and Social Psychology, 78*(3), 524–536.

Baillargeon, R. (1987). Object permanence in 3½- and 4½-month-old infants. *Developmental Psychology, 23*(5), 655–664.

Baillargeon, R. (2004). Infants' reasoning about hidden objects: Evidence for event-general and event-specific expectations. *Developmental Science, 7*(4), 391–414.

Baillargeon, R., & Graber, M. (1987). Where's the rabbit? 5-month-old infants' representation of the height of a hidden object. *Cognitive Development, 2*(4), 375–392.

Baillargeon, R., & Graber, M. (1988). Evidence of location memory in 8-month-old infants in a nonsearch AB task. *Developmental Psychology, 24*(4), 502–511.

Baillargeon, R., Graber, M., DeVos, J., & Black, J. (1990). Why do young infants fail to search for hidden objects? *Cognition, 36*(3), 255–284.

Baillargeon, R., Li, J., Gertner, Y., & Wu, D. (2011). How do infants reason about physical events? In U. Goswami (Ed.), *The Wiley-Blackwell handbook of childhood cognitive development* (2nd ed., pp. 11–48). Wiley-Blackwell.

Baillargeon, R., Spelke, E. S., & Wasserman, S. (1985). Object permanence in five-month-old infants. *Cognition, 20*(3), 191–208.

Bair, D. (2004). *Jung: A biography*. Back Bay Books.

Baird, B., Mota-Rolim, S. A., & Dresler, M. (2019). The cognitive neuroscience of lucid dreaming. *Neuroscience & Biobehavioral Reviews, 100*, 305–323. https://doi.org/10.1016/j.neubiorev.2019.03.008

Baker, D. B., & Benjamin, L. T., Jr. (2012). Concluding thoughts on internationalizing the history of psychology. In D. B. Baker (Ed.), *The Oxford handbook of the history of psychology: Global perspectives* (pp. 616–624). Oxford University Press.

Baker, F. C., & Driver, H. S. (2004). Self-reported sleep across the menstrual cycle in young, healthy women. *Journal of Psychosomatic Research, 56*(2), 239–243.

Baker, F. C., & Driver, H. S. (2007). Circadian rhythms, sleep, and the menstrual cycle. *Sleep Medicine, 8*(6), 613–622.

Baker, J. R., Bezance, J. B., Zellaby, E., & Aggleton, J. P. (2004). Chewing gum can produce context-dependent effects upon memory. *Appetite, 43*(2), 207–210.

Baker, K. D., Loughman, A., Spencer, S. J., & Reichelt, A. C. (2017). The impact of obesity and hypercaloric diet consumption on anxiety and emotional behavior across the lifespan. *Neuroscience & Biobehavioral Reviews, 83*, 173–182.

Baker, L. A., Raine, A., Liu, J., & Jacobson, K. C. (2008). Differential genetic and environmental influences on reactive and proactive aggression in children. *Journal of Abnormal Child Psychology, 36*(8), 1265–1278.

Baker, L. D., Frank, L. L., Foster-Schubert, K., Green, P. S., Wilkinson, C. W., McTiernan, A., Plymate, S. R., Fishel, M. A., Watson, G. S., Cholerton, B. A., Duncan, G. E., Mehta, P. D., & Craft, S. (2010). Effects of aerobic exercise on mild cognitive impairment: A controlled trial. *Archives of Neurology, 67*(1), 71.

Baker, M. C. (2001). Syntax. In M. Aronoff & J. Rees-Miller (Eds.), *The handbook of linguistics* (pp. 265–294). Blackwell.

Balch, W. R., Bowman, K., & Mohler, L. A. (1992). Music-dependent memory in immediate and delayed word recall. *Memory & Cognition, 20*(1), 21–28.

Balch, W. R., & Lewis, B. S. (1996). Music-dependent memory: The roles of tempo change and mood mediation. *Journal of Experimental Psychology: Learning, Memory, and Cognition, 22*(6), 1354–1363.

Baldwin, D., & Meyer, M. (2007). How inherently social is language? In E. Hoff & M. Shatz (Eds.), *Blackwell handbook of language development* (pp. 87–106). Blackwell.

Ball, H. L., Hooker, E., & Kelly, P. J. (1999). Where will the baby sleep? Attitudes and practices of new and experienced parents regarding cosleeping with their newborn infants. *American Anthropologist, 101*(1), 143–151.

Ball-Rokeach, S. J. (2016). The politics of studying media violence: Reflections 30 years after the violence commission. In R. Wei (Ed.), *Refining milestone mass communications theories for the 21st century* (pp. 102–117). Routledge.

Balon, R., Martini, S., & Singareddy, R. K. (2004). Patient perspective on collaborative treatment. *Psychiatric Services, 55*(8), 945–946.

Baltes, P. B., Lindenberger, U., & Staudinger, U. M. (2006). Life span theory in developmental psychology. In R. M. Lerner (Vol. Ed.), *Handbook of child psychology* (6th ed., Vol. 1, pp. 569–664). Wiley.

Banack, H. R., Stokes, A., Fox, M. P., Hovey, K. M., Feliciano, E. M. C., LeBlanc, E. S., Bird, C., Caan, B. J., Kroenke, C. H., Allison, M. A., Going, S. B., Snetselaar, L., Cheng, T.-Y. D., Chlebowski, R. T., Stefanick, M. L., LaMonte, M. J., & Wactawski-Wende, J. (2018). Stratified probabilistic bias analysis for body mass index–related exposure misclassification in postmenopausal women. *Epidemiology, 29*(5), 604–613.

Banaji, M. R., & Heiphetz, L. (2010). Attitudes. In S. T. Fiske, D. T. Gilbert, & G. Lindzey (Eds.), *Handbook of social psychology* (5th ed., Vol. 1, pp. 353–393). Wiley.

Bandelow, B., & Baldwin, D. S. (2010). Pharmacotherapy for panic disorder. In D. J. Stein, E. Hollander, & B. O. Rothbaum (Eds.), *Textbook of anxiety disorders* (2nd ed., pp. 399–416). American Psychiatric Publishing.

Bandelow, B., Sagebiel, A., Belz, M., Görlich, Y., Michaelis, S., & Wedekind, D. (2018). Enduring effects of psychological treatments for anxiety disorders: Meta-analysis of follow-up studies. *The British Journal of Psychiatry, 212*(6), 333–338.

Bandettini, P. A. (2012). Twenty years of functional MRI: The science and the stories. *Neuroimage, 62*(2), 575–588.

Bandura, A. (1965). Influence of models' reinforcement contingencies on the acquisition of imitative responses. *Journal of Social Psychology, 1*(6), 589–595.

Bandura, A. (1977a). Self-efficacy: Toward a unifying theory of behavioral change. *Psychological Review, 84*(2), 191–215.

Bandura, A. (1977b). *Social learning theory*. Prentice Hall.

Bandura, A. (1982). Self-efficacy mechanism in human agency. *American Psychologist, 37*(2), 122–147.

Bandura, A. (1986). *Social foundations of thought and action: A social-cognitive theory*. Prentice-Hall.

Bandura, A. (1997). *Self-efficacy: The exercise of control*. W. H. Freeman.

Bandura, A. (2001). Social-cognitive theory: An agentic perspective. *Annual Review of Psychology, 52*, 1–26.

Bandura, A., Ross, D., & Ross, S. A. (1961). Transmission of aggression through imitation of aggressive models. *Journal of Abnormal and Social Psychology, 63*(3), 575–582.

Bandura, A., Ross, D., & Ross, S. A. (1963). Imitation of film-mediated aggressive models. *Journal of Abnormal and Social Psychology, 66*(1), 3–11.

Banerjee, S. C., Greene, K., Yanovitzky, I., Bagdasarov, Z., Choi, S. Y., & Magsamen-Conrad, K. (2015). Adolescent egocentrism and indoor tanning: Is the relationship direct or mediated? *Journal of Youth Studies, 18*(3), 357–375.

Bani, M., Russo, S., Ardenghi, S., Rampoldi, G., Wickline, V., Nowicki, S., & Strepparava, M. G. (2021). Behind the mask: Emotion recognition in healthcare students. *Medical Science Educator, 31*(4), 1–5. https://doi.org/10.1007/s40670-021-01317-8

Banich, M. T. (2009). Executive function: The search for an integrated account. *Current Directions in Psychological Science, 18*(2), 89–94.

Banker, B. S., & Gaertner, S. L. (1998). Achieving stepfamily harmony: An intergroup-relations approach. *Journal of Family Psychology, 12*(3), 310–325.

Banuazizi, A., & Movahedi, S. (1975). Interpersonal dynamics in a simulated prison: A methodological analysis. *American Psychologist, 30*(2), 152–160.

Baptista, J. P., & Gradim, A. (2020). Understanding fake news consumption: A review. *Social Sciences, 9*(10), 185. https://doi.org/10.3390/socsci9100185

Baquet, D. (2017, December 3). The strongest thing a man can do is cry. *The New York Times Style Magazine*, pp. 132–139. https://www.nytimes.com/interactive/2017/11/29/t-magazine/jay-z-dean-baquet-interview.html

Barabasz, A. F., & Barabasz, M. (2008). Hypnosis and the brain. In M. R. Nash & A. J. Barnier (Eds.), *The Oxford handbook of hypnosis: Theory, research, and practice* (pp. 337–364). Oxford University Press.

Barad, M. (2005). Fear extinction in rodents: Basic insight to clinical promise. *Current Opinion in Neurobiology, 15*(6), 710–715.

Barash, D. P. (1983). Sociobiology and behavior (2nd ed.). Elsevier.

Barbaresi, W. J., Weaver, A. L., Voigt, R. G., Killian, J. M., & Katusic, S. K. (2018). Comparing methods to determine persistence of childhood ADHD into adulthood: A prospective, population-based study. *Journal of Attention Disorders, 22*(6), 571–580.

Barber, C. (2008). *Comfortably numb: How psychiatry is medicating a nation*. Pantheon.

Barber, J. P., & Solomonov, N. (2016). Psychodynamic theories. In J. C. Norcross, G. R. VandenBos, & D. K. Freedheim (Eds.), *APA handbook of clinical psychology* (Vol. 2, pp. 53–78). American Psychological Association.

Barcella, L. (2021). What happened to Hannah Upp? The mystery around the young woman's disappearance continues. https://www.aetv.com/real-crime/what-happened-to-hannah-upp-the-mystery-around-the-young-womans-disappearance-continues

Barchard, K. A., Grob, K. E., & Roe, M. J. (2017). Is sadness blue? The problem of using figurative language for emotions on psychological tests. *Behavior Research Methods, 49*(2), 443–456.

Bard, P. (1928). A diencephalic mechanism for the expression of rage with special reference to the central nervous system. *American Journal of Physiology, 84*, 490–513.

Bard, P. (1934). The neuro-humoral basis of emotional reactions. In C. Murchinson (Ed.), *Handbook of general experimental psychology* (pp. 264–311). Clark University Press.

Bard, P., & Rioch, D. M. (1937). A study of four cats deprived of neocortex and additional portions of the forebrain. *The Johns Hopkins Medical Journal, 60*, 73–153.

Bardia, A., Bauer, B. A., & Loprinzi, C. L. (2009). Cancer. In B. P. Jacobs & K. Gundling (Eds.), *The ACP evidence-based guide to complementary and alternative medicine* (pp. 77–100). American College of Physicians.

Barenbaum, N. B., & Winter, D. G. (2008). History of modern personality theory and research. In O. P. John, R. W. Robins, & L. A. Pervin (Eds.), *Handbook of personality: Theory and research* (3rd ed., pp. 3–27). Guilford Press.

Barker, E. T., & Galambos, N. L. (2003). Body dissatisfaction of adolescent girls and boys: Risk and resource factors. *The Journal of Early Adolescence, 23*(2), 141–165.

Barkil-Oteo, A. (2013). Collaborative care for depression in primary care: How psychiatry could "troubleshoot" current treatments and practices. *The Yale Journal of Biology and Medicine, 86*(2), 139–146. https://www.ncbi.nlm.nih.gov/pmc/articles/PMC36704

Barkley, R. A. (1997). Behavioral inhibition, sustained attention, and executive functions: Constructing a unifying theory of ADHD. *Psychological Bulletin, 121*(1), 65–94.

Barkley, R. A. (2015). Etiologies of ADHD. In R. A. Barkley (Ed.), Attention-deficit *hyperactivity disorder: A handbook for diagnosis and treatment* (4th ed., pp. 356–390). Guilford Press.

Barlett, C. P., Gentile, D. A., Chng, G., Li, D., & Chamberlin, K. (2018). Social media use and cyberbullying perpetration: A longitudinal analysis. *Violence and Gender, 5*(3), 191–197.

Barlow, D. H. (2002). *Anxiety and its disorders: The nature and treatment of anxiety and panic* (2nd ed.). Guilford Press.

Barlow, D. H. (2021). *Clinical handbook of psychological disorders: A step-by-step treatment manual* (6th ed.). Guilford.

Barlow, D. H., Allen, L. B., & Basden, S. L. (2007). Psychological treatments for panic disorders, phobias, and generalized anxiety disorder. In P. E. Nathan & J. M. Gorman (Eds.), *A guide to treatments that work* (3rd ed., pp. 351–394). Oxford University Press.

Barlow, D. H., Bullis, J. R., Comer, J. S., & Ametaj, A. A. (2013). Evidence-based psychological treatments: An update and a way forward. *Annual Review of Clinical Psychology, 9*, 1–27.

Barlow, D. H., Curreri, A. J., & Woodard, L. S. (2021). Neuroticism and disorders of emotion: A new synthesis. *Current Directions in Psychological Science, 30*(5), 410–417. https://doi.org/10.1177/09637214211030253

Barnes, A. (2004). Race, schizophrenia, and admission to state psychiatric hospitals. *Administration and Policy in Mental Health, 31*(3), 241–252.

Barnes, D. E., & Yaffe, K. (2011). The projected effect of risk factor reduction on Alzheimer's disease prevalence. *The Lancet: Neurology, 10*(9), 819–828.

Barnes, P. M., Powell-Griner, E., McFann, K., & Nahin, R. L. (2004, June). Complementary and alternative medicine use among adults: United States, 2002. *Seminars in Integrative Medicine, 2*(2), 54–71.

Barnes, S., Brown, K. W., Krusemark, E., Campbell, W. K., & Rogge, R. D. (2007). The role of mindfulness in romantic relationship satisfaction and responses to relationship stress. *Journal of Marital and Family Therapy, 33*(4), 482–500.

Barnett, J. E. (2017). Unavoidable incidental contacts and multiple relationships in rural practice. In O. Zur (Ed.), *Multiple relationships in psychotherapy and counseling* (pp. 97–107). Routledge.

Barnett, J. E. (2018). Integrating technological advances into clinical training and practice: The future is now! *Clinical Psychology: Science and Practice*, e12233.

Barnett, J. E., & Kolmes, K. (2016). The practice of tele-mental health: Ethical, legal, and clinical issues for practitioners. *Practice Innovations, 1*(1), 53–66.

Barnier, A. J., & Nash, M. R. (2008). Introduction: A roadmap for explanation, a working definition. In M. R. Nash & A. J. Barnier (Eds.), *The Oxford handbook of hypnosis: Theory, research, and practice* (pp. 1–20). Oxford University Press.

Barnwell, S. S., McCann, R., & McCutcheon, S. (2018). Competence of the psychologist. In L. F. Campbell, F. Millan, & J. N. Martin (Eds.), *A telepsychology casebook: Using technology ethically and effectively in your professional practice* (pp. 7–26). American Psychological Association.

Baron-Cohen, S. (1995). *Mindblindness: An essay on autism and theory of mind*. MIT Press.

Baron-Cohen, S. (2000). Theory of mind and autism: A review. *International Review of Research in Mental Retardation, 23*, 169–184.

Baron-Cohen, S., Jolliffe, T., Mortimore, C., & Robertson, M. (1997). Another advanced test of theory of mind: Evidence from very high functioning adults with autism or Asperger syndrome. *Journal of Child Psychology and Psychiatry, 38*(7), 813–822.

Baron-Cohen, S., Leslie, A. M., & Frith, U. (1985). Does the autistic child have a "theory of mind"? *Cognition, 21*(1), 37–46.

Barr, H., Bookstein, F., O'Malley, K., Connor, P., Huggins, J., & Streissguth, A. (2006). Binge drinking during pregnancy as a predictor of psychiatric disorders on the Structured Clinical Interview for DSM-IV in young adult offspring. *American Journal of Psychiatry, 163*(6), 1061–1065.

Barr, J. T. (2005). History and development of contact lenses. In E. S. Bennett & B. A. Weissman (Eds.), *Clinical contact lens practice* (pp. 1–10). Lippincott Williams & Wilkins.

Barrash, J., Tranel, D., & Anderson, S. W. (2000). Acquired personality disturbances associated with bilateral damage to the ventromedial prefrontal region. *Developmental Neuropsychology, 18*(3), 355–381.

Barreto, M., Victor, C., Hammond, C., Eccles, A., Richins, M. T., & Qualter, P. (2021). Loneliness around the world: Age, gender, and cultural differences in loneliness. *Personality and Individual Differences, 169*, 110066. https://doi.org/10.1016/j.paid.2020.110066

Barrett, E. S., Vitek, W., Mbowe, O., Thurston, S. W., Legro, R. S., Alvero, R., Baker, V., Bates, G. W., Casson, P., Coutifaris, C., Eisenberg, E., Hansen, K., Krawetz, S., Robinson, R., Rosen, M., Usadi, R., Zhang, H., Santoro, N., & Diamond, M. (2018). Allostatic load, a measure of chronic physiological stress, is associated with pregnancy outcomes, but not fertility, among women with unexplained infertility. *Human Reproduction, 33*(9), 1757–1766.

Barrett, L., Dunbar, R., & Lycett, J. (2002). *Human evolutionary psychology*. Palgrave.

Barrett, L. F., & Bliss-Moreau, E. (2009). She's emotional. He's having a bad day: Attributional explanations for emotion stereotypes. *Emotion, 9*(5), 649–658.

Barrick, M. R., & Mount, M. K. (1991). The Big Five personality dimensions and job performance: A meta-analysis. *Personnel Psychology, 44*(1), 1–26.

Barringer, M., & Saenz, A. (2007). Promoting positive school environments: A career in school psychology. In R. J. Sternberg (Ed.), *Career paths in psychology: Where your degree can take you* (2nd ed., pp. 227–248). American Psychological Association.

Barrouillet, P., Gavens, N., Vergauwe, E., Gaillard, V., & Camos, V. (2009). Working memory span development: A time-based resource-sharing model account. *Developmental Psychology, 45*(2), 477.

Barry, E. (2022, March 18). How long should it take to grieve? Psychiatry has come up with an answer. *The New York Times*. https://www.nytimes.com/2022/03/18/health/prolonged-grief-disorder.html

Barsaglini, A., Sartori, G., Benetti, S., Pettersson-Yeo, W., & Mechelli, A. (2014). The effects of psychotherapy on brain function: A systematic and critical review. *Progress in Neurobiology, 114*, 1–14.

Barsalou, L. W. (1983). Ad hoc categories. *Memory Cognition, 11*(3), 211–227.

Barsalou, L. W. (1985). Ideals, central tendency, and frequency of instantiation as determinants of graded structure in categories. *Journal of Experimental Psychology: Learning, Memory, and Cognition, 11*(4), 629–654.

Barsalou, L. W. (2003). Situated simulation in the human conceptual system. *Language and Cognitive Processes, 18*(5–6), 513–562.

Barsalou, L. W. (2012). The human conceptual system. In M. Spivey, K. McRae, & M. Joanisse (Eds.), *The Cambridge handbook of psycholinguistics* (pp. 239–258). Cambridge University Press.

Bartels, M., Rietveld, M. J. H., Van Baal, G. C. M., & Boomsma, D. I. (2002). Genetic and environmental influences on the development of intelligence. *Behavior Genetics, 32*(4), 237–249.

Bartley, E. J., & Fillingim, R. B. (2013). Sex differences in pain: A brief review of clinical and experimental findings. *British Journal of Anaesthesia, 111*(1), 52–58. https://doi.org/10.1093/bja/aet127

Bartone, P. T., Eid, J., & Hystad, S. W. (2016). Training hardiness for stress resilience. In N. Maheshwari & V. Kumar (Eds.), *Military psychology: Concepts, trends and interventions* (pp. 231–248). Sage.

Bartone, P. T., Johnsen, B. H., Eid, J., Hystad, S. W., & Laberg, J. C. (2017). Hardiness, avoidance coping, and alcohol consumption in war veterans: A moderated-mediation study. *Stress and Health, 33*(5), 498–507.

Bartoshuk, L. M., Duffy, V. B., & Miller, I. J. (1994). PTC/PROP tasting: Anatomy, psychophysics, and sex effects. *Physiology & Behavior, 56*(6), 1165–1171.

Bartsch, K., & Wellman, H. M. (1997). *Children talk about the mind*. Oxford University Press.

Barušs, I. (2003). *Alterations of consciousness: An empirical analysis for social scientists*. American Psychological Association.

Baruth, L.G., & Manning, M.L. (1992). *Multicultural education of children and adolescents*. Allyn & Bacon.

Baryshnikov, I., Joffe, G., Koivisto, M., Melartin, T., Aaltonen, K., Suominen, K., Rosenström, T., Näätänen, P., Karpov, B., Heikkinen, M., & Isometsä, E. (2017). Relationships between self-reported childhood traumatic experiences, attachment style, neuroticism and features of borderline personality disorders in patients with mood disorders. *Journal of Affective Disorders, 210*, 82–89.

Basile, K. C. (2005). Sexual violence in the lives of girls and women. In K. A. Kendall-Tackett (Ed.), *Handbook of women, stress, and trauma* (pp. 101–122). Brunner-Routledge.

Basow, S. A. (2010). Gender in the classroom. In J. C. Chrisler & D. R. McCreary (Eds.), *Handbook of gender research in psychology* (pp. 277–295). Springer Science+Business Media.

Bassok, M., & Novick, L. R. (2012). Problem solving. In K. J. Holyoak & R. G. Morrison (Eds.), *The Oxford handbook of thinking and reasoning* (pp. 413–432). Oxford University Press.

Batson, C. D., & Shaw, L. L. (1991). Evidence for altruism: Toward a pluralism of prosocial motives. *Psychological Inquiry, 2*(2), 107–122.

Batty, G. D., Deary, I. J., Fawns-Ritchie, C., Gale, C. R., & Altschul, D. (2021). Pre-pandemic cognitive function and COVID-19 vaccine hesitancy: Cohort study. *Brain, Behavior, and Immunity, 95*, 100–105. https://doi.org/10.1016/j.bbi.2021.05.016

Batty, G. D., Deary, I. J., & Gottfredson, L. S. (2007). Premorbid (early life) IQ and later mortality risk: Systematic review. *Annals of Epidemiology, 17*(4), 278–288.

Bauer, A. J., & Just, M. A. (2017). A brain-based account of "basic-level" concepts. *NeuroImage, 161*, 196–205.

Bauer, P. J., Larkina, M., & Deocampo, J. (2011). Early memory development. In U. Goswami (Ed.), *The Wiley-Blackwell handbook of childhood cognitive development* (2nd ed., pp. 153–179). Wiley-Blackwell.

Baumann, N., & Pham Dinh, D. (2001). Biology of oligodendrocyte and myelin in the mammalian central nervous system. *Physiological, 81*(2), 871–927.

Baumeister, A., & Francis, J. (2002). Historical development of the dopamine hypothesis of schizophrenia. *Journal of the History of the Neurosciences, 11*(3), 265–277.

Baumeister, R. F. (2013). Writing a literature review. In M. J. Prinstein (Ed.), *The portable mentor: Expert guide to a successful career in psychology* (pp. 119–132). Springer.

Baumeister, R. F., & Leary, M. R. (1995). The need to belong: Desire for interpersonal attachments as a fundamental human motivation. *Psychological Bulletin, 117*(3), 497–529.

Bäuml, K. H. (1996). Revisiting an old issue: Retroactive interference as a function of the degree of original and interpolated learning. *Psychonomic Bulletin & Review, 3*(3), 380–384.

Baumrind, D. (1966). Effects of authoritative parental control on child behavior. *Child Development, 37*(4), 887–907.

Baumrind, D. (1967). Child care practices anteceding three patterns of preschool behavior. *Genetic Psychology Monographs, 75*(1), 43–88.

Baumrind, D. (1971). Current patterns of parental authority. *Developmental Psychology Monographs, 4*(1, Pt. 2), 1–103.

Baumrind, D. (1972). An exploratory study of socialization effects on black children: Some black–white comparisons. *Child Development, 43*(1), 261–267.

Baumrind, D. (1978). Parental disciplinary patterns and social competence in children. *Youth & Society, 9*(3), 239–276.

Baumrind, D. (1996). The discipline controversy revisited. *Family Relations, 45*(4), 405–414.

Baumrind, D. (2013). Authoritative parenting revisited: History and current status. In R. E. Larzelere, A. S. Morris, & A. W. Harrist (Eds.), *Authoritative parenting: Synthesizing nurturance and discipline for optimal child development* (pp. 11–34). American Psychological Association.

Bavelier, D., Green, C. S., & Dye, M. W. G. (2009). Exercising your brain: Training-related brain plasticity. In M. S. Gazzaniga (Ed.), *The cognitive neurosciences* (4th ed., pp. 153–164). MIT Press.

Baxter, A. J., Brugha, T. S., Erskine, H. E., Scheurer, R. W., Vos, T., & Scott, J. G. (2015). The epidemiology and global burden of autism spectrum disorders. *Psychological Medicine, 45*(3), 601–613.

Baxter, L. R., Schwartz, J. M., Bergman, K. S., Szuba, M. P., Guze, B. H., Mazziotta, J. C., Alazraki, A., Selin, C. E., Ferng, H.-K., Munford, P., & Phelps, M. E. (1992). Caudate glucose metabolic rate changes with both drug and behavior therapy for obsessive-compulsive disorder. *Archives of General Psychiatry, 49*(9), 681–689.

Bazin, N., & Perruchet, P. (1996). Implicit and explicit associative memory in patients with schizophrenia. *Schizophrenia Research, 22*(3), 241–248.

Bear, M. F., & Abraham, W. C. (1996). Long-term depression in hippocampus. *Annual Review of Neuroscience, 19*(1), 437–462.

Beattie, G., Laliberté, J. W. P., & Oreopoulos, P. (2018). Thrivers and divers: Using non-academic measures to predict college success and failure. *Economics of Education Review, 62*, 170–182.

Beauchaine, T. P., & Hayden, E. P. (2016). Child and adolescent disorders. In J. C. Norcross, G. R. VandenBox, & D. K. Freedheim (Eds.), *APA handbook of clinical psychology* (Vol. 4, pp. 135–171). American Psychological Association.

Beauchaine, T. P., Hinshaw, S. P., & Gatzke-Kopp, L. (2008). Genetic and environmental influences on behavior. In T. P. Beauchaine & S. P. Hinshaw (Eds.), *Child and adolescent psychopathology* (pp. 58–90). Wiley.

Beauchamp-Turner, D. L., & Levinson, D. M. (1992). Effects of meditation on stress, health, and affect. *Medical Psychotherapy: An International Journal, 5*, 123–131.

Beaudoin, M., & Desrichard, O. (2011). Are memory self-efficacy and memory performance related? A meta-analysis. *Psychological Bulletin, 137*(2), 211–241.

Bebbington, P., & Kuipers, E. (2008). Psychosocial factors. In K. T. Meuser & D. V. Jeste (Eds.), *Clinical handbook of schizophrenia* (pp. 74–81). Guilford Press.

Bechara, A., & Damasio, A. R. (2005). The somatic marker hypothesis: A neural theory of economic decision. *Games and Economic Behavior, 52*(2), 336–372.

Bechara, A., Damasio, H., Tranel, D., & Damasio, A. R. (1997). Deciding advantageously before knowing the advantageous strategy. *Science, 275*(5304), 1293–1295.

Beck, A. T. (1976). *Cognitive therapy and the emotional disorders*. International Universities Press.

Beck, A. T., & Haigh, E. A. (2014). Advances in cognitive theory and therapy: The generic cognitive model. *Annual Review of Clinical Psychology, 10*, 1–24.

Beck, A. T., Rush, A. J., Shaw, B. F., & Emery, G. (1979). *Cognitive therapy of depression*. Guilford Press.

Beck, J. S. (1995). *Cognitive therapy: Basics and beyond*. Guilford Press.

Beck, J. S. (2002). Beck therapy approach. In M. Hersen & W. Sledge (Eds.), *Encyclopedia of psychotherapy* (Vol. 1, pp. 155–163). Academic Press.

Beck, R. C., & McBee, W. (1995). Mood-dependent memory for generated and repeated words: Replication and extension. *Cognition & Emotion, 9*(4), 289–307.

Becker, A. E., Burwell, R. A., Gilman, S. E., Herzog, D. B., & Hamburg, P. (2002). Eating behaviours and attitudes following prolonged exposure to television among ethnic Fijian adolescent girls. *British Journal of Psychiatry, 180*, 509–514.

Becker, C. B., Wilson, C., Williams, A., Kelly, M., McDaniel, L., & Elmquist, J. (2010). Peer-facilitated cognitive dissonance versus healthy weight eating disorders prevention: A randomized comparison. *Body Image, 7*(4), 280–288.

Becker, J. T., & Overman, A. A. (2002). The memory deficit in Alzheimer's disease. In A. D. Baddeley, M. D. Kopelman, & B. A. Wilson (Eds.), *The handbook of memory disorders* (2nd ed., pp. 569–589). Wiley.

Bee, M. A., & Micheyl, C. (2008). The "cocktail party problem": What is it? How can it be solved? And why should animal behaviorists study it? *Journal of Comparative Psychology, 122*(3), 235–251.

Beevers, C. G. (2005). Cognitive vulnerability to depression: A dual process model. *Clinical Psychology Review, 25*(7), 975–1002.

Bégin, C., Carbonneau, E., Gagnon-Girouard, M. P., Mongeau, L., Paquette, M. C., Turcotte, M., & Provencher, V. (2018). Eating-related and psychological outcomes of Health at Every Size intervention in health and social services centers across the province of Québec. *American Journal of Health Promotion, 33*(2), 248–258. https://doi.org/0890117118786326

Bègue, L., Subra, B., Arvers, P., Muller, D., Bricout, V., & Zorman, M. (2009). A message in a bottle: Extrapharmacological effects of alcohol on aggression. *Journal of Experimental Social Psychology, 45*(1), 137–142.

Behne, T., Carpenter, M., Call, J., & Tomasello, M. (2005). Unwilling versus unable: Infants' understanding of intentional action. *Developmental Psychology, 41*(2), 328–337.

Behnke, S. H., & Jones, S. E. (2012). Ethics and ethics codes for psychologists. In S. J. Knapp (Ed.), *APA handbook of ethics in psychology* (Vol. 1, pp. 43–74). American Psychological Association.

Beidel, D. C., & Turner, S. M. (2007). *Shy children, phobic adults: Nature and treatment of social anxiety disorder* (2nd ed.). American Psychological Association.

Beijers, R., Cassidy, J., Lustermans, H., & de Weerth, C. (2018). Parent-infant room sharing during the first months of life: Longitudinal links with behavior during middle childhood. *Child Development, 90*(4), 1350–1367. https://doi.org/10.1111/cdev.13146

Beins, B. C. (2012). Jean Piaget: Theorist of the child's mind. In W. E. Pickren, D. A. Dewsbury, & M. Wertheimer (Eds.), *Portraits of pioneers in developmental psychology* (pp. 89–107). Psychology Press.

Beins, B., & Beins, A. (2008). *Effective writing in psychology: Papers, posters, and presentations*. Blackwell.

Beitman, B. D., & Manring, J. (2009). Theory and practice of psychotherapy integration. In G. O. Gabbard (Ed.), *Textbook of psychotherapeutic treatments* (pp. 705–726). American Psychiatric Publishing.

Békés, V., & Aafjes-van Doorn, K. (2020). Psychotherapists' attitudes toward online therapy during the COVID-19 pandemic. *Journal of Psychotherapy Integration, 30*(2), 238–247. https://doi.org/10.1037/int0000214

Bekkers, R. (2007). Intergenerational transmission of volunteering. *Acta Sociologica, 50*(2), 99–114.

Belanger, H. G., Spiegel, E., & Vanderploeg, R. D. (2010). Neuropsychological performance following a history of multiple self-reported concussions: A meta-analysis. *Journal of the International Neuropsychological Society, 16*(2), 262–267.

Bélanger, L., Vallières, A., Ivers, H., Moreau, V., Lavigne, G., & Morin, C. M. (2007). Meta-analysis of sleep changes in control groups of insomnia treatment trials. *Journal of Sleep Research, 16*(1), 77–84.

Belgrave, F. Z., & Allison, K. W. (2014). *African American psychology: From Africa to America* (3rd ed.). Sage.

Belicki, D., & Belicki, K. (1982). Nightmares in a university population. *Sleep Research, 11*, 116.

Belicki, K. (1992a). Nightmare frequency versus nightmare distress: Relations to psychopathology and cognitive style. *Journal of Abnormal Psychology, 101*(3), 592–597.

Belicki, K. (1992b). The relationship of nightmare frequency to nightmare suffering with implications for treatment and research. *Dreaming, 2*(3), 143–148.

Bell, C. G., Walley, A. J., & Froguel, P. (2005). The genetics of human obesity. *Nature Reviews Genetics, 6*(3), 221–234.

Bell, M. C., & McDevitt, M. A. (2014). Conditioned reinforcement. In F. K. McSweeney & E. S. Murphy (Eds.), *The Wiley-Blackwell handbook of operant and classical conditioning* (pp. 221–248). Wiley.

Belleville, G., Dubé-Frenette, M., & Rousseau, A. (2018). Efficacy of imagery rehearsal therapy and cognitive behavioral therapy in sexual assault victims with posttraumatic stress disorder: A randomized controlled trial. *Journal of Traumatic Stress, 31*(4), 591–601.

Bellieni, C. V., Severi, F., Bocchi, C., Caparelli, N., Bagnoli, F., Buonocore, G., & Petraglia, F. (2005). Blink-startle reflex habituation in 30–34-week low-risk fetuses. *Journal of Perinatal Medicine, 33*(1), 33–37.

Belsky, J., & Fearon, R. P. (2002). Early attachment security, subsequent maternal sensitivity, and later child development: Does continuity in development depend upon continuity of caregiving? *Attachment & Human Development, 4*(3), 361–387.

Belsky, J., & Pluess, M. (2009). Beyond diathesis stress: Differential susceptibility to environmental influences. *Psychological Bulletin, 135*(6), 885–908.

Belsky, J., Steinberg, L., & Draper, P. (1991). Childhood experience, interpersonal development, and reproductive strategy: An evolutionary theory of socialization. *Child Development, 62*(4), 647–670.

Bem, D. J. (1967). Self-perception: An alternative interpretation of cognitive dissonance phenomena. *Psychological Review, 74*(3), 183–200.

Bender, P. K., Plante, C., & Gentile, D. A. (2018). The effects of violent media content on aggression. *Current Opinion in Psychology, 19*, 104–108.

Benders, T., & Altvater-Mackensen, N. (2017). Before the word: Acquiring a phoneme inventory. In G. Westermann & N. Mani (Eds.), *Early word learning* (pp. 15–28). Routledge.

Beniczky, S., Kéri, S., Vörös, E., Ungureán, A., Benedek, G., Janka, Z., & Vécsei, L. (2002). Complex hallucinations following occipital lobe damage. *European Journal of Neurology, 9*(2), 175–176.

Benjafield, J. G. (2012). *Psychology: A concise history*. Oxford University Press.

Benjafield, J. G. (2015). *A history of psychology* (3rd. ed.). Oxford University Press.

Benjamin, A. J., Jr., Kepes, S., & Bushman, B. J. (2017). Effects of weapons on aggressive thoughts, angry feelings, hostile appraisals, and aggressive behavior: A meta-analytic review of the weapons effect literature. *Personality and Social Psychology Review, 22(4), 347–377.* https://doi.org/1088868317725419.

Benjamin, G. A. H., & Beck, C. J. (2018). Major legal cases that have influenced mental health ethics. In M. M. Leach & E. R. Welfel (Eds.), *The Cambridge handbook of applied psychological ethics* (pp. 429–451). Cambridge University Press.

Benjamin, L. T. (2006). *A history of psychology in letters*. Blackwell.

Benjamin, L. T., Jr. (2005). A history of clinical psychology as a profession in America (and a glimpse at its future). *Annual Review of Clinical Psychology, 1*, 1–30.

Benjamin, L. T., Jr. (2007). *A brief history of modern psychology*. Blackwell.

Benjamin, L. T., Jr., & Baker, D. B. (2012). The internationalization of psychology: A history. In D. B. Baker (Ed.), *The Oxford handbook of the history of psychology: Global perspectives* (pp. 1–17). Oxford University Press.

Benjamin, L. T., Jr., & Crouse, E. M. (2002). The American Psychological Association's response to *Brown v. Board of Education*: The case of Kenneth B. Clark. *American Psychologist, 57*(1), 38–50.

Benner, A. D., Wang, Y., Shen, Y., Boyle, A. E., Polk, R., & Cheng, Y.-P. (2018). Racial/ethnic discrimination and well-being during adolescence: A meta-analytic review. *American Psychologist, 73*(7), 855–883. https://doi.org/10.1037/amp0000204

Bennett, M. (1999). Introduction. In M. Bennett (Ed.), *Developmental psychology: Achievements and prospects* (pp. 1–12). Psychology Press.

Bennett, T., & Holloway, K. (2017). Motives for illicit prescription drug use among university students: A systematic review and meta-analysis. *International Journal of Drug Policy, 44*, 12–22.

Ben-Porath, Y. S., & Tellegen, A. (2008). *Minnesota Multiphasic Personality Inventory-2: Restructured Form manual*. Pearson.

Bensmaia, S. (2010). Tactile acuity. In E. B. Goldstein (Ed.), *Encyclopedia of perception* (pp. 947–950). Sage.

Benson, K., & Flory, K. (2017). Symptoms of depression and ADHD in relation to stimulant medication misuse among college students. *Substance Use & Misuse, 52*(14), 1937–1945.

Benson, K., Flory, K., Humphreys, K. L., & Lee, S. S. (2015). Misuse of stimulant medication among college students: A comprehensive review and meta-analysis. *Clinical Child and Family Psychology Review, 18*(1), 50–76.

Benson, K., Woodlief, D. T., Flory, K., Siceloff, E. R., Coleman, K., & Lamont, A. (2018). Is ADHD, independent of ODD, associated with whether and why college students misuse stimulant medication? *Experimental and Clinical Psychopharmacology, 26*(5), 476–487.

Benware, C. A., & Deci, E. L. (1984). Quality of learning with an active versus passive motivational set. *American Educational Research Journal, 21*(4), 755–765.

Benyamani, Y. (2011). Health and illness perception. In H. S. Friedman (Ed.), *The Oxford handbook of health psychology* (pp. 281–314). Oxford University Press.

Beran, T. N., McLaughlin, K., Al Ansari, A., & Kassam, A. (2013). Conformity of behaviors among medical students: Impact on performance of knee arthrocentesis in simulation. *Advances in Health Sciences Education: Theory and Practice, 18*(4), 589–596.

Berge, J. M., Wall, M., Loth, K., & Neumark-Sztainer, D. (2010). Parenting style as a predictor of adolescent weight and weight-related behaviors. *Journal of Adolescent Health, 46*(4), 331–338.

Berger, R., Brenick, A., Lawrence, S. E., Coco, L., & Abu-Raiya, H. (2018). Comparing the effectiveness and durability of contact- and skills-based prejudice reduction approaches. *Journal of Applied Developmental Psychology, 59*, 46–53.

Bergin, D. A., & Cooks, H. C. (2002). High school students of color talk about accusations of "acting white." *The Urban Review, 34*(2), 113–134.

Bergkvist, L., & Zhou, K. Q. (2016). Celebrity endorsements: A literature review and research agenda. *International Journal of Advertising, 35*(4), 642–663. https://doi.org/10.1080/02650487.2015.1137537

Bering, J. M., & Bjorklund, D. F. (2007). The serpent's gift: Evolutionary psychology and consciousness. In P. D. Zelazo, M. Moscovitch, & E. Thompson (Eds.), *The Cambridge handbook of consciousness* (pp. 597–630). Cambridge University Press.

Berk, E. (2008a). Leptin. In K. Keller (Ed.), *Encyclopedia of obesity* (Vol. 2, pp. 425–426). Sage.

Berk, E. (2008b). Thrifty gene hypothesis. In K. Keller (Ed.), *Encyclopedia of obesity* (Vol. 2, pp. 743–745). Sage.

Berkowitz, L. (1989). Frustration-aggression hypothesis: Examination and reformulation. *Psychological Bulletin, 106*(1), 59–73.

Berkowitz, L. (1993). *Aggression: Its causes, consequences, and control*. McGraw-Hill.

Berkowitz, L., & Harmon-Jones, E. (2004). Toward an understanding of the determinants of anger. *Emotion, 4*(2), 107–130.

Berlan, E. D., Corliss, H. L., Field, A. E., Goodman, E., & Austin, S. B. (2010). Sexual orientation and bullying among adolescents in the Growing Up Today Study. *Journal of Adolescent Health, 46*(4), 366–371.

Berlin, B. O., & Kay, P. D. (1969). *Basic color terms*. University of California Press.

Berlyne, D. E. (1960). *Conflict, arousal, and curiosity*. McGraw-Hill.

Bermudes, R. A., Wright, J. H., & Casey, D. (2009). Techniques of cognitive-behavioral therapy. In G. O. Gabbard (Ed.), *Textbook of psychotherapeutic treatments* (pp. 201–237). American Psychiatric Publishing.

Bernal, G., & Gomez-Arroyo, K. (2017). Family therapy: Theory and practice. In A. J. Consoli, L. E. Beutler, & B. Bongar (Eds.), *Comprehensive textbook of psychotherapy: Theory and practice* (2nd ed., pp. 239–253). Oxford University Press.

Bernal, G., Jiménez-Chafey, M. I., & Domenech Rodríguez, M. M. (2009). Cultural adaptation of treatments: A resource for considering culture in evidence-based practice. *Professional Psychology: Research and Practice, 40*(4), 361–368. https://doi.org/10.1037/a0016401

Bernstein, D. (2018). Flashbulb memories and social identity. In O. Luminet & A. Curci (Eds.), *Flashbulb memories: New challenges and future perspectives* (2nd ed., pp. 182–200). Routledge.

Bernstein, I. L. (1978). Learned taste aversions in children receiving chemotherapy. *Science, 200*(4347), 1302–1303.

Bernstein, I. L. (1999). Taste aversion learning: A contemporary perspective. *Nutrition, 15*(3), 229–234.

Bernstein, I. L., & Webster, M. M. (1985). Learned food aversions: A consequence of cancer chemotherapy. In T. G. Burish, S. M. Levy, & B. E. Meyerowitz (Eds.), *Cancer, nutrition, and eating behavior* (pp. 103–116). Lawrence Erlbaum.

Berntsen, D. (1996). Involuntary autobiographical memories. *Applied Cognitive Psychology, 10*(5), 435–454.

Berntsen, D. (2001). Involuntary memories of emotional events: Do memories of traumas and extremely happy events differ? *Applied Cognitive Psychology, 15*(7), S135–S158.

Berrettini, W., & Lohoff, F. W. (2017). Genetics of bipolar and unipolar disorders. In R. J. DeRubeis & D. R. Strunk (Eds.), *The Oxford handbook of mood disorders* (pp. 111–119). Oxford University Press.

Berry, J. W. (1970). Marginality, stress and ethnic identification in an acculturated Aboriginal community. *Journal of Cross-Cultural Psychology, 1*(3), 239–252.

Berry, J. W. (1980). Acculturation as varieties of adaptation. In A. Padilla (Ed.), *Acculturation: Theory, models and findings* (pp. 9–25). Westview Press.

Berry, J. W. (2003). Conceptual approaches to acculturation. In K. M. Chun, P. B. Organista, & G. Marin (Eds.), *Acculturation: Advances in theory, measurement, and applied research* (pp. 17–37). American Psychological Association.

Berry, J. W. (2006a). Contexts of acculturation. In D. L. Sam & J. W. Berry (Eds.), *The Cambridge handbook of acculturation psychology* (pp. 27–42). Cambridge University Press.

Berry, J. W. (2006b). Stress perspectives on acculturation. In D. L. Sam & J. W. Berry (Eds.), *The Cambridge handbook of acculturation psychology* (pp. 43–57). Cambridge University Press.

Berry, J. W. (2015). Acculturation. In J. E. Grusec & P. D. Hastings (Eds.), *Handbook of socialization: Theory and research* (pp. 520–538). Guilford Press.

Berry, J. W. (2017). Theories and models of acculturation. In S. J. Schwartz & J. B. Unger (Eds.), *The Oxford handbook of acculturation and health* (pp. 15–28). Oxford University Press.

Berry, J. W., & Sam, D. L. (1997). Acculturation and adaptation. In J. W. Berry, M. H. Segal, & C. Kagitöibasi (Eds.), *Handbook of cross-cultural psychology* (Vol. 3, pp. 293–326). Allyn & Bacon.

Berry, J. W., Kim, U., Minde, T., & Mok, D. (1987). Comparative studies of acculturative stress. *International Migration Review, 21*(3), 491–511.

Berry, K. M., Erickson, D. J., Berger, A. T., Wahlstrom, K., Iber, C., Full, K. M., Redline, S., & Widome, R. (2021). Association of delaying school start time with sleep–wake behaviors among adolescents. *Journal of Adolescent Health*. https://doi.org/10.1016/j.jadohealth.2021.04.030

Berryhill, M. B., Halli-Tierney, A., Culmer, N., Williams, N., Betancourt, A., King, M., & Ruggles, H. (2018). Videoconferencing psychological therapy and anxiety: A systematic review. *Family Practice, 36*(1), 53–63.

Bertrand, M., & Mullainathan, S. (2003). Are Emily and Greg more employable than Lakisha and Jamal? A field experiment on labor market discrimination. *American Economics Review, 94*(4), 991–1013.

Best, P., Manktelow, R., & Taylor, B. (2014). Online communication, social media and adolescent wellbeing: A systematic narrative review. *Children and Youth Services Review, 41*, 27–36.

Betancourt, H., & López, S. R. (1993). The study of culture, ethnicity, and race in American psychology. *American Psychologist, 48*(6), 629–637.

Betz, D. E., Ramsey, L. R., & Sekaquaptewa, D. (2013). Gender stereotype threat among women and girls. In M. K. Ryan & N. R. Branscombe (Eds.), *The Sage handbook of gender and psychology* (pp. 428–450). Sage.

Beyers, W., & Seiffge-Krenke, I. (2010). Does identity precede intimacy? Testing Erikson's theory on romantic development in emerging adults of the 21st century. *Journal of Adolescent Research, 25*(3), 387–415.

Bezdek, M. A., Gerrig, R. J., Wenzel, W. G., Shin, J., Revill, K. P., & Schumacher, E. H. (2015). Neural evidence that suspense narrows attentional focus. *Neuroscience, 303*, 338–345.

Bhawuk, D. P. S. (2018). Individualism and collectivism. In Y. Y. Kim (Gen. Ed.) & K. L. McKay-Semmler (Assoc. Ed.), *The international encyclopedia of intercultural communication* (Vol. 2, pp. 920–929). John Wiley & Sons. https://doi.org/10.1002/9781118783665

Bhutani, S., Dellen, M. R. V., & Cooper, J. A. (2021). Longitudinal weight gain and related risk behaviors during the COVID-19 pandemic in adults in the US. *Nutrients, 13*(2), 671. https://doi.org/10.3390/nu13020671

Bibok, M. B., Müller, U., & Carpendale, J. I. M. (2009). Childhood. In U. Müller, J. I. M. Carpendale, & L. Smith (Eds.), *The Cambridge companion to Piaget* (pp. 229–254). Cambridge University Press.

Bichakjian, B. H. (2017). Language evolution: How language was built and made to evolve. *Language Sciences, 63*, 119–129.

Bickerton, D. (1992). *Language and species*. University of Chicago Press.

Bickerton, D. (2009). *Adam's tongue: How humans made language, how language made humans*. Hill and Wang.

Bickerton, D. (2013). The evolution of language. In D. Reisberg (Ed.), *The Oxford handbook of cognitive psychology* (pp. 524–538). Oxford University Press.

Bickerton, D., & Szathmáry, E. (Eds.). (2009). *Biological foundations and origin of syntax*. MIT Press.

Biggs, A., Brough, P., & Drummond, S. (2017). Lazarus and Folkman's psychological stress and coping theory. In C. L. Cooper & J. C. Quick (Eds.), *The handbook of stress and health: A guide to research and practice* (pp. 351–364). Wiley-Blackwell.

Birbiglia, M. (2011). *Sleepwalk with me: And other painfully true stories*. Simon & Schuster.

Birditt, K. S., Fingerman, K. L., & Almeida, D. M. (2005). Age differences in exposure and reactions to interpersonal tensions: A daily diary study. *Psychology and Aging, 20*(2), 330.

Birman, D., & Simon, C. D. (2014). Acculturation research: Challenges, complexities, and possibilities. In F. T. L. Leong (Ed.), *APA handbook of multicultural psychology* (Vol. 1, pp. 207–230). American Psychological Association.

Birney, D. P., Citron-Pousty, J. H., Lutz, D. J., & Sternberg, R. J. (2005). The development of cognitive and intellectual abilities. In M. H. Bornstein & M. E. Lamb (Eds.), *Developmental science: An advanced textbook* (5th ed., pp. 327–358). Lawrence Erlbaum.

Bishop, S. R., Lau, M., Shapiro, S., Carlson, L., Anderson, N. D., Carmody, J., Devins, G. (2004). Mindfulness: A proposed operational definition. *Clinical Psychology: Science and Practice, 11*(3), 230–241.

Biswas-Diener, R., & Diener, E. (2001). Making the best of a bad situation: Satisfaction in the slums of Calcutta. *Social Indicators Research, 55*(3), 329–352.

Bjerkeset, O., Romundstad, P., Evans, J., & Gunnell, D. (2008). Association of adult body mass index and height with anxiety, depression, and suicide in the general population: The HUNT Study. *American Journal of Epidemiology, 167*(2), 193–202.

Bjork, E. L., Bjork, R. A., & Anderson, M. C. (1998). Varieties of goal-directed forgetting. In J. M. Golding & C. Macleod (Eds.), *Intentional forgetting: Interdisciplinary approaches* (pp. 103–137). Erlbaum.

Bjork, R. A. (1972). Theoretical implications of directed forgetting. In A. W. Melton & E. Martin (Eds.), *Coding processes in human memory* (pp. 217–235). V. M. Winston.

Bjork, R. A. (1978). The updating of human memory. In G. H. Bower (Ed.), *The psychology of learning and motivation* (Vol. 12, pp. 235–259). Academic Press.

Bjork, R. A. (1989). Retrieval inhibition as an adaptive mechanism in human memory. In H. L. Roediger & F. I. M. Craik (Eds.), *Varieties of memory and consciousness: Essays in honor of Endel Tulving* (pp. 309–330). Erlbaum.

Bjork, R. A. (2011). On the symbiosis of remembering, forgetting, and learning. In A. S. Benjamin (Ed.), *Successful remembering and successful forgetting: A Festschrift in honor of Robert A. Bjork* (pp. 1–22). Psychology Press.

Bjork, R. A. (2014). Forgetting as a friend of learning. In D. S. Lindsay, C. M. Kelley, A. P. Yonelinas, & H. L. Roediger III (Eds.), *Remembering* (pp. 39–52). Psychology Press.

Bjørkløf, G. H., Engedal, K., Selbæk, G., Kouwenhoven, S. E., & Helvik, A. S. (2013). Coping and depression in old age: A literature review. *Dementia and Geriatric Cognitive Disorders, 35*(3–4), 121–154.

Björkqvist, K. (2018). Gender differences in aggression. *Current Opinion in Psychology, 19*, 39–42.

Blackwell, L. S., Trzesniewski, K. H., & Dweck, C. S. (2007). Implicit theories of intelligence predict achievement across an adolescent transition: A longitudinal study and an intervention. *Child Development, 78*(1), 246–263.

Blair, R. J. R. (2007). The amygdala and ventromedial prefrontal cortex in morality and psychopathy. *Trends in Cognitive Sciences, 11*(9), 387–392.

Blake, J. J., Keith, V. M., Luo, W., Le, H., & Salter, P. (2017). The role of colorism in explaining African American females' suspension risk. *School Psychology Quarterly, 32*(1), 118–130. https://doi.org/10.1037/spq0000173

Blakey, S. M., & Abramowitz, J. S. (2018). Obsessive-compulsive disorder. In J. Hunsley & E. J. Mash (Eds.), *A guide to assessments that work* (2nd ed., pp. 311–328). Oxford University Press.

Blanchard, R. J., Blanchard, D. C., Griebel, G., & Nutt, D. (2008). Introduction to the handbook on fear and anxiety. In R. J. Blanchard, D. C. Blanchard, G. Griebel, & D. Nutt (Eds.), *Handbook of anxiety and fear* (pp. 3–7). Elsevier.

Blanck, P., Perleth, S., Heidenreich, T., Kröger, P., Ditzen, B., Bents, H., & Mander, J. S. (2018). Effects of mindfulness exercises as stand-alone intervention on symptoms of anxiety and depression: Systematic review and meta-analysis. *Behaviour Research and Therapy, 102*, 25–35.

Blanco, C., Schneier, F. R., Vesga-Lopez, O., & Liebowitz, M. R. (2010). Pharmacotherapy for social anxiety disorder. In D. J. Stein, E. Hollander, & B. O. Rothbaum (Eds.), *Textbook of anxiety disorders* (2nd ed., pp. 471–499). American Psychiatric Publishing.

Blanton, J. S. (2007). In the halls of business: Consulting psychology as a career. In R. J. Sternberg (Ed.), *Career paths in psychology: Where your degree can take you* (2nd ed., pp. 259–278). American Psychological Association.

Blashfield, R. K., & Burgess, D. R. (2007). Classification provides an essential basis for organizing mental disorders. In S. O. Lilienfeld & W. T. O'Donohue (Eds.), *The great ideas of clinical science: 17 principles that every mental health professional should understand* (pp. 93–117). Routledge.

Blashfield, R. K., Flanagan, E., & Raley, K. (2010). Themes in the evolution of the 20th-century DSMs. In T. Millon, R. F. Krueger, & E. Simonsen (Eds.), *Contemporary directions in psychopathology: Scientific foundations of the DSM-IV and ICD-11* (pp. 53–71). Guilford Press.

Blashfield, R. K., Keeley, J. W., & Burgess, D. R. (2009). Classification. In P. H. Blaney & T. Millon (Eds.), *Oxford textbook of psychopathology* (pp. 35–57). Oxford University Press.

Blashfield, R. K., Keeley, J. W., Flanagan, E. H., & Miles, S. R. (2014). The cycle of classification: DSM-I through DSM-5. *Annual Review of Clinical Psychology, 10*, 25–51.

Blass, T. (Ed.). (1999a). *Obedience to authority: Current perspectives on the Milgram paradigm*. Lawrence Erlbaum.

Blass, T. (1999b). The Milgram paradigm after 35 years: Some things we now know about obedience to authority. *Journal of Applied Social Psychology, 29*(5), 955–978.

Blass, T. (2004). *The man who shocked the world: The life and legacy of Stanley Milgram*. Basic Books.

Blass, T. (2009). *The man who shocked the world: The life and legacy of Stanley Milgram* (Paperback ed.). Basic Books.

Blass, T., & Schmitt, C. (2001). The nature of perceived authority in the Milgram paradigm: Two replications. *Current Psychology, 20*(2), 115–121.

Blazer, D. (2013). Neurocognitive disorders in DSM-5. *American Journal of Psychiatry, 170*(6), 585–587.

Bleidorn, W., & Hopwood, C. J. (2019). Stability and change in personality traits over the lifespan. In D. P. McAdams, R. L. Shiner, & J. L. Tackett (Eds.), *Handbook of personality development* (pp. 237–254). Guilford Press.

Bliss, T. V., & Collingridge, G. L. (1993). A synaptic model of memory: Long-term potentiation in the hippocampus. *Nature, 361*(6407), 31–39.

Block, J. (1995). A contrarian view of the five-factor approach to personality description. *Psychological Bulletin, 117*(2), 187–215.

Bloedon, L. T., & Szapary, P. O. (2009). Coronary heart disease. In B. P. Jacobs & K. Gundling (Eds.), *The ACP evidence-based guide to complementary and alternative medicine* (pp. 161–200). American College of Physicians.

Blood, A. J., & Zatorre, R. J. (2001). Intensely pleasurable responses to music correlate with activity in brain regions implicated in reward and emotion. *Proceedings of the National Academy of Sciences, 98*(20), 11818–11823.

Bloom, B., Jones, L. I., & Freeman, G. (2013). Summary health statistics for U.S. children: National Health Interview Survey, 2012. *Vital and Health Statistics, 10*(258), 1–81.

Bloom, P. (2002). *How children learn the meanings of words*. MIT Press.

Blow, F. C., Zeber, J. E., McCarthy, J. F., Valenstein, M., Gillon, L., & Bingham, C. R. (2004). Ethnicity and diagnostic patterns in veterans with psychoses. *Social Psychiatry and Psychiatric Epidemiology, 39*(10), 841–851.

Blowers, G. (2006). Origins of scientific psychology in China 1899–1949. In A. C. Brock (Ed.), *Internationalizing the history of psychology* (pp. 94–111). New York University Press.

Bluck, S., Alea, N., & Demiray, B. (2010). You get what you need: The psychosocial functions of remembering. In J. H. Mace (Ed.), *The act of remembering* (pp. 284–307). Wiley-Blackwell.

Blum, D. (2002). *Love at Goon Park: Harry Harlow and the science of affection*. Perseus.

Blumberg, M. S., & Rattenborg, N. C. (2017). Decomposing the evolution of sleep: Comparative and developmental approaches. In J. Kaas (Ed.), *Evolution of nervous systems* (Vol. 2, pp. 523–545). Elsevier.

Blume, A. W., Lovato, L. V., Thyken, B. N., & Denny, N. (2012). The relationship of microaggressions with alcohol use and anxiety among ethnic minority college students in a historically White institution. *Cultural Diversity and Ethnic Minority Psychology, 18*(1), 45–54.

Blumenthal, A. L. (1997). Wilhelm Wundt. In W. G. Bringmann, H. E. Lück, R. Miller, & C. E. Early (Eds.), *A pictorial history of psychology* (pp. 117–125). Quintessence Publishing.

Blumenthal, A. L. (2002). A reappraisal of Wilhelm Wundt. In W. E. Pickren & D. A. Dewsbury (Eds.), *Evolving perspectives on the history of psychology* (pp. 65–78). American Psychological Association.

Blustein, D. L., Thompson, M. N., Kozan, S., & Allan, B. A. (2021). Intersecting losses and integrative practices: Work and mental health during the COVID-19 era and beyond. *Professional Psychology: Research and Practice, 52*(5), 523–532. https://doi.org/10.1037/pro0000425

Bobbitt-Zeher, D., Downey, D. B., & Merry, J. (2016). Number of siblings during childhood and the likelihood of divorce in adulthood. *Journal of Family Issues, 37*(15), 2075–2094.

Bochner, S. (1994). Cross-cultural differences in the self-concept: A test of Hofstede's individualism/collectivism distinction. *Journal of Cross-Cultural Psychology, 25*(2), 273–283.

Bockting, W. O., Miner, M. H., Swinburne Romine, R. E., Hamilton, A., & Coleman, E. (2013). Stigma, mental health, and resilience in an online sample of the U.S. transgender population. *American Journal of Public Health, 103*(5), 943–951.

Boecker, H., Sprenger, T., Spilker, M. E., Henriksen, G., Koppenhoefer, M., Wagner, K. J., Valet, M., Berthele, A., & Tolle, T. R. (2008). The runner's high: Opioidergic mechanisms in the human brain. *Cerebral Cortex, 18*(11), 2523–2531.

Boehm, J. K., & Kubzansky, L. D. (2012). The heart's content: The association between positive psychological well-being and cardiovascular health. *Psychological Bulletin, 138*(4), 655–691.

Boehm, J. K., Lyubomirsky, S., & Sheldon, K. M. (2011). A longitudinal experimental study comparing the effectiveness of happiness-enhancing strategies in Anglo Americans and Asian Americans. *Cognition & Emotion, 25*(7), 1263–1272.

Boerner, K., Stroebe, M., Schut, H., & Wortman, C. B. (2015). Theories of grief and bereavement. In N. Pachana (Ed.), *Encyclopedia of geropsychology* (pp. 1–10). Springer.

Bogdan, A., Bouchareb, B., & Touitou, Y. (2001). Ramadan fasting alters endocrine and neuroendocrine circadian patterns. Meal-time as a synchronizer in humans? *Life Sciences, 68*(14), 1607–1615.

Bogle, K. (2008). *Hooking up*. New York University Press.

Bohart, A. C., & Tallman, K. (1999). *How clients make therapy work: The process of active self-healing*. American Psychological Association.

Bohlmeijer, E., Prenger, R., Taal, E., & Cuijpers, P. (2010). The effects of mindfulness-based stress reduction therapy on mental health of adults with a chronic medical disease: A meta-analysis. *Journal of Psychosomatic Research, 68*(6), 539–544.

Bohlmeijer, E., Roemer, M., Cuijpers, P., & Smit, F. (2007). The effects of reminiscence on psychological well-being in older adults: A meta-analysis. *Aging and Mental Health, 11*(3), 291–300.

Bohlmeijer, E., Smit, F., & Cuijpers, P. (2003). Effects of reminiscence and life review on late-life depression: A meta-analysis. *International Journal of Geriatric Psychiatry, 18*(12), 1088–1094.

Boksem, M. A., & Smidts, A. (2015). Brain responses to movie trailers predict individual preferences for movies and their population-wide commercial success. *Journal of Marketing Research, 52*(4), 482–492.

Bolger, D. J., Perfetti, C. A., & Schneider, W. (2005). Cross-cultural effect on the brain revisited: Universal structures plus writing system variation. *Human Brain Mapping, 25*(1), 92–104.

Bolzan, S., Bolzan, J., & Rother, C. (2011). *My life, deleted: A memoir*. HarperCollins.

Bombak, A., Monaghan, L. F., & Rich, E. (2018). Dietary approaches to weight-loss, Health at Every Size® and beyond: Rethinking the war on obesity. *Social Theory & Health, 17*, 89–108. https://doi.org/10.1057/s41285-018-0070-9

Bonanno, G. A. (2004). Loss, trauma, and human resilience: Have we underestimated the human capacity to thrive after extremely aversive events? *American Psychologist, 59*(1), 20–28.

Bonanno, G. A. (2009). *The other side of sadness: What the new science of bereavement tells us about life after loss*. Basic Books.

Bonanno, G. A., Galea, S., Bucciarelli, A., & Vlahov, D. (2007). What predicts psychological resilience after disaster? The role of demographics, resources, and life stress. *Journal of Consulting and Clinical Psychology, 75*(5), 671–682.

Bonanno, G. A., Goorin, L., & Coifman, K. G. (2008). Sadness and grief. In M. Lewis, J. M. Haviland-Jones, & L. F. Barrett (Eds.), *Handbook of emotions* (3rd ed., pp. 797–810). Guilford Press.

Bond, A. E., Wagler, K., & Anestis, M. D. (2021). Essential workers: Past month suicidal ideation and COVID-19 stress. *Journal of Clinical Psychology, 77*(12), 2849–2859. https://doi.org/10.1002/jclp.23276

Bond, M. H. (2004). Culture and aggression—from context to coercion. *Personality and Social Psychology Review, 8*(1), 62–78.

Bond, R., & Smith, P. B. (1996). Culture and conformity: A meta-analysis of studies using Asch's (1952b, 1956) line judgment task. *Psychological Bulletin, 119*(1), 111.

Bonnie, R. J., & Scott, E. S. (2013). The teenage brain: Adolescent brain research and the law. *Current Directions in Psychological Science, 22*(2), 158–161.

Booth, A. L., & Kee, H. J. (2009). Birth order matters: The effect of family size and birth order on educational attainment. *Journal of Population Economics, 22*(2), 367–397.

Booth-Kewley, S., & Friedman, H. S. (1987). Psychological predictors of heart disease: A quantitative review. *Psychological Bulletin, 101*(3), 343–362.

Booth-Kewley, S., & Vickers, R. R. (1994). Associations between major domains of personality and health behavior. *Journal of Personality, 62*(3), 281–298.

Borbély, A. A. (1982). A two-process model of sleep regulation. *Human Neurobiology, 1*(3), 195–204.

Borca, G., Bina, M., Keller, P. S., Gilbert, L. R., & Begotti, T. (2015). Internet use and developmental tasks: Adolescents' point of view. *Computers in Human Behavior, 52*, 49–58.

Borghuis, J., Denissen, J. J., Oberski, D., Sijtsma, K., Meeus, W. H., Branje, S., Koot, H. M., & Bleidorn, W. (2017). Big Five personality stability, change, and codevelopment across adolescence and early adulthood. *Journal of Personality and Social Psychology, 113*(4), 641.

Born, J., Rasch, B., & Gais, S. (2006). Sleep to remember. *Neuroscientist, 12*(5), 410–424.

Bornstein, M. H. (1999). Human infancy: Past, present, future. In M. Bennett (Ed.), *Developmental psychology: Achievements and prospects* (pp. 13–35). Psychology Press.

Bornstein, M. H., Arterberry, M. E., & Mash, C. (2005). Perceptual development. In M. H. Bornstein & M. E. Lamb (Eds.), *Developmental science: An advanced textbook* (5th ed., pp. 283–325). Lawrence Erlbaum.

Bornstein, M. H., & Bradley, R. H. (2003). *Socioeconomic status, parenting, and child development*. Lawrence Erlbaum.

Bornstein, R. F. (1989). Exposure and affect: Overview and meta-analysis of research, 1968–1987. *Psychological Bulletin, 106*(2), 265–289.

Boroditsky, L. (2011). How language shapes thought. *Scientific American, 304*(2), 62–65.

Boroditsky, L. (2012). How the languages we speak shape the ways we think: The FAQs. In M. Spivey, M. Joanisse, & K. McRae (Eds.), *The Cambridge handbook of psycholinguistics* (pp. 615–632). Cambridge University Press.

Boroditsky, L., & Gaby, A. (2006). East of Tuesday: Representing time in absolute space. In *Proceedings of the 28th Annual Meeting of the Cognitive Science Society, Vancouver, BC, Canada*. Lawrence Erlbaum.

Boroditsky, L., Schmidt, L. S., & Phillips, W. (2003). Sex, syntax, and semantics. In D. Gentner & S. Goldin-Meadow (Eds.), *Language in mind: Advances in the study of language and thought* (pp. 61–80). MIT Press.

Bos, J. E., Bles, W., & Groen, E. L. (2008). A theory on visually induced motion sickness. *Displays, 29*(2), 47–57.

Bosch, J. A., Engeland, C. G., Cacioppo, J. T., & Marucha, P. T. (2007). Depressive symptoms predict mucosal wound healing. *Psychosomatic Medicine, 69*(7), 597–605.

Bosma, H., & Gerlsma, C. (2003). From early attachment relations to the adolescent and adult organization of self. In J. Valsiner & K. Connolly (Eds.), *Handbook of developmental psychology* (pp. 450–488). Sage.

Bostwick, W. B., Boyd, C. J., Hughes, T. L., West, B. T., & McCabe, S. E. (2014). Discrimination and mental health among lesbian, gay, and bisexual adults in the United States. *American Journal of Orthopsychiatry, 84*(1), 35–45.

Boswell, J. F., Iles, B. R., Gallagher, M. W., & Farchione, T. J. (2017). Behavioral activation strategies in cognitive-behavioral therapy for anxiety disorders. *Psychotherapy, 54*(3), 231–236.

Boswell, J. F., Sharpless, B. A., Greenberg, L. S., Heatherington, L., Huppert, J. D., Barber, J. P., Goldfried, M., & Castonguay, L. G. (2011). Schools of psychotherapy and the beginnings of a scientific approach. In D. H. Barlow (Ed.), *The Oxford handbook of clinical psychology* (pp. 98–127). Oxford University Press.

Both, S., Brauer, M., & Laan, E. (2011). Classical conditioning of sexual response in women: A replication study. *The Journal of Sexual Medicine, 8*(11), 3116–3131.

Bottoms, B. L., Shaver, P. R., & Goodman, G. S. (1996). An analysis of ritualistic and religion-related child abuse allegations. *Law and Human Behavior, 20*(1), 1–34.

Bouchard, C., Tremblay, A., Després, J. P., Thériault, G., Nadeauf, A., Lupien, P. J., ... Fournier, G. (1994). The response to exercise with constant energy intake in identical twins. *Obesity Research, 2*(5), 400–410.

Bouchard, T. J., Jr. (2004). Genetic influence on human psychological traits: A survey. *Current Directions in Psychological Science, 13*(4), 148–151.

Bouchard, T. J. (2013). The Wilson effect: The increase in heritability of IQ with age. *Twin Research and Human Genetics, 16*(05), 923–930.

Bouchard, T. J., & McGue, M. (1981). Familial studies of intelligence: A review. *Science, 212*(4498), 1055–1059.

Bouchard, T. J., & McGue, M. (2003). Genetic and environmental influences on human psychological differences. *Journal of Neurobiology, 54*(1), 4–45.

Bouchard, T. J., Lykken, D. T., McGue, M., Segal, N. L., & Tellegen, A. (1990). Sources of human psychological differences: The Minnesota study of twins reared apart. *Science, 250*(4978), 223–228.

Boulougouris, J. C., Marks, I. M., & Marset, P. (1971). Superiority of flooding (implosion) to desensitisation for reducing pathological fear. *Behaviour Research and Therapy, 9*(1), 7–16.

Bowen, S., Vietan, C., Witkiewitz, K., & Carroll, H. (2015). A mindfulness-based approach to addiction. In K. W. Brown, J. D. Creswell, & R. M. Ryan (Eds.), *Handbook of mindfulness: Theory, research, and practice* (pp. 387–404). Guilford Press.

Bower, G. H. (1981). Mood and memory. *American Psychologist, 36*(2), 129–148.

Bower, G. H. (2000). A brief history of memory research. In E. Tulving & F. I. M. Craik (Eds.), *The Oxford handbook of memory* (pp. 3–32). Oxford University Press.

Bowers, J. S., & Davis, C. J. (2004). Is speech perception modular or interactive? *Trends in Cognitive Sciences, 8*(1), 3–5.

Bowlby, J. (1969). *Attachment and loss* (Vol. 1). Basic Books.

Bowlby, J. (1973). *Attachment and loss* (Vol. 2). Basic Books.

Bowlby, J. (1988). *A secure base*. Basic Books.

Bowleg, L. (2020). We're not all in this together: On COVID-19, intersectionality, and structural inequality. *American Journal of Public Health, 110*(7), 917–917. https://doi.org/10.2105/AJPH.2020.305766

Bowler, D. M. (1992). "Theory of mind" in Asperger's syndrome. *Journal of Child Psychology and Psychiatry, 33*(5), 877–893.

Boyce, C. J., Daly, M., Hounkpatin, H. O., & Wood, A. M. (2017). Money may buy happiness, but often so little that it doesn't matter. *Psychological Science, 28*(4), 544-546. https://doi.org/10.1177/0956797616672271

Boylan, J. F. (2003). *She's not there: A life in two genders*. Broadway Books.

Boyle, G. J. (2008). Critique of the Five-Factor Model of personality. In G. J. Boyle, G. Matthews, & D. H. Saklofske (Eds.), *The Sage handbook of personality theory and assessment* (Vol. 1, pp. 295–312). Sage.

Boynton-Jarrett, R., Wright, R. J., Putnam, F. W., Lividoti Hibert, E., Michels, K. B., Forman, M. R., & Rich-Edwards, J. (2013). Childhood abuse and age at menarche. *Journal of Adolescent Health, 52*(2), 241–247.

Boysen, G. A., Wells, A. M., & Dawson, K. J. (2016). Instructors' use of trigger warnings and behavior warnings in Abnormal Psychology. *Teaching of Psychology, 43*(4), 334–339.

Bozarth, J. D. (1997). Empathy from the framework of client-centered theory and the Rogerian hypothesis. In A. C. Bohart & L. S. Greenberg (Eds.), *Empathy reconsidered: New directions in psychotherapy* (pp. 81–102). American Psychological Association.

Bozarth, J. D., Zimring, F. M., & Tausch, R. (2002). Client-centered therapy: The evolution of a revolution. In D. J. Cain & J. Seeman (Eds.), *Humanistic psychotherapies: Handbook of research and practice* (pp. 147–188). American Psychological Association.

Brabender, V. A. (2002). *Introduction to group therapy*. Wiley.

Bracha, H. S., & Maser, J. D. (2008). Anxiety and posttraumatic stress disorder in the context of human brain evolution: A role for theory in DSM-V? *Clinical Psychology: Science and Practice, 15*(1), 91–97.

Bracken, B. A., & McCallum, S. (2009). Universal Nonverbal Intelligence Test (UNIT). In J. A. Naglieri & S. Goldstein (Eds.), *Practitioner's guide to assessing intelligence and achievement* (pp. 291–313). Wiley.

Bradbury, T. N., & Miller, G. A. (1985). Season of birth in schizophrenia: A review of evidence, methodology, and etiology. *Psychological Bulletin, 98*(3), 569–594.

Bradley, R., Conklin, C. Z., & Westen, D. (2007). Borderline personality disorder. In W. O'Donohue, K. A. Fowler, & S. O. Lilienfeld (Eds.), *Personality disorders: Toward the DSM-V* (pp. 167–201). Sage.

Brand, A., Behrend, O., Marquardt, T., McAlpine, D., & Grothe, B. (2002). Precise inhibition is essential for microsecond interaural time difference coding. *Nature, 417*(6888), 543–547.

Brand, B. L., Sar, V., Stavropoulos, P., Krüger, C., Korzekwa, M., Martínez-Taboas, A., & Middleton, W. (2016). Separating fact from fiction: An empirical examination of six myths about dissociative identity disorder. *Harvard Review of Psychiatry, 24*(4), 257–270.

Brand, M., Eggers, C., Reinhold, N., Fujiwara, E., Kessler, J., Heiss, W. D., & Markowitsch, H. J. (2009). Functional brain imaging in 14 patients with dissociative amnesia reveals right inferolateral prefrontal hypometabolism. *Psychiatry Research: Neuroimaging, 174*(1), 32–39.

Brand, M., & Markowitsch, H. J. (2010). Aspects of forgetting in psychogenic amnesia. In S. Della Sala (Ed.), *Forgetting* (pp. 239–251). Psychology Press.

Branje, S. J., van Doorn, M., van der Valk, I., & Meeus, W. (2009). Parent-adolescent conflicts, conflict resolution types, and adolescent adjustment. *Journal of Applied Developmental Psychology, 30*(2), 195–204.

Braslow, J. (1997). *Mental ills and bodily cures: Psychiatric treatment in the first half of the twentieth century*. University of California Press.

Bray, G. A. (2004). Medical consequences of obesity. *The Journal of Clinical Endocrinology & Metabolism, 89*(6), 2583–2589.

Bray, N. W., Pieruccini-Faria, F., Bartha, R., Doherty, T. J., Nagamatsu, L. S., & Montero-Odasso, M. (2021). The effect of physical exercise on functional brain network connectivity in older adults with and without cognitive impairment. A systematic review. *Mechanisms of Ageing and Development, 196*(6), 111493. https://doi.org/10.1016/j.mad.2021.111493

Brazelton, T. B., Koslowski, B., Main, M., Lewis, M., & Rosenblum, L. A. (1974). *The origins of reciprocity: The early mother-infant interaction*. Wiley-Interscience.

Brebion, G., Amador, X., Smith, M. J., & Gorman, J. M. (1997). Mechanisms underlying memory impairment in schizophrenia. *Psychological Medicine, 27*(2), 383–393.

Breggin, P. R. (2008). *Brain-disabling treatments in psychiatry: Drugs, electroshock, and the psychopharmaceutical complex* (2nd ed.). Springer.

Breinbauer, H. A., Anabalón, J. L., Gutierrez, D., Cárcamo, R., Olivares, C., & Caro, J. (2012). Output capabilities of personal music players and assessment of preferred listening levels of test subjects: Outlining recommendations for preventing music-induced hearing loss. *The Laryngoscope, 122*(11), 2549–2556.

Breland, K., & Breland, M. (1961). The misbehavior of organisms. *American Psychologist, 16*(11), 661–664.

Brelet, L., Ginet, M., Colomb, C., Jund, R., & Désert, M. (2018). Memory for cars among a female population: Is the cognitive interview beneficial in reducing stereotype threat? *Journal of Police and Criminal Psychology*, 1–12.

Bremner, J. D. (1999). Does stress damage the brain? *Biological Psychiatry, 45*(7), 797–805.

Bremner, J. D., & Charney, D. S. (2010). Neural circuits in fear and anxiety. In D. J. Stein, E. Hollander, & B. O. Rothbaum (Eds.), *Textbook of anxiety disorders* (2nd ed., pp. 55–71). American Psychiatric Publishing.

Brennan, P. A. (2010). Pheromones. In E. B. Goldstein (Ed.), *Encyclopedia of perception* (pp. 801–805). Sage.

Brenner, R. A., Simons-Morton, B. G., Bhaskar, B., Revenis, M., Das, A., & Clemens, J. D. (2003). Infant-parent bed sharing in an inner-city population. *Archives of Pediatrics & Adolescent Medicine, 157*(1), 33–39.

Breslau, N. (2009). The epidemiology of trauma, PTSD, and other posttrauma disorders. *Trauma, Violence, & Abuse, 10*(3), 198–210.

Brewer, M. B. (1988). A dual-process model of impression formation. In R. S. Wyer, Jr., & T. K. Srull (Eds.), *Advances in social cognition* (Vol. 1, pp. 1–36). Lawrence Erlbaum.

Brewer, M. B. (2007). The social psychology of intergroup relations: Social categorization, ingroup bias, and outgroup prejudice. In A. W. Kruglanski & E. T. Higgins (Eds.), *Social psychology: Handbook of basic principles* (2nd ed., pp. 695–715). Guilford Press.

Brewer, M. B., & Chen, Y. R. (2007). Where (who) are collectives in collectivism? Toward conceptual clarification of individualism and collectivism. *Psychological Review, 114*(1), 133–151.

Brewer, M. B., & Silver, M. (2006). Ingroup bias as a function of task characteristics. *European Journal of Social Psychology, 8*(3), 393–400.

Brick, J., & Erickson, C. K. (2013). *Drugs, the brain, and behavior: The pharmacology of drug use disorders*. Routledge.

Briere, J., Agee, E., & Dietrich, A. (2016). Cumulative trauma and current posttraumatic stress disorder status in general population and inmate samples. *Psychological Trauma: Theory, Research, Practice, and Policy, 8*(4), 439–446.

Brimeyer, T. M., & Smith, W. L. (2012). Religion, race, social class, and gender differences in dating and hooking up among college students. *Sociological Spectrum, 32*(5), 462–473.

Bringmann, W. G., Voss, U., & Ungerer, G. A. (1997). Wundt's laboratories. In W. G. Bringmann, H. E. Lück, R. Miller, & C. E. Early (Eds.), *A pictorial history of psychology* (pp. 126–132). Quintessence Publishing.

Briton, N. J., & Hall, J. A. (1995). Beliefs about female and male nonverbal communication. *Sex Roles, 32*(1–2), 79–90.

Britton, J. C., & Rauch, S. L. (2009). Neuroanatomy and neuroimaging of anxiety disorders. In M. M. Antony & M. B. Stein (Eds.), *Oxford handbook of anxiety and related disorders* (pp. 97–110). Oxford University Press.

Broadbent, D. E., & Gregory, M. (1964). Accuracy of recognition for speech presented to the right and left ears. *Quarterly Journal of Experimental Psychology, 16*(4), 359–360.

Broadbent, E., Ellis, C. J., Thomas, J., Gamble, G., & Petrie, K. J. (2009a). Further development of an illness perception intervention for myocardial infarction patients: A randomized controlled trial. *Journal of Psychosomatic Research, 67*(1), 17–23.

Broadbent, E., Ellis, C. J., Thomas, J., Gamble, G., & Petrie, K. J. (2009b). Can an illness perception intervention reduce illness anxiety in spouses of myocardial infarction patients? A randomized controlled trial. *Journal of Psychosomatic Research, 67*(1), 11–15.

Broadbent, E., Kahokehr, A., Booth, R. J., Thomas, J., Windsor, J. A., Buchanan, C. M., Wheeler, B. R. L., Sammour, T., & Hill, A. G. (2012). A brief relaxation intervention reduces stress and improves surgical wound healing response: A randomised trial. *Brain, Behavior, and Immunity, 26*(2), 212–217.

Broadbent, E., Petrie, K. J., Alley, P. G., & Booth, R. J. (2003). Psychological stress impairs early wound repair following surgery. *Psychosomatic Medicine, 65*(5), 865–869.

Broberg, D. J., & Bernstein, I. L. (1987). Candy as a scapegoat in the prevention of food aversions in children receiving chemotherapy. *Cancer, 60*(9), 2344–2347.

Brochu, P. M., & Morrison, M. A. (2007). Implicit and explicit prejudice toward overweight and average-weight men and women: Testing their correspondence and relation to behavioral intentions. *The Journal of Social Psychology, 147*(6), 681–706.

Brock, A. C. (2006). Introduction. In A. C. Brock (Ed.), *Internationalizing the history of psychology* (pp. 1–15). New York University Press.

Brockway, M., Benzies, K., & Hayden, K. A. (2017). Interventions to improve breastfeeding self-efficacy and resultant breastfeeding rates: A systematic review and meta-analysis. *Journal of Human Lactation, 33*(3), 486–499.

Brodal, P. (2010). *The central nervous system: Structure and function*. Oxford University Press.

Brody, A. L., Saxena, A. L., Saxena, S., Stoessel, P., Gillies, L. A., Alborzian, S., Phelps, M. E., Huang, S. C., Wu, H. M., Ho, M. L., Au, S. C., Maidment, K, & Baxter, L. R., Jr. (2001). Regional brain metabolic changes in patients with major depression treated with either paroxetine or interpersonal therapy: Preliminary findings. *Archives of General Psychiatry, 58*(7), 631–640.

Brody, L. R. (2000). The socialization of gender differences in emotional expression: Display rules, infant temperament, and differentiation. In A. H. Fischer (Ed.), *Gender and emotion: Social psychological perspectives* (pp. 24–47). Cambridge University Press.

Brody, L. R., & Hall, J. A. (2008). Gender and emotion in context. In M. Lewis, J. M. Haviland-Jones, & L. F. Barrett (Eds.), *Handbook of emotions* (3rd ed., pp. 395–408). Guilford Press.

Brody, L. R., & Hall, J. A. (2010). Gender, emotion, and socialization. In J. C. Chrisler & D. R. McCreary (Eds.), *Handbook of gender research in psychology* (Vol. 1, pp. 429–454). Springer.

Brom, M., Both, S., Laan, E., Everaerd, W., & Spinhoven, P. (2014). The role of conditioning, learning and dopamine in sexual behavior: A narrative review of animal and human studies. *Neuroscience & Biobehavioral Reviews, 38*, 38–59.

Brom, M., Laan, E., Everaerd, W., Spinhoven, P., & Both, S. (2015). Extinction of aversive classically conditioned human sexual response. *The Journal of Sexual Medicine, 12*(4), 916–935.

Brooks, D. (2007, October 26). The outsourced brain. *The New York Times*. https://www.nytimes.com/2007/10/26/opinion/26brooks.html

Brooks, L. R. (1978). Nonanalytic concept formation and memory for instances. In E. Rosch & B. B. Lloyd (Eds.), *Cognition and categorizations* (pp. 169–211). Erlbaum.

Brooks, R., & Meltzoff, A. N. (2005). The development of gaze following and its relation to language. *Developmental Science, 8*(6), 535–543.

Brooks, S. J., & Stein, D. J. (2015). A systematic review of the neural bases of psychotherapy for anxiety and related disorders. *Dialogues in Clinical Neuroscience, 17*(3), 261–279. https://doi.org/10.31887/DCNS.2015.17.3/sbrooks

Brose, A., Scheibe, S., & Schmiedek, F. (2013). Life contexts make a difference: Emotional stability in younger and older adults. *Psychology and Aging, 28*(1), 148–159.

Brougham, R. R., Zail, C. M., Mendoza, C. M., & Miller, J. R. (2009). Stress, sex differences, and coping strategies among college students. *Current Psychology, 28*(2), 85–97.

Brown, A. S., Begg, M. D., Gravenstein, S., Schaefer, C. A., Wyatt, R. J., Bresnahan, M., Babulas, V. P., & Susser, E. S. (2004). Serologic evidence of prenatal influenza in the etiology of schizophrenia. *Archives of General Psychiatry, 61*(8), 774–780.

Brown, B. B., & Larson, J. (2009). Peer relationships in adolescence. In R. M. Lerner & L. Steinberg (Eds.), *Handbook of adolescent psychiatry* (3rd ed., Vol. 2, pp. 74–103). Wiley.

Brown, D. L., & Pomerantz, A. M. (2011). Multicultural incompetence and other unethical behaviors: Perceptions of therapist practices. *Ethics & Behavior, 21*(6), 498–508.

Brown, E. G., Gallagher, S., & Creaven, A. M. (2018). Loneliness and acute stress reactivity: A systematic review of psychophysiological studies. *Psychophysiology, 55*(5), e13031.

Brown, G. D. A., & Lewandowsky, S. (2010). Forgetting in memory models: Arguments against trace decay and consolidation failure. In S. Della Sala (Ed.), *Forgetting* (pp. 49–75). Psychology Press.

Brown, G. D., Neath, I., & Chater, N. (2007). A temporal ratio model of memory. *Psychological Review, 114*(3), 539–576.

Brown, J. (1958). Some tests of the decay theory of immediate memory. *Quarterly Journal of Experimental Psychology, 10*(1), 12–21.

Brown, J. S. (1965). Generalization and discrimination. In D. I. Mostofsky (Ed.), *Stimulus generalization* (pp. 7–23). Stanford University Press.

Brown, K. W. (2015). Mindfulness training to enhance positive functioning. In K. W. Brown, J. D. Creswell, & R. M. Ryan (Eds.), *Handbook of mindfulness: Theory, research, and practice* (pp. 311–328). Guilford Press.

Brown, K. W., Creswell, J. D., & Ryan, R. M. (2015). Introduction: The evolution of mindfulness science. In K. W. Brown, J. D. Creswell, & R. M. Ryan (Eds.), *Handbook of mindfulness: Theory, research, and practice* (pp. 1–8). Guilford Press.

Brown, K. W., Goodman, R. J., & Inzlicht, M. (2012). Dispositional mindfulness and the attenuation of neural responses to emotional stimuli. *Social Cognitive and Affective Neuroscience, 8*(1), 93–99.

Brown, K. W., & Ryan, R. M. (2004). Perils and promise in defining and measuring mindfulness: Observations from experience. *Clinical Psychology: Science and Practice, 11*(3), 242–248.

Brown, L. H., & Roodin, P. A. (2003). Grandparent-grandchild relationships and the life-course perspective. In J. Demick & C. Andreoletti (Eds.), *Handbook of adult development* (pp. 459–474). Springer Science+Business Media.

Brown, L. S. (2006). The neglect of lesbian, gay, bisexual, and transgendered clients. In J. C. Norcross, L. E. Beutler, & R. F. Levant (Eds.), *Evidence-based practices in mental health: Debate and dialogue on the fundamental questions* (pp. 346–353). American Psychological Association.

Brown, L. S. (2008). *Cultural competence in trauma therapy: Beyond the flashback*. American Psychological Association.

Brown, R. H., Cannon, S. C., & Rowland, L. P. (2013). Diseases of the nerve and motor unit. In E. R. Kandel, J. H. Schwartz, T. M. Jessell, S. A. Siegelbaum, & A. J. Hudspeth (Eds.), *Principles of neural science* (5th ed., pp. 307–331). McGraw-Hill.

Brown, R. T., Abrahamson, D. J., Baker, D. C., Bevins, R. A., Grus, C. L., Hoover, M., LeVine, E. S., Lincoln, A. J., & Foster, E. O. (2021). The revised 2019 standards for psychopharmacological training: Model education and training program in psychopharmacology for prescriptive authority. *American Psychologist, 76*(1), 154–164. https://doi.org/10.1037/amp0000729

Brown, R., & Kulik, J. (1977). Flashbulb memories. *Cognition, 5*(1), 73–99.

Brown, S. C., & Craik, F. I. M. (2000). Encoding and retrieval of information. In E. Tulving & F. I. M. Craik (Eds.), *The Oxford handbook of memory* (pp. 93–107). Oxford University Press.

Brown, T. A., & Lawrence, A. E. (2009). Generalized anxiety disorder and obsessive-compulsive disorder. In P. H. Blaney & T. Millon (Eds.), *Oxford textbook of psychopathology* (2nd ed., pp. 146–175). Oxford University Press.

Brown, T. A., & Naragon-Gainey, K. (2013). Evaluation of the unique and specific contributions of dimensions of the triple vulnerability model to the prediction of DSM-IV anxiety and mood disorder constructs. *Behavior Therapy, 44*(2), 277–292.

Brown, Z., & Tiggemann, M. (2021, January 26). Celebrity influence on body image and eating disorders: A review. *Journal of Health Psychology*. https://doi.org/10.1177/1359105320988312

Browne, K. D., & Hamilton-Giachritsis, C. (2005). The influence of violent media on children and adolescents: A public-health approach. *The Lancet, 365*(9460), 702–710.

Browne, T. K. (2017). A role for philosophers, sociologists and bioethicists in revising the DSM: A philosophical case conference. *Philosophy, Psychiatry, & Psychology, 24*(3), 187–201.

Brownell, K. D. (2004). *The LEARN program for weight management* (10th ed.). American Health Publishing.

Brownell, K. D., & Salovey, P. (2007). Health psychology: Where psychological, biological, and social factors intersect. In R. J. Sternberg (Ed.), *Career paths in psychology: Where your degree can take you* (2nd ed., pp. 307–327). American Psychological Association.

Bruce, J. M., & Echemendia, R. J. (2009). History of multiple self-reported concussions is not associated with reduced cognitive abilities. *Neurosurgery, 64*(1), 100–106.

Bruder, K. J. (1997). William James: America's premier psychologist. In W. G. Bringmann, H. E. Lück, R. Miller, & C. E. Early (Eds.), *A pictorial history of psychology* (pp. 66–70). Quintessence Publishing.

Brugger, P. (2010). Phantom limb. In E. B. Goldstein (Ed.), *Encyclopedia of perception* (pp. 796–799). Sage.

Brugman, B. C., Burgers, C., & Steen, G. J. (2017). Recategorizing political frames: A systematic review of metaphorical framing in experiments on political communication. *Annals of the International Communication Association, 41*(2), 181–197.

Bruine de Bruin, W. (2005). Save the last dance for me: Unwanted serial position effects in jury evaluations. *Acta Psychologica, 118*(3), 245–260.

Brumariu, L. E., & Kerns, K. A. (2011). Parent-child attachment in early and middle childhood. In P. K. Smith & C. H. Hart (Eds.), *The Wiley-Blackwell handbook of childhood social development* (2nd ed., pp. 319–336). Wiley-Blackwell.

Brumm, H., & Slabbekoorn, H. (2005). Acoustic communication in noise. *Advances in the Study of Behavior, 35*(35), 151–209.

Bruner, J. (1981). The social context of language acquisition. *Language & Communication, 1*(2), 155–178.

Bruner, J. S. (1975). The ontogenesis of speech acts. *Journal of Child Language, 2*(1), 1–19.

Bruner, M. W., McLaren, C. D., Sutcliffe, J. T., Gardner, L. A., Lubans, D. R., Smith, J. J., & Vella, S. A. (2021). The effect of sport-based interventions on positive youth development: A systematic review and meta-analysis. *International Review of Sport and Exercise Psychology*. https://doi.org/10.1080/1750984X.2021.1875496

Bruni, F. (2009). *Born round: The secret history of a full-time eater*. Penguin.

Brunt, L. (2008). *Sote hue log*: In and out of sleep in India. In L. Brunt & B. Steger (Eds.), *Worlds of sleep* (pp. 153–174). Frank & Timme.

Bruschi, T. (2014, June 10). From Super Bowl to stroke—and back again. *Men's Health*. http://www.menshealth.com/health/tedy-bruschi-stroke

Bryant, P. A., Trinder, J., & Curtis, N. (2004). Sick and tired: Does sleep have a vital role in the immune system? *Nature Reviews Immunology, 4*(6), 457–467.

Bryant, R. A. (2008). Hypnosis and anxiety: Early interventions. In M. R. Nash & A. J. Barnier (Eds.), *The Oxford handbook of hypnosis: Theory, research, and practice* (pp. 535–548). Oxford University Press.

Bryant, R. A., Nickerson, A., Creamer, M., O'Donnell, M., Forbes, D., Galatzer-Levy, I., McFarlane, A. C., & Silove, D. (2015). Trajectory of post-traumatic stress following traumatic injury: 6-year follow-up. *The British Journal of Psychiatry, 206*(5), 417–423.

Brzezinski, A., Vangel, M. G., Wurtman, R. J., Norrie, G., Zhdanova, I., Ben-Shushan, A., & Ford, I. (2005). Effects of exogenous melatonin on sleep: A meta-analysis. *Sleep Medicine Reviews, 9*(1), 41–50.

Buchanan, T. (2002). Online assessment: Desirable or dangerous? *Professional Psychology: Research and Practice, 33*(2), 148–154.

Buchanan, T., & Smith, J. L. (1999). Using the Internet for psychological research: Personality testing on the World Wide Web. *British Journal of Psychology, 90*(1), 125–144.

Buchsbaum, G., & Gottschalk, A. (1983). Trichromacy, opponent colours coding and optimum colour information transmission in the retina. *Proceedings of the Royal Society of London. Series B: Biological Sciences, 220*(1218), 89–113.

Buck, R. (1980). Nonverbal behavior and the theory of emotion: The facial feedback hypothesis. *Journal of Personality and Social Psychology, 38*(5), 811–824.

Buckley, K. W. (1989). *Mechanical man: John B. Watson and the beginnings of behaviorism*. Guilford Press.

Buddin, R. (2014). Gender gaps in high school GPA and ACT scores (ACT Research & Policy Information Brief 2014-12). http://www.act.org/research/researchers/briefs/pdf/2014-12.pdf

Budge, S. L., & Wampold, B. E. (2015). The relationship: How it works. In O. C. G. Gelo, A. Pritz, & B. Rieken (Eds.), *Psychotherapy research: Foundations, process, and outcomes* (pp. 213–228). Springer.

Bugental, J. F. (1964). The third force in psychology. *Journal of Humanistic Psychology, 4*(1), 19–25.

Bühner, M., König, C. J., Pick, M., & Krumm, S. (2006). Working memory dimensions as differential predictors of the speed and error aspect of multitasking performance. *Human Performance, 19*(3), 253–275.

Buhrmester, D. (1990). Intimacy of friendship, interpersonal competence, and adjustment during preadolescence and adolescence. *Child Development, 61*(4), 1101–1111.

Buijzen, M., van der Molen, J. H. W., & Sondij, P. (2007). Parental mediation of children's emotional responses to a violent news event. *Communication Research, 34*(2), 212–230.

Bukowski, W. M., Hoza, B., & Boivin, M. (1993). Popularity, friendship, and emotional adjustment during early adolescence. *New Directions for Child and Adolescent Development, 1993*(60), 23–37.

Bulik, C. M., Sullivan, P. F., Tozzi, F., Furberg, H., Lichtenstein, P., & Pedersen, N. L. (2006). Prevalence, heritability, and prospective risk factors for anorexia nervosa. *Archives of General Psychiatry, 63*(3), 305–312.

Bulkeley, K., & Kahan, T. L. (2008). The impact of September 11 on dreaming. *Consciousness and Cognition, 17*(4), 1248–1256.

Bullock, J. L., Lockspeiser, T., del Pino-Jones, A., Richards, R., Teherani, A., & Hauer, K. E. (2020). They don't see a lot of people my color: A mixed methods study of racial/ethnic stereotype threat among medical students on core clerkships. *Academic Medicine, 95*(11S), S58–S66. https://doi.org/10.1097/ACM.0000000000003628

Burgener, E., & Thomsen, M. (2018). Prevalence and changes of food stores in Arkansas food deserts: 2009–2015. *Journal of the Academy of Nutrition and Dietetics, 118*(9), A77.

Burger, J. M. (2009). Replicating Milgram: Would people still obey today? *American Psychologist, 64*(1), 1–11.

Burger, J. M., & Caputo, D. (2015). The low-ball compliance procedure: A meta-analysis. *Social Influence, 10*(4), 214–220.

Burgoine, T., Forouhi, N. G., Griffin, S. J., Brage, S., Wareham, N. J., & Monsivais, P. (2016). Does neighborhood fast-food outlet exposure amplify inequalities in diet and obesity? A cross-sectional study, 2. *The American Journal of Clinical Nutrition, 103*(6), 1540–1547.

Burkart, J. M., Schubiger, M. N., & van Schaik, C. P. (2017). The evolution of general intelligence. *Behavioral and Brain Sciences, 40*, e195.

Burke, D. M., Locantore, J. K., Austin, A. A., & Chae, B. (2004). Cherry pit primes Brad Pitt: Homophone priming effects on young and older adults' production of proper names. *Psychological Science, 15*(3), 164–170.

Burke, J., O'Campo, P., Salmon, C., & Walker, R. (2009). Pathways connecting neighborhood influences and mental well-being: Socioeconomic position and gender differences. *Social Science & Medicine, 68*(7), 1294–1304.

Burlingame, G. M., & Baldwin, S. (2011). Treatment modalities: Group therapy. In J. C. Norcross, G. R. Vandenbos, & D. K. Freedheim (Eds.), *History of psychotherapy: Continuity and change* (2nd ed., pp. 505–515). American Psychological Association.

Burlingame, G. M., McClendon, D. T., & Yang, C. (2018). Cohesion in group therapy: A meta-analysis. *Psychotherapy, 55*(4), 384–398.

Burman, D., Buysse, D. J., & Reynolds, C. F., III. (2015). Treatment of sleep disorders. In P. E. Nathan & J. M. Gorman (Eds.), *A guide to treatments that work* (pp. 659–698). Oxford University Press.

Burnett, D. (2013, November 29). Online IQ tests: Are they valid? *The Guardian*. http://www.theguardian.com/science/2013/nov/29/iq-tests-online-are-they-valid

Burnham, M. M. (2013). Co-sleeping and self-soothing during infancy. In A. R. Wolfson & H. Montgomery-Downs (Eds.), *The Oxford handbook of infant, child, and adolescent sleep and behavior* (pp. 127–139). Oxford University Press.

Burnham, M. M., & Gaylor, E. E. (2011). Sleep environment of young children in post-industrial societies. In M. El-Sheikh (Ed.), *Sleep and development: Familial and socio-cultural considerations* (pp. 195–218). Oxford University Press.

Burns, W. J., Rey, J., & Burns, K. A. (2008). Psychopharmacology as practiced by psychologists. In M. Hersen & A. M. Gross (Eds.), *Handbook of clinical psychology* (Vol. 1, pp. 663–692). Wiley.

Burt, D. B., Zembar, M. J., & Niederehe, G. (1995). Depression and memory impairment: A meta-analysis of the association, its pattern, and specificity. *Psychological Bulletin, 117*(2), 285–305.

Burton, C. M., Marshal, M. P., Chisolm, D. J., Sucato, G. S., & Friedman, M. S. (2013). Sexual minority-related victimization as a mediator of mental health disparities in sexual minority youth: A longitudinal analysis. *Journal of Youth and Adolescence, 42*(3), 394–402.

Bus, A. G., Van Ijzendoorn, M. H., & Pellegrini, A. D. (1995). Joint book reading makes for success in learning to read: A meta-analysis on intergenerational transmission of literacy. *Review of Educational Research, 65*(1), 1–21.

Buscemi, J., & Spring, B. (2015). Evidence-based practice in psychology. In R. L. Cautin & S. O. Lilienfeld (Eds.), *The encyclopedia of clinical psychology* (pp. 1147–1153). Wiley-Blackwell.

Bushdid, C., Magnasco, M. O., Vosshall, L. B., & Keller, A. (2014). Humans can discriminate more than 1 trillion olfactory stimuli. *Science, 343*(6177), 1370–1372.

Bushman, B. J., & Anderson, C. A. (2001). Media violence and the American public: Scientific facts versus media misinformation. *American Psychologist, 56*(6–7), 477–489.

Bushman, B. J., & Anderson, C. A. (2015). Understanding causality in the effects of media violence. *American Behavioral Scientist, 59*(14), 1807–1821.

Bushman, B. J., & Cooper, H. M. (1990). Effects of alcohol on human aggression: An integrative research review. *Psychological Bulletin, 107*(3), 341–354.

Bushman, B. J., & Huesmann, L. R. (2010). Aggression. In S. T. Fiske, D. T. Gilbert, & G. Lindzey (Eds.), *Handbook of social psychology* (5th ed.), Volume 2, pp. 833–863. Wiley.

Bushnell, I. W. R. (2001). Mother's face recognition in newborn infants: Learning and memory. *Infant and Child Development, 10*(1–2), 67–74.

Bushnell, I. W. R., Sai, F., & Mullin, J. T. (1989). Neonatal recognition of the mother's face. *British Journal of Developmental Psychology, 7*(1), 3–15.

Buss, D. M. (1989). Sex differences in human mate preferences: Evolutionary hypotheses tested in 37 cultures. *Behavioral and Brain Sciences, 12*(1), 1–49.

Buss, D. M. (1994). *The evolution of desire: Strategies of human mating*. Basic Books.

Buss, D. M. (1995). Psychological sex differences: Origins through sexual selection. *American Psychologist, 50*(3), 164–168.

Buss, D. M. (2005). *The murderer next door: Why the mind is designed to kill*. Penguin Press.

Buss, D. M., & Duntley, J. D. (2006). The evolution of aggression. In M. Schaller, J. A. Simpson, & D. T. Kenrick (Eds.), *Evolution and social psychology* (pp. 263–285). Psychology Press.

Buss, D. M., Larsen, R. J., Westen, D., & Semmelroth, J. (1992). Sex differences in jealousy: Evolution, physiology, and psychology. *Psychological Science, 3*(4), 251–255.

Bussey, K. (2013). Gender development. In M. K. Ryan & N. R. Branscombe (Eds.), *The Sage handbook of gender and psychology* (pp. 81–99). Sage.

Bussey, K., & Bandura, A. (1999). Social cognitive theory of gender development and differentiation. *Psychological Review, 106*(4), 676–713.

Butcher, J. N. (2010). Personality assessment from the nineteenth to the early twenty-first century: Past achievements and contemporary challenges. *Annual Review of Clinical Psychology, 6*, 1–20.

Butcher, J. N. (2011). *A beginner's guide to the MMPI-2* (3rd ed.). American Psychological Association.

Butcher, J. N. (2012). 25 historical highlights: Significant contributions for use of the MMPI/MMPI-2 in personnel applications. http://mmpi.umn.edu/documents/Highlights%20in%20Using%20the%20MMPI%20in%20personnel%20evaluations.pdf

Butcher, J. N., & Beutler, L. E. (2003). The MMPI-2. In L. E. Beutler & G. Groth-Marnat (Eds.), *Integrative assessment of adult personality* (2nd ed., pp. 157–191). Guilford Press.

Butcher, J. N., & Williams, C. L. (2009). Personality assessment with the MMPI-2: Historical roots, international adaptations, and current challenges. *Applied Psychology: Health and Well-Being, 1*(1), 105–135.

Butcher, J. N., Mosch, S. C., Tsai, J., & Nezami, E. (2006). Cross-cultural applications of the MMPI-2. In J. N. Butcher (Ed.), *MMPI-2: A practitioner's guide* (pp. 505–537). American Psychological Association.

Butler, E. A., Egloff, B., Wilhelm, F. H., Smith, N. C., Erickson, E. A., & Gross, J. J. (2003). The social consequences of expressive suppression. *Emotion, 3*(1), 48–67.

Butzlaff, R. L., & Hooley, J. M. (1998). Expressed emotion and psychiatric relapse: A meta-analysis. *Archives of General Psychiatry, 55*(6), 547–552.

Buunk, B. P., Angleitner, A., Oubaid, V., & Buss, D. M. (1996). Sex differences in jealousy in evolutionary and cultural perspective: Tests from the Netherlands, Germany, and the United States. *Psychological Science, 7*(6), 359–363.

Buunk, B. P., Collins, R. L., Taylor, S. E., VanYperen, N. W., & Dakof, G. A. (1990). The affective consequences of social comparison: Either direction has its ups and downs. *Journal of Personality and Social Psychology, 59*(6), 1238–1249.

Bybee, J., & McClelland, J. L. (2005). Alternatives to the combinatorial paradigm of linguistic theory based on domain general principles of human cognition. *The Linguistic Review, 22*(2–4), 381–410.

Cabaniss, D. L., Cherry, S., Douglas, C. J., & Schwartz, A. R. (2011). *Psychodynamic psychotherapy: A clinical manual*. Wiley.

Cabrita, M., Lamers, S. M., Trompetter, H. R., Tabak, M., & Vollenbroek-Hutten, M. M. (2017). Exploring the relation between positive emotions and the functional status of older adults living independently: A systematic review. *Aging & Mental Health, 21*(11), 1121–1128.

Caccavale, J. (2013). Mental healthcare professionals need to boycott the DSM-5. *The Clinical Practitioner, 8*(4), 1–3.

Cacciari, C., & Padovani, R. (2012). The development of figurative language. In M. Spivey, M. Joanisse, & K. McRae (Eds.), *The Cambridge handbook of psycholinguistics* (pp. 505–522). Cambridge University Press.

Caceres, A., Hall, D. L., Zelaya, F. O., Williams, S. C., & Mehta, M. A. (2009). Measuring fMRI reliability with the intra-class correlation coefficient. *Neuroimage, 45*(3), 758–768.

Cacioppo, J. T., & Berntson, G. C. (2011). The brain, homeostasis, and health: Balancing demands of the internal and external milieu. In H. S. Friedman (Ed.), *The Oxford handbook of health psychology* (pp. 121–137). Oxford University Press.

Cacioppo, J. T., Hawkley, L. C., & Berntson, G. G. (2003). The anatomy of loneliness. *Current Directions in Psychological Science, 12*(3), 71–74.

Cadinu, M., Maass, A., Rosabianca, A., & Kiesner, J. (2005). Why do women underperform under stereotype threat? Evidence for the role of negative thinking. *Psychological Science, 16*(7), 572–578.

Cain, D. J. (2002). Defining characteristics, history, and evolution of humanistic psychotherapies. In D. J. Cain & J. Seeman (Eds.), *Humanistic psychotherapies: Handbook of research and practice* (pp. 3–54). American Psychological Association.

Cain, D. J. (2010). *Person-centered psychotherapies*. American Psychological Association.

Cain, W. S. (1982). Odor identification by males and females: Predictions vs performance. *Chemical Senses, 7*(2), 129–142.

Cairns, R. B., & Cairns, B. D. (2006). The making of developmental psychology. In R. M. Lerner (Vol. Ed.), *Handbook of child psychology* (6th ed., Vol. 1, pp. 89–165). Wiley.

Calem, M., Bromis, K., McGuire, P., Morgan, C., & Kempton, M. J. (2017). Meta-analysis of associations between childhood adversity and hippocampus and amygdala volume in non-clinical and general population samples. *NeuroImage: Clinical, 14*, 471–479.

Calfee, R. (2007). Learning about learning: Psychologists in schools of education. In R. J. Sternberg (Ed.), *Career paths in psychology: A guide for graduate students and research assistants* (pp. 35–49). American Psychological Association.

Calkins, H. (2021). Online therapy is here to stay. *Monitor on Psychology, 52*(1), 78–82. https://www.apa.org/monitor/2021/01/trends-online-therapy

Calle, E. E., Rodriguez, C., Walker-Thurmond, K., & Thun, M. J. (2003). Overweight, obesity, and mortality from cancer in a prospectively studied cohort of U.S. adults. *New England Journal of Medicine, 348*(17), 1625–1638.

Calvert, S. L., Appelbaum, M., Dodge, K. A., Graham, S., Nagayama Hall, G. C., Hamby, S., ... Hedges, L. V. (2017). The American Psychological Association Task Force assessment of violent video games: Science in the service of public interest. *American Psychologist, 72*(2), 126–143.

Calvillo, D. P., & Mills, N. V. (2020). Bilingual witnesses are more susceptible to the misinformation effect in their less proficient language. *Current Psychology, 39*, 673–680.

Camacho, G., Reinka, M. A., & Quinn, D. M. (2020). Disclosure and concealment of stigmatized identities. *Current Opinion in Psychology, 31*, 28–32. https://doi.org/10.1016/j.copsyc.2019.07.031

Camara, W. J., Nathan, J. S., & Puente, A. E. (2000). Psychological test usage: Implications in professional psychology. *Professional Psychology: Research and Practice, 31*(2), 141–154.

Cameron, A. Y. (2015). Dialectical behavior therapy. In R. L. Cautin & S. O. Lilienfeld (Eds.), *The encyclopedia of clinical psychology* (pp. 873–878). Wiley-Blackwell.

Campbell, L. F., & Norcross, J. C. (2018). Do you see what we see? Psychology's response to technology in mental health. *Clinical Psychology: Science and Practice, 25*, e12237.

Campbell, L. F., Millán, F. A., & Martin, J. N. (Eds.). (2018). *A telepsychology casebook: Using technology ethically and effectively in your professional practice*. American Psychological Association. https://doi.org/10.1037/0000046-000

Campbell, W. H., & Rohrbaugh, R. M. (2006). *The biopsychosocial formulation manual: A guide for mental health professionals*. Routledge.

Campos, B., Ullman, J. B., Aguilera, A., & Schetter, C. D. (2014). Familism and psychological health: The intervening role of closeness and social support. *Cultural Diversity and Ethnic Minority Psychology, 20*(2), 191–201. https://doi.org/10.1037/a0034094

Camras, L. A., Malatesta, C., & Izard, C. E. (1991). The development of facial expression in infancy. In R. Feldman & B. Rime (Eds.), *Fundamentals of nonverbal behavior* (pp. 73–105). Cambridge University Press.

Candel, I., & Merckelbach, H. (2003). Fantasy proneness and thought suppression as predictors of Medical Student Syndrome. *Personality and Individual Differences, 35*(1), 519–524.

Cannon, W. B. (1927). The James-Lange theory of emotions: A critical examination and an alternative theory. *American Journal of Psychology, 39*, 106–124.

Cannon, W. B. (1931). Against the James–Lange and the thalamic theories of emotions. *Psychological Review, 38*(4), 281–295.

Cannon, W. B. (1932). *The wisdom of the body*. Norton.

Cantor, J. (2004). "I'll never have a clown in my house"—Why movie horror lives on. *Poetics Today, 25*(2), 283–304.

Cantor, J. (2011). Fear reactions and the mass media. In K. Döveling, C. Sheve, & E. Konijn (Eds.), *The Routledge handbook of emotions and mass media* (pp. 148–165). Routledge.

Cantor, J., Byrne, S., Moyer-Gusé, E., & Riddle, K. (2010). Descriptions of media-induced fright reactions. *Journal of Children and Media, 4*(1), 1–17.

Canuto, A., Weber, K., Baertschi, M., Andreas, S., Volkert, J., Dehoust, M. C., Sehner, S., Suling, A., Wegscheider, K., Ausín, B., Crawford, M. J., Da Ronch, C., Grassi, L., Hershkovitz., Y., Munoz, M., Quirk, A., Rotenstein, O., Santos-Olmo, A. B., Shalev, A., ... Härter, M. (2018). Anxiety disorders in old age: Psychiatric comorbidities, quality of life, and prevalence according to age, gender, and country. *The American Journal of Geriatric Psychiatry, 26*(2), 174–185.

Capaldi, E. J., & Proctor, R. W. (2003). Current and future trends in experimental psychology. In S. F. Davis (Ed.), *Handbook of research methods in experimental psychology* (pp. 24–38). Blackwell.

Capellini, I., Nunn, C. L., McNamara, P., Preston, B. T., & Barton, R. A. (2008). Energetic constraints, not predation, influence the evolution of sleep patterning in mammals. *Functional Ecology, 22*(5), 847–853.

Caplan, P. J. (1992). Gender issues in the diagnosis of mental disorder. *Women & Therapy, 12*(4), 71–82.

Caplan, P. J. (1995). *They say you're crazy: How the world's most powerful psychiatrists decide who's normal*. Addison-Wesley.

Caplan, P. J., & Cosgrove, L. (Eds.). (2004). *Bias in psychiatric diagnosis*. Jason Aronson.

Caporael, L. R. (2007). Evolutionary theory for social and cultural psychology. In A. W. Kruglanski & E. T. Higgins (Eds.), *Social psychology: Handbook of basic principles* (2nd ed., pp. 3–18). Guilford Press.

Cappeliez, P., & Webster, J. D. (2017). Introduction to the special section: Reminiscence through a cultural lens. *The International Journal of Reminiscence and Life Review, 4*(2), 46–47.

Caprara, G. V., Vecchione, M., Alessandri, G., Gerbino, M., & Barbaranelli, C. (2011). The contribution of personality traits and self-efficacy beliefs to academic achievement: A longitudinal study. *British Journal of Educational Psychology, 81*(1), 78–96.

Cara, E. (2016). *Health at Every Size movement: What proponents say vs. what science says*. Medical Daily. https://www.medicaldaily.com/health-every-size-obesity-weight-loss-science-383008

Carbado, D. W., Crenshaw, K. W., Mays, V. M., & Tomlinson, B. (2013). Intersectionality. *Du Bois Review: Social Science Research on Race, 10*(2), 303–312.

Carbon, C. C. (2020). Wearing face masks strongly confuses counterparts in reading emotions. *Frontiers in Psychology, 11*, 2526. https://doi.org/10.3389/fpsyg.2020.566886

Carbone, E. G., & Echols, E. T. (2017). Effects of optimism on recovery and mental health after a tornado outbreak. *Psychology & Health, 32*(5), 530–548.

Card, N. A., & Little, T. D. (2007). Longitudinal modeling of developmental processes. *International Journal of Behavioral Development, 31*(4), 297–302.

Card, N. A., Stucky, B. D., Sawalani, G. M., & Little, T. D. (2008). Direct and indirect aggression during childhood and adolescence: A meta-analytic review of gender differences, intercorrelations, and relations to maladjustment. *Child Development, 79*(5), 1185–1229.

Cárdenas, M., & Barrientos, J. E. (2008). The attitudes toward lesbians and gay men scale (ATLG): Adaptation and testing the reliability and validity in Chile. *Journal of Sex Research, 45*(2), 140–149.

Cárdenas, M., Barrientos, J., & Gómez, F. (2018). Determinants of heterosexual men's attitudes toward gay men and lesbians in Chile. *Journal of Gay & Lesbian Mental Health, 22*(2), 105–119.

Cardno, A. G., & Gottesman, I. I. (2000). Twin studies of schizophrenia: From bow-and-arrow concordances to Star Wars Mx and functional genomics. *American Journal of Medical Genetics, 97*(1), 12–17.

Carew, T. J., Hawkins, R. D., & Kandel, E. R. (1983). Differential classical conditioning of a defensive withdrawal reflex in *Aplysia californica*. *Science, 219*(4583), 397–400.

Carew, T. J., Walters, E. T., & Kandel, E. R. (1981). Classical conditioning in a simple withdrawal reflex in *Aplysia californica*. *The Journal of Neuroscience, 1*(12), 1426–1437.

Carl, E., Stein, A. T., Levihn-Coon, A., Pogue, J. R., Rothbaum, B., Emmelkamp, P., Asmundson, G. J. G., Carlbring, P., & Powers, M. B. (2019). Virtual reality exposure therapy for anxiety and related disorders: A meta-analysis of randomized controlled trials. *Journal of Anxiety Disorders, 61*, 27–36.

Carli, L. L. (1990). Gender, language, and influence. *Journal of Personality and Social Psychology, 59*(5), 941–951.

Carli, L. L. (2013). Gendered communication and social influence. In M. K. Ryan & N. R. Branscombe (Eds.), *The Sage handbook of gender and psychology* (pp. 199–215). Sage.

Carlo, G., White, R. M., Streit, C., Knight, G. P., & Zeiders, K. H. (2018). Longitudinal relations among parenting styles, prosocial behaviors, and academic outcomes in US Mexican adolescents. *Child Development, 89*(2), 577–592.

Carlson, E. N., & Oltmanns, T. F. (2018). Is it adaptive for people with personality problems to know how their romantic partner perceives them? The effect of meta-accuracy on romantic relationship satisfaction. *Journal of Personality Disorders, 32*(3), 374–391.

Carlson, L. A. (2010). Top-down and bottom-up processing. In E. B. Goldstein (Ed.), *Encyclopedia of perception* (pp. 1011–1014). Sage.

Carlson, L. E. (2015). Mindfulness-based interventions for physical conditions: A selective review. In K. W. Brown, J. D. Creswell, & R. M. Ryan (Eds.), *Handbook of mindfulness: Theory, research, and practice* (pp. 405–425). Guilford Press.

Carlson, L. E., Speca, M., Patel, K. D., & Goodey, E. (2003). Mindfulness-based stress reduction in relation to quality of life, mood, symptoms of stress, and immune parameters in breast and prostate cancer outpatients. *Psychosomatic Medicine, 65*(4), 571–581.

Carlson, M., Marcus-Newhall, A., & Miller, N. (1990). Effects of situational aggression cues: A quantitative review. *Journal of Personality and Social Psychology, 58*(4), 622–633.

Carmody, J. (2015). Reconceptualizing mindfulness: The psychological principles of attending in mindfulness practice and their role in well-being. In K. W. Brown, J. D. Creswell, & R. M. Ryan (Eds.), *Handbook of mindfulness: Theory, research, and practice* (pp. 62–80). Guilford Press.

Carnagey, N. L., Anderson, C. A., & Bushman, B. J. (2007). The effect of video game violence on physiological desensitization to real-life violence. *Journal of Experimental Social Psychology, 43*(3), 489–496.

Carney, S. Cowen, P., Geddes, J., Goodwin, G., Rogers, R., Dearness, K., ... Scott, A. (2003). Efficacy and safety of electroconvulsive therapy in depressive disorders: A systematic review and meta-analysis. *The Lancet, 361*(9360), 799–808.

Carpendale, J. I. M. (2009). Piaget's theory of moral development. In U. Müller, J. I. M. Carpendale, & L. Smith (Eds.), *The Cambridge companion to Piaget* (pp. 270–286). Cambridge University Press.

Carpendale, J. I. M., & Lewis, C. (2010). The development of social understanding: A relational perspective. In W. F. Overton (Ed.), *Handbook of life-span development* (Vol. 1, pp. 584–627). Wiley.

Carpenter, M. (2011). Social cognition and social motivations in infancy. In U. Goswami (Ed.), *The Wiley-Blackwell handbook of childhood cognitive development* (2nd ed., pp. 106–128). Wiley-Blackwell.

Carpenter, M., Akhtar, N., & Tomasello, M. (1998). Fourteen- through 18-month-old infants differentially imitate intentional and accidental actions. *Infant Behavior and Development, 21*(2), 315–330.

Carpenter, R. J. (1997). Margaret Floy Washburn. In W. G. Bringmann, H. E. Lück, R. Miller, & C. E. Early (Eds.), *A pictorial history of psychology* (pp. 187–190). Quintessence Publishing.

Carr, A. (2008). *What works with children, adolescents, and adults? A review of research on the effectiveness of psychotherapy*. Routledge.

Carraher, T. N., Carraher, D. W., & Schliemann, A. D. (1985). Mathematics in the streets and in schools. *British Journal of Developmental Psychology, 3*(1), 21–29.

Carras, C. (2018, June 6). Kate Spade's husband issues statement: She "suffered from depression and anxiety." *Variety*. https://variety.com/2018/biz/news/kate-spade-husband-death-statement-1202834789/

Carrier, M., & Pashler, H. (1992). The influence of retrieval on retention. *Memory & Cognition, 20*(6), 633–642.

Carrillo, J., Corning, A. F., Dennehy, T. C., & Crosby, F. J. (2011). Relative deprivation: Understanding the dynamics of discontent. In D. Chadee (Ed.), *Theories in social psychology* (pp. 140–160). Wiley-Blackwell.

Carroll, A. E. (2017, July 17). Can psychedelics be therapy? Allow research to find out. *The New York Times*. https://www.nytimes.com/2017/07/17/upshot/can-psychedelics-be-therapy-allow-research-to-find-out.html

Carroll, J. B. (1993). *Human cognitive abilities: A survey of factor-analytic studies*. Cambridge University Press.

Carroll, L. (2013). Problem-focused coping. In M. D. Gellman & J. R. Turner (Eds.), *Encyclopedia of Behavioral Medicine* (pp. 1540–1541). Springer Science+Business Media.

Carskadon, M. A., & Dement, W. C. (1996). Normal human sleep: An overview. In M. H. Kryger, T. Roth, & W. C. Dement (Eds.), *Principles and practice of sleep medicine* (pp. 16–25). Saunders.

Carskadon, M. A., Acebo, C., & Jenni, O. G. (2004). Regulation of adolescent sleep: Implications for behavior. *Annals of the New York Academy of Sciences, 1021*(1), 276–291.

Carskadon, M. A., & Tarokh, L. (2013). Developmental changes in circadian timing and sleep: Adolescence and emerging adulthood. In A. R. Wolfson & H. Montgomery-Downs (Eds.), *The Oxford handbook of infant, child, and adolescent sleep and behavior* (pp. 70–79). Oxford University Press.

Carskadon, M. A., Vieira, C., & Acebo, C. (1993). Association between puberty and delayed phase preference. *Sleep, 16*, 258–262.

Carsley, D., Khoury, B., & Heath, N. L. (2018). Effectiveness of mindfulness interventions for mental health in schools: A comprehensive meta-analysis. *Mindfulness, 9*(3), 693–707.

Carson, J. W., Carson, K. M., Gil, K. M., & Baucom, D. H. (2004). Mindfulness-based relationship enhancement. *Behavior Therapy, 35*(3), 471–494.

Carson, S. H., Peterson, J. B., & Higgins, D. M. (2005). Reliability, validity, and factor structure of the creative achievement questionnaire. *Creativity Research Journal, 17*(1), 37–50.

Carstairs-McCarthy, A. (2001). Origins of language. In M. Aronoff & J. Rees-Miller (Eds.), *The handbook of linguistics* (pp. 1–18). Blackwell.

Carstens, E. (2010). Itch, tickle, and tingle. In E. B. Goldstein (Ed.), *Encyclopedia of perception* (pp. 509–512). Sage.

Carstensen, L. L., & DeLiema, M. (2018). The positivity effect: A negativity bias in youth fades with age. *Current Opinion in Behavioral Sciences, 19*, 7–12.

Carstensen, L. L., Pasupathi, M., Mayr, U., & Nesselroade, J. R. (2000). Emotional experience in everyday life across the adult life span. *Journal of Personality and Social Psychology, 79*(4), 644–655.

Carstensen, L. L., Turan, B., Scheibe, S., Ram, N., Ersner-Hershfield, H., Samanez-Larkin, G. R., Brooks, K. P., & Nesselroade, J. R. (2011). Emotional experience improves with age: Evidence based on over 10 years of experience sampling. *Psychology and Aging, 26*(1), 21–33.

Carter, N. T., Dalal, D. K., Boyce, A. S., O'Connell, M. S., Kung, M. C., & Delgado, K. M. (2014). Uncovering curvilinear relationships between conscientiousness and job performance: How theoretically appropriate measurement makes an empirical difference. *Journal of Applied Psychology, 99*(4), 564–586.

Carter, N., Ulfberg, J., Nyström, B., & Edling, C. (2003). Sleep debt, sleepiness and accidents among males in the general population and male professional drivers. *Accident Analysis & Prevention, 35*(4), 613–617.

Cartwright, M., Wardle, J., Steggles, N., Simon, A. E., Croker, H., & Jarvis, M. J. (2003). Stress and dietary practices in adolescents. *Health Psychology, 22*(4), 362–369.

Cartwright, R. (2005). Dreaming as a mood regulation system. In M. Kryger, T. Roth, & W. Dement (Eds.), *Principles and practice of sleep medicine* (4th ed., pp. 565–572). Elsevier Saunders.

Cartwright, R. D. (2006). Sleepwalking. In T. L. Lee-Chiong (Ed.), *Sleep: A comprehensive handbook* (pp. 429–434). Wiley-Liss.

Cartwright, R., Luten, A., Young, M., Mercer, P., & Bears, M. (1998a). Role of REM sleep and dream affect in overnight mood regulation: A study of normal volunteers. *Psychiatry Research, 81*(1), 1–8.

Cartwright, R., Young, M. A., Mercer, P., & Bears, M. (1998b). Role of REM sleep and dream variables in the prediction of remission from depression. *Psychiatry Research, 80*(3), 249–255.

Carver, C. (2013). Coping. In M. D. Gellman & J. R. Turner (Eds.), *Encyclopedia of behavioral medicine* (pp. 496–500). Springer Science+Business Media.

Carver, C. S., & Connor-Smith, J. (2010). Personality and coping. *Annual Review of Psychology, 61*, 679–704.

Carver, C. S., & Scheier, M. F. (2017). Optimism, coping, and well being. In C. L. Cooper & J. C. Quick (Eds.), *The handbook of stress and health: A guide to research and practice* (pp. 400–414). Wiley-Blackwell.

Carver, C. S., & Vargas, S. (2011). Stress, coping, and health. In H. S. Friedman (Ed.), *The Oxford handbook of health psychology* (pp. 162–188). Oxford University Press.

Carver, K., Joyner, K., & Udry, J. R. (2003). National estimates of adolescent romantic relationships. In P. Florsheim (Ed.), *Adolescent romantic relations and sexual behavior: Theory, research, and practical implications* (pp. 23–56). Lawrence Erlbaum.

Casados, A. T. (2017). Reducing the stigma of mental illness: Current approaches and future directions. *Clinical Psychology: Science and Practice, 24*(3), 306–323. https://doi.org/10.1111/cpsp.12206

Casagrande, M., Favieri, F., Tambelli, R., & Forte, G. (2020). The enemy who sealed the world: Effects quarantine due to the COVID-19 on sleep quality, anxiety, and psychological distress in the Italian population. *Sleep Medicine, 75*, 12–20. https://doi.org/10.1016/j.sleep.2020.05.011

Casellas-Grau, A., Ochoa, C., & Ruini, C. (2017). Psychological and clinical correlates of posttraumatic growth in cancer: A systematic and critical review. *Psycho-oncology, 26*(12), 2007–2018.

Cashel, M. L. (2002). Child and adolescent psychological assessment: Current clinical practices and the impact of managed care. *Professional Psychology: Research and Practice, 33*(5), 446–453.

Caskey-Sirmons, L. A., & Hickerson, N. P. (1977). Semantic shift and bilingualism: Variation in the color terms of five languages. *Anthropological Linguistics, 19*(8), 358–367.

Caspi, A., Harrington, H., Milne, B., Amell, J., Theodore, R. F., & Moffitt, T. E. (2003). Children's behavioral styles at age 3 are linked to their adult personality traits at age 26. *Journal of Personality, 71*(4), 495–514.

Caspi, A., & Shiner, R. L. (2006). Personality development. In N. Eisenberg (Vol. Ed.), *Handbook of child psychology* (6th ed., Vol. 3, pp. 300–365). Wiley.

Cass, K., McGuire, C., Bjork, I., Sobotka, N., Walsh, K., & Mehler, P. S. (2020). Medical complications of anorexia nervosa. *Psychosomatics, 61*(6), 625–631. https://doi.org/10.1016/j.psym.2020.06.020

Castano, E. (2012). Antisocial behavior in individuals and groups: An empathy-focused approach. In K. Deaux & M. Snyder (Eds.), *The Oxford handbook of personality and social psychology* (pp. 419–445). Oxford University Press.

Castelnuovo, G., Pietrabissa, G., Manzoni, G. M., Cattivelli, R., Rossi, A., Novelli, M., Varallo, G., & Molinari, E. (2017). Cognitive behavioral therapy to aid weight loss in obese patients: Current perspectives. *Psychology Research and Behavior Management, 10*, 165–173.

Castle, D. J., & Buckley, P. F. (2008). *Schizophrenia*. Oxford University Press.

Castro, F. G., Barrera, M., Jr., & Holleran Steiker, L. K. (2010). Issues and challenges in the design of culturally adapted evidence-based interventions. *Annual Review of Clinical Psychology, 6*, 213–239.

Cattell, J. M. (1895). Proceedings of the Third Annual Meeting of the American Psychological Association. *Psychological Review, 2*, 149–172.

Cattell, R. B. (1943). The description of personality: Basic traits resolved into clusters. *The Journal of Abnormal and Social Psychology, 38*(4), 476–506.

Cattell, R. B. (1971). *Abilities: Their structure, growth, and action*. Houghton Mifflin.

Cautin, R. L. (2011). A century of psychotherapy, 1860–1960. In J. C. Norcross, G. R. Vandenbos, & D. K. Freedheim (Eds.), *History of psychotherapy: Continuity and change* (2nd ed., pp. 3–38). American Psychological Association.

Cavanaugh, J. C. & Whitbourne, S. K. (2003). Research methods in adult development. In J. Demick & C. Andreoletti (Eds.), *Handbook of adult development* (pp. 85–100). Kluwer.

Cawley, J. (2011). The economics of obesity. In J. H. Cawley (Ed.), *The Oxford handbook of the social science of obesity* (pp. 120–137). Oxford University Press.

Ceci, S. J., Peters, D., & Plotkin, J. (1985). Human subjects review, personal values, and the regulation of social science research. *American Psychologist, 40*(9), 994–1002.

Celeghin, A., Diano, M., Bagnis, A., Viola, M., & Tamietto, M. (2017). Basic emotions in human neuroscience: Neuroimaging and beyond. *Frontiers in Psychology, 8*, 1432.

Centers for Disease Control and Prevention. (2012). Fast stats: Body measurements. http://www.cdc.gov/nchs/fastats/body-measurements.htm

Centers for Disease Control and Prevention. (2014). Prevalence of autism spectrum disorder among children aged 8 years—Autism and developmental disabilities monitoring network, 11 sites, United States, 2010. *Morbidity and Mortality Weekly Report, Surveillance Summaries, 63*(2), 1–21.

Centers for Disease Control and Prevention. (2015). *About adult BMI*. http://www.cdc.gov/healthyweight/assessing/bmi/adult_bmi/#Definition

Centers for Disease Control and Prevention. (2017). Short sleep duration among US adults. https://www.cdc.gov/sleep/data_statistics.html

Cerasoli, C. P., Nicklin, J. M., & Ford, M. T. (2014). Intrinsic motivation and extrinsic incentives jointly predict performance: A 40-year meta-analysis. *Psychological Bulletin, 140*(4), 980–1008.

Cernoch, J. M., & Porter, R. H. (1985). Recognition of maternal axillary odors by infants. *Child Development, 56*(6), 1593–1598.

Cervero, F. (2013). III. Pain research: What have we learned and where are we going. *British Journal of Anaesthesia, 111*(1), 6–8.

Cesarani, D. (2004). *Eichmann: His life and crimes*. Heinemann.

Ceschi, A., Costantini, A., Sartori, R., Weller, J., & Di Fabio, A. (2018). Dimensions of decision-making: An evidence-based classification of heuristics and biases. *Personality and Individual Differences, 146*, 188–200. https://doi.org/10.1016/j.paid.2018.07.033

Chae, D. H., Nuru-Jeter, A. M., Lincoln, K. D., & Jacob Arriola, K. R. (2012). Racial discrimination, mood disorders, and cardiovascular disease among black Americans. *Annals of Epidemiology, 22*(2), 104–111.

Chae, Y., Kulkofsky, S., & Wang, Q. (2006). What happened in our pizza game?: Memory of a staged event in Korean and European American preschoolers. In F. Columbus (Ed.), *Frontiers in cognitive psychology* (pp. 71–89). Nova Science Publishers.

Chagnon, N. A. (1988). Life histories, blood revenge, and warfare in a tribal population. *Science, 239*(4843), 985–992.

Chakravarthy, M. V., & Booth, F. W. (2004). Eating, exercise, and "thrifty" genotypes: Connecting the dots toward an evolutionary understanding of modern chronic diseases. *Journal of Applied Physiology, 96*(1), 3–10.

Chaloupka, F. J. (2011). Lessons for obesity policy from the tobacco wars. In J. H. Cawley (Ed.), *The Oxford handbook of the social science of obesity* (pp. 620–638). Oxford University Press.

Chambless, D. L. (2002). Beware the dodo bird: The dangers of overgeneralization. *Clinical Psychology: Science and Practice, 9*(1), 13–16.

Chambless, D. L., Baker, M. J., Baucom, D. H., Beutler, L. E., Calhoun, K. S., Crits-Christoph, P., Daiuto, A., DeRubeis, R. J., Detweiler, J., Haaga, D., Johnson, S. B., McCurry, S. M., Mueser, K., Pope, K. S., Sanderson, W. C., Shoham, V., Stickle, T., Williams, D. A., & Woody, S. R. (1998). Update on empirically validated therapies, II. *The Clinical Psychologist, 51*(1), 3–13.

Chambless, D. L., & Ollendick, T. H. (2001). Empirically supported psychological interventions: Controversies and evidence. *Annual Review of Psychology, 52*(1), 685–716.

Chamorro-Premuzic, T., Kallias, A., & Hsu, A. (2014). What type of movie person are you? Understanding individual differences in film preferences and uses: A psychographic approach. In J. C. Kaufman & D. K. Simonton (Eds.), *The social science of cinema* (pp. 87–122). Oxford University Press.

Chan, A. S., & Cistulli, P. A. (2009). Oral appliance treatment of obstructive sleep apnea: An update. *Current Opinion in Pulmonary Medicine, 15*(6), 591–596.

Chan, A., & Poulin, F. (2007). Monthly changes in the composition of friendship networks in early adolescence. *Merrill-Palmer Quarterly, 53*(4), 578–602.

Chan, T. W., & Koo, A. (2011). Parenting style and youth outcomes in the UK. *European Sociological Review, 27*(3), 385–399.

Chan, Y. Y., Lo, W. Y., Yang, S. N., Chen, Y. H., & Lin, J. G. (2015). The benefit of combined acupuncture and antidepressant medication for depression: A systematic review and meta-analysis. *Journal of Affective Disorders, 176*, 106–117.

Chance, S., Gaunet, F., Beall, A., & Loomis, J. (1998). Locomotion mode affects the updating of objects encountered during travel: The contribution of vestibular and proprioceptive inputs to path integration. *Presence, 7*(2), 168–178.

Chandler, J., & Schwarz, N. (2009). How extending your middle finger affects your perception of others: Learned movements influence concept accessibility. *Journal of Experimental Social Psychology, 45*(1), 123–128.

Chandra, A, Mosher, W. D., & Copen, C. (2011). Sexual behavior, sexual attraction, and sexual identity in the United States: Data from the 2006–2008 National Survey of Family Growth. *National Health Statistics Report, 36*, 1–36.

Chang, E. C., & Sanna, L. J. (2003). Introduction: Beyond virtue and vice in personality: Classical themes and current trends. In E. C. Chang & L. J. Sanna (Eds.), *Virtue, vice, and personality: The complexity of behavior* (pp. xix–xxvi). American Psychological Association.

Chang, W. J., O'Connell, N. E., Beckenkamp, P. R., Alhassani, G., Liston, M. B., & Schabrun, S. M. (2018). Altered primary motor cortex structure, organization, and function in chronic pain: A systematic review and meta-analysis. *The Journal of Pain, 19*(4), 341–359.

Changizi, M. A., Zhang, Q., & Shimojo, S. (2006). Bare skin, blood and the evolution of primate colour vision. *Biology Letters, 2*(2), 217–221.

Chaplin, T. M. (2015). Gender and emotion expression: A developmental contextual perspective. *Emotion Review, 7*(1), 14–21.

Chaplin, T. M., & Aldao, A. (2013). Gender differences in emotion expression in children: A meta-analytic review. *Psychological Bulletin, 139*(4), 735–765.

Chapman, B. P., Roberts, B., Lyness, J., & Duberstein, P. (2013). Personality and physician-assessed illness burden in older primary care patients over 4 years. *American Journal of Geriatric Psychiatry, 21*(8), 737–746.

Charland, L. C. (2018). Lost in myth, lost in translation: Philippe Pinel's 1809 medico-philosophical treatise on mental alienation. *International Journal of Mental Health, 47*(3), 245–249.

Charles, S. T., Gatz, M., Kato, K., & Pedersen, N. L. (2008). Physical health 25 years later: The predictive ability of neuroticism. *Health Psychology, 27*(3), 369–378.

Charles, S. T., Luong, G., Almeida, D. M., Ryff, C., Sturm, M., & Love, G. (2010). Fewer ups and downs: Daily stressors mediate age differences in negative affect. *The Journals of Gerontology Series B: Psychological Sciences and Social Sciences, 65*(3), 279–286.

Charlson, F. J., Ferrari, A. J., Santomauro, D. F., Diminic, S., Stockings, E., Scott, J. G., McGrath, J. J., & Whiteford, H. A. (2018). Global epidemiology and burden of schizophrenia: Findings from the global burden of disease study 2016. *Schizophrenia Bulletin, 44*(6), 1195–1203.

Charnley, B. (1991). Self portrait series 18th May 1991. http://www.bryancharnley.info/self-portraits-2/charnley_self_portrait_series_09/

Chase, W. G., & Simon, H. A. (1973). Perception in chess. *Cognitive Psychology, 4*(1), 55–81.

Chater, N., Heit, E., & Oaksford, M. (2005). Reasoning. In K. Lamberts & R. L. Goldstone (Eds.), *Handbook of cognition* (pp. 297–320). Sage.

Chatfield, T. (2012, July 4). Google Glass and the rise in outsourcing our memories. *BBC Future.* http://www.bbc.com/future/story/20120703-outsourcing-our-memories on September 7, 2013

Cheah, C. S., Leung, C. Y., Tahseen, M., & Schultz, D. (2009). Authoritative parenting among immigrant Chinese mothers of preschoolers. *Journal of Family Psychology, 23*(3), 311–320.

Chen, C., Frey, C. B., & Presidente, G. (2021). Culture and contagion: Individualism and compliance with COVID-19 policy. *Journal of Economic Behavior & Organization, 190*, 191–200. https://doi.org/10.1016/j.jebo.2021.07.026

Chen, C., Xue, G., Mei, L., Chen, C., & Dong, Q. (2009). Cultural neurolinguistics. *Progress in Brain Research, 178*, 159–171.

Chen, E., Bazargan-Hejazi, S., Ani, C., Hindman, D., Pan, D., Ebrahim, G., Shirazi, A., & Banta, J. E. (2021). Schizophrenia hospitalization in the US 2005–2014: Examination of trends in demographics, length of stay, and cost. *Medicine, 100*(15), e25206. https://doi.org/10.1097/MD.0000000000025206

Chen, F. R., Rothman, E. F., & Jaffee, S. R. (2017). Early puberty, friendship group characteristics, and dating abuse in US girls. *Pediatrics, 139*(6), e20162847.

Chen, F. T., Hopman, R. J., Huang, C. J., Chu, C. H., Hillman, C. H., Hung, T. M., & Chang, Y. K. (2020). The effect of exercise training on brain structure and function in older adults: A systematic review based on evidence from randomized control trials. *Journal of Clinical Medicine, 9*(4), 914. https://doi.org/10.3390/jcm9040914

Chen, H. (2006). Flow on the net—detecting Web users' positive affects and their flow states. *Computers in Human Behavior, 22*(2), 221–233.

Chen, H., Carlson, R. A., & Wyble, B. (2018). Is source information automatically available in working memory? *Psychological Science, 29*(4), 645–655.

Chen, H., Wigand, R. T., & Nilan, M. S. (1999). Optimal experience of web activities. *Computers in Human Behavior, 15*(5), 585–608.

Chen, H., Wigand, R. T., & Nilan, M. (2000). Exploring web users' optimal flow experiences. *Information Technology & People, 13*(4), 263–281.

Chen, J. H., & Shiu, C. S. (2017). Sexual orientation and sleep in the US: A national profile. *American Journal of Preventive Medicine, 52*(4), 433–442. https://doi.org/10.1016/j.amepre.2016.10.039

Chen, J. Q., & Gardner, H. (2018). Assessment from the perspective of multiple-intelligences theory. In D. P. Flanagan & E. M. McDonough (Eds.), *Contemporary intellectual assessment: Theories, tests, and issues* (4th ed., pp. 164–173). Guilford Press.

Chen, X., Chung, J., Lechcier-Kimel, R., & French, D. (2011). Culture and social development. In P. K. Smith & C. H. Hart (Eds.), *The Wiley-Blackwell handbook of childhood social development* (2nd ed., pp. 141–160). Wiley-Blackwell.

Chen, X., Hastings, P. D., Rubin, K. H., Chen, H., Cen, G., & Stewart, S. L. (1998). Child-rearing attitudes and behavioral inhibition in Chinese and Canadian toddlers: A cross-cultural study. *Developmental Psychology, 34*(4), 677–686.

Chen, X., Kaspar, V., Zhang, Y., Wang, L., & Zheng, S. (2004). Peer relationships among Chinese and North American boys: A cross-cultural perspective. In N. Way & J. Chu (Eds.), *Adolescent boys: Exploring diverse cultures of boyhood* (pp. 197–218). New York University Press.

Chen, X. P., Liu, D., & Portnoy, R. (2012). A multilevel investigation of motivational cultural intelligence, organizational diversity climate, and cultural sales: Evidence from U.S. real estate firms. *Journal of Applied Psychology, 97*(1), 93–106.

Chen, X., Rubin, K. H., and Sun, Y. (1992). Social reputation and peer relationships in Chinese and Canadian children: A cross-cultural study. *Child Development, 63*(6), 1336–1343.

Cheney, T. (2009). *Manic: A Memoir*. HarperCollins.

Cheng, C., Cheung, S.-F., Chio, J. H., & Chan, M.-P. (2013). Cultural meaning of perceived control: A meta-analysis of locus of control and psychological symptoms across 18 cultural regions. *Psychological Bulletin, 139*(1), 152–188.

Cheng, Y. H., Roach, G. D., & Petrilli, R. (2014). Current and future directions in clinical fatigue management: An update for emergency medicine practitioners. *Emergency Medicine Australasia, 26*(6), 640–644.

Cherry, E. C. (1953). Some experiments on the recognition of speech, with one and with two ears. *The Journal of the Acoustical Society of America, 25*(5), 975–979.

Cheryan, S., Ziegler, S. A., Montoya, A. K., & Jiang, L. (2017). Why are some STEM fields more gender balanced than others? *Psychological Bulletin, 143*(1), 1–35.

Chesney, E., Goodwin, G. M., & Fazel, S. (2014). Risks of all-cause and suicide mortality in mental disorders: A meta-review. *World Psychiatry, 13*(2), 153–160. https://doi.org/10.1002/wps.20128

Chesney, M. A., & Rosenman, R. H. (1980). Type A behavior in the work setting. In C. L. Cooper & R. Payne (Eds.), *Current concerns in occupational stress* (pp. 187–212). John Wiley.

Chess, S, & Thomas, A. (1991). Temperament and the concept of goodness of fit. In J. Strelau & A. Angleitner (Eds.), *Explorations in temperament: International perspectives on theory and measurement* (pp. 15-28). Plenum Press.

Chess, S., & Thomas, A. (1986). *Temperament in clinical practice*. Guilford Press.

Chevallier, C. (2012). Theory of mind and autism: Revisiting Baron-Cohen et al.'s Sally-Anne study. In A. M. Slater & P. C. Quinn (Eds.), *Developmental psychology: Revisiting the classic studies* (pp. 148–163). Sage.

Chevallier, C., Noveck, I., Happé, F., & Wilson, D. (2011). What's in a voice? Prosody as a test case for the theory of mind account of autism. *Neuropsychologia, 49*(3), 507–517.

Chiang, H. (2015). Translating culture and psychiatry across the Pacific: How koro became culture-bound. *History of Science, 53*(1), 102–119.

Chiao, J., & Harada, T. (2008). Cultural neuroscience of consciousness: From visual perception to self-awareness. *Journal of Consciousness Studies, 15*(10–11), 58–69.

Chiappelli, F. (2012). Fundamentals: Evidence-based practice in complementary and alternative medicine- perspectives, protocols, problems, and potentials. In S. Rastogi, F. Chiappelli, M. H. Ramchandani & R. H. Singh, *Evidence-based practice in complementary and alternative medicine*, pp. 3–29. Springer.

Chiaro, G., Caletti, M. T., & Provini, F. (2015). Treatment of sleep-related eating disorder. *Current Treatment Options in Neurology, 17*(8), 33.

Chida, Y., & Steptoe, A. (2008). Positive psychological well-being and mortality: A quantitative review of prospective observational studies. *Psychosomatic Medicine, 70*(7), 741–756.

Chidiac, C. W. (2019). An update on the medical consequences of anorexia nervosa. *Current Opinion in Pediatrics, 31*(4), 448–453. https://doi.org/10.1097/MOP.0000000000000755

Chien, G. C. C., & Bolash, R. (2017). Phantom limb pain. In J. Pope & T. Deer (Eds.), *Treatment of chronic pain conditions* (pp. 283–286). Springer.

Chiesa, A., & Serretti, A. (2011). Mindfulness-based cognitive therapy for psychiatric disorders: A systematic review and meta-analysis. *Psychiatry Research, 187*(3), 441–453.

Chihuly, D. (2007). *Team Chihuly*. Portland Press.

Chisholm, J. S., Quinlivan, J. A., Petersen, R. W., & Coall, D. A. (2005). Early stress predicts age at menarche and first birth, adult attachment, and expected lifespan. *Human Nature, 16*(3), 233–265.

Chiu, L. H. (1972). A cross-cultural comparison of cognitive styles in Chinese and American children. *International Journal of Psychology, 7*(4), 235–242.

Cho, S., Crenshaw, K. W., & McCall, L. (2013). Toward a field of intersectionality studies: Theory, applications, and praxis. *Signs: Journal of Women in Culture and Society, 38*(4), 785–810.

Chodorow, N. J. (1978). *The reproduction of mothering*. University of California Press.

Chodorow, N. J. (1989). *Feminism and psychoanalytic theory*. Yale University Press.

Choi, J., & Silverman, I. (2003). Processes underlying sex differences in route-learning strategies in children and adolescents. *Personality and Individual Differences, 34*(7), 1153–1166.

Cholewiak, R. W., & Cholewiak, S. A. (2010). Cutaneous perception. In E. B. Goldstein (Ed.), *Encyclopedia of perception* (pp. 343–348). Sage.

Chomsky, N. (1959). A review of B. F. Skinner's verbal behavior. *Language, 35*(1), 26–58.

Chomsky, N. (1995). *The minimalist program* (Vol. 28). MIT Press.

Chou, H. T. G., & Edge, N. (2012). "They are happier and having better lives than I am": The impact of using Facebook on perceptions of others' lives. *Cyberpsychology, Behavior, and Social Networking, 15*(2), 117–121.

Chou, T., Carpenter, A. L., Kerns, C. E., Elkins, R. M., Green, J. G., & Comer, J. S. (2017). Disqualified qualifiers: Evaluating the utility of the revised DSM-5 definition of potentially traumatic events among area youth following the Boston marathon bombing. *Depression and Anxiety, 34*(4), 367–373.

Chrisler, J. C., & Barney, A. (2017). Sizeism is a health hazard. *Fat Studies, 6*(1), 38–53.

Christiansen, M. H., & Kirby, S. (Eds.). (2003). *Language evolution*. Oxford University Press.

Christie, B. R., Swann, S. E., Fox, C. J., Froc, D., Lieblich, S. E., Redila, V., & Webber, A. (2005). Voluntary exercise rescues deficits in spatial memory and long-term potentiation in prenatal ethanol-exposed male rats. *European Journal of Neuroscience, 21*(6), 1719–1726.

Christoforou, C., Papadopoulos, T. C., Constantinidou, F., & Theodorou, M. (2017). Your brain on the movies: A computational approach for predicting box-office performance from viewer's brain responses to movie trailers. *Frontiers in Neuroinformatics, 11*, 72.

Christophel, T. B., Klink, P. C., Spitzer, B., Roelfsema, P. R., & Haynes, J. D. (2017). The distributed nature of working memory. *Trends in Cognitive Sciences, 21*(2), 111–124.

Chrysikou, E. G. (2006). When shoes become hammers: Goal-derived categorization training enhances problem-solving performance. *Journal of Experimental Psychology: Learning, Memory, and Cognition, 32*(4), 935–942.

Chu, J., Leino, A., Pflum, S., & Sue, S. (2016). A model for the theoretical basis of cultural competency to guide psychotherapy. *Professional Psychology: Research and Practice, 47*(1), 18–29.

Chua, H. F., Boland, J. E., & Nisbett, R. E. (2005). Cultural variation in eye movements during scene perception. *Proceedings of the National Academy of Sciences of the United States of America, 102*(35), 12629–12633.

Chun, C. A., Enomoto, K., & Sue, S. (1996). Health care issues among Asian Americans. In P. M. Kato & T. Mann (Eds.), *Handbook of diversity issues in health psychology* (pp. 347–365). Springer Science+Business Media.

Chun, C., Moos R. H., & Cronkite, R. C. (2006). Culture: A fundamental context for the stress and coping paradigm. In P. T. P. Wong and L. C. J. Wong (Eds.), *Handbook of multicultural perspectives on stress and coping* (pp. 29–54). Plenum Press.

Chun, M. M., & Wolfe, J. M. (2001). Visual attention. In E. B. Goldstein (Ed.), *Blackwell handbook of perception* (pp. 272–310). Blackwell.

Chung, F. F., Yao, C. C. C., & Wan, G. H. (2005). The associations between menstrual function and life style/working conditions among nurses in Taiwan. *Journal of Occupational Health, 47*(2), 149–156.

Cialdini, R. B., & Goldstein, N. J. (2004). Social influence: Compliance and conformity. *Annual Review of Psychology, 55*, 591–621.

Cialdini R. B., & Trost, M. R. (1998). Social influence: Social norms, conformity, and compliance. In D. T. Gilbert, S. T. Fiske, & G. Lindzey (Eds.), *The handbook of social psychology* (4th ed., Vol. 2, pp. 151–192). McGraw-Hill.

Cialdini, R. B., Vincent, J. E., Lewis, S. K., Catalan, J., Wheeler, D., & Darby, B. L. (1975). Reciprocal concessions procedure for inducing compliance: The door-in-the-face technique. *Journal of Personality and Social Psychology, 31*(2), 206–215.

Cingel, D. P., & Olsen, M. K. (2018). Getting over the hump: Examining curvilinear relationships between adolescent self-esteem and Facebook use. *Journal of Broadcasting & Electronic Media, 62*(2), 215–231.

Cingel, D. P., Krcmar, M., & Olsen, M. K. (2015). Exploring predictors and consequences of personal fable ideation on Facebook. *Computers in Human Behavior, 48*(7), 28–35. https://doi.org/10.1016/j.chb.2015.01.017

Ciocanel, O., Power, K., Eriksen, A., & Gillings, K. (2017). Effectiveness of positive youth development interventions: A meta-analysis of randomized controlled trials. *Journal of Youth and Adolescence, 46*(3), 483–504.

Cipani, E., & Schock, K. M. (2007). *Functional behavioral assessment, diagnosis, and treatment*. Springer.

Cirillo, P., Gold, A. K., Nardi, A. E., Ornelas, A. C., Nierenberg, A. A., Camprodon, J., & Kinrys, G. (2019). Transcranial magnetic stimulation in anxiety and trauma-related disorders: A systematic review and meta-analysis. *Brain and Behavior, 9*(6), e01284. https://doi.org/10.1002/brb3.1284

Civitarese, G. (2014). *The necessary dream: New theories and techniques of interpretation in psychoanalysis*. Routledge.

Claparède, E. (1911). Recognition et moiïté. *Archives de Psychologie, 11*, 79–90.

Claridge, G. (1995). *Origins of mental illness: Temperament, deviance, and disorder*. Malor.

Clark, D. A., & Beck, A. T. (2010). *Cognitive therapy of anxiety disorders*. Guilford Press.

Clark, D. A., Hollifield, M., Leahy, R., & Beck, J. (2009). Theory of cognitive therapy. In G. O. Gabbard (Ed.), *Textbook of psychotherapeutic treatments* (pp. 165–200). American Psychiatric Publishing.

Clark, H. H. (1992). *Arenas of language use*. University of Chicago Press.

Clark, K. B., & Clark, M. K. (1939). The development of consciousness of self and the emergence of racial identification in Negro preschool children. *The Journal of Social Psychology, 10*(4), 591–599. https://doi.org/10.1080/00224545.1939.9713394

Clark, K. B., & Clark, M. P. (1947). Racial identification and preference in Negro children. In T. M. Newcomb & E. L. Hartley (Eds.), *Readings in social psychology*. Holt, Rinehart & Winston.

Clark, L. A., Watson, D., & Mineka, S. (1994). Temperament, personality, and the mood and anxiety disorders. *Journal of Abnormal Psychology, 103*(1), 103–116.

Clark, P., Hinton, W. J., & Grames, H. A. (2016). Therapists' perspectives of the co-therapy experience in a training setting. *Contemporary Family Therapy, 38*(2), 159–171.

Clarke, A. T. (2006). Coping with interpersonal stress and psychosocial health among children and adolescents: A meta-analysis. *Journal of Youth and Adolescence, 35*(1), 10–23.

Clarkin, J. F., Widiger, T. A., Frances, A., Hurt, S. W., & Gilmore, M. (1983). Prototypic typology and the borderline personality disorder. *Journal of Abnormal Psychology, 92*(3), 263–275.

Clarkin, J., Yeomanns, F., & Kernberg, O. (2006). *Psychotherapy for borderline personality disorder: Focusing on object relations*. American Psychiatric Association Publishing.

Clary, W. F., Burstin, K. J., & Carpenter, J. S. (1984). Multiple personality and borderline personality disorder. *Psychiatric Clinics of North America, 7*(1), 89–99.

Clegg, J. M., Wen, N., & Legare, C. H. (2017). Is non-conformity WEIRD? Cultural variation in adults' beliefs about children's competency and conformity. *Journal of Experimental Psychology: General, 146*(3), 428.

Clément, F., & Dukes, D. (2017). Social appraisal and social referencing: Two components of affective social learning. *Emotion Review, 9*(3), 253–261.

Clement, S., Schauman, O., Graham, T., Maggioni, F., Evans-Lacko, S., Bezborodovs, N., Morgan, C., Rüsch, N., Brown, J. S. L., & Thornicroft, G. (2015). What is the impact of mental health–related stigma on help-seeking? A systematic review of quantitative and qualitative studies. *Psychological Medicine, 45*(1), 11–27. https://doi.org/10.1017/S0033291714000129

Clements-Nolle, K., Marx, R., Guzman, R., & Katz, M. (2001). HIV prevalence, risk behaviors, health care use, and mental health status of transgender persons: Implications for public health intervention. *American Journal of Public Health, 91*(6), 915–921.

Clemow, D. B., & Walker, D. J. (2014). The potential for misuse and abuse of medications in ADHD: A review. *Postgraduate Medicine, 126*(5), 64–81. https://doi.org/10.3810/pgm.2014.09.2801

Climo, A. H., & Stewart, A. J. (2003). Eldercare and personality development in middle age. In J. Demick & C. Andreoletti (Eds.), *Handbook of adult development* (pp. 443–458). Kluwer.

Clinton, H. R., & Hyman, S. (1999). Mental illness is a disease. In T. I. Rodeff & L. K. Egendorf (Eds.), *How should mental illness be defined?* (pp. 37–41). Greenhaven Press.

Coates, R. D. (2011) (Ed.). *Covert racism: Theories, institutions, and experiences*. Brill Publishers.

Coburn, K., Lauterbach, E., Boutros, N., Black, K., Arciniegas, D., & Coffey, C. (2006). The value of quantitative electroencephalography in clinical psychiatry: A report by the Committee on Research of the American Neuropsychiatric Association. *Journal of Neuropsychiatry and Clinical Neurosciences, 18*(4), 460–500.

Cochran, S. D., & Mays, V. M. (2013). Sexual orientation and mental health. In C. J. Patterson & A. R. D'Augelli (Eds.), *Handbook of psychology and sexual orientation* (pp. 204–222). Oxford University Press.

Cochran, S. D., Sullivan, J. G., & Mays, V. M. (2003). Prevalence of mental disorders, psychological distress, and mental health services use among lesbian, gay, and bisexual adults in the United States. *Journal of Consulting and Clinical Psychology, 71*(1), 53–61.

Cohen, B. E., Edmondson, D., & Kronish, I. M. (2015). State of the art review: Depression, stress, anxiety, and cardiovascular disease. *American Journal of Hypertension, 28*(11), 1295–1302.

Cohen, D., & Gunz, A. (2002). As seen by the other...: Perspectives on the self in the memories and emotional perceptions of Easterners and Westerners. *Psychological Science, 13*(1), 55–59.

Cohen, L. B., & Cashon, C. H. (2006). Infant cognition. In D. Kuhn & R. Siegler (Vol. Eds.), *Handbook of child psychology* (6th ed., Vol. 2, pp. 214–251). Wiley.

Cohen, L. L., Greco, L., & Martin, S. (2013). Presenting your research. In M. J. Prinstein (Ed.), *The portable mentor: Expert guide to a successful career in psychology* (pp. 133–143). Springer.

Cohen, N., Moynihan, J. A., & Ader, R. (1994). Pavlovian conditioning of the immune system. *International Archives of Allergy and Immunology, 105*(2), 101–106.

Cohen, R., Newton-John, T., & Slater, A. (2017). The relationship between Facebook and Instagram appearance-focused activities and body image concerns in young women. *Body Image, 23*, 183–187. https://doi.org/10.1016/j.bodyim.2017.10.002

Cohen, S. (2004). Social relationships and health. *American Psychologist, 59*(8), 676–684.

Cohen, S., Doyle, W. J., Turner, R., Alper, C. M., & Skoner, D. P. (2003). Sociability and susceptibility to the common cold. *Psychological Science, 14*(5), 389–395.

Cohen, S., & Pressman, S. D. (2006). Positive affect and health. *Current Directions in Psychological Science, 15*(3), 122–125.

Cohen, S., Tyrrell, D. A., & Smith, A. P. (1991). Psychological stress and susceptibility to the common cold. *New England Journal of Medicine, 325*(9), 606–612.

Cohen, S., Tyrrell, D. A., & Smith, A. P. (1993). Negative life events, perceived stress, negative affect, and susceptibility to the common cold. *Journal of Personality and Social Psychology, 64*(1), 131–140.

Cohen, S., & Williamson, G. M. (1991). Stress and infectious disease in humans. *Psychological Bulletin, 109*(1), 5–24.

Cohen-Filipic, J. (2015). Dual relationship/conflict of interest. In R. L. Cautin & S. O. Lilienfeld (Eds.), *The encyclopedia of clinical psychology* (pp. 978–984). Wiley-Blackwell.

Cohn, A. (2001). Phonology. In M. Aronoff & J. Rees-Miller (Eds.), *The handbook of linguistics* (pp. 180–212). Blackwell.

Coid, J., Yang, N., Tyrer, P., Roberts, S., & Ullrich. S. (2006). Prevalence and correlates of personality disorder in Great Britain. *British Journal of Psychiatry, 188*(5), 423–431.

Coker, L. A., & Widiger, T. A. (2005). Personality disorders. In J. E. Maddux & B. A. Winstead (Eds.), *Psychopathology: Foundations for a contemporary understanding* (pp. 223–252). Lawrence Erlbaum.

Colcombe, S. J., Erickson, K. I., Scalf, P. E., Kim, J. S., Prakash, R., McAuley, E., Elavsky, S., Marquez, D. X., Hu, L., & Kramer, A. F. (2006). Aerobic exercise training increases brain volume in aging humans. *The Journals of Gerontology Series A: Biological Sciences and Medical Sciences, 61*(11), 1166–1170.

Cole, E. R. (2009). Intersectionality and research in psychology. *American Psychologist, 64*(3), 170–180.

Cole, M. (2005). Culture in development. In M. H. Bornstein & M. E. Lamb (Eds.), *Developmental science: An advanced textbook* (5th ed., pp. 45–101). Lawrence Erlbaum.

Cole, M. (2006). Culture and cognitive development in phylogenic, historical, and ontogenic perspective. In D. Kuhn & R. Siegler (Vol. Eds.), *Handbook of child psychology* (6th ed., Vol. 2, pp. 636–683). Wiley.

Coleman, S. R. (1997). B. F. Skinner: Maverick, inventor, behaviorist, critic. In W. G. Bringmann, H. E. Lück, R. Miller, & C. E. Early (Eds.), *A pictorial history of psychology* (pp. 206–213). Quintessence Publishing.

Coles, N. A., Larsen, J. T., & Lench, H. C. (2019). A meta-analysis of the facial feedback literature: Effects of facial feedback on emotional experience are small and variable. *Psychological Bulletin, 145*(6), 610–651. https://doi.org/10.1037/bul0000194

Coles, R. (Ed.). (2000). *The Erik Erikson reader*. W. W. Norton.

Colich, N. L., Rosen, M. L., Williams, E. S., & McLaughlin, K. A. (2020). Biological aging in childhood and adolescence following experiences of threat and deprivation: A systematic review and meta-analysis. *Psychological Bulletin, 146*(9), 721–764. https://doi.org/10.1037/bul0000270

Collins, R. L., Elliott, M. N., Berry, S. H., Kanouse, D. E., Kunkel, D., Hunter, S. B., & Miu, A. (2004). Watching sex on television predicts adolescent initiation of sexual behavior. *Pediatrics, 114*(3), e280–e289.

Collins, W. A., & Steinberg, L. (2006). Adolescent development in interpersonal context. In N. Eisenberg (Vol. Ed.), *Handbook of child psychology* (6th ed., Vol. 3, pp. 1003–1067). Wiley.

Colman, P. (2007). *Breaking the chains: The crusade of Dorothea Lynde Dix*. ASJA Press.

Colodro-Conde, L., Couvy-Duchesne, B., Whitfield, J. B., Streit, F., Gordon, S., Kemper, K. E., Yengo, L., Zheng, Z., Trzaskowski, M., de Zeeuw, E. L., Nivard, M. G., Das, M., Neale, R. E., MacGregor, S., Olsen, C. M., Whiteman, D. C., Boomsma, D. I., Yang, J., Rietschel, M., McGrath, J. J., Medland, S. E., & Martin, N. G. (2018). Association between population density and genetic risk for schizophrenia. *JAMA Psychiatry, 75*(9), 901–910.

Colom, R., Martínez-Molina, A., Shih, P. C., & Santacreu, J. (2010). Intelligence, working memory, and multitasking performance. *Intelligence, 38*(6), 543–551.

Coltheart, M. (1980). Iconic memory and visible persistence. *Perception & Psychophysics, 27*(3), 183–228.

Coltrane, S., & Messineo, M. (2000). The perpetuation of subtle prejudice: Race and gender imagery in 1990s television advertising. *Sex Roles, 42*(5–6), 363–389.

Comas-Diaz, L. (2011). Multicultural approaches to psychotherapy. In J. C. Norcross, G. R. Vandenbos, & D. K. Freedheim (Eds.), *History of psychotherapy: Continuity and change* (2nd ed., pp. 243–268). American Psychological Association.

Comas-Diaz, L. (2012). *Multicultural care: A clinician's guide to cultural competence*. American Psychological Association.

Comas-Díaz, L., & Brown, L. S. (2016). Multicultural theories. In J. C. Norcross, G. R. VandenBos, & D. K. Freedheim (Eds.), *APA handbook of clinical psychology* (Vol. 2, pp. 213–240). American Psychological Association.

Common Sense Census. (2015). *The Common Sense Census*. https://www.commonsensemedia.org/sites/default/files/uploads/research/census_researchreport.pdf

Compas, B. E., Jaser, S. S., Bettis, A. H., Watson, K. H., Gruhn, M. A., Dunbar, J. P., Williams, E., & Thigpen, J. C. (2017). Coping, emotion regulation, and psychopathology in childhood and adolescence: A meta-analysis and narrative review. *Psychological Bulletin, 143*(9), 939–991.

Compton, R. P., & Berning, A. (2015, February). *Drug and alcohol crash risk* (Traffic Safety Facts, Research Note DOT HS 812 117). National Highway Traffic Safety Administration.

Conde, L. C., Couvy-Duchesne, B., Zhu, G., Meyer-Lindenberg, A., Rietschel, M., Medland, S., Whitfield, J., & Martin, N. (2017). Higher genetic risk for schizophrenia is associated with living in urban and populated areas. *European Neuropsychopharmacology, 27*(Suppl. 3), S488.

Condon, J., Luszcz, M., & McKee, I. (2018). The transition to grandparenthood: A prospective study of mental health implications. *Aging & Mental Health, 22*(3), 336–343.

Cone, J. E., Vaughan, L. M., Huete, A., & Samuels, S. J. (1998). Reproductive health outcomes among female flight attendants: An exploratory study. *Journal of Occupational and Environmental Medicine, 40*(3), 210–216.

Conklin, Q. A., Crosswell, A. D., Saron, C. D., & Epel, E. S. (2018). Meditation, stress processes, and telomere biology. *Current Opinion in Psychology, 28*, 92–101.

Connelly, B. S., & Ones, D. S. (2010). Another perspective on personality: Meta-analytic integration of observers' accuracy and predictive validity. *Psychological Bulletin, 136*(6), 1092.

Connolly, J., Craig, W., Goldberg, A., & Pepler, D. (2004). Mixed-gender groups, dating, and romantic relationships in early adolescence. *Journal of Research on Adolescence, 14*(2), 185–207.

Connolly, J., Friedlander, L., Pepler, D., Craig, W., & Laporte, L. (2010). The ecology of adolescent dating aggression: Attitudes, relationships, media use, and socio-demographic risk factors. *Journal of Aggression, Maltreatment & Trauma, 19*(5), 469–491.

Connolly, J. A., & McIsaac, C. (2009). Romantic relationships in adolescence. In R. M. Lerner & L. Steinberg (Eds.), *Handbook of adolescent psychology* (3rd ed., Vol. 2, pp. 104–151). Wiley.

Connolly, J., & McIsaac, C. (2011). Romantic relationships in adolescence. In M. K. Underwood & L. H. Rosen (Eds.), *Social development: Relationships in infancy, childhood, and adolescence* (pp. 180–203). Guilford Press.

Connolly, J. J., Kavanagh, E. J., & Viswesvaran, C. (2007). The convergent validity between self and observer ratings of personality: A meta-analytic review. *International Journal of Selection and Assessment, 15*(1), 110–117.

Connolly, S. L., & Alloy, L. B. (2018). Negative event recall as a vulnerability for depression: Relationship between momentary stress-reactive rumination and memory for daily life stress. *Clinical Psychological Science, 6*(1), 32–47.

Conover, E. A., & Polifka, J. E. (2011, August). The art and science of teratogen risk communication. *American Journal of Medical Genetics Part C: Seminars in Medical Genetics, 157*(3), 227–233.

Constantine, M. G. (2002). Predictors of satisfaction with counseling: Racial and ethnic minority clients' attitudes toward counseling and ratings of their counselors' general and multicultural counseling competence. *Journal of Counseling Psychology, 49*(2), 255–263.

Constantino, M. J., Glass, C. R., Arnkoff, D. B., Ametrano, R. M., & Smith, J. Z. (2011). Expectations. In J. C. Norcross (Ed.), *Psychotherapy relationships that work: Evidence-based responsiveness* (2nd ed., pp. 354–376). Oxford University Press.

Constantino, M. J., Lembke, A., Fischer, C., & Arnow, B. A. (2006). Adult depression: Features, burdens, models, and interventions. In T. G. Plante (Ed.), *Mental disorders of the new millennium* (Vol. 1, pp. 139–166). Praeger.

Constantino, M. J., Visl⊠, A., Coyne, A. E., & Boswell, J. F. (2018). A meta-analysis of the association between patients' early treatment outcome expectation and their posttreatment outcomes. *Psychotherapy, 55*(4), 473–485.

Contrada, R. J., Ashmore, R. D., Gary, M. L., Coups, E., Egeth, J. D., Sewell, A., Ewell K., Goyal, T. M., & Chasse, V. (2000). Ethnicity-related sources of stress and their effects on well-being. *Current Directions in Psychological Science, 9*(4), 136–139.

Contrada, R. J., Ashmore, R. D., Gary, M. L., Coups, E., Egeth, J. D., Sewell, A., Ewell K., Goyal, T. M., & Chasse, V. (2001). Measures of ethnicity-related stress: Psychometric properties, ethnic group differences, and associations with well-being. *Journal of Applied Social Psychology, 31*(9), 1775–1820.

Contrada, R. J., & Baum, A. (2011). *The handbook of stress science: Biology, psychology, and health*. Springer.

Conway, M. A. (2008). Exploring episodic memory. In E. Dere, A. Easton, L. Nadel, & J. P. Huston (Eds.), *Handbook of episodic memory* (pp. 19–29). Elsevier Science.

Conway, M. A., Wang, Q., Hanyu, K., & Haque, S. (2005). A cross-cultural investigation of autobiographical memory on the universality and cultural variation of the reminiscence bump. *Journal of Cross-Cultural Psychology, 36*(6), 739–749.

Cook, E. W., Hodes, R. L., & Lang, P. J. (1986). Preparedness and phobia: Effects of stimulus content on human visceral conditioning. *Journal of Abnormal Psychology, 95(3)*, 195–207.

Cook, J. M., Biyanova, T., & Coyne, J. C. (2009). Influential psychotherapy figures, authors, and books: An Internet survey of over 2,000 psychotherapists. *Psychotherapy: Theory, Research, Practice, Training, 46*(1), 42–51.

Cook, J. M., Biyanova, T., Elhai, J., Schnurr, P. P., & Coyne, J. C. (2010). What do psychotherapists really do in practice? An Internet study of over 2,000 practitioners. *Psychotherapy: Theory, Research, Practice, Training, 47*(2), 260–267.

Cook, K. (2014). *Kitty Genovese: The murder, the bystanders, the crime that changed America*. W. W. Norton.

Cooksey-Stowers, K., Schwartz, M. B., & Brownell, K. D. (2017). Food swamps predict obesity rates better than food deserts in the United States. *International Journal of Environmental Research and Public Health, 14*(11), 1366. https://doi.org/10.3390/ijerph14111366

Cooper, C. L., & Dewe, P. (2004). *Stress: A brief history*. Blackwell.

Cooper, H., & Goodnough, A. (2009, July 30). Over beers, no apologies, but plans to have lunch." *The New York Times*. http://www.nytimes.com/2009/07/31/us/politics/31obama.html

Cooper, J. (1999). Unwanted consequences and the self: In search of the motivation for dissonance reduction. In E. Harmon-Jones & J. Mills (Eds.), *Cognitive dissonance: Progress on a pivotal theory in social psychology* (pp. 149–173). American Psychological Association.

Cooper, J. (2007). *Cognitive dissonance: 50 years of a classic theory*. Sage.

Cooper, J. (2012). Cognitive dissonance theory. In P. A. M. Van Lange, A. W. Kruglanski, & E. T. Higgins (Eds.), *Handbook of theories of social psychology* (Vol. 1, pp. 377–397). Sage.

Cooper, L., & Bright, J. (2001). Individual differences in reactions to stress. In F. Jones & J. Bright (Eds.), *Stress: Myth, theory and research* (pp. 111–131). Pearson Education Ltd.

Copeland, W. E., Angold, A., Costello, E. J., & Egger, H. (2013). Prevalence, comorbidity, and correlates of DSM-5 proposed disruptive mood dysregulation disorder. *American Journal of Psychiatry, 170*(2), 173–179.

Copenhaver, A., & Ferguson, C. J. (2018). Selling violent video game solutions: A look inside the APA's internal notes leading to the creation of the APA's 2005 resolution on violence in video games and interactive media. *International Journal of Law and Psychiatry, 57*, 77–84. https://doi.org/ 10.1016/j.ijlp.2018.01.004

Copp, H. L., & Koehler, W. J. (2017). Peer attitudes toward LGBT-identified university students as mediated by demographic factors. *Journal of Gay & Lesbian Mental Health, 21*(4), 277–291.

Corballis, M. C. (2007). The evolution of consciousness. In P. D. Zelazo, M. Moscovitch, & E. Thompson (Eds.), *The Cambridge handbook of consciousness* (pp. 571–596). Cambridge University Press.

Corcoran, K., Crusius, J., & Mussweiler, T. (2011). Social comparison: Motives, standards, and mechanisms. In D. Chadee (Ed.), *Theories in social psychology* (pp. 119–139). Wiley-Blackwell.

Corey, G., & Corey, M. S. (2016). Group psychotherapy. In J. C. Norcross, G. R. VandenBos, & D. K. Freedheim (Eds.), *APA handbook of clinical psychology* (Vol. 3, pp. 289–306). American Psychological Association.

Corkin, S. (2013). *Permanent present tense: The unforgettable life of the amnesic patient, H. M.* Basic Books.

Cornblatt, B. A., Green, M. F., Walker, E. F., & Mittal, V. A. (2009). Schizophrenia: Etiology and neurocognition. In P. H. Blaney & T. Millon (Eds.), *Oxford textbook of psychopathology* (2nd ed., pp. 298–332). Oxford University Press.

Cornette, M. M., Strauman, T. J., Abramson, L. Y., & Busch, A. M. (2009). Self-discrepancy and suicidal ideation. *Cognition and Emotion, 23*(3), 504–527.

Corney, W. J., & Richards, C. H. (2005). A comparative analysis of the desirability of work characteristics: Chile versus the United States. *International Journal of Management, 22*(2), 159–165. https://www.proquest.com/openview/f3d45dd094d74b51c466f4dae5c84a90/1?pq-origsite=gscholar&cbl=5703

Corrigan, P. (2004). How stigma interferes with mental health care. *American Psychologist, 59*(7), 614–625. https://doi.org/10.1037/0003-066X.59.7.614

Corrigan, P. W. (2007). How clinical diagnosis might exacerbate the stigma of mental illness. *Social Work, 52*(1), 31–39. https://doi.org/10.1093/sw/52.1.31

Corrigan, P. W. (2014). Afterword: A critical eye for stigma change. In P. W. Corrigan (Ed.), *The stigma of disease and disability* (pp. 297–301). American Psychological Association.

Corrigan, P. W., Bink, A. B., Schmidt, A., Jones, N., & Rüsch, N. (2016). What is the impact of self-stigma? Loss of self-respect and the "why try" effect. *Journal of Mental Health, 25*(1), 10–15. https://doi.org/10.3109/09638237.2015.1021902

Corrigan, P. W., Larson, J. E., & Rüsch, N. (2009). Self-stigma and the "why try" effect: Impact on life goals and evidence-based practices. *World Psychiatry, 8*(2), 75. https://doi.org/10.1002/j.2051-5545.2009.tb00218.x

Corrigan, P. W., Morris, S. B., Michaels, P. J., Rafacz, J. D., & Rüsch, N. (2012). Challenging the public stigma of mental illness: A meta-analysis of outcome studies. Psychiatric Services, 63(10), 963–973. https://doi.org/10.1176/appi.ps.201100529

Corrigan, P. W., Nieweglowski, K., & Sayer, J. (2019). Self-stigma and the mediating impact of the "why try" effect on depression. *Journal of Community Psychology, 47*(3), 698–705. https://doi.org/10.1002/jcop.22144

Corrigan, P. W., River, L. P., Lundin, R. K., Penn, D. L., Uphoff-Wasowski, K., Campion, J., Mathisen, J., Gagnon, C., Bergman, M., Goldstein, H., & Kubiak, M. A. (2001). Three strategies for changing attributions about severe mental illness. *Schizophrenia Bulletin, 27*(2), 187–195. https://doi.org/10.1093/oxfordjournals.schbul.a006865

Corrigan, P. W., & Watson, A. C. (2005). Mental illness and dangerousness: Fact or misperception, and implications for stigma. In P. W. Corrigan (Ed.), *On the stigma of mental illness: Practical strategies for research and social change* (pp. 165–179). American Psychological Association.

Cortese, S., Kelly, C., Chabernaud, C., Proal, E., Adriana Di Martino, M. D., Milham, M. P., & Castellanos, F. X. (2012). Toward systems neuroscience of ADHD: A meta-analysis of 55 fMRI studies. *American Journal of Psychiatry, 169*(10), 1038–1055.

Costa, P. A., Pereira, H., & Leal, I. (2015). "The contact hypothesis" and attitudes toward same-sex parenting. *Sexuality Research and Social Policy, 12*(2), 125–136.

Costa, P. T., & McCrae, R. R. (1985). *The NEO personality inventory*. Psychological Assessment Resources.

Costa, P. T., & McCrae, R. R. (1992a). Four ways five factors are basic. *Personality and Individual Differences, 13*(6), 653–665.

Costa, P. T., & McCrae, R. R. (1992b). *Revised NEO personality inventory (NEO) PI-R and NEO five-factor inventory: Professional manual*. Psychological Assessment Resources.

Costa, P. T., & Widiger, T. A. (2001). *Personality disorders and the five-factor model of personality* (2nd ed.). American Psychological Association.

Costa, P. T., Jr., & McCrae, R. R. (2008). The NEO inventories. In R. P. Archer & S. R. Smith (Eds.), *Personality assessment* (pp. 213–246). Routledge.

Costa, P. T., Jr., & McCrae, R. R. (2017). The NEO Inventories as instruments of psychological theory. In T. A. Widiger (Ed.), *The Oxford handbook of the Five Factor Model* (pp. 11–38). Oxford University Press.

Costa, P., Jr., Terracciano, A., & McCrae, R. R. (2001). Gender differences in personality traits across cultures: Robust and surprising findings. *Journal of Personality and Social Psychology, 81*(2), 322–331.

Côté, J. E. (2009). Identity formation and self-development in adolescence. In R. M. Lerner & L. Steinberg (Eds.), *Handbook of adolescent psychology* (3rd ed., Vol. 1, pp. 266–304). Wiley.

Côté, J. E. (2014). The dangerous myth of emerging adulthood: An evidence-based critique of a flawed developmental theory. *Applied Developmental Science, 18*(4), 177–188.

Côté, J., & Bynner, J. M. (2008). Changes in the transition to adulthood in the UK and Canada: The role of structure and agency in emerging adulthood. *Journal of Youth Studies, 11*(3), 251–268.

Côté, S., Lopes, P. N., Salovey, P., & Miners, C. T. (2010). Emotional intelligence and leadership emergence in small groups. *The Leadership Quarterly, 21*(3), 496–508.

Côté, S. M., Vaillancourt, T., Barker, E. D., Nagin, D., & Tremblay, R. E. (2007). The joint development of physical and indirect aggression: Predictors of continuity and change during childhood. *Development and Psychopathology, 19*(1), 37–55.

Courtin, E., & Knapp, M. (2017). Social isolation, loneliness and health in old age: A scoping review. *Health & Social Care in the Community, 25*(3), 799–812.

Couture, S., & Penn, D. (2003). Interpersonal contact and the stigma of mental illness: A review of the literature. *Journal of Mental Health, 12*(3), 291–305. https://doi.org/10.1080/09638231000118276

Couturier, J., & Lock, J. (2006). Eating disorders: Anorexia nervosa, bulimia nervosa, and binge eating disorder. In T. G. Plante (Ed.), *Mental disorders of the new millennium* (Vol. 3, pp. 135–156). Praeger.

Covre, P., Baddeley, A. D., Hitch, G. J., & Bueno, O. F. A. (2018). Maintaining task set against distraction: The role of working memory in multitasking. *Psychology & Neuroscience, 12*(1). https://doi.org/10.1037/pne0000152

Cowan, N. (1988). Evolving conceptions of memory storage, selective attention, and their mutual constraints within the human information-processing system. *Psychological Bulletin, 104*(2), 163–191.

Cowan, N. (2001). The magical number 4 in short-term memory: A reconsideration of mental storage capacity. *Behavioral and Brain Sciences, 24*(1), 87–114.

Cowan, N. (2005). *Working memory capacity*. Psychology Press.

Cowan, N. (2008). What are the differences between long-term, short-term, and working memory? *Progress in Brain Research, 169*, 323–338.

Cowan, N. (2010). The magical mystery four: How is working memory capacity limited, and why? *Current Directions in Psychological Science, 19*(1), 51–57.

Cowart, B. J., & Rawson, N. E. (2001). Olfaction. In E. B. Goldstein (Ed.), *Blackwell handbook of perception* (pp. 567–635). Blackwell.

Cowell, J. M., Lee, K., Malcolm-Smith, S., Selcuk, B., Zhou, X., & Decety, J. (2017). The development of generosity and moral cognition across five cultures. *Developmental Science, 20*(4), e12403.

Coyne, S. M., Linder, J. R., Rasmussen, E. E., Nelson, D. A., & Birkbeck, V. (2016). Pretty as a princess: Longitudinal effects of engagement with Disney princesses on gender stereotypes, body esteem, and prosocial behavior in children. *Child Development, 87*(6), 1909–1925.

Coyne, S. M., Padilla-Walker, L. M., Holmgren, H. G., Davis, E. J., Collier, K. M., Memmott-Elison, M. K., & Hawkins, A. J. (2018). A meta-analysis of prosocial media on prosocial behavior, aggression, and empathic concern: A multidimensional approach. *Developmental Psychology, 54*(2), 331–347.

Cozolino, L. J. (2008). *The healthy aging brain: Sustaining attachment, attaining wisdom*. W. W. Norton.

Cozolino, L. (2010). *The neuroscience of psychotherapy: Healing the social brain* (2nd ed.). Norton

Cozolino, L. J. (2017). *The neuroscience of psychotherapy: Healing the social brain* (3rd ed.). Norton.

Craddock, N., & Jones, I. (1999). Genetics of bipolar disorder. *Journal of Medical Genetics, 36*(8), 585–594.

Craig, S. L., & McInroy, L. (2014). You can form a part of yourself online: The influence of new media on identity development and coming out for LGBTQ youth. *Journal of Gay & Lesbian Mental Health, 18*(1), 95–109.

Craig, C., Overbeek, R., Condon, M., & Rinaldo, S. B. (2016). A relationship between temperature and aggression in NFL football penalties. *Journal of Sport and Health Sciences, 5*(2), 205–210. https://doi.org/10.1016/j.jshs.2015.01.001

Craighead, W. E., Ritschel, L. A., Arnarson, E. O., & Gillespie, C. F. (2008). Major depressive disorder. In W. E. Craighead, D. J. Milkowitz, & L. W. Craighead (Eds.), *Psychopathology: History, diagnosis, and empirical foundations* (pp. 279–328). Wiley.

Craik, F. I. M. (2002). Levels of processing: Past, present—and future? *Memory, 10*(5–6), 305–318.

Craik, F. I. M. (2007). Encoding: A cognitive perspective. In H. L. Roediger, Y. Dudai, & S. M. Fitzpatrick (Eds.), *Science of memory: Concepts* (pp. 129–135). Oxford University Press.

Craik, F. I. M., & Lockhart, R. S. (1972). Levels of processing: A framework for memory research. *Journal of Verbal Learning and Verbal Behavior, 11*(6), 671–684.

Craik, F. I. M., & Tulving, E. (1975). Depth of processing and the retention of words in episodic memory. *Journal of Experimental Psychology: General, 104*(3), 268–294.

Craik, F. I. M., & Watkins, M. J. (1973). The role of rehearsal in short-term memory. *Journal of Verbal Learning and Verbal Behavior, 12*(6), 599–607.

Crane, C. A., Godleski, S. A., Przybyla, S. M., Schlauch, R. C., & Testa, M. (2016). The proximal effects of acute alcohol consumption on male-to-female aggression: A meta-analytic review of the experimental literature. *Trauma, Violence, & Abuse, 17*(5), 520–531.

Crane, R. S. (2017). Implementing mindfulness in the mainstream: Making the path by walking it. *Mindfulness, 8*(3), 585–594.

Crano, W. D., & Lac, A. (2012). The evolution of research methodologies in social psychology: A historical analysis. In A. W. Kruglanski & W. Stroebe (Eds.), *Handbook of the history of social psychology* (pp. 159–174). Psychology Press.

Craske, M. G. (2010). *Cognitive-behavioral therapy*. American Psychological Association.

Craske, M. G., & Barlow, D. H. (2008). Panic disorder and agoraphobia. In D. H. Barlow (Ed.), *Clinical handbook of psychological disorders: A step-by-step treatment manual* (4th ed., pp. 1–64). Guilford Press.

Craske, M. G., Rauch, S. L., Ursano, R., Prenoveau, J., Pine, D. S., & Zinbarg, R. E. (2009). What is an anxiety disorder? *Depression and Anxiety, 26*(12), 1066–1085.

Crawford, C. (1998). The theory of evolution in the study of human behavior: An introduction and overview. In C. Crawford & D. L. Krebs (Eds.), *Handbook of evolutionary psychology: Ideas, issues, and applications* (pp. 3–43). Lawrence Erlbaum.

Credé, M., Roch, S. G., & Kieszczynka, U. M. (2010). Class attendance in college: A meta-analytic review of the relationship of class attendance with grades and student characteristics. *Review of Educational Research, 80*(2), 272–295.

Crenshaw, K. (1989). Demarginalizing the intersection of race and sex: A black feminist critique of antidiscrimination doctrine, feminist theory and antiracist politics. *University of Chicago Legal Forum, 139*(1), 139–168.

Crenshaw, K. (1991). Mapping the margins: Intersectionality, identity politics, and violence against women of color. *Stanford Law Review, 43*(6), 1241–1299.

Crespo, C. J., Smit, E., Troiano, R. P., Bartlett, S. J., Macera, C. A., & Andersen, R. E. (2001). Television watching, energy intake, and obesity in U.S. children: Results from the third National Health and Nutrition Examination Survey, 1988–1994. *Archives of Pediatrics & Adolescent Medicine, 155*(3), 360–365.

Creswell, J. D., Way, B. M., Eisenberger, N. I., & Lieberman, M. D. (2007). Neural correlates of dispositional mindfulness during affect labeling. *Psychosomatic Medicine, 69*(6), 560–565.

Crews, D. J., & Landers, D. M. (1987). A meta-analytic review of aerobic fitness and reactivity to psychosocial stressors. *Medicine & Science in Sports & Exercise, 19*(5), 114–120.

Crick, N. R., & Grotpeter, J. K. (1995). Relational aggression, gender, and social-psychological adjustment. *Child Development, 66*(3), 710–722.

Crisler, M. C., Brooks, J. O., Ogle, J. H., Guirl, C. D., Alluri, P., & Dixon, K. K. (2008). Effect of wireless communication and entertainment devices on simulated driving performance. *Transportation Research Record: Journal of the Transportation Research Board, 2069*(1), 48–54.

Crisp, R. J., & Maitner, A. T. (2011). Social categorization theories: From culture to cognition. In D. Chadee (Ed.), *Theories in social psychology* (pp. 232–249). Wiley-Blackwell.

Crispim, C., & Mota, M. (2018, June 29). New perspectives on chrononutrition. *Biological Rhythm Research, 50*(1), 1–15.

Crits-Christoph, P., Gibbons, M. B. C., Hamilton, J., Ring-Kurtz, S., & Gallop, R. (2011). The dependability of alliance assessments: The alliance–outcome correlation is larger than you might think. *Journal of Consulting and Clinical Psychology, 79*(3), 267–278.

Crittenden, K. S. (1991). Asian self-effacement or feminine modesty? Attributional patterns of women university students in Taiwan. *Gender & Society, 5*(1), 98–117.

Crivelli, C., Russell, J. A., Jarillo, S., & Fernández-Dols, J. M. (2017). Recognizing spontaneous facial expressions of emotion in a small-scale society of Papua New Guinea. *Emotion, 17*(2), 337–347.

Crocetti, E., Klimstra, T., Keijsers, L., Hale, W. W., III, & Meeus, W. (2009). Anxiety trajectories and identity development in adolescence: A five-wave longitudinal study. *Journal of Youth and Adolescence, 38*(6), 839–849.

Crocker, J., & Park, L. E. (2004). The costly pursuit of self-esteem. *Psychological Bulletin, 130*(3), 392–414.

Crocq, M. A. (2015). A history of anxiety: From Hippocrates to DSM. *Dialogues in Clinical Neuroscience, 17*(3), 319–325.

Croizet, J. C., & Claire, T. (1998). Extending the concept of stereotype threat to social class: The intellectual underperformance of students from low socioeconomic backgrounds. *Personality and Social Psychology Bulletin, 24*(6), 588–594.

Crow, S. J., & Brandenburg, B. (2010). Diagnosis, assessment, and treatment planning for bulimia nervosa. In C. M. Grilo & J. E. Mitchell (Eds.), *The treatment of eating disorders: A clinical handbook* (pp. 28–43). Guilford Press.

Crowder, R. G., & Green, R. L. (2000). Serial learning: Cognition and behavior. In E. Tulving & F. I. M. Craik (Eds.), *The Oxford handbook of memory* (pp. 125–135). Oxford University Press.

Crowe, E., & Higgins, E. T. (1997). Regulatory focus and strategic inclinations: Promotion and prevention in decision-making. *Organizational Behavior and Human Decision Processes, 69*(2), 117–132.

Crowe, S. F., Matthews, C., & Walkenhorst, E. (2007). Relationship between worry, anxiety and thought suppression and the components of working memory in a non-clinical sample. *Australian Psychologist, 42*(3), 170–177.

Crowne, K. A. (2008). What leads to cultural intelligence? *Business Horizons, 51*(5), 391–399.

Crum, A. J., Salovey, P., & Achor, S. (2013). Rethinking stress: The role of mindsets in determining the stress response. *Journal of Personality and Social Psychology, 104*(4), 716–733.

Crystal, D. (2008). *Txtng: The gr8 db8*. Oxford University Press.

Csikszentmihalyi, M. (1975). *Beyond boredom and anxiety*. Jossey-Bass.

Csikszentmihalyi, M. (1990). *Flow: The psychology of optimal experience* (Vol. 3, pp. 13–36). Harper & Row.

Csupak, B., Sommer, J. L., Jacobsohn, E., & El-Gabalawy, R. (2018). A population-based examination of the co-occurrence and functional correlates of chronic pain and generalized anxiety disorder. *Journal of Anxiety Disorders, 56*, 74–80.

Cuijpers, P., Quero, S., Noma, H., Ciharova, M., Miguel, C., Karyotaki, E., Cipriani, A., Cristea, I. A., & Furukawa, T. A. (2021). Psychotherapies for depression: A network meta-analysis covering efficacy, acceptability and long-term outcomes of all main treatment types. *World Psychiatry, 20*(2), 283–293. https://doi.org/10.1002/wps.20860

Cuijpers, P., Reijnders, M., & Huibers, M. J. (2018). The role of common factors in psychotherapy outcomes. *Annual Review of Clinical Psychology, 15*, 207–231. https://doi.org/10.1146/annurev-clinpsy-050718-095424

Cuijpers, P., Van Straten, A., & Warmerdam, L. (2007). Behavioral activation treatments of depression: A meta-analysis. *Clinical Psychology Review, 27*(3), 318–326.

Cummings, N. A. (2007). Treatment and assessment take place in an economic context, always. In S. O. Lilienfeld & W. T. O'Donohue (Eds.), *The great ideas of clinical science: 17 principles that every mental health professional should understand* (pp. 163–184). Routledge.

Curci, A., Lanciano, T., Maddalena, C., Mastandrea, S., & Sartori, G. (2015). Flashbulb memories of the Pope's resignation: Explicit and implicit measures across differing religious groups. *Memory, 23*(4), 529–544.

Curci, A., & Luminet, O. (2006). Follow-up of a cross-national comparison on flashbulb and event memory for the September 11th attacks. *Memory, 14*(3), 329–344.

Curci, A., & Luminet, O. (2009). General conclusions. In O. Luminet & A. Curci (Eds.), *Flashbulb memories: New issues and new perspectives* (pp. 269–276). Psychology Press.

Curcio, G., Ferrara, M., & De Gennaro, L. (2006). Sleep loss, learning capacity and academic performance. *Sleep Medicine Reviews, 10*(5), 323–337.

Curry, K. T., & Hanson, W. E. (2010). National survey of psychologists' test feedback training, supervision, and practice: A mixed methods study. *Journal of Personality Assessment, 92*(4), 327–336.

Curtis, R. C., & Miller, K. (1986). Believing another likes or dislikes you: Behaviors making the beliefs come true. *Journal of Personality and Social Psychology, 51*(2), 284.

Cury, F., Da Fonseca, D., Zahn, I., & Elliot, A. (2008). Implicit theories and IQ test performance: A sequential mediational analysis. *Journal of Experimental Social Psychology, 44*(3), 783–791.

Cushner, K., & Mahon, J. (2009). Intercultural competence in teacher education. In D. K. Deardorff (Ed.), *The Sage handbook of intercultural competence* (pp. 304–320). Sage.

Czeisler, C. A., & Dijk, D.-J. (2001). Human circadian physiology and sleep–wake regulation. In J. S. Takahashi, F. W. Turek, & R. Y. Moore (Eds.), *Circadian clocks* (pp. 531–569). Kluwer Academic/Plenum.

Czeisler, C. A., Duffy, J. F., Shanahan, T. L., Brown, E. N., Mitchell, J. F., Rimmer, D. W., & Kronauer, R. E. (1999). Stability, precision, and near 24-hour period of the human circadian pacemaker. *Science, 284*(5423), 2177–2181.

D'Amour, S., Bos, J. E., & Keshavarz, B. (2017). The efficacy of airflow and seat vibration on reducing visually induced motion sickness. *Experimental Brain Research, 235*(9), 2811–2820.

Da Fonseca, D., Cury, F., Fakra, E., Rufo, M., Poinso, F., Bounoua, L., & Huguet, P. (2008). Implicit theories of intelligence and IQ test performance in adolescents with Generalized Anxiety Disorder. *Behaviour Research and Therapy, 46*(4), 529–536.

Dabul, A. J., Bernal, M. E., & Knight, G. P. (1995). Allocentric and idiocentric self-description and academic achievement among Mexican American and Anglo American adolescents. *The Journal of Social Psychology, 135*(5), 621–630.

Dahling, J. J. (2017). Exhausted, mistreated, or indifferent? Explaining deviance from emotional display rules at work. *European Journal of Work and Organizational Psychology, 26*(2), 171–182.

Dai, H., & Hao, J. (2019). Sleep deprivation and chronic health conditions among sexual minority adults. *Behavioral Sleep Medicine, 17*(3), 254–268. https://doi.org/10.1080/15402002.2017.1342166

Dale, K. R., Raney, A. A., Janicke, S. H., Sanders, M. S., & Oliver, M. B. (2017). YouTube for good: A content analysis and examination of elicitors of self-transcendent media. *Journal of Communication, 67*(6), 897–919.

Daley, A. (2008). Exercise and depression: A review of reviews. *Journal of Clinical Psychology in Medical Settings, 15*(2), 140–147.

Daley, C. E., & Onwuegbuzie, A. J. (2011). Race and intelligence. In R. J. Sternberg & S. B. Kaufman (Eds.), *The Cambridge handbook of intelligence* (pp. 293–308). Cambridge University Press.

Dalgleish, T. (2004). The emotional brain. *Nature Reviews Neuroscience, 5*(7), 583–589.

Dalgleish, T., & Cox, S. G. (2002). Memory and emotional disorder. In A. D. Baddeley, M. D. Kopelman, & B. A. Wilson (Eds.), *The handbook of memory disorders* (2nd ed., pp. 437–449). Wiley.

Dallam, S. J. (2005). Health issues associated with violence against women. In K. A. Kendall-Tackett (Ed.), *Handbook of women, stress, and trauma* (pp. 159–180). Brunner-Routledge.

Dalrymple, K. L., Guadiano, B. A., & Weinstock, L. M. (2015). Efficacy versus effectiveness research. In R. L. Cautin & S. O. Lilienfeld (Eds.), *The encyclopedia of clinical psychology* (pp. 1015–1021). Wiley-Blackwell.

Dalton, M. A., Beach, M. L., Adachi-Mejia, A. M., Raymond, M., Matzkin, A. L., Sargent, J. D., Heatherton, T. F., & Titus, L. (2009). Early exposure to movie smoking predicts established smoking by older teens and young adults. *Pediatrics, 123*(4), 551–558.

Daly, M., & Robinson, E. (2021). Psychological distress and adaptation to the COVID-19 crisis in the United States. *Journal of Psychiatric Research, 136*, 603–609. https://doi.org/10.1016/j.jpsychires.2020.10.035

Daly, M., & Wilson, M. (1988). *Homicide*. Aldine Transaction.

Damasio, A. R. (1994). *Descartes' error: Emotion, rationality and the human brain*. Putnam.

Damasio, H., Grabowski, T., Frank, R., Galaburda, A. M., & Damasio, A. R. (1994). The return of Phineas Gage: Clues about the brain from the skull of a famous patient. *Science, 264*(5162), 1102–1105.

Damian, R. I., & Roberts, B. W. (2015). The associations of birth order with personality and intelligence in a representative sample of US high school students. *Journal of Research in Personality, 58*, 96–105.

Damian, R. I., Su, R., Shanahan, M., Trautwein, U., & Roberts, B. W. (2015). Can personality traits and intelligence compensate for background disadvantage? Predicting status attainment in adulthood. *Journal of Personality and Social Psychology, 109*(3), 473–489.

Damon, W. (2004). What is positive youth development? *The Annals of the American Academy of Political and Social Science, 591*(1), 13–24.

Dan, A., Mondal, T., Chakraborty, K., Chaudhuri, A., & Biswas, A. (2017). Clinical course and treatment outcome of Koro: A follow up study from a Koro epidemic reported from West Bengal, India. *Asian Journal of Psychiatry, 26*, 14–20.

Dana, R. H. (2005). *Multicultural assessment: Principles, applications, and examples*. Lawrence Erlbaum.

Daniels, D., & Plomin, R. (1985). Origins of individual differences in infant shyness. *Developmental Psychology, 21*(1), 118–121.

Daniels, E. A., & Zurbriggen, E. L. (2016). "It's not the right way to do stuff on Facebook": An investigation of adolescent girls' and young women's attitudes toward sexualized photos on social media. *Sexuality & Culture, 20*(4), 936–964.

Daniels, H. (1996). Introduction: Psychology in a social world. In H. Daniels (Ed.), *An introduction to Vygotsky* (pp. 1–27). Routledge.

Daniels, H. (2011). Vygotsky and psychology. In U. Goswami (Ed.), *The Wiley-Blackwell handbook of childhood cognitive development* (2nd ed., pp. 673–696). Wiley-Blackwell.

Daniels, S. R., Arnett, D. K., Eckel, R. H., Gidding, S. S., Hayman, L. L., Kumanyika, S., Robinson, T. N., Scott, B. J., St Jeor, S., & Williams, C. L. (2005). Overweight in children and adolescents: Pathophysiology, consequences, prevention, and treatment. *Circulation, 111*(15), 1999–2012.

Danion, J., Huron, C., Rizzo, L., & Vidaihet, P. (2004). Emotion, memory, and conscious awareness in schizophrenia. In D. Reisberg & P. Hertel (Eds.), *Memory and emotion* (pp. 217–241). Oxford University Press.

Danner, F., & Phillips, B. (2008). Adolescent sleep, school start times, and teen motor vehicle crashes. *Journal of Clinical Sleep Medicine: Official Publication of the American Academy of Sleep Medicine, 4*(6), 533.

Danoff-Burg, S., & Revenson, T. A. (2005). Benefit-finding among patients with rheumatoid arthritis: Positive effects on interpersonal relationships. *Journal of Behavioral Medicine, 28*(1), 91–103.

Danquah, M. N. (1999). *Willow weep for me: A black woman's journey through depression*. One World/Ballantine.

Danquah, M. N. (2002). Writing the wrongs of identity. In N. Casey (Ed.), *Unholy ghost: Writers on depression* (pp. 173–180). Perennial.

Danziger, K. (2006). Universalism and indigenization in the history of modern psychology. In A. C. Brock (Ed.), *Internationalizing the history of psychology* (pp. 208–225). New York University Press.

Danziger, K., & Ballantyne, P. (1997). Psychological experiments. In W. G. Bringmann, H. E. Lück, R. Miller, & C. E. Early (Eds.), *A pictorial history of psychology* (pp. 233–239). Quintessence Publishing.

Darcangelo, S. (2012). Fetishism: Psychotherapy and theory. In D. R. Laws & W. T. O'Donohue (Eds.), *Sexual deviance: Theory, assessment, and treatment* (2nd ed., pp. 108–118). Guilford Press.

Darley, J. M., & Latané, B. (1968). Bystander intervention in emergencies: Diffusion of responsibility. *Journal of Personality and Social Psychology, 8*(4, Pt. 1), 377–383.

Darwin, C. (1877). Biographical sketch of an infant. *Mind, 2*, 285–294.

Das, J. P. (2014). *Consciousness quest: Where East meets West: On mind, meditation, and neural correlates*. Sage.

Dasgupta, N., & Rivera, L. M. (2008). When social context matters: The influence of long-term contact and short-term exposure to admired outgroup members on implicit attitudes and behavioral intentions. *Social Cognition, 26*(1), 112–123.

Dauvilliers, Y., Arnulf, I., & Mignot, E. (2007). Narcolepsy with cataplexy. *The Lancet, 369*(9560), 499–511.

Dauvilliers, Y., & Bayard, S. (2012). Hypersomnia and narcolepsy. In C. M. Morin & C. A. Espie (Eds.), *The Oxford handbook of sleep and sleep disorders* (pp. 690–706). Oxford University Press.

Dauvilliers, Y., Montplaisir, J., Molinari, N., Carlander, B., Ondze, B., Besset, A., & Billiard, M. (2001). Age at onset of narcolepsy in two large populations of patients in France and Quebec. *Neurology, 57*(11), 2029–2033.

David, D., & Mellman, T. A. (1997). Dreams following Hurricane Andrew. *Dreaming, 7*(3), 209–214. https://doi.org/10.1037/h0094475

David, D., Cotet, C., Matu, S., Mogoase, C., & Stefan, S. (2018). 50 years of rational-emotive and cognitive-behavioral therapy: A systematic review and meta-analysis. *Journal of Clinical Psychology, 74*(3), 304–318.

David, D. O., Sucală, M., Coteă, C., Şoflău, R., & Vălenaş, S. (2019). Empirical research in REBT theory and practice. In M. Bernard & W. Dryden (Eds.), *Advances in REBT*. Springer. https://doi.org/10.1007/978-3-319-93118-0_5

David, E. J. R., Okazaki, S., & Giroux, D. (2014). A set of guiding principles to advance multicultural psychology and its major concepts. In F. T. L. Leong, L. Comas-Diaz, G. C. Nagaayama-Hall, V. C. McLoyd, & J. E. Trimble (Eds.), *APA handbook of multicultural psychology* (Vol. 1, pp. 85–104). American Psychological Association.

Davidson, J. E., & Kemp, I. A. (2011). Contemporary models of intelligence. In R. J. Sternberg & S. B. Kaufman (Eds.), *The Cambridge handbook of intelligence* (pp. 58–84). Cambridge University Press.

Davidson, K. W., Mostofsky, E., & Whang, W. (2010). Don't worry, be happy: Positive affect and reduced 10-year incident coronary heart disease: The Canadian Nova Scotia Health Survey. *European Heart Journal, 31*(9), 1065–1070.

Davidson, P. S. R. (2008). The cognitive and neural bases of flashbulb memories. In E. Dere, A. Easton, L. Nadel, & J. P. Huston (Eds.), *Handbook of episodic memory* (pp. 81–97). Elsevier Science.

Davidson, R. J., Kabat-Zinn, J., Schumacher, J., Rosenkranz, M., Muller, D., Santorelli, S. F., & Sheridan, J. F. (2003). Alterations in brain and immune function produced by mindfulness meditation. *Psychosomatic Medicine, 65*(4), 564–570.

Davies, E., & Lea, S. E. (1995). Student attitudes to student debt. *Journal of Economic Psychology, 16*(4), 663–679.

Davies, G., & Hine, S. (2007). Change blindness and eyewitness testimony. *The Journal of Psychology, 141*(4), 423–434.

Davies, P. T., Sturge-Apple, M. L., & Martin, M. J. (2013). Family discord and child health: An emotional security formulation. In N. S. Landale, S. M. McHale, & A. Booth (Eds.), *Families and child health* (National Symposium on Family Issues, pp. 45–74). Springer Science+Business Media.

Daviglus, M. L., Plassman, B. L., Pirzada, A., Bell, C. C., Bowen, P. E., Burke, J. R., Connolly, E. S., Jr., Dunbar-Jacob, J. M., Granieri, E. C., McGarry, K., Patel, D., Trevisan, M., & Williams, J. W., Jr. (2011). Risk factors and preventive interventions for Alzheimer disease: State of the science. *Archives of Neurology, 68*(9), 1185–1190.

Davila, J., Hershenberg, R., Feinstein, B. A., Gorman, K., Bhatia, V., & Starr, L. R. (2012). Frequency and quality of social networking among young adults: Associations with depressive symptoms, rumination, and corumination. *Psychology of Popular Media Culture, 1*(2), 72–86.

Davis, B., Stafford, M. B. R., & Pullig, C. (2014). How gay-straight alliance groups mitigate the relationship between gay-bias victimization and adolescent suicide attempts. *Journal of the American Academy of Child & Adolescent Psychiatry, 53*(12), 1271–1278.

Davis, C. G., & Nolen-Hoeksema, S. (2009). Making sense of loss, perceiving benefits, and posttraumatic growth. In S. J. Lopez & C. R. Snyder (Eds.), *Oxford handbook of positive psychology* (pp. 641–651). Oxford University Press.

Davis, D. E., DeBlaere, C., Owen, J., Hook, J. N., Rivera, D. P., Choe, E., Van Tongeren, D. R., Worthington, E. L. Jr., & Placeres, V. (2018). The multicultural orientation framework: A narrative review. *Psychotherapy, 55*(1), 89–100.

Davis, D. R., Kurti, A. N., Skelly, J. M., Redner, R., White, T. J., & Higgins, S. T. (2016). A review of the literature on contingency management in the treatment of substance use disorders, 2009–2014. *Preventive Medicine, 92*, 36–46.

Davis, D., & Loftus, E. F. (2007). Internal and external sources of misinformation in adult witness memory. In M. P. Toglia, J. D. Read, D. F. Ross, & R. C. L. Lindsay (Eds.), *The Handbook of eyewitness psychology* (pp. 195–237). Lawrence Erlbaum.

Davis, J. H., & Thompson, E. (2015). Developing attention and decreasing affective bias: Toward a cross-cultural cognitive science of mindfulness. In K. W. Brown, J. D. Creswell, & R. M. Ryan (Eds.), *Handbook of mindfulness: Theory, research, and practice* (pp. 42–61). Guilford Press.

Davis, J. I., Senghas, A., & Ochsner, K. N. (2009). How does facial feedback modulate emotional experience? *Journal of Research in Personality, 43*(5), 822–829.

Davis, K., Christodoulou, J., Seider, S., & Gardner, H. (2011). The theory of multiple intelligences. In R. J. Sternberg & S. B. Kaufman (Eds.), *The Cambridge handbook of intelligence* (pp. 485–503). Cambridge University Press.

Davis, M. C., Matthews, K. A., & Twamley, E. W. (1999). Is life more difficult on Mars or Venus? A meta-analytic review of sex differences in major and minor life events. *Annals of Behavioral Medicine, 21*(1), 83–97.

Davison, G. C., & Lazarus, A. A. (2007). Clinical case studies are important in the science and practice of psychotherapy. In S. O. Lilienfeld & W. T. O'Donohue (Eds.), *The great ideas of clinical science: 17 principles that every mental health professional should understand* (pp. 149–162). Routledge.

Davison, K. K., Markey, C., & Birch, L. (2000). Etiology of body dissatisfaction and weight concerns among 5-year-old girls. *Appetite, 35*(2), 143–151.

Dawson, A. F., Brown, W. W., Anderson, J., Datta, B., Donald, J. N., Hong, K., Allan, S., Mole, T. B., Jones, P. B., & Galante, J. (2020). Mindfulness-based interventions for university students: a systematic review and meta-analysis of randomised controlled trials. *Applied Psychology: Health and Well-Being, 12*(2), 384–410. https://doi.org/10.1111/aphw.12188

Dawson, G. (2008). Early behavioral intervention, brain plasticity, and the prevention of autism spectrum disorder. *Development and Psychopathology, 20*(3), 775–803.

Dawson, G. (2013). Dramatic increase in autism prevalence parallels explosion of research into its biology and causes. *JAMA, 70*(1), 9–10.

de Abreu Costa, M., de Oliveira, G. S. D. A., Tatton-Ramos, T., Manfro, G. G., & Salum, G. A. (2018). Anxiety and stress-related disorders and mindfulness-based interventions: A systematic review and multilevel meta-analysis and meta-regression of multiple outcomes. *Mindfulness, 10*, 996–1005.

de Bruin, E. J., van Run, C., Staaks, J., & Meijer, A. M. (2017). Effects of sleep manipulation on cognitive functioning of adolescents: A systematic review. *Sleep Medicine Reviews, 32*, 45–57.

de Castro, J. M. (1994). Family and friends produce greater social facilitation of food intake than other companions. *Physiology & Behavior, 56*(3), 445–455. https://doi.org/10.1016/0031-9384(94)90286-0

de Felice, G., Giuliani, A., Halfon, S., Andreassi, S., Paoloni, G., & Orsucci, F. F. (2019). The misleading dodo bird verdict: How much of the outcome variance is explained by common and specific factors? *New Ideas in Psychology, 54*, 50–55.

De Fruyt, F. (1997). Gender and individual differences in adult crying. *Personality and Individual Differences, 22*(6), 937–940.

De Fruyt, F., De Clercq, B., De Bolle, M., Wille, B., Markon, K., & Krueger, R. F. (2013). General and maladaptive traits in a five-factor framework for DSM-5 in a university student sample. *Assessment, 20*(3), 295–307.

De Houwer, J., Thomas, S., & Baeyens, F. (2001). Association learning of likes and dislikes: A review of 25 years of research on human evaluative conditioning. *Psychological Bulletin, 127*(6), 853–869.

De Koninck, J. D. (2012). Sleep, dreams, and dreaming. In C. M. Morin & C. A. Espie (Eds.), *The Oxford handbook of sleep and sleep disorders* (pp. 150–171). Oxford University Press.

de León-Vázquez, C. D., Villalobos-Hernández, A., Rivera-Márquez, J. A., & Unikel-Santoncini, C. (2018). Effect of parental criticism on disordered eating behaviors in male and female university students in Mexico City. *Eating and Weight Disorders, 24*(5), 853–860. https://doi.org/10.1007/s40519-018-0564-4

de Mejia, E. G., & Ramirez-Mares, M. V. (2014). Impact of caffeine and coffee on our health. *Trends in Endocrinology & Metabolism, 25*(10), 489–492.

De Pauw, S. S. W. (2017). Childhood personality and temperament. In T. A. Widiger (Ed.), *The Oxford handbook of the Five Factor Model* (pp. 243–280). Oxford University Press.

de Ridder, D., & Gillebaart, M. (2022). How food overconsumption has hijacked our notions about eating as a pleasurable activity. *Current Opinion in Psychology, 46*, 101324. https://doi.org/10.1016/j.copsyc.2022.101324

De Vries, R. E., de Vries, A., de Hoogh, A., & Feij, J. (2009). More than the Big Five: Egoism and the HEXACO model of personality. *European Journal of Personality, 23*(8), 635–654.

de Waal, F. B. (2008). Putting the altruism back into altruism: The evolution of empathy. *Annual Review of Psychology, 59*, 279–300.

Dean, M. L. (1980). Presentation order effects in product taste tests. *The Journal of Psychology, 105*(1), 107–110.

DeAndrea, D. C., Shaw, A. S., & Levine, T. R. (2010). Online language: The role of culture in self-expression and self-construal on Facebook. *Journal of Language and Social Psychology, 29*(4), 425–442.

DeAngelis, T. (2017, Fall). Prescriptive authority: Renewed action in the states. *APA Practice Organization: Good Practice*, 16–18.

DeAngelis, T. (2021a). Dark clouds, silver linings. *APA Monitor on Psychology, 52*(5), 88. https://www.apa.org/monitor/2021/07/numbers-silver-linings

DeAngelis, T. (2021b). Pandemic leads more young people to lose jobs, move in with their parents. *APA Monitor on Psychology, 52*(2), 80. https://www.apa.org/monitor/2021/03/numbers-young-people

Deary, I. J., Spinath, F. M., & Bates, T. C. (2006). Genetics of intelligence. *European Journal of Human Genetics, 14*(6), 690–700.

Deary, I. J., Strand, S., Smith, P., & Fernandes, C. (2007). Intelligence and educational achievement. *Intelligence, 35*(1), 13–21.

Deater-Deckard, K., Dodge, K. A., Bates, J. E., & Pettit, G. S. (1996). Physical discipline among African American and European American mothers: Links to children's externalizing behaviors. *Developmental Psychology, 32*(6), 1065–1072.

DeBacker, T. K., Heddy, B. C., Kershen, J. L., Crowson, H. M., Looney, K., & Goldman, J. A. (2018). Effects of a one-shot growth mindset intervention on beliefs about intelligence and achievement goals. *Educational Psychology, 38*(6), 711–733.

Debarnot, U., Castellani, E., Valenza, G., Sebastiani, L., & Guillot, A. (2011). Daytime naps improve motor imagery learning. *Cognitive, Affective, & Behavioral Neuroscience, 11*(4), 541–550.

Debiec, J., & LeDoux, J. E. (2009). The amygdala networks of fear: From animal models to human psychopathology. In D. McKay, J. S. Abramowitz, S. Taylor, & G. J. G. Asmundson (Eds.), *Current perspectives on the anxiety disorders: Implications for DSM-V and beyond* (pp. 107–126). Springer.

DeCasper, A. J., & Fifer, W. P. (1980). Of human bonding: Newborns prefer their mothers' voices. *Science, 208*(4448), 1174–1176.

DeCasper, A. J., & Spence, M. J. (1986). Prenatal maternal speech influences newborns' perception of speech sounds. *Infant Behavior and Development, 9*(2), 133–150.

Deci, E. L., Koestner, R., & Ryan, R. M. (1999). A meta-analytic review of experiments examining the effects of extrinsic rewards on intrinsic motivation. *Psychological Bulletin, 125*(6), 627–668.

Deci, E. L., & Ryan, R. M. (2012). Motivation, personality, and development within embedded social contexts: An overview of self-determination theory. In R. M. Ryan (Ed.), *The Oxford handbook of human motivation* (pp. 85–110). Oxford University Press.

Dehaene, S. (2011). *The number sense: How the mind creates mathematics*. Oxford University Press.

Dehaene, S., Lau, H., & Kouider, S. (2017). What is consciousness, and could machines have it? *Science, 358*(6362), 486–492.

Dehaene, S., Spelke, E., Pinel, P., Stanescu, R., & Tsivkin, S. (1999). Sources of mathematical thinking: Behavioral and brain-imaging evidence. *Science, 284*(5416), 970–974.

Dehaene-Lambertz, G., Dehaene, S., & Hertz-Pannier, L. (2002). Functional neuroimaging of speech perception in infants. *Science, 298*(5600), 2013–2015.

Dehn, M. J. (2008). *Working memory and academic learning: Assessment and intervention*. John Wiley.

Del Vicario, M., Vivaldo, G., Bessi, A., Zollo, F., Scala, A., Caldarelli, G., & Quattrociocchi, W. (2016). Echo chambers: Emotional contagion and group polarization on Facebook. *Scientific Reports, 6*, 37825.

DeLeon, P. H., Kenkel, M. B., Gray, J. M. O., & Sammons, M. T. (2011). Emerging policy issues for psychology: A key to the future of the profession. In D. H. Barlow (Ed.), *The Oxford handbook of clinical psychology* (pp. 34–51). Oxford University Press.

Delgado, M. R., Labouliere, C. D., & Phelps, E. A. (2006). Fear of losing money? Aversive conditioning with secondary reinforcers. *Social Cognitive and Affective Neuroscience, 1*(3), 250–259.

Delgado, P. L., & Moreno, F. A. (2006). Neurochemistry of mood disorders. In D. J. Stein, D. J. Kupfer, & A. F. Schatzberg (Eds.), The American Psychiatric Publishing textbook of mood disorders (pp. 101–116). American Psychiatric Association Publishing.

Dell, D. M., Schmidt, L. D., & Meara, N. M. (2006). Applying for approval to conduct research with human participants. In F. T. L. Leong & J. T. Austin (Eds.), The psychology research handbook: A guide for graduate students and research assistants (2nd ed., pp. 175–185). Sage.

Dell'Osso, L., Abelli, M., Carpita, B., Pini, S., Castellini, G., Carmassi, C., & Ricca, V. (2016). Historical evolution of the concept of anorexia nervosa and relationships with orthorexia nervosa, autism, and obsessive–compulsive spectrum. *Neuropsychiatric Disease and Treatment, 12,* 1651–1660.

Dellis, N. (2012). Watch memory champion trick his brain. YouTube. http://www.youtube.com/watch?v=KxD_XQ7ItyA

Deloitte. (2017). Device addition shifts to device etiquette. https://www2.deloitte.com/content/dam/Deloitte/us/Documents/technology-media-telecommunications/us-tmt-global-mobile-consumer-survey-2017-infographic.pdf

DeLongis, A., Folkman, S., & Lazarus, R. S. (1988). The impact of daily stress on health and mood: Psychological and social resources as mediators. *Journal of Personality and Social Psychology, 54*(3), 486–495.

Delorme, A., Poncet, M., & Fabre-Thorpe, M. (2018). Briefly flashed scenes can be stored in long-term memory. *Frontiers in Neuroscience, 12,* 688.

Demaree, H. A., Schmeichel, B. J., Robinson, J. L., Pu, J., Everhart, D. E., & Berntson, G. G. (2006). Up- and down-regulating facial disgust: Affective, vagal, sympathetic, and respiratory consequences. *Biological Psychology, 71*(1), 90–99.

DeMatteo, D., Marczyk, G., Krauss, D. A., & Burl, J. (2009). Educational and training models in forensic psychology. *Training and Education in Professional Psychology, 3*(3), 184–201.

Dement, J., Welch, L. S., Ringen, K., Cranford, K., & Quinn, P. (2018). Hearing loss among older construction workers: Updated analyses. *American Journal of Industrial Medicine, 61*(4), 326–335.

Dement, W. (1960). The effect of dream deprivation. *Science, 131*(3415), 1705–1707.

Dement, W., & Kleitman, N. (1957). The relation of eye movement during sleep to dream activity: An objective method for the study of dreaming. *Journal of Experimental Psychology, 53*(5), 330–346.

DeMers, S. T., & Siegel, A. M. (2016). Legal and statutory regulations. In J. C. Norcross, G. R. VandenBos, & D. K. Freedheim (Eds.), *APA handbook of clinical psychology* (Vol. 5, pp. 375–393). American Psychological Association.

Demiray, B., & Freund, A. M. (2015). Michael Jackson, Bin Laden and I: Functions of positive and negative, public and private flashbulb memories. *Memory, 23*(4), 487–506.

Denes-Raj, V., & Epstein, S. (1994). Conflict between intuitive and rational processing: When people behave against their better judgment. *Journal of Personality and Social Psychology, 66*(5), 819–829.

Deng, W., Aimone, J. B., & Gage, F. H. (2010). New neurons and new memories: How does adult hippocampal neurogenesis affect learning and memory? *Nature Reviews Neuroscience, 11*(5), 339–350.

Denko, T. C., & Thase, M. E. (2006). Psychopharmacological interventions. In M. Hersen & J. C. Thomas (Eds.), *Comprehensive handbook of personality and psychopathology* (Vol. 2, pp. 503–518). Wiley.

Dennerstein, L., Dudley, E., & Guthrie, J. (2002). Empty nest or revolving door: A prospective study of women's quality of life in midlife during the phase of children leaving and reentering the home. *Psychological Medicine, 32*(3), 545–550.

Dennhardt, A. A., Yurasek, A. M., & Murphy, J. G. (2015). Motivational interviewing. In R. L. Cautin & S. O. Lilienfeld (Eds.), *The encyclopedia of clinical psychology* (pp. 1908–1913). Wiley-Blackwell.

Denollet, J. (2000). Type D personality: A potential risk factor refined. *Journal of Psychosomatic Research, 49*(4), 255–266.

Deo, M. S., & Lymburner, J. A. (2011). Personality traits and psychological health concerns: The search for Psychology Student Syndrome. *Teaching of Psychology, 38*(3), 155–157.

DePrince, A. P., Brown, L. S., Cheit, R. E., Freyd, J. J., Gold, S. N., Pezdek, K., & Quina, K. (2012). Motivated forgetting and misremembering: Perspectives from betrayal trauma theory. In R. F. Belli (Ed.), *True and false recovered memories: Toward a reconciliation of the debate* (pp. 193–242). Springer.

DeRubeis, R. J., Keefe, J. R., & Beck, A. T. (2019). Cognitive therapy. In K. S. Dobson & D. J. A. Dozois (Eds.), *Handbook of cognitive-behavioral therapies* (4th ed., pp. 218–248). Guilford Press.

DeRubeis, R. J., Siegle, G. J., & Hollon, S. D. (2008). Cognitive therapy versus medication for depression: Treatment outcomes and neural mechanisms. *Nature Reviews Neuroscience, 9*(10), 788–796.

DeRubeis, R. J., Strunk, D. R., & Lorenzo-Luaces, L. (2016). Mood disorders. In J. C. Norcross, G. R. VandenBos, & D. K. Freedheim (Eds.), *APA handbook of clinical psychology: Vol. 4. Psychopathology and health* (pp. 31–60). American Psychological Association.

DeSantis, A. D., Webb, E. M., & Noar, S. M. (2008). Illicit use of prescription ADHD medications on a college campus: A multimethodological approach. *Journal of American College Health, 57*(3), 315–324.

Dessel, A. B., Goodman, K. D., & Woodford, M. R. (2017). LGBT discrimination on campus and heterosexual bystanders: Understanding intentions to intervene. *Journal of Diversity in Higher Education, 10*(2), 101–116.

Deutsch, M., & Gerard, H. B. (1955). A study of normative and informative social influences upon individual judgment. *Journal of Abnormal and Social Psychology, 51*(3), 629–636.

Devereux, P. G., Miller, M. K., & Kirshenbaum, J. M. (2021). Moral disengagement, locus of control, and belief in a just world: Individual differences relate to adherence to COVID-19 guidelines. *Personality and Individual Differences, 182,* 111069. https://doi.org/10.1016/j.paid.2021.111069

Dewald, P. A. (1964). *Psychotherapy: A dynamic approach.* Basic Books.

Dewar, M., Cowan, N., & Della Sala, S. (2010). Forgetting due to retroactive interference in amnesia: Findings and implications. In S. Della Sala (Ed.), *Forgetting* (pp. 185–209). Psychology Press.

DeYoung, C. G., & Allen, T. A. (2019). Personality neuroscience. In D. P. McAdams, R. L. Shiner, & J. L. Tackett (Eds.), *Handbook of personality development* (pp. 79–105). Guilford Press.

DeYoung, C. G., Hirsh, J. B., Shane, M. S., Papademetris, X., Rajeevan, N., & Gray, J. R. (2010). Testing predictions from personality neuroscience brain structure and the Big Five. *Psychological Science, 21*(6), 820–828.

Dhanani, L. Y., & Franz, B. (2021). Why public health framing matters: An experimental study of the effects of COVID-19 framing on prejudice and xenophobia in the United States. *Social Science & Medicine, 269,* 113572. https://doi.org/10.1016/j.socscimed.2020.113572

Dhawan, N., Roseman, I. J., Naidu, R. K., Thapa, K., & Rettek, S. I. (1995). Self-concepts across two cultures: India and the United States. *Journal of Cross-Cultural Psychology, 26*(6), 606–621.

Di Lorenzo, P. M., & Rosen, A. M. (2010). Taste. In E. B. Goldstein (Ed.), *Encyclopedia of perception* (pp. 952–957). Sage.

Diamond, D., Yeomans, F. E., Stern, B. L., & Kernberg, O. F. (2022). *Treating pathological narcissism with transference-focused psychotherapy.* Guilford Publications.

Diamond, L. M. (2000). Sexual identity, attractions, and behavior among young sexual-minority women over a 2-year period. *Developmental Psychology, 36*(2), 241–250.

Diamond, L. M. (2005). A new view of lesbian subtypes: Stable versus fluid identity trajectories over an 8-year period. *Psychology of Women Quarterly, 29*(2), 119–128.

Diamond, L. M. (2007). A dynamical systems approach to the development and expression of female same-sex sexuality. *Perspectives on Psychological Science, 2*(2), 142–161.

Diamond, L. M. (2008). Female bisexuality from adolescence to adulthood: Results from a 10-year longitudinal study. *Developmental Psychology, 44*(1), 5.

Diamond, L. M. (2009). *Sexual fluidity: Understanding women's love and desire.* Harvard University Press.

Diamond, L. M. (2013). Concepts of female sexual orientation. In C. J. Patterson & A. R. D'Augelli (Eds.), *Handbook of psychology and sexual orientation* (pp. 3–17). Oxford University Press.

Diamond, M. C., Law, F., Rhodes, H., Lindner, B., Rosenzweig, M. R., Krech, D., & Bennett, E. L. (1966). Increases in cortical depth and glia numbers in rats subjected to enriched environment. *Journal of Comparative Neurology, 128*(1), 117–125.

Diamond, M. C., Lindner, B., Johnson, R., Bennett, E. L., & Rosenzweig, M. R. (1975). Difference in occipital cortical synapses from environmentally enriched, impoverished, and standard colony rats. *Journal of Neuroscience Research, 1*(2), 109–119.

Dickerson, B. C. (2007). Advances in functional magnetic resonance imaging: Technology and clinical applications. *Neurotherapeutics, 4*(3), 360–370.

Dickson, N., Paul, C., & Herbison, P. (2003). Same-sex attraction in a birth cohort: Prevalence and persistence in early adulthood. *Social Science & Medicine, 56*(8), 1607–1615.

Dickter, D. N. (2006). Basic statistical analyses. In F. T. L. Leong & J. T. Austin (Eds.), *The psychology research handbook* (pp. 293–305). Sage.

DiClemente, C. C., & Prochaska, J. O. (1982). Self-change and therapy change of smoking behavior: A comparison of processes of change in cessation and maintenance. *Addictive Behaviors, 7*(2), 133–142.

Didie, E. R. (2015). Interpersonal psychotherapy (IPT). In R. L. Cautin & S. O. Lilienfeld (Eds.), *The encyclopedia of clinical psychology* (pp. 1540–1545). Wiley-Blackwell.

Diekelmann, S., & Born, J. (2010). The memory function of sleep. *Nature Reviews Neuroscience, 11*(2), 114–126.

Diekman, A. B., Brown, E. R., Johnston, A. M., & Clark, E. K. (2010). Seeking congruity between goals and roles: A new look at why women opt out of science, technology, engineering, and mathematics careers. *Psychological Science, 21*(8), 1051–1057.

Diekman, A. B., & Eagly, A. H. (2008). Of men, women, and motivation: A role congruity account. In J. Y. Shah & W. L. Gardner (Eds.), *Handbook of motivation science* (pp. 434–447). Guilford Press.

Diener, E., & Biswas-Diener, R. (2002). Will money increase subjective well-being? *Social Indicators Research, 57*(2), 119–169.

Diener, E., & Chan, M. Y. (2011). Happy people live longer: Subjective well-being contributes to health and longevity. *Applied Psychology: Health and Well-Being, 3*(1), 1–43.

Diener, E., & Diener, M. (2009). Cross-cultural correlates of life satisfaction and self-esteem. In E. Diener (Ed.), *Culture and well-being: The collected works of Ed Diener* (pp. 71–91). Springer Science+Business Media.

Diener, E., & Suh, E. (2003). National differences in subjective well-being. In D. Kahneman, E. Diener, & N. Schwarz (Eds.), *Well-being: The foundations of hedonic psychology* (pp. 434–450). Russell Sage Foundation.

Diener, E., Sandvik, E., Seidlitz, L., & Diener, M. (1993). The relationship between income and subjective well-being: Relative or absolute? *Social Indicators Research, 28*(3), 195–223.

Dietz, T. L. (2000). Disciplining children: Characteristics associated with the use of corporal punishment. *Child Abuse & Neglect, 24*(12), 1529–1542.

Díez-Izquierdo, A., Cassanello, P., Cartanyà, A., Matilla-Santander, N., Santamaria, A. B., & Martinez-Sanchez, J. M. (2018a). Knowledge and attitudes toward thirdhand smoke among parents with children under 3 years in Spain. *Pediatric Research, 84,* 645–649.

Díez-Izquierdo, A., Cassanello-Peñarroya, P., Lidón-Moyano, C., Matilla-Santander, N., Balaguer, A., & Martínez-Sánchez, J. M. (2018b). Update on thirdhand smoke: A comprehensive systematic review. *Environmental Research, 167,* 341–371.

DiGiuseppe, R., David, D., & Venezia, R. (2016). Cognitive theories. In J. C. Norcross, G. R. VandenBos, & D. K. Freedheim (Eds.), *APA handbook of clinical psychology* (Vol. 2, pp. 145–182). American Psychological Association.

DiGiuseppe, R. A., & Doyle, K. A. (2019). Rational emotive behaviour therapy. In K. S. Dobson & D. J. A. Dozois (Eds.), *Handbook of cognitive-behavioral therapies* (4th ed., pp. 191–217). Guilford Press.

Digman, J. M. (1990). Personality structure: Emergence of the five-factor model. *Annual Review of Psychology, 41,* 417–440.

Digman, J. M. (1996). The curious history of the five-factor model. In J. S. Wiggins (Ed.), *The five-factor model of personality: Theoretical perspectives* (pp. 1–20). Guilford Press.

Dijk, D.-J., & Lazar, A. S. (2012). The regulation of human sleep and wakefulness: Sleep homeostasis and circadian rhythmicity. In C. M. Morin & C. A. Espie (Eds.), *The Oxford handbook of sleep and sleep disorders* (pp. 38–60). Oxford University Press.

Dijk, D.-J., Duffy, J. F., Riel, E., Shanahan, T. L., & Czeisler, C. A. (1999). Ageing and the circadian and homeostatic regulation of human sleep during forced desynchrony of rest, melatonin and temperature rhythms. *The Journal of Physiology, 516*(2), 611–627.

Dijk, D.-J., Groeger, J. A., Stanley, N., & Deacon, S. (2010). Age-related reduction in daytime sleep propensity and nocturnal slow wave sleep. *Sleep, 33*(2), 211.

Dillard, J. P., Hunter, J. E., & Burgoon, M. (1984). Sequential-request persuasive strategies: Meta-analysis of foot-in-the-door and door-in-the-face. *Human Communication Research, 10*(4), 461–488.

Dillon, K. P., & Bushman, B. J. (2017). Effects of exposure to gun violence in movies on children's interest in real guns. *JAMA Pediatrics, 171*(11), 1057–1062.

Dimaggio, G., & Shahar, G. (2017). Behavioral activation as a common mechanism of change across different orientations and disorders. *Psychotherapy, 54*(3), 221–224.

Dimberg, U., Andréasson, P., & Thunberg, M. (2011). Emotional empathy and facial reactions to facial expressions. *Journal of Psychophysiology, 25*(1), 26–31.

Dimberg, U., & Lundquist, L. O. (1990). Gender differences in facial reactions to facial expressions. *Biological Psychology, 30*(2), 151–159.

Dimberg, U., & Thunberg, M. (2012). Empathy, emotional contagion, and rapid facial reactions to angry and happy facial expressions. *Psych Journal, 1*(2), 118–127.

Dimeff, L. A., Paves, A. P., Skutch, J. M., & Woodcock, E. A. (2011). Shifting paradigms in clinical psychology: How innovative technologies are shaping treatment delivery. In D. H. Barlow (Ed.), *The Oxford handbook of clinical psychology* (pp. 618–648). Oxford University Press.

Dimidjian, S., Barrera, M., Jr., Martell, C., Munoz, R. F., & Lewinsohn, P. M. (2011). The origins and current status of behavioral activation treatments for depression. *Annual Review of Clinical Psychology, 7,* 1–38.

Dimidjian, S., & Linehan, M. M. (2009). Mindfulness practice. In W. T. O'Donohue & J. E. Fisher (Eds.), *General principles and empirically supported techniques of cognitive behavior therapy* (pp. 425–434). Wiley.

Dimler, L. M., & Natsuaki, M. N. (2015). The effects of pubertal timing on externalizing behaviors in adolescence and early adulthood: A meta-analytic review. *Journal of Adolescence, 45,* 160–170.

Dinehart, M. E., Hayes, J. E., Bartoshuk, L. M., Lanier, S. L., & Duffy, V. B. (2006). Bitter taste markers explain variability in vegetable sweetness, bitterness, and intake. *Physiology & Behavior, 87*(2), 304–313.

Dinges, D. F., & Broughton, R. (1989). *Sleep and alertness: Chronobiological, behavioral, and medical aspects of napping*. Raven Press.

Dinges, D. F., Pack, F., Williams, K., Gillen, K. A., Powell, J. W., Ott, G. E., Aptowicz, C., & Pack, A. I. (1997). Cumulative sleepiness, mood disturbance and psychomotor vigilance performance decrements during a week of sleep restricted to 4–5 hours per night. *Sleep: Journal of Sleep Research & Sleep Medicine, 20*(4), 267–277.

Dirix, C. E. H., Nijhuis, J. G., Jongsma, H. W., and Hornstra, G. (2009). Aspects of fetal learning and memory. *Child Development, 80*(4), 1251–1258. https://doi.org/10.1111/j.1467-8624.2009.01329.x

Dirks, M. A., Persram, R., Recchia, H. E., & Howe, N. (2015). Sibling relationships as sources of risk and resilience in the development and maintenance of internalizing and externalizing problems during childhood and adolescence. *Clinical Psychology Review, 42,* 145–155.

Dixon, J. S., Coyne, A. E., Duff, K., & Ready, R. E. (2021). Predictors of cognitive decline in a multi-racial sample of midlife women: A longitudinal study. *Neuropsychology, 35*(5), 514–528. https://doi.org/10.1037/neu0000743

do Nascimento, I. C., & Ulrich, H. (2015). Basic studies on neural stem cells in the brain. In L. Zhao & J. H. Zhang (Eds.), *Cellular therapy for stroke and CNS injuries* (pp. 3–16). Springer International.

Dobalian, A., & Rivers, P. A. (2008). Racial and ethnic disparities in the use of mental health services. *The Journal of Behavioral Health Services & Research, 35*(2), 128–141.

Dobson, K. S. (2012). *Cognitive therapy*. American Psychological Association.

Dobson, K. S., & Hamilton, K. E. (2008). Cognitive restructuring: Behavioral tests of negative cognitions. In W. T. O'Donohue & J. E. Fisher (Eds.), *Cognitive behavior therapy: Applying empirically supported techniques in your practice* (2nd ed., pp. 96–100). Wiley.

Dodge, B., Herbenick, D., Friedman, M. R., Schick, V., Fu, T. C. J., Bostwick, W., Bartelt, E., Muñoz-Laboy, M., Pletta, D., Reece, M., & Sandfort, T. G. (2016). Attitudes toward bisexual men and women among a nationally representative probability sample of adults in the United States. *PLoS One, 11*(10), e0164430.

Dodgen, D., Fowler, R. D., & Williams-Nickelson, C. (2013). Getting involved in professional organizations: A gateway to career advancement. In M. J. Prinstein (Ed.), *The portable mentor: Expert guide to a successful career in psychology* (pp. 257–267). Springer.

Doherty, R. W. (1997). The emotional contagion scale: A measure of individual differences. *Journal of Nonverbal Behavior, 21*(2), 131–154.

Dolder, C. R. (2008). Side effects of antipsychotics. In K. T. Mueser & D. V. Jeste (Eds.), *Clinical handbook of schizophrenia* (pp. 168–177). Guilford Press.

Dolinski, D. (2000). On inferring one's beliefs from one's attempt and consequences for subsequent compliance. *Journal of Personality and Social Psychology, 78*(2), 260–272.

Domínguez, D. J. F., Lewis, E. D., Turner, R., & Egan, G. F. (2009). The brain in culture and culture in the brain: A review of core issues in neuroanthropology. *Progress in Brain Research, 178,* 43–64.

Dominy, N. J., & Lucas, P. W. (2001). Ecological importance of trichromatic vision to primates. *Nature, 410*(6826), 363–366.

Donahoe, J. W. (1998). Positive reinforcement: The selection of behavior. In W. O'Donohue (Ed.), *Learning and behavior therapy* (pp. 169–187). Allyn & Bacon.

Donnerstein, E., & Wilson, D. W. (1976). Effects of noise and perceived control on ongoing and subsequent aggressive behavior. *Journal of Personality and Social Psychology, 34*(5), 774–781.

Donoghue, J. P., Suner, S., & Sanes, J. N. (1990). Dynamic organization of primary motor cortex output to target muscles in adult rats. II. Rapid reorganization following motor nerve lesions. *Experimental Brain Research, 79*(3), 492–503.

Donohue, G., & Keogh, B. (2021). Do we need to revisit our thinking on electroconvulsive therapy? *Journal of Psychiatric and Mental Health Nursing, 28*(3), 307–308. https://doi.org/10.1111/jpm.12719

Donovan, J., & Zucker, C. (2016). *In a different key: The story of autism*. Crown Publishers.

Donovan, R. A., Galban, D. J., Grace, R. K., Bennett, J. K., & Felicié, S. Z. (2013). Impact of racial macro-and microaggressions in black women's lives: A preliminary analysis. *Journal of Black Psychology, 39*(2), 185–196.

Dor, A. (2013). Don't stay out late! Mom, I'm twenty-eight: Emerging adults and their parents under one roof. *International Journal of Social Science Studies, 1*(1), 37–46.

Dorofaeff, T. F., & Denny, S. (2006). Sleep and adolescence. Do New Zealand teenagers get enough? *Journal of Paediatrics and Child Health, 42*(9), 515–520.

Dosher, B., & Lu, Z-L. (2010). Attention: Selective. In E. B. Goldstein (Ed.), *Encyclopedia of perception* (pp. 100–103). Sage.

Doty, R. L. (2010). Olfaction. In E. B. Goldstein (Ed.), *Encyclopedia of perception* (pp. 657–661). Sage.

Doty, R. L. (2012). Olfactory dysfunction in Parkinson disease. *Nature Reviews Neurology, 8*(6), 329–339.

Doty, R. L., Applebaum, S., Zusho, H., & Settle, R. G. (1985). Sex differences in odor identification ability: A cross-cultural analysis. *Neuropsychologia, 23*(5), 667–672.

Doty, R. L., & Kamath, V. (2014). The influences of age on olfaction: A review. *Frontiers in Psychology, 5,* 20. https://doi.org/10.3389/fpsyg.2014.00020

Dougherty, D. D., Rauch, S. L., & Jenike, M. A. (2015). Treatments for obsessive-compulsive disorder. In P. E. Nathan & J. M. Gorman (Eds.), *A guide to treatments that work* (4th ed., pp. 545–570). Oxford University Press.

Dovidio, J. F., Brown, C. E., Heltman, K., Ellyson, S. L., & Keating, C. F. (1988a). Power displays between women and men in discussions of gender-linked tasks: A multichannel study. *Journal of Personality and Social Psychology, 55*(4), 580–587.

Dovidio, J. F., Ellyson, S. L., Keating, C. F., Heltman, K., & Brown, C. E. (1988b). The relationship of social power to visual displays of dominance between men and women. *Journal of Personality and Social Psychology, 54*(2), 233–242.

Dovidio, J. F., & Gaertner, S. L. (2010). Intergroup bias. In S. T. Fiske, D. T. Gilbert, & G. Lindzey (Eds.), *Handbook of social psychology* (5th ed., Vol. 2, pp. 1084–1121). Wiley.

Dovidio, J. F., Gaertner, S. L., & Kawakami, K. (2003). Intergroup contact: The past, present, and the future. *Group Processes & Intergroup Relations, 6*(1), 5–21. https://doi.org/10.1177/1368430203006001009

Dovidio, J. F., Gaertner, S. L., & Saguy, T. (2009). Commonality and the complexity of "we": Social attitudes and social change. *Personality and Social Psychology Review, 13*(1), 3–20.

Dovidio, J. F., Newheiser, A., & Leyens, J. (2012). A history of intergroup relations research. In A. W. Kruglanski & W. Stroebe (Eds.), *Handbook of the history of social psychology* (pp. 407–429). Psychology Press.

Dowling, W. J. (2001). Perception of music. In E. B. Goldstein (Ed.), *Blackwell handbook of perception* (pp. 469–498). Blackwell.

Downar, J., & Kapur, S. (2008). Biological theories. In K. T. Meuser & D. V. Jeste (Eds.), *Clinical handbook of schizophrenia* (pp. 25–34). Guilford Press.

Downey, D. B., & Vogt Yuan, A. S. (2005). Sex differences in school performance during high school: Puzzling patterns and possible explanations. *The Sociological Quarterly, 46*(2), 299–321.

Doyle, A. B., Lawford, H., and Markiewicz, D. (2009). Attachment style with mother, father, best friend, and romantic partner during adolescence. *Journal of Research on Adolescence, 19*(4), 690–714.

Dozois, D. J. A., & Brinker, J. K. (2015). Cognitive therapies. In R. L. Cautin & S. O. Lilienfeld (Eds.), *The encyclopedia of clinical psychology* (pp. 656–665). Wiley-Blackwell.

Draaisma, D. (2000). *Metaphors of memory: A history of ideas about the mind*. Cambridge University Press.

Drake, C. L., Roehrs, T., Richardson, G., Walsh, J. K., & Roth, T. (2004). Shift work sleep disorder: Prevalence and consequences beyond that of symptomatic day workers. *Sleep, 27*(8), 1453–1462.

Drescher, J. (2010). Queer diagnoses: Parallels and contrasts in the history of homosexuality, gender variance, and the Diagnostic and Statistical Manual. *Archives of Sexual Behavior, 39*(2), 427–460.

Dresser, N. (2005). *Multicultural manners: Essential rules of etiquette for the 21st century*. John Wiley.

Drews, F. A., Yazdani, H., Godfrey, C. N., Cooper, J. M., & Strayer, D. L. (2009). Text messaging during simulated driving. *Human Factors: The Journal of the Human Factors and Ergonomics Society, 51*(5), 762–770.

Dreyfuss, J. H. (2010). Thirdhand smoke identified as potent, enduring carcinogen. *CA: A Cancer Journal for Clinicians, 60*(4), 203–204.

Driver, H. S. (2012). Sleep and gender: The paradox of sex and sleep? In C. M. Morin & C. A. Espie (Eds.), *The Oxford handbook of sleep and sleep disorders* (pp. 266–288). Oxford University Press.

Dror, O. E. (2014). The Cannon–Bard thalamic theory of emotions: A brief genealogy and reappraisal. *Emotion Review, 6*(1), 13–20.

Drossel, C., Garrison-Diehn, C. G., & Fisher, J. E. (2008). Contingency management interventions. In W. T. O'Donohue & J. E. Fisher (Eds.), *Cognitive behavior therapy: Applying empirically supported techniques in your practice* (2nd ed., pp. 116–122). Wiley.

Drotar, D., Wu, Y. P., & Rohan, J. M. (2013). How to write an effective journal article review. In M. J. Prinstein (Ed.), *The portable mentor: Expert guide to a successful career in psychology* (pp. 163–173). Springer.

Drouin, M. A. (2011). College students' text messaging, use of textese and literacy skills. *Journal of Computer Assisted Learning, 27*(1), 67–75.

Drozdick, L. W., Raiford, S. E., Wahlstrom, D., & Weiss, L. G. (2018). The Wechsler Adult Intelligence Scale–Fourth Edition and the Wechsler Memory Scale–Fourth Edition. In D. P. Flanagan & E. M. McDonough (Eds.), *Contemporary intellectual assessment: Theories, tests, and issues* (4th ed., pp. 486–511). Guilford Press.

Druckman, J. N., Levendusky, M. S., & McLain, A. (2018). No need to watch: How the effects of partisan media can spread via interpersonal discussions. *American Journal of Political Science, 62*(1), 99–112.

Dryden, W. (1995). *Brief rational emotive behaviour therapy*. Wiley.

Dryden, W. (2009). *Understanding emotional problems: The REBT perspective*. Routledge.

Dryden, W. (2015). Albert Ellis. In R. L. Cautin & S. O. Lilienfeld (Eds.), *The encyclopedia of clinical psychology* (pp. 1025–1027). Wiley-Blackwell.

Du, J., Zhang, D., Yin, Y., Zhang, X., Li, J., Liu, D., Pan, F., & Chen, W. (2016). The personality and psychological stress predict major adverse cardiovascular events in patients with coronary heart disease after percutaneous coronary intervention for five years. *Medicine, 95*(15), e3364.

Dubessy, A. L., Leu-Semenescu, S., Attali, V., Maranci, J. B., & Arnulf, I. (2016). Sexsomnia: A specialized non-REM parasomnia? *Sleep, 40*(2), zsw043.

du Bois-Reymond, M. (2016). Emerging adulthood theory under scrutiny. *Emerging Adulthood, 4*(4), 242–243.

Duboué, E. R., Keene, A. C., & Borowsky, R. L. (2011). Evolutionary convergence on sleep loss in cavefish populations. *Current Biology, 21*(8), 671–676.

Duckworth, A. L., & Seligman, M. E. (2006). Self-discipline gives girls the edge: Gender in self-discipline, grades, and achievement test scores. *Journal of Educational Psychology, 98*(1), 198–208.

Duckworth, K., Halpern, J. H., Schutt, R. K., & Gillespie, C. (2003). Use of schizophrenia as a metaphor in U.S. newspapers. *Psychiatric Services, 54*(10), 1402–1404.

Dudai, Y. (1997). How big is human memory, or, on being just useful enough. *Learning & Memory, 3,* 341–365.

Duffy, J. F., & Dijk, D.-J. (2002). Getting through to circadian oscillators: Why use constant routines? *Journal of Biological Rhythms, 17*(1), 4–13.

Duffy, J. F., Rimmer, D. W., & Czeisler, C. A. (2001). Association of intrinsic circadian period with morningness–eveningness, usual wake time, and circadian phase. *Behavioral Neuroscience, 115*(4), 895–899.

Duffy, J. F., & Wright, K. P. (2005). Entrainment of the human circadian system by light. *Journal of Biological Rhythms, 20*(4), 326–338.

Duffy, V. B., & Bartoshuk, L. M. (2000). Food acceptance and genetic variation in taste. *Journal of the American Dietetic Association, 100*(6), 647–655.

Dugan, J. W., Weatherly, R. A., Girod, D. A., Barber, C. E., & Tsue, T. T. (2014). A longitudinal study of emotional intelligence training for otolaryngology residents and faculty. *JAMA Otolaryngology–Head & Neck Surgery, 140*(8), 720–726.

Dugas, M. J., Charette, C. A., & Gervais, N. J. (2018). Generalized anxiety disorder. In J. Hunsley & E. J. Mash (Eds.), *A guide to assessments that work* (2nd ed., pp. 293–310). Oxford University Press.

Duhigg, J. M., Rostosky, S. S., Gray, B. E., & Wimsatt, M. K. (2010). Development of heterosexuals into allies: A qualitative exploration. *Sexuality Research and Social Policy, 7,* 2–14.

Duits, P., Cath, D. C., Lissek, S., Hox, J. J., Hamm, A. O., Engelhard, I. M., van den Hout, M. A., & Baas, J. M. (2015). Updated meta-analysis of classical fear conditioning in the anxiety disorders. *Depression and Anxiety, 32*(4), 239–253.

Dum, R. P., & Strick, P. L. (2009). Basal ganglia and cerebellar circuits with the cerebral cortex. In M. S. Gazzaniga (Ed.), *The cognitive neurosciences* (4th ed., pp. 553–564). MIT Press.

Duncan, L. A., Schaller, M., & Park, J. H. (2009). Perceived vulnerability to disease: Development and validation of a 15-item self-report instrument. *Personality and Individual Differences, 47*(6), 541–546.

Dunietz, G. L., Matos-Moreno, A., Singer, D. C., Davis, M. M., O'Brien, L. M., & Chervin, R. D. (2017). Later school start times: What informs parent support or opposition? *Journal of Clinical Sleep Medicine, 13*(07), 889–897.

Dunn, E. W., Wilson, T. D., & Gilbert, D. T. (2003). Location, location, location: The misprediction of satisfaction in housing lotteries. *Personality and Social Psychology Bulletin, 29*(11), 1421–1432.

Dunn, T. M., & Bratman, S. (2016). On orthorexia nervosa: A review of the literature and proposed diagnostic criteria. *Eating Behaviors, 21*, 11–17.

Duran-Bonavila, S., Morales-Vives, F., Cosi, S., & Vigil-Colet, A. (2017). How impulsivity and intelligence are related to different forms of aggression. *Personality and Individual Differences, 117*, 66–70.

Durand, V. M., & Wang, M. (2011). Clinical trials. In J. C. Thomas & M. Hersen (Eds.), *Understanding research in clinical and counseling psychology* (2nd ed., pp. 201–227). Taylor & Francis.

Durkee, M. I., & Williams, J. L. (2015). Accusations of acting white: Links to black students' racial identity and mental health. *Journal of Black Psychology, 41*(1), 26–48.

Durkin, K., & Nugent, B. (1998). Kindergarten children's gender-role expectations for television actors. *Sex Roles, 38*(5–6), 387–402.

Durlach, P. J. (2004). Change blindness and its implications for complex monitoring and control systems design and operator training. *Human–Computer Interaction, 19*(4), 423–451.

Duschinsky, R. (2015). The emergence of the disorganized/disoriented (D) attachment classification, 1979–1982. *History of Psychology, 18*(1), 32–46.

Dweck, C. S., & Grant, H. (2008). Self-theories, goals, and meaning. In J. Y. Shah & W. L. Gardner (Eds.), *Handbook of motivation science* (pp. 405–416). Guilford Press.

Dweck, C. S., & Leggett, E. L. (1988). A social-cognitive approach to motivation and personality. *Psychological Review, 95*(2), 256–273.

Dworkin, S. H. (2013). Bisexual identities. In C. J. Patterson & A. R. D'Augelli (Eds.), *Handbook of psychology and sexual orientation* (pp. 31–41). Oxford University Press.

Dwyer, L. A., Bolger, N., Laurenceau, J. P., Patrick, H., Oh, A. Y., Nebeling, L. C., & Hennessy, E. (2017). Autonomous motivation and fruit/vegetable intake in parent–adolescent dyads. *American Journal of Preventive Medicine, 52*(6), 863–871.

Eagly, A. H. (1987). *Sex differences in social behavior: A social-role interpretation*. Lawrence Erlbaum.

Eagly, A. H. (2013). The science and politics of comparing women and men: A reconsideration. In M. K. Ryan & N. R. Branscombe (Eds.), *The Sage handbook of gender and psychology* (pp. 11–28). Sage.

Eagly, A. H., & Crowley, M. (1986). Gender and helping behavior: A meta-analytic review of the social psychological literature. *Psychological Bulletin, 100*(3), 283–308.

Eagly, A. H., & Diekman, A. B. (2003). The malleability of sex differences in response to changing social roles. In L. G. Aspinwall & U. M. Staudinger (Eds.), *A psychology of human strengths* (pp. 103–115). American Psychological Association.

Eagly, A. H., & Wood, W. (1999). The origins of sex differences in human behavior: Evolved dispositions versus social roles. *American Psychologist, 54*(6), 408–423.

Eagly, A. H., Wood, W., & Diekman, A. B. (2000). Social role theory of sex differences and similarities: A current appraisal. In T. Eckes & H. M. Trautner (Eds.), *The developmental social psychology of gender* (pp. 123–174). Lawrence Erlbaum.

Eakin, L., Minde, K., Hechtman, L., Ochs, E., Krane, E., Bouffard, R., & Looper, K. (2004). The marital and family functioning of adults with ADHD and their spouses. *Journal of Attention Disorders, 8*(1), 1–10.

Earley, P. C., & Ang, S. (2003). *Cultural intelligence: Individual interactions across cultures*. Stanford University Press.

Earley, P. C., & Mosakowski, E. (2004). Cultural intelligence. *Harvard Business Review, 82*(10), 139–146.

Eastwick, P. W., Finkel, E. J., Krishnamurti, T., & Loewenstein, G. (2008). Mispredicting distress following romantic breakup: Revealing the time course of the affective forecasting error. *Journal of Experimental Social Psychology, 44*(3), 800–807. https://doi.org/10.1016/j.jesp.2007.07.001

Eastwick, P. W., Finkel, E. J., Mochon, D., & Ariely, D. (2007). Selective versus unselective romantic desire: Not all reciprocity is created equal. *Psychological Science, 18*(4), 317–319.

Eatock, R. A. (2010). Auditory receptors and transduction. In E. B. Goldstein (Ed.), *Encyclopedia of perception* (pp. 183–186). Sage.

Eaton, W. W., & Chen, C. (2006). Epidemiology. In J. A. Lieberman, T. S. Stroup, & D. O. Perkins (Eds.), *The American Psychiatric Publishing textbook of schizophrenia* (pp. 17–37). American Psychiatric Association Publishing.

Ebbinghaus, H. (1885). *Memory: A contribution to experimental psychology*. Dover.

Ebel, M. D., Rudolph, I., Keinki, C., Hoppe, A., Muecke, R., Micke, O., Muenstedt, K., & Huebner, J. (2015). Perception of cancer patients of their disease, self-efficacy and locus of control and usage of complementary and alternative medicine. *Journal of Cancer Research and Clinical Oncology, 141*(8), 1449–1455.

Eberth, J., & Sedlmeier, P. (2012). The effects of mindfulness meditation: A meta-analysis. *Mindfulness, 3*(3), 174–189.

Ebner, N. C. (2008). Age of face matters: Age-group differences in ratings of young and old faces. *Behavior Research Methods, 40*(1), 130–136.

Ebner, N. C., Freund, A. M., & Baltes, P. B. (2006). Developmental changes in personal goal orientation from young to late adulthood: From striving for gains to maintenance and prevention of losses. *Psychology and Aging, 21*(4), 664–678.

Ebrecht, M., Hextall, J., Kirtley, L. G., Taylor, A., Dyson, M., & Weinman, J. (2004). Perceived stress and cortisol levels predict speed of wound healing in healthy male adults. *Psychoneuroendocrinology, 29*(6), 798–809.

Eccleston, C., & Crombez, G. (1999). Pain demands attention: A cognitive–affective model of the interruptive function of pain. *Psychological Bulletin, 125*(3), 356–366.

Eckert, D. J., Malhotra, A., & Jordan, A. S. (2009). Mechanisms of apnea. *Progress in Cardiovascular Diseases, 51*(4), 313–323.

Eckler, P., Kalyango, Y., & Paasch, E. (2017). Facebook use and negative body image among US college women. *Women & Health, 57*(2), 249–267.

Economos, C. D., Brownson, R. C., DeAngelis, M. A., Foerster, S. B., Foreman, C. T., Gregson, J., Kumanyika, S. K., & Pate, R. R. (2001). What lessons have been learned from other attempts to guide social change? *Nutrition Reviews, 59*(3), S40–S56.

Economos, C. D., & Sliwa, S. A. (2011). Community interventions. In J. H. Cawley (Ed.), *The Oxford handbook of the social science of obesity* (pp. 713–740). Oxford University Press.

Edenfield, T. M., & Blumenthal, J. A. (2011). Exercise and stress reduction. In A. Baum & R. Contrada (Eds.), *The handbook of stress science: Biology, psychology, and health* (pp. 301–319). Springer.

Egger, G., & Swinburn, B. (1997). An "ecological" approach to the obesity pandemic. *BMJ: British Medical Journal, 315*(7106), 477–479.

Ehlers, A. (1993). Somatic symptoms and panic attacks: A retrospective study of learning experiences. *Behaviour Research and Therapy, 31*(3), 269–278.

Ehrenwald, J. (Ed.). (1991). *The history of psychotherapy*. Aronson.

Ehrlich, P., & Feldman, M., (2003). Genes and cultures. *Current Anthropology, 44*(1), 87–107.

Eibl-Eibesfeldt, I. (1973). The expressive behaviour of the deaf-and-blind born. In M. von Cranach & I. Vine (Eds.), *Social communication and movement* (pp. 163–194). Academic Press.

Eich, E. (1995a). Searching for mood dependent memory. *Psychological Science, 6*(2), 67–75.

Eich, E. (1995b). Mood as a mediator of place dependent memory. *Journal of Experimental Psychology: General, 124*(3), 293–308.

Eich, E. (2007). Context: Mood, memory, and the concept of context. In H. L. Roediger, Y. Dudai, & S. M. Fitzpatrick (Eds.). *Science of memory: Concepts* (pp. 107–110). Oxford University Press.

Eichenbaum, H. (2010). Memory systems. *Wiley Interdisciplinary Reviews: Cognitive Science, 1*(4), 478–490.

Eichstaedt, J. C., Schwartz, H. A., Kern, M. L., Park, G., Labarthe, D. R., Merchant, R. M., Jha, S., Agrawal, M., Dziurzynski, L., Sap, M., Weeg, C., Larson, E. E., Ungar, L. H., & Seligman, M. E. (2015). Psychological language on Twitter predicts county-level heart disease mortality. *Psychological Science, 26*(2), 159–169.

Eid, M., & Diener, E. (2001). Norms for experiencing emotions in different cultures: Inter- and intranational differences. *Journal of Personality and Social Psychology, 81*(5), 869–885.

Eisen, J. L., Yip, A. G., Mancebo, M. C., Pinto, A., & Rasmussen, S. A. (2010). Phenomenology of obsessive-compulsive disorder. In D. J. Stein, E. Hollander, & B. O. Rothbaum (Eds.), *Textbook of anxiety disorders* (2nd ed., pp. 261–286). American Psychiatric Association Publishing.

Eisenberg, M. E., Neumark-Sztainer, M. S., & Perry, C. (2005). The role of social norms and friends' influences on unhealthy weight-control behaviors among adolescent girls. *Social Science & Medicine, 60*(6), 1165–1173.

Eisenberg, N., Fabes, R. A., Miller, P. A., Fultz, J., Shell, R., Mathy, R. M., & Reno, R. R. (1989). Relation of sympathy and distress to prosocial behavior: A multimethod study. *Journal of Personality and Social Psychology, 57*(1), 55–66.

Eisenberg, N., Morris, A. S., McDaniel, B., & Spinrad, T. L. (2009). Moral cognitions and prosocial responding in adolescence. In R. M. Lerner & L. Steinberg (Eds.), *Handbook of adolescent psychology* (3rd ed., Vol. 1, pp. 229–265). Wiley.

Eisenberger, N. I., Lieberman, M. D., & Williams, K. D. (2003). Does rejection hurt? An fMRI study of social exclusion. *Science, 302*(5643), 290–292.

Eiser, J. R. (2012). A history of social judgment research. In A. W. Kruglanski & W. Stroebe (Eds.), *Handbook of the history of social psychology* (pp. 219–241). Psychology Press.

Ekman, P. (1972). Universal and cultural differences in facial expression of emotion. In J. R. Cole (Ed.), *Nebraska Symposium on Motivation* (Vol. 19, pp. 207–283). University of Nebraska Press.

Ekman, P. (Ed.). (1974). *Darwin and facial expression*. Academic Press.

Ekman, P. (1993). Facial expression and emotion. *American Psychologist, 48*(4), 384–392.

Ekman, P. (2003). *Emotions revealed: Recognizing faces and feelings to improve communication and emotional life*. Times Books.

Ekman, P., & Cordaro, D. (2011). What is meant by calling emotions basic. *Emotion Review, 3*(4), 364–370.

Ekman, P., & Friesen, W. (1971). Constants across culture in the face and emotion. *Journal of Personality and Social Psychology, 17*(2), 124–129.

Ekman, P., Friesen, W. V., O'Sullivan, M., Chan, A., Diacoyanni-Tarlatiz, I., Heider, K., ... Ricci-Pitti, P. E. (1987). Universals and cultural differences in the judgements of facial expressions of emotion. *Journal of Personality and Social Psychology, 53*(4), 712–717.

Ekstrand, B. R. (1972). To sleep, perchance to dream: About why we forget. In C. Duncan, P. L. Sechrest, & A. W. Melton (Eds.), *Human memory; Festschrift for Benton J. Underwood* (pp. 59–82). Appleton-Century-Crofts.

Elbert, T., Pantev, C., Wienbruch, C., Rockstroh, B., & Taub, E. (1995). Increased cortical representation of the fingers of the left hand in string players. *Science, 270*(5234), 305–307.

Elder, G. H., Jr., & Shanahan, M. J. (2006). The life course and human development. In R. M. Lerner (Vol. Ed.), *Handbook of child psychology* (6th ed., Vol. 1, pp. 665–715). Wiley.

Elderton, A., Berry, A., & Chan, C. (2017). A systematic review of posttraumatic growth in survivors of interpersonal violence in adulthood. *Trauma, Violence, & Abuse, 18*(2), 223–236.

Eley, T. C. (2009). The genetic basis of anxiety disorders. In G. Andrews, D. S. Charney, P. J. Sirovatka, & D. A. Regier (Eds.), *Stress-induced and fear circuitry disorders: Refining the research agenda for DSM-V* (pp. 145–158). American Psychiatric Association.

Elfenbein, H. A. (2013). Nonverbal dialects and accents in facial expressions of emotion. *Emotion Review, 5*(1), 90–96.

Elfenbein, H. A. (2017). Emotional dialects in the language of emotion. In J. Fernandez-Dols & J. A. Russell (Eds.), *The science of facial expression* (p. 479). Oxford University Press.

Elfenbein, H. A., & Ambady, N. (2002). On the universality and cultural specificity of emotion recognition: A meta-analysis. *Psychological Bulletin, 128*(2), 203–235.

Elfenbein, H. A., Beaupré, M., Lévesque, M., & Hess, U. (2007). Toward a dialect theory: Cultural differences in the expression and recognition of posed facial expressions. *Emotion, 7*(1), 131–146.

Elflein, J. (2021). Number of U.S. adults who received mental health treatment or counseling in the past year from 2002 to 2020. https://www.statista.com/statistics/794027/mental-health-treatment-counseling-past-year-us-adults/#statisticContainer

Elgar, F. J., Donnelly, P. D., Michaelson, V., Gariépy, G., Riehm, K. E., Walsh, S. D., & Pickett, W. (2018). Corporal punishment bans and physical fighting in adolescents: An ecological study of 88 countries. *BMJ Open, 8*(9), e021616.

Elias, A., Thomas, N., & Sackeim, H. A. (2021). Electroconvulsive therapy in mania: A review of 80 years of clinical experience. *American Journal of Psychiatry, 178*(3), 229–239. https://doi.org/10.1176/appi.ajp.2020.20030238

Eliason, M. J. (2001). Substance abuse counselor's attitudes regarding lesbian, gay, bisexual, and transgendered clients. *Journal of Substance Abuse, 12*(4), 311–328.

Elkind, D. (1967). Egocentrism in adolescence. *Child Development, 38*(4), 1025–1034.

Elkind, D. (1985). Egocentrism redux. *Developmental Review, 5*(3), 218–226.

Elkins, D. N. (2016). *The human elements of psychotherapy: A nonmedical model of emotional healing*. American Psychological Association.

Elkins, G., & Perfect, M. (2008). Hypnosis for health-compromising behaviors. In M. R. Nash & A. J. Barnier (Eds.), *The Oxford handbook of hypnosis: Theory, research, and practice* (pp. 569–592). Oxford, UK: Oxford University Press.

Ellemers, N. (2018). Gender stereotypes. *Annual Review of Psychology, 69*, 275–298.

Ellenbogen, J. M., Hulbert, J. C., Stickgold, R., Dinges, D. F., & Thompson-Schill, S. L. (2006). Interfering with theories of sleep and memory: Sleep, declarative memory, and associative interference. *Current Biology, 16*(13), 1290–1294.

Elliot, A. J., Heffner, K. L., Mooney, C. J., Moynihan, J. A., & Chapman, B. P. (2018). Social relationships and inflammatory markers in the MIDUS cohort: The role of age and gender differences. *Journal of Aging and Health, 30*(6), 904–923.

Elliot, A. J., McGregor, H. A., & Gable, S. (1999). Achievement goals, study strategies, and exam performance: A mediational analysis. *Journal of Educational Psychology, 91*(3), 549–563.

Elliott, E. S., & Dweck, C. S. (1988). Goals: An approach to motivation and achievement. *Journal of Personality and Social Psychology, 54*(1), 5–12.

Elliott, J. L., & Gentile, J. R. (1986). The efficacy of a mnemonic technique for learning disabled and nondisabled adolescents. *Journal of Learning Disabilities, 19*(4), 237–241.

Elliott, K., Barker, K. K., & Hunsley, J. (2015). Dodo bird verdict in psychotherapy. In R. L. Cautin & S. O. Lilienfeld (Eds.), *The encyclopedia of clinical psychology* (pp. 944–948). Wiley-Blackwell.

Elliott, M. L., Knodt, A. R., Ireland, D., Morris, M. L., Poulton, R., Ramrakha, S., Sison, M. L., Moffitt, T. E., Caspi, A., & Hariri, A. R. (2020). What is the test-retest reliability of common task-functional MRI measures? New empirical evidence and a meta-analysis. *Psychological Science, 31*(7), 792–806. https://doi.org/10.1177/0956797620916786

Elliott, R., Bohart, A. C., Watson, J. C., & Greenberg, L. S. (2011). Empathy. In J. C. Norcross (Ed.), *Psychotherapy relationships that work: Evidence-based responsiveness* (2nd ed., pp. 132–152). Oxford University Press.

Elliott, R., Bohart, A. C., Watson, J. C., & Murphy, D. (2018). Therapist empathy and client outcome: An updated meta-analysis. *Psychotherapy, 55*(4), 399–410.

Ellis, A. (1962). *Reason and emotion in psychotherapy*. Lyle Stuart.

Ellis, A. (2008). Cognitive restructuring of the disputing of irrational beliefs. In W. T. O'Donohue & J. E. Fisher (Eds.), *Cognitive behavior therapy: Applying empirically supported techniques in your practice* (2nd ed., pp. 91–95). Wiley.

Ellis, A., & Ellis, D. J. (2011). *Rational emotive behavior therapy*. American Psychological Association.

Ellis, A., & Grieger, R. (1977). *Handbook of rational-emotive therapy*. Springer.

Ellis, A., & Harper, R. A. (1975). *A new guide to rational living*. Wilshire.

Ellis, W. E., & Dumas, T. M. (2019). Peers over parents? How peer relationships influence dating violence. In D. A. Wolfe & J. R. Temple (Eds.), *Adolescent dating violence* (pp. 105–133). Academic Press.

Ellison, C. G. (1991). Religious involvement and subjective well-being. *Journal of Health and Social Behavior, 32*(1), 80–99.

Ellison, K. (2010). *Buzz: A year of paying attention*. Voice.

Elman, J. L., Bates, E. A., Johnson, M. H., Karmiloff-Smith, A., Parisi, D., & Plunkett, K. (1996). *Rethinking innateness*. MIT Press.

Elmore, K. C., & Luna-Lucero, M. (2017). Light bulbs or seeds? How metaphors for ideas influence judgments about genius. *Social Psychological and Personality Science, 8*(2), 200–208.

Emerson, C. (1983). The outer word and inner speech: Bakhtin, Vygotsky, and the internalization of language. *Critical Inquiry, 10*(2), 245–264.

Emmelkamp, P. M. G., & Kamphuis, J. H. (2002). Aversion relief. In M. Hersen & W. Sledge (Eds.), *Encyclopedia of psychotherapy* (Vol. 1, pp. 139–143). Academic Press.

Emmelkamp, P. M., & Meyerbröker, K. (2021). Virtual reality therapy in mental health. *Annual Review of Clinical Psychology, 17*, 495–519. https://doi.org/10.1146/annurev-clinpsy-081219-115923

Emmelkamp, P. M., & Wessels, H. (1975). Flooding in imagination vs flooding in vivo: A comparison with agoraphobics. *Behaviour Research and Therapy, 13*(1), 7–15.

Emmelkamp, P. M. G., & Wittchen, H. (2009). Specific phobias. In G. Andrews, D. S. Charney, P. J. Sirovatka, & D. A. Regier (Eds.), *Stress-induced and fear circuitry disorders: Refining the research agenda for DSM-V* (pp. 77–101). American Psychiatric Association.

Emmons, R. A., & McCullough, M. E. (2003). Counting blessings versus burdens: An experimental investigation of gratitude and subjective well-being in daily life. *Journal of Personality and Social Psychology, 84*(2), 377–389.

Emond, J. A., Longacre, M. R., Drake, K. M., Titus, L. J., Hendricks, K., MacKenzie, T., Harris, J. L., Carroll, J. E., Cleveland, L. P., Langeloh, G., & Dalton, M. A. (2019). Exposure to child-directed TV advertising and preschoolers' intake of advertised cereals. *American Journal of Preventive Medicine, 56*(2), e35–e43. https://doi.org/10.1016/j.amepre.2018.09.015

Encinosa, W. E., Bernard, D. M., Du, D., & Steiner, C. A. (2009). Recent improvements in bariatric surgery outcomes. *Medical Care, 47*(5), 531–535.

Encinosa, W., Du, D., & Bernard, D. (2011). Anti-obesity drugs and bariatric surgery. In J. H. Cawley (Ed.), *The Oxford handbook of the social science of obesity* (pp. 792–807). Oxford University Press.

Endo, T., Roth, C., Landolt, H. P., Werth, E., Aeschbach, D., Achermann, P., & Borbély, A. A. (1998). Selective REM sleep deprivation in humans: Effects on sleep and sleep EEG. *American Journal of Physiology – Regulatory, Integrative and Comparative Physiology, 274*(4), R1186–R1194.

Endo, Y., Heine, S. J., & Lehman, D. R. (2000). Culture and positive illusions in close relationships: How my relationships are better than yours. *Personality and Social Psychology Bulletin, 26*(12), 1571–1586.

Endresen, I. M., & Olweus, D. (2001). Self-reported empathy in Norwegian adolescents: Sex differences, age trends, and relationship to bullying. In A. C. Bohart, & D. J. Stipek (Eds.), *Constructive & destructive behavior: Implications for family, school, and society* (pp. 147–165). American Psychological Association.

Engel, J. (2008). *American therapy: The rise of psychotherapy in the United States*. Gotham Books.

Engeln, R., Loach, R., Imundo, M. N., & Zola, A. (2020). Compared to Facebook, Instagram use causes more appearance comparison and lower body satisfaction in college women. *Body Image, 34*, 38–45. https://doi.org/10.1016/j.bodyim.2020.04.007

Engle, R. W. (2002). Working memory capacity as executive attention. *Current Directions in Psychological Science, 11*(1), 19–23.

English, T., John, O. P., & Gross, J. J. (2013). Emotion regulation in close relationships. In J. A. Simpson & L. Campbell (Eds.), *The Oxford handbook of close relationships* (pp. 500–513). Oxford University Press.

Eonta, A. M., Christon, L. M., Hourigan, S. E., Ravindran, N., Vrana, S. R., & Southam-Gerow, M. A. (2011). Using everyday technology to enhance evidence-based treatments. *Professional Psychology: Research and Practice, 42*(6), 513–520.

Epstein, R. A., Patai, E. Z., Julian, J. B., & Spiers, H. J. (2017). The cognitive map in humans: Spatial navigation and beyond. *Nature Neuroscience, 20*(11), 1504–1513.

Epstein, S. (1991). Cognitive-experiential self-theory: An integrative theory of personality. In R. Curtis (Ed.), *The self with others: Convergences in psychoanalytic, social, and personality psychology* (pp. 111–137). Guilford Press.

Epstein, S. (1994). Trait theory as personality theory: Can a part be as great as the whole? *Psychological Inquiry, 5*(2), 120–122.

Er, N. (2003). A new flashbulb memory model applied to the Marmara earthquake. *Applied Cognitive Psychology, 17*(5), 503–517.

Erdley, C. A., & Day, H. J. (2017). Friendship in childhood and adolescence. In M. Hojjat & A. Moyer (Eds.), *The psychology of friendship* (pp. 3–19). Oxford University Press.

Erekson, D. M., & Lambert, M. J. (2015). Client-centered therapy. In R. L. Cautin & S. O. Lilienfeld (Eds.), *The encyclopedia of clinical psychology* (pp. 532–537). Wiley-Blackwell.

Erhart, S. M., Young, A. S., Marder, S. R., & Mintz, J. (2005). Clinical utility of magnetic resonance imaging radiographs for suspected organic syndromes in adult psychiatry. *Journal of Clinical Psychiatry, 66*(8), 968–973.

Erickson, J. J., Martinengo, G., & Hill, E. J. (2010). Putting work and family experiences in context: Differences by family life stage. *Human Relations, 63*(7), 955–979.

Erickson, K. I., & Kramer, A. F. (2009). Aerobic exercise effects on cognitive and neural plasticity in older adults. *British Journal of Sports Medicine, 43*(1), 22–24.

Erickson, K. I., Voss, M. W., Prakash, R. S., Basak, C., Szabo, A., Chaddock, L., ... Kramer, A. F. (2011). Exercise training increases size of hippocampus and improves memory. *Proceedings of the National Academy of Sciences, 108*(7), 3017–3022.

Eriksen, I. M., & Lyng, S. T. (2018). Relational aggression among boys: Blind spots and hidden dramas. *Gender and Education, 30*(3), 396–409.

Eriksen, K., & Kress, V. E. (2005). *Beyond the DSM story: Ethical quandaries, challenges, and best practices*. Sage.

Erikson, E. H. (1946). Ego development and historical change—clinical notes. *Psychoanalytic Study of the Child, 2*, 359–396.

Erikson, E. H. (1950). *Childhood and society*. Norton.

Erikson, E. H. (1959). *Identity and the life cycle*. International Universities Press.

Erikson, E. H. (1968). *Identity, youth and crisis*. Norton.

Erikson, E. H., & Erikson, J. M. (1998). *The life cycle completed (extended version)*. Norton.

Eriksson, P. S., Perfilieva, E., Björk-Eriksson, T., Alborn, A. M., Nordborg, C., Peterson, D. A., & Gage, F. H. (1998). Neurogenesis in the adult human hippocampus. *Nature Medicine, 4*(11), 1313–1317.

Erlacher, D. (2012). Lucid dreaming in sports. In D. Barrett & P. McNamara (Eds.), *Encyclopedia of sleep and dreams* (pp. 400–401). Greenwood.

Ernst, E., Pittler, M. H., & Wider, B. (2006). *The desktop guide to complementary and alternative medicine: An evidence-based approach* (2nd ed.). Mosby Elsevier.

Eron, L. D., Huesmann, L. R., Lefkowitz, M. M., & Walder, L. O. (1972). Does television violence cause aggression? *American Psychologist, 27*(4), 253–263.

Ershadi, M., Goldstein, T. R., Pochedly, J., & Russell, J. A. (2018). Facial expressions as performances in mime. *Cognition and Emotion, 32*(3), 494–503.

Erskine, H. E., & Whiteford, H. A. (2018). Epidemiology of binge eating disorder. *Current Opinion in Psychiatry, 31*(6), 462–470.

Erwin, E. (Ed.). (2002). *The Freud encyclopedia: Theory, therapy, and culture*. Routledge.

Escudero, V., & Friedlander, M. L. (2017). *Therapeutic alliances with families*. Springer.

Eshel, N., & Roiser, J. P. (2010). Reward and punishment processing in depression. *Biological Psychiatry, 68*(2), 118 –124. https://doi.org/10.1016/j.biopsych.2010.01.027

Eshun, S., & Gurung, R. A. R. (Eds.). (2009). *Culture and mental health: Sociocultural influences, theory, and practice*. Wiley-Blackwell.

Espelage, D. L., Van Ryzin, M. J., & Holt, M. K. (2018). Trajectories of bully perpetration across early adolescence: Static risk factors, dynamic covariates, and longitudinal outcomes. *Psychology of Violence, 8*(2), 141–150.

Espie, C. A., & Morin, C. M. (2012). Introduction: Historical landmarks and current status of sleep research and practice. In C. M. Morin & C. A. Espie (Eds.), *The Oxford handbook of sleep and sleep disorders* (pp. 1–9). Oxford University Press.

Essau, C. A., Lewinsohn, P. M., Lim, J. X., Moon-Ho, R. H., & Rohde, P. (2018). Incidence, recurrence and comorbidity of anxiety disorders in four major developmental stages. *Journal of Affective Disorders, 228*, 248–253.

Esterling, B. A., Kiecolt-Glaser, J. K., Bodnar, J. C., & Glaser, R. (1994). Chronic stress, social support, and persistent alterations in the natural killer cell response to cytokines in older adults. *Health Psychology, 13*(4), 291–298.

Etale, A., Jobin, M., & Siegrist, M. (2018). Tap versus bottled water consumption: The influence of social norms, affect and image on consumer choice. *Appetite, 121*, 138–146.

Etchegoyen, A. (1993). Latency: A reappraisal. *International Journal of Psycho-analysis, 74*(Pt. 2), 347–357.

Etkin, A., Pittenger, C., Polan, H. J., & Kandel, E. R. (2005). Toward a neurobiology of psychotherapy: Basic science and clinical applications. *Journal of Neuropsychiatry and Clinical Neurosciences, 17*(2), 145–158.

Euling, S. Y., Selevan, S. G., Pescovitz, O. H., & Skakkebaek, N. E. (2008). Role of environmental factors in the timing of puberty. *Pediatrics, 121*(Suppl. 3), S167–S171.

Evans, D. (2009). *Rage against the meshugenah: Why it takes balls to go nuts: A memoir*. Penguin Books.

Evans, J. S. B. T. (2012). Dual-process theories of deductive reasoning: Facts and fallacies. In K. J. Holyoak & R. G. Morrison (Eds.), *The Oxford handbook of thinking and reasoning* (pp. 115–133). Oxford University Press.

Evans, J. S. B. T. (2013). Reasoning. In D. Reisberg (Ed.), *The Oxford handbook of cognitive psychology* (pp. 635–649). Oxford University Press.

Evans, J. S. B. T. (2018). Dual-process theories. In L. J. Ball & V. A. Thompson (Eds.), *Routledge international handbook of thinking and reasoning* (pp. 151–166). Routledge.

Evans, J. S. B. T., & Over, D. E. (1996). *Rationality and reasoning*. Psychology Press.

Evans, J. S. B. T., & Stanovich, K. E. (2013). Dual-process theories of higher cognition advancing the debate. *Perspectives on Psychological Science, 8*(3), 223–241.

Evans, R. I. (1968). *B. F. Skinner: The man and his ideas*. Dutton.

Everitt, B. J., & Robbins, T. W. (2005). Neural systems of reinforcement for drug addiction: From actions to habits to compulsion. *Nature Neuroscience, 8*(11), 1481–1489.

Ewert, J. P. (1987). Neuroethology of releasing mechanisms: Prey-catching in toads. *Behavioral Brain Science, 10*(3), 337–405.

Exner, J. E., Jr. (1986). *The Rorschach: A comprehensive system* (2nd ed.). Wiley.

Exton, M. S., von Auer, A. K., Buske-Kirschbaum, A., Stockhorst, U., Göbel, U., & Schedlowski, M. (2000). Pavlovian conditioning of immune function: Animal investigation and the challenge of human application. *Behavioural Brain Research, 110*(1), 129–141.

Eyde, L. D. (2000). Other responsibilities to participants. In B. D. Sales & S. Folkman (Eds.), *Ethics in research with human participants* (pp. 61–73). American Psychological Association.

Eyler, L. T. (2008). Brain imaging. In K. T. Meuser & D. V. Jeste (Eds.), *Clinical handbook of schizophrenia*, pp. 35–43. Guilford.

Eysenck, H. J. (1952). The effects of psychotherapy: An evaluation. *Journal of Consulting Psychology, 16*(6), 319–324.

Fabbri-Destro, M., & Rizzolatti, G. (2008). Mirror neurons and mirror systems in monkeys and humans. *Physiology, 23*(3), 171–179.

Fabel, K., & Kempermann, G. (2008). Physical activity and the regulation of neurogenesis in the adult and aging brain. *Neuromolecular Medicine, 10*(2), 59–66.

Fabiano, F., & Haslam, N. (2020). Diagnostic inflation in the DSM: A meta-analysis of changes in the stringency of psychiatric diagnosis from DSM-III to DSM-5. *Clinical Psychology Review, 80*, 101889. https://doi.org/10.1016/j.cpr.2020.101889

Fairburn, C. G., Cooper, Z., Doll, H. A., Norman, P., & O'Connor, M. (2000). The natural course of bulimia nervosa and binge eating disorder in young women. *Archives of General Psychiatry, 57*(7), 659–665.

Faith, M. S., Butryn, M., Wadden, T. A., Fabricatore, A., Nguyen, A. M., & Heymsfield, S. B. (2011). Evidence for prospective associations among depression and obesity in population-based studies. *Obesity Reviews, 12*(5), e438–e453.

Falbe, J., Willett, W. C., Rosner, B., & Field, A. E. (2017). Body mass index, new modes of TV viewing and active video games. *Pediatric Obesity, 12*(5), 406–413.

Falconier, M. K., Nussbeck, F., Bodenmann, G., Schneider, H., & Bradbury, T. (2015). Stress from daily hassles in couples: Its effects on intradyadic stress, relationship satisfaction, and physical and psychological well-being. *Journal of Marital and Family Therapy, 41*(2), 221–235.

Falls, W. A. (1998). Extinction: A review of the theory and the evidence suggesting that memories are not erased with nonreinforcement. In W. O'Donohue (Ed.), *Learning and behavior therapy* (pp. 205–229). Allyn & Bacon.

Famy, C., Streissguth, A. P., & Unis, A. S. (1998). Mental illness in adults with fetal alcohol syndrome or fetal alcohol effects. *American Journal of Psychiatry, 155*(4), 552–554.

Fancher, R. E., & Rutherford, A. (2012). *Pioneers of psychology: A history* (4th ed.). Norton.

Fancher, R. T. (1995). *Cultures of healing: Correcting the image of American mental health care.* W. H. Freeman.

Fanselow, M. S., & Sterlace, S. R. (2014). Pavlovian fear conditioning: Function, cause, and treatment. In F. K. McSweeney & E. S. Murphy (Eds.), *The Wiley-Blackwell handbook of operant and classical conditioning* (pp. 117–142). Wiley.

Fantz, R. L., Fagan, J. F., & Miranda, S. B. (1975). Early visual selectivity: As function of pattern variables, previous exposure, age from birth and conception, and expected cognitive deficit. In L. B. Cohen & P. Salapatek (Eds.), *Infant perception: From sensation to cognition* (Vol. 1, pp. 249–346). Elsevier.

Farah, M. J. (2010). *Neuroethics: An introduction with readings*. MIT Press.

Faraone, S. V., Rostain, A. L., Montano, C. B., Mason, O., Antshel, K. M., & Newcorn, J. H. (2020). Systematic review: Nonmedical use of prescription stimulants: Risk factors, outcomes, and risk reduction strategies. *Journal of the American Academy of Child & Adolescent Psychiatry, 59*(1), 100–112. https://doi.org/10.1016/j.jaac.2019.06.012

Faravelli, C., Furukawa, T. A., & Truglia, E. (2009). Panic disorder. In G. Andrews, D. S. Charney, P. J. Sirovatka, & D. A. Regier (Eds.), *Stress-induced and fear circuitry disorders: Refining the research agenda for DSM-V* (pp. 31–58). American Psychiatric Association.

Farber, B. A., & Doolin, E. M. (2011). Positive regard and affirmation. In J. C. Norcross (Ed.), *Psychotherapy relationships that work: Evidence-based responsiveness* (2nd ed., pp. 168–186). Oxford University Press.

Farber, B. A., Suzuki, J. Y., & Lynch, D. A. (2018). Positive regard and psychotherapy outcome: A meta-analytic review. *Psychotherapy, 55*(4), 411–423.

Fardouly, J., Diedrichs, P. C., Vartanian, L. R., & Halliwell, E. (2015). Social comparisons on social media: The impact of Facebook on young women's body image concerns and mood. *Body Image, 13,* 38–45.

Fardouly, J., Pinkus, R. T., & Vartanian, L. R. (2017). The impact of appearance comparisons made through social media, traditional media, and in person in women's everyday lives. *Body Image, 20,* 31–39.

Fardouly, J., & Vartanian, L. R. (2015). Negative comparisons about one's appearance mediate the relationship between Facebook usage and body image concerns. *Body Image, 12,* 82–88.

Fardouly, J., Willburger, B. K., & Vartanian, L. R. (2018). Instagram use and young women's body image concerns and self-objectification: Testing mediational pathways. *New Media & Society, 20*(4), 1380–1395.

Farley, S. D., Ashcraft, A. M., Stasson, M. F., & Nusbaum, R. L. (2010). Nonverbal reactions to conversational interruption: A test of complementarity theory and the status/gender parallel. *Journal of Nonverbal Behavior, 34*(4), 193–206.

Farley, S. D., Hughes, S. M., & LaFayette, J. N. (2013). People will know we are in love: Evidence of differences between vocal samples directed toward lovers and friends. *Journal of Nonverbal Behavior, 37*(3), 123–138.

Farreras, I. G., Routh, D. K., & Cautin, R. L. (2016). History of clinical psychology following World War II. In J. C. Norcross, G. R. VandenBos, & D. K. Freedheim (Eds.), *APA handbook of clinical psychology* (Vol. 1, pp. 19–40). American Psychological Association.

Farver, J. A. M., Kim, Y. K., & Lee, Y. (1995). Cultural differences in Korean- and Anglo-American preschoolers' social interaction and play behaviors. *Child Development, 66*(4), 1088–1099.

Fast, D. K., & Conry, J. (2004). The challenge of fetal alcohol syndrome in the criminal legal system. *Addiction Biology, 9*(2), 161–166.

Fast, D. K., & Conry, J. (2009). Fetal alcohol spectrum disorders and the criminal justice system. *Developmental Disabilities Research Reviews, 15*(3), 250–257.

Fast, D. K., Conry, J., & Loock, C. A. (1999). Identifying fetal alcohol syndrome among youth in the criminal justice system. *Journal of Developmental and Behavioral Pediatrics, 20*(5), 370–372.

Fatania, J., & Mercer, T. (2017). Nonspecific retroactive interference in children and adults. *Advances in Cognitive Psychology, 13*(4), 314–322.

Fattoracci, E. S. M., Revels-Macalinao, M., & Huynh, Q.-L. (2021). Greater than the sum of racism and heterosexism: Intersectional microaggressions toward racial/ethnic and sexual minority group members. *Cultural Diversity and Ethnic Minority Psychology, 27*(2), 176–188. https://doi.org/10.1037/cdp0000329

Fazio, R. H. (1990). Multiple processes by which attitudes guide behavior: The MODE model as an integrative framework. In M. P. Zanna (Ed.), *Advances in experimental social psychology* (pp. 75–109). Academic Press.

Fazio, R. H., & Olson, M. A. (2003). Implicit measures in social cognition research: Their meaning and use. *Annual Review of Psychology, 54*(1), 297–327.

Feather, N. T. (1988). Moral judgement and human values. *British Journal of Social Psychology, 27*(3), 239–246.

Feder, K., Michaud, D., McNamee, J., Fitzpatrick, E., Davies, H., & Leroux, T. (2017). Prevalence of hazardous occupational noise exposure, hearing loss, and hearing protection usage among a representative sample of working Canadians. *Journal of Occupational and Environmental Medicine, 59*(1), 92–113.

Federn, E. (1997). Sigmund Freud: A biographical sketch. In W. G. Bringmann, H. E. Lück, R. Miller, & C. E. Early (Eds.), *A pictorial history of psychology* (pp. 391–394). Quintessence Publishing.

Fehr, B. (2019). Everyday conceptions of love. In R. J. Sternberg & K. Sternberg (Eds.), *The new psychology of love* (2nd ed., pp. 154–182). Cambridge University Press.

Feigenbaum, E. A., & Simon, H. A. (1962). A theory of the serial position effect. *British Journal of Psychology, 53*(3), 307–320.

Feigin, S., Owens, G., & Goodyear-Smith, F. (2018). Theories of human altruism: A systematic review. *Journal of Psychiatry and Brain Functions, 1*(1), 5.

Feinberg, I., & Campbell, I. G. (2010). Sleep EEG changes during adolescence: An index of a fundamental brain reorganization. *Brain and Cognition, 72*(1), 56–65.

Feinberg, I., & Floyd, T. C. (1979). Systematic trends across the night in human sleep cycles. *Psychophysiology, 16*(3), 283–291.

Feingold, A. (1994). Gender differences in personality: A meta-analysis. *Psychological Bulletin, 116*(3), 429–456.

Feld, G. B., & Born, J. (2017). Sculpting memory during sleep: Concurrent consolidation and forgetting. *Current Opinion in Neurobiology, 44,* 20–27.

Felitti, V. J., Anda, R. F., Nordenberg, D., Williamson, D. F., Spitz, A. M., Edwards, V., Koss, M. P., & Marks, J. S. (1998). Relationship of childhood abuse and household dysfunction to many of the leading causes of death in adults: The Adverse Childhood Experiences (ACE) Study. *American Journal of Preventive Medicine, 14*(4), 245–258.

Felson, R. B., & Palmore, C. (2018). Biases in blaming victims of rape and other crime. *Psychology of Violence, 8*(3), 390–399.

Fenson, L., Dale, P. S., Reznick, J. S., Bates, E., Thal, D. J., & Pethick, S. J. (1994). Variability in early communicative development. *Monographs of the Society for Research in Child Development, 59*(5), 1–173.

Ferber, S., & Karnath, H. O. (1999). Parietal and occipital lobe contributions to perception of straight ahead orientation. *Journal of Neurology, Neurosurgery & Psychiatry, 67*(5), 572–578.

Ferdenzi, C., Roberts, S. C., Schirmer, A., Delplanque, S., Cekic, S., Porcherot, C., Cayeux, I., Sander, D., & Grandjean, D. (2013). Variability of affective responses to odors: Culture, gender, and olfactory knowledge. *Chemical Senses, 38*(2), 175–186.

Ferdowsian, H., Durham, D., & Brüne, M. (2013). Mood and anxiety disorders in chimpanzees (*Pan troglodytes*): A response to Rosati et al. (2012). *Journal of Comparative Psychology, 127*(3), 337–340. https://doi.org/10.1037/a0032823

Ferguson, C. J. (2013). Spanking, corporal punishment and negative long-term outcomes: A meta-analytic review of longitudinal studies. *Clinical Psychology Review, 33*(1), 196–208.

Ferguson, C. J. (2018). Violent video games, sexist video games, and the law: Why can't we find effects? *Annual Review of Law and Social Science, 14,* 411–426.

Ferguson, C. J., & Beresin, E. (2017). Social science's curious war with pop culture and how it was lost: The media violence debate and the risks it holds for social science. *Preventive Medicine, 99,* 69–76.

Ferguson, C. J., & Colwell, J. (2018). A meaner, more callous digital world for youth? The relationship between violent digital games, motivation, bullying, and civic behavior among children. *Psychology of Popular Media Culture, 7*(3), 202–215.

Ferguson, C. J., Copenhaver, A., & Markey, P. (2020). Reexamining the findings of the American Psychological Association's 2015 task force on violent media: A meta-analysis. *Perspectives on Psychological Science, 15*(6), 1423–1443. https://doi.org/10.1177/1745691620927666

Ferguson, C. J., & Kilburn, J. (2009). The public health risks of media violence: A meta-analytic review. *The Journal of Pediatrics, 154(5),* 759–763.

Ferguson, C. J., & Kilburn, J. (2010). Much ado about nothing: The misestimation and overinterpretation of violent video game effects in eastern and western nations: Comment on Anderson et al. (2010). *Psychological Bulletin, 136*(2), 182–187.

Ferguson, C. J., Miguel, C. S., Garza, A., & Jerabeck, J. M. (2012). A longitudinal test of video game violence influences on dating and aggression: A 3-year longitudinal study of adolescents. *Journal of Psychiatric Research, 46*(2), 141–146.

Ferguson, K. A., Cartwright, R., Rogers, R., & Schmidt-Nowara, W. (2006). Oral appliances for snoring and obstructive sleep apnea: A review. *Sleep, 29*(2), 244.

Fergusson, D. M., Horwood, L. J., & Beautrais, A. L. (1999). Is sexual orientation related to mental health problems and suicidality in young people? *Archives of General Psychiatry, 56*(10), 876–880.

Fergusson, D. M., Horwood, L. J., Ridder, E. M., & Beautrais, A. L. (2005). Sexual orientation and mental health in a birth cohort of young adults. *Psychological Medicine, 35*(7), 971–981.

Fernald, A. (1994). Human material vocalizations to infants as biologically relevant signals: An evolutionary perspective. In P. Bloom (Ed.), *Language acquisition: Core readings* (pp. 51–94). MIT Press.

Fernandez, A., Dobson, K., & Kazantzis, N. (2021). Cognitive therapy. In A. Wenzel (Ed.), Handbook of cognitive behavioral therapy: Overview and approaches (pp. 417–443). *American Psychological Association.* https://doi.org/10.1037/0000218-014https://doi.org/10.1037/0000218-014

Fernandez, E., & Turk, D. C. (1995). The scope and significance of anger in the experience of chronic pain. *Pain, 61*(2), 165–175.

Fernandez, E., Woldgabreal, Y., Day, A., Pham, T., Gleich, B., & Aboujaoude, E. (2021). Live psychotherapy by video versus in-person: A meta-analysis of efficacy and its relationship to types and targets of treatment. *Clinical Psychology & Psychotherapy, 28*(6), 1535–1549. https://doi.org/10.1002/cpp.2594

Fernández-Dols, J., & Russell, J. A. (2017). Introduction. In J. Fernandez-Dols & J. A. Russell (Eds.), *The science of facial expression* (pp. 3–14). Oxford University Press.

Ferracioli-Oda, E., Qawasmi, A., & Bloch, M. H. (2014). Meta-analysis: Melatonin for the treatment of primary sleep disorders. *FOCUS, 12*(1), 73–79.

Ferrari, P. F., & Coudé, G. (2018). Mirror neurons, embodied emotions, and empathy. In K. Z. Meyza & E. Knapska (Eds.), *Neuronal correlates of empathy: From rodent to human* (pp. 67–77). Academic Press.

Festinger, L. (1954). A theory of social comparison processes. *Human Relations, 7,* 117–140.

Festinger, L. (1957). *A theory of cognitive dissonance*. Row, Peterson.

Festinger, L. (1964). *Conflict, decision, and dissonance*. Stanford University Press.

Festinger, L., & Carlsmith, M. M. (1959). Cognitive consequences of forced compliance. *Journal of Abnormal and Social Psychology, 58*(2), 203–210.

Fetner, T., & Kush, K. (2008). Gay-straight alliances in high schools social predictors of early adoption. *Youth & Society, 40*(1), 114–130.

Feybesse, C., & Hatfield, E. (2019). Passionate love. In R. J. Sternberg & K. Sternberg (Eds.), *The new psychology of love* (2nd ed., pp. 183–207). Cambridge University Press.

Fiechtner, L., Block, J., Duncan, D. T., Gillman, M. W., Gortmaker, S. L., Melly, S. J., ... Taveras, E. M. (2013). Proximity to supermarkets associated with higher body mass index among overweight and obese preschool-age children. *Preventive Medicine, 56*(3), 218–221.

Field, A. E., & Kitos, N. (2010). Eating and weight concerns in eating disorders. In W. S. Agras (Ed.), *The Oxford handbook of eating disorders* (pp. 206–222). Oxford University Press.

Field, A. E., Austin, S. B., Strigel-Moore, R., Taylor, C. B., Camargo, C. A., Jr., Laird, N., & Colditz, G. (2005). Weight concerns and weight control behaviors of adolescents and their mothers. *Archives of Pediatric and Adolescent Medicine, 159*(12), 1121–1126.

Field, A. E., Camargo, C. A., Taylor, C. B., Berkey, C. S., & Colditz, G. A. (1999a). Relation of peer and media influence to the development of purging behaviors among preadolescent and adolescent girls. *Archives of Pediatric & Adolescent Medicine, 153*(11), 1184–1189.

Field, A., Cheung, L., Wolf, A., Herzog, D., Gortmaker, S., & Colditz, G. (1999b). Exposure to the mass media and weight concerns among girls. *Pediatrics, 103*(3), E36.

Field, T. M. (1979). Visual and cardiac responses to animate and inanimate faces by young term and preterm infants. *Child Development, 50*(1), 188–194.

Fielder, R. L., & Carey, M. P. (2010). Predictors and consequences of sexual "hookups" among college students: A short-term prospective study. *Archives of Sexual Behavior, 39*(5), 1105–1119.

Fielder, R. L., Walsh, J. L., Carey, K. B., & Carey, M. P. (2013). Predictors of sexual hookups: A theory-based, prospective study of first-year college women. *Archives of Sexual Behavior, 42*(8), 1425–1441.

Fields, H. L. (2011). The doctor's dilemma: Opiate analgesics and chronic pain. *Neuron, 69*(4), 591–594.

Fields, L., Didehbani, N., Hart Jr, J., & Cullum, C. M. (2020). No linear association between number of concussions or years played and cognitive outcomes in retired NFL players. *Archives of Clinical Neuropsychology, 35*(3), 233–239. https://doi.org/10.1093/arclin/acz008

Fields, R. D. (2016, January 1). Does TV rot your brain? *Scientific American Mind*. https://www.scientificamerican.com/article/does-tv-rot-your-brain/

Figueiro, M. G., Nagare, R., & Price, L. L. A. (2018). Non-visual effects of light: How to use light to promote circadian entrainment and elicit alertness. *Lighting Research & Technology, 50*(1), 38–62.

Figuereo, V., & Calvo, R. (2021, March 31). Racialization and psychological distress among US Latinxs. *Journal of Racial and Ethnic Health Disparities*, 1–9. https://doi.org/10.1007/s40615-021-01026-3

Filley, C. M. (2013). White matter. In D. B. Arciniegas, C. A. Anderson, & C. M. Filley (Eds.), *Behavioral neurology & neuropsychiatry* (pp. 47–58). Cambridge University Press.

Finer, L. B., & Zolna, M. R. (2011). Unintended pregnancy in the United States: Incidence and disparities, 2006. *Contraception, 84*(5), 478–485.

Fingerman, K. L., Pitzer, L. M., Chan, W., Birditt, K., Franks, M. M., & Zarit, S. (2011). Who gets what and why? Help middle-aged adults provide to parents and grown children. *The Journals of Gerontology Series B: Psychological Sciences and Social Sciences, 66*(1), 87–98.

Fink, D. S., Lowe, S., Cohen, G. H., Sampson, L. A., Ursano, R. J., Gifford, R. K., Fullerton, C. S., & Galea, S. (2017). Trajectories of posttraumatic stress symptoms after civilian or deployment traumatic event experiences. *Psychological Trauma: Theory, Research, Practice, and Policy, 9*(2), 138–146.

Fink, M. (2001). Convulsive therapy: A review of the first 55 years. *Journal of Affective Disorders, 63*(1–3), 1–15.

Fink, M. (2009). *Electroconvulsive therapy: A guide for professionals and their patients*. Oxford University Press.

Finkelstein, E., & Yang, H. K. (2011). Obesity and medical costs. In J. H. Cawley (Ed.), *The Oxford handbook of the social science of obesity* (pp. 495–501). Oxford University Press.

Fiori, M., & Vesely-Maillefer, A. K. (2018). Emotional intelligence as an ability: Theory, challenges, and new directions. In K. Keefer, J. Parker, & D. Saklofske (Eds.), *Emotional intelligence in education* (pp. 23–47). Springer.

Fischer, A. H., & Manstead, A. S. (2000). The relation between gender and emotions in different cultures. In A. Fischer (Ed.), *Gender and emotion: Social psychological perspectives* (pp. 71–94). University of Cambridge Press.

Fischer, A. H., & Manstead, A. S. R. (2008). Social functions of emotion. In M. Lewis, J. M. Haviland-Jones, & L. F. Barrett (Eds.), *Handbook of emotions* (3rd ed., pp. 456–468). Guilford Press.

Fischer, A., & Evers, C. (2013). The social basis of emotion in men and women. In M. K. Ryan & N. R. Branscombe (Eds.), *The Sage handbook of gender and psychology* (pp. 183–198). Sage.

Fischer, A., & Tsai, L. (2009). Counteracting molecular pathways regulating the reduction of fear: Implications for the treatment of anxiety disorders. In P. J. Shiromani, T. M. Keane, & J. E. LeDoux (Eds.), *Post-traumatic stress disorder: Basic science and clinical practice* (pp. 79–104). Humana Press.

Fischer, B., Gooch, J., Goldman, B., Kurdyak, P., & Rehm, J. (2014). Non-medical prescription opioid use, prescription opioid-related harms and public health in Canada: An update 5 years later. *The Canadian Journal of Public Health, 105*(2), e146–e149.

Fischer, K. W., & Bidell, T. R. (2006). Dynamic development of action and thought. In R. M. Lerner (Vol. Ed.), *Handbook of child psychology* (6th ed., Vol. 1, pp. 313–399). Wiley.

Fischer, S., Nater, U. M., & Laferton, J. A. (2016). Negative stress beliefs predict somatic symptoms in students under academic stress. *International Journal of Behavioral Medicine, 23*(6), 746–751.

Fischman, M. W. (2000). Informed consent. In B. D. Sales & S. Folkman (Eds.), *Ethics in research with human participants* (pp. 35–48). American Psychological Association.

Fish, M., Stifter, C. A., & Belsky, J. (1991). Conditions of continuity and discontinuity in infant negative emotionality: Newborn to five months. *Child Development, 62*(6), 1525–1537.

Fisher, A. K., Moore, D. J., Simmons, C., & Allen, S. C. (2017). Teaching social workers about microaggressions to enhance understanding of subtle racism. *Journal of Human Behavior in the Social Environment, 27*(4), 346–355. https://doi.org/10.1080/10911359.2017.1289877

Fisher, C. B., & Fried, A. A. (2003). Internet-mediated psychological services and the American Psychological Association ethics code. *Psychotherapy: Theory, Research, Practice, Training, 40*(1–2), 103–111.

Fisher, C. B., & Vacanti-Shova, K. (2012). The responsible conduct of psychological research: An overview of ethical principles, APA ethics code standards, and federal regulations. In S. J. Knapp (Ed.), *APA handbook of ethics in psychology* (Vol. 2, pp. 335–369). American Psychological Association.

Fisher, D. A., Hill, D. L., Grube, J. W., Bersamin, M. M., Walker, S., & Gruber, E. L. (2009). Televised sexual content and parental mediation: Influences on adolescent sexuality. *Media Psychology, 12*(2), 121–147.

Fisher, M. A. (2012). Confidentiality and record keeping. In S. J. Knapp (Ed.), *APA handbook of ethics in psychology* (Vol. 1, pp. 333–375). American Psychological Association.

Fisher, R. P., & Craik, F. I. M. (1977). Interaction between encoding and retrieval operations in cued recall. *Journal of Experimental Psychology: Human Learning and Memory, 3*(6), 701.

Fishman, D. B. (2016). Behavioral theories. In J. C. Norcross, G. R. VandenBos, & D. K. Freedheim (Eds.), *APA handbook of clinical psychology* (Vol. 2, pp. 79–116). American Psychological Association.

Fiske, D. W., & Maddi, S. R. (1961). A conceptual framework. In D. W. Fiske & S. R. Maddi (Eds.), *Function of varied experience* (pp. 11–56). Dorsey.

Fiske, S. T. (2008). Core social motivations: Views from the couch, consciousness, classroom, computers and collectives. In J. Y. Shah & W. L. Gardner (Eds.), *Handbook of motivation science* (pp. 3–27). Guilford Press.

Fiske, S. T. (2010). *Social beings: Core motives in social psychology* (2nd ed.). Wiley.

Fiske, S. T. (2012). The continuum model and the stereotype content model. In P. A. M. Van Lange, A. W. Kruglanski, & E. T. Higgins (Eds.), *Handbook of theories of social psychology* (Vol. 1, pp. 267–288). Sage.

Fiske, S. T., & Neuberg, S. L. (1990). A continuum of impression formation, from category-based to individuating process: Influences of information and motivation on attention and interpretation. *Advances in Experimental Social Psychology, 23*(C), 1–74.

Fitch, W. T. (2012). Innateness and human language: A biological perspective. In M. Tallerman & K. R. Gibson (Eds.), *The Oxford handbook of language evolution* (pp. 143–156). Oxford University Press.

Fitch, W. T. (2018). The biology and evolution of speech: A comparative analysis. *Annual Review of Linguistics, 4*, 255–279.

FitzGerald, C., & Hurst, S. (2017). Implicit bias in healthcare professionals: A systematic review. *BMC Medical Ethics, 18*(1), 19.

Fitzpatrick, J. F., & Bringmann, W. G. (1997). Charles Darwin and psychology. In W. G. Bringmann, H. E. Lück, R. Miller, & C. E. Early (Eds.), *A pictorial history of psychology* (pp. 51–52). Quintessence Publishing.

Fivush, R., Bohanek, J. B., Marin, K., & Sales, J. M. (2009). Emotional memory and memory for emotions. In O. Luminet & A. Curci (Eds.), *Flashbulb memories: New issues and new perspectives* (pp. 163–184). Psychology Press.

Flanagan, D. P., McGrew, K. S., & Ortiz, S. O. (2000). *The Wechsler Intelligence Scales and Gf-Gc theory: A contemporary approach to interpretation*. Allyn & Bacon.

Flanagan, D. P., Ortiz, S. O., & Alfonso, V. C. (2013). *Essentials of cross-battery assessment*. John Wiley & Sons.

Flannelly, K. J. (2017). *Religious beliefs, evolutionary psychiatry, and mental health in America*. Springer.

Flash, G., & Ritz, D. (2008). *The adventures of Grandmaster Flash: My life, my beats*. Broadway Books.

Fleischman, A., & Nguyen, T. (2018). *Flavor bombs: The umami ingredients that make taste explode*. Houghton Mifflin Harcourt.

Fletcher, G. J., Simpson, J. A., & Boyes, A. D. (2006). Accuracy and bias in romantic relationships: An evolutionary and social psychological analysis. In M. Schaller, J. A. Simpson, & D. T. Kenrick (Eds.), *Evolution and social psychology* (pp. 189–209). Psychology Press.

Flett, J. A., Hayne, H., Riordan, B. C., Thompson, L. M., & Conner, T. S. (2019). Mobile mindfulness meditation: A randomised controlled trial of the effect of two popular apps on mental health. *Mindfulness, 10*(5), 863–876. https://doi.org/10.1007/s12671-018-1050-9

Flier, J. S. (2004). Obesity wars: Molecular progress confronts an expanding epidemic. *Cell, 116*(2), 337–350.

Floderus-Myrhed, B., Pedersen, N., & Rasmuson, I. (1980). Assessment of heritability for personality, based on a short-form of the Eysenck personality inventory: A study of 12,898 twin pairs. *Behavioral Genetics, 10*(2), 153–162. https://doi.org/10.1007/BF01066265

Flohr, E. L., Erwin, E., Croy, I., & Hummel, T. (2017). Sad man's nose: Emotion induction and olfactory perception. *Emotion, 17*(2), 369–378.

Flor, H. (2002). Phantom-limb pain: Characteristics, causes, and treatment. *The Lancet Neurology, 1*(3), 182–189.

Flor, H., Nikolajsen, L., & Jensen, T. S. (2006). Phantom limb pain: A case of maladaptive CNS plasticity? *Nature Reviews Neuroscience, 7*(11), 873–881.

Flora, S. R. (2004). *The power of reinforcement*. State University of New York Press.

Flückiger, C., Del Re, A. C., Wampold, B. E., & Horvath, A. O. (2018). The alliance in adult psychotherapy: A meta-analytic synthesis. *Psychotherapy, 55*(4), 316–340.

Flynn, J. R. (1984). The mean IQ of Americans: Massive gains 1932 to 1978. *Psychological Bulletin, 95*(1), 29–51.

Flynn, J. R. (1987). Massive IQ gains in 14 nations: What IQ tests really measure. *Psychological Bulletin, 101*(2), 171–191.

Flynn, J. R. (2011). Secular changes in intelligence. In R. J. Sternberg & S. B. Kaufman (Eds.), *The Cambridge handbook of intelligence* (pp. 647–665). Cambridge University Press.

Foa, E. B., & McLean, C. P. (2015). The efficacy of exposure therapy for anxiety-related disorders and its underlying mechanisms: The case of OCD and PTSD. *Annual Review of Clinical Psychology, 12*, 1–28.

Fodor, N., & Gaynor, F. (1950). *Freud: Dictionary of psychoanalysis*. Barnes & Noble Books.

Foell, J., & Flor, H. (2013). Phantom limb pain. In R. J. Moore (Ed.), *Handbook of pain and palliative care* (pp. 417–430). Springer.

Foer, J. (2011). *Moonwalking with Einstein: The art and science of remembering everything*. Penguin Press.

Foley, D., Ancoli-Israel, S., Britz, P., & Walsh, J. (2004). Sleep disturbances and chronic disease in older adults: Results of the 2003 National Sleep Foundation Sleep in America Survey. *Journal of Psychosomatic Research, 56*(5), 497–502.

Foley, R. (1995). The adaptive legacy of human evolution: A search for the environment of evolutionary adaptedness. *Evolutionary Anthropology: Issues, News, and Reviews, 4*(6), 194–203.

Folk, A. L., Wagner, B. E., Hahn, S. L., Larson, N., Barr-Anderson, D. J., & Neumark-Sztainer, D. (2021). Changes to physical activity during a global pandemic: A mixed methods analysis among a diverse population-based sample of emerging adults in the US. *International Journal of Environmental Research and Public Health, 18*(7), 3674. https://doi.org/10.3390/ijerph18073674

Folkman, S. (1997). Positive psychological states and coping with severe stress. *Social Science & Medicine, 45*(8), 1207–1221.

Folkman, S. (2011). Stress, health, and coping: An overview. In S. Folkman, *Oxford handbook of stress, health, and coping* (pp. 3–11). Oxford University Press.

Folkman, S., & Moskowitz, J. T. (2000). Positive affect and the other side of coping. *American Psychologist, 55*(6), 647–654.

Folkman, S., & Moskowitz, J. T. (2004). Coping: Pitfalls and promise. *Annual Review of Psychology, 55*, 745–774.

Folkman, S., Lazarus, R. S., Dunkel-Schetter, C., DeLongis, A., & Gruen, R. J. (1986). Dynamics of a stressful encounter: Cognitive appraisal, coping, and encounter outcomes. *Journal of Personality and Social Psychology, 50*(5), 992–1003.

Follette, V. M., & Hazlett-Stevens, H. (2016). Mindfulness and acceptance theories. In J. C. Norcross, G. R. VandenBos, & D. K. Freedheim (Eds.), *APA handbook of clinical psychology* (Vol. 2, pp. 273–302). American Psychological Association.

Fong, C. J., Acee, T. W., & Weinstein, C. E. (2018). A person-centered investigation of achievement motivation goals and correlates of community college student achievement and persistence. *Journal of College Student Retention: Research, Theory & Practice, 20*(3), 369–387.

Fong, J. (2012, December 7). Eye-opener: Why do pupils dilate in response to emotional states? *Scientific American*. http://www.scientificamerican.com/article/eye-opener-why-do-pupils-dilate

Fonzo, G. A., Goodkind, M. S., Oathes, D. J., Zaiko, Y. V., Harvey, M., Peng, K. K., Weiss, M. E., Thompson, A. L., Zack, S. E., Lindley, S. E., Arnow, B. A., Jo, B., Rothbaum, B. O., & Etkin, A. (2021). Amygdala and insula connectivity changes following psychotherapy for posttraumatic stress disorder: A randomized clinical trial. *Biological Psychiatry, 89*(9), 857–867. https://doi.org/10.1016/j.biopsych.2020.11.021

Forcier, K., Stroud, L. R., Papandonatos, G. D., Hitsman, B., Reiches, M., Krishnamoorthy, J., & Niaura, R. (2006). Links between physical fitness and cardiovascular reactivity and recovery to psychological stressors: A meta-analysis. *Health Psychology, 25*(6), 723–739.

Ford, E. (2007). *What you must think of me: A firsthand account of one teenager's experience with social anxiety disorder*. Oxford University Press.

Fordham, S., & Ogbu, J. U. (1986). Black students' school success: Coping with the "burden of 'acting white'." *The Urban Review, 18*(3), 176–206.

Forman, E. M., Juarascio, A. S., Martin, L. M., & Herbert, J. D. (2015). Acceptance and commitment therapy (ACT). In R. L. Cautin & S. O. Lilienfeld (Eds.), *The encyclopedia of clinical psychology* (pp. 10–17). Wiley-Blackwell.

Fornazieri, M. A., Doty, R. L., Bezerra, T. F. P., de Rezende Pinna, F., Costa, F. O., Voegels, R. L., & Silveira-Moriyama, L. (2019). Relationship of socioeconomic status to olfactory function. *Physiology & Behavior, 198*, 84–89. https://doi.org/10.1016/j.physbeh.2018.10.011

Forsyth, J. P., & Eifert, G. H. (2016). *The mindfulness & acceptance workbook for anxiety* (2nd ed.). New Harbinger.

Forsyth, J. P., Fuse, T., & Acheson, D. T. (2009). Interoceptive exposure for panic disorder. In W. O'Donohue & J. E. Fisher (Eds.), *General principles and empirically supported techniques of cognitive behavior therapy* (pp. 394–406). Wiley.

Fortner, B. V., and Neimeyer, R. A. (1999). Death anxiety in older adults: A quantitative review. *Death Studies, 23*(5), 387–411.

Foshee, V. A., Benefield, T. S., Reyes, H. L. M., Ennett, S. T., Faris, R., Chang, L. Y., Hussong, A., & Suchindran, C. M. (2013). The peer context and the development of the perpetration of adolescent dating violence. *Journal of Youth and Adolescence, 42*(4), 471–486.

Foster, G. D., Wadden, T. A., Makris, A. P., Davidson, D., Sanderson, R. S., Allison, D. B., & Kessler, A. (2003). Primary care physicians' attitudes about obesity and its treatment. *Obesity Research, 11*(10), 1168–1177.

Foster, J. K. (2009). *Memory: A very short introduction*. Oxford University Press.

Fothergill, E., Guo, J., Howard, L., Kerns, J. C., Knuth, N. D., Brychta, R., Chen, K. Y., Skarulis, M. C., Walter, M., Walter, P. J., & Hall, K. D. (2016). Persistent metabolic adaptation 6 years after "The Biggest Loser" competition. *Obesity, 24*(8), 1612–1619.

Fouad, N. A., & Arredondo, P. (2007). *Becoming culturally oriented: Practical advice for psychologists and educators*. American Psychological Association.

Fournier, J. C., & Tang, T. Z. (2017). Personality and depression. In R. J. DeRubeis & D. R. Strunk (Eds.), *The Oxford handbook of mood disorders* (pp. 154–164). Oxford University Press.

Fowler, C. A., & Magnuson, J. S. (2012). Speech perception. In M. J. Spivey, K. McRae, & M. F. Joanisse (Eds.), *The Cambridge handbook of psycholinguistics* (pp. 3–25). Cambridge University Press.

Fox, N. A., Henderson, H. A., Pérez-Edgar, K., & White, L. K. (2008). The biology of temperament: An integrative approach. In C. A. Nelson & M. Luciana (Eds.), *Handbook of developmental cognitive neuroscience* (2nd ed., pp. 839–853). MIT Press.

Fox, N. A., & Pine, D. S. (2012). Temperament and the emergence of anxiety disorders. *Journal of the American Academy of Child and Adolescent Psychiatry, 51*(2), 125–128.

Fox, R., Lehmkuhle, S. W., & Bush, R. C. (1977). Stereopsis in the falcon. *Science, 197*(4298), 79–81.

Frances, A. (2012, December 2). DSM-5 is guide not bible—ignore its ten worst changes. http://www.psychologytoday.com/blog/dsm5-in-distress/201212/dsm-5-is-guide-not-bible-ignore-its-ten-worst-changes

Frances, A. (2013). *Saving normal: An insider's revolt against out-of-control psychiatric diagnosis, DSM-5, Big Pharma, and the medicalization of ordinary life*. HarperCollins.

Frances, A., & Batstra, L. (2013). Why so many epidemics of childhood mental disorder? *Journal of Developmental & Behavioral Pediatrics, 34*(4), 291–292.

Francis, L. A., Ventura, A. K., Marini, M., & Birch, L. L. (2007). Parent overweight predicts daughters' increase in BMI and disinhibited overeating from 5 to 13 years. *Obesity, 15*(6), 1544–1553.

Frank, E., & Levenson, J. C. (2011). *Interpersonal psychotherapy*. American Psychological Association.

Frank, J. D. (1961). *Persuasion and healing*. Johns Hopkins University Press.

Frank, M. G. (2006a). The function of sleep. In T. L. Lee-Chiong (Ed.), *Sleep: A comprehensive handbook* (pp. 45–48). Wiley-Liss.

Frank, M. G. (2006b). The mystery of sleep function: Current perspectives and future directions. *Reviews in the Neurosciences, 17*(4), 375–392.

Frank, M. G. (2010). The function(s) of sleep. In J. W. Winkelman & D. T. Plante (Eds.), *Foundations of psychiatric sleep medicine* (pp. 59–78). Cambridge University Press.

Frankenberger, K. D. (2000). Adolescent egocentrism: A comparison among adolescents and adults. *Journal of Adolescence, 23*(3), 343–354.

Franklin, A., & Ritz, D. (1999). *Aretha: From these roots*. Villard.

Franklin, K. A., & Lindberg, E. (2015). Obstructive sleep apnea is a common disorder in the population—a review on the epidemiology of sleep apnea. *Journal of Thoracic Disease, 7*(8), 1311–1322.

Fraser, S. (Ed.). (1995). *The bell curve wars: Race, intelligence, and the future of America*. Basic Books.

Fredricks, J. A., & Eccles, J. S. (2006). Is extracurricular participation associated with beneficial outcomes? Concurrent and longitudinal relations. *Developmental Psychology, 42*(4), 698.

Fredrickson, B. L. (2001). The role of positive emotions in positive psychology: The broaden-and-build theory of positive emotions. *American Psychologist, 56*(3), 218–226.

Fredrickson, B. L., & Branigan, C. (2005). Positive emotions broaden the scope of attention and thought-action repertoires. *Cognition & Emotion, 19*(3), 313–332.

Fredrickson, B. L., & Cohn, M. A. (2008). Positive emotions. In M. Lewis, J. M. Haviland-Jones, & L. F. Barrett (Eds.), *Handbook of emotions* (3rd ed., pp. 777–796). Guilford Press.

Fredrickson, B. L., & Joiner, T. (2018). Reflections on positive emotions and upward spirals. *Perspectives on Psychological Science, 13*(2), 194–199.

Fredrickson, B. L., Roberts, T. A., Noll, S. M., Quinn, D. M., & Twenge, J. M. (1998). That swimsuit becomes you: Sex differences in self-objectification, restrained eating, and math performance. *Journal of Personality and Social Psychology, 75*(1), 269–284.

Freeman, E. W. (2017). Premenstrual dysphoric disorder. In R. J. DeRubeis & D. R. Strunk (Eds.), *The Oxford handbook of mood disorders* (pp. 238–253). Oxford University Press.

Freeman, J. B., Rule, N. O., Adams, R. B., Jr., & Ambady, N. (2009a). Culture shapes a mesolimbic response to signals of dominance and subordination that associates with behavior. *Neuroimage, 47*(1), 353–359.

Freeman, J. B., Rule, N. O., & Ambady, N. (2009b). The cultural neuroscience of person perception. *Progress in Brain Research, 178*, 191–201.

Freeman, K. A. (2002). Modeling. In M. Hersen & W. Sledge (Eds.), *Encyclopedia of psychotherapy* (Vol. 2, pp. 147–154). Academic Press.

Freeman, K. A., & Eagle, R. F. (2011). Single-subject research designs. In J. C. Thomas & M. Hersen (Eds.), *Understanding research in clinical and counseling psychology* (2nd ed., pp. 129–154). Taylor & Francis.

Freijy, T., & Kothe, E. J. (2013). Dissonance-based interventions for health behaviour change: A systematic review. *British Journal of Health Psychology, 18*(2), 310–337.

French, D., Pidada, S., & Victor, A. (2005). Friendships of Indonesian and United States youth. *International Journal of Behavioral Development, 29*(4), 304–313.

French, S. E., & Chávez, N. R. (2010). The relationship of ethnicity-related stressors and Latino ethnic identity to well-being. *Hispanic Journal of Behavioral Sciences, 32*(3), 410–428.

French, S. E., Tran, N., & Chávez, N. R. (2013). Exploring the effect of in-group and out-group race-related stressors on anxiety among Asian Pacific Islander American students. *Journal of Applied Social Psychology, 43*(S2), E339–E350.

Freud, A. (1936). *The ego and the mechanisms of defense*. International Universities Press.

Freud, S. (1900). *The interpretation of dreams*. Hogarth Press.

Freud, S. (1905). *Three essays on the theory of sexuality*. Hogarth Press.

Freud, S. (1922). *A general introduction to psychoanalysis*. Boni and Liveright.

Freud, S. (1923/1990). *The ego and the id (Standard Edition)* (pp. 1–66). W. W. Norton.

Freud, S. (1932/1990). *New introductory lectures on psycho-analysis (Standard Edition)* (pp. 1–182). W. W. Norton.

Freund, A. M., & Ebner, N. C. (2005). The aging self: Shifting from promoting gains to balancing losses. In W. Greve, K. Rothermund, & D. Wentura (Eds.), *The adaptive self: Personal continuity and intentional self-development* (pp. 185–202). Hogrefe & Huber.

Freund, A. M., Hennecke, M., & Mustafić, M. (2012). On gains and losses, means, and ends: Goal orientation and goal focus across adulthood. In R. M. Ryan (Ed.), *The Oxford handbook of human motivation* (pp. 280–302). Oxford University Press.

Freund, A. M., Hennecke, M., & Riediger, M. (2010). Age-related differences in outcome and process goal focus. *European Journal of Developmental Psychology, 7*(2), 198–222.

Frey, J. A., & Hall, A. (2021). *Motivational Interviewing for mental health clinicians: A toolkit for skills enhancement*. PESI Publishing.

Frey, L. C. & Spitz, M. C. (2013). Electroencephalography. In D. B. Arciniegas, C. A. Anderson & C. M. Filley (Eds.). *Behavioral neurology and neuropsychology* (pp. 442–458). Cambridge University Press.

Fridlund, A. J., Beck, H. P., Goldie, W. D., & Irons, G. (2012). Little Albert: A neurologically impaired child. *History of Psychology, 15*(4), 302–327. https://doi.org/10.1037/a0026720

Fried, A. L. (2012). Ethics in psychological research: Guidelines and regulations. In H. Cooper (Ed.), *APA handbook of research methods in psychology* (Vol. 1, pp. 55–74). American Psychological Association.

Fried, C. B., & Aronson, E. (1995). Hypocrisy, misattribution, and dissonance reduction. *Personality and Social Psychology Bulletin, 21*(9), 925–933.

Friedlander, M. L., Escudero, V., Welmers-van de Poll, M. J., & Heatherington, L. (2018). Meta-analysis of the alliance–outcome relation in couple and family therapy. *Psychotherapy, 55*(4), 356–371.

Friedman, E. M., Love, G. D., Rosenkranz, M. A., Urry, H. L., Davidson, R. J., Singer, B. H., & Ryff, C. D. (2007). Socioeconomic status predicts objective and subjective sleep quality in aging women. *Psychosomatic Medicine, 69*(7), 682–691.

Friedman, H. S. (2011). Personality, disease, and self-healing. In H. S. Friedman (Ed.), *The Oxford handbook of health psychology* (pp. 215–240). Oxford University Press.

Friedman, H. S., & Booth-Kewley, S. (1987). The "disease-prone personality": A meta-analytic view of the construct. *American Psychologist, 42*(6), 539–555.

Friedman, H. S., Tucker, J. S., Tomlinson-Keasey, C., Schwartz, J. E., Wingard, D. L., & Criqui, M. H. (2003). Does childhood personality predict longevity? *Journal of Personality and Social Psychology, 65*(1), 176–185.

Friedman, H., & Martin, L. R. (2011). *The Longevity Project: Surprising discoveries for health and long life from the landmark eight-decade study*. Hudson Street Press.

Friedman, M. J. (2009). PTSD and other posttraumatic syndromes. In D. McKay, J. S. Abramowitz, S. Taylor, & G. J. G. Asmundson (Eds.), *Current perspectives on the anxiety disorders: Implications for DSM-V and beyond* (pp. 377–410). Springer.

Friedman, M. R., Coulter, R. W., Silvestre, A. J., Stall, R., Teplin, L., Shoptaw, S., ... Plankey, M. W. (2017). Someone to count on: Social support as an effect modifier of viral load suppression in a prospective cohort study. *AIDS Care, 29*(4), 469–480.

Friedman, M., & Rosenman, R. H. (1959). Association of specific overt behavior pattern with blood and cardiovascular findings: Blood cholesterol level, blood clotting time, incidence of arcus senilis, and clinical coronary artery disease. *JAMA, 169*(12), 1286–1296.

Friesdorf, R., Conway, P., & Gawronski, B. (2015). Gender differences in responses to moral dilemmas: A process dissociation analysis. *Personality and Social Psychology Bulletin, 41*(5), 696–713.

Frijda, N. H. (2008). The psychologists' point of view. In M. Lewis, J. M. Haviland-Jones, & L. F. Barrett (Eds.), *Handbook of emotions* (3rd ed., pp. 68–87). Guilford Press.

Frishman, L. J. (2001). Basic visual processes. In E. B. Goldstein (Ed.), *Blackwell handbook of perception* (pp. 53–91). Blackwell.

Frison, E., & Eggermont, S. (2016). Exploring the relationships between different types of Facebook use, perceived online social support, and adolescents' depressed mood. *Social Science Computer Review, 34*(2), 153–171.

FritoLay. (2016). *Tostitos Original Restaurant Style Tortilla Chips: Nutrition facts*. http://www.fritolay.com/snacks/product-page/tostitos

Fritz, M. M., Walsh, L. C., & Lyubomirsky, S. (2017). Staying happier. In M. D. Robinson & M. Eid (Eds.), *The happy mind: Cognitive contributions to well-being* (pp. 95–114). Springer International.

Froh, J. J., Kashdan, T. B., Ozimkowski, K. M., & Miller, N. (2009). Who benefits the most from a gratitude intervention in children and adolescents? Examining positive affect as a moderator. *The Journal of Positive Psychology, 4*(5), 408–422.

Froh, J. J., Sefick, W. J., & Emmons, R. A. (2008). Counting blessings in early adolescents: An experimental study of gratitude and subjective well-being. *Journal of School Psychology, 46*(2), 213–233.

Frorer, P., Hazzan, O., & Manes, M. (1997). Revealing the faces of abstraction. *International Journal of Computers for Mathematical Learning, 2*(3), 217–228.

Froy, O. (2010). Metabolism and circadian rhythms—implications for obesity. *Endocrine Reviews, 31*(1), 1–24.

Fruzzetti, A. E., McLean, C., & Erikson, K. M. (2019). Mindfulness and acceptance interventions in cognitive-behavioral therapy. In K. S. Dobson & D. J. A. Dozois (Eds.), *Handbook of cognitive-behavioral therapies* (4th ed., pp. 271–296). Guilford Press.

Frydenberg, E., & Lewis, R. (1993). Boys play sport and girls turn to others: Age, gender and ethnicity as determinants of coping. *Journal of Adolescence, 16*(3), 253–266.

Fryer, S. L., Crocker, N. A., & Mattson, S. N. (2008). Exposure to teratogenic agents as a risk factor for psychopathology. In T. P. Beauchaine & S. P. Hinshaw (Eds.), *Child and adolescent psychopathology* (pp. 180–207). Wiley.

Fryer, S. L., McGee, C. L., Matt, G. E., Riley, E. P., & Mattson, S. N. (2007). Evaluation of psychopathological conditions in children with heavy prenatal alcohol exposure. *Pediatrics, 119*(3), e733–e741.

Fuchs, A. H. (2002). Contributions of American mental philosophers to psychology in the United States. In W. E. Pickren & D. A. Dewsbury (Eds.), *Evolving perspectives on the history of psychology* (pp. 79–100). American Psychological Association.

Fuchs, C. (2017). *Social media: A critical introduction* (2nd ed.). Sage.
Fuertes, J. N., Stracuzzi, T. I., Bennett, J., Scheinholtz, J., Mislowack, A., Hersh, M., & Cheng, D. (2006). Therapist multicultural competency: A study of therapy dyads. *Psychotherapy: Theory, Research, Practice, Training, 43*(4), 480–490.
Fukuyama, M., Puig, A., Baggs, A., & Wolf, C. P. (2014). Religion and spirituality. In F. T. L. Leong (Ed.), *APA handbook of multicultural psychology* (Vol. 1, pp. 519–534). American Psychological Association.
Fuligni, A. J., & Hardway, C. (2006). Daily variation in adolescents' sleep, activities, and psychological well-being. *Journal of Research on Adolescence, 16*(3), 353–378.
Funder, D. C. (2008). Persons, situations, and person-situation interactions. In O. P. John, R. W. Robins, & L. A. Pervin (Eds.), *Handbook of personality: Theory and research* (3rd ed., pp. 568–580). Guilford Press.
Funder, D. C., & Fast, L. A. (2010). Personality in social psychology. In S. T. Fiske, D. T. Gilbert, & G. Lindzey (Eds.), *Handbook of social psychology* (5th ed., Vol. 1, pp. 668–697). Wiley.
Funder, D. C., & Fast, L. A. (2010). Personality in social psychology. In S. T. Fiske, D. T. Gilbert, & G. Lindzey (Eds.), *Handbook of social psychology* (5th ed., Vol. 1, pp. 668–697). Wiley.
Fung, J. (2011). Cultural psychological perspectives on social development in childhood. In P. K. Smith & C. H. Hart (Eds.), *The Wiley-Blackwell handbook of childhood social development* (2nd ed., pp. 100–118). Wiley-Blackwell.
Furmark, T., Tillfors, M., Marteinsdottir, I., Fischer, H., Pissiota, A., Långström, B., & Fredrikson, M. (2002). Common changes in cerebral blood flow in patients with social phobia treated with citalopram or cognitive-behavioral therapy. *Archives of General Psychiatry, 59*(5), 425–433.
Furnham, A., & Cheng, H. (2017). Factors affecting adult trait neuroticism in a nationally representative sample. *Psychiatry Research, 256*, 253–257.
Furr, R. M. & Funder, D. C. (2021). Persons, situations, and person-situation interactions. In O. P. John & R. W. Robbins (Eds.), *Handbook of personality: Theory and research* (4th ed.), pp. 667–685. Guilford.
Fürst, G., & Grin, F. (2018). Multilingualism and creativity: A multivariate approach. *Journal of Multilingual and Multicultural Development, 39*(4), 341–355.
Furumoto, L. (1995). Christine Ladd-Franklin's color theory: Strategy for claiming scientific authority. In H. E. Adler & R. W. Rieber (Eds.), *Aspects of the history of psychology in America: 1892–1992* (pp. 91–100). New York Academy of Sciences; American Psychological Association. https://doi.org/10.1037/10503-006
Furumoto, L., & Scarborough, E. (2002). Placing women in the history of psychology: The first American women psychologists. In W. E. Pickren & D. A. Dewsbury (Eds.), *Evolving perspectives on the history of psychology* (pp. 527–543). Washington, DC: American Psychological Association.
Gabbard, G. O. (2001). Psychotherapy in Hollywood cinema. *Australasian Psychiatry, 9*(4), 365–369.
Gabbard, G. O. (2005). Major modalities: Psychoanalytic/psychodynamic. In G. O. Gabbard, J. S. Beck, & J. Holmes (Eds.), *Oxford textbook of psychotherapy* (pp. 3–14). Oxford University Press.
Gabbard, G. O. (2009a). Foreword. In R. A. Levy & J. S. Ablon (Eds.), *Handbook of evidence-based psychodynamic psychotherapy: Bridging the gap between science and practice* (pp. vii–ix). Humana.
Gabbard, G. O. (2009b). Techniques of psychodynamic psychotherapy. In G. O. Gabbard (Ed.), *Textbook of psychotherapeutic treatments* (pp. 43–67). American Psychiatric Publishing.
Gabbard, G. O. (2009c). What is a "good enough" termination? *Journal of the American Psychoanalytical Association, 57*(3), 575–594. https://doi.org/10.1177/0003065109340678
Gabbay, M., Kelly, Z., Reedy, J., & Gastil, J. (2018). Frame-induced group polarization in small discussion networks. *Social Psychology Quarterly, 81*(3), 248–271.
Gabig, C. S. (2014). Language development in middle and late childhood and adolescence. In S. Levey (Ed.), *Introduction to language development* (pp. 211–246). Plural Publishing.
Gable, S. L., & Haidt, J. (2005). What (and why) is positive psychology? *Review of General Psychology, 9*(2), 103–110.
Gabrieli, J. D., Poldrack, R. A., & Desmond, J. E. (1998). The role of left prefrontal cortex in language and memory. *Proceedings of the National Academy of Sciences, 95*(3), 906–913.
Gabrielli, J., Traore, A., Stoolmiller, M., Bergamini, E., & Sargent, J. D. (2016). Industry television ratings for violence, sex, and substance use. *Pediatrics, 138*(3), e20160487.
Gabrielsson, A., Whaley, J., & Sloboda, J. (2016). Peak experiences in music. In S. Hallam, I. Cross, & M. Thaut (Eds.), *The Oxford handbook of music psychology* (2nd ed., pp 745–758). Oxford University Press.
Gaertner. S. L., & Dovidio, J. F. (2012). The common ingroup identity model. In P. A. M. Van Lange, A. W. Kruglanski, & E. T. Higgins (Eds.), *Handbook of theories of social psychology* (Vol. 2, pp. 439–457). Sage.
Gaertner, S. L., Dovidio, J. F., & Bachman, B. A. (1996). Revisiting the contact hypothesis: The induction of a common ingroup identity. *International Journal of Intercultural Relations, 20*(3), 271–290.
Gage, F. H. (2000). Mammalian neural stem cells. *Science, 287*(5457), 1433–1438.
Gais, S., Lucas, B., & Born, J. (2006). Sleep after learning aids memory recall. *Learning and Memory, 13*(3), 259–262.
Gál, É., Ştefan, S., & Cristea, I. A. (2020). The efficacy of mindfulness meditation apps in enhancing users' well-being and mental health related outcomes: A meta-analysis of randomized controlled trials. *Journal of Affective Disorders, 279*, 131–142. https://doi.org/10.1016/j.jad.2020.09.134
Galak, J., & Redden, J. P. (2018). The properties and antecedents of hedonic decline. *Annual Review of Psychology, 69*, 1–25.
Galambos, N. L., Berenbaum, S. A., & McHale, S. M. (2009). Gender development in adolescence. In R. M. Lerner & L. M. Steinberg (Eds.), *Handbook of adolescent psychology* (3rd ed., Vol. 1, pp. 305–357). Wiley.
Galambos, N. L., & Martínez, M. L. (2007). Poised for emerging adulthood in Latin America: A pleasure for the privileged. *Child Development Perspectives, 1*(2), 109–114.
Galatzer-Levy, I. R., Huang, S. H., & Bonanno, G. A. (2018). Trajectories of resilience and dysfunction following potential trauma: A review and statistical evaluation. *Clinical Psychology Review, 63*, 41–55.
Galatzer-Levy, R. M., Bachrach, H., Skolnikoff, A., & Waldron, S. (2000). *Does psychoanalysis work?* Yale University Press.
Galbraith, N., Moss, T., Galbraith, V., & Purewal, S. (2018). A systematic review of the traits and cognitions associated with use of and belief in complementary and alternative medicine (CAM). *Psychology, Health & Medicine, 23*(7), 854–869. https://doi.org/10.1080/13548506.2018.1442010
Galinsky, A. M., Ward, B. W., Joestl, S. S., & Dahlhamer, J. M. (2018). Sleep duration, sleep quality, and sexual orientation: Findings from the 2013–2015 National Health Interview Survey. *Sleep Health, 4*(1), 56–62. https://doi.org/10.1016/j.sleh.2017.10.004
Gallagher, D., & Grimm, L. R. (2018). Making an impact: The effects of game making on creativity and spatial processing. *Thinking Skills and Creativity, 28*, 138–149.
Gallagher, S., Phillips, A. C., Drayson, M. T., & Carroll, D. (2009). Parental caregivers of children with developmental disabilities mount a poor antibody response to pneumococcal vaccination. *Brain, Behavior, and Immunity, 23*(3), 338–346.
Gallant, S. J., & Hamilton, J. A. (1988). On a premenstrual psychiatric diagnosis: What's in a name? *Professional Psychology: Research and Practice, 19*(3), 271–278.
Gallo, K. P., Comer, J. S., & Barlow, D. H. (2013). Single-case experimental designs and small pilot trial designs. In J. S. Comer & P. C. Kendall (Eds.), *The Oxford handbook of research strategies for clinical psychology* (pp. 24–39). Oxford University Press.
Galvin, B. M., Randel, A. E., Collins, B. J., & Johnson, R. E. (2018). Changing the focus of locus (of control): A targeted review of the locus of control literature and agenda for future research. *Journal of Organizational Behavior, 39*(7), 820–833.
Gambla, W. C., Fernandez, A. M., Gassman, N. R., Tan, M. C. B., & Daniel, C. L. (2017). College tanning behaviors, attitudes, beliefs, and intentions: A systematic review of the literature. *Preventive Medicine, 105*, 77–87.
Gamble, A. L., Harvey, A. G., & Rapee, R. M. (2010). Specific phobia. In D. J. Stein, E. Hollander, & B. O. Rothbaum (Eds.), *Textbook of anxiety disorders* (2nd ed., pp. 525–543). American Psychiatric Association.
Gandour, J. (2005). Neurophonetics of tone. In K. Brown (Ed.), *Encyclopedia of language and linguistics* (2nd ed.). Elsevier.
Gangestad, S. W. (2019). Evolutionary perspectives. In K. Deaux & M. Snyder (Eds.), *The Oxford handbook of personality and social psychology* (2nd ed., pp. 133–160). Oxford University Press.
Gangestad, S. W., & Scheyd, G. J. (2005). The evolution of human physical attractiveness. *Annual Review of Anthropology, 34*, 523–548.
Ganster, D. C., Schaubroeck, J., Sime, W. E., & Mayes, B. T. (1991). The nomological validity of the Type A personality among employed adults. *Journal of Applied Psychology, 76*(1), 143–168.
Gantz, W., Schwartz, N., Angelini, J. R., & Rideout, V. (2007). *Food for thought: Television food advertising to children in the United States*. Menlo Park, CA: Henry J. Kaiser Family Foundation.
Ganz, C. (2021, March 16). How honest can Demi Lovato be? *The New York Times*. https://www.nytimes.com/2021/03/16/arts/music/demi-lovato-interview.htmlhttps://www.nytimes.com/2021/03/16/arts/music/demi-lovato-interview.html
Garcia, F., & Gracia, E. (2009). Is always authoritative the optimum parenting style? Evidence from Spanish families. *Adolescence, 44*(173), 101–131.
Garcia, J., Brett. L. P., & Rusiniak, K. W. (1989). Limits of Darwinian conditioning. In S. B. Klein & R. R. Mowrer (Eds.), *Contemporary learning theories: Instrumental conditioning theory and the impact of biological constraints on learning* (pp. 237–275). Lawrence Erlbaum.
Garcia, J., Ervin, F. R., & Koelling, R. A. (1966). Learning with prolonged delay of reinforcement. *Psychonomic Science, 5*, 121–122.
Garcia, J., & Gustavson, A. R. (1997). Carl R. Gustavson (1946–1996): Pioneering wildlife psychologist. *APS Observer, 10*(1), 34–35.
Garcia, J., & Koelling, R. A. (1966). Relation of cue to consequence in avoidance learning. *Psychonomic Science, 4*, 123–124.
Garcia, O. F., Lopez-Fernandez, O., & Serra, E. (2021). Raising Spanish children with an antisocial tendency: Do we know what the optimal parenting style is? *Journal of Interpersonal Violence, 36*(13–14), 6117–6144. https://doi.org/10.1177/0886260518818426
Garcia, S. E. (2020, June 17). Where did BIPOC come from? *The New York Times*. https://www.nytimes.com/article/what-is-bipoc.html
García, S., Martínez-Cengotitabengoa, M., López-Zurbano, S., Zorrilla, I., López, P., Vieta, E., & González-Pinto, A. (2016). Adherence to antipsychotic medication in bipolar disorder and schizophrenic patients: A systematic review. *Journal of Clinical Psychopharmacology, 36*(4), 355–371.
García-Hermoso, A., Hormazábal-Aguayo, I., Fernández-Vergara, O., Olivares, P. R., & Oriol-Granado, X. (2020). Physical activity, screen time and subjective well-being among children. *International Journal of Clinical and Health Psychology, 20*(2), 126–134. https://doi.org/10.1016/j.ijchp.2020.03.001
Gardiner, J. M. (2007). Retrieval: On its essence and related concepts. In H. L. Roediger, Y. Dudai, & S. M. Fitzpatrick (Eds.), *Science of memory: Concepts* (pp. 221–224). Oxford University Press.
Gardiner, J. M., & Atema, J. (2010). The function of bilateral odor arrival time differences in olfactory orientation of sharks. *Current Biology, 20*(13), 1187–1191.
Gardiner, J. M., Gawlik, B., & Richardson-Klavehn, A. (1994). Maintenance rehearsal affects knowing, not remembering; elaborative rehearsal affects remembering, not knowing. *Psychonomic Bulletin & Review, 1*(1), 107–110.
Gardner, E. P., & Johnson, K. O. (2013). The somatosensory system: Receptors and central pathways. In E. R. Kandel, J. H. Schwartz, T. M. Jessell, S. A. Siegelbaum, & A. J. Hudspeth (Eds.), *Principles of neural science* (5th ed., pp. 475–497). McGraw-Hill.
Gardner, H. (1985). *Frames of mind: The theory of multiple intelligences*. Basic Books.
Gardner, H. (1995). Cracking open the IQ box. In S. Fraser (Ed.), *The bell curve wars: Race, intelligence, and the future of America* (pp. 23–35). Basic Books.
Gardner, H. (1999). *The disciplined mind: What all students should understand*. Simon & Schuster.
Gardner, H. (2006). *Multiple intelligences: New horizons in theory and* practice. Basic Books.
Gardner, M. P., Wansink, B., Kim, J., & Park, S. B. (2014). Better moods for better eating? How mood influences food choice. *Journal of Consumer Psychology, 24*(3), 320–335.
Garfinkel-Castro, A., Kim, K., Hamidi, S., & Ewing, R. (2017). Obesity and the built environment at different urban scales: Examining the literature. *Nutrition Reviews, 75*(suppl_1), 51–61.
Gariépy, G., Janssen, I., Sentenac, M., & Elgar, F. J. (2018). School start time and the healthy weight of adolescents. *Journal of Adolescent Health, 63*(1), 69–73.
Garland, A. F., Lau, A. S., Yeh, M., McCabe, K. M., Hough, R. L., & Landsverk, J. A. (2014). Racial and ethnic differences in utilization of mental health services among high-risk youths. *American Journal of Psychiatry, 162*(7), 1336–1343.
Garland, D. J., & Barry, J. R. (1990). Sport expertise: The cognitive advantage. *Perceptual and Motor Skills, 70*(3 Pt 2), 1299–1314.
Garland, D. J., & Barry, J. R. (1991). Cognitive advantage in sport: The nature of perceptual structures. *The American Journal of Psychology, 104*(2), 211–228.
Garlovsky, J. K., Overton, P. G., & Simpson, J. (2016). Psychological predictors of anxiety and depression in Parkinson's disease: A systematic review. *Journal of Clinical Psychology, 72*(10), 979–998.
Garn, S. N., & Newton, R. A. (1988). Kinesthetic awareness in subjects with multiple ankle sprains. *Physical Therapy, 68*(11), 1667–1671.
Garner, L. E., Steinberg, E. J., & McKay, D. (2021). Exposure therapy. In A. Wenzel (Ed.), *Handbook of cognitive behavioral therapy: Overview and approaches* (pp. 275–312). American Psychological Association. https://doi.org/10.1037/0000218-010
Garnham, A. (2005). Language comprehension. In K. Lamberts & R. L. Goldstone (Eds.), *Handbook of cognition* (pp. 241–254). SAGE.

Garrett, B. (2015). *Brain & behavior: An introduction to biological psychology* (4th ed.). Sage.

Garrido, M., & Velasquez, R. (2006). Interpretation of Latino/Latina MMPI-2 profiles: Review and application of empirical findings and cultural-linguistic considerations. In J. N. Butcher (Ed.), *MMPI-2: A practitioner's guide* (pp. 477–504). American Psychological Association.

Garry, M., Hope, L., Zajac, R., Verrall, A. J., & Robertson, J. M. (2021). Contact tracing: A memory task with consequences for public health. *Perspectives on Psychological Science, 16*(1), 175–187. https://doi.org/10.1177/1745691620978205

Garske, J. P., & Anderson, T. (2003). Toward a science of psychotherapy research: Present status and evaluation. In S. O. Lilienfeld, S. J. Lynn, & J. M. Lohr (Eds.), *Science and pseudoscience in clinical psychology* (pp. 145–175). Guilford Press.

Gask, L. (2018). In defence of the biopsychosocial model. *The Lancet Psychiatry, 5*(7), 548–549.

Gates, G. J. (2013). Demographic perspectives on sexual orientation. In C. J. Patterson & A. R. D'Augelli (Eds.), *Handbook of psychology and sexual orientation* (pp. 69–86). Oxford University Press.

Gates, G. J., & Newport, F. (2013). Gallup Special Report: New estimates of the LGBT population in the United States. http://williamsinstitute.law.ucla.edu/research/census-lgbt-demographics-studies/gallup-lgbt-pop-feb-2013/

Gathercole, S. E. (2007). Working memory: What it is, and what it is not. In H. L. Roediger, Y. Dudai, & S. M. Fitzpatrick (Eds.), *Science of memory: Concepts* (pp. 155–158). Oxford University Press.

Gathercole, S. E., & Alloway, T. (2008). Working memory and classroom learning. In S. K. Thurman & C. A. Fiorello (Eds.), *Applied cognitive research in K-3 classrooms* (pp. 17–40). Routledge.

Gathercole, S. E., Pickering, S. J., Knight, C., & Stegmann, Z. (2004). Working memory skills and educational attainment: Evidence from national curriculum assessments at 7 and 14 years of age. *Applied Cognitive Psychology, 18*(1), 1–16.

Gau, S. F., & Soong, W. T. S. (1999). Psychiatric comorbidity of adolescents with sleep terrors or sleepwalking: A case-control study. *Australian and New Zealand Journal of Psychiatry, 33*(5), 734–739.

Gauci, M., Husband, A. J., Saxarra, H., & King, M. G. (1994). Pavlovian conditioning of nasal tryptase release in human subjects with allergic rhinitis. *Physiology & Behavior, 55*(5), 823–825.

Gautam, S., Bulley, A., von Hippel, W., & Suddendorf, T. (2017). Affective forecasting bias in preschool children. *Journal of Experimental Child Psychology, 159*, 175–184.

Gauthier, I. (2010). Face perception: Physiological. In E. B. Goldstein (Ed.), *Encyclopedia of perception* (pp. 449–452). Sage.

Gauthier, I. (2018). Domain-specific and domain-general individual differences in visual object recognition. *Current Directions in Psychological Science, 27*(2), 97–102.

Gay, P. (Ed.). (1995). *The Freud reader.* W. W. Norton.

Gay, P., Weaver, T., Loube, D., & Iber, C. (2006). Evaluation of positive airway pressure treatment for sleep-related breathing disorders in adults. *Sleep, 29*(3), 381–401.

Gazelle, H., & Ladd, G. W. (2003). Anxious solitude and peer exclusion: A diathesis–stress model of internalizing trajectories in childhood. *Child Development, 74*(1), 257–278.

Gazzaniga, M. S. (1998). The split brain revisited. *Scientific American, 279*(1), 50–55.

Gazzaniga, M. S. (2005). Forty-five years of split-brain research and still going strong. *Nature Reviews Neuroscience, 6*(8), 653–659.

Gazzaniga, M. S. (2018). *The consciousness instinct: Unraveling the mystery of how the brain makes the mind.* Farrar, Straus & Giroux.

Gazzaniga, M. S., Bogen, J. E., & Sperry, R. W. (1962). Some functional effects of sectioning the cerebral commissures in man. *Proceedings of the National Academy of Sciences of the United States of America, 48*(10), 1765–1769.

Geen, R. G., & McCown, E. J. (1984). Effects of noise and attack on aggression and physiological arousal. *Motivation and Emotion, 8*(3), 231–241.

Gegenfurtner, K. (2010). Color perception: Physiological. In E. B. Goldstein (Ed.), *Encyclopedia of perception* (pp. 270–275). Sage.

Gegenfurtner, K. R., & Kiper, D. C. (2003). Color vision. *Annual Review of Neuroscience, 26*(1), 181–206.

Geher, G. & Kaufman, S. B. (2011). Mating intelligence. In R. J. Sternberg & S. B. Kaufman (Eds.), *Cambridge handbook of intelligence*, pp. 603–621. Cambridge University Press.

Gehlbach, H., Brinkworth, M. E., King, A. M., Hsu, L. M., McIntyre, J., & Rogers, T. (2016). Creating birds of similar feathers: Leveraging similarity to improve teacher–student relationships and academic achievement. *Journal of Educational Psychology, 108*(3), 342.

Gehrman, P., Findley, J., & Perlis, M. (2012). Insomnia I: Etiology and conceptualization. In C. M. Morin & C. A. Espie (Eds.), *The Oxford handbook of sleep and sleep disorders* (pp. 405–427). Oxford University Press.

Gelernter, J., & Stein, M. B. (2009). Heritability and genetics of anxiety disorders. In M. M. Antony & M. B. Stein (Eds.), *Oxford handbook of anxiety and related disorders* (pp. 87–96). Oxford University Press.

Gelfand, M. J., Erez, M., & Aycan, Z. (2007). Cross-cultural organizational behavior. *Annual Review of Psychology*, 58, 479–514.

Geller, J., Toftness, A. R., Armstrong, P. I., Carpenter, S. K., Manz, C. L., Coffman, C. R., & Lamm, M. H. (2018). Study strategies and beliefs about learning as a function of academic achievement and achievement goals. *Memory, 26*(5), 683–690.

Gelman, S. A., & Kalish, C. W. (2006). Conceptual development. In D. Kuhn & R. Siegler (Vol. Eds.), *Handbook of child psychology* (6th ed., Vol. 2, pp. 687–733). Wiley.

Gelso, C. J. (2006). Applying theories to research: The interplay of theory and research in science. In F. T. L. Leong & J. T. Austin (Eds.), *The psychology research handbook: A guide for graduate students and research assistants* (2nd ed., pp. 455–464). Sage.

Gelso, C. J. (2010). The diversity status of the psychotherapist: Editorial introduction. *Psychotherapy: Theory, Research, Practice, Training, 47*(2), 143.

Gendron, M. (2017). Revisiting diversity: Cultural variation reveals the constructed nature of emotion perception. *Current Opinion in Psychology, 17*, 145–150.

Gendron, M., Crivelli, C., & Barrett, L. F. (2018). Universality reconsidered: Diversity in making meaning of facial expressions. *Current Directions in Psychological Science, 27*(4), 211–219.

Genta, F. D., Rodrigues Neto, G. B., Sunfeld, J. P. V., Porto, J. F., Xavier, A. D., Moreno, C. R., Lorenzi-Filho, G., & Genta, P. R. (2021). COVID-19 pandemic impact on sleep habits, chronotype, and health-related quality of life among high school students: A longitudinal study. *Journal of Clinical Sleep Medicine, 17*(7), 1371–1377. https://doi.org/10.5664/jcsm.9196

Gentile, A., Boca, S., & Giammusso, I. (2018). "You play like a woman!" Effects of gender stereotype threat on women's performance in physical and sport activities: A meta-analysis. *Psychology of Sport and Exercise, 39*, 95–103. https://doi.org/10.1016/j.psychsport.2018.07.013

Gentile, D. A., Bender, P. K., & Anderson, C. A. (2017). Violent video game effects on salivary cortisol, arousal, and aggressive thoughts in children. *Computers in Human Behavior, 70*, 39–43.

Gentner, D., & Kurtz, K. J. (2005). Relational categories. In W. K. Ahn, R. L. Goldstone, B. C. Love, A. B. Markman, & P. Wolff (Eds.), *Categorization inside and outside the laboratory: Essays in honor of Douglas L. Medin* (pp. 151–175). American Psychological Association.

Georgakis, M. K., Thomopoulos, T. P., Diamantaras, A. A., Kalogirou, E. I., Skalkidou, A., Daskalopoulou, S. S., & Petridou, E. T. (2016). Association of age at menopause and duration of reproductive period with depression after menopause: A systematic review and meta-analysis. *JAMA Psychiatry, 73*(2), 139–149.

George, J. M. (2000). Emotions and leadership: The role of emotional intelligence. *Human Relations, 53*(8), 1027–1055.

George, L. (2007). Foreword: The haunted animal. In R. Noll (Ed.), *The encyclopedia of schizophrenia and other psychotic disorders* (3rd ed., iv–vi). Facts on File.

George, M. S., Nahas, Z., Bohning, D. E., Kozel, F. A., Anderson, B., Mu, C., Borckardt, J., & Li, X. (2006). Vagus nerve stimulation and deep brain stimulation. In D. J. Stein, D. J. Kupfer, & A. F. Schatzberg (Eds.), *The American Psychiatric Publishing textbook of mood disorders* (pp. 337–349). American Psychiatric Publishing.

Georgieff, M. K., Tran, P. V., & Carlson, E. S. (2018). Atypical fetal development: Fetal alcohol syndrome, nutritional deprivation, teratogens, and risk for neurodevelopmental disorders and psychopathology. *Development and Psychopathology, 30*(3), 1063–1086.

Gerardi, M., Rothbaum, B. O., Ressler, K., Heekin, M., & Rizzo, A. (2008). Virtual reality exposure therapy using a virtual Iraq: Case report. *Journal of Traumatic Stress, 21*(2), 209–213.

Gerber, A. J., & Gonzalez, M. Z. (2013). Structural and functional brain imaging in clinical psychology. In J. S. Comer & P. C. Kendall (Eds.), *The Oxford handbook of research strategies for clinical psychology* (pp. 165–187). Oxford University Press.

Gerber, J. P., Wheeler, L., & Suls, J. (2018). A social comparison theory meta-analysis 60+ years on. *Psychological Bulletin, 144*(2), 177–197.

Gerdes, A. B. M., Uhl, G., & Alpers, G. W. (2009). Spiders are special: Fear and disgust evoked by pictures of arthropods. *Evolution and Human Behavior, 30*(1), 66–73.

Gerhardt, H. C., & Bee, M. A. (2006). Recognition and localization of acoustic signals. In P. M. Narins, A. S. Feng, R. R. Fay, & A. N. Popper (Eds.), *Hearing and sound communication in amphibians* (pp. 113–146). Springer.

Gerhart, B., & Fang, M. (2015). Pay, intrinsic motivation, extrinsic motivation, performance, and creativity in the workplace: Revisiting long-held beliefs. *Annual Review of Organizational Psychology and Organizational Behavior, 2*(1), 489–521.

Gerken, L. (2007). Acquiring linguistic structure. In E. Hoff & M. Shatz (Eds.), *Blackwell handbook of language development* (pp. 173–190). Blackwell.

Germain, A. (2012). Parasomnias I: Nightmares. In C. M. Morin & C. A. Espie (Eds.), *The Oxford handbook of sleep and sleep disorders* (pp. 555–576). Oxford University Press.

Germer, C. K. (2005). Mindfulness: What is it? What does it matter? In C. K. Germer, R. D. Siegel, & P. R. Fulton (Eds.), *Mindfulness and psychotherapy* (pp. 3–27). Guilford Press.

Geronimus, A. T., Hicken, M. T., Pearson, J. A., Seashols, S. J., Brown, K. L., & Cruz, T. D. (2010). Do U.S. black women experience stress-related accelerated biological aging? *Human Nature, 21*(1), 19–38.

Gershman, S. J., & Daw, N. D. (2017). Reinforcement learning and episodic memory in humans and animals: An integrative framework. *Annual Review of Psychology, 68*, 101–128.

Gershoff, E. T. (2002). Corporal punishment by parents and associated child behaviors and experiences: A meta-analytic and theoretical review. *Psychological Bulletin, 128*(4), 539–579.

Gershoff, E. T. (2008). *Report on physical punishment in the United States: What research tells us about its effects on children.* Center for Effective Discipline.

Gershoff, E. T. (2010). More harm than good: A summary of scientific research on the intended and unintended effects of corporal punishment on children. *Law and Contemporary Problems, 73*(2), 31–56.

Gershoff, E. T., & Bitensky, S. H. (2007). The case against corporal punishment of children: Converging evidence from social science research and international human rights law and implications for U.S. public policy. *Psychology, Public Policy, and Law, 13*(4), 231–272.

Gershoff, E. T., Goodman, G. S., Miller-Perrin, C. L., Holden, G. W., Jackson, Y., & Kazdin, A. E. (2018). The strength of the causal evidence against physical punishment of children and its implications for parents, psychologists, and policymakers. *American Psychologist, 73*(5), 626.

Gerstorf, D., Ram, N., Mayraz, G., Hidajat, M., Lindenberger, U., Wagner, G. G., & Schupp, J. (2010). Late-life decline in well-being across adulthood in Germany, the United Kingdom, and the United States: Something is seriously wrong at the end of life. *Psychology and Aging, 25*(2), 477.

Gervais, M. M., & Fessler, D. M. (2017). On the deep structure of social affect: Attitudes, emotions, sentiments, and the case of "contempt." *Behavioral and Brain Sciences, 40*, 1–18.

Gesser, G., Wong, P. T., & Reker, G. T. (1987). Death attitudes across the life-span: The development and validation of the Death Attitude Profile (DAP). *OMEGA—Journal of Death and Dying, 18*(2), 113–128.

Gethin, R. (2015). Buddhist conceptualizations of mindfulness. In K. W. Brown, J. D. Creswell, & R. M. Ryan (Eds.), *Handbook of mindfulness: Theory, research, and practice* (pp. 9–41). Guilford Press.

Gevirtz, R. N., Alhassoon, O. M., & Miller, B. P. (2016). Biomedical treatments. In J. C. Norcross, G. R. VandenBos, & D. K. Freedheim (Eds.), *APA handbook of clinical psychology* (Vol. 3, pp. 373–386). American Psychological Association.

Ghandour, B. M., Donner, M., Ross-Nash, Z., Hayward, M., Pinto, M., & DeAngelis, T. (2018). Perfectionism in past and present anorexia nervosa. *North American Journal of Psychology, 20*(3), 671–690.

Gharaibeh, N. M. (2005). The psychiatrist's image in commercially available American movies. *Acta Psychiatrica Scandinavica, 111*(4), 316–319.

Gheysen, F., Poppe, L., DeSmet, A., Swinnen, S., Cardon, G., De Bourdeaudhuij, I., Chastin, S., & Fias, W. (2018). Physical activity to improve cognition in older adults: Can physical activity programs enriched with cognitive challenges enhance the effects? A systematic review and meta-analysis. *International Journal of Behavioral Nutrition and Physical Activity, 15*(1), 1–13. https://doi.org/10.1186/s12966-018-0697-x

Ghezzi, P. M., Wilson, G. R., Tarbox, R. S. F., & MacAlesse, K. R. (2008). Guidelines for developing and managing a token economy. In W. T. O'Donohue & J. E. Fisher (Eds.), *Cognitive behavior therapy: Applying empirically supported techniques in your practice* (2nd ed., pp. 565–570). Wiley.

Ghildayal, N., Johnson, P. J., Evans, R. L., & Kreitzer, M. J. (2016). Complementary and alternative medicine use in the US adult low back pain population. *Global Advances in Health and Medicine, 5*(1), 69–78.

Ghiselin, M. T. (1974). *The economy of nature and the evolution of sex.* University of California Press.

Gianaros, P. J., & Wager, T. D. (2015). Brain-body pathways linking psychological stress and physical health. *Current Directions in Psychological Science, 24*(4), 313–321.

Giannotti, F., Cortesi, F., Sebastiani, T., & Vagnoni, C. (2008). Sleep practices and habits in children across different cultures. In A. Ivanenkno (Ed.), *Sleep and psychiatric disorders in children and adolescents* (pp. 37–48). Informa Healthcare USA.

Gibbons, M. B. C., Crits-Christoph, P., Barber, J. P., & Schamberger, M. (2007). Insight in psychotherapy: A review of empirical literature. In L. G. Castonguay & C. E. Hill (Eds.), *Insight in psychotherapy* (pp. 143–165). American Psychological Association.

Gibbs, R. W., Jr., Wilson, N. L., & Bryant, G. A. (2012). Figurative language: Normal adult cognitive research. In M. Spivey, M. Joanisse, & K. McRae (Eds.), *The Cambridge handbook of psycholinguistics* (pp. 465–484). Cambridge University Press.

Gibson, D., Benabe, J., Watters, A., Oakes, J., & Mehler, P. (2021). Personality characteristics and medical impact of stimulant laxative abuse in eating disorder patients—a pilot study. Journal of Eating Disorders, 9(146). https://doi.org/10.1186/s40337-021-00502-9

Gibson, E. S., Powles, A. C., Thabane, L., O'Brien, S., Molnar, D. S., Trajanovic, N., & Chilcott-Tanser, L. (2006). "Sleepiness" is serious in adolescence: Two surveys of 3235 Canadian students. *BMC Public Health, 6*(116), 1–9.

Gibson, K. R. (2012). Tool-dependent foraging strategies and the origin of language. In M. Tallerman & K. R. Gibson (Eds.), *The Oxford handbook of language evolution* (pp. 340–342). Oxford University Press.

Gibson, K. R., & Tallerman, M. (2012). Introduction to part III: The prehistory of language: When and why did language evolve? In M. Tallerman & K. R. Gibson (Eds.), *The Oxford handbook of language evolution* (pp. 239–249). Oxford University Press.

Gil, K. M., Carson, J. W., Porter, L. S., Scipio, C., Bediako, S. M., & Orringer, E. (2004). Daily mood and stress predict pain, health care use, and work activity in African American adults with sickle-cell disease. *Health Psychology, 23*(3), 267–274.

Gilbert, A. N. (2008). *What the nose knows: The science of scent in everyday life*. Crown Publishers.

Gilbert, D. (2006). *Stumbling on happiness*. Knopf.

Gilbert, D. T., & Malone, P. S. (1995). The correspondence bias. *Psychological Bulletin, 117*(1), 21.

Gilbert, D. T., & Wilson, T. D. (2000). Miswanting. In J. P. Forgas (Ed.), *Feeling and thinking: The role of affect in social cognition* (pp. 178–197). Cambridge University Press.

Gilbert, D. T., & Wilson, T. D. (2007). Prospection: Experiencing the future. *Science, 317*(5843), 1351–1354.

Gilbert, D. T., Pinel, E. C., Wilson, T. D., Blumberg, S. T., & Wheatley, T. P. (1998). Durability bias in affective forecasting. *Journal of Personality and Social Psychology, 75*, 617–638.

Gilbertson-White, S., Campbell, G., Ward, S., Sherwood, P., & Donovan, H. (2017). Coping with pain severity, distress, and consequences in women with ovarian cancer. *Cancer Nursing, 40*(2), 117.

Gillespie, G. (1997). Hypnopompic imagery and visual dream experience. *Dreaming, 7*(3), 187–194.

Gillespie, W. H. (1971). Aggression and instinct theory. *The International Journal of Psychoanalysis, 52*, 155–160.

Gilligan, C. (1982). *In a different voice: Psychological theory and women's development.* Harvard University Press.

Gilligan, C. (1987). Moral orientation and moral development. In E. F. Kittay & D. T. Meyers (Eds.), *Women and moral theory* (pp. 19–33). Rowman & Littlefield.

Gilligan, C. (1992). *Meeting at the crossroads: Women's psychology and girls' development*. Harvard University Press.

Gilligan, C., & Wiggins, G. (1987). The origins of morality in early childhood relationships. In J. Kagan & S. Lamb (Eds.), *The emergence of morality in young children* (pp. 277–305). University of Chicago Press.

Gillihan, S. J., & Foa, E. B. (2016). Exposure-based interventions for adult anxiety disorders, obsessive-compulsive disorder, and posttraumatic stress disorder. In C. M. Nezu & A. M. Nezu (Eds.), *The Oxford handbook of cognitive and behavioral therapies* (pp. 96–117). Oxford University Press.

Gillon, W. (2007). *Person-centered counseling psychology: An introduction*. Sage.

Gilman, S. E., Rende, R., Boergers, J., Abrams, D. B., Buka, S. L., & Clark, M. A. (2009). Parental smoking and adolescent initiation: An intergenerational perspective on tobacco control. *Pediatrics, 123*(2), 274–281.

Gilovich, T., & Savitsky, K. (2002). Like goes with like: The role of representativeness in erroneous and pseudo-scientific beliefs. In T. Gilovich, D. W. Griffin, & D. Kahneman (Eds.), *Heuristics and biases: The psychology of intuitive judgment* (pp. 617–624). Cambridge University Press.

Gilovich, T., Kumar, A., & Jampol, L. (2015). A wonderful life: Experiential consumption and the pursuit of happiness. *Journal of Consumer Psychology, 25*(1), 152–165.

Gim, R. H., Atkinson, D. R., & Kim, S. J. (1991). Asian-American acculturation, counselor ethnicity and cultural sensitivity, and ratings of counselors. *Journal of Counseling Psychology, 38*(1), 57–62.

Ginter, E., Glauser, A., & Richmond, B. O. (1994). Loneliness, social support, and anxiety among two South Pacific cultures. *Psychological Reports, 74*(3), 875–879.

Givrad, S. (2016). Dream theory and science: A review. *Psychoanalytic Inquiry, 36*(3), 199–213.

GLAAD. (2018). GLAAD media reference guide—lesbian/gay/bisexual glossary of terms. https://www.glaad.org/reference/lgbtq

Glaser, R., Kiecolt-Glaser, J. K., Marucha, P. T., MacCallum, R. C., Laskowski, B. F., & Malarkey, W. B. (1999). Stress-related changes in proinflammatory cytokine production in wounds. *Archives of General Psychiatry, 56*(5), 450–456.

Glasman, L. R., & Albarracín, D. (2006). Forming attitudes that predict future behavior: A meta-analysis of the attitude-behavior relation. *Psychological Bulletin, 132*(5), 778–822.

Glass, C., & Minnotte, K. L. (2010). Recruiting and hiring women in STEM fields. *Journal of Diversity in Higher Education, 3*(4), 218–229.

Gleaves, D. H., May, M. C., & Cardena E. (2001). An examination of the diagnostic validity of dissociative identity disorder. *Clinical Psychology Review, 21*(4), 577–608.

Gleeson, S. (1991). Response acquisition. In I. H. Iverson & K. A. Lattal (Eds.), *Experimental analysis of behavior* (Pt. 1, pp. 63–86). Elsevier.

Gleitman, L., & Papafragou, A. (2013). Relations between language and thought. In D. Reisberg (Ed.), *The Oxford handbook of cognitive psychology* (pp. 504–523). Oxford University Press.

Globus, A., Rosenzweig, M. R., Bennett, E. L., & Diamond, M. C. (1973). Effects of differential experience on dendritic spine counts in rat cerebral cortex. *Journal of Comparative and Physiological Psychology, 82*(2), 175.

Glucksberg, S. (1989). Metaphors in conversation: How are they understood? Why are they used? *Metaphor and Symbol, 4*(3), 125–143.

Glucksberg, S., & Weisberg, R. W. (1966). Verbal behavior and problem solving: Some effects of labeling in a functional fixedness problem. *Journal of Experimental Psychology, 71*(5), 659–664.

Glueckauf, R. L., Maheu, M. M., Drude, K. P., Wells, B. A., Wang, Y., Gustafson, D. J., & Nelson, E. L. (2018). Survey of psychologists' telebehavioral health practices: Technology use, ethical issues, and training needs. *Professional Psychology: Research and Practice, 49*(3), 205–219.

Gobet, F., & Clarkson, G. (2004). Chunks in expert memory: Evidence for the magical number four—or is it two? *Memory, 12*(6), 732–747.

Gobet, F., & Simon, H. A. (1998). Expert chess memory: Revisiting the chunking hypothesis. *Memory, 6*(3), 225–255.

Gobet, F., Lane, P. C., Croker, S., Cheng, P. C., Jones, G., Oliver, I., & Pine, J. M. (2001). Chunking mechanisms in human learning. *Trends in Cognitive Sciences, 5*(6), 236–243.

Gocłowska, M. A., Damian, R. I., & Mor, S. (2018). The diversifying experience model: Taking a broader conceptual view of the multiculturalism–creativity link. *Journal of Cross-Cultural Psychology, 49*(2), 303–322.

Godden, D. R., & Baddeley, A. D. (1975). Context-dependent memory in two natural environments: On land and underwater. *British Journal of Psychology, 66*(3), 325–331.

Godfrey-Smith, P. (2017). *Other minds: The octopus, the sea and the deep origins of consciousness*. William Collins.

Godijn, R., & Theeuwes, J. (2012). Overt is no better than covert when rehearsing visuo-spatial information in working memory. *Memory & Cognition, 40*(1), 52–61.

Goebel, M. U., Meykadeh, N., Kou, W., Schedlowski, M., & Hengge, U. R. (2008). Behavioral conditioning of antihistamine effects in patients with allergic rhinitis. *Psychotherapy and Psychosomatics, 77*(4), 227–234.

Goetz, T., Frenzel, A., Pekrun, R., & Hall, N. (2005). Emotional intelligence in the context of learning and achievement. In R. Schulze & R. D. Roberts (Eds.), *Emotional intelligence: An international handbook* (pp. 233–253). Hogrefe & Huber.

Goetzel, R. Z., Kowlessar, N., Rormer, E. C., Pei, X., Tabrizi, M., Liss-Levinson, R. C., Samoly, D., & Waddell, J. (2011). Workplace obesity prevention programs. In J. H. Cawley (Ed.), *The Oxford handbook of the social science of obesity* (pp. 683–712). Oxford University Press.

Goffman, E. (1963). *Stigma: Notes on the management of spoiled identity*. Prentice-Hall.

Gold, E. B., Bromberger, J., Crawford, S., Samuels, S., Greendale, G. A., Harlow, S. D., & Skurnick, J. (2001). Factors associated with age at natural menopause in a multiethnic sample of midlife women. *American Journal of Epidemiology, 153*(9), 865–874.

Gold, J. R. (1996). *Key concepts in psychotherapy integration*. Plenum Press.

Gold, J., & Stricker, G. (2017). Psychodynamic therapies in historical perspective. In A. J. Consoli, L. E. Beutler, & B. Bongar (Eds.), *Comprehensive textbook of psychotherapy: Theory and practice* (2nd ed., pp. 31–44). Oxford University Press.

Goldapple, K., Segal, Z., Garson, C., Lau, M., Bieling, P., Kennedy, S., & Mayberg, H. (2004). Modulation of cortical-limbic pathways in major depression: Treatment-specific effects of cognitive behavior therapy. *Archives of General Psychiatry, 61*(1), 34–41.

Goldberg, P. (2012). Process, resistance, and interpretation. In G. O. Gabbard, B. E. Litowitz, & P. Williams (Eds.), *Textbook of psychoanalysis* (2nd ed., pp. 283–302). American Psychiatric Publishing.

Goldberg, S. B., & Hoyt, W. T. (2015). Group as social microcosm: Within-group interpersonal style is congruent with outside group relational tendencies. *Psychotherapy, 52*(2), 195–204.

Goldberg, S. B., Tucker, R. P., Greene, P. A., Davidson, R. J., Wampold, B. E., Kearney, D. J., & Simpson, T. L. (2018). Mindfulness-based interventions for psychiatric disorders: A systematic review and meta-analysis. Clinical Psychology Review, 59(2), 52–60. https://doi.org/10.1016/j.cpr.2017.10.011

Goldberg, S. H. (2012). Transference. In G. O. Gabbard, B. E. Litowitz, & P. Williams (Eds.), *Textbook of psychoanalysis* (2nd ed., pp. 65–78). American Psychiatric Publishing.

Goldberg, W. A., & Keller, M. A. (2007). Co-sleeping during infancy and early childhood: Key findings and future directions. *Infant and Child Development, 16*(4), 457–469. https://doi.org/10.1002/icd.522

Goldenberg, H., & Goldenberg, I. (2007). *Family therapy: An overview* (7th ed.). Brooks/Cole.

Goldfried, M. R. (1995). *From cognitive-behavior therapy to psychotherapy integration: An evolving view*. Springer.

Goldin-Meadow, S. (2005). *The resilience of language: What gesture creation in deaf children can tell us about how all children learn language*. Psychology Press.

Goldscheider, F., & Goldscheider, C. (1999). *The changing transition to adulthood: Leaving and returning home*. Sage.

Goldstein, E. B. (2001a). Cross-talk between psychophysics and physiology in the study of perception. In E. B. Goldstein (Ed.), *Blackwell handbook of perception* (pp. 1–23). Blackwell.

Goldstein, E. B. (2001b). Pictorial perception and art. In E. B. Goldstein (Ed.), *Blackwell handbook of perception* (pp. 344–378). Blackwell.

Goldstein, E. B. (2010a). Constancy. In E. B. Goldstein (Ed.), *Encyclopedia of perception* (pp. 309–313). Sage.

Goldstein, E. B. (2010b). Vision. In E. B. Goldstein (Ed.), *Encyclopedia of perception* (pp. 1044–1048). Sage.

Goldstein, G. (2008). Intellectual evaluation. In M. Hersen & A. M. Gross (Eds.), *Handbook of clinical psychology* (Vol. 1, pp. 395–421). Wiley.

Goldstein, M. H., & Schwade, J. A. (2008). Social feedback to infants' babbling facilitates rapid phonological learning. *Psychological Science, 19*(5), 515–523.

Goldstein, M. H., & West, M. J. (1999). Consistent responses of human mothers to prelinguistic infants: The effect of prelinguistic repertoire size. *Journal of Comparative Psychology, 113*(1), 52–58.

Goldstein, M. H., King, A. P., & West, M. J. (2003). Social interaction shapes babbling: Testing parallels between birdsong and speech. *Proceedings of the National Academy of Sciences, 100*(13), 8030–8035.

Goldwater, M. B., Markman, A. B., & Stilwell, C. H. (2011). The empirical case for role-governed categories. *Cognition, 118*(3), 359–376.

Goleman, D. (1998). *Working with emotional intelligence*. Random House.

Goleman, D. (2006). *Emotional intelligence: Why it can matter more than IQ*. Random House.

Golinkoff, R. M., Shuff-Bailey, M., Olguin, R., & Ruan, W. (1995). Young children extend novel words at the basic level: Evidence for the principle of categorical scope. *Developmental Psychology, 31*(3), 494–507.

Gollenberg, A. L., Liu, F., Brazil, C., Drobnis, E. Z., Guzick, D., Overstreet, J. W., Redmon, J. B., Sparks, A., Wang, C., & Swan, S. H. (2010). Semen quality in fertile men in relation to psychosocial stress. *Fertility and Sterility, 93*(4), 1104–1111.

Gomersall, P., & Baguley, D. (2010). Audition: Disorders. In E. B. Goldstein (Ed.), *Encyclopedia of perception* (pp. 141–145). Sage.

Gómez, A. M. (2011). Testing the cycle of violence hypothesis: Child abuse and adolescent dating violence as predictors of intimate partner violence in young adulthood. *Youth & Society, 43*(1), 171–192.

Gómez, R. L., & Gerken, L. (2000). Infant artificial language learning and language acquisition. *Trends in Cognitive Sciences, 4*(5), 178–186.

Gone, J. P., & Kirmayer, L. J. (2010). On the wisdom of considering culture and context in psychopathology. In T. Millon, R. F. Krueger, & E. Simonsen (Eds.), *Contemporary directions in psychopathology: Scientific foundations of the DSM-V and ICD-11* (pp. 72–96). Guilford Press.

Gong, X., Wong, N., & Wang, D. (2018). Are gender differences in emotion culturally universal? Comparison of emotional intensity between Chinese and German samples. *Journal of Cross-Cultural Psychology, 49*(6), 993–1005.

Gonzales, A. L., & Hancock, J. T. (2011). Mirror, mirror on my Facebook wall: Effects of exposure to Facebook on self-esteem. *Cyberpsychology, Behavior, and Social Networking, 14*(1–2), 79–83.

Gonzales, P. M., Blanton, H., & Williams, K. J. (2002). The effects of stereotype threat and double-minority status on the test performance of Latino women. *Personality and Social Psychology Bulletin, 28*(5), 659–670.

Good, B. J., & Hinton, D. E. (2009). Introduction: Panic disorder in cross-cultural and historical perspective. In D. E. Hinton & B. J. Good (Eds.), *Culture and panic disorder* (pp. 1–28). Stanford University Press.

Goodale, M. A. (2011). Transforming vision into action. *Vision Research, 51*(13), 1567–1587.

Goodale, M. A., & Humphrey, G. K. (2001). Separate visual systems for action and perception. In E. B. Goldstein (Ed.), *Blackwell handbook of perception* (pp. 311–343). Blackwell.

Goodale, M. A., & Milner, A. D. (1992). Separate visual pathways for perception and action. *Trends in Neurosciences, 15*(1), 20–25.

Goodale, M. A., & Milner, A. D. (2013). *Sight unseen: An exploration of conscious and unconscious vision* (2nd ed.). Oxford University Press.

Goodale, M. A., & Westwood, D. A. (2004). An evolving view of duplex vision: Separate but interacting cortical pathways for perception and action. *Current Opinion in Neurobiology, 14*(2), 203–211.

Goodheart, L. B. (2003). *Mad Yankees: The Hartford Retreat for the Insane and nineteenth-century psychiatry*. University of Massachusetts Press.

Goodman, G. S., Magnussen, S., Andersson, J., Endestad, T., Løkken, L., & Moestue, A. C. (2007). Memory illusions and false memories in the real world. In S. Magnussen & T. Helstrup (Eds.), *Everyday memory* (pp. 157–182). Psychology Press.

Goodwin, C. J. (2003). Psychology's experimental foundations. In S. F. Davis (Ed.), *Handbook of research methods in experimental psychology* (pp. 3–23). Blackwell.

Goodwin, C. J. (2012). United States. In D. B. Baker (Ed.), *The Oxford handbook of the history of psychology: Global perspectives* (pp. 571–593). Oxford University Press.

Goodwin, R. D., & Friedman, H. S. (2006). Health status and the five-factor personality traits in a nationally representative sample. *Journal of Health Psychology, 11*(5), 643–654.

Goodwin, R. D., Jocobi, F., Bittner, A., & Wittchen, H. (2006). Epidemiology of mood disorders. In D. J. Stein, D. J. Kupfer, & A. F. Schatzberg (Eds.), *The American Psychiatric Publishing textbook of mood disorders* (pp. 33–54). American Psychiatric Association Publishing.

Gopinath, B., Sue, C. M., Kifley, A., & Mitchell, P. (2012). The association between olfactory impairment and total mortality in older adults. *The Journals of Gerontology, Series A: Biological Sciences and Medical Sciences, 67*(2), 204–209.

Gopnik, A., & Meltzoff, A. N. (1997). *Words, thoughts, and theories*. MIT Press.

Gorassini, D. R., & Olson, J. M. (1995). Does self-perception change explain the foot-in-the-door effect? *Journal of Personality and Social Psychology, 69*(1), 91–105.

Gordon, J., & Abramov, I. (2001). Color vision. In E. B. Goldstein (Ed.), *Blackwell handbook of perception* (pp. 92–127). Blackwell.

Gordon, R. A. (2000). *Eating disorders: Anatomy of a social epidemic* (2nd ed.). Blackwell.

Gore, W. L., & Widiger, T. A. (2013). The DSM-5 dimensional trait model and five-factor models of general personality. *Journal of Abnormal Psychology, 122*(3), 816–821.

Goren, C. C., Sarty, M., & Wu, P. Y. (1975). Visual following and pattern discrimination of face-like stimuli by newborn infants. *Pediatrics, 56*(4), 544–549.

Gott, J., Rak, M., Bovy, L., Peters, E., van Hooijdonk, C. F., Mangiaruga, A., Varatheeswaran, R., Chaabou, M., Gorman, L., Wilson, S., Weber, F., Talamini, L., Steiger, A., & Dresler, M. (2020). Sleep fragmentation and lucid dreaming. *Consciousness and Cognition, 84*, 102988. https://doi.org/10.1016/j.concog.2020.102988

Gottesman, I. I. (1991). *Schizophrenia genesis: The origins of madness*. W. H. Freeman.

Gottesman, I. I. (2001). Psychopathology through a life span–genetic prism. *American Psychologist, 56*(11), 867–878.

Gottesmann, C. (2013). *Henri Piéron and Nathaniel Kleitman, two major figures of 20th century sleep research*. Nova Biomedical.

Gottfredson, L. S., & Deary, I. J. (2004). Intelligence predicts health and longevity, but why? *Current Directions in Psychological Science, 13*(1), 1–4.

Gottfried, J. A., Vaala, S. E., Bleakley, A., Hennessy, M., & Jordan, A. (2013). Does the effect of exposure to TV sex on adolescent sexual behavior vary by genre? *Communication Research, 40*(1), 73–95.

Gottlieb, D. A., & Begej, E. L. (2014). Principles of Pavlovian conditioning: Description, content, function. In F. K. McSweeney & E. S. Murphy (Eds.), *The Wiley-Blackwell handbook of operant and classical conditioning* (pp. 3–26). Wiley.

Gouin, J. P., & Kiecolt-Glaser, J. K. (2011). The impact of psychological stress on wound healing: Methods and mechanisms. *Immunology and Allergy Clinics of North America, 31*(1), 81–93.

Gould, J. L., & Gould, C. G. (1994). *The animal mind*. Scientific American Library.

Goyal, M., Singh, S., Sibinga, E. M., Gould, N. F., Rowland-Seymour, A., Sharma, R., ... Ranasinghe, P. D. (2014). Meditation programs for psychological stress and well-being: A systematic review and meta-analysis. *JAMA Internal Medicine, 174*(3), 357–368.

Göz, I., Çeven, Z. I., & Tekcan, A. I. (2017). Urban–rural differences in children's earliest memories. *Memory, 25*(2), 214–219.

Grabe, S., Ward, L. M., & Hyde, J. S. (2008). The role of the media in body image concerns among women: A meta-analysis of experimental and correlational studies. *Psychological Bulletin, 134*(3), 460–476.

Gradisar, M., & Short, M. A. (2013). Sleep hygiene and environment: Role of technology. In A. R. Wolfson & H. Montgomery-Downs (Eds.), *The Oxford handbook of infant, child, and adolescent sleep and behavior* (pp. 113–126). Oxford University Press.

Graham, C. A., Mercer, C. H., Tanton, C., Jones, K. G., Johnson, A. M., Wellings, K., & Mitchell, K. R. (2017). What factors are associated with reporting lacking interest in sex and how do these vary by gender? Findings from the third British National Survey of Sexual Attitudes and Lifestyles. *BMJ Open, 7*(9), e016942.

Graham, G., Sauer, J. D., Akehurst, L., Smith, J., & Hillstrom, A. P. (2018). CCTV observation: The effects of event type and instructions on fixation behaviour in an applied change blindness task. *Applied Cognitive Psychology, 32*(1), 4–13.

Graham, J. R., & Roemer, L. (2015). Multicultural issues in training and practice. In R. L. Cautin & S. O. Lilienfeld (Eds.), *The encyclopedia of clinical psychology* (pp. 1921–1926). Wiley-Blackwell.

Granato, H. F., Sewart, A. R., Vinograd, M., & McFarr, L. (2021). Dialectical behavior therapy. In A. Wenzel (Ed.), *Handbook of cognitive behavioral therapy: Overview and approaches* (pp. 539–565). American Psychological Association. https://doi.org/10.1037/0000218-018

Grandin, J. M., & Hedderich, N. (2009). International competence in engineering. In D. K. Deardorff (Ed.), *The Sage handbook of intercultural competence* (pp. 362–373). Sage.

Granic, I., Lobel, A., & Engels, R. C. (2014). The benefits of playing video games. *American Psychologist, 69*(1), 66.

Grant, A. M., & Ashford, S. J. (2008). The dynamics of proactivity at work. *Research in Organizational Behavior, 28*, 3–34.

Grant, J. M., Mottet, L. A., Tanis, J., Herman, J. L., Harrison, J., & Keisling, M. (2010). *National Transgender Discrimination Survey Report on health and health care*. National Center for Transgender Equality and National Gay and Lesbian Task Force.

Grant, P., Young, P. R., & DeRubeis, R. J. (2005). Cognitive and behavioral therapies. In G. O. Gabbard, J. S. Beck, & J. Holmes (Eds.), *Oxford textbook of psychotherapy* (pp. 15–25). Oxford University Press.

Gray, J. A. (1979). *Ivan Pavlov*. Viking Press.

Gray, J. A. (1987). *The psychology of fear and stress* (2nd ed.). Cambridge University Press.

Gray, J., Kaslow, N., & Allbaugh, L. (2020). Introduction to the special issue: Advocacy in public service settings. *Psychological Services, 17*(S1), 1–4. http://dx.doi.org/10.1037/ser0000497

Graybiel, A. M., & Mink, J. W. (2009). *The cognitive neurosciences*. MIT Press.

Grayling, A. C. (2002, June 22). Scientist or storyteller? *The Guardian*. https://www.theguardian.com/books/2002/jun/22/socialsciences.gender

Green, B. G. (2004). Temperature perception and nociception. *Journal of Neurobiology, 61*(1), 13–29.

Green, C. (2017). Usage-based linguistics and the magic number four. *Cognitive Linguistics, 28*(2), 209–237.

Green, C. D., & Groff, P. R. (2003). *Early psychological thought: Ancient accounts of mind and soul*. Praeger.

Green, C. S., & Bavelier, D. (2007). Action-video-game experience alters the spatial resolution of vision. *Psychological Science, 18*(1), 88–94. https://doi.org/ 10.1111/j.1467-9280.2007.01853.x

Greenberg, A. E., & Mogilner, C. (2021). Consumer debt and satisfaction in life. *Journal of Experimental Psychology: Applied, 27*(1), 57–68. https://doi.org/10.1037/xap0000276

Greenberg, D. M., Matz, S. C., Schwartz, H. A., & Fricke, K. R. (2021). The self-congruity effect of music. *Journal of Personality and Social Psychology, 121*(1), 137–150. https://doi.org/10.1037/pspp0000293

Greenberg, G. (2013). *The book of woe: The DSM and the unmaking of psychiatry*. Blue Rider Press.

Greene, C. M., Nash, R. A., & Murphy, G. (2021). Misremembering Brexit: Partisan bias and individual predictors of false memories for fake news stories among Brexit voters. *Memory*, 29(5) 587–604. https://doi.org/10.1080/09658211.2021.1923754

Greene, G. (2008). *Insomniac*. University of California Press.

Greene, K., Krcmar, M., Walters, L. H., Rubin, D. L., & Hale, L. (2000). Targeting adolescent risk-taking behaviors: The contributions of egocentrism and sensation-seeking. *Journal of Adolescence, 23*(4), 439–461.

Greene, R. L. (1986). Sources of recency effects in free recall. *Psychological Bulletin, 99*(2), 221–228.

Greene, R. L. (1987). Effects of maintenance rehearsal on human memory. *Psychological Bulletin, 102*(3), 403–413.

Greene, R. L., & Clopton, J. R. (2004). Minnesota Multiphasic Personality Inventory-2 (MMPI-2). In M. W. Maruish (Ed.), *The use of psychological testing for treatment planning and outcomes assessment* (3rd ed., Vol. 3, pp. 449–477). Lawrence Erlbaum.

Greener, M. (2017). Are culture-bound syndromes on the verge of extinction? *Progress in Neurology and Psychiatry, 21*(1), 30–32.

Greenlee, M. W., Werner, J. S., & Wagner, C. (2018). An introduction to the special issue "Seeing Colors." *i-Perception, 9*(5), 1–2.

Greeno, C. G., & Wing, R. R. (1994). Stress-induced eating. *Psychological Bulletin, 115*(3), 444–464.

Greenstein, L. (2015). Maybe Modern Family isn't so modern after all. https://www.nami.org/Blogs/NAMI-Blog/October-2015/Maybe-Modern-Family-Isn't-So-Modern-After-All

Greenwald, A. G., Poehlman, T. A., Uhlmann, E. L., & Banaji, M. R. (2009). Understanding and using the Implicit Association Test: III. Meta-analysis of predictive validity. *Journal of Personality and Social Psychology, 97*(1), 17–41.

Gregory, R. J. (2004). *Psychological testing: History, principles, and applications*. Allyn & Bacon.

Grey, N., & Holmes, E. A. (2008). "Hotspots" in trauma memories in the treatment of post-traumatic stress disorder: A replication. *Memory, 16*(7), 788–796.

Gribble, K., Marinelli, K. A., Tomori, C., & Gross, M. S. (2020). Implications of the COVID-19 pandemic response for breastfeeding, maternal caregiving capacity and infant mental health. *Journal of Human Lactation, 36*(4), 591–603. https://doi.org/10.1177/0890334420949514

Griffin, D. W., Gonzalez, R., Koehler, D. J., & Gilovich, T. (2012). Judgmental heuristics: A historical overview. In K. J. Holyoak & R. G. Morrison (Eds.), *The Oxford handbook of thinking and reasoning* (pp. 322–345). Oxford University Press.

Griffiths, B. (2001). Have you paxiled lately? *Annals of the American Psychotherapy Association, 4*, 9.

Griffiths, K. M., Carron-Arthur, B., Parsons, A., & Reid, R. (2014). Effectiveness of programs for reducing the stigma associated with mental disorders: A meta-analysis of randomized controlled trials. World Psychiatry, 13(2), 161–175. https://doi.org.10.1002/wps.20129

Griggs, R. A. (2015). Coverage of the Phineas Gage story in introductory psychology textbooks: Was Gage no longer Gage? *Teaching of Psychology, 42*(3), 195–202.

Grigorenko, E. L. (2007). Working as a psychologist in a medical school. In R. J. Sternberg (Ed.), *Career paths in psychology: Where your degree can take you* (2nd ed., pp. 69–81). American Psychological Association.

Grill-Spector, K., Weiner, K. S., Kay, K., & Gomez, J. (2017). The functional neuroanatomy of human face perception. *Annual Review of Vision Science, 3*(1), 167–196.

Grinde, B. (2018). Did consciousness first evolve in the amniotes? *Psychology of Consciousness: Theory, Research, and Practice, 5*(3), 239–257.

Griner, D., & Smith, T. B. (2006). Culturally adapted mental health intervention: A meta-analytic review. *Psychotherapy: Theory, Research, Practice, Training, 43*(4), 531–548.

Groeger, J. A., Zijlstra, F. R. H., & Dijk, D.-J. (2004). Sleep quantity, sleep difficulties and their perceived consequences in a representative sample of some 2000 British adults. *Journal of Sleep Research, 13*(4), 359–371.

Groesz, L. M., Levine, M. P., & Murnen, S. K. (2002). The effect of experimental presentation of thin media images on body satisfaction: A meta-analytic review. *International Journal of Eating Disorders, 31*(1), 1–16.

Grogan-Kaylor, A., Ma, J., & Graham-Bermann, S. A. (2018). The case against physical punishment. *Current Opinion in Psychology, 19*, 22–27.

Groh, A. M., Narayan, A. J., Bakermans-Kranenburg, M. J., Roisman, G. I., Vaughn, B. E., Fearon, R. P., & van IJzendoorn, M. H. (2017). Attachment and temperament in the early life course: A meta-analytic review. *Child Development, 88*(3), 770–795.

Grohol, J. (2013). Top 25 psychiatric prescriptions for 2013. *PsychCentral*. https://psychcentral.com/lib/top-25-psychiatric-medication-prescriptions-for-2013/

Grohol, J. M. (2019). Top 25 psychiatric medications for 2018. *PsychCentral*. https://psychcentral.com/blog/top-25-psychiatric-medications-for-2018

Gros-Louis, J., West, M. J., Goldstein, M. H., & King, A. P. (2006). Mothers provide differential feedback to infants' prelinguistic sounds. *International Journal of Behavioral Development, 30*(6), 509–516.

Gross, C. L., & Marcussen, K. (2017). Postpartum depression in mothers and fathers: The role of parenting efficacy expectations during the transition to parenthood. *Sex Roles, 76*(5–6), 290–305.

Gross, J. J. (1998a). Antecedent-and response-focused emotion regulation: Divergent consequences for experience, expression, and physiology. *Journal of Personality and Social Psychology, 74*(1), 224–237.

Gross, J. J. (1998b). The emerging field of emotion regulation: An integrative review. *Review of General Psychology, 2*(3), 271–299.

Gross, J. J. (2008). Emotion regulation. In M. Lewis, J. M. Haviland-Jones, & L. F. Barrett (Eds.), *Handbook of emotions* (3rd ed., pp. 497–512). Guilford Press.

Gross, J. J. (2014). Emotion regulation: Conceptual and empirical foundations. In J. J. Gross (Ed.), *Handbook of emotion regulation* (2nd ed., pp. 3–20). Guilford Press.

Gross, J. J., & John, O. P. (2003). Individual differences in two emotion regulation processes: Implications for affect, relationships, and well-being. *Journal of Personality and Social Psychology, 85*(2), 348–362.

Gross, J. J., & Levenson, R. W. (1993). Emotional suppression: Physiology, self-report, and expressive behavior. *Journal of Personality and Social Psychology, 64*(6), 970.

Gross, J. J., & Levenson, R. W. (1997). Hiding feelings: The acute effects of inhibiting negative and positive emotion. *Journal of Abnormal Psychology, 106*(1), 95–103.

Gross, J. T., Stern, J. A., Brett, B. E., & Cassidy, J. (2017). The multifaceted nature of prosocial behavior in children: Links with attachment theory and research. *Social Development, 26*(4), 661–678.

Grossman, P. (2011). Defining mindfulness by how poorly I think I pay attention during everyday awareness and other intractable problems for psychology's (re)invention of mindfulness: Comment on Brown et al. (2011). *Psychological Assessment, 23*(4), 1034–1040.

Grossman, P., & Van Dam, N. T. (2011). Mindfulness, by any other name&: Trials and tribulations of sati in western psychology and science. Contemporary Buddhism, 12(01), 219–239.

Grossman, P., Niemann, L., Schmidt, S., & Walach, H. (2004). Mindfulness-based stress reduction and health benefits: A meta-analysis. *Journal of Psychosomatic Research, 57*(1), 35–43.

Grossmann, I., Na, J., Varnum, M. E., Park, D. C., Kitayama, S., & Nisbett, R. E. (2010). Reasoning about social conflicts improves into old age. *Proceedings of the National Academy of Sciences, 107*(16), 7246–7250.

Gruber, J., Prinstein, M. J., Clark, L. A., Rottenberg, J., Abramowitz, J. S., Albano, A. M., Aldao, A., Borelli, J. L., Chung, T., Davila, J., Forbes, E. E., Gee, D. G., Hall, G. C. N., Hallion, L. S., Hinshaw, S. P., Hofmann, S. G., Hollon, S. D., Joormann, J., Kazdin, A. E., Klein, D. N., & Weinstock, L. M. (2021). Mental health and clinical psychological science in the time of COVID-19: Challenges, opportunities, and a call to action. *American Psychologist, 76*(3), 409–426. https://doi.org/10.1037/amp0000707

Gruber, R., Saha, S., Somerville, G., Boursier, J., & Wise, M. S. (2020). The impact of COVID-19 related school shutdown on sleep in adolescents: A natural experiment. *Sleep Medicine, 76*, 33–35. https://doi.org/10.1016/j.sleep.2020.09.015

Grundmann, F., Epstude, K., & Scheibe, S. (2021). Face masks reduce emotion-recognition accuracy and perceived closeness. *PloS ONE, 16*(4), e0249792. https://doi.org/10.1371/journal.pone.0249792

Grusec, J. E., Hastings, P., & Almas, A. (2011). Prosocial behavior. In P. K. Smith & C. H. Hart (Eds.), *The Wiley-Blackwell handbook of childhood social development* (2nd ed., pp. 549–566). Wiley-Blackwell.

Gu, J., Strauss, C., Bond, R., & Cavanagh, K. (2015). How do mindfulness-based cognitive therapy and mindfulness-based stress reduction improve mental health and wellbeing? A systematic review and meta-analysis of meditation studies. *Clinical Psychology Review, 37*, 1–12.

Guadiano, B. A. (2008). Cognitive behavioural therapies: Achievements and challenges. *Evidence-Based Mental Health, 11*(1), 5–7.

Gualtieri, S., & Denison, S. (2018). The development of the representativeness heuristic in young children. *Journal of Experimental Child Psychology, 174*, 60–76.

Guéguen, N., & De Gail, M. A. (2003). The effect of smiling on helping behavior: Smiling and good Samaritan behavior. *Communication Reports, 16*(2), 133–140.

Guéguen, N., & Jacob, C. (2001). Fund-raising on the web: The effect of an electronic foot-in-the-door on donation. *CyberPsychology & Behavior, 4*(6), 705–709.

Guilleminault, C., Moscovitch, A., Yuen, K., & Poyares, D. (2002). Atypical sexual behavior during sleep. *Psychosomatic Medicine, 64*(2), 328–336.

Guillin, O., Abi-Dargham, A., & Laruelle, M. (2007). Neurobiology of dopamine in schizophrenia. In A. Abi-Dargham & O. Guillin (Eds.), *Integrating the neurobiology of schizophrenia* (pp. 1–39). Elsevier.

Gulerce, A. (2006). History of psychology in Turkey as a sign of diverse modernization and global psychologization. In A. C. Brock (Ed.), *Internationalizing the history of psychology* (pp. 75–93). New York University Press.

Gunaratana, B. H. (2014). *Mindfulness in plain English (20th anniversary edition)*. Wisdom.

Gunderson, J. G. (2001). *Borderline personality disorder: A clinical guide*. American Psychiatric Association Press.

Güngör, D., Bornstein, M. H., De Leersnyder, J., Cote, L., Ceulemans, E., & Mesquita, B. (2013). Acculturation of personality: A three-culture study of Japanese, Japanese Americans, and European Americans. *Journal of Cross-Cultural Psychology, 44*(5), 701–718. https://doi.org/10.1177/0022022112470749

Gupta, A., Elheis, M., & Pansari, K. (2004). Imaging in psychiatric illnesses. *International Journal of Clinical Practice, 58*(9), 850–858.

Gupta, P., & Cohen, N. J. (2002). Theoretical and computational analysis of skill learning, repetition priming, and procedural memory. *Psychological Review, 109*(2), 401–448.

Gurstelle, E. B., & De Oliveira, J. L. (2004). Daytime parahypnagogia: A state of consciousness that occurs when we almost fall asleep. *Medical Hypotheses, 62*(2), 166–168.

Gurung, R. A. R. (2014). *Health psychology: A cultural approach*. (3rd ed.). Wadsworth Cengage Learning.

Gurung, R. A. R., & Neufeld, G. (Eds.). (2022). Introduction: The introductory psychology initiative. In R. A. R. Gurung & G. Neufeld (Eds.), *Transforming introductory psychology: Expert advice on teacher training, course design, and student success* (pp. 3–6). American Psychological Association. https://doi.org/10.1037/0000260-001

Güss, C. D., Tuason, M. T., Göltenboth, N., & Mironova, A. (2018). Creativity through the eyes of professional artists in Cuba, Germany, and Russia. *Journal of Cross-Cultural Psychology, 49*(2), 261–289.

Gustavson, C. R., Garcia, J., Hankins, W. G., & Rusiniak, K. W. (1974). Coyote predation control by aversive conditioning. *Science, 184*(4136), 581–583.

Gustavson, C. R., Holzer, G. A., Gustavson, J. C., & Vakoch, D. L. (1982). An evaluation of phenol methylcarbamates as taste aversion producing agents in caged blackbirds. *Applied Animal Ethology, 8*(6), 551–559.

Gustavson, C. R., Kelly, D. J., Seeney, M., & Garcia, J. (1976). Prey lithium aversions I: Coyotes and wolves. *Behavioral Biology, 17*(1), 61–72.

Gutheil, T. G., & Brodsky, A. (2008). *Preventing boundary violations in clinical practice*. Guilford Press.

Guthrie, R. V. (2004). *Even the rat was white: A historical view of psychology* (2nd ed.). Allyn & Bacon.

Gwaltney, C. J., Metrik, J., Kahler, C. W., & Shiffman, S. (2009). Self-efficacy and smoking cessation: A meta-analysis. *Psychology of Addictive Behaviors, 23*(1), 56–66.

Gyani, A., Shafran, R., Myles, P., & Rose, S. (2014). The gap between science and practice: How therapists make their clinical decisions. *Behavior Therapy, 45*(2), 199–211.

Haagen-Dazs. (2021). Vanilla ice cream. https://www.haagendazs.us/products/ice-cream/vanilla-ice-cream

Hackel, L. S., & Ruble, D. N. (1992). Changes in the marital relationship after the first baby is born: Predicting the impact of expectancy disconfirmation. *Journal of Personality and Social Psychology, 62*(6), 944.

Hackman, J. R., & Katz, N. (2010). Group behavior and performance. In S. T. Fiske, D. T. Gilbert, & G. Lindzey (Eds.), *Handbook of social psychology* (5th ed., Vol. 2, pp. 1208–1251). Wiley.

Hackney, C. M. (2010). Auditory processing: Peripheral. In E. B. Goldstein (Ed.), *Encyclopedia of perception* (pp. 180–183). Sage.

Hafer, C. L., & Begue, L. (2005). Experimental research on just-world theory: Problems, developments, and future challenges. *Psychological Bulletin, 131*(1), 128–167.

Hafner, H., & an der Heiden, W. (2008). Course and outcome. In K. T. Mueser & D. V. Jeste (Eds.), *Clinical handbook of schizophrenia* (pp. 100–113). Guilford Press.

Hagenauer, M. H., Perryman, J. I., Lee, T. M., & Carskadon, M. A. (2009). Adolescent changes in the homeostatic and circadian regulation of sleep. *Developmental Neuroscience, 31*(4), 276–284.

Hager, E. R., Cockerham, A., O'Reilly, N., Harrington, D., Harding, J., Hurley, K. M., & Black, M. M. (2017). Food swamps and food deserts in Baltimore City, MD, USA: Associations with dietary behaviours among urban adolescent girls. *Public Health Nutrition, 20*(14), 2598–2607. https://doi.org/10.1017/S1368980016002123

Haglund, K. A., & Fehring, R. J. (2010). The association of religiosity, sexual education, and parental factors with risky sexual behaviors among adolescents and young adults. *Journal of Religion and Health, 49*(4), 460–472.

Haidt, J. (2017). The unwisest idea on campus: Commentary on Lilienfeld (2017). *Perspectives on Psychological Science, 12*(1), 176–177.

Hair, N. L., Hanson, J. L., Wolfe, B. L., & Pollak, S. D. (2015). Association of child poverty, brain development, and academic achievement. *JAMA Pediatrics, 169*(9), 822–829.

Hajibayova, L., & Jacob, E. K. (2017). Factors influencing user-generated vocabularies: How basic are basic level terms? *Knowledge Organization, 42*(2), 102–112.

Hakulinen, C., Pulkki-Råback, L., Jokela, M., Ferrie, J. E., Aalto, A. M., Virtanen, M., Kivimäki, M., Vahtera, J., & Elovainio, M. (2016). Structural and functional aspects of social support as predictors of mental and physical health trajectories: Whitehall II cohort study. *Journal of Epidemiology Community Health, 70*(7), 710–715.

Halberstadt, A. G., Cooke, A. N., Garner, P. W., Hughes, S. A., Oertwig, D., & Neupert, S. D. (2020). Racialized emotion recognition accuracy and anger bias of children's faces. *Emotion*. Advance online publication. https://doi.org/10.1037/emo0000756

Hald, G. M., Seaman, C., & Linz, D. (2014). Sexuality and pornography. In D. Tolman, L. Diamond, J. Bauermeister, W. George, J. Pfaus, & M. Ward (Eds.), *APA handbook of sexuality and psychology: Contextual approaches* (Vol. 2, pp. 3–35). American Psychological Association.

Hale, L., & Guan, S. (2015). Screen time and sleep among school-aged children and adolescents: A systematic literature review. *Sleep Medicine Reviews, 21*, 50–58.

Halfon, S. (2021). Psychodynamic technique and therapeutic alliance in prediction of outcome in psychodynamic child psychotherapy. *Journal of Consulting and Clinical Psychology, 89*(2), 96–109. https://doi.org/10.1037/ccp0000620

Halford, G. S., & Andrews, G. (2006). Reasoning and problem solving. In D. Kuhn & R. Siegler (Vol. Eds.), *Handbook of child psychology* (6th ed., Vol. 2, pp. 557–608). Wiley.

Halim, M. L., Ruble, D. N., & Tamis-LeMonda, C. S. (2013). Four-year-olds' beliefs about how others regard males and females. *British Journal of Developmental Psychology, 31*(1), 128–135.

Hall, A. (2005). Audience personality and the selection of media and media genres. *Media Psychology, 7*(4), 377–398.

Hall, C. C. I. (1997). Cultural malpractice: The growing obsolescence of psychology with the changing U.S. population. *American Psychologist, 52*(6), 642–651.

Hall, C. C. I. (2014). The evolution of the revolution: The successful establishment of multicultural psychology. In F. T. L. Leong (Ed.), *APA handbook of multicultural psychology* (Vol. 1, pp. 3–18). American Psychological Association.

Hall, J. A. (2006). Women's and men's nonverbal communication: Similarities, differences, stereotypes, and origins. In V. Manusov & M. L. Patterson (Eds.), *The Sage handbook of nonverbal communication* (pp. 201–218). Sage.

Hall, J. A., Carter, J. D., & Horgan, T. G. (2000). Gender differences in nonverbal communication of emotion. In A. H. Fischer (Ed.), *Gender and emotion: Social psychological perspectives* (pp. 97–117). Cambridge University Press.

Hall, M., Levenson, J., & Hasler, B. (2012). Sleep and emotion. In C. M. Morin & C. A. Espie (Eds.), *The Oxford handbook of sleep and sleep disorders* (pp. 131–149). Oxford University Press.

Haller, D. L., & Acosta, M. C. (2010). Characteristics of pain patients with opioid-use disorder. *Psychosomatics, 51*(3), 257–266.

Haller, H., Winkler, M. M., Klose, P., Dobos, G., Kuemmel, S., & Cramer, H. (2017). Mindfulness-based interventions for women with breast cancer: An updated systematic review and meta-analysis. *Acta Oncologica, 56*(12), 1665–1676.

Halpern, D. F. (2012). *Sex differences in cognitive abilities* (4th ed). Psychology Press.

Halpern, D. F. (2017). Whither psychology. *Perspectives on Psychological Science, 12*(4), 665–668.

Halpern, D. F., Beninger, A. S., & Straight, C. A. (2011). Sex differences in intelligence. In R. J. Sternberg & S. B. Kaufman (Eds.), *The Cambridge handbook of intelligence* (pp. 253–272). Cambridge University Press.

Halvari, A. E. M., Halvari, H., Williams, G. C., & Deci, E. L. (2017). Predicting dental attendance from dental hygienists' autonomy support and patients' autonomous motivation: A randomised clinical trial. *Psychology & Health, 32*(2), 127–144.

Hambrick, D. Z., Kane, M. J., & Engle, R. W. (2005). The role of working memory in higher-level cognition: Domain-specific versus domain-general perspectives. In R. Sternberg & J. E. Pretz (Eds.), *Cognition and intelligence: Identifying the mechanisms of the mind* (pp. 104–121). Cambridge University Press.

Hambrick, D. Z., & Meinz, E. J. (2011). Limits on the predictive power of domain-specific experience and knowledge in skilled performance. *Current Directions in Psychological Science, 20*(5), 275–279.

Hambrick, D. Z., Oswald, F. L., Darowski, E. S., Rench, T. A., & Brou, R. (2010). Predictors of multitasking performance in a synthetic work paradigm. *Applied Cognitive Psychology, 24*(8), 1149–1167.

Hamer, M., Taylor, A., & Steptoe, A. (2006). The effect of acute aerobic exercise on stress related blood pressure responses: A systematic review and meta-analysis. *Biological Psychology, 71*(2), 183–190.

Hames, J. L., Bell, D. J., Perez-Lima, L. M., Holm-Denoma, J. M., Rooney, T., Charles, N. E., Thompson, S. M., Mehlenbeck, R. S., Tawfik, S. H., Fondacaro, K. M., Simmons, K. T., & Hoersting, R. C. (2020). Navigating uncharted waters: Considerations for training clinics in the rapid transition to telepsychology and telesupervision during COVID-19. *Journal of Psychotherapy Integration, 30*(2), 348–365. https://doi.org/10.1037/int0000224

Hamilton, W. D. (1964). The genetical evolution of social behaviour. I. *Journal of Theoretical Biology, 7*(1), 1–16.

Hamm, M. P., Newton, A. S., Chisholm, A., Shulhan, J., Milne, A., Sundar, P., Ennis, H., Scott, S. D., & Hartling, L. (2015). Prevalence and effect of cyberbullying on children and young people: A scoping review of social media studies. *JAMA Pediatrics, 169*(8), 770–777.

Hammen, C., & Watkins, E. (2008). *Depression* (2nd ed.). Psychology Press.

Hampton, J. A. (1995). Testing the prototype theory of concepts. *Journal of Memory and Language, 34*(5), 686–708.

Hampton, J. A. (2016). Categories, prototypes, and exemplars. In N. Riemer (Ed.), *The Routledge handbook of semantics* (pp. 125–141). Routledge.

Hanh, T. N. (1975). *The miracle of mindfulness: An introduction to the practice of meditation*. Beacon Press.

Haninger, K., & Thompson, K. M. (2004). Content and ratings of teen-rated video games. *The Journal of the American Medical Association, 291*(7), 856–865.

Hankin, B. L., Wetter, E., & Cheely, C. (2008). Sex differences in child and adolescent depression: A developmental psychopathological approach. In J. R. Z. Abela & B. L. Hankin (Eds.), *Handbook of depression in children and adolescents* (pp. 377–414). Guilford Press.

Hankivsky, O., & Kapilashrami, A. (2020). Intersectionality offers a radical rethinking of Covid-19. *BMJ, 20*(09), 26. https://laptrinhx.com/news/intersectionality-offers-a-radical-rethinking-of-covid-19-dmwoLpm/amp/

Hanley, G., Piazza, C., Fisher, W., & Maglieri, K. (2005). On the effectiveness of and preference for punishment and extinction components of function-based interventions. *Journal of Applied Behavior Analysis, 38*(1), 51–65.

Hannah, A., & Murachver, T. (2007). Gender preferential responses to speech. *Journal of Language and Social Psychology, 26*(3), 274–290.

Hannon, E. E., & Trainor, L. J. (2007). Music acquisition: Effects of enculturation and formal training on development. *Trends in Cognitive Sciences, 11*(11), 466–472.

Hannon, E. E., & Trehub, S. E. (2005a). Metrical categories in infancy and adulthood. *Psychological Science, 16*(1), 48–55.

Hannon, E. E., & Trehub, S. E. (2005b). Tuning in to musical rhythms: Infants learn more readily than adults. *Proceedings of the National Academy of Sciences of the United States of America, 102*(35), 12639–12643.

Hansen, S. N., Schendel, D. E., & Parner, E. T. (2015). Explaining the increase in the prevalence of autism spectrum disorders: The proportion attributable to changes in reporting practices. *JAMA Pediatrics, 169*(1), 56–62.

Hansenne, M., & Christophe, V. (2019). Further evidences of the role of personality on affective forecasting. *Polish Psychological Bulletin*, 270–274. https://doi.org/10.24425/ppb.2019.130700

Hanson, J., & Hackman, D. A. (2012). Cognitive neuroscience and disparities in socioeconomic status. In B. Wolfe (Ed.), *The biological consequences of socioeconomic inequalities* (pp. 158–186). Russell Sage Foundation.

Harackiewicz, J. M., Barron, K. E., Pintrich, P. R., Elliot, A. J., & Thrash, T. M. (2002a). Revision of achievement goal theory: Necessary and illuminating. *Journal of Educational Psychology, 94*(3), 638–645.

Harackiewicz, J. M., Barron, K. E., Tauer, J. M., Carter, S. M., & Elliot, A. J. (2000). Short-term and long-term consequences of achievement goals: Predicting interest and performance over time. *Journal of Educational Psychology, 92*(2), 316–330.

Harackiewicz, J. M., Barron, K. E., Tauer, J. M., & Elliot, A. J. (2002b). Predicting success in college: A longitudinal study of achievement goals and ability measures as predictors of interest and performance from freshman year through graduation. *Journal of Educational Psychology, 94*(3), 562–575.

Harbaugh, E., & Lindsey, E. W. (2015). Attitudes toward homosexuality among young adults: Connections to gender role identity, gender-typed activities, and religiosity. *Journal of Homosexuality, 62*(8), 1098–1125.

Harding, S. R., Flannelly, K. J., Weaver, A. J., & Costa, K. G. (2005). The influence of religion on death anxiety and death acceptance. *Mental Health, Religion & Culture, 8*(4), 253–261.

Hardy, M. S., & Calhoun, L. G. (1997). Psychological distress and the "medical student syndrome" in abnormal psychology students. *Teaching of Psychology, 24*(3), 192–193.

Hareli, S., & Hess, U. (2017). Facial expressions and emotion. *Encyclopedia of Personality and Individual Differences*, 1–7.

Harkins, S. G., & Jackson, J. M. (1985). The role of evaluation in eliminating social loafing. *Personality and Social Psychology Bulletin, 11*(4), 457–465.

Harlow, H. F. (1958). The nature of love. *American Psychologist, 13*, 673–685.

Harlow, H. F., & Harlow, M. (1962). Social deprivation in monkeys. *Scientific American, 207*, 136–146.

Harlow, H. F., & Zimmerman, R. (1958). The development of affection in infant monkeys. *Proceedings of the American Philosophical Society, 102*(5), 501–509.

Harlow, H. F., & Zimmerman, R. (1959). Affectional responses in the infant monkey. *Science, 130*(3373), 421–432.

Harmon-Jones, E., & Mills, J. (1999). An introduction to cognitive dissonance theory and an overview of current perspectives on the theory. In E. Harmon-Jones & J. Mills (Eds.), *Cognitive dissonance: Progress on a pivotal theory in social psychology* (pp. 3–21). American Psychological Association.

Harrell, S. P. (2000). A multidimensional conceptualization of racism-related stress: Implications for the well-being of people of color. *American Journal of Orthopsychiatry, 70*(1), 42–57.

Harrington, A. (2008). *The cure within: A history of mind-body medicine*. W. W. Norton.

Harris Interactive & Witeck-Combs. (2010). *The lesbian, gay, bisexual, and transgender population at a glance*. Harris Interactive.

Harris, A. (2012). Transference, countertransference, and the real relationship. In G. O. Gabbard, B. E. Litowitz, & P. Williams (Eds.), *Textbook of psychoanalysis* (2nd ed., pp. 255–268). American Psychiatric Publishing.

Harris, C., & Alvarado, N. (2005). Facial expressions, smile types, and self-report during humour, tickle, and pain. *Cognition & Emotion, 19*(5), 655–669.

Harris, G. (2011, March 5). Talk doesn't pay, so psychiatry turns instead to drug therapy. *The New York Times*. http://www.nytimes.com/2011/03/06/health/policy/06 doctors.html?_r=1&pagewanted=all

Harris, P. E., Cooper, K. L., Relton, C., & Thomas, K. J. (2012). Prevalence of complementary and alternative medicine (CAM) use by the general population: A systematic review and update. *International Journal of Clinical Practice, 66*(10), 924–939.

Harrison, K., & Cantor, J. (1999). Tales from the screen: Enduring fright reactions to scary media. *Media Psychology, 1*(2), 97–116.

Harrison, Y. (2012). The functions of sleep. In C. M. Morin & C. A. Espie (Eds.), *The Oxford handbook of sleep and sleep disorders* (pp. 61–74). Oxford University Press.

Harrow, M., Hansford, B. G., & Astrachan-Fletcher, E. B. (2009). Locus of control: Relation to schizophrenia, to recovery, and to depression and psychosis—A 15-year longitudinal study. *Psychiatry Research, 168*(3), 186–192.

Hart, C. N., Jelalian, E., & Raynor, H. A. (2020). Behavioral and social routines and biological rhythms in prevention and treatment of pediatric obesity. *American Psychologist, 75*(2), 152–162. https://doi.org/10.1037/amp0000599

Hartman, J. D., Patock-Peckham, J. A., Corbin, W. R., Gates, J. R., Leeman, R. F., Luk, J. W., & King, K. M. (2015). Direct and indirect links between parenting styles, self-concealment (secrets), impaired control over drinking and alcohol-related outcomes. *Addictive Behaviors, 40*, 102–108.

Hartmann, M., Kopf, S., Kircher, C., Faude-Lang, V., Djuric, Z., Augstein, F., Friederich, H.-C., Kieser, M., Bierhaus, A., Humpert, P. M., Herzog, W., & Nawroth, P. P. (2012). Sustained effects of a mindfulness-based stress-reduction intervention in type 2 diabetic patients: Design and first results of a randomized controlled trial (the Heidelberger Diabetes and Stress-Study). *Diabetes Care, 35*(5), 945–947.

Hartup, W. W. (1999). Peer experience and its developmental significance. In M. Bennett (Ed.), *Developmental psychology: Achievements and prospects* (pp. 106–125). Psychology Press.

Hartz, A. J., Rupley, D. C., Kalkhoff, R. D., & Rimm, A. A. (1983). Relationship of obesity to diabetes: Influence of obesity level and body fat distribution. *Preventive Medicine, 12*(2), 351–357.

Hartzler, B. M. (2014). Fatigue on the flight deck: The consequences of sleep loss and the benefits of napping. *Accident Analysis & Prevention, 62*, 309–318.

Harvey, R. D., Tennial, R. E., & Hudson Banks, K. (2017). The development and validation of a colorism scale. *Journal of Black Psychology, 43*(7), 740–764. https://doi.org/10.1177/0095798417690054

Harwood, K., McLean, N., & Durkin, K. (2007). First-time mothers' expectations of parenthood: What happens when optimistic expectations are not matched by later experiences? *Developmental Psychology, 43*(1), 1–12.

Hasher, L., & Zacks, R. T. (1979). Automatic and effortful processes in memory. *Journal of Experimental Psychology: General, 108*(3), 356–388.

Hasher, L., & Zacks, R. T. (1984). Automatic processing of fundamental information: The case of frequency of occurrence. *American Psychologist, 39*(12), 1372–1388.

Haslam, N., & Levy, S. R. (2006). Essentialist beliefs about homosexuality: Structure and implications for prejudice. *Personality and Social Psychology Bulletin, 32*(4), 471–485.

Hatfield, E., & Rapson, R. (1993). *Love, sex, and intimacy: The psychology, biology, and history*. HarperCollins.

Hatfield, E., & Sprecher, S. (1986). Measuring passionate love in intimate relationships. *Journal of Adolescence, 9*(4), 383–410.

Hatfield, E., Luckhurst, C., & Rapson, R. L. (2010). Sexual motives: Cultural, evolutionary, and social psychological perspectives. *Sexuality & Culture, 14*(3), 173–190.

Hattie, J. (1992). *Self-concept*. Lawrence Erlbaum.

Hatzenbuehler, M. L., & McLaughlin, K. A. (2017). Sex, sexual orientation, and depression. In R. J. DeRubeis & D. R. Strunk (Eds.), *The Oxford handbook of mood disorders* (pp. 49–59). Oxford University Press.

Hatzenbuehler, M. L., McLaughlin, K. A., Keyes, K. M., & Hasin, D. S. (2010). The impact of institutional discrimination on psychiatric disorders in lesbian, gay, and bisexual populations: A prospective study. *American Journal of Public Health, 100*(3), 452–459.

Hauck, F. R., Signore, C., Fein, S. B., & Raju, T. N. (2008). Infant sleeping arrangements and practices during the first year of life. *Pediatrics, 122*(Suppl. 2), S113–S120.

Haus, E. L., & Smolensky, M. H. (2013). Shift work and cancer risk: Potential mechanistic roles of circadian disruption, light at night, and sleep deprivation. *Sleep Medicine Reviews, 17*(4), 273–284.

Hauser, D. J., & Schwarz, N. (2015). The war on prevention: Bellicose cancer metaphors hurt (some) prevention intentions. *Personality and Social Psychology Bulletin, 41*(1), 66–77.

Hawkins, R. D., Clark, G. A., & Kandel, E. R. (2006). Brief communications: Operant conditioning of gill withdrawal in *Aplysia*. *The Journal of Neuroscience, 26*(9), 2443–2448.

Hay, D. F. (2017). The early development of human aggression. *Child Development Perspectives, 11*(2), 102–106.

Hay, P. (2021). Is orthorexia nervosa a healthy way of being or a mental health disorder? Commentary on He et al.(2020). *International Journal of Eating Disorders, 54*(2), 222–224. https://doi.org/10.1002/eat.23465

Hayashi, M., Watanabe, M., & Hori, T. (1999). The effects of a 20 min nap in the mid-afternoon on mood, performance and EEG activity. *Clinical Neurophysiology, 110*(2), 272–279.

Hayatbini, N., & Oberle, C. D. (2019). Are orthorexia nervosa symptoms associated with cognitive inflexibility? *Psychiatry Research, 271*, 464–468.

Haycock, D. A. (2014). *Murderous minds: Exploring the criminal psychopathic brain: Neurological imaging and the manifestation of evil*. Pegasus Books.

Hayes, J. P., Morey, R. A., Petty, C. M., Seth, S., Smoski, M. J., McCarthy, G., & LaBar, K. S. (2010). Staying cool when things get hot: Emotion regulation modulates neural mechanisms of memory encoding. *Frontiers in Human Neuroscience, 4*, 1–10.

Hayes, S. C. (2004). Acceptance and commitment therapy and the new behavior therapies: Mindfulness, acceptance, and relationship. In S. C. Hayes, V. M. Follette, & M. M. Linehan (Eds.), *Mindfulness and acceptance: Expanding the cognitive-behavioral tradition* (pp. 1–29). Guilford Press.

Hayes, S. C., Strosahl, K., & Wilson, K. G. (2012). *Acceptance and commitment therapy: The process and practice of mindful change* (2nd ed.). Guilford Press.

Hayes, S. C., Villatte, M., Levin, M., & Hildebrandt, M. (2011). Open, aware, and active: Contextual approaches as an emerging trend in the behavioral and cognitive therapies. *Annual Review of Clinical Psychology, 7*, 141–168.

Hayes, S., Hirsch, C., & Mathews, A. (2008). Restriction of working memory capacity during worry. *Journal of Abnormal Psychology, 117*(3), 712– 717.

Hayes-Skelton, J. A., & Wadsworth, L. P. (2015). Mindfulness in the treatment of anxiety. In K. W. Brown, J. D. Creswell, & R. M. Ryan (Eds.), *Handbook of mindfulness: Theory, research, and practice* (pp. 367–386). Guilford Press.

Haynes, S. N., & Kaholokula, J. K. (2008). Behavioral assessment. In M. Hersen & A. M. Gross (Eds.), *Handbook of clinical psychology* (Vol. 1, pp. 495–522). Wiley.

Hays, P. A. (1996). Addressing the complexities of culture and gender in counseling. *Journal of Counseling & Development, 74*(4), 332–338. https://doi.org/10.1002/j.1556-6676.1996.tb01876.x

Hays, P. A. (2008). *Addressing cultural complexities in practice: Assessment, diagnosis, and therapy* (2nd ed.). American Psychological Association.

Hays, P. A. (2013). *Connecting across cultures*. Sage. https://us.sagepub.com/en-us/nam/connecting-across-cultures/book237541

Hays, P. A. (2022). *Addressing cultural complexities in counseling and clinical practice: An intersectional approach* (4th ed.). American Psychological Association. https://www.apa.org/pubs/books/addressing-cultural-complexities-counseling-clinical-practice?tab=1

Hazlett-Stevens, H., & Craske, M. G. (2008). Live (in vivo) exposure. In W. T. O'Donohue & J. E. Fisher (Eds.), *Cognitive behavior therapy: Applying empirically supported techniques in your practice* (2nd ed., pp. 309–316). Wiley.

Hazlett-Stevens, H., Pruitt, L. D., & Collins, A. (2009). Phenomenology of generalized anxiety disorder. In M. M. Antony & M. B. Stein (Eds.), *Oxford handbook of anxiety and related disorders* (pp. 47–55). Oxford University Press.
He, S. (2010). Selective adaptation. In E. B. Goldstein (Ed.), *Encyclopedia of perception* (pp. 879–881). Sage.
Head, L. S., & Gross, A. M. (2008). Systematic desensitization. In W. T. O'Donohue & J. E. Fisher (Eds.), *Cognitive behavior therapy: Applying empirically supported techniques in your practice* (2nd ed., pp. 542–549). Wiley.
Head, L. S., & Gross, A. M. (2009). Systematic desensitization. In W. O'Donohue & J. E. Fisher (Eds.), *General principles and empirically supported techniques of cognitive behavior therapy* (pp. 640–647). Wiley.
Heaps, C. M., & Nash, M. (2001). Comparing recollective experience in true and false autobiographical memories. *Journal of Experimental Psychology: Learning, Memory, and Cognition, 27*(4), 920–930.
Heatherton, T. F., & Sargent, J. D. (2009). Does watching smoking in movies promote teenage smoking? *Current Directions in Psychological Science, 18*(2), 63–67.
Hebl, M. R., & Turchin, J. M. (2005). The stigma of obesity: What about men? *Basic and Applied Social Psychology, 27*(3), 267–275.
Heckhausen, J., & Heckhausen, H. (2018). Development of motivation. In J. Heckhausen & H. Heckhausen (Eds.), *Motivation and action* (pp. 679–743). Springer.
Hedegaard, M. (1992). The zone of proximal development as basis for instruction. In L. C. Moll (Ed.), *Vygotsky and education: Instructional implications and applications of sociohistorical psychology* (pp. 349–371). Cambridge University Press.
Hedges, L. V., & Nowell, A. (1995). Sex differences in mental test scores, variability, and numbers of high-scoring individuals. *Science, 269*(5220), 41–45.
Hedman-Lagerlöf, M., Hedman-Lagerlöf, E., & Öst, L. G. (2018). The empirical support for mindfulness-based interventions for common psychiatric disorders: A systematic review and meta-analysis. *Psychological Medicine, 48*(13), 2116–2129.
Hegarty, J. D., Baldessarine, R. J., Tohen, M., Waternaux, C., & Oepen, G. (1994). One hundred years of schizophrenia: A meta-analysis of the outcome literature. *American Journal of Psychiatry, 151*(10), 1409–1416.
Hegarty, M., & Waller, D. A. (2005). Individual differences in spatial abilities. In A. Miyake & P. Shah (Eds.), *The Cambridge handbook of visuospatial thinking* (pp. 121–169). Cambridge University Press.
Hegarty, P., & Pratto, F. (2001). Sexual orientation beliefs: Their relationship to anti-gay attitudes and biological determinist arguments. *Journal of Homosexuality, 41*(1), 121–135.
Heiby, E. M., & Haynes, S. N. (2004). Introduction to behavioral assessment. In S. N. Haynes & E. M. Heiby (Eds.), *Comprehensive handbook of psychological assessment: Behavioral assessment* (Vol. 3, pp. 3–18). Wiley.
Heider, F. (1958). *The psychology of interpersonal relations*. Wiley.
Heine, S. J., & Lehman, D. R. (1995). Cultural variation in unrealistic optimism: Does the West feel more vulnerable than the East? *Journal of Personality and Social Psychology, 68*(4), 595–607.
Heine, S. J., Kitayama, S., Lehman, D. R., Takata, T., Ide, E., Leung, C., & Matsumoto, H. (2001). Divergent consequences of success and failure in Japan and North America: An investigation of self-improving motivations and malleable selves. *Journal of Personality and Social Psychology, 81*(4), 599–615.
Heine, S. J., Lehman, D. R., Markus, H. R., & Kitayama, S. (1999). Is there a universal need for positive self-regard? *Psychological Review, 106*(4), 766–794.
Heinze, J. E., & Horn, S. S. (2009). Intergroup contact and beliefs about homosexuality in adolescence. *Journal ofYouth and Adolescence, 38*(7), 937–951.
Heinze, J. E., Kruger, D. J., Reischl, T. M., Cupal, S., & Zimmerman, M. A. (2015). Relationships among disease, social support, and perceived health: A lifespan approach. *American Journal of Community Psychology, 56*(3–4), 268–279.
Held, Lisa. (2010). Profile of Leta Hollingworth. In A. Rutherford (Ed.), Psychology's feminist voices multimedia internet archive. https://feministvoices.com/profiles/leta-hollingworth
Helgeson, V. S. (2011). Gender, stress, and coping. In S. Folkman (Ed.), *Oxford handbook of stress, health, and coping* (pp. 63–85). Oxford University Press.
Heller, S. B., Shah, A. K., Guryan, J., Ludwig, J., Mullainathan, S., & Pollack, H. A. (2017). Thinking, fast and slow? Some field experiments to reduce crime and dropout in Chicago. *The Quarterly Journal of Economics, 132*(1), 1–54.
Helliwell, J. F., Huang, H., & Wang, S. (2017a). The social foundations of world happiness. In J. Helliwell, R., Layard, & J. Sachs (Eds.), *World happiness report 2017* (Chapter 2). Sustainable Development Solutions Network.
Helliwell, J. F., Huang, H., Wang, S., & Norton, M. (2021). World happiness, trust and deaths under COVID-19. In J. F. Helliwell, H. Huang, S. Wang, & M. Norton (Eds.), *World happiness report 2021*. Sustainable Development Solutions Network. https://happiness-report.s3.amazonaws.com/2021/WHR+21_Ch2.pdf
Helliwell, J., Layard, R., & Sachs, J. (2017b). *World happiness report 2017.* Sustainable Development Solutions Network.
Helm, A. F., & Spencer, R. M. (2019). Television use and its effects on sleep in early childhood. *Sleep Health, 5*(3), 241–247. https://doi.org/10.1016/j.sleh.2019.02.009
Helm, R. K., McCormick, M. J., & Reyna, V. F. (2018). Expert decision making: A fuzzy-trace theory perspective. In L. J. Ball & V. A. Thompson (Eds.), *Routledge international handbook of thinking and reasoning* (pp. 289–303). Routledge.
Helmholtz, H. V. (1852). LXXXI. On the theory of compound colours. *Philosophical Magazine Series 4, 4*(28), 519–534.
Helms, J. E. (2006). Fairness is not validity or cultural bias in racial-group assessment: A quantitative perspective. *American Psychologist, 61*(8), 845–859.
Helms, J. L., & Rogers, D. T. (2015). *Majoring in psychology: Achieving your educational and career goals* (2nd ed.). Wiley-Blackwell.
Helstrup, T., De Beni, R., Cornoldi, C., & Koriat, A. (2007). Memory pathways: Involuntary and voluntary processes in retrieving personal memories. In S. Magnussen & T. Helstrup (Eds.), *Everyday memory* (pp. 291–315). Psychology Press.
Helwig, C. C., & Turiel, E. (2011). Children's social and moral reasoning. In P. K. Smith & C. H. Hart (Eds.), *The Wiley-Blackwell handbook of childhood social development* (2nd ed., pp. 567–583). Wiley-Blackwell.
Helzner, E. P., Cauley, J. A., Pratt, S. R., Wisniewski, S. R., Zmuda, J. M., Talbott, E. O., de Rekeneire, N., Harris, T. B., Rubin, S. M., Simonsick, E. M.,Tylavsky, F. A., & Newman, A. B. (2005). Race and sex differences in age-related hearing loss: The Health, Aging and Body Composition Study. *Journal of the American Geriatrics Society, 53*(12), 2119–2127.
Henderlong, J., & Lepper, M. R. (2002). The effects of praise on children's intrinsic motivation: A review and synthesis. *Psychological Bulletin, 128*(5), 774–795.
Henderson, V. R., & Kelly, B. (2005). Food advertising in the age of obesity: Content analysis of food advertising on general market and African American television. *Journal of Nutrition Education and Behavior, 37*(4), 191–196.
Hendry, L. B., & Kloep, M. (2007). Conceptualizing emerging adulthood: Inspecting the emperor's new clothes? *Child Development Perspectives, 1*(2), 74–79.
Henry J. Kaiser Family Foundation. (2014). Population distribution by race/ethnicity. http://kff.org/other/state-indicator/distribution-by-raceethnicity/
Henry, L. A. (2001). How does the severity of a learning disability affect working memory performance? *Memory, 9*(4–6), 233–247.
Hensley, C. J., Otani, H., & Knoll, A. R. (2018). Reducing negative emotional memories by retroactive interference. *Cognition and Emotion, 33*(4), 801–815.
Hepper, P. (2003). Prenatal psychological and behavioural development. In J. Valsiner & K. Connolly (Eds.), *Handbook of developmental psychology* (pp. 91–113). Sage.
Hepper, P. G., Dornan, J. C., & Lynch, C. (2012). Sex differences in fetal habituation. *Developmental Science, 15*(3), 373–383.
Herbst-Damm, K. L., & Kulik, J. A. (2005). Volunteer support, marital status, and the survival times of terminally ill patients. *Health Psychology, 24*(2), 225–229.
Herek, G. M. (2000). Sexual prejudice and gender: Do heterosexuals' attitudes toward lesbians and gay men differ? *Journal of Social Issues, 56*(2), 251–266.
Herek, G. M., Norton, A. T., Allen, T. J., & Sims, C. L. (2010). Demographic, psychological, and social characteristics of self-identified lesbian, gay, and bisexual adults in a U.S. probability sample. *Sexuality Research and Social Policy, 7*(3), 176–200.
Hering, E. (1878). *Zur lehre vom lichtsinne* (Vol. 68). Kaiserlichen Akademie der Wissenschaften.
Hering, E. (1964). *Outlines of a theory of the light sense* (L. M. Hurvich & D. Jameson, Trans.). Harvard University Press.
Herman, K. M., Hopman, W. M., & Sabiston, C. M. (2015). Physical activity, screen time and self-rated health and mental health in Canadian adolescents. *Preventive Medicine, 73*, 112–116.
Hernandez, K. M., Mahoney, A., & Pargament, K. I. (2014). Sexuality and religion. In D. L. Tolman & L. M. Diamond (Eds.), *APA handbook of sexuality and psychology* (Vol. 2, pp. 425–447). American Psychological Association.
Hernández-Díaz, S., Werler, M. M., Walker, A. M., & Mitchell, A. A. (2000). Folic acid antagonists during pregnancy and the risk of birth defects. *New England Journal of Medicine, 343*(22), 1608–1614.
Herrnstein, R. J., & Murray, C. (1994). *Bell curve: Intelligence and class structure in American life*. Free Press.
Hershey, D. A., Jacobs-Lawson, J. M., & Wilson, T. L. (2006). Research as a script. In F. T. L. Leong & J. T. Austin (Eds.), *The psychology research handbook: A guide for graduate students and research assistants* (2nd ed., pp. 3–22). Sage.
Hershey, D. A., Wilson, T. L., & Mitchell-Copeland, J. (1996). Conceptions of the psychological research process: Script variation as a function of training and experience. *Current Psychology, 14*(4), 293–312.
Hershner, S. (2013). Impact of sleep on the challenges of safe driving in young adults. In A. R. Wolfson & H. Montgomery-Downs (Eds.), *The Oxford handbook of infant, child, and adolescent sleep and behavior* (pp. 441–455). Oxford University Press.
Hertel, P. (2004). Memory for emotional and nonemotional events in depression: A question of habit? In D. Reisberg & P. Hertel (Eds.), *Memory and emotion* (pp. 186–216). Oxford University Press.
Hertenstein, E., Voinescu, B., & Riemann, D. (2017). The treatment of insomnia: The state of the science and practice. In D. David, S. J. Lynn, & G. H. Montgomery (Eds.), *Evidence based psychotherapy* (pp. 465–506). Wiley.
Herts, K. L., Khaled, M. M., & Stanton, A. L. (2017). Correlates of self-efficacy for disease management in adolescent/young adult cancer survivors: A systematic review. *Health Psychology, 36*(3), 192–205.
Herz, R. S. (1997). The effects of cue distinctiveness on odor-based context-dependent memory. *Memory & Cognition, 25*(3), 375–380.
Hespos, S. J., & Baillargeon, R. (2008). Young infants' actions reveal their developing knowledge of support variables: Converging evidence for violation-of-expectation findings. *Cognition, 107*(1), 304–316.
Hespos, S. J., & Baillargeon, R. (2008). Young infants' actions reveal their developing knowledge of support variables: Converging evidence for violation-of-expectation findings. *Cognition, 107*(1), 304–316.
Hess, T. M., Auman, C., Colcombe, S. J., & Rahhal, T. A. (2003). The impact of stereotype threat on age differences in memory performance. *The Journals of Gerontology Series B: Psychological Sciences and Social Sciences, 58*(1), P3–P11.
Hess, U., Adams, R. B., Simard, A., Stevenson, M. T., & Kleck, R. E. (2012). Smiling and sad wrinkles: Age-related changes in the face and the perception of emotions and intentions. *Journal of Experimental Social Psychology, 48*(6), 1377–1380.
Hess, U., & Thibault, P. (2009). Darwin and emotion expression. *American Psychologist, 64*(2), 120–128.
Hetherington, M. M. (2019). The portion size effect and overconsumption-towards downsizing solutions for children and adolescents-an update. *Nutrition Bulletin, 44*(2), 130–137. https://doi.org/10.1111/nbu.12375
Hetherington, M. M., & Blundell-Birtill, P. (2018). The portion size effect and overconsumption-towards downsizing solutions for children and adolescents. *Nutrition Bulletin, 43*(1), 61–68. https://doi.org/10.1111/nbu.12307
Hettema, J., Steele, J., & Miller, W. R. (2005). Motivational interviewing. *Annual Review of Clinical Psychology, 1*, 91–111.
Hettich, P. (2014). APA Guidelines for the Undergraduate Psychology Major, Version 2.0: Your covert career counselor. *Psychology Student Network*. https://www.apa.org/ed/precollege/psn/2014/09/career-counselor
Heyes, C. (2010). Where do mirror neurons come from? *Neuroscience & Biobehavioral Reviews, 34*(4), 575–583.
Heyman, G. D., & Dweck, C. S. (1992). Achievement goals and intrinsic motivation: Their relation and their role in adaptive motivation. *Motivation and Emotion, 16*(3), 231–247.
Heyman, G. D., & Lee, K. (2012). Moral development: Revisiting Kohlberg's stages. In A. M. Slater & P. C. Quinn (Eds.), *Developmental psychology: Revisiting the classic studies* (pp. 164–175). Sage.
Heyman, G. D., Fu, G., & Lee, K. (2008). Reasoning about the disclosure of success and failure to friends among children in the United States and China. *Developmental Psychology, 44*(4), 908.
Hick, S. F. (2008). Cultivating therapeutic relationships: The role of mindfulness. In S. F. Hick & T. Bien (Eds.), *Mindfulness and the therapeutic relationship* (pp. 3–18). Guilford Press.
Hickok, G., & Poeppel, D. (2007). The cortical organization of speech processing. *Nature Reviews Neuroscience, 8*(5), 393–402.
Hiemstra, M., de Leeuw, R. N., Engels, R. C., & Otten, R. (2017). What parents can do to keep their children from smoking: A systematic review on smoking-specific parenting strategies and smoking onset. *Addictive Behaviors, 70*, 107–128.
Hieronymus, F., Lisinski, A., Eriksson, E., & Østergaard, S. D. (2021). Do side effects of antidepressants impact efficacy estimates based on the Hamilton Depression Rating Scale? A pooled patient-level analysis. *Translational Psychiatry, 11*(1), 1–9. https://doi.org/10.1038/s41398-021-01364-0
Higgins, E. T. (1997). Beyond pleasure and pain. *American Psychologist, 52*(12), 1280–1300.
Higgins, E. T. (2000). Making a good decision: Value from fit. *American Psychologist, 55*(11), 1217–1230.

Higgins, E. T. (2002). How self-regulation creates distinct values: The case of promotion and prevention decision making. *Journal of Consumer Psychology, 12*(3), 177–191.

Higgins, E. T. (2008). Regulatory fit. In J. Y. Shah & W. L. Gardner (Eds.), *Handbook of motivation science* (pp. 356–372). Guilford Press.

Higgins, E. T. (2011). *Beyond pleasure and pain: How motivation works*. Oxford University Press.

Higgs, S., & Ruddock, H. (2020) Social influences on eating. In Meiselman, H. (ed.)., *Handbook of Eating and Drinking*. Springer, Cham. https://doi.org/10.1007/978-3-030-14504-0_27

Hilgard, E. R., Leary, D. E., & McGuire, G. R. (1991). The history of psychology: A survey and critical assessment. *Annual Review of Psychology, 42*(1), 79–107.

Hill, A. K., Dawood, K., & Puts, D. A. (2013). Biological foundations of sexual orientation. In C. J. Patterson & A. R. D'Augelli (Eds.), *Handbook of psychology and sexual orientation* (pp. 55–68). Oxford University Press.

Hill, C. E., & Knox, S. (2010). The use of dreams in modern psychotherapy. *International Review of Neurobiology, 92*, 291–317.

Hill, D. C., Moss, R. H., Sykes-Muskett, B., Conner, M., & O'Connor, D. B. (2018). Stress and eating behaviors in children and adolescents: Systematic review and meta-analysis. *Appetite, 123*, 14–22.

Hill, N. E. & Redding, A. (2021). The real reason young adults seem slow to "grow up": It's not a new developmental stage; it's the economy. *The Atlantic*, April 28, 2021. https://www.theatlantic.com/family/archive/2021/04/real-reason-young-adults-seem-slow-grow/618733/

Himmel, S., & Himmel, L. (2009). *Hungry: A mother and daughter fight anorexia*. Berkley Books.

Hinduja, S. (2008). Deindividuation and Internet software piracy. *CyberPsychology & Behavior, 11*(4), 391–398.

Hinduja, S., & Patchin, J. W. (2010). Cyberbullying identification, prevention, and response. http://www.cyberbullying.us/Cyberbullying_Identification_Prevention_Response_Fact_Sheet.pdf

Hinshaw, S. P. (2007). *The mark of shame: Stigma of mental illness and an agenda for change*. Oxford University Press.

Hinshaw, S. P. (2017). *Another kind of madness: A journey through the stigma and hope of mental illness*. St. Martin's Press.

Hinshaw, S. P., & Ellison, K. (2016). *ADHD: What everyone needs to know*. Oxford University Press.

Hinshaw, S. P., Heller, T., & McHale, J. P. (1992). Covert antisocial behavior in boys with attention-deficit hyperactivity disorder: External validation and effects of methylphenidate. *Journal of Consulting and Clinical Psychology, 60*(2), 274–281.

Hinshaw, S. P., & Scheffler, R. M. (2014). *The ADHD explosion: Myths, medication, money, and today's push for performance*. Oxford University Press.

Hinton, D. E., Hsia, C., Park, L., Rasmussen, A., & Pollack, M. H. (2009). Cultural anthropology and anxiety diagnoses. In D. McKay, J. S. Abramowitz, S. Taylor, & G. J. G. Asmundson (Eds.), *Current perspectives on the anxiety disorders: Implications for DSM-V and beyond* (pp. 245–274). Springer.

Hipson, W. E., & Séguin, D. G. (2016). Is good fit related to good behaviour? Goodness of fit between daycare teacher-child relationships, temperament, and prosocial behaviour. *Early Child Development and Care, 186*(5), 785–798.

Hirshkowitz, M., & Lee-Chiong, T. (2006). Positive airway pressure therapy for obstructive sleep apnea. In T. L. Lee-Chiong (Ed.), *Sleep: A comprehensive handbook* (pp. 355–364). Wiley-Liss.

Hirst, W., & Meksin, R. (2018). Aligning flashbulb memories and collective memories. In O. Luminet & A. Curci (Eds.), *Flashbulb memories: New challenges and future perspectives* (2nd ed., pp. 201–218). Routledge.

His Holiness the Dalai Lama. (2011). *Beyond religion: Ethics for a whole world*. Houghton-Mifflin.

Ho, S. C., Chong, H. Y., Chaiyakunapruk, N., Tangiisuran, B., & Jacob, S. A. (2016). Clinical and economic impact of non-adherence to antidepressants in major depressive disorder: A systematic review. *Journal of Affective Disorders, 193*, 1–10.

Hoagland, H. (1930). The Weber–Fechner law and the all-or-none theory. *The Journal of General Psychology, 3*(3), 351–373.

Hobson, J. A. (2009). REM sleep and dreaming: Towards a theory of protoconsciousness. *Nature Reviews Neuroscience, 10*(11), 803–813.

Hobson, J. A., & McCarley R. W. (1977). The brain as a dream state generator: An activation-synthesis hypothesis of the dream process. *American Journal of Psychiatry, 134*(12), 1335–1348.

Hock, R. R. (2013). Preface. In R. R. Hock, *Forty studies that changed psychology: Explorations into the history of psychological research* (7th ed., pp. xi–xviii). Pearson.

Hodapp, R. M., Evans, D. W., and Gray, F. L. (1999). Intellectual development in children with Down syndrome. In J. Rondal, J. Perera, & L. Nadel (Eds.), *Down syndrome: A review of current knowledge* (pp. 124–132). Whurr.

Hodapp, R. M., Griffin, M. M., Burke, M. M., & Fisher, M. H. (2011). Intellectual disabilities. In R. J. Sternberg & S. B. Kaufman (Eds.), *The Cambridge handbook of intelligence* (pp. 193–209). Cambridge University Press.

Hodges, E. V., Boivin, M., Vitaro, F., & Bukowski, W. M. (1999). The power of friendship: Protection against an escalating cycle of peer victimization. *Developmental Psychology, 35*(1), 94–101.

Hodges, J. R. (2000). Memory in the dementias. In E. Tulving & F. I. M. Craik (Eds.), *The Oxford handbook of memory* (pp. 441–459). Oxford University Press.

Hoehl, S., Hellmer, K., Johansson, M., & Gredebäck, G. (2017). Itsy bitsy spider ...: Infants react with increased arousal to spiders and snakes. *Frontiers in Psychology, 8*, 1710.

Hoekstra, S. J., Harris, R. J., & Helmick, A. L. (1999). Autobiographical memories about the experience of seeing frightening movies in childhood. *Media Psychology, 1*(2), 117–140.

Hoelter, L. (2009). Divorce and separation. In D. Carr (Ed.), *Encyclopedia of the life course and human development* (Vol. 2, pp. 100–104). Gale/Cengage.

Hoerger, M., Chapman, B., & Duberstein, P. (2016). Realistic affective forecasting: The role of personality. *Cognition and Emotion, 30*(7), 1304–1316.

Hofer, M. A. (2010). Evolutionary concepts of anxiety. In D. J. Stein, E. Hollander, & B. O. Rothbaum (Eds.), *Textbook of anxiety disorders* (2nd ed., pp. 129–145). American Psychiatric Association.

Hoffmann, H. (2017). Situating human sexual conditioning. *Archives of Sexual Behavior, 46*(8), 2213–2229.

Hoffmann, H., Goodrich, D., Wilson, M., & Janssen, E. (2014). The role of classical conditioning in sexual compulsivity: A pilot study. *Sexual Addiction & Compulsivity, 21*(2), 75–91.

Hoffmann, H., Janssen, E., & Turner, S. L. (2004). Classical conditioning of sexual arousal in women and men: Effects of varying awareness and biological relevance of the conditioned stimulus. *Archives of Sexual Behavior, 33*(1), 43–53.

Hoffmann, H., Peterson, K., & Garner, H. (2012). Field conditioning of sexual arousal in humans. *Socioaffective Neuroscience & Psychology, 2*(1), 17336.

Hofmann, S. G., Alpers, G. W., & Pauli, P. (2009a). Phenomenology of panic and phobic disorders. In M. M. Antony & M. B. Stein (Eds.), *Oxford handbook of anxiety and related disorders* (pp. 34–46). Oxford University Press.

Hofmann, S. G., Asmundson, G. J., & Beck, A. T. (2013). The science of cognitive therapy. *Behavior Therapy, 44*(2), 199–212.

Hofmann, S. G., Richey, J. A., Sawyer, A., Asnaani, A., & Rief, W. (2009b). Social anxiety disorder and the DSM-V. In D. McKay, J. S. Abramowitz, S. Taylor, & G. J. G. Asmundson (Eds.), *Current perspectives on the anxiety disorders: Implications for DSM-V and beyond* (pp. 411–430). Springer.

Hofmann, S. G., Sawyer, A. T., Witt, A. A., & Oh, D. (2010). The effect of mindfulness-based therapy on anxiety and depression: A meta-analytic review. *Journal of Consulting and Clinical Psychology, 78*(2), 169–183.

Hofstede, G. (1980). *Culture's consequences*. Sage.

Hofstede, G. H. (2001). *Culture's consequences: Comparing values, behaviors, institutions and organizations across nations* (2nd ed.). Sage.

Hofstede, G., Hofstede, G. J., & Minkov, M. (1997). *Cultures and organizations*. McGraw-Hill.

Hofstede, G. H., Hofstede, G. J., & Minkov, M. (2010). *Cultures and organizations: Software of the mind: International cooperation and its importance for survival* (3rd ed., rev. and expanded). McGraw-Hill.

Hofstede, G. J., Pedersen, P., & Hofstede, G. H. (2002). *Exploring culture: Exercises, stories, and synthetic cultures*. Intercultural Press.

Hogg, M. A. (2010). Influence and leadership. In S. T. Fiske, D. T. Gilbert, & G. Lindzey (Eds.), *Handbook of social psychology* (5th ed., Vol. 2, pp. 1166–1207). Wiley.

Hogg, M. A., Terry, D. J., & White, K. M. (1995). A tale of two theories: A critical comparison of identity theory with social identity theory. *Social Psychology Quarterly, 58*(4), 255–269.

Høglend, P., & Hagtvet, K. (2019). Change mechanisms in psychotherapy: Both improved insight and improved affective awareness are necessary. *Journal of Consulting and Clinical Psychology, 87*(4). https://doi.org/10.1037/ccp0000381

Holbrook, A. L., Sterrett, D., Johnson, T. P., & Krysan, M. (2016). Racial disparities in political participation across issues: The role of issue-specific motivators. *Political Behavior, 38*(1), 1–32.

Holbrook, B. D., & Rayburn, W. F. (2014). Teratogenic risks from exposure to illicit drugs. *Obstetrics and Gynecology Clinics, 41*(2), 229–239.

Holder, A. M. (2019). Microaggressions: Workplace interventions. In G. C. Torino, D. P. Rivera, C. M. Capodilupo, K. L. Nadal, & D. W. Sue (Eds.), *Microaggression theory: Influence and implications* (pp. 259–275). Wiley.

Holland, A., & Andre, T. (1987). Participation in extracurricular activities in secondary school: What is known, what needs to be known? *Review of Educational Research, 57*(4), 437–466.

Holland, G., & Tiggemann, M. (2016). A systematic review of the impact of the use of social networking sites on body image and disordered eating outcomes. *Body Image, 17*, 100–110.

Holland, G., & Tiggemann, M. (2017). "Strong beats skinny every time": Disordered eating and compulsive exercise in women who post fitspiration on Instagram. *International Journal of Eating Disorders, 50*(1), 76–79. https://doi.org/10.1002/eat.22559

Holland, P. C., & Rescorla, R. A. (1975). Second-order conditioning with food unconditioned stimulus. *Journal of Comparative & Physiological Psychology, 88*(1), 459–467.

Holliday, B. G. (2009). The history and visions of African American psychology: Multiple pathways to place, space, and authority. *Cultural Diversity and Ethnic Minority Psychology, 15*(4), 317–337.

Hollifield, M., Sinclair-Lian, N., Warner, T. D., & Hammerschlag, R. (2007). Acupuncture for posttraumatic stress disorder: A randomized controlled pilot trial. *The Journal of Nervous and Mental Disease, 195*(6), 504–513.

Hollingworth, A. (2009). Memory for real-world scenes. In J. R. Brockmole (Ed.), *The visual world in memory* (pp. 89–116). Psychology Press.

Hollins, M. (2010). Texture perception: Tactile. In E. B. Goldstein (Ed.), *Encyclopedia of perception* (pp. 987–991). Sage.

Hollis, C. (2003). Developmental precursors of child- and adolescent-onset schizophrenia and affective psychoses: Diagnostic specificity and continuity with symptom dimensions. *British Journal of Psychiatry, 182*, 37–44.

Hollon, S. D., & DiGiuseppe, R. (2011). Cognitive theories of psychotherapy. In J. C. Norcross, G. R. Vandenbos, & D. K. Freedheim (Eds.), *History of psychotherapy: Continuity and change* (2nd ed., pp. 203–242). American Psychological Association.

Holmes, E. A., Grey, N., & Young, K. A. (2005). Intrusive images and "hotspots" of trauma memories in posttraumatic stress disorder: An exploratory investigation of emotions and cognitive themes. *Journal of Behavior Therapy and Experimental Psychiatry, 36*(1), 3–17.

Holmes, M., & Newman, M. G. (2006). Generalized anxiety disorder. In M. Hersen & J. C. Thomas (Eds.), *Comprehensive handbook of personality and psychopathology* (Vol. 2, pp. 101–120). Wiley.

Holmes, T. H., & Masuda, M. (1973). Life changes and illness susceptibility. In J. Scott & E. Senay (Eds.), *Separation and depression: Clinical and research aspects* (pp. 161–186). American Association for the Advancement of Science.

Holmes, T. H., & Rahe, R. H. (1967). The social readjustment rating scale. *Journal of Psychosomatic Research, 11*(2), 213–218.

Holmqvist, R. (2016). Client and therapist reports: Symptom reduction, functional improvement, and the therapeutic alliance. In S. Maltzman (Ed.), *The Oxford handbook of treatment processes and outcomes in psychology: A multidisciplinary, biopsychosocial approach* (pp. 449–464). Oxford University Press.

Holroyd, K. A., & Lazarus, R. S. (1982). Stress, coping, and somatic adaptation. In L. Goldberger & S. Breznitz (Eds.), *Handbook of stress: Theoretical and clinical aspects* (pp. 21–35). Free Press.

Holson, L. M. (2018, October 3). Psychedelic mushrooms are closer to medicinal use (it's not just your imagination). The New York Times. Retrieved from https://www.nytimes.com/2018/10/03/science/magic-mushrooms-psilocybin-scheduleiv.html

Holt, R. R. (1999). Empiricism and the Thematic Apperception Test: Validity is the payoff. In L. Gieser & M. I. Stein (Eds.), *Evocative images: The Thematic Apperception Test and the art of projection* (pp. 99–105). American Psychological Association.

Holt-Lunstad, J., Smith, T. B., Baker, M., Harris, T., & Stephenson, D. (2015). Loneliness and social isolation as risk factors for mortality: A meta-analytic review. *Perspectives on Psychological Science, 10*(2), 227–237.

Homan, K. J., Houlihan, D., Ek, K., & Wanzek, J. (2012). Cultural differences in the levels of rewards between adolescents from America, Australia, Tanzania, Denmark, Honduras, Korea, and Spain. *International Journal of Psychological Studies, 4*(2), 264–272.

Hong, J. H., Omur-Ozbek, O., Stanek, B. T., Dietrich, A. M., Duncan, S. E., Lee, Y. W., & Lesser, G. (2009). Taste and odor abnormalities in cancer patients. *The Journal of Supportive Oncology, 7*(2), 58–65.

Hook, J. N., Davis, D. E., Owen, J., Worthington, E. L., Jr., & Utsey, S. O. (2013). Cultural humility: Measuring openness to culturally diverse clients. *Journal of Counseling Psychology, 60*(3), 353–366.

Hook, J. N., Davis, D., Owen, J., & DeBlaere, C. (2017). *Cultural humility: Engaging diverse identities in therapy*. American Psychological Association. https://doi.org/10.1037/0000037-000

Hook, J. N., Davis, D. E., Owen, J., Worthington, E. L., Jr., & Utsey, S. O. (2013). Cultural humility: Measuring openness to culturally diverse clients. *Journal of Counseling Psychology, 60*(3), 353–366.

Hooley, J. M. (2009). Schizophrenia: Interpersonal functioning. In P. H. Blaney & T. Millon (Eds.), *Oxford textbook of psychopathology* (2nd ed., pp. 333–360). Oxford University Press.

Hooley, J. M., & St. Germain, S. (2008). Borderline personality disorder. In W. E. Craighead, D. J. Miklowitz, & L. W. Craighead (Eds.), *Psychopathology: History, diagnosis, and empirical foundations* (pp. 598–630). Wiley.

Hooper, R. (2018). *Superhuman: Life at the extremes of our capacity*. Simon & Schuster.

Hopkins, C., Surda, P., Vaira, L. A., Lechien, J. R., Safarian, M., Saussez, S., & Kumar, N. (2021, February). Six month follow-up of self-reported loss of smell during the COVID-19 pandemic. *Rhinology, 59*(1), 26–31. https://doi.org/10.4193/rhin20.544

Hopko, D. R., Ryba, M. M., McIndoo, C., & File, A. (2016). Behavioral activation. In C. M. Nezu & A. M. Nezu (Eds.), *The Oxford handbook of cognitive and behavioral therapies* (pp. 229–263). Oxford University Press.

Hopper, K., Harrison, G., Janca, A., Sartorius, N., & Wiersman, D. (2007). Conclusion. In K. Hopper, G. Harrison, A. Janca, & N. Sartorius (Eds.), *Recovery from schizophrenia: An international perspective* (pp. 277–282). Oxford University Press.

Hopwood, C. J., Kotov, R., Krueger, R. F., Watson, D., Widiger, T. A., Althoff, R. R., Ansell, E. B., Bach, B., Baby, R. M., Blais, M. A., Bornovalova, M. A., Chmielewski, M., Cicero, D. C., Conway, C., de Clerq, B., De Fruyt, F., Docherty, A. R., Eaton, N. R., Edens, J. F., ... Zimmermann, J. (2018). The time has come for dimensional personality disorder diagnosis. *Personality and Mental Health, 12*(1), 82–86.

Horenstein, A., Kaplan, S. C., Butler, R. M., & Heimberg, R. G. (2021). Social anxiety moderates the relationship between body mass index and motivation to avoid exercise. *Body Image, 36*, 185–192. https://doi.org/10.1016/j.bodyim.2020.11.010

Horita, Y., & Takezawa, M. (2018). Cultural differences in strength of conformity explained through pathogen stress: A statistical test using hierarchical Bayesian estimation. *Frontiers in Psychology, 9*, 1921.

Horn, J. L., & Cattell, R. B. (1966). Refinement and test of the theory of fluid and crystallized general intelligences. *Journal of Educational Psychology, 57*(5), 253–270.

Horn, J. L., & Noll, J. (1997). Human cognitive capabilities: Gf-Gc theory. In D. P. Flanagan, J. L. Genshaft, & P. L. Harrison (Eds.), *Contemporary intellectual assessment: Theories, tests, and issues* (pp. 53–91). Guilford Press.

Horn, J. P., & Swanson, L. W. (2013). The autonomic motor system and the hypothalamus. In E. R. Kandel, J. H. Schwartz, T. M. Jessell, S. A. Siegelbaum, & A. J. Hudspeth (Eds.), *Principles of neural science* (5th ed., pp. 1056–1078). McGraw-Hill.

Horne, J., & Reyner, L. (1999). Vehicle accidents related to sleep: A review. *Occupational and Environmental Medicine, 56*(5), 289–294.

Hornsey, M. J., & Hogg, M. A. (2000). Subgroup relations: A comparison of mutual intergroup differentiation and common ingroup identity models of prejudice reduction. *Personality and Social Psychology Bulletin, 26*(2), 242–256.

Horowitz, S. S. (2012). *The universal sense: How hearing shapes the mind*. Bloomsbury.

Horsley, R. R., Osborne, M., Norman, C., & Wells, T. (2012). High-frequency gamblers show increased resistance to extinction following partial reinforcement. *Behavioural Brain Research, 229*(2), 438–442.

Horvath, A. O., Del Re, A. C., Flückiger, C., & Symonds, D. (2011). Alliance in individual psychotherapy. In J. C. Norcross (Ed.), *Psychotherapy relationships that work: Evidence-based responsiveness* (2nd ed., pp. 25–69). Oxford University Press.

Horwitz, A. V. (2015). The DSM-5 and the continuing transformation of normal sadness into depressive disorder. *Emotion Review, 7*(3), 209–215.

Horwitz, A. V. (2017). Social context, biology, and the definition of disorder. *Journal of Health and Social Behavior, 58*(2), 131–145.

Horwitz, A. V., & Wakefield, J. C. (2007). *The loss of sadness: How psychiatry transformed normal sorrow into depressive disorder*. Oxford University Press.

Horwitz, A. V., Wakefield, J. C., & Lorenzo-Luaces, L. (2017). History of depression. In R. J. DeRubeis & D. R. Strunk (Eds.), *The Oxford handbook of mood disorders* (pp. 11–23). Oxford University Press.

Hosking, S. G., Young, K. L., & Regan, M. A. (2009). The effects of text messaging on young drivers. *Human Factors: The Journal of the Human Factors and Ergonomics Society, 51*(4), 582–592.

Hothersall, D. (2004). *History of psychology* (4th ed.). Random House.

House, J. S., Landis, K. R., & Umberson, D. (1988). Social relationships and health. *Science, 241*(4865), 540–545.

Houston, B., & Snyder, C. R. (1988). *Type A behavior pattern: Research, theory, and intervention*. Wiley.

Houston, D. M., Hay-McCutcheon, M. J., Bergeson, T. R., & Miyamoto, R. T. (2010). Cochlear implants: Technology. In E. B. Goldstein (Ed.), *Encyclopedia of perception* (pp. 245–249). Sage.

Howard, D. E., Debnam, K. J., & Wang, M. Q. (2013). Ten-year trends in physical dating violence victimization among U.S. adolescent females. *Journal of School Health, 83*(6), 389–399.

Howard, M. E., Desai, A. V., Grunstein, R. R., Hukins, C., Armstrong, J. G., Joffe, D., Swann, P., Campbell, D. A., & Pierce, R. J. (2004). Sleepiness, sleep-disordered breathing, and accident risk factors in commercial vehicle drivers. *American Journal of Respiratory and Critical Care Medicine, 170*(9), 1014–1021.

Howard, M., Muris, P., Loxton, H., & Wege, A. (2017). Anxiety-proneness, anxiety symptoms, and the role of parental overprotection in young South African children. *Journal of Child and Family Studies, 26*(1), 262–270.

Howe, L. C., & Krosnick, J. A. (2017). Attitude strength. *Annual Review of Psychology, 68*, 327–351.

Howe, M. L., & Malone, C. (2011). Mood-congruent true and false memory: Effects of depression. *Memory, 19*(2), 192–201.

Howell, A. J., Passmore, H. A., & Holder, M. D. (2016). Implicit theories of well-being predict well-being and the endorsement of therapeutic lifestyle changes. *Journal of Happiness Studies, 17*(6), 2347–2363.

Howell, M. J., Schenck, C. H., & Crow, S. J. (2009). A review of nighttime eating disorders. *Sleep Medicine Reviews, 13*(1), 23–34.

Howland, R. H. (2005). Biological bases of psychopathology. In J. E. Maddux & B. A. Winstead (Eds.), *Psychopathology* (pp. 109–124). Lawrence Erlbaum.

Hoza, B., Mrug, S., Pelham, W. E., Greiner, A. R., & Gnagy, E. M. (2003). A friendship intervention for children with attention-deficit/hyperactivity disorder: Preliminary findings. *Journal of Attention Disorders, 6*(3), 87–98.

Hruby, A., & Hu, F. B. (2015). The epidemiology of obesity: A big picture. *Pharmacoeconomics, 33*(7), 673–689.

Hsiao, S. (2010). Cutaneous perception: Physiology. In E. B. Goldstein (Ed.), *Encyclopedia of perception* (pp. 348–354). Sage.

Hsueh, Y., & Guo, B. (2012). China. In D. B. Baker (Ed.), *The Oxford handbook of the history of psychology: Global perspectives* (pp. 81–124). Oxford University Press.

Hu, Y., Parde, C. J., Hill, M. Q., Mahmood, N., & O'Toole, A. J. (2018). First impressions of personality traits from body shapes. *Psychological Science, 29*(12), 1969–1983.

Huang, C. M., & Park, D. (2013). Cultural influences on Facebook photographs. *International Journal of Psychology, 48*(3), 334–343.

Huang, W., Ramsey, K. M., Marcheva, B., & Bass, J. (2011). Circadian rhythms, sleep, and metabolism. *The Journal of Clinical Investigation, 121*(6), 2133–2141.

Huber, L., & Wilkinson, A. (2010). Evolutionary approach. In E. B. Goldstein (Ed.), *Encyclopedia of perception* (pp. 401–405). Sage.

Hublin, C., & Kaprio, J. (2003). Genetic aspects and genetic epidemiology of parasomnias. *Sleep Medicine Reviews, 7*(5), 413–421.

Hublin, C., Kaprio, J., Partinen, M., Heikkila, K., & Koskenvuo, M. (1997). Prevalence and genetics of sleepwalking: A population-based twin study. *Neurology, 48*(1), 177–181.

Hudson, J. I., Coit, C. E., Lalonde, J. K., & Pope, H. G. (2012). By how much will the proposed new DSM-5 criteria increase the prevalence of binge eating disorder? *International Journal of Eating Disorders, 45*(1), 139–141.

Hudson, J. L., & Rapee, R. M. (2009). Familial and social environments in the etiology and maintenance of anxiety disorders. In M. M. Antony & M. B. Stein (Eds.), *Oxford handbook of anxiety and related disorders* (pp. 173–189). Oxford University Press.

Huesmann, L. R. (1986). Psychological processes promoting the relation between exposure to media violence and aggressive behavior by the viewer. *Journal of Social Issues, 42*(3), 125–139.

Huesmann, L. R. (2010). Nailing the coffin shut on doubts that violent video games stimulate aggression: Comment on Anderson et al. (2010). *Psychological Bulletin, 136*(2), 179–181.

Huesmann, L. R., Dubow, E. F., & Boxer, P. (2009). Continuity of aggression from childhood to early adulthood as a predictor of life outcomes: Implications for the adolescent-limited and life-course-persistent models. *Aggressive Behavior, 35*(2), 136–149.

Huesmann, L. R., & Kirwil, L. (2007). Why observing violence increases the risk of violent behavior by the observer. In D. J. Flannery, A. T. Vazsonyi, & I. D. Waldman (Eds.), *The Cambridge handbook of violent behavior and aggression* (pp. 545–570). Cambridge University Press.

Huesmann, L. R., & Miller, L. S. (1994). Long-term effects of repeated exposure to media violence in childhood. In L. R. Huesmann (Ed.), *Aggressive behavior: Current perspective* (pp. 153–186). Plenum Press.

Huesmann, L. R., & Moise, J. (1998). The stability and continuity of aggression from early childhood to young adulthood. In D. J. Flannery & C. R. Huff (Eds.), *Youth violence: Prevention, intervention, and social policy* (pp. 73–95). American Psychiatric Press.

Huey, S. J., Jr., Tilley, J. L., Jones, E. O., & Smith, C. A. (2014). The contribution of cultural competence to evidence-based care for ethnically diverse populations. *Annual Review of Clinical Psychology, 10*, 305–338.

Hui, B. P. H., Ng, J. C. K., Berzaghi, E., Cunningham-Amos, L. A., & Kogan, A. (2020). Rewards of kindness? A meta-analysis of the link between prosociality and well-being. *Psychological Bulletin, 146*(12), 1084–1116. https://doi.org/10.1037/bul0000298

Hui, C. H., & Triandis, H. C. (1986). Individualism-collectivism: A study of cross-cultural researchers. *Journal of Cross-Cultural Psychology, 17*(2), 225–248.

Hull, C. (1943). *Principles of behavior*. Appleton-Century-Crofts.

Hull, C. L. (1952). *A behavior system*. Yale University Press.

Hulse, S. H. (2002). Auditory scene analysis in animal communication. *Advances in the Study of Behavior, 31*, 163–200.

Hummel, K. L., Bizar-Stanton, B., Packman, W., & Koocher, G. P. (2017). Ethics and legal matters in psychotherapy. In A. J. Consoli, L. E. Beutler, & B. Bongar (Eds.), *Comprehensive textbook of psychotherapy: Theory and practice* (2nd ed., pp. 480–496). Oxford University Press.

Hummer, K., Vannatta, J., & Thompson, D. (2011). Locus of control and metabolic control of diabetes: A meta-analysis. *The Diabetes Educator, 37*(1), 104–110.

Hummert, M. L. (2014). Age changes in facial morphology, emotional communication, and age stereotyping. In P. Verhaeghen & C. K. Hertzog (Eds.), *The Oxford handbook of emotion, social cognition, and problem solving in adulthood* (pp. 47–60). Oxford University Press.

Humphrey, L., Clifford, D., & Morris, M. N. (2015). Health at Every Size college course reduces dieting behaviors and improves intuitive eating, body esteem, and anti-fat attitudes. *Journal of Nutrition Education and Behavior, 47*(4), 354–360.

Humphreys, G. W., & Riddoch, M. J. (2001). The neuropsychology of visual object and space perception. In E. B. Goldstein (Ed.), *Blackwell handbook of perception* (pp. 204–236). Blackwell.

Hunt, A., & Rhodes, T. (2018). The new famous: Deconstructing African American girl fights on social media. In K. McQueeney & A. Girgenti-Malone (Eds.), *Girls, aggression, and intersectionality: Transforming the discourse of "mean girls" in the United States* (pp. 106–122). Routledge.

Hunt, J. M. (1965). Intrinsic motivation and its role in psychological development. In D. Levine (Ed.), *Nebraska symposium on motivation* (Vol. 13, pp. 189–282). University of Nebraska Press.

Hunt, M. M. (1993). *The story of psychology*. Doubleday.

Hunt, M. M. (2007). *The story of psychology* (2nd ed.). Anchor.

Huntemann, N., & Morgan, M. (2012). Media and identity development. In D. G. Singer & J. L. Singer (Eds.), *Handbook of children and the media* (2nd ed., pp. 303–319). Sage.

Hunter, M. S. (1990). Psychological and somatic experience of the menopause: A prospective study. *Psychosomatic Medicine, 52*(3), 357–367.

Hupbach, A., Weinberg, J. L., & Shiebler, V. L. (2018). Forget-me, forget-me-not: Evidence for directed forgetting in preschoolers. *Cognitive Development, 45*, 24–30.

Hupp, S., & Jewell, J. (2015). *Great myths of child development*. Wiley-Blackwell.

Hurley, R., Flashman, L., Chow, T., & Taber, K. (2010). The brainstem: Anatomy, assessment, and clinical syndromes. *Journal of Neuropsychiatry and Clinical Neurosciences, 22*(1), iv–7.

Hurley, R. A., Lucas, D. M., & Taber, K. H. (2013). Structural neuroimaging. In D. B. Arciniegas, C. A. Anderson, & C. M. Filley (Eds.), *Behavioral neurology & neuropsychiatry* (pp. 415–429). Cambridge University Press.

Hurley, R. A., Taber, K. H., Zhang, J., & Hayman, L. A. (1999). Neuropsychiatric presentation of multiple sclerosis. *Journal of Neuropsychiatry and Clinical Neurosciences, 11*(1), 5–7.

Hursh, S. R., & Drummond, S. (2017). Eliminating the controlled napping policy at CSX is a blow to public safety. *Sleep, 40*(10).

Hurtz, G. M., & Donovan, J. J. (2000). Personality and job performance: The Big Five revisited. *Journal of Applied Psychology, 85*(6), 869–879.

Huttenlocher, P. R., & Dabholkar, A. S. (1997). Regional differences in synaptogenesis in human cerebral cortex. *Journal of Comparative Neurology, 387*(2), 167–178.

Huwaë, S., & Schaafsma, J. (2018). Cross-cultural differences in emotion suppression in everyday interactions. *International Journal of Psychology, 53*(3), 176–183.

Huynh, V. W. (2012). Ethnic microaggressions and the depressive and somatic symptoms of Latino and Asian American adolescents. *Journal of Youth and Adolescence, 41*(7), 831–846.

Hwang, W.-C., & Goto, S. (2008). The impact of perceived racial discrimination on the mental health of Asian American and Latino college students. *Cultural Diversity and Ethnic Minority Psychology, 14*(4), 326–335. https://doi.org/10.1037/1099-9809.14.4.326

Hyde, J. S. (2005). The gender similarities hypothesis. *American Psychologist, 60*(6), 581–592.

Hyde, J. S. (2014). Gender similarities and differences. *Annual Review of Psychology, 65*, 373–398.

Hyde, J. S., Lindberg, S. M., Linn, M. C., Ellis, A. B., & Williams, C. C. (2008). Gender similarities characterize math performance. *Science, 321*(5888), 494–495.

Hyde, J. S., & Mezulis, A. H. (2020). Gender differences in depression: Biological, affective, cognitive, and sociocultural factors. *Harvard Review of Psychiatry, 28*(1), 4–13. https://doi.org/10.1097/HRP.0000000000000230

Hyman, I. E., Wulff, A. N., & Thomas, A. K. (2018). Crime blindness: How selective attention and inattentional blindness can disrupt eyewitness awareness and memory. *Policy Insights from the Behavioral and Brain Sciences*. https://doi.org/10.1177/2372732218786749.

Hymel, S., Closson, L. M., Caravita, S. C. S., & Vaillancourt, T. (2011). Social status among peers: From sociometric attraction to peer acceptance to perceived popularity. In P. K. Smith & C. H. Hart (Eds.), *The Wiley-Blackwell handbook of childhood social development* (2nd ed., pp. 375–392). Wiley-Blackwell.

Iacoboni, M. (2009). Imitation, empathy, and mirror neurons. *Annual Review of Psychology, 60*, 653–670.

Ikeda, M., Iwanaga, M., & Seiwa, H. (1996). Test anxiety and working memory system. *Perceptual and Motor Skills, 82*(3, Part 2), 1223–1231.

Illes, J., Moser, M. A., McCormick, J. B., Racine, E., Blakeslee, S., Caplan, A., Hayden, E. C., Ingram, J., Lohwater, T., McKnight, P., Nicholson, C., Phillips, A., Sauvé, K. D., Snell, E., Weiss, S. (2009). Neurotalk: Improving the communication of neuroscience research. *Nature Reviews Neuroscience, 11*(1), 61–69.

Imai, L., & Gelfand, M. J. (2010). The culturally intelligent negotiator: The impact of cultural intelligence (CQ) on negotiation sequences and outcomes. *Organizational Behavior and Human Decision Processes, 112*(2), 83–98.

Ingham, A. G., Levinger, G., Graves, J., & Peckham, V. (1974). The Ringelmann effect: Studies of group size and group performance. *Journal of Experimental Social Psychology, 10*(4), 371–384.

Ingraham, C. (2015, February 9). How just a couple drinks make your odds of a car crash skyrocket. *Washington Post*. http://www.washingtonpost.com/blogs/wonkblog/wp/2015/02/09/how-just-a-couple-drinks-make-your-odds-of-a-car-crash-skyrocket/

Innes, C. A. (1988). *Drug use and crime*. U.S. Department of Justice.

Inoue, Y. (2015). Sleep-related eating disorder and its associated conditions. *Psychiatry and Clinical Neurosciences, 69*(6), 309–320.

Institute of Medicine. (2006). *Food marketing to children and youth: Threat or opportunity?* National Academies Press.

Ippolito, P. M. (2011). Regulation of food advertising. In J. H. Cawley (Ed.), *The Oxford handbook of the social science of obesity* (pp. 741–751). Oxford University Press.

Irish, D. P., Lundqvist, K. F., & Nelsen, V. J. (Eds.). (1993). *Ethnic variations in dying, death, and grief: Diversity in universality*. Routledge.

Irving, J. A., Farb, N. A. S., & Segal, Z. V. (2015). Mindfulness-based cognitive therapy for chronic depression. In K. W. Brown, J. D. Creswell, & R. M. Ryan (Eds.), *Handbook of mindfulness: Theory, research, and practice* (pp. 348–366). Guilford Press.

Irwin, D. E., & Thomas, L. E. (2008). Visual sensory memory. In S. J. Luck & A. Hollingworth (Eds.), *Visual memory* (pp. 9–41). Oxford University Press.

Irwin, M. R. (2008). Human psychoneuroimmunology: 20 years of discovery. *Brain, Behavior, and Immunity, 22*(2), 129–139.

Isen, A. M. (2008). Some ways in which positive affect influences decision making and problem solving. In M. Lewis, J. M. Haviland-Jones, & L. F. Barrett (Eds.), *Handbook of emotions* (3rd ed., pp. 548–573). Guilford Press.

Ishikawa-Takata, K., Ohta, T., & Tanaka, H. (2003). How much exercise is required to reduce blood pressure in essential hypertensives: A dose–response study. *American Journal of Hypertension, 16*(8), 629–633.

Israel, T., & Mohr, J. J. (2004). Attitudes toward bisexual women and men: Current research, future directions. *Journal of Bisexuality, 4*(12), 117–134.

Itzkoff, D. (2014, August 11). Robin Williams, Oscar-winning comedian, dies at 63. *The New York Times*.

Ivanenko, A., & Larson, K. (2013). Nighttime distractions: Fears, nightmares, and parasomnias. In A. R. Wolfson & H. Montgomery-Downs (Eds.), *The Oxford handbook of infant, child, and adolescent sleep and behavior* (pp. 347–361). Oxford University Press.

Iverach, L., Menzies, R. G., & Menzies, R. E. (2014). Death anxiety and its role in psychopathology: Reviewing the status of a transdiagnostic construct. *Clinical Psychology Review, 34*(7), 580–593.

Iverson, G. L., Brooks, B. L., Lovell, M. R., & Collins, M. W. (2006). No cumulative effects for one or two previous concussions. *British Journal of Sports Medicine, 40*(1), 72–75.

Iverson, G. L., Gaetz, M., Lovell, M. R., & Collins, M. W. (2004). Cumulative effects of concussion in amateur athletes. *Brain Injury, 18*(5), 433–443.

Iyadurai, L., Visser, R. M., Lau-Zhu, A., Porcheret, K., Horsch, A., Holmes, E. A., & James, E. L. (2019). Intrusive memories of trauma: A target for research bridging cognitive science and its clinical application. *Clinical Psychology Review, 69*, 67–82.

Iyengar, S., & Westwood, S. J. (2015). Fear and loathing across party lines: New evidence on group polarization. *American Journal of Political Science, 59*(3), 690–707.

Izuma, K., Aoki, R., Shibata, K., & Nakahara, K. (2019). Neural signals in amygdala predict implicit prejudice toward an ethnic outgroup. *NeuroImage, 189*, 341–352.

Jackendoff, R. (2012). Language. In K. Frankish & W. M. Ramsey (Eds.), *The Cambridge handbook of cognitive science* (pp. 171–192). Cambridge University Press.

Jackson, J. J., & Hill, P. L. (2019). Lifespan development of conscientiousness. In D. P. McAdams, R. L. Shiner, & J. L. Tackett (Eds.), *Handbook of personality development* (pp. 153–170). Guilford Press.

Jackson, S. A. (1995). Factors influencing the occurrence of flow state in elite athletes. *Journal of Applied Sport Psychology, 7*(2), 138–166.

Jackson, S. A. (2012). Flow. In R. M. Ryan (Ed.), *The Oxford handbook of human motivation* (pp. 127–140). Oxford University Press.

Jackson, S. A., & Csikszentmihalyi, M. (1999). *Flow in sports: The keys to optimal experiences and performances*. Human Kinetics.

Jacobi, C., & Fittig, E. (2010). Psychosocial risk factors for eating disorders. In W. S. Agras (Ed.), *The Oxford handbook of eating disorders* (pp. 123–136). Oxford University Press.

Jacobs, B., & Gundling, K. (2009). Complementary and alternative medicine: Definitions and patterns of use. In B. P. Jacobs & K. Gundling (Eds.), *The ACP evidence-based guide to complementary and alternative medicine* (pp. 3–22). American College of Physicians.

Jacobs, G. D., Pace-Schott, E. F., Stickgold, R., & Otto, M. W. (2004). Cognitive behavior therapy and pharmacotherapy for insomnia: A randomized controlled trial and direct comparison. *Archives of Internal Medicine, 164*(17), 1888–1896.

Jacobs, G. H. (2009). Evolution of colour vision in mammals. *Philosophical Transactions of the Royal Society B: Biological Sciences, 364*(1531), 2957–2967.

Jacobson, B. H., Chen, H. C., Cashel, C., & Guerrero, L. (1997). The effect of T'ai Chi Chuan training on balance, kinesthetic sense, and strength. *Perceptual and Motor Skills, 84*(1), 27–33.

Jadva, V., Hines, M., & Golombok, S. (2010). Infants' preferences for toys, colors, and shapes: Sex differences and similarities. *Archives of Sexual Behavior, 39*(6), 1261–1273.

Jaeger, C. B., Levin, D. T., & Porter, E. (2017). Justice is (change) blind: Applying research on visual metacognition in legal settings. *Psychology, Public Policy, and Law, 23*(2), 259–279.

Jaffee, S., & Hyde, J. S. (2000). Gender differences in moral orientation: A meta-analysis. *Psychological Bulletin, 126*(5), 703–726.

Jagers, R. J., Morgan-Lopez, A. A., Howard, T. L., Browne, D. C., & Flay, B. R. (2007). Mediators of the development and prevention of violent behavior. *Prevention Science, 8*(3), 171–179.

Jahrami, H., BaHammam, A. S., Bragazzi, N. L., Saif, Z., Faris, M., & Vitiello, M. V. (2021). Sleep problems during the COVID-19 pandemic by population: A systematic review and meta-analysis. *Journal of Clinical Sleep Medicine, 17*(2), 299–313. https://doi.org/10.5664/jcsm.8930

Jaimes, A., Larose-Hébert, K., & Moreau, N. (2015). Current trends in theoretical orientation of psychologists: The case of Quebec clinicians. *Journal of Clinical Psychology, 71*(10), 1042–1048.

Jakobsen, K. V. (2012). Applying for academic positions. In P. J. Giordano, S. F. Davis, & C. A. Licht (Eds.), *Your graduate training in psychology: Effective strategies for success* (pp. 279–294). Sage.

James, C. (2009). *Young people, ethics, and the new digital media: A synthesis from the GoodPlay Project*. MIT Press.

James, S. E., Herman, J. L., Rankin, S., Keisling, M., Mottet, L., & Anafi, M. (2016). *Executive summary of the report of the 2015 U.S. Transgender Survey*. National Center for Transgender Equality.

James, S. M., Honn, K. A., Gaddameedhi, S., & Van Dongen, H. P. (2017). Shift work: Disrupted circadian rhythms and sleep—implications for health and well-being. *Current Sleep Medicine Reports, 3*(2), 104–112.

James, W. (1884). What is an emotion? *Mind, 9*, 188–205.

James, W. (1890). *The principles of psychology, in two volumes*. Henry Holt and Company.

Jamieson, J. P., Mendes, W. B., & Nock, M. K. (2013). Improving acute stress responses: The power of reappraisal. *Current Directions in Psychological Science, 22*(1), 51–56.

Jamieson, J. P., Nock, M. K., & Mendes, W. B. (2012). Mind over matter: Reappraising arousal improves cardiovascular and cognitive responses to stress. *Journal of Experimental Psychology: General, 141*(3), 417–422.

Jang, K. L., Livesley, W. J., & Vernon, P. A. (1996). Heritability of the Big Five personality dimensions and their facets: A twin study. *Journal of Personality, 64*(3), 577–591.

Janis, I. L. (1982). *Groupthink: Psychological studies of policy decisions and fiascoes*. Houghton Mifflin.

Jarnecke, A. M., & South, S. C. (2017). Behavior and molecular genetics of the Five Factor Model. In T. A. Widiger (Ed.), *The Oxford handbook of the Five Factor Model* (pp. 301–318). Oxford University Press.

Javitt, D. C., & Laruelle, M. (2006). Neurochemical theories. In J. A. Lieberman, T. S. Stroup, & D. O. Perkins (Eds.), *The American Psychiatric Publishing textbook of schizophrenia* (pp. 85–116). American Psychiatric Association.

Jeffery, R. W., Wing, R. R., Sherwood, N. E., & Tate, D. F. (2003). Physical activity and weight loss: Does prescribing higher physical activity goals improve outcome? *The American Journal of Clinical Nutrition, 78*(4), 684–689.

Jenni, O. G., & O'Connor, B. B. (2005). Children's sleep: An interplay between culture and biology. *Pediatrics, 115*(Suppl. 1), 204–216.

Jensen, M. P., & Patterson, D. R. (2008). Hypnosis in the relief of pain and pain disorders. In M. R. Nash & A. J. Barnier (Eds.), *The Oxford handbook of hypnosis: Theory, research, and practice* (pp. 503–534). Oxford, UK: Oxford University Press.

Jeon, M., Dimitriou, D., & Halstead, E. J. (2021). A systematic review on cross-cultural comparative studies of sleep in young populations: The roles of cultural factors. *International Journal of Environmental Research and Public Health, 18*(4), 2005. https://doi.org/10.3390/ijerph18042005

Jeong, S. H. (2007). Effects of news about genetics and obesity on controllability attribution and helping behavior. *Health Communication, 22*(3), 221–228.

Jessell, T. M., & Sanes, J. R. (2013). Differentiation and survival of nerve cells. In E. R. Kandel, J. H. Schwartz, T. M. Jessell, S. A. Siegelbaum, & A. J. Hudspeth (Eds.), *Principles of neural science* (5th ed., pp. 1187–1208). McGraw-Hill.

Jessor, R. (2018). Reflections on six decades of research on adolescent behavior and development. *Journal of Youth and Adolescence, 47*, 473–476.

Jetten, J., & Hornsey, M. J. (2014). Deviance and dissent in groups. *Annual Review of Psychology, 65*(1), 461–485.

Jewett, M. E., Wyatt, J. K., Ritz-De Cecco, A., Khalsa, S. B., Dijk, D.-J., & Czeisler, C. A. (1999). Time course of sleep inertia dissipation in human performance and alertness. *Journal of Sleep Research, 8*(1), 1–8.

Ji, J., Zöller, B., Sundquist, K., & Sundquist, J. (2012). Increased risks of coronary heart disease and stroke among spousal caregivers of cancer patients. *Circulation, 125*(14), 1742–1747.

Ji, L. J., Peng, K., & Nisbett, R. E. (2000). Culture, control, and perception of relationships in the environment. *Journal of Personality and Social Psychology, 78*(5), 943–955.

Ji, L. J., Zhang, Z., & Nisbett, R. E. (2004). Is it culture or is it language? Examination of language effects in cross-cultural research on categorization. *Journal of Personality and Social Psychology, 87*(1), 57–65.

Ji, X., Li, J., & Liu, J. (2018). The relationship between midday napping and neurocognitive function in early adolescents. *Behavioral Sleep Medicine*, 1–15.

Jiang, X. L., & Cillessen, A. H. (2005). Stability of continuous measures of sociometric status: A meta-analysis. *Developmental Review, 25*(1), 1–25.

Jiang, Y. V., Makovski, T., & Shim, W. M. (2009). Visual memory for features, conjunctions, objects, and locations. In J. R. Brockmole (Ed.), *The visual world in memory* (pp. 33–65). Psychology Press.

Johanson, A., Risberg, J., Tucker, D. M., & Gustafson, L. (2006). Changes in frontal lobe activity with cognitive therapy for spider phobia. *Applied Neuropsychology, 13*(1), 34–41.

Johansson, P., Høglend, P., Ulberg, R., Amlo, S., Marble, A., Bøgwald, K., Sørbye, O., Sjaastad, M. C., & Heyerdahl, O. (2010). The mediating role of insight for long-term improvements in psychodynamic therapy. *Journal of Consulting and Clinical Psychology, 78*(3), 438–448.

John, O. P. (2021). History, measurement, and conceptual elaboration of the big-five trait taxonomy: The paradigm matures. In O. P. John & R. W. Robbins (Eds.), *Handbook of personality: Theory and research* (4th ed.), pp. 35–82. Guilford.

John, O. P., & Gross, J. J. (2004). Healthy and unhealthy emotion regulation: Personality processes, individual differences, and life span development. *Journal of Personality, 72*(6), 1301–1334.

John, O. P., Naumann, L. P., & Soto, C. J. (2008). Paradigm shift to the integrative Big Five trait taxonomy: History, measurement, and conceptual issues. In O. P. John, R. W. Robins, &

L. A. Pervin (Eds.), *Handbook of personality: Theory and research* (3rd ed., pp. 114–158). Guilford Press.

Johnson, J. G., Cohen, P., Kasen, S., & Brook, J. S. (2006). Dissociative disorders among adults in the community, impaired functioning, and axis I and II comorbidity. *Journal of Psychiatric Research, 40*(2), 131–140.

Johnson, K. E. (2013). Culture, expertise, and mental categories. In D. Reisberg (Ed.), *The Oxford handbook of cognitive psychology* (pp. 330–345). Oxford University Press.

Johnson, K. E., & Mervis, C. B. (1997). Effects of varying levels of expertise on the basic level of categorization. *Journal of Experimental Psychology: General, 126*(3), 248–277.

Johnson, K. E., Sol, K., Sprague, B. N., Cadet, T., Muñoz, E., & Webster, N. J. (2020). The impact of region and urbanicity on the discrimination–cognitive health link among older Blacks. *Research in Human Development, 17*(1), 4–19. https://doi.org/10.1080/15427609.2020.1746614

Johnson, K. J., & Fredrickson, B. L. (2005). "We all look the same to me": Positive emotions eliminate the own-race bias in face recognition. *Psychological Science, 16*(11), 875–881.

Johnson, K. L., & Tassinary, L. G. (2007). Compatibility of basic social perceptions determines perceived attractiveness. *Proceedings of the National Academy of Sciences, 104*(12), 5246–5251.

Johnson, M. H., Dziurawiec, S., Ellis, H., & Morton, J. (1991). Newborns' preferential tracking of face-like stimuli and its subsequent decline. *Cognition, 40*(1), 1–19.

Johnson, M. K., Hashtroudi, S., & Lindsay, D. S. (1993). Source monitoring. *Psychological Bulletin, 114*(1), 3–28.

Johnson, S. B., Riis, J. L., & Noble, K. G. (2016). State of the art review: Poverty and the developing brain. *Pediatrics, 137*(4), e20153075.

Johnson, S. L., Cuellar, A. K., & Miller, C. (2009). Bipolar and unipolar depression: A comparison of clinical phenomenology, biological vulnerability, and psychosocial predictors. In I. H. Gotlib & C. L. Hammen (Eds.), *Handbook of depression* (2nd ed., pp. 142–162). Guilford Press.

Johnson, T. P., Shavitt, S., & Holbrook, A. L. (2011). Survey response styles across cultures. In D. Matsumoto & F. J. R. van de Vijver (Eds.), *Cross-cultural research methods in psychology* (pp. 130–177). Cambridge University Press.

Johnson, W. B., & Johnson, S. J. (2016). Unavoidable and mandated multiple relationships in military settings. In O. Zur (Ed.), *Multiple relationships in psychotherapy and counseling* (pp. 61–72). Routledge.

Johnston, E., & Johnson, A. (2017). Balancing life and work by unbending gender: Early American women psychologists' struggles and contributions. *Journal of the History of the Behavioral Sciences, 53*(3), 246–264. https://doi.org/10.1002/jhbs.21862

Johnston, J. M. (1972). Punishment of human behavior. *American Psychologist, 27*(11), 1033.

Johnstone, T., Somerville, L. H., Alexander, A. L., Oakes, T. R., Davidson, R. J., Kalin, N. H., & Whalen, P. J. (2005). Stability of amygdala BOLD response to fearful faces over multiple scan sessions. *Neuroimage, 25*(4), 1112–1123.

Jokela, M. (2018). Personality as a'determinant of health behaviors and chronic diseases: Review of meta-analytic evidence. In C. D. Ryff & R. F. Krueger (Eds.), *The Oxford handbook of integrative health science* (pp. 317–332). Oxford University Press.

Jokela, M., Pulkki-Råback, L., Elovainio, M., & Kivimäki, M. (2014). Personality traits as risk factors for stroke and coronary heart disease mortality: Pooled analysis of three cohort studies. *Journal of Behavioral Medicine, 37*(5), 881–889.

Jolley, D., & Douglas, K. M. (2017). Prevention is better than cure: Addressing anti-vaccine conspiracy theories. *Journal of Applied Social Psychology, 47*(8), 459-469.

Jolliffe, D., & Farrington, D. P. (2006). Examining the relationship between low empathy and bullying. *Aggressive Behavior, 32*(6), 540–550.

Jolliffe, D., & Farrington, D. P. (2011). Is low empathy related to bullying after controlling for individual and social background variables? *Journal of Adolescence, 34*(1), 59–71.

Jones, B. C., Little, A. C., Burt, D. M., & Perrett, D. I. (2004). When facial attractiveness is only skin deep. *Perception, 33*(5), 569–576.

Jones, C. M. (2013). Heroin use and heroin use risk behaviors among nonmedical users of prescription opioid pain relievers—United States, 2002–2004 and 2008–2010. *Drug and Alcohol Dependence, 132*(1), 95–100.

Jones, D., & Hill, K. (1993). Criteria of facial attractiveness in five populations. *Human Nature, 4*(3), 271–296.

Jones, E. E., & Harris, V. A. (1967). The attribution of attitudes. *Journal of Experimental Social Psychology, 3*(1), 1–24.

Jones, G. V., & Martin, M. (2004). Orientation illusions in memory. In R. F. Pohl (Ed.), *Cognitive illusions: A handbook on fallacies and biases in thinking, judgement, and memory* (pp. 293–308). Psychology Press.

Jones, K. L., & Streissguth, A. P. (2010). Fetal alcohol syndrome and fetal alcohol spectrum disorders: A brief history. *Journal of Psychiatry and Law, 38*(4), 373–382.

Jones, K., Bertsch, A., Ondracek, J., & Saeed, M. (2016). Don't mess with Coca-Cola: Introducing New Coke reveals flaws in decision-making within the Coca-Cola Company. *GE-International Journal of Management and Research, 4*(10), 70–98.

Jones, L. A. (2010). Temperature perception. In E. B. Goldstein (Ed.), *Encyclopedia of perception* (pp. 983–987). Sage.

Jones, L. L., Wurm, L. H., Norville, G. A., & Mullins, K. L. (2020). Sex differences in emoji use, familiarity, and valence. *Computers in Human Behavior, 108*, 106305. https://doi.org/10.1016/j.chb.2020.106305

Jones-Corneille, L. R., Stack, R. M., & Wadden, T. A. (2011). Behavioral treatment of obesity. In J. H. Cawley (Ed.), *The Oxford handbook of the social science of obesity* (pp. 771–791). Oxford University Press.

Jongsma, H. E., & Jones, P. B. (2018). Weaving causal explanations of schizophrenia in urban areas: The role of gene-environment selection. *JAMA Psychiatry, 75*(9), 878–880.

Joormann, J. (2009). Cognitive aspects of depression. In I. H. Gotlib & C. L. Hammen (Eds.), *Handbook of depression* (2nd ed., pp. 298–321). Guilford Press.

Jorm, A. F., Korten, A. E., Jacomb, P. A., Rodgers, B., & Pollitt, P. (1997). Beliefs about the helpfulness of interventions for mental disorders: A comparison of general practitioners, psychiatrists and clinical psychologists. *Australian and New Zealand Journal of Psychiatry, 31*(6), 844–851.

Jorm, A. F., & Reavley, N. J. (2014). Public belief that mentally ill people are violent: Is the USA exporting stigma to the rest of the world? *Australian & New Zealand Journal of Psychiatry, 48*(3), 213–215.

Josephson, B. R. (1996). Mood regulation and memory: Repairing sad moods with happy memories. *Cognition & Emotion, 10*(4), 437–444.

Josephson, W. L. (1987). Television violence and children's aggression: Testing the priming, social script, and disinhibition predictions. *Journal of Personality and Social Psychology, 53*(5), 882–890.

Jouvet, M., Michel, F., & Courjon, J. (1959). On a stage of rapid cerebral electrical activity in the course of physiological sleep. *Comptes Rendus des Séances de la Société de Biologie et de Ses Filiales, 153*, 1024–1028.

Joy, J., McClure, N., Hepper, P. G., & Cooke, I. (2012). Fetal habituation in assisted conception. *Early Human Development, 88*(6), 431–436.

Jozkowski, K. N., Peterson, Z. D., Sanders, S. A., Dennis, B., & Reece, M. (2014). Gender differences in heterosexual college students' conceptualizations and indicators of sexual consent: Implications for contemporary sexual assault prevention education. *The Journal of Sex Research, 51*(8), 904–916.

Judge, T. A., & Zapata, C. P. (2015). The person–situation debate revisited: Effect of situation strength and trait activation on the validity of the Big Five personality traits in predicting job performance. *Academy of Management Journal, 58*(4), 1149–1179.

Junco, R. (2012). Too much face and not enough books: The relationship between multiple indices of Facebook use and academic performance. *Computers in Human Behavior, 28*(1), 187–198.

Junco, R. (2013a). Inequalities in Facebook use. *Computers in Human Behavior, 29*(6), 2328–2336.

Junco, R. (2013b). Comparing actual and self-reported measures of Facebook use. *Computers in Human Behavior, 29*(3), 626–631.

Jung, C. G. (1963). *Memories, dreams, reflections*. Random House.

Jung, C. G. (1964). *Man and his symbols*. Doubleday.

Jung, C. G. (1971). *Psychological types*. Princeton University Press.

Jung, Y. S., Paik, H., Min, S.-H., Choo, H., Seo, M., Bahk, J.-H., & Seo, J.-H. (2017). Calling the patient's own name facilitates recovering from general anaesthesia: A randomised double-blind trial. *Anaesthesia, 72*(2), 197–200. https://doi.org/10.1111/anae.13688

Juntunen, C., Quincer, M. A., & Unsworth, S. K. P. M. (2018). Ethics in a rural context. In M. M. Leach & E. R. Welfel (Eds.), *The Cambridge handbook of applied psychological ethics* (pp. 93–114). Cambridge University Press.

Kabat-Zinn, J. (1994). *Wherever you go, there you are: Mindfulness meditation in everyday life*. Hyperion.

Kabat-Zinn, J. (2018). *Meditation is not what you think*. Hachette.

Kaeser, P. S., & Regehr, W. G. (2017). The readily releasable pool of synaptic vesicles. *Current Opinion in Neurobiology, 43*, 63–70.

Kagan, J., & Fox, N. A. (2006). Biology, culture, and temperamental biases. In N. Eisenberg (Vol. Ed.), *Handbook of child psychology* (6th ed., Vol. 3, pp. 167–225). Wiley.

Kagan, J., & Snidman, N. (1999). Early childhood predictors of adult anxiety disorders. *Biological Psychiatry, 46*(11), 1536–1541.

Kagan, J., & Snidman, N. C. (2004). *The long shadow of temperament*. Belknap Press of Harvard University Press.

Kagan, J., Snidman, N., Arcus, D., & Reznick, J. S. (1994). *Galen's prophecy: Temperament in human nature*. Basic Books.

Kahana, M. J. (2000). Contingency analyses of memory. In E. Tulving & F. I. M. Craik (Eds.), *The Oxford handbook of memory* (pp. 59–72). Oxford University Press.

Kahneman, D. (1999). Objective happiness. In D. Kahneman, E. Diener, & N. Schwarz (Eds.), *Well-being: The foundations of hedonic psychology* (pp. 758–774). Russell Sage Foundation.

Kahneman, D. (2000). New challenges to the rationality assumption. In D. Kahneman & A. Tversky (Eds.), *Choices, values, and frames* (pp. 758–774). Russell Sage Foundation.

Kahneman, D., & Fredrick, S. (2002). Representativeness revisited: Attribute substitution in intuitive judgement. In T. Gilovich, D. W. Griffin, & D. Kahneman (Eds.), *Heuristics and biases: The psychology of intuitive judgment* (pp. 49–81). Cambridge University Press.

Kahneman, D., & Fredrick, S. (2005). A model of heuristic judgement. In K. J. Holyoak & R. G. Morrison (Eds.), *The Cambridge handbook of thinking and reasoning* (pp. 267–293). Cambridge University Press.

Kahneman, D., Fredrickson, B. L., Schreiber, C. A., & Redelmeier, D. A. (1993). When more pain is preferred to less: Adding a better end. *Psychological Science, 4*(6), 401–405.

Kahneman, D., & Tversky, A. (1972). Subjective probability: A judgment of representativeness. *Cognitive Psychology, 3*(3), 430–454.

Kahneman, D., & Tversky, A. (1973). On the psychology of prediction. *Psychology Review, 80*(4), 237–251.

Kahneman, D., & Tversky, A. (1979). Prospect theory: An analysis of decision under risk. *Econometrica, 47*(2), 263–291. http://www.jstor.org/stable/1914185

Kahneman, D., & Tversky, A. (1996). On the reality of cognitive illusions. *Psychological Review, 103*(3), 582–591.

Kahneman, D., & Tversky, A. (2000). *Choices, values, and frames*. Cambridge University Press.

Kaiser, J., Hanschmidt, F., & Kersting, A. (2021). The association between therapeutic alliance and outcome in internet-based psychological interventions: A meta-analysis. *Computers in Human Behavior, 114*, 106512. https://doi.org/10.1016/j.chb.2020.106512

Kalaska, J. F., & Rizzolatti, G. (2013). Voluntary movement: The primary motor cortex. In E. R. Kandel, J. H. Schwartz, T. M. Jessell, S. A. Siegelbaum, & A. J. Hudspeth (Eds.), *Principles of neural science* (5th ed., pp. 835–864). McGraw-Hill.

Kallam, M., Hoernicke, P. A., & Coser, P. G. (1994). Native Americans and behavioral disorders. In R. L. Peterson, & S. Ishii-Jordan, *Multicultural issues in the education of students with behavioral disorders* (pp. 126–137). Brookline Press.

Kalmuss, D., Davidson, A., & Cushman, L. (1992). Parenting expectations, experiences, and adjustment to parenthood: A test of the violated expectations framework. *Journal of Marriage and the Family, 54*(3), 516–526.

Kalpidou, M., Costin, D., & Morris, J. (2011). The relationship between Facebook and the well-being of undergraduate college students. *Cyberpsychology, Behavior, and Social Networking, 14*(4), 183–189.

Kamphaus, R. W., & Kroncke, A. P. (2004). "Back to the future" of the Stanford-Binet Intelligence Scales. In M. Hersen (Ed.-in-Chief), *Comprehensive handbook of psychological assessment* (Vol. 1, pp. 77–86). Wiley.

Kanazawa, S. (2017). Possible evolutionary origins of human female sexual fluidity. *Biological Reviews, 92*(3), 1251–1274.

Kandel, E. R., & Siegelbaum, S. A. (2013). Cellular mechanisms of implicit memory storage and the biological basis of individuality. In E. R. Kandel, J. H. Schwartz, T. M. Jessell, S. A. Siegelbaum, & A. J. Hudspeth (Eds.), *Principles of neural science* (5th ed., pp. 1461–1486). McGraw-Hill.

Kandel, E. R., & Siegelbaum, S. A. (2013). Cellular mechanisms of implicit memory storage and the biological basis of individuality. In E. R. Kandel, J. H. Schwartz, T. M. Jessell, S. A. Siegelbaum, & A. J. Hudspeth (Eds.), *Principles of neural science* (5th ed., pp. 1461–1486). McGraw-Hill.

Kandel, E. R., Barres, B. A., & Hudspeth, A. J. (2013). Nerve cells, neural circuitry, and behavior. In E. R. Kandel, J. H. Schwartz, T. M. Jessell, S. A. Siegelbaum, & A. J. Hudspeth (Eds.), Principles of neural science (5th ed., pp. 21–38). McGraw-Hill.

Kandler, C., & Zapko-Willmes, A. (2017). Theoretical perspectives on the interplay of nature and nurture in personality development. In J. Specht (Ed.), *Personality development across the lifespan* (pp. 101–115). Academic Press.

Kanner, A. D., Coyne, J. C., Schaefer, C., & Lazarus, R. S. (1981). Comparison of two modes of stress measurement: Daily hassles and uplifts versus major life events. *Journal of Behavioral Medicine, 4*(1), 1–39.

Kanwisher, N. (2017). The quest for the FFA and where it led. *Journal of Neuroscience, 37*(5), 1056–1061.

Kanwisher, N., McDermott, J., & Chun, M. M. (1997). The fusiform face area: A module in human extrastriate cortex specialized for face perception. *The Journal of Neuroscience, 17*(11), 4302–4311.

Kapen, S. (2006). Medical treatment of obstructive sleep apnea: Life-style changes, weight reduction, and postural therapy. In T. L. Lee-Chiong (Ed.), *Sleep: A comprehensive handbook* (pp. 337–346). Wiley-Liss.

Kaplan, A., & Midgley, C. (1997). The effect of achievement goals: Does level of perceived academic competence make a difference? *Contemporary Educational Psychology, 22*(4), 415–435.

Kaplan, K. A., & Harvey, A. G. (2013). Behavioral treatment of insomnia in bipolar disorder. *American Journal of Psychiatry, 170*(7), 716–720.

Kaplowitz, P. B. (2008). Link between body fat and the timing of puberty. *Pediatrics, 121*(Suppl. 3), S208–S217.

Kapur, N., Thompson, P., Kartsounis, L. D., & Abbott, P. (1998). Retrograde amnesia: Clinical and methodological caveats. *Neuropsychologia, 37*(1), 27–30.

Kapur, S., Craik, F. I., Tulving, E., Wilson, A. A., Houle, S., & Brown, G. M. (1994). Neuroanatomical correlates of encoding in episodic memory: Levels of processing effect. *Proceedings of the National Academy of Sciences, 91*(6), 2008–2011.

Karau, S. J., & Williams, K. D. (1993). Social loafing: A meta-analytic review and theoretical integration. *Journal of Personality and Social Psychology, 65*(4), 681–706.

Karazsia, B. T., Murnen, S. K., & Tylka, T. L. (2017). Is body dissatisfaction changing across time? A cross-temporal meta-analysis. *Psychological Bulletin, 143*(3), 293.

Karni, A., Tanne, D., Rubenstein, B. S., Askenasy, J. J., & Sagi, D. (1994). Dependence on REM sleep of overnight improvement of a perceptual skill. *Science, 265*(5172), 679–682.

Karon, B. P., & Widener, A. J. (1995). Psychodynamic therapies in historical perspective: "Nothing human do I consider alien to me." In B. Bongar & L. E. Beutler (Eds.), *Comprehensive textbook of psychotherapy: Theory and practice* (pp. 24–47). Oxford University Press.

Karpiak, C. P., Norcross, J. C., & Wedding, D. (2016). Evolution of theory in clinical psychology. In J. C. Norcross, G. R. VandenBos, & D. K. Freedheim (Eds.), *APA handbook of clinical psychology* (Vol. 2, pp. 3–18). American Psychological Association.

Karver, M. S., De Nadai, A. S., Monahan, M., & Shirk, S. R. (2018). Meta-analysis of the prospective relation between alliance and outcome in child and adolescent psychotherapy. *Psychotherapy, 55*(4), 341–355.

Kaslow, F. W. (2011). Treatment modalities: Family therapy. In J. C. Norcross, G. R. Vandenbos, & D. K. Freedheim (Eds.), *History of psychotherapy: Continuity and change* (2nd ed., pp. 497–504). American Psychological Association.

Kaslow, N. J., Davis, S. P., & Smith, C. O. (2009). Biological and psychosocial interventions for depression in children and adolescents. In I. H. Gotlib & C. L. Hammen (Eds.), *Handbook of depression* (2nd ed., pp. 642–671). Guilford Press.

Kassan, L. D. (1999). *Second opinions: Sixty psychotherapy patients evaluate their therapists*. Aronson.

Kasser, T., & Ryan, R. M. (1993). A dark side of the American dream: Correlates of financial success as a central life aspiration. *Journal of Personality and Social Psychology, 65*(2), 410.

Kasser, T., & Ryan, R. M. (1996). Further examining the American dream: Differential correlates of intrinsic and extrinsic goals. *Personality and Social Psychology Bulletin, 22*(3), 280–287.

Kastendieck, T., Zillmer, S., & Hess, U. (2021). (Un) mask yourself! Effects of face masks on facial mimicry and emotion perception during the COVID-19 pandemic. *Cognition and Emotion*, 1–11. https://doi.org/10.1080/02699931.2021.1950639

Katz, D. L. (2012). Why I can't quite be OK with "Okay at any size." Retrieved from https://www.huffpost.com/entry/obesity-crisis_b_1967677

Katz, J. (2016). *Speaking American*. Houghton Mifflin Harcourt.

Katz, J. (2017, August 10). Short answers to hard questions about the opioid crisis. *The New York Times*. https://www.nytimes.com/interactive/2017/08/03/upshot/opioid-drug-overdose-epidemic.html

Katzman, D. K., Kanbur, N. O., & Steinegger, C. M. (2010). Medical screening and management of eating disorders in adolescents. In W. S. Agras (Ed.), *The Oxford handbook of eating disorders* (pp. 267–291). Oxford University Press.

Kaufman, J. C., & Beghetto, R. A. (2009). Beyond big and little: The Four C model of creativity. *Review of General Psychology, 13*(1), 1–12.

Kaufman, J. C., Kaufman, S. B., & Plucker, J. A. (2013). Contemporary theories of intelligence. In D. Reisberg (Ed.), *The Oxford handbook of cognitive psychology* (pp. 811–822). Oxford University Press.

Kaufman, S. B., DeYoung, C. G., Gray, J. R., Jiménez, L., Brown, J., & Mackintosh, N. (2010). Implicit learning as an ability. *Cognition, 116*(3), 321–340.

Kaufman, S. B., Reynolds, M. R., Liu, X., Kaufman, A. S., & McGrew, K. S. (2012). Are cognitive *g* and academic achievement *g* one and the same *g*: An exploration on the Woodcock–Johnson and Kaufman tests. *Intelligence, 40*(2), 123–138.

Kavanau, J. L. (2004). Sleep researchers need to bring Darwin on board: Elucidating functions of sleep via adaptedness and natural selection. *Medical Hypotheses, 62*(2), 161–165.

Kavanau, J. L. (2005). Evolutionary approaches to understanding sleep. *Sleep Medicine Reviews, 9*(2), 141–152.

Kavanau, J. L. (2006). Is sleep's "supreme mystery" unraveling? An evolutionary analysis of sleep encounters no mystery; nor does life's earliest sleep, recently discovered in jellyfish. *Medical Hypotheses, 66*(1), 3–9.

Kavanau, J. L. (2008). Sleepless in the sea. *Science (Letters), 322*(5901), 527.

Kay, P., & Regier, T. (2006). Language, thought and color: Recent developments. *Trends in Cognitive Sciences, 10*(2), 51–54.

Kay, P., & Regier, T. (2007). Color naming universals: The case of Berinmo. *Cognition, 102*(2), 289–298.

Kaye, J. M., & Lightman, S. L. (2005). Psychological stress and endocrine axes. In K. Vedhara & M. Irwin (Eds.), *Human psychoneuroimmunology* (pp. 25–52). Oxford University Press.

Kaye, W. H., & Oberndorfer, T. (2010). Appetitive regulation in anorexia nervosa and bulimia nervosa. In W. S. Agras (Ed.), *The Oxford handbook of eating disorders* (pp. 75–102). Oxford University Press.

Kayyal, M. H., & Russell, J. A. (2013). Americans and Palestinians judge spontaneous facial expressions of emotion. *Emotion, 13*(5), 891–904.

Kazdin, A. E. (1978). *History of behavior modification: Experimental foundations of contemporary research*. University Park Press.

Kazdin, A. E. (2011). *Single-case research designs: Methods for clinical and applied settings* (2nd ed.). Oxford University Press.

Kazdin, A. E. (2013). Publishing your research. In M. J. Prinstein (Ed.), *The portable mentor: Expert guide to a successful career in psychology* (pp. 145–161). Springer.

Kealey, D. J. (1989). A study of cross-cultural effectiveness: Theoretical issues, practical applications. *International Journal of Intercultural Relations, 13*(3), 387–428.

Kean, S. (2014). *The tale of the dueling neurosurgeons: The history of the human brain as revealed by true stories of trauma, madness, and recovery*. Little, Brown.

Keane, T. M., Fairbank, J. A., Caddell, J. M., & Zimering, R. T. (1989). Implosive (flooding) therapy reduces symptoms of PTSD in Vietnam combat veterans. *Behavior Therapy, 20*(2), 245–260.

Keane, T. M., Marx, B. P., & Sloan, D. M. (2009). Post-traumatic stress disorder: Definition, prevalence, and risk factors. In P. J. Shiromani, T. M. Keane, & J. E. LeDoux (Eds.), *Post-traumatic stress disorder: Basic science and clinical practice* (pp. 1–19). Humana.

Kearney, C. A., & Vecchio, J. (2002). Contingency management. In M. Hersen & W. Sledge (Eds.), *Encyclopedia of psychotherapy* (Vol. 1, pp. 525–532). Academic Press.

Keblusek, L., Giles, H., & Maass, A. (2017). Communication and group life: How language and symbols shape intergroup relations. *Group Processes & Intergroup Relations, 20*(5), 632–643.

Keck, P. E., Jr., & McElroy, S. L. (2006). Lithium and mood stabilizers. In D. J. Stein, D. J. Kupfer, & A. F. Schatzberg (Eds.), *The American Psychiatric Publishing textbook of mood disorders* (pp. 281–290). American Psychiatric Publishing.

Keck, P. E., Jr., & McElroy, S. L. (2007). Pharmacological treatments for bipolar disorder. In P. E. Nathan & J. M. Gorman (Eds.), *A guide to treatments that work* (3rd ed., pp. 323–350). Oxford University Press.

Keefe, R. S. E., & Eesley, C. E. (2006). Neurocognitive impairments. In J. A. Lieberman, T. S. Stroup, & D. O. Perkins (Eds.), *The American Psychiatric Publishing textbook of schizophrenia* (pp. 245–260). American Psychiatric Association Publishing.

Keel, P. K. (2010). Epidemiology and course of eating disorders. In W. S. Agras (Ed.), *The Oxford handbook of eating disorders* (pp. 25–32). Oxford University Press.

Keel, P. K., & McCormick, L. (2010). Diagnosis, assessment, and treatment planning for anorexia nervosa. In C. M. Grilo & J. E. Mitchell (Eds.), *The treatment of eating disorders: A clinical handbook* (pp. 3–27). Guilford Press.

Keen, E. (2001). *A history of ideas in American psychology*. Praeger.

Keen, R. E., & Berthier, N. E. (2004). Continuities and discontinuities in infants' representation of objects and events. *Advances in Child Development and Behavior, 32*, 243–279.

Keene, A. C., & Duboue, E. R. (2018). The origins and evolution of sleep. *Journal of Experimental Biology, 221*(11), jeb159533.

Keeping, J. (2006). How does the bird build its nest? Instincts as embodied meaning. *Phenomenology and the Cognitive Sciences, 5*(2), 171–195.

Kegl, J., Senghas, A., & Coppola, M. (1999). Creations through contact: Sign language emergence and sign language change in Nicaragua. In M. DeGraff (Ed.), *Language creation and language change* (pp. 179–237). MIT Press.

Kehoe, E. J., & Macrae, M. (1998). Classical conditioning. In W. O'Donohue (Ed.), *Learning and behavior therapy* (pp. 36–58). Allyn & Bacon.

Keil, F. (2006). Cognitive science and cognitive development. In D. Kuhn & R. Siegler (Vol. Eds.), *Handbook of child psychology* (6th ed., Vol. 2, pp. 609–635). Wiley.

Keith, K. D. (2012). Visual illusions and ethnocentrism: Exemplars for teaching cross-cultural concepts. *History of Psychology, 15*(2), 171–176.

Keles, S., Idsøe, T., Friborg, O., Sirin, S., & Oppedal, B. (2017). The longitudinal relation between daily hassles and depressive symptoms among unaccompanied refugees in Norway. *Journal of Abnormal Child Psychology, 45*(7), 1413–1427.

Keller, A., Litzelman, K., Wisk, L. E., Maddox, T., Cheng, E. R., Creswell, P. D., & Witt, W. P. (2012). Does the perception that stress affects health matter? The association with health and mortality. *Health Psychology, 31*(5), 677–684.

Keller, M. A., & Goldberg, W. A. (2004). Co-sleeping: Help or hindrance for young children's independence? *Infant and Child Development, 13*(5), 369–388.

Keller, M. C., & Miller, G. (2006). Resolving the paradox of common, harmful, heritable mental disorders: Which evolutionary genetic models work best? *Behavioral and Brain Sciences, 29*(4), 385–404.

Kelley, A. E., & Berridge, K. C. (2002). The neuroscience of natural rewards: Relevance to addictive drugs. *The Journal of Neuroscience, 22*(9), 3306–3311.

Kelley, H. H. (1950). The warm-cold variable in first impressions of persons. *Journal of Personality, 18*(4), 431–439.

Kelley, H. H. (1973). The processes of causal attribution. *American Psychologist, 28*(2), 107–128.

Kellman, P. J., & Arterberry, M. E. (2006). Infant visual perception. In D. Kuhn & R. Siegler (Vol. Eds.), *Handbook of child psychology* (6th ed., Vol. 2, pp. 109–160). Wiley.

Kellner, C. H. (2019). *Handbook of ECT*. Cambridge University Press.

Kelly, Y., Zilanawala, A., Sacker, A., Hiatt, R., & Viner, R. (2017). Early puberty in 11-year-old girls: Millennium Cohort Study findings. *Archives of Disease in Childhood, 102*(3), 232–237.

Keltner, D., & Kring, A. M. (1998). Emotion, social function, and psychopathology. *Review of General Psychology, 2*(3), 320–342.

Kemeny, M. E. (2011). Psychoneuroimmunology. In H. S. Friedman (Ed.), *The Oxford handbook of health psychology* (pp. 138–161). Oxford University Press.

Kemp, N. (2010). Texting versus txtng: Reading and writing text messages, and links with other linguistic skills. *Writing Systems Research, 2*(1), 53–71.

Kemp, N., & Bushnell, C. (2011). Children's text messaging: Abbreviations, input methods, and links with literacy. *Journal of Computer Assisted Learning, 27*(1), 18–27.

Kempermann, G., Kuhn, H. G., & Gage, F. H. (1997). More hippocampal neurons in adult mice living in an enriched environment. *Nature, 386*(6624), 493–495.

Kendall-Tackett, K. A. (2005a). Introduction: Women's experiences of stress and trauma. In K. A. Kendall-Tackett (Ed.), *Handbook of women, stress, and trauma* (pp. 1–5). Brunner-Routledge.

Kendall-Tackett, K. A. (2005b). Caught in the middle: Stress in the lives of young adult women. In K. A. Kendall-Tackett (Ed.), *Handbook of women, stress, and trauma* (pp. 33–52). Brunner-Routledge.

Kendall-Tackett, K. A. (2005c). Trauma associated with perinatal events: Birth experience, prematurity, and childbearing loss. In K. A. Kendall-Tackett (Ed.), *Handbook of women, stress, and trauma* (pp. 53–74). Brunner-Routledge.

Kendi, I. X. (2019). *How to be an antiracist*. One World.

Kendler, K. S. (2018). Classification of psychopathology: Conceptual and historical background. *World Psychiatry, 17*(3), 241.

Kendler, K. S., & Diehl, S. R. (1993). The genetics of schizophrenia: A current genetic-epidemiologic perspective. *Schizophrenia Bulletin, 19*(2), 261–285.

Kendler, K. S., & Myers, J. (2010). The genetic and environmental relationship between major depression and the five-factor model of personality. *Psychological Medicine, 40*(5), 801–806.

Kendler, K. S., Myers, J., Potter, J., & Opalesky, J. (2009). A Web-based study of personality, psychopathology and substance use in twin, other relative and relationship pairs. *Twin Research and Human Genetics, 12*(2), 137–141.

Keng, S. L., Smoski, M. J., & Robins, C. J. (2011). Effects of mindfulness on psychological health: A review of empirical studies. *Clinical Psychology Review, 31*(6), 1041–1056.

Kennedy, W. (2012, May 12). Congregations find themselves stronger after storm. *The Joplin Globe.* http://www.joplinglobe.com/topstories/x1640795676/Congregations-find-themselves-stronger-after-storm

Kenny, M. C., Abreu, R. L., Marchena, M. T., Helpingstine, C., Lopez-Griman, A., & Mathews, B. (2017). Legal and clinical guidelines for making a child maltreatment report. *Professional Psychology: Research and Practice, 48*(6), 469–480.

Kenny, M. E. (1987). The extent and function of parental attachment among first-year college students. *Journal of Youth and Adolescence, 16*(1), 17–29.

Kenny, M. E., & Barton, C. E. (2003). Attachment theory and research: Contributions for understanding late adolescent and young adult development. In J. Demick & C. Andreoletti (Eds.), *Handbook of adult development* (pp. 371–390). Springer Science+Business Media.

Kenny, M. E., & Donaldson, G. A. (1991). Contributions of parental attachment and family structure to the social and psychological functioning of first-year college students. *Journal of Counseling Psychology, 38*(4), 479.

Kenny, M. E., & Perez, V. (1996). Attachment and psychological well-being among racially and ethnically diverse first-year college students. *Journal of College Student Development, 37*(5), 527–535.

Kenny, M. E., & Sirin, S. R. (2006). Parental attachment, self-worth, and depressive symptoms among emerging adults. *Journal of Counseling & Development, 84*(1), 61–71.

Kenrick, D. T. (2012). Evolutionary theory and human social behavior. In P. A. M. Van Lange, A. W. Kruglanski, & E. T. Higgins (Eds.), *Handbook of theories of social psychology* (Vol. 1, pp. 11–31). Sage.

Kent, K. M., Pelham, W. E., Jr., Molina, B. S., Sibley, M. H., Waschbusch, D. A., Yu, J., Gnagy, E. M., Biswas, A., Babinski, D. E., & Karch, K. M. (2011). The academic experience of male high school students with ADHD. *Journal of Abnormal Child Psychology, 39*(3), 451–462.

Kent, P. (2017). Fluid intelligence: A brief history. *Applied Neuropsychology: Child, 6*(3), 193–203.

Keppel, G., & Underwood, B. J. (1962). Proactive inhibition in short-term retention of single items. *Journal of Verbal Learning and Verbal Behavior, 1*(3), 153–161.

Kerckhoff, A. C. (2003). From student to worker. In J. T. Mortimer & M. J. Shanahan (Eds.), *Handbook of the life course* (pp. 251–267). Kluwer.

Kern, D. M., Auchincloss, A. H., Robinson, L. F., Stehr, M. F., & Pham-Kanter, G. (2017). Healthy and unhealthy food prices across neighborhoods and their association with neighborhood socioeconomic status and proportion Black/Hispanic. *Journal of Urban Health, 94*(4), 494–505.

Kern, L., & Kokina, A. (2008). Using positive reinforcement to decrease challenging behavior. In J. K. Luiselli, D. C. Russo, W. P. Christian, & S. W. Wilczynski (Eds.), *Effective practices for children with autism* (pp. 413–432). Oxford University Press.

Kern, M. L., & Friedman, H. S. (2008). Do conscientious individuals live longer? A quantitative review. *Health Psychology, 27*(5), 505–512.

Kern, M. L., & Friedman, H. S. (2017). *The Oxford handbook of the five factor model.* Oxford.

Kernberg, O. F. (2004). *Contemporary controversies in psychoanalytic theories, techniques, and their applications.* Yale University Press.

Kersh, R., & Morone, J. (2011). Obesity politics and policy. In J. H. Cawley (Ed.), *The Oxford handbook of the social science of obesity* (pp. 158–172). Oxford University Press.

Kesselring, T. (2009). The mind's staircase revisited. In U. Müller, J. I. M. Carpendale, & L. Smith (Eds.), *The Cambridge companion to Piaget* (pp. 371–399). Cambridge University Press.

Kessler, R. C. (2018). Trauma and PTSD in the United States. In C. B. Nemeroff & C. R. Marmar (Eds.), *Post-traumatic stress disorder* (pp. 109–132). Oxford University Press.

Kessler, R. C., & Wang, P. S. (2009). Epidemiology of depression. In I. H. Gotlib & C. L. Hammen (Eds.), *Handbook of depression* (2nd ed., pp. 5–22). Guilford Press.

Kessler, R. C., Adler, L., Barkley, R., Biederman, J., Conners, C. K., Demler, O., Faraone, S. V., Greenhill, L. L., Howes, M. J., Secnik, K., Spencer, T., Ustun, T. B., Walters, E. E., & Zaslavsky, A. M. (2006). The prevalence and correlates of adult ADHD in the United States: Results from the National Comorbidity Survey Replication. *American Journal of Psychiatry, 163*(4), 716–723.

Kessler, R. C., Berglund, P. A., Chiu, W. T., Deitz, A. C., Hudson, J. I., Shahly, V., ... Xavier, M. (2013). The prevalence and correlates of binge eating disorder in the World Health Organization World Mental Health Surveys. *Biological Psychiatry, 73*(9), 904–914.

Kessler, R. C., Berglund, P. A., Chiu, W., Demler, O., Glantz, M., Lane, M. C., Jin, R., Merikangas, K. R., Nock, M., Olfson, M., Pincus, H. A., Walters, E. E., Wang, P. S., & Wells, K. B. (2008). The national comorbidity survey replication (NCS-R): Cornerstone in improving mental health and mental health care in the United States. In R. C. Kessler & T. B. Ustun (Eds.), *The WHO World Mental Health Surveys: Global perspectives on the epidemiology of mental disorders* (pp. 165–209). Cambridge University Press.

Kessler, R. C., Berglund, P., Demler, O., Jin, R., Merikangas, K. R., & Walters, E. E. (2005a). Lifetime prevalence and age-of-onset distributions of DSM-IV disorders in the National Comorbidity Survey Replication. *Archives of General Psychiatry, 62*(7), 593–602.

Kessler, R. C., Chiu, W. T., Demler, O., & Walters, E. E. (2005b). Prevalance, severity, and comorbidity of 12-month DSM-IV disorders in the National Comorbidity Survey Replication (NCS-R). *Archives of General Psychiatry, 62*(6), 617–709.

Kessler, R. C., Ruscio, A. M., Shear, K., & Wittchen, H. (2009). Epidemiology of anxiety disorders. In M. M. Antony & M. B. Stein (Eds.), *Oxford handbook of anxiety and related disorders* (pp. 19–33). Oxford University Press.

Ketter, T. A., & Wang, P. W. (2010). DSM-IV-TR diagnosis of bipolar disorders. In T. A. Ketter (Ed.), *Handbook of diagnosis and treatment of bipolar disorders* (pp. 11–37). American Psychiatric Publishing.

Keyes, L., Small, E., & Nikolova, S. (2020). The complex relationship between colorism and poor health outcomes with African Americans: A systematic review. *Analyses of Social Issues and Public Policy, 20*(1), 676–697. https://doi.org/10.1111/asap.12223

Keysers, C., & Gazzola, V. (2018). Neural correlates of empathy in humans, and the need for animal models. In K. Z. Meyza & E. Knapska (Eds.), *Neuronal correlates of empathy: From rodent to human* (pp. 37–52). Academic Press.

Kharkhurin, A. V., & Samadpour Motalleebi, S. N. (2008). The impact of culture on the creative potential of American, Russian, and Iranian college students. *Creativity Research Journal, 20*(4), 404–411.

Khazan, I. Z. (2013). *The clinical handbook of biofeedback: A step-by-step for training and practice with mindfulness.* Wiley-Blackwell.

Khoshaba, D. M., & Maddi, S. R. (2001). *HardiTraining.* Hardiness Institute.

Khoury, B., Langer, E. J., & Pagnini, F. (2014). The DSM: Mindful science or mindless power? A critical review. *Frontiers in Psychology, 5*, 602.

Khoury, B., Lecomte, T., Fortin, G., Masse, M., Therien, P., Bouchard, V., & Hofmann, S. G. (2013). Mindfulness-based therapy: A comprehensive meta-analysis. *Clinical Psychology Review, 33*(6), 763–771.

Kidd, G., Jr. (2010). Auditory thresholds. In E. B. Goldstein (Ed.), *Encyclopedia of perception* (pp. 197–200). Sage.

Kiecolt-Glaser, J. K., Bane, C., Glaser, R., & Malarkey, W. B. (2003). Love, marriage, and divorce: Newlyweds' stress hormones foreshadow relationship changes. *Journal of Consulting and Clinical Psychology, 71*(1), 176–188.

Kiecolt-Glaser, J. K., Glaser, R., Cacioppo, J. T., MacCallum, R. C., Snydersmith, M., Kim, C., & Malarkey, W. B. (1997). Marital conflict in older adults: Endocrinological and immunological correlates. *Psychosomatic Medicine, 59*(4), 339–349.

Kiecolt-Glaser, J. K., Glaser, R., Gravenstein, S., Malarkey, W. B., & Sheridan, J. (1996). Chronic stress alters the immune response to influenza virus vaccine in older adults. *Proceedings of the National Academy of Sciences, 93*(7), 3043–3047.

Kiecolt-Glaser, J. K., Marucha, P. T., Mercado, A. M., Malarkey, W. B., & Glaser, R. (1995). Slowing of wound healing by psychological stress. *The Lancet, 346*(8984), 1194–1196.

Kihlstrom, J. F. (2002). To honor Kraepelin: From symptoms to pathology in the diagnosis of mental illness. In L. E. Beutler & M. L. Malik (Eds.), *Rethinking the DSM: A psychological perspective* (pp. 279–303). American Psychological Association.

Kihlstrom, J. F. (2005). Is hypnosis an altered state of consciousness or what? *Contemporary Hypnosis, 22*(1), 34–38.

Kihlstrom, J. F. (2007). Consciousness in hypnosis. In P. D. Zelazo, M. Moscovitch, & E. Thompson (Eds.), *The Cambridge handbook of consciousness* (pp. 445–480). Cambridge University Press.

Kihlstrom, J. F. (2008). The domain of hypnosis, revisited. In M. R. Nash & A. J. Barnier (Eds.), *The Oxford handbook of hypnosis: Theory, research, and practice* (pp. 21–52). Oxford University Press.

Kiken, L. G., Lundberg, K. B., & Fredrickson, B. L. (2017). Being present and enjoying it: Dispositional mindfulness and savoring the moment are distinct, interactive predictors of positive emotions and psychological health. *Mindfulness, 8*(5), 1280–1290.

Kilmer, J. R., Geisner, I. M., Gasser, M. L., & Lindgren, K. P. (2015). Normative perceptions of non-medical stimulant use: Associations with actual use and hazardous drinking. *Addictive Behaviors, 42*, 51–56.

Kim, A. S. N., Shakory, S., Azad, A., Popovic, C., & Park, L. (2020). Understanding the impact of attendance and participation on academic achievement. *Scholarship of Teaching and Learning in Psychology, 6*(4), 272–284. https://doi.org/10.1037/stl0000151

Kim, D. J., Davis, E. P., Sandman, C. A., Glynn, L., Sporns, O., O'Donnell, B. F., & Hetrick, W. P. (2019). Childhood poverty and the organization of structural brain connectome. *NeuroImage, 184*, 409–416.

Kim, E. K. (2012, November 30). Cop who bought shoes for homeless man "really didn't think about the money." *Today News.* http://todaynews.today.com/news/2012/11/30/15568550-cop-who-bought-shoes-for-homeless-man-really-didnt-think-about-the-money?lite

Kim, E. S., Hagan, K. A., Grodstein, F., DeMeo, D. L., De Vivo, I., & Kubzansky, L. D. (2017). Optimism and cause-specific mortality: A prospective cohort study. *American Journal of Epidemiology, 185*(1), 21–29.

Kim, H. S., Sherman, D. K., & Taylor, S. E. (2008). Culture and social support. *American Psychologist, 63*(6), 518–526.

Kim, J. E., & Moen, P. (2001). Is retirement good or bad for subjective well-being? *Current Directions in Psychological Science, 10*(3), 83–86.

Kim, J. E., & Moen, P. (2002). Retirement transitions, gender, and psychological well-being: A life-course, ecological model. *The Journals of Gerontology Series B: Psychological Sciences and Social Sciences, 57*(3), P212–P222.

Kim, J. L., Lynn Sorsoli, C., Collins, K., Zylbergold, B. A., Schooler, D., & Tolman, D. L. (2007). From sex to sexuality: Exposing the heterosexual script on primetime network television. *Journal of Sex Research, 44*(2), 145–157.

Kim, N., & Wojcieszak, M. (2018). Intergroup contact through online comments: Effects of direct and extended contact on outgroup attitudes. *Computers in Human Behavior, 81*, 63–72.

Kim, U. E., Triandis, H. C., Kâğitçibaşi, ö. E., Choi, S. C. E., & Yoon, G. E. (Eds.). (1994). *Individualism and collectivism: Theory, method, and applications.* Sage.

Kim, Y. J. (2006). The role of regulatory focus in message framing in antismoking advertisements for adolescents. *Journal of Advertising, 35*(1), 143–151.

Kim, Y., Park, I., Kang, S., Kim, Y., Park, I., & Kang, S. (2018). Age and gender differences in health risk perception. *Central European Journal of Public Health, 26*(1), 54–59.

Kimble, G. A. (1981). *Biological and cognitive constraints on learning.* American Psychological Association.

Kimmel, R. J., Roy-Byrne, P. P., & Cowley, D. S. (2015). Pharmacological treatments for panic disorder, generalized anxiety disorder, specific phobia, and social anxiety disorder. In P. E. Nathan & J. M. Gorman (Eds.), *A guide to treatments that work* (4th ed., pp. 463–506). Oxford University Press.

Kimura, D. (1967). Functional asymmetry of the brain in dichotic listening. *Cortex, 3*(2), 163–178.

King, A. R., Ratzak, A., Ballantyne, S., Knutson, S., Russell, T. D., Pogalz, C. R., & Breen, C. M. (2018). Differentiating corporal punishment from physical abuse in the prediction of lifetime aggression. *Aggressive Behavior, 44*(3), 306–315.

King, L. A. (2001). The health benefits of writing about life goals. *Personality and Social Psychology Bulletin, 27*(7), 798–807.

Kingdon, D. G., & Turkington, D. (2005). *Cognitive therapy of schizophrenia.* Guilford Press.

Kingery, J. N., & Erdley, C. A. (2007). Peer experience as predictors of adjustment across the middle school transition. *Education and Treatment of Children, 30*(2), 73–88.

Kingery, J. N., Erdley, C. A., & Marshall, K. C. (2011). Peer acceptance and friendship as predictors of early adolescents' adjustment across the middle school transition. *Merrill-Palmer Quarterly, 57*(3), 215–243.

Kingsley, R. C., & Hall, V. C. (1967). Training conservation through the use of learning sets. *Child Development, 38*(4), 1111–1126.

Kinnish, K. K., Strassberg, D. S., & Turner, C. W. (2005). Sex differences in the flexibility of sexual orientation: A multidimensional retrospective assessment. *Archives of Sexual Behavior, 34*(2), 173–183.

Kinsella, E. L., Ritchie, T. D., & Igou, E. R. (2015). Zeroing in on heroes: A prototype analysis of hero features. *Journal of Personality and Social Psychology, 108*(1), 114–127.

Kinzler, K. D. (2021). Language as a social cue. *Annual Review of Psychology, 72*, 241–264. https://doi.org/10.1146/annurev-psych-010418-103034

Kinzler, K. D., Corriveau, K. H., & Harris, P. L. (2011). Children's selective trust in native-accented speakers. *Developmental Science, 14*(1), 106–111.

Kinzler, K. D., Shutts, K., DeJesus, J., & Spelke, E. S. (2009). Accent trumps race in guiding children's social preferences. *Social Cognition, 27*(4), 623–634.

Kirby, M., Maggi, S., & D'Angiulli, A. (2011). School start times and the sleep–wake cycle of adolescents: A review and critical evaluation of available evidence. *Educational Researcher, 40*(2), 56–61.

Kirmayer, L. J., & Jarvis, G. E. (2006). Depression across cultures. In D. J. Stein, D. J. Kupfer, & A. F. Schatzberg (Eds.), *The American Psychiatric Publishing textbook of mood disorders* (pp. 699–716). American Psychiatric Association Publishing.

Kirmayer, L. J., Adeponle, A., & Dzokoto, V. A. A. (2018). Varieties of global psychology: Cultural diversity and constructions of the self. In S. Fernando & R. Moodley (Eds.), *Global Psychologies* (pp. 21–37). Palgrave Macmillan.

Kirsch, A. C., & Murnen, S. K. (2015). "Hot" girls and "cool dudes": Examining the prevalence of the heterosexual script in American children's television media. *Psychology of Popular Media Culture, 4*(1), 18–30.

Kirsch, I., & Braffman, W. (2001). Imaginative suggestibility and hypnotizability. *Current Directions in Psychological Science, 10*(2), 57–61.

Kirschbaum, C., & Hellhammer, D. H. (1994). Salivary cortisol in psychoneuroendocrine research: Recent developments and applications. *Psychoneuroendocrinology, 19*(4), 313–333.

Kirschbaum, C., Tietze, A., Skoluda, N., & Dettenborn, L. (2009). Hair as a retrospective calendar of cortisol production—increased cortisol incorporation into hair in the third trimester of pregnancy. *Psychoneuroendocrinology, 34*(1), 32–37.

Kirsh, S. J. (2012). *Children, adolescents, and media violence: A critical look at the research*. Sage.

Kisilevsky, B. S., Stack, D. M., & Muir, D. W. (1991). Fetal and infant response to tactile stimulation. In M. J. S. Weiss & P. R. Zelazo (Eds.), *Newborn attention: Biological constraints and the influence of experience* (pp. 63–98). Ablex.

Kitayama, S., Duffy, S., Kawamura, T., & Larsen, J. T. (2003). Perceiving an object and its context in different cultures: A cultural look at new look. *Psychological Science, 14*(3), 201–206.

Kite, M. E., & Bryant-Lees, K. B. (2016). Historical and contemporary attitudes toward homosexuality. *Teaching of Psychology, 43*(2), 164–170.

Kito, M. (2005). Self-disclosure in romantic relationships and friendships among American and Japanese college students. *The Journal of Social Psychology, 145*(2), 127–140.

Klahr, D. (2012). Revisiting Piaget: A perspective from studies of children's problem-solving abilities. In A. M. Slater & P. C. Quinn (Eds.), *Developmental psychology: Revisiting the classic studies* (pp. 56–70). Sage.

Klass, D., & Hutch, R. A. (1985). Elisabeth Kubler-Ross as a religious leader. *OMEGA—Journal of Death and Dying, 16*(2), 89–109.

Klatzky, R. L., & Lederman, S. J. (2010). Haptics. In E. B. Goldstein (Ed.), *Encyclopedia of perception* (pp. 477–481). Sage.

Klein, D. N., & Black, S. R. (2017). Persistent depressive disorder. In R. J. DeRubeis & D. R. Strunk (Eds.), *The Oxford handbook of mood disorders* (pp. 238–253). Oxford University Press.

Klein, D. N., Shankman, S. A., & McFarland, B. R. (2006). Classification of mood disorders. In D. J. Stein, D. J. Kupfer, & A. F. Schatzberg (Eds.), *The American Psychiatric Publishing textbook of mood disorders* (pp. 17–32). American Psychiatric Association Publishing.

Klein, R. P., & Jennings, K. D. (1979). Responses to social and inanimate stimuli in early infancy. *The Journal of Genetic Psychology, 135*(1), 3–9.

Kleinke, C. (2002). *Coping with life challenges*. Waveland Press.

Kleinman, N. L., Brook, R. A., Doan, J. F., Melkonian, A. K., & Baran, R. W. (2009). Health benefit costs and absenteeism due to insomnia from the employer's perspective: A retrospective, case-control, database study. *The Journal of Clinical Psychiatry, 70*(8), 1098–1104.

Kleitman, N. (1963). *Sleep and wakefulness*. University of Chicago Press.

Kleitman, N., & Kleitman, E. (1953). Effect of non-twenty-four-hour routines of living on oral temperature and heart rate. *Journal of Applied Physiology, 6*(5), 283–291.

Klenk, M. M., Strauman, T. J., & Higgins, E. T. (2011). Regulatory focus and anxiety: A self-regulatory model of GAD-depression comorbidity. *Personality and Individual Differences, 50*(7), 935–943.

Klerman, G. L., Weissman, M. M., Rounsaville, B. J., & Chevron, E. S. (1984). *Interpersonal psychotherapy of depression*. Basic Books.

Klinesmith, J., Kasser, T., & McAndrew, F. T. (2006). Guns, testosterone, and aggression: An experimental test of a mediational hypothesis. *Psychological Science, 17*(7), 568–571.

Kloep, M., & Hendry, L. B. (2010). Letting go or holding on? Parents' perceptions of their relationships with their children during emerging adulthood. *British Journal of Developmental Psychology, 28*(4), 817–834. https://doi.org/10.1348/026151009X480581

Kloep, M., & Hendry, L. B. (2011). A systemic approach to the transitions to adulthood. In J. J. Arnett, M. Kloep, L. B. Hendry, & J. L. Tanner (Eds.), *Debating emerging adulthood: Stage or process?* (pp. 53–76). Oxford University Press.

Klump, K. L., Miller, K., Keel, P., McGue, M., & Iacono, W. (2001). Genetic and environmental influence on anorexia nervosa symptoms in a population-based twin sample. *Psychological Medicine, 31*(4), 737–740.

Knapp, S. J., & VandeCreek, L. D. (2006). *Practical ethics for psychologists: A positive approach*. American Psychological Association.

Kneeland, T. W., & Warren, C. A. B. (2002). *Pushbutton psychiatry: A history of electroshock in America*. Praeger.

Knobloch, L. K., Miller, L. E., Sprecher, S., Wenzel, A., & Harvey, J. (2008). Uncertainty and relationship initiation. In S. Sprecher, A. Wenzel, & J. Harvey (Eds.), *Handbook of relationship initiation* (pp. 121–134). Psychology Press.

Knobloch-Westerwick, S., Mothes, C., & Polavin, N. (2020). Confirmation bias, ingroup bias, and negativity bias in selective exposure to political information. *Communication Research, 47*(1), 104–124. https://doi.org/10.1177/0093650217719596

Knoll, J., & Matthes, J. (2017). The effectiveness of celebrity endorsements: A meta-analysis. *Journal of the Academy of Marketing Science, 45*, 55–75. https://doi.org/10.1007/s11747-016-0503-8

Knopf, A. (2017). Vaccines do not cause autism: Pediatricians fight back against anti-science. *The Brown University Child and Adolescent Behavior Letter, 33*(S2), 1–2. https://doi.org/10.1002/cbl.30195

Knopf, A. (2021). Time to remember: Vaccines don't cause autism. *The Brown University Child and Adolescent Behavior Letter, 37*(7), 9–10. https://doi.org/10.1002/cbl.30559

Knudsen, E. I. (2018). Neural circuits that mediate selective attention: A comparative perspective. *Trends in Neurosciences, 41*(11), 789–805.

Knutsson, A. (2003). Health disorders of shift workers. *Occupational Medicine, 53*(2), 103–108.

Kobak, R. (2012). Attachment and early social deprivation: Revisiting Harlow's monkey studies. In A. M. Slater & P. C. Quinn (Eds.), *Developmental psychology: Revisiting the classic studies* (pp. 10–23). Sage.

Kobau, R., Seligman, M. E., Peterson, C., Diener, E., Zack, M. M., Chapman, D., & Thompson, W. (2011). Mental health promotion in public health: Perspectives and strategies from positive psychology. *American Journal of Public Health, 101*(8), e1–e9.

Koenig, M., & Cole, C. (2013). Early word learning. In D. Reisberg (Ed.), *The Oxford handbook of cognitive psychology* (pp. 492–503). Oxford University Press.

Koerner, K. (2012). *Doing dialectical behavior therapy: A practical guide*. Guilford Press.

Koester, J., & Siegelbaum, S. A. (2013a). Membrane potential and the passive electrical properties of the neuron. In E. R. Kandel, J. H. Schwartz, T. M. Jessell, S. A. Siegelbaum, & A. J. Hudspeth (Eds.), *Principles of neural science* (5th ed., pp. 126–147). McGraw-Hill.

Koester, J., & Siegelbaum, S. A. (2013b). Propagated signaling: The action potential. In E. R. Kandel, J. H. Schwartz, T. M. Jessell, S. A. Siegelbaum, & A. J. Hudspeth (Eds.), *Principles of neural science* (5th ed., pp. 148–171). McGraw-Hill.

Koestner, R., Zuckerman, M., & Koestner, J. (1987). Praise, involvement, and intrinsic motivation. *Journal of Personality and Social Psychology, 53*(2), 383–390.

Kohlberg, L. (1963). The development of children's orientations toward a moral order. *Human Development, 51*(1), 8–20.

Kohlberg, L. (1973a). The claim to moral adequacy of a highest stage of moral judgment. *The Journal of Philosophy, 70*(18), 630–646.

Kohlberg, L. (1973b). The contribution of developmental psychology to education—examples from moral education. *Educational Psychologist, 10*(1), 2–14.

Kohlberg, L. (1974). Education, moral development and faith. *Journal of Moral Education, 4*(1), 5–16.

Kohlberg, L. (1981). *The philosophy of moral development: Moral stages and the idea of justice*. Harper & Row.

Kohlberg, L. (1984). *Essays on moral development* (Vol. II). Harper & Row.

Kohlberg, L., & Candee, D. (1984). The relationship of moral judgment to moral action. In W. Kirtines & J. Gerwitz (Eds.), *Morality, moral behavior, and moral development* (pp. 52–73). Wiley.

Kohler, W. (1924). *The mentality of apes*. Harcourt.

Kohli, R., Arteaga, N., & McGovern, E. R. (2019). "Compliments" and "jokes": Unpacking racial microaggressions in the K–12 classroom. In G. C. Torino, D. P. Rivera, C. M. Capodilupo, K. L. Nadal, & D. W. Sue (Eds.), *Microaggression theory: Influence and implications* (pp. 276–290). Wiley.

Kohout, J. L., & Pate, W. E., II. (2013). Employment and trends in psychology. In M. J. Prinstein (Ed.), *The portable mentor: Expert guide to a successful career in psychology* (pp. 343–361). New York, NY: Springer.

Kok, B. E., Coffey, K. A., Cohn, M. A., Catalino, L. I., Vacharkulksemsuk, T., Algoe, S. B., Brantley, M., & Fredrickson, B. L. (2013). How positive emotions build physical health: Perceived positive social connections account for the upward spiral between positive emotions and vagal tone. *Psychological Science, 24*(7), 1123–1132.

Kolb, B., & Gibb, R. (2011). Brain plasticity and behaviour in the developing brain. *Journal of the Canadian Academy of Child and Adolescent Psychiatry, 20*(4), 265.

Kolb, B., & Whishaw, I. Q. (1998). Brain plasticity and behavior. *Annual Review of Psychology, 49*(1), 43–64.

Kolden, G. G., Klein, M. H., Wang, C., & Austin, S. B. (2011). Congruence/genuineness. In J. C. Norcross (Ed.), *Psychotherapy relationships that work: Evidence-based responsiveness* (2nd ed., 187–202). Oxford University Press.

Kolden, G. G., Wang, C. C., Austin, S. B., Chang, Y., & Klein, M. H. (2018). Congruence /genuineness: A meta-analysis. *Psychotherapy, 55*(4), 424–433.

Koltko-Rivera, M. E. (1998). Maslow's "transhumanism": Was transpersonal psychology conceived as "a psychology without people in it"? *Journal of Humanistic Psychology, 38*(1), 71–80.

Koltko-Rivera, M. E. (2006). Rediscovering the later version of Maslow's hierarchy of needs: Self-transcendence and opportunities for theory, research, and unification. *Review of General Psychology, 10*(4), 302–317.

Komarraju, M., Karau, S. J., & Schmeck, R. R. (2009). Role of the Big Five personality traits in predicting college students' academic motivation and achievement. *Learning and Individual Differences, 19*(1), 47–52.

Koncz, A., Demetrovics, Z., & Takacs, Z. K. (2021). Meditation interventions efficiently reduce cortisol levels of at-risk samples: A meta-analysis. *Health Psychology Review, 15*(1), 56–84. https://doi.org/10.1080/17437199.2020.1760727

Kong, L., Fang, M., Ma, T., Li, G., Yang, F., Meng, Q., Li, Y., &Li, P. (2018). Positive affect mediates the relationships between resilience, social support and posttraumatic growth of women with infertility. *Psychology, Health & Medicine, 23*(6), 707–716.

Konijn, E. A., Bijvank, M. N., & Bushman, B. J. (2007). I wish I were a warrior: The role of wishful identification in effects of violent video games on aggression in adolescent boys. *Developmental Psychology, 43*(4), 1038–1044.

Koocher, G. P. (2009). Any minute now but far far away: Electronically mediated mental health. *Clinical Psychology: Science and Practice, 16*(3), 339–342.

Koocher, G. P. (2013). Ethical considerations in clinical psychology research. In J. S. Comer & P. C. Kendall (Eds.), *The Oxford handbook of research strategies for clinical psychology* (pp. 395–412). Oxford University Press.

Koocher, G. P., & Campbell, L. F. (2016). Professional ethics in the United States. In J. C. Norcross, G. R. VandenBos, & D. K. Freedheim (Eds.), *APA handbook of clinical psychology* (Vol. 5, pp. 301–337). American Psychological Association.

Koocher, G. P., & Daniel, J. H. (2012). Treating children and adolescents. In S. J. Knapp (Ed.), *APA handbook of ethics in psychology* (Vol. 2, pp. 3–14). American Psychological Association.

Koocher, G. P., & Keith-Spiegel, P. (2016). *Ethics in psychology and the mental health professions: Standards and cases*. Oxford University Press.

Koole, S. L. (2009). The psychology of emotion regulation: An integrative review. *Cognition and Emotion, 23*(1), 4–41.

Kopelman, M. D. (2002a). Psychogenic amnesia. In A. D. Baddeley, M. D. Kopelman, & B. A. Wilson (Ed.), *The handbook of memory disorders* (2nd ed., pp. 451–471). Wiley.

Kopelowicz, A., Liberman, R. P., & Zarate, R. (2007). Psychosocial treatments for schizophrenia. In P. E. Nathan & J. M. Gorman (Eds.), *A guide to treatments that work* (3rd ed., pp. 243–269). Oxford University Press.

Korchmaros, J. D., & Kenny, D. A. (2001). Emotional closeness as a mediator of the effect of genetic relatedness on altruism. *Psychological Science, 12*(3), 262–265.

Korchmaros, J. D., & Kenny, D. A. (2006). An evolutionary and close-relationship model of helping. *Journal of Social and Personal Relationships, 23*(1), 21–43.

Koriat, A. (2000). Control processes in remembering. In E. Tulving & F. I. M. Craik (Eds.), *The Oxford handbook of memory* (pp. 333–346). Oxford University Press.

Kornienko, O., Santos, C. E., Martin, C. L., & Granger, K. L. (2016). Peer influence on gender identity development in adolescence. *Developmental Psychology, 52*(10), 1578–1592.

Kornstein, S. G., & Sloan, D. M. E. (2006). Depression and gender. In D. J. Stein, D. J. Kupfer, & A. F. Schatzberg (Eds.), *The American Psychiatric Publishing textbook of mood disorders* (pp. 687–698). American Psychiatric Association Publishing.

Korzekwa, M. I., Dell, P. F., Links, P. S., Thabane, L., & Fougere, P. (2009). Dissociation in borderline personality disorder: A detailed look. *Journal of Trauma & Dissociation, 10*(3), 346–367.

Kosic, A. (2006). Personality and individual factors in acculturation. In D. L. Sam & J. W. Berry (Eds.), *The Cambridge handbook of acculturation psychology* (pp. 113–128). Cambridge University Press.

Koslowsky, M., & Pindek, S. (2011). Impression management: Influencing perceptions of self. In D. Chadee (Ed.), *Theories in social psychology* (pp. 280–296). Wiley-Blackwell.

Koterba, E. A., Ponti, F., & Ligman, K. (2021). "Get out of my selfie!" Narcissism, gender, and motives for self-photography among emerging adults. *Psychology of Popular Media, 10*(1), 98–104. https://doi.org/10.1037/ppm0000272

Kotov, R., Gamez, W., Schmidt, F., & Watson, D. (2010). Linking "big" personality traits to anxiety, depressive, and substance use disorders: A meta-analysis. *Psychological Bulletin, 136*(5), 768–821.

Kounios, J., & Beeman, M. (2009). The *Aha!* moment: The cognitive neuroscience of insight. *Current Directions in Psychological Science, 18*(4), 210–216.

Kowler, E., & Collewijin, H. (2010). Eye movements: Behavioral. In E. B. Goldstein (Ed.), *Encyclopedia of perception* (pp. 421–425). Sage.

Kozusznik, M. W., Rodríguez, I., & Peiró, J. M. (2015). Eustress and distress climates in teams: Patterns and outcomes. *International Journal of Stress Management, 22*(1), 1–23.

Kraaykamp, G., & Van Eijck, K. (2005). Personality, media preferences, and cultural participation. *Personality and Individual Differences, 38*(7), 1675–1688.

Kraemer, H. C. (2010). Concepts and methods for researching categories and dimensions in psychiatric diagnosis. In T. Millon, R. F. Krueger, & E. Simonsen (Eds.), *Contemporary directions in psychopathology: Scientific foundations of the DSM-V and ICD-11* (pp. 337–349). Guilford Press.

Kraft, C., & Mayeux, L. (2018). Associations among friendship jealousy, peer status, and relational aggression in early adolescence. *The Journal of Early Adolescence, 38*(3), 385–407.

Kraha, A., & Boals, A. (2014). Why so negative? Positive flashbulb memories for a personal event. *Memory, 22*(4), 442–449.

Krakauer, J. W., Ghazanfar, A. A., Gomez-Marin, A., MacIver, M. A., & Poeppel, D. (2017). Neuroscience needs behavior: Correcting a reductionist bias. *Neuron, 93*(3), 480–490.

Krakow, B., Hollifield, M., Johnston, L., Koss, M., Schrader, R., Warner, T. D., & Prince, H. (2001). Imagery rehearsal therapy for chronic nightmares in sexual assault survivors with posttraumatic stress disorder: A randomized controlled trial. *The Journal of the American Medical Association, 286*(5), 537–545.

Krakow, B., & Zadra, A. (2006). Clinical management of chronic nightmares: Imagery rehearsal therapy. *Behavioral Sleep Medicine, 4*(1), 45–70.

Kramer, D. (2003). The ontogeny of wisdom in its variations. In J. Demick & C. Andreoletti (Eds.), *Handbook of adult development* (pp. 131–152). Kluwer.

Kramer, J. (2007). Is abstraction the key to computing? *Communications of the ACM, 50*(4), 36–42.

Kramer, M. (2006). Biology of dreaming. In T. L. Lee-Chiong (Ed.), *Sleep: A comprehensive handbook* (pp. 31–36). Wiley-Liss.

Krans, J., Woud, M. L., Näring, G., Becker, E. S., & Holmes, E. A. (2010). Exploring involuntary recall in posttraumatic stress disorder from an information processing perspective: Intrusive images of trauma. In J. H. Mace (Ed.), *The act of remembering* (pp. 311–336). Wiley-Blackwell.

Kraus, M. W., Huang, C., & Keltner, D. (2010). Tactile communication, cooperation, and performance: An ethological study of the NBA. *Emotion, 10*(5), 745–749.

Kraus, R. (2004). Ethical and legal considerations for providers of mental health services online. In R. Kraus, J. Zack, & G. Stricker (Eds.), *Online counseling: A handbook for mental health professionals* (pp. 123–144). Elsevier.

Kraus, S. J. (1995). Attitudes and the prediction of behavior: A meta-analysis of the empirical literature. *Personality and Social Psychology Bulletin, 21*(1), 58–75.

Krause, A. J., Simon, E. B., Mander, B. A., Greer, S. M., Saletin, J. M., Goldstein-Piekarski, A. N., & Walker, M. P. (2017). The sleep-deprived human brain. *Nature Reviews Neuroscience, 18*(7), 404–418.

Krause, M. A., & Domjan, M. (2017). Ethological and evolutionary perspectives on Pavlovian conditioning. In J. Call (Ed.), *APA handbook of comparative psychology: Vol. 2. Perception, learning, and cognition* (pp. 247–266). American Psychological Association.

Krcmar, M., & Kean, L. G. (2005). Uses and gratifications of media violence: Personality correlates of viewing and liking violent genres. *Media Psychology, 7*(4), 399–420.

Krcmar, M., van der Meer, A., & Cingel, D. P. (2015). Development as an explanation for and predictor of online self-disclosure among Dutch adolescents. *Journal of Children and Media, 9*(2), 194–211. https://doi.org/10.1080/17482798.2015.1015432

Krebs, D. L., & Denton, K. (2005). Toward a more pragmatic approach to morality: A critical evaluation of Kohlberg's model. *Psychological Review, 112*(3), 629.

Krebs, P., Norcross, J. C., Nicholson, J. M., & Prochaska, J. O. (2018). Stages of change and psychotherapy outcomes: A review and meta-analysis. *Journal of Clinical Psychology, 74*(11), 1964–1979.

Krech, D., Rosenzweig, M. R., & Bennett, E. L. (1966). Environmental impoverishment, social isolation and changes in brain chemistry and anatomy. *Physiology & Behavior, 1*(2), 99–104.

Kreitzer, M. J., Gross, C. R., Ye, X., Russas, V., & Treesak, C. (2005). Longitudinal impact of mindfulness meditation on illness burden in solid-organ transplant recipients. *Progress in Transplantation, 15*(2), 166–172.

Kremer, P., Elshaug, C., Leslie, E., Toumbourou, J. W., Patton, G. C., & Williams, J. (2014). Physical activity, leisure-time screen use and depression among children and young adolescents. *Journal of Science and Medicine in Sport, 17*(2), 183–187.

Kreuger, K. A., & Dayan, P. (2009). Flexible shaping: How learning in small steps helps. *Cognition, 110*(3), 380–394.

Kring, A. M., & Gordon, A. H. (1998). Sex differences in emotion: Expression, experience, and physiology. *Journal of Personality and Social Psychology, 74*(3), 686–703.

Krippner, S., & Weinhold, J. (2002). Gender differences in a content analysis study of 608 dream reports from research participants in the United States. *Social Behavior and Personality: An International Journal, 30*(4), 399–409. https://doi.org/10.2224/sbp.2002.30.4.399

Kris, A. O. (2012). Unconscious processes. In G. O. Gabbard, B. E. Litowitz, & P. Williams (Eds.), *Textbook of psychoanalysis* (2nd ed., pp. 53–64). American Psychiatric Publishing.

Kroeger, R. A., & Smock, P. J. (2014). Cohabitation: Recent research and implications. In J. Treas, J. Scott, & M. Richards (Eds.), *The Wiley Blackwell companion to the sociology of families* (pp. 217–235). Wiley-Blackwell.

Krueger, R. F. (2008). Behavioral genetics and personality: A new look at the integration of nature and nurture. In O. P. John, R. W. Robins, & L. A. Pervin (Eds.), *Handbook of personality: Theory and research* (3rd ed., pp. 287–310). Guilford Press.

Krueger, R. F., Kotov, R., Watson, D., Forbes, M. K., Eaton, N. R., Ruggero, C. J., ... Bagby, R. M. (2018). Progress in achieving quantitative classification of psychopathology. *World Psychiatry, 17*(3), 282–293.

Kruglanski, A. W., & Stroebe, W. (2012). The making of social psychology. In A. W. Kruglanski & W. Stroebe (Eds.), *Handbook of the history of social psychology* (pp. 3–18). Psychology Press.

Kruglanski, A. W., Fishbach, A., Woolley, K., Bélanger, J. J., Chernikova, M., Molinario, E., & Pierro, A. (2018). A structural model of intrinsic motivation: On the psychology of means-ends fusion. *Psychological Review, 125*(2), 165–182.

Kruglanski, A. W., Jasko, K., Chernikova, M., Milyavsky, M., Babush, M., Baldner, C., & Pierro, A. (2015). The rocky road from attitudes to behaviors: Charting the goal systemic course of actions. *Psychological Review, 122*(4), 598–620.

Krumbholz, K., Patterson, R. D., & Pressnitzer, D. (2000). The lower limit of pitch as determined by rate discrimination. *The Journal of the Acoustical Society of America, 108*(3), 1170–1180.

Krupnick, J. L. (2017). Gender differences in trauma types and themes in veterans with posttraumatic stress disorder. *Journal of Loss and Trauma, 22*(6), 514–525.

Kruschke, J. K. (2005). Category learning. In K. Lamberts & R. L. Goldstone (Eds.), *Handbook of cognition* (pp. 183–201). Sage.

Kruse, E., & Sweeny, K. (2018). Comment: Well-being can improve health by shaping stress appraisals. *Emotion Review, 10*(1), 63–65.

Kubala, K. H., Christianson, J. P., Kaufman, R. D., Watkins, L. R., & Maier, S. F. (2012). Short- and long-term consequences of stressor controllability in adolescent rats. *Behavioural Brain Research, 234*(2), 278–284.

Kübler-Ross, E. (1969). *On death and dying*. Macmillan.

Kuehlwein, K. T. (1993). A survey and update of cognitive therapy systems. In K. T. Kuehlwein & H. Rosen (Eds.), *Cognitive therapies in action* (pp. 1–32). Jossey-Bass.

Kuh, G. D., Cruce, T. M., Shoup, R., Kinzie, J., & Gonyea, R. M. (2008). Unmasking the effects of student engagement on first-year college grades and persistence. *The Journal of Higher Education, 79*(5), 540–563.

Kuhl, P. K. (2004). Early language acquisition: Cracking the speech code. *Nature Reviews Neuroscience, 5*(11), 831–843.

Kuhl, P. K., & Damasio, A. R. (2013). Language. In E. R. Kandel, J. H. Schwartz, T. M. Jessell, S. A. Siegelbaum, & A. J. Hudspeth (Eds.), *Principles of neural science* (5th ed., pp. 1353–1372). McGraw-Hill.

Kuhlmann, T., Ludwin, S., Prat, A., Antel, J., Brück, W., & Lassmann, H. (2017). An updated histological classification system for multiple sclerosis lesions. *Acta Neuropathologica, 133*(1), 13–24.

Kuhn, D. (2009). Adolescent thinking. In R. M. Lerner & L. Steinberg (Eds.), *Handbook of adolescent psychology* (3rd ed., Vol. 1, pp. 152–186). Wiley.

Kuhn, D., & Franklin, S. (2006). The second decade: What develops (and how). In D. Kuhn & R. Siegler (Vol. Eds.), *Handbook of child psychology* (6th ed., Vol. 2, pp. 953–993). Wiley.

Kuhn, D., Langer, J., Kohlberg, L., & Haan, N. S. (1977). The development of formal operations in logical and moral judgment. *Genetic Psychology Monographs, 95*(1), 97–188.

Kulkofsky, S., Wang, Q., Conway, M. A., Hou, Y., Aydin, C., Mueller-Johnson, K., & Williams, H. (2011). Cultural variation in the correlates of flashbulb memories: An investigation in five countries. *Memory, 19*(3), 233–240.

Kunkel, D., & Castonguay, J. (2012). Children and advertising: Content, comprehension, and consequences. In D. G. Singer & J. L. Singer (Eds.), *Handbook of children and the media* (2nd ed., pp. 395–418). Thousand Oaks, CA: Sage.

Kunst-Wilson, W. R., & Zajonc, R. B. (1980). Affective discrimination of stimuli that cannot be recognized. *Science, 207*(4430), 557–558.

Kupers, T. A. (2001). Psychotherapy with men in prison. In G. R. Brooks & G. E. Good (Eds.), *The new handbook of psychotherapy and counseling with men: A comprehensive guide to settings, problems, and treatment approaches*, Vol. 1 & 2 (pp. 170–184). Jossey-Bass/Wiley.

Kupfer, D. J., Kuhl, E. A., & Regier, D. A. (2013). DSM-5—the future arrived. *JAMA, 309*(16), 1691–1692.

Kupper, N., & Denollet, J. (2018). Type D personality as a risk factor in coronary heart disease: A review of current evidence. *Current Cardiology Reports, 20*(11), 104.

Kurdi, B., Seitchik, A. E., Axt, J. R., Carroll, T. J., Karapetyan, A., Kaushik, N., & Banaji, M. R. (2018). Relationship between the implicit association test and intergroup behavior: A meta-analysis. *American Psychologist*. https://doi.org/10.1037/amp0000364

Kuriyan, A. B., Pelham, W. E., Jr., Molina, B. S., Waschbusch, D. A., Gnagy, E. M., Sibley, M. H., Babinski, D. E., Walther, C., Cheong, J., Yu, J., & Kent, K. M. (2013). Young adult educational and vocational outcomes of children diagnosed with ADHD. *Journal of Abnormal Child Psychology, 41*(1), 27–41.

Kurtz, K. J., Boukrina, O., & Gentner, D. (2013). Comparison promotes learning and transfer of relational categories. *Journal of Experimental Psychology: Learning, Memory, and Cognition, 39*(4), 1303–1310.

Kurzban, R., Tooby, J., & Cosmides, L. (2001). Can race be erased? Coalitional computation and social categorization. *Proceedings of the National Academy of Sciences, 98*(26), 15387–15392.

Kutchins, H., & Kirk, S. A. (1997). *Making us crazy: DSM: The psychiatric bible and the creation of mental disorders*. Free Press.

Kuther, T. L., & Morgan, R. D. (2013). *Careers in psychology: Opportunities in a changing world* (4th ed.). Thomson/Wadsworth.

Kutscher, E. C. (2008). Antipsychotics. In K. T. Mueser & D. V. Jeste (Eds.), *Clinical handbook of schizophrenia* (pp. 159–167). Guilford Press.

Kuvaas, B., Buch, R., Weibel, A., Dysvik, A., & Nerstad, C. G. (2017). Do intrinsic and extrinsic motivation relate differently to employee outcomes? *Journal of Economic Psychology, 61*, 244–258.

Kvavilashvili, L., & Mandler, G. (2004). Out of one's mind: A study of involuntary semantic memories. *Cognitive Psychology, 48*(1), 47–94.

Kwan, I., Dickson, K., Richardson, M., MacDowall, W., Burchett, H., Stansfield, C., Brunton, G., Sutcliffe, K., & Thomas, J. (2020). Cyberbullying and children and young people's mental health: a systematic map of systematic reviews. *Cyberpsychology, Behavior, and Social Networking, 23*(2), 72–82. https://doi.org/10.1089/cyber.2019.0370

Kwok, C. S., Kontopantelis, E., Kuligowski, G., Gray, M., Muhyaldeen, A., Gale, C. P., Peat, G. M., Cleator, J., Chew-Graham, C., Loke, Y. K., & Mamas, M. A. (2018). Self-reported sleep duration and quality and cardiovascular disease and mortality: A dose-response meta-analysis. *Journal of the American Heart Association, 7*(15), e008552.

Kwok, D. W., Harris, J. A., & Boakes, R. A. (2017). Timing of interfering events in one-trial serial overshadowing of a taste aversion. *Learning & Behavior, 45*(2), 124–134.

Kwong, A. S. F., Pearson, R. M., Adams, M. J., Northstone, K., Tilling, K., Smith, D., Fawns-Ritchie, C., Bould, H., Warne, N., Zammit, S., Gunnell, D. J., Moran, P. A., Micali, N., Reichenberg, A., Hickman, M., Rai, D., Haworth, S., Campbell, A., Altschul, D., Flaig, R., & Timpson, N. (2021). Mental health before and during the COVID-19 pandemic in two longitudinal UK population cohorts. *The British Journal of Psychiatry, 218*(6), 334–343. https://doi.org/10.1192/bjp.2020.242

Kyle, U. G., Genton, L., Slosman, D. O., & Pichard, C. (2001). Fat-free and fat mass percentiles in 5225 healthy subjects aged 15 to 98 years. *Nutrition, 17*(7), 534–541.

La Gerche, A., & Prior, D. L. (2007). Exercise—is it possible to have too much of a good thing? *Heart, Lung and Circulation, 16*(3), S102–S104.

Laar, C. V., Levin, S., Sinclair, S., & Sidanius, J. (2005). The effect of university roommate contact on ethnic attitudes and behavior. *Journal of Experimental Social Psychology, 41*(4), 329–345.

LaBerge, S. (1985). *Lucid dreaming*. Ballantine.
LaBerge, S. (1988). The psychophysiology of lucid dreaming. In J. Gackenbach & S. LaBerge (Eds.), *Conscious mind, sleeping brain: Perspectives on lucid dreaming* (pp. 135–153). Plenum Press.
LaBerge, S. (2000). Lucid dreaming: Evidence and methodology. *Behavioral and Brain Sciences, 23*(06), 962–964.
LaBerge, S. (2007). Lucid dreaming. In D. Barrett & P. McNamara (Eds.), *The new science of dreaming* (Vol. 2, pp. 307–328). Praeger.
Labov, W., Ash, S., & Boberg, C. (2006). *The Atlas of North American English: Phonetics, phonology, and sound change*. Mouton de Gruyter.
Labyak, S., Lava, S., Turek, F., & Zee, P. (2002). Effects of shiftwork on sleep and menstrual function in nurses. *Health Care for Women International, 23*(6–7), 703–714.
LaCaille, R., & Taylor, M. (2013). Stress, exercise. In M. D. Gellman & J. R. Turner (Eds.), *Encyclopedia of behavioral medicine* (pp. 1908–1910). Springer Science+Business Media.
Lacasse, J. R., & Leo, J. (2015). Antidepressants and the chemical imbalance theory of depression. *The Behavior Therapist, 38*(7), 206–213.
Lacewing, M. (2014). Psychodynamic psychotherapy, insight, and therapeutic action. *Clinical Psychology: Science and Practice, 21*(2), 154–171.
Lack, L. C., & Wright, H. R. (2012). Circadian rhythm disorders I: Phase-advanced and phase-delayed syndromes. In C. M. Morin & C. A. Espie (Eds.), *The Oxford handbook of sleep and sleep disorders* (pp. 597–625). Oxford University Press.
Lackner, J. R. (2010a). Kinesthesia. In E. B. Goldstein (Ed.), *Encyclopedia of perception* (pp. 513–517). Sage.
Lackner, J. R. (2010b). Proprioception. In E. B. Goldstein (Ed.), *Encyclopedia of perception* (pp. 832–836). Sage.
Lackner, J. R. (2010c). Vestibular system. In E. B. Goldstein (Ed.), *Encyclopedia of perception* (pp. 1025–1029). Sage.
Lacks, P., Bertelson, A. D., Sugerman, J., & Kunkel, J. (1983). The treatment of sleep-maintenance insomnia with stimulus-control techniques. *Behaviour Research and Therapy, 21*(3), 291–295.
Ladd, G. W., Kochenderfer, B. J., & Coleman, C. C. (1997). Classroom peer acceptance, friendship, and victimization: Distinct relational systems that contribute uniquely to children's school adjustment? *Child Development, 68*(6), 1181–1197.
LaFarge, L. (2012). Defense and resistance. In G. O. Gabbard, B. E. Litowitz, & P. Williams (Eds.), *Textbook of psychoanalysis* (2nd ed., pp. 93–104). American Psychiatric Publishing.
Laflamme, N., Cisbani, G., Préfontaine, P., Srour, Y., Bernier, J., St-Pierre, M. K., & Rivest, S. (2018). mCSF-induced microglial activation prevents myelin loss and promotes its repair in a mouse model of multiple sclerosis. *Frontiers in Cellular Neuroscience, 12*, 178. https:/doi .org/10.3389/fncel.2018.00178
Laganière, C., Gaudreau, H., Pokhvisneva, I., Atkinson, L., Meaney, M., & Pennestri, M. (2018). Sleepwalking and sleeptalking in children: Associations with emotional/behavioral problems and sleep quality. *Sleep, 41*(Suppl. 1), A293.
LaGasse, L. L., Derauf, C., Smith, L. M., Newman, E., Shah, R., Neal, C., Arria, A., Huestis, M. A., DellaGrotta, S., Lin, H., Dansereau, L. M., & Lester, B. M. (2012). Prenatal methamphetamine exposure and childhood behavior problems at 3 and 5 years of age. *Pediatrics, 129*(4), 681–688.
Lagerspetz, K. M., Björkqvist, K., & Peltonen, T. (1988). Is indirect aggression typical of females? Gender differences in aggressiveness in 11- to 12-year-old children. *Aggressive Behavior, 14*(6), 403–414.
Laird-Johnson, P. N. (2012). Inference in mental models. In K. J. Holyoak & R. G. Morrison (Eds.), *The Oxford handbook of thinking and reasoning* (pp. 134–154). Oxford University Press.
Lakoff, G. (2016). *Moral politics: How liberals and conservatives think* (3rd ed.). University of Chicago Press.
Lalancette, M. F., & Standing, L. (1990). Asch fails again. *Social Behavior and Personality: An International Journal, 18*(1), 7–12.
Lally, J., & MacCabe, J. H. (2015). Antipsychotic medication in schizophrenia: A review. *British Medical Bulletin, 114*(1), 169–179.
Lalumiere, M. L., & Quinsey, V. L. (1998). Pavlovian conditioning of sexual interests in human males. *Archives of Sexual Behavior, 27*(3), 241–252.
Lam, S. P., Fong, S. Y., Ho, C. K., Yu, M. W., & Wing, Y. K. (2008). Parasomnia among psychiatric outpatients: A clinical, epidemiologic, cross-sectional study. *The Journal of Clinical Psychiatry, 69*(9), 1374–1382.
Lamb, M. E., & Lewis, C. (2005). The role of parent-child relationships in child development. In M. H. Bornstein & M. E. Lamb (Eds.), *Developmental science: An advanced textbook* (5th ed., pp. 429–468). Lawrence Erlbaum.
Lambert, M. J. (2011). Psychotherapy research and its achievements. In J. C. Norcross, G. R. Vandenbos, & D. K. Freedheim (Eds.), *History of psychotherapy: Continuity and change* (2nd ed., pp. 299–332). American Psychological Association.
Lambert, M. J. (2013). The efficacy and effectiveness of psychotherapy. In M. J. Lambert (Ed.), *Bergin & Garfield's handbook of psychotherapy and behavior change* (6th ed.). Wiley.
Lambert, M. J., & Ogles, B. M. (2004). The efficacy and effectiveness of psychotherapy. In M. J. Lambert (Ed.), *Bergin and Garfield's handbook of psychotherapy and behavior change* (5th ed., pp. 139–193). Wiley.
Lambert, M. J., & Simon, W. (2008). The therapeutic relationship: Central and essential in psychotherapy outcome. In S. F. Hick & T. Bien (Eds.), *Mindfulness and the therapeutic relationship* (pp. 19–33). Guilford Press.
Lambert, T. A., Kahn, A. S., & Apple, K. J. (2003). Pluralistic ignorance and hooking up. *Journal of Sex Research, 40*(2), 129–133.
Lamblin, M., Murawski, C., Whittle, S., & Fornito, A. (2017). Social connectedness, mental health and the adolescent brain. *Neuroscience & Biobehavioral Reviews, 80*, 57–68.
Lamont, R. A., Swift, H. J., & Abrams, D. (2015). A review and meta-analysis of age-based stereotype threat: Negative stereotypes, not facts, do the damage. *Psychology and Aging, 30*(1), 180–193. https://doi.org/10.1037/a0038586
Lamontagne, S. J., Pizzagalli, D. A., & Olmstead, M. C. (2021). Does inflammation link stress to poor COVID-19 outcome? *Stress and Health, 37*(3), 401–414. https://doi.org/10.1002/smi.3017
Lanciano, T., Curci, A., Matera, G., & Sartori, G. (2018). Measuring the flashbulb-like nature of memories for private events: The flashbulb memory checklist. *Memory, 26*(8), 1053–1064.
Landauer, T. K. (2011). Distributed learning and the size of memory: A 50-year spacing odyssey. In A. S. Benjamin (Ed.), *Successful remembering and successful forgetting: A Festschrift in honor of Robert A. Bjork* (pp. 49–69). Psychology Press.
Landauer, T. K., & Bjork, R. A. (1978). Optimum rehearsal patterns and name learning. In M. Gruneberg, P. E. Morris, & R. N. Sykes (Eds.), *Practical aspects of memory* (pp. 625–632). Academic Press.
Landrine, H., & Klonoff, E. A. (1996). Traditional African-American family practices: Prevalence and correlates. *The Western Journal of Black Studies, 20*, 59–62.
Landry, N., Gifford, R., Milfont, T. L., Weeks, A., & Arnocky, S. (2018). Learned helplessness moderates the relationship between environmental concern and behavior. *Journal of Environmental Psychology, 55*, 18–22.
Lane, C. (2007). *Shyness: How normal behavior became a sickness*. Yale University Press.
Lane, R. C., & Harris, M. (2008). Psychodynamic psychotherapy. In M. Hersen & A. M. Gross (Eds.), *Handbook of clinical psychology* (Vol. 1, pp. 525–550). Wiley.
Lang, J., Erickson, W. W., & Jing-Schmidt, Z. (2021). # MaskOn!# MaskOff! Digital polarization of mask-wearing in the United States during COVID-19. *PloS ONE, 16*(4), e0250817. https://doi .org/10.1371/journal.pone.0250817
Lang, P. J. (1994). The varieties of emotional experience: A meditation on James–Lange theory. *Psychological Review, 101*(2), 211–221.
Lang, P. J., Greenwald, M. K., Bradley, M. M., & Hamm, A. O. (1993). Looking at pictures: Affective, facial, visceral, and behavioral reactions. *Psychophysiology, 30*(3), 261–273.
Lange, B. P., Zaretsky, E., Schwarz, S., & Euler, H. A. (2013). Words won't fail: Experimental evidence on the role of verbal proficiency in mate choice. *Journal of Language and Social Psychology, 33*(5), 482–499.
Lange, S., Probst, C., Gmel, G., Rehm, J., Burd, L., & Popova, S. (2018). Global prevalence of fetal alcohol spectrum disorder among children and youth: A systematic review and meta-analysis. *Obstetrical & Gynecological Survey, 73*(4), 189–191.
Langenbucher, J., & Nathan, P. E. (2006). Diagnosis and classification. In M. Hersen & J. C. Thomas (Eds.), *Comprehensive handbook of personality and psychopathology* (Vol. 2, pp. 3–20). Wiley.
Langford, P. E. (2005). *Vygotsky's developmental and educational psychology*. Psychology Press.
Langlois, J. H., & Roggman, L. A. (1990). Attractive faces are only average. *Psychological Science, 1*(2), 115–121.
LaPiere, R. T. (1934). Attitudes vs. actions. *Social Forces, 13*(2), 230–237.
LaPointe, L. L. (2013). *Paul Broca and the origins of language in the brain*. Plural Publishing.
Lappin, S. (2001). An introduction to formal semantics. In M. Aronoff & J. Rees-Miller (Eds.), *The handbook of linguistics* (pp. 369–393). Blackwell.
Lara, M. A. (2008). Women and depression: The influence of gender in major depressive disorder. In S. A. Aguilar-Gaxiola & T. P. Gullotta (Eds.), *Depression in Latinos: Assessment, treatment, and prevention* (pp. 239–261). Springer Science+Business Media.
Large, M. M., Ryan, C. J., Singh, S. P., Paton, M. B., & Nielssen, O. B. (2011). The predictive value of risk categorization in schizophrenia. *Harvard Review of Psychiatry, 19*(1), 25–33.
Larrick, R. P., Timmerman, T. A., Carton, A. M., & Abrevaya, J. (2011). Temper, temperature, and temptation: Heat-related retaliation in baseball. *Psychological Science, 22*(4), 423–428.
Larsen, S. E., & Pacella, M. L. (2016). Comparing the effect of DSM-congruent traumas vs. DSM-incongruent stressors on PTSD symptoms: A meta-analytic review. *Journal of Anxiety Disorders, 38*, 37–46.
Larson, M. C., Gunnar, M. R., & Hertsgaard, L. (1991). The effects of morning naps, car trips, and maternal separation on adrenocortical activity in human infants. *Child Development, 62*(2), 362–372.
Larson, R. W. (2000). Toward a psychology of positive youth development. *American Psychologist, 55*(1), 170.
Larson, S. (2018, Fall). Considerations when using mental health apps. *APA Practice Organization: Good Practice*, 18–19.
Larsson, M., Arshamian, A., & Kärnekull, C. (2017). Odor-based context dependent memory. In A. Buettner (Ed.), *Springer handbook of odor* (pp. 105–106). Springer.
Larzelere, R. E., & Kuhn, B. R. (2005). Comparing child outcomes of physical punishment and alternative disciplinary tactics: A meta-analysis. *Clinical Child and Family Psychology Review, 8*(1), 1–37.
Laserna, C. M., Seih, Y. T., & Pennebaker, J. W. (2014). Um … Who like says you know: Filler word use as a function of age, gender, and personality. *Journal of Language and Social Psychology, 33*(3), 328–338.
Lash, S. J., Eisler, R. M., & Southard, D. R. (1995). Sex differences in cardiovascular reactivity as a function of the appraised gender relevance of the stressor. *Behavioral Medicine, 21*(2), 86–94.
Lash, S. J., Gillespie, B. L., Eisler, R. M., & Southard, D. R. (1991). Sex differences in cardiovascular reactivity: Effects of the gender relevance of the stressor. *Health Psychology, 10*(6), 392–398.
Laska, K. M., & Wampold, B. E. (2014). Ten things to remember about common factor theory. *Psychotherapy, 51*(4), 519–524.
Lass, J. W., Bennett, P. J., Peterson, M. A., & Sekuler, A. B. (2017). Effects of aging on figure-ground perception: Convexity context effects and competition resolution. *Journal of Vision, 17*(2), 15.
Latané, B., & Darley, J. M. (1968). Group inhibition of bystander intervention in emergencies. *Journal of Personality and Social Psychology, 10*(3), 215–221.
Latané, B., & Darley, J. M. (1970). *The unresponsive bystander: Why doesn't he help?* Appleton-Century Crofts.
Latané, B., Williams, K., & Harkins, S. (1979). Many hands make light the work: The causes and consequences of social loafing. *Journal of Personality and Social Psychology, 37*(6), 822–832.
LaTour, K. A., LaTour, M. S., & Wansink, B. (2018). The impact of supertasters on taste test and marketing outcomes: How an innate characteristic shapes taste, preference, experience, and behavior. *Journal of Advertising, 58*(2), 1–15. https://doi.org/10.2501/JAR-2017-030
Latz, S., Wolf, A. W., & Lozoff, B. (1999). Cosleeping in context: Sleep practices and problems in young children in Japan and the United States. *Archives of Pediatrics & Adolescent Medicine, 153*(4), 339–346.
Lau, R. W., & Cheng, S. T. (2011). Gratitude lessens death anxiety. *European Journal of Ageing, 8*(3), 169–175.
Lauer, J. E., Ilksoy, S. D., & Lourenco, S. F. (2018). Developmental stability in gender-typed preferences between infancy and preschool age. *Developmental Psychology, 54*(4), 613–620.
Lauer, J., Black, D. W., & Keen, P. (1993). Multiple personality disorder and borderline personality disorder: Distinct entities or variations on a common theme? *Annals of Clinical Psychiatry, 5*(2), 129–134.
Laumann, E. O. (1994). *The social organization of sexuality: Sexual practices in the United States*. University of Chicago Press.
Laumann, E. O., Ellingson, S., Mahay, J., Paik, A., & Youm, Y. (2004). *Sexual organization of the city*. University of Chicago Press.
Laursen, B., & Collins, W. A. (2009). Parent-child relationships during adolescence. In R. M. Lerner & L. Steinberg (Eds.), *Handboook of adolescent psychology* (3rd ed., Vol. 2, pp. 3–42). Wiley.
Lavie, C. J., Milani, R. V., & Ventura, H. O. (2009). Obesity and cardiovascular disease: Risk factor, paradox, and impact of weight loss. *Journal of the American College of Cardiology, 53*(21), 1925–1932.
LaVoie, D. J., Mertz, H. K., & Richmond, T. L. (2007). False memory susceptibility in older adults: Implications for the elderly eyewitness. In M. P. Toglia, J. D. Read, D. F. Ross, & R. C. L. Lindsay

(Eds.), *The handbook of eyewitness psychology: Memory for events* (Vol. I, pp. 605–625). Psychology Press.
Lawless, H. T. (2001). Taste. In E. B. Goldstein (Ed.), *Blackwell handbook of perception* (pp. 601–635). Blackwell.
Lawrence, A. E., Rosellini, A. J., & Brown, T. A. (2009). Classification of anxiety disorders: Treatment implications. In J. Abramowitz, D. McKay, S. Taylor, & G. Asmundson (Eds.), *Current perspectives on the anxiety disorders: Implications for DSM-V and beyond* (pp. 453–475). Springer.
Lawrence, K., Campbell, R., & Skuse, D. (2015). Age, gender and puberty influence the development of facial emotion recognition. *Frontiers in Psychology, 6*, 761.
Lawson, T. J. (2007). *Scientific perspectives on pseudoscience and the paranormal: Readings for general psychology*. Pearson Prentice Hall.
Lawson, W. B. (2008). Schizophrenia in African Americans. In K. T. Mueser & D. V. Jeste (Eds.), *Clinical handbook of schizophrenia* (pp. 616–623). Guilford Press.
Lawton, C. A. (1994). Gender differences in way-finding strategies: Relationship to spatial ability and spatial anxiety. *Sex Roles, 30*(1112), 765–779.
Lawton, C. A., & Kallai, J. (2002). Gender differences in wayfinding strategies and anxiety about wayfinding: A cross-cultural comparison. *Sex Roles, 47*(910), 389–401.
Layous, K., Nelson, S. K., & Lyubomirsky, S. (2013). What is the optimal way to deliver a positive activity intervention? The case of writing about one's best possible selves. *Journal of Happiness Studies, 14*(2), 635–654.
Lazarus, R. S. (1964). A laboratory approach to the dynamics of psychological stress. *American Psychologist, 19*(6), 400–411.
Lazarus, R. S. (1982). Thoughts on the relations between emotion and cognition. *American Psychologist, 37*(9), 1019–1024.
Lazarus, R. S. (1984). On the primacy of cognition. *American Psychologist, 39*(2), 124–129.
Lazarus, R. S. (1993). From psychological stress to the emotions: A history of changing outlooks. *Annual Review of Psychology, 44*, 1–22.
Lazarus, R. S. (1999). *Stress and emotion: A new synthesis*. Springer.
Lazarus, R. S., & Alfert, E. (1964). Short-circuiting of threat by experimentally altering cognitive appraisal. *The Journal of Abnormal and Social Psychology, 69*(2), 195–205.
Lazarus, R. S., DeLongis, A., Folkman, S., & Gruen, R. (1985). Stress and adaptational outcomes: The problem of confounded measures. *American Psychologist, 40*(7), 770–779.
Lazer, D. M., Baum, M. A., Benkler, Y., Berinsky, A. J., Greenhill, K. M., Menczer, F., Metzger, M. J., Nyhan, B., Pennycook, G., Rothschild, D., Schudson, M., Sloman, S. A., Sunstein, C. R., Thorson, E. A., Watts, D. J., & Zittrain, J. L. (2018). The science of fake news. *Science, 359*(6380), 1094–1096.
Le Grand, R., Mondloch, C. J., Maurer, D., & Brent, H. P. (2001). Neuroperception: Early visual experience and face processing. *Nature, 410*(6831), 890.
Le Grand, R., Mondloch, C. J., Maurer, D., & Brent, H. P. (2004). Impairment in holistic face processing following early visual deprivation. *Psychological Science, 15*(11), 762–768.
Le, H., Oh, I. S., Robbins, S. B., Ilies, R., Holland, E., & Westrick, P. (2011). Too much of a good thing: Curvilinear relationships between personality traits and job performance. *Journal of Applied Psychology, 96*(1), 113–133.
Leach, M. J., & Page, A. T. (2015). Herbal medicine for insomnia: A systematic review and meta-analysis. *Sleep Medicine Reviews, 24*, 1–12.
Leader, L. R. (2016). The potential value of habituation in the fetus. In N. Reissland & B. Kisilevsky (Eds.), *Fetal development* (pp. 189–209). Springer.
Leahey, T. M., LaRose, J. G., Lanoye, A., Fava, J. L., & Wing, R. R. (2017). Secondary data analysis from a randomized trial examining the effects of small financial incentives on intrinsic and extrinsic motivation for weight loss. *Health Psychology and Behavioral Medicine, 5*(1), 129–144.
Leahy, A., Clayman, C., Mason, I., Lloyd, G., & Epstein, O. (1997). Computerised biofeedback games: A new method for teaching stress management and its use in irritable bowel syndrome. *Journal of the Royal College of Physicians of London, 32*(6), 552–556.
Leahy, R. L. (2003). *Cognitive therapy techniques: A practitioner's guide*. Guilford Press.
Leahy, R. L. (2017). *Cognitive therapy techniques: A practitioner's guide* (2nd ed.). Guilford Press.
Leaper, C., & Robnett, R. D. (2011). Women are more likely than men to use tentative language, aren't they? A meta-analysis testing for gender differences and moderators. *Psychology of Women Quarterly, 35*(1), 129–142.
Leary, D. E. (2002). William James and the art of human understanding. In W. E. Pickren & D. A. Dewsbury (Eds.), *Evolving perspectives on the history of psychology* (pp. 101–120). American Psychological Association.
Leary, D. E. (2003). A profound and radical change: How William James inspired the reshaping of American psychology. In R. J. Sternberg (Ed.), *The anatomy of impact: What makes the great works of psychology great* (pp. 19–42). American Psychological Association.
Leary, M. R., & Cox, C. B. (2008). Belongingness motivation: A mainspring of social action. In J. Y. Shah & W. L. Gardner (Eds.), *Handbook of motivation science* (pp. 27–40). Guilford Press.
Leary, M. R., Koch, E. J., & Hechenbleikner, N. R. (2001). Emotional response to interpersonal responses to interpersonal rejections. In M. R. Leary (Ed.), *Interpersonal rejection* (pp. 145–166). Oxford University Press.
Leary, M. R., Kowalski, R. M., Smith, L., & Phillips, S. (2003). Teasing, rejection, and violence: Case studies of the school shootings. *Aggressive Behavior, 29*(3), 202–214.
LeBoeuf, R. A., & Shafir, E. (2012). Decision making. In K. J. Holyoak & R. G. Morrison (Eds.), *The Oxford handbook of thinking and reasoning* (pp. 301–321). Oxford University Press.
Lebow, J. (2006). *Research for the psychotherapist: From science to practice*. Routledge.
Lebow, J. L., & Stroud, C. B. (2016). Family therapy. In J. C. Norcross, G. R. VandenBos, & D. K. Freedheim (Eds.), *APA handbook of clinical psychology* (Vol. 3, pp. 327–349). American Psychological Association.
Lebowitz, E. R., Leckman, J. F., Silverman, W. K., & Feldman, R. (2016). Cross-generational influences on childhood anxiety disorders: Pathways and mechanisms. *Journal of Neural Transmission, 123*(9), 1053–1067.
Lechner, S. C., Tennen, H., & Affleck, G. (2009). Benefit-finding and growth. In S. J. Lopez & C. R. Snyder (Eds.), *Oxford handbook of positive psychology* (pp. 633–640). Oxford University Press.
LeCuyer, E., Swanson, D., Cole, R., & Kitzman, H. (2011). Effect of African- and European-American maternal attitudes and limit-setting strategies on children's self-regulation. *Research in Nursing and Health, 34*(6), 468–482.
Ledley, D. R., Erwin, B. A., & Heimberg, R. G. (2008). Social anxiety disorder. In W. E. Craighead, D. J. Milkowitz, & L. W. Craighead (Eds.), *Psychopathology: History, diagnosis, and empirical foundations* (pp. 198–233). Wiley.
LeDoux, J. E. (1996). *The emotional brain: The mysterious underpinnings of emotional life*. Simon & Schuster.
LeDoux, J. E. (2007). Consolidation: Challenging the traditional view. In H. L. Roediger, Y. Dudai, & S. M. Fitzpatrick (Eds.), *Science of memory: Concepts* (pp. 171–175). Oxford University Press.
LeDoux, J. E., & Damasio, A. R. (2013). Emotions and feelings. In E. R. Kandel, J. H. Schwartz, T. M. Jessell, S. A. Siegelbaum, & A. J. Hudspeth (Eds.), *Principles of neural science* (5th ed., pp. 1079–1094). McGraw-Hill.
LeDoux, J. E., Schiller, D., & Cain, C. (2009). Emotional reaction and action: From threat processing to goal-directed behavior. In M. S. Gazzaniga (Ed.), *The cognitive neurosciences* (4th ed., pp. 905–924). MIT Press.
Lee, B. B. (2010). Retinal anatomy. In E. B. Goldstein (Ed.), *Encyclopedia of perception* (pp. 868–871). Sage.
Lee, C. (2002). The impact of belonging to a high school gay/straight alliance. *The High School Journal, 85*(3), 13–26.
Lee, E. (Ed.). (1997). *Working with Asian Americans: A guide for clinicians*. Guilford Press.
Lee, E. A. E., & Troop-Gordon, W. (2011). Peer processes and gender role development: Changes in gender atypicality related to negative peer treatment and children's friendships. *Sex Roles, 64*(12), 90–102.
Lee, E. B., Pierce, B. G., Twohig, M. P., & Levin, M. E. (2021). Acceptance and commitment therapy. In A. Wenzel (Ed.), *Handbook of cognitive behavioral therapy: Overview and approaches* (pp. 567–594). American Psychological Association. https://doi.org/10.1037/0000218-019
Lee, E., & Mock, M. R. (2005). Asian families: An overview. In M. McGoldrick, J. Giordano, & N. Garcia-Preto (Eds.), *Ethnicity and family therapy* (3rd ed., pp. 269–289). Guilford Press.
Lee, F., Hallahan, M., & Herzog, T. (1996). Explaining real-life events: How culture and domain shape attributions. *Personality and Social Psychology Bulletin, 22*, 732–741.
Lee, H. B., Offidani, E., Ziegelstein, R. C., Bienvenu, O. J., Samuels, J., Eaton, W. W., & Nestadt, G. (2014). Five-factor model personality traits as predictors of incident coronary heart disease in the community: A 10.5-year cohort study based on the Baltimore epidemiologic catchment area follow-up study. *Psychosomatics, 55*(4), 352–361.
Lee, K. A., & Rosen, L. A. (2012). Sleep and human development. In C. M. Morin & C. A. Espie (Eds.), *The Oxford handbook of sleep and sleep disorders* (pp. 75–94). Oxford University Press.
Lee, M., & Seo, M. (2018). Effect of direct and indirect contact with mental illness on dangerousness and social distance. *International Journal of Social Psychiatry, 64*(2), 112–119.
Lee, S. A., & Liang, Y. J. (2019). Robotic foot-in-the-door: Using sequential-request persuasive strategies in human-robot interaction. *Computers in Human Behavior, 90*, 351–356.
Lee-Chiong, T., & Sateia, M. (2006). Pharmacologic therapy of insomnia. In T. L. Lee-Chiong (Ed.), *Sleep: A comprehensive handbook* (pp. 125–132). Wiley-Liss.
Lee-Won, R. J., Shim, M., Joo, Y. K., & Park, S. G. (2014). Who puts the best "face" forward on Facebook? Positive self-presentation in online social networking and the role of self-consciousness, actual-to-total Friends ratio, and culture. *Computers in Human Behavior, 39*, 413–423.
LeFebvre, A., & Huta, V. (2021). Age and gender differences in eudaimonic, hedonic, and extrinsic motivations. *Journal of Happiness Studies, 22*(5), 2299–2321. https://doi.org/10.1007/s10902-020-00319-4
Leger, D. (1994). The cost of sleep-related accidents: A report for the National Commission on Sleep Disorders Research. *Sleep, 17*(1), 84–93.
Leger, D. (2012). A socioeconomic perspective of sleep disorders (insomnia and obstructive sleep apnea). In C. M. Morin & C. A. Espie (Eds.), *The Oxford handbook of sleep and sleep disorders* (pp. 324–347). Oxford University Press.
Legerstee, M. (1992). A review of the animate-inanimate distinction in infancy: Implications for models of social and cognitive knowing. *Early Development and Parenting, 1*(2), 59–67.
Legerstee, M. (1994), The role of familiarity and sound in the development of person and object permanence. *British Journal of Developmental Psychology, 12*(4), 455–468. https://doi.org/10.1111/j.2044-835X
Legerstee, M., Pomerleau, A., Malcuit, G., & Feider, H. (1987). The development of infants' responses to people and a doll: Implications for research in communication. *Infant Behavior and Development, 10*(1), 81–95.
Legewie, J., & DiPrete, T. A. (2012). School context and the gender gap in educational achievement. *American Sociological Review, 77*(3), 463–485.
Lehman, A. F., Kreyenbuhl, J., Buchanan, R. W., Dickerson, F. B., Dixon, L. B., Goldberg, R., ... Steinwachs, D. M. (2004). The schizophrenia patient outcomes research team (PORT): Updated treatment recommendations 2003. *Schizophrenia Bulletin, 30*(2), 193–217.
Leiblum, S., Wiegel, M., & Brickle, F. (2003). Sexual attitudes of U.S. and Canadian medical students: The role of ethnicity, gender, religion and acculturation. *Sexual and Relationship Therapy, 18*(4), 473–491.
Leigh, B. C. (1989). Reasons for having and avoiding sex: Gender, sexual orientation, and relationship to sexual behavior. *Journal of Sex Research, 26*(2), 199–209.
Leigh, E., & Hirsch, C. R. (2011). Worry in imagery and verbal form: Effect on residual working memory capacity. *Behaviour Research and Therapy, 49*(2), 99–105.
Leighty, K. A., Grand, A. P., Pittman Courte, V. L., Maloney, M. A., & Bettinger, T. L. (2013). Relational responding by eastern box turtles (*Terrapene carolina*) in a series of color discrimination tasks. *Journal of Comparative Psychology, 127*(3), 256–264.
Lemm, K. M. (2006). Positive associations among interpersonal contact, motivation, and implicit and explicit attitudes toward gay men. *Journal of Homosexuality, 51*(2), 79–99.
Lenhart, A. (2015). Chapter 4: Social media and friendships. In *Teens, technology, and friendships*. http://www.pewinternet.org/2015/08/06/chapter-4-social-media-and-friendships/
Lenzenweger, M. F., & Clarkin, J. F. (Eds.). (2005). *Major theories of personality disorder*. Guilford Press.
Lenzenweger, M. F., Lane, M. C., Loranger, A. W., & Kessler, R. C. (2007). DSM-IV personality disorders in the National Comorbidity Survey Replication (NCS-R). *Biological Psychiatry, 62*(6), 553–564.
Leonard, L., & Dawson, D. (2018). The marginalisation of dreams in clinical psychological practice. *Sleep Medicine Reviews, 42*, 10–18.
Leong, F. T. L. (2009). Guest editor's introduction: History of racial and ethnic minority psychology. *Cultural Diversity and Ethnic Minority Psychology, 15*(4), 315–316.
Leong, F. T. L. (2014). Introduction. In F. T. L. Leong (Ed.), *APA handbook of multicultural psychology* (Vol. 1, pp. xxi–xxvii). American Psychological Association.
Leong, F. T. L., Holliday, B. G., Trimble, J. E., Padilla, A., & McCubbin, L. (2012a). Ethnic minority psychology. In I. Weiner (Ed.-in-Chief) & D. Freedheim (Vol. Ed.), *Handbook of psychology* (2nd ed., Vol. 1). Wiley.
Leong, F. T. L., & Kalibetseva, Z. (2013). Clinical research with culturally diverse populations. In J. S. Comer & P. C. Kendall (Eds.), *The Oxford handbook of research strategies for clinical psychology* (pp. 413–433). Oxford University Press.
Leong, F. T. L., & Okazaki, S. (2009). History of Asian American psychology. *Cultural Diversity and Ethnic Minority Psychology, 15*(4), 352–362.
Leong, F. T. L., Schmitt, N., & Lyons, B. J. (2012). Developing testable and important research questions. In H. Cooper (Ed.), *APA handbook of research methods in psychology: Vol. 1. Foundations, planning, measures, and psychometrics* (pp. 119–132). American Psychological Association.

Leong, F. T., Pickren, W. E., & Tang, L. C. (2012b). A history of cross-cultural clinical psychology, and its importance to mental health today. In E. C. Chang & C. A. Downey (Eds.), *Handbook of race and development in mental health* (pp. 11–26). Springer Science+Business Media.

Leppanen, J., Sedgewick, F., Treasure, J., & Tchanturia, K. (2018). Differences in the Theory of Mind profiles of patients with anorexia nervosa and individuals on the autism spectrum: A meta-analytic review. *Neuroscience & Biobehavioral Reviews, 90*, 146–163.

Lepper, M. R., Ross, L., & Lau, R. R. (1986). Persistence of inaccurate beliefs about the self: Perseverance effects in the classroom. *Journal of Personality and Social Psychology, 50*(3), 482–491.

Lerman, D. C., & Toole, L. M. (2011). Developing function-based punishment procedures for problem behavior. In W. W. Fisher, C. C. Piazza, & H. S. Roane (Eds.), *Handbook of applied behavior analysis* (pp. 348–369). Guilford Press.

Lerner, J. V., Phelps, E., Forman, Y., & Bowers, E. P. (2009). Positive youth development. In R. M. Lerner & L. Steinberg (Eds.), *Handbook of adolescent psychology* (3rd ed., Vol. 1, pp. 524–558). Wiley.

Lerner, M. J. (1965). Evaluation of performance as a function of performer's reward and attractiveness. *Journal of Personality and Social Psychology, 1*(4), 355–360.

Lerner, M. J., & Miller, D. T. (1978). Just world research and the attribution process: Looking back and ahead. *Psychological Bulletin, 85*(5), 1030–1051.

Lerner, R. M. (2006). Developmental science, developmental systems, and contemporary theories of human development. In R. M. Lerner (Vol. Ed.), *Handbook of child psychology* (6th ed., Vol. 1, pp. 1–17). Wiley.

Lerner, R. M., & Steinberg, L. (2009). The scientific study of adolescent development: Historical and contemporary perspectives. In R. M. Lerner & L. Steinberg (Eds.), *Handbook of adolescent psychology* (3rd ed., Vol. 1, pp. 3–14). Wiley.

Lerner, R. M., Theokas, C., & Bobek, D. L. (2005). Concepts and theories of human development: Historical and contemporary dimensions. In M. H. Bornstein & M. E. Lamb (Eds.), *Developmental science: An advanced textbook* (5th ed., pp. 3–44). Lawrence Erlbaum.

Leserman, J., Jackson, E. D., Petitto, J. M., Golden, R. N., Silva, S. G., Perkins, D. O., ... Evans, D. L. (1999). Progression to AIDS: The effects of stress, depressive symptoms, and social support. *Psychosomatic Medicine, 61*(3), 397–406.

Lesku, J. A., Rattenborg, N. C., & Amlaner, C. J., Jr. (2006). The evolution of sleep: A phylogenetic approach. In T. L. Lee-Chiong (Ed.), *Sleep: A comprehensive handbook* (pp. 49–62). Wiley-Liss.

Leu, J., Mesquita, B., Ellsworth, P. C., ZhiYong, Z., Huijuan, Y., Buchtel, E., Karasawa, M., & Masuda, T. (2010). Situational differences in dialectical emotions: Boundary conditions in a cultural comparison of North Americans and East Asians. *Cognition and Emotion, 24*(3), 419–435.

Leung, A. K. Y., & Cohen, D. (2007). The soft embodiment of culture: Camera angles and motion through time and space. *Psychological Science, 18*(9), 824–830.

Leung, A. K. Y., Maddux, W. W., Galinsky, A. D., & Chiu, C. Y. (2008). Multicultural experience enhances creativity: The when and how. *American Psychologist, 63*(3), 169–181.

Leung, J., Pachana, N. A., & McLaughlin, D. (2014). Social support and health-related quality of life in women with breast cancer: A longitudinal study. *Psycho-oncology, 23*(9), 1014–1020. https://doi.org/10.1002/pon.3523

Levey, S. (2013). *Introduction to language development*. Plural Publishing.

Levin, A. (2017, July 27). Psychologist prescribing bills defeated in many states. *Psychiatry News*. https://doi.org/10.1176/appi/pn.2017.8a2

Levin, D. S., Thurman, S. K., & Kiepert, M. H. (2010). More than just a memory: The nature and validity of working memory in educational settings. In G. M. Davies & D. B. Wright (Eds.), *Current issues in applied memory research* (pp. 72–95). Psychology Press.

Levin, H. S., & Hanten, G. (2002). Posttraumatic amnesia and residual memory deficit after closed head injury. In A. D. Baddeley, M. D. Kopelman, & B. A. Wilson (Eds.), *The handbook of memory disorders* (2nd ed., pp. 381–411). Wiley.

Levin, I. P. (1987). Associative effects of information framing. *Bulletin of the Psychonomic Society, 25*(2), 85–86.

Levin, I. P., Schnittjer, S. K., & Thee, S. L. (1988). Information framing effects in social and personal decisions. *Journal of Experimental Social Psychology, 24*(6), 520–529.

Levin, S., Van Laar, C., & Sidanius, J. (2003). The effects of ingroup and outgroup friendships on ethnic attitudes in college: A longitudinal study. *Group Processes & Intergroup Relations, 6*(1), 76–92.

Levine, J. M. & Kerr, N. L. (2007). Inclusion and exclusion: Implications for group processes. In A. W. Kruglanski & E. T. Higgins (Eds.), *Social psychology: Handbook of basic principles* (pp. 759–784). The Guilford Press.

Levine, J. M., & Moreland, R. L. (2012). A history of small group research. In A. W. Kruglanski & W. Stroebe (Eds.), *Handbook of the history of social psychology* (pp. 383–405). Psychology Press.

Levine, M. P., & Murnen, S. K. (2009). "Everybody knows that mass media are/are not [pick one] a cause of eating disorders": A critical review of evidence for a causal link between media, negative body image, and disordered eating in females. *Journal of Social & Clinical Psychology, 28*(1), 9–42.

Levine, M. P., & Smolak, L. (2010). Cultural influences on body image and the eating disorders. In W. S. Agras (Ed.), *The Oxford handbook of eating disorders* (pp. 223–246). Oxford University Press.

Levine, M. W. (2001). Principles of neural processing. In E. B. Goldstein (Ed.), *Blackwell handbook of perception* (pp. 24–52). Blackwell.

Levis, D. J. (2008). The prolonged exposure techniques of implosive (flooding) therapy. In W. T. O'Donohue & J. E. Fisher (Eds.), *Cognitive behavior therapy: Applying empirically supported techniques in your practice* (2nd ed., pp. 272–282). Wiley.

Levis, D. J. (2008). The prolonged exposure techniques of implosive (flooding) therapy. In W. T. O'Donohue & J. E. Fisher (Eds.), *Cognitive behavior therapy: Applying empirically supported techniques in your practice* (2nd ed., pp. 272–282). Wiley.

Levis, D. J., & Carrera, R. (1967). Effects of ten hours of implosive therapy in the treatment of outpatients: A preliminary report. *Journal of Abnormal Psychology, 72*(6), 504.

Levitch, C. F., Zimmerman, M. E., Lubin, N., Kim, N., Lipton, R. B., Stewart, W. F., & Lipton, M. L. (2018). Recent and long-term soccer heading exposure is differentially associated with neuropsychological function in amateur players. Journal of the International Neuropsychological Society, 24(2), 147–155.

Levitin, D. J., & Tirovolas, A. K. (2010). Music cognition and perception. In E. B. Goldstein (Ed.), *Encyclopedia of perception* (pp. 599–606). Sage.

Levorato, M. C., & Cacciari, C. (2002). The creation of new figurative expressions: Psycholinguistic evidence in Italian children, adolescents and adults. *Journal of Child Language, 29*(01), 127–150.

Levorato, M. C., Nesi, B., & Cacciari, C. (2004). Reading comprehension and understanding idiomatic expressions: A developmental study. *Brain and Language, 91*(3), 303–314.

Levy, K. N., & Johnson, B. N. (2016). Personality disorders. In J. C. Norcross, G. R. VandenBos, & D. K. Freedheim (Eds.), *APA handbook of clinical psychology: Vol. 4. Psychopathology and health* (pp. 173–208). American Psychological Association.

Lewes, K. (1995). *Psychoanalysis and male homosexuality*. Jason Aronson.

Lewis, B. H., Legato, M., & Fisch, H. (2006). Medical implications of the male biological clock. *JAMA: The Journal of the American Medical Association, 296*(19), 2369–2371.

Lewis, C., & Carpendale, J. (2011). Social cognition. In P. K. Smith & C. H. Hart (Eds.), *The Wiley-Blackwell handbook of childhood social development* (2nd ed., pp. 531–548). Wiley-Blackwell.

Lewis, M. (2008). The emergence of human emotions. In M. Lewis, J. M. Haviland-Jones, & L. F. Barrett (Eds.), *Handbook of emotions* (3rd ed., pp. 304–319). Guilford Press.

Lewis, M. B. (2012). Exploring the positive and negative implications of facial feedback. *Emotion, 12*(4), 852–859.

Lewis, M., & Thomas, D. (1990). Cortisol release in infants in response to inoculation. *Child Development, 61*(1), 50–59.

Lewis, N. A., Jr., & Sekaquaptewa, D. (2016). Beyond test performance: A broader view of stereotype threat. *Current Opinion in Psychology, 11*, 40–43.

Lewis, S. W., & Buchanan, R. W. (2007). *Fast facts: Schizophrenia* (3rd ed.). Health Press.

Lewis, T. T., Cogburn, C. D., & Williams, D. R. (2015). Self-reported experiences of discrimination and health: Scientific advances, ongoing controversies, and emerging issues. *Annual Review of Clinical Psychology, 11*, 407–440.

Lewkowicz, D. J. (2010). Nature and nurture in perception. In E. B. Goldstein (Ed.), *Encyclopedia of perception* (pp. 610–615). Sage.

Li, J., Wang, Y. J., Zhang, M., Xu, Z. Q., Gao, C. Y., Fang, C. Q., Yan, J. C., Zhou, H. D., & Chongqing Ageing Study Group. (2011). Vascular risk factors promote conversion from mild cognitive impairment to Alzheimer disease. *Neurology, 76*(17), 1485–1491.

Li, N. P., Bailey, J. M., Kenrick, D. T., & Linsenmeier, J. A. (2002). The necessities and luxuries of mate preferences: Testing the tradeoffs. *Journal of Personality and Social Psychology, 82*(6), 947–955.

Li, P., Jin, Z., & Tan, L. H. (2004). Neural representations of nouns and verbs in Chinese: An fMRI study. *NeuroImage, 21*(4), 1533–1541.

Li, W., Luxenberg, E., Parrish, T., & Gottfried, J. A. (2006). Learning to smell the roses: Experience-dependent neural plasticity in human piriform and orbitofrontal cortices. *Neuron, 52*(6), 1097–1108.

Li, Y., & Epley, N. (2009). When the best appears to be saved for last: Serial position effects on choice. *Journal of Behavioral Decision Making, 22*(4), 378–389.

Li, Y., Wang, X., Lin, X., & Hajli, M. (2018). Seeking and sharing health information on social media: A net valence model and cross-cultural comparison. *Technological Forecasting and Social Change, 126*, 28–40.

Libby, D., & Chaparro, A. (2009, October). Text messaging versus talking on a cell phone: A comparison of their effects on driving performance. *Proceedings of the Human Factors and Ergonomics Society Annual Meeting, 53*(18), 1353–1357.

Lichstein, K. L., Vander Wal, G. S., & Dillon, H. R. (2012). Insomnia III: Therapeutic approaches. In C. M. Morin & C. A. Espie (Eds.), *The Oxford handbook of sleep and sleep disorders* (pp. 453–470). Oxford University Press.

Lichtenberger, E. O., & Kaufman, A. S. (2009). *Essentials of WAIS-IV assessment*. Wiley.

Lichtenfeld, S., Maier, M. A., Buechner, V. L., & Elliot, A. J. (2018). Ambient green and creativity. *Creativity Research Journal, 30*(3), 305–309.

Lichtenstein, P., Carlström, E., Råstam, M., Gillberg, C., & Anckarsäter, H. (2010). The genetics of autism spectrum disorders and related neuropsychiatric disorders in childhood. *American Journal of Psychiatry, 167*(11), 1357–1363.

Lichtenstein, P., Yip, B. H., Björk, C., Pawitan, Y., Cannon, T. D., Sullivan, P. F., & Hultman, C. M. (2009). Common genetic determinants of schizophrenia and bipolar disorder in Swedish families: A population-based study. *The Lancet, 373*(9659), 234–239.

Lieberman, J. A., Stroup, T. S., McEvoy, J. P., Swartz, M. S., Rosenheck, R. A., Perkins, D. O., Keefe, R. S. E., Davis, S. M., Davis, C. E., Lebowitz, B. D., Severe, J., Hsaiao, J. K., Clinical Antipsychotic Trials of Intervention Effectiveness (CATIE) Investigators. (2005). Effectiveness of antipsychotic drugs in patients with chronic schizophrenia. *New England Journal of Medicine, 353*(12), 1209–1223.

Lieberman, J. A., Stroup, T. S., & Perkins, D. O. (2006). Preface. In J. A. Lieberman, T. S. Stroup, & D. O. Perkins (Eds.), *The American Psychiatric Publishing textbook of schizophrenia* (p. xvii). American Psychiatric Association Publishing.

Lilienfeld, S. O. (2010). *50 great myths of popular psychology: Shattering widespread misconceptions about human behavior*. Wiley-Blackwell.

Lilienfeld, S. O. (2017a). Microaggressions: Strong claims, inadequate evidence. *Perspectives on Psychological Science, 12*(1), 138–169.

Lilienfeld, S. O. (2017b). Through a glass, darkly: Microaggressions and psychological science. *Perspectives on Psychological Science, 12*(1), 178–180.

Lilienfeld, S. O. (2018). Foreword: Navigating a post-truth world. Ten enduring lessons from the study of pseudoscience. In A. B. Kaufman & J. C. Kaufman (Eds.), *Pseudoscience: The conspiracy against science* (pp. xi–xvii). MIT Press.

Lilienfeld, S. O. (2020). Microaggression research and application: Clarifications, corrections, and common ground. *Perspectives on Psychological Science, 15*(1), 27–37. https://doi.org/10.1177/1745691619867117

Lilienfeld, S. O., & Lynn, S. J. (2003). Dissociative identity disorder: Multiple personalities, multiple controversies. In S. O. Lilienfeld, S. J. Lynn, & J. M. Mohr (Eds.), *Science and pseudoscience in clinical psychology* (pp. 109–142). Guilford Press.

Lilienfeld, S. O., Lynn, S. J., & Lohr, J. M. (Eds.). (2015). *Science and pseudoscience in clinical psychology* (2nd ed.). Guilford Press.

Lilienfeld, S. O., Lynn, S. J., Ruscio, J., & Beyerstein, B. L. (2010). *50 great myths of popular psychology*. Wiley-Blackwell.

Lilienfeld, S. O., Wood, J. M., & Garb, H. N. (2000). The scientific status of projective techniques. *Psychological Science in the Public Interest, 1*(2), 27–66.

Lillard, A. S. (2017). Why do the children (pretend) play? *Trends in Cognitive Sciences, 21*(11), 826–834.

Lim, J., & Dinges, D. F. (2010). A meta-analysis of the impact of short-term sleep deprivation on cognitive variables. *Psychological Bulletin, 136*(3), 375–389.

Lima, M. A., Silva, M., Oliveira, R. V., Soares, C. N., Takano, C. L., Azevedo, A. E., Moraes, R. L., Rezende, R. B., Chagas, I. T., Espíndola, O., Leite, A. C., & Araujo, A. (2020). Smell dysfunction in COVID-19 patients: More than a yes–no question. *Journal of the Neurological Sciences, 418*, 117107. https://doi.org/10.1016/j.jns.2020.117107

Lima, S. L., Rattenborg, N. C., Lesku, J. A., & Amlaner, C. J. (2005). Sleeping under the risk of predation. *Animal Behaviour, 70*(4), 723–736.

Lin, C. L., Liu, T. C., Chung, C. H., & Chien, W. C. (2018). Risk of pneumonia in patients with insomnia: A nationwide population-based retrospective cohort study. *Journal of Infection and Public Health, 11*(2), 270–274.

Lin, L., Conroy, J., & Ghaness, A. (2020). Datapoint: Psychology's workforce is becoming more diverse. *Monitor on Psychology, 51*(8), 19. https://www.apa.org/monitor/2020/2020-11-monitor.pdf.

Lin, M. I. B., & Huang, Y. P. (2017). The impact of walking while using a smartphone on pedestrians' awareness of roadside events. *Accident Analysis & Prevention, 101*, 87–96.

Lin, P. (2016). Risky behaviors: Integrating adolescent egocentrism with the theory of planned behavior. *Review of General Psychology, 20*(4), 392–398.

Lind, M. (1995). Brave new right. In S. Fraser (Ed.), *The bell curve wars: Race, intelligence, and the future of America* (pp. 172–178). Basic Books.

Linda, W. P., & McGrath, R. E. (2017). The current status of prescribing psychologists: Practice patterns and medical professional evaluations. *Professional Psychology: Research and Practice, 48*(1), 38–45.

Lindeman, M. I., Crandall, A. K., & Finkelstein, L. M. (2017). The effects of messages about the causes of obesity on disciplinary action decisions for overweight employees. *The Journal of Psychology, 151*(4), 345–358.

Linden, D. (2012). *The biology of psychological disorders*. Palgrave Macmillan.

Linden, D. E. J. (2006). How psychotherapy changes the brain: The contribution of functional neuroimaging. *Molecular Psychiatry, 11*(6), 528–538.

Linden, D. J. (1994). Long-term synaptic depression in the mammalian brain. *Neuron, 12*(3), 457–472.

Linden, D. J. (2015). *Touch: The science of hand, heart, and mind*. Penguin.

Linden, D. J., & Connor, J. A. (1995). Long-term synaptic depression. *Annual Review of Neuroscience, 18*(1), 319–357.

Linden-Carmichael, A. N., & Lau-Barraco, C. (2017). A daily diary examination of caffeine mixed with alcohol among college students. *Health Psychology, 36*(9), 881–889.

Lindenmayer, J. P., & Khan, A. (2006). Psychopathology. In J. A. Lieberman, T. S. Stroup, & D. O. Perkins (Eds.), *The American Psychiatric Publishing textbook of schizophrenia* (pp. 187–221). American Psychiatric Association.

Lindsey, D. T., & Brown, A. M. (2002). Color naming and the phototoxic effects of sunlight on the eye. *Psychological Science, 13*(6), 506–512.

Lindsey, D. T., & Brown, A. M. (2006). Universality of color names. *Proceedings of the National Academy of Sciences of the United States of America, 103*(44), 16608–16613.

Linehan, M. M. (1993a). *Cognitive-behavioral treatment of borderline personality disorder*. Guilford Press.

Linehan, M. M. (1993b). *Skills training manual for treating borderline personality disorder*. Guilford Press.

Link, B. G., & Stuart, H. (2017). On revisiting some origins of the stigma concept as it applies to mental illness. In W. Gaebel, W. Rössler, & N. Sartorius (Eds.), *The stigma of mental illness—End of the story?* (pp. 3–28). Springer International Publishing Sweden.

Linton, S. J. (2000). A review of psychological risk factors in back and neck pain. *Spine, 25*(9), 1148–1156.

Lippa, R. A. (2007). The preferred traits of mates in a cross-national study of heterosexual and homosexual men and women: An examination of biological and cultural influences. *Archives of Sexual Behavior, 36*(2), 193–208.

Lipsey, M. W., & Wilson, D. B. (1993). The efficacy of psychological, educational, and behavioral treatment: Confirmation from meta-analysis. *American Psychologist, 48*(12), 1181–1209.

Lipsey, M. W., Wilson, D. B., Cohen, M. A., & Derzon, J. H. (1997). Is there a causal relationship between alcohol use and violence? *Recent Developments in Alcoholism, 13*, 245–282.

Lipsitz, J. D., & Markowitz, J. C. (2016). Interpersonal theory. In J. C. Norcross, G. R. VandenBos, & D. K. Freedheim (Eds.), *APA handbook of clinical psychology* (Vol. 2, pp. 183–212). American Psychological Association.

Lipton, M. L., Kim, N., Zimmerman, M. E., Kim, M., Stewart, W. F., Branch, C. A., & Lipton, R. B. (2013). Soccer heading is associated with white matter microstructural and cognitive abnormalities. *Radiology, 268*(3), 850–857.

Lissek, S., & Grillon, C. (2010). Overgeneralization of conditioned fear in the anxiety disorders: Putative memorial mechanisms. *Journal of Psychology, 218*(2), 146–148.

Lissek, S., Powers, A. S., McClure, E. B., Phelps, E. A., Woldehawariat, G., Gillon, C., & Pine, D. S. (2005). Classical fear conditioning in the anxiety disorders: A meta-analysis. *Behaviour Research and Therapy, 43*(11), 1391–1424.

Little, C. A. (2018). Teaching strategies to support the education of gifted learners. In S. I. Pfeiffer, E. Shaunessy-Dedrick, & M. Foley-Nicpon (Eds.), *APA handbook of giftedness and talent* (pp. 371–385). American Psychological Association.

Little, D. M., Arciniegas, D. B., & Hart, J., Jr. (2013). Electroencephalography. In D. B. Arciniegas, C. A. Anderson, & C. M. Filley (Eds.), *Behavioral neurology & neuropsychiatry* (pp. 442–458). Cambridge University Press.

Little, T. D., Card, N. A., Preacher, K. J., & McConnell, E. (2009). Modeling longitudinal data from research on adolescence. In R. M. Lerner & L. Steinberg (Eds.), *Handbook of adolescent psychology* (3rd ed., Vol. 1, pp. 15–54). Wiley.

Liu, D., Kirschner, P. A., & Karpinski, A. C. (2017). A meta-analysis of the relationship of academic performance and social network site use among adolescents and young adults. *Computers in Human Behavior, 77*, 148–157. https://doi.org/10.1016/j.chb.2017.08.039

Liu, S., Liu, P., Wang, M., & Zhang, B. (2021). Effectiveness of stereotype threat interventions: A meta-analytic review. *Journal of Applied Psychology, 106*(6), 921–949. https://doi.org/10.1037/apl0000770

Liu, T. Z., Xu, C., Rota, M., Cai, H., Zhang, C., Shi, M. J., Yuan, R.-X., Weng, H., Meng, X.-Y., Kwong, J. S. W., & Sun, X. (2017). Sleep duration and risk of all-cause mortality: A flexible, non-linear, meta-regression of 40 prospective cohort studies. *Sleep Medicine Reviews, 32*, 28–36.

Liu, T., & Csikszentmihalyi, M. (2020). Flow among introverts and extraverts in solitary and social activities. *Personality and Individual Differences, 167*, 110197. https://doi.org/10.1016/j.paid.2020.110197

Liverant, G. I., Stoddard, J. A., Meuret, A. E., & Barlow, D. H. (2007). Clinical science and the revolution in psychological treatment: The example of anxiety disorders. In T. A. Treat, R. R. Bootzin, & T. B. Baker (Eds.), *Psychological clinical science: Papers in honor of Richard M. McFall* (pp. 77–103). Routledge.

Livermore, D. A. (2015). *Leading with cultural intelligence: The real secret to success*. AMACOM.

Livingstone, M. (2014). *Vision and art: The biology of seeing*. Abrams.

Llaneza, P., García-Portilla, M. P., Llaneza-Suárez, D., Armott, B., & Pérez-López, F. R. (2012). Depressive disorders and the menopause transition. *Maturitas, 71*(2), 120–130.

Lobel, A., Engels, R. C. M. E., Stone, L. L., & Granic, I. (2017). Gaining a competitive edge: Longitudinal associations between children's competitive video game playing, conduct problems, peer relations, and prosocial behavior. *Psychology of Popular Media Culture, 8*(1), 76–87. http://dx.doi.org/10.1037/ppm0000159

Locher, P., Unger, R., Sociedade, P., & Wahl, J. (1993). At first glance: Accessibility of the physical attractiveness stereotype. *Sex Roles, 28*(11), 729–743.

Locke, A. E., Kahali, B., Berndt, S. I., Justice, A. E., Pers, T. H., Day, F. R., Powell, C., Vedantam, S., Buchkovich, M. L., Yang, J., Croteau-Chonka, D. C., Esko, T., Fall, T., Ferreira, T., Gustafsson, S., Kutalik, Z., Luan, J., Mägi, R., Randall, J. C., Winkler, T. W., ... Speliotes, E. K. (2015). Genetic studies of body mass index yield new insights for obesity biology. *Nature, 518*(7538), 197.

Locke, J. L. (2012). Displays of vocal and verbal complexity: A fitness account of language, situated in development. In M. Tallerman & K. R. Gibson (Eds.), *The Oxford handbook of language evolution* (pp. 328–339). Oxford University Press.

Lockhart, R. S. (2000). Methods of memory research. In E. Tulving & F. I. M. Craik (Eds.), *The Oxford handbook of memory* (pp. 45–57). Oxford University Press.

Lodhi, P. H., Deo, S., & Belhekar, V. M. (2002). The five-factor model of personality. In R. R. McCrae & J. Allik (Eds.), *The five-factor model of personality across cultures* (pp. 227–248). Springer Science+Business Media.

Loebach, J. L., Conway, C. M., & Pisoni, D. B. (2010). Attention: Cognitive influences. In E. B. Goldstein (Ed.), *Encyclopedia of perception* (pp. 138–141). Sage.

Loeber, R., & Hay, D. (1997). Key issues in the development of aggression and violence from childhood to early adulthood. *Annual Review of Psychology, 48*(1), 371–410.

Loehlin, J. C., & Nichols, R. C. (1976). *Heredity, environment, & personality: A study of 850 sets of twins*. University of Texas Press.

Loewenstein, G. (1994). The psychology of curiosity: A review and reinterpretation. *Psychological Bulletin, 116*(1), 75–98.

Loftus, E. F. (2005). Planting misinformation in the human mind: A 30-year investigation of the malleability of memory. *Learning & Memory, 12*(4), 361–366.

Loftus, E. F., & Cahill, L. (2007). Memory distortion: From misinformation to rich false memory. In H. L. Roediger & J. S. Nairne (Eds.), *The foundation of remembering* (pp. 413– 425). Psychology Press.

Loftus, E. F., & Palmer, J. C. (1974). Reconstruction of automobile destruction: An example of the interaction between language and memory. *Journal of Verbal Learning and Verbal Behavior, 13*(5), 585–589.

Loftus, E. F., & Pickrell, J. E. (1995). The formation of false memories. *Psychiatric Annals, 25*(12), 720–725.

Logue, A. W. (1979). Taste aversion and the generality of the laws of learning. *Psychological Bulletin, 86*(2), 276–296.

Lohmann, R. I. (2007). Dreams and ethnography. In D. Barrett & P. McNamara (Eds.), *The new science of dreaming* (Vol. 3, pp. 35–70). Praeger.

Lohse, T., Rohrmann, S., Richard, A., Bopp, M., Faeh, D., & Swiss National Cohort Study Group. (2017). Type A personality and mortality: Competitiveness but not speed is associated with increased risk. *Atherosclerosis, 262*, 19–24.

Long, G. M. (1980). Iconic memory: A review and critique of the study of short-term visual storage. *Psychological Bulletin, 88*(3), 785–820.

Long, J. E., Jr. (2005). Power to prescribe: The debate over prescription privileges for psychologists and the legal issues implicated. *Law and Psychology Review, 29*, 243–260.

Longo, D. L., Duffey, P. L., Kopp, W. C., Heyes, M. P., Alvord, W. G., Sharfman, W. H., Schmidt, P. J., Rubinow, D. R., & Rosenstein, D. L. (1999). Conditioned immune response to interferon-γ in humans. *Clinical Immunology, 90*(2), 173–181.

Loonis, R. F., Brincat, S. L., Antzoulatos, E. G., & Miller, E. K. (2017). A meta-analysis suggests different neural correlates for implicit and explicit learning. *Neuron, 96*(2), 521–534.

Loos, R. J., & Janssens, A. C. J. (2017). Predicting polygenic obesity using genetic information. *Cell Metabolism, 25*(3), 535–543.

Lorenzo-Luaces, L., German, R. E., & DeRubeis, R. J. (2015). It's complicated: The relation between cognitive change procedures, cognitive change, and symptom change in cognitive therapy for depression. *Clinical Psychology Review, 41*, 3–15.

Lotze, M., Grodd, W., Birbaumer, N., Erb, M., Huse, E., & Flor, H. (1999). Does use of a myoelectric prosthesis prevent cortical reorganization and phantom limb pain? *Nature Neuroscience, 2*(6), 501–502.

Love, K. (2018). Everyone is going through something. https://www.theplayerstribune.com/en-us/articles/kevin-love-everyone-is-going-through-something

Lozano-Blasco, R., Cortés-Pascual, A., & Latorre-Martínez, M. P. (2020). Being a cybervictim and a cyberbully—the duality of cyberbullying: A meta-analysis. *Computers in Human Behavior, 111*, 106444. https://doi.org/10.1016/j.chb.2020.106444

Lubart, T. (1999). Cross-cultural perspectives on creativity. In R. J. Sternberg (Ed.), *The Cambridge handbook of creativity* (pp. 265–278). Cambridge University Press.

Luborsky, L., Rosenthal, R., Diguer, L., Andrusyna, T. P., Berman, J. S., Levitt, J. T., Seligman, D. A., & Krause, E. (2002). The dodo bird verdict is alive and well—mostly. *Clinical Psychology: Science and Practice, 9*(1), 2–12.

Luborsky, L., Singer, J., & Luborsky, L. (1975). Comparative studies of psychotherapies: Is it true that "everyone has won and all must have prizes"? *Archives of General Psychiatry, 32*(8), 995–1008.

Lucas, R. E., Clark, A. E., Georgellis, Y., & Diener, E. (2003). Reexamining adaptation and the set point model of happiness: Reactions to changes in marital status. *Journal of Personality and Social Psychology, 84*(3), 527–539.

Lucas, R. E., & Diener, E. (2008). Subjective well-being. In M. Lewis, J. M. Haviland-Jones, & L. F. Barrett (Eds.), *Handbook of emotions* (3rd ed., pp. 471–484). Guilford Press.

Lukatela, G., & Turvey, M. T. (1994a). Visual lexical access is initially phonological: 1. Evidence from associative priming by words, homophones, and pseudohomophones. *Journal of Experimental Psychology: General, 123*(2), 107–128.

Lukatela, G., & Turvey, M. T. (1994b). Visual lexical access is initially phonological: 2. Evidence from phonological priming by homophones and pseudohomophones. *Journal of Experimental Psychology: General, 123*(4), 331–353.

Luminet, O., & Curci, A. (2009). Introduction. In O. Luminet & A. Curci (Eds.), *Flashbulb memories: New issues and new perspectives* (pp. 1–9). Psychology Press.

Luminet, O., Curci, A., Marsh, E. J., Wessel, I., Constantin, T., Gencoz, F., & Yogo, M. (2004). The cognitive, emotional, and social impacts of the September 11 attacks: Group differences in memory for the reception context and the determinants of flashbulb memory. *The Journal of General Psychology, 131*(3), 197–224.

Lund, E. M. (2020). Even more to handle: Additional sources of stress and trauma for clients from marginalized racial and ethnic groups in the United States during the COVID-19 pandemic. *Counselling Psychology Quarterly, 34*(3–4), 321–330. https://doi.org/10.1080/09515070.2020.1766420

Lundström, J. N., Gonçalves, M., Esteves, F., & Olsson, M. J. (2003). Psychological effects of subthreshold exposure to the putative human pheromone 4,16-androstadien-3-one. *Hormones and Behavior, 44*(5), 395–401.

Lungu, A., & Linehan, M. M. (2016). Dialectical behavior therapy: A comprehensive multi- and transdiagnostic intervention. In C. M. Nezu & A. M. Nezu (Eds.), *The Oxford handbook of cognitive and behavioral therapies* (pp. 200–214). Oxford University Press.

Lunt, P. (2009). *Stanley Milgram: Shaper of obedience*. Palgrave Macmillan.

Lupien, S. J., de Leon, M., De Santi, S., Convit, A., Tarshish, C., Nair, N. P. V., Thakur, M., McEwen, B. S., Hauger, R. L., & Meaney, M. J. (1998). Cortisol levels during human aging predict hippocampal atrophy and memory deficits. *Nature Neuroscience, 1*(1), 69–73.

Lupien, S. J., McEwen, B. S., Gunnar, M. R., & Heim, C. (2009). Effects of stress throughout the lifespan on the brain, behaviour and cognition. *Nature Reviews Neuroscience, 10*(6), 434–445.

Lustgarten, S. D., & Elhai, J. D. (2018). Technology use in mental health practice and research: Legal and ethical risks. *Clinical Psychology: Science and Practice, 25*(2), e12234.

Lutsey, P. L., Misialek, J. R., Mosley, T. H., Gottesman, R. F., Punjabi, N. M., Shahar, E., MacLehose, R., Ogilvie, R. P., Knopman, D., & Alonso, A. (2018). Sleep characteristics and risk of dementia and Alzheimer's disease: The Atherosclerosis Risk in Communities Study. *Alzheimer's & Dementia, 14*(2), 157–166.

Luxton, D. D., Nelson, E., & Maheu, M. M. (2016). *A practitioner's guide to telemental health: How to conduct legal, ethical, and evidence-based telepractice*. American Psychological Association.

Lyamin, O. I., Manger, P. R., Ridgway, S. H., Mukhametov, L. M., & Siegel, J. M. (2008). Cetacean sleep: An unusual form of mammalian sleep. *Neuroscience & Biobehavioral Reviews, 32*(8), 1451–1484.

Lydecker, J. A., & Grilo, C. M. (2017). Children of parents with BED have more eating behavior disturbance than children of parents with obesity or healthy weight. *International Journal of Eating Disorders, 50*(6), 648–656.

Lynch, M. P., & Eilers, R. E. (1991). Children's perception of native and nonnative musical scales. *Music Perception: An Interdisciplinary Journal, 9*(1), 121–131.

Lynch, M. P., & Eilers, R. E. (1992). A study of perceptual development for musical tuning. *Perception & Psychophysics, 52*(6), 599–608.

Lynch, M. P., Eilers, R. E., Oller, D. K., & Urbano, R. C. (1990). Innateness, experience, and music perception. *Psychological Science, 4*(1). https://doi.org/10.1111/j.1467-9280.1990.tb00213.x

Lynn, R., & Martin, T. (1997). Gender differences in extraversion, neuroticism, and psychoticism in 37 nations. *The Journal of Social Psychology, 137*(3), 369–373.

Lynn, R., Fuerst, J., & Kirkegaard, E. O. (2018). Regional differences in intelligence in 22 countries and their economic, social and demographic correlates: A review. *Intelligence, 69*, 24–36. https://doi.org/10.1016/j.intell.2018.04.004

Lyons, H. Z., Bieschke, K. J., Dendy, A. K., Worthington, R. L., & Georgemiller, R. (2010). Psychologists' competence to treat lesbian, gay and bisexual clients: State of the field and strategies for improvement. *Professional Psychology: Research and Practice, 41*(5), 424–434.

Lyubomirsky, S., & Layous, K. (2013). How do simple positive activities increase well-being? *Current Directions in Psychological Science, 22*(1), 57–62.

Lyubomirsky, S., Dickerhoof, R., Boehm, J. K., & Sheldon, K. M. (2011). Becoming happier takes both a will and a proper way: An experimental longitudinal intervention to boost well-being. *Emotion, 11*(2), 391–402.

Lyubomirsky, S., King, L., & Diener, E. (2005). The benefits of frequent positive affect: Does happiness lead to success? *Psychological Bulletin, 131*(6), 803–855.

MacCann, C., Ziegler, M., & Roberts, R. D. (2012). Faking in personality assessments: Reflections and recommendations. In M. Ziegler, C. MacCann, & R. D. Roberts (Eds.), *New perspectives on faking in personality assessment* (pp. 309–329). Oxford University Press.

Maccoby, E. E. (1998). *The two sexes: Growing up apart, coming together*. Harvard University Press.

MacDonald, G., & Leary, M. R. (2005). Why does social exclusion hurt? The relationship between social and physical pain. *Psychological Bulletin, 131*(2), 202–223.

MacDonald, J. (2018). Hearing lips and seeing voices: The origins and development of the "McGurk effect" and reflections on audio-visual speech perception over the last 40 years. *Multisensory Research, 31*(1–2), 7–18.

Mace, J. H. (2004). Involuntary autobiographical memories are highly dependent on abstract cuing: The Proustian view is incorrect. *Applied Cognitive Psychology, 18*(7), 893–899.

Mace, J. H. (2010). The act of remembering the past: An overview. In J. H. Mace (Ed.), *The act of remembering: Toward an understanding of how we remember the past* (pp. 3–10). Wiley-Blackwell.

Mack, A. (2003). Inattentional blindness: Looking without seeing. *Current Directions in Psychological Science, 12*(5), 180–184.

Mackintosh, N. J. (2011). History of theories and measurement of intelligence. In R. J. Sternberg & S. B. Kaufman (Eds.), *The Cambridge handbook of intelligence* (pp. 3–19). Cambridge University Press.

MacLean, C. R., Walton, K. G., Wenneberg, S. R., Levitsky, D. K., Mandarino, J. P., Waziri, R., Hillis, S. L., & Schneider, R. H. (1997). Effects of the transcendental meditation program on adaptive mechanisms: Changes in hormone levels and responses to stress after 4 months of practice. *Psychoneuroendocrinology, 22*(4), 277–295.

MacLeod, C. M. (1988). Forgotten but not gone: Savings for pictures and words in long-term memory. *Journal of Experimental Psychology: Learning, Memory, and Cognition, 14*(2), 195–212.

MacLeod, C., & Mathews, A. (2004). Selective memory effects in anxiety disorders: An overview of research findings and their implications. In D. Reisberg & P. Hertel (Eds.), *Memory and emotion* (pp. 155–185). Oxford University Press.

MacLeod, M. D., & Hulbert, J. C. (2011). Sleep, retrieval inhibition, and the resolving power of human memory. In A. S. Benjamin (Ed.), *Successful remembering and successful forgetting: A Festschrift in honor of Robert A. Bjork* (pp. 133–152). Psychology Press.

Macmillan, M. (2000a). *An odd kind of fame: Stories of Phineas Gage*. MIT Press.

Macmillan, M. (2000b). Restoring Phineas Gage: A 150th retrospective. *Journal of the History of the Neurosciences, 9*(1), 46–66.

Macmillan, M., & Lena, M. L. (2010). Rehabilitating Phineas Gage. *Neuropsychological Rehabilitation, 20*(5), 641–658.

MacMullin, K., Jerry, P., & Cook, K. (2020). Psychotherapist experiences with telepsychotherapy: Pre COVID-19 lessons for a post COVID-19 world. *Journal of Psychotherapy Integration, 30*(2), 248–264. https://doi.org/10.1037/int0000213

Macrae, C. N., & Quadflieg, S. (2010). Perceiving people. In S. T. Fiske, D. T. Gilbert, & G. Lindzey (Eds.), *Handbook of social psychology* (5th ed., Vol. 1, pp. 428–463). Wiley.

MacWhinney, B. (2001). First language acquisition. In M. Aronoff & J. Rees-Miller (Eds.), *The handbook of linguistics* (pp. 466–487). Blackwell.

Maddi, S. R. (1987). Hardiness training at Illinois Bell Telephone. In J. P. Opatz (Ed.), *Health promotion evaluation* (pp. 101–115). National Wellness Institute.

Maddi, S. R. (2002). The story of hardiness: Twenty years of theorizing, research, and practice. *Consulting Psychology Journal: Practice and Research, 54*(3), 173–185.

Maddi, S. R. (2017). Hardiness as a pathway to resilience under stress. In U. Kumar (Ed.), *The Routledge international handbook of psychosocial resilience* (pp. 104–110). Routledge.

Maddi, S. R., & Harvey, R. H. (2006). Hardiness considered across cultures. In P. T. P. Wong & L. C. J. Wong (Eds.), *Handbook of multicultural perspectives on stress and coping* (pp. 409–426). Springer Science+Business Media.

Maddi, S. R., & Hightower, M. (1999). Hardiness and optimism as expressed in coping patterns. *Consulting Psychology Journal: Practice and Research, 51*(2), 95–105.

Maddi, S. R., & Kobasa, S. C. (1984). *The hardy executive: Health under stress*. Dow Jones-Irwin.

Maddi, S. R., Khoshaba, D. M., Jensen, K., Carter, E., Lu, J. L., & Harvey, R. H. (2002). Hardiness training for high risk undergraduates. *NACADA Journal, 22*(1), 45–55.

Maddi, S. R., Matthews, M. D., Kelly, D. R., Villarreal, B. J., Gundersen, K. K., & Savino, S. C. (2017). The continuing role of hardiness and grit on performance and retention in West Point cadets. *Military Psychology, 29*(5), 355–358.

Maddock, J. (2004). The relationship between obesity and the prevalence of fast food restaurants: State-level analysis. *American Journal of Health Promotion, 19*(2), 137–143.

Maddox, K. B., & Gray, S. A. (2002). Cognitive representations of Black Americans: Reexploring the role of skin tone. *Personality and Social Psychology Bulletin, 28*(2), 250–259. https://doi.org/10.1177/0146167202282010

Maddux, J. E., Gosselin, J. T., & Winstead, B. A. (2005). Conceptions of psychopathology: A social constructionist perspective. In J. E. Maddux & B. A. Winstead (Eds.), *Psychopathology* (pp. 3–18). Lawrence Erlbaum.

Madigan, S., Browne, D., Racine, N., Mori, C., & Tough, S. (2019). Association between screen time and children's performance on a developmental screening test. *JAMA Pediatrics, 173*(3), 244–250. https://doi.org/10.1001/jamapediatrics.2018.5056

Madon, S., Guyll, M., Buller, A. A., Scherr, K. C., Willard, J., & Spoth, R. (2008). The mediation of mothers' self-fulfilling effects on their children's alcohol use: Self-verification, informational conformity, and modeling processes. *Journal of Personality and Social Psychology, 95*(2), 369–384.

Madsen, H. B., & Kim, J. H. (2016). Ontogeny of memory: An update on 40 years of work on infantile amnesia. *Behavioural Brain Research, 298*(Part A), 4–14.

Madsen, K. M., Hviid, A., Vestergaard, M., Schendel, D., Wohlfarhrt, J., Thorsen, P., Olsen, J., & Melbye, M. (2002). A population-based study of measles, mumps, and rubella vaccination and autism. *New England Journal of Medicine, 347*(19), 1477–1482.

Maehr, M. L., & Midgley, C. (1991). Enhancing student motivation: A schoolwide approach. *Educational Psychologist, 26*(3–4), 399–427.

Maertens, R., Roozenbeek, J., Basol, M., & van der Linden, S. (2021). Long-term effectiveness of inoculation against misinformation: Three longitudinal experiments. *Journal of Experimental Psychology: Applied, 27*(1), 1–16. https://doi.org/10.1037/xap0000315

Maes, H. H., Neale, M. C., & Eaves, L. J. (1997). Genetic and environmental factors in relative body weight and human adiposity. *Behavior Genetics, 27*(4), 325–351.

Maffetone, P., & Khopkar, M. (2018). The overfat pandemic in India. *Global Epidemic Obesity, 6*(1), 2.

Maffetone, P. B., Rivera-Dominguez, I., & Laursen, P. B. (2017a). Overfat and underfat: New terms and definitions long overdue. *Frontiers in Public Health, 4*, 279.

Maffetone, P. B., Rivera-Dominguez, I., & Laursen, P. B. (2017b). Overfat adults and children in developed countries: The public health importance of identifying excess body fat. *Frontiers in Public Health, 5*, 190.

Magai, C. (2001). Emotions over the lifespan. In J. E. Birren & K. W. Schaie (Eds.), *Handbook of the psychology of aging* (5th ed., pp. 310–344). Academic Press.

Magai, C. (2008). Long-lived emotions: A life course perspective on emotional development. In M. Lewis, J. M. Haviland-Jones, & L. F. Barrett (Eds.), *Handbook of emotions* (3rd ed., pp. 376–392). Guilford Press.

Magga, O. H. (2006). Diversity in Saami terminology for reindeer, snow, and ice. *International Social Science Journal, 58*(157), 25–34.

Maggiolini, A., Di Lorenzo, M., Falotico, E., & Morelli, M. (2020). The typical dreams in the life cycle. *International Journal of Dream Research, 13*(1), 17–28. https://doi.org/10.11588/ijodr.2020.1.61558

Magill, M., Apodaca, T. R., Borsari, B., Gaume, J., Hoadley, A., Gordon, R. E. F., Tonigan, J. S., & Moyers, T. (2018). A meta-analysis of motivational interviewing process: Technical, relational, and conditional process models of change. *Journal of Consulting and Clinical Psychology, 86*(2), 140–157.

Magliozzi, T., & Magliozzi, R. (2011, February 25). Hitting brake and gas is bad move. http://blog.nwautos.com/2011/02/hitting_brake_and_gas_is_bad_move.html

Magnusson, D., & Stattin, H. (2006). The person in context: A holistic-interactionistic approach. In R. M. Lerner (Vol. Ed.), *Handbook of child psychology* (6th ed., Vol. 1, pp. 400–464). Wiley.

Maguire, E. A., Gadian, D. G., Johnsrude, I. S., Good, C. D., Ashburner, J., Frackowiak, R. S., & Frith, C. D. (2000). Navigation-related structural change in the hippocampi of taxi drivers. *Proceedings of the National Academy of Sciences, 97*(8), 4398–4403.

Magyar-Moe, J. L., Owens, R. L., & Conoley, C. W. (2015). Positive psychological interventions in counseling: What every counseling psychologist should know. *The Counseling Psychologist, 43*(4), 508–557.

Magyaródi, T., & Oláh, A. (2015). A cross-sectional survey study about the most common solitary and social flow activities to extend the concept of optimal experience. *Europe's Journal of Psychology, 11*(4), 632–650. https://doi.org/10.5964/ejop.v11i4.866

Maheu, M. M., Pulier, M. L., Wilhelm, F. H., McMenamin, J. P., & Brown-Connolly, N. E. (2005). *The mental health professional and the new technologies: A handbook for practice today*. Lawrence Erlbaum.

Mahmoud, A. B., Reisel, W. D., Hack-Polay, D., & Fuxman, L. (2021). No one is safe! But who's more susceptible? Locus of control moderates pandemic perceptions' effects on job insecurity and psychosocial factors amongst MENA hospitality frontliners: A PLS-SEM approach. *BMC Public Health, 21*(1), 1–13. https://doi.org/10.1186/s12889-021-12071-2

Mahoney, J. L., Vandell, D. L., Simpkins, S., & Zarrett, N. (2009). Adolescent out-of-school activities. In R. M. Lerner & L. Steinberg (Eds.), *Handbook of adolescent psychology* (3rd ed., Vol. 2, pp. 228–269). Wiley.

Mahoney, M. M. (2010). Shift work, jet lag, and female reproduction. *International Journal of Endocrinology*, 813764. https://doi.org/10.1155/2010/813764

Mai, Q. D., Hill, T. D., Vila-Henninger, L., & Grandner, M. A. (2018). Employment insecurity and sleep disturbance: Evidence from 31 European countries. *Journal of Sleep Research, 28*(1), e12763.

Maier, C., Laumer, S., Eckhardt, A., & Weitzel, T. (2015). Giving too much social support: Social overload on social networking sites. *European Journal of Information Systems, 24*(5), 447–464.

Maier, N. R. F. (1931). Reasoning in humans. II. The solution of a problem and its appearance in consciousness. *Journal of Comparative Psychology, 12*(2), 181–194. https://doi.org/10.1037/h0071361

Maier, S. F., Seligman, M. E. P., & Solomon, R. L. (1969). Pavlovian fear conditioning and learned helplessness. In B. A. Campbell & R. M. Church (Eds.), *Punishment and aversive behavior* (pp. 299–343). Appleton-Century-Crofts.

Main, M., & Solomon, J. (1986). Discovery of a new, insecure-disorganized/disoriented attachment pattern. In M. Yogman & T. B. Brazelton (Eds.), *Affective development in infancy* (pp. 95–124). Ablex.

Main, M., & Solomon, J. (1990). Procedures for identifying infants as disorganised/disoriented during the Ainsworth strange situation. In M. T. Greenberg, D. Cicchetti, & E. M. Cummings (Eds.), *Attachment in the preschool years* (pp. 121–160). University of Chicago Press.

Maiorano, A., Lasalvia, A., Sampogna, G., Pocai, B., Ruggeri, M., & Henderson, C. (2017). Reducing stigma in media professionals: Is there room for improvement? Results from a systematic review. *The Canadian Journal of Psychiatry, 62*(10), 702–715.

Majdandžić, M., de Vente, W., Colonnesi, C., & Bögels, S. M. (2018). Fathers' challenging parenting behavior predicts less subsequent anxiety symptoms in early childhood. *Behaviour Research and Therapy, 109*, 18–28.

Major, B., Dovidio, J. F., Link, B. G., & Calabrese, S. K. (2018). Stigma and its implications for health: Introduction and overview. In B. Major, J. F. Dovidio, & B. G. Link (Eds.), *The Oxford handbook of stigma, discrimination, and health* (pp. 3–28). Oxford University Press.

Makin, T. R., & Flor, H. (2020). Brain (re) organisation following amputation: Implications for phantom limb pain. *NeuroImage, 218*, 116943. https://doi.org/10.1016/j.neuroimage.2020.116943

Malark, A. (2017). Sexuality, religion, and atheism in psychodynamic treatment. *Psychology of Sexual Orientation and Gender Diversity, 4*(4), 412–421.

Malarkey, W. B., Kiecolt-Glaser, J. K., Pearl, D., & Glaser, R. (1994). Hostile behavior during marital conflict alters pituitary and adrenal hormones. *Psychosomatic Medicine, 56*(1), 41–51.

Malatesta, C. Z., & Haviland, J. M. (1982). Learning display rules: The socialization of emotion expression in infancy. *Child Development, 53*(4), 991–1003.

Malenka, R. C., & Bear, M. F. (2004). LTP and LTD: An embarrassment of riches. *Neuron, 44*(1), 5–21.

Malenka, R. C., & Nicoll, R. A. (1999). Long-term potentiation—a decade of progress? *Science, 285*(5435), 1870–1874.

Malgady, R. G., & Colon-Malgady, G. (2008). Building community test norms: Considerations for ethnic minority populations. In L. A. Suzuki & J. G. Ponterotto (Eds.), *Handbook of multicultural assessment: Clinical, psychological, and educational applications* (3rd ed., pp. 34–51). Wiley.

Malgady, R. G., Costantino, G., & Rogler, L. H. (1984). Development of a thematic apperception test ([temas]) for urban Hispanic children. *Journal of Consulting and Clinical Psychology, 52*(6), 986–996. https://doi.org/10.1037/0022-006X.52.6.986

Malizia, A. L., & Nutt, D. (2008). Principles and findings from human imaging of anxiety disorders. In R. J. Blanchard, D. C. Blanchard, G. Griebel, & D. Nutt (Eds.), *Handbook of anxiety and fear* (pp. 437–454). Elsevier.

Malle, B. F. (2006). The actor-observer asymmetry in attribution: A (surprising) meta-analysis. *Psychological Bulletin, 132*(6), 895–919.

Malle, B. F. (2011). Attribution theories: How people make sense of behavior. In D. Chadee (Ed.), *Theories in social psychology* (pp. 72–95). Wiley-Blackwell.

Malleret, G., Alarcon, J. M., Martel, G., Takizawa, S., Vronskaya, S., Yin, D., Chen, I. Z., Kandel, E. R., & Shumyatsky, G. P. (2010). Bidirectional regulation of hippocampal long-term synaptic plasticity and its influence on opposing forms of memory. *Journal of Neuroscience, 30*(10), 3813–3825.

Malone, C. M., Gibson, A., & Isom, D. L. (2020). Tell-Me-A-Story (TEMAS). In Bernardo J. Carducci, Christopher S. Nave, Christopher S. Nave (Eds.), *The Wiley Encyclopedia of personality and individual differences: Measurement and assessment*, pp. 377–379. https://doi.org/10.1002/9781118970843.ch132

Malone, J. C. (2009). *Psychology: Pythagoras to present*. MIT Press.

Malouff, J. M., Thorsteinsson, E. B., Schutte, N. S., Bhullar, N., & Rooke, S. E. (2010). The Five-Factor Model of personality and relationship satisfaction of intimate partners: A meta-analysis. *Journal of Research in Personality, 44*(1), 124–127.

Malouff, J., Thorsteinsson, E., Schutte, N., & Rooke, S. E. (2009). Effects of vicarious punishment: A meta-analysis. *The Journal of General Psychology, 136*(3), 271–286.

Manago, A. M., Ward, L. M., Lemm, K. M., Reed, L., & Seabrook, R. (2014). Facebook involvement, objectified body consciousness, body shame, and sexual assertiveness in college women and men. *Sex Roles, 72*(12), 1–14.

Manber, R., & Bootzin, R. R. (1997). Sleep and the menstrual cycle. *Health Psychology, 16*(3), 209–214.

Mancke, F., Schmitt, R., Winter, D., Niedtfeld, I., Herpertz, S. C., & Schmahl, C. (2018). Assessing the marks of change: How psychotherapy alters the brain structure in women with borderline personality disorder. *Journal of Psychiatry & Neuroscience, 43*(3), 171–181.

Mandell, B., & Pherwani, S. (2003). Relationship between emotional intelligence and transformational leadership style: A gender comparison. *Journal of Business and Psychology, 17*(3), 387–404.

Mandelman, S. D., & Grigorenko, E. L. (2011). Intelligence: Genes, environments, and their interactions. In R. J. Sternberg & S. B. Kaufman (Eds.), *The Cambridge handbook of intelligence* (pp. 85–106). Cambridge University Press.

Mandler, G. (1980). Recognizing: The judgment of previous occurrence.*Psychological Review, 87*(3), 252–271.

Manenschijn, L., van Kruysbergen, R. G., de Jong, F. H., Koper, J. W., & van Rossum, E. F. (2011). Shift work at young age is associated with elevated long-term cortisol levels and body mass index. *The Journal of Clinical Endocrinology & Metabolism, 96*(11), E1862–E1865.

Maner, J. K., Luce, C. L., Neuberg, S. L., Cialdini, R. B., Brown, S., & Sagarin, B. J. (2002). The effects of perspective taking on motivations for helping: Still no evidence for altruism. *Personality and Social Psychology Bulletin, 28*(11), 1601–1610.

Mangan, M. A. (2004). A phenomenology of problematic sexual behavior occurring in sleep. *Archives of Sexual Behavior, 33*(3), 287–293.

Mangelsdorf, S., Gunnar, M., Kestenbaum, R., Lang, S., & Andreas, D. (1990). Infant proneness-to-distress temperament, maternal personality, and mother–infant attachment: Associations and goodness of fit. *Child Development, 61*(3), 820–831.

Manlove, J., Logan, C., Moore, K. A., & Ikramullah, E. (2008). Pathways from family religiosity to adolescent sexual activity and contraceptive use. *Perspectives on Sexual and Reproductive Health, 40*(2), 105–117.

Manning, R., Levine, M., & Collins, A. (2007). The Kitty Genovese murder and the social psychology of helping: The parable of the 38 witnesses. *American Psychologist, 62*(6), 555–562.

Manson, J. H., & Perry, S. (2013). Personality structure, sex differences, and temporal change and stability in wild white-faced capuchins (*Cebus capucinus*). *Journal of Comparative Psychology, 127*(3), 299–311. https://doi.org/10.1037/a0031316

Manto, M. (2010). *Cerebellar disorders: A practical approach to diagnosis and management*. Cambridge University Press.

Mantonakis, A., Rodero, P., Lesschaeve, I., & Hastie, R. (2009). Order in choice effects of serial position on preferences. *Psychological Science, 20*(11), 1309–1312.

Maquet, P., Péters, J. M., Aerts, J., Delfiore, G., Degueldre, C., Luxen, A., & Franck, G. (1996). Functional neuroanatomy of human rapid-eye-movement sleep and dreaming. *Nature, 383*(6596), 163–166.

Marceau, K., Zahn-Waxler, C., Shirtcliff, E. A., Schreiber, J. E., Hastings, P., & Klimes-Dougan, B. (2015). Adolescents', mothers', and fathers' gendered coping strategies during conflict: Youth and parent influences on conflict resolution and psychopathology. *Development and Psychopathology, 27*(4pt1), 1025–1044.

Marcia, J. E. (1966). Development and validation of ego-identity status. *Journal of Personality and Social Psychology, 3*(5), 551.

Marcia, J. E. (1980). Identity in adolescence. *Handbook of Adolescent Psychology, 9*, 159–187.

Marcus, G. (2004). *The birth of the mind: How a tiny number of genes creates the complexities of human thought*. Basic Books.

Marcus, G. F., Vijayan, S., Rao, S. B., & Vishton, P. M. (1999). Rule learning by seven-month-old infants. *Science, 283*(5398), 77–80.

Marczyk, G. R., DeMatteo, D., & Festinger, D. (2005). *Essentials of research design and methodology*. John Wiley & Sons.

Marczyk, G., Krauss, D. A., & Burl, J. (2012). Educational and training models in forensic psychology. In C. R. Bartol & A. M. Bartol (Eds.), *Current perspectives in forensic psychology and criminal behavior* (pp. 2–10). Sage.

Marden, J. R., Tchetgen Tchetgen, E. J., Kawachi, I., & Glymour, M. M. (2017). Contribution of socioeconomic status at 3 life-course periods to late-life memory function and decline: Early and late predictors of dementia risk. *American Journal of Epidemiology, 186*(7), 805–814. https://doi.org/10.1093/aje/kwx155

Mares, D. M., & Moffett, K. W. (2016). Climate change and interpersonal violence: A "global" estimate and regional inequities. *Climatic Change, 135*(2), 297–310.

Mareschal, D., & Kaufman, J. (2012). Object permanence in infancy: Revisiting Baillargeon's drawbridge study. In A. M. Slater & P. C. Quinn (Eds.), *Developmental psychology: Revisiting the classic studies* (pp. 86–100). Sage.

Marian, V., & Kaushanskaya, M. (2004). Self-construal and emotion in bicultural bilinguals. *Journal of Memory and Language, 51*(2), 190–201.

Marian, V., & Neisser, U. (2000). Language-dependent recall of autobiographical memories. *Journal of Experimental Psychology: General, 129*(3), 361.

Markiewicz, D., Lawford, H., Doyle, A. B., & Haggart, N. (2006). Developmental differences in adolescents' and young adults' use of mothers, fathers, best friends, and romantic partners to fulfill attachment needs. *Journal of Youth and Adolescence, 35*(1), 121–134.

Markin, R. D., & Kasten, J. (2015). Group psychotherapy. In R. L. Cautin & S. O. Lilienfeld (Eds.), *The encyclopedia of clinical psychology* (pp. 1358–1363). Wiley-Blackwell.

Markman, A. B. (1999). *Knowledge representation*. Lawrence Erlbaum.

Markman, A. B., & Rein, J. R. (2013). The nature of mental concepts. In D. Reisberg (Ed.), *The Oxford handbook of cognitive psychology* (pp. 321–329). Oxford University Press.

Markowitz, J. C., & Weissman, M. M. (2012). Interpersonal psychotherapy: Past, present and future. *Clinical Psychology and Psychotherapy, 19*(2), 99–105.

Marks, I., & Cavanagh, K. (2009). Computer-aided psychological treatments: Evolving issues. *Annual Review of Clinical Psychology, 5*, 121–141.

Marks, R. J., De Foe, A., & Collett, J. (2020). The pursuit of wellness: Social media, body image and eating disorders. *Children and Youth Services Review, 119*, 105659. https://doi.org/10.1016/j.childyouth.2020.105659

Maron, E., Hettema, J. M., & Shilk, J. (2008). The genetics of human anxiety disorders. In R. J. Blanchard, D. C. Blanchard, G. Griebel, & D. Nutt (Eds.), *Handbook of anxiety and fear* (pp. 475–510). Elsevier.

Marsh, A. A., Stoycos, S. A., Brethel-Haurwitz, K. M., Robinson, P., VanMeter, J. W., & Cardinale, E. M. (2014). Neural and cognitive characteristics of extraordinary altruists. *Proceedings of the National Academy of Sciences, 111*(42), 15036–15041.

Marshall, G. D., & Zimbardo, P. G. (1979). Affective consequences of inadequately explained physiological arousal. *Journal of Personality and Social Psychology, 37*(6), 970–988.

Marshall, L., & Born, J. (2007). The contribution of sleep to hippocampus-dependent memory consolidation. *Trends in Cognitive Sciences, 11*(10), 442–450.

Marshall, W. L. (1985). The effects of variable exposure in flooding therapy. *Behavior Therapy, 16*(2), 117–135.

Marshall-Lee, E., Hinger, C., Popovic, R., Roberts, T. M., & Prempeh, L. (2020). Social justice advocacy in mental health services: Consumer, community, training, and policy perspectives. *Psychological Services, 17*(S1), 12–21. https://doi.org/10.1037/ser0000349

Marsland, A. L., Walsh, C., Lockwood, K., & John-Henderson, N. A. (2017). The effects of acute psychological stress on circulating and stimulated inflammatory markers: A systematic review and meta-analysis. *Brain, Behavior, and Immunity, 64*, 208–219.

Martell, B. A., O'Connor, P. G., Kerns, R. D., Becker, W. C., Morales, K. H., Kosten, T. R., & Fiellin, D. A. (2007). Systematic review: Opioid treatment for chronic back pain: Prevalence, efficacy, and association with addiction. *Annals of Internal Medicine, 146*(2), 116–127.

Marti, A., Moreno-Aliaga, M. J., Hebebrand, J., & Martinez, J. A. (2004). Genes, lifestyles and obesity. *International Journal of Obesity, 28*(Suppl. 3), S29–S36.

Martí, E. (2003). Strengths and weaknesses of cognition over preschool years. In J. Valsiner & K. Connolly (Eds.), *Handbook of developmental psychology* (pp. 114–140). Sage.

Martin, A., & Chao, L. L. (2001). Semantic memory and the brain: Structure and processes. *Current Opinion in Neurobiology, 11*(2), 194–201.

Martin, C. L., Andrews, N. C., England, D. E., Zosuls, K., & Ruble, D. N. (2017). A dual identity approach for conceptualizing and measuring children's gender identity. *Child Development, 88*(1), 167–182.

Martin, C. L., & Ruble, D. N. (2010). Patterns of gender development. *Annual Review of Psychology, 61*, 353–381.

Martin, J. K., Pescosolido, B. A., & Tuch, S. A. (2000). Of fear and loathing: The role of "disturbing behavior," labels, and causal attributions in shaping public attitudes toward people with mental illness. *Journal of Health and Social Behavior, 41*(2), 208–223. https://doi.org/10.2307/2676306

Martin, J. N., Millán, F., & Campbell, L. F. (2020). Telepsychology practice: Primer and first steps. *Practice Innovations, 5*(2), 114–127. https://doi.org/10.1037/pri0000111

Martini, D. N., & Broglio, S. P. (2018). Long-term effects of sport concussion on cognitive and motor performance: A review. *International Journal of Psychophysiology, 132*, 25–30.

Martire, L. M., & Helgeson, V. S. (2017). Close relationships and the management of chronic illness: Associations and interventions. *American Psychologist, 72*(6), 601–612.

Martz, M. E., Patrick, M. E., & Schulenberg, J. E. (2015). Alcohol mixed with energy drink use among US 12th-grade students: Prevalence, correlates, and associations with unsafe driving. *Journal of Adolescent Health, 56*(5), 557–563.

Marucha, P. T., Kiecolt-Glaser, J. K., & Favagehi, M. (1998). Mucosal wound healing is impaired by examination stress. *Psychosomatic Medicine, 60*(3), 362–365.

Maruish, M. E. (2008). The clinical interview. In R. P. Archer & S. R. Smith (Eds.), *Personality assessment* (pp. 37–80). Routledge.

Marx, R. F. (2017, September 29). A teacher vanishes again. This time, in the Virgin Islands. *The New York Times*. https://www.nytimes.com/2017/09/29/nyregion/missing-teacher-virgin-islands.html

Marx, R. F., & Didziulis, V. (2009, February 27). A life, interrupted. *The New York Times.* http://www.nytimes.com/2009/03/01/nyregion/thecity/01miss.html?pagewanted=1&_r=3&ref=nyregion

Masih, T., Dimmock, J. A., Epel, E. S., & Guelfi, K. J. (2017). Stress-induced eating and the relaxation response as a potential antidote: A review and hypothesis. *Appetite, 118*, 136–143.

Maski, K., Steinhart, E., Holbrook, H., Katz, E. S., Kapur, K., & Stickgold, R. (2017). Impaired memory consolidation in children with obstructive sleep disordered breathing. *PLoS ONE, 12*(11), e0186915.

Maslach, C. (1979). Negative emotional biasing of unexplained arousal. *Journal of Personality and Social Psychology, 37*(6), 953–969.

Maslow, A. H. (1943). A theory of human motivation. *Psychological Review, 50*(4), 370–396.

Maslow, A. H. (1954). *Motivation and personality.* Harper.

Maslow, A. H. (1967). A theory of metamotivation: The biological rooting of the value-life. *Journal of Humanistic Psychology, 7*(2), 93–127.

Maslow, A. H. (1968). *Toward a psychology of being* (2nd ed.). Van Nostrand.

Maslow, A. H. (1969). The farther reaches of human nature. *Journal of Transpersonal Psychology, 1*(1), 1–9.

Maslow, A. H. (1970). *Religions, values, and peak-experiences.* Viking Press.

Maslow, A. H. (1971). *The farther reaches of human nature.* Viking Press.

Mason, N. S., & Chaney, J. M. (1996). Bulimia nervosa in undergraduate women: Factors associated with internalization of the sociocultural standard of thinness. *Applied and Preventive Psychology, 5*(4), 249–259.

Mason, T. B., Barrington-Trimis, J., & Leventhal, A. M. (2021). Eating to cope with the COVID-19 pandemic and body weight change in young adults. *Journal of Adolescent Health, 68*(2), 277–283. https://doi.org/10.1016/j.jadohealth.2020.11.011

Massen, C., & Vaterrodt-Plunnecke, B. (2006). The role of proactive interference in mnemonic techniques. *Memory, 14*(2), 189–196.

Mast, M. S., & Sczesny, S. (2010). Gender, power, and nonverbal behavior. In J. C. Chrisler & D. R. McCreary (Eds.), *Handbook of gender research in psychology* (Vol. 1, pp. 411–425). Springer Science+Business Media.

Masten, A. S. (2004). Regulatory processes, risk, and resilience in adolescent development. *Annals of the New York Academy of Sciences, 1021*(1), 310–319.

Masten, A. S. (2006). Developmental psychopathology: Pathways to the future. *International Journal of Behavioral Development, 30*(1), 47–54.

Masuda, T. (2010). Cultural effects on visual perception. In E. B. Goldstein (Ed.), *Encyclopedia of perception* (pp. 339–343). Sage.

Masuda, T., & Nisbett, R. E. (2001). Attending holistically versus analytically: Comparing the context sensitivity of Japanese and Americans. *Journal of Personality and Social Psychology, 81*(5), 922–934.

Masuda, T., & Nisbett, R. E. (2006). Culture and change blindness. *Cognitive Science, 30*(2), 381–399.

Mather, G. (2011). *Essentials of sensation and perception.* Routledge.

Mathers, C., Smith, A., & Concha, M. (2000). Global burden of hearing loss in the year 2000. *Global Burden of Disease, 18*, 1–30.

Mathes, J., & Schredl, M. (2013). Gender differences in dream content: Are they related to personality? *International Journal of Dream Research, 6*(2), 104–109. https://doi.org/10.11588/ijodr.2013.2.10954

Matheson, D. M., Killen, J. D., Wang, Y., Varady, A., & Robinson, T. N. (2004). Children's food consumption during television viewing. *The American Journal of Clinical Nutrition, 79*(6), 1088–1094.

Mathews, C. A. (2009). Phenomenology of obsessive-compulsive disorder. In M. M. Antony & M. B. Stein (Eds.), *Oxford handbook of anxiety and related disorders* (pp. 56–64). Oxford University Press.

Mathias, K. C., Rolls, B. J., Birch, L. L., Kral, T. V., Hanna, E. L., Davey, A., & Fisher, J. O. (2012). Serving larger portions of fruits and vegetables together at dinner promotes intake of both foods among young children. *Journal of the Academy of Nutrition and Dietetics, 112*(2), 266–270.

Mathy, F., & Feldman, J. (2012). What's magic about magic numbers? Chunking and data compression in short-term memory. *Cognition, 122*(3), 346–362.

Matos, L., Lens, W., Vansteenkiste, M., & Mouratidis, A. (2017). Optimal motivation in Peruvian high schools: Should learners pursue and teachers promote mastery goals, performance-approach goals or both? *Learning and Individual Differences, 55*, 87–96.

Matser, J. T., Kessels, A. G. H., Lezak, M. D., & Troost, J. (2001). A dose-response relation of headers and concussions with cognitive impairment in professional soccer players. *Journal of Clinical and Experimental Neuropsychology, 23*(6), 770–774.

Matson, J. L., Rieske, R. D., & Williams, L. W. (2013). The relationship between autism spectrum disorders and attention-deficit/hyperactivity disorder: An overview. *Research in Developmental Disabilities, 34*(9), 2475–2484.

Matsumoto, D. (1990). Cultural similarities and differences in display rules. *Motivation and Emotion, 14*(3), 195–214.

Matsumoto, D. (2003). Cross-cultural research. In S. F. Davis (Ed.), *Handbook of research methods in experimental psychology* (pp. 189–208). Blackwell.

Matsumoto, D., Consolacion, T., Yamada, H., Suzuki, R., Franklin, B., Paul, S., Ray, R., & Uchida, H. (2002). American-Japanese cultural differences in judgements of emotional expressions of different intensities. *Cognition & Emotion, 16*(6), 721–747.

Matsumoto, D., Keltner, D., Shiota, M. N., O'Sullivan, M., & Frank, M. (2008a). Facial expressions of emotion. In M. Lewis, J. M. Haviland-Jones, & L. F. Barrett (Eds.), *Handbook of emotions* (3rd. ed., pp. 211–234). Guilford Press.

Matsumoto, D., Yoo, S. H., & Fontaine, J. (2008b). Mapping expressive differences around the world: The relationship between emotional display rules and individualism versus collectivism. *Journal of Cross-Cultural Psychology, 39*(1), 55–74.

Matsumoto, D., Yoo, S. H., & Nakagawa, S. (2008c). Culture, emotion regulation, and adjustment. *Journal of Personality and Social Psychology, 94*(6), 925–937.

Matsumoto, D., & Willingham, B. (2006). The thrill of victory and the agony of defeat: Spontaneous expressions of medal winners of the 2004 Athens Olympic Games. *Journal of Personality and Social Psychology, 91*(3), 568–581.

Matsumoto, D., & Willingham, B. (2009). Spontaneous facial expressions of emotion of congenitally and noncongenitally blind individuals. *Journal of Personality and Social Psychology, 96*(1), 1–10.

Matt, G. E., Hoh, E., Quintana, P. J., Zakarian, J. M., & Arceo, J. (2018). Cotton pillows: A novel field method for assessment of thirdhand smoke pollution. *Environmental Research, 168*, 206–210.

Matt, G. E., Quintana, P. J., Fortmann, A. L., Zakarian, J. M., Galaviz, V. E., Chatfield, D. A., Hoh, E., Hovell, M. F., & Winston, C. (2014). Thirdhand smoke and exposure in California hotels: Non-smoking rooms fail to protect non-smoking hotel guests from tobacco smoke exposure. *Tobacco Control, 23*(3), 264–272.

Matt, G. E., Quintana, P. J., Zakarian, J. M., Fortmann, A. L., Chatfield, D. A., Hoh, E., & Hovell, M. F. (2010). When smokers move out and non-smokers move in: Residential thirdhand smoke pollution and exposure. Tobacco Control, 20(1), e1. https://doi.org/1136/tc.2010.037382

Matt, G. E., Quintana, P. J., Zakarian, J. M., Hoh, E., Hovell, M. F., Mahabee-Gittens, M., Watanabe, K., Datuin, K., Vue, C., & Chatfield, D. A. (2017). When smokers quit: Exposure to nicotine and carcinogens persists from thirdhand smoke pollution. *Tobacco Control, 26*(5), 548–556.

Matt, G. E., Vazquez, C., & Campbell, W. K. (1992). Mood-congruent recall of affectively toned stimuli: A meta-analytic review. *Clinical Psychology Review, 12*(2), 227–255.

Mattes, R. D. (1997). The taste for salt in humans. *The American Journal of Clinical Nutrition, 65*(2), 692S–697S.

Matthews, J. R., & Matthews, L. H. (2012). Applying for clinical and other applied positions. In P. J. Giordano, S. F. Davis, & C. A. Licht (Eds.), *Your graduate training in psychology: Effective strategies for success* (pp. 295–306). Sage.

Matthews, K. A., Wing, R. R., Kuller, L. H., Meilahn, E. N., Kelsey, S. F., Costello, E. J., & Caggiula, A. W. (1990). Influences of natural menopause on psychological characteristics and symptoms of middle-aged healthy women. *Journal of Consulting and Clinical Psychology, 58*(3), 345–351.

Mattson, M. P. (2012). Energy intake and exercise as determinants of brain health and vulnerability to injury and disease. *Cell Metabolism, 16*(6), 706–722.

Mattson, S. N., & Riley, E. P. (1998). A review of the neurobehavioral deficits in children with fetal alcohol syndrome or prenatal exposure to alcohol. *Alcoholism: Clinical and Experimental Research, 22*(2), 279–294.

Mattys, S. L. (2013). Speech perception. In D. Reisberg (Ed.), *The Oxford handbook of cognitive psychology* (pp. 391–411). Oxford University Press.

Matud, M. P. (2004). Gender differences in stress and coping styles. *Personality and Individual Differences, 37*(7), 1401–1415.

Maurer, D., Lewis, T. L., & Mondloch, C. J. (2005). Missing sights: Consequences for visual cognitive development. *Trends in Cognitive Sciences, 9*(3), 144–151.

Mauriello, L. M., Johnson, S. S., & Prochaska, J. M. (2017). Meeting patients where they are at: Using a stage approach to facilitate engagement. In J. W. O'Donohue & C. Snipes (Eds.), *Practical strategies and tools to promote treatment engagement* (pp. 25–44). Springer International.

Maury, E., Ramsey, K. M., & Bass, J. (2010). Circadian rhythms and metabolic syndrome from experimental genetics to human disease. *Circulation Research, 106*(3), 447–462.

Mauss, I. B., Levenson, R. W., McCarter, L., Wilhelm, F. H., & Gross, J. J. (2005). The tie that binds? Coherence among emotion experience, behavior, and physiology. *Emotion, 5*(2), 175–190.

May, A. L., Kim, J. Y., McHale, S. M., & Crouter, A. (2006). Parent–adolescent relationships and the development of weight concerns from early to late adolescence. *International Journal of Eating Disorders, 39*(8), 729–740.

May, C. P., Dein, A., & Ford, J. (2020). New insights into the formation and duration of flashbulb memories: Evidence from medical diagnosis memories. *Applied Cognitive Psychology, 34*(5), 1154–1165. https://doi.org/10.1002/acp.3704

Mayberry, M. L., & Espelage, D. L. (2007). Associations among empathy, social competence, & reactive/proactive aggression subtypes. *Journal of Youth and Adolescence, 36*(6), 787–798.

Mayer, J. D., & Salovey, P. (1997). What is emotional intelligence? In P. Salovey & D. J. Sluyter (Eds.), *Emotional development and emotional intelligence: Educational implications* (pp. 3–31). Basic Books.

Mayer, J. D., Roberts, R. D., & Barsade, S. G. (2008). Human abilities: Emotional intelligence. *Annual Review of Psychology, 59*, 507–536.

Mayer, R. E. (2011). Intelligence and achievement. In R. J. Sternberg & S. B. Kaufman (Eds.), *The Cambridge handbook of intelligence* (pp. 738–747). Cambridge University Press.

Mayer, R. E. (2013). Problem solving. In D. Reisberg (Ed.), *The Oxford handbook of cognitive psychology* (pp. 769–778). Oxford University Press.

Mayes, A. R. (2000). Selective memory disorders. In E. Tulving & F. I. M. Craik (Eds.), *The Oxford handbook of memory* (pp. 427–440). Oxford University Press.

Mayes, A. R. (2002). Theories of anterograde amnesia. In A. D. Baddeley, M. D. Kopelman, & B. A. Wilson (Eds.), *The handbook of memory disorders* (2nd ed., pp. 167–187). Wiley.

Mayhew, G., & Harris, F. (1979). Decreasing self-injurious behavior: Punishment with citric acid and reinforcement of alternative behavior. *Behavior Modification, 3*(3), 322–336.

Mayo Clinic Staff. (2017, March 8). Caffeine: How much is too much? https://www.mayoclinic.org/healthy-lifestyle/nutrition-and-healthy-eating/in-depth/caffeine/art-20045678

Mayopoulos, G. A., Ein-Dor, T., Dishy, G. A., Nandru, R., Chan, S. J., Hanley, L. E., Kaimal, A. J., & Dekel, S. (2021). COVID-19 is associated with traumatic childbirth and subsequent mother-infant bonding problems. *Journal of Affective Disorders, 282*, 122–125. https://doi.org/10.1016/j.jad.2020.12.101

Mays, V. M., & Ghavami, N. (2018). History, aspirations, and transformations of intersectionality: Focusing on gender. In C. B. Travis, J. W. White, A. Rutherford, W. S. Williams, S. L. Cook, & K. F. Wyche (Eds.), *APA handbook of the psychology of women: History, theory, and battlegrounds* (APA Handbooks in Psychology series, pp. 541–566). American Psychological Association.

Mazzucchelli, T., Kane, R., & Rees, C. (2009). Behavioral activation treatments for depression in adults: A meta-analysis and review. *Clinical Psychology: Science and Practice, 16*(4), 383–411.

McAdams, D. P. (1992). The five-factor model *in* personality: A critical appraisal. *Journal of Personality, 60*(2), 329–361.

McAleavey, A. A., & Castonguay, L. G. (2014). Insight as a common and specific impact of psychotherapy: Therapist-reported exploratory, directive, and common factor interventions. *Psychotherapy, 51*(2), 283–294.

McAlpine, D. (2010). Auditory localization: Physiology. In E. B. Goldstein (Ed.), *Encyclopedia of perception* (pp. 167–170). Sage.

McAndrew, F. T., & Jeong, H. S. (2012). Who does what on Facebook? Age, sex, and relationship status as predictors of Facebook use. *Computers in Human Behavior, 28*(6), 2359–2365.

McBride, C., Farvolden, P., & Swallow, S. R. (2007). Major depressive disorder and cognitive schemas. In L. P. Riso, P. L. du Toit, D. J. Stein, & J. E. Young (Eds.), *Cognitive schemas and core beliefs in psychological problems: A scientist-practitioner guide* (pp. 11–39). American Psychological Association.

McBurney, D. H. (2010a). Evolutionary approach: Perceptual adaptations. In E. B. Goldstein (Ed.), *Encyclopedia of perception* (pp. 405–407). Sage.

McBurney, D. H. (2010b). Extrasensory perception. In E. B. Goldstein (Ed.), *Encyclopedia of perception* (pp. 411–413). Sage.

McCabe, D. P., & Castel, A. D. (2008). Seeing is believing: The effect of brain images on judgments of scientific reasoning. *Cognition, 107*(1), 343–352.

McCabe, J. (2009). Racial and gender microaggressions on a predominantly-White campus: Experiences of Black, Latina/o and White undergraduates. *Race, Gender & Class, 16* (1–2), 133–151.

McCabe, S. E., Teter, C. J., Boyd, C. J., Wilens, T. E., & Schepis, T. S. (2018). Sources of prescription medication misuse among young adults in the United States: The role of educational status. *The Journal of Clinical Psychiatry, 79*(2), 17m11958.

McCallum, R. S., & Bracken, B. A. (2005). The Universal Nonverbal Intelligence Test: A multidimensional measure of intelligence. In D. P. Flanagan & P. L. Harrison (Eds.), *Contemporary intellectual assessment: Theories, tests, and issues* (2nd ed., pp. 425–440). Guilford Press.

McCallum, R. S., & Bracken, B. A. (2018). The Universal Nonverbal Intelligence Test, second edition: A multidimensional nonverbal alternative for cognitive assessment. In D. P. Flanagan & E. M. McDonough (Eds.), *Contemporary intellectual assessment: Theories, tests, and issues* (4th ed., pp. 567–584). Guilford Press.

McCartan, R., Elliott, M. A., Pagani, S., Finnegan, E., & Kelly, S. W. (2018). Testing the effects of explicit and implicit bidimensional attitudes on objectively measured speeding behaviour. *British Journal of Social Psychology, 57*(3), 630–651.

McCarthy, M., Chen, C. C., & McNamee, R. C. (2018). Novelty and usefulness trade-off: Cultural cognitive differences and creative idea evaluation. *Journal of Cross-Cultural Psychology, 49*(2), 171–198.

McClellan, J., & King, M. C. (2010). Genomic analysis of mental illness. *JAMA, 303*(24), 2523–2524.

McClellan, M. J., Osbaldiston, R., Wu, R., Yeager, R., Monroe, A. D., McQueen, T., & Dunlap, M. H. (2021). The effectiveness of telepsychology with veterans: A meta-analysis of services delivered by videoconference and phone. *Psychological Services*. Advance online publication. https://doi.org/10.1037/ser0000522

McClelland, D. C. (1961). *Achieving society*. Van Nostrand.

McClintock, S. M., Ranginwala, N., & Husain, M. M. (2008). Electroconvulsive therapy. In K. T. Mueser & D. V. Jeste (Eds.), *Clinical handbook of schizophrenia* (pp. 196–204). Guilford Press.

McClintock, S. M., Reti, I. M., Carpenter, L. L., McDonald, W. M., Dubin, M., Taylor, S. F., Cook, I. A., O'Reardon, J., Husain, M. M., Wall, C., Krystal, A. D., Sampson, S. M., Morales, O., Nelson, B. G., Latoussakis, V., George, M. S., Lisanby, S. H., National Network of Depression Centers rTMS Task Group, & American Pyschiatric Association Council on Research Task Force of Novel Biomarkers and Treatments. (2018). Consensus recommendations for the clinical application of repetitive transcranial magnetic stimulation (rTMS) in the treatment of depression. *The Journal of Clinical Psychiatry, 79*(1), 16cs10905. https://doi.org/10.4088/JCP.16cs10905

McCord, C., Bernhard, P., Walsh, M., Rosner, C., & Console, K. (2020). A consolidated model for telepsychology practice. *Journal of Clinical Psychology, 76*(6), 1060–1082. https://doi.org/10.1002/jclp.22954

McCrae, R. R., & Costa, P. T. (1994). The stability of personality: Observations and evaluations. *Current Directions in Psychological Science, 3*(6). https://doi.org/10.1111/1467-8721.ep10770693

McCrae, R. R., & Costa, P. T. (1996). Toward a new generation of personality theories: Theoretical contexts for the five-factor model. In J. S. Wiggins (Ed.). *The five-factor model of personality: Theoretical perspectives* (pp. 51–87). Guilford Press.

McCrae, R. R., & Costa, P. T. (2003). *Personality in adulthood: A five-factor theory perspective* (2nd ed.). Guilford Press.

McCrae, R. R., & Costa, P. T., Jr. (2008). The five-factor theory of personality. In O. P. John, R. W. Robins, & L. A. Pervin (Eds.), *Handbook of personality: Theory and research* (3rd ed., pp. 159–181). Guilford Press.

McCrae, R. R., & Costa, P. T. (2013). Introduction to the empirical and theoretical status of the five-factor model of personality traits. In T. A. Widiger & P. T. Costa (Eds.), *Personality disorders and the five-factor model of personality* (3rd ed., pp. 15–27). American Psychological Association.

McCreary, M. L., Cunningham, J. N., Ingram, K. M., & Fife, J. E. (2006). Stress, culture, and racial socialization: Making an impact. In P. T. P. Wong & L. C. J. Wong (Eds.), *Handbook of multicultural perspectives on stress and coping* (pp. 487–514). Springer Science+Business Media.

McCrink, K., & Shaki, S. (2016). Culturally inconsistent spatial structure reduces learning. *Acta Psychologica, 169*, 20–26. http://doi.org/10.1016/j.actpsy.2016.05.007

McDonald, C. (2018). Genetic risk in adult family members of patients with bipolar disorder. In J. C. Soares, C. Walss-Bass, & P. Brambilla (Eds.), *Bipolar disorder vulnerability* (pp. 69–96). Elsevier.

McDonough, E. M., Flanagan, D. P., Sy, M., & Alfonso, V. C. (2017). Specific learning disorder. In S. Goldstein & M. DeVries (Eds.), *Handbook of DSM-5 disorders in children and adolescents* (pp. 77–104). Springer.

McElhaney, K. B., Allen, J. P., Stephenson, J. C., & Hare, A. L. (2009). Attachment and autonomy during adolescence. In R. M. Lerner & L. Steinberg (Eds.), *Handbook of adolescent psychology* (3rd ed., Vol. 1, pp. 358–403). Wiley.

McElwain, N. L., Booth-LaForce, C., Lansford, J. E., Wu, X., & Justin Dyer, W. (2008). A process model of attachment–friend linkages: Hostile attribution biases, language ability, and mother–child affective mutuality as intervening mechanisms. *Child Development, 79*(6), 1891–1906.

McEwen, B. S. (1999). Stress and hippocampal plasticity. *Annual Review of Neuroscience, 22*(1), 105–122.

McEwen, B. S. (2004). How sex and stress hormones regulate the structural and functional plasticity of the hippocampus. In M. S. Gazzaniga (Ed.), *The new cognitive neurosciences III* (pp. 171–182). MIT Press.

McEwen, B., & Lasley, E. N. (2002). Allostatic load: When protection gives way to damage. In B. McEwen & E. N. Lasley, *The end of stress as we know it* (pp. 99–109). National Academies Press.

McFarlane, A. C. (2010). Phenomenology of posttraumatic stress disorder. In D. J. Stein, E. Hollander, & B. O. Rothbaum (Eds.), *Textbook of anxiety disorders* (2nd ed., pp. 547–565). American Psychiatric Publishing.

McGaughey, S. L., Iverson, R. D., & De Cieri, H. (1997). A multi-method analysis of work-related preferences in three nations: Implications for inter-and intra-national human resource management. *International Journal of Human Resource Management, 8*(1), 1–17.

McGhee, P. E., & Frueh, T. (1980). Television viewing and the learning of sex-role stereotypes. *Sex Roles, 6*(2), 179–188.

McGlynn, F. D. (2002). Systematic desensitization. In M. Hersen & W. Sledge (Eds.), *Encyclopedia of psychotherapy* (Vol. 2, pp. 755–764). Academic Press.

McGoldrick, M., Giordano, J., & Garcia-Preto, N. (Eds.). (2005). *Ethnicity and family therapy* (3rd ed.). Guilford Press.

McGrath, R. E. (2004). Saving our psychosocial souls. *American Psychologist, 59*(7), 644–645.

McGrath, R. E. (2010). Prescriptive authority for psychologists. *Annual Review of Clinical Psychology, 6*, 21–47.

McGuire, P. K., Murray, R. M., & Shah, G. M. S. (1993). Increased blood flow in Broca's area during auditory hallucinations in schizophrenia. *The Lancet, 342*(8873), 703–706.

McGurk, H., & MacDonald, J. (1976). Hearing lips and seeing voices. *Nature, 264*(5588), 746–748.

McHale, S. M., Crouter, A. C., & Whiteman, S. D. (2003). The family contexts of gender development in childhood and adolescence. *Social Development, 12*(1), 125–148.

McHugh, M. C., & Hambaugh, J. (2010). She said, he said: Gender language and power. In J. C. Chrisler & D. R. McCreary (Eds.), Handbook of gender research in psychology (Vol. 1, pp. 379–410). Springer Science+Business Media.

McHugh, M. C., & Kasardo, A. E. (2012). Anti-fat prejudice: The role of psychology in explication, education and eradication. *Sex Roles, 66*(9–10), 617–627.

McHugh, P. R. (1995). Resolved: Multiple personality disorder is an individually and socially created artifact. *Journal of the American Academy of Child and Adolescent Psychiatry, 34*(7), 957–959.

McIntosh, D. N. (1996). Facial feedback hypotheses: Evidence, implications, and directions. *Motivation and Emotion, 20*(2), 121–147.

McIntosh, D. N., Zajonc, R. B., Vig, P. S., & Emerick, S. W. (1997). Facial movement, breathing, temperature, and affect: Implications of the vascular theory of emotional efference. *Cognition & Emotion, 11*(2), 171–196.

McKay, D. (2016). Anxiety disorders. In J. C. Norcross, G. R. VandenBos, & D. K. Freedheim (Eds.), *APA handbook of clinical psychology: Vol. 4. Psychopathology and health* (pp. 61–96). American Psychological Association.

McKeever, P. M., & Clark, L. (2017). Delayed high school start times later than 8:30 am and impact on graduation rates and attendance rates. *Sleep Health, 3*(2), 119–125.

McKenna, J. J., & McDade, T. (2005). Why babies should never sleep alone: A review of the co-sleeping controversy in relation to SIDS, bedsharing and breast feeding. *Paediatric Respiratory Reviews, 6*(2), 134–152.

McKenna, M., & Pereboom, D. (2016). *Free will: A contemporary introduction*. Routledge.

McKenna, P. J., McKay, A. P., & Laws, K. (2000). Memory in functional psychosis. In G. E. Berrios & J. R. Hodges (Eds.), *Memory disorders in psychiatric practice*. Cambridge University Press.

McKenna, P., Ornstein, T., & Baddeley, A. D. (2002). Schizophrenia. In A. D. Baddeley, M. D. Kopelman, & B. A. Wilson (Eds.), *The handbook of memory disorders* (2nd ed., pp. 413–435). Wiley.

McKenzie, C. R. M. (2005). Reasoning. In K. Lamberts & R. L. Goldstone (Eds.), *Handbook of cognition* (pp. 321–338). Sage.

McKitrick, D. S., & Li, S. T. (2008). Multicultural treatment. In M. Hersen & A. M. Gross (Eds.), *Handbook of clinical psychology* (Vol. 1, pp. 724–751). Wiley.

McKnight-Eily, L. R., Eaton, D. K., Lowry, R., Croft, J. B., Presley-Cantrell, L., & Perry, G. S. (2011). Relationships between hours of sleep and health-risk behaviors in U.S. adolescent students. *Preventive Medicine, 53*(4), 271–273.

McLean, R. (2003). *Recovered, not cured: A journey through schizophrenia*. Allen & Unwin.

McLeod, K., & DiCola, P. (2011). *Creative license: The law and culture of digital sampling*. Duke University Press.

McMahan, D. L., & Braun, E. (2017). *Meditation, Buddhism, and science*. Oxford University Press.

McMullan, R. D., Berle, D., Arnáez, S., & Starcevic, V. (2019). The relationships between health anxiety, online health information seeking, and cyberchondria: Systematic review and meta-analysis. *Journal of Affective Disorders, 245*, 270–278.

McNally, R. J. (1987). Preparedness and phobias: A review. *Psychological Bulletin, 101*(2), 283–303.

McWhorter, J. (2013a). Is texting killing the English language? *Time*. https://ideas.time.com/2013/04/25/is-texting-killing-the-english-language/

McWhorter, J. (2013b). Txtng is killing language. JK!!!. *TED*. Long Beach, California. https://www.ted.com/talks/john_mcwhorter_txtng_is_killing_language_jk

Mead, K. M., & Ball, L. J. (2007). Music tonality and context-dependent recall: The influence of key change and mood mediation. *European Journal of Cognitive Psychology, 19*(1), 59–79.

Means, M. K., & Edinger, J. D. (2006). Nonpharmacologic therapy of insomnia. In T. L. Lee-Chiong (Ed.), *Sleep: A comprehensive handbook* (pp. 133–136). Wiley-Liss.

Medin, D. L., & Schaffer, M. M. (1978). Context theory of classification learning. *Psychological Review, 85*(3), 207–238.

Medin, D. L., Ross, N., Atran, S., Burnett, R. C., & Blok, S. V. (2002). Categorization and reasoning in relation to culture and expertise. *Psychology of Learning and Motivation, 41*, 1–41.

Medin, D. L., Unsworth, S. J., & Hirschfeld, L. (2007). Culture, categorization, and reasoning. In S. Kitayama & D. Cohen (Eds.), *Handbook of cultural psychology* (pp. 615–644). Guilford Press.

Medina, J. (2014). *Brain rules: 12 principles for surviving and thriving at work, home and school*. (2nd ed.). Pear Press.

Mednick, S. C., Nakayama, K., Cantero, J. L., Atienza, M., Levin, A. A., Pathak, N., & Stickgold, R. (2002). The restorative effect of naps on perceptual deterioration. *Nature Neuroscience, 5*(7), 677–681.

Mednick, S., Nakayama, K., & Stickgold, R. (2003). Sleep-dependent learning: A nap is as good as a night. *Nature Neuroscience, 6*(7), 697–698.

Medwed, D. S. (2007). *Wrongful convictions and the DNA revolution: Twenty-five years of freeing the innocent*. Cambridge University Press.

Meece, J. L., & Holt, K. (1993). A pattern analysis of students' achievement goals. *Journal of Educational Psychology, 85*(4), 582–590.

Mehler, P. S., Birmingham, C. L., Crow, S. J., & Jahraus, J. P. (2010). Medical complications of eating disorders. In C. M. Grilo & J. E. Mitchell (Eds.), *The treatment of eating disorders: A clinical handbook* (pp. 66–80). Guilford Press.

Mehta-Raghavan, N. S., Wert, S. L., Morley, C., Graf, E. N., & Redei, E. E. (2017). Nature and nurture: Environmental influences on a genetic rat model of depression. *Translational Psychiatry, 6*(3), e770.

Meintjes, E. M., Jacobson, J. L., Molteno, C. D., Gatenby, J. C., Warton, C., Cannistraci, ... Jacobson, S. W. (2010). An fMRI study of number processing in children with fetal alcohol syndrome. *Alcoholism: Clinical and Experimental Research, 34*(8), 1450–1464.

Meinz, E. J., & Hambrick, D. Z. (2010). Deliberate practice is necessary but not sufficient to explain individual differences in piano sight-reading skill: The role of working memory capacity. *Psychological Science, 21*(7), 914–919.

Meixner, J. B., Jr. (2015). Applications of neuroscience in criminal law: Legal and methodological issues. *Current Neurology and Neuroscience Reports, 15*(2), 1–10.

Melchert, T. P. (2011). *Foundations of professional psychology: The end of theoretical orientations and the emergence of the biopsychosocial approach*. Elsevier.

Melnyk, L., Crossman, A. M., & Scullin, M. H. (2007). The suggestibility of children's memory. In M. P. Toglia, J. D. Read, D. F. Ross, & R. C. L. Lindsay (Eds.), *The handbook of eyewitness psychology: Memory for events* (Vol. I, pp. 401–427). Psychology Press.

Melton, G. B., Petrila, J., Poythress, N. G., Slobogin, C., Otto, R. K., Mossman, D., & Condie, L. O. (2018). *Psychological evaluations for the courts: A handbook for mental health professionals and lawyers* (4th ed.). Guilford Press.

Meltzoff, A. N. (2011). Social cognition and the origins of imitation, empathy, and theory of mind. In U. Goswami (Ed.), *The Wiley-Blackwell handbook of childhood cognitive development* (2nd ed., pp. 49–75). Wiley-Blackwell.

Melzack, R., & Casey, K. L. (1968). Sensory, motivational, and central control determinants of pain. In D. R. Kenshalo (Ed.), *The skin senses* (pp. 423–439). Charles C. Thomas Publisher.

Melzack, R., & Wall, P. D. (1967). Pain mechanisms: A new theory. *Survey of Anesthesiology, 11*(2), 89–90.

Melzack, R., & Wall, P. D. (2008). *The challenge of pain* (2nd ed.). Penguin.

Menaker, M., Murphy, Z. C., & Sellix, M. T. (2013). Central control of peripheral circadian oscillators. *Current Opinion in Neurobiology, 23*(5), 741–746.

Mendell, L. M. (2014). Constructing and deconstructing the gate theory of pain. *Pain, 155*(2), 210–216.

Mendoza-Denton, N. (2008). *Homegirls: Language and cultural practice among Latina youth gangs.* Blackwell.

Menni, C., Valdes, A. M., Freidin, M. B., Sudre, C. H., Nguyen, L. H., Drew, D. A., Ganesh, S., Varsavsky, T., Cardoso, M. J., Moustafa, J. S. E., Visconti, A., Hysi, P., Bowyer, R. C. E., Mangino, M., Falchi, M., Wolf, J., Ourselin, S., Chan, A. T., Steves, C. J., & Spector, T. D. (2020). Real-time tracking of self-reported symptoms to predict potential COVID-19. *Nature Medicine, 26*(7), 1037–1040. https://doi.org/10.1038/s41591-020-0916-2

Menon, U. (2003). Morality and context: A study of Hindu understandings. In J. Valsiner & K. Connolly (Eds.), *Handbook of developmental psychology* (pp. 431–449). Sage.

Mensinger, J. L., Tylka, T. L., & Calamari, M. E. (2018). Mechanisms underlying weight status and healthcare avoidance in women: A study of weight stigma, body-related shame and guilt, and healthcare stress. *Body Image, 25*, 139–147.

Mental health: Does therapy help? (1995, November). *Consumer Reports*, 734–739.

Mercado, T., Alvarez, A., & Herranz, J. M. (2014). The fracking debate in the media: The role of citizen platforms as sources of information. *ESSACHESS—Journal for Communication Studies, 7*(1), 45–62.

Mercier, M., Vinchon, F., Pichot, N., Bonetto, E., Bonnardel, N., Girandola, F., & Lubart, T. (2021). COVID-19: A boon or a bane for creativity? *Frontiers in Psychology, 11*, 601150. https://doi.org/10.3389/fpsyg.2020.601150

Merino, H., Senra, C., & Ferreiro, F. (2016). Are worry and rumination specific pathways linking neuroticism and symptoms of anxiety and depression in patients with generalized anxiety disorder, major depressive disorder and mixed anxiety-depressive disorder? *PLoS One, 11*(5), e0156169.

Mesquita, B., & Karasawa, M. (2002). Different emotional lives. *Cognition & Emotion, 16*(1), 127–141.

Mesquita, B., & Leu, J. (2007). The cultural psychology of emotion. In S. Kitayama & D. Cohen (Eds.), *Handbook of cultural psychology* (pp. 734–759). Guilford Press.

Messer, S. B., & Wampold, B. E. (2002). Let's face facts: Common factors are more potent than specific therapy ingredients. *Clinical Psychology: Science and Practice, 9*(1), 21–25.

Messerly, J. G. (2009). Piaget's biology. In U. Müller, J. I. M. Carpendale, & L. Smith (Eds.), *The Cambridge companion to Piaget* (pp. 94–109). Cambridge University Press.

Meston, C. M., & Buss, D. M. (2007). Why humans have sex. *Archives of Sexual Behavior, 36*(4), 477–507.

Metzger, A. M. (1979). A Q-methodological study of the Kubler-Ross stage theory. *OMEGA—Journal of Death and Dying, 10*(4), 291–301.

Meyer, A., Kegley, M., & Klein, D. N. (2021). Overprotective parenting mediates the relationship between early childhood ADHD and anxiety symptoms: Evidence from a cross-sectional and longitudinal study. *Journal of Attention Disorders, 26*(2), 319–327. https://doi.org/10.1177/1087054720978552

Meyer, G. J. (2004). The reliability and validity of the Rorschach and Thematic Apperception Test (TAT) compared to other psychological and medical procedures: An analysis of systematically gathered evidence. In M. J. Hilsenroth & D. L. Segal (Eds.), *Comprehensive handbook of psychological assessment: Personality assessment* (Vol. 2, pp. 315–342). Wiley.

Meyer, I. H. (2003). Prejudice, social stress, and mental health in lesbian, gay, and bisexual populations: Conceptual issues and research evidence. *Psychological Bulletin, 129*(5), 674–697.

Meyer, O. L., & Takeuchi, D. T. (2014). Help seeking and service utilization. In F. T. L. Leong (Ed.), *APA handbook of multicultural psychology* (Vol. 2, pp. 529–541). American Psychological Association.

Meyer, O. L., Zane, N., Cho, Y. I., & Takeuchi, D. T. (2009). Use of specialty mental health services by Asian Americans with psychiatric disorders. *Journal of Consulting and Clinical Psychology, 77*(5), 1000–1005.

Mheidly, N., Fares, M. Y., Zalzale, H., & Fares, J. (2020). Effect of face masks on interpersonal communication during the COVID-19 pandemic. *Frontiers in Public Health, 8*, 898. https://doi.org/10.3389/fpubh.2020.582191

Miao, C., Humphrey, R. H., & Qian, S. (2017a). Are the emotionally intelligent good citizens or counterproductive? A meta-analysis of emotional intelligence and its relationships with organizational citizenship behavior and counterproductive work behavior. *Personality and Individual Differences, 116*, 144–156.

Miao, C., Humphrey, R. H., & Qian, S. (2017b). A meta-analysis of emotional intelligence and work attitudes. *Journal of Occupational and Organizational Psychology, 90*(2), 177–202.

Miao, C., Humphrey, R. H., & Qian, S. (2018). A cross-cultural meta-analysis of how leader emotional intelligence influences subordinate task performance and organizational citizenship behavior. *Journal of World Business, 53*(4), 463–474.

Michael, M. T. (2019). Why aren't more philosophers interested in Freud? Re-evaluating philosophical arguments against psychoanalysis. *Philosophia, 47*, 959–976.

Michaels, M. S., Chu, C., & Joiner, T. E., Jr. (2017). Suicide. In R. J. DeRubeis & D. R. Strunk (Eds.), *The Oxford handbook of mood disorders* (pp. 60–70). Oxford University Press.

Michel, J. S., Kotrba, L. M., Mitchelson, J. K., Clark, M. A., & Baltes, B. B. (2011). Antecedents of work–family conflict: A meta-analytic review. *Journal of Organizational Behavior, 32*(5), 689–725.

Micozzi, M. S. (2011). *Fundamentals of complementary and alternative medicine* (4th ed.). Saunders/Elsevier.

Miczek, K. A., de Almeida, R. M., Kravitz, E. A., Rissman, E. F., de Boer, S. F., & Raine, A. (2007). Neurobiology of escalated aggression and violence. *The Journal of Neuroscience, 27*(44), 11803–11806.

Mihura, J. L., Meyer, G. J., Bombel, G., & Dumitrascu, N. (2015). Standards, accuracy, and questions of bias in Rorschach meta-analyses: Reply to Wood, Garb, Nezworski, Lilienfeld, and Duke (2015). *Psychological Bulletin, 141*(3), 250–260.

Mihura, J. L., Meyer, G. J., Dumitrascu, N., & Bombel, G. (2013). The validity of individual Rorschach variables: Systematic reviews and meta-analyses of the comprehensive system. *Psychological Bulletin, 139*(3), 548–605.

Mihura, J. L., Roy, M., & Graceffo, R. A. (2017). Psychological assessment training in clinical psychology doctoral programs. *Journal of Personality Assessment, 99*(2), 153–164.

Mikami, A. Y. (2010). The importance of friendship for youth with attention-deficit/hyperactivity disorder. *Clinical Child and Family Psychology Review, 13*(2), 181–198.

Mikels, J. A., Reed, A. E., Hardy, L. N., & Löckenhoff, C. E. (2014). Positive emotions across the adult life span. In M. M. Tugade, M. N. Shiota, & L. D. Kirby (Eds.), *Handbook of positive emotions* (pp. 256–255). Guilford Press.

Miklowitz, D. J. (2009). Pharmacotherapy and psychosocial treatments for bipolar disorder. In I. H. Gotlib & C. L. Hammen (Eds.), *Handbook of depression* (2nd ed., pp. 604–623). Guilford Press.

Miklowitz, D. J., & Craighead, W. E. (2007). Psychosocial treatments for bipolar disorder. In P. E. Nathan & J. M. Gorman (Eds.), *A guide to treatments that work* (3rd ed., pp. 309–322). Oxford University Press.

Miklowitz, D. J., & Johnson, S. L. (2008). Bipolar disorder. In W. E. Craighead, D. J. Milkowitz, & L. W. Craighead (Eds.), *Psychopathology: History, diagnosis, and empirical foundations* (pp. 366–401). Wiley.

Miles, C., & Hardman, E. (1998). State-dependent memory produced by aerobic exercise. *Ergonomics, 41*(1), 20–28.

Miles, D. R., & Carey, G. (1997). Genetic and environmental architecture of human aggression. *Journal of Personality and Social Psychology, 72*(1), 207–217.

Miles-Novelo, A., & Anderson, C. A. (2019). Climate change and psychology: Effects of rapid global warming on violence and aggression. *Current Climate Change Reports, 5*, 36–46.

Miletich, R. S. (2009). Positron emission tomography for neurologists. *Neurologic Clinics, 27*(1), 61–88, viii.

Milgram, D. (2011). How to recruit women and girls to the science, technology, engineering, and math (STEM) classroom. *Technology and Engineering Teacher, 71*(3), 4–11.

Milgram, S. (1963). Behavioral study of obedience. *Journal of Abnormal and Social Psychology, 67*(4), 371–378.

Milgram, S. (1965). Some conditions of obedience and disobedience to authority. *Human Relations, 18*(1), 57–76.

Milgram, S. (1974). *Obedience to authority: An experimental view.* Harper and Row.

Miller, A. E., Mehak, A., Trolio, V., & Racine, S. E. (2021). Impact of the COVID-19 pandemic on the psychological health of individuals with mental health conditions: A mixed methods study. *Journal of Clinical Psychology*. https://doi.org/10.1002/jclp.23250

Miller, A., & Hom, H. L. (1990). Influence of extrinsic and ego incentive value on persistence after failure and continuing motivation. *Journal of Educational Psychology, 82*(3), 539–545.

Miller, D. J., & Thelen, M. H. (1986). Knowledge and beliefs about confidentiality in psychotherapy. *Professional Psychology Research and Practice, 17*(1), 15–19.

Miller, G. A. (1956). The magical number seven, plus or minus two: Some limits on our capacity for processing information. *Psychological Review, 63*(2), 81–97.

Miller, K. E., Quigley, B. M., Eliseo-Arras, R. K., & Ball, N. J. (2016). Alcohol mixed with energy drink use as an event-level predictor of physical and verbal aggression in bar conflicts. *Alcoholism: Clinical and Experimental Research, 40*(1), 161–169.

Miller, L., & Gur, M. (2002). Religiousness and sexual responsibility in adolescent girls. *Journal of Adolescent Health, 31*(5), 401–406.

Miller, N., & Pollock, V. E. (1996). Alcohol and aggression: A meta-analysis on the moderating effects of inhibitory cues, triggering events, and self-focused attention. *Psychological Bulletin, 120*(1), 60–62.

Miller, P. A., & Eisenberg, N. (1988). The relation of empathy to aggressive and externalizing/antisocial behavior. *Psychological Bulletin, 103*(3), 324–344.

Miller, P. A., & Eisenberg, N. (1988). The relation of empathy to aggressive and externalizing/antisocial behavior. *Psychological Bulletin, 103*(3), 324–344.

Miller, P. H. (2011). Piaget's theory: Past, present, and future. In U. Goswami (Ed.), *The Wiley-Blackwell handbook of childhood cognitive development* (2nd ed., pp. 649–672). Wiley-Blackwell.

Miller, P. H. (2011). Piaget's theory: Past, present, and future. In U. Goswami (Ed.), *The Wiley-Blackwell handbook of childhood cognitive development* (2nd ed., pp. 649–672). Wiley-Blackwell.

Miller, P. H. (2011). Piaget's theory: Past, present, and future. In U. Goswami (Ed.), *The Wiley-Blackwell handbook of childhood cognitive development* (2nd ed., pp. 649–672). Wiley-Blackwell.

Miller, R. (2011). *Vygotsky in perspective.* Cambridge University Press.

Miller, R. L. (2003). Ethical issues in psychological research with human participants. In S. F. Davis (Ed.), *Handbook of research methods in experimental psychology* (pp. 127–150). Blackwell.

Miller, R. M., Marriott, D., Trotter, J., Hammond, T., Lyman, D., Call, T., Walker, B., Christensen, N., Haynie, D., Badura, Z., Homan, M., & Edwards, J. G. (2018). Running exercise mitigates the negative consequences of chronic stress on dorsal hippocampal long-term potentiation in male mice. *Neurobiology of Learning and Memory, 149*, 28–38.

Miller, T. Q., Turner, C. W., Tindale, R. S., Posavac, E. J., & Dugoni, B. L. (1991). Reasons for the trend toward null findings in research on Type A behavior. *Psychological Bulletin, 110*(3), 469–485.

Miller, W. R., & Moyers, T. B. (2017). Motivational interviewing and the clinical science of Carl Rogers. *Journal of Consulting and Clinical Psychology, 85*(8), 757–766.

Miller, W. R., & Rollnick, S. (2013). *Motivational interviewing: Helping people change* (3rd ed.). Guilford Press.

Miller, W. R., & Rose, G. R. (2009). Toward a theory of motivational interviewing. *American Psychologist, 64*(6), 527–537.

Miller, W. R., & Rose, G. S. (2015). Motivational interviewing and decisional balance: Contrasting responses to client ambivalence. *Behavioural and Cognitive Psychotherapy, 43*(02), 129–141.

Millett, D. (2001). Hans Berger: From psychic energy to the EEG. *Perspectives in Biology and Medicine, 44*(4), 522–542.

Milling, L. S., Gover, M. C., & Moriarty, C. L. (2018a). The effectiveness of hypnosis as an intervention for obesity: A meta-analytic review. *Psychology of Consciousness: Theory, Research, and Practice, 5*(1), 29–45. https://doi.org/10.1037/cns0000139

Milling, L. S., Valentine, K. E., McCarley, H. S., & LoStimolo, L. M. (2018b). A meta-analysis of hypnotic interventions for depression symptoms: High hopes for hypnosis? *American Journal of Clinical Hypnosis, 61*(3), 227–243. https://doi.org/10.1080/00029157.2018.1489777

Millon, T. (2004). *Personality disorders and modern life* (2nd ed.). Wiley.

Millon, T. (2009). Personality and its disorders: Structural models, mathematical methods, and theoretical conceptions. In P. H. Blaney & T. Millon (Eds.), *Oxford textbook of psychopathology* (2nd ed., 551–585). Oxford University Press.

Mills, J. A. (1998). *Control: A history of behavioral psychology.* New York University Press.

Mills, J. S., Musto, S., Williams, L., & Tiggemann, M. (2018). "Selfie" harm: Effects on mood and body image in young women. *Body Image, 27*, 86–92.

Milner, A. D., & Goodale, M. A. (2008). Two visual systems re-viewed. *Neuropsychologia, 46*(3), 774–785.

Milner, A., Krnjacki, L., & LaMontagne, A. D. (2016). Age and gender differences in the influence of social support on mental health: A longitudinal fixed-effects analysis using 13 annual waves of the HILDA cohort. *Public Health, 140*, 172–178.

Milner, C. E., & Cote, K. A. (2009). Benefits of napping in healthy adults: Impact of nap length, time of day, age, and experience with napping. *Journal of Sleep Research, 18*(2), 272–281.

Mindell, J. A., Meltzer, L. J., Carskadon, M. A., & Chervin, R. D. (2009). Developmental aspects of sleep hygiene: Findings from the 2004 National Sleep Foundation Sleep in America Poll. *Sleep Medicine, 10*(7), 771–779.

Mindell, J. A., & Owens, J. A. (2015). *A clinical guide to pediatric sleep: Diagnosis and management of sleep problems* (3rd ed.). Wolters Kluwer.

Mineka, S., & Cook, M. (1993). Mechanisms involved in the observational conditioning of fear. *Journal of Experimental Psychology: General, 122*(1), 23–38.

Ming, G. L., & Song, H. (2011). Adult neurogenesis in the mammalian brain: Significant answers and significant questions. *Neuron, 70*(4), 687–702.

Minkov, M. (2013). *Cross-cultural analysis: The science and art of comparing the world's modern societies and their cultures*. Sage.

Minkov, M. (2018). A revision of Hofstede's model of national culture: Old evidence and new data from 56 countries. *Cross Cultural & Strategic Management, 25*(2), 231–256.

Minkov, M., & Hofstede, G. (2010). Hofstede's fifth dimension: New evidence from the World Values Survey. *Journal of Cross-Cultural Psychology, 43*(1), 3–14.

Minkov, M., & Hofstede, G. (2011). The evolution of Hofstede's doctrine. *Cross Cultural Management: An International Journal, 18*(1), 10–20.

Minuchin, S. (1974). *Families and family therapy*. Harvard University Press.

Minzenberg, M., Yoon, J. H., & Cameron, S. C. (2008). Schizophrenia. In R. E. Hales & S. Yudofsky (Eds.), *Textbook of clinical psychiatry* (pp. 407–456). American Psychiatric Association Publishing.

Mio, J. S., Barker-Hackett, L., & Tumambing, J. S. (2009). *Multicultural psychology: Understanding our diverse communities* (2nd ed.). McGraw-Hill.

Mirsalimi, H. (2010). Perspectives of an Iranian psychologist practicing in America. *Psychotherapy: Theory, Research, Practice, Training, 47*(2), 151–161.

Misailidi, P. (2006). Young children's display rule knowledge: Understanding the distinction between apparent and real emotions and the motives underlying the use of display rules. *Social Behavior and Personality: An International Journal, 34*(10), 1285–1296.

Mischel, W. (1979). On the interface of cognition and personality: Beyond the person–situation debate. *American Psychologist, 34*(9), 740–754.

Mischel, W., & Shoda, Y. (1995). A cognitive-affective system theory of personality: Reconceptualizing situations, dispositions, dynamics, and invariance in personality structure. *Psychological Review, 102*(2), 246–268.

Missler, M., Stroebe, M., Geurtsen, L., Mastenbroek, M., Chmoun, S., & van der Houwen, K. (2011). Exploring death anxiety among elderly people: A literature review and empirical investigation. *OMEGA—Journal of Death and Dying, 64*(4), 357–379.

Mitamura, C., Leu, J., Campos, B., Boccagno, C., & Tugade, M. M. (2014). Traversing affective boundaries: Examining cultural norms for positive emotions. In M. M. Tugade, M. N. Shiota, & L. D. Kirby (Eds.), *Handbook of positive emotions* (pp. 229–240). Guilford Press.

Mitchell, B. A., & Gee, E. M. (1996). "Boomerang kids" and midlife parental marital satisfaction. *Family Relations, 45*(4), 442–448.

Mitchell, B. A., & Lovegreen, L. D. (2009). The empty nest syndrome in midlife families: A multi-method exploration of parental gender differences and cultural dynamics. *Journal of Family Issues, 30*(12), 1651–1670.

Mitchell, B. A., & Wister, A. V. (2015). Midlife challenge or welcome departure? Cultural and family-related expectations of empty nest transitions. *The International Journal of Aging and Human Development, 81*(4), 260–280.

Mitchell, J. E., & Crow, S. J. (2010). Medical comorbidities or eating disorders. In W. S. Agras (Ed.), *The Oxford handbook of eating disorders* (pp. 259–268). Oxford University Press.

Mitchell, K. J., & Johnson, M. K. (2000). Source monitoring: Attributing mental experiences. In E. Tulving & F. I. M. Craik (Eds.), *The Oxford handbook of memory* (pp. 179–195). Oxford University Press.

Mitchell, S. A., & Black, M. J. (1995). *Freud and beyond: A history of modern psychoanalytic thought*. Basic Books.

Mithen, S. (2012). Musicality and language. In M. Tallerman & K. R. Gibson (Eds.), *The Oxford handbook of language evolution* (pp. 296–298). Oxford University Press.

Miu, A. S., & Yeager, D. S. (2015). Preventing symptoms of depression by teaching adolescents that people can change: Effects of a brief incremental theory of personality intervention at 9-month follow-up. *Clinical Psychological Science, 3*(5), 726–743.

Miyamoto, Y., & Ryff, C. D. (2011). Cultural differences in the dialectical and non-dialectical emotional styles and their implications for health. *Cognition and Emotion, 25*(1), 22–39.

Miyamoto, Y., & Wilken, B. (2013). Cultural differences and their mechanisms. In D. Reisberg (Ed.), *The Oxford handbook of cognitive psychology* (pp. 970–987). Oxford University Press.

Miyazaki, S., Liu, C. Y., & Hayashi, Y. (2017). Sleep in vertebrate and invertebrate animals, and insights into the function and evolution of sleep. *Neuroscience Research, 118*, 3–12.

Mize, J. L., & Kliewer, W. (2017). Domain-specific daily hassles, anxiety, and delinquent behaviors among low-income, urban youth. *Journal of Applied Developmental Psychology, 53*, 31–39.

Moayedi, M., & Davis, K. D. (2013). Theories of pain: From specificity to gate control. *Journal of Neurophysiology, 109*(1), 5–12.

Modinos, G., Ormel, J., & Aleman, A. (2010). Individual differences in dispositional mindfulness and brain activity involved in reappraisal of emotion. *Social Cognitive and Affective Neuroscience, 5*(4), 369–377.

Moe, A., & De Beni, R. (2004). Studying passages with the loci method: Are subject-generated more effective than experimenter-supplied loci pathways? *Journal of Mental Imagery, 28*, 75–86.

Moe, A., & De Beni, R. (2005). Stressing the efficacy of the loci method: Oral presentation and the subject-generation of the loci pathway with expository passages. *Applied Cognitive Psychology, 19*(1), 95–106.

Moein, S. T., Hashemian, S. M., Mansourafshar, B., Khorram-Tousi, A., Tabarsi, P., & Doty, R. L. (2020, August). Smell dysfunction: A biomarker for COVID-19. *International Forum of Allergy & Rhinology, 10*(8), 944–950. https://doi.org/10.1002/alr.22587

Moen, P., & Roehling, P. (2005). *The career mystique: Cracks in the American dream*. Rowman & Littlefield.

Moffitt, T. E., Caspi, A., Belsky, J., & Silva, P. A. (1992). Childhood experience and the onset of menarche: A test of a sociobiological model. *Child Development, 63*(1), 47–58.

Mogil, J.S. (2020). Qualitative sex differences in pain processing: Emerging evidence of a biased literature. *Nature Reviews Neuroscience, 21*, 353–365. https://doi.org/10.1038/s41583-020-0310-6

Mohr, J. J., & Rochlen, A. B. (1999). Measuring attitudes regarding bisexuality in lesbian, gay male, and heterosexual populations. *Journal of Counseling Psychology, 46*(3), 353–369.

Molina, B. S., Howard, A. L., Swanson, J. M., Stehli, A., Mitchell, J. T., Kennedy, T. M., Epstein, J. N., Arnold, L. E., Hechtman, L., Vitiello, B., & Hoza, B. (2018). Substance use through adolescence into early adulthood after childhood-diagnosed ADHD: Findings from the MTA longitudinal study. *Journal of Child Psychology and Psychiatry, 59*(6), 692–702.

Moline, M. L., Broch, L., Zak, R., & Gross, V. (2003). Sleep in women across the life cycle from adulthood through menopause. *Sleep Medicine Reviews, 7*(2), 155–177.

Moller, H., & Pedersen, C. S. (2004). Hearing at low and infrasonic frequencies. *Noise and Health, 6*(23), 37–57.

Mollon, J. D., Pokorny, J., & Knoblauch, K. (Eds.). (2003). *Normal and defective colour vision*. Oxford University Press.

Mols, F., & Denollet, J. (2010). Type D personality among noncardiovascular patient populations: A systematic review. *General Hospital Psychiatry, 32*(1), 66–72.

Moltz, H. (1965). Contemporary instinct theory and the fixed action pattern. *Psychological Review, 72*(1), 27–47.

Monat, A., Lazarus, R. S., & Reevy, G. (2007). Introduction. In A. Monat, R. S. Lazarus, & G. Reevy (Eds.), *The Praeger handbook on stress and coping*, pp. xxvii–xxxvi. Praeger.

Mondimore, F. M. (2006). *Depression, the mood disease* (3rd ed.). Johns Hopkins University Press.

Mondloch, C. J., Lewis, T. L., Budreau, D. R., Maurer, D., Dannemiller, J. L., Stephens, B. R., & Kleiner-Gathercoal, K. A. (1999). Face perception during early infancy. *Psychological Science, 10*(5), 419–422.

Monk Jr., E. P. (2021). The unceasing significance of colorism: skin tone stratification in the United States. *Daedalus, 150*(2), 76–90. https://doi.org/10.1162/daed_a_01847

Monk, T. H. (2012). Sleep and human performance. In C. M. Morin & C. A. Espie (Eds.), *The Oxford handbook of sleep and sleep disorders* (pp. 95–109). Oxford University Press.

Monk, T. H., Petrie, S. R., Hayes, A. J., & Kupfer, D. J. (1994). Regularity of daily life in relation to personality, age, gender, sleep quality and circadian rhythms. *Journal of Sleep Research, 3*(4), 196–205.

Monroe, S. M., & Simons, A. D. (1991). Diathesis-stress theories in the context of life stress research: Implications for the depressive disorders. *Psychological Bulletin, 110*(3), 406–425.

Montag, C., & Panksepp, J. (2017). Primary emotional systems and personality: An evolutionary perspective. *Frontiers in Psychology, 8*, 464.

Montoro, J. P. & Ceballo, R. Latinx adolescents facing multiple stressors and the protective role of familismo. *Cultural Diversity and Ethnic Minority Psychology, 27*(4), 705–716. https://doi.org/10.1037/cdp0000461

Montoya, R. M., & Horton, R. S. (2012). A meta-analytic investigation of the processes underlying the similarity-attraction effect. *Journal of Social and Personal Relationships, 30*(1), 64–94.

Montoya, R. M., Horton, R. S., & Kirchner, J. (2008). Is actual similarity necessary for attraction? A meta-analysis of actual and perceived similarity. *Journal of Social and Personal Relationships, 25*(6), 889–922.

Montoya, R. M., Horton, R. S., Vevea, J. L., Citkowicz, M., & Lauber, E. A. (2017). A re-examination of the mere exposure effect: The influence of repeated exposure on recognition, familiarity, and liking. *Psychological Bulletin, 143*(5), 459–498.

Mook, D. (2004). *Classic experiments in psychology*. Greenwood Press.

Moore, B. A., & Krakow, B. (2007). Imagery rehearsal therapy for acute posttraumatic nightmares among combat soldiers in Iraq. *The American Journal of Psychiatry, 164*(4), 683–684.

Moore, B. C. J. (2001a). Basic auditory processes. In E. B. Goldstein (Ed.), *Blackwell handbook of perception* (pp. 379–407). Blackwell.

Moore, B. C. J. (2001b). Loudness, pitch, and timbre. In E. B. Goldstein (Ed.), *Blackwell handbook of perception* (pp. 408–436). Blackwell.

Moore, B. C. J. (2010). Audition. In E. B. Goldstein (Ed.), *Encyclopedia of perception* (pp. 133–138). Sage.

Moore, B. C. J. (2012). *An introduction to the psychology of hearing*. Emerald.

Moore, B. E., & Fine, B. D. (Eds). (1990). *Psychoanalytic terms & concepts*. American Psychoanalytic Association.

Moore, P. S., March, J. S., Albano, A. M., & Thienemann, M. (2010). Anxiety disorders in children and adolescents. In D. J. Stein, E. Hollander, & B. O. Rothbaum (Eds.), *Textbook of anxiety disorders* (2nd ed., pp. 629–649). American Psychiatric Association Publishing.

Moore, R. Y. (2006). Biological rhythms and sleep. In T. L. Lee-Chiong (Ed.), *Sleep: A comprehensive handbook* (pp. 25–30). Wiley-Liss.

Morabia, A., & Costanza, M. C. (1998). World Health Organization collaborative study of neoplasia and steroid contraceptives: International variability in ages at menarche, first livebirth, and menopause. *American Journal of Epidemiology, 148*(12), 1195–1205.

Moradi, B., & Grzanka, P. R. (2017). Using intersectionality responsibly: Toward critical epistemology, structural analysis, and social justice activism. *Journal of Counseling Psychology, 64*(5), 500–513.

Moran, R. T., Abramson, N. R., & Moran, S. V. (2014). *Managing cultural differences* (9th ed.). Routledge.

Moran, R. T., Youngdahl, W. E., & Moran, S. V. (2009). Intercultural competence in business. In D. K. Deardorff (Ed.), *The Sage handbook of intercultural competence* (pp. 287–303). Sage.

Moreland, R. L., & Beach, S. R. (1992). Exposure effects in the classroom: The development of affinity among students. *Journal of Experimental Social Psychology, 28*(3), 255–276.

Morelli, G., Rogoff, B., & Angelillo, C. (2003). Cultural variation in young children's access to work or involvement in specialised child-focused activities. *International Journal of Behavioral Development, 27*(3), 264–274.

Moretti, R. J., & Rossini, E. D. (2004). The Thematic Apperception Test (TAT). In M. J. Hilsenroth & D. L. Segal (Eds.), *Comprehensive handbook of psychological assessment: Personality assessment* (Vol. 2, pp. 356–371). Wiley.

Morey, L. C., & Hopwood, C. J. (2008). Objective personality evaluation. In M. Hersen & A. M. Gross (Eds.), *Handbook of clinical psychology* (Vol. 1, pp. 451–474). Wiley.

Morey, L. C., & Hopwood, C. J. (2019). Expert preferences for categorical, dimensional, and mixed/hybrid approaches to personality disorder diagnosis. *Journal of Personality Disorders*, 1–8. https://doi.org/10.1521/pedi_2019_33_398

Morgan, A. J., Reavley, N. J., Ross, A., San Too, L., & Jorm, A. F. (2018). Interventions to reduce stigma towards people with severe mental illness: Systematic review and meta-analysis. *Journal of Psychiatric Research, 103*, 120–133. https://doi.org/10.1016/j.jpsychires.2018.05.017

Morgan, C. D., & Murray, H. A. (1935). A method for investigating fantasies: The Thematic Apperception Test. *Archives of Neurology and Psychiatry, 34*(2), 289–306.

Morgan, E. S., & Scheibe, S. (2014). Reconciling cognitive decline and increased well-being with age: The role of increased emotion regulation efficiency. In P. Verhaeghen & C. K. Hertzog (Eds.), *The Oxford handbook of emotion, social cognition, and problem solving in adulthood* (pp. 155–173). Oxford University Press.

Morgan, K. (2012). The epidemiology of sleep. In C. M. Morin & C. A. Espie (Eds.), *The Oxford handbook of sleep and sleep disorders* (pp. 303–323). Oxford University Press.

Morgan, L. P. K., & Roemer, L. (2015). Mindfulness/meditation. In R. L. Cautin & S. O. Lilienfeld (Eds.), *The encyclopedia of clinical psychology* (pp. 1830–1839). Wiley-Blackwell.

Morgan, L., & Wren, Y. E. (2018). A systematic review of the literature on early vocalizations and babbling patterns in young children. *Communication Disorders Quarterly, 40*(1), 3–16. https://doi.org/10.1177/1525740118760215.

Morgan, P. L., Farkas, G., Hillemeier, M. M., Pun, W. H., & Maczuga, S. (2018). Kindergarten children's executive functions predict their second-grade academic achievement and behavior. *Child Development, 90*(5), 1802–1816. https://doi.org/10.1111/cdev.13095

Morgan, R. D., & Cohen, L. M. (2008). Clinical and counseling psychology: Can differences be gleaned from printed recruiting materials? *Training and Education in Professional Psychology, 2*(3), 156.

Morganstern, K. P. (1973). Implosive therapy and flooding procedures: A critical review. *Psychological Bulletin, 79*(5), 318.

Mori, D., Chaiken, S., & Pliner, P. (1987). "Eating lightly" and the self-presentation of femininity. *Journal of Personality and Social Psychology, 53*(4), 693–702.

Morken, I. S., Røysamb, E., Nilsen, W., & Karevold, E. B. (2018). Body dissatisfaction and depressive symptoms on the threshold to adolescence: Examining gender differences in depressive symptoms and the impact of social support. *The Journal of Early Adolescence, 39*(6), 0272431618791280.

Morland, K., Roux, A. V. D., & Wing, S. (2006). Supermarkets, other food stores, and obesity: The atherosclerosis risk in communities study. *American Journal of Preventive Medicine, 30*(4), 333–339.

Morland, K., Wing, S., & Roux, A. D. (2002a). The contextual effect of the local food environment on residents' diets: The atherosclerosis risk in communities study. *American Journal of Public Health, 92*(11), 1761–1768.

Morland, K., Wing, S., Roux, A. D., & Poole, C. (2002b). Neighborhood characteristics associated with the location of food stores and food service places. *American Journal of Preventive Medicine, 22*(1), 23–29.

Morling, B., & Kitayama, S. (2008). Culture and motivation. In J. Y. Shah & W. L. Gardner (Eds.), *Handbook of motivation science* (pp. 417–433). Guilford Press.

Moroń, M., & Biolik-Moroń, M. (2021). Trait emotional intelligence and emotional experiences during the COVID-19 pandemic outbreak in Poland: A daily diary study. *Personality and Individual Differences, 168*, 110348. https://doi.org/10.1016/j.paid.2020.110348

Morrell, C. H., Gordon-Salant, S., Pearson, J. D., Brant, L. J., & Fozard, J. L. (1996). Age- and gender-specific reference ranges for hearing level and longitudinal changes in hearing level. *The Journal of the Acoustical Society of America, 100*(4), 1949–1967.

Morris, M. R., Hoeflich, C. C., Nutley, S., Ellingrod, V. L., Riba, M. B., & Striley, C. W. (2021). Use of psychiatric medication by college students: A decade of data. *Pharmacotherapy: The Journal of Human Pharmacology and Drug Therapy, 41*(4), 350–358. https://doi.org/10.1002/phar.2513

Morrison, E. R., Bain, H., Pattison, L., & Whyte-Smith, H. (2018). Something in the way she moves: Biological motion, body shape, and attractiveness in women. *Visual Cognition*, 26(6), 405–411.

Morrison, J. (2008). *The first interview* (3rd ed.). Guilford Press.

Morrison, S. J., & Demorest, S. M. (2009). Cultural restraints on music perception and cognition. In J. Y. Chaio (Ed.), *Cultural neuroscience: Cultural influences on brain function* (pp. 67–77). Elsevier.

Mortensen, P. B., Pedersen, C. B., Westergaard, T., Wohlfahrt, J., Ewald, H., Mors, O., Andersen, P. K., & Melbye, M. (1999). Effects of family history and place and season of birth on the risk of schizophrenia. *New England Journal of Medicine, 340*(8), 603–608.

Morton, J., & Johnson, M. H. (1991). CONSPEC and CONLERN: A two-process theory of infant face recognition. *Psychological Review, 98*(2), 164–181.

Mosak, H. H., & Maniacci, M. (1999). *A primer of Adlerian psychology: The analytic-behavioral-cognitive psychology of Alfred Adler*. Brunner/Mazel.

Moscovitch, M., Cabeza, R., Winocur, G., & Nadel, L. (2016). Episodic memory and beyond: The hippocampus and neocortex in transformation. *Annual Review of Psychology, 67*, 105–134.

Mosher, D. K., Hook, J. N., Captari, L. E., Davis, D. E., DeBlaere, C., & Owen, J. (2017). Cultural humility: A therapeutic framework for engaging diverse clients. *Practice Innovations, 2*(4), 221–233. https://doi.org/10.1037/pri0000055

Moshman, D. (2003). Developmental change in adulthood. In J. Demick & C. Andreoletti (Eds.), *Handbook of adult development* (pp. 43–62). Springer Science+Business Media.

Moshman, D. (2009). Adolescence. In U. Müller, J. I. M. Carpendale, & L. Smith (Eds.), *The Cambridge companion to Piaget* (pp. 255–269). Cambridge University Press.

Moskovich, A., Hunger, J., & Mann, T. (2011). The psychology of obesity. In J. H. Cawley (Ed.), *The Oxford handbook of the social science of obesity* (pp. 87–104). Oxford University Press.

Moskowitz, J. T., & Saslow, L. R. (2014). Health and psychology: The importance of positive affect. In M. M. Tugade, M. N. Shiota, & L. D. Kirby (Eds.), *Handbook of positive emotions* (pp. 413–431). Guilford Press.

Moss, C. F., & Surlykke, A. (2001). Auditory scene analysis by echolocation in bats. *The Journal of the Acoustical Society of America, 110*(4), 2207–2226.

Mouton, A. R., & Montijo, M. N. (2017). Love, passion, and peak experience: A qualitative study on six continents. *The Journal of Positive Psychology, 12*(3), 263–280.

Moynihan, R., & Cassels, A. (2005). *Selling sickness*. Nation Books.

Mozaffarian, D., Hao, T., Rimm, E. B., Willett, W. C., & Hu, F. B. (2011). Changes in diet and lifestyle and long-term weight gain in women and men. *New England Journal of Medicine, 364*(25), 2392–2404.

Mu, Q., Mishory, A., Johnson, K. A., Nahas, Z., Kozel, F. A., Yamanaka, K., Bohning, D. E., & George, M. S. (2005). Decreased brain activation during a working memory task at rested baseline is associated with vulnerability to sleep deprivation. *Sleep, 28*(4), 433–446.

Mueser, K. T., & Duva, S. M. (2011). Schizophrenia. In D. H. Barlow (Ed.), *The Oxford handbook of clinical psychology* (pp. 469–503). Oxford University Press.

Mueser, K. T., & Jeste, D. V. (2008). Preface. In K. T. Mueser & D. V. Jeste (Eds.), *Clinical handbook of schizophrenia* (pp. xii–xvi). Guilford Press.

Mueser, K. T., & Roe, D. (2016). Schizophrenia disorders. In J. C. Norcross, G. R. VandenBox, & D. K. Freedheim (Eds.), *APA handbook of clinical psychology* (Vol. 4, pp. 225–251). American Psychological Association.

Mueser, K. T., Bolton, E., & McGurk, S. R. (2006). Schizophrenia. In M. Hersen & J. C. Thomas (Eds.), *Comprehensive handbook of personality and psychopathology* (Vol. 2, pp. 262–277). Wiley.

Mueser, K. T., Deavers, F., Penn, D. L., & Cassisi, J. E. (2013). Psychosocial treatments for schizophrenia. *Annual Review of Clinical Psychology, 9*, 465–497.

Mukherjee, D., Filipowicz, A. L. S., Vo, K., Satterthwaite, T. D., & Kable, J. W. (2020). Reward and punishment reversal-learning in major depressive disorder. *Journal of Abnormal Psychology, 129*(8), 810–823. https://doi.org/10.1037/abn0000641

Mulder, R., Murray, G., & Rucklidge, J. (2017). Common versus specific factors in psychotherapy: Opening the black box. *The Lancet Psychiatry, 4*(12), 953–962.

Mullen, B., & Hu, L. T. (1989). Perceptions of ingroup and outgroup variability: A meta-analytic integration. *Basic and Applied Social Psychology, 10*(3), 233–252.

Mullen, B., Brown, R., & Smith, C. (1992). Ingroup bias as a function of salience, relevance, and status: An integration. *European Journal of Social Psychology, 22*(2), 103–122.

Mullen, M. K. (1994). Earliest recollections of childhood: A demographic analysis. *Cognition, 52*(1), 55–79.

Müller, M. J. (2013). Depressive attribution style and stressor uncontrollability increase perceived pain intensity after electric skin stimuli in healthy young men. *Pain Research & Management, 18*(4), 203–206.

Müller, U. (2009). Infancy. In U. Müller, J. I. M. Carpendale, & L. Smith (Eds.), *The Cambridge companion to Piaget* (pp. 200–228). Cambridge University Press.

Müller, U., & Racine, T. P. (2010). The development of representation and concepts. In W. F. Overton (Ed.), *Handbook of life-span development* (Vol. 1, pp. 346–390). Wiley.

Mundasad, S. (2017). "Fat but fit is a big fat myth." https://www.bbc.com/news/health-39936138

Munger, S. D. (2010). Olfactory receptors and transduction. In E. B. Goldstein (Ed.), *Encyclopedia of perception* (pp. 699–703). Sage.

Munoz, R. F., & Mendelson, T. (2005). Toward evidence-based interventions for diverse populations: The San Francisco General Hospital prevention and treatment manuals. *Journal of Consulting and Clinical Psychology, 73*(5), 790–799.

Munoz-Rubke, F., Olson, D., Will, R., & James, K. H. (2018). Functional fixedness in tool use: Learning modality, limitations and individual differences. *Acta Psychologica, 190*, 11–26.

Murayama, K., Elliot, A. J., & Friedman, R. (2012). Achievement goals. In R. M. Ryan (Ed.), *The Oxford handbook of human motivation* (pp. 191–207). Oxford University Press.

Murdock, B. B., Jr. (1962). The serial position effect of free recall. *Journal of Experimental Psychology, 64*(5), 482–488.

Murphey, R. J., Ruprecht, M. J., Baggio, P., & Nunes, D. L. (1979). The use of mild punishment in combination with reinforcement of alternate behaviors to reduce the self-injurious behavior of a profoundly retarded individual. *Research and Practice for Persons with Severe Disabilities, 4*(2), 187–195.

Murphy, E. S., & Lupfer, G. J. (2014). Basic principles of operant conditioning. In F. K. McSweeney & E. S. Murphy (Eds.), *The Wiley-Blackwell handbook of operant and classical conditioning* (pp. 167–194). Wiley.

Murphy, G. L. (2002). *The big book of concepts*. MIT Press.

Murphy, G. L. (2016a). Explaining the basic-level concept advantage in infants ... or is it the superordinate-level advantage? In B. H. Ross (Ed.), *Psychology of learning and motivation* (Vol. 64, pp. 57–92). Academic Press.

Murphy, G. L. (2016b). Is there an exemplar theory of concepts? *Psychonomic Bulletin & Review, 23*(4), 1035–1042.

Murphy, G. L., & Hoffman, A. B. (2012). Concepts. In K. Frankish & W. M. Ramsey (Eds.), *The Cambridge handbook of cognitive science* (pp. 151–170). Cambridge University Press.

Murphy, G., Lynch, L., Loftus, E., & Egan, R. (2021). Push polls increase false memories for fake news stories. *Memory, 29*(1), 1–15. https://doi.org/10.1080/09658211.2021.1934033

Murphy, J. M., & Pomerantz, A. M. (2016). Informed consent: An adaptable question format for telepsychology. *Professional Psychology: Research and Practice, 47*(5), 330–339.

Murphy, S. E., Capitão, L. P., Giles, S. L., Cowen, P. J., Stringaris, A., & Harmer, C. J. (2021). The knowns and unknowns of SSRI treatment in young people with depression and anxiety: Efficacy, predictors, and mechanisms of action. *The Lancet Psychiatry, 8*(9), 824–835. https://doi.org/10.1016/S2215-0366(21)00154-1

Murr, J., Hummel, T., Ritschel, G., & Croy, I. (2018). Individual significance of olfaction: A comparison between normosmic and dysosmic people. *Psychosomatics, 59*(3), 283–292.

Murray, C. J. L., & Lopez, A. D. (Eds.). (1996). *The global burden of disease: A comprehensive assessment of mortality and disability from diseases, injuries, and risk factors in 1990 and projected to 2020*. Harvard University Press.

Murray, D. J. (1988). *A history of Western psychology* (2nd ed.). Prentice Hall.

Murray, H. A. (1943). *Thematic Apperception Test: Manual*. Harvard University Press.

Murray, M., Dordevic, A. L., & Bonham, M. P. (2017). Systematic review and meta-analysis: The impact of multicomponent weight management interventions on self-esteem in overweight and obese adolescents. *Journal of Pediatric Psychology, 42*(4), 379–394.

Murtagh, D. R., & Greenwood, K. M. (1995). Identifying effective psychological treatments for insomnia: A meta-analysis. *Journal of Consulting and Clinical Psychology, 63*(1), 79–89.

Must, A., & Evans, E. W. (2011). The epidemiology of obesity. In J. H. Cawley (Ed.), *The Oxford handbook of the social science of obesity* (pp. 9–34). Oxford University Press.

Must, A., Hollander, S. A., & Economos, C. D. (2006). Childhood obesity: A growing public health concern. *Expert Review of Endocrinology and Metabolism, 1*(2), 233–254.

Must, A., Spadano, J., Coakley, E. H., Field, A. E., Colditz, G., & Dietz, W. H. (1999). The disease burden associated with overweight and obesity. *JAMA, 282*(16), 1523–1529.

Mustanski, B., Andrews, R., & Puckett, J. A. (2016). The effects of cumulative victimization on mental health among lesbian, gay, bisexual, and transgender adolescents and young adults. *American Journal of Public Health, 106*(3), 527–533.

Muzina, D. J., & Calabrese, J. R. (2006). Guidelines for the treatment of bipolar disorder. In D. J. Stein, D. J. Kupfer, & A. F. Schatzberg (Eds.), *The American Psychiatric Publishing textbook of mood disorders* (pp. 463–483). American Psychiatric Publishing.

Myers, D. G., & Bishop, G. D. (1970). Discussion effects on racial attitudes. *Science, 169*(3947), 778–779.

Myers, D. G., & Diener, E. (2018). The scientific pursuit of happiness. *Perspectives on Psychological Science, 13*(2), 218–225.

Myers, D. G., & Lamm, H. (1976). The group polarization phenomenon. *Psychological Bulletin, 83*(4), 602.

Myles, S., Lea, R. A., Ohashi, J., Chambers, G. K., Weiss, J. G., Hardouin, E., Engelken, J., Macartney-Coxson, D. P., Eccles, D. A., Naka, I., Kimura, R., Inaoka, T., Matsumura, Y., & Stoneking, M. (2011). Testing the thrifty gene hypothesis: The Gly482Ser variant in PPARGC1A is associated with BMI in Tongans. *BMC Medical Genetics, 12*(1), 10. https://doi.org/10.1186/1471-2350-12-10

Nadal, K. L. (2013). *That's so gay! Microaggressions and the lesbian, gay, bisexual, and transgender community*. American Psychological Association.

Nadal, K. L. (2014). A guide to responding to microaggressions. *CUNY Forum, 2*(1), 71–76. https://friendsnrc.org/wp-content/uploads/2021/05/A_Guide_to_Responding_to_Microaggressions.pdf

Nadal, K. L., Issa, M. A., Leon, J., Meterko, V., Wideman, M., & Wong, Y. (2011a). Sexual orientation microaggressions: "Death by a thousand cuts" for lesbian, gay, and bisexual youth. *Journal of LGBT Youth, 8*(3), 234–259.

Nadal, K. L., Whitman, C. N., Davis, L. S., Erazo, T., & Davidoff, K. C. (2016). Microaggressions toward lesbian, gay, bisexual, transgender, queer, and genderqueer people: A review of the literature. *The Journal of Sex Research, 53*(4–5), 488–508.

Nadal, K. L., Wong, Y., Griffin, K., Sriken, J., Vargas, V., Wideman, M., & Kolawole, A. (2011c). Microaggressions and the multiracial experience. *International Journal of Humanities and Social Sciences, 1*(7), 36–44.

Nadal, K. L., Wong, Y., Issa, M. A., Meterko, V., Leon, J., & Wideman, M. (2011b). Sexual orientation microaggressions: Processes and coping mechanisms for lesbian, gay, and bisexual individuals. *Journal of LGBT Issues in Counseling, 5*(1), 21–46.
Nadkarni, A., & Hofmann, S. G. (2012). Why do people use Facebook? *Personality and Individual Differences, 52*(3), 243–249.
Nagaraja, A. S., Sadaoui, N. C., Dorniak, P. L., Lutgendorf, S. K., & Sood, A. K. (2016). SnapShot: Stress and disease. *Cell Metabolism, 23*(2), 388–388e1.
Nagata, D. K., & Trierweiler, S. J. (2006). Revising a research manuscript. In F. T. L. Leong & J. T. Austin (Eds.), *The psychology research handbook: A guide for graduate students and research assistants* (pp. 370–380). Sage.
Nagata, J. M., Garber, A. K., Tabler, J., Murray, S. B., & Bibbins-Domingo, K. (2018). Disordered eating behaviors among overweight/obese young adults and future cardiometabolic risk in the National Longitudinal Study of Adolescent to Adult Health. *Journal of Adolescent Health, 62*(2), S17–S18.
Naglieri, J. A., & Bornstein, B. T. (2003). Intelligence and achievement: Just how correlated are they? *Journal of Psychoeducational Assessment, 21*(3), 244–260.
Naglieri, J. A., Drasgow, F., Schmit, M., Handler, L., Prifitera, A., Margolis, A., & Velasquez, R. (2004). Psychological testing on the Internet: New problems, old issues. *American Psychologist, 59*(3), 150–162.
Nahmod, N. G., Lee, S., Buxton, O. M., Chang, A. M., & Hale, L. (2017). High school start times after 8:30 am are associated with later wake times and longer time in bed among teens in a national urban cohort study. *Sleep Health, 3*(6), 444–450.
Nail, P. R., & Boniecki, K. A. (2011). Inconsistency in cognition: Cognitive dissonance. In D. Chadee (Ed.), *Theories in social psychology* (pp. 44–71). Wiley-Blackwell.
Nairne, J. S., & Rescorla, R. A. (1981). Second-order conditioning with diffuse auditory reinforcers in the pigeon. *Learning and Motivation, 12*(1), 65–91.
Nakajima, K., Minami, T., & Nakauchi, S. (2017). Interaction between facial expression and color. *Scientific Reports, 7*, 41019.
Nakamura, A., Yamada, T., Goto, A., Kato, T., Ito, K., Abe, Y., Kachi, T., & Kakigi, R. (1998). Somatosensory homunculus as drawn by MEG. *Neuroimage, 7*(4), 377–386.
Nakatani, E., Nakgawa, A., Ohara, Y., Goto, S., Uozumi, N., Iwakiri, M., Yamamoto, Y., Motomura, K., Iikura, Y., & Yamagami, T. (2003). Effects of behavior therapy on regional cerebral blood flow in obsessive-compulsive disorder. *Psychiatry Research: Neuroimaging, 124*(2), 113–120.
Nakayama, K. (2001). Modularity in perception, its relation to cognition and knowledge. In E. B. Goldstein (Ed.), *Blackwell handbook of perception* (pp. 737–759). Blackwell.
Nakayama, M., Ueda, Y., Taylor, P. M., Tominaga, H., & Uchida, Y. (2017). Cultural psychology as a form of memory research. In T. Tsukiura & S. Umeda (Eds.), *Memory in a social context* (pp. 281–295). Springer.
Nam, S. K., Choi, S. I., Lee, J. H., Lee, M. K., Kim, A. R., & Lee, S. M. (2013). Psychological factors in college students' attitudes toward seeking professional psychological help: A meta-analysis. *Professional Psychology: Research and Practice, 44*(1), 37–45. https://doi.org/10.1037/a0029562
Nargund, V. H. (2015). Effects of psychological stress on male fertility. *Nature Reviews Urology, 12*(7), 373–382.
Nascimento, S. S., Oliveira, L. R., & DeSantana, J. M. (2018). Correlations between brain changes and pain management after cognitive and meditative therapies: A systematic review of neuroimaging studies. *Complementary Therapies in Medicine, 39*, 137–145.
Nash, M. R. (2008). Foundations of clinical hypnosis. In M. R. Nash & A. J. Barnier (Eds.), *The Oxford handbook of hypnosis: Theory, research, and practice* (pp. 487–502). Oxford University Press.
Naslund, J. A., Aschbrenner, K. A., Marsch, L. A., & Bartels, S. J. (2016). The future of mental health care: Peer-to-peer support and social media. *Epidemiology and Psychiatric Sciences, 25*(2), 113–122.
Naslund, J. A., Whiteman, K. L., McHugo, G. J., Aschbrenner, K. A., Marsch, L. A., & Bartels, S. J. (2017). Lifestyle interventions for weight loss among overweight and obese adults with serious mental illness: A systematic review and meta-analysis. *General Hospital Psychiatry, 47*, 83–102.
Nasrallah, H. A. (2017). Prescribing is the culmination of extensive medical training and psychologists don't qualify. *Current Psychiatry, 16*(6), 11–16.
Nathan, D. (2011). *Sybil exposed*. Free Press.
Nathan, P. E., & Gorman, J. M. (Eds.). (2007). *A guide to treatments that work* (3rd ed.). Oxford University Press.
Nathan, P. W. (1976). The gate-control theory of pain: A critical review. *Brain, 99*(1), 123–158.
National Center for Transgender Equality. (2014). Transgender terminology. http://www.transequality.org/sites/default/files/docs/resources/TransTerminology_2014.pdf
National Institute on Deafness and Other Communication Disorders. (2017). Cochlear implants. https://www.nidcd.nih.gov/health/cochlear-implants
National Public Radio. (2014, August 29). J Dilla's lost scrolls. http://www. npr.org/2014/08/29/344255548/j-dillas-lost-scrolls
National Sleep Foundation. (2011). *2011 Sleep in America poll*. National Sleep Foundation.
National Vital Statistics. (2010). Births, marriages, divorces, deaths: Provisional data for November 2009. *National Vital Statistics Reports, 58*(23), 1–5.
Natsuaki, M. N., & Yates, T. M. (2021). Adolescent acne and disparities in mental health. *Child Development Perspectives, 15*(1), 37–43. https://doi.org/10.1111/cdep.12397
Nave, C. S., Sherman, R. A., Funder, D. C., Hampson, S. E., & Goldberg, L. R. (2010). On the contextual independence of personality: Teachers' assessments predict directly observed behavior after four decades. *Social Psychological and Personality Science, 1*(4), 327–334.
Naveh-Benjamin, M., & Jonides, J. (1984). Maintenance rehearsal: A two-component analysis. *Journal of Experimental Psychology: Learning, Memory, and Cognition, 10*(3), 369–385.
Nawrot, P., Jordan, S., Eastwood, J., Rotstein, J., Hugenholtz, A., & Feeley, M. (2003). Effects of caffeine on human health. *Food Additives & Contaminants, 20*(1), 1–30.
Neel, J. V. (1962). Diabetes mellitus: A "thrifty" genotype rendered detrimental by "progress"? *American Journal of Human Genetics, 14*(4), 353–362.
Neel, J. V. (1999). The "thrifty genotype" in 1998. *Nutrition Reviews, 57*(5), 2–9.
Neimark, E. D. (1975). Longitudinal development of formal operations thought. *Genetic Psychology Monographs, 91*(2), 171–225.
Neimeyer, G. J., Taylor, J. M., Wear, D. M., & Buyukgoze-Kavas, A. (2011). How special are the specialties? Workplace settings in counseling and clinical psychology in the United States. *Counselling Psychology Quarterly, 24*(1), 43–53.
Neimeyer, R. A., Currier, J. M., Coleman, R., Tomer, A., & Samuel, E. (2011). Confronting suffering and death at the end of life: The impact of religiosity, psychosocial factors, and life regret among hospice patients. *Death Studies, 35*(9), 777–800.
Neisser, U. (1987). From direct perception to conceptual structure. In U. Neisser (Ed.), *Concepts and conceptual development: Ecological and intellectual factors in categorization* (pp. 11–24). Cambridge University Press.
Neisser, U., & Libby, L. K. (2000). Remembering life experiences. In E. Tulving & F. I. M. Craik (Eds.), *The Oxford handbook of memory* (pp. 315–332). Oxford University Press.
Neisser, U., Boodoo, G., Bouchard, T. J., Jr., Boykin, A. W., Brody, N., Ceci, S. J., & Urbina, S. (1996). Intelligence: Knowns and unknowns. *American Psychologist, 51*(2), 77–101.
Nelson, C. A., III, Thomas, K. M., & De Haan, M. (2006). Neural bases of cognitive development. In D. Kuhn & R. Siegler (Vol. Eds.), *Handbook of child psychology* (6th ed., Vol. 2, pp. 3–57). Wiley.
Nelson, D. I., Nelson, R. Y., Concha-Barrientos, M., & Fingerhut, M. (2005). The global burden of occupational noise-induced hearing loss. *American Journal of Industrial Medicine, 48*(6), 446–458.
Nelson, E. A. S., Taylor, B. J., Jenik, A., Vance, J., Walmsley, K., Pollard, K., Freemantle, M., Ewing, D., Einspieler, C., Engele, H., Ritter, P., Hildes-Ripstein, G. E., Arancibia, M., Ji, X., Li, H., Bedard, C., Helweg-Larsen, K., Sidenius, K., Karlqvist, S., Poets, C., & & ICCPS Study Group. (2001). International child care practices study: Infant sleeping environment. *Early Human Development, 62*(1), 43–55.
Nelson, E. L., & Bui, T. (2010). Rural telepsychology services for children and adolescents. *Journal of Clinical Psychology, 66*(5), 490–501. https://doi.org/10.1002/jclp.20682
Nelson, K. (2018). The cultural construction of memory in early childhood. In B. Wagoner (Ed.), *Handbook of culture and memory* (pp. 185–208). Oxford University Press.
Nelson, M. D., & Tumpap, A. M. (2017). Posttraumatic stress disorder symptom severity is associated with left hippocampal volume reduction: A meta-analytic study. *CNS Spectrums, 22*(4), 363–372.
Nelson, S. K., & Lyubomirsky, S. (2014). Finding happiness: Tailoring positive activities for optimal well-being benefits. In M. M. Tugade, M. N. Shiota, & L. D. Kirby (Eds.), *Handbook of positive emotions* (pp. 275–293). Guilford Press.
Nelson, T. O. (1985). Ebbinghaus's contribution to the measurement of retention: Savings during relearning. *Journal of Experimental Psychology: Learning, Memory, and Cognition, 11*(3), 472–479.
Nemeroff, C. B., & Schatzberg, A. F. (2007). Pharmacological treatments for unipolar depression. In P. E. Nathan & J. M. Gorman (Eds.), *A guide to treatments that work* (3rd ed., pp. 271–287). Oxford University Press.
Nemeth, C. J., Connell, J. B., Rogers, J. D., & Brown, K. S. (2001). Improving decision making by means of dissent. *Journal of Applied Social Psychology, 31*(1), 48–58.
Nemeth, C., & Rogers, J. (2011). Dissent and the search for information. *British Journal of Social Psychology, 35*(1), 67–76.
Nesi, J., & Prinstein, M. J. (2015). Using social media for social comparison and feedback-seeking: Gender and popularity moderate associations with depressive symptoms. *Journal of Abnormal Child Psychology, 43*(8), 1427–1438.
Nesse, R. M. (2005). Natural selection and the regulation of defenses: A signal detection analysis of the smoke detector principle. *Evolution and Human Behavior, 26*(1), 88–105.
Nesse, R. M. (2019a). *Good reasons for bad feelings: Insights from the frontier of evolutionary psychiatry*. Dutton.
Nesse, R. M. (2019b). The smoke detector principle: Signal detection and optimal defense regulation. *Evolution, Medicine, and Public Health, 2019*(1), 1.
Nettle, D. (2007). *Personality: What makes you the way you are*. Oxford University Press.
Nettle, D. (2011). Evolutionary perspectives on the five-factor model of personality. In D. M. Buss & P. H. Hawley (Eds.), *The evolution of personality and individual differences* (pp. 5–28). Oxford University Press.
Neubauer, A. C., & Freudenthaler, H. H. (2005). Models of emotional intelligence. In R. Schulze & R. D. Roberts (Eds.), *Emotional intelligence: An international handbook* (pp. 31–50). Hogrefe & Huber.
Neuberg, S. L., & Cottrell, C. A. (2006). Evolutionary bases of prejudices. In M. Schaller, J. A. Simpson, & D. T. Kenrick (Eds.), *Evolution and social psychology* (pp. 163–187). Psychology Press.
Neuberg, S. L., & Schaller, M. (2016). An evolutionary threat-management approach to prejudices. *Current Opinion in Psychology, 7*, 1–5.
Neuberg, S. L., Kenrick, D. T., & Schaller, M. (2010). Evolutionary social psychology. In S. T. Fiske, D. T. Gilbert, & G. Lindzey (Eds.), *Handbook of social psychology* (5th ed., Vol. 2, pp. 761–796). John Wiley & Sons.
Neupert, S. D., Almeida, D. M., & Charles, S. T. (2007). Age differences in reactivity to daily stressors: The role of personal control. *The Journals of Gerontology Series B: Psychological Sciences and Social Sciences, 62*(4), P216–P225.
Neuschatz, J. S., Lampinen, J. M., Toglia, M. P., Payne, D. G., & Cisneros, E. P. (2007). False memory research: History, theory, and applied applications. In M. P. Toglia, J. D. Read, D. F. Ross, & R. C. L. Lindsay (Eds.), *The handbook of eyewitness psychology: Memory for events* (Vol. I, pp. 239–260). Psychology Press.
Neville, H., & Sur, M. (2009). Introduction. In M. S. Gazzaniga (Ed.), *The cognitive neurosciences* (4th ed., pp. 89–90). MIT Press.
Newberg, A. B. (2010). The neurobiology of meditation. In D. A. Monti & B. D. Beitman (Eds.), *Integrative psychiatry* (pp. 339–358). Oxford University Press.
Newby-Clark, I. R. (2004). Getting ready for the bad times: Self-esteem and anticipatory coping. *European Journal of Social Psychology, 34*(3), 309–316.
Newey, C. A., & Hood, B. M. (2004). Determinants of shift-work adjustment for nursing staff: The critical experience of partners. *Journal of Professional Nursing, 20*(3), 187–195.
Newland, R. P., & Crnic, K. A. (2017). Developmental risk and goodness of fit in the mother-child relationship: Links to parenting stress and children's behaviour problems. *Infant and Child Development, 26*(2), e1980.
Newman, C. F. (2006). Bipolar disorder. In M. Hersen & J. C. Thomas (Eds.), *Comprehensive handbook of personality and psychopathology* (Vol. 2, pp. 244–261). Wiley.
Newman, C. F. (2016). Cognitive restructuring/cognitive therapy. In C. M. Nezu & A. M. Nezu (Eds.), *The Oxford handbook of cognitive and behavioral therapies* (pp. 118–141). Oxford University Press.
Newman, K. S. (2012). *The accordion family: Boomerang kids, anxious parents, and the private toll of global competition*. Beacon Press.
Newman, L. C., & Larsen, R. J. (Eds.). (2011). *Taking sides: Clashing views in personality psychology*. McGraw-Hill.
Newman, M. G., Lafreniere, L. S., & Shin, K. E. (2017). Cognitive-behavioral therapies in historical perspective. In A. J. Consoli, L. E. Beutler, & B. Bongar (Eds.), *Comprehensive textbook of psychotherapy: Theory and practice* (2nd ed., pp. 61–75). Oxford University Press.
Newport, F., & Gates, G. J. (2015). San Francisco Metro area ranks highest in LGBT percentage. http://www.gallup.com/poll/182051/san-francisco-metro-area-ranks-highest-lgbt-percentage.aspx?utm_source=Social%20Issues&utm_medium=newsfeed&utm_campaign=tiles
Neyer, F. J., & Lang, F. R. (2003). Blood is thicker than water: Kinship orientation across adulthood. *Journal of Personality and Social Psychology, 84*(2), 310–321.

Nezu, A. M. (2010). Cultural influences on the process of conducting psychotherapy: Personal reflections of an ethnic minority psychologist. *Psychotherapy: Theory, Research, Practice, Training, 47*(2), 169–176.

Ng, K. Y., Van Dyne, L., & Ang, S. (2012). Cultural intelligence: A review, reflections, and recommendations for future research. In A. M. Ryan, F. T. L. Leong, & F. L. Oswald (Eds.), *Conducting multinational research: Applying organizational psychology in the workplace* (pp. 29–58). American Psychological Association.

Ng, T. W. H., Sorensen, K. L., & Eby, L. T. (2006). Locus of control at work: A meta-analysis. *Journal of Organizational Behavior, 27*(8), 1057–1087.

Nguyen, B. H., Pérusse, D., Paquet, J., Petit, D., Boivin, M., Tremblay, R. E., & Montplaisir, J. (2008). Sleep terrors in children: A prospective study of twins. *Pediatrics, 122*(6), e1164–e1167.

Nguyen, H. H. (2006). Acculturation in the United States. In D. L. Sam & J. W. Berry (Eds.), *The Cambridge handbook of acculturation psychology* (pp. 311–330). Cambridge University Press.

Nguyen, J., Liu, M. A., Patel, R. J., Tahara, K., & Nguyen, A. L. (2016). Use and interest in complementary and alternative medicine among college students seeking healthcare at a university campus student health center. *Complementary Therapies in Clinical Practice, 24*, 103–108.

Nicholls, R. E., Alarcon, J. M., Malleret, G., Carroll, R. C., Grody, M., Vronskaya, S., & Kandel, E. R. (2008). Transgenic mice lacking NMDAR-dependent LTD exhibit deficits in behavioral flexibility. *Neuron, 58*(1), 104–117.

Nichols, K., & Graves, S. L., Jr. (2018). Training in strength-based intervention and assessment methodologies in APA-accredited psychology programs. *Psychology in the Schools, 55*(1), 93–100.

Nicholson, N., Cole, S. G., & Rocklin, T. (1985). Conformity in the Asch situation: A comparison between contemporary British and U.S. university students. *British Journal of Social Psychology, 24*(1), 59–63.

Nickels, N., Kubicki, K., & Maestripieri, D. (2017). Sex differences in the effects of psychosocial stress on cooperative and prosocial behavior: Evidence for 'flight or fight' in males and 'tend and befriend' in females. *Adaptive Human Behavior and Physiology, 3*(2), 171–183.

Nicolaus, L. K., Hoffman, T. E., & Gustavson, C. R. (1982). Taste aversion conditioning in free-ranging raccoons (*Procyon lotor*). *Northwest Science, 56*, 165–169.

Nicoll, R. A. (2017). A brief history of long-term potentiation. *Neuron, 93*(2), 281–290.

Nielsen, T. A. (1995). Describing and modeling hypnagogic imagery using a systematic self-observation procedure. *Dreaming, 5*(2), 75–94.

Nielsen, T. A. (2000). A review of mentation in REM and NREM sleep: "Covert" REM sleep as a possible reconciliation of two opposing models. *Behavioral and Brain Sciences, 23*(06), 851–866.

Nielsen, T. A. (2004). Chronobiological features of dream production. *Sleep Medicine Reviews, 8*(5), 403–424.

Niemeier, H. M., Raynor, H. A., Lloyd-Richardson, E. E., Rogers, M. L., & Wing, R. R. (2006). Fast food consumption and breakfast skipping: Predictors of weight gain from adolescence to adulthood in a nationally representative sample. *Journal of Adolescent Health, 39*(6), 842–849.

Niemiec, C. P., Ryan, R. M., & Deci, E. L. (2009). The path taken: Consequences of attaining intrinsic and extrinsic aspirations in post-college life. *Journal of Research in Personality, 43*(3), 291–306.

Nikitin, J., & Freund, A. M. (2018). Feeling loved and integrated or lonely and rejected in everyday life: The role of age and social motivation. *Developmental Psychology, 54*(6), 1186–1198.

Nikitin, J., Schoch, S., & Freund, A. M. (2014). The role of age and motivation for the experience of social acceptance and rejection. *Developmental Psychology, 50*(7), 1943–1950.

Nippold, M. A., & Duthie, J. K. (2003). Mental imagery and idiom comprehension: A comparison of school-age children and adults. *Journal of Speech, Language, and Hearing Research, 46*(4), 788–799.

Nisbet, E. C., & Kamenchuk, O. (2019). The psychology of state-sponsored disinformation campaigns and implications for public diplomacy. *The Hague Journal of Diplomacy, 14*(1–2), 65–82. https://doi.org/10.1163/1871191X-11411019

Nisbet, E. C., & Kamenchuk, O. (2021). Russian news media, digital media, informational learned helplessness, and belief in COVID-19 misinformation. *International Journal of Public Opinion Research*, edab011. https://doi.org/10.1093/ijpor/edab011doi.org/10.1093/ijpor/edab011

Nisbett, R. (1995). Race, IQ, and scientism. In S. Fraser (Ed.), *The bell curve wars: Race, intelligence, and the future of America* (pp. 36–57). Basic Books.

Nisbett, R. (2003). *The geography of thought: How Asians and Westerners think differently ... and why*. Free Press.

Nisbett, R. E., & Masuda, T. (2003). Culture and point of view. *Proceedings of the National Academy of Sciences, 100*(19), 11163–11170.

Nisbett, R. E., & Miyamoto, Y. (2005). The influence of culture: Holistic versus analytic perception. *Trends in Cognitive Sciences, 9*(10), 467–473.

Nisbett, R. E., Aronson, J., Blair, C., Dickens, W., Flynn, J., Halpern, D. F., & Turkheimer, E. (2012). Intelligence: New findings and theoretical developments. *American Psychologist, 67*(2), 130–159.

Nisenson, L., Berenbaum, H., & Good, T. (2001). The development of interpersonal relationships in individuals with schizophrenia. *Psychiatry, 64*(2), 111–125.

Nishida, M., Pearsall, J., Buckner, R. L., & Walker, M. P. (2009). REM sleep, prefrontal theta, and the consolidation of human emotional memory. *Cerebral Cortex, 19*(5), 1158–1166.

Niu, W. (2020). Intelligence in worldwide perspective: A twenty-first-century update. In R. J. Sternberg (Ed.), *The Cambridge handbook of intelligence* (pp. 893–915). Cambridge University Press.

Niu, W., & Brass, J. (2011). Intelligence in worldwide perspective. In R. J. Sternberg & S. B. Kaufman (Eds.), *The Cambridge handbook of intelligence* (pp. 623–646). Cambridge University Press.

Niu, W., & Sternberg, R. J. (2001). Cultural influences on artistic creativity and its evaluation. *International Journal of Psychology, 36*(4), 225–241.

Nixon, A. E., Bruk-Lee, V., & Spector, P. E. (2017). Grin and bear it? Employees' use of surface acting during co-worker conflict. *Stress and Health, 33*(2), 129–142.

Noah, T., Schul, Y., & Mayo, R. (2018). When both the original study and its failed replication are correct: Feeling observed eliminates the facial-feedback effect. *Journal of Personality and Social Psychology, 114*(5), 657–664. https://doi.org/10.1037/pspa0000121

Noar, S. M., Benac, C. N., & Harris, M. S. (2007). Does tailoring matter? Meta-analytic review of tailored print health behavior change interventions. *Psychological Bulletin, 133*(4), 673–693.

Nobler, M. S., & Sackeim, H. A. (2006). Electroconvulsive therapy and transcranial magnetic stimulation. In D. J. Stein, D. J. Kupfer, & A. F. Schatzberg (Eds.), *The American Psychiatric Publishing textbook of mood disorders* (pp. 317–336). American Psychiatric Publishing.

Nobler, M. S., & Sackeim, H. A. (2006). Electroconvulsive therapy and transcranial magnetic stimulation. In D. J. Stein, D. J. Kupfer, & A. F. Schatzberg (Eds.), *The American Psychiatric Publishing textbook of mood disorders* (pp. 317–336). American Psychiatric Publishing.

Nolen-Hoeksema, S. (2000). The role of rumination in depressive disorders and mixed anxiety/depressive symptoms. *Journal of Abnormal Psychology, 109*(3), 504–511.

Nolen-Hoeksema, S., & Hilt, L. M. (2009). Gender differences in depression. In I. H. Gotlib & C. L. Hammen (Eds.), *Handbook of depression* (2nd ed., pp. 386–404). Guilford Press.

Nolen-Hoeksema, S., Stice, E., Wade, E., & Bohon, C. (2007). Reciprocal relations between rumination and bulimic, substance abuse, and depressive symptoms in female adolescents. *Journal of Abnormal Psychology, 116*(1), 198–207.

Noll, J. G., Trickett, P. K., Long, J. D., Negriff, S., Susman, E. J., Shalev, I., Li, J. C., & Putnam, F. W. (2017). Childhood sexual abuse and early timing of puberty. *Journal of Adolescent Health, 60*(1), 65–71.

Noll, R. (2007). *The encyclopedia of schizophrenia and other psychotic disorders* (3rd ed.). Facts on File.

Nolte, J. (2008). *The human brain: An introduction to its functional anatomy* (6th ed.). Mosby.

Norcross, J. C. (2000). Clinical versus counseling psychology: What's the diff? *Eye on Psi Chi, 5*(1), 20–22.

Norcross, J. C. (2005). A primer on psychotherapy integration. In J. C. Norcross & M. R. Goldfried (Eds.), *Handbook of psychotherapy integration* (2nd ed., pp. 3–24). Oxford University Press.

Norcross, J. C., Beutler, L. E., & Goldfried, M. R. (2019). Cognitive-behavioral therapy and psychotherapy integration. In K. S. Dobson & D. J. A. Dozois (Eds.), *Handbook of cognitive-behavioral therapies* (4th ed., pp. 318–345). Guilford Press.

Norcross, J. C., Freedheim, D. K., & Vandenbos, G. R. (2011). Into the future: Retrospect and prospect in psychotherapy. In J. C. Norcross, G. R. Vandenbos, & D. K. Freedheim (Eds.), *History of psychotherapy: Continuity and change* (2nd ed., pp. 743–760). American Psychological Association.

Norcross, J. C., Goldfried, M. R., & Arigo, D. (2016). Integrative theories. In J. C. Norcross, G. R. VandenBos, & D. K. Freedheim (Eds.), *APA handbook of clinical psychology* (Vol. 2, pp. 303–332). American Psychological Association.

Norcross, J. C., Hogan, T. P., Koocher, G. P., & Maggio, L. A. (2017). *Clinician's guide to evidence-based practices: Behavioral health and addictions* (2nd ed.). Oxford University Press.

Norcross, J. C., & Karpiak, C. P. (2012). Clinical psychologists in the 2010s: 50 years of the APA Division of Clinical Psychology. *Clinical Psychology: Science and Practice, 19*(1), 1–12.

Norcross, J. C., Karpiak, C. P., & Santoro, S. O. (2005). Clinical psychologists across the years: The division of clinical psychology from 1960 to 2003. *Journal of Clinical Psychology, 61*(12), 1467–1483.

Norcross, J. C., Kohout, J. L., & Wicherski, M. (2005). Graduate study in psychology: 1971–2004. *American Psychologist, 60*(9), 959–975.

Norcross, J. C., & Lambert, M. J. (2011). Evidence-based therapy relationships. In J. C. Norcross (Ed.), *Psychotherapy relationships that work: Evidence-based responsiveness* (2nd ed., pp. 3–21). Oxford University Press.

Norcross, J. C., & Newman, C. F. (1992). Psychotherapy integration: Setting the context. In J. C. Norcross & M. R. Goldfried (Eds.), *Handbook of psychotherapy integration* (pp. 3–45). Basic Books.

Norcross, J. C., Pfund, R. A., & Cook, D. M. (2021). The predicted future of psychotherapy: A decennial e-Delphi poll. *Professional Psychology: Research and Practice*. Advance online publication. https://doi.org/10.1037/pro0000431

Norcross, J. C., & Wampold, B. E. (2011). Evidence-based therapy relationships: Research conclusions and clinical practices. In J. C. Norcross (Ed.), *Psychotherapy relationships that work: Evidence-based responsiveness* (2nd ed., pp. 423–430). Oxford University Press.

Nordby, V. J., & Hall, C. S. (1974). *A guide to psychologists and their concepts*. W. H. Freeman.

Nordstroem, A. L., Talbot, D., Bernasconi, C., Berardo, C. G., & Lalonde, J. (2017). Burden of illness of people with persistent symptoms of schizophrenia: A multinational cross-sectional study. *International Journal of Social Psychiatry, 63*(2), 139–150.

Norem, J. K. (2003). Pessimism: Accentuating the positive possibilities. In E. C. Chang & L. J. Sanna (Eds.), *Virtue, vice, and personality: The complexity of behavior* (pp. 91–104). American Psychological Association.

Norem, J. K. (2008). Defensive pessimism, anxiety, and the complexity of evaluating self-regulation. *Social and Personality Psychology Compass, 2*(1), 121–134.

Norem, J. K. (2010). Resisting the hegemony of the five-factor model: There is plenty of personality outside the FFA. *Psychological Inquiry, 21*(1), 65–68.

Norem, J. K., & Cantor, N. (1986). Defensive pessimism: Harnessing anxiety as motivation. *Journal of Personality and Social Psychology, 51*(6), 1208–1217.

Norenzayan, A., Choi, I., & Peng, K. (2007). Perception and cognition. In S. Kitayama & D. Cohen (Eds.), *Handbook of cultural psychology* (pp. 569–594). Guilford Press.

Normand, S., Ambrosoli, J., Guiet, J., Soucisse, M. M., Schneider, B. H., Maisonneuve, M. F., Lee, M. D., & Tassi, F. (2017). Behaviors associated with negative affect in the friendships of children with ADHD: An exploratory study. *Psychiatry Research, 247*, 222–224.

Norris, S. C., Gleaves, D. H., & Hutchinson, A. D. (2019). Anorexia nervosa and perfectionism: A meta-analysis. *International Journal of Eating Disorders, 52*(3), 219–229.

Nosofsky, R. M., Clark, S. E., & Shin, H. J. (1989). Rules and exemplars in categorization, identification, and recognition. *Journal of Experimental Psychology: Learning, Memory, and Cognition, 15*(2), 282–304.

Nosofsky, R. M., & Johansen, M. K. (2000). Exemplar-based accounts of "multiple-system" phenomena in perceptual categorization. *Psychonomic Bulletin and Review, 7*(3), 375–402.

Nowak, A. L. V., & Hale, H. M. (2012). Prevalence of complementary and alternative medicine use among US college students: A systematic review. *American Journal of Health Education, 43*(2), 116–126.

Nowak, A. L. V., DeGise, J., Daugherty, A., O'Keefe, R., Seward, S., Jr., Setty, S., & Tang, F. (2015). Prevalence and predictors of complementary and alternative medicine (CAM) use among Ivy League college students: Implications for student health services. *Journal of American College Health, 63*(6), 362–372.

Nucci, L. P., & Gingo, M. (2011). The development of moral reasoning. In U. Goswami (Ed.), *The Wiley-Blackwell handbook of childhood cognitive development* (2nd ed., pp. 420–445). Wiley-Blackwell.

Nurminen, T. (1998). Shift work and reproductive health. *Scandinavian Journal of Work, Environment & Health, 24*(Suppl. 23), 28–34.

Nutt, D., & Carhart-Harris, R. (2021). The current status of psychedelics in psychiatry. *JAMA Psychiatry, 78*(2), 121–122. https://doi.org/10.1001/jamapsychiatry.2020.2171

Nyberg, D., Wright, C., & Kirk, J. (2020). Fracking the future: The temporal portability of frames in political contests. *Organization Studies, 41*(2), 175–196. https://doi.org/10.1177/0170840618814568

Nyklíček, I., & Kuijpers, K. F. (2008). Effects of mindfulness-based stress reduction intervention on psychological well-being and quality of life: Is increased mindfulness indeed the mechanism? *Annals of Behavioral Medicine, 35*(3), 331–340.

Oakley, D. A. (2008). Hypnosis, trance, and suggestion: Evidence from neuroimaging. In M. R. Nash & A. J. Barnier (Eds.), *The Oxford handbook of hypnosis: Theory, research, and practice* (pp. 365–392). Oxford University Press.

Oaksford, M., Chater, N., & Stewart, N. (2012). Reasoning and decision making. In K. Frankish & W. M. Ramsey (Eds.), *The Cambridge handbook of cognitive science* (pp. 131–150). Cambridge, UK: Cambridge University Press.

Oas, P. T. (2010). Current status on corporal punishment with children: What the literature says. *The American Journal of Family Therapy, 38*(5), 413–420.

Oberauer, K., Lewandowsky, S., Awh, E., Brown, G. D., Conway, A., Covan, N., Donkin, C., Farrell, S., Hitch, G. J., Hurlstone, M. J., Ma, W. J., Morey, C. C., Nee, D. E., Schweppe, J., Vergauwe, E., & Ward, G. (2018). Benchmarks for models of short term and working memory. *Psychological Bulletin, 144*(9), 885–958.

O'Boyle, E. H., Humphrey, R. H., Pollack, J. M., Hawver, T. H., & Story, P. A. (2011). The relation between emotional intelligence and job performance: A meta-analysis. *Journal of Organizational Behavior, 32*(5), 788–818.

O'Brien, K. S., Latner, J. D., Ebneter, D., & Hunter, J. A. (2013). Obesity discrimination: The role of physical appearance, personal ideology, and anti-fat prejudice. *International Journal of Obesity, 37*(3), 455–460.

O'Brien, W. H., Haynes, S. N., & Kaholokula, J. K. (2016). Behavioral assessment and the functional analysis. In C. M. Nezu & A. M. Nezu (Eds.), *The Oxford handbook of cognitive and behavioral therapies* (pp. 44–61). Oxford University Press.

O'Brien, W. H., & Tabaczynski, T. (2007). Unstructured interviewing. In M. Hersen & J. C. Thomas (Eds.), *Handbook of clinical interviewing with children* (pp. 16–29). Sage.

Ocampo-Garcés, A., Molina, E., Rodríguez, A., & Vivaldi, E. A. (2000). Homeostasis of REM sleep after total and selective sleep deprivation in the rat. *Journal of Neurophysiology, 84*(5), 2699–2702.

O'Connor, A., Ladebue, A., Peterson, J., Davis, R., Jung Grant, S., McCreight, M., & Lambert-Kerzner, A. (2018). Creating and testing regulatory focus messages to enhance medication adherence. *Chronic Illness, 15*(2), 124–137. https://doi.org/10.1177/1742395317753882

O'Connor, M. G., & Kaplan, E. F. (2003). Age-related changes in memory. In J. Demick & C. Andreoletti (Eds.), *Handbook of adult development* (pp. 121–130). Springer Science+Business Media.

O'Connor, M. J., Shah, B., Whaley, S., Cronin, P., Gunderson, B., & Graham, J. (2002). Psychiatric illness in a clinical sample of children with prenatal alcohol exposure. *The American Journal of Drug and Alcohol Abuse, 28*(4), 743–754.

O'Connor, M., & Verfaillie, M. (2002). The amnesic syndrome: Overview and subtypes. In A. D. Baddeley, M. D. Kopelman, & B. A. Wilson (Eds.), *The handbook of memory disorders* (2nd ed., pp. 145–166). Wiley.

O'Connor, S. M., Burt, S. A., VanHuysse, J. L., & Klump, K. L. (2016). What drives the association between weight-conscious peer groups and disordered eating? Disentangling genetic and environmental selection from pure socialization effects. *Journal of Abnormal Psychology, 125*(3), 356.

Oderda, G. M., Lake, J., Rüdell, K., Roland, C. L., & Masters, E. T. (2015). Economic burden of prescription opioid misuse and abuse: A systematic review. *Journal of Pain & Palliative Care Pharmacotherapy, 29*(4), 388–400.

O'Donohue, W. (2009). A brief history of cognitive behavior therapy: Are there troubles ahead? In W. T. O'Donohue & J. E. Fisher (Eds.), *General principles and empirically supported techniques of cognitive behavior therapy* (pp. 1–14). Wiley.

Ofen-Noy, N., Dudai, Y., & Karni, A. (2003). Skill learning in mirror reading: How repetition determines acquisition. *Cognitive Brain Research, 17*(2), 507–521.

Ogden, J. (2012, January 16). HM, the man with no memory. *Psychology Today.* https://www.psychologytoday.com/blog/trouble-in-mind/201201/hm-the-man-no-memory

Ogletree, S. M., Fancher, J., & Gill, S. (2014). Gender and texting: Masculinity, femininity, and gender role ideology. *Computers in Human Behavior, 37*, 49–55.

Ogloff, J. R. P. (Ed.). (2002). *Taking psychology and law into the twenty-first century.* Kluwer Academic/Plenum Press.

Oh, D., Shafir, E., & Todorov, A. (2020). Economic status cues from clothes affect perceived competence from faces. *Nature Human Behaviour, 4*(3), 287–293. https://doi.org/10.1038/s41562-019-0782-4

Oh, J., Stewart, A. E., & Phelps, R. E. (2017). Topics in the *Journal of Counseling Psychology*, 1963–2015. *Journal of Counseling Psychology, 64*(6), 604–615.

O'Hara, R. E., Gibbons, F. X., Gerrard, M., Li, Z., & Sargent, J. D. (2012). Greater exposure to sexual content in popular movies predicts earlier sexual debut and increased sexual risk taking. *Psychological Science, 23*(9), 984–993.

Ohashi, M. M., & Yamaguchi, S. (2004). Super-ordinary bias in Japanese self-predictions of future life events. *Asian Journal of Social Psychology, 7*(2), 169–185.

Ohayon, M. M., & Guilleminault, C. (2006). Epidemiology of sleep disorders. In T. L. Lee-Chiong (Ed.), *Sleep: A comprehensive handbook* (pp. 73–82). Wiley-Liss.

Ohayon, M. M., Carskadon, M. A., Guilleminault, C., & Vitiello, M. V. (2004). Meta-analysis of quantitative sleep parameters from childhood to old age in healthy individuals: Developing normative sleep values across the human lifespan. *Sleep, 27*(7), 1255–1274.

Ohayon, M. M., Guilleminault, C., & Priest, R. G. (1999). Night terrors, sleepwalking, and confusional arousals in the general population: Their frequency and relationship to other sleep and mental disorders. *Journal of Clinical Psychiatry, 60*(4), 268–276.

Ohayon, M. M., Priest, R. G., Zulley, J., Smirne, S., & Paiva, T. (2002). Prevalence of narcolepsy symptomatology and diagnosis in the European general population. *Neurology, 58*(12), 1826–1833.

Ohst, B., & Tuschen-Caffier, B. (2018). Catastrophic misinterpretation of bodily sensations and external events in panic disorder, other anxiety disorders, and healthy subjects: A systematic review and meta-analysis. *PLoS One, 13*(3), e0194493.

Oishi, S. (2002). The experiencing and remembering of well-being: A cross-cultural analysis. *Personality and Social Psychology Bulletin, 28*(10), 1398–1406.

Oishi, S., Kushlev, K., & Benet-Martinez, V. (2021). Culture and personality: Current directions. In O. P. John & R. W. Robbins (Eds.), *Handbook of personality: Theory and research* (4th ed.), pp. 686–703. Guilford.

Ojeda, L., Navarro, R. L., Meza, R. R., & Arbona, C. (2012). Too Latino and not Latino enough: The role of ethnicity-related stressors on Latino college students' life satisfaction. *Journal of Hispanic Higher Education, 11*(1), 14–28.

Okaichi, Y., & Okaichi, H. (2001). Music discrimination by rats. *Japanese Journal of Animal Psychology, 51*(1), 29–34.

Okami, P., Weisner, T., & Olmstead, R. (2002). Outcome correlates of parent-child bedsharing: An eighteen-year longitudinal study. *Journal of Developmental & Behavioral Pediatrics, 23*(4), 244–253.

O'Kelly, M. E., & Collard, J. J. (2016). Rational emotive behavior therapy. In C. M. Nezu & A. M. Nezu (Eds.), *The Oxford handbook of cognitive and behavioral therapies* (pp. 142–159). Oxford University Press.Olatunji, B. O., & Feldman, G. (2008). Cognitive-behavioral therapy. In M. Hersen & A. M. Gross (Eds.), *Handbook of clinical psychology* (Vol. 1, pp. 551–584). Wiley.

Olaya, B., Domènech-Abella, J., Moneta, M. V., Lara, E., Caballero, F. F., Rico-Uribe, L. A., & Haro, J. M. (2017). All-cause mortality and multimorbidity in older adults: The role of social support and loneliness. *Experimental Gerontology, 99*, 120–126.

Olejniczak, P. (2006). Neurophysiologic basis of EEG. *Journal of Clinical Neurophysiology, 23*(3), 186–189.

Olff, M., Langeland, W., Draijer, N., & Gersons, B. P. (2007). Gender differences in posttraumatic stress disorder. *Psychological Bulletin, 133*(2), 183–204.

Olfson, M., Marcus, S. C., Tedeschi, M., & Wan, G. J. (2006). Continuity of antidepressant treatment for adults with depression in the United States. *American Journal of Psychiatry, 163*(1), 101–108.

Oliva, R., Morys, F., Horstmann, A., Castiello, U., & Begliomini, C. (2019). The impulsive brain: Neural underpinnings of binge eating behavior in normal-weight adults. *Appetite, 136*, 33–49.

Oliver, B. R., & Plomin, R. (2007). Twins' Early Development Study (TEDS): A multivariate, longitudinal genetic investigation of language, cognition and behavior problems from childhood through adolescence. *Twin Research and Human Genetics, 10*(01), 96–105.

Oliver, G., & Wardle, J. (1999). Perceived effects of stress on food choice. *Physiology & Behavior, 66*(3), 511–515.

Oliver, M. B., & Hyde, J. S. (1993). Gender differences in sexuality: A meta-analysis. *Psychological Bulletin, 114*(1), 29–51.

Oliver, M. B., Raney, A. A., Slater, M. D., Appel, M., Hartmann, T., Bartsch, A., Schneider, F. M., Janicke-Bowles, S. H., Krämer, N., Mares, M.-L., Vorderer, P., Reiger, D., Dale, K. R., & Das, E. (2018). Self-transcendent media experiences: Taking meaningful media to a higher level. *Journal of Communication, 68*(2), 380–389.

Olkin, R., & Taliaferro, G. (2006). Evidence-based practices have ignored people with disabilities. In J. C. Norcross, L. E. Beutler, & R. F. Levant (Eds.), *Evidence-based practices in mental health: Debate and dialogue on the fundamental questions* (pp. 353–359). American Psychological Association.

Ollendick, T. H., Alvarez, H. K., & Greene, R. W. (2004). Behavioral assessment: History of underlying concepts and methods. In S. N. Haynes & E. M. Heiby (Eds.), *Comprehensive handbook of psychological assessment* (Vol. 3, pp. 19–34). Wiley.

Ollendick, T. H., Weist, M. D., Borden, M. C., & Greene, R. W. (1992). Sociometric status and academic, behavioral, and psychological adjustment: A five-year longitudinal study. *Journal of Consulting and Clinical Psychology, 60*(1), 80–87.

Oller, D. K. (2000). *The emergence of the speech capacity.* Lawrence Erlbaum.

Olson, C. R., & Colby, C. L. (2013). The organization of cognition. In E. R. Kandel, J. H. Schwartz, T. M. Jessell, S. A. Siegelbaum, & A. J. Hudspeth (Eds.), *Principles of neural science* (5th ed., pp. 392–411). McGraw-Hill.

Olson, I. R., & Marshuetz, C. (2005). Facial attractiveness is appraised in a glance. *Emotion, 5*(4), 498–502.

Olson, M. A., & Fazio, R. H. (2009). Implicit and explicit measures of attitude: The perspective of the MODE model. In R. E. Petty, R. H. Fazio, & P. Brinol (Eds.), *Attitudes: Insights for the new implicit measures* (pp. 19–63). Psychology Press.

Olson-Ayala, L. A., & Patrick, C. J. (2018). Clinical aspects of antisocial personality disorder. In W. J. Livesley & R. Larstone (Eds.), *Handbook of personality disorders: Theory, research, and treatment* (2nd ed., pp. 444–458). Guilford Press.

Olszewski-Kubilius, P., & Corwith, S. (2018). Poverty, academic achievement, and giftedness: A literature review. *Gifted Child Quarterly, 62*(1), 37–55.

O'Malley, D., Quigley, E. M., Dinan, T. G., & Cryan, J. F. (2011). Do interactions between stress and immune responses lead to symptom exacerbations in irritable bowel syndrome? *Brain, Behavior, and Immunity, 25*(7), 1333–1341.

Oman, C. M. (1990). Motion sickness: A synthesis and evaluation of the sensory conflict theory. *Canadian Journal of Physiology and Pharmacology, 68*(2), 294–303.

Oman, D., Shapiro, S. L., Thoresen, C. E., Plante, T. G., & Flinders, T. (2008). Meditation lowers stress and supports forgiveness among college students: A randomized controlled trial. *Journal of American College Health, 56*(5), 569–578.

O'Neal, J. M. (1984). First person account: Finding myself and loving it. *Schizophrenia Bulletin, 10*(1), 109–110.Ong, A. D., & Allaire, J. C. (2005). Cardiovascular intraindividual variability in later life: The influence of social connectedness and positive emotions. *Psychology and Aging, 20*(3), 476–485.

Ong, A. D., & Burrow, A. L. (2017). Microaggressions and daily experience: Depicting life as it is lived. *Perspectives on Psychological Science, 12*(1), 173–175.

Ong, A. D., Burrow, A. L., Fuller-Rowell, T. E., Ja, N. M., & Sue, D. W. (2013). Racial microaggressions and daily well-being among Asian Americans. *Journal of Counseling Psychology, 60*(2), 188–199.

Onken, L. S. (2015). Cognitive training: Targeting cognitive processes in the development of behavioral interventions. *Clinical Psychological Science, 3*(1), 39–44.

Opfer, J. E., & Gelman, S. A. (2011). Development of the animate-inanimate distinction. In U. Goswami (Ed.), *The Wiley-Blackwell handbook of childhood cognitive development* (2nd ed., pp. 213–238). Wiley-Blackwell.

O'Philbin, L., Woods, B., Farrell, E. M., Spector, A. E., & Orrell, M. (2018). Reminiscence therapy for dementia: An abridged Cochrane systematic review of the evidence from randomized controlled trials. *Expert Review of Neurotherapeutics, 18*(9), 715–727.Ophoff, D., Slaats, M. A., Boudewyns, A., Glazemakers, I., Van Hoorenbeeck, K., & Verhulst, S. L. (2018). Sleep disorders during childhood: A practical review. *European Journal of Pediatrics, 177*(5), 641–648.

Orcutt, H. K., Bonanno, G. A., Hannan, S. M., & Miron, L. R. (2014). Prospective trajectories of posttraumatic stress in college women following a campus mass shooting. *Journal of Traumatic Stress, 27*(3), 249–256.

Ordway, M. R., Sadler, L. S., Jeon, S., O'Connell, M., Banasiak, N., Fenick, A. M., Crowley, A. A., Canapari, C., & Redeker, N. S. (2020). Sleep health in young children living with socioeconomic adversity. *Research in Nursing & Health, 43*(4), 329–340. https://doi.org/10.1002/nur.22023

O'Regan, J. K., Rensink, R. A., & Clark, J. J. (1999). Change-blindness as a result of "mudsplashes." *Nature, 398*(6722), 34.

Organ, A., & Fedoroff, J. P. (2015). Sexsomnia: Sleep sex research and its legal implications. *Current Psychiatry Reports, 17*(5), 34.

Orioli, G., Bremner, A. J., & Farroni, T. (2018). Multisensory perception of looming and receding objects in human newborns. *Current Biology, 28*(22), R1294–R1295.

Orlick, T., Zhou, Q. Y., & Partington, J. (1990). Co-operation and conflict within Chinese and Canadian kindergarten settings. *Canadian Journal of Behavioural Science, 22*(1), 20–25.

Orlinsky, D. E. (2017). Unity and diversity among psychotherapies. In A. J. Consoli, L. E. Beutler, & B. Bongar (Eds.), *Comprehensive textbook of psychotherapy: Theory and practice* (2nd ed., pp. 11–30). Oxford University Press.

Orlinsky, D. E., & Howard, K. I. (1995). Unity and diversity among psychotherapies: A comparative perspective. In B. Bongar & L. E. Beutler (Eds.), *Comprehensive textbook of psychotherapy: Theory and practice* (pp. 3–23). Oxford University Press.

Ormont, L. R. (1992). *The group therapy experience: From theory to practice*. St. Martin's Press.

Ornstein, R. M., Rosen, D. S., Mammel, K. A., Callahan, S. T., Forman, S., Jay, M. S., Fisher, M., Rome, E., & Walsh, B. T. (2013). Distribution of eating disorders in children and adolescents using the proposed DSM-5 criteria for feeding and eating disorders. *Journal of Adolescent Health, 53*(2), 303–305.

Orsillo, S. M., Danitz, S. B., & Roemer, L. (2016). Mindfulness- and acceptance-based cognitive and behavioral therapies. In C. M. Nezu & A. M. Nezu (Eds.), *The Oxford handbook of cognitive and behavioral therapies* (pp. 172–199). Oxford University Press.

Orth, U., Erol, R. Y., & Luciano, E. C. (2018). Development of self-esteem from age 4 to 94 years: A meta-analysis of longitudinal studies. *Psychological Bulletin, 144*(10), 1045–1080. http://doi.org/10.1037/bul0000161

Orth, U., & Robins, R. W. (2019). Development of self-esteem across the lifespan. In D. P. McAdams, R. L. Shiner, & J. L. Tackett (Eds.), *Handbook of personality development* (pp. 328–344). Guilford Press.

Ortiz, S. O., & Dynda, A. M. (2005). Use of intelligence tests with culturally and linguistically diverse populations. In D. P. Flanagan & P. L. Harrison (Eds.), *Contemporary intellectual assessment: Theories, tests, and issues* (2nd ed., pp. 545–556). Guilford Press.

Osby, U., Brandt, L., Correia, N., Ekbom, A., & Sparen, P. (2001). Excess mortality in bipolar and unipolar disorder in Sweden. *Archives of General Psychiatry, 58*(9), 844–850.

Osipow, S. H. (2006). Dealing with journal editors and reviewers. In F. T. L. Leong & J. T. Austin (Eds.), *The psychology research handbook: A guide for graduate students and research assistants* (pp. 381–386). Sage.

Oskovi-Kaplan, Z. A., Buyuk, G. N., Ozgu-Erdinc, A. S., Keskin, H. L., Ozbas, A., & Tekin, O. M. (2021). The effect of COVID-19 pandemic and social restrictions on depression rates and maternal attachment in immediate postpartum women: A preliminary study. *Psychiatric Quarterly, 92*(2), 675–682. https://doi.org/10.1007/s11126-020-09843-1

Österman, K., Björkqvist, K., & Wahlbeck, K. (2014). Twenty-eight years after the complete ban on the physical punishment of children in Finland: Trends and psychosocial concomitants. *Aggressive Behavior, 40*(6), 568–581.

Ostir, G. V., Markides, K. S., Peek, M. K., & Goodwin, J. S. (2001). The association between emotional well-being and the incidence of stroke in older adults. *Psychosomatic Medicine, 63*(2), 210–215.

Ó Súilleabháin, P. S., Howard, S., & Hughes, B. M. (2018). Openness to experience and adapting to change: Cardiovascular stress habituation to change in acute stress exposure. *Psychophysiology, 55*(5), e13023.Oswald, T. K., Rumbold, A. R., Kedzior, S. G., & Moore, V. M. (2020). Psychological impacts of "screen time" and "green time" for children and adolescents: A systematic scoping review. *PloS ONE, 15*(9), e0237725. https://doi.org/10.1371/journal.pone.0237725

Otake, K., Shimai, S., Tanaka-Matsumi, J., Otsui, K., & Fredrickson, B. L. (2006). Happy people become happier through kindness: A counting kindnesses intervention. *Journal of Happiness Studies, 7*(3), 361–375.

Ott, D. L., & Michailova, S. (2018). Cultural intelligence: A review and new research avenues. *International Journal of Management Reviews, 20*(1), 99–119.

Otto, M. W., & Applebaum, A. J. (2011). The nature and treatment of bipolar disorder and the bipolar spectrum. In D. H. Barlow (Ed.), *The Oxford handbook of clinical psychology* (pp. 294–310). Oxford University Press.

Otto, R. K., Buffington-Vollum, J. K., & Edens, J. F. (2003). Child custody evaluation. In A. M. Goldstein (Ed.), *Handbook of psychology* (Vol. 11, pp. 179–208). Wiley.

Otto, R. K., & Heilbrun, K. (2002). The practice of forensic psychology: A look toward the future in light of the past. *American Psychologist, 57*(1), 5–18.

Ouellette, S. C., & DiPlacido, J. (2001). Personality's role in the protection and enhancement of health: Where the research has been, where it is stuck, how it might move. In A. Baum, T. A. Revenson, & J. Singer (Eds.), *Handbook of health psychology* (pp. 175–193). Lawrence Erlbaum.

Overmier, J. B., & LoLordo, V. M. (1998). Learned helplessness. In W. O'Donohue (Ed.), *Learning and behavior therapy* (pp. 352–373). Allyn & Bacon.

Overmier, J. B., & Seligman, M. E. P. (1967). Effects of inescapable shock on subsequent escape and avoidance responding. *Journal of Comparative and Physiological Psychology, 63*(1), 28–33.

Overton, W. F. (2006). Developmental psychology: Philosophy, concepts, methodology. In R. M. Lerner (Vol. Ed.), *Handbook of child psychology* (6th ed., Vol. 1, pp. 18–88). Wiley.

Overton, W. F. (2010). Life-span development: Concepts and issues. In W. F. Overton (Ed.), *Handbook of life-span development* (Vol. 1, pp. 1–29). Wiley.

Ovington, L. A., Saliba, A. J., Moran, C. C., Goldring, J., & MacDonald, J. B. (2018). Do people really have insights in the shower? The when, where and who of the aha! moment. *The Journal of Creative Behavior, 52*(1), 21–34.

Owen, J., & Fincham, F. D. (2011). Young adults' emotional reactions after hooking up encounters. *Archives of Sexual Behavior, 40*(2), 321–330.

Owen, J., Tao, K. W., & Drinane, J. M. (2019). Microaggressions: Clinical impact and psychological harm. In G. C. Torino, D. P. Rivera, C. M. Capodilupo, K. L. Nadal, & D. W. Sue (Eds.), *Microaggression theory: Influence and implications* (pp. 65–85). Wiley.

Owen, J., Tao, K. W., Imel, Z. E., Wampold, B. E., & Rodolfa, E. (2014). Addressing racial and ethnic microaggressions in therapy. *Professional Psychology: Research and Practice, 45*(4), 283–290.

Owen, J. J., Tao, K., Leach, M. M., & Rodolfa, E. (2011). Clients' perceptions of their psychotherapists' multicultural orientation. *Psychotherapy (Chic), 48*(3), 274–282.

Owens, E. B., & Hinshaw, S. P. (2019). Adolescent mediators of unplanned pregnancy among women with and without childhood ADHD. *Journal of Clinical Child & Adolescent Psychology, 49*(2), 229–238. https://doi.org/10.1080/15374416.2018.1547970

Owens, E. B., Cardoos, S. L., & Hinshaw, S. P. (2015). Developmental progression and gender differences. In R. A. Barkley (Ed.). *Attention-deficit hyperactivity disorder: A handbook for diagnosis and treatment* (4th ed., pp. 223–255). New York, NY: Guilford Press.

Owens, E. B., Zalecki, C., Gillette, P., & Hinshaw, S. P. (2017). Girls with childhood ADHD as adults: Cross-domain outcomes by diagnostic persistence. *Journal of Consulting and Clinical Psychology, 85*(7), 723–736.

Owens, J. A., Belon, K., & Moss, P. (2010). Impact of delaying school start time on adolescent sleep, mood, and behavior. *Archives of Pediatrics & Adolescent Medicine, 164*(7), 608–614.

Owings-Fonner, N. (2020). Telepsychology expands to meet demand. *Monitor on Psychology, 51*(4). https://www.apa.org/monitor/2020/06/covid-telepsychology

Oyserman, D. (2017). Culture three ways: Culture and subcultures within countries. *Annual Review of Psychology, 68*, 435–463.

Oyserman, D., Coon, H. M., & Kemmelmeier, M. (2002). Rethinking individualism and collectivism: Evaluation of theoretical assumptions and meta-analyses. *Psychological Bulletin, 128*(1), 3–72.

Ozer, D. J., & Benet-Martinez, V. (2006). Personality and the prediction of consequential outcomes. *Annual Review of Psychology, 57*, 401–421.

Ozturk, M. B., & Berber, A. (2020). Racialised professionals' experiences of selective incivility in organisations: A multi-level analysis of subtle racism. *Human Relations, 75*(2), 213–239. https://doi.org/10.1177/0018726720957727

Pace, B. T., Dembe, A., Soma, C. S., Baldwin, S. A., Atkins, D. C., & Imel, Z. E. (2017). A multivariate meta-analysis of motivational interviewing process and outcome. *Psychology of Addictive Behaviors, 31*(5), 524–533.

Pachankis, J. E., & Bränström, R. (2018). Hidden from happiness: Structural stigma, sexual orientation concealment, and life satisfaction across 28 countries. *Journal of Consulting and Clinical Psychology, 86*(5), 403–415. https://doi.org/10.1037/ccp0000299

Pachankis, J. E., Mahon, C. P., Jackson, S. D., Fetzner, B. K., & Bränström, R. (2020). Sexual orientation concealment and mental health: A conceptual and meta-analytic review. *Psychological Bulletin, 146*(10), 831–871. https://doi.org/10.1037/bul0000271

Packer, D. J. (2009). Avoiding groupthink: Whereas weakly identified members remain silent, strongly identified members dissent about collective problems. *Psychological Science, 20*(5), 546–548.

Packer, D. J., Fujita, K., & Chasteen, A. L. (2014). The motivational dynamics of dissent decisions: A goal-conflict approach. *Social Psychological and Personality Science, 5*(1), 27–34.

Packer, D. J., Miners, C. T., & Ungson, N. D. (2018). Benefiting from diversity: How groups' coordinating mechanisms affect leadership opportunities for marginalized individuals. *Journal of Social Issues, 74*(1), 56–74.

Padgett, D. K., Patrick, C., Burns, B. J., & Schlesinger, H. J. (1994). Ethnicity and the use of outpatient mental health services in a national insured population. *American Journal of Public Health, 84*(2), 222–226.

Padilla, A. M., & Borrero, N. E. (2006). Acculturative stress. In P. T. P. Wong & L. C. J. Wong (Eds.), *Handbook of multicultural perspectives on stress and coping* (pp. 299–318). Springer Science+Business Media.

Padilla, A. M., & Olmedo, E. (2009). Synopsis of key persons, events, and associations in the history of Latino psychology. *Cultural Diversity and Ethnic Minority Psychology, 15*(4), 363–373.

Padilla-Walker, L. M., Coyne, S. M., Collier, K. M., & Nielson, M. G. (2015). Longitudinal relations between prosocial television content and adolescents' prosocial and aggressive behavior: The mediating role of empathic concern and self-regulation. *Developmental Psychology, 51*(9), 1317–1328.

Pagani, L., Tremblay, R., Nagin, D., Zoccolillo, M., Vitaro, F., & McDuff, P. (2004). Risk factor models for adolescent verbal and physical aggression toward mothers. *International Journal of Behavioral Development, 28*(6), 528–537.

Pagani, L., Tremblay, R. E., Nagin, D., Zoccolillo, M., Vitaro, F., & McDuff, P. (2009). Risk factor models for adolescent verbal and physical aggression toward fathers. *Journal of Family Violence, 24*(3), 173–182.

Page, J., Lustenberger, C., & Fröhlich, F. (2018). Social, motor, and cognitive development through the lens of sleep network dynamics in infants and toddlers between 12 and 30 months of age. *Sleep, 41*(4), zsy024.

Page, L., & Page, K. (2010). Last shall be first: A field study of biases in sequential performance evaluation on the Idol series. *Journal of Economic Behavior & Organization, 73*(2), 186–198.

Pager, D., & Shepherd, H. (2008). The sociology of discrimination: Racial discrimination in employment, housing, credit, and consumer markets. *Annual Review of Sociology, 34*, 181–209.

Pagliano, P. J. (2012). *The multisensory handbook: A guide for children and adults with sensory learning disabilities*. Routledge.

Pagura, J., Cox, B. J., & Enns, M. W. (2009). Personality factors in the anxiety disorders. In M. M. Antony & M. B. Stein (Eds.), *Oxford handbook of anxiety and related disorders* (pp. 190–208). Oxford University Press.

Paine, S. J., Gander, P. H., Harris, R., & Reid, P. (2004). Who reports insomnia? Relationships with age, sex, ethnicity, and socioeconomic deprivation. *Sleep, 27*(6), 1163–1169.

Pakenham, K. I. (2011). Benefit-finding and sense-making in chronic illness. In S. Folkman (Ed.), *Oxford handbook of stress, health, and coping* (pp. 242–268). Oxford University Press.

Pakkenberg, B., & Gundersen, H. J. G. (1997). Neocortical neuron number in humans: Effect of sex and age. *Journal of Comparative Neurology, 384*(2), 312–320.

Paller, K. A., Creery, J. D., and Schechtman, E. (2021). Memory and sleep: How sleep cognition can change the waking mind for the better. *Annual Review of Psychology, 72*(1), 123–150. https://doi.org/10.1146/annurev-psych-010419-050815

Palmiero, M., Nakatani, C., & van Leeuwen, C. (2017). Visual creativity across cultures: A comparison between Italians and Japanese. *Creativity Research Journal, 29*(1), 86–90.

Palomares, J. K. S., & Young, A. W. (2018). Facial first impressions of partner preference traits: Trustworthiness, status, and attractiveness. *Social Psychological and Personality Science, 9*(8), 990–1000.

Panksepp, J., Siviy, S., & Normansell, L. A. (1985). Brain opioids and social emotion. In M. Reite & T. Field (Eds.), *The psychobiology of attachment and separation* (pp. 3–49). Academic Press.

Pantalone, D. W., Iwamasa, G. Y., & Martell, C. R. (2010). Cognitive-behavioral therapy with diverse populations. In K. Dobson (Ed.). *Handbook of cognitive-behavioral therapies* (pp. 445–462). Guilford Press.

Papafragou, A. (2007). Space and language-cognition interface. In P. Carruthers, S. Laurence, & S. Stich (Eds.), *The innate mind: Foundations and the future* (pp. 272–292). Oxford University Press.

Papagno, C. (1998). Transient retrograde amnesia associated with impaired naming of living categories. *Cortex, 34*(1), 111–121.

Papp, L. A. (2010). Phenomenology of generalized anxiety disorder. In D. J. Stein, E. Hollander, & B. O. Rothbaum (Eds.), *Textbook of anxiety disorders* (2nd ed., pp. 159–171). American Psychiatric Association Publishing.

Paquette, V., Lévesque, J., Mensour, B., Leroux, J. M., Beaudoin, G., Bourgouin, P., & Beauregard, M. (2003). "Change the mind and you change the brain": Effects of cognitive-behavioral therapy on the neural correlates of spider phobia. *Neuroimage, 18*(2), 401–409.

Paranjpe, A. C. (2006). From tradition through colonialism to globalization: Reflections on the history of psychology in India. In A. C. Brock (Ed.), *Internationalizing the history of psychology* (pp. 56–74). New York University Press.

Parcesepe, A. M., & Cabassa, L. J. (2013). Public stigma of mental illness in the United States: A systematic literature review. *Administration and Policy in Mental Health and Mental Health Services Research, 40*(5), 384–399. https://doi.org/10.1007/s10488-012-0430-z

Pardo, J. V., Lee, J. T., Sheikh, S. A., Surerus-Johnson, C., Shah, H., Munch, K. R., Carlis, J. V., Lewis, S. M., Kuskowski, M. A., & Dysken, M. W. (2007). Where the brain grows old: Decline in anterior cingulate and medial prefrontal function with normal aging. *Neuroimage, 35*(3), 1231–1237.

Pargament, K. I. (2011). Religion and coping: The current state of knowledge. In S. Folkman (Ed.), *Oxford handbook of stress, health, and coping* (pp. 269–288). Oxford University Press.

Paris, J. (2004). Gender differences in personality traits and disorders. *Current Psychiatry Reports, 6*(5), 71–74.

Paris, J. (2007). The nature of borderline personality disorder: Multiple dimensions, multiple symptoms, but one category. *Journal of Personality Disorders, 21*(5), 457–473.
Paris, J. (2009). Borderline personality disorder. In P. H. Blaney & T. Millon (Eds.), *Oxford textbook of psychopathology* (2nd ed., pp. 723–737). Oxford University Press.
Paris, J. (2013a). Preface. In J. Paris & J. Phillips (Eds.), *Making the DSM-5: Concepts and controversies* (pp. v–vi). Springer Science+Business Media.
Paris, J. (2013b). *The intelligent clinician's guide to DSM-5.* Oxford University Press.
Paris, J. (2018). Clinical features of borderline personality disorder. In W. J. Livesley & R. Larstone (Eds.), *Handbook of personality disorders: Theory, research, and treatment* (2nd ed., pp. 419–425). Guilford Press.
Park, C. L. (2011). Meaning, coping, and health and well-being. In S. Folkman (Ed.), *Oxford handbook of stress, health, and coping* (pp. 227–241). Oxford University Press.
Park, C. L., Finkelstein-Fox, L., Russell, B. S., Fendrich, M., Hutchison, M., & Becker, J. (2021). Psychological resilience early in the COVID-19 pandemic: Stressors, resources, and coping strategies in a national sample of Americans. *American Psychologist.* Advance online publication. https://doi.org/10.1037/amp0000813
Park, D. C., Lautenschlager, G., Hedden, T., Davidson, N. S., Smith, A. D., & Smith, P. K. (2002). Models of visuospatial and verbal memory across the adult life span. *Psychology and Aging, 17*(2), 299–320.
Park, E. J., Kikutani, M., Yogo, M., Suzuki, N., & Lee, J. H. (2018). Influence of culture on categorical structure of emotional words: Comparison between Japanese and Korean. *Journal of Cross-Cultural Psychology, 49*(9), 1340–1357.
Park, H., & Reder, L. M. (2004). Moses illusion. In R. F. Pohl (Ed.), *Cognitive illusions: A handbook on fallacies and biases in thinking, judgement, and memory* (pp. 275–291). Psychology Press.
Park, N., Lee, S., & Kim, J. H. (2012). Individuals' personal network characteristics and patterns of Facebook use: A social network approach. *Computers in Human Behavior, 28*(5), 1700–1707.
Parker, J. G., & Asher, S. R. (1987). Peer relations and later personal adjustment: Are low-accepted children at risk? *Psychological Bulletin, 102*(3), 357–389.
Parker, J. G., & Asher, S. R. (1993). Friendship and friendship quality in middle childhood: Links with peer group acceptance and feelings of loneliness and social dissatisfaction. *Developmental Psychology, 29*(4), 611–621.
Parker, L. A. (2014). Conditioned taste aversion learning: Relationship to nausea and conditioned disgust. In F. K. McSweeney & E. S. Murphy (Eds.), *The Wiley-Blackwell handbook of operant and classical conditioning* (pp. 97–116). Wiley.
Parrott, D. J., & Eckhardt, C. I. (2018). Effects of alcohol on human aggression. *Current Opinion in Psychology, 19,* 1–5.
Parrott, W. G., & Gleitman, H. (1989). Infants' expectations in play: The joy of peek-a-boo. *Cognition & Emotion, 3*(4), 291–311.
Parsons, C. E., Crane, C., Parsons, L. J., Fjorback, L. O., & Kuyken, W. (2017). Home practice in mindfulness-based cognitive therapy and mindfulness-based stress reduction: A systematic review and meta-analysis of participants' mindfulness practice and its association with outcomes. *Behaviour Research and Therapy, 95,* 29–41.
Pascalis, O., de Schonen, S., Morton, J., Deruelle, C., & Fabre-Grenet, M. (1995). Mother's face recognition by neonates: A replication and an extension. *Infant Behavior and Development, 18*(1), 79–85.
Pascoe, M. C., Thompson, D. R., Jenkins, Z. M., & Ski, C. F. (2017). Mindfulness mediates the physiological markers of stress: Systematic review and meta-analysis. *Journal of Psychiatric Research, 95,* 156–178.
Pascual, A., Carpenter, C. J., Guéguen, N., & Girandola, F. (2016). A meta-analysis of the effectiveness of the low-ball compliance-gaining procedure. *Revue Européenne de Psychologie Appliquée/European Review of Applied Psychology, 66*(5), 261–267.
Pascual, A., & Guéguen, N. (2005). Foot-in-the-door and door-in-the-face: A comparative meta-analytic study. *Psychological Reports, 96*(1), 122–128.
Pascual-Leone, A., & Torres, F. (1993). Sensorimotor cortex representation of the reading finger in Braille readers: An example of activity-induced cerebral plasticity in humans. *Brain, 116*(1), 39–52.
Pass, J. J. (2007). Industrial/organizational (I/O) psychology as a career: Improving workforce performance and retention. In R. J. Sternberg (Ed.), *Career paths in psychology: Where your degree can take you* (2nd ed., pp. 249–257). American Psychological Association.
Pasterski, V., Golombok, S., & Hines, M. (2011). Sex differences in social behavior. In P. K. Smith & C. H. Hart (Eds.), *The Wiley-Blackwell handbook of childhood social development* (2nd ed., pp. 281–298). Wiley-Blackwell.
Patchin, J. W. (2016). 2016 Cyberbullying data. Cyberbullying Research Center. https://cyberbullying.org/2016-cyberbullying-data
Patel, K. C. (2012). Eastern traditions, consciousness, and spirituality. In L. J. Miller (Ed.), *The Oxford handbook of psychology and spirituality* (pp. 343– 359). Oxford University Press.
Patihis, L., Ho, L. Y., Loftus, E. F., & Herrera, M. E. (2021). Memory experts' beliefs about repressed memory. *Memory, 29*(6), 823–828. https://doi.org/10.1080/09658211.2018.1532521
Patrick, C. J. (2007). Antisocial personality disorder and psychopathy. In W. O'Donohue, K. A. Fowler, & S. O. Lilienfeld (Eds.), *Personality disorders: Toward the DSM-V* (pp. 109–166). Sage.
Patrick, C. J., & Brislin, S. J. (2018). Theoretical perspectives on psychopathy and antisocial personality disorder. In W. J. Livesley & R. Larstone (Eds.), *Handbook of personality disorders: Theory, research, and treatment* (2nd ed., pp. 426–443). Guilford Press.
Patterson, C. J., & Potter, E. C. (2019). Sexual orientation and sleep difficulties: A review of research. *Sleep Health, 5*(3), 227–235. https://doi.org/10.1016/j.sleh.2019.02.004
Patterson, C. J., & Potter, E. C. (2020). Sexual orientation and sleep difficulties: Evidence from the National Health and Nutrition Examination (NHANES). *Journal of Bisexuality, 20*(1), 1–18. https://doi.org/10.1080/15299716.2020.1729288
Patterson, J. (2016). Aubrey Plaza: "Things take on a different meaning when death comes so close." *The Guardian.* https://www.theguardian.com/culture/2016/aug/04/aubrey-plaza-mike-dave-different-meaning-death-so-close
Pattie, F. A. (1994). *Mesmer and animal magnetism: A chapter in the history of medicine.* Edmonston.
Paul, G. L. (2007). Psychotherapy outcome can be studied scientifically. In S. O. Lilienfeld & W. T. O'Donohue (Eds.), *The great ideas of clinical science: 17 principles that every mental health professional should understand* (pp. 119–147). Routledge.
Paulhus, D. L., Trapnell, P. D., & Chen, D. (1999). Birth order effects on personality and achievement within families. *Psychological Science, 10*(6), 482–488.
Paunonen, S. V., & Jackson, D. N. (2000). What is beyond the big five? Plenty! *Journal of Personality, 68*(5), 821–835.
Paus, T. (2009). Brain development. In R. M. Lerner & L. Steinberg (Eds.), *Handbook of adolescent psychology* (3rd ed., Vol. 1, pp. 95–115). Wiley.
Pause, B. M., Sojka, B., Krauel, K., Fehm-Wolfsdorf, G., & Ferstl, R. (1996). Olfactory information processing during the course of the menstrual cycle. *Biological Psychology, 44*(1), 31–54.
Pavlov, I. P. (1927). *Conditioned reflexes: An investigation of the physiological activity of the cerebral cortex.* Oxford University Press.
Pavlov, I. P. (1928). *Lectures on conditioned reflexes.* Liveright.
Pazzona, R., Guicciardi, M., & Murgia, M. (2018). The inattentional blindness in soccer referees. *Medicina Dello Sport, 71*(71), 216–225.
Pearce, L. J., & Field, A. P. (2016), The impact of "scary" TV and film on children's internalizing emotions: A meta-analysis. *Human Communication Research, 42*(1), 98–121.
Pearce, L., & Cooper, J. (2021). Fostering COVID-19 safe behaviors using cognitive dissonance. Basic and Applied *Social Psychology, 43*(5), 267–282. https://doi.org/10.1080/01973533.2021.1953497
Pearce, S. (2019). "It was the small things": Using the concept of racial microaggressions as a tool for talking to new teachers about racism. *Teaching and Teacher Education, 79,* 83–92.
Pearson, J. D., Morrell, C. H., Gordon-Salant, S., Brant, L. J., Metter, E. J., Klein, L. L., & Fozard, J. L. (1995). Gender differences in a longitudinal study of age-associated hearing loss. *The Journal of the Acoustical Society of America, 97*(2), 1196–1205.
Pearson, K. G., & Gordon, J. E. (2013). Spinal reflexes. In E. R. Kandel, J. H. Schwartz, T. M. Jessell, S. A. Siegelbaum, & A. J. Hudspeth (Eds.), *Principles of neural science* (5th ed., pp. 790–811). McGraw-Hill.
Pearson, P. (2008). *A brief history of anxiety [yours and mine].* Bloomsbury USA.
Pedersen, C. B. (2015). Persons with schizophrenia migrate towards urban areas due to the development of their disorder or its prodromata. *Schizophrenia Research, 168*(1–2), 204–208.
Pedersen, D. M., & Wheeler, J. (1983). The Müller-Lyer illusion among Navajos. *The Journal of Social Psychology, 121*(1), 3–6.
Pedersen, N. L., McClearn, G. E., Plomin, R., & Nesselroade, J. R. (1991). The Swedish adoption/twin study of aging: An update. *Acta Geneticae Medicae et Gemellologiae: Twin Research, 40*(1), 7–20.
Pedersen, N. L., Plomin, R., McClearn, G. E., & Friberg, L. (1988). Neuroticism, extraversion, and related traits in adult twins reared apart and reared together. *Journal of Personality and Social Psychology, 55*(6), 950–957.
Pedersen, P. (1990). The multicultural perspective as a fourth force in counseling. *Journal of Mental Health Counseling, 12*(1), 93–95.
Pedersen, P. (1999). *Multiculturalism as a fourth force.* Brunner/Mazel.
Pedersen, P. B. (2008). Ethics, competence, and professional issues in cross-cultural counseling. In P. B. Pedersen, J. G. Draguns, W. J. Lonner, & J. E. Trimble (Eds.), *Counseling across cultures* (6th ed., pp. 5–20). Sage.
Pedersen, S. S., & Denollet, J. (2003). Type D personality, cardiac events, and impaired quality of life: A review. *European Journal of Cardiovascular Prevention & Rehabilitation, 10*(4), 241–248.
Pedersen, S. S., & Denollet, J. (2006). Is Type D personality here to stay? Emerging evidence across cardiovascular disease patient groups. *Current Cardiology Reviews, 2*(3), 205–213.
Pederson, E., Danziger, E., Wilkins, D., Levinson, S., Kita, S., & Senft, G. (1998). Semantic typology and spatial conceptualization. *Language, 74*(3), 557–589.
Peigneux, P., Schmitz, R., & Urbain, C. (2010). Sleeping and forgetting. In S. Della Sala (Ed.), *Forgetting* (pp. 165–184). Psychology Press.
Peigneux, P., Urbain, C., & Schmitz, R. (2012). Sleep and the brain. In C. M. Morin & C. A. Espie (Eds.), *The Oxford handbook of sleep and sleep disorders* (pp. 11–37). Oxford University Press.
Peiris, N., Blasini, M., Wright, T., & Colloca, L. (2018). The placebo phenomenon: A narrow focus on psychological models. *Perspectives in Biology and Medicine, 61*(3), 388–400.
Pelayo, R., & Lopes, M. C. (2006). Narcolepsy. In T. L. Lee-Chiong (Ed.), *Sleep: A comprehensive handbook* (pp. 145–150). Wiley-Liss.
Pelham III, W. E., Page, T. F., Altszuler, A. R., Gnagy, E. M., Molina, B. S., & Pelham Jr, W. E. (2020). The long-term financial outcome of children diagnosed with ADHD. *Journal of Consulting and Clinical Psychology, 88*(2), 160–171. https://doi.org/10.1037/ccp0000461
Pellegrini, A. D., Long, J. D., Roseth, C. J., Bohn, C. M., & Van Ryzin, M. (2007). A short-term longitudinal study of preschoolers' (*Homo sapiens*) sex segregation: The role of physical activity, sex, and time. *Journal of Comparative Psychology, 121*(3), 282–289.
Penades, R., Boget, T., Lomena, F., Mateos, J. J., Catalan, R., Gasto, C., & Salamero, M. (2002). Could the hypofrontality pattern in schizophrenia be modified through neuropsychological rehabilitation? *Acta Psychiatrica Scandinavica, 105*(3), 202–208.
Penev, P. D. (2007). Sleep deprivation and energy metabolism: To sleep, perchance to eat? *Current Opinion in Endocrinology, Diabetes and Obesity, 14*(5), 374–381.
Peng, P., Barnes, M., Wang, C., Wang, W., Li, S., Swanson, H. L., Dardick, W., & Tao, S. (2018). A meta-analysis on the relation between reading and working memory. *Psychological Bulletin, 144*(1), 48.
Penhollow, T., Young, M., & Bailey, W. (2007). Relationship between religiosity and "hooking up" behavior. *American Journal of Health Education, 38*(6), 338–345.
Penley, J. A., Tomaka, J., & Wiebe, J. S. (2002). The association of coping to physical and psychological health outcomes: A meta-analytic review. *Journal of Behavioral Medicine, 25*(6), 551–603.
Penney, T. L., & Kirk, S. F. (2015). The Health at Every Size paradigm and obesity: Missing empirical evidence may help push the reframing obesity debate forward. *American Journal of Public Health, 105*(5), e38–e42.
Penny, H., & Haddock, G. (2007). Anti-fat prejudice among children: The "mere proximity" effect in 5–10 year olds. *Journal of Experimental Social Psychology, 43*(4), 678–683.
Pennycook, G., McPhetres, J., Zhang, Y., Lu, J. G., & Rand, D. G. (2020). Fighting COVID-19 misinformation on social media: Experimental evidence for a scalable accuracy-nudge intervention. *Psychological Science, 31*(7), 770-780. https://doi.org/10.1177/0956797620939054
Pennycook, G., & Rand, D. G. (2020). Who falls for fake news? The roles of bullshit receptivity, overclaiming, familiarity, and analytic thinking. *Journal of Personality, 88*(2), 185–200. https://doi.org/10.1111/jopy.12476
Pentina, I., Bailey, A. A., & Zhang, L. (2018). Exploring effects of source similarity, message valence, and receiver regulatory focus on Yelp review persuasiveness and purchase intentions. *Journal of Marketing Communications, 24*(2), 125–145.
Peplau, L. A. (2003). Human sexuality: How do men and women differ? *Current Directions in Psychological Science, 12*(2), 37–40.
Peplau, L. A., & Fingerhut, A. W. (2007). The close relationships of lesbians and gay men. *Annual Review of Psychology, 58,* 405–424.
Peplau, L. A., & Garnets, L. D. (2000). A new paradigm for understanding women's sexuality and sexual orientation. *Journal of Social Issues, 56*(2), 330–350.
Peppard, P. E., & Hagen, E. W. (2018). The last 25 years of obstructive sleep apnea epidemiology—and the next 25? *American Journal of Respiratory and Critical Care Medicine, 197*(3), 310–312.
Pepperberg, I. M., Koepke, A., Livingston, P., Girard, M., & Hartsfield, L. A. (2013). Reasoning by inference: Further studies on exclusion in grey parrots (*Psittacus erithacus*). *Journal of Comparative Psychology, 127*(3), 272–281.

Perales, M. A., Drake, E. K., Pemmaraju, N., & Wood, W. A. (2016). Social media and the adolescent and young adult (AYA) patient with cancer. *Current Hematologic Malignancy Reports, 11*(6), 449–455.

Pérez, J. C., Petrides, K. V., & Furnham, A. (2005). Measuring trait emotional intelligence. In R. Schulze & R. D. Roberts (Eds.), *Emotional intelligence: An international handbook* (pp. 181–201). Hogrefe & Huber.

Perez-Albeniz, A., & de Paul, J. (2003). Dispositional empathy in high- and low-risk parents for child physical abuse. *Child Abuse & Neglect, 27*(7), 769–780.

Pérez-Rojas, A. E., Lockard, A. J., Bartholomew, T. T., Janis, R. A., Carney, D. M., Xiao, H., Youn, S. J., Scofield, B. E., Locke, B. D., Castonguay, L. G., & Hayes, J. A. (2017). Presenting concerns in counseling centers: The view from clinicians on the ground. *Psychological Services, 14*(4), 416–427.

Perlis, M. L., Giles, D. E., Mendelson, W. B., Bootzin, R. R., & Wyatt, J. K. (1997). Psychophysiological insomnia: The behavioural model and a neurocognitive perspective. *Journal of Sleep Research, 6*(3), 179–188.

Pernanen, K. (1991). *Alcohol in human violence*. Guilford Press.

Perner, J. (1999). Theory of mind. In M. Bennett (Ed.), *Developmental psychology: Achievements and prospects* (pp. 205–230). Psychology Press.

Perner, J., Leekam, S. R., & Wimmer, H. (1987). Three-year-olds' difficulty with false belief: The case for a conceptual deficit. *British Journal of Developmental Psychology, 5*(2), 125–137.

Perri, M. G., & Corsica, J. A. (2002). Improving the maintenance of weight lost in behavioral treatment of obesity. In *Handbook of obesity treatment* (pp. 357–379). Guilford Press.

Perrin, J. S., Hervé, P. Y., Leonard, G., Perron, M., Pike, G. B., Pitiot, A., Richer, L., Veillette, S., Pausova, Z., & Paus, T. (2008). Growth of white matter in the adolescent brain: Role of testosterone and androgen receptor. *The Journal of Neuroscience, 28*(38), 9519–9524.

Perry, B. L., Harp, K. L., & Oser, C. B. (2013). Racial and gender discrimination in the stress process: Implications for African American women's health and well-being. *Sociological Perspectives, 56*(1), 25–48.

Perszyk, D. R., & Waxman, S. R. (2018). Linking language and cognition in infancy. *Annual Review of Psychology, 69*, 231–250.

Pervin, L. A. (1994). A critical analysis of current trait theory. *Psychological Inquiry, 5*(2), 103–113.

Pesant, N., & Zadra, A. (2004). Working with dreams in therapy: What do we know and what should we do? *Clinical Psychology Review, 24*(5), 489–512.

Pescosolido, B. A. (2013). The public stigma of mental illness: What do we think; what do we know; what can we prove? *Journal of Health and Social behavior, 54*(1), 1–21. https://doi.org/10.1177/0022146512471197

Pescosolido, B. A. (2013). The public stigma of mental illness: What do we think; what do we know; what can we prove? *Journal of Health and Social behavior, 54*(1), 1–21. https://doi.org/10.1177/0022146512471197

Pescosolido, B. A., Manago, B., & Monahan, J. (2019). Evolving public views on the likelihood of violence from people with mental illness: Stigma and its consequences. *Health Affairs, 38*(10), 1735–1743. https://10.1377/hlthaff.2019.00702

Pescosolido, B. A., Martin, J. K., Lang, A., & Olafsdottir, S. (2008). Rethinking theoretical approaches to stigma: A framework integrating normative influences on stigma (FINIS). *Social Science & Medicine, 67*(3), 431–440. https://doi.org/10.1016/j.socscimed.2008.03.018

Pescosolido, B. A., Medina, T. R., Martin, J. K., & Long, J. S. (2013). The "backbone" of stigma: Identifying the global core of public prejudice associated with mental illness. *American Journal of Public Health, 103*(5), 853–860. https://doi.org/10.2105/AJPH.2012.301147

Pesonen, A. K., Lipsanen, J., Halonen, R., Elovainio, M., Sandman, N., Mäkelä, J. M., Béchard, D., Ollila,, H. M., & Kuula, L. (2020). Pandemic dreams: Network analysis of dream content during the COVID-19 lockdown. *Frontiers in Psychology, 11*, 2569. https://doi.org/10.3389/fpsyg.2020.573961

Pesta, B. J., Bertsch, S., McDaniel, M. A., Mahoney, C. B., & Poznanski, P. J. (2012). Differential epidemiology: IQ, neuroticism, and chronic disease by the 50 U.S. states. *Intelligence, 40*(2), 107–114.

Peter, B. (2005). Gassner's exorcism—not Mesmer's magnetism—is the real predecessor of modern hypnosis. *International Journal of Clinical and Experimental Hypnosis, 53*(1), 1–12.

Peter, M., Vingerhoets, A. J., & Van Heck, G. L. (2001). Personality, gender, and crying. *European Journal of Personality, 15*(1), 19–28.

Peters, A. J., Liu, H., & Komiyama, T. (2017). Learning in the rodent motor cortex. *Annual Review of Neuroscience, 40*, 77–97.

Peters, R., & McGee, R. (1982). Cigarette smoking and state-dependent memory. *Psychopharmacology, 76*(3), 232–235.

Petersen, J., & Hyde, J. S. (2010a). Gender differences in sexuality. In J. C. Chrisler & D. R. McCreary (Eds.), *Handbook of gender research in psychology* (Vol. 1, pp. 471–491). Springer Science+Business Media.

Petersen, J. L., & Hyde, J. S. (2010b). A meta-analytic review of research on gender differences in sexuality, 1993–2007. *Psychological Bulletin, 136*(1), 21–38.

Peterson, C. (2006). Writing rough drafts. In F. T. L. Leong & J. T. Austin (Eds.), *The psychology research handbook: A guide for graduate students and research assistants* (pp. 360–370). Sage.

Peterson, L. R. (1966). Short-term verbal memory and learning. *Psychological Review, 73*(3), 193–207.

Peterson, L., & Peterson, M. J. (1959). Short-term retention of individual verbal items. *Journal of Experimental Psychology, 58*(3), 193–198.

Peterson, M. A. (2001). Object perception. In E. B. Goldstein (Ed.), *Blackwell handbook of perception* (pp. 168–203). Oxford, UK: Blackwell.

Petit, D., Pennestri, M. H., Paquet, J., Desautels, A., Zadra, A., Vitaro, F., & Montplaisir, J. (2015). Childhood sleepwalking and sleep terrors: A longitudinal study of prevalence and familial aggregation. *JAMA Pediatrics, 169*(7), 653–658.

Petraglia, J., Bhatia, M., & Drapeau, M. (2017). Ten principles to guide psychodynamic technique with defense mechanisms: An examination of theory, research, and clinical implications. *Journal of Psychology and Psychotherapy*, 7(288), 2161–0487.

Petrides, K. V., Mikolajczak, M., Mavroveli, S., Sanchez-Ruiz, M. J., Furnham, A., & Pérez-González, J. C. (2016). Developments in trait emotional intelligence research. *Emotion Review, 8*(4), 335–341.

Petrie, K. J., Cameron, L. D., Ellis, C. J., Buick, D., & Weinman, J. (2002). Changing illness perceptions after myocardial infarction: An early intervention randomized controlled trial. *Psychosomatic Medicine, 64*(4), 580–586.

Petrie, K., & Weinman, J. (2006). Why illness perceptions matter. *Clinical Medicine, 6*(6), 536–539.

Petry, N. M., Alessi, S. M., & Rash, C. J. (2013). Contingency management treatments decrease psychiatric symptoms. *Journal of Consulting and Clinical Psychology, 81*(5), 926–931.

Petry, N. M., & O'Brien, C. P. (2013). Internet gaming disorder and the DSM-5 [Editorial]. *Addiction, 108*(7), 1186–1187. https://doi.org/10.1111/add.12162

Petscher, E. S., Rey, C., & Bailey, J. S. (2009). A review of empirical support for differential reinforcement of alternative behavior. *Research in Developmental Disabilities, 30*(3), 409–425.

Pettigrew, T. F. (1997). Generalized intergroup contact effects on prejudice. *Personality and Social Psychology Bulletin, 23*(2), 173–185.

Pettigrew, T. F., & Tropp, L. R. (2006). A meta-analytic test of intergroup contact theory. *Journal of Personality and Social Psychology, 90*(5), 751–783.

Petty, R. E., & Briñol, P. (2012). The elaboration likelihood model. In P. A. M. Van Lange, A. W. Kruglanski, & E. T. Higgins (Eds.), *Handbook of theories of social psychology* (Vol. 1, pp. 224–245). Sage.

Petty, R. E., & Cacioppo, J. T. (1986). The elaboration likelihood model of persuasion. *Advances in Experimental Social Psychology, 19*(1), 123–205.

Petty, R. E., Fazio, R. H., & Brinol, P. (Eds.). (2009a). *Attitudes: Insights from the new implicit measures*. Psychology Press.

Petty, R. E., Fazio, R. H., & Brinol, P. (2009b). The new implicit measures. In R. E. Petty, R. H. Fazio, & P. Brinol (Eds.), *Attitudes: Insights from the new implicit measures* (pp. 3–18). Psychology Press.

Petty, R. E., Haugtvedt, C. P., & Smith, S. M. (1995). Elaboration as a determinant of attitude strength: Creating attitudes that are persistent, resistant, and predictive of behavior. In R. E. Petty & J. A. Krosnick (Eds.), *Attitude strength: Antecedents and consequences* (pp. 93–130). Erlbaum Associates.

Petty, R. E., Wegener, D. T., & Fabrigar, L. R. (1997). Attitudes and attitude change. *Annual Review of Psychology, 48*(1), 609–647.

Pew Research Center. (2018). Demographic and economic trends in urban, suburban and rural communities. https://www.pewresearch.org/social-trends/2018/05/22/demographic-and-economic-trends-in-urban-suburban-and-rural-communities/

Pew Research Center. (2019). In U.S., decline of Christianity continues at rapid pace. http://www.pewforum.org/2019/10/17/in-u-s-decline-of-christianity-continues-at-rapid-pace/

Pfiffner, L. J., & Haack, L. M. (2015). Nonpharmacologic treatments for childhood attention-deficit/hyperactivity disorder and their combination with medication. In P. E. Nathan & J. M. Gorman (Eds.), *A guide to treatments that work* (4th ed., pp. 55–84). Oxford University Press.

Phan, K. L., Wager, T., Taylor, S. F., & Liberzon, I. (2002). Functional neuroanatomy of emotion: A meta-analysis of emotion activation studies in PET and fMRI. *Neuroimage, 16*(2), 331–348.

Phelps, E. A. (2006). Emotion and cognition: Insights from studies of the human amygdala. *Annual Review of Psychology, 57*, 27–53.

Phelps, E. A., & LeDoux, J. E. (2005). Contributions of the amygdala to emotion processing: From animal models to human behavior. *Neuron, 48*(2), 175–187.

Phelps, L., Johnston, L. S., Jimenez, D. P., Wilczenski, F. L., Andrea, R. K., & Healy, R. W. (1993). Figure preference, body dissatisfaction, and body distortion in adolescence. *Journal of Adolescent Research, 8*(3), 297–310.

Phillips, J. (2013). The conceptual status of DSM-5 diagnoses. In J. Paris & J. Phillips (Eds.), *Making the DSM-5: Concepts and controversies* (pp. 159–175). Springer Science+Business Media.

Phillips, K. (2009, July 23). Blogtalk: Gates, Obama, race and the police. *The New York Times*. http://thecaucus.blogs.nytimes.com/2009/07/23/blogtalk-gates-obama-race-and-the-police/

Philpot, L. M., Ramar, P., Roellinger, D. L., Barry, B. A., Sharma, P., & Ebbert, J. O. (2021). Changes in social relationships during an initial "stay-at-home" phase of the COVID-19 pandemic: A longitudinal survey study in the US. *Social Science & Medicine, 274*, 113779. https://doi.org/10.1016/j.socscimed.2021.113779

Photos, V. I., Michel, B. D., & Nock, M. K. (2008). Single-case research. In M. Hersen & A. M. Gross (Eds.), *Handbook of clinical psychology* (Vol. 1, pp. 224–245). Wiley.

Piaget, J. (1924). *Judgment and reasoning in the child*. Kegan Paul.

Piaget, J. (1926). *The language and thought of the child*. Harcourt, Brace.

Piaget, J. (1929). *The child's conception of the world*. Routledge and Kegan Paul.

Piaget, J. (1936/1952). *The origins of intelligence in children*. International University Press.

Piaget, J. (1954). *The construction of reality in the child*. Basic Books.

Piaget, J. (1983). Piaget's theory. In P. Mussen (Ed.), *Handbook of child psychology* (4th ed., Vol. 1, pp. 103–128). Wiley.

Piaget, J., & Inhelder, B. (1969). *The psychology of the child*. Basic Books.

Picillo, M., De Rosa, A., Pellecchia, M. T., Criscuolo, C., Amboni, M., Erro, R., Bonifati, V., De Michele, G., & Barone, P. (2015). Olfaction in homozygous and heterozygous SYNJ1 Arg258Gln mutation carriers. *Movement Disorders Clinical Practice, 2*(4), 413–416.

Pickles, J. O. (2013). *An introduction to the physiology of hearing* (4th ed.). Brill.

Pickrell, J. E., Bernstein, D. M., & Loftus, E. F. (2004). Misinformation effect. In R. F. Pohl (Ed.), *Cognitive illusions: Handbook on fallacies and biases in thinking, judgement, and memory* (pp. 345–361). Psychology Press.

Pickren, W. E., & Burchett, C. (2014). Making psychology inclusive: A history of education and training for diversity in American psychology. In F. T. L. Leong, L. Comas-Díaz, G. C. Nagayama Hall, V. C. McLoyd, & J. E. Trimble (Eds.), *APA handbook of multicultural psychology* (APA Handbooks in Psychology series, Vol. 2, pp. 3–18). American Psychological Association.

Pickren, W. E., & Rutherford, A. (2010). *A history of modern psychology in context*. Wiley.

Pierangelo, R., & Giuliani, G. A. (2008). *Classroom management for students with emotional and behavioral disorders: A step-by-step guide for educators*. Corwin Press.

Pierre, J. M. (2013). Overdiagnosis, underdiagnosis, synthesis: A dialectic for psychiatry and the DSM. In J. Paris & J. Phillips (Eds.), *Making the DSM-5: Concepts and controversies* (pp. 105–124). Springer Science+Business Media.

Piet, J., & Hougaard, E. (2011). The effect of mindfulness-based cognitive therapy for prevention of relapse in recurrent major depressive disorder: A systematic review and meta-analysis. *Clinical Psychology Review, 31*(6), 1032–1040.

Pieterse, A. L., Todd, N. R., Neville, H. A., & Carter, R. T. (2012). Perceived racism and mental health among Black American adults: A meta-analytic review. *Journal of Counseling Psychology, 59*(1), 1–9. https://doi.org/10.1037/a0026208

Pilch, I., Baran, L., Bolek-Kochanowska, M., Bożek, M., Friedrich, W., Hyla, M., & Sikora, J. (2018). Situational suppression use and social hierarchy in non-individualistic and hierarchic society: A replication study. *Journal of Research in Personality, 74*, 114–123.

Pilcher, J. J., & Walters, A. S. (1997). How sleep deprivation affects psychological variables related to college students' cognitive performance. *Journal of American College Health, 46*(3), 121–126.

Piliavin, I. M., Rodin, J., & Piliavin, J. A. (1969). Good samaritanism: An underground phenomenon? *Journal of Personality and Social Psychology, 13*(4), 289–299.

Pilkington, K., Kirkwood, G., Rampes, H., Cummings, M., & Richardson, J. (2007). Acupuncture for anxiety and anxiety disorders—a systematic literature review. *Acupuncture in Medicine, 25*(1–2), 1–10.

Pilkington, K., Kirkwood, G., Rampes, H., Fisher, P., & Richardson, J. (2006). Homeopathy for anxiety and anxiety disorders: A systematic review of the research. *Homeopathy, 95*(3), 151–162.

Pillemer, D. B. (2009). "Hearing the news" versus "being there": Comparing flashbulb memories and recall of first-hand experiences. In O. Luminet & A. Curci (Eds.), *Flashbulb memories: New issues and new perspectives* (pp. 125–140). Psychology Press.

Pinar, C., Fontaine, C. J., Triviño-Paredes, J., Lottenberg, C. P., Gil-Mohapel, J., & Christie, B. R. (2017). Revisiting the flip side: Long-term depression of synaptic efficacy in the hippocampus. *Neuroscience & Biobehavioral Reviews, 80*, 394–413.

Pinciotti, C. M., & Orcutt, H. K. (2021). Understanding gender differences in rape victim blaming: The power of social influence and just world beliefs. *Journal of Interpersonal Violence, 36*(1–2), 255–275. https://doi.org/10.1177/0886260517725736

Pinel, J. P. J. (2011). *Biopsychology* (8th ed.). Allyn & Bacon.

Pinel, J. P., Assanand, S., & Lehman, D. R. (2000). Hunger, eating, and ill health. *American Psychologist, 55*(10), 1105–1116.

Pinker, S. (1994). *The language instinct.* HarperCollins.

Pinna, M., Manchia, M., Oppo, R., Scano, F., Pillai, G., Loche, A. P., Salis, P., & Minnai, G. P. (2018). Clinical and biological predictors of response to electroconvulsive therapy (ECT): A review. *Neuroscience Letters, 669*, 32–42.

Pinquart, M. (2016). Associations of parenting styles and dimensions with academic achievement in children and adolescents: A meta-analysis. *Educational Psychology Review, 28*(3), 475–493.

Pinquart, M. (2017). Associations of parenting dimensions and styles with externalizing problems of children and adolescents: An updated meta-analysis. *Developmental Psychology, 53*(5), 873–932.

Pinquart, M., & Kauser, R. (2018). Do the associations of parenting styles with behavior problems and academic achievement vary by culture? Results from a meta-analysis. *Cultural Diversity and Ethnic Minority Psychology, 24*(1), 75–100.

Pinto, D. J., Brumberg, J. C., & Simons, D. J. (2000). Circuit dynamics and coding strategies in rodent somatosensory cortex. *Journal of Neurophysiology, 83*(3), 1158–1166.

Pintrich, P. R., & De Groot, E. V. (1990). Motivational and self-regulated learning components of classroom academic performance. *Journal of Educational Psychology, 82*(1), 33–40.

Piskor, E. (2013). *Hip hop family tree* (Vol. 1). Fantagraphics.

Pitman, R. K., Altman, B., Greenwald, E., & Longpre, R. E. (1991). Psychiatric complications during flooding therapy for posttraumatic stress disorder. *Journal of Clinical Psychiatry, 52*(1), 17–20.

Plana-Ripoll, O., Pedersen, C. B., & McGrath, J. J. (2018). Urbanicity and risk of schizophrenia—New studies and old hypotheses. *JAMA Psychiatry, 75*(7), 687–688.

Plante, C., Anderson, C. A., Allen, J. J., Groves, C. L., & Gentile, D. A. (2020). *Game on!: Sensible answers about video games and media violence.* Zengen LLC.

Platt, J. M., Colich, N. L., McLaughlin, K. A., Gary, D., & Keyes, K. M. (2017). Transdiagnostic psychiatric disorder risk associated with early age of menarche: A latent modeling approach. *Comprehensive Psychiatry, 79*, 70–79.

Plaud, J. J., & Martini, J. R. (1999). The respondent conditioning of male sexual arousal. *Behavior Modification, 23*(2), 254–268.

Plester, B., Wood, C., & Bell, V. (2008). Txt msg n school literacy: Does texting and knowledge of text abbreviations adversely affect children's literacy attainment? *Literacy, 42*(3), 137–144.

Plester, B., Wood, C., & Joshi, P. (2009). Exploring the relationship between children's knowledge of text message abbreviations and school literacy outcomes. *British Journal of Developmental Psychology, 27*(1), 145–161.

Pleyer, M. (2017). Protolanguage and mechanisms of meaning construal in interaction. *Language Sciences, 63*, 69–90.

Pliner, P., Bell, R., Hirsch, E. S., & Kinchla, M. (2006). Meal duration mediates the effect of "social facilitation" on eating in humans. *Appetite, 46*(2), 189–198. https://doi.org/10.1016/j.appet.2005.12.003

Pliner, P., & Chaiken, S. (1990). Eating, social motives, and self-presentation in women and men. Journal of Experimental Social Psychology, 26(3), 240–254.

Pliszka, S. R. (2015). Comorbid psychiatric disorders in children with ADHD. In R. A. Barkley (Ed.), *Attention-deficit hyperactivity disorder: A handbook for diagnosis and treatment* (4th ed., pp. 140–168). Guilford Press.

Plomin, R., & Dale, P. S. (2000). Genetics and early language development: A UK study of twins. In D. V. M. Bishop & L. B. Leonard (Eds.), *Speech and language impairments in children: Causes, characteristics, intervention and outcome* (pp. 35–51). Psychology Press,

Plomin, R., & von Stumm, S. (2018). The new genetics of intelligence. *Nature Reviews Genetics, 19*(3), 148–159.

Plutchik, R. (2001). The nature of emotions. *American Scientist, 89*(4), 344–350.

Plutchik, R. (2003). *Emotions and life: Perspectives from psychology, biology, and evolution.* American Psychological Association.

Pohl, R. F. (2004a). Effects of labeling. In R. F. Pohl (Ed.), *Cognitive illusions: A handbook on fallacies and biases in thinking, judgement, and memory* (pp. 327–344). Psychology Press.

Pohl, R. F. (2004b). Hindsight bias. In R. F. Pohl (Ed.), *Cognitive illusions: A handbook on fallacies and biases in thinking, judgement, and memory* (pp. 363–378). Psychology Press.

Polanczyk, G., de Lima, M. S., Horta, B. L., Biederman, J., & Rohde, L. A. (2007). The worldwide prevalence of ADHD: A systematic review and metaregression analysis. *American Journal of Psychiatry, 164*(6), 942–948.

Polanczyk, G. V., Willcutt, E. G., Salum, G. A., Kieling, C., & Rohde, L. A. (2014). ADHD prevalence estimates across three decades: An updated systematic review and meta-regression analysis. *International Journal of Epidemiology, 43*(2), 434–442.

Pole, N., Fields, L., & D'Andrea, W. (2016). Stress and trauma disorders. In J. C. Norcross, G. R. VandenBos, & D. K. Freedheim (Eds.), *APA handbook of clinical psychology: Vol. 4. Psychopathology and health* (pp. 97–134). American Psychological Association.

Poletti, B., Tagini, S., Brugnera, A., Parolin, L., Pievani, L., Ferrucci, R., Compare, A., & Silani, V. (2020). Telepsychotherapy: A leaflet for psychotherapists in the age of COVID-19. A review of the evidence. *Counselling Psychology Quarterly*, 1–16. https://doi.org/10.1080/09515070.2020.1769557

Poling, A., Ehrhardt, K. E., & Ervin, R. A. (2002). Positive punishment. In M. Hersen & W. Sledge (Eds.), *Encyclopedia of psychotherapy* (Vol. 2, pp. 359–366). Academic Press.

Poling, A., Weetjens, B. J., Cox, C., Beyene, N., Bach, H., & Sully, A. (2010). Teaching giant African pouched rats to find landmines: Operant conditioning with real consequences. *Behavior Analysis in Practice, 3*(2), 19.

Poling, A., Weetjens, B. J., Cox, C., Beyene, N. W., & Sully, A. (2011). Using giant African pouched rats (*Cricetomys gambianus*) to detect landmines. *The Psychological Record, 60*(4), 11.

Polinko, N. K., & Popovich, P. M. (2001). Evil thoughts but angelic actions: Responses to overweight job applicants. *Journal of Applied Social Psychology, 31*(5), 905–924.

Polk, D. M. (2011). Evaluating fairness: Critical assessment of equity theory. In D. Chadee (Ed.), *Theories in social psychology* (pp. 163–190). Wiley-Blackwell.

Pollack, M. H., & Simon, N. M. (2009). Pharmacotherapy for panic disorder and agoraphobia. In M. M. Antony & M. B. Stein (Eds.), *Oxford handbook of anxiety and related disorders* (pp. 295–307). Oxford University Press.

Pollack, M. H., Smoller, J. W., Otto, M. W., Hoge, E., & Simon, N. (2010). Phenomenology of panic disorder. In D. J. Stein, E. Hollander, & B. O. Rothbaum (Eds.), *Textbook of anxiety disorders* (2nd ed., pp. 367–379). American Psychiatric Association Publishing.

Pollan, M. (2018). *How to change your mind: What the new science of psychedelics teaches us about consciousness, dying, addiction, depression, and transcendence.* Penguin Random House.

Pollard, M. A., & Courage, M. L. (2017). Working memory capacity predicts effective multitasking. *Computers in Human Behavior, 76*, 450–462.

Polman, J., Orobio de Castro, B., & Van Aken, M. (2008). Experimental study of the differential effects of playing versus watching violent video games on children's aggressive behavior. *Aggressive Behavior, 34*(3), 256–264.

Polsky, J. Y., Moineddin, R., Dunn, J. R., Glazier, R. H., & Booth, G. L. (2016). Absolute and relative densities of fast-food versus other restaurants in relation to weight status: Does restaurant mix matter? *Preventive Medicine, 82*, 28–34.

Pomerantz, A. M. (2005). Increasingly informed consent: Discussing distinct aspects of psychotherapy at different points in time. *Ethics & Behavior, 15*(4), 351–360.

Pomerantz, A. M. (2012). Informed consent to psychotherapy (empowered collaboration). In S. J. Knapp (Ed.), *APA handbook of ethics in psychology* (Vol. 1., pp. 311–332). American Psychological Association.

Pomerantz, A. M. (2015). Informed consent, psychotherapy. In R. L. Cautin & S. O. Lilienfeld (Eds.), *The encyclopedia of clinical psychology* (pp. 1467–1470). Wiley-Blackwell.

Pomerantz, A. M. (2017). Informed consent and psychotherapy. In A. Wenzel (Ed.), *The Sage encyclopedia of abnormal and clinical psychology* (Vol. 4, pp. 1799–1800). Sage.

Pomerantz, A. M., & Handelsman, M. M. (2004). Informed consent revisited: An updated written question format. *Professional Psychology: Research and Practice, 35*(2), 201–205.

Pomerantz, A. M., & Seely, E. A. (2000). Under what conditions is individual psychotherapy distressing to clients' romantic partners? An empirical analogue study. *Journal of Contemporary Psychotherapy, 30*, 255–260.

Pomerantz, J. R., & Portillo, M. C. (2010). Perceptual organization: Vision. In E. B. Goldstein (Ed.), *Encyclopedia of perception* (pp. 786–790). Sage.

Poole, J. M. L., & Crow, B. E. (2018). Confidentiality of data and information. In L. F. Campbell, F. Millan, & J. N. Martin (Eds.), *A telepsychology casebook: Using technology ethically and effectively in your professional practice* (pp. 69–82). American Psychological Association.

Poole, K. L., Van Lieshout, R. J., & Schmidt, L. A. (2017). Exploring relations between shyness and social anxiety disorder: The role of sociability. *Personality and Individual Differences, 110*, 55–59.

Pope, K. S. (1994). *Sexual involvement with therapists: Patient assessment, subsequent therapy, forensics.* American Psychological Association.

Pope, K. S. (2011). Ethical issues in clinical psychology. In D. H. Barlow (Ed.), *The Oxford handbook of clinical psychology* (pp. 184–209). Oxford University Press.

Pope, K. S., & Vasquez, M. J. T. (2016). *Ethics in psychotherapy and counselling: A practical guide* (5th ed.). Wiley.

Popenoe, D. (2009). Cohabitation, marriage, and child wellbeing: A cross-national perspective. *Society, 46*(5), 429–436.

Popova, S., Lange, S., Probst, C., Gmel, G., & Rehm, J. (2017). Estimation of national, regional, and global prevalence of alcohol use during pregnancy and fetal alcohol syndrome: A systematic review and meta-analysis. *The Lancet Global Health, 5*(3), e290–e299.

Popova, S., Lange, S., Shield, K., Mihic, A., Chudley, A. E., Mukherjee, R. A., ... Rehm, J. (2016). Comorbidity of fetal alcohol spectrum disorder: A systematic review and meta-analysis. *The Lancet, 387*(10022), 978–987.

Popova, S., Patra, J., Mohapatra, S., Fischer, B., & Rehm, J. (2009). How many people in Canada use prescription opioids non-medically in general and street drug using populations? *Canadian Journal of Public Health/Revue Canadienne de Santé Publique, 100*(2), 104–108.

Popple, A. (2010). Individual differences in perception. In E. B. Goldstein (Ed.), *Encyclopedia of perception* (pp. 492–495). Sage.

Popplestone, J. A., & McPherson, M. W. (1998). *An illustrated history of American psychology* (2nd ed.). University of Akron Press.

Poran, M. A. (2002). Denying diversity: Perceptions of beauty and social comparison processes among Latina, Black, and White women. *Sex Roles, 47*(1), 65–81.

Poropat, A. E. (2009). A meta-analysis of the five-factor model of personality and academic performance. *Psychological Bulletin, 135*(2), 322–338.

Portaluppi, F., Tiseo, R., Smolensky, M. H., Hermida, R. C., Ayala, D. E., & Fabbian, F. (2012). Circadian rhythms and cardiovascular health. *Sleep Medicine Reviews, 16*(2), 151–166.

Porter, E., Chambless, D. L., Keefe, J. R., Allred, K. M., & Brier, M. J. (2019). Social anxiety disorder and perceived criticism in intimate relationships: Comparisons with normal and clinical control groups. *Behavior Therapy, 50*(1), 241–253.

Porter, J., Anand, T., Johnson, B., Khan, R. M., & Sobel, N. (2005). Brain mechanisms for extracting spatial information from smell. *Neuron, 47*(4), 581–592.

Porter, S., Yuille, J. C., & Lehman, D. R. (1999). The nature of real, implanted, and fabricated memories for emotional childhood events. *Law and Human Behavior, 23*(5), 517–537.

Posner, M. I., & Keele, S. W. (1970). Retention of abstract ideas. *Journal of Experimental Psychology, 83*(2), 304–308.

Post, R. M., & Weiss, S. R. (1997). Emergent properties of neural systems: How focal molecular neurobiological alterations can affect behavior. *Development and Psychopathology, 9*(4), 907–929.

Postman, L., & Phillips, L. W. (1965). Short-term temporal changes in free recall. *Quarterly Journal of Experimental Psychology, 17*(2), 132–138.

Pot, G. K. (2018). Sleep and dietary habits in the urban environment: The role of chrono-nutrition. *Proceedings of the Nutrition Society, 77*(3), 189–198.

Poteat, V. P. (2015). Individual psychological factors and complex interpersonal conditions that predict LGBT-affirming behavior. *Journal of Youth and Adolescence, 44*(8), 1494–1507.

Poteat, V. P., Calzo, J. P., & Yoshikawa, H. (2018). Gay–Straight Alliance involvement and youths' participation in civic engagement, advocacy, and awareness-raising. *Journal of Applied Developmental Psychology, 56*, 13–20. https://doi.org/10.1016/j.appdev.2018.01.001

Potenza, M. N. (2006). Should addictive disorders include non-substance-related conditions? *Addiction, 101*(S1), 142–151.

Potter, W. Z., Padich, R. A., Rudorfer, M. V., & Krishnan, K. R. R. (2006). Tricyclics, tetracyclics, and monoamine oxidase inhibitors. In D. J. Stein, D. J. Kupfer, & A. F. Schatzberg (Eds.), *The American Psychiatric Publishing textbook of mood disorders* (pp. 251–262). American Psychiatric Publishing.

Powell, D., & Dixon, M. (2011). Does SMS text messaging help or harm adults' knowledge of standard spelling? *Journal of Computer Assisted Learning, 27*(1), 58–66.

Powell, L. M., Auld, M. C., Chaloupka, F. J., O'Malley, P. M., & Johnston, L. D. (2007). Access to fast food and food prices: Relationship with fruit and vegetable consumption and overweight among adolescents. *Advances in Health Economics and Health Services Research, 17*, 23–48.

Powell, L. M., & Bao, Y. (2009). Food prices, access to food outlets and child weight. *Economics & Human Biology*, *7*(1), 64–72.

Powell, L. M., & Chaloupka, F. J. (2009). Food prices and obesity: Evidence and policy implications for taxes and subsidies. *Milbank Quarterly*, *87*(1), 229–257.

Power, M., & Brewin, C. R. (2011). From Freud to cognitive science: A contemporary account of the unconscious. *British Journal of Clinical Psychology*, *30*(4), 289–310.

Powers, M. B., & Rothbaum, B. O. (2019). Recent advances in virtual reality therapy for anxiety and related disorders: Introduction to the special issue. *Journal of Anxiety Disorders*, *61*, 1–2.

Premack, D. (2010). Why humans are unique: Three theories. *Perspectives on Psychological Science*, *5*(1), 22–32. https://doi.org/10.1177/1745691609356782

Prescott, J. (2010). Taste: Supertasters. In E. B. Goldstein (Ed.), *Encyclopedia of perception* (pp. 964–967). Sage.

Prescott, J., Bell, G. A., Gillmore, R., Yoshida, M., O'Sullivan, M., Korac, S., & Yamazaki, K. (1997). Cross-cultural comparisons of Japanese and Australian responses to manipulations of sweetness in foods. *Food Quality and Preference*, *8*(1), 45–55.

Pressley, T., & Ha, C. (2021). Teaching during a pandemic: United States teachers' self-efficacy during COVID-19. *Teaching and Teacher Education*, *106*, 103465. https://doi.org/10.1016/j.tate.2021.103465

Pressman, S. D., Acevedo, A. M., Hammond, K. V., & Kraft-Feil, T. L. (2020). Smile (or grimace) through the pain? The effects of experimentally manipulated facial expressions on needle-injection responses. *Emotion*. Advance online publication. https://doi.org/10.1037/emo0000913

Pressman, S. D., Cohen, S., Miller, G. E., Barkin, A., Rabin, B. S., & Treanor, J. J. (2005). Loneliness, social network size, and immune response to influenza vaccination in college freshmen. *Health Psychology*, *24*(3), 297–306.

Pressman, S. D., Kraft, T. L., & Cross, M. P. (2015). It's good to do good and receive good: The impact of a "pay it forward" style kindness intervention on giver and receiver well-being. *The Journal of Positive Psychology*, *10*(4), 293–302.

Pressnitzer, D., Patterson, R. D., & Krumbholz, K. (2001). The lower limit of melodic pitch. *The Journal of the Acoustical Society of America*, *109*(5), 2074–2084.

Pretzer, J., & Beck, J. S. (2004). Cognitive therapy of personality disorders: Twenty years of progress. In R. L. Leahy (Ed.), *Contemporary cognitive therapy: Theory, research, and practice* (pp. 299–318). Guilford Press.

Preuss, T. M. (2009). The cognitive neuroscience of human uniqueness. In M. S. Gazzaniga (Ed.), *The cognitive neurosciences* (4th ed., pp. 49–66). MIT Press.

Pribram, K. H. (1960). A review of theory in physiological psychology. *Annual Review of Psychology*, *11*(1), 1–40.

Pridmore, B. (2007). World memory champion Ben Pridmore on Central News. https://www.youtube.com/watch?v=Yp9qF-SjJZk

Prieler, M. (2016). Gender stereotypes in Spanish- and English-language television advertisements in the United States. *Mass Communication and Society*, *19*(3), 275–300.

Priess, H. A., & Hyde, J. S. (2010). Gender and academic abilities and preferences. In J. C. Chrisler & D. R. McCreary (Eds.), *Handbook of gender research in psychology* (Vol. 1, pp. 297–316). Springer Science+Business Media.

Prigerson, H. G., Kakarala, S., Gang, J., & Maciejewski, P. K. (2021). History and status of prolonged grief disorder as a psychiatric diagnosis. *Annual Review of Clinical Psychology*, *17*, 109–126. https://doi.org/10.1146/annurev-clinpsy-081219-093600

Prinstein, M. J., & La Greca, A. M. (2003). Peer crowd affiliation and internalizing distress in childhood and adolescence: A longitudinal follow-back study. *Journal of Research on Adolescence*, *12*(3), 325–351.

Prinstein, M. J., Choukas-Bradley, S. C., & Guan, K. (2013). Deciding to apply and successfully gaining admission to graduate schools in psychology. In M. J. Prinstein (Ed.), *The portable mentor: Expert guide to a successful career in psychology* (pp. 13–44). Springer.

Prislin, R., & Crano, W. D. (2012). A history of social influence research. In A. W. Kruglanski & W. Stroebe (Eds.), *Handbook of the history of social psychology* (pp. 321–339). Psychology Press.

Privette, G. (1983). Peak experience, peak performance, and flow: A comparative analysis of positive human experiences. *Journal of Personality and Social Psychology*, *45*(6), 1361–1368.

Prochaska, J. O., DiClemente, C. C., & Norcross, J. C. (1992). In search of how people change: Applications to addictive behaviors. *American Psychologist*, *47*(9), 1102–1114. https://doi.org/10.1037//0003-066x.47.9.1102

Prochaska, J. O., & Norcross, J. C. (2018). *Systems of psychotherapy: A transtheoretical analysis* (9th ed.). Oxford University Press.

Prochaska, J. O., & Velicer, W. F. (1997). The transtheoretical model of health behavior change. *American Journal of Health Promotion*, *12*(1), 38–48.

Prosek, E. A., Giordano, A. L., Turner, K. D., Bevly, C. M., Reader, E. A., LeBlanc, Y., Molina, C. E., Vera, R. A., & Garber, S. A. (2018). Prevalence and correlates of stimulant medication misuse among the collegiate population. *Journal of College Student Psychotherapy*, *32*(1), 10–22.

Pryor, K. (2009). *Reaching the animal mind: Clicker training and what it teaches us about all animals*. Scribner.

Pryor, K., & Ramirez, K. (2014). Modern animal training: A transformative technology. In F. K. McSweeney & E. S. Murphy (Eds.), *The Wiley-Blackwell handbook of operant and classical conditioning* (pp. 455–482). Wiley.

Pryzgoda, J., & Chrisler, J. C. (2000). Definitions of gender and sex: The subtleties of meaning. *Sex Roles*, *43*(78), 553–569.

Przybylski, A. K., & Weinstein, N. (2019). Violent video game engagement is not associated with adolescents' aggressive behaviour: Evidence from a registered report. *Royal Society Open Science*, *6*(2), 171474.

Puhl, R., & Brownell, K. D. (2012). Bias, discrimination, and obesity. *Obesity Research*, *9*(12), 788–805.

Puhl, R. M., Himmelstein, M. S., & Pearl, R. L. (2020). Weight stigma as a psychosocial contributor to obesity. *American Psychologist*, *75*(2), 274–289. https://doi.org/10.1037/amp0000538

Puhl, R. M., Lessard, L. M., Larson, N., Eisenberg, M. E., & Neumark-Stzainer, D. (2020). Weight stigma as a predictor of distress and maladaptive eating behaviors during COVID-19: Longitudinal findings from the EAT study. *Annals of Behavioral Medicine*, *54*(10), 738–746. https://doi.org/10.1093/abm/kaaa077

Purdon, C. (2021). Cognitive restructuring. In A. Wenzel (Ed.), *Handbook of cognitive behavioral therapy: Overview and approaches* (pp. 207–234). American Psychological Association. https://doi.org/10.1037/0000218-008

Puterman, E., Weiss, J., Lin, J., Schilf, S., Slusher, A. L., Johansen, K. L., & Epel, E. S. (2018). Aerobic exercise lengthens telomeres and reduces stress in family caregivers: A randomized controlled trial. *Psychoneuroendocrinology*, *98*, 245–252.

Pyers, J. E., Senghas, A., & Senghas, R. J. (2014). The emergence of Nicaraguan sign language: Questions of development, acquisition, and evolution. In S. T. Parker, J. Langer, & C. Milbrath (Eds.), *Biology and knowledge revisited* (pp. 305–324). Routledge.

Qasim, A., Turcotte, M., de Souza, R. J., Samaan, M. C., Champredon, D., Dushoff, J., Speakman, J. R., & Meyre, D. (2018). On the origin of obesity: Identifying the biological, environmental and cultural drivers of genetic risk among human populations. *Obesity Reviews*, *19*(2), 121–149.

Qasrawi, S. O., Pandi-Perumal, S. R., & BaHammam, A. S. (2017). The effect of intermittent fasting during Ramadan on sleep, sleepiness, cognitive function, and circadian rhythm. *Sleep and Breathing*, *21*(3), 577–586.

Quaglia, J. T., Brown, K. W., Lindsay, E. K., Creswell, J. D., & Goodman, R. J. (2015). From conceptualization to operationalization of mindfulness. In K. W. Brown, J. D. Creswell, & R. M. Ryan (Eds.), *Handbook of mindfulness: Theory, research, and practice* (pp. 151–170). Guilford Press.

Quek, Y. H., Tam, W. W., Zhang, M. W., & Ho, R. C. (2017). Exploring the association between childhood and adolescent obesity and depression: A meta-analysis. *Obesity Reviews*, *18*(7), 742–754.

Querido, J. G., Warner, T. D., & Eyberg, S. M. (2002). Parenting styles and child behavior in African American families of preschool children. *Journal of Clinical Child and Adolescent Psychology*, *31*(2), 272–277.

Quesenberry, C. P., Caan, B., & Jacobson, A. (1998). Obesity, health services use, and health care costs among members of a health maintenance organization. *Archives of Internal Medicine*, *158*(5), 466–472.

Quinn, P. C. (2011). Born to categorize. In U. Goswami (Ed.), *The Wiley-Blackwell handbook of childhood cognitive development* (2nd ed., pp. 129–152). Wiley-Blackwell.

Quintana, S. M. (2011). Ethnicity, race, and children's social development. In P. K. Smith & C. H. Hart (Eds.), *The Wiley-Blackwell handbook of childhood social development* (2nd ed., pp. 299–316). Wiley-Blackwell.

Ra, Y. A., & Trusty, J. (2017). Impact of social support and coping on acculturation and acculturative stress of East Asian international students. *Journal of Multicultural Counseling and Development*, *45*(4), 276–291.

Rabin, B. S. (2005). Introduction to immunology and immune-endocrine interactions. In K. Vedhara & M. Irwin (Eds.), *Human psychoneuroimmunology* (pp. 1–24). Oxford University Press.

Rabkin, J. G., McElhiney, M., Moran, P., Acree, M., & Folkman, S. (2009). Depression, distress and positive mood in late-stage cancer: A longitudinal study. *Psycho-oncology*, *18*(1), 79–86.

Raboteg-Saric, Z., & Sakic, M. (2014). Relations of parenting styles and friendship quality to self-esteem, life satisfaction and happiness in adolescents. *Applied Research in Quality of Life*, *9*(3), 749–765.

Racine, E., Bar-Ilan, O., & Illes, J. (2005). fMRI in the public eye. *Nature Reviews Neuroscience*, *6*(2), 159–164.

Racine, E., Waldman, S., Rosenberg, J., & Illes, J. (2010). Contemporary neuroscience in the media. *Social Science & Medicine*, *71*(4), 725–733.

Raffel, G. (1936). Two determinants of the effect of primacy. *The American Journal of Psychology*, *48*(4), 654–657.

Raiford, S. E. (2018). The Wechsler Intelligence Scale for Children, fifth edition integrated. In D. P. Flanagan & E. M. McDonough (Eds.), *Contemporary intellectual assessment: Theories, tests, and issues* (4th ed., pp. 302–332). Guilford Press.

Raiford, S. E., Coalson, D. L., Saklofske, D. H., & Weiss, L. G. (2010). Practical issues in WAIS-IV administration and scoring. In L. G. Weiss, D. H. Saklofske, D. Coalson, & S. E. Raiford (Eds.), *WAIS-IV clinical use and interpretation: Scientist-practitioner perspectives* (pp. 25–60). Elsevier.

Raine, A. (2013). *The anatomy of violence: The biological roots of crime*. Pantheon Books.

Raine, A., Buchsbaum, M., & LaCasse, L. (1997). Brain abnormalities in murderers indicated by positron emission tomography. *Biological Psychiatry*, *42*(6), 495–508.

Raine, A., Reynolds, C., Venables, P. H., Mednick, S. A., & Farrington, D. P. (1998). Fearlessness, stimulation-seeking, and large body size at age 3 years as early predispositions to childhood aggression at age 11 years. *Archives of General Psychiatry*, *55*(8), 745.

Rainville, P., & Price, D. D. (2003). Hypnosis phenomenology and the neurobiology of consciousness. *International Journal of Clinical and Experimental Hypnosis*, *51*(2), 105–129.

Raitanen, J., Sandberg, S., & Oksanen, A. (2017). The bullying-school shooting nexus: Bridging master narratives of mass violence with personal narratives of social exclusion. *Deviant Behavior*, *40*(1), 96–109.

Rakic, P., Arellano, J. L., & Breuing, J. (2009). Development of the primate cerebral cortex. In M. S. Gazzaniga (Ed.), *The cognitive neurosciences* (4th ed., pp. 7–28). MIT Press.

Rakic, P., Eugenius, S., Ang, B. C., & Breuing, J. (2004). Setting the stage for cognition: Genesis of the primate cerebral cortex. In M. S. Gazzaniga (Ed.), *The new cognitive neurosciences III* (pp. 33–50). MIT Press.

Rakison, D. H. (In press). Do 5-month-old infants possess an evolved detection mechanism for snakes, sharks, and rats? *Journal of Cognition and Development*.

Rakison, D. H., & Poulin-Dubois, D. (2001). Developmental origin of the animate–inanimate distinction. *Psychological Bulletin*, *127*(2), 209–228.

Rakow, T., & Skylark, W. J. (2018). Judgement heuristics. In L. J. Ball & V. A. Thompson (Eds.), *Routledge international handbook of thinking and reasoning* (pp. 451–471). Routledge.

Rama, A. N., Cho, S. C., & Kushida, C. A. (2006). Normal human sleep. In T. L. Lee-Chiong (Ed.), *Sleep: A comprehensive handbook* (pp. 3–10). Wiley-Liss.

Ramachandran, V. S., & Hirstein, W. (1998). The perception of phantom limbs. The D. O. Hebb lecture. *Brain*, *121*(9), 1603–1630.

Ramírez, N., Lytle, S. R., Fish, M., & Kuhl, P. K. (2018). Parent coaching at 6 and 10 months improves language outcomes at 14 months: A randomized controlled trial. *Developmental Science*, *22*(3), e12762.

Ramírez-Esparza, N., García-Sierra, A., and Kuhl, P. K. (2014). Look who's talking: Speech style and social context in language input to infants are linked to concurrent and future speech development. *Developmental Science*, *17*(6), 880–891.

Ramírez-Esparza, N., García-Sierra, A., & Kuhl, P. K. (2017). Look who's talking NOW! Parentese speech, social context, and language development across time. *Frontiers in Psychology*, *8*, 1008.

Ramos, K. D., & Youngclarke, D. M. (2006). Parenting advice books about child sleep: Cosleeping and crying it out. *Sleep*, *29*(12), 1616.

Rand, R. (2004). *Dancing away an anxious mind: A memoir about overcoming panic disorder*. University of Wisconsin Press.

Randall, W. L. (2007). From computer to compost: Rethinking our metaphors for memory. *Theory & Psychology*, *17*(5), 611–633.

Ranganath, C., Libby, L. A., & Wong, L. (2012). Human learning and memory. In K. Frankish & W. M. Ramsey (Eds.), *The Cambridge handbook of cognitive science* (pp. 112–130). Cambridge University Press.

Ranzini, G., & Hoek, E. (2017). To you who (I think) are listening: Imaginary audience and impression management on Facebook. *Computers in Human Behavior*, *75*(10), 228–235. https://doi.org/10.1016/j.chb.2017.04.047

Rao, M., Afshin, A., Singh, G., & Mozaffarian, D. (2013). Do healthier foods and diet patterns cost more than less healthy options? A systematic review and meta-analysis. *BMJ Open, 3*(12), e004277. https://doi.org/10.1136/bmjopen-2013-004277

Rapee, R. M. (1993). The utilisation of working memory by worry. *Behaviour Research and Therapy, 31*(6), 617–620.

Rapee, R. M., Kennedy, S., Ingram, M., Edwards, S., & Sweeney, L. (2005). Prevention and early intervention of anxiety disorders in inhibited preschool children. *Journal of Consulting and Clinical Psychology, 73*(3), 488–497.

Rapee, R. M., Schniering, C. A., & Hudson, J. L. (2009). Anxiety disorders during childhood and adolescence: Origins and treatment. *Annual Review of Clinical Psychology, 5*, 311–341.

Rash, J. A., Matsuba, M. K., & Prkachin, K. M. (2011). Gratitude and well-being: Who benefits the most from a gratitude intervention? *Applied Psychology: Health and Well-Being, 3*(3), 350–369.

Rashid, T. (2015). Positive psychotherapy: A strength-based approach. *The Journal of Positive Psychology, 10*(1), 25–40.

Raskin, J. D. (2018). What might an alternative to the DSM suitable for psychotherapists look like? *Journal of Humanistic Psychology, 59*(3), 368–375. https://doi.org/10.1177/0022167818761919

Raskin, J. D., & Gayle, M. C. (2016). DSM-5: Do psychologists really want an alternative? *Journal of Humanistic Psychology, 56*(5), 439–456.

Ratcliff, R., & Van Dongen, H. (2018). The effects of sleep deprivation on item and associative recognition memory. *Journal of Experimental Psychology: Learning, Memory, and Cognition, 44*(2), 193–208.

Rattenborg, N. C. (2007). Response to commentary on evolution of slow-wave sleep and palliopallial connectivity in mammals and birds: A hypothesis. *Brain Research Bulletin, 72*(4), 187–193.

Rattenborg, N. C., Lima, S. L., & Amlaner, C. J. (1999). Facultative control of avian unihemispheric sleep under the risk of predation. *Behavioural Brain Research, 105*(2), 163–172.

Rattenborg, N. C., Martinez-Gonzalez, D., & Lesku, J. A. (2009). Avian sleep homeostasis: Convergent evolution of complex brains, cognition and sleep functions in mammals and birds. *Neuroscience & Biobehavioral Reviews, 33*(3), 253–270.

Raup, J. L., & Myers, J. E. (1989). The empty nest syndrome: Myth or reality? *Journal of Counseling & Development, 68*(2), 180–183.

Raver, J. L., & Van Dyne, L. (2018). Developing cultural intelligence. In K. G. Brown (Ed.), *The Cambridge handbook of workplace training and employee development* (pp. 407–440). Cambridge University Press.

Rayner, K. (1998). Eye movements in reading and information processing: 20 years of research. *Psychological Bulletin, 124*(3), 372–422.

Rayner, K., & Pollatsek, A. (2010). Eye movements and reading. In E. B. Goldstein (Ed.), *Encyclopedia of perception* (pp. 433–416). Sage.

Rayner, K., Li, X., Williams, C. C., Cave, K. R., & Well, A. D. (2007). Eye movements during information processing tasks: Individual differences and cultural effects. *Vision Research, 47*(21), 2714–2726.

Read, J., Renton, J., Harrop, C., Geekie, J., & Dowrick, C. (2020). A survey of UK general practitioners about depression, antidepressants and withdrawal: Implementing the 2019 Public Health England report. *Therapeutic Advances in Psychopharmacology, 10*, 1–14. https://doi.org/10.1177/2045125320950124

Reale, S., Hamilton, J., Akparibo, R., Hetherington, M. M., Cecil, J. E., & Caton, S. J. (2019). The effect of food type on the portion size effect in children aged 2–12 years: A systematic review and meta-analysis. *Appetite, 137*, 47–61. https://doi.org/10.1016/j.appet.2019.01.025

Reangsing, C., Rittiwong, T., & Schneider, J. K. (2021). Effects of mindfulness meditation interventions on depression in older adults: A meta-analysis. *Aging & Mental Health, 25*(7), 1181–1190. https://doi.org/10.1080/13607863.2020.1793901

Redelmeier, D. A., Katz, J., & Kahneman, D. (2003). Memories of colonoscopy: A randomized trial. *Pain, 104*(1), 187–194.

Redick, T. S., Shipstead, Z., Meier, M. E., Montroy, J. J., Hicks, K. L., Unsworth, N., Kane, M. J., Hambrick, D. Z., & Engle, R. W. (2016). Cognitive predictors of a common multitasking ability: Contributions from working memory, attention control, and fluid intelligence. *Journal of Experimental Psychology: General, 145*(11), 1473–1492.

Redmond, D. (2012, July 27). *Derek Redmond: The day that changed my life.* DailyMail.com. http://www.dailymail.co.uk/femail/article-2179361/Derek-Redmond-The-day-changed-life.html

Reed, C. L. (2010). Body perception. In E. B. Goldstein (Ed.), *Encyclopedia of perception* (pp. 216–220). Sage.

Reed, C. L., Stone, V. E., Bozova, S., & Tanaka, J. (2003). The body-inversion effect. *Psychological Science, 14*(4), 302–308.

Reed, C. L., Stone, V. E., Grubb, J. D., & McGoldrick, J. E. (2006). Turning configural processing upside down: Part and whole body postures. *Journal of Experimental Psychology: Human Perception and Performance, 32*(1), 73–87.

Reed, J., Hirsh-Pasek, K., & Golinkoff, R. M. (2017). Learning on hold: Cell phones sidetrack parent-child interactions. *Developmental Psychology, 53*(8), 1428–1436.

Reed, S. K. (1972). Pattern recognition and categorization. *Cognitive Psychology, 3*(3), 382–407.

Regan, B. C., Julliot, C., Simmen, B., Vienot, F., Charles-Dominique, P., & Mollon, J. D. (2001). Fruits, foliage and the evolution of primate colour vision. *Philosophical Transactions of the Royal Society of London B: Biological Sciences, 356*(1407), 229–283.

Reger, G. M., Holloway, K. M., Candy, C., Rothbaum, B. O., Difede, J., Rizzo, A. A., & Gahm, G. A. (2011). Effectiveness of virtual reality exposure therapy for active duty soldiers in a military mental health clinic. *Journal of Traumatic Stress, 24*(1), 93–96.

Reger, M. A., & Gahm, G. A. (2009). A meta-analysis of the effects of Internet- and computer-based cognitive-behavioral treatments for anxiety. Journal of Clinical Psychology, 65(1), 53–75.

Regier, D. A., Kuhl, E. A., & Kupfer, D. J. (2013). The DSM-5: Classification and criteria changes. *World Psychiatry, 12*(2), 92–98.

Regier, T., Kay, P., & Cook, R. S. (2005). Focal colors are universal after all. *Proceedings of the National Academy of Sciences of the United States of America, 102*(23), 8386–8391.

Reich, S. M., & Vandell, D. L. (2011). The interplay between parents and peers as socializing influences in children's development. In P. K. Smith & C. H. Hart (Eds.), *The Wiley-Blackwell handbook of childhood social development* (2nd ed., pp. 263–280). Wiley-Blackwell.

Reid, A., Maldonado, C. C., & Baker, F. C. (2002). Sleep behavior of South African adolescents. *Sleep, 25*(4), 423–427.

Reid, K. J., & Zee, P. C. (2004). Circadian rhythm disorders. *Seminars in Neurology, 24*(3), 315–325.

Reifman, A., Larrick, R., & Fein, S. (1991). Temper and temperature on the diamond: The heat-aggression relationship in major league baseball. *Personality and Social Psychology Bulletin, 17*(5), 580–585.

Reiger, T., Kay, P., Gilbert, A. L., & Ivry, R. B. (2010). Language and thought. Which side are you on anyway? In B. Malt & P. Wolff (Eds.), *Words and the mind: How words capture human experience* (pp. 165–182). Oxford University Press.

Reinders, A., & Veltman, D. (2021). Dissociative identity disorder: Out of the shadows at last? *The British Journal of Psychiatry, 219*(2), 413–414. https://doi.org/10.1192/bjp.2020.168

Reinecke, L., Aufenanger, S., Beutel, M. E., Dreier, M., Quiring, O., Stark, B., Wölfling, K., & Müller, K. W. (2017). Digital stress over the life span: The effects of communication load and internet multitasking on perceived stress and psychological health impairments in a German probability sample. *Media Psychology, 20*(1), 90–115.

Reiner, R. (2008). Integrating a portable biofeedback device into clinical practice for patients with anxiety disorders: Results of a pilot study. *Applied Psychophysiology and Biofeedback, 33*(1), 55–61.

Reinhardt, A., & Rossmann, C. (2021). Age-related framing effects: Why vaccination against COVID-19 should be promoted differently in younger and older adults. *Journal of Experimental Psychology: Applied.* Advance online publication. https://doi.org/10.1037/xap0000378

Reis, H. T., & Gosling, S. D. (2010). Social psychological methods outside the laboratory. In S. T. Fiske, D. T. Gilbert, & G. Lindzey (Eds.), *Handbook of social psychology* (5th ed., Vol. 1, pp. 82–114). Wiley.

Reis, H. T., & Holmes, J. G. (2019). Perspectives on the situation. In K. Deaux & M. Snyder (Eds.), *The Oxford handbook of personality and social psychology* (2nd ed., pp. 67–96). Oxford University Press.

Reis, S. M., & McCoach, D. B. (2000). The underachievement of gifted students: What do we know and where do we go? *Gifted Child Quarterly, 44*(3), 152–170.

Reis, S. M., & Renzulli, J. S. (2011). Intellectual giftedness. In R. J. Sternberg & S. B. Kaufman (Eds.), *The Cambridge handbook of intelligence* (pp. 235–252). Cambridge University Press.

Reisberg, D., & Heuer, F. (2004). Memory for emotional events. In D. Reisberg & P. Hertel (Eds.), *Memory and emotion* (pp. 3–41). Oxford University Press.

Reisberg, D., & Heuer, F. (2007). The influence of emotion on memory in forensic settings. In M. P. Toglia, J. D. Read, D. F. Ross, & R. C. L. Lindsay (Eds.), *The handbook of eyewitness psychology: Memory for events* (Vol. I, pp. 81–116). Psychology Press.

Reisenzein, R. (1983). The Schachter theory of emotion: Two decades later. *Psychological Bulletin, 94*(2), 239–264.

Reisman, J. M. (1991). *A history of clinical psychology* (2nd ed.). Hemisphere.

Remes, O., Brayne, C., Van Der Linde, R., & Lafortune, L. (2016). A systematic review of reviews on the prevalence of anxiety disorders in adult populations. *Brain and Behavior, 6*(7), e00497.

Renner, J., Stafford, D., Lawson, A., McKinnon, J., Friot, E., & Kellogg, D. (1976). *Research, teaching, and learning with the Piaget model.* University of Oklahoma Press.

Renner, M. J., & Rosenzweig, M. R. (1987). *Enriched and impoverished environments: Effects on brain and behavior recent research in psychology.* Springer-Verlag.

Renninger, K. A., & Hidi, S. (2011). Revisiting the conceptualization, measurement, and generation of interest. *Educational Psychologist, 46*(3), 168–184.

Renninger, K. A., & Su, S. (2012). Interest and its development. In R. M. Ryan (Ed.), *The Oxford handbook of human motivation* (pp. 167–190). Oxford University Press.

Rensink, R. A. (2000). Seeing, sensing, and scrutinizing. *Vision Research, 40*(10), 1469–1487.

Rensink, R. A. (2010). Change detection. In E. B. Goldstein (Ed.), *Encyclopedia of perception* (pp. 241–244). Sage.

Rensink, R. A. (2013). Perception and attention. In D. Reisberg (Ed.), *Oxford handbook of cognitive psychology* (pp. 97–116). Oxford University Press.

Renzulli, J. S., & Park, S. (2002). *Giftedness and high school dropouts: Personal, family, and school-related factors* (RM02168). University of Connecticut, National Research Center on the Gifted and Talented.

Rescorla, R. A. (1976). Second-order conditioning of Pavlovian conditioned inhibition. *Learning and Motivation, 7(2)*, 161–172.

Rescorla, R. A. (1980). *Pavlovian second-order conditioning: Studies in associative learning.* Lawrence Erlbaum.

Rescorla, R. A. (1988a). Behavioral studies of Pavlovian conditioning. *Annual Review of Neuroscience, 11*, 329–352.

Rescorla, R. A. (1988b). Pavlovian conditioning: It's not what you think. *American Psychologist, 43*(3), 151–160.

Rescorla, R. A. (1997). Spontaneous recovery after Pavlovian conditioning with multiple outcomes. *Animal Learning & Behavior, 25*(1), 99–107.

Resick, P. A., Monson, C. M., & Rizvi, S. L. (2008). Posttraumatic stress disorder. In D. H. Barlow (Ed.), *Clinical handbook of psychological disorders: A step-by-step treatment manual* (4th ed., pp. 65–122). Guilford Press.

Resnick, R. J. (2005). Attention deficit hyperactivity disorder in teens and adults: They don't all outgrow it. *Journal of Clinical Psychology, 61*(5), 529–533.

Resnick, R. J., & Norcross, J. C. (2002). Prescription privileges for psychologists: Scared to death? *Clinical Psychology: Science and Practice, 9*(3), 270–274.

Rettie, H., & Daniels, J. (2021). Coping and tolerance of uncertainty: Predictors and mediators of mental health during the COVID-19 pandemic. *American Psychologist, 76*(3), 427–437. https://doi.org/10.1037/amp0000710

Reuter, J., Raedler, T., Rose, M., Hand, I., Gläscher, J., & Büchel, C. (2005). Pathological gambling is linked to reduced activation of the mesolimbic reward system. *Nature Neuroscience, 8*(2), 147–148.

Revonsuo, A. (2018). *Foundations of consciousness.* Routledge.

Reynolds, G. D., & Roth, K. C. (2018). The development of attentional biases for faces in infancy: A developmental systems perspective. *Frontiers in Psychology, 9*, 222.

Reynolds, G. H. (2017, September 5). Hurricane Harvey revealed the awesome power of real people. *USA Today.* https://www.usatoday.com/story/opinion/2017/09/05/hurricane-harvey-houston-flood-demonstrates-power-ordinary-americans-glenn-harlan-reynolds-column/631375001/

Reynolds, S. A., & Ebben, M. R. (2017). The cost of insomnia and the benefit of increased access to evidence-based treatment: Cognitive behavioral therapy for insomnia. *Sleep Medicine Clinics, 12*(1), 39–46.

Rhee, E., Uleman, J. S., Lee, H. K., & Roman, R. J. (1995). Spontaneous self-descriptions and ethnic identities in individualistic and collectivistic cultures. *Journal of Personality and Social Psychology, 69*(1), 142–152.

Rhee, S. H., & Waldman, I. D. (2002). Genetic and environmental influences on antisocial behavior: A meta-analysis of twin and adoption studies. *Psychological Bulletin, 128*(3), 490–529.

Rhodes, G. (2006). The evolutionary psychology of facial beauty. *Annual Review of Psychology, 57*, 199–226.

Ricciardelli, L. A. (1992). Creativity and bilingualism. *The Journal of Creative Behavior, 26*(4), 242–254.

Richard, D. C. S., & Lauterbach, D. (2003). Computers in the training and practice of behavioral assessment. In S. N. Haynes & E. M. Heiby (Eds.), *Comprehensive handbook of psychological assessment* (Vol. 3, pp. 222–245). Wiley.

Richards, J. M., & Gross, J. J. (2000). Emotion regulation and memory: The cognitive costs of keeping one's cool. *Journal of Personality and Social Psychology, 79*(3), 410–424.

Richards, J. M., & Gross, J. J. (2006). Personality and emotional memory: How regulating emotion impairs memory for emotional events. *Journal of Research in Personality, 40*(5), 631–651.
Richardson, A., Field, T., Newton, R., & Bendell, D. (2012). Locus of control and prenatal depression. *Infant Behavior and Development, 35*(4), 662–668.
Richardson, G. S. (2006). Shift work sleep disorder. In T. L. Lee-Chiong (Ed.), *Sleep: A comprehensive handbook* (pp. 395–400). Wiley-Liss.
Richelle, M. N. (1993). *B. F. Skinner: A reappraisal*. Psychology Press.
Richerson, G. B., Aston-Jones, G., & Saper, C. B. (2013). The modulatory functions of the brain stem. In E. R. Kandel, J. H. Schwartz, T. M. Jessell, S. A. Siegelbaum, & A. J. Hudspeth (Eds.), *Principles of neural science* (5th ed., pp. 1038–1055). McGraw-Hill.
Richman, L. S., & Leary, M. R. (2009). Reactions to discrimination, stigmatization, ostracism, and other forms of interpersonal rejection: A multimotive model. *Psychological Review, 116*(2), 365–383.
Richter, A. (2003). Sleeping time in early Chinese literature. In B. Steger & L. Brunt (Eds.), *Night-time and sleep in Asia and the West: Exploring the dark side of life* (pp. 24–44). University of Vienna Press.
Rideout, V. J., Foehr, U. G., & Roberts, D. F. (2010). *Generation M2: Media in the lives of 8- to 18-year-olds*. Henry J. Kaiser Family Foundation.
Rideout, V., & Hamel, E. (2006). *The media family: Electronic media in the lives of infants, toddlers, preschoolers and their parents*. Henry J. Kaiser Family Foundation.
Riediger, M., & Freund, A. M. (2008). Me against myself: Motivational conflicts and emotional development in adulthood. *Psychology and Aging, 23*(3), 479–494.
Riediger, M., & Rauers, A. (2014). Do everyday affective experiences differ throughout childhood? A review of ambulatory-assessment evidence. In P. Verhaeghen & C. K. Hertzog (Eds.), *The Oxford handbook of emotion, social cognition, and problem solving in adulthood* (pp. 61–81). Oxford University Press.
Riediger, M., Schmiedek, F., Wagner, G. G., & Lindenberger, U. (2009). Seeking pleasure and seeking pain: Differences in prohedonic and contra-hedonic motivation from adolescence to old age. *Psychological Science, 20*(12), 1529–1535.
Riediger, M., Schmiedek, F., Wagner, G. G., & Lindenberger, U. (2009). Seeking pleasure and seeking pain: Differences in prohedonic and contra-hedonic motivation from adolescence to old age. *Psychological Science, 20*(12), 1529–1535.
Riemann, D., & Nissen, C. (2012). Sleep and psychotropic drugs. In C. M. Morin & C. A. Espie (Eds.), *The Oxford handbook of sleep and sleep disorders* (pp. 190–222). Oxford University Press.
Rienecke, R. D. (2018). Expressed emotion and eating disorders: An updated review. *Current Psychiatry Reviews, 14*(2), 84–98.
Riffin, C., Ong, A. D., & Bergeman, C. S. (2014). Positive emotions and health in adulthood and later life. In P. Verhaeghen & C. K. Hertzog (Eds.), *The Oxford handbook of emotion, social cognition, and problem solving in adulthood* (pp. 115–127). Oxford University Press.
Riggs, D. W., Worth, A., & Bartholomaeus, C. (2018). The transition to parenthood for Australian heterosexual couples: Expectations, experiences and the partner relationship. *BMC Pregnancy and Childbirth, 18*(1), 342.
Riley, E. P., & McGee, C. L. (2005). Fetal alcohol spectrum disorders: An overview with emphasis on changes in brain and behavior. *Experimental Biology and Medicine, 230*(6), 357–365.
Rilling, J. K. (2006). Human and nonhuman primate brains: Are they allometrically scaled versions of the same design? *Evolutionary Anthropology: Issues, News, and Reviews, 15*(2), 65–77.
Rimé, B., Mesquita, B., Boca, S., & Philippot, P. (1991). Beyond the emotional event: Six studies on the social sharing of emotion. *Cognition & Emotion, 5*(5–6), 435–465.
Rimfeld, K., Kovas, Y., Dale, P. S., & Plomin, R. (2016). True grit and genetics: Predicting academic achievement from personality. *Journal of Personality and Social Psychology, 111*(5), 780–789.
Rindermann, H., Becker, D., & Coyle, T. R. (2017). Survey of expert opinion on intelligence: The Flynn effect and the future of intelligence. *Personality and Individual Differences, 106*, 242–247.
Rindermann, H., Flores-Mendoza, C., & Woodley, M. A. (2012). Political orientations, intelligence and education. *Intelligence, 40*(2), 217–225.
Rinderu, M. I., Bushman, B. J., & Van Lange, P. A. (2018). Climate, aggression, and violence (CLASH): A cultural-evolutionary approach. *Current Opinion in Psychology, 19*, 113–118.
Riper, H., & Cuijpers, P. J. (2016). Telepsychology and eHealth. In J. C. Norcross, G. R. VandenBos, & D. K. Freedheim (Eds.), *APA handbook of clinical psychology* (Vol. 3, pp. 451–463). American Psychological Association.
Rips, L. J., Smith, E. E., & Medin, D. L. (2012). Concepts and categories: Memory, meaning, and metaphysics. In K. J. Holyoak and R. G. Morrison (Eds.), *The Oxford handbook of thinking and reasoning* (pp. 177–209). Oxford University Press.
Rivadeneyra, R. (2011). Gender and race portrayals on Spanish-language television. *Sex Roles, 65*(3–4), 208–222.
Rivera, L. M. (2010). Acculturation. In J. G. Ponterotto, J. M. Casas, L. A. Suzuki, & C. M. Alexander (Eds.), *Handbook of multicultural counseling* (3rd ed., pp. 331–341). Sage.
Rivkees, S. A. (2003). Developing circadian rhythmicity in infants. *Pediatrics, 112*(2), 373–381.
Rizvi, S. L., & King, A. M. (2019). Dialectical behaviour therapy: A comprehensive cognitive-behavioral treatment for borderline personality disorder, emotion dysregulation, and difficult-to-treat behaviors. In K. S. Dobson & D. J. A. Dozois (Eds.), *Handbook of cognitive-behavioral therapies* (4th ed., pp. 297–317). Guilford Press.
Rizzi, T. S., & Posthuma, D. (2013). Genes and intelligence. In D. Reisberg (Ed.), *The Oxford handbook of cognitive psychology* (pp. 823–841). Oxford University Press.
Rizzolatti, G., & Craighero, L. (2004). The mirror-neuron system. *Annual Review of Neuroscience, 27*, 169–192.
Rizzolatti, G., & Kalaska, J. F. (2013). Voluntary movement: The parietal and premotor cortex. In E. R. Kandel, J. H. Schwartz, T. M. Jessell, S. A. Siegelbaum, & A. J. Hudspeth (Eds.), *Principles of neural science* (5th ed., pp. 865–893). McGraw-Hill.
Rizzolatti, G., & Strick, P. L. (2013). Cognitive functions of the premotor systems. In E. R. Kandel, J. H. Schwartz, T. M. Jessell, S. A. Siegelbaum, & A. J. Hudspeth (Eds.), *Principles of neural science* (5th ed., pp. 412–425). McGraw-Hill.
Robbins, S. B., Lauver, K., Le, H., Davis, D., Langley, R., & Carlstrom, A. (2004). Do psychosocial and study skill factors predict college outcomes? A meta-analysis. *Psychological Bulletin, 130*(2), 261.
Roberson, D. (2005). Color categories are culturally diverse in cognition as well as in language. *Cross-Cultural Research, 39*(1), 56–71.
Roberson, D., & Hanley, J. R. (2010). An account of the relationship between language and thought in the color domain. In B. C. Malt & P. Wolff (Eds.), *Words and the mind: How words capture human experience* (pp. 183–198). Oxford University Press.
Roberson, D., Davidoff, J., Davies, I. R., & Shapiro, L. R. (2004). The development of color categories in two languages: A longitudinal study. *Journal of Experimental Psychology: General, 133*(4), 554–571.
Roberson, D., Davidoff, J., Davies, I. R., & Shapiro, L. R. (2005a). Color categories: Evidence for the cultural relativity hypothesis. *Cognitive Psychology, 50*(4), 378–411.
Roberson, D., Davies, I. R., Corbett, G. G., & Vandervyver, M. (2005b). Free-sorting of colors across cultures: Are there universal grounds for grouping? *Journal of Cognition and Culture, 5*(3), 349–386.
Roberson, D., Davies, I., & Davidoff, J. (2000). Color categories are not universal: Replications and new evidence from a stone-age culture. *Journal of Experimental Psychology: General, 129*(3), 369–398.
Robert, G., & Zadra, A. (2008). Measuring nightmare and bad dream frequency: Impact of retrospective and prospective instruments. *Journal of Sleep Research, 17*(2), 132–139.
Roberto, C. A., & Brownell, K. D. (2011). The imperative of changing public policy to address obesity. In J. H. Cawley (Ed.), *The Oxford handbook of the social science of obesity* (pp. 587–608). Oxford University Press.
Roberto, C. A., Swinburn, B., Hawkes, C., Huang, T. T. K., Costa, S. A., Ashe, M., Zwicker, L., Cawley, J. H., & Brownell, K. D. (2015). Patchy progress on obesity prevention: Emerging examples, entrenched barriers, and new thinking. *The Lancet, 385*(9985), 2400–2409.
Roberts, A., Cash, T., Feingold, A., & Johnson, B. T. (2006). Are black-white differences in females' body dissatisfaction decreasing? A meta-analytic review. *Journal of Consulting and Clinical Psychology, 74*(6), 1121–1131.
Roberts, B. W. (1997). Plaster or plasticity: Are adult work experiences associated with personality change in women? *Journal of Personality, 65*(2), 205–232. https://doi.org/10.1111/j.1467-6494.1997.tb00953.x
Roberts, B. W., Robins, R. W., Trzesniewski, K. H., & Caspi, A. (2003). Personality trait development in adulthood. In J. T. Mortimer & M. J. Shanahan (Eds.), *Handbook of the life course* (pp. 579–595). Kluwer.
Roberts, B. W., Wood, D., & Caspi, A. (2008). The development of personality traits in adulthood. In O. P. John, R. W. Robins, & L. A. Pervin (Eds.), *Handbook of personality: Theory and research* (3rd ed., pp. 375–398). Guilford Press.
Roberts, D. F., Foehr, U. G., Rideout, V. J., & Brodie, M. (1999). *Kids and media @ the new millennium: A comprehensive national analysis of children's media use*. Henry J. Kaiser Family Foundation.
Roberts, S. O., & Rizzo, M. T. (2021). The psychology of American racism. *American Psychologist, 76*(3), 475–487. https://doi.org/10.1037/amp0000642
Roberts, W., Milich, R., & Barkley, R. A. (2015). Primary symptoms, diagnostic criteria, subtyping, and prevalence of ADHD. In R. A. Barkley (Ed.), *Attention-deficit hyperactivity disorder: A handbook for diagnosis and treatment* (4th ed., pp. 51–80). Guilford Press.
Robillard, R., Dion, K., Pennestri, M. H., Solomonova, E., Lee, E., Saad, M., Murkar, A., Godbout, R., Edwards, J. D., Quilty, L., Daros, A. R., Bhatia, R., & Kendzerska, T. (2021). Profiles of sleep changes during the COVID-19 pandemic: Demographic, behavioural and psychological factors. *Journal of Sleep Research, 30*(1), e13231. https://doi.org/10.1111/jsr.13231
Robiner, W. N., Bearman, D. L., Berman, M., Grove, W. M., Colon, E., & Armstrong, J. (2002). Prescriptive authority for psychologists: A looming health hazard? *Clinical Psychology: Science and Practice, 9*(3), 231–248.
Robiner, W. N., Tompkins, T. L., & Hathaway, K. M. (2020). Prescriptive authority: Psychologists' abridged training relative to other professions' training. Clinical Psychology: Science and Practice, 27(1), e12309. https://doi.org/10.1111/cpsp.12309
Robins, R. W., & Pals, J. L. (2002). Implicit self-theories in the academic domain: Implications for goal orientation, attributions, affect, and self-esteem change. *Self and Identity, 1*(4), 313–336.
Robins, R. W., Caspi, A., & Moffitt, T. E. (2002). It's not just who you're with, it's who you are: Personality and relationship experiences across multiple relationships. *Journal of Personality, 70*(6), 925–964. https://doi.org/10.1111/1467-6494.05028
Robinson, A., Bonnette, A., Howard, K., Ceballos, N., Dailey, S., Lu, Y., & Grimes, T. (2019). Social comparisons, social media addiction, and social interaction: An examination of specific social media behaviors related to major depressive disorder in a millennial population. *Journal of Applied Biobehavioral Research, 24*(1), e12158.
Robinson, D. N. (1997). Aristotle and psychology. In W. G. Bringmann, H. E. Lück, R. Miller, & C. E. Early (Eds.), *A pictorial history of psychology* (pp. 3–7). Quintessence Publishing.
Robinson, E., McFarland-Lesser, I., Patel, Z., & Jones, A. (2022). Downsizing food: A systematic review and meta-analysis examining the effect of reducing served food portion sizes on daily energy intake and body weight. *British Journal of Nutrition*, 1–39. https://doi.org/10.1017/S0007114522000903
Robinson, M. D., & Johnson, J. T. (1997). Is it emotion or is it stress? Gender stereotypes and the perception of subjective experience. *Sex Roles, 36*(3–4), 235–258.
Robinson-Wood, T. L. (2009). Extending cultural understanding beyond race and ethnicity. In C. C. Lee, D. A. Burnhill, A. L. Butler, C. P. Hipolito-Delgado, M. Humphrey, O. Munoz, & H. Shin (Eds.), *Elements of culture in counseling* (pp. 31–41). Pearson.
Röcke, C., Li, S. C., & Smith, J. (2009). Intraindividual variability in positive and negative affect over 45 days: Do older adults fluctuate less than young adults? *Psychology and Aging, 24*(4), 863–878.
Rockstuhl, T., & Ng, K.-Y. (2008). The effects of cultural intelligence on interpersonal trust in multicultural teams. In S. Ang & L. Van Dyne (Eds.), *Handbook of cultural intelligence: Theory, measurement, and applications* (pp. 206–220). Sharpe.
Rodríguez, I., Kozusznik, M. W., & Peiró, J. M. (2013). Development and validation of the Valencia Eustress-Distress Appraisal Scale. *International Journal of Stress Management, 20*(4), 279–308.
Roe, D., Lysaker, P. H., & Yanos, P. T. (2014). Overcoming stigma. In P. W. Corrigan (Ed.), *The stigma of disease and disability* (pp. 269–282). American Psychological Association.
Roediger, H. L., & Gallo, D. A. (2004). Associative memory illusions. In R. F. Pohl (Ed.), *Cognitive illusions: A handbook on fallacies and biases in thinking, judgement, and memory* (pp. 309–326). Psychology Press.
Roediger, H. L., & Karpicke, J. D. (2011). Intricacies of spaced retrieval: A resolution. In A. S. Benjamin (Ed.), *Successful remembering and successful forgetting: A Festschrift in honor of Robert A. Bjork* (pp. 23–47). Psychology Press.
Roediger, H. L., & McDermott, K. B. (2000). Distortions of memory. In E. Tulving & F. I. M. Craik (Eds.), *The Oxford handbook of memory* (pp. 149–162). Oxford University Press.
Roediger, H. L., III. (2007). Teaching, research, and more: Psychologists in an academic career. In R. J. Sternberg (Ed.), *Career paths in psychology: Where your degree can take you* (2nd ed., pp. 9–33). American Psychological Association.
Roediger, H. L., Weinstein, Y., & Agarwal, P. K. (2010). Forgetting: Preliminary considerations. In S. Della Sala (Ed.), *Forgetting* (pp. 1–22). Psychology Press.
Roemer, L., & Orsillo, S. M. (2009). *Mindfulness- and acceptance-based behavioral therapies in practice*. Guilford Press.
Roemer, L., Molina, S., & Borkovec, T. D. (1997). An investigation of worry content among generally anxious individuals. *The Journal of Nervous & Mental Disease, 185*(5), 314–319.
Roenneberg, T., Kumar, C. J., & Merrow, M. (2007). The human circadian clock entrains to sun time. *Current Biology, 17*(2), R44–R45.
Roese, N. J., Pennington, G. L., Coleman, J., Janicki, M., Li, N. P., & Kenrick, D. T. (2006). Sex differences in regret: All for love or some for lust? *Personality and Social Psychology Bulletin, 32*(6), 770–780.

Roest, A. M., de Vries, Y. A., Lim, C. C., Wittchen, H. U., Stein, D. J., Adamowski, T., Al-Hamzawi, A., Bromet, E. J., Viana, M. C., de Girolamo, G., Demyttenaere, K., Florescu, S., Gureje, O., Haro, J. M., Hu, C., Karam, E. G., Caldas-de-Almeida, J. M., Kawakami, N., Lépine, J. P., ... WHO World Mental Health Survey Collaborators. (2019). A comparison of DSM-5 and DSM-IV agoraphobia in the World Mental Health Surveys. *Depression and Anxiety, 36*(6), 499–510. https://doi.org/10.1002/da.22885

Roffman, J. L., Marci, C. D., Glick, D. M., Dougherty, D. D., & Rauch, S. L. (2005). Neuroimaging and the functional neuroanatomy of psychotherapy. *Psychological Medicine, 35*(10), 1385–1398.

Roger, P. R., & Stone, G. (2014). Counseling vs. clinical. http://www.div17.org/about/what-is-counseling-psychology/counseling-vs-clinical/

Rogers, A. (2018). Carl Rogers: Absence and presence in the contemporary landscape. In R. House, D. Kalisch, & J. Maidman (Eds.), *Humanistic psychology: Current trends and future prospects* (pp. 149–159). Routledge.

Rogers, C. R. (1957). The necessary and sufficient conditions of therapeutic personality change. *Journal of Consulting Psychology, 21*(2), 95–103.

Rogers, C. R. (1959). Client-centered therapy. In S. Arieti (Ed.), *American handbook of psychiatry* (Vol. 3). Basic Books.

Rogers, C. R. (1961). *On becoming a person*. Houghton-Mifflin.

Rogers, C. R. (1980). *A way of being*. Houghton-Mifflin.

Rogers, C. R. (1986). Reflection of feelings and transference. *Person-Centered Review, 1*, 375–377.

Rogers-Sirin, L., Melendez, F., Refano, C., & Zegarra, Y. (2015). Immigrant perceptions of therapists' cultural competence: A qualitative investigation. *Professional Psychology: Research and Practice, 46*(4), 258–269.

Rogoff, B. (2003). *The cultural nature of human development*. Oxford University Press.

Rohde, T. E., & Thompson, L. A. (2007). Predicting academic achievement with cognitive ability. *Intelligence, 35*(1), 83–92.

Rohrer, J. M., Egloff, B., & Schmukle, S. C. (2015). Examining the effects of birth order on personality. *Proceedings of the National Academy of Sciences, 112*(46), 14224–14229.

Roland, J. L., Snyder, A. Z., Hacker, C. D., Mitra, A., Shimony, J. S., Limbrick, D. D., & Leuthardt, E. C. (2017). On the role of the corpus callosum in interhemispheric functional connectivity in humans. *Proceedings of the National Academy of Sciences, 114*(50), 13278–13283.

Rolland, J. S., & Walsh, F. (2009). Family systems theory and practice. In G. O. Gabbard (Ed.), *Textbook of psychotherapeutic treatments* (pp. 499–531). American Psychiatric Publishing.

Rollman, G. B. (2010). Pain: Cognitive and contextual influences. In E. B. Goldstein (Ed.), *Encyclopedia of perception* (pp. 716–720). Sage.

Romans, S. E., Martin, J. M., Gendall, K., & Herbison, G. P. (2003). Age of menarche: The role of some psychosocial factors. *Psychological Medicine, 33*(5), 933–939.

Romero, A., & Piña-Watson, B. (2017). Acculturative stress and bicultural stress: Psychological measurement and mental health. In S. J. Schwartz & J. B. Unger (Eds.), *The Oxford handbook of acculturation and health* (pp. 119–134). Oxford University Press.

Ronningstam, E. (2009). Narcissistic personality disorder. In P. H. Blaney & T. Millon (Eds.), *Oxford textbook of psychopathology* (2nd ed., pp. 752–771). Oxford University Press.

Room, R., Babor, T., & Rehm, J. (2005). Alcohol and public health. *The Lancet, 365*(9458), 519–530.

Rosch, E. (1975). Cognitive representations of semantic categories. *Journal of Experimental Psychology: General, 104*(3), 192–233.

Rosch, E., & Mervis, C. B. (1975). Family resemblances: Studies in the internal structure of categories. *Cognitive Psychology, 7*(4), 573–605.

Rosch, E., Mervis, C. B., Gray, W. D., Johnson, D. M., & Boyes-Braem, P. (1976). Basic objects in natural categories. *Cognitive Psychology, 8*(3), 382–439.

Rose, A. J. (2002). Co-rumination in the friendships of girls and boys. *Child Development, 73*(6), 1830–1843.

Rose, A. J., Carlson, W., & Waller, E. M. (2007). Prospective associations of co-rumination with friendship and emotional adjustment: Considering the socioemotional trade-offs of co-rumination. *Developmental Psychology, 43*(4), 1019–1031.

Rose, L. T., & Fischer, K. W. (2009). Dynamic development: A neo-Piagetian approach. In U. Müller, J. I. M. Carpendale, & L. Smith (Eds.), *The Cambridge companion to Piaget* (pp. 400–421). Cambridge University Press.

Rose, N. S., & Abi-Rached, J. M. (2013). *Neuro: The new brain sciences and the management of the mind*. Princeton University Press.

Rose, N. S., Craik, F. I., & Buchsbaum, B. R. (2015). Levels of processing in working memory: Differential involvement of frontotemporal networks. *Journal of Cognitive Neuroscience, 27*(3), 522–532.

Rose, T., Kaser-Boyd, N., & Maloney, M. P. (2001). *Essentials of Rorschach assessment*. Wiley.

Rosen, L. D., Chang, J., Erwin, L., Carrier, L. M., & Cheever, N. A. (2010). The relationship between "textisms" and formal and informal writing among young adults. *Communication Research, 37*(3), 420–440.

Rosenberg, J., & Tunney, R. J. (2008). Human vocabulary use as display. *Evolutionary Psychology, 6*(3), 538–549.

Rosenfeld, G. W. (2009). *Beyond evidence-based psychotherapy: Fostering the eight sources of change in child and adolescent treatment*. Routledge.

Rosenman, R. H., Brand, R. J., Jenkins, C. D., Friedman, M., Straus, R., & Wurm, M. (1975). Coronary heart disease in the Western Collaborative Group Study: Final follow-up experience of 8 1/2 years. *JAMA, 233*(8), 872–877.

Rosenman, R. H., Friedman, M., Straus, R., Wurm, M., Kositchek, R., Hahn, W., & Werthessen, N. T. (1964). A predictive study of coronary heart disease: The Western Collaborative Group Study. *JAMA, 189*(1), 15–22.

Rosenthal, L. (2016). Incorporating intersectionality into psychology: An opportunity to promote social justice and equity. *American Psychologist, 71*(6), 474–485.

Rosenthal, L., & Lobel, M. (2011). Explaining racial disparities in adverse birth outcomes: Unique sources of stress for Black American women. *Social Science & Medicine, 72*(6), 977–983.

Rosenthal, L., Merlotti, L., Roehrs, T. A., & Roth, T. (1991). Enforced 24-hour recovery following sleep deprivation. *Sleep, 14*(5), 448–453.

Rosenzweig, M. R., Krech, D., Bennett, E. L., & Diamond, M. C. (1962). Effects of environmental complexity and training on brain chemistry and anatomy: A replication and extension. *Journal of Comparative and Physiological Psychology, 55*(4), 429–437. https://doi.org/10.1037/h0041137

Rosenzweig, S. (1936). Some implicit common factors in diverse methods of psychotherapy. *American Journal of Orthopsychiatry, 6*(3), 422–425.

Rosete, D., & Ciarrochi, J. (2005). Emotional intelligence and its relationship to workplace performance outcomes of leadership effectiveness. *Leadership & Organization Development Journal, 26*(5), 388–399.

Rosner, R. I. (2015). Beck, Aaron T. In R. L. Cautin & S. O. Lilienfeld (Eds.), *The encyclopedia of clinical psychology* (pp. 293–296). Wiley-Blackwell.

Rosner, R. I. (2018). History and the topsy-turvy world of psychotherapy. *History of Psychology, 21*(3), 177–186.

Rosnow, R. L., Rotheram-Borus, M. J., Ceci, S. J., Blanck, P. D., & Koocher, G. P. (1993). The Institutional Review Board as a mirror of scientific and ethical standards. *American Psychologist, 48*(7), 821–826.

Rosqvist, J., Thomas, J. C., & Truax, P. (2011). Effectiveness versus efficacy studies. In J. C. Thomas & M. Hersen (Eds.), *Understanding research in clinical and counseling psychology* (2nd ed., pp. 319–354). Taylor & Francis.

Ross, A. M., Morgan, A. J., Jorm, A. F., & Reavley, N. J. (2018). A systematic review of the impact of media reports of severe mental illness on stigma and discrimination, and interventions that aim to mitigate any adverse impact. *Social Psychiatry and Psychiatric Epidemiology, 54*(1), 11–31.

Ross, C. A. (1997). *Dissociative identity disorder: Diagnosis, clinical features, and treatment of multiple personality* (2nd ed.). Wiley.

Ross, L. (1977). The intuitive psychologist and his shortcomings: Distortions in the attribution process. *Advances in Experimental Social Psychology, 10*, 173–220.

Ross, L., & Nisbett, R. E. (1991). *The person and the situation*. McGraw-Hill.

Ross, L., Lepper, M., & Ward, A. (2010). History of social psychology: Insights, challenges, and contributions to theory and application. In S. T. Fiske, D. T. Gilbert, & G. Lindzey (Eds.), *Handbook of social psychology* (5th ed., Vol. 1, pp. 3–50). Wiley.

Ross, M., & Wang, Q. (2010). Why we remember and what we remember: Culture and autobiographical memory. *Perspectives on Psychological Science, 5*(4), 401–409.

Ross, M., Xun, W. E., & Wilson, A. E. (2002). Language and the bicultural self. *Personality and Social Psychology Bulletin, 28*(8), 1040–1050.

Rossini, P. M., Martino, G., Narici, L., Pasquarelli, A., Peresson, M., Pizzella, V., Tecchio, F., Torrioli, G., & Romani, G. L. (1994). Short-term brain "plasticity" in humans: Transient finger representation changes in sensory cortex somatotopy following ischemic anesthesia. *Brain Research, 642*(1–2), 169–177.

Rostosky, S. S., Regnerus, M. D., & Wright, M. L. C. (2003). Coital debut: The role of religiosity and sex attitudes in the Add Health Survey. *Journal of Sex Research, 40*(4), 358–367.

Rotenberg, K. J., Betts, L. R., Eisner, M., & Ribeaud, D. (2012). Social antecedents of children's trustworthiness. *Infant and Child Development, 21*(3), 310–322.

Roth, A., & Fonagy, P. (2005). *What works for whom? A critical review of psychotherapy research* (2nd ed.). Guilford Press.

Roth, D. A., Eng, W., & Heimberg, R. G. (2002). Cognitive behavior therapy. In M. Hersen & W. Sledge (Eds.), *Encyclopedia of psychotherapy* (Vol. 1, pp. 451–458). Academic Press.

Rothbart, M. K. (2007). Temperament, development, and personality. *Current Directions in Psychological Science, 16*(4), 207–212.

Rothbart, M. K., & Bates, J. E. (2006). Temperament. In N. Eisenberg (Vol. Ed.), *Handbook of child psychology* (6th ed., Vol. 3, pp. 99–166). Wiley.

Rothbart, M. K., Ahadi, S. A., & Evans, D. E. (2000). Temperament and personality: Origins and outcomes. *Journal of Personality and Social Psychology, 78*(1), 122–135.

Rothbaum, F., Weisz, J. R., & Snyder, S. S. (1982). Changing the world and changing the self: A two-process model of perceived control. *Journal of Personality and Social Psychology, 42*(1), 5–37.

Rothstein, H. R. (2012). Accessing relevant literature. In H. Cooper (Ed.), *APA handbook of research methods in psychology* (Vol. 1, pp. 133–144). American Psychological Association.

Rothstein, M. G., & Goffin, R. D. (2006). The use of personality measures in personnel selection: What does current research support? *Human Resource Management Review, 16*(2), 155–180.

Rotter, J. B. (1966). Generalized expectancies for internal versus external control of reinforcement. *Psychological Monographs, 80*(1), 1–28.

Rotter, J. B. (1975). Some problems and misconceptions related to the construct of internal versus external control of reinforcement. *Journal of Consulting and Clinical Psychology, 43*(1), 56–67.

Rotter, J. B. (1989). Internal versus external control of reinforcement: A case history of a variable. *American Psychologist, 45*(4), 489–493.

Roubinov, D. S., Hagan, M. J., Boyce, W. T., Essex, M. J., & Bush, N. R. (2017). Child temperament and teacher relationship interactively predict cortisol expression: The prism of classroom climate. *Development and Psychopathology, 29*(5), 1763–1775.

Rounsefell, K., Gibson, S., McLean, S., Blair, M., Molenaar, A., Brennan, L., Truby, H., & McCaffrey, T. A. (2020). Social media, body image and food choices in healthy young adults: A mixed methods systematic review. *Nutrition & Dietetics, 77*(1), 19–40. https://doi.org/10.1111/1747-0080.12581

Rousseau, A., & Eggermont, S. (2018). Television and preadolescents' objectified dating script: Consequences for self- and interpersonal objectification. *Mass Communication and Society, 21*(1), 71–93.

Routh, D. K. (1996). Lightner Witmer and the first 100 years of clinical psychology. *American Psychologist, 51*(3), 244–247.

Routh, D. K. (2011). A history of clinical psychology. In D. H. Barlow (Ed.), *The Oxford handbook of clinical psychology* (pp. 23–33). Oxford University Press.

Rowa, K., McCabe, R. E., & Antony, M. M. (2018). Specific phobia and social anxiety disorder. In J. Hunsley & E. J. Mash (Eds.), *A guide to assessments that work* (2nd ed., pp. 242–265). Oxford University Press.

Roysircar, G. (2013). Multicultural assessment: Individual and contextual dynamic sizing. In F. T. L. Leong (Ed.), *APA handbook of multicultural psychology* (Vol. 1, pp. 141–160). American Psychological Association.

Rozental, A., Castonguay, L., Dimidjian, S., Lambert, M., Shafran, R., Andersson, G., & Carlbring, P. (2018). Negative effects in psychotherapy: Commentary and recommendations for future research and clinical practice. *BJPsych Open, 4*(4), 307–312. https://doi.org/10.1192/bjo.2018.42

Rozental, A., Kottorp, A., Boettcher, J., Andersson, G., & Carlbring, P. (2016). Negative effects of psychological treatments: An exploratory factor analysis of the negative effects questionnaire for monitoring and reporting adverse and unwanted events. *PLoS One, 11*(6), e0157503. https://doi.org/10.1371/journal.pone.0157503

Rozgonjuk, D., Levine, J. C., Hall, B. J., & Elhai, J. D. (2018). The association between problematic smartphone use, depression and anxiety symptom severity, and objectively measured smartphone use over one week. *Computers in Human Behavior, 87*, 10–17.

Rubin, D. C., & Kontis, T. C. (1983). A schema for common cents. *Memory & Cognition, 11*(4), 335–341.

Rubin, K. H., Bukowski, W. M., & Parker, J. G. (2006). Peer interactions, relationships, and groups. In N. Eisenberg (Vol. Ed.), *Handbook of child psychology* (6th ed., Vol. 3, pp. 571–645). Wiley.

Rubin, K. H., Coplan, R., Chen, X., Buskirk, A. A., & Wojslawowicz, J. C. (2005). Peer relationships in childhood. In M. H. Bornstein & M. E. Lamb (Eds.), *Developmental science: An advanced textbook* (5th ed., pp. 469–512). Lawrence Erlbaum.

Rubin, R. (Host). (2020). *RZA (No. 49)* [Audio podcast episode]. Broken Record Podcast, Broken Record. https://brokenrecordpodcast.com/episode-49-

Rubinstein, G., & Strul, S. (2007). The Five Factor Model (FFM) among four groups of male and female professionals. *Journal of Research in Personality, 41*(4), 931–937.

Ruble, D. N., & Martin, C. L. (1998). Gender development. In W. Damon & N. Eisenberg (Eds.), *Handbook of child psychology* (5th ed., Vol. 3, pp. 933–1016). Wiley.

Ruble, D. N., Martin, C. L., & Berenbaum, S. A. (2006). Gender development. In N. Eisenberg, W. Damon, & R. M. Lerner (Eds.), *Handbook of child psychology* (6th ed., Vol. 3, pp. 858–932). Wiley.

Ruch, W. (1995). Will the real relationship between facial expression and affective experience please stand up: The case of exhilaration. *Cognition & Emotion, 9*(1), 33–58.

Ruddy, N. B., Borresen, D. A., & Gunn, W. B., Jr. (2008). *The collaborative psychotherapist: Creating reciprocal relationships with medical professionals.* American Psychological Association.

Rudmin, F. W. (2003). Critical history of the acculturation psychology of assimilation, separation, integration, and marginalization. *Review of General Psychology, 7*(1), 3–37.

Rudmin, F. W., & Ahmadzadeh, V. (2001). Psychometric critique of acculturation psychology: The case of Iranian migrants in Norway. *Scandinavian Journal of Psychology, 42*(1), 41–56.

Rudolph, C. W., Wells, C. L., Weller, M. D., & Baltes, B. B. (2009). A meta-analysis of empirical studies of weight-based bias in the workplace. *Journal of Vocational Behavior, 74*(1), 1–10.

Rudolph, U., Roesch, S., Greitemeyer, T., & Weiner, B. (2004). A meta-analytic review of help giving and aggression from an attributional perspective: Contributions to a general theory of motivation. *Cognition and Emotion, 18*(6), 815–848.

Rueger, S. Y., Malecki, C. K., & Demaray, M. K. (2010). Relationship between multiple sources of perceived social support and psychological and academic adjustment in early adolescence: Comparisons across gender. *Journal of Youth and Adolescence, 39*(1), 47–61.

Rueger, S. Y., Malecki, C. K., Pyun, Y., Aycock, C., & Coyle, S. (2016). A meta-analytic review of the association between perceived social support and depression in childhood and adolescence. *Psychological Bulletin, 142*(10), 1017.

Rule, N. O., Freeman, J. B., & Ambady, N. (2013). Culture in social neuroscience: A review. *Social Neuroscience, 8*(1), 3–10.

Rummell, C. M., & Joyce, N. R. (2010). "So wat do u want to wrk on 2day?": The ethical implications of online counseling. *Ethics & Behavior, 20*(6), 482–496.

Runco, M. A. (2018). Creative thinking. In L. J. Ball & V. A. Thompson (Eds.), *Routledge international handbook of thinking and reasoning* (pp. 472–486). Routledge.

Rüsch, N. & Xu, Z. (2017). Strategies to reduce mental illness stigma. In W. Gaebel, W. Rössler, & N. Sartorius (Eds.), *The stigma of mental illness—end of the story?* (pp. 451–468). Springer International Publishing Sweden.

Russac, R. J., Gatliff, C., Reece, M., & Spottswood, D. (2007). Death anxiety across the adult years: An examination of age and gender effects. *Death Studies, 31*(6), 549–561.

Russell, G. F. M. (1979). Bulimia nervosa: An ominous variant of anorexia nervosa. *Psychological Medicine, 9*(3), 429–448.

Russell, J. A. (1994). Is there universal recognition of emotion from facial expressions? A review of the cross-cultural studies. *Psychological Bulletin, 115*(1), 102–141.

Russell, J. A. (2017a). Toward a broader perspective on facial expressions. In J. Fernández-Dols & J. A. Russell (Eds.), *The science of facial expression* (pp. 93–106). Oxford University Press.

Russell, J. A. (2017b). Cross-cultural similarities and differences in affective processing and expression. In M. Jeon (Ed.), *Emotions and affect in human factors and human-computer interaction* (pp. 123–141). Academic Press.

Russell, S. T., & Consolacion, T. B. (2003). Adolescent romance and emotional health in the United States: Beyond binaries. *Journal of Clinical Child and Adolescent Psychology, 32*(4), 499–508.

Russell, S. T., & Fish, J. N. (2016). Mental health in lesbian, gay, bisexual, and transgender (LGBT) youth. *Annual Review of Clinical Psychology, 12*, 465–487.

Russell, S. T., Muraco, A., Subramaniam, A., & Laub, C. (2009). Youth empowerment and high school gay-straight alliances. *Journal of Youth and Adolescence, 38*(7), 891–903.

Rusting, C. L., & DeHart, T. (2000). Retrieving positive memories to regulate negative mood: Consequences for mood-congruent memory. *Journal of Personality and Social Psychology, 78*(4), 737.

Rutan, J. S., & Shay, J. J. (2017). Group therapy: Theory and practice. In A. J. Consoli, L. E. Beutler, & B. Bongar (Eds.), *Comprehensive textbook of psychotherapy: Theory and practice* (2nd ed., pp. 223–238). Oxford University Press.

Rutherford, A. (2009). *Beyond the box: B. F. Skinner's technology of behavior from laboratory to life, 1950s–1970s*. University of Toronto Press.

Rutherford, A., & Milar, K. (2017). "The difference being a woman made": *Untold Lives* in personal and intellectual context. *Journal of the History of the Behavioral Sciences, 53*(3), 221–227. https://doi.org/10.1002/jhbs.21860

Rutledge, T., Reis, S. E., Olson, M., Owens, J., Kelsey, S. F., Pepine, C. J., Mankad, S., Rogers, W. J., Bairey Merz, C. N., Sopko, G., Cornell, C. E., Sharaf, B., Matthews, K. A., & National Heart, Lung, and Blood Institute. (2004). Social networks are associated with lower mortality rates among women with suspected coronary disease: The National Heart, Lung, and Blood Institute-sponsored Women's Ischemia Syndrome Evaluation study. *Psychosomatic Medicine, 66*(6), 882–888.

Rutter, M. (2000). Psychosocial influences: Critiques, findings, and research needs. *Development and Psychopathology, 12*(3), 375–405.

Rutter, M. (2006). *Genes and behavior: Nature–nurture interplay explained*. Blackwell.

Rutter, M. (2011). Biological and experiential influences on psychological development. In D. P. Keating (Ed.), *Nature and nurture in early child development* (pp. 7–44). Cambridge University Press.

Ryan, L., Hoscheidt, S., & Nadel, L. (2008). Perspectives on episodic and semantic memory retrieval. In E. Dere, A. Easton, L. Nadel, & J. P. Huston (Eds.), *Handbook of episodic memory* (pp. 5–18). Elsevier Science.

Ryan, R. M. (2012). Motivation and the organization of human behavior: Three reasons for the reemergence of a field. In R. M. Ryan (Ed.), *The Oxford handbook of human motivation* (pp. 2–12). Oxford University Press.

Ryan, R. M., & Deci, E. L. (2000a). Self-determination theory and the facilitation of intrinsic motivation, social development, and well-being. *American Psychologist, 55*(1), 68–78.

Ryan, R. M., & Deci, E. L. (2000b). Intrinsic and extrinsic motivations: Classic definitions and new directions. *Contemporary Educational Psychology, 25*(1), 54–67.

Ryan, R. M., & Deci, E. L. (2003). On assimilating identities to the self: A self-determination theory perspective on internalization and integrity within cultures. In M. R. Leary & J. P. Tangney (Eds.), *Handbook of self and identity* (pp. 254–274). Guilford Press.

Ryan, R. M., & Deci, E. L. (2017). *Self-determination theory: Basic psychological needs in motivation, development, and wellness*. Guilford Press.

Ryan, R. M., Connell, J. P., & Plant, R. W. (1990). Emotions in nondirected text learning. *Learning and Individual Differences, 2*(1), 1–17.

Ryan, R. M., Domenico, S. I. D., Ryan, W. S., & Deci, E. L. (2017). Pervasive influences on wellness and thriving: Cultural, political, and economic contexts and the support of basic psychological needs. In F. Guay, H. W. Marsh, D. M. McInerney, & R. G. Craven (Eds.), *Self: Driving positive psychology and well-being* (International Advances in Self Research series, pp. 199–231). IAP Information Age Publishing.

Rychtarik, R. G., Silverman, W. K., Van Landingham, W. P., & Prue, D. M. (1984). Treatment of an incest victim with implosive therapy: A case study. *Behavior Therapy, 15*(4), 410–420.

Rycroft, C. (1968). *A critical dictionary of psychoanalysis*. Nelson.

Ryder, A. G., Alden, L. E., & Paulhus, D. L. (2000). Is acculturation unidimensional or bidimensional? A head-to-head comparison in the prediction of personality, self-identity, and adjustment. *Journal of Personality and Social Psychology, 79*(1), 49–65.

Ryder, A. G., Zhao, Y., & Chentsova-Dutton, Y. E. (2017). Disordered mood in cultural-historical context. In R. J. DeRubeis & D. R. Strunk (Eds.), *The Oxford handbook of mood disorders* (pp. 71–82). Oxford University Press.

Rygh, J. L., & Sanderson, W. C. (2004). *Treating generalized anxiety disorder: Evidence-based strategies, tools, and techniques*. Guilford Press.

Rymarczyk, K., Zurawski, Ł., Jankowiak-Siuda, K., & Szatkowska, I. (2016). Emotional empathy and facial mimicry for static and dynamic facial expressions of fear and disgust. *Frontiers in Psychology, 7*, 1853.

Rzeszutek, M. (2017). Social support and posttraumatic growth in a longitudinal study of people living with HIV: The mediating role of positive affect. *European Journal of Psychotraumatology, 8*(1), 1412225.

Saarenpaa-Heikkila, O. A., Rintahaka, P. J., Laippala, P. J., & Koivikko, M. J. (1995). Sleep habits and disorders in Finnish schoolchildren. *Journal of Sleep Research, 4*(3), 173–182.

Sachs, G. S. (2004). Strategies for improving treatment of bipolar disorder: Integration of measurement and management. *Acta Psychiatrica Scandinavica Supplementum, 110*(422), 7–17.

Sackett, P. R. (2012). Faking in personality assessments: Where do we stand? In M. Ziegler, C. MacCann, & R. D. Roberts (Eds.), *New perspectives on faking in personality assessment* (pp. 330–344). Oxford University Press.

Sadeh, A. V. I., Mindell, J. A., Luedtke, K., & Wiegand, B. (2009). Sleep and sleep ecology in the first 3 years: A web-based study. *Journal of Sleep Research, 18*(1), 60–73.

Sadler, P. M., Sonnert, G., Hazari, Z., & Tai, R. (2012). Stability and volatility of STEM career interest in high school: A gender study. *Science Education, 96*(3), 411–427.

Sadowsky, J. (2016). *Electroconvulsive therapy in America*. Routledge.

Sadri, G., & Robertson, I. T. (1993). Self-efficacy and work-related behaviour: A review and meta-analysis. *Applied Psychology: An International Review, 42*(2), 139–152.

Safdar, S., Friedlmeier, W., Matsumoto, D., Yoo, S. H., Kwantes, C. T., Kakai, H., & Shigemasu, E. (2009). Variations of emotional display rules within and across cultures: A comparison between Canada, USA, and Japan. *Canadian Journal of Behavioural Science, 41*(1), 1–10.

Saffran, J. R., & Thiessen, E. D. (2003). Pattern induction by infant language learners. *Developmental Psychology, 39*(3), 484.

Safran, J. D., Abreu, I., Ogilvie, J., & DeMaria, A. (2011), Does psychotherapy research influence the clinical practice of researcher–clinicians? *Clinical Psychology: Science and Practice, 18*(4), 357–371.

Sagarin, B. J., Vaughn Becker, D., Guadagno, R. E., Nicastle, L. D., & Millevoi, A. (2003). Sex differences (and similarities) in jealousy: The moderating influence of infidelity experience and sexual orientation of the infidelity. *Evolution and Human Behavior, 24*(1), 17–23.

Saha, S., Chant, D., Welham, J., & McGrath, J. (2005). The systematic review of the prevalence of schizophrenia. *PLoS Med, 2*(5), e141.

Saiphoo, A. N., Halevi, L. D., & Vahedi, Z. (2020). Social networking site use and self-esteem: A meta-analytic review. *Personality and Individual Differences, 153*. https://doi.org/10.1016/j.paid.2019.109639

Sajatovic, M., Madhusoodanan, S., & Fuller, M. A. (2008). Clozapine. In K. T. Mueser & D. V. Jeste (Eds.), *Clinical handbook of schizophrenia* (pp. 178–185). Guilford Press.

Sakai, Y., Kumano, H., Nishikawa, M., Sakano, Y., Kaiya, H., Imabayashi, E., Ohnishi, T., Matsuda, H., Yasuda, A., Sato, A., Diksic, M., & Kuboki, T. (2006). Changes in cerebral glucose utilization in patients with panic disorder treated with cognitive-behavioral therapy. *Neuroimage, 33*(1), 218–226.

Sakaki, M., Yagi, A., & Murayama, K. (2018). Curiosity in old age: A possible key to achieving adaptive aging. *Neuroscience & Biobehavioral Reviews, 88*, 106–116.

Saks, E. R. (2007). *The center cannot hold: My journey through madness*. Hyperion Books.

Sala, G., & Gobet, F. (2017). Experts' memory superiority for domain-specific random material generalizes across fields of expertise: A meta-analysis. *Memory & Cognition, 45*(2), 183–193.

Sala, M., Shankar Ram, S., Vanzhula, I. A., & Levinson, C. A. (2020). Mindfulness and eating disorder psychopathology: A meta-analysis. *International Journal of Eating Disorders, 53*(6), 834–851. https://doi.org/10.1002/eat.23247

Salem, T., Winer, E. S., Jordan, D. G., & Dorr, M. M. (2019). Doubting the diagnosis but seeking a talking cure: An experimental investigation of causal explanations for depression and willingness to accept treatment. *Cognitive Therapy and Research, 43*(6), 971–985. https://doi.org/10.1007/s10608-019-10027-w

Sallis, J. F., Adams, M. A., & Ding, D. (2011). Physical activity and the built environment. In J. H. Cawley (Ed.), *The Oxford handbook of the social science of obesity* (pp. 433–451). Oxford University Press.

Salmon, P. (2001). Effects of physical exercise on anxiety, depression, and sensitivity to stress: A unifying theory. *Clinical Psychology Review, 21*(1), 33–61.

Salovey, P. (2005). Foreword. In R. Schulze & R. D. Roberts (Eds.), *Emotional intelligence: An international handbook* (pp. v–x). Hogrefe & Huber.

Salovey, P., & Mayer, J. D. (1989). Emotional intelligence. *Imagination, Cognition, and Personality, 9*(3), 185–211.

Salthouse, T. A. (2009). When does age-related cognitive decline begin? *Neurobiology of Aging, 30*(4), 507–514.

Salthouse, T. A., & Babcock, R. L. (1991). Decomposing adult age differences in working memory. *Developmental Psychology, 27*(5), 763–776.

Salti, M., Harel, A., & Marti, S. (2019). Conscious perception: Time for an update? *Journal of Cognitive Neuroscience, 31*(1), 1–7.

Salvy, S. J., Jarrin, D., Paluch, R., Irfan, N., & Pliner, P. (2007). Effects of social influence on eating in couples, friends and strangers. *Appetite, 49*(1), 92–99.

Sam, D. L., & Berry, J. W. (2006). Introduction. In D. L. Sam & J. W. Berry (Eds.), *The Cambridge handbook of acculturation psychology* (pp. 1–10). Cambridge University Press.

Samaras, K. (2008). Twin studies and genetics of obesity. In K. Keller (Ed.), *Encyclopedia of obesity* (Vol. 2, pp. 759–760). Sage.

Sammons, M. T. (2011). Treatment modalities: Pharmacotherapy. In J. C. Norcross, G. R. Vandenbos, & D. K. Freedheim (Eds.), *History of psychotherapy: Continuity and change* (2nd ed., pp. 516–532). American Psychological Association.

Sammons, M. T. (2016). Prescribing psychology and pharmacotherapy. In J. C. Norcross, G. R. VandenBos, & D. K. Freedheim (Eds.), *APA handbook of clinical psychology* (Vol. 1, pp. 305–322). American Psychological Association.

Samuel, S., Cole, G., & Eacott, M. J. (2019). Grammatical gender and linguistic relativity: A systematic review. *Psychonomic Bulletin & Review, 26*(6), 1767–1786. https://doi.org/10.3758/s13423-019-01652-3

Samuels, D. V., Rosenthal, R., Lin, R., Chaudhari, S., & Natsuaki, M. N. (2020). Acne vulgaris and risk of depression and anxiety: A meta-analytic review. *Journal of the American Academy of Dermatology, 83*(2), 532–541. https://doi.org/10.1016/j.jaad.2020.02.040

Samuels, N., Gropp, C., Singer, S. R., & Oberbaum, M. (2008). Acupuncture for psychiatric illness: A literature review. *Behavioral Medicine, 34*(2), 55–64.

Sánchez, F. J., & Vilain, E. (2013). Transgender identities: Research and controversies. In C. J. Patterson & A. R. D'Augelli (Eds.), *Handbook of psychology and sexual orientation* (pp. 42–54). Oxford University Press.

Sand, S. (2017). How contemporary psychoanalysis contributes to LGBT psychology: Examining and addressing gender fluidity and diversity as we slide toward 21st-century transformations. In R. Ruth & E. Santacruz (Eds.), *LGBT Psychology and mental health: Emerging research and advances* (pp. 69–86). Praeger.

Sanders, K. A., & Bruce, N. W. (1997). A prospective study of psychosocial stress and fertility in women. *Human Reproduction, 12*(10), 2324–2329.

Sanders, M. H., & Givelber, R. J. (2006). Overview of obstructive sleep apnea in adults. In T. L. Lee-Chiong (Ed.), *Sleep: A comprehensive handbook* (pp. 231–240). Wiley-Liss.

Sandler, J., & Freud, A. (1985). *The analysis of defense: The ego and the mechanisms of defense revisited.* International Universities Press.

Sandstrom, M. J., Cillessen, A. H., & Eisenhower, A. (2003). Children's appraisal of peer rejection experiences: Impact on social and emotional adjustment. *Social Development, 12*(4), 530–550.

Sandy, C. J., Gosling, S. D., & Durant, J. (2013). Predicting consumer behavior and media preferences: The comparative validity of personality traits and demographic variables. *Psychology & Marketing, 30*(11), 937–949.

Sanes, J. N., & Donoghue, J. P. (2000). Plasticity and primary motor cortex. *Annual Review of Neuroscience, 23*(1), 393–415.

Sanes, J. N., Suner, S., & Donoghue, J. P. (1990). Dynamic organization of primary motor cortex output to target muscles in adult rats. I. Long-term patterns of reorganization following motor or mixed peripheral nerve lesions. *Experimental Brain Research, 79*(3), 479–491.

Sanes, J. N., Wang, J., & Donoghue, J. P. (1992). Immediate and delayed changes of rat motor cortical output representation with new forelimb configurations. *Cerebral Cortex, 2*(2), 141–152.

Sanes, J. R., & Jessell, T. M. (2013a). The growth and guidance of axons. In E. R. Kandel, J. H. Schwartz, T. M. Jessell, S. A. Siegelbaum, & A. J. Hudspeth (Eds.), *Principles of neural science* (5th ed., pp. 1209–1232). McGraw-Hill.

Sanes, J. R., & Jessell, T. M. (2013b). Formation and elimination of synapses. In E. R. Kandel, J. H. Schwartz, T. M. Jessell, S. A. Siegelbaum, & A. J. Hudspeth (Eds.), *Principles of neural science* (5th ed., pp. 1233–1258). McGraw-Hill.

Sanes, J. R., & Jessell, T. M. (2013c). Experience and the refinement of synaptic connections. In E. R. Kandel, J. H. Schwartz, T. M. Jessell, S. A. Siegelbaum, & A. J. Hudspeth (Eds.), *Principles of neural science* (5th ed., pp. 1259–1283). McGraw-Hill.

Sanes, J. R., & Jessell, T. M. (2013d). Repairing the damaged brain. In E. R. Kandel, J. H. Schwartz, T. M. Jessell, S. A. Siegelbaum, & A. J. Hudspeth (Eds.), *Principles of neural science* (5th ed., pp. 1284–1305). McGraw-Hill.

Sanghani, S. N., Petrides, G., & Kellner, C. H. (2018). Electroconvulsive therapy (ECT) in schizophrenia: A review of recent literature. *Current Opinion in Psychiatry, 31*(3), 213–222. https://doi.org/10.1097/YCO.0000000000000418

Sanson, A., Hemphill, S. A., Yarmurlu, B., & McClowry, S. (2011). Temperament and social development. In P. K. Smith & C. H. Hart (Eds.), *The Wiley-Blackwell handbook of childhood social development* (2nd ed., pp. 227–245). Wiley-Blackwell.

Santos, M. M., Puspitasari, A. J., Nagy, G. A., & Kanter, J. W. (2021). Behavioral activation. In A. Wenzel (Ed.), *Handbook of cognitive behavioral therapy: Overview and approaches* (pp. 235–273). American Psychological Association. https://doi.org/10.1037/0000218-009

Saper, C. B., Lumsden, A. G. S., & Richerson, G. B. (2013). The sensory, motor, and reflex functions of the brain stem. In E. R. Kandel, J. H. Schwartz, T. M. Jessell, S. A. Siegelbaum, & A. J. Hudspeth (Eds.), *Principles of neural science* (5th ed., pp. 1019–1037). McGraw-Hill.

Saper, C. B., Lumsden, A. G. S., & Richerson, G. B. (2013). The sensory, motor, and reflex functions of the brain stem. In E. R. Kandel, J. H. Schwartz, T. M. Jessell, S. A. Siegelbaum, & A. J. Hudspeth (Eds.), *Principles of neural science* (5th ed., pp. 1019–1037). McGraw-Hill.

Saper, C. B., Scammell, T. E., & Lu, J. (2005). Hypothalamic regulation of sleep and circadian rhythms. *Nature, 437*(7063), 1257–1263.

Şar, V., Dorahy, M. J., & Krüger, C. (2017). Revisiting the etiological aspects of dissociative identity disorder: A biopsychosocial perspective. *Psychology Research and Behavior Management, 10,* 137–146. https://doi.org/10.2147/PRBM.S113743

Sasaki, J. Y., & Kim, H. S. (2017). Nature, nurture, and their interplay: A review of cultural neuroscience. *Journal of Cross-Cultural Psychology, 48*(1), 4–22.

Sassler, S., & Miller, A. (2017). *Cohabitation nation: Gender, class, and the remaking of relationships.* University of California Press.

Satel, S. L., & Lilienfeld, S. O. (2013). *Brainwashed: The seductive appeal of mindless neuroscience.* Basic Books.

Satpute, A. B., Nook, E. C., Narayanan, S., Shu, J., Weber, J., & Ochsner, K. N. (2016). Emotions in "black and white" or shades of gray? How we think about emotion shapes our perception and neural representation of emotion. *Psychological Science, 27*(11), 1428–1442.

Sauce, B., & Matzel, L. D. (2018). The paradox of intelligence: Heritability and malleability coexist in hidden gene-environment interplay. *Psychological Bulletin, 144*(1), 26–47.

Saucier, D. M., Green, S. M., Leason, J., MacFadden, A., Bell, S., & Elias, L. J. (2002). Are sex differences in navigation caused by sexually dimorphic strategies or by differences in the ability to use the strategies? *Behavioral Neuroscience, 116*(3), 403–410.

Saucier, D., & Ehresman, C. (2010). The physiology of sex differences. In J. C. Chrisler & D. R. McCreary (Eds.), *Handbook of gender research in psychology* (Vol. 1, pp. 215–233). Springer Science+Business Media.

Saucier, G., Hampson, S. E., & Goldberg, L. R. (2000). Cross-language studies of lexical personality factors. In S. E. Hampson (Ed.), *Advances in personality psychology,* Vol. 1, pp. 1–36. Psychology Press.

Saucier, G., & Srivastava, S. (2015). What makes a good structural model of personality? Evaluating the Big Five and alternatives. In M. Mikulincer & P. R. Shaver (Eds.), *APA Handbook of personality and social psychology* (Vol. 4, pp. 283–305). American Psychological Association.

Sauer-Zavala, S. Barlow, D. H. (2021). *Neuroticism: A new framework for emotional disorders and their treatment.* Guilford Press.

Sauer-Zavala, S., Wilner, J. G., & Barlow, D. H. (2017). Addressing neuroticism in psychological treatment. *Personality Disorders: Theory, Research, and Treatment, 8*(3), 191–198.

Saunders, H. (2012, May 2). See photos of J Dilla's recently discovered record collection. *Paste Magazine.* http://www.pastemagazine.com/blogs/awesome_of_the_day/2012/05/record-store-owner-finds-j-dillas-record-collection-home-tapes.html

Saunders, J. F., & Eaton, A. A. (2018). Snaps, selfies, and shares: How three popular social media platforms contribute to the sociocultural model of disordered eating among young women. *Cyberpsychology, Behavior, and Social Networking, 21*(6), 343–354.

Saxton, M. (2010). *Child language: Acquisition and development.* Sage.

Sayegh, C. S., Huey, S. J., Jr., Zara, E. J., & Jhaveri, K. (2017). Follow-up treatment effects of contingency management and motivational interviewing on substance use: A meta-analysis. *Psychology of Addictive Behaviors, 31*(4), 403–414.

Sayette, M. A., & Norcross, J. C. (2018). *Insider's guide to graduate programs in clinical and counseling psychology: 2018/2019 edition.* Guilford Press.

Scalera, G., & Bavieri, M. (2008). Role of conditioned taste aversion on the side effects of chemotherapy in cancer patients. In S. Reilly & T. R. Schachtman (Eds.), *Conditioned taste aversion: Neural and behavioral processes* (pp. 513–542). Oxford University Press.

Scarborough, E. & Furumoto, L. (1987). *Untold lives: The first generation of American women psychologists.* Columbia University Press.

Scarpelli, S., Alfonsi, V., Mangiaruga, A., Musetti, A., Quattropani, M. C., Lenzo, V., Freda, M. F., Lemmo, D., Vegni, E., Lidia, B., Saita, E., Cattivelli, R., Castelnuovo, G., Plazzi, G., De Gennaro, L., & Franceschini, C. (2021). Pandemic nightmares: Effects on dream activity of the COVID-19 lockdown in Italy. *Journal of Sleep Research,* e13300. https://doi.org/10.1111/jsr.13300

Schaafsma, S. M., Pfaff, D. W., Spunt, R. P., & Adolphs, R. (2015). Deconstructing and reconstructing theory of mind. *Trends in Cognitive Sciences, 19*(2), 65–72.

Schachtman, T. R., Walker, J., & Fowler, S. (2011). Effects of conditioning in advertising. In T. R. Schachtman & S. S. Reilly (Eds.), *Associative learning and conditioning theory: Human and non-human applications* (pp. 481–506). Oxford University Press.

Schacter, D. L. (2001). *The seven sins of memory: How the mind forgets and remembers.* Houghton Mifflin.

Schacter, D. L., & Wagner, A. D. (2013). Learning and memory. In E. R. Kandel, J. H. Schwartz, T. M. Jessell, S. A. Siegelbaum, & A. J. Hudspeth (Eds.), *Principles of neural science* (5th ed., pp. 1441–1460). McGraw-Hill.

Schacter, D. L., Wagner, A. D., & Buckner, R. L. (2000). Memory systems of 1999. In E. Tulving & F. I. M. Craik (Eds.), *The Oxford handbook of memory* (pp. 627–643). Oxford University Press.

Schacter, H. L., & Juvonen, J. (2017). Depressive symptoms, friend distress, and self-blame: Risk factors for adolescent peer victimization. *Journal of Applied Developmental Psychology, 51,* 35–43.

Schaefer, J. D., Caspi, A., Belsky, D. W., Harrington, H., Houts, R., Israel, S., ... Moffitt, T. E. (2015). Early-life intelligence predicts midlife biological age. *Journals of Gerontology Series B: Psychological Sciences and Social Sciences, 71*(6), 968–977.

Schafe, G. E., & LeDoux, J. E. (2004). The neural basis of fear. In M. S. Gazzaniga (Ed.), *The new cognitive neurosciences III* (pp. 987–1004). MIT Press.

Schaffer, M., Clark, S., & Jeglic, E. L. (2009). The role of empathy and parenting style in the development of antisocial behaviors. *Crime & Delinquency, 55*(4), 586–599.

Schaie, K. W. (2012). *Developmental influences on adult intelligence: The Seattle longitudinal study.* Oxford University Press.

Schaller, M., & Cialdini, R. B. (1988). The economics of empathic helping: Support for a mood management motive. *Journal of Experimental Social Psychology, 24*(2), 163–181.

Schank, J. A., Helbok, C. M., Haldeman, D. C., & Gallardo, M. E. (2010). Challenges and benefits of ethical small-community practice. *Professional Psychology: Research and Practice, 41*(6), 502–510.

Schank, J., Slater, R., Banerjee-Stevens, D., & Skovholt, T. M. (2003). Ethics of multiple and overlapping relationships. In W. O'Donohue & K. Ferguson (Eds.), *Handbook of professional ethics for psychologists: Issues, questions, and controversies* (pp. 181–193). Thousand Oaks, CA: Sage.

Scheier, M. F., & Carver, C. S. (1985). Optimism, coping, and health: Assessment and implications of generalized outcome expectancies. *Health Psychology, 4*(3), 219–247.

Scheier, M. F., & Carver, C. S. (2018). Dispositional optimism and physical health: A long look back, a quick look forward. *American Psychologist, 73*(9), 1082–1094.

Scheier, M. F., Swanson, J. D., Barlow, M. A., Greenhouse, J. B., Wrosch, C., & Tindle, H. A. (2021). Optimism versus pessimism as predictors of physical health: A comprehensive reanalysis of dispositional optimism research. *American Psychologist, 76*(3), 529–548. https://doi.org/10.1037/amp0000666

Schenck, C. H., & Mahowald, M. W. (1994). Review of nocturnal sleep-related eating disorders. *International Journal of Eating Disorders, 15*(4), 343–356.

Schenck, C. H., Arnulf, I., & Mahowald, M. W. (2007). Sleep and sex: What can go wrong? A review of the literature on sleep related disorders and abnormal sexual behaviors and experiences. *Sleep, 30*(6), 683–702.

Schenck, C. H., Hurwitz, T. D., O'Connor, K. A., & Mahowald, M. W. (1993). Additional categories of sleep-related eating disorders and the current status of treatment. *Sleep, 16*(5), 457–466.

Schepis, T. S., Buckner, J. D., Klare, D. L., Wade, L. R., & Benedetto, N. (2021). Predicting college student prescription stimulant misuse: An analysis from ecological momentary assessment. *Experimental and Clinical Psychopharmacology, 29*(6), 580–586. https://doi.org/10.1037/pha0000386

Scher, C. D., Steidtmann, D., Luxton, D., & Ingram, R. E. (2006). Specific phobia: A common problem, rarely treated. In T. G. Plante (Ed.), *Mental disorders of the new millennium* (pp. 245–263). Praeger.

Scherer, L. D., McPhetres, J., Pennycook, G., Kempe, A., Allen, L. A., Knoepke, C. E., Tate, C. E., & Matlock, D. D. (2021). Who is susceptible to online health misinformation? A test of four psychosocial hypotheses. *Health Psychology, 40*(4), 274–284.https://doi.org/10.1037/hea0000978

Schiffer, L. P., & Roberts, T. (2018). The paradox of happiness: Why are we not doing what we know makes us happy? *The Journal of Positive Psychology, 13*(3), 252–259. http://doi.org/10.1080/17439760.2017.1279209

Schiller, D., Eichenbaum, H., Buffalo, E. A., Davachi, L., Foster, D. J., Leutgeb, S., & Ranganath, C. (2015). Memory and space: Towards an understanding of the cognitive map. *Journal of Neuroscience, 35*(41), 13904–13911.

Schindler, R. M. (1992). The real lesson of New Coke: The value of focus groups for predicting the effects of social influence. *Marketing Research, 4*(4), 22–27.

Schirillo, J. A. (2010). Gestalt approach. In E. B. Goldstein (Ed.), *Encyclopedia of perception* (pp. 469–472). Sage.

Schlegel, A. (2009). Cross-cultural issues in the study of adolescent development. In R. M. Lerner & L. Steinberg (Eds.), *Handbook of adolescent psychology* (3rd ed., Vol. 2, pp. 570–589). Wiley.

Schloss, J. G. (2004). *Making beats: The art of sample-based hip-hop.* Wesleyan University Press.

Schmader, T., & Johns, M. (2003). Converging evidence that stereotype threat reduces working memory capacity. *Journal of Personality and Social Psychology, 85*(3), 440–452.

Schmader, T., Johns, M., & Forbes, C. (2008). An integrated process model of stereotype threat effects on performance. *Psychological Review, 115*(2), 336–356.

Schmajuk, N. A. (2001). Hippocampal dysfunction in schizophrenia. *Hippocampus, 11*(5), 599–613.

Schmidt, F. L., & Hunter, J. (2004). General mental ability in the world of work: Occupational attainment and job performance. *Journal of Personality and Social Psychology, 86*(1), 162–173.

Schmidt, M. H. (2014). The energy allocation function of sleep: A unifying theory of sleep, torpor, and continuous wakefulness. *Neuroscience & Biobehavioral Reviews, 47*, 122–153.

Schmidt, P. J., Murphy, J. H., Haq, N., Rubinow, D. R., & Danaceau, M. A. (2004). Stressful life events, personal losses, and perimenopause-related depression. *Archives of Women's Mental Health, 7*(1), 19–26.

Schmidt, S. R. (2007). Unscrambling the effects of emotion and distinctiveness on memory. In H. L. Roediger & J. S. Nairne (Eds.), *The foundation of remembering* (pp. 141–158). Psychology Press.

Schmitt, M. T., Branscombe, N. R., Postmes, T., & Garcia, A. (2014). The consequences of perceived discrimination for psychological well-being: A meta-analytic review. *Psychological Bulletin, 140*(4), 921–948. https://doi.org/10.1037/a0035754

Schmitz, S. (1997). Gender-related strategies in environmental development: Effects of anxiety on wayfinding in and representation of a three-dimensional maze. *Journal of Environmental Psychology, 17*(3), 215–228.

Schneider, B. H., Atkinson, L., & Tardif, C. (2001). Child–parent attachment and children's peer relations: A quantitative review. *Developmental Psychology, 37*(1), 86–100.

Schneider, B. H., Benenson, J., Fülöp, M., Berkics, M., & Sándor, M. (2011). Cooperation and competition. In P. K. Smith & C. H. Hart (Eds.), *The Wiley-Blackwell handbook of childhood social development* (2nd ed., pp. 472–490). Wiley-Blackwell.

Schneider, G. E. (2014). *Brain structure and its origins: In development and in evolution of behavior and the mind*. MIT Press.

Schneider, M. C., Holman, M. R., Diekman, A. B., & McAndrew, T. (2016). Power, conflict, and community: How gendered views of political power influence women's political ambition. *Political Psychology, 37*(4), 515–531.

Schneider, R., Lotz, C., & Sparfeldt, J. R. (2018). Smart, confident, interested: Contributions of intelligence, self-concept, and interest to elementary school achievement. *Learning and Individual Differences, 62*, 23–35.

Schneider, W. J., & McGrew, K. S. (2018). The Cattell-Horn-Carroll theory of cognitive abilities. In D. P. Flanagan & E. M. McDonough (Eds.), *Contemporary intellectual assessment: Theories, tests, and issues* (4th ed., pp. 73–163). Guilford Press.

Schnupp, J., Nelken, I., & King, A. (2012). *Auditory neuroscience: Making sense of sound*. MIT Press.

Schoenemann, P. T. (2006). Evolution of the size and functional areas of the human brain. *Annual Review of Anthropology, 35*, 379–406.

Schoenemann, P. T., Sheehan, M. J., & Glotzer, L. D. (2005). Prefrontal white matter volume is disproportionately larger in humans than in other primates. *Nature Neuroscience, 8*(2), 242–252.

Scholer, A. A., & Higgins, E. T. (2012). Too much of a good thing? Trade-offs in promotion and prevention focus. In R. M. Ryan (Ed.), *The Oxford handbook of human motivation* (pp. 65–84). Oxford University Press.

Schooler, J. W., & Eich, E. (2000). Memory for emotional events. In E. Tulving & F. I. M. Craik (Eds.), *The Oxford handbook of memory* (pp. 379–392). Oxford University Press.

Schore, A. N. (2001). Effects of a secure attachment relationship on right brain development, affect regulation, and infant mental health. *Infant Mental Health Journal, 22*(1–2), 7–66.

Schredl, M., & Bulkeley, K. (2020). Dreaming and the COVID-19 pandemic: A survey in a U.S. sample. *Dreaming, 30*(3), 189–198. https://doi.org/10.1037/drm0000146

Schredl, M., Ciric, P., Götz, S., & Wittmann, L. (2004). Typical dreams: Stability and gender differences. *The Journal of Psychology, 138*(6), 485–494. https://doi.org/10.3200/JRLP.138.6.485-494

Schreer, G. E., Smith, S., & Thomas, K. (2009). "Shopping while Black": Examining racial discrimination in a retail setting. *Journal of Applied Social Psychology, 39*(6), 1432–1444.

Schreiber, F. R. (1973). *Sybil*. Warner Books.

Schroder, H. S., Duda, J. M., Christensen, K., Beard, C., & Björgvinsson, T. (2020). Stressors and chemical imbalances: Beliefs about the causes of depression in an acute psychiatric treatment sample. *Journal of Affective Disorders, 276*, 537–545. https://doi.org/10.1016/j.jad.2020.07.061

Schroeder, D. A., Stephens, E., Colgan, D., Hunsinger, M., Rubin, D., & Christopher, M. S. (2018). A brief mindfulness-based intervention for primary care physicians: A pilot randomized controlled trial. *American Journal of Lifestyle Medicine, 12*(1), 83–91.

Schubert, C. R., Cruickshanks, K. J., Nondahl, D. M., Klein, B. E., Klein, R., & Fischer, M. E. (2013). Association of exercise with lower long-term risk of olfactory impairment in older adults. *JAMA Otolaryngology—Head & Neck Surgery, 139*(10), 1061–1066.

Schultheis, H., & Carlson, L. A. (2013). Spatial reasoning. In D. Reisberg (Ed.), *The Oxford handbook of cognitive psychology* (pp. 719–732). Oxford University Press.

Schultheiss, O. C., & Pang, J. S. (2007). Measuring implicit motives. In R. W. Robins, R. C. Fraley, & R. F. Krueger (Eds.), *Handbook of research methods in personality psychology* (pp. 322–344). Guilford Press.

Schultz, R. T. (2005). Developmental deficits in social perception in autism: The role of the amygdala and fusiform face area. *International Journal of Developmental Neuroscience, 23*(2), 125–141.

Schulz, R., & Beach, S. R. (1999). Caregiving as a risk factor for mortality: The Caregiver Health Effects Study. *The Journal of the American Medical Association, 282*(23), 2215–2219.

Schulze, R., Roberts, R. D., Zeidner, M., & Matthews, G. (2005). Theory, measurement, and applications of emotional intelligence: Frames of reference. In R. Schulze & R. D. Roberts (Eds.), *Emotional intelligence: An international handbook* (pp. 3–30). Hogrefe & Huber.

Schumer, M. C., Lindsay, E. K., & Creswell, J. D. (2018). Brief mindfulness training for negative affectivity: A systematic review and meta-analysis. *Journal of Consulting and Clinical Psychology, 86*(7), 569–583.

Schutte, N. S., Malouff, J. M., Thorsteinsson, E. B., Bhullar, N., & Rooke, S. E. (2007). A meta-analytic investigation of the relationship between emotional intelligence and health. *Personality and Individual Differences, 42*(6), 921–933.

Schvey, N. A., Sbrocco, T., Bakalar, J. L., Ress, R., Barmine, M., Gorlick, J., Pine, A., Stephens, M., & Tanofsky-Kraff, M. (2017). The experience of weight stigma among gym members with overweight and obesity. *Stigma and Health, 2*(4), 292–306. https://doi.org/10.1037/sah0000062

Schwaba, T. (2019). The structure, measurement, and development of openness to experience across adulthood. In D. P. McAdams, R. L. Shiner, & J. L. Tackett (Eds.), *Handbook of personality development* (pp. 185–200). Guilford Press.

Schwaba, T., & Bleidorn, W. (2018). Individual differences in personality change across the adult life span. *Journal of Personality, 86*(3), 450–464.

Schwartz, B. G., McDonald, S. A., & Kloner, R. A. (2013). Super Bowl outcome's association with cardiovascular death. *Clinical Research in Cardiology, 102*(11), 807–811.

Schwartz, B., & Sommers, R. (2013). Affective forecasting and well-being. In D. Reisberg (Ed.), *The Oxford handbook of cognitive psychology* (pp. 704–718). Oxford University Press.

Schwartz, C., Lange, C., Hachefa, C., Cornil, Y., Nicklaus, S., & Chandon, P. (2020). Effects of snack portion size on anticipated and experienced hunger, eating enjoyment, and perceived healthiness among children. *International Journal of Behavioral Nutrition and Physical Activity, 17*(1), 1–14. https://doi.org/10.1186/s12966-020-00974-z

Schwartz, J. H., & Javitch, J. A. (2013). Neurotransmitters. In E. R. Kandel, J. H. Schwartz, T. M. Jessell, S. A. Siegelbaum, & A. J. Hudspeth (Eds.), *Principles of neural science* (5th ed., pp. 289–306). McGraw-Hill.

Schwartz, M. S., & Andrasik, F. (2005). *Biofeedback: A practitioner's guide* (3rd ed.). Guilford Press.

Schwartz, M. W., & Porte, D. (2005). Diabetes, obesity, and the brain. *Science, 307*(5708), 375–379.

Schwartz, M., Acosta, L., Hung, Y. L., Padilla, M., & Enciso, R. (2018). Effects of CPAP and mandibular advancement device treatment in obstructive sleep apnea patients: A systematic review and meta-analysis. *Sleep and Breathing, 22*(3), 555–568.

Schwartz, S. J. (2016). Turning point for a turning point: Advancing emerging adulthood theory and research. *Emerging Adulthood, 4*(5), 307–317.

Schwarz, A. (2016). *ADHD nation: Children, doctors, Big Pharma, and the making of an American epidemic*. Scribner.

Schwarz, J. F., Åkerstedt, T., Lindberg, E., Gruber, G., Fischer, H., & Theorell-Haglöw, J. (2017). Age affects sleep microstructure more than sleep macrostructure. *Journal of Sleep Research, 26*(3), 277–287. https://doi.org/10.1111/jsr.12478

Schwarz, N. (2015). Metacognition. In M. Mikulincer, P. R. Shaver, E. Borgida, & J. A. Bargh (Eds.), *APA handbook of personality and social psychology, Vol. 1. Attitudes and social cognition* (pp. 203–229). American Psychological Association. https://doi.org/10.1037/14341-006

Schwarzer, R. (2011). Health behavior change. In H. S. Friedman (Ed.), *The Oxford handbook of health psychology* (pp. 591–611). Oxford University Press.

Schwarzer, R., & Leppin, A. (1991). Social support and health: A theoretical and empirical overview. *Journal of Social and Personal Relationships, 8*(1), 99–127.

Schwebel, D. C., Stavrinos, D., Byington, K. W., Davis, T., O'Neal, E. E., & De Jong, D. (2012). Distraction and pedestrian safety: How talking on the phone, texting, and listening to music impact crossing the street. *Accident Analysis & Prevention, 45*, 266–271.

Schweickert, R., & Boruff, B. (1986). Short-term memory capacity: Magic number or magic spell? *Journal of Experimental Psychology: Learning, Memory, and Cognition, 12*(3), 419–425.

Scott, K. M., Bruffaerts, R., Simon, G. E., Alonso, J., Angermeyer, M., de Girolamo, G., Demyttenaere, K., Kessler, R. C. (2008). Obesity and mental disorders in the general population: Results from the world mental health surveys. *International Journal of Obesity, 32*(1), 192–200.

Scott, L., & O'Hara, M. W. (1993). Self-discrepancies in clinically anxious and depressed university students. *Journal of Abnormal Psychology, 102*(2), 282–287.

Scoville, W. B., & Milner, B. (1957). Loss of recent memory after bilateral hippocampal lesions. *Journal of Neurology, Neurosurgery, and Psychiatry, 20*(1), 11–21.

Scullin, M. K., Fairley, J., Decker, M. J., & Bliwise, D. L. (2017). The effects of an afternoon nap on episodic memory in young and older adults. *Sleep, 40*(5), zsx035.

Sedgwick, H. A. (2001). Visual space perception. In E. B. Goldstein (Ed.), *Blackwell handbook of perception* (pp. 128–167). Blackwell.

Sedlmeier, P., Eberth, J., Schwarz, M., Zimmermann, D., Haarig, F., Jaeger, S., & Kunze, S. (2012). The psychological effects of meditation: A meta-analysis. *Psychological Bulletin, 138*(6), 1139–1171.

Seeman, T. E. (1996). Social ties and health: The benefits of social integration. *Annals of Epidemiology, 6*(5), 442–451.

Segal, N. L. (2011). Twin, adoption, and family methods as approaches to the evolution of individual differences. In D. M. Buss & P. H. Hawley (Eds.), *The evolution of personality and individual differences* (pp. 303–337). Oxford University Press.

Segal, Z. V., Williams, J. M. G., & Teasdale, J. D. (2012). *Mindfulness-based cognitive therapy for depression: A new approach for preventing relapse* (2nd ed.). Guilford Press.

Segall, M., Campbell, D., & Herskovits, M. J. (1966). The influence of culture on visual perception. In H. Toch & C. Smith (Eds.), *Social Perception*, 1–5. Bobbs-Merrill.

Segall, M., Campbell, D., & Herskovits, M. J. (1966). The influence of culture on visual perception. In H. Toch & C. Smith (Eds.), *Social Perception*, 1–5. Bobbs-Merrill.

Segerstrom, S. C., & Miller, G. E. (2004). Psychological stress and the human immune system: A meta-analytic study of 30 years of inquiry. *Psychological Bulletin, 130*(4), 601–630.

Segerstrom, S. C., Taylor, S. E., Kemeny, M. E., & Fahey, J. L. (1998). Optimism is associated with mood, coping, and immune change in response to stress. *Journal of Personality and Social Psychology, 74*(6), 1646–1655.

Segrin, C., McNelis, M., & Pavlich, C. A. (2018). Indirect effects of loneliness on substance use through stress. *Health Communication, 33*(5), 513–518.

Sehatzadeh, S., Daskalakis, Z. J., Yap, B., Tu, H. A., Palimaka, S., Bowen, J. M., & O'Reilly, D. J. (2019). Unilateral and bilateral repetitive transcranial magnetic stimulation for treatment-resistant depression: A meta-analysis of randomized controlled trials over 2 decades. *Journal of Psychiatry & Neuroscience, 44*(3), 151. https://doi.org/10.1503/jpn.180056

Seibert, A., & Kerns, K. (2015). Early mother-child attachment: Longitudinal prediction to the quality of peer relationships in middle childhood. *International Journal of Behavioral Development, 39*(2), 130–138.

Sekeres, M. J., Winocur, G., & Moscovitch, M. (2018). The hippocampus and related neocortical structures in memory transformation. *Neuroscience Letters, 680*, 39–53. https://doi.org/10.1016/j.neulet.2018.05.006

Seligman, M. (2018). PERMA and the building blocks of well-being. *The Journal of Positive Psychology, 13*(4), 333–335.

Seligman, M. E. (2004). *Authentic happiness: Using the new positive psychology to realize your potential for lasting fulfillment*. Simon & Schuster.

Seligman, M. E. P. (1970). On the generality of the laws of learning. *Psychological Review, 77*(5), 406–418.

Seligman, M. E. P. (1971). Phobias and preparedness. *Behavior Therapy, 2*(3), 307–320.

Seligman, M. E. P. (1975). *Helplessness: On depression, development, and death*. Freeman.

Seligman, M. E. P. (1991). *Learned optimism*. Knopf.

Seligman, M. E. P. (1995). The effectiveness of psychotherapy: The *Consumer Reports* survey. *American Psychologist, 50*(12), 965–974.

Seligman, M. E. P. (2011). *Flourish: A visionary new understanding of happiness and well-being*. Free Press.

Seligman, M. E. P., & Czikszentmihalyi, M. (2000). Positive psychology: An introduction. *American Psychologist, 55*(1), 5–14.

Seligman, M. E. P., & Hager, J. L. (1972). Sauce-béarnaise syndrome. *Psychology Today, 6*, 59.

Seligman, M. E. P., & Maier, S. F. (1967). Failure to escape traumatic shock. *Journal of Experimental Psychology, 74*(1), 1–9.

Seligman, M. E., Rashid, T., & Parks, A. C. (2006). Positive psychotherapy. *American Psychologist, 61*(8), 774–788.

Seligman, M. E., Steen, T. A., Park, N., & Peterson, C. (2005). Positive psychology progress: Empirical validation of interventions. *American Psychologist, 60*(5), 410–421.

Sell, C. S. (2014). *Chemistry and the sense of smell*. Wiley.

Sellbom, M., Fischler, G. L., & Ben-Porath, Y. S. (2007). Identifying MMPI-2 predictors of police officer integrity and misconduct. *Criminal Justice and Behavior, 34*(8), 985–1004.

Selten, J. P., van Os, J., & Cantor-Graae, E. (2016). The social defeat hypothesis of schizophrenia: Issues of measurement and reverse causality. *World Psychiatry, 15*(3), 294.

Selye, H. (1936). A syndrome produced by diverse noxious agents. *Nature, 138*(32), 659–661.

Selye, H. (1952). *The story of the adaptation syndrome: Told in the form of informal, illustrated lectures*. Acta.

Selye, H. (1956). *The stress of life*. McGraw-Hill.

Semendeferi, K., Armstrong, E., Schleicher, A., Zilles, K., & Van Hoesen, G. W. (2001). Prefrontal cortex in humans and apes: A comparative study of area 10. *American Journal of Physical Anthropology, 114*(3), 224–241.

Semino, E. (2021). "Not soldiers but fire-fighters"–metaphors and COVID-19. *Health Communication, 36*(1), 50–58. https://doi.org/10.1080/10410236.2020.1844989

Senghas, A., Kita, S., & Özyürek, A. (2004). Children creating core properties of language: Evidence from an emerging sign language in Nicaragua. *Science, 305*(5691), 1779–1782.

Senko, C., Durik, A. M., & Harackiewicz, J. M. (2008). Historical perspectives and new directions in achievement goal theory: Understanding the effects of mastery and performance-approach goals. In J. Y. Shah & W. L. Gardner (Eds.), *Handbook of motivation science* (pp. 100–113). Guilford Press.

Sergeant, M. J., Dickins, T. E., Davies, M. N., & Griffiths, M. D. (2006). Aggression, empathy and sexual orientation in males. *Personality and Individual Differences, 40*(3), 475–486.

Serido, J., Almeida, D. M., & Wethington, E. (2004). Chronic stressors and daily hassles: Unique and interactive relationships with psychological distress. *Journal of Health and Social Behavior, 45*(1), 17–33.

Sewart, A. R., & Craske, M. G. (2018). Panic disorder and agoraphobia. In J. Hunsley & E. J. Mash (Eds.), *A guide to assessments that work* (2nd ed., pp. 266–292). Oxford University Press.

Sewell, H. (2009). *Working with ethnicity, race, and culture in mental health: A handbook for practitioners*. Jessica Kingsley.

Sexton, T. L., & Stanton, M. (2016). Systems theories. In J. C. Norcross, G. R. VandenBos, & D. K. Freedheim (Eds.), *APA handbook of clinical psychology* (Vol. 2, pp. 213–240). American Psychological Association.

Shackelford, T. K., Schmitt, D. P., & Buss, D. M. (2005). Universal dimensions of human mate preferences. *Personality and Individual Differences, 39*(2), 447–458.

Shackman, A. J., & Fox, A. S. (2016). Contributions of the central extended amygdala to fear and anxiety. *Journal of Neuroscience, 36*(31), 8050–8063.

Shah, M., Khan, M., & Doty, R. L. (2010). Olfactory central processing. In E. B. Goldstein (Ed.), *Encyclopedia of perception* (pp. 685–690). Sage.

Shahin, I., & Einarson, A. (2011). Knowledge transfer and translation: Examining how teratogen information is disseminated. *Birth Defects Research. Part A, Clinical and Molecular Teratology, 91*(11), 956–961.

Shakkottai, V. G., Batla, A., Bhatia, K., Dauer, W. T., Dresel, C., Niethammer, M., & Hess, E. J. (2017). Current opinions and areas of consensus on the role of the cerebellum in dystonia. The Cerebellum, 16(2), 577–594.

Shalev, A. Y., & Marmar, C. R. (2018). Conceptual history of post-traumatic stress disorder. In C. B. Nemeroff & C. R. Marmar (Eds.), *Post-traumatic stress disorder* (pp. 3–30). Oxford University Press.

Shamey R., & Kuehni, R. G. (2020). Ladd-Franklin, Christine 1847–1930. In *Pioneers of color science*. Springer. https://doi.org/10.1007/978-3-319-30811-1_48

Shams, L. (2010). Multimodal interactions: Visual–auditory. In E. B. Goldstein (Ed.), *Encyclopedia of perception* (pp. 593–599). Sage.

Shan, Z. Y., Liu, J. Z., Sahgal, V., Wang, B., & Yue, G. H. (2005). Selective atrophy of left hemisphere and frontal lobe of the brain in old men. *The Journals of Gerontology. Series A, Biological Sciences and Medical Sciences, 60*(2), 165–174.

Shane, S. A. (1992). Why do some societies invent more than others? *Journal of Business Venturing, 7*(1), 29–46.

Shane, S. (1993). Cultural influences on national rates of innovation. *Journal of Business Venturing, 8*(1), 59–73.

Shang, A., Huwiler-Müntener, K., Nartey, L., Jüni, P., Dörig, S., Sterne, J. A., Pewsner, D., & Egger, M. (2005). Are the clinical effects of homoeopathy placebo effects? Comparative study of placebo-controlled trials of homoeopathy and allopathy. *The Lancet, 366*(9487), 726–732.

Shannon, L. M., & Begley, T. M. (2008). Antecedents of the four-factor model of cultural intelligence. In S. Ang & L. Van Dyne (Eds.), *Handbook of cultural intelligence: Theory, measurement, and applications* (pp. 41–55). Sharpe.

Shapiro, C. M., Trajanovic, N. N., & Fedoroff, J. P. (2003). Sexsomnia—a new parasomnia? *Canadian Journal of Psychiatry, 48*(5), 311–317.

Shapiro, D. A., & Shapiro, D. (1982). Meta-analysis of comparative therapy outcome studies: A replication and refinement. *Psychological Bulletin, 92*(3), 581–604.

Shapiro, E. (1999). Cotherapy. In J. R. Price, D. R. Hescheles, & A. R. Price (Eds.), *A guide to starting psychotherapy groups* (pp. 53–61). Academic Press.

Shapiro, S. L. (2009). The integration of mindfulness and psychology. *Journal of Clinical Psychology, 65*(6), 555–560.

Shapiro, S. L. (2009a). Mediation and positive psychology. In S. J. Lopez & C. R. Snyder (Eds.), *Oxford handbook of positive psychology* (pp. 601–610). Oxford University Press.

Shapiro, S. L. (2009b). The integration of mindfulness and psychology. *Journal of Clinical Psychology, 65*(6), 555–560.

Shapiro, S. L., & Carlson, L. E. (2017). *The art and science of mindfulness: Integrating mindfulness into psychology and the helping professions*. American Psychological Association.

Shapiro, S. L., & Jazaieri, H. (2015). Mindfulness-based stress reduction for healthy stressed adults. In K. W. Brown, J. D. Creswell, & R. M. Ryan, *Handbook of mindfulness: Theory, research, and practice* (pp. 269–282). Guilford Press.

Shapiro, S. L., & Walsh, R. (2003). An analysis of recent meditation research and suggestions for future directions. *The Humanistic Psychologist, 31*(2–3), 86–114.

Sharif, Z., Bradford, D., Stroup, S., & Lieberman, J. (2007). Pharmacological treatment of schizophrenia. In P. E. Nathan & J. M. Gorman (Eds.), *A guide to treatments that work* (3rd ed., pp. 203–241). Oxford University Press.

Shaw, J. (2014, March–April). *The price of healthy eating*. Harvard Magazine. http://harvardmagazine.com/2014/03/the-price-of-healthy-eating

Shedler, J. (2015). Where is the evidence for "evidence-based" therapy? *The Journal of Psychological Therapies in Primary Care, 4*(1), 47–59.

Shedler, J., & Westen, D. (2004). Dimensions of personality pathology: An alternative to the five-factor model. *American Journal of Psychiatry, 161*(10), 1743–1754.

Sheehan, L., Nieweglowski, K., & Corrigan, P. W. (2017). Structures and types of stigma. In W. Gaebel, W. Rössler, & N. Sartorius (Eds.), *The stigma of mental illness—end of the story?* (pp. 43–66). Springer International Publishing Sweden.

Sheeran, P., & Webb, T. L. (2016). The intention–behavior gap. *Social and Personality Psychology Compass, 10*(9), 503–518.

Sheldon, K. M., Boehm, J. K., & Lyubomirsky, S. (2012). Variety is the spice of happiness: The hedonic adaptation prevention (HAP) model. In I. Boniwell & S. David (Eds.), *Oxford handbook of happiness* (pp. 901–914). Oxford University Press.

Sheldon, K. M., Ryan, R. M., Deci, E. L., & Kasser, T. (2004). The independent effects of goal contents and motives on well-being: It's both what you pursue and why you pursue it. *Personality and Social Psychology Bulletin, 30*(4), 475–486.

Sheldon, P. (2013). Examining gender differences in self-disclosure on Facebook versus face-to-face. *The Journal of Social Media in Society, 2*(1), 88–105.

Sheldon, P., Rauschnabel, P. A., Antony, M. G., & Car, S. (2017). A cross-cultural comparison of Croatian and American social network sites: Exploring cultural differences in motives for Instagram use. *Computers in Human Behavior, 75*, 643–651.

Shelton, R. C., & Lester, N. (2006). Selective serotonin reuptake inhibitors and newer antidepressants. In D. J. Stein, D. J. Kupfer, & A. F. Schatzberg (Eds.), *The American Psychiatric Publishing textbook of mood disorders* (pp. 263–280). American Psychiatric Publishing.

Shenger-Krestovnikova, N. R. (1921). Contributions to the physiology of differentiation of visual stimuli, and determination of limit of differentiation by the visual analyzer of the dog. *Bulletin of Institute of Lesgaft* (iii).

Shensa, A., Escobar-Viera, C. G., Sidani, J. E., Bowman, N. D., Marshal, M. P., & Primack, B. A. (2017). Problematic social media use and depressive symptoms among U.S. young adults: A nationally-representative study. *Social Science and Medicine, 182*, 150–157. https://doi.org/10.1016/j.socscimed.2017.03.061

Sher, A. E. (2006). Upper airway surgery for obstructive sleep apnea. In T. L. Lee-Chiong (Ed.), *Sleep: A comprehensive handbook* (pp. 365–372). Wiley-Liss.

Shergill, S. S., Brammer, M. J., Williams, S. C., Murray, R. M., & McGuire, P. K. (2000). Mapping auditory hallucinations in schizophrenia using functional magnetic resonance imaging. *Archives of General Psychiatry, 57*(11), 1033.

Sherif, M. (1936). *The psychology of social norms*. Harper.

Shi, L., Chen, S. J., Ma, M. Y., Bao, Y. P., Han, Y., Wang, Y. M., Shi, J., Vitiello, M. V., & Lu, L. (2018). Sleep disturbances increase the risk of dementia: A systematic review and meta-analysis. *Sleep Medicine Reviews, 40*, 4–16.

Shields, G. S., Sazma, M. A., McCullough, A. M., & Yonelinas, A. P. (2017). The effects of acute stress on episodic memory: A meta-analysis and integrative review. *Psychological Bulletin, 143*(6), 636.

Shields, J. P., Cohen, R., Glassman, J. R., Whitaker, K., Franks, H., & Bertolini, I. (2013). Estimating population size and demographic characteristics of lesbian, gay, bisexual, and transgender youth in middle school. *Journal of Adolescent Health, 52*(2), 248–250.

Shiffrin, R. M., & Nosofsky, R. M. (1994). Seven plus or minus two: A commentary on capacity limitations. *Psychological Review, 101*(2), 357–360.

Shikatani, B., Fracalanza, K., & Antony, M. M. (2015). Behavior therapies. In R. L. Cautin & S. O. Lilienfeld (Eds.), *The encyclopedia of clinical psychology* (pp. 354–365). Wiley-Blackwell.

Shim, J. W., & Paul, B. (2007). Effects of personality types on the use of television genre. *Journal of Broadcasting & Electronic Media, 51*(2), 287–304.

Shiner, R. L. (2019). Negative emotionality and neuroticism from childhood through adulthood. In D. P. McAdams, R. L. Shiner, & J. L. Tackett (Eds.), *Handbook of personality development* (pp. 137–152). Guilford Press.

Shinfuku, M., Kishimoto, T., Uchida, H., Suzuki, T., Mimura, M., & Kikuchi, T. (2019). Effectiveness and safety of long-term benzodiazepine use in anxiety disorders: A systematic review and meta-analysis. *International Clinical Psychopharmacology, 34*(5), 211–221. https://doi.org/10.1097/YIC.0000000000000276

Shiota, M. N. (2014). The evolutionary perspective in positive emotion research. In M. M. Tugade, M. N. Shiota, & L. D. Kirby (Eds.), *Handbook of positive emotions* (pp. 44–59). Guilford Press.

Shiraev, E. (2011). *A history of psychology: A global perspective*. Sage.

Shizgal, P. B., & Hyman, S. E. (2013). Homeostasis, motivation, and addictive states. In E. R. Kandel, J. H. Schwartz, T. M. Jessell, S. A. Siegelbaum, & A. J. Hudspeth (Eds.), *Principles of neural science* (5th ed., pp. 1095–1115). McGraw-Hill.

Shlomo, S. B., Taubman-Ben-Ari, O., Findler, L., Sivan, E., & Dolizki, M. (2010). Becoming a grandmother: Maternal grandmothers' mental health, perceived costs, and personal growth. *Social Work Research, 34*(1), 45–57.

Shochat, T., Flint-Bretler, O., & Tzischinsky, O. (2010). Sleep patterns, electronic media exposure and daytime sleep-related behaviours among Israeli adolescents. *Acta Paediatrica, 99*(9), 1396–1400.

Shonkoff, J. P., Boyce, W. T., & McEwen, B. S. (2009). Neuroscience, molecular biology, and the childhood roots of health disparities: Building a new framework for health promotion and disease prevention. *The Journal of the American Medical Association, 301*(21), 2252–2259.

Shorter, E. (1997). *A history of psychiatry: From the era of the asylum to the age of Prozac*. Wiley.

Shorter, E., & Healy, D. (2007). *Shock therapy: A history of electroconvulsive treatment in mental illness*. Rutgers University Press.

Shrager, Y., & Squire, L. R. (2009). Medial temporal lobe function and human memory. In M. S. Gazzaniga (Ed.), *The cognitive neurosciences* (4th ed., pp. 675–690). MIT Press.

Shu, F., McAbee, S. T., & Ayman, R. (2017). The HEXACO personality traits, cultural intelligence, and international student adjustment. *Personality and Individual Differences, 106*, 21–25.

Shu, L. L., Gino, F., & Bazerman, M. H. (2011). Dishonest deed, clear conscience: When cheating leads to moral disengagement and motivated forgetting. *Personality and Social Psychology Bulletin, 37*(3), 330–349.

Shulman, R. G. (2013). *Brain imaging: What it can (and cannot) tell us about consciousness*. Oxford University Press.

Shweder, R. A., & Bourne, E. J. (1982). Does the concept of the person vary cross-culturally? In A. Marsella & G. White (Eds.), *Cultural conceptions of mental health and therapy* (pp. 97–137). Reidel.

Shweder, R. A., Goodnow, J. J., Hatano, G., LeVine, R. A., Markus, H. R., & Miller, P. J. (2006). The cultural psychology of development: One mind, many mentalities. In R. M. Lerner (Ed.), *Handbook of child psychology* (6th ed., Vol. 1, pp. 716–792). Wiley.

Shweder, R. A., Jensen, L. A., & Goldstein, W. M. (1995). Who sleeps by whom revisited: A method for extracting the moral goods implicit in practice. *New Directions for Child and Adolescent Development, 1995*(67), 21–39.

Sibley, C. G., & Duckitt, J. (2008). Personality and prejudice: A meta-analysis and theoretical review. *Personality and Social Psychology Review, 12*(3), 248–279.

Sidani, J. E., Shensa, A., Hoffman, B., Hanmer, J., & Primack, B. A. (2016). The association between social media use and eating concerns among US young adults. *Journal of the Academy of Nutrition and Dietetics, 116*(9), 1465–1472.

Sidani, J. E., Shensa, A., Hoffman, B., Hanmer, J., & Primack, B. A. (2016). The association between social media use and eating concerns among US young adults. *Journal of the Academy of Nutrition and Dietetics, 116*(9), 1465–1472.

Siegel, D. J. (2018). *Aware*. Penguin Random House.

Siegel, J. M. (2005). Clues to the functions of mammalian sleep. *Nature, 437*(7063), 1264–1271.

Siegel, J. M. (2009). Sleep viewed as a state of adaptive inactivity. *Nature Reviews Neuroscience, 10*(10), 747–753.
Siegelbaum, S. A., & Kandel, E. R. (2013a). Overview of synaptic transmission. In E. R. Kandel, J. H. Schwartz, T. M. Jessell, S. A. Siegelbaum, & A. J. Hudspeth (Eds.), *Principles of neural science* (5th ed., pp. 177–188). McGraw-Hill.
Siegelbaum, S. A., & Kandel, E. R. (2013b). Prefrontal cortex, hippocampus, and the biology of explicit memory storage. In E. R. Kandel, J. H. Schwartz, T. M. Jessell, S. A. Siegelbaum, & A. J. Hudspeth (Eds.), *Principles of neural science* (5th ed., pp. 1487–1522). McGraw-Hill.
Siegelbaum, S. A., Kandel, E. R., & Sudhof, T. C. (2013a). Neurotransmitter release. In E. R. Kandel, J. H. Schwartz, T. M. Jessell, S. A. Siegelbaum, & A. J. Hudspeth (Eds.), *Principles of neural science* (5th ed., pp. 260–288). McGraw-Hill.
Siegelbaum, S. A., Kandel, E. R., & Yuste, R. (2013b). Synaptic integration in the central nervous system. In E. R. Kandel, J. H. Schwartz, T. M. Jessell, S. A. Siegelbaum, & A. J. Hudspeth (Eds.), *Principles of neural science* (5th ed., pp. 210–235). McGraw-Hill.
Siev, J., & Chambless, D. L. (2007). Specificity of treatment effects: Cognitive therapy and relaxation for generalized anxiety and panic disorders. *Journal of Consulting and Clinical Psychology, 75*(4), 513–522.
Signorielli, N. (2012). Television's gender-role images and contribution to stereotyping. In D. G. Singer & J. L. Singer (Eds.), *Handbook of children and the media* (2nd ed., pp. 321–339). Sage.
Sigurvinsdottir, R., Thorisdottir, I. E., & Gylfason, H. F. (2020). The impact of COVID-19 on mental health: The role of locus on control and Internet use. *International Journal of Environmental Research and Public Health, 17*(19), 6985. https://doi.org/10.3390/ijerph17196985
Silber, M. H., Ancoli-Israel, S., Bonnet, M. H., Chokroverty, S., Grigg-Damberger, M. M., Hirshkowitz, M., & Iber, C. (2007). The visual scoring of sleep in adults. *Journal of Clinical Sleep Medicine, 3*(2), 121–131.
Silbersweig, D. A., Stern, E., Frith, C., Cahill, C., Holmes, A., Grootoonk, S., Seaward, J., McKenna, P., Chua, S. E., Schnorr, L., Jones, T., & Frackowiak, R. S. J. (1995). A functional neuroanatomy of hallucinations in schizophrenia. *Nature, 378*, 176–179.
Silke, A. (2003). Deindividuation, anonymity, and violence: Findings from Northern Ireland. *The Journal of Social Psychology, 143*(4), 493–499.
Silove, D., Baker, J. R., Mohsin, M., Teesson, M., Creamer, M., O'Donnell, M., Forbes, D., Carragher, N., Slad, T., Mills, K., Bryant, R., McFarlane, A., Steel, Z., Felmingham, K., & Rees, S. (2017). The contribution of gender-based violence and network trauma to gender differences in post-traumatic stress disorder. *PLoS ONE, 12*(2), e0171879.
Silva, E. J., & Duffy, J. F. (2008). Sleep inertia varies with circadian phase and sleep stage in older adults. *Behavioral Neuroscience, 122*(4), 928–935.
Silverman, W. H. (1996). Cookbooks, manuals, and paint-by-numbers: Psychotherapy in the 90s. *Psychotherapy: Theory, Research, Practice, Training, 33*(2), 207–215.
Silvia, P. J. (2008). Interest—The curious emotion. *Current Directions in Psychological Science, 17*(1), 57–60.
Silvia, P. J. (2012). Curiosity and motivation. In R. M. Ryan (Ed.), *The Oxford handbook of human motivation* (pp. 157–166). Oxford University Press.
Silvia, P. J., Martin, C., & Nusbaum, E. C. (2009). A snapshot of creativity: Evaluating a quick and simple method for assessing divergent thinking. *Thinking Skills and Creativity, 4*(2), 79–85.
Simmonds-Buckley, M., Kellett, S., & Waller, G. (2019). Acceptability and efficacy of group behavioral activation for depression among adults: A meta-analysis. *Behavior Therapy, 55*(5), 864–885. https://doi.org/10.1016/j.beth.2019.01.003
Simmons, B. L., & Nelson, D. L. (2007). Eustress at work: Extending the holistic stress model. In B. L. Simmons & D. L. Nelson (Eds.), *Positive organizational behaviour* (pp. 40–53). Sage.
Simms, A., & Nichols, T. (2014). Social loafing: A review of the literature. *Journal of Management Policy and Practice, 15*(1), 58–67.
Simms, L. J., Williams, T. F., & Nus, E. (2017). Assessment of the Five Factor Model. In T. A. Widiger (Ed.), *The Oxford handbook of the Five Factor Model* (pp. 353–380). Oxford University Press.
Simon, B., & Mummendey, A. (2012). Perceptions of relative group size and group homogeneity: We are the majority and they are all the same. *European Journal of Social Psychology, 20*(4), 351–356.
Simon, D. A., & Bjork, R. A. (2001). Metacognition in motor learning. *Journal of Experimental Psychology: Learning, Memory, and Cognition, 27*(4), 907.
Simon, G. E., Von Korff, M., Saunders, K., Miglioretti, D. L., Crane, P. K., Van Belle, G., & Kessler, R. C. (2006). Association between obesity and psychiatric disorders in the U.S. adult population. *Archives of General Psychiatry, 63*(7), 824–830.
Simon, L. (1998). *Genuine reality: A life of William James*. Harcourt Brace.
Simone, A. N., Marks, D. J., Bédard, A. C., & Halperin, J. M. (2018). Low working memory rather than ADHD symptoms predicts poor academic achievement in school-aged children. *Journal of Abnormal Child Psychology, 46*(2), 277–290.
Simonetti, V., Durante, A., Ambrosca, R., Arcadi, P., Graziano, G., Pucciarelli, G., Simeone, S., Vellone, E., Alvaro, R., & Cicolini, G. (2021). Anxiety, sleep disorders and self-efficacy among nurses during COVID-19 pandemic: A large cross-sectional study. *Journal of Clinical Nursing, 30*(9–10), 1360–1371. https://doi.org/10.1111/jocn.15685
Simon-Rusinowitz, L., Krach, C. A., Marks, L. N., Piktialis, D., & Wilson, L. B. (1996). Grandparents in the workplace: The effects of economic and labor trends. *Generations—Journal of the American Society on Aging, 20*(1), 41–44.
Simons, D. J., & Ambinder, M. S. (2005). Change blindness theory and consequences. *Current Directions in Psychological Science, 14*(1), 44–48.
Simons, D. J., & Chabris, C. F. (1999). Gorillas in our midst: Sustained inattentional blindness for dynamic events. *Perception-London, 28*(9), 1059–1074.
Simons, D. J., & Levin, D. T. (1997). Change blindness. *Trends in Cognitive Sciences, 1*(7), 261–267.
Simons, D. J., & Rensink, R. A. (2005). Change blindness: Past, present, and future. *Trends in Cognitive Sciences, 9*(1), 16–20.
Simonsen, E. (2010). The integration of categorical and dimensional approaches to psychopathology. In T. Millon, R. F. Krueger, & E. Simonsen (Eds.), *Contemporary directions in psychopathology: Scientific foundations of the DSM-V and ICD-11* (pp. 350–361). Guilford Press.
Simonton, D. K. (2008). Bilingualism and creativity. In J. Altarriba & R. R. Heredia (Eds.), *An introduction to bilingualism: Principles and processes* (pp. 147–166). Lawrence Erlbaum.
Simonton, D. K., & Damian, R. I. (2013). Creativity. In D. Reisberg (Ed.), *The Oxford handbook of cognitive psychology* (pp. 795–809). Oxford University Press.
Simpkins, C. A., & Simpkins, A. M. (2009). *Meditation for therapists and their clients*. W. W. Norton.
Simpson, S., Richardson, L., Pietrabissa, G., Castelnuovo, G., & Reid, C. (2021). Videotherapy and therapeutic alliance in the age of COVID-19. *Clinical Psychology & Psychotherapy, 28*(2), 409–421. https://doi.org/10.1002/cpp.2521
Sin, N. L., & Lyubomirsky, S. (2009). Enhancing well-being and alleviating depressive symptoms with positive psychology interventions: A practice-friendly meta-analysis. *Journal of Clinical Psychology, 65*(5), 467–487.
Sinclair, R. C., Hoffman, C., Mark, M. M., Martin, L. L., & Pickering, T. L. (1994). Construct accessibility and the misattribution of arousal: Schachter and Singer revisited. *Psychological Science, 5*(1), 15–19.
Sindermann, C., Elhai, J. D., & Montag, C. (2020). Predicting tendencies towards the disordered use of Facebook's social media platforms: On the role of personality, impulsivity, and social anxiety. *Psychiatry Research, 285*, 112793. https://doi.org/10.1016/j.psychres.2020.112793
Singer, D. G., & Revenson, T. A. (1996). *A Piaget primer* (Rev. ed.). Plume.
Sinha, P., Ostrovsky, Y., & Russell, R. (2010). Face perception. In E. B. Goldstein (Ed.), *Encyclopedia of perception* (pp. 445–449). Sage.
Sink, A., & Mastro, D. (2017). Depictions of gender on primetime television: A quantitative content analysis. *Mass Communication and Society, 20*(1), 3–22.
Sivertsen, B., Omvik, S., Pallesen, S., Bjorvatn, B., Havik, O. E., Kvale, G., & Nordhus, I. H. (2006). Cognitive behavioral therapy vs zopiclone for treatment of chronic primary insomnia in older adults: A randomized controlled trial. *Journal of the American Medical Association, 295*(24), 2851–2858.
Skelton, R. M. (Ed.). (2006). *The Edinburgh international encyclopaedia of psychoanalysis*. Edinburgh University Press.
Skibbe, L. E., Justice, L. M., Zucker, T. A., & McGinty, A. S. (2008). Relations among maternal literacy beliefs, home literacy practices, and the emergent literacy skills of preschoolers with specific language impairment. *Early Education and Development, 19*(1), 68–88.
Skinner, B. F. (1938). *The behavior of organisms: An experimental analysis*. Appleton-Century.
Skinner, B. F. (1961). Teaching machines. *Scientific American, 205*(5), 91–102.
Skinner, B. F. (1971). *Beyond freedom and dignity*. Bantam/Vintage.
Skinner, B. F. (1974). *About behaviorism*. Random House.
Skinner, B. F. (1976). *Walden two* (Reissued ed.). Macmillan.
Slater, A., & Johnson, S. P. (1998). Visual sensory and perceptual abilities of the newborn: Beyond the blooming, buzzing confusion. In F. Simion & G. Butterworth (Eds.), *The development of sensory, motor and cognitive capacities in early infancy* (pp. 121–141). Psychology Press.
Slavin, L. A., Rainer, K. L., McCreary, M. L., & Gowda, K. K. (1991). Toward a multicultural model of the stress process. *Journal of Counseling & Development, 70*(1), 156–163.
Sleiman, M., Gundel, L. A., Pankow, J. F., Jacob, P., Singer, B. C., & Destaillats, H. (2010). Formation of carcinogens indoors by surface-mediated reactions of nicotine with nitrous acid, leading to potential thirdhand smoke hazards. *Proceedings of the National Academy of Sciences, 107*(15), 6576–6581.
Sloman, S. A. (1996). The empirical case for two systems of reasoning. *Psychological Bulletin, 119*(1), 3–22.
Slovic, P. (1975). Choice between equally valued alternatives. *Journal of Experimental psychology: Human Perception and Performance, 1*(3), 280–287.
Small, S. (2021). *Forgetting: The benefits of not remembering*. Crown.
Small, S. A., & Heeger, D. J. (2013). Functional imaging of cognition. In E. R. Kandel, J. H. Schwartz, T. M. Jessell, S. A. Siegelbaum, & A. J. Hudspeth (Eds.), *Principles of neural science* (5th ed., pp. 426–441). McGraw-Hill.
Smallheer, B. A., Vollman, M., & Dietrich, M. S. (2018). Learned helplessness and depressive symptoms following myocardial infarction. *Clinical Nursing Research, 27*(5), 597–616.
Smetana, J. G., & Villalobos, M. (2009). Social cognitive development in adolescence. In R. M. Lerner & L. Steinberg (Eds.), *Handbook of adolescent psychology* (3rd ed., Vol. 1, pp. 187–228). Wiley.
Smillie, L. D., Kern, M. L., & Uljarevic, M. (2019). Extraversion: Description, development, and mechanisms. In D. P. McAdams, R. L. Shiner, & J. L. Tackett (Eds.), *Handbook of personality development* (pp. 118–136). Guilford Press.
Smirle, C. (2013). *Profile–Rosalie Rayner*. Psychology's feminist voices. https://www.feministvoices.com/rosalie-rayner/
Smith, A. R., Hames, J. L., & Joiner, T. E. (2013). Status update: Maladaptive Facebook usage predicts increases in body dissatisfaction and bulimic symptoms. *Journal of Affective Disorders, 149*(1), 235–240.
Smith, D., & Cummins, S. (2011). Food deserts. In J. H. Cawley (Ed.), *The Oxford handbook of the social science of obesity* (pp. 452–462). Oxford University Press.
Smith, E. E., & Medin, D. L. (1981). *Categories and concepts* (pp. 51–83). Harvard University Press.
Smith, J. D., & Minda, J. P. (1998). Prototypes in the mist: The early epochs of category learning. *Journal of Experimental Psychology: Learning, Memory, and Cognition, 24*(6), 1411–1436.
Smith, J. D., & Minda, J. P. (2000). Thirty categorization results in search of a model. *Journal of Experimental Psychology: Learning, Memory, and Cognition, 26*(1), 3–27.
Smith, J. P., Hardy, S. T., Hale, L. E., & Gazmararian, J. A. (2019). Racial disparities and sleep among preschool aged children: A systematic review. *Sleep Health, 5*(1), 49–57. https://doi.org/10.1016/j.sleh.2018.09.010
Smith, K. (2012). Against homeopathy—A utilitarian perspective. *Bioethics, 26*(8), 398–409.
Smith, K. D., Keating, J. P., & Stotland, E. (1989). Altruism reconsidered: The effect of denying feedback on a victim's status to empathic witnesses. *Journal of Personality and Social Psychology, 57*(4), 641.
Smith, L. (2009). Introduction II. Jean Piaget: From boy to man. In U. Müller, J. I. M. Carpendale, & L. Smith (Eds.), *The Cambridge companion to Piaget* (pp. 18–27). Cambridge University Press.
Smith, L. D. (1996). Conclusion: Situating B. F. Skinner and behaviorism in American culture. In L. D. Smith & W. R. Woodward (Eds.), *B. F. Skinner and behaviorism in American culture* (pp. 294–315). Lehigh University Press.
Smith, M. L., & Glass, G. V. (1977). Meta-analysis of psychotherapy outcome studies. *American Psychologist, 32*(9), 752–760.
Smith, M. L., Glass, G. V., & Miller, T. I. (1980). *The benefits of psychotherapy*. Johns Hopkins University Press.
Smith, M. T., Perlis, M. L., Park, A., Smith, M. S., Pennington, J., Giles, D. E., & Buysse, D. J. (2002). Comparative meta-analysis of pharmacotherapy and behavior therapy for persistent insomnia. *American Journal of Psychiatry, 159*(1), 5–11.
Smith, P. B. (2011). Cross-cultural perspectives on identity. In S. Schwartz, K. Luyckx, & V. Vignoles (Eds.), *Handbook of identity theory and research* (pp. 249–265). Springer.
Smith, P. B., Ahmad, A. H., Owe, E., Celikkol, G. C., Ping, H., Gavreliuc, A., Chobthamkit, P., Rizwan, M., Chen, S. X., Teh, H. B., & Vignoles, V. L. (2016). Nation-level moderators of the extent to which self-efficacy and relationship harmony predict students' depression and life satisfaction: Evidence from 10 cultures. *Journal of Cross-Cultural Psychology, 47*(6), 818–834.
Smith, P. J., Blumenthal, J. A., Hoffman, B. M., Cooper, H., Strauman, T. A., Welsh-Bohmer, K., Browndyke, J. N., & Sherwood, A. (2010). Aerobic exercise and neurocognitive performance: A meta-analytic review of randomized controlled trials. *Psychosomatic Medicine, 72*(3), 239–252.
Smith, R. A., & Davis, S. F. (2003). The changing face of research methods. In S. F. Davis (Ed.), *Handbook of research methods in experimental psychology* (pp. 106–126). Blackwell.

Smith, R. S., Guilleminault, C., & Efron, B. (1997). Sports, sleep, and circadian rhythms: Circadian rhythms and enhanced athletic performance in the National Football League. *Sleep, 20*(5), 362–365.

Smith, S. M., & Vela, E. (2001). Environmental context-dependent memory: A review and meta-analysis. *Psychonomic Bulletin & Review, 8*(2), 203–220.

Smith, S. M., & Ward T. B. (2012). Cognition and the creation of ideas. In K. J. Holyoak & R. G. Morrison (Eds.), *The Oxford handbook of thinking and reasoning* (pp. 456–474). Oxford University Press.

Smith, S. M., Handy, J. D., Hernandez, A., & Jacoby, L. L. (2018, February 1). Context specificity of automatic influences of memory. *Journal of Experimental Psychology: Learning, Memory, and Cognition, 44*(10). http://doi.org/10.1037/xlm0000523

Smith, S. R., & Archer, R. P. (2008). Introducing personality assessment. In R. P. Archer & S. R. Smith (Eds.), *Personality assessment* (pp. 1–35). Routledge.

Smith, T. W., & MacKenzie, J. (2006). Personality and risk of physical illness. *Annual Review of Clinical Psychology, 2*, 435–467.

Smits, J. A. J., O'Cleirigh, C. M., & Otto, M. W. (2006). Panic and agoraphobia. In M. Hersen & J. C. Thomas (Eds.), *Comprehensive handbook of personality and psychopathology* (Vol. 2, pp. 121–137). Wiley.

Smoller, J. W., Gardner-Schuster, E., & Misiaszek, M. (2008). Genetics of anxiety: Would the genome recognize the DSM? *Depression and Anxiety, 25*(4), 368–377.

Smyth, J. M., Sliwinski, M. J., Zawadzki, M. J., Scott, S. B., Conroy, D. E., Lanza, S. T., Marcusson-Clavertz, D., Kim, J., Stawski, R. S., Stoney, C. M., Buxton, O. M., Sciamanna, C. N., Green, P. M., Almeida, D. M. (2018). Everyday stress response targets in the science of behavior change. *Behaviour Research and Therapy, 101*, 20–29.

Snarey, J. R. (2012). Lawrence Kohlberg: Moral biography, moral psychology, and moral pedagogy. In W. E. Pickren, D. A. Dewsbury, & M. Wertheimer (Eds.), *Portraits of pioneers in developmental psychology* (pp. 277–296). Psychology Press.

Snast, I., Reiter, O., Atzmony, L., Leshem, Y. A., Hodak, E., Mimouni, D., & Pavlovsky, L. (2018). Psychological stress and psoriasis: A systematic review and meta-analysis. *British Journal of Dermatology, 178*(5), 1044–1055.

Snell, J., van Leipsig, S., Grainger, J., & Meeter, M. (2018). OB1-reader: A model of word recognition and eye movements in text reading. *Psychological Review, 125*(6), 969–984. http://dx.doi.org/10.1037/rev0000119

Snodderly, D. M. (2018). Visual discriminations encountered in food foraging by a neotropical primate: Implications for the evolution of color vision. In E. H. Burtt Jr. (Ed.), *The behavioral significance of color* (pp. 237–285). Routledge.

Snowden, L. R. (2007). Explaining mental health treatment disparities: Ethnic and cultural differences in family involvement. *Culture, Medicine and Psychiatry, 31*(3), 389–402.

Snowden, L. R. (2012). Health and mental health policies' role in better understanding and closing African American–White American disparities in treatment access and quality of care. *American Psychologist, 67*(7), 524–531.

Snowden, L. R., & Yamada, A. M. (2005). Cultural differences in access to care. *Annual Review of Clinical Psychology, 1*, 143–166.

Snowden, L. R., Masland, M., & Guerrero, R. (2007). Federal civil rights policy and mental health treatment access for persons with limited English proficiency. *American Psychologist, 62*(2), 109–117.

Snowden, L. R., Masland, M. C., Peng, C. J., Lou, C. W. M., & Wallace, N. T. (2011). Limited English proficient Asian Americans: Threshold language policy and access to mental health treatment. *Social Science & Medicine, 72*(2), 230–237.

Snowling, M. J., & Hulme, C. (Eds.). (2008). *The science of reading: A handbook* (Vol. 9). Wiley.

Snyder, C. M. (1975). *The lady and the president: The letters of Dorothea Dix and Millard Fillmore*. The University Press of Kentucky.

Snyder, C. R., Lopez, S. J., & Pedrotti, J. T. (2011). *Positive psychology: The scientific and practical explorations of human strengths* (2nd ed.). Sage.

Snyder, M., & Deaux, K. (2012). Personality and social psychology: Crossing boundaries and integrating perspectives. In K. Deaux & M. Snyder (Eds.), *The Oxford handbook of personality and social psychology* (pp. 3–9). Oxford University Press.

Sobkowicz, P., Thelwall, M., Buckley, K., Paltoglou, G., & Sobkowicz, A. (2013). Lognormal distributions of user post lengths in Internet discussions—A consequence of the Weber-Fechner law? *EPJ Data Science, 2*(1), 1–20.

Society for Community Research and Action. (2016). What we do. http://www.scra27.org/what-we-do/

Söderkvist, S., Ohlén, K., & Dimberg, U. (2018). How the experience of emotion is modulated by facial feedback. *Journal of Nonverbal Behavior, 42*(1), 129–151.

Sokal, M. M. (2002). Origins and early years of the American Psychological Association, 1890–1906. In W. E. Pickren & D. A. Dewsbury (Eds.), *Evolving perspectives on the history of psychology* (pp. 141–168). American Psychological Association.

Sokol, R. L., Qin, B., & Poti, J. M. (2017). Parenting styles and body mass index: A systematic review of prospective studies among children. *Obesity Reviews, 18*(3), 281–292.

Sokolov, A. A., Miall, R. C., & Ivry, R. B. (2017). The cerebellum: Adaptive prediction for movement and cognition. *Trends in Cognitive Sciences, 21*(5), 313–332.

Soldz, S., & Vaillant, G. E. (1999). The Big Five personality traits and the life course: A 45-year longitudinal study. *Journal of Research in Personality, 33*(2), 208–232.

Solomon, B. C., & Jackson, J. J. (2014). Why do personality traits predict divorce? Multiple pathways through satisfaction. *Journal of Personality and Social Psychology, 106*(6), 978–996.

Solomon, R. C. (2008). The philosophy of emotions. In M. Lewis, J. M. Haviland-Jones, & L. F. Barrett (Eds.), *Handbook of emotions* (3rd ed., pp. 3–16). Guilford Press.

Somary, K., & Strieker, G. (1998). Becoming a grandparent: A longitudinal study of expectations and early experiences as a function of sex and lineage. *The Gerontologist, 38*(1), 53–61.

Somerville, L. H. (2013). The teenage brain sensitivity to social evaluation. *Current Directions in Psychological Science, 22*(2), 121–127.

Sommers-Flanagan, J., & Sommers-Flanagan, R. (2009). *Clinical interviewing* (4th ed.). Wiley.

Sommers-Flanagan, R. (2012). Boundaries, multiple roles, and the professional relationship. In S. J. Knapp (Ed.), *APA handbook of ethics in psychology* (Vol. 1, pp. 241–277). American Psychological Association.

Son, L. K. (2004). Spacing one's study: Evidence for a metacognitive control strategy. *Journal of Experimental Psychology: Learning, Memory, and Cognition, 30*(3), 601.

Son, L. K. (2005). Metacognitive control: Children's short-term versus long-term study strategies. *The Journal of General Psychology, 132*(4), 347–364.

Son, L. K., & Kornell, N. (2008). Research on the allocation of study time: Key studies from 1890 to the present (and beyond). In J. Dunlosky & R. A. Bjork (Eds.), *Handbook of metamemory and memory* (pp. 333–351). Psychological Press.

Song, H., Kempermann, G., Wadiche, L. O., Zhao, C., Schinder, A. F., & Bischofberger, J. (2005). New neurons in the adult mammalian brain: Synaptogenesis and functional integration. *The Journal of Neuroscience, 25*(45), 10366–10368.

Sonnby-Borgström, M. (2002). Automatic mimicry reactions as related to differences in emotional empathy. *Scandinavian Journal of Psychology, 43*(5), 433–443.

Sonne, J. L. (2012). Sexualized relationships. In S. J. Knapp (Ed.), *APA handbook of ethics in psychology* (Vol. 1, pp. 295–310). American Psychological Association.

Søraas, A., Bø, R., Kalleberg, K. T., Støer, N. C., Ellingjord-Dale, M., & Landrø, N. I. (2021). Self-reported memory problems 8 months after COVID-19 infection. *JAMA Network Open, 4*(7), e2118717-e2118717. https://doi.org/10.1001/jamanetworkopen.2021.18717

Soraci, S. A., Carlin, M. T., Read, J. D., Pogoda, T. K., Wakeford, Y., Cavanagh, S., & Shin, L. (2007). Psychological impairment, eyewitness testimony, and false memories: Individual differences. In M. P. Toglia, J. D. Read, D. F. Ross, & R. C. L. Lindsay (Eds.), *The handbook of eyewitness psychology: Memory for events* (Vol. I, pp. 261–297). Psychology Press.

Sorce, J. F., Emde, R. N., Campos, J. J., & Klinnert, M. D. (1985). Maternal emotional signaling: Its effect on the visual cliff behavior of 1-year-olds. *Developmental Psychology, 21*(1), 195–200.

Sorensen, N., Nagda, B. A., Gurin, P., & Maxwell, K. E. (2009). Taking a "hands on" approach to diversity in higher education: A critical-dialogic model for effective intergroup interaction. *Analyses of Social Issues and Public Policy, 9*(1), 3–35.

Sorkin, D., Rook, K. S., & Lu, J. L. (2002). Loneliness, lack of emotional support, lack of companionship, and the likelihood of having a heart condition in an elderly sample. *Annals of Behavioral Medicine, 24*(4), 290–298.

Sorkin, J. D., Muller, D. C., & Andres, R. (1999). Longitudinal change in height of men and women: Implications for interpretation of the body mass index: The Baltimore longitudinal study of aging. *American Journal of Epidemiology, 150*(9), 969–977.

Sorokowski, P., Karwowski, M., Misiak, M., Marczak, M. K., Dziekan, M., Hummel, T., & Sorokowska, A. (2019). Sex differences in human olfaction: A meta-analysis. *Frontiers in Psychology, 10*, 242. https://doi.org/10.3389/fpsyg.2019.00242

Soto, A., Smith, T. B., Griner, D., Domenech Rodríguez, M., & Bernal, G. (2018). Cultural adaptations and therapist multicultural competence: Two meta-analytic reviews. *Journal of Clinical Psychology, 74*(11), 1907–1923.

Soto-Faraco, S., & Alsius, A. (2009). Deconstructing the McGurk–MacDonald illusion. *Journal of Experimental Psychology: Human Perception and Performance, 35*(2), 580–587.

Soto-Rubio, A., Giménez-Espert, M. D. C., & Prado-Gascó, V. (2020). Effect of emotional intelligence and psychosocial risks on burnout, job satisfaction, and nurses' health during the Covid-19 pandemic. *International Journal of Environmental Research and Public Health, 17*(21), 7998. https://doi.org/10.3390/ijerph17217998

Sourander, A. (2001). Emotional and behavioural problems in a sample of Finnish three-year-olds. *European Child & Adolescent Psychiatry, 10*(2), 98–104.

Sousa, A. M., Meyer, K. A., Santpere, G., Gulden, F. O., & Sestan, N. (2017). Evolution of the human nervous system function, structure, and development. *Cell, 170*(2), 226–247.

Soussignan, R. (2002). Duchenne smile, emotional experience, and autonomic reactivity: A test of the facial feedback hypothesis. *Emotion, 2*(1), 52–74.

South, S. C., Oltmanns, T. F., & Krueger, R. F. (2011). The spectrum of personality disorders. In D. H. Barlow (Ed.), *The Oxford handbook of clinical psychology* (pp. 530–550). Oxford University Press.

Spangler, J. G., Song, E. Y., Egan, K. L., Wagoner, K. G., Reboussin, B. A., Wolfson, M., & Sutfin, E. L. (2018). Correlates of alcohol mixed with energy drink use among first year college students: Clinical and research implications. *Journal of Caffeine and Adenosine Research, 8*(3), 107–112.

Sparkman, D. J., Eidelman, S., & Blanchar, J. C. (2016). Multicultural experiences reduce prejudice through personality shifts in openness to experience. *European Journal of Social Psychology, 46*(7), 840–853. https://doi.org/10.1002/ejsp.2189

Sparr, L. F., & Pitman, R. K. (2007). PTSD and the law. In M. J. Friedman, T. M. Keane, & P. A. Resick (Eds.), *Handbook of PTSD: Science and practice* (pp. 449–468). Guilford Press.

Sparrenberger, F., Cichelero, F. T., Ascoli, A. M., Fonseca, F. P., Weiss, G., Berwanger, O., Fuchs, S. C., Moreira, L. B., & Fuchs, F. D. (2009). Does psychosocial stress cause hypertension? A systematic review of observational studies. *Journal of Human Hypertension, 23*(1), 12–19.

Speakman, J. R. (2013). Evolutionary perspectives on the obesity epidemic: Adaptive, maladaptive, and neutral viewpoints. *Annual Review of Nutrition, 33*, 289–317.

Speakman, J. R., Levitsky, D. A., Allison, D. B., Bray, M. S., de Castro, J. M., Clegg, D. J., Clapham, J. C., Dulloo, A. G., Gruer, L., Haw, S., Hebebrand, J., Hetherington, M. M., Higgs, S., Jebb, S. A., Loos, R. J. F., Luckman, S., Luke, A., Mohammed-Ali, V., O'Rahilly, S., Pereira, M., Perusse, L., … Westerterp-Plantenga, M. S. (2011). Set points, settling points and some alternative models: Theoretical options to understand how genes and environments combine to regulate body adiposity. *Disease Models & Mechanisms, 4*(6), 733–745.

Spear, N. E. (2007). Retrieval: Properties and effects. In H. L. Roediger, Y. Dudai, & S. M. Fitzpatrick (Eds.), *Science of memory: Concepts* (pp. 215–219). Oxford University Press.

Spearman, C. (1904). "General intelligence," objectively determined and measured. *The American Journal of Psychology, 15*(2), 201–292.

Spearman, C. (1923). *The nature of "intelligence" and the principles of cognition*. Macmillan.

Speekenbring, M., & Shanks, D. R. (2013). Decision making. In D. Reisberg (Ed.), *The Oxford handbook of cognitive psychology* (pp. 682–703). Oxford University Press.

Spence, S. H., Donovan, C. L., March, S., Gamble, A., Anderson, R. E., Prosser, S., & Kenardy, J. (2011). A randomized controlled trial of online versus clinic-based CBT for adolescent anxiety. Journal of Consulting and Clinical Psychology, 79(5), 629–642.

Spencer, S. J., Logel, C., & Davies, P. G. (2016). Stereotype threat. *Annual Review of Psychology, 67*, 415–437.

Spencer, S. J., Steele, C. M., & Quinn, D. M. (1999). Stereotype threat and women's math performance. *Journal of Experimental Social Psychology, 35*(1), 4–28.

Sperling, G. (1960). The information available in brief visual presentations. *Psychological Monographs: General and Applied, 74*(11), 1–29.

Sperry, L. (2016). *Handbook of diagnosis and treatment of the DSM-5 personality disorders* (3rd ed.). Taylor & Francis.

Spiegel, D. (2003). Negative and positive visual hypnotic hallucinations: Attending inside and out. *International Journal of Clinical and Experimental Hypnosis, 51*(2), 130–146.

Spiegler, M. D. (2016). *Contemporary behavior therapy* (6th ed.). Cengage.

Spiegler, M. D., & Guevremont, D. C. (2010). *Contemporary behavior therapy* (5th ed.). Wadsworth.

Spielman, A. J., Saskin, P., & Thorpy, M. J. (1987). Treatment of chronic insomnia by restriction of time in bed. *Sleep, 10*(1), 45–56.

Spiner, T. (January/February 2021). 2021 trends report. *Monitor on Psychology, 52*(1), 2. https://www.apa.org/monitor/2021/01

Spokas, M. E., Rodebaugh, T. L., & Heimburg, R. G. (2008). Treatment research. In M. Hersen & A. M. Gross (Eds.), *Handbook of clinical psychology* (Vol. 1, pp. 300–338). Wiley.

Spoormaker, V. I., & Lancee, J. (2012). Lucid dreaming therapy for nightmares. In D. Barrett & P. McNamara (Eds.), *Encyclopedia of sleep and dreams: The evolution, function, nature, and mysteries of slumber* (Vol. 1, pp. 401–403). Greenwood.

Sprecher, S. (1987). The effects of self-disclosure given and received on affection for an intimate partner and stability of the relationship. *Journal of Social and Personal Relationships, 4*(2), 115–127.

Sprecher, S., & Regan, P. C. (2007). Passionate and companionate love in courting and young married couples. *Sociological Inquiry, 68*(2), 163–185.

Spring, B., & Neville, K. (2011). Evidence-based practice in clinical psychology. In D. H. Barlow (Ed.), *The Oxford handbook of clinical psychology* (pp. 128–149). Oxford University Press.

Spunt, R. P., & Adolphs, R. (2017). A new look at domain specificity: Insights from social neuroscience. *Nature Reviews Neuroscience, 18*(9), 559.

Squire, L. R. (1992). Memory and the hippocampus: A synthesis from findings with rats, monkeys, and humans. *Psychological Review, 99*(2), 195–231.

Squire, L. R. (2004). Memory systems of the brain: A brief history and current perspective. *Neurobiology of Learning and Memory, 82*(3), 171–177.

Squire, L. R., & Zola, S. M. (1996). Structure and function of declarative and nondeclarative memory systems. *Proceedings of the National Academy of Sciences, 93*(24), 13515–13522.

Srihari, A., Shanmukananda, P., Kumar, L. S. D., & John, S. (2021). Analysis of potential risk of hearing loss among students using personal audio devices. *National Journal of Physiology, Pharmacy and Pharmacology, 11*(5), 462–465. https://doi.org/10.5455/njppp.2021.11.11301202027122020

Srivastava, S., John, O. P., Gosling, S. D., & Potter, J. (2003). Development of personality in early and middle adulthood: Set like plaster or persistent change? *Journal of Personality and Social Psychology, 84*(5), 1041–1053.

Srivastava, S., Tamir, M., McGonigal, K. M., John, O. P., & Gross, J. J. (2009). The social costs of emotional suppression: A prospective study of the transition to college. *Journal of Personality and Social Psychology, 96*(4), 883–897.

Sroufe, L. A. (2005). Attachment and development: A prospective, longitudinal study from birth to adulthood. *Attachment & Human Development, 7*(4), 349–367.

Sroufe, L. A., Egeland, B., Carlson, E. A., & Collins, W. A. (2005). *The development of the person: The Minnesota study of risk and adaptation from birth to adulthood*. Guilford Press.

Srull, T. K., & Wyer, R. S. (1979). The role of category accessibility in the interpretation of information about persons: Some determinants and implications. *Journal of Personality and Social Psychology, 37*(10), 1660–1672.

Stachl, C., Au, Q., Schoedel, R., Gosling, S. D., Harari, G. M., Buschek, D., Völkel, S. T., Schuwerk, T., Oldemeier, M., Ullmann, T., Hussmann, H., Bischl, B., & Bühner, M. (2020). Predicting personality from patterns of behavior collected with smartphones. *Proceedings of the National Academy of Sciences, 117*(30), 17680–17687. https://doi.org/10.1073/pnas.1920484117

Stadler, M. A., & Frensch, P. A. (Eds.). (1998). *Handbook of implicit learning*. Sage.

Stagner, R. (1988). *A history of psychological theories*. Macmillan.

Stahl, S. M. (2012). Psychotherapy as an epigenetic "drug": Psychiatric therapeutics target symptoms linked to malfunctioning brain circuits with psychotherapy as well as with drugs. *Journal of Clinical Pharmacy and Therapeutics, 37*(3), 249–253.

Stajkovic, A. D., Bandura, A., Locke, E. A., Lee, D., & Sergent, K. (2018). Test of three conceptual models of influence of the Big Five personality traits and self-efficacy on academic performance: A meta-analytic path-analysis. *Personality and Individual Differences, 120*, 238–245.

Stake, J. E., & Eisele, H. (2010). Gender and personality. In J. C. Chrisler & D. R. McCreary (Eds.), *Handbook of gender research in psychology* (Vol. 1, pp. 19–40). Springer Science+Business Media.

Stalder, D. R. (2005). Learning and motivational benefits of acronym use in introductory psychology. *Teaching of Psychology, 32*(4), 222–228.

Stam, K. R., & Stanton, J. M. (2010). Events, emotions, and technology: Examining acceptance of workplace technology changes. *Information Technology & People, 23*(1), 23–53.

Stanar, D. (2021). The vital significance of military ethics. *Journal of Military Ethics*, 1–14. https://doi.org/10.1080/15027570.2021.2011913

Staniloiu, A., Markowitsch, H. J., Sarlon, J., & Kordon, A. (2018). Migration and dissociative amnesia. *Psychological Applications and Trends*, 44–48.

Stanovich, K. (2011). *Rationality and the reflective mind*. Oxford University Press.

Stanovich, K. E. (2013). *How to think straight about psychology* (10th ed.). Pearson.

Starcevic, V., & Aboujaoude, E. (2015). Cyberchondria, cyberbullying, cybersuicide, cybersex: "New" psychopathologies for the 21st century? *World Psychiatry, 14*(1), 97–100.

Stathopoulou, G., Powers, M. B., Berry, A. C., Smits, J. A., & Otto, M. W. (2006). Exercise interventions for mental health: A quantitative and qualitative review. *Clinical Psychology: Science and Practice, 13*(2), 179–193.

Statista. (2018). Reach of leading social media and networking sites used by teenagers and young adults in the United States as of February 2017. https://www.statista.com/statistics/199242/social-media-and-networking-sites-used-by-us-teenagers/

Stattin, H., & Klackenberg, G. (1992). Discordant family relations in intact families: Developmental tendencies over 18 years. *Journal of Marriage and the Family, 54*(4), 940–956.

Steele, C. M. (1997). A threat in the air: How stereotypes shape intellectual identity and performance. *American Psychologist, 52*(6), 613–629.

Steele, C. M. (2010). *Whistling Vivaldi: And other clues to how stereotypes affect us*. W. W. Norton.

Steele, C. M., & Aronson, J. A. (2004). Stereotype threat does not live by Steele and Aronson alone. *American Psychologist, 59*(1), 47–48.

Steenari, M. R., Vuontela, V., Paavonen, E. J., Carlson, S., Fjällberg, M., & Aronen, E. T. (2003). Working memory and sleep in 6- to 13-year-old schoolchildren. *Journal of the American Academy of Child & Adolescent Psychiatry, 42*(1), 85–92.

Steenhuis, I., & Poelman, M. (2017). Portion size: latest developments and interventions. *Current Obesity Reports, 6*(1), 10–17. https://doi.org/10.1007/s13679-017-0239-x

Steensma, T. D., Kreukels, B. P., de Vries, A. L., & Cohen-Kettenis, P. T. (2013). Gender identity development in adolescence. *Hormones and Behavior, 64*(2), 288–297.

Steere, J., & Cooper, P. J. (1993). The effects on eating of dietary restraint, anxiety, and hunger. *International Journal of Eating Disorders, 13*(2), 211–219.

Steger, B. (2003). Negotiating sleep patterns in Japan. In B. Steger & L. Brunt (Eds.), *Night-time and sleep in Asia and the West: Exploring the dark side of life* (pp. 65–86). University of Vienna Press.

Steger, B., & Brunt, L. (2003). Introduction: Into the night and the world of sleep. In B. Steger & L. Brunt (Eds.), *Night-time and sleep in Asia and the West: Exploring the dark side of life* (pp. 1–23). University of Vienna Press.

Steiger, H., & Bruce, K. R. (2009). Eating disorders. In P. H. Blaney & T. Millon (Eds.), *Oxford textbook of psychopathology* (2nd ed., pp. 431–451). Oxford University Press.

Steiger, V. R., Brühl, A. B., Weidt, S., Delsignore, A., Rufer, M., Jäncke, L., Herwig, U., & Hänggi, J. (2017). Pattern of structural brain changes in social anxiety disorder after cognitive behavioral group therapy: A longitudinal multimodal MRI study. *Molecular Psychiatry, 22*(8), 1164–1171.

Stein, A., Carl, E., Cuijpers, P., Karyotaki, E., & Smits, J. (2021). Looking beyond depression: A meta-analysis of the effect of behavioral activation on depression, anxiety, and activation. *Psychological Medicine, 51*(9), 1491–1504. https://doi.org/10.1017/S0033291720000239

Stein, D. J., & Nesse, R. M. (2015). Normal and abnormal anxiety in the age of DSM-5 and ICD-11. *Emotion Review, 7*(3), 223–229.

Stein, D. J., & Williams, D. (2010). Cultural and social aspects of anxiety disorders. In D. J. Stein, E. Hollander, & B. O. Rothbaum (Eds.), *Textbook of anxiety disorders* (2nd ed., pp. 717–729). American Psychiatric Association.

Stein, S. (2008). Genetics. In K. Keller (Ed.), *Encyclopedia of obesity* (Vol. 2, pp. 321–325). Sage.

Stein, S. J., & Bartone, P. T. (2020). *Hardiness: Making stress work for you to achieve your life goals*. John Wiley & Sons.

Steinberg, L. (1981). Transformations in family relations at puberty. *Developmental Psychology, 17*(6), 833–840.

Steinberg, L. (1990). Interdependence in the family: Autonomy, conflict, and harmony in the parent–adolescent relationships. In S. S. Feldman & G. Elliott (Eds.), *At the threshold: The developing adolescent* (pp. 255–276). Harvard University Press.

Steinberg, L., & Silk, J. S. (2002). Parenting adolescents. In M. H. Bornstein (Ed.), *Handbook of parenting* (Vol. 1, pp. 103–133). Lawrence Erlbaum.

Steinberg, L., Elmen, J. D., & Mounts, N. S. (1989). Authoritative parenting, psychosocial maturity, and academic success among adolescents. *Child Development, 60*(6), 1424–1436.

Steinberg, L., Lamborn, S. D., Dornbusch, S. M., & Darling, N. (1992). Impact of parenting practices on adolescent achievement: Authoritative parenting, school involvement, and encouragement to succeed. *Child Development, 63*(5), 1266–1281.

Steinberg, L., Mounts, N. S., Lamborn, S. D., & Dornbusch, S. M. (1991). Authoritative parenting and adolescent adjustment across varied ecological niches. *Journal of Research on Adolescence, 1*(1), 19–36.

Steiner, A. M., & Fletcher, P. C. (2017). Sandwich generation caregiving: A complex and dynamic role. *Journal of Adult Development, 24*(2), 133–143.

Steiner, J. E. (1977). Facial expressions of the neonate infant indicating the hedonics of food-related chemical stimuli. In J. M. Weiffenbach (Ed.), *Taste and development: The genesis of sweet preference* (pp. 173–188). Department of Health, Education, and Welfare.

Stephan, W. G., & Stephan, C. W. (2000). An integrated threat theory of prejudice. In S. Oskamp (Ed.), *Reducing prejudice and discrimination* (pp. 23–45). Lawrence Erlbaum.

Stephan, Y., Sutin, A. R., Bayard, S., & Terracciano, A. (2017). Subjective age and sleep in middle-aged and older adults. *Psychology & Health, 32*(9), 1140–1151. https://doi.org/10.1080/08870446.2017.1324971

Steptoe, A., Leigh, E. S., & Kumari, M. (2011). Positive affect and distressed affect over the day in older people. *Psychology and Aging, 26*(4), 956–965.

Steptoe, A., Lipsey, Z., & Wardle, J. (1998). Stress, hassles and variations in alcohol consumption, food choice and physical exercise: A diary study. *British Journal of Health Psychology, 3*(1), 51–63.

Stern, J. A., Fraley, R. C., Jones, J. D., Gross, J. T., Shaver, P. R., & Cassidy, J. (2018). Developmental processes across the first two years of parenthood: Stability and change in adult attachment style. *Developmental Psychology, 54*(5), 975–988.

Sternberg, R. J. (1999). The theory of successful intelligence. *Review of General Psychology, 3*(4), 292–316.

Sternberg, R. J. (2000). The concept of intelligence. In R. J. Sternberg (Ed.), *Handbook of intelligence* (pp. 3–15). Cambridge University Press.

Sternberg, R. J. (2006). The nature of creativity. *Creativity Research Journal, 18*(1), 87–99.

Sternberg, R. J. (2011). Individual differences in cognitive development. In U. Goswami (Ed.), *The Wiley-Blackwell handbook of childhood cognitive development* (2nd ed., pp. 749–774). Wiley-Blackwell.

Sternberg, R. J. (2018). Speculations on the role of successful intelligence in solving contemporary world problems. *Journal of Intelligence, 6*(1), 4.

Sternberg, R. J., & Lubart, T. I. (1991). An investment theory of creativity and its development. *Human Development, 34*(1), 1–31.

Sternberg, R. J., & Sternberg, K. (2010). *The psychologist's companion: A guide to writing scientific papers for students and researchers* (5th ed.). Cambridge University Press.

Sterns, H. L., & Huyck, M. H. (2001). The role of work in midlife. In M. E. Lachman (Ed.), *Handbook of midlife development* (pp. 447–486). Wiley.

Sternthal, M. J., Jun, H. J., Earls, F., & Wright, R. J. (2010). Community violence and urban childhood asthma: A multilevel analysis. *European Respiratory Journal, 36*(6), 1400–1409.

Stevens, G., Owens, D., & Schaefer, E. C. (1990). Education and attractiveness in marriage choices. *Social Psychology Quarterly, 53*(1), 62–70.

Stevens, W. D., Kravitz, D. J., Peng, C. S., Tessler, M. H., & Martin, A. (2017). Privileged functional connectivity between the visual word form area and the language system. *Journal of Neuroscience, 37*(21), 5288–5297.

Stewart, D. G. & Davis, K. L. (2008). Neuropathology. In K. T. Mueser & D. V. Jeste (Eds.), *Clinical handbook of schizophrenia*, pp. 44–54. Guilford.

Stewart, J. W., Quitkin, F. M., & Davies, C. (2006). Atypical depression, dysthymia, and cyclothymia. In D. J. Stein, D. J. Kupfer, & A. F. Schatzberg (Eds.), *The American Psychiatric Publishing textbook of mood disorders* (pp. 547–560). American Psychiatric Association.

Stewart, R. E., Stirman, S. W., & Chambless, D. L. (2012). A qualitative investigation of practicing psychologists' attitudes toward research-informed practice: Implications for dissemination strategies. *Professional Psychology: Research and Practice, 43*(2), 100–109.

Stewart, W. (2008). *A biographical dictionary of psychologists, psychiatrists and psychotherapists*. McFarland.

Stewart, W. F., Kim, N., Ifrah, C., Sliwinski, M., Zimmerman, M. E., Kim, M., & Lipton, M. L. (2018). Heading frequency is more strongly related to cognitive performance than unintentional head impacts in amateur soccer players. Frontiers in Neurology, 9, 240.

Stewart, W. F., Ricci, J. A., Chee, E., Hahn, S. R., & Morganstein, D. (2003). Cost of lost productive work time among U.S. workers with depression. *Journal of the American Medical Association, 289*(23), 3135–3144.

Stice, E. (2002). Risk and maintenance factors for eating pathology: A meta-analytic review. *Psychological Bulletin, 128*(5), 825–848.

Stice, E., Marti, C. N., & Rohde, P. (2013). Prevalence, incidence, impairment, and course of the proposed DSM-5 eating disorder diagnoses in an 8-year prospective community study of young women. *Journal of Abnormal Psychology, 122*(2), 445–457.

Stice, E., Ragan, J., & Randall, P. (2004). Prospective relations between social support and depression: Differential direction of effects for parent and peer support? *Journal of Abnormal Psychology, 113*(1), 155–159.

Stice, E., Rohde, P., & Shaw, H. (2016). Eating disorders. In J. C. Norcross, G. R. VandenBos, & D. K. Freedheim (Eds.), *APA handbook of clinical psychology: Vol. 4. Psychopathology and health* (pp. 275–294). American Psychological Association.

Stockman, A. (2010). Color mixing. In E. B. Goldstein (Ed.), *Encyclopedia of perception* (pp. 262–264). Sage.

Stoffregen, T. A., & Riccio, G. E. (1991). An ecological critique of the sensory conflict theory of motion sickness. *Ecological Psychology, 3*(3), 159–194.

Stoller, M. K. (1994). Economic effects of insomnia. *Clinical Therapeutics, 16*(5), 873–897.

Stone, A. A., & Brownell, K. D. (1994). The stress-eating paradox: Multiple daily measurements in adult males and females. *Psychology and Health, 9*(6), 425–436.

Stone, C. B., & Jay, A. C. V. (2018). A comparison of flashbulb memories for positive and negative events and their biopsychosocial functions. In O. Luminet & A. Curci (Eds.), *Flashbulb memories: New challenges and future perspectives* (2nd ed., pp. 161–181). Routledge.

Stone, J., & Fernandez, N. C. (2008). To practice what we preach: The use of hypocrisy and cognitive dissonance to motivate behavior change. *Social and Personality Psychology Compass, 2*(2), 1024–1051.

Stone, M. H. (1997). *Healing the mind: A history of psychiatry from antiquity to the present.* W. W. Norton.

Stoppelbein, L., McRae, E., & Greening, L. (2017). A longitudinal study of hardiness as a buffer for posttraumatic stress symptoms in mothers of children with cancer. *Clinical Practice in Pediatric Psychology, 5*(2), 149–160.

Stothard, E. R., McHill, A. W., Depner, C. M., Birks, B. R., Moehlman, T. M., Ritchie, H. K., Guzzetti, J. R., Chinoy, E. D., LeBourgeois, M. K., Axelsson, J., & Wright, K. P., Jr. (2017). Circadian entrainment to the natural light-dark cycle across seasons and the weekend. *Current Biology, 27*(4), 508–513.

Strack, F., & Mussweiler, T. (1997). Explaining the enigmatic anchoring effect: Mechanisms of selective accessibility. *Journal of Personality and Social Psychology, 73*(3), 437–446.

Strahler, J., Hermann, A., Walter, B., & Stark, R. (2018). Orthorexia nervosa: A behavioral complex or a psychological condition? *Journal of Behavioral Addictions, 7*(4), 1143–1156.

Straker, G. (2013). Continuous traumatic stress: Personal reflections 25 years on. *Peace and Conflict: Journal of Peace Psychology, 19*(2), 209–217.

Straker, G., Moosa, F., & Team, S. C. (1988). Post-traumatic stress disorder: A reaction to state-supported child abuse and neglect. *Child Abuse & Neglect, 12*(3), 383–395.

Strakowski, S. M., & Shelton, R. C. (2006). Antipsychotic medications. In D. J. Stein, D. J. Kupfer, & A. F. Schatzberg (Eds.), *The American Psychiatric Publishing textbook of mood disorders* (pp. 291–304). American Psychiatric Publishing.

Straube, T., Glauer, M., Dilger, S., Mentzel, H. J., & Miltner, W. H. (2006). Effects of cognitive-behavioral therapy on brain activation in specific phobia. *Neuroimage, 29*(1), 125–135.

Straud, C. L., & McNaughton-Cassill, M. (2018). Self-blame and stress in undergraduate college students: The mediating role of proactive coping. *Journal of American College Health, 67*(4), 367–373.

Strauman, T. J. (1989). Self-discrepancies in clinical depression and social phobia: Cognitive structures that underlie emotional disorders? *Journal of Abnormal Psychology, 98*(1), 14–22.

Strauman, T. J. (2002). Self-regulation and depression. *Self and Identity, 1*(2), 151–157.

Straus, M. A., & Stewart, J. H. (1999). Corporal punishment by American parents: National data on prevalence, chronicity, severity, and duration, in relation to child and family characteristics. *Clinical Child and Family Psychology Review, 2*(2), 55–70.

Strenze, T. (2007). Intelligence and socioeconomic success: A meta-analytic review of longitudinal research. *Intelligence, 35*(5), 401–426.

Striano, J. (1988). *Can psychotherapists hurt you?* Professional Press.

Stricker, G. (2010). *Psychotherapy integration.* American Psychological Association.

Strijbos, D., & Glas, G. (2018). Self-knowledge in personality disorder: Self-referentiality as a stepping stone for psychotherapeutic understanding. *Journal of Personality Disorders, 32*(3), 295–310.

Stroebe, M., Schut, H., & Boerner, K. (2017). Cautioning health-care professionals: Bereaved persons are misguided through the stages of grief. *OMEGA—Journal of Death and Dying, 74*(4), 455–473.

Strohmetz, D. B., Rind, B., Fisher, R., & Lynn, M. (2006). Sweetening the till: The use of candy to increase restaurant tipping. *Journal of Applied Social Psychology, 32*(2), 300–309.

Strong, T. (2017). *Medicalizing counselling.* Palgrave Macmillan.

Stronge, S., Greaves, L. M., Milojev, P., West-Newman, T., Barlow, F. K., & Sibley, C. G. (2015). Facebook is linked to body dissatisfaction: Comparing users and non-users. *Sex Roles, 73*(5–6), 200–213.

Strosahl, K. D., & Robinson, P. J. (2017). *The mindfulness & acceptance workbook for depression* (2nd ed.). New Harbinger.

Stroud, L. R., Papandonatos, G. D., D'Angelo, C. M., Brush, B., and Lloyd-Richardson, E. E. (2017). Sex differences in biological response to peer rejection and performance challenge across development: A pilot study. *Physiological Behavior, 169*, 224–233. https://doi.org/10.1016/j.physbeh.2016.12.005

Stroud, L. R., Salovey, P., & Epel, E. S. (2002). Sex differences in stress responses: Social rejection versus achievement stress. *Biological Psychiatry, 52*(4), 318–327.

Stroup, T. S., Kraus, J. E., & Marder, S. R. (2006). Pharmacotherapies. In J. A. Lieberman, T. S. Stroup, & D. O. Perkins (Eds.), *The American Psychiatric Publishing textbook of schizophrenia* (pp. 303–325). American Psychiatric Publishing.

Strube, M. J., Miles, M. E., & Finch, W. H. (1981). The social facilitation of a simple task: Field tests of alternative explanations. *Personality and Social Psychology Bulletin, 7*(4), 701–707.

Strunk, D. S., & Sasso, K. E. (2017). Phenomenology and course of mood disorders. In R. J. DeRubeis & D. R. Strunk (Eds.), *The Oxford handbook of mood disorders* (pp. 37–48). Oxford University Press.

Strupp, H. H. (1996). The tripartite model and the Consumer Reports study. *American Psychologist, 51*(10), 1017–1024.

Strupp, H. H., & Hadley, S. W. (1977). A tripartite model of mental health and therapeutic outcomes: With special reference to negative effects in psychotherapy. *American Psychologist, 32*(3), 187–196.

Stryker, S., & Statham, A. (1986). Symbolic interaction and role theory. In G. Lindzey & E. Aronson (Eds.), *The handbook of social psychology* (3rd ed., Vol. 1, pp. 311–378). Random House.

Stuart, S. (2017). Interpersonal psychotherapy in historical perspective. In A. J. Consoli, L. E. Beutler, & B. Bongar (Eds.), *Comprehensive textbook of psychotherapy: Theory and practice* (2nd ed., pp. 121–136). Oxford University Press.

Stubbe, M., & Holmes, J. (1995). You know, eh and other "exasperating expressions": An analysis of social and stylistic variation in the use of pragmatic devices in a sample of New Zealand English. *Language & Communication, 15*(1), 63–88.

Stumbrys, T., & Erlacher, D. (2016). Applications of lucid dreams and their effects on the mood upon awakening. *International Journal of Dream Research, 9*(2), 146–150.

Stunkard, A. J., Foch, T. T., & Hrubec, Z. (1986a). A twin study of human obesity. *JAMA, 256*(1), 51–54.

Stunkard, A. J., Sørensen, T. I., Hanis, C., Teasdale, T. W., Chakraborty, R., Schull, W. J., & Schulsinger, F. (1986b). An adoption study of human obesity. *New England Journal of Medicine, 314*(4), 193–198.

Sturm, R. (2002). The effects of obesity, smoking, and drinking on medical problems and costs. *Health Affairs, 21*(2), 245–253.

Sturm, R., & Datar, A. (2005). Body mass index in elementary school children, metropolitan area food prices and food outlet density. *Public Health, 119*(12), 1059–1068.

Sturmey, P., Ward-Horner, J., Marroquin, M., & Doran, E. (2007). Operant and respondent behavior. In P. Sturmey (Ed.), *Functional analysis in clinical treatment* (pp. 23–50). Elsevier.

Stuve, P., & Salinas, J. A. (2002). Token economy. In M. Hersen & W. Sledge (Eds.), *Encyclopedia of psychotherapy* (Vol. 2, pp. 821–827). Academic Press.

Suarez, L. M., Bennett, S. M., Goldstein, C. R., & Barlow, D. H. (2009). Understanding anxiety disorders from a "triple vulnerability" framework. In M. M. Antony & M. B. Stein (Eds.), *Oxford handbook of anxiety and related disorders* (pp. 153–172). Oxford University Press.

Subrahmanyam, K., & Greenfield, P. (2012). Digital media and youth: Games, Internet, and development. In D. G. Singer & J. L. Singer (Eds.), *Handbook of children and the media* (2nd ed., pp. 75–96). Sage.

Subrahmanyam, K., & Šmahel, D. (2012). *Digital youth: The role of media in development.* Springer.

Sue, D. W. (2010a). *Microaggressions and marginality: Manifestation, dynamics, and impact.* Wiley.

Sue, D. W. (2010b). *Microaggressions in everyday life: Race, gender, and sexual orientation.* Wiley.

Sue, D. W. (2017). Microaggressions and "evidence" empirical or experiential reality? *Perspectives on Psychological Science, 12*(1), 170–172.

Sue, D. W., Calle, C. Z., Mendez, N., Alsaidi, S., & Glaeser, E. (2021). *Microintervention strategies: What you can do to disarm and dismantle individual and systemic racism and bias.* Wiley.

Sue, D. W., Capodilupo, C. M., Torino, G. C., Bucceri, J. M., Holder, A., Nadal, K. L., & Esquilin, M. (2007). Racial microaggressions in everyday life: Implications for clinical practice. *American Psychologist, 62*(4), 271–286.

Sue, D. W., Ivey, A. E., & Pedersen, P. B. (1996). *A theory of multicultural counseling and therapy.* Brooks/Cole.

Sue, D. W., & Sue, D. (2016). *Counseling the culturally diverse* (7th ed.). Wiley.

Sue, S. (1998). In search of cultural competence in psychotherapy and counseling. *American Psychologist, 53*(4), 440–448.

Sue, S. (2006). Cultural competency: From philosophy to research and practice. *Journal of Community Psychology, 34*(2), 237–245.

Sue, S., & Consolacion, T. B. (2003). Clinical psychology issues among Asian/Pacific Islander Americans. In J. S. Mio & G. Y. Iwamasa (Eds.), *Culturally diverse mental health: The challenges of research and resistance* (pp. 173–189). Brunner-Routledge.

Sue, S., & Sue, D. (2008). *Counseling the culturally diverse* (5th ed.). Wiley.

Sue, S., & Sue, D. (2012). *Counseling the culturally diverse* (6th ed.). Wiley.

Sue, S., & Zane, N. (2006). Ethnic minority populations have been neglected by evidence-based practices. In J. C. Norcross, L. E. Beutler, & R. F. Levant (Eds.), *Evidence-based practices in mental health: Debate and dialogue on the fundamental questions* (pp. 329–337). American Psychological Association.

Sugden, N. A., & Marquis, A. R. (2017). Meta-analytic review of the development of face discrimination in infancy: Face race, face gender, infant age, and methodology moderate face discrimination. *Psychological Bulletin, 143*(11), 1201–1244.

Sugden, N. A., & Moulson, M. C. (2018). These are the people in your neighbourhood: Consistency and persistence in infants' exposure to caregivers', relatives', and strangers' faces across contexts. *Vision Research.* https://doi.org/10.1016/j.visres.2018.09.005

Suh, E., Diener, E., Oishi, S., & Triandis, H. C. (1998). The shifting basis of life satisfaction judgments across cultures. *Journal of Personality and Social Psychology, 74*(2), 482–493.

Suh, J., Horvitz, E., White, R. W., & Althoff, T. (2021, March). Population-scale study of human needs during the covidCOVID-19 pandemic: Analysis and implications. Proceedings of the 14th ACM International Conference on Web Search and Data Mining, pp. 4–-12. https://doi.org/10.1145/3437963.3441788

Sulaiman, A. H., Husain, R., & Seluakumaran, K. (2014). Evaluation of early hearing damage in personal listening device users using extended high-frequency audiometry and otoacoustic emissions. *European Archives of Oto-Rhino-Laryngology, 271*(6), 1463–1470.

Sulaiman, A. H., Seluakumaran, K., & Husain, R. (2013). Hearing risk associated with the usage of personal listening devices among urban high school students in Malaysia. *Public Health, 127*(8), 710–715.

Sullivan, B. F., & Pomerantz, A. M. (2017). Forensic psychology. In A. M. Pomerantz, *Clinical Psychology: Science, Practice, and Culture* (4th ed.). Sage.

Sullivan, P. F., Daly, M. J., & O'Donovan, M. (2012). Genetic architectures of psychiatric disorders: The emerging picture and its implications. *Nature Reviews Genetics, 13*(8), 537–551.

Sullivan, S. A., & Birch, L. L. (1990). Pass the sugar, pass the salt: Experience dictates preference. *Developmental Psychology, 26*(4), 546–551.

Sulloway, F. J. (1996). *Born to rebel: Birth order, family dynamics, and creative lives.* Pantheon.

Sulloway, F. J. (2001). Birth order, sibling competition, and human behavior. In H. R. Holcomb III (Ed.), *Conceptual challenges in evolutionary psychology: Innovative research strategies* (pp. 39–83). Kluwer Academic.

Sulloway, F. J. (2009). Sources of scientific innovation: A meta-analytic approach. *Perspectives on Psychological Science, 4*(5), 455–459.

Sulloway, F. J. (2011). Why siblings are like Darwin's finches: Birth order, sibling competition, and adaptive divergence within the family. In D. M. Buss & P. H. Hawley (Eds.), *The evolution of personality and individual differences* (pp. 86–120). Oxford University Press.

Sulloway, F. J., & Zweigenhaft, R. L. (2010). Birth order and risk taking in athletics: A meta-analysis and study of major league baseball. *Personality and Social Psychology Review, 14*(4), 402–416.

Suls, J., & Wheeler, L. (2012). Social comparison theory. In P. A. M. Van Lange, A. W. Kruglanski, & E. T. Higgins (Eds.), *Handbook of theories of social psychology* (Vol. 1, pp. 460–482). Sage.

Sultan, R. S., Correll, C. U., Schoenbaum, M., King, M., Walkup, J. T., & Olfson, M. (2018). National patterns of commonly prescribed psychotropic medications to young people. *Journal of Child and Adolescent Psychopharmacology, 28*(3), 158–165. https://doi.org/10.1089/cap.2017.0077

Summerfield, Q. (1992). Lipreading and audio-visual speech perception. *Philosophical Transactions of the Royal Society of London. Series B: Biological Sciences, 335*(1273), 71–78.

Sun, Y., Mensah, F. K., Azzopardi, P., Patton, G. C., & Wake, M. (2017). Childhood social disadvantage and pubertal timing: A national birth cohort from Australia. *Pediatrics, 139*(6), e20164099.

Sundberg, M. L., Michael, J., Partington, J. W., & Sundberg, C. A. (1996). The role of automatic reinforcement in early language acquisition. *The Analysis of Verbal Behavior, 13*(1), 21–37.

Sunstein, C. R. (2018). *Republic: Divided democracy in the age of social media.* Princeton University Press.

Super, C. M., & Harkness, S. (2013). Culture and children's sleep. In A. R. Wolfson & H. Montgomery-Downs (Eds.), *The Oxford handbook of infant, child, and adolescent sleep and behavior* (pp. 81–98). Oxford University Press.

Surawski, M. K., & Ossoff, E. P. (2006). The effects of physical and vocal attractiveness on impression formation of politicians. *Current Psychology, 25*(1), 15–27.

Susman, E. J., & Dorn, L. D. (2009). Puberty: Its role in development. In R. M. Lerner & L. Steinberg (Eds.), *Handbook of adolescent psychology* (3rd ed., Vol. 1, pp. 116–151). Wiley.

Susser, E., & Opler, M. (2006). Prenatal events that influence schizophrenia. In T. Sharma & P. D. Harvey (Eds.), *The early course of schizophrenia* (pp. 3–18). Oxford University Press.

Sutherland, P. A. (1992). *Cognitive development today: Piaget and his critics*. Sage.

Suzuki, L. A., & Ponterotto, J. G. (Eds.). (2008). *Handbook of multicultural assessment: Clinical, psychological, and educational applications* (3rd ed.). Jossey-Bass.

Suzuki, L. A., Short, E. L., & Lee, C. S. (2011). Racial and ethnic group differences in intelligence in the United States. In R. J. Sternberg & S. B. Kaufman (Eds.), *The Cambridge handbook of intelligence* (pp. 273–292). Cambridge University Press.

Suzuki, W. A. (2009). Comparative analysis of the cortical afferents, intrinsic projections, and interconnections of the parahippocampal region in monkeys and rats. In M. S. Gazzaniga (Ed.), *The cognitive neurosciences* (4th ed., pp. 659–674). MIT Press.

Swain, J., Hancock, K., Hainsworth, C., & Bowman, J. (2013). Acceptance and commitment therapy in the treatment of anxiety: A systematic review. *Clinical Psychology Review, 33*(8), 965–978.

Swami, V. (2015). Cultural influences on body size ideals: Unpacking the impact of westernisation and modernisation. *European Psychologist, 20*(1), 44–51.

Swanson, H. L., & Berninger, V. W. (1996). Individual differences in children's working memory and writing skill. *Journal of Experimental Child Psychology, 63*(2), 358–385.

Swartz, H. A., & Markowitz, J. C. (2009). Techniques of individual interpersonal psychotherapy. In G. O. Gabbard (Ed.), *Textbook of psychotherapeutic treatments* (pp. 309–338). American Psychiatric Publishing.

Swartz, K. L. (2007). *Depression and anxiety: Your personal guide to prevention, diagnosis, and treatment (The Johns Hopkins white papers)*. Johns Hopkins Medicine.

Sweeney, T. J. (1998). *Adlerian counseling and psychotherapy: A practitioner's approach* (5th ed.). Routledge.

Syed, M. (2015). Emerging adulthood: Developmental stage, theory, or nonsense. In J. J. Arnett (Ed.), *The Oxford handbook of emerging adulthood* (pp. 11–25). Oxford University Press.

Sylvester, B. D., Jackson, B., & Beauchamp, M. R. (2018). The effects of variety and novelty on physical activity and healthy nutritional behaviors. In A. J. Elliot (Ed.), *Advances in motivation science* (Vol. 5, pp. 169–202). Elsevier.

Symms, M., Jäger, H. R., Schmierer, K., & Yousry, T. A. (2004). A review of structural magnetic resonance neuroimaging. *Journal of Neurology, Neurosurgery & Psychiatry, 75*(9), 1235–1244.

Sysko, R., & Alavi, S. (2018). Eating disorders. In J. Hunsley & E. J. Mash (Eds.), *A guide to assessments that work* (2nd ed., pp. 293–310). Oxford University Press.

Sysko, R., & Wilson, G. T. (2011). Eating disorders. In D. H. Barlow (Ed.), *The Oxford handbook of clinical psychology* (pp. 387–404). Oxford University Press.

Taber, K. H., Wen, C., Khan, A., & Hurley, R. A. (2004). The limbic thalamus. *Journal of Neuropsychiatry and Clinical Neurosciences, 16*(2), 127–132.

Tackett, J. L., Hernandez, M. M., & Eisenberg, N. (2019). Agreeableness. In D. P. McAdams, R. L. Shiner, & J. L. Tackett (Eds.), *Handbook of personality development* (pp. 171–184). Guilford Press.

Tafarodi, R. W., & Smith, A. J. (2001). Individualism–collectivism and depressive sensitivity to life events: The case of Malaysian sojourners. *International Journal of Intercultural Relations, 25*(1), 73–88.

Taherkhani, S., Moztarzadeh, F., Seraj, J. M., Nazari, S. S. H., Taherkhani, F., Gharehdaghi, J., Okazi, A., & Pouraghaei, S. (2015). Iran Smell Identification Test (Iran-SIT): A modified version of the University of Pennsylvania Smell Identification Test (UPSIT) for Iranian population. *Chemosensory Perception, 8*(4), 183–191. https://doi.org/10.1007/s12078-015-9192-9

Tahiri, M., Mottillo, S., Joseph, L., Pilote, L., & Eisenberg, M. J. (2012). Alternative smoking cessation aids: A meta-analysis of randomized controlled trials. *The American Journal of Medicine, 125*(6), 576–584.

Taiana, C. (2006). Transatlantic migration of the disciplines of the mind: Examination of the reception of Wundt's and Freud's theories in Argentina. In A. C. Brock (Ed.), *Internationalizing the history of psychology* (pp. 34–55). New York University Press.

Tait, D. M., & Carroll, J. (2010). Color deficiency. In E. B. Goldstein (Ed.), *Encyclopedia of perception* (pp. 257–262). Sage.

Takahashi, K., Oishi, T., & Shimada, M. (2017). Is J smiling? Cross-cultural study on recognition of emoticon's emotion. *Journal of Cross-Cultural Psychology, 48*(10), 1578–1586.

Takahashi, M., & Kaida, K. (2006). Napping. In T. L. Lee-Chiong (Ed.), *Sleep: A comprehensive handbook* (pp. 197–202). Wiley-Liss.

Takashima, A., Bakker, I., Van Hell, J. G., Janzen, G., & McQueen, J. M. (2017). Interaction between episodic and semantic memory networks in the acquisition and consolidation of novel spoken words. *Brain and Language, 167*, 44–60.

Takeuchi, D. T., Chun, C. A., Gong, F., & Shen, H. (2002). Cultural expressions of distress. *Health, 6*(2), 221–236.

Takeuchi, H., & Kawashima, R. (2016). Neural mechanisms and children's intellectual development: Multiple impacts of environmental factors. *The Neuroscientist, 22*(6), 618–631.

Takeuchi, H., Taki, Y., Hashizume, H., Asano, K., Asano, M., Sassa, Y., Yokota, S., Kotozaki, Y., & Kawashima, R. (2015). The impact of television viewing on brain structures: Cross-sectional and longitudinal analyses. *Cerebral Cortex, 25*(5), 1188–1197.

Talarico, J. M., & Rubin, D. C. (2009). Flashbulb memories result from ordinary memory processes and extraordinary event characteristics. In O. Luminet & A. Curci (Eds.), *Flashbulb memories: New issues and new perspectives* (pp. 79–97). Psychology Press.

Tallis, F. (1998). *Changing minds: The history of psychotherapy as an answer to human suffering*. Cassell.

Tallis, F. (2004). *Love sick: Love as a mental illness*. Thunder's Mouth Press.

Tallis, R. C. (1996). Burying Freud. *The Lancet, 347*(9902), 669–671.

Tam, K. P., & Chan, H. W. (2017). Environmental concern has a weaker association with pro-environmental behavior in some societies than others: A cross-cultural psychology perspective. *Journal of Environmental Psychology, 53*, 213–223.

Tamres, L. K., Janicki, D., & Helgeson, V. S. (2002). Sex differences in coping behavior: A meta-analytic review and an examination of relative coping. *Personality and Social Psychology Review, 6*(1), 2–30.

Tan, J. J. X., Kraus, M. W., Carpenter, N. C., & Adler, N. E. (2020). The association between objective and subjective socioeconomic status and subjective well-being: A meta-analytic review. *Psychological Bulletin, 146*(11), 970–1020. https://doi.org/10.1037/bul0000258

Tan, K. A. (2019). The effects of personal susceptibility and social support on internet addiction: An application of Adler's theory of individual psychology. *International Journal of Mental Health and Addiction, 17*, 806–816. https://doi.org/10.1007/s11469-018-9871-2

Tan, L. H., Spinks, J. A., Gao, J. H., Liu, H. L., Perfetti, C. A., Xiong, J., & Fox, P. T. (2000). Brain activation in the processing of Chinese characters and words: A functional MRI study. *Human Brain Mapping, 10*(1), 16–27.

Tanaka, J. W., & Taylor, M. (1991). Object categories and expertise: Is the basic level in the eye of the beholder? *Cognitive Psychology, 23*(3), 457–482.

Tang, C. S. K., Lai, F. D. M., & Chung, T. K. (1997). Assessment of sexual functioning for Chinese college students. *Archives of Sexual Behavior, 26*(1), 79–90.

Tang, M., Hofreiter, S., Reiter-Palmon, R., Bai, X., & Murugavel, V. (2021). Creativity as a means to well-being in times of COVID-19 pandemic: Results of a cross-cultural study. *Frontiers in Psychology, 12*, 265. https://doi.org/10.3389/fpsyg.2021.601389

Tang, N., Bensman, L., & Hatfield, E. (2012). The impact of culture and gender on sexual motives: Differences between Chinese and North Americans. *International Journal of Intercultural Relations, 36*(2), 286–294.

Tang, S. S. S., & Freyd, J. J. (2012). Betrayal trauma and gender differences in posttraumatic stress. *Psychological Trauma: Theory, Research, Practice, and Policy, 4*(5), 469–478.

Tang, Y. Y., & Liu, Y. (2009). Numbers in the cultural brain. *Progress in Brain Research, 178*, 151–157.

Tangkiatkumjai, M., Boardman, H., & Walker, D. M. (2020). Potential factors that influence usage of complementary and alternative medicine worldwide: A systematic review. *BMC Complementary Medicine and Therapies, 20*(1), 1–15. https://doi.org/10.1186/s12906-020-03157-2

Tanimoto, H., Heisenberg, M., & Gerber, B. (2004). Experimental psychology: Event timing turns punishment to reward. *Nature, 430*(7003), 983–983.

Tannock, R. (2013). Rethinking ADHD and LD in DSM-5 proposed changes in diagnostic criteria. *Journal of Learning Disabilities, 46*(1), 5–25.

Taquet, M., Luciano, S., Geddes, J. R., & Harrison, P. J. (2021). Bidirectional associations between COVID-19 and psychiatric disorder: Retrospective cohort studies of 62 354 COVID-19 cases in the USA. *The Lancet Psychiatry, 8*(2), 130–140. https://doi.org/10.1016/S2215-0366(20)30462-4

Taras, H., & Potts-Datema, W. (2005). Sleep and student performance at school. *Journal of School Health, 75*(7), 248–254.

Tardif, T., Fletcher, P., Liang, W., Zhang, Z., Kaciroti, N., & Marchman, V. A. (2008). Baby's first 10 words. *Developmental Psychology, 44*(4), 929–938.

Tarique, I., & Takeuchi, R. (2008). Developing cultural intelligence: The roles of international nonwork experiences. In S. Ang & L. Van Dyne (Eds.), *Handbook of cultural intelligence: Theory, measurement, and applications* (pp. 56–70). Sharpe.

Tate, R. L. (2002). Emotional and social consequences of memory disorders. In A. D. Baddeley, M. D. Kopelman, & B. A. Wilson (Eds.), *The handbook of memory disorders* (2nd ed., pp. 785–808). Wiley.

Taubman-Ben-Ari, O., Shlomo, S. B., & Findler, L. (2018). The transition to grandparenthood: A chance to promote well-being and personal growth in later life. In M. Demir & N. Sümer (Eds.), *Close relationships and happiness across cultures* (pp. 87–103). Springer.

Taylor, B. E. S. (2007). *ADHD & me: What I learned from lighting fires at the dinner table*. New Harbinger.

Taylor, D. M. (2006). *Schizophrenia in focus*. Pharmaceutical Press.

Taylor, D., Gehrman, P., Dautovich, N. D., Lichstein, K. L., & McCrae, C. S. (2014). *Handbook of insomnia*. Springer Healthcare.

Taylor, J. C., Wiggett, A. J., & Downing, P. E. (2017). fMRI analysis of body and body part representations in the extrastriate and fusiform body areas. *Journal of Neurophysiology, 98*, 1626–1633.

Taylor, S. (2002). Exposure. In M. Hersen & W. Sledge (Eds.), *Encyclopedia of psychotherapy* (Vol. 1, pp. 755–759). Academic Press.

Taylor, S. E. (2011a). Affiliation and stress. In S. Folkman (Ed.), *Oxford handbook of stress, health, and coping* (pp. 86–100). Oxford University Press.

Taylor, S. E. (2011b). Social support: A review. In H. S. Friedman (Ed.), *The Oxford handbook of health psychology* (pp. 189–214). Oxford University Press.

Taylor, S. E., Kemeny, M. E., Reed, G. M., Bower, J. E., & Gruenewald, T. L. (2000a). Psychological resources, positive illusions, and health. *American Psychologist, 55*(1), 99–109.

Taylor, S. E., Klein, L. C., Lewis, B. P., Gruenewald, T. L., Gurung, R. A., & Updegraff, J. A. (2000b). Biobehavioral responses to stress in females: Tend-and-befriend, not fight-or-flight. *Psychological Review, 107*(3), 411.

Taylor, S. E., Sherman, D. K., Kim, H. S., Jarcho, J., Takagi, K., & Dunagan, M. S. (2004). Culture and social support: Who seeks it and why? *Journal of Personality and Social Psychology, 87*(3), 354–367.

Taylor, S., Cox, B. J., & Asmundson, G. J. G. (2009). Anxiety disorders: Panic and phobias. In P. H. Blaney & Theodore Millon (Eds.), *Oxford textbook of psychopathology* (2nd ed., pp. 119–145). Oxford University Press.

Taylor, V. J., & Walton, G. M. (2011). Stereotype threat undermines academic learning. *Personality and Social Psychology Bulletin, 37*(8), 1055–1067.

te Poel, F., Baumgartner, S. E., Hartmann, T., & Tanis, M. (2016). The curious case of cyberchondria: A longitudinal study on the reciprocal relationship between health anxiety and online health information seeking. *Journal of Anxiety Disorders, 43*, 32–40.

Teachman, J., Tedrow, L., & Kim, G. (2013). The demography of families. In G. W. Peterson & K. R. Bush (Eds.), *Handbook of marriage and the family* (3rd ed. pp. 39–63). Springer Science+Business Media.

Tedeschi, R., Blevins, C., & Riffle, O. (2017). Posttraumatic growth: A brief history and evaluation. In M. A. Warren & S. I. Donaldson (Eds.), *Scientific advances in positive psychology* (pp. 131–163). Praeger.

Tefft, B. C. (2014, November). Prevalence of motor vehicle crashes involving drowsy drivers, United States, 2009–2013. AAA Foundation for Traffic Safety. https://aaafoundation.org/wp-content/uploads/2017/12/PrevalenceofMVCDrowsyDriversReport.pdf

Teglasi, H. (2010). *Essentials of TAT and other storytelling assessments* (2nd ed.). Wiley.

Teigen, K. H. (1994). Yerkes-Dodson: A law for all seasons. *Theory & Psychology, 4*(4), 525–547.

Teitcher, A. (2011). Weaving functional brain imaging into the tapestry of evidence: A case for functional neuroimaging in federal criminal courts. *Fordham Law Review, 80*(1), 355–401.

Teixeira, P. J., Carraça, E. V., Marques, M. M., Rutter, H., Oppert, J. M., De Bourdeaudhuij, I., Lakerveld, J., & Brug, J. (2015). Successful behavior change in obesity interventions in adults: A systematic review of self-regulation mediators. *BMC Medicine, 13*(1), 84.

Tekampe, J., van Middendorp, H., Meeuwis, S. H., van Leusden, J. W., Pacheco-Lopez, G., Hermus, A. R., & Evers, A. W. (2017). Conditioning immune and endocrine parameters in humans: A systematic review. *Psychotherapy and Psychosomatics, 86*(2), 99–107.

Tellegen, A., Lykken, D. T., Bouchard, T. J., Wilcox, K. J., Segal, N. L., & Rich, S. (1988). Personality similarity in twins reared apart and together. *Journal of Personality and Social Psychology, 54*(6), 1031–1039.

Temoshok, L. (1986). Personality, coping style, emotion and cancer: Towards an integrative model. *Cancer Surveys, 6*(3), 545–567.

Temoshok, L., Heller, B. W., Sagebiel, R. W., Blois, M. S., Sweet, D. M., DiClemente, R. J., & Gold, M. L. (1985). The relationship of psychosocial factors to prognostic indicators in cutaneous malignant melanoma. *Journal of Psychosomatic Research, 29*(2), 139–153.

Templer, K. J., Tay, C., & Chandrasekar, N. A. (2006). Motivational cultural intelligence, realistic job preview, realistic living conditions preview, and cross-cultural adjustment. *Group & Organization Management, 31*(1), 154–173.
Tennen, H., Affleck, G., Armeli, S., & Carney, M. A. (2000). A daily process approach to coping: Linking theory, research, and practice. *American Psychologist, 55*(6), 626–636.
Tennen, H., Affleck, G., & Zautra, A. (2006). Depression history and coping with chronic pain: A daily process analysis. *Health Psychology, 25*(3), 370–379.
Terlizzi, E. P., & Zablotsky, B. (2020). *Mental health treatment among adults: United States, 2019*. NCHS Data Brief, no 380. National Center for Health Statistics. 2020. https://www.cdc.gov/nchs/products/databriefs/db380.htm
Terman, D. M. (2012). Self psychology. In G. O. Gabbard, B. E. Litowitz, & P. Williams (Eds.), *Textbook of psychoanalysis* (2nd ed., pp. 199–210). American Psychiatric Publishing.
Tervalon, M., & Murray-Garcia, J. (1998). Cultural humility versus cultural competence: A critical distinction in defining physician training outcomes in multicultural education. *Journal of Health Care for the Poor and Underserved, 9*(2), 117–125. https://doi.org/10.1353/hpu.2010.0233
Tesser, A., & Martin, L. (2005). Reviewing empirical submissions to journals. In R. J. Sternberg (Ed.), *Reviewing scientific works in psychology* (pp. 3–29). American Psychological Association.
Teti, D. M., & Teti, L. O. (1996). Infant-parent relationships. In N. Vanzetti & S. Duck (Eds.), *A lifetime of relationships* (pp. 77–104). Brooks/Cole.
Tett, R. P., Freund, K. A., Christiansen, N. D., Fox, K. E., & Coaster, J. (2012). Faking on self-report emotional intelligence and personality tests: Effects of faking opportunity, cognitive ability, and job type. *Personality and Individual Differences, 52*(2), 195–201.
Teufel, M., Stephan, K., Kowalski, A., Käsberger, S., Enck, P., Zipfel, S., & Giel, K. E. (2013). Impact of biofeedback on self-efficacy and stress reduction in obesity: A randomized controlled pilot study. *Applied Psychophysiology and Biofeedback, 38*(3), 177–184.
Thaler, N. S., Thames, A. D., Cagigas, X. E., & Norman, M. A. (2015). IQ testing and the African American client. In L. T. Benuto & B. D. Leany (Eds.), *Guide to psychological assessment with African American clients* (pp. 63–77). Springer.
Thalmann, M., Souza, A. S., & Oberauer, K. (2018). How does chunking help working memory? *Journal of Experimental Psychology: Learning, Memory, and Cognition, 45*(1). https://doi.org/10.1037/xlm0000578
Thapar, A., Cooper, M., Eyre, O., & Langley, K. (2013). Practitioner review: What have we learnt about the causes of ADHD? *Journal of Child Psychology and Psychiatry, 54*(1), 3–16.
Thase, M. E. (2006). Major depressive disorder. In M. Hersen & J. C. Thomas (Eds.), *Comprehensive handbook of personality and psychopathology* (Vol. 2, pp. 207–230). Wiley.
The New York Times. (2013, April 22). 4:09:03: A moment from the Boston Marathon. http://www.nytimes.com/interactive/2013/04/22/sports/boston-moment.html
Thedinga, H. K., Zehl, R., & Thiel, A. (2021). Weight stigma experiences and self-exclusion from sport and exercise settings among people with obesity. *BMC Public Health, 21*(1), 1–18. https://doi.org/10.1186/s12889-021-10565-7
Theokas, C., & Bloch, M. (2006). *Out-of-school time is critical for children: Who participates in programs?* (Research-to-Results Fact Sheet. Publication #2006-20). Child Trends.
Theorell-Haglöw, J., Miller, C. B., Bartlett, D. J., Yee, B. J., Openshaw, H. D., & Grunstein, R. R. (2018). Gender differences in obstructive sleep apnea, insomnia and restless legs syndrome in adults—what do we know? A clinical update. *Sleep Medicine Reviews, 38*, 28–38. https://doi.org/10.1016/j.smrv.2017.03.003
Theriault, M., De Beaumont, L., Tremblay, S., Lassonde, M., & Jolicoeur, P. (2011). Cumulative effects of concussions in athletes revealed by electrophysiological abnormalities on visual working memory. *Journal of Clinical and Experimental Neuropsychology, 33*(1), 30–41.
Thibodeau, P. H., Crow, L., & Flusberg, S. J. (2017a). The metaphor police: A case study of the role of metaphor in explanation. *Psychonomic Bulletin & Review, 24*(5), 1375–1386.
Thibodeau, P. H., Hendricks, R. K., & Boroditsky, L. (2017b). How linguistic metaphor scaffolds reasoning. *Trends in Cognitive Sciences, 21*(11), 852–863.
Thiedke, C. C. (2001). Sleep disorders and sleep problems in childhood. *American Family Physician, 63*(2), 277–284.
Thiel, K. J. & Dretsch, M. N. (2011). The basics of the stress response: A historical context and introduction. In C. D. Conrad (Ed.), *The handbook of stress*. Wiley-Blackwell.
Thomas, A., & Chess, S. (1977). *Temperament and development*. Brunner/Mazel.
Thomas, A., Chess, S., & Birch, H. G. (1970). The origin of personality. *Scientific American, 223*(2), 102–109.
Thomas, M. L. (2011). Detection of female mating status using chemical signals and cues. *Biological Reviews, 86*(1), 1–13.
Thomas, M. S., & Johnson, M. H. (2008). New advances in understanding sensitive periods in brain development. *Current Directions in Psychological Science, 17*(1), 1–5.
Thomassen, Å. G., Hystad, S. W., Johnsen, B. H., Johnsen, G. E., & Bartone, P. T. (2018). The effect of hardiness on PTSD symptoms: A prospective mediational approach. *Military Psychology, 30*(2), 142–151.
Thompson, B. (2013). Overview of traditional/classical statistical approaches. In T. D. Little (Ed.), *The Oxford handbook of quantitative methods: Vol. 2. Statistical analysis* (pp. 7–25). Oxford University Press.
Thompson, D., Brown, J. B., Nichols, G. A., Elmer, P. J., & Oster, G. (2001). Body mass index and future healthcare costs: A retrospective cohort study. *Obesity Research, 9*(3), 210–218.
Thompson, E. M., & Morgan, E. M. (2008). "Mostly straight" young women: Variations in sexual behavior and identity development. *Developmental Psychology, 44*(1), 15–21.
Thompson, K. (2009, July 21). Harvard professor arrested at home. *The Washington Post*. http://www.washingtonpost.com/wp-dyn/content/article/2009/07/20/AR2009072001358.html
Thompson, K. M., & Haninger, K. (2001). Violence in E-rated video games. *JAMA, 286*(5), 591–598.
Thompson, P. (1980). Margaret Thatcher: A new illusion. *Perception, 9*, 483–484.
Thompson, R. A. (1998). Early sociopersonality development. In W. Damon & N. Eisenberg (Eds.), *Handbook of child psychology* (5th ed., Vol. 3, pp. 25–104). Wiley.
Thompson, R. A. (2006). The development of the person: Social understanding, relationships, conscience, self. In N. Eisenberg (Vol. Ed.), *Handbook of child psychology* (6th ed., Vol. 3, pp. 24–98). Wiley.
Thompson, R. J., Spectre, A., Insel, P. S., Mennin, D., Gotlib, I. H., & Gruber, J. (2017). Positive and negative affective forecasting in remitted individuals with bipolar I disorder, and major depressive disorder, and healthy controls. *Cognitive Therapy and Research, 41*(5), 673–685.
Thompson, T. (2014). Autism and behavior analysis: History and current status. In F. K. McSweeney & E. S. Murphy (Eds.), *The Wiley-Blackwell handbook of operant and classical conditioning* (pp. 483–508). Wiley.
Thomson, D. M., & Tulving, E. (1970). Associative encoding and retrieval: Weak and strong cues. *Journal of Experimental Psychology, 86*(2), 255–262.
Thorleifsdottir, B., Björnsson, J. K., Benediktsdottir, B., Gislason, T. H., & Kristbjarnarson, H. (2002). Sleep and sleep habits from childhood to young adulthood over a 10-year period. *Journal of Psychosomatic Research, 53*(1), 529–537.
Thorndike, E. (1898). Animal intelligence: An experimental study of the associative processes in animals. *Psychological Review Monograph Supplement, 2*(4), 1–109.
Thorndike, E. (1900). The associative processes in animals. In *Biological lectures delivered at the Marine Biological Laboratory of Woods Hole 1899* (pp. 61–91). Ginn & Company.
Thorndike, E. (1911). *Animal intelligence*. Macmillan Company.
Thorndike, E. (1927). The law of effect. *The American Journal of Psychology, 39*, 212–222.
Thornhill, R., & Gangestad, S. W. (1999). Facial attractiveness. *Trends in Cognitive Sciences, 3*(12), 452–460.
Thornton, M. A., & Conway, A. R. (2013). Working memory for social information: Chunking or domain-specific buffer? *NeuroImage, 70*, 233–239.
Thorpy, M. J. (2010). History of sleep and man. In C. P. Pollak, M. J. Thorpy, & J. Yager (Eds.), *The encyclopedia of sleep and sleep disorders* (3rd ed., pp. xvii–xxxviii). Infobase.
Thurstone, L. L. (1938). *Primary mental abilities*. University of Chicago Press.
Tietzel, A. J., & Lack, L. C. (2002). The recuperative value of brief and ultra-brief naps on alertness and cognitive performance. *Journal of Sleep Research, 11*(3), 213–218.
Tifferet, S., & Vilnai-Yavetz, I. (2014). Gender differences in Facebook self-presentation: An international randomized study. *Computers in Human Behavior, 35*, 388–399.
Tiggemann, M., Anderberg, I., & Brown, Z. (2020). # Loveyourbody: The effect of body positive Instagram captions on women's body image. *Body Image, 33*, 129–136. https://doi.org/10.1016/j.bodyim.2020.02.015
Tiggemann, M., Hayden, S., Brown, Z., & Veldhuis, J. (2018). The effect of Instagram "likes" on women's social comparison and body dissatisfaction. *Body Image, 26*, 90–97.
Tiggemann, M., & Slater, A. (2013). NetGirls: The Internet, Facebook, and body image concern in adolescent girls. *International Journal of Eating Disorders, 46*(6), 630–633.
Tik, M., Sladky, R., Luft, C. D. B., Willinger, D., Hoffmann, A., Banissy, M. J., ... Windischberger, C. (2018). Ultra-high-field fMRI insights on insight: Neural correlates of the Aha!-moment. *Human Brain Mapping, 39*(8), 3241–3252.
Till, B. D., & Priluck, R. L. (2000). Stimulus generalization in classical conditioning: An initial investigation and extension. *Psychology & Marketing, 17*(1), 55–72.
Tiller, J. M., Sloane, G., Schmidt, U., Troop, N., Power, M., & Treasure, J. L. (1997). Social support in patients with anorexia nervosa and bulimia nervosa. *International Journal of Eating Disorders, 21*(1), 31–38.
Timmers, M., Fischer, A. H., & Manstead, A. S. (1998). Gender differences in motives for regulating emotions. *Personality and Social Psychology Bulletin, 24*(9), 974–985.
Timmers, M., Fischer, A., & Manstead, A. (2003). Ability versus vulnerability: Beliefs about men's and women's emotional behaviour. *Cognition & Emotion, 17*(1), 41–63.
Timney, B. (2010). Animal depth perception. In E. B. Goldstein (Ed.), *Encyclopedia of perception* (pp. 50–52). Sage.
Timney, B., & Keil, K. (1999). Local and global stereopsis in the horse. *Vision Research, 39*(10), 1861–1867.
Tindale, C. W. (2007). *Fallacies and argument appraisal*. Cambridge University Press.
Tinterow, M. M. (1970). *Foundations of hypnosis: From Mesmer to Freud*. Charles C. Thomas.
Tirodkar, M. A., & Jain, A. (2003). Food messages on African American television shows. *American Journal of Public Health, 93*(3), 439–441.
Toates, F. (2009). *Burrhus F. Skinner: Shaper of behaviour*. Palgrave Macmillan.
Todes, D. P. (2014). *Ivan Pavlov: A Russian life in science*. Oxford University Press.
Toelch, U., & Dolan, R. J. (2015). Informational and normative influences in conformity from a neurocomputational perspective. *Trends in Cognitive Sciences, 19*(10), 579–589.
Toepfer, S. M., Cichy, K., & Peters, P. (2012). Letters of gratitude: Further evidence for author benefits. *Journal of Happiness Studies, 13*(1), 187–201.
Tokumoto, J. (2009). Human immunodeficiency virus. In B. P. Jacobs & K. Gundling (Eds.), *The ACP evidence-based guide to complementary and alternative medicine* (pp. 201–222). American College of Physicians.
Tolin, D. F., & Foa, E. B. (2006). Sex differences in trauma and posttraumatic stress disorder: A quantitative review of 25 years of research. *Psychological Bulletin, 132*(6), 959–992.
Tolin, D. F., Gilliam, C. M., & Dufresne, D. (2010). The economic and social burden of anxiety disorders. In D. J. Stein, E. Hollander, & B. O. Rothbaum (Eds.), *Textbook of anxiety disorders* (2nd ed., pp. 731–746). American Psychiatric Association.
Tolman, E. C. (1923). The nature of instinct. *Psychological Bulletin, 20*(4), 200–218.
Tolman, E. C. (1932). *Purposive behavior in animals and man*. Century.
Tolman, E. C. (1948). Cognitive maps in rats and men. *Psychological Review, 55*(4), 189–208.
Tolman, E. C., & Honzik, C. H. (1930). Introduction and removal of reward, and maze performance in rats. *University of California Publications in Psychology, 4*, 257–275.
Tomaka, J., & Blascovich, J. (1994). Effects of justice beliefs on cognitive appraisal of and subjective physiological, and behavioral responses to potential stress. *Journal of Personality and Social Psychology, 67*(4), 732–740.
Tomasello, M. (2004). Syntax or semantics? Response to Lidz et al. *Cognition, 93*(2), 139–140.
Tomasello, M., Carpenter, M., Call, J., Behne, T., & Moll, H. (2005). Understanding and sharing intentions: The origins of cultural cognition. *Behavioral and Brain Sciences, 28*(5), 675–690.
Tomiyama, A. J., Hunger, J. M., Nguyen-Cuu, J., & Wells, C. (2016). Misclassification of cardiometabolic health when using body mass index categories in NHANES 2005-2012. *International Journal of Obesity, 40*(5), 883–886.
Tomova, L., Wang, K. L., Thompson, T., Matthews, G. A., Takahashi, A., Tye, K. M., & Saxe, R. (2020). Acute social isolation evokes midbrain craving responses similar to hunger. *Nature Neuroscience, 23*(12), 1597–1605. https://doi.org/10.1038/s41593-020-00742-z
Toomey, R. B., Ryan, C., Diaz, R. M., & Russell, S. T. (2011). High school gay–straight alliances (GSAs) and young adult well-being: An examination of GSA presence, participation, and perceived effectiveness. *Applied Developmental Science, 15*(4), 175–185.
Toplak, M. E. (2018). The development of rational thinking: Insights from the heuristics and biases literature and dual process models. In L. J. Ball & V. A. Thompson (Eds.), *Routledge international handbook of thinking and reasoning* (pp. 542–558). Routledge.
Topolinski, S., & Reber, R. (2010). Gaining insight into the "Aha" experience. *Current Directions in Psychological Science, 19*(6), 402–405.
Toppari, J., & Juul, A. (2010). Trends in puberty timing in humans and environmental modifiers. *Molecular and Cellular Endocrinology, 324*(1), 39–44.
Torres, A., Vidal, A., Puig, O., Boget, T., & Salamero, M. (2006). Gender differences in cognitive functions and influence of sex hormones. *Actas Españolas Psiquiatría, 34*(6), 408–415.
Torres, L., Driscoll, M. W., & Burrow, A. L. (2010). Racial microaggressions and psychological functioning among highly achieving African-Americans: A mixed-methods approach. *Journal of Social and Clinical Psychology, 29*(10), 1074–1099.

Torrey, E. F. (1986). *Witchdoctors and psychiatrists: The common roots of psychotherapy and its future*. Perennial Library.

Torrey, E. F. (2008). *The insanity offense: How America's failure to treat the seriously mentally ill endangers its citizens*. W. W. Norton.

Torrey, E. F., Miller, J., Rawlings, R., & Yolken, R. H. (1997). Seasonality of births in schizophrenia and bipolar disorder: A review of the literature. *Schizophrenia Research, 28*(1), 1–38.

Tossell, C. C., Kortum, P., Shepard, C., Barg-Walkow, L. H., Rahmati, A., & Zhong, L. (2012). A longitudinal study of emoticon use in text messaging from smartphones. *Computers in Human Behavior, 28*(2), 659–663.

Tov, W., & Diener, E. (2007). Culture and subjective well-being. In S. Kitayama & D. Cohen (Eds.), *Handbook of cultural psychology* (pp. 691–713). Guilford Press.

Townsend, J. M., & Wasserman, T. H. (2011). Sexual hookups among college students: Sex differences in emotional reactions. *Archives of Sexual Behavior, 40*(6), 1173–1181.

Traig, J. (2004). *Devil in the details: Scenes from an obsessive girlhood*. Little, Brown.

Tramer, M. (1929). Uber die biologische, bedeutung des geburtsmonates, insbesondere für die psychoseerkrankung. *Archive für Neurologie und Psychiatrie, 24*, 17–24.

Treffert, D. A., & Christensen, D. D. (2009, December 23). Inside the mind of a savant. *Scientific American*. http://www.scientificamerican.com/article.cfm?id=inside-the-mind-repost

Tremblay, R. E. (2011). Origins, development, and prevention of aggressive behavior. In D. P. Keating (Ed.), *Nature and nurture in early child development* (pp. 169–187). Cambridge University Press.

Tremblay, R. E., & Nagin, D. S. (2005). The developmental origins of physical aggression in humans. In R. E. Tremblay, W. W. Hartuup, & J. Archer (Eds.), *Developmental origins of aggression* (pp. 83–106). Guilford Press.

Tremmel, M., Gerdtham, U. G., Nilsson, P. M., & Saha, S. (2017). Economic burden of obesity: A systematic literature review. *International Journal of Environmental Research and Public Health, 14*(4), 435.

Triandis, H. C. (1995). *Individualism & collectivism*. Westview Press.

Triandis, H. C. (2001). Individualism–collectivism and personality. *Journal of Personality, 69*(6), 907–924.

Triandis, H. C. (2007). Culture and psychology: A history of the study of their relationship. In S. Kitayama & D. Cohen (Eds.), *Handbook of cultural psychology* (pp. 59–76). Guilford Press.

Triandis, H. C., Bontempo, R., Villareal, M. J., Asai, M., & Lucca, N. (1988). Individualism and collectivism: Cross-cultural perspectives on self-ingroup relationships. *Journal of Personality and Social Psychology, 54*(2), 323–338.

Tribbensee, N. E., & Claiborn, C. D. (2003). Confidentiality in psychotherapy and related contexts. In W. O'Donohue & K. Ferguson (Eds.), *Handbook of professional ethics for psychologists: Issues, questions, and controversies* (pp. 287–300). Sage.

Trimble, J. E., & Clearing-Sky, M. (2009). An historical profile of American Indians and Alaska natives in psychology. *Cultural Diversity and Ethnic Minority Psychology, 15*(4), 338–351.

Trinidad, D. R., & Johnson, C. A. (2002). The association between emotional intelligence and early adolescent tobacco and alcohol use. *Personality and Individual Differences, 32*(1), 95–105.

Trockel, M. T., Barnes, M. D., & Egget, D. L. (2000). Health-related variables and academic performance among first-year college students: Implications for sleep and other behaviors. *Journal of American College Health, 49*(3), 125–131.

Tropp, L. R., & Barlow, F. K. (2018). Making advantaged racial groups care about inequality: Intergroup contact as a route to psychological investment. *Current Directions in Psychological Science*, 0963721417743282.

Truax, P. (2002). Behavioral case conceptualization for adults. In M. Hersen (Ed.), *Clinical behavior therapy: Adults and children* (pp. 3–36). Wiley.

Truax, P., & Thomas, J. C. (2003). Effectiveness versus efficacy studies: Issues, designs, and methodologies. In J. C. Thomas & M. Hersen (Eds.), *Understanding research in clinical and counseling psychology* (pp. 342–378). Lawrence Erlbaum.

Truscott, D. (2010). *Becoming an effective psychotherapist: Adopting a theory of psychotherapy that's right for you and your client*. American Psychological Association.

Tryon, W. W. (2008). History and theoretical foundations. In M. Hersen & A. M. Gross (Eds.), *Handbook of clinical psychology* (Vol. 1, pp. 3–37). Wiley.

Tsai, J., El-Gabalawy, R., Sledge, W. H., Southwick, S. M., & Pietrzak, R. H. (2015). Post-traumatic growth among veterans in the USA: Results from the national health and resilience in veterans study. *Psychological Medicine, 45*(1), 165–179.

Tsai, S. F., Ku, N. W., Wang, T. F., Yang, Y. H., Shih, Y. H., Wu, S. Y., Lee, C.-W., Yu, M., Yang, T.-T., & Kuo, Y. M. (2018). Long-term moderate exercise rescues age-related decline in hippocampal neuronal complexity and memory. *Gerontology, 64*(6), 1–11.

Tu, H.-W, & Hampton, R. R. (2013). One-trial memory and habit contribute independently to matching-to-sample performance in rhesus monkeys (*Macaca mulatta*). *Journal of Comparative Psychology, 127*(3), 319–328.

Tuber, S. (2012). *Understanding personality through projective testing*. Jason Aronson.

Tudor, K., & Worrall, M. (2006). *Person-centered therapy: A clinical philosophy*. Routledge.

Tugade, M. M. (2011). Positive emotions and coping: Examining dual-process models of resilience. In S. Folkman (Ed.), *Oxford handbook of stress, health, and coping* (pp. 186–199). Oxford University Press.

Tugade, M. M., Shiota, M. N., & Kirby, L. D. (Eds.). (2014). Handbook of positive emotions. Guilford Press.

Tulving, E. (1972). Episodic and semantic memory. In E. Tulving & W. Donaldson (Eds.), *Organization of memory* (pp. 381–403). Academic Press.

Tulving, E. (1976). Ecphoric processes in recall and recognition. In J. Brown (Ed.), *Recall and recognition* (pp. 37–73). Wiley.

Tulving, E. (1983). *Elements of episodic memory*. Clarendon Press.

Tulving, E. (1998). Neurocognitive processes of human memory. In C. von Euler, I. Lundberg, & R. Llinas (Eds.), *Basic mechanisms in cognition and language* (pp. 261–281). Elsevier.

Tulving, E. (2007). Are there 256 different kinds of memory? In H. L. Roediger & J. S. Nairne (Eds.), *The foundation of remembering* (pp. 39–52). Psychology Press.

Tulving, E., & Osler, S. (1968). Effectiveness of retrieval cues in memory for words. *Journal of Experimental Psychology, 77*(4), 593–601.

Tulving, E., & Thomson, D. M. (1973). Encoding specificity and retrieval processes in episodic memory. *Psychological Review, 80*(5), 352–373.

Tuma, R. S. (2010). Thirdhand smoke: Studies multiply, catchy name raises awareness. *Journal of the National Cancer Institute, 102*(14), 1004–1005.

Tuorila, H. (2010). Taste and food preferences. In E. B. Goldstein (Ed.), *Encyclopedia of perception* (pp. 969–973). Sage.

Turiel, E. (2002). *The culture of morality: Social development, context, and conflict*. Cambridge University Press.

Turiel, E. (2006). The development of morality. In N. Eisenberg (Vol. Ed.), *Handbook of child psychology* (6th ed., Vol. 3, pp. 789–857). Wiley.

Turiel, E. (2008). The development of children's orientations toward moral, social, and personal orders: More than a sequence in development. *Human Development, 51*(1), 21–39.

Turiel, E. (2010). The development of morality: Reasoning, emotions, and resistance. In W. F. Overton (Ed.), *Handbook of life-span development* (Vol. 1, pp. 554–583). Wiley.

Turiel, E. (2015). Moral development. In W. F. Overton & P. C. Molenaar (Eds.), *Handbook of child psychology: Vol. 1. Theory & method* (7th ed., pp. 484–522). John Wiley & Sons.

Turk, D. C., & Melzack, R. (2011). The measurement of pain and the assessment of people experiencing pain. In D. C. Turk & R. Melzack (Eds.), *Handbook of pain assessment* (3rd ed., pp. 3–16). Guilford Press.

Turkington, C., & Harris, J. R. (2001). *The encyclopedia of memory and memory disorders* (2nd ed.). Facts on File.

Turner, C. W., Layton, J. F., & Simons, L. S. (1975). Naturalistic studies of aggressive behavior: Aggressive stimuli, victim visibility, and horn honking. *Journal of Personality and Social Psychology, 31*(6), 1098–1107.

Turow, J. (2012). Nurses and doctors in prime time series: The dynamics of depicting professional power. *Nursing Outlook, 60*(5), S4–S11.

Tversky, A., & Kahneman, D. (1971). Belief in the law of small numbers. *Psychological Bulletin, 76*(2), 105–110.

Tversky, A., & Kahneman, D. (1973). Availability: A heuristic for judging frequency and probability. *Cognitive Psychology, 5*(2), 207–232.

Tversky, A., & Kahneman, D. (1974). Judgment under uncertainty: Heuristics and biases. *Science, 185*(4157), 1124–1131.

Tversky, A., & Kahneman, D. (1981). The framing of decisions and the psychology of choice. *Science, 211*(4481), 453–458.

Tversky, A., & Kahneman, D. (1982). Judgments of and by representativeness. In D. Kahneman, P. Slovic, & A. Tversky (Eds.), *Judgment under uncertainty: Heuristics and biases* (pp. 84–98). Cambridge University Press.

Tversky, A., & Kahneman, D. (1986). Rational choice and the framing of decisions. *Journal of Business, 59*(4), S251–S278.

Tweed, R. G., & Conway, L. G., III. (2006). Coping strategies and culturally influenced beliefs about the world. In P. T. P. Wong & L. C. J. Wong (Eds.), *Handbook of multicultural perspectives on stress and coping* (pp. 133–154). Springer Science+Business Media.

Tweed, R. G., White, K., & Lehman, D. R. (2004). Culture, stress, and coping internally- and externally-targeted control strategies of European Canadians, East Asian Canadians, and Japanese. *Journal of Cross-Cultural Psychology, 35*(6), 652–668.

Twenge, J. M., & Campbell, S. M. (2008). Generational differences in psychological traits and their impact on the workplace. *Journal of Managerial Psychology, 23*(8), 862–877.

Twenge, J. M., & Cooper, A. B. (2020). The expanding class divide in happiness in the United States, 1972–2016. *Emotion*. Advance online publication. https://doi.org/10.1037/emo0000774

Twenge, J. M., & Joiner, T. E. (2020). Mental distress among US adults during the COVID-19 pandemic. *Journal of Clinical Psychology, 76*(12), 2170–2182. https://doi.org/10.1002/jclp.23064

Twenge, J. M., Gentile, B., DeWall, C. N., Ma, D., Lacefield, K., & Schurtz, D. R. (2010). Birth cohort increases in psychopathology among young Americans, 1938–2007: A cross-temporal meta-analysis of the MMPI. *Clinical Psychology Review, 30*(2), 145–154.

Twenge, J. M., Martin, G. N., & Campbell, W. K. (2018). Decreases in psychological well-being among American adolescents after 2012 and links to screen time during the rise of smartphone technology. *Emotion, 18*(6), 765–780.

Twenge, J. M., Sherman, R. A., & Wells, B. E. (2016). Changes in American adults' reported same-sex sexual experiences and attitudes, 1973–2014. *Archives of Sexual Behavior, 45*(7), 1713–1730.

Twenge, J. M., Zhang, L., & Im, C. (2004). It's beyond my control: A cross-temporal meta-analysis of increasing externality in locus of control, 1960–2002. *Personality and Social Psychology Review, 8*(3), 308–319.

Twomey, J., LaGasse, L., Derauf, C., Newman, E., Shah, R., Smith, L., Arria, A., Huestis, M., DellaGrotta, S., Roberts, M., Dansereau, L., Neal., C., & Lester, B. (2013). Prenatal methamphetamine exposure, home environment, and primary caregiver risk factors predict child behavioral problems at 5 years. *American Journal of Orthopsychiatry, 83*(1), 64–72. https://doi.org/10.1111/ajop.12007

Tzeng, O. J. (1973). Positive recency effect in a delayed free recall. *Journal of Verbal Learning and Verbal Behavior, 12*(4), 436–439.

U.S. Census Bureau (2016). Educational attainment in the United States: 2015. https://www.census.gov/content/dam/Census/library/publications/2016/demo/p20-578.pdf

U.S. Census Bureau. (2011). Statistical abstract of the United States. Section 1: Population. http://www.census.gov/prod/2011pubs/11statab/pop.pdf

U.S. Census Bureau. (2015). Census Bureau reports at least 350 languages spoken in U.S. homes. https://www.census.gov/newsroom/archives/2015-pr/cb15-185.html

U.S. Census Bureau. (2017a). American community survey. https://www.census.gov/programs-surveys/acs/

U.S. Census Bureau. (2017b). Quick facts: United States. https://www.census.gov/quickfacts/fact/table/US/RHI125217

U.S. Census Bureau. (2018). Americans with disabilities: 2014. https://www.census.gov/content/dam/Census/library/publications/2018/demo/p70-152.pdf

U.S. Census Bureau. (2018). Historical marital status tables: Table MS-2 estimated median age at first marriage, by sex: 1890 to the present. https://www.census.gov/data/tables/time-series/demo/families/marital.html?#

U.S. Census Bureau. (2019). QuickFacts. https://www.census.gov/quickfacts/fact/table/US/PST045219

U.S. Census Bureau. (2021). Historical population density data (1910–2020). https://www.census.gov/data/tables/time-series/dec/density-data-text.html

U.S. Department of Agriculture. (2014). Food expenditures: Table 13. http://www.ers.usda.gov/data-products/food-expenditures.aspx

U.S. Department of Health and Human Services. (2018). What is the US opioid epidemic? https://www.hhs.gov/opioids/about-the-epidemic/index.html

U.S. Department of Health and Human Services. (2021). Opioid crisis statistics. https://www.hhs.gov/opioids/about-the-epidemic/opioid-crisis-statistics/index.html

Uchida, M., Spencer, T. J., Faraone, S. V., & Biederman, J. (2015). Adult outcome of ADHD: An overview of results from the MGH Longitudinal Family Studies of Pediatrically and Psychiatrically Referred Youth With and Without ADHD of Both Sexes. *Journal of Attention Disorders, 22*(6), 523–534. https://doi.org/10.1177/1087054715604360

Uchida, Y., & Kitayama, S. (2009). Happiness and unhappiness in east and west: Themes and variations. *Emotion, 9*(4), 441–456.

Uchida, Y., Norasakkunkit, V., & Kitayama, S. (2004). Cultural constructions of happiness: Theory and empirical evidence. *Journal of Happiness Studies, 5*(3), 223–239.

Uchino, B. N. (2006). Social support and health: A review of physiological processes potentially underlying links to disease outcomes. *Journal of Behavioral Medicine, 29*(4), 377–387.

Ucros, C. G. (1989). Mood state-dependent memory: A meta-analysis. *Cognition and Emotion, 3*(2), 139–169.

Udry, J. R., & Chantala, K. (2006). Masculinity–femininity predicts sexual orientation in men but not in women. *Journal of Biosocial Science, 38*(6), 797–809.

Uhls, Y. T., Ellison, N. B., & Subrahmanyam, K. (2017). Benefits and costs of social media in adolescence. *Pediatrics, 140*(Suppl. 2), S67–S70.

UK ECT Review Group. (2003). Efficacy and safety of electroconvulsive therapy in depressive disorders: A systematic review and meta-analysis. *The Lancet, 361*(9360), 799–808.

Uleman, J. S., & Saribay, S. A. (2012). Initial impressions of others. In K. Deaux & M. Snyder (Eds.), *The Oxford handbook of personality and social psychology* (pp. 337–366). Oxford University Press.

Ulian, M. D., Aburad, L., da Silva Oliveira, M. S., Poppe, A. C. M., Sabatini, F., Perez, I., Gualano, B., Benatti, F. B., Pinto, A. J., Roble, O. J., Vessoni, A., de Morais Sato, P., Unsain, R. F., Scagliusi, F. B. (2018a). Effects of Health at Every Size® interventions on health-related outcomes of people with overweight and obesity: A systematic review. *Obesity Reviews, 19*(12), 1659–1666.

Ulian, M. D., Pinto, A. J., de Morais Sato, P., Benatti, F. B., de Campos-Ferraz, P. L., Coelho, D., Roble, O. J., Sabatini, F., Perez, I., Aburad, L., Vessoni, A., & Unsain, R. F. (2018b). Effects of a new intervention based on the Health at Every Size approach for the management of obesity: The "Health and Wellness in Obesity" study. *PLoS One, 13*(7), e0198401.

Underwood, B. J. (1957). Interference and forgetting. *Psychological Review, 64*(1), 49–60.

Underwood, M. K., Brown, B. B., & Ehrenreich, S. E. (2018). Social media and peer relations. In W. M. Bukowski, B. Laursen, & K. H. Rubin (Eds.), *Handbook of peer interactions, relationships, and groups* (2nd ed., pp. 533–551). Guilford Press.

Urban, E. J., Charles, S. T., Levine, L. J., & Almeida, D. M. (2018). Depression history and memory bias for specific daily emotions. *PLoS ONE, 13*(9), e0203574.

Urbina, S. (2011). Tests of intelligence. In R. J. Sternberg & S. B. Kaufman (Eds.), *The Cambridge handbook of intelligence* (pp. 20–38). Cambridge University Press.

Ursin, R., Bjorvatn, B., & Holsten, F. (2005). Sleep duration, subjective sleep need, and sleep habits of 40- to 45-year-olds in the Hordaland Health Study. *Sleep, 28*(10), 1260–1269.

Ustun, T. B., & Sartorius, N. (Eds.). (1995). *Mental illness in general health care: An international study*. Wiley.

Vagi, K. J., Rothman, E. F., Latzman, N. E., Tharp, A. T., Hall, D. M., & Breiding, M. J. (2013). Beyond correlates: A review of risk and protective factors for adolescent dating violence perpetration. *Journal of Youth and Adolescence, 42*(4), 633–649.

Vago, D. R., & Silbersweig, D. A. (2012). Self-awareness, self-regulation, and self-transcendence (S-ART): A framework for understanding the neurobiological mechanisms of mindfulness. *Frontiers in Human Neuroscience, 6*, 296.

Vahia, I. V., & Cohen, C. I. (2008). Psychopathology. In K. T. Meuser & D. V. Jeste (Eds.), *Clinical handbook of schizophrenia* (pp. 82–90). Guilford Press.

Vai, B., Mazza, M. G., Delli Colli, C., Foiselle, M., Allen, B., Benedetti, F., Borsini, A., Casanova Dias, M., Tamouza, R., Leboyer, M., Benros, M. E., Branchi, I., Fusar-Poli, P., & De Picker, L. J. (2021). Mental disorders and risk of COVID-19 related mortality, hospitalization and intensive care unit admission: A systematic review and meta-analysis. *The Lancet, 8*(9), 797–812. http://doi.org/10.2139/ssrn.3832645

Valdivieso-Mora, E., Peet, C. L., Garnier-Villarreal, M., Salazar-Villanea, M. & Johnson, D. K. (2016). A systematic review of the relationship between familism and mental health outcomes in Latino population. *Frontiers in Psychology, 7*. https://doi.org/10.3389/fpsyg.2016.01632

Valente, D., Theurel, A., & Gentaz, E. (2017). The role of visual experience in the production of emotional facial expressions by blind people: A review. *Psychonomic Bulletin & Review, 25*(2), 483–497.

Valentine, K. E., Milling, L. S., Clark, L. J., & Moriarty, C. L. (2019). The efficacy of hypnosis as a treatment for anxiety: A meta-analysis. *International Journal of Clinical and Experimental Hypnosis, 67*(3), 336–363. https://doi.org/10.1080/00207144.2019.1613863

Valentino, K., Nuttall, A. K., Comas, M., Borkowski, J. G., & Akai, C. E. (2012). Intergenerational continuity of child abuse among adolescent mothers: Authoritarian parenting, community violence, and race. *Child Maltreatment, 17*, 172–181.

Valenza, E., Simion, F., Cassia, V. M., & Umiltà, C. (1996). Face preference at birth. *Journal of Experimental Psychology: Human Perception and Performance, 22*(4), 892–903.

Vallat, R., & Ruby, P. M. (2019). Is it a good idea to cultivate lucid dreaming? *Frontiers in Psychology, 10*, 2585. https://doi.org/10.3389/fpsyg.2019.02585

Vallières, A., & Bastille-Denis, E. (2012). Circadian rhythm disorders II: Jet lag. In C. M. Morin & C. A. Espie (Eds.), *The Oxford handbook of sleep and sleep disorders* (pp. 648–665). Oxford University Press.

Van Ameringen, M., Mancini, C., & Patterson, B. (2009). Pharmacotherapy for social anxiety disorder and specific phobia. In M. M. Antony & M. B. Stein (Eds.), *Oxford handbook of anxiety and related disorders* (pp. 321–333). Oxford University Press.

van Bergen, E., van Zuijen, T., Bishop, D., & de Jong, P. F. (2017). Why are home literacy environment and children's reading skills associated? What parental skills reveal. *Reading Research Quarterly, 52*(2), 147–160.

van de Vijver, F. J. R., & Matsumoto, D. (2011). Introduction to the methodological issues associated with cross-cultural research. In D. Matsumoto & F. J. R. van de Vijver (Eds.), *Cross-cultural research methods in psychology* (pp. 1–14). Cambridge University Press.

Van den Berg, P., Paxton, S. J., Keery, H., Wall, M., Guo, J., & Neumark-Sztainer, D. (2007). Body dissatisfaction and body comparison with media images in males and females. *Body Image, 4*(3), 257–268.

Van den Bulck, J. (2004). Television viewing, computer game playing, and Internet use and self-reported time to bed and time out of bed in secondary-school children. *Sleep, 27*(1), 101–104.

van der Hart, O., & Nijenhuis, E. R. S. (2009). Dissociative disorders. In P. H. Blaney & Theodore Millon (Eds.), *Oxford textbook of psychopathology* (2nd ed., 452–481). Oxford University Press.

van der Linden, D., Pekaar, K. A., Bakker, A. B., Schermer, J. A., Vernon, P. A., Dunkel, C. S., & Petrides, K. V. (2017). Overlap between the general factor of personality and emotional intelligence: A meta-analysis. *Psychological Bulletin, 143*(1), 36.

van der Linden, D., Scholte, R. H., Cillessen, A. H., Nijenhuis, J. T., & Segers, E. (2010). Classroom ratings of likeability and popularity are related to the Big Five and the general factor of personality. *Journal of Research in Personality, 44*(5), 669–672.

van der Linden, S., Leiserowitz, A., Rosenthal, S., & Maibach, E. (2017). Inoculating the public against misinformation about climate change. *Global Challenges, 1*(2), 1600008. https://doi.org/10.1002/gch2.201600008

van der Veer, R., & Valsiner, J. (Eds.). (1994). *The Vygotsky reader*. Blackwell.

van Dijk, W. W., van Dillen, L. F., Rotteveel, M., & Seip, E. C. (2017). Looking into the crystal ball of our emotional lives: Emotion regulation and the overestimation of future guilt and shame. *Cognition and Emotion, 31*(3), 616–624.

Van Dongen, H. P., Maislin, G., Mullington, J. M., & Dinges, D. F. (2003). The cumulative cost of additional wakefulness: Dose-response effects on neurobehavioral functions and sleep physiology from chronic sleep restriction and total sleep deprivation. *Sleep, 26*(2), 117–126.

Van Erum, J., Van Dam, D., & De Deyn, P. P. (2017). Sleep and Alzheimer's disease: A pivotal role for the suprachiasmatic nucleus? *Sleep Medicine Reviews, 40*, 17–27.

van Harmelen, A. L., Gibson, J. L., St Clair, M. C., Owens, M., Brodbeck, J., Dunn, V., Lewis, G., Croudace, T., Jones, P. B., Kievit, R. A., & Goodyer, I. M. (2016). Friendships and family support reduce subsequent depressive symptoms in at-risk adolescents. *PLoS One, 11*(5), e0153715.

van Harmelen, A. L., Kievit, R. A., Ioannidis, K., Neufeld, S., Jones, P. B., Bullmore, E., Dolan, R., NSPN Consortium, Fonagy, P., & Goodyer, I. (2017). Adolescent friendships predict later resilient functioning across psychosocial domains in a healthy community cohort. *Psychological Medicine, 47*(13), 2312–2322.

Van Horn, D. H. A., Wenzel, A., & Britton, P. C. (2021). Motivational interviewing. In A. Wenzel (Ed.), *Handbook of cognitive behavioral therapy: Overview and approaches* (pp. 313–347). American Psychological Association. https://doi.org/10.1037/0000218-011

Van Horn, J. D. (2004). Cognitive neuroimaging: History, developments, and directions. In M. S. Gazzaniga (Ed.), *The new cognitive neurosciences III* (pp. 1281–1294). MIT Press.

van Kessel, P., Baronavski, C., Scheller, A., & Smith, A. (2020). In their own words, Americans describe the struggles and silver linings of the COVID-19 pandemic. https://www.pewresearch.org/2021/03/05/in-their-own-words-americans-describe-the-struggles-and-silver-linings-of-the-covid-19-pandemic/

Van Kessel, P., Baronavski, C., Scheller, A., & Smith, A. (2021). In their own words, Americans describe the struggles and silver linings of the COVID-19 pandemic. *Pew Research Center.* https://www.pewresearch.org/2021/03/05/in-their-own-words-americans-describe-the-struggles-and-silver-linings-of-the-covid-19-pandemic/

van Maanen, A., Meijer, A. M., Smits, M. G., & Oort, F. J. (2017). Classical conditioning for preserving the effects of short melatonin treatment in children with delayed sleep: A pilot study. *Nature and Science of Sleep, 9*, 67.

Van Os, J., Hanseen, M., & Bak, M. (2003). Do urbanicity and familial liability co-participate in causing psychosis? *American Journal of Psychiatry, 160*(3), 477–482.

Van Os, J., Hanseen, M., van Bijl, R., & Vollebergh, W. (2001). Prevalence of psychotic disorder and community level of psychotic symptoms. *Archives of General Psychiatry, 58*(7), 663–668.

van Os, J., Kenis, G., & Rutten, B. P. (2010). The environment and schizophrenia. *Nature, 468*(7321), 203.

van Praag, H., Christie, B. R., Sejnowski, T. J., & Gage, F. H. (1999). Running enhances neurogenesis, learning, and long-term potentiation in mice. *Proceedings of the National Academy of Sciences, 96*(23), 13427–13431.

van Praag, H., Kempermann, G., & Gage, F. H. (2000). Neural consequences of environmental enrichment. *Nature Reviews Neuroscience, 1*(3), 191–198.

van Praag, H., Schinder, A. F., Christie, B. R., Toni, N., Palmer, T. D., & Gage, F. H. (2002). Functional neurogenesis in the adult hippocampus. *Nature, 415*(6875), 1030–1034.

Van Rooy, D. L., & Viswesvaran, C. (2004). Emotional intelligence: A meta-analytic investigation of predictive validity and nomological net. *Journal of Vocational Behavior, 65*(1), 71–95.

Van Solinge, H., & Henkens, K. (2005). Couples' adjustment to retirement: A multi-actor panel study. *The Journals of Gerontology. Series B, Psychological Sciences and Social Sciences, 60*(1), S11–S20.

Van Solinge, H., & Henkens, K. (2007). Involuntary retirement: The role of restrictive circumstances, timing, and social embeddedness. *The Journals of Gerontology: Series B: Psychological Sciences and Social Sciences, 62*(5), S295–S303.

van Vugt, M. K. (2015). Cognitive benefits of mindfulness meditation. In K. W. Brown, J. D. Creswell, & R. M. Ryan (Eds.), *Handbook of mindfulness: Theory, research, and practice* (pp. 190–207). Guilford Press.

Van Vugt, M., & Van Lange, P. A. M. (2006). The altruism puzzle: Psychological adaptations for prosocial behavior. In M. Schaller, J. A. Simpson, & D. T. Kenrick (Eds.), *Evolution and social psychology* (pp. 237–261). Psychology Press.

van Winkel, M., Wichers, M., Collip, D., Jacobs, N., Derom, C., Thiery, E., Myin-Germeys, I., & Peeters, F. (2017). Unraveling the role of loneliness in depression: The relationship between daily life experience and behavior. *Psychiatry, 80*(2), 104–117.

Van, H. C., Guinand, N., Damis, E., Mansbach, A. L., Poncet, A., Hummel, T., & Landis, B. N. (2018). Olfactory stimulation may promote oral feeding in immature newborn: A randomized controlled trial. *European Archives of Oto-Rhino-Laryngology, 275*(1), 125–129.

Vanasse, A., Blais, L., Courteau, J., Cohen, A. A., Roberge, P., Larouche, A., Grignon, S., Fleury, M.-J., Lesage, A., Demers, M.-F., Roy, M.-A., Carrier, J.-D., & Delorme, A. (2016). Comparative effectiveness and safety of antipsychotic drugs in schizophrenia treatment: a real-world observational study. *Acta Psychiatrica Scandinavica, 134*(5), 374–384. https://doi.org/10.1111/acps.12621

Vandewater, E. A., & Wartella, E. A. (2011). Food marketing, television, and video games. In J. H. Cawley (Ed.), *The Oxford handbook of the social science of obesity* (pp. 350–366). Oxford University Press.

VanHuysse, J. L., Burt, S. A., O'Connor, S. M., Thompson, J. K., & Klump, K. L. (2016). Socialization and selection effects in the association between weight conscious peer groups and thin-ideal internalization: A co-twin control study. *Body Image, 17*, 1–9.

Vargas-Alvarez, M., Navas-Carretero, S., Palla, L., Martínez, J. A., & Almiron-Roig, E. (2021). Impact of portion control tools on portion size awareness, choice and intake: Systematic review and meta-analysis. *Nutrients, 13*(6), 1978. https://doi.org/10.3390/nu13061978

Vargha-Khadem, F., Gadian, D. G., Watkins, K. E., Connelly, A., Van Paesschen, W., & Mishkin, M. (1997). Differential effects of early hippocampal pathology on episodic and semantic memory. *Science, 277*(5324), 376–380.

Varker, T., Brand, R. M., Ward, J., Terhaag, S., & Phelps, A. (2018). Efficacy of synchronous telepsychology interventions for people with anxiety, depression, posttraumatic stress disorder, and adjustment disorder: A rapid evidence assessment. *Psychological Services, 16(4), 621–635.* https://doi.org/10.1037/ser0000239

Varshney, M., Mahapatra, A., Krishnan, V., Gupta, R., & Deb, K. S. (2016). Violence and mental illness: What is the true story? *Journal of Epidemiology and Community Health, 70*(3), 223–225.

Vartanian, L. R., Herman, C. P., & Polivy, J. (2007). Consumption stereotypes and impression management: How you are what you eat. *Appetite, 48*(3), 265–277.

Vartanian, L. R., Pinkus, R. T., & Smyth, J. M. (2018). Experiences of weight stigma in everyday life: Implications for health motivation. *Stigma and Health, 3*(2), 85–92. https://doi.org/10.1037/sah0000077

Vartanian, L. R., Spanos, S., Herman, C. P., & Polivy, J. (2015). Modeling of food intake: A meta-analytic review. *Social Influence, 10*(3), 119–136. https://doi.org/10.1080/15534510.2015.1008037

Vasquez, M. (2015). Ethics code, APA. (2015). In R. L. Cautin & S. O. Lilienfeld (Eds.), *The encyclopedia of clinical psychology* (pp. 1124–1126). Wiley-Blackwell.

Vasquez, M. J. T. (2010). Ethics in multicultural counseling practice. In J. G. Ponterotto, J. M. Casas, L. A. Suzuki, & C. M. Alexander (Eds.), *Handbook of multicultural counseling* (3rd ed., pp. 127–145). Sage.

Vaux, B. (2003). *American dialects*. Choices. http://www.choicesmagazine.org/magazine/pdf/article_115.pdf

Vazire, S., & Carlson, E. N. (2010). Self-knowledge of personality: Do people know themselves? *Social and Personality Psychology Compass, 4*(8), 605–620.

Vecera, S. P., & Lee, H. (2010). Vision: Cognitive influences. In E. B. Goldstein (Ed.), *Encyclopedia of perception* (pp. 1048–1053). Sage.

Vedhara, K., & Irwin, M. (2005). *Human psychoneuroimmunology*. Oxford University Press.

Velasquez, P. A. E., & Montiel, C. J. (2018). Reapproaching Rogers: A discursive examination of client-centered therapy. *Person-Centered & Experiential Psychotherapies, 17*(3), 253–269.

Velayudhan, L., Pritchard, M., Powell, J. F., Proitsi, P., & Lovestone, S. (2013). Smell identification function as a severity and progression marker in Alzheimer's disease. *International Psychogeriatrics, 25*(7), 1157–1166.

Velmans, M. (2009). How to define consciousness: And how not to define consciousness. *Journal of Consciousness Studies, 16*(5), 139–156.

Venturo-Conerly, K. E., Fitzpatrick, O. M., Horn, R. L., Ugueto, A. M., & Weisz, J. R. (2021). Effectiveness of youth psychotherapy delivered remotely: A meta-analysis. *American Psychologist*. Advance online publication. https://doi.org/10.1037/amp0000816

Verduyn, P., Lee, D. S., Park, J., Shablack, H., Orvell, A., Bayer, J., Ybarra, O., Jonides, J., & Kross, E. (2015). Passive Facebook usage undermines affective well-being: Experimental and longitudinal evidence. *Journal of Experimental Psychology: General, 144*(2), 480.

Verhaeghen, P., & Salthouse, T. A. (1997). Meta-analyses of age–cognition relations in adulthood: Estimates of linear and nonlinear age effects and structural models. *Psychological Bulletin, 122*(3), 231–249.

Verheijen, G. P., Burk, W. J., Stoltz, S. E., van den Berg, Y. H., & Cillessen, A. H. (2018). Friendly fire: Longitudinal effects of exposure to violent video games on aggressive behavior in adolescent friendship dyads. *Aggressive Behavior, 44*(3), 257–267.

Vervoort, L., & Blusiewicz, T. (2020). Free will and (in) determinism in the brain. *Theoria: An International Journal for Theory, History and Foundations of Science, 35*(3), 345–364. https://www.jstor.org/stable/26936764

Veselka, L., Schermer, J. A., & Vernon, P. A. (2011). Beyond the Big Five: The Dark Triad and the supernumerary personality inventory. *Twin Research and Human Genetics, 14*(2), 158–168.

Vetter, C., & Scheer, F. A. (2017). Circadian biology: Uncoupling human body clocks by food timing. *Current Biology, 27*(13), R656–R658.

Viamontes, G. I., & Beitman, B. D. (2009). Brain processes informing psychotherapy. In G. O. Gabbard (Ed.), *Textbook of psychotherapeutic treatments* (pp. 781–808). American Psychiatric Publishing.

Vilanova, F., Beria, F. M., Costa, Â. B., & Koller, S. H. (2017). Deindividuation: From Le Bon to the social identity model of deindividuation effects. *Cogent Psychology, 4*(1), 1308104.

Villa, M., & Reitman, D. (2007). Overview of interviewing strategies with children, parents, and teachers. In M. Hersen & J. C. Thomas (Eds.), *Handbook of clinical interviewing with children* (pp. 2–15). Sage.

Villamar, A. J., Donohue, B. C., & Allen, D. N. (2008). Applied behavior analysis. In M. Hersen & A. M. Gross (Eds.), *Handbook of clinical psychology* (Vol. 1, pp. 161–170). Wiley.

Villamarin-Salomon, R. M., & Brustoloni, J. C. (2010). Using reinforcement to strengthen users' secure behaviors. In *Proceedings of the 28th International Conference on Human Factors in Computing Systems* (pp. 363–372).

Villanueva, L., Montoya-Castilla, I., & Prado-Gasco, V. (2017). The importance of trait emotional intelligence and feelings in the prediction of perceived and biological stress in adolescents: Hierarchical regressions and fsQCA models. *Stress, 20*(4), 355–362.

Vimal, R. (2009). Meanings attributed to the term "consciousness": An overview. *Journal of Consciousness Studies, 16*(5), 9–27.

Vingerhoets, A. J., & Bylsma, L. M. (2016). The riddle of human emotional crying: A challenge for emotion researchers. *Emotion Review, 8*(3), 207–217.

Vingerhoets, A. J., & Scheirs, J. (2000). Sex differences in crying: Empirical findings and possible explanations. *Gender and Emotion: Social Psychological Perspectives, 2*, 143–165.

Vingerhoets, A. J., Cornelius, R. R., Van Heck, G. L., & Becht, M. C. (2000). Adult crying: A model and review of the literature. *Review of General Psychology, 4*(4), 354–377.

Virnig, B., Huang, Z., Lurie, N., Musgrave, D., McBean, A. M., & Dowd, B. (2004). Does Medicare managed care provide equal treatment for mental illness across races? *Archives of General Psychiatry, 61*(2), 201–205.

Visser, S. N., Danielson, M. L., Bitsko, R. H., Holbrook, J. R., Kogan, M. D., Ghandour, R. M., Perou, R., & Blumberg, S. J. (2014). Trends in the parent-report of health care provider-diagnosed and medicated attention-deficit/hyperactivity disorder: United States, 2003–2011. *Journal of the American Academy of Child & Adolescent Psychiatry, 53*(1), 34–46.

Visu-Petra, L., Cheie, L., Benga, O., & Alloway, T. P. (2011). Effects of anxiety on memory storage and updating in young children. *International Journal of Behavioral Development, 35*(1), 38–47.

Visu-Petra, L., Miclea, M., & Visu-Petra, G. (2013). Individual differences in anxiety and executive functioning: A multidimensional view. *International Journal of Psychology, 48*(4), 649–659.

Viswesvaran, C., & Ones, D. S. (1999). Meta-analyses of fakability estimates: Implications for personality measurement. *Educational and Psychological Measurement, 59*(2), 197–210.

Vits, S., Cesko, E., Enck, P., Hillen, U., Schadendorf, D., & Schedlowski, M. (2011). Behavioural conditioning as the mediator of placebo responses in the immune system. *Philosophical Transactions of the Royal Society B: Biological Sciences, 366*(1572), 1799–1807.

Vivian-Taylor, J., & Hickey, M. (2014). Menopause and depression: Is there a link? *Maturitas, 79*(2), 142–146.

Vlassova, A., & Pearson, J. (2018). Unconscious decisional learning improves unconscious information processing. *Cognition, 176*, 131–139.

Vogel, G. W. (1991). Sleep-onset mentation. In S. J. Ellman & J. Antrobus (Eds.), *The mind in sleep* (pp. 125–136). Wiley.

Vogele, C., & Gibson, E. L. (2010). Mood, emotions, and eating disorders. In W. S. Agras (Ed.), *The Oxford handbook of eating disorders* (pp. 180–205). Oxford University Press.

Vogler, G. P., Sørensen, T. I., Stunkard, A. J., Srinivasan, M. R., & Rao, D. C. (1995). Influences of genes and shared family environment on adult body mass index assessed in an adoption study by a comprehensive path model. *International Journal of Obesity and Related Metabolic Disorders, 19*(1), 40–45.

Volkow, N., Benveniste, H., & McLellan, A. T. (2018). Use and misuse of opioids in chronic pain. *Annual Review of Medicine, 69*, 451–465.

Vøllestad, J., Nielsen, M. B., & Nielsen, G. H. (2012). Mindfulness- and acceptance-based interventions for anxiety disorders: A systematic review and meta-analysis. *British Journal of Clinical Psychology, 51*(3), 239–260.

Volz, K., Leonhart, R., Stark, R., Vaitl, D., & Ambach, W. (2017). Psychophysiological correlates of the misinformation effect. *International Journal of Psychophysiology, 117*, 1–9.

von Hofsten, C. (2003). On the development of perception and action. In J. Valsiner & K. Connolly (Eds.), *Handbook of developmental psychology* (pp. 114–140). Sage.

Vonofakou, C., Hewstone, M., & Voci, A. (2007). Contact with out-group friends as a predictor of meta-attitudinal strength and accessibility of attitudes toward gay men. *Journal of Personality and Social Psychology, 92*(5), 804–820.

Vorona, R. D., Szklo-Coxe, M., Wu, A., Dubik, M., Zhao, Y., & Ware, J. C. (2011). Dissimilar teen crash rates in two neighboring southeastern Virginia cities with different high school start times. *Journal of Clinical Sleep Medicine, 7*(2), 145–151.

Voss, J. L. (2009). Long-term associative memory capacity in man. *Psychonomic Bulletin & Review, 16*(6), 1076–1081.

Voss, M. W., Nagamatsu, L. S., Liu-Ambrose, T., & Kramer, A. F. (2011). Exercise, brain, and cognition across the life span. *Journal of Applied Physiology, 111*(5), 1505–1513.

Voss, M. W., Prakash, R. S., Erickson, K. I., Basak, C., Chaddock, L., Kim, J. S., Alves, H., Heo, S., Szabo, A. N., White, S. M., Wójcicki, T. R., Mailey, E. L., Gothe, N., Olson, E. A., McAuley, E., & Kramer, A. F. (2010). Plasticity of brain networks in a randomized intervention trial of exercise training in older adults. *Frontiers in Aging Neuroscience, 2*, 32.

Vouloumanos, A., & Werker, J. F. (2004). Tuned to the signal: The privileged status of speech for young infants. *Developmental Science, 7*(3), 270–276.

Vouloumanos, A., & Werker, J. F. (2007). Listening to language at birth: Evidence for a bias for speech in neonates. *Developmental Science, 10*(2), 159–164.

Vouloumanos, A., Hauser, M. D., Werker, J. F., & Martin, A. (2010). The tuning of human neonates' preference for speech. *Child Development, 81*(2), 517–527.

Vouloumanos, A., Kiehl, K. A., Werker, J. F., & Liddle, P. F. (2001). Detection of sounds in the auditory stream: Event-related fMRI evidence for differential activation to speech and nonspeech. *Journal of Cognitive Neuroscience, 13*(7), 994–1005.

Vrangalova, Z., & Savin-Williams, R. C. (2012). Mostly heterosexual and mostly gay/lesbian: Evidence for new sexual orientation identities. *Archives of Sexual Behavior, 41*(1), 85–101.

Vroom, V. H. (2007). Teaching the managers of tomorrow: Psychologists in business schools. In R. J. Sternberg (Ed.), *Career paths in psychology: Where your degree can take you* (2nd ed., pp. 51–67). American Psychological Association.

Vurbic, D., & Bouton, M. E. (2014). A contemporary behavioral perspective on extinction. In F. K. McSweeney & E. S. Murphy (Eds.), *The Wiley-Blackwell handbook of operant and classical conditioning* (pp. 53–76). Wiley.

Vyas, M. V., Garg, A. X., Iansavichus, A. V., Costella, J., Donner, A., Laugsand, L. E., & Hackam, D. G. (2012). Shift work and vascular events: Systematic review and meta-analysis. *BMJ, 345*, e4800. https://doi.org/10.1136/bmj.e4800

Vygotsky, L. (1986). *Thought and language* (Rev. ed., A. Kozulin, Trans.). MIT Press.

Vygotsky, L. S. (1978). Interaction between learning and development. In M. Cole, S. Scribner, & E. Souberman (Eds.), *Mind in society: The development of higher psychological processes* (Rev. ed., pp. 79–91). Harvard University Press.

Wachtel, P. L. (1977). *Psychoanalysis and behavior therapy: Toward an integration*. Basic Books.

Wacker, D. P., Harding, J., Berg, W., Cooper-Brown, L. J., & Barretto, A. (2009). Punishment. In W. T. O'Donohue & J. E. Fisher (Eds.), *General principles and empirically supported techniques of cognitive behavior therapy* (pp. 506–512). Wiley.

Wadden, T. A. (1995). Characteristics of successful weight loss maintainers. In D. B. Allison & F. X. Pi-Sunyer (Eds.), *Obesity treatment: Establishing goals, improving outcomes, and reviewing the research agenda* (pp. 103–111). Plenum Press.

Wadden, T. A., Butryn, M. L., & Wilson, C. (2007). Lifestyle modification for the management of obesity. *Gastroenterology, 132*(6), 2226–2238.

Wade, D. T., & Halligan, P. W. (2017). The biopsychosocial model of illness: A model whose time has come. *Clinical Rehabilitation, 31*(8), 995–1004.

Wade, K. A., Garry, M., Read, J. D., & Lindsay, D. S. (2002). A picture is worth a thousand lies: Using false photographs to create false childhood memories. *Psychonomic Bulletin & Review, 9*(3), 597–603.

Wade, T. D. (2010). Genetic influences on eating and the eating disorders. In W. S. Agras (Ed.), *The Oxford handbook of eating disorders* (pp. 103–122). Oxford University Press.

Wager, T. D., & Atlas, L. Y. (2015). The neuroscience of placebo effects: Connecting context, learning and health. *Nature Reviews Neuroscience, 16*(7), 403–418.

Wagner, A. D., Schacter, D. L., Rotte, M., Koutstaal, W., Maril, A., Dale, A. M., Rosen, B. R., & Buckner, R. L. (1998). Building memories: Remembering and forgetting of verbal experiences as predicted by brain activity. *Science, 281*(5380), 1188–1191.

Wagner, B. C., & Petty, R. E. (2011). The elaboration likelihood model of persuasion: Thoughtful and non-thoughtful social influence. In D. Chadee (Ed.), *Theories in social psychology* (pp. 96–116). Wiley-Blackwell.

Wagner, P. S., & Spiro, C. S. (2005). *Divided minds: Twin sisters and their journey through schizophrenia*. St. Martin's Press.

Wagner, R. K., & Sternberg, R. J. (1985). Practical intelligence in real-world pursuits: The role of tacit knowledge. *Journal of Personality and Social Psychology, 49*(2), 436–458.

Wagner, U., Gais, S., & Born, J. (2001). Emotional memory formation is enhanced across sleep intervals with high amounts of rapid eye movement sleep. *Learning & Memory, 8*(2), 112–119.

Wahlstrom, D., Raiford, S. E., Breaux, K. C., Zhu, J., & Weiss, L. G. (2018). The Wechsler Preschool and Primary Scale of Intelligence, fourth edition, Wechsler intelligence scale for children, fifth edition, and Wechsler individual achievement test, third edition. In D. P. Flanagan & E. M. McDonough (Eds.), *Contemporary intellectual assessment: Theories, tests, and issues* (4th ed., pp. 245–282). Guilford Press.

Wahlstrom, K. L. (2002a). Accommodating the sleep patterns of adolescents within current educational structures: An uncharted path. In M. A. Carskadon (Ed.), *Adolescent sleep patterns: Biological, social, and psychological influences* (pp. 172–197). Cambridge University Press.

Wahlstrom, K. (2002b). Changing times: Findings from the first longitudinal study of later high school start times. *NASSP Bulletin, 86*(633), 3–21.

Wahlstrom, K. L., Berger, A. T., & Widome, R. (2017). Relationships between school start time, sleep duration, and adolescent behaviors. *Sleep Health, 3*(3), 216–221.

Wakefield, J. C. (2013). DSM-5: An overview of changes and controversies. *Clinical Social Work Journal*, 41(2), 139–154.

Wakefield, J. C., & Demazeux, S. (2016). *Sadness or depression? International perspectives on the depression epidemic and its meaning*. Springer.

Wakefield, J. C., Horwitz, A. V., & Lorenzo-Luaces, L. (2017). Uncomplicated depression as normal sadness: Rethinking the boundary between normal and disordered depression. In R. J. DeRubeis & D. R. Strunk (Eds.), *The Oxford handbook of mood disorders* (pp. 83–94). Oxford University Press.

Walburn, J., Vedhara, K., Hankins, M., Rixon, L., & Weinman, J. (2009). Psychological stress and wound healing in humans: A systematic review and meta-analysis. *Journal of Psychosomatic Research, 67*(3), 253–271.

Walburn, J., Vedhara, K., & Weinman, J. (2018). The psychobiology of wound healing. In P. N. Murphy (Ed.), *The Routledge international handbook of psychobiology* (pp. 25–36). Routledge.

Waldroff, K. (2020). As the U.S. stays home, psychology moves online. *Monitor on Psychology, 51*(4). https://www.apa.org/monitor/2020/06/covid-psychology-online

Walker, E., & Lewine, R. J. (1990). Prediction of adult-onset schizophrenia from childhood home movies of the patients. *American Journal of Psychiatry, 147*(8), 1052–1056.

Walker, L. J. (2006). Gender and morality. In M. Killen & J. G. Smetana (Eds.), *Handbook of moral development* (pp. 93–115). Lawrence Erlbaum.

Walker, M. (2017). *Why we sleep*. Scribner.

Walker, M. P. (2012). The role of sleep in neurocognitive function. In C. M. Morin & C. A. Espie (Eds.), *The Oxford handbook of sleep and sleep disorders* (pp. 110–130). Oxford University Press.

Wallace, D. S., Paulson, R. M., Lord, C. G., & Bond, C. F., Jr. (2005). Which behaviors do attitudes predict? Meta-analyzing the effects of social pressure and perceived difficulty. *Review of General Psychology, 9*(3), 214–227.

Wallace, M. N. (2010). Auditory system: Structure. In E. B. Goldstein (Ed.), *Encyclopedia of perception* (pp. 194–196). Sage.

Wallace, P. M., & Gotlib, I. H. (1990). Marital adjustment during the transition to parenthood: Stability and predictors of change. *Journal of Marriage and Family, 52*(1), 21–29.

Walle, E. A., Reschke, P. J., & Knothe, J. M. (2017). Social referencing: Defining and delineating a basic process of emotion. *Emotion Review, 9*(3), 245–252.

Waller, D., Loomis, J. M., & Haun, D. B. (2004). Body-based senses enhance knowledge of directions in large-scale environments. *Psychonomic Bulletin & Review, 11*(1), 157–163.

Wallis, D. J., & Hetherington, M. M. (2009). Emotions and eating: Self-reported and experimentally induced changes in food intake under stress. *Appetite, 52*(2), 355–362.

Walls, N. E., Kane, S. B., & Wisneski, H. (2010). Gay-straight alliances and school experiences of sexual minority youth. *Youth & Society, 41*(3), 307–332.

Walsh, J. J., Barnes, J. D., Cameron, J. D., Goldfield, G. S., Chaput, J. P., Gunnell, K. E., Ledoux, A.-A., Zemek, R. L., & Tremblay, M. S. (2018). Associations between 24 hour movement behaviours and global cognition in US children: A cross-sectional observational study. *The Lancet Child & Adolescent Health, 2*(11), 783–791. https://doi.org/10.1016/S2352-4642(18)30278-5

Walsh, R., & Shapiro, S. L. (2006). The meeting of meditative disciplines and Western psychology: A mutually enriching dialogue. *American Psychologist, 61*(3), 227–239.

Walters, G. D., & Espelage, D. L. (2018). Resurrecting the empathy–bullying relationship with a pro-bullying attitudes mediator: The Lazarus effect in mediation research. *Journal of Abnormal Child Psychology, 46*(6), 1229–1239.

Walters, R. H., & Demkow, L. (1963). Timing of punishment as a determinant of response inhibition. *Child Development, 34*(1), 207–214.

Walvoord, E. C. (2010). The timing of puberty: Is it changing? Does it matter? *Journal of Adolescent Health, 47*(5), 433–439.

Wampold, B. E. (2001). *The great psychotherapy debate: Models, methods, and findings*. Lawrence Erlbaum.

Wampold, B. E. (2006). Designing a research study. In F. T. L. Leong & J. T. Austin (Eds.), *The psychology research handbook: A guide for graduate students and research assistants* (pp. 93–103). Sage.

Wampold, B. E. (2010a). *The basics of psychotherapy: An introduction to theory and practice*. American Psychological Association.

Wampold, B. E. (2010b). The research evidence for the common factors model: A historically situated perspective. In B. L. Duncan, S. D. Miller, B. E. Wampold, & M. A. Hubble (Eds.), *The heart & soul of change: Delivering what works in therapy* (2nd ed., pp. 49–81). American Psychological Association.

Wampold, B. E. (2015). How important are the common factors in psychotherapy? An update. *World Psychiatry, 14*(3), 270–277.

Wampold, B. E., & Imel, Z. E. (2015). *The great psychotherapy debate* (2nd ed.). Routledge.

Wang, A. Y., & Thomas, M. H. (2000). Looking for long-term effects on serial recall: The legacy of Simonides. *American Journal of Psychology, 113*(3), 331–340.

Wang, C. W., Chan, C. H., Ho, R. T., Chan, J. S., Ng, S. M., & Chan, C. L. (2014). Managing stress and anxiety through qigong exercise in healthy adults: A systematic review and meta-analysis of randomized controlled trials. *BMC Complementary and Alternative Medicine, 14*(1), 8.

Wang, F. (2008). Motivation and English achievement: An exploratory and confirmatory factor analysis of a new measure for Chinese students of English learning. *North American Journal of Psychology, 10*(3), 633–646.

Wang, H., Braun, C., & Enck, P. (2017). How the brain reacts to social stress (exclusion): A scoping review. *Neuroscience & Biobehavioral Reviews, 80*, 80–88.

Wang, H., Braun, C., & Enck, P. (2017). How the brain reacts to social stress (exclusion): A scoping review. *Neuroscience & Biobehavioral Reviews, 80*, 80–88.

Wang, H., Lin, S. L., Leung, G. M., & Schooling, C. M. (2016). Age at onset of puberty and adolescent depression: "Children of 1997" birth cohort. *Pediatrics, 137*(6), e20153231.

Wang, H., Qi, H., Wang, B. S., Cui, Y. Y., Zhu, L., Rong, Z. X., & Chen, H. Z. (2008). Is acupuncture beneficial in depression: A meta-analysis of 8 randomized controlled trials? *Journal of Affective Disorders, 111*(2), 125–134.

Wang, J. (2007). Mental health treatment dropout and its correlates in a general population sample. *Medical Care, 45*(3), 224–229.

Wang, J., Leu, J., & Shoda, Y. (2011). When the seemingly innocuous "stings": Racial microaggressions and their emotional consequences. *Personality and Social Psychology Bulletin, 37*(12), 1666–1678.

Wang, M. T., & Degol, J. L. (2017). Gender gap in science, technology, engineering, and mathematics (STEM): Current knowledge, implications for practice, policy, and future directions. *Educational Psychology Review, 29*(1), 119–140.

Wang, P. S., & Kessler, R. C. (2006). Global burden of mood disorders. In D. J. Stein, D. J. Kupfer, & A. F. Schatzberg (Eds.), *The American Psychiatric Publishing textbook of mood disorders* (pp. 55–68). American Psychiatric Association Publishing.

Wang, Q. (2004). The emergence of cultural self-constructs: Autobiographical memory and self-description in European American and Chinese children. *Developmental Psychology, 40*(1), 3–15.

Wang, Q. (2006). Earliest recollections of self and others in European American and Taiwanese young adults. *Psychological Science, 17*(8), 708–714.

Wang, Q. (2013). *The autobiographical self in time and culture*. Oxford University Press.

Wang, Q. (2018). Studying cognitive development in cultural context: A multi-level analysis approach. *Developmental Review, 50*(Part A), 54–64.

Wang, Q. (2021). The cultural foundation of human memory. *Annual Review of Psychology, 72*, 151–179. https://doi.org/10.1146/annurev-psych-070920-023638

Wang, Q., & Aydin, C. (2009). Cultural issues in flashbulb memory. In O. Luminet & A. Curci (Eds.), *Flashbulb memories: New issues and new perspectives* (pp. 247–268). Psychology Press.

Wang, Q., & Aydin, C. (2009). Cultural issues in flashbulb memory. In O. Luminet & A. Curci (Eds.), *Flashbulb memories: New issues and new perspectives* (pp. 247–268). Psychology Press.

Wang, Q., & Conway, M. A. (2004). The stories we keep: Autobiographical memory in American and Chinese middle-aged adults. *Journal of Personality, 72*(5), 911–938.

Wang, Q., Conway, M. A., & Hou, Y. (2004). Infantile amnesia: A cross-cultural investigation. *Cognitive Sciences, 1*(1), 123–135.

Wang, Q., Hou, Y., Koh, J. B. K., Song, Q., & Yang, Y. (2018). Culturally motivated remembering: The moderating role of culture for the relation of episodic memory to well-being. *Clinical Psychological Science, 6*(6), 860–871.

Wang, Q., & Ross, M. (2005). What we remember and what we tell: The effects of culture and self-priming on memory representations and narratives. *Memory, 13*(6), 594–606.

Wang, S., Yu, R., Tyszka, J. M., Zhen, S., Kovach, C., Sun, S., Huang, Y., Hurlemann, R., Ross, I. B., Chung, J. M., Mamelak, A. N., Adolphs, R., & Rutishauser, U. (2017). The human amygdala parametrically encodes the intensity of specific facial emotions and their categorical ambiguity. *Nature Communications, 8*, 14821.

Wapner, S., & Demick, J. (2003). Adult development: The holistic, developmental, and systems-oriented perspective. In J. Demick & C. Andreoletti (Eds.), *Handbook of adult development* (pp. 63–84). Springer Science+Business Media.

Warburton, W. A., Williams, K. D., & Cairns, D. R. (2006). When ostracism leads to aggression: The moderating effects of control deprivation. *Journal of Experimental Social Psychology, 42*(2), 213–220.

Ward, C., & Geeraert, N. (2016). Advancing acculturation theory and research: The acculturation process in its ecological context. *Current Opinion in Psychology, 8*, 98–104.

Ward, C., Leong, C. H., & Low, M. (2004). Personality and sojourner adjustment: An exploration of the big five and the cultural fit proposition. *Journal of Cross-Cultural Psychology, 35*(2), 137–151.

Ward, L. M., & Friedman, K. (2006). Using TV as a guide: Associations between television viewing and adolescents' sexual attitudes and behavior. *Journal of Research on Adolescence, 16*(1), 133–156.

Ward, L. M., Epstein, M., Caruthers, A., & Merriwether, A. (2011). Men's media use, sexual cognitions, and sexual risk behavior: Testing a mediational model. *Developmental Psychology, 47*(2), 592–602.

Ward, L. M., Erickson, S., Lippman, J., & Giaccardi, S. (2016). Sexual media content and effects. In J. Nussbaum (Ed.), Oxford research encyclopedia of communication. http://oxfordre.com/communication/view/10.1093/acrefore/9780190228613.001.0001/acrefore-9780190228613-e-2

Ward, L. M., Reed, L., Trinh, S. L., & Foust, M. (2014). Sexuality and entertainment media. In D. L. Tolman & L. M. Diamond (Eds.), *APA handbook of sexuality and psychology* (Vol. 2, pp. 373–423). American Psychological Association.

Ward, N. S., Oakley, D. A., Frackowiak, R. S. J., & Halligan, P. W. (2003). Differential brain activations during intentionally simulated and subjectively experienced paralysis. *Cognitive Neuropsychiatry, 8*(4), 295–312.

Wardle, J., & Cooke, L. (2005). The impact of obesity on psychological well-being. *Best Practice & Research Clinical Endocrinology & Metabolism, 19*(3), 421–440.

Wardle, J., Herrera, M. L., Cooke, L., & Gibson, E. L. (2003). Modifying children's food preferences: The effects of exposure and reward on acceptance of an unfamiliar vegetable. *European Journal of Clinical Nutrition, 57*(2), 341–348.

Warner, L. R., Settles, I. H., & Shields, S. A. (2018). Intersectionality theory in the psychology of women. In C. B. Travis, J. W. White, A. Rutherford, W. S. Williams, S. L. Cook, & K. F. Wyche (Eds.), *APA handbook of the psychology of women: History, theory, and battlegrounds* (APA Handbooks in Psychology series, pp. 521–539). American Psychological Association.

Warner, R. (2004). *Recovery from schizophrenia* (3rd ed.). Brunner-Routledge.

Wartella, E., & Robb, M. (2007). Young children, new media. *Journal of Children and Media, 1*(1), 35–44.

Warwick-Evans, L. A., Symons, N., Fitch, T., & Burrows, L. (1998). Evaluating sensory conflict and postural instability: Theories of motion sickness. *Brain Research Bulletin, 47*(5), 465–469.

Wason, P. C., & Johnson-Laird, P. N. (1972). *Psychology of reasoning: Structure and content*. Harvard University Press.

Wasow, T. (2001). Generative grammar. In M. Aronoff & J. Rees-Miller (Eds.), *The handbook of linguistics* (pp. 295–318). Blackwell.

Wasserman, J. D., & Tulsky, D. S. (2005). A history of intelligence assessment. In D. P. Flanagan & P. L. Harrison (Eds.), *Contemporary intellectual assessment: Theories, tests, and issues* (2nd ed., pp. 3–22). Guilford Press.

Watkins, C. E., Campbell, V. L., Nieberding, R., & Hallmark, R. (1995). Contemporary practice of psychological assessment by clinical psychologists. *Professional Psychology: Research and Practice, 26*(1), 54–60.

Watkins, P. C., Grimm, D. L., & Kolts, R. (2004). Counting your blessings: Positive memories among grateful persons. *Current Psychology, 23*(1), 52–67.

Watkins, P. C., Mathews, A., Williamson, D. A., & Fuller, R. D. (1992). Mood-congruent memory in depression: Emotional priming or elaboration? *Journal of Abnormal Psychology, 101*(3), 581–586.

Watkins, P. C., Vache, K., Verney, S. P., Muller, S., & Mathews, A. (1996). Unconscious mood-congruent memory bias in depression. *Journal of Abnormal Psychology, 105*(1), 34–41.

Watson, D., & Casillas, A. (2003). Neuroticism: Adaptive and maladaptive features. In E. C. Chang & L. J. Sanna (Eds.), *Virtue, vice, and personality: The complexity of behavior* (pp. 145–161). American Psychological Association.

Watson, J. B. (1913). Psychology as the behaviorist views it. *Psychological Review, 20*(2), 158–177.

Watson, J. B. (1914). *Behavior: An introduction to comparative psychology*. Henry Holt.

Watson, J. B. (1924). *Behaviorism*. People's Institute.

Watson, J. C., & Bohart, A. (2015). Humanistic/existential/phenomenological psychotherapy. In R. L. Cautin & S. O. Lilienfeld (Eds.), *The encyclopedia of clinical psychology* (pp. 1416–1425). Wiley-Blackwell.

Watson, J. C., & Schneider, K. (2016). Humanistic-existential theories. In J. C. Norcross, G. R. VandenBos, & D. K. Freedheim (Eds.), *APA handbook of clinical psychology* (Vol. 2, pp. 117–144). American Psychological Association.

Watson, J., & Pos, A. E. (2017). Humanistic and experiential perspectives. In R. J. DeRubeis & D. R. Strunk (Eds.), *The Oxford handbook of mood disorders* (pp. 459–468). Oxford University Press.

Watson, R. I. (1973). Investigation into deindividuation using a cross-cultural survey technique. *Journal of Personality and Social Psychology, 25*(3), 342–345.

Watson, R. I., Sr., & Evans, R. B. (1991). *The great psychologists*. HarperCollins.

Watt, H. M. G. (2010). Gender and occupational choice. In J. C. Chrisler & D. R. McCreary (Eds.), *Handbook of gender research in psychology* (pp. 379–400). Springer Science+Business Media.

Watters, E. (2010). *Crazy like us: The globalization of the American psyche*. Free Press.

Waxman, S. R., & Leddon, E. M. (2011). Early word-learning and conceptual development: Everything had a name, and each name gave birth to a new thought. In U. Goswami (Ed.), *The Wiley-Blackwell handbook of childhood cognitive development* (2nd ed., pp. 180–208). Wiley-Blackwell.

Way, N. (2006). The cultural practice of close friendships among urban adolescents in the United States. In X. Chen, D. French, & B. Schneider (Eds.), *Peer relationships in cultural context* (pp. 403–425). Cambridge University Press.

Wear, D., Aultman, J. M., Varley, J. D., & Zarconi, J. (2006). Making fun of patients: Medical students' perceptions and use of derogatory and cynical humor in clinical settings. *Academic Medicine, 81*(5), 454–462.

Wearing, D. (2005). *Forever today: A memoir of love and amnesia*. Doubleday.

Weathers, F. W. (2018). DSM-5 diagnostic criteria for PTSD. In C. B. Nemeroff & C. R. Marmar (Eds.), *Post-traumatic stress disorder* (pp. 31–48). Oxford University Press.

Weaver, J. B. (2003). Individual differences in television viewing motives. *Personality and Individual Differences, 35*(6), 1427–1437.

Weaver, T. E., & Ye, L. (2012). Sleep-related breathing disorders. In C. M. Morin & C. A. Espie (Eds.), *The Oxford handbook of sleep and sleep disorders* (pp. 666–689). Oxford University Press.

Webb, T. L., Lindquist, K. A., Jones, K., Avishai, A., & Sheeran, P. (2018). Situation selection is a particularly effective emotion regulation strategy for people who need help regulating their emotions. *Cognition and Emotion, 32*(2), 231–248.

Webb, T. L., Miles, E., & Sheeran, P. (2012). Dealing with feeling: A meta-analysis of the effectiveness of strategies derived from the process model of emotion regulation. *Psychological Bulletin, 138*(4), 775–808.

Webb, W. B., & Agnew, H. W., Jr. (1974). Regularity in the control of the free-running sleep-wakefulness rhythm. *Aerospace Medicine, 45*(7), 701–704.

Weber, B. (2009, December 26). Kim Peek, inspiration for "Rain Man," dies at 58. *The New York Times*. http://www.nytimes.com/2009/12/27/us/27peek.html?_r=2&

Weber, N., & Brewer, N. (2003). Expert memory: The interaction of stimulus structure, attention, and expertise. *Applied Cognitive Psychology, 17*(3), 295–308.

Webster, G. D., Graber, J. A., Gesselman, A. N., Crosier, B. S., & Schember, T. O. (2014). A life history theory of father absence and menarche: A meta-analysis. *Evolutionary Psychology, 12*(2), 147470491401200202.

Webster, M. (2010). Color perception. In E. B. Goldstein, *Encyclopedia of perception* (pp. 266–270). Sage.

Weems, C. F., Russell, J. D., Banks, D. M., Graham, R. A., Neill, E. L., & Scott, B. G. (2014). Memories of traumatic events in childhood fade after experiencing similar less stressful events: Results from two natural experiments. *Journal of Experimental Psychology: General, 143*(5), 2046–2055.

Weems, C. F., Scott, B. G., Banks, D. M., & Graham, R. A. (2012). Is TV traumatic for all youths? The role of preexisting posttraumatic-stress symptoms in the link between disaster coverage and stress. *Psychological Science, 23*(11), 1293–1297.

Wegenek, A. R., Buskist, W., & American Psychological Association. (2010). *The insider's guide to the psychology major: Everything you need to know about the degree and profession*. American Psychological Association.

Wehling, E. (2018). Politics and framing: How language impacts political thought. In C. Cotter & D. Perrin (Eds.), *The Routledge handbook of language and media* (pp. 136–150). Routledge.

Wehrens, S. M., Christou, S., Isherwood, C., Middleton, B., Gibbs, M. A., Archer, S. N., Skene, D. J., & Johnston, J. D. (2017). Meal timing regulates the human circadian system. *Current Biology, 27*(12), 1768–1775.

Weimer, S. M., Dise, T. L., Evers, P. B., Ortiz, M. A., Welidaregay, W., & Steinmann, W. C. (2002). Prevalence, predictors, and attitudes toward cosleeping in an urban pediatric center. *Clinical Pediatrics, 41*(6), 433–438.

Weinberg, R. (2004). *94: Derek and dad finish Olympic 400 together.* http://espn.go.com/espn/espn25/story?page=moments/94./

Weiner, B. (1993). On sin versus sickness: A theory of perceived responsibility and social motivation. *American Psychologist, 48*(9), 957–965.

Weiner, B., Perry, R. P., & Magnusson, J. (1988). An attributional analysis of reactions to stigmas. *Journal of Personality and Social Psychology, 55*(5), 738–748.

Weiner, D. B. (1994). "Le geste de Pinel": The history of a psychiatric myth. In M. S. Micale & R. Porter (Eds.), *Discovering the history of psychiatry* (pp. 232–247). Oxford University Press.

Weiner, I. B. (2004). Rorschach inkblot method. In M. W. Maruish (Ed.), *The use of psychological testing for treatment planning and outcomes assessment* (3rd ed., Vol. 3, pp. 553–587). Lawrence Erlbaum.

Weiner, I. B. (2016). Individual psychotherapy. In J. C. Norcross, G. R. VandenBos, & D. K. Freedheim (Eds.), *APA handbook of clinical psychology* (Vol. 3, pp. 269–288). American Psychological Association.

Weingarten, C. P., & Strauman, T. J. (2015). Neuroimaging for psychotherapy research: Current trends. *Psychotherapy Research, 25*(2), 185–213.

Weinstein, E. C., & Selman, R. L. (2016). Digital stress: Adolescents' personal accounts. *New Media & Society, 18*(3), 391–409.

Weinstein, E. C., Selman, R. L., Thomas, S., Kim, J. E., White, A. E., & Dinakar, K. (2016). How to cope with digital stress: The recommendations adolescents offer their peers online. *Journal of Adolescent Research, 31*(4), 415–441.

Weinstein, N., & Ryan, R. M. (2010). When helping helps: Autonomous motivation for prosocial behavior and its influence on well-being for the helper and recipient. *Journal of Personality and Social Psychology, 98*(2), 222–244.

Weisberg, D. S., Keil, F. C., Goodstein, J., Rawson, E., & Gray, J. R. (2008). The seductive allure of neuroscience explanations. *Journal of Cognitive Neuroscience, 20*(3), 470–477.

Weisberg, R. W. (2015). Toward an integrated theory of insight in problem solving. *Thinking & Reasoning, 21*(1), 5–39.

Weisberg, R. W. (2018a). Problem solving. In L. J. Ball & V. A. Thompson (Eds.), *Routledge international handbook of thinking and reasoning* (pp. 607–623). Routledge.

Weisberg, R. W. (2018b). Reflections on a personal journey studying the psychology of creativity. In R. J. Sternberg & J. C. Kaufman (Eds.), *The nature of human creativity* (pp. 351–373). Cambridge University Press.

Weisenberger, J. M. (2001). Cutaneous perception. In E. B. Goldstein (Ed.), *Blackwell handbook of perception* (pp. 535–566). Blackwell.

Weiss, S. J. (2014). Instrumental and classical conditioning: Intersections, interactions, and stimulus control. In F. K. McSweeney & E. S. Murphy (Eds.), *The Wiley-Blackwell handbook of operant and classical conditioning* (pp. 417–450). Wiley.

Weissman, M. M. (1995). *Mastering depression: A patient's guide to interpersonal psychotherapy*. Graywind.

Weissmark, M. S., & Giacomo, D. A. (1998). *Doing psychotherapy effectively*. University of Chicago Press.

Weisz, J. R., Rothbaum, F. M., & Blackburn, T. C. (1984). Standing out and standing in: The psychology of control in America and Japan. *American Psychologist, 39*(9), 955–969.

Welchman, K. (2000). *Erik Erikson: His life, work and significance*. Open University Press.

Welfel, E. R., Werth, J. L., Jr., & Benjamin, G. A. H. (2012). Treating clients who threaten others or themselves. In S. J. Knapp (Ed.), *APA handbook of ethics in psychology* (Vol. 1, pp. 377–400). American Psychological Association.

Wellman, H. M. (2011). Developing a theory of mind. In U. Goswami (Ed.), *The Wiley-Blackwell handbook of childhood cognitive development* (2nd ed., pp. 258–284). Wiley-Blackwell.

Wellman, H. M., Cross, D., & Watson, J. (2003). Meta-analysis of theory-of-mind development: The truth about false belief. *Child Development, 72*(3), 655–684.

Wells, W. R. (1923). The anti-instinct fallacy. *Psychological Review, 30*(3), 228–234.

Wentzel, K. R. (2003). Sociometric status and adjustment in middle school: A longitudinal study. *The Journal of Early Adolescence, 23*(1), 5–28.

Wentzel, K. R., Barry, C. M., & Caldwell, K. A. (2004). Friendships in middle school: Influences on motivation and school adjustment. *Journal of Educational Psychology, 96*(2), 195–203.

Wenzel, A. (2017). Cognitive-behavioral therapies in practice. In A. J. Consoli, L. E. Beutler, & B. Bongar (Eds.), *Comprehensive textbook of psychotherapy: Theory and practice* (2nd ed., pp. 76–90). Oxford University Press.

Wenzlaff, R. M., Meier, J. S., & Salas, D. M. (2002). Thought suppression and memory biases during and after depressive moods. *Cognition & Emotion, 16*, 403–422.

Wermter, A. K., Laucht, M., Schimmelmann, B. G., Banaschweski, T., Sonuga-Barke, E. J., Rietschel, M., & Becker, K. (2010). From nature versus nurture, via nature and nurture, to gene × environment interaction in mental disorders. *European Child & Adolescent Psychiatry, 19*(3), 199–210.

Werner, S., & Thies, B. (2000). Is "change blindness" attenuated by domain-specific expertise? An expert–novices comparison of change detection in football images. *Visual Cognition, 7*(1–3), 163–173.

Werner-Seidler, A., Tan, L., & Dalgleish, T. (2017). The vicissitudes of positive autobiographical recollection as an emotion regulation strategy in depression. *Clinical Psychological Science, 5*(1), 26–36.

Werth, J. L., Hastings, S. L., & Riding-Malon, R. (2010). Ethical challenges of practicing in rural areas. *Journal of Clinical Psychology, 66*(5), 537–548.

Werth, R. (2006). Visual functions without the occipital lobe or after cerebral hemispherectomy in infancy. *European Journal of Neuroscience, 24*(10), 2932–2944.

Wertheimer, M. (2012). *A brief history of psychology* (5th ed.). Psychology Press.

Wertsch, J. V., & Tulviste, P. (1992). L. S. Vygotsky and contemporary developmental psychology. *Developmental Psychology, 28*(4), 548–557.

Wertz, A. T., Ronda, J. M., Czeisler, C. A., & Wright, K. P. (2006). Effects of sleep inertia on cognition. *JAMA, 295*(2), 159–164.

Wessely, S. (2008). How shyness became social phobia. *The Lancet, 371*(9618), 1063–1064.

West, C., & Zimmerman, D. H. (1983). Small insults: A study of interruptions in cross-sex conversations between unacquainted persons. In B. Thorne, C. Kramarae, & N. Henley (Eds.), *Language, gender and society* (pp. 102–117). Newbury House.

West, M. A. (1987). Traditional and psychological perspectives on meditation. In M. A. West (Ed.), *The psychology of meditation* (pp. 5–22). Oxford University Press.

Westbrook, G. L. (2013). Seizures and epilepsy. In E. R. Kandel, J. H. Schwartz, T. M. Jessell, S. A. Siegelbaum, & A. J. Hudspeth (Eds.), *Principles of neural science* (5th ed., pp. 1116–1139). McGraw-Hill.

Westbrook, J. I., Raban, M. Z., Walter, S. R., & Douglas, H. (2018). Task errors by emergency physicians are associated with interruptions, multitasking, fatigue and working memory capacity: A prospective, direct observation study. *BMJ Quality and Safety, 27*(8), 655–663. https://doi.org/10.1136/bmjqs-2017-007333

Westen, D., Gabbard, G. O., & Ortigo, K. M. (2008). Psychoanalytic approaches to personality. In O. P. John, R. W. Robins, & L. A. Pervin (Eds.), *Handbook of personality: Theory and research* (3rd ed., pp. 61–113). Guilford Press.

Westen, D., Novotny, C. M., & Thompson-Brenner, H. (2004). The empirical status of empirically supported psychotherapies: Assumptions, findings, and reporting in controlled clinical trials. *Psychological Bulletin, 130*(4), 631–663.

Westerhof, G. J., & Bohlmeijer, E. T. (2014). Celebrating fifty years of research and applications in reminiscence and life review: State of the art and new directions. *Journal of Aging Studies, 29*, 107–114.

Westerwick, A., Johnson, B. K., & Knobloch-Westerwick, S. (2017). Confirmation biases in selective exposure to political online information: Source bias vs. content bias. *Communication Monographs, 84*(3), 343–364.

Wever, R. A. (1984). Sex differences in human circadian rhythms: Intrinsic periods and sleep fractions. *Experientia, 40*(11), 1226–1234.

Weyrauch, D., Schwartz, M., Hart, B., Klug, M. G., & Burd, L. (2017). Comorbid mental disorders in fetal alcohol spectrum disorders: A systematic review. *Journal of Developmental & Behavioral Pediatrics, 38*(4), 283–291.

Wheeler, L., Reis, H., & Nezlek, J. B. (1983). Loneliness, social interaction, and sex roles. *Journal of Personality and Social Psychology, 45*(4), 943–953.

Wheeler, M. A. (2000). Episodic memory and autonoetic awareness. In E. Tulving & F. I. M. Craik (Eds.), *The Oxford handbook of memory* (pp. 597–608). Oxford University Press.

Whillans, A. V., Weidman, A. C., & Dunn, E. W. (2016). Valuing time over money is associated with greater happiness. *Social Psychological and Personality Science, 7*(3), 213–222.

Whitaker, R. (2015). The triumph of American psychiatry: How it created the modern therapeutic state. *European Journal of Psychotherapy & Counselling, 17*(4), 326–341.

White, B. P., Becker-Blease, K. A., & Grace-Bishop, K. (2006). Stimulant medication use, misuse, and abuse in an undergraduate and graduate student sample. *Journal of American College Health, 54*(5), 261–268.

Whitehurst, G. J., Falco, F. L., Lonigan, C. J., Fischel, J. E., DeBaryshe, B. D., Valdez-Menchaca, M. C., & Caulfield, M. (1988). Accelerating language development through picture book reading. *Developmental Psychology, 24*(4), 552–559.

Whiteman, S. D., McHale, S. M. and Crouter, A. C. (2003), What parents learn from experience: The first child as a first draft? *Journal of Marriage and Family, 65*(3), 608–621.

Whiting, B. B., & Edwards, C. P. (1988). *Children of different worlds: The formation of social behavior*. Harvard University Press.

Whiting, S., Buoncristiano, M., Gelius, P., Abu-Omar, K., Pattison, M., Hyska, J., Duleva, V., Musić Milanović, S., Zamrazilová, H., Hejgaard, T., Rasmussen, M., Nurk, E., Shengelia, L., Kelleher, C. C., Heinen, M. M., Spinelli, A., Nardone, P., Abildina, A., Abdrakhmanova, S., … & Breda, J. (2021). Physical activity, screen time, and sleep duration of children aged 6–9 years in 25 countries: An analysis within the WHO European Childhood Obesity Surveillance Initiative (COSI) 2015–2017. *Obesity Facts, 14*(1), 32–44. https://doi.org/10.1159/000511263

Whitmer, R. A., Gunderson, E. P., Barrett-Connor, E., Quesenberry, C. P., Jr., & Yaffe, K. (2005). Obesity in middle age and future risk of dementia: A 27 year longitudinal population based study. *BMJ: British Medical Journal, 330*(7504), 1360–1362.

Whitney, P., & Rosen, P. J. (2013). Sleep deprivation and performance: The role of working memory. In T. P. Alloway & R. G. Alloway (Eds.), *Working memory: The connected intelligence* (pp. 175–186). Psychology Press.

Whittaker, E., & Kowalski, R. M. (2015). Cyberbullying via social media. *Journal of School Violence, 14*(1), 11–29.

Whooley, O., & Horwitz, A. V. (2013). The paradox of professional success: Grand ambition, furious resistance, and the derailment of the DSM-5 revision process. In J. Paris & J. Phillips (Eds.), *Making the DSM-5: Concepts and controversies* (pp. 75–92). Springer Science+Business Media.

Whorf, B. L. (1956). *Language, thought, and reality* (J. Carroll, Ed.). MIT Press.

Wicke, P., & Bolognesi, M. M. (2020). Framing COVID-19: How we conceptualize and discuss the pandemic on Twitter. *PloS One, 15*(9), e0240010. https://doi.org/10.1371/journal.pone.0240010

Wickwire, E. M., Shaya, F. T., & Scharf, S. M. (2016). Health economics of insomnia treatments: The return on investment for a good night's sleep. *Sleep Medicine Reviews, 30*, 72–82.

Widiger, T. A. (2005). Classification and diagnosis: Historical development and contemporary issues. In J. E. Maddux & B. A. Winstead (Eds.), *Psychopathology* (pp. 63–83). Lawrence Erlbaum.

Widiger, T. A. (2017). Introduction. In T. A. Widiger (Ed.), *The Oxford handbook of the Five Factor Model* (pp. 1–10). Oxford University Press.

Widiger, T. A., & Costa, P. T. (2012). *Personality disorders and the five-factor model of personality* (3rd ed.). American Psychological Association.

Widiger, T. A., & Edmundson, M. (2011). Diagnoses, dimensions, and DSM-5. In D. H. Barlow (Ed.), *The Oxford handbook of clinical psychology* (pp. 254–278). Oxford University Press.

Widiger, T. A., & Lowe, J. R. (2010). Personality disorders. In M. M. Antony & D. H. Barlow (Eds.), *Handbook of assessment and treatment planning for psychological disorders* (2nd ed., pp. 571–605). Guilford Press.

Widiger, T. A., & Mullins-Sweatt, S. (2008). Personality disorders. In A. Tasman, J. Kay, J. A. Lieberman, M. B. First, & M. Maj (Eds.), *Psychiatry* (3rd ed., Vol. 2, pp. 1718–1753). Wiley.

Widiger, T. A., & Trull, T. J. (2007). Plate tectonics in the classification of personality disorder: Shifting to a dimensional model. *American Psychologist, 62*(2), 71–83.

Widom, C. S., Czaja, S. J., Kozakowski, S. S., & Chauhan, P. (2018). Does adult attachment style mediate the relationship between childhood maltreatment and mental and physical health outcomes? *Child Abuse & Neglect, 76*, 533–545.

Widome, R., Berger, A. T., Iber, C., Wahlstrom, K., Laska, M. N., Kilian, G., Redline, S., & Erickson, D. J. (2020). Association of delaying school start time with sleep duration, timing, and quality among adolescents. *JAMA Pediatrics, 174*(7), 697–704. https://doi:10.1001/jamapediatrics.2020.0344

Wiemers, U. S., Sauvage, M. M., & Wolf, O. T. (2014). Odors as effective retrieval cues for stressful episodes. *Neurobiology of Learning and Memory, 112*, 230–236.

Wierson, M., Long, P. J., & Forehand, R. L. (1993). Toward a new understanding of early menarche: The role of environmental stress in pubertal timing. *Adolescence, 28*(112), 913–924.

Wilcox, L. M., & Allison, R. S. (2010). Binocular vision and stereopsis. In E. B. Goldstein (Ed.), *Encyclopedia of perception* (pp. 208–212). Sage.

Wilcutt, E. G. (2012). The prevalence of DSM-IV attention-deficit/hyperactivity disorder: A meta-analytic review. *Neurotherapeutics, 9*(3), 490–499.

Wild, S. H., Roglic, G., Green, A., Sicree, R., & King, H. (2004). Global prevalence of diabetes: Estimates for the year 2000 and projections for 2030. *Diabetes Care, 27*(5), 1047–1053.

Wiley, R. E., & Berman, S. L. (2013). Adolescent identity development and distress in a clinical sample. *Journal of Clinical Psychology, 69*(12), 1299–1304. https://doi.org/10.1002/jclp.22004

Wilgus, J., & Wilgus, B. (2009). Face to face with Phineas Gage. *Journal of the History of the Neurosciences, 18*(3), 340–345.

Wilkinson, S., & DeJong, M. (2021). Dissociative identity disorder: A developmental perspective. *BJPsych Advances, 27*(2), 96–98. https://doi.org/10.1192/bja.2020.35

Willcutt, E. G., & Pennington, B. F. (2000). Psychiatric comorbidity in children and adolescents with reading disability. *Journal of Child Psychology and Psychiatry, 41*(08), 1039–1048.

Williams, A. A., & Marquez, B. A. (2015). The lonely selfie king: Selfies and the conspicuous prosumption of gender and race. *International Journal of Communication, 9*(1), 1775–1787.

Williams, A. D., & Moulds, M. L. (2010). The content, nature, and persistence of intrusive memories in depression. In J. H. Mace (Ed.), *The act of remembering: Toward an understanding of how we recall the past* (pp. 361–383). Wiley-Blackwell.

Williams, C. L., & Butcher, J. N. (2011). *A beginner's guide to the MMPI-A*. American Psychological Association.

Williams, D. R., Lawrence, J. A., & Davis, B. A. (2019). Racism and health: Evidence and needed research. *Annual Review of Public Health, 40*, 105–125. https://doi.org/10.1146/annurev-publhealth-040218-043750

Williams, G. C., Cox, E. M., Hedberg, V. A., & Deci, E. L. (2000). Extrinsic life goals and health-risk behaviors in adolescents. *Journal of Applied Social Psychology, 30*(8), 1756–1771.

Williams, G. C., Freedman, Z. R., & Deci, E. L. (1998). Supporting autonomy to motivate patients with diabetes for glucose control. *Diabetes Care, 21*(10), 1644–1651.

Williams, G. C., Grow, V. M., Freedman, Z. R., Ryan, R. M., & Deci, E. L. (1996). Motivational predictors of weight loss and weight-loss maintenance. *Journal of Personality and Social Psychology, 70*(1), 115–126.

Williams, G. C., McGregor, H., Sharp, D., Kouides, R. W., Lévesque, C. S., Ryan, R. M., & Deci, E. L. (2006a). A self-determination multiple risk intervention trial to improve smokers' health. *Journal of General Internal Medicine, 21*(12), 1288–1294.

Williams, G. C., McGregor, H. A., Sharp, D., Lévesque, C., Kouides, R. W., Ryan, R. M., & Deci, E. L. (2006b). Testing a self-determination theory intervention for motivating tobacco cessation: Supporting autonomy and competence in a clinical trial. *Health Psychology, 25*(1), 91–101.

Williams, K., Harkins, S. G., & Latané, B. (1981). Identifiability as a deterrent to social loafing: Two cheering experiments. *Journal of Personality and Social Psychology, 40*(2), 303–311.

Williams, K. A., Kolar, M. M., Reger, B. E., & Pearson, J. C. (2001). Evaluation of a wellness-based mindfulness stress reduction intervention: A controlled trial. *American Journal of Health Promotion, 15*(6), 422–432.

Williams, M. T. (2020). Microaggressions: Clarification, evidence, and impact. *Perspectives on Psychological Science, 15*(1), 3–26. https://doi.org/10.1177/1745691619827499

Williams, M., Davids, K., Burwitz, L., & Williams, J. (1993). Cognitive knowledge and soccer performance. *Perceptual and Motor Skills, 76*(2), 579–593.

Williams, R. L. (1972). *The BITCH Test (Black Intelligence Test of Cultural Homogeneity)*. Williams and Associates.

Williams, T., Connolly, J., Pepler, D., & Craig, W. (2003). Questioning and sexual minority adolescents: High school experiences of bullying, sexual harassment and physical abuse. *Canadian Journal of Community Mental Health, 22*(2), 47–58.

Willinger, M., Ko, C. W., Hoffman, H. J., Kessler, R. C., & Corwin, M. J. (2003). Trends in infant bed sharing in the United States, 1993–2000: The National Infant Sleep Position study. *Archives of Pediatrics & Adolescent Medicine, 157*(1), 43–49.

Willis, J. O., Dumont, R., & Kaufman, A. S. (2011). Factor-analytic models of intelligence. In R. J. Sternberg & S. B. Kaufman (Eds.), *The Cambridge handbook of intelligence* (pp. 39–57). Cambridge University Press.

Willis, M. S., Esqueda, C. W., & Schacht, R. N. (2008). Social perceptions of individuals missing upper front teeth. *Perceptual and Motor Skills, 106*(2), 423–435.

Willis, M., & Smith, R. (2021). Sexual consent across diverse behaviors and contexts: Gender differences and nonconsensual sexual experiences. *Journal of Interpersonal Violence*, https://doi.org/10.1177/08862605211044101

Willis, R. W., & Edwards, J. A. (1969). A study of the comparative effectiveness of systematic desensitization and implosive therapy. *Behaviour Research and Therapy, 7*(4), 387–395.

Wilson, R. S., de Leon, C. F. M., Bienias, J. L., Evans, D. A., & Bennett, D. A. (2004). Personality and mortality in old age. *The Journals of Gerontology Series B: Psychological Sciences and Social Sciences, 59*(3), P110–P116.

Wilson, T. D., Aronson, E., & Carlsmith, K. (2010). The art of laboratory experimentation. In S. T. Fiske, D. T. Gilbert, & G. Lindzey (Eds.), *Handbook of social psychology* (5th ed., Vol.1, pp. 51–82). Wiley.

Wilson, T. D., Wheatley, T., Meyers, J. M., Gilbert, D. T., & Axsom, D. (2000). Focalism: A source of durability bias in affective forecasting. *Journal of Personality and Social Psychology, 78*(5), 821–836.

Wimmer, H., & Perner, J. (1983). Beliefs about beliefs: Representation and constraining function of wrong beliefs in young children's understanding of deception. *Cognition, 13*(1), 103–128.

Windholz, G. (1997). Ivan P. Pavlov: An overview of his life and psychological work. *American Psychologist, 52*(9), 941–946.

Winer, J. P., Parent, J., Forehand, R., & Breslend, N. L. (2016). Interactive effects of psychosocial stress and early pubertal timing on youth depression and anxiety: Contextual amplification in family and peer environments. *Journal of Child and Family Studies, 25*(5), 1375–1384.

Winerman, L. (2017). By the numbers: APA at its 125th anniversary: A snapshot of the association in its quasquicentennial year. *Monitor on Psychology, 48*(5), 80.

Wingate, L. (2011). Black Intelligence Test of Cultural Homogeneity. In S. Goldstein & J. A. Naglieri (Eds.), *Encyclopedia of child behavior and development* (pp. 261–262). Springer.

Winickoff, J. P., Friebely, J., Tanski, S. E., Sherrod, C., Matt, G. E., Hovell, M. F., & McMillen, R. C. (2009). Beliefs about the health effects of "thirdhand" smoke and home smoking bans. *Pediatrics, 123*(1), e74–e79.

Winkelman, J. W. (1998). Clinical and polysomnographic features of sleep-related eating disorder. *The Journal of Clinical Psychiatry, 59*(1), 14–19.

Winocur, G., McDonald, R. M., & Moscovitch, M. (2001). Anterograde and retrograde amnesia in rats with large hippocampal lesions. *Hippocampus, 11*(1), 18–26.

Winpenny, E. M., Marteau, T. M., & Nolte, E. (2013). Exposure of children and adolescents to alcohol marketing on social media websites. *Alcohol and Alcoholism, 49*(2), 154–159.

Winston, J. S., Gottfried, J. A., Kilner, J. M., & Dolan, R. J. (2005). Integrated neural representations of odor intensity and affective valence in human amygdala. *The Journal of Neuroscience, 25*(39), 8903–8907.

Winter, W. C., Hammond, W. R., Green, N. H., Zhang, Z., & Bliwise, D. L. (2009). Measuring circadian advantage in Major League Baseball: A 10-year retrospective study. *International Journal of Sports Physiology and Performance, 4*(3), 394–401.

Winton, W. M. (1987). Do introductory textbooks present the Yerkes-Dodson Law correctly? *American Psychologist, 42*(2), 202–203.

Wirtz, P. H., & von Känel, R. (2017). Psychological stress, inflammation, and coronary heart disease. *Current Cardiology Reports, 19*(11), 1–10. https://doi.org/10.1007/s11886-017-0919-x

Wise, E. A., Price, D. D., Myers, C. D., Heft, M. W., & Robinson, M. E. (2002). Gender role expectations of pain: Relationship to experimental pain perception. *Pain, 96*(3), 335–342. https://doi.org/10.1016/S0304-3959(01)00473-0

Wise, M. J. (2018). Naps and sleep deprivation: Why academic libraries should consider adding nap stations to their services for students. *New Review of Academic Librarianship, 24*(2), 192–210.

Witcomb, G. L., Bouman, W. P., Claes, L., Brewin, N., Crawford, J. R., & Arcelus, J. (2018). Levels of depression in transgender people and its predictors: Results of a large matched control study with transgender people accessing clinical services. *Journal of Affective Disorders, 235*, 308–315.

Witt, S. D. (2000). The influence of peers on children's socialization to gender roles. *Early Child Development and Care, 162*(1), 1–7. https://doi.org/10.1080/0300443001620101

Wixted, J. (2010). The role of retroactive interference and consolidation in everyday forgetting. In S. Della Sala (Ed.), *Forgetting* (pp. 285–312). Psychology Press.

Wolf, A. W., Lozoff, B., Latz, S., & Paludetto, R. (1996). Parental theories in the management of young children's sleep in Japan, Italy, and the United States. In S. Harkness & C. M. Super (Eds.), *Parent's cultural belief systems: Their origins, expressions, and consequences* (pp. 364–384). Guilford Press.

Wolfe, B. E. (2012). Healing the research–practice split: Let's start with me. *Psychotherapy, 49*(2), 101–108.

Wolf-Meyer, M. (2013). Where have all our naps gone? Or Nathaniel Kleitman, the consolidation of sleep, and the historiography of emergence. *Anthropology of Consciousness, 24*(2), 96–116.

Wolfson, A. R., & Carskadon, M. A. (2003). Understanding adolescents' sleep patterns and school performance: A critical appraisal. *Sleep Medicine Reviews, 7*(6), 491–506.

Wolfson, A. R., & O'Malley, E. B. (2012). Sleep-related problems in adolescence and emerging adulthood. In C. M. Morin & C. A. Espie (Eds.), *The Oxford handbook of sleep and sleep disorders* (pp. 746–768). Oxford University Press.

Wolfson, A. R., & Richards, M. (2011). Young adolescents: Struggles with insufficient sleep. In M. El-Sheikh (Ed.), *Sleep and development: Familial and socio-cultural considerations* (pp. 265–299). Oxford University Press.

Wolfson, A. R., Spaulding, N. L., Dandrow, C., & Baroni, E. M. (2007). Middle school start times: The importance of a good night's sleep for young adolescents. *Behavioral Sleep Medicine, 5*(3), 194–209.

Wolf-Wendel, L., Ward, K., & Kinzie, J. (2009). A tangled web of terms: The overlap and unique contribution of involvement, engagement, and integration to understanding college student success. *Journal of College Student Development, 50*(4), 407–428.

Wolitzky, D. L. (2016). Psychoanalytic theories. In J. C. Norcross, G. R. VandenBos, & D. K. Freedheim (Eds.), *APA handbook of clinical psychology* (Vol. 2, pp. 19–52). American Psychological Association.

Wolman, D. (2012). The split brain: A tale of two halves. *Nature, 483*(7389), 260–263.

Wolpe, J. (1958). *Psychotherapy by reciprocal inhibition*. Stanford University Press.

Wolpe, J. (1969). *The practice of behavior therapy*. Pergamon Press.

Wolpert, D. M., Pearson, K. G., & Ghez, C. P. J. (2013). The organization and planning of movement. In E. R. Kandel, J. H. Schwartz, T. M. Jessell, S. A. Siegelbaum, & A. J. Hudspeth (Eds.), *Principles of neural science* (5th ed., pp. 743–767). McGraw-Hill.

Wolters, C. A. (2004). Advancing achievement goal theory: Using goal structures and goal orientations to predict students' motivation, cognition, and achievement. *Journal of Educational Psychology, 96*(2), 236–250.

Wong, C. C. Y., Correa, A., Robinson, K., & Lu, Q. (2017). The roles of acculturative stress and social constraints on psychological distress in Hispanic/Latino and Asian immigrant college students. *Cultural Diversity and Ethnic Minority Psychology, 23*(3), 398–406.

Wong, G., Derthick, A. O., David, E. J. R., Saw, A., & Okazaki, S. (2014). The what, the why, and the how: A review of racial microaggressions research in psychology. *Race and Social Problems, 6*(2), 181–200.

Wong-Padoongpatt, G., Zane, N., Okazaki, S., & Saw, A. (2017). Decreases in implicit self-esteem explain the racial impact of microaggressions among Asian Americans. *Journal of Counseling Psychology, 64*(5), 574–583.

Wood, A. M., Froh, J. J., & Geraghty, A. W. (2010). Gratitude and well-being: A review and theoretical integration. *Clinical Psychology Review, 30*(7), 890–905.

Wood, C., Jackson, E., Hart, L., Plester, B., & Wilde, L. (2011). The effect of text messaging on 9- and 10-year-old children's reading, spelling and phonological processing skills. *Journal of Computer Assisted Learning, 27*(1), 28–36.

Wood, J. M., Garb, H. N., & Nezworski, M. T. (2007). Psychometrics: Better measurement makes better clinicians. In S. O. Lilienfeld & W. T. O'Donohue (Eds.), *The great ideas of clinical science: 17 principles that every mental health professional should understand* (pp. 77–92). Routledge.

Wood, J. M., Nezworski, M. T., Lilienfeld, S. O., & Garb, H. N. (2003). *What's wrong with the Rorschach?* Jossey-Bass.

Wood, M. A., Bukowski, W. M., & Lis, E. (2016). The digital self: How social media serves as a setting that shapes youth's emotional experiences. *Adolescent Research Review, 1*(2), 163–173.

Wood, N., & Cowan, N. (1995). The cocktail party phenomenon revisited: How frequent are attention shifts to one's name in an irrelevant auditory channel? *Journal of Experimental Psychology: Learning, Memory, and Cognition, 21*(1), 255–260.

Wood, W., & Eagly, A. H. (2010). Gender. In S. T. Fiske, D. T. Gilbert, & G. Lindzey (Eds.), *Handbook of social psychology* (5th ed., Vol. 1, pp. 629–667). Wiley.

Woodbury, D., & Black, I. B. (2004). Stem cell plasticity: Overview and perspective. In M. S. Gazzaniga (Ed.), *The cognitive neurosciences III* (pp. 161–170). MIT Press.

Woody, S. R., & Nosen, E. (2009). Psychological models of phobic disorders and panic. In M. M. Antony & M. B. Stein (Eds.), *Oxford handbook of anxiety and related disorders* (pp. 209–224). Oxford University Press.

Wool, Z. H. (2013). War sick: Meaningful illness and military victimhood. *Focaal: Journal of Global and Historical Anthropology, 66*, 139–147.

Workman, M. (2018). An empirical study of social media exchanges about a controversial topic: Confirmation bias and participant characteristics. *The Journal of Social Media in Society, 7*(1), 381–400.

World Health Organization. (2003). *Joint WHO/FAO Expert Consultation on Diet, Nutrition, and the Prevention of Chronic Disease*. Author.

Worringham, C. J., & Messick, D. M. (1983). Social facilitation of running: An unobtrusive study. *The Journal of Social Psychology, 121*(1), 23–29.

Worthen, J. B., & Hunt, R. R. (2011). *Mnemonology: Mnemonics for the 21st century*. Psychology Press.

Worthen, M. G. (2014). The interactive impacts of high school gay-straight alliances (GSAs) on college student attitudes toward LGBT individuals: An investigation of high school characteristics. *Journal of Homosexuality, 61*(2), 217–250.

Worthman, C. M. (2011). Developmental cultural ecology of sleep. In M. El-Sheikh (Ed.), *Sleep and development: Familial and socio-cultural considerations* (pp. 167–194). Oxford University Press.

Wozniak, R. H. (1997). Behaviorism. In W. G. Bringmann, H. E. Lück, R. Miller, & C. E. Early (Eds.), *A pictorial history of psychology* (pp. 198–205). Quintessence Publishing.

Wray, A. (1998). Protolanguage as a holistic system for social interaction. *Language & Communication, 18*(1), 47–67.

Wray, A. (2000). Holistic utterances in protolanguage: The link from primates to humans. In C. Knight, M. Studdert-Kennedy, & J. R. Hurford (Eds.), *The evolutionary emergence of language: Social function and the origins of linguistic form* (pp. 285–302). Cambridge University Press.

Wren, A. M., Seal, L. J., Cohen, M. A., Brynes, A. E., Frost, G. S., Murphy, K. G., Dhillo, W. S., Ghatei, M. A., & Bloom, S. R. (2001). Ghrelin enhances appetite and increases food intake in humans. *Journal of Clinical Endocrinology and Metabolism, 86*(12), 5992–5995.

Wright, A. G. C. (2017). Factor analytic support for the Five Factor Model. In T. A. Widiger (Ed.), *The Oxford handbook of the Five Factor Model* (pp. 217–242). Oxford University Press.

Wright, C. V., Beattie, S. G., Galper, D. I., Church, A. S., Bufka, L. F., Brabender, V. M., & Smith, B. L. (2017). Assessment practices of professional psychologists: Results of a national survey. *Professional Psychology: Research and Practice, 48*(2), 73.

Wright, K. P., McHill, A. W., Birks, B. R., Griffin, B. R., Rusterholz, T., & Chinoy, E. D. (2013). Entrainment of the human circadian clock to the natural light-dark cycle. *Current Biology, 23*(16), 1554–1558.

Wright, P., Albarracin, D., Brown, R. D., Li, H., He, G., & Liu, Y. (2008). Dissociated responses in the amygdala and orbitofrontal cortex to bottom-up and top-down components of emotional evaluation. *Neuroimage, 39*(2), 894–902.

Wright, R. J., Mitchell, H., Visness, C. M., Cohen, S., Stout, J., Evans, R., & Gold, D. R. (2004). Community violence and asthma morbidity: The inner-city asthma study. *American Journal of Public Health, 94*(4), 625–632.

Wright, S. C., Aron, A., McLaughlin-Volpe, T., & Ropp, S. A. (1997). The extended contact effect: Knowledge of cross-group friendships and prejudice. *Journal of Personality and Social Psychology, 73*(1), 73–90.

Wrzus, C., & Roberts, B. W. (2017). Processes of personality development in adulthood: The TESSERA framework. *Personality and Social Psychology Review, 21*(3), 253–277.

Wu, G. (2002). Evaluation of the effectiveness of Tai Chi for improving balance and preventing falls in the older population—A review. *Journal of the American Geriatrics Society, 50*(4), 746–754.

Wu, Y., Kang, R., Yan, Y., Gao, K., Li, Z., Jiang, J., Chi, X., & Xia, L. (2018). Epidemiology of schizophrenia and risk factors of schizophrenia-associated aggression from 2011 to 2015. *Journal of International Medical Research, 46*(10), 4039–4049.

Wyart, C., Webster, W. W., Chen, J. H., Wilson, S. R., McClary, A., Khan, R. M., & Sobel, N. (2007). Smelling a single component of male sweat alters levels of cortisol in women. *The Journal of Neuroscience, 27*(6), 1261–1265.

Wykes, T., Brammer, M., Mellers, J., Bray, P., Reeder, C., Williams, C., & Corner, J. (2002). Effects on the brain of a psychological treatment: Cognitive remediation therapy: Functional magnetic resonance imaging in schizophrenia. *British Journal of Psychiatry, 181*(2), 144–152.

Wymbs, B., Molina, B., Pelham, W., Cheong, J., Gnagy, E., Belendiuk, K., Walkter, C., Babinski, D., & Waschbusch, D. (2012). Risk of intimate partner violence among young adult males with childhood ADHD. *Journal of Attention Disorders, 16*(5), 373–383.

Wynn, K. (1992). Addition and subtraction by human infants. *Nature, 358*(6389), 749–750.

Wyrwicka, W. (2000). *Conditioning: Situation versus intermittent stimulus*. Transaction.

Xie, W., Campbell, S., & Zhang, W. (2020). Working memory capacity predicts individual differences in social-distancing compliance during the COVID-19 pandemic in the United States. *Proceedings of the National Academy of Sciences, 117*(30), 17667–17674. https://doi.org/10.1073/pnas.2008868117

Xu, J., Murphy, S. L., Kochanek, K. D., Bastian, B., & Arias, E. (2018). Deaths: Final data for 2016. In National Vital Statistics Reports (Vol. 67, No. 5). Washington, DC: U.S. Department of Health and Human Services, Centers for Disease Control and Prevention, National Center for Health Statistics, National Vital Statistics System. https://www.cdc.gov/nchs/data/nvsr/nvsr67/nvsr67_05.pdf

Yaden, D. B., Eichstaedt, J. C., Schwartz, H. A., Kern, M. L., Le Nguyen, K. D., Wintering, N. A., ... Newberg, A. B. (2016). The language of ineffability: Linguistic analysis of mystical experiences. *Psychology of Religion and Spirituality, 8*(3), 244–252.

Yaden, D. B., Haidt, J., Hood, R. W., Jr., Vago, D. R., & Newberg, A. B. (2017). The varieties of self-transcendent experience. *Review of General Psychology, 21*(2), 143–160.

Yager, J. (2010). The sociology of sleep. In C. P. Pollak, M. J. Thorpy, & J. Yager, *The encyclopedia of sleep and sleep disorders* (3rd ed., pp. xxxix–xliii). Infobase.

Yagiz, O., & Izadpanah, S. (2013). Language, culture, idioms, and their relationship with the foreign language. *Journal of Language Teaching and Research, 4*(5), 953.

Yalch, M. M., & Hopwood, C. J. (2017). Target-, informant-, and meta-perceptual ratings of maladaptive traits. *Psychological Assessment, 29*(9), 1142–1156.

Yalom, I. D. (1983). *Inpatient group psychotherapy*. Basic Books.

Yalom, I. D., & Lezcz, M. (2020). *The theory and practice of group psychotherapy* (6th ed.). Hachette.

Yamaguchi, S., & Ninomiya, K. (1999). Umami and food palatability. In R. Teranishi, E. L. Wick, & I. Hornstein (Eds.), *Flavor chemistry: Thirty years of progress* (pp. 423–432). Springer Science+Business Media.

Yan, H., Ding, Y., & Guo, W. (2020). Mental health of pregnant and postpartum women during the coronavirus disease 2019 pandemic: A systematic review and meta-analysis. *Frontiers in Psychology, 11*, 3324. https://doi.org/10.3389/fpsyg.2020.617001

Yang, C. K., Kim, J. K., Patel, S. R., & Lee, J. H. (2005). Age-related changes in sleep/wake patterns among Korean teenagers. *Pediatrics, 115*(Suppl. 1), 250–256.

Yang, Y., & Raine, A. (2009). Prefrontal structural and functional brain imaging findings in antisocial, violent, and psychopathic individuals: A meta-analysis. *Psychiatry Research: Neuroimaging, 174*(2), 81–88.

Yanos, P. T. (2018). *Written off: Mental health stigma and the loss of human potential*. Cambridge University Press.

Yapko, M. D. (2008). Hypnotic approaches to treating depression. In M. R. Nash & A. J. Barnier (Eds.), *The Oxford handbook of hypnosis: Theory, research, and practice* (pp. 549–568). Oxford University Press.

Yardley, L. (1992). Motion sickness and perception: A reappraisal of the sensory conflict approach. *British Journal of Psychology, 83*(4), 449–471.

Yarkoni, T. (2009). Big correlations in little studies: Inflated fMRI correlations reflect low statistical power—Commentary on Vul et al. (2009). *Perspectives on Psychological Science, 4*(3), 294–298.

Yasnitsky, A. (2012). Lev Vygotsky: Philologist and defectologist, a sociointellectual biography. In W. E. Pickren, D. A. Dewsbury, & M. Wertheimer (Eds.), *Portraits of pioneers in developmental psychology* (pp. 109–133). Psychology Press.

Ye, B., Zhou, X., Im, H., Liu, M., Wang, X. Q., & Yang, Q. (2020). Epidemic rumination and resilience on college students' depressive symptoms during the COVID-19 pandemic: The mediating role of fatigue. *Frontiers in Public Health, 8*, 858. https://doi.org/10.3389/fpubh.2020.560983

Yeager, D. S., Hanselman, P., Walton, G. M., Murray, J. S., Crosnoe, R., Muller, C., Tipton, E., Schneider, B., Hulleman, C. S., Hinojosa, C. P., Paunesku, D., Romero, C., Flint, K., Roberts, A., Trott, J., Iachan, R., Buontempo, J., Yang, S. M., Carvalho, C. M., Hahn, P. R., ... Dweck, C. S. (2019). A national experiment reveals where a growth mindset improves achievement. *Nature, 573*(7774), 364–369. https://doi.org/10.1038/s41586-019-1466-y

Yeh, C. J., Arora, A. K., & Wu, K. A. (2006). A new theoretical model of collectivistic coping. In P. T. P. Wong and L. C. J. Wong (Eds.), *Handbook of multicultural perspectives on stress and coping* (pp. 55–72). Springer Science+Business Media.

Yeh, C., & Inose, M. (2002). Difficulties and coping strategies of Chinese, Japanese and Korean immigrant students. *Adolescence, 37*(145), 69–82.

Yeh, M. A., Jewell, R. D., & Thomas, V. L. (2017). The stigma of mental illness: Using segmentation for social change. *Journal of Public Policy & Marketing, 36*(1), 97–116. https://doi.org/10.1509/jppm.13.125

Yeo, D. J., Wilkey, E. D., & Price, G. R. (2017). The search for the number form area: A functional neuroimaging meta-analysis. *Neuroscience & Biobehavioral Reviews, 78*, 145–160.

Yerkes, R. M., & Dodson, J. D. (1908). The relation of strength of stimulus to rapidity of habit-formation. *Journal of Comparative Neurological Psychology, 18*(5), 459–482.

Yeshurun, Y., Lapid, H., Haddad, R., Gelstein, S., Arzi, A., Sela, L., & Sobel, N. (2009). Olfaction: From percept to molecule. In M. S. Gazzaniga (Ed.), *The cognitive neurosciences* (4th ed., pp. 321–342). MIT Press.

Yih, J., Uusberg, A., Taxer, J. L., & Gross, J. J. (2018). Better together: A unified perspective on appraisal and emotion regulation. *Cognition and Emotion, 33*(1), 41–47.

Yoon, J. A., Han, D. H., Noh, J. Y., Kim, M. H., Son, G. H., Kim, K., Kim, C.-J., Pak, Y. K., & Cho, S. (2012). Meal time shift disturbs circadian rhythmicity along with metabolic and behavioral alterations in mice. *PLoS ONE, 7*(8), e44053.

Yost, W. A. (2001). Auditory, localization, and scene perception. In E. B. Goldstein (Ed.), *Blackwell handbook of perception* (pp. 437–468). Blackwell.

Yost, W. A. (2010). Audition: Pitch perception. In E. B. Goldstein (Ed.), *Encyclopedia of perception* (pp. 151–154). Sage.

Young, C. A., Haffejee, B., & Corsun, D. L. (2018). Developing cultural intelligence and empathy through diversified mentoring relationships. *Journal of Management Education, 42*(3), 319–346.

Young, K. S., & Anderson, M. R. (2019). Microaggressions in higher education: Embracing educative spaces. In G. C. Torino, D. P. Rivera, C. M. Capodilupo, K. L. Nadal, & D. W. Sue (Eds.), *Microaggression theory: Influence and implications* (pp. 291–305). Wiley.

Young, L. R., & Nestle, M. (2002). The contribution of expanding portion sizes to the US obesity epidemic. *American Journal of Public Health, 92*(2), 246–249.
Young, L. R., & Nestle, M. (2007). Portion sizes and obesity: Responses of fast-food companies. *Journal of Public Health Policy, 28*(2), 238–248.
Young, M. E. (2016). The problem with categorical thinking by psychologists. *Behavioural Processes, 123*, 43–53.
Young, S. D. (2012). *Psychology at the movies*. Wiley-Blackwell.
Young, T. (1802). The Bakerian lecture: On the theory of light and colours. *Philosophical Transactions of the Royal Society of London, 92*(1802), 12–48.
Young, T., & Peppard, P. E. (2005). Clinical presentation of OSAS: Gender does matter. *Sleep, 28*(3), 293–295.
Young, T., Skatrud, J., & Peppard, P. E. (2004). Risk factors for obstructive sleep apnea in adults. *JAMA, 291*(16), 2013–2016.
Yu, Y., Peng, L., Tang, T., Chen, L., Li, M., & Wang, T. (2014). Effects of emotion regulation and general self-efficacy on posttraumatic growth in Chinese cancer survivors: Assessing the mediating effect of positive affect. *Psychooncology, 23*(4), 473–478.
Yuki, M., Maddux, W. W., & Masuda, T. (2007). Are the windows to the soul the same in the East and West? Cultural differences in using the eyes and mouth as cues to recognize emotions in Japan and the United States. *Journal of Experimental Social Psychology, 43*(2), 303–311.
Yzerbyt, V., & Demoulin, S. (2010). Intergroup relations. In S. T. Fiske, D. T. Gilbert, & G. Lindzey (Eds.), *Handbook of social psychology* (5th ed., Vol. 2, pp. 1024–1083). Wiley.
Zachar, P. (2018). Diagnostic nomenclatures in the mental health professions as public policy. *Journal of Humanistic Psychology 59*(3), 438–445. https://doi.org/10.1177/0022167818793002.
Zachar, P., & Kendler, K. S. (2010). Philosophical issues in the classification of psychopathology. In T. Millon, R. F. Krueger, & E. Simonsen (Eds.), *Contemporary directions in psychopathology: Scientific foundations of the DSM-V and ICD-11* (pp. 127–148). Guilford Press.
Zachar, P., & Kendler, K. S. (2014). A diagnostic and statistical manual of mental disorders history of premenstrual dysphoric disorder. *The Journal of Nervous and Mental Disease, 202*(4), 346–352.
Zachary, Z., Brianna, F., Brianna, L., Garrett, P., Jade, W., Alyssa, D., & Mikayla, K. (2020). Self-quarantine and weight gain related risk factors during the COVID-19 pandemic. *Obesity Research & Clinical Practice, 14*(3), 210–216. https://doi.org/10.1016/j.orcp.2020.05.004
Zacks, R. T., & Hasher, L. (2002). Frequency processing: A twenty-five year perspective. In P. Sedlmeier & T. Betsch (Eds.), *Etc.: Frequency processing and cognition* (pp. 21–36). Oxford.
Zacks, R. T., Hasher, L., & Sanft, H. (1982). Automatic encoding of event frequency: Further findings. *Journal of Experimental Psychology: Learning, Memory, and Cognition, 8*(2), 106.
Zadra, A., & Pilon, M. (2012). Parasomnias II: Sleep terrors and somnambulism. In C. M. Morin & C. A. Espie (Eds.), *The Oxford handbook of sleep and sleep disorders* (pp. 577–596). Oxford University Press.
Zadra, A., Hébert-Tremblay, L., Trudeau, S., Desautels, A., & Montplaisir, J. (2018). Patients' self-reported precipitating factors for sleepwalking. *Sleep, 41*(Suppl. 1), A255.
Zagorsky, J. L. (2007). Do you have to be smart to be rich? The impact of IQ on wealth, income and financial distress. *Intelligence, 35*(5), 489–501.
Zahodne, L. B., Manly, J. J., Smith, J., Seeman, T., & Lachman, M. E. (2017). Socioeconomic, health, and psychosocial mediators of racial disparities in cognition in early, middle, and late adulthood. *Psychology and Aging, 32*(2), 118–130. https://doi.org/10.1037/pag0000154
Zahodne, L. B., Sol, K., & Kraal, Z. (2019). Psychosocial pathways to racial/ethnic inequalities in late-life memory trajectories. *The Journals of Gerontology: Series B, 74*(3), 409–418. https://doi.org/10.1093/geronb/gbx113
Zajac, K., Ginley, M. K., Chang, R., & Petry, N. M. (2017). Treatments for Internet gaming disorder and Internet addiction: A systematic review. *Psychology of Addictive Behaviors, 31*(8), 979–994. https://doi.org/10.1037/adb0000315
Zajonc, R. B. (1968). Attitudinal effects of mere exposure. *Journal of Personality and Social Psychology, 9*(2), 1–27.
Zajonc, R. B. (1980). Feeling and thinking: Preferences need no inferences. *American Psychologist, 35*(2), 151–175.
Zajonc, R. B. (1984). On the primacy of affect. *American Psychologist, 39*(2), 117–123.
Zajonc, R. B., Murphy, S. T., & Inglehart, M. (1989). Feeling and facial efference: Implications of the vascular theory of emotion. *Psychological Review, 96*(3), 395–416.
Zald, D. H. (2003). The human amygdala and the emotional evaluation of sensory stimuli. *Brain Research Reviews, 41*(1), 88–123.
Zanker, J. M. (2010). *Sensation, perception and action: An evolutionary perspective*. Palgrave Macmillan.
Zapata Sola, A., Kreuch, T., Landers, R. N., Hoyt, T., & Butcher, J. N. (2009). Personality assessment in personnel selection using the MMPI-2: A cross-cultural comparison. *International Journal of Clinical and Health Psychology, 9*(2), 287–298.
Zautra, A. J., & Reich, J. W. (2011). Resilience: The meanings, methods, and measures of a fundamental characteristic of human adaptation. In S. Folkman (Ed.), *Oxford handbook of stress, health, and coping* (pp. 173–185). Oxford University Press.
Zea, M. C., & Nakamura, N. (2014). Sexual orientation. In F. T. L. Leong (Ed.), *APA handbook of multicultural psychology* (Vol. 1, pp. 395–410). Washington, DC: American Psychological Association.
Zebroff, D. (2018). Youth texting: Help or hindrance to literacy? *Education and Information Technologies, 23*(1), 341–356.
Zebroff, D., & Kaufman, D. (2017). Texting, reading, and other daily habits associated with adolescents' literacy levels. *Education and Information Technologies, 22*(5), 2197–2216.
Zeidan, F. (2015). The neurobiology of mindfulness meditation. In K. W. Brown, J. D. Creswell, & R. M. Ryan (Eds.), *Handbook of mindfulness: Theory, research, and practice* (pp. 171–189). Guilford Press.
Zeidan, F., Martucci, K. T., Kraft, R. A., Gordon, N. S., McHaffie, J. G., & Coghill, R. C. (2011). Brain mechanisms supporting the modulation of pain by mindfulness meditation. *Journal of Neuroscience, 31*(14), 5540–5548.
Zeidan, F., Martucci, K. T., Kraft, R. A., McHaffie, J. G., & Coghill, R. C. (2013). Neural correlates of mindfulness meditation-related anxiety relief. *Social Cognitive and Affective Neuroscience, 9*(6), 751–759.
Zelazo, P. D., & Lee, W. S. C. (2010). Brain development: An overview. In W. F. Overton (Ed.), *Handbook of life-span development* (Vol. 1, pp. 89–114). Wiley.
Zeligman, M., Varney, M., Grad, R. I., & Huffstead, M. (2018). Posttraumatic growth in individuals with chronic illness: The role of social support and meaning making. *Journal of Counseling & Development, 96*(1), 53–63.
Zellner, D. A. (2010). Multimodal interactions: Color-chemical. In E. B. Goldstein (Ed.), *Encyclopedia of perception* (pp. 584–585). Sage.
Zellner, D. A. (2013). Color–odor interactions: A review and model. *Chemosensory Perception, 6*(4), 155–169.
Zellner, D. A., Bartoli, A. M., & Eckard, R. (1991). Influence of color on odor identification and liking ratings. *The American Journal of Psychology, 104*(4), 547–561.
Zeman, J., & Garber, J. (1996). Display rules for anger, sadness, and pain: It depends on who is watching. *Child Development, 67*(3), 957–973.
Zerach, G., Karstoft, K. I., & Solomon, Z. (2017). Hardiness and sensation seeking as potential predictors of former prisoners of wars' posttraumatic stress symptoms trajectories over a 17-year period. *Journal of Affective Disorders, 218*, 176–181.
Zettler, I., Schild, C., Lilleholt, L., Kroencke, L., Utesch, T., Moshagen, M., Böhm, R., Back, M. D., & Geukes, K. (2021, April 5). The role of personality in COVID-19-related perceptions, evaluations, and behaviors: Findings across five samples, nine traits, and 17 criteria. *Social Psychological and Personality Science*, 19485506211001680. https://doi.org/10.1177/19485506211001680
Zhang, W., Gao, F., Gross, J., Shrum, L. J., & Hayne, H. (2021). How does social distancing during COVID-19 affect negative moods and memory? *Memory, 29*(1), 90–97. https://doi.org/10.1080/09658211.2020.1857774
Zhang, X., Wang, G., Wang, H., Wang, X., Ji, T., Hou, D., Wu, J., Sun, J., & Zhu, B. (2020). Spouses' perceptions of and attitudes toward female menopause: A mixed-methods systematic review. *Climacteric, 23*(2), 148–157. https://doi.org/10.1080/13697137.2019.1703937
Zhang, X., Zong, B., Zhao, W., & Li, L. (2021). Effects of mind–body exercise on brain structure and function: A systematic review on MRI studies. *Brain Sciences, 11*(2), 205. https://doi.org/10.3390/brainsci11020205
Zhang, Y., Ma, Y., Chen, S., Liu, X., Kang, H. J., Nelson, S., & Bell, S. (2019). Long-term cognitive performance of retired athletes with sport-related concussion: A systematic review and meta-analysis. *Brain Sciences, 9*(8), 199. https://doi.org/10.3390/brainsci9080199
Zhang, Z. J., Chen, H. Y., Yip, K. C., Ng, R., & Wong, V. T. (2010). The effectiveness and safety of acupuncture therapy in depressive disorders: Systematic review and meta-analysis. *Journal of Affective Disorders, 124*(1), 9–21.
Zhao, L. R. (2015). Neural stem cells in response to microenvironment changes inside and outside of the brain. In L. Zhao & J. H. Zhang (Eds.), *Cellular therapy for stroke and CNS injuries* (pp. 17–32). Springer.
Zheng, D., Ni, X. L., & Luo, Y. J. (2019). Selfie posting on social networking sites and female adolescents' self-objectification: The moderating role of imaginary audience ideation. *Sex Roles, 80*(5), 325–331. https://doi.org/10.1007/s11199-018-0937-1
Zhou, W., Yang, X., Chen, K., Cai, P., He, S., & Jiang, Y. (2014). Chemosensory communication of gender through two human steroids in a sexually dimorphic manner. *Current Biology, 24*(10), 1091–1095.
Zhou, X., Guo, J., Lu, G., Chen, C., Xie, Z., Liu, J., & Zhang, C. (2020). Effects of mindfulness-based stress reduction on anxiety symptoms in young people: A systematic review and meta-analysis. *Psychiatry Research, 289*, 113002. https://doi.org/10.1016/j.psychres.2020.113002
Zhou, X., Hetrick, S. E., Cuijpers, P., Qin, B., Barth, J., Whittington, C. J., Cohen, D., Del Giovane, C., Liu, Y., Michael, K. D., Zhang, Y., Weisz, J. R., & Xie, P. (2015). Comparative efficacy and acceptability of psychotherapies for depression in children and adolescents: A systematic review and network meta-analysis. *World Psychiatry, 14*(2), 207–222. https://doi.org/10.1002/wps.20217
Ziegler, M., MacCann, C., & Roberts, R. D. (2012). Faking: Knowns, unknowns, and points of contention. In M. Ziegler, C. MacCann, & R. D. Roberts (Eds.), *New perspectives on faking in personality assessment* (pp. 3–16). Oxford University Press.
Zilboorg, G., & Henry, G. W. (1941). *A history of medical psychology*. W. W. Norton.
Zimbardo, P. G. (1972). Pathology of imprisonment. *Society, 9*(6), 4–8.
Zimbardo, P. G., Haney, C., Banks, W. C., & Jaffe, D. (1973, April 8). The mind is a formidable jailer: A Pirandellian prison. *New York Times Magazine*. http://www.nytimes.com/1973/04/08/archives/a-pirandellian-prison-the-mind-is-a-formidable-jailer.html?_r=0
Zimmerman, A. G., & Ybarra, G. J. (2016). Online aggression: The influences of anonymity and social modeling. *Psychology of Popular Media Culture, 5*(2), 181–193.
Zimmermann, J., & Neyer, F. J. (2013). Do we become a different person when --hitting the road? Personality development of sojourners. *Journal of Personality and Social Psychology, 105*(3), 515–530. https://doi.org/10.1037/a0033019
Zinbarg, R. E., Uliaszek, A. A., & Lewis, A. R. (2009). Anxiety. In R. E. Ingram (Ed.), *The international encyclopedia of depression* (pp. 27–30). Springer.
Zoellner, L. A., Abramowitz, J. S., Moore, S. A., & Slagle, D. M. (2008). Flooding. In W. T. O'Donohue & J. E. Fisher (Eds.), *Cognitive behavior therapy: Applying empirically supported techniques in your practice* (2nd ed., pp. 202–210). Wiley.
Zoellner, L. A., Abramowitz, J. S., Moore, S. A., & Slagle, D. M. (2008). Flooding. In W. T. O'Donohue & J. E. Fisher (Eds.), *Cognitive behavior therapy: Applying empirically supported techniques in your practice* (2nd ed., pp. 202–210). Wiley.
Zohar, D., Tzischinsky, O., Epstein, R., & Lavie, P. (2005). The effects of sleep loss on medical residents' emotional reactions to work events: A cognitive-energy model. *Sleep, 28*(1), 47–54.
Zosuls, K. M., Miller, C. F., Ruble, D. N., Martin, C. L., & Fabes, R. A. (2011). Gender development research in sex roles: Historical trends and future directions. *Sex Roles, 64*(11–12), 826–842.
Zuckerman, M. (1999). *Vulnerability to psychopathology: A biosocial model*. American Psychological Association.
Zur, O. (2007). *Boundaries in psychotherapy: Ethical and clinical explorations*. American Psychological Association.
Zur, O. (2009). Therapeutic boundaries and effective therapy: Exploring the relationships. In W. O'Donohue & S. R. Graybar (Eds.), *Handbook of contemporary psychotherapy: Toward an improved understanding of effective psychotherapy* (pp. 341–357). Thousand Oaks, CA: Sage.
Zur, O. (Ed.). (2017). *Multiple relationships in psychotherapy and counseling: Unavoidable, common, and mandatory dual relations in therapy*. Routledge.
Zuraikat, F. M., Smethers, A. D., & Rolls, B. J. (2019). Potential moderators of the portion size effect. *Physiology & Behavior, 204*, 191–198. https://doi.org/10.1016/j.physbeh.2019.02.043
Zuroff, D. C., Kelly, A. C., Leybman, M. J., Blatt, S. J., & Wampold, B. E. (2010). Between-therapist and within-therapist differences in the quality of the therapeutic relationship: Effects on maladjustment and self-critical perfectionism. *Journal of Clinical Psychology, 66*(7), 681–697.
Zysberg, L., & Zisberg, A. (2020). Days of worry: Emotional intelligence and social support mediate worry in the COVID-19 pandemic. *Journal of Health Psychology*, 1359105320949935. https://doi.org/10.1177/1359105320949935
Zywiczynski, P., Gontier, N., & Wacewicz, S. (2017). The evolution of (proto-) language: Focus on mechanisms. *Language Sciences, 63*, 1–11.

Name Index

Page numbers preceded by A indicate the Appendix.

Subject Index

Page numbers followed by f indicate figures; page numbers followed by t indicate tables; and page numbers preceded by A indicate the Appendix.